HISTORICAL STATISTICS
OF THE
UNITED STATES

HISTORICAL STATISTICS
OF THE
UNITED STATES

Earliest Times to the Present

MILLENNIAL EDITION

VOLUME FIVE

PART E
GOVERNANCE AND INTERNATIONAL RELATIONS

Editors in Chief

Susan B. Carter

Scott Sigmund Gartner

Michael R. Haines

Alan L. Olmstead

Richard Sutch

Gavin Wright

CAMBRIDGE
UNIVERSITY PRESS

CAMBRIDGE UNIVERSITY PRESS
Cambridge, New York, Melbourne, Madrid, Cape Town, Singapore, São Paulo

Cambridge University Press
40 West 20th Street, New York, NY 10011-4211, USA

http://www.cambridge.org
Information on this title: www.cambridge.org/9780521817912

First published 2006

Printed in the United States of America

A catalog record for this publication is available from the British Library.

Library of Congress Cataloging in Publication Data

Historical statistics of the United States : earliest times to the present / Susan B. Carter ... [et al.]. – Millennial ed.
    p. cm.
    Rev. update of: Historical statistics of the United States, colonial times to 1970. Bicentennial ed. Washington : U.S. Dept. of Commerce, Bureau of the Census, 1975.
    Includes bibliographical references and index.
    ISBN 0-521-81791-9 (set)
    1. United States – Statistics.   I. Carter, Susan B.   II. Historical statistics of the United States, colonial times to 1970.   III. Title.

HA202.H57 2006
317.3 – dc22   2005027089

ISBN-13 978-0-521-81791-2 (set of five volumes hardback)
ISBN-10 0-521-81791-9 (set of five volumes hardback)

ISBN-13 978-0-521-58496-8 (volume 1 hardback)
ISBN-10 0-521-58496-5 (volume 1 hardback)

ISBN-13 978-0-521-58540-8 (volume 2 hardback)
ISBN-10 0-521-58540-6 (volume 2 hardback)

ISBN-13 978-0-521-81790-5 (volume 3 hardback)
ISBN-10 0-521-81790-0 (volume 3 hardback)

ISBN-13 978-0-521-85389-7 (volume 4 hardback)
ISBN-10 0-521-85389-3 (volume 4 hardback)

ISBN-13 978-0-521-85390-3 (volume 5 hardback)
ISBN-10 0-521-85390-7 (volume 5 hardback)

ISBN-13 978-0-511-13297-1 (on-line edition)
ISBN-10 0-511-13297-2 (on-line edition)

SUMMARY CONTENTS

DETAILED CONTENTS OF VOLUME FIVE

GUIDE TO THE MILLENNIAL EDITION

Monty Hindman and Richard Sutch

Editions and Copyright

Previous editions. This is the fourth edition of *Historical Statistics of the United States*. The U.S. Bureau of the Census published the prior editions in 1949, 1960, and 1975, the last known as the Bicentennial Edition. Cambridge University Press publishes this, the Millennial Edition, with the permission of the Census Bureau. Some of the data and table documentation presented here are used without explicit quotation, but with permission, from the earlier editions. The Census Bureau takes no responsibility for the design of this edition or the accuracy of its content, which rests solely with the contributors, the editors, and Cambridge University Press.

Electronic edition. This edition of *Historical Statistics of the United States* is available in electronic form from Cambridge University Press. A compact disk containing the Bicentennial Edition of *Historical Statistics of the United States* is also available from the Press.

Copyright. Permission to quote or reprint copyright material should be obtained directly from the copyright owner. Much of the data reproduced in this work were originally published by agencies of the U.S. government and are in the public domain. Generally speaking, original data that have been published elsewhere under copyright protection may be freely used for educational, scholarly, or journalistic purposes (but not commercial purposes) with proper citation to the original source under the fair use provision of U.S. copyright law. Cambridge University Press has made every effort to secure, where necessary, permission to reproduce protected material. In almost every case the permission requested was freely granted. In a few instances, however, the copyright owner requested a specific citation. These citations may be found in the listing of Copyright Citations at the end of Volume 5.

Data Revisions and Updates

Reproduction and revision of data from prior editions. Although this volume provides many data series from prior editions of *Historical Statistics of the United States*, users should be aware that some data from these editions have subsequently been revised. Our contributors sought to present the most recently available data, and thus users probably will wish to use the data presented here rather than that in previous editions. In some cases, data from the earlier editions were judged to be unreliable or obsolete and were not reproduced.

Data updates. The data series in *Historical Statistics of the United States* do not have a uniform end date; instead, each table reports the data available at the time the contributor compiled the data. Many series in these volumes are continued on a regular basis with periodic updates and revisions by the agency, group, or individual responsible for the original data. Figures for many of the current series are presented in the *Statistical Abstract of the United States*, published annually by the U.S. Bureau of the Census. The updating of industrial statistics will be complicated by the switch in 1997 from the Standard Industrial Classification (SIC) system to the North American Industrial Classification System (NAICS); see the Introduction to Part D.

Additional data. In many cases, additional data can be found in the source documents, in references mentioned in the table documentation or chapter essays, and through the Internet sites of the groups or agencies noted in the sources for the data presented here.

Errors. In a work as large as this, errors of both commission and omission are likely to have occurred. Users who discover errors are urged to communicate them to Cambridge University Press, 40 West 20th Street, New York, New York 10011-4211, USA.

Data Selection

General principles. The criteria for the selection of data to be included in this edition varied broadly, depending on the particular subject matter. Generally, summary measures or aggregates at gross levels and immediately below were given highest priority for inclusion. Below such levels, selection was governed by the interplay of the following: the amount of space already devoted to a particular subject; the attempt to achieve a relatively balanced presentation among subject fields; whether other data already covered a particular topic; the quantity and quality of the data available; and the extent to which the data might enhance the value of other material in the book. During the early phases of the project these selection criteria were conveyed to our contributors, upon whose judgment we ultimately relied.

Data reliability. Our contributors have attempted to select data that they consider to be generally reliable and to reproduce faithfully the data reported in their sources. They have also provided citations and technical descriptions to assist users in making independent assessments of both the data's reliability and their suitability for a project at hand.

Original versus derived data. Primary emphasis was placed on the presentation of original, unmodified figures rather than derived data because they offer greater flexibility to users. Derived data – for example, averages, percentages, ratios, and index numbers – were provided if they were the accepted standard for presentation (for example, unemployment rates), if the table contributor judged that the derived data would be particularly helpful, or if the use of derived data saved a significant amount of space.

Topical coverage. Because the last thirty years have witnessed the expansion of data collection into areas that were only inadequately covered, if at all, in the 1970s, this edition has a broader topical scope than its predecessors. A tentative list of topics emerged after extensive discussions between the project's editors in chief and Cambridge University Press. The outline was widely circulated to scholars, reference librarians, and government statistical bureaus. After a revision of that outline, the project recruited contributors, who offered additional suggestions. What emerged from this process was an outline for the project that was both designed by the profession and feasible to accomplish.

Temporal coverage. Contributors were asked to take the data series under their charge as far backward and forward in time as possible. They were also encouraged to include important lapsed series – those that begin and terminate in the past – because such series are sometimes available only in out-of-print documents. Most data series in *Historical Statistics of the United States* provide annual or decennial data spanning at least twenty years, with the main exceptions being for special topics (the colonial period and the Confederate States of America), for newly developed series providing the only data available to represent an important subject field, and for short series that served as important extensions of longer series.

Data frequency. Annual data were given preference for inclusion, but certain series are presented only for years in which a national census was conducted and, in some instances, only for scattered dates, as dictated by data availability. When both annual figures and benchmark data exist, both series are sometimes shown. A major exception was made for Chapter Cb, which presents many of its series on a monthly or quarterly basis. Although this volume mainly provides annual data, underlying data are sometimes available more frequently from the original sources.

Geographical coverage. The data in *Historical Statistics of the United States* generally cover the nation as a whole, defined by the recognized borders of the country for the year in question. As new states were admitted to the Union, the coverage of the typical statistical series in this volume expands to include the new additions, without any special notation in the table documentation. The documentation should be consulted to determine if such changes in the boundaries of the United States are likely to have affected the series. When the year of a state's inclusion in a series differs significantly from its year of statehood, this fact was noted in the documentation whenever possible. Refer to Appendix 2 for the dates of statehood.

Subnational data. Because of limitations of space, data are generally not shown for regions, states, or localities. The underlying sources sometimes provide data in finer geographical detail than shown here. Some tables provide data for U.S. census regions or divisions; see Appendix 2 for more information on such regional classifications.

Outlying areas. In almost all cases, outlying areas are not included in the national totals reported here. Refer to Chapter Ef for additional information on such areas.

Organization of the Volume

Arrangement of the data. In this edition of *Historical Statistics of the United States,* data are arranged by broad subjects in five parts, each published in a separate volume and each volume containing several chapters. The tables in most chapters are further organized into various subsections (see the Detailed Table of Contents in each volume).

Essays. Each chapter is introduced by one or more essays that provide a general guide to the data, the sources, and the historical trends that have been emphasized in the scholarly literature. They contain a list of references that may be consulted by those interested in more detail.

Series identifiers. Each data series is assigned a unique alphanumeric identifier. The two letters in the identifier indicate the chapter in which the series resides. Within a chapter, series are numbered sequentially. Sets of contiguous series are identified by means of a series range (for example, series Da42–47). Source citations and table documentation are linked to the data series by means of such identifiers, which may be preferred over page numbers for use in reference citations.

Table identifiers. An entire table is identified by the range of series that it contains. For example, the first two tables in the chapter on vital statistics contain ten and twenty series, respectively; thus, they are identified as Table Ab1–10 and Table Ab11–30. Similarly, a group of contiguous tables is identified by a series range. Using the same example, these two tables could be referred to jointly as Tables Ab1–30.

Table Documentation

Table contributors. Each table provides the names of the contributors who selected, collected, and described the data. The editorial staff also reviewed the data and table documentation for accuracy, completeness, and clarity of presentation.

Sources. In most cases, full citations are given for data sources; however, when numerous issues of a publication were used, the source citations are usually limited to "annual issues" or similar notations. When data are reproduced from the Bicentennial Edition, the source citation lists the original source rather than the Bicentennial Edition, except under special circumstances.

Unpublished data. Nearly all the data reported here have been previously published or accepted for publication. Rare exceptions for previously unpublished data were allowed if a contributor felt that the data were particularly important and if peer review accepted the data for inclusion.

Integrated Public Use Microdata Series. A number of series reported in this edition are extracted from the Integrated Public Use Microdata Series (IPUMS). The IPUMS is composed of representative samples drawn from the returns of the decennial censuses of the population. All censuses from 1850 to 1990 are included, with the exception of 1930, which is under development, and 1890, the manuscripts for which were destroyed by fire. The IPUMS data and documentation are available over the Internet.*

Internet sources. Some data series in *Historical Statistics of the United States* are based on electronic sources; however, owing to the fleeting nature of specific Internet addresses or Web-based

---

* Steven Ruggles, Matthew Sobek, et al., *Integrated Public Use Microdata Series: Version 2.0* (Historical Census Projects, University of Minnesota, 1997).

file names, we do not use them when identifying sources. Instead, we use more general phrasing to direct users to the Internet source.

Table documentation. Most tables are accompanied by documentation defining relevant terms and concepts, providing methodological and historical background, noting unusual values or comparability issues, explaining methods used to calculate derived data, and providing references to sources containing more detailed data or more extensive discussion. Unlike prior editions, which consolidated table documentation at the beginning of chapters, this edition locates the documentation with the tables, the intent being to increase its visibility, convenience, and thus use. Many tables are fully self-documenting, without cross references to other parts of this work; however, when cross references to other tables or essays are provided, the user is encouraged to follow those references.

Footnotes. There is no sharp demarcation between the type of information conveyed in the ordinary table documentation and that conveyed in the footnotes. Roughly speaking, footnotes are used for two purposes: to draw attention to issues of particular importance (footnotes as warnings) or to comment on matters related to specific columns, rows, or cells in a table.

Footnote order. Within a table, footnotes are numbered sequentially as follows: first the general footnotes that apply to the entire table; then left-to-right across the table header (the footnotes governing specific series); and finally footnotes attached to the table stub and the data area, proceeding in top-to-bottom, then left-to-right fashion (as used here, the directional terms apply to tables with standard page orientation). A footnote's first appearance within a table determines its position within the sequential numbering.

Total and subtotals. In most cases, a table's header structure will clearly indicate the total–subtotal relationships among the series. The typical practice in this volume is to provide the total series first, followed by its components. Often the sum of the components will equal the total, perhaps with small deviations attributable to rounding or other causes; however, sometimes the breakdowns provided in a table are not exhaustive, and the components will add to an amount less than the total. Users should consult the table documentation and exercise caution in this regard.

Race and ethnicity. Many tables provide disaggregations by race or ethnicity. This volume typically uses the terms "white," "black," "Asian" (or "Asian American"), "Indian" (or "Amerindian" or "Native American"), and "Hispanic." Note that a person identified as Hispanic may be of any race. See the essay on definitions and measurement of race and ethnicity in the Introduction to Part A for a discussion of racial classification and identification as it applies to the collection of historical statistics in the United States.

Dates

Date ranges. Throughout the table documentation and the chapter essays, date ranges are inclusive: for example, 1964–1987 includes both 1964 and 1987.

Year of record. The identification of the year of record – in other words, the precise meaning of the years shown in a table stub – was complicated by the failure of some sources to state whether the data were prepared on a calendar year, fiscal year, or some other basis; by changes in the year of record over time; and, in some instances, by imprecision or silence in the source concerning the beginning or ending date for the year of record. Table contributors

attempted to clarify such matters, but ambiguity remains in some tables.

Transition quarters. Sometimes the year of record changes in the middle of a table, and values are provided for the "transition quarter" – the gap between the end of the old year of record and beginning of the new. In such cases, users will see a (TQ) designation in the table stub. Nearly all transition quarters in this volume are associated with the year 1976, when the federal government changed the end of its fiscal year from June 30 to September 30. In rare cases, the (TQ) designation will be for a transition period that is not actually a quarter, but some other fraction of a year.

Units, Measures, and Monetary Values

Units of measure. Series are usually expressed in the units reported in the original source. In some cases, however, units were converted to make two or more data series comparable, or to create a single series when splicing data from multiple sources. The approach taken in these volumes was to restrict the units information to true *measures* and to rely on the table title and layered headers to convey other details about the things being counted or measured. Sometimes series are expressed in units too complex for pithy statement; in these rare cases, a generic unit of measure is given, with further elaboration left to the table documentation.

Billion and trillion. The American and Canadian definitions of billion (10^9) and trillion (10^{12}) are used throughout, not the definitions used in England, Germany, and many other countries.

Index numbers. Some series are expressed in terms of index numbers. In such cases, the base period of the index is provided where the unit of measure would normally be found. For a discussion of index numbers, see the essay on prices and price indexes in Chapter Cc and the essay on national income and product in Chapter Ca.

Weights and measures. Most data series are expressed in American units (the U.S. Customary System) rather than metric units (the International System). For a discussion of these two systems and for conversion information, see Appendix 1.

Monetary values. Unless otherwise noted, monetary values are expressed in current or nominal terms – in other words, the actual historical values (usually U.S. dollars), not adjusted for previous or subsequent changes in prices. This standard was adopted to avoid attaching the word "current" or "nominal" to every reference to a monetary unit. When monetary values have been adjusted in some fashion, this is stated explicitly and the relevant base period is given. For a discussion of monetary values, see Appendix 1 and the essay on prices and price indexes in Chapter Cc.

Data Values

Data precision and significant digits. In making decisions regarding the precision with which data values should be presented, fidelity to sources was our primary consideration. Thus, the underlying data files for *Historical Statistics of the United States* – available in the electronic edition – retain the full precision provided by table contributors, even though this level of detail might be deemed excessive by scientific standards for the reporting of significant digits. In most cases, the detail comes straight from the sources themselves; therefore, exact reproduction provides a valuable check for researchers wanting to trace the provenance of a number or hunt down an anomaly. In other cases, excessive precision comes from spreadsheet calculations made by table contributors (for example, in the computation of derived data). Here, too, we did not impose our judgments concerning the appropriate precision and instead retained the full detail provided by contributors. Users should note that historical sources sometimes change the precision with which they report data over time. Also, some tables contain series reported in the sources at different levels of detail but that, for ease of comparison, are provided here in consistent units. The usual indication of varying precision – whether in a single series or across multiple series within a table – is a run of data values with trailing zeros, either before or after the decimal point. In such cases, users will need to exercise judgment concerning the precision of the data.

Decimal precision for display purposes. While the underlying data files retain all of the detail provided by table contributors, the data displayed in the print edition of *Historical Statistics of the United States* are shown in rounded fashion, typically with no more than three digits following the decimal point. Similarly, tables generated for display purposes by the electronic edition are formatted using the same rounding conventions; however, the underlying files available for downloading provide the values at full precision.

Zero values and (Z). A zero in a data series means exactly that: a reported value of zero. In some cases, an underlying data value may be so small that it rounds to zero when displayed at the level of decimal precision chosen for the series. In such cases, a (Z) marker is used rather than a zero value. Stated more precisely, the (Z) notation indicates a *nonzero value that is not shown or possibly not known*. In the former case – a nonzero value not shown – (Z) means that the value falls below the threshold of our rounding convention: the number rounds to zero, as displayed in this volume (full precision for such values is available through the electronic edition). In the latter case – a nonzero value not known – (Z) means that the original source did not provide a specific value. Owing to these complexities, the meaning of the (Z) marker is specifically documented in every table that uses the device.

Dash as a data value. The "—" marker means that a value is not being reported. There are several possible reasons: the data are not available anywhere; the data were not provided in the source but conceivably could be found with sufficient research; the data were available in the source but the table contributor decided that they should not be reported (for example, unreliable data); or the data might conceivably be reported as a zero, but the table contributor decided for conceptual reasons to represent it as "no value reported" (for example, if a category or program covered by the series did not yet exist). Some sources do not carefully distinguish between zero values and missing data. Table contributors attempted to eliminate such confusion, but in some cases the "—" marker could mean that the value, if shown, would be zero.

Historical Statistics
of the
United States

Millennial Edition
Volume 5

Part E
Governance and International Relations

CHAPTER Ea

Government Finance and Employment

Editor: John Joseph Wallis

GOVERNMENT FINANCE AND EMPLOYMENT

John Joseph Wallis

One of the most prominent features of modern economies and societies is the significant role played by government. In the United States, government purchases of goods and service (federal, state, and local governments combined) composed 18 percent of gross domestic product (GDP) in 2000 (series Ca79). This chapter traces the growth and changing shape of American government from 1787 to the end of the twentieth century through its most visible and quantifiable aspects: the revenues it collects, the expenditures it makes, the debts it incurs, and the people it employs. Government does much more than is reflected in financial and employment data, of course. Those government records do not reflect laws, regulations, and politics, but they are the framework on which any study of American government must be built.

The History of the Accounts

The United States has not one government but many. Counting all of the governments in the United States is a daunting task. In 1940, when the first complete count was made, there were 155,116 governments: one national government, 48 state governments, 3,050 county governments, 16,220 municipal governments, 18,919 township and town governments, 108,579 school districts, and 8,299 special districts (Table Ea1–9). Over the course of the twentieth century, the number of governments declined with the consolidation of school districts, which shrank to only 14,556 in 1992, but this decrease was offset by an increase in the number of special districts, which rose to 33,131 in 1992. There are no estimates of the number of governments before 1900. Because knowing how many governments there are to count is a prerequisite to knowing that you have counted all of the governments, there are no complete counts of government activity in the United States before the census of governments taken in 1902.

Although the national government and every state published financial records in every year, systematic collection of government financial data by the national government did not begin until the 1850s. The census gathered information on state, county, and other local governments. Initially, their primary area of concern was public debt and the level of taxation, and the results were published in a series of census volumes with various titles, all something close to "Wealth, Debt, and Taxation."[1] Coverage in succeeding censuses improved, but it was not until the Census of 1902 that the census attempted complete coverage of all governments in the United States. The Census of 1902, therefore, is the starting point for the financial statistics on national, state, and local governments presented in this chapter.

The 1902 Census was followed by similar, but less complete, censuses in 1913, 1922, and 1927. These censuses were less complete in their coverage of governments (excluding small local governments) and in their coverage of functions (excluding some types of expenditures and revenues). More complete, but still partial, censuses were conducted in 1932 and 1942. Legislation mandating a complete census every five years was passed in 1952, but funding for the 1952 Census was not forthcoming. The first postwar Census of Governments was conducted in 1957. They have been conducted every five years since.

The tables for the twentieth century begin with the years 1902, 1913, 1922, 1927, and 1932, because those are the years for which data are available. Between 1932 and 1952, accounts are presented for every other year, with intercensal years based on estimates. Since 1952, the Census of Governments has collected extensive samples of government activity every year, including information on every state, all counties, and major municipal governments. Annual estimates of government finance at every level of government are available after 1952.

Readers interested in general histories of government finance in the United States can consult Dewey (1968 [1934]) or Studenski and Kroos (1963); nothing comparable to those books is available for the late twentieth century. All the data on federal, state, and local government finance in Tables Ea1–583 are taken from the Census of Governments. This information is available electronically at the Census of Governments Internet site. A complete description of the current Census of Governments methods can be found in "Federal, State, and Local Governments Government Finance and Employment Classification Manual," *Census of Governments, 1997*. The most complete discussion of all the twentieth-century data can be found in "Historical Statistics on Government Finance and Employment," *Census of Governments, 1982*. The material on federal government finance (Tables Ea584–826) is taken from various federal government sources. As discussed in the next section, the accounting concepts used vary over time, and readers with

Acknowledgments

John Wallis thanks Henry Wulf and Donna Hirsch of the Census of Governments for invaluable help with the original census data. Phillip Schuler and Luning Yu were tireless in their efforts to prepare tables and documentation. Monty Hindman asked the right questions, found the inconsistencies, and patiently reminded me of deadlines missed. Finally, the National Science Foundation has financed my research on state and local government public finance, which underlies this entire chapter.

[1] Late nineteenth-century census data can be found in U.S. Department of the Interior (1866, 1872, 1884, and 1895) and U.S. Bureau of Census (1907 and 1915).

specific interest in how these data are created should consult the references in the source notes to the individual tables. Information on government employment (Tables Ea827–965) is limited to the federal government before 1940. After 1940, information on government employment by level of government and type of employment is available through the Census of Governments. Federal government employment statistics are taken from Congressional, Civil Service Commission, and Bureau of Labor Statistics sources. Revisions to the official series made by Johnson and Libecap (1994) have also been included.

Terms and Concepts

Revenues, expenditures, and debt seem like straightforward concepts. Upon examining the tables in this chapter in detail, however, some problems arise. For example, Tables Ea132–159, Ea348–384, and Ea489–518 give total revenues for federal, state, and local governments, respectively. But those three numbers do not add up to the total revenues for all governments combined given in Table Ea24–51 How can that be? To answer that question and to understand something of the nature of the government accounts, we need to consider three problems: time, multiple governments, and governments with multiple budgets.

The first problem stems from the fact that government activity spans long periods of time but that financial accounts must be constructed for arbitrary periods, such as a year. Suppose that a government decides to build a bridge for $1,000,000. It finances construction of the bridge by issuing $1,000,000 in 5 percent bonds in year 1 and builds the bridge in year 1. Then in year 2 it levies $1,050,000 in taxes and pays off the bonds. In the first year, this government had revenues of $1,000,000 from loans and spent $1,000,000 on bridge construction. In the second year, this government had $1,050,000 in tax revenues and expenditures of $1,050,000 in loan repayments. Over the two-year period, this government collected $2,050,000 in revenues from all sources and spent $2,050,000 on expenditures for all functions.

This doesn't make sense. This government built a $1,000,000 bridge, paid $50,000 in interest, and levied $1,050,000 in taxes to pay for the two expenditures. Counting all the money that a government receives in a given year as revenues, or all the money that a government spends in a given year as expenditures, produces double counting. In the case of government borrowing and loan repayment, the problem is dealt with by the following rules: Government revenues do not include revenues from loans, and government expenditures do not include expenditures for the repayment of loan principle.

This accounting convention eliminates double counting, and it produces the concept of a budget deficit (as in series Ea586). If a government borrows money to balance its budget, since loans are not included in revenues, the amount by which expenditures exceed revenues is the current budget deficit. In subsequent years, repayments of the loan principle are not treated as expenditures, although interest payments are. When loans are being repaid, the result is a budget surplus (all else being equal). This can produce a somewhat confusing outcome because the government has a surplus but no extra money (all the surplus is going to repay debt). The concepts of budget deficits and surpluses are net concepts; the government cannot have a deficit and a surplus in the same year. They are the change in "net debt." Over time, the accumulated deficits produce a "government debt," which is the total amount

of debt owed in a given year. This is not the same as a government deficit, which refers to the amount borrowed (repaid) in a given year. Accumulated surpluses that are not used for debt repayment produce government assets (in the form of bank deposits, currency holdings, other financial assets, land, public buildings, and so forth).

The second problem introduced by time is how and when to account for revenues and expenditures. This problem is analogous to the record of your household income and expenses kept in your checkbook and the record of your income and expenses kept by the bank. Every day, you record deposits and checks in your checkbook. Every month the bank sends you a statement that lists the deposits and checks they have credited and debited to your account and the dates of the transactions. Even if the amounts in your checkbook agree exactly with the bank numbers, the dates in your checkbook for checks issued will not agree with the bank statement's dates for checks redeemed: the timing of the two accounts will be different.

Governments typically have the following arrangement. The treasurer keeps accounts of the checks written, often called warrants. The treasurer's accounts are like your checkbook. Another government office or official, often called a comptroller or an auditor, does an independent verification of the warrants that have actually been paid. The auditor's accounts are like your bank statement. The two accounts are reconciled by the amount of warrants outstanding. Over time the two accounts give the same results, but in individual years they can look very different. The distinction is important historically because the federal government accounts presented in Tables Ea584–593 and Ea636–643 are based on warrants issued for 1789–1915, daily Treasury statements for 1916–1939, a consolidated cash basis for 1940–1953, and the unified budget concept beginning 1954. These accounting methods are discussed later in this chapter. The differences between them are essentially differences in timing and how interfund transfers are accounted for.

In general, the accounts that follow are organized on the basis of warrants redeemed. That is, they are like your bank statements rather than your checkbook. They record transactions when money is received or warrants are paid, not when warrants are issued. This is a basic concept in the Census of Governments accounts that are used in Tables Ea1–583.

The third major issue arises because there are multiple levels of government in the United States, and, particularly at the local level, these multiple governments are serving the same geographic area. From the very beginning of our history, governments have transferred funds to one another. The most common example is federal government grants to the states. The first grant was embodied in the Northwest Ordinance, which gave public land to states for the support of education. When the federal government gives money to a state, how is that to be treated in the accounts? If grants are counted both as expenditures of the federal government and revenues of the state government, then the total of government expenditures will double count grants. There are four possible ways to control for double counting. Grants can be credited to the granting or to the receiving government, and this can be done for both revenues and expenditures. None of the four ways is more "true" than the others, but two are regularly used in public finance. Typically, when considering revenues, grants are credited to the granting government (grants received are subtracted from the gross revenues of the recipient government). This measure is called direct revenues because it reflects only revenues raised directly by the recipient government, as opposed to total revenues, which reflect all the nonloan receipts of the government. Expenditures are typically calculated by crediting the grants to the recipient government (grants made are subtracted from the granting government). This is why the sum of total expenditures for federal, state, and local governments exceeds the sum for total expenditures in Table Ea24–51, which gives revenues for all three levels of government combined. In Table Ea24–51, grants have been netted out.

Intergovernmental grants and other transactions occur between state and local governments and, importantly, among the multiple levels of local government. One of the most common forms of local government is the school district, and school districts often receive subsidies from state, county, or municipal governments. This poses a serious obstacle to getting an accurate picture of government activity in the nineteenth century. Not only must information be gathered on thousands of local governments, but the financial relationship between those governments needs to be sorted out to avoid double counting. In Tables Ea1–583, all local government revenues and expenditures are net of grants.

The next major problem is the existence of multiple accounts within governments. The Social Security fund of the federal government provides an example. Individuals pay payroll taxes into the Social Security fund. The amount of taxes paid into the fund usually exceeds the payments made to Social Security recipients. The fund invests its surplus receipts in federal government bonds. This creates a situation where the federal government is borrowing from itself: bonds are issued to the Social Security fund, which holds them, and interest is paid from the general fund of the federal government to the Social Security fund. Should the bonds held by the Social Security fund be counted as part of the national debt? Should interest payments to the Social Security fund be counted as expenditures of the federal government? And if so, should those interest payments be counted as the revenues of the Social Security fund, and thus of the federal government?

In general, interfund transfers within governments are not treated as revenues or expenditures. Over time, the federal government accounts in Tables Ea584–826 have used a variety of different methods to "consolidate" or "unify" the accounts of the different funds within the federal government. The details of those accounting methods can be found in the sources cited in the notes to the tables. Careful students of government should always be aware, however, that different agencies of the federal government (as well as state and local governments) do not all use the same budget concepts. Over the last several decades of the twentieth century, there has been an ongoing debate over the treatment of the Social Security fund surplus (or deficit) in the federal accounts. Because Social Security payroll taxes reflect a claim on future government expenditures, some argue that the "surplus" in the fund is not really a surplus at all, but funds set aside to cover future government liabilities (here the issue of time raises its head again). At times, the Office of Management and Budget in the executive branch and the Congressional Budget Office in the legislative branch have used different methods of accounting for Social Security (and other items), producing two very different versions of the federal accounts. Table Ea726–730 distinguishes between debt held by the public and debt held by federal agencies.

The last complication is publicly owned or operated businesses, which go under a number of names. Many local governments own and operate public utilities such as water and sewer systems, and the federal government owns and operates several large corporations to provide services in the market for home mortgages and student loans. How should the accounts of these business enterprises be incorporated into the government accounts? In the early years of the twentieth century, the receipts of most public enterprises were treated as revenues, and their expenses were treated as expenditures. Since the 1930s, the net earnings of most public enterprises are treated as an item in "other" revenues.

Tables Ea1–583 are taken from the Census of Governments accounts for the twentieth century. In these accounts, every effort has been made to consolidate all intergovernmental and intragovernmental transactions. These accounts reflect all the money paid into and paid out of governments in the United States in a given fiscal year. Tables Ea584–826 reflect the different accounting systems used by the federal government over time.

Government History: The Long View

War Finance

Four prominent historical patterns stand out in these tables. The first is the effect of wars on federal government finance. Tables Ea584–587 and Ea679–682 report federal government revenues, expenditures, and debt from 1787 to 1992. Expenditures have sharp peaks in 1812–1816 (the War of 1812), 1863–1865 (the Civil War), 1918–1919 (World War I), and 1943–1945 (World War II). The expenditure peaks are matched by revenue humps. That is, the sharp increases in wartime expenditures are matched by increases in revenues that continue for several years after the war is over. War finance involves both taxing and borrowing, as can be seen by the rising size of the budget deficit in wartime, as well as the persistently higher levels of federal debt following the wars. Expenditures for defense are reflected in two ways in the accounts. The first is direct expenditures for defense, and the second is interest on federal government debt, both in Tables Ea636–643 and Ea698–703 (this is a good example of why repayment of debt principal should not be included in expenditures). In most years, federal government expenditures on defense and interest are well over 50 percent of federal government expenditures, and in and after wars, they are well over 75 percent. Until the end of the 1930s, federal government finances were dominated by the pattern of expenditures, revenues, and debts required by war finance.

The Era of State Finance

Other patterns in government finance extend back into the nineteenth century. Over the nation's history, government finance has gone through three distinct systems. Each era was characterized by one level of government taking the lead in promoting economic development, and each era was characterized by a dominant source of government revenue. The first financial system lasted from 1790 until about 1842. In this period, state governments took the active lead in promoting economic development through infrastructure investment and legal innovation to promote corporations and banks. Infrastructure investment and land sales offered governments the opportunity to collect "asset income." State governments were uniquely situated to charter corporations and create asset income in the process. Given the national government's unwillingness to participate in transportation improvements, states took the lead in those investments as well.

Complete data are not available for state and local governments in the nineteenth century (see the estimates in Davis and Legler 1966). Tables Ea-A and Ea-B present estimates of federal, state, and local revenues per capita at decade intervals in the nineteenth century, as well as the level of government debt at selected dates.

TABLE Ea-A Government revenues, by level of government – per capita and as a share of gross national product: 1800–1900

Year	Dollars per capita				Total as a percentage of GNP
	Federal	State	Local	Total	
1800	1.96	0.42	—	—	—
1810	1.80	0.36	—	—	—
1820	2.52	0.56	—	—	—
1830	2.07	0.54	—	—	—
1840	1.50	0.88	1.23	3.60	4.0
1850	1.93	0.99	1.23	4.14	4.2
1860	3.32	1.72	2.17	7.20	5.4
1870	9.82	2.34	5.48	17.64	8.4
1880	6.39	1.70	4.98	13.07	5.7
1890	5.74	1.84	5.96	13.55	6.4
1900	6.42	2.43	8.83	17.68	7.2

Sources

Wallis (2000) and Sylla, Legler, and Wallis (1993).

TABLE Ea-B Government debt, by level of government: 1838–1902

Year	Debt (million dollars)			Percentage of total		
	State	Local	National	State	Local	National
1838	172	25	3	86.0	12.5	1.5
1841	190	25	5	86.4	11.4	2.3
1870	352	516	2,436	10.7	15.6	73.7
1880	297	826	2,090	9.2	25.7	65.0
1890	228	905	1,122	10.1	40.1	49.8
1902	230	1,877	1,178	7.0	57.1	35.9

Sources

Wallis (2000) and Sylla, Legler, and Wallis (1993).

The clearest indicator of state government activity in the nineteenth century is government debt. In the early nineteenth century up to 1842, state governments promoted banking through government ownership and assistance, and transportation through the construction and subsidy of turnpikes, canals, and railroads. In the late 1820s and 1830s there was a canal "boom." By 1841, state government borrowing for banks, canals, and railroads had increased state debt to the point that it was roughly eight times that of the national and local governments combined. State investments in transportation and banking, along with taxation of business, enabled many states on the eastern seaboard to eliminate their property taxes by the middle of the 1830s (Sylla and Wallis 1998; Wallis 2001). The high level of debt created serious problems for state governments in the economic depression that began in 1839. By the summer of 1842, eight states and the territory of Florida were in default on their debts. In the 1840s and 1850s, constitutional changes in many states made it more difficult for states to borrow money and make investments in social infrastructure.

In the early nineteenth century, the federal government usually collected more taxes than state governments, and most of those taxes went to direct military expenditures or interest on debt. With the exception of a few years with extraordinary revenues from land sales in the mid-1810s and mid-1830s, customs revenues on imported goods accounted for more than 80 percent of all federal government revenues (Table Ea588–593). Local government revenues are imperfectly estimated and appear to fall between federal revenues and state revenues. The evidence we have suggests that local government relied heavily on the property tax. As the nineteenth century progressed, local governments became larger.

The Era of Local Finance

The second financial system began to unfold in the 1840s (Legler, Sylla, and Wallis 1988). It was dominated by local governments and property taxation. Local governments grew in size and importance and took over most of the important infrastructure investment in education, roads, water systems, sewer systems, and public utilities. Property taxes continued to be the most important source of local and state finance. By 1902, local debt was $1.877 billion, about eight times the amount of total state debt. National debt was $1.178 billion in 1902, consisting primarily of debt from the Civil War (Table Ea125–131). In rough terms, local government revenues were about 40 percent higher than state revenues in 1840; in 1902, they were 4.6 time state revenues (Table Ea10–23). Local government revenues exceeded national government revenues, $858 million to $653 million. By 1900, local governments had clearly become the most active level of government in the United States.

Property taxes came to dominate the state and local revenue structure after 1842 as well. State property taxes were roughly 16 percent of revenues in the years between 1835 and 1841 (Wallis 2000, 2001); by 1902, property taxes accounted for 57 percent of all state revenues (Table Ea348–384). The continued reliance of states on the property tax was, in part, the result of the constitutional changes begun in the 1840s. State debt limitations typically established procedures for new debt issue that effectively required states to raise property taxes to fund debt. The property tax had always been a mainstay of local finance, and in 1902 property taxes were 73 percent of all revenues raised at the local level (Table Ea489–518). Overall, property taxes accounted for 42 percent of all revenues at the national, state, and local levels combined and were the single most important source of government revenue in the country (Table Ea24–51). Customs revenues continued to be the most important source of federal revenues, providing more than half of all federal revenues in most years through the end of the nineteenth century.

The Era of Federal Finance

On the eve of the Great Depression, local governments collected more than half of the tax revenues collected by all governments; they had incurred a debt for their investments equal to the national debt that remained from World War I, and property taxes were more than 40 percent of all government revenues. The Great Depression and New Deal ushered in the third financial system. This system had two expenditure components: a federal system of domestic economic programs (including infrastructure investment), funded by national grants and administered by state and local governments, and a national system of national defense and old-age

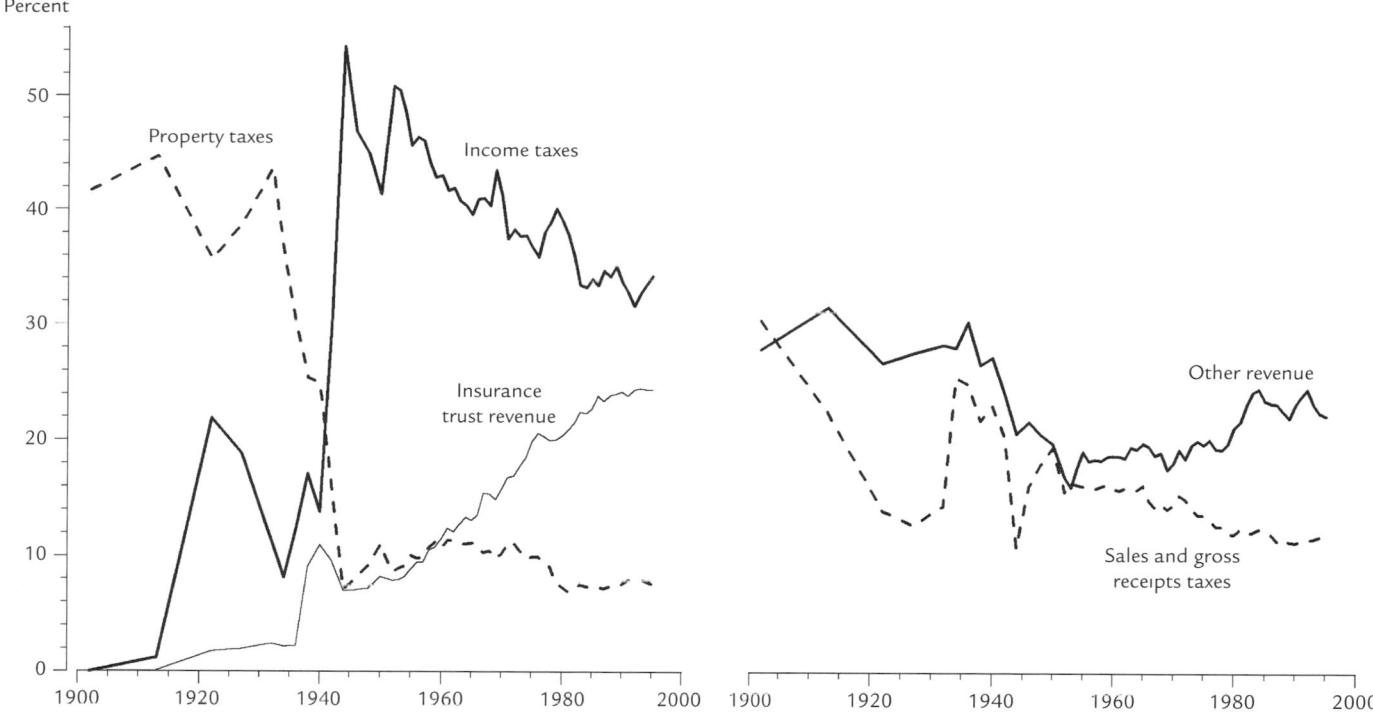

FIGURE Ea-C   Total government revenue, by source: 1902–1995

Source

Computed from Table Ea21 51.

Documentation

In this graph, "other revenue" consists of the following: other taxes (series Ea34), charges and miscellaneous revenue (series Ea35), and utility and liquor store revenue (series Ea38).

security. Income and sales taxes became the most important source of government revenue at the national and state levels (see Figure Ea-C). Even though this system has not been static, the basic relationships among national, state, and local governments remained in place for the rest of the twentieth century.

During the 1930s, the relative fiscal importance of national and local governments shifted substantially, and the national government became the largest level of government (Table Ea10–23). This change had two distinct parts: the federal system and the national system. The federal system provided welfare services, agricultural price supports, and public works projects and was financed through intergovernmental grants. Franklin D. Roosevelt and the New Deal Democrats constructed a federal system in which the national government collected revenue and the states administered expenditures. Cooperative federalism became the norm for intergovernmental relationships, and national grants to state and local governments, which had been extremely small before 1933, grew to 9.4 percent of national expenditures in 1940, 15.4 percent in 1977, and 16 percent in 1995 (Tables Ea10–23 and Ea220–246). National grants now account for roughly 16 percent of state and local revenues (Table Ea247–275), and grants from federal and state governments account for more than one third of all local government revenues (Table Ea489–518). A system of central revenue collection and decentralized expenditure and administration became the standard model for administering programs in education, highways, water and sewage systems, and public welfare.

The national system was built around the two responsibilities assumed by the national government during the New Deal and World War II: Social Security and a permanently large military establishment. The national government has always been primarily responsible for the national defense. Yet, even though expenditures for the military services and the expense of servicing and retiring war debt had occupied a large share of the national budget prior to 1940 – usually 40 to 50 percent of all spending even in peacetime – these expenditures exceeded 1 percent of gross national product (GNP) only during the Civil War and World War I. After World War II, military expenditures commanded between 5 and 7 percent of GDP each year until the late 1980s, as the nation fought cold and hot wars and the acceptable level of peacetime military preparedness increased. At the same time, commitments made during the New Deal to Social Security, together with the later commitments to Medicare and Medicaid, steadily required more resources. Outlays for Social Security, Medicaid, and Medicare were 4.5, 1.2, and 2.6 percent of GNP, respectively, in 1997 (Tables Ea171–219 and Ea698–703).

The growing importance of the federal government was associated with the growing importance of income taxes, broadly understood to include individual, corporate, and payroll taxes at both the national and the state level. One effect of the Depression was the adoption of new sales and income taxes between 1929 and 1933. National income tax collections actually fell between 1929 and 1933 and then rose through the rest of the 1930s. Income tax collections jumped during World War II when the income tax was dramatically expanded by the reduction in personal deductions, increases in marginal tax rates, and the beginning of withholding. The country emerged from the war with a completely different revenue structure, one that has remained largely in place until the present. The importance of the income tax for government revenue overall can be seen in Table Ea24–51 and for the federal government is illustrated in Tables Ea132–159, Ea588–593, and Ea683–697. Details on the federal income tax can be found in Tables Ea594–635 and Ea731–826.

Once income and payroll taxes had risen to prominence, the national government had an advantage in collecting revenues. Through the administration of the Social Security payroll tax, the national government possessed an enormous amount of information on wages and salaries, information critical to the administration of a broad-based income tax, and had experience with the administrative machinery necessary to put an income tax in place. State and local governments could piggyback on the IRS information, but as small jurisdictions they are relatively more constrained by the mobility of business and labor. In 1992, personal and corporate income taxes were $716 billion, of which 80 percent was collected by the national government, 18 percent by state governments, and only 2 percent by local governments. An additional $394 billion in Social Security payroll taxes was collected by the national government. Together, income and payroll taxes accounted for 49 percent of the $2.266 trillion in government revenues in 1992.

In 1902, property taxes were the most important source of state revenues. The ability to tax automobiles and gasoline provided states with an important new source of sales tax revenues, and by taking advantage of the information provided by the federal income tax, states were able to levy their own income taxes. By 1940, property taxes had fallen to less than 10 percent of state revenues, replaced by sales and income taxes. In the 1990s, property taxes were less than 2 percent of all state revenues, while sales taxes were roughly 26 percent and income taxes were 20 percent of state revenues (Table Ea348–384). On the other hand, property taxes continued to be the single most important source of local revenues to the end of the century (Table Ea171–219).

Sources of Government Growth in the Twentieth Century

A simple way to look at the sources of government growth is to calculate the increase in the size of government over time, and then to allocate the increase in government revenues and expenditures among different revenue sources and expenditure functions. This is done in Table Ea-D, using the data in Tables Ea24–51 and Ea61–124.

The first four columns of the top panel show the share of growth in all government revenues attributable to the growth in each revenue source, for three thirty-year periods and for the entire ninety-year period from 1902 to 1992. In the early part of the century, growth in property taxes was the most important source of new government revenue, but over the second half of the century, income taxes and insurance trust revenues (primarily Social Security and unemployment compensation payroll taxes) are the most important sources of new government revenue. The last three columns present the share of total revenue accounted for by each revenue source in 1902 and 1992, and the ratio of those shares. Over the course of the twentieth century, revenue sources where this ratio is less than one fell in relative importance. Because there were no income taxes or insurance trust revenues in 1902, the ratio of their shares cannot be calculated.

The lower panel of Table Ea-D does the same for expenditures. The first four columns show the share in the growth of all government expenditures attributable to each expenditure function. Over the course of the twentieth century, the three largest sources of government expenditure growth were Social Security, defense, and education, with each contributing roughly the same amount to overall expenditure growth. The functions that have grown smaller as a share of government expenditures are the post office, veterans' benefits, and transportation.

Over the course of the twentieth century, government in the United States became much larger. The sources of government

TABLE Ea-D Sources of government growth, by revenue source and expenditure function: 1902–1992

Revenue source or expenditure function	Percentage of growth explained by each source or function				Percentage of total accounted for by each source or function		
	1902–1932	1932–1962	1962–1992	1902–1992	1902	1992	Ratio: 1992 to 1902
Revenue							
Property taxes	44	9	8	8	42	8	0.19
Sales and gross receipts taxes	11	16	11	12	30	12	0.38
Individual income taxes	6	30	26	26	—	26	—
Corporate income taxes	8	13	5	5	—	5	—
Charges and miscellaneous revenue	16	11	20	19	15	19	1.25
Utility and liquor store revenue	5	3	3	3	4	3	0.76
Insurance trust revenue	3	13	25	24	—	24	—
Total explained	**92**	**96**	**97**	**97**	**91**	**97**	**—**
Expenditure							
Defense	5	33	13	14	10	14	1.42
Education	19	13	14	14	16	14	0.89
Welfare	4	3	9	8	2	8	3.29
Health	5	3	4	4	4	4	1.15
Interest	11	5	11	10	6	10	1.75
Other insurance trust	2	5	5	5	—	5	—
Social Security and medical	0	8	17	16	—	16	—
Total explained	**46**	**70**	**73**	**73**	**38**	**73**	**—**

Sources
Computed from Tables Ea24–51 and Ea61–124.

revenue changed dramatically. In 1902, there was no income tax, individual or corporate, and no payroll taxes for Social Security and unemployment compensation. In 1992, income and payroll taxes made up 55 percent of all government revenues. On the expenditure side, however, things have not changed nearly as much, with the exception of the growth of the welfare system and the expansion of old-age pensions through Social Security. Defense made up 10 percent of expenditures in 1902 and 14 percent in 1992; education accounted for 16 percent in 1902 and 14 percent in 1992; health was 4 percent in 1902 and 4 percent in 1992; and interest on government debt represented 6 percent in 1902 and 10 percent in 1992. American government has grown enormously, changed radically in some ways, and remained very much the same in others.

References

Davis, Lance E., and John B. Legler. 1966. "Interrelations between Government Activities and Economic Growth: The Government in the American Economy, 1815–1902: A Quantitative Study." *Journal of Economic History* 26 (4): 514–52.

Dewey, Davis R. 1968 [1934]. *Financial History of the United States,* 12th edition. Augustus Kelley.

Johnson, Ronald N., and Gary D. Libecap. 1994. *The Federal Civil Service System and the Problem of Bureaucracy.* University of Chicago Press.

Legler, John B., Richard E. Sylla, and John Joseph Wallis. 1988. "U.S. City Finances and the Growth of Government, 1850–1902." *Journal of Economic History* 48: 347–56.

Studenski, Paul, and Herman E. Kroos. 1963. *Financial History of the United States.* McGraw-Hill.

Sylla, Richard E., John B. Legler, and John Joseph Wallis. 1993. *State and Local Government [United States]: Source and Uses of Funds, City and County Data, Nineteenth Century,* computer file number 9728, Inter-University Consortium for Political and Social Research.

Sylla, Richard E., and John Joseph Wallis. 1998. "The Anatomy of a Sovereign Debt Crisis." *Japan and the World Economy* 10: 267–93.

U.S. Bureau of the Census. 1907. *Wealth, Debt, and Taxation: 1902.* Government Printing Office.

U.S. Bureau of the Census. 1915. *Wealth, Debt, and Taxation: 1913,* volumes 1 and 2. U.S. Government Printing Office.

U.S. Department of the Interior. 1866. *Statistics of the United States in 1860.* Government Printing Office.

U.S. Department of the Interior. 1872. *The Statistics of the Wealth and Industry of the United States.* Government Printing Office.

U.S. Department of the Interior, Census Office. 1884. *Valuation, Taxation, and Public Indebtedness in the United States: 1880.* Government Printing Office.

U.S. Department of the Interior, Census Office. 1895. *Report on Wealth, Debt and Taxation,* part 2, *Valuation and Taxation.* Government Printing Office.

Wallis, John Joseph. 2000. "American Government Finance in the Long Run: 1790 to 1990." *Journal of Economic Perspectives* 14: 61–82.

Wallis, John Joseph. 2001. "A History of the Property Tax in America." In Wallace E. Oates, editor. *Property Taxation and Local Government Finance.* Lincoln Institute of Land Policy.

FEDERAL, STATE, AND LOCAL GOVERNMENT FINANCES – CENSUS OF GOVERNMENTS

John Joseph Wallis

TABLE Ea1–9   Governments, by level and type: 1942–1992

Contributed by John Joseph Wallis

| | | | | Local | | | | | |
	Total	National	State	Total	County	Municipal	Township and town	School districts	Special districts
	Ea1	Ea2	Ea3	Ea4	Ea5	Ea6	Ea7	Ea8	Ea9
Year	Number	Number	Number	Number	Number	Number	Number	Number	Number
1942	155,116	1	48	155,067	3,050	16,220	18,919	108,579	8,299
1952 [1]	116,807	1	50	116,756	3,052	16,807	17,202	67,355	12,340
1957 [1]	102,392	1	50	102,341	3,050	17,215	17,198	50,454	14,424
1962	91,237	1	50	91,186	3,043	18,000	17,142	34,678	18,323
1967	81,299	1	50	81,248	3,049	18,048	17,105	21,782	21,264
1972	78,269	1	50	78,218	3,044	18,517	16,991	15,781	23,885
1977	79,913	1	50	79,862	3,042	18,862	16,822	15,174	25,962
1982	81,831	1	50	81,780	3,041	19,076	16,734	14,851	28,078
1987	83,237	1	50	83,186	3,042	19,200	16,691	14,721	29,532
1992	86,743	1	50	86,692	3,043	19,296	16,666	14,556	33,131

[1] Adjusted to include units in Alaska and Hawai'i, which adopted statehood in 1959.

Source

Figures are from data files provided by the Census of Governments. For pub-lished versions through 1982, see U.S. Department of Commerce, "Historical Statistics on Government Finance and Employment," in *Census of Governments, 1982*, volume 6, pp. 225–64.

TABLE Ea10–23   Total government revenue and expenditure, by level: 1902–1995

Contributed by John Joseph Wallis

| | Revenue | | | | Expenditure | |
	Total	Federal	State	Local	Total	Federal
	Ea10	Ea11	Ea12	Ea13	Ea14	Ea15
Fiscal year	Thousand dollars	Thousand dollars	Thousand dollars	Thousand dollars	Thousand dollars	Thousand dollars
1902	1,694,000	653,000	183,000	858,000	1,660,000	565,000
1913	2,980,000	962,000	360,000	1,658,000	3,215,000	958,000
1922	9,322,000	4,261,000	1,234,000	3,827,000	9,297,000	3,645,000
1927	12,191,000	4,469,000	1,994,000	5,728,000	11,220,000	3,410,000
1932	10,289,000	2,634,000	2,274,000	5,381,000	12,437,000	4,034,000
1934	11,300,000	3,886,000	2,452,000	4,962,000	12,807,000	4,965,000
1936	13,588,000	5,176,000	3,265,000	5,147,000	16,758,000	8,257,000
1938	17,484,000	7,226,000	4,612,000	5,646,000	17,675,000	7,687,000
1940	17,804,000	7,000,000	5,012,000	5,792,000	20,417,000	9,177,000
1942	28,352,000	16,062,000	6,012,000	6,278,000	45,576,000	34,662,000
1944	64,778,000	51,399,000	6,714,000	6,665,000	109,947,000	99,448,000
1946	61,532,000	46,405,000	7,712,000	7,416,000	79,707,000	65,640,000
1948	67,005,000	47,254,000	10,086,000	9,666,000	55,081,000	33,821,000
1950	66,680,000	43,527,000	11,480,000	11,673,000	70,334,000	42,429,000
1952	100,245,000	71,798,000	14,330,000	14,117,000	99,847,000	68,984,000
1953	104,781,000	74,239,000	15,218,000	15,323,000	110,054,000	77,117,000
1954	108,255,000	75,835,000	15,951,000	16,468,000	111,332,000	74,725,000
1955	106,404,000	71,915,000	16,678,000	17,811,000	110,717,000	70,342,000
1956	119,651,000	81,294,000	18,903,000	19,453,000	115,796,000	72,644,000
1957	129,151,000	87,066,000	20,728,000	21,357,000	125,463,000	77,910,000
1958	130,403,000	86,006,000	21,427,000	22,970,000	134,931,000	81,219,000
1959	133,085,000	85,459,000	22,912,000	24,714,000	145,748,000	87,177,000
1960	153,135,000	99,800,000	26,094,000	27,243,000	151,288,000	90,289,000
1961	158,774,000	101,341,000	27,821,000	29,612,000	164,875,000	97,852,000
1962	168,100,000	106,441,000	30,115,000	31,544,000	176,240,000	105,693,000
1963	181,192,000	114,557,000	32,750,000	33,885,000	186,058,000	110,298,000
1964	192,451,000	120,959,000	35,703,000	35,788,000	196,431,000	115,852,000

TABLE Ea10–23 Total government revenue and expenditure, by level: 1902–1995
Contributed by John Joseph Wallis

	Revenue				Expenditure	
	Total	Federal	State	Local	Total	Federal
	Ea10	Ea11	Ea12	Ea13	Ea14	Ea15
Fiscal year	Thousand dollars	Thousand dollars	Thousand dollars	Thousand dollars	Thousand dollars	Thousand dollars
1965	202,585,000	125,837,000	38,507,000	38,242,000	205,682,000	118,996,000
1966	225,547,000	141,142,000	43,000,000	41,404,000	224,813,000	129,907,000
1967	252,562,000	161,351,000	46,793,000	44,419,000	257,799,000	151,821,000
1968	265,639,000	165,239,000	52,525,000	47,875,000	282,645,000	166,411,000
1969	312,638,000	199,637,000	59,809,000	53,192,000	308,344,000	176,744,000
1970	333,810,000	205,562,000	68,691,000	59,557,000	332,985,000	184,933,000
1971	342,482,000	202,537,000	73,424,000	66,521,000	369,423,000	198,657,000
1972	382,935,310	223,378,000	84,358,059	75,199,251	399,099,142	208,602,000
1973	432,164,488	253,697,000	97,107,890	81,359,598	436,967,076	231,502,000
1974	484,658,618	288,519,000	107,645,281	88,494,337	478,339,888	252,649,000
1975	519,598,917	302,501,000	119,206,244	97,891,673	560,130,865	291,889,000
1976	570,997,152	323,224,000	139,104,124	108,669,028	625,076,477	322,028,000
1977	657,205,778	381,780,000	155,799,298	119,626,480	682,491,867	359,324,000
1978	731,736,685	429,722,000	171,549,931	130,464,754	747,172,215	401,857,000
1979	829,328,279	499,601,000	189,874,400	139,852,879	832,513,884	452,140,000
1980	932,198,054	563,690,000	212,635,251	155,872,803	958,656,087	526,329,000
1981	1,075,387,444	658,954,000	240,042,286	176,391,158	1,109,814,363	624,640,000
1982	1,146,270,792	685,835,000	261,732,939	198,702,853	1,233,263,485	710,469,000
1983	1,181,182,206	677,817,000	284,933,537	218,431,669	1,346,476,005	781,578,000
1984	1,307,482,525	752,421,000	315,636,835	239,424,690	1,427,673,024	829,173,000
1985	1,418,781,230	804,877,000	349,529,743	264,374,487	1,580,813,648	924,889,000
1986	1,515,657,107	845,378,000	382,733,690	287,545,417	1,696,120,835	980,769,000
1987	1,679,165,267	950,144,000	414,412,573	314,608,694	1,811,732,910	1,037,143,000
1988	1,775,999,234	1,009,484,000	434,184,462	332,330,772	1,920,097,382	1,093,906,000
1989	1,917,735,704 [1]	1,089,757,000	471,165,491	356,813,213	2,030,753,224	1,142,821,000
1990	2,046,997,599	1,151,685,000	505,842,733	389,469,866	2,218,825,620	1,246,131,000
1991	2,124,211,491	1,197,448,000	516,414,406	410,349,085	2,379,168,661	1,319,364,000
1992	2,266,764,769	1,255,952,000	573,593,425	437,219,344	2,494,424,256	1,341,275,000
1993	2,377,235,218	1,305,071,000	616,940,179	455,224,039	2,575,969,756	1,365,873,000
1994	2,511,555,862	1,395,556,000	637,184,080	478,815,782	2,673,005,696	1,412,364,000
1995	2,680,424,110	1,491,271,000	690,845,885	498,307,225	2,818,796,004	1,471,033,000

	Expenditure		As a percentage of total					
			Revenue			Expenditure		
	State	Local	Federal	State	Local	Federal	State	Local
	Ea16	Ea17	Ea18	Ea19	Ea20	Ea21	Ea22	Ea23
Fiscal year	Thousand dollars	Thousand dollars	Percent	Percent	Percent	Percent	Percent	Percent
1902	136,000	959,000	38.6	10.8	50.7	34.0	8.2	57.8
1913	297,000	1,960,000	32.3	12.1	55.6	29.8	9.2	61.0
1922	1,085,000	4,567,000	45.7	13.2	41.1	39.2	11.7	49.1
1927	1,451,000	6,359,000	36.7	16.4	47.0	30.4	12.9	56.7
1932	2,028,000	6,375,000	25.6	22.1	52.3	32.4	16.3	51.3
1934	2,143,000	5,699,000	34.4	21.7	43.9	38.8	16.7	44.5
1936	2,445,000	6,056,000	38.1	24.0	37.9	49.3	14.6	36.1
1938	3,082,000	6,906,000	41.3	26.4	32.3	43.5	17.4	39.1
1940	3,555,000	7,685,000	39.3	28.2	32.5	45.0	17.4	37.6
1942	3,563,000	7,351,000	56.7	21.2	22.1	76.1	7.8	16.1
1944	3,319,000	7,180,000	79.4	10.4	10.3	90.5	3.0	6.5
1946	4,974,000	9,093,000	75.4	12.5	12.1	82.4	6.2	11.4
1948	7,897,000	13,363,000	70.5	15.1	14.4	61.4	14.3	24.3
1950	10,864,000	17,041,000	65.3	17.2	17.5	60.3	15.5	24.2
1952	10,790,000	20,073,000	71.6	14.3	14.1	69.1	10.8	20.1
1953	11,466,000	21,471,000	70.9	14.5	14.6	70.1	10.4	19.5
1954	13,008,000	23,599,000	70.1	14.7	15.2	67.1	11.7	21.2

Note appears at end of table

(continued)

TABLE Ea10–23   Total government revenue and expenditure, by level: 1902–1995 *Continued*

	Expenditure		As a percentage of total					
			Revenue			Expenditure		
	State	Local	Federal	State	Local	Federal	State	Local
	Ea16	Ea17	Ea18	Ea19	Ea20	Ea21	Ea22	Ea23
Fiscal year	Thousand dollars	Thousand dollars	Percent	Percent	Percent	Percent	Percent	Percent
1955	14,371,000	26,004,000	67.6	15.7	16.7	63.5	13.0	23.5
1956	15,148,000	28,004,000	67.9	15.8	16.3	62.7	13.1	24.2
1957	16,796,000	30,757,000	67.4	16.1	16.5	62.1	13.4	24.5
1958	19,991,000	33,721,000	66.0	16.4	17.6	60.2	14.8	25.0
1959	22,436,000	36,136,000	64.2	17.2	18.6	59.8	15.4	24.8
1960	22,152,000	38,847,000	65.2	17.0	17.8	59.7	14.6	25.7
1961	24,578,000	42,445,000	63.8	17.5	18.7	59.4	14.9	25.7
1962	25,495,000	45,053,000	63.3	17.9	18.8	60.0	14.5	25.6
1963	27,698,000	48,062,000	63.2	18.1	18.7	59.3	14.9	25.8
1964	29,616,000	50,964,000	62.9	18.6	18.6	59.0	15.1	25.9
1965	31,465,000	55,221,000	62.1	19.0	18.9	57.9	15.3	26.9
1966	34,195,000	60,711,000	62.6	19.1	18.4	57.8	15.2	27.0
1967	39,704,000	66,274,000	63.9	18.5	17.6	58.9	15.4	25.7
1968	44,304,000	71,930,000	62.2	19.8	18.0	58.9	15.7	25.5
1969	49,448,000	82,152,000	63.9	19.1	17.0	57.3	16.0	26.6
1970	56,163,000	91,889,000	61.6	20.6	17.8	55.5	16.9	27.6
1971	66,200,000	104,566,000	59.1	21.4	19.4	53.8	17.9	28.3
1972	72,497,325	117,999,817	58.3	22.0	19.6	52.3	18.2	29.6
1973	78,013,610	127,451,466	58.7	22.5	18.8	53.0	17.9	29.2
1974	86,193,242	139,497,646	59.5	22.2	18.3	52.8	18.0	29.2
1975	106,904,685	161,337,180	58.2	22.9	18.8	52.1	19.1	28.8
1976	123,067,559	179,980,918	56.6	24.4	19.0	51.5	19.7	28.8
1977	128,765,247	194,402,620	58.1	23.7	18.2	52.7	18.9	28.5
1978	136,544,926	208,770,289	58.7	23.4	17.8	53.8	18.3	27.9
1979	148,690,147	231,683,737	60.2	22.9	16.9	54.3	17.9	27.8
1980	173,307,542	259,019,545	60.5	22.8	16.7	54.9	18.1	27.0
1981	198,347,660	286,826,703	61.3	22.3	16.4	56.3	17.9	25.8
1982	211,386,194	311,408,291	59.8	22.8	17.3	57.6	17.1	25.3
1983	232,782,048	332,115,957	57.4	24.1	18.5	58.1	17.3	24.7
1984	242,808,738	355,691,286	57.6	24.1	18.3	58.1	17.0	24.9
1985	269,171,337	386,753,311	56.7	24.6	18.6	58.5	17.0	24.5
1986	292,267,062	423,084,773	55.8	25.3	19.0	57.8	17.2	24.9
1987	314,420,921	460,168,989	56.6	24.7	18.7	57.3	17.4	25.4
1988	333,005,115	491,186,267	56.8	24.5	18.7	57.1	17.3	25.6
1989	359,661,315	528,270,909	56.8	24.6	18.6	56.3	17.7	26.0
1990	397,290,778	575,403,842	56.3	24.7	19.0	56.2	17.9	25.9
1991	442,295,272	617,509,389	56.4	24.3	19.3	55.5	18.6	26.0
1992	498,774,398	654,374,858	55.4	25.3	19.3	53.8	20.0	26.2
1993	529,167,089	680,929,667	54.9	26.0	19.2	53.0	20.5	26.4
1994	550,276,118	710,365,578	55.6	25.4	19.1	52.8	20.6	26.6
1995	596,325,152	751,437,852	55.6	25.8	18.6	52.2	21.2	26.7

[1] The total presented here equals the sum of the components and differs from the total presented in the source.

Source

Figures are from data files provided by the Census of Governments. For published versions through 1982, see U.S. Department of Commerce, "Historical Statistics on Government Finance and Employment," in *Census of Governments, 1982*, volume 6, pp. 225–64.

Documentation

See the text for Table Ea24–51.

TABLE Ea24–51   Total government revenue, by source: 1902–1995

Contributed by John Joseph Wallis

			General				
					Taxes		
						Sales and gross receipts	
	Total revenue	Total	Total	Property	Total	General sales	Custom duties
	Ea24	Ea25	Ea26	Ea27	Ea28	Ea29	Ea30
Fiscal year	Thousand dollars	Thousand dollars	Thousand dollars	Thousand dollars	Thousand dollars	Thousand dollars	Thousand dollars
1902	1,694,000	1,632,000	1,373,000	706,000	515,000	—	243,000
1913	2,980,000	2,862,000	2,271,000	1,332,000	670,000	—	310,000
1922	9,322,000	8,894,000	7,387,000	3,321,000	1,306,000	—	318,000
1927	12,191,000	11,551,000	9,451,000	4,730,000	1,558,000	—	585,000
1932	10,289,000	9,578,000	7,977,000	4,487,000	1,485,000	—	311,000
1934	11,300,000	10,463,000	8,854,000	4,076,000	2,885,000	—	299,000
1936	13,588,000	12,533,000	10,583,000	4,093,000	3,389,000	—	372,000
1938	17,484,000	15,023,000	12,949,000	4,440,000	3,815,000	—	343,000
1940	17,804,000	14,858,000	12,688,000	4,430,000	4,109,000	—	331,000
1942	28,352,000	24,347,000	20,793,000	4,537,000	5,776,000	—	369,000
1944	64,778,000	58,617,000	49,095,000	4,604,000	7,012,000	—	417,000
1946	61,532,000	55,130,000	46,380,000	4,986,000	9,950,000	—	424,000
1948	67,005,000	59,666,000	51,218,000	6,126,000	12,092,000	—	403,000
1950	66,680,000	58,486,000	51,100,000	7,349,000	12,997,000	—	407,000
1952	100,245,000	89,230,000	79,066,000	8,652,000	15,689,000	2,598,000	532,000
1953	104,781,000	93,124,000	83,704,000	9,375,000	17,279,000	2,860,000	596,000
1954	108,255,000	95,844,000	84,476,000	9,967,000	17,643,000	2,948,000	542,000
1955	106,404,000	93,264,000	81,072,000	10,735,000	17,221,000	3,090,000	585,000
1956	119,651,000	104,494,000	91,593,000	11,749,000	19,160,000	3,582,000	602,000
1957	129,151,000	112,723,000	98,632,000	12,864,000	20,594,000	4,029,000	735,000
1958	130,403,000	112,466,000	98,387,000	14,047,000	21,102,000	4,206,000	782,000
1959	133,085,000	114,178,000	99,636,000	14,983,000	21,769,000	4,444,000	925,000
1960	153,135,000	130,618,000	113,120,000	16,405,000	24,452,000	5,177,000	1,105,000
1961	158,774,000	133,969,000	116,331,000	18,002,000	25,112,000	5,431,000	982,000
1962	168,100,000	142,397,000	123,816,000	19,054,000	26,922,000	6,069,000	1,142,000
1963	181,192,000	152,314,000	131,078,000	20,089,000	28,671,000	6,604,000	1,205,000
1964	192,451,000	160,740,000	138,292,000	21,241,000	30,538,000	7,254,000	1,252,000
1965	202,585,000	169,691,000	144,953,000	22,583,000	32,904,000	7,981,000	1,442,000
1966	225,547,000	188,368,000	160,742,000	24,670,000	33,726,000	9,225,000	1,767,000
1967	252,562,000	206,696,000	176,121,000	26,047,000	36,336,000	10,124,000	1,901,000
1968	265,639,000	217,323,000	185,126,000	27,747,000	39,186,000	11,645,000	2,038,000
1969	312,638,000	258,242,000	222,708,000	30,673,000	44,345,000	14,038,000	2,319,000
1970	333,810,000	272,480,000	232,877,000	34,054,000	48,619,000	16,128,000	2,430,000
1971	342,482,000	275,669,000	232,252,000	37,852,000	52,660,000	17,812,000	2,591,000
1972	382,935,310	308,321,463	263,342,945	42,877,189	57,618,639	20,345,981	3,287,000
1973	432,164,488	344,419,027	286,131,637	45,282,538	61,768,584	22,992,171	3,188,000
1974	484,658,618	383,133,898	314,784,652	47,704,699	66,631,896	26,314,019	3,450,000
1975	519,598,917	402,877,200	331,435,023	51,490,941	70,904,790	29,101,627	4,289,000
1976	570,997,152	438,299,477	358,226,932	57,001,463	76,264,522	32,043,914	4,496,000
1977	657,205,778	506,324,419	419,778,200	62,527,223	83,820,515	36,367,540	5,394,000
1978	731,736,685	565,583,090	468,161,079	66,421,967	93,049,273	41,472,895	6,823,000
1979	829,328,279	640,499,955	524,403,549	64,943,568	100,961,148	46,558,597	7,688,000
1980	932,198,054	716,629,027	574,243,640	68,498,743	111,960,588	51,327,616	7,436,000
1981	1,075,387,444	820,814,308	650,228,139	74,969,444	134,532,420	55,641,390	8,161,000
1982	1,146,270,792	866,392,435	671,514,820	82,067,442	139,287,948	60,573,300	8,917,000
1983	1,181,182,206	878,633,439	665,615,467	89,104,863	144,717,638	64,889,896	8,727,000
1984	1,307,482,525	975,308,267	735,022,816	96,456,745	163,556,342	75,211,609	11,463,000
1985	1,418,781,230	1,050,480,599	804,403,541	103,756,624	175,534,711	84,295,648	12,176,000
1986	1,515,657,107	1,106,860,104	844,977,186	111,709,287	182,050,563	90,694,713	13,420,000
1987	1,679,165,267	1,236,520,042	944,202,978	121,202,638	192,513,686	96,602,538	15,138,000
1988	1,775,999,234	1,298,855,848	998,340,719	132,212,301	209,056,331	105,237,831	16,317,000
1989	1,917,491,819	1,400,517,613	1,084,500,032	142,524,733	218,542,635	112,597,602	16,450,000
1990	2,046,997,599	1,493,178,661	1,133,885,648	155,613,321	231,854,755	121,286,594	16,810,000
1991	2,124,211,491	1,557,212,898	1,167,337,132	167,999,489	244,065,228	125,448,814	16,034,000
1992	2,266,764,769	1,651,352,462	1,218,900,016	180,336,841	262,013,143	131,979,152	17,480,000
1993	2,377,235,218	1,730,096,745	1,307,232,495	189,743,930	277,115,859	138,822,010	18,931,000
1994	2,511,555,862	1,828,747,088	1,403,908,938	197,141,008	296,387,301	149,039,888	20,264,000
1995	2,680,424,110	1,955,775,201	1,504,991,796	203,451,246	312,453,397	160,166,175	19,438,000

(continued)

TABLE Ea24–51 Total government revenue, by source: 1902–1995 *Continued*

	General						
	Taxes				Charges and miscellaneous		
		Income					
	Total	Individual	Corporate	Other	Total	Charges	Miscellaneous
	Ea31	Ea32	Ea33	Ea34	Ea35	Ea36	Ea37
Fiscal year	Thousand dollars	Thousand dollars	Thousand dollars	Thousand dollars	Thousand dollars	Thousand dollars	Thousand dollars
1902	0	0	0	152,000	259,000	—	—
1913	35,000	0	35,000	234,000	591,000	—	—
1922	2,040,000	—	—	720,000	1,507,000	—	—
1927	2,300,000	949,000	1,351,000	863,000	2,100,000	—	—
1932	1,156,000	479,000	677,000	849,000	1,601,000	—	—
1934	920,000	485,000	435,000	973,000	1,609,000	—	—
1936	1,677,000	819,000	858,000	1,424,000	1,950,000	—	—
1938	2,993,000	1,495,000	1,498,000	1,701,000	2,074,000	—	—
1940	2,462,000	1,183,000	1,279,000	1,687,000	2,170,000	—	—
1942	8,480,000	3,481,000	4,999,000	2,000,000	3,554,000	—	—
1944	35,231,000	20,043,000	15,188,000	2,248,000	9,522,000	—	—
1946	28,859,000	16,579,000	12,280,000	2,585,000	8,750,000	—	—
1948	30,118,000	19,848,000	10,270,000	2,882,000	8,448,000	—	—
1950	27,614,000	16,533,000	11,081,000	3,140,000	7,386,000	—	—
1952	50,991,000	28,919,000	22,072,000	3,734,000	10,163,000	8,049,000	2,115,000
1953	52,936,000	30,881,000	22,055,000	4,114,000	9,420,000	7,173,000	2,249,000
1954	52,548,000	30,669,000	21,879,000	4,318,000	11,369,000	8,300,000	3,068,000
1955	48,588,000	29,984,000	18,604,000	4,528,000	12,192,000	8,833,000	3,359,000
1956	55,495,000	33,725,000	21,770,000	5,189,000	12,900,000	9,096,000	3,804,000
1957	59,525,000	37,374,000	22,151,000	5,649,000	14,091,000	10,583,000	3,508,000
1958	57,575,000	36,483,000	21,092,000	5,663,000	14,079,000	10,086,000	3,992,000
1959	57,023,000	38,713,000	18,310,000	5,861,000	14,542,000	10,540,000	4,001,000
1960	65,852,000	43,178,000	22,674,000	6,411,000	17,499,000	12,451,000	5,047,000
1961	66,171,000	43,951,000	22,220,000	7,046,000	17,637,000	12,805,000	4,833,000
1962	70,439,000	48,608,000	21,831,000	7,401,000	18,581,000	13,670,000	4,911,000
1963	73,941,000	50,857,000	23,084,000	8,377,000	21,235,000	15,448,000	5,788,000
1964	77,676,000	52,488,000	25,188,000	8,837,000	22,448,000	16,279,000	6,170,000
1965	80,272,000	52,882,000	27,390,000	9,194,000	24,739,000	17,648,000	7,091,000
1966	92,317,000	60,206,000	32,111,000	10,029,000	27,626,000	19,189,000	8,439,000
1967	103,549,000	67,351,000	36,198,000	10,189,000	30,575,000	21,084,000	9,491,000
1968	107,217,000	76,034,000	31,183,000	10,976,000	32,197,000	22,182,000	10,017,000
1969	136,015,000	96,157,000	39,858,000	11,675,000	35,534,000	24,784,000	10,750,000
1970	137,791,000	101,224,000	36,567,000	12,413,000	39,603,000	26,273,000	13,330,000
1971	128,339,000	98,130,000	30,209,000	13,401,000	43,417,000	29,329,000	14,088,000
1972	146,545,399	109,963,561	36,581,838	16,301,718	44,978,518	31,368,620	13,609,898
1973	162,816,506	121,239,512	41,576,994	16,264,009	58,287,390	37,739,093	20,548,297
1974	183,077,565	138,443,047	44,634,518	17,370,492	68,349,246	41,511,628	26,837,618
1975	191,103,252	143,840,152	47,263,100	17,936,040	71,442,237	45,156,313	26,285,924
1976	204,859,685	156,177,988	48,681,697	20,101,262	80,072,545	51,852,432	28,220,113
1977	250,037,083	185,971,274	64,065,809	23,393,379	86,546,219	56,227,063	30,319,156
1978	284,854,596	214,164,300	70,690,296	23,835,243	97,422,011	61,836,044	35,585,967
1979	332,577,310	254,772,786	77,804,524	25,921,523	116,096,406	70,426,100	45,670,306
1980	364,070,095	286,148,764	77,921,331	29,714,214	142,385,387	80,132,026	62,253,361
1981	407,257,923	331,977,426	75,280,497	33,468,352	170,586,169	90,533,600	80,052,569
1982	413,084,490	348,849,164	64,235,326	37,074,940	194,877,615	103,203,307	91,674,308
1983	395,346,574	344,066,927	51,279,647	36,446,392	213,017,972	113,172,024	99,845,948
1984	434,517,438	360,483,897	74,033,541	40,492,291	240,285,451	133,340,177	106,945,274
1985	481,762,589	401,279,403	80,483,186	43,349,617	246,077,058	135,314,626	110,762,432
1986	506,461,057	423,323,912	83,137,145	44,756,279	261,882,918	143,691,020	118,191,898
1987	582,842,354	476,491,727	106,350,627	47,644,300	292,317,064	164,321,717	127,995,347
1988	607,388,977	489,530,539	117,858,438	49,683,110	300,515,129	174,624,604	125,890,525
1989	672,709,848	543,497,192	129,212,656	50,722,816	316,017,581	180,898,430	135,119,151
1990	689,597,059	572,523,737	117,073,322	56,820,513	359,293,013	204,417,659	154,875,354
1991	697,496,277	577,167,832	120,328,445	57,776,138	389,875,766	211,527,530	178,348,236
1992	716,253,089	592,102,837	124,150,252	60,296,943	432,452,446	227,786,683	204,665,763
1993	776,852,698	632,915,406	143,937,292	63,520,008	422,864,250	243,963,881	178,900,369
1994	840,569,436	671,864,920	168,704,516	69,811,193	424,838,150	257,836,144	167,002,006
1995	916,583,409	728,173,595	188,409,814	72,503,744	450,783,405	267,922,415	182,860,990

TABLE 24–51   Total government revenue, by source: 1902–1995 *Continued*

		Utility and liquor store					
		Utility					
Fiscal year	Total	Total	Water	Electric	Gas	Transit	Liquor store
	Ea38	Ea39	Ea40	Ea41	Ea42	Ea43	Ea44
	Thousand dollars	Thousand dollars	Thousand dollars	Thousand dollars	Thousand dollars	Thousand dollars	Thousand dollars
1902	62,000	60,000	56,000	3,000	1,000	0	2,000
1913	116,000	116,000	99,000	16,000	1,000	0	0
1922	266,000	266,000	175,000	72,000	6,000	13,000	0
1927	403,000	403,000	247,000	111,000	10,000	35,000	0
1932	463,000	463,000	317,000	111,000	10,000	25,000	0
1934	590,000	499,000	342,000	115,000	10,000	32,000	91,000
1936	747,000	558,000	369,000	131,000	17,000	41,000	189,000
1938	877,000	605,000	371,000	169,000	18,000	47,000	272,000
1940	998,000	704,000	401,000	220,000	25,000	58,000	294,000
1942	1,277,000	887,000	439,000	251,000	27,000	170,000	390,000
1944	1,633,000	1,066,000	521,000	305,000	32,000	208,000	567,000
1946	2,033,000	1,169,000	556,000	348,000	38,000	227,000	864,000
1948	2,511,000	1,565,000	640,000	474,000	52,000	399,000	946,000
1950	2,712,000	1,808,000	705,000	574,000	61,000	468,000	904,000
1952	3,108,000	2,071,000	839,000	683,000	70,000	479,000	1,037,000
1953	3,324,000	2,237,000	939,000	713,000	85,000	500,000	1,087,000
1954	3,496,000	2,403,000	971,000	787,000	90,000	554,000	1,093,000
1955	3,688,000	2,609,000	1,092,000	870,000	104,000	544,000	1,079,000
1956	3,854,000	2,718,000	1,162,000	887,000	127,000	542,000	1,136,000
1957	4,127,000	2,944,000	1,235,000	1,011,000	157,000	541,000	1,183,000
1958	4,211,000	3,041,000	1,256,000	1,096,000	173,000	516,000	1,170,000
1959	4,536,000	3,320,000	1,388,000	1,178,000	190,000	565,000	1,216,000
1960	4,877,000	3,613,000	1,529,000	1,307,000	196,000	581,000	1,264,000
1961	5,116,000	3,856,000	1,621,000	1,450,000	197,000	588,000	1,260,000
1962	5,308,000	4,026,000	1,725,000	1,422,000	236,000	643,000	1,282,000
1963	5,790,000	4,474,000	1,865,000	1,728,000	242,000	639,000	1,316,000
1964	5,975,000	4,616,000	1,917,000	1,718,000	266,000	715,000	1,359,000
1965	6,355,000	4,908,000	2,004,000	1,833,000	295,000	776,000	1,447,000
1966	6,619,000	5,069,000	2,115,000	1,911,000	300,000	743,000	1,550,000
1967	6,911,000	5,246,000	2,187,000	1,881,000	319,000	860,000	1,665,000
1968	7,502,000	5,683,000	2,313,000	2,119,000	332,000	919,000	1,819,000
1969	7,840,000	5,931,000	2,464,000	2,166,000	366,000	934,000	1,908,000
1970	8,614,000	6,608,000	2,687,000	2,385,000	401,000	1,135,000	2,006,000
1971	9,359,000	7,276,000	2,980,000	2,644,000	439,000	1,213,000	2,083,000
1972	9,828,273	7,700,733	3,171,464	2,831,019	436,404	1,261,846	2,127,540
1973	10,897,601	8,621,598	3,463,401	3,355,030	535,981	1,267,186	2,276,003
1974	11,747,523	9,392,073	3,712,052	3,762,593	551,214	1,366,214	2,355,450
1975	13,334,934	10,867,284	4,142,177	4,689,262	625,178	1,410,667	2,467,650
1976	15,126,332	12,572,928	4,463,077	5,819,137	724,668	1,566,046	2,553,404
1977	17,541,015	14,990,850	4,995,345	7,142,381	862,238	1,990,886	2,550,165
1978	20,011,482	17,252,258	5,512,059	8,675,475	1,008,554	2,056,170	2,759,224
1979	22,628,517	19,730,480	6,249,831	9,938,477	1,296,679	2,245,493	2,898,037
1980	25,559,447	22,358,861	6,765,752	11,387,176	1,808,756	2,397,177	3,200,586
1981	29,895,616	26,617,125	7,717,612	13,714,634	2,219,838	2,965,041	3,278,491
1982	34,040,011	30,697,066	8,472,461	16,027,491	2,670,730	3,526,384	3,342,945
1983	37,254,155	33,943,059	9,528,164	17,822,871	3,046,919	3,545,105	3,311,096
1984	40,613,586	37,373,901	10,466,984	19,613,735	3,501,467	3,791,715	3,239,685
1985	44,772,026	41,536,534	11,979,703	21,767,248	3,573,130	4,216,453	3,235,492
1986	47,162,720	43,850,149	13,260,170	22,845,860	3,291,135	4,452,984	3,312,571
1987	50,167,729	46,809,362	14,402,746	24,672,325	2,970,976	4,763,315	3,358,367
1988	52,515,781	49,225,618	15,314,515	26,239,582	2,905,124	4,766,397	3,290,163
1989	56,224,957	52,909,768	16,767,400	28,186,841	2,929,647	5,025,880	3,315,189
1990	58,642,454	55,201,882	17,674,155	29,268,197	3,043,413	5,216,117	3,440,572
1991	60,736,278	57,165,113	18,034,149	30,489,473	3,012,652	5,628,839	3,571,165
1992	63,239,911	59,608,105	19,464,412	31,421,710	3,056,038	5,665,945	3,631,806
1993	65,245,971	61,604,650	20,450,540	31,985,302	3,333,573	5,835,235	3,641,321
1994	70,075,062	66,468,546	22,692,069	33,807,601	3,712,533	6,256,343	3,606,516
1995	72,270,882	68,633,703	23,879,068	34,626,919	3,588,145	6,539,571	3,637,179

(continued)

TABLE 24–51   Total government revenue, by source: 1902–1995   *Continued*

			Insurance trust				
			Unemployment compensation			Social Security and medical insurance	
Fiscal year	Total	Employee retirement	Total	Payroll taxes	Workers' compensation		Other
	Ea45	Ea46	Ea47	Ea48	Ea49	Ea50	Ea51
	Thousand dollars	Thousand dollars	Thousand dollars	Thousand dollars	Thousand dollars	Thousand dollars	Thousand dollars
1902	0	0	0	0	—	0	0
1913	2,000	2,000	0	0	—	0	0
1922	162,000	59,000	0	0	—	0	103,000
1927	237,000	92,000	0	0	—	0	145,000
1932	248,000	126,000	0	0	—	0	122,000
1934	247,000	136,000	0	0	—	0	111,000
1936	308,000	158,000	23,000	23,000	—	0	127,000
1938	1,584,000	182,000	731,000	706,000	—	387,000	284,000
1940	1,948,000	214,000	931,000	896,000	—	538,000	265,000
1942	2,728,000	285,000	1,218,000	1,159,000	—	869,000	356,000
1944	4,528,000	498,000	1,518,000	1,432,000	—	1,260,000	1,252,000
1946	4,369,000	571,000	1,282,000	1,154,000	—	1,201,000	1,315,000
1948	4,828,000	672,000	1,337,000	1,193,000	—	1,616,000	1,203,000
1950	5,482,000	965,000	1,190,000	1,042,000	173,000	2,107,000	1,046,000
1952	7,907,000	1,253,000	1,612,000	1,452,000	224,000	3,547,000	1,270,000
1953	8,333,000	1,332,000	1,571,000	1,389,000	249,000	4,060,000	1,120,000
1954	8,914,000	1,502,000	1,488,000	1,284,000	270,000	4,554,000	1,100,000
1955	9,452,000	1,622,000	1,345,000	1,156,000	279,000	5,087,000	1,120,000
1956	11,303,000	1,872,000	1,536,000	1,350,000	292,000	6,442,000	1,161,000
1957	12,301,000	2,130,000	1,799,000	1,588,000	344,000	6,857,000	1,171,000
1958	13,726,000	2,365,000	1,807,000	1,587,000	340,000	8,044,000	1,168,000
1959	14,371,000	2,671,000	1,935,000	1,754,000	331,000	8,294,000	1,141,000
1960	17,642,000	2,902,000	2,476,000	2,295,000	363,000	10,656,000	1,243,000
1961	19,690,000	3,223,000	2,669,000	2,473,000	402,000	12,131,000	1,265,000
1962	20,395,000	3,475,000	2,967,000	2,802,000	416,000	12,289,000	1,246,000
1963	23,088,000	3,798,000	3,331,000	3,150,000	459,000	14,195,000	1,305,000
1964	25,735,000	4,117,000	3,404,000	3,197,000	498,000	16,386,000	1,330,000
1965	26,539,000	4,494,000	3,387,000	3,145,000	530,000	16,742,000	1,386,000
1966	30,558,000	4,870,000	3,476,000	3,188,000	557,000	20,023,000	1,633,000
1967	38,956,000	5,492,000	3,422,000	3,057,000	617,000	27,663,000	1,763,000
1968	40,814,000	6,240,000	3,103,000	2,685,000	656,000	29,029,000	1,785,000
1969	46,557,000	7,133,000	3,174,000	2,683,000	714,000	33,649,000	1,887,000
1970	52,716,000	8,206,000	3,224,000	2,654,000	770,000	38,485,000	2,032,000
1971	57,454,000	9,364,000	3,215,000	2,617,000	863,000	41,909,000	2,101,000
1972	64,785,574	10,624,579	3,712,741	3,248,930	916,660	47,341,000	2,190,594
1973	76,847,860	12,316,059	5,076,444	4,621,341	1,047,975	56,070,000	2,337,382
1974	89,777,197	13,302,437	6,442,412	5,858,320	1,218,241	66,059,000	2,755,107
1975	103,386,723	14,981,054	8,479,000	5,478,929	1,405,977	75,617,000	2,903,692
1976	117,571,343	17,364,643	15,284,000	6,291,958	1,667,583	80,320,000	2,935,117
1977	133,340,344	20,071,944	15,464,586	8,727,094	2,039,338	92,495,000	3,269,476
1978	146,142,113	22,153,901	13,361,703	10,142,632	2,649,233	104,502,000	3,475,276
1979	166,199,807	25,309,101	13,135,130	12,011,424	3,276,085	120,522,000	3,957,491
1980	190,009,580	29,059,583	13,689,698	11,835,400	3,604,269	139,370,000	4,286,030
1981	224,677,520	34,251,585	18,732,198	11,386,269	3,579,148	163,834,000	4,280,589
1982	245,838,346	38,244,743	17,103,393	12,142,831	3,993,365	181,598,000	4,898,845
1983	265,294,612	46,831,072	21,740,459	13,061,668	4,160,424	187,189,000	5,373,657
1984	291,560,672	50,613,014	16,949,179	17,368,912	4,391,508	213,520,000	6,086,971
1985	323,528,605	57,803,523	17,860,533	18,578,522	4,984,635	236,565,000	6,314,914
1986	361,634,283	73,906,494	18,487,811	18,935,912	5,668,722	257,263,000	6,308,256
1987	392,477,496	83,977,004	19,129,064	17,796,353	6,481,660	275,874,000	7,015,768
1988	424,627,605	82,262,122	17,467,502	17,943,337	7,373,060	310,023,000	7,501,921
1989	460,749,249	85,597,736	19,905,164	17,465,650	8,250,788	339,493,000	7,502,561
1990	495,176,484	98,668,525	18,540,960	15,586,449	9,049,646	361,684,000	7,233,353
1991	506,262,315	91,651,826	18,209,351	14,899,370	10,257,667	378,510,000	7,633,471
1992	552,172,396	110,510,752	27,153,195	15,995,375	11,749,994	394,268,000	8,490,455
1993	581,892,502	117,738,103	34,713,445	18,683,005	12,977,095	407,860,000	8,603,859
1994	612,733,712	118,843,989	29,928,482	21,074,649	13,376,298	441,983,000	8,601,943
1995	652,378,027	127,034,119	37,248,702	33,452,393	13,161,333	466,367,000	8,566,873

TABLE 24–51 Total government revenue, by source: 1902–1995 *Continued*

Source

Figures are from data files provided by the Census of Governments. For published versions through 1982, see U.S. Department of Commerce, "Historical Statistics on Government Finance and Employment," in *Census of Governments, 1982*, volume 6, pp. 225–64.

Documentation

Except as noted, duplicative transactions between governments are excluded. Also, unless noted, revenues and expenditures are "direct" or "own-source." In other words, the figures do not include revenues from, or expenditures for, intergovernmental grants.

General revenues and expenditures exclude utility, liquor store, and insurance trust finances.

There is an inconsistency between the federal revenue data and the state-local expenditure data. Federal intergovernmental revenue is less than state-local intergovernmental transfers (expenditures) to the federal government.

Unless noted otherwise, federal Social Security and medical insurance expenditures cover Old-Age Survivors, Disability, and Health Insurance (OASDHI) and Medicare.

Alaska is included beginning 1960; Hawai'i beginning 1961.

Series Ea45. Excludes interest on federal securities held by federal agencies and funds.

TABLE Ea52–60 Total government expenditure, by character and object: 1902–1995

Contributed by John Joseph Wallis

		Capital outlays							
Fiscal year	Total expenditure	Salaries and wages	Total	Construction	Other	Current operations	Assistance and subsidies	Interest on debt	Insurance trust
	Ea52	Ea53	Ea54	Ea55	Ea56	Ea57	Ea58	Ea59	Ea60
	Thousand dollars	Thousand dollars	Thousand dollars	Thousand dollars	Thousand dollars	Thousand dollars	Thousand dollars	Thousand dollars	Thousand dollars
1902	1,660,000	700,000	—	202,000	—	1,350,000	—	108,000	0
1913	3,215,000	1,427,000	—	561,000	—	2,451,000	—	196,000	7,000
1922	9,297,000	3,303,000	—	1,397,000	—	6,398,000	—	1,418,000	84,000
1927	11,220,000	4,255,000	—	2,095,000	—	7,560,000	—	1,426,000	139,000
1932	12,437,000	4,729,000	—	1,876,000	—	8,968,000	—	1,422,000	171,000
1934	12,807,000	5,338,000	—	2,155,000	—	8,888,000	—	1,571,000	193,000
1936	16,758,000	6,353,000	—	2,427,000	—	12,551,000	—	1,558,000	222,000
1938	17,675,000	7,047,000	—	2,662,000	—	12,835,000	—	1,624,000	554,000
1940	20,417,000	7,649,000	—	3,139,000	—	14,624,000	—	1,686,000	968,000
1942	45,576,000	10,966,000	—	8,232,000	—	34,625,000	—	1,732,000	986,000
1944	109,947,000	26,760,000	—	5,117,000	—	101,201,000	—	2,786,000	842,000
1946	79,707,000	28,413,000	—	2,536,000	—	70,356,000	—	4,422,000	2,392,000
1948	55,081,000	17,345,000	—	4,376,000	—	43,226,000	—	4,866,000	2,614,000
1950	70,334,000	20,530,000	—	6,840,000	—	51,584,000	—	5,017,000	6,894,000
1952	99,847,000	29,766,000	24,873,000	9,723,000	15,151,000	56,112,000	8,387,000	4,986,000	5,489,000
1953	110,054,000	33,070,000	26,403,000	10,498,000	15,904,000	63,051,000	8,933,000	5,660,000	6,006,000
1954	111,332,000	33,538,000	27,369,000	11,739,000	15,631,000	62,468,000	8,296,000	5,713,000	7,484,000
1955	110,717,000	34,916,000	28,736,000	12,612,000	16,125,000	58,110,000	8,966,000	5,904,000	9,002,000
1956	115,796,000	37,573,000	26,363,000	12,771,000	13,592,000	64,065,000	9,261,000	6,531,000	9,576,000
1957	125,463,000	39,486,000	28,866,000	13,783,000	15,084,000	68,994,000	9,460,000	6,873,000	11,269,000
1958	134,931,000	41,857,000	30,838,000	14,922,000	15,916,000	71,663,000	10,252,000	7,653,000	14,524,000
1959	145,748,000	44,994,000	32,228,000	16,385,000	15,843,000	78,979,000	10,629,000	7,283,000	16,631,000
1960	151,288,000	47,136,000	31,946,000	15,832,000	16,114,000	81,687,000	10,369,000	9,690,000	17,596,000
1961	164,875,000	50,215,000	32,320,000	16,987,000	15,333,000	91,758,000	10,896,000	9,710,000	20,191,000
1962	176,240,000	54,153,000	35,220,000	17,298,000	17,922,000	98,146,000	11,660,000	9,586,000	21,628,000
1963	186,058,000	57,268,000	36,581,000	18,233,000	18,349,000	104,106,000	11,750,000	10,335,000	23,285,000
1964	196,431,000	61,361,000	36,905,000	19,420,000	17,485,000	111,496,000	12,750,000	11,119,000	24,161,000
1965	205,682,000	65,724,000	33,876,000	20,977,000	12,900,000	122,481,000	12,493,000	11,952,000	24,880,000
1966	224,813,000	72,963,000	39,981,000	22,411,000	17,569,000	130,488,000	13,363,000	12,857,000	28,126,000
1967	257,799,000	81,270,000	42,101,000	23,832,000	18,269,000	153,458,000	14,694,000	13,985,000	33,561,000
1968	282,645,000	89,375,000	47,057,000	24,772,000	22,285,000	165,515,000	16,450,000	15,496,000	38,127,000
1969	308,344,000	99,068,000	47,246,000	26,836,000	20,410,000	181,547,000	18,288,000	17,663,000	43,600,000
1970	332,985,000	110,499,000	47,519,000	28,402,000	19,118,000	197,020,000	20,764,000	19,160,000	48,521,000
1971	369,423,000	120,107,000	48,823,000	31,051,000	17,773,000	214,713,000	25,357,000	22,503,000	58,028,000
1972	399,099,142	133,764,427	55,442,669	33,221,195	22,221,474	226,955,370	28,004,525	24,061,089	64,635,489
1973	436,967,076	142,729,207	55,343,914	32,866,992	22,476,922	249,412,305	30,725,402	26,159,923	75,325,532
1974	478,339,888	154,213,739	57,249,900	35,650,665	21,599,235	269,843,889	33,213,864	31,290,212	86,742,023
1975	560,130,865	163,700,000	66,621,979	42,960,764	23,661,215	305,212,531	43,970,705	35,091,762	109,233,888
1976	625,076,477	180,391,018	71,630,919	45,222,678	26,408,241	335,331,054	47,739,422	40,987,456	129,387,626
1977	682,491,867	193,182,245	75,160,445	43,763,224	31,397,221	367,995,902	48,837,374	46,413,393	144,084,753
1978	747,172,215	211,630,047	81,058,237	44,720,089	36,338,148	403,901,194	54,016,434	53,373,874	154,822,476
1979	832,513,884	227,519,137	93,150,983	51,728,821	41,422,162	446,964,672	57,311,166	64,230,767	170,856,296

(continued)

TABLE Ea52–60   Total government expenditure, by character and object: 1902–1995

Contributed by John Joseph Wallis

| | | Capital outlays | | | | | | | |
Fiscal year	Total expenditure	Salaries and wages	Total	Construction	Other	Current operations	Assistance and subsidies	Interest on debt	Insurance trust
	Ea52	Ea53	Ea54	Ea55	Ea56	Ea57	Ea58	Ea59	Ea60
	Thousand dollars	Thousand dollars	Thousand dollars	Thousand dollars	Thousand dollars	Thousand dollars	Thousand dollars	Thousand dollars	Thousand dollars
1980	958,656,087	250,886,104	99,385,478	58,409,671	40,975,807	517,009,611	63,997,918	78,890,482	199,372,598
1981	1,109,814,363	272,453,382	116,499,477	62,310,290	54,189,187	584,819,393	68,552,879	101,021,098	238,921,516
1982	1,233,263,485	295,855,258	129,474,110	61,681,837	67,792,273	640,948,117	69,151,945	126,136,795	267,552,518
1983	1,346,476,005	314,019,391	148,477,699	61,813,965	86,663,734	688,601,445	74,055,102	137,913,188	297,428,571
1984	1,427,673,024	330,439,108	143,093,968	63,209,429	79,884,539	758,495,456	78,141,325	143,647,537	304,294,738
1985	1,580,813,648	357,151,546	156,912,066	71,185,360	85,726,706	832,592,615	83,387,185	179,098,167	328,823,615
1986	1,696,120,835	379,675,901	176,124,409	79,833,634	96,290,775	897,765,784	86,963,295	188,537,141	346,730,206
1987	1,811,732,910	403,996,458	195,712,776	86,565,473	109,147,303	963,217,093	89,003,243	196,542,192	367,257,606
1988	1,920,097,382	430,601,176	197,850,693	89,065,548	108,785,145	1,027,052,210	96,103,966	210,922,043	388,168,470
1989	2,030,753,224	456,136,143	211,733,668	95,824,690	115,908,978	1,072,796,734	101,831,797	229,767,482	414,623,543
1990	2,218,825,620	487,089,779	220,992,797	98,566,138	122,426,659	1,190,146,748	106,601,784	246,866,048	454,218,243
1991	2,379,168,661	520,694,908	227,225,220	107,144,724	120,080,496	1,282,688,025	118,420,533	256,675,374	494,159,509
1992	2,494,424,256	544,874,239	229,615,101	113,214,182	116,400,919	1,325,539,165	129,598,049	264,727,293	544,944,648
1993	2,575,969,756	558,872,250	222,227,297	109,813,725	112,413,572	1,366,771,688	138,318,749	263,597,275	585,054,747
1994	2,673,005,696	573,267,598	217,327,843	111,639,607	105,688,236	1,422,148,814	148,137,463	267,147,405	618,244,171
1995	2,818,796,004	593,341,826	225,024,430	119,941,692	105,082,738	1,471,733,755	156,758,948	299,648,191	665,630,680

Source

Figures are from data files provided by the Census of Governments. For published versions through 1982, see U.S. Department of Commerce, "Historical Statistics on Government Finance and Employment," in *Census of Governments, 1982,* volume 6, pp. 225–64.

Documentation

See the text for Table Ea24–51.

In order to compute total expenditures under a different revenue concept, use the data from Table Ea125–131 on the change in debt during the year. See the essay in this chapter for additional information on this matter.

Series Ea59. Includes interest on debt of utilities operated by local governments.

TABLE Ea61–124   Total government expenditure, by function: 1902–1995

Contributed by John Joseph Wallis

				General						
		Federal defense and international relations					Education			
Fiscal year	Total	Total	Total	Military service	Space research and technology	Postal service	Total	Local schools	Higher education	Other
	Ea61	Ea62	Ea63	Ea64	Ea65	Ea66	Ea67	Ea68	Ea69	Ea70
	Thousand dollars	Thousand dollars	Thousand dollars	Thousand dollars	Thousand dollars	Thousand dollars	Thousand dollars	Thousand dollars	Thousand dollars	Thousand dollars
1902	1,660,000	1,578,000	165,000	162,000	0	126,000	258,000	238,000	13,000	7,000
1913	3,215,000	3,022,000	250,000	245,000	0	270,000	582,000	522,000	49,000	11,000
1922	9,297,000	8,854,000	875,000	864,000	0	553,000	1,713,000	1,541,000	143,000	29,000
1927	11,220,000	10,590,000	616,000	599,000	0	711,000	2,243,000	2,017,000	196,000	30,000
1932	12,437,000	11,748,000	721,000	702,000	0	794,000	2,325,000	2,033,000	251,000	41,000
1934	12,807,000	12,086,000	553,000	541,000	0	651,000	2,005,000	1,612,000	188,000	205,000
1936	16,758,000	15,835,000	932,000	916,000	0	751,000	2,365,000	1,885,000	250,000	230,000
1938	17,675,000	16,273,000	1,041,000	1,021,000	0	776,000	2,653,000	2,152,000	288,000	213,000
1940	20,417,000	18,125,000	1,590,000	1,567,000	0	808,000	2,827,000	2,270,000	312,000	245,000
1942	45,576,000	43,483,000	26,555,000	22,633,000	0	878,000	2,696,000	2,204,000	317,000	175,000
1944	109,947,000	107,823,000	85,503,000	74,670,000	0	1,085,000	2,805,000	2,318,000	406,000	81,000
1946	79,707,000	75,582,000	50,461,000	42,677,000	0	1,381,000	3,711,000	2,861,000	422,000	428,000
1948	55,081,000	50,088,000	16,075,000	10,642,000	0	1,715,000	7,721,000	4,308,000	950,000	2,463,000
1950	70,334,000	60,701,000	18,355,000	12,118,000	0	2,270,000	9,647,000	5,843,000	1,170,000	2,634,000
1952	99,847,000	91,291,000	48,187,000	38,962,000	0	2,612,000	9,598,000	6,862,000	1,267,000	1,469,000
1953	110,054,000	100,733,000	53,583,000	43,847,000	0	2,686,000	10,117,000	7,822,000	1,361,000	934,000
1954	111,332,000	100,365,000	49,265,000	40,519,000	0	2,669,000	11,196,000	8,947,000	1,418,000	831,000
1955	110,717,000	97,828,000	43,472,000	33,782,000	0	2,726,000	12,710,000	10,129,000	1,570,000	1,012,000
1956	115,796,000	102,156,000	43,388,000	35,553,000	0	2,899,000	14,160,000	11,165,000	1,814,000	1,182,000
1957	125,463,000	109,765,000	47,500,000	39,073,000	0	3,034,000	15,099,000	11,657,000	2,206,000	1,236,000
1958	134,931,000	115,714,000	47,626,000	38,998,000	89,000	3,327,000	16,836,000	13,032,000	2,582,000	1,222,000
1959	145,748,000	124,217,000	49,688,000	41,230,000	145,000	3,499,000	18,119,000	14,034,000	2,920,000	1,165,000
1960	151,288,000	128,600,000	48,922,000	41,340,000	395,000	3,730,000	19,404,000	15,166,000	3,202,000	1,036,000
1961	164,875,000	139,161,000	51,210,000	43,068,000	735,000	4,025,000	21,214,000	16,608,000	3,570,000	1,036,000
1962	176,240,000	149,159,000	55,172,000	46,950,000	1,242,000	4,101,000	22,814,000	17,739,000	4,042,000	1,032,000
1963	186,058,000	156,840,000	56,386,000	47,973,000	2,529,000	4,402,000	24,527,000	18,802,000	4,470,000	1,255,000
1964	196,431,000	166,088,000	57,326,000	49,341,000	4,140,000	4,775,000	27,342,000	20,399,000	5,278,000	1,665,000
1965	205,682,000	173,745,000	55,810,000	48,385,000	5,058,000	5,261,000	29,613,000	21,966,000	5,863,000	1,785,000
1966	224,813,000	189,406,000	60,832,000	53,770,000	5,869,000	5,706,000	34,837,000	25,091,000	7,207,000	2,539,000
1967	257,799,000	216,888,000	74,638,000	66,782,000	5,359,000	6,227,000	40,214,000	27,590,000	8,932,000	3,691,000
1968	282,645,000	236,348,000	83,874,000	76,747,000	4,645,000	6,485,000	43,614,000	29,305,000	10,214,000	4,093,000
1969	308,344,000	255,924,000	84,496,000	77,179,000	4,189,000	6,993,000	50,377,000	33,752,000	11,551,000	5,074,000
1970	332,985,000	275,017,000	84,253,000	76,550,000	3,691,000	7,722,000	55,771,000	37,461,000	12,924,000	5,385,000
1971	369,423,000	301,096,000	83,147,000	75,876,000	3,334,000	8,683,000	63,818,000	41,766,000	14,785,000	7,266,000
1972	399,099,142	323,065,300	81,719,000	74,456,000	3,369,000	9,366,000	70,376,217	46,670,381	15,861,270	7,844,566
1973	436,967,076	348,606,888	83,004,000	72,137,000	3,270,000	9,572,000	74,889,205	48,788,871	17,369,320	8,731,014
1974	478,339,888	377,192,221	85,444,000	79,066,000	3,289,000	11,235,000	81,653,070	53,059,162	18,883,654	9,710,254
1975	560,130,865	433,611,341	93,877,000	86,645,000	3,314,000	12,678,000	95,011,129	61,485,257	21,702,445	11,823,427
1976	625,076,477	476,146,273	100,414,000	91,009,000	3,691,000	13,748,000	107,542,271	67,673,568	24,303,730	15,564,973
1977	682,491,867	514,217,140	105,596,000	97,824,000	4,008,000	14,641,000	111,793,765	71,546,137	25,972,295	14,275,333
1978	747,172,215	566,072,018	114,811,000	105,782,000	3,983,000	15,271,000	120,147,569	76,702,639	28,390,637	15,054,293
1979	832,513,884	630,812,044	128,529,000	118,268,000	4,177,000	16,581,000	129,427,201	83,385,150	30,058,856	15,983,195
1980	958,656,087	723,092,851	149,459,000	137,500,000	4,892,000	18,177,000	143,829,804	92,930,007	33,919,259	16,980,538
1981	1,109,814,363	827,876,830	174,564,000	160,747,000	5,523,000	20,466,000	158,012,259	100,534,479	38,114,279	19,363,501
1982	1,233,263,485	917,298,655	204,275,000	189,273,000	6,181,000	21,761,000	165,766,461	105,761,428	41,569,919	18,435,114
1983	1,346,476,005	996,235,571	228,763,000	213,159,000	6,816,000	23,561,000	176,648,678	112,945,179	43,820,105	19,883,394
1984	1,427,673,024	1,068,316,743	248,040,000	229,113,000	7,203,000	26,619,000	188,603,629	120,895,748	47,612,902	20,094,979
1985	1,580,813,648	1,192,191,910	288,736,000	265,232,000	7,346,000	28,898,000	205,893,974	131,986,576	52,316,006	21,591,392
1986	1,696,120,835	1,284,093,697	312,183,000	288,454,000	7,275,000	30,985,000	224,399,505	145,110,764	56,535,108	22,753,633
1987	1,811,732,910	1,375,367,194	319,084,000	296,915,000	7,450,000	32,243,000	240,646,646	156,910,098	60,072,709	23,663,839
1988	1,920,097,382	1,461,880,257	329,993,000	306,474,000	8,866,000	33,892,000	256,960,417	169,694,203	62,687,689	24,578,525
1989	2,030,753,224	1,542,620,386	346,338,000	320,844,000	10,806,000	36,472,000	280,713,223	185,170,700	67,550,270	27,992,253
1990	2,218,825,620	1,686,806,855	344,069,000	316,087,000	12,063,000	39,065,000	305,552,071	202,009,431	73,418,284	30,124,356
1991	2,379,168,661	1,804,005,074	366,112,000	335,849,000	13,514,000	43,102,000	329,494,355	217,642,750	78,748,664	33,102,941
1992	2,494,424,256	1,864,165,586	351,684,000	320,168,000	13,550,000	44,890,000	346,787,916	227,273,362	84,127,578	35,386,976
1993	2,575,969,756	1,906,431,982	344,008,000	311,006,000	13,873,000	44,528,000	368,165,080	240,310,015	88,108,569	39,746,496
1994	2,673,005,696	1,963,599,028	333,380,000	300,578,000	13,553,000	46,110,000	376,525,956	246,981,375	90,871,177	38,673,404
1995	2,818,796,004	2,058,930,343	327,231,000	293,972,000	13,316,000	49,482,000	404,932,664	264,240,479	97,048,481	43,643,704

(continued)

TABLE Ea61–124 Total government expenditure, by function: 1902–1995 *Continued*

		General								
		Social services and income maintenance								
		Public welfare				Health and hospitals			Employment security administration	Veteran services
			Assistance programs							
	Libraries	Total	Categorical	Noncategorical	Other	Total	Hospitals	Health		
	Ea71	Ea72	Ea73	Ea74	Ea75	Ea76	Ea77	Ea78	Ea79	Ea80
Fiscal year	Thousand dollars	Thousand dollars	Thousand dollars	Thousand dollars	Thousand dollars	Thousand dollars	Thousand dollars	Thousand dollars	Thousand dollars	Thousand dollars
1902	—	41,000	11,000	—	30,000	63,000	45,000	18,000	—	141,000
1913	—	57,000	17,000	—	40,000	113,000	80,000	33,000	—	177,000
1922	—	128,000	57,000	—	71,000	352,000	287,000	65,000	—	505,000
1927	—	161,000	79,000	—	82,000	431,000	347,000	84,000	—	579,000
1932	—	445,000	366,000	—	79,000	583,000	462,000	121,000	—	928,000
1934	—	979,000	796,000	—	183,000	535,000	416,000	119,000	—	508,000
1936	—	997,000	731,000	—	266,000	592,000	461,000	131,000	—	1,699,000
1938	—	1,233,000	483,000	485,000	265,000	678,000	496,000	182,000	—	590,000
1940	—	1,314,000	611,000	438,000	265,000	732,000	537,000	195,000	—	501,000
1942	—	1,285,000	761,000	345,000	179,000	714,000	517,000	197,000	—	481,000
1944	—	1,150,000	842,000	166,000	142,000	857,000	568,000	289,000	—	530,000
1946	—	1,435,000	1,014,000	216,000	205,000	1,142,000	762,000	380,000	—	2,588,000
1948	—	2,144,000	1,473,000	357,000	314,000	1,934,000	1,398,000	536,000	—	3,926,000
1950	—	2,964,000	2,010,000	538,000	416,000	2,711,000	2,050,000	661,000	—	3,258,000
1952	118,000	2,830,000	2,033,000	303,000	494,000	3,199,000	2,460,000	739,000	238,000	2,570,000
1953	136,000	2,956,000	2,167,000	272,000	517,000	3,246,000	2,548,000	698,000	—	2,823,000
1954	145,000	3,103,000	2,234,000	308,000	561,000	3,368,000	2,676,000	692,000	316,000	2,913,000
1955	153,000	3,210,000	2,278,000	329,000	603,000	3,428,000	2,721,000	707,000	—	3,058,000
1956	—	3,184,000	2,319,000	244,000	621,000	3,739,000	3,068,000	671,000	388,000	3,185,000
1957	199,000	3,534,000	2,538,000	195,000	801,000	4,151,000	3,416,000	735,000	424,000	3,224,000
1958	—	3,866,000	2,700,000	275,000	891,000	4,566,000	3,805,000	761,000	520,000	3,576,000
1959	—	4,193,000	2,897,000	301,000	995,000	5,067,000	4,074,000	993,000	651,000	3,706,000
1960	278,000	4,462,000	3,006,000	310,000	1,146,000	5,244,000	4,213,000	1,031,000	549,000	3,801,000
1961	368,000	4,779,000	3,084,000	335,000	1,360,000	5,681,000	4,549,000	1,132,000	636,000	4,049,000
1962	353,000	5,147,000	3,266,000	258,000	1,623,000	6,135,000	4,791,000	1,344,000	727,000	4,224,000
1963	399,000	5,599,000	3,416,000	249,000	1,934,000	6,689,000	5,149,000	1,540,000	740,000	3,961,000
1964	401,000	5,880,000	3,491,000	226,000	2,163,000	7,079,000	5,461,000	1,618,000	834,000	4,208,000
1965	444,000	6,420,000	3,697,000	234,000	2,489,000	7,672,000	5,867,000	1,805,000	894,000	4,210,000
1966	486,000	6,965,000	3,829,000	236,000	2,900,000	8,362,000	6,297,000	2,065,000	1,108,000	4,531,000
1967	518,000	9,592,000	4,388,000	266,000	4,938,000	9,457,000	6,951,000	2,506,000	1,210,000	4,448,000
1968	573,000	11,245,000	4,849,000	349,000	6,047,000	10,579,000	7,801,000	2,778,000	1,378,000	4,773,000
1969	634,000	14,730,000	5,737,000	446,000	8,547,000	11,930,000	8,593,000	3,337,000	1,572,000	5,097,000
1970	700,000	17,517,000	6,917,000	480,000	10,120,000	13,588,000	9,693,000	3,895,000	1,790,000	5,455,000
1971	762,000	20,446,000	8,662,000	610,000	11,174,000	14,834,000	11,141,000	3,693,000	2,031,000	6,476,000
1972	816,011	23,604,556	9,846,771	697,753	13,060,032	17,189,178	12,796,643	4,392,535	2,291,087	6,932,843
1973	877,195	26,966,873	10,375,470	761,030	15,830,373	18,748,058	13,661,941	5,086,117	2,524,764	7,401,255
1974	967,540	31,030,757	11,557,128	722,226	18,751,403	21,683,460	15,189,364	6,494,096	2,730,322	7,679,218
1975	1,118,770	39,402,960	14,117,930	871,726	24,413,304	24,842,225	17,387,598	7,454,627	3,245,935	8,960,576
1976	1,249,117	45,128,787	15,638,040	1,073,022	28,417,725	27,570,216	18,948,463	8,621,753	3,468,453	9,353,035
1977	1,406,890	49,432,855	16,217,199	1,274,185	31,941,471	30,546,884	21,274,569	9,272,315	3,690,786	10,219,026
1978	1,517,507	54,337,831	18,090,659	1,357,946	34,889,226	33,087,028	22,837,994	10,249,034	3,942,872	10,829,710
1979	1,674,666	59,240,130	17,807,041	1,293,716	40,139,373	37,150,540	25,736,765	11,413,775	4,099,110	11,606,303
1980	2,025,627	64,764,246	19,583,229	1,336,446	43,844,571	43,309,469	29,207,790	14,101,679	4,536,792	12,503,951
1981	2,045,190	74,642,596	21,516,229	1,516,736	51,609,631	47,377,405	32,131,564	15,245,841	5,075,431	13,832,969
1982	2,197,593	78,780,380	22,054,593	1,672,423	55,053,364	53,225,742	36,243,353	16,982,389	5,408,868	15,022,798
1983	2,499,222	83,906,097	23,778,754	2,201,147	57,926,196	56,126,854	38,980,752	17,146,102	5,897,187	15,891,688
1984	2,710,517	88,424,444	23,913,780	2,313,186	62,197,478	59,295,429	41,157,908	18,137,521	6,122,711	16,118,572
1985	2,965,929	94,757,337	25,833,797	2,498,541	66,424,999	63,600,667	43,400,742	20,199,925	6,317,119	16,988,881
1986	3,263,501	99,574,593	27,893,856	2,636,488	69,044,249	68,628,897	45,559,356	23,069,541	6,578,220	17,260,785
1987	3,662,578	106,406,521	29,451,591	2,627,033	74,327,897	72,604,593	47,970,170	24,634,423	6,774,691	17,217,454
1988	3,775,747	115,113,302	31,496,555	2,623,472	80,993,275	78,788,865	51,497,040	27,291,825	7,166,110	18,474,281
1989	4,250,451	126,132,182	33,558,076	2,818,695	89,755,411	85,091,301	55,259,913	29,831,388	7,352,169	18,815,198
1990	4,527,814	140,733,581	35,033,319	2,923,808	102,776,454	92,486,739	58,895,004	33,591,735	7,716,354	17,504,682
1991	4,839,137	167,680,579	41,044,800	3,214,100	123,421,679	102,816,950	63,829,346	38,987,604	8,192,688	19,163,313
1992	5,191,062	202,875,467	47,144,656	3,380,401	152,350,410	108,626,882	69,576,282	39,050,600	9,171,776	20,490,014
1993	4,959,447	218,707,371	51,182,098	3,406,415	164,118,858	119,172,613	73,438,966	45,733,647	9,587,023	21,362,681
1994	5,465,133	236,033,425	54,455,256	3,595,643	177,982,526	125,596,498	76,451,773	49,144,725	9,860,807	22,057,076
1995	5,894,677	250,355,515	55,110,253	3,521,604	191,723,658	132,467,445	79,916,472	52,550,973	9,591,014	21,759,109

TABLE Ea61–124   Total government expenditure, by function: 1902–1995   *Continued*

						General					
	Public safety						Transportation				
				Corrections		Protective inspection and regulation					
	Police	Fire	Total	Institutions	Other		Highways	Air	Parking	Water	Transit
	Ea81	Ea82	Ea83	Ea84 [1]	Ea85	Ea86	Ea87	Ea88 [2,3]	Ea89	Ea90 [2,3]	Ea91
Fiscal year	Thousand dollars	Thousand dollars	Thousand dollars	Thousand dollars	Thousand dollars	Thousand dollars	Thousand dollars	Thousand dollars	Thousand dollars	Thousand dollars	Thousand dollars
1902	50,000	40,000	—	—	—	—	175,000	0	—	22,000	0
1913	92,000	76,000	—	—	—	—	419,000	0	—	90,000	0
1922	204,000	158,000	—	—	—	—	1,296,000	1,000	—	301,000	0
1927	290,000	203,000	—	—	—	—	1,819,000	1,000	—	253,000	0
1932	349,000	210,000	—	—	—	—	1,766,000	10,000	—	188,000	0
1934	306,000	189,000	—	—	—	—	1,829,000	20,000	—	193,000	0
1936	331,000	205,000	—	—	—	—	1,945,000	39,000	—	230,000	0
1938	378,000	231,000	—	—	—	—	2,150,000	42,000	—	224,000	0
1940	386,000	235,000	—	—	—	—	2,177,000	53,000	—	321,000	0
1942	444,000	236,000	—	—	—	—	1,765,000	220,000	—	670,000	0
1944	497,000	251,000	—	—	—	—	1,215,000	207,000	—	4,534,000	0
1946	549,000	294,000	—	—	—	—	1,680,000	98,000	—	1,092,000	0
1948	724,000	406,000	—	—	—	—	3,071,000	136,000	—	414,000	0
1950	864,000	488,000	—	—	—	—	3,872,000	214,000	—	410,000	0
1952	1,080,000	586,000	365,000	—	—	—	4,714,000	352,000	—	718,000	0
1953	1,160,000	598,000	—	—	—	—	5,053,000	385,000	—	920,000	0
1954	1,254,000	653,000	427,000	—	—	—	5,586,000	372,000	—	765,000	0
1955	1,358,000	694,000	—	—	—	—	6,520,000	359,000	—	707,000	0
1956	1,486,000	737,000	500,000	—	—	—	7,035,000	405,000	—	818,000	0
1957	1,623,000	810,000	549,000	—	—	—	7,931,000	508,000	—	862,000	0
1958	1,769,000	873,000	573,000	—	—	—	8,702,000	524,000	—	885,000	0
1959	1,880,000	914,000	708,000	—	—	—	9,726,000	733,000	—	1,022,000	0
1960	2,030,000	995,000	722,000	—	—	—	9,565,000	842,000	—	1,142,000	0
1961	2,210,000	1,087,000	810,000	—	—	—	9,995,000	1,065,000	—	1,273,000	0
1962	2,326,000	1,124,000	841,000	—	—	—	10,508,000	1,082,000	83,000	1,388,000	0
1963	2,491,000	1,186,000	873,000	—	—	—	11,300,000	1,099,000	112,000	1,410,000	0
1964	2,586,000	1,222,000	939,000	—	—	—	11,828,000	1,109,000	114,000	1,404,000	0
1965	2,792,000	1,306,000	1,033,000	—	—	—	12,348,000	1,198,000	108,000	1,529,000	0
1966	3,033,000	1,376,000	1,077,000	—	—	—	12,895,000	1,226,000	128,000	1,673,000	0
1967	3,331,000	1,499,000	1,199,000	—	—	—	14,032,000	1,326,000	144,000	1,886,000	0
1968	3,700,000	1,623,000	1,335,000	—	—	—	14,654,000	1,360,000	105,000	1,983,000	0
1969	4,242,000	1,793,000	1,457,000	—	—	—	15,738,000	1,630,000	137,000	1,993,000	0
1970	4,903,000	2,024,000	1,709,000	—	—	—	16,746,000	2,065,000	158,000	1,904,000	0
1971	6,050,000	2,303,000	1,979,000	—	—	—	18,262,000	3,176,000	159,000	1,534,000	0
1972	6,963,061	2,579,037	2,222,715	—	—	—	19,260,992	3,697,631	171,164	1,556,865	0
1973	7,802,948	2,804,000	2,523,345	—	—	—	18,885,837	3,147,308	205,054	1,755,566	0
1974	8,276,980	3,036,776	2,987,355	—	—	—	20,188,770	2,922,269	214,003	1,859,222	0
1975	9,620,803	3,522,000	3,577,578	—	—	—	22,839,688	3,166,315	301,879	2,079,286	0
1976	10,734,679	3,897,534	4,004,136	—	—	—	24,200,807	3,358,767	333,920	2,086,285	0
1977	11,788,365	4,412,298	4,603,821	2,148,706	2,455,115	1,637,427	23,322,891	3,369,197	298,181	2,331,568	184,913
1978	12,877,046	4,801,757	5,317,145	2,462,641	2,854,504	1,888,537	24,885,728	3,834,098	269,653	2,284,354	183,500
1979	13,931,499	5,146,503	5,924,423	2,768,907	3,155,516	2,076,133	28,858,094	4,205,065	324,011	2,841,738	252,483
1980	15,232,702	5,718,232	6,834,503	3,303,223	3,531,280	2,317,612	33,745,286	5,070,979	343,053	3,278,418	290,815
1981	16,851,018	6,335,761	7,805,898	3,771,173	4,034,725	2,556,994	34,909,137	6,994,072	377,345	4,675,252	234,691
1982	18,511,354	7,025,556	8,891,988	4,398,893	4,493,095	2,787,350	35,096,249	5,442,028	406,483	3,495,013	299,500
1983	20,279,612	7,582,075	10,263,483	4,935,598	5,327,885	2,967,185	37,214,925	5,384,502	454,483	3,532,991	319,626
1984	21,353,992	8,201,727	11,768,901	5,859,629	5,909,272	3,233,321	40,210,823	6,663,454	483,985	3,140,338	340,209
1985	24,386,316	8,916,631	13,558,627	6,926,231	6,632,396	3,530,205	45,822,995	7,152,822	591,729	3,353,160	231,471
1986	26,228,458	9,586,526	15,755,343	8,093,078	7,662,265	4,078,692	49,936,228	7,855,947	682,460	3,415,447	275,946
1987	28,778,362	10,452,893	17,561,907	8,827,643	8,734,264	4,417,026	52,977,963	8,736,994	760,559	3,722,110	241,544
1988	30,933,791	11,752,856	20,153,958	11,268,961	8,884,997	4,723,810	55,997,868	9,536,812	784,884	3,953,771	262,146
1989	32,722,661	11,932,217	22,500,451	12,671,538	9,828,913	5,080,913	58,880,619	10,180,001	754,578	4,071,867	401,729
1990	35,920,606	13,186,081	26,229,201	14,702,059	11,527,142	5,570,328	61,913,330	10,982,626	749,235	4,524,378	369,687
1991	38,941,685	13,796,137	29,297,376	16,658,168	12,639,208	6,008,078	65,601,616	12,390,199	813,557	4,865,664	376,603
1992	42,134,625	14,751,172	31,229,627	17,417,585	13,812,042	6,272,041	68,164,483	14,146,649	874,455	4,619,741	430,304
1993	43,762,822	15,372,647	32,052,809	18,073,881	13,978,928	6,353,983	68,988,567	15,504,158	697,892	5,121,233	351,853
1994	45,972,621	16,122,797	34,857,345	19,994,937	14,862,408	6,637,861	72,758,398	15,896,319	729,078	5,476,350	363,596
1995	47,916,532	17,009,481	38,921,854	22,793,376	16,128,478	7,236,299	77,839,526	15,085,419	800,118	5,016,348	322,320

Notes appear at end of table

(continued)

TABLE Ea61–124 Total government expenditure, by function: 1902–1995 *Continued*

	General										
	Environment and housing										
	Natural resources								State and local sanitation		
		Agriculture									
	Total	Total	Farm income stabilization	Fish and game	Forestry	Other	Parks and recreation	Housing and community development	Total	Sewage	Solid waste
	Ea92	Ea93	Ea94	Ea95	Ea96	Ea97	Ea98	Ea99	Ea100	Ea101	Ea102
Fiscal year	Thousand dollars	Thousand dollars	Thousand dollars	Thousand dollars	Thousand dollars	Thousand dollars	Thousand dollars	Thousand dollars	Thousand dollars	Thousand dollars	Thousand dollars
1902	17,000	—	0	—	—	—	29,000	0	51,000	—	—
1913	44,000	—	0	—	—	—	57,000	0	97,000	—	—
1922	140,000	—	0	—	—	—	85,000	1,000	189,000	—	—
1927	206,000	—	0	—	—	—	153,000	1,000	312,000	—	—
1932	326,000	—	0	—	—	—	147,000	0	223,000	—	—
1934	1,241,000	—	382,000	—	—	—	126,000	3,000	177,000	—	—
1936	2,158,000	—	602,000	—	—	—	104,000	71,000	204,000	—	—
1938	2,089,000	—	326,000	—	—	—	130,000	109,000	226,000	—	—
1940	2,730,000	—	694,000	—	—	—	162,000	267,000	207,000	—	—
1942	2,468,000	—	929,000	—	—	—	128,000	622,000	229,000	—	—
1944	2,731,000	—	1,532,000	—	—	—	123,000	574,000	245,000	—	—
1946	3,111,000	—	2,012,000	—	—	—	179,000	221,000	370,000	—	—
1948	2,223,000	—	592,000	—	—	—	243,000	245,000	670,000	—	—
1950	5,005,000	—	2,712,000	—	—	—	304,000	573,000	834,000	—	—
1952	3,252,000	—	638,000	—	—	—	324,000	875,000	992,000	—	—
1953	4,816,000	—	2,271,000	—	—	—	374,000	768,000	908,000	—	—
1954	6,377,000	—	3,863,000	—	—	—	424,000	742,000	1,058,000	—	—
1955	6,338,000	—	3,892,000	—	—	—	509,000	611,000	1,142,000	—	—
1956	6,630,000	—	4,118,000	—	—	—	541,000	562,000	1,326,000	835,000	492,000
1957	6,137,000	—	3,283,000	—	—	—	608,000	624,000	1,443,000	906,000	537,000
1958	6,160,000	—	2,890,000	—	—	—	685,000	801,000	1,505,000	933,000	572,000
1959	7,966,000	—	4,559,000	—	—	—	729,000	838,000	1,609,000	1,011,000	598,000
1960	7,087,000	—	3,404,000	—	—	—	770,000	1,142,000	1,727,000	1,103,000	624,000
1961	9,756,000	—	5,508,000	—	—	—	857,000	1,320,000	1,774,000	1,103,000	672,000
1962	10,468,000	—	5,963,000	—	—	—	886,000	1,701,000	1,958,000	1,272,000	686,000
1963	9,602,000	—	4,993,000	—	—	—	978,000	1,756,000	2,187,000	1,464,000	723,000
1964	10,042,000	—	4,989,000	—	—	—	1,022,000	2,037,000	2,267,000	1,515,000	752,000
1965	11,121,000	—	5,803,000	—	—	—	1,104,000	2,198,000	2,360,000	1,567,000	793,000
1966	10,301,000	—	4,203,000	—	—	—	1,187,000	2,415,000	2,571,000	1,707,000	864,000
1967	10,145,000	—	3,496,000	—	—	—	1,291,000	2,413,000	2,523,000	1,635,000	888,000
1968	9,200,000	—	2,598,000	—	—	—	1,412,000	2,841,000	2,707,000	1,732,000	975,000
1969	10,024,000	—	2,933,000	—	—	—	1,645,000	2,505,000	2,969,000	1,895,000	1,074,000
1970	11,469,000	—	4,261,000	—	—	—	1,888,000	3,189,000	3,413,000	2,167,000	1,246,000
1971	13,740,000	—	5,227,000	—	—	—	2,109,000	4,351,000	4,087,000	2,646,000	1,441,000
1972	14,571,367	—	4,895,000	—	—	—	2,318,139	5,136,832	4,845,944	3,259,222	1,586,722
1973	16,710,016	—	5,970,000	—	—	—	2,560,700	6,929,914	5,321,344	3,603,809	1,717,535
1974	17,357,632	—	4,079,000	—	—	—	2,950,649	5,876,925	5,995,188	4,080,301	1,914,887
1975	18,066,879	—	2,447,000	—	—	—	3,461,616	5,851,341	7,438,293	5,262,293	2,176,000
1976	16,958,219	—	1,339,000	—	—	—	3,864,224	5,435,116	8,239,553	5,937,310	2,302,243
1977	22,383,770	6,148,740	2,245,000	540,677	2,399,670	13,294,683	5,697,887	5,599,497	9,425,234	7,051,720	2,373,514
1978	26,632,129	8,601,601	3,606,000	586,424	1,660,292	15,783,812	6,731,760	6,044,099	9,869,241	7,141,863	2,727,378
1979	30,294,957	9,647,305	3,667,000	649,699	2,174,583	17,823,370	7,422,567	8,032,116	11,787,444	8,795,399	2,992,045
1980	35,243,157	13,363,845	5,994,000	707,195	2,276,911	18,895,206	8,184,259	12,141,567	13,214,358	9,892,321	3,322,037
1981	43,599,263	15,740,295	7,180,000	828,638	2,480,086	24,550,244	8,535,772	13,893,907	14,898,220	11,121,401	3,776,819
1982	45,541,117	19,293,819	8,474,000	898,489	2,311,784	23,037,025	8,876,291	16,493,940	14,940,214	10,806,209	4,134,005
1983	54,757,232	30,616,977	19,371,000	921,346	2,373,468	20,845,441	9,479,832	14,375,128	15,603,463	11,239,056	4,364,407
1984	65,296,655	40,095,446	27,957,000	1,013,876	2,401,607	21,785,726	9,882,451	17,608,284	16,225,085	11,515,530	4,709,555
1985	60,433,643	32,687,917	18,937,000	1,077,604	2,642,253	24,025,869	10,718,228	18,591,777	17,397,964	12,185,960	5,212,004
1986	67,694,838	42,447,118	28,214,000	1,146,372	2,572,104	21,529,244	11,618,420	19,209,888	19,141,856	13,307,328	5,834,528
1987	93,005,615	67,201,256	50,177,000	1,189,364	2,607,900	22,007,095	12,521,276	21,307,900	21,647,340	15,147,941	6,499,399
1988	90,119,064	62,605,227	46,151,000	1,294,884	3,231,060	22,987,893	13,669,762	25,223,519	23,678,593	16,328,592	7,350,001
1989	64,353,132	35,786,664	19,156,000	1,391,711	3,480,350	23,694,407	14,640,933	28,230,393	25,772,606	17,038,864	8,733,742
1990	80,915,027	50,903,631	38,131,000	1,498,226	3,372,531	25,140,639	16,006,628	32,430,337	28,452,664	18,308,853	10,143,811
1991	56,949,248	27,562,275	14,954,000	1,581,505	3,441,036	24,364,432	17,718,189	33,345,593	31,013,616	19,675,544	11,338,072
1992	64,359,150	31,438,121	19,665,000	1,699,799	3,467,209	27,754,021	17,985,330	32,941,165	36,051,698	21,008,588	15,043,110
1993	63,378,523	28,559,287	16,708,000	1,776,999	4,461,817	28,580,420	18,312,491	31,356,659	38,330,540	22,784,869	15,545,671
1994	64,624,396	26,837,710	15,620,000	1,833,958	3,679,746	32,272,982	18,829,588	35,716,295	38,521,649	21,623,860	16,897,789
1995	54,994,187	15,757,589	5,297,000	1,932,462	3,639,289	33,664,847	20,138,496	36,720,779	41,283,902	23,583,401	17,700,501

TABLE Ea61–124   Total government expenditure, by function: 1902–1995   *Continued*

	General								
	General administration								
	Financial administration and general control	Financial administration	Judicial	Legislative	Public buildings	Central staff	Interest on general debt	Miscellaneous commercial activities	Other
	Ea103 [4]	Ea104 [4]	Ea105 [4]	Ea106 [4]	Ea107 [4]	Ea108 [4]	Ea109 [5]	Ea110	Ea111 [2,4]
Fiscal year	Thousand dollars	Thousand dollars	Thousand dollars	Thousand dollars	Thousand dollars	Thousand dollars	Thousand dollars	Thousand dollars	Thousand dollars
1902	175,000	—	—	—		—	97,000	—	128,000
1913	256,000	—	—	—	—	—	170,000	—	272,000
1922	439,000	—	—	—	—	—	1,370,000	—	544,000
1927	526,000	—	—	—	—	—	1,348,000	—	737,000
1932	601,000	—	—	—	—	—	1,323,000	—	809,000
1934	533,000	—	—	—	—	—	1,473,000	—	765,000
1936	662,000	—	—	—	—	—	1,455,000	—	1,095,000
1938	725,000	—	—	—	—	—	1,513,000	—	1,485,000
1940	739,000	—	—	—	—	—	1,552,000	—	1,524,000
1942	828,000	—	—	—	—	—	1,591,000	—	1,673,000
1944	1,087,000	—	—	—	—	—	2,650,000	—	1,779,000
1946	1,163,000	—	—	—	—	—	4,286,000	—	1,821,000
1948	1,325,000	—	—	—	—	—	4,722,000	—	2,394,000
1950	1,555,000	—	—	—	—	—	4,862,000	—	2,515,000
1952	1,801,000	—	—	—	—	—	4,814,000	—	2,066,000
1953	1,866,000	—	—	—	—	—	5,477,000	—	2,861,000
1954	1,997,000	—	—	—	308,000	—	5,515,000	—	2,220,000
1955	2,060,000	—	—	—	371,000	—	5,684,000	—	3,089,000
1956	2,235,000	—	—	—	363,000	—	6,297,000	—	2,641,000
1957	2,405,000	—	—	—	429,000	—	6,603,000	—	2,497,000
1958	2,536,000	—	—	—	493,000	—	7,360,000	—	2,935,000
1959	2,750,000	—	—	—	567,000	—	6,959,000	—	3,315,000
1960	2,859,000	—	—	—	533,000	—	9,332,000	—	3,602,000
1961	3,025,000	1,608,000	—	—	590,000	—	9,309,000	—	3,983,000
1962	3,187,000	1,705,000	—	—	602,000	—	9,173,000	—	4,519,000
1963	3,362,000	1,820,000	—	—	638,000	—	9,881,000	—	5,371,000
1964	3,585,000	1,957,000	—	—	654,000	—	10,649,000	—	5,299,000
1965	3,842,000	2,074,000	—	—	831,000	—	11,430,000	—	5,994,000
1966	4,105,000	2,178,000	—	—	856,000	—	12,278,000	—	6,445,000
1967	4,537,000	2,387,000	—	—	931,000	—	13,405,000	—	7,494,000
1968	4,966,000	2,566,000	—	—	1,037,000	—	14,873,000	—	8,423,000
1969	5,563,000	2,885,000	—	—	1,209,000	—	16,992,000	—	9,218,000
1970	6,370,000	3,284,000	—	—	1,287,000	—	18,411,000	—	10,281,000
1971	—	3,612,000	—	—	1,405,000	—	21,688,000	—	13,110,000
1972	—	4,067,765	—	—	1,528,737	—	23,142,942	—	15,338,217
1973	—	4,614,083	—	—	1,682,418	—	25,117,357	—	21,293,648
1974	—	4,787,573	—	—	1,902,068	—	30,116,363	760,258	22,247,823
1975	—	5,996,266	—	—	2,314,417	—	33,787,091	1,087,149	28,050,145
1976	—	6,574,402	—	—	2,557,327	—	39,574,753	1,153,326	31,008,346
1977	—	7,258,062	1,565,069	470,495	2,441,662	5,495,065	44,509,659	140,117	25,946,756
1978	—	8,240,513	2,467,464	1,033,003	2,561,055	4,917,784	51,312,689	143,980	31,848,966
1979	—	9,351,229	2,739,662	1,126,305	2,829,058	5,403,726	61,755,186	174,963	33,849,932
1980	—	10,227,705	3,178,613	1,262,946	3,018,141	6,076,800	76,032,843	228,786	37,954,187
1981	—	10,943,521	3,265,660	1,378,953	3,229,744	6,869,088	97,641,170	271,575	41,070,939
1982	—	11,980,530	5,481,288	1,548,711	3,285,585	5,869,943	121,975,820	301,484	46,429,369
1983	—	13,208,705	8,126,431	1,620,482	3,625,490	4,988,950	132,871,241	289,556	49,180,453
1984	—	14,258,336	8,833,866	1,772,350	3,859,338	5,187,908	137,905,368	319,679	48,633,371
1985	—	15,548,463	10,566,125	1,884,783	4,105,160	5,095,528	172,708,044	323,770	51,770,562
1986	—	17,296,904	11,393,842	1,991,843	4,106,314	5,632,900	181,230,629	282,486	56,530,229
1987	—	18,697,828	12,374,225	2,124,339	4,847,669	6,091,449	188,046,209	294,538	60,669,965
1988	—	20,453,616	13,852,374	2,347,834	4,788,278	6,668,641	202,437,351	307,611	67,203,996
1989	—	22,125,045	15,535,861	2,469,665	5,145,335	6,937,005	220,882,725	356,676	73,675,450
1990	—	24,200,095	17,388,500	2,675,700	5,643,399	7,638,499	237,691,095	366,794	110,234,404
1991	—	27,204,023	19,372,798	2,853,285	6,051,485	8,699,785	247,375,594	352,958	126,062,563
1992	—	29,093,292	20,879,085	2,949,712	6,056,315	9,022,942	255,077,047	325,006	103,534,630
1993	—	30,970,620	21,672,532	2,973,148	5,995,216	8,928,840	253,894,544	266,584	97,783,106
1994	—	32,364,816	22,643,217	3,026,787	6,482,286	9,456,452	257,623,268	315,224	106,598,790
1995	—	34,823,913	24,528,153	3,101,737	7,071,992	9,908,159	290,195,143	293,650	110,692,911

Notes appear at end of table

(continued)

TABLE Ea61–124 Total government expenditure, by function: 1902–1995 *Continued*

	Utility and liquor store							Insurance trust					
		Utility							Employee	Unemployment	Workers'	Social Security and medical	
	Total	Total	Water	Electric	Gas	Transit	Liquor store	Total	retirement	compensation	compensation	insurance	Other
	Ea112	Ea113	Ea114	Ea115	Ea116	Ea117	Ea118	Ea119	Ea120	Ea121	Ea122	Ea123	Ea124
Fiscal year	Thousand dollars	Thousand dollars	Thousand dollars	Thousand dollars	Thousand dollars	Thousand dollars	Thousand dollars	Thousand dollars	Thousand dollars	Thousand dollars	Thousand dollars	Thousand dollars	Thousand dollars
1902	82,000	80,000	71,000	8,000	1,000	0	2,000	0	0	—	—	—	0
1913	186,000	186,000	159,000	25,000	1,000	1,000	0	7,000	7,000	—	—	—	0
1922	359,000	359,000	255,000	75,000	4,000	25,000	0	84,000	36,000	—	—	—	48,000
1927	491,000	491,000	349,000	94,000	10,000	38,000	0	139,000	64,000	—	—	—	75,000
1932	518,000	518,000	320,000	92,000	7,000	99,000	0	171,000	103,000	—	—	—	68,000
1934	528,000	457,000	292,000	102,000	6,000	57,000	71,000	193,000	135,000	—	—	—	58,000
1936	701,000	553,000	344,000	117,000	11,000	81,000	148,000	222,000	157,000	—	—	—	65,000
1938	848,000	636,000	385,000	156,000	13,000	82,000	212,000	554,000	193,000	202,000	—	5,000	154,000
1940	1,324,000	1,090,000	404,000	257,000	18,000	411,000	234,000	968,000	209,000	509,000	—	16,000	234,000
1942	1,106,000	804,000	368,000	216,000	19,000	201,000	302,000	986,000	247,000	386,000	—	110,000	243,000
1944	1,281,000	822,000	355,000	227,000	25,000	215,000	459,000	842,000	298,000	70,000	—	185,000	289,000
1946	1,733,000	1,014,000	426,000	305,000	36,000	247,000	719,000	2,393,000	503,000	985,000	—	321,000	584,000
1948	2,379,000	1,612,000	628,000	438,000	47,000	499,000	767,000	2,614,000	541,000	821,000	—	512,000	740,000
1950	2,739,000	2,005,000	849,000	534,000	52,000	570,000	734,000	6,894,000	629,000	1,980,000	133,000	726,000	3,426,000
1952	3,067,000	2,246,000	973,000	631,000	61,000	581,000	821,000	5,488,000	831,000	1,022,000	157,000	1,983,000	1,495,000
1953	3,316,000	2,457,000	1,084,000	723,000	68,000	582,000	859,000	6,005,000	948,000	1,008,000	170,000	2,728,000	1,151,000
1954	3,482,000	2,577,000	1,150,000	751,000	90,000	586,000	905,000	7,485,000	1,090,000	1,648,000	183,000	3,276,000	1,288,000
1955	3,886,000	3,023,000	1,479,000	819,000	125,000	600,000	863,000	9,001,000	1,152,000	1,990,000	196,000	4,333,000	1,330,000
1956	4,065,000	3,119,000	1,461,000	895,000	128,000	636,000	946,000	9,577,000	1,332,000	1,383,000	209,000	5,361,000	1,292,000
1957	4,428,000	3,494,000	1,584,000	1,102,000	156,000	652,000	934,000	11,271,000	1,534,000	1,633,000	230,000	6,515,000	1,359,000
1958	4,693,000	3,720,000	1,624,000	1,260,000	150,000	686,000	973,000	14,523,000	1,773,000	2,979,000	246,000	8,043,000	1,482,000
1959	4,901,000	3,923,000	1,764,000	1,273,000	174,000	711,000	978,000	16,631,000	1,936,000	3,523,000	259,000	9,388,000	1,525,000
1960	5,088,000	4,066,000	1,881,000	1,244,000	191,000	750,000	1,022,000	17,595,000	2,161,000	2,639,000	283,000	10,798,000	1,714,000
1961	5,523,000	4,532,000	2,106,000	1,461,000	210,000	755,000	992,000	20,192,000	2,339,000	3,715,000	305,000	11,889,000	1,944,000
1962	5,453,000	4,445,000	2,077,000	1,378,000	219,000	771,000	1,008,000	21,628,000	2,642,000	3,019,000	335,000	13,669,000	1,963,000
1963	5,932,000	4,899,000	2,209,000	1,572,000	228,000	891,000	1,033,000	23,286,000	2,874,000	2,927,000	360,000	15,015,000	2,110,000
1964	6,184,000	5,067,000	2,255,000	1,614,000	251,000	948,000	1,117,000	24,160,000	3,170,000	2,772,000	374,000	15,830,000	2,014,000
1965	7,058,000	5,886,000	2,505,000	1,983,000	272,000	1,127,000	1,172,000	24,879,000	3,455,000	2,413,000	394,000	16,618,000	1,999,000
1966	7,282,000	6,042,000	2,716,000	1,949,000	263,000	1,114,000	1,240,000	28,126,000	3,915,000	1,981,000	409,000	19,793,000	2,028,000
1967	7,350,000	6,006,000	2,587,000	1,847,000	287,000	1,285,000	1,344,000	33,560,000	4,584,000	2,012,000	457,000	23,919,000	2,588,000
1968	8,170,000	6,721,000	2,740,000	2,123,000	299,000	1,559,000	1,449,000	38,127,000	4,979,000	2,126,000	481,000	27,951,000	2,590,000
1969	8,820,000	7,316,000	3,019,000	2,216,000	332,000	1,750,000	1,505,000	43,600,000	5,641,000	2,089,000	507,000	32,474,000	2,889,000
1970	9,447,000	7,820,000	3,211,000	2,486,000	370,000	1,753,000	1,627,000	48,521,000	6,399,000	2,816,000	551,000	35,828,000	2,927,000
1971	10,300,000	8,675,000	3,432,000	2,816,000	410,000	2,018,000	1,625,000	58,026,000	7,414,000	4,803,000	529,000	41,959,000	3,321,000
1972	11,398,353	9,715,084	3,739,652	3,281,198	403,802	2,290,432	1,683,269	64,635,489	8,573,918	4,860,749	642,964	46,949,000	3,608,858
1973	13,034,656	11,203,769	4,084,324	3,760,603	493,351	2,865,491	1,830,887	75,325,532	10,378,337	4,153,625	736,602	56,371,000	3,685,968
1974	14,405,644	12,486,898	4,669,237	4,151,719	504,608	3,161,334	1,918,746	86,742,023	12,347,587	4,752,869	829,006	64,688,000	4,124,561
1975	17,285,636	15,276,454	5,439,936	5,279,905	579,772	3,976,841	2,009,182	109,233,888	14,569,719	12,378,000	909,859	76,587,000	4,789,310
1976	19,542,578	17,451,298	5,929,099	6,429,170	661,100	4,431,929	2,091,280	129,387,626	16,774,197	18,121,000	1,070,266	88,300,000	5,122,163
1977	24,189,974	22,094,161	6,380,513	9,312,532	803,071	5,598,045	2,095,813	144,084,753	19,219,649	14,876,807	1,326,063	103,177,000	5,485,234
1978	26,277,721	23,960,424	6,884,321	10,587,718	915,345	5,573,040	2,317,297	154,822,476	21,778,210	10,937,196	1,422,552	115,005,000	5,679,518
1979	30,845,544	28,429,338	8,068,538	12,664,653	1,231,445	6,464,702	2,416,206	170,856,296	24,806,221	9,028,033	1,703,742	129,177,000	6,141,300
1980	36,190,638	33,599,199	9,227,513	15,015,946	1,714,707	7,641,033	2,591,439	199,372,598	28,869,638	12,282,600	1,976,811	149,451,000	6,792,549
1981	43,016,017	40,289,791	10,582,266	17,870,579	2,229,756	9,607,190	2,726,226	238,921,516	33,558,641	18,190,386	2,043,011	177,520,000	7,609,478
1982	48,412,312	45,570,599	11,408,258	20,446,411	2,566,390	11,149,540	2,841,713	267,552,518	37,485,977	18,472,010	2,524,442	201,204,000	7,866,089
1983	52,811,863	49,995,463	12,453,908	22,222,709	3,007,745	12,311,101	2,816,400	297,428,571	40,253,527	24,605,447	2,867,956	221,489,000	8,212,641
1984	55,061,543	52,320,660	12,579,505	23,206,055	3,343,704	13,191,396	2,740,883	304,294,738	44,021,295	14,277,628	3,093,277	234,517,000	8,385,538
1985	59,798,123	56,975,167	14,297,760	25,341,478	3,467,916	13,868,013	2,822,956	328,823,615	47,719,594	15,170,083	3,462,152	253,594,000	8,877,786
1986	65,296,932	62,430,342	16,195,860	28,182,170	3,291,450	14,760,862	2,866,590	346,730,206	50,747,100	15,067,895	3,618,676	267,923,000	9,373,535
1987	69,108,110	66,172,409	18,466,637	28,951,042	2,895,114	15,859,616	2,935,701	367,257,606	55,593,708	15,412,132	4,288,454	282,212,000	9,751,312
1988	70,048,655	67,211,390	18,863,929	29,046,861	2,824,542	16,476,058	2,837,265	388,168,470	60,496,132	13,205,828	4,849,194	299,475,000	10,142,316
1989	73,509,295	70,637,775	20,524,366	30,177,608	2,840,923	17,094,878	2,871,520	414,623,543	64,385,469	12,951,837	5,318,374	321,335,000	10,632,863
1990	77,800,522	74,874,709	22,101,397	30,996,783	2,988,742	18,787,787	2,925,813	454,218,243	69,782,896	16,586,338	6,372,855	350,435,000	11,041,154
1991	81,004,078	77,999,375	23,560,543	31,090,032	2,969,530	20,379,270	3,004,703	494,159,509	75,745,090	22,222,392	7,337,666	376,933,000	11,921,361
1992	85,314,022	82,224,046	24,833,879	32,518,602	3,077,733	21,793,832	3,089,976	544,944,648	80,344,844	32,973,355	7,844,385	410,855,000	12,927,064
1993	84,483,027	81,421,482	24,621,180	32,230,911	3,273,135	21,296,256	3,061,545	585,054,747	86,894,181	35,479,045	8,874,325	440,994,000	12,813,196
1994	91,162,497	88,177,901	26,617,294	33,829,381	3,509,894	24,221,332	2,984,596	618,244,171	92,388,355	28,706,671	8,851,525	472,461,000	15,836,620
1995	94,234,981	91,214,778	28,040,858	34,021,256	3,433,922	25,718,742	3,020,203	665,630,680	100,222,170	35,282,966	8,356,094	505,709,000	16,060,450

TABLE Ea61–124   Total government expenditure, by function: 1902–1995   *Continued*

[1] Through 1976, included with other general expenditures, series Ea111, or with other long-term debt outstanding, not shown in this table.

[2] Through 1950, state and local amounts for air transportation and water transportation and terminals are included under series Ea111.

[3] Includes parking facilities and transit subsidies.

[4] Through 1970, series Ea103 includes all expenditures on general government administration; thereafter (and earlier for some functions), individual activities are reported separately. Some activities reported separately may have been included under other general expenditures during the earlier period.

[5] Excludes interest on federal securities held by federal agencies and funds.

Source
Figures are from data files provided by the Census of Governments. For published versions through 1982, see U.S. Department of Commerce, "Historical Statistics on Government Finance and Employment," in *Census of Governments, 1982*, volume 6, pp. 225–64.

Documentation
See the text for Table Ea24–51.

TABLE Ea125–131   Total government debt, by level: 1902–1996

Contributed by John Joseph Wallis

	Outstanding at end of fiscal year				Change during year		
	Total	Federal	State	Local	Federal	State	Local
	Ea125	Ea126	Ea127	Ea128	Ea129	Ea130	Ea131
Fiscal year	Thousand dollars	Thousand dollars	Thousand dollars	Thousand dollars	Thousand dollars	Thousand dollars	Thousand dollars
1902	3,285,000	1,178,000	230,000	1,877,000	−44,000	11,000	—
1913	5,607,000	1,193,000	379,000	4,035,000	−1,000	47,000	—
1922	33,072,000	22,963,000	1,131,000	8,978,000	−1,014,000	230,000	1,216,000
1927	33,393,000	18,512,000	1,971,000	12,910,000	−1,131,000	145,000	929,000
1932	38,692,000	19,487,000	2,832,000	16,373,000	2,686,000	223,000	9,000
1934	45,982,000	27,053,000	3,248,000	15,681,000	4,514,000	167,000	−826,000
1936	53,253,000	33,779,000	3,413,000	16,061,000	3,008,000	−9,000	306,000
1938	56,601,000	37,165,000	3,343,000	16,093,000	740,000	−32,000	6,000
1940	63,251,000	42,968,000	3,590,000	16,693,000	2,528,000	58,000	162,000
1942	91,759,000	72,422,000	3,257,000	16,080,000	23,461,000	−233,000	−337,000
1944	218,482,000	201,003,000	2,776,000	14,703,000	64,307,000	−214,000	−1,080,000
1946	285,339,000	269,422,000	2,353,000	13,564,000	10,740,000	−154,000	−600,000
1948	270,948,000	252,292,000	3,676,000	14,980,000	−5,994,000	708,000	1,133,000
1950	281,472,000	257,357,000	5,285,000	18,830,000	4,587,000	1,137,000	1,979,000
1952	289,205,000	259,105,000	6,874,000	23,226,000	3,883,000	652,000	1,332,000
1953	299,852,000	266,071,000	7,824,000	25,957,000	6,966,000	950,000	2,731,000
1954	310,190,000	271,260,000	9,600,000	29,331,000	5,189,000	1,776,000	3,374,000
1955	318,641,000	274,374,000	11,198,000	33,069,000	3,114,000	1,598,000	3,738,000
1956	321,619,000	272,751,000	12,890,000	35,978,000	−1,623,000	1,692,000	2,909,000
1957	323,566,000	270,527,000	13,738,000	39,301,000	−2,224,000	848,000	3,323,000
1958	334,530,000	276,343,000	15,394,000	42,793,000	5,816,000	1,656,000	3,492,000
1959	348,816,000	284,706,000	16,930,000	47,180,000	8,363,000	1,536,000	4,387,000
1960	356,286,000	286,331,000	18,543,000	51,412,000	1,625,000	1,613,000	4,232,000
1961	363,994,000	288,971,000	19,993,000	55,030,000	2,640,000	1,450,000	3,618,000
1962	379,479,000	298,201,000	22,023,000	59,255,000	9,230,000	2,030,000	4,225,000
1963	393,312,000	305,860,000	23,176,000	64,276,000	7,659,000	1,153,000	5,021,000
1964	403,935,000	311,713,000	25,041,000	67,181,000	5,853,000	1,865,000	2,905,000
1965	416,786,000	317,274,000	27,034,000	72,478,000	5,561,000	1,993,000	5,297,000
1966	426,958,000	319,907,000	29,564,000	77,487,000	2,633,000	2,530,000	5,009,000
1967	439,880,000	326,221,000	32,472,000	81,187,000	6,314,000	2,908,000	3,700,000
1968	468,736,000	347,578,000	35,666,000	85,492,000	21,357,000	3,194,000	4,305,000
1969	487,268,000	353,720,000	39,555,000	93,995,000	6,142,000	3,889,000	8,503,000
1970	514,489,000	370,919,000	42,008,000	101,563,000	17,199,000	2,453,000	7,568,000
1971	568,286,000	409,459,000	47,793,000	111,034,000	38,540,000	5,785,000	9,471,000
1972	612,479,466	437,321,000	54,453,436	120,705,030	27,862,000	6,660,436	9,671,030
1973	656,902,643	468,418,000	59,374,951	129,109,692	31,097,000	4,921,515	8,404,662
1974	692,850,849	486,235,000	65,296,227	141,319,622	17,817,000	5,921,276	12,209,930
1975	764,054,377	544,129,000	72,127,377	147,798,000	57,894,000	6,831,150	6,478,378
1976	871,815,323	631,283,000	84,825,000	155,707,323	87,154,000	12,697,623	7,909,323
1977	968,794,248	709,136,000	90,199,895	169,458,353	77,853,000	5,374,895	13,751,030
1978	1,060,856,007	780,423,000	102,568,904	177,864,103	71,287,000	12,369,009	8,405,750
1979	1,137,852,860	833,750,000	111,739,943	192,362,917	53,327,000	9,171,039	14,498,814

(continued)

TABLE Ea125–131   Total government debt, by level: 1902–1996   *Continued*

	Outstanding at end of fiscal year				Change during year		
	Total	Federal	State	Local	Federal	State	Local
	Ea125	Ea126	Ea127	Ea128	Ea129	Ea130	Ea131
Fiscal year	Thousand dollars	Thousand dollars	Thousand dollars	Thousand dollars	Thousand dollars	Thousand dollars	Thousand dollars
1980	1,249,919,055	914,316,000	121,957,862	213,645,193	80,566,000	10,217,919	21,282,276
1981	1,367,830,881	1,003,939,000	134,846,537	229,045,344	89,623,000	12,888,675	15,400,151
1982	1,551,565,046	1,146,986,000	147,470,100	257,108,946	143,047,000	12,623,563	28,063,602
1983	1,836,386,890	1,381,886,000	167,289,946	287,210,944	234,900,000	19,819,846	30,101,998
1984	2,083,063,678	1,576,734,000	186,376,896	319,952,782	194,848,000	19,086,950	32,741,838
1985	2,396,084,199	1,827,451,000	211,916,930	356,716,269	250,717,000	25,540,034	36,763,487
1986	2,788,380,867	2,129,506,000	247,715,163	411,159,704	302,055,000	35,798,233	54,443,435
1987	3,081,204,608	2,354,073,000	265,551,412	461,580,196	224,567,000	17,836,249	50,420,492
1988	3,369,614,598	2,614,581,000	276,786,404	478,247,194	260,508,000	11,234,992	16,666,998
1989	3,680,189,130	2,881,112,000	295,500,265	503,576,865	266,531,000	18,713,861	25,329,671
1990	4,124,078,815	3,266,073,000	318,253,891	539,751,924	384,961,000	22,753,626	36,175,059
1991	4,598,765,466	3,683,054,000	345,554,047	570,157,419	416,981,000	27,300,156	30,405,495
1992	5,058,480,632	4,082,871,000	372,319,136	603,290,496	399,817,000	26,765,089	33,133,077
1993	5,453,857,475	4,436,171,000	389,721,038	627,965,437	353,300,000	17,401,902	24,674,941
1994	5,795,952,279	4,721,292,000	410,998,326	663,661,953	285,121,000	21,277,288	35,696,516
1995	6,116,315,314	5,000,945,000	427,239,150	688,131,164	279,653,000	16,240,824	24,469,211
1996	—	—	452,392,009	717,322,308	—	25,152,859	29,191,144

Source

Figures are from data files provided by the Census of Governments. For published versions through 1982, see U.S. Department of Commerce, "Historical Statistics on Government Finance and Employment," in *Census of Governments, 1982*, volume 6, pp. 225–64.

Documentation

See the text for Table Ea24–51.

TABLE Ea132–159 Federal government revenue, by source: 1902–1995
Contributed by John Joseph Wallis

				General revenue						
					Taxes					
						Sales and gross receipts				
									Select sales	
Fiscal year	Total revenue	Direct	Intergovernmental	Total	Own-source	Total	Total	Custom duties	Total	Motor fuel
	Ea132	Ea133	Ea134	Ea135	Ea136	Ea137	Ea138	Ea139	Ea140	Ea141
	Million dollars	Million dollars	Million dollars	Million dollars	Million dollars	Million dollars	Million dollars	Million dollars	Million dollars	Million dollars
1902	653	653	0	653	653	513	487	243	244	0
1913	962	962	0	962	962	662	612	310	302	0
1922	4,221	4,261	0	4,221	4,221	3,371	1,152	318	834	0
1927	4,469	4,469	0	4,396	4,396	3,364	1,088	585	503	0
1932	2,634	2,634	0	2,542	2,542	1,813	733	311	422	0
1934	3,886	3,886	0	3,801	3,801	2,942	1,877	299	1,578	203
1936	5,176	5,176	0	5,086	5,086	3,882	1,905	372	1,533	177
1938	7,226	7,226	0	6,595	6,595	5,344	2,021	343	1,678	204
1940	7,000	7,000	0	6,194	6,194	4,878	2,127	331	1,796	226
1942	16,062	16,062	0	14,788	14,788	12,265	3,425	369	3,056	370
1944	51,399	51,399	0	48,663	48,663	40,321	4,723	417	4,306	271
1946	46,405	46,405	0	43,629	43,629	36,286	6,964	424	6,540	406
1948	47,254	47,254	0	44,277	44,277	37,876	7,650	403	7,247	479
1950	43,527	43,527	0	40,061	40,061	35,186	7,843	407	7,436	534
1952	71,798	71,798	0	66,615	66,615	59,744	9,332	532	8,800	720
1953	74,239	74,239	0	68,687	68,687	62,796	10,352	596	9,756	906
1954	75,835	75,835	0	69,798	69,798	62,409	10,367	542	9,825	845
1955	71,915	71,915	0	65,322	65,322	57,589	9,578	585	8,994	972
1956	81,294	81,294	0	73,162	73,162	65,226	10,469	682	9,787	1,055
1957	87,066	87,066	0	78,403	78,403	69,815	11,127	735	10,392	1,498
1958	86,006	86,006	0	76,112	76,112	68,007	11,273	782	10,491	1,592
1959	85,459	85,459	0	75,249	75,249	67,257	11,332	925	10,407	1,656
1960	99,800	99,800	0	87,088	87,088	77,003	12,603	1,105	11,498	1,984
1961	101,341	101,341	0	87,062	87,062	77,470	12,649	982	11,667	2,333
1962	106,441	106,441	0	92,016	92,016	82,262	13,428	1,142	12,286	2,451
1963	114,557	114,557	0	98,145	98,145	86,797	14,215	1,205	13,010	2,558
1964	120,959	120,959	0	102,300	102,300	90,507	14,776	1,252	13,524	2,697
1965	125,837	125,837	0	106,720	106,720	93,710	15,786	1,442	14,344	2,792
1966	141,142	141,142	0	118,547	118,547	104,095	14,641	1,767	12,874	2,955
1967	161,351	161,351	0	130,869	130,869	115,121	15,806	1,901	13,905	3,178
1968	165,239	165,239	0	133,240	133,240	117,554	16,275	2,038	14,236	3,325
1969	199,637	199,637	0	162,845	162,845	145,996	17,826	2,319	15,506	3,508
1970	205,562	205,562	0	163,582	163,582	146,082	18,297	2,430	15,867	3,776
1971	202,537	202,537	0	156,887	156,887	137,277	19,427	2,591	16,836	3,918
1972	223,378	223,378	0	172,122	172,122	153,733	20,101	3,287	16,814	4,167
1973	253,697	253,697	0	193,461	193,461	165,030	19,722	3,188	16,534	4,402
1974	289,016	288,519	497	217,781	217,284	184,112	20,534	3,450	17,084	4,609
1975	303,745	302,501	1,244	222,984	221,740	189,970	21,090	4,289	16,801	4,475
1976	324,555	323,224	1,331	239,044	237,713	201,414	21,718	4,496	17,222	4,636
1977	383,155	381,780	1,375	284,987	283,612	243,842	23,180	5,394	17,786	4,903
1978	431,280	429,722	1,558	320,773	319,215	274,519	25,453	6,823	18,630	5,083
1979	500,927	499,601	1,326	373,754	372,428	318,932	26,714	7,688	19,026	5,188
1980	565,477	563,690	1,787	419,123	417,336	350,781	32,034	7,436	24,598	4,887
1981	660,758	658,954	1,804	489,509	487,705	405,714	48,561	8,161	40,400	4,678
1982	687,647	685,835	1,812	497,833	496,021	405,125	45,675	8,917	36,758	4,950
1983	679,663	677,817	1,846	483,733	481,887	381,179	44,471	8,727	35,744	5,784
1984	754,016	752,421	1,595	531,109	529,514	414,829	49,459	11,463	37,996	10,714
1985	806,808	804,877	1,931	560,449	558,518	454,037	49,159	12,176	36,983	11,614
1986	847,516	845,378	2,138	580,611	578,473	471,898	47,046	13,420	33,626	11,641
1987	952,631	950,144	2,487	667,004	664,517	539,400	48,423	15,138	33,285	11,952
1988	1,012,343	1,009,484	2,859	692,555	689,696	562,600	52,604	16,317	36,287	12,876
1989	1,092,660	1,089,757	2,903	743,359	740,456	615,853	52,527	16,450	36,077	14,372
1990	1,154,596	1,151,685	2,911	783,390	780,479	632,267	53,970	16,810	37,160	13,077
1991	1,200,682	1,197,448	3,234	812,339	809,105	641,982	58,495	16,034	42,461	16,917
1992	1,259,383	1,255,952	3,431	854,821	851,390	659,041	64,282	17,480	46,802	19,865
1993	1,308,369	1,305,071	3,298	890,414	887,116	712,932	67,467	18,931	48,536	20,223
1994	1,398,775	1,395,556	3,219	946,968	943,749	778,380	72,759	20,264	52,495	26,441
1995	1,494,331	1,491,271	3,060	1,018,102	1,015,042	844,415	75,185	19,438	55,747	28,669

(continued)

TABLE Ea132–159   Federal government revenue, by source: 1902–1995   *Continued*

				General revenue						
			Taxes						Charges and miscellaneous	
	Sales and gross receipts				Income					
	Select sales									
	Alcoholic beverage	Tobacco	Other	Total	Individual	Corporation	Other	Total	General charges	Miscellaneous
	Ea142	Ea143	Ea144	Ea145	Ea146	Ea147	Ea148	Ea149	Ea150	Ea151
Fiscal year	Million dollars	Million dollars	Million dollars	Million dollars	Million dollars	Million dollars	Million dollars	Million dollars	Million dollars	Million dollars
1902	187	49	8	0	0	0	26	140	—	—
1913	223	77	2	35	0	35	15	300	—	—
1922	44	270	520	1,939	—	—	280	850	—	—
1927	20	376	107	2,138	879	1,259	138	1,032	—	—
1932	8	398	16	1,003	405	598	77	730	—	—
1934	248	424	703	791	405	386	274	859	—	—
1936	493	499	364	1,411	666	745	566	1,204	—	—
1938	556	567	351	2,610	1,277	1,333	713	1,251	—	—
1940	613	607	350	2,082	959	1,123	669	1,316	—	—
1942	1,037	779	870	7,932	3,205	4,727	908	2,523	—	—
1944	1,592	986	1,457	34,438	19,701	14,737	1,160	8,342	—	—
1946	2,479	1,156	2,499	27,990	16,157	11,833	1,332	7,343	—	—
1948	2,203	1,297	3,268	28,983	19,305	9,678	1,243	6,401	—	—
1950	2,165	1,325	3,412	26,233	15,745	10,488	1,110	4,875	—	—
1952	2,549	1,565	3,966	49,147	27,921	21,226	1,265	6,871	5,786	1,085
1953	2,781	1,655	4,414	51,054	29,816	21,238	1,390	5,891	4,744	1,149
1954	2,716	1,580	4,684	50,643	29,542	21,101	1,399	7,390	5,626	1,764
1955	2,694	1,571	3,757	46,608	28,747	17,861	1,403	7,733	5,861	1,872
1956	2,846	1,607	4,279	53,068	32,188	20,880	1,689	7,936	5,717	2,219
1957	2,893	1,669	4,332	56,787	35,620	21,167	1,901	8,588	6,807	1,781
1958	2,860	1,728	4,311	54,798	34,724	20,074	1,936	8,105	5,929	2,176
1959	2,915	1,798	4,038	54,028	36,719	17,309	1,897	7,992	5,877	2,115
1960	3,106	1,927	4,481	62,209	40,715	21,494	2,191	10,085	7,132	2,953
1961	3,124	1,986	4,224	62,292	41,338	20,954	2,529	9,592	7,101	2,491
1962	3,248	2,022	4,565	66,094	45,571	20,523	2,740	9,754	7,395	2,359
1963	3,345	2,075	5,032	69,167	47,588	21,579	3,415	11,347	8,347	3,001
1964	3,478	2,048	5,301	72,190	48,697	23,493	3,541	11,793	8,788	3,006
1965	3,667	2,142	5,743	74,253	48,792	25,461	3,671	13,010	9,247	3,763
1966	3,698	2,066	4,155	85,519	55,446	30,073	3,935	14,452	9,817	4,635
1967	3,958	2,077	4,692	95,497	61,526	33,971	3,818	15,748	10,602	5,146
1968	4,269	2,122	4,520	97,391	68,726	28,665	3,888	15,686	10,397	5,290
1969	4,534	2,138	5,326	123,927	87,249	36,678	4,243	16,848	11,479	5,369
1970	4,726	2,094	5,271	123,241	90,412	32,829	4,544	17,500	11,401	6,099
1971	4,781	2,207	5,930	113,015	86,230	26,785	4,835	19,610	12,444	7,166
1972	5,089	2,207	5,351	126,903	94,737	32,166	6,729	18,389	12,481	5,908
1973	5,129	2,277	4,726	139,398	103,246	36,152	5,910	28,431	16,808	11,623
1974	5,339	2,437	4,699	157,572	118,952	38,620	6,006	33,172	18,343	14,829
1975	5,331	2,315	4,680	163,007	122,386	40,621	5,873	31,770	19,568	12,202
1976	5,413	2,488	4,685	173,012	131,603	41,409	6,684	36,299	22,532	13,767
1977	5,387	2,399	5,097	211,617	156,725	54,892	9,045	39,770	25,054	14,716
1978	5,594	2,451	5,502	240,940	180,988	59,952	8,126	44,696	27,135	17,561
1979	5,629	2,496	5,713	283,518	217,841	65,677	8,700	53,496	30,957	22,539
1980	5,685	2,446	11,580	308,669	244,069	64,600	10,078	66,555	35,759	30,796
1981	5,667	2,584	27,471	346,688	285,551	61,137	10,465	81,991	40,296	41,695
1982	5,439	2,539	23,830	347,318	298,111	49,207	12,132	90,896	46,283	44,613
1983	5,613	4,140	20,207	325,960	288,938	37,022	10,748	100,708	50,547	50,161
1984	5,381	4,664	17,237	352,848	295,955	56,893	12,522	114,685	64,318	50,367
1985	5,376	4,483	15,510	392,249	330,918	61,331	12,629	104,481	60,992	43,489
1986	5,601	4,608	11,776	412,102	348,959	63,143	12,750	106,575	63,291	43,284
1987	6,135	4,937	10,261	476,483	392,557	83,926	14,494	125,117	76,875	48,242
1988	5,830	4,523	13,058	495,376	401,181	94,195	14,620	127,096	80,081	47,015
1989	5,810	4,290	11,605	548,981	445,690	103,291	14,345	124,603	76,322	48,281
1990	5,753	4,268	14,062	560,391	466,884	93,507	17,906	148,212	88,877	59,335
1991	7,227	4,782	13,535	565,913	467,827	98,086	17,574	167,123	86,292	80,831
1992	7,907	5,190	13,840	576,735	476,465	100,270	18,024	192,349	89,482	102,867
1993	7,704	5,700	14,909	627,200	509,680	117,520	18,265	174,184	94,613	79,571
1994	7,600	5,744	12,710	683,440	543,055	140,385	22,181	165,369	96,670	68,699
1995	7,523	5,878	13,677	747,247	590,243	157,004	21,983	170,627	95,860	74,767

TABLE Ea132–159   Federal government revenue, by source: 1902–1995   *Continued*

			Insurance trust					
			Unemployment compensation		Other			
Fiscal year	Total	Employee retirement	Total	Payroll taxes	Total	Railroad retirement	Veteran life insurance	Other
	Ea152	Ea153	Ea154	Ea155	Ea156	Ea157	Ea158	Ea159
	Million dollars	Million dollars	Million dollars	Million dollars	Million dollars	Million dollars	Million dollars	Million dollars
1902	0	0	0	0	0	0	0	0
1913	0	0	0	0	0	0	0	0
1922	40	14	0	0	26	0	26	0
1927	73	25	0	0	48	0	48	0
1932	91	33	0	0	58	0	58	0
1934	85	29	0	0	56	0	56	0
1936	90	33	0	0	57	0	57	0
1938	631	39	0	0	592	146	59	387
1940	806	45	46	46	715	121	56	538
1942	1,274	90	76	76	1,108	141	98	869
1944	2,736	270	109	109	2,357	263	834	1,260
1946	2,776	282	117	117	2,377	283	893	1,201
1948	2,977	239	131	131	2,607	557	434	1,616
1950	3,466	359	10	10	3,097	550	440	2,107
1952	5,183	418	10	10	4,755	735	473	3,547
1953	5,552	423	15	15	5,113	625	428	4,060
1954	6,037	432	18	18	5,587	603	430	4,554
1955	6,594	442	16	16	6,136	599	450	5,087
1956	8,132	577	31	31	7,524	641	441	6,442
1957	8,663	644	74	74	7,943	616	472	6,857
1958	9,894	677	90	90	9,126	575	507	8,044
1959	10,210	770	102	102	9,338	525	519	8,294
1960	12,712	769	153	153	11,790	607	527	10,656
1961	14,279	866	150	150	13,263	571	561	12,131
1962	14,425	877	147	147	13,401	564	548	12,289
1963	16,412	946	150	150	15,317	559	563	14,195
1964	18,659	1,006	144	144	17,508	593	529	16,386
1965	19,117	1,071	143	143	17,903	636	525	16,742
1966	22,595	1,126	139	139	21,329	683	623	20,023
1967	30,482	1,220	137	137	29,126	795	668	27,663
1968	31,999	1,375	131	131	30,493	858	606	29,029
1969	36,793	1,479	126	126	35,188	939	600	33,649
1970	41,980	1,713	123	123	40,144	980	679	38,485
1971	45,650	1,913	119	119	43,618	1,044	665	41,909
1972	51,256	2,054	112	112	49,090	1,082	667	47,341
1973	60,236	2,144	113	113	57,979	1,250	659	56,070
1974	71,235	2,299	713	713	68,223	1,508	656	66,059
1975	80,761	2,508	324	324	77,929	1,625	687	75,617
1976	85,511	2,756	101	101	82,654	1,656	678	80,320
1977	98,168	2,906	169	169	95,093	1,908	690	92,495
1978	110,507	3,129	204	204	107,174	1,975	697	104,502
1979	127,173	3,386	194	194	123,593	2,409	662	120,522
1980	146,354	3,619	161	161	142,574	2,534	670	139,370
1981	171,249	3,869	162	162	167,218	2,711	673	163,834
1982	189,814	4,102	181	181	185,531	3,185	748	181,598
1983	195,930	4,305	158	158	191,467	3,561	717	187,189
1984	222,907	4,433	190	190	218,284	4,055	709	213,520
1985	246,359	4,592	221	221	241,546	4,330	651	236,565
1986	266,905	4,541	221	221	262,143	4,194	686	257,263
1987	285,627	4,486	204	204	280,937	4,337	726	275,874
1988	319,788	4,444	195	195	315,149	4,423	703	310,023
1989	349,301	4,424	201	201	344,676	4,488	695	339,493
1990	371,206	4,401	100	100	366,705	4,352	669	361,684
1991	388,343	4,446	184	184	383,713	4,461	742	378,510
1992	404,562	4,658	134	134	399,770	4,608	894	394,268
1993	417,955	4,684	64	64	413,207	4,451	896	407,860
1994	451,807	4,540	27	27	447,240	4,386	871	441,983
1995	476,229	4,439	24	24	471,766	4,551	848	466,367

(continued)

TABLE Ea132–159   Federal government revenue, by source: 1902–1995   *Continued*

Source

Data in this table are taken from spreadsheets provided by the Census of Governments. Published versions of the data through 1982 can be found in U.S. Department of Commerce, "Historical Statistics on Government Finance and Employment." in *Census of Governments, 1982,* volume 6, pp. 225–64.

Documentation

See the text for Table Ea24–51.

Series Ea159. Includes Social Security, medical insurance, and other insurance trust expenditures not elsewhere classified.

TABLE Ea160–170   Federal government expenditure, by character and object: 1902–1995

Contributed by John Joseph Wallis

				Direct							
	Total expenditure	Salaries and wages	Intergovernmental	Total	Current operation	Capital outlay			Assistance and subsidies	Interest on debt	Insurance trust
						Total	Construction	Other			
	Ea160	Ea161	Ea162	Ea163	Ea164 [1]	Ea165	Ea166	Ea167 [1]	Ea168 [1]	Ea169	Ea170
Fiscal year	Million dollars	Million dollars	Million dollars	Million dollars	Million dollars	Million dollars	Million dollars	Million dollars	Million dollars	Million dollars	Million dollars
1902	572	160	7	565	498	—	38	—	—	29	0
1913	970	401	12	958	816	—	119	—	—	23	0
1922	3,763	919	118	3,645	2,487	—	161	—	—	988	9
1927	3,533	1,110	123	3,410	2,442	—	174	—	—	764	30
1932	4,266	1,188	232	4,034	3,083	—	318	—	—	582	51
1934	5,941	2,144	976	4,965	3,186	—	985	—	—	734	60
1936	9,165	2,797	908	8,257	6,312	—	1,162	—	—	717	66
1938	8,449	3,023	762	7,687	5,552	—	1,124	—	—	840	171
1940	10,061	3,347	884	9,177	6,686	—	1,311	—	—	899	281
1942	35,549	6,451	887	34,662	26,276	—	6,991	—	—	1,026	369
1944	100,520	21,772	1,072	99,448	92,254	—	4,555	—	—	2,151	488
1946	66,534	22,468	894	65,640	59,123	—	1,566	—	—	3,865	1,086
1948	35,592	8,915	1,771	33,821	26,790	—	1,291	—	—	4,323	1,417
1950	44,800	10,487	2,371	42,429	31,839	—	1,671	—	—	4,404	4,515
1952	71,568	17,721	2,585	68,984	37,579	17,437	3,337	14,100	5,916	4,262	3,790
1953	79,990	19,970	2,873	77,117	43,086	18,498	3,735	14,763	6,376	4,863	4,294
1954	77,692	19,195	2,967	74,725	40,986	18,244	4,001	14,244	5,637	4,796	5,061
1955	73,441	19,377	3,099	70,342	34,947	18,030	3,564	14,467	6,282	4,845	6,238
1956	75,991	20,454	3,347	72,644	38,582	14,956	3,416	11,540	6,595	5,311	7,200
1957	81,783	20,779	3,873	77,910	40,983	16,250	3,396	12,854	6,660	5,497	8,520
1958	86,054	21,071	4,835	81,219	40,775	16,852	3,218	13,634	7,119	6,116	10,356
1959	93,531	22,466	6,355	87,177	45,581	16,877	3,662	13,215	7,329	5,543	11,847
1960	97,284	22,691	6,994	90,289	45,336	16,842	3,480	13,362	6,884	7,662	13,565
1961	104,863	23,754	7,011	97,852	51,923	16,229	3,773	12,456	7,324	7,485	14,892
1962	113,428	25,424	7,735	105,693	55,410	18,429	3,673	14,756	7,952	7,162	16,740
1963	118,805	26,237	8,507	110,298	57,728	18,635	3,752	14,884	7,979	7,682	18,273
1964	125,949	28,051	10,097	115,852	61,809	17,818	4,031	13,787	8,865	8,293	19,067
1965	130,059	29,629	11,062	118,996	68,552	13,209	4,472	8,737	8,366	8,940	19,930
1966	143,022	32,904	13,115	129,907	70,276	17,652	4,610	13,041	9,048	9,589	23,342
1967	166,849	36,819	15,027	151,821	85,618	17,868	4,470	13,398	9,679	10,373	28,283
1968	184,464	40,379	18,053	166,411	90,204	21,326	3,972	17,354	10,801	11,607	32,474
1969	196,165	43,373	19,421	176,744	95,369	19,006	3,932	15,074	11,562	13,260	37,547
1970	208,190	47,501	23,257	184,933	99,105	17,869	4,150	13,719	12,674	14,037	41,248
1971	225,837	49,546	27,180	198,657	102,884	15,686	4,081	11,605	15,253	16,599	48,235
1972	242,186	53,917	33,584	208,602	100,130	20,816	4,801	16,015	16,456	17,114	54,086
1973	272,770	56,557	41,268	231,502	110,308	20,072	4,616	15,456	18,538	18,332	64,252
1974	295,503	60,160	42,854	252,649	115,034	19,166	5,109	14,057	21,924	22,450	74,075
1975	341,517	57,532	49,628	291,889	124,237	21,798	6,605	15,193	32,824	25,005	88,025
1976	389,798	63,925	67,770	322,028	130,944	25,100	6,924	18,176	35,245	29,306	101,433
1977	432,162	66,852	72,838	359,324	142,346	30,006	7,429	22,577	35,760	33,276	117,936
1978	479,297	73,927	77,440	401,857	154,678	36,289	8,521	27,768	40,263	39,330	131,297
1979	535,345	78,415	83,205	452,140	172,798	39,955	8,403	31,552	43,267	48,768	147,352
1980	617,165	86,990	90,836	526,329	209,199	36,492	6,918	29,574	48,776	61,286	170,576
1981	719,249	93,553	94,609	624,640	241,196	48,903	7,360	41,543	51,692	80,510	202,339
1982	796,483	104,285	86,014	710,469	265,891	62,835	8,177	54,658	51,817	101,816	228,110
1983	874,264	109,641	92,686	781,578	286,634	80,744	8,796	71,948	55,371	108,735	250,094
1984	928,188	111,173	99,015	829,173	324,919	72,456	9,387	63,069	58,447	109,209	264,142

Note appears at end of table

TABLE Ea160–170 Federal government expenditure, by character and object: 1902–1995 *Continued*

	Total expenditure	Salaries and wages	Intergovernmental	Direct			Capital outlay			Assistance and subsidies	Interest on debt	Insurance trust
				Total	Current operation	Total	Construction	Other			
	Ea160	Ea161	Ea162	Ea163	Ea164 [1]	Ea165	Ea166	Ea167 [1]	Ea168 [1]	Ea169	Ea170
Fiscal year	Million dollars	Million dollars	Million dollars	Million dollars	Million dollars	Million dollars	Million dollars	Million dollars	Million dollars	Million dollars	Million dollars
1985	1,032,131	120,331	107,242	924,889	360,281	77,014	10,532	66,482	62,680	140,281	284,633
1986	1,096,401	123,054	115,632	980,769	386,388	85,647	11,866	73,781	64,375	144,167	300,192
1987	1,148,654	129,262	111,511	1,037,143	412,126	96,871	12,403	84,468	65,537	146,155	316,454
1988	1,214,812	134,912	118,906	1,095,906	435,791	93,531	10,468	83,063	72,176	158,119	336,289
1989	1,270,068	138,562	127,247	1,142,821	432,256	99,790	11,788	88,002	76,857	174,288	359,630
1990	1,383,692	146,436	137,561	1,246,131	490,016	97,891	9,422	88,469	79,375	187,952	390,897
1991	1,479,509	154,289	160,145	1,319,364	520,681	95,575	10,491	85,084	87,965	195,142	420,001
1992	1,527,311	161,551	186,036	1,341,275	497,115	93,095	10,920	82,175	96,622	199,713	454,730
1993	1,570,503	162,536	204,630	1,365,873	490,847	86,328	9,661	76,667	103,655	198,795	486,248
1994	1,630,283	162,658	217,919	1,412,364	494,250	79,827	9,648	70,179	112,842	202,663	522,782
1995	1,704,421	162,392	233,388	1,471,033	486,041	73,584	9,930	63,654	119,892	233,225	558,291

[1] Through 1950, amounts for other capital outlay and assistance and subsidies are included under current operation.

Source

Figures are from data files provided by the Census of Governments. For published versions through 1982, see U.S. Department of Commerce, "Historical Statistics on Government Finance and Employment," in *Census of Governments, 1982*, volume 6, pp. 225–64.

Documentation

See the text for Table Ea24–51.

In order to compute total expenditures under a different revenue concept, use the data from Table Ea125–131 on the change in debt during the year. See the essay in this chapter for additional information on this matter.

TABLE Ea171–219   Federal government expenditure, by function: 1902–1995

Contributed by John Joseph Wallis

				Direct							
					General						
						Federal defense and international relations		Space research	Postal		
Fiscal year	Total expenditure	General	Intergovernmental	Total	Total	Total	Military	and technology	service	Education	Libraries
	Ea171	Ea172	Ea173	Ea174	Ea175	Ea176	Ea177	Ea178	Ea179	Ea180	Ea181
	Million dollars	Million dollars	Million dollars	Million dollars	Million dollars	Million dollars	Million dollars	Million dollars	Million dollars	Million dollars	Million dollars
1902	—	572	572	7	565	565	165	162	0	126	3
1913	—	970	970	12	958	958	250	245	0	270	5
1922	—	3,763	3,754	118	3,645	3,636	875	864	0	553	8
1927	—	3,533	3,503	123	3,410	3,380	616	599	0	711	8
1932	—	4,266	4,215	232	4,034	3,983	721	702	0	794	14
1934	—	5,941	5,881	976	4,965	4,905	553	541	0	651	174
1936	—	9,165	9,099	908	8,257	8,191	932	916	0	751	188
1938	—	8,449	8,278	762	7,687	7,516	1,041	1,021	0	776	162
1940	—	10,061	9,780	884	9,177	8,896	1,590	1,567	0	808	189
1942	—	35,549	35,180	887	34,662	34,293	26,555	22,633	0	878	110
1944	—	100,520	100,032	1,072	99,448	98,960	85,503	74,670	0	1,085	12
1946	—	66,534	65,448	894	65,640	64,554	50,461	42,677	0	1,381	355
1948	—	35,592	34,175	1,771	33,821	32,404	16,075	10,642	0	1,715	2,342
1950	—	44,800	40,285	2,371	42,429	37,914	18,355	12,118	0	2,270	2,470
1952	—	71,568	67,778	2,585	68,984	65,193	48,187	38,962	0	2,612	1,280
1953	—	79,990	75,696	2,873	77,117	72,823	53,583	43,847	0	2,686	727
1954	—	77,692	72,631	2,967	74,725	69,664	49,265	40,519	0	2,669	639
1955	—	73,441	67,203	3,099	70,342	64,104	43,472	35,782	0	2,726	802
1956	—	75,991	68,792	3,347	72,644	65,445	43,388	35,553	0	2,899	940
1957	—	81,783	73,263	3,873	77,910	69,390	47,500	39,073	0	3,034	964
1958	—	86,054	75,698	4,835	81,219	70,863	47,626	38,998	89	3,327	917
1959	—	93,531	81,685	6,355	87,177	75,330	49,688	41,230	145	3,499	836
1960	—	97,284	83,719	6,994	90,289	76,724	48,922	41,340	395	3,730	685
1961	—	104,863	89,971	7,011	97,852	82,960	51,210	43,068	735	4,025	640
1962	—	113,428	96,689	7,735	105,693	88,953	55,172	46,950	1,242	4,101	598
1963	—	118,805	100,532	8,507	110,298	92,025	56,386	47,973	2,529	4,402	751
1964	—	125,949	106,882	10,097	115,852	96,786	57,326	49,341	4,140	4,775	1,056
1965	—	130,059	110,129	11,062	118,996	99,067	55,810	48,385	5,058	5,261	1,050
1966	—	143,022	119,679	13,115	129,907	106,564	60,832	53,770	5,869	5,706	1,550
1967	—	166,849	138,566	15,027	151,821	123,538	74,638	66,782	5,359	6,227	2,295
1968	—	184,464	151,990	18,053	166,411	133,937	83,874	76,747	4,645	6,485	2,456
1969	—	196,165	158,618	19,421	176,744	139,197	84,496	77,179	4,189	6,993	3,139
1970	—	208,190	166,942	23,257	184,933	143,685	84,253	76,550	3,691	7,722	3,053
1971	—	225,837	177,602	27,180	198,657	150,422	83,147	75,876	3,334	8,683	4,405
1972	—	242,186	188,100	33,584	208,602	154,516	81,719	74,456	3,369	9,366	4,563
1973	—	272,770	208,518	41,268	231,502	167,250	83,004	72,137	3,270	9,572	5,176
1974	—	295,503	221,428	42,854	252,649	178,574	85,444	79,066	3,289	11,235	5,820
1975	—	341,517	253,492	49,628	291,889	203,864	93,877	86,645	3,314	12,678	7,153
1976	—	389,798	288,365	67,770	322,028	220,595	100,414	91,009	3,691	13,748	10,326
1977	128	432,162	314,226	72,838	359,324	241,388	105,596	97,824	4,008	14,641	9,014
1978	156	479,297	348,000	77,440	401,857	270,560	114,811	105,782	3,983	15,271	9,390
1979	170	535,345	387,993	83,205	452,140	304,788	128,529	118,268	4,177	16,581	9,979
1980	332	617,165	446,589	90,836	526,329	355,753	149,459	137,500	4,892	18,177	10,619
1981	180	719,249	516,910	94,609	624,640	422,301	174,564	160,747	5,523	20,466	12,228
1982	185	796,483	568,373	86,014	710,469	482,359	204,275	189,273	6,181	21,761	11,484
1983	286	874,264	624,170	92,686	781,578	531,484	228,763	213,159	6,816	23,561	12,773
1984	298	928,188	664,046	99,015	829,173	565,031	248,040	229,113	7,203	26,619	12,496
1985	266	1,032,131	747,498	107,242	924,889	640,256	288,736	265,232	7,346	28,898	13,208
1986	316	1,096,401	796,209	115,632	980,769	680,577	312,183	288,454	7,275	30,985	13,581
1987	365	1,148,654	832,200	111,511	1,037,143	720,689	319,084	296,915	7,450	32,243	14,028
1988	275	1,214,812	878,523	118,906	1,095,906	759,617	329,993	306,474	8,866	33,892	14,277
1989	467	1,270,068	910,438	127,247	1,142,821	783,191	346,338	320,844	10,806	36,472	16,815
1990	426	1,383,692	992,795	137,561	1,246,131	855,234	344,069	316,087	12,063	39,065	17,404
1991	397	1,479,509	1,059,508	160,145	1,319,364	899,363	366,112	335,849	13,514	43,102	20,192
1992	478	1,527,311	1,072,581	186,036	1,341,275	886,545	351,684	320,168	13,550	44,890	22,136
1993	297	1,570,503	1,084,255	204,630	1,365,873	879,625	344,008	311,006	13,873	44,528	25,878
1994	511	1,630,283	1,107,501	217,919	1,412,364	889,582	333,380	300,578	13,553	46,110	23,239
1995	610	1,704,421	1,146,130	233,388	1,471,033	912,742	327,231	293,972	13,316	49,482	26,660

TABLE Ea171–219   Federal government expenditure, by function: 1902–1995   *Continued*

	General							
	Social services and income maintenance							
	Public welfare			Health and hospitals			Employee security administration	Veteran services
	Total expenditure	Categorical cash assistance	Other	Total	Hospitals	Health		
	Ea182	Ea183	Ea184	Ea185	Ea186	Ea187	Ea188	Ea189
Fiscal year	Million dollars	Million dollars	Million dollars	Million dollars	Million dollars	Million dollars	Million dollars	Million dollars
1902	4	0	—	3	2	1	0	141
1913	5	0	—	5	1	4	0	177
1922	9	0	—	94	87	7	0	425
1927	10	0	—	76	68	8	0	579
1932	1	0	—	127	113	14	0	928
1934	90	0	—	117	107	10	—	508
1936	170	0	—	125	110	15	—	1,699
1938	164	0	—	127	96	31	—	590
1940	158	0	—	123	87	36	—	501
1942	60	0	—	123	85	38	—	480
1944	17	0	—	201	100	101		529
1946	26	0	—	324	195	129	—	2,534
1948	45	0	—	705	461	244	—	3,293
1950	24	0	—	963	666	297	—	2,796
1952	42	10	—	1,014	715	299	60	2,428
1953	42	8	—	956	685	271	—	2,710
1954	43	10	—	959	714	245	126	2,811
1955	42	9	—	905	667	238	—	2,997
1956	45	9	—	967	752	215	173	3,097
1957	49	13	36	1,032	797	235	190	3,186
1958	48	11	—	1,104	844	260	250	3,455
1959	57	11	—	1,343	932	411	348	3,645
1960	58	9	—	1,450	978	472	236	3,689
1961	59	9	—	1,595	1,053	542	285	3,965
1962	63	9	54	1,793	1,118	675	328	4,129
1963	118	37	—	2,008	1,178	830	329	3,941
1964	114	13	—	2,169	1,290	879	408	4,189
1965	105	7	—	2,309	1,340	969	437	4,190
1966	208	7	—	2,452	1,328	1,124	608	4,510
1967	1,374	7	1,367	2,817	1,392	1,425	663	4,425
1968	1,388	32	—	3,033	1,519	1,514	772	4,740
1969	2,620	46	—	3,410	1,582	1,828	905	5,046
1970	2,837	15	—	3,919	1,830	2,089	1,021	5,388
1971	2,220	53	2,167	3,629	2,055	1,574	1,086	6,411
1972	2,488	52	2,436	4,167	2,350	1,817	1,155	6,882
1973	3,385	67	3,318	4,904	2,550	2,354	1,243	7,353
1974	6,286	2,315	3,971	5,738	2,696	3,042	1,422	7,523
1975	12,212	5,530	6,682	5,996	2,955	3,041	1,732	8,598
1976	13,694	5,950	7,744	6,884	3,222	3,662	1,892	9,289
1977	14,904	6,151	8,753	7,508	3,733	3,775	1,985	10,165
1978	16,659	7,700	8,959	8,135	4,189	3,946	2,179	10,776
1979	18,822	7,182	11,640	8,933	4,698	4,235	2,293	11,553
1980	19,212	7,998	11,214	11,136	5,421	5,715	2,528	12,443
1981	22,395	8,683	13,712	11,277	5,802	5,475	2,799	13,776
1982	22,564	9,047	13,517	12,507	5,998	6,509	3,123	14,959
1983	24,749	10,087	14,662	12,377	6,529	5,848	3,424	15,817
1984	23,715	9,468	14,247	12,966	7,105	5,861	3,567	16,020
1985	25,234	10,931	14,303	14,020	7,531	6,489	3,725	16,876
1986	25,790	11,666	14,124	15,093	7,573	7,520	3,871	17,139
1987	26,187	12,588	13,599	15,517	7,786	7,731	4,023	17,088
1988	28,656	14,236	14,420	16,849	8,045	8,804	4,313	18,340
1989	31,170	15,643	15,527	17,334	8,187	9,147	4,405	18,669
1990	33,447	15,661	17,786	17,852	8,483	9,369	4,702	17,353
1991	40,716	19,338	21,378	21,707	9,425	12,282	4,943	19,006
1992	47,722	23,278	24,444	20,054	10,435	9,619	5,455	20,320
1993	51,609	26,137	25,472	24,318	10,875	13,443	5,642	21,198
1994	56,204	29,736	26,468	25,167	11,351	13,816	5,790	21,878
1995	57,246	29,831	27,415	26,521	11,990	14,531	5,645	21,553

(continued)

TABLE Ea171–219   Federal government expenditure, by function: 1902–1995 *Continued*

					Direct							
					General							
	Public safety				Transportation			Environment and housing				
		Corrections							Natural resources			
										Agriculture		
Police	Total	Institutions	Other	Highways	Air	Water	Total	Total		Farm income stabilization	Forestry	Other
Ea190	Ea191	Ea192	Ea193	Ea194	Ea195	Ea196	Ea197	Ea198		Ea199	Ea200	Ea201
Million dollars	Million dollars	Million dollars	Million dollars	Million dollars	Million dollars	Million dollars	Million dollars	Million dollars		Million dollars	Million dollars	Million dollars

Fiscal year	Police Ea190	Total Ea191	Institutions Ea192	Other Ea193	Highways Ea194	Air Ea195	Water Ea196	Total Ea197	Total Ea198	Farm income stabilization Ea199	Forestry Ea200	Other Ea201
1902	0	—	—	—	0	0	22	8	—	0	—	—
1913	3	—	—	—	0	0	90	30	—	0	—	—
1922	14	—	—	—	2	1	301	79	—	0	—	—
1927	20	—	—	—	10	1	253	112	—	0	—	—
1932	31	—	—	—	25	10	188	161	—	0	—	—
1934	15	—	—	—	320	20	193	1,082	—	382	—	—
1936	17	—	—	—	520	39	230	1,965	—	602	—	—
1938	19	—	—	—	500	42	224	1,867	—	326	—	—
1940	21	—	—	—	604	53	321	2,512	—	694	—	—
1942	50	—	—	—	275	220	670	2,254	—	929	—	—
1944	83	—	—	—	15	207	4,534	2,499	—	1,532	—	—
1946	70	—	—	—	8	98	1,092	2,809	—	2,012	—	—
1948	80	—	—	—	35	136	414	1,727	—	592	—	—
1950	88	—	—	—	69	214	410	4,335	—	2,712	—	—
1952	141	28	—	28	64	240	622	2,476	—	638	—	—
1953	122	—	—	—	66	286	764	4,111	2,479	2,271	113	1,519
1954	124	30	—	30	60	259	570	5,615	4,107	3,863	127	1,381
1955	129	—	—	—	68	245	553	5,545	4,108	3,892	128	1,309
1956	156	33	—	33	82	234	618	5,724	4,476	4,118	148	1,100
1957	155	34	—	34	115	276	675	5,205	3,759	3,283	162	1,284
1958	159	39	—	39	135	270	666	5,161	3,516	2,890	180	1,465
1959	170	37	—	37	134	425	781	6,890	4,996	4,559	219	1,675
1960	173	44	—	44	137	500	905	5,898	3,786	3,404	229	1,883
1961	193	47	—	47	151	643	980	8,429	5,961	5,508	326	2,142
1962	196	51	—	51	151	709	1,096	9,097	6,499	5,963	287	2,311
1963	209	55	—	55	165	736	1,097	8,014	5,320	4,993	311	2,383
1964	220	56	—	56	164	750	1,113	8,207	5,349	4,989	378	2,480
1965	243	59	—	59	127	783	1,253	9,260	6,194	5,803	461	2,605
1966	257	57	—	57	125	802	1,355	8,262	4,654	4,203	472	3,136
1967	282	60	—	60	100	860	1,567	7,801	4,194	3,496	603	3,004
1968	290	65	—	65	173	844	1,576	6,729	3,187	2,598	597	2,945
1969	341	66	—	66	321	907	1,532	7,472	3,685	2,933	606	3,181
1970	409	83	—	83	319	1,096	1,460	8,737	5,110	4,261	753	2,874
1971	822	94	—	94	167	2,115	1,030	10,658	6,065	5,227	1,178	3,415
1972	958	111	—	111	240	2,419	1,034	11,449	5,823	4,895	1,435	4,191
1973	1,023	140	—	140	271	1,729	1,155	13,432	7,046	5,970	1,631	4,755
1974	988	182	—	182	243	1,622	1,234	13,697	5,162	4,079	1,788	6,747
1975	1,095	203	—	203	312	1,718	1,337	13,844	3,959	2,447	1,924	7,961
1976	1,204	220	—	220	294	1,858	1,381	12,296	3,255	1,339	2,127	6,914
1977	1,343	245	—	245	265	2,021	1,574	18,335	4,635	2,245	1,972	11,728
1978	1,571	336	—	336	277	2,217	1,530	22,407	6,968	3,606	1,222	14,217
1979	1,724	390	—	390	418	2,299	1,797	25,589	7,884	3,667	1,702	16,003
1980	1,739	387	—	387	434	2,570	2,110	29,734	11,397	5,994	1,775	16,562
1981	1,904	413	—	413	306	4,251	3,167	37,424	13,518	7,180	1,916	21,990
1982	2,000	422	—	422	576	2,578	2,122	38,974	16,874	8,474	1,741	20,359
1983	2,322	480	—	480	560	2,371	2,075	47,675	28,076	19,371	1,791	17,808
1984	2,092	681	—	681	792	3,079	1,811	57,876	37,444	27,957	1,828	18,604
1985	3,430	720	—	720	834	3,409	1,860	52,077	29,812	18,937	2,006	20,259
1986	3,543	798	—	798	568	3,599	1,690	58,621	39,350	28,214	1,864	17,407
1987	4,036	924	—	924	623	3,823	1,971	83,063	63,959	50,177	1,908	17,196
1988	4,657	1,168	967	201	377	4,186	2,112	79,881	59,254	46,151	2,362	18,265
1989	4,952	1,303	1,076	227	776	4,428	2,149	53,261	32,164	19,156	2,497	18,600
1990	5,344	1,594	1,332	262	856	4,499	2,556	68,585	46,963	38,131	2,363	19,259
1991	6,170	1,941	1,646	295	665	5,157	2,817	44,374	23,498	14,954	2,291	18,585
1992	6,703	2,411	2,070	341	813	5,871	2,721	51,501	27,281	19,665	2,493	21,727
1993	7,356	2,422	2,108	314	619	6,214	2,953	50,143	24,231	16,708	3,486	22,426
1994	7,328	2,587	2,253	334	691	6,482	2,848	50,637	22,465	15,620	2,696	25,476
1995	6,862	3,065	2,698	367	731	6,688	2,707	39,743	11,283	5,297	2,466	25,994

TABLE Ea171–219 Federal government expenditure, by function: 1902–1995 *Continued*

	Direct							
	General							
	Environment and housing			General administration				
Fiscal year	Parks and recreation	Housing and community development	Sanitation	Financial administration and general control	Financial administration	Judicial	Legislative	Other financial administration
	Ea202	Ea203	Ea204	Ea205 [1]	Ea206 [1]	Ea207 [1]	Ea208 [1]	Ea209 [1]
	Million dollars	Million dollars	Million dollars	Million dollars	Million dollars	Million dollars	Million dollars	Million dollars
1902	—	0	—	34	—	—	—	—
1913	—	0	—	45	—	—	—	—
1922	—	1	—	126	—	—	—	—
1927	—	1	—	114	—	—	—	—
1932	—	0	—	131	—	—	—	—
1934	—	3	—	101	—	—	—	—
1936	—	71	—	162	—	—	—	—
1938	—	106	—	183	—	—	—	—
1940	—	37	—	178	—	—	—	—
1942	—	386	—	250	—	—	—	—
1944	—	528	—	488	—	—	—	—
1946	—	107	—	460	—	—	—	—
1948	—	69	—	445	—	—	—	—
1950	—	121	—	514	—	—	—	—
1952	—	106	—	608	—	—	—	—
1953	—	138	—	602	—	—	—	—
1954	—	131	—	622	—	—	—	—
1955	—	112	—	607	—	—	—	—
1956	—	125	—	675	—	—	—	—
1957	—	119	—	680	—	—	—	—
1958	—	200	—	693	—	—	—	—
1959	—	223	—	747	—	—	—	—
1960	—	284	—	746	—	—	—	—
1961	—	377	—	788	591	—	—	—
1962	—	548	—	850	641	—	—	—
1963	—	509	—	923	701	—	—	—
1964	—	895	—	1,016	777	—	—	—
1965	—	948	—	1,069	807	—	—	—
1966	—	1,009	—	1,131	845	—	—	—
1967	—	944	—	1,224	919	—	—	—
1968	—	1,209	—	1,319	956	—	—	—
1969	—	603	—	1,458	1,079	—	—	—
1970	—	1,051	—	1,688	1,254	—	—	—
1971	—	1,797	—	—	1,341	—	—	540
1972	—	2,403	—	—	1,567	—	—	678
1973	—	3,765	—	—	1,803	—	—	741
1974	—	2,416	—	—	1,623	—	—	825
1975	—	2,392	—	—	2,402	—	—	878
1976	—	2,284	—	—	2,614	—	—	1,066
1977	782	2,212	—	—	2,769	0	0	1,273
1978	1,462	2,345	—	—	2,948	441	533	443
1979	1,527	3,308	—	—	3,280	483	554	491
1980	1,664	6,080	—	—	3,509	591	643	587
1981	1,472	6,808	—	—	3,714	616	678	679
1982	1,375	7,910	—	—	3,875	729	761	675
1983	1,430	5,870	—	—	4,420	1,119	776	747
1984	1,539	8,325	—	—	4,756	1,185	869	746
1985	1,558	8,214	—	—	5,077	2,129	882	221
1986	1,454	7,925	—	—	5,400	2,090	900	229
1987	1,503	9,538	—	—	5,826	2,271	943	190
1988	1,600	11,969	—	—	6,865	2,639	1,051	136
1989	1,714	13,492	—	—	7,132	2,949	1,056	153
1990	1,681	16,951	—	—	7,983	3,281	1,181	265
1991	1,788	16,698	—	—	10,209	3,995	1,232	284
1992	1,984	15,482	2,649	—	10,762	4,415	1,368	300
1993	2,135	12,582	2,717	—	11,647	4,680	1,393	284
1994	2,154	15,817	2,857	—	11,788	4,766	1,368	336
1995	2,250	15,212	2,711	—	12,444	5,360	1,336	276

Note appears at end of table

(continued)

TABLE Ea171–219   Federal government expenditure, by function: 1902–1995 *Continued*

						Direct				
	General						Insurance trust			
									Other		
	Interest on general debt	General revenue sharing	Other	Total	Employee retirement	Unemployment compensation	Total	Social Security and medical insurance	Railroad retirement	Veteran life insurance
	Ea210	Ea211	Ea212	Ea213	Ea214	Ea215	Ea216	Ea217	Ea218	Ea219
Fiscal year	Million dollars	Million dollars	Million dollars	Million dollars	Million dollars	Million dollars	Million dollars	Million dollars	Million dollars	Million dollars
1902	29	0	30	0	0	0	0	0	0	0
1913	23	0	55	0	0	0	0	0	0	0
1922	988	0	160	9	6	0	3	0	0	3
1927	764	0	105	30	14	0	16	0	0	16
1932	582	0	270	51	28	0	23	0	0	23
1934	734	0	344	60	39	0	21	0	0	21
1936	717	0	605	66	44	0	22	0	0	22
1938	840	0	875	171	64	0	107	5	80	22
1940	899	0	902	281	69	15	197	16	113	68
1942	1,026	0	956	369	78	9	282	110	126	46
1944	2,151	0	1,108	488	103	1	384	185	134	65
1946	3,865	0	964	1,086	266	17	803	321	152	330
1948	4,323	0	1,000	1,417	244	62	1,111	512	222	377
1950	4,404	0	881	4,515	268	131	4,116	26	302	3,088
1952	4,262	0	1,023	3,789	300	49	3,440	1,983	384	1,073
1953	4,863	0	1,167	4,294	363	98	3,833	2,728	460	645
1954	4,796	0	945	5,061	411	140	4,510	3,276	485	749
1955	4,845	0	1,056	6,237	430	206	5,601	4,333	570	698
1956	5,311	0	978	7,201	507	106	6,588	5,361	599	628
1957	5,497	0	679	8,521	591	133	7,797	6,515	670	612
1958	6,116	0	608	10,355	699	222	9,434	8,043	719	672
1959	5,543	0	819	11,847	792	248	10,807	9,388	768	651
1960	7,662	0	1,210	13,564	896	275	12,393	10,798	916	679
1961	7,485	0	1,353	14,893	956	252	13,685	11,889	982	814
1962	7,162	0	1,667	16,740	1,064	211	15,465	13,669	1,024	772
1963	7,682	0	2,171	18,273	1,183	167	16,923	15,015	1,064	844
1964	8,293	0	1,895	19,066	1,326	134	17,606	15,830	1,092	684
1965	8,940	0	2,165	19,929	1,447	115	18,367	16,618	1,116	633
1966	9,589	0	2,242	23,343	1,696	88	21,559	19,793	1,194	572
1967	10,373	0	2,529	28,283	1,976	71	26,236	23,919	1,257	1,060
1968	11,607	0	2,732	32,474	2,150	76	30,248	27,951	1,388	909
1969	13,260	0	2,439	37,547	2,420	97	35,030	32,474	1,533	1,023
1970	14,037	0	2,921	41,248	2,770	93	38,385	35,828	1,586	971
1971	16,599	0	2,344	48,235	3,259	95	44,881	41,959	1,889	1,033
1972	17,114	0	2,834	54,086	3,806	120	50,160	46,949	2,107	1,104
1973	18,332	0	6,952	64,252	4,555	73	59,624	56,371	2,419	834
1974	22,450	0	6,537	74,075	5,709	50	68,316	64,688	2,649	979
1975	25,005	0	9,118	88,025	7,127	67	80,831	76,587	3,052	1,192
1976	29,306	0	8,134	101,433	8,352	218	92,863	88,300	3,448	1,115
1977	33,276	6	9,338	117,936	9,653	180	108,103	103,177	3,768	1,158
1978	39,330	7	13,353	131,297	11,004	197	120,096	115,005	3,950	1,141
1979	48,768	7	13,116	147,352	12,533	142	134,677	129,177	4,238	1,262
1980	61,286	6	15,616	170,576	14,862	212	155,502	149,451	4,671	1,380
1981	80,510	11	17,140	202,339	17,864	258	184,217	177,520	5,246	1,451
1982	101,816	6	21,501	228,110	19,673	346	208,091	201,204	5,297	1,590
1983	108,735	6	24,332	250,094	20,999	433	228,662	221,489	5,610	1,563
1984	109,209	7	21,140	264,142	22,106	218	241,818	234,517	5,682	1,619
1985	140,281	8	21,247	284,633	23,306	175	261,152	253,594	5,818	1,740
1986	144,167	8	23,352	300,192	24,226	181	275,785	267,923	5,969	1,893
1987	146,155	0	23,838	316,454	25,991	164	290,299	282,212	6,148	1,939
1988	158,119	0	29,396	336,289	28,371	113	307,805	299,475	6,343	1,987
1989	174,288	0	33,062	359,630	29,491	90	330,049	321,335	6,672	2,042
1990	187,952	0	66,125	390,897	31,428	87	359,382	350,435	6,847	2,100
1991	195,142	0	79,202	420,001	33,624	87	386,290	376,933	7,168	2,189
1992	199,713	0	53,563	454,730	33,987	86	420,657	410,855	7,401	2,401
1993	198,795	0	44,334	486,248	35,232	70	450,946	440,994	7,592	2,360
1994	202,663	0	51,428	522,782	36,723	83	485,976	472,461	10,958	2,557
1995	233,225	0	51,868	558,291	38,795	79	519,417	505,709	11,177	2,531

TABLE Ea171–219   Federal government expenditure, by function: 1902–1995   *Continued*

[1] Through 1970, series Ea205 includes all expenditures on general government administration; thereafter (and earlier for some functions), individual activities are reported separately. Some activities reported separately may have been included under other general expenditures during the earlier period.

Source

Figures are from data files provided by the Census of Governments. For published versions through 1982, see U.S. Department of Commerce, "Historical Statistics on Government Finance and Employment," in *Census of Governments, 1982,* volume 6, pp. 225–64.

Documentation

See the text for Table Ea24–51.

TABLE Ea220–246   Federal intergovernmental expenditure, by function: 1902–1995

Contributed by John Joseph Wallis

					Social services and income maintenance							Transportation		
					Public welfare			Health and hospitals						
	Total	General revenue sharing	Education	Libraries	Total	Categorical assistance	Other	Total	Hospitals	Health	Employee security administration	Highways	Air	Water
	Ea220	Ea221	Ea222	Ea223	Ea224	Ea225	Ea226	Ea227	Ea228	Ea229	Ea230	Ea231	Ea232	Ea233
Fiscal year	Million dollars	Million dollars	Million dollars	Million dollars	Million dollars	Million dollars	Million dollars	Million dollars	Million dollars	Million dollars	Million dollars	Million dollars	Million dollars	Million dollars
1902	7	0	1	—	1	—	—	—	—	—	0	0	—	—
1913	12	0	3	—	2	—	—	—	—	—	0	0	—	—
1922	118	0	7	—	1	—	—	—	—	—	0	92	—	—
1927	123	0	10	—	1	—	—	—	—	—	0	83	—	—
1932	232	0	12	—	1	—	—	—	—	—	0	191	—	—
1934	976	0	61	—	495	—	—	12	—	—	1	279	—	—
1936	908	0	147	—	290	—	—	—	—	—	—	285	—	—
1938	762	0	112	—	218		—	14	—	—	46	264	—	—
1940	884	0	154	—	278		—	—	—	—	62	195	—	—
1942	887	0	76	—	383		—	—	—	—	—	164	—	—
1944	1,072	0	193	—	420	—	—	60	—	—	36	147	—	—
1946	894	0	149	—	424	—	—	—	—	—	75	79	—	—
1948	1,771	0	418	—	724	—	—	55	—	—	158	318	—	—
1950	2,371	0	369	—	1,131	—	—	—	—	—	—	429	—	—
1952	2,585	0	436	—	1,181	—	—	134	—	—	182	415	—	—
1953	2,873	0	508	—	1,332	—	—	116	—	—	196	510	—	—
1954	2,967	0	475	—	1,439	—	—	92	—	—	198	530	17	—
1955	3,099	0	521	—	1,429	—	—	74	—	—	187	589	8	—
1956	3,347	0	535	—	1,458	—	—	88	—	—	224	732	16	—
1957	3,873	0	604	—	1,557	—	—	111	32	79	245	944	20	—
1958	4,835	0	653	—	1,799	—	—	110	—	—	288	1,478	42	—
1959	6,355	0	826	—	1,973	—	—	121	—	—	298	2,575	56	—
1960	6,994	0	950	—	2,070	—	—	135	—	—	325	2,905	56	—
1961	7,011	0	1,030	—	2,178	—	—	154	—	—	370	2,586	64	—
1962	7,735	0	1,169	—	2,448	2,423	25	168	—	—	461	2,748	57	—
1963	8,507	0	1,115	—	2,752	—	—	184	—	—	342	2,981	51	—
1964	10,097	0	1,371	—	2,973	—	—	278	—	—	415	3,628	64	—
1965	11,062	0	1,677	—	3,098	—	—	292	—	—	413	3,997	70	—
1966	13,115	0	3,014	—	3,579	—	—	323	—	—	486	3,953	54	—
1967	15,027	0	3,920	—	4,234	4,148	85	409	119	290	564	4,059	61	0
1968	18,053	0	4,727	—	5,407	—	—	718	—	—	592	4,291	74	—
1969	19,421	0	4,775	—	6,358	—	—	654	—	—	616	4,352	102	—
1970	23,257	0	5,844	—	7,574	—	—	931	—	—	664	4,608	82	—
1971	27,180	0	5,907	—	9,825	9,587	238	672	105	567	721	4,738	70	17
1972	33,584	0	6,250	—	13,251	13,038	213	1,177	96	1,081	756	4,741	119	25
1973	41,268	6,636	6,791	—	12,097	11,870	227	1,610	202	1,408	804	4,807	231	21
1974	42,854	6,106	7,496	—	12,837	12,564	273	1,138	205	933	822	4,555	253	22
1975	49,628	6,130	8,959	—	14,352	13,855	497	2,052	151	1,901	998	4,754	305	28
1976	67,770	6,238	7,967	—	17,225	16,497	728	2,264	257	2,007	1,228	6,243	294	61
1977	72,838	6,758	9,027	157	19,520	18,569	951	2,353	106	2,247	1,532	6,173	381	95
1978	77,440	6,823	10,204	206	20,051	18,879	1,172	2,464	108	2,356	1,538	6,197	719	323
1979	83,205	6,848	11,401	253	25,456	22,567	2,889	2,919	151	2,768	1,584	7,395	632	190

(continued)

TABLE Ea220–246 Federal intergovernmental expenditure, by function: 1902–1995 *Continued*

					Social services and income maintenance							Transportation		
					Public welfare			Health and hospitals			Employee security administration			
	Total	General revenue sharing	Education	Libraries	Total	Categorical assistance	Other	Total	Hospitals	Health		Highways	Air	Water
	Ea220	Ea221	Ea222	Ea223	Ea224	Ea225	Ea226	Ea227	Ea228	Ea229	Ea230	Ea231	Ea232	Ea233
Fiscal year	Million dollars	Million dollars	Million dollars	Million dollars	Million dollars	Million dollars	Million dollars	Million dollars	Million dollars	Million dollars	Million dollars	Million dollars	Million dollars	Million dollars
1980	90,836	6,829	12,889	123	28,494	24,322	4,172	3,440	123	3,317	1,862	9,457	613	76
1981	94,609	5,133	12,708	78	34,405	28,708	5,697	3,767	134	3,633	2,066	9,253	472	46
1982	86,014	4,569	11,971	124	34,414	28,617	5,797	3,231	138	3,093	2,122	8,000	339	36
1983	92,686	4,614	14,434	74	34,376	29,688	4,688	3,682	144	3,538	2,452	8,851	459	25
1984	99,015	4,567	15,690	37	37,972	32,668	5,304	4,070	163	3,907	2,339	10,204	695	24
1985	107,242	4,584	16,870	38	40,983	35,508	5,475	4,357	213	4,144	2,533	12,469	780	24
1986	115,632	5,113	18,023	47	44,544	39,004	5,540	4,615	227	4,388	2,536	14,370	853	22
1987	111,511	0	17,988	60	47,821	43,131	4,690	4,775	227	4,548	2,501	12,858	917	18
1988	118,906	0	19,539	47	51,253	46,472	4,781	5,412	261	5,151	2,604	14,065	819	18
1989	127,247	0	21,670	65	56,410	51,391	5,019	6,070	302	5,768	2,760	13,441	1,120	17
1990	137,561	0	22,757	125	60,456	56,937	3,519	6,795	366	6,429	2,804	14,233	1,205	4
1991	160,145	0	24,537	130	78,419	69,932	8,487	6,500	371	6,129	3,052	14,611	1,516	2
1992	186,036	0	26,821	187	94,760	86,272	8,488	7,625	314	7,311	3,565	15,490	1,652	7
1993	204,630	0	29,190	156	105,521	94,972	10,549	8,336	462	7,874	3,667	16,860	1,906	8
1994	217,919	0	26,752	107	114,908	102,082	12,826	9,257	435	8,822	3,355	19,199	1,602	2
1995	233,388	0	28,524	129	120,628	109,621	11,007	9,875	602	9,273	3,451	19,745	1,796	1

	Public safety		Environment and housing							General administration			
				Natural resources			Parks and recreation	Housing and community development					
	Police	Corrections	Total	Agriculture	Forestry	Other			Sanitation	Financial	Judicial	Other	Other
	Ea234	Ea235	Ea236	Ea237	Ea238	Ea239	Ea240	Ea241	Ea242	Ea243	Ea244	Ea245	Ea246
Fiscal year	Million dollars	Million dollars	Million dollars	Million dollars	Million dollars	Million dollars	Million dollars	Million dollars	Million dollars	Million dollars	Million dollars	Million dollars	Million dollars
1902	—	—	—	—	—	—	—	0	0	—	—	—	5
1913	—	—	—	—	—	—	—	0	0	—	—	—	7
1922	—	—	—	—	—	—	—	0	0	—	—	—	18
1927	—	—	—	—	—	—	—	0	0	—	—	—	29
1932	—	—	—	—	—	—	—	0	0	—	—	—	28
1934	—	—	—	—	—	—	—	0	0	—	—	—	128
1936	—	—	—	—	—	—	—	—	0	—	—	—	186
1938	—	—	—	—	—	—	—	—	0	—	—	—	108
1940	—	—	—	—	—	—	—	—	0	—	—	—	195
1942	—	—	—	—	—	—	—	—	0	—	—	—	264
1944	—	—	—	—	—	—	—	—	0	—	—	—	216
1946	—	—	—	—	—	—	—	—	0	—	—	—	167
1948	—	—	—	—	—	—	—	—	0	—	—	—	98
1950	—	—	—	—	—	—	—	—	0	—	—	—	442
1952	—	—	119	—	—	—	—	11	0	—	—	—	107
1953	—	—	66	—	—	—	—	—	0	—	—	—	145
1954	—	—	70	—	—	—	—	—	0	—	—	—	146
1955	—	—	88	—	—	—	—	—	0	—	—	—	203
1956	—	—	92	—	—	—	—	88	0	—	—	—	114
1957	—	—	122	—	—	—	—	114	0	—	—	—	156
1958	—	—	118	—	—	—	—	200	0	—	—	—	147
1959	—	—	120	—	—	—	—	184	0	—	—	—	202
1960	—	—	127	—	—	—	—	226	0	—	—	—	200
1961	—	—	132	—	—	—	—	278	0	—	—	—	219
1962	—	—	142	—	—	—	—	352	0	—	—	—	190
1963	—	—	164	—	—	—	—	371	0	—	—	—	547
1964	—	—	177	—	—	—	—	564	0	—	—	—	627
1965	—	—	187	—	—	—	—	676	0	—	—	—	652
1966	—	—	218	—	—	—	—	607	0	—	—	—	881
1967	1	6	238	—	—	—	—	670	0	0	—	—	865
1968	—	—	273	—	—	—	—	787	0	—	—	—	1,184
1969	—	—	305	—	—	—	—	921	0	—	—	—	1,338

TABLE Ea220–246   Federal intergovernmental expenditure, by function: 1902–1995   *Continued*

	Public safety		Environment and housing							General administration			
	Police	Corrections	Natural resources				Parks and recreation	Housing and community development	Sanitation	Financial	Judicial	Other	Other
			Total	Agriculture	Forestry	Other							
	Ea234	Ea235	Ea236	Ea237	Ea238	Ea239	Ea240	Ea241	Ea242	Ea243	Ea244	Ea245	Ea246
Fiscal year	Million dollars	Million dollars	Million dollars	Million dollars	Million dollars	Million dollars	Million dollars	Million dollars	Million dollars	Million dollars	Million dollars	Million dollars	Million dollars
1970	—	—	295	—	—	—	—	1,609	0	—	—	—	1,650
1971	1	10	563	230	159	174	—	1,611	0	0	—	0	3,045
1972	1	15	624	241	116	267	—	1,981	0	0	—	0	4,644
1973	1	18	670	259	130	281	—	2,121	0	0	—	0	5,461
1974	104	23	750	271	79	400	—	2,391	0	0	—	0	6,357
1975	87	26	887	300	100	487	—	2,734	0	0	—	0	8,316
1976	93	30	957	324	111	522	—	2,820	0	0	—	0	22,350
1977	134	40	967	334	67	566	2	2,914	0	0	0	0	22,785
1978	141	19	1,294	356	152	786	34	2,969	0	0	0	17	24,441
1979	180	18	1,506	395	141	970	56	6,399	0	0	0	17	18,351
1980	202	21	1,634	289	150	1,195	80	6,093	0	0	0	16	19,007
1981	214	23	2,150	454	139	1,557	69	6,065	0	0	0	18	18,142
1982	153	28	2,183	480	107	1,596	92	5,716	0	0	0	7	13,029
1983	119	30	2,093	540	44	1,509	127	9,730	0	0	0	0	11,620
1984	1	40	2,628	630	54	1,944	131	8,817	0	0	0	0	11,800
1985	65	72	2,415	562	124	1,729	94	10,841	0	0	0	0	11,117
1986	101	64	2,349	594	17	1,738	75	11,237	0	0	0	0	11,683
1987	195	70	2,050	598	77	1,375	70	10,652	0	0	0	0	11,536
1988	297	90	2,153	644	73	1,436	65	11,436	0	0	0	0	11,108
1989	355	115	2,229	720	114	1,395	69	11,814	0	0	0	0	11,112
1990	322	140	2,215	723	214	1,278	67	12,320	0	0	2,117	0	12,001
1991	555	181	2,175	759	76	1,340	78	13,501	0	99	2,389	0	12,400
1992	697	235	2,437	816	125	1,496	80	16,405	2,712	81	2,962	0	10,320
1993	724	268	2,496	846	75	1,575	85	18,739	2,513	115	3,170	0	10,876
1994	741	254	2,686	899	104	1,683	91	21,099	2,405	41	3,463	0	11,957
1995	1,750	285	2,664	910	81	1,673	95	25,139	2,869	50	3,875	0	12,512

Source

Figures are from data files provided by the Census of Governments. For published versions through 1982, see U.S. Department of Commerce, "Historical Statistics on Government Finance and Employment," in *Census of Governments, 1982*, volume 6, pp. 225–64.

Documentation

See the text for Table Ea24–51.

TABLE Ea247–275   State and local government revenue, by source: 1902–1995

Contributed by John Joseph Wallis

				Direct						
					General					
						Taxes				
								Sales and gross receipts		
Fiscal year	Total revenue	General	Intergovernmental, from federal	Total	Total	Total	Property	Total	General	Select
	Ea247	Ea248	Ea249	Ea250	Ea251	Ea252	Ea253	Ea254	Ea255	Ea256
	Thousand dollars	Thousand dollars	Thousand dollars	Thousand dollars	Thousand dollars	Thousand dollars	Thousand dollars	Thousand dollars	Thousand dollars	Thousand dollars
1902	1,048,000	986,000	7,000	1,041,000	979,000	860,000	706,000	28,000	—	—
1913	2,030,000	1,912,000	12,000	2,018,000	1,900,000	1,609,000	1,332,000	58,000	—	—
1922	5,169,000	4,781,000	108,000	5,061,000	4,673,000	4,016,000	3,321,000	154,000	—	—
1927	7,838,000	7,271,000	116,000	7,722,000	7,155,000	6,087,000	4,730,000	470,000	—	—
1932	7,887,000	7,267,000	232,000	7,655,000	7,035,000	6,164,000	4,487,000	752,000	—	—
1934	8,430,000	7,678,000	1,016,000	7,414,000	6,662,000	5,912,000	4,076,000	1,008,000	—	—
1936	9,360,000	8,395,000	948,000	8,412,000	7,447,000	6,701,000	4,093,000	1,484,000	—	—
1938	11,058,000	9,228,000	800,000	10,258,000	8,428,000	7,605,000	4,440,000	1,794,000	—	—
1940	11,749,000	9,609,000	945,000	10,804,000	8,664,000	7,810,000	4,430,000	1,982,000	—	—
1942	13,148,000	10,418,000	858,000	12,290,000	9,560,000	8,528,000	4,537,000	2,351,000	—	—
1944	14,333,000	10,908,000	954,000	13,379,000	9,954,000	8,774,000	4,604,000	2,289,000	—	—
1946	15,983,000	12,356,000	855,000	15,128,000	11,501,000	10,094,000	4,986,000	2,986,000	—	—
1948	21,613,000	17,250,000	1,861,000	19,752,000	15,389,000	13,342,000	6,126,000	4,442,000	—	—
1950	25,639,000	20,911,000	2,486,000	23,153,000	18,425,000	15,914,000	7,349,000	5,154,000	—	—
1952	31,013,000	25,181,000	2,566,000	28,447,000	22,615,000	19,323,000	8,652,000	6,357,000	2,598,000	3,759,000
1953	33,411,000	27,307,000	2,870,000	30,541,000	24,437,000	20,908,000	9,375,000	6,927,000	2,860,000	4,067,000
1954	35,386,000	29,012,000	2,966,000	32,420,000	26,046,000	22,067,000	9,967,000	7,276,000	2,948,000	4,330,000
1955	37,619,000	31,073,000	3,131,000	34,489,000	27,942,000	23,483,000	10,735,000	7,643,000	3,090,000	4,553,000
1956	41,692,000	34,667,000	3,335,000	38,357,000	31,332,000	26,368,000	11,749,000	8,691,000	3,582,000	5,108,000
1957	45,929,000	38,164,000	3,843,000	42,085,000	34,320,000	28,817,000	12,864,000	9,467,000	4,029,000	5,438,000
1958	49,262,000	41,219,000	4,865,000	44,397,000	36,354,000	30,380,000	14,047,000	9,829,000	4,206,000	5,622,000
1959	54,002,000	45,306,000	6,377,000	47,626,000	38,929,000	32,379,000	14,983,000	10,437,000	4,444,000	5,993,000
1960	60,311,000	50,505,000	6,974,000	53,336,000	43,530,000	36,117,000	16,405,000	11,849,000	5,177,000	6,672,000
1961	64,564,000	54,037,000	7,131,000	57,433,000	46,907,000	38,861,000	18,002,000	12,463,000	5,431,000	7,031,000
1962	69,530,000	58,252,000	7,871,000	61,659,000	50,381,000	41,554,000	19,054,000	13,494,000	6,069,000	7,426,000
1963	75,357,000	62,891,000	8,722,000	66,635,000	54,169,000	44,281,000	20,089,000	14,456,000	6,604,000	7,852,000
1964	81,494,000	68,443,000	10,002,000	71,492,000	58,440,000	47,785,000	21,241,000	15,762,000	7,254,000	8,509,000
1965	87,777,000	74,000,000	11,029,000	76,748,000	62,971,000	51,243,000	22,583,000	17,118,000	7,981,000	9,137,000
1966	97,619,000	83,036,000	13,214,000	84,405,000	69,822,000	56,647,000	24,670,000	19,085,000	9,225,000	9,860,000
1967	106,581,000	91,197,000	15,370,000	91,211,000	75,827,000	61,000,000	26,047,000	20,530,000	10,124,000	10,408,000
1968	117,581,000	101,264,000	17,181,000	100,400,000	84,083,000	67,572,000	27,747,000	22,911,000	11,645,000	11,265,000
1969	132,153,000	114,550,000	19,153,000	113,001,000	95,397,000	76,712,000	30,673,000	26,519,000	14,038,000	12,481,000
1970	150,106,000	130,756,000	21,857,000	128,248,000	108,898,000	86,795,000	34,054,000	30,322,000	16,128,000	14,194,000
1971	166,090,000	144,927,000	26,146,000	139,945,000	118,782,000	94,975,000	37,852,000	33,233,000	17,812,000	15,420,000
1972	190,899,000	167,541,153	31,341,690	159,557,310	136,199,463	109,609,945	42,877,189	37,517,639	20,345,981	17,171,658
1973	217,731,297	190,221,836	39,263,809	178,467,488	150,958,027	121,101,637	45,282,538	42,046,584	22,992,171	19,054,413
1974	237,959,976	207,670,256	41,820,358	196,139,618	165,849,898	130,672,652	47,704,699	46,097,896	26,314,019	19,783,877
1975	264,131,470	228,170,813	47,033,553	217,097,917	181,137,260	141,465,023	51,490,941	49,814,790	29,101,627	20,713,163
1976	303,362,385	256,175,710	55,589,233	247,773,152	200,586,477	156,812,932	57,001,463	54,546,522	32,043,914	22,502,608
1977	337,869,862	285,156,503	62,444,084	275,425,778	222,712,419	175,936,200	62,527,223	60,640,515	36,367,540	24,272,975
1978	371,607,090	315,960,495	69,592,405	302,014,685	246,368,090	193,642,079	66,421,967	67,596,273	41,472,895	26,123,378
1979	404,891,107	343,235,783	75,163,828	329,727,279	268,071,955	205,471,549	64,943,568	74,247,148	46,558,597	27,688,551
1980	451,536,599	382,321,572	83,028,545	368,508,054	299,293,027	223,462,640	68,498,743	79,926,588	51,327,616	28,598,972
1981	506,727,811	423,403,675	90,294,367	416,433,444	333,109,308	244,514,139	74,969,444	85,971,420	55,641,390	30,330,030
1982	547,717,920	457,653,563	87,282,128	460,435,792	370,371,435	266,389,820	82,067,442	93,612,948	60,573,300	33,039,648
1983	593,371,721	486,752,954	90,006,515	503,365,206	396,746,439	284,436,467	89,104,863	100,246,638	64,889,896	35,356,742
1984	651,996,807	542,729,549	96,935,282	555,061,525	445,794,267	320,193,816	96,456,745	114,097,342	75,211,609	38,885,733
1985	720,062,166	598,120,535	106,157,936	613,904,230	491,962,599	350,366,541	103,756,624	126,375,711	84,295,648	42,080,063
1986	783,377,916	641,485,913	113,098,809	670,279,107	528,387,104	373,079,186	111,709,287	135,004,563	90,694,713	44,309,850
1987	843,878,724	686,860,499	114,857,457	729,021,267	572,003,042	404,802,978	121,202,638	144,090,686	96,602,538	47,488,148
1988	884,116,964	726,761,578	117,601,730	766,515,234	609,159,848	435,740,719	132,212,301	156,452,331	105,237,831	51,214,500
1989	953,802,436	786,129,230	125,823,732	827,978,704	660,305,498	468,890,917	142,400,237	166,335,997	112,673,222	53,662,775
1990	1,032,114,523	849,501,585	136,801,924	895,312,599	712,699,661	501,618,648	155,613,321	177,884,755	121,286,594	56,598,161
1991	1,080,862,400	902,206,807	154,098,909	926,763,491	748,107,898	525,355,132	167,999,489	185,570,228	125,448,814	60,121,414
1992	1,189,987,099	979,136,792	179,174,330	1,010,812,769	799,962,462	559,859,016	180,336,841	197,731,143	131,979,152	65,751,991
1993	1,270,826,852	1,041,643,379	198,662,634	1,072,164,218	842,980,745	594,300,495	189,743,930	209,648,859	138,822,010	70,826,849
1994	1,331,492,151	1,100,490,377	215,492,289	1,115,999,862	884,998,088	625,528,938	197,141,008	223,628,301	149,039,888	74,588,413
1995	1,417,924,528	1,169,504,619	228,771,418	1,189,153,110	940,733,201	660,576,796	203,451,246	237,268,397	160,166,175	77,102,222

TABLE Ea247–275   State and local government revenue, by source: 1902–1995   *Continued*

					Direct					
				General				Utility and liquor store		
	Taxes			Charges and miscellaneous				Utility		
	Income									
	Individual	Corporate	Other	Total	Charges	Miscellaneous	Total	Total	Water	Electric
	Ea257	Ea258	Ea259	Ea260	Ea261	Ea262	Ea263	Ea264	Ea265	Ea266
Fiscal year	Thousand dollars	Thousand dollars	Thousand dollars	Thousand dollars	Thousand dollars	Thousand dollars	Thousand dollars	Thousand dollars	Thousand dollars	Thousand dollars
1902	0	0	126,000	119,000	—	—	62,000	60,000	56,000	3,000
1913	0	0	219,000	291,000	—	—	116,000	116,000	99,000	16,000
1922	43,000	58,000	440,000	657,000	—	—	266,000	266,000	175,000	72,000
1927	70,000	92,000	725,000	1,068,000	—	—	403,000	403,000	247,000	111,000
1932	74,000	79,000	772,000	871,000	—	—	463,000	463,000	317,000	111,000
1934	80,000	49,000	699,000	750,000	—	—	590,000	499,000	342,000	115,000
1936	153,000	113,000	858,000	746,000	—	—	747,000	558,000	369,000	131,000
1938	218,000	165,000	988,000	823,000	—	—	877,000	605,000	371,000	169,000
1940	224,000	156,000	1,018,000	854,000	—	—	998,000	704,000	401,000	220,000
1942	276,000	272,000	1,092,000	1,031,000	—	—	1,277,000	887,000	439,000	251,000
1944	342,000	451,000	1,088,000	1,180,000	—	—	1,633,000	1,066,000	521,000	305,000
1946	422,000	447,000	1,253,000	1,407,000	—	—	2,033,000	1,169,000	556,000	348,000
1948	543,000	592,000	1,639,000	2,047,000	—	—	2,511,000	1,565,000	640,000	474,000
1950	788,000	593,000	2,030,000	2,511,000	—	—	2,712,000	1,808,000	705,000	574,000
1952	998,000	846,000	2,470,000	3,292,000	2,263,000	1,030,000	3,108,000	2,071,000	839,000	683,000
1953	1,065,000	817,000	2,724,000	3,529,000	2,429,000	1,100,000	3,324,000	2,237,000	939,000	713,000
1954	1,127,000	778,000	2,919,000	3,979,000	2,674,000	1,304,000	3,496,000	2,403,000	971,000	787,000
1955	1,237,000	744,000	3,124,000	4,459,000	2,972,000	1,487,000	3,688,000	2,609,000	1,092,000	870,000
1956	1,538,000	890,000	3,500,000	4,964,000	3,379,000	1,585,000	3,854,000	2,718,000	1,162,000	887,000
1957	1,754,000	984,000	3,748,000	5,503,000	3,776,000	1,727,000	4,127,000	2,944,000	1,235,000	1,011,000
1958	1,759,000	1,018,000	3,727,000	5,974,000	4,157,000	1,816,000	4,211,000	3,041,000	1,256,000	1,096,000
1959	1,994,000	1,001,000	3,964,000	6,550,000	4,663,000	1,886,000	4,536,000	3,320,000	1,388,000	1,178,000
1960	2,463,000	1,180,000	4,220,000	7,414,000	5,319,000	2,094,000	4,877,000	3,613,000	1,529,000	1,307,000
1961	2,613,000	1,266,000	4,517,000	8,045,000	5,704,000	2,342,000	5,116,000	3,856,000	1,621,000	1,450,000
1962	3,037,000	1,308,000	4,661,000	8,827,000	6,275,000	2,552,000	5,308,000	4,026,000	1,725,000	1,422,000
1963	3,269,000	1,505,000	4,962,000	9,888,000	7,101,000	2,787,000	5,790,000	4,474,000	1,865,000	1,728,000
1964	3,791,000	1,695,000	5,296,000	10,655,000	7,491,000	3,164,000	5,975,000	4,616,000	1,917,000	1,718,000
1965	4,090,000	1,929,000	5,523,000	11,729,000	8,401,000	3,328,000	6,355,000	4,908,000	2,004,000	1,833,000
1966	4,760,000	2,038,000	6,094,000	13,174,000	9,372,000	3,804,000	6,619,000	5,069,000	2,115,000	1,911,000
1967	5,825,000	2,227,000	6,371,000	14,827,000	10,482,000	4,345,000	6,911,000	5,246,000	2,187,000	1,881,000
1968	7,308,000	2,518,000	7,088,000	16,511,000	11,785,000	4,727,000	7,502,000	5,683,000	2,313,000	2,119,000
1969	8,908,000	3,180,000	7,432,000	18,686,000	13,305,000	5,381,000	7,840,000	5,931,000	2,464,000	2,166,000
1970	10,812,000	3,738,000	7,869,000	22,103,000	14,872,000	7,231,000	8,614,000	6,608,000	2,687,000	2,385,000
1971	11,900,000	3,424,000	8,566,000	23,807,000	16,885,000	6,922,000	9,359,000	7,276,000	2,980,000	2,644,000
1972	15,226,561	4,415,838	9,572,718	26,589,518	18,887,620	7,701,898	9,828,273	7,700,733	3,171,464	2,831,019
1973	17,993,512	5,424,994	10,354,009	29,856,390	20,931,093	8,925,297	10,897,601	8,621,598	3,463,401	3,355,030
1974	19,491,047	6,014,518	11,364,492	35,177,246	23,168,628	12,008,618	11,747,523	9,392,073	3,712,052	3,762,593
1975	21,454,152	6,642,100	12,063,040	39,672,237	25,588,313	14,083,924	13,334,934	10,867,284	4,142,177	4,689,262
1976	24,574,988	7,272,697	13,417,262	43,773,545	29,320,432	14,453,113	15,126,332	12,572,928	4,463,077	5,819,137
1977	29,246,274	9,173,809	14,348,379	46,776,219	31,173,063	15,603,156	17,541,015	14,990,850	4,995,345	7,142,381
1978	33,176,300	10,738,296	15,709,243	52,726,011	34,701,044	18,024,967	20,011,482	17,252,258	5,512,059	8,675,475
1979	36,931,786	12,127,524	17,221,523	62,600,406	39,469,100	23,131,306	22,628,517	19,730,480	6,249,831	9,938,477
1980	42,079,764	13,321,331	19,636,214	75,830,387	44,373,026	31,457,361	25,559,447	22,358,861	6,765,752	11,387,176
1981	46,426,426	14,143,497	23,003,352	88,595,169	50,237,600	38,357,569	29,895,616	26,617,125	7,717,612	13,714,634
1982	50,738,164	15,028,326	24,942,940	103,981,615	56,920,307	47,061,308	34,040,011	30,697,066	8,472,461	16,027,491
1983	55,128,927	14,257,647	25,698,392	112,309,972	62,625,024	49,684,948	37,254,155	33,943,059	9,528,164	17,822,871
1984	64,528,897	17,140,541	27,970,291	125,600,451	69,022,177	56,578,274	40,613,586	37,373,901	10,466,984	19,613,735
1985	70,361,403	19,152,186	30,720,617	141,596,058	74,322,626	67,273,432	44,772,026	41,536,534	11,979,703	21,767,248
1986	74,364,912	19,994,145	32,006,279	155,307,918	80,400,020	74,907,898	47,162,720	43,850,149	13,260,170	22,845,860
1987	83,934,727	22,424,627	33,150,300	167,200,064	87,446,717	79,753,347	50,167,729	46,809,362	14,402,746	24,672,325
1988	88,349,539	23,663,438	35,063,110	173,419,129	94,543,604	78,875,525	52,515,781	49,225,618	15,314,515	26,239,582
1989	97,805,749	25,925,885	36,423,049	191,414,581	104,576,430	86,838,151	56,224,957	52,909,768	16,767,400	28,186,841
1990	105,639,737	23,566,322	38,914,513	211,081,013	115,540,659	95,540,354	58,642,454	55,201,882	17,674,155	29,268,197
1991	109,340,832	22,242,445	40,202,138	222,752,766	125,235,530	97,517,236	60,736,278	57,165,113	18,034,149	30,489,473
1992	115,637,837	23,880,252	42,272,943	240,103,446	138,304,683	101,798,763	63,239,911	59,608,105	19,464,412	31,421,710
1993	123,235,406	26,417,292	45,255,008	248,680,250	149,350,881	99,329,369	65,245,971	61,604,650	20,450,540	31,985,302
1994	128,809,920	28,319,516	47,630,193	259,469,150	161,166,144	98,303,006	70,075,062	66,468,546	22,692,069	33,807,601
1995	137,930,595	31,405,814	50,520,744	280,156,405	172,062,415	108,093,990	72,270,882	68,633,703	23,879,068	34,626,919

(continued)

TABLE Ea247–275   State and local government revenue, by source: 1902–1995 *Continued*

			Direct					
Utility and liquor store			Insurance trust					
Utility					Unemployment compensation		Workers' compensation	Other
Gas	Transit	Liquor store	Total	Employee retirement	Total	Payroll taxes		
Ea267	Ea268	Ea269	Ea270	Ea271	Ea272	Ea273	Ea274	Ea275
Fiscal year	Thousand dollars	Thousand dollars	Thousand dollars	Thousand dollars	Thousand dollars	Thousand dollars	Thousand dollars	Thousand dollars	Thousand dollars
1902	1,000	0	2,000	0	0	0	0	—	0
1913	1,000	0	0	2,000	2,000	0	0	—	0
1922	6,000	13,000	0	122,000	45,000	0	0	—	77,000
1927	10,000	35,000	0	164,000	67,000	0	0	—	97,000
1932	10,000	25,000	0	157,000	93,000	0	0	—	64,000
1934	10,000	32,000	91,000	162,000	107,000	0	0	—	55,000
1936	17,000	41,000	189,000	218,000	125,000	23,000	23,000	—	70,000
1938	18,000	47,000	272,000	953,000	143,000	731,000	706,000	—	79,000
1940	25,000	58,000	294,000	1,142,000	169,000	885,000	850,000	—	88,000
1942	27,000	170,000	390,000	1,454,000	195,000	1,142,000	1,083,000	—	117,000
1944	32,000	208,000	567,000	1,792,000	228,000	1,409,000	1,323,000	—	155,000
1946	38,000	227,000	864,000	1,593,000	289,000	1,165,000	1,037,000	—	139,000
1948	52,000	399,000	946,000	1,851,000	433,000	1,206,000	1,062,000	—	212,000
1950	61,000	468,000	904,000	2,016,000	606,000	1,180,000	1,032,000	173,000	56,000
1952	70,000	479,000	1,037,000	2,724,000	835,000	1,602,000	1,442,000	224,000	62,000
1953	85,000	500,000	1,087,000	2,781,000	909,000	1,556,000	1,374,000	249,000	67,000
1954	90,000	554,000	1,093,000	2,877,000	1,070,000	1,470,000	1,266,000	270,000	67,000
1955	104,000	544,000	1,079,000	2,858,000	1,180,000	1,329,000	1,141,000	279,000	71,000
1956	127,000	542,000	1,136,000	3,171,000	1,295,000	1,505,000	1,318,000	292,000	79,000
1957	157,000	541,000	1,183,000	3,638,000	1,486,000	1,725,000	1,514,000	344,000	83,000
1958	173,000	516,000	1,170,000	3,832,000	1,688,000	1,717,000	1,497,000	340,000	86,000
1959	190,000	565,000	1,216,000	4,161,000	1,901,000	1,833,000	1,652,000	331,000	97,000
1960	196,000	581,000	1,264,000	4,930,000	2,133,000	2,323,000	2,142,000	363,000	109,000
1961	197,000	588,000	1,260,000	5,411,000	2,357,000	2,519,000	2,323,000	402,000	133,000
1962	236,000	643,000	1,282,000	5,970,000	2,598,000	2,820,000	2,655,000	416,000	134,000
1963	242,000	639,000	1,316,000	6,676,000	2,852,000	3,181,000	3,000,000	459,000	183,000
1964	266,000	715,000	1,359,000	7,076,000	3,111,000	3,260,000	3,054,000	498,000	208,000
1965	295,000	776,000	1,447,000	7,422,000	3,423,000	3,244,000	3,002,000	530,000	225,000
1966	300,000	743,000	1,550,000	7,964,000	3,744,000	3,337,000	3,049,000	557,000	327,000
1967	319,000	860,000	1,665,000	8,474,000	4,272,000	3,285,000	2,920,000	617,000	300,000
1968	332,000	919,000	1,819,000	8,815,000	4,865,000	2,972,000	2,554,000	656,000	321,000
1969	366,000	934,000	1,908,000	9,764,000	5,654,000	3,049,000	2,557,000	714,000	348,000
1970	401,000	1,135,000	2,006,000	10,736,000	6,493,000	3,101,000	2,531,000	770,000	373,000
1971	439,000	1,213,000	2,083,000	11,804,000	7,451,000	3,096,000	2,498,000	863,000	392,000
1972	436,404	1,261,846	2,127,540	13,529,574	8,570,579	3,600,741	3,136,930	916,660	441,594
1973	535,981	1,267,186	2,276,003	16,611,860	10,172,059	4,963,444	4,508,341	1,047,975	428,382
1974	551,214	1,366,214	2,355,450	18,542,197	11,003,437	5,729,412	5,145,320	1,218,241	591,107
1975	625,178	1,410,667	2,467,650	22,625,723	12,473,054	8,155,000	5,154,929	1,405,977	591,692
1976	724,668	1,566,046	2,553,404	32,060,343	14,608,643	15,183,000	6,190,958	1,667,583	601,117
1977	862,238	1,990,886	2,550,165	35,172,344	17,165,944	15,295,586	8,558,094	2,039,338	671,476
1978	1,008,554	2,056,170	2,759,224	35,635,113	19,024,901	13,157,703	9,938,632	2,649,233	803,276
1979	1,296,679	2,245,493	2,898,037	39,026,807	21,923,101	12,941,130	11,817,424	3,276,085	886,491
1980	1,808,756	2,397,177	3,200,586	43,655,580	25,440,583	13,528,698	11,674,400	3,604,269	1,082,030
1981	2,219,838	2,965,041	3,278,491	53,428,520	30,382,585	18,570,198	11,224,269	3,579,148	896,589
1982	2,670,730	3,526,384	3,342,945	56,024,346	34,142,743	16,922,393	11,961,831	3,993,365	965,845
1983	3,046,919	3,545,105	3,311,096	69,364,612	42,526,072	21,582,459	12,903,668	4,160,424	1,095,657
1984	3,501,467	3,791,715	3,239,685	68,653,672	46,180,014	16,759,179	17,178,912	4,391,508	1,322,971
1985	3,573,130	4,216,453	3,235,492	77,169,605	53,211,523	17,639,533	18,357,522	4,984,635	1,333,914
1986	3,291,135	4,452,984	3,312,571	94,729,283	69,365,494	18,266,811	18,714,912	5,668,722	1,428,256
1987	2,970,976	4,763,315	3,358,367	106,850,496	79,491,004	18,925,064	17,592,353	6,481,660	1,952,768
1988	2,905,124	4,766,397	3,290,163	104,839,605	77,818,122	17,272,502	17,748,337	7,373,060	2,375,921
1989	2,929,647	5,025,880	3,315,189	111,448,249	81,173,736	19,704,164	17,264,650	8,250,788	2,319,561
1990	3,043,413	5,216,117	3,440,572	123,970,484	94,267,525	18,440,960	15,486,449	9,049,646	2,212,353
1991	3,012,652	5,628,839	3,571,165	117,919,315	87,205,826	18,025,351	14,715,370	10,257,667	2,430,471
1992	3,056,038	5,665,945	3,631,806	147,610,396	105,852,752	27,019,195	15,861,375	11,749,994	2,988,455
1993	3,333,573	5,835,235	3,641,321	163,937,502	113,054,103	34,649,445	18,619,005	12,977,095	3,256,859
1994	3,712,533	6,256,343	3,606,516	160,926,712	114,303,989	29,901,482	21,047,649	13,376,298	3,344,943
1995	3,588,145	6,539,571	3,637,179	176,149,027	122,595,119	37,224,702	33,428,393	13,161,333	3,167,873

TABLE Ea247–275   State and local government revenue, by source: 1902–1995   *Continued*

Source
Figures are from data files provided by the Census of Governments. For published versions through 1982, see U.S. Department of Commerce, "Historical Statistics on Government Finance and Employment," in *Census of Governments, 1982*, volume 6, pp. 225–64.

Documentation
See the text for Table Ea24–51.

TABLE Ea276–286   State and local government expenditure, by character and object: 1902–1996

Contributed by John Joseph Wallis

			Direct							
						Capital outlay				
Total expenditure	Salaries and wages	Intergovernmental	Total	Current operation	Total	Construction	Other	Assistance and subsidies	Interest on debt	Insurance trust
Ea276	Ea277	Ea278	Ea279	Ea280	Ea281	Ea282	Ea283	Ea284	Ea285	Ea286
Fiscal year	Thousand dollars	Thousand dollars	Thousand dollars	Thousand dollars	Thousand dollars	Thousand dollars	Thousand dollars	Thousand dollars	Thousand dollars	Thousand dollars
1902	1,095,000	540,000	—	1,095,000	796,000	205,000	164,000	41,000	15,000	79,000	0
1913	2,257,000	1,026,000	—	2,257,000	1,505,000	548,000	442,000	106,000	24,000	173,000	7,000
1922	5,652,000	2,384,000	—	5,652,000	3,477,000	1,518,000	1,236,000	282,000	152,000	430,000	75,000
1927	7,810,000	3,145,000	—	7,810,000	4,590,000	2,356,000	1,921,000	435,000	93,000	662,000	109,000
1932	8,403,000	3,541,000	—	8,403,000	5,179,000	1,876,000	1,558,000	318,000	388,000	840,000	120,000
1934	7,842,000	3,194,000	—	7,842,000	4,650,000	1,407,000	1,170,000	237,000	815,000	837,000	133,000
1936	8,501,000	3,556,000	—	8,501,000	5,228,000	1,524,000	1,265,000	259,000	752,000	841,000	156,000
1938	9,988,000	4,024,000	—	9,988,000	5,969,000	1,858,000	1,538,000	320,000	994,000	784,000	383,000
1940	11,240,000	4,302,000	—	11,240,000	6,176,000	2,515,000	1,828,000	687,000	1,075,000	787,000	687,000
1942	10,914,000	4,515,000	—	10,913,000	7,027,000	1,477,000	1,241,000	236,000	1,086,000	706,000	617,000
1944	10,499,000	4,988,000	—	10,498,000	7,803,000	709,000	562,000	147,000	997,000	635,000	354,000
1946	14,067,000	5,945,000	—	14,067,000	9,630,000	1,305,000	970,000	334,000	1,269,000	557,000	1,306,000
1948	21,260,000	8,430,000	—	21,261,000	13,345,000	3,725,000	3,085,000	640,000	2,451,000	543,000	1,197,000
1950	27,905,000	10,043,000	—	27,905,000	15,856,000	6,047,000	5,169,000	879,000	3,010,000	613,000	2,379,000
1952	30,863,000	12,045,000	—	30,863,000	18,533,000	7,436,000	6,386,000	1,051,000	2,472,000	724,000	1,698,000
1953	32,937,000	13,100,000	—	32,936,000	19,965,000	7,905,000	6,763,000	1,142,000	2,558,000	797,000	1,711,000
1954	36,607,000	14,343,000	—	36,605,000	21,482,000	9,125,000	7,738,000	1,386,000	2,659,000	916,000	2,423,000
1955	40,375,000	15,539,000	—	40,376,000	23,163,000	10,706,000	9,048,000	1,658,000	2,684,000	1,059,000	2,764,000
1956	43,152,000	17,118,000	—	43,152,000	25,483,000	11,407,000	9,354,000	2,053,000	2,666,000	1,220,000	2,376,000
1957	47,553,000	18,707,000	—	47,552,000	28,011,000	12,616,000	10,387,000	2,230,000	2,800,000	1,376,000	2,749,000
1958	53,712,000	20,786,000	—	53,712,000	30,888,000	13,986,000	11,704,000	2,282,000	3,133,000	1,537,000	4,168,000
1959	58,572,000	22,528,000	—	58,573,000	33,398,000	15,351,000	12,723,000	2,628,000	3,300,000	1,740,000	4,784,000
1960	60,999,000	24,445,000	—	60,999,000	36,351,000	15,104,000	12,352,000	2,752,000	3,485,000	2,028,000	4,031,000
1961	67,023,000	26,461,000	—	67,023,000	39,835,000	16,091,000	13,214,000	2,877,000	3,573,000	2,225,000	5,299,000
1962	70,547,000	28,729,000	—	70,547,000	42,736,000	16,791,000	13,625,000	3,166,000	3,708,000	2,424,000	4,888,000
1963	75,760,000	31,031,000	—	75,760,000	46,378,000	17,946,000	14,481,000	3,465,000	3,771,000	2,653,000	5,012,000
1964	80,579,000	33,310,000	—	80,579,000	49,687,000	19,087,000	15,389,000	3,698,000	3,885,000	2,826,000	5,094,000
1965	86,686,000	36,095,000	—	86,685,000	53,929,000	20,667,000	16,505,000	4,163,000	4,127,000	3,012,000	4,950,000
1966	94,906,000	40,059,000	—	94,907,000	60,212,000	22,330,000	17,801,000	4,528,000	4,315,000	3,268,000	4,782,000
1967	105,978,000	44,451,000	—	105,978,000	67,840,000	24,233,000	19,362,000	4,871,000	5,015,000	3,612,000	5,278,000
1968	116,234,000	48,996,000	—	116,233,000	75,311,000	25,731,000	20,800,000	4,931,000	5,649,000	3,889,000	5,653,000
1969	131,600,000	55,695,000	—	131,600,000	86,178,000	28,240,000	22,904,000	5,336,000	6,726,000	4,403,000	6,053,000
1970	148,052,000	62,998,000	—	148,051,000	97,915,000	29,650,000	24,252,000	5,399,000	8,090,000	5,123,000	7,273,000
1971	170,766,000	70,561,000	—	170,767,000	111,829,000	33,137,000	26,970,000	6,168,000	10,104,000	5,904,000	9,793,000
1972	190,497,142	79,847,427	—	190,497,142	126,825,370	34,626,669	28,420,195	6,206,474	11,548,525	6,947,089	10,549,489
1973	205,465,076	86,172,207	—	205,465,076	139,104,305	35,271,914	28,250,992	7,020,922	12,187,402	7,827,923	11,073,532
1974	226,032,082	94,053,739	341,194	225,690,888	154,809,889	38,083,900	30,541,665	7,542,235	11,289,864	8,840,212	12,667,023
1975	269,216,645	106,168,000	974,780	268,241,865	180,975,531	44,823,979	36,355,764	8,468,215	11,146,705	10,086,762	21,208,888
1976	304,228,057	116,466,018	1,179,580	303,048,477	204,387,054	46,530,919	38,298,678	8,232,241	12,494,422	11,681,456	27,954,626
1977	324,554,117	126,330,245	1,386,250	323,167,867	225,649,902	45,154,445	36,334,224	8,820,221	13,077,374	13,137,393	26,148,753
1978	346,787,653	137,703,047	1,472,438	345,315,215	249,223,194	44,769,237	36,199,089	8,570,148	13,753,434	14,043,874	23,525,476
1979	381,867,140	149,104,137	1,493,256	380,373,884	274,166,672	53,195,983	43,325,821	9,870,162	14,044,166	15,462,767	23,504,296
1980	434,073,391	163,896,104	1,746,304	432,327,087	307,810,611	62,893,478	51,491,671	11,401,807	15,221,918	17,604,482	28,796,598
1981	487,047,370	178,900,382	1,873,007	485,174,363	343,623,393	67,596,477	54,950,290	12,646,187	16,860,879	20,511,098	36,582,516
1982	524,587,774	191,570,258	1,793,289	522,794,485	375,057,117	66,639,110	53,504,837	13,134,273	17,334,945	24,320,795	39,442,518
1983	566,662,933	204,378,391	1,764,928	564,898,005	401,967,445	67,733,699	53,017,965	14,715,734	18,684,102	29,178,188	47,334,571
1984	600,222,142	219,266,108	1,722,118	598,500,024	433,576,456	70,637,968	53,822,429	16,815,539	19,694,325	34,438,537	40,152,738

(continued)

TABLE Ea276–286   State and local government expenditure, by character and object: 1902–1996 *Continued*

				Direct							
						Capital outlay					
Fiscal year	Total expenditure	Salaries and wages	Intergovernmental	Total	Current operation	Total	Construction	Other	Assistance and subsidies	Interest on debt	Insurance trust
	Ea276	Ea277	Ea278	Ea279	Ea280	Ea281	Ea282	Ea283	Ea284	Ea285	Ea286
	Thousand dollars	Thousand dollars	Thousand dollars	Thousand dollars	Thousand dollars	Thousand dollars	Thousand dollars	Thousand dollars	Thousand dollars	Thousand dollars	Thousand dollars
1985	657,888,116	236,820,546	1,963,468	655,924,648	472,311,615	79,898,066	60,653,360	19,244,706	20,707,185	38,817,167	44,190,615
1986	717,457,666	256,621,901	2,105,831	715,351,835	511,377,784	90,477,409	67,967,634	22,509,775	22,588,295	44,370,141	46,538,206
1987	777,045,448	274,734,458	2,455,538	774,589,910	551,091,093	98,841,776	74,162,473	24,679,303	23,466,243	50,387,192	50,803,606
1988	826,848,709	295,689,176	2,657,327	824,191,382	591,261,210	104,319,693	78,597,548	25,722,145	23,927,966	52,803,043	51,879,470
1989	890,863,307	317,574,143	2,931,083	887,932,224	640,540,734	111,943,668	84,036,690	27,906,978	24,974,797	55,479,482	54,993,543
1990	975,939,985	340,653,779	3,245,365	972,694,620	700,130,748	123,101,797	89,144,138	33,957,659	27,226,784	58,914,048	63,321,243
1991	1,063,270,462	366,405,908	3,465,801	1,059,804,661	762,007,025	131,650,220	96,653,724	34,996,496	30,455,533	61,533,374	74,158,509
1992	1,156,781,435	383,323,239	3,632,179	1,153,149,256	828,424,165	136,520,101	102,294,182	34,225,919	32,976,049	65,014,293	90,214,648
1993	1,213,723,590	396,336,250	3,626,834	1,210,096,756	875,924,688	135,899,297	100,152,725	35,746,572	34,663,749	64,802,275	98,806,747
1994	1,264,289,223	410,609,598	3,647,527	1,260,641,696	927,898,814	137,500,843	101,991,607	35,509,236	35,295,463	64,484,405	95,462,171
1995	1,351,437,907	430,949,826	3,674,903	1,347,763,004	985,692,755	151,440,430	110,011,692	41,428,738	36,866,948	66,423,191	107,339,680
1996	1,397,634,473	447,638,265	3,920,141	1,393,714,332	1,021,155,474	158,910,981	116,075,753	42,835,228	36,153,660	68,743,465	108,750,752

Source

Data in this table are taken from spreadsheets provided by the Census of Governments. Published versions of the data through 1982 can be found in U.S. Department of Commerce, "Historical Statistics on Government Finance and Employment." in *Census of Governments, 1982,* volume 6, pp. 225-64.

Documentation

See the text for Table Ea24–51.

In order to compute total expenditures under a different revenue concept, use the data from Table Ea125–131 on the change in debt during the year. See the essay in this chapter for additional information on this matter.

Series Ea285. Includes interest on debt of utilities operated by local governments.

TABLE Ea287–347   State and local government expenditure, by function: 1902–1995

Contributed by John Joseph Wallis

	Total expenditure	General	Intergovernmental	Total	Direct General Education					
					Total	Total	Total	Elementary	Higher education	Other	Libraries
	Ea287	Ea288	Ea289	Ea290	Ea291	Ea292	Ea293	Ea294	Ea295	Ea296
Fiscal year	Thousand dollars	Thousand dollars	Thousand dollars	Thousand dollars	Thousand dollars	Thousand dollars	Thousand dollars	Thousand dollars	Thousand dollars	Thousand dollars
1902	1,095,000	1,013,000	0	1,095,000	1,013,000	255,000	238,000	13,000	4,000	—
1913	2,257,000	2,064,000	0	2,257,000	2,064,000	577,000	522,000	49,000	6,000	—
1922	5,652,000	5,218,000	0	5,652,000	5,218,000	1,705,000	1,541,000	143,000	21,000	—
1927	7,810,000	7,210,000	0	7,810,000	7,210,000	2,235,000	2,017,000	196,000	22,000	—
1932	8,403,000	7,765,000	0	8,403,000	7,765,000	2,311,000	2,033,000	251,000	27,000	—
1934	7,842,000	7,181,000	0	7,842,000	7,181,000	1,831,000	1,612,000	188,000	31,000	—
1936	8,501,000	7,644,000	0	8,501,000	7,644,000	2,177,000	1,885,000	250,000	42,000	—
1938	9,988,000	8,757,000	0	9,988,000	8,757,000	2,491,000	2,152,000	288,000	51,000	—
1940	11,240,000	9,229,000	0	11,240,000	9,229,000	2,638,000	2,270,000	312,000	56,000	—
1942	10,914,000	9,190,000	0	10,914,000	9,190,000	2,586,000	2,204,000	317,000	65,000	—
1944	10,499,000	8,863,000	0	10,499,000	8,863,000	2,793,000	2,318,000	406,000	69,000	—
1946	14,067,000	11,028,000	0	14,067,000	11,028,000	3,356,000	2,861,000	422,000	73,000	—
1948	21,260,000	17,684,000	0	21,260,000	17,684,000	5,379,000	4,308,000	950,000	121,000	—
1950	27,905,000	22,787,000	0	27,905,000	22,787,000	7,177,000	5,843,000	1,170,000	164,000	—
1952	30,863,000	26,098,000	0	30,863,000	26,098,000	8,318,000	6,862,000	1,267,000	189,000	118,000
1953	32,937,000	27,910,000	0	32,937,000	27,910,000	9,390,000	7,822,000	1,361,000	207,000	136,000
1954	36,607,000	30,701,000	0	36,607,000	30,701,000	10,557,000	8,947,000	1,418,000	192,000	145,000
1955	40,375,000	33,724,000	0	40,375,000	33,724,000	11,907,000	10,129,000	1,570,000	210,000	153,000
1956	43,152,000	36,711,000	0	43,152,000	36,711,000	13,220,000	11,165,000	1,814,000	241,000	—
1957	47,553,000	40,375,000	0	47,553,000	40,375,000	14,134,000	11,657,000	2,206,000	272,000	199,000
1958	53,712,000	44,851,000	0	53,712,000	44,851,000	15,919,000	13,032,000	2,582,000	305,000	—
1959	58,572,000	48,887,000	0	58,572,000	48,887,000	17,283,000	14,034,000	2,920,000	329,000	—
1960	60,999,000	51,876,000	0	60,999,000	51,876,000	18,719,000	15,166,000	3,202,000	351,000	278,000
1961	67,023,000	56,201,000	0	67,023,000	56,201,000	20,574,000	16,608,000	3,570,000	396,000	368,000
1962	70,547,000	60,206,000	0	70,547,000	60,206,000	22,216,000	17,739,000	4,043,000	434,000	353,000
1963	75,760,000	64,815,000	0	75,760,000	64,815,000	23,776,000	18,802,000	4,470,000	504,000	399,000
1964	80,579,000	69,302,000	0	80,579,000	69,302,000	26,286,000	20,399,000	5,278,000	609,000	401,000
1965	86,686,000	74,678,000	0	86,686,000	74,678,000	28,563,000	21,966,000	5,863,000	735,000	444,000
1966	94,906,000	82,843,000	0	94,906,000	82,843,000	33,287,000	25,091,000	7,207,000	989,000	486,000
1967	105,978,000	93,350,000	0	105,978,000	93,350,000	37,919,000	27,590,000	8,932,000	1,397,000	518,000
1968	116,234,000	102,411,000	0	116,234,000	102,411,000	41,158,000	29,305,000	10,214,000	1,637,000	573,000
1969	131,600,000	116,728,000	0	131,600,000	116,728,000	47,238,000	33,752,000	11,551,000	1,935,000	634,000
1970	148,052,000	131,332,000	0	148,052,000	131,332,000	52,718,000	37,461,000	12,924,000	2,332,000	700,000
1971	170,766,000	150,674,000	0	170,766,000	150,674,000	59,413,000	41,766,000	14,785,000	2,861,000	762,000
1972	190,497,142	168,549,300	0	190,497,142	168,549,300	65,813,217	46,670,381	15,861,270	3,281,566	816,011
1973	205,465,076	181,356,888	0	205,465,076	181,356,888	69,713,205	48,788,871	17,369,320	3,555,014	877,195
1974	226,032,082	198,959,415	341,194	225,690,888	198,618,221	75,833,070	53,059,162	18,883,654	3,890,254	967,540
1975	269,216,645	230,722,121	974,780	268,241,865	229,747,341	87,858,129	61,485,257	21,702,445	4,670,427	1,118,770
1976	304,228,057	256,730,853	1,179,580	303,048,477	255,551,273	97,216,271	67,673,568	24,303,730	5,238,973	1,249,117
1977	324,554,117	274,215,390	1,386,250	323,167,867	272,829,140	102,779,765	71,546,137	25,972,295	5,261,333	1,278,890
1978	346,787,653	296,984,456	1,472,438	345,315,215	295,512,018	110,757,569	76,702,639	28,390,637	5,664,293	1,361,507
1979	381,867,140	327,517,300	1,493,256	380,373,884	326,024,044	119,448,201	83,385,150	30,058,856	6,004,195	1,504,666
1980	434,073,391	369,086,155	1,746,304	432,327,087	367,339,851	133,210,804	92,930,007	33,919,259	6,361,538	1,693,627
1981	487,047,370	407,448,837	1,873,007	485,174,363	405,575,830	145,784,259	100,534,479	38,114,279	7,135,501	1,865,190
1982	524,587,774	436,732,944	1,793,289	522,794,485	434,939,655	154,282,461	105,761,428	41,569,919	6,951,114	2,012,593
1983	566,662,933	466,516,499	1,764,928	564,898,005	464,751,571	163,875,678	112,945,179	43,820,105	7,110,394	2,213,222
1984	600,222,142	505,007,861	1,722,118	598,500,024	503,285,743	176,107,629	120,895,748	47,612,902	7,598,979	2,412,517
1985	657,888,116	553,899,378	1,963,468	655,924,648	551,935,910	192,685,974	131,986,576	52,316,006	8,383,392	2,699,929
1986	717,457,666	605,622,528	2,105,831	715,351,835	603,516,697	210,818,505	145,110,764	56,535,108	9,172,633	2,947,501
1987	777,045,448	657,133,732	2,455,538	774,589,910	654,678,194	226,618,646	156,910,098	60,072,709	9,635,839	3,297,578
1988	826,848,709	704,920,584	2,657,327	824,191,382	702,263,257	242,683,417	169,694,203	62,687,689	10,301,525	3,500,747
1989	890,863,307	762,360,469	2,931,083	887,932,224	759,429,386	263,898,223	185,170,700	67,550,270	11,177,253	3,783,451
1990	975,939,985	834,818,220	3,245,365	972,694,620	831,572,855	288,148,071	202,009,431	73,418,284	12,720,356	4,101,814
1991	1,063,270,462	908,107,875	3,465,801	1,059,804,661	904,642,074	309,302,355	217,642,750	78,748,664	12,910,941	4,442,137
1992	1,156,781,435	981,252,765	3,632,179	1,153,149,256	977,620,586	324,651,916	227,273,362	84,127,578	13,250,976	4,713,062
1993	1,213,723,590	1,030,433,816	3,626,834	1,210,096,756	1,026,806,982	342,287,080	240,310,015	88,108,569	13,868,496	4,662,447
1994	1,264,289,223	1,077,664,555	3,647,527	1,260,641,696	1,074,017,028	353,286,956	246,981,375	90,871,177	15,434,404	4,954,133
1995	1,351,437,907	1,149,863,246	3,674,903	1,347,763,004	1,146,188,343	378,272,664	264,240,479	97,048,481	16,983,704	5,284,677

(continued)

TABLE Ea287–347   State and local government expenditure, by function: 1902–1995 *Continued*

										Direct			
										General			
					Social services and income maintenance							Public safety	
	Public welfare												
		Cash assistance				Health and hospitals		Employment security administration				
	Total	Categorical	Noncategorical	Other	Total	Hospitals	Health		Veterans' services	Police	Fire
	Ea297	Ea298	Ea299	Ea300	Ea301	Ea302	Ea303	Ea304	Ea305	Ea306	Ea307
Fiscal year	Thousand dollars	Thousand dollars	Thousand dollars	Thousand dollars	Thousand dollars	Thousand dollars	Thousand dollars	Thousand dollars	Thousand dollars	Thousand dollars	Thousand dollars
1902	37,000	11,000	—	26,000	60,000	43,000	17,000	0	0	50,000	40,000
1913	52,000	17,000	—	35,000	108,000	79,000	29,000	0	0	89,000	76,000
1922	119,000	57,000	—	62,000	258,000	200,000	58,000	0	80,000	190,000	158,000
1927	151,000	79,000	—	72,000	355,000	279,000	76,000	0	0	270,000	203,000
1932	444,000	366,000	—	78,000	456,000	349,000	107,000	0	0	318,000	210,000
1934	889,000	796,000	—	93,000	418,000	309,000	109,000	1,000	0	291,000	189,000
1936	827,000	731,000	—	96,000	467,000	351,000	116,000	3,000	0	314,000	205,000
1938	1,069,000	483,000	485,000	101,000	551,000	400,000	151,000	48,000	0	359,000	231,000
1940	1,156,000	611,000	438,000	107,000	609,000	450,000	159,000	64,000	0	365,000	235,000
1942	1,225,000	761,000	345,000	119,000	591,000	432,000	159,000	59,000	1,000	394,000	236,000
1944	1,133,000	842,000	166,000	125,000	656,000	468,000	188,000	35,000	1,000	414,000	251,000
1946	1,409,000	1,014,000	216,000	179,000	818,000	567,000	251,000	60,000	54,000	479,000	294,000
1948	2,099,000	1,473,000	357,000	269,000	1,229,000	937,000	292,000	150,000	633,000	644,000	406,000
1950	2,940,000	2,010,000	538,000	392,000	1,748,000	1,384,000	364,000	172,000	462,000	776,000	488,000
1952	2,788,000	2,023,000	303,000	462,000	2,185,000	1,745,000	440,000	178,000	142,000	939,000	586,000
1953	2,914,000	2,159,000	272,000	483,000	2,290,000	1,863,000	427,000	187,000	113,000	1,038,000	598,000
1954	3,060,000	2,224,000	308,000	528,000	2,409,000	1,962,000	447,000	190,000	102,000	1,130,000	653,000
1955	3,168,000	2,269,000	329,000	570,000	2,524,000	2,053,000	471,000	207,000	61,000	1,229,000	694,000
1956	3,139,000	2,310,000	244,000	585,000	2,772,000	2,316,000	456,000	215,000	88,000	1,330,000	737,000
1957	3,485,000	2,525,000	195,000	765,000	3,119,000	2,619,000	500,000	234,000	38,000	1,468,000	810,000
1958	3,818,000	2,689,000	275,000	854,000	3,462,000	2,961,000	501,000	270,000	121,000	1,610,000	873,000
1959	4,136,000	2,886,000	301,000	949,000	3,724,000	3,142,000	582,000	303,000	61,000	1,710,000	914,000
1960	4,404,000	2,997,000	310,000	1,097,000	3,794,000	3,235,000	559,000	313,000	112,000	1,857,000	995,000
1961	4,720,000	3,075,000	335,000	1,310,000	4,086,000	3,496,000	590,000	351,000	84,000	2,017,000	1,087,000
1962	5,084,000	3,257,000	258,000	1,569,000	4,342,000	3,673,000	669,000	399,000	95,000	2,130,000	1,124,000
1963	5,481,000	3,379,000	249,000	1,853,000	4,681,000	3,971,000	710,000	411,000	20,000	2,282,000	1,186,000
1964	5,766,000	3,478,000	226,000	2,062,000	4,910,000	4,171,000	739,000	426,000	19,000	2,366,000	1,222,000
1965	6,315,000	3,690,000	234,000	2,391,000	5,361,000	4,525,000	836,000	457,000	20,000	2,549,000	1,306,000
1966	6,757,000	3,822,000	236,000	2,699,000	5,910,000	4,969,000	941,000	500,000	21,000	2,776,000	1,376,000
1967	8,218,000	4,381,000	266,000	3,571,000	6,640,000	5,559,000	1,081,000	547,000	23,000	3,049,000	1,499,000
1968	9,857,000	4,817,000	349,000	4,691,000	7,546,000	6,282,000	1,264,000	606,000	33,000	3,410,000	1,623,000
1969	12,110,000	5,691,000	446,000	5,973,000	8,520,000	7,011,000	1,509,000	667,000	51,000	3,901,000	1,793,000
1970	14,679,000	6,902,000	480,000	7,297,000	9,669,000	7,863,000	1,806,000	769,000	67,000	4,494,000	2,024,000
1971	18,226,000	8,609,000	610,000	9,007,000	11,205,000	9,086,000	2,119,000	945,000	65,000	5,228,000	2,303,000
1972	21,116,556	9,794,771	697,753	10,624,032	13,022,178	10,446,643	2,575,535	1,136,087	50,843	6,005,061	2,579,037
1973	23,581,873	10,308,470	761,030	12,512,373	13,844,058	11,111,941	2,732,117	1,281,764	48,255	6,779,948	2,804,000
1974	24,744,757	9,242,128	722,226	14,780,403	15,945,460	12,493,364	3,452,096	1,308,322	156,218	7,288,980	3,036,776
1975	27,190,960	8,587,930	871,726	17,731,304	18,846,225	14,432,598	4,413,627	1,513,935	362,576	8,525,803	3,522,000
1976	31,434,787	9,688,040	1,073,022	20,673,725	20,686,216	15,726,463	4,959,753	1,576,453	64,035	9,530,679	3,897,534
1977	34,528,855	10,066,199	1,274,185	23,188,471	23,038,884	17,541,569	5,497,315	1,705,786	54,000	10,445,365	4,412,298
1978	37,678,831	10,390,659	1,357,946	25,930,226	24,952,028	18,648,994	6,303,034	1,763,872	53,710	11,306,046	4,801,757
1979	40,418,130	10,625,041	1,293,716	28,499,373	28,217,540	21,038,765	7,178,775	1,806,110	53,303	12,207,499	5,146,503
1980	45,552,246	11,585,229	1,336,446	32,630,571	32,173,469	23,786,790	8,386,679	2,008,792	60,951	13,493,702	5,718,232
1981	52,247,596	12,833,229	1,516,736	37,897,631	36,100,405	26,329,564	9,770,841	2,276,431	56,969	14,947,018	6,335,761
1982	56,216,380	13,007,593	1,672,423	41,536,364	40,718,742	30,245,353	10,473,389	2,285,868	63,798	16,511,354	7,025,556
1983	59,157,097	13,691,754	2,201,147	43,264,196	43,749,854	32,451,752	11,298,102	2,473,187	74,688	17,957,612	7,582,075
1984	64,709,444	14,445,780	2,313,186	47,950,478	46,329,429	34,052,908	12,276,521	2,555,711	98,572	19,261,992	8,201,727
1985	69,523,337	14,902,797	2,498,541	52,121,999	49,580,667	35,869,742	13,710,925	2,592,119	112,881	20,956,316	8,916,631
1986	73,784,593	16,227,856	2,636,488	54,920,249	53,535,897	37,986,356	15,549,541	2,707,220	121,785	22,685,458	9,586,526
1987	80,219,521	16,863,591	2,627,033	60,728,897	57,087,593	40,184,170	16,903,423	2,751,691	129,454	24,742,362	10,452,893
1988	86,457,302	17,260,555	2,623,472	66,573,275	61,939,865	43,452,040	18,487,825	2,853,110	134,281	26,276,791	11,752,856
1989	94,962,182	17,915,076	2,818,695	74,228,411	67,757,301	47,072,913	20,684,388	2,947,169	146,198	27,770,661	11,932,217
1990	107,286,581	19,372,319	2,923,808	84,990,454	74,634,739	50,412,004	24,222,735	3,014,354	151,682	30,576,606	13,186,081
1991	126,964,579	21,706,800	3,214,100	102,043,679	81,109,950	54,404,346	26,705,604	3,249,688	157,313	32,771,685	13,796,137
1992	155,153,467	23,866,656	3,380,401	127,906,410	88,572,882	59,141,282	29,431,600	3,716,776	170,014	35,431,625	14,751,172
1993	167,098,371	25,045,098	3,406,415	138,646,858	94,854,613	62,563,966	32,290,647	3,945,023	164,681	36,406,822	15,372,647
1994	179,829,425	24,719,256	3,595,643	151,514,526	100,429,498	65,100,773	35,328,725	4,070,807	179,076	38,644,621	16,122,797
1995	193,109,515	25,279,253	3,521,604	164,308,658	105,946,445	67,926,472	38,019,973	3,946,014	206,109	41,054,532	17,009,481

TABLE Ea287–347   State and local government expenditure, by function: 1902–1995   *Continued*

		Direct							
		General							
	Public safety				Transportation				
		Corrections		Protective inspection and regulation					
	Total	Institutions	Other		Highways	Air	Parking	Water	Transit
	Ea308	Ea309	Ea310	Ea311	Ea312	Ea313	Ea314	Ea315	Ea316
Fiscal year	Thousand dollars	Thousand dollars	Thousand dollars	Thousand dollars	Thousand dollars	Thousand dollars	Thousand dollars	Thousand dollars	Thousand dollars
1902	—	—	—	—	175,000	—	—	—	—
1913	—	—	—	—	419,000	—	—	—	—
1922	—	—	—	—	1,294,000	—	—	—	—
1927	—	—	—	—	1,809,000	—	—	—	—
1932	—	—	—	—	1,741,000	—	—	—	—
1934	—	—	—	—	1,509,000	—	—	—	—
1936	—	—	—	—	1,425,000	—	—	—	—
1938	—	—	—	—	1,650,000	—	—	—	—
1940	—	—	—	—	1,573,000	—	—	—	—
1942	—	—	—	—	1,490,000	—	—	—	—
1944	—	—	—	—	1,200,000	—	—	—	—
1946	—	—	—	—	1,672,000	—	—	—	—
1948	—	—	—	—	3,036,000	—	—	—	—
1950	—	—	—	—	3,803,000	—	—	—	—
1952	337,000	—	—	—	4,650,000	112,000	—	96,000	0
1953	365,000	—	—	—	4,987,000	99,000	—	156,000	0
1954	397,000	—	—	—	5,527,000	113,000	—	195,000	0
1955	435,000	—	—	—	6,452,000	114,000	—	154,000	0
1956	467,000	—	—	—	6,953,000	171,000	—	200,000	0
1957	515,000	—	—	—	7,816,000	232,000	—	187,000	0
1958	534,000	—	—	—	8,567,000	254,000	—	219,000	0
1959	671,000	—	—	—	9,592,000	308,000	—	241,000	0
1960	678,000	—	—	—	9,428,000	342,000	—	237,000	0
1961	763,000	—	—	—	9,844,000	422,000	—	293,000	0
1962	790,000	—	—	—	10,357,000	373,000	83,000	292,000	0
1963	818,000	—	—	—	11,135,000	363,000	112,000	313,000	0
1964	883,000	—	—	—	11,664,000	359,000	114,000	291,000	0
1965	974,000	—	—	—	12,221,000	415,000	108,000	276,000	0
1966	1,020,000	—	—	—	12,770,000	424,000	128,000	318,000	0
1967	1,139,000	—	—	—	13,932,000	466,000	144,000	319,000	0
1968	1,270,000	—	—	—	14,481,000	516,000	105,000	407,000	0
1969	1,391,000	—	—	—	15,417,000	723,000	137,000	461,000	0
1970	1,626,000	—	—	—	16,427,000	969,000	158,000	444,000	0
1971	1,885,000	—	—	—	18,095,000	1,061,000	159,000	504,000	0
1972	2,111,715	—	—	—	19,020,992	1,278,631	171,164	522,865	0
1973	2,383,345	—	—	—	18,614,837	1,418,308	205,054	600,566	0
1974	2,805,355	—	—	—	19,945,770	1,300,269	214,003	625,222	0
1975	3,374,578	—	—	—	22,527,688	1,448,315	301,879	742,286	0
1976	3,784,136	—	—	—	23,906,807	1,500,767	333,920	705,285	0
1977	4,358,821	2,148,706	2,210,115	1,637,427	23,057,891	1,348,197	298,181	757,568	184,913
1978	4,981,145	2,462,641	2,518,504	1,888,537	24,608,728	1,617,098	269,653	754,354	183,500
1979	5,534,423	2,768,907	2,765,516	2,076,133	28,440,094	1,906,065	324,011	1,044,738	252,483
1980	6,447,503	3,303,223	3,144,280	2,317,612	33,311,286	2,500,979	343,053	1,168,418	290,815
1981	7,392,898	3,771,173	3,621,725	2,556,994	34,603,137	2,743,072	377,345	1,508,252	234,691
1982	8,469,988	4,398,893	4,071,095	2,787,350	34,520,249	2,864,028	406,483	1,373,013	299,500
1983	9,783,483	4,935,598	4,847,885	2,967,185	36,654,925	3,013,502	454,483	1,457,991	319,626
1984	11,087,901	5,859,629	5,228,272	3,233,321	39,418,823	3,584,454	483,985	1,329,338	340,209
1985	12,838,627	6,926,231	5,912,396	3,530,205	44,988,995	3,743,822	591,729	1,493,160	231,471
1986	14,957,343	8,093,078	6,864,265	4,078,692	49,368,228	4,256,947	682,460	1,725,447	275,946
1987	16,637,907	8,827,643	7,810,264	4,417,026	52,354,963	4,913,994	760,559	1,751,110	241,544
1988	18,985,958	10,301,961	8,683,997	4,723,810	55,620,868	5,350,812	784,884	1,841,771	262,146
1989	21,197,451	11,595,538	9,601,913	5,080,913	58,104,619	5,752,001	754,578	1,922,867	401,729
1990	24,635,201	13,370,059	11,265,142	5,570,328	61,057,330	6,483,626	749,235	1,968,378	369,687
1991	27,356,376	15,012,168	12,344,208	6,008,078	64,936,616	7,233,199	813,557	2,048,664	376,603
1992	28,818,627	15,347,585	13,471,042	6,272,041	67,351,483	8,275,649	874,455	1,898,741	430,304
1993	29,630,809	15,965,881	13,664,928	6,353,983	68,369,567	9,290,158	697,892	2,168,233	351,853
1994	32,270,345	17,741,937	14,528,408	6,637,861	72,067,398	9,414,319	729,078	2,628,350	363,596
1995	35,856,854	20,095,376	15,761,478	7,236,299	77,108,526	8,397,419	800,118	2,309,348	322,320

(continued)

TABLE Ea287-347   State and local government expenditure, by function: 1902–1995 *Continued*

	Direct								
	General								
	Environmental and housing								
	Natural resources							Sanitation	
	Total	Agriculture	Fish and game	Forestry	Other	Parks and recreation	Housing and community development	Total	Sewage	Solid waste
	Ea317	Ea318	Ea319	Ea320	Ea321	Ea322	Ea323	Ea324	Ea325	Ea326
Fiscal year	Thousand dollars	Thousand dollars	Thousand dollars	Thousand dollars	Thousand dollars	Thousand dollars	Thousand dollars	Thousand dollars	Thousand dollars	Thousand dollars
1902	9,000	—	—	—	—	29,000	0	51,000	—	—
1913	14,000	—	—	—	—	57,000	0	97,000	—	—
1922	61,000	—	—	—	—	85,000	0	189,000	—	—
1927	94,000	—	—	—	—	153,000	0	312,000	—	—
1932	165,000	—	—	—	—	147,000	0	223,000	—	—
1934	159,000	—	—	—	—	126,000	0	177,000	—	—
1936	193,000	—	—	—	—	104,000	0	204,000	—	—
1938	222,000	—	—	—	—	130,000	3,000	226,000	—	—
1940	218,000	—	—	—	—	162,000	230,000	207,000	—	—
1942	214,000	—	—	—	—	128,000	236,000	229,000	—	—
1944	232,000	—	—	—	—	123,000	46,000	245,000	—	—
1946	302,000	—	—	—	—	179,000	114,000	370,000	—	—
1948	496,000	—	—	—	—	243,000	176,000	670,000	—	—
1950	670,000	—	—	—	—	304,000	452,000	834,000	—	—
1952	776,000	—	—	—	—	324,000	769,000	992,000	—	—
1953	705,000	—	—	—	—	374,000	631,000	908,000	—	—
1954	762,000	—	—	—	—	424,000	611,000	1,058,000	—	—
1955	793,000	—	—	—	—	509,000	499,000	1,142,000	—	—
1956	906,000	—	—	—	—	541,000	437,000	1,326,000	835,000	492,000
1957	932,000	—	—	—	—	608,000	505,000	1,443,000	906,000	537,000
1958	999,000	—	—	—	—	685,000	601,000	1,505,000	933,000	572,000
1959	1,076,000	—	—	—	—	729,000	615,000	1,609,000	1,011,000	598,000
1960	1,189,000	—	—	—	—	770,000	858,000	1,727,000	1,103,000	624,000
1961	1,327,000	—	—	—	—	857,000	943,000	1,774,000	1,103,000	672,000
1962	1,371,000	—	—	—	—	886,000	1,153,000	1,958,000	1,272,000	686,000
1963	1,588,000	—	—	—	—	978,000	1,247,000	2,187,000	1,464,000	723,000
1964	1,835,000	—	—	—	—	1,022,000	1,142,000	2,267,000	1,515,000	752,000
1965	1,861,000	—	—	—	—	1,104,000	1,250,000	2,360,000	1,567,000	793,000
1966	2,039,000	—	—	—	—	1,187,000	1,406,000	2,571,000	1,707,000	864,000
1967	2,344,000	—	—	—	—	1,291,000	1,469,000	2,523,000	1,635,000	888,000
1968	2,471,000	—	—	—	—	1,412,000	1,632,000	2,707,000	1,732,000	975,000
1969	2,552,000	—	—	—	—	1,645,000	1,902,000	2,969,000	1,895,000	1,074,000
1970	2,732,000	—	—	—	—	1,888,000	2,138,000	3,413,000	2,167,000	1,246,000
1971	3,082,000	—	—	—	—	2,109,000	2,554,000	4,087,000	2,646,000	1,441,000
1972	3,122,367	—	—	—	—	2,318,139	2,733,832	4,845,944	3,259,222	1,586,722
1973	3,278,016	—	—	—	—	2,560,700	3,164,914	5,321,344	3,603,809	1,717,535
1974	3,660,632	—	—	—	—	2,950,649	3,460,925	5,995,188	4,080,301	1,914,887
1975	4,222,879	—	—	—	—	3,461,616	3,459,341	7,438,293	5,262,293	2,176,000
1976	4,662,219	—	—	—	—	3,864,224	3,151,116	8,239,553	5,937,310	2,302,243
1977	4,048,770	1,513,740	540,677	427,670	1,566,683	4,915,887	3,387,497	9,425,234	7,051,720	2,373,514
1978	4,225,129	1,633,601	586,424	438,292	1,566,812	5,269,760	3,699,099	9,869,241	7,141,863	2,727,378
1979	4,705,957	1,763,305	649,699	472,583	1,820,370	5,895,567	4,724,116	11,787,444	8,795,399	2,992,045
1980	5,509,157	1,966,845	707,195	501,911	2,333,206	6,520,259	6,061,567	13,214,358	9,892,321	3,322,037
1981	6,175,263	2,222,295	828,638	564,086	2,560,244	7,063,772	7,085,907	14,898,220	11,121,401	3,776,819
1982	6,567,117	2,419,819	898,489	570,784	2,678,025	7,501,291	8,583,940	14,940,214	10,806,209	4,134,005
1983	7,082,232	2,540,977	921,346	582,468	3,037,441	8,049,832	8,505,128	15,603,463	11,239,056	4,364,407
1984	7,420,655	2,651,446	1,013,876	573,607	3,181,726	8,343,451	9,283,284	16,225,085	11,515,530	4,709,555
1985	8,356,643	2,875,917	1,077,604	636,253	3,766,869	9,160,228	10,377,777	17,397,964	12,185,960	5,212,004
1986	9,073,838	3,097,118	1,146,372	708,104	4,122,244	10,164,420	11,284,888	19,141,856	13,307,328	5,834,528
1987	9,942,615	3,242,256	1,189,364	699,900	4,811,095	11,018,276	11,769,900	21,647,340	15,147,941	6,499,399
1988	10,238,064	3,351,227	1,294,884	869,060	4,722,893	12,069,762	13,254,519	23,678,593	16,328,592	7,350,001
1989	11,092,132	3,622,664	1,391,711	983,350	5,094,407	12,926,933	14,738,393	25,772,606	17,038,864	8,733,742
1990	12,330,027	3,940,631	1,498,226	1,009,531	5,881,639	14,325,628	15,479,337	28,452,664	18,308,853	10,143,811
1991	12,575,248	4,064,275	1,581,505	1,150,036	5,779,432	15,930,189	16,647,593	31,013,616	19,675,544	11,338,072
1992	12,858,150	4,157,121	1,699,799	974,209	6,027,021	16,001,330	17,459,165	33,402,698	21,008,588	12,394,110
1993	13,235,523	4,328,287	1,776,999	975,817	6,154,420	16,177,491	18,774,659	35,613,540	22,784,869	12,828,671
1994	13,987,396	4,372,710	1,833,958	983,746	6,796,982	16,675,588	19,899,295	35,664,649	21,623,860	14,040,789
1995	15,251,187	4,474,589	1,932,462	1,173,289	7,670,847	17,888,496	21,508,779	38,572,902	23,583,401	14,989,501

TABLE Ea287–347   State and local government expenditure, by function: 1902–1995   *Continued*

	Direct								
	General								
	Government administration and general control								
	Financial administration and general control	Financial administration	Judicial	Legislative	General public building	Central staff	Interest	Miscellaneous commercial activities	Other
	Ea327 [1]	Ea328 [1]	Ea329 [1]	Ea330 [1]	Ea331 [1]	Ea332 [1]	Ea333	Ea334	Ea335
Fiscal year	Thousand dollars	Thousand dollars	Thousand dollars	Thousand dollars	Thousand dollars	Thousand dollars	Thousand dollars	Thousand dollars	Thousand dollars
1902	141,000	—	—	—	—	—	68,000	—	98,000
1913	211,000	—	—	—	—	—	147,000	—	217,000
1922	313,000	—	—	—	—	—	382,000	—	384,000
1927	412,000	—	—	—	—	—	584,000	—	632,000
1932	470,000	—	—	—	—	—	741,000	—	539,000
1934	432,000	—	—	—	—	—	739,000	—	420,000
1936	500,000	—	—	—	—	—	738,000	—	487,000
1938	542,000	—	—	—	—	—	673,000	—	562,000
1940	561,000	—	—	—	—	—	653,000	—	558,000
1942	578,000	—	—	—	—	—	565,000	—	658,000
1944	599,000	—	—	—	—	—	499,000	—	636,000
1946	703,000	—	—	—	—	—	421,000	—	797,000
1948	880,000	—	—	—	—	—	399,000	—	1,244,000
1950	1,041,000	—	—	—	—	—	458,000	—	1,462,000
1952	1,193,000	—	—	30,000	—	—	552,000	—	1,043,000
1953	1,263,000	—	—	39,000	—	—	614,000	—	1,142,000
1954	1,375,000	—	—	32,000	308,000	—	718,000	—	1,275,000
1955	1,452,000	—	—	43,000	371,000	—	838,000	—	1,393,000
1956	1,560,000	—	—	41,000	363,000	—	986,000	—	1,663,000
1957	1,725,000	—	—	57,000	429,000		1,106,000		1,818,000
1958	1,843,000	—	—	46,000	493,000	—	1,244,000		2,327,000
1959	2,003,000	—		64,000	567,000	—	1,416,000	—	2,496,000
1960	2,113,000	—	—	52,000	533,000	—	1,670,000	—	2,392,000
1961	2,237,000	1,017,000	—	77,000	590,000	—	1,824,000	—	2,630,000
1962	2,338,000	1,064,000	—	63,000	602,000	—	2,011,000	—	2,851,000
1963	2,439,000	1,119,000	—	88,000	638,000	—	2,199,000	—	3,200,000
1964	2,567,000	1,180,000	—	71,000	654,000	—	2,356,000	—	3,406,000
1965	2,773,000	1,267,000	—	98,000	831,000	—	2,490,000	—	3,831,000
1966	2,974,000	1,333,000	—	90,000	856,000	—	2,690,000	—	4,203,000
1967	3,313,000	1,468,000	—	128,000	931,000	—	3,032,000	—	4,965,000
1968	3,647,000	1,610,000	—	130,000	1,037,000	—	3,266,000	—	5,691,000
1969	4,105,000	1,806,000	—	167,000	1,209,000	—	3,732,000	—	6,780,000
1970	4,682,000	2,030,000	—	179,000	1,287,000	—	4,374,000	—	7,361,000
1971	—	2,271,000	—	225,000	1,405,000	—	5,089,000	—	10,001,000
1972	—	2,500,765	—	236,131	1,528,737	—	6,028,942	—	11,590,086
1973	—	2,811,083	—	289,167	1,682,418	—	6,785,357	—	13,311,481
1974	—	3,164,573	—	321,459	1,902,068	—	7,666,363	760,258	14,564,364
1975	—	3,594,266	—	388,497	2,314,417	—	8,782,091	1,087,149	17,665,648
1976	—	3,960,402	—	411,454	2,557,327	—	10,268,753	1,153,326	21,396,892
1977	—	4,489,062	1,565,069	470,495	2,441,662	4,222,065	11,233,659	140,117	16,602,756
1978	—	5,292,513	2,026,464	500,003	2,561,055	4,474,784	11,982,689	143,980	18,488,966
1979	—	6,071,229	2,256,662	572,305	2,829,058	4,912,726	12,987,186	174,963	20,726,932
1980	—	6,718,705	2,587,613	619,946	3,018,141	5,489,800	14,746,843	228,786	22,333,187
1981	—	7,229,521	2,649,660	700,953	3,229,744	6,190,088	17,131,170	271,575	23,919,939
1982	—	8,105,530	4,752,288	787,711	3,285,585	5,194,943	20,159,820	301,484	24,922,369
1983	—	8,788,705	7,007,431	844,482	3,625,490	4,241,950	24,136,241	289,556	24,842,453
1984	—	9,502,336	7,648,866	903,350	3,859,338	4,441,908	28,696,368	319,679	27,486,371
1985	—	10,471,463	8,437,125	1,002,783	4,105,160	4,874,528	32,427,044	323,770	30,515,562
1986	—	11,896,904	9,303,842	1,091,843	4,106,314	5,403,900	37,063,629	282,486	33,170,229
1987	—	12,871,828	10,103,225	1,181,339	4,847,669	5,901,449	41,891,209	294,538	36,831,965
1988	—	13,588,616	11,213,374	1,296,834	4,788,278	6,532,641	44,318,351	307,611	37,807,996
1989	—	14,993,045	12,586,861	1,413,665	5,145,335	6,784,005	46,594,725	356,676	40,613,450
1990	—	16,217,095	14,107,500	1,494,700	5,643,399	7,373,499	49,739,095	366,794	44,109,404
1991	—	16,995,023	15,377,798	1,621,285	6,051,485	8,415,785	52,233,594	352,958	46,860,563
1992	—	18,331,292	16,464,085	1,581,712	6,056,315	8,722,942	55,364,047	325,006	49,971,630
1993	—	19,323,620	16,992,532	1,580,148	5,995,216	8,644,840	55,099,544	266,584	53,449,106
1994	—	20,576,816	17,877,217	1,658,787	6,482,286	9,120,452	54,960,268	315,224	55,170,790
1995	—	22,379,913	19,168,153	1,765,737	7,071,992	9,632,159	56,970,143	293,650	58,824,911

Notes appear at end of table

TABLE Ea287–347 State and local government expenditure, by function: 1902–1995 *Continued*

	Direct											
	Utility and liquor store							Insurance trust				
		Utilities					Liquor store		Employee retirement	Unemployment compensation	Workers' compensation	Other
	Total	Total	Water	Electric	Gas	Transit		Total				
	Ea336	Ea337	Ea338	Ea339	Ea340	Ea341	Ea342	Ea343	Ea344	Ea345	Ea346	Ea347
Fiscal year	Thousand dollars	Thousand dollars	Thousand dollars	Thousand dollars	Thousand dollars	Thousand dollars	Thousand dollars	Thousand dollars	Thousand dollars	Thousand dollars	Thousand dollars	Thousand dollars
1902	82,000	80,000	71,000	8,000	1,000	0	2,000	0	0	0	0	0
1913	186,000	186,000	159,000	25,000	1,000	1,000	0	7,000	7,000	0	—	0
1922	359,000	359,000	255,000	75,000	4,000	25,000	0	75,000	30,000	0	—	45,000
1927	491,000	491,000	349,000	94,000	10,000	38,000	0	109,000	50,000	0	—	59,000
1932	518,000	518,000	320,000	92,000	7,000	99,000	0	120,000	75,000	0	—	45,000
1934	528,000	457,000	292,000	102,000	6,000	57,000	71,000	133,000	96,000	0	—	37,000
1936	701,000	553,000	344,000	117,000	11,000	81,000	148,000	156,000	113,000	0	—	43,000
1938	848,000	636,000	385,000	156,000	13,000	82,000	212,000	383,000	129,000	202,000	—	52,000
1940	1,324,000	1,090,000	404,000	257,000	18,000	411,000	234,000	687,000	140,000	494,000	—	53,000
1942	1,106,000	804,000	368,000	216,000	19,000	201,000	302,000	617,000	169,000	377,000	—	71,000
1944	1,281,000	822,000	355,000	227,000	25,000	215,000	459,000	354,000	195,000	69,000	—	90,000
1946	1,733,000	1,014,000	426,000	305,000	36,000	247,000	719,000	1,307,000	237,000	968,000	—	102,000
1948	2,379,000	1,612,000	628,000	438,000	47,000	499,000	767,000	1,197,000	297,000	759,000	—	141,000
1950	2,739,000	2,005,000	849,000	534,000	52,000	570,000	734,000	2,379,000	361,000	1,849,000	133,000	36,000
1952	3,067,000	2,246,000	973,000	631,000	61,000	581,000	821,000	1,698,000	530,000	973,000	157,000	38,000
1953	3,316,000	2,457,000	1,084,000	723,000	68,000	582,000	859,000	1,711,000	585,000	910,000	170,000	46,000
1954	3,482,000	2,577,000	1,150,000	751,000	90,000	586,000	905,000	2,423,000	679,000	1,507,000	183,000	54,000
1955	3,886,000	3,023,000	1,479,000	819,000	125,000	600,000	863,000	2,764,000	722,000	1,784,000	196,000	62,000
1956	4,065,000	3,119,000	1,461,000	895,000	128,000	636,000	946,000	2,376,000	825,000	1,277,000	209,000	65,000
1957	4,428,000	3,494,000	1,584,000	1,102,000	156,000	652,000	934,000	2,750,000	943,000	1,500,000	230,000	77,000
1958	4,693,000	3,720,000	1,624,000	1,260,000	150,000	686,000	973,000	4,168,000	1,074,000	2,757,000	246,000	91,000
1959	4,901,000	3,923,000	1,764,000	1,273,000	174,000	711,000	978,000	4,784,000	1,144,000	3,275,000	259,000	106,000
1960	5,088,000	4,066,000	1,881,000	1,244,000	191,000	750,000	1,022,000	4,031,000	1,265,000	2,364,000	283,000	119,000
1961	5,523,000	4,532,000	2,106,000	1,461,000	210,000	755,000	992,000	5,299,000	1,383,000	3,463,000	305,000	148,000
1962	5,453,000	4,445,000	2,077,000	1,378,000	219,000	771,000	1,008,000	4,888,000	1,578,000	2,808,000	335,000	167,000
1963	5,932,000	4,899,000	2,209,000	1,572,000	228,000	891,000	1,033,000	5,013,000	1,691,000	2,760,000	360,000	202,000
1964	6,184,000	5,067,000	2,255,000	1,614,000	251,000	948,000	1,117,000	5,094,000	1,844,000	2,638,000	374,000	238,000
1965	7,058,000	5,886,000	2,505,000	1,983,000	272,000	1,127,000	1,172,000	4,950,000	2,008,000	2,298,000	394,000	250,000
1966	7,282,000	6,042,000	2,716,000	1,949,000	263,000	1,114,000	1,240,000	4,783,000	2,219,000	1,893,000	409,000	262,000
1967	7,350,000	6,006,000	2,587,000	1,847,000	287,000	1,285,000	1,344,000	5,277,000	2,608,000	1,941,000	457,000	271,000
1968	8,170,000	6,721,000	2,740,000	2,123,000	299,000	1,559,000	1,449,000	5,653,000	2,829,000	2,050,000	481,000	293,000
1969	8,820,000	7,316,000	3,019,000	2,216,000	332,000	1,750,000	1,505,000	6,053,000	3,221,000	1,992,000	507,000	333,000
1970	9,447,000	7,820,000	3,211,000	2,486,000	370,000	1,753,000	1,627,000	7,273,000	3,629,000	2,723,000	551,000	370,000
1971	10,300,000	8,675,000	3,432,000	2,816,000	410,000	2,018,000	1,625,000	9,791,000	4,155,000	4,708,000	529,000	399,000
1972	11,398,353	9,715,084	3,739,652	3,281,198	403,802	2,290,432	1,683,269	10,549,489	4,767,918	4,740,749	642,964	397,858
1973	13,034,656	11,203,769	4,084,324	3,760,603	493,351	2,865,491	1,830,887	11,073,532	5,823,337	4,080,625	736,602	432,968
1974	14,405,644	12,486,898	4,669,237	4,151,719	504,608	3,161,334	1,918,746	12,667,023	6,638,587	4,702,869	829,006	496,561
1975	17,285,636	15,276,454	5,439,936	5,279,905	579,772	3,976,841	2,009,182	21,208,888	7,442,719	12,311,000	909,859	545,310
1976	19,542,578	17,451,298	5,929,099	6,429,170	661,100	4,431,929	2,091,280	27,954,626	8,422,197	17,903,000	1,070,266	559,163
1977	24,189,974	22,094,161	6,380,513	9,312,532	803,071	5,598,045	2,095,813	26,148,753	9,566,649	14,696,807	1,326,063	559,234
1978	26,277,721	23,960,424	6,884,321	10,587,718	915,345	5,573,040	2,317,297	23,525,476	10,774,210	10,740,196	1,422,552	588,518
1979	30,845,544	28,429,338	8,068,538	12,664,653	1,231,445	6,464,702	2,416,206	23,504,296	12,273,221	8,886,033	1,703,742	641,300
1980	36,190,638	33,599,199	9,227,513	15,015,946	1,714,707	7,641,033	2,591,439	28,796,598	14,007,638	12,070,600	1,976,811	741,549
1981	43,016,017	40,289,791	10,582,266	17,870,579	2,229,756	9,607,190	2,726,226	36,582,516	15,694,641	17,932,386	2,043,011	912,478
1982	48,412,312	45,570,599	11,408,258	20,446,411	2,566,390	11,149,540	2,841,713	39,442,518	17,812,977	18,126,010	2,524,442	979,089
1983	52,811,863	49,995,463	12,453,908	22,222,709	3,007,745	12,311,101	2,816,400	47,334,571	19,254,527	24,172,447	2,867,956	1,039,641
1984	55,061,543	52,320,660	12,579,505	23,206,055	3,343,704	13,191,396	2,740,883	40,152,738	21,915,295	14,059,628	3,093,277	1,084,538
1985	59,798,123	56,975,167	14,297,760	25,341,478	3,467,916	13,868,013	2,822,956	44,190,615	24,413,594	14,995,083	3,462,152	1,319,786
1986	65,296,932	62,430,342	16,195,860	28,182,170	3,291,450	14,760,862	2,866,590	46,538,206	26,521,100	14,886,895	3,618,676	1,511,535
1987	69,108,110	66,172,409	18,466,637	28,951,042	2,895,114	15,859,616	2,935,701	50,803,606	29,602,708	15,248,132	4,288,454	1,664,312
1988	70,048,655	67,211,390	18,863,929	29,046,861	2,824,542	16,476,058	2,837,265	51,879,470	32,125,132	13,092,828	4,849,194	1,812,316
1989	73,509,295	70,637,775	20,524,366	30,177,608	2,840,923	17,094,878	2,871,520	54,993,543	34,894,469	12,861,837	5,318,374	1,918,863
1990	77,800,522	74,874,709	22,101,397	30,996,783	2,988,742	18,787,787	2,925,813	63,321,243	38,354,896	16,499,338	6,372,855	2,094,154
1991	81,004,078	77,999,375	23,560,543	31,090,032	2,969,530	20,379,270	3,004,703	74,158,509	42,121,090	22,135,392	7,337,666	2,564,361
1992	85,314,022	82,224,046	24,833,879	32,518,602	3,077,733	21,793,832	3,089,976	90,214,648	46,357,844	32,887,355	7,844,385	3,125,064
1993	84,483,027	81,421,482	24,621,180	32,230,911	3,273,135	21,296,256	3,061,545	98,806,747	51,662,181	35,409,045	8,874,325	2,861,196
1994	91,162,497	88,177,901	26,617,294	33,829,381	3,509,894	24,221,332	2,984,596	95,462,171	55,665,355	28,623,671	8,851,525	2,321,620
1995	94,234,981	91,214,778	28,040,858	34,021,256	3,433,922	25,718,742	3,020,203	107,339,680	61,427,170	35,203,966	8,356,094	2,352,450

TABLE Ea287–347   State and local government expenditure, by function: 1902–1995   *Continued*

[1] Through 1970, series Ea327 includes all expenditures on general government administration; thereafter (and earlier for some functions), individual activities are reported separately. Some activities reported separately may have been included under other general expenditures during the earlier period.

Source

Figures are from data files provided by the Census of Governments. For pub-lished versions through 1982, see U.S. Department of Commerce, "Historical Statistics on Government Finance and Employment," in *Census of Governments, 1982*, volume 6, pp. 225–64.

Documentation

See the text for Table Ea24–51.

TABLE Ea348–384   State government revenue, by source: 1902–1996

Contributed by John Joseph Wallis

	Intergovernmental					Direct	General	Taxes		Sales and gross receipts		Select	
													Motor
	Total revenue	General	Total	From federal	From local	Total	Total	Total	Property	Total	General	Total	fuel
	Ea348	Ea349	Ea350	Ea351	Ea352	Ea353	Ea354	Ea355	Ea356	Ea357	Ea358	Ea359	Ea360
Fiscal year	Thousand dollars	Thousand dollars	Thousand dollars	Thousand dollars	Thousand dollars	Thousand dollars	Thousand dollars	Thousand dollars	Thousand dollars	Thousand dollars	Thousand dollars	Thousand dollars	Thousand dollars
1902	192,000	190,000	9,000	3,000	6,000	183,000	181,000	156,000	82,000	28,000	0	28,000	0
1913	376,000	376,000	16,000	6,000	10,000	360,000	360,000	301,000	140,000	55,000	0	55,000	0
1922	1,360,000	1,254,000	126,000	99,000	27,000	1,234,000	1,128,000	947,000	348,000	134,000	0	134,000	13,000
1927	2,152,000	2,015,000	158,000	107,000	51,000	1,994,000	1,857,000	1,608,000	370,000	445,000	0	445,000	259,000
1932	2,541,000	2,423,000	267,000	222,000	45,000	2,274,000	2,156,000	1,890,000	328,000	726,000	7,000	719,000	527,000
1934	3,421,000	3,212,000	969,000	933,000	36,000	2,452,000	2,243,000	1,979,000	273,000	978,000	173,000	805,000	565,000
1936	4,023,000	3,672,000	758,000	719,000	39,000	3,265,000	2,914,000	2,618,000	228,000	1,394,000	364,000	1,030,000	687,000
1938	5,293,000	4,141,000	681,000	633,000	48,000	4,612,000	3,460,000	3,132,000	244,000	1,674,000	447,000	1,227,000	777,000
1940	5,737,000	4,382,000	725,000	667,000	58,000	5,012,000	3,657,000	3,313,000	260,000	1,852,000	499,000	1,353,000	839,000
1942	6,870,000	5,132,000	858,000	802,000	56,000	6,012,000	4,274,000	3,903,000	264,000	2,218,000	632,000	1,585,000	940,000
1944	7,695,000	5,465,000	981,000	926,000	55,000	6,714,000	4,484,000	4,071,000	243,000	2,153,000	720,000	1,433,000	684,000
1946	8,576,000	6,284,000	865,000	802,000	63,000	7,712,000	5,419,000	4,937,000	249,000	2,803,000	899,000	1,905,000	886,000
1948	11,826,000	9,257,000	1,740,000	1,643,000	97,000	10,086,000	7,517,000	6,743,000	276,000	4,042,000	1,478,000	2,563,000	1,259,000
1950	13,903,000	11,262,000	2,423,000	2,275,000	148,000	11,480,000	8,839,000	7,930,000	307,000	4,670,000	1,670,000	2,999,000	1,544,000
1952	16,815,000	13,429,000	2,485,000	2,329,000	156,000	14,330,000	10,944,000	9,857,000	370,000	5,730,000	2,229,000	3,501,000	1,870,000
1953	17,979,000	14,511,000	2,761,000	2,570,000	191,000	15,218,000	11,750,000	10,552,000	365,000	6,209,000	2,433,000	3,776,000	2,019,000
1954	18,834,000	15,299,000	2,883,000	2,668,000	215,000	15,951,000	12,417,000	11,089,000	391,000	6,573,000	2,540,000	4,034,000	2,218,000
1955	19,667,000	16,194,000	2,988,000	2,762,000	226,000	16,678,000	13,205,000	11,597,000	412,000	6,864,000	2,637,000	4,227,000	2,353,000
1956	22,199,000	18,389,000	3,296,000	3,027,000	269,000	18,903,000	15,093,000	13,375,000	467,000	7,801,000	3,036,000	4,765,000	2,687,000
1957	24,656,000	20,382,000	3,927,000	3,500,000	427,000	20,728,000	16,454,000	14,531,000	479,000	8,436,000	3,373,000	5,062,000	2,828,000
1958	26,191,000	21,772,000	4,764,000	4,461,000	302,000	21,427,000	17,008,000	14,919,000	532,000	8,750,000	3,507,000	5,243,000	2,919,000
1959	29,164,000	24,448,000	6,252,000	5,888,000	364,000	22,912,000	18,196,000	15,848,000	566,000	9,287,000	3,697,000	5,589,000	3,058,000
1960	32,838,000	27,363,000	6,745,000	6,382,000	363,000	26,094,000	20,618,000	18,036,000	607,000	10,510,000	4,302,000	6,208,000	3,335,000
1961	34,603,000	28,693,000	6,782,000	6,412,000	370,000	27,821,000	21,911,000	19,057,000	631,000	11,031,000	4,510,000	6,521,000	3,431,000
1962	37,595,000	31,157,000	7,480,000	7,108,000	373,000	30,115,000	23,677,000	20,561,000	640,000	12,038,000	5,111,000	6,928,000	3,665,000
1963	40,993,000	33,882,000	8,243,000	7,832,000	411,000	32,750,000	25,639,000	22,117,000	688,000	12,873,000	5,539,000	7,334,000	3,851,000
1964	45,167,000	37,648,000	9,464,000	9,046,000	417,000	35,703,000	28,184,000	24,243,000	722,000	13,957,000	6,084,000	7,874,000	4,059,000
1965	48,827,000	40,930,000	10,320,000	9,874,000	447,000	38,507,000	30,610,000	26,126,000	766,000	15,059,000	6,711,000	8,348,000	4,300,000
1966	55,246,000	46,757,000	12,246,000	11,743,000	503,000	43,000,000	34,511,000	29,380,000	834,000	17,044,000	7,873,000	9,172,000	4,627,000
1967	61,082,000	52,071,000	14,289,000	13,616,000	673,000	46,793,000	37,782,000	31,926,000	862,000	18,575,000	8,923,000	9,652,000	4,837,000
1968	68,460,000	59,132,000	15,935,000	15,228,000	707,000	52,525,000	43,197,000	36,400,000	912,000	20,979,000	10,441,000	10,537,000	5,178,000
1969	77,584,000	67,312,000	17,775,000	16,907,000	868,000	59,809,000	49,537,000	41,931,000	981,000	24,050,000	12,443,000	11,606,000	5,644,000
1970	88,939,000	77,755,000	20,248,000	19,252,000	995,000	68,691,000	57,507,000	47,962,000	1,092,000	27,254,000	14,177,000	13,076,000	6,283,000
1971	97,233,000	85,099,000	23,809,000	22,754,000	1,054,000	73,424,000	61,290,000	51,541,000	1,126,000	29,570,000	15,473,000	14,097,000	6,628,000
1972	112,339,318	98,631,995	27,981,259	26,790,503	1,190,756	84,358,059	70,650,736	59,870,369	1,257,173	33,250,447	17,618,951	15,631,496	7,216,216
1973	129,808,265	113,132,711	32,700,375	31,361,000	1,339,375	97,107,890	80,432,336	68,069,264	1,312,371	37,122,569	19,792,894	17,329,675	8,057,793
1974	140,815,514	122,327,392	33,170,233	31,632,094	1,538,139	107,645,281	89,157,159	74,206,938	1,301,298	40,556,197	22,611,751	17,944,446	8,206,632
1975	157,033,466	134,611,347	37,827,222	36,147,553	1,679,669	119,206,244	96,784,125	80,154,888	1,451,154	43,346,313	24,780,056	18,566,257	8,255,483
1976	183,821,043	152,117,660	44,716,919	42,012,871	2,704,048	139,104,124	107,400,741	89,255,517	2,117,901	47,390,733	27,332,726	20,058,007	8,659,726
1977	204,426,221	169,125,766	48,626,923	45,889,689	2,737,234	155,799,298	120,498,843	101,084,645	2,259,796	52,362,328	30,895,901	21,466,427	9,088,264
1978	225,011,116	189,099,414	53,461,185	50,199,706	3,261,479	171,549,931	135,638,229	113,261,134	2,364,183	58,270,203	35,279,902	22,990,301	9,501,349
1979	246,961,795	207,950,703	57,087,395	54,548,137	2,539,258	189,874,400	150,863,308	124,865,493	2,490,112	63,668,351	39,505,479	24,162,872	9,980,104
1980	276,961,730	233,592,124	64,326,479	61,892,384	2,434,095	212,635,251	169,265,645	137,075,178	2,892,105	67,854,790	43,167,534	24,687,256	9,721,569
1981	310,827,996	258,159,197	70,785,710	67,867,768	2,917,942	240,042,286	187,373,487	149,737,943	2,949,281	72,751,233	46,412,126	26,339,107	9,733,528
1982	330,898,732	275,111,180	69,165,793	66,026,345	3,139,448	261,732,939	205,945,387	162,607,135	3,115,511	78,788,928	50,356,889	28,432,039	10,473,023
1983	357,661,062	290,479,711	72,727,525	68,985,473	3,742,052	284,933,537	217,752,186	171,440,020	3,280,844	83,894,609	53,639,404	30,255,205	10,793,330
1984	397,086,640	330,740,178	81,449,805	76,140,229	5,309,576	315,636,835	249,290,373	196,795,248	3,861,655	95,801,167	62,563,602	33,237,565	12,395,562
1985	439,416,467	365,834,969	89,886,724	84,433,788	5,452,936	349,529,743	275,948,245	215,893,155	3,984,180	105,419,355	69,632,708	35,786,647	13,344,397
1986	481,307,474	393,503,416	98,573,784	92,666,253	5,907,531	382,733,690	294,929,632	228,081,788	4,352,932	112,376,718	74,805,816	37,570,902	14,126,153
1987	516,793,232	419,063,001	102,380,659	95,462,932	6,917,727	414,412,573	316,682,342	246,509,508	4,700,120	119,365,418	79,230,293	40,135,125	15,707,472
1988	541,425,816	445,138,028	107,241,354	100,478,229	6,763,125	434,184,462	337,896,674	264,145,836	5,021,399	130,330,397	87,079,049	43,251,348	17,210,686
1989	586,930,723	482,721,055	115,765,232	108,235,243	7,529,989	471,165,491	366,955,823	284,412,634	5,292,776	138,569,077	93,489,922	45,079,155	18,105,711

TABLE Ea348–384   State government revenue, by source: 1902–1996   *Continued*

		Intergovernmental				Direct							
							General						
								Taxes					
										Sales and gross receipts			
												Select	
		Total	From	From									Motor
Total revenue	General	Total	federal	local	Total	Total	Total	Property	Total	General	Total	fuel
Ea348	Ea349	Ea350	Ea351	Ea352	Ea353	Ea354	Ea355	Ea356	Ea357	Ea358	Ea359	Ea360
Fiscal year	Thousand dollars	Thousand dollars	Thousand dollars	Thousand dollars	Thousand dollars	Thousand dollars	Thousand dollars	Thousand dollars	Thousand dollars	Thousand dollars	Thousand dollars	Thousand dollars	Thousand dollars
1990	632,171,562	517,429,481	126,328,829	118,352,725	7,976,104	505,842,733	391,100,652	300,488,565	5,848,175	147,069,349	99,701,944	47,367,405	19,379,238
1991	659,948,013	551,721,744	143,533,607	134,926,318	8,607,289	516,414,406	408,188,137	310,561,109	6,227,751	153,534,721	103,165,478	50,369,243	20,638,959
1992	743,521,591	608,804,311	169,928,166	159,067,541	10,860,625	573,593,425	438,876,145	331,179,823	7,363,812	164,135,284	108,712,128	55,423,156	22,252,877
1993	805,196,100	653,564,419	188,255,921	177,272,643	10,983,278	616,940,179	465,308,498	353,849,819	7,796,392	174,543,210	114,634,988	59,908,222	23,568,474
1994	841,701,928	692,298,133	204,517,848	191,450,553	13,067,295	637,184,080	487,780,285	373,319,379	8,386,000	185,871,031	123,005,615	62,865,416	24,489,699
1995	906,404,245	739,023,944	215,558,360	202,485,216	13,073,144	690,845,885	523,465,584	399,147,005	9,518,305	196,850,450	132,236,159	64,614,291	25,439,721
1996	966,808,121	770,516,099	221,368,813	207,984,481	13,384,332	745,439,308	549,147,286	418,390,240	9,973,524	206,114,816	139,363,248	66,751,568	25,988,277

					Direct						
					General						
				Taxes					Charges and miscellaneous		
Sales and gross receipts					Income						
Select											
Alcoholic beverages	Tobacco products	Other	Motor vehicle and operators' licenses	Total	Individual	Corporate	Other	Total	Charges	Miscellaneous	
Ea361	Ea362	Ea363	Ea364	Ea365	Ea366	Ea367	Ea368	Ea369	Ea370	Ea371 [1]	
Fiscal year	Thousand dollars	Thousand dollars	Thousand dollars	Thousand dollars	Thousand dollars	Thousand dollars	Thousand dollars	Thousand dollars	Thousand dollars	Thousand dollars	Thousand dollars
1902	0	0	28,000	0	0	0	0	0	46,000	25,000	—	—
1913	2,000	0	53,000	5,000	0	0	0	101,000	59,000	—	—
1922	0	0	121,000	152,000	101,000	43,000	58,000	212,000	181,000	—	—
1927	0	0	186,000	301,000	162,000	70,000	92,000	330,000	249,000	—	—
1932	0	19,000	173,000	335,000	153,000	74,000	79,000	348,000	266,000	—	—
1934	62,000	25,000	153,000	305,000	129,000	80,000	49,000	294,000	264,000	—	—
1936	126,000	44,000	173,000	360,000	266,000	153,000	113,000	370,000	296,000	—	—
1938	176,000	55,000	219,000	359,000	383,000	218,000	165,000	472,000	328,000	—	—
1940	193,000	97,000	224,000	387,000	361,000	206,000	155,000	453,000	344,000	—	—
1942	257,000	130,000	258,000	431,000	518,000	249,000	269,000	472,000	370,000	—	—
1944	267,000	159,000	323,000	394,000	762,000	316,000	446,000	519,000	413,000	—	—
1946	402,000	198,000	419,000	439,000	831,000	389,000	442,000	615,000	482,000	—	—
1948	425,000	337,000	542,000	593,000	1,084,000	499,000	585,000	748,000	774,000	—	—
1950	420,000	414,000	621,000	755,000	1,310,000	724,000	586,000	888,000	909,000	626,000	283,000
1952	442,000	449,000	740,000	924,000	1,751,000	913,000	838,000	1,082,000	1,087,000	728,000	360,000
1953	465,000	469,000	823,000	1,013,000	1,779,000	969,000	810,000	1,186,000	1,198,000	804,000	394,000
1954	463,000	464,000	889,000	1,098,000	1,776,000	1,004,000	772,000	1,251,000	1,328,000	863,000	465,000
1955	471,000	459,000	944,000	1,184,000	1,831,000	1,094,000	737,000	1,306,000	1,608,000	953,000	655,000
1956	546,000	515,000	1,017,000	1,295,000	2,264,000	1,374,000	890,000	1,548,000	1,718,000	1,092,000	626,000
1957	569,000	556,000	1,109,000	1,368,000	2,547,000	1,563,000	984,000	1,701,000	1,923,000	1,240,000	683,000
1958	566,000	616,000	1,142,000	1,415,000	2,562,000	1,544,000	1,018,000	1,660,000	2,089,000	1,400,000	689,000
1959	599,000	675,000	1,257,000	1,492,000	2,765,000	1,764,000	1,001,000	1,738,000	2,348,000	1,575,000	772,000
1960	650,000	923,000	1,300,000	1,573,000	3,389,000	2,209,000	1,180,000	1,957,000	2,583,000	1,783,000	800,000
1961	688,000	1,001,000	1,401,000	1,641,000	3,621,000	2,355,000	1,266,000	2,133,000	2,854,000	1,959,000	895,000
1962	740,000	1,075,000	1,448,000	1,667,000	4,036,000	2,728,000	1,308,000	2,180,000	3,116,000	2,198,000	918,000
1963	793,000	1,124,000	1,566,000	1,780,000	4,461,000	2,956,000	1,505,000	2,315,000	3,523,000	2,462,000	1,061,000
1964	864,000	1,196,000	1,755,000	1,917,000	5,110,000	3,415,000	1,695,000	2,537,000	3,942,000	2,747,000	1,194,000
1965	917,000	1,284,000	1,847,000	2,021,000	5,586,000	3,657,000	1,929,000	2,694,000	4,483,000	3,123,000	1,360,000
1966	985,000	1,541,000	2,019,000	2,236,000	6,326,000	4,288,000	2,038,000	2,940,000	5,131,000	3,606,000	1,526,000
1967	1,041,000	1,615,000	2,159,000	2,311,000	7,136,000	4,909,000	2,227,000	3,042,000	5,856,000	4,197,000	1,659,000
1968	1,138,000	1,886,000	2,335,000	2,485,000	8,749,000	6,231,000	2,518,000	3,275,000	6,797,000	4,891,000	1,906,000
1969	1,246,000	2,056,000	2,660,000	2,685,000	10,707,000	7,527,000	3,180,000	3,508,000	7,606,000	5,460,000	2,146,000

Note appears at end of table

(continued)

TABLE Ea348–384   State government revenue, by source: 1902–1996   *Continued*

										Direct		
										General		
					Taxes						Charges and miscellaneous	
	Sales and gross receipts						Income					
		Select										
	Alcoholic beverages	Tobacco products	Other	Motor vehicle and operators' licenses	Total	Individual	Corporate	Other	Total	Charges	Miscellaneous
	Ea361	Ea362	Ea363	Ea364	Ea365	Ea366	Ea367	Ea368	Ea369	Ea370	Ea371 [1]
Fiscal year	Thousand dollars	Thousand dollars	Thousand dollars	Thousand dollars	Thousand dollars	Thousand dollars	Thousand dollars	Thousand dollars	Thousand dollars	Thousand dollars	Thousand dollars
1970	1,420,000	2,308,000	3,065,000	2,955,000	12,921,000	9,183,000	3,738,000	3,740,000	9,545,000	6,102,000	3,443,000
1971	1,527,000	2,536,000	3,406,000	3,174,000	13,577,000	10,153,000	3,424,000	4,094,000	9,749,000	7,066,000	2,683,000
1972	1,683,998	2,831,122	3,900,160	3,340,135	17,411,754	12,995,916	4,415,838	4,610,860	10,780,367	7,820,345	2,960,022
1973	1,817,302	3,112,378	4,342,202	3,636,519	21,012,076	15,587,082	5,424,994	4,985,729	12,363,072	8,609,093	3,753,979
1974	1,909,154	3,249,794	4,578,866	3,754,832	23,092,449	17,077,931	6,014,518	5,502,162	14,950,221	9,597,392	5,352,829
1975	1,963,420	3,285,851	5,061,503	3,940,941	25,460,889	18,818,789	6,642,100	5,955,591	16,629,237	10,436,508	6,192,729
1976	2,057,193	3,462,306	5,878,782	4,356,101	28,720,592	21,447,895	7,272,697	6,670,190	18,145,224	11,652,470	6,492,754
1977	2,119,750	3,500,226	6,758,187	4,587,230	34,666,319	25,492,510	9,173,809	7,208,972	19,414,198	12,076,129	7,338,069
1978	2,286,383	3,653,733	7,548,836	4,835,878	39,843,118	29,104,822	10,738,296	7,947,752	22,377,095	13,554,485	8,822,610
1979	2,400,322	3,640,466	8,141,980	5,155,288	44,749,975	32,622,451	12,127,524	8,801,767	25,997,815	14,859,270	11,138,545
1980	2,477,569	3,737,798	8,750,320	5,325,041	50,410,812	37,089,481	13,321,331	10,592,430	32,190,467	16,544,821	15,645,646
1981	2,613,421	3,893,171	10,098,987	5,695,070	55,038,732	40,895,235	14,143,497	13,303,627	37,635,544	18,774,872	18,860,672
1982	2,722,195	3,955,155	11,281,666	6,035,920	59,669,226	45,667,517	14,001,709	14,997,550	43,338,252	21,043,167	22,295,085
1983	2,743,092	4,000,992	12,717,791	6,288,699	62,941,070	49,788,567	13,152,503	15,034,798	46,312,166	23,182,046	23,130,120
1984	2,900,195	4,149,028	13,792,780	6,920,876	74,453,605	58,942,227	15,511,378	15,757,945	52,495,125	25,737,868	26,757,257
1985	3,031,347	4,362,083	15,048,820	7,779,934	81,539,145	63,907,951	17,631,194	17,170,541	60,055,090	27,497,810	32,557,280
1986	3,072,009	4,449,756	15,922,984	8,368,853	85,822,623	67,416,629	18,405,994	17,160,662	66,847,844	29,987,167	36,860,677
1987	3,108,918	4,591,453	16,727,282	9,068,256	96,693,549	76,216,412	20,477,137	16,682,165	70,172,834	31,900,381	38,272,453
1988	3,188,780	4,841,851	18,010,031	9,612,680	101,740,762	80,133,347	21,607,415	17,440,598	73,750,838	34,421,214	39,329,624
1989	3,117,812	5,053,660	18,801,972	10,185,485	112,683,277	88,817,680	23,865,597	17,682,019	82,543,189	38,552,780	43,990,409
1990	3,191,150	5,540,620	19,256,397	10,674,745	117,827,362	96,076,243	21,751,119	19,068,934	90,612,087	42,745,259	47,866,828
1991	3,400,402	5,980,154	20,349,728	10,996,835	119,635,778	99,278,910	20,356,868	20,166,024	97,627,028	47,334,317	50,292,711
1992	3,590,510	6,118,679	23,461,090	11,659,227	126,846,128	104,994,892	21,851,236	21,175,372	107,696,322	52,941,024	54,755,298
1993	6,745,652	6,231,502	26,533,343	12,519,115	136,310,353	112,115,039	24,195,314	22,680,749	111,458,679	57,383,789	54,074,890
1994	6,836,176	6,717,102	28,048,155	12,893,071	142,819,958	117,127,800	25,692,158	23,349,319	114,460,906	61,017,673	53,443,233
1995	3,597,128	7,347,647	28,229,795	13,559,242	154,685,144	125,610,125	29,075,019	24,533,864	124,318,579	64,782,625	59,535,954
1996	3,666,690	7,337,848	29,758,753	13,847,973	162,862,402	133,546,718	29,315,684	25,591,525	130,757,046	67,258,797	63,498,249

							Direct						
	Utility and liquor store							Insurance trust					
		Utility								Unemployment compensation			
	Total	Total	Water	Electric	Gas	Transit	Liquor store	Total	Employee retirement	Total	Payroll taxes	Workers' compensation	Other
	Ea372	Ea373 [1]	Ea374	Ea375	Ea376	Ea377	Ea378	Ea379	Ea380	Ea381	Ea382	Ea383	Ea384
Fiscal year	Thousand dollars	Thousand dollars	Thousand dollars	Thousand dollars	Thousand dollars	Thousand dollars	Thousand dollars	Thousand dollars	Thousand dollars	Thousand dollars	Thousand dollars	Thousand dollars	Thousand dollars
1902	2,000	—	—	—	—	—	2,000	0	0	0	0	—	0
1913	0	—	—	—	—	—	0	0	0	0	0	—	0
1922	0	—	—	—	—	—	0	106,000	29,000	0	0	—	77,000
1927	0	—	—	—	—	—	0	137,000	40,000	0	0	—	97,000
1932	0	—	—	—	—	—	0	118,000	54,000	0	0	—	64,000
1934	90,000	—	—	—	—	—	90,000	119,000	64,000	0	0	—	55,000
1936	183,000	—	—	—	—	—	183,000	168,000	75,000	23,000	23,000	—	70,000
1938	262,000	—	—	—	—	—	262,000	890,000	85,000	726,000	702,000	—	79,000
1940	281,000	—	—	—	—	—	281,000	1,074,000	108,000	878,000	844,000	—	88,000
1942	373,000	—	—	—	—	—	373,000	1,366,000	115,000	1,134,000	1,076,000	—	117,000
1944	528,000	—	—	—	—	—	528,000	1,702,000	142,000	1,405,000	1,319,000	—	155,000

TABLE Ea348–384   State government revenue, by source: 1902–1996 *Continued*

							Direct						
	Utility and liquor store							Insurance trust					
		Utility									Unemployment compensation		
	Total	Total	Water	Electric	Gas	Transit	Liquor store	Total	Employee retirement	Total	Payroll taxes	Workers' compensation	Other
	Ea372	Ea373 [1]	Ea374	Ea375	Ea376	Ea377	Ea378	Ea379	Ea380	Ea381	Ea382	Ea383	Ea384
Fiscal year	Thousand dollars	Thousand dollars	Thousand dollars	Thousand dollars	Thousand dollars	Thousand dollars	Thousand dollars	Thousand dollars	Thousand dollars	Thousand dollars	Thousand dollars	Thousand dollars	Thousand dollars
1946	798,000	—	—	—	—	—	798,000	1,494,000	193,000	1,162,000	1,034,000	—	139,000
1948	857,000	—	—	—	—	—	857,000	1,711,000	296,000	1,203,000	1,059,000	—	212,000
1950	810,000	—	—	—	—	—	810,000	1,831,000	425,000	1,176,000	1,028,000	173,000	57,000
1952	924,000	—	—	—	—	—	924,000	2,462,000	579,000	1,597,000	1,438,000	224,000	62,000
1953	967,000	—	—	—	—	—	967,000	2,501,000	634,000	1,551,000	1,370,000	249,000	67,000
1954	974,000	—	—	—	—	—	974,000	2,560,000	757,000	1,466,000	1,263,000	270,000	67,000
1955	962,000	—	—	—	—	—	962,000	2,511,000	837,000	1,325,000	1,138,000	279,000	70,000
1956	1,019,000	—	—	—	—	—	1,019,000	2,791,000	919,000	1,500,000	1,315,000	292,000	80,000
1957	1,065,000	—	—	—	—	—	1,065,000	3,209,000	1,063,000	1,719,000	1,510,000	344,000	83,000
1958	1,058,000	—	—	—	—	—	1,058,000	3,361,000	1,224,000	1,711,000	1,493,000	340,000	86,000
1959	1,085,000	—	—	—	—	—	1,085,000	3,631,000	1,376,000	1,827,000	1,647,000	331,000	97,000
1960	1,128,000	—	—	—	—	—	1,128,000	4,347,000	1,558,000	2,316,000	2,136,000	363,000	110,000
1961	1,119,000	—	—	—	—	—	1,119,000	4,791,000	1,745,000	2,511,000	2,317,000	402,000	133,000
1962	1,134,000	—	—	—	—	—	1,134,000	5,304,000	1,942,000	2,812,000	2,649,000	416,000	134,000
1963	1,161,000	—	—	—	—	—	1,161,000	5,950,000	2,136,000	3,171,000	2,992,000	459,000	184,000
1964	1,195,000	—	—	—	—	—	1,195,000	6,324,000	2,369,000	3,250,000	3,046,000	498,000	207,000
1965	1,270,000	—	—	—	—	—	1,270,000	6,627,000	2,638,000	3,234,000	2,994,000	530,000	225,000
1966	1,361,000	—	—	—	—	—	1,361,000	7,128,000	2,918,000	3,326,000	3,040,000	557,000	327,000
1967	1,470,000	—	—	—	—	—	1,470,000	7,541,000	3,351,000	3,273,000	2,911,000	617,000	300,000
1968	1,557,000	—	—	—	—	—	1,557,000	7,771,000	3,831,000	2,963,000	2,547,000	656,000	321,000
1969	1,663,000	—	—	—	—	—	1,663,000	8,609,000	4,509,000	3,039,000	2,550,000	714,000	347,000
1970	1,748,000	—	—	—	—	—	1,748,000	9,437,000	5,205,000	3,090,000	2,524,000	770,000	372,000
1971	1,814,000	—	—	—	—	—	1,814,000	10,320,000	5,981,000	3,084,000	2,490,000	863,000	392,000
1972	1,904,190	—	—	—	—	—	1,904,190	11,803,133	6,856,694	3,588,185	3,127,534	916,660	441,594
1973	1,985,380	—	—	—	—	—	1,985,380	14,690,174	8,266,976	4,946,841	4,494,515	1,047,975	428,382
1974	2,049,354	—	—	—	—	—	2,049,354	16,438,768	8,918,634	5,710,786	5,129,360	1,218,241	591,107
1975	2,129,283	—	—	—	—	—	2,129,283	20,292,836	10,182,167	8,113,000	5,134,737	1,405,977	591,692
1976	2,195,974	—	—	—	—	—	2,195,974	29,507,409	12,170,709	15,068,000	6,165,921	1,667,583	601,117
1977	2,935,791	691,726	6,235	377,468	0	308,023	2,244,065	32,364,664	14,440,542	15,213,308	8,522,736	2,039,338	671,476
1978	3,349,994	962,069	7,094	633,335	0	321,640	2,387,925	32,561,708	16,025,843	13,083,356	9,894,470	2,649,233	803,276
1979	3,641,053	1,136,566	7,831	792,617	0	336,118	2,504,487	35,370,039	18,341,129	12,866,334	11,761,128	3,276,085	886,491
1980	4,069,025	1,303,584	9,462	931,848	0	362,274	2,765,441	39,300,581	21,145,878	13,468,404	11,615,657	3,604,269	1,082,030
1981	4,627,970	1,823,132	18,619	1,309,172	0	495,341	2,804,838	48,040,829	25,122,412	18,442,680	11,167,477	3,579,148	896,589
1982	4,939,556	2,085,218	21,237	1,466,821	0	597,160	2,854,338	50,847,996	29,034,773	16,854,013	11,910,851	3,993,365	965,845
1983	5,209,592	2,390,417	30,191	1,686,941	0	673,285	2,819,175	61,971,759	35,235,959	21,479,719	12,848,493	4,160,424	1,095,657
1984	5,396,902	2,638,051	32,419	1,863,701	0	741,931	2,758,851	60,949,560	38,563,631	16,671,450	17,109,571	4,391,508	1,322,971
1985	5,673,999	2,920,535	32,593	2,040,606	0	847,336	2,753,464	67,907,499	43,993,141	17,595,809	18,276,207	4,984,635	1,333,914
1986	5,714,116	2,907,292	58,599	1,970,334	241	878,118	2,806,824	82,089,942	56,820,176	18,172,788	18,632,383	5,668,722	1,428,256
1987	5,796,947	2,964,381	68,586	1,909,312	241	986,242	2,832,566	91,933,284	64,659,506	18,839,350	17,521,362	6,481,660	1,952,768
1988	5,796,423	3,029,871	71,631	1,990,467	230	967,543	2,766,552	90,491,365	63,555,717	17,186,667	17,675,081	7,373,060	2,375,921
1989	6,035,491	3,247,787	89,064	2,114,294	5,925	1,038,504	2,787,704	98,174,177	67,964,005	19,639,823	17,214,269	8,250,788	2,319,561
1990	6,212,521	3,305,135	109,606	2,116,218	5,251	1,074,060	2,907,386	108,529,560	78,897,842	18,369,719	15,428,562	9,049,646	2,212,353
1991	6,473,775	3,460,359	113,813	2,216,170	7,286	1,123,090	3,013,416	101,752,494	71,112,560	17,951,796	14,654,940	10,257,667	2,430,471
1992	6,567,314	3,511,541	123,993	2,256,475	5,279	1,125,794	3,055,773	128,149,966	86,490,190	26,921,327	15,785,312	11,749,994	2,988,455
1993	6,745,652	3,675,192	126,627	2,397,047	6,411	1,145,107	3,070,460	144,886,029	94,209,613	34,442,462	18,510,379	12,977,095	3,256,859
1994	6,836,176	3,784,363	136,038	2,423,623	6,939	1,217,763	3,051,813	142,567,619	96,139,103	29,707,275	20,922,547	13,376,298	3,344,943
1995	6,918,632	3,845,228	144,696	2,437,774	6,119	1,256,639	3,073,404	160,461,669	107,091,584	37,040,879	33,239,594	13,161,333	3,167,873
1996	7,078,796	3,919,223	121,098	2,482,643	7,673	1,307,809	3,159,573	189,213,226	139,316,425	33,684,503	29,868,287	13,483,687	2,728,611

[1] Through 1976, utility revenue reported miscellaneous general revenue, series Ea371.

Source

Figures are from data files provided by the Census of Governments. For published versions through 1982, see U.S. Department of Commerce, "Historical Statistics on Government Finance and Employment," in *Census of Governments, 1982*, volume 6, pp. 225–64.

Documentation

See the text for Table Ea24–51.

TABLE Ea385–395 State government expenditure, by character and object: 1902–1996

Contributed by John Joseph Wallis

				Direct							
	Total expenditure	Salaries and wages	Intergovernmental	Total	Current operation	Capital outlay			Assistance and subsidies	Interest on debt	Insurance trust
						Total	Construction	Other			
	Ea385	Ea386	Ea387	Ea388	Ea389	Ea390	Ea391	Ea392	Ea393	Ea394	Ea395
Year	Thousand dollars	Thousand dollars	Thousand dollars	Thousand dollars	Thousand dollars	Thousand dollars	Thousand dollars	Thousand dollars	Thousand dollars	Thousand dollars	Thousand dollars
1902	188,000	65,000	52,000	136,000	114,000	2,000	2,000	0	10,000	10,000	0
1913	388,000	125,000	91,000	297,000	218,000	48,000	42,000	6,000	17,000	14,000	0
1922	1,397,000	343,000	312,000	1,085,000	562,000	302,000	263,000	39,000	122,000	45,000	54,000
1927	2,047,000	465,000	596,000	1,451,000	762,000	492,000	430,000	62,000	43,000	83,000	71,000
1932	2,829,000	616,000	801,000	2,028,000	982,000	786,000	686,000	100,000	83,000	114,000	63,000
1934	3,461,000	576,000	1,318,000	2,143,000	985,000	619,000	540,000	79,000	356,000	119,000	64,000
1936	3,862,000	685,000	1,417,000	2,445,000	1,192,000	634,000	553,000	81,000	416,000	124,000	79,000
1938	4,598,000	848,000	1,516,000	3,082,000	1,503,000	701,000	612,000	89,000	448,000	128,000	302,000
1940	5,209,000	902,000	1,654,000	3,555,000	1,570,000	737,000	643,000	94,000	517,000	130,000	601,000
1942	5,343,000	961,000	1,780,000	3,563,000	1,827,000	642,000	560,000	82,000	466,000	122,000	505,000
1944	5,161,000	1,061,000	1,842,000	3,319,000	2,134,000	330,000	288,000	42,000	527,000	101,000	226,000
1946	7,066,000	1,240,000	2,092,000	4,974,000	2,701,000	368,000	292,000	75,000	663,000	84,000	1,158,000
1948	11,181,000	1,960,000	3,283,000	7,897,000	3,837,000	1,456,000	1,268,000	188,000	1,499,000	86,000	1,020,000
1950	15,082,000	2,450,000	4,217,000	10,864,000	4,450,000	2,237,000	1,966,000	272,000	1,891,000	109,000	2,177,000
1952	15,834,000	2,956,000	5,044,000	10,790,000	5,201,000	2,658,000	2,323,000	336,000	1,374,000	144,000	1,413,000
1953	16,850,000	3,232,000	5,384,000	11,466,000	5,570,000	2,847,000	2,472,000	375,000	1,471,000	162,000	1,416,000
1954	18,686,000	3,491,000	5,679,000	13,008,000	5,915,000	3,347,000	2,831,000	515,000	1,457,000	193,000	2,096,000
1955	20,357,000	3,795,000	5,986,000	14,371,000	6,265,000	3,992,000	3,404,000	589,000	1,451,000	251,000	2,411,000
1956	21,686,000	4,132,000	6,538,000	15,148,000	6,776,000	4,564,000	3,872,000	692,000	1,513,000	311,000	1,984,000
1957	24,235,000	4,473,000	7,440,000	16,796,000	7,358,000	5,163,000	4,318,000	845,000	1,611,000	351,000	2,313,000
1958	28,080,000	5,063,000	8,089,000	19,991,000	8,187,000	5,946,000	5,022,000	924,000	1,787,000	396,000	3,675,000
1959	31,125,000	5,474,000	8,689,000	22,436,000	8,804,000	7,059,000	5,937,000	1,122,000	1,862,000	453,000	4,259,000
1960	31,596,000	5,914,000	9,443,000	22,152,000	9,567,000	6,607,000	5,509,000	1,098,000	1,982,000	536,000	3,461,000
1961	34,693,000	6,524,000	10,114,000	24,578,000	10,419,000	6,865,000	5,699,000	1,166,000	2,009,000	584,000	4,701,000
1962	36,402,000	7,051,000	10,906,000	25,495,000	11,290,000	7,214,000	5,960,000	1,254,000	2,118,000	635,000	4,238,000
1963	39,583,000	7,722,000	11,885,000	27,698,000	12,449,000	8,110,000	6,717,000	1,393,000	2,112,000	721,000	4,306,000
1964	42,583,000	8,408,000	12,968,000	29,616,000	13,492,000	8,820,000	7,263,000	1,558,000	2,175,000	765,000	4,364,000
1965	45,639,000	9,257,000	14,174,000	31,465,000	14,930,000	9,307,000	7,600,000	1,707,000	2,236,000	822,000	4,170,000
1966	51,123,000	10,561,000	16,928,000	34,195,000	16,855,000	10,193,000	8,287,000	1,906,000	2,301,000	894,000	3,952,000
1967	58,760,000	12,011,000	19,056,000	39,704,000	20,201,000	11,544,000	9,550,000	1,994,000	2,665,000	1,026,000	4,268,000
1968	66,254,000	13,799,000	21,950,000	44,304,000	23,379,000	12,210,000	10,053,000	2,158,000	2,960,000	1,128,000	4,626,000
1969	74,227,000	15,592,000	24,779,000	49,448,000	27,052,000	12,701,000	10,610,000	2,091,000	3,509,000	1,275,000	4,911,000
1970	85,055,000	17,786,000	28,892,000	56,163,000	30,971,000	13,295,000	11,185,000	2,110,000	4,387,000	1,499,000	6,010,000
1971	98,840,000	19,921,000	32,640,000	66,200,000	35,846,000	14,736,000	12,446,000	2,289,000	5,531,000	1,761,000	8,327,000
1972	109,256,571	22,688,458	36,759,246	72,497,325	39,790,239	15,286,000	13,021,967	2,264,033	6,336,617	2,135,239	8,949,230
1973	118,835,745	24,161,207	40,822,135	78,013,610	44,838,305	14,676,914	12,326,992	2,349,922	6,897,374	2,434,152	9,166,865
1974	132,134,353	26,344,002	45,941,111	86,193,242	50,802,721	15,416,985	12,654,509	2,762,476	6,520,706	2,863,161	10,589,669
1975	158,883,009	30,296,000	51,978,324	106,904,685	60,792,531	17,306,979	14,442,764	2,864,215	6,673,361	3,271,542	18,860,272
1976	180,925,801	32,855,535	57,858,242	123,067,559	68,174,833	18,008,649	15,285,050	2,723,599	7,289,747	4,139,704	25,454,626
1977	191,225,150	35,779,773	62,459,903	128,765,247	75,683,317	16,964,162	13,803,454	3,160,708	7,555,515	5,136,265	23,425,988
1978	203,832,186	40,518,891	67,287,260	136,544,926	86,152,619	16,063,867	13,260,282	2,803,585	8,340,693	5,493,105	20,494,642
1979	224,653,127	43,781,717	75,962,980	148,690,147	94,533,213	19,123,946	15,929,865	3,194,081	8,874,207	6,048,033	20,110,748
1980	257,811,993	48,792,921	84,504,451	173,307,542	108,130,998	23,325,066	19,736,347	3,588,719	9,817,816	7,052,537	24,981,125
1981	291,527,209	53,072,382	93,179,549	198,347,660	122,794,209	24,285,624	20,631,981	3,653,643	10,889,397	8,157,112	32,221,318
1982	310,129,170	56,626,522	98,742,976	211,386,194	133,152,143	23,302,938	19,397,222	3,905,716	10,866,929	9,400,451	34,663,733
1983	333,668,950	60,347,578	100,886,902	232,782,048	143,917,910	23,101,445	18,368,280	4,733,165	11,874,765	11,707,802	42,180,126
1984	351,181,926	65,196,325	108,373,188	242,808,738	156,922,257	25,485,947	19,507,362	5,978,585	12,386,123	13,737,605	34,276,806
1985	390,742,488	70,570,673	121,571,151	269,171,337	172,124,243	30,656,897	23,877,199	6,779,698	12,841,719	15,608,441	37,940,037
1986	424,233,320	76,095,575	131,966,258	292,267,062	186,098,123	34,577,839	26,557,244	8,020,595	14,162,129	17,600,707	39,828,264
1987	455,699,593	81,211,431	141,278,672	314,420,921	199,806,290	37,208,661	28,174,048	9,034,613	14,705,345	19,384,984	43,315,641
1988	484,666,981	86,931,345	151,661,866	333,005,115	213,249,468	40,666,881	31,421,064	9,245,817	14,999,984	20,207,528	43,881,254
1989	525,076,730	94,447,951	165,415,415	359,661,315	232,963,877	43,121,446	33,611,736	9,509,710	15,420,690	21,160,452	46,994,850
1990	572,318,410	100,834,008	175,027,632	397,290,778	258,046,266	45,524,240	34,803,447	10,720,793	16,901,709	22,366,846	54,451,717
1991	628,835,510	107,678,874	186,540,238	442,295,272	287,079,068	47,937,389	37,647,332	10,290,057	18,875,874	24,189,437	64,213,504
1992	701,600,905	112,685,119	202,826,507	498,774,398	323,297,347	50,125,540	39,000,537	11,125,003	20,511,030	25,481,962	79,358,519
1993	743,261,971	115,283,209	214,094,882	529,167,089	345,323,798	50,152,233	39,603,947	10,548,286	21,884,198	24,828,881	86,977,979
1994	775,039,735	120,331,720	224,763,617	550,276,118	368,008,681	52,894,706	41,648,940	11,245,766	22,192,001	24,493,580	82,687,150
1995	837,081,992	125,431,931	240,756,840	596,325,152	396,035,029	57,828,938	46,113,125	11,715,813	23,511,134	25,258,533	93,691,518
1996	859,599,139	129,577,236	252,004,998	607,594,141	405,526,560	58,927,174	46,933,500	11,993,674	23,312,951	26,175,439	93,652,017

TABLE Ea385–395   State government expenditure, by character and object: 1902–1996   *Continued*

Source

Figures are from data files provided by the Census of Governments. For published versions through 1982, see U.S. Department of Commerce, "Historical Statistics on Government Finance and Employment," in *Census of Governments, 1982*, volume 6, pp. 225–64.

Documentation

See the text for Table Ea24–51.

In order to compute total expenditures under a different revenue concept, use the data from Table Ea125–131 on the change in debt during the year. See the essay in this chapter for additional information on this matter.

TABLE Ea396–456   State government expenditure, by function: 1902–1995
Contributed by John Joseph Wallis

		Intergovernmental				Direct					
							General				
								Education			
Year	Total expenditure	General	Total	To local	To federal	Total	Total	Total	Elementary	Higher education	Other
	Ea396	Ea397	Ea398	Ea399	Ea400	Ea401	Ea402	Ea403	Ea404	Ea405	Ea406
	Thousand dollars	Thousand dollars	Thousand dollars	Thousand dollars	Thousand dollars	Thousand dollars	Thousand dollars	Thousand dollars	Thousand dollars	Thousand dollars	Thousand dollars
1902	188,000	186,000	52,000	52,000	0	136,000	134,000	17,000	0	13,000	4,000
1913	388,000	388,000	91,000	91,000	0	297,000	297,000	55,000	0	49,000	6,000
1922	1,397,000	1,343,000	312,000	312,000	0	1,085,000	1,031,000	164,000	0	143,000	21,000
1927	2,047,000	1,976,000	596,000	596,000	0	1,451,000	1,380,000	218,000	0	196,000	22,000
1932	2,829,000	2,766,000	801,000	801,000	0	2,028,000	1,965,000	278,000	17,000	234,000	27,000
1934	3,461,000	3,327,000	1,318,000	1,318,000	0	2,143,000	2,009,000	228,000	20,000	177,000	31,000
1936	3,862,000	3,640,000	1,417,000	1,417,000	0	2,445,000	2,223,000	297,000	24,000	231,000	42,000
1938	4,598,000	4,092,000	1,516,000	1,516,000	0	3,082,000	2,576,000	347,000	28,000	268,000	51,000
1940	5,209,000	4,384,000	1,654,000	1,654,000	0	3,555,000	2,730,000	375,000	29,000	290,000	56,000
1942	5,343,000	4,549,000	1,780,000	1,780,000	0	3,563,000	2,769,000	391,000	30,000	296,000	65,000
1944	5,161,000	4,508,000	1,842,000	1,842,000	0	3,319,000	2,666,000	489,000	40,000	380,000	69,000
1946	7,066,000	5,245,000	2,092,000	2,092,000	0	4,974,000	3,153,000	518,000	48,000	397,000	73,000
1948	11,181,000	9,469,000	3,283,000	3,283,000	0	7,897,000	6,186,000	1,081,000	65,000	895,000	121,000
1950	15,082,000	12,250,000	4,217,000	4,217,000	0	10,864,000	8,033,000	1,358,000	87,000	1,107,000	164,000
1952	15,834,000	13,697,000	5,044,000	5,044,000	0	10,790,000	8,653,000	1,494,000	125,000	1,180,000	189,000
1953	16,850,000	14,678,000	5,384,000	5,384,000	0	11,466,000	9,294,000	1,634,000	150,000	1,277,000	207,000
1954	18,686,000	15,788,000	5,679,000	5,679,000	0	13,008,000	10,109,000	1,715,000	199,000	1,324,000	192,000
1955	20,357,000	17,176,000	5,986,000	5,986,000	0	14,371,000	11,190,000	1,905,000	227,000	1,468,000	210,000
1956	21,686,000	18,857,000	6,538,000	6,538,000	0	15,148,000	12,319,000	2,138,000	219,000	1,678,000	241,000
1957	24,235,000	21,086,000	7,440,000	7,440,000	0	16,796,000	13,647,000	2,342,000	112,000	1,958,000	272,000
1958	28,080,000	23,537,000	8,089,000	8,089,000	0	19,991,000	15,449,000	2,728,000	117,000	2,305,000	305,000
1959	31,125,000	26,006,000	8,689,000	8,689,000	0	22,436,000	17,318,000	3,093,000	150,000	2,614,000	329,000
1960	31,596,000	27,228,000	9,443,000	9,443,000	0	22,152,000	17,784,000	3,396,000	189,000	2,856,000	351,000
1961	34,693,000	29,118,000	10,114,000	10,114,000	0	24,578,000	19,004,000	3,792,000	226,000	3,170,000	396,000
1962	36,402,000	31,281,000	10,906,000	10,906,000	0	25,495,000	20,375,000	4,270,000	202,000	3,634,000	434,000
1963	39,583,000	34,377,000	11,885,000	11,885,000	0	27,698,000	22,491,000	4,718,000	222,000	3,992,000	504,000
1964	42,583,000	37,242,000	12,968,000	12,968,000	0	29,616,000	24,275,000	5,465,000	207,000	4,649,000	609,000
1965	45,639,000	40,446,000	14,174,000	14,174,000	0	31,465,000	26,273,000	6,181,000	189,000	5,258,000	735,000
1966	51,123,000	46,090,000	16,928,000	16,928,000	0	34,195,000	29,162,000	7,572,000	231,000	6,353,000	988,000
1967	58,760,000	53,305,000	19,056,000	19,056,000	0	39,704,000	34,249,000	9,384,000	300,000	7,728,000	1,357,000
1968	66,254,000	60,395,000	21,950,000	21,950,000	0	44,304,000	38,446,000	10,957,000	339,000	8,982,000	1,637,000
1969	74,227,000	68,023,000	24,779,000	24,779,000	0	49,448,000	43,244,000	12,304,000	365,000	10,004,000	1,935,000
1970	85,055,000	77,642,000	28,892,000	28,892,000	0	56,163,000	48,749,000	13,780,000	437,000	11,011,000	2,332,000
1971	98,840,000	89,118,000	32,640,000	32,640,000	0	66,200,000	56,478,000	15,800,000	491,000	12,448,000	2,861,000
1972	109,256,571	98,812,543	36,759,246	36,759,246	0	72,497,325	62,053,297	17,152,667	490,559	13,380,562	3,281,546
1973	118,835,745	108,086,178	40,822,135	40,822,135	0	78,013,610	67,264,043	18,282,944	479,741	14,248,320	3,554,883
1974	132,134,353	119,891,358	45,941,111	45,599,917	341,194	86,193,242	73,950,247	19,753,336	467,835	15,395,269	3,890,232
1975	158,883,009	138,303,991	51,978,324	51,003,544	974,780	106,904,685	86,325,667	22,902,063	535,565	17,696,105	4,670,393
1976	180,925,801	153,689,853	57,858,242	56,678,662	1,179,580	123,067,559	95,831,611	25,546,240	600,105	19,707,164	5,238,971
1977	191,225,150	164,350,899	62,459,903	61,073,666	1,386,237	128,765,247	101,890,996	27,072,707	650,769	21,165,804	5,256,134
1978	203,832,186	179,802,319	67,287,260	65,814,882	1,472,378	136,544,926	112,515,059	29,576,709	653,602	23,259,191	5,663,916
1979	224,653,127	200,517,338	75,962,980	74,469,765	1,493,215	148,690,147	124,554,358	31,516,720	833,128	24,679,813	6,003,779
1980	257,811,993	228,222,861	84,504,451	82,758,150	1,746,301	173,307,542	143,718,410	35,250,601	963,970	27,926,670	6,359,961
1981	291,527,209	253,653,877	93,179,549	91,306,569	1,872,980	198,347,660	160,474,328	39,663,515	1,040,070	31,488,163	7,135,282
1982	310,129,170	269,327,205	98,742,976	96,949,692	1,793,284	211,386,194	170,584,229	42,300,895	1,053,752	34,296,029	6,951,114
1983	333,668,950	284,691,416	100,886,902	99,122,081	1,764,821	232,782,048	183,804,514	44,584,376	977,870	36,496,112	7,110,394
1984	351,181,926	309,774,929	108,373,188	106,651,073	1,722,115	242,808,738	201,401,741	48,572,849	958,188	40,015,682	7,598,979
1985	390,742,488	345,047,045	121,571,151	119,607,683	1,963,468	269,171,337	223,475,894	53,667,466	1,019,949	44,264,125	8,383,392
1986	424,233,320	376,457,068	131,966,258	129,860,427	2,105,831	292,267,062	244,490,810	58,259,774	1,158,919	47,928,222	9,172,633
1987	455,699,593	403,942,284	141,278,672	138,823,310	2,455,362	314,420,921	262,663,612	61,647,377	1,301,257	50,710,281	9,635,839
1988	484,666,981	432,178,781	151,661,866	149,008,885	2,652,981	333,005,115	280,516,915	64,109,734	1,398,394	52,409,815	10,301,525
1989	525,076,730	469,268,608	165,415,415	162,485,793	2,929,622	359,661,315	303,853,193	68,582,652	1,417,044	55,988,355	11,177,253
1990	572,318,410	508,284,090	175,027,632	171,783,998	3,243,634	397,290,778	333,256,458	75,496,551	1,798,462	60,977,733	12,720,356
1991	628,835,510	554,900,684	186,540,238	183,075,874	3,464,364	442,295,272	368,360,446	80,468,304	1,997,405	65,559,958	12,910,941
1992	701,600,905	612,629,116	202,826,507	199,217,596	3,608,911	498,774,398	409,802,609	86,376,990	2,221,660	70,904,354	13,250,976
1993	743,261,971	646,908,256	214,094,882	210,469,831	3,625,051	529,167,089	432,813,374	90,367,707	2,530,291	73,968,920	13,868,496
1994	775,039,735	682,643,230	224,763,617	221,160,170	3,603,447	550,276,118	457,879,613	94,895,692	2,333,945	77,127,809	15,433,938
1995	837,081,992	733,282,090	240,756,840	237,140,009	3,616,831	596,325,152	492,525,250	101,509,904	2,187,243	82,338,957	16,983,704

TABLE Ea396–456   State government expenditure, by function: 1902–1995   *Continued*

					Direct				
					General				
					Social services and income maintenance				
		Public welfare							
			Cash assistance			Health and hospitals			
	Libraries	Total	Categorical	Noncategorical	Other	Total	Hospitals	Health	Employment security administration	Veterans' services
	Ea407	Ea408	Ea409	Ea410	Ea411	Ea412	Ea413	Ea414	Ea415	Ea416
Year	Thousand dollars	Thousand dollars	Thousand dollars	Thousand dollars	Thousand dollars	Thousand dollars	Thousand dollars	Thousand dollars	Thousand dollars	Thousand dollars
1902	—	10,000	—	—	—	32,000	28,000	4,000	—	0
1913	—	16,000	—	—	—	53,000	47,000	6,000	—	0
1922	—	38,000	—	—	—	125,000	105,000	20,000	—	80,000
1927	—	40,000	—	—	—	170,000	146,000	24,000	—	0
1932	—	74,000	—	—	—	215,000	181,000	34,000	—	0
1934	—	363,000	—	—	—	203,000	167,000	36,000	1,000	0
1936	—	422,000	—	—	—	221,000	180,000	41,000	3,000	0
1938	—	453,000	257,000	165,000	—	268,000	209,000	59,000	48,000	0
1940	—	527,000	321,000	170,000	—	300,000	236,000	64,000	64,000	0
1942	—	523,000	414,000	72,000	—	299,000	235,000	64,000	59,000	1,000
1944	—	577,000	506,000	32,000	—	331,000	253,000	78,000	35,000	1,000
1946	—	680,000	589,000	35,000	—	424,000	308,000	116,000	60,000	54,000
1948	—	962,000	820,000	58,000	—	663,000	533,000	130,000	150,000	633,000
1950	—	1,566,000	1,337,000	92,000	—	947,000	788,000	159,000	172,000	462,000
1952	7,000	1,410,000	1,192,000	37,000	181,000	1,132,000	968,000	164,000	178,000	142,000
1953	8,000	1,534,000	1,307,000	37,000	190,000	1,184,000	1,014,000	170,000	187,000	113,000
1954	7,000	1,548,000	1,298,000	32,000	218,000	1,276,000	1,089,000	187,000	190,000	102,000
1955	7,000	1,600,000	1,321,000	44,000	235,000	1,338,000	1,145,000	193,000	207,000	61,000
1956	—	1,603,000	1,364,000	37,000	202,000	1,470,000	1,268,000	202,000	215,000	88,000
1957	—	1,826,000	1,481,000	49,000	296,000	1,571,000	1,373,000	198,000	234,000	38,000
1958	—	1,944,000	1,563,000	55,000	326,000	1,760,000	1,549,000	211,000	270,000	121,000
1959	—	2,124,000	1,683,000	66,000	375,000	1,850,000	1,627,000	223,000	303,000	61,000
1960	17,000	2,221,000	1,728,000	76,000	417,000	1,896,000	1,664,000	232,000	313,000	112,000
1961	19,000	2,311,000	1,767,000	78,000	466,000	2,059,000	1,799,000	260,000	351,000	84,000
1962	21,000	2,509,000	1,863,000	61,000	584,000	2,161,000	1,878,000	283,000	399,000	95,000
1963	22,000	2,712,000	1,909,000	60,000	743,000	2,330,000	2,006,000	324,000	411,000	20,000
1964	22,000	2,796,000	1,935,000	59,000	800,000	2,464,000	2,127,000	337,000	426,000	19,000
1965	30,000	2,998,000	1,970,000	62,000	964,000	2,701,000	2,317,000	384,000	457,000	20,000
1966	37,000	3,138,000	1,986,000	57,000	1,096,000	2,966,000	2,533,000	433,000	500,000	21,000
1967	49,000	4,291,000	2,243,000	54,000	1,994,000	3,358,000	2,857,000	501,000	545,000	23,000
1968	52,000	5,122,000	2,421,000	57,000	2,644,000	3,832,000	3,233,000	599,000	606,000	33,000
1969	55,000	6,464,000	2,827,000	91,000	3,545,000	4,258,000	3,582,000	676,000	665,000	51,000
1970	54,000	8,203,000	3,534,000	145,000	4,524,000	4,788,000	4,002,000	786,000	767,000	67,000
1971	60,000	10,518,000	4,464,000	183,000	5,872,000	5,400,000	4,487,000	913,000	942,000	65,000
1972	63,353	12,247,362	5,088,849	191,767	6,966,746	6,008,418	4,902,465	1,105,953	1,132,659	50,843
1973	66,134	14,146,574	5,556,293	223,179	8,367,102	6,505,986	5,367,305	1,138,681	1,277,482	48,255
1974	71,379	15,168,554	4,983,572	211,624	9,973,358	7,494,555	6,083,442	1,411,113	1,303,845	156,218
1975	86,468	17,457,467	4,661,175	325,137	12,471,155	8,968,046	7,016,419	1,951,627	1,509,254	362,576
1976	99,230	20,156,880	5,203,271	353,116	14,600,493	9,850,600	7,725,736	2,124,864	1,570,062	64,035
1977	96,939	22,645,986	5,308,014	510,511	16,827,461	11,208,817	8,621,610	2,587,207	1,698,200	54,026
1978	106,810	25,729,126	5,712,386	623,478	19,393,262	12,318,597	9,248,800	3,069,797	1,757,022	53,710
1979	121,830	28,742,484	6,146,661	602,137	21,993,686	13,785,823	10,220,658	3,565,165	1,799,117	53,303
1980	127,337	33,242,074	6,830,793	686,780	25,724,501	15,666,614	11,277,115	4,389,499	2,001,385	60,951
1981	140,026	38,580,262	7,579,296	799,187	30,201,779	18,027,229	12,696,657	5,330,572	2,269,037	56,969
1982	146,508	41,512,785	7,337,181	874,819	33,300,785	19,235,136	13,874,169	5,360,967	2,277,865	63,798
1983	194,474	44,876,140	7,883,663	1,199,901	35,792,576	20,465,556	14,733,396	5,732,160	2,463,570	74,688
1984	198,331	49,121,685	8,296,821	1,153,943	39,670,921	21,566,964	15,226,683	6,340,281	2,545,614	98,572
1985	234,846	52,634,970	8,388,226	1,147,646	43,099,098	23,210,992	15,940,093	7,270,899	2,581,828	112,881
1986	259,917	56,166,156	9,277,006	1,161,172	45,727,978	25,498,887	17,128,217	8,370,670	2,696,787	121,785
1987	288,152	61,269,681	9,589,783	1,139,943	50,539,955	27,202,364	17,994,906	9,207,458	2,741,100	129,454
1988	302,543	66,570,017	9,803,307	1,152,738	55,613,972	29,381,389	19,586,158	9,795,231	2,841,813	134,281
1989	260,014	73,135,873	9,923,391	1,256,273	61,956,209	32,359,726	21,310,584	11,049,142	2,936,827	146,198
1990	261,736	83,335,930	10,671,835	1,299,217	71,364,878	35,542,842	22,551,710	12,991,132	3,003,319	151,682
1991	281,635	100,114,370	11,965,218	1,376,023	86,773,129	38,503,833	24,384,116	14,119,717	3,238,133	157,313
1992	288,174	125,908,339	13,512,854	1,269,184	111,126,301	41,643,763	26,005,299	15,638,464	3,702,371	170,014
1993	273,605	137,076,671	14,417,054	1,254,908	121,404,709	44,601,350	27,427,892	17,173,458	3,930,349	164,681
1994	270,410	148,244,289	13,756,930	1,454,507	133,032,852	46,995,543	28,063,775	18,931,768	4,056,438	178,847
1995	280,167	160,420,559	14,021,280	1,423,763	144,975,516	49,486,716	28,882,739	20,603,977	3,932,011	206,109

(continued)

TABLE Ea396–456   State government expenditure, by function: 1902–1995 *Continued*

					Direct				
					General				
		Public safety					Transportation		
		Corrections			Protective inspection				
	Police	Total	Institutions	Other	and regulation	Highways	Air	Water	Transit
	Ea417	Ea418	Ea419	Ea420	Ea421	Ea422	Ea423	Ea424	Ea425
Year	Thousand dollars	Thousand dollars	Thousand dollars	Thousand dollars	Thousand dollars	Thousand dollars	Thousand dollars	Thousand dollars	Thousand dollars
1902	0	14,000	—	—	—	4,000	—	—	—
1913	1,000	28,000	—	—	—	26,000	—	—	—
1922	4,000	64,000	—	—	—	303,000	—	—	—
1927	7,000	64,000	—	—	—	514,000	—	—	—
1932	15,000	87,000	—	—	—	843,000	—	—	—
1934	15,000	70,000	—	—	—	738,000	—	—	—
1936	19,000	73,000	—	—	—	754,000	—	—	—
1938	30,000	85,000	—	—	—	815,000	—	—	—
1940	34,000	86,000	—	—	—	793,000	—	—	—
1942	40,000	80,000	—	—	—	790,000	—	—	—
1944	41,000	83,000	—	—	—	540,000	—	—	—
1946	45,000	97,000	—	—	—	613,000	—	—	—
1948	65,000	153,000	—	—	—	1,510,000	—	—	—
1950	85,000	198,000	—	—	—	2,058,000	—	—	—
1952	106,000	223,000	—	—	143,000	2,556,000	—	—	—
1953	119,000	238,000	—	—	154,000	2,781,000	7,000	39,000	—
1954	130,000	250,000	—	—	167,000	3,254,000	7,000	41,000	—
1955	139,000	268,000	—	—	175,000	3,899,000	6,000	34,000	—
1956	159,000	295,000	—	—	191,000	4,367,000	6,000	50,000	—
1957	179,000	328,000	—	—	209,000	4,875,000	6,000	54,000	—
1958	214,000	370,000	—	—	231,000	5,507,000	17,000	63,000	—
1959	228,000	413,000	—	—	245,000	6,414,000	24,000	89,000	—
1960	245,000	425,000	—	—	259,000	6,070,000	26,000	80,000	—
1961	261,000	479,000	—	—	277,000	6,230,000	36,000	78,000	—
1962	276,000	508,000	—	—	295,000	6,635,000	35,000	91,000	—
1963	297,000	536,000	—	—	317,000	7,425,000	33,000	82,000	—
1964	315,000	586,000	—	—	331,000	7,850,000	40,000	89,000	—
1965	348,000	632,000	—	—	354,000	8,214,000	46,000	104,000	—
1966	385,000	664,000	—	—	384,000	8,624,000	45,000	147,000	—
1967	441,000	747,000	—	—	425,000	9,423,000	65,000	121,000	—
1968	516,000	838,000	—	—	461,000	9,819,000	67,000	186,000	—
1969	585,000	914,000	—	—	513,000	10,414,000	89,000	198,000	—
1970	688,000	1,051,000	—	—	572,000	11,044,000	178,000	173,000	—
1971	797,000	1,194,000	—	—	621,000	12,304,000	148,000	161,000	—
1972	899,528	1,308,700	—	—	677,000	12,746,711	144,387	158,926	—
1973	1,016,948	1,474,949	—	—	766,000	12,071,732	243,734	168,390	—
1974	1,145,212	1,728,752	—	—	873,000	12,635,737	223,721	172,158	—
1975	1,313,803	2,099,796	—	—	989,000	14,258,084	283,849	212,274	—
1976	1,411,743	2,359,867	—	—	1,069,000	14,859,661	289,624	233,379	—
1977	1,569,440	2,759,363	2,148,706	610,657	1,175,523	13,853,092	188,479	259,575	102,641
1978	1,683,276	3,157,013	2,462,641	694,372	1,324,881	14,657,862	244,499	235,877	145,341
1979	1,824,500	3,574,623	2,768,907	805,716	1,433,574	17,078,929	257,840	304,131	209,225
1980	2,060,296	4,212,491	3,303,223	909,268	1,563,671	20,661,232	360,069	360,106	217,566
1981	2,269,604	4,816,736	3,771,173	1,045,563	1,724,382	20,687,746	315,969	509,066	175,340
1982	2,396,178	5,523,619	4,398,893	1,124,726	1,904,854	20,103,020	345,559	513,151	216,055
1983	2,622,363	6,287,247	4,935,598	1,351,649	2,033,146	21,153,386	332,687	426,429	206,153
1984	2,793,088	7,160,810	5,859,629	1,301,181	2,228,871	23,152,800	385,939	401,546	255,589
1985	3,113,667	8,369,883	6,926,231	1,443,652	2,436,738	27,134,722	473,195	534,353	110,162
1986	3,328,373	9,855,289	8,093,078	1,762,211	2,718,047	30,190,965	454,106	548,460	140,656
1987	3,635,756	10,771,157	8,827,643	1,943,514	2,885,581	31,488,145	476,140	535,321	104,905
1988	3,914,111	12,286,666	10,301,961	1,984,705	3,047,285	33,731,664	453,683	482,120	129,464
1989	4,138,238	13,825,208	11,595,538	2,229,670	3,309,689	35,317,731	507,380	632,482	151,510
1990	4,486,510	15,897,848	13,370,059	2,527,789	3,544,983	36,464,434	635,442	504,329	178,107
1991	4,785,299	17,806,641	15,012,168	2,794,473	3,867,346	38,911,306	759,431	487,040	182,911
1992	4,863,131	18,401,186	15,347,585	3,053,601	4,083,156	40,477,769	963,205	504,210	189,484
1993	4,960,517	19,091,342	15,965,881	3,125,461	4,157,368	42,056,000	914,852	572,395	130,378
1994	5,324,906	21,266,053	17,741,937	3,524,116	4,353,486	43,812,093	788,197	634,871	118,929
1995	5,734,937	24,091,069	20,095,376	3,995,693	4,764,255	46,892,834	782,978	603,537	100,354

TABLE Ea396–456   State government expenditure, by function: 1902–1995   *Continued*

	Direct									
	General									
	Environment and housing									
		Natural resources				Parks and recreation	Housing and community development	Sanitation		
	Total	Agriculture	Fish and game	Forestry	Other			Total	Sewage	Solid waste
	Ea426	Ea427	Ea428	Ea429	Ea430	Ea431	Ea432	Ea433	Ea434	Ea435
Year	Thousand dollars	Thousand dollars	Thousand dollars	Thousand dollars	Thousand dollars	Thousand dollars	Thousand dollars	Thousand dollars	Thousand dollars	Thousand dollars
1902	9,000	—	—	—	—	—	—	—	—	—
1913	14,000	—	—	—	—	—	—	—	—	—
1922	61,000	—	—	—	—	—	—	—	—	—
1927	94,000	—	—	—	—	—	—	—	—	—
1932	119,000	—	—	—	—	—	—	—	—	—
1934	85,000	—	—	—	—	—	—	—	—	—
1936	93,000	—	—	—	—	—	—	—	—	—
1938	128,000	—	—	—	—	—	—	—	—	—
1940	144,000	—	—	—	—	—	—	—	—	—
1942	159,000	—	—	—	—	—	—	—	—	—
1944	164,000	—	—	—	—	—	—	—	—	—
1946	207,000	—	—	—	—	—	—	—	—	—
1948	344,000	—	—	—	—	—	—	—	—	—
1950	468,000	—	—	—	—	—	—	—	—	—
1952	539,000	—	—	—	—	—	4,000	—	—	—
1953	531,000	—	—	—	—	—	2,000	—	—	—
1954	563,000	—	—	—	—	—	2,000	—	—	—
1955	597,000	—	—	—	—	—	2,000	—	—	—
1956	670,000	—	—	—	—	—	2,000	—	—	—
1957	688,000	—	—	—	—	—	2,000	—	—	—
1958	733,000	—	—	—	—	—	2,000	—	—	—
1959	813,000	—	—	—	—	—	3,000	—	—	—
1960	842,000	—	—	—	—	—	8,000	—	—	—
1961	906,000	—	—	—	—	—	7,000	—	—	—
1962	973,000	—	—	—	—	—	8,000	—	—	—
1963	1,097,000	—	—	—	—	—	12,000	—	—	—
1964	1,185,000	—	—	—	—	—	17,000	—	—	—
1965	1,343,000	—	—	—	—	—	23,000	—	—	—
1966	1,532,000	—	—	—	—	—	24,000	—	—	—
1967	1,801,000	—	—	—	—	—	28,000	—	—	—
1968	1,954,000	—	—	—	—	—	20,000	—	—	—
1969	2,035,000	—	—	—	—	—	15,000	—	—	—
1970	2,158,000	—	—	—	—	—	23,000	—	—	—
1971	2,484,000	—	—	—	—	—	32,000	—	—	—
1972	2,469,713	—	—	—	—	—	34,039	—	—	—
1973	2,623,383	—	—	—	—	—	263,836	—	—	—
1974	2,917,038	—	—	—	—	—	382,171	—	—	—
1975	3,367,815	—	—	—	—	—	406,668	—	—	—
1976	3,640,878	—	—	—	—	—	272,431	—	—	—
1977	3,083,351	1,513,740	540,677	427,670	601,264	1,025,114	177,864	240,316	240,316	0
1978	3,240,742	1,633,601	586,424	438,292	582,425	1,012,591	164,694	299,549	299,549	0
1979	3,594,116	1,763,305	649,699	472,583	708,529	1,153,498	213,937	307,174	307,174	0
1980	4,124,376	1,966,845	707,195	501,911	948,425	1,273,523	330,505	334,306	334,306	0
1981	4,724,596	2,222,295	828,638	564,086	1,109,577	1,328,755	401,913	345,151	345,151	0
1982	5,164,537	2,419,819	898,489	570,784	1,275,445	1,361,617	487,961	358,860	358,860	0
1983	5,544,982	2,540,977	921,346	582,468	1,500,191	1,461,560	655,357	202,643	202,643	0
1984	5,662,144	2,651,446	1,013,876	573,607	1,423,215	1,387,655	817,862	245,706	245,706	0
1985	6,394,909	2,875,917	1,077,604	636,253	1,805,135	1,572,736	1,034,089	328,128	328,128	0
1986	6,897,457	3,097,118	1,146,372	708,104	1,945,863	1,733,461	1,188,786	341,330	341,330	0
1987	7,354,216	3,242,256	1,189,364	699,900	2,222,696	1,875,881	1,308,389	405,548	405,548	0
1988	7,793,663	3,351,227	1,294,884	869,060	2,278,492	2,013,714	1,524,659	798,488	554,920	243,568
1989	8,599,878	3,622,664	1,391,711	983,350	2,602,153	2,351,007	1,802,570	1,196,671	576,009	620,662
1990	9,434,914	3,940,631	1,498,226	1,009,531	2,986,526	2,470,706	1,723,570	1,526,211	635,611	890,600
1991	9,724,468	4,064,275	1,581,505	1,150,036	2,928,652	2,743,599	1,759,100	1,993,939	832,677	1,161,262
1992	9,921,875	4,157,121	1,699,799	974,209	3,090,746	2,687,651	1,605,553	2,228,906	908,048	1,320,858
1993	10,514,232	4,328,287	1,776,999	975,817	3,433,129	2,672,197	1,797,493	2,400,762	1,097,017	1,303,745
1994	11,150,501	4,372,710	1,833,958	983,746	3,960,087	2,799,215	2,044,792	2,688,605	1,318,462	1,370,143
1995	11,980,412	4,474,589	1,932,462	1,173,289	4,400,072	2,964,508	2,085,136	3,120,423	1,462,387	1,658,036

(continued)

TABLE Ea396–456   State government expenditure, by function: 1902–1995 *Continued*

					Direct			
					General			
		Administration and general control						
Year	Financial administration and general control	Financial administration	Judicial	Legislative	General public building	Other	Interest	Miscellaneous commercial activities	Other
	Ea436 [1]	Ea437 [1]	Ea438 [1]	Ea439 [1]	Ea440 [1]	Ea441 [1]	Ea442	Ea443	Ea444
	Thousand dollars	Thousand dollars	Thousand dollars	Thousand dollars	Thousand dollars	Thousand dollars	Thousand dollars	Thousand dollars	Thousand dollars
1902	23,000	—	—	—	—	—	10,000	—	15,000
1913	38,000	—	—	—	—	—	14,000	—	52,000
1922	69,000	—	—	—	—	—	45,000	—	78,000
1927	96,000	—	—	—	—	—	83,000	—	94,000
1932	114,000	—	—	—	—	—	114,000	—	106,000
1934	108,000	—	—	—	—	—	119,000	—	79,000
1936	130,000	—	—	—	—	—	124,000	—	87,000
1938	146,000	—	—	—	—	—	128,000	—	128,000
1940	151,000	—	—	—	—	—	130,000	—	126,000
1942	164,000	—	—	—	—	—	122,000	—	141,000
1944	162,000	—	—	—	—	—	101,000	—	142,000
1946	192,000	—	—	—	—	—	84,000	—	179,000
1948	266,000	—	—	—	—	—	86,000	—	273,000
1950	317,000	—	—	—	—	—	109,000	—	293,000
1952	361,000	—	—	—	—	—	144,000	18,000	196,000
1953	399,000	—	—	39,000	52,000	—	162,000	18,000	184,000
1954	419,000	—	—	32,000	54,000	—	193,000	20,000	225,000
1955	447,000	—	—	43,000	80,000	—	251,000	21,000	233,000
1956	477,000	—	—	41,000	85,000	—	311,000	20,000	257,000
1957	531,000	350,000	—	57,000	78,000	—	351,000	20,000	393,000
1958	569,000	384,000	—	46,000	96,000	—	396,000	20,000	484,000
1959	619,000	407,000	—	64,000	120,000	—	453,000	185,000	401,000
1960	654,000	442,000	—	52,000	120,000	—	536,000	244,000	440,000
1961	726,000	472,000	—	77,000	120,000	—	584,000	318,000	486,000
1962	763,000	509,000	—	63,000	130,000	—	635,000	175,000	526,000
1963	830,000	537,000	—	88,000	135,000	—	721,000	113,000	815,000
1964	871,000	577,000	—	71,000	149,000	—	765,000	105,000	929,000
1965	948,000	605,000	—	98,000	157,000	—	822,000	104,000	948,000
1966	1,024,000	655,000	—	90,000	196,000	—	894,000	79,000	1,126,000
1967	1,175,000	734,000	—	128,000	236,000	—	1,026,000	189,000	1,158,000
1968	1,310,000	810,000	—	130,000	274,000	—	1,128,000	223,000	1,322,000
1969	1,496,000	905,000	—	167,000	294,000	—	1,275,000	244,000	1,669,000
1970	1,720,000	1,022,000	—	179,000	340,000	—	1,499,000	252,000	1,732,000
1971	—	1,131,000	—	225,000	365,000	—	1,761,000	300,000	2,170,000
1972	—	1,222,000	—	236,131	407,600	—	2,135,239	454,827	2,503,194
1973	—	1,380,492	—	289,167	428,530	—	2,434,152	655,276	3,120,079
1974	—	1,583,595	—	321,459	508,242	—	2,863,161	727,915	3,920,199
1975	—	1,783,903	—	388,497	567,827	—	3,271,542	1,045,410	5,051,325
1976	—	1,945,013	—	411,454	566,177	—	4,139,704	1,124,400	6,221,233
1977	—	2,223,105	670,900	470,495	557,016	618,571	4,956,225	111,331	5,071,920
1978	—	2,459,921	1,056,991	500,003	587,870	682,610	5,268,224	112,613	6,138,528
1979	—	2,691,907	1,274,883	572,305	652,854	761,150	5,790,371	149,915	6,690,149
1980	—	2,993,648	1,584,976	619,946	725,671	914,601	6,762,766	201,461	8,068,238
1981	—	3,271,597	1,533,519	700,953	803,263	1,056,117	7,843,553	224,773	9,004,257
1982	—	3,668,682	1,832,517	787,711	867,443	1,151,937	9,015,320	238,042	9,110,179
1983	—	4,135,860	2,698,833	844,482	932,965	586,203	11,251,722	165,526	9,604,166
1984	—	4,428,414	3,028,280	903,350	931,889	545,148	13,137,238	186,114	11,645,283
1985	—	4,946,671	3,398,705	1,002,783	952,658	618,844	14,982,498	176,855	13,451,315
1986	—	5,768,278	3,727,315	1,091,843	959,332	675,184	16,876,111	143,765	14,848,746
1987	—	6,364,772	3,972,834	1,181,339	1,106,339	713,582	18,586,799	143,863	16,474,917
1988	—	6,887,955	4,492,794	1,296,834	1,119,987	771,695	19,366,822	145,301	16,920,233
1989	—	7,571,452	4,979,190	1,413,665	1,250,543	823,499	20,354,863	248,306	17,958,021
1990	—	8,515,291	5,443,719	1,494,700	1,360,037	892,998	21,531,818	240,397	19,118,384
1991	—	8,992,615	5,919,570	1,621,285	1,453,331	955,584	23,392,876	223,817	20,016,700
1992	—	9,649,001	6,326,165	1,581,712	1,369,278	949,310	24,621,220	200,425	21,089,721
1993	—	10,433,242	6,644,044	1,580,148	1,465,587	1,011,491	24,018,529	195,993	21,782,441
1994	—	11,287,141	6,904,352	1,657,867	1,330,584	1,020,714	23,719,182	234,120	22,102,786
1995	—	12,619,472	7,533,740	1,765,737	1,738,311	1,123,373	24,485,426	210,746	24,092,536

Note appears at end of table

TABLE Ea396–456   State government expenditure, by function: 1902–1995 *Continued*

		Direct										
	Utility and liquor store							Insurance trust				
		Utility							Employee retirement	Unemployment compensation	Workers' compensation	Other
	Total	Total	Water	Electric	Gas	Transit	Liquor store	Total				
	Ea445	Ea446	Ea447	Ea448	Ea449	Ea450	Ea451	Ea452	Ea453	Ea454	Ea455	Ea456
Year	Thousand dollars	Thousand dollars	Thousand dollars	Thousand dollars	Thousand dollars	Thousand dollars	Thousand dollars	Thousand dollars	Thousand dollars	Thousand dollars	Thousand dollars	Thousand dollars
1902	2,000	—	—	—	—	—	2,000	0	0	0	0	0
1913	0	—	—	—	—	—	0	0	0	0	0	0
1922	0	—	—	—	—	—	0	54,000	9,000	0	—	45,000
1927	0	—	—	—	—	—	0	71,000	12,000	0	—	59,000
1932	0	—	—	—	—	—	0	63,000	18,000	0	—	45,000
1934	70,000	—	—	—	—	—	70,000	64,000	27,000	0	—	37,000
1936	143,000	—	—	—	—	—	143,000	79,000	36,000	0	—	43,000
1938	204,000	—	—	—	—	—	204,000	302,000	48,000	202,000	—	52,000
1940	224,000	—	—	—	—	—	224,000	601,000	56,000	492,000	—	53,000
1942	288,000	—	—	—	—	—	288,000	505,000	65,000	369,000	—	71,000
1944	426,000	—	—	—	—	—	426,000	226,000	71,000	65,000	—	90,000
1946	663,000	—	—	—	—	—	663,000	1,159,000	92,000	965,000	—	102,000
1948	691,000	—	—	—	—	—	691,000	1,020,000	123,000	756,000	—	141,000
1950	654,000	—	—	—	—	—	654,000	2,177,000	163,000	1,845,000	133,000	36,000
1952	723,000	—	—	—	—	—	723,000	1,413,000	247,000	971,000	157,000	38,000
1953	757,000	—	—	—	—	—	757,000	1,416,000	292,000	908,000	170,000	46,000
1954	803,000	—	—	—	—	—	803,000	2,096,000	355,000	1,504,000	183,000	54,000
1955	770,000	—	—	—	—	—	770,000	2,411,000	373,000	1,780,000	196,000	62,000
1956	845,000	—	—	—	—	—	845,000	1,984,000	437,000	1,273,000	209,000	65,000
1957	836,000	—	—	—	—	—	836,000	2,313,000	511,000	1,495,000	230,000	77,000
1958	869,000	—	—	—	—	—	869,000	3,675,000	587,000	2,751,000	246,000	91,000
1959	860,000	—	—	—	—	—	860,000	4,259,000	626,000	3,268,000	259,000	106,000
1960	907,000	—	—	—	—	—	907,000	3,461,000	700,000	2,359,000	283,000	119,000
1961	873,000	—	—	—	—	—	873,000	4,700,000	791,000	3,456,000	305,000	148,000
1962	882,000	—	—	—	—	—	882,000	4,237,000	933,000	2,802,000	335,000	167,000
1963	900,000	—	—	—	—	—	900,000	4,307,000	995,000	2,750,000	360,000	202,000
1964	977,000	—	—	—	—	—	977,000	4,364,000	1,125,000	2,627,000	374,000	238,000
1965	1,022,000	—	—	—	—	—	1,022,000	4,170,000	1,238,000	2,288,000	394,000	250,000
1966	1,081,000	—	—	—	—	—	1,081,000	3,953,000	1,398,000	1,884,000	409,000	262,000
1967	1,187,000	—	—	—	—	—	1,187,000	4,268,000	1,606,000	1,934,000	457,000	271,000
1968	1,233,000	—	—	—	—	—	1,233,000	4,626,000	1,810,000	2,042,000	481,000	293,000
1969	1,293,000	—	—	—	—	—	1,293,000	4,912,000	2,088,000	1,984,000	507,000	333,000
1970	1,404,000	—	—	—	—	—	1,404,000	6,010,000	2,376,000	2,713,000	551,000	370,000
1971	1,395,000	—	—	—	—	—	1,395,000	8,325,000	2,705,000	4,692,000	529,000	399,000
1972	1,494,798	—	—	—	—	—	1,494,798	8,949,230	3,186,618	4,721,790	642,964	397,858
1973	1,582,702	—	—	—	—	—	1,582,702	9,166,865	3,941,772	4,055,523	736,602	432,968
1974	1,653,326	—	—	—	—	—	1,653,326	10,589,669	4,591,257	4,672,845	829,006	496,561
1975	1,718,746	—	—	—	—	—	1,718,746	18,860,272	5,160,103	12,245,000	909,859	545,310
1976	1,781,322	—	—	—	—	—	1,781,322	25,454,626	6,045,197	17,780,000	1,070,266	559,163
1977	3,448,263	1,631,328	21,034	981,864	0	628,430	1,816,935	23,425,988	6,929,837	14,610,854	1,326,063	559,234
1978	3,535,225	1,544,366	22,329	889,175	0	632,862	1,990,859	20,494,642	7,811,275	10,672,297	1,422,552	588,518
1979	4,025,041	1,956,686	49,898	1,147,641	0	759,147	2,068,355	20,110,748	8,937,384	8,828,322	1,703,742	641,300
1980	4,608,007	2,401,463	90,639	1,285,135	0	1,025,689	2,206,544	24,981,125	10,256,548	12,006,217	1,976,811	741,549
1981	5,652,014	3,346,782	99,170	1,736,002	0	1,511,610	2,305,232	32,221,318	11,419,411	17,846,418	2,043,011	912,478
1982	6,138,232	3,730,336	74,350	1,812,629	0	1,843,357	2,407,896	34,663,733	13,133,479	18,026,723	2,524,442	979,089
1983	6,797,408	4,416,660	112,543	2,097,167	0	2,206,950	2,380,748	42,180,126	14,204,398	24,068,131	2,867,956	1,039,641
1984	7,130,191	4,816,787	64,876	1,960,010	0	2,791,901	2,313,404	34,276,806	16,111,802	13,987,189	3,093,277	1,084,538
1985	7,755,406	5,364,388	69,367	2,045,017	0	3,250,004	2,391,018	37,940,037	18,229,691	14,928,408	3,462,152	1,319,786
1986	7,947,988	5,530,151	87,570	2,109,785	209	3,332,587	2,417,837	39,828,264	19,877,501	14,820,552	3,618,676	1,511,535
1987	8,441,668	5,971,374	109,356	2,155,166	190	3,706,662	2,470,294	43,315,641	22,188,816	15,174,059	4,288,454	1,664,312
1988	8,606,946	6,229,177	101,907	2,279,952	190	3,847,128	2,377,769	43,881,254	24,196,008	13,023,736	4,849,194	1,812,316
1989	8,813,272	6,409,929	128,345	2,345,641	4,569	3,931,374	2,403,343	46,994,850	26,966,399	12,791,214	5,318,374	1,918,863
1990	9,582,603	7,131,079	135,781	2,470,159	4,005	4,521,134	2,451,524	54,451,717	29,562,155	16,422,553	6,372,855	2,094,154
1991	9,721,322	7,217,361	147,108	2,503,737	4,460	4,562,056	2,503,961	64,213,504	32,294,947	22,016,530	7,337,666	2,564,361
1992	9,613,270	7,036,147	209,125	2,531,919	3,221	4,291,882	2,577,123	79,358,519	35,628,389	32,760,681	7,844,385	3,125,064
1993	9,375,736	6,817,221	187,740	2,551,050	4,295	4,074,136	2,558,515	86,977,979	40,045,028	35,197,430	8,874,325	2,861,196
1994	9,709,355	7,214,483	176,430	2,599,770	4,587	4,433,696	2,494,872	82,687,150	43,047,608	28,466,397	8,851,525	2,321,620
1995	10,108,384	7,585,965	177,733	2,589,489	4,419	4,814,324	2,522,419	93,691,518	47,950,959	35,032,015	8,356,094	2,352,450

(continued)

TABLE Ea396–456   State government expenditure, by function: 1902–1995   *Continued*

[1] Through 1970, series Ea436 includes all expenditures on general government administration; thereafter (and earlier for some functions), individual activities are reported separately. Some activities reported separately may have been included under other general expenditures during the earlier period.

Source

Data in this table are taken from spreadsheets provided by the Census of Governments. Published versions of the data through 1982 can be found in U.S. Department of Commerce, "Historical Statistics on Government Finance and Employment." in *Census of Governments, 1982,* volume 6, pp. 225–64.

Documentation

See the text for Table Ea24–51.

TABLE Ea457–488   State intergovernmental expenditure, by function: 1902–1995

Contributed by John Joseph Wallis

						Social services and income maintenance		
							Health and hospitals	
Fiscal year	Total expenditure	To local	To federal	Education	Libraries	Public welfare	Total	Hospitals	Health
	Ea457	Ea458	Ea459	Ea460	Ea461	Ea462	Ea463	Ea464	Ea465
	Thousand dollars	Thousand dollars	Thousand dollars	Thousand dollars	Thousand dollars	Thousand dollars	Thousand dollars	Thousand dollars	Thousand dollars
1902	52,000	52,000	0	45,000	—	0	—	—	—
1913	91,000	91,000	0	82,000	—	0	—	—	—
1922	312,000	312,000	0	202,000	—	4,000	—	—	—
1927	596,000	596,000	0	292,000	—	6,000	—	—	—
1932	801,000	801,000	0	398,000	—	28,000	—	—	—
1934	1,318,000	1,318,000	0	434,000	—	211,000	—	—	—
1936	1,417,000	1,417,000	0	573,000	—	245,000	—	—	—
1938	1,516,000	1,516,000	0	656,000	—	346,000	—	—	—
1940	1,654,000	1,654,000	0	700,000	—	420,000	—	—	—
1942	1,780,000	1,780,000	0	790,000	—	390,000	12,000	—	—
1944	1,842,000	1,842,000	0	861,000	—	368,000	16,000	—	—
1946	2,092,000	2,092,000	0	953,000	—	376,000	23,000	—	—
1948	3,283,000	3,283,000	0	1,554,000	—	648,000	37,000	—	—
1950	4,217,000	4,217,000	0	2,054,000	—	792,000	95,000	—	—
1952	5,044,000	5,044,000	0	2,523,000	2,000	976,000	125,000	—	—
1953	5,384,000	5,384,000	0	2,737,000	3,000	981,000	130,000	—	—
1954	5,679,000	5,679,000	0	2,930,000	4,000	1,004,000	126,000	—	—
1955	5,986,000	5,986,000	0	3,150,000	4,000	1,046,000	125,000	—	—
1956	6,538,000	6,538,000	0	3,541,000	—	1,069,000	132,000	72,000	60,000
1957	7,440,000	7,440,000	0	4,212,000	—	1,136,000	142,000	73,000	69,000
1958	8,089,000	8,089,000	0	4,598,000	—	1,247,000	150,000	82,000	67,000
1959	8,689,000	8,689,000	0	4,957,000	—	1,409,000	161,000	91,000	71,000
1960	9,443,000	9,443,000	0	5,461,000	7,000	1,483,000	176,000	95,000	81,000
1961	10,114,000	10,114,000	0	5,963,000	11,000	1,602,000	184,000	100,000	84,000
1962	10,906,000	10,906,000	0	6,474,000	14,000	1,777,000	191,000	95,000	96,000
1963	11,885,000	11,885,000	0	6,993,000	17,000	1,919,000	207,000	107,000	101,000
1964	12,968,000	12,968,000	0	7,664,000	18,000	2,108,000	235,000	120,000	115,000
1965	14,174,000	14,174,000	0	8,351,000	28,000	2,436,000	241,000	120,000	122,000
1966	16,928,000	16,928,000	0	10,177,000	45,000	2,882,000	275,000	114,000	161,000
1967	19,056,000	19,056,000	0	11,845,000	63,000	2,897,000	301,000	116,000	185,000
1968	21,950,000	21,950,000	0	13,321,000	80,000	3,527,000	371,000	141,000	231,000
1969	24,779,000	24,779,000	0	14,858,000	82,000	4,402,000	446,000	156,000	289,000
1970	28,892,000	28,892,000	0	17,085,000	73,000	5,003,000	567,000	161,000	406,000
1971	32,640,000	32,640,000	0	19,292,000	84,000	5,760,000	751,000	158,000	593,000
1972	36,759,246	36,759,246	0	21,195,345	91,934	6,943,634	954,705	147,239	807,466
1973	40,822,135	40,822,135	0	23,315,651	88,521	7,531,738	844,071	109,399	734,672
1974	45,941,111	45,599,917	341,194	27,106,812	100,797	7,369,108	948,172	125,602	822,570
1975	51,978,324	51,003,544	974,780	31,110,237	128,462	8,101,451	1,189,563	78,168	1,111,395
1976	57,858,242	56,678,662	1,179,580	34,083,711	129,338	9,476,411	1,260,051	95,738	1,164,313
1977	62,459,903	61,073,666	1,386,237	36,964,306	139,091	10,133,404	1,397,944	120,350	1,277,594
1978	67,287,260	65,814,882	1,472,378	40,125,488	154,944	10,047,049	1,564,734	114,922	1,449,812
1979	75,962,980	74,469,765	1,493,215	46,195,698	165,053	10,155,152	1,743,661	77,678	1,665,983
1980	84,504,451	82,758,150	1,746,301	52,688,101	180,566	10,977,467	2,188,388	92,751	2,095,637
1981	93,179,549	91,306,569	1,872,980	57,257,373	192,360	12,882,475	2,565,117	65,156	2,499,961
1982	98,742,976	96,949,692	1,793,284	60,683,583	207,804	13,744,417	2,886,054	63,975	2,822,079
1983	100,886,902	99,122,081	1,764,821	63,118,351	169,167	12,668,359	3,091,912	60,973	3,030,939
1984	108,373,188	106,651,073	1,722,115	67,484,926	206,217	13,627,522	3,414,884	51,394	3,363,490
1985	121,571,151	119,607,683	1,963,468	74,936,970	239,645	14,628,859	4,383,846	41,914	4,341,932
1986	131,966,258	129,860,427	2,105,831	81,929,467	288,592	16,298,296	4,660,304	51,308	4,608,996
1987	141,278,672	138,823,310	2,455,362	88,253,298	297,174	17,184,138	4,928,569	53,502	4,875,067
1988	151,661,866	149,008,885	2,652,981	95,390,536	319,890	17,664,585	5,490,580	83,851	5,406,729
1989	165,415,415	162,485,793	2,929,622	104,601,291	399,906	19,614,348	6,242,209	103,684	6,138,525
1990	175,027,632	171,783,998	3,243,634	109,438,131	428,965	21,635,018	7,122,724	85,331	7,037,393
1991	186,540,238	183,075,874	3,464,364	116,179,860	414,222	24,341,214	7,373,496	81,391	7,292,105
1992	202,826,507	199,217,596	3,608,911	124,939,025	395,706	29,511,968	7,983,564	119,887	7,863,677
1993	214,094,882	210,469,831	3,625,051	131,179,517	408,399	31,339,777	8,709,651	106,623	8,603,028
1994	224,763,617	221,160,170	3,603,447	135,420,690	427,085	34,189,235	9,550,300	119,437	9,430,863
1995	240,756,840	237,140,009	3,616,831	147,939,148	459,593	34,365,957	10,516,487	255,858	10,260,629

(continued)

TABLE Ea457–488   State intergovernmental expenditure, by function: 1902–1995   *Continued*

	Public safety			Transportation				Environment and housing				
									Natural resources			
Fiscal year	Police	Corrections	Protective inspection and regulation	Highways	Air	Water	Transit	Total	Agriculture	Fish and game	Forestry	Other
	Ea466	Ea467 [1]	Ea468	Ea469	Ea470	Ea471	Ea472	Ea473	Ea474	Ea475	Ea476	Ea477
	Thousand dollars	Thousand dollars	Thousand dollars	Thousand dollars	Thousand dollars	Thousand dollars	Thousand dollars	Thousand dollars	Thousand dollars	Thousand dollars	Thousand dollars	Thousand dollars
1902	—	—	—	2,000	—	—	—	—	—	—	—	—
1913	—	—	—	4,000	—	—	—	—	—	—	—	—
1922	—	—	—	70,000	—	—	—	—	—	—	—	—
1927	—	—	—	197,000	—	—	—	—	—	—	—	—
1932	—	—	—	229,000	—	—	—	—	—	—	—	—
1934	—	—	—	247,000	—	—	—	—	—	—	—	—
1936	—	—	—	285,000	—	—	—	—	—	—	—	—
1938	—	—	—	317,000	—	—	—	—	—	—	—	—
1940	—	—	—	332,000	—	—	—	—	—	—	—	—
1942	—	—	—	344,000	—	—	—	1,000	—	—	—	—
1944	—	—	—	298,000	—	—	—	1,000	—	—	—	—
1946	—	—	—	339,000	—	—	—	2,000	—	—	—	—
1948	—	—	—	507,000	—	—	—	2,000	—	—	—	—
1950	—	—	—	610,000	—	—	—	9,000	—	—	—	—
1952	2,000	2,000	0	728,000	—	—	—	9,000	—	—	—	—
1953	3,000	0	0	803,000	10,000	—	—	11,000	—	—	—	—
1954	3,000	2,000	0	871,000	8,000	—	—	9,000	—	—	—	—
1955	2,000	3,000	0	911,000	6,000	—	—	14,000	—	—	—	—
1956	2,000	3,000	0	984,000	6,000	—	—	11,000	—	—	—	—
1957	3,000	5,000	0	1,082,000	8,000	0	0	11,000	—	—	—	—
1958	4,000	6,000	0	1,167,000	16,000	0	0	16,000	—	—	—	—
1959	3,000	7,000	0	1,207,000	17,000	0	0	18,000	—	—	—	—
1960	6,000	8,000	0	1,247,000	24,000	1,000	0	20,000	—	—	—	—
1961	5,000	9,000	0	1,266,000	20,000	1,000	0	18,000	—	—	—	—
1962	5,000	16,000	0	1,327,000	22,000	1,000	0	19,000	—	—	—	—
1963	6,000	14,000	0	1,416,000	18,000	1,000	0	28,000	—	—	—	—
1964	4,000	18,000	0	1,524,000	18,000	1,000	0	23,000	—	—	—	—
1965	5,000	21,000	6,000	1,630,000	19,000	2,000	0	38,000	—	—	—	—
1966	5,000	27,000	7,000	1,725,000	15,000	6,000	0	36,000	—	—	—	—
1967	5,000	31,000	6,000	1,861,000	23,000	4,000	0	46,000	—	—	—	—
1968	23,000	36,000	7,000	2,029,000	29,000	7,000	0	51,000	—	—	—	—
1969	36,000	45,000	10,000	2,109,000	40,000	12,000	0	61,000	—	—	—	—
1970	53,000	53,000	8,000	2,439,000	47,000	5,000	0	64,000	—	—	—	—
1971	68,000	63,000	12,000	2,507,000	42,000	8,000	0	64,000	—	—	—	—
1972	83,689	80,037	8,000	2,633,417	33,826	7,263	0	124,992	—	—	—	—
1973	101,125	78,291	13,000	2,953,424	54,126	4,709	0	101,430	—	—	—	—
1974	116,850	82,812	13,000	3,211,455	52,882	3,996	0	136,083	—	—	—	—
1975	109,583	102,860	10,000	3,224,861	82,389	9,001	0	185,956	—	—	—	—
1976	157,274	120,129	21,000	3,240,806	78,892	9,212	0	222,245	—	—	—	—
1977	120,378	123,015	13,142	3,631,108	46,274	16,877	430,316	125,225	33,999	2,021	13,842	75,363
1978	142,873	118,100	12,222	3,821,135	84,627	12,217	591,667	170,313	42,574	3,536	28,604	95,599
1979	209,695	195,222	19,770	4,148,573	89,622	28,601	631,250	213,975	44,748	2,150	29,106	137,971
1980	203,056	236,697	19,210	4,382,716	102,483	22,916	777,317	221,382	32,909	2,877	32,481	153,115
1981	288,611	276,748	18,413	4,751,449	117,319	44,197	988,524	283,759	48,387	2,718	37,643	195,011
1982	334,083	365,583	22,585	5,028,072	83,855	37,361	1,198,245	320,760	51,939	3,793	41,216	223,812
1983	379,805	455,905	31,003	5,277,447	98,048	38,233	1,183,219	288,967	48,780	3,300	47,074	189,813
1984	346,649	571,190	35,629	5,686,834	134,063	54,222	1,534,136	282,462	47,607	6,879	47,092	180,884
1985	404,265	801,169	33,127	6,019,069	164,500	65,127	1,678,783	362,935	69,737	5,782	56,776	230,640
1986	385,321	915,475	42,588	6,470,049	144,983	23,734	1,738,936	414,720	57,248	7,640	47,288	302,544
1987	412,150	932,465	39,788	6,784,699	221,085	25,502	2,065,710	461,604	68,226	7,272	62,923	323,183
1988	594,107	1,016,244	36,023	6,949,190	203,400	22,494	2,410,153	515,953	74,747	8,242	53,774	379,190
1989	607,639	1,192,320	79,515	7,376,173	203,995	31,701	2,499,567	469,956	80,315	13,890	61,440	314,311
1990	679,431	1,368,631	72,938	7,784,316	278,567	32,966	2,346,066	474,111	78,317	9,429	66,251	320,114
1991	721,058	1,433,091	71,813	8,126,477	311,856	30,967	2,649,762	531,666	81,227	15,861	108,324	326,254
1992	631,241	1,688,593	90,080	8,480,871	423,708	28,843	3,593,215	598,789	65,426	13,836	120,387	399,140
1993	642,967	1,712,117	91,693	9,298,624	377,863	25,464	3,682,397	698,290	61,319	20,701	123,919	492,351
1994	675,424	1,868,682	87,381	9,622,849	388,858	33,937	3,526,210	714,859	66,878	15,098	131,816	501,067
1995	716,427	1,977,969	94,008	10,481,616	469,043	25,167	3,877,285	553,500	58,676	17,897	88,221	388,706

Note appears at end of table

TABLE Ea457–488   State intergovernmental expenditure, by function: 1902–1995 *Continued*

		Environment and housing				Administration and general control					
			Sanitation			Administration					
Fiscal year	Parks and recreation	Housing and community development	Total	Sewerage	Solid waste	Financial	Judicial	Other	General support	Utility	Other
	Ea478	Ea479	Ea480	Ea481	Ea482	Ea483	Ea484	Ea485	Ea486	Ea487	Ea488
	Thousand dollars	Thousand dollars	Thousand dollars	Thousand dollars	Thousand dollars	Thousand dollars	Thousand dollars	Thousand dollars	Thousand dollars	Thousand dollars	Thousand dollars
1902	—	—	—	—	—	—	—	—	5,000	—	0
1913	—	—	—	—	—	—	—	—	5,000	—	0
1922	—	—	—	—	—	—	—	—	35,000	—	1,000
1927	—	—	—	—	—	—	—	—	98,000	—	3,000
1932	—	—	—	—	—	—	—	—	140,000	—	6,000
1934	—	—	—	—	—	—	—	—	145,000	—	281,000
1936	—	—	—	—	—	—	—	—	163,000	—	151,000
1938	—	—	—	—	—	—	—	—	180,000	—	17,000
1940	—	—	—	—	—	—	—	—	181,000	—	21,000
1942	—	—	—	—	—	—	—	—	224,000	—	19,000
1944	—	—	—	—	—	—	—	—	274,000	—	24,000
1946	—	—	—	—	—	—	—	—	357,000	—	42,000
1948	—	—	—	—	—	—	—	—	428,000	—	107,000
1950	—	—	—	—	—	—	—	—	482,000	—	175,000
1952	—	8,000	—	—	—	—	—	—	549,000	—	120,000
1953	—	11,000	—	—	—	—	—	—	592,000	—	103,000
1954	—	12,000	—	—	—	—	—	—	600,000	—	110,000
1955	—	13,000	—	—	—	—	—	—	591,000	—	121,000
1956	—	18,000	—	—	—	—	—	—	631,000	—	141,000
1957	—	17,000	—	—	—	4,000	—	—	668,000	—	152,000
1958	—	21,000	—	—	—	4,000	—	—	687,000	—	173,000
1959	—	26,000	—	—	—	4,000	—	—	725,000	—	155,000
1960	—	26,000	—	—	—	5,000	—	—	806,000	—	173,000
1961	—	30,000	—	—	—	5,000	—	—	821,000	—	179,000
1962	—	35,000	—	—	—	3,000	—	—	839,000	—	183,000
1963	—	43,000	—	—	—	5,000	—	—	1,012,000	—	206,000
1964	—	48,000	—	—	—	5,000	—	—	1,053,000	—	249,000
1965	—	57,000	—	—	—	5,000	—	—	1,102,000	—	233,000
1966	—	60,000	—	—	—	5,000	—	—	1,361,000	—	302,000
1967	—	67,000	—	—	—	6,000	—	—	1,585,000	—	316,000
1968	—	83,000	—	—	—	9,000	—	—	1,993,000	—	384,000
1969	—	92,000	—	—	—	8,000	—	—	2,135,000	—	443,000
1970	—	97,000	—	—	—	10,000	—	—	2,958,000	—	430,000
1971	—	143,000	—	—	—	14,000	—	—	3,258,000	—	574,000
1972	—	115,122	—	—	—	13,435	—	—	3,752,327	—	721,520
1973	—	166,035	—	—	—	12,638	—	—	4,279,646	—	1,277,730
1974	—	162,703	—	—	—	10,541	—	—	4,803,875	—	1,822,025
1975	—	224,921	—	—	—	8,405	—	—	5,129,333	—	2,361,302
1976	—	192,361	—	—	—	10,322	—	—	5,673,843	—	3,182,647
1977	135,160	174,734	495,739	495,739	—	18,241	77,850	20,537	6,372,543	—	2,024,019
1978	220,469	172,692	388,500	388,500	—	22,364	61,489	29,542	6,819,438	—	2,727,397
1979	239,424	209,886	497,278	497,278	—	31,492	175,400	28,354	8,224,338	—	2,760,536
1980	271,717	270,913	439,288	439,288	—	37,563	75,767	36,853	8,643,789	—	2,728,262
1981	287,322	286,368	476,249	476,249	—	59,058	86,013	42,598	9,570,248	—	2,705,348
1982	308,520	290,344	562,631	562,631	—	66,066	101,336	35,134	10,044,372	—	2,422,171
1983	218,578	347,685	567,849	567,849	—	70,456	125,867	15,116	10,364,144	—	2,376,791
1984	193,813	488,045	459,427	459,427	—	88,094	168,950	8,182	10,744,740	—	2,843,203
1985	237,881	505,588	583,670	583,670	—	72,629	195,104	15,812	12,319,623	—	3,922,549
1986	277,248	683,368	669,848	669,848	—	86,943	265,993	6,666	13,383,912	—	3,279,815
1987	259,256	820,912	564,114	564,114	—	93,854	313,901	9,501	14,245,089	—	3,365,863
1988	354,422	1,025,387	879,390	870,046	9,344	80,790	346,661	13,690	14,896,991	—	3,451,380
1989	238,251	1,140,267	731,872	717,094	14,778	100,616	459,530	13,839	15,749,681	—	3,662,739
1990	323,117	1,132,490	871,359	794,339	77,020	100,809	542,759	10,402	16,565,106	8,993	3,810,733
1991	333,787	1,067,445	869,100	761,246	107,854	108,121	837,350	20,872	16,977,032	14,956	4,126,093
1992	328,519	1,062,020	862,454	709,143	153,311	101,992	1,174,355	16,841	16,368,139	29,246	4,517,338
1993	334,498	1,032,137	860,173	708,967	151,206	97,696	1,176,207	20,776	17,690,986	30,466	4,685,184
1994	395,639	1,099,052	949,827	705,910	243,917	88,967	1,121,974	15,267	18,017,293	34,799	6,535,289
1995	438,426	1,381,353	963,839	702,994	260,845	141,922	1,141,879	14,018	18,996,435	42,354	6,160,414

(continued)

TABLE Ea457–488   State intergovernmental expenditure, by function: 1902–1995   *Continued*

[1] Includes only non-institutional corrections.

Source

Figures are from data files provided by the Census of Governments. For published versions through 1982, see U.S. Department of Commerce, "Historical Statistics on Government Finance and Employment," in *Census of Governments, 1982*, volume 6, pp. 225–64.

Documentation

See the text for Table Ea24–51.

Series Ea487. Intergovernmental expenditures for utilities were not reported until 1976.

TABLE Ea489–518   Local government revenue, by source: 1902–1995

Contributed by John Joseph Wallis

		Intergovernmental				Direct			
							General		
								Taxes	
Fiscal year	Total revenue	General	Total	From federal	From state	Total	Total	Total	Property
	Ea489	Ea490	Ea491	Ea492	Ea493	Ea494	Ea495	Ea496	Ea497
	Thousand dollars	Thousand dollars	Thousand dollars	Thousand dollars	Thousand dollars	Thousand dollars	Thousand dollars	Thousand dollars	Thousand dollars
1902	914,000	854,000	56,000	4,000	52,000	858,000	798,000	704,000	624,000
1913	1,755,000	1,637,000	97,000	6,000	91,000	1,658,000	1,540,000	1,308,000	1,192,000
1922	4,148,000	3,866,000	321,000	9,000	312,000	3,827,000	3,545,000	3,069,000	2,973,000
1927	6,333,000	5,903,000	605,000	9,000	596,000	5,728,000	5,298,000	4,479,000	4,360,000
1932	6,192,000	5,690,000	811,000	10,000	801,000	5,381,000	4,879,000	4,274,000	4,159,000
1934	6,363,000	5,820,000	1,401,000	83,000	1,318,000	4,962,000	4,419,000	3,933,000	3,803,000
1936	6,793,000	6,179,000	1,646,000	229,000	1,417,000	5,147,000	4,533,000	4,083,000	3,865,000
1938	7,329,000	6,651,000	1,683,000	167,000	1,516,000	5,646,000	4,968,000	4,473,000	4,196,000
1940	7,724,000	6,939,000	1,932,000	278,000	1,654,000	5,792,000	5,007,000	4,497,000	4,170,000
1942	8,114,000	7,122,000	1,836,000	56,000	1,780,000	6,278,000	5,286,000	4,625,000	4,273,000
1944	8,535,000	7,340,000	1,870,000	28,000	1,842,000	6,665,000	5,470,000	4,703,000	4,361,000
1946	9,561,000	8,227,000	2,145,000	53,000	2,092,000	7,416,000	6,082,000	5,157,000	4,737,000
1948	13,167,000	11,373,000	3,501,000	218,000	3,283,000	9,666,000	7,872,000	6,599,000	5,850,000
1950	16,101,000	14,014,000	4,428,000	211,000	4,217,000	11,673,000	9,586,000	7,984,000	7,042,000
1952	19,398,000	16,952,000	5,281,000	237,000	5,044,000	14,117,000	11,671,000	9,466,000	8,282,000
1953	21,007,000	18,371,000	5,684,000	300,000	5,384,000	15,323,000	12,687,000	10,356,000	9,010,000
1954	22,402,000	19,562,000	5,933,000	298,000	5,635,000	16,468,000	13,629,000	10,978,000	9,577,000
1955	24,166,000	21,092,000	6,355,000	368,000	5,987,000	17,811,000	14,737,000	11,886,000	10,323,000
1956	26,352,000	23,137,000	6,899,000	309,000	6,590,000	19,453,000	16,238,000	12,992,000	11,282,000
1957	29,021,000	25,531,000	7,664,000	343,000	7,321,000	21,357,000	17,866,000	14,286,000	12,385,000
1958	31,348,000	27,723,000	8,378,000	404,000	7,974,000	22,970,000	19,345,000	15,461,000	13,514,000
1959	33,602,000	29,621,000	8,888,000	489,000	8,399,000	24,714,000	20,733,000	16,531,000	14,417,000
1960	37,358,000	33,027,000	10,114,000	592,000	9,522,000	27,243,000	22,912,000	18,081,000	15,798,000
1961	40,516,000	35,899,000	10,904,000	719,000	10,185,000	29,612,000	24,995,000	19,804,000	17,370,000
1962	43,185,000	38,346,000	11,642,000	763,000	10,879,000	31,544,000	26,705,000	20,993,000	18,414,000
1963	46,573,000	41,218,000	12,689,000	890,000	11,799,000	33,885,000	28,530,000	22,164,000	19,401,000
1964	49,617,000	44,084,000	13,829,000	956,000	12,873,000	35,788,000	30,256,000	23,542,000	20,519,000
1965	53,408,000	47,528,000	15,165,000	1,155,000	14,010,000	38,242,000	32,362,000	25,116,000	21,817,000
1966	59,268,000	53,172,000	17,863,000	1,472,000	16,391,000	41,404,000	35,310,000	27,267,000	23,836,000
1967	64,608,000	58,235,000	20,188,000	1,753,000	18,434,000	44,419,000	38,045,000	29,074,000	25,186,000
1968	70,171,000	63,181,000	22,295,000	1,954,000	20,342,000	47,875,000	40,886,000	31,171,000	26,835,000
1969	79,274,000	71,943,000	26,082,000	2,245,000	23,837,000	53,192,000	45,861,000	34,781,000	29,692,000
1970	89,082,000	80,916,000	29,525,000	2,605,000	26,920,000	59,557,000	51,392,000	38,833,000	32,963,000
1971	100,993,000	91,964,000	34,473,000	3,391,000	31,081,000	66,521,000	57,491,000	43,434,000	36,726,000
1972	114,893,852	105,243,328	39,694,601	4,551,187	35,143,414	75,199,251	65,548,727	49,739,576	41,620,016
1973	129,225,407	118,391,500	47,865,809	7,902,809	39,963,000	81,359,598	70,525,691	53,032,373	43,970,167
1974	143,368,978	131,567,380	54,874,641	10,188,264	44,686,377	88,494,337	76,692,739	56,465,714	46,403,401
1975	159,845,557	146,307,019	61,953,884	10,886,000	51,067,884	97,891,673	84,353,135	61,310,135	50,039,787
1976	178,414,514	162,931,222	69,745,486	13,576,362	56,169,124	108,669,028	93,185,736	67,557,415	54,883,562
1977	196,457,848	179,044,944	76,831,368	16,554,395	60,276,973	119,626,480	102,213,576	74,851,555	60,267,427
1978	214,518,674	194,783,781	84,053,920	19,392,699	64,661,221	130,464,754	110,729,861	80,380,945	64,057,784
1979	234,630,155	211,985,923	94,777,276	20,615,691	74,161,585	139,852,879	117,208,647	80,606,056	62,453,456
1980	258,298,246	232,452,825	102,425,443	21,136,161	81,289,282	155,872,803	130,027,382	86,387,462	65,606,638
1981	287,834,451	257,179,114	111,443,293	22,426,599	89,016,694	176,391,158	145,735,821	94,776,196	72,020,163
1982	315,321,536	281,044,731	116,618,683	21,255,783	95,362,900	198,702,853	164,426,048	103,782,685	78,951,931
1983	337,831,010	298,393,594	119,399,341	21,021,042	98,378,299	218,431,669	178,994,253	112,996,447	85,824,019
1984	366,039,263	323,118,467	126,614,573	20,795,053	105,819,520	239,424,690	196,503,894	123,398,568	92,595,090
1985	402,478,796	354,118,663	138,104,309	21,724,148	116,380,161	264,374,487	216,014,354	134,473,386	99,772,444
1986	434,801,864	380,713,919	147,256,447	20,432,556	126,823,891	287,545,417	233,457,472	144,997,398	107,356,355
1987	470,872,069	411,584,075	156,263,375	19,394,525	136,868,850	314,608,694	255,320,700	158,293,470	116,502,518
1988	495,044,201	433,976,603	162,713,429	17,123,501	145,589,928	332,330,772	271,263,174	171,594,883	127,190,902
1989	532,053,756	468,590,218	175,240,543	17,588,489	157,652,054	356,813,213	293,349,675	184,478,283	137,107,461
1990	578,195,066	510,324,209	188,725,200	18,449,199	170,276,001	389,469,866	321,599,009	201,130,083	149,765,146
1991	612,181,816	541,752,492	201,832,731	19,172,591	182,660,140	410,349,085	339,919,761	214,794,023	161,771,738
1992	655,215,792	579,082,765	217,996,448	20,106,789	197,889,659	437,219,344	361,086,317	228,679,193	172,973,029
1993	681,910,413	604,358,621	226,686,374	21,389,991	205,296,383	455,224,039	377,672,247	240,450,676	181,947,538
1994	720,899,894	639,301,915	242,084,112	24,041,736	218,042,376	478,815,782	397,217,803	252,209,559	188,755,008
1995	757,400,420	676,360,812	259,093,195	26,286,202	232,806,993	498,307,225	417,267,617	261,429,791	193,932,941

(continued)

TABLE Ea489-518   Local government revenue, by source: 1902–1995   *Continued*

					Direct					
					General					
				Taxes						
	Sales and gross receipts			Income				Charges and miscellaneous		
	Total	General	Select	Total	Individual	Corporate	Other	Total	Charges	Miscellaneous
	Ea498	Ea499	Ea500	Ea501	Ea502 [1]	Ea503 [1]	Ea504	Ea505	Ea506	Ea507
Fiscal year	Thousand dollars	Thousand dollars	Thousand dollars	Thousand dollars	Thousand dollars	Thousand dollars	Thousand dollars	Thousand dollars	Thousand dollars	Thousand dollars
1902	0	—	—	0	0	0	80,000	94,000	—	—
1913	3,000	—	—	0	0	0	113,000	232,000	—	—
1922	20,000	—	—	0	0	0	76,000	476,000	—	—
1927	25,000	—	—	0	0	0	94,000	819,000	—	—
1932	26,000	—	—	0	0	0	89,000	605,000	—	—
1934	30,000	—	—	0	0	0	100,000	486,000	—	—
1936	90,000	—	—	0	0	0	128,000	450,000	—	—
1938	120,000	—	—	0	0	0	157,000	495,000	—	—
1940	130,000	—	—	19,000	18,000	1,000	178,000	510,000	—	—
1942	133,000	—	—	30,000	27,000	3,000	189,000	661,000	—	—
1944	136,000	—	—	31,000	26,000	5,000	175,000	767,000	—	—
1946	183,000	—	—	38,000	33,000	5,000	199,000	925,000	—	—
1948	400,000	—	—	51,000	44,000	7,000	298,000	1,273,000	—	—
1950	484,000	—	—	71,000	64,000	7,000	387,000	1,602,000	—	—
1952	627,000	369,000	258,000	93,000	85,000	8,000	464,000	2,205,000	1,535,000	670,000
1953	718,000	427,000	291,000	103,000	96,000	7,000	525,000	2,331,000	1,625,000	706,000
1954	703,000	408,000	296,000	129,000	123,000	6,000	569,000	2,651,000	1,811,000	839,000
1955	779,000	453,000	326,000	150,000	143,000	7,000	634,000	2,851,000	2,019,000	832,000
1956	889,000	546,000	343,000	164,000	164,000	0	657,000	3,246,000	2,287,000	959,000
1957	1,031,000	656,000	376,000	191,000	191,000	0	679,000	3,580,000	2,536,000	1,044,000
1958	1,079,000	699,000	379,000	215,000	215,000	0	653,000	3,885,000	2,757,000	1,127,000
1959	1,150,000	747,000	404,000	230,000	230,000	0	734,000	4,202,000	3,088,000	1,114,000
1960	1,339,000	875,000	464,000	254,000	254,000	0	690,000	4,831,000	3,536,000	1,294,000
1961	1,432,000	921,000	510,000	258,000	258,000	0	744,000	5,192,000	3,745,000	1,447,000
1962	1,456,000	958,000	498,000	309,000	309,000	0	814,000	5,711,000	4,077,000	1,634,000
1963	1,583,000	1,065,000	518,000	313,000	313,000	0	867,000	6,365,000	4,639,000	1,726,000
1964	1,806,000	1,170,000	635,000	376,000	376,000	0	841,000	6,714,000	4,744,000	1,970,000
1965	2,059,000	1,270,000	789,000	433,000	433,000	0	807,000	7,245,000	5,278,000	1,968,000
1966	2,041,000	1,352,000	688,000	472,000	472,000	0	918,000	8,044,000	5,766,000	2,278,000
1967	1,956,000	1,201,000	756,000	916,000	916,000	0	1,016,000	8,971,000	6,285,000	2,686,000
1968	1,932,000	1,204,000	728,000	1,077,000	1,077,000	0	1,327,000	9,714,000	6,894,000	2,821,000
1969	2,470,000	1,595,000	875,000	1,381,000	1,381,000	0	1,238,000	11,080,000	7,845,000	3,235,000
1970	3,068,000	1,951,000	1,118,000	1,629,000	1,629,000	0	1,173,000	12,558,000	8,770,000	3,788,000
1971	3,662,000	2,339,000	1,323,000	1,747,000	1,747,000	0	1,299,000	14,058,000	9,819,000	4,239,000
1972	4,267,192	2,727,030	1,540,162	2,230,645	2,230,645	0	1,621,723	15,809,151	11,067,275	4,741,876
1973	4,924,015	3,199,277	1,724,738	2,406,430	2,406,430	0	1,731,761	17,493,318	12,322,000	5,171,318
1974	5,541,699	3,702,268	1,839,431	2,413,116	2,413,116	0	2,107,498	20,227,025	13,571,236	6,655,789
1975	6,468,477	4,321,571	2,146,906	2,635,363	2,635,363	0	2,166,508	23,043,000	15,151,805	7,891,195
1976	7,155,789	4,711,188	2,444,601	3,127,093	3,127,093	0	2,390,971	25,628,321	17,667,962	7,960,359
1977	8,278,187	5,471,639	2,806,548	3,753,764	3,753,764	0	2,552,177	27,362,021	19,096,934	8,265,087
1978	9,326,070	6,192,993	3,133,077	4,071,478	4,071,478	0	2,925,613	30,348,916	21,146,559	9,202,357
1979	10,578,797	7,053,118	3,525,679	4,309,335	4,309,335	0	3,264,468	36,602,591	24,609,830	11,992,761
1980	12,071,798	8,160,082	3,911,716	4,990,283	4,990,283	0	3,718,743	43,639,920	27,828,205	15,811,715
1981	13,220,187	9,229,264	3,990,923	5,531,191	5,531,191	0	4,004,655	50,959,625	31,462,728	19,496,897
1982	14,824,020	10,216,411	4,607,609	6,097,264	5,070,647	1,026,617	3,909,470	60,643,363	35,877,140	24,766,223
1983	16,352,029	11,250,492	5,101,537	6,445,504	5,340,360	1,105,144	4,374,895	65,997,806	39,442,978	26,554,828
1984	18,296,175	12,648,007	5,648,168	7,215,833	5,586,670	1,629,163	5,291,470	73,105,326	43,284,309	29,821,017
1985	20,956,356	14,662,940	6,293,416	7,974,444	6,453,452	1,520,992	5,770,142	81,540,968	46,824,816	34,716,152
1986	22,627,845	15,888,897	6,738,948	8,536,434	6,948,283	1,588,151	6,476,764	88,460,074	50,412,853	38,047,221
1987	24,725,268	17,372,245	7,353,023	9,665,805	7,718,315	1,947,490	7,399,879	97,027,230	55,546,336	41,480,894
1988	26,121,934	18,158,782	7,963,152	10,272,215	8,216,192	2,056,023	8,009,832	99,668,291	60,122,390	39,545,901
1989	27,766,920	19,183,300	8,583,620	11,048,357	8,988,069	2,060,288	8,555,545	108,871,392	66,023,650	42,847,742
1990	30,815,406	21,584,650	9,230,756	11,378,697	9,563,494	1,815,203	9,170,834	120,468,926	72,795,400	47,673,526
1991	32,035,507	22,283,336	9,752,171	11,947,499	10,061,922	1,885,577	9,039,279	125,125,738	77,901,213	47,224,525
1992	33,595,859	23,267,024	10,328,835	12,671,961	10,642,945	2,029,016	9,438,344	132,407,124	85,363,659	47,043,465
1993	35,105,649	24,187,022	10,918,627	13,342,345	11,120,367	2,221,978	10,055,144	137,221,571	91,967,092	45,254,479
1994	37,757,270	26,034,273	11,722,997	14,309,478	11,682,120	2,627,358	11,387,803	145,008,244	100,148,471	44,859,773
1995	40,417,947	27,930,016	12,487,931	14,651,265	12,320,470	2,330,795	12,427,638	155,837,826	107,279,790	48,558,036

Note appears at end of table

TABLE Ea489–518   Local government revenue, by source: 1902–1995   *Continued*

		Direct									
	Utility and liquor store							Insurance trust			
		Utility								Unemployment compensation	
	Total	Total	Water	Electric	Gas	Transit	Liquor store	Total	Employee retirement	Total	Payroll taxes
	Ea508	Ea509	Ea510	Ea511	Ea512	Ea513	Ea514	Ea515	Ea516	Ea517 [2]	Ea518
Fiscal year	Thousand dollars	Thousand dollars	Thousand dollars	Thousand dollars	Thousand dollars	Thousand dollars	Thousand dollars	Thousand dollars	Thousand dollars	Thousand dollars	Thousand dollars
1902	60,000	60,000	56,000	3,000	1,000	0	0	0	0	0	0
1913	116,000	116,000	99,000	16,000	1,000	0	0	2,000	2,000	0	0
1922	266,000	266,000	175,000	72,000	6,000	13,000	0	16,000	16,000	0	0
1927	403,000	403,000	247,000	111,000	10,000	35,000	0	27,000	27,000	0	0
1932	463,000	463,000	317,000	111,000	10,000	25,000	0	39,000	39,000	0	0
1934	500,000	499,000	342,000	115,000	10,000	32,000	1,000	43,000	43,000	0	0
1936	564,000	558,000	369,000	131,000	17,000	41,000	6,000	50,000	50,000	0	0
1938	615,000	605,000	371,000	169,000	18,000	47,000	10,000	63,000	58,000	5,000	4,000
1940	717,000	704,000	401,000	220,000	25,000	58,000	13,000	68,000	61,000	7,000	6,000
1942	904,000	887,000	439,000	251,000	27,000	170,000	17,000	88,000	80,000	8,000	7,000
1944	1,105,000	1,066,000	521,000	305,000	32,000	208,000	39,000	90,000	86,000	4,000	4,000
1946	1,235,000	1,169,000	556,000	348,000	38,000	227,000	66,000	99,000	96,000	3,000	3,000
1958	1,654,000	1,565,000	640,000	474,000	52,000	399,000	89,000	140,000	137,000	3,000	3,000
1950	1,902,000	1,808,000	705,000	574,000	61,000	468,000	94,000	185,000	181,000	4,000	4,000
1952	2,184,000	2,071,000	839,000	683,000	70,000	479,000	113,000	262,000	256,000	5,000	4,000
1953	2,357,000	2,237,000	939,000	713,000	85,000	500,000	120,000	280,000	275,000	5,000	4,000
1954	2,522,000	2,403,000	971,000	787,000	90,000	554,000	119,000	317,000	313,000	4,000	3,000
1955	2,726,000	2,609,000	1,092,000	870,000	104,000	544,000	117,000	347,000	343,000	4,000	3,000
1956	2,835,000	2,718,000	1,162,000	887,000	127,000	542,000	117,000	380,000	376,000	5,000	3,000
1957	3,062,000	2,944,000	1,235,000	1,011,000	157,000	541,000	118,000	429,000	423,000	6,000	4,000
1958	3,153,000	3,041,000	1,256,000	1,096,000	173,000	516,000	112,000	471,000	464,000	6,000	4,000
1959	3,451,000	3,320,000	1,388,000	1,178,000	190,000	565,000	131,000	530,000	525,000	6,000	5,000
1960	3,749,000	3,613,000	1,529,000	1,307,000	196,000	581,000	136,000	583,000	575,000	7,000	6,000
1961	3,997,000	3,856,000	1,621,000	1,450,000	197,000	588,000	141,000	620,000	612,000	8,000	6,000
1962	4,174,000	4,026,000	1,725,000	1,422,000	236,000	643,000	148,000	665,000	656,000	8,000	6,000
1963	4,629,000	4,474,000	1,865,000	1,728,000	242,000	639,000	155,000	726,000	716,000	10,000	8,000
1964	4,780,000	4,616,000	1,917,000	1,718,000	266,000	715,000	164,000	752,000	742,000	10,000	7,000
1965	5,085,000	4,908,000	2,004,000	1,833,000	295,000	776,000	177,000	795,000	785,000	10,000	8,000
1966	5,258,000	5,069,000	2,115,000	1,911,000	300,000	743,000	189,000	837,000	826,000	11,000	9,000
1967	5,441,000	5,246,000	2,187,000	1,881,000	319,000	860,000	195,000	933,000	921,000	12,000	9,000
1968	5,945,000	5,683,000	2,313,000	2,119,000	332,000	919,000	262,000	1,044,000	1,034,000	9,000	7,000
1969	6,176,000	5,931,000	2,464,000	2,166,000	366,000	934,000	245,000	1,155,000	1,145,000	10,000	7,000
1970	6,866,000	6,608,000	2,687,000	2,385,000	401,000	1,135,000	258,000	1,299,000	1,288,000	11,000	7,000
1971	7,545,000	7,276,000	2,980,000	2,644,000	439,000	1,213,000	269,000	1,484,000	1,470,000	12,000	8,000
1972	7,924,083	7,700,733	3,171,464	2,831,019	436,404	1,261,846	223,350	1,726,441	1,713,885	12,556	9,396
1973	8,912,221	8,621,598	3,463,401	3,355,030	535,981	1,267,186	290,623	1,921,686	1,905,083	16,603	13,826
1974	9,698,169	9,392,073	3,712,052	3,762,593	551,214	1,366,214	306,096	2,103,429	2,084,803	18,626	15,960
1975	11,205,651	10,867,284	4,142,177	4,689,262	625,178	1,410,667	338,367	2,332,887	2,290,887	42,000	20,192
1976	12,930,358	12,572,928	4,463,077	5,819,137	724,668	1,566,046	357,430	2,552,934	2,437,934	115,000	25,037
1977	14,605,224	14,299,124	4,989,110	6,764,913	862,238	1,682,863	306,100	2,807,680	2,725,402	82,278	35,358
1978	16,661,488	16,290,189	5,504,965	8,042,140	1,008,554	1,734,530	371,299	3,073,405	2,999,058	74,347	44,162
1979	18,987,464	18,593,914	6,242,000	9,145,860	1,296,679	1,909,375	393,550	3,656,768	3,581,972	74,796	56,296
1980	21,490,422	21,055,277	6,756,290	10,455,328	1,808,756	2,034,903	435,145	4,354,999	4,294,705	60,294	58,743
1981	25,267,646	24,793,993	7,698,993	12,405,462	2,219,838	2,469,700	473,653	5,387,691	5,260,173	127,518	56,792
1982	29,100,455	28,611,848	8,451,224	14,560,670	2,670,730	2,929,224	488,607	5,176,350	5,107,970	68,380	50,980
1983	32,044,563	31,552,642	9,497,973	16,135,930	3,046,919	2,871,820	491,921	7,392,853	7,290,113	102,740	55,175
1984	35,216,684	34,735,850	10,434,565	17,750,034	3,501,467	3,049,784	480,834	7,704,112	7,616,383	87,729	69,341
1985	39,098,027	38,615,999	11,947,110	19,726,642	3,573,130	3,369,117	482,028	9,262,106	9,218,382	43,724	81,315
1986	41,448,604	40,942,857	13,201,571	20,875,526	3,290,894	3,574,866	505,747	12,639,341	12,545,318	94,023	82,529
1987	44,370,782	43,844,981	14,334,160	22,763,013	2,970,735	3,777,073	525,801	14,917,212	14,831,498	85,714	70,991
1988	46,719,358	46,195,747	15,242,884	24,249,115	2,904,894	3,798,854	523,611	14,348,240	14,262,405	85,835	73,256
1989	50,189,466	49,661,981	16,678,336	26,072,547	2,923,722	3,987,376	527,485	13,274,072	13,209,731	64,341	50,381
1990	52,429,933	51,896,747	17,564,549	27,151,979	3,038,162	4,142,057	533,186	15,440,924	15,369,683	71,241	57,887
1991	54,262,503	53,704,754	17,920,336	28,273,303	3,005,366	4,505,749	557,749	16,166,821	16,093,266	73,555	60,430
1992	56,672,597	56,096,564	19,340,419	29,165,235	3,050,759	4,540,151	576,033	19,460,430	19,362,562	97,868	76,063
1993	58,500,319	57,929,458	20,323,913	29,588,255	3,327,162	4,690,128	570,861	19,051,473	18,844,490	206,983	108,626
1994	63,238,886	62,684,183	22,556,031	31,383,978	3,705,594	5,038,580	554,703	18,359,093	18,164,886	194,207	125,102
1995	65,352,250	64,788,475	23,734,372	32,189,145	3,582,026	5,282,932	563,775	15,687,358	15,503,535	183,823	188,799

Note appears on next page

(continued)

TABLE Ea489–518   Local government revenue, by source: 1902–1995   *Continued*

[1] Minor amounts of corporation income tax are included under individual income tax.
[2] Washington, D.C., only.

Source
Figures are from data files provided by the Census of Governments. For published versions through 1982, see U.S. Department of Commerce, "Historical Statistics on Government Finance and Employment," in *Census of Governments, 1982*, volume 6, pp. 225–64.

Documentation
See the text for Table Ea24–51.

TABLE Ea519–529   Local government expenditure, by character and object: 1902–1995

Contributed by John Joseph Wallis

	Total			Direct							
	Total	Salaries and wages	Intergovernmental	Total	Current operation	Capital outlay			Assistance and subsidies	Interest on debt	Insurance trust
						Total	Construction	Other			
	Ea519	Ea520	Ea521 [1]	Ea522 [1]	Ea523	Ea524	Ea525	Ea526	Ea527	Ea528	Ea529
Fiscal year	Thousand dollars	Thousand dollars	Thousand dollars	Thousand dollars	Thousand dollars	Thousand dollars	Thousand dollars	Thousand dollars	Thousand dollars	Thousand dollars	Thousand dollars
1902	959,000	475,000	—	959,000	682,000	203,000	162,000	41,000	5,000	69,000	0
1913	1,960,000	901,000	—	1,960,000	1,287,000	500,000	400,000	100,000	7,000	159,000	8,000
1922	4,567,000	2,041,000	—	4,567,000	2,915,000	1,216,000	973,000	243,000	30,000	385,000	21,000
1927	6,359,000	2,680,000	—	6,359,000	3,828,000	1,864,000	1,491,000	373,000	50,000	579,000	38,000
1932	6,375,000	2,925,000	—	6,375,000	4,197,000	1,090,000	872,000	218,000	305,000	726,000	57,000
1934	5,699,000	2,618,000	—	5,699,000	3,665,000	788,000	630,000	158,000	459,000	718,000	69,000
1936	6,056,000	2,871,000	—	6,056,000	4,036,000	890,000	712,000	178,000	336,000	717,000	77,000
1938	6,906,000	3,176,000	—	6,906,000	4,466,000	1,157,000	926,000	231,000	546,000	656,000	81,000
1940	7,685,000	3,400,000	—	7,685,000	4,606,000	1,778,000	1,185,000	593,000	558,000	657,000	86,000
1942	7,351,000	3,554,000	—	7,351,000	5,200,000	835,000	681,000	154,000	620,000	584,000	112,000
1944	7,180,000	3,927,000	—	7,180,000	5,669,000	379,000	274,000	105,000	470,000	534,000	128,000
1946	9,093,000	4,705,000	—	9,093,000	6,929,000	937,000	678,000	259,000	606,000	473,000	148,000
1948	13,363,000	6,470,000	—	13,363,000	9,508,000	2,269,000	1,817,000	452,000	952,000	457,000	177,000
1950	17,041,000	7,593,000	—	17,041,000	11,406,000	3,810,000	3,203,000	607,000	1,119,000	504,000	202,000
1952	20,229,000	9,089,000	156,000	20,073,000	13,333,000	4,778,000	4,063,000	715,000	1,097,000	580,000	285,000
1953	21,662,000	9,868,000	191,000	21,471,000	14,393,000	5,058,000	4,291,000	767,000	1,089,000	635,000	296,000
1954	23,814,000	10,851,000	215,000	23,599,000	15,567,000	5,778,000	4,907,000	871,000	1,203,000	723,000	327,000
1955	26,230,000	11,744,000	226,000	26,004,000	16,898,000	6,713,000	5,644,000	1,069,000	1,232,000	807,000	353,000
1956	28,273,000	12,986,000	269,000	28,004,000	18,707,000	6,843,000	5,482,000	1,361,000	1,153,000	910,000	392,000
1957	31,057,000	14,234,000	300,000	30,757,000	20,653,000	7,454,000	6,069,000	1,385,000	1,189,000	1,025,000	436,000
1958	34,023,000	15,723,000	302,000	33,721,000	22,701,000	8,040,000	6,682,000	1,358,000	1,346,000	1,141,000	493,000
1959	36,341,000	17,055,000	205,000	36,136,000	24,594,000	8,292,000	6,786,000	1,506,000	1,438,000	1,287,000	525,000
1960	39,056,000	18,531,000	209,000	38,847,000	26,785,000	8,497,000	6,843,000	1,654,000	1,503,000	1,492,000	570,000
1961	42,641,000	19,937,000	196,000	42,445,000	29,416,000	9,226,000	7,515,000	1,711,000	1,564,000	1,641,000	598,000
1962	45,279,000	21,678,000	226,000	45,053,000	31,446,000	9,577,000	7,665,000	1,912,000	1,590,000	1,789,000	651,000
1963	48,309,000	23,309,000	247,000	48,062,000	33,929,000	9,836,000	7,764,000	2,072,000	1,659,000	1,932,000	706,000
1964	51,199,000	24,902,000	235,000	50,964,000	36,197,000	10,267,000	8,127,000	2,140,000	1,709,000	2,061,000	730,000
1965	55,482,000	26,838,000	262,000	55,221,000	38,999,000	11,360,000	8,905,000	2,456,000	1,891,000	2,191,000	780,000
1966	60,994,000	29,498,000	283,000	60,711,000	43,357,000	12,137,000	9,514,000	2,622,000	2,014,000	2,374,000	830,000
1967	66,648,000	32,439,000	374,000	66,274,000	47,639,000	12,689,000	9,811,000	2,877,000	2,349,000	2,587,000	1,008,000
1968	72,357,000	35,197,000	427,000	71,930,000	51,932,000	13,521,000	10,747,000	2,773,000	2,689,000	2,761,000	1,027,000
1969	82,698,000	40,103,000	546,000	82,152,000	59,126,000	15,539,000	12,294,000	3,245,000	3,217,000	3,128,000	1,141,000
1970	92,522,000	45,212,000	633,000	91,889,000	66,943,000	16,355,000	13,067,000	3,289,000	3,703,000	3,624,000	1,263,000
1971	105,167,000	50,640,000	601,000	104,566,000	75,983,000	18,402,000	14,524,000	3,878,000	4,573,000	4,142,000	1,466,000
1972	118,566,633	57,158,969	566,816	117,999,817	87,035,131	19,340,669	15,398,228	3,942,441	5,211,908	4,811,850	1,600,259
1973	128,253,016	62,011,000	801,550	127,451,466	94,266,000	20,595,000	15,924,000	4,671,000	5,290,028	5,393,771	1,906,667
1974	140,386,724	67,709,737	889,078	139,497,646	104,007,168	22,666,915	17,887,156	4,779,759	4,769,158	5,977,051	2,077,354
1975	162,615,412	75,872,000	1,278,232	161,337,180	120,183,000	27,517,000	21,913,000	5,604,000	4,473,344	6,815,220	2,348,616
1976	181,802,608	83,610,483	1,821,690	179,980,918	136,212,221	28,522,270	23,013,628	5,508,642	5,204,675	7,541,752	2,500,000
1977	196,306,643	90,550,472	1,904,023	194,402,620	149,966,585	28,190,283	22,530,770	5,659,513	5,521,859	8,001,128	2,722,765
1978	211,083,200	97,184,156	2,312,911	208,770,289	163,070,575	28,705,370	22,938,807	5,766,563	5,412,741	8,550,769	3,030,834
1979	233,322,905	105,322,420	1,639,168	231,683,737	179,633,459	34,072,037	27,395,956	6,676,081	5,169,959	9,414,734	3,393,548
1980	260,777,021	115,103,183	1,757,476	259,019,545	199,679,613	39,568,412	31,755,324	7,813,088	5,404,102	10,551,945	3,815,473
1981	288,570,902	125,828,000	1,744,199	286,826,703	220,829,184	43,310,853	34,318,309	8,992,544	5,971,482	12,353,986	4,361,198
1982	313,364,924	134,943,736	1,956,633	311,408,291	241,904,974	43,336,172	34,107,615	9,228,557	6,468,016	14,920,344	4,778,785
1983	335,120,909	144,030,813	3,004,952	332,115,957	258,049,535	44,632,254	34,649,685	9,982,569	6,809,337	17,470,386	5,154,445
1984	359,287,798	154,069,783	3,596,512	355,691,286	276,654,199	45,152,021	34,315,067	10,836,954	7,308,202	20,700,932	5,875,932

TABLE Ea519–529 Local government expenditure, by character and object: 1902–1995 *Continued*

	Total			Direct							
	Total	Salaries and wages	Intergovernmental	Total	Current operation	Capital outlay — Total	Construction	Other	Assistance and subsidies	Interest on debt	Insurance trust
	Ea519	Ea520	Ea521 [1]	Ea522 [1]	Ea523	Ea524	Ea525	Ea526	Ea527	Ea528	Ea529
Fiscal year	Thousand dollars	Thousand dollars	Thousand dollars	Thousand dollars	Thousand dollars	Thousand dollars	Thousand dollars	Thousand dollars	Thousand dollars	Thousand dollars	Thousand dollars
1985	390,782,860	166,249,873	4,029,549	386,753,311	300,187,372	49,241,169	36,776,161	12,465,008	7,865,466	23,208,726	6,250,578
1986	427,875,282	180,526,326	4,790,509	423,084,773	325,279,661	55,899,570	41,410,390	14,489,180	8,426,166	26,769,434	6,709,942
1987	465,420,093	193,523,027	5,251,104	460,168,989	351,284,803	61,633,115	45,988,425	15,644,690	8,760,898	31,002,208	7,487,965
1988	496,346,456	208,757,831	5,160,189	491,186,267	378,011,742	63,652,812	47,176,484	16,476,328	8,927,982	32,595,515	7,998,216
1989	533,172,518	223,126,192	4,901,609	528,270,909	407,576,857	68,822,222	50,424,954	18,397,268	9,554,107	34,319,030	7,998,693
1990	581,240,047	239,819,771	5,836,205	575,403,842	442,084,482	77,577,557	54,340,691	23,236,866	10,325,075	36,547,202	8,869,526
1991	622,910,530	258,727,034	5,401,141	617,509,389	474,927,957	83,712,831	59,006,392	24,706,439	11,579,659	37,343,937	9,945,005
1992	661,744,403	270,638,120	7,369,545	654,374,858	505,126,818	86,394,561	63,293,645	23,100,916	12,465,019	39,532,331	10,856,129
1993	688,289,388	281,053,041	7,359,721	680,929,667	530,600,890	85,747,064	60,548,778	25,198,286	12,779,551	39,973,394	11,828,768
1994	719,138,389	290,277,878	8,772,811	710,365,578	559,890,133	84,606,137	60,342,667	24,263,470	13,103,462	39,990,825	12,775,021
1995	759,368,076	305,517,895	7,930,224	751,437,852	589,657,726	93,611,492	63,898,567	29,712,925	13,355,814	41,164,658	13,648,162

[1] Through 1950, minor amounts of intergovernmental expenditure are not separated, and are included under total direct expenditures.

Source

Figures are from data files provided by the Census of Governments. For published versions through 1982, see U.S. Department of Commerce, "Historical Statistics on Government Finance and Employment," in *Census of Governments, 1982*, volume 6, pp. 225–64.

Documentation

See the text for Table Ea24–51.

In order to compute total expenditures under a different revenue concept, use the data from Table Ea125–131 on the change in debt during the year. See the essay in this chapter for additional information on this matter.

Series Ea521. Covers intergovernmental expenditures to states.

Series Ea528. Includes interest on debt of utilities operated by local governments.

TABLE Ea530–583 Local government expenditure, by function: 1902–1995

Contributed by John Joseph Wallis

	Intergovernmental and direct		Intergovernmental			Direct					
								General			
									Education		
	Total	General	Total	To state	To federal	Total	Total	Total	Elementary	Higher education	Other
	Ea530	Ea531	Ea532 [1]	Ea533	Ea534	Ea535 [1]	Ea536	Ea537	Ea538	Ea539	Ea540
Fiscal year	Thousand dollars	Thousand dollars	Thousand dollars	Thousand dollars	Thousand dollars	Thousand dollars	Thousand dollars	Thousand dollars	Thousand dollars	Thousand dollars	Thousand dollars
1902	959,000	879,000	—	—	0	959,000	879,000	238,000	238,000	—	0
1913	1,960,000	1,767,000	—	—	0	1,960,000	1,767,000	522,000	522,000	—	0
1922	4,567,000	4,187,000	—	—	0	4,567,000	4,187,000	1,541,000	1,541,000	—	0
1927	6,359,000	5,830,000	—	—	0	6,359,000	5,830,000	2,017,000	2,017,000	—	0
1932	6,375,000	5,800,000	—	—	0	6,375,000	5,800,000	2,033,000	2,016,000	17,000	0
1934	5,699,000	5,172,000	—	—	0	5,699,000	5,172,000	1,603,000	1,592,000	11,000	0
1936	6,056,000	5,421,000	—	—	0	6,056,000	5,421,000	1,880,000	1,861,000	19,000	0
1938	6,906,000	6,181,000	—	—	0	6,906,000	6,181,000	2,144,000	2,124,000	20,000	0
1940	7,685,000	6,499,000	—	—	0	7,685,000	6,499,000	2,263,000	2,241,000	22,000	0
1942	7,351,000	6,421,000	—	—	0	7,351,000	6,421,000	2,195,000	2,174,000	21,000	0
1944	7,180,000	6,197,000	—	—	0	7,180,000	6,197,000	2,304,000	2,278,000	26,000	0
1946	9,093,000	7,875,000	—	—	0	9,093,000	7,875,000	2,838,000	2,813,000	25,000	0
1948	13,363,000	11,498,000	—	—	0	13,363,000	11,498,000	4,298,000	4,243,000	55,000	0
1950	17,041,000	14,754,000	—	—	0	17,041,000	14,754,000	5,819,000	5,756,000	63,000	0
1952	20,229,000	17,600,000	156,000	156,000	0	20,073,000	17,444,000	6,824,000	6,737,000	87,000	0
1953	21,662,000	18,807,000	191,000	191,000	0	21,471,000	18,616,000	7,756,000	7,672,000	84,000	0
1954	23,814,000	20,808,000	215,000	215,000	0	23,599,000	20,593,000	8,842,000	8,748,000	94,000	0
1955	26,230,000	22,760,000	226,000	226,000	0	26,004,000	22,534,000	10,003,000	9,902,000	102,000	0
1956	28,273,000	24,661,000	269,000	269,000	0	28,004,000	24,392,000	11,082,000	10,946,000	136,000	0
1957	31,057,000	27,029,000	300,000	300,000	0	30,757,000	26,729,000	11,793,000	11,545,000	248,000	0
1958	34,023,000	29,705,000	302,000	302,000	0	33,721,000	29,403,000	13,192,000	12,915,000	277,000	0
1959	36,341,000	31,775,000	205,000	205,000	0	36,136,000	31,570,000	14,190,000	13,884,000	306,000	0

Notes appear at end of table

(continued)

TABLE Ea530–583   Local government expenditure, by function: 1902–1995 *Continued*

	Intergovernmental and direct		Intergovernmental			Direct					
							General				
								Education			
Fiscal year	Total	General	Total	To state	To federal	Total	Total	Total	Elementary	Higher education	Other
	Ea530	Ea531	Ea532 [1]	Ea533	Ea534	Ea535 [1]	Ea536	Ea537	Ea538	Ea539	Ea540
	Thousand dollars	Thousand dollars	Thousand dollars	Thousand dollars	Thousand dollars	Thousand dollars	Thousand dollars	Thousand dollars	Thousand dollars	Thousand dollars	Thousand dollars
1960	39,056,000	34,301,000	209,000	209,000	0	38,847,000	34,092,000	15,323,000	14,977,000	346,000	0
1961	42,641,000	37,393,000	196,000	196,000	0	42,445,000	37,197,000	16,782,000	16,382,000	400,000	0
1962	45,279,000	40,057,000	226,000	226,000	0	45,053,000	39,831,000	17,946,000	17,538,000	408,000	0
1963	48,309,000	42,571,000	247,000	247,000	0	48,062,000	42,324,000	19,058,000	18,580,000	478,000	0
1964	51,199,000	45,262,000	235,000	235,000	0	50,964,000	45,027,000	20,822,000	20,192,000	630,000	0
1965	55,482,000	48,667,000	262,000	262,000	0	55,221,000	48,405,000	22,382,000	21,777,000	605,000	0
1966	60,994,000	53,963,000	283,000	283,000	0	60,711,000	53,680,000	25,715,000	24,860,000	855,000	0
1967	66,648,000	59,475,000	374,000	374,000	0	66,274,000	59,101,000	28,534,000 [4]	27,290,000	1,204,000	40,000
1968	72,357,000	64,393,000	427,000	427,000	0	71,930,000	63,966,000	30,200,000	28,966,000	1,233,000	0
1969	82,698,000	74,029,000	546,000	546,000	0	82,152,000	73,483,000	34,934,000	33,387,000	1,547,000	0
1970	92,522,000	83,215,000	633,000	633,000	0	91,889,000	82,582,000	38,938,000	37,024,000	1,914,000	0
1971	105,167,000	94,797,000	601,000	601,000	0	104,566,000	94,196,000	43,613,000	41,275,000	2,337,000	0
1972	118,566,633	107,062,819	566,816	566,816	0	117,999,817	106,496,003	48,660,550	46,179,822	2,480,708	20
1973	128,253,016	114,894,395	801,550	801,550	0	127,451,466	114,092,845	51,430,261	48,309,130	3,121,000	131
1974	140,386,724	125,557,052	889,078	889,078	0	139,497,646	124,667,974	56,079,734	52,591,327	3,488,385	22
1975	162,615,412	144,699,906	1,278,232	1,278,232	0	161,337,180	143,421,674	64,956,066	60,949,692	4,006,340	34
1976	181,802,608	161,541,352	1,821,690	1,821,690	0	179,980,918	159,719,662	71,670,031	67,073,463	4,596,566	2
1977	196,306,643	172,842,167	1,904,023	1,904,010	13	194,402,620	170,938,144	75,707,058	70,895,368	4,806,491	5,199
1978	211,083,200	185,309,870	2,312,911	2,312,851	60	208,770,289	182,996,959	81,180,860	76,049,037	5,131,446	377
1979	233,322,905	203,108,854	1,639,168	1,639,127	41	231,683,737	201,469,686	87,931,481	82,552,022	5,379,043	416
1980	260,777,021	225,378,917	1,757,476	1,757,473	3	259,019,545	223,621,441	97,960,203	91,966,037	5,992,589	1,577
1981	288,570,902	246,845,701	1,744,199	1,744,172	27	286,826,703	245,101,502	106,120,744	99,494,409	6,626,116	219
1982	313,364,924	266,312,059	1,956,633	1,956,628	5	311,408,291	264,355,426	111,981,566	104,707,676	7,273,890	0
1983	335,120,909	283,952,009	3,004,952	3,004,845	107	332,115,957	280,947,057	119,291,302	111,967,309	7,323,993	0
1984	359,287,798	305,480,514	3,596,512	3,596,509	3	355,691,286	301,884,002	127,534,780	119,937,560	7,597,220	0
1985	390,782,860	332,489,565	4,029,549	4,029,549	0	386,753,311	328,460,016	139,018,508	130,966,627	8,051,881	0
1986	427,875,282	363,816,396	4,790,509	4,790,509	0	423,084,773	359,025,887	152,558,731	143,951,845	8,606,886	0
1987	465,420,093	397,265,686	5,251,104	5,250,928	176	460,168,989	392,014,582	164,971,269	155,608,841	9,362,428	0
1988	496,346,456	426,906,531	5,160,189	5,155,843	4,346	491,186,267	421,746,342	178,573,683	168,295,809	10,277,874	0
1989	533,172,518	460,477,802	4,901,609	4,900,148	1,461	528,270,909	455,576,193	195,315,571	183,753,656	11,561,915	0
1990	581,240,047	504,152,602	5,836,205	5,834,474	1,731	575,403,842	498,316,397	212,651,520	200,210,969	12,440,551	0
1991	622,910,530	541,682,769	5,401,141	5,399,704	1,437	617,509,389	536,281,628	228,834,051	215,645,345	13,188,706	0
1992	661,744,403	575,187,522	7,369,545	7,346,277	23,268	654,374,858	567,817,977	238,274,926	225,051,702	13,223,224	0
1993	688,289,388	601,353,329	7,359,721	7,357,938	1,783	680,929,667	593,993,608	251,919,373	237,779,724	14,139,649	0
1994	719,138,389	624,910,226	8,772,811	8,728,731	44,080	710,365,578	616,137,415	258,391,264	244,647,430	13,743,368	466
1995	759,368,076	661,593,317	7,930,224	7,872,152	58,072	751,437,852	653,663,093	276,762,760	262,053,236	14,709,524	0

			Direct							
			General							
			Social services and income maintenance							
		Public welfare					Health and hospitals			
			Cash assistance							
	Libraries	Total	Categorical	Noncategorical	Institutional	Other	Total	Hospitals	Health	Employee security administration
	Ea541	Ea542	Ea543	Ea544	Ea545	Ea546	Ea547	Ea548	Ea549	Ea550
Fiscal year	Thousand dollars	Thousand dollars	Thousand dollars	Thousand dollars	Thousand dollars	Thousand dollars	Thousand dollars	Thousand dollars	Thousand dollars	Thousand dollars
1902	—	27,000	—	—	—	27,000	28,000	15,000	13,000	0
1913	—	36,000	—	—	—	36,000	55,000	32,000	23,000	0
1922	—	81,000	—	—	—	81,000	133,000	95,000	38,000	0
1927	—	111,000	—	—	—	111,000	185,000	133,000	52,000	0
1932	—	370,000	—	—	—	370,000	241,000	168,000	73,000	0
1934	—	526,000	—	—	—	526,000	215,000	142,000	73,000	0

TABLE Ea530–583   Local government expenditure, by function: 1902–1995   *Continued*

					Direct				
					General				
					Social services and income maintenance				
		Public welfare				Health and hospitals			
		Cash assistance							
Libraries	Total	Categorical	Noncategorical	Institutional	Other	Total	Hospitals	Health	Employee security administration
Ea541	Ea542	Ea543	Ea544	Ea545	Ea546	Ea547	Ea548	Ea549	Ea550
Fiscal year — Thousand dollars	Thousand dollars	Thousand dollars	Thousand dollars	Thousand dollars	Thousand dollars	Thousand dollars	Thousand dollars	Thousand dollars	Thousand dollars
1936 —	405,000	—	—	—	405,000	246,000	171,000	75,000	0
1938 —	616,000	226,000	320,000	—	70,000	283,000	191,000	92,000	0
1940 —	629,000	290,000	268,000	—	71,000	309,000	214,000	95,000	0
1942 —	702,000	347,000	273,000	—	82,000	292,000	197,000	95,000	0
1944 —	556,000	336,000	134,000	—	86,000	325,000	215,000	110,000	0
1946 —	729,000	425,000	181,000	—	123,000	394,000	259,000	135,000	0
1948 —	1,137,000	653,000	299,000	—	185,000	566,000	404,000	162,000	0
1950 —	1,374,000	673,000	446,000	—	255,000	801,000	596,000	205,000	0
1952 111,000	1,378,000	831,000	266,000	—	281,000	1,053,000	777,000	276,000	0
1953 128,000	1,380,000	853,000	236,000	—	291,000	1,107,000	849,000	258,000	0
1954 138,000	1,512,000	927,000	276,000	—	309,000	1,133,000	873,000	260,000	0
1955 146,000	1,568,000	947,000	285,000	—	336,000	1,185,000	908,000	277,000	0
1956 187,000	1,536,000	946,000	207,000	—	383,000	1,302,000	1,048,000	254,000	0
1957 199,000	1,659,000	1,043,000	146,000	—	470,000	1,549,000	1,246,000	303,000	0
1958 224,000	1,874,000	1,126,000	220,000	—	528,000	1,704,000	1,412,000	292,000	0
1959 243,000	2,012,000	1,203,000	235,000	—	574,000	1,874,000	1,515,000	359,000	0
1960 261,000	2,183,000	1,269,000	234,000	—	680,000	1,898,000	1,571,000	327,000	0
1961 349,000	2,409,000	1,308,000	257,000	—	844,000	2,027,000	1,697,000	330,000	0
1962 332,000	2,575,000	1,394,000	197,000	—	984,000	2,181,000	1,795,000	386,000	0
1963 377,000	2,769,000	1,470,000	189,000		1,110,000	2,351,000	1,965,000	386,000	0
1964 379,000	2,970,000	1,543,000	167,000		1,260,000	2,446,000	2,044,000	402,000	0
1965 414,000	3,317,000	1,719,000	171,000	—	1,427,000	2,660,000	2,208,000	452,000	0
1966 449,000	3,620,000	1,836,000	179,000	—	1,605,000	2,944,000	2,436,000	508,000	0
1967 469,000	3,927,000	2,138,000	212,000	—	1,577,000	3,283,000	2,703,000	580,000	2,000
1968 521,000	4,735,000	2,396,000	292,000	—	2,047,000	3,715,000	3,049,000	666,000	0
1969 579,000	5,646,000	2,863,000	354,000	—	2,429,000	4,262,000	3,429,000	833,000	2,000
1970 646,000	6,477,000	3,368,000	335,000	—	2,774,000	4,880,000	3,861,000	1,019,000	2,000
1971 702,000	7,708,000	4,145,000	428,000	—	3,135,000	5,806,000	4,600,000	1,206,000	3,000
1972 752,658	8,869,194	4,705,922	505,986	—	3,657,286	7,013,760	5,544,178	1,469,582	3,428
1973 811,061	9,435,299	4,752,177	537,851	—	4,145,271	7,338,072	5,744,636	1,593,436	4,282
1974 896,161	9,576,203	4,258,556	510,602	—	4,807,045	8,450,905	6,409,922	2,040,983	4,477
1975 1,032,302	9,733,493	3,926,755	546,589	—	5,260,149	9,878,179	7,416,179	2,462,000	4,681
1976 1,149,887	11,277,907	4,484,769	719,906	—	6,073,232	10,835,616	8,000,727	2,834,889	6,391
1977 1,181,951	11,882,869	4,758,185	763,674	70,522	6,290,488	11,830,067	8,919,959	2,910,108	7,586
1978 1,254,697	11,949,705	4,678,273	734,468	80,438	6,456,526	12,633,431	9,400,194	3,233,237	6,850
1979 1,382,836	11,675,646	4,478,380	691,579	76,171	6,429,516	14,431,717	10,818,107	3,613,610	6,993
1980 1,566,290	12,310,172	4,754,436	649,666	68,461	6,837,609	16,506,855	12,509,675	3,997,180	7,407
1981 1,725,164	13,667,334	5,253,933	717,549	82,988	7,612,864	18,073,176	13,632,907	4,440,269	7,394
1982 1,866,085	14,703,595	5,670,412	797,604	91,497	8,144,082	21,483,606	16,371,184	5,112,422	8,003
1983 2,018,748	14,280,957	5,808,091	1,001,246	109,939	7,361,681	23,284,298	17,718,356	5,565,942	9,617
1984 2,214,186	15,587,759	6,148,959	1,159,243	113,532	8,166,025	24,762,465	18,826,225	5,936,240	10,097
1985 2,465,083	16,888,367	6,514,571	1,350,895	139,659	8,883,242	26,369,675	19,929,649	6,440,026	10,291
1986 2,687,584	17,618,437	6,950,850	1,475,316	159,736	9,032,535	28,037,010	20,858,139	7,178,871	10,433
1987 3,009,426	18,949,840	7,273,808	1,487,090	214,819	9,974,123	29,885,229	22,189,264	7,695,965	10,591
1988 3,198,204	19,887,285	7,457,248	1,470,734	226,555	10,732,748	32,558,476	23,865,882	8,692,594	11,297
1989 3,523,437	21,826,309	7,991,685	1,562,422	253,723	12,018,479	35,397,575	25,762,329	9,635,246	10,342
1990 3,840,078	23,950,651	8,700,484	1,624,591	282,792	13,342,784	39,091,897	27,860,294	11,231,603	11,035
1991 4,160,502	26,850,209	9,741,582	1,838,077	300,815	14,969,735	42,606,117	30,020,230	12,585,887	11,555
1992 4,424,888	29,245,128	10,353,802	2,111,217	282,868	16,497,241	46,929,119	33,135,983	13,793,136	14,405
1993 4,388,842	30,021,700	10,628,044	2,151,507	145,741	17,096,408	50,253,263	35,136,074	15,117,189	14,674
1994 4,683,723	31,585,136	10,962,326	2,141,136	157,444	18,324,230	53,433,955	37,036,998	16,396,957	14,369
1995 5,004,510	32,688,956	11,257,973	2,097,841	167,282	19,165,860	56,459,729	39,043,733	17,415,996	14,003

(continued)

TABLE Ea530–583 Local government expenditure, by function: 1902–1995 *Continued*

					Direct						
					General						
	Transportation					Public safety				Environment and housing	
	Highways	Air	Parking	Water	Transit	Police	Fire	Corrections	Protective inspection and regulation	Natural resources	Parks and recreation
	Ea551	Ea552	Ea553	Ea554	Ea555	Ea556	Ea557	Ea558	Ea559	Ea560	Ea561
Fiscal year	Thousand dollars	Thousand dollars	Thousand dollars	Thousand dollars	Thousand dollars	Thousand dollars	Thousand dollars	Thousand dollars	Thousand dollars	Thousand dollars	Thousand dollars
1902	171,000	—	—	—	0	50,000	40,000	—	—	0	29,000
1913	393,000	—	—	—	0	88,000	76,000	—	—	0	57,000
1922	991,000	—	—	—	0	186,000	158,000	—	—	0	85,000
1927	1,295,000	—	—	—	0	263,000	203,000	—	—	0	153,000
1932	898,000	—	—	—	0	303,000	210,000	—	—	46,000	147,000
1934	771,000	—	—	—	0	276,000	189,000	—	—	74,000	126,000
1936	671,000	—	—	—	0	295,000	205,000	—	—	100,000	104,000
1938	835,000	—	—	—	0	329,000	231,000	—	—	94,000	130,000
1940	780,000	—	—	—	0	331,000	235,000	—	—	74,000	162,000
1942	700,000	—	—	—	0	354,000	236,000	—	—	55,000	128,000
1944	660,000	—	—	—	0	373,000	251,000	—	—	68,000	123,000
1946	1,059,000	—	—	—	0	434,000	294,000	—	—	95,000	179,000
1948	1,526,000	—	—	—	0	579,000	406,000	—	•	152,000	243,000
1950	1,745,000	—	—	—	0	691,000	488,000	—	—	202,000	304,000
1952	2,094,000	—	—	—	0	833,000	586,000	114,000	—	237,000	324,000
1953	2,207,000	92,000	—	117,000	0	919,000	598,000	127,000	—	173,000	374,000
1954	2,272,000	106,000	—	155,000	0	1,000,000	653,000	147,000	—	199,000	424,000
1955	2,553,000	108,000	—	120,000	0	1,091,000	694,000	167,000	—	196,000	509,000
1956	2,586,000	165,000	—	150,000	0	1,172,000	737,000	172,000	—	236,000	541,000
1957	2,941,000	225,000	—	133,000	0	1,290,000	810,000	187,000	—	244,000	608,000
1958	3,060,000	237,000	—	156,000	0	1,396,000	873,000	164,000	—	246,000	685,000
1959	3,178,000	284,000	—	152,000	0	1,482,000	914,000	258,000	—	263,000	729,000
1960	3,358,000	316,000	—	157,000	0	1,612,000	995,000	253,000	—	347,000	770,000
1961	3,614,000	386,000	—	215,000	0	1,756,000	1,087,000	284,000	—	421,000	857,000
1962	3,722,000	338,000	83,000	201,000	0	1,854,000	1,124,000	282,000	—	398,000	886,000
1963	3,710,000	330,000	112,000	231,000	0	1,985,000	1,186,000	282,000	—	491,000	978,000
1964	3,814,000	319,000	114,000	202,000	0	2,051,000	1,222,000	297,000	—	650,000	1,022,000
1965	4,007,000	369,000	108,000	172,000	0	2,201,000	1,306,000	343,000	—	518,000	1,104,000
1966	4,146,000	380,000	128,000	171,000	0	2,391,000	1,376,000	356,000	—	507,000	1,187,000
1967	4,510,000	400,000	144,000	198,000	0	2,609,000	1,499,000	392,000	—	542,000	1,291,000
1968	4,663,000	448,000	105,000	220,000	0	2,894,000	1,623,000	432,000	—	517,000	1,412,000
1969	5,003,000	634,000	137,000	263,000	0	3,316,000	1,793,000	477,000	—	517,000	1,645,000
1970	5,383,000	791,000	158,000	271,000	0	3,806,000	2,024,000	575,000	—	574,000	1,888,000
1971	5,792,000	913,000	159,000	343,000	0	4,430,000	2,303,000	691,000	—	597,000	2,109,000
1972	6,274,281	1,134,244	171,164	363,939	0	5,105,533	2,579,037	803,015	—	652,654	2,318,139
1973	6,543,105	1,174,574	205,054	432,176	0	5,763,000	2,804,000	908,396	—	654,633	2,560,700
1974	7,310,033	1,076,548	214,003	453,064	0	6,143,768	3,036,776	1,076,603	—	743,594	2,950,649
1975	8,269,604	1,164,466	301,879	530,012	0	7,212,000	3,522,000	1,274,782	—	855,064	3,461,616
1976	9,047,146	1,211,143	333,920	471,906	0	8,118,936	3,897,534	1,424,269	—	1,021,341	3,864,224
1977	9,204,799	1,159,718	298,181	497,993	82,272	8,875,925	4,412,298	1,599,458	461,904	965,419	3,890,773
1978	9,950,866	1,372,599	269,653	518,477	38,159	9,622,770	4,801,757	1,824,132	563,656	984,387	4,257,169
1979	11,361,165	1,648,225	324,011	740,607	43,258	10,382,999	5,146,503	1,959,800	642,559	1,111,841	4,742,069
1980	12,650,054	2,140,910	343,053	808,312	73,249	11,433,406	5,718,232	2,235,012	753,941	1,384,781	5,246,736
1981	13,915,391	2,427,103	377,345	999,186	59,351	12,677,414	6,335,761	2,576,162	832,612	1,450,667	5,735,017
1982	14,417,229	2,518,469	406,483	859,862	83,445	14,115,176	7,025,556	2,946,369	882,496	1,402,580	6,139,674
1983	15,501,539	2,680,815	454,483	1,031,562	113,473	15,335,249	7,582,075	3,496,236	934,039	1,537,250	6,588,272
1984	16,266,023	3,198,515	483,985	927,792	84,620	16,468,904	8,201,727	3,927,091	1,004,450	1,758,511	6,955,796
1985	17,854,273	3,270,627	591,729	958,807	121,309	17,842,649	8,916,631	4,468,744	1,093,467	1,961,734	7,587,492
1986	19,177,263	3,802,841	682,460	1,176,987	135,290	19,357,085	9,586,526	5,102,054	1,360,645	2,176,381	8,430,959
1987	20,866,818	4,437,854	760,559	1,215,789	136,639	21,106,606	10,452,893	5,866,750	1,531,445	2,588,399	9,142,395
1988	21,889,204	4,897,129	784,884	1,359,651	132,682	22,362,680	11,752,856	6,699,292	1,676,525	2,444,401	10,056,048
1989	22,786,888	5,244,621	754,578	1,290,385	250,219	23,632,423	11,932,217	7,372,243	1,771,224	2,492,254	10,575,926
1990	24,592,896	5,848,184	749,235	1,464,049	191,580	26,090,096	13,186,081	8,737,353	2,025,345	2,895,113	11,854,922
1991	26,025,310	6,473,768	813,557	1,561,624	193,692	27,986,386	13,796,137	9,549,735	2,140,732	2,850,780	13,186,590
1992	26,873,714	7,312,444	874,455	1,394,531	240,820	30,568,494	14,751,172	10,417,441	2,188,885	2,936,275	13,313,679
1993	26,313,567	8,375,306	697,892	1,595,838	221,475	31,446,305	15,372,647	10,539,467	2,196,615	2,721,291	13,505,294
1994	28,255,305	8,626,122	729,078	1,993,479	244,667	33,319,715	16,122,797	11,004,292	2,284,375	2,836,895	13,876,373
1995	30,215,692	7,614,441	800,118	1,705,811	221,966	35,319,595	17,009,481	11,765,785	2,472,044	3,270,775	14,923,988

TABLE Ea530–583   Local government expenditure, by function: 1902–1995   *Continued*

				Direct								
				General								
	Environment and housing			Administration and general control								
Fiscal year	Housing and community development	Sanitation			Financial administration and general control	Financial administration	Judicial	General public building	Other	Interest on general debt	Miscellaneous commercial activities	Other
		Total	Sewerage	Solid waste								
	Ea562	Ea563	Ea564	Ea565	Ea566 [2]	Ea567	Ea568	Ea569	Ea570	Ea571	Ea572	Ea573
	Thousand dollars	Thousand dollars	Thousand dollars	Thousand dollars	Thousand dollars	Thousand dollars	Thousand dollars	Thousand dollars	Thousand dollars	Thousand dollars	Thousand dollars	Thousand dollars
1902	0	51,000	—	—	118,000	—	—	—	—	58,000	—	69,000
1913	0	97,000	—	—	173,000	—	—	—	—	133,000	—	137,000
1922	0	189,000	—	—	244,000	—	—	—	—	337,000	—	242,000
1927	0	312,000	—	—	316,000	—	—	—	—	501,000	—	474,000
1932	0	223,000	—	—	356,000	—	—	—	—	627,000	—	346,000
1934	0	177,000	—	—	324,000	—	—	—	—	620,000	—	271,000
1936	0	204,000	—	—	370,000	—	—	—	—	614,000	—	327,000
1938	3,000	226,000	—	—	396,000	—	—	—	—	545,000	—	349,000
1940	230,000	207,000	—	—	410,000	—	—	—	—	523,000	—	346,000
1942	236,000	229,000	—	—	414,000	—	—	—	—	443,000	—	437,000
1944	46,000	245,000	—	—	437,000	—	—	—	—	398,000	—	411,000
1946	114,000	370,000	—	—	511,000	—	—	—	—	337,000	—	521,000
1948	176,000	670,000	—	—	614,000	—	—	—	—	313,000	—	818,000
1950	452,000	834,000	—	—	724,000	—	—	—	—	349,000	—	971,000
1952	766,000	992,000	—	—	832,000	—	—	—	—	408,000	—	892,000
1953	628,000	908,000	—	—	864,000	—	—	—	—	452,000	—	786,000
1954	609,000	1,058,000	—	—	956,000	—	—	254,000	—	525,000	—	864,000
1955	497,000	1,142,000	—	—	1,005,000	—	—	291,000	—	587,000	—	963,000
1956	435,000	1,326,000	835,000	492,000	1,083,000	—	—	278,000	—	675,000	—	1,007,000
1957	503,000	1,443,000	906,000	537,000	1,195,000	—	—	351,000	—	755,000	—	1,195,000
1958	599,000	1,505,000	933,000	572,000	1,274,000	—	—	397,000	—	848,000	—	1,366,000
1959	612,000	1,609,000	1,011,000	598,000	1,384,000	—	—	447,000	—	963,000	—	1,423,000
1960	850,000	1,727,000	1,103,000	624,000	1,459,000	—	—	413,000	—	1,134,000	—	1,449,000
1961	936,000	1,774,000	1,103,000	672,000	1,512,000	545,000	—	470,000	—	1,240,000	—	1,548,000
1962	1,145,000	1,958,000	1,272,000	686,000	1,574,000	554,000	—	472,000	—	1,376,000	—	1,856,000
1963	1,235,000	2,187,000	1,464,000	723,000	1,608,000	582,000	—	503,000	—	1,478,000	—	1,956,000
1964	1,125,000	2,267,000	1,515,000	752,000	1,697,000	604,000	—	505,000	—	1,590,000	—	2,040,000
1965	1,227,000	2,360,000	1,567,000	793,000	1,825,000	662,000	—	674,000	—	1,668,000	—	2,424,000
1966	1,382,000	2,571,000	1,707,000	864,000	1,950,000	678,000	—	660,000	—	1,796,000	—	2,611,000
1967	1,441,000	2,523,000	1,635,000	888,000	2,139,000	734,000	—	695,000	—	2,007,000	—	3,191,000
1968	1,613,000	2,707,000	1,732,000	975,000	2,337,000	800,000	—	763,000	—	2,138,000	—	3,686,000
1969	1,887,000	2,969,000	1,895,000	1,074,000	2,609,000	901,000	—	915,000	—	2,457,000	—	4,353,000
1970	2,115,000	3,413,000	2,167,000	1,246,000	2,961,000	1,007,000	—	947,000	—	2,875,000	—	4,805,000
1971	2,522,000	4,087,000	2,646,000	1,441,000	—	1,141,000	—	1,040,000	—	3,328,000	—	6,909,000
1972	2,699,793	4,845,944	3,259,222	1,586,722	—	1,278,765	—	1,121,137	—	3,893,703	—	7,955,065
1973	2,901,078	5,321,344	3,603,809	1,717,535	—	1,430,591	—	1,253,888	—	4,351,205	—	8,770,126
1974	3,078,754	5,995,188	4,080,301	1,914,887	—	1,580,978	—	1,393,826	—	4,803,202	32,343	9,771,165
1975	3,052,673	7,438,293	5,262,293	2,176,000	—	1,810,363	—	1,746,590	—	5,510,549	41,739	11,625,323
1976	2,878,685	8,239,553	5,937,310	2,302,243	—	2,015,389	—	1,991,150	—	6,129,049	28,926	14,106,659
1977	3,209,633	9,184,918	6,811,404	2,373,514	—	2,265,957	894,169	1,884,646	3,603,494	6,277,434	28,786	11,530,836
1978	3,534,405	9,569,692	6,842,314	2,727,378	—	2,832,592	969,473	1,973,185	3,792,174	6,714,465	31,367	12,350,438
1979	4,510,179	11,480,270	8,488,225	2,992,045	—	3,379,322	981,779	2,176,204	4,151,576	7,196,815	25,048	14,036,783
1980	5,731,062	12,880,052	9,558,015	3,322,037	—	3,725,057	1,002,637	2,292,470	4,575,199	7,984,077	27,325	14,264,949
1981	6,683,994	14,553,069	10,776,250	3,776,819	—	3,957,924	1,116,141	2,426,481	5,133,971	9,287,617	46,802	14,915,682
1982	8,095,979	14,581,354	10,447,349	4,134,005	—	4,436,848	2,919,771	2,418,142	4,043,006	11,144,500	63,442	15,812,190
1983	7,849,771	15,400,820	11,036,413	4,364,407	—	4,652,845	4,308,598	2,692,525	3,655,747	12,884,519	124,030	15,238,287
1984	8,465,422	15,979,379	11,269,824	4,709,555	—	5,073,922	4,620,586	2,927,449	3,896,760	15,559,130	133,565	15,841,088
1985	9,343,688	17,069,836	11,857,832	5,212,004	—	5,524,792	5,038,420	3,152,502	4,255,684	17,444,546	146,915	17,064,247
1986	10,096,102	18,800,526	12,965,998	5,834,528	—	6,128,626	5,576,527	3,146,982	4,728,716	20,187,518	138,721	18,321,483
1987	10,461,511	21,241,792	14,742,393	6,499,399	—	6,507,056	6,130,391	3,741,330	5,187,867	23,304,410	150,675	20,357,048
1988	11,729,860	22,880,105	15,773,672	7,106,433	—	6,700,661	6,720,580	3,668,291	5,760,946	24,951,529	162,310	20,887,763
1989	12,935,823	24,575,935	16,462,855	8,113,080	—	7,421,593	7,607,671	3,894,792	5,960,506	26,239,862	108,370	22,655,429
1990	13,755,767	26,926,453	17,673,242	9,253,211	—	7,701,804	8,663,781	4,283,362	6,480,501	28,207,277	126,397	24,991,020
1991	14,888,493	29,019,677	18,842,867	10,176,810	—	8,002,408	9,458,228	4,598,154	7,460,201	28,840,718	129,141	26,843,863
1992	15,853,612	31,173,792	20,100,540	11,073,252	—	8,682,291	10,137,920	4,687,037	7,773,632	30,742,827	124,581	28,881,909
1993	16,977,166	33,212,778	21,687,852	11,524,926	—	8,890,378	10,348,488	4,529,629	7,633,349	31,081,015	70,591	31,666,665
1994	17,854,503	32,976,044	20,305,398	12,670,646	—	9,289,675	10,972,865	5,151,702	8,099,738	31,241,086	81,104	33,069,153 [5]
1995	19,423,643	35,452,479	22,121,014	13,331,465	—	9,760,441	11,634,413	5,333,681	8,508,786	32,484,717	82,904	34,732,375

Notes appear at end of table

(continued)

TABLE Ea530–583   Local government expenditure, by function: 1902–1995   *Continued*

	Direct									
	Utility and liquor store							Insurance trust		
		Utility								Unemployment compensation
	Total	Total	Water	Electric	Gas	Transit	Liquor store	Total	Employee retirement	
	Ea574	Ea575	Ea576	Ea577	Ea578	Ea579	Ea580	Ea581	Ea582	Ea583 [3]
Fiscal year	Thousand dollars	Thousand dollars	Thousand dollars	Thousand dollars	Thousand dollars	Thousand dollars	Thousand dollars	Thousand dollars	Thousand dollars	Thousand dollars
1902	80,000	80,000	71,000	8,000	1,000	0	0	0	0	0
1913	186,000	186,000	159,000	25,000	1,000	1,000	0	7,000	7,000	0
1922	359,000	359,000	255,000	75,000	4,000	25,000	0	21,000	21,000	0
1927	491,000	491,000	349,000	94,000	10,000	38,000	0	38,000	38,000	0
1932	518,000	518,000	320,000	92,000	7,000	99,000	0	57,000	57,000	0
1934	458,000	457,000	292,000	102,000	6,000	57,000	1,000	69,000	69,000	0
1936	558,000	553,000	344,000	117,000	11,000	81,000	5,000	77,000	77,000	0
1938	644,000	636,000	385,000	156,000	13,000	82,000	8,000	81,000	81,000	0
1940	1,100,000	1,090,000	404,000	257,000	18,000	411,000	10,000	86,000	84,000	2,000
1942	818,000	804,000	368,000	216,000	19,000	201,000	14,000	112,000	104,000	8,000
1944	855,000	822,000	355,000	227,000	25,000	215,000	33,000	128,000	124,000	4,000
1946	1,070,000	1,014,000	426,000	305,000	36,000	247,000	56,000	148,000	145,000	3,000
1948	1,688,000	1,612,000	628,000	438,000	47,000	499,000	76,000	177,000	174,000	3,000
1950	2,085,000	2,005,000	849,000	534,000	52,000	570,000	80,000	202,000	198,000	4,000
1952	2,344,000	2,246,000	973,000	631,000	61,000	581,000	98,000	285,000	283,000	2,000
1953	2,559,000	2,457,000	1,084,000	723,000	68,000	582,000	102,000	295,000	293,000	2,000
1954	2,679,000	2,577,000	1,150,000	751,000	90,000	586,000	102,000	327,000	324,000	3,000
1955	3,116,000	3,023,000	1,479,000	819,000	125,000	600,000	93,000	353,000	349,000	4,000
1956	3,220,000	3,119,000	1,461,000	895,000	128,000	636,000	101,000	392,000	388,000	4,000
1957	3,592,000	3,494,000	1,584,000	1,102,000	156,000	652,000	98,000	437,000	432,000	5,000
1958	3,824,000	3,720,000	1,624,000	1,260,000	150,000	686,000	104,000	493,000	487,000	6,000
1959	4,041,000	3,923,000	1,764,000	1,273,000	174,000	711,000	118,000	525,000	518,000	7,000
1960	4,181,000	4,066,000	1,881,000	1,244,000	191,000	750,000	115,000	570,000	565,000	5,000
1961	4,651,000	4,532,000	2,106,000	1,461,000	210,000	755,000	119,000	599,000	592,000	7,000
1962	4,571,000	4,445,000	2,077,000	1,378,000	219,000	771,000	126,000	651,000	645,000	6,000
1963	5,032,000	4,899,000	2,209,000	1,572,000	228,000	891,000	133,000	706,000	696,000	10,000
1964	5,207,000	5,067,000	2,255,000	1,614,000	251,000	948,000	140,000	730,000	719,000	11,000
1965	6,036,000	5,886,000	2,505,000	1,983,000	272,000	1,127,000	150,000	780,000	770,000	10,000
1966	6,201,000	6,042,000	2,716,000	1,949,000	263,000	1,114,000	159,000	830,000	821,000	9,000
1967	6,163,000	6,006,000	2,587,000	1,847,000	287,000	1,285,000	157,000	1,009,000	1,002,000	7,000
1968	6,937,000	6,721,000	2,740,000	2,123,000	299,000	1,559,000	216,000	1,027,000	1,019,000	8,000
1969	7,528,000	7,316,000	3,019,000	2,216,000	332,000	1,750,000	212,000	1,141,000	1,133,000	8,000
1970	8,043,000	7,820,000	3,211,000	2,486,000	370,000	1,753,000	223,000	1,263,000	1,253,000	10,000
1971	8,905,000	8,675,000	3,432,000	2,816,000	410,000	2,018,000	230,000	1,466,000	1,450,000	16,000
1972	9,903,555	9,715,084	3,739,652	3,281,198	403,802	2,290,432	188,471	1,600,259	1,581,300	18,959
1973	11,451,954	11,203,769	4,084,324	3,760,603	493,351	2,865,491	248,185	1,906,667	1,881,565	25,102
1974	12,752,318	12,486,898	4,669,237	4,151,719	504,608	3,161,334	265,420	2,077,354	2,047,330	30,024
1975	15,566,890	15,276,454	5,439,936	5,279,905	579,772	3,976,841	290,436	2,348,616	2,282,616	66,000
1976	17,761,256	17,451,298	5,929,099	6,429,170	661,100	4,431,929	309,958	2,500,000	2,377,000	123,000
1977	20,741,711	20,462,833	6,359,479	8,330,668	803,071	4,969,615	278,878	2,722,765	2,636,812	85,953
1978	22,742,496	22,416,058	6,861,992	9,698,543	915,345	4,940,178	326,438	3,030,834	2,962,935	67,899
1979	26,820,503	26,472,652	8,018,640	11,517,012	1,231,445	5,705,555	347,851	3,393,548	3,335,837	57,711
1980	31,582,631	31,197,736	9,136,874	13,730,811	1,714,707	6,615,344	384,895	3,815,473	3,751,090	64,383
1981	37,364,003	36,943,009	10,483,096	16,134,577	2,229,756	8,095,580	420,994	4,361,198	4,275,230	85,968
1982	42,274,080	41,840,263	11,333,908	18,633,782	2,566,390	9,306,183	433,817	4,778,785	4,679,498	99,287
1983	46,014,455	45,578,803	12,341,365	20,125,542	3,007,745	10,104,151	435,652	5,154,445	5,050,129	104,316
1984	47,931,352	47,503,873	12,514,629	21,246,045	3,343,704	10,399,495	427,479	5,875,932	5,803,493	72,439
1985	52,042,717	51,610,779	14,228,393	23,296,461	3,467,916	10,618,009	431,938	6,250,578	6,183,903	66,675
1986	57,348,944	56,900,191	16,108,290	26,072,385	3,291,241	11,428,275	448,753	6,709,942	6,643,599	66,343
1987	60,666,442	60,201,035	18,357,281	26,795,876	2,894,924	12,152,954	465,407	7,487,965	7,413,892	74,073
1988	61,441,709	60,982,213	18,762,022	26,766,909	2,824,352	12,628,930	459,496	7,998,216	7,929,124	69,092
1989	64,696,023	64,227,846	20,396,021	27,831,967	2,836,354	13,163,504	468,177	7,998,693	7,928,070	70,623
1990	68,217,919	67,743,630	21,965,616	28,526,624	2,984,737	14,266,653	474,289	8,869,526	8,792,741	76,785
1991	71,282,756	70,782,014	23,413,435	28,586,295	2,965,070	15,817,214	500,742	9,945,005	9,826,143	118,862
1992	75,700,752	75,187,899	24,624,754	29,986,683	3,074,512	17,501,950	512,853	10,856,129	10,729,455	126,674
1993	75,107,291	74,604,261	24,433,440	29,679,861	3,268,840	17,222,120	503,030	11,828,768	11,617,153	211,615
1994	81,453,142	80,963,418	26,440,864	31,229,611	3,505,307	19,787,636	489,724	12,775,021	12,617,747	157,274
1995	84,126,597	83,628,813	27,863,125	31,431,767	3,429,503	20,904,418	497,784	13,648,162	13,476,211	171,951

TABLE Ea530–583   Local government expenditure, by function: 1902–1995   *Continued*

[1] Through 1950, minor amounts of intergovernmental expenditure to states are included under total direct expenditures.

[2] Through 1970, series Ea566 includes all expenditures on general government administration; thereafter (and earlier for some functions), individual activities are reported separately. Some activities reported separately may have been included under other general expenditures during the earlier period.

[3] Washington, D.C., only.

[4] Includes minor amounts of expenditure by municipalities on behalf of school districts, not shown separately.

[5] Includes $229,000 spent on veterans' services.

Source

Data in this table are taken from spreadsheets provided by the Census of Governments. Published versions of the data through 1982 can be found in U.S. Department of Commerce, "Historical Statistics on Government Finance and Employment." in *Census of Governments, 1982*, volume 6, pp. 225–64.

Documentation

See the text for Table Ea24–51.

FEDERAL GOVERNMENT FINANCES

John Joseph Wallis

TABLE Ea584–587   Federal government finances – revenue, expenditure, and debt: 1789–1939[1, 2]

Contributed by John Joseph Wallis

Fiscal year	Revenue Ea584 [3] Thousand dollars	Expenditure Ea585 [3] Thousand dollars	Surplus or deficit Ea586 Thousand dollars	Public debt Ea587 Thousand dollars	Fiscal year	Revenue Ea584 [3] Thousand dollars	Expenditure Ea585 [3] Thousand dollars	Surplus or deficit Ea586 Thousand dollars	Public debt Ea587 Thousand dollars
1789–1791 [4]	4,419	4,269	150	77,228	1845	29,970	22,937	7,033	15,925
1792	3,670	5,080	−1,410	80,359	1846	29,700	27,767	1,933	15,550
1793	4,653	4,482	171	78,427	1847	26,496	57,281	−30,786	38,827
1794	5,432	6,991	−1,559	80,748	1848	35,736	45,377	−9,641	47,045
1795	6,115	7,540	−1,425	83,762	1849	31,208	45,052	−13,844	63,062
1796	8,378	5,727	2,651	82,064	1850	43,603	39,543	4,060	63,453
1797	8,689	6,134	2,555	79,229	1851	52,559	47,709	4,850	68,305
1798	7,900	7,677	224	78,409	1852	49,847	44,195	5,652	66,199
1799	7,547	9,666	−2,120	82,976	1853	61,587	48,184	13,403	59,805
1800	10,849	10,786	63	83,038	1854	73,800	58,045	15,755	42,244
1801	12,935	9,395	3,541	80,713	1855	65,351	59,743	5,608	35,588
1802	14,996	7,862	7,134	77,055	1856	74,057	69,571	4,486	31,974
1803	11,064	7,852	3,212	86,427	1857	68,965	67,796	1,170	28,701
1804	11,826	8,719	3,107	82,312	1858	46,655	74,185	−27,530	44,913
1805	13,561	10,506	3,054	75,723	1859	53,486	69,071	−15,585	58,498
1806	15,560	9,804	5,756	69,218	1860	56,065	63,131	−7,066	64,844
1807	16,398	8,354	8,044	65,196	1861	41,510	66,547	−25,037	90,582
1808	17,061	9,932	7,128	57,023	1862	51,987	474,762	−422,774	524,178
1809	7,773	10,281	−2,507	53,173	1863	112,697	714,741	−602,043	1,119,774
1810	9,384	8,157	1,228	48,006	1864	264,627	865,323	−600,696	1,815,831
1811	14,424	8,058	6,365	45,210	1865	333,715	1,297,555	−963,841	2,677,929
1812	9,801	20,281	−10,480	55,963	1866	558,033	520,809	37,223	2,755,764
1813	14,340	31,682	−17,341	81,488	1867	490,634	357,543	133,091	2,650,168
1814	11,182	34,721	−23,539	99,834	1868	405,638	377,340	28,298	2,583,446
1815	15,729	32,708	−16,979	127,335	1869	370,944	322,865	48,078	2,545,111
1816	47,678	30,587	17,091	123,492	1870	411,255	309,654	101,602	2,436,453
1817	33,099	21,844	11,255	103,467	1871	383,324	292,177	91,147	2,322,052
1818	21,585	19,825	1,760	95,530	1872	374,107	277,518	96,589	2,209,991
1819	24,603	21,464	3,140	91,016	1873	333,738	290,345	43,393	2,151,210
1820	17,881	18,261	−380	89,987	1874	304,979	302,634	2,345	2,159,933
1821	14,573	15,811	−1,237	93,547	1875	288,000	274,623	13,377	2,156,277
1822	20,232	15,000	5,232	90,876	1876	294,096	265,101	28,995	2,130,846
1823	20,541	14,707	5,834	90,270	1877	281,406	241,334	40,072	2,107,760
1824	19,381	20,327	−945	83,788	1878	257,764	236,964	20,800	2,159,418
1825	21,841	15,857	5,984	81,054	1879	273,827	266,948	6,879	2,298,913
1826	25,260	17,036	8,225	73,987	1880	333,527	267,643	65,884	2,090,909
1827	22,966	16,139	6,827	67,475	1881	360,782	260,713	100,069	2,019,286
1828	24,764	16,395	8,369	58,421	1882	403,525	257,981	145,544	1,856,916
1829	24,828	15,203	9,624	48,565	1883	398,288	265,408	132,879	1,721,959
1830	24,844	15,143	9,701	39,123	1884	348,520	244,126	104,394	1,625,307
1831	28,527	15,248	13,279	24,322	1885	323,691	260,227	63,464	1,578,551
1832	31,866	17,289	14,577	7,012	1886	336,440	242,483	93,957	1,555,660
1833	33,948	23,018	10,931	4,760	1887	371,403	267,932	103,471	1,465,485
1834	21,792	18,628	3,164	38	1888	379,266	267,925	111,341	1,384,632
1835	35,430	17,573	17,857	38	1889	387,050	299,289	87,761	1,249,471
1836	50,827	30,868	19,959	337	1890	403,081	318,041	85,040	1,122,397
1837	24,954	37,243	−12,289	3,308	1891	392,612	365,774	26,839	1,005,807
1838	26,303	33,865	−7,562	10,434	1892	354,938	345,023	9,914	968,219
1839	31,483	26,899	4,584	3,573	1893	385,820	383,478	2,342	961,432
1840	19,480	24,318	−4,837	5,251	1894	306,355	367,525	−61,170	1,016,898
1841	16,860	26,566	−9,706	13,594					
1842	19,976	25,206	−5,230	20,201					
1843	8,303	11,858	−3,555	32,743					
1844	29,321	22,338	6,984	23,462					

Notes appear at end of table

TABLE Ea584–587   Federal government finances – revenue, expenditure, and debt: 1789–1939   *Continued*

Fiscal year	Revenue Ea584 [3] Thousand dollars	Expenditure Ea585 [3] Thousand dollars	Surplus or deficit Ea586 Thousand dollars	Public debt Ea587 Thousand dollars	Fiscal year	Revenue Ea584 [3] Thousand dollars	Expenditure Ea585 [3] Thousand dollars	Surplus or deficit Ea586 Thousand dollars	Public debt Ea587 Thousand dollars
1895	324,729	356,195	−31,466	1,096,913	1920	6,648,898	6,357,677	291,222	24,299,321
1896	338,142	352,179	−14,037	1,222,729	1921	5,570,790	5,061,785	509,005	23,977,451
1897	347,722	365,774	−18,052	1,226,794	1922	4,025,901	3,289,404	736,496	22,963,382
1898	405,321	443,369	−38,047	1,232,743	1923	3,852,795	3,140,287	712,508	22,349,707
1899	515,961	605,072	−89,112	1,436,701	1924	3,871,214	2,907,847	963,367	21,250,813
1900	567,241	520,861	46,380	1,263,417	1925	3,640,805	2,923,762	717,043	20,516,194
1901	587,685	524,617	63,068	1,221,572	1926	3,795,108	2,929,964	865,144	19,643,216
1902	562,478	485,234	77,244	1,178,031	1927	4,012,794	2,857,429	1,155,365	18,511,907
1903	561,881	517,006	44,875	1,159,406	1928	3,900,329	2,961,245	939,083	17,604,293
1904	541,087	583,660	−42,573	1,136,259	1929	3,861,589	3,127,199	734,391	16,931,088
1905	544,275	567,279	−23,004	1,132,357	1930	4,057,884	3,320,211	737,673	16,185,310
1906	594,984	570,202	24,782	1,142,523	1931	3,115,557	3,577,434	−461,877	16,801,281
1907	665,860	579,129	86,732	1,147,178	1932	1,923,892	4,659,182	−2,735,290	19,487,002
1908	601,862	659,196	−57,334	1,177,690	1933	1,996,844	4,598,496	−2,601,652	22,538,673
1909	604,320	693,744	−89,423	1,148,315	1934	3,014,970	6,644,602	−3,629,632	27,053,141
1910	675,512	693,617	−18,105	1,146,940	1935	3,705,956	6,497,008	−2,791,052	28,700,893
1911	701,833	691,202	10,631	1,153,985	1936	3,997,059	8,421,608	−4,424,549	33,778,543
1912	692,609	689,881	2,728	1,193,839	1937	4,955,613	7,733,033	−2,777,421	36,424,614
1913	714,463	714,864	−401	1,193,048	1938	5,588,012	6,764,628	−1,176,617	37,164,740
1914	725,117	725,525	−408	1,188,235	1939	4,979,066	8,841,224	−3,862,158	40,439,532
1915	683,417	746,093	−62,676	1,191,264					
1916	761,445	712,967	48,478	1,225,146					
1917	1,100,500	1,953,857	−853,357	2,975,619					
1918	3,645,240	12,677,359	−9,032,120	12,455,225					
1919	5,130,042	18,492,665	−13,362,623	25,484,506					

[1] Refunds of receipts are excluded starting 1913; comparable data are not available for prior years.

[2] Certain interfund transactions are excluded starting 1932; for prior years, the amounts of such transactions are insignificant.

[3] Through 1912, total; thereafter, net.

[4] Total for three-year period, except for series Ea587.

Source

U.S. Department of the Treasury, *Statistical Appendix to the Annual Report of the Secretary of the Treasury* (1970), pp. 8–13 and 60–61, and (1971), pp. 8–12.

Documentation

General Note for the Federal Government Finances Tables

Figures in Tables Ea584–661 and Ea679–730 are based on categories used by the federal government to report its financial data. "Internal revenue" refers to taxes that are raised from taxes within the borders of the United States. It is in contrast to "customs," which are taxes on foreign trade, and certain "other" revenues, such as land sales, trust revenues, sale of government assets, and other transactions. The budget concepts used by the federal government have changed over time. The figures in these tables differ from those reported for the federal government in Tables Ea10–246, which are constructed using Census of Government budget concepts. See the essay in this chapter for additional information on such matters.

Table Ea584–587

Figures exclude receipts from borrowing and expenditures for debt repayment.

Series Ea584. See Table Ea588–593 for a breakdown of this series.

Series Ea585. See Table Ea636–643 for a breakdown of this series, as well as additional data covering 1940–1970.

Series Ea587. Figures are as of end of period.

TABLE Ea588–593   Federal government revenue, by source: 1789–1939[1, 2]

Contributed by John Joseph Wallis

				Other receipts		Refunds, transfers, interfund transactions
	Total	Customs	Internal revenue	Total	Sales of public lands	
	Ea588 [3]	Ea589	Ea590	Ea591	Ea592	Ea593
Fiscal year	Thousand dollars	Thousand dollars	Thousand dollars	Thousand dollars	Thousand dollars	Thousand dollars
1789–1791 [4]	4,419	4,399	—	19	—	—
1792	3,670	3,443	209	18	—	—
1793	4,653	4,255	338	60	—	—
1794	5,432	4,801	274	357	—	—
1795	6,115	5,588	338	188	—	—
1796	8,378	6,568	475	1,334	5	—
1797	8,689	7,550	575	564	84	—
1798	7,900	7,106	644	150	12	—
1799	7,547	6,610	779	157	(Z)	—
1800	10,849	9,081	809	958	(Z)	—
1801	12,935	10,751	1,048	1,137	168	—
1802	14,996	12,438	622	1,936	189	—
1803	11,064	10,479	215	370	166	—
1804	11,826	11,099	51	677	488	—
1805	13,561	12,936	22	602	540	—
1806	15,560	14,668	20	872	765	—
1807	16,398	15,846	13	539	466	—
1808	17,061	16,364	8	689	648	—
1809	7,773	7,296	4	473	442	—
1810	9,384	8,583	7	793	697	—
1811	14,424	13,313	2	1,108	1,040	—
1812	9,801	8,959	5	837	710	—
1813	14,340	13,225	5	1,111	836	—
1814	11,182	5,999	1,663	3,520	1,136	—
1815	15,729	7,283	4,678	3,768	1,288	—
1816	47,678	36,307	5,125	6,246	1,718	—
1817	33,099	26,283	2,678	4,138	1,991	—
1818	21,585	17,176	955	3,454	2,607	—
1819	24,603	20,284	230	4,090	3,274	—
1820	17,881	15,006	106	2,769	1,636	—
1821	14,573	13,004	69	1,500	1,213	—
1822	20,232	17,590	68	2,575	1,804	—
1823	20,541	19,088	34	1,418	917	—
1824	19,381	17,878	35	1,468	984	—
1825	21,841	20,099	26	1,716	1,216	—
1826	25,260	23,341	22	1,898	1,394	—
1827	22,966	19,712	20	3,234	1,496	—
1828	24,764	23,206	17	1,541	1,018	—
1829	24,828	22,682	15	2,131	1,517	—
1830	24,844	21,922	12	2,910	2,329	—
1831	28,527	24,224	7	4,295	3,211	—
1832	31,866	28,465	12	3,389	2,623	—
1833	33,948	29,033	3	4,913	3,968	—
1834	21,792	16,215	4	5,573	4,858	—
1835	35,430	19,391	10	16,028	14,758	—
1836	50,827	23,410	(Z)	27,416	24,877	—
1837	24,954	11,169	5	13,779	6,776	—
1838	26,303	16,159	2	10,141	3,082	—
1839	31,483	23,138	3	8,342	7,076	—
1840	19,480	13,500	2	5,979	3,293	—
1841	16,860	14,487	3	2,370	1,366	—
1842	19,976	18,188	(Z)	1,788	1,336	—
1843	8,303	7,047	(Z)	1,256	898	—
1844	29,321	26,184	2	3,136	2,060	—
1845	29,970	27,528	4	2,438	2,077	—
1846	29,700	26,713	3	2,984	2,694	—
1847	26,496	23,748	(Z)	2,748	2,498	—
1848	35,736	31,757	(Z)	3,978	3,329	—
1849	31,208	28,347	(Z)	2,861	1,689	—

Notes appear at end of table

TABLE Ea588–593   **Federal government revenue, by source: 1789–1939**   *Continued*

				Other receipts		Refunds, transfers, interfund transactions
	Total	Customs	Internal revenue	Total	Sales of public lands	
	Ea588 [3]	Ea589	Ea590	Ea591	Ea592	Ea593
Fiscal year	Thousand dollars	Thousand dollars	Thousand dollars	Thousand dollars	Thousand dollars	Thousand dollars
1850	43,603	39,669	(Z)	3,935	1,860	—
1851	52,559	49,018	(Z)	3,542	2,352	—
1852	49,847	47,339	(Z)	2,507	2,043	—
1853	61,587	58,932	(Z)	2,655	1,667	—
1854	73,800	64,224	(Z)	9,576	8,471	—
1855	65,351	53,026	(Z)	12,325	11,497	—
1856	74,057	64,023	(Z)	10,034	8,918	—
1857	68,965	63,876	(Z)	5,089	3,829	—
1858	46,655	41,790	(Z)	4,866	3,514	—
1859	53,486	49,566	(Z)	3,921	1,757	—
1860	56,065	53,188	(Z)	2,877	1,779	—
1861	41,510	39,582	(Z)	1,928	871	—
1862	51,987	49,056	(Z)	2,931	152	—
1863	112,697	69,060	37,641	5,997	168	—
1864	264,627	102,316	109,741	52,569	588	—
1865	333,715	84,928	209,464	39,322	997	—
1866	558,033	179,047	309,227	69,759	665	—
1867	490,634	176,418	266,028	48,189	1,164	—
1868	405,638	164,465	191,088	50,086	1,349	—
1869	370,944	180,048	158,356	32,539	4,020	—
1870	411,255	194,538	184,900	31,817	3,350	—
1871	383,324	206,270	143,098	33,955	2,389	—
1872	374,107	216,370	130,642	27,094	2,576	—
1873	333,738	188,090	113,729	31,919	2,882	—
1874	304,979	163,104	102,410	39,465	1,852	—
1875	288,000	157,168	110,007	20,825	1,414	—
1876	294,096	148,072	116,701	29,323	1,129	—
1877	281,406	130,956	118,630	31,820	976	—
1878	257,764	130,171	110,582	17,012	1,080	—
1879	273,827	137,250	113,562	23,016	925	—
1880	333,527	186,522	124,009	22,995	1,017	—
1881	360,782	198,160	135,264	27,358	2,202	—
1882	403,525	220,411	146,498	36,617	4,753	—
1883	398,288	214,706	144,720	38,861	7,956	—
1884	348,520	195,067	121,586	31,866	9,811	—
1885	323,691	181,472	112,499	29,720	5,706	—
1886	336,440	192,905	116,806	26,729	5,631	—
1887	371,403	217,287	118,823	35,293	9,254	—
1888	379,266	219,091	124,297	35,878	11,202	—
1889	387,050	223,833	130,882	32,336	8,039	—
1890	403,081	229,669	142,607	30,806	6,358	—
1891	392,612	219,522	145,686	27,404	4,030	—
1892	354,938	177,453	153,971	23,514	3,262	—
1893	385,820	203,355	161,028	21,437	3,182	—
1894	306,355	131,819	147,111	27,426	1,674	—
1895	324,729	152,159	143,422	29,149	1,103	—
1896	338,142	160,022	146,763	31,358	1,006	—
1897	347,722	176,554	146,689	24,479	865	—
1898	405,321	149,575	170,901	84,846	1,243	—
1899	515,961	206,128	273,437	36,395	1,678	—
1900	567,241	233,165	295,328	38,748	2,837	—
1901	587,685	238,585	307,181	41,919	2,965	—
1902	562,478	254,445	271,880	36,153	4,144	—
1903	561,881	284,480	230,810	46,591	8,926	—
1904	541,087	261,275	232,904	46,908	7,453	—
1905	544,275	261,799	234,096	48,380	4,859	—
1906	594,984	300,252	249,150	45,582	4,880	—
1907	665,860	332,233	269,667	63,960	7,879	—
1908	601,862	286,113	251,711	64,038	9,732	—
1909	604,320	300,712	246,213	57,396	7,701	—

Notes appear at end of table   (continued)

TABLE Ea588–593 Federal government revenue, by source: 1789–1939 *Continued*

	Total	Customs	Internal revenue	Other receipts Total	Sales of public lands	Refunds, transfers, interfund transactions
	Ea588 [3]	Ea589	Ea590	Ea591	Ea592	Ea593
Fiscal year	Thousand dollars	Thousand dollars	Thousand dollars	Thousand dollars	Thousand dollars	Thousand dollars
1910	675,512	333,683	289,934	51,895	6,356	—
1911	701,833	314,497	322,529	64,807	5,732	—
1912	692,609	311,322	321,612	59,675	5,393	—
1913	714,463	318,891	344,417	60,803	2,910	−9,648
1914	725,117	292,320	380,041	62,312	2,572	−9,556
1915	683,417	209,787	415,670	72,455	2,167	−14,494
1916	761,445	213,186	512,702	56,647	1,888	−21,089
1917	1,100,500	225,962	809,366	88,996	1,893	−23,825
1918	3,645,240	179,998	3,186,034	298,550	1,969	−19,343
1919	5,130,042	184,458	4,315,285	652,514	1,405	−22,215
1920	6,648,898	322,903	5,405,032	966,631	1,910	−45,667
1921	5,570,790	308,564	4,596,426	719,943	1,530	−54,143
1922	4,025,901	356,443	3,213,253	539,408	895	−83,203
1923	3,852,795	561,929	2,624,473	820,734	657	−154,341
1924	3,871,214	545,638	2,795,157	671,250	522	−140,831
1925	3,640,805	547,561	2,589,176	643,412	624	−139,343
1926	3,795,108	579,430	2,837,639	545,686	754	−167,648
1927	4,012,794	605,500	2,869,414	654,480	621	−116,601
1928	3,900,329	568,986	2,794,971	678,391	385	−142,019
1929	3,861,589	602,263	2,938,019	492,968	315	−171,661
1930	4,057,884	587,001	3,039,295	551,646	396	−120,058
1931	3,115,557	378,354	2,429,781	381,504	230	−74,082
1932	1,923,892	327,755	1,561,006	116,964	170	−81,834
1933	1,996,844	250,750	1,604,424	224,523	103	−82,853
1934	3,014,970	313,434	2,640,604	161,516	99	−100,584
1935	3,705,956	343,353	3,277,690	179,424	87	−94,512
1936	3,997,059	386,812	3,512,852	216,293	74	−118,898
1937	4,955,613	486,357	4,597,140	210,094	71	−337,978
1938	5,588,012	359,187	5,674,318	208,156	96	−653,649
1939	4,979,066	318,837	5,161,221	187,765	248	−688,758

(Z) Less than $500.

[1] Refunds of receipts are excluded starting 1913; comparable data are not available for prior years.

[2] Certain interfund transactions are excluded starting 1932; for prior years, the amounts of such transactions are insignificant.

[3] Through 1912, total; thereafter, net.

[4] Total for three-year period.

Source

Series Ea592. U.S. Department of the Treasury, *Annual Report of the Secretary of the Treasury* (1946), pp. 422–3.

All other series. U.S. Department of the Treasury, *Statistical Appendix to the Annual Report of the Secretary of the Treasury* (1970), pp. 8–13 and 60–61, and (1971), pp. 8–12.

Documentation

See the text for Table Ea584–587 for a general note on the federal government finances tables.

Figures exclude receipts from borrowing.

Series Ea588. Equals series Ea584.

TABLE Ea594–608 Federal government internal tax revenue, by source: 1863–1940

Contributed by John Joseph Wallis

Fiscal year	Income			Employment	Estate and gift	Total	Alcohol	Tobacco	Total	Excise			Admissions	Telephone and teletype services	Capital stock
	Total	Individual	Corporate							Manufacturers					
										Automobiles and accessories	Tires, tubes, tread rubber	Gasoline and lubricants			
	Ea594	Ea595	Ea596	Ea597	Ea598	Ea599	Ea600	Ea601	Ea602	Ea603	Ea604	Ea605	Ea606	Ea607	Ea608
	Thousand dollars	Thousand dollars	Thousand dollars	Thousand dollars	Thousand dollars	Thousand dollars	Thousand dollars	Thousand dollars	Thousand dollars	Thousand dollars	Thousand dollars	Thousand dollars	Thousand dollars	Thousand dollars	Thousand dollars
1863	41,003	—	—	—	57	—	6,805	3,098	16,525	—	—	—	—	—	—
1864	116,966	—	—	—	311	—	32,619	8,592	36,223	—	—	—	—	—	—
1865	210,856	—	—	—	547	—	22,466	11,401	73,318	—	—	—	—	—	—
1866	310,120	—	—	—	1,171	—	38,489	16,531	127,231	—	—	—	—	—	—
1867	265,065	—	—	—	1,865	—	39,600	19,765	91,531	—	—	—	—	—	—
1868	190,375	—	—	—	2,823	—	24,612	18,730	61,550	—	—	—	—	—	—
1869	159,124	—	—	—	2,435	—	51,171	23,431	3,345	—	—	—	—	—	—
1870	184,303	—	—	—	3,092	—	61,925	31,351	3,017	—	—	—	—	—	—
1871	143,198	—	—	—	2,505	—	53,671	33,759	3,532	—	—	—	—	—	—
1872	130,890	—	—	—	—	—	57,734	33,736	4,516	—	—	—	—	—	—
1873	113,504	—	—	—	—	—	61,424	34,386	1,267	—	—	—	—	—	—
1874	102,191	—	—	—	—	—	58,749	33,243	625	—	—	—	—	—	—
1875	110,072	—	—	—	—	—	61,226	37,303	864	—	—	—	—	—	—
1876	116,768	—	—	—	—	—	65,998	39,795	509	—	—	—	—	—	—
1877	118,549	—	—	—	—	—	66,950	41,107	238	—	—	—	—	—	—
1878	110,654	—	—	—	—	—	60,358	40,092	430	—	—	—	—	—	—
1879	113,450	—	—	—	—	—	63,300	40,135	299	—	—	—	—	—	—
1880	123,982	—	—	—	—	—	74,015	38,870	228	—	—	—	—	—	—
1881	135,230	—	—	—	—	—	80,854	42,855	49	—	—	—	—	—	—
1882	146,523	—	—	—	—	—	86,027	47,392	82	—	—	—	—	—	—
1883	144,553	—	—	—	—	—	91,269	42,104	72	—	—	—	—	—	—
1884	121,590	—	—	—	—	—	94,990	26,062	24	—	—	—	—	—	—
1885	112,421	—	—	—	—	—	85,742	26,407	23	—	—	—	—	—	—
1886	116,903	—	—	—	—	—	88,769	27,907	24	—	—	—	—	—	—
1887	118,837	—	—	—	—	—	87,752	30,108	22	—	—	—	—	—	—
1888	124,326	—	—	—	—	—	92,630	30,662	10	—	—	—	—	—	—
1889	130,894	—	—	—	—	—	98,036	31,867	6	—	—	—	—	—	—
1890	142,595	—	—	—	—	—	107,696	33,959	9	—	—	—	—	—	—
1891	146,035	—	—	—	—	—	111,901	32,796	4	—	—	—	—	—	—
1892	153,858	—	—	—	—	—	121,347	31,000	2	—	—	—	—	—	—
1893	161,005	—	—	—	—	—	127,269	31,890	7	—	—	—	—	—	—
1894	147,168	—	—	—	—	—	116,674	28,618	2	—	—	—	—	—	—
1895	143,246	—	—	—	—	—	111,503	29,705	(Z)	—	—	—	—	—	—
1896	146,831	—	—	—	—	—	114,454	30,712	1	—	—	—	—	—	—
1897	146,620	—	—	—	—	—	114,481	30,710	9	—	—	—	—	—	—
1898	170,867	—	—	—	—	—	132,062	36,231	1	—	—	—	—	—	—
1899	273,485	—	—	—	1,235	—	167,928	52,493	5	—	—	—	—	—	—
1900	295,316	—	—	—	2,884	—	183,420	59,355	3	—	—	—	—	—	—
1901	306,872	—	—	—	5,212	—	191,698	62,482	1	—	—	—	—	—	—
1902	271,868	—	—	—	4,843	—	193,127	51,938	—	—	—	—	—	—	—
1903	230,741	—	—	—	5,357	—	179,501	43,515	—	—	—	—	—	—	—
1904	232,904	—	—	—	2,072	—	184,893	44,656	—	—	—	—	—	—	—

Note appears at end of table

(continued)

TABLE Ea594–608 Federal government internal tax revenue, by source: 1863–1940 *Continued*

| | Income | | | | | Excise | | | Manufacturers | | | | | | |
| | Total | Individual | Corporate | Employment | Estate and gift | Total | Alcohol | Tobacco | Total | Automobiles and accessories | Tires, tubes, tread rubber | Gasoline and lubricants | Admissions | Telephone and teletype services | Capital stock |
Fiscal year	Ea594	Ea595	Ea596	Ea597	Ea598	Ea599	Ea600	Ea601	Ea602	Ea603	Ea604	Ea605	Ea606	Ea607	Ea608
	Thousand dollars	Thousand dollars	Thousand dollars	Thousand dollars	Thousand dollars	Thousand dollars	Thousand dollars	Thousand dollars	Thousand dollars	Thousand dollars	Thousand dollars	Thousand dollars	Thousand dollars	Thousand dollars	Thousand dollars
1905	234,188	—	—	—	774	—	186,319	45,660	—	—	—	—	—	—	—
1906	249,103	—	—	—	142	—	199,036	48,423	—	—	—	—	—	—	—
1907	269,664	—	—	—	50	—	215,905	51,811	—	—	—	—	—	—	—
1908	251,666	—	—	—	—	—	199,966	49,863	—	—	—	—	—	—	—
1909	246,213	—	—	—	—	—	192,324	51,887	—	—	—	—	—	—	—
1910	289,957	—	—	—	—	—	208,602	58,118	—	—	—	—	—	—	—
1911	322,526	—	—	—	—	—	219,648	67,006	—	—	—	—	—	—	—
1912	321,616	—	—	—	—	—	219,660	70,590	—	—	—	—	—	—	—
1913	344,424	—	—	—	—	—	230,146	76,789	—	—	—	—	—	—	—
1914	380,009	—	—	—	—	—	226,180	79,987	—	—	—	—	—	—	—
1915	415,681	—	—	—	—	—	223,949	79,957	—	—	—	—	—	—	—
1916	512,723	67,944	56,994	—	—	—	247,454	88,064	4,219	—	—	—	—	—	—
1917	809,394	180,108	207,274	—	6,077	—	284,009	103,202	775	—	—	—	26,357	6,299	10,472
1918	3,698,956	—	—	—	47,453	—	443,840	156,189	36,637	—	—	—	50,920	17,902	24,996
1919	3,850,150	—	—	—	82,030	—	483,051	206,003	79,400	—	—	—	76,721	27,677	28,776
1920	5,407,580	—	—	—	103,636	—	139,871	295,809	267,969	—	—	—	89,731	28,442	93,020
1921	4,595,357	—	—	—	154,043	—	82,623	255,219	229,398	—	—	—	73,385	29,272	81,526
1922	3,197,451	—	—	—	139,419	—	45,609	270,759	174,361	—	—	—	70,175	30,381	80,612
1923	2,621,745	—	—	—	126,705	—	30,358	309,015	185,117	—	—	—	77,713	34,662	81,568
1924	2,796,179	—	—	—	102,967	—	27,586	325,639	200,922	—	—	—	30,908	—	87,472
1925	2,584,140	845,426	916,233	—	108,940	—	25,905	345,247	140,877	—	—	—	23,981	—	90,003
1926	2,836,000	879,124	1,094,980	—	119,216	—	26,452	370,666	150,220	—	—	—	17,941	—	97,386
1927	2,865,683	911,940	1,308,013	—	100,340	—	21,196	376,170	66,850	—	—	—	17,725	—	8,970
1928	2,790,536	882,727	1,291,846	—	60,087	—	15,308	396,450	51,952	—	—	—	6,083	—	8,689
1929	2,939,054	1,095,541	1,235,733	—	61,897	539,927	12,777	434,445	5,712	—	—	—	4,231	—	5,956
1930	3,040,146	1,146,845	1,263,414	—	64,770	565,070	11,695	450,339	2,665	—	—	—	2,779	—	—
1931	2,428,229	833,648	1,026,393	—	48,078	520,110	10,432	444,277	138	—	—	—	1,859	—	47
1932	1,557,729	427,191	629,566	—	47,422	453,550	8,704	398,579	87	—	—	—	—	—	—
1933	1,619,839	352,574	394,218	—	34,310	838,738	43,174	402,739	243,600	17,825	14,980	141,162	15,521	14,565	—
1934	2,672,239	419,509	400,146	—	113,138	1,287,854	258,911	425,169	385,291	43,271	27,630	227,830	14,614	19,251	80,168
1935	3,299,436	527,113	578,678	—	212,112	1,363,802	411,022	459,179	342,145	50,617	26,638	189,332	15,380	19,741	91,508
1936	3,520,208	674,416	753,032	48	378,840	1,547,293	505,464	501,166	382,716	62,311	32,208	204,443	17,112	21,098	94,943
1937	4,653,195	1,091,741	1,088,101	265,745	305,548	1,764,561	594,245	552,254	450,581	84,382	40,819	227,996	19,740	24,570	137,499
1938	5,658,765	1,286,312	1,342,718	742,660	416,874	1,730,853	567,979	568,182	417,152	58,051	31,567	235,213	20,801	23,977	139,349
1939	5,181,574	1,028,834	1,156,281	740,429	360,716	1,768,113	587,800	580,159	396,975	56,666	34,819	237,516	19,471	24,094	127,203
1940	5,340,452	982,017	1,147,592	833,521	360,071	1,884,512	624,253	608,518	447,152	77,847	41,555	257,420	21,888	26,368	132,739

(Z) Less than $500.

Sources

Internal Revenue Service Annual Report (1863–1940), and *Historical Statistics of the United States* (1975), series Y 358–372, which were based on the following: U.S. Department of the Treasury, *Annual Report of the Secretary of the Treasury* (1929), pp. 419–24; *Annual Report of the Secretary of the Treasury* (1946), pp. 406–9; and *Statistical Appendix to Annual Report of the Treasury* (1970), pp. 46–51.

Documentation

See the text for Table Ea584–587 for a general note on the federal government finances tables.

TABLE Ea609–635　Federal government internal tax revenue, by source: 1940–1999

Contributed by John Joseph Wallis

	Total		Income							Employment			
	Overall	Excluding excises not collected by IRS	Total	Individual			Corporate			Total	Old Age, Disability, and Hospital Insurance	Unemployment Insurance	Railroad Retirement
				Total	Withheld by employers	Other	Total	Regular	Exempt organization business				
	Ea609 [1]	Ea610 [1]	Ea611	Ea612	Ea613	Ea614	Ea615	Ea616	Ea617	Ea618	Ea619	Ea620	Ea621
Fiscal year	Thousand dollars	Thousand dollars	Thousand dollars	Thousand dollars	Thousand dollars	Thousand dollars	Thousand dollars	Thousand dollars	Thousand dollars	Thousand dollars	Thousand dollars	Thousand dollars	Thousand dollars
1940	5,180,703	—	2,102,599	982,017	—	—	1,120,582	—	—	833,521	605,350	106,123	122,048
1941	7,001,975	—	3,269,643	1,417,655	—	—	1,851,988	—	—	925,857	687,328	100,658	137,871
1942	11,091,157	—	6,332,073	3,262,800	—	—	3,069,273	—	—	1,185,362	895,336	119,617	170,409
1943	16,208,474	—	10,464,769	5,943,917	—	—	4,520,852	—	—	1,498,706	1,131,546	156,008	211,152
1944	22,435,004	—	15,721,716	10,437,570	—	—	5,284,146	—	—	1,738,373	1,290,025	183,337	265,011
1945	22,016,670	—	13,649,809	8,770,094	—	—	4,879,715	—	—	1,779,178	1,307,931	186,489	284,758
1946	22,548,737	—	13,486,896	8,846,947	—	—	4,639,949	—	—	1,700,828	1,237,825	178,745	284,258
1947	35,485,426	—	25,398,393	19,343,297	9,842,282	9,501,015	6,055,096	—	—	2,024,365	1,458,934	185,876	379,555
1948	41,539,909	—	30,849,281	20,997,781	11,533,577	9,464,204	9,851,500	—	—	2,381,342	1,612,721	208,508	560,113
1949	40,245,962	—	29,394,466	18,051,822	10,055,502	7,996,320	11,342,544	—	—	2,476,113	1,687,151	226,228	562,734
1950	38,862,097	—	27,912,894	17,153,308	9,888,976	7,264,332	10,759,586	—	—	2,644,574	1,873,401	223,135	548,038
1951	50,445,685	—	37,384,878	22,997,309	13,089,770	9,907,539	14,337,569	—	—	3,627,479	2,810,749	236,952	579,778
1952	65,009,585	—	50,741,017	29,274,107	17,929,047	11,345,060	21,466,910	21,466,873	37	4,464,263	3,584,025	259,616	620,622
1953	69,686,536	—	54,130,732	32,536,217	21,132,275	11,403,942	21,594,515	21,594,251	264	4,718,403	3,816,252	273,182	628,969
1954	69,919,988	—	54,360,013	32,813,691	22,077,113	10,736,578	21,546,322	21,545,632	690	5,107,623	4,218,520	283,882	605,221
1955	71,044,996	—	53,602,363	35,337,642	24,015,676	11,321,966	18,264,721	18,262,571	2,150	7,295,784	6,336,805	324,656	634,323
1956	75,107,380	—	56,636,164	35,337,642	24,015,676	11,321,966	21,298,522	21,297,167	1,355	7,295,784	6,336,805	324,656	634,323
1957	80,156,485	—	60,560,425	39,029,772	26,727,543	12,302,229	21,530,653	21,528,031	2,622	7,580,521	6,634,457	330,034	616,020
1958	79,971,456	—	59,101,874	38,568,559	27,040,911	11,527,648	20,533,315	20,531,116	2,199	8,644,385	7,733,223	335,880	575,282
1959	79,792,529	—	58,826,253	40,734,744	29,001,375	11,733,369	18,091,509	18,088,669	2,840	8,853,744	8,004,355	324,020	525,369
1960	91,774,806	—	67,125,126	44,945,712	31,674,588	13,271,124	22,179,414	22,177,310	2,104	11,158,589	10,210,550	341,108	606,931
1961	94,401,081	—	67,917,940	46,153,000	32,977,654	13,175,346	21,764,940	21,761,747	3,193	12,502,451	11,586,283	345,356	570,812
1962	99,440,839	—	71,945,305	50,649,594	36,246,109	14,403,485	21,295,711	21,293,717	1,994	12,708,171	11,686,231	457,629	564,311
1963	105,925,395	—	75,323,714	52,987,580	38,718,702	14,268,878	22,336,134	22,334,205	1,929	15,004,487	13,484,379	948,464	571,644
1964	112,260,258	—	78,891,217	54,590,354	39,258,881	15,331,473	24,300,863	24,298,959	1,904	17,002,505	15,557,783	850,858	593,864
1965	114,434,633	—	79,792,016	53,660,682	36,840,394	16,820,288	26,131,334	26,128,635	2,699	17,104,306	15,846,073	622,499	635,734
1966	128,879,961	—	92,131,794	61,297,551	42,811,381	18,486,170	30,834,243	30,831,126	3,117	20,256,133	19,005,488	567,014	683,631
1967	148,379,460	—	104,288,421	69,370,595	50,520,874	18,849,721	34,917,826	34,914,910	2,916	26,958,241	25,562,638	602,745	792,858
1968	153,636,837	—	108,148,565	78,252,045	57,300,546	20,951,499	29,896,520	29,893,255	3,265	28,085,898	26,620,648	606,802	858,448
1969	187,919,557	—	135,778,051	97,440,406	70,182,175	27,258,231	38,337,645	38,332,032	5,613	33,068,657	31,489,943	640,030	938,684
1970	195,722,094	—	138,688,568	103,651,585	77,416,070	26,235,515	35,036,983	35,032,183	4,800	37,449,188	35,692,198	776,139	980,851
1971	191,647,199	—	131,072,374	100,752,421	76,490,128	24,262,293	30,319,953	30,313,195	6,758	39,918,690	37,902,403	972,409	1,043,878
1972	209,855,764	—	143,804,732	108,879,186	83,200,366	25,678,820	34,925,546	34,916,132	9,414	43,714,001	41,617,156	1,024,069	1,072,776
1973	237,787,204	—	164,157,315	125,112,006	98,092,726	27,019,280	39,045,309	39,032,707	12,602	52,081,708	49,514,852	1,315,997	1,250,859
1974	268,952,255	—	184,648,093	142,903,650	112,091,799	30,811,851	41,744,443	41,725,250	19,193	62,093,633	59,105,066	1,480,574	1,507,993
1975	294,822,725	—	203,146,098	157,399,438	123,103,137	34,296,301	45,746,660	45,723,608	23,052	70,140,809	67,136,584	1,388,082	1,616,143
1976	310,822,818	—	211,320,658	163,888,780	127,757,804	36,130,976	47,431,878	47,392,422	39,456	76,694,901	73,346,484	1,625,205	1,723,212
1977	358,139,419	—	246,805,067	186,755,263	144,672,331	42,082,932	60,049,804	60,015,704	34,100	86,076,316	82,257,211	1,910,302	1,908,803
1978	399,776,388	—	278,438,289	213,058,143	165,254,230	47,803,913	65,380,146	65,344,150	35,996	97,291,652	92,630,407	2,642,014	2,019,231
1979	460,412,187	—	322,993,732	251,545,856	195,331,016	56,214,840	71,447,876	71,408,891	38,985	112,849,875	107,525,982	2,958,000	2,365,893

Notes appear at end of table

(continued)

TABLE Ea609–635   Federal government internal tax revenue, by source: 1940–1999   Continued

	Total		Total	Income			Corporate			Employment			
	Overall [1]	Excluding excises not collected by IRS [1]		Individual Total	Withheld by employers	Other	Total	Regular	Exempt organization business	Total	Old Age, Disability, and Hospital Insurance	Unemployment Insurance	Railroad Retirement
Fiscal year	Ea609	Ea610 [1]	Ea611	Ea612	Ea613	Ea614	Ea615	Ea616	Ea617	Ea618	Ea619	Ea620	Ea621
	Thousand dollars	Thousand dollars	Thousand dollars	Thousand dollars	Thousand dollars	Thousand dollars	Thousand dollars	Thousand dollars	Thousand dollars	Thousand dollars	Thousand dollars	Thousand dollars	Thousand dollars
1980	519,375,275	—	359,927,392	287,547,782	223,801,608	63,746,174	72,379,610	72,346,551	33,059	128,330,480	122,486,499	3,309,000	2,534,981
1981	606,799,101	—	406,583,303	332,850,146	256,006,407	76,843,739	73,733,157	73,692,166	40,991	152,885,816	146,529,366	3,645,456	2,710,994
1982	632,240,503	—	418,599,768	352,608,936	267,513,089	85,095,847	65,990,832	65,926,131	64,701	168,717,936	162,137,919	3,351,128	3,228,889
1983	627,246,793	—	411,407,522	349,627,967	266,043,347	83,584,620	61,779,555	61,734,430	45,125	173,847,855	166,420,846	4,311,582	3,115,427
1984	680,475,233	—	437,071,049	362,891,679	278,983,806	83,907,873	74,179,370	74,129,397	49,973	199,210,028	189,515,975	6,052,023	3,642,030
1985	742,871,542	—	474,072,327	396,659,558	298,975,371	97,684,187	77,412,769	77,342,976	69,793	225,214,568	215,590,990	5,671,797	3,951,781
1986	782,251,811	—	497,406,391	416,964,771	314,838,340	102,126,431	80,441,620	80,288,596	153,024	243,978,380	234,879,738	5,265,002	3,833,640
1987	886,290,589	—	568,311,470	465,452,486	322,495,330	142,957,156	102,858,984	102,614,712	244,272	277,000,469	266,616,935	6,232,000	4,151,534
1988	945,459,303	935,106,594	583,349,120	473,666,566	341,467,682	132,198,884	109,682,554	109,393,550	289,004	318,038,990	307,594,215	6,178,000	4,266,775
1989	1,023,551,771	1,013,322,133	632,746,070	515,731,505	361,418,569	154,312,936	117,014,565	116,743,148	271,417	345,625,586	336,809,068	4,692,520	4,123,997
1990	1,066,515,193	1,056,365,652	650,244,947	540,228,408	388,416,444	151,811,964	110,016,539	109,712,541	303,998	367,219,321	357,545,552	5,515,998	4,157,771
1991	1,098,977,301	1,086,851,401	660,475,444	546,876,876	404,183,687	142,693,189	113,598,568	113,310,389	288,179	384,451,220	374,743,589	5,474,000	4,233,631
1992	1,133,923,812	1,120,799,558	675,673,952	557,723,156	408,380,909	149,342,247	117,950,796	117,571,285	379,511	400,080,904	389,967,051	5,754,998	4,358,855
1993	1,190,672,149	1,176,685,625	717,321,668	585,774,158	431,002,453	154,771,705	131,547,510	131,204,785	342,725	411,510,516	401,687,664	5,561,301	4,261,551
1994	1,290,244,979	1,276,466,776	774,023,837	619,819,153	—	—	154,204,684	—	—	443,831,352	—	—	—
1995	1,390,049,207	1,375,731,835	850,201,510	675,779,337	—	—	174,422,173	—	—	465,405,305	—	—	—
1996	1,500,352,063	1,486,546,674	934,368,068	745,313,276	—	—	189,054,791	—	—	492,365,178	—	—	—
1997	1,637,155,071	1,623,272,071	1,029,513,216	825,020,880	—	—	204,492,336	—	—	528,596,833	—	—	—
1998	1,782,997,023	1,769,408,739	1,141,335,868	928,025,857	—	—	213,270,011	—	—	557,799,193	—	—	—
1999	1,917,642,125	1,904,151,888	1,218,510,654	1,002,185,765	—	—	216,324,889	—	—	598,669,865	—	—	—

	Estate and gift			Excise										
	Total	Estate	Gift	Total Overall [1]	Excluding excises not collected by IRS [1]	Excises collected by BATF [1]	Alcohol and tobacco Total [2]	Alcohol	Tobacco	Gasoline [3]	Diesel and special motor fuel [4]	Telephone and teletype services	Air transportation	Other
Fiscal year	Ea622	Ea623	Ea624	Ea625	Ea626	Ea627	Ea628	Ea629	Ea630	Ea631	Ea632	Ea633	Ea634	Ea635
	Thousand dollars	Thousand dollars	Thousand dollars	Thousand dollars	Thousand dollars	Thousand dollars	Thousand dollars	Thousand dollars	Thousand dollars	Thousand dollars	Thousand dollars	Thousand dollars	Thousand dollars	Thousand dollars
1940	360,071	330,886	29,185	1,884,512	—	—	1,232,771	624,253	608,518	226,187	(Z)	26,368	11,511	387,675
1941	407,058	355,194	51,864	2,399,417	—	—	1,518,133	820,056	698,077	343,021	(Z)	27,331	12,481	498,451
1942	432,540	340,323	92,217	3,141,182	—	—	1,829,499	1,048,517	780,982	369,587	(Z)	75,023	34,854	832,219
1943	447,496	414,531	32,965	3,797,503	—	—	2,347,503	1,423,646	923,857	288,786	(Z)	158,161	183,360	819,693
1944	511,211	473,466	37,745	4,463,704	—	—	2,607,258	1,618,775	988,483	271,217	(Z)	231,474	385,021	968,734
1945	643,055	596,137	46,918	5,944,628	—	—	3,242,011	2,309,866	932,145	405,563	(Z)	341,587	471,556	1,483,911
1946	676,833	629,601	47,232	6,684,180	—	—	3,691,684	2,526,165	1,165,519	405,695	(Z)	380,082	461,695	1,745,024
1947	779,291	708,794	70,497	7,283,377	—	—	3,712,530	2,474,762	1,237,768	433,676	(Z)	417,691	536,693	2,182,787
1948	899,345	822,380	76,965	7,409,941	—	—	3,555,607	2,255,327	1,300,280	478,638	(Z)	468,776	582,299	2,324,621
1949	796,538	735,781	60,757	7,578,845	—	—	3,532,482	2,210,607	1,321,875	503,647	(Z)	535,910	607,743	2,399,063

	Estate and gift			Total			Excise							
							Alcohol and tobacco							
Fiscal year	Total	Estate	Gift	Overall	Excluding excises not collected by IRS	Excises collected by BATF [1]	Total [2]	Alcohol	Tobacco	Gasoline [3]	Diesel and special motor fuel [4]	Telephone and teletype services	Air transportation	Other
	Ea622	Ea623	Ea624	Ea625 [1]	Ea626 [1]	Ea627	Ea628 [2]	Ea629	Ea630	Ea631 [3]	Ea632 [4]	Ea633	Ea634	Ea635
	Thousand dollars	Thousand dollars	Thousand dollars	Thousand dollars	Thousand dollars	Thousand dollars	Thousand dollars	Thousand dollars	Thousand dollars	Thousand dollars	Thousand dollars	Thousand dollars	Thousand dollars	Thousand dollars
1950	706,226	657,441	48,785	7,598,403	—	—	3,547,666	2,219,202	1,328,464	526,732	(Z)	559,620	568,850	2,395,535
1951	729,730	638,523	91,207	8,703,598	—	—	3,927,204	2,546,808	1,380,396	569,048	(Z)	644,980	643,905	2,918,461
1952	833,147	750,591	82,556	8,971,158	—	—	4,114,282	2,549,120	1,565,162	713,174	7,138	705,770	690,644	2,740,150
1953	891,284	784,590	106,694	9,946,117	—	—	4,435,836	2,780,925	1,654,911	890,575	15,091	775,873	735,390	3,093,252
1954	935,122	863,344	71,778	9,517,230	—	—	4,363,241	2,783,012	1,580,229	836,392	17,969	771,981	672,699	2,854,448
1955	936,267	848,492	87,775	9,210,582	—	—	4,314,053	2,742,840	1,571,213	954,558	22,692	520,449	631,962	2,766,768
1956	1,171,237	1,053,867	117,370	10,004,195	—	—	4,534,071	2,920,574	1,613,497	1,030,397	24,464	557,233	701,163	3,156,867
1957	1,377,999	1,253,071	124,928	10,637,540	—	—	4,647,245	2,973,195	1,674,050	1,455,952	39,454	613,209	727,295	3,154,385
1958	1,410,925	1,277,052	133,873	10,814,272	—	—	4,680,482	2,946,461	1,734,021	1,636,529	46,061	650,186	723,941	3,076,973
1959	1,352,983	1,235,823	117,160	10,759,549	—	—	4,808,912	3,002,095	1,806,816	1,700,253	52,528	690,436	378,256	3,129,164
1960	1,626,348	1,439,259	187,089	11,864,743	—	—	5,125,218	3,193,714	1,931,504	2,014,403	71,869	738,297	258,649	3,656,307
1961	1,916,392	1,745,480	170,912	12,064,298	—	—	5,203,918	3,212,801	1,991,117	2,370,303	88,856	827,302	265,955	3,307,964
1962	2,035,187	1,796,227	238,960	12,752,176	—	—	5,367,018	3,341,282	2,025,736	2,412,714	105,178	843,478	263,377	3,760,411
1963	2,187,457	1,971,614	215,843	13,409,737	—	—	5,520,893	3,441,655	2,079,237	2,497,316	113,012	880,605	234,388	4,163,523
1964	2,416,304	2,110,992	305,312	13,950,232	—	—	5,630,044	3,577,499	2,052,545	2,618,370	128,079	910,196	106,349	4,557,194
1965	2,745,533	2,454,332	291,201	14,792,778	—	—	5,921,228	3,772,634	2,148,594	2,687,135	152,188	1,078,937	126,139	4,827,151
1966	3,093,922	2,646,968	446,954	13,398,112	—	—	5,888,334	3,814,373	2,073,956	2,824,189	159,326	907,917	139,755	3,478,591
1967	3,014,406	2,728,580	285,826	14,118,392	—	—	6,155,592	4,075,723	2,079,869	2,932,894	182,147	1,101,853	170,374	3,575,532
1968	3,081,979	2,710,254	371,725	14,320,395	—	—	6,409,514	4,287,237	2,122,277	3,030,792	201,918	1,105,478	199,304	3,373,389
1969	3,530,064	3,136,691	393,373	15,542,785	—	—	6,693,145	4,555,560	2,137,585	3,186,239	224,657	1,316,378	223,687	3,898,679
1970	3,680,076	3,241,321	438,755	15,904,262	—	—	6,840,594	4,746,382	2,094,212	3,430,076	257,712	1,469,562	250,802	3,655,516
1971	3,784,283	3,352,641	431,642	16,871,852	—	—	7,007,067	4,800,482	2,206,585	3,547,678	271,141	1,624,533	470,380	3,951,053
1972	5,489,969	5,126,522	363,447	16,847,062	—	—	7,317,274	5,110,001	2,207,273	3,741,160	307,446	1,650,499	586,995	3,243,688
1973	4,975,862	4,338,924	636,938	16,572,319	—	—	7,426,464	5,149,513	2,276,951	3,927,535	344,719	1,885,228	660,929	2,327,444
1974	5,100,674	4,659,825	440,849	17,109,855	—	—	7,795,482	5,358,477	2,437,005	4,087,669	384,291	1,892,731	758,016	2,191,666
1975	4,688,078	4,312,657	375,421	16,847,740	—	—	7,665,948	5,350,853	2,315,090	3,980,412	381,616	2,023,744	850,567	1,945,453
1976	5,408,141	4,944,575	463,566	17,399,118	—	—	7,913,376	5,399,055	2,514,321	4,180,860	400,915	1,879,268	932,209	2,092,490
1977	7,425,326	5,649,460	1,775,866	17,832,710	—	—	7,805,134	5,406,633	2,398,501	4,322,077	450,580	1,708,778	1,070,694	2,475,447
1978	5,381,499	5,242,080	139,419	18,664,948	—	—	8,063,628	5,612,715	2,450,913	4,444,484	492,381	1,656,736	1,245,112	2,762,607
1979	5,519,075	5,344,176	174,899	19,049,505	—	—	8,143,441	5,647,924	2,495,517	4,525,065	517,371	1,362,193	1,425,656	3,075,779
1980	6,498,381	6,282,247	216,134	24,619,022	—	—	8,151,184	5,704,763	2,446,416	4,218,147	523,523	1,117,834	1,748,837	8,859,497
1981	6,910,386	6,694,641	215,745	40,419,596	—	—	8,272,270	5,688,413	2,583,857	4,017,956	557,024	998,503	1,326,829	25,257,014
1982	8,143,373	8,035,335	108,038	36,779,426	—	—	7,999,305	5,459,810	2,539,495	4,214,373	599,262	919,749	1,154,818	21,891,919
1983	6,225,877	6,077,202	148,675	35,765,539	—	—	9,774,663	5,634,853	4,139,810	4,904,580	755,841	1,048,317	1,898,787	17,383,351
1984	6,176,667	6,024,985	151,682	38,017,489	—	—	10,066,077	5,402,467	4,663,610	9,021,518	1,579,175	2,034,965	2,456,713	12,859,041
1985	6,579,702	6,303,418	276,284	37,004,945	—	—	9,881,293	5,398,100	4,483,193	9,062,387	2,439,853	2,307,607	2,589,818	10,723,987
1986	7,194,955	6,814,417	380,538	33,672,085	—	—	10,233,303 [5]	5,647,485	4,596,756	8,857,380	2,672,914	2,339,153	2,707,534	6,861,801
1987	7,667,670	7,164,681	502,989	33,310,980	—	—	11,097,677	5,791,352	4,573,015	8,931,668	2,901,245	2,522,062	2,913,249	4,945,079
1988	7,784,445	7,348,679	435,766	36,286,749	25,934,040	10,352,709	10,352,709	5,829,876	4,522,533	9,237,330	3,294,140	2,555,082	3,145,422	7,702,066
1989	8,973,146	8,143,689	829,457	36,206,971	25,977,333	10,229,638	10,229,638	5,939,358	4,290,280	9,852,121	4,023,191	2,820,528	3,569,447	5,712,046

Notes appear at end of table

(continued)

TABLE Ea609–635   Federal government internal tax revenue, by source: 1940–1999   *Continued*

Fiscal year	Estate and gift			Overall	Total			Alcohol and tobacco		Excise				
	Total	Estate	Gift		Excluding excises not collected by IRS	Excises collected by BATF	Total	Alcohol	Tobacco	Gasoline	Diesel and special motor fuel	Telephone and teletype services	Air transportation	Other
	Ea622	Ea623	Ea624	Ea625 [1]	Ea626 [1]	Ea627 [1]	Ea628 [2]	Ea629	Ea630	Ea631 [3]	Ea632 [4]	Ea633	Ea634	Ea635
	Thousand dollars	Thousand dollars	Thousand dollars	Thousand dollars	Thousand dollars	Thousand dollars	Thousand dollars	Thousand dollars	Thousand dollars	Thousand dollars	Thousand dollars	Thousand dollars	Thousand dollars	Thousand dollars
1990	11,761,938	9,633,736	2,128,202	37,288,986	27,139,445	10,149,541	10,149,541	5,752,448	4,270,717	9,589,584	3,296,030	3,075,209	3,400,513	7,778,109
1991	11,473,141	10,237,247	1,235,894	42,577,496	30,451,596	12,125,900	12,125,900	7,226,686	4,781,936	12,675,100	3,958,519	2,952,522	4,299,627	6,565,828
1992	11,479,116	10,411,450	1,067,666	46,689,841	33,565,587	13,124,254	13,124,254	7,875,435	5,189,516	14,759,324	4,071,929	3,173,000	4,661,757	6,899,577
1993	12,890,965	11,433,495	1,457,470	48,949,000	34,962,476	13,986,524	13,986,524	7,759,603	5,700,009	14,753,020	4,287,926	3,351,600	4,623,948	7,945,982
1994	15,606,793	—	—	56,782,997	43,004,794	13,778,203	13,778,203	7,629,943	5,803,199	19,794,300	6,395,500	3,774,000	5,303,000	7,737,994
1995	15,144,394	—	—	59,297,999	44,980,627	14,317,372	14,317,372	7,603,396	5,910,874	19,918,500	6,733,100	3,825,700	5,518,700	8,984,627
1996	17,591,817	—	—	56,027,000	42,221,611	13,805,389	13,805,389	7,582,336	5,795,442	19,653,800	7,091,500	4,243,400	1,777,900	9,455,011
1997	20,356,401	—	—	58,688,621	44,805,621	13,883,000	13,883,000	7,609,020	5,873,314	20,836,000	7,160,800	4,706,800	4,666,000	7,436,021
1998	24,630,962	—	—	59,231,000	45,642,716	13,588,284	13,588,284	7,524,705	5,672,035	20,644,998	7,497,816	4,747,227	7,410,547	5,342,128
1999	28,385,607	—	—	72,076,000	58,585,763	13,490,237	13,490,237	7,712,200	5,300,499	21,236,659	7,895,919	5,248,965	7,978,397	16,225,823

(Z) Less than $500.

[1] See text regarding excises collected by the Bureau of Alcohol, Tobacco, and Firearms and the Customs Service, beginning in 1988.

[2] Beginning in 1987, total includes taxes not shown by type.

[3] Beginning in 1992, includes only excise taxes on gasoline. Before 1992, includes small amounts for gasohol and lubricating oils.

[4] Beginning in 1992, includes only excise taxes on diesel fuel, excluding trains and intercity buses. Before 1992, includes gasohol and gasoline used in noncommercial aviation.

[5] In the source, the sum of the detailed amounts for alcohol and tobacco exceed the total.

Documentation

See the text for Table Ea584–587 for a general note on the federal government finances tables.

Series Ea609–610 and Ea625–626. Starting with fiscal year 1988 (alcohol and tobacco) and the second quarter of fiscal year 1991 (firearms), excise taxes on alcohol, tobacco, and firearms were collected by the Bureau of Alcohol, Tobacco, and Firearms and the Customs Service. Previously, these taxes were collected by the Internal Revenue Service. Excises collected by the Bureau of Alcohol, Tobacco, and Firearms and the Customs Service are excluded from series Ea610 and Ea626.

Series Ea622. Prior to 1916, entitled "legacies, successions, inheritances" taxes.

Sources

Internal Revenue Service Annual Report (1940–1983). Internal Revenue Service, *Statistics of Income Bulletin* (1984–2001).

TABLE Ea636–643 Federal government expenditure, by major function: 1789–1970

Contributed by John Joseph Wallis

		Defense					Other	
	Total	Total (Department of Defense)	Army	Navy	Air Force	Interest on public debt	Total	Veterans' compensation and pensions
	Ea636	Ea637	Ea638	Ea639	Ea640	Ea641	Ea642	Ea643
Fiscal year	Thousand dollars	Thousand dollars	Thousand dollars	Thousand dollars	Thousand dollars	Thousand dollars	Thousand dollars	Thousand dollars
1789–1791 [1]	4,269	—	633	1	—	2,349	1,286	176
1792	5,080	—	1,101	(Z)	—	3,202	777	109
1793	4,482	—	1,130	—	—	2,772	580	80
1794	6,991	—	2,639	61	—	3,490	800	81
1795	7,540	—	2,481	411	—	3,189	1,459	69
1796	5,727	—	1,260	275	—	3,195	997	101
1797	6,134	—	1,039	383	—	3,300	1,412	92
1798	7,677	—	2,010	1,381	—	3,053	1,232	105
1799	9,666	—	2,467	2,858	—	3,186	1,155	95
1800	10,786	—	2,561	3,449	—	3,375	1,402	64
1801	9,395	—	1,673	2,111	—	4,413	1,197	74
1802	7,862	—	1,179	916	—	4,125	1,642	85
1803	7,852	—	822	1,215	—	3,849	1,966	63
1804	8,719	—	875	1,190	—	4,267	2,388	80
1805	10,506	—	713	1,598	—	4,149	4,047	82
1806	9,804	—	1,224	1,650	—	3,723	3,206	82
1807	8,354	—	1,289	1,722	—	3,370	1,974	71
1808	9,932	—	2,901	1,884	—	3,428	1,719	83
1809	10,281	—	3,346	2,428	—	2,866	1,641	88
1810	8,157	—	2,294	1,654	—	2,845	1,363	84
1811	8,058	—	2,033	1,966	—	2,466	1,594	75
1812	20,281	—	11,818	3,959	—	2,451	2,052	91
1813	31,682	—	19,652	6,447	—	3,599	1,984	87
1814	34,721	—	20,351	7,311	—	4,593	2,466	90
1815	32,708	—	14,794	8,660	—	5,755	3,499	70
1816	30,587	—	16,012	3,908	—	7,213	3,453	189
1817	21,844	—	8,004	3,315	—	6,389	4,136	297
1818	19,825	—	5,623	2,954	—	6,016	5,232	891
1819	21,464	—	6,506	3,848	—	5,164	5,946	2,416
1820	18,261	—	2,630	4,388	—	5,126	6,116	3,208
1821	15,811	—	4,461	3,319	—	5,087	2,943	243
1822	15,000	—	3,112	2,224	—	5,173	4,491	1,948
1823	14,707	—	3,097	2,504	—	4,923	4,183	1,781
1824	20,327	—	3,341	2,905	—	4,997	9,085	1,499
1825	15,857	—	3,660	3,049	—	4,367	4,781	1,309
1826	17,036	—	3,943	4,219	—	3,973	4,900	1,557
1827	16,139	—	3,939	4,264	—	3,486	4,450	976
1828	16,395	—	4,146	3,919	—	3,099	5,232	851
1829	15,203	—	4,724	3,309	—	2,543	4,627	950
1830	15,143	—	4,767	3,239	—	1,914	5,223	1,363
1831	15,248	—	4,842	3,856	—	1,384	5,166	1,171
1832	17,289	—	5,446	3,956	—	773	7,114	1,184
1833	23,018	—	6,704	3,901	—	304	12,108	4,589
1834	18,628	—	5,696	3,956	—	202	8,773	3,364
1835	17,573	—	5,759	3,865	—	58	7,891	1,955
1836	30,868	—	12,169	5,808	—	—	12,891	2,883
1837	37,243	—	13,683	6,647	—	—	16,914	2,672
1838	33,865	—	12,897	6,132	—	15	14,821	2,156
1839	26,899	—	8,917	6,182	—	400	11,400	3,143
1840	24,318	—	7,097	6,114	—	175	10,932	2,604
1841	26,566	—	8,806	6,001	—	285	11,474	2,388
1842	25,206	—	6,612	8,397	—	774	9,423	1,379
1843 [2]	11,858	—	2,957	3,728	—	524	4,649	843
1844	22,338	—	5,179	6,498	—	1,834	8,826	2,031
1845	22,937	—	5,753	6,297	—	1,040	9,847	2,397
1846	27,767	—	10,793	6,455	—	843	9,676	1,810
1847	57,281	—	38,306	7,901	—	1,119	9,956	1,748
1848	45,377	—	25,502	9,408	—	2,391	8,076	1,211
1849	45,052	—	14,853	9,787	—	3,566	16,846	1,330

Notes appear at end of table

(continued)

TABLE Ea636–643 Federal government expenditure, by major function: 1789–1970 *Continued*

		Defense					Other	
	Total	Total (Department of Defense)	Army	Navy	Air Force	Interest on public debt	Total	Veterans' compensation and pensions
	Ea636	Ea637	Ea638	Ea639	Ea640	Ea641	Ea642	Ea643
Fiscal year	Thousand dollars	Thousand dollars	Thousand dollars	Thousand dollars	Thousand dollars	Thousand dollars	Thousand dollars	Thousand dollars
1850	39,543	—	9,400	7,905	—	3,782	18,456	1,870
1851	47,709	—	11,812	9,006	—	3,697	23,195	2,290
1852	44,195	—	8,225	8,953	—	4,000	23,017	2,404
1853	48,184	—	9,947	10,919	—	3,666	23,652	1,778
1854	58,045	—	11,734	10,799	—	3,071	32,442	1,238
1855	59,743	—	14,774	13,312	—	2,314	29,342	1,450
1856	69,571	—	16,948	14,092	—	1,954	36,577	1,298
1857	67,796	—	19,262	12,748	—	1,678	34,108	1,312
1858	74,185	—	25,485	13,985	—	1,567	33,148	1,217
1859	69,071	—	23,244	14,643	—	2,638	28,546	1,220
1860	63,131	—	16,410	11,515	—	3,177	32,029	1,103
1861	66,547	—	22,981	12,421	—	4,000	27,144	1,036
1862	474,762	—	394,368	42,668	—	13,190	24,535	853
1863	714,741	—	599,299	63,222	—	24,730	27,490	1,079
1864	865,323	—	690,792	85,726	—	53,685	35,119	4,984
1865	1,297,555	—	1,031,323	122,613	—	77,398	66,221	16,339
1866	520,809	—	284,450	43,324	—	133,068	59,968	15,605
1867	357,543	—	95,224	31,034	—	143,782	87,503	20,937
1868	377,340	—	123,247	25,776	—	140,424	87,894	23,782
1869	322,865	—	78,502	20,001	—	130,694	93,668	28,477
1870	309,654	—	57,656	21,780	—	129,235	100,982	28,340
1871	292,177	—	35,800	19,431	—	125,577	111,370	34,444
1872	277,518	—	35,372	21,250	—	117,358	103,538	28,533
1873	290,345	—	46,323	23,526	—	104,751	115,745	29,359
1874	302,634	—	42,314	30,933	—	107,120	122,268	29,038
1875	274,623	—	41,121	21,498	—	103,094	108,912	29,456
1876	265,101	—	38,071	18,963	—	100,243	107,824	28,257
1877	241,334	—	37,083	14,960	—	97,125	92,167	27,964
1878	236,964	—	32,154	17,365	—	102,501	84,944	27,137
1879	266,948	—	40,426	15,125	—	105,328	106,069	35,121
1880	267,643	—	38,117	13,537	—	95,758	120,231	56,777
1881	260,713	—	40,466	15,687	—	82,509	122,051	50,059
1882	257,981	—	43,570	15,032	—	71,077	128,302	61,345
1883	265,408	—	48,911	15,283	—	59,160	142,053	66,013
1884	244,126	—	39,430	17,293	—	54,578	132,826	55,429
1885	260,227	—	42,671	16,021	—	51,386	150,149	56,102
1886	242,483	—	34,324	13,908	—	50,580	143,671	63,405
1887	267,932	—	38,561	15,141	—	47,742	166,488	75,029
1888	267,925	—	38,522	16,926	—	44,715	167,761	80,289
1889	299,289	—	44,435	21,379	—	41,001	192,473	87,625
1890	318,041	—	44,583	22,006	—	36,099	215,352	106,937
1891	365,774	—	48,720	26,114	—	37,547	253,393	124,416
1892	345,023	—	46,895	29,174	—	23,378	245,576	134,583
1893	383,478	—	49,642	30,136	—	27,264	276,436	159,358
1894	367,525	—	54,568	31,701	—	27,841	253,415	141,177
1895	356,195	—	51,805	28,798	—	30,978	244,615	141,395
1896	352,179	—	50,831	27,148	—	35,385	238,816	139,434
1897	365,774	—	48,950	34,562	—	37,791	244,471	141,053
1898	443,369	—	91,992	58,824	—	37,585	254,968	147,452
1899	605,072	—	229,841	63,942	—	39,897	271,392	139,395
1900	520,861	—	134,775	55,953	—	40,160	289,973	140,877
1901	524,617	—	144,616	60,507	—	32,343	287,151	139,324
1902	485,234	—	112,272	67,803	—	29,108	276,051	138,489
1903	517,006	—	118,630	82,618	—	28,556	287,202	138,426
1904	583,660	—	165,200	102,956	—	24,646	290,857	142,559
1905	567,279	—	126,094	117,550	—	24,591	299,044	141,774
1906	570,202	—	137,326	110,474	—	24,309	298,093	141,035
1907	579,129	—	149,775	97,128	—	24,481	307,744	139,310
1908	659,196	—	175,840	118,037	—	21,426	343,893	153,892
1909	693,744	—	192,487	115,546	—	21,804	363,907	161,710

Notes appear at end of table

TABLE Ea636–643   Federal government expenditure, by major function: 1789–1970   *Continued*

		Defense					Other	
	Total	Total (Department of Defense)	Army	Navy	Air Force	Interest on public debt	Total	Veterans' compensation and pensions
	Ea636	Ea637	Ea638	Ea639	Ea640	Ea641	Ea642	Ea643
Fiscal year	Thousand dollars	Thousand dollars	Thousand dollars	Thousand dollars	Thousand dollars	Thousand dollars	Thousand dollars	Thousand dollars
1910	693,617	—	189,823	123,174		21,343	359,277	160,696
1911	691,202	—	197,199	119,938	—	21,311	352,753	157,981
1912	689,881	—	184,123	135,592	—	22,616	347,550	153,591
1913	714,864	—	202,129	133,263	—	22,899	356,573	175,085
1914	725,525	—	208,349	139,682	—	22,864	354,630	173,440
1915	746,093	—	202,060	141,836	—	22,903	379,295	164,388
1916	712,967	—	183,176	153,854	—	22,901	353,036	159,302
1917	1,953,857	—	377,941	239,633	—	24,743	1,311,541	160,318
1918	12,677,359	—	4,869,955	1,278,840	—	189,743	6,338,820	181,138
1919	18,492,665	—	9,009,076	2,002,311	—	619,216	6,862,063	221,615
1920	6,357,677	—	1,621,953	736,021	—	1,020,252	2,979,451	213,344
1921	5,061,785	—	1,118,076	650,374	—	999,145	2,294,190	260,611
1922	3,289,404	—	457,756	476,775	—	991,001	1,363,872	252,577
1923	3,140,287	—	397,051	333,201	—	1,055,924	1,354,111	264,148
1924	2,907,847	—	357,017	332,249	—	940,603	1,277,978	228,262
1925	2,923,762	—	370,981	346,137	—	881,807	1,324,837	218,321
1926	2,929,964	—	364,090	312,743	—	831,938	1,421,193	207,190
1927	2,857,429	—	369,114	318,909	—	787,020	1,382,386	230,556
1928	2,961,245	—	400,990	331,335	—	731,764	1,497,156	229,401
1929	3,127,199	—	425,946	364,562	—	678,330	1,658,361	229,781
1930	3,320,211	—	464,854	374,164	—	659,348	1,821,846	220,609
1931	3,577,434	—	486,142	353,768	—	611,560	2,125,964	234,402
1932	4,659,182	—	476,305	357,518	—	599,277	3,226,082	232,521
1933	4,598,496	—	434,621	349,373	—	689,365	3,125,137	234,990
1934	6,644,602	—	408,587	296,927	—	756,617	5,182,470	319,322
1935	6,497,008	—	487,995	436,266	—	820,926	4,751,821	373,805
1936	8,421,608	—	618,587	528,882	—	749,397	6,524,742	399,066
1937	7,733,033	—	628,104	556,674	—	866,384	5,681,871	396,047
1938	6,764,628	—	644,264	596,130	—	926,281	4,597,954	402,779
1939	8,841,224	—	695,256	672,722	—	940,540	6,532,705	416,721
1940	9,055,269	—	907,160	891,485	—	1,040,936	6,215,689	429,178
1941	13,254,948	—	3,938,943	2,313,058	—	1,110,693	5,892,255	433,148
1942	34,036,861	—	14,325,508	8,579,589	—	1,260,085	9,871,679	431,294
1943	79,367,714	—	42,525,563	20,888,349	—	1,808,160	14,145,642	442,394
1944	94,986,002	—	49,438,330	26,537,634	—	2,608,980	16,401,058	494,959
1945	98,302,937	—	50,490,102	30,047,152	—	3,616,686	14,148,997	772,190
1946	60,326,042	—	27,986,769	15,164,412	—	4,721,959	12,452,902	1,261,415
1947	38,923,379	—	9,172,139	5,597,203	—	4,957,922	19,196,115	1,929,226
1948	32,955,232	—	7,698,556	4,284,619	—	5,211,102	15,760,955	2,080,130
1949	39,474,413	—	7,862,397	4,434,706	1,690,461	5,339,396	20,147,453	2,153,828
1950	39,544,037	—	5,789,468	4,129,546	3,520,633	5,749,913	20,354,478	2,222,926
1951	43,970,284	—	8,635,939	5,862,549	6,358,604	5,612,655	17,500,538	2,171,475
1952	65,303,201	—	17,452,710	10,231,265	12,851,619	5,859,263	18,908,343	2,177,893
1953	74,119,798	—	17,054,333	11,874,830	15,085,228	6,503,580	23,601,826	2,420,140
1954	70,889,744	40,625,674	—	—	—	6,382,486	23,881,584	2,481,514
1955	68,509,184	35,629,779	—	—	—	6,370,362	26,509,044	2,680,834
1956	70,460,329	35,692,897	—	—	—	6,786,599	27,980,833	2,797,509
1957	76,740,583	38,719,035	—	—	—	7,244,193	30,777,355	2,869,989
1958	82,575,093	39,916,689	—	—	—	7,606,774	35,051,629	3,104,494
1959	92,104,459	44,602,920	—	—	—	7,592,769	39,908,769	3,274,568
1960	92,223,354	43,968,848 [3]	—	—	—	9,179,589	39,074,917	3,368,224
1961	97,794,579	45,688,376 [3]	—	—	—	8,957,242	43,148,961	3,621,506
1962	106,812,594	49,283,445 [3]	—	—	—	9,119,760	48,409,389	3,704,671
1963	111,311,144	49,242,562	—	—	—	9,895,304	52,173,279	3,871,438
1964	118,583,708	50,702,893	—	—	—	10,665,858	57,214,957	3,961,206
1965	118,429,745	47,179,329	—	—	—	11,346,455	59,903,961	4,109,144
1966	134,651,927	55,445,394	—	—	—	12,013,863	67,192,670	4,214,289
1967	158,254,257	68,762,932	—	—	—	13,391,068	76,100,256	4,301,855
1968	178,832,655	78,672,894	—	—	—	14,573,008	85,586,754	4,605,253
1969	184,556,043	79,144,789	—	—	—	16,588,237	88,823,017	4,879,320
1970	196,587,786	78,360,168	—	—	—	19,303,670	98,923,948	5,307,901

Notes appear at end of table

(continued)

TABLE Ea636–643   Federal government expenditure, by major function: 1789–1970   *Continued*

(Z) Less than $500.

[1] Totals for three-year period.

[2] First six months only.

[3] Includes military assistance.

Sources

All series except series Ea643. U.S. Department of the Treasury, *Statistical Appendix to Annual Report of the Secretary of the Treasury* (1970), pp. 8–16.

Series Ea643. 1789–1946, Department of the Treasury, *Annual Report*, (1946), pp. 422–32; 1947–1970, U.S. Office of Management and Budget (formerly Bureau of the Budget), *Budget of the United States Government* (annual issues, 1949–1970).

Documentation

See the text for Table Ea584–587 for a general note on the federal government finances tables.

For 1789–1842, data are for years ending December 31; thereafter, June 30. Data for 1789–1953 are administrative budget figures; thereafter, unified budget figures.

Series Ea636. Equals series Ea585. Effective January 3, 1949, amounts refunded by the government, principally for overpayment of taxes, are reported as deductions from total receipts rather than as outlays. Also, effective July 1, 1948, payments to the Treasury, principally by wholly owned government corporations for retirement of capital stock and for disposition of earnings, are excluded in reporting both budget receipts and outlays. Neither change affects the budget surplus or deficit. Figures beginning with fiscal 1913 have been adjusted accordingly for comparability.

Series Ea638. Formerly War Department.

Series Ea642. Includes interest payments by government corporations and other business-type activities on securities issued by the Treasury. Beginning in 1954, undistributed intrabudgetary transactions are deducted from the total. Beginning in 1932, interfund transactions are deducted from the total.

Series Ea643. Excludes education and training.

TABLE Ea644–649   Federal government expenditure, by major function: 1900–1939

Contributed by John Joseph Wallis

Fiscal year	Total	Major national security	International affairs and finance	Veterans' service and benefits	Interest	Other
	Ea644	Ea645	Ea646	Ea647	Ea648	Ea649
	Million dollars	Million dollars	Million dollars	Million dollars	Million dollars	Million dollars
1900	521	191	—	141	40	149
1901	525	206	—	139	32	148
1902	485	180	—	138	29	138
1903	517	202	—	138	29	148
1904	584	268	—	143	25	148
1905	567	244	—	142	25	156
1906	570	247	—	141	24	158
1907	579	247	—	139	24	169
1908	659	294	—	154	21	190
1909	694	308	—	162	22	202
1910	694	284	—	161	21	228
1911	691	283	—	158	21	229
1912	690	284	5	154	23	224
1913	715	293	5	175	23	219
1914	725	298	5	173	23	226
1915	746	297	5	176	23	245
1916	713	305	6	171	23	208
1917	1,954	602	891	171	25	265
1918	12,662	7,110	4,748	235	198	371
1919	18,448	13,548	3,500	324	616	460
1920	6,357	3,997	435	332	1,024	569
1921	5,058	2,581	83	646	999	749
1922	3,285	929	10	686	991	669
1923	3,137	680	14	747	1,056	640
1924	2,890	647	15	676	941	611
1925	2,881	591	15	741	882	652
1926	2,888	586	17	772	832	681
1927	2,837	578	17	786	787	669
1928	2,933	656	12	806	731	728
1929	3,127	696	14	812	719	886
1930	3,320	734	14	821	697	1,054
1931	3,578	733	16	1,040	628	1,161
1932	4,659	703	19	985	619	2,333
1933	4,623	648	16	863	701	2,395
1934	6,694	540	12	557	770	4,815
1935	6,521	711	19	607	826	4,358
1936	8,494	914	18	2,350	756	4,456
1937	7,756	937	18	1,137	872	4,792
1938	6,792	1,030	19	581	933	4,229
1939	8,858	1,075	20	560	950	6,254

Source

Historical Statistics of the United States (1975), series Y 466–471, which were based on unpublished data from the U.S. Bureau of the Budget.

Documentation

See the text for Table Ea584–587 for a general note on the federal government finances tables.

Series Ea646. Through 1911, included under other outlays.

TABLE Ea650–661   Federal government debt, by type: 1791–1970

Contributed by John Joseph Wallis

					Principal						Computed interest charge and rate	
	Total					Interest-bearing						
				Non-interest-bearing			Bonds					
	Amount	Per capita	Matured	bearing	Total	U.S. savings	Other	Treasury bills	Treasury notes	Special issues	Interest charge	Rate
	Ea650 [1]	Ea651	Ea652	Ea653	Ea654	Ea655	Ea656	Ea657 [2]	Ea658 [3]	Ea659	Ea660	Ea661
Fiscal year	Million dollars	Dollars	Million dollars	Million dollars	Million dollars	Million dollars	Million dollars	Million dollars	Million dollars	Million dollars	Million dollars	Percent
1791	75.5	18.64	—	—	—	—	—	—	—	—	—	—
1792	77.2	18.51	—	—	—	—	—	—	—	—	—	—
1793	80.4	18.69	—	—	—	—	—	—	—	—	—	—
1794	78.4	17.71	—	—	—	—	—	—	—	—	—	—
1795	80.7	17.70	—	—	—	—	—	—	—	—	—	—
1796	83.8	17.82	—	—	—	—	—	—	—	—	—	—
1797	82.1	16.94	—	—	—	—	—	—	—	—	—	—
1798	79.2	15.88	—	—	—	—	—	—	—	—	—	—
1799	78.4	15.25	—	—	—	—	—	—	—	—	—	—
1800	83.0	15.66	—	—	—	—	—	—	—	—	—	—
1801	83.0	15.21	—	—	—	—	—	—	—	—	—	—
1802	80.7	14.33	—	—	—	—	—	—	—	—	—	—
1803	77.1	13.26	—	—	—	—	—	—	—	—	—	—
1804	86.4	14.43	—	—	—	—	—	—	—	—	—	—
1805	82.3	13.32	—	—	—	—	—	—	—	—	—	—
1806	75.7	11.87	—	—	—	—	—	—	—	—	—	—
1807	69.2	10.51	—	—	—	—	—	—	—	—	—	—
1808	65.2	9.59	—	—	—	—	—	—	—	—	—	—
1809	57.0	8.14	—	—	—	—	—	—	—	—	—	—
1810	58.2	8.05	—	—	—	—	—	—	—	—	—	—
1811	48.0	6.46	—	—	—	—	—	—	—	—	—	—
1812	45.2	5.91	—	—	—	—	—	—	—	—	—	—
1813	56.0	7.11	—	—	—	—	—	—	—	—	—	—
1814	81.5	10.08	—	—	—	—	—	—	—	—	—	—
1815	99.8	12.02	—	—	—	—	—	—	—	—	—	—
1816	127.3	14.91	—	—	—	—	—	—	—	—	—	—
1817	123.5	14.05	—	—	—	—	—	—	—	—	—	—
1818	103.5	11.42	—	—	—	—	—	—	—	—	—	—
1819	95.5	10.23	—	—	—	—	—	—	—	—	—	—
1820	91.0	9.46	—	—	—	—	—	—	—	—	—	—
1821	90.0	9.09	—	—	—	—	—	—	—	—	—	—
1822	93.5	9.18	—	—	—	—	—	—	—	—	—	—
1823	90.9	8.66	—	—	—	—	—	—	—	—	—	—
1824	90.3	8.36	—	—	—	—	—	—	—	—	—	—
1825	83.8	7.54	—	—	—	—	—	—	—	—	—	—
1826	81.1	7.08	—	—	—	—	—	—	—	—	—	—
1827	74.0	6.27	—	—	—	—	—	—	—	—	—	—
1828	67.5	5.55	—	—	—	—	—	—	—	—	—	—
1829	58.4	4.66	—	—	—	—	—	—	—	—	—	—
1830	48.6	3.76	—	—	—	—	—	—	—	—	—	—
1831	39.1	2.95	—	—	—	—	—	—	—	—	—	—
1832	24.3	1.78	—	—	—	—	—	—	—	—	—	—
1833	7.0	0.50	—	—	—	—	—	—	—	—	—	—
1834	4.8	0.33	—	—	—	—	—	—	—	—	—	—
1835	(Z)	(Z)	—	—	—	—	—	—	—	—	—	—
1836	(Z)	(Z)	—	—	—	—	—	—	—	—	—	—
1837	0.4	0.02	—	—	—	—	—	—	—	—	—	—
1838	3.3	0.20	—	—	—	—	—	—	—	—	—	—
1839	10.4	0.63	—	—	—	—	—	—	—	—	—	—
1840	3.6	0.21	—	—	—	—	—	—	—	—	—	—
1841	5.3	0.30	—	—	—	—	—	—	—	—	—	—
1842	13.6	0.75	—	—	—	—	—	—	—	—	—	—
1843	32.7	1.76	—	—	—	—	—	—	—	—	—	—
1844	23.5	1.22	—	—	—	—	—	—	—	—	—	—

Notes appear at end of table

TABLE Ea650–661   Federal government debt, by type: 1791–1970 *Continued*

					Principal						Computed interest charge and rate	
	Total					Interest-bearing						
				Non-interest-			Bonds					
	Amount	Per capita	Matured	bearing	Total	U.S. savings	Other	Treasury bills	Treasury notes	Special issues	Interest charge	Rate
	Ea650 [1]	Ea651	Ea652	Ea653	Ea654	Ea655	Ea656	Ea657 [2]	Ea658 [3]	Ea659	Ea660	Ea661
Fiscal year	Million dollars	Dollars	Million dollars	Million dollars	Million dollars	Million dollars	Million dollars	Million dollars	Million dollars	Million dollars	Million dollars	Percent
1845	15.9	0.81	—	—	—	—	—	—	—	—	—	—
1846	15.6	0.77	—	—	—	—	—	—	—	—	—	—
1847	38.8	1.85	—	—	—	—	—	—	—	—	—	—
1848	47.0	2.17	—	—	—	—	—	—	—	—	—	—
1849	63.1	2.81	—	—	—	—	—	—	—	—	—	—
1850	63.5	2.73	—	—	—	—	—	—	—	—	—	—
1851	68.3	2.83	—	—	—	—	—	—	—	—	—	—
1852	65.2	2.61	—	—	—	—	—	—	—	—	—	—
1853	59.8	2.31	0.2	—	59.6	—	—	—	—	—	—	—
1854	42.2	1.57	0.2	—	42.0	—	—	—	—	—	—	—
1855	35.6	1.28	0.2	—	35.4	—		—	—	—	2.3	—
1856	32.0	1.12	0.2	—	31.8	—	—	—	—	—	1.9	—
1857	28.7	0.98	0.2	—	28.5	—	—	—	—	—	1.7	—
1858	44.9	1.49	0.2	—	44.7	—	—	—	—	—	2.4	—
1859	58.5	1.90	0.2	—	58.3	—	—	—	—	—	3.1	—
1860	64.8	2.06	0.2	—	64.7	—	—	—	—	—	3.4	—
1861	90.6	2.81	0.2	—	90.4	—	—	—	—	—	5.1	—
1862	524.2	15.94	0.2	158.6	365.4	—	—	—	—	—	22.0	—
1863	1,119.8	33.32	0.2	411.8	707.8	—	—	—	—	—	41.9	—
1864	1,815.8	52.82	0.4	455.4	1,360.0	—	—	—	—	—	78.9	—
1865	2,677.9	76.12	2.1	458.1	2,217.7	—	—	—	—	—	137.7	—
1866	2,755.8	76.44	4.4	429.2	2,322.1		—	—	—	—	146.1	—
1867	2,650.2	71.68	1.7	409.5	2,239.0		—	—	—	—	138.9	—
1868	2,583.4	68.19	1.2	390.9	2,191.3	—	—	—	—	—	128.5	—
1869	2,545.1	65.48	5.1	388.5	2,151.5	—	—	—	—	—	125.5	—
1870	2,436.5	61.06	3.6	397.0	2,035.9	—	—	—	—	—	118.8	—
1871	2,322.1	56.62	1.9	399.4	1,920.7	—	—	—	—	—	111.9	—
1872	2,210.0	52.54	7.9	401.3	1,800.8	—	—	—	—	—	104.0	—
1873	2,151.2	49.77	51.9	402.8	1,696.5	—	—	—	—	—	98.1	—
1874	2,159.9	48.62	3.2	431.8	1,724.9	—	—	—	—	—	98.8	—
1875	2,156.3	47.40	11.4	436.2	1,708.7	—	—	—	—	—	96.9	—
1876	2,130.8	45.87	3.9	430.3	1,696.7	—	—	—	—	—	96.1	—
1877	2,107.8	44.47	16.6	393.2	1,697.9	—	—	—	—	—	93.2	—
1878	2,159.4	44.69	5.6	373.1	1,780.7	—	—	—	—	—	94.7	—
1879	2,298.9	46.67	37.0	374.2	1,887.7	—	—	—	—	—	83.8	—
1880	2,090.9	41.60	7.6	373.3	1,710.0	—	1,709	1	—	—	79.7	—
1881	2,019.3	39.24	6.7	387.0	1,625.6	—	1,625	1	—	—	75.0	—
1882	1,856.9	35.11	16.3	390.8	1,449.8	—	1,449	(Z)	—	—	57.4	—
1883	1,722.0	31.63	7.8	389.9	1,324.2	—	1,324	(Z)	—	—	51.4	—
1884	1,625.3	29.11	19.7	393.1	1,212.6	—	1,212	(Z)	—	—	47.9	—
1885	1,578.6	27.63	4.1	392.3	1,182.2	—	1,182	(Z)	—	—	47.0	—
1886	1,555.7	26.70	9.7	413.9	1,132.0	—	1,132	(Z)	—	—	45.5	—
1887	1,465.5	24.69	6.1	451.7	1,007.7	—	1,008	(Z)	—	—	41.8	—
1888	1,384.6	22.84	2.5	445.6	936.5	—	936	(Z)	—	—	39.0	—
1889	1,249.5	20.19	1.9	431.7	815.9	—	816	(Z)	—	—	33.8	—
1890	1,122.4	17.80	1.8	409.3	711.3	—	711	(Z)	—	—	29.4	—
1891	1,005.8	15.61	1.6	393.7	610.5	—	610	(Z)	—	—	23.6	—
1892	968.2	14.69	2.8	380.4	585.0	—	585	(Z)	—	—	22.9	—
1893	961.4	14.25	2.1	374.3	585.0	—	585	(Z)	—	—	22.9	—
1894	1,016.9	14.76	1.9	380.0	635.0	—	635	(Z)	—	—	25.4	—
1895	1,096.9	15.65	1.7	379.0	716.2	—	716	(Z)	—	—	29.1	—
1896	1,222.7	17.18	1.6	373.7	847.4	—	847	(Z)	—	—	34.4	—
1897	1,226.8	16.94	1.3	378.1	847.4	—	847	(Z)	—	—	34.4	—
1898	1,232.7	16.75	1.3	384.1	847.4	—	847	(Z)	—	—	34.4	—
1899	1,436.7	19.21	1.2	389.4	1,046.0	—	1,046	(Z)	—	—	40.8	—

Notes appear at end of table

(continued)

TABLE Ea650–661   Federal government debt, by type: 1791–1970   *Continued*

	Total				Principal			Interest-bearing				Computed interest charge and rate	
				Non-interest-bearing		Bonds							
	Amount	Per capita	Matured		Total	U.S. savings	Other	Treasury bills	Treasury notes	Special issues	Interest charge	Rate	
	Ea650 [1]	Ea651	Ea652	Ea653	Ea654	Ea655	Ea656	Ea657 [2]	Ea658 [3]	Ea659	Ea660	Ea661	
Fiscal year	Million dollars	Dollars	Million dollars	Million dollars	Million dollars	Million dollars	Million dollars	Million dollars	Million dollars	Million dollars	Million dollars	Percent
1900	1,263.4	16.60	1.2	238.8	1,023.5	—	1,023	(Z)	—	—	33.5	—
1901	1,221.6	15.75	1.4	233.0	987.1	—	987	(Z)	—	—	29.8	—
1902	1,178.0	14.88	1.3	245.7	931.1	—	913	(Z)	—	—	27.5	—
1903	1,159.4	14.38	1.2	243.7	914.5	—	915	(Z)	—	—	25.5	—
1904	1,136.3	13.83	2.0	239.1	895.2	—	895	(Z)	—	—	24.2	—
1905	1,132.4	13.51	1.4	235.8	895.2	—	895	(Z)	—	—	24.2	—
1906	1,142.5	13.37	1.1	246.2	895.2	—	895	(Z)	—	—	23.2	—
1907	1,147.2	13.18	1.1	251.3	894.8	—	895	(Z)	—	—	21.6	—
1908	1,177.7	13.28	4.1	276.1	897.5	—	883	14	—	—	21.1	—
1909	1,148.3	12.69	2.9	232.1	913.3	—	913	—	—	—	21.3	—
1910	1,146.9	12.41	2.1	231.5	913.3	—	913	—	—	—	21.3	—
1911	1,154.0	12.29	1.9	236.8	915.4	—	915	—	—	—	21.3	—
1912	1,193.8	12.52	1.8	228.3	963.8	—	964	—	—	—	22.8	—
1913	1,193.0	12.27	1.7	225.7	965.7	—	966	—	—	—	22.8	—
1914	1,188.2	11.99	1.6	218.7	968.0	—	968	—	—	—	22.9	—
1915	1,191.3	11.85	1.5	220.0	969.8	—	970	—	—	—	22.9	—
1916	1,225.1	12.02	1.5	252.1	971.6	—	967	—	4	—	23.1	2.38
1917	2,975.6	28.81	14.2	248.8	2,712.5	—	2,412	273	27	—	83.6	3.12
1918	12,455.3	120.68	20.2	237.5	12,197.5	—	9,911	1,706	369	—	468.6	3.91
1919	25,484.5	243.84	11.2	236.4	25,236.9	—	17,188	3,625	4,422	—	1,054.2	4.18
1920	24,299.3	228.25	6.7	230.1	24,062.5	—	16,218	2,769	5,075	—	1,016.6	4.23
1921	23,977.5	220.91	10.7	227.9	23,738.9	—	16,119	2,700	4,920	—	1,029.9	4.34
1922	22,963.4	208.67	25.3	227.8	22,710.3	—	15,965	1,829	4,916	—	962.9	4.24
1923	22,349.7	199.65	98.7	243.9	22,007.0	—	16,535	1,031	4,441	—	927.3	4.21
1924	21,250.8	186.23	30.3	239.3	20,981.2	—	16,025	808	4,148	—	877.0	4.18
1925	20,516.2	177.12	30.3	275.0	20,210.9	—	16,842	533	2,740	95	829.7	4.11
1926	19,643.2	167.32	13.4	246.1	19,383.8	—	16,928	453	1,799	204	793.4	4.09
1927	18,511.9	155.52	14.7	244.5	18,252.7	—	15,222	686	1,986	359	722.7	3.96
1928	17,604.3	146.08	45.3	241.3	17,317.7	—	13,021	1,252	2,582	462	671.4	3.88
1929	16,931.1	139.05	50.7	241.4	16,638.9	—	12,125	1,640	2,267	607	656.7	3.95
1930	16,185.3	131.51	31.7	231.7	15,921.9	—	12,111	1,420	1,626	764	606.0	3.81
1931	16,801.3	135.45	51.8	229.9	16,519.6	—	13,531	2,246	452	291	589.0	3.57
1932	19,487.0	156.10	60.1	265.7	19,161.3	—	14,250	3,341	1,261	309	671.6	3.51
1933	22,538.7	179.48	65.9	315.1	22,157.6	—	14,223	3,063	4,548	323	742.2	3.35
1934	27,053.1	214.07	54.3	518.4	26,480.5	—	16,510	2,921	6,653	396	842.3	3.18
1935	28,700.9	225.55	230.7	825.0	27,645.2	62	14,874	2,053	10,023	633	750.7	2.72
1936	33,778.5	263.79	169.4	620.4	32,988.8	316	18,312	2,354	11,381	626	838.0	2.56
1937	36,424.6	282.74	118.5	506.0	35,800.1	800	20,522	2,303	10,617	1,558	924.3	2.58
1938	37,164.7	286.27	141.4	447.5	36,575.9	1,238	22,361	1,154	9,147	2,676	947.1	2.59
1939	40,439.5	308.98	142.3	411.3	39,886.0	1,868	25,698	1,308	7,243	3,770	1,036.9	2.60
1940	42,967.5	325.63	204.6	386.4	42,376.5	2,905	27,012	1,302	6,383	4,775	1,094.6	2.58
1941	48,961.4	367.80	205.0	369.0	48,387.4	4,314	30,652	1,603	5,698	6,120	1,218.2	2.52
1942	72,422.4	540.79	98.3	355.7	71,968.4	10,188	38,588	5,604	9,703	7,885	1,644.5	2.29
1943	136,696.1	1,018.26	140.5	1,175.3	135,380.3	21,256	58,164	28,425	16,663	10,871	2,678.8	1.98
1944	201,003.4	1,512.61	200.9	1,259.2	199,543.4	34,606	80,132	43,557	26,962	14,287	3,849.3	1.93
1945	258,682.2	1,952.60	268.7	2,056.9	256,356.6	45,586	107,149	51,177	33,633	18,812	4,963.7	1.94
1946	269,422.1	1,923.70	376.4	934.8	268,110.9	49,035	119,929	51,843	24,972	22,332	5,350.8	2.00
1947	258,286.4	1,800.58	230.9	2,942.1	255,113.4	51,367	121,607	41,071	13,702	27,366	5,374.4	2.11
1948	252,292.2	1,726.93	279.8	1,949.1	250,063.3	53,274	114,464	36,345	15,769	30,211	5,455.5	2.18
1949	252,770.4	1,700.27	244.8	1,764.0	250,761.6	56,260	112,306	40,964	8,456	32,776	5,605.9	2.24
1950	257,357.4	1,694.61	264.8	1,883.2	255,209.4	57,536	104,490	31,951	28,876	32,356	5,612.7	2.20
1951	255,222.0	1,657.48	512.0	1,858.2	252,851.8	57,572	93,881	23,123	43,624	34,653	5,739.6	2.27
1952	259,105.2	1,656.76	418.7	1,823.6	256,862.9	57,685	90,221	45,642	25,575	37,739	5,981.4	2.33
1953	266,071.1	1,673.87	298.4	1,826.6	263,946.0	57,886	95,084	35,561	34,878	40,538	6,431.0	2.44
1954	271,259.6	1,675.64	437.2	1,912.6	268,909.8	58,061	93,660	37,920	37,039	42,229	6,298.1	2.34

Notes appear at end of table

TABLE Ea650–661   Federal government debt, by type: 1791–1970   *Continued*

					Principal							Computed interest charge and rate	
	Total					Interest-bearing							
							Bonds						
	Amount	Per capita	Matured	Non-interest-bearing	Total	U.S. savings	Other	Treasury bills	Treasury notes	Special issues	Interest charge	Rate
	Ea650 [1]	Ea651	Ea652	Ea653	Ea654	Ea655	Ea656	Ea657 [2]	Ea658 [3]	Ea659	Ea660	Ea661
Fiscal year	Million dollars	Dollars	Million dollars	Million dollars	Million dollars	Million dollars	Million dollars	Million dollars	Million dollars	Million dollars	Million dollars	Percent
1955	274,374.2	1,662.18	588.6	2,044.4	271,741.3	58,365	94,133	33,350	42,642	43,250	6,387.2	2.35
1956	272,750.8	1,622.67	666.1	2,201.7	269,883.1	57,497	94,210	37,111	35,952	45,114	6,949.7	2.58
1957	270,527.2	1,580.30	529.2	1,512.4	268,485.6	54,622	92,170	43,893	30,973	46,827	7,325.1	2.73
1958	276,343.2	1,586.82	597.3	1,048.3	274,697.6	51,984	100,725	55,326	20,416	46,246	7,245.2	2.64
1959	284,705.9	1,607.28	476.5	2,396.1	281,833.4	50,503	93,401	65,860	27,314	44,756	8,065.9	2.87
1960	286,330.8	1,590.91	444.6	2,645.0	283,241.2	47,544	88,250	51,065	51,483	44,899	9,316.1	3.30
1961	288,970.9	1,579.15	349.4	2,950.0	285,671.6	47,514	86,796	50,062	56,257	45,043	8,761.5	3.07
1962	298,200.8	1,605.21	437.6	3,321.2	294,442.0	47,607	79,915	56,518	65,464	44,939	9,518.9	3.24
1963	305,859.6	1,622.74	310.4	3,595.5	301,953.7	48,314	86,619	69,891	52,328	44,801	10,119.3	3.36
1964	311,712.9	1,630.80	295.3	4,061.0	307,356.6	49,299	92,962	51,028	67,436	46,627	10,900.4	3.56
1965	317,273.9	1,639.44	292.3	3,868.8	313,112.8	50,043	107,183	54,537	52,699	48,650	11,466.6	3.68
1966	319,907.1	1,635.72	307.7	4,168.4	315,431.1	50,537	105,439	57,348	50,987	51,120	12,516.4	3.99
1967	326,220.9	1,652.11	284.3	3,650.7	322,286.0	51,213	100,243	64,899	49,774	56,155	12,952.9	4.04
1968	347,578.4	1,743.13	254.0	2,923.9	344,400.5	51,712	93,789	65,580	73,793	59,526	15,403.8	4.50
1969	353,720.3	1,756.44	460.7	1,530.1	351,729.4	51,711	81,430	69,039	82,761	66,790	17,086.6	4.89
1970	370,918.7	1,818.37	366.0	1,527.2	369,025.5	51,281	65,551	78,050	97,821	76,323	20,338.9	5.56

(Z) Series Ea650: less than $50,000. Series Ea651: less than $0.005. Series Ea657: less than $500,000.

[1] Figures for 1791–1852 are not entirely comparable with later figures.

[2] Includes certificates of indebtedness. For 1880–1907, includes refunding certificates of deposit.

[3] For 1918–1929, includes old Treasury (War) savings securities.

Sources

Series Ea650–654. U.S. Department of the Treasury, *Statistical Appendix to Annual Report of the Secretary of the Treasury* (1970), pp. 60–1.

Series Ea655–659. 1880–1915, U.S. Department of the Treasury, unpublished data; 1916–1970, *Annual Report* (1946), p. 459; *Annual Report* (1958), pp. 472–3; *Annual Report* (1967), p. 506; and *Statistical Appendix* (1970), p. 66.

Series Ea660–661. 1855 and 1892–1915: U.S. Bureau of Foreign and Domestic Commerce, *Statistical Abstract of the United States* (1921), p. 829; 1856–1891 and 1916–1970: U.S. Department of the Treasury, *Annual Report* (1891), p. XCIV; U.S. Department of the Treasury, *Annual Report* (1946), p. 546; and U.S. Department of the Treasury, *Statistical Appendix* (1970), pp. 220–1.

Documentation

See the text for Table Ea584–587 for a general note on the federal government finances tables.

Figures represent gross federal debt outstanding. See Table Ea662–678 for data after 1967 presented using a different categorization.

Series Ea651. Equals series Ea650 divided by series Aa7, U.S. resident population.

Series Ea653. Includes old demand notes; U.S. notes (gold reserve deducted since 1900); postal currency and fractional currency, less the amounts officially estimated to have been destroyed; and also the deposits held by the Treasury for the retirement of Federal Reserve bank notes and for national bank notes of national banks that failed, are in liquidation, and are reducing circulation, which, prior to 1890, were not included in the published debt statements. Does not include gold, silver, or currency certificates, or Treasury notes of 1890, for redemption of which an exact equivalent of the respective kinds of money or bullion is held in the Treasury.

Series Ea654. Excludes bonds issued to Pacific Railways (provision was made by law to secure the Treasury against both principal and interest) and the Navy pension fund (which was not a debt, the principal being the property of the United States). The Statement of the Public Debt included the railroad bonds from issuance and the Navy fund from September 1, 1896, until the Statement of June 30, 1890.

Series Ea656. Includes Treasury, Panama Canal, Depositary, and U.S. retirement bonds.

Series Ea659. Comprises special issues to government agencies and trust funds.

TABLE Ea662–678   Federal government debt, by type: 1967–2000

Contributed by John Joseph Wallis

Fiscal year	Total Amount Ea662 (Million dollars)	Total Per capita Ea663 (Dollars)	Total Ea664 (Million dollars)	Marketable Total Ea665 [1] (Million dollars)	Marketable Treasury bills Ea666 (Million dollars)	Marketable Treasury notes Ea667 (Million dollars)	Marketable Treasury bonds Ea668 (Million dollars)	Marketable Other Ea669 (Million dollars)	Total Ea670 (Million dollars)	U.S. savings bonds Ea671 (Million dollars)	Foreign government Ea672 (Million dollars)	Gov. account series Total Ea673 (Million dollars)	Gov.-sponsored enterprises Ea674 (Million dollars)	State and local government Ea675 [2] (Million dollars)	Other Ea676 [2] (Million dollars)	Non-int.-bearing Total Ea677 [3] (Million dollars)	Matured debt not paying interest Ea678 (Million dollars)
1967	326,221	1,652	322,286	210,672	64,145 [4]	49,108	97,418	0	111,614	51,213	1,514	56,155	18,400	—	2,731	3,935	284
1968	347,578	1,743	344,401	226,592	64,440	71,073	91,079	0	117,808	51,712	3,741	59,526	21,600	—	2,828	3,178	254
1969	353,720	1,756	351,729	226,107	68,356	78,946	78,805	0	125,623	51,711	4,070	66,790	30,600	—	3,051	1,991	461
1970	370,918	1,818	369,026	232,599	76,154	93,489	62,956	0	136,426	51,281	4,755	76,323	38,900	—	4,068	1,892	365
1971	398,130	1,925	396,289	245,473	86,677	104,807	53,989	0	150,816	53,003	9,270	82,784	40,000	—	5,759	1,841	322
1972	427,260	2,042	425,360	257,202	94,648	113,419	49,135	0	168,158	55,921	18,985	89,598	43,500	—	3,654	1,901	380
1973	458,142	2,168	456,353	262,971	100,061	117,840	45,071	0	193,382	59,418	28,524	101,738	59,800	—	3,701	1,788	255
1974	475,060	2,227	473,238	266,575	105,019	128,419	33,137	0	206,663	61,921	25,011	115,442	76,400	—	4,289	1,822	277
1975	533,189	2,475	532,122	315,606	128,569	150,257	36,779	0	216,516	65,482	23,216	124,173	78,800	—	3,644	1,067	338
1976	620,433	2,852	619,254	392,581	161,198	191,758	39,626	0	226,673	69,733	21,500	130,557	81,200	—	4,883	1,179	460
1977	698,840	3,180	697,629	443,508	156,091	241,692	45,724	0	254,121	75,411	21,799	140,113	88,200	—	16,797	1,211	462
1978	771,544	3,474	766,971	485,155	160,936	267,865	56,355	0	281,816	79,798	21,680	153,271	111,300	—	27,067	4,573	3,787
1979	826,519	3,681	819,007	506,693	161,378	274,242	71,073	0	312,314	80,440	28,115	176,360	135,500	—	27,400	7,512	6,668
1980	907,701	3,995	906,402	594,506	199,832	310,903	83,772	0	311,896	72,727	25,158	189,848	159,900	—	24,164	1,299	393
1981	997,855	4,349	996,495	683,209	223,388	363,643	96,178	0	313,286	68,017	20,499	201,052	190,400	—	23,718	1,360	406
1982	1,142,035	4,930	1,140,883	824,422	277,900	442,890	103,631	0	316,461	67,274	14,641	210,462	205,400	—	24,085	1,151	420
1983	1,377,211	5,891	1,375,751	1,024,000	340,733	557,525	125,742	0	351,751	70,024	11,450	234,684	206,800	—	35,593	1,459	738
1984	1,572,267	6,667	1,559,570	1,176,556	356,798	661,687	158,070	0	383,015	72,832	8,806	259,534	237,200	—	41,843	12,696	12,006
1985	1,823,103	7,663	1,821,010	1,360,179	384,220	776,449	199,510	0	460,831	77,011	6,638	313,928	257,800	62,778	476	2,093	1,421
1986	2,125,304	8,851	2,122,684	1,564,329	410,730	896,884	241,716	15,000	558,355	85,551	4,128	365,872	273,000	102,367	437	2,619	1,942
1987	2,350,277	9,700	2,347,750	1,675,980	378,263	1,005,127	277,590	15,000	671,769	97,004	4,350	440,658	303,200	129,029	728	2,527	1,828
1988	2,602,338	10,644	2,599,877	1,802,905	398,451	1,089,578	299,875	15,000	796,972	106,176	6,320	536,455	348,100	147,596	425	2,460	1,745
1989	2,857,431	11,577	2,836,309	1,892,763	406,597	1,133,193	337,974	15,000	943,546	114,025	6,818	663,677	373,300	158,580	446	21,122	20,392
1990	3,233,313	12,953	3,210,943	2,092,759	482,454	1,218,081	377,224	15,000	1,118,184	122,152	36,041	779,412	393,700	161,248	19,331	22,370	21,612
1991	3,665,303	14,488	3,662,759	2,390,660	564,589	1,387,717	423,354	15,000	1,272,099	133,512	41,639	908,406	402,900	158,117	30,425	2,544	1,766
1992	4,064,621	15,846	4,061,801	2,677,476	634,287	1,566,349	461,840	15,000	1,384,325	148,266	37,039	1,011,020	443,100	157,570	30,430	2,819	1,978
1993	4,411,489	16,973	4,408,567	2,904,910	658,381	1,734,161	497,367	15,000	1,503,657	167,024	42,459	1,114,289	523,700	149,449	30,436	2,922	1,974
1994	4,692,750	17,835	4,689,524	3,091,602	697,295	1,867,507	511,800	15,000	1,597,922	176,413	41,996	1,211,689	700,600	137,386	30,438	3,226	2,117
1995	4,973,983	18,680	4,950,644	3,260,447	742,462	1,980,343	522,643	15,000	1,690,197	181,181	40,950	1,324,270	806,500	113,368	19,331	23,339	22,031
1996	5,224,811	19,395	5,220,790	3,418,371	761,232	2,098,670	543,549	15,000	1,802,419	184,147	37,488	1,454,690	896,900	95,674	30,420	4,021	1,766
1997	5,413,146	19,854	5,407,528	3,439,616	701,909	2,122,172	576,151	39,384	1,967,912	182,665	34,939	1,608,478	995,300	111,863	29,967	5,618	—
1998	5,526,193	20,033	5,518,681	3,331,030	637,648	2,009,115	610,444	73,823	2,187,651	180,816	35,079	1,777,329	1,273,600	164,431	29,996	7,512	—
1999	5,656,271	20,270	5,647,241	3,232,998	653,165	1,828,775	643,695	107,363	2,414,242	180,019	30,970	2,005,166	1,591,700	168,091	29,996	9,030	—
2000	5,674,178	20,112	5,622,092	2,992,752	616,174	1,611,326	635,263	129,989	2,629,341	177,724	25,431	2,242,900	1,825,800	153,288	29,998	52,086	—

1 Beginning 1986, includes federal financing securities not shown separately, in the amount of $15,000 million.

2 Through 1984, figures for series Ea675 are included with series Ea676.

3 Includes debt issued for the International Monetary Fund; after 1975 this debt is excluded from totals.

4 Includes $5,610 million of certificates of indebtedness.

TABLE Ea662–678   Federal government debt, by type: 1967–2000   *Continued*

Sources

Series Ea662–673 and Ea675–678. Through 1974: U.S. Treasury Department, "Daily Statement of the United States Treasury"; 1975–2000: U.S. Treasury Department, "Monthly Statement of the Public Debt."

Series Ea674. Federal Reserve Board, "Flow of Funds Accounts of the United States" (2002).

Documentation

See the text for Table Ea584–587 for a general note on the federal government finances tables.

Figures represent gross federal debt outstanding. See Table Ea650–661 for earlier data that is presented under a somewhat different categorization.

The fiscal year ended June 30 through 1976; September 30 thereafter.

Series Ea663. Equals series Ea662 divided by series Aa7, U.S. resident population.

Series Ea669. Includes $15,000 million in federal financing bank bonds beginning in 1986, and inflation-indexed Treasury bills and notes beginning in 1997.

Series Ea673–674. Series Ea673 comprises special issues to government agencies and trust funds. Series Ea674 – a subset of series Ea673 – includes debt issued by federal home loan banks, the Federal National Mortgage Association, the Federal Home Loan Mortgage Association, the farm credit system, the financing corporation, the Resolution Funding Corporation, and the Student Loan Marketing Association.

Series Ea676. Includes nonmarketable certificates of indebtedness, notes, bonds, and bills in the Treasury foreign dollar-denominated and foreign-currency-denominated issues.

FEDERAL GOVERNMENT FINANCES – OFFICE OF MANAGEMENT AND BUDGET

John Joseph Wallis

TABLE Ea679–682   Federal government finances – revenue, expenditure, and debt: 1940–1999[1]   [OMB]

Contributed by John Joseph Wallis

Fiscal year	Revenue Ea679 Million dollars	Expenditure Ea680 Million dollars	Surplus or deficit Ea681 Million dollars	Gross federal debt Ea682 Million dollars	Fiscal year	Revenue Ea679 Million dollars	Expenditure Ea680 Million dollars	Surplus or deficit Ea681 Million dollars	Gross federal debt Ea682 Million dollars
1940	6,548	9,468	−2,920	50,696	1975	279,090	332,332	−53,242	541,925
1941	8,712	13,653	−4,941	57,531	1976	298,060	371,792	−73,732	628,970
1942	14,634	35,137	−20,503	79,200	(TQ)	81,232	96,000	15,000	643,561
1943	24,001	78,555	−54,554	142,648	1977	355,559	409,218	−53,659	706,398
1944	43,747	91,304	−47,557	204,079	1978	399,561	458,746	−59,186	776,602
1945	45,159	92,712	−47,553	260,123	1979	463,302	503,485	−40,183	829,471
1946	39,296	55,232	−15,936	270,991	1980	517,112	590,947	−73,835	909,050
1947	38,514	34,496	4,018	257,149	1981	599,272	678,249	−78,976	994,845
1948	41,560	29,764	11,796	252,031	1982	617,766	745,755	−127,989	1,137,345
1949	39,415	38,835	580	252,610	1983	600,562	808,380	−207,818	1,371,710
1950	39,443	42,562	−3,119	256,853	1984	666,486	851,874	−185,388	1,564,657
1951	51,616	45,514	6,102	255,288	1985	734,088	946,423	−212,334	1,817,521
1952	66,167	67,686	−1,519	259,097	1986	769,215	990,460	−221,245	2,120,629
1953	69,608	76,101	−6,493	265,963	1987	854,353	1,004,122	−149,769	2,346,125
1954	69,701	70,855	−1,154	270,812	1988	909,303	1,064,489	−155,187	2,601,307
1955	65,451	68,444	−2,993	274,366	1989	991,190	1,143,671	−152,481	2,868,039
1956	74,587	70,640	3,947	272,693	1990	1,031,969	1,253,198	−221,229	3,206,564
1957	79,990	76,578	3,412	272,252	1991	1,055,041	1,324,403	−269,361	3,598,485
1958	79,636	82,405	−2,769	279,666	1992	1,091,279	1,381,684	−290,404	4,002,123
1959	79,249	92,098	−12,849	287,465	1993	1,154,401	1,409,512	−255,110	4,351,403
1960	92,492	92,191	301	290,525	1994	1,258,627	1,461,902	−203,275	4,643,691
1961	94,388	97,723	−3,335	292,648	1995	1,351,830	1,515,837	−164,007	4,921,005
1962	99,676	106,821	−7,146	302,928	1996	1,453,062	1,560,572	−107,510	5,181,921
1963	106,560	111,316	−4,756	310,324	1997	1,579,292	1,601,282	−21,990	5,369,694
1964	112,613	118,528	−5,915	316,059	1998	1,721,798	1,652,619	69,179	5,478,711
1965	116,817	118,228	−1,411	322,318	1999	1,827,454	1,702,875	124,579	5,606,087
1966	130,835	134,532	−3,698	328,498					
1967	148,822	157,464	−8,643	340,445					
1968	152,973	178,134	−25,161	368,685					
1969	186,882	183,640	3,242	365,769					
1970	192,807	195,649	−2,842	380,921					
1971	187,139	210,172	−23,033	408,176					
1972	207,309	230,681	−23,373	435,936					
1973	230,799	245,707	−14,908	466,291					
1974	263,224	269,359	−6,135	483,893					

(TQ) Transition quarter.

[1] Data for 1940–1954 are consolidated cash statement figures; thereafter, unified budget figures.

Source

Office of Management and Budget (OMB), Historical Tables, *Budget of the U.S. Government* (2001), Tables 1.1 and 7.1.

Documentation

See the text for Table Ea584–587 for a general note on the federal government finances tables.

These figures do not match similar data presented in *Historical Statistics of the United States* (1975). This table is based on OMB budget concepts, which after 1934 diverge from those used in *Historical Statistics* (1975).

Through 1976, data are for fiscal years ending June 30; thereafter, September 30.

Series Ea682. Debt measured at the end of the fiscal year.

TABLE Ea683–697 Federal government revenue, by source: 1934–1999 [OMB]

Contributed by John Joseph Wallis

	Income taxes			Social insurance taxes and contributions				Excise taxes			Miscellaneous receipts				
	Total	Individual	Corporate	Total	Employment	Unemployment and insurance	Other retirement	Total	Federal funds	Trust funds	Total	Estate and gift taxes	Customs duties and fees	Federal reserve deposits	Other
	Ea683	Ea684	Ea685	Ea686	Ea687	Ea688	Ea689	Ea690	Ea691	Ea692	Ea693	Ea694	Ea695	Ea696	Ea697
Fiscal year	Million dollars	Million dollars	Million dollars	Million dollars	Million dollars	Million dollars	Million dollars	Million dollars	Million dollars	Million dollars	Million dollars	Million dollars	Million dollars	Million dollars	Million dollars
1934	2,955	420	364	30	—	—	—	1,354	—	—	788	—	—	—	—
1935	3,609	527	529	31	—	—	—	1,439	—	—	1,084	—	—	—	—
1936	3,923	674	719	52	—	—	—	1,631	—	—	847	—	—	—	—
1937	5,387	1,092	1,038	580	—	—	—	1,876	—	—	801	—	—	—	—
1938	6,751	1,286	1,287	1,541	—	—	—	1,863	—	—	773	—	—	—	—
1939	6,295	1,029	1,127	1,593	—	—	—	1,871	—	—	675	—	—	—	—
1940	6,548	892	1,197	1,785	725	1,015	45	1,977	1,977	—	698	353	331	—	14
1941	8,712	1,314	2,124	1,940	827	1,056	57	2,552	2,552	—	781	403	365	—	14
1942	14,634	3,263	4,719	2,452	1,064	1,299	89	3,399	3,399	—	801	420	369	—	11
1943	24,001	6,505	9,557	3,044	1,338	1,477	229	4,096	4,096	—	800	441	308	—	50
1944	43,747	19,705	14,838	3,473	1,557	1,644	272	4,759	4,759	—	972	507	417	—	48
1945	45,159	18,372	15,988	3,451	1,592	1,568	291	6,265	6,255	—	1,083	637	341	—	105
1946	39,296	16,098	11,883	3,115	1,517	1,316	282	6,998	6,998	—	1,202	668	424	—	109
1947	38,514	17,935	8,615	3,422	1,835	1,329	259	7,211	7,211	—	1,331	771	477	15	69
1948	41,560	19,315	9,678	3,751	2,168	1,343	239	7,356	7,356	—	1,461	890	403	100	68
1949	39,415	15,552	11,192	3,781	2,246	1,205	330	7,502	7,532	—	1,388	780	367	187	54
1950	39,443	15,755	10,449	4,338	2,648	1,332	358	7,550	7,550	—	1,351	698	407	192	55
1951	51,616	21,616	14,101	5,674	3,688	1,609	377	8,648	8,648	—	1,578	708	609	189	72
1952	66,167	27,934	21,226	6,445	4,315	1,712	418	8,852	8,852	—	1,710	818	533	278	81
1953	69,608	29,816	21,238	6,820	4,722	1,675	423	9,877	9,877	—	1,857	881	596	298	81
1954	69,701	29,542	21,101	7,208	5,192	1,561	455	9,945	9,945	—	1,905	934	542	341	88
1955	65,451	28,747	17,861	7,862	5,981	1,449	431	9,131	9,131	—	1,850	924	585	251	90
1956	74,587	32,188	20,880	9,320	7,059	1,690	571	9,929	9,929	—	2,270	1,161	682	287	140
1957	79,990	35,620	21,167	9,997	7,405	1,950	642	10,534	9,055	1,479	2,672	1,365	735	434	139
1958	79,636	34,724	20,074	11,239	8,624	1,933	682	10,638	8,612	2,026	2,961	1,393	782	664	123
1959	79,249	36,719	17,309	11,722	8,821	2,131	770	10,578	8,504	2,074	2,921	1,333	925	491	171
1960	92,492	40,715	21,494	14,683	11,248	2,667	768	11,676	9,137	2,539	3,923	1,606	1,105	1,093	119
1961	94,388	41,338	20,954	16,439	12,679	2,903	857	11,860	9,063	2,798	3,796	1,896	982	788	130
1962	99,676	45,571	20,523	17,046	12,835	3,337	875	12,534	9,585	2,949	4,001	2,016	1,142	718	125
1963	106,560	47,588	21,579	19,804	14,746	4,112	946	13,194	9,915	3,279	4,395	2,167	1,205	828	194
1964	112,613	48,697	23,493	21,963	16,959	3,997	1,007	13,731	10,211	3,519	4,731	2,394	1,252	947	139
1965	116,817	48,792	25,461	22,242	17,358	3,803	1,081	14,570	10,911	3,659	5,753	2,716	1,442	1,372	222
1966	130,835	55,446	30,073	25,546	20,662	3,755	1,129	13,062	9,145	3,917	6,708	3,066	1,767	1,713	163
1967	148,822	61,526	33,971	32,619	27,823	3,575	1,221	13,719	9,278	4,441	6,987	2,978	1,901	1,805	302
1968	152,973	68,726	28,665	33,923	29,224	3,346	1,354	14,079	9,700	4,379	7,580	3,051	2,038	2,091	400
1969	186,882	87,249	36,678	39,015	34,236	3,328	1,451	15,222	10,585	4,637	8,718	3,491	2,319	2,662	247
1970	192,807	90,412	32,829	44,362	39,133	3,464	1,765	15,705	10,352	5,354	9,499	3,644	2,430	3,266	158
1971	187,139	86,230	26,785	47,325	41,699	3,674	1,952	16,614	10,510	6,104	10,185	3,735	2,591	3,533	325
1972	207,309	94,737	32,166	52,574	46,120	4,357	2,097	15,477	9,506	5,971	12,355	5,436	3,287	3,252	380
1973	230,799	103,246	36,153	63,115	54,876	6,051	2,187	16,260	9,836	6,424	12,026	4,917	3,188	3,495	425
1974	263,224	118,952	38,620	75,071	65,888	6,837	2,347	16,844	9,743	7,100	13,737	5,035	3,334	4,845	523

(continued)

TABLE Ea683–697　Federal government revenue, by source: 1934–1999　[OMB]　Continued

	Income taxes			Social insurance taxes and contributions				Excise taxes			Miscellaneous receipts				
	Total	Individual	Corporate	Total	Employment	Unemployment and insurance	Other retirement	Total	Federal funds	Trust funds	Total	Estate and gift taxes	Customs duties and fees	Federal reserve deposits	Other
Fiscal year	Ea683	Ea684	Ea685	Ea686	Ea687	Ea688	Ea689	Ea690	Ea691	Ea692	Ea693	Ea694	Ea695	Ea696	Ea697
	Million dollars	Million dollars	Million dollars	Million dollars	Million dollars	Million dollars	Million dollars	Million dollars	Million dollars	Million dollars	Million dollars	Million dollars	Million dollars	Million dollars	Million dollars
1975	279,090	122,386	40,621	84,534	75,199	6,771	2,565	16,551	9,400	7,151	14,998	4,611	3,676	5,777	935
1976	298,060	131,603	41,409	90,769	79,901	8,054	2,814	16,963	10,612	6,351	17,317	5,216	4,074	5,451	2,576
(TQ)	81,232	38,801	8,460	25,219	21,801	2,698	720	4,473	2,520	1,953	4,279	1,455	1,212	1,500	111
1977	355,559	157,626	54,892	106,485	92,199	11,312	2,974	17,548	9,648	7,900	19,008	7,327	5,150	5,908	623
1978	399,561	180,988	59,952	120,967	103,881	13,850	3,237	18,376	10,054	8,323	19,278	5,285	6,573	6,641	778
1979	463,302	217,841	65,677	138,939	120,058	15,387	3,494	18,745	9,808	8,937	22,101	5,411	7,439	8,327	925
1980	517,112	244,069	64,600	157,803	138,748	15,336	3,719	24,329	15,563	8,766	26,311	6,389	7,174	11,767	981
1981	599,272	285,917	61,137	182,720	162,973	15,763	3,984	40,839	34,128	6,711	28,659	6,787	8,083	12,834	956
1982	617,766	297,744	49,207	201,498	180,686	16,600	4,212	36,311	28,670	7,641	33,006	7,991	8,854	15,186	975
1983	600,562	288,938	37,022	208,994	185,766	18,799	4,429	35,300	24,086	11,214	30,309	6,053	8,655	14,492	1,108
1984	666,486	298,415	56,893	239,376	209,658	25,138	4,580	37,361	22,279	15,082	34,440	6,010	11,370	15,684	1,376
1985	734,088	334,531	61,331	265,163	234,646	25,758	4,759	35,992	19,097	16,894	37,072	6,422	12,079	17,059	1,512
1986	769,215	348,959	63,143	283,901	255,062	24,098	4,742	32,919	16,053	16,866	40,292	6,958	13,327	18,374	1,634
1987	854,353	392,557	83,926	303,318	273,028	25,575	4,715	32,457	14,844	17,613	42,095	7,493	15,085	16,817	2,701
1988	909,303	401,181	94,508	334,335	305,093	24,584	4,658	35,227	16,185	19,042	44,051	7,594	16,198	17,163	3,096
1989	991,190	445,690	103,291	359,416	332,859	22,011	4,546	34,386	13,147	21,239	48,407	8,745	16,334	19,604	3,724
1990	1,031,969	466,884	93,507	380,047	353,891	21,635	4,522	35,345	15,591	19,754	56,186	11,500	16,707	24,319	3,659
1991	1,055,041	467,827	98,086	396,016	370,526	20,922	4,568	42,402	18,275	24,127	50,710	11,138	15,949	19,158	4,465
1992	1,091,279	475,964	100,270	413,689	385,491	23,410	4,788	45,569	21,836	23,733	55,787	11,143	17,359	22,920	4,364
1993	1,154,401	509,680	117,520	428,300	396,939	26,556	4,805	48,057	24,522	23,535	50,844	12,577	18,802	14,908	4,557
1994	1,258,627	543,055	140,385	461,475	428,810	28,004	4,661	55,225	31,226	23,999	58,487	15,225	20,099	18,023	5,141
1995	1,351,830	590,244	157,004	484,473	451,045	28,878	4,550	57,484	26,941	30,543	62,625	14,763	19,301	23,378	5,183
1996	1,453,062	656,417	171,824	509,414	476,361	28,584	4,469	54,014	25,447	28,567	61,393	17,189	18,670	20,477	5,057
1997	1,579,292	737,466	182,293	539,371	506,751	28,202	4,418	56,924	27,831	29,093	63,238	19,845	17,928	19,636	5,829
1998	1,721,798	828,586	188,677	571,831	540,014	27,484	4,333	57,673	21,665	36,008	75,031	24,076	18,297	24,540	8,118
1999	1,827,454	879,480	184,680	611,833	580,880	26,480	4,473	70,414	19,293	51,121	81,047	27,782	18,336	25,917	9,012

(TQ) Transition quarter.

Source

U.S. Office of Management and Budget (OMB), Historical Tables, *Budget of the United States Government* (2001), Tables 2.1, 2.4, and 2.5.

Documentation

See the text for Table Ea584–587 for a general note on the federal government finances tables.

Series Ea683. Totals reflect interfund and intergovernmental transactions or other functions, not shown separately.

Series Ea684. Beginning in 1989, includes trust fund receipts for catastrophic health insurance.

Series Ea685. Beginning in 1987, includes trust fund receipts for the hazardous substance superfund.

Series Ea687. Employment taxes include Old-Age and Survivors Insurance (OASI), Disability Insurance (DI, beginning in 1957), Hospital Insurance (HI, beginning in 1966), and the Railroad Social Security Equivalent account (beginning in 1986).

Series Ea691. Includes alcohol and tobacco excise revenues. Also includes crude oil windfall excise revenues (beginning in 1980), telephone excise revenues (beginning in 1984), ozone-depleting chemicals excise (beginning in 1990), and transportation fuels excise (beginning in 1991).

Series Ea692. Trust fund excise revenues include highway funds from 1957 on. They also include airport and airway excises since 1971; black lung disability since 1978; hazardous substance response superfund and inland waterway excises since 1981; postclosure liability (hazardous waste) excises since 1984; aquatic resource excises since 1984; leaking underground storage tank excises since 1987; vaccine injury compensation excises since 1988; and oil spill liability excises since 1990.

Series Ea696. Deposits of earnings by the Federal Reserve System.

Series Ea697. Beginning in 1984, includes universal service fund receipts.

TABLE Ea698–703   Federal government expenditure, by major function: 1934–1999   [OMB]

Contributed by John Joseph Wallis

				Other		
	Total	Defense	Interest on public debt	Total	Veterans' compensation and pensions	Social Security
	Ea698	Ea699	Ea700	Ea701	Ea702	Ea703
Fiscal year	Million dollars	Million dollars	Million dollars	Million dollars	Million dollars	Million dollars
1934	6,541	—	—	—	—	—
1935	6,412		—	—	—	—
1936	8,228	—	—	—	—	—
1937	7,580	—	—	—	—	—
1938	6,840	—	—	—	—	—
1939	9,141	—	—	—	—	—
1940	9,468	1,660	899	6,909	570	28
1941	13,653	6,435	943	6,275	560	91
1942	35,137	25,658	1,052	8,427	501	137
1943	78,555	66,699	1,529	10,327	276	177
1944	91,304	79,143	2,219	9,942	−126	217
1945	92,712	82,965	3,112	6,635	110	267
1946	55,232	42,681	4,111	8,440	2,465	358
1947	34,496	12,808	4,204	17,484	6,344	466
1948	29,764	9,105	4,341	16,318	6,457	558
1949	38,835	13,150	4,523	21,162	6,599	657
1950	42,562	13,724	4,812	24,026	8,834	781
1951	45,514	23,566	4,665	17,283	5,526	1,565
1952	67,686	46,089	4,701	16,896	5,341	2,063
1953	76,101	52,802	5,156	18,143	4,519	2,717
1954	70,855	49,266	4,811	16,778	4,613	3,352
1955	68,444	42,729	4,850	20,865	4,675	4,427
1956	70,640	42,523	5,079	23,038	4,891	5,478
1957	76,578	45,430	5,354	25,794	5,005	6,661
1958	82,405	46,815	5,604	29,986	5,350	8,219
1959	92,098	49,015	5,762	37,321	5,443	9,737
1960	92,191	48,130	6,947	37,114	5,441	11,602
1961	97,723	49,601	6,716	41,406	5,705	12,474
1962	106,821	52,345	6,889	47,587	5,619	14,365
1963	111,316	53,400	7,740	50,176	5,514	15,788
1964	118,528	54,757	8,199	55,572	5,675	16,620
1965	118,228	50,620	8,591	59,017	5,716	17,460
1966	134,532	58,111	9,386	67,035	5,916	20,694
1967	157,464	71,417	10,268	75,779	6,735	21,725
1968	178,134	81,926	11,090	85,118	7,032	23,854
1969	183,640	82,497	12,699	88,444	7,631	27,298
1970	195,649	81,692	14,380	99,577	8,669	30,270
1971	210,172	78,872	14,841	116,459	9,768	35,872
1972	230,681	79,174	15,478	136,029	10,720	40,157
1973	245,707	76,681	17,349	151,677	12,003	49,090
1974	269,359	79,347	21,449	168,563	13,374	55,867
1975	332,332	86,509	23,244	222,579	16,584	64,658
1976	371,792	89,619	26,727	255,446	18,419	73,899
(TQ)	95,975	22,269	6,949	66,757	3,960	19,763
1977	409,218	97,241	29,901	282,076	18,022	85,061
1978	458,746	104,495	35,458	318,793	18,961	93,861
1979	504,032	116,342	42,636	345,054	19,914	104,073
1980	590,947	133,995	52,538	404,414	21,169	118,547
1981	678,249	157,513	68,774	451,962	22,973	139,584
1982	745,755	185,309	85,044	475,402	23,938	155,964
1983	808,385	209,903	89,828	508,654	24,824	170,724
1984	851,874	227,413	111,123	513,338	25,588	178,223
1985	946,423	252,748	129,504	564,171	26,262	188,623
1986	990,460	273,375	136,047	581,038	26,327	198,757
1987	1,004,122	281,999	138,652	583,471	26,750	207,353
1988	1,064,489	290,361	151,838	622,290	29,386	219,341
1989	1,143,671	303,559	169,018	671,094	30,031	232,542

(continued)

TABLE Ea698–703   Federal government expenditure, by major function: 1934–1999   [OMB]
Continued

			Interest on	Other		
	Total	Defense	public debt	Total	Veterans' compensation and pensions	Social Security
Fiscal year	Ea698	Ea699	Ea700	Ea701	Ea702	Ea703
	Million dollars	Million dollars	Million dollars	Million dollars	Million dollars	Million dollars
1990	1,253,198	299,331	184,380	769,487	29,058	248,623
1991	1,324,403	273,292	194,482	856,629	31,305	269,015
1992	1,381,684	298,350	199,373	883,961	34,064	287,585
1993	1,409,512	291,086	198,736	919,690	35,671	304,585
1994	1,461,902	281,642	202,957	977,303	37,584	319,565
1995	1,515,837	272,066	232,169	1,011,602	37,890	335,846
1996	1,560,572	265,753	241,090	1,053,729	36,985	349,676
1997	1,601,282	270,505	244,016	1,086,761	39,313	365,257
1998	1,652,619	268,456	241,153	1,143,010	41,781	379,225
1999	1,702,875	274,873	229,735	1,198,267	43,212	390,041

(TQ) Transition quarter.

Source

U.S. Office of Management and Budget, Historical Tables, *Budget of the United States Government* (2001), Tables 1.1 and 3.1.

Documentation

See the text for Table Ea584–587 for a general note on the federal government finances tables.

TABLE Ea704–725   Federal government expenditure, by function: 1940–1999   [OMB]

Contributed by John Joseph Wallis

				General science, space,		Administration of	General	Human resources			
	Total	Defense	International affairs	and technology	Agriculture	justice	government	Total	Education, training, employment, and social services	Health	Medicare
	Ea704	Ea705	Ea706	Ea707	Ea708	Ea709	Ea710	Ea711	Ea712	Ea713	Ea714
Fiscal year	Million dollars	Million dollars	Million dollars	Million dollars	Million dollars	Million dollars	Million dollars	Million dollars	Million dollars	Million dollars	Million dollars
1940	9,468	1,660	51	—	369	81	274	4,139	1,972	55	—
1941	13,653	6,435	145	—	339	92	306	4,158	1,592	60	—
1942	35,137	25,658	968	4	344	117	397	3,599	1,062	71	—
1943	78,555	66,699	1,286	1	343	154	673	2,659	375	92	—
1944	91,304	79,143	1,449	48	1,275	192	900	1,928	160	174	—
1945	92,712	82,965	1,913	111	1,635	178	581	1,859	134	211	—
1946	55,232	42,681	1,935	34	610	176	825	5,493	85	201	—
1947	34,496	12,808	5,791	5	814	176	1,114	9,909	102	177	—
1948	29,764	9,105	4,566	1	69	170	1,045	9,868	191	162	—
1949	38,835	13,150	6,052	48	1,924	184	824	10,805	178	197	—
1950	42,562	13,724	4,673	55	2,049	193	986	14,221	241	268	—
1951	45,514	23,566	3,647	51	−323	218	1,097	11,001	235	323	—
1952	67,686	46,089	2,691	49	176	267	1,163	11,745	339	347	—
1953	76,101	52,802	2,119	49	2,253	243	1,209	11,836	441	336	—
1954	70,855	49,266	1,596	46	1,817	257	799	13,076	370	307	—
1955	68,444	42,729	2,223	74	3,514	256	651	14,908	445	291	—
1956	70,640	42,523	2,414	79	3,486	302	1,201	16,052	591	359	—
1957	76,578	45,430	3,147	122	2,288	303	1,360	18,161	590	479	—
1958	82,405	46,815	3,364	141	2,411	325	655	22,288	643	541	—
1959	92,098	49,015	3,144	294	4,509	356	926	24,892	789	685	—
1960	92,191	48,130	2,988	599	2,623	366	1,184	26,184	968	795	—
1961	97,723	49,601	3,184	1,042	2,641	400	1,354	29,838	1,063	913	—
1962	106,821	52,345	5,639	1,723	3,562	429	1,049	31,630	1,241	1,198	—
1963	111,316	53,400	5,308	3,051	4,384	465	1,230	33,522	1,458	1,451	—
1964	118,528	54,757	4,945	4,897	4,609	489	1,518	35,294	1,555	1,788	—
1965	118,228	50,620	5,273	5,823	3,955	535	1,499	36,576	2,140	1,791	—
1966	134,532	58,111	5,580	6,717	2,447	563	1,603	43,257	4,363	2,543	64
1967	157,464	71,417	5,566	6,233	2,990	618	1,719	51,272	6,453	3,351	2,748
1968	178,134	81,926	5,301	5,524	4,545	659	1,757	59,375	7,634	4,390	4,649
1969	183,640	82,497	4,600	5,020	5,826	766	1,939	66,410	7,548	5,162	5,695

TABLE Ea704–725　Federal government expenditure, by function: 1940–1999　[OMB]　*Continued*

			General				Human resources			
		International	science, space,		Administration of	General		Education, training, employment, and		
	Total	Defense	affairs	and technology	Agriculture	justice	government	Total	social services	Health	Medicare
	Ea704	Ea705	Ea706	Ea707	Ea708	Ea709	Ea710	Ea711	Ea712	Ea713	Ea714
Fiscal year	Million dollars	Million dollars	Million dollars	Million dollars	Million dollars	Million dollars	Million dollars	Million dollars	Million dollars	Million dollars	Million dollars
1970	195,649	81,692	4,330	4,511	5,166	959	2,320	75,349	8,634	5,907	6,213
1971	210,172	78,872	4,159	4,182	4,290	1,306	2,442	91,901	9,849	6,843	6,622
1972	230,681	79,174	4,781	4,175	5,259	1,653	2,960	107,211	12,529	8,674	7,479
1973	245,707	76,681	4,149	4,032	4,854	2,141	9,774	119,522	12,745	9,356	8,052
1974	269,359	79,347	5,710	3,980	2,230	2,470	10,032	135,783	12,457	10,733	9,639
1975	332,332	86,509	7,097	3,991	3,036	2,955	10,408	173,245	16,022	12,930	12,875
1976	371,792	89,619	6,433	4,373	3,170	3,328	9,747	203,594	18,910	15,734	15,834
(TQ)	95,975	22,269	2,458	1,162	983	891	3,895	52,065	5,169	3,924	4,264
1977	409,218	97,241	6,353	4,736	6,787	3,605	12,833	221,895	21,104	17,302	19,345
1978	458,746	104,495	7,482	4,926	11,357	3,813	12,015	242,329	26,710	18,524	22,768
1979	504,032	116,342	7,459	5,235	11,236	4,173	12,293	267,574	30,223	20,494	26,495
1980	590,947	133,995	12,714	5,832	8,839	4,584	13,028	313,374	31,843	23,169	32,090
1981	678,249	157,513	13,104	6,469	11,323	4,769	11,429	362,022	33,709	26,866	39,149
1982	745,755	185,309	12,300	7,200	15,944	4,712	10,914	388,681	27,029	27,445	46,567
1983	808,385	209,903	11,848	7,935	22,901	5,105	11,235	426,003	26,606	28,641	52,588
1984	851,874	227,413	15,876	8,317	13,613	5,663	11,817	432,042	27,579	30,417	57,540
1985	946,423	252,748	16,176	8,627	25,565	6,270	11,588	471,822	29,342	33,542	65,822
1986	990,460	273,375	14,152	8,976	31,449	6,572	12,564	481,594	30,585	35,936	70,164
1987	1,004,122	281,999	11,649	9,216	26,606	7,553	7,560	502,200	29,724	39,967	75,120
1988	1,064,489	290,361	10,471	10,841	17,210	9,236	9,465	533,402	31,938	44,487	78,878
1989	1,143,671	303,559	9,573	12,838	16,919	9,474	9,249	568,684	36,674	48,390	84,964
1990	1,253,198	299,331	13,764	14,444	11,958	9,993	10,575	619,329	38,755	57,716	98,102
1991	1,324,403	273,292	15,851	16,111	15,183	12,276	11,719	689,667	43,354	71,183	104,489
1992	1,381,684	298,350	16,107	16,409	15,205	14,426	13,039	772,440	45,248	89,497	119,024
1993	1,409,512	291,086	17,248	17,030	20,363	14,955	13,086	827,533	50,012	99,415	130,552
1994	1,461,902	281,642	17,083	16,227	15,046	15,256	11,345	869,410	46,307	107,122	144,747
1995	1,515,837	272,066	16,434	16,724	9,778	16,216	13,998	923,765	54,263	115,418	159,855
1996	1,560,572	265,753	13,496	16,709	9,159	17,548	12,004	958,232	52,001	119,378	174,225
1997	1,601,282	270,505	15,228	17,174	9,032	20,173	12,891	1,002,336	53,008	123,843	190,016
1998	1,652,619	268,456	13,109	18,219	12,206	22,832	15,709	1,033,426	54,954	131,442	192,822
1999	1,702,875	274,873	15,243	18,125	23,011	25,924	15,757	1,058,722	56,241	141,074	190,447

	Human resources			Physical resources							
			Veterans' benefits and			Natural resources and	Commerce		Community and regional		Undistributed offsetting
	Income security	Social Security	services	Total	Energy	environment	and housing	Transportation	development	Net interest	receipts
	Ea715	Ea716	Ea717	Ea718	Ea719	Ea720	Ea721	Ea722	Ea723	Ea724	Ea725
Fiscal year	Million dollars	Million dollars	Million dollars	Million dollars	Million dollars	Million dollars	Million dollars	Million dollars	Million dollars	Million dollars	Million dollars
1940	1,514	28	570	2,312	88	997	550	392	285	899	−317
1941	1,855	91	560	1,782	91	817	398	353	123	943	−547
1942	1,828	137	501	3,892	156	819	1,521	1,283	113	1,052	−894
1943	1,739	177	276	6,433	116	726	2,151	3,220	219	1,529	−1,221
1944	1,503	217	−126	5,471	65	642	624	3,901	238	2,219	−1,320
1945	1,137	267	110	1,747	25	455	−2,630	3,654	243	3,112	−1,389
1946	2,384	358	2,465	836	41	482	−1,857	1,970	200	4,111	−1,468
1947	2,820	466	6,344	1,227	18	700	−923	1,130	302	4,204	−1,552
1948	2,499	558	6,457	2,243	292	780	306	787	78	4,341	−1,643
1949	3,174	657	6,599	3,104	341	1,080	800	916	−33	4,523	−1,779
1950	4,097	781	8,834	3,667	327	1,308	1,035	967	30	4,812	−1,817
1951	3,352	1,565	5,526	3,924	383	1,310	1,228	956	47	4,665	−2,332
1952	3,655	2,063	5,341	4,182	474	1,233	1,278	1,124	73	4,701	−3,377
1953	3,823	2,717	4,519	4,005	425	1,289	910	1,264	117	5,156	−3,571
1954	4,434	3,352	4,613	2,584	432	1,007	−184	1,229	100	4,811	−3,397

(continued)

TABLE Ea704–725   Federal government expenditure, by function: 1940–1999   [OMB]   *Continued*

	Human resources			Physical resources						Net interest	Undistributed offsetting receipts
	Income security	Social Security	Veterans' benefits and services	Total	Energy	Natural resources and environment	Commerce and housing	Transportation	Community and regional development		
	Ea715	Ea716	Ea717	Ea718	Ea719	Ea720	Ea721	Ea722	Ea723	Ea724	Ea725
Fiscal year	Million dollars	Million dollars	Million dollars	Million dollars	Million dollars	Million dollars	Million dollars	Million dollars	Million dollars	Million dollars	Million dollars
1955	5,071	4,427	4,675	2,732	325	940	92	1,246	129	4,850	−3,493
1956	4,734	5,478	4,891	3,092	174	870	506	1,450	92	5,079	−3,589
1957	5,427	6,661	5,005	4,559	240	1,098	1,424	1,662	135	5,354	−4,146
1958	7,535	8,219	5,350	5,188	348	1,407	930	2,334	169	5,604	−4,385
1959	8,239	9,737	5,443	7,813	382	1,632	1,933	3,655	211	5,762	−4,613
1960	7,378	11,602	5,441	7,991	464	1,559	1,618	4,126	224	6,947	−4,820
1961	9,683	12,474	5,705	7,754	510	1,779	1,203	3,987	275	6,716	−4,807
1962	9,207	14,365	5,619	8,831	604	2,044	1,424	4,290	469	6,889	−5,274
1963	9,311	15,788	5,514	8,013	530	2,251	62	4,596	574	7,740	−5,797
1964	9,657	16,620	5,675	9,528	572	2,364	418	5,242	933	8,199	−5,708
1965	9,469	17,460	5,716	11,264	699	2,531	1,157	5,763	1,114	8,591	−5,908
1966	9,678	20,694	5,916	13,410	612	2,719	3,245	5,730	1,105	9,386	−6,542
1967	10,261	21,725	6,735	14,674	782	2,869	3,979	5,936	1,108	10,268	−7,294
1968	11,816	23,854	7,032	16,002	1,037	2,988	4,280	6,316	1,382	11,090	−8,045
1969	13,076	27,298	7,631	11,869	1,010	2,900	−119	6,526	1,552	12,699	−7,986
1970	15,655	30,270	8,669	15,574	997	3,065	2,112	7,008	2,392	14,380	−8,632
1971	22,946	35,872	9,768	18,286	1,035	3,915	2,366	8,052	2,917	14,841	−10,107
1972	27,650	40,157	10,720	19,574	1,296	4,241	2,222	8,392	3,423	15,478	−9,583
1973	28,276	49,090	12,003	20,614	1,237	4,775	931	9,066	4,605	17,349	−13,409
1974	33,713	55,867	13,374	25,106	1,303	5,697	4,705	9,172	4,229	21,449	−16,749
1975	50,176	64,658	16,584	35,449	2,916	7,346	9,947	10,918	4,322	23,244	−13,602
1976	60,799	73,899	18,419	39,188	4,204	8,184	7,619	13,739	5,442	26,727	−14,386
(TQ)	14,985	19,763	3,960	9,512	1,129	2,524	931	3,358	1,569	6,949	−4,206
1977	61,060	85,061	18,022	40,746	5,770	10,032	3,093	14,829	7,021	29,901	−14,879
1978	61,505	93,861	18,961	52,591	7,992	10,983	6,254	15,521	11,841	35,458	−15,720
1979	66,376	104,073	19,914	54,559	9,180	12,135	4,686	18,079	10,480	42,636	−17,476
1980	86,557	118,547	21,169	65,985	10,156	13,858	9,390	21,329	11,252	52,538	−19,942
1981	99,742	139,584	22,973	70,886	15,166	13,568	8,206	23,379	10,568	68,774	−28,041
1982	107,737	155,964	23,938	61,752	13,527	12,998	6,256	20,625	8,347	85,044	−26,099
1983	122,621	170,724	24,824	57,604	9,353	12,672	6,681	21,334	7,564	89,828	−33,976
1984	112,694	178,223	25,588	57,967	7,073	12,593	6,959	23,669	7,673	111,123	−31,957
1985	128,230	188,623	26,262	56,821	5,609	13,357	4,337	25,838	7,680	129,504	−32,698
1986	119,824	198,757	26,327	58,738	4,690	13,639	5,059	28,117	7,233	136,047	−33,007
1987	123,286	207,353	26,750	55,142	4,072	13,363	6,435	26,222	5,051	138,652	−36,455
1988	129,373	219,341	29,386	68,632	2,297	14,606	19,164	27,272	5,294	151,838	−36,967
1989	136,082	232,542	30,031	81,568	2,706	16,182	29,710	27,608	5,362	169,018	−37,212
1990	147,076	248,623	29,058	126,039	3,341	17,080	67,600	29,485	8,532	184,380	−36,615
1991	170,321	269,015	31,305	135,179	2,436	18,559	76,271	31,099	6,813	194,482	−39,356
1992	197,022	287,585	34,064	75,616	4,500	20,025	10,919	33,332	6,841	199,373	−39,280
1993	207,297	304,585	35,671	46,860	4,319	20,239	−21,853	35,004	9,149	198,736	−37,386
1994	214,085	319,565	37,584	70,708	5,219	21,026	−4,228	38,066	10,625	202,957	−37,772
1995	220,493	335,846	37,890	59,142	4,936	21,915	−17,808	39,350	10,749	232,169	−44,455
1996	225,967	349,676	36,985	64,201	2,839	21,524	−10,472	39,565	10,745	241,090	−37,620
1997	230,899	365,257	39,313	59,900	1,475	21,227	−14,624	40,767	11,055	244,016	−49,973
1998	233,202	379,225	41,781	74,703	1,270	22,300	1,014	40,343	9,776	241,153	−47,194
1999	237,707	390,041	43,212	81,930	912	23,968	2,647	42,533	11,870	229,735	−40,445

(TQ) Transition quarter.

Source

U.S. Office of Management and Budget, Historical Tables, *Budget of the United States Government* (2001), Table 3.1.

Documentation

See the text for Table Ea584–587 for a general note on the federal government finances tables.

TABLE Ea726-730   Federal government debt, by where held: 1939-1999   [OMB]
Contributed by John Joseph Wallis

		Held by						Held by		
		Federal government accounts	Public					Federal government accounts	Public		
	Total		Total	Federal Reserve system	Other		Total		Total	Federal Reserve system	Other
	Ea726	Ea727	Ea728	Ea729	Ea730		Ea726	Ea727	Ea728	Ea729	Ea730
Fiscal year	Million dollars	Million dollars	Million dollars	Million dollars	Million dollars	Fiscal year	Million dollars	Million dollars	Million dollars	Million dollars	Million dollars
1939	48,156	6,735	41,421	2,551	38,870	1970	380,921	97,723	283,198	57,714	225,484
1940	50,696	7,924	42,772	2,458	40,314	1971	408,176	105,140	303,037	65,518	237,519
1941	57,531	9,308	48,223	2,180	46,043	1972	435,936	113,559	322,377	71,426	250,951
1942	79,200	11,447	67,753	2,640	65,113	1973	466,291	125,381	340,910	75,181	265,729
1943	142,648	14,882	127,766	7,149	120,617	1974	483,893	140,194	343,699	80,648	263,051
1944	204,079	19,283	184,796	14,899	169,897	1975	541,925	147,225	394,700	84,993	309,707
1945	260,123	24,941	235,182	21,792	213,390	1976	628,970	151,566	477,404	94,714	382,690
1946	270,991	29,130	241,861	23,783	218,078	(TQ)	643,561	148,052	495,509	96,702	398,807
1947	257,149	32,810	224,339	21,872	202,467	1977	706,398	157,295	549,103	105,004	444,099
1948	252,031	35,761	216,270	21,366	194,904	1978	776,602	169,477	607,125	115,480	491,645
1949	252,610	38,288	214,322	19,343	194,979	1979	829,471	189,161	640,310	115,594	524,716
1950	256,853	37,830	219,023	18,331	200,692	1980	909,050	197,118	711,932	120,846	591,086
1951	255,288	40,962	214,326	22,982	191,344	1981	994,845	205,418	789,427	124,466	664,961
1952	259,097	44,339	214,758	22,906	191,852	1982	1,137,345	212,740	924,605	134,497	790,108
1953	265,963	47,580	218,383	24,746	193,637	1983	1,371,710	234,392	1,137,318	155,527	981,791
1954	270,812	46,313	224,499	25,037	199,462	1984	1,564,657	257,611	1,307,046	155,122	1,151,924
1955	274,366	47,751	226,616	23,607	203,009	1985	1,817,521	310,163	1,507,357	169,806	1,337,551
1956	272,693	50,537	222,156	23,758	198,398	1986	2,120,629	379,878	1,740,750	190,855	1,549,895
1957	272,252	52,931	219,320	23,035	196,285	1987	2,346,125	456,203	1,889,922	212,040	1,677,881
1958	279,666	53,329	226,336	25,438	200,898	1988	2,601,307	549,487	2,051,819	229,218	1,822,601
1959	287,465	52,764	234,701	26,044	208,657	1989	2,868,039	677,084	2,190,956	220,088	1,970,868
1960	290,525	53,686	236,840	26,523	210,317	1990	3,206,564	794,733	2,411,831	234,410	2,177,421
1961	292,648	54,291	238,357	27,253	211,104	1991	3,598,485	909,179	2,689,306	258,591	2,430,715
1962	302,928	54,918	248,010	29,663	218,347	1992	4,002,123	1,002,050	3,000,073	296,397	2,703,676
1963	310,324	56,345	253,978	32,027	221,951	1993	4,351,403	1,102,647	3,248,755	325,653	2,923,103
1964	316,059	59,210	256,849	34,794	222,055	1994	4,643,691	1,210,242	3,433,449	355,150	3,078,299
1965	322,318	61,540	260,778	39,100	221,678	1995	4,921,005	1,316,208	3,604,797	374,114	3,230,683
1966	328,498	64,784	263,714	42,169	221,545	1996	5,181,921	1,447,392	3,734,529	390,924	3,343,605
1967	340,445	73,819	266,626	46,719	219,907	1997	5,369,694	1,596,862	3,772,832	424,518	3,348,314
1968	368,685	79,140	289,545	52,230	237,315	1998	5,478,711	1,757,090	3,721,621	458,182	3,263,439
1969	365,769	87,661	278,108	54,095	224,013	1999	5,606,087	1,973,160	3,632,927	496,644	3,136,283

(TQ) Transition quarter.

Figures represent gross federal debt.

Source
U.S. Office of Management and Budget, Historical Tables, *Budget of the United States Government* (2001), Table 7.1.

Documentation
See the text for Table Ea584-587 for a general note on the federal government finances tables.

FEDERAL INCOME TAX RETURNS AND RATES

John Joseph Wallis

TABLE Ea731–739   Federal income tax returns – corporate: 1909–1991

Contributed by John Joseph Wallis

			Active corporations						Inactive corporation returns
		All returns			Returns with net income				
	Total returns	Returns	Receipts	Net income (less deficit)	Returns	Receipts	Net income	Income tax	
	Ea731	Ea732	Ea733 [1]	Ea734	Ea735	Ea736 [1]	Ea737	Ea738 [2]	Ea739 [3]
Fiscal year	Number	Number	Thousand dollars	Thousand dollars	Number	Thousand dollars	Thousand dollars	Thousand dollars	Number
1909	262,490	262,490	—	—	52,498	—	3,590,000	20,960	—
1910	270,202	270,202	—	—	54,040	—	3,761,000	33,512	—
1911	288,352	288,352	—	—	55,129	—	3,503,000	28,583	—
1912	305,336	305,336	—	—	61,116	—	4,151,000	35,006	—
1913	316,909	316,909	—	—	188,866	—	4,714,000	43,128	—
1914	299,445	299,445	—	—	174,205	—	3,940,000	39,145	—
1915	366,443	366,443	—	—	190,911	—	5,310,000	56,994	—
1916	341,253	341,253	35,327,631 [4]	8,109,005	206,984	32,531,097	8,765,909	171,805	—
1917	351,426	351,426	84,693,239 [4]	10,100,753	232,079	79,540,005	10,730,360	503,698	—
1918	317,579	317,579	86,464,281 [4]	7,671,739	202,061	79,706,659	8,361,511	653,198	—
1919	320,198	320,198	99,918,749 [4]	8,415,872	209,634	88,261,006	9,411,418	743,536	—
1920	345,595	345,595	118,205,562 [4]	5,873,231	203,233	93,824,225	7,902,655	636,508	—
1921	356,397	356,397	91,249,274 [4]	457,829	171,239	60,051,123	4,336,048	366,444	—
1922	382,883	382,883	100,920,515 [4]	4,770,035	212,535	80,331,680	6,963,811	775,310	—
1923	398,933	398,933	119,019,865	6,307,974	233,339	97,793,737	8,321,529	937,106	—
1924	417,421	417,421	119,746,703	5,362,726	236,389	97,560,316	7,586,652	881,550	—
1925	430,072	430,072	134,779,997	7,621,056	252,334	114,086,725	9,583,684	1,170,331	—
1926	455,320	455,320	142,629,445	7,504,693	258,134	118,420,378	9,673,403	1,229,797	—
1927	475,031	425,675	144,899,177	6,510,145	259,849	115,732,970	8,981,884	1,130,674	49,356
1928	495,892	443,611	153,304,973	8,226,617	268,783	127,787,507	10,617,741	1,184,142	52,281
1929	509,436	456,021	161,158,206	8,739,758	269,430	130,064,831	11,653,886	1,193,436	53,415
1930	518,736	463,036	136,588,320	1,551,218	221,420	89,910,937	6,428,813	711,704	55,700
1931	516,404	459,704	108,056,952	−3,287,545	175,898	52,267,013	3,683,368	398,994	56,700
1932	508,636	451,884	81,637,988	−5,643,574	82,646	31,855,431	2,153,113	285,576	56,752
1933	504,080	446,842	84,234,006	−2,547,367	109,786	46,906,664	2,985,972	416,093	57,238
1934	528,898	469,804	101,489,954	−94,170	145,101	63,118,536	4,275,197	588,375	59,094
1935	533,631	477,113	114,649,717	1,695,950	164,231	77,638,952	5,164,723	710,156	56,518
1936	530,779	478,857	132,722,602	7,326,218	203,161	105,011,693	9,478,241	1,169,765	51,922
1937	529,097	477,838	142,443,379	7,353,991	192,028	109,202,739	9,634,837	1,232,837	51,259
1938	520,501	471,032	120,453,946	3,672,882	169,884	80,267,477	6,525,979	853,578	49,469
1939	515,960	469,617	132,878,224	6,734,565	199,479	105,658,338	8,826,713	1,216,450	46,343
1940	516,783	473,042	148,236,787	8,919,429	220,977	125,180,472	11,203,224	2,144,292	43,741
1941	509,066	468,906	190,432,017	16,332,542	264,628	175,181,820	18,111,095	3,744,568	40,160
1942	479,677	442,665	217,680,512	23,051,611	269,942	206,160,215	24,052,358	4,337,728	37,012
1943	455,894	420,521	249,592,493	27,819,245	283,735	240,766,898	28,717,966	4,479,166	35,373
1944	446,796	412,467	262,200,531	26,304,481	288,904	252,962,944	27,123,741	4,353,620	34,329
1945	454,460	421,125	255,447,753	21,138,957	303,019	239,045,611	22,165,206	4,182,705	33,335
1946	526,363	491,152	288,954,237	25,192,886	359,310	265,597,448	27,184,592	8,606,695	35,211
1947	587,683	551,807	367,745,578	31,422,728	382,531	343,273,851	33,381,291	10,981,482	35,876
1948	630,670	594,243	410,965,648	34,425,024	395,860	379,309,471	36,273,250	11,920,260	36,427
1949	649,957	614,842	393,449,692	28,194,837	384,772	350,168,722	30,576,517	9,817,308	35,115
1950	665,992	629,314	458,130,069	42,613,304	426,283	430,687,780	44,140,741	15,929,488	36,678
1951	687,310	652,376	517,039,183	43,545,590	439,047	479,243,451	45,333,173	19,623,441	34,934
1952	705,497	672,071	531,307,298	38,456,179	442,577	486,441,344	40,431,697	17,596,969	33,426
1953	730,974	697,975	558,242,262	39,484,687	441,767	506,450,081	41,819,445	18,255,625	32,999
1954	754,019	722,805	554,822,450	36,328,435	441,177	484,727,486	39,572,830	16,823,241	31,214
1955	842,125	807,303	642,248,036	47,478,271	513,270	584,975,387	50,328,887	21,740,890	34,822
1956	924,961	885,747	679,868,168	46,884,912	559,710	614,857,002	50,184,217	21,364,290	39,214
1957	984,516	940,147	720,413,567	44,476,464	572,936	625,621,466	48,664,002	20,581,934	44,369
1958	1,032,632	990,381	735,338,092	38,522,869	611,131	632,342,814	43,489,773	18,814,304	42,251
1959	1,119,835	1,074,120	816,799,884	46,797,267	670,581	719,416,050	51,651,374	22,524,687	45,715

Notes appear at end of table

TABLE Ea731–739   Federal income tax returns – corporate: 1909–1991   *Continued*

		Active corporations							
		All returns			Returns with net income				Inactive corporation returns
	Total returns	Returns	Receipts	Net income (less deficit)	Returns	Receipts	Net income	Income tax	
	Ea731	Ea732	Ea733 [1]	Ea734	Ea735	Ea736 [1]	Ea737	Ea738 [2]	Ea739 [3]
Fiscal year	Number	Number	Thousand dollars	Thousand dollars	Number	Thousand dollars	Thousand dollars	Thousand dollars	Number
1960	1,187,642	1,140,574	849,131,939	43,505,174	670,239	724,451,248	50,382,345	21,866,299	47,068
1961	1,240,759	1,190,286	873,177,644	45,893,900	715,589	750,598,885	52,401,331	22,188,057	50,473
1962	1,318,757	1,268,042	949,305,342	49,606,038	783,195	825,254,516	56,248,301	23,930,297	50,715
1963	1,381,677	1,323,187	1,008,742,704	54,284,740	808,045	887,327,015	61,315,228	26,298,372	58,490
1964	1,437,209	1,373,517	1,086,739,483	61,575,194	858,515	968,052,709	68,734,651	27,856,983	63,692
1965	1,490,103	1,423,980	1,194,600,662	73,889,821	915,311	1,079,661,387	80,796,801	31,661,573	66,123
1966	1,537,857	1,468,725	1,306,517,897	80,527,706	939,846	1,180,714,247	87,740,224	34,449,174	69,132
1967	1,609,900	1,534,360	1,374,598,532	78,181,729	988,906	1,221,446,354	86,653,746	33,301,013	75,540
1968	1,614,768	1,541,670	1,507,785,705	85,961,988	999,328	1,349,977,425	95,102,002	39,694,253	73,098
1969	1,737,877	1,658,820	1,680,482,985	80,218,685	1,045,520	1,461,061,949	93,432,590	39,374,125	79,057
1970	1,747,629	1,665,477	1,750,776,503	64,050,106	1,008,337	1,453,122,279	83,710,924	33,293,018	82,152
1971	1,804,127	1,733,332	1,906,007,776	79,700,323	1,063,940	1,620,755,731	96,688,311	37,510,264	70,795
1972	1,887,041	1,812,760	2,171,209,849	96,760,642	1,140,182	1,895,095,856	112,798,221	42,890,248	74,281
1973	1,980,593	1,904,670	2,557,688,950	120,446,898	1,203,356	2,265,525,480	138,324,272	52,438,603	75,923
1974	2,042,996	1,965,894	3,089,701,363	145,997,808	1,207,396	2,646,541,904	171,166,224	66,112,989	77,102
1975	2,099,816	2,023,647	3,198,627,860	142,636,826	1,226,208	2,702,584,664	169,483,336	66,144,308	76,169
1976	2,158,779	2,082,200	3,635,471,982	185,419,106	1,273,535	3,152,050,626	210,406,400	83,291,815	76,579
1977	2,328,450	2,241,887	4,128,304,478	219,243,043	1,424,528	3,655,771,492	245,274,490	96,340,453	86,563
1978	2,469,992	2,376,779	4,714,602,615	246,867,473	1,523,648	4,204,361,186	274,519,721	107,888,445	93,213
1979	2,652,282	2,556,794	5,598,689,129	284,615,731	1,586,485	4,890,972,248	321,649,761	120,047,034	95,488
1980	2,843,247	2,710,538	6,361,284,012	239,006,542	1,596,632	5,173,865,707	296,787,201	105,142,436	132,709
1981	2,937,045	2,812,420	7,026,351,839	213,648,962	1,597,298	5,461,362,076	301,440,778	102,257,851	124,625
1982	3,047,235	2,925,933	7,024,097,766	154,334,143	1,608,357	5,202,373,378	274,352,942	86,766,154	121,302
1983	3,119,175	2,999,071	7,135,494,059	188,313,928	1,676,288	5,437,650,190	296,932,146	92,218,567	120,104
1984	3,326,521	3,170,743	7,860,711,226	232,900,596	1,777,770	6,081,937,505	349,179,415	107,968,407	155,778
1985	3,430,164	3,277,219	8,398,278,426	240,119,020	1,820,120	6,420,237,212	363,867,384	111,340,839	152,945
1986	3,615,039	3,428,515	8,669,378,501	269,530,240	1,907,738	6,679,365,666	408,860,760	111,140,137	186,524
1987	3,849,764	3,612,133	9,580,720,701	328,223,710	1,995,452	7,246,439,617	465,234,737	118,484,975	237,631
1988	3,784,935	3,562,789	10,264,867,461	412,982,753	1,908,799	8,167,955,799	555,850,912	131,367,397	222,146
1989	3,834,480	3,627,863	10,934,973,405	389,010,675	1,921,805	8,403,467,360	556,332,401	127,754,021	206,617
1990	3,919,329	3,716,650	11,409,520,074	370,632,632	1,910,670	8,597,755,190	552,526,789	128,185,666	202,679
1991	4,002,724	3,802,788	11,436,474,767	344,859,794	1,942,450	8,369,035,947	535,816,622	121,121,231	199,936

[1] For 1918–1924, railroads and other public utility corporations frequently reported only net income, resulting in understatements estimated at $5 billion in 1918 and 1919 and nearly twice that amount in 1920 and 1921.

[2] See text for changes in the series over time.

[3] Through 1926, inactive corporation returns included among those reporting no net income.

[4] Figures represent gross income. "Total receipts" is not available separately for returns with and without net income.

Sources
Historical Statistics of the United States (1975), series Y 381–392 (based on U.S. Internal Revenue Service, 1909–1915, *Annual Report of the Commissioner of Internal Revenue*, various issues; and 1916–1970, *Statistics of Income, Corporation Income Tax Returns*, annual issues), along with data supplied by the Internal Revenue Service.

Documentation
Series Ea738. For 1941–1943, includes a small amount of surtax from returns with no net income but with partially tax-exempt interest from government obligations. For 1941–1970, includes a small amount of tax from returns with no net income because of special provisions for insurance companies. For 1963–1970, includes tax from recomputing prior year investment credit; for 1967–1970, includes the surcharge; and for 1969–1970, includes the additional tax for preferences.

TABLE Ea740–747   Federal income tax returns – individual: 1940–1992

Contributed by John Joseph Wallis

	All returns			Returns with adjusted gross income				Returns without adjusted gross income
	Total	Taxable	Nontaxable	Returns	Adjusted gross income	Taxable income	Income tax (after credits)	
	Ea740	Ea741 [1]	Ea742 [2]	Ea743	Ea744	Ea745	Ea746 [1, 3, 4]	Ea747 [2]
Fiscal year	Number	Number	Number	Number	Thousand dollars	Thousand dollars	Thousand dollars	Number
1940	14,598,074	7,437,261	7,160,813	—	—	—	1,440,967	—
1941	25,770,089	17,502,587	8,267,502	—	—	—	3,815,415	—
1942	36,456,110	27,637,051	8,819,059	—	—	—	8,823,041	—
1943	43,506,553	40,222,699	3,283,854	—	—	—	14,449,441	—
1944	47,111,495	42,354,468	4,757,027	46,919,590	116,714,736	—	16,216,401	191,905
1945	49,932,783	42,650,502	7,282,281	49,750,991	120,301,131	—	17,050,378	181,792
1946	52,816,547	37,915,696	14,900,651	52,600,470	134,330,006	—	16,075,913	216,077
1947	55,099,008	41,578,524	13,520,484	54,799,936	150,295,275	—	18,076,281	299,072
1948	52,072,006	36,411,248	15,660,758	51,745,697	164,173,861	—	15,441,529	326,309
1949	51,814,124	35,628,295	16,185,829	51,301,910	161,373,205	—	14,538,141	512,214
1950	53,060,098	38,186,682	14,873,416	52,655,564	179,874,478	—	18,374,922	404,534
1951	55,447,009	42,648,610	12,798,399	55,042,597	203,097,033	—	24,227,780	404,412
1952	56,528,817	43,876,273	12,652,544	56,107,089	216,087,449	—	27,802,831	421,728
1953	57,838,184	45,223,151	12,615,033	57,415,885	229,863,409	—	29,430,659	422,299
1954	56,747,008	42,633,060	14,113,948	56,306,704	230,235,855	115,331,301	26,665,753	440,304
1955	58,250,188	44,689,065	13,561,123	57,818,164	249,429,182	128,020,111	29,613,722	432,024
1956	59,197,004	46,258,646	12,938,358	58,798,843	268,583,814	141,532,061	32,732,132	398,161
1957	59,825,121	46,865,315	12,959,806	59,407,673	281,308,431	149,363,077	34,393,639	417,448
1958	59,085,182	45,652,134	13,433,048	58,700,924	282,166,418	149,337,414	34,335,652	384,258
1959	60,271,297	47,496,913	12,774,384	59,838,162	306,616,924	166,540,616	38,645,299	433,135
1960	61,027,931	48,060,985	12,966,946	60,592,712	316,557,566	171,627,771	39,464,156	435,219
1961	61,499,420	48,582,765	12,916,655	61,067,589	330,935,737	181,779,732	42,225,498	431,831
1962	62,712,386	50,092,363	12,620,023	62,290,595	349,860,992	195,320,479	44,902,840	421,791
1963	63,943,236	51,323,221	12,620,015	63,511,244	370,270,618	209,090,323	48,203,580	431,992
1964	65,375,601	51,306,338	14,069,263	64,943,284	398,212,083	229,875,078	47,152,855	432,317
1965	67,596,300	53,700,794	13,895,506	67,198,928	430,663,209	255,082,124	49,529,695	397,372
1966	70,160,425	56,709,076	13,451,349	69,786,185	470,271,721	286,296,994	56,087,084	374,240
1967	71,651,909	58,672,938	12,978,971	71,282,525	506,641,751	315,108,212	62,919,958	369,384
1968	73,728,708	61,288,708	12,440,000	73,347,156	556,304,955	352,799,662	76,637,902	381,552
1969	75,834,388	63,721,394	12,112,994	75,375,731	605,578,947	388,153,971	86,568,215	458,657
1970	74,279,831	59,317,371	14,962,460	73,862,448	634,250,263	401,154,285	83,909,314	417,383
1971	74,576,407	59,916,372	14,660,035	74,146,785	676,334,156	413,986,534	85,409,237	429,622
1972	77,572,730	60,869,017	16,703,713	77,132,295	748,924,765	445,589,847	93,576,113	440,435
1973	80,692,587	64,267,162	16,425,425	80,248,984	830,653,262	511,929,462	108,083,776	443,603
1974	83,340,190	67,334,767	16,005,423	82,794,391	910,803,189	573,605,736	123,607,102	545,799
1975	82,229,332	61,490,737	20,338,595	81,585,541	954,089,426	595,492,866	124,526,297	643,791
1976	84,670,389	64,421,367	20,738,595	84,123,626	1,060,805,806	674,866,988	141,801,470	546,763
1977	86,634,640	64,381,138	22,253,502	86,066,234	1,165,776,870	938,968,454	159,796,824	568,406
1978	89,771,551	68,688,305	21,083,246	89,247,480	1,309,918,739	1,062,190,322	188,232,537	524,071
1979	92,694,302	71,694,983	20,999,319	92,152,198	1,474,781,366	1,157,247,646	214,494,519	542,104
1980	93,902,469	73,906,244	19,996,225	93,238,823	1,626,554,501	1,279,985,360 [5]	250,341,440	663,646
1981	95,396,123	76,724,724	18,671,399	94,586,878	1,791,115,516	1,410,880,665	284,128,989	809,245
1982	95,337,432	77,035,432	18,302,132	94,426,498	1,875,871,710	1,473,348,899	277,597,290	910,934
1983	96,321,310	78,016,323	18,304,987	95,330,713	1,969,599,862	1,544,872,497	274,181,323	990,597
1984	99,438,708	81,639,509	17,799,199	98,435,000	2,173,227,608	1,701,365,731	301,923,057	1,003,708
1985	101,660,287	82,846,420	18,813,867	100,625,484	2,343,988,823	1,820,740,833 [5]	325,710,254	1,034,803
1986	103,045,170	83,967,413	19,077,757	102,087,623	2,524,123,612	1,947,024,584 [5]	367,287,213	957,547
1987	106,996,270	86,723,796	20,272,474	106,154,761	2,813,727,901	1,850,597,119 [6]	369,202,757	841,509
1988	109,708,280	87,135,332	22,572,948	108,872,859	3,124,156,072	2,069,966,980	412,869,909	835,420
1989	112,135,673	89,178,355	22,957,318	111,321,721	3,298,857,991	2,173,345,881	432,939,998	822,952
1990	113,717,138	89,862,434	23,854,704	112,812,262	3,451,237,012	2,263,661,230	447,126,703	904,876
1991	114,730,123	88,733,587	25,996,536	113,804,104	3,516,141,520	2,284,087,935	448,429,593	926,020
1992	113,604,503	86,731,946	26,872,557	112,652,759	3,629,129,550	2,395,695,907	476,238,785	961,744

[1] Includes minimum tax or alternate minimum tax, 1970–1992.

[2] Includes returns with no information, 1944–1952 and 1957.

[3] Through 1943, figures represent tax before credits. Also, includes defense tax (1940–1941) and victory tax (1943).

[4] Beginning 1970, includes amounts reported on returns with no adjusted gross income.

[5] Includes amounts "taxed" at zero percent.

[6] Includes standard deductions for age 65 or older, or for blindness.

Sources

Historical Statistics of the United States (1975), series Y 393–401 (based on U.S. Internal Revenue Service, *Statistics of Income, Individual Income Tax Returns*, annual issues), along with data supplied by the Internal Revenue Service.

TABLE Ea748–757   Federal income tax returns – individual: 1913–1943

Contributed by John Joseph Wallis

	Returns with net income						Returns without net income			
	Returns									
	Total	Taxable	Nontaxable	Total income	Net income	Income tax	Returns	Total income	Net deficit	Income tax
	Ea748 [1]	Ea749	Ea750	Ea751	Ea752	Ea753 [2]	Ea754	Ea755	Ea756	Ea757
Fiscal year	Number	Number	Number	Thousand dollars	Thousand dollars	Thousand dollars	Number	Thousand dollars	Thousand dollars	Thousand dollars
1913 [3]	357,598	—	—	—	3,900,000	28,254	—	—	—	—
1914	357,515	—	—	—	4,000,000	41,046	—	—	—	—
1915	336,652	—	—	—	4,600,000	67,944	—	—	—	—
1916	437,036	362,970	74,066	8,349,902	6,298,578	173,387	—	—	—	—
1917	3,472,890	2,707,234	765,656	14,538,146 [4]	13,407,303	691,493	—	—	—	—
1918	4,425,114	3,392,863	1,032,251	17,745,761	15,924,639	1,127,722	—	—	—	—
1919	5,332,760	4,231,181	1,101,579	22,437,686	19,859,491	1,269,630	—	—	—	—
1920	7,259,944	5,518,310	1,741,634	26,690,270	23,735,629	1,075,054	—	—	—	—
1921	6,662,176	3,589,985	3,072,191	23,328,782	19,577,213	719,387	—	—	—	—
1922	6,787,481	3,681,249	3,106,232	24,871,908	21,336,213	861,057	—	—	—	—
1923	7,698,321	4,270,121	3,428,200	29,247,593	24,777,466	661,666	—	—	—	—
1924	7,369,788	4,489,698	2,880,090	29,578,997	25,656,153	704,265	—	—	—	—
1925	4,171,051	2,501,166	1,669,885	25,272,035	21,894,576	734,555	—	—	—	—
1926	4,138,092	2,470,990	1,667,102	25,447,436	21,958,506	732,471	—	—	—	—
1927	4,101,547	2,440,941	1,660,606	26,208,561	22,545,091	830,639	—	—	—	—
1928	4,070,851	2,523,063	1,547,788	28,987,634	25,226,327	1,164,254	72,829	420,649	499,213	—
1929	4,044,327	2,458,049	1,586,278	29,844,758	24,800,736	1,001,938	92,545	902,251	1,025,130	—
1930	3,707,509	2,037,645	1,669,864	22,319,446	18,118,635	476,715	144,867	1,204,383	1,539,452	—
1931	3,225,924	1,525,546	1,700,378	17,268,451	13,604,996	246,127	184,583	1,299,750	1,936,878	—
1932	3,877,430	1,936,095	1,941,335	14,392,080	11,655,909	329,962	206,293	831,592	1,480,922	—
1933	3,723,558	1,747,740	1,975,818	13,393,825	11,008,638	374,120	168,449	725,817	1,141,331	—
1934	4,094,420	1,795,920	2,298,500	15,092,960	12,796,802	511,400	104,170	344,055	412,859	—
1935	4,575,012	2,110,890	2,464,122	17,316,505	14,909,812	657,439	94,609	288,653	381,353	—
1936	5,413,499	2,861,108	2,552,391	21,888,373	19,240,110	1,214,017	73,272	248,530	286,632	—
1937	6,301,833	3,326,912	2,974,921	23,891,481	20,941,302	1,093,163	83,904	250,394	308,518	—
1938	6,150,776	2,995,664	3,155,112	21,549,277	18,660,929	726,120	100,233	318,769	354,156	615
1939	7,570,320	3,896,418	3,673,902	25,816,147	22,938,918	890,934	82,461	228,690	284,327	300
1940	14,598,074	7,437,261	7,160,813	40,277,645	36,309,719	1,440,967	112,697	239,583	311,385	473
1941	25,770,089	17,502,587	8,267,502	63,841,047	58,527,217 [5]	3,815,415	99,828	264,032	292,023	2,326
1942	36,456,110	27,637,051	8,819,059	85,876,118	78,589,729 [5]	8,823,041	163,136	181,486	198,598	—
1943	43,506,553	40,222,699	3,283,854	106,614,214	99,209,862 [5]	14,449,441	215,485	170,866	225,683	643

[1] Through 1936, includes fiduciary returns with net income filed on form 1040.

[2] For 1924–1931, tax after earned income credit in capital loss credit; for 1932–1933, after capital loss credit only; for 1943, after form tax credit and tax paid at source. Includes defense tax (1940–1941) and victory tax (1943).

[3] Last ten months of the year.

[4] Somewhat understated because net income was used also as total income on returns with income of $1,000 to $2,000.

[5] Total income on form 1040A was also used as net income.

Source

U.S. Internal Revenue Service, *Statistics of Income, Individual Income Tax Returns* (annual issues).

TABLE Ea758-772 Federal income tax rates, by income group – average rates: 1913–1970

Contributed by John Joseph Wallis

Tax year	Year of revenue act (Ea758)	Taxable income													
		$600 (Ea759)	$1,000 (Ea760)	$2,000 (Ea761)	$3,000 (Ea762)	$5,000 (Ea763)	$6,000 (Ea764)	$8,000 (Ea765)	$10,000 (Ea766)	$15,000 (Ea767)	$20,000 (Ea768)	$25,000 (Ea769)	$50,000 (Ea770)	$100,000 (Ea771)	$1,000,000 (Ea772) [1]
		Percent	Percent	Percent	Percent	Percent	Percent	Percent	Percent	Percent	Percent	Percent	Percent	Percent	Percent
1913 [2]	1913	—	—	—	—	0.4	0.5	0.6	0.7	0.8	0.9	1.1	1.5	2.5	6.0
1914	1913	—	—	—	—	0.4	0.5	0.6	0.7	0.8	0.9	1.1	1.5	2.5	6.0
1915	1913	—	—	—	—	0.4	0.5	0.6	0.7	0.8	0.9	1.1	1.5	2.5	6.0
1916	1916	—	—	—	—	0.8	1.0	1.3	1.4	1.6	1.7	2.0	2.7	3.9	10.0
1917	1917	—	—	1.0	1.3	2.4	2.8	3.4	4.0	5.1	6.1	7.3	10.4	16.2	47.5
1918	1918	—	—	3.0	4.0	4.8	6.2	8.1	9.5	11.9	13.8	15.4	22.3	35.2	70.3
1919	1918	—	—	2.0	2.7	3.2	4.2	5.6	6.7	8.7	10.4	11.8	18.5	31.3	66.3
1920	1918	—	—	2.0	2.7	3.2	4.2	5.6	6.7	8.7	10.4	11.8	18.5	31.3	66.3
1921	1921	—	—	2.0	2.7	3.2	4.2	5.6	6.7	8.7	10.4	11.8	18.5	31.3	66.3
1922	1921	—	—	2.0	2.7	3.2	4.0	5.3	6.0	7.6	9.0	10.6	17.4	30.2	55.1
1923	1921	—	—	1.5	2.0	2.4	3.0	3.9	4.5	5.7	6.8	7.9	13.1	22.7	41.3
1924	1924	—	—	0.8	1.0	1.2	1.5	1.9	2.3	3.9	5.2	6.5	12.3	22.7	43.0
1925 [9]	1926	—	—	0.3	0.6	0.8	0.9	1.3	1.5	2.6	3.5	4.9	9.9	16.1	24.1
1926	1926	—	—	0.3	0.6	0.8	0.9	1.3	1.5	2.6	3.5	4.9	9.9	16.1	24.1
1927	1926	—	—	0.3	0.6	0.8	0.9	1.3	1.5	2.6	3.5	4.9	9.9	16.1	24.1
1928	1928	—	—	0.3	0.6	0.8	0.9	1.3	1.5	2.6	3.5	4.4	9.3	15.8	24.1
1929 [3]	1928	—	—	0.1	0.2	0.3	0.4	0.7	0.9	1.9	2.8	3.7	8.5	14.9	23.1
1930	1928	—	—	0.3	0.6	0.8	0.9	1.3	1.5	2.6	3.5	4.4	9.3	15.8	24.1
1931	1928	—	—	0.3	0.6	0.8	0.9	1.3	1.5	2.6	3.5	4.4	9.3	15.8	24.1
1932	1932	—	—	2.0	2.7	3.2	4.0	5.3	6.0	7.6	9.0	10.6	17.4	30.2	57.1
1933	1932	—	—	2.0	2.7	3.2	4.0	5.3	6.0	7.6	9.0	10.6	17.4	30.2	57.1
1934	1934	—	—	1.6	2.3	2.8	3.6	4.7	5.6	7.4	9.2	11.2	18.7	31.4	57.2
1935	1934	—	—	1.6	2.3	2.8	3.6	4.7	5.6	7.4	9.2	11.2	18.7	31.4	57.2
1936 [10]	1936	—	—	1.6	2.3	2.8	3.6	4.7	5.6	7.4	9.2	11.2	18.7	33.4	68.0
1937 [10]	1936	—	—	1.6	2.3	2.8	3.6	4.7	5.6	7.4	9.2	11.2	18.7	33.4	68.0
1938 [10]	1938	—	—	1.6	2.3	2.8	3.6	4.7	5.6	7.4	9.2	11.2	18.7	33.4	68.0
1939 [10]	1938	—	—	1.6	2.3	2.8	3.6	4.7	5.6	7.4	9.2	11.2	18.7	33.4	68.0
1940 [4]	1940	—	0.4	2.2	2.8	3.4	4.3	5.6	6.9	9.8	13.3	17.0	29.4	44.3	71.8
1941	1941	—	2.1	5.9	7.4	9.7	10.8	12.9	14.9	20.0	24.6	28.9	41.8	53.2	73.3
1942 [5]	1942	2.5	8.9	13.7	15.7	18.4	19.6	21.8	23.9	29.1	34.1	38.5	51.6	64.6	85.5
1943 [5,6]	1942	2.8	10.7	16.7	19.1	22.1	23.4	25.7	27.8	33.1	38.1	42.6	56.1	69.7	90.0
1944	1944	3.8	11.5	17.3	19.5	22.1	23.3	25.4	27.6	32.9	37.9	42.4	55.9	69.9	90.0
1945	1944	3.8	11.5	17.3	19.5	22.1	23.3	25.4	27.6	32.9	37.9	42.4	55.9	69.9	90.0
1946	1945	3.2	9.5	14.3	16.2	18.4	19.5	21.5	23.5	28.5	33.2	37.5	50.3	63.5	84.0
1947	1945	3.2	9.5	14.3	16.2	18.4	19.5	21.5	23.5	28.5	33.2	37.5	50.3	63.5	84.0
1948	1948	—	6.6	11.6	13.6	16.2	17.3	19.3	21.2	26.0	30.4	34.4	46.4	58.8	77.0
1949	1948	—	6.6	11.6	13.6	16.2	17.3	19.3	21.2	26.0	30.4	34.4	46.4	58.8	77.0
1950	1950	—	7.0	12.2	14.3	16.9	18.0	20.0	22.0	26.9	31.5	35.6	48.0	60.8	80.0
1951 [7]	1951	—	8.2	14.3	16.6	19.3	20.6	22.7	24.9	30.2	35.4	39.9	53.5	67.3	87.2
1952 [7]	1951	—	8.9	15.5	18.1	21.0	22.4	24.9	27.2	33.1	38.8	43.8	56.9	69.7	88.0
1953 [7]	1951	—	8.9	15.5	18.1	21.0	22.4	24.9	27.2	33.1	38.8	43.8	56.9	69.7	88.0
1954 [7]	1954	—	8.0	14.0	16.3	18.9	20.1	22.2	24.4	29.7	34.7	39.2	52.8	66.8	86.9
1955	1954	—	8.0	14.0	16.3	18.9	20.1	22.2	24.4	29.7	34.7	39.2	52.8	66.8	86.9
1956	1954	—	8.0	14.0	16.3	18.9	20.1	22.2	24.4	29.7	34.7	39.2	52.8	66.8	86.9
1957	1954	—	8.0	14.0	16.3	18.9	20.1	22.2	24.4	29.7	34.7	39.2	52.8	66.8	86.9
1958	1954	—	8.0	14.0	16.3	18.9	20.1	22.2	24.4	29.7	34.7	39.2	52.8	66.8	86.9
1959	1954	—	8.0	14.0	16.3	18.9	20.1	22.2	24.4	29.7	34.7	39.2	52.8	66.8	86.9

Tax year	Year of revenue act Ea758 Year	\$600 Ea759 Percent	\$1,000 Ea760 Percent	\$2,000 Ea761 Percent	\$3,000 Ea762 Percent	\$5,000 Ea763 Percent	\$6,000 Ea764 Percent	\$8,000 Ea765 Percent	\$10,000 Ea766 Percent	\$15,000 Ea767 Percent	\$20,000 Ea768 Percent	\$25,000 Ea769 Percent	\$50,000 Ea770 Percent	\$100,000 Ea771 Percent	\$1,000,000 Ea772 [1] Percent
1960	1954	—	8.0	14.0	16.3	18.9	20.1	22.2	24.4	29.7	34.7	39.2	52.8	66.8	86.9
1961	1954	—	8.0	14.0	16.3	18.9	20.1	22.2	24.4	29.7	34.7	39.2	52.8	66.8	86.9
1962	1954	—	8.0	14.0	16.3	18.9	20.1	22.2	24.4	29.7	34.7	39.2	52.8	66.8	86.9
1963	1954	—	8.0	14.0	16.3	18.9	20.1	22.2	24.4	29.7	34.7	39.2	52.8	66.8	86.9
1964	1964	—	6.4	11.6	14.0	16.7	17.8	19.8	21.8	26.4	30.8	35.0	47.1	58.9	75.1
1965	1964	—	5.6	10.4	12.9	15.6	16.6	18.5	20.2	24.7	29.0	32.9	44.5	55.1	68.5
1966	1964	—	5.6	10.4	12.9	15.6	16.6	18.5	20.2	24.7	29.0	32.9	44.5	55.1	68.5
1967	1964	—	5.6	10.4	12.9	15.6	16.6	18.5	20.2	24.7	29.0	32.9	44.5	55.1	68.5
1968 [8]	1964	—	5.6	11.0	13.8	16.7	17.9	19.9	21.7	26.6	31.2	35.4	47.8	59.2	73.6
1969 [8]	1964	—	5.6	11.1	14.2	17.1	18.3	20.4	22.2	27.2	31.9	36.2	48.9	60.6	75.4
1970 [8]	1969	—	5.3	10.4	13.0	15.8	17.0	18.9	20.6	25.3	29.7	33.7	45.5	56.4	70.2

Taxable income

[1] Takes into account the following maximum effective rate limitations: 1944–1945, 90 percent; 1946–1947, 85.5 percent; 1948–1949, 77 percent; 1950, 80 percent; 1951, 87.2 percent; 1952–1953, 88 percent; 1954–1957, 87 percent.

[2] Beginning March 1.

[3] Normal tax rates of 1928 Act were reduced for 1929 only by Joint Resolution of Congress.

[4] Includes defense tax.

[5] Tax liabilities unadjusted for transition to current payment basis.

[6] Includes net victory tax. Computed by assuming that deductions are 10 percent of victory tax net income (that is, that victory tax net income is ten ninths of selected net income).

[7] Excludes self-employment tax.

[8] Includes income tax surcharge, generally 7.5 percent in 1968, 10 percent in 1969, and 2.5 percent in 1970, except in low-income tax brackets.

[9] Provisions of 1926 Act were retroactive to 1925.

[10] Rates and exemptions for 1936 and 1938 Acts were identical and resulted in the same tax liabilities.

Source

Historical Statistics of the United States (1975), series 412–425, which were based on unpublished data from the U.S. Department of the Treasury.

Documentation

Tax rates are based on actual tax liabilities for the amount of taxable income shown. Taxable income is gross income minus deductions. All rates are calculated for a single individual with one exemption. All rates are average tax rates: taxes paid divided by taxable income. Tax rates apply only to the specific amount of taxable income given in the table. Tax rates apply to income intervals. The incomes reported in the table do not duplicate the actual tax intervals, and so tax rates for incomes between the specific figures used in the tables may vary.

Series Ea758. Indicates the year of the governing revenue act.

TABLE Ea773–826   Federal income tax rates, by income group – average and marginal rates: 1968–2000
Contributed by John Joseph Wallis

Average tax rate, by taxable income

Tax year	$1,000 Ea773 Percent	$2,000 Ea774 Percent	$4,000 Ea775 Percent	$6,000 Ea776 Percent	$8,000 Ea777 Percent	$10,000 Ea778 Percent	$15,000 Ea779 Percent	$20,000 Ea780 Percent	$25,000 Ea781 Percent	$30,000 Ea782 Percent	$35,000 Ea783 Percent	$40,000 Ea784 Percent	$45,000 Ea785 Percent	$50,000 Ea786 Percent	$60,000 Ea787 Percent	$70,000 Ea788 Percent	$80,000 Ea789 Percent	$90,000 Ea790 Percent
1968	14.5	15.5	17.3	18.8	20.4	21.9	26.3	30.4	34.1	37.2	39.6	41.7	43.5	45.2	48.0	50.3	52.2	54.0
1969	14.5	15.5	17.3	18.8	20.4	21.9	26.3	30.4	34.1	37.2	39.6	41.7	43.5	45.2	48.0	50.3	52.2	54.0
1970	14.5	15.5	17.3	18.8	20.4	21.9	26.3	30.4	34.1	37.2	39.6	41.7	43.5	45.2	48.0	50.3	52.2	54.0
1971	14.5	15.5	17.3	18.5	19.9	20.9	23.3	26.2	28.8	31.3	33.7	36.0	38.2	40.4	44.0	46.8	49.2	51.3
1972	14.5	15.5	17.3	18.5	19.9	20.9	23.3	26.2	28.8	31.3	33.7	36.0	38.2	40.4	44.0	46.8	49.2	51.3
1973	14.5	15.5	17.3	18.5	19.9	20.9	23.3	26.2	28.8	31.3	33.7	36.0	38.2	40.4	44.0	46.8	49.2	51.3
1974	14.5	15.5	17.3	18.5	19.9	20.9	23.3	26.2	28.8	31.3	33.7	36.0	38.2	40.4	44.0	46.8	49.2	51.3
1975	14.5	15.5	17.3	18.5	19.9	20.9	23.3	26.2	28.8	31.3	33.7	36.0	38.2	40.4	44.0	46.8	49.2	51.3
1976	14.7	15.6	17.4	18.6	20.0	21.0	23.5	26.2	28.8	31.3	33.7	36.0	38.2	40.4	44.0	46.8	49.2	51.3
1977	0.0	0.0	6.9	10.9	13.4	15.4	19.1	22.2	25.2	28.0	30.5	33.0	35.4	37.7	41.7	44.8	47.4	49.7
1978	0.0	0.0	6.9	10.9	13.4	15.4	19.1	22.2	25.2	28.0	30.5	33.0	35.4	37.7	41.7	44.8	47.4	49.7
1979	0.0	0.0	6.3	10.0	12.2	13.9	17.4	20.9	23.8	26.5	29.2	31.6	34.0	36.1	39.9	43.2	45.7	48.1
1980	0.0	0.0	6.3	10.0	12.2	13.9	17.4	20.9	23.8	26.5	29.2	31.6	34.0	36.1	39.9	43.2	45.7	48.1
1981	0.0	0.0	6.3	10.0	12.2	13.9	17.4	20.9	23.8	26.5	29.2	31.6	34.0	36.1	39.9	43.2	45.7	48.1
1982	0.0	0.0	5.1	8.8	10.8	12.3	12.3	18.8	21.4	23.9	26.3	28.5	30.7	32.6	35.5	37.6	39.1	40.4
1983	0.0	0.0	5.0	8.2	9.9	11.2	14.0	16.8	19.3	21.6	23.8	25.8	27.8	29.5	32.5	35.0	36.8	38.3
1984	0.0	0.0	4.8	7.8	9.5	10.8	13.3	16.0	18.3	20.4	22.4	24.4	26.2	27.8	30.6	33.1	35.0	36.6
1985	0.0	0.0	4.5	7.5	9.3	10.5	13.1	15.6	17.8	19.8	21.8	23.8	25.6	27.2	29.9	32.5	34.4	36.0
1986	0.0	0.0	4.3	7.3	9.1	10.3	12.8	15.2	17.4	19.4	21.4	23.3	24.9	26.7	29.2	31.9	33.9	35.5
1987	11.0	11.4	13.2	13.8	14.1	14.3	14.5	16.7	19.0	21.2	23.2	24.6	25.8	26.7	28.4	29.9	31.0	31.8
1988	15.0	15.0	15.0	15.0	15.0	15.0	15.0	16.4	18.7	20.3	21.4	22.2	23.0	24.0	25.5	26.6	27.4	27.9
1989	15.0	15.0	15.0	15.0	15.0	15.0	15.0	15.9	18.4	20.0	21.1	22.0	22.7	23.7	25.2	26.3	27.2	27.8
1990	15.0	15.0	15.0	15.0	15.0	15.0	15.0	15.4	17.9	19.6	20.8	21.7	22.4	23.2	24.9	26.0	26.9	27.6
1991	15.0	15.0	15.0	15.0	15.0	15.0	15.0	15.0	17.4	19.2	20.4	21.4	22.1	22.8	24.1	25.1	25.8	26.4
1992	15.0	15.0	15.0	15.0	15.0	15.0	15.0	15.0	16.8	18.7	20.0	21.0	21.8	22.4	23.8	24.8	25.6	26.2
1993	15.0	15.0	15.0	15.0	15.0	15.0	15.0	15.0	16.5	18.4	19.8	20.8	21.6	22.3	23.5	24.6	25.4	26.0
1994	15.0	15.0	15.0	15.0	15.0	15.0	15.0	15.0	16.2	18.1	19.6	20.6	21.4	22.1	23.3	24.4	25.2	25.9
1995	15.0	15.0	15.0	15.0	15.0	15.0	15.0	15.0	15.9	17.9	19.3	20.4	21.3	21.9	23.1	24.2	25.1	25.7
1996	15.0	15.0	15.0	15.0	15.0	15.0	15.0	15.0	15.5	17.6	19.1	20.2	21.1	21.8	22.9	24.1	24.9	25.6
1997	15.0	15.0	15.0	15.0	15.0	15.0	15.0	15.0	15.2	17.3	18.8	20.0	20.9	21.6	22.7	23.9	24.8	25.4
1998	15.0	15.0	15.0	15.0	15.0	15.0	15.0	15.0	15.0	17.0	18.6	19.8	20.7	21.4	22.5	23.7	24.6	25.3
1999	15.0	15.0	15.0	15.0	15.0	15.0	15.0	15.0	15.0	16.8	18.4	19.6	20.6	21.3	22.4	23.5	24.5	25.2
2000	15.0	15.0	15.0	15.0	15.0	15.0	15.1	15.0	15.0	16.6	18.3	19.5	20.4	21.2	22.3	23.4	24.4	25.1

Marginal tax rate, by taxable income

Tax year	$1,000 Ea800 Percent	$2,000 Ea801 Percent	$4,000 Ea802 Percent	$6,000 Ea803 Percent	$8,000 Ea804 Percent	$10,000 Ea805 Percent	$15,000 Ea806 Percent	$20,000 Ea807 Percent	$25,000 Ea808 Percent
1968	16	19	22	25	28	32	39	48	50
1969	16	19	22	25	28	32	39	48	50
1970	16	19	22	25	28	32	39	48	50
1971	16	19	21	24	25	27	29	38	40
1972	16	19	21	24	25	27	29	38	40
1973	16	19	21	24	25	27	29	38	40
1974	16	19	21	24	25	27	29	38	40
1975	16	19	21	24	25	27	29	38	40
1976	16	18	21	23	25	26	31	38	40
1977	0	0	17	19	21	24	29	34	40
1978	0	0	17	19	21	24	29	34	40
1979	0	0	15	18	19	21	30	34	39
1980	0	0	16	18	19	21	30	34	39
1981	0	0	16	18	19	21	30	34	39
1982	0	0	14	16	17	19	23	31	35
1983	0	0	13	15	15	17	24	28	32
1984	0	0	12	14	15	16	23	26	30
1985	0	0	12	14	15	16	20	26	30
1986	0	0	12	14	15	16	20	26	26
1987	11	15	15	15	15	15	15	28	28
1988	15	15	15	15	15	15	15	28	28
1989	15	15	15	15	15	15	15	28	28
1990	15	15	15	15	15	15	15	28	28
1991	15	15	15	15	15	15	15	15	28
1992	15	15	15	15	15	15	15	15	28
1993	15	15	15	15	15	15	15	15	28
1994	15	15	15	15	15	15	15	15	28
1995	15	15	15	15	15	15	15	15	28
1996	15	15	15	15	15	15	15	15	28
1997	15	15	15	15	15	15	15	15	28
1998	15	15	15	15	15	15	15	15	15
1999	15	15	15	15	15	15	15	15	15
2000	15	15	15	15	15	15	15	15	15

Average tax rate, by taxable income

Tax year	$100,000 Ea791 Percent	$125,000 Ea792 Percent	$150,000 Ea793 Percent	$175,000 Ea794 Percent	$200,000 Ea795 Percent	$300,000 Ea796 Percent	$400,000 Ea797 Percent	$500,000 Ea798 Percent	$1,000,000 Ea799 Percent
1968	55.5	58.4	60.3	61.7	62.7	65.2	66.4	67.1	68.5
1969	55.5	58.4	60.3	61.7	62.7	65.2	66.4	67.1	68.5
1970	55.5	58.4	60.3	61.7	62.7	65.2	66.4	67.1	68.5
1971	53.1	56.5	58.7	60.3	61.5	64.4	65.8	66.6	68.3
1972	53.1	56.5	58.7	60.3	61.5	64.4	65.8	66.6	68.3
1973	53.1	56.5	58.7	60.3	61.5	64.4	65.8	66.6	68.3
1974	53.1	56.5	58.7	60.3	61.5	64.4	65.8	66.6	68.3
1975	53.1	56.5	58.7	60.3	61.5	64.4	65.8	66.6	68.3
1976	53.1	56.5	58.7	60.3	61.5	64.4	65.8	66.6	68.3
1977	51.6	55.2	57.7	59.5	60.8	63.9	65.4	66.3	68.2
1978	51.6	55.2	57.7	59.5	60.8	63.9	65.4	66.3	68.2
1979	50.1	53.9	56.6	58.5	59.9	63.3	65.0	66.0	68.0
1980	50.1	53.9	56.6	58.5	59.9	63.3	65.0	66.0	68.0
1981	50.1	53.9	56.6	58.5	59.9	63.3	65.0	66.0	68.0
1982	41.3	43.1	44.2	45.0	45.7	47.1	47.8	48.3	49.1
1983	39.5	41.6	43.0	44.0	44.7	46.5	47.4	47.9	48.9
1984	37.9	40.3	42.0	43.1	44.0	46.0	47.0	47.6	48.8
1985	37.4	40.0	41.6	42.8	43.7	45.8	46.9	47.5	48.7
1986	37.0	39.6	41.3	42.6	43.5	45.7	46.7	47.4	48.7
1987	32.5	33.7	34.5	35.1	35.5	36.5	37.0	37.3	37.9
1988	28.0	28.0	28.0	28.0	28.0	28.0	28.0	28.0	28.0
1989	28.0	28.0	28.0	28.0	28.0	28.0	28.0	28.0	28.0
1990	28.0	28.0	28.0	28.0	28.0	28.0	28.0	28.0	28.0
1991	26.9	27.7	28.3	28.6	28.9	29.6	30.0	30.2	30.6
1992	26.7	27.5	28.1	28.5	28.8	29.6	29.9	30.1	30.6
1993	26.5	27.6	29.0	30.4	30.5	33.2	34.8	35.8	37.7
1994	26.4	27.5	28.9	30.3	30.4	33.1	34.8	35.7	37.7
1995	26.3	27.5	28.9	29.9	30.7	33.0	34.6	35.6	37.6
1996	26.1	27.3	28.7	29.8	30.5	32.8	34.5	35.5	37.6
1997	26.0	27.0	28.5	29.6	30.4	32.6	34.4	35.4	37.5
1998	25.9	26.9	28.3	29.4	30.2	32.4	34.2	35.3	37.4
1999	25.8	26.8	28.2	29.3	30.1	32.3	34.1	35.2	37.4
2000	25.7	26.7	28.0	29.2	30.0	32.2	34.0	35.1	37.4

TABLE Ea773–826   Federal income tax rates, by income group – average and marginal rates: 1968–2000   *Continued*

Marginal tax rate, by taxable income

Tax year	$30,000 Ea809 Percent	$35,000 Ea810 Percent	$40,000 Ea811 Percent	$45,000 Ea812 Percent	$50,000 Ea813 Percent	$60,000 Ea814 Percent	$70,000 Ea815 Percent	$80,000 Ea816 Percent	$90,000 Ea817 Percent	$100,000 Ea818 Percent	$125,000 Ea819 Percent	$150,000 Ea820 Percent	$175,000 Ea821 Percent	$200,000 Ea822 Percent	$300,000 Ea823 Percent	$400,000 Ea824 Percent	$500,000 Ea825 Percent	$1,000,000 Ea826 Percent
1968	53	55	58	60	62	64.0	66.0	68.0	69.0	70.0	70.0	70.0	70.0	70.0	70.0	70.0	70.0	70.0
1969	53	55	58	60	62	64.0	66.0	68.0	69.0	70.0	70.0	70.0	70.0	70.0	70.0	70.0	70.0	70.0
1970	53	55	58	60	62	64.0	66.0	68.0	69.0	70.0	70.0	70.0	70.0	70.0	70.0	70.0	70.0	70.0
1971	45	50	55	60	62	64.0	66.0	68.0	69.0	70.0	70.0	70.0	70.0	70.0	70.0	70.0	70.0	70.0
1972	45	50	55	60	62	64.0	66.0	68.0	69.0	70.0	70.0	70.0	70.0	70.0	70.0	70.0	70.0	70.0
1973	45	50	55	60	62	64.0	66.0	68.0	69.0	70.0	70.0	70.0	70.0	70.0	70.0	70.0	70.0	70.0
1974	45	50	55	60	62	64.0	66.0	68.0	69.0	70.0	70.0	70.0	70.0	70.0	70.0	70.0	70.0	70.0
1975	45	50	55	60	62	64.0	66.0	68.0	69.0	70.0	70.0	70.0	70.0	70.0	70.0	70.0	70.0	70.0
1976	45	50	55	60	62	64.0	66.0	68.0	69.0	70.0	70.0	70.0	70.0	70.0	70.0	70.0	70.0	70.0
1977	45	50	50	55	60	62.0	64.0	66.0	68.0	69.0	70.0	70.0	70.0	70.0	70.0	70.0	70.0	70.0
1978	45	50	50	55	60	62.0	64.0	66.0	68.0	69.0	70.0	70.0	70.0	70.0	70.0	70.0	70.0	70.0
1979	44	49	49	55	55	63.0	63.0	63.0	68.0	68.0	70.0	70.0	70.0	70.0	70.0	70.0	70.0	70.0
1980	44	49	49	55	55	63.0	63.0	63.0	68.0	68.0	70.0	70.0	70.0	70.0	70.0	70.0	70.0	70.0
1981	44	49	49	55	55	63.0	63.0	63.0	68.0	68.0	70.0	70.0	70.0	70.0	70.0	70.0	70.0	70.0
1982	40	44	44	50	50	50.0	50.0	50.0	50.0	50.0	50.0	50.0	50.0	50.0	50.0	50.0	50.0	50.0
1983	36	40	40	45	45	50.0	50.0	50.0	50.0	50.0	50.0	50.0	50.0	50.0	50.0	50.0	50.0	50.0
1984	34	38	38	42	42	48.0	48.0	48.0	50.0	50.0	50.0	50.0	50.0	50.0	50.0	50.0	50.0	50.0
1985	30	34	38	42	42	48.0	48.0	48.0	50.0	50.0	50.0	50.0	50.0	50.0	50.0	50.0	50.0	50.0
1986	30	34	38	42	42	48.0	48.0	48.0	50.0	50.0	50.0	50.0	50.0	50.0	50.0	50.0	50.0	50.0
1987	35	35	35	35	35	38.5	38.5	38.5	38.5	38.5	38.5	38.5	38.5	38.5	38.5	38.5	38.5	38.5
1988	28	28	28	33	33	33.0	33.0	33.0	33.0	28.0	28.0	28.0	28.0	28.0	28.0	28.0	28.0	28.0
1989	28	28	28	33	33	33.0	33.0	33.0	33.0	28.0	28.0	28.0	28.0	28.0	28.0	28.0	28.0	28.0
1990	28	28	28	28	33	33.0	33.0	33.0	33.0	28.0	28.0	28.0	28.0	28.0	28.0	28.0	28.0	28.0
1991	28	28	28	28	31	31.0	31.0	31.0	31.0	31.0	31.0	31.0	31.0	31.0	31.0	31.0	31.0	31.0
1992	28	28	28	28	28	31.0	31.0	31.0	31.0	31.0	31.0	31.0	31.0	31.0	31.0	31.0	31.0	31.0
1993	28	28	28	28	28	31.0	31.0	31.0	31.0	31.0	36.0	36.0	36.0	36.0	39.6	39.6	39.6	39.6
1994	28	28	28	28	28	31.0	31.0	31.0	31.0	31.0	36.0	36.0	36.0	36.0	39.6	39.6	39.6	39.6
1995	28	28	28	28	28	31.0	31.0	31.0	31.0	31.0	36.0	36.0	36.0	36.0	39.6	39.6	39.6	39.6
1996	28	28	28	28	28	31.0	31.0	31.0	31.0	31.0	36.0	36.0	36.0	36.0	39.6	39.6	39.6	39.6
1997	28	28	28	28	28	31.0	31.0	31.0	31.0	31.0	36.0	36.0	36.0	36.0	39.6	39.6	39.6	39.6
1998	28	28	28	28	28	28.0	31.0	31.0	31.0	31.0	31.0	36.0	36.0	36.0	39.6	39.6	39.6	39.6
1999	28	28	28	28	28	28.0	31.0	31.0	31.0	31.0	31.0	36.0	36.0	36.0	39.6	39.6	39.6	39.6
2000	28	28	28	28	28	28.0	31.0	31.0	31.0	31.0	31.0	36.0	36.0	36.0	39.6	39.6	39.6	39.6

Source

Tax tables from Internal Revenue Services 1040 forms (various years).

Documentation

Taxes are based on all income earned in the calendar year. Taxable income is income subject to tax after all deductions are taken: gross income minus deductions. Both average and marginal tax apply only to the specific amount of taxable income given in the table. Tax rates apply to income intervals. The incomes reported in the table do not duplicate the actual tax intervals, and so tax rates for incomes between the specific figures used in the tables may vary.

GOVERNMENT EMPLOYMENT

John Joseph Wallis

TABLE Ea827–869 Government employees, by level and type of government: 1940–1999[1],[2]

Contributed by John Joseph Wallis

	Employees										Education			
	All												State and local	
			State and local		Local									
Fiscal year	Total	Federal (civilian)	Total	State	Total	County	Municipal	Township	Special district	School district	Total	Federal (civilian)	Total	State
	Ea827	Ea828	Ea829	Ea830	Ea831	Ea832	Ea833	Ea834	Ea835	Ea836	Ea837	Ea838	Ea839	Ea840
	Thousand	Thousand	Thousand	Thousand	Thousand	Thousand	Thousand	Thousand	Thousand	Thousand	Thousand	Thousand	Thousand	Thousand
1940	4,474	1,128	3,346	—	—	—	—	—	—	—	—	—	1,320	—
1941	4,970	1,598	3,372	—	—	—	—	—	—	—	—	—	1,320	—
1942	5,915	2,664	3,251	—	—	—	—	—	—	—	—	—	1,320	—
1943	6,358	3,166	3,192	—	—	—	—	—	—	—	—	—	1,320	—
1944	6,537	3,365	3,172	—	—	—	—	—	—	—	—	—	1,311	—
1945	6,556	3,375	3,181	—	—	—	—	—	—	—	—	—	1,267	—
1946	6,001	2,434	3,567	804	2,762	417	1,155	257	—	934	—	—	1,457	233
1947	5,791	2,002	3,789	909	2,880	434	1,202	282	—	962	—	—	1,529	271
1948	6,042	2,076	3,966	963	3,002	469	1,249	298	—	986	—	—	1,581	286
1949	6,203	2,047	4,156	1,037	3,119	476	1,281	307	—	1,056	—	—	1,658	306
1950	6,402	2,117	4,285	1,057	3,228	500	1,311	317	—	1,102	—	—	1,723	312
1951	6,802	2,515	4,287	1,070	3,218	505	1,297	280	—	1,136	—	—	1,759	316
1952	7,105	2,583	4,522	1,060	3,461	573	1,341	189	123	1,234	1,884	11	1,872	293
1953	7,048	2,385	4,663	1,082	3,580	597	1,382	308	—	1,293	1,959	11	1,949	294
1954	7,232	2,373	4,859	1,149	3,710	628	1,420	297	—	1,365	2,059	9	2,050	310
1955	7,432	2,378	5,054	1,199	3,855	648	1,436	315	—	1,455	2,181	12	2,169	333
1956	7,685	2,410	5,275	1,268	4,007	674	1,485	199	120	1,533	2,286	3	2,283	353
1957[3]	8,047	2,439	5,608	1,300	4,307	726	1,539	244	150	1,651	2,470	9	2,461	375
1958	8,297	2,405	5,892	1,408	4,484	738	1,594	549	—	1,752	2,600	11	2,589	406
1959	8,487	2,399	6,088	1,454	4,634	767	1,636	599	—	1,820	2,756	11	2,745	443
1960	8,808	2,421	6,387	1,527	4,860	788	1,692	581	—	1,921	2,930	12	2,918	474
1961	9,100	2,484	6,616	1,625	4,992	821	1,734	427	—	2,049	3,062	12	3,050	518
1962	9,388	2,539	6,849	1,680	5,169	862	1,696	245	204	2,161	3,236	12	3,224	555
1963	9,736	2,548	7,188	1,775	5,413	875	1,782	476	—	2,300	3,448	11	3,437	602
1964	10,064	2,528	7,536	1,873	5,663	936	1,817	474	—	2,436	3,687	13	3,674	656
1965	10,589	2,588	8,001	2,028	5,973	979	1,884	510	—	2,598	3,974	14	3,960	739
1966	11,388	2,861	8,527	2,211	6,316	1,043	1,971	543	—	2,850	4,422	18	4,313	866
1967	11,867	2,993	8,874	2,335	6,539	1,077	1,993	315	234	2,919	4,568	18	4,550	940
1968	12,342	2,984	9,358	2,495	6,864	1,151	2,112	315	258	3,028	4,847	18	4,829	1,037
1969	12,685	2,969	9,716	2,614	7,102	1,163	2,165	330	269	3,176	5,079	18	5,061	1,112
1970	13,028	2,881	10,147	2,755	7,392	1,229	2,244	330	275	3,316	5,316	19	5,297	1,182
1971	13,316	2,872	10,444	2,832	7,612	1,270	2,273	342	291	3,436	5,501	20	5,481	1,223
1972	13,759	2,795	10,964	2,957	7,869	1,342	2,348	363	303	3,587	5,646	20	5,733	1,267
1973	14,139	2,786	11,353	3,013	8,339	1,451	2,471	374	350	3,694	5,922	21	5,901	1,280
1974	14,628	2,874	11,754	3,155	8,599	1,490	2,491	379	374	3,866	6,188	25	6,163	1,357

Notes appear at end of table

(continued)

TABLE Ea827–869   Government employees, by level and type of government: 1940–1999   *Continued*

	Employees										Education			
	All												State and local	
			State and local											
					Local									
Fiscal year	Total	Federal (civilian)	Total	State	Total	County	Municipal	Township	Special district	School district	Total	Federal (civilian)	Total	State
	Ea827	Ea828	Ea829	Ea830	Ea831	Ea832	Ea833	Ea834	Ea835	Ea836	Ea837	Ea838	Ea839	Ea840
	Thousand	Thousand	Thousand	Thousand	Thousand	Thousand	Thousand	Thousand	Thousand	Thousand	Thousand	Thousand	Thousand	Thousand
1975	14,973	2,890	12,084	3,271	8,813	1,563	2,506	392	383	3,969	6,294	22	6,272	1,400
1976	15,012	2,843	12,169	3,343	8,826	1,600	2,443	401	398	3,985	6,330	22	6,308	1,434
1977	15,459	2,848	12,611	3,491	9,120	1,761	2,469	415	399	4,127	6,570	22	6,549	1,484
1978	15,628	2,885	12,743	3,539	9,204	1,768	2,509	411	403	4,113	6,582	24	6,559	1,508
1979	15,971	2,869	13,102	3,699	9,403	1,804	2,553	401	445	4,200	6,756	24	6,732	1,577
1980	16,213	2,898	13,315	3,753	9,562	1,853	2,561	394	484	4,270	6,867	19	6,841	1,599
1981	15,968	2,865	13,103	3,726	9,377	1,808	2,469	386	492	4,222	6,786	18	6,768	1,603
1982	15,918	2,848	13,013	3,764	9,249	1,824	2,460	377	502	4,194	6,749	16	6,749	1,638
1983	16,034	2,874	13,159	3,816	9,344	1,811	2,424	379	519	4,211	6,807	16	6,791	1,666
1984	16,436	2,942	13,494	3,898	9,595	1,872	2,434	386	516	4,387	7,037	15	7,022	1,708
1985	16,690	3,021	13,669	3,984	9,685	1,891	2,467	392	519	4,416	7,119	15	7,104	1,764
1986	16,933	3,019	13,913	4,068	9,846	1,926	2,494	400	524	4,502	7,253	14	7,240	1,800
1987	17,212	3,091	14,121	4,115	10,076	1,963	2,541	393	529	4,627	7,404	15	7,389	1,804
1988	17,588	3,112	14,476	4,236	10,240	2,024	2,570	415	552	4,679	7,525	14	7,510	1,854
1989	17,879	3,114	14,765	4,365	10,400	2,085	2,569	405	568	4,774	7,698	14	7,684	1,925
1990	18,369	3,105	15,263	4,503	10,760	2,167	2,642	418	585	4,950	7,971	13	7,958	1,984
1991	18,554	3,103	15,452	4,521	10,930	2,196	2,662	415	612	5,045	8,086	14	8,072	1,999
1992	18,164	3,047	15,117	4,587	10,531	2,251	2,638	410	646	4,582	—	14	7,642	2,027
1993	18,823	2,999	15,824	4,673	11,151	—	—	—	—	—	—	—	—	—
1994	19,420	2,952	16,468	4,694	11,775	—	—	—	—	—	—	—	—	—
1995	19,521	2,895	16,626	4,719	11,906	—	—	—	—	—	—	—	—	—
1997 [4]	19,540	2,807	16,733	4,733	12,000	2,425	2,755	455	691	5,675	8,969	—	10,947	2,114
1998 [4]	19,854	2,765	17,089	4,758	12,331	—	—	—	—	—	—	—	—	—
1999 [4]	20,306	2,799	17,506	4,818	12,689	—	—	—	—	—	—	—	—	—

	Employees										Full-time equivalents			
	Education					Other than education – state and local					All			
	State and local							Local					State and local	
	Local													
Fiscal year	Total	County	Municipal	Township	Special district	Total	State	Total	County	Municipal	Total	Federal (civilian)	Total	State
	Ea841	Ea842	Ea843	Ea844	Ea845	Ea846	Ea847	Ea848	Ea849	Ea850	Ea851	Ea852	Ea853	Ea854
	Thousand	Thousand	Thousand	Thousand	Thousand	Thousand	Thousand	Thousand	Thousand	Thousand	Thousand	Thousand	Thousand	Thousand
1940	—	—	—	—	—	2,026	551	1,475	345	887	—	—	—	—
1941	—	—	—	—	—	2,052	547	1,505	335	901	—	—	—	—
1942	—	—	—	—	—	1,931	503	1,428	333	872	—	—	—	—
1943	—	—	—	—	—	1,872	464	1,408	322	858	—	—	—	—
1944	—	—	—	—	—	1,861	456	1,405	329	855	—	—	—	—

TABLE (Employees, in thousands) / Full-time equivalents (in thousands)

Fiscal year	Education — state and local, Local: Total	County	Municipal	Township	Special district	Other than education — state and local: Total	State	Local: Total	County	Municipal	Full-time equivalents, All: Total	Federal (civilian)	State and local: Total	State
	Ea841	Ea842	Ea843	Ea844	Ea845	Ea846	Ea847	Ea848	Ea849	Ea850	Ea851	Ea852	Ea853	Ea854
	Thousand	Thousand	Thousand	Thousand	Thousand	Thousand	Thousand	Thousand	Thousand	Thousand	Thousand	Thousand	Thousand	Thousand
1945	—	—	—	—	—	1,914	473	1,441	316	879	—	—	—	—
1946	1,224	—	—	—	—	2,110	571	1,538	361	955	—	—	—	—
1947	1,258	—	—	—	—	2,260	638	1,622	375	996	—	—	—	—
1948	1,295	—	—	—	—	2,385	677	1,707	406	1,039	—	—	—	—
1949	1,352	—	—	—	—	2,497	731	1,767	410	1,082	—	—	—	—
1950	1,411	—	—	—	—	2,562	745	1,817	429	1,106	—	—	—	—
1951	1,443	—	—	—	—	2,528	754	1,775	435	1,102	—	—	3,815	973
1952	1,580	—	—	39	—	2,649	767	1,881	454	1,154	—	—	4,012	958
1953	1,654	—	—	—	—	2,714	788	1,926	473	1,187	—	—	4,126	966
1954	1,740	—	—	—	—	2,809	839	1,970	497	1,220	—	—	4,309	1,024
1955	1,835	—	—	—	—	2,885	866	2,020	512	1,238	—	—	4,487	1,081
1956	1,930	—	—	48	—	2,992	915	2,077	530	1,277	—	—	4,687	1,136
1957 [3]	2,086	104	220	53	—	3,147	925	2,221	562	1,319	7,133	2,340	4,793	1,154
1958	2,183	—	—	—	—	3,303	1,002	2,301	564	1,369	—	—	5,171	1,259
1959	2,302	—	—	—	—	3,343	1,011	2,332	568	1,399	—	—	5,342	1,302
1960	2,444	—	—	—	—	3,469	1,053	2,416	571	1,439	—	—	5,570	1,353
1961	2,532	177	261	70	—	3,566	1,107	2,460	654	1,448	8,428	2,470	5,845	1,435
1962	2,670	—	—	—	—	3,625	1,125	2,499	686	1,434	—	—	5,958	1,478
1963	2,835	—	—	—	—	3,751	1,173	2,578	698	1,498	—	—	6,282	1,558
1964	3,018	—	—	—	—	3,862	1,217	2,645	737	1,514	—	—	6,586	1,639
1965	3,221	—	—	—	—	4,041	1,289	2,752	767	1,560	9,489	2,552	6,937	1,751
1966	3,447	—	—	—	—	4,214	1,345	2,869	805	1,613	10,030	2,767	7,263	1,864
1967	3,610	245	360	86	—	4,324	1,395	2,929	832	1,633	10,364	2,908	7,454	1,946
1968	3,792	269	398	96	—	4,530	1,458	3,072	881	1,714	10,780	2,901	7,879	2,085
1969	3,949	261	417	95	—	4,655	1,502	3,153	902	1,747	11,053	2,893	8,160	2,179
1970	4,115	279	429	92	—	4,850	1,573	3,277	949	1,815	11,338	2,810	8,528	2,302
1971	4,258	292	435	95	—	4,963	1,609	3,354	978	1,838	—	—	8,806	2,384
1972	4,367	306	441	107	—	5,231	1,690	3,502	1,036	1,907	—	—	9,237	2,487
1973	4,621	330	479	118	—	5,452	1,733	3,718	1,121	1,992	—	—	9,578	2,547
1974	4,805	334	482	123	—	5,591	1,798	3,794	1,156	2,309	—	—	9,852	2,653
1975	4,872	335	447	121	—	5,812	1,871	3,941	1,228	2,059	—	—	10,098	2,744
1976	4,875	346	422	122	—	5,861	1,909	3,951	1,254	2,021	—	—	10,206	2,799
1977	5,065	369	421	127	—	6,062	2,007	4,055	1,392	2,048	—	—	10,591	2,903
1978	5,051	391	425	123	—	6,184	2,031	4,153	1,377	2,084	—	—	10,724	2,966
1979	5,156	403	432	121	—	6,370	2,122	4,247	1,401	2,121	—	—	10,944	3,072
1980	5,241	423	431	120	—	6,474	2,154	4,321	1,430	2,130	—	—	11,047	3,106
1981	5,165	417	413	115	—	6,335	2,123	4,212	1,391	2,056	—	—	10,917	3,087
1982	5,111	426	401	111	(Z)	6,264	2,126	4,138	1,398	2,059	—	—	10,862	3,080
1983	5,125	433	373	112	(Z)	6,368	2,150	4,219	1,378	2,051	—	—	10,885	3,116
1984	5,314	454	364	113	(Z)	6,472	2,190	4,281	1,418	2,070	—	—	11,143	3,177

Notes appear at end of table

(continued)

TABLE Ea827–869   Government employees, by level and type of government: 1940–1999   *Continued*

	Employees										Full-time equivalents			
	Education					Other than education – state and local					All			
	State and local							Local					State and local	
		Local												
	Total	County	Municipal	Township	Special district	Total	State	Total	County	Municipal	Total	Federal (civilian)	Total	State
Fiscal year	Ea841	Ea842	Ea843	Ea844	Ea845	Ea846	Ea847	Ea848	Ea849	Ea850	Ea851	Ea852	Ea853	Ea854
	Thousand	Thousand	Thousand	Thousand	Thousand	Thousand	Thousand	Thousand	Thousand	Thousand	Thousand	Thousand	Thousand	Thousand
1985	5,340	451	364	112	(Z)	6,565	2,220	4,345	1,440	2,103	—	—	11,853	3,437
1986	5,439	459	368	115	(Z)	6,673	2,268	4,407	1,467	2,126	—	—	12,101	3,479
1987	5,584	471	380	117	(Z)	6,732	2,311	4,492	1,492	2,161	—	—	12,404	3,606
1988	5,656	482	382	118	(Z)	6,966	2,382	4,584	1,542	2,188	—	—	12,723	3,709
1989	5,759	494	379	117	(Z)	7,081	2,440	4,641	1,591	2,190	—	—	13,080	3,840
1990	5,974	510	402	118	(Z)	7,305	2,519	4,786	1,657	2,240	—	—	13,186	3,829
1991	6,074	515	401	138	1	7,380	2,523	4,856	1,681	2,261	—	—	13,182	3,836
1992	5,616	522	401	113	26	7,475	2,560	4,915	1,729	2,237	—	—	13,443	3,891
1993	—	—	—	—	—	—	—	—	—	—	—	—	13,912	3,917
1994	—	—	—	—	—	—	—	—	—	—	—	—	14,091	3,971
1995	—	—	—	—	—	—	—	—	—	—	—	—	14,214	3,987
1997 [4]	6,844	608	434	—	—	5,786	2,619	5,156	1,817	2,321	16,952	—	—	—
1998 [4]	—	—	—	—	—	—	—	—	—	—	—	—	—	—
1999 [4]	—	—	—	—	—	—	—	—	—	—	—	—	—	—

Full-time equivalents

	All								Education						
	State and local								State and local						
	Local										Local				
	Total	County	Municipal	Township	Special district	School district	Total	Federal (civilian)	Total	State	Total	County	Municipal	Township	Special district
Fiscal year	Ea855	Ea856	Ea857	Ea858	Ea859	Ea860	Ea861	Ea862	Ea863	Ea864	Ea865	Ea866	Ea867	Ea868	Ea869
	Thousand	Thousand	Thousand	Thousand	Thousand	Thousand	Thousand	Thousand	Thousand	Thousand	Thousand	Thousand	Thousand	Thousand	Thousand
1940	—	—	—	—	—	—	—	—	—	—	—	—	—	—	—
1941	—	—	—	—	—	—	—	—	—	—	—	—	—	—	—
1942	—	—	—	—	—	—	—	—	—	—	—	—	—	—	—
1943	—	—	—	—	—	—	—	—	—	—	—	—	—	—	—
1944	—	—	—	—	—	—	—	—	—	—	—	—	—	—	—
1945	—	—	—	—	—	—	—	—	—	—	—	—	—	—	—
1946	—	—	—	—	—	—	—	—	—	—	—	—	—	—	—
1947	—	—	—	—	—	—	—	—	—	—	—	—	—	—	—
1948	—	—	—	—	—	—	—	—	—	—	—	—	—	—	—
1949	—	—	—	—	—	—	—	—	—	—	—	—	—	—	—
1950	—	—	—	—	—	—	—	—	—	—	—	—	—	—	—
1951	2,843	458	1,145	179	—	1,060	—	—	1,577	—	—	—	—	—	—
1952	3,054	538	1,175	196	—	1,146	—	—	1,678	—	—	—	—	—	—
1953	3,160	561	1,200	203	—	1,197	—	—	1,737	—	—	—	—	—	—
1954	3,284	587	1,234	199	—	1,264	—	—	1,826	—	—	—	—	—	—

Full-time equivalents (in Thousand)

Column groupings:
- **All → State and local:** Ea855 = Total; **Local:** Ea856 = County, Ea857 = Municipal, Ea858 = Township, Ea859 = Special district, Ea860 = School district, Ea861 = Total
- **All → Federal (civilian):** Ea862
- **Education → State and local:** Ea863 = Total, Ea864 = State; **Local:** Ea865 = Total, Ea866 = County, Ea867 = Municipal, Ea868 = Township, Ea869 = Special district

Fiscal year	Ea855 S&L Total	Ea856 County	Ea857 Municipal	Ea858 Township	Ea859 Special dist.	Ea860 School dist.	Ea861 Local Total	Ea862 Federal (civ.)	Ea863 Educ Total	Ea864 Educ State	Ea865 Educ Local Total	Ea866 Educ County	Ea867 Educ Municipal	Ea868 Educ Township	Ea869 Educ Special dist.
1955	3,406	604	1,252	209	—	1,341	—	—	1,935	—	—	—	—	—	—
1956	3,551	632	1,292	213	—	1,415	—	—	2,032	—	—	—	—	—	—
1957 [3]	3,638	647	1,297	122	120	1,452	—	—	2,093	258	1,834	—	—	—	—
1958	3,912	678	1,372	289	—	1,572	—	—	2,270	—	—	—	—	—	—
1959	4,039	703	1,406	288	—	1,635	—	—	2,396	—	—	—	—	—	—
1960	4,217	728	1,447	302	—	1,729	—	—	2,525	—	—	—	—	—	—
1961	4,410	760	1,491	149	152	1,836	—	—	2,652	—	—	—	—	—	—
1962	4,480	784	1,486	145	165	1,901	—	—	2,730	390	2,340	151	227	62	—
1963	4,724	804	1,549	154	161	2,056	—	—	2,948	422	2,526	—	—	—	—
1964	4,947	859	1,584	165	176	2,164	—	—	3,132	460	2,671	—	—	—	—
1965	5,186	893	1,638	177	191	2,287	—	—	3,337	508	2,829	—	—	—	—
1966	5,399	948	1,701	181	200	2,369	—	—	3,543	575	2,968	—	—	—	—
1967	5,509	973	1,715	175	196	2,449	—	—	3,658	620	3,039	208	306	76	—
1968	5,795	1,034	1,813	185	207	2,555	—	—	3,898	694	3,204	—	—	—	—
1969	5,981	1,053	1,858	191	221	2,656	—	—	4,063	746	3,316	—	—	—	—
1970	6,226	1,098	1,922	192	228	2,786	—	—	4,258	803	3,455	—	—	—	—
1971	6,422	1,153	1,960	200	244	2,865	—	—	4,403	841	3,562	—	—	—	—
1972	6,750	1,242	2,029	215	283	2,981	—	—	4,585	861	3,729	—	—	—	—
1973	7,031	1,318	2,109	232	298	3,074	—	—	4,751	887	3,863	—	—	—	—
1974	7,199	1,343	2,127	233	312	3,183	—	—	4,901	795	4,106	—	—	—	—
1975	7,354	1,408	2,142	237	324	3,243	—	—	4,952	952	4,000	—	—	—	—
1976	7,407	1,448	2,107	245	335	3,272	—	—	5,003	973	4,030	—	—	—	—
1977	7,688	1,582	2,168	241	346	3,350	—	—	5,134	1,005	4,102	—	—	—	—
1978	7,758	1,606	2,163	245	351	3,393	—	—	5,202	1,016	4,187	—	—	—	—
1979	7,871	1,621	2,190	250	374	3,435	—	—	5,291	1,046	4,245	—	—	—	—
1980	7,941	1,651	2,166	249	406	3,468	—	—	5,341	1,063	4,278	351	360	101	(Z)
1981	7,830	1,609	2,111	245	413	3,453	—	—	5,302	1,063	4,240	344	346	98	(Z)
1982	7,782	1,616	2,088	238	414	3,426	—	—	5,230	1,050	4,163	345	322	94	(Z)
1983	7,769	1,601	2,060	242	438	3,428	—	—	5,237	1,072	4,165	345	300	94	(Z)
1984	7,966	1,645	2,090	239	437	3,555	—	—	5,395	1,091	4,304	356	300	95	(Z)
1985	8,415	—	—	—	—	—	—	—	—	—	—	—	—	—	—
1986	8,621	1,737	2,191	247	451	3,800	—	—	5,852	1,256	4,595	379	320	99	(Z)
1987	8,798	1,777	2,223	260	461	3,872	—	—	5,979	1,264	4,704	395	337	114	(Z)
1988	9,014	1,838	2,251	263	472	3,973	—	—	6,125	1,309	4,816	401	342	103	(Z)
1989	9,239	1,896	2,268	265	497	4,087	—	—	6,297	1,360	4,937	409	341	103	(Z)
1990	9,356	1,957	2,295	271	509	4,207	—	—	6,486	1,418	5,067	423	338	104	(Z)
1991	9,346	1,986	2,303	267	525	4,275	—	—	6,541	1,404	5,137	425	338	117	(Z)
1992	9,552	2,031	2,341	267	561	4,146	6,443	13	6,430	1,394	5,036	432	361	99	18
1993	9,996	—	—	—	—	—	—	—	—	—	—	—	—	—	—
1994	10,119	—	—	—	—	—	—	—	—	—	—	—	—	—	—
1995	—	—	—	—	—	—	—	—	—	—	—	—	—	—	—
1997 [4]	10,227	2,181	2,407	293	585	4,763	7,262	—	7,250	1,484	5,057	440	343	—	—
1998 [4]	—	—	—	—	—	—	—	—	—	—	—	—	—	—	—
1999 [4]	—	—	—	—	—	—	—	—	—	—	—	—	—	—	—

Notes appear on next page

TABLE Ea827–869   Government employees, by level and type of government: 1940–1999 *Continued*

(Z) Less than 500.

[1] For 1946–1966, during most years data for townships and special districts, when available, were calculated together and are shown under townships.

[2] Prior to 1953, federal figures are as of September 30.

[3] As of April 30.

[4] Data for March.

Sources

U.S. Department of Commerce, "Historical Statistics on Governmental Finances & Employment," *1982 Census of Governments*, number 4, Tables 6 and 7, pp. 230–31; and data on public employment (for various years) obtained directly from the Census of Governments.

Documentation

All figures are for the month of October, except as noted.

Complete local government data were collected in 1957, 1962, 1967, 1972, 1977, 1982, 1987, 1992, and 1997. All other years are samples subject to sampling variation.

Federal figures cover civilian employees, including those outside the continental United States. Federal payroll figures represent pay for the number of working days in month specified. Thus, changes in amount of payroll reflect in part differences in number of work days covered.

The local totals for education employees include local school district employees shown under all employees.

TABLE Ea870–893   Monthly government payroll, by level and type of government: 1940–1999[1, 2]

Contributed by John Joseph Wallis

											Education	
				All employees								
				State and local								
							Local					
		Federal (civilian)	Total	State	Total	County	Municipal	Township	Special district	School district	Total	Federal (civilian)
	Total											
	Ea870	Ea871	Ea872	Ea873	Ea874	Ea875	Ea876	Ea877	Ea878	Ea879	Ea880	Ea881
Fiscal year	Million dollars	Million dollars	Million dollars	Million dollars	Million dollars	Million dollars	Million dollars	Million dollars	Million dollars	Million dollars	Million dollars	Million dollars
1940	566	177	389	—	—	—	—	—	—	—	—	—
1941	649	254	395	—	—	—	—	—	—	—	—	—
1942	880	486	394	—	—	—	—	—	—	—	—	—
1943	1,084	673	412	—	—	—	—	—	—	—	—	—
1944	1,103	685	418	—	—	—	—	—	—	—	—	—
1945	1,110	642	468	—	—	—	—	—	—	—	—	—
1946	1,156	572	584	128	456	58	206	25	—	166	—	—
1947	1,184	481	702	161	542	68	236	35	—	202	—	—
1948	1,329	534	795	185	610	78	266	43	—	223	353	—
1949	1,406	539	867	210	657	86	277	44	—	249	385	—
1950	1,528	613	915	218	696	93	290	47	—	267	—	—
1951	1,865	857	1,008	246	762	101	315	48	—	299	—	—
1952	1,980	856	1,124	260	863	124	345	25	31	339	507	4
1953	2,014	793	1,221	279	942	141	368	58	—	376	556	3
1954	2,103	785	1,318	301	1,018	152	396	60	—	410	603	3
1955	2,265	846	1,419	326	1,093	162	414	64	—	453	666	4
1956	2,509	944	1,566	367	1,199	176	450	69	—	504	736	1
1957 [3]	2,533	919	1,615	388	1,242	184	461	37	40	520	—	—
1958	2,977	1,091	1,886	447	1,439	213	511	105	—	618	911	5
1959	3,114	1,073	2,042	485	1,556	229	548	109	—	670	1,004	5
1960	3,333	1,118	2,215	524	1,691	249	583	118	—	735	—	—
1961	3,634	1,214	2,420	586	1,834	272	630	60	60	812	1,211	6
1962	3,966	1,347	2,619	635	1,985	295	662	60	68	899	1,337	7
1963	4,264	1,423	2,840	696	2,144	311	708	65	68	992	1,470	6
1964	4,572	1,475	3,097	761	2,336	346	761	72	79	1,080	1,616	8
1965	4,884	1,484	3,400	849	2,551	377	818	81	87	1,189	1,786	8
1966	5,463	1,665	3,798	975	2,823	414	892	87	97	1,333	2,041	11
1967	6,056	1,842	4,213	1,106	3,108	465	972	96	100	1,475	2,256	12
1968	6,889	2,137	4,752	1,257	3,495	532	1,097	107	115	1,644	2,558	13
1969	7,588	2,335	5,252	1,431	3,822	572	1,196	114	124	1,816	2,845	15
1970	8,334	2,428	5,906	1,612	4,294	640	1,361	122	140	2,032	3,472	16
1971	8,911	2,529	6,382	1,742	4,641	722	1,482	138	152	2,146	3,402	19
1972	9,950	2,710	7,240	1,937	5,303	857	1,654	166	198	2,428	3,705	19
1973	11,027	3,012	8,015	2,158	5,857	952	1,855	192	234	2,623	4,205	20
1974	12,086	3,294	8,792	2,410	6,382	1,057	1,985	200	258	2,882	4,648	28
1975	13,224	3,584	9,640	2,653	6,987	1,183	2,129	215	300	3,160	4,985	24
1976	13,924	3,565	10,359	2,894	7,465	1,295	2,235	237	327	3,371	5,338	28
1977	15,338	3,918	11,420	3,195	8,225	1,489	2,412	250	367	3,707	5,874	29
1978	16,483	4,344	12,139	3,483	8,656	1,564	2,535	269	392	3,897	6,216	30
1979	18,077	4,728	13,349	3,869	9,480	1,726	2,729	291	463	4,272	6,791	34
1980	19,946	5,216	14,730	4,285	10,445	1,935	2,951	330	546	4,683	7,491	40
1981	21,193	5,239	15,954	4,668	11,287	2,083	3,222	349	612	5,021	8,035	33
1982	23,124	5,394	17,214	5,022	12,192	2,287	3,425	377	678	5,403	8,562	35
1983	24,525	5,959	18,223	5,346	12,878	2,387	3,640	398	724	5,729	9,045	37
1984	26,904	7,137	19,767	5,815	13,952	2,596	3,872	421	780	6,283	9,873	38
1985	28,945	7,580	21,365	6,329	15,036	2,819	4,191	446	834	6,746	10,722	38
1986	30,670	7,561	23,109	6,810	16,298	3,009	4,407	474	892	7,517	11,717	37
1987	32,382	7,924	24,745	7,263	17,482	3,258	4,687	508	938	7,768	12,352	37
1988	34,203	7,976	26,227	7,842	18,385	3,532	4,979	556	1,020	8,298	13,161	37
1989	36,763	8,636	28,127	8,443	19,684	3,855	5,274	599	1,104	8,852	14,062	38
1990	39,228	8,999	30,229	9,083	21,146	4,192	5,564	642	1,197	9,551	15,116	37
1991	41,237	9,687	31,550	9,437	22,113	4,404	5,784	664	1,287	9,975	15,724	41
1992	42,804	9,937	32,437	9,750	22,686	4,722	6,238	704	1,414	9,609	—	—
1993	44,972	10,433	34,540	10,288	24,252	—	—	—	—	—	—	—
1994	46,118	9,686	36,433	10,554	25,878	—	—	—	—	—	—	—
1995	47,458	9,744	37,714	10,927	26,787	—	—	—	—	—	—	—
1997 [4]	49,406	9,994	39,412	11,413	27,999	5,750	7,146	869	1,654	12,579	19,818	—
1998 [4]	51,569	10,115	41,454	11,845	29,608	—	—	—	—	—	—	—
1999 [4]	54,363	10,478	43,886	12,565	31,321	—	—	—	—	—	—	—

Notes appear at end of table   (continued)

TABLE Ea870–893 Monthly government payroll, by level and type of government: 1940–1999 *Continued*

	Education							Other than education – state and local				
	State and local									Local		
			Local									
	Total	State	Total	County	Municipal	Township	Special district	Total	State	Total	County	Municipal
	Ea882	Ea883	Ea884	Ea885	Ea886	Ea887	Ea888	Ea889	Ea890	Ea891	Ea892	Ea893
Fiscal year	Million dollars	Million dollars	Million dollars	Million dollars	Million dollars	Million dollars	Million dollars	Million dollars	Million dollars	Million dollars	Million dollars	Million dollars
1940	175	—	—	—	—	—	—	214	59	155	34	105
1941	175	—	—	—	—	—	—	220	62	158	35	108
1942	175	—	—	—	—	—	—	219	60	159	35	110
1943	176	—	—	—	—	—	—	236	64	172	37	119
1944	172	—	—	—	—	—	—	246	64	182	39	125
1945	200	—	—	—	—	—	—	268	73	195	43	133
1946	260	35	226	—	—	6	—	324	93	230	51	160
1947	319	45	274	—	—	6	—	384	116	268	58	181
1948	353	51	302	—	—	7	—	442	134	308	67	206
1949	385	59	326	—	—	7	—	482	151	331	74	220
1950	409	61	348	—	—	8	—	505	157	348	79	230
1951	453	68	385	—	—	10	—	556	178	378	86	254
1952	503	65	438	—	—	10	—	621	195	426	97	283
1953	552	69	483	—	—	11	—	669	210	459	110	301
1954	600	73	527	19	—	12	—	718	227	491	119 [5]	324
1955	662	83	579	23	—	13	—	757	243	514	138 [5]	337
1956	734	93	641	22	—	15	—	831	273	558	155 [5]	365
1957 [3]	758	111	663	27	—	15	—	857	277	580	158 [5]	376
1958	906	122	784	—	—	—	—	980	325	655	—	418
1959	999	139	860	—	—	—	—	1,042	346	696	—	446
1960	1,095	151	944	52	113	—	—	1,120	373	747	198	471
1961	1,205	177	1,028	61	129	27	—	1,215	409	806	212	502
1962	1,325	202	1,123	67	128	29	—	1,294	433	861	229	534
1963	1,464	230	1,234	70	138	33	—	1,377	466	910	241	570
1964	1,608	258	1,350	81	154	36	—	1,489	504	986	265	607
1965	1,778	290	1,488	89	170	40	—	1,623	559	1,063	288	649
1966	2,020	353	1,677	101	188	45	—	1,778	622	1,146	313	703
1967	2,244	406	1,838	245	360	47	—	1,969	699	1,270	221	611
1968	2,545	477	2,068	138	229	57	—	2,207	780	1,428	394	868
1969	2,831	554	2,276	138	265	57	—	2,422	876	1,546	434	931
1970	3,170	630	2,539	149	299	60	—	2,737	982	1,755	490	1,062
1971	3,382	1,223	4,258	175	315	65	—	3,000	519	383	547	1,167
1972	3,814	1,260	4,367	194	341	76	—	3,426	677	936	663	1,313
1973	4,185	1,280	4,621	233	415	92	—	3,830	878	1,236	719	1,441
1974	4,580	932	3,688	241	425	98	—	4,212	1,478	2,694	816	1,560
1975	4,960	1,022	3,939	252	425	102	—	4,680	1,631	3,048	932	1,705
1976	5,310	1,112	4,208	285	431	111	—	5,049	1,782	3,257	1,010	1,804
1977	5,846	1,237	4,516	321	442	117	—	5,574	1,958	3,709	1,169	1,970
1978	6,186	1,333	4,853	357	478	122	—	5,953	2,150	3,803	1,207	2,056
1979	6,757	1,451	5,306	391	514	130	—	6,592	2,418	4,174	1,335	2,215
1980	7,451	1,608	5,843	444	564	153	—	7,279	2,677	4,603	1,491	2,387
1981	8,002	1,768	6,234	479	583	153	—	7,952	2,900	5,053	1,604	2,640
1982	8,545	1,873	6,652	513	581	156	(Z)	8,670	3,149	5,540	1,774	2,844
1983	9,007	1,985	7,019	544	581	166	(Z)	9,216	3,361	5,859	1,843	3,059
1984	9,835	2,178	7,657	594	604	178	(Z)	9,932	3,637	6,295	2,002	3,268
1985	10,684	2,444	8,240	655	655	187	(Z)	10,681	3,885	6,796	2,164	3,536
1986	11,680	2,584	9,097	701	683	200	(Z)	11,429	4,226	7,202	2,308	3,724
1987	12,452	2,758	9,557	787	789	216	(Z)	12,293	4,505	7,925	2,471	3,898
1988	13,125	2,929	10,196	824	843	237	(Z)	13,102	4,914	8,189	2,707	4,136
1989	14,024	3,175	10,849	882	869	250	(Z)	14,104	5,268	8,836	2,973	4,405
1990	15,078	3,426	11,652	954	889	264	(Z)	15,151	5,657	9,494	3,238	4,675
1991	15,683	3,551	12,132	982	906	275	24	15,867	5,886	9,981	3,423	4,878
1992	15,688	3,724	11,964	1,027	1,040	292	27	—	—	—	—	—
1993	—	—	—	—	—	—	—	—	—	—	—	—
1994	—	—	—	—	—	—	—	—	—	—	—	—
1995	—	—	—	—	—	—	—	—	—	—	—	—
1997 [4]	19,722	4,372	15,401	1,307	1,161	359	54	19,690	7,041	12,598	4,443	5,985
1998 [4]	—	—	—	—	—	—	—	—	—	—	—	—
1999 [4]	—	—	—	—	—	—	—	—	—	—	—	—

TABLE Ea870–893   Monthly government payroll, by level and type of government: 1940–1999   *Continued*

(Z) Less than $50,000.

[1] For 1946–1970, during most years data for townships and special districts, when available, were calculated together and are shown under townships.

[2] Prior to 1953, federal figures are as of September 30.

[3] As of April 30.

[4] Data for March.

[5] Differs from *Historical Statistics of the United States* (1975); figures were calculated as the difference between total and education payroll.

Sources

1940–1967. U.S. Bureau of the Census, "Historical Statistics on Governmental Finance and Employment," *U.S. Census of Governments: 1967*, volume 6, number 5, pp. 1–133.

1968–1970. U.S. Bureau of the Census, *Public Employment* (annual issues).

1971–1999. U.S. Department of Commerce, "Historical Statistics on Governmental Finances and Employment," *1982 Census of Governments*, number 4, Tables 6 and 7; and data on public employment (for various years) obtained directly from the Census of Governments.

Documentation

See the text for Table Ea827–869.

TABLE Ea894–903   Federal government employees, by government branch and location relative to the capital: 1816–1992

Contributed by John Joseph Wallis

	Total		Location relative to Washington, D.C., and surrounding area		Government branch					
					Executive					
	All	Competitive civil service (classified)	Inside	Outside	Total	Defense	Post Office	Other	Legislative	Judicial
	Ea894 [1,2]	Ea895	Ea896 [3]	Ea897 [3]	Ea898 [1]	Ea899 [4]	Ea900	Ea901	Ea902	Ea903 [5]
Fiscal year	Number	Number	Number	Number	Number	Number	Number	Number	Number	Number
1816	4,837	—	535	4,302	4,479	190	3,341	938	243	115
1821	6,914	—	603	6,311	6,526	161	4,766	1,599	252	136
1831	11,491	—	666	10,825	11,067	377	8,764	1,926	289	135
1841	18,038	—	1,014	17,024	17,550	598	14,290	2,662	332	156
1851	26,274	—	1,533	24,741	25,713	403	21,391	3,919	384	177
1861	36,672	—	2,199	34,473	36,106	946	30,269	4,891	393	173
1871	51,020	—	6,222	44,798	50,155	1,183	36,696	12,276	618	247
1881	100,020	—	13,124	86,896	94,679	16,297	56,421	21,961	2,579	2,762
1884 [6]	131,208	13,780	—	—	—	—	—	—	—	—
1885 [6]	134,476	15,590	—	—	—	—	—	—	—	—
1886 [6]	137,825	17,273	—	—	—	—	—	—	—	—
1887 [6]	141,260	19,345	—	—	—	—	—	—	—	—
1888	150,035	22,577	—	—	—	—	—	—	—	—
1889	159,356	29,650	—	—	—	—	—	—	—	—
1890	162,644	30,626	—	—	—	—	—	—	—	—
1891	166,000	33,873	20,834	136,608	150,844	20,561	95,449	34,834	3,867	2,731
1892	171,000	37,523	—	—	—	—	—	—	—	—
1893	176,000	43,915	—	—	—	—	—	—	—	—
1894	180,000	45,821	—	—	—	—	—	—	—	—
1895	189,000	54,222	—	—	—	—	—	—	—	—
1896	190,494	87,044	—	—	—	—	—	—	—	—
1897	192,000	85,886	—	—	—	—	—	—	—	—
1898	199,839	89,306	—	—	—	—	—	—	—	—
1899	208,000	93,144	—	—	—	—	—	—	—	—
1900	230,755	94,893	—	—	—	—	—	—	—	—
1901	256,000	106,205	28,044	211,432	231,056	44,524	136,192	50,340	5,690	2,730
1902	277,589	107,990	—	—	—	—	—	—	—	—
1903	301,000	135,453	—	—	—	—	—	—	—	—
1904	290,858	154,093	—	—	—	—	—	—	—	—
1905	300,000	171,807	—	—	—	—	—	—	—	—
1906	326,855	184,178	—	—	—	—	—	—	—	—
1907	337,751	194,323	—	—	—	—	—	—	—	—
1908	356,754	206,637	34,647	322,107	348,479	50,665	199,904	97,910	5,825	2,450
1909	372,379	234,940	35,936	336,443	364,078	54,425	205,360	104,293	5,891	2,410
1910	388,708	222,278	38,911	349,797	380,428	58,320	209,005	113,103	5,910	2,370
1911	395,905	227,657	39,782	356,123	387,673	60,283	211,546	115,844	5,902	2,330
1912	400,150	217,392	38,555	361,595	391,918	60,015	214,770	117,133	5,942	2,290
1913	396,494	282,597	38,975	357,519	388,217	55,476	213,103	119,638	6,037	2,240
1914	401,887	292,460	40,016	361,871	393,555	57,989	212,973	122,593	6,132	2,200

Notes appear at end of table   (continued)

TABLE Ea894–903   Federal government employees, by government branch and location relative to the capital: 1816–1992 *Continued*

	Total		Location relative to Washington, D.C., and surrounding area		Government branch					
						Executive				
	All	Competitive civil service (classified)	Inside	Outside	Total	Defense	Post Office	Other	Legislative	Judicial
	Ea894 [1,2]	Ea895	Ea896 [3]	Ea897 [3]	Ea898 [1]	Ea899 [4]	Ea900	Ea901	Ea902	Ea903 [5]
Fiscal year	Number	Number	Number	Number	Number	Number	Number	Number	Number	Number
1915	395,429	292,291	41,281	354,148	387,294	58,286	212,012	116,996	5,975	2,160
1916	399,381	296,926	41,804	357,577	391,133	63,395	212,215	115,523	6,128	2,120
1917	438,500	326,899	48,313	390,187	429,727	91,982	215,883	121,862	6,693	2,080
1918	854,500	642,432	120,835	733,665	844,480	—	—	—	7,980	2,040
1919 [7]	794,271	592,961	106,073	688,198	784,180	—	—	—	8,091	2,000
1920 [8]	655,265	497,603	94,110	561,155	645,408	237,212	242,400	165,796	7,897	1,960
1921 [8]	561,142	448,112	82,416	478,726	550,020	138,293	251,300	160,427	9,202	1,920
1922	543,507	420,688	73,645	469,862	532,210	107,126	260,100	164,984	9,417	1,880
1923	536,900	411,398	70,062	466,838	525,746	94,001	268,951	162,794	9,314	1,840
1924	543,484	415,593	68,000	475,484	532,048	92,331	279,679	160,038	9,636	1,800
1925	553,045	423,538	67,563	485,482	541,792	94,772	284,550	162,470	9,493	1,760
1926	548,713	422,300	64,722	483,991	537,251	92,208	288,573	156,470	9,742	1,720
1927	547,127	422,998	63,814	483,313	535,599	85,717	291,249	158,633	9,848	1,680
1928	560,772	431,763	65,506	495,266	549,238	94,005	293,023	162,210	9,894	1,640
1929	579,559	445,957	68,266	511,293	567,721	103,098	295,695	168,928	10,240	1,598
1930	601,319	462,083	73,032	528,287	588,951	103,462	297,895	187,594	10,620	1,748
1931	609,746	468,050	76,303	533,443	596,745	107,980	297,159	191,606	11,192	1,809
1932	605,496	467,161	73,455	532,041	592,560	100,420	296,136	196,004	11,159	1,777
1933	603,587	456,096	70,261	533,326	590,984	101,228	286,935	202,821	10,847	1,756
1934	698,649	450,592	94,244	604,405	685,108	133,092	281,770	270,246	11,667	1,874
1935	780,582	455,229	108,673	671,909	765,712	147,188	275,483	343,041	12,970	1,900
1936	867,432	498,725	122,937	744,495	850,395	148,369	281,314	420,712	14,976	2,061
1937	895,993	532,073	117,020	778,973	878,214	160,737	304,852	412,625	15,609	2,170
1938	882,226	562,909	120,744	761,482	864,534	163,457	311,440	389,637	15,609	2,083
1939	953,891	662,832	129,314	824,577	935,797	195,997	314,478	425,322	15,802	2,292
1940	1,042,420	726,895	139,770	902,650	1,022,853	256,025	323,481	443,347	17,099	2,468
1941	1,437,682	990,233	190,588	1,247,094	1,416,444	556,073	335,008	525,363	18,712	2,526
1942	2,296,384	—	276,352	2,020,032	2,272,082	1,291,093	338,090	642,899	21,657	2,645
1943	3,299,414	—	284,665	3,014,749	3,273,887	2,200,064	339,005	734,818	22,903	2,624
1944	3,332,356	—	276,758	3,055,598	3,304,379	2,246,454	374,758	683,167	25,314	2,663
1945	3,816,310	—	264,770	3,551,540	3,786,645	2,634,575	416,314	735,756	26,959	2,706
1946	2,696,529	—	242,263	2,454,266	2,665,520	1,416,225	453,953	795,342	27,946	3,063
1947	2,111,001	1,692,065	213,515	1,897,486	2,082,258	859,142	445,683	777,433	25,669	3,074
1948	2,071,009	1,707,220	214,544	1,856,465	2,043,981	870,962	474,911	698,108	23,551	3,477
1949	2,102,109	1,771,927	225,901	1,876,208	2,075,148	879,875	501,743	693,530	23,382	3,579
1950	1,960,708	1,656,803	223,312	1,737,396	1,934,040	753,149	484,679	696,212	22,896	3,772
1951	2,482,666	2,144,882	265,980	2,216,686	2,455,901	1,235,498	482,281	738,122	22,835	3,930
1952	2,600,612	2,247,692	261,569	2,339,043	2,574,132	1,337,095	507,779	729,258	22,517	3,963
1953	2,558,416	2,138,899	242,678	2,315,738	2,532,150	1,332,068	506,555	693,527	22,312	3,954
1954	2,407,676	1,992,057	228,501	2,179,175	2,381,659	1,208,892	507,135	665,632	21,972	4,045
1955	2,397,309	2,004,853	231,873	2,165,436	2,371,462	1,186,580	511,613	673,269	21,711	4,136
1956	2,398,736	2,042,007	232,707	2,166,029	2,372,266	1,179,836	508,587	683,843	22,115	4,355
1957	2,417,565	2,067,285	236,330	2,181,235	2,390,561	1,160,915	521,198	708,448	22,340	4,664
1958	2,382,491	2,032,944	230,271	2,152,220	2,355,292	1,097,095	538,416	719,781	22,347	4,852
1959	2,382,807	2,042,034	234,358	2,148,449	2,355,054	1,078,178	549,951	726,925	22,853	4,900
1960 [9]	2,398,704	2,050,938	239,873	2,158,831	2,370,826	1,047,120	562,868	760,838	22,886	4,992
1961	2,435,804	2,096,635	246,266	2,189,538	2,407,025	1,042,407	582,447	782,171	23,621	5,158
1962	2,514,197	2,159,050	257,350	2,256,847	2,484,655	1,069,543	588,477	826,635	23,974	5,568
1963	2,527,960	2,164,163	266,737	2,261,223	2,497,699	1,050,007	587,161	860,531	24,523	5,738
1964	2,500,503	2,153,658	269,993	2,230,510	2,469,645	1,029,756	585,313	854,576	25,048	5,810
1965	2,527,915	2,154,992	279,997	2,247,918	2,496,064	1,033,775	595,512	866,777	25,947	5,904
1966	2,759,019	2,367,100	299,429	2,459,590	2,726,144	1,138,126	675,423	912,595	26,908	5,967
1967	3,002,461	2,485,863	318,608	2,683,853	2,967,964	1,302,605	716,603	948,756	28,178	6,319
1968	3,055,212	2,569,752	329,879	2,725,333	3,019,976	1,316,977	730,977	972,022	28,675	6,561
1969	3,076,414	2,549,506	328,077	2,748,337	3,040,129	1,341,587	739,002	959,540	29,577	6,708

Notes appear at end of table

TABLE Ea894–903   Federal government employees, by government branch and location relative to the capital: 1816–1992   *Continued*

	Total		Location relative to Washington, D.C., and surrounding area		Government branch					
					Executive					
	All	Competitive civil service (classified)	Inside	Outside	Total	Defense	Post Office	Other	Legislative	Judicial
	Ea894 [1,2]	Ea895	Ea896 [3]	Fa897 [3]	Ea898 [1]	Ea899 [4]	Ea900	Ea901	Ea902	Ea903 [5]
Fiscal year	Number	Number	Number	Number	Number	Number	Number	Number	Number	Number
1970 [9]	2,981,574	2,453,292	327,369	2,654,205	2,943,818	1,219,125	741,216	983,477	30,869	6,887
1971	2,922,841	2,297,935	334,250	2,588,591	2,882,675	1,154,313	728,911	999,451	32,436	7,730
1972	2,865,193	1,615,091	334,617	2,530,576	2,823,061	1,107,739	706,400	1,008,922	33,889	8,243
1973	2,824,244	1,595,428	334,809	2,489,435	2,780,576	1,052,639	697,932	1,030,005	34,928	8,740
1974	2,893,118	1,648,741	343,335	2,549,783	2,847,070	1,070,004	707,202	1,069,864	36,558	9,490
1975	2,896,944	1,663,228	352,786	2,544,158	2,848,014	1,041,829	699,174	1,107,011	38,531	10,399
1976	2,883,134	1,661,714	357,808	2,525,326	2,832,641	1,007,735	675,653	1,149,253	39,234	11,259
1977	2,893,334	1,652,229	360,464	2,532,870	2,840,148	1,008,690	658,390	1,173,068	40,715	12,471
1978	2,929,100	1,679,532	365,576	2,563,524	2,874,547	999,696	650,320	1,224,531	41,474	13,079
1979	2,949,614	1,750,136	370,952	2,578,662	2,895,007	978,690	665,980	1,250,337	41,114	13,493
1980 [9]	3,121,783	1,749,809	376,083	2,745,700	3,065,686	987,890	666,228	1,411,568	41,357	14,740
1981	2,947,651	1,731,239	367,225	2,580,426	2,891,844	1,008,462	664,691	1,218,691	40,467	15,340
1982	2,917,149	1,727,778	353,864	2,563,285	2,860,806	1,045,388	667,782	1,147,636	40,588	15,755
1983	2,920,514	1,729,775	356,427	2,564,087	2,863,071	1,049,388	663,012	1,150,671	41,061	16,382
1984	2,983,618	1,735,603	363,190	2,620,428	2,925,326	1,071,299	707,857	1,146,170	41,209	17,083
1985	3,060,415	1,749,584	360,024	2,700,391	3,001,540	1,099,290	752,126	1,150,124	40,921	17,954
1986	3,061,695	1,731,525	350,700	2,710,995	3,005,153	1,087,255	791,685	1,126,213	37,815	18,727
1987	3,128,654	1,759,126	355,337	2,773,317	3,069,539	1,098,965	819,650	1,150,924	39,309	19,806
1988	3,126,187	1,750,295	357,489	2,768,698	3,065,560	1,060,476	833,281	1,171,803	39,504	21,123
1989	3,166,578	1,772,421	362,133	2,804,445	3,105,678	1,075,396	834,258	1,196,024	39,237	21,663
1990 [9]	3,508,463	1,773,436	367,080	3,141,383	3,446,119	1,052,951	823,181	1,569,987	39,204	23,140
1991	3,138,147	1,768,902	375,727	2,762,420	3,073,729	1,019,792	816,541	1,237,396	39,747	24,671
1992	3,134,915	1,778,885	383,754	2,751,161	3,066,699	1,011,582	799,529	1,255,588	40,627	27,589

[1] Excludes employees of the Central Intelligence Agency, the National Security Agency (beginning 1960), and the Defense Intelligence Agency (as of November 1984).

[2] Figures for 1884–1907 are from Johnson and Libecap (1994).

[3] Geographical composition changes over time; see text.

[4] Prior to 1947, covers the War and Navy Departments. Beginning in 1881, includes mechanics and other workmen at army arsenals and navy yards.

[5] Estimated for 1908–1928.

[6] Figures for 1884–1887 cover the following periods, respectively: July 16, 1883, to January 15, 1884; January 16, 1884, to January 15, 1885; January 16, 1885, to January 15, 1886; and January 16, 1886, to June 30, 1887.

[7] As of July 31.

[8] As of November 11.

[9] Includes the following numbers of temporary census workers: 437,000 in 1960, 396,000 in 1970, 153,709 in 1980, and 361,329 in 1990.

Sources

All series, 1816–1970, except as noted: U.S. Civil Service Commission, unpublished data. The data for 1816–1891, Civil Service Commission, *Official Register of the United States*; for 1901–1911, Civil Service Commission, *Annual Report* and *Official Register*; for 1908–1970, Civil Service Commission, *Annual Report* and *Federal Civilian Manpower Statistics*, formerly titled *Monthly Report of Federal Employment*, and supplemented throughout by Civil Service Commission records.

Series Ea894, 1884–1907. Ronald N. Johnson and Gary D. Libecap, *The Federal Civil Service System and the Problem of Bureaucracy* (University of Chicago Press, 1994), data underlying Figures 3.1 and 3.2, pp. 60, 61. These data are based on U.S. House of Representatives, Subcommittee on Manpower

and Civil Service of the Committee on Post Office and Civil Service, 94th Congress, 2nd session, December 1976, "History of Civil Service Merit Systems of the United States and Selected Foreign Countries," p. 305.

All series, 1971–1992. Office of Personnel Management, Monthly Report of Federal Civilian Employment (SF113-A).

Documentation

Figures represent paid civilian employment. Data are as of June 30, except as noted

Series Ea894. Figures for 1884–1907 are from Johnson and Libecap (1994). *Historical Statistics of the United States* (1975) presented values during this period only for 1891 (157,442) and 1901 (239,476). Because the breakdowns by location and branch are from *Historical Statistics* rather than Johnson and Libecap, the total and the subtotals presented here do not agree for these two years.

Series Ea896–897. Through June 1941, series Ea896 covers the District of Columbia only. Thereafter it includes the following: beginning in July 1941, Alexandria city, Arlington County, and part of Fairfax County, Virginia, along with parts of Montgomery and Prince Georges Counties, Maryland; beginning in 1950, all of Fairfax County, Virginia, and all of Montgomery and Prince Georges Counties, Maryland; beginning in 1952, Falls Church city, Virginia; beginning in 1965, Fairfax city, Virginia; beginning in 1967, Loudoun and Prince William Counties, Virginia; beginning in 1976, Charles County, Maryland, along with Manassas and Manassas Park cities, Virginia; and beginning in 1983, Calvert and Frederick Counties, Maryland, and Stafford County, Virginia.

TABLE Ea904–915   Federal government employees and average pay: 1948–1992[1]

Contributed by John Joseph Wallis

	Employees						Average annual pay					
	Total	General schedule	Crafts, protective, and custodial schedule	Wage system	Postal pay system	Other	Total	General schedule	Crafts, protective, and custodial schedule	Wage system	Postal pay system	Other
	Ea904	Ea905	Ea906	Ea907	Ea908	Ea909	Ea910	Ea911	Ea912	Ea913	Ea914	Ea915
Fiscal year	Thousand	Thousand	Thousand	Thousand	Thousand	Thousand	Dollars	Dollars	Dollars	Dollars	Dollars	Dollars
1948	1,696	703	104	486	340	64	2,905	3,018	2,267	2,731	2,819	3,267
1949	1,764	723	106	502	361	72	3,259	3,401	2,624	3,000	3,241	3,522
1950	1,628	702	99	430	362	35	3,504	3,788	2,807	3,133	3,488	4,502
1951	2,121	886	119	719	348	49	3,481	3,700	2,814	3,245	3,523	4,302
1952	2,379	1,076	—	851	352	100	3,775	4,043	—	3,350	4,002	3,718
1953	2,344	1,014	—	803	431	97	3,937	4,144	—	3,685	3,916	3,942
1954	2,214	975	—	711	434	95	4,047	4,225	—	3,862	3,955	4,022
1955	2,255	993	—	731	434	97	4,250	4,602	—	3,790	4,196	4,356
1956	2,264	950	—	768	441	106	4,398	4,749	—	4,012	4,330	4,331
1957	2,272	971	—	747	447	108	4,540	4,848	—	4,275	4,326	4,490
1958	2,231	962	—	700	461	108	5,031	5,510	—	4,531	4,808	4,945
1959	2,239	970	—	688	474	107	5,165	5,611	—	4,742	4,837	5,292
1960	2,237	973	—	667	483	114	5,273	5,705	—	4,935	4,854	5,344
1961	2,291	1,007	—	663	503	118	5,664	6,216	—	5,086	5,292	5,775
1962	2,372	1,058	—	676	517	120	5,739	6,286	—	5,202	5,283	5,907
1963	2,387	1,084	—	658	521	125	6,149	6,808	—	5,358	5,744	6,298
1964	2,370	1,090	—	627	524	130	6,479	7,293	—	5,530	5,889	6,618
1965	2,398	1,112	—	621	534	131	6,868	7,707	—	5,887	6,219	7,032
1966	2,574	1,189	—	681	570	135	6,920	7,904	—	5,508	6,437	7,426
1967	2,784	1,252	—	757	605	170	7,014	8,148	—	5,538	6,574	6,805
1968	2,868	1,302	—	737	639	190	7,426	8,654	—	5,835	6,932	6,857
1969	2,879	1,299	—	746	657	178	7,980	9,367	—	6,249	7,343	7,461
1970	2,806	1,287	—	674	673	172	9,234	11,065	—	6,976	8,120	8,741
1971	2,766	1,298	—	632	664	172	10,062	11,809	—	7,695	9,054	9,459
1972	2,682	1,281	—	604	665	131	11,285	12,588	—	8,461	10,059	11,862
1973	2,538	1,302	—	547	550	139	12,037	13,204	—	9,194	11,543	12,297
1974	2,547	1,322	—	536	553	136	12,518	13,704	—	10,071	11,937	12,985
1975	2,582	1,349	—	528	566	139	13,529	14,483	—	11,197	13,329	13,951
1976	2,557	1,358	—	515	548	136	14,576	15,343	—	12,489	14,360	15,687
1977	2,502	1,390	—	470	528	113	15,874	16,230	—	14,517	15,322	19,704
1978	2,483	1,396	—	462	522	103	17,186	17,578	—	15,816	16,561	21,172
1979	2,488	1,397	—	457	529 [2]	105	18,496	18,715	—	16,926	—	22,383
1980	2,500	1,402	—	456	528	113	19,446	19,910	—	17,970	18,344	24,825
1981	2,475	1,395	—	446	506	127	21,115	21,833	—	19,557	19,089	26,777
1982	2,502	1,400	—	449	530 [2]	123	22,839	22,975	—	20,550	—	29,627
1983	2,499	1,393	—	430	547	128	24,074	24,178	—	21,500	24,612	31,544
1984	2,520	1,407	—	420	561	132	25,211	25,282	—	22,393	25,504	33,453
1985	2,590	1,450	—	418	586	136	26,139	26,186	—	23,288	26,559	34,413
1986	2,616	1,462	—	409	606	139	26,369	26,274	—	23,837	26,744	34,814
1987	2,625	1,457	—	391	633	143	27,429	27,375	—	24,330	26,925	36,443
1988	2,661	1,480	—	383	647	151	28,211	28,114	—	24,965	28,465	37,393
1989	2,682	1,494	—	374	666 [2]	148	29,618	29,655	—	25,462	—	39,764
1990	2,697	1,506	—	369	661	161	31,174	31,239	—	26,565	31,992	41,149
1991	2,665	1,499	—	328	651	187	33,340	33,288	—	27,543	33,186	43,926
1992	2,685	1,537	—	328	634 [2]	186	35,357	35,254	—	28,852	—	42,689

[1] See text for a discussion of changes in employee pay systems and data coverage.

[2] Full-time employees in the postal service were estimated as 80 percent of all postal employees, as reported by the Bureau of Labor Statistics.

Sources

1848–1970: U.S. Civil Service Commission, *Pay Structure of the Federal Civil Service* (annual issues), Table 2.

1971–1992: *Statistical Abstract of the United States* (1972), Table 641; (1975), Table 407; (1976), Table 411; (1978), Table 460; (1979), Table 466; (1980), Table 474; (1984), Table 539; (1990), Table 525; and (1993), Table 537.

Documentation

These series cover paid civilian employment in full-time positions in the federal government

This table excludes employees of Congress and federal courts, maritime seamen of the Department of Commerce, and a small number for whom rates were not reported. The figures exclude military personnel but include civilian employees of the military departments. Employees of the District of Columbia are not included because they are considered employees of a local government.

TABLE Ea904–915 **Federal government employees and average pay: 1948–1992** *Continued*

Prior to 1954, only executive branch employees are shown; later data include all legislative branch employees except employees of Congress.

The data for 1948–1951 include only those employees in the conterminous United States; later data are worldwide figures.

Average annual pay is calculated as the arithmetic mean of annual rates and other rates converted to annual equivalents.

Figures are as of June 30, except for 1949 (July 1).

Series Ea907 and Ea914. Data on the crafts, protective, and custodial schedule are shown for 1948–1951. Beginning in 1956, this schedule was discontinued and, under the amended Classification Act of 1949, approximately one third of crafts, protective, and custodial employees were classified under the general schedule, and two thirds were classified under the wage system.

Series Ea908 and Ea914. Does not include postal substitutes as full-time employees until 1953. Postal seasonal Christmas assistants are not included.

Series Ea909 and Ea915. Beginning in 1952, includes foreign nationals employed overseas.

TABLE Ea916–965   Government employment and compensation, by level and major function of government: 1929–2000   [BEA]

Contributed by John Joseph Wallis

	Employment													Full-time equivalents			
	Employees														Federal		
		Federal					State and local								General government		
		General government				Government enterprise		General government				Government enterprise					
	Total	Total	Total	Military	Civilian, except work relief	Work relief		Total	Total	Education	Work relief	Other		Total	Total	Total	Military
Year	Ea916	Ea917	Ea918	Ea919	Ea920	Ea921	Ea922	Ea923	Ea924	Ea925	Ea926	Ea927	Ea928	Ea929	Ea930	Ea931	Ea932
	Thousand	Thousand	Thousand	Thousand	Thousand	Thousand	Thousand	Thousand	Thousand	Thousand	Thousand	Thousand	Thousand	Thousand	Thousand	Thousand	Thousand
1929	3,611	981	644	267	377	—	337	2,630	2,509	1,067	1,442	—	121	3,152	847	548	267
1930	3,779	1,034	695	310	385	—	339	2,745	2,618	1,095	1,503	20	127	3,287	893	593	310
1931	4,133	1,019	683	296	387	—	336	3,114	2,984	1,105	1,580	299	130	3,369	874	576	296
1932	4,373	1,006	673	290	383	—	333	3,367	3,249	1,093	1,564	592	118	3,331	861	564	290
1933	5,901	1,470	1,135	294	370	471	335	4,431	4,317	1,069	1,524	1,724	114	3,841	1,237	937	294
1934	6,820	2,227	1,868	357	371	1,140	359	4,593	4,473	1,069	1,570	1,834	120	4,700	1,738	1,415	357
1935	7,150	2,209	1,835	449	396	990	374	4,941	4,815	1,097	1,621	2,097	126	5,001	1,799	1,463	449
1936	8,050	4,993	4,612	521	438	3,653	381	3,057	2,922	1,118	1,713	91	135	6,120	3,514	3,171	521
1937	7,192	4,085	3,698	517	474	2,707	387	3,107	2,967	1,149	1,762	56	140	5,503	2,834	2,485	517
1938	8,197	4,987	4,583	507	504	3,572	404	3,210	3,070	1,180	1,871	19	140	6,127	3,360	2,994	507
1939	8,020	4,754	4,342	560	566	3,216	412	3,266	3,123	1,207	1,877	39	143	6,114	3,312	2,937	560
1940	7,917	4,652	4,227	642	793	2,792	425	3,265	3,104	1,194	1,872	38	161	6,251	3,412	3,023	642
1941	8,572	5,281	4,829	944	1,693	2,192	452	3,291	3,119	1,256	1,846	17	172	7,282	4,419	3,988	944
1942	10,486	7,252	6,765	1,702	4,154	909	487	3,234	3,063	1,264	1,794	5	171	9,714	6,906	6,457	1,702
1943	15,293	12,155	11,611	2,497	9,029	85	544	3,138	2,965	1,256	1,709	—	173	14,810	12,078	11,573	2,497
1944	17,527	14,405	13,885	2,520	11,365	—	520	3,122	2,956	1,256	1,700	—	166	17,079	14,366	13,885	2,520
1945	17,431	14,258	13,722	2,420	11,302	—	536	3,173	3,007	1,273	1,734	38	166	16,954	14,217	13,722	2,420
1946	9,311	5,902	5,294	1,822	3,472	—	608	3,409	3,236	1,347	1,889	17	173	8,698	5,770	5,195	1,758
1947	7,483	3,808	3,268	1,436	1,832	—	540	3,675	3,481	1,445	2,036	5	194	6,697	3,528	3,018	1,386
1948	7,894	4,007	3,437	1,428	2,009	—	570	3,887	3,657	1,504	2,153	—	230	6,744	3,460	2,922	1,378
1949	8,516	4,462	3,857	1,448	2,409	—	605	4,054	3,815	1,581	2,234	—	239	7,207	3,684	3,114	1,397
1950	8,802	4,603	4,016	1,468	2,548	—	587	4,199	3,947	1,636	2,311	—	252	7,432	3,783	3,230	1,417
1951	10,358	6,131	5,519	1,817	3,702	—	612	4,227	3,967	1,684	2,283	—	260	9,267	5,535	4,957	1,753
1952	11,102	6,737	6,081	1,910	4,171	—	656	4,365	4,067	1,762	2,305	—	298	10,043	6,175	5,555	1,843
1953	11,123	6,611	5,976	1,823	4,153	—	635	4,512	4,209	1,851	2,358	—	303	10,013	5,989	5,390	1,760
1954	11,114	6,394	5,759	1,702	4,057	—	635	4,720	4,415	1,946	2,469	—	305	9,855	5,669	5,070	1,643
1955	11,182	6,234	5,601	1,711	3,890	—	633	4,948	4,637	2,076	2,561	—	311	9,745	5,393	4,796	1,651
1956	11,414	6,202	5,563	1,738	3,825	—	639	5,212	4,900	2,199	2,701	—	312	9,840	5,270	4,667	1,678
1957	11,709	6,277	5,618	1,734	3,884	—	659	5,432	5,117	2,310	2,807	—	315	10,035	5,263	4,641	1,674
1958	11,756	6,044	5,373	1,691	3,682	—	671	5,712	5,375	2,430	2,945	—	337	10,077	5,062	4,429	1,632
1959	11,940	6,030	5,349	1,721	3,628	—	681	5,910	5,516	2,559	2,957	—	394	10,343	5,010	4,367	1,656
1960	12,275	6,090	5,390	1,770	3,620	—	700	6,185	5,777	2,732	3,045	—	408	10,621	5,055	4,394	1,704
1961	12,632	6,200	5,481	1,772	3,709	—	719	6,432	6,022	2,863	3,159	—	410	10,983	5,157	4,479	1,705
1962	12,992	6,349	5,618	1,833	3,785	—	731	6,643	6,228	3,012	3,216	—	415	11,391	5,409	4,721	1,764
1963	13,247	6,302	5,568	1,852	3,716	—	734	6,945	6,521	3,214	3,307	—	424	11,599	5,351	4,660	1,782
1964	13,683	6,382	5,641	1,838	3,803	—	741	7,301	6,861	3,431	3,430	—	440	11,939	5,360	4,663	1,767

	Employment													Full-time equivalents			
	Employees															Federal	
	Federal						State and local									General government	
		General government						General government									
Year	Total	Total	Total	Military	Civilian, except work relief	Work relief	Government enterprise	Total	Total	Education	Work relief	Other	Government enterprise	Total	Total	Total	Military
	Ea916	Ea917	Ea918	Ea919	Ea920	Ea921	Ea922	Ea923	Ea924	Ea925	Ea926	Ea927	Ea928	Ea929	Ea930	Ea931	Ea932
	Thousand	Thousand	Thousand	Thousand	Thousand	Thousand	Thousand	Thousand	Thousand	Thousand	Thousand	Thousand	Thousand	Thousand	Thousand	Thousand	Thousand
1965	14,115	6,387	5,625	1,856	3,769	—	762	7,728	7,276	3,705	3,571	—	452	12,316	5,389	4,675	1,787
1966	15,322	7,057	6,222	1,978	4,244	—	835	8,265	7,830	4,049	3,751	—	465	13,293	5,988	5,206	1,889
1967	16,169	7,497	6,623	2,100	4,523	—	874	8,672	8,199	4,321	3,878	—	473	14,006	6,450	5,630	2,023
1968	16,670	7,551	6,669	2,112	4,557	—	882	9,119	8,625	4,582	4,043	—	494	14,456	6,531	5,700	2,039
1969	16,995	7,492	6,599	2,083	4,516	—	893	9,503	8,931	4,828	4,163	—	512	14,716	6,484	5,640	2,019
1970	17,068	7,129	6,217	2,042	4,175	—	912	9,939	9,404	5,060	4,344	—	535	14,691	6,094	5,232	1,959
1971	17,044	6,717	5,807	2,002	3,805	—	910	10,327	9,778	5,298	4,480	—	549	14,659	5,715	4,849	1,947
1972	17,036	6,308	5,427	2,017	3,410	—	881	10,728	10,164	5,467	4,697	—	564	14,677	5,344	4,505	1,952
1973	17,287	6,174	5,293	2,001	3,292	—	881	11,113	10,524	5,641	4,883	—	589	14,886	5,194	4,360	1,921
1974	17,647	6,146	5,251	2,049	3,202	—	895	11,501	10,879	5,858	5,021	—	622	15,158	5,161	4,311	1,966
1975	18,000	6,060	5,183	2,075	3,108	—	877	11,940	11,280	6,052	5,228	—	660	15,464	5,116	4,283	1,988
1976	17,997	5,934	5,080	2,085	2,995	—	854	12,063	11,400	6,124	5,276	—	663	15,542	5,067	4,253	2,000
1977	18,169	5,871	5,027	2,090	2,937	—	844	12,298	11,638	6,251	5,387	—	660	15,670	5,047	4,239	2,000
1978	18,492	5,881	5,031	2,117	2,914	—	850	12,611	11,922	6,292	5,630	—	689	16,009	5,065	4,249	2,029
1979	18,902	5,881	5,016	2,126	2,890	—	865	13,021	12,289	6,361	5,928	—	732	16,144	5,047	4,220	2,031
1980	19,273	6,010	5,140	2,221	2,919	—	870	13,263	12,506	6,481	6,025	—	757	16,288	5,111	4,278	2,069
1981	19,148	6,006	5,133	2,131	3,002	—	873	13,142	12,389	6,466	5,923	—	753	16,165	5,135	4,296	2,037
1982	19,149	6,084	5,207	2,113	3,094	—	877	13,065	12,367	6,421	5,886	—	758	16,171	5,141	4,319	2,026
1983	19,172	6,095	5,246	2,117	3,129	—	849	13,077	12,315	6,478	5,837	—	762	16,055	5,130	4,334	2,026
1984	19,428	6,196	5,316	2,143	3,173	—	880	13,232	12,459	6,581	5,878	—	773	16,264	5,230	4,395	2,067
1985	19,795	6,311	5,401	2,180	3,221	—	910	13,484	12,652	6,759	5,933	—	792	16,617	5,275	4,442	2,098
1986	20,170	6,384	5,427	2,164	3,263	—	957	13,786	12,981	6,940	6,041	—	805	16,955	5,268	4,445	2,088
1987	20,550	6,475	5,493	2,190	3,303	—	982	14,075	13,258	6,992	6,266	—	817	17,237	5,314	4,489	2,121
1988	20,906	6,470	5,465	2,192	3,273	—	1,005	14,436	13,608	7,257	6,351	—	828	17,642	5,336	4,487	2,156
1989	21,284	6,483	5,471	2,207	3,264	—	1,012	14,801	13,955	7,458	6,497	—	846	18,045	5,354	4,498	2,176
1990	21,779	6,532	5,520	2,315	3,205	—	1,012	15,247	14,382	7,668	6,714	—	865	18,340	5,345	4,486	2,221
1991	21,802	6,349	5,356	2,211	3,145	—	993	15,453	14,581	7,785	6,796	—	872	18,383	5,260	4,411	2,198
1992	21,839	6,177	5,211	2,231	2,980	—	966	15,662	14,835	7,885	6,950	—	827	18,327	5,060	4,240	2,181
1993	21,853	5,931	4,977	2,177	2,800	—	954	15,922	15,095	8,067	7,028	—	827	18,261	4,829	4,046	2,136
1994	21,911	5,720	4,748	2,100	2,648	—	972	16,191	15,342	8,223	7,119	—	849	18,248	4,661	3,866	2,051
1995	21,965	5,560	4,570	2,026	2,544	—	990	16,405	15,549	8,388	7,161	—	856	18,335	4,530	3,722	1,984
1996	21,935	5,387	4,397	1,951	2,446	—	990	16,548	15,704	8,522	7,182	—	844	18,328	4,378	3,575	1,913
1997	22,053	5,265	4,275	1,899	2,376	—	990	16,788	15,954	8,736	7,218	—	834	18,435	4,269	3,476	1,869
1998	22,262	5,194	4,200	1,878	2,322	—	994	17,068	16,227	8,928	7,299	—	841	18,604	4,207	3,416	1,845
1999	22,539	5,139	4,147	1,856	2,291	—	992	17,400	16,545	9,148	7,398	—	854	18,739	4,164	3,370	1,821
2000	22,996	5,235	4,260	1,976	2,284	—	975	17,761	16,891	9,382	7,509	—	870	19,102	4,262	3,478	1,931

(continued)

TABLE Ea916–965   Government employment and compensation, by level and major function of government: 1929–2000   [BEA]   Continued

	Employment									Compensation					
	Full-time equivalents									Total employee compensation					
	Federal				State and local						Federal				
	General government				General government							General government			
	Civilian, except work relief	Work relief	Government enterprise	Total	Total	Education	Work relief	Other	Government enterprise	Total	Total	Total	Military	Civilian	Government enterprise
Year	Ea933	Ea934	Ea935	Ea936	Ea937	Ea938	Ea939	Ea940	Ea941	Ea942	Ea943	Ea944	Ea945	Ea946	Ea947
	Thousand	Thousand	Thousand	Thousand	Thousand	Thousand	Thousand	Thousand	Thousand	Thousand dollars	Thousand dollars	Thousand dollars	Thousand dollars	Thousand dollars	Thousand dollars
1929	281	—	299	2,305	2,195	1,030	1,165	—	110	5,121	1,488	907	—	—	581
1930	283	—	300	2,394	2,278	1,057	1,217	4	116	5,346	1,529	945	—	—	584
1931	280	—	298	2,495	2,378	1,067	1,267	44	117	5,457	1,534	952	—	—	582
1932	274	—	297	2,470	2,366	1,056	1,223	87	104	5,182	1,456	912	—	—	544
1933	270	373	300	2,604	2,505	1,032	1,174	299	99	5,357	1,680	1,195	—	—	485
1934	271	787	323	2,962	2,857	1,031	1,223	603	105	6,306	2,269	1,729	—	—	540
1935	286	728	336	3,202	3,092	1,059	1,268	765	110	6,762	2,420	1,806	—	—	614
1936	316	2,334	343	2,606	2,487	1,080	1,352	55	119	8,150	4,274	3,612	—	—	662
1937	341	1,627	349	2,669	2,544	1,110	1,401	33	125	7,816	3,732	3,057	—	—	675
1938	357	2,130	366	2,767	2,641	1,139	1,496	6	126	8,571	4,250	3,552	—	—	698
1939	381	1,996	375	2,802	2,674	1,166	1,497	11	128	8,573	4,183	3,464	—	—	719
1940	592	1,789	389	2,839	2,693	1,176	1,506	11	146	8,815	4,288	3,542	—	—	746
1941	1,680	1,364	431	2,863	2,705	1,190	1,509	6	158	10,552	5,887	5,079	—	—	808
1942	4,154	601	449	2,808	2,655	1,186	1,467	2	153	16,381	11,612	10,694	—	—	918
1943	9,029	47	505	2,732	2,577	1,169	1,408	—	155	27,091	22,092	20,953	—	—	1,139
1944	11,365	—	481	2,713	2,564	1,158	1,406	—	149	33,780	28,502	27,314	—	—	1,188
1945	11,302	—	495	2,737	2,589	1,166	1,423	—	148	36,947	31,217	29,969	—	—	1,248
1946	3,437	—	575	2,928	2,771	1,215	1,556	—	157	24,281	17,680	16,188	—	—	1,490
1947	1,632	—	510	3,169	2,992	1,299	1,693	—	177	19,608	11,770	10,305	—	—	1,465
1948	1,544	—	538	3,284	3,073	1,350	1,723	—	211	20,393	11,232	9,556	—	—	1,676
1949	1,717	—	570	3,523	3,302	1,420	1,882	—	221	22,685	12,536	10,679	5,078	5,601	1,857
1950	1,813	—	553	3,649	3,415	1,463	1,952	—	234	23,935	13,030	11,095	5,401	5,694	1,935
1951	3,204	—	578	3,732	3,486	1,506	1,980	—	246	30,741	18,722	16,582	7,161	9,421	2,140
1952	3,712	—	620	3,868	3,584	1,576	2,008	—	284	35,016	21,708	19,275	8,036	11,239	2,433
1953	3,630	—	599	4,024	3,732	1,650	2,082	—	292	35,913	21,441	19,075	7,952	11,123	2,366
1954	3,427	—	599	4,186	3,893	1,726	2,167	—	293	36,598	20,713	18,346	7,495	10,851	2,367
1955	3,145	—	597	4,352	4,052	1,824	2,228	—	300	38,604	21,493	18,958	8,133	10,825	2,535
1956	2,989	—	603	4,570	4,268	1,925	2,343	—	302	41,224	22,293	19,604	8,821	10,783	2,689
1957	2,967	—	622	4,772	4,467	2,027	2,440	—	305	44,012	23,086	20,227	9,261	10,966	2,859
1958	2,797	—	633	5,015	4,695	2,131	2,564	—	320	47,584	24,512	21,325	10,113	11,212	3,187
1959	2,711	—	643	5,333	4,958	2,384	2,574	—	375	49,872	24,990	21,728	10,357	11,371	3,262
1960	2,690	—	661	5,566	5,178	2,530	2,648	—	388	53,546	26,142	22,604	11,106	11,498	3,538
1961	2,774	—	678	5,826	5,432	2,650	2,782	—	394	57,324	27,428	23,657	11,858	11,799	3,771
1962	2,957	—	688	5,982	5,582	2,743	2,839	—	400	61,593	29,157	25,211	12,642	12,569	3,946
1963	2,878	—	691	6,248	5,840	2,930	2,910	—	408	65,954	30,770	26,483	13,467	13,016	4,287
1964	2,896	—	697	6,579	6,155	3,125	3,030	—	424	71,543	33,094	28,535	14,373	14,162	4,559
1965	2,888	—	714	6,927	6,491	3,339	3,152	—	436	76,943	34,870	29,986	15,138	14,848	4,884
1966	3,317	—	782	7,305	6,860	3,573	3,287	—	445	86,740	39,623	34,304	16,678	17,626	5,319
1967	3,607	—	820	7,556	7,107	3,729	3,378	—	449	96,287	43,528	37,875	18,127	19,748	5,653
1968	3,661	—	831	7,925	7,455	3,928	3,527	—	470	107,744	48,186	41,903	20,050	21,853	6,283
1969	3,621	—	844	8,232	7,745	4,112	3,633	—	487	118,439	51,739	44,862	21,323	23,539	6,877

	Employment									Compensation					
	Full-time equivalents									Total employee compensation					
	Federal			State and local							Federal				
	General government			General government								General government			
	Civilian, except work relief	Work relief	Government enterprise	Total	Total	Education	Work relief	Other	Government enterprise	Total	Total	Total	Military	Civilian	Government enterprise
Year	Ea933	Ea934	Ea935	Ea936	Ea937	Ea938	Ea939	Ea940	Ea941	Ea942	Ea943	Ea944	Ea945	Ea946	Ea947
	Thousand	Thousand	Thousand	Thousand	Thousand	Thousand	Thousand	Thousand	Thousand	Thousand dollars	Thousand dollars	Thousand dollars	Thousand dollars	Thousand dollars	dollars
1970	3,273	—	862	8,597	8,087	4,290	3,797	—	510	132,213	56,551	48,335	23,429	24,906	8,216
1971	2,902	—	866	8,944	8,417	4,477	3,940	—	527	144,935	60,559	51,659	26,028	25,631	8,900
1972	2,553	—	839	9,333	8,791	4,653	4,138	—	542	158,279	64,980	55,384	27,952	27,422	9,596
1973	2,439	—	834	9,692	9,127	4,832	4,295	—	565	172,189	67,764	57,434	29,362	28,072	10,330
1974	2,345	—	850	9,997	9,400	4,981	4,419	—	597	189,045	73,978	62,044	32,515	29,529	11,934
1975	2,295	—	833	10,348	9,713	5,100	4,613	—	635	211,840	82,080	68,384	36,788	31,596	13,696
1976	2,253	—	814	10,475	9,834	5,163	4,671	—	641	230,448	88,144	73,307	40,349	32,958	14,837
1977	2,239	—	808	10,623	9,989	5,244	4,745	—	634	250,994	96,019	79,930	45,386	34,544	16,089
1978	2,220	—	816	10,944	10,279	5,302	4,977	—	665	273,169	103,038	85,758	48,977	36,781	17,280
1979	2,189	—	827	11,097	10,396	5,280	5,116	—	701	297,731	110,882	91,808	52,377	39,431	19,074
1980	2,209	—	833	11,177	10,451	5,250	5,201	—	726	331,580	124,228	102,536	58,228	44,308	21,692
1981	2,259	—	839	11,030	10,309	5,206	5,103	—	721	366,094	140,088	115,089	63,610	51,479	24,999
1982	2,293	—	822	11,030	10,293	5,153	5,140	—	737	395,828	151,006	125,308	67,625	57,683	25,698
1983	2,308	—	796	10,925	10,195	5,170	5,025	—	730	421,782	159,725	132,317	71,414	60,903	27,408
1984	2,328	—	835	11,034	10,292	5,226	5,066	—	742	460,320	178,730	149,362	75,444	73,918	29,368
1985	2,344	—	833	11,342	10,578	5,411	5,167	—	764	497,813	190,438	158,952	79,595	79,357	31,486
1986	2,357	—	823	11,687	10,905	5,609	5,296	—	782	526,704	195,041	163,082	81,260	81,822	31,959
1987	2,368	—	825	11,923	11,129	5,648	5,481	—	794	558,764	204,493	170,292	85,397	84,895	34,201
1988	2,331	—	849	12,306	11,499	5,918	5,581	—	807	596,548	215,365	177,973	91,463	86,510	37,392
1989	2,322	—	856	12,691	11,862	6,112	5,750	—	829	634,462	224,556	185,701	96,989	88,712	38,855
1990	2,265	—	859	12,995	12,151	6,250	5,901	—	844	682,574	236,666	193,865	103,263	90,597	42,801
1991	2,213	—	849	13,123	12,274	6,308	5,966	—	849	721,770	250,602	205,860	110,426	95,434	44,742
1992	2,059	—	820	13,267	12,404	6,377	6,027	—	863	752,960	258,642	210,697	115,822	94,875	47,945
1993	1,910	—	783	13,432	12,571	6,479	6,092	—	861	777,509	259,362	211,929	122,196	89,733	47,433
1994	1,815	—	795	13,587	12,710	6,595	6,115	—	877	802,963	259,572	209,935	123,851	86,084	49,637
1995	1,738	—	808	13,805	12,922	6,769	6,153	—	883	824,180	257,688	206,903	123,674	83,229	50,785
1996	1,662	—	803	13,950	13,079	6,887	6,192	—	871	849,625	263,231	211,001	124,935	86,066	52,230
1997	1,607	—	793	14,166	13,304	7,070	6,234	—	862	882,629	266,816	213,247	127,331	85,916	53,569
1998	1,571	—	791	14,397	13,528	7,226	6,302	—	869	915,052	270,161	215,262	129,828	85,434	54,899
1999	1,549	—	794	14,575	13,699	7,359	6,340	—	876	954,139	277,790	221,797	134,869	86,928	55,993
2000	1,547	—	784	14,840	13,953	7,556	6,397	—	887	1,008,972	293,671	233,438	142,648	90,790	60,233

(continued)

TABLE Ea916–965 Government employment and compensation, by level and major function of government: 1929–2000 [BEA] *Continued*

	Total employee compensation					Compensation — Average annual wages and salary												
	Total	State and local				All government	Federal						Total	State and local				
		General government			Government enterprise		Total	General government				Government enterprise		Total	General government			Government enterprise
		Total	Education	Other				Total	Military	Civilian, except work relief	Work relief					Education	Work relief	Other	
	Ea948	Ea949	Ea950	Ea951	Ea952	Ea953	Ea954	Ea955	Ea956	Ea957	Ea958	Ea959	Ea960	Ea961	Ea962	Ea963	Ea964	Ea965
Year	Thousand dollars	Thousand dollars	Thousand dollars	Thousand dollars	Thousand dollars	Dollars	Dollars	Dollars	Dollars	Dollars	Dollars	Dollars	Dollars	Dollars	Dollars	Dollars	Dollars	Dollars
1929	3,633	3,456	—	—	177	1,574	1,673	1,547	1,933	1,181	—	1,903	1,538	1,534	1,517	1,549	—	1,600
1930	3,817	3,630	—	—	187	1,576	1,632	1,492	1,768	1,191	—	1,907	1,555	1,553	1,528	1,576	1,000	1,595
1931	3,923	3,737	—	—	186	1,568	1,673	1,549	1,895	1,182	—	1,913	1,532	1,530	1,536	1,541	1,045	1,573
1932	3,726	3,565	—	—	161	1,499	1,603	1,504	1,824	1,164	—	1,791	1,462	1,459	1,470	1,479	1,057	1,529
1933	3,677	3,531	—	—	146	1,344	1,302	1,213	1,673	1,070	954	1,577	1,364	1,361	1,365	1,413	1,140	1,455
1934	4,037	3,884	—	—	153	1,297	1,263	1,178	1,717	1,070	971	1,635	1,317	1,313	1,329	1,391	1,128	1,438
1935	4,342	4,178	—	—	164	1,305	1,295	1,183	1,759	1,154	839	1,780	1,311	1,305	1,358	1,425	1,034	1,473
1936	3,876	3,696	—	—	180	1,290	1,186	1,112	1,896	1,152	931	1,869	1,431	1,428	1,395	1,457	1,345	1,487
1937	4,084	3,889	—	—	195	1,367	1,270	1,188	1,797	1,132	1,007	1,851	1,471	1,467	1,435	1,493	1,455	1,536
1938	4,321	4,121	—	—	200	1,348	1,221	1,149	1,832	1,120	991	1,811	1,502	1,499	1,476	1,517	1,333	1,563
1939	4,390	4,185	—	—	205	1,348	1,214	1,137	1,843	1,134	939	1,819	1,506	1,503	1,473	1,530	909	1,578
1940	4,527	4,289	—	—	238	1,354	1,205	1,125	1,894	1,025	883	1,820	1,534	1,530	1,507	1,552	909	1,610
1941	4,665	4,388	—	—	277	1,399	1,292	1,239	1,970	1,113	889	1,777	1,565	1,555	1,534	1,574	1,000	1,734
1942	4,769	4,473	—	—	296	1,645	1,652	1,632	2,226	1,485	965	1,949	1,626	1,609	1,588	1,628	1,000	1,908
1943	4,999	4,663	—	—	336	1,797	1,808	1,792	2,628	1,565	1,064	2,168	1,749	1,725	1,688	1,756	—	2,142
1944	5,278	4,938	—	—	340	1,930	1,943	1,929	2,677	1,763	—	2,372	1,861	1,838	1,817	1,855	—	2,255
1945	5,730	5,370	—	—	360	2,059	2,069	2,057	2,646	1,931	—	2,412	2,004	1,981	1,975	1,986	—	2,405
1946	6,601	6,195	—	—	406	2,380	2,491	2,490	2,904	2,279	—	2,492	2,162	2,139	2,127	2,149	—	2,554
1947	7,838	7,338	—	—	500	2,615	2,831	2,843	3,180	2,556	—	2,763	2,375	2,350	2,374	2,331	—	2,791
1948	9,161	8,521	—	—	640	2,818	2,957	2,949	3,256	2,676	—	2,996	2,673	2,650	2,666	2,638	—	3,000
1949	10,149	9,442	—	—	707	2,888	3,016	2,995	3,481	2,599	—	3,132	2,754	2,727	2,805	2,668	—	3,158
1950	10,905	10,145	—	—	760	3,043	3,238	3,220	3,632	2,897	—	3,345	2,841	2,817	2,934	2,729	—	3,201
1951	12,019	11,159	—	—	859	3,152	3,227	3,189	3,924	2,788	—	3,554	3,041	3,013	3,147	2,911	—	3,435
1952	13,308	12,252	5,574	6,678	1,056	3,322	3,372	3,326	4,202	2,891	—	3,789	3,241	3,209	3,327	3,116	—	3,655
1953	14,472	13,334	6,096	7,238	1,138	3,427	3,456	3,412	4,412	2,927	—	3,855	3,385	3,353	3,478	3,254	—	3,795
1954	15,885	14,698	6,797	7,901	1,187	3,540	3,531	3,487	4,508	2,997	—	3,908	3,551	3,523	3,685	3,393	—	3,925
1955	17,111	15,838	7,402	8,435	1,274	3,753	3,816	3,777	4,804	3,237	—	4,136	3,675	3,644	3,788	3,526	—	4,087
1956	18,931	17,620	8,320	9,301	1,310	3,941	4,016	3,986	5,024	3,402	—	4,247	3,855	3,832	4,018	3,679	—	4,179
1957	20,926	19,556	9,373	10,185	1,368	4,085	4,103	4,076	5,205	3,439	—	4,305	4,064	4,047	4,288	3,848	—	4,308
1958	23,072	21,578	10,470	11,108	1,494	4,376	4,491	4,464	5,779	3,697	—	4,678	4,260	4,246	4,561	3,985	—	4,456
1959	24,882	23,133	11,514	11,619	1,749	4,450	4,611	4,593	5,851	3,824	—	4,733	4,299	4,298	4,453	4,154	—	4,315
1960	27,404	25,470	12,979	12,491	1,934	4,628	4,756	4,725	6,072	3,872	—	4,964	4,511	4,506	4,687	4,334	—	4,572
1961	29,896	27,934	14,321	13,613	1,962	4,774	4,861	4,818	6,453	3,813	—	5,145	4,698	4,707	4,914	4,511	—	4,561
1962	32,436	30,243	15,784	14,459	2,193	4,943	4,923	4,867	6,644	3,807	—	5,307	4,962	4,958	5,209	4,716	—	5,013
1963	35,184	32,857	17,463	15,394	2,327	5,171	5,219	5,143	6,993	3,997	—	5,732	5,131	5,127	5,361	4,891	—	5,191
1964	38,449	35,873	19,345	16,528	2,576	5,434	5,578	5,510	7,518	4,284	—	6,034	5,317	5,303	5,565	5,033	—	5,524
1965	42,073	39,294	21,285	18,009	2,779	5,672	5,844	5,769	7,858	4,477	—	6,336	5,538	5,520	5,757	5,270	—	5,807
1966	47,117	44,115	24,255	19,860	3,002	5,893	5,984	5,927	8,170	4,650	—	6,366	5,818	5,800	6,046	5,533	—	6,085
1967	52,759	49,530	27,377	22,153	3,229	6,170	6,063	5,999	8,259	4,732	—	6,499	6,262	6,250	6,503	5,971	—	6,452
1968	59,558	55,898	31,126	24,772	3,660	6,684	6,605	6,526	9,002	5,148	—	7,143	6,749	6,725	7,019	6,398	—	7,123
1969	66,700	62,599	34,635	27,964	4,101	7,171	7,099	7,017	9,690	5,526	—	7,652	7,227	7,202	7,504	6,860	—	7,624

Compensation

	Total employee compensation					Average annual wages and salary											
		State and local					Federal					State and local				
		General government					General government					General government			
Year	Total	Total	Education	Other	Government enterprise	All government	Total	Total	Military	Civilian, except work relief	Work relief	Government enterprise	Total	Total	Education	Work relief	Other	Government enterprise
	Ea948	Ea949	Ea950	Ea951	Ea952	Ea953	Ea954	Ea955	Ea956	Ea957	Ea958	Ea959	Ea960	Ea961	Ea962	Ea963	Ea964	Ea965
	Thousand dollars	Thousand dollars	Thousand dollars	Thousand dollars	Thousand dollars	Dollars	Dollars	Dollars	Dollars	Dollars	Dollars	Dollars	Dollars	Dollars	Dollars	Dollars	Dollars	Dollars
1970	75,662	71,058	39,337	31,721	4,604	7,974	8,146	8,042	10,921	8,319	—	8,774	7,852	7,831	8,170	7,449	—	8,182
1971	84,376	79,236	43,653	35,583	5,140	8,642	9,012	8,998	11,769	9,139	—	9,090	8,405	8,379	8,676	8,042	—	8,827
1972	93,299	87,693	48,020	39,673	5,606	9,387	10,298	10,333	12,597	9,603	—	10,106	8,866	8,837	9,139	8,497	—	9,334
1973	104,425	97,987	53,073	44,914	6,438	9,988	11,004	11,006	13,464	9,070	—	10,993	9,443	9,399	9,623	9,147	—	10,159
1974	115,067	107,708	57,893	49,815	7,359	10,581	11,716	11,641	14,083	9,594	—	12,095	9,994	9,937	10,089	9,767	—	10,891
1975	129,760	121,245	66,041	55,204	8,515	11,387	12,587	12,448	15,201	10,064	—	13,299	10,794	10,732	11,007	10,428	—	11,745
1976	142,304	133,094	72,788	60,306	9,210	12,144	13,375	13,156	16,238	10,420	—	14,517	11,549	11,493	11,849	11,100	—	12,393
1977	154,975	145,127	79,013	66,114	9,848	12,917	14,215	13,977	17,474	10,854	—	15,463	12,301	12,237	12,539	11,904	—	13,301
1978	170,131	159,041	85,014	74,027	11,090	13,732	15,303	15,075	18,909	11,570	—	16,489	13,005	12,929	13,222	12,617	—	14,176
1979	186,849	174,499	92,983	81,516	12,350	14,676	16,241	15,968	19,903	12,316	—	17,634	13,964	13,904	14,408	13,384	—	14,857
1980	207,352	193,213	101,898	91,315	14,139	16,039	17,622	17,229	21,212	13,498	—	19,639	15,315	15,241	15,781	14,697	—	16,373
1981	226,006	210,371	110,661	99,710	15,635	17,668	19,598	19,085	23,021	15,537	—	22,224	16,770	16,677	17,136	16,209	—	18,093
1982	244,822	227,768	119,407	108,361	17,054	19,000	21,074	20,691	24,434	17,384	—	23,089	18,036	17,952	18,539	17,363	—	19,210
1983	262,057	243,489	126,680	116,809	18,568	20,213	22,038	21,474	25,295	18,120	—	25,113	19,356	19,241	19,479	18,996	—	20,971
1984	281,590	261,668	136,887	124,781	19,922	21,386	23,150	22,609	26,412	19,232	—	25,998	20,551	20,439	20,770	20,098	—	22,101
1985	307,375	285,303	150,017	135,286	22,072	22,479	24,279	23,681	27,327	20,418	—	27,463	21,641	21,508	21,846	21,154	—	23,487
1986	331,663	308,066	162,928	145,138	23,597	23,391	25,042	24,451	28,092	21,225	—	28,238	22,647	22,509	22,868	22,129	—	24,564
1987	354,271	329,614	173,480	156,134	24,657	24,495	26,022	25,284	28,941	22,009	—	30,034	23,815	23,703	24,291	23,097	—	25,379
1988	381,183	354,623	186,343	168,280	26,560	25,557	27,375	26,621	30,457	23,072	—	31,363	24,768	24,628	24,911	24,327	—	26,773
1989	409,906	381,571	200,423	181,148	28,335	26,583	28,212	27,454	31,389	23,845	—	31,985	25,896	25,757	26,022	25,475	—	27,882
1990	445,908	415,502	218,022	197,480	30,406	28,176	29,989	29,108	32,554	25,729	—	34,588	27,431	27,302	27,613	26,973	—	29,281
1991	471,168	439,244	230,555	208,689	31,924	29,678	32,067	31,261	34,798	27,748	—	36,258	28,720	28,593	28,989	28,175	—	30,555
1992	494,318	461,065	240,884	220,181	33,253	30,975	34,266	33,158	36,506	29,611	—	39,998	29,719	29,613	29,868	29,343	—	31,248
1993	518,147	483,892	253,509	230,383	34,255	32,029	36,142	35,171	39,070	30,810	—	41,160	30,550	30,448	30,690	30,190	—	32,041
1994	543,391	507,050	265,530	241,520	36,341	33,094	37,529	36,534	41,254	31,199	—	42,370	31,572	31,454	31,459	31,449	—	33,282
1995	566,492	528,907	278,484	250,423	37,585	33,962	38,541	37,650	42,619	31,977	—	42,646	32,460	32,338	32,221	32,467	—	34,248
1996	586,394	548,416	290,650	257,766	37,978	34,974	40,101	39,190	44,587	32,978	—	44,156	33,365	33,242	33,176	33,314	—	35,220
1997	615,813	576,759	307,530	269,229	39,054	36,032	41,493	40,571	46,079	34,166	—	45,532	34,387	34,252	34,077	34,450	—	36,477
1998	644,891	604,420	323,707	280,713	40,471	37,235	42,666	41,719	47,487	34,945	—	46,755	35,648	35,517	35,346	35,713	—	37,684
1999	676,349	634,016	340,484	293,532	42,333	38,650	44,287	43,522	49,766	36,181	—	47,533	37,040	36,902	36,620	37,228	—	39,208
2000	715,301	670,666	361,349	309,317	44,635	40,228	45,887	44,512	50,050	37,601	—	51,987	38,603	38,453	37,968	39,025	—	40,967

Sources

U.S. Bureau of Economic Analysis, National Income and Product Accounts (available through the Bureau of Economic Analysis (BEA) Internet site), as follows: series Ea916–928, "Full-Time and Part-Time Employees, by Industry," Tables 6.4A, 6.4B, and 6.4C; series Ea929–941, "Full-Time Equivalent Employees, by Industry," Tables 6.5A, 6.5B, and 6.5C; series Ea942–952, "Compensation of Employees, by Industry," Tables 6.2A, 6.2B, and 6.2C; and series Ea953–965, "Wage and Salary Accruals, by Industry," Tables 6.3A, 6.3B, and 6.3C.

Documentation

Figures are annual averages of monthly data.

Federal military figures include the Coast Guard.

For more information on the source, see U.S. Bureau of Economic Analysis, "Improved Estimates of the national income and product accounts for 1929–99: Results of the Comprehensive Revision," *Survey of Current Business* (April 2000), pp. 11–16.

Series Ea942–952. Figures are totals of all compensation paid to government employees in the calendar year, including wages, salaries, and insurance trust expenditures.

TABLE Ea966–985   Government employees, by level, branch, and major function of government: 1939–1999   [BLS]

Contributed by Susan B. Carter

				Federal							
			Government branch						Industry division		
			Executive								
	Total	Total	Total	Defense Department	U.S. Postal Service	Other	Legislative	Judicial	Manufacturing	Transportation	Service
	Ea966	Ea967	Ea968	Ea969	Ea970	Ea971	Ea972	Ea973	Ea974	Ea975	Ea976
Year	Thousand	Thousand	Thousand	Thousand	Thousand	Thousand	Thousand	Thousand	Thousand	Thousand	Thousand
1939	3,995	905	887	183	318	386	16	2	—	—	—
1940	4,202	996	977	251	326	400	17	2	—	—	—
1941	4,660	1,340	1,319	518	338	463	19	2	—	—	—
1942	5,483	2,213	2,189	1,272	346	572	21	3	—	—	—
1943	6,080	2,905	2,879	1,881	366	633	23	3	—	—	—
1944	6,043	2,928	2,900	1,868	405	627	25	3	—	—	—
1945	5,944	2,808	2,778	1,705	436	637	27	3	—	—	—
1946	5,595	2,254	2,223	1,030	469	724	28	3	—	—	—
1947	5,474	1,892	1,864	689	467	708	25	3	—	—	—
1948	5,650	1,863	1,836	707	494	635	24	3	—	—	—
1949	5,856	1,908	1,881	733	523	624	24	4	—	—	—
1950	6,026	1,928	1,901	737	513	652	23	4	—	—	—
1951	6,389	2,302	2,276	1,101	518	657	23	4	—	—	—
1952	6,609	2,420	2,394	1,199	538	656	23	4	—	—	—
1953	6,645	2,305	2,279	1,131	527	622	22	4	—	—	—
1954	6,751	2,188	2,162	1,027	529	605	22	4	—	—	—
1955	6,914	2,187	2,162	1,028	530	604	22	4	—	—	—
1956	7,278	2,209	2,183	1,034	535	614	22	4	—	—	—
1957	7,616	2,217	2,190	1,007	551	632	22	5	—	—	—
1958	7,839	2,191	2,164	960	563	641	22	5	—	—	—
1959	8,083	2,233	2,205	966	575	665	23	5	—	—	—
1960	8,353	2,270	2,243	941	587	715	23	5	—	—	—
1961	8,594	2,279	2,251	944	597	711	23	5	—	—	—
1962	8,890	2,340	2,311	963	597	750	24	6	—	—	—
1963	9,225	2,358	2,328	949	598	781	24	6	—	—	—
1964	9,596	2,348	2,318	934	600	784	25	6	—	—	—
1965	10,074	2,378	2,347	939	614	794	25	6	—	—	—
1966	10,784	2,564	2,532	1,024	681	827	26	6	—	—	—
1967	11,391	2,719	2,685	1,109	714	863	27	6	—	—	—
1968	11,839	2,737	2,702	1,107	724	871	28	7	—	—	—
1969	12,195	2,758	2,722	1,126	732	864	29	7	—	—	—
1970	12,554	2,731	2,694	1,044	736	914	30	7	—	—	—
1971	12,881	2,696	2,657	1,009	726	921	31	8	—	—	—
1972	13,334	2,684	2,643	995	698	950	33	8	—	—	—
1973	13,732	2,663	2,621	961	693	967	34	9	—	—	—
1974	14,170	2,724	2,679	964	705	1,010	36	9	—	—	—
1975	14,686	2,748	2,700	955	697	1,049	37	10	—	—	—
1976	14,871	2,733	2,684	929	671	1,084	38	11	129	36	357
1977	15,127	2,727	2,676	918	654	1,104	39	12	134	40	376
1978	15,672	2,753	2,700	910	649	1,141	40	13	124	46	380
1979	15,947	2,773	2,720	895	661	1,163	40	13	125	43	360
1980	16,241	2,866	2,812	893	661	1,257	40	15	124	41	405
1981	16,031	2,772	2,717	913	661	1,144	39	15	130	42	393
1982	15,837	2,739	2,684	939	662	1,082	39	16	133	42	396
1983	15,869	2,774	2,712	947	685	1,085	40	16	136	41	405
1984	16,024	2,807	2,751	963	703	1,086	39	17	135	40	406
1985	16,394	2,875	2,819	988	743	1,087	39	18	132	40	411
1986	16,693	2,899	2,844	983	789	1,072	37	19	125	40	411
1987	17,010	2,943	2,886	985	810	1,090	38	20	124	43	425
1988	17,386	2,971	2,912	964	831	1,117	38	21	118	41	414
1989	17,779	2,988	2,928	973	832	1,123	38	21	115	36	395

TABLE Ea966-985   Government employees, by level, branch, and major function of government: 1939-1999   [BLS]
Continued

		Federal									
		Government branch							Industry division		
		Executive									
	Total	Total	Defense Department	U.S. Postal Service	Other	Legislative	Judicial	Manufacturing	Transportation	Service	
	Ea966	Ea967	Ea968	Ea969	Ea970	Ea971	Ea972	Ea973	Ea974	Ea975	Ea976
Year	Thousand	Thousand	Thousand	Thousand	Thousand	Thousand	Thousand	Thousand	Thousand	Thousand	Thousand
1990	18,304	3,085	3,025	951	819	1,255	38	23	115	36	398
1991	18,402	2,966	2,903	921	807	1,175	38	25	107	35	395
1992	18,645	2,969	2,903	917	792	1,194	39	27	101	33	396
1993	18,841	2,915	2,849	870	788	1,191	38	28	88	29	390
1994	19,128	2,870	2,807	825	818	1,164	36	28	76	24	385
1995	19,305	2,822	2,760	779	843	1,137	34	28	66	22	379
1996	19,419	2,757	2,696	740	856	1,100	32	29	55	21	372
1997	19,557	2,699	2,638	698	858	1,082	31	30	51	14	361
1998	19,823	2,686	2,625	665	867	1,092	31	31	50	14	356
1999	20,170	2,669	2,607	640	873	1,094	30	32	49	14	360

	State				Local				
	Total	Hospital	Education	General administration	Total	Transportation and public utility	Hospital	Education	General administration
	Ea977	Ea978	Ea979	Ea980	Ea981	Ea982	Ea983	Ea984	Ea985
Year	Thousand	Thousand	Thousand	Thousand	Thousand	Thousand	Thousand	Thousand	Thousand
1939	—	—	—	—	—	—	—	—	—
1940	—	—	—	—	—	—	—	—	—
1941	—	—	—	—	—	—	—	—	—
1942	—	—	—	—	—	—	—	—	—
1943	—	—	—	—	—	—	—	—	—
1944	—	—	—	—	—	—	—	—	—
1945	—	—	—	—	—	—	—	—	—
1946	—	—	—	—	—	—	—	—	—
1947	—	—	—	—	—	—	—	—	—
1948	—	—	—	—	—	—	—	—	—
1949	—	—	—	—	—	—	—	—	—
1950	—	—	—	—	—	—	—	—	—
1951	—	—	—	—	—	—	—	—	—
1952	—	—	—	—	—	—	—	—	—
1953	—	—	—	—	—	—	—	—	—
1954	—	—	—	—	—	—	—	—	—
1955	1,168	—	308	—	3,558	—	—	1,792	—
1956	1,250	—	334	—	3,819	—	—	1,928	—
1957	1,328	—	363	—	4,071	—	—	2,073	—
1958	1,415	—	389	—	4,232	—	—	2,165	—
1959	1,484	—	420	—	4,366	—	—	2,250	—
1960	1,536	—	448	—	4,547	—	—	2,369	—
1961	1,607	—	474	—	4,708	—	—	2,468	—
1962	1,668	—	511	—	4,881	—	—	2,581	—
1963	1,747	—	557	—	5,121	—	—	2,738	—
1964	1,856	—	609	—	5,392	—	—	2,906	—
1965	1,996	—	679	—	5,700	—	—	3,102	—
1966	2,141	—	775	—	6,080	—	—	3,375	—
1967	2,302	—	873	—	6,371	—	—	3,572	—
1968	2,442	—	958	—	6,660	—	—	3,736	—
1969	2,533	—	1,042	—	6,904	—	—	3,874	—
1970	2,664	—	1,104	—	7,158	—	—	4,004	—
1971	2,747	—	1,149	—	7,437	—	—	4,188	—
1972	2,859	459	1,188	711	7,790	497	467	4,363	2,175
1973	2,923	472	1,205	726	8,146	512	477	4,537	2,326
1974	3,039	483	1,267	751	8,407	533	483	4,692	2,396

(continued)

TABLE Ea966–985   Government employees, by level, branch, and major function of government: 1939–1999   [BLS]
Continued

	State				Local				
	Total	Hospital	Education	General administration	Total	Transportation and public utility	Hospital	Education	General administration
	Ea977	Ea978	Ea979	Ea980	Ea981	Ea982	Ea983	Ea984	Ea985
Year	Thousand	Thousand	Thousand	Thousand	Thousand	Thousand	Thousand	Thousand	Thousand
1975	3,179	503	1,323	797	8,758	555	489	4,834	2,566
1976	3,273	518	1,371	827	8,865	555	492	4,899	2,613
1977	3,377	538	1,385	879	9,023	550	494	4,974	2,685
1978	3,474	541	1,367	969	9,446	572	535	5,075	2,897
1979	3,541	538	1,378	1,006	9,633	594	571	5,107	2,969
1980	3,610	530	1,398	1,040	9,765	596	604	5,210	2,964
1981	3,640	515	1,420	1,062	9,619	561	622	5,216	2,871
1982	3,640	494	1,433	1,098	9,458	518	635	5,169	2,834
1983	3,662	471	1,450	1,141	9,434	490	644	5,139	2,856
1984	3,734	459	1,488	1,193	9,482	492	623	5,196	2,869
1985	3,832	449	1,540	1,261	9,687	496	608	5,344	2,926
1986	3,893	438	1,561	1,340	9,901	491	601	5,484	3,003
1987	3,967	439	1,586	1,410	10,100	490	606	5,598	3,077
1988	4,076	446	1,621	1,485	10,339	487	619	5,722	3,181
1989	4,182	442	1,668	1,560	10,609	479	632	5,875	3,282
1990	4,305	426	1,730	1,652	10,914	455	646	6,042	3,419
1991	4,355	417	1,768	1,684	11,081	445	653	6,136	3,483
1992	4,408	419	1,799	1,709	11,267	451	665	6,220	3,546
1993	4,488	414	1,834	1,747	11,438	454	673	6,353	3,565
1994	4,576	407	1,882	1,783	11,682	459	673	6,479	3,651
1995	4,635	395	1,919	1,818	11,849	458	669	6,606	3,675
1996	4,606	376	1,911	1,824	12,056	454	648	6,748	3,733
1997	4,582	360	1,904	1,821	12,276	453	632	6,918	3,766
1998	4,612	346	1,922	1,840	12,525	454	630	7,085	3,812
1999	4,695	342	1,968	1,879	12,806	460	631	7,272	3,875

Sources

U.S. Bureau of Labor Statistics (BLS), *Employment, Hours, and Earnings: United States, 1909–94*, Bulletin number 2445, two volumes (1994). U.S. Bureau of Labor Statistics, *Employment, Hours, and Earnings: United States, 1990–95*, Bulletin number 2465 (1995). U.S. Bureau of Labor Statistics, *National Employment, Hours, and Earnings*, Internet site. Also see the periodical, *Employment and Earnings*, published monthly by the BLS.

Documentation

Figures cover civilian employees only.

See the text for Table Ba840–848.

Series Ea966. Equals series Ba848. See the latter for data covering the period 1919–1938.

Series Ea967. Equals the sum of series Ea968 and Ea972–973.

CHAPTER Eb
Elections and Politics

Editor: John P. McIver

ELECTIONS AND POLITICS

John P. McIver

Although elections are not a sufficient condition for democracy, competitive elections are necessary for, and often the most visible evidence of, the operation of democratic governments.[1] Certainly, in the United States, competitive elections signal the degree to which American government operates democratically. Nonetheless, the evolution of elections in America and the impact of these elections on the operation of American political institutions yield a story that occasionally raises questions about the success of the grand American experiment. The involvement of state and federal courts in settling the presidential election of 2000 certainly challenged the belief that elections and electoral rules settle all political disputes. But despite these shortcomings, America remains the most visible example worldwide of how democratic elections operate.[2]

This chapter summarizes American electoral history from its immediate postcolonial days through the end of the twentieth century. In doing so, it explores the determinants of many historical patterns and offers a brief review of the interactions between electoral outcomes and other political developments. The principal sections of this essay detail the expansion of the voting franchise, its exercise by the mass public, and its impact on the operation of the American national government. The final section provides a picture of the American electorate in interelection periods by examining public opinion over the past fifty years.

Voting Rights

The story of the evolution of "universal suffrage" in the United States is a long and somewhat painful tale when told from a contemporary perspective.[3] It is a narrative full of fits and starts that begins with a quite limited conception of government by property owners and evolves through the slow legal enfranchisement of economic, racial, gender, and age groups. The tale proceeds not in a straight line and often not even as one of "two steps forward, one step back." Rather, each incorporated group ultimately won the right to vote as the culmination of a long series of battles fought in Congress, state legislatures, and state and federal courts, and often on the streets of America through public action.

The history of the U.S. Constitution provides a formal glimpse of the spread of voting rights to different segments of the American populace. In the Constitution (Article 1, Section 4), the power to establish rules governing the participation of voters was left to the states, with the exception that Congress might step in to alter those rules in the future. This provision would play a key role in the many alterations made to the right to vote.

In the ratified Constitution, the public had the right to vote only for members of the House of Representatives. Senators were originally chosen by state legislatures, and the President by electors selected by the states. Only with the ratification of the Seventeenth Amendment in 1913 did the American public gain the right to elect their senators. Choosing the President and Vice President, however, remains a task left to the electoral college.[4] The variety of methods by which the electors were originally chosen is detailed in Table Eb123–148. But by 1836, all states, with the exception of South Carolina, moved to a system of statewide popular elections (the South Carolina legislature continued to choose its electors until 1860). Indirectly, the public, through its selection of state electors, chooses each President.

The opportunity to vote for candidates to national offices has been expanded many times since the approval of the original Constitution. The Fourteenth Amendment (1868) and the Fifteenth Amendment (1870) provide voting rights to male citizens of all races, colors, or previous conditions of servitude. The Nineteenth

---

[1] Among the many works linking elections and democracy are Dahl (1956, 1989); Gastil (1978); Bollen (1980, 1993); Bollen and Grandjean (1981); and Gurr, Jaggers, and Moore (1990).

[2] Perhaps the claim to "be" a democracy is misplaced, as Czechoslovak President Václav Havel explained in his address to a joint session of the U.S. Congress in February 1990: "As long as people are people, democracy in the full sense of the word will always be no more than an ideal; one may approach it as one would a horizon, in ways that may be better or worse, but it can never be fully attained. In this sense you are also merely approaching democracy" (Mueller 1999).

Acknowledgments

John P. McIver thanks Monty Hindman for his assistance in the production of this chapter and the associated data series.

[3] Despite the Founders' fear that the public might not be up to the task of governing, the importance of the right to vote is emphasized today. Indeed, this right is trumpeted by the Immigration and Naturalization Service. One of the standard 100 questions asked on the citizenship test is, "What is the most important right guaranteed to U.S. citizens?" The official answer is "the right to vote" (Internet site of the U.S. Department of Justice).

[4] Article 2, Section 1 lays out the original details. Failures of the electoral college (notably the difficult resolution of the election of 1800) led reformers to enact the Twelfth Amendment by 1804. The term "electoral college" does not appear in the Constitution. Article 2 and the Twelfth Amendment refer to "electors," but not to the "electoral college." In the early 1800s, the term "electoral college" came into general usage as the unofficial designation for the group of citizens selected to cast votes for President and Vice President.

TABLE Eb-A   Constitutional extensions of the right to vote, by state: 1869–1984

State	15th Amendment: male suffrage for all races	19th Amendment: female suffrage	23rd Amendment: presidential electors for Washington, D.C.	24th Amendment: suffrage cannot be denied for failure to pay taxes	26th Amendment: suffrage for 18- to 20-year-olds
Alabama	—	September 8, 1953 [1,2]	—	—	June 30, 1971
Alaska	—	—	February 10, 1961	February 11, 1963	April 8, 1971
Arizona	—	February 12, 1920	March 10, 1961	—[2]	May 14, 1971
Arkansas	March 15, 1869	July 28, 1919	—[2]	—	March 30, 1971
California	March 4, 1962 [1,2]	November 1, 1919	January 19, 1961	February 7, 1963	April 19, 1971
Colorado	—	December 15, 1919	February 8, 1961	February 21, 1963	April 27, 1971
Connecticut	May 19, 1869	September 14, 1920 [1]	March 9, 1961	March 20, 1963	March 23, 1971
Delaware	February 12, 1901 [1,2]	March 6, 1923 [1,2]	February 20, 1961	May 1, 1963	March 23, 1971
Florida	June 14, 1869	May 13, 1969 [1]	—	April 18, 1963	—
Georgia	February 2, 1870	February 20, 1970 [1,2]	—	—	October 4, 1971 [1]
Hawai'i	—	—	June 23, 1960	March 6, 1963	March 24, 1971
Idaho	—	February 11, 1920	January 31, 1961	March 8, 1963	March 30, 1971
Illinois	March 5, 1869	June 10, 1919	March 14, 1961	November 14, 1962	June 29, 1971
Indiana	May 14, 1869	January 16, 1920	March 3, 1961	February 19, 1963	April 8, 1971
Iowa	February 3, 1870	July 2, 1919	March 16, 1961	April 24, 1963	March 30, 1971
Kansas	January 19, 1870	June 16, 1919	March 29, 1961	March 28, 1963	April 7, 1971
Kentucky	March 18, 1976 [1,2]	January 6, 1920	—	June 27, 1963	—
Louisiana	March 5, 1869	June 11, 1970 [1,2]	—	—	April 17, 1971
Maine	March 11, 1869	November 5, 1919	January 31, 1961	January 16, 1964	April 9, 1971
Maryland	—[2]	March 29, 1941 [1,2]	January 30, 1961	February 6, 1963	April 8, 1971
Massachusetts	March 12, 1869	June 25, 1919	August 22, 1960	March 28, 1963	March 24, 1971
Michigan	March 8, 1869	June 10, 1919	March 8, 1961	February 20, 1963	April 7, 1971
Minnesota	January 13, 1870	September 8, 1919	January 31, 1961	February 27, 1963	March 23, 1971
Mississippi	January 17, 1870	March 22, 1984 [1,2]	—	—[2]	—
Missouri	January 7, 1870	July 3, 1919	March 20, 1961	May 13, 1963	June 14, 1971
Montana	—	August 2, 1919	February 6, 1961	January 28, 1963	March 29, 1971
Nebraska	February 17, 1870	August 2, 1919	March 15, 1961	April 4, 1963	April 2, 1971
Nevada	March 1, 1869	February 7, 1920	February 2, 1961	March 19, 1963	—
New Hampshire	July 1, 1869	September 10, 1919	March 29, 1961	June 12, 1963	May 13, 1971
New Jersey	February 15, 1871 [1,2]	February 9, 1920	December 19, 1960	December 3, 1962	April 3, 1971
New Mexico	—	February 21, 1920	February 1, 1961	March 5, 1963	—
New York	April 14, 1869 [3]	June 16, 1919	January 17, 1961	February 4, 1963	June 2, 1971
North Carolina	March 5, 1869	May 6, 1971 [1]	—	—	July 1, 1971
North Dakota	—	December 1, 1919	—	March 7, 1963	—
Ohio	January 27, 1870	June 16, 1919 [2]	March 29, 1961	February 27, 1963	June 30, 1971
Oklahoma	—	February 28, 1920	March 21, 1961	—	July 1, 1971
Oregon	February 24, 1959 [1]	January 13, 1920	January 27, 1961	January 25, 1963	June 4, 1971
Pennsylvania	March 25, 1869	June 24, 1919	February 28, 1961	March 25, 1963	April 27, 1971
Rhode Island	January 18, 1870	January 6, 1920	March 22, 1961	February 14, 1963	May 27, 1971
South Carolina	March 15, 1869	July 1, 1969 [1,2]	—	—	April 28, 1971
South Dakota	—	December 4, 1919	February 6, 1961	January 23, 1964	—
Tennessee	—[2]	August 18, 1920	March 6, 1961	March 21, 1963	March 23, 1971
Texas	February 18, 1870 [1]	June 28, 1919	—	—	April 27, 1971
Utah	—	October 2, 1919	February 21, 1961	February 20, 1963	—
Vermont	October 20, 1869	February 8, 1921 [1]	March 15, 1961	March 15, 1963	April 16, 1971
Virginia	October 8, 1869	February 21, 1952 [1,2]	—	February 25, 1977 [1]	July 8, 1971
Washington	—	March 22, 1920	February 9, 1961	March 14, 1963	March 23, 1971
West Virginia	April 3, 1869	March 10, 1920	February 9, 1961	February 1, 1963	April 28, 1971
Wisconsin	April 9, 1869	June 10, 1919	February 21, 1961	March 26, 1963	June 22, 1971
Wyoming	—	January 27, 1920	February 13, 1961	—	July 8, 1971 [1]

[1] Ratified by state after completion of federal ratification process.

[2] Rejected proposed amendment during federal ratification.

[3] Rejected amendment after previously ratifying.

Source
"U.S. Constitution [Annotated]," in *U.S. Code Annotated* (Westlaw, 1980), annotations to the Constitutional Amendments specified.

Documentation
The amendments shown in this table were ratified by three fourths of the states and then certified by the United States on the following dates:

Fifteenth Amendment: February 17, 1870; certified March 30, 1870
Nineteenth Amendment: August 18, 1920; certified August 26, 1920
Twenty-third Amendment: March 29, 1961; certified April 3, 1961
Twenty-fourth Amendment: January 23, 1964; certified February 4, 1964
Twenty-sixth Amendment: July 1, 1971; certified July 5, 1971
When no date is provided, it means that the state did not ratify (or ultimately rejected) the amendment in question.

Amendment (1920) prevents states from denying women the right to vote. The Twenty-third Amendment (1961) provided representation to the residents of the District of Columbia for the purpose of voting for the President and Vice President. The Twenty-sixth Amendment (1971) extended the right to vote to citizens between the ages of 18 and 20, beginning with the election of 1972 (see Table Eb-A).

But constitutional amendments do not always operate as intended. Although the formal recognition of voting rights by their incorporation into the Constitution of the United States might seem to suggest universal acceptance of the right to vote for all designated groups of citizens, American political history suggests that such actions did not always result in their intended consequences – at least not immediately. The extension of constitutional rights to black men, all women, and young Americans was not uncontroversial.

In some instances, states actively opposed the extension of voting rights. In others, they simply did not act. Even after the ratification of each amendment, some states continued to express their opposition to the extension of voting rights. It took almost 100 years for California and Oregon to ratify the Fifteenth Amendment, and Kentucky took even longer. Every state has now ratified the right of women to vote, but nine bitterly opposed the extension of the franchise in 1920, and others refused to vote on the amendment, certain the outcome would be "no." These contrarian states only grudgingly accepted this amendment (Mississippi was the last state to approve the Nineteenth Amendment, in 1984). The Old South clearly opposed national intervention into its electoral processes with the passage of the Twenty-fourth Amendment. Few Southern states approved the amendment banning poll taxes, and few have ratified the amendment to this day. Virginia has had a change of heart, finally ratifying this amendment in 1977.

The history of the extension of the franchise to women during the latter half of the nineteenth century up to the final passage of the Nineteenth Amendment in 1920 illustrates the slow process by which voting rights are won. Women first gained the right to vote in school elections, where they were presumed to be informed about and able to comprehend the issues. Eventually, property requirements to voting were lifted, which removed barriers to women, whose property was commonly judged to be the property of their husbands. Slowly, women gained the right to vote on tax and bond issues and in municipal and county elections. Presidential suffrage was the last hurdle to universal suffrage. Of course, ratification of the Nineteenth Amendment did not guarantee the right to vote immediately. Although the required thirty-six states approved the amendment by late August 1920, women in at least two states were not permitted to vote in the 1920 election because of state registration laws. Then existing laws of Georgia and Mississippi required voters to register four months prior to the election.

Constitutional amendments do not control all aspects of election law. In the absence of direct federal involvement, states regulate elections. In response to constitutional changes, states restricted access to the ballot box through property and economic qualifications, residency expectations, alien voting restrictions, white-only voting requirements, poll taxes, and literacy tests. But states could also be "first movers" in extending the right to vote, as the history of female suffrage suggests.[5]

In the face of state opposition, intervention by the national government to ensure the right to vote was often required. Such actions ranged from informal pressures to the passage of legislation. Executive power, expressed as police and military authority, was occasionally necessary to enforce national laws. The U.S. Congress acted to enfranchise voters denied access to the voting booth by state restrictions. The Voting Rights Act of 1965 (and later extensions) is the most visible expression of legislative power dedicated to protect these constitutional rights. Similarly, the federal courts have acted to prevent the dilution of voting rights.[6] Numerous court rulings have supported the rights of minorities to be free of state encumbrances to their right to vote.

The U.S. Supreme Court has not only acted to ensure expansion of the franchise to millions of Americans, but also worked to protect the value of that franchise. Throughout much of the first half of the twentieth century, the Court refused to decide "political questions" – in other words, legal disputes that dealt with the operation of the legislative and executive departments of the federal government. Most notably, the Court avoided the issue of apportionment, the manner in which seats in the Congress were distributed (see *Colegrove v. Green*, 328 US 549 (1946)). But beginning in 1960, the Supreme Court became involved in a series of cases that would alter the structure of political competition by mandating adherence to the principle of "one person, one vote."[7] The spillover from these initial forays into the reapportionment debate has been to embroil the Court (and the lower federal courts) in a long series of partisan battles over the design of federal, state, and local electoral districts.

Voter Participation

Extending the right to vote to an increasing number of America's citizens provided *opportunity* for electoral participation. Opportunity does not always translate into action. While more voters did go to the polls in response to constitutional expansion of voting rights, more ballots cast did not necessarily mean that an increasing proportion of eligible voters were participating in elections. The expansion of suffrage may produce declining turnout rates if new voters participate less frequently than longtime voters. In this section, historical participation rates are examined.

Voter turnout is among the most basic statistics reflecting the health of American democracy. Concerns about democracy in the United States arise with the recognition that modern voter turnout is quite low. Barely 50 percent of individuals in the eligible electorate turn out to vote for the President, and many fewer vote in other races and at other times. Whether in historical perspective or in comparison to the voting rates of other democratic nations, modern Americans vote less often.[8] Some believe low turnout indicates

---

[5] Rusk (2001) provides the state-specific historical details behind these many restrictions and permissions (see especially pp. 13–36).

[6] Some of the landmark decisions are *Ex Parte Siebold* 100 US 371 (1880), *Smith v. Allwright* 321 US 649 (1944), *South Carolina v. Katzenbach* 383 US 301 (1966), *United Jewish Organization v. Carey* 430 US 144 (1977), and *Rogers v. Lodge* 458 US 613 (1982).

[7] Some of the important cases are *Gomillion v. Lightfoot* 364 US 339 (1960), *Baker v. Carr* 369 US 186 (1962), *Wesberry v. Sanders* 376 US 1 (1964), and *Reynolds v. Sims* 377 US 533 (1964).

[8] Comparison of American voter participation in our national elections with the voting behavior of citizens of other major democratic nations shows (with few exceptions) that Americans turn out at much lower rates than voters in other nations. The common explanation for this discrepancy is the more rigid institutional impediments to voting found in American election laws (Wolfinger and Rosenstone 1980; Powell 1986; Jackman 1987).

general disengagement of the American public from the political process. Indeed, the low turnout in the last election of the millennium came close to producing a constitutional crisis. Public ambivalence produced an electoral "tie" between George W. Bush and Albert Gore. The public became energized only when the likelihood of a tie became evident.

Turnout: A "Simple" Concept

Operationalizing voter participation is more slippery than it first appears. Voter turnout is effectively reported as a "rate" – a fraction or percentage of the population who participate in an election by casting ballots for candidates.

$$\text{Turnout} = \frac{\text{Voters}}{\text{Population}}$$

where:

Voters = number of voters casting ballots for all candidates

Population = number of individuals eligible to vote in the election

It would seem straightforward to compute both of these counts. It is not – especially in attempting to estimate turnout historically. Furthermore, these two counts may not fully help us to understand why voter turnout rises or declines.

Most explanations of turnout in the United States focus on impediments to voting. Access to the voting booth is provided only to those members of the eligible electorate who choose to register their interest in voting. In this manner, turnout may be conceived as the product of two ratios:

$$\text{Turnout} = \frac{\text{Voters}}{\text{Registered}} \times \frac{\text{Registered}}{\text{Population}}$$

where:

Registered = the number of individuals registered to vote

Conceptualizing turnout as the product of two ratios helps us to understand some of the reasons why voters may not turn out. Of course, recent experience suggests that institutional barriers are not the only obstacles preventing Americans from voting. New national registration laws (for example, the "Motor Voter Law"), the easing of date and time restrictions, alternative registration methods, and campaigns to register voters in many states have failed to stimulate significant increases in turnout in the last several elections. Many new registrants, disinterested in politics, would have been nonregistrants without the easing of registration rules. These individuals, while now registered, have a hard time making it to the polling place on election day.[9]

In any case, attempts to measure voter participation encounter significant problems with both the numerator of the first ratio and denominator of the second.[10] The bottom line in estimating turnout is that we do not have accurate historical counts of either voters or populations.

---

[9] For additional commentary and evidence of the effectiveness of the "Motor Voter Law," see Franklin and Grier (1996), Knack (1995), Knack and White (1998), Timpone (1998), and Martinez and Hill (1999).

[10] This is not to say that registration counts are without problems (Claggett 1990), but here they serve only to illustrate the conceptual underpinnings of turnout rates.

The Numerator: Voters

Lacking a count of the number of *voters*, turnout is typically calculated on the basis of the number of *votes* recorded for the highest office in the jurisdiction counting ballots. The presumption is that the number of votes cast for the most important office reasonably reflects the total number of voters participating. In presidential election years, the total number of votes is typically the number of votes cast for all presidential candidates. What we miss by taking this approach is several different sets of voters whose intents may differ widely.

> Voters who participate but do not vote for all offices (especially the one at the top of the ticket).
>
> Disqualified voters: those who appear at the polling place and are not allowed to vote for legal reasons or are prevented from voting by legal or illegal means.
>
> Disqualified ballots: ballots mis-marked by the voter or mis-scored by the counter.
>
> Abstainers: those who intend to make a political statement by their nonparticipation.[11]

Because none of these voters are systematically recorded by state election officials, the vote count that serves as the numerator in any calculation of turnout is an undercount of the actual number of voters. What we do not know is by what extent this numerator misrepresents the total number of individuals who express their preferences in any given election. Recent research suggests the national undercount is on the general order of 2 to 3 percent, but the percentage may range far more widely in local electorates (McDonald and Popkin 2001; McDonald 2002).

Yet even if we had an accurate assessment of all of the components of the "undercount," we would have to recognize that the numerator – number of votes cast – is still imperfect. Counts are subject to a variety of recording errors, some intentional and others not. Incomplete counts may be recorded and not corrected. Records may be lost. Voting machines may not work properly. False results may be reported as true vote counts.[12] All of these problems have occurred in American electoral history.

The Denominator: Population

At first blush, this component of turnout is less subject to manipulation. Yet the measure of population used in estimating voter turnout is flawed or misunderstood.

The first issue is conceptual. Whom do we want to consider as the base population for estimating turnout? Should turnout be calculated as a proportion of those eligible to vote during the period for which turnout is calculated? Or, when making historical comparisons of turnout, should the base be some standard against

---

[11] By not choosing, some abstainers wish to indicate that they oppose the choices offered to them by the political system. Anthony Downs (1957) argued for such "rational abstention" as a political critique of the lack of choice among candidates commonly offered by the two-party system.

[12] Vote fraud – whether the stuffing of ballot boxes, the intentional loss of ballots, the certification of ineligible supporters, and the decertification of eligible opponents – produces both over- and undercounts. Believed to be a particularly vexing problem in the nineteenth century, modern examples abound. Republicans often claim deceased Chicagoans won Illinois and the 1960 presidential election for John Kennedy. Democrats will long claim mishandling of ballots from Democratic counties in the 2000 Florida presidential election count.

which all eras can be judged equally? For example, turnout in the 1850s could be calculated as votes cast divided by (1) an 1850 definition of the eligible population, (2) a 2000 definition of the eligible population, or even (3) a "gold standard," a hypothetical definition of a fully eligible society. Normally, turnout is estimated as current vote count divided by current voting age population, and these estimates are often the basis for concerns about the contemporary turnout rates. But if turnout were calculated as current vote divided by modern definitions of voter eligibility or some ideal eligible population, a much more optimistic view of contemporary turnout would likely emerge.

Operationally, "accurate" population estimates are produced only once per decade. To call the Census Bureau's decennial census of the U.S. population accurate likely strains credibility, but by treating it as a preliminary approximation, a reasonable estimate of the vote-eligible population may be produced. In modern times, the Census Bureau and local agencies do provide intercensus estimates of some jurisdictions. Typically, intercensus population estimates may rely on the most immediate census, the prior census, or some extrapolation across two or more time periods.

In estimating turnout, it is important to recognize that the population eligible to vote is not the same as the population count produced by the Census Bureau. The first section of this essay outlined the slow legal expansion of franchise. Yet the history of voting is replete with local obstacles that constitutional changes by themselves could not overcome. The passage of laws without enforcement and the enactment of local laws to contradict federal edicts play a large role in establishing who could and could not vote. Only continuing efforts by the federal government served to change practices.

Although modern America operates on the premise that universal suffrage exists, not all residents or even all citizens of the United States have the right to vote. Most of those without the right to vote have little political voice and consequently little chance of having this right extended to them. Commonly overlooked is the startlingly large number of American citizens who have been disenfranchised by their criminal activity.[13] Institutionalized persons may not be eligible, or may not be able to vote if eligible. Other residents are not enfranchised because of their lack of citizenship. Both legal and illegal immigrants reside in the United States without access to the basic opportunity to decide who will make the laws governing their lives (Harper-Ho 2000). In addition, a popular movement today lobbies for the "rights of the disabled." Such voters are not legally barred from voting, yet simple obstacles often block their access to the voting booth (Schriner, Ochs, and Shields 1997). Finally, residents of the District of Columbia have no representation in Congress.[14] Additional counting errors arise in mis-identifying the residential location of military personnel. All of these sources of population may or may not be included in the population figures used to estimate turnout. Errors committed in estimating voter populations impact assessments of voter turnout.

Consequently, a recent set of papers argues that the denominator typically used in estimating voter turnout – voting age population (VAP) – is simply not adequate. McDonald and Popkin insist that the appropriate theoretical denominator is voting *eligible* population (VEP) (McDonald and Popkin 2001; McDonald 2002). After adjustment of official population figures for ineligible citizens located in the states who are counted and eligible citizens residing abroad who are not counted, the dramatic falloff in presidential turnout observed during the past thirty years disappears. The decline is due to the sharp increase in recent years in the number of persons of voting age population who are not eligible. McDonald notes that an "astonishing" 19.8 percent of the California VAP are noncitizens (McDonald 2002). But the number of noncitizens varies widely by state, with eighteen states having noncitizen populations that total less than 2 percent of the VAP.

Estimates of Voter Turnout

Voter turnout estimates for American presidential elections based on Walter Dean Burnham's work are presented in Table Eb62–113. Table Eb114–122 reports competing estimates of presidential turnout offered by Jerrold Rusk, who makes a special effort to incorporate the history of voter eligibility exclusions and inclusions to more closely approximate VAP (Rusk 2001).

All turnout estimates have their imperfections. They are based on imperfect counts and approximating assumptions. Different historical estimates of both the numerator (the number of voters) and the denominator (population) affect the results.[15] But most track quite closely, and none give a decidedly different image of the approximate turnout and turnout trends of American voters.[16] Again, the exception here is the work of McDonald and Popkin, which offers a more optimistic assessment of voter turnout, one that quite reasonably reflects a reassessment of the population component of turnout estimates (McDonald and Popkin 2001; McDonald 2002).

Presidential turnout rates rise and decline throughout American history. More than 80 percent of enfranchised Americans participated during the latter half of the nineteenth century. Only about 50 percent turned out to vote in the 2000 election. Most contemporary commentary focuses on this recent "failure" of the American electorate to exercise their franchise by participating in presidential elections. Yet modern turnout rates, although low, are not uncommon historically. The next section offers some specific insights into why rates are high or low during particular periods, but a broadbrush understanding of turnout motivated by political interest is appropriate here. Anthony Downs offers an analytic explanation captured more fully by Benjamin Page. Downs insists that turnout is a rational act: if there are benefits to be gained from voting, individuals will vote. If not, voters will not turn out (Downs 1957). Page picks up this theme in investigating American presidential elections (Page 1978). When the presidential race consists of a

---

[13] For a history of the disenfranchisement of felons and a debate over the impact of this policy, see Harvard Law Review (1989), Shapiro (1993), Harvey (1994), Love and Kuzma (1996), Fellner and Mauer (1998), and Preuhs (1999).

[14] On October 16, 2000, the Supreme Court summarily affirmed a decision by a special three-judge panel denying the residents of the District of Columbia the right to vote for members of the House of Representatives. See *Alexander v. Mineta* (69 USLW 3268) and *Adams v. Clinton* (69 USLW 3268).

[15] Table Eb149–153 presents one estimate of the national vote count from which different estimates of voter turnout could be computed with alternative estimates of the voting population.

[16] The U.S. Census Bureau also estimates voter turnout. Their turnout figures are consistently lower, in large part a function of a less restrictive definition of VAP. Since 1964, the Census Bureau has provided a second, survey-based estimate of voter participation based on the Current Population Survey (CPS). These data produce turnout rates significantly higher than the Rusk or Burnham estimates. One interpretation – consistent with National Election Survey findings – is that survey respondents exaggerate their voting activity.

contest between Tweedledum and Tweedledee, voters have no incentive to vote. The outcome, regardless of who is elected, will be the same. In contrast, when the candidates offer widely different programs to the voters such that who is elected does matter, voters have a reason to pay attention to the campaign and participate on election day. Throughout history, political parties have offered different options. "Choices" offered to the public matter. When one candidate's campaign "echoes" another's, elections do not matter and voters do not turn out.

Turnout for nonpresidential elections falls well below presidential election turnout, particularly in the modern era. Table Eb260–263 extends the congressional vote count series reported in the previous edition of *Historical Statistics of the United States* (1975). Table Eb114–122 reports Rusk's estimates of turnout for congressional races. Rusk's narrower conception of VAP produces a slightly higher turnout rate each year, but the trends are the same.[17] Relatively few Americans participate in midterm elections today, with turnout rates hovering around 40 percent. Yet the historical record shows a different picture in early times. From the 1830s through the First World War, more than half of all eligible voters turned out for midterm elections. It was not uncommon for two thirds of the electorate to participate in these races.

Series Eb208 and Eb260 allow comparison of total votes cast in presidential and "midterm" congressional election years.[18] Voters consistently cast fewer votes for House candidates than they do for the presidential contestants. Commenting on the "saw blade" pattern of voter turnout from one presidential election to the next with interspersed midterm elections, Campbell invoked the theory of "surge and decline" of electorates to explain the participation pattern so regularly observed among Americans (Campbell 1966; also see Kramer 1971; Kernell 1977; Campbell 1987; Erikson 1990; Jacobson 1990; Coleman 1997). This theory is consistent with the Downs and Page perspectives on presidential voting: as voter interest peaks during presidential elections, so too does voter turnout. With less excitement to pull marginal voters to the polls, core and typically partisan constituencies dominate participation in midterm elections.

Ultimately, commentary on American voter turnout turns on a "glass half-empty or glass half-full" assessment of contemporary participation. Voter turnout in modern American presidential elections hovers around 50 percent of the electorate, and turnout in most other races at most other times is a fraction of presidential election turnout. Yet in contrast to the few citizens who were both eligible to vote and willing to do so 200 years ago, more than 100 million Americans voted for George W. Bush, Albert Gore, Ralph Nader, or the several minor party candidates in the 2000 election.

Figure Eb-B dramatically illustrates these two patterns and the conundrum for analysts. It is easy to be critical of the decline in voter turnout. Yet the history of the expansion of the franchise, although difficult at times, has broadened the definition of the electorate far beyond the comprehension of the Founding Fathers.

The two-sided assessment of turnout continues in comparisons made to other democratic countries. U.S. turnout appears to be quite low. Indeed, if the United States operated under election rules existing in other nations, it would fall perilously close to having

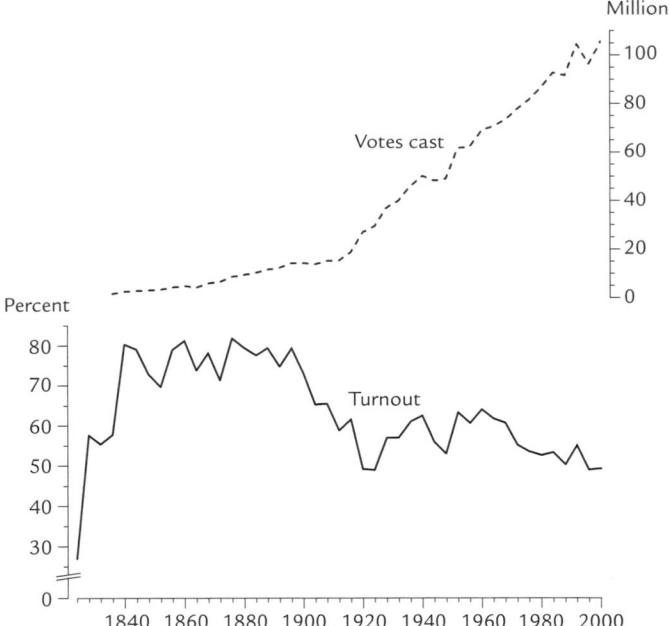

FIGURE Eb-B   Voter participation in presidential elections: 1824–2000

Sources
Series Eb62 and Eb208.

elections without results. For example, Serbia's 2002 presidential election was declared null and void because turnout fell below 50 percent. Yet if we consider turnout by just those voters who are registered to vote, U.S. turnout is substantially higher. Overall turnout by registered Americans in recent elections hovered between 65 and 70 percent, with turnout in some states approaching levels equivalent to European participation rates. Yet even a more positive view of voter participation rates based on registered voters leaves the United States near the bottom in comparison to established democracies in Western Europe. Interestingly, however, voter turnout declined throughout the world during the 1990s (International Institute for Democracy and Electoral Assistance 2003).

Explaining Historical Variations in Turnout

The turnout roller coaster that is Figure Eb-B represents not only the impact of legal changes to the franchise but also the inner workings of national, state, and local politics combined with the wide assortment of exogenous shocks to the American political system. The surge in national voter turnout observed in the 1828 election of Andrew Jackson clearly represents the impact of a shift in state election laws to adult white male suffrage. The subsequent development of mass-based parties during the 1830s produced a sea change in electoral competition from the narrow elite-based era that preceded it. This new party system supported and encouraged the participation of American white males. Slavery, and the economic, social, and moral issues that accompanied it, polarized the nation and spurred further partisan competition. Dramatic demographic changes – a consequence of westward expansion, economic opportunity, and immigration – also altered the nature of political competition. Periods of economic hardship and competition between groups spurred political struggles and inspired public participation.

---

[17] For more discussion of VAP, see the text for Table Eb114–122.

[18] Alternatively, series Eb114 and Eb117 allow comparison of turnout rates between presidential and "midterm" congressional election years.

Internal, regional, and finally world war inspired lively debate and fueled interest in politics.

Changes in the late nineteenth and early twentieth centuries, however, seemed to stifle public involvement. The period from 1890 to 1920 represents an era of massive immigration (rivaled only by the influx of new immigrants during the last twenty years of the twentieth century) in which new citizens – not socialized to participation in politics – joined the ranks of the American electorate. Turnout fell from 80 percent down to 50 percent in thirty years. Voter turnout during the 1920s rivals modern voting patterns. Low turnout and declining partisan allegiances seen during this era set the stage for the politically tumultuous 1930s and the rewriting of the American party system. The onset of the Great Depression shifted the balance of political power from Republicans to Franklin Roosevelt and Congressional Democrats and sparked a revival of relevance of the parties as their differences came to be seen more starkly. Over the last forty years, however, public involvement in national elections gradually declined as campaigns became "candidate-centered" (Wattenberg 1987, 1991) and parties withered as objects of voter attachment to the political system. Whether the limited turnout rates observed in the late twentieth century presages new changes in political competition remains for future assessment.

Hidden in the big picture are a variety of subplots. The emancipation of blacks and their enfranchisement was very quickly followed by new restrictions. "Jim Crow" laws were written to discriminate against blacks. Given full support by the Supreme Court's infamous *Plessy v. Ferguson* decision (*Plessy v. Ferguson*, 163 US 537 (1896)), white supremacy movements throughout the South prevented many blacks from fully participating in the political system until the 1960s.

Explanations for the rise and decline of voter participation throughout American history range far beyond simply identifying the legal and extralegal expansions and contractions of the franchise. They also unfortunately range far beyond the scope of this essay. Even an answer to the restricted question "Did changes to the franchise increase aggregate participation while lowering participation rates?" is not easy to come by. Many believe the expanding right to vote has had precisely the effect of lowering turnout rates while increasing turnout. Academic debate over the decline in voter turnout during the early years of the twentieth century broadly pits social conditions against legal and institutional restrictions as the key explanation for the downturn in voter participation.[19] Likely both perspectives are right – and wrong. The explanations are complex, and single-variable answers are not viable.

Explanations of turnout rates based solely on legal shifts in the right to vote have been criticized as inadequate or incomplete. For example, was enfranchisement of women the reason why turnout declined precipitously in the 1920s? Kleppner argued, to the contrary, that political context, most reasonably operationalized as electoral competition, is the basis for a significant portion of the 1920 reduction in voter turnout.[20] Turnout by men as well as women declined during this era. Furthermore, the lack of a common pattern of reduced voting across states and across time suggests that female suffrage is not the definitive explanation for the downturn in turnout.

Similarly, recent declines in voter turnout are often blamed on the 1972 expansion of the franchise, the granting of voting rights to 18- to 20-year-olds. Historically, the youngest cohorts in the electorate have turned out at significantly lower rates than other age groups. The enactment of the Twenty-sixth Amendment exacerbated this tendency, although the campaign of 1992 appeared to have energized young voters more than any election in the last thirty years. Sole blame for recent declines in turnout cannot be placed at the feet of young voters.

Of recent institutional changes that have had positive effects on voter turnout, none may have been so important as the Voting Rights Act of 1965, which produced major changes in voter registration in the South. From 1960 to 1970, voter registration rose 8.1 percentage points among white voters (from 61.1 to 69.2 percent). But the real impact of this law was to improve opportunities for minority voters. During this decade the proportion of black citizens registered to vote more then doubled, rising from 29.1 percent to 62.0 percent. These changes were not uniform. The largest improvements occurred in states with very low black registration rates at the start of the decade. South Carolina and Alabama registration figures for blacks rose 309 percent and 382 percent, respectively. In Mississippi the percentage of black citizens registered to vote rose from 5.2 percent to 71 percent, an astounding 1,265 percent increase in registered voters over the decade. By the end of the decade, most of the South continued to show higher white registration rates, although the differences between races shrank markedly. The lone exception was Texas, in which the proportion of black voters exceeded the registration rates of white voters by 1970.

Yet progress toward racial neutrality in voter registration of the 1960s was short lived. During the next decade, minority registration rates fell, while white registration rates increased, tripling the gap between white and black voter registration by 1980. White registration increases may be attributable to "blacklash" against newly enfranchised blacks. Mississippi, for one, engaged in patently illegal registrations. According to the statistics of the Southern Regional Council's Voter Education Project, more than 100 percent of white Mississippians were registered to vote in 1980 (*Statistical Abstract*, 1981, p. 495).

While institutional explanations do not always satisfy, it is not the case that social and demographic change is the alternative explanation for turnout decline. For example, despite the apparent correlation between immigration and voter turnout, Tuckel and Maisel find little evidence directly tying immigration to the reduced participation by electorates at the turn of the century (Tuckel and Maisel 1994). Although county-level data point to low turnout in areas populated by immigrants, these data capture primarily patterns in rural voting. Examination of ward data in urban areas indicates, in fact, that voting rates were higher in places with large foreign-born populations. The potential to grab control of power in urban areas created justification for voters to participate in the political arena.

Apportionment and Popular Votes versus Electoral Votes

Despite the popular perception that the public chooses the President, Article 2, Section 1 of the U.S. Constitution establishes electors for that task in a process referred to by most as the "electoral

---

[19] Burnham (1965, 1970, 1974), as compared to Converse (1972, pp. 263–337) and Rusk (1970). Also see Dugan and Taggart (1995).

[20] Kleppner (1982b). Kleppner would be a kindred spirit to Page.

college."[21] At present, each state selects, by popular vote, a group of electors equal in number to its total of members of Congress. The District of Columbia also has three presidential electors granted by the Twenty-third Amendment, adopted in 1961. After the general election, those selected as electors meet in their respective states to vote for President and Vice President. The 2000 election again shows the relevance of the electoral college vote. For the fourth time in U.S. history, a candidate who did not win the popular vote was elected President.

A state's representation in both the electoral college and the U.S. House of Representatives is governed by its share of the national population, which is affected by population growth and interstate migration. Relative changes in population – together with the principle of "one person, one vote" – produce a reapportionment of the House and the electoral college each decade (for apportionment, see Tables Eb1–61; for votes in the electoral college, see Tables Eb149–207).

Research on American Elections: Realignment to Divided Government

The voting statistics reported in Tables Eb62–122 and Eb149–267 tell a second critical story about American political history, a story about the ebb and flow of support for the major political parties. With the publication of V. O Key's influential papers on "critical elections" and "secular realignments," the study of elections turned to focus on theories of realignment (Key 1955, 1959). Realignments – shifts in the balance of partisan power in the electorate and the institutions of government – were observed to occur with predictable regularity: forty-year cycles of one-party dominance broken or confirmed by cataclysmic "critical" elections (Burnham 1965, 1970; Ladd and Hadley 1978; McCormick 1982, 1986). The elections of 1860, 1892, and 1932 changed the face of Washington politics. The observed periodicity of realignments has spawned a variety of hypotheses to explain their strength and duration. By the late 1960s a new realignment was expected.

It never happened – at least not in the way realignments had occurred previously. As a result, many political scientists and historians questioned the value of realignment theories (Lichtman 1982; Carmines and Stimson 1989; Shafer 1991; Aldrich and Niemi 1996; Aldrich 1999; Shea 1999). The failure of cyclical theories to predict the next period of party dominance has yielded to alternative visions of the future, with political scientists offering a menu of dealignment, the end of realignment, punctuated equilibria, a sixth-party system, and a "baseless" party system among the options. Historians have taken the failures of realignment theory in a different direction. Silbey, drawing on his earlier collaborations with Benson and Field, finds "political eras" a more satisfying construct capable of extending analysis to normal periods of American politics. In a similar vein, Shafer offers the notion of "electoral order" as a concept capable of bringing coherence to the discussion of American political history (Silbey 1991; Shafer 1991).

In place of realignment, the focus in political science has shifted to the study of "divided" government, the control of the executive by one party sharing power with the other major party in command of one or both of the chambers of the legislature. Attention is directed primarily at the partisan control of the institutions of government, although those seeking explanation for patterns of divided government still look to elections and the behavior of voters to explain the reasons why governments cannot be unified under the direction of a single political party.

Some may see this shift to divided government as simply a shift in the historical focus point. Rather than study the periods immediately after critical elections when government is unified behind a dominant party, scholars now look to the end of periods of party dominance and focus on those times when competition becomes more heated and control by a single party is not a given. Yet the picture political history offers up is not so obvious, especially as our attention moves from the national level to state political competition. The first half of the twentieth century, a period of unified government, tends to dominate expectations of "normalcy." Yet this period is unique in American history. Fiorina notes the common occurrences of divided government throughout the nineteenth century, in contrast to the unified governments of the first half of the twentieth century (Fiorina 1996). The last thirty years are more typical than we often believe (see Table Eb296–308 for the partisan divisions within the national government).

Whether we study American political history from the perspective of realignment and critical elections, from the perspective of political periods, or with divided government the common pattern for periods of normal politics, we are looking at the same data with different lenses. The Gestalt principle of figure and ground (most often recognized in visual form as optical illusion – a picture of two faces or a vase) serves as a reasonable analogy for our perception of American political history as one "most usefully" examined as critical elections, stable party periods, or shared control of national government. Each perspective offers a different insight into the operation of the American democracy.

Institutional Time Series

A realignment perspective on American political history is not based solely on the behavior of the voting public. The operation of government over broad periods of American history can be traced by examining major changes in national and local institutions, changes most typically represented by the extensive and dramatic shift in power within our governing institutions from one major political party to another. Certainly authors describing realignments recognize this institutional component (Burnham 1965; Lowi 1967; Huntington 1981; Sundquist 1983; Lichtman 1976; Clubb, Flanigan, and Zingale 1980; Brady 1988; Morone 1990; Jillson 1994).

Examination of the control of the institutions of the national government focuses attention on the partisan divisions within the U.S. Congress, as well as the party affiliation of the sitting President (see Table Eb296–308).[22] Although the President often has a different perspective on public policy than his colleagues in the Congress, it is quite clear that party is the glue that holds the federal system together. It is simply far easier to find common ground in

---

[21] According to Vile (1996), the constitutional provision establishing the electoral college has been the focus of more constitutional amending activity than any other, except for the often-proposed equal rights for women amendment.

[22] Similarly the study of state policy making concentrates on the partisan divisions in the state legislature and the party affiliation of the governor (Fiorina 1996).

enacting laws when both institutions are populated by members of the same political party with similar ideological preferences.[23]

Partisan control presumably has some impact on the nature of government policy. Both chambers of the U.S. Congress are organized by their respective majorities. Seat margin in the House of Representatives and Senate influences the composition of committees as well as the flexibility with which leadership can attend both to programmatic direction and to constituency needs of its members. The importance of party unity for the passage of legislative agendas increases when majority status grows more tenuous.

Congressional Bills and Resolutions

Do realignments presage policy shifts (Brady 1988)? Is unified government critical for advancing legislative agendas (Sundquist 1988–1989)? Does divided government promote deadlock (Burns 1963, 1966)? The evidence is surprisingly mixed, and the debate is likely to continue (Mayhew 1991; Jones 1994).

Simple questions about congressional activity in the face of interchamber party division or division between the party controlling the Congress and the party of the President may be answered by comparing Tables Eb268–278 and Eb296–308. Table Eb268–278 provides information on the number of bills and resolutions considered and enacted in each Congress.

Care must be exercised in comparing counts of bill and resolution introductions and enactments across historical periods. Significant differences exist in the length and breadth of the subject matter covered at different points in time. A single omnibus bill may substitute for many individual topic bills. The abrupt reduction in the number of private bills enacted into law beginning with the 60th Congress was the result of combining many private bills, particularly pension bills, into omnibus enactments.

The number of bills enacted is also affected by the nature and timing of congressional reforms (Adler 2002). In 1855 Congress established the U.S. Court of Claims to examine and resolve contractual claims made against the United States government. In 1946, in response to the dramatic rise in private legislation following the First World War, Congress banned several types of private legislation in the Legislative Reform Act.[24] Prior to then, private legislation had occupied considerable congressional time, precluding consideration of public legislation. Its virtual elimination dramatically shifted the balance of activity back to a focus on public bills and resolutions.

Presidential Vetoes

Conflict between Congress and the President is most visible in the veto process represented in Table Eb279–284. The number of bills vetoed is often a function of the partisan division across these institutions (Copeland 1983; Shields and Huang 1995). Periods of divided government typically presage more vetoes than eras

in which a single political party claims both Congress and the presidency. Yet intraparty disagreements also promote conflict over legislation even when Congress and the President are of the same partisan affiliation.

In modern times, presidential vetoes have come most often when a Republican President has faced off against a Democratic Congress. Presidents Eisenhower, Nixon, Ford, and Reagan confronted Congress over a number of important bills (Watson 1993; Cameron 2000). Only Eisenhower carried the day without significant losses. While Congress was able to override Eisenhower's veto only twice, the other modern Republican Presidents lost approximately 25 percent of their constitutional disagreements with Congress over legislation.

The subsequent success or failure of Congress to override the presidential veto is a function not only of partisan differences between President and Congress but also of the magnitude of partisan divisions within each chamber (Rohde and Simon 1985). Presidents who face an extraordinary majority of the opposing party face long odds in vetoing legislation. But such majorities are rare. The loyalty of members of the President's party makes building the two-thirds vote necessary to override a veto quite difficult under most circumstances.

Presidential Success

Summary measures of the President's success in passing his program are reported in Table Eb285–295. Scores are constructed by Congressional Quarterly Press based on roll call votes on bills for which the President has taken a stand in favor or in opposition. A number of caveats must be acknowledged when using such scores to infer how good a job the President is doing, how well the President and Congress work together, or which chamber works best with the President. Problems affecting inferences of presidential success include:

Bills killed in committee are not counted.

Bills passed or defeated on voice vote are not counted.

All votes are equally weighted, regardless of importance.

Bills are weighted by the number of votes taken.

The two chambers of Congress may disagree on a bill (which may not be the same bill).

Amendments will differ across chambers.

Owing to such considerations, the operational "presidential success" score has been roundly criticized, but few simple alternatives exist (Edwards 1985; Pritchard 1986; Collier and Sullivan 1995).

Nonetheless, many scholars substitute alternative measures in their attempts to examine the interactions between President and Congress. Peterson, Mayhew, Jones, Howell, and others have identified different classes of legislation as more or less important and hence worth more or less in interpreting how successful the branches of government are in working together or legislating "alone" (Peterson 1989; Mayhew 1991; Jones 1994; Howell, Adler, et al. 2000). Typically this work evaluates legislation subjectively and ordinally, ranking bills on a simple scale from "landmark" to "mundane."

Contemporary research on presidential success focuses on the conditions underlying success or failure – for example, control of the Congress by the President's party, or the magnitude of a Congressional majority. Consequently, the discussion of presidential

---

[23] There are, of course, exceptions to this general rule. The inability of New Deal Democrats to enact civil rights legislation lay in the split within the Democratic party. Similarly, the precursors to realigning elections have often been a result of a political party's inability to deal with intraparty disagreements over the key issue of the day.

[24] "Private bills deal with specific individuals, corporations, institutions, and so forth, as distinguished from public bills which deal with classes only" (Sensenbrenner 1999).

success highlights the link between divided government (Table Eb296–308) and the passage of the presidential program (Table Eb285–295). The conclusion of this literature is that no single conclusion exists (Chamberlain 1946; Moe and Teel 1970; Edwards 1989; Peterson 1989; Mayhew 1991; Jones 1994). At different points in time, the Congress is shown to be more or less supportive and the President more or less successful.

More constructively, Peterson and Jones recognize that no institution can enact law on its own: lawmaking proceeds best when the President and Congress "work together" (Peterson 1989; Jones 1994). Indeed, a focus on institutional success may misread the reality of American government. Such a perspective is simply myopic. Furthermore, the inability of any single institution to be successful on its own does not preclude all politicians from claiming credit for political successes. And with the apparent exception of Harry Truman – who famously declared "the buck stops here" – all elected officials seek to avoid blame for policy failures.

Public Opinion on Politics

The advent of public opinion polling – first as commercial enterprise and later as academic and scientific exercise – has transformed our ability to understand the nature of the aggregate political statistics that have been collected since the founding of the Republic. Beginning with the regular efforts of Gallup, Harris, Crossley, and Roper in the 1930s, Americans have faced a steady barrage of pollsters wondering about their assessments of the state of the nation, the performance of the President, and myriad problems that have faced the nation, from the condition of the economy to the world at war (Converse 1987). Following World War II, academic survey researchers, many of them recruited from the federal bureaucracy, joined commercial pollsters in the streets and later on telephones to query Americans about their opinions on political and social issues of the day.

Early public opinion research concentrated on current events. More recently, academic researchers and commercial survey firms have recognized the value of time series survey data for assessing contemporary opinions (Page and Shapiro 1992; Mayer 1993). Only with the perspective offered by prior opinions can the current mood of the country be evaluated. The answer to the question "Is the glass half full or half empty?" is partially answered by knowing whether it used to be full or empty.

This short discussion cannot do full justice to the many facets of public opinion that have been the focus of study by survey researchers. Rather, it offers a brief history of the basic partisan attachments of the public, a summary of popular stands on issues in broad ideological terms, and a description of public judgments of presidential performance in office over the past fifty years.

Party Identification

The occasional subject of speculation prior to the Second World War, the partisan and ideological leanings of Americans moved to center stage in the postwar era. Both political and academic interest in the hearts and minds of Americans stimulated this data collection. McCarthy-era investigations into the political preferences of Americans – particularly the radical, fascist, and communist tendencies of some – reinforced perceptions that underlying political predispositions play an important role in the decisions Americans made in going to the polls on election day.

Although questions about the political predispositions of the public have been asked in public opinion polls for almost seventy years, attention to the critical nature of party identification is largely the result of the emphasis placed on it by researchers at the University of Michigan. The defining moment for this tradition was the 1960 publication of *The American Voter* by Campbell, Converse, et al., who insisted on the centrality of party attachment in the decisions of Americans facing the ballot box (also see Campbell, Gurin, and Miller 1954; Campbell, Converse, et al. 1966; and Miller and Shanks 1996).

The standard survey approach to measuring party identification is the question "Generally speaking, do you usually think of yourself a Republican, a Democrat, an Independent, or what?" Academic researchers with the flexibility of asking more questions than commercial surveyors typically add one of two follow-ups. For those who respond to the initial question that they believe themselves to be a member of one major party or the other, the second question is "Do you believe yourself to be a strong [Democrat/Republican] or a weak [Democrat/Republican]?" For those who declare their independence from the two dominant parties in response to the first question, the next question is, "Do you lean toward the Democratic Party or the Republican Party?" The combination of these three questions produces a seven-point index ranking party identification from strong Democrat at one extreme to strong Republican at the other (see Table Eb309–316). These three questions can also serve to rank respondents on the strength of their partisan identification: a "pure" independent, an independent leaning toward a party, a weakly identified party member, or a strong supporter of a party.

The post–World War II era began with a plurality of Americans identifying with the Democratic Party. Representing the continuance of the New Deal coalition, almost twice as many Americans identified with the Democratic Party as with the Republican Party throughout the 1950s and 1960s. The high point of Democratic Party support among the general public occurred during the Johnson landslide of 1964, when 52 percent of Americans claimed to identify with the party of the President. It should be emphasized that party identification does not by itself determine election outcomes. For example, despite these general predispositions of the electorate, the immense popularity of Dwight David Eisenhower led to Republican control of the White House for almost half of these two decades. Election outcomes hinge on turnout rates among party groups, as well as success in attracting independents and members of the opposition while retaining party identifiers.

The late 1960s and early 1970s represent a watershed period in modern American politics. Public dissatisfaction with government, reflected in concerns about civil rights, the environment, the war in Vietnam, and election tactics produced significant shifts in the attachments of the public to the major parties. Within the span of eight years, both parties lost supporters and the number of "Independent" Americans grew dramatically. By 1974, Democrat and Independent were the responses of about 40 percent of the public, while barely one fifth of those polled identified with the Republican Party, an apparently unattractive alternative in the wake of the resignation of President Nixon in August 1974.

The Republican Party won back some of their support and gained adherents among new voters during the next twenty years. However, 1994 proved to be the high point of Republican support. Despite recent success in both chambers of Congress, the party has not won more converts. The 2000 electorate is composed of a plurality of Independents. Democrats remain the larger party, with Republican support falling to barely one fourth of the public.

Elections have changed over time, and parties seem to play a lesser role in the decisions of voters today. Candidates themselves emphasize this change. Recognizing the strategic need to capture the independent voter, rarely do candidates advertise their party affiliation. Campaigns promote voting for the candidate. Consequently, "the person, not the party" is the rationale underlying many voter decisions in this candidate-centered era (Wattenberg 1998). Nonetheless, in less visible races, lack of information means that party remains a key clue for voters.

Political Ideology and Policy Mood

The ideological identification of the American public has been investigated by pollsters in a variety of ways. Modern questions vary from the Gallup and media versions (for example, "How would you describe your views on most political matters? Generally, do you think of yourself as liberal, moderate, or conservative?") to academic versions that solicit greater variation.

Contemporary America is populated by citizens who describe themselves as "conservative" far more often than they call themselves "liberal." Yet more popular than either choice is the American preference for "moderate" or "middle of the road." The self-identified ideological preferences of Americans shift very slowly, with only minor aggregate change over time.[25]

Yet citizen ideological self-identification does not always point definitively to the public's preferences for individual policies. The mass public is rarely as constrained as political elites in the clustering and consistency of their attitudes about political actors, institutions, and policies (Converse 1964; Erikson, Mackuen, and Stimson 2002; Stimson 1999).

Recently, Stimson has provided a classification of the ideological "mood" of the American public based on their issue positions (see series Eb317) (Stimson 1999). This series is much more volatile than ideological self-identification and clearly shows the ebb and flow of public anticipation of and reaction to public policy. Stimson argues that American public opinion defines a zone of acceptable behavior for its political leaders, with public preferences regulating the extremes to which government officials may go. As policies near the extremes, public pressures pull them back toward the mainstream. Thus, we see in these policy mood data a tendency for public opinion to swing against what is often seen as the prevailing political tendency. As an example, the public mood swung in a decidedly liberal direction throughout the Reagan presidency.

Presidential Approval

For better or worse, the "buck" often stops at the White House. Americans typically judge their government by their President. This perspective – which might be thought of as government personalized – is commonly found among children (Greenstein 1965; Easton and Dennis 1969), and even though adults have much more complex images of the government, their impressions are often formed in response to presidential action or inaction in national and world events.

Since the mid-1930s, public opinion polls have regularly asked Americans what they thought about the performance of the incumbent President (Edwards and Gallup 1990). Although individual assessments of a sitting President can be quite detailed, the query used by the Gallup organization throughout this period is straightforward: Do you approve or disapprove of the way President [name of incumbent] has handled his job as President? Despite the limitations of this question (and two follow-up questions often asked of his specific handling of the economy and of foreign affairs), it remains a key indicator of general levels of public support for the President and an indicator of presidential "power" (Neustadt 1960; Brace and Hinckley 1992).

Annual averages of public responses to the Gallup presidential job approval question for the period 1948–2000 are reported in Table Eb318–328. The degree of variation around these annual averages is reflected in the highest and lowest support reported for any individual poll for each year. Although the individual polls are not reported in the series, Figure Eb-C does show the intra-annual variation in public support for the President and highlights the degree of variation surrounding the annual averages.

Common patterns in this series have been observed by many scholars. With few exceptions, to be popular as President is to be popular early in the administration. The political "honeymoon" of newly elected leaders is quite visibly captured in the graph of public support for each administration from Truman to Clinton. This initial approval is usually followed by a decline in popularity. George Herbert Walker Bush is the clear exception. Unlike the common pattern with other Presidents, Bush's approval rating steadily increased during his first three years in office. His fourth-year crash in the polls, from the highest job approval rating ever recorded, was closely followed by only the second electoral defeat of an incumbent President in the last seventy years.

In addition to the commonly noted deterioration of support as the President's electoral coalition gradually unwinds, a "rally round the flag" effect has often been observed at times of international crisis (Mueller 1970; Hurwitz and Peffley 1987). Upturns in presidential approval occur during wars and external threats to American national security. That this public response is widely recognized often breeds cynicism about presidential decisions to participate in foreign affairs.

As Neustadt observed, the power of the President is the "power to persuade" (Neustadt 1960). This power to persuade Congress is often a function of the standing the President has with the general public. In both the examination of presidential support and in the passage of particular legislation, public opinion has often been considered a key explanatory variable.[26]

The Future of Survey Data

Clearly, the value of survey data will increase as the collection of these data expands over time. A number of common difficulties arise in the use of public opinion time series data. Often unconsidered, but perhaps the most common difficulty, is the lack of easily accessible data archives for polling data. Some of these data are

---

[25] Fifty years of these self-identifications can be found within the Continuity Guide to the American National Elections, available at the Internet site of the National Election Studies (NES).

[26] The work of Mueller (1973), Zeidenstein (1983, 1985), Ostrom and Simon (1985), Rivers and Rose (1985), Edwards (1989), Bond and Fleisher (1990), Canes-Wrone and de Marchi (2002), and Erikson, Mackuen, and Stimson (2002) provides a small sample of the research examining the interrelationships of public preferences and national government policies mediated by the critical standing of the President.

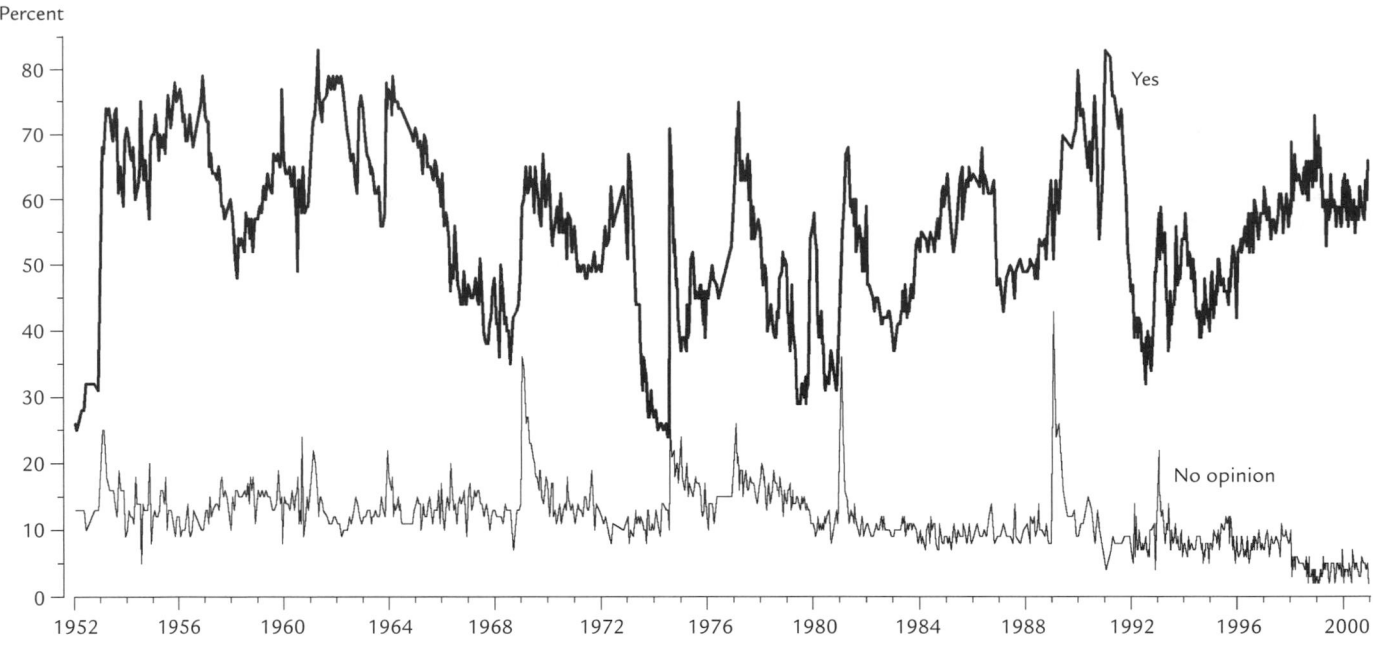

FIGURE Eb-C   Presidential approval: 1952–2000

Sources

George C. Edwards III and Alec M. Gallup, *Presidential Approval: A Sourcebook* (Johns Hopkins University Press, 1990); Lyn Ragsdale, *Vital Statistics on the*

Presidency: Washington to Clinton (Congressional Quarterly Press, 1996); *The Gallup Poll Monthly* (October 2000): 10–12.

lost, while others are merely lost from easy public access. Other common problems arising in the analysis of public opinion data collected over long periods of time include the following: lack of consistent wording; alteration of word meaning; changing sampling techniques; changing interviewing techniques; and "house" (survey organization) effects (Converse and Schuman 1984; Smith 1987).

Each of these problems arises in the analysis of any of the extended time series of public opinion. Indeed, the reader will notice that many of the series reported here could have begun with the first Gallup surveys of 1935 and 1936. They do not, in large part, because these early surveys suffer from enough weaknesses that they were set aside as potentially not comparable with more contemporary data. Early polls, especially those conducted prior to the 1948 campaign, often chose samples with less scientific rigor than we insist on today. Early surveys did not strive for simple demographic balance. Some Southern samples, for example, exclude black respondents. Other surveys did not use probability sampling strategies that allow reasonable inferences to be drawn from the collected survey responses.

But despite their limitations, these time series of public preferences provide critical insights that are simply not observed in the historical time series of elections and institutional control that dominate discussions of political periods in American history. These series help to define the context within which political parties compete for votes. Similarly, they define for the party in office, as well as for their future challengers, the nature of the public agenda to which successful politicians must speak. This is not to insist that public preferences are exogenous in all instances. Politicians by their words and by their actions can affect both the centrality and evaluation of government for the public agenda. But politicians evade the majority of the public at their own peril over the long haul.

Conclusion

The statistical series reported in this chapter represent the story of American politics over the past 200 years. Elections serve as mechanisms linking voter preferences with government officials whose decisions produce public policies. Party groups act as key aggregators of those preferences and the principal means by which governments are organized and policies enacted. For this reason alone, many of the series are about the behavior or preferences of partisans, either in the general public or the political elite.

Multiple stories may be told with these data. Some observers take the position that politicians in government lead the public into accepting the outcomes of the political process. This process may be viewed as benign (with citizens educated by their political leaders) or malevolent (where leadership manipulates citizens). In either case, elections may be seen to follow the decisions of political elites. Others will find a more optimistic image within the details of these historical trends: elections select leaders who deliver democratically chosen policy outcomes. From this perspective, politicians, feeling the call of the reelection imperative, respond to the preferences of their constituents. Within the diverse community that is America, majority preferences are enacted without fear of majority tyranny, as once expressed by the authors of the Federalist Papers. A third set of scholars may find that these data only produce further evidence of the "paradox of modern democracy": despite a mostly uninformed public, the United States has survived as a relatively stable democracy for more than 200 years (Delli Carpini and Keeter 1996).

These data will not definitively answer the question, "Which portrayal is correct?" But there is enough here to stimulate both sides of the debate. The degree to which the American experiment has successfully produced a democratic polity remains an open and important question.

At the same time, American political history is not well represented as a straight-line extrapolation of trends. Unique events have played (and will continue to play) enormously important roles in defining opportunities for parties and political leaders, while influencing the public's view of their generation's problems and successes. Some of these events are set out in Table Eb-D. The assassination of Presidents, the clash of armies, the crash of markets and economies, and the attack of terrorists seem destined to define eras in American politics. Extraordinary events complicate our explanations of historical paths. They do not, however, make drawing inferences about political history impossible. These data provide the basis for expectations and baselines for understanding deviations from the past.

TABLE Eb-D   Chronology of U.S. elections and politics: 1775–2000

1775	The Revolutionary War begins.
1776	The Second Continental Congress adopts the Declaration of Independence.
1781	The Articles of Confederation are ratified.
1783	The Treaty of Paris ends the Revolutionary War.
1787	Shay's Rebellion in western Massachusetts.
1787	Constitutional Convention convenes in Philadelphia.
1788	The Constitution is ratified.
1789	George Washington is elected as the first President of the United States.
1789	The First Congress convenes in New York City.
1789	The Federal Judiciary Act establishes a six-member U.S. Supreme Court, as well as a district and circuit court system. John Jay is chosen as the first Chief Justice of the Supreme Court.
1791	The Bill of Rights is ratified.
1791	Washington, D.C., is established as the site for the U.S. capital.
1792	The Democratic–Republican Party organizes in opposition to the "Federalist" establishment.
1794	The Whiskey Rebellion breaks out in western Pennsylvania among farmers who oppose the collection of the tax on liquor and stills.
1795	Jay's Treaty provides for withdrawal of British forces from the Northwest Territory by June 1, 1796, in exchange for payments of war debts to British citizens.
1795	In response to the Supreme Court's 1793 decision in *Chisholm v. Georgia*, the Eleventh Amendment is ratified to prevent citizens of one state from suing another state in the federal courts.
1795	John Rutledge serves as acting Chief Justice following Jay's resignation, but the Senate refuses to confirm him.
1796	Oliver Ellsworth is confirmed as Chief Justice.
1796	John Adams (Federalist) is elected President.
1798	The Alien and Sedition Acts are enacted.
1800	Congress convenes in Washington, D.C., for the first time.
1800	Thomas Jefferson is chosen as the President over incumbent John Adams in a contested election that is decided in the House of Representatives.
1801	The War with Tripoli begins and will last until 1805.
1801	John Marshall begins 34 years as Chief Justice.
1803	In *Marbury v. Madison,* the Supreme Court rules that an act of Congress is null and void when it conflicts with provisions of the U.S. Constitution.
1803	The Louisiana purchase ($15 million) doubles the land area of the United States.
1804	Passage of the Twelfth Amendment: election of President and Vice President on separate ballots.
1804	The House of Representatives votes to impeach Supreme Court Justice Samuel Chase, but the Senate does not convict.
1808	The Osage, a Sioux tribe, sign the Osage Treaty ceding their lands in what is now Missouri and Arkansas to the United States.
1808	James Madison (Democratic–Republican) is elected President.
1810	The Supreme Court declares a state law unconstitutional for the first time (*Fletcher v. Peck*).
1812	The War of 1812 begins.
1816	In *Martin v. Hunter's Lessee*, the Supreme Court asserts its authority over state courts as interpreter of the Constitution and acts of Congress.
1816	James Monroe (Democratic–Republican) is elected President.
1819	In *McCulloch v. Maryland*, the Supreme Court interprets the "necessary and proper" clause of Article 1 to provide the implied power to carry out the duties of the federal government enumerated in the Constitution. This case dramatically defines the distribution of power in the federal system: when state and federal law conflict, federal law is supreme.
1820	The Missouri Compromise balances slave and free states admitted to the union. Missouri is admitted as a slave state, but no slavery will be permitted anywhere north of Missouri's southern border.
1823	President Monroe announces the Monroe Doctrine: the United States will not tolerate European interference in the Western Hemisphere.
1824	John Quincy Adams (Democratic–Republican), son of John Adams, is elected President in a contested election that ends in the House of Representatives. Speaker of the House Henry Clay uses his influence to elect Adams, an action bitterly resented by candidate Andrew Jackson, whose 99 electoral votes make him a logical choice. Adams names Clay his Secretary of State.

(continued)

TABLE Eb-D   Chronology of U.S. elections and politics: 1775–2000   *Continued*

1824	In *Gibbons v. Ogden*, the Supreme Court expands the scope of federal authority by defining the government's ability to regulate interstate commerce.
1828	Andrew Jackson (Democrat) is elected President.
1830	President Andrew Jackson signs the Indian Removal Act authorizing the move of several tribes to western lands.
1831	Nat Turner leads a slave uprising in which 70 whites are killed; 100 blacks are killed in a search for Turner.
1831	Alexis de Tocqueville and his friend Gustave de Beaumont spend nine months touring America. The book that de Tocqueville writes after this trip, *Democracy in America*, would be published in 1835.
1832	South Carolina Ordinance of Nullification. Based on John Calhoun's theory of states' rights, South Carolina attempts to nullify certain acts of the Congress of the United States.
1834	The Whig Party is formed.
1836	Roger Taney is confirmed as Chief Justice.
1836	Santa Anna leads 3,000 men in a siege of the Alamo, killing all 187 Texans inside.
1836	Martin Van Buren (Democrat) is elected President.
1838	The Underground Railroad is organized.
1839	The Spanish slave ship *Amistad*, carrying fifty three slaves, is taken over in a mutiny by their leader, Cinque. Before the Supreme Court, John Quincy Adams argues their right to be freed.
1840	William Henry Harrison (Whig) is elected President but catches pneumonia during his inauguration. He survives only one month.
1841	Vice President John Tyler (Whig) assumes the presidency on Harrison's death in April.
1844	James K. Polk (Democrat) is elected President.
1846	At President Polk's request, on May 11 Congress declares the United States at war with Mexico.
1848	The Mexican War ends with the Treaty of Guadalupe Hidalgo. In exchange for $15 million and the settling of $3.25 million in American claims, Mexico cedes some 500,000 square miles of its territory in the western and southwestern United States.
1848	Lucretia Mott and Elizabeth Cady Stanton organize the first American women's rights convention in Seneca Falls, New York, where the Declaration of Sentiments was signed.
1848	Zachary Taylor (Whig) is elected President.
1849	Harriet Tubman (1820–1913) escapes to the North and begins working with the Underground Railroad.
1850	The Fugitive Slave Act provides for the return of slaves brought to free states.
1850	The Compromise of 1850 admits California as a free state and Texas as a slave state; New Mexico and Utah are organized with no restrictions on slavery.
1850	Millard Fillmore (Whig) assumes the presidency with the death of Zachary Taylor.
1852	Franklin Pierce (Democrat) is elected President, defeating the last significant Whig presidential candidate, Winfield Scott.
1854	The Kansas–Nebraska Act passes, allowing "popular sovereignty"; the net effect was to negate the Missouri Compromise (1820).
1854	The Republican Party is established (Ripon, Wisconsin).
1856	James Buchanan (Democrat) is elected President.
1857	*Dred Scott v. Sandford* decision by the Supreme Court. After being brought to free territory by his owner, Scott sued for his freedom, but the Court ruled that he had never ceased to be a slave, denied that he was a citizen, and denied him the right to sue.
1859	John Brown leads an abolitionist raid on the federal arsenal at Harper's Ferry, West Virginia.
1860	Abraham Lincoln is elected President.
1860	South Carolina votes to secede from the Union.
1861	An attack on Fort Sumter off the coast of Charleston, South Carolina, on April 12 signals the beginning of the Civil War.
1863	The Emancipation Proclamation is signed January 1.
1864	Salmon Chase is confirmed as Chief Justice.
1865	The Ku Klux Klan (KKK) is founded to maintain white supremacy through intimidation and violence.
1865	The Freedmen's Bureau is formed during Reconstruction to assist freed slaves in the South.
1865	The Civil War ends when Lee surrenders to Grant at Appomattox Court House.
1865	On April 14th, Lincoln is shot by John Wilkes Booth and dies the following day. Andrew Johnson becomes President.
1865	The Thirteenth Amendment abolishes slavery.
1866	The Civil Rights Act grants citizenship to native-born Americans, except Indians.
1867	Secretary of State Seward purchases Alaska from Russia for $7.2 million. Congressional critics call this "Seward's Folly."
1867	Congress passes the Reconstruction Acts of 1867. The ten ex-Confederate states still without federal representation must eliminate all racial barriers to suffrage as a precondition for readmission.
1868	The Fourteenth Amendment grants full citizenship to all individuals born or naturalized in the United States, except Native Americans. It precludes states from making laws to restrict the rights of citizens of the United States.
1868	The impeachment trial of President Andrew Johnson ends in his acquittal.
1868	Civil War veteran General Ulysses S. Grant (Republican) is elected President.
1869	The Union Pacific–Central Pacific transcontinental railroad is completed as the two lines meet at Promontory Point, Utah.
1869	Wyoming territory passes the first woman's suffrage act.
1869	The number of justices on the Supreme Court rises from seven to nine.
1869	Elizabeth Cady Stanton is elected president of the National Woman Suffrage Association, which demands federal voting rights for women. Susan B. Anthony is elected president of the American Equal Rights Association.
1870	The Fifteenth Amendment establishes the right of African-American men to vote.

TABLE Eb-D Chronology of U.S. elections and politics: 1775–2000 _Continued_

1870	Congress enacts the "Ku Klux Klan Act of 1870" or "Enforcement Act" to stop Southern white resistance to the power African Americans have gained during Reconstruction.
1870	The Department of Justice is created.
1874	Morrison Waite becomes Chief Justice.
1875	The Civil Rights Act grants equal access to public accommodations.
1875	The Supreme Court decision of _Minor v. Happersett_ allows states to set suffrage requirements and denies women voting rights.
1876	Ignoring warnings of a massed Sioux army of 2,000 to 4,000 men, Custer and 250 soldiers attack the forces of Sitting Bull and Crazy Horse at the Little Big Horn. Custer and all of his men die in the attack.
1876	The presidential election fails to produce a decisive outcome, sending the contest to the House of Representatives.
1877	The Electoral Commission Bill authorizes a committee of fifteen to decide the election between Hayes and Tilden. The committee's votes split along party lines. On March 3, Hayes is announced as President after House Republicans agree, among other concessions, to pull out federal troops from the South.
1880	James A. Garfield (Republican) is elected President.
1881	President Garfield is shot on July 2. After Garfield's death on September 19, Chester A. Arthur becomes President.
1883	The Pendleton Civil Service Act is passed to reform the corruption in the civil service.
1883	In what are known as the Civil Rights cases, the Supreme Court declares the Civil Rights Act of 1875 unconstitutional.
1884	Grover Cleveland (Democrat) is elected President (for the first time).
1886	To celebrate the centennial of the Declaration of Independence, the Statue of Liberty is dedicated in New York harbor as an international symbol of political freedom.
1887	The Interstate Commerce Act is passed.
1888	The Senate confirms Melville Fuller as the Chief Justice of the Supreme Court.
1888	Benjamin Harrison (Republican) is elected President.
1890	The Sherman Anti-Trust Law is enacted.
1890	The last major armed conflict between Native Americans and the U.S. Army takes place at Wounded Knee Creek, South Dakota.
1891	The Populist Party is formed in Cincinnati, Ohio.
1891	The Judiciary (Evarts) Act establishes the U.S. Courts of Appeals.
1892	Ellis Island opens as a federal immigration station. More than twelve million immigrants will pass through its doors during its sixty-two years in operation.
1892	Grover Cleveland (Democrat) is elected President (for the second time).
1893	Panic of 1893. This economic crisis and the three-year depression that follows produce a realignment of the political parties, solidifying Republican control over the presidency and Congress.
1893	In Hawai'i, Queen Liliuokalani's government is overthrown; Hawai'i becomes a U.S. protectorate despite President Cleveland's opposition.
1894	In Chicago, after the Pullman Palace Car Company reduces wages, workers strike (May 11 to August 3). A general sympathy strike ensues on June 26. Despite protests by Illinois Governor John P. Altgeld, deputy marshals and U.S. troops are called out to quell the strikers.
1896	The Supreme Court validates the principle of "separate but equal" in _Plessy v. Ferguson_.
1896	William McKinley (Republican) defeats William Jennings Bryan to win election as President of the United States.
1898	The explosion and sinking of the battleship _Maine_ in Havana harbor results in 260 deaths. It becomes a justification for the Spanish–American War.
1901	President McKinley is shot by Leon Czolgosz in Buffalo, New York. He dies of his wounds on September 14, and Vice President Theodore Roosevelt is sworn in as President.
1903	The Hay–Buneau–Varilla treaty establishes the Panama Canal Zone.
1905	The Niagara Movement is founded to fight for school integration and voting rights and to assist African-American political candidates; forerunner of the National Association for the Advancement of Colored People (NAACP).
1906	Race riot in Greensburg, Indiana – the first of many in reaction to the migration of African Americans to the North.
1908	William Howard Taft (Republican) is elected President.
1909	W. E. B. DuBois founds the NAACP to fight for civil rights through legal action and education.
1910	Associate Justice Edward White is promoted to Chief Justice.
1910	Speaker of the House Joseph Cannon is stripped of most of his powers. Committees, party caucuses, and seniority play important new roles in the organization of Congress.
1912	The _Farm Journal_ magazine straw poll predicts the presidential election.
1912	Woodrow Wilson (Democrat) is elected President.
1913	The Sixteenth Amendment is ratified, providing for a graduated national income tax. The Underwood–Simmons Tariff Act implements the newly approved income tax.
1913	The Seventeenth Amendment is ratified, providing for the direct election of senators.
1913	The Federal Reserve Act establishes a regional federal bank system to promote economic development and stabilization.
1914	The Clayton Antitrust Act and the Federal Trade Commission Act are enacted to define the scope of federal intervention in the economy.

(continued)

TABLE Eb-D Chronology of U.S. elections and politics: 1775–2000 *Continued*

1914	The Panama Canal opens for shipping.
1915	Refounding of the Ku Klux Klan.
1916	The *Literary Digest* begins predicting elections based on magazine straw polls.
1916	The first Jewish Supreme Court justice, Louis Brandeis, is confirmed.
1917	Saying that "the world must be made safe for democracy," Wilson asks Congress to declare war on Germany (April 2).
1917	Rule XXII (cloture) is adopted by the Senate to limit debate.
1919	Signing of the Versailles Treaty, which the Senate later refuses to ratify.
1920	The Eighteenth Amendment goes into effect January 16, prohibiting the manufacture, sale, or transportation of intoxicating liquors.
1920	The Nineteenth Amendment grants voting rights to women.
1920	The American Civil Liberties Union (ACLU) is established.
1920	Warren G. Harding (Republican) is elected President.
1921	William Howard Taft becomes the first former President to serve as Chief Justice.
1921	With the Budget and Accounting Act, Congress creates the General Accounting Office as a legislative agency and the Bureau of the Budget (later the Office of Management and Budget) as an executive agency.
1923	President Harding dies in office. Calvin Coolidge is sworn in as President on August 3.
1923	The Teapot Dome scandal erupts as the deal between Harry F. Sinclair of Mammoth Oil and Secretary of the Interior Albert B. Fall is revealed. Fall is the first cabinet member in U.S. history to go to jail.
1924	American Indians are granted citizenship and the right to vote.
1925	Judiciary Act of 1925. Congress grants the Supreme Court control of its docket through writs of certiorari.
1928	Herbert Hoover (Republican) is elected President of the United States, defeating Democratic Party challenger Alfred E. Smith.
1929	The stock market crash marks the beginning of the Great Depression.
1930	Charles Evans Hughes replaces Taft as Chief Justice.
1932	In an election that changes the face of American politics, Franklin D. Roosevelt (Democrat) is elected President and the Democratic Party wins the majority of both chambers of the Congress.
1933	The Twentieth Amendment is adopted, reducing the "lame duck" period, with Congress to assemble January 3 and presidential terms to begin January 20. Also, presidential succession is modified.
1933	The Twenty-first Amendment is ratified, repealing the Eighteenth Amendment.
1933	Roosevelt's "First 100 Days" begins the establishment of a new federal bureaucracy. Among the agencies established are the Agricultural Adjustment Administration (AAA), the Civilian Conservation Corps (CCC), the Federal Deposit Insurance Corporation (FDIC), the Immigration and Naturalization Service (INS), the National Resources Planning Board, the Rural Electrification Administration, and the Tennessee Valley Authority (TVA).
1934	Additional pieces of the New Deal bureaucracy established this year include the Securities and Exchange Commission (SEC), the Federal Communications Commission (FCC), the National Archives, the Federal Housing Administration (FHA), and the National Mediation Board.
1935	The American Institute of Public Opinion (AIPO) is founded by George Gallup.
1935	The Federal Bureau of Investigation (FBI), the National Bureau of Labor Relations, the Federal Power Commission, and the Social Security Board are established.
1936	*Literary Digest* preelection straw poll mispredicts Alf Landon as the winner. New pollsters Gallup, Roper, and Crossley, employing scientific samples, correctly predict Roosevelt's reelection.
1937	President Roosevelt's "Court packing" plan is announced.
1937	In a series of decisions, the Supreme Court upholds key elements of Roosevelt's New Deal (*West Coast Hotel v. Parrish*; *NLRB v. Jones & Laughlin Steel*; *Steward Machine Co. v. Davis*; and *Helvering v. Davis*).
1938	*United States v. Carolene Products* announces the standards for the selective incorporation of the Bill of Rights. The Court asserts the power to carefully scrutinize laws that threaten the integrity of the political process or deny due process on the basis of "suspect classifications" such as race, religion, and gender.
1939	Congress passes the Reorganization Act, expanding the White House staff and giving Roosevelt authority to create the Executive Office of the President and reorganize the federal departments.
1941	Japan attacks U.S. ships at Pearl Harbor, and the United States enters World War II.
1941	Harlan Stone becomes Chief Justice.
1942	Congress of Racial Equality (CORE) is founded to fight for civil rights using nonviolent, direct-action protests.
1942	Executive Order 9066 forces more than 100,000 Japanese Americans into detention camps.
1944	In *Smith v. Allright*, the Supreme Court declares the Southern Democratic "all white primary" unconstitutional and invalidates the doctrine that political parties, being private associations, could exclude blacks (or any others they chose to exclude) from their nominating processes.
1944	In *Korematsu v. United States*, the Supreme Court permits citizens to be imprisoned based on their race.
1945	President Franklin Roosevelt dies. Vice President Harry Truman succeeds him in office.
1945	The U.S. drops atomic bombs on Hiroshima and Nagasaki. World War II ends.
1945	Harry S. Truman (Democrat) is elected President.
1946	Fred Vinson becomes Chief Justice.
1946	The Legislative Reorganization Act restructures the congressional committee system.

TABLE Eb-D Chronology of U.S. elections and politics: 1775–2000 *Continued*

1947	Congress passes the Taft–Hartley Act (also known as the Labor–Management Relations Act) over Truman's veto. This law restricted union access to the workplace and union political activity. It also permitted the federal government to seek injunctions against any work stoppage that threatened "national health or safety."
1947	The Marshall Plan is announced to help rebuild postwar Europe.
1948	Harry S. Truman is reelected President, contrary to the predictions of opinion pollsters famously captured in a "Dewey Wins" newspaper headline.
1948	President Truman ends segregation in the U.S. military.
1949	The North Atlantic Treaty is approved by the U.S. Senate.
1950	The Korean War begins.
1951	The Twenty-second Amendment is ratified: Presidents are limited to two elected terms.
1952	Dwight D. Eisenhower is elected President.
1953	Earl Warren becomes Chief Justice.
1954	In *Brown v. Board of Education of Topeka*, the Supreme Court overturns the principle of "separate but equal" that had been established by *Plessy v. Ferguson*.
1955	Rosa Parks begins the Montgomery bus boycott.
1957	President Eisenhower sends U.S. Army troops to Little Rock, Arkansas, to enforce the desegregation of schools.
1957	The Southern Christian Leadership Conference (SCLC) is founded to coordinate localized Southern efforts to fight for civil rights.
1960	Sit-in at the F. W. Woolworth lunch counter in Greensboro, North Carolina (February 1).
1960	Hundreds of university students stage a sit-in at downtown stores in Nashville, Tennessee, to protest segregated lunch counters.
1960	The Student Nonviolent Coordinating Committee (SNCC) is founded to coordinate student-led efforts to end segregation.
1960	The Civil Rights Act reaffirms voting rights for all Americans.
1960	The first televised presidential debates match Republican Vice President Richard Nixon against Democratic Senator John F. Kennedy.
1960	John F. Kennedy (Democrat) is elected President.
1961	The Twenty-third Amendment extends suffrage to the District of Columbia for presidential elections.
1961	Integrated groups of protesters join Freedom Rides on buses across the South to protest segregation.
1962	The Supreme Court asserts the right to establish standards for voting districts in *Baker v. Carr*.
1962	Cuban Missile Crisis.
1962	César Chávez establishes the National Farm Workers Association.
1963	Hundreds of thousands of Americans take part in the March on Washington to call for racial equality.
1963	President Kennedy is assassinated by Lee Harvey Oswald, and Lyndon Johnson is sworn in as President.
1964	The Twenty-fourth Amendment prohibits laws that used failure to pay taxes (notably poll taxes) as a reason for denying individuals the right to vote; the amendment applies to national elections.
1964	The Civil Rights Act outlaws discrimination in public accommodations and by employers.
1964	The Organization for Afro-American Unity (OAU) is formed to promote closer ties between African Americans and Africa.
1964	Congress passes the Gulf of Tonkin Resolution.
1964	In *Wesberry v. Sanders* and *Reynolds v. Sims*, the Supreme Court establishes the principle of "one person, one vote" in reapportioning congressional and state legislative districts.
1965	The Voting Rights Act nullifies local laws and practices that prevent minorities from voting.
1965	Malcolm X is assassinated.
1966	In *South Carolina v. Katzenbach*, the Supreme Court upholds the constitutionality of the Voting Rights Act of 1965.
1966	In *Harper v. State Board of Elections*, the Supreme Court extends the Twenty-fourth Amendment (prohibition against denying voting rights on the basis of the failure to pay taxes); the amendment now applies not just to national elections, but to state and local elections as well.
1967	The Twenty-fifth Amendment modifies presidential and vice presidential succession and establishes procedures for presidential disability.
1967	Thurgood Marshall becomes the first black citizen to serve as a Supreme Court justice.
1968	Martin Luther King Jr. is assassinated.
1968	The Civil Rights Act outlaws discrimination in the sale or rental of housing.
1968	Richard M. Nixon (Republican) defeats Vice President Hubert Humphrey to win election as President.
1969	Warren Burger becomes Chief Justice.
1970	The Civil Rights Act of 1970 prohibited the use of literacy tests as a requirement for voting lowered the minimum voting age from 21 to 18 in all federal and state elections, and lowered the minimum residence requirement for voting in presidential elections to a uniform thirty days. The Act is upheld by the Supreme Court in *Oregon v. Mitchell*.
1970	The Legislative Reorganization Act of 1970 encouraged open committee meetings, required written rules and public or recorded votes, permitted media coverage of committee hearings, and safeguarded the rights of minority party members.
1971	Ratification of the Twenty-sixth Amendment, which lowers the voting age minimum from 21 to 18.
1971	Congress consolidates earlier efforts at campaign finance reform in passing the Federal Election Campaign Act (FECA).

(continued)

TABLE Eb-D Chronology of U.S. elections and politics: 1775–2000 *Continued*

1972	The bungled burglary of the Democratic Party headquarters at the Watergate Hotel during the Nixon reelection campaign haunts the President and the Republican Party for many years.
1973	The War Powers Act is passed by Congress over the veto of President Nixon.
1973	The Supreme Court expands a right to privacy with its decision in *Roe v. Wade*, legalizing abortion.
1973	The House of Representatives accepts a subcommittee "Bill of Rights," decentralizing power by granting subcommittees the authority to hold hearings and act on matters referred to them.
1974	President Richard Nixon resigns in the wake of congressional investigations. Vice President Gerald R. Ford assumes office.
1974	Congress amends the 1971 FECA to set limits on campaign contributions by individuals, political parties, and political action committees (PACs). The 1974 amendments also establish an independent agency – the Federal Election Commission (FEC) – to enforce the law, facilitate disclosure, and administer the public funding program.
1974	Congress passes the Congressional Budget and Impoundment Control Act to reassert the role of the House and Senate in the budget process.
1975	The Senate changes its cloture rule, loosening the requirement to end filibusters from two thirds to three fifths of those present and voting.
1976	In *Buckley v. Valeo*, the Supreme Court rules that federal government limits on campaign spending violate First Amendment guarantees of free speech.
1976	James Earl ("Jimmy") Carter Jr. (Democrat) defeats President Gerald Ford in the first post-Watergate presidential election.
1979	The American embassy in Tehran is seized by Iranian students on November 4, 1979. A rescue attempt fails (April 24, 1980), and the ensuing stalemate over American hostages at the embassy is not resolved until Ronald Reagan's inauguration.
1980	Ronald Reagan (Republican) defeats incumbent Jimmy Carter to become President.
1981	Sandra Day O'Connor becomes the first woman member of the Supreme Court.
1983	The legislative veto is ruled unconstitutional in *Immigration and Naturalization Service v. Chadha*.
1986	Associate Justice William Rehnquist is promoted to Chief Justice.
1988	Vice President George Herbert Walker Bush (Republican) is elected President.
1991	U.S. success in the Gulf War against Iraq pushes President Bush's public approval to the highest level recorded for an American President since the end of the Second World War.
1992	The Twenty-seventh Amendment is ratified, requiring a built-in delay for any law affecting the pay of members of Congress; such laws do not take effect until after the next election for the House of Representatives.
1992	George H. W. Bush loses his reelection bid, and William Clinton (Democrat) is elected President.
1993	Congress passes the National Voter Registration Act of 1993 ("Motor Voter Law"), to become effective January 1, 1995.
1994	Republicans win control of Congress for the first time in forty years.
1996	Congress authorizes a "line item" veto for the President.
1998	President William Clinton becomes the second President to be impeached by the House of Representatives; he is acquitted in the Senate trial.
1998	In *Clinton v. City of New York*, the Supreme Court declares the presidential line item veto unconstitutional.
2000	Texas Governor George W. Bush (Republican) defeats Democrat Vice President Albert Gore in a presidential election conceded only after the U.S. Supreme Court, in a 5–4 decision, prevented ballot recounts in Florida.

Sources

Arthur M. Schlesinger Jr., *The Almanac of American History* (Barnes and Noble, 1993).

Lee Epstein, Jeffrey A. Segal, et al., *The Supreme Court Compendium: Data, Decisions, and Developments* (Congressional Quarterly Press, 1996).

Donna M. Campbell, "Brief Timeline of American Literature and Events: Pre-1620 to 1920," downloaded from Campbell's Web page at the Internet site of Gonzaga University.

Smithsonian Institution, "American History Timeline" and "Political History," in *Encyclopedia Smithsonian*, downloaded from the Institution's Internet site.

Brian Balogh, Joanna Grisinger, and Phillip Zelikow, "Making Democracy Work: A Brief History of Federal Executive Reorganization" (Miller Center of Public Affairs, University of Virginia, 2002), downloaded from the Internet site of the Miller Center of Public Affairs at the University of Virginia.

Joint Committee on the Organization of Congress, "Organization of the Congress" (1993), downloaded from the Internet site of the U.S. House of Representatives.

References

Adler, E. Scott. 2002. *Why Congressional Reforms Fail*. University of Chicago Press.

Aldrich, John H. 1999. "Political Parties in a Critical Era." *American Politics Quarterly* 27: 9–32.

Aldrich, John H., and Richard G. Niemi. 1996. "The Sixth American Party System: Electoral Change, 1952–1992." In S. Craig, editor. *Broken Contract: Changing Relationships between Americans and Their Government*. Westview Press.

Bollen, Kenneth. 1980. "Issues in the Comparative Measurement of Political Democracy." *American Sociological Review* 45: 370–90.

Bollen, Kenneth. 1993. "Liberal Democracy: Validity and Method Factors in Cross-National Measures." *American Journal of Political Science* 37: 1207–30.

Bollen, Kenneth, and Burke D. Grandjean. 1981. "The Dimension(s) of Democracy: Further Issues in the Measurement and Effects of Political Democracy." *American Sociological Review* 46: 651–9.

Bond, Jon R., and Richard Fleisher. 1990. *The President in the Legislative Arena*. University of Chicago Press.

Brace, Paul, and Barbara Hinckley. 1992. *Follow the Leader: Opinion Polls and the Modern Presidents*. HarperCollins.

Brady, David W. 1988. *Critical Elections and Congressional Policy Making.* Stanford University Press.

Burnham, Walter Dean. 1955. *Presidential Ballots, 1836 to 1892.* Johns Hopkins University Press and Oxford University Press.

Burnham, Walter Dean. 1965. "The Changing Shape of the American Political University." *American Political Science Review* 59: 1–40.

Burnham, Walter Dean. 1970. *Critical Elections and the Mainsprings of American Politics.* Norton.

Burnham, Walter Dean. 1970/1979. "State-Level Congressional, Gubernatorial and Senatorial Election Data for the United States, 1824–1972." Inter-university Consortium for Political and Social Research (computer file).

Burnham, Walter Dean. 1974. "Theory and Voting Research: Some Reflections on Converse's 'Change in the American Electorate.'" *American Political Science Review* 68: 1002–23.

Burnham, Walter Dean. 1975. "Elections and Politics: Series Y1–271." In *Historical Statistics of the United States.* U.S. Government Printing Office.

Burnham, Walter Dean. 1980/1987. "Partisan Division of American State Governments, 1834–1985." Inter-university Consortium for Political and Social Research (computer file).

Burnham, Walter Dean. 1994. "Pattern Recognition and 'Doing' Political History: Art, Science or Bootless Enterprise?" In Lawrence C. Dodd and Calvin Jillson, editors. *The Dynamics of American Politics: Approaches and Interpretations.* Westview Press.

Burns, James McGregor. 1963. *The Deadlock of Democracy: Four-Party Politics in America.* Prentice Hall.

Burns, James McGregor. 1966. *Congress on Trial: The Legislative Process and the Administrative State.* Gordian Press.

Cameron, Charles M. 2000. *Veto Bargaining: Presidents and the Politics of Negative Power.* Cambridge University Press.

Campbell, Angus. 1966. "Surge and Decline: A Study of Electoral Change." In Angus Campbell, Philip E. Converse, et al., editors. *Elections and the Political Order.* Wiley.

Campbell, Angus, Philip E. Converse, et al., editors. 1960. *The American Voter.* Wiley.

Campbell, Angus, Philip E. Converse, et al. 1966. *Elections and the Political Order.* Wiley.

Campbell, Angus, Gerald Gurin, and Warren E. Miller. 1954. *The Voter Decides.* Row, Peterson.

Campbell, Bruce A., and Richard J. Trilling, editors. 1979. *Realignment in American Politics: Toward a Theory.* University of Texas Press.

Campbell, James E. 1987. "The Revised Theory of Surge and Decline." *American Journal of Political Science* 31: 965–79.

Canes-Wrone, Brandice, and Scott de Marchi. 2002. "Presidential Approval and Legislative Success." *Journal of Politics* 64: 491–509.

Carmines, Edward G., and James A. Stimson. 1989. *Issue Evolution: Race and the Transformation of American Politics.* Princeton University Press.

Chamberlain, Lawrence H. 1946. *The President, Congress, and Legislation.* Columbia University Press.

Claggett, William. 1990. "Reported and Validated Voter Registration." *American Politics Quarterly* 18: 197–207.

Clubb, Jerome M., William H. Flanigan, and Nancy H. Zingale. 1980. *Partisan Realignment: Voters, Parties and Government in American History.* Sage.

Coleman, John J. 1997. "The Importance of Being Republican: Forecasting Party Fortunes in House Midterm Elections." *Journal of Politics* 59: 497–519.

Collier, Kenneth, and Terry Sullivan. 1995. "New Evidence Undercutting the Linkage of Approval with Presidential Support and Influence." *Journal of Politics* 57: 197–209.

Converse, Jean M. 1987. *Survey Research in the United States: Roots and Emergence.* University of California Press.

Converse, Jean, and Howard Schuman. 1984. "The Manner of Inquiry: An Analysis of Survey Question Form across Organizations and over Time." In C. F. Turner and E. Martin, editors. *Surveying Subjective Phenomena,* volume 2. Russell Sage.

Converse, Philip E. 1964. "The Nature of Belief Systems in Mass Publics." In David Apter, editor. *Ideology and Discontent.* Free Press.

Converse, Philip E. 1972. "Change in the American Electorate." In Angus Campbell and Philip E. Converse, editors. *The Human Meaning of Social Change.* Russell Sage.

Copeland, Gary. 1983. "When Congress and the President Collide: Why Presidents Veto Legislation." *Journal of Politics* 45: 696–710.

Dahl, Robert A. 1956. *A Preface to Democratic Theory.* University of Chicago Press.

Dahl, Robert A. 1989. *Democracy and Its Critics.* Yale University Press.

Delli Carpini, Michael X., and Scott Keeter. 1996. *What Americans Know about Politics and Why It Matters.* Yale University Press.

Downs, Anthony. 1957. *An Economic Theory of Democracy.* Harper and Row.

Dugan, William E., and William A. Taggart. 1995. "The Changing Shape of the American Political Universe Revisited." *Journal of Politics* 57: 469–82.

Easton, David, and Jack Dennis. 1969. *Children in the Political System.* McGraw-Hill.

Edwards, George C., III. 1985. "Measuring Presidential Success in Congress: Alternative Approaches." *Journal of Politics* 47: 667–85.

Edwards, George C., III. 1989. *At the Margins: Presidential Leadership in Congress.* Yale University Press.

Edwards, George C., III, and Alec M. Gallup. 1990. *Presidential Approval: A Sourcebook.* Johns Hopkins University Press.

Erikson, Robert S. 1990. "Economic Conditions and the Congressional Vote: A Review of Macrolevel Evidence." *American Journal of Political Science* 34: 373–99.

Erikson, Robert S., Michael Mackuen, and James A. Stimson. 2002. *The Macro Polity.* Cambridge University Press.

Fellner, Jamie, and Marc Mauer. 1998. *Losing the Vote: The Impact of Felony Disenfranchisement Laws in the United States.* Human Rights Watch.

Fiorina, Morris P. 1996. *Divided Government,* 2nd edition. Allyn and Bacon.

Franklin, Daniel P., and Eric E. Grier. 1996. "Effects of Motor Voter Legislation: Voter Turnout, Registration, and Partisan Trends in the 1992 Presidential Election." *American Politics Quarterly* 25: 104–17.

Gastil, Raymond D. 1978. *Freedom in the World: Political Rights and Civil Liberties.* Freedom House.

Greenstein, Fred I. 1965. *Children and Politics.* Yale University Press.

Gurr, Ted Robert, Keith Jaggers, and Will H. Moore. 1990. "The Transformation of the Western State: The Growth of Democracy, Autocracy and State Power since 1800." *Studies in Comparative International Development* 25: 73–108.

Harper-Ho, Virginia. 2000. "Noncitizen Voting Rights: The History, the Law and Current Prospects for Change." *Law and Inequality* 18 (2): 271.

Harvard Law Review. 1989. "The Disenfranchisement of Ex-Felons: Citizenship, Criminality and the Purity of the Ballot Box." *Harvard Law Review* 102: 1300–17.

Harvey, Alice E. 1994. "Ex-Felons Disenfranchisement and Its Influence on the Black Vote: The Need for a Second Look." *University of Pennsylvania Law Review* 142: 1145–89.

Howell, William, E. Scott Adler, et al. 2000. "Measuring the Institutional Performance of Congress in the Post-war Era: Surges and Slumps in the Production of Legislation, 1945–1994." *Legislative Studies Quarterly* 25: 285–312.

Huntington, Samuel P. 1981. *American Politics: The Promise of Disharmony.* Harvard University Press.

Hurwitz, Jon, and Mark Peffley. 1987. "The Means and Ends of Foreign Policy as Determinants of Presidential Support." *American Journal of Political Science* 31: 236–58.

International Institute for Democracy and Electoral Assistance (IDEA). 2003. "Voter Turnout from 1945 to Date." Downloaded from the institute's Internet site.

Jackman, Robert W. 1987. "Political Institutions and Voter Turnout in Industrial Democracies." *American Political Science Review* 81: 405–24.

Jacobson, Gary C. 1990. "Does the Economy Matter in Midterm Elections?" *American Journal of Political Science* 34: 400–4.

Jillson, Calvin. 1994. "Patterns and Periodicity in American National Politics." In Lawrence C. Dodd and Calvin Jillson, editors. *The Dynamics of American Politics: Approaches and Interpretations.* Westview Press.

Jones, Charles O. 1994. *The Presidency in a Separated System.* Brookings Institution Press.

Kernell, Samuel. 1977. "Presidential Popularity and Negative Voting: An Alternative Explanation of the Midterm Congressional Decline of the President's Party." *American Political Science Review* 71: 44–66.

Key, V. O., Jr. 1955. "A Theory of Critical Elections." *Journal of Politics* 17: 3–18.

Key, V. O., Jr. 1959. "Secular Realignment and the Party System." *Journal of Politics* 21: 198–210.

Kleppner, Paul. 1982a. *The Dynamics of Electoral Turnout, 1870–1980.* Praeger.

Kleppner, Paul. 1982b. "Were Women to Blame? Female Suffrage and Voter Turnout." *Journal of Interdisciplinary History* 12: 621–43.

Knack, Stephen. 1995. "Does 'Motor Voter' Work? Evidence from State-Level Data." *Journal of Politics* 57: 796–811.

Knack, Stephen, and James White. 1998. "Did States' Motor Voter Programs Help the Democrats?" *American Politics Quarterly* 26 (3): 344–65.

Kramer, Gerald H. 1971. "Short-term Fluctuations in U.S. Voting Behavior, 1896–1964." *American Political Science Review* 65: 131–43.

Ladd, Everett Carll, Jr., and Charles Hadley. 1978. *Transformations of the American Party System*, 2nd edition. Norton.

Lichtman, Allan J. 1976. "Critical Election Theory and the Reality of American Presidential Politics, 1916–1940." *American Historical Review* 81: 317–50.

Lichtman, Allan J. 1982. "The End of Realignment Theory? Toward a New Research Program for American Political History." *Historical Methods* 15: 170–88.

Love, Margaret C., and Susan M. Kuzma. 1996. *Civil Disabilities of Convicted Felons: A State-by-State Survey.* U.S. Department of Justice.

Lowi, Theodore J. 1967. "The Public Philosophy: Interest Group Liberalism." *American Political Science Review* 61: 5–24.

Martinez, Michael D., and David Hill. 1999. "Did Motor Voter Work?" *American Politics Quarterly* 27 (3): 296–315.

Mayer, William G. 1993. *The Changing American Mind: How and Why American Public Opinion Changed between 1960 and 1988.* University of Michigan Press.

Mayhew, David. 1991. *Divided We Govern: Party Control, Lawmaking, and Investigations, 1946–1990.* Yale University Press.

McCormick, Richard L. 1982. "The Realignment System in American History." *Journal of Interdisciplinary History* 13: 85–105.

McCormick, Richard L. 1986. *The Party Period and Public Policy: American Politics from the Age of Jackson to the Progressive Era.* Oxford University Press.

McDonald, Michael P. 2002. "The Turnout Rate among Eligible Voters for U.S. States, 1980–2000." *State Politics and Policy Quarterly* 2: 199–212.

McDonald, Michael P., and Samuel Popkin. 2001. "The Myth of the Vanishing Voter." *American Political Science Review* 95: 963–74.

Miller, Warren E., and J. Merrill Shanks. 1996. *The New American Voter.* Harvard University Press.

Moe, Ronald C., and Steven C. Teel. 1970. "Congress as Policymaker: A Necessary Reappraisal." *Political Science Quarterly* 85: 443–70.

Morone, James A. 1990. *The Democratic Wish: Popular Participation and the Limits of American Government.* Basic Books.

Mueller, John E. 1970. "Presidential Popularity from Truman to Johnson." *American Political Science Review* 64: 18–34.

Mueller, John E. 1973. *War, Presidents and Public Opinion.* Wiley.

Mueller, John E. 1999. "Democracy: Optimal Illusions and Grim Realities." Center for the Study of Democracy, University of California, Irvine.

Neustadt, Richard E. 1960. *Presidential Power.* Wiley.

Ostrom, Charles W., Jr., and Dennis M. Simon. 1985. "Promise and Performance: A Dynamic Model." *American Political Science Review* 79: 334–58.

Page, Benjamin I. 1978. *Choices and Echoes in Presidential Elections.* University of Chicago Press.

Page, Benjamin I., and Robert Y. Shapiro. 1992. *The Rational Public: Fifty Years of Trends in American Policy Preferences.* University of Chicago Press.

Peterson, Mark A. 1989. *Legislating Together: The White House and Capitol Hill from Eisenhower to Reagan.* Harvard University Press.

Powell, G. Bingham, Jr. 1986. "The American Voter in Comparative Perspective." *American Political Science Review* 80: 17–43.

Preuhs, Robert. 1999. "Civil Disabilities: Explaining State Restrictions on the Political Participation of Convicted Felons." Presented at the 1998 annual meetings of the Midwest Political Science Association.

Pritchard, Anita. 1986. "An Evaluation of CQ Presidential Support Scores: The Relationship between Presidential Election Results and Congressional Voting Decisions." *American Journal of Political Science* 30: 480–95.

Rivers, Douglas, and Nancy L. Rose. 1985. "Passing the President's Program: Public Opinion and Presidential Influence in Congress." *American Journal of Political Science* 29: 183–96.

Rohde, David W., and Dennis M. Simon. 1985. "Presidential Vetoes and Congressional Response: A Study of Institutional Conflict." *American Journal of Political Science* 29: 397–427.

Rusk, Jerrold G. 1970. "The Effect of the Australian Ballot Reform on Split Ticket Voting: 1876–1908." *American Political Science Review* 64: 1220–38.

Rusk, Jerrold G. 2001. *A Statistical History of the American Electorate.* Congressional Quarterly Press.

Schriner, Kay, Lisa A. Ochs, and Todd G. Shields. 1997. "The Last Suffrage Movements: Voting Rights for Persons with Cognitive and Emotional Disabilities." *Publius* 27: 75.

Sensenbrenner, F. James, Jr. 1999. "Extension of Remarks: The History of the Private Calendar and the Consideration of Private Bills." U.S. House of Representatives, April 21.

Shafer, Byron E. 1991. *The End of Realignment? Interpreting American Electoral Eras.* University of Wisconsin Press.

Shapiro, Andrew L. 1993. "Note: Challenging Criminal Disenfranchisement under the Voting Rights Act: A New Strategy." *Yale Law Journal* 103: 537–66.

Shea, Daniel M. 1999. "The Passing of Realignment and the Advent of the 'Base-less' Party System." *American Politics Quarterly* 27: 33–57.

Shields, Todd G., and Chi Huang. 1995. "Presidential Vetoes: An Event Count Model." *Political Research Quarterly* 48: 559–72.

Silbey, Joel H. 1991. *The American Political Nation, 1838–1893.* Stanford University Press.

Smith, Tom W. 1987. "The Art of Asking Questions, 1936–1985." *Public Opinion Quarterly* 51: S95–S108.

Stimson, James A. 1999. *Public Opinion in America: Moods, Cycles and Swings*, 2nd edition. Westview Press.

Sundquist, James L. 1983. *Dynamics of the Party System: Alignment and Realignment of Political Parties in the United States*, revised edition. Brookings Institution Press.

Sundquist, James L. 1988–1989. "Needed: A Political Theory for the New Era of Coalition Government in the United States." *Political Science Quarterly* 103: 613–35.

Timpone, Richard J. 1998. "Structure, Behavior, and Voter Turnout in the United States." *American Political Science Review* 92: 145–58.

Tuckel, Peter, and Richard Maisel. 1994. "Voter Turnout among European Immigrants to the United States." *Journal of Interdisciplinary History* 24: 407–30.

Vile, John R. 1996. *Encyclopedia of Constitutional Amendments, Proposed Amendments and Amending Issues, 1789–1995.* ABC-CLIO.

Watson, Richard A. 1993. *Presidential Vetoes and Public Policy.* University Press of Kansas.

Wattenberg, Martin P. 1987. "The Hollow Realignment: Partisan Change in a Candidate-Centered Era." *Public Opinion Quarterly* 51: 58–74.

Wattenberg, Martin P. 1991. *The Rise of Candidate-Centered Politics: Presidential Elections of the 1980s.* Harvard University Press.

Wattenberg, Martin P. 1998. *The Decline of American Political Parties: 1952–1996.* Harvard University Press.

Wolfinger, Raymond E., and Steven J. Rosenstone. 1980. *Who Votes?* Yale University Press.

Zeidenstein, Harvey. 1983. "Varying Relationships between Presidents' Popularity and Their Legislative Success: A Futile Search for Patterns." *Presidential Studies Quarterly* 13: 530–50.

Zeidenstein, Harvey. 1985. "Presidents' Popularity and Their Wins and Losses on Major Issues in Congress: Does One Have Greater Influence over the Other?" *Presidential Studies Quarterly* 15: 287–300.

APPORTIONMENT

John P. McIver

TABLE Eb1–56   Apportionment of the House of Representatives: 1787–2000

Contributed by John P. McIver

Decade	Date of apportionment act (Eb1)	Congresses (Eb2)	States (Eb3) Number	Apportionment population — Total (Eb4) Thousand	Per representative (Eb5) Number	Representatives — Total (Eb6)	Alabama (Eb7)	Alaska (Eb8)	Arizona (Eb9)	Arkansas (Eb10)	California (Eb11)	Colorado (Eb12)	Connecticut (Eb13)	Delaware (Eb14)	Florida (Eb15)	Georgia (Eb16)	Hawai'i (Eb17)	Idaho (Eb18)
1787	Constitution 1789	1st–2nd	13	—	30,000	65	—	—	—	—	—	—	5	1	—	3	—	—
1790	Apr 14, 1792	3rd–7th	15	3,616	34,436	105	—	—	—	—	—	—	7	1	—	2	—	—
1800	Jan 14, 1802	8th–12th	16	4,880	34,609	141	—	—	—	—	—	—	7	1	—	4	—	—
1810	Dec 21, 1811	13th–17th	17	6,584	36,377	181	1[8]	—	—	—	—	—	7	2	—	6	—	—
1820	Mar 7, 1822	18th–22nd	24	8,972	42,124	213	3	—	—	—	—	—	6	1	—	7	—	—
1830	May 22, 1832	23rd–27th	24	11,931	49,712	240	5	—	—	1[8]	—	—	6	1	—	9	—	—
1840	June 25, 1842	28th–32nd	26	15,908	71,338	223	7	—	—	1	—	—	4	1	1[8]	8	—	—
1850	May 23, 1850 [3]	33rd–37th	31	21,767	93,020	234	7	—	—	2	2[8]	—	4	1	1	8	—	—
1860	May 23, 1850 [4]	38th–42nd	34	29,550	122,614	241	6	—	—	3	3	—	4	1	1	7	—	—
1870	Feb 2, 1872 [5]	43rd–47th	37	38,116	130,533	292	8	—	—	4	4	1[8]	4	1	2	9	—	—
1880	Feb 25, 1882	48th–52nd	38	49,371	151,912	325	8	—	—	5	6	1	4	1	2	10	—	1[8]
1890	Feb 7, 1891	53rd–57th	44	61,909	173,901	356	9	—	—	6	7	2	4	1	2	11	—	1
1900	Jan 16, 1901	58th–62nd	45	74,563	193,167	386	9	—	—	7	8	3	5	1	3	11	—	1
1910	Aug 8, 1911	63rd–67th	48	91,604	210,583	435	10	—	1[9]	7	11	4	5	1	4	12	—	2
1920 [2]	Aug 8, 1911	68th–72nd	48	—	—	435	10	—	1	7	11	4	5	1	4	12	—	2
1930	Jun 18, 1929	73rd–77th	48	122,093	280,675	435	9	—	1	7	20	4	6	1	5	10	—	2
1940	Nov 15, 1941	78th–82nd	48	131,006	301,164	435	9	—	2	7	23	4	6	1	6	10	—	2
1950	Nov 15, 1941	83rd–87th	48	149,895	334,587	435	9	1[8]	2	6	30	4	6	1	8	10	1[8]	2
1960	Nov 15, 1941	88th–92nd	50	178,559	410,481	435	8	1	3	4	38	4	6	1	12	10	2	2
1970	Nov 15, 1941	93rd–97th	50	204,053 [6]	469,088 [7]	435	7	1	4	4	43	5	6	1	15	10	2	2
1980	Nov 15, 1941	98th–102nd	50	225,867	519,235	435	7	1	5	4	45	6	6	1	19	10	2	2
1990	Nov 15, 1941	103rd–107th	50	249,023	572,466 [7]	435	7	1	6	4	52	6	6	1	23	11	2	2
2000	Nov 15, 1941	108th–	50	281,424	646,952	435	7	1	8	4	53	7	5	1	25	13	2	2

Notes appear at end of table

(continued)

TABLE Eb1-56 Apportionment of the House of Representatives: 1787–2000 *Continued*

Representatives

Decade	Illinois	Indiana	Iowa	Kansas	Kentucky	Louisiana	Maine	Maryland	Massachusetts	Michigan	Minnesota	Mississippi	Missouri	Montana	Nebraska	Nevada	New Hampshire	New Jersey	New Mexico
	Eb19	Eb20	Eb21	Eb22	Eb23	Eb24	Eb25	Eb26	Eb27	Eb28	Eb29	Eb30	Eb31	Eb32	Eb33	Eb34	Eb35	Eb36	Eb37
	Number	Number	Number	Number	Number	Number	Number	Number	Number	Number	Number	Number	Number	Number	Number	Number	Number	Number	Number
1787	—	—	—	—	—	—	—	6	8	—	—	—	—	—	—	—	3	4	—
1790	—	—	—	—	2	—	—	8	14	—	—	—	—	—	—	—	4	5	—
1800	—	—	—	—	6	—	—	9	17	—	—	—	—	—	—	—	5	6	—
1810	1[8]	1[8]	—	—	10	1[8]	7[10]	9	13	—	—	1[8]	—	—	—	—	6	6	—
1820	1	3	—	—	12	3	7	9	13	—	—	1	1[8]	—	—	—	6	6	—
1830	3	7	—	—	13	3	8	8	12	1[8]	—	2	2	—	—	—	5	6	—
1840	7	10	2[8]	—	10	4	7	6	10	3	—	4	5	—	—	—	4	5	—
1850	9	11	2	—	10	4	6	6	11	4	2[8]	5	7	—	—	—	3	5	—
1860	14	11	6	1[8]	9	5	5	5	10	6	2	5	9	—	1[8]	1[8]	3	5	—
1870	19	13	9	3	10	6	5	6	11	9	3	6	13	—	1	1	3	7	—
1880	20	13	11	7	11	6	4	6	12	11	5	7	14	1[8]	3	1	2	7	—
1890	22	13	11	8	11	6	4	6	13	12	7	7	15	1	6	1	2	8	—
1900	25	13	11	8	11	7	4	6	14	12	9	8	16	1	6	1	2	10	—
1910	27	13	11	8	11	8	4	6	16	13	10	8	16	2	6	1	2	12	1[8]
1920[2]	27	13	11	8	11	8	4	6	16	13	10	8	16	2	6	1	2	12	1
1930	27	12	9	7	9	8	3	6	15	17	9	7	13	2	5	1	2	14	1
1940	26	11	8	6	9	8	3	6	14	17	9	7	13	2	4	1	2	14	2
1950	25	11	8	6	8	8	3	7	14	18	9	6	11	2	4	1	2	14	2
1960	24	11	7	5	7	8	2	8	12	19	8	5	10	2	3	1	2	15	2
1970	24	11	6	5	7	8	2	8	12	19	8	5	10	2	3	1	2	15	2
1980	22	10	6	5	7	8	2	8	11	18	8	5	9	2	3	2	2	14	3
1990	20	10	5	4	6	7	2	8	10	16	8	5	9	1	3	2	2	13	3
2000	19	9	5	4	6	7	2	8	10	15	8	4	9	1	3	3	2	13	3

Representatives

Decade	New York	North Carolina	North Dakota	Ohio	Oklahoma	Oregon	Pennsylvania	Rhode Island	South Carolina	South Dakota	Tennessee	Texas	Utah	Vermont	Virginia	Washington	West Virginia	Wisconsin	Wyoming
	Eb38	Eb39	Eb40	Eb41	Eb42	Eb43	Eb44	Eb45	Eb46	Eb47	Eb48	Eb49	Eb50	Eb51	Eb52	Eb53	Eb54	Eb55	Eb56
	Number	Number	Number	Number	Number	Number	Number	Number	Number	Number	Number	Number	Number	Number	Number	Number	Number	Number	Number
1787	6	5	—	—	—	—	8	1	5	—	—	—	—	—	10	—	—	—	—
1790	10	10	—	—	—	—	13	2	6	—	1[8]	—	—	2[8]	19	—	—	—	—
1800	17	12	—	1[8]	—	—	18	2	8	—	3	—	—	4	22	—	—	—	—
1810	27	13	—	6	—	—	23	2	9	—	6	—	—	6	23	—	—	—	—
1820	34	13	—	14	—	—	26	2	9	—	9	—	—	5	22	—	—	—	—
1830	40	13	—	19	—	—	28	2	9	—	13	—	—	5	21	—	—	—	—
1840	34	9	—	21	—	—	24	2	7	—	11	2[8]	—	4	15	—	—	2[8]	—
1850	33	8	—	21	—	1[8]	25	2	6	—	10	2	—	3	13	—	—	3	—
1860	31	7	—	19	—	1	24	2	4	—	8	4	—	3	11	—	3[8]	6	—
1870	33	8	—	20	—	1	27	2	5	—	10	6	—	3	9	—	3	8	—
1880	34	9	1[8]	21	—	1	28	2	7	2[8]	10	11	—	2	10	1[8]	4	9	1[8]
1890	34	9	1	21	—	2	30	2	7	2	10	13	1[8]	2	10	2	4	10	1
1900	37	10	2	21	5[8]	2	32	2	7	2	10	16	1	2	10	3	5	11	1
1910	43	10	3	22	8	3	36	3	7	3	10	18	2	2	10	5	6	11	1
1920[2]	43	10	3	22	8	3	36	3	7	3	10	18	2	2	10	5	6	11	1

Representatives

Decade	New York Eb38 Number	North Carolina Eb39 Number	North Dakota Eb40 Number	Ohio Eb41 Number	Oklahoma Eb42 Number	Oregon Eb43 Number	Pennsylvania Eb44 Number	Rhode Island Eb45 Number	South Carolina Eb46 Number	South Dakota Eb47 Number	Tennessee Eb48 Number	Texas Eb49 Number	Utah Eb50 Number	Vermont Eb51 Number	Virginia Eb52 Number	Washington Eb53 Number	West Virginia Eb54 Number	Wisconsin Eb55 Number	Wyoming Eb56 Number
1930	45	11	2	24	9	3	34	2	6	2	9	21	2	1	9	6	6	10	1
1940	45	12	2	23	8	4	33	2	6	2	10	21	2	1	9	6	6	10	1
1950	43	12	2	23	6	4	30	2	6	2	9	22	2	1	10	7	6	10	1
1960	41	11	2	24	6	4	27	2	6	2	9	23	2	1	10	7	5	10	1
1970	39	11	1	23	6	4	25	2	6	2	8	24	2	1	10	7	4	9	1
1980	34	11	1	21	6	5	23	2	6	1	9	27	3	1	10	8	4	9	1
1990	31	12	1	19	6	5	21	2	6	1	9	30	3	1	11	9	3	9	1
2000	29	13	1	18	5	5	19	2	6	1	9	32	3	1	11	9	3	8	1

[1] Excludes the population of the District of Columbia; the population of the territories; prior to 1940, the number of Indians not taxed; and prior to 1870, two fifths of the slave population. In 1970 and 1990, includes selected segments of Americans abroad.

[2] No reapportionment; see text.

[3] Amended by the Act of July 30, 1852.

[4] Amended by the Act of March 4, 1862.

[5] Amended by the Act of May 30, 1872.

[6] Includes 1,575,000 persons in population abroad.

[7] Ratio of resident population to representatives was 465,468 in 1970 and 570,352 in 1990.

[8] Assigned after apportionment.

[9] Included in apportionment act in anticipation of statehood.

[10] Included in the twenty members originally assigned to Massachusetts but credited to Maine after its admission as a state, March 15, 1820 (3 Stat. L 555).

Sources

1789–1968: *Historical Statistics of the United States* (1975), series Y215–271, which are based on U.S. Bureau of the Census, *U.S. Census of Population: 1970*, volume 1, p. viii.

1970–1997: Census/1990 CPH-2-1, Census of Population and Housing Unit Counts, Tables A and B.

2000: U.S. Census Bureau Internet site, release date: December 28, 2000.

Documentation

The original assignment of representatives for each state, to be in effect until after the first enumeration of the population, is defined in the United States Constitution, Article 1, Section 2. Thereafter, the addition and reapportionment of seats occurred with Congress action on the report of the census and with the entry of new states into the Union.

The population figures used for apportionment purposes are those determined by each decennial enumeration. Prior to the passage of the Fourteenth Amendment, representatives were apportioned among the states "according to their respective numbers, which shall be determined by adding to the whole number of free persons, including those bound to service for a term of years, and excluding Indians not taxed, three-fifths of all other persons" (Article 1, Section 2). In effect, censuses between 1790 and 1860 included three fifths of slaves in the apportionment population. Following the passage of the Fourteenth Amendment in 1868, representatives have been apportioned "among the several States according to their respective numbers, counting the whole number of persons in each State, excluding Indians not taxed." At the time of the 1940 apportionment, it was determined that there were no longer any Indians who would be classed as "not taxed" under apportionment law.

In 1970, for the first time, the following classes of persons abroad were allocated to their home states for inclusion in the apportionment population: (1) members of the armed forces; (2) civilian employees of any federal department or agency who were citizens of the United States or who had a home state; (3) spouses and children who were living abroad with persons classified in groups 1 and 2 above; and (4) other relatives living abroad in groups 1 and 2 who were citizens of the United States or who had a home state. Similar efforts were made to assign Americans abroad to their home states in 1990 and 2000. For detailed information about apportionment methods, see House Report 91-1314, "The Decennial Population Census and Congressional Apportionment, 1970"; the U.S. Census Bureau, Population Division, "Congressional Apportionment – Historical Perspective"; and David C. Huckabee, "The House Apportionment Process in Theory and Practice," Congressional Research Service, October 10, 2000.

Each decade shown in the table represents the ten-year period affected by the census conducted during that year. For example, the information given for 1790 reflects the apportionment of representatives to Congress for the Third through the Seventh Congresses, or 1792 through 1801. The first two Congresses predate a counting of the United States population. Representation was apportioned under Article 1, Section 2 of the Constitution.

Total House membership, series Eb6, is shown as of the date of the fixing of the new House apportionment. The series for individual states, however, include members added for new states admitted during the subsequent decade. Consequently, the total of all state representatives in series Eb7–56 will show the number of representatives serving at the end of the apportionment decade. The precise date of statehood and the subsequent representation of the state in the Congress may be found by referring to Table Ap-E in Appendix 2. Major boundary changes affecting state representation in the House occurred in 1820, when Maine separated from Massachusetts, and in 1863, when West Virginia separated from Virginia.

The minimum ratio of population to representatives is 30,000, as stated in the Constitution, Article 1, Section 2. Prior to 1850, apportionment ratios were chosen arbitrarily; from 1850 to 1900, ratios were the apportionment population of the United States divided by a predetermined number of representatives; from 1910 on, apportionment ratios were computed by dividing a fixed number (435) of representatives into the apportionment population.

No reapportionment was made following the 1920 Census. Congress, being unable to reach agreement for allotting representation without further increasing the size of the House, failed to reapportion seats among the states. See Laurence F. Schmeckebier, *Congressional Apportionment* (Brookings Institution, 1941).

No change in total House membership has been made since 1912; however, the legislation granting statehood to Alaska and Hawai'i allotted one representative to each of those states and thus increased the total of members to 437 for the period 1960–1962. The total reverted to 435 after reapportionment following the 1960 Census.

TABLE Eb57–61 Apportionment population and number of representatives, by state: 2002

Contributed by John P. McIver

State	Apportionment population Eb57	Number of apportioned representatives based on 2000 Census Eb58	Change from 1990 Census apportionment Eb59	Population per representative Eb60	Percentage deviation from equal representation Eb61
	Number	Number	Number	Number	Percent
All States	281,424,177	435	—	646,952	—
Alabama	4,461,130	7	0	637,304	−1.49
Alaska	628,933	1	0	628,933	−2.79
Arizona	5,140,683	8	2	642,585	−0.67
Arkansas	2,679,733	4	0	669,933	3.55
California	33,930,798	53	1	640,204	−1.04
Colorado	4,311,882	7	1	615,983	−4.79
Connecticut	3,409,535	5	−1	681,907	5.40
Delaware	785,068	1	0	785,068	21.35
Florida	16,028,890	25	2	641,156	−0.90
Georgia	8,206,975	13	2	631,306	−2.42
Hawai'i	1,216,642	2	0	608,321	−5.97
Idaho	1,297,274	2	0	648,637	0.26
Illinois	12,439,042	19	−1	654,686	1.20
Indiana	6,090,782	9	−1	676,754	4.61
Iowa	2,931,923	5	0	586,385	−9.36
Kansas	2,693,824	4	0	673,456	4.10
Kentucky	4,049,431	6	0	674,905	4.32
Louisiana	4,480,271	7	0	640,039	−1.07
Maine	1,277,731	2	0	638,866	−1.25
Maryland	5,307,886	8	0	663,486	2.56
Massachusetts	6,355,568	10	0	635,557	−1.76
Michigan	9,955,829	15	−1	663,722	2.59
Minnesota	4,925,670	8	0	615,709	−4.83
Mississippi	2,852,927	4	−1	713,232	10.24
Missouri	5,606,260	9	0	622,918	−3.72
Montana	905,316	1	0	905,316	39.94
Nebraska	1,715,369	3	0	571,790	−11.62
Nevada	2,002,032	3	1	667,344	3.15
New Hampshire	1,238,415	2	0	619,208	−4.29
New Jersey	8,424,354	13	0	648,027	0.17
New Mexico	1,823,821	3	0	607,940	−6.03
New York	19,004,973	29	−2	655,344	1.30
North Carolina	8,067,673	13	1	620,590	−4.07
North Dakota	643,756	1	0	643,756	−0.49
Ohio	11,374,540	18	−1	631,919	−2.32
Oklahoma	3,458,819	5	−1	691,764	6.93
Oregon	3,428,543	5	0	685,709	5.99
Pennsylvania	12,300,670	19	−2	647,404	0.07
Rhode Island	1,049,662	2	0	524,831	−18.88
South Carolina	4,025,061	6	0	670,844	3.69
South Dakota	756,874	1	0	756,874	16.99
Tennessee	5,700,037	9	0	633,337	−2.10
Texas	20,903,994	32	2	653,250	0.97
Utah	2,236,714	3	0	745,571	15.24
Vermont	609,890	1	0	609,890	−5.73
Virginia	7,100,702	11	0	645,518	−0.22
Washington	5,908,684	9	0	656,520	1.48
West Virginia	1,813,077	3	0	604,359	−6.58
Wisconsin	5,371,210	8	−1	671,401	3.78
Wyoming	495,304	1	0	495,304	−23.44

Source

U.S. Census Bureau Internet site, release date: December 28, 2000.

Documentation

Article 1, Section 2 of the Constitution of the United States apportions membership in the U.S. House of Representatives according to state population. The original sixty-five members of the House were divided among the thirteen states by the "best guess" of the Constitutional Convention and subject to the first "enumeration" to be conducted within three years. The Constitution requires recounting the population every ten years with each census resulting in the redistribution of seats according to contemporary population counts.

The 2000 Census serves as the basis for reapportionment of the state representation in the House of Representatives for the decade 2002–2011.

In recent years, extensive public debate has centered on the processes by which Americans are counted by the Census Bureau. The limitations of existing methodology in reaching certain population subgroups prompted claims by different states and different groups that the counting process was biased against their interests. A variety of proposals to change the way in which the population of states and other census areas are estimated were debated. However, in deciding a lawsuit brought to prevent the use of these alternative techniques, the U.S. Supreme Court ruled that the apportionment population counts cannot reflect the use of statistical sampling to correct for overcounting or undercounting (*Department of Commerce v. House of Representatives*, 525 U.S. 316, 1999).

Series Eb57. Includes the resident population for the fifty states, as ascertained by the Twenty-second Decennial Census under Title 13, United States Code, and counts of overseas U.S. military and federal civilian employees (and their dependents living with them) allocated to their home state, as reported by the employing federal agencies. The apportionment population excludes the population of the District of Columbia.

Series Eb61. While equal representation in the House of Representatives is the goal of reapportionment, the clustering of population into states precludes all citizens from having equal weight in the Congress. Without state boundaries, it would be theoretically possible to draw congressional districts such that each congressman and woman represented 646,952 citizens. State boundaries, however, produce deviations from this norm. These deviations (in percentages) are reported here. For example, Montana's single representative serves 40 percent more citizens and Wyoming's representative 23 percent fewer citizens than the "average" member of the House of Representatives.

VOTER TURNOUT

John P. McIver

TABLE Eb62–113 Voter turnout in presidential elections, by state: 1824–2000[1]

Contributed by John P. McIver

Year	United States	Alabama	Alaska	Arizona	Arkansas	California	Colorado	Connecticut	Delaware	District of Columbia	Florida	Georgia	Hawai'i	Idaho	Illinois	Indiana	Iowa
	Eb62	Eb63	Eb64	Eb65	Eb66	Eb67	Eb68	Eb69	Eb70	Eb71	Eb72	Eb73	Eb74	Eb75	Eb76	Eb77	Eb78
	Percent	Percent	Percent	Percent	Percent	Percent	Percent	Percent	Percent	Percent	Percent	Percent	Percent	Percent	Percent	Percent	Percent
1824	26.9	49.1	—	—	—	—	—	14.9	—	—	—	—	—	—	24.3	37.1	—
1828	57.6	54.6	—	—	—	—	—	27.2	—	—	—	31.8	—	—	52.4	68.7	—
1832	55.4	31.5	—	—	—	—	—	46.0	67.1	—	—	29.0	—	—	46.0	71.9	—
1836	57.8	64.9	—	—	28.9	—	—	52.3	69.5	—	—	61.8	—	—	43.5	69.2	—
1840	80.2	89.7	—	—	67.6	—	—	75.7	82.3	—	—	88.8	—	—	86.0	84.4	—
1844	78.9	80.3	—	—	63.5	—	—	80.0	85.3	—	—	92.6	—	—	76.0	84.7	—
1848	72.7	69.7	—	—	55.9	75.7	—	72.3	80.4	—	64.0	86.0	—	—	70.5	78.5	90.7
1852	69.6	45.3	—	—	48.6	81.6	—	72.3	75.0	—	56.9	54.8	—	—	64.7	80.3	80.2
1856	78.9	71.0	—	—	60.2	71.2	—	81.8	78.5	—	77.6	82.8	—	—	72.4	88.3	87.0
1860	81.2	78.7	—	—	79.5	71.2	—	73.3	79.5	—	79.5	85.1	—	—	80.5	89.4	94.2
1864 [3]	73.8	—	—	—	—	64.6	—	76.3	79.8	—	—	—	—	—	—	82.9	95.4
1868 [3]	78.1	77.9	—	—	49.0	72.3	—	80.1	84.3	—	—[4]	73.2	—	—	69.2	92.5	97.7
1872	71.3	79.6	—	—	67.6	57.9	—	71.3	73.3	—	77.0	55.2	—	—	76.7	85.3	79.0
1876	81.8	72.8	—	—	64.7	75.9	—[4]	82.0	73.4	—	93.5	63.5	—	—	75.0	94.6	99.1
1880	79.4	58.8	—	—	59.5	67.1	57.4	81.4	81.9	—	85.9	49.4	—	—	87.5	94.4	93.7
1884	77.5	54.2	—	—	59.1	68.8	52.4	79.9	76.0	—	83.1	41.0	—	—	89.9	92.2	90.0
1888	79.3	56.6	—	—	68.9	76.5	57.4	85.5	58.3	—	85.0	37.6	—	—	84.4	93.3	87.9
1892	74.7	68.5	—	—	55.0	73.8	54.6	85.4	80.4	—	35.3	53.1	—	63.1	82.9	89.0	88.5
1896	79.3	51.9	—	—	48.2	75.0	65.2	83.3	54.5	—	40.0	34.3	—	76.1	86.0	95.1	96.1
1900	73.2	38.9	—	—	40.8	69.9	71.2	79.7	81.9	—	29.9	24.4	—	77.8	95.7	92.1	91.0
1904	65.2	24.2	—	—	33.8	61.7	71.0	80.5	82.0	—	24.4	23.8	—	65.3	89.9	89.7	79.7
1908	65.4	21.5	—	—	40.2	60.2	65.4	76.3	86.2	—	26.2	22.0	—	65.8	80.5	89.9	77.6
1912	58.8	22.6	—	38.6	30.7	46.9	59.1	71.5	84.1	—	24.2	18.9	—	59.8	81.6	77.8	74.2
1916	61.6	24.3	—	48.7	40.0	58.0	60.5	73.8	86.1	—	33.8	23.7	—	67.4	74.7	81.9	75.0
1920	49.2	20.6	—	46.8	20.9	47.2	56.0	58.7	75.1	—	30.3	10.5	—	61.1	66.8	71.0	64.5
1924	48.9	13.5	—	44.4	15.3	50.8	62.5	57.9	58.1	—	17.0	11.5	—	65.2	60.5	70.7	68.4
1928	56.9	19.1	—	47.9	21.4	59.0	68.4	72.6	75.3	—	33.0	15.7	—	66.0	64.1	74.9	68.9
1932	56.9	17.5	—	55.1	22.1	64.0	75.3	70.8	76.3	—	30.5	16.5	—	74.4	73.4	78.9	69.1
1936	61.0	18.8	—	52.0	17.3	66.0	75.5	74.6	79.3	—	31.3	17.7	—	71.8	74.6	78.7	73.5
1940	62.5	18.9	—	57.0	18.2	73.4	79.7	77.2	79.4	—	40.9	17.7	—	77.0	81.6	81.1	75.5
1944	55.9	15.0	—	42.2	19.3	65.1	67.9	73.9	56.9	—	33.5	17.6	—	64.5	82.2	71.7	64.3
1948	53.0	12.6	—	45.4	21.9	63.2	64.5	71.9	58.5	—	34.1	21.4	—	63.1	74.8	67.2	62.4
1952	63.3	24.2	—	53.9	36.9	69.4	76.2	80.9	78.4	—	47.6	31.9	—	78.2	70.3	75.7	75.8
1956	60.6	27.6	—	47.8	38.0	64.0	69.2	75.8	72.7	—	43.6	31.3	—	75.2	76.0	73.7	74.0
1960	64.0	31.2	59.2	53.8	41.1	67.9	71.7	77.1	74.5	—	50.0	32.9	58.9	80.6	72.4	76.9	76.8
1964	61.7	36.1	48.0	56.8	51.2	66.1	67.6	71.3	59.5	39.4	51.9	45.3	52.4	75.2	76.5	71.7	70.0
1968	60.6	52.8	53.0	50.6	54.1	62.0	64.0	68.8	58.7	34.7	53.8	44.7	53.3	71.9	72.6	69.5	67.9
1972	55.2	43.3	46.9	47.4	48.1	59.5	59.5	66.2	52.1	30.4	48.6	37.3	49.4	63.3	69.3	60.8	64.0
1976	53.5	46.3	48.1	46.1	51.1	50.4	58.8	62.8	57.2	32.2	49.2	42.0	46.7	60.7	62.3	60.1	63.1
1980	52.6	48.8	57.8	44.7	51.4	49.0	56.0	61.0	54.5	35.5	48.6	41.3	43.6	68.0	59.4	57.7	63.0
1984	53.3	50.3	58.8	45.3	52.3	49.3	55.7	60.3	56.0	41.8	48.3	41.9	44.7	60.9	57.8	56.4	63.3
1988	50.3	46.7	54.2	44.9	48.2	46.5	57.2	57.1	51.0	38.4	42.6	39.1	44.0	59.9	57.9	53.6	59.7
1992	55.1	54.8	63.8	52.9	53.6	49.4	60.8	64.4	55.5	48.7	51.0	46.4	43.1	64.3	54.2	54.8	65.3
1996	49.0	50.4	56.6	64.5	58.0	58.6	55.3	52.0	56.4	48.3	46.5	51.2	49.0	54.2	52.6	54.3	48.9
2000	49.3	50.0	66.4	42.3	47.8	44.1	56.8	58.4	56.4	49.1	50.6	44.1	40.5	54.5	52.8	49.4	60.8

Notes appear at end of table

(continued)

TABLE Eb62–113   Voter turnout in presidential elections, by state: 1824–2000   Continued

Year	Kansas Eb79 Percent	Kentucky Eb80 Percent	Louisiana Eb81 Percent	Maine Eb82 Percent	Maryland Eb83 Percent	Massachusetts Eb84 Percent	Michigan Eb85 Percent	Minnesota Eb86 Percent	Mississippi Eb87 Percent	Missouri Eb88 Percent	Montana Eb89 Percent	Nebraska Eb90 Percent	Nevada Eb91 Percent	New Hampshire Eb92 Percent	New Jersey Eb93 Percent	New Mexico Eb94 Percent	New York Eb95 Percent
1824	—	25.4	—	19.1	53.7	29.0	—	—	41.3	19.8	—	—	—	18.0	35.6	—	—
1828	—	70.7	36.2	42.7	70.3	25.7	—	—	56.6	54.0	—	—	—	74.3	71.0	—	80.2
1832	—	74.0	22.3	66.2	55.7	39.4	—	—	28.0	41.0	—	—	—	70.1	68.8	—	84.2
1836	—	61.1	19.2	37.7	67.6	43.4	35.0	—	64.4	36.1	—	—	—	38.2	69.2	—	70.5
1840	—	74.3	39.4	83.7	84.5	66.7	84.9	—	88.2	75.1	—	—	—	86.3	80.4	—	91.9
1844	—	80.7	47.1	71.3	81.4	65.8	79.8	—	86.1	77.8	—	—	—	68.9	87.2	—	92.1
1848	—	73.9	51.1	68.4	76.0	64.6	74.5	—	80.7	62.5	—	—	—	67.4	82.7	—	79.6
1852	—	64.2	48.7	61.2	72.8	57.8	71.3	—	61.7	46.3	—	—	—	65.7	79.8	—	84.7
1856	—	76.7	53.6	78.1	80.0	69.8	81.1	—	78.3	54.7	—	—	—	87.9	83.1	—	89.9
1860	—	74.1	58.6	68.9	81.1	65.8	80.0	74.9	89.5	69.1	—	—	—	80.7	89.4	—	95.5
1864 [3]	31.8	44.0	—	73.2	57.7	63.8	66.2	57.5	—	36.3	—	—	157.5	84.3	81.0	—	89.3
1868 [3]	51.3	69.9	75.9	74.4	72.6	66.9	77.4	71.1	—	43.0	—	46.1	73.7	82.3	89.5	—	91.7
1872	77.8	66.2	76.4	57.9	75.0	62.0	64.0	67.5	71.1	66.6	—	43.7	74.4	80.9	81.4	—	80.5
1876	65.7	80.9	77.9	71.5	82.7	72.3	78.0	71.3	79.7	76.6	—	53.0	90.0	92.0	94.8	—	89.6
1880	80.8	75.5	50.3	85.0	79.8	71.2	75.5	68.9	50.1	78.0	—	67.7	76.5	93.3	95.4	—	89.3
1884	85.1	70.8	49.8	75.0	79.9	69.3	76.0	68.2	49.2	77.0	—	67.8	61.6	87.4	88.6	—	87.5
1888	88.2	81.1	50.0	71.7	84.8	71.7	80.9	76.3	43.8	81.8	—	75.9	71.4	90.2	91.9	—	92.3
1892	80.7	73.8	45.1	63.5	79.9	74.6	73.2	66.6	18.8	77.4	74.2	66.2	70.1	85.8	90.3	—	86.3
1896	85.5	89.2	35.8	63.0	87.3	70.6	95.3	75.2	22.1	88.5	73.8	74.1	69.2	78.1	88.4	—	84.3
1900	91.2	87.0	21.7	56.0	85.9	67.4	89.0	76.7	16.9	83.1	75.3	80.2	71.4	83.9	85.9	—	84.6
1904	78.1	77.7	15.6	49.5	69.6	67.6	78.9	64.3	15.6	74.9	65.8	70.1	59.2	81.6	83.6	—	83.3
1908	82.5	84.0	19.8	53.2	70.9	65.1	75.9	66.1	16.5	79.7	61.9	77.8	92.1	80.8	82.4	—	79.7
1912	76.3	74.6	19.3	63.4	64.8	63.4	69.8	61.2	15.1	74.9	63.3	77.1	68.1	78.2	69.1	59.6	72.1
1916	65.8	82.8	21.6	65.1	68.1	62.8	72.9	65.0	20.0	81.5	68.0	84.5	73.6	77.3	70.7	77.8	71.6
1920	58.0	71.8	14.1	46.9	52.3	53.3	55.1	59.5	9.4	67.6	61.4	55.7	61.0	67.5	59.1	62.3	56.4
1924	64.1	61.0	12.4	44.9	41.0	56.6	53.7	62.0	12.0	63.3	59.2	63.8	56.1	67.4	60.7	61.8	56.3
1928	65.9	67.7	20.1	60.2	56.8	74.0	56.3	68.5	15.2	69.1	65.3	71.5	63.0	77.8	75.6	60.3	68.3
1932	71.1	67.4	23.4	66.3	51.2	69.5	62.0	66.2	13.8	70.9	70.3	72.1	73.2	77.5	72.0	69.7	66.1
1936	76.6	59.9	27.3	64.4	58.1	75.9	62.1	69.7	14.4	77.3	70.8	75.6	69.1	77.8	75.0	68.7	72.6
1940	75.1	59.5	29.4	65.0	57.2	78.7	66.6	72.3	14.7	74.4	72.2	75.4	75.7	79.6	76.1	66.6	75.7
1944	62.2	51.9	25.1	57.3	46.7	71.0	63.7	63.0	15.0	62.2	59.0	67.9	64.8	73.5	69.1	48.8	70.9
1948	65.0	47.9	27.5	49.0	41.7	71.5	55.6	65.7	16.0	61.0	62.3	58.2	64.0	70.3	63.0	53.4	65.0
1952	71.7	57.0	40.2	63.1	57.5	75.0	68.5	72.6	23.8	71.8	71.8	71.9	69.7	79.2	72.3	60.5	71.2
1956	67.4	60.5	36.0	61.8	54.6	72.0	71.1	68.7	21.0	68.8	71.6	67.6	65.9	74.4	68.9	56.8	67.9
1960	71.8	60.5	45.1	74.0	58.3	76.9	72.7	77.1	25.7	72.6	71.7	72.1	61.0	80.2	71.8	64.5	66.9
1964	63.6	54.8	47.1	65.0	54.7	68.4	66.2	73.7	34.1	65.2	70.6	66.6	60.0	71.4	69.2	62.8	64.4
1968	63.4	51.3	54.9	66.4	55.2	66.4	64.9	71.7	53.3	64.9	68.4	60.0	55.9	68.5	65.8	60.0	59.7
1972	59.5	48.0	44.0	60.3	49.8	62.0	59.4	68.6	44.2	57.3	67.6	56.4	49.5	63.6	59.8	57.7	56.3
1976	58.8	48.0	48.7	63.7	49.3	61.7	58.8	71.5	48.0	57.3	63.3	56.2	44.2	57.3	57.7	53.4	50.7
1980	56.8	50.0	53.1	64.6	50.0	59.0	59.9	70.1	52.0	58.7	65.1	56.8	41.2	57.2	54.9	51.0	47.9
1984	57.4	51.2	55.6	64.9	51.1	57.0	58.0	68.6	52.7	57.8	65.8	56.6	41.2	53.1	56.5	51.9	50.9
1988	54.9	48.8	54.2	61.5	48.5	56.7	54.2	66.2	51.3	55.5	63.8	57.7	42.5	55.2	52.5	49.8	47.5
1992	62.9	53.4	58.8	72.9	53.6	60.1	61.5	71.8	52.4	62.1	68.4	63.4	50.1	64.2	56.1	50.8	50.5
1996	49.2	54.5	57.4	58.1	64.3	57.7	54.2	56.3	61.1	56.1	56.6	45.9	46.0	49.5	46.7	42.7	47.5
2000	54.1	51.6	54.2	67.4	51.5	56.9	57.5	68.8	48.6	57.5	61.5	56.5	43.8	62.5	51.0	47.4	49.3 [5]

Year	North Carolina Eb96	North Dakota Eb97	Ohio Eb98	Oklahoma Eb99	Oregon Eb100	Pennsylvania Eb101	Rhode Island Eb102	South Carolina Eb103[2]	South Dakota Eb104	Tennessee Eb105	Texas Eb106	Utah Eb107	Vermont Eb108	Virginia Eb109	Washington Eb110	West Virginia Eb111	Wisconsin Eb112	Wyoming Eb113
	Percent	Percent	Percent	Percent	Percent	Percent	Percent	Percent	Percent	Percent	Percent	Percent	Percent	Percent	Percent	Percent	Percent	Percent
1824	41.8	—	34.8	—	—	18.8	12.0	—	—	28.3	—	—	—	11.6	—	—	—	—
1828	56.9	—	75.9	—	—	56.5	17.1	—	—	55.0	—	—	54.5	27.7	—	—	—	—
1832	31.3	—	73.9	—	—	52.3	26.3	—	—	31.3	—	—	50.0	31.1	—	—	—	—
1836	53.0	—	75.5	—	—	53.1	23.8	—	—	57.3	—	—	52.5	35.2	—	—	—	—
1840	82.4	—	84.5	—	—	77.5	33.2	—	—	39.7	—	—	73.8	54.7	—	—	—	—
1844	78.8	—	83.6	—	—	77.3	45.1	—	—	39.8	—	—	70.8	54.2	—	—	—	—
1848	71.4	—	77.5	—	—	76.3	41.1	—	—	33.4	69.6	—	70.5	47.3	—	—	58.3	—
1852	65.8	—	80.6	—	—	72.6	57.8	—	—	72.9	42.6	—	63.5	63.3	—	—	59.6	—
1856	66.7	—	82.3	—	—	80.8	62.9	—	—	32.9	58.1	—	72.5	67.8	—	—	80.8	—
1860	70.9	—	83.3	—	97.8	78.4	59.4	—	—	30.9	67.4	—	63.0	71.5	—	—	79.0	—
1864[3]	—	—	87.6	—	91.8	85.0	53.8	—	—	—	—	—	77.0	—	—	51.6	66.8	—
1868[3]	91.2	—	90.4	—	85.8	88.3	46.6	79.6	—	39.7	—	—	75.9	—	—	58.0	79.8	—
1872	71.9	—	84.4	—	60.5	68.6	40.2	60.4	—	66.2	56.3	—	69.1	66.2	—	61.2	70.6	—
1876	90.1	—	94.4	—	70.4	83.5	49.4	101.0	—	74.6	54.6	—	83.3	77.6	—	83.6	83.9	—
1880	83.0	—	94.4	—	79.1	88.8	48.7	83.9	—	75.1	68.8	—	81.6	64.1	—	82.6	82.4	—
1884	86.3	—	93.4	—	63.0	82.3	48.1	43.0	—	73.1	80.2	—	70.5	81.7	—	86.7	82.2	—
1888	85.2	—	91.9	—	53.5	83.0	53.4	35.0	—	77.6	78.3	—	71.4	83.2	—	94.5	81.1	—
1892	78.0	56.6	86.2	—	58.4	75.7	63.0	29.1	70.7	64.0	79.4	—	50.4	75.3	67.3	90.3	76.8	47.7
1896	85.3	63.1	95.5	—	69.9	81.8	59.2	25.2	78.0	70.8	88.3	79.4	57.5	71.0	63.1	93.6	84.9	50.7
1900	70.2	65.2	91.5	—	58.3	75.0	56.2	18.0	85.4	56.6	61.4	84.5	57.9	59.6	64.9	91.3	77.5	51.1
1904	46.1	61.4	83.1	—	47.6	74.3	63.4	18.4	73.0	47.7	29.6	78.4	50.7	27.7	60.9	89.2	72.0	50.8
1908	52.0	73.2	87.5	71.5	47.3	71.8	62.4	20.6	69.5	48.1	33.6	73.0	48.9	27.4	59.0	86.9	68.7	49.2
1912	46.1	60.8	74.8	57.4	51.8	64.4	62.7	14.6	61.9	45.1	30.8	66.4	56.8	25.7	50.8	81.9	68.7	50.3
1916	49.8	77.7	76.5	60.4	54.2	63.4	65.8	17.5	60.9	46.6	35.0	79.5	58.2	27.1	54.7	83.6	70.2	54.9
1920	44.6	67.4	62.6	48.6	52.3	42.8	57.9	8.6	56.6	35.4	21.7	69.6	45.3	19.4	52.4	71.7	52.3	52.3
1924	35.9	63.8	57.8	47.4	55.3	45.8	66.3	6.4	59.4	23.3	25.8	69.7	51.3	18.1	51.2	75.2	57.3	71.0
1928	43.1	72.4	66.9	50.5	57.7	62.7	68.9	8.5	72.0	25.7	24.8	73.4	56.8	24.0	56.6	76.4	65.9	68.7
1932	44.0	74.5	65.5	54.4	60.7	53.1	71.7	12.5	76.5	26.5	27.2	80.0	66.6	22.1	64.2	81.9	65.1	74.9
1936	47.4	78.0	71.8	56.4	62.5	72.5	78.0	12.5	77.5	30.0	24.8	77.9	68.5	23.0	66.5	84.9	68.9	74.0
1940	42.7	78.4	75.4	60.5	67.1	67.6	75.6	10.1	79.5	30.6	30.1	83.1	66.8	22.1	70.6	83.0	72.4	74.8
1944	38.0	61.5	66.9	52.8	58.4	59.8	65.0	9.8	59.3	28.2	28.2	75.0	56.9	22.3	67.0	65.5	65.7	63.3
1948	35.4	61.6	58.4	52.5	56.5	56.0	66.0	12.8	63.3	28.7	26.0	76.0	54.5	21.6	63.2	65.8	59.8	59.6
1952	51.3	75.5	69.7	68.6	69.6	66.5	79.8	29.1	74.4	47.7	43.5	82.9	66.8	29.9	71.2	76.3	72.5	72.5
1956	47.4	71.3	66.4	61.4	71.1	65.5	73.2	24.7	74.7	45.9	37.9	77.2	66.5	31.8	70.4	74.6	67.8	67.4
1960	54.1	79.1	71.3	64.3	72.4	70.7	77.3	31.4	78.8	50.4	42.4	78.9	72.9	34.4	74.1	77.9	73.5	73.9
1964	51.9	72.9	65.3	62.4	67.2	66.6	69.3	38.7	75.4	51.5	44.1	78.0	67.0	41.6	67.2	73.0	68.6	74.1
1968	54.1	70.0	62.7	60.0	64.6	64.3	65.6	46.0	72.8	53.2	48.2	75.2	62.9	50.5	64.3	69.3	65.6	65.3
1972	42.8	68.3	57.3	56.7	62.1	56.0	61.0	38.2	69.4	43.5	45.0	69.4	60.7	44.7	63.1	62.5	62.5	64.4
1976	43.0	67.2	55.1	54.9	61.3	54.2	59.7	40.2	64.1	48.7	46.3	68.4	55.7	47.0	59.8	57.2	66.5	58.6
1980	43.5	64.8	55.4	52.3	61.5	51.9	58.6	40.6	67.6	48.8	44.9	64.6	57.8	47.6	57.5	52.9	67.2	53.2
1984	47.3	63.6	58.0	52.9	62.5	54.3	55.5	40.9	63.9	49.4	47.4	61.6	60.7	50.7	58.6	52.5	63.8	54.9
1988	43.5	63.2	55.0	50.9	58.5	50.2	52.5	39.4	62.9	45.3	45.7	60.5	59.1	47.9	53.8	48.1	61.6	55.1
1992	50.3	66.7	60.2	59.1	65.9	54.1	59.0	45.1	66.6	52.2	48.5	63.6	67.5	52.7	60.0	49.7	68.9	61.0
1996	45.0	45.8	41.5	42.6	48.0	47.1	47.5	47.1	47.7	45.6	45.1	47.5	56.9	49.9	41.2	47.0	49.7	62.9
2000	50.2	60.4	55.8	48.8	60.6	53.7	54.3	46.5	58.4	49.2	43.1	52.6	64.0	52.0	56.9	45.8	66.1	61.0

Notes appear on next page

(continued)

TABLE Eb62–113   Voter turnout in presidential elections, by state: 1824–2000   *Continued*

[1] See text regarding potential discontinuity in the series beginning 1972.

[2] For 1840–1860, South Carolina chose electors through its legislature.

[3] Confederate states did not participate in the election of 1864. Also, Mississippi, Texas, and Virginia did not participate in the election of 1868.

[4] Three Republican electoral votes were cast through the state legislature rather than by popular vote.

[5] Excluding 138,216 miscellaneous write-in, blank, and void votes compiled as one total.

Sources

1824–1968: Walter Dean Burnham, in *Historical Statistics of the United States* (1975), series Y27–78.

1970–1996: compiled by U.S. Bureau of the Census and printed in *Statistical Abstract of the United States*, annual. Population data are from U.S. Bureau of the Census, *Current Population Reports*, P25-1117 and Statistical Brief SB/96-2; votes-cast data are from Elections Research Center, *America Votes*, biennial.

2000: State-by-state presidential vote totals from the Federal Election Commission (FEC), Federal Elections 2000; downloaded from the FEC Internet site. Voting age population estimates are based on "Projections of the Population of Voting Age, for States, by Race, November 7, 2000," Internet release date: July 31, 2000, available from the Internet site of the U.S. Census Bureau.

Documentation

Figures are the number of voters as a percentage of eligible voters. It is not possible to achieve precise statements of the number of eligible voters, often referred to as voting age population (VAP). Consequently, the data in this table are clearly approximations, and should be read throughout with that point in mind. This table description is derived from the notes provided by Walter Dean Burnham for *Historical Statistics of the United States* (1975), series Y27–78. See series Eb114 for alternative estimates of voter turnout in presidential elections.

Under the U.S. Constitution, state laws govern the eligibility of voters to cast ballots for candidates. Article 1, Section 4 and Article 2, Section 1 of the Constitution grant the power to state legislatures to establish the "Times, Places and Manner" of holding elections for senators and representatives. Article 2, Section 1 similarly establishes state legislatures as the institution to determine the "manner" by which electors of the President are appointed.

Each of the states is the sole judge of the electoral procedures within its jurisdiction, subject only to constitutional amendments, congressional legislation enacted pursuant to such amendments or other portions of the Constitution, and federal judicial decisions. Only the most salient of such interventions are mentioned here, specifically as they apply to the composition of the potentially eligible electorate:

The Reconstruction Act of March 2, 1867, which (with the Supplemental Act of March 23, 1867) required that the ten ex-Confederate states still without federal representation eliminate all racial barriers to suffrage as a precondition for readmission.

The Fifteenth Amendment to the Constitution (1870) (and subsequent implementing legislation of 1870, 1871, and 1875), which forbade either the states or the federal government to deny the right of citizens to vote "on account of race, color, or previous condition of servitude."

The Nineteenth Amendment to the Constitution (1920), which enfranchised women on the same constitutional terms as men.

The Supreme Court's invalidation of the white primary and of the doctrine that political parties, being private associations, could exclude blacks or any others they chose to exclude from their nominating processes (*Smith v. Allright*, 321 U.S. 649, 1944).

The Twenty-third Amendment to the Constitution (1961), extending presidential suffrage to the District of Columbia.

The Twenty-fourth Amendment to the Constitution (1964), prohibiting the levying of a poll tax or any other tax as a prerequisite to voting in federal elections.

The Civil Rights Act of 1965, suspending all literacy tests in Alabama, Alaska, Georgia, Louisiana, Mississippi, South Carolina, Virginia, forty counties in North Carolina, and one county in Arizona, and establishing federal registrars in the affected areas.

The Civil Rights Act of 1970, which continued suspension for another five years and extended it to all literacy tests, lowered the minimum voting age from 21 to 18 in all federal and state elections, and lowered the minimum residence requirement for voting in presidential elections to a uniform thirty days.

The Twenty-sixth Amendment to the Constitution (1971), which formally reaffirmed the lowering of the voting age minimum from 21 to 18 years.

Every estimate of voting turnout is a ratio between a numerator and a denominator. Errors in estimates may occur because of errors in the numerator, the denominator, or both. Problems with the numerator include the following: fraudulent ballot-box stuffing; fraudulent suppression of returns, or failure of subdivisions to report within the legal time limit; compiling or reporting errors, without fraudulent intent; and available returns that may be significantly fragmentary because the original records were lost.

Problems with the denominator (that is, the population base), relate primarily to its derivation. The components of the denominator, the estimated eligible population, alone can be developed more or less accurately for all states and time periods, but even these have very significant problems. In general, the denominator estimates are much more precise from 1900 on than they are for years prior to that date. The reason for this lies in the changing nature of census reporting of critical components that enter the calculation.

Information that has been compiled into the denominator falls into the following classifications: (1) age cohorts; (2) sex by age for and following every point at which women were enfranchised by state law or by the Nineteenth Amendment; (3) race, which substantially means adding the black adult male population to the denominator base in 1868 (ten Southern states) or 1870; and (4) citizenship status, reported separately as "male citizens" in 1870, and in more detail beginning with the 1900 Census.

One final remark should be made about method of computing the size of the eligible voting age population. In the absence of any better estimation, the biennial figures are compiled on the basis of linear interpolation between one decennial census year and the next. Obviously, patterns of population growth and decline are never perfectly linear and may deviate widely from that assumption. This is a problem in the "mining-camp" states of the West. Fortunately, the linear model does not appear sharply inconsistent with reality in well-settled states. In any event, no known alternative appears to exist throughout most of American political and demographic history except in those few states that published adequate censuses falling between federal census years.

The following possible elements of a denominator have not been compiled in generating this estimate of voter turnout, although they have entered into state legislation regulating eligibility to vote: (1) literacy of the adult male/adult population; (2) taxpaying components of the adult male/adult population; and (3) other components that define those legally entitled to vote at any given time. Many of such devices were deliberately employed, particularly between 1890 and 1965, to prevent access of racial and ethnic minorities to the voting booth. Rusk's estimates in Table Eb114–122 attempt to account for these exclusions.

Note that the 1972–2000 figures are drawn from the Census Bureau estimates of voting age population and votes cast as recorded in biennial volumes of *America Votes*. There is some potential for discontinuity in the series, although 1960s decade presidential election turnout estimates for both sources differ by only 0.2 to 0.3 percent.

TABLE Eb114–122   Voter turnout in presidential and congressional elections – national, South, and non-South: 1824–1998

Contributed by John P. McIver

Year	President			House of Representatives			Senate		
	Overall	Non-South	South	Overall	Non-South	South	Overall	Non-South	South
	Eb114	Eb115	Eb116	Eb117	Eb118	Eb119	Eb120	Eb121	Eb122
	Percent	Percent	Percent	Percent	Percent	Percent	Percent	Percent	Percent
1824	26.7	26.7	26.7	42.1	43.0	27.6	—	—	—
1826	—	—	—	46.5	45.5	66.2	—	—	—
1828	55.2	59.0	42.0	57.1	55.0	74.9	—	—	—
1830	—	—	—	54.4	51.2	83.1	—	—	—
1832	54.4	61.1	29.8	59.1	57.0	77.4	—	—	—
1834	—	—	—	62.1	60.6	73.7	—	—	—
1836	54.4	55.8	49.1	57.5	56.0	69.3	—	—	—
1838	—	—	—	69.9	68.8	78.0	—	—	—
1840	77.5	78.1	75.3	69.9	70.6	65.1	—	—	—
1842	—	—	—	62.1	60.9	69.0	—	—	—
1844	74.5	74.6	74.5	71.8	71.6	73.4	—	—	—
1846	—	—	—	58.9	57.2	69.8	—	—	—
1848	67.3	66.9	68.7	63.5	62.4	69.9	—	—	—
1850	—	—	—	56.6	55.2	71.3	—	—	—
1852	63.2	64.1	59.1	62.0	60.9	72.7	—	—	—
1854	—	—	—	60.2	57.8	73.6	—	—	—
1856	70.9	71.1	69.8	67.9	68.1	66.6	—	—	—
1858	—	—	—	62.1	61.6	65.8	—	—	—
1860	72.1	71.7	73.7	70.4	70.2	82.6	—	—	—
1862	—	—	—	56.3	56.3	—	—	—	—
1864	66.2	66.2	—	61.9	62.9	30.3	—	—	—
1866	—	—	—	62.4	62.8	48.1	—	—	—
1868	71.8	72.9	66.2	69.6	72.4	57.6	—	—	—
1870	—	—	—	66.8	67.2	64.9	—	—	—
1872	72.2	73.9	66.9	74.0	75.7	68.7	—	—	—
1874	—	—	—	65.0	65.6	63.0	—	—	—
1876	82.9	85.3	75.0	81.3	84.0	71.9	—	—	—
1878	—	—	—	65.3	70.3	49.3	—	—	—
1880	80.5	85.6	64.7	79.3	84.5	63.2	—	—	—
1882	—	—	—	66.1	70.6	51.8	—	—	—
1884	78.8	83.4	64.1	77.6	82.6	61.5	—	—	—
1886	—	—	—	64.0	70.5	42.9	—	—	—
1888	80.9	86.2	63.8	79.9	85.1	62.3	—	—	—
1890	—	—	—	64.9	70.6	45.3	—	—	—
1892	76.2	81.3	58.9	74.9	79.9	57.6	—	—	—
1894	—	—	—	67.4	73.4	46.9	—	—	—
1896	79.7	86.2	57.4	78.1	84.3	56.9	—	—	—
1898	—	—	—	60.0	67.8	33.7	—	—	—
1900	73.6	82.6	43.3	72.2	81.2	41.8	—	—	—
1902	—	—	—	55.4	64.9	23.8	—	—	—
1904	65.4	76.3	29.0	63.7	74.3	28.3	—	—	—
1906	—	—	—	51.1	60.7	18.6	—	—	—
1908	65.5	75.8	30.7	63.6	73.8	28.9	—	—	—
1910	—	—	—	51.3	60.4	20.4	—	—	—
1912	58.8	67.4	27.8	55.7	64.0	25.8	57.5	57.5	—
1914	—	—	—	50.1	58.5	18.5	54.6	60.4	17.6
1916	61.9	69.3	31.7	59.0	66.0	30.0	61.4	66.6	31.4
1918	—	—	—	40.0	46.0	14.8	37.9	50.0	15.6
1920	49.2	57.3	21.7	47.0	54.5	21.3	49.4	55.4	20.3
1922	—	—	—	35.8	42.6	12.4	38.9	43.5	14.1
1924	48.8	57.5	18.8	45.0	53.0	17.8	43.2	58.4	18.3
1926	—	—	—	32.8	39.8	8.3	35.8	41.2	9.1
1928	56.7	66.3	23.3	52.7	61.8	21.1	56.1	62.6	21.6
1930	—	—	—	36.7	43.7	12.4	34.6	47.7	12.9
1932	56.8	66.2	24.2	53.6	62.3	23.6	56.3	62.9	23.1
1934	—	—	—	44.6	53.8	13.0	48.3	55.1	12.9
1936	61.1	71.7	24.8	57.6	67.7	23.0	51.5	69.6	22.4
1938	—	—	—	46.9	57.4	11.2	50.2	57.9	12.7
1940	62.9	73.6	26.3	58.8	69.2	23.6	62.3	69.8	23.8
1942	—	—	—	34.0	42.0	7.0	29.9	44.1	7.2

(continued)

TABLE Eb114–122 Voter turnout in presidential and congressional elections – national, South, and non-South: 1824–1998 Continued

	President			House of Representatives			Senate		
	Overall	Non-South	South	Overall	Non-South	South	Overall	Non-South	South
	Eb114	Eb115	Eb116	Eb117	Eb118	Eb119	Eb120	Eb121	Eb122
Year	Percent	Percent	Percent	Percent	Percent	Percent	Percent	Percent	Percent
1944	56.0	65.3	24.4	52.6	61.7	21.7	56.1	63.1	22.2
1946	—	—	—	38.7	47.0	10.5	41.8	48.1	10.2
1948	53.1	61.4	25.1	50.0	58.4	21.3	45.6	60.7	21.7
1950	—	—	—	42.5	51.2	12.6	46.8	53.1	16.2
1952	63.5	70.8	38.6	59.6	67.7	32.4	62.3	68.1	33.3
1954	—	—	—	43.0	51.0	16.2	39.0	53.5	16.5
1956	61.4	68.8	36.7	57.5	66.1	29.4	59.7	66.6	28.0
1958	—	—	—	44.6	53.4	14.7	48.5	55.3	16.7
1959	—	—	—	—	—	—	54.7	54.7	—
1960	65.2	72.5	41.4	61.3	69.4	33.6	57.5	72.2	35.0
1962	—	—	—	47.6	54.6	24.1	49.6	55.2	24.3
1964	63.3	68.6	46.3	59.6	65.7	39.5	63.2	67.7	42.9
1966	—	—	—	46.6	52.1	28.7	44.5	54.1	29.5
1968	62.5	65.8	52.1	57.1	61.8	41.8	59.7	63.0	45.6
1970	—	—	—	46.3	50.5	30.8	50.2	53.0	37.0
1972	56.4	60.4	44.6	52.9	57.3	36.9	53.0	60.0	43.1
1974	—	—	—	38.0	41.6	24.0	39.6	42.6	27.5
1976	55.3	58.1	47.5	51.5	54.7	40.6	53.4	55.6	45.3
1978	—	—	—	37.3	40.4	25.7	36.9	43.0	28.1
1980	55.1	57.5	48.6	50.8	53.6	40.6	52.8	54.5	46.1
1982	—	—	—	41.1	44.0	31.3	43.0	45.4	34.5
1984	56.4	58.4	51.1	52.5	55.1	43.5	54.8	59.1	48.9
1986	—	—	—	36.5	38.4	30.1	39.6	40.2	37.8
1988	53.4	55.7	47.7	49.3	51.6	41.6	52.5	54.0	47.4
1990	—	—	—	36.2	38.3	29.6	37.6	43.2	30.2
1992	58.6	60.8	53.1	54.7	56.7	48.3	55.4	57.9	46.3
1994	—	—	—	39.8	41.6	34.0	41.9	42.9	38.6
1996	52.1	54.0	47.8	49.4	51.3	43.3	50.4	54.5	45.7
1998	—	—	—	37.1	39.8	28.5	39.6	40.7	36.1

Source

Jerrold G. Rusk, *A Statistical History of the American Electorate* (Congressional Quarterly Press, 2001), Tables 3-3, 3-5, and 3-8.

Documentation

Turnout may be defined simply as the number of votes cast as a percentage of the population eligible to vote. Yet many different estimates of turnout exist. Variations in both the numerator and denominator play significant roles in determining the result.

As Burnham did in his estimates of voter turnout for *Historical Statistics of the United States* (1975), series Y27–78 (see Table Eb62–113), Rusk uses votes cast as the numerator; but even here estimates differ.

Estimates of the denominator, voting age population (VAP), are more problematic for students of voter turnout. Defining the eligible population (given both federal constitutional "requirements" as well as myriad local and state legal variations) and estimating its size become more difficult the further back in time one proceeds. Extrapolations are required between censuses. Many of the electoral restrictions and legal and social constraints that define the actual voting population are detailed in Rusk (2001), Chapter 2. In this regard, Rusk may have made additional adjustments to VAP not included in the Burnham estimates. Rusk relies heavily on the work of John J. Stucker in estimating the eligible population. See Stucker, "The Impact of Woman Suffrage on Patterns of Voter Participation" (Ph.D. dissertation, University of Michigan, 1973).

Contemporary alternatives to both the Burnham and Rusk estimates exist in current practice of the U.S. Census Bureau. The Census Bureau offers at least two estimates of voter turnout, one similar to the Burnham and Rusk definitions that relies on the Census's own estimate of VAP each election year, and a second based on the Current Population Survey (CPS). The Census Bureau turnout figures are consistently lower than both Rusk's series Eb114 and Burnham's series Eb62 for the period 1932–1960 and than Rusk's data throughout the latter half of the twentieth century – in large part a function of a less restrictive definition of VAP. On the other hand, relying on the November supplement to the Current Population Survey (CPS), the Census has also produced survey-based estimates of voter turnout. These data produce turnout rates significantly higher than Rusk's or Burnham's and suggest that survey respondents exaggerate their voting activity. The CPS samples do, however, allow investigators to understand the correlates of turnout in greater detail than possible with aggregate data. Also see the following technical reports from the American National Election Studies (NES) – available at the NES Internet site – which document problems with exaggerated self-reporting of voting by survey respondents: Santa Traugott, "Validating Self-Reported Vote: 1964–1988" (August 1989), NES Technical Report number 34; Stanley Presser, Michael W. Traugott, and Santa Traugott, "Vote 'Over' Reporting in Surveys: The Records or the Respondents?" (November 1990), NES Technical Report number 39; and Michael W. Traugott, Santa Traugott, and Stanley Presser, "Revalidation of Self-Reported Vote" (May 1992), NES Technical Report number 42.

Estimates for the 1788–1820 period are also provided by Rusk (2001).

In this table the South consists of the eleven states of the Old Confederacy: Alabama, Arkansas, Florida, Georgia, Louisiana, Mississippi, North Carolina, South Carolina, Tennessee, Texas, and Virginia.

PRESIDENTIAL AND CONGRESSIONAL ELECTIONS

John P. McIver

TABLE Eb123–148   Methods used by states to select presidential electors: 1788–1836[1]

Contributed by John P. McIver

	Delaware	Pennsylvania	New Jersey	Georgia	Connecticut	Massachusetts	Maryland	South Carolina	New Hampshire	Virginia	New York	North Carolina	Rhode Island	Vermont
	Eb123	Eb124	Eb125	Eb126	Eb127	Eb128	Eb129 [2]	Eb130	Eb131	Eb132	Eb133	Eb134	Eb135	Eb136
Year	—	—	—	—	—	—	—	—	—	—	—	—	—	—
1788 [4]	D 3 [5]	G	L	L	L	D 8; L [6]	G	L	G; L [11]	D 12	—	—	—	—
1792	L	G	L	L	L	D 4; L [7]	G	L	G [12]	D 21	L	L [14]	L	L
1796	L	G	L	G	L	D 14; L [8]	D 10	L	G; L [11]	D 21	L	D 12	L	L
1800	L	L	L	L	L	L	D 10	L	L	G	L	D 12	G	L
1804	L	G	G	L	L	D 17; A 2	D 9	L	G	G	L	D 14	G	L
1808	L	G	G	L	L	L	D 9	L	G	G	L	D 14	G	L
1812	L	G	L	L	L	D 6 [9]	D 9	L	G	G	L	L	G	L
1816	L	G	G	L	L	L	D 9	L	G	G	L	G	G	L
1820	L	G	G	L	G	D 13; A 2	D 9	L	G	G	L	G	G	L
1824	L	G	G	L	G	G	D 9	L	G	G	L	G	G	L
1828	L	G	G	G	G	G	D 9	L	G	G	D 30; E [13]	G	G	G
1832	G	G	G	G	G	G	D 4 [10]	L	G	G	G	G	G	G
1836	G	G	G	G	G	G	G	L	G	G	G	G	G	G

	Kentucky	Tennessee	Ohio	Louisiana	Indiana	Mississippi	Illinois	Alabama	Maine	Missouri	Arkansas	Michigan
	Eb137 [3]	Eb138	Eb139	Eb140	Eb141	Eb142	Eb143	Eb144	Eb145	Eb146	Eb147	Eb148
Year	—	—	—	—	—	—	—	—	—	—	—	—
1788 [4]	—	—	—	—	—	—	—	—	—	—	—	—
1792	D 4	—	—	—	—	—	—	—	—	—	—	—
1796	D 4	E [16]	—	—	—	—	—	—	—	—	—	—
1800	D 4	E [16]	—	—	—	—	—	—	—	—	—	—
1804	D 2	D 5	G	—	—	—	—	—	—	—	—	—
1808	D 2	D 5	G	—	—	—	—	—	—	—	—	—
1812	D 3	D 8	G	L	—	—	—	—	—	—	—	—
1816	D 3	D 8	G	L	L	—	—	—	—	—	—	—
1820	D 3	D 8	G	L	L	G	D 3	L	D 7; A 2	L	—	—
1824	D 3 [15]	D 11	G	L	G	G	D 3	G	D 7; A 2	D 3	—	—
1828	G	D 11	G	G	G	G	G	G	D 7; A 2	G	—	—
1832	G	G	G	G	G	G	G	G	G	G	—	—
1836	G	G	G	G	G	G	G	G	G	G	G	G

[1] The designations used in the table are shown here. When two designations are given for a state, a combination of methods is used; details are often provided in the notes. When a number is paired with a designation, it indicates either the number of districts into which the state was divided (in the case of "D" designations), or the number of electors elected at large (in the case of "A" designations).

- L   by legislature
- G   by voters, on general ticket
- D   by voters, in districts
- A   by voters, in the state at large
- E   by electors

[2] For 1804–1828, eleven electors were chosen; two of the districts elected two members each.

[3] For 1804–1820, each district elected four electors.

[4] 1788–1789.

[5] Each qualified voter voted for one elector. The three electors who received the most votes in the state were elected.

[6] Each of the eight districts chose two electors, from which the General Court (that is, the legislature) selected one. It also elected two electors at large.

[7] Two of the districts voted for five members each, and two for three members each. A majority of votes was necessary for a choice. In case of a failure to elect by popular vote, the General Court supplied the deficiency. In the election of 1792, the people chose five electors and the General Court, eleven.

[8] A majority of votes was necessary for a popular choice. Deficiencies were filled by the General Court, as in 1792. It also chose two electors at large. In 1796 it chose nine electors, and the people, seven.

[9] One district chose six electors; one, five electors; one, four electors; two, three electors each; and one, one elector.

[10] One district chose four electors; one, three electors; one, two electors; and one, one elector.

[11] A majority of the popular vote was necessary for a choice. In case of a failure to elect, the legislature supplied the deficiency.

[12] A majority of votes was necessary for a choice. In case of a failure to elect one or more electors, a second election was held by the people, at which choice was made from the candidates in the first election who had the most votes. The number of candidates in the second election was limited to twice the number of electors wanted.

[13] One district elected three electors; two, two electors each; and twenty-seven, one elector each. The thirty-four electors thus elected chose two presidential electors.

[14] Members of the legislature residing in each district chose three electors.

[15] Two districts chose five electors each, and one chose four electors.

[16] Three presidential electors were chosen – one each for the districts of Washington, Hamilton, and Mero. Three "electors" for each county in the state were appointed by the legislature, and the "electors" residing in each of the three districts chose one of the three presidential electors.

(continued)

TABLE Eb123-148   Methods used by states to select presidential electors: 1788-1836 *Continued*

Source

Historical Statistics of the United States (1975), series Y1-26, which are based on Charles O. Paullin, *Atlas of the Historical Geography of the United States* (Carnegie Institution of Washington and American Geographical Society of New York, 1932), p. 89.

Documentation

The presidential electors of each state are selected, according to the Constitution, "in such manner as the legislature thereof may direct." The development of political party direction of the electoral college was not anticipated in the Constitution and, during the early years of the republic, electors were chosen in the several states by a number of different devices. The principal methods were election by the state legislature itself, by state electors popularly chosen to elect presidential electors, and by direct popular vote for the electors. With few exceptions, presidential electors have been elected by popular vote since 1828. The legislature of South Carolina, however, continued to elect presidential electors until 1860. Since the Civil War, legislatures have chosen electors only twice: Florida in 1868, and Colorado in 1876.

TABLE Eb149-153   Electoral and popular votes cast for President, by candidate: 1789-2000[1,2]

Contributed by John P. McIver

	Number of states	Presidential candidate	Candidate's political party	Votes received by candidate	
				Electoral	Popular
	Eb149	Eb150	Eb151	Eb152	Eb153
Year	Number	—	—	Number	Number
1789	10	George Washington	—	69	—
		John Adams	—	34	—
		John Jay	—	9	—
		R. H. Harrison	—	6	—
		John Rutledge	—	6	—
		John Hancock	—	4	—
		George Clinton	—	3	—
		Samuel Huntington	—	2	—
		John Milton	—	2	—
		James Armstrong	—	1	—
		Benjamin Lincoln	—	1	—
		Edward Telfair	—	1	—
		(Not voted)	—	12	—
1792	15	George Washington	Federalist	132	—
		John Adams	Federalist	77	—
		George Clinton	Democratic Republican	50	—
		Thomas Jefferson	—	4	—
		Aaron Burr	—	1	—
1796	16	John Adams	Federalist	71	—
		Thomas Jefferson	Democratic Republican	68	—
		Thomas Pinckney	Federalist	59	—
		Aaron Burr	Anti-Federalist	30	—
		Samuel Adams	Democratic Republican	15	—
		Oliver Ellsworth	Federalist	11	—
		George Clinton	Democratic Republican	7	—
		John Jay	Independent Federalist	5	—
		James Iredell	Federalist	3	—
		George Washington	Federalist	2	—
		John Henry	Independent	2	—
		S. Johnston	Independent Federalist	2	—
		C. C. Pinckney	Independent Federalist	1	—
1800	16	Thomas Jefferson	Democratic Republican	73	—
		Aaron Burr	Democratic Republican	73	—
		John Adams	Federalist	65	—
		C. C. Pinckney	Federalist	64	—
		John Jay	Federalist	1	—
1804	17	Thomas Jefferson	Democratic Republican	162	—
		C. C. Pinckney	Federalist	14	—
1808	17	James Madison	Democratic Republican	122	—
		C. C. Pinckney	Federalist	47	—
		George Clinton	Independent Republican	6	—
		(Not voted)	—	1	—
1812	18	James Madison	Democratic Republican	128	—
		De Witt Clinton	Fusion	89	—
		(Not voted)	—	1	—

Notes appear at end of table

TABLE Eb149–153 Electoral and popular votes cast for President, by candidate: 1789–2000 *Continued*

Year	Number of states	Presidential candidate	Candidate's political party	Votes received by candidate	
				Electoral	Popular
	Eb149	Eb150	Eb151	Eb152	Eb153
	Number	—	—	Number	Number
1816	19	James Monroe	Republican	183	—
		Rufus King	Federalist	34	—
		(Not voted)	—	4	—
1820	24	James Monroe	Republican	231	—
		John Q. Adams	Independent Republican	1	—
		(Not voted)	—	3	—
1824	24	John Q. Adams	No distinct party designation	84 [3]	108,740
		Andrew Jackson	No distinct party designation	99 [3]	153,544
		Henry Clay	No distinct party designation	37	47,136
		W. H. Crawford	No distinct party designation	41	46,618
1828	24	Andrew Jackson	Democratic	178	647,286
		John Q. Adams	National Republican	83	508,064
1832	24	Andrew Jackson	Democratic	219	687,502
		Henry Clay	National Republican	49	530,189
		William Wirt	Anti-Masonic	7	—
		John Floyd	Nullifiers	11	—
		(Not voted)	—	2	—
1836	26	Martin Van Buren	Democratic	170	765,483
		William H. Harrison	Whig	73	739,795 [12]
		Hugh L. White	Whig	26	739,795 [12]
		Daniel Webster	Whig	14	739,795 [12]
		W. P. Mangum	Anti-Jackson	11	—
1840	26	William H. Harrison	Whig	234	1,274,624
		Martin Van Buren	Democratic	60	1,127,781
1844	26	James K. Polk	Democratic	170	1,338,464
		Henry Clay	Whig	105	1,300,097
		James G. Birney	Liberty	0	62,300
1848	30	Zachary Taylor	Whig	163	1,360,967
		Lewis Cass	Democratic	127	1,222,342
		Martin Van Buren	Free Soil	0	291,263
1852	31	Franklin Pierce	Democratic	254	1,601,117
		Winfield Scott	Whig	42	1,385,453
		John P. Hale	Free Soil	0	155,825
1856	31	James Buchanan	Democratic	174	1,832,955
		John C. Fremont	Republican	114	1,339,932
		Millard Fillmore	American	8	871,731
1860	33	Abraham Lincoln	Republican	180	1,865,593
		J. C. Breckinridge	Democratic (Southern)	72	848,356
		Stephen A. Douglas	Democratic	12	1,382,713
		John Bell	Constitutional Union	39	592,906
1864	36	Abraham Lincoln	Republican	212	2,206,938
		George B. McClellan	Democratic	21	1,803,787
		(Not voted)	—	81	—
1868	37	Ulysses S. Grant	Republican	214	3,013,421
		Horatio Seymour	Democratic	80	2,706,829
		(Not voted)	—	23	—
1872	37	Ulysses S. Grant	Republican	286	3,596,745
		Horace Greeley	Democratic	3 [4]	2,843,446
		Charles O'Connor	Straight Democratic	0	29,489
		Thomas A. Hendricks	Independent-Democratic	42	—
		B. Gratz Brown	Democratic	18	—
		Charles J. Jenkins	Democratic	2	—
		David Davis	Democratic	1	—
		(Not voted)	—	17	—
1876	38	Rutherford B. Hayes	Republican	185	4,036,572
		Samuel J. Tilden	Democratic	184	4,284,020
		Peter Cooper	Greenback	0	81,737
1880	38	James A. Garfield	Republican	214	4,453,295
		Winfield S. Hancock	Democratic	155	4,414,082
		James B. Weaver	Greenback-Labor	0	308,578
		Neal Dow	Prohibition	0	10,305

Notes appear at end of table

(continued)

TABLE Eb149–153   Electoral and popular votes cast for President, by candidate: 1789–2000 Continued

	Number of states	Presidential candidate	Candidate's political party	Votes received by candidate	
				Electoral	Popular
	Eb149	Eb150	Eb151	Eb152	Eb153
Year	Number	—	—	Number	Number
1884	38	Grover Cleveland	Democratic	219	4,879,507
		James G. Blaine	Republican	182	4,850,293
		Benjamin F. Butler	Greenback-Labor	0	175,370
		John P. St. John	Prohibition	0	150,369
1888	38	Benjamin Harrison	Republican	233	5,447,129
		Grover Cleveland	Democratic	168	5,537,857
		Clinton B. Fisk	Prohibition	0	249,506
		Anson J. Streeter	Union Labor	0	146,935
1892	44	Grover Cleveland	Democratic	277	5,555,426
		Benjamin Harrison	Republican	145	5,182,690
		James B. Weaver	People's	22	1,029,846
		John Bidwell	Prohibition	0	264,133
		Simon Wing	Socialist Labor	0	21,164
1896	45	William McKinley	Republican	271	7,102,246
		William J. Bryan	Democratic	176 [5]	6,492,559
		John M. Palmer	National Democratic	0	133,148
		Joshua Levering	Prohibition	0	132,007
		Charles H. Hatchett	Socialist Labor	0	36,274
		Charles E. Bentley	Nationalist	0	13,969
1900	45	William McKinley	Republican	292	7,218,491
		William J. Bryan	Democratic	155 [5]	6,356,734
		John C. Wooley	Prohibition	0	208,914
		Eugene V. Debs	Socialist	0	87,814
		Wharton Barker	People's	0	50,373
		Joseph F. Malloney	Socialist Labor	0	39,739
1904	45	Theodore Roosevelt	Republican	336	7,628,461
		Alton B. Parker	Democratic	140	5,084,223
		Eugene V. Debs	Socialist	0	402,283
		Silas C. Swallow	Prohibition	0	258,536
		Thomas E. Watson	People's	0	117,183
		Charles H. Corregan	Socialist Labor	0	31,249
1908	46	William H. Taft	Republican	321	7,675,320
		William J. Bryan	Democratic	162	6,412,294
		Eugene V. Debs	Socialist	0	420,793
		Eugene W. Chafin	Prohibition	0	253,840
		Thomas L. Hisgen	Independence	0	82,872
		Thomas E. Watson	People's	0	29,100
		August Gillhaus	Socialist Labor	0	14,021
1912	48	Woodrow Wilson	Democratic	435	6,296,547
		Theodore Roosevelt	Progressive	88	4,118,571
		William H. Taft	Republican	8	3,486,720
		Eugene V. Debs	Socialist	0	900,672
		Eugene W. Chafin	Prohibition	0	206,275
		Arthur E. Reimer	Socialist Labor	0	28,750
1916	48	Woodrow Wilson	Democratic	277	9,127,695
		Charles E. Hughes	Republican	254	8,533,507
		A. L. Benson	Socialist	0	585,113
		J. Frank Hanly	Prohibition	0	220,506
		Arthur E. Reimer	Socialist Labor	0	13,403
1920	48	Warren G. Harding	Republican	404	16,153,115
		James M. Cox	Democratic	127	9,133,092
		Eugene V. Debs	Socialist	0	915,490
		Parley P. Christensen	Farmer-Labor	0	265,229
		Aaron S. Watkins	Prohibition	0	189,339
		James E. Ferguson	American	0	48,098
		William W. Cox	Socialist Labor	0	30,594
		Robert C. Macauley	Single Tax	0	5,833
		Unnamed nominee	(Texas)	0	27,309
		Scattered votes	—	0	514

Notes appear at end of table

(continued)

TABLE Eb149–153 Electoral and popular votes cast for President, by candidate: 1789–2000 *Continued*

Year	Number of states	Presidential candidate	Candidate's political party	Votes received by candidate	
				Electoral	Popular
	Eb149	Eb150	Eb151	Eb152	Eb153
	Number	—	—	Number	Number
1924	48	Calvin Coolidge	Republican	382	15,719,921
		John W. Davis	Democratic	136	8,386,704
		Robert I. LaFollette	Progressive	13	4,832,532
		Herman P. Faris	Prohibition	0	56,292
		Frank T. Johns	Socialist Labor	0	34,174
		William Z. Foster	Workers	0	33,360
		Gilbert O. Nations	American	0	24,340
		William J. Wallace	Commonwealth Land	0	2,948
		Scattered votes	—	0	4,752
1928	48	Herbert C. Hoover	Republican	444	21,437,277
		Alfred E. Smith	Democratic	87	15,007,698
		Norman Thomas	Socialist	0	265,583
		William Z. Foster	Communist	0	46,896
		Verne L. Reynolds	Socialist Labor	0	21,586
		William F. Varney	Prohibition	0	20,101
		Frank E. Webb	Farmer-Labor	0	6,390
		Scattered votes	—	0	420
1932	48	Franklin D. Roosevelt	Democratic	472	22,829,501
		Herbert C. Hoover	Republican	59	15,760,684
		Norman Thorn	Socialist	0	884,649
		William Z. Foster	Communist	0	103,253
		William D. Upshaw	Prohibition	0	81,872
		William H. Harvey	Liberty	0	53,247
		Verne L. Reynolds	Socialist Labor	0	34,043
		Jacob Coxey	Farmer-Labor	0	7,431
		John Zahnd	National	0	1,645
		James R. Cox	Jobless	0	740
		Unnamed nominee	(Texas and Arizona)	0	166
		Scattered votes	—	0	1,528
1936	48	Franklin D. Roosevelt	Democratic	523	27,757,333
		Alfred M. Landon	Republican	8	16,684,231
		William Lemke	Union	0	892,267
		Norman Thorn	Socialist	0	187,833
		Earl Browder	Communist	0	80,171
		D. Leigh Colvin	Prohibition	0	37,677
		John W. Aiken	Socialist Labor	0	12,829
		William Pelley	Christian	0	1,598
		Scattered votes	—	0	824
1940	48	Franklin D. Roosevelt	Democratic	449	27,313,041
		Wendell L. Willkie	Republican	82	22,348,480
		Norman Thomas	Socialist	0	116,410
		Roger Q. Babson	Prohibition	0	58,708
		Earl Browder	Communist	0	46,259
		John W. Aiken	Socialist Labor	0	14,892
		Alfred Knutson	(North Dakota)	0	545
		Scattered votes	—	0	2,083
1944	48	Franklin D. Roosevelt	Democratic	432	25,612,610
		Thomas E. Dewey	Republican	99	22,017,617
		Norman Thomas	Socialist	0	79,003
		Claude A. Watson	Prohibition	0	74,799
		Edward A. Teichert	Socialist Labor	0	45,191
		Gerald Smith	American First	0	1,780
		Uncommitted electors	(Texas and South Carolina)	0	143,243
		Scattered votes	—	0	2,447
1948	48	Harry S. Truman	Democratic	303	24,179,345
		Thomas E. Dewey	Republican	189	21,991,291
		Strom Thurmond	States' Rights	39	1,176,125
		Henry Wallace	Progressive	0	1,157,326
		Norman Thomas	Socialist	0	139,572
		Claude A. Watson	Prohibition	0	103,900
		Edward A. Teichert	Socialist Labor	0	29,241
		Farrel Dobbs	Socialist Workers	0	13,614
		Scattered votes	—	0	3,412

(continued)

TABLE Eb149–153 Electoral and popular votes cast for President, by candidate: 1789–2000 *Continued*

Year	Number of states	Presidential candidate	Candidate's political party	Votes received by candidate	
				Electoral	Popular
	Eb149	Eb150	Eb151	Eb152	Eb153
Year	Number	—	—	Number	Number
1952	48	Dwight D. Eisenhower	Republican	442	33,936,234
		Adlai E. Stevenson	Democratic	89	27,314,992
		Vincent Hallinan	Progressive	0	140,023
		Stuart Hamblen	Prohibition	0	72,949
		Eric Hass	Socialist Labor	0	30,267
		Darlington Hoopes	Socialist	0	20,203
		Douglas A. MacArthur	Constitution	0	17,205
		Farrell Dobbs	Socialist Workers	0	10,312
		Two other named candidates	Four other minor parties	0	21,408
		Scattered votes	—	0	4,530
1956	48	Dwight D. Eisenhower	Republican	457	35,590,472
		Adlai E. Stevenson	Democratic	73 [6]	26,022,752
		T. Coleman Andrews	States' Rights	0	111,178
		Eric Hass	Socialist Labor	0	44,450
		Enoch A. Holtwick	Prohibition	0	41,937
		Five other named candidates	Five other minor parties	0	14,417
		Unnamed nominee	(Alabama, Louisiana, Mississippi, and South Carolina)	0	196,318
		Scattered votes	—	0	5,384
1960	50	John F. Kennedy	Democratic	303 [7]	34,226,731
		Richard M. Nixon	Republican	219	34,108,157
		Eric Hass	Socialist Labor	0	47,522
		Rutherford L. Decker	Prohibition	0	46,203
		Orval E. Faubus	National States' Rights	0	44,977
		Farrell Dobbs	Socialist Workers	0	40,165
		Charles L. Sullivan	Constitution	0	18,162
		Five other named candidates	Five other minor parties	0	17,565
		Unnamed nominee	(Louisiana, Mississippi, and Michigan)	0	286,359
		Scattered votes	—	0	2,378
1964	50	Lyndon B. Johnson	Democratic	486	43,129,566
		Barry M. Goldwater	Republican	52	27,178,188
		Eric Hass	Socialist Labor	0	45,219
		Clifton DeBerry	Socialist Workers	0	32,720
		E. Harold Munn	Prohibition	0	23,267
		Three other named candidates	Three other minor parties	0	12,032
		Unnamed nominee	(Alabama)	0	210,732
		Scattered votes	—	0	12,868
1968	50	Richard M. Nixon	Republican	301	31,785,480
		Hubert H. Humphrey	Democratic	191	31,275,166
		George C. Wallace	American Independent	46	9,906,473
		Henning A. Blomen	Socialist Labor	0	52,588
		Dick Gregory	—	0	47,133 [13]
		Fred Halstead	Socialist Workers	0	41,388
		Eldridge Cleaver	Peace and Freedom	0	36,563
		Eugene J. McCarthy	—	0	25,552 [14]
		E. Harold Munn	Prohibition	0	15,123
		Five other named candidates	Five other minor parties	0	2,777
		Unnamed nominee	—	0	12,430
		Scattered votes	—	0	11,192
1972	50	Richard M. Nixon	Republican	520	47,169,911
		George S. McGovern	Democratic	17	29,170,383
		John G. Schmitz	American	0	1,099,482
		Benjamin Spock	People's	0	78,756
		Linda Jenness	Socialist Workers	0	66,677
		Louis Fisher	Socialist Labor	0	53,814
		Gus Hall	Communist	0	25,595
		E. Harold Munn	Prohibition	0	13,505
		Three other named candidates	Three other minor parties	0 [8]	5,636
		Scattered write-in votes	—	0	34,795

Notes appear at end of table

(continued)

TABLE Eb149–153 Electoral and popular votes cast for President, by candidate: 1789–2000 *Continued*

Year	Number of states	Presidential candidate	Candidate's political party	Votes received by candidate — Electoral	Votes received by candidate — Popular
	Eb149	Eb150	Eb151	Eb152	Eb153
Year	Number	—	—	Number	Number
1976	50	Jimmy Carter	Democratic	297	40,830,763
		Gerald Ford	Republican	240 [9]	39,147,793
		Eugene J. McCarthy	Independent	0	756,691
		Roger L. MacBride	Libertarian	0	173,011
		Lester G. Maddox	American Independent	0	170,531
		Thomas J. Anderson	American	0	160,773
		Peter Camejo	Socialist Workers	0	91,314
		Gus Hall	Communist	0	58,992
		Margaret Wright	People's	0	49,024
		Lyndon H. LaRouche	U.S. Labor	0	40,043
		Benjamin C. Bubar	Prohibition	0	15,934
		Four other named candidates	Four other minor parties	0	16,051
		Scattered write-in votes		—	39,861
		None of these candidates		—	5,108
1980	50	Ronald Reagan	Republican	489	43,904,153
		Jimmy Carter	Democratic	49	35,483,883
		John B. Anderson	Independent	0	5,720,060
		Edward E. Clark	Libertarian	0	921,299
		Barry Commoner	Citizens	0	234,294
		Gus Hall	Communist	0	45,023
		John Rarick	American Independent	0	41,268
		Clifton DeBerry	Socialist Workers	0	38,737
		Ellen McCormack	Right to Life	0	32,327
		Maureen Smith	Peace and Freedom	0	18,116
		Deidre Griswold	Workers World	0	13,300
		Ten other named candidates	Nine other minor parties	0	39,244
		Scattered write-in votes		—	13,185
		Unnamed nominee	Minnesota for America	0	6,139
		None of these candidates		—	4,193
1984	50	Ronald Reagan	Republican	525	54,455,075
		Walter Mondale	Democratic	13	37,577,185
		David Bergland	Libertarian	0	228,314
		Lyndon H. LaRouche	Independent	0	78,807
		Sonia Johnson	Citizens	0	72,200
		Bob Richards	Populist	0	66,336
		Dennis L. Serrette	Alliance	0	46,868
		Gus Hall	Communist	0	36,386
		Mel Mason	Socialist Workers	0	24,706
		Larry Holmes	Workers World	0	17,985
		Delmar Dennis	American	0	13,161
		Ed Winn	Workers League	0	10,801
		Four other named candidates	Four other minor parties	0	7,445
		Scattered write-in votes		—	13,623
		None of these candidates		—	3,950
1988	50	George H. W. Bush	Republican	426	48,886,097
		Michael Dukakis	Democratic	111 [10]	41,809,074
		Ron Paul	Libertarian	0	432,179
		Lenora B. Fulani	New Alliance	0	217,219
		David Duke	Populist	0	47,047
		Eugene J. McCarthy	Consumer	0	30,905
		James Griffin	American Independent	0	27,818
		Lyndon H. LaRouche	National Economic Recovery	0	25,562
		William Mara	Right-to-Life	0	20,504
		Ed Winn	Workers League	0	18,693
		James Warren	Socialist Workers	0	15,604
		Herbert Lewin	Peace and Freedom	0	10,370
		Seven other named candidates	Seven other minor parties	0	25,762
		Scattered write-in votes		—	21,041
		None of these candidates		—	6,934

Notes appear at end of table

(continued)

TABLE Eb149–153   Electoral and popular votes cast for President, by candidate: 1789–2000 *Continued*

Year	Number of states	Presidential candidate	Candidate's political party	Votes received by candidate	
				Electoral	Popular
	Eb149	Eb150	Eb151	Eb152	Eb153
	Number	—	—	Number	Number
1992	50	William Clinton	Democratic	370	44,909,326
		George H. W. Bush	Republican	168	39,103,882
		H. Ross Perot	Independent	0	19,741,657
		Andre V. Marrou	Libertarian	0	291,627
		James Gritz	America First	0	107,014
		Lenora B. Fulani	New Alliance	0	73,714
		Howard Phillips	Taxpayers	0	43,434
		John Hagelin	Natural Law	0	39,179
		Ron Daniels	Peace and Freedom	0	27,961
		Lyndon H. LaRouche	Economic Recovery	0	26,333
		James Warren	Socialist Workers	0	23,096
		Twelve other named candidates	Twelve other minor parties	0	21,213
		Scattered write-in votes		—	14,041
		None of these candidates	(Nevada)	0	2,537 [15]
1996	50	William Clinton	Democratic	379	47,402,357
		Robert Dole	Republican	159	39,198,755
		H. Ross Perot	Reform	0	8,085,402
		Ralph Nader	Green	0	685,040
		Harry Browne	Libertarian	0	485,798
		Howard Phillips	U.S. Taxpayers	0	184,658
		John Hagelin	Natural Law	0	113,668
		Monica Moorehead	Workers World	0	29,083
		Marsha Feinland	Peace and Freedom	0	25,332
		Charles Collins	Independent	0	8,930
		James Harris	Socialist Workers	0	8,476
		Ten other named candidates	Ten other minor parties	0	19,647
		Scattered write-in votes		0	25,118
		None of these candidates		0	5,608
2000	50	George W. Bush	Republican	271	50,455,156
		Al Gore	Democratic	266	50,992,335
		Ralph Nader	Green	0	2,882,738
		Patrick Buchanan	Reform/Independent	0	449,077
		Harry Browne	Libertarian	0	384,429
		Howard Phillips	Constitution	0	98,020
		John Hagelin	Natural Law/Reform/Independent	0	83,525
		Nine other named candidates	Other minor parties	0	27,104
		Scattered write-in votes		—	20,767
		None of these candidates		1 [11]	3,315 [15]

[1] Prior to the election of 1804, each elector voted for two candidates for President; the one reviewing the highest number of votes, if a majority, was declared elected President, the next highest, Vice President. This provision was modified by adoption of the Twelfth Amendment, which was declared ratified by the legislatures of three fourths of the states in a proclamation of the Secretary of State, September 25, 1804.

[2] Prior to 1920 the table excludes unpledged tickets and minor candidates polling under 10,000 votes. Various party labels may have been used by a candidate in different states; the more important of these are listed in the table.

[3] No candidate having a majority in the electoral college, the election was decided in the House of Representatives.

[4] Greeley died shortly after the election and presidential electors supporting him cast their votes as indicated, including three for Greeley, which were not counted.

[5] Includes a variety of joint tickets with People's Party electors committed to Bryan.

[6] One Democratic elector in Alabama voted for Walter Jones.

[7] Six Democratic electors in Alabama, all eight unpledged Democratic electors in Mississippi, and one Republican elector in Oklahoma voted for Senator Harry F. Byrd.

[8] One electoral vote was cast for John Hospers, Libertarian Party candidate for President, who received 3,673 popular votes.

[9] One electoral vote was cast for Ronald Reagan.

[10] One electoral vote was cast for Lloyd Bentsen, Vice Presidential candidate of the Democratic Party.

[11] The District of Columbia electors cast two electoral votes for Al Gore. Its third vote was not cast.

[12] Whig tickets were pledged to various candidates in various states. The value for popular vote represents the combined figure for Whigs in 1836.

[13] Total vote for Gregory includes write-in votes as well as votes for the Freedom and Peace Party, the Peace Freedom Alternative, the Peace and Freedom Party, and the New Party.

[14] Total vote for McCarthy includes write-in votes as well as votes for the Alternative in November Party and the New Party.

[15] Nevada permits voters to select "none of the candidates."

Sources

1789–1968. Walter Dean Burnham, series Y79–83, in *Historical Statistics of the United States* (1975). Original source material includes the following: 1789–1832, Edward Stanwood, *A History of the Presidency*, 2 volumes (Houghton Mifflin, 1928), various pages; 1836–1892, Walter Dean Burnham, *Presidential Ballots, 1816–1892* (Johns Hopkins University Press, 1955), pp. 246–57, 887–9; 1896–1916, Edgar Eugene Robinson, *The Presidential Vote* (Stanford University Press, 1934), pp. 46, 402.

1972–2000. Alice V. McGillivray, Richard M. Scammon, and Rhodes Cook, *America at the Polls, 1960–2000, John F. Kennedy to George W. Bush: A Handbook of American Presidential Election Statistics* (Congressional Quarterly Press, 2001).

Documentation

The election of the President is provided for in the U.S. Constitution. Article 2, Section 1 establishes an electoral college with electors from each state

TABLE Eb149–153   Electoral and popular votes cast for President, by candidate: 1789–2000   *Continued*

appointed for each presidential election. The number of electors, and therefore of electoral votes, is "equal to the whole number of Senators and Representatives to which the State may be entitled in Congress." The method of casting the electoral vote was modified in 1804 by the adoption of the Twelfth Amendment. With the ratification of the Twenty-third Amendment, the District of Columbia became eligible to choose electors beginning in 1964.

In four elections the entire electoral vote of certain states remained uncast: (a) 1789 – no electoral vote was cast in New York because the legislature failed to agree on electors; (b) 1864 – no vote in the Confederate states (Alabama, Arkansas, Florida, Georgia, Louisiana, Mississippi, North and South Carolina, Tennessee, Texas, and Virginia); (c) 1868 – no vote in Mississippi, Texas, and Virginia because these states had not yet been readmitted to the Union; (d) 1872 – the vote of Arkansas was rejected, the count of the popular vote in Louisiana was disputed, and the votes of both sets of electors were rejected by Congress.

In some states, state laws bind electors to vote for the candidate whom they endorsed. This restriction may come with a variety of penalties attached for failing to vote as promised. Other states do not bind electors. Nonetheless, few electors vote contrary to their pledges and in no instances have such votes affected the outcome of the presidential contest. The footnotes identify individual instances in which electors have chosen to vote contrary to their public pledges.

In addition to the sources given, the following references were used in compiling the data for Tables Eb149–259: U.S. Congress, Clerk of the House of Representatives, *Platforms of the Two Great Political Parties, 1932 to 1944*, pp. 437–47, and *Statistics of the Presidential and Congressional Elections*, various issues; Julius F. Prufer and Stanley J. Folmesbee, *American Political Parties and Presidential Elections* (McKinley, 1928); Charles O. Paullin, *Atlas of the Historical Geography of the United States* (Carnegie Institution of Washington and American Geographical Society of New York, 1932), pp. 88–104; U.S. Bureau of the Census, *Vote Cast in Presidential and Congressional Elections, 1928–1944*.

TABLE Eb154–207   Electoral votes cast for President, by party and state: 1804–2000
Contributed by John P. McIver

	By party			By state														
	Democratic	Republican	Other	Alabama	Alaska	Arizona	Arkansas	California	Colorado	Connecticut	Delaware	District of Columbia	Florida	Georgia	Hawai'i	Idaho	Illinois	Indiana
Year	Eb154	Eb155	Eb156	Eb157	Eb158	Eb159	Eb160	Eb161	Eb162	Eb163	Eb164	Eb165	Eb166	Eb167	Eb168	Eb169	Eb170	Eb171
	Number	Number	Number	Number	Number	Number	Number	Number	Number	Number	Number	Number	Number	Number	Number	Number	Number	Number
1804	—	—	—	—	—	—	—	—	—	9 F	3 F	—	—	6 DR	—	—	—	—
1808	—	—	—	—	—	—	—	—	—	9 F	3 F	—	—	6 DR	—	—	—	—
1812	—	—	—	—	—	—	—	—	—	9 C	4 C	—	—	8 DR	—	—	—	—
1816	—	—	—	—	—	—	—	—	—	9 F	3 F [16]	—	—	8 DR	—	—	—	3 DR
1820	—	—	—	3 DR	—	—	—	—	—	9 DR	4 DR	—	—	8 DR	—	—	3 DR	3 DR
1824 [1]	—	—	—	5 Jackson	—	—	—	—	—	8 Adams	— [17]	—	—	9 Crawford	—	—	3 DR	5 Jackson [20]
1828	—	—	—	5 D	—	—	—	—	—	8 NR	3 NR	—	—	9 D	—	—	3 D	5 D
1832	—	—	—	7 D	—	—	—	—	—	8 NR	3 NR	—	—	11 D	—	—	5 D	9 D
1836 [2]	—	—	—	7 D	—	—	3 D	—	—	8 D	3 W	—	—	11 W	—	—	5 D	9 W
1840	—	—	—	7 D	—	—	3 D	—	—	8 W	3 W	—	—	11 W	—	—	5 D	9 W
1844	—	—	—	9 D	—	—	3 D	—	—	6 W	3 W	—	—	10 D	—	—	9 D	12 D
1848	—	—	—	9 D	—	—	3 D	—	—	6 W	3 W	—	3 W	10 W	—	—	9 D	12 D
1852	—	—	—	9 D	—	—	4 D	4 D	—	6 D	3 D	—	3 D	10 D	—	—	11 D	13 D
1856	—	—	—	9 D	—	—	4 D	4 D	—	6 R	3 D	—	3 D	10 D	—	—	11 D	13 D
1860	84 [7]	180	39 [9]	9 SD	—	—	4 SD	4 R	—	6 R	3 SD	—	3 SD	10 SD	—	—	11 R	13 R
1864 [3]	21	212	0	—	—	—	—	5 R	—	6 R	3 D	—	—	—	—	—	16 R	13 R
1868 [4]	80	214	0	8 R	—	—	5 R	5 R	—	6 R	3 D	—	3 R	9 D	—	—	16 R	13 R
1872 [5]	63	286	0	10 R	—	—	—	6 R	—	6 R	3 R	—	4 R	8 D [19]	—	—	21 R	15 R
1876	184	185	0	10 D	—	—	6 D	6 R	3 R	6 D	3 D	—	4 R	11 D	—	—	21 R	15 D
1880	155 [8]	214	0	10 D	—	—	6 D	1 R; 5 D	3 R	6 R	3 D	—	4 D	11 D	—	—	21 R	15 R
1884	219	182	0	10 D	—	—	7 D	8 R	3 R	6 D	3 D	—	4 D	12 D	—	—	22 R	15 D
1888	168	233	0	10 D	—	—	7 D	8 R	3 R	6 D	3 D	—	4 D	12 D	—	—	22 R	15 R
1892	277	145	22 [10]	11 D	—	—	8 D	1 R; 8 D	4 PP	6 D	3 D	—	4 D	13 D	—	3 PP	24 D	15 D
1896 [6]	176 [6]	271	0	11 D	—	—	8 D	8 R; 1 D	4 D	6 R	3 R	—	4 D	13 D	—	3 D	24 R	15 R
1900	155	292	0	11 D	—	—	8 D	9 R	4 D	6 R	3 R	—	4 D	13 D	—	3 D	24 R	15 R
1904	140	336	0	11 D	—	—	9 D	10 R	5 R	7 R	3 R	—	5 D	13 D	—	3 R	27 R	15 R
1908	162	321	0	11 D	—	—	9 D	10 R	5 D	7 R	3 R	—	5 D	13 D	—	3 R	27 R	15 R
1912	435	8	88 [11]	12 D	—	3 D	9 D	2 D; 11 PR	6 D	7 D	3 D	—	6 D	14 D	—	4 D	29 D	15 D
1916	277	254	0	12 D	—	3 D	9 D	13 D	6 D	7 R	3 R	—	6 D	14 D	—	4 D	29 R	15 R
1920	127	404	0	12 D	—	3 R	9 D	13 R	6 R	7 R	3 R	—	6 D	14 D	—	4 R	29 R	15 R
1924	136	382	13	12 D	—	3 R	9 D	13 R	6 R	7 R	3 R	—	6 D	14 D	—	4 R	29 R	15 R
1928	87	444	0	12 D	—	3 R	9 D	13 R	6 R	7 R	3 R	—	6 R	14 D	—	4 R	29 R	15 R
1932	472	59	0	11 D	—	3 D	9 D	22 D	6 D	8 R	3 D	—	7 D	12 D	—	4 D	29 D	14 D
1936	523	8	0	11 D	—	3 D	9 D	22 D	6 D	8 D	3 D	—	7 D	12 D	—	4 D	29 D	14 D
1940	449	82	0	11 D	—	3 D	9 D	22 D	6 R	8 D	3 D	—	7 D	12 D	—	4 D	29 D	14 R
1944	432	99	0	11 D	—	4 D	9 D	25 D	6 R	8 D	3 D	—	8 D	12 D	—	4 D	28 D	14 R
1948	303	189	39 [12]	11 SR	—	4 D	9 D	25 D	6 D	8 R	3 R	—	8 D	12 D	—	4 D	28 D	13 D
1952	89	442	0	11 D	—	4 R	8 D	32 R	6 R	8 R	3 R	—	10 R	12 D	—	4 R	27 R	13 R
1956	73	457	1	10 D [14]	—	4 R	8 D	32 R	6 R	8 R	3 R	—	10 R	12 D	—	4 R	27 R	13 R
1960	303	219	15	5 D [15]	3 R	4 R	8 D	32 R	6 R	8 D	3 D	—	10 R	12 D	3 D	4 R	27 D	13 R
1964	486	52	0	10 R	3 D	5 R	6 D	40 D	6 D	8 D	3 D	3 D	14 D	12 R	4 D	4 D	26 D	13 D
1968	191	301	46 [13]	10 A	3 R	5 R	6 A	40 R	6 R	8 D	3 R	3 D	14 R	12 A	4 D	4 R	26 R	13 R
1972	17	520	1	9 R	3 R	6 R	6 R	45 R	7 R	8 R	3 R	3 D	17 R	12 R	4 R	4 R	26 R	13 R
1976	297	240	0	9 D	3 R	6 R	6 D	45 R	7 R	8 R	3 D	3 D	17 D	12 D	4 D	4 R	26 R	13 R
1980	49	489	0	9 R	3 R	6 R	6 R	45 R	7 R	8 R	3 R	3 D	17 R	12 D	4 D	4 R	26 R	13 R
1984	13	525	0	9 R	3 R	7 R	6 R	47 R	8 R	8 R	3 R	3 D	21 R	12 R	4 R	4 R	24 R	12 R
1988	111	426	1	9 R	3 R	7 R	6 R	47 R	8 R	8 R	3 R	3 D	21 R	12 R	4 D	4 R	24 R	12 R
1992	370	168	0	9 R	3 R	8 R	6 D	54 D	8 D	8 D	3 D	3 D	25 R	13 D	4 D	4 R	22 D	12 R
1996	379	159	0	9 R	3 R	8 D	6 D	54 D	8 R	8 D	3 D	3 D	25 D	13 R	4 D	4 R	22 D	12 R
2000	266	271	1	9 R	3 R	8 R	6 R	54 D	8 R	8 D	3 D	2 D [18]	25 R	13 R	4 D	4 R	22 D	12 R

By state

Year	Iowa Eb172	Kansas Eb173	Kentucky Eb174	Louisiana Eb175	Maine Eb176	Maryland Eb177	Massachusetts Eb178	Michigan Eb179	Minnesota Eb180	Mississippi Eb181	Missouri Eb182	Montana Eb183	Nebraska Eb184	Nevada Eb185	New Hampshire Eb186	New Jersey Eb187	New Mexico Eb188	New York Eb189
	Number	Number	Number	Number	Number	Number	Number	Number	Number	Number	Number	Number	Number	Number	Number	Number	Number	Number
1804	—	—	8 DR	—	—	2 F; 9 DR	19 DR	—	—	—	—	—	—	—	7 DR	8 DR	—	19 DR
1808	—	—	7 DR [16]	—	—	2 F; 9 DR	19 F	—	—	—	—	—	—	—	7 F	8 DR	—	13 DR [27]
1812	—	—	12 DR	3 DR	—	5 C; 6 DR	22 C	—	—	—	—	—	—	—	8 C	8 C	—	29 C
1816	—	—	12 DR	3 DR	—	8 DR [22]	22 F	—	—	—	—	—	—	—	8 DR	8 DR	—	29 DR
1820	—	—	12 DR	3 DR	9 DR	11 DR	15 DR	—	—	2 DR [16]	3 DR [26]	—	—	—	7 DR	8 DR	—	29 DR
1824 [1]	—	—	14 Clay	— [21]	9 Adams	— [23]	15 Adams	—	—	3 Jackson	3 Clay	—	—	—	8 Adams	8 Jackson	—	— [28]
1828	—	—	14 D	5 D	8 NR; 1 D	6 NR; 5 D	15 NR	—	—	3 D	3 D	—	—	—	8 NR	8 NR	—	16 NR; 20 D
1832	—	—	15 NR	5 D	10 D	5 NR; 3 D [24]	14 NR	—	—	4 D	4 D	—	—	—	7 D	8 D	—	42 D
1836 [2]	—	—	15 W	5 D	10 D	10 W	14 W	3 D	—	4 D	4 D	—	—	—	7 D	8 W	—	42 D
1840	—	—	15 W	5 W	10 W	10 W	14 W	3 W	—	4 W	4 D	—	—	—	7 D	8 W	—	42 W
1844	—	—	12 W	6 D	9 D	8 W	12 W	5 D	—	6 D	7 D	—	—	—	6 D	7 W	—	36 D
1848	4 D	—	12 W	6 W	9 D	8 W	12 W	5 D	—	6 D	7 D	—	—	—	6 D	7 W	—	36 W
1852	4 D	—	12 W	6 D	8 D	8 D	13 W	6 D	—	7 D	9 D	—	—	—	5 D	7 D	—	35 D
1856	4 R	—	12 D	6 D	8 R	8 A	13 R	6 R	—	7 D	9 D	—	—	—	5 R	7 D	—	35 R
1860	4 R	—	12 CU	6 SD	8 R	8 SD	13 R	6 R	4 R	7 SD	9 D	—	—	—	5 R	4 R; 3 D	—	35 R
1864 [3]	8 R	3 R	11 D	—	7 R	7 R	12 R	8 R	4 R	—	11 R	—	—	2 R	5 R	7 D	—	33 R
1868 [4]	8 R	3 R	11 D	7 D	7 R	7 D	12 R	8 R	4 R	—	11 R	—	3 R	3 R	5 R	7 D	—	33 D
1872 [5]	11 R	5 R	12 D	—	7 R	8 D	13 R	11 R	5 R	8 R	15 D	—	3 R	3 R	5 R	9 R	—	35 R
1876	11 R	5 R	12 D	8 R	7 R	8 D	13 R	11 R	5 R	8 D	15 D	—	3 R	3 R	5 R	9 D	—	35 D
1880	11 R	5 R	12 D	8 D	7 R	8 D	13 R	11 R	5 R	8 D	15 D	—	3 R	3 D	5 R	9 D	—	35 R
1884	13 R	9 R	13 D	8 D	6 R	8 D	14 R	13 R	7 R	9 D	16 D	—	5 R	3 R	4 R	9 D	—	36 D
1888	13 R	9 R	13 D	8 D	6 R	8 D	14 R	13 R	7 R	9 D	16 D	—	5 R	3 R	4 R	9 D	—	36 R
1892	13 R	10 PP	13 D	8 D	6 R	8 D	15 R	9 R; 5 D	9 R	9 D	17 D	3 R	8 R	3 PP	4 R	10 D	—	36 D
1896 [6]	13 R	10 D	12 R; 1 D	8 D	6 R	8 R	15 R	14 R	9 R	9 D	17 D	3 D	8 D	3 D	4 R	10 R	—	36 R
1900	13 R	10 R	13 D	8 D	6 R	8 R	15 R	14 R	9 R	9 D	17 D	3 D	8 R	3 D	4 R	10 R	—	36 R
1904	13 R	10 R	13 D	9 D	6 R	1 R; 7 D	16 R	14 R	11 R	10 D	18 R	3 R	8 R	3 R	4 R	12 R	—	39 R
1908	13 R	10 R	13 D	9 D	6 R	2 R; 6 D	16 R	14 R	11 R	10 D	18 R	3 R	8 D	3 D	4 R	12 R	—	39 R
1912	13 D	10 D	13 D	10 D	6 D	8 D	18 D	15 PR	12 PR	10 D	18 D	4 D	8 D	3 D	4 D	14 D	3 D	45 D
1916	13 R	10 D	13 D	10 D	6 R	8 D	18 R	15 R	12 R	10 D	18 D	4 D	8 D	3 D	4 D	14 R	3 D	45 R
1920	13 R	10 R	13 D	10 D	6 R	8 R	18 R	15 R	12 R	10 D	18 R	4 R	8 R	3 R	4 R	14 R	3 R	45 R
1924	13 R	10 R	13 R	10 D	6 R	8 R	18 R	15 R	12 R	10 D	18 R	4 R	8 R	3 R	4 R	14 R	3 R	45 R
1928	13 R	10 R	13 R	10 D	6 R	8 R	18 D	15 R	12 R	10 D	18 R	4 R	8 R	3 R	4 R	14 R	3 R	45 R
1932	11 D	9 D	11 D	10 D	5 R	8 D	17 D	19 D	11 D	9 D	15 D	4 D	7 D	3 D	4 R	16 D	3 D	47 D
1936	11 D	9 D	11 D	10 D	5 R	8 D	17 D	19 D	11 D	9 D	15 D	4 D	7 D	3 D	4 D	16 D	3 D	47 D
1940	11 R	9 R	11 D	10 D	5 R	8 D	17 D	19 R	11 D	9 D	15 D	4 D	7 R	3 D	4 D	16 D	3 D	47 D
1944	10 R	8 R	11 D	10 D	5 R	8 D	16 D	19 R	11 D	9 D	15 D	4 D	6 R	3 D	4 D	16 D	4 D	47 D
1948	10 D	8 R	11 D	10 SR	5 R	8 R	16 D	19 R	11 D	9 SR	15 D	4 D	6 R	3 D	4 R	16 R	4 D	47 R
1952	10 R	8 R	10 D	10 D	5 R	9 R	16 R	20 R	11 R	8 D	13 R	4 R	6 R	3 R	4 R	16 R	4 R	45 R
1956	10 R	8 R	10 R	10 R	5 R	9 R	16 R	20 R	11 R	8 D	13 D	4 R	6 R	3 R	4 R	16 R	4 R	45 R
1960	10 R	8 R	10 R	10 D	5 R	9 D	16 D	20 D	11 D	— [25]	13 D	4 R	6 R	3 D	4 R	16 D	4 D	45 D
1964	9 D	7 D	9 D	10 R	4 D	10 D	14 D	21 D	10 D	7 R	12 D	4 D	5 D	3 D	4 D	17 D	4 D	43 D
1968	9 R	7 R	9 R	10 A	4 D	10 D	14 D	21 D	10 D	7 A	12 R	4 R	5 R	3 R	4 R	17 R	4 R	43 D
1972	8 R	7 R	9 R	10 R	4 R	10 R	14 D	21 R	10 R	7 R	12 R	4 R	5 R	3 R	4 R	17 R	4 R	41 R
1976	8 R	7 R	9 D	10 D	4 R	10 D	14 D	21 R	10 D	7 D	12 D	4 R	5 R	3 R	4 R	17 R	4 R	41 D
1980	8 R	7 R	9 R	10 R	4 R	10 D	14 R	21 R	10 D	7 R	12 R	4 R	5 R	3 R	4 R	17 R	4 R	41 R
1984	8 R	7 R	9 R	10 R	4 R	10 R	13 R	20 R	10 D	7 R	11 R	4 R	5 R	4 R	4 R	16 R	5 R	36 R
1988	8 D	7 R	9 R	10 R	4 R	10 R	13 D	20 R	10 D	7 R	11 R	4 R	5 R	4 R	4 R	16 R	5 R	36 R
1992	7 D	6 R	8 D	9 D	4 D	10 D	12 D	18 D	10 D	7 R	11 D	3 D	5 R	4 D	4 D	15 D	5 D	33 D
1996	7 D	6 R	8 D	9 D	4 D	10 D	12 D	18 D	10 D	7 R	11 D	3 R	5 R	4 D	4 D	15 D	5 D	33 D
2000	7 D	6 R	8 R	9 R	4 D	10 D	12 D	18 D	10 D	7 R	11 R	3 R	5 R	4 R	4 R	15 D	5 D	33 D

Notes appear at end of table

(continued)

TABLE Eb154–207 Electoral votes cast for President, by party and state: 1804–2000 Continued

By state

Year	North Carolina Eb190	North Dakota Eb191	Ohio Eb192	Oklahoma Eb193	Oregon Eb194	Pennsylvania Eb195	Rhode Island Eb196	South Carolina Eb197	South Dakota Eb198	Tennessee Eb199	Texas Eb200	Utah Eb201	Vermont Eb202	Virginia Eb203	Washington Eb204	West Virginia Eb205	Wisconsin Eb206	Wyoming Eb207
	Number	Number	Number	Number	Number	Number	Number	Number	Number	Number	Number	Number	Number	Number	Number	Number	Number	Number
1804	14 DR	—	3 DR	—	—	20 DR	4 DR	10 DR	—	5 DR	—	—	6 DR	24 DR	—	—	—	—
1808	3 F; 11 DR	—	3 DR	—	—	20 DR	4 F	10 DR	—	5 DR	—	—	6 DR	24 DR	—	—	—	—
1812	15 DR	—	7 DR [16]	—	—	25 DR	4 C	11 DR	—	8 DR	—	—	8 DR	25 DR	—	—	—	—
1816	15 DR	—	8 DR	—	—	25 DR	4 DR	11 DR	—	8 DR	—	—	8 DR	25 DR	—	—	—	—
1820	15 DR	—	8 DR	—	—	24 DR [16]	4 DR	11 DR	—	7 DR [16]	—	—	8 DR	25 DR	—	—	—	—
1824 [1]	15 Jackson	—	16 Clay	—	—	28 Jackson	4 Adams	11 Jackson	—	11 Jackson	—	—	7 Adams	24 Crawford	—	—	—	—
1828	15 D	—	16 D	—	—	28 D	4 NR	11 D	—	11 D	—	—	7 NR	24 D	—	—	—	—
1832	15 D	—	21 D	—	—	30 D	4 NR	11 N	—	15 D	—	—	7 AM	23 D	—	—	—	—
1836 [2]	15 D	—	21 W	—	—	30 D	4 D	11 D	—	15 W	—	—	7 W	23 D	—	—	—	—
1840	15 W	—	21 W	—	—	30 W	4 W	11 D	—	15 W	—	—	7 W	23 D	—	—	—	—
1844	11 W	—	23 W	—	—	26 D	4 W	9 D	—	13 W	—	—	6 W	17 D	—	—	—	—
1848	11 W	—	23 D	—	—	26 W	4 W	9 D	—	13 W	4 D	—	6 W	17 D	—	—	4 D	—
1852	10 D	—	23 D	—	—	27 D	4 D	8 D	—	12 W	4 D	—	5 W	15 D	—	—	5 D	—
1856	10 D	—	23 R	—	—	27 D	4 R	8 D	—	12 D	4 D	—	5 R	15 D	—	—	5 R	—
1860	10 SD	—	23 R	—	3 R	27 R	4 R	8 SD	—	12 CU	4 SD	—	5 R	15 CU	—	—	5 R	—
1864 [3]	—	—	21 R	—	3 R	26 R	4 R	—	—	—	—	—	5 R	—	—	5 R	8 R	—
1868 [4]	9 R	—	21 R	—	3 D	26 R	4 R	6 R	—	10 R	—	—	5 R	—	—	5 R	8 R	—
1872 [5]	10 R	—	22 R	—	3 R	29 R	4 R	7 R	—	12 D	8 D	—	5 R	11 R	—	5 R	10 R	—
1876	10 D	—	22 R	—	3 R	29 R	4 R	7 R	—	12 D	8 D	—	5 R	11 D	—	5 D	10 R	—
1880	10 D	—	22 R	—	3 R	29 R	4 R	7 D	—	12 D	8 D	—	5 R	11 D	—	5 D	10 R	—
1884	11 D	—	23 R	—	3 R	30 R	4 R	9 D	—	12 D	13 D	—	4 R	12 D	—	6 D	11 R	—
1888	11 D	—	23 R	—	3 R	30 R	4 R	9 D	—	12 D	13 D	—	4 R	12 D	—	6 D	11 R	—
1892	11 D	1 R; 1 D; 1 PP	22 R; 1 D	—	3 R; 1 PP	32 R	4 R	9 D	4 R	12 D	15 D	—	4 R	12 D	4 R	6 D	12 D	3 R
1896 [6]	11 D	3 R	23 R	—	4 R	32 R	4 R	9 D	4 D	12 D	15 D	3 D	4 R	12 D	4 D	6 R	12 R	3 D
1900	11 D	3 R	23 R	—	4 R	32 R	4 R	9 D	4 R	12 D	15 D	3 R	4 R	12 D	4 R	6 R	12 R	3 R
1904	12 D	4 R	23 R	—	4 R	34 R	4 R	9 D	4 R	12 D	18 D	3 R	4 R	12 D	5 R	7 R	13 R	3 R
1908	12 D	4 R	23 R	7 D	4 R	34 R	4 R	9 D	4 R	12 D	18 D	3 R	4 R	12 D	5 R	7 R	13 R	3 R
1912	12 D	5 D	24 D	10 D	5 D	38 PR	5 D	9 D	5 PR	12 D	20 D	4 R	4 R	12 D	7 PR	8 D	13 D	3 D
1916	12 D	5 D	24 D	10 D	5 R	38 R	5 R	9 D	5 R	12 D	20 D	4 D	4 R	12 D	7 D	7 R; 1 D	13 R	3 D
1920	12 D	5 R	24 R	10 R	5 R	38 R	5 R	9 D	5 R	12 R	20 D	4 R	4 R	12 D	7 R	8 R	13 R	3 R
1924	12 D	5 R	24 R	10 D	5 R	38 R	5 R	9 D	5 R	12 D	20 D	4 R	4 R	12 D	7 R	8 R	13 PR	3 R
1928	12 R	5 R	24 R	10 R	5 R	38 R	5 D	9 D	5 R	12 R	20 R	4 R	4 R	12 R	7 R	8 R	13 R	3 R
1932	13 D	4 D	26 D	11 D	5 D	36 R	4 D	8 D	4 D	11 D	23 D	4 D	3 R	11 D	8 D	8 D	12 D	3 D
1936	13 D	4 D	26 D	11 D	5 D	36 D	4 D	8 D	4 D	11 D	23 D	4 D	3 R	11 D	8 D	8 D	12 D	3 D
1940	13 D	4 D	26 D	11 D	5 D	36 D	4 D	8 D	4 R	11 D	23 D	4 D	3 R	11 D	8 D	8 D	12 D	3 D
1944	14 D	4 R	25 R	10 D	6 D	35 D	4 D	8 D	4 R	12 D	23 D	4 D	3 R	11 D	8 D	8 D	12 R	3 R
1948	14 D	4 R	25 D	10 D	6 R	35 R	4 D	8 SR	4 R	11 D; 1 SR	23 D	4 D	3 R	11 D	8 D	8 D	12 D	3 D
1952	14 D	4 R	25 R	8 R	6 R	32 R	4 R	8 D	4 R	11 R	24 R	4 R	3 R	12 R	9 R	8 D	12 R	3 R
1956	14 D	4 R	25 R	8 R	6 R	32 R	4 R	8 D	4 R	11 R	24 R	4 R	3 R	12 R	9 R	8 R	12 R	3 R
1960	14 D	4 R	25 R	7 R [29]	6 R	32 D	4 D	8 D	4 R	11 R	24 D	4 R	3 R	12 R	9 R	8 D	12 R	3 R
1964	13 D	4 D	26 D	8 D	6 D	29 D	4 D	8 R	4 D	11 D	25 D	4 D	3 D	12 D	9 D	7 D	12 D	3 D
1968	12 R; 1 A	4 R	26 R	8 R	6 R	29 D	4 D	8 R	4 R	11 R	25 D	4 R	3 R	12 R	9 D	7 D	12 R	3 R
1972	13 R	3 R	25 R	8 R	6 R	27 R	4 R	8 R	4 R	10 R	26 R	4 R	3 R	11 R [30]	9 R	6 R	11 R	3 R
1976	13 D	3 R	25 D	8 R	6 R	27 D	4 D	8 D	4 R	10 D	26 D	4 R	3 R	12 R	8 R; 1 D [31]	6 D	11 D	3 R
1980	13 R	3 R	25 R	8 R	6 R	27 R	4 D	8 R	4 R	10 R	26 R	4 R	3 R	12 R	9 R	6 D	11 R	3 R
1984	13 R	3 R	23 R	8 R	7 R	25 R	4 R	8 R	3 R	11 R	29 R	5 R	3 R	12 R	10 R	6 R	11 R	3 R
1988	13 R	3 R	23 R	8 R	7 D	25 R	4 D	8 R	3 R	11 R	29 R	5 R	3 R	12 R	10 D	5 D [32]	11 D	3 R
1992	14 R	3 R	21 D	8 R	7 D	23 D	4 D	8 R	3 R	11 D	32 R	5 R	3 D	13 R	11 D	5 D	11 D	3 R
1996	14 R	3 R	21 D	8 R	7 D	23 D	4 D	8 R	3 R	11 D	32 R	5 R	3 D	13 R	11 D	5 D	11 D	3 R
2000	14 R	3 R	21 R	8 R	7 D	23 D	4 D	8 R	3 R	11 R	32 R	5 R	3 D	13 R	11 D	5 R	11 D	3 R

1 In the 1824 election, party lines were so indistinct that names of the individual candidates are shown here.

2 Whig electors divided their votes among Harrison (73), White (26), and Webster (14).

3 Confederate states did not participate in the election.

4 Mississippi, Texas, and Virginia did not participate in the election.

5 Electoral votes for Arkansas and Louisiana were not counted. Owing to the death of Greeley, Democratic electors divided their votes among Hendricks (42), Brown (18), Jenkins (2), and Davis (1).

6 Electors classed here as Democratic were elected in many states on joint Democratic and People's Party fusion tickets.

7 Democratic electoral votes were split between candidates John Breckinridge (72) and Stephen Douglas (12).

8 Georgia's electoral votes arrived late. If not counted, the total for Democratic presidential candidate Winfield Hancock is 144.

9 Major party totals exclude 39 electoral votes cast for John Bell, Constitutional Union party candidate, as follows: Kentucky, 12; Tennessee, 12; Virginia, 15.

10 Major party totals exclude 22 electoral votes cast for James Weaver as follows: Colorado, 4; Idaho, 3; Kansas, 10; North Dakota, 1; Nevada, 3; Oregon, 1.

11 Major party totals exclude 88 electoral votes cast for Theodore Roosevelt, Progressive "Bull Moose" candidate, as follows: California, 11; Michigan, 15; Minnesota, 12; Pennsylvania, 38; South Dakota, 5; Washington, 7.

12 Major party totals exclude 39 electoral votes cast for States' Rights Democratic candidates as follows: Alabama, 11; Louisiana, 10; Mississippi, 9; South Carolina, 8; Tennessee, 1.

13 Major party totals exclude 46 electoral votes cast for George C. Wallace as follows: Alabama, 10; Arkansas, 6; Georgia, 12; Louisiana, 10; Mississippi, 7; North Carolina, 1.

14 One elector voted for Walter Jones.

15 Six electors voted for Harry F. Byrd.

16 One elector did not vote.

17 Two electors voted for Crawford and one for Adams.

18 The District of Columbia has three electoral votes. Two were cast for Gore. One vote was an abstention.

19 Excludes three votes for Greeley, which were not counted.

20 Two electors voted for Jackson and one for Adams.

21 Three electors voted for Jackson and two for Adams.

22 Three electors did not vote.

23 Seven electors voted for Jackson, three for Adams, and one for Crawford.

24 Two electors did not vote.

25 Eight electors voted for Harry F. Byrd.

26 One elector voted for John Quincy Adams.

27 Six electors voted for George Clinton.

28 Twenty-six electors voted for Adams, five for Crawford, four for Clay, and one for Jackson.

29 One elector voted for Harry F. Byrd

30 One elector voted for John Hospers.

31 One elector voted for Ronald Reagan.

32 One elector voted for Lloyd Bentsen for President.

Sources

1804–1968. Walter Dean Burnham, series Y84–134, in *Historical Statistics of the United States* (1975). Original source material includes the following: 1789–1832, Edward Stanwood, *A History of the Presidency,* 2 volumes (Houghton Mifflin, 1928), various pages; 1836–1892, Walter Dean Burnham, *Presidential Ballots, 1836–1892* (Johns Hopkins University Press, 1955), pp. 246–57, 887–9; 1896–1916, Edgar Eugene Robinson, *The Presidential Vote* (Stanford University Press, 1934), pp. 46, 402.

1972–2000. Alice V. McGillivray, Richard M. Scammon, and Rhodes Cook, *America at the Polls, 1920–2000, John F. Kennedy to George W. Bush: A Handbook of American Presidential Election Statistics* (Congressional Quarterly Press, 2001).

Additional source material was obtained from the USConstitution.net Internet site.

Documentation

See the text for Table Eb149–153.

Electoral votes are cast by electors chosen in individual states. This table highlights the support of state delegations for each presidential candidate.

Electoral votes are shown for each presidential candidate using these letter symbols for the various political parties:

A	American
AJ	Anti-Jackson
AM	Anti-Masonic
C	Coalition
CU	Constitutional Union
D	Democratic
DR	Democratic–Republican
F	Federalist
N	Nullification
NR	National Republican
PP	People's Party
PR	Progressive
R	Republican
SD	Southern Democratic
SR	States' Rights
W	Whig

TABLE Eb208–259 Popular votes cast for President, by state and political party: 1836–2000

Contributed by John P. McIver

Year and party	United States Eb208	Alabama Eb209	Alaska Eb210	Arizona Eb211	Arkansas Eb212	California Eb213	Colorado Eb214	Connecticut Eb215	Delaware Eb216	District of Columbia Eb217	Florida Eb218	Georgia Eb219	Hawai'i Eb220	Idaho Eb221	Illinois Eb222	Indiana Eb223	Iowa Eb224	Kansas Eb225
	Thousand	Thousand	Thousand	Thousand	Thousand	Thousand	Thousand	Thousand	Thousand	Thousand	Thousand	Thousand	Thousand	Thousand	Thousand	Thousand	Thousand	Thousand
1836	1,505	37	—	—	4	—	—	38	9	—	—	47	—	—	33	74	—	—
Democratic	765	21	—	—	2	—	—	19	4	—	—	23	—	—	18	32	—	—
Whig	740	17	—	—	1	—	—	19	5	—	—	24	—	—	15	41	—	—
1840	2,412	63	—	—	12	—	—	57	11	—	—	72	—	—	93	117	—	—
Democratic	1,128	34	—	—	7	—	—	25	5	—	—	32	—	—	47	52	—	—
Whig	1,275	29	—	—	5	—	—	32	6	—	—	40	—	—	46	65	—	—
1844	2,701	63	—	—	15	—	—	65	12	—	—	86	—	—	108	140	—	—
Democratic	1,338	37	—	—	10	—	—	30	6	—	—	44	—	—	59	70	—	—
Whig	1,300	26	—	—	6	—	—	33	6	—	—	42	—	—	46	68	—	—
1848	2,879	62	—	—	17	—	—	62	12	—	7	92	—	—	125	153	22	—
Democratic	1,222	31	—	—	9	—	—	27	6	—	3	45	—	—	56	75	11	—
Whig	1,361	30	—	—	8	—	—	30	6	—	4	48	—	—	53	70	10	—
1852	3,162	44	—	—	20	77	—	67	13	—	7	62	—	—	155	184	35	—
Democratic	1,601	27	—	—	12	41	—	33	6	—	4	35	—	—	80	95	18	—
Whig	1,385	15	—	—	7	36	—	30	6	—	3	17	—	—	65	81	16	—
1856	4,045	75	—	—	33	110	—	81	14	—	11	99	—	—	239	235	90	—
Democratic	1,833	47	—	—	22	53	—	35	8	—	6	57	—	—	106	119	36	—
Republican	1,340	0	—	—	0	21	—	43	0	—	0	0	—	—	96	94	44	—
American	872	29	—	—	11	36	—	3	6	—	5	42	—	—	38	22	9	—
1860	4,690	90	—	—	54	120	—	80	16	—	13	107	—	—	337	272	128	—
Democratic	1,383	14	—	—	5	38	—	17	1	—	0	12	—	—	158	116	55	—
Republican	1,866	0	—	—	0	39	—	43	4	—	0	0	—	—	171	139	70	—
Constitutional Union	593	28	—	—	20	9	—	3	4	—	5	43	—	—	5	5	2	—
Southern Democrat	848	49	—	—	29	34	—	16	7	—	8	52	—	—	2	12	1	—
1864	4,011	0	—	—	0	106	—	87	17	—	0	0	—	—	348	280	135	21
Democratic	1,804	0	—	—	0	44	—	42	9	—	0	0	—	—	159	130	48	4
Republican	2,207	0	—	—	0	62	—	45	8	—	0	0	—	—	190	150	86	17
1868	5,720	149	—	—	41	109	—	99	19	—	0	160	—	—	448	344	194	44
Democratic	2,707	72	—	—	19	54	—	48	11	—	0	103	—	—	198	167	74	14
Republican	3,013	76	—	—	22	55	—	51	8	—	0	57	—	—	250	177	120	30
1872	6,460	170	—	—	79	96	—	96	22	—	33	143	—	—	430	350	205	100
Democratic	2,843	79	—	—	38	41	—	46	10	—	15	76	—	—	185	164	71	33
Republican	3,597	90	—	—	41	54	—	50	11	—	18	63	—	—	242	186	132	67
1876	8,422	172	—	—	97	156	—	122	24	—	48	181	—	—	553	430	295	124
Democratic	4,284	103	—	—	58	76	—	62	13	—	24	130	—	—	259	214	112	38
Republican	4,037	69	—	—	39	79	—	59	11	—	24	51	—	—	277	207	174	78
1880	9,217	152	—	—	109	164	54	133	29	—	52	157	—	—	622	471	323	201
Democratic	4,414	91	—	—	61	80	25	64	15	—	28	103	—	—	277	226	106	60
Republican	4,453	56	—	—	42	80	28	67	14	—	24	54	—	—	318	232	184	122
1884	10,053	154	—	—	126	197	64	137	30	—	60	143	—	—	673	495	377	266
Democratic	4,880	93	—	—	73	89	28	67	17	—	32	94	—	—	312	245	178	90
Republican	4,850	59	—	—	51	102	36	66	13	—	28	48	—	—	337	239	197	154
1888	11,383	175	—	—	157	250	91	154	30	—	67	142	—	—	748	537	404	331
Democratic	5,538	117	—	—	86	118	37	75	16	—	40	100	—	—	348	261	180	103
Republican	5,447	57	—	—	60	125	50	75	13	—	27	40	—	—	370	263	212	183
1892	12,061	233	—	—	148	270	96	165	37	—	35	221	—	19	874	552	443	325
Democratic	5,555	138	—	—	88	118	—	82	19	—	30	129	—	0	426	263	196	0
Republican	5,183	9	—	—	47	118	39	77	18	—	0	48	—	9	399	254	220	157
People's	1,030	85	—	—	12	25	54	4	0	—	5	42	—	11	22	22	21	163

Year and party	United States Eb208	Alabama Eb209	Alaska Eb210	Arizona Eb211	Arkansas Eb212	California Eb213	Colorado Eb214	Connecticut Eb215	Delaware Eb216	District of Columbia Eb217	Florida Eb218	Georgia Eb219	Hawai'i Eb220	Idaho Eb221	Illinois Eb222	Indiana Eb223	Iowa Eb224	Kansas Eb225
	Thousand	Thousand	Thousand	Thousand	Thousand	Thousand	Thousand	Thousand	Thousand	Thousand	Thousand	Thousand	Thousand	Thousand	Thousand	Thousand	Thousand	Thousand
1896	13,907	195	—	—	140	299	187	174	32	—	46	156	—	30	1,088	637	521	336
Democratic	6,493	130	—	—	101	123	159	57	13	—	31	93	—	23	465	306	224	172
Republican	7,102	56	—	—	38	147	26	110	17	—	11	59	—	6	607	324	289	159
1900	13,968	160	—	—	128	303	221	180	42	—	40	121	—	58	1,132	663	530	352
Democratic	6,357	97	—	—	81	125	123	74	19	—	28	81	—	29	503	310	209	161
Republican	7,218	56	—	—	45	165	93	103	23	—	7	34	—	27	598	335	308	186
1904	13,521	109	—	—	117	332	244	191	44	—	39	130	—	73	1,076	682	486	329
Democratic	5,084	80	—	—	64	89	100	73	19	—	27	84	—	18	328	274	149	86
Republican	7,628	22	—	—	48	205	135	111	24	—	8	24	—	48	633	369	308	213
1908	14,884	105	—	—	152	387	264	190	48	—	49	132	—	98	1,155	721	495	376
Democratic	6,412	74	—	—	88	127	127	68	22	—	31	72	—	36	451	338	201	161
Republican	7,675	26	—	—	57	214	124	113	25	—	11	41	—	53	630	349	275	197
1912	15,037	118	—	23	124	678	266	190	49	—	52	121	—	106	1,146	654	492	365
Democratic	6,297	82	—	10	69	283	114	75	23	—	36	94	—	34	405	282	185	144
Republican	3,487	10	—	3	24	4	58	68	16	—	4	6	—	33	254	151	120	75
Progressive	4,119	23	—	7	22	284	72	34	9	—	5	21	—	26	386	162	162	120
1916	18,531	131	—	58	168	1,000	294	214	52	—	81	160	—	135	2,193	719	515	628
Democratic	9,128	99	—	33	112	466	179	100	25	—	56	128	—	70	950	334	221	314
Republican	8,534	29	—	21	47	463	102	107	26	—	15	11	—	55	1,153	341	279	276
1920	26,748	234	—	67	183	943	292	366	95	—	145	149	—	136	2,095	1,263	895	570
Democratic	9,130	156	—	30	106	229	105	121	40	—	91	106	—	47	534	511	228	185
Republican	16,143	75	—	37	72	625	173	229	53	—	45	43	—	89	1,420	696	635	369
1924	29,086	165	—	74	139	1,282	342	400	90	—	109	165	—	148	2,470	1,272	972	662
Democratic	8,385	113	—	26	85	106	75	110	33	—	62	123	—	24	577	492	160	156
Republican	15,718	43	—	31	41	733	195	246	52	—	31	30	—	70	1,453	703	537	408
Progressive	4,831	8	—	17	13	425	70	42	5	—	9	13	—	54	432	72	274	98
1928	36,812	249	—	91	202	1,797	392	553	105	—	254	231	—	154	3,107	1,421	1,010	713
Democratic	15,016	128	—	39	123	614	133	252	35	—	102	130	—	53	1,313	563	379	193
Republican	21,392	121	—	53	78	1,162	254	297	69	—	144	65	—	100	1,769	848	624	514
1932	39,732	242	—	118	219	2,266	457	594	113	—	275	256	—	187	3,408	1,575	1,037	790
Democratic	22,810	205	—	79	190	1,324	251	282	54	—	206	234	—	109	1,882	862	598	423
Republican	15,759	35	—	36	27	848	190	288	57	—	69	20	—	71	1,433	677	414	348
1936	45,643	276	—	124	179	2,638	489	691	128	—	327	293	—	200	3,957	1,651	1,143	859
Democratic	27,753	238	—	87	147	1,767	295	382	79	—	249	255	—	126	2,283	935	622	462
Republican	16,675	35	—	33	32	836	181	279	54	—	78	37	—	66	1,570	692	488	394
1940	49,891	294	—	150	200	3,269	549	782	135	—	485	313	—	235	4,218	1,783	1,215	860
Democratic	27,308	251	—	95	157	1,878	266	418	75	—	359	265	—	128	2,150	874	579	365
Republican	22,321	42	—	54	42	1,351	280	361	61	—	126	24	—	107	2,047	899	632	489
1944	47,969	245	—	138	213	3,521	505	832	125	—	483	328	—	208	4,036	1,672	1,053	734
Democratic	25,607	199	—	81	149	1,989	234	435	68	—	339	268	—	107	2,079	781	500	287
Republican	22,015	45	—	56	64	1,513	269	391	57	—	143	57	—	100	1,939	876	547	442
1948	48,794	215	—	177	242	4,022	515	884	139	—	578	419	—	215	3,984	1,656	1,038	789
Democratic	24,179	0	—	95	150	1,913	267	423	68	—	282	255	—	107	1,995	808	522	352
Republican	21,991	41	—	78	51	1,895	240	438	70	—	194	77	—	102	1,961	821	494	423
States' Rights	1,176	171	—	0	40	1	0	0	0	—	90	85	—	0	0	0	0	0
1952	61,551	426	—	261	405	5,142	630	1,097	174	—	989	656	—	276	4,481	1,955	1,269	896
Democratic	27,315	275	—	109	226	2,198	246	482	83	—	445	457	—	95	2,014	802	452	273
Republican	33,936	149	—	152	177	2,897	380	611	90	—	544	199	—	181	2,457	1,136	809	616
1956	62,034	497	—	290	407	5,466	657	1,117	178	—	1,126	670	—	273	4,407	1,975	1,235	866
Democratic	26,023	281	—	113	213	2,420	258	405	79	—	480	445	—	106	1,776	784	502	296
Republican	35,590	196	—	177	186	3,028	394	712	98	—	644	223	—	167	2,623	1,183	729	567

(continued)

Notes appear at end of table

TABLE Eb208–259 Popular votes cast for President, by state and political party: 1836–2000 Continued

Year and party	United States Eb208	Alabama Eb209	Alaska Eb210	Arizona Eb211	Arkansas Eb212	California Eb213	Colorado Eb214	Connecticut Eb215	Delaware Eb216	District of Columbia Eb217	Florida Eb218	Georgia Eb219	Hawai'i Eb220	Idaho Eb221	Illinois Eb222	Indiana Eb223	Iowa Eb224	Kansas Eb225
	Thousand	Thousand	Thousand	Thousand	Thousand	Thousand	Thousand	Thousand	Thousand	Thousand	Thousand	Thousand	Thousand	Thousand	Thousand	Thousand	Thousand	Thousand
1960	68,838	570	61	398	429	6,507	736	1,223	197	—	1,544	733	185	300	4,757	2,135	1,274	929
Democratic	34,227	324	30	177	215	3,224	331	657	100	—	749	459	92	139	2,378	952	551	363
Republican	34,108	238	31	221	185	3,260	402	566	96	—	795	274	92	162	2,369	1,175	722	561
1964	70,645	690	67	481	560	7,058	777	1,219	201	199	1,854	1,139	207	292	4,703	2,092	1,185	858
Democratic	43,130	211[1]	44	238	314	4,172	476	826	123	170	949	523	163	149	2,797	1,171	733	464
Republican	27,178	479	23	243	243	2,879	297	391	78	29	906	617	44	144	1,906	911	449	387
1968	73,212	1,050	83	487	620	7,252	811	1,256	214	171	2,188	1,250	236	291	4,620	2,124	1,168	873
Democratic	31,275	197	35	171	188	3,244	335	622	89	140	677	334	141	89	2,040	807	477	303
Republican	31,785	147	38	267	191	3,468	409	557	97	31	887	380	91	165	2,175	1,068	619	479
American Independent	9,906	691	10	47	241	487	61	77	28	0	624	536	3	37	391	243	66	89
1972	77,719	1,006	95	623	651	8,368	954	1,384	236	163	2,583	1,175	270	310	4,723	2,126	1,226	916
Democratic	29,170	257	33	199	200	3,476	330	555	92	128	718	290	101	81	1,913	709	496	270
Republican	47,170	729	55	403	449	4,602	597	811	140	35	1,858	881	169	199	2,788	1,405	706	620
1976	81,556	1,183	124	743	768	7,867	1,082	1,382	236	169	3,151	1,467	291	344	4,719	2,220	1,279	958
Democratic	40,831	659	44	296	499	3,742	460	648	123	138	1,636	979	147	127	2,271	1,015	620	430
Republican	39,148	504	72	419	268	3,882	584	719	110	28	1,470	484	140	204	2,364	1,184	633	503
1980	86,515	1,342	158	874	838	8,587	1,184	1,406	236	175	3,687	1,597	303	437	4,750	2,242	1,318	980
Democratic	35,484	637	42	247	398	3,084	368	542	106	131	1,419	891	136	110	1,981	844	509	326
Republican	43,904	654	86	530	403	4,525	652	677	111	24	2,047	654	130	291	2,358	1,256	676	567
1984	92,653	1,442	208	1,026	884	9,505	1,295	1,467	255	211	4,180	1,776	336	411	4,819	2,233	1,320	1,022
Democratic	37,577	552	62	334	339	3,923	455	570	102	180	1,449	707	147	109	2,086	841	606	333
Republican	54,455	873	138	681	535	5,467	822	891	152	29	2,730	1,069	185	298	2,707	1,377	703	677
1988	91,595	1,378	200	1,172	828	9,887	1,372	1,443	250	193	4,302	1,810	354	409	4,559	2,169	1,226	993
Democratic	41,809	550	73	454	349	4,702	621	677	109	159	1,657	715	192	147	2,216	861	671	423
Republican	48,886	816	119	703	467	5,055	728	750	140	28	2,619	1,081	159	254	2,311	1,298	545	554
1992	104,425	1,688	259	1,487	951	11,132	1,569	1,616	290	228	5,314	2,321	373	482	5,050	2,306	1,355	1,157
Democratic	44,909	690	78	543	506	5,121	630	682	126	193	2,073	1,009	179	137	2,453	848	586	390
Republican	39,104	804	102	572	337	3,631	563	578	102	21	2,173	995	137	203	1,734	989	505	450
Independent	19,742	183	73	354	99	2,296	366	349	59	10	1,053	310	53	130	841	456	253	312
1996	96,278	1,534	242	1,404	884	10,019	1,511	1,393	271	186	5,304	2,299	360	492	4,311	2,136	1,234	1,074
Democratic	47,402	662	80	653	475	5,120	671	736	140	158	2,547	1,054	205	165	2,342	887	620	388
Republican	39,199	769	123	622	325	3,828	692	483	99	17	2,245	1,081	114	257	1,587	1,007	493	583
Reform	8,085	92	26	112	70	698	100	140	29	4	484	146	27	63	346	224	105	93
2000	105,397	1,666	286	1,532	922	10,966	1,741	1,460	328	202	5,963	2,597	368	502	4,742	2,199	1,316	1,072
Democratic	50,992	693	79	685	422	5,861	738	816	180	172	2,912	1,116	205	139	2,589	902	639	399
Republican	50,455	941	167	782	473	4,567	884	561	137	18	2,913	1,420	138	337	2,019	1,246	634	622

Year and party	Kentucky Eb226	Louisiana Eb227	Maine Eb228	Maryland Eb229	Massachusetts Eb230	Michigan Eb231	Minnesota Eb232	Mississippi Eb233	Missouri Eb234	Montana Eb235	Nebraska Eb236	Nevada Eb237	New Hampshire Eb238	New Jersey Eb239	New Mexico Eb240	New York Eb241	North Carolina Eb242
	Thousand	Thousand	Thousand	Thousand	Thousand	Thousand	Thousand	Thousand	Thousand	Thousand	Thousand	Thousand	Thousand	Thousand	Thousand	Thousand	Thousand
1836	69	7	38	48	78	12	—	20	18	—	—	—	25	52	—	306	50
Democratic	33	4	23	22	35	7	—	10	11	—	—	—	19	26	—	167	27
Whig	37	4	15	26	42	6	—	10	7	—	—	—	6	26	—	139	24
1840	91	19	93	62	126	44	—	37	53	—	—	—	59	64	—	442	79
Democratic	33	8	46	29	52	21	—	17	30	—	—	—	33	31	—	213	34
Whig	59	11	47	34	73	23	—	20	23	—	—	—	26	33	—	226	46

Year and party	Kentucky	Louisiana	Maine	Maryland	Massachusetts	Michigan	Minnesota	Mississippi	Missouri	Montana	Nebraska	Nevada	New Hampshire	New Jersey	New Mexico	New York	North Carolina
	Eb226	Eb227	Eb228	Eb229	Eb230	Eb231	Eb232	Eb233	Eb234	Eb235	Eb236	Eb237	Eb238	Eb239	Eb240	Eb241	Eb242
	Thousand	Thousand	Thousand	Thousand	Thousand	Thousand	Thousand	Thousand	Thousand	Thousand	Thousand	Thousand	Thousand	Thousand	Thousand	Thousand	Thousand
1844	113	27	85	69	130	56	—	46	73	—	—	—	49	76	—	486	82
Democratic	52	14	46	33	52	28	—	26	41	—	—	—	27	37	—	238	39
Whig	61	13	34	36	68	24	—	20	31	—	—	—	18	38	—	232	43
1848	115	34	87	72	134	65	—	52	73	—	—	—	50	78	—	456	80
Democratic	49	15	40	34	35	31	—	27	40	—	—	—	28	37	—	114	36
Whig	67	18	35	38	61	24	—	26	33	—	—	—	15	40	—	219	44
1852	111	36	82	75	125	83	—	45	69	—	—	—	51	84	—	525	79
Democratic	54	19	42	40	45	42	—	27	39	—	—	—	29	44	—	263	40
Whig	57	17	33	35	53	34	—	18	30	—	—	—	15	39	—	235	39
1856	133	43	110	87	167	126	—	59	106	—	—	—	70	100	—	597	85
Democratic	70	22	39	39	39	52	—	34	58	—	—	—	32	47	—	196	48
Republican	0	0	67	0	108	72	—	0	0	—	—	—	37	28	—	276	0
American	63	21	3	47	20	2	—	24	49	—	—	—	0	24	—	125	37
1860	146	51	101	93	169	155	35	69	165	—	—	—	66	121	—	677	96
Democratic	26	8	30	6	34	65	12	4	59	—	—	—	26	63	—	314	3
Republican	1	0	63	2	107	88	22	0	17	—	—	—	38	58	—	363	0
Constitutional Union	66	20	2	42	22	0	—	25	58	—	—	—	0	0	—	0	45
Southern Democrat	53	23	6	42	6	1	1	40	31	—	—	—	2	0	—	0	49
1864	90	0	115	70	175	160	42	0	104	—	—	16	69	129	—	731	0
Democratic	63	0	47	32	49	72	17	0	31	—	—	7	33	68	—	362	0
Republican	27	0	68	37	127	89	25	0	73	—	—	10	36	61	—	369	0
1868	155	114	113	93	196	226	72	0	152	—	15	12	68	163	—	850	181
Democratic	116	80	42	62	59	97	28	0	66	—	6	5	31	83	—	430	85
Republican	39	33	70	30	136	129	44	0	87	—	10	6	38	80	—	420	97
1872	189	129	91	135	199	222	91	129	271	—	25	15	69	168	—	830	165
Democratic	100	57	29	68	65	79	35	47	151	—	8	6	31	77	—	387	70
Republican	89	72	61	67	133	139	56	82	119	—	17	8	37	92	—	441	95
1876	260	146	116	164	259	317	124	165	351	—	58	20	80	220	—	1,016	234
Democratic	160	71	50	92	109	141	49	112	202	—	17	9	39	116	—	522	125
Republican	97	75	66	72	150	167	73	53	145	—	32	10	42	104	—	490	108
1880	267	103	144	173	283	353	151	116	397	—	87	18	86	246	—	1,104	241
Democratic	149	65	65	94	112	132	53	76	209	—	29	10	41	123	—	535	125
Republican	106	38	74	79	165	185	94	34	154	—	55	9	45	121	—	556	116
1884	276	109	130	186	303	403	190	121	441	—	134	13	84	261	—	1,167	268
Democratic	153	63	52	97	122	150	70	78	236	—	54	6	39	128	—	563	143
Republican	118	46	72	86	147	193	112	44	203	—	77	7	43	123	—	562	125
1888	344	116	128	211	345	475	262	115	521	—	203	12	91	304	—	1,320	286
Democratic	184	85	50	106	152	213	104	85	262	—	80	5	43	152	—	636	148
Republican	155	31	74	100	184	236	143	29	236	—	108	7	46	144	—	650	135
1892	341	114	116	213	391	467	268	53	542	44	200	11	89	336	—	1,337	278
Democratic	175	88	48	114	177	202	101	41	268	18	24	1	42	171	—	655	133
Republican	136	26	63	93	203	223	123	1	228	19	87	3	46	156	—	609	101
People's	24	0	3	1	3	20	30	10	41	7	83	7	0	1	—	16	45
1896	446	101	118	251	402	546	342	70	674	53	223	10	84	371	—	1,424	330
Democratic	218	77	35	105	106	237	140	63	364	42	115	8	21	134	—	551	175
Republican	218	22	80	137	279	293	194	5	305	10	103	2	57	221	—	820	154
1900	468	68	108	264	415	544	316	58	684	64	241	10	92	401	—	1,548	292
Democratic	235	54	38	122	157	211	113	51	352	37	114	6	35	165	—	678	158
Republican	227	14	66	136	239	316	190	6	314	25	122	4	55	222	—	822	133

Notes appear at end of table

(continued)

TABLE Eb208–259 Popular votes cast for President, by state and political party: 1836–2000 *Continued*

Year and party	Kentucky Eb226	Louisiana Eb227	Maine Eb228	Maryland Eb229	Massachusetts Eb230	Michigan Eb231	Minnesota Eb232	Mississippi Eb233	Missouri Eb234	Montana Eb235	Nebraska Eb236	Nevada Eb237	New Hampshire Eb238	New Jersey Eb239	New Mexico Eb240	New York Eb241	North Carolina Eb242
	Thousand	Thousand	Thousand	Thousand	Thousand	Thousand	Thousand	Thousand	Thousand	Thousand	Thousand	Thousand	Thousand	Thousand	Thousand	Thousand	Thousand
1904	436	54	97	224	445	520	293	59	644	64	226	12	90	432	—	1,618	208
Democratic	217	48	28	109	166	134	55	53	296	22	53	4	34	165	—	684	124
Republican	205	5	65	109	258	362	217	3	321	35	139	7	54	245	—	860	82
1908	490	76	106	239	457	538	330	67	716	69	267	25	90	467	—	1,638	252
Democratic	244	64	35	116	156	175	109	60	347	29	131	11	34	183	—	667	137
Republican	235	9	67	117	266	333	196	4	347	32	127	11	53	265	—	870	115
1912	453	79	130	232	489	548	334	64	699	80	249	20	88	434	49	1,588	244
Democratic	219	60	51	113	174	150	106	57	331	28	109	8	35	179	20	656	144
Republican	116	4	27	55	156	151	64	2	208	19	54	3	33	89	18	455	29
Progressive	102	9	48	58	142	213	126	4	124	22	73	6	18	146	8	390	69
1916	520	93	136	262	532	647	387	86	787	178	287	33	89	494	67	1,706	290
Democratic	270	80	64	138	248	284	179	80	398	101	159	18	44	211	34	759	168
Republican	242	6	70	117	269	333	180	4	369	67	118	12	44	269	31	869	121
1920	919	126	198	428	994	1,038	736	82	1,332	179	383	27	159	904	106	2,899	538
Democratic	456	88	59	181	277	231	143	69	575	57	120	10	63	257	47	781	305
Republican	452	39	136	236	681	756	519	12	727	109	248	15	95	611	58	1,871	233
1924	814	122	192	359	1,130	1,160	822	112	1,310	174	464	27	165	1,086	114	3,264	482
Democratic	376	93	42	148	281	152	56	100	575	34	137	6	57	298	49	951	284
Republican	397	25	138	162	703	875	421	8	648	74	219	11	99	675	55	1,820	191
Progressive	38	4	11	47	141	122	339	3	84	66	106	10	9	109	10	475	7
1928	941	216	262	528	1,578	1,372	971	152	1,501	194	547	32	197	1,548	118	4,406	635
Democratic	381	165	81	224	793	397	396	125	663	79	198	14	81	616	48	2,090	286
Republican	558	51	180	301	776	965	561	26	834	113	346	18	115	925	70	2,193	349
1932	983	269	298	511	1,580	1,665	1,003	146	1,610	216	570	41	206	1,630	151	4,689	712
Democratic	581	249	129	314	800	872	601	140	1,025	127	359	29	101	806	95	2,535	498
Republican	395	19	167	184	737	740	364	5	565	78	201	13	104	775	54	1,938	208
1936	923	330	304	625	1,840	1,805	1,130	162	1,829	231	608	44	218	1,819	169	5,596	839
Democratic	539	293	126	390	943	1,017	699	157	1,111	160	347	32	108	1,084	106	3,293	616
Republican	370	37	169	231	769	700	350	4	698	64	248	12	105	719	62	2,181	223
1940	968	372	321	660	2,027	2,086	1,251	176	1,834	248	616	53	235	1,974	183	6,302	823
Democratic	557	320	156	385	1,077	1,033	644	168	958	146	264	32	125	1,016	104	3,252	609
Republican	410	52	164	270	940	1,040	596	7	871	100	352	21	110	945	79	3,027	214
1944	868	349	296	608	1,961	2,205	1,126	180	1,572	207	563	54	230	1,964	152	6,317	791
Democratic	473	282	141	315	1,035	1,107	590	169	807	113	233	30	120	988	81	3,304	527
Republican	392	68	155	293	921	1,084	527	12	761	93	330	25	110	961	71	2,988	263
1948	823	416	265	597	2,107	2,110	1,212	192	1,579	224	489	62	231	1,950	187	6,177	791
Democratic	467	136	112	287	1,152	1,003	693	19	917	119	224	31	108	895	105	2,780	459
Republican	341	73	150	295	909	1,039	484	5	655	97	265	29	121	981	80	2,841	259
States' Rights	10	204	0	2	0	0	0	168	0	0	0	0	(Z)	0	0	0	70
1952	993	652	352	902	2,383	2,799	1,379	286	1,892	265	610	82	273	2,419	239	7,128	1,211
Democratic	496	345	119	395	1,084	1,231	608	173	930	106	188	32	107	1,016	106	3,105	653
Republican	495	307	232	499	1,292	1,552	763	113	959	157	422	51	166	1,374	132	3,953	558
1956	1,054	618	352	933	2,349	3,080	1,340	248	1,833	271	577	97	267	2,484	254	7,096	1,166
Democratic	476	244	102	373	948	1,360	618	144	918	116	199	41	90	850	106	2,748	591
Republican	572	329	249	560	1,393	1,714	719	61	914	155	378	56	177	1,607	147	4,346	575

Year and party	Kentucky	Louisiana	Maine	Maryland	Massachusetts	Michigan	Minnesota	Mississippi	Missouri	Montana	Nebraska	Nevada	New Hampshire	New Jersey	New Mexico	New York	North Carolina
	Eb226	Eb227	Eb228	Eb229	Eb230	Eb231	Eb232	Eb233	Eb234	Eb235	Eb236	Eb237	Eb238	Eb239	Eb240	Eb241	Eb242
	Thousand	Thousand	Thousand	Thousand	Thousand	Thousand	Thousand	Thousand	Thousand	Thousand	Thousand	Thousand	Thousand	Thousand	Thousand	Thousand	Thousand
1960	1,124	808	422	1,055	2,469	3,318	1,542	298	1,934	278	613	107	296	2,773	311	7,291	1,369
Democratic	522	407	181	566	1,487	1,687	780	108	972	135	233	55	138	1,385	156	3,830	713
Republican	603	231	241	490	977	1,620	758	74	962	142	381	52	158	1,363	154	3,446	655
1964	1,046	896	381	1,116	2,345	3,203	1,554	409	1,818	279	584	135	288	2,848	329	7,166	1,425
Democratic	670	387	262	731	1,786	2,137	991	53	1,164	164	307	79	184	1,868	194	4,913	800
Republican	373	509	119	385	550	1,060	560	357	654	113	277	56	104	964	133	2,244	625
1968	1,056	1,097	393	1,235	2,332	3,306	1,589	655	1,810	274	537	154	297	2,875	327	6,792	1,587
Democratic	398	310	217	538	1,469	1,593	858	151	791	114	171	61	131	1,264	130	3,378	464
Republican	462	258	169	518	767	1,371	659	89	812	139	321	73	155	1,325	170	3,008	627
American Independent	193	530	6	179	87	332	69	415	206	20	45	20	11	262	26	359	496
1972	1,067	1,051	417	1,354	2,459	3,490	1,742	646	1,856	318	576	182	334	2,997	386	7,166	1,519
Democratic	371	298	161	506	1,333	1,459	802	127	697	120	170	66	116	1,102	141	2,951	439
Republican	676	687	256	829	1,112	1,962	898	505	1,154	184	406	116	214	1,846	236	4,193	1,055
1976	1,167	1,278	483	1,440	2,548	3,654	1,950	769	1,954	329	608	202	340	3,014	418	6,534	1,679
Democratic	616	661	232	760	1,429	1,697	1,070	381	998	149	234	92	148	1,445	201	3,390	927
Republican	532	587	236	673	1,030	1,894	819	367	927	174	360	101	186	1,510	211	3,101	742
1980	1,295	1,549	523	1,540	2,524	3,910	2,052	893	2,100	364	641	248	384	2,976	457	6,202	1,856
Democratic	616	708	221	726	1,054	1,662	954	429	931	118	167	67	109	1,147	168	2,728	876
Republican	635	793	239	681	1,058	1,915	873	441	1,074	207	420	155	222	1,547	251	2,894	915
1984	1,369	1,707	553	1,676	2,559	3,802	2,084	941	2,123	384	652	287	389	3,218	514	6,807	2,175
Democratic	540	652	215	788	1,240	1,530	1,036	352	849	147	188	92	120	1,261	202	3,120	824
Republican	822	1,037	337	880	1,311	2,252	1,033	582	1,274	232	460	189	267	1,934	307	3,665	1,346
1988	1,323	1,628	555	1,714	2,633	3,669	2,097	932	2,294	366	661	350	451	3,100	520	6,486	2,134
Democratic	580	717	244	826	1,401	1,676	1,109	364	1,302	169	259	133	164	1,320	244	3,348	890
Republican	734	884	307	876	1,195	1,965	962	558	1,385	190	398	206	281	1,743	270	3,082	1,237
1992	1,493	1,790	679	1,985	2,774	4,275	2,348	982	2,392	411	738	506	538	3,344	570	6,927	2,612
Democratic	665	816	263	989	1,319	1,871	1,021	400	1,054	155	217	189	209	1,436	262	3,444	1,114
Republican	617	733	207	707	805	1,555	748	488	811	144	344	176	202	1,357	213	2,347	1,135
Independent	204	211	207	281	631	825	563	86	519	107	174	133	121	522	92	1,091	358
1996	1,389	1,784	606	1,781	2,557	3,849	2,193	894	2,158	407	677	464	499	3,076	556	6,316	2,516
Democratic	637	928	313	966	1,572	1,990	1,120	394	1,026	168	237	204	246	1,652	273	3,756	1,108
Republican	623	713	186	682	718	1,481	766	440	890	180	363	199	196	1,103	233	1,933	1,226
Reform	120	123	86	116	227	337	258	52	217	55	71	44	48	262	32	503	168
2000	1,544	1,766	652	2,020	2,703	4,233	2,439	994	2,560	411	697	609	569	3,187	599	6,822	2,911
Democratic	639	792	320	1,141	1,616	2,170	1,168	405	1,111	137	232	280	266	1,789	287	4,108	1,258
Republican	872	928	287	814	879	1,953	1,110	573	1,190	240	434	302	274	1,284	286	2,403	1,631

Year and party	North Dakota	Ohio	Oklahoma	Oregon	Pennsylvania	Rhode Island	South Carolina	South Dakota	Tennessee	Texas	Utah	Vermont	Virginia	Washington	West Virginia	Wisconsin	Wyoming
	Eb243	Eb244	Eb245	Eb246	Eb247	Eb248	Eb249	Eb250	Eb251	Eb252	Eb253	Eb254	Eb255	Eb256	Eb257	Eb258	Eb259
	Thousand	Thousand	Thousand	Thousand	Thousand	Thousand	Thousand	Thousand	Thousand	Thousand	Thousand	Thousand	Thousand	Thousand	Thousand	Thousand	Thousand
1836	—	203	—	—	179	6	—	—	62	—	—	35	54	—	—	—	—
Democratic	—	97	—	—	91	3	—	—	26	—	—	14	30	—	—	—	—
Whig	—	106	—	—	87	3	—	—	36	—	—	21	23	—	—	—	—
1840	—	273	—	—	288	9	—	—	108	—	—	51	86	—	—	—	—
Democratic	—	124	—	—	144	3	—	—	48	—	—	18	44	—	—	—	—
Whig	—	148	—	—	144	5	—	—	60	—	—	32	43	—	—	—	—

Notes appear at end of table

(continued)

TABLE Eb208–259   Popular votes cast for President, by state and political party: 1836–2000   *Continued*

Year and party	North Dakota Eb243	Ohio Eb244	Oklahoma Eb245	Oregon Eb246	Pennsylvania Eb247	Rhode Island Eb248	South Carolina Eb249	South Dakota Eb250	Tennessee Eb251	Texas Eb252	Utah Eb253	Vermont Eb254	Virginia Eb255	Washington Eb256	West Virginia Eb257	Wisconsin Eb258	Wyoming Eb259
	Thousand	Thousand	Thousand	Thousand	Thousand	Thousand	Thousand	Thousand	Thousand	Thousand	Thousand	Thousand	Thousand	Thousand	Thousand	Thousand	Thousand
1844	—	312	—	—	331	12	—	—	120	—	—	49	96	—	—	—	—
Democratic	—	149	—	—	167	5	—	—	60	—	—	18	51	—	—	—	—
Whig	—	155	—	—	160	7	—	—	60	—	—	27	45	—	—	—	—
1848	—	329	—	—	369	11	—	—	122	17	—	48	92	—	—	39	—
Democratic	—	155	—	—	173	4	—	—	58	12	—	11	47	—	—	15	—
Whig	—	139	—	—	185	7	—	—	64	5	—	23	45	—	—	14	—
1852	—	353	—	—	386	17	—	—	115	20	—	44	133	—	—	62	—
Democratic	—	169	—	—	199	9	—	—	57	15	—	13	74	—	—	32	—
Whig	—	153	—	—	179	8	—	—	59	5	—	22	59	—	—	21	—
1856	—	386	—	—	460	20	—	—	140	48	—	51	150	—	—	120	—
Democratic	—	171	—	—	231	7	—	—	74	32	—	11	90	—	—	53	—
Republican	—	187	—	—	148	11	—	—	—	—	—	40	—	—	—	66	—
American	—	28	—	—	82	2	—	—	66	16	—	1	60	—	—	1	—
1860	—	443	—	14	476	20	—	—	144	63	—	45	167	—	—	152	—
Democratic	—	187	—	3	17	8	—	—	11	0	—	9	16	—	—	65	—
Republican	—	232	—	5	268	12	—	—	0	—	—	34	2	—	—	86	—
Constitutional Union	—	12	—	—	13	—	—	—	69	15	—	2	74	—	—	0	—
Southern Democrat	—	11	—	5	179	0	—	—	64	48	—	0	74	—	—	1	—
1864	—	471	—	18	574	23	—	—	—	—	—	56	—	—	34	145	—
Democratic	—	206	—	8	277	9	—	—	—	—	—	13	—	—	10	63	—
Republican	—	266	—	10	296	14	—	—	—	—	—	42	—	—	23	80	—
1868	—	519	—	20	656	20	108	—	82	—	—	56	—	—	49	194	—
Democratic	—	238	—	11	314	6	45	—	26	—	—	12	—	—	20	85	—
Republican	—	280	—	11	342	13	62	—	57	—	—	44	—	—	29	109	—
1872	—	529	—	20	562	19	95	—	181	116	—	52	185	—	62	192	—
Democratic	—	244	—	8	213	5	23	—	95	68	—	11	92	—	30	86	—
Republican	—	282	—	12	349	14	72	—	86	48	—	41	93	—	32	105	—
1876	—	659	—	30	755	26	183	—	223	151	—	65	237	—	100	257	—
Democratic	—	323	—	14	362	11	91	—	133	106	—	20	141	—	57	124	—
Republican	—	331	—	15	385	16	92	—	90	45	—	44	96	—	42	130	—
1880	—	725	—	41	875	29	171	—	243	241	—	65	212	—	113	266	—
Democratic	—	341	—	20	407	11	112	—	130	156	—	18	96	—	57	114	—
Republican	—	375	—	21	445	18	58	—	108	57	—	46	84	—	46	144	—
1884	—	785	—	53	900	33	93	—	259	326	—	59	285	—	132	320	—
Democratic	—	368	—	25	395	12	70	—	134	226	—	17	145	—	67	146	—
Republican	—	400	—	27	473	19	22	—	124	93	—	40	139	—	63	161	—
1888	—	839	—	62	998	41	80	—	304	364	—	63	304	—	159	355	—
Democratic	—	395	—	27	447	18	66	—	159	236	—	17	152	—	79	155	—
Republican	—	416	—	33	526	22	14	—	139	94	—	45	150	—	78	177	—
1892	36	851	—	78	1,003	53	71	71	266	423	—	56	292	88	171	371	17
Democratic	0	405	—	14	452	24	55	9	136	240	—	16	164	30	84	177	0
Republican	18	405	—	35	516	27	13	35	101	75	—	38	113	37	80	171	8
People's	18	15	—	27	9	0	2	27	24	101	—	0	12	19	4	10	8
1896	47	1,014	—	97	1,194	55	66	83	318	539	78	64	295	94	202	447	21
Democratic	21	477	—	45	427	14	59	41	164	369	65	10	155	52	94	166	10
Republican	26	526	—	49	728	37	7	41	149	163	13	51	135	39	105	268	10
1900	58	1,040	—	84	1,173	57	51	96	274	422	93	56	264	108	221	442	25
Democratic	21	475	—	33	424	20	47	40	145	268	45	13	146	45	99	159	10
Republican	36	544	—	47	713	34	4	55	123	131	47	43	116	57	120	266	14

Year and party	North Dakota Eb243	Ohio Eb244	Oklahoma Eb245	Oregon Eb246	Pennsylvania Eb247	Rhode Island Eb248	South Carolina Eb249	South Dakota Eb250	Tennessee Eb251	Texas Eb252	Utah Eb253	Vermont Eb254	Virginia Eb255	Washington Eb256	West Virginia Eb257	Wisconsin Eb258	Wyoming Eb259
	Thousand	Thousand	Thousand	Thousand	Thousand	Thousand	Thousand	Thousand	Thousand	Thousand	Thousand	Thousand	Thousand	Thousand	Thousand	Thousand	Thousand
1904	70	1,004	—	90	1,237	69	56	101	243	233	102	52	131	145	240	443	31
Democratic	14	345	—	17	338	25	53	22	132	167	33	10	81	28	101	124	9
Republican	53	600	—	60	841	42	3	72	105	51	62	40	48	102	133	280	20
1908	95	1,122	256	111	1,265	72	66	115	257	298	109	53	137	184	258	454	36
Democratic	33	503	127	38	447	25	62	40	136	218	43	11	83	58	111	167	15
Republican	58	572	107	63	746	44	4	68	118	69	61	40	53	106	138	248	21
1912	86	1,037	253	137	1,218	78	50	117	253	302	112	63	137	322	264	400	42
Democratic	30	425	119	47	396	30	48	49	133	220	37	15	90	87	113	164	15
Republican	23	278	91	35	273	28	1	—	60	29	42	23	23	70	57	131	15
Progressive	26	230	—	38	445	17	1	59	55	27	24	22	22	114	79	62	9
1916	115	1,164	292	262	1,297	88	64	129	273	373	143	64	154	381	290	447	52
Democratic	55	604	148	120	522	40	62	59	153	287	84	23	103	183	140	192	28
Republican	53	514	97	127	704	45	2	64	117	65	54	40	49	167	143	221	22
1920	204	2,021	489	239	1,853	168	67	182	428	486	146	90	231	399	510	701	55
Democratic	37	780	218	80	504	55	64	36	207	288	57	21	142	157	221	113	17
Republican	160	1,182	248	144	1,218	107	2	111	219	115	82	68	87	223	282	499	35
1924	199	2,016	528	279	2,145	210	51	204	301	656	157	103	224	422	584	841	80
Democratic	14	478	256	68	409	77	49	27	159	483	47	16	140	43	257	68	13
Republican	95	1,176	226	143	1,401	125	1	101	131	130	77	80	73	220	289	312	42
Progressive	90	358	41	68	308	8	1	75	11	43	33	6	10	151	37	454	25
1928	240	2,508	618	320	3,160	237	69	262	353	708	177	135	305	501	643	1,017	83
Democratic	107	864	219	109	1,077	119	63	103	157	340	81	44	140	157	264	450	29
Republican	131	1,628	394	205	2,055	118	3	158	195	367	95	90	165	336	376	544	53
1932	256	2,610	705	369	2,859	266	104	288	390	856	207	137	298	615	744	1,115	97
Democratic	178	1,302	516	214	1,296	147	102	184	259	753	117	56	204	353	405	707	54
Republican	72	1,228	188	136	1,454	115	2	99	127	98	85	79	90	209	331	348	40
1936	274	3,012	750	414	4,138	310	115	296	477	850	217	144	335	692	830	1,259	103
Democratic	163	1,747	501	267	2,354	164	114	160	328	742	150	62	235	460	503	803	63
Republican	73	1,128	245	123	1,690	125	2	126	147	103	65	81	98	207	325	381	39
1940	281	3,320	826	481	4,078	321	100	308	523	1,117	248	143	347	794	868	1,406	112
Democratic	124	1,733	474	258	2,171	182	95	131	352	905	154	64	236	462	496	705	59
Republican	155	1,587	349	220	1,890	139	2	177	169	212	93	78	109	322	372	679	53
1944	220	3,153	722	480	3,795	299	103	232	511	1,144	248	125	388	856	716	1,339	101
Democratic	100	1,571	401	249	1,940	175	91	97	309	816	150	54	242	487	393	650	49
Republican	119	1,582	319	225	1,835	123	5	135	200	192	98	72	145	362	323	675	52
1948	221	2,936	722	524	3,735	328	143	250	550	1,250	276	123	419	905	749	1,277	101
Democratic	96	1,453	453	243	1,752	189	34	118	270	824	149	46	201	476	429	647	52
Republican	115	1,446	269	261	1,902	136	5	130	203	303	124	76	172	386	316	591	48
States' Rights	(Z)	0	0	0	0	0	103	0	74	114	0	0	43	0	0	0	0
1952	270	3,701	949	695	4,581	414	341	294	893	2,076	330	154	620	1,103	874	1,607	129
Democratic	77	1,600	431	271	2,146	203	73	90	444	969	135	43	269	493	454	622	48
Republican	192	2,100	518	421	2,416	211	68	204	446	1,103	194	110	349	599	420	980	81
1956	254	3,702	859	736	4,577	388	301	294	939	1,955	334	153	698	1,151	831	1,551	124
Democratic	97	1,440	386	329	1,982	162	136	122	457	860	118	43	268	523	382	587	50
Republican	157	2,263	474	406	2,585	226	76	172	462	1,081	216	110	386	620	449	955	75

Notes appear at end of table

(continued)

TABLE Eb208–259 Popular votes cast for President, by state and political party: 1836–2000 Continued

Year and party	North Dakota Eb243	Ohio Eb244	Oklahoma Eb245	Oregon Eb246	Pennsylvania Eb247	Rhode Island Eb248	South Carolina Eb249	South Dakota Eb250	Tennessee Eb251	Texas Eb252	Utah Eb253	Vermont Eb254	Virginia Eb255	Washington Eb256	West Virginia Eb257	Wisconsin Eb258	Wyoming Eb259
	Thousand	Thousand	Thousand	Thousand	Thousand	Thousand	Thousand	Thousand	Thousand	Thousand	Thousand	Thousand	Thousand	Thousand	Thousand	Thousand	Thousand
1960	278	4,162	903	776	5,007	406	387	306	1,052	2,311	375	167	771	1,242	838	1,729	141
Democratic	124	1,944	370	367	2,556	258	198	128	481	1,168	169	69	362	599	442	831	63
Republican	154	2,218	533	408	2,440	148	189	178	557	1,121	205	98	405	629	396	895	77
1964	258	3,969	932	786	4,823	390	525	293	1,144	2,627	401	163	1,042	1,259	792	1,692	143
Democratic	150	2,498	520	501	3,131	315	216	163	635	1,663	220	108	558	780	538	1,050	81
Republican	108	1,471	413	283	1,674	75	309	130	509	959	182	55	481	470	254	638	62
1968	248	3,960	943	820	4,748	385	667	281	1,249	3,079	423	161	1,361	1,304	754	1,692	127
Democratic	95	1,701	302	359	2,259	247	197	118	351	1,267	157	70	442	616	374	749	45
Republican	139	1,791	450	408	2,090	122	254	150	473	1,228	239	85	590	589	308	810	71
American Independent	14	467	192	50	379	16	215	13	425	584	27	5	322	97	73	128	11
1972	281	4,095	1,030	928	4,592	416	674	307	1,201	3,471	478	187	1,457	1,471	762	1,853	146
Democratic	100	1,559	247	393	1,797	195	187	140	357	1,154	126	68	439	568	277	810	44
Republican	174	2,442	759	487	2,715	220	477	166	813	2,299	324	117	988	837	485	989	100
1976	297	4,112	1,092	1,030	4,621	411	803	301	1,476	4,072	541	188	1,697	1,556	751	2,104	156
Democratic	136	2,012	532	490	2,329	228	451	147	826	2,082	182	81	814	717	436	1,040	62
Republican	153	2,001	546	492	2,206	181	346	152	634	1,953	338	102	837	778	315	1,005	93
1980	302	4,284	1,150	1,182	4,562	416	894	328	1,618	4,542	604	213	1,866	1,742	738	2,273	177
Democratic	79	1,752	402	457	1,938	198	430	104	783	1,881	124	82	752	650	367	982	49
Republican	194	2,207	696	571	2,262	155	442	198	788	2,511	440	95	990	865	334	1,089	111
1984	309	4,548	1,256	1,227	4,845	410	969	318	1,712	5,398	630	235	2,147	1,884	736	2,212	189
Democratic	104	1,825	385	536	2,228	197	344	116	712	1,949	155	96	796	807	328	996	53
Republican	200	2,679	862	686	2,584	212	616	200	990	3,433	469	136	1,337	1,052	405	1,199	133
1988	297	4,394	1,171	1,202	4,536	405	986	313	1,636	5,427	647	243	2,192	1,865	653	2,192	177
Democratic	128	1,940	483	616	2,195	225	370	146	680	2,353	207	116	860	934	341	1,127	67
Republican	167	2,417	678	560	2,300	178	606	165	947	3,037	428	124	1,309	904	310	1,047	107
1992	308	4,940	1,390	1,463	4,960	453	1,203	336	1,983	6,154	744	290	2,559	2,288	684	2,531	201
Democratic	99	1,985	473	621	2,239	213	480	125	934	2,282	183	134	1,039	993	331	1,041	68
Republican	136	1,894	593	476	1,792	132	578	137	841	2,496	323	88	1,151	731	242	931	79
Independent	71	1,036	320	354	903	105	139	73	200	1,355	203	66	349	542	109	544	51
1996	266	4,534	1,207	1,378	4,506	390	1,152	324	1,894	5,612	666	258	2,417	2,254	636	2,196	212
Democratic	125	1,860	582	538	1,801	105	573	151	864	2,736	362	80	1,138	841	234	845	105
Republican	107	2,148	488	650	2,216	233	506	139	909	2,460	222	138	1,091	1,123	328	1,072	78
Reform	33	483	131	121	431	44	64	31	106	379	66	31	160	201	72	227	26
2000	288	4,702	1,234	1,534	4,913	409	1,383	316	2,076	6,408	771	294	2,739	2,487	648	2,599	218
Democratic	95	2,184	474	720	2,486	250	566	119	982	2,434	203	149	1,217	1,248	295	1,243	60
Republican	174	2,350	744	714	2,281	131	786	191	1,062	3,800	515	120	1,437	1,109	336	1,237	148

(Z) Less than 500.

[1] 210,733 votes were cast for unpledged Democratic Party electors and thus were not necessarily votes for the Democratic nominee Lyndon Johnson. U.S. total does not include the Alabama vote.

Sources

1824–1968. Walter Dean Burnham, series Y135–186, in *Historical Statistics of the United States* (1975). Original source material includes the following: 1789–1832, Edward Stanwood, *A History of the Presidency*, 2 volumes (Houghton Mifflin, 1928), various pages; 1836–1892, Walter Dean Burnham, *Presidential Ballots, 1816–1892* (Johns Hopkins University Press, 1955), pp. 246–57, 887–9; 1896–1916, Edgar Eugene Robinson, *The Presidential Vote* (Stanford University Press, 1934), pp. 46, 402. 1972–2000, Alice V. McGillivray, Richard M. Scammon, and Rhodes Cook, *America at the Polls, 1960–2000, John F. Kennedy to George W. Bush: A Handbook of American Presidential Election Statistics* (Congressional Quarterly Press, 2001).

Documentation

See the text for Table Eb149–153.

The American electoral college system creates a presidential election not as a single national election but as a series of state elections in which a successful candidate must win sufficient individual contests to accumulate an absolute majority of electoral votes. This table summarizes the popular votes cast in support of the major party candidates by state.

The vote listed is normally that of the highest candidate for presidential elector for each party. The Democratic vote in 1896 and 1900 includes a variety of joint elector tickets with the People's Party, and party totals generally include votes cast for the presidential candidate under designations other than that of the party itself.

TABLE Eb260-263   Votes cast for House candidates, by political party: 1896-2000[1]

Contributed by John P. McIver

Year	Total Eb260 Thousand	Republican Eb261 Thousand	Democratic Eb262 Thousand	Other Eb263 Thousand	Year	Total Eb260 Thousand	Republican Eb261 Thousand	Democratic Eb262 Thousand	Other Eb263 Thousand
1896	14,652	6,845	6,339	1,468	1956	58,610	28,533	29,951	126
1898	11,513	5,258	5,373	882	1958	44,984	19,565	25,306	112
1900	13,626	6,973	6,086	567	1960	63,110	28,625	34,222	263
1902	10,654	5,250	4,980	424	1962	50,634	24,021	26,467	146
1904	12,697	6,837	5,298	562	1964	67,154	28,288	38,549	317
1906	10,552	5,350	4,659	543	1966	53,143	25,635	27,044	463
1908	14,021	6,975	6,466	580	1968	66,285	32,142	33,244	900
1910	11,669	5,427	5,536	706	1970	54,173	24,415	28,923	835
1912	13,517	4,602	6,128	2,787	1972	71,270	33,104	36,828	1,338
1914	13,275	5,650	5,727	1,898	1974	52,391	21,281	30,159	951
1916	16,140	7,810	7,468	862	1976	74,262	31,242	41,741	1,279
1918	12,579	6,600	5,421	558	1978	55,332	24,849	29,688	795
1920	25,214	14,773	9,038	1,403	1980	77,995	37,370	39,338	1,287
1922	20,409	10,548	9,131	730	1982	64,514	27,799	35,696	1,019
1924	26,884	14,932	10,854	1,098	1984	83,231	38,956	43,539	736
1926	20,435	11,643	8,284	508	1986	59,619	26,532	32,540	547
1928	33,906	19,163	14,361	382	1988	81,786	37,175	43,662	949
1930	24,777	13,032	11,044	701	1990	61,513	27,648	32,565	1,300
1932	37,657	15,575	20,540	1,542	1992	96,239	43,833	48,964	3,442
1934	32,256	13,558	17,385	1,313	1994	69,770	36,590	31,698	1,482
1936	42,886	17,003	23,944	1,939	1996	89,863	43,902	43,626	2,335
1938	36,236	17,047	17,612	1,577	1998	65,897	31,482	32,255	2,160
1940	46,951	21,393	24,092	1,466	2000	99,456	46,738	46,593	6,125
1942	28,074	14,203	12,934	937					
1944	45,103	21,303	22,808	992					
1946	34,398	18,400	15,221	777					
1948	45,933	20,920	23,820	1,193					
1950	40,342	19,750	19,785	807					
1952	57,723	28,470	28,715	538					
1954	42,749	20,095	22,453	200					

[1] State law in Arkansas, Florida, and Oklahoma does not require tabulation of votes for unopposed candidates.

Sources

1896-1950: Governmental Affairs Institute, unpublished data. Figures adapted by Richard M. Scammon from Cortez A. M. Ewing, *Congressional Elections, 1896-1944* (University of Oklahoma Press, 1947), and from unpublished worksheets used in its preparation and the biennial reports of the Clerk of the House of Representatives giving statistics of Congressional voting; 1952-1962: U.S. Bureau of the Census, *Congressional District Data Book* (Districts of the 88th Congress); 1964-1996: Governmental Affairs Institute, *America Votes*, biennial; 1998: *Statistical Abstract of the United States*. 2000: Federal Election Commission (FEC), Federal Elections 2000, downloaded from the FEC Internet site.

Documentation

Article 1, Section 2 of the U.S. Constitution establishes a House composed of representatives from each state chosen by the state's electorate. The number of members in each state delegation is a function of the apportionment process (see Tables Eb1-61).

All representatives face the electorate every two years. This table presents a summation of all votes cast for each major political party. Unlike proportional representation systems common in other democratic nations, however, the single-member plurality ("winner take all") election system does not directly translate national vote totals into seats in the lower chamber of the national legislature (see Table Eb296-308 for seats won by each party).

Historical sources disagree as to the total number of party votes cast in each biennial election. For any given election year it is possible to find two or more alternative vote totals in the following sources: *Statistical Abstract of the United States* (annual); Jerrold G. Rusk, *A Statistical History of the American Electorate* (Congressional Quarterly Press, 2001); Clerk of the U.S. House of Representatives, statistics on presidential and congressional elections (biennial), available from the Internet site of the Clerk of the House; and the Federal Election Commission, which provides data through its Internet site.

Variations reflect publication of data prior to corrections, state laws on data publication, inclusion or exclusion of special elections, counts of minor party votes, and typographical errors. Overall differences are typically not very large.

Election returns for individual races can be found in the following: Rusk (2001); Ewing (1947); *Congressional Elections, 1896-1944* (Congressional Quarterly Press, 1998); and the Internet site of the Clerk of the House.

TABLE Eb264–267   Votes cast for Senate candidates, by political party: 1912–2000

Contributed by John P. McIver

Year	Total Eb264 Thousand	Democrat Eb265 Thousand	Republican Eb266 Thousand	Other Eb267 Thousand	Year	Total Eb264 Thousand	Democrat Eb265 Thousand	Republican Eb266 Thousand	Other Eb267 Thousand
1912	1,329	589	532	208	1960	31,784	17,639	14,014	130
1914	10,894	4,369	4,457	2,068	1962	39,186	19,674	19,319	194
1916	12,025	5,348	5,988	689	1964	52,703	30,035	22,209	459
1918	6,272	2,949	3,021	301	1966	25,798	12,357	13,171	270
1920	19,511	7,376	10,577	1,558	1968	50,827	25,059	24,169	1,599
1922	15,650	7,114	7,505	1,031	1970	48,528	25,371	19,509	3,647
1924	14,529	6,167	7,645	717	1972	37,825	17,235	19,832	758
1926	16,170	7,223	8,570	377	1974	40,938	22,638	16,421	1,879
1928	26,046	10,647	14,347	1,052	1976	58,862	32,003	24,879	1,981
1930	13,011	6,751	5,784	476	1978	28,387	14,334	13,549	505
1932	28,522	15,637	11,354	1,531	1980	58,636	29,890	27,003	1,743
1934	25,145	12,463	10,969	1,712	1982	51,596	28,042	22,694	860
1936	21,342	11,797	8,049	1,497	1984	45,464	22,220	22,851	393
1938	27,972	14,424	12,932	615	1986	48,262	24,290	23,488	484
1940	35,803	16,962	17,194	1,646	1988	67,432	35,279	31,341	812
1942	13,551	6,330	6,693	528	1990	33,067	17,022	15,533	513
1944	34,765	18,403	16,173	189	1992	69,983	35,184	31,870	2,929
1946	27,254	11,988	14,984	281	1994	56,771	25,633	28,889	2,249
1948	22,600	12,751	9,663	186	1996	49,030	23,501	24,212	1,317
1950	32,181	15,611	16,167	403	1998	53,799	26,925	25,719	1,156
1952	44,802	20,603	23,264	935	2000	79,315	36,788	36,730	5,797
1954	20,550	11,436	8,839	275					
1956	43,853	22,499	21,259	95					
1958	37,429	20,855	16,172	403					
1959	165	78	87	0					

Sources

1912–1998: Jerrold G. Rusk, *A Statistical History of the American Electorate* (Congressional Quarterly Press, 2001), Table 6-3, p. 378.

2000: "Federal Elections 2000," Internet site of the Federal Election Commission.

Documentation

Article 1, Section 3 of the U.S. Constitution establishes a Senate composed of two senators from each state chosen by the state's legislature. Legislative appointment of senators, however, became the subject of considerable partisan bickering and charges of corruption. The result was often political deadlocks and vacant Senate seats.

The impetus for reform began as early as 1826, when direct election of senators was first proposed. In the 1870s, voters petitioned the House of Representatives for a popular election. Each year, from 1893 to 1902, a constitutional amendment to elect senators by popular vote was proposed in Congress. On May 13, 1912, Congress finally approved an amendment to Article 1, Section 3 mandating popular election of senators. This amendment was quickly ratified by the states as the Seventeenth Amendment to the U.S. Constitution, with the necessary approval voted on April 8, 1913.

Prior to ratification, senators were elected in several Western states by popular majority vote. In the early 1900s, Oregon pioneered direct election and experimented with different measures over several years until it succeeded in 1907. Soon after, Nebraska followed suit. By 1912, as many as twenty-nine states elected senators, either as nominees of their party's primary or in a general election. Final ratification institutionalized this practice everywhere for the 1914 elections.

For more details on the history of the direct election of senators, see Richard A. Baker, *The Senate of the United States: A Bicentennial History* (Krieger, 1988); Robert C. Byrd, "Direct Election of Senators," in *The Senate 1789–1989*, volume 1 (U.S. Government Printing Office, 1988); and "Direct Election of Senators," available from the Internet site of the U.S. Senate.

For concerns about the consistency of these data across sources, see the text for Table Eb260–263.

CONGRESSIONAL LEGISLATION

John P. McIver

TABLE Eb268–278   Congressional bills and resolutions: 1789–2000
Contributed by John P. McIver

		Measures introduced			Measures passed						
				Joint		Public			Private		
	Congress	Total	Bills	resolutions	Total	Total	Bills	Resolutions	Total	Bills	Resolutions
	Eb268	Eb269	Eb270	Eb271	Eb272	Eb273	Eb274	Eb275 [1]	Eb276	Eb277	Eb278 [1]
Dates	Number	Number	Number	Number	Number	Number	Number	Number	Number	Number	Number
Mar 1789–Mar 1791	1	144	144	—	118	108	94	14	10	8	2
Mar 1791–Mar 1793	2	105	105	—	77	65	64	1	12	12	0
Mar 1793–Mar 1795	3	122	122	—	127	103	94	9	24	24	0
June 1795–Mar 1797	4	132	132	—	85	75	72	3	10	10	0
Mar 1797–Mar 1799	5	234	234	—	155	137	135	2	18	18	0
Dec 1799–Mar 1801	6	157	157	—	112	100	94	6	12	12	0
Mar 1801–Mar 1803	7	161	161	—	95	80	78	2	15	15	0
Oct 1803–Mar 1805	8	217	217	—	111	93	90	3	18	18	0
Mar 1805–Mar 1807	9	219	219	—	106	90	88	2	16	16	0
Oct 1807–Mar 1809	10	266	266	—	105	88	87	1	17	17	0
Mar 1809–Mar 1811	11	348	348	—	119	94	91	3	25	25	0
Mar 1811–Mar 1813	12	406	406	—	209	170	163	7	39	39	0
Mar 1813–Mar 1815	13	400	400	—	273	185	167	18	88	88	0
Dec 1815–Mar 1817	14	465	465	—	298	173	163	10	125	124	1
Mar 1817–Mar 1819	15	507	507	—	257	156	136	20	101	101	0
Dec 1819–Mar 1821	16	480	480	—	208	117	109	8	91	91	0
Dec 1821–Mar 1823	17	492	492	—	238	136	130	6	102	102	0
Dec 1823–Mar 1825	18	498	481	17	335	141	137	4	194	194	0
Mar 1825–Mar 1827	19	622	609	13	266	153	147	6	113	113	0
Dec 1827–Mar 1829	20	632	612	20	235	134	126	8	101	100	1
Mar 1829–Mar 1831	21	856	842	14	369	152	143	9	217	217	0
Dec 1831–Mar 1833	22	1,000	976	24	462	191	175	16	271	270	1
Dec 1833–Mar 1835	23	993	946	47	390	128	121	7	262	262	0
Dec 1835–Mar 1837	24	1,107	1,055	52	459	144	130	14	315	314	1
Mar 1837–Mar 1839	25	1,631	1,566	65	532	150	138	12	382	376	6
Dec 1839–Mar 1841	26	1,122	1,081	41	147	55	50	5	92	90	2
Mar 1841–Mar 1843	27	1,210	1,146	64	524	201	178	23	323	317	6
Dec 1843–Mar 1845	28	1,085	979	106	279	142	115	27	137	131	6
Mar 1845–Mar 1847	29	1,051	956	95	303	142	117	25	161	146	15
Dec 1847–Mar 1849	30	1,433	1,305	128	446	176	142	34	270	254	16
Mar 1849–Mar 1851	31	1,080	978	102	167	109	88	21	58	51	7
Mar 1851–Mar 1853	32	1,167	1,011	156	306	137	113	24	169	156	13
Mar 1853–Mar 1855	33	1,660	1,552	108	540	188	161	27	352	329	23
Dec 1855–Mar 1857	34	1,608	1,515	93	433	157	127	30	276	265	11
Mar 1857–Mar 1859	35	1,686	1,544	142	312	129	100	29	183	174	9
Mar 1859–Mar 1861	36	1,746	1,595	151	370	157	131	26	213	192	21
Mar 1861–Mar 1863	37	1,661	1,370	291	521	428	335	93	93	66	27
Mar 1863–Mar 1865	38	1,708	1,402	306	515	411	318	93	104	79	25
Mar 1865–Mar 1867	39	2,348	1,864	484	714	427	306	121	287	228	59
Mar 1867–Mar 1869	40	3,723	3,003	720	765	354	226	128	411	380	31
Mar 1869–Mar 1871	41	5,314	4,466	848	769	470	313	157	299	235	64
Mar 1871–Mar 1873	42	5,943	5,725	218	1,012	531	515	16	481	479	2
Mar 1873–Mar 1875	43	6,434	6,252	182	859	415	392	23	444	441	3
Mar 1875–Mar 1877	44	6,230	6,001	229	580	278	251	27	302	292	10
Mar 1877–Mar 1879	45	8,735	8,413	322	746	303	255	48	443	430	13
Mar 1879–Mar 1881	46	10,067	9,481	586	650	372	288	84	278	250	28
Mar 1881–Mar 1883	47	10,704	10,194	510	761	419	330	89	342	317	25
Dec 1883–Mar 1885	48	11,443	10,961	482	969	284	219	65	685	678	7
Mar 1885–Mar 1887	49	15,002	14,618	384	1,452	424	367	57	1,028	1,025	3
Dec 1887–Mar 1889	50	17,078	16,664	414	1,824	570	508	62	1,254	1,246	8
Mar 1889–Mar 1891	51	19,630	19,163	467	2,251	611	531	80	1,640	1,633	7
Dec 1891–Mar 1893	52	14,893	14,518	375	722	398	347	51	324	318	6
Mar 1893–Mar 1895	53	12,226	11,796	430	711	463	374	89	248	235	13
Dec 1895–Mar 1897	54	14,585	14,114	471	948	434	356	78	514	504	10
Mar 1897–Mar 1899	55	18,463	17,817	646	1,437	552	449	103	885	880	5

Note appears at end of table

(continued)

TABLE Eb268–278 Congressional bills and resolutions: 1789–2000 *Continued*

		Measures introduced			Measures passed						
							Public			Private	
	Congress	Total	Bills	Joint resolutions	Total	Total	Bills	Resolutions	Total	Bills	Resolutions
	Eb268	Eb269	Eb270	Eb271	Eb272	Eb273	Eb274	Eb275 [1]	Eb276	Eb277	Eb278 [1]
Dates	Number	Number	Number	Number	Number	Number	Number	Number	Number	Number	Number
Dec 1899–Mar 1901	56	20,893	20,409	484	1,942	443	383	60	1,499	1,498	1
Mar 1901–Mar 1903	57	25,460	25,007	453	2,790	480	423	57	2,310	2,309	1
Mar 1903–Mar 1905	58	26,851	26,504	347	4,041	575	502	73	3,466	3,465	1
Mar 1905–Mar 1907	59	34,879	34,524	355	7,024	775	692	83	6,249	6,248	1
Dec 1907–Mar 1909	60	38,388	37,981	407	646	411	350	61	235	234	1
Mar 1909–Mar 1911	61	44,363	43,921	442	884	595	526	69	289	286	3
Apr 1911–Mar 1913	62	38,032	37,459	573	716	530	457	73	186	180	6
Mar 1913–Mar 1915	63	30,053	29,367	686	700	417	342	75	283	271	12
Dec 1915–Mar 1917	64	30,052	29,438	614	684	458	400	58	226	221	5
May 1917–Dec 1919	65	22,594	21,919	675	453	405	349	56	48	48	0
May 1919–Mar 1921	66	21,967	21,222	745	594	470	401	69	124	120	4
Apr 1921–Mar 1923	67	19,889	19,133	756	930	654	549	105	276	275	1
Dec 1923–Mar 1925	68	17,462	16,884	578	996	707	632	75	289	286	3
Dec 1925–Mar 1927	69	23,799	23,250	549	1,423	879	808	71	544	537	7
Dec 1927–Mar 1929	70	23,897	23,238	659	1,722	1,145	1,037	108	577	568	9
Apr 1929–Mar 1931	71	24,453	23,652	801	1,522	1,009	869	140	513	512	1
Dec 1931–Mar 1933	72	21,382	20,501	881	843	516	442	74	327	326	1
Mar 1933–June 1934	73	14,370	13,774	596	975	539	486	53	436	434	2
Jan 1935–June 1936	74	18,754	17,819	935	1,724	987	851	136	737	730	7
Jan 1937–June 1938	75	16,156	15,120	1,036	1,759	919	788	131	840	835	5
Jan 1939–Jan 1941	76	16,105	15,174	931	1,662	1,005	894	111	657	651	6
Jan 1941–Dec 1942	77	11,334	10,793	541	1,485	850	850	—	635	635	—
Jan 1943–Dec 1944	78	8,334	7,845	489	1,157	568	568	—	589	589	—
Jan 1945–Aug 1946	79	10,330	9,748	582	1,625	733	733	—	892	892	—
Jan 1947–Dec 1948	80	10,797	10,108	689	1,363	906	906	—	457	457	—
Jan 1949–Jan 1951	81	14,988	14,219	769	2,024	921	921	—	1,103	1,103	—
Jan 1951–July 1952	82	12,730	12,062	668	1,617	594	594	—	1,023	1,023	—
Jan 1953–Dec 1954	83	14,952	14,181	771	1,783	781	781	—	1,002	1,002	—
Jan 1955–July 1956	84	17,687	16,782	905	1,921	1,028	1,028	—	893	893	—
Jan 1957–Aug 1958	85	19,112	18,205	907	1,720	936	936	—	784	784	—
Jan 1959–Sept 1960	86	18,261	17,230	1,031	1,292	800	800	—	492	492	—
Jan 1961–Oct 1962	87	18,376	17,230	1,146	1,569	885	885	—	684	684	—
Jan 1963–Oct 1964	88	17,480	16,079	1,401	1,026	666	666	—	360	360	—
Jan 1965–Oct 1966	89	24,003	22,483	1,520	1,283	810	810	—	473	473	—
Jan 1967–Oct 1968	90	26,460	24,786	1,674	1,002	640	640	—	362	362	—
Jan 1969–Jan 1971	91	26,303	24,631	1,672	941	695	695	—	246	246	—
Jan 1971–Oct 1972	92	22,969	21,363	1,606	768	607	607	—	161	161	—
Jan 1973–Dec 1974	93	23,369	21,950	1,446	774	651	651	—	123	123	—
Jan 1975–Oct 1976	94	21,096	19,762	1,334	729	588	588	—	141	141	—
Jan 1977–Oct 1978	95	19,387	18,045	1,342	803	633	633	—	170	170	—
Jan 1979–Dec 1980	96	12,583	11,722	861	736	613	613	—	123	123	—
Jan 1981–Dec 1982	97	11,490	10,582	908	529	473	473	—	56	56	—
Jan 1983–Oct 1984	98	11,156	10,134	1,022	677	623	623	—	54	54	—
Jan 1985–Oct 1986	99	9,885	8,697	1,188	483	466	466	—	17	17	—
Jan 1987–Oct 1988	100	9,588	8,515	1,073	761	713	713	—	48	48	—
Jan 1989–Oct 1990	101	6,664	5,977	687	666	650	650	—	16	16	—
Jan 1991–Oct 1992	102	6,775	6,212	563	609	589	589	—	20	20	—
Jan 1993–Dec 1994	103	8,544	7,883	661	473	465	465	—	8	8	—
Jan 1995–Oct 1996	104	6,808	6,545	263	337	333	333	—	4	4	—
Jan 1997–Oct 1998	105	7,732	7,532	200	404	394	394	—	10	10	—
Jan 1999–Dec 2000	106	9,158	8,968	190	604	580	580	—	24	24	—

[1] Once distinguished, public and private resolutions are reported only as public and private laws beginning with the 77th Congress.

Sources

1789–1968: *Historical Statistics of the United States* (1975), series Y189–198, which were based on U.S. Congress, *Calendars of the United States House of Representatives and History of Legislation*; Library of Congress, Legislative Reference Service, unpublished tabulations; U.S. Congress, *Congressional Record*, various issues; 1968–1992: *Statistical Abstract of the United States*, annual; 1993–2000: "Resume of Congressional Activity," available at the Internet site of the Library of Congress.

Session dates are from *Congressional Directory* (biennial), available online at the Internet site of the U.S. Government Printing Office.

Documentation

Some measure of the activities of the U.S. Congress can be gained from the number of bills and resolutions that have been introduced. Congress considers two types of bills – public and private. A public bill is one that affects the public generally. A bill that affects only a specified individual or a private entity is called a private bill. A typical private bill is used to help individuals who face immigration and naturalization problems or companies asserting claims for payment of a government contract. The abrupt reduction in the

TABLE Eb268–278   **Congressional bills and resolutions: 1789–2000** *Continued*

number of private bills enacted into law beginning with the 60th Congress was the result of combining many private bills, particularly pension bills, into omnibus enactments.

Congress also operates by passing joint resolutions, concurrent resolutions, and simple resolutions. There is little practical difference between a bill and a joint resolution, and the two forms are often used interchangeably. Both are subject to the same procedures – except for a joint resolution proposing an amendment to the Constitution. Joint resolutions may originate either in the House of Representatives or in the Senate. By contrast, concurrent and simple resolutions normally are not "legislative" in character (*INS v. Chadha*,

462 U.S. 919 (1983)). These types of resolutions are not "presented" to the President for approval, but are used merely for expressing facts, principles, opinions, and purposes of the two houses. Because these are not legislative actions, the figures reported here exclude simple and concurrent resolutions. For more information, see Charles W. Johnson, "How Our Laws Are Made," Parliamentarian, U.S. House of Representatives (2000), also available at the Internet site of the Library of Congress.

See the text for Table Eb296–308 for additional information about the dates in the table stub and the length of each Congress.

TABLE Eb279–284   **Congressional bills vetoed: 1789–2001**

Contributed by John P. McIver

Years	President	Total	Bills vetoed		Vetoes sustained	Bills passed over presidential veto
			Regular vetoes	Pocket vetoes		
	Eb279	Eb280	Eb281	Eb282	Eb283	Eb284
	—	Number	Number	Number	Number	Number
1789–1797	Washington	2	2	0	2	0
1797–1801	John Adams	0	0	0	0	0
1801–1809	Jefferson	0	0	0	0	0
1809–1817	Madison	7	5	2	7	0
1817–1825	Monroe	1	1	0	1	0
1825–1829	John Q. Adams	0	0	0	0	0
1829–1837	Jackson	12	5	7	12	0
1837–1841	Van Buren	1	0	1	1	0
1841	W. H. Harrison	0	0	0	0	0
1841–1845	Tyler	10	6	4	9	1
1845–1849	Polk	3	2	1	3	0
1849–1850	Taylor	0	0	0	0	0
1850–1853	Fillmore	0	0	0	0	0
1853–1857	Pierce	9	9	—	4	5
1857–1861	Buchanan	7	4	3	7	0
1861–1865	Lincoln	7	2	5	7	0
1865–1869	A. Johnson	29	21	8	14	15
1869–1877	Grant	93	45	48	89	4
1877–1881	Hayes	13	12	1	12	1
1881	Garfield	0	0	0	0	0
1881–1885	Arthur	12	4	8	11	1
1885–1889	G. Cleveland	414	304	110	412	2
1889–1893	B. Harrison	44	19	25	43	1
1893–1897	G. Cleveland	170	42	128	165	5
1897–1901	McKinley	42	6	36	42	0
1901–1909	T. Roosevelt	82	42	40	81	1
1909–1913	Taft	39	30	9	38	1
1913–1921	Wilson	44	33	11	38	6
1921–1923	Harding	6	5	1	6	0
1923–1929	Coolidge	50	20	30	46	4
1929–1933	Hoover	37	21	16	34	3
1933–1945	F. Roosevelt	635	372	263	626	9
1945–1953	Truman	250	180	70	238	12
1953–1961	Eisenhower	181	73	108	179	2
1961–1963	Kennedy	21	12	9	21	0
1963–1969	L. Johnson	30	16	14	30	0
1969–1974	Nixon	43	26	17	36	7
1974–1977	Ford	66	48	18	54	12
1977–1981	Carter	31	13	18	29	2
1981–1989	Reagan	78	39	39	69	9
1989–1993	G. H. W. Bush	44	29	15 [1]	43	1
1993–2001	Clinton	36	36	0	34	2

[1] President George H. W. Bush attempted to pocket veto two bills during intrasession recesses. Congress considers both bills as enacted into law. A count of pocket vetoes from President Bush's perspective would increase the number reported here by two.

Sources

1789–1968: *Historical Statistics of the United States* (1975), series Y199–203, which were based on U.S. Congress, Senate Library, *Presidential Vetoes, 1789–1968*; U.S. Congress, *Calendars of the United States House of Representatives and History of Legislation*, annual.

1970–1999: Gary L. Galemore, "Presidential Vetoes, 1789–Present: A Summary View," Congressional Research Service reports, available at the Internet site of the U.S. House of Representatives, Committee on Rules (updated November 4, 2000).

Documentation

Article 1, Section 7 of the U.S. Constitution described the formal manner under which the Congress and the President share lawmaking authority.

"Every Bill which shall have passed the House of Representatives and the Senate, shall, before it becomes a Law, be presented to the President of the United States; If he approves he shall sign it, but if not he shall return it, with his Objections to that House in which it shall have originated, who shall enter the Objections at large on their journal, and proceed to reconsider it."

The term "veto," which does not appear in the Constitution, indicates the action of the President when he disapproves a bill and returns it with his objections. These regular vetoes differ from pocket vetoes, which result when a bill fails to become law because the President has not signed it within ten days but cannot return it with objections because the Congress has adjourned during the same period.

For a bill to pass over a veto, both the House of Representatives and the Senate must vote to override the veto. The vote to override a Presidential veto requires a two-thirds vote in each chamber.

TABLE Eb285–295   Presidential victories and support scores in Congress, and partisan roll call voting: 1953–2000

Contributed by John P. McIver

		Presidential victories in Congress				Presidential support scores in Congress				Partisan roll call voting	
		House votes on which the President took a position		Senate votes on which the President took a position		House		Senate			
	President	Number	Percentage of victories	Number	Percentage of victories	Democrats	Republicans	Democrats	Republicans	House	Senate
	Eb285	Eb286	Eb287	Eb288	Eb289	Eb290	Eb291	Eb292	Eb293	Eb294	Eb295
Year	—	Number	Percent	Number	Percent	Percent	Percent	Percent	Percent	Percent	Percent
1953	Eisenhower	34	91.2	49	87.8	55	80	55	78	—	—
1954	Eisenhower	38	78.9	77	77.9	54	80	45	82	38	47
1955	Eisenhower	41	63.4	52	84.6	58	67	65	85	41	30
1956	Eisenhower	34	73.5	65	67.7	58	79	44	80	44	53
1957	Eisenhower	60	58.3	57	78.9	54	60	60	80	59	36
1958	Eisenhower	50	74.0	98	76.5	63	65	51	77	40	44
1959	Eisenhower	54	55.6	121	50.4	44	76	44	80	55	48
1960	Eisenhower	43	65.1	86	65.1	49	63	52	76	53	37
1961	Kennedy	65	83.1	124	80.6	81	41	73	42	50	62
1962	Kennedy	60	85.0	125	85.6	83	47	76	48	46	41
1963	Kennedy	71	83.1	115	89.6	84	36	77	52	49	47
1964	Johnson	52	88.5	97	87.6	84	42	73	52	55	36
1965	Johnson	112	93.8	162	92.6	83	46	75	55	52	42
1966	Johnson	103	91.3	125	68.8	81	45	71	53	41	50
1967	Johnson	127	75.6	165	81.2	80	51	73	63	36	35
1968	Johnson	103	83.5	164	68.9	77	59	64	57	35	32
1969	Nixon	47	72.3	72	76.4	56	65	55	74	31	36
1970	Nixon	65	84.6	91	71.4	64	79	56	74	27	35
1971	Nixon	57	82.5	82	69.5	53	79	48	76	38	42
1972	Nixon	37	81.1	46	54.3	56	74	52	77	27	36
1973	Nixon	125	48.0	185	52.4	39	67	42	70	42	40
1974	Nixon [1]	53	67.9	83	54.2	52	71	44	65	29 [2]	44 [2]
1974	Ford [1]	54	59.3	68	57.4	48	59	45	67	29 [2]	44 [2]
1975	Ford	89	50.6	93	71.0	40	67	53	76	48	48
1976	Ford	51	43.1	53	64.2	36	70	47	73	36	37
1977	Carter	79	74.7	88	76.1	69	46	77	58	42	42
1978	Carter	112	69.6	151	84.8	67	40	74	47	33	45
1979	Carter	145	71.7	161	81.4	70	37	75	51	47	47
1980	Carter	117	76.9	116	73.3	71	44	71	50	38	46
1981	Reagan	76	72.4	128	88.3	46	72	52	84	37	48
1982	Reagan	77	55.8	119	83.2	43	70	46	77	36	43
1983	Reagan	82	47.6	85	85.9	30	74	45	77	56	44
1984	Reagan	113	52.2	77	85.7	37	64	45	81	47	40
1985	Reagan	80	45.0	102	71.6	31	69	36	80	61	50
1986	Reagan	90	33.3	83	80.7	26	69	39	90	57	52
1987	Reagan	99	33.3	78	56.4	26	65	38	67	64	41
1988	Reagan	104	32.7	88	64.8	28	61	51	73	47	42
1989	G. H. W. Bush	86	50.0	101	73.3	38	72	56	84	55	35
1990	G. H. W. Bush	108	32.4	93	63.4	26	65	39	72	49	54
1991	G. H. W. Bush	111	43.2	83	67.5	35	74	42	84	55	49
1992	G. H. W. Bush	105	37.1	60	53.4	27	75	33	75	64	53
1993	Clinton	102	87.3	89	85.4	79	40	89	30	65	67
1994	Clinton	78	87.2	62	85.5	79	48	89	44	62	52
1995	Clinton	133	26.3	102	49.0	79	22	84	29	73	69
1996	Clinton	79	53.2	59	57.6	78	39	85	38	56	62
1997	Clinton	75	38.7	63	71.4	73	31	87	61	50	62
1998	Clinton	82	36.6	72	66.7	78	27	86	42	56	56
1999	Clinton	82	35.4	45	42.2	73	23	84	34	47	63
2000	Clinton	69	49.3	40	65.0	73	27	89	46	43	49

[1] In 1974, Richard Nixon and Gerald Ford split the year as President.

[2] Figures represent the calendar year partisan division in the chambers of Congress without regard for the presidential terms of office.

Sources

Congressional Quarterly Almanac, annual editions. *Congressional Quarterly Weekly Report.* Also reported in Harold W. Stanley and Richard G. Niemi, *Vital Statistics on American Politics, 1999–2000* (Congressional Quarterly Press, 2000), and in Norman J. Ornstein, Thomas E. Mann, and Michael J. Malbin, *Vital Statistics on Congress* (Congressional Quarterly Press, 2002).

Documentation

Minor variations exist across sources owing to corrections and rounding decisions.

Series Eb286–289. Presidential victories represent the success with which Presidents push their legislative agenda through the U.S. Congress. These

TABLE Eb285–295   Presidential victories and support scores in Congress, and partisan roll call voting: 1953–2000
Continued

series indicate the number of congressional votes on which the President took a position, along with the percentage of these votes that went favorably for the President.

Series Eb290–293. Within each chamber, Presidents receive more or less support from members of each party. Presidential support scores represent the percentage of votes by the members of each party in agreement with the President's position on all bills on which the President took a public position. The base is the total number of votes cast on all bills on which the President took a position.

Series Eb294–295. These figures represent the percentage of all roll call votes on which a majority of the Democrats voted against a majority of the Republicans.

PARTY AFFILIATION AND PUBLIC OPINION

John P. McIver

TABLE Eb296–308 Political party affiliations in Congress and the presidency: 1789–2002

Contributed by John P. McIver

		House of Representatives					Senate						President	
		Majority party		Minority party		Other parties – representatives	Majority party		Minority party		Other parties – senators			
Congress		Party	Representatives	Party	Representatives		Party	Senators	Party	Senators		Party	Name
Number			Number		Number	Number		Number		Number	Number		
Years	Eb296	Eb297	Eb298	Eb299	Eb300	Eb301	Eb302	Eb303	Eb304	Eb305	Eb306	Eb307	Eb308
1789–1791	1	Ad	38	Op	26	0	Ad	17	Op	9	0	F	Washington
1791–1793	2	F	37	DR	33	0	F	16	DR	13	0	F	Washington
1793–1795	3	DR	57	F	48	0	F	17	DR	13	0	F	Washington
1795–1797	4	F	54	DR	52	0	F	19	DR	13	0	F	Washington
1797–1799	5	F	58	DR	48	0	F	20	DR	12	0	F	J. Adams
1799–1801	6	F	64	DR	42	0	F	19	DR	13	0	F	J. Adams
1801–1803	7	DR	69	F	36	0	DR	18	F	13	0	DR	Jefferson
1803–1805	8	DR	102	F	39	0	DR	25	F	9	0	DR	Jefferson
1805–1807	9	DR	116	F	25	0	DR	27	F	7	0	DR	Jefferson
1807–1809	10	DR	118	F	24	0	DR	28	F	6	0	DR	Jefferson
1809–1811	11	DR	94	F	48	0	DR	28	F	6	0	DR	Madison
1811–1813	12	DR	108	F	36	0	DR	30	F	6	0	DR	Madison
1813–1815	13	DR	112	F	68	0	DR	27	F	9	0	DR	Madison
1815–1817	14	DR	117	F	65	0	DR	25	F	11	0	DR	Madison
1817–1819	15	DR	141	F	42	0	DR	34	F	10	0	DR	Monroe
1819–1821	16	DR	156	F	27	0	DR	35	F	7	0	DR	Monroe
1821–1823	17	DR	158	F	25	0	DR	44	F	4	0	DR	Monroe
1823–1825	18	DR	187	F	26	0	DR	44	F	4	0	DR	Monroe
1825–1827	19	Ad	105	J	97	0	Ad	26	J	20	0	C	J. Q. Adams
1827–1829	20	J	119	Ad	94	0	J	28	Ad	20	0	C	J. Q. Adams
1829–1831	21	D	139	NR	74	0	D	26	NR	22	0	D	Jackson
1831–1833	22	D	141	NR	58	14	D	25	NR	21	2	D	Jackson
1833–1835	23	D	147	AM	53	60	D	20	NR	20	8	D	Jackson
1835–1837	24	D	145	W	98	0	D	27	W	25	0	D	Jackson
1837–1839	25	D	108	W	107	24	D	30	W	18	4	D	Van Buren
1839–1841	26	D	124	W	118	0	D	28	W	22	0	D	Van Buren
1841–1843	27	W	133	D	102	6	W	28	D	22	2	W	Harrison/Tyler
1843–1845	28	D	142	W	79	1	W	28	D	25	1	W	Tyler
1845–1847	29	D	143	W	77	6	D	31	W	25	0	D	Polk
1847–1849	30	W	115	D	108	4	D	36	W	21	1	D	Polk
1849–1851	31	D	112	W	109	9	D	35	W	25	2	W	Taylor/Fillmore
1851–1853	32	D	140	W	88	5	D	35	W	24	3	W	Fillmore
1853–1855	33	D	159	W	71	4	D	38	W	22	2	D	Pierce
1855–1857	34	R	108	D	83	43	D	40	R	15	5	D	Pierce
1857–1859	35	D	118	R	92	26	D	36	R	20	8	D	Buchanan

Series Eb296–308. Party affiliation and public opinion – political party control of Congress and the presidency

		House of Representatives					Senate					President	
		Majority party		Minority party		Other parties – representatives	Majority party		Minority party		Other parties – senators		
Congress	Years	Party	Representatives	Party	Representatives	Number	Party	Senators	Party	Senators	Number	Party	Name
Eb296		Eb297	Eb298	Eb299	Eb300	Eb301	Eb302	Eb303	Eb304	Eb305	Eb306	Eb307	Eb308
Number		—	Number	—	Number	Number	—	Number	—	Number	Number	—	—
36	1859–1861	R	114	D	92	31	D	36	R	26	4	D	Buchanan
37	1861–1863	R	105	D	43	30	R	31	D	10	8	R	Lincoln
38	1863–1865	R	102	D	75	9	R	36	D	9	5	R	Lincoln
39	1865–1867	U	149	D	42	0	U	42	D	10	0	R	Lincoln/A. Johnson
40	1867–1869	R	143	D	49	0	R	42	D	11	0	R	A. Johnson
41	1869–1871	R	149	D	63	0	R	56	D	11	0	R	Grant
42	1871–1873	R	134	D	104	5	R	52	D	17	5	R	Grant
43	1873–1875	R	194	D	92	14	R	49	D	19	5	R	Grant
44	1875–1877	D	169	R	109	14	R	45	D	29	2	R	Grant
45	1877–1879	D	153	R	140	0	R	39	D	36	1	R	Hayes
46	1879–1881	D	149	R	130	14	D	42	R	33	1	R	Hayes
47	1881–1883	R	147	D	135	11	R	37	D	37	1	R	Garfield/Arthur
48	1883–1885	D	197	R	118	10	R	38	D	36	2	R	Arthur
49	1885–1887	D	183	R	140	2	R	43	D	34	0	D	Cleveland
50	1887–1889	D	169	R	152	4	R	39	D	37	0	D	Cleveland
51	1889–1891	R	166	D	159	0	R	39	D	37	0	R	B. Harrison
52	1891–1893	D	235	R	88	9	R	47	D	39	2	R	B. Harrison
53	1893–1895	D	218	R	127	11	D	44	R	38	3	D	Cleveland
54	1895–1897	R	244	D	105	7	R	43	D	39	6	D	Cleveland
55	1897–1899	R	204	D	113	40	R	47	D	34	7	R	McKinley
56	1899–1901	R	185	D	163	9	R	53	D	26	8	R	McKinley
57	1901–1903	R	197	D	151	9	R	55	D	31	4	R	McKinley/T. Roosevelt
58	1903–1905	R	208	D	178	0	R	57	D	33	0	R	T. Roosevelt
59	1905–1907	R	250	D	136	0	R	57	D	33	0	R	T. Roosevelt
60	1907–1909	R	222	D	164	0	R	61	D	31	0	R	T. Roosevelt
61	1909–1911	R	219	D	172	0	R	61	D	32	0	R	Taft
62	1911–1913	D	228	R	161	1	R	51	D	41	0	R	Taft
63	1913–1915	D	291	R	127	17	D	51	R	44	1	D	Wilson
64	1915–1917	D	230	R	196	9	D	56	R	40	0	D	Wilson
65	1917–1919	D	216	R	210	6	D	53	R	42	0	D	Wilson
66	1919–1921	R	240	D	190	3	R	49	D	47	0	D	Wilson
67	1921–1923	R	301	D	131	1	R	59	D	37	0	R	Harding
68	1923–1925	R	225	D	205	5	R	51	D	43	2	R	Coolidge
69	1925–1927	R	247	D	183	4	R	56	D	39	1	R	Coolidge
70	1927–1929	R	237	D	195	3	R	49	D	46	1	R	Coolidge
71	1929–1931	R	267	D	167	1	R	56	D	39	1	R	Hoover
72	1931–1933	D	220	R	214	1	R	48	D	47	1	R	Hoover
73	1933–1934	D	310	R	117	5	D	60	R	35	1	D	F. Roosevelt
74	1935–1936	D	319	R	103	10	D	69	R	25	2	D	F. Roosevelt
75	1937–1938	D	331	R	89	13	D	76	R	16	4	D	F. Roosevelt
76	1939–1940	D	261	R	164	4	D	69	R	23	4	D	F. Roosevelt
77	1941–1942	D	268	R	162	5	D	66	R	28	2	D	F. Roosevelt
78	1943–1944	D	218	R	208	4	D	58	R	37	1	D	F. Roosevelt
79	1945–1946	D	242	R	190	2	D	56	R	38	1	D	Truman
80	1947–1948	R	245	D	188	1	R	51	D	45	0	D	Truman

Notes and codes appear at end of table

(continued)

TABLE Eb296–308   Political party affiliations in Congress and the presidency: 1789–2002

		House of Representatives					Senate						President	
		Majority party		Minority party		Other parties – representatives	Majority party		Minority party		Other parties – senators			
Years	Congress	Party	Representatives	Party	Representatives		Party	Senators	Party	Senators		Party	Name
	Eb296	Eb297	Eb298	Eb299	Eb300	Eb301	Eb302	Eb303	Eb304	Eb305	Eb306	Eb307	Eb308
	Number	–	Number	–	Number	Number	–	Number	–	Number	Number	–	–
1949–1950	81	D	263	R	171	1	D	54	R	42	0	D	Truman
1951–1952	82	D	234	R	199	1	D	49	R	47	0	D	Truman
1953–1954	83	R	221	D	211	1	R	48	D	47	1	R	Eisenhower
1955–1956	84	D	232	R	203	0	D	48	R	47	1	R	Eisenhower
1957–1958	85	D	233	R	200	0	D	49	R	47	0	R	Eisenhower
1959–1960 [1]	86	D	283	R	153	0	D	64	R	34	0	R	Eisenhower
1961–1962	87	D	263	R	174	0	D	65	R	35	0	D	Kennedy
1963–1964	88	D	258	R	177	0	D	67	R	33	0	D	Kennedy/L. Johnson
1965–1966	89	D	295	R	140	0	D	68	R	32	0	D	L. Johnson
1967–1968	90	D	247	R	187	0	D	64	R	36	0	D	L. Johnson
1969–1970	91	D	245	R	189	0	D	57	R	43	0	R	Nixon
1971–1972 [2]	92	D	254	R	180	0	D	54	R	44	2	R	Nixon
1973–1974 [2,3]	93	D	239	R	192	1	D	56	R	42	2	R	Nixon/Ford
1975–1976 [4]	94	D	291	R	144	0	D	60	R	37	2	R	Ford
1977–1978 [5]	95	D	292	R	143	0	D	61	R	38	1	D	Carter
1979–1980 [5]	96	D	276	R	157	0	D	58	R	41	1	D	Carter
1981–1982 [5]	97	D	243	R	192	0	R	53	D	46	1	R	Reagan
1983–1984	98	D	269	R	165	0	R	54	D	46	0	R	Reagan
1985–1986	99	D	252	R	182	0	R	53	D	47	0	R	Reagan
1987–1988	100	D	258	R	177	0	D	55	R	45	0	R	Reagan
1989–1990	101	D	259	R	174	0	D	55	R	45	0	R	G. H. W. Bush
1991–1992 [6]	102	D	267	R	167	1	D	56	R	44	0	R	G. H. W. Bush
1993–1994 [6]	103	D	258	R	176	1	D	57	R	43	0	D	Clinton
1995–1996 [7]	104	R	230	D	204	0	R	53	D	47	0	D	Clinton
1997–1998	105	R	227	D	207	0	R	55	D	45	0	D	Clinton
1999–2000	106	R	222	D	212	1	R	54	D	45	1	D	Clinton
2001–2002 [8]	107	R	221	D	212	2	R	50	D	50	0	R	G. W. Bush

[1] Excludes Hawai'i: two senators (one Republican, one Democrat) and one representative (Democrat) seated August 1959.

[2] Senate had one Independent and one Conservative-Republican.

[3] House had one Independent-Democrat.

[4] Senate had one Independent, one Conservative-Republican, and one undecided.

[5] Senate had one Independent.

[6] House had one Independent-Socialist.

[7] Senator Richard Shelby switched parties the day after the election. Thus the November election produced a Senate split 52–48, but Shelby's defection gave the Republicans a 53–47 majority on opening day of the 104th Congress.

[8] "Unified" government during the 2001–2002 period reflects an evenly split Senate organized by the Republican Party, which held the vice presidency and the tie-breaking vote. The defection of Senator James Jeffords in May 2001 shifted control of the Senate to the Democratic Party.

Sources

1st to 74th Congresses: Library of Congress, Legislative Reference Service, "Political Trends – Both Houses of Congress – 1789–1944" (typewritten tabulation based on *Encyclopedia Americana*, 1936 edi-

tion, volume 7, pp. 516–18, for the 1st to 69th Congresses; and on Harold R. Bruce, *American Parties and Politics*, 3rd edition (Henry Holt, 1936), pp. 174–9, for the 70th to 74th Congresses). 75th to 91st Congresses: U.S. Congress, Congressional Directory, annual volumes. 90th to 107th Congresses: *Statistical Abstract of the United States*, annual volumes.

Documentation

Figures are for the beginning of the first session of each Congress.

"Modern democracy is unthinkable save in terms of the parties" (E. E. Schattschneider, *Party Government* (Holt, Rinehart & Winston, 1942, p. 1)). This assessment is often echoed. Indeed, it is generally recognized today that popular government operates only through the agency of organized political parties. During the early development of the United States, party alignments and the function of political parties were neither fully appreciated nor provided for. Indeed, Federalist Paper number 10 is often portrayed as a diatribe against parties, although "factions," against which Madison railed, encompasses a conception of interest narrower than that held by most mass parties. Despite the absence of formal recognition of political parties in the Constitution, they developed quickly during the formative period, representing the diversity of opinion among and within the states.

TABLE Eb296–308 Political party affiliations in Congress and the presidency: 1789–2002 *Continued*

Although America's political system is usually thought of as a two-party system, the history of American politics is populated with many political parties that have contested elections and won seats in Congress. The abbreviations used in the table for these "major" historical political parties are as follows:

Ad	Administration
AM	Anti-Masonic
C	Coalition
D	Democratic
DR	Democratic–Republican
F	Federalist
J	Jacksonian
NR	National Republican
Op	Opposition
R	Republican
U	Unionist
W	Whig

In the classification by party, the titles of parties during early years have been so designated as to be recognizable in the records of the periods concerned, and also to show the thread of continuity that tends to run from early alignments into the present two-party system. Inasmuch as the party of Thomas Jefferson (generally known at the time as the Republican Party) has with a considerable measure of continuity survived to the present time as the Democratic Party, the name later accepted by the Jeffersonian Republicans of "Democratic–Republican" is used in the table to avoid any confusion of the early Jeffersonian Republican Party with the present-day Republican Party. Opposed to the early Republican Party was the Federalist Party, which was dominant in the first national administration and which, with interruptions, can be traced tenuously by elements of popular support through the National Republican, the Whig, and the Free Soil parties to the Republican Party of today.

In the table stub, the two years listed reflect the first and last years of the associated Congress. Prior to the passage of the Twentieth Amendment, Congress might extend its session, as "lame ducks," into a third calendar year. On its ratification in early 1933, the Twentieth Amendment specified the end of the Congressional term as noon on the third of January, and the Congress effectively ends the prior year.

Note that minor fluctuations in the number of Party members in each chamber occur across sources. This reflects timing of the counts, certification and challenges of election results, and partisan defection during the course of the Congress.

TABLE Eb309–316   Party identification – percentage identifying themselves
as Democrats or Republicans: 1952–2000

Contributed by John P. McIver

	Democrat		Independent			Republican		
	Strong	Not so strong	Closer to Democratic Party	Independent	Closer to Republican Party	Not so strong	Strong	Apolitical
	Eb309	Eb310	Eb311	Eb312	Eb313	Eb314	Eb315	Eb316
Year	Percent	Percent	Percent	Percent	Percent	Percent	Percent	Percent
1952	22	25	10	6	7	14	14	3
1954	22	25	9	7	6	14	13	4
1956	21	23	6	9	8	14	15	4
1958	27	22	7	7	5	16	11	4
1960	20	25	6	10	7	14	16	2
1962	23	23	7	8	6	16	12	4
1964	27	25	9	8	6	14	11	1
1966	18	28	9	12	7	15	10	1
1968	20	25	10	11	9	15	10	1
1970	20	24	10	13	8	15	9	1
1972	15	26	11	13	10	13	10	1
1974	17	21	13	15	9	14	8	3
1976	15	25	12	15	10	14	9	1
1978	15	24	14	14	10	13	8	3
1980	18	23	11	13	10	14	9	2
1982	20	24	11	11	8	14	10	2
1984	17	20	11	11	12	15	12	2
1986	18	22	10	12	11	15	10	2
1988	17	18	12	11	13	14	14	2
1990	20	19	12	10	12	15	10	2
1992	18	18	14	12	12	14	11	1
1994	15	19	13	11	12	15	15	1
1996	18	19	14	9	12	15	12	1
1998	19	18	14	11	11	16	10	2
2000	19	15	15	12	13	12	12	1

Source

National Election Studies (NES), "NES Guide to Public Opinion and Electoral Behavior," available at the NES Internet site. This question is variable VCF0301 in the NES Cumulative Data File data set. Weight variable VCF0009A was used to produce this table. The table was generated by NES staff on September 3, 2001.

Documentation

Party identification represents the attachments of a citizen to the major political parties. It is a staple underlying almost all assessments of American voting behavior. Angus Campbell, Philip E. Converse, et al., in *The American Voter* (Wiley, 1960), describe party identification: "Only in the exceptional case does the sense of individual attachment to partly reflect a formal membership or active connection with a party apparatus. Nor does it simply denote a voting record, although the influence of party allegiance on electoral behavior is strong. Generally this tie is a psychological identification, which can persist without legal recognition or evidence of formal membership and even without a consistent record of party support. Most Americans have this sense of attachment with one party or the other" (p. 121).

The standard measure of party identification is a series of three questions. Respondents are asked for a baseline attachment, after which one of two follow-up questions is asked. If the respondent indicates an attachment to one of the two major parties, he or she is asked about the strength of that attachment. If the respondent is independent of the major parties or identifies some connection to a minor party, the follow-up is designed to determine to which of the two major parties the respondent feels closer. Responses to these questions produce a seven-point party identification scale ranging from strong Democrat to strong Republican.

The baseline party identification question is worded as follows: "Generally speaking, do you usually think of yourself as a Republican, a Democrat, an Independent, or what?" If the respondent indicated a preference for the Republican or Democratic parties, the second question is "Would you call yourself a strong [Republican/Democrat] or a not very strong [Republican/Democrat]?" If the respondent identifies him- or herself as "Independent," "other," or (in 1966 and later years) as having "no pref-

erence," then he or she is asked, "Do you think of yourself as closer to the Republican or Democratic party?"

Party identification is often reported as a three-point scale in which the seven response combinations to these questions are collapsed in one of two ways. Version 1 essentially adopts the response to the base question as a summary of an individual's party attachment and collapses the categories as follows: (1) strong and not-so-strong Democrats; (2) the three independent categories; and (3) strong and not-so-strong Republicans. Version 2 is based on substantial empirical evidence that leaning independents are often more partisan in their political behavior than weak party identifiers and, thus, combines the categories as follows: (1) strong and not-so-strong Democrats, plus independents identified as closer to the Democratic party; (2) independents closer to neither party; and (3) strong and not-so-strong Republicans, plus independents identified as closer to the Republican party.

Responses to the party identification series have also been combined in another way to indicate "strength of partisanship." This scale folds the seven-point scale at its pure independent midpoint. The resulting index runs from independent to strong partisan: (1) independent, closer to neither party; (2) independent, close to one party or the other; (3) not-so-strong Democrats and Republicans; and (4) strong Democrats and Republicans.

Commercial and media pollsters typically employ only the first question in measuring the party attachments of Americans. Extended time series have been constructed for national or state level electorates using such poll data. See Michael B. Mackuen, Robert S. Erikson, and James A. Stimson, "Macropartisanship," *American Political Science Review* 83 (1989): 1125–42; Robert S. Erikson, Michael Mackuen, and James A. Stimson, *The Macro Polity* (Cambridge University Press, 2002); and Donald Green, Bradley Palmquist, and Eric Schickler, "Macropartisanship: A Replication and Critique," *American Political Science Review* 92 (1998): 883–900. State-level partisanship is reported in Robert S. Erikson, Gerald C. Wright, and John P. McIver, *Statehouse Democracy* (Cambridge University Press, 1993); and Gerald C. Wright, John P. McIver, et al., "Stability and Change in State Electorates, Carter through Clinton" (paper presented at the Midwest Political Science Association meeting, Chicago, April 2000).

TABLE Eb317   Policy mood: 1952–2000

Contributed by John P. McIver

Year	Policy mood Eb317 Number	Year	Policy mood Eb317 Number	Year	Policy mood Eb317 Number	Year	Policy mood Eb317 Number	Year	Policy mood Eb317 Number
1952	50.700	1965	62.334	1975	56.555	1985	59.411	1995	66.542
1953	54.710	1966	63.492	1976	54.639	1986	60.950	1996	60.685
1954	53.477	1967	63.351	1977	54.023	1987	62.142	1997	60.998
1955	58.382	1968	63.819	1978	53.524	1988	63.632	1998	60.086
1956	60.407	1969	59.324	1979	52.495	1989	65.397	1999	60.113
1957	61.132	1970	60.929	1980	52.446	1990	66.403	2000	59.663
1958	65.312	1971	61.834	1981	53.408	1991	66.882		
1959	65.662	1972	59.708	1982	55.259	1992	65.738		
1960	64.824	1973	58.552	1983	58.882	1993	64.718		
1961	70.294	1974	58.661	1984	59.698	1994	61.959		
1962	69.271								
1963	66.541								
1964	63.878								

Source

James A. Stimson, *Public Opinion in America: Moods, Cycles and Swings*, 2nd edition (Westview Press, 1999). Data are available at Stimson's Internet site through the University of North Carolina at Chapel Hill.

Documentation

Policy mood is a concept and an operational measure of public preferences over the contemporary political issues. It is designed to capture trends in liberal and conservative sentiment among the general public.

Survey marginals – the aggregated responses of all respondents to individual questions – are collected from a variety of commercial and academic sources including the Roper Center, Harris Interactive, the Survey Research Center of the University of Michigan (American National Election Study), and the National Opinion Research Center (General Social Survey). Only questions that have been repeatedly administered are used to calculate policy mood. Almost 150 questions asked in more than 2,000 surveys from 1952 to 2000 are used to construct this index. Domestic questions include items on attitudes about the death penalty, federal income taxes, Social Security, racial integration, labor unions, birth control, handguns, big business, aid to public schools, equal opportunity and affirmative action, subsidized medical care, the environment, and the problems of big cities, among others.

Policy mood in its simplest light is the smoothed weighted average of the liberal versus conservative marginals of the American public over the past half-century. Higher scores represent more liberal public policy preferences. Lower scores represent more conservative preferences.

Several alternative approaches to computing policy mood exist. This series represents the Dynamic Recursion method. A detailed discussion of this complex algorithm (and the alternatives) for constructing policy mood may be found in Stimson (1999), "Appendix 1: An Algorithm for Estimating Mood."

Data constraints for the first twenty years of the series preclude detailed analysis of the components of policy mood. As the set of available survey marginals expanded during the middle to late 1960s, it is increasingly possible to identify and estimate components of policy mood that move somewhat independently of this broad measure. Stimson (1999, Appendix 2) has generated similar indexes of public policy preferences for education, health, race, urban problems and welfare, size of government, civil liberties, military spending, the environment, and abortion rights.

TABLE Eb318–328   Presidential approval: 1945–2000

Contributed by John P. McIver

			Percentage approving or disapproving of President's job performance								
			Mean of survey results during the year			Highest or lowest survey result during the year					
						Approving		Disapproving		No opinion given	
	President	Number of surveys conducted	Approving	Disapproving	No opinion given	Lowest	Highest	Lowest	Highest	Lowest	Highest
	Eb318	Eb319	Eb320	Eb321	Eb322	Eb323	Eb324	Eb325	Eb326	Eb327	Eb328
Year	—	Number	Percent	Percent	Percent	Percent	Percent	Percent	Percent	Percent	Percent
1945	Truman	3	81.3	8.7	10.0	75	87	3	14	9	11
1946	Truman	5	44.6	40.6	14.8	32	63	22	53	12	18
1947	Truman	5	54.8	30.4	14.8	48	60	23	39	13	17
1948	Truman	2	37.5	48.5	14.0	36	39	47	50	14	14
1949	Truman	4	58.5	24.5	17.0	51	69	17	31	14	19
1950	Truman	8	40.4	40.5	19.0	37	46	32	45	15	25
1951	Truman	10	28.3	56.1	15.6	23	36	49	61	12	19
1952	Truman	6 [1]	28.5	59.2	12.5	25	32	55	62	10	13
1953	Eisenhower	12	68.8	14.3	16.9	59	74	7	25	9	25
1954	Eisenhower	17	65.8	21.5	12.7	57	75	17	26	5	20
1955	Eisenhower	13	71.3	15.5	13.2	66	76	11	21	9	18
1956	Eisenhower	13	72.8	16.5	10.7	68	79	11	20	9	14
1957	Eisenhower	14	64.4	21.4	14.2	57	73	14	27	11	18
1958	Eisenhower	16	54.7	30.3	15.0	48	60	27	36	10	18
1959	Eisenhower	14	63.7	21.7	14.6	57	77	14	27	8	19
1960	Eisenhower	16 [1]	61.3	24.5	14.3	49	66	18	33	9	24
1961	Kennedy	14	76.2	9.6	14.2	72	83	5	14	11	22
1962	Kennedy	13	71.8	16.7	11.5	61	79	10	25	9	15
1963	Kennedy	13 [2]	63.4	24.2	12.5	56	74	14	31	11	15
1964	Johnson	14	74.4	11.7	13.9	69	79	5	19	11	18
1965	Johnson	19	65.9	20.8	13.3	59	71	15	26	10	17
1966	Johnson	16	50.9	35.3	13.9	44	64	24	47	9	20
1967	Johnson	17	44.0	42.1	13.9	38	51	35	50	10	17
1968	Johnson	12 [1]	41.8	46.1	12.1	35	50	38	52	7	14
1969	Nixon	18 [3]	61.2	16.7	22.1	56	67	5	29	14	36
1970	Nixon	18	56.9	29.2	13.9	51	64	22	34	11	18
1971	Nixon	13	50.0	36.5	13.5	48	56	32	39	10	19
1972	Nixon	10	56.2	33.2	10.6	49	62	28	39	8	12
1973	Nixon	20	41.8	47.4	10.8	27	67	25	63	8	13
1974	Nixon	9 [4]	25.7	62.4	11.9	24	28	59	66	9	14
1974	Ford	7 [4]	54.3	25.1	20.6	42	71	3	41	17	26
1975	Ford	19	42.9	40.5	16.6	37	52	33	46	12	24
1976	Ford	8 [1]	46.9	40.0	13.1	45	50	36	45	10	15
1977	Carter	23	63.1	19.3	17.6	54	75	8	30	14	26
1978	Carter	25	45.6	38.1	16.3	39	55	27	44	12	20
1979	Carter	23	37.3	48.6	14.1	29	54	35	58	11	17
1980	Carter	16 [1]	41.1	48.1	10.8	31	58	32	58	8	13
1981	Reagan	19	57.5	28.4	14.1	49	68	13	41	9	36
1982	Reagan	19	44.3	45.4	10.3	41	59	30	50	9	12
1983	Reagan	18	44.1	45.6	10.3	37	54	37	54	8	12
1984	Reagan	19	55.4	35.4	9.2	52	62	30	39	7	12
1985	Reagan	15	60.3	30.5	9.2	52	65	24	37	7	11
1986	Reagan	11	61.5	28.5	10.0	47	68	23	44	8	14
1987	Reagan	9	48.0	42.3	9.7	43	51	41	46	8	14
1988	Reagan	13 [1]	50.8	38.5	10.7	48	54	35	43	8	14
1989	G. H. W. Bush	8	65.0	15.6	19.4	51	71	6	20	9	43
1990	G. H. W. Bush	10	68.4	20.5	11.1	54	80	11	36	8	15
1991	G. H. W. Bush	10	69.2	22.8	8.0	50	83	11	41	4	9
1992	G. H. W. Bush	23 [1]	39.8	52.3	8.0	32	47	47	59	5	14
1993	Clinton	27	48.6	41.1	10.3	37	58	20	50	6	22
1994	Clinton	28	46.3	46.2	7.5	39	58	35	54	5	9
1995	Clinton	21	47.6	43.1	9.3	42	53	38	48	5	12
1996	Clinton	24	54.5	37.9	7.5	42	60	31	49	5	10
1997	Clinton	19	58.3	33.4	8.4	54	62	28	37	6	11
1998	Clinton	42	63.6	32.0	4.4	58	73	25	37	2	10
1999	Clinton	37	61.6	34.5	3.8	53	70	27	42	2	7
2000	Clinton	25 [1]	59.5	36.4	4.1	55	64	32	40	2	7

TABLE Eb318–328   Presidential approval: 1945–2000   *Continued*

[1] One or more post-election polls occurring after the election of a new President were dropped from the annual estimate for the sitting President.

[2] Two post-assassination polls about Johnson were dropped from the annual estimate.

[3] One pre-inauguration poll on the outgoing President was dropped from the annual estimate.

[4] The sixteen polls in 1974 are divided between Nixon and Ford and reported separately.

Sources

George C. Edwards III and Alec M. Gallup, *Presidential Approval: A Sourcebook* (Johns Hopkins University Press, 1990); Lyn Ragsdale, *Vital Statistics on the Presidency: Washington to Clinton* (Congressional Quarterly Press, 1996); *The Gallup Poll Monthly* (October 2000): 10–12.

Documentation

Richard Neustadt, in *Presidential Power* (Wiley, 1960), argues that presidential power is the power to persuade. Underlying the President's ability to persuade all of the other actors in the American government, including members of his own administration, is an ability to claim support of the American people.

Since the mid-1930s, survey organizations, most notably Gallup, have tracked the degree to which the public has approved of the performance of the President. Since 1945, the standard question wording originally formulated for the Gallup Poll (and adopted by many others) has been "Do you approve or disapprove of the way [PRESIDENT'S NAME] is handling his job as President?"

This table is meant to represent public judgment of the job performance of the sitting President. Series Eb320–322 present the average percentage approval and disapproval of the President (as well as the percentage of those uncertain or unwilling to express their opinion). The percentages are calculated by equally weighting each survey reported by the Gallup survey organization during the year. These means may be influenced by the number, distribution, and timing of the surveys. The figures in series Eb323–328 are the high and low single survey results for the year.

Gallup regularly chose to omit the presidential approval question during presidential election campaigns. These series does not include public reaction to Presidents during their last three months in office following the election of a new officeholder in order to preclude confusion over whose performance is really being evaluated and to discount any halo effects caused by the imminent departure of the previous President or the impending arrival of the new one.

For time series describing the reactions of various demographic groups to presidential performance, see Edwards and Gallup (1990) or Ragsdale (1996) for data from the Truman through Clinton presidencies, or the *Gallup Poll Monthly* for contemporary evaluations of the President. Edwards and Gallup report these data for each survey, whereas Ragsdale provides quarterly summaries for demographic groups.

Beginning in the mid-1970s, Gallup interviewers asked two follow-up questions designed to elicit a distinction between public reactions to the economy versus foreign policy performance. Question wording on these series changed after Carter's term as President, which makes long-term historical trend analysis difficult. Current question wordings mirror the general question: (a) "Do you approve or disapprove of the way [PRESIDENT'S NAME] is handling the nation's economy?" (b) "Do you approve or disapprove of the way [PRESIDENT'S NAME] is handling foreign affairs?"

These assessments are summarized in Ragsdale (1996) from Nixon's final days through the Clinton years. See the *Gallup Poll Monthly* for contemporary evaluations of the presidential handling of the economy and foreign affairs.

Additional discussion of presidential approval polls may be found in the following: Paul Brace and Barbara Hinckley, *Follow the Leader: Opinion Polls and the Modern Presidents* (Basic Books, 1992); Richard A. Brody, *Assessing the President: The Media, Elite Opinion and Public Support* (Stanford University Press, 1991); and John E. Mueller, *War Presidents and Public Opinion* (Wiley, 1973).

CHAPTER Ec

Crime, Law Enforcement, and Justice

Editor: Douglas Eckberg

Associate Editor: Richard Sutch

CRIME AND VICTIMIZATION

Douglas Eckberg

Three quarters of a century ago Edwin Sutherland flatly declared, "statistics of crime are known as the most unreliable and the most difficult of all statistics" (Sutherland 1924). The sentiment was not new then, and observations on problems with crime statistics remain staples of criminology and sociology textbooks today. This was not just an academic observation either. Crime statistics are important to policymakers and ordinary citizens as well as to academics. The amount of crime is a basic fact that allows us to compare our society with others, helps us know how our society has changed over time, and provides evidence to help determine what social conditions and what social policies are useful for minimizing disorder.

The quantity of crime – the total count, the categories, and the rates – remains shrouded to a degree that would seem intolerable to people in most other fields. We face a "dark figure" of crime, where the number of unknown or unknowable criminal events "haunts all attempts to estimate crime rates even in the present; for the past it is multiplied enormously" (Lane 1992, p. 39). This "dark figure" is analogous to the one facing astrophysicists. They know that there is a vast mass of "dark matter" in space, but not how much. How much dark matter determines whether the universe ends in fire or ice. For crime, the "dark figure" mocks our ability to know important things about our society and its development.

Many scholars have worked to quantify the level and trend of crime in the United States. This essay sketches some of that research and discusses the strengths and weaknesses of the results. It barely touches the immense problems of counting crime before the advent of regularly gathered and published criminal statistics. There is a lively tradition of scholarship devoted to that topic, but

Acknowledgments

Douglas Eckberg thanks the following people and institutions for providing data. Gary Kleck supplied published and unpublished data on firearm availability and possession. Marie Pees of the Bureau of the Census provided unpublished data on custody in training schools for juvenile delinquents and in detention centers, from a special tabulation of 1990 Census data. Eric Monkkonen and Roger Lane shared historical homicide data for New York City and Philadelphia. Stewart Tolnay and E. M. Beck provided data on lynching in ten Southern states, while W. Fitzhugh Brundage provided data on the state of Virginia and additional data on the state of Georgia. The Federal Bureau of Investigation provided unpublished data on crimes and arrests. The work was made possible by a sabbatical leave granted the author by Winthrop University.

it is beyond the scope of this essay.[1] This discussion does not discuss white collar crime either, which is even more poorly measured than violent and property crime. Except for a few historical series, this essay does not deal with city and state differences in crime rates and trends, though evidence suggests that these regional differences are large. It focuses instead on the sources of unrecorded crime, on data development efforts aimed at bringing crime to light, and on the U.S. system of national crime statistics.

Social and Psychological Factors in the Measurement of Crime

The social world is, for the most part, invisible to its inhabitants. Any one of us can witness only a small fraction of the events that occur within it. Some important aspects of societies, such as average life spans, total homicides, cannot be witnessed by a single individual because they are summations of large numbers of events occurring in diverse places and times. Nothing that happens outside our immediate range of vision and hearing, whether because of distance, closed doors, the presence of gatekeepers, or privacy rights, can be known directly, and the more pronounced the distance or other barriers, the more difficult it is to see.

Because they can carry severe consequences, criminal and deviant actions are even more difficult to observe than are other social actions. Offenders are not the only participants who wish to conceal crime. Bystanders may want to avoid involvement; friends may want to avoid injuring their intimates; victims may fear retaliation or want to avoid the humiliation, pity, derision, or gawking curiosity that can accompany victimization. Victims may feel it is not worth the effort to report a crime.

People also misrepresent crime by reporting events that are not criminal or that did not occur. One reason is to hide a different crime, as when a theft is claimed in order to hide insurance fraud. People also make false accusations to exact revenge and to avoid embarrassment. Perhaps the best known historical example of false accusation is the case of the "Scottsboro Boys," where a group of nine young black men were convicted in 1931 of raping two white women solely on the basis of the women's testimony. At subsequent retrials one of the women recanted her earlier testimony, but the men were convicted again (Goodman 1994; Carter 1979).

When there are great social strains, it is possible for even fairly bizarre accounts to be given credence by the public and by law enforcement officials. Witch crazes in eighteenth-century New England fall into this category. In late-twentieth-century society,

---

[1] Some of this work is conveniently presented in Gurr (1989).

the form of story called the "urban legend" commonly involves an alleged recent, local crime that can be found to be an old story, existing in diverse communities, with no clear basis in fact (for example, the legend of razors in Halloween apples) (Best and Horiuchi 1985). Urban legends and beliefs similar to them seldom affect criminal statistics, but at certain times they can lead to arrests, prosecutions, and imprisonment. In the past two decades, there has been a surprisingly widespread belief in "Satanic" cults that practice sexual molestation of small children, the memories of which the children repress. People have been convicted and imprisoned on such charges, even when the evidence was sparse and contradictory. In the social science community, the majority opinion is that most – if not all – of the alleged events never occurred (Richardson, Best, and Bromley 1991; Loftus 1979; Loftus and Ketcham 1994). These are extreme examples of the way in which shared social beliefs shape and distort crime statistics.

The police also distort crime statistics. They misrepresent the criminal behavior of others and engage in criminal behavior themselves. There are a number of reasons for this. Many police appear to believe that following official standards interferes with the performance of their jobs. In addition, the danger in police work and the need for mutual trust and reliance breed powerful internal solidarity. The "blue wall of silence," which draws much commentary, can hide such criminal behaviors of police as use of excessive force and manipulation of charges and evidence in ways that affect specific crime rates and racial and ethnic differences in crime rates (see, for example, Barker and Carter 1990). Moreover, police work offers opportunities for graft. Overall, then, the reason crime generates "the most unreliable and the most difficult" statistics is that so many different actors have such strong reasons to mislead.

It is easy to see why many are motivated to misrepresent deviant or criminal behavior. What about those who want to give accurate accounts of what they have witnessed? One of the surprising findings of social science research is that they mislead as well. It has been known for over half a century that when people gossip or pass rumors, the accounts they pass become shorter and simpler – a handful of details are played up to the exclusion of other, potentially important points. Accounts change to fit the social expectations of the tellers. A biased and oversimplified picture replaces a more accurate account (Allport and Postman 1975). One cause of this is limitations in human perception. Eyewitnesses cannot agree on even basic information about offenders, victims, or circumstances. Witnesses are profoundly suggestible (Wells and Loftus 1984). The longer the chain of information-passers is, the greater the distortion and simplification of the original message will be. More new and incorrect elements enter. The final message comes to mirror social expectations.

Defining Criminal Behavior

Which behaviors are considered criminal depends upon culture institutions. Changes in culture and the law mean changes in measured crime. For example, in New York at the opening of the twentieth century, there was a large increase in convictions for rape (Sutherland 1924, p. 32). This was caused not by an increase in sexual assaults on women, but by a legal change that raised the age of sexual consent for girls from 10 to 18 years and by the institutional fact that statutory rape was included with forcible rape.

Statutory rapes are not included in modern criminal statistics such as the FBI's Uniform Crime Report rape statistics reported in series Ec4. The modern statistics refer to forcible rapes only.

Cultural change can affect crime statistics even in the absence of legal change. Roger Lane argues that much of the increase in arrests in late-nineteenth-century Massachusetts was caused not by an increase in crime but by an increasing intolerance toward disorderliness (Lane 1968). Eric Monkkonen and Jeffrey Adler document similar developments at other times and places (Monkkonen 1981; Adler 2001).

Homicide is arguably the most consistently defined of all crimes. Yet the definition of homicide has changed substantially over the past century. Much of the surge in homicides in early-twentieth-century cities can be attributed to a growth in social sensitivity to death by violence and a change in the way many deaths were categorized. Auto accident deaths, which were on the increase, often were ruled homicides. Police changed their method of reporting deaths. In the nineteenth century, they had worked diligently to avoid calling an action a murder; in the early twentieth century, they began calling more deaths wrongful murder (Lane 1989; Weiner and Zahn 1989; Adler 2001).

Early vital statistics counts of deaths by homicide did not regularly distinguish between felonious and justifiable homicides. Most justifiable homicides are killings by the police. Today the FBI tabulates police killings separately, and vital statistics tables allow "legal intervention" deaths to be broken out from homicide totals. In the 1920s, perhaps a quarter to a third of all homicides was "justifiable" according to the definition then in use. Thus, the high level of the homicide rate in the early part of the twentieth century, as shown in series Ec192, does not necessarily imply a high murder rate. It could mean a large number of "justifiable" killings by police, which are excluded from contemporary murder counts. But recognition of this problem requires recognition of another problem: standards of police conduct have changed greatly over time. Today, although the overall homicide rate is about the same as it was in the 1920s, justifiable homicides by police are only about 2 percent of the total (Federal Bureau of Investigation 1998, p. 24). Judged by today's standards, police of earlier eras would be judged grossly reckless and negligent in their use of deadly force. Many early "justifiable" homicides would now be ruled felonious.

Changes in social organization affect crime statistics. This is because both the formal and the informal (therefore often hidden) criteria by which an event is assigned to some recognizable category vary by time and place. Cultural differences play a role here, but social rules of classification are also important. For one who views every abortion as murder, the U.S. murder rate is very much higher than official statistics suggest.

Public sensibilities are volatile and laws can change. The United States whipsawed from rates of drinking and drunkenness far above those of today to a change in the Constitution outlawing the sale of alcohol, then to Prohibition's repeal. Drunk-driving laws have grown much more stringent in recent years. Until recently, gambling was illegal in most of the nation; today many states promote it, at least in the form of state lotteries. Civil rights for black Americans were very different during slavery, Reconstruction, the Jim Crow era, and the era of the Civil Rights movement. It is again legal in several states to carry concealed firearms. The United States did, then did not, and now does execute criminals – in some states at least.

Laws and mores concerning sex and reproduction are perhaps the most volatile aspects of public and private life. Laws regulating acts, ages, circumstances, and appropriate partners seem always contested. This is the social basis of ongoing controversies about contraception, abortion, reproductive technology, divorce, homosexuality, and sexuality in the arts, where competing social movement organizations line up against one another in what have been called "culture wars" (Hunter 1991; Bolton 1992). Until the 1960s, racial intermarriage was illegal in most Southern states; the ban was not removed from the South Carolina constitution until 1998. The age of sexual consent in most states is now typically 16 or older, and people are serving prison terms for statutory rape, but in some of the same states a child of 13 can (with parental permission) marry. In this social scene, it has to be hard to understand the meaning of even well-documented changes in rates of arrests, convictions, or incarcerations, in terms of the private activities of masses of people.

The Administration of Criminal Justice

The U.S. criminal justice system is characterized by substantial decentralization. Each state runs its own system, with its own criminal codes, modes of organization, and funding. Within states, most counties, cities, and other governmental bodies have their own law enforcement agencies (police departments, sheriff's office, and so forth). As a result, determining lines of authority can at times be contentious. This is partly because authority is divided along geographic lines but also because social considerations must be taken into account (for example, state police typically will pursue different forms of crime than will local police, though this itself varies from state to state). Court systems and prisons likewise vary from state to state because of the evolution of their development. Thus, Michael Hindus found that by the late 1800s Massachusetts had developed a fairly unified statewide prison system, but that in South Carolina authority was jealously held at the county level (Hindus 1980). Overriding all of this is the separate federal justice system, which itself has a large number of agencies, with often crosscutting jurisdiction.

Gathering basic information on crimes is made difficult by this hodge-podge of agencies. State agencies cannot be compelled to provide criminal statistics to the Federal Bureau of Investigation (FBI); however, they do so in a voluntary arrangement. Some states require that all agencies submit criminal statistics to a central statewide agency, and those states submit crime data from that agency. From other states, though, individual local agencies provide data, and some, particularly very small police departments that encounter few crimes, find the process not worth the effort. Crimes that are reported must be coded to FBI standards, which may be difficult when the statutes of the state differ greatly from the norm.

Consequently, the highly decentralized character of the American criminal justice system is the source of much of the inconsistency in the U.S. crime statistics, as will become apparent later in this essay. The system requires that data be collected by local agencies and then forwarded to the FBI, sometimes going first to a state agency. Because local agencies differ in their official and unofficial approaches to crime, these numbers are not fully comparable with one another.

Crime Statistics

In the United States, crime statistics were first collected in a handful of large cities and in one or two states, notably Massachusetts, well over a century ago. The development of comprehensive crime statistics gained momentum in the second quarter of the twentieth century. The statistics have improved in detail and accuracy, and the speed of improvement has increased. Nonetheless, the obstacles to complete tabulation remain formidable.

The first comprehensive national measures of criminal activity refer to prison inmates. This is the phenomenon most distantly removed from the original criminal action; therefore, if one is interested in tracing crime trends themselves, this is the statistic most likely to misrepresent crime. On the other hand, incarceration is a phenomenon that is interesting in its own right.

The decennial censuses began publishing statistics on prisoners in 1850. (See Table Ec-A for a chronology of important events in crime and criminal statistics.) Since then, there have been several

TABLE Ec-A Important events in crime and criminal statistics: 1850–2001

1850	The first prison and mortality statistics are gathered in the decennial U.S. Census.
1870	The U.S. Department of Justice is established, with the Attorney General as its head. There had been Attorneys General in the cabinet since 1789, but none had headed a department.
1880	The U.S. Death Registration Area is organized. It encompasses only Massachusetts, New Jersey, the District of Columbia, and nineteen cities.
1892	The Lizzie Borden Case. In Fall River, Massachusetts, the father and stepmother of Lizzie Borden are killed with an axe. Borden is accused and, in the most sensational and controversial trial of the time, acquitted.
1892	Tuskegee University archives record 230 lynching deaths, the most for any year in U.S. history.
1900	The first year of mortality data (including data on suicides and homicides) for the U.S. Death Registration Area are published by the Bureau of the Census in Mortality Statistics. The data cover ten states, the District of Columbia, and hundreds of U.S. cities.
1908	The Federal Bureau of Investigation (FBI) is founded. It is a division of the U.S. Department of Justice and is charged with investigating violations of federal law.
1918	The Eighteenth Amendment to the U.S. Constitution prohibits the manufacture, transportation, or sale of alcoholic beverages.
1919	The Volstead Act (the National Prohibition Act) passes Congress, outlawing the production and sale of alcoholic beverages. The act takes effect in 1920.
1924	Congress authorizes creation of the Federal Bureau of Prisons.
1926	The first year of publication of annual statistics on state and federal prisoners is published by the Census Bureau. The data later are named "National Prisoner Statistics." Publication shifts to the Federal Bureau of Prisons in 1950 and to the Bureau of Justice Statistics and its predecessor in 1970.

(continued)

TABLE Ec-A   Important events in crime and criminal statistics: 1850–2001 *Continued*

1930	The International Association of Chiefs of Police creates the "Uniform Crime Reports" to ensure reliable tabulation of crimes. The FBI assumes stewardship, and the first report covers August 1930.
1931	The Scottsboro Case. A group of nine young black men are accused, and convicted, of raping two white women, in what appears to have been a clear case of false accusation. The case leads to four trials but, although the defendants are thrice sentenced to death, none is executed. The last "Scottsboro Boy" leaves prison in 1950.
1932	The Lindbergh Kidnapping. The infant son of Charles A. and Anne Morrow Lindbergh is kidnapped and dies of a fractured skull. Bruno Richard Hauptmann, an illegal German immigrant with a criminal record, is convicted of the crime and executed. The case is as much a media event as the O. J. Simpson trial in the 1990s, and the result is ultimately as controversial.
1933	The Twenty-First Amendment to the U.S. Constitution repeals the Eighteenth Amendment, which had instituted Prohibition.
1933	Texas is admitted to the U.S. Death Registration Area, so that for the first time the Registration Area encompasses the entire nation.
1943	Austin Porterfield (Texas Christian University) conducts the first survey of juvenile delinquency.
1950	The decennial U.S. Census counts the number of juveniles in custody, categorized by race, sex, age, and type of institution.
1950	Ethel and Julius Rosenberg, along with several others, are charged with having provided U.S. atomic secrets to the Soviet Union beginning in 1944. They are convicted and are executed in 1953.
1951	Senator Estes Kefauver publishes *Crime in America*, about the influence of "the mob" in national affairs. The book is based on records of the Senate Crime Investigating Committee of 1950–1951, also known as the Kefauver Committee. The work sets the stage for a national debate on the nature of organized crime.
1956	The Children's Bureau (U. S. Department of Health, Education, and Welfare) conducts the first regular survey of juvenile institutions.
1958	The FBI aggregates Uniform Crime Reports crime counts and rates to the national level.
1964	The Civil Rights Act of 1964, a comprehensive act, bars unequal application of voting requirements, bars discrimination in public accommodations, authorizes the Attorney General of the United States to file suits to force desegregation, authorizes withdrawal of federal funds from programs that practice discrimination, outlaws employment discrimination in any business exceeding twenty-five people, and creates the Equal Employment Opportunities Commission.
1964	Civil Rights workers James Chaney, Andrew Goodman, and Michael Schwerner are murdered in rural Mississippi, in what Tuskegee University records categorize as the last official lynching in the United States. This is one of several outrages that influence passage of the Voting Rights Act of 1965.
1971	The first National Household Survey on Drug Abuse is undertaken by the National Commission on Marijuana and Drug Abuse. The survey is taken over by the National Institute on Drug Abuse in 1974, and by the Office of Applied Studies of the Substance Abuse and Mental Health Services Administration in 1992.
1971	A prison riot at the Attica Correctional Facility in New York leaves forty-three dead. Of these forty-three, thirty-nine – including ten hostages – are killed when the prison is retaken by New York authorities.
1972	In the case of *Furman v. Georgia*, the U.S. Supreme Court rules that Georgia's – and by extension most states' – death penalty laws are unconstitutional. This and a set of related cases end capital punishment in the United States until 1977.
1973	The first annual National Crime Victimization Survey is undertaken by the Bureau of Justice Statistics (U.S. Department of Justice).
1975	The first annual "Monitoring the Future" survey of drug use and delinquency by high school seniors in conducted by University of Michigan researchers Lloyd D. Johnston, Patrick M. O'Malley, and Jerald Bachman.
1978	Theodore Kaczynski, later known as the Unabomber, sends the first of sixteen bombs over eighteen years, killing three people and seriously injuring nearly a dozen. Kaczynski, who is highly intelligent but found to be mentally ill, pleads guilty in 1998 and receives four life sentences.
1989	Charles Keating Jr. is indicted on charges of fraudulently diverting more than $1 billion in the failure of Lincoln Savings and Loan Association, the most prominent savings and loan (S&L) failure of the 1982–1991 S&L crisis. The crisis ultimately costs taxpayers approximately $150 billion. Keating is convicted in 1993, appeals the conviction, and in 1999 pleads guilty to embezzling just under $1 million.
1993	Twelve-year-old Polly Klaas is abducted from a slumber party by Richard Allen Davis and murdered. The case leads to California's passing of the first state "three strikes" law, in which long sentences are mandated for repeat offenders with convictions of even fairly minor crimes.
1994	Nicole Brown Simpson, the ex-wife of retired football star O. J. Simpson, and her friend Ronald Goldman are found stabbed to death. Simpson is charged with the crime. He is acquitted in a 1995 trial that is surrounded by intense media coverage, but in a later civil trial he is found responsible for the deaths.
1995	The number of people incarcerated in federal or state prisons tops 1,000,000.
1995	The Alfred P. Murrah Federal Building in Oklahoma City, Oklahoma, is bombed, killing 168 people and injuring more than 500. In 1997, Timothy McVeigh is convicted of the crime and sentenced to death. Terry Nichols is convicted of conspiracy and involuntary manslaughter and is sentenced to life in prison, and Michael Fortier, who testifies for the prosecution, receives a short sentence after a plea-bargain agreement.
2001	Terrorists associated with Al Qaeda, a fundamentalist Islamic organization headquartered in Afghanistan and headed by Osama Bin Laden, crash hijacked jetliners into the World Trade Center in New York City, the Pentagon in Washington, D.C., and a field in rural Pennsylvania. The two main towers of the World Trade Center collapse and more than 2,800 people are killed in the most deadly and expensive act of terrorism recorded on U.S. soil.

different data collection programs. The most important and comprehensive, the National Prisoner Statistics series, was begun by the Census Bureau in 1926. This is a voluntary program in which penal institutions supply statistics on prisoner admissions, releases, "movements," and executions (for descriptions of these data, see Cahalan 1986; Langan 1991).

It would seem almost too easy a matter to collect data on prisoners. They are – literally – a captive population, inherently easy to count. That is far from the case, though, mainly because of problems resulting from federalism. Over the years it has proven difficult to get the many prisons throughout the country – each operated by a local jurisdiction – to provide the required information. The situation worsened in the early 1970s, when often over a third of states provided no admissions-series figures (see Langan 1991).

There are, moreover, gaps in which one or another regularly reported datum simply ceases to be reported for a time. One finds these gaps in federal as well as state data. For example, there are no published admissions series data for 1951–1959, 1961, 1963, 1965–1969, and 1971–1973. From 1990 through 1992, *Correctional Populations in the United States*, the annual volume of National Prisoner Statistics, issued no release statistics or statistics on "returned" prisoners (mainly people who had previously been paroled or on probation) for federal prisons. As "new" data are found, updated figures replace older ones for some items but not others. This means that official data on prisoners is in a constant state of revision. The partial revisions of the prisoners data is the reason why many subtotals of crime statistics in the tables shown here do not always add to the total.

The available data, displayed in Figure Ec-B, bring to light two important facts about incarceration. First, there has been a profound increase in the rate of state and federal admissions of prisoners, beginning in the mid-1970s and continuing to the early 1990s. Second, the incarceration rate of nonwhites is much higher than that of whites, with the gap increasing since the mid-1970s.

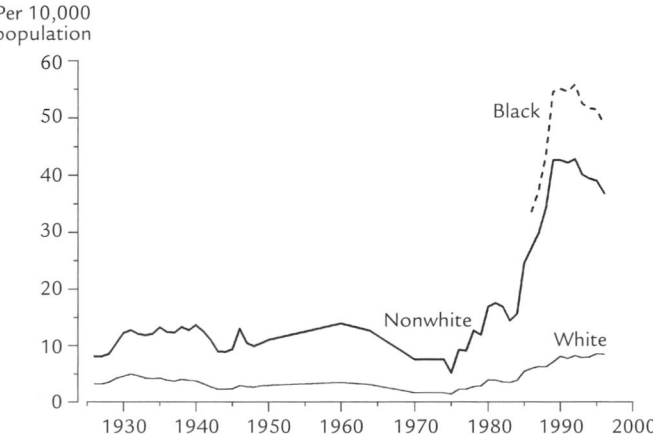

FIGURE Ec-B   Sentenced prisoners admitted to state and federal institutions as a share of population, by race: 1926–1996

Sources
Series Ec311–312 and Ec314 expressed as a share of series Aa113, Aa116, and Aa119, respectively. Beginning 1986, the number of nonwhite prisoners is calculated as the sum of series Ec312–313.

Documentation
Figures cover sentenced prisoners admitted to state and federal institutions for whom racial data are available.

Do these increased incarceration rates mean that crime, too, has increased? The answer is probably no. Scholars who have studied the matter believe that the steep rise in imprisonment reflects changes in legal policy. This has led to a greater number of arrests for behaviors that, in the past, would have been ignored or dealt with administratively. Prison sentences, further, are now prescribed for activities that in the past would have been dealt with via parole, probation, or fines.

The lack of good early data is similar for purely juvenile facilities. The census has provided counts of juveniles in various types of youth facilities since 1950, but the first trial survey of public institutions for delinquents was undertaken by the Children's Bureau of the old Department of Health, Education, and Welfare in 1953. The first comprehensive survey had to wait until 1956 (Children's Bureau 1958). It received completed questionnaires from only 78 percent of the institutions surveyed, though in later years, as it became an almost annual survey, the response rate rose to 90 to 95 percent. Following reorganization in the late 1960s and early 1970s, the surveys – now considered censuses of juvenile institutions – were taken over by the Justice Department, and data were collected by the Census Bureau. Coverage of what came to be called the "children in custody" series was then expanded to include short-term holding facilities and private juvenile institutions, and became a biennial survey. Coverage of public institutions is almost universal today, but there remains some difficulty in collecting data from private facilities. For example, in 1991 the response rate for private juvenile facilities was only 84 percent, and there were about 8 percent outright refusals to cooperate (Table Ec402–425).

In the absence of nationwide data on crimes, scholars have looked for clues about trends in criminal activity in the vital statistics that include homicide and suicide as causes of death. Mortality questions were first asked in the Census of 1850, but the responses were judged at the time to be unreliable. The "death registration area" was established in 1880, as part of a movement promoting continuous official reporting of deaths (Census Bureau 1906, p. lv).

Table Ec190–198 displays official statistics on homicide and suicide counts and rates beginning with 1900. For the early years, these official numbers are known to be misleading. The compilers admitted that data for the subcategories of violent deaths (deaths by "external causes") – homicide, suicide, and specific types of accident – were poor, calling them "incorrect and absolutely misleading" (Census Bureau 1906, p. lv). The problem was that it was common to list a physical cause of death (for example, poison) without specifying whether the death was accidental or intentional. Most death certificates provided no place to indicate crime, so the compilers at the Census Bureau had to make the determination. They categorized 97,805 "suspicious" deaths as "accidents" in the five years from 1900 through 1904 (Wilbur 1916). In some cases, they sent death reports back to the originating officials for more information. They also developed a new model death certificate, and by the time they published the death tables for 1907, they appear to have resolved this problem (Eckberg 1995).

A second problem is that the death registration area did not encompass the entire nation until 1933. The earliest states in the area were primarily Northeastern and upper Midwestern states that had relatively low rates of homicide. Southern and Western states, which had higher rates, were late to enter. The admission over time of these high-homicide states created a false impression of rising homicide rates.

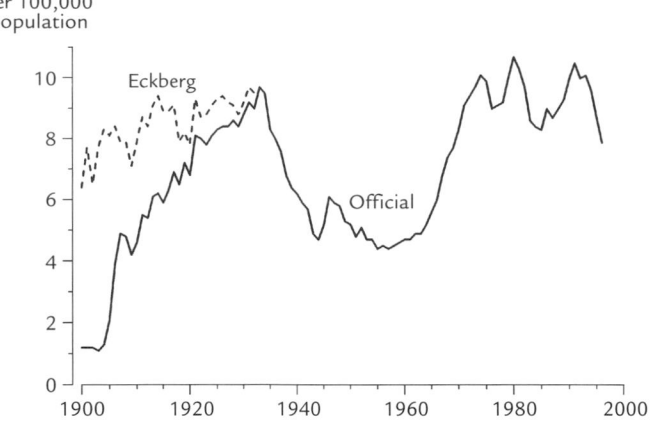

Per 100,000 population

FIGURE Ec-C   Homicide rate: 1900–1996

Sources
Series Ec191–192.

Figure Ec-C shows the official national homicide rate and a separate series designed to correct for the two problems described previously. If the corrected figures are accurate, then the rate of killing early in the century was on the order of six times the rate originally published and not far out of line with rates today.

Figure Ec-C reflects a substantial increase in the homicide rate beginning in the 1960s, with several peak years of rates above 10 killings per 100,000 population. This high level would support imprisonment statistics in that it points toward a great increase in lawlessness in the latter part of the century. Note that homicide is a comparatively rare crime, normally claiming fewer than 20,000 victims per year and accounting for perhaps half that many incarcerations. By itself, it could not cause the explosion in imprisonment rates shown in Figure Ec-B.

Gathering data on crime from police departments themselves began in the early 1930s, at about the same time that the death registration area became complete. Today these statistics are presented in the FBI's Uniform Crime Reports or UCR, the most important element of which is the annual publication, *Crime in the United States*. The UCR is the single most closely watched measure of the crime level and trends in the United States.

The development of the UCR was led by the FBI in a cooperative arrangement with local and state law enforcement agencies. A major innovation was to record, along with records of arrests, "crimes known to police." To qualify for inclusion in the report, police do not need to arrest a suspect; they merely indicate that crimes have been reported. The FBI also instituted a focus on seven important and reasonably well-defined "index crimes." These index crimes are murder or non-negligent manslaughter, rape, aggravated assault, robbery, burglary, motor vehicle theft, and larceny or theft. In recent years the UCR has included arson as an index crime, but a great many jurisdictions do not yet report it. The index crimes let the FBI develop a standard measure of the amount of serious personal crime and monitor trends. The number of these index crimes reported each year since 1960 and the crime rate for the nation as a whole are presented in Tables Ec1–20. Index crimes tabulated by urban police departments for the years 1937 through 1957 are reported in Table Ec21–29. The FBI keeps records on over thirty types of crimes. The statistics are published in annual issues of *Crime in America*.

Even though they are heavily used, the accuracy of UCR data has long been questioned. First, the UCR data are known to seriously underreport the total quantity of crime because only the most serious charge in a given incident is recorded (Maltz 1999). For example, an armed robbery might result in charges of robbery and carrying a concealed weapon, but the UCR would record only the robbery. This is called the "hierarchy rule." It was implemented to simplify record-keeping, but one of the consequences is that minor crimes are underreported.

Moreover, the UCR faces predictable problems securing regular and timely cooperation from local and state agencies in a decentralized governmental structure. For a number of years, the main tables in *Crime in the United States* drew on data from only a subset of cities because there was fairly slow progress toward cooperation with agencies in small towns and rural areas. There were also problems of categorization and organization. In an effort to solve these problems, the entire system was reorganized in the late 1950s. The FBI no longer considers data collected before 1960 to be reliable. To address remaining weaknesses in the data, the FBI has been developing a new system, the National Incident-Based Reporting System (NIBRS), to replace the present UCR. It will keep a complete record of each individual incident so that minor offenses will be better represented in national crime statistics (Federal Bureau of Investigation 1998, pp. 1–4).

Problems in gaining prompt cooperation from local agencies still remain. *Crime in the United States* never gets complete statistics from all jurisdictions. In 1997, for example, 7.1 percent of the population of Metropolitan Statistical Areas (MSAs), 22.6 percent of the population of cities outside of MSAs, and 22.9 percent of the population from rural counties were not covered by agencies that returned completed crime reports. For various reasons, complete data were not available for Illinois, Kansas, Kentucky, Montana, New Hampshire, and Vermont. Indiana, Mississippi, Missouri, New Mexico, Ohio, South Dakota, and Tennessee are notable for the large proportions of their populations not covered by reporting agencies. Kansas has not provided complete state totals since 1994. States converting from the older reporting system to NIBRS have run into problems gathering and presenting crime data that fit UCR protocols. There also remain problems with definitions used in categorizing crime. Since 1984, Illinois has not collected data on forcible rape that fit UCR guidelines. Many agencies in Illinois follow different rules than the UCR on the categorization of other offenses, so that a correction factor has to be employed before figures can be compared with those of other states (Federal Bureau of Investigation 1998).

A sizable fraction of UCR crime data for any given year, then, are imputed, which is to say that estimates are used in place of counts. These are calculated primarily by applying proportional trend figures from reporting agencies to nonreporting agencies that are similar in size and type of jurisdiction (Federal Bureau of Investigation 1998, pp. 401–2). There are ongoing discussions about the best imputing methods to use (Maltz 1999).

Figure Ec-D shows the trend of UCR crime rates for the violent index crimes (criminal homicide, rape, robbery, and aggravated assault) and the property index crimes (burglary, larceny-theft, and motor vehicle theft). There were significant increases in both property and violent crimes known to police in the period during which homicides and imprisonments began their accelerated growth in the mid-1970s. Since the 1990s, however, both crime indexes turn downward, while imprisonment counts continue to rise.

FIGURE Ec-D   Rates of property and violent crimes known to police: 1960–1997

Sources

Series Ec12 and Ec17.

Documentation

For display purposes, the two lines are plotted on different scales because the rate of property crime is so much higher than the rate of violent crime.

The trend for arrest statistics is similar to that of crimes known to police (Tables Ec30–141), namely, rising from the 1960s through some part of the 1980s or early 1990s, then leveling off or even dropping significantly. In all, it is clear that the increase in prison populations through the late 1990s is not attributable to an increase in the number of crimes reported to police or in amounts of victimization (see the discussion in the next paragraph). The issue has been subject to substantial discussion, and it appears to grow from a variety of changes in U.S. public policy toward arrests and imprisonment.

In the early 1970s, a second federal crime measure appeared, the National Crime Victimization Survey (NCVS) of the Bureau of Justice Statistics (BJS). The NCVS is a survey (in recent years of over 80,000 individuals in some 43,000 households) that has been conducted annually since 1973. Responses are shown in Tables Ec142–181. These surveys are administered following principles of scientific survey research in which probability samples of people are selected and then questioned about their experiences with criminal victimization and with delinquency. Interviewers tried to avoid the biases built into the rest of the criminal justice reporting system in which only some people report certain crimes. In addition, by going directly to the public, the data collectors ended reliance on law enforcement agencies entirely. Because it is an alternative or supplement to UCR's crimes "known to police," it employs categories similar to those in the crime index: rape, robbery, simple and aggravated assault, theft or larceny, burglary, and motor vehicle theft. It is similar to the National Household Survey on Drug Abuse (NHSDA) in that it covers only people age 12 and older. Additionally, "households" do not include merchant vessels, military barracks, or institutions such as prisons, and the surveys do not cover commercial crime or homicide (Rand 1998).

Nonetheless, even these steps do not completely eliminate the possibility of bias. First, it is virtually impossible to select a perfectly representative sample from a complex society like the United States. Then, after the sample is drawn, those who refuse to cooperate further complicate the interpretation of the findings. Even though one may "weight" data to adjust for over- or underrepresentation of people with various characteristics, there is always the possibility that those who do not cooperate are simply different from those who do.

Another issue is the reliability of self-reported activities. Research has shown that people misreport many of their activities, including their voting behavior, contributions to charity, amounts of photocopying, and church attendance (Bradburn, Rips, and Shevell 1987; Presser and Traugott 1992; Goldstone and Chin 1993; Bishop and Fisher 1995; Marler and Hadaway 1999). Gary Kleck argues that people underreport gun ownership to researchers (Kleck 1991, pp. 455–60). Thus, it seems likely that people would misrepresent their illegal activities and shameful experiences to strangers in surveys.

The concern with self-reported victimization and delinquency is not just that it understates the total amount of the activity, for if it could be shown that it did so by a certain proportion, then one could easily estimate the true amount. The concern is that the amount of concealment might be different for people of different races, ethnic groups, regions, classes, sexes, and so forth, either masking or exaggerating average group differences.

With many types of victimless crime, though, self-reports may be almost the only way to determine the prevalence in the general population. Also, since the first pioneering self-report survey in the 1940s (Porterfield 1943), survey respondents have seemed quite willing to reveal sensitive information about themselves, once rapport has been established, especially if methods are used to assure the respondents of the anonymity of their answers. Moreover, close inspection of the results does not reveal many systematic problems (Hindelang, Hirschi, and Weis 1981), though black youths are more likely than others to underreport officially recorded delinquency. Most questioning in self-report studies is fairly general and focuses on minor deviance that people might not feel uncomfortable reporting, though there are some exceptions (for example, Wright and Rossi 1986; Elliot, Ageton, et al. 1983). Thus, it is common to use the results of such surveys to trace general trends.

There are two fairly long-term self-reported delinquency series that focus on recreational drug use. The first, the Monitoring the Future (MFT) program, has been surveying the drug use of high school seniors every spring since 1975 (and youths of other ages for a considerably shorter time). The results of this program are displayed in Tables Ec1015–1126. The investigators are aware of potential biases, but they believe that false and misleading answers are minimized, and they give several reasons to think this; however, they note differences in the propensity to answer questions (for example, black males are more likely than others not to answer questions on drug use). About a third of schools in the samples refuse to participate and must be replaced. If these schools had particularly difficult drug problems, the effect would be to underreport drug use. Noncooperation by students is another problem. About 17 percent of sampled students did not complete questionnaires in the most recent year, mostly because of absenteeism and conflicts with school trips.

The MTF program surveys the same grades year after year, so results are comparable across cohorts. Because it surveys only high school seniors, however, it can tell us little about drug use among, say, middle-aged adults. Also, because the survey is done during class, it does not catch students who have dropped out, have been expelled or suspended, or skip school on the survey day. As a group, we would expect such people to be more involved with drugs than the group of teens attending school.[2]

A more broadly based drug survey is the NHSDA, which dates from 1971, with consistent statistics beginning in 1979. The results of these surveys are displayed in Tables Ec951–1014. The NHSDA surveys a representative sample of noninstitutionalized, civilian households, to provide data representative of the U.S. population age 12 and older (excluding military personnel, people in prisons, hospitals, and other institutions, and homeless people who do not live in shelters).

The two surveys attempt to provide figures on the amount of drug use, by specific types of drugs and for various subgroups in the population. Because their sampling is so different, their findings can be used as checks on each other. Nonetheless, both miss those who want to be missed or cannot be found, as for example those in criminal subcultures. Neither of them independently assesses the actions of their respondents. It is generally believed that the trends they uncover follow trends in the general population fairly accurately, though both probably understate the total amount of drug use.

Illicit drug use is one common form of delinquent behavior, and it can be used as an indicator of the general lawlessness of the population. If we think of illicit drug use in this way, we find that neither the MTF surveys of seniors nor the NHSDA support the idea that lawlessness was increasing during the period of rising "crimes known to police" or imprisonments. Figure Ec-E plots the trend. It shows that both surveys indicate a remarkable decrease in the rate of illicit drug use in the general population since the 1970s, a drop of over 50 percent. MTF data do show a rebound in the early 1990s, though not to the level of use during the late 1970s.

In addition to the drug-use questions, the MTF program includes a series of questions about the types and number of other delinquent acts students have committed in the course of the year, including vandalism, trespassing, theft, and injury of another person. No details on incidents are gathered, and no items refer to sexual offenses or homicides, but students are asked about actions that could be charged as such serious offenses as assault, larceny, auto theft, and robbery. Responses are shown in Tables Ec601–650.

It is difficult to know the extent to which the total amount of delinquency is understated by these measures. One calculation suggests that the understatement may be relatively small. If self-reported delinquency is compared with self-reported victimization in similar categories (for example, theft of possessions worth more or less than $50), one finds that the proportion of students admitting to having performed such acts is roughly equal to the proportion of students who report being victimized in school. The *number* of delinquent acts that are admitted, though, is far fewer than the number of victimization experiences reported.

For drug use there are some new, alternative sources that offer contrasts with the findings of general surveys, by surveying different populations using different methods. The most ambitious such project is the Arrestee Drug Abuse Monitoring program (ADAM, previously called Drug Use Forecasting) that surveys prisoners

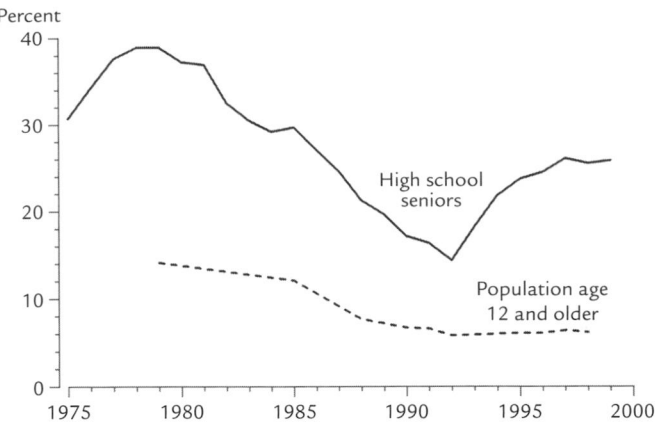

FIGURE Ec-E   Use of illicit drugs – percentage of survey respondents reporting use in the past month: 1975–1999

Sources
Series Ec969 and Ec1029.

in several dozen cities. Persons just arrested answer a series of questions and submit to urinalysis. The program is voluntary, assurances about confidentiality are given, and uniformed officers are not used to gather the information. Although one might well ask how "voluntary" this will seem to a person just arrested, about 20 percent of prisoners do refuse to participate.

For the general population, NHSDA data on drug use within "the past thirty days" indicates that about 6 percent admit to using any drug, 5 percent admit to using marijuana, and under 1 percent admit to using cocaine. In contrast, 1998 ADAM data show a median city rate of cocaine use of 37 percent for men and 40 percent for women. Because cocaine is detectable for only about three days after ingestion, the share of arrestees who use cocaine regularly could well be higher. About a third of inmates tested positive for marijuana, and about two thirds tested positive for at least one drug (Arrestee Drug Abuse Monitoring Program 1999). These rates of drug use among arrestees are six to fifty times the level in the general population. One possible explanation for the extraordinarily high rates of drug use recorded for arrestees is that prisoners have fewer opportunities than those in the general population to disguise their drug use, but the most recent ADAM annual report finds that juvenile prisoners who are in school have substantially lower rates of drug use – 40 to 70 percent lower – than juvenile prisoners who are not in school (Arrestee Drug Abuse Monitoring Program 1999, p. 4). Most professionals interpret the findings to mean that serious, chronic offenders are also likely to be heavy users of many different illicit drugs (Weis 1986).

In principle, researchers should be able to "triangulate" different, fairly independent methods to get some kind of summary figure on phenomena like drug use. In fact, it would seem that this would be essential for the measurement of hidden deviance. However, the differences in methods, in the subpopulations studied, in statistical assumptions, and so forth, have thus far yielded disappointing results. This was symbolized by a 1997 White House drug strategy report that presented the number of "habitual" cocaine users in the United States as *both* 582,000 and 2.2 million, based on NHSDA and ADAM data, respectively (Leen 1998).

Victimization surveys face similar problems with sampling and questioning. Take, for example, the National Crime Victimization Survey, the most highly regarded and long-term survey of crime in the United States. The weaknesses in the NCVS system are well known. It misses that part of the population most likely to be victimized – those who do not have any permanent residence, or who cannot or do not want to be found. For aggravated assaults and rapes, the NCVS figures appear to exclude many attacks by non-strangers that do not result in injuries. Research has shown the opposite as well – that some of the crimes reported, particularly of assaults and rapes by strangers, do not fit the legal criteria for those crimes (Gove, Hughes, and Geerken 1985).

In an effort to correct these problems and following recommendations by the National Academy of Sciences, the NCVS was redesigned in 1992 to stimulate the recollection of respondents and to allow more precise, less subjective responses (Kindermann, Lynch, and Cantor 1997). Both the earlier and later forms were used that year, for sake of comparison. The effect of the redesign was dramatic. Only three types of crime did not show significant rate increases under the new research procedures: robbery, theft, and motor vehicle theft. The reported amount of rape, particularly, was 157 percent higher using the new procedures than using the old ones, reflecting mostly an increased reporting of non-stranger, attempted (but not completed) incidents that were not reported to the police. For violent crime overall, the increases were greater for whites and other racial groups than for blacks, for more affluent people than for poorer people, for middle-aged people than for younger or older people, and for suburbanites than for urban or rural dwellers. Overall, people who were thought least likely to fall prey to criminal victimization were most likely to underreport in the old system (Kindermann, Lynch, and Cantor 1997, pp. 2–4). A sizeable fraction of the victimization gap between groups was shown to be an artifact of differences in their response patterns. The impact of the redesign on reported race differentials for rape was particularly dramatic. The redesigned NCVS now finds relatively small black–white differences.

The NCVS redesign has also helped to resolve a long standing puzzle regarding racial differences in the UCR crimes known to police and self-reported delinquency surveys. UCR data show blacks to be dramatically overrepresented in many crimes; self-reported delinquency studies find only small racial differences. Was the difference caused by a biased criminal justice system or by some other artifact? It could be a result of the fact that most self-report studies usually concentrate on more minor offenses or that black respondents excessively misrepresent their delinquent activities, or it might be a problem of sampling because many self-report studies use high school students and blacks have higher drop-out rates than whites. In the late 1970s, Michael Hindelang showed that victimization statistics mostly supported arrest statistics, though a portion of the racial gap in arrests for rape, simple assault, and aggravated assault could be attributed to the racial bias of the police and the criminal justice system (Hindelang 1978). Because the NVCS redesign led to a reduction in the racial gap in victimization, it probably will lead to a reexamination of the extent of racial bias among police and in the criminal justice system more generally.

It is interesting to compare the picture of crime painted by the NCVS and UCR data. We would expect the two measures to display different pictures of the level and perhaps trend in crime because they were constructed on different bases. The UCR measure, "crimes known to police," understates less serious crime through its hierarchy rule. Because the NCVS records all incidents, the number of minor crimes it shows is undoubtedly more accurate than is the number reported by individuals to the police. Because

the NCVS includes criminal actions that were not reported to the police, this would lead to a difference from the UCR even without the hierarchy rule.

Series Ec11 along with series Ec160 and Ec165 present the level and trend in the crime rate as measured by these two statistics. As we would expect, the NCVS reports a much higher level of crime in all years than does the UCR. The magnitude of the difference may come as a surprise, though. In some cases it is as large as a factor of ten. The large difference between the two measures does not necessarily mean that the police are doing a poor job. It may be the case, as Wesley Skogan put the matter, that most victimizations are not "notable events." The majority are property crimes in which the perpetrators are never detected, the financial stakes are small, and the costs of calling the police greatly outweigh the benefits (Skogan 1981). Another possible explanation for the large difference between the two measures is that many victimizations are considered by the victim to be private matters. We know that many rapes and assaults perpetuated by intimates are viewed in this way.

Except for the most recent years, trends in the two sorts of data also differ. Crimes reported to police rise while reported victimizations fall. The fall in the victimization rate is the most pronounced trend. (It should be noted that the 1992 questionnaire redesign does not lead to a "bump" in victimization rates because a correction factor is now applied to all previous years' rates to ensure comparability.) These differences are apparent across the full range of property and violent crimes. According to the UCR figures, property crime rates increased until the early 1980s and then slowly subsided, while the NCVS finds declining rates of property crime across virtually the entire period. The NCVS shows a slight downward trend in overall violent crime, whereas the UCR finds an explosion in violent crime up to the early 1990s. The general findings are that the NCVS reports much more crime than does the UCR, but the quarter-century trends are the opposite until the decade of the 1990s.

The rape statistics deserve special discussion. In the past, the reporting rate for rape was extremely low. Police statistics may seriously misrepresent both rates and trends. This is apparently what happened in the 1970s and 1980s. From 1973 through 1992, *Crime in the United States* showed a 76.1 percent increase in the rate of reported rapes, which was taken by many as indicating a profound increase in sexual violence in the nation (series Ec4). The NCVS reports across the same period, however, showed a 55.6 percent *decrease* in rape rates (series Ec161). Because it is based on a sample, NCVS figures tend to fluctuate, but even using a three-year (1990–1992) average for rape shows almost a 39 percent decrease from the 1973 figure. Much of the rise in rapes known to police can be attributed to a dramatic increase in the proportion of rapes reported to police and treated by the police as assaults. Figure Ec-F shows the dramatic divergence between the two measures of rape up through the early 1990s, with UCR figures rising and NCVS figures declining. Beginning in the early 1990s, both measures begin to decline together. (It should be repeated that NCVS data do not record victimizations among children younger than 12, so its rate may be artificially elevated; this should not affect general trends, however.) Also, to return to the general question of trends in lawlessness, the rape statistics do not indicate the increase in lawlessness since the mid-1970s that appears indicated in the sentencing statistics. Like the drug-use data, they point toward decreased lawlessness.

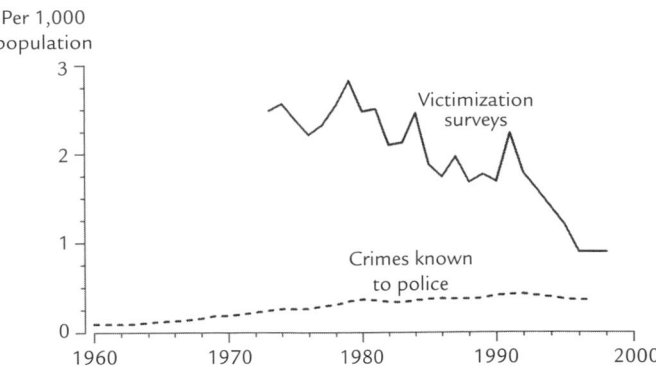

FIGURE Ec-F   Rape rates: 1960–1998

Sources

Series Ec14 and Ec161.

Documentation

Note that the National Crime Victimization Survey covers the population age 12 and older, while crimes known to police are expressed relative to the entire population.

Conclusion

Criminal statistics remain difficult and unreliable, but not completely so. The frustrations that people who got a glimpse of the hidden world of crime experienced led to technical innovations that introduced light. By the 1930s, homicide victimization was well documented. By the 1990s, we had good quantitative evidence on especially difficult-to-measure crimes such as rape and drug use.

Some cautions are warranted though. There are problems that are very difficult to address in principle, and even if all major problems with contemporary criminal data are overcome, we will still face problems tracing most crime trends very far into the past. The UCR statistics are not hopeless; they and the redesigned victimization statistics tend ever more to point in the same direction with respect to trends in personal crime – that it is downward in the United States. If one gives up the dream of counting every single offense and is willing to settle for figures that seem in principle reasonably close to the hidden reality, then one can say that a lot is known about the amounts of different sorts of crime, about the people who commit them, and about the people who are victimized.

Differences in regional laws and policies remain problems. Co-operation between local or state and federal authorities is never complete. Police discretion at the scene and prosecutorial discretion affect the totals. There will, then, continue to be an element of indeterminacy in crime figures. These can be minimized in much the same way that differences in interpretation of activities have been minimized in the NCVS. The NIBRS, when it is completely developed, should substantially expand the amount of crime data available to scholars and law enforcement officials. Even now, the fact that the UCR figures include many estimates for nonreporting agencies does not appear to bias estimates of national trends (Maltz 1999).

The NCVSs have profited from focused attempts to draw information from the population. The professional staff within the Department of Justice, the National Academy of Sciences, and academic criminologists believe that the combination of random selection, regular contact over a period of years, and better interview

protocols have improved the quality of these data. These data can help deal with the problem of unreported or unrecorded crime, but of course they still have the problems of sampling and voluntarism. The sample never fully represents the entire population. The people it misses – those who are homeless, in transit, in hiding, or unco-operative – are those most likely to be both victims and offenders. The data show the victimization experiences of the broad middle part of the population.

Even though self-report data are the weakest link in efforts to estimate personal crime, they have an important role to play, especially with measuring victimless crime. There are limits to the degree of honesty one can expect in the population, and self-reported delinquency always should be considered to understate the true amount of crime. We should not expect people to report delinquent or criminal actions more accurately than they report, say, church attendance. In principle, ways of estimating the degree of underreporting of delinquency can be developed, thereby allowing the derivation of correction factors. The work of Fendrich and Vaughn is an excellent example of what might be done along these lines (Fendrich and Vaughn 1994). They compared self-reports of "lifetime" drug use for specific cohorts across time and discovered a progressive tendency to underreport youthful drug use as people age. Such evidence could be used to adjust the self-reported data and develop more accurate measures.

Efforts to improve the quality of the historical crime record face greater challenges. Take the example of the reformulated NCVS. Recall that almost all forms of crime were found to be more common under the new survey protocols than under the old ones. The estimated rate of rape was 157 percent higher. So what shall be done with findings from the years 1973–1991? The decision was to take the rate (and count) of rape for each of those years and multiply it by the ratio estimator (correction factor) of 2.57 (Rand, Lynch, and Cantor 1997, pp. 6–8). The corrected figures are now published for the earlier years and are included in Table Ec160–168. Although this is not the only approach one could take, it is straightforward and should be reasonably accurate for nearby years. Yet, the further in time one moves from the year in which the figure was calculated, the greater is the likelihood that the figure is inappropriate. Relationships change; consequently, there is a great deal of uncertainty about the estimates for early years in the series. This kind of uncertainty exists whenever data collection procedures change. Because of the desire to implement improved procedures, we can expect further changes in data collection procedures in the future. Whenever this happens, it will introduce problems for comparing figures from different years.

The problem of comparing data collected using different methods complicates all historical work on crime trends. New York, Boston, and Philadelphia have the longest sets of criminal records. They began recording crimes in the eighteenth century.[3] Eric Monkkonen has developed a two-century homicide data series for New York City (Monkkonen 1989). Midwestern and Northeastern states started to publish crime statistics in the nineteenth century. In the South and West, especially in rural districts, there is little good-quality data before the Second World War. Consider statistics on homicide, the most easily counted crime. Texas did not collect death data that met even the minimal criteria needed for admission

---

[3] For a discussion and analysis of these city statistics, see Lane (1968, 1979); Monkkonen (1981, 1989).

to the U.S. death registration area until 1933. South Carolina's death data were considered admissible in 1916; however, years later registration officials published extended tables showing how poorly its data collection compared with that of Vermont (Census Bureau 1924, pp. 97–108). Indeed a recent detailed study of crime in post-Reconstruction South Carolina – hardly the most remote or decentralized of the Old South states – finds that its main newspaper missed probably one third of its murders and that records in the state archives are missing over half (Eckberg 2001). Fragmentary evidence suggests that the further south and west one traveled and the more rural the district was, the higher was the rate of murder (see Montell 1986; Vandal 1991, 1994; McKanna 1995; McGrath 1989). The record is even less clear for other crimes. Overall, the severe limitations in crime data mean that it is very difficult to generalize about crime in America as a whole before the middle of the twentieth century.

One should mention an exception to such a lack of data. In the case of lynching, usually the most public form of homicide, records drawn mainly from news accounts, and now housed at Tuskegee University, have long been the main data source for scholars. It has been long known that the Tuskegee data are somewhat unreliable, about when or where an incident took place and about whether it was indeed a "lynching" (see the discussion in Tolnay and Beck 1995). Stewart Tolnay and E. M. Beck have gathered the most comprehensive state-by-state lynching data series, using modern methods, not for the entire nation but for ten Southern states. W. Fitzhugh Brundage has added lynchings for Virginia (Brundage 1993). In Figure Ec-G are plotted year-by-year totals from Tables Ec251–289. It is clear that they parallel each other very closely. The new data series, which excludes Texas and all Northern and Western states, has slightly fewer lynchings, year-by-year, across the entire period.

Roger Lane attributes our difficulties in counting crimes, even in the rare "settled late nineteenth-century American cities, in the Northeast or West, with established police forces and recording procedures" to two main causes (Lane 1992, p. 39). The first of these he calls "prejudice," referring to the prejudices that directed the passing of laws, arrests, and record keeping of nineteenth-century record keepers, but also referring to the ideological positions of modern scholars who take sides on the meaning of the old records. He does not find the first cause unsolvable, but the second one almost causes him to throw up his hands. This is that dark figure, the "holes in the historical record," caused by differences in categorization, lacunae in recording, indifference by authorities, changes in laws, and uncertainties about the sizes of populations and subpopulations, to name some factors (Lane 1992, p. 30). His complaint reads much like Sutherland's, and he believes we cannot in principle know with certainty if there was proportionately more, or less, of most types of crime in the past than now. He is willing to hazard guesses (his term) about broad quantitative changes in *some* offenses – murder of adults, theft, assault, perhaps robbery. The general trend of Lane's and Eric Monkkonen's findings on urban homicide, the best documented crime, is that it declined from the mid-nineteenth century to roughly the end of the century and then grew until the 1930s (Lane 1992; Monkkonen 1980, 1989). Lane is unwilling to discuss rape, except to speculate that it may have been common among working girls and step-children. He is similarly disinclined to discuss infanticide or abortion (Lane 1992, pp. 45–7). Infanticide, which he calls a "wild card," was often hard to detect, rarely acknowledged, and seldom prosecuted. It almost never led to a conviction. Many infant murders were a form of ex post facto abortions, replacing the ordinary ones that had been legal until the 1860s and that were mostly hidden afterward. Infanticides and abortions thus coexisted in a legal shadow land, with no clear line separating them. To develop estimates, one needs some kind of record with a known basis. Here the record is both mostly blank *and* murky. The other crimes – the ones that make up the bulk of the crime record – are much more difficult and much less reliable, though there is some historical record even for them. It remains to be seen what can be done with them.

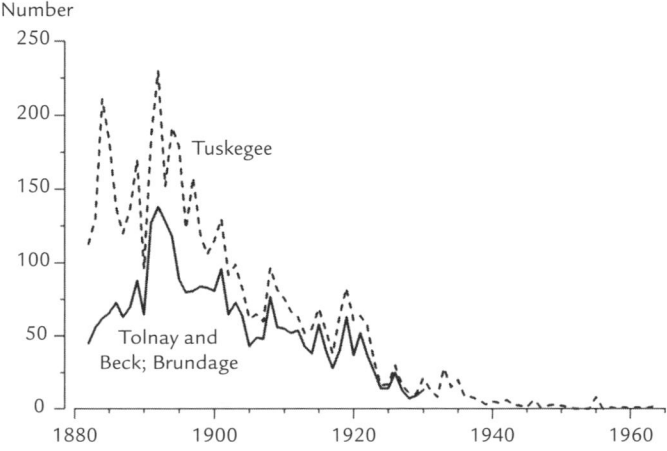

FIGURE Ec-G   Victims of lynching: 1882–1964

Sources
Series Ec251 and Ec254.

Documentation
The figures in series Ec251 present national totals for the reported white and black victims of lynching. Those in series Ec254 (Tolnay and Beck 1995; Brundage 1993) present totals of known victims of lynching (all races) in eleven Southern states.

References

Adler, Jeffrey. 2001. "'Halting the Slaughter of the Innocents': The Civilizing Process and the Surge in Violence in Turn-of-Century Chicago." *Social Science History* 25: 29–52.

Allport, Gordon, and Leo Postman. 1975 [1948]. *The Psychology of Rumor.* Russell and Russell.

Arrestee Drug Abuse Monitoring Program. 1999. *1998 Annual Report on Drug Use among Adult and Juvenile Arrestees.* National Institute of Justice.

Barker, Tom, and David Carter. 1990. "Fluffing Up the Evidence and Covering Your Ass: Some Conceptual Notes on Police Lying." *Deviant Behavior* 11: 61–73.

Best, Joel, and Gerald Horiuchi. 1985. "The Razor Blade in the Apple." *Social Problems* 32: 488–99.

Bishop, G. F., and B. S. Fisher. 1995. "Secret Ballots and Self-Reports in an Exit-Poll Experiment." *Public Opinion Quarterly* 59: 568–88.

Bolton, Richard, editor. 1992. *Culture Wars: Documents from the Recent Controversies in the Arts.* New Press.

Bradburn, N., L. J. Rips, and S. K. Shevell. 1987. "Answering Autobiographical Questions: The Impact of Memory and Inferences on Surveys." *Science* 236: 157–61.

Brundage, W. Fitzhugh. 1993. *Lynching in the New South: Georgia and Virginia, 1880–1930.* University of Illinois Press.

Bureau of Justice Statistics. 1998. *Sourcebook of Criminal Justice Statistics 1997.* U.S. Government Printing Office.

Cahalan, Margaret Werner. 1986. *Historical Corrections Statistics in the United States, 1850–1984.* NCJ-102529. Bureau of Justice Statistics.

Carter, Dan T. 1979. *Scottsboro: A Tragedy of the American South*. Revised edition. Louisiana State University Press.

Census Bureau. 1906. *Mortality Statistics: 1900–1904*. U.S. Government Printing Office.

Census Bureau. 1924. *Mortality Statistics: 1921*. U.S. Government Printing Office.

Children's Bureau. 1958. *Statistics on Public Institutions for Delinquent Children: 1956*. Statistical series number 48. U.S. Department of Health, Education and Welfare.

Eckberg, Douglas Lee. 1995. "Estimates of Early Twentieth-Century U.S. Homicide Rates: An Econometric Forecasting Approach." *Demography* 32: 1–16.

Eckberg, Douglas Lee. 2001. "Stalking the Elusive Homicide: A Capture-Recapture Approach to the Estimation of Post-Reconstruction South Carolina Killings." *Social Science History* 25: 67–92.

Elliot, Delbert S., Suzanne S. Ageton, et al. 1983. *The Prevalence and Incidence of Delinquent Behavior: 1976–1980*. The National Youth Survey Report, number 26. Behavioral Research Institute.

Federal Bureau of Investigation. 1998. *Crime in the United States, 1997*. Uniform Crime Reports. U.S. Government Printing Office.

Fendrich, M., and C. M. Vaughn. 1994. "Diminished Lifetime Substance Abuse over Time: An Inquiry into Differential Underreporting." *Public Opinion Quarterly* 58: 96–123.

Goldstone, R. L., and C. Chin. 1993. "Dishonesty in Self-Report of Copies Made: Moral Relativity and the Copy Machine." *Basic and Applied Social Psychology* 14: 19–32.

Goodman, James. 1994. *Stories of Scottsboro*. Pantheon.

Gove, Walter R., Michael Hughes, and Michael Geerken. 1985. "Are Uniform Crime Reports a Valid Indicator of Index Crimes? An Affirmative Answer with Minor Qualifications." *Criminology* 23: 451–501.

Gurr, Ted Robert, editor. 1989. *Violence in America*, volume 1, *The History of Crime*. Sage.

Hindelang, Michael J., Travis Hirschi, and Joseph G. Weis. 1981. *Measuring Delinquency*. Sage.

Hindelang, Michael. 1978. "Race and Involvement in Common Law Personal Crimes." *American Sociological Review* 43: 93–109.

Hindus, Michael S. 1980. *Prison and Plantation: Crime, Justice and Authority in Massachusetts and South Carolina, 1767–1878*. University of North Carolina Press.

Hunter, James D. 1991. *Culture Wars: The Struggle to Define America*. Basic Books.

Kindermann, Charles, James A. Lynch, and David Cantor. 1997. *Effects of the Redesign on Victimization Estimates*. National Crime Victimization Survey. Bureau of Justice Statistics.

Kleck, Gary. 1991. *Point Blank: Guns and Violence in America*. Aldine de Gruyter.

Lane, Roger. 1968. "Crime and Criminal Statistics in Nineteenth Century Massachusetts." *Journal of Social History* 2: 156–63.

Lane, Roger. 1979. *Violent Death in the City: Suicide, Accident, and Murder in Nineteenth Century Philadelphia*. Harvard University Press.

Lane, Roger. 1989. "On the Social Meaning of Homicide Trends in America." In Ted Robert Gurr, editor. *Violence in America*, volume 1, *The History of Crime*. Sage.

Lane, Roger. 1992. "Urban Police and Crime in Nineteenth-Century America." In Michael Tonry and Norval Morris, editors. *Modern Policing: Crime and Justice, A Review of Research*, volume 15. University of Chicago Press.

Langan, Patrick A. 1991. *Race of Prisoners Admitted to State and Federal Institutions, 1926–86*. NCJ-125618. Bureau of Justice Statistics.

Leen, Jeff. 1998. "Number Jumble Clouds Judgment of Drug War: Differing Surveys, Analyses Yield Unreliable Data." *Washington Post*, January 2, p. A01.

Loftus, Elizabeth. 1979. *Eye Witness Testimony*. Harvard University Press.

Loftus, Elizabeth, and Katherine Ketcham. 1994. *The Myth of Repressed Memory: False Memories and Allegations of Sexual Abuse*. St. Martin's Press.

Maltz, Michael D. 1999. *Bridging Gaps in Police Crime Data*. NCJ-176365. Bureau of Justice Statistics.

Marler, Penny Long, and C. Kirk Hadaway. 1999. "Testing the Attendance Gap in a Conservative Church." *Sociology of Religion* 60: 175–86.

McGrath, Roger D. 1989. "Violence and Lawlessness on the Western Frontier." In Ted Robert Gurr, editor. *Violence in America*, volume 1, *The History of Crime*. Sage.

McKanna, Clare V., Jr. 1995. "Alcohol, Handguns, and Homicide in the American West." *Western Historical Quarterly* 26: 455–82.

Monkkonen, Eric H. 1980. "The Quantitative Historical Study of Crime and Criminal Justice." In James A. Inciardi and Charles E. Faupel, editors. *History and Crime: Implication for Criminal Justice Policy*. Sage.

Monkkonen, Eric H. 1981. *Police in Urban America: 1860–1920*. Cambridge University Press.

Monkkonen, Eric H. 1989. "Diverging Homicide Rates: England and the United States." In Ted Robert Gurr, editor. *Violence in America*, volume 1, *The History of Crime*. Sage.

Montell, William Lynwood. 1986. *Killings: Folk Justice in the Upper South*. University Press of Kentucky.

Porterfield, Austin L. 1943. "Delinquency and Its Outcome in Court and College." *American Journal of Sociology* 49: 199–208.

Presser, Stanley, and M. Traugott. 1992. "Little White Lies and Social Science Models." *Public Opinion Quarterly* 56: 77–86.

Rand, Michael, James A. Lynch, and David Cantor. 1997. *Criminal Victimization, 1973–95*. National Crime Victimization Surveys. Bureau of Justice Statistics.

Rand, Michael. 1998. *Criminal Victimization 1997: Changes 1996–97, with Trends 1993–97. A National Crime Victimization Survey Report*. Bureau of Justice Statistics.

Richardson, James T., Joel Best, and David G. Bromley, editors. 1991. *The Satanism Scare*. Aldine de Gruyter.

Skogan, Welsey. 1981. "Assessing the Behavioral Context of Victimization." *Journal of Criminal Law and Criminology* 72: 727–42.

Sutherland, Edwin H. 1924. *Criminology*. J. B. Lippincott.

Tolnay, Stewart E., and E. M. Beck. 1995. *A Festival of Violence: An Analysis of Southern Lynchings, 1882–1930*. University of Illinois Press

Vandal, Gilles. 1991. "'Bloody Caddo': White Violence against Blacks in a Louisiana Parish, 1865–1876." *Journal of Social History* 25: 373–88.

Vandal, Gilles. 1994. "Black Violence in Post–Civil War Louisiana." *Journal of Interdisciplinary History* 25: 45–64.

Weiner, Neil Alan, and Margaret A. Zahn. 1989. "Violence Arrests in the City: The Philadelphia Story, 1857–1980." In Ted Robert Gurr, editor. *Violence in America*, volume 1, *The History of Crime*. Sage.

Weis, Joseph G. 1986. "Issues in the Measurement of Criminal Careers." In Alfred Blumstein, J. Cohen, et al., editors. *Criminal Careers and "Career Criminals."* National Academy Press.

Wells, Gary L., and Elizabeth Loftus, editors. 1984. *Eye Witness Testimony: Psychological Perspectives*. Harvard University Press.

Wilbur, Cressy L. 1916. *The Federal Registration Service of the United States*. U.S. Government Printing Office.

Wright, James D., and Peter H. Rossi. 1986. *Armed and Considered Dangerous: A Survey of Felons and Their Firearms*. Aldine de Gruyter.

LAW ENFORCEMENT, COURTS, AND THE JUSTICE SYSTEM

Richard Sutch

Law enforcement and the administration of justice take place at all three levels of government – federal, state, and local – and involve all three branches of government – executive, legislative, and judicial. Federal and state legislatures and local governments pass laws that make certain behavior illegal (such as child employment) and that compel certain other behavior (such as child school attendance). The executive branch of government is responsible for the management of law enforcement agencies, prosecuting attorneys, and penal institutions. The judicial branch embraces a system of courts that try to decide the outcomes of cases brought before them. The executive branch also has the authority to pardon convicted criminals or to reduce their sentences.

Law Enforcement

Disincentives to break the law are, for the most part, inherent in the law-making process. The laws themselves commonly prescribe the punishment for those convicted of breaking the law, although the discretion left to prosecutors and judges is generally quite broad. The number of police officers, the resources provided to law enforcement and the prosecutors, and the capacity of the criminal justice system all influence the risk that lawbreakers will be caught, convicted, and punished. There are also extra-legal disincentives to engage in criminal activity. Criminals surprised in the act may be injured or killed by private citizens or police officers. It is sometimes argued that the right of Americans to own firearms is itself deterrence to criminal activity (see Tables Ec1127–1158).

Statutes passed by Congress or state legislatures and ordinances – laws passed by local governments – specify whether a violation is subject to criminal or civil penalties. Criminal acts are investigated by the police. The accused is subject to arrest and, if found guilty, may be punished by fines, imprisonment, or both. By contrast, in the case of a breach of civil law, the injured party is compelled to bring a suit in a court. The defendant in a civil case, if the judgment is unfavorable, may be fined or compelled to make restitution but cannot be imprisoned.

Criminal law enforcement can be divided into three parts: investigation of crimes and arrests of persons suspected of committing them, prosecution of those charged with crime, and punishment or treatment of persons convicted of crime. The first function is the responsibility of law enforcement agencies (police departments, sheriffs' offices, and so forth). Prosecutors, advised by grand juries, are responsible for charging and trying in court those accused of breaking the law. To be convicted of breaking a criminal law, it must be established that the defendant intended to act unlawfully. After the defendant is convicted, the courts set the punishment and other conditions that must be met. If punishment entails incarceration or execution, the penal system carries out the court's orders. A probation system oversees any court-ordered constraints on activities on those released from or excused from imprisonment.

Civil law is governed by the American common law system, under which enforcement is initiated when the aggrieved party files suit in court. The complaining party, the plaintiff, has the burden of demonstrating that the claim is legitimate. Typically, such cases involve a dispute over property rights, breach of contract, or violation of tort law. Disputes over family issues, such as divorce and child custody, are also subject to civil procedures. The plaintiff formally seeks a judicial resolution of his or her claims against the defending party, although the majority of cases are settled by negotiation before trial. In civil law the losing party might be held responsible even if the consequences of the action were unintentional. For example, one might be financially responsible for damage caused by an accident.

Each state has its own criminal and civil laws, though there are substantial similarities across jurisdictions. Many of the states' civil codes are adapted from model statutes. Similarly, even though the organization, methods of finance, and procedural rules may vary among justice systems, they have much in common with one another. Within each state, the enforcement of the criminal law is predominantly the responsibility of local agencies. Police departments, prosecutors, and courts are in most instances either municipal or county agencies. To a large extent, even the correctional processes, such as probation and misdemeanor imprisonment, are functions administered by local authorities. Direct state responsibility is largely confined to providing penal institutions for those offenders convicted and committed to long-term imprisonment. Data on law enforcement officers are presented in Table Ec1353–1355.

Courts

The bulk of civil and criminal litigation in the country is commenced and determined in the various state and local courts. Only when the U.S. Constitution and acts of Congress specifically confer jurisdiction upon the federal courts may civil or criminal litigation be heard and decided by them. Generally, the federal courts have jurisdiction over the following types of cases: suits or proceedings by or against the United States; civil actions between private parties arising under the Constitution, laws, or treaties of the United States; civil actions between private litigants who are citizens of different states; civil cases involving admiralty, maritime, or prize jurisdiction; and all matters in bankruptcy.

There are several types of courts with varying degrees of legal jurisdiction. These jurisdictions include original, appellate, general, and limited or special. A court of original jurisdiction is one having the authority initially to try a case and pass judgment on the law and the facts; a court of appellate jurisdiction is one with the legal authority to review cases and hear appeals; a court of general jurisdiction is a trial court of unlimited original jurisdiction in civil or criminal cases (also called a major trial court); a court of limited or special jurisdiction is a trial court with legal authority over only a particular class of cases, such as probate, juvenile, or traffic cases.

The federal courts of original jurisdiction are known as the U.S. district courts. One or more of these courts is established in every state, and one each is located in Puerto Rico, the Virgin Islands, and Guam. Appeals from the district courts are taken to intermediate appellate courts, of which there are eleven, known as U.S. courts of appeals. The Supreme Court of the United States is the final and highest appellate court in the federal system of courts. Comprehensive information on the business of the federal courts is collected by the Administrative Office of the U.S. Courts and is published in the *Annual Report of the Director* and in *Juror Utilization in United States Courts*. Statistics on the caseload of the federal courts is available annually since 1940.

Statistics on state court cases and the outcome of prosecutions are incomplete for the country as a whole, although data are available for many states individually. The only national compilations of such statistics were made by the Census Bureau for 1932–1945 covering a maximum of thirty-two states and by the Bureau of Justice Statistics for 1986, 1988, 1990, and 1992 based on a nationally representative sample survey (see Tables Ec1159–1352).

Correctional Institutions and Prisoners

Penal institutions include jails, state and federal prisons, and various juvenile facilities. A jail is a facility to hold persons pending adjudication of their case or to incarcerate persons after conviction for a period of one year or less. Jails are typically operated by local law enforcement agencies. A prison is a confinement facility with authority over adults sentenced to imprisonment for a period longer than one year. State or federal authorities typically operate prisons. Juvenile residence facilities have a variety of names including reformatories, correctional facilities, and detention centers. Some states maintain state hospitals for the criminally insane. Persons under care or custody in institutions at the time of the census enumeration are classified as inmates of the institution regardless of their length of stay in the place and regardless of the number of people there. In the Bureau of Census classification, institutions are a subcategory of group quarters (see Chapter Ae). Incarceration statistics are presented in Tables Ec298–327 and Ec358–425. Data on executions are presented in Table Ec343–357.

CRIMES AND ARRESTS

Douglas Eckberg

TABLE Ec1–10   Estimated crimes known to police, by type of offense: 1960–1997

Contributed by Douglas Eckberg

	Violent crimes						Property crimes			
	Total	Total	Murders	Rapes	Robberies	Aggravated assaults	Total	Burglaries	Larcenies and thefts	Motor vehicle thefts
	Ec1	Ec2	Ec3	Ec4	Ec5	Ec6	Ec7	Ec8	Ec9	Ec10
Year	Number	Number	Number	Number	Number	Number	Number	Number	Number	Number
1960	3,384,200	288,460	9,110	17,190	107,840	154,320	3,095,700	912,100	1,855,400	328,200
1961	3,488,000	289,390	8,740	17,220	106,670	156,760	3,198,600	949,600	1,913,000	336,000
1962	3,752,200	301,510	8,530	17,550	110,860	164,570	3,450,700	994,300	2,089,600	366,800
1963	3,109,500	316,970	8,640	17,650	116,470	174,210	3,792,500	1,086,400	2,297,800	408,300
1964	4,564,600	364,220	9,360	21,420	130,390	203,050	4,200,400	1,213,200	2,514,400	472,800
1965	4,739,400	387,390	9,960	23,410	138,690	215,330	4,352,000	1,282,500	2,572,600	496,900
1966	5,223,500	430,180	11,040	25,820	157,990	235,330	4,793,300	1,410,100	2,822,000	561,200
1967	5,903,400	499,930	12,240	27,620	202,910	257,160	5,403,500	1,632,100	3,111,600	659,800
1968	6,720,200	595,010	13,800	31,670	262,840	286,700	6,125,200	1,858,900	3,482,700	783,600
1969	7,410,900	661,870	14,760	37,170	298,850	311,090	6,749,000	1,981,900	3,888,600	878,500
1970	8,098,000	738,820	16,000	37,990	349,860	334,970	7,359,200	2,205,000	4,225,800	928,400
1971	8,588,000	816,500	17,780	42,260	387,700	368,760	7,771,700	2,399,300	4,424,200	948,200
1972	8,248,800	834,900	18,670	46,850	376,290	393,090	7,413,900	2,375,500	4,151,200	887,200
1973	8,718,100	875,910	19,640	51,400	384,220	420,650	7,842,200	2,565,500	4,347,900	928,800
1974	10,253,400	974,720	20,710	55,400	442,400	456,210	9,278,700	3,039,200	5,262,500	977,100
1975	11,292,400	1,039,710	20,510	56,090	470,500	492,620	10,252,700	3,265,300	5,977,700	1,009,600
1976	11,349,700	1,004,210	18,780	57,080	427,810	500,530	10,345,500	3,108,700	6,270,800	966,000
1977	10,984,500	1,029,580	19,120	63,500	412,610	534,350	9,955,000	3,071,500	5,905,700	977,700
1978	11,209,000	1,085,550	19,560	67,610	426,930	571,460	10,123,400	3,128,300	5,991,000	1,004,100
1979	12,249,500	1,208,030	21,460	76,390	480,700	629,480	11,041,500	3,327,700	6,601,000	1,112,800
1980	13,408,300	1,344,520	23,040	82,990	565,840	672,650	12,063,700	3,795,200	7,136,900	1,131,700
1981	13,423,800	1,361,820	22,520	82,500	592,910	663,900	12,061,900	3,779,700	7,194,400	1,087,800
1982	12,974,400	1,322,390	21,010	78,770	553,130	669,480	11,652,000	3,447,100	7,142,500	1,062,400
1983	12,108,600	1,258,090	19,310	78,920	506,570	653,290	10,850,500	3,129,900	6,712,800	1,007,900
1984	11,881,800	1,273,280	18,960	84,230	485,010	685,350	10,608,500	2,984,400	6,591,900	1,032,200
1985	12,431,400	1,328,800	18,980	88,670	497,870	723,250	11,102,600	3,073,300	6,926,400	1,102,900
1986	13,211,900	1,489,170	20,610	91,460	542,780	834,320	11,722,700	3,241,400	7,257,200	1,224,100
1987	13,508,700	1,484,000	20,100	91,110	517,700	855,090	12,024,700	3,236,200	7,499,900	1,288,700
1988	13,923,100	1,566,220	20,680	92,490	542,970	910,090	12,356,900	3,218,100	7,705,900	1,432,900
1989	14,251,400	1,646,040	21,500	94,500	578,330	951,710	12,605,400	3,168,200	7,872,400	1,564,800
1990	14,475,600	1,820,130	23,440	102,560	639,270	1,054,860	12,655,500	3,073,900	7,945,700	1,635,900
1991	14,872,900	1,911,770	24,700	106,590	687,730	1,092,740	12,961,100	3,157,200	8,142,200	1,661,700
1992	14,438,200	1,932,270	23,760	109,060	672,480	1,126,970	12,505,900	2,979,900	7,915,200	1,610,800
1993	14,141,800	1,926,020	24,530	106,010	659,870	1,135,610	12,218,800	2,834,800	7,820,900	1,563,100
1994	13,989,500	1,857,670	23,330	102,220	618,950	1,113,180	12,131,900	2,712,800	7,879,800	1,539,300
1995	13,862,700	1,798,790	21,610	97,470	580,510	1,099,210	12,063,900	2,593,800	7,997,700	1,472,400
1996	13,493,900	1,688,540	19,650	96,250	535,590	1,037,050	11,805,300	2,506,400	7,904,700	1,394,200
1997	13,175,100	1,634,770	18,210	96,120	497,950	1,022,490	11,540,300	2,461,100	7,725,500	1,353,700

Source

Crime in the United States (U.S. Department of Justice, Federal Bureau of Investigation Uniform Crime Reports, annual issues). Compiled in *Source-book of Criminal Justice Statistics 1998* (U.S. Bureau of Justice Statistics, 1999), Table 3.114.

Documentation

The Uniform Crime Reporting (UCR) data displayed in this table are gathered via a cooperative arrangement between the Federal Bureau of Investigation (FBI) and local or state law enforcement agencies, which forward monthly counts of offenses to the FBI. In the case of incomplete data, if an agency forwards between seven and twelve monthly reports, year-to-year changes are estimated based on the data forwarded. In the case of an agency forwarding fewer than seven monthly reports, year-to-year changes are estimated on the basis of data from similarly sized jurisdictions. In 1995, for example, data were estimated for 2.9 percent of agencies in Metropolitan Statistical Areas,

9.6 percent of agencies in other cities, and 12 percent of agencies in rural areas. Florida and Kentucky did not report usable data in 1988; their totals were estimated. Illinois (1985 to 1995) and Michigan and Minnesota (1993) did not provide forcible rape figures in accordance with UCR guidelines, so their rape totals were estimated. Several states have had little or no data available during their change to the new National Incident-Based Reporting System. For them, estimation techniques specific to each state were employed. For further information on classification and counting rules, see *Uniform Crime Reporting Handbook* (U.S. Government Printing Office, 1984).

Series Ec1. The estimated number of crimes is not the total of all crimes, but the total of all "index" crimes. These include four types of "violent" crime and three types of "property" crime. On the basis of these estimates, the FBI tracks trends in criminal behavior in the United States. Property crime estimates are rounded to the nearest 100 offenses, and violent crime estimates

(continued)

TABLE Ec1–10   Estimated crimes known to police, by type of offense: 1960–1997 *Continued*

are rounded to the nearest ten offenses. Because of information that develops over time, estimated crime totals for any given year change somewhat (usually upward) for several years following initial publication of totals. Because of weaknesses in earlier data-gathering procedures, the FBI no longer supplies crime data gathered prior to 1960.

Series Ec2. Violent index crimes include criminal homicide, forcible rape, robbery, and aggravated assault.

Series Ec3. Criminal homicide includes murder and nonnegligent manslaughter: the willful (nonnegligent) killing of one human being by another, excluding deaths by negligence, attempts to kill, assaults to kill, suicides, accidental deaths, and justifiable homicides. Manslaughter by gross negligence is not included in crime index totals.

Series Ec4. Forcible rape is the carnal knowledge of a female forcibly and against her will, including attempts or assaults to rape. The crime index excludes statutory offenses in which no force is used but the victim is under the age of consent.

Series Ec5. Robbery is the taking or attempting to take anything of value from the care, custody, or control of a person or persons by force or threat of force or violence and/or by putting the victim in fear.

Series Ec6. Aggravated assault is an unlawful attack by one person upon another for the purpose of inflicting severe or aggravated bodily injury. It is usually accompanied by the use of a weapon or by means likely to produce death or great bodily harm. Simple assaults are excluded.

Series Ec7. Property index crimes include burglary, larceny-theft, and motor vehicle theft.

Series Ec8. Burglary, or breaking and entering, is the unlawful entry of a structure to commit a felony or a theft. Attempted forcible entry is included.

Series Ec9. Larceny-theft is the unlawful taking, carrying, leading, or riding away of property from the possession or constructive possession of another. Motor vehicle theft is excluded from this category. Larceny is theft of property worth at least $50. Attempted larcenies are included.

Series Ec10. Motor vehicle theft is theft or attempted theft of a motor vehicle. Such a vehicle is self-propelled and runs on a surface rather than on rails. Thefts of motorboats, construction equipment, airplanes, and farming equipment are excluded.

TABLE Ec11–20   Estimated rate of crimes known to police, by type of offense: 1960–1997

Contributed by Douglas Eckberg

	All crimes	Violent crimes					Property crimes			
		Total	Murders	Rapes	Robberies	Aggravated assaults	Total	Burglaries	Larcenies and thefts	Motor vehicle thefts
	Ec11	Ec12	Ec13	Ec14	Ec15	Ec16	Ec17	Ec18	Ec19	Ec20
Year	Per 100,000	Per 100,000	Per 100,000	Per 100,000	Per 100,000	Per 100,000	Per 100,000	Per 100,000	Per 100,000	Per 100,000
1960	1,887.2	160.9	5.1	9.6	60.1	86.1	1,726.3	508.6	1,034.7	183.0
1961	1,906.1	158.1	4.8	9.4	58.3	85.7	1,747.9	518.9	1,045.4	183.6
1962	2,019.8	162.3	4.6	9.4	59.7	88.6	1,857.5	535.2	1,124.8	197.4
1963	2,180.3	168.2	4.6	9.4	61.8	92.4	2,012.1	576.4	1,219.1	216.6
1964	2,388.1	190.6	4.9	11.2	68.2	106.2	2,197.5	634.7	1,315.5	247.4
1965	2,449.0	200.2	5.1	12.1	71.7	111.3	2,248.8	662.7	1,329.3	256.8
1966	2,670.8	220.0	5.6	13.2	80.8	120.3	2,450.9	721.0	1,442.9	286.9
1967	2,989.7	253.2	6.2	14.0	102.8	130.2	2,736.5	826.6	1,575.8	334.1
1968	3,370.2	298.4	6.9	15.9	131.8	143.8	3,071.8	932.3	1,746.6	393.0
1969	3,680.0	328.7	7.3	18.5	148.4	154.5	3,351.3	984.1	1,930.9	436.2
1970	3,984.5	363.5	7.9	18.7	172.1	164.8	3,621.0	1,084.9	2,079.3	456.8
1971	4,164.7	396.0	8.6	20.5	188.0	178.8	3,768.8	1,163.5	2,145.5	459.8
1972	3,961.4	401.0	9.0	22.5	180.7	188.8	3,560.4	1,140.8	1,993.6	426.1
1973	4,154.4	417.4	9.4	24.5	183.1	200.5	3,737.0	1,222.5	2,071.9	442.6
1974	4,850.4	461.1	9.8	26.2	209.3	215.8	4,389.3	1,437.7	2,489.5	462.2
1975	5,298.5	487.8	9.6	26.3	220.8	231.1	4,810.7	1,532.1	2,804.8	473.7
1976	5,287.3	467.8	8.8	26.6	199.3	233.2	4,819.5	1,448.2	2,921.3	450.0
1977	5,077.6	475.9	8.8	29.4	190.7	247.0	4,601.7	1,419.8	2,729.9	451.9
1978	5,140.3	497.8	9.0	31.0	195.8	262.1	4,642.5	1,434.6	2,747.4	460.5
1979	5,565.5	548.9	9.7	34.7	218.4	286.0	5,016.6	1,511.9	2,999.1	505.6
1980	5,950.0	596.6	10.2	36.8	251.1	298.5	5,353.3	1,684.1	3,167.0	502.2
1981	5,858.2	594.3	9.8	36.0	258.7	289.7	5,263.9	1,649.5	3,139.7	474.7
1982	5,603.6	571.1	9.1	34.0	238.9	289.2	5,032.5	1,488.8	3,084.8	458.8
1983	5,175.0	537.7	8.3	33.7	216.5	279.2	4,637.4	1,337.7	2,868.9	430.8
1984	5,031.3	539.2	7.9	35.7	205.4	290.2	4,492.1	1,263.7	2,791.3	437.1
1985	5,207.1	556.6	7.9	37.1	208.5	302.9	4,650.5	1,287.3	2,901.2	462.0
1986	5,480.4	617.7	8.6	37.9	225.1	346.1	4,862.6	1,344.6	3,010.3	507.8
1987	5,550.0	609.7	8.3	37.4	212.7	351.3	4,940.3	1,329.6	3,081.3	529.4
1988	5,664.2	637.2	8.4	37.6	220.9	370.2	5,027.1	1,309.2	3,134.9	582.9
1989	5,741.0	663.7	8.7	38.1	233.0	383.4	5,077.9	1,276.3	3,171.3	630.4

TABLE Ec11-20   Estimated rate of crimes known to police, by type of offense: 1960-1997   *Continued*

	All crimes	Violent crimes						Property crimes			
		Total	Murders	Rapes	Robberies	Aggravated assaults	Total	Burglaries	Larcenies and thefts	Motor vehicle thefts
	Ec11	Ec12	Ec13	Ec14	Ec15	Ec16	Ec17	Ec18	Ec19	Ec20
Year	Per 100,000	Per 100,000	Per 100,000	Per 100,000	Per 100,000	Per 100,000	Per 100,000	Per 100,000	Per 100,000	Per 100,000
1990	5,820.3	731.8	9.4	41.2	257.0	424.1	5,088.5	1,235.9	3,194.8	657.8
1991	5,897.8	758.1	9.8	42.3	272.2	433.3	5,139.7	1,252.0	3,228.8	659.0
1992	5,660.2	757.5	9.3	42.8	263.6	441.8	4,902.7	1,168.2	3,103.0	631.5
1993	5,484.4	746.8	9.5	41.1	255.9	440.3	4,734.6	1,099.2	3,032.4	606.1
1994	5,373.5	713.6	9.0	39.3	237.7	427.6	4,660.0	1,042.0	3,026.7	591.3
1995	5,275.9	684.6	8.2	37.1	220.9	418.3	4,591.3	987.1	3,043.8	560.4
1996	5,086.6	636.5	7.4	36.3	201.9	390.9	4,450.1	944.8	2,979.7	525.6
1997	4,922.7	610.8	6.8	35.9	186.1	382.0	4,311.9	919.6	2,886.5	505.8

Source

Crime in the United States (U.S. Department of Justice, Federal Bureau of Investigation Uniform Crime Reports, annual issues). Compiled in *Sourcebook of Criminal Justice Statistics 1998* (U.S. Bureau of Justice Statistics, 1999), Table 3.114.

Documentation

See the text for Table Ec1-10 for a description of the source and definitions of crimes.

All rates are expressed per 100,000 population.

TABLE Ec21-29   Crimes known to urban police, by type of offense: 1937-1957

Contributed by Douglas Eckberg

	Total	Criminal homicides	Homicides by negligence	Rapes	Robberies	Aggravated assaults	Burglaries	Larcenies and thefts	Motor vehicle thefts
	Ec21	Ec22	Ec23	Ec24	Ec25	Ec26	Ec27	Ec28	Ec29
Year	Number	Number	Number	Number	Number	Number	Number	Number	Number
1937	605,447	2,479	1,978	3,047	26,696	19,841	137,757	325,974	87,675
1938	613,062	2,133	1,428	2,967	27,836	18,765	138,939	346,178	74,816
1939	637,514	2,223	1,229	3,235	26,347	19,063	145,208	369,442	70,767
1940	661,988	2,208	1,469	3,207	25,269	20,312	146,361	391,812	71,350
1941	661,132	2,295	1,852	3,513	24,212	20,736	138,043	393,615	76,866
1942	619,165	2,278	1,698	3,903	22,903	22,914	123,642	372,664	69,163
1943	604,554	2,030	1,428	4,349	22,636	22,126	127,368	342,337	82,280
1944	621,925	2,141	1,424	4,592	22,301	25,698	132,768	346,060	86,941
1945	702,720	2,361	1,723	5,042	27,671	28,026	156,835	375,488	105,574
1946	745,282	2,629	1,724	5,225	31,028	30,228	171,029	405,829	97,590
1947	708,014	2,535	1,481	5,268	29,395	31,004	164,709	396,798	76,824
1948	704,410	2,533	1,450	4,987	27,850	31,014	163,965	402,543	70,068
1949	734,925	2,332	1,308	5,137	29,693	32,144	173,312	422,583	68,416
1950	736,721	2,370	1,544	4,994	25,909	32,350	170,708	425,325	73,521
1951	779,458	2,302	1,557	5,306	26,086	31,884	169,209	457,977	85,137
1952	809,267	2,471	1,688	5,302	28,644	36,136	181,216	460,921	92,889
1953	845,208	2,439	1,599	5,449	31,813	38,064	191,339	476,771	97,734
1954	876,275	2,352	1,573	5,339	34,139	37,976	206,426	497,201	91,269
1955	884,682	2,410	1,643	5,910	30,675	38,785	202,660	505,011	97,588
1956	1,003,641	2,502	1,766	6,502	31,471	39,439	218,248	586,969	116,744
1957	1,096,337	2,533	1,722	6,752	34,641	39,833	247,845	632,215	130,796

Source

U.S. Federal Bureau of Investigation, Uniform Crime Reports for the United States, *Annual Bulletin* 28 (2) (1957): 85. Reprinted from *Historical Statistics of the United States: From Colonial Times to the Present* (1975), Chapter H, Series 962-970, p. 413.

Documentation

The data reported in this table are gathered via a cooperative arrangement between the Federal Bureau of Investigation (FBI) and local or state law enforcement agencies, begun in the early 1930s. Until a reorganization of data collection that was instituted following a review of practices in 1957, satisfactory national data were not available. Consequently, the present data are from a set of 353 cities with 25,000 or more population with cooperating police departments. The FBI no longer supplies crime data gathered prior to 1960.

See the text for Table Ec1-10 for descriptions of crimes. Exceptions are noted here.

Series Ec21. The estimated number of total crimes is not the total of all crimes, but the total of all index crimes. These include four types of violent crime and three types of property crime. Violent index crimes include criminal homicide, forcible rape, robbery, and aggravated assault. Property index crimes include burglary, larceny-theft, and motor vehicle theft. It is on the basis of these statistics that the FBI tracks trends in criminal behavior in the United States.

Series Ec22. Criminal homicide includes murder and nonnegligent manslaughter: the willful (nonnegligent) killing of one human being by another, excluding deaths by negligence, attempts to kill, assaults to kill, suicides, accidental deaths, and justifiable homicides.

Series Ec23. Homicide by negligence is not included in crime index totals, though it is included in this table.

TABLE Ec30–53 Reported arrests, by race, ethnicity, sex, and age: 1960–1997

Contributed by Douglas Eckberg

											Agencies categorizing arrests by sex and age	
		Agencies categorizing arrests by ethnicity										
			Arrests reported									
	Number of agencies	Population served	Total	Whites	Blacks	American Indians	Chinese ancestry	Japanese ancestry	Asian ancestry	Unstated ancestry	Number of agencies	Population served
	Ec30	Ec31	Ec32	Ec33	Ec34	Ec35	Ec36	Ec37	Ec38	Ec39	Ec40	Ec41
Year	Number	Number	Number	Number	Number	Number	Number	Number	Number	Number	Number	Number
1960	3,576	108,990,288	4,063,138	2,775,469	1,169,176	84,607	1,992	4,362	—	27,532	3,576	108,990,288
1961	3,912	102,432,449	4,088,639	2,815,482	1,145,505	93,890	1,811	3,630	—	28,321	3,942	112,445,711
1962	4,087	121,196,890	4,384,234	2,981,645	1,259,664	100,013	2,076	3,278	—	37,558	4,087	121,196,890
1963	3,954	114,390,526	4,497,282	3,052,835	1,300,668	106,332	2,003	2,723	—	32,721	3,987	123,032,201
1964	3,945	116,994,800	4,714,235	3,230,033	1,335,320	105,316	2,560	3,715	—	37,291	3,983	126,525,053
1965	4,028	117,508,077	4,766,278	3,251,450	1,355,043	113,423	1,295	2,973	—	42,094	4,047	126,564,363
1966	4,026	123,106,594	4,973,968	3,417,603	1,399,118	111,955	1,841	3,675	—	39,776	4,048	132,389,995
1967	4,263	128,695,804	5,361,196	3,700,194	1,486,517	122,783	2,155	3,549	—	45,998	4,302	138,480,685
1968	4,502	127,550,089	5,437,099	3,762,505	1,491,161	124,779	1,677	4,196	—	52,781	4,533	136,646,814
1969	4,486	129,466,100	5,757,101	3,959,175	1,611,672	125,320	1,952	3,687	—	55,295	4,510	138,705,074
1970	4,516	127,205,723	6,007,543	4,217,283	1,601,751	129,534	2,488	4,029	—	52,458	5,073	145,013,723
1971	5,445	140,598,228	6,708,850	4,686,724	1,807,973	140,701	3,285	3,940	—	66,227	5,490	149,491,360
1972	6,174	151,482,551	6,885,475	4,784,397	1,892,929	130,628	4,607	3,449	—	69,465	6,264	160,996,698
1973	5,857	146,246,813	6,706,172	4,695,896	1,816,278	116,336	3,647	4,060	—	69,955	5,946	156,356,205
1974	6,196	135,531,033	6,708,577	4,759,868	1,743,691	105,219	4,111	5,118	—	90,570	6,279	145,584,197
1975	7,481	147,550,663	6,983,990	5,166,616	1,641,203	111,456	4,065	3,867	—	56,783	7,528	156,854,427
1976	7,209	155,273,264	7,362,880	5,234,255	1,929,416	97,042	4,008	4,480	—	93,679	7,253	164,566,449
1977	7,452	162,022,810	7,719,393	5,501,755	2,003,061	97,199	5,572	4,671	—	107,135	7,479	163,288,064
1978	9,200	187,413,578	9,056,583	6,290,190	2,450,930	95,398	7,755	5,431	—	206,879	9,213	187,544,197
1979	9,794	183,894,765	8,916,523	6,407,349	2,235,177	97,138	6,089	7,592	—	163,178	9,833	183,941,066
1980	8,170	169,352,293	8,263,395	6,055,025	2,067,596	91,342	—	—	49,432	—	8,178	169,439,406
1981	10,340	185,626,249	9,343,218	6,789,030	2,407,308	90,881	—	—	55,999	—	10,382	186,013,133
1982	9,789	186,479,714	10,000,078	7,070,374	2,777,145	91,845	—	—	60,714	—	9,832	187,346,458
1983	10,765	200,117,650	10,247,859	7,291,129	2,796,038	93,736	—	—	66,956	—	10,827	200,692,319
1984	10,667	198,971,910	10,028,918	7,145,273	2,722,151	97,685	—	—	63,809	—	10,696	199,475,004
1985	11,245	205,510,618	10,495,781	7,422,263	2,888,209	112,583	—	—	72,726	—	11,263	206,269,125
1986	10,703	201,993,002	10,677,084	7,468,261	3,029,747	107,540	—	—	71,536	—	10,747	202,817,764
1987	10,545	201,675,183	10,750,309	7,386,639	3,168,129	116,916	—	—	78,625	—	10,616	202,336,839
1988	10,040	191,163,901	10,234,507	6,984,022	3,057,417	110,051	—	—	83,017	—	10,077	192,274,780
1989	10,478	198,545,092	11,175,708	7,543,883	3,456,702	113,712	—	—	61,411	—	10,502	199,098,217
1990	10,676	204,563,914	11,773,484	8,123,531	3,427,443	125,416	—	—	97,094	—	10,765	204,543,366
1991	10,120	190,135,349	10,870,100	7,375,143	3,276,433	116,718	—	—	101,806	—	10,192	193,454,113
1992	11,038	217,263,153	12,346,974	8,192,873	3,903,221	131,694	—	—	119,186	—	11,058	217,754,521
1993	10,273	213,651,060	11,899,043	7,836,083	3,821,240	127,122	—	—	114,598	—	10,277	213,705,457
1994	10,694	208,034,970	11,928,600	7,952,469	3,725,103	127,643	—	—	123,385	—	10,699	208,080,875
1995	10,037	206,762,449	12,029,689	7,927,340	3,840,758	131,868	—	—	129,723	—	10,039	206,782,546
1996	10,027	196,000,398	11,392,544	7,636,964	3,479,226	144,199	—	—	132,155	—	10,032	195,852,942
1997	9,721	183,239,000	10,516,707	7,061,803	3,201,014	132,734	—	—	121,156	—	9,271	183,240,000

TABLE Ec30–53   Reported arrests, by race, ethnicity, sex, and age: 1960–1997   *Continued*

Agencies categorizing arrests by sex and age

Arrests reported

	Total	Sex		Age								
		Males	Females	Under 18	18–24	25–29	30–34	35–39	40–44	45–49	50 and older	Unknown age
	Ec42	Ec43	Ec44	Ec45	Ec46	Ec47	Ec48	Ec49	Ec50	Ec51	Ec52	Ec53
Year	Number	Number	Number	Number	Number	Number	Number	Number	Number	Number	Number	Number
1960	4,281,141	3,823,534	457,607	611,323	793,487	449,351	473,803	486,811	425,449	366,247	672,472	2,198
1961	4,359,654	3,883,020	476,634	641,106	835,491	453,346	466,920	484,755	429,630	363,385	682,335	2,686
1962	4,603,509	4,088,763	514,746	730,154	872,320	464,657	474,252	500,941	459,891	376,163	722,626	2,515
1963	4,748,729	4,208,022	540,707	839,520	917,848	463,321	460,425	494,609	467,623	374,424	727,800	3,158
1964	5,020,939	4,436,007	584,932	1,029,699	1,011,452	471,337	453,336	481,416	466,677	369,581	734,738	2,703
1965	5,054,550	4,451,487	603,063	1,080,319	1,053,639	462,894	431,482	464,582	456,566	372,195	724,426	8,447
1966	5,173,827	4,540,904	632,923	1,175,855	1,124,986	472,369	422,132	431,034	432,774	378,246	727,084	9,347
1967	5,615,992	4,912,632	703,360	1,362,743	1,297,864	510,817	433,038	442,479	454,309	384,700	728,297	1,745
1968	5,716,583	4,976,097	740,486	1,492,639	1,389,783	524,879	419,969	414,923	427,377	363,097	682,984	932
1969	6,045,542	5,212,711	832,831	1,538,371	1,563,675	579,333	442,767	420,048	430,565	376,525	693,374	884
1970	6,637,819	5,682,850	954,969	1,675,546	1,804,590	653,618	486,310	447,243	448,344	393,499	728,044	625
1971	7,052,194	5,995,844	1,056,350	1,820,664	1,960,046	702,583	514,917	460,030	450,522	398,554	739,648	5,230
1972	7,200,908	6,111,729	1,089,179	1,837,347	2,014,558	757,144	548,062	463,460	444,934	391,716	730,093	13,594
1973	6,970,012	5,906,077	1,063,935	1,835,168	1,995,709	737,299	524,898	427,952	400,435	360,457	679,408	8,686
1974	7,056,630 [1]	5,928,766	1,127,864	1,912,515	2,136,917	784,731	521,382	404,999	365,417	323,395	597,467	8,617
1975	7,330,207 [1]	6,173,258	1,156,949	1,905,642	2,285,816	857,759	556,116	422,636	364,468	323,735	602,721	9,541
1976	7,905,457 [1]	6,658,011	1,247,446	1,969,316	2,496,556	987,202	617,302	467,814	389,668	336,881	637,549	2,703
1977	7,763,069 [1]	6,507,312	1,255,757	1,865,684	2,506,239	993,734	635,505	461,781	373,140	313,439	609,022	4,281
1978	9,129,391 [1]	7,679,383	1,450,008	2,139,195	3,031,170	1,198,360	774,102	548,730	422,103	343,517	667,197	4,544
1979	8,947,826 [1]	7,539,519	1,408,307	2,001,048	3,078,375	1,210,509	785,095	535,876	396,935	311,805	619,025	8,665
1980	8,270,472	6,964,216	1,306,256	1,739,117	2,899,410	1,185,003	771,716	490,860	356,560	271,040	545,758	—
1981	9,362,363	7,851,704	1,510,659	1,859,849	3,253,143	1,410,884	937,294	585,065	407,990	301,096	607,042	—
1982	10,062,343	8,425,163	1,637,180	1,804,688	3,527,245	1,623,271	1,068,314	667,773	447,450	311,804	611,798	—
1983	10,287,309	8,581,823	1,705,486	1,725,746	3,512,582	1,736,797	1,155,532	730,066	480,983	325,604	619,999	—
1984	10,060,207	8,372,979	1,687,228	1,674,154	3,333,794	1,735,321	1,174,456	750,596	482,999	316,232	592,655	—
1985	10,545,992	8,712,003	1,833,989	1,815,895	3,412,594	1,850,509	1,257,473	812,826	498,261	317,551	580,883	—
1986	10,733,319	8,877,240	1,856,079	1,810,728	3,425,972	1,928,198	1,330,449	865,823	500,588	314,276	557,285	—
1987	10,795,869	8,881,528	1,914,341	1,781,240	3,356,992	1,977,845	1,415,921	904,908	528,330	316,171	514,462	—
1988	10,316,956	8,479,344	1,837,612	1,677,993	3,168,622	1,891,671	1,399,454	893,055	522,264	301,751	462,146	—
1989	11,212,475	9,184,764	2,027,711	1,733,165	3,419,684	2,064,895	1,579,109	1,013,130	588,925	333,403	480,156	—
1990	11,730,700	9,574,467	2,156,233	1,839,942	3,534,527	2,091,569	1,666,106	1,095,067	646,410	356,590	500,489	—
1991	11,097,094	9,027,424	2,069,670	1,824,774	3,263,711	1,894,745	1,589,353	1,068,876	647,272	342,478	465,885	—
1992	12,372,307	10,033,641	2,338,666	2,037,625	3,484,376	2,045,568	1,816,501	1,274,565	769,748	413,096	530,828	—
1993	11,917,326	9,610,549	2,306,777	2,060,643	3,268,696	1,876,315	1,745,846	1,271,552	768,086	416,185	510,003	—
1994	11,960,804	9,574,232	2,386,572	2,220,633	3,188,583	1,774,044	1,725,536	1,308,153	803,192	437,743	502,920	—
1995	12,060,727	9,612,576	2,448,151	2,227,169	3,154,943	1,742,694	1,715,966	1,377,895	857,360	473,515	511,185	—
1996	11,417,547	9,058,818	2,358,729	2,159,321	3,002,033	1,589,978	1,530,126	1,310,839	842,977	480,482	501,791	—
1997	10,544,624	8,261,870	2,282,754	1,969,407	2,811,460	1,444,067	1,360,528	1,224,147	814,282	455,339	465,394	—

[1] The sum of adult arrests by age is fewer than the reported total. See text.

Sources

Crime in the United States (U.S. Department of Justice, Federal Bureau of Investigation Uniform Crime Reports, annual reports), and data provided by the FBI.

Documentation

The table presents all known arrests, by age, sex, and ethnicity, since 1960, as collected by the Uniform Crime Reporting program of the Federal Bureau of Investigation (FBI). Data are of arrests, not individuals, so an individual may be represented in more than one arrest. Not all jurisdictions provide data in any given year, and fewer jurisdictions tabulate data on race or ethnicity than do so for sex and age, so the data are known to be incomplete. Data are updated, and the most recent available data are reported here.

Series Ec42. The sum of adult arrests by age categories, plus adults of unknown ages, is fewer than the reported total of adult arrests by 1,190 in 1974, 1,770 in 1975, 466 in 1976, 244 in 1977, 473 in 1978, and 493 in 1979.

TABLE Ec54–97   Arrests of juveniles, by race, ethnicity, and index offense: 1964–1997

Contributed by Douglas Eckberg

	Agencies categorizing arrests by ethnicity		Arrests of juveniles for												
			Criminal homicide						Forcible rape					
	Number	Population served	Whites	Blacks	American Indians	Japanese or Chinese ancestry	Asian ancestry	Unreported ancestry	Whites	Blacks	American Indians	Japanese or Chinese ancestry	Asian ancestry	Unreported ancestry
	Ec54	Ec55	Ec56	Ec57	Ec58	Ec59	Ec60	Ec61	Ec62	Ec63	Ec64	Ec65	Ec66	Ec67
Year	Number	Number	Number	Number	Number	Number	Number	Number	Number	Number	Number	Number	Number	Number
1964	3,945	116,994,800	209	278	7	1	—	7	719	1,009	11	0	—	12
1965	4,028	117,508,077	192	295	3	1	—	14	666	1,233	14	2	—	37
1966	4,026	123,106,594	253	401	7	0	—	12	756	1,196	8	1	—	30
1967	4,263	128,695,804	259	479	5	2	—	9	913	1,302	11	1	—	26
1968	4,502	127,550,089	314	620	5	0	—	16	987	1,382	7	1	—	34
1969	4,486	129,466,100	245	770	8	3	—	21	1,066	1,682	16	4	—	29
1970	4,516	127,205,723	337	852	2	0	—	26	1,099	1,712	17	2	—	23
1971	5,445	140,598,228	367	880	10	0	—	30	1,218	1,785	28	2	—	37
1972	6,174	151,482,551	651	1,224	8	4	—	62	1,098	1,723	13	1	—	39
1973	5,857	146,246,813	460	922	17	10	—	20	1,470	1,918	35	2	—	59
1974	6,196	135,931,033	508	774	20	8	—	39	1,543	1,740	28	7	—	57
1975	7,481	147,550,663	579	627	11	2	—	5	1,508	1,412	15	2	—	44
1976	7,209	155,273,264	598	727	11	4	—	47	1,512	1,785	36	4	—	48
1977	7,452	162,022,810	707	710	9	2	—	65	1,666	2,009	28	5	—	47
1978	9,200	187,413,578	771	798	7	5	—	65	1,780	2,344	16	2	—	112
1979	9,794	183,894,765	846	721	13	1	—	59	1,868	2,422	33	4	—	66
1980	8,170	169,352,293	810	646	10	—	9	—	1,563	2,040	33	—	28	—
1981	10,340	185,626,249	825	876	5	—	18	—	1,652	2,292	14	—	9	—
1982	9,789	186,479,714	744	796	18	—	19	—	1,730	2,337	34	—	28	—
1983	10,765	200,117,650	667	656	10	—	12	—	1,815	2,509	28	—	21	—
1984	10,667	198,971,910	672	612	7	—	7	—	2,116	2,651	33	—	17	—
1985	11,245	205,510,618	655	706	5	—	12	—	2,342	2,602	32	—	22	—
1986	10,703	201,993,002	713	755	14	—	24	—	2,193	2,748	27	—	27	—
1987	10,545	201,675,183	671	880	16	—	24	—	2,076	2,776	20	—	26	—
1988	10,040	191,163,901	737	1,038	9	—	25	—	1,987	2,132	23	—	28	—
1989	10,478	198,545,092	814	1,348	11	—	25	—	2,314	2,307	33	—	27	—
1990	10,676	204,563,914	1,037	1,599	10	—	28	—	2,558	2,344	34	—	43	—
1991	10,120	190,135,349	1,069	1,590	14	—	33	—	2,638	2,231	22	—	41	—
1992	11,038	217,263,153	1,202	1,780	11	—	31	—	2,816	2,517	53	—	48	—
1993	10,273	213,651,060	1,229	2,183	16	—	41	—	2,941	2,466	38	—	32	—
1994	10,694	208,034,970	1,202	1,848	16	—	48	—	2,693	2,075	60	—	45	—
1995	10,037	206,762,449	1,090	1,650	24	—	48	—	2,388	2,102	28	—	38	—
1996	10,026	195,804,943	858	1,251	14	—	61	—	2,348	1,807	39	—	34	—
1997	9,271	183,239,000	697	997	8	—	29	—	2,129	1,603	30	—	29	—

Arrests of juveniles for

	Robbery						Aggravated assault						Burglary		
	Whites	Blacks	American Indians	Japanese or Chinese ancestry	Asian ancestry	Unreported ancestry	Whites	Blacks	American Indians	Japanese or Chinese ancestry	Asian ancestry	Unreported ancestry	Whites	Blacks	American Indians
	Ec68	Ec69	Ec70	Ec71	Ec72	Ec73	Ec74	Ec75	Ec76	Ec77	Ec78	Ec79	Ec80	Ec81	Ec82
Year	Number	Number	Number	Number	Number	Number	Number	Number	Number	Number	Number	Number	Number	Number	Number
1964	3,540	7,608	52	8	—	96	4,926	5,508	50	14	—	95	61,862	27,856	638
1965	3,288	7,982	25	4	—	153	4,661	5,765	70	5	—	121	62,950	30,058	546
1966	3,602	8,942	64	10	—	134	5,675	6,136	76	22	—	100	69,785	32,818	555
1967	4,148	11,396	45	11	—	173	6,784	7,171	95	19	—	100	82,880	37,865	785
1968	5,237	13,334	69	6	—	184	6,961	7,710	111	8	—	170	89,305	43,874	843
1969	5,259	16,172	98	21	—	274	7,748	8,579	88	20	—	216	86,966	45,695	814
1970	5,804	16,215	113	43	—	315	8,182	8,871	127	32	—	225	87,409	44,598	990
1971	6,437	18,211	163	18	—	359	9,832	10,604	153	18	—	271	96,857	46,217	1,151
1972	7,051	20,720	151	10	—	363	12,025	11,892	149	60	—	270	106,883	48,499	1,044
1973	8,700	20,979	171	39	—	454	12,910	11,871	151	65	—	273	118,303	50,530	1,228
1974	9,915	20,340	149	47	—	601	14,594	10,913	175	41	—	353	135,070	53,409	1,304

TABLE Ec54–97   Arrests of juveniles, by race, ethnicity, and index offense: 1964–1997   *Continued*

Arrests of juveniles for

	Robbery						Aggravated assault						Burglary		
	Whites	Blacks	American Indians	Japanese or Chinese ancestry	Asian ancestry	Unreported ancestry	Whites	Blacks	American Indians	Japanese or Chinese ancestry	Asian ancestry	Unreported ancestry	Whites	Blacks	American Indians
	Ec68	Ec69	Ec70	Ec71	Ec72	Ec73	Ec74	Ec75	Ec76	Ec77	Ec78	Ec79	Ec80	Ec81	Ec82
Year	Number	Number	Number	Number	Number	Number	Number	Number	Number	Number	Number	Number	Number	Number	Number
1975	11,620	18,386	167	52	—	245	16,737	10,465	233	37	—	259	154,214	50,755	1,562
1976	10,355	16,550	116	50	—	482	17,833	11,302	237	37	—	406	140,295	52,048	1,137
1977	12,550	21,607	140	56	—	634	19,904	11,820	240	43	—	264	144,735	53,374	1,189
1978	13,821	30,651	105	66	—	1,664	23,273	14,227	247	65	—	945	165,162	63,318	1,259
1979	14,059	25,150	166	77	—	777	24,109	12,968	293	79	—	366	152,741	55,506	1,318
1980	12,564	25,554	117	—	289	—	21,186	11,899	255	—	176	—	135,225	48,858	1,344
1981	12,355	27,114	114	—	271	—	21,378	12,823	228	—	181	—	136,909	49,864	1,280
1982	11,346	24,522	110	—	331	—	20,423	12,997	267	—	197	—	122,179	46,790	1,203
1983	10,379	24,404	105	—	307	—	19,997	13,266	226	—	202	—	114,492	42,101	1,025
1984	9,326	22,448	79	—	282	—	19,817	14,137	233	—	218	—	104,020	34,898	1,102
1985	9,920	21,439	95	—	257	—	21,029	15,101	303	—	256	—	110,906	35,091	1,146
1986	9,517	20,334	99	—	229	—	21,356	16,548	273	—	285	—	102,611	33,892	1,069
1987	8,503	18,766	103	—	279	—	20,628	17,208	292	—	289	—	97,693	31,597	1,134
1988	8,248	16,587	103	—	328	—	20,575	18,005	331	—	368	—	82,705	26,749	1,075
1989	10,068	20,218	101	—	307	—	24,661	21,399	345	—	414	—	84,165	26,266	1,147
1990	12,222	22,275	110	—	380	—	29,655	23,663	404	—	572	—	88,120	26,573	1,245
1991	13,549	22,469	155	—	508	—	30,166	22,400	360	—	569	—	84,242	24,166	1,275
1992	15,809	25,948	172	—	624	—	36,798	29,148	462	—	668	—	93,898	29,251	1,213
1993	15,960	27,705	173	—	659	—	37,423	29,993	583	—	797	—	86,261	27,919	1,365
1994	17,162	28,937	219	—	728	—	38,666	29,895	643	—	906	—	85,321	27,854	1,362
1995	17,449	28,808	241	—	742	—	37,604	29,348	661	—	910	—	77,758	26,631	1,287
1996	15,684	23,075	193	—	836	—	33,729	23,065	598	—	863	—	74,527	23,303	1,327
1997	11,835	15,529	173	—	514	—	31,185	20,067	506	—	736	—	65,867	21,892	1,095

Arrests of juveniles for

	Burglary			Larceny-theft						Motor vehicle theft					
	Japanese or Chinese ancestry	Asian ancestry	Unreported ancestry	Whites	Blacks	American Indians	Japanese or Chinese ancestry	Asian ancestry	Unreported ancestry	Whites	Blacks	American Indians	Japanese or Chinese ancestry	Asian ancestry	Unreported ancestry
	Ec83	Ec84	Ec85	Ec86	Ec87	Ec88	Ec89	Ec90	Ec91	Ec92	Ec93	Ec94	Ec95	Ec96	Ec97
Year	Number	Number	Number	Number	Number	Number	Number	Number	Number	Number	Number	Number	Number	Number	Number
1964	159	—	1,138	134,784	59,595	1,139	332	—	2,227	44,981	15,879	426	121	—	859
1965	143	—	1,454	138,279	60,414	1,004	316	—	2,347	42,013	15,826	397	108	—	1,128
1966	165	—	1,414	151,761	64,492	1,102	376	—	2,085	45,731	16,784	451	111	—	794
1967	212	—	1,621	163,058	70,890	1,272	454	—	2,417	48,276	20,616	461	131	—	923
1968	190	—	1,847	167,936	75,770	1,410	565	—	2,850	47,626	23,922	433	132	—	1,183
1969	180	—	1,479	172,813	81,857	1,509	591	—	2,852	45,157	24,731	529	185	—	1,286
1970	161	—	1,490	188,454	82,271	1,894	699	—	3,136	42,288	21,845	651	141	—	1,049
1971	189	—	1,741	209,370	85,174	2,174	764	—	3,199	42,328	20,277	592	108	—	902
1972	198	—	1,741	224,603	91,448	1,999	836	—	3,686	42,206	19,384	681	88	—	866
1973	183	—	1,880	222,008	94,059	2,155	770	—	3,530	44,328	18,930	789	111	—	923
1974	247	—	2,425	261,220	103,091	2,262	921	—	4,916	44,171	15,678	533	123	—	1,099
1975	206	—	1,702	276,178	98,336	2,792	658	—	3,081	43,443	11,418	755	80	—	579
1976	231	—	2,692	256,849	109,621	2,434	830	—	6,044	41,686	12,554	509	83	—	1,350
1977	224	—	2,658	255,377	110,990	2,588	865	—	5,695	47,855	13,130	602	109	—	1,318
1978	349	—	5,450	286,602	128,384	2,985	1,050	—	7,761	52,926	15,574	657	142	—	2,245
1979	323	—	2,746	287,029	112,291	3,046	999	—	6,926	49,720	14,577	695	127	—	1,455
1980	—	1,366	—	251,931	101,756	3,525	—	4,329	—	36,606	13,111	502	—	617	—
1981	—	1,436	—	262,764	107,923	3,123	—	4,440	—	32,763	11,045	413	—	469	—
1982	—	1,492	—	248,843	110,767	3,255	—	4,709	—	28,208	9,875	364	—	450	—
1983	—	1,224	—	256,033	112,349	3,295	—	4,475	—	25,824	9,808	306	—	465	—
1984	—	1,072	—	252,614	109,305	3,766	—	4,194	—	26,296	10,544	374	—	389	—
1985	—	1,306	—	275,925	112,653	4,492	—	5,282	—	30,644	13,563	472	—	499	—
1986	—	1,274	—	273,767	108,335	4,295	—	5,353	—	33,145	18,691	549	—	643	—
1987	—	1,398	—	275,340	102,680	3,981	—	6,149	—	34,785	22,175	569	—	927	—
1988	—	1,568	—	252,367	92,205	4,037	—	6,370	—	36,224	25,336	528	—	1,117	—
1989	—	1,165	—	256,602	91,189	4,421	—	4,428	—	41,171	31,165	794	—	1,052	—

(continued)

TABLE Ec54–97   Arrests of juveniles, by race, ethnicity, and index offense: 1964–1997 *Continued*

Arrests of juveniles for

	Burglary			Larceny-theft						Motor vehicle theft					
	Japanese or Chinese ancestry	Asian ancestry	Unreported ancestry	Whites	Blacks	American Indians	Japanese or Chinese ancestry	Asian ancestry	Unreported ancestry	Whites	Blacks	American Indians	Japanese or Chinese ancestry	Asian ancestry	Unreported ancestry
	Ec83	Ec84	Ec85	Ec86	Ec87	Ec88	Ec89	Ec90	Ec91	Ec92	Ec93	Ec94	Ec95	Ec96	Ec97
Year	Number	Number	Number	Number	Number	Number	Number	Number	Number	Number	Number	Number	Number	Number	Number
1990	—	1,599	—	280,408	94,770	4,569	—	6,566	—	45,186	30,494	699	—	1,349	—
1991	—	1,747	—	269,845	91,153	4,212	—	6,731	—	42,126	29,404	695	—	1,292	—
1992	—	2,002	—	295,785	103,213	4,901	—	7,907	—	45,091	33,008	754	—	1,343	—
1993	—	1,763	—	275,766	103,326	5,038	—	8,249	—	42,863	33,362	865	—	1,541	—
1994	—	1,584	—	287,916	111,520	5,170	—	8,775	—	41,171	29,951	880	—	1,342	—
1995	—	1,564	—	280,722	109,269	5,174	—	8,912	—	38,088	27,314	1,017	—	1,424	—
1996	—	1,622	—	269,470	96,379	5,745	—	9,075	—	32,218	21,301	826	—	1,452	—
1997	—	1,492	—	243,734	89,524	4,957	—	7,978	—	27,348	17,281	712	—	882	—

Sources

Crime in the United States (U.S. Department of Justice, Federal Bureau of Investigation Uniform Crime Reports, annual reports), and data provided by the FBI.

Documentation

The data reported in this table are gathered via a cooperative arrangement between the Federal Bureau of Investigation (FBI) and local or state law enforcement agencies, who forward monthly counts of offenses to the FBI. Not all jurisdictions provide data every year, and not all report arrests by the ethnicity of the defendant. This table provides arrests in reporting jurisdictions that do provide ethnic data. Counts are of arrests, not individuals, so an individual may be represented in more than one arrest.

The table does not present arrests for all crimes, but only for index crimes. These include four types of violent crime and three types of property crime. On the basis of these statistics, the FBI tracks trends in criminal behavior in the United States. Because of weaknesses in earlier data-gathering procedures, the FBI no longer supplies crime data gathered prior to 1960.

See the text for Table Ec1–10 for descriptions of crimes.

TABLE Ec98–141   Arrests of adults, by race, ethnicity, and index offense: 1964–1997

Contributed by Douglas Eckberg

	Agencies categorizing arrests by ethnicity		Arrests of adults for												
			Criminal homicide						Forcible rape						
	Number	Population served	Whites	Blacks	American Indians	Japanese or Chinese ancestry	Asian ancestry	Unreported ancestry	Whites	Blacks	American Indians	Japanese or Chinese ancestry	Asian ancestry	Unreported ancestry
	Ec98	Ec99	Ec100	Ec101	Ec102	Ec103	Ec104	Ec105	Ec106	Ec107	Ec108	Ec109	Ec110	Ec111
Year	Number	Number	Number	Number	Number	Number	Number	Number	Number	Number	Number	Number	Number	Number
1964	3,945	116,994,800	2,282	3,152	53	7	—	49	3,995	3,450	64	6	—	85
1965	4,028	117,508,077	2,498	3,424	43	7	—	62	3,851	3,446	71	4	—	50
1966	4,026	123,106,594	2,722	3,880	62	5	—	54	4,572	3,790	61	3	—	80
1967	4,263	128,695,804	2,996	4,439	46	12	—	67	4,889	4,154	74	3	—	111
1968	4,502	127,550,089	3,329	5,154	90	4	—	114	5,137	4,119	80	8	—	107
1969	4,486	129,466,100	3,639	5,910	64	7	—	133	5,528	5,244	66	7	—	150
1970	4,516	127,205,723	4,081	5,860	72	8	—	136	5,755	4,930	85	10	—	97
1971	5,445	140,598,228	4,425	7,443	78	11	—	187	6,300	6,060	118	5	—	121
1972	6,174	151,482,551	4,873	7,501	102	19	—	172	6,675	5,402	97	11	—	181
1973	5,857	146,246,813	5,073	7,385	105	15	—	142	7,698	6,692	161	11	—	166
1974	6,196	135,931,033	5,248	7,206	106	19	—	296	7,237	6,398	149	10	—	249
1975	7,481	147,550,663	5,553	6,287	131	24	—	108	8,249	6,123	164	11	—	159
1976	7,209	155,273,264	5,800	6,894	100	13	—	218	8,643	7,541	137	16	—	249
1977	7,452	162,022,810	6,109	7,026	115	20	—	256	9,600	8,707	181	22	—	264
1978	9,200	187,413,578	7,349	7,960	124	21	—	489	10,832	10,511	197	26	—	546
1979	9,794	183,894,765	7,669	7,328	126	23	—	288	11,762	10,793	185	24	—	287
1980	8,170	169,352,293	7,315	7,009	109	—	112	—	10,925	9,894	174	—	130	—
1981	10,340	185,626,249	8,393	8,088	104	—	119	—	11,788	10,649	173	—	186	—
1982	9,789	186,479,714	8,264	8,378	123	—	133	—	12,000	11,654	210	—	186	—
1983	10,765	200,117,650	8,169	8,279	104	—	130	—	13,183	12,212	190	—	156	—
1984	10,667	198,971,910	8,043	7,508	101	—	120	—	14,023	12,506	196	—	157	—

TABLE Ec98–141   Arrests of adults, by race, ethnicity, and index offense: 1964–1997   *Continued*

	Agencies categorizing arrests by ethnicity		Arrests of adults for												
			Criminal homicide						Forcible rape					
	Number	Population served	Whites	Blacks	American Indians	Japanese or Chinese ancestry	Asian ancestry	Unreported ancestry	Whites	Blacks	American Indians	Japanese or Chinese ancestry	Asian ancestry	Unreported ancestry
	Ec98	Ec99	Ec100	Ec101	Ec102	Ec103	Ec104	Ec105	Ec106	Ec107	Ec108	Ec109	Ec110	Ec111
Year	Number	Number	Number	Number	Number	Number	Number	Number	Number	Number	Number	Number	Number	Number
1985	11,245	205,510,618	7,377	7,457	112	—	113	—	14,358	12,874	210	—	161	—
1986	10,703	201,993,002	7,515	7,742	133	—	104	—	14,046	12,702	214	—	147	—
1987	10,545	201,675,183	6,971	7,866	115	—	135	—	13,576	12,330	251	—	153	—
1988	10,040	191,163,901	6,611	7,907	95	—	122	—	13,043	11,396	213	—	164	—
1989	10,478	198,545,092	6,741	8,767	109	—	74	—	13,414	11,878	220	—	152	—
1990	10,676	204,563,914	7,275	9,046	123	—	138	—	15,475	12,040	215	—	233	—
1991	10,120	190,135,349	7,023	9,214	132	—	139	—	13,969	11,473	242	—	203	—
1992	11,038	217,263,153	7,526	9,938	97	—	137	—	15,778	12,093	245	—	245	—
1993	10,273	213,651,060	7,206	10,134	117	—	179	—	15,640	11,432	285	—	230	—
1994	10,694	208,034,970	6,531	8,598	110	—	176	—	14,080	10,374	271	—	286	—
1995	10,037	206,762,449	6,611	8,335	120	—	187	—	13,030	9,959	239	—	257	—
1996	10,026	195,804,943	5,457	6,746	152	—	158	—	11,649	8,549	232	—	264	—
1997	9,271	183,239,000	4,648	6,197	86	—	97	—	10,738	7,185	207	—	194	—

	Arrests of adults for														
	Robbery						Aggravated assault						Burglary		
	Whites	Blacks	American Indians	Japanese or Chinese ancestry	Asian ancestry	Unreported ancestry	Whites	Blacks	American Indians	Japanese or Chinese ancestry	Asian ancestry	Unreported ancestry	Whites	Blacks	American Indians
	Ec112	Ec113	Ec114	Ec115	Ec116	Ec117	Ec118	Ec119	Ec120	Ec121	Ec122	Ec123	Ec124	Ec125	Ec126
Year	Number	Number	Number	Number	Number	Number	Number	Number	Number	Number	Number	Number	Number	Number	Number
1964	13,499	14,759	265	45	—	222	27,700	31,753	500	34	—	485	56,395	27,268	810
1965	13,366	14,601	263	25	—	252	28,022	30,930	499	32	—	462	55,765	29,890	753
1966	13,359	16,611	283	24	—	222	31,970	33,180	580	40	—	480	57,599	28,986	658
1967	15,658	20,571	321	15	—	270	36,460	35,784	589	58	—	598	66,355	36,327	831
1968	16,622	23,792	416	13	—	326	40,105	39,612	715	39	—	712	69,956	37,919	854
1969	16,677	28,434	389	21	—	441	43,322	42,880	777	64	—	827	70,530	40,162	864
1970	18,035	28,780	425	36	—	497	49,356	41,438	993	82	—	789	78,655	41,896	849
1971	20,431	38,016	468	46	—	637	55,492	49,199	1,241	84	—	1,057	98,898	53,247	1,247
1972	21,924	40,079	549	90	—	654	62,139	51,920	1,249	173	—	1,184	94,270	49,950	1,013
1973	22,625	38,701	472	65	—	655	64,754	51,608	1,197	86	—	1,118	93,827	47,518	1,100
1974	25,324	39,601	558	78	—	880	71,002	51,506	1,505	120	—	1,601	107,080	53,085	1,352
1975	28,283	34,460	577	64	—	356	81,855	50,762	1,852	171	—	1,233	127,333	53,236	1,531
1976	27,357	38,663	450	81	—	993	81,649	55,452	1,712	128	—	1,488	118,150	58,909	1,215
1977	32,017	40,962	480	124	—	967	92,120	61,701	1,767	187	—	1,421	123,663	62,134	1,379
1978	36,316	49,293	576	153	—	2,310	114,015	81,155	1,911	321	—	4,704	141,874	70,905	1,494
1979	37,633	46,062	561	138	—	1,042	123,476	76,998	2,256	318	—	1,990	149,855	69,973	1,631
1980	38,036	47,000	530	—	528	—	117,808	69,439	2,095	—	982	—	152,519	73,504	1,632
1981	40,570	55,707	516	—	570	—	127,876	76,608	1,849	—	1,210	—	166,820	85,160	1,610
1982	41,134	59,000	519	—	600	—	133,612	86,845	1,997	—	1,269	—	168,499	90,704	1,728
1983	38,217	59,290	642	—	524	—	134,139	89,451	2,043	—	1,367	—	164,681	88,221	1,765
1984	36,227	56,546	453	—	469	—	134,953	90,984	1,927	—	1,333	—	153,257	80,332	1,710
1985	35,701	55,921	454	—	415	—	131,545	91,614	2,229	—	1,412	—	156,550	79,758	1,899
1986	37,220	62,200	490	—	434	—	151,860	104,339	2,232	—	1,479	—	158,301	84,646	1,817
1987	35,396	59,191	457	—	457	—	153,689	104,320	2,573	—	1,653	—	153,151	85,956	1,956
1988	32,728	57,081	451	—	429	—	155,900	109,364	2,749	—	1,889	—	140,741	80,416	1,764
1989	35,326	66,598	382	—	432	—	178,711	123,150	2,810	—	1,978	—	150,625	88,592	1,771
1990	41,533	68,889	376	—	659	—	205,471	131,175	3,184	—	2,293	—	154,388	83,608	1,809
1991	38,887	65,576	467	—	728	—	191,820	123,230	2,867	—	2,539	—	142,013	75,648	1,602
1992	43,615	73,449	439	—	800	—	226,986	152,549	3,207	—	3,001	—	154,590	87,549	1,652
1993	40,593	70,167	465	—	941	—	220,806	149,833	3,236	—	3,463	—	141,468	80,244	1,616
1994	37,968	60,457	520	—	1,042	—	226,391	146,523	3,409	—	3,681	—	130,916	70,495	1,513
1995	38,058	58,720	466	—	1,028	—	233,075	150,890	3,536	—	4,205	—	125,889	69,456	1,525
1996	33,669	49,337	468	—	998	—	202,102	127,029	3,446	—	4,135	—	110,688	56,961	1,599
1997	26,844	38,128	378	—	578	—	196,147	116,117	3,303	—	3,407	—	101,233	50,888	1,474

(continued)

TABLE Ec98–141   Arrests of adults, by race, ethnicity, and index offense: 1964–1997   *Continued*

Arrests of adults for

	Burglary			Larceny-theft						Motor vehicle theft					
	Japanese or Chinese ancestry	Asian ancestry	Unreported ancestry	Whites	Blacks	American Indians	Japanese or Chinese ancestry	Asian ancestry	Unreported ancestry	Whites	Blacks	American Indians	Japanese or Chinese ancestry	Asian ancestry	Unreported ancestry
	Ec127	Ec128	Ec129	Ec130	Ec131	Ec132	Ec133	Ec134	Ec135	Ec136	Ec137	Ec138	Ec139	Ec140	Ec141
Year	Number	Number	Number	Number	Number	Number	Number	Number	Number	Number	Number	Number	Number	Number	Number
1964	99	—	523	109,393	52,156	1,603	274	—	1,398	22,680	10,303	598	40	—	290
1965	68	—	627	110,654	49,919	1,581	226	—	1,205	22,410	10,609	531	31	—	342
1966	87	—	637	115,052	54,211	1,465	311	—	1,452	23,887	11,761	511	46	—	406
1967	103	—	760	130,853	61,707	1,580	428	—	1,665	26,270	14,237	537	42	—	387
1968	85	—	946	135,769	66,660	1,681	381	—	1,918	26,748	17,571	531	52	—	609
1969	96	—	1,096	152,939	80,040	2,250	525	—	2,337	28,064	20,319	542	47	—	718
1970	107	—	954	180,505	91,192	2,169	578	—	2,316	28,914	20,014	528	57	—	583
1971	127	—	1,405	229,185	112,158	2,791	739	—	3,404	34,699	22,685	682	158	—	830
1972	174	—	1,376	221,394	110,995	2,556	911	—	3,514	29,267	19,381	643	63	—	697
1973	152	—	1,415	219,939	114,789	2,894	899	—	3,530	28,453	17,956	622	48	—	621
1974	143	—	1,956	254,310	127,069	3,224	1,135	—	5,519	28,636	15,573	577	83	—	762
1975	161	—	1,149	305,220	144,389	4,025	1,119	—	5,454	30,163	13,496	687	32	—	374
1976	155	—	1,932	305,237	175,561	3,615	1,127	—	7,073	31,242	16,044	517	53	—	795
1977	171	—	1,903	313,895	172,095	3,763	1,346	—	6,870	36,620	18,503	602	74	—	635
1978	286	—	4,887	371,058	200,018	4,523	1,613	—	9,960	43,259	24,063	659	92	—	2,278
1979	298	—	2,005	395,522	194,806	5,434	1,531	—	9,055	44,923	22,835	698	92	—	907
1980	—	951	—	389,467	193,644	5,958	—	5,437	—	39,818	21,590	575	—	501	—
1981	—	1,156	—	451,692	237,932	6,078	—	6,420	—	42,588	23,169	522	—	475	—
1982	—	1,179	—	487,180	268,606	6,383	—	7,586	—	44,258	24,114	582	—	428	—
1983	—	1,095	—	499,403	275,570	6,785	—	7,735	—	43,642	24,203	550	—	497	—
1984	—	973	—	478,361	265,435	7,620	—	6,197	—	43,982	24,677	552	—	434	—
1985	—	1,156	—	524,985	275,649	9,513	—	7,335	—	46,090	26,193	673	—	565	—
1986	—	1,180	—	537,901	281,833	8,971	—	6,900	—	49,266	31,368	597	—	482	—
1987	—	1,194	—	550,446	299,012	9,334	—	7,617	—	52,455	34,356	727	—	541	—
1988	—	1,344	—	514,446	291,742	8,715	—	7,358	—	54,552	38,730	638	—	633	—
1989	—	915	—	548,407	326,069	8,470	—	6,577	—	59,934	46,403	662	—	469	—
1990	—	1,362	—	586,018	307,756	8,891	—	8,815	—	59,832	40,535	580	—	972	—
1991	—	1,610	—	537,811	306,966	8,949	—	9,652	—	54,013	40,299	596	—	920	—
1992	—	1,716	—	575,284	338,160	9,368	—	10,107	—	57,024	42,589	603	—	1,104	—
1993	—	1,755	—	529,836	329,356	8,218	—	9,864	—	54,791	40,874	652	—	1,295	—
1994	—	1,813	—	510,572	297,034	7,884	—	10,003	—	54,224	36,723	699	—	1,455	—
1995	—	1,743	—	502,122	301,783	7,854	—	10,512	—	53,716	37,767	774	—	1,601	—
1996	—	1,834	—	463,655	265,007	8,661	—	10,824	—	43,724	33,059	787	—	1,278	—
1997	—	1,623	—	423,794	244,522	7,897	—	10,061	—	39,968	27,922	616	—	1,219	—

Sources

Crime in the United States (U.S. Department of Justice, Federal Bureau of Investigation Uniform Crime Reports, annual reports), and data provided by the FBI.

Documentation

See the text for Table Ec54–97 for a description of the data source. See the text for Table Ec1–10 for definitions of crimes.

TABLE Ec142–159   Estimated number and rate of criminal victimization, by type of offense: 1973–1992
[Original National Crime Victimization Survey]

Contributed by Douglas Eckberg

	Estimated incidents								
	Personal victimization						Property victimization		
	Female rape	All rapes	Robbery	Aggravated assault	Simple assault	Personal larceny	Burglary	Household larceny	Motor vehicle theft
	Ec142	Ec143	Ec144	Ec145	Ec146	Ec147	Ec148	Ec149	Ec150
Year	Number	Number	Number	Number	Number	Number	Number	Number	Number
1973	151,700	155,730	1,107,800	1,654,800	2,432,300	14,907,600	6,458,700	7,537,350	1,343,900
1974	159,400	163,010	1,198,700	1,735,500	2,412,700	15,889,000	6,720,600	8,933,130	1,358,400
1975	146,400	153,740	1,147,100	1,631,300	2,640,600	16,293,600	6,743,700	9,223,020	1,433,000
1976	129,300	145,190	1,110,600	1,695,200	2,648,200	16,519,400	6,663,400	9,300,850	1,234,600
1977	141,900	154,240	1,083,100	1,737,900	2,926,300	16,933,000	6,764,900	9,418,280	1,296,800
1978	153,000	171,050	1,038,500	1,707,800	3,023,700	17,050,300	6,704,000	9,351,940	1,365,100
1979	171,200	191,740	1,115,900	1,768,500	3,082,400	16,382,300	6,685,400	10,630,100	1,392,800

TABLE Ec142–159   Estimated number and rate of criminal victimization, by type of offense: 1973–1992
[Original National Crime Victimization Survey]   Continued

	Estimated incidents								
	Personal victimization						Property victimization		
	Female rape	All rapes	Robbery	Aggravated assault	Simple assault	Personal larceny	Burglary	Household larceny	Motor vehicle theft
	Ec142	Ec143	Ec144	Ec145	Ec146	Ec147	Ec148	Ec149	Ec150
Year	Number	Number	Number	Number	Number	Number	Number	Number	Number
1980	151,400	173,770	1,209,100	1,706,900	3,040,500	15,300,200	6,972,500	10,467,990	1,380,800
1981	169,700	177,540	1,380,800	1,795,800	3,228,200	15,862,800	7,394,000	10,176,500	1,439,000
1982	140,500	152,570	1,333,700	1,754,300	3,218,600	15,553,000	6,662,800	9,704,640	1,376,900
1983	137,900	154,170	1,149,170	1,517,310	3,082,770	14,657,300	6,063,140	9,113,690	1,263,620
1984	164,480	179,890	1,116,680	1,727,300	3,017,180	13,789,000	5,642,860	8,750,200	1,340,310
1985	130,850	138,490	984,810	1,605,170	3,094,170	13,473,810	5,594,420	8,702,910	1,270,170
1986	122,200	129,940	1,009,160	1,542,870	2,833,480	13,235,190	5,556,600	8,455,220	1,355,860
1987	134,300	148,450	1,045,960	1,587,460	3,014,190	13,574,720	5,704,550	8,788,250	1,472,850
1988	119,780	127,370	1,048,000	1,741,380	2,992,800	14,056,390	5,776,780	8,419,020	1,634,070
1989	122,740	135,410	1,091,830	1,664,710	2,969,080	13,829,450	5,352,310	8,955,470	1,820,120
1990	106,660	130,260	1,149,710	1,600,670	3,128,130	12,975,320	5,147,740	8,304,190	1,967,540
1991	153,120	174,010	1,203,020	1,634,390	3,575,420	12,885,380	5,186,570	8,701,790	2,136,350
1992	83,080	140,930	1,225,510	1,848,530	3,406,160	12,210,830	4,757,420	8,101,150	1,958,780

	Estimated rates								
	Personal victimization (per 1,000 persons age 12 and older)						Property victimization (per 1,000 households)		
	Female rape	All rape	Robbery	Aggravated assault	Simple assault	Personal larceny	Burglary	Household larceny	Motor vehicle theft
	Ec151	Ec152	Ec153	Ec154	Ec155	Ec156	Ec157	Ec158	Ec159
Year	Per 1,000	Per 1,000	Per 1,000	Per 1,000	Per 1,000	Per 1,000	Per 1,000	Per 1,000	Per 1,000
1973	1.8	0.9	6.7	10.1	14.8	91.1	91.7	107.0	19.1
1974	1.8	1.0	7.2	10.4	14.4	95.1	93.1	123.8	18.8
1975	1.7	0.9	6.8	9.6	15.6	96.0	91.7	125.4	19.5
1976	1.4	0.8	6.5	9.9	15.4	96.1	88.9	124.1	16.5
1977	1.6	0.9	6.2	10.0	16.8	97.3	88.5	123.3	17.0
1978	1.7	1.0	5.9	9.7	17.2	96.8	86.0	119.9	17.5
1979	1.8	1.1	6.3	9.9	17.3	91.9	84.1	133.7	17.5
1980	1.6	0.9	6.6	9.3	16.5	83.0	84.3	126.5	16.7
1981	1.8	1.0	7.4	9.6	17.3	85.1	87.9	121.0	17.1
1982	1.4	0.8	7.1	9.3	17.1	82.5	78.2	113.9	16.2
1983	1.4	0.8	6.0	8.0	16.2	76.9	70.0	105.2	14.6
1984	1.6	0.9	5.8	9.0	15.7	71.8	64.1	99.4	15.2
1985	1.3	0.7	5.1	8.3	15.9	69.4	62.7	97.5	14.2
1986	1.2	0.7	5.1	7.9	14.4	67.5	61.5	93.5	15.0
1987	1.3	0.8	5.3	8.0	15.2	68.7	62.1	95.7	16.0
1988	1.2	0.6	5.3	8.7	15.0	70.5	61.9	90.2	17.5
1989	1.2	0.7	5.4	8.5	15.1	70.2	56.4	94.4	19.2
1990	1.0	0.6	5.7	8.4	16.5	63.8	53.8	86.7	20.5
1991	1.4	0.9	5.9	8.0	17.5	63.1	53.9	90.4	22.2
1992	0.8	0.7	5.9	9.0	16.5	59.2	48.9	83.2	20.1

Source
Criminal Victimization in the United States: 1973–1992 Trends, A National Crime Victimization Report, NCJ-147006 (U.S. Department of Justice, 1994).

Documentation
See the text for Table Ec160–168 for a description of the source, the National Crime Victimization Survey.

Personal victimization data are for persons age 12 and older.

The methodology of the survey was revised in 1993, producing a substantial increase in rates of victimization in most categories. The data reported in this table were gathered prior to the changed form of the survey. In publications in 1993 and subsequent years, a simple ratio estimator is used to adjust these data to the findings gathered using the newer methodology: each is multiplied by the ratio of the rate determined from the new method to the rate determined by the old method. Because it is possible that this may mislead the reader, it was decided to report the original findings in this table.

See the text for Table Ec160–168 for descriptions of crimes. Exceptions are noted here.

Series Ec142 and Ec151. Female rape is the carnal knowledge of a female through the use of force or the threat of force. Attempted rapes are included. Statutory rape (without force) is excluded.

Series Ec143 and Ec152. Rape is the carnal knowledge of a person through the use of force or the threat of force. Both heterosexual and homosexual rapes are included, though in Uniform Crime Report data only rapes of females are included. Attempted rapes are included. Statutory rape (without force) is excluded.

Series Ec147 and Ec156. Personal larceny is theft or attempted theft of property or cash by stealth, either with contact (but without force or threat of force) or without direct contact between the victim and the offender.

Series Ec149 and Ec158. Household larceny is theft or attempted theft of property or cash from a residence or the immediate vicinity of a residence. For the theft to occur within a house, the thief must have a legal right to be in the house (such as a maid, delivery person, or guest), since unlawful or forcible entry constitutes burglary.

TABLE Ec160–168   Estimated rate of criminal victimization, by type of offense: 1973–1998
[Redesigned National Crime Victimization Survey]
Contributed by Douglas Eckberg

	Violent crime (per 1,000 population age 12 and older)					Property crime (per 1,000 households)			
	Total	Rape	Robbery	Aggravated assault	Simple assault	Total	Burglary	Theft	Motor vehicle theft
	Ec160	Ec161	Ec162	Ec163	Ec164	Ec165	Ec166	Ec167	Ec168
Year	Per 1,000	Per 1,000	Per 1,000	Per 1,000	Per 1,000	Per 1,000	Per 1,000	Per 1,000	Per 1,000
1973	47.7	2.5	6.7	12.5	25.9	519.9	110.0	390.8	19.1
1974	48.0	2.6	7.2	12.9	25.3	551.5	111.8	421.0	18.8
1975	48.4	2.4	6.8	11.9	27.2	553.6	110.0	424.1	19.5
1976	48.0	2.2	6.5	12.2	27.0	544.2	106.7	421.0	16.5
1977	50.4	2.3	6.2	12.4	29.4	544.1	106.2	420.9	17.0
1978	50.6	2.6	5.9	12.0	30.0	532.6	103.1	412.0	17.5
1979	51.7	2.8	6.3	12.3	30.3	531.8	100.9	413.4	17.5
1980	49.4	2.5	6.6	11.4	28.8	496.1	101.4	378.0	16.7
1981	52.3	2.5	7.4	12.0	30.3	497.2	105.9	374.1	17.2
1982	50.7	2.1	7.1	11.5	29.8	468.3	94.1	358.0	16.2
1983	46.5	2.1	6.0	9.9	28.3	428.4	84.0	329.8	14.6
1984	46.4	2.5	5.8	10.8	27.2	399.2	76.9	307.1	15.2
1985	45.2	1.9	5.1	10.3	27.9	385.4	75.2	296.0	14.2
1986	42.0	1.7	5.1	9.8	25.3	372.7	73.8	284.0	15.0
1987	44.0	2.0	5.3	10.0	26.7	379.6	74.6	289.0	16.0
1988	44.1	1.7	5.3	10.8	26.3	378.4	74.3	286.7	17.5
1989	43.3	1.8	5.4	10.3	25.8	373.4	67.7	286.5	19.2
1990	44.1	1.7	5.7	9.8	26.9	348.9	64.5	263.8	20.6
1991	48.8	2.2	5.9	9.9	30.6	353.7	64.6	266.8	22.2
1992	47.9	1.8	6.1	11.1	28.9	325.3	58.6	248.2	18.5
1993	49.1	1.6	6.0	12.0	29.4	318.9	58.2	241.7	19.0
1994	51.2	1.4	6.3	11.9	31.5	310.2	56.3	235.1	18.8
1995	46.1	1.2	5.4	9.5	29.9	290.5	49.3	224.3	16.9
1996	41.6	0.9	5.2	8.8	26.6	266.4	47.2	205.7	13.5
1997	38.8	0.9	4.3	8.6	24.9	248.3	44.6	189.9	13.8
1998	36.0	0.9	4.0	7.5	23.5	217.4	38.5	168.1	10.8

Source
U.S. Bureau of Justice Statistics Web site, "Key Facts at a Glance," October 1999.

Documentation
Violent crime rates are for persons age 12 and older.

The National Crime Victimization Survey annually surveys more than 90,000 individuals, age 12 and over, in 45,000–50,000 households. It includes people living in group quarters such as dormitories, rooming houses, and religious group dwellings but excludes crew members of merchant vessels, armed forces personnel in barracks, and institutionalized persons. U.S. citizens living abroad and foreign nationals living in the United States are excluded. Each housing unit remains in the sample for three years and is subject to seven interviews at six-month intervals.

Following a review of methodology by the National Academy of Sciences, and by the American Statistical Association's Committee on Law and Justice Statistics, a major redesign in methodology was instituted in 1993. Primarily these revisions involved changes to the screening section, designed to better stimulate recall of victimizations and to diminish the effects of subjective interpretations of survey questions. In addition, questions on the nature and consequences of victimization were added. When compared with the old method, there was a substantial increase in rates for most victimization categories. For example, the estimated number of rapes increased by 157 percent; assaults, by 57 percent; burglaries, by 20 percent; and thefts, by 27 percent. The new method has a larger impact on estimates of non-stranger crimes, attempted crimes, and crimes not reported to police, than on estimates of crimes by strangers, completed crimes, and crime reported to police. It increased victim recounting more for whites, for people between the ages of 33 and 44, for persons with household incomes above $15,000, and for suburban residents (see *Effects of the Redesign on Victimization Estimates*, NCJ-164381, U.S. Department of Justice, 1997).

The data reported in this table, from 1992 to 1998, were gathered using the redesigned survey. Pre-1992 rates for each type of victimization were adjusted using a simple ratio estimator: each was multiplied by the ratio of the rate determined from the new method to the rate determined by the old method. Suitable caution should therefore be used in interpreting earlier findings, but the general trends are unchanged. Criminal victimization as determined by the earlier method can be found in Table Ec142–159.

Series Ec160. Total violent criminal victimizations are the sum of criminal homicides, rapes, robberies, simple assaults, and aggravated assaults. Criminal homicides are found in the Federal Bureau of Investigation's Uniform Crime Reports – reported in Tables Ec1–20 – and include murder and non-negligent manslaughter.

Series Ec161. Rape, as used here, is the carnal knowledge of a person forcibly and against his or her will, including attempts or assaults to rape. It includes both heterosexual and homosexual rapes, though in Uniform Crime Report data it includes only rapes of females.

Series Ec162. Robbery is attempted or completed theft, directly from a person, of property or cash, by force or threat of force, with or without a weapon.

Series Ec163. Aggravated assault is an attack or attempted attack with a weapon, whether or not an injury occurred, or an attack without a weapon in which a serious injury results. Serious injury includes broken bones, lost teeth, internal injuries, loss of consciousness, or any injury requiring two or more days of hospitalization.

Series Ec164. Simple assault is attempted attack without a weapon, or an attack without a weapon that results either in minor injury or in undetermined injury requiring less than two days of hospitalization. Minor injury includes bruises, black eyes, cuts, scratches, or swelling.

Series Ec165. Total property crime victimization is the sum of burglaries, thefts, and motor vehicle thefts.

TABLE Ec160–168   Estimated rate of criminal victimization, by type of offense: 1973–1998
   [Redesigned National Crime Victimization Survey]   *Continued*

Series Ec166. Burglary is unlawful or forcible entry or attempted entry of a residence. Burglary usually, but not always, involves theft.

Series Ec167. Theft is completed or attempted theft of property or cash without personal contact.

Series Ec168. Motor vehicle theft is stealing or unauthorized taking of a motor vehicle, including attempted thefts. A motor vehicle is an automobile, truck, motorcycle, or any other motorized vehicle legally allowed on public roads and highways.

TABLE Ec169–177   Rate of violent crime victimization, by sex and age: 1973–1998
   [Redesigned National Crime Victimization Survey]

Contributed by Douglas Eckberg

	Male	Female	Age						
			12–15	16–19	20–24	25–34	35–49	50–64	65 and older
	Ec169	Ec170	Ec171	Ec172	Ec173	Ec174	Ec175	Ec176	Ec177
Year	Per 1,000	Per 1,000	Per 1,000	Per 1,000	Per 1,000	Per 1,000	Per 1,000	Per 1,000	Per 1,000
1973	68.0	31.4	81.8	81.7	87.6	52.4	38.8	17.2	9.1
1974	69.4	31.3	77.5	90.6	83.5	58.6	37.5	15.5	9.5
1975	66.8	33.1	80.3	85.7	80.9	59.5	36.9	17.8	8.3
1976	65.8	33.3	76.4	88.8	79.7	61.5	35.9	16.1	8.1
1977	71.1	32.4	83.0	90.2	86.2	63.5	35.8	16.8	8.0
1978	70.0	32.8	83.7	91.7	91.1	60.5	35.8	15.0	8.4
1979	69.7	35.3	78.5	93.4	98.4	66.3	38.2	13.6	6.2
1980	68.1	33.0	72.5	91.3	94.1	60.0	37.4	15.6	7.2
1981	70.9	36.5	86.0	90.7	93.7	65.8	41.6	17.3	8.3
1982	66.9	36.9	75.6	94.4	93.8	69.6	38.6	13.8	6.1
1983	61.7	32.4	75.4	86.3	82.0	62.2	36.5	11.9	5.9
1984	60.6	33.4	78.2	90.0	87.5	56.6	37.9	13.2	5.2
1985	59.5	31.6	79.6	89.4	82.0	56.5	35.6	13.0	4.8
1986	54.3	30.9	77.1	80.8	80.1	52.0	36.0	10.8	4.8
1987	56.8	32.0	87.2	92.4	85.5	51.9	34.7	11.4	5.2
1988	55.0	34.4	83.7	95.9	80.2	53.2	39.1	13.4	4.4
1989	56.8	31.4	92.5	98.2	78.8	52.8	37.3	10.5	4.2
1990	57.6	32.0	101.1	99.1	86.1	55.2	34.4	9.9	3.7
1991	64.5	33.4	94.5	122.6	103.6	54.3	37.2	12.5	4.0
1992	59.3	37.2	111.0	103.7	95.2	56.8	38.1	13.2	5.2
1993	59.8	40.7	115.5	114.2	91.6	56.9	42.5	15.2	5.9
1994	61.1	43.0	118.6	123.9	100.4	59.1	41.3	17.6	4.6
1995	55.7	38.1	113.1	106.6	85.8	58.5	35.7	12.9	6.4
1996	49.9	34.6	95.0	102.8	74.5	51.2	32.9	15.7	4.9
1997	45.8	33.0	87.9	96.3	68.0	47.0	32.3	14.6	4.4
1998	43.1	30.4	82.4	91.2	67.5	41.6	30.0	15.4	2.8

Source
U.S. Bureau of Justice Statistics Web site, "Key Facts at a Glance," October 1999.

Documentation
Rates are expressed per 1,000 population.

   See the text for Tables Ec160–168 and Ec178–181 for a description of the sources, the National Crime Victimization Survey, and the Uniform Crime Reports (UCR).

   Violent crimes are forcible rape, robbery, simple and aggravated assault, and criminal homicide. See the text for Table Ec1–10 for a discussion of these crimes. The series include the estimated rates of rapes, robberies, and simple and aggravated assaults, derived from data gathered by the victimization survey, plus the rates of homicides reported in the UCR.

TABLE Ec178–181   Measures of serious violent crime – estimated crimes, victimizations reported, crimes recorded, and arrests: 1973–1998

Contributed by Douglas Eckberg

Year	Estimate of total violent crimes	Victimizations reported to the police	Crimes recorded by the police	Arrests for violent crimes	Year	Estimate of total violent crimes	Victimizations reported to the police	Crimes recorded by the police	Arrests for violent crimes
	Ec178	Ec179	Ec180	Ec181		Ec178	Ec179	Ec180	Ec181
	Number	Number	Number	Number		Number	Number	Number	Number
1973	3,590,500	1,861,000	715,900	392,700	1990	3,500,600	1,949,200	1,556,800	722,400
1974	3,800,000	2,030,000	791,000	462,900	1991	3,712,000	2,133,000	1,632,700	738,200
1975	3,594,700	1,976,100	844,100	441,100	1992	3,987,000	2,161,000	1,657,300	722,700
1976	3,613,300	2,039,600	822,800	414,600	1993	4,191,000	2,218,500	1,648,100	716,100
1977	3,662,500	1,966,800	845,700	438,500	1994	4,116,000	2,110,800	1,605,600	778,800
1978	3,626,100	1,879,800	894,100	469,900	1995	3,493,500	1,848,600	1,549,900	796,200
1979	3,834,800	2,020,500	998,700	467,700	1996	3,260,000	1,740,400	1,444,600	729,900
1980	3,794,400	2,037,500	1,108,300	482,900	1997	3,039,000	1,741,800	1,405,200	717,800
1981	4,101,700	2,217,900	1,125,000	496,600	1998	2,776,800	1,587,900	1,319,800	675,900
1982	3,926,200	2,232,700	1,108,300	547,400					
1983	3,455,500	1,877,400	1,064,900	516,600					
1984	3,683,300	2,003,500	1,081,800	501,600					
1985	3,358,400	1,926,500	1,126,700	506,800					
1986	3,284,700	1,900,200	1,268,800	565,000					
1987	3,424,900	1,987,800	1,265,300	568,100					
1988	3,563,000	1,942,000	1,336,700	600,000					
1989	3,533,700	1,847,800	1,405,000	666,100					

Source

U.S. Bureau of Justice Statistics Web site, "Key Facts at a Glance," October 1999.

Documentation

The measures of violent crime come from two data sources: (1) the National Crime Victimization Survey (see the text for Table Ec160–168 for a discussion of this source) and (2) the Uniform Crime Reports (UCR), which collect information on crimes and arrests reported by law enforcement authorities to the Federal Bureau of Investigation (FBI) (see the text for Table Ec1–10 for a discussion of this source).

Serious violent crimes are forcible rape, robbery, aggravated assault, and criminal homicide. See the text for Table Ec160–168 for a discussion of these crimes.

Series Ec178. Total violent crime is the estimated number of rapes, robberies, and aggravated assaults, derived from data gathered by the victimiza-

tion surveys as described in the notes to Table Ec160-168, plus all homicides as reported in the FBI's Uniform Crime Reports (UCR).

Series Ec179. Victimizations reported to the police are the number of rapes, robberies, and aggravated assaults that victims reported to the police, derived from data gathered by the victimization surveys, plus all homicides reported by police to the FBI.

Series Ec180. Crimes recorded by the police are the number of homicides, forcible rapes, robberies, and aggravated assaults reported by law enforcement agencies to the FBI and included in the UCR, but excluding commercial robberies and those involving children younger than age 12.

Series Ec181. Arrests for violent crimes are the number of persons arrested for homicide, forcible rape, robbery, or aggravated assault, as reported by law enforcement agencies to the FBI.

HOMICIDES AND SUICIDES

Douglas Eckberg

TABLE Ec182–189   Reported suicides and suicide rates, by sex and mode of death: 1900–1997[1,2]

Contributed by Douglas Eckberg

		Reported suicides						
						Suicides by		
	Crude suicide rates	Total	Male	Female	Poisoning	Hanging or strangulation	Firearms and explosives	Unstated means
	Ec182	Ec183	Ec184	Ec185	Ec186	Ec187	Ec188	Ec189
Year	Per 100,000	Number	Number	Number	Number	Number	Number	Number
1900	10.2	2,036	1,568	468	619	409	449	559
1901	10.4	2,105	1,567	538	636	411	439	619
1902	10.3	2,124	1,589	535	626	382	449	667
1903	11.3	2,371	1,807	564	791	413	520	647
1904	12.2	2,611	1,976	635	838	518	585	670
1905	13.5	2,940	2,208	732	843	541	741	815
1906	12.8	4,323	3,368	955	1,257	692	1,230	1,144
1907	14.5	5,027	3,861	1,166	1,454	780	1,522	1,271
1908	16.8	6,506	5,045	1,461	1,803	1,016	1,931	1,756
1909	16.0	7,061	5,481	1,580	1,989	1,092	2,017	1,963
1910 [3]	15.3	7,283	5,621	1,662	1,955	1,160	2,173	1,995
1911 [3]	16.0	8,612	6,637	1,975	2,567	1,291	2,559	2,195
1912 [3]	15.6	8,549	6,603	1,946	2,419	1,341	2,462	2,327
1913 [3]	15.4	8,932	6,914	2,018	2,469	1,300	2,609	2,554
1914 [3]	16.1	9,802	7,522	2,280	2,657	1,468	2,950	2,727
1915 [3]	16.2	10,011	7,712	2,299	2,178	1,634	3,266	2,933
1916	13.7	9,181	7,069	2,112	1,814	1,434	3,066	2,867
1917 [4]	13.0	9,157	6,880	2,277	1,645	1,488	3,057	2,967
1918 [4,5]	12.3	9,713	7,247	2,466	1,411	1,624	3,372	3,278
1919	11.5	9,543	6,968	2,575	1,500	1,716	3,204	3,123
1920	10.2	8,790	6,364	2,426	1,368	1,611	3,078	2,733
1921	12.4	10,906	8,430	2,476	3,045	1,934	4,015	1,912
1922	11.7	10,876	8,259	2,617	3,231	1,880	3,831	1,934
1923	11.5	11,096	8,344	2,752	3,229	2,049	3,825	1,993
1924	11.9	11,846	9,100	2,746	3,544	2,102	4,197	2,003
1925	12.0	12,209	9,297	2,912	3,628	2,259	4,209	2,113
1926	12.6	13,082	9,894	3,188	4,046	2,371	4,469	2,196
1927	13.2	14,096	10,831	3,265	4,505	2,516	4,864	2,211
1928	13.5	15,390	11,905	3,485	4,794	2,851	5,366	2,379
1929	13.9	16,045	12,305	3,740	5,074	2,901	5,565	2,505
1930	15.6	18,323	14,319	4,004	5,541	3,268	6,735	2,779
1931	16.8	19,807	15,662	4,145	5,972	3,560	7,409	2,866
1932	17.4	20,646	16,453	4,193	6,225	3,615	7,940	2,866
1933	15.9	19,993	15,785	4,208	5,835	3,543	7,798	2,817
1934	14.9	18,828	14,564	4,264	5,334	3,517	7,296	2,681
1935	14.3	18,214	13,942	4,272	5,247	3,399	6,830	2,738
1936	14.3	18,294	13,971	4,323	5,241	3,528	6,771	2,754
1937	15.0	19,294	14,793	4,501	5,485	3,795	7,073	2,941
1938	15.3	19,802	15,376	4,426	5,756	3,756	7,357	2,933
1939	14.1	18,511	14,259	4,252	5,405	3,504	6,944	2,658
1940	14.4	18,907	14,466	4,441	5,623	3,554	7,073	2,657
1941	12.8	17,102	12,903	4,199	4,892	3,340	6,385	2,485
1942	12.0	16,117	12,189	3,928	4,136	3,433	6,117	2,431
1943	10.2	13,725	10,014	3,711	3,434	3,045	5,076	2,170
1944	10.0	13,231	9,497	3,734	3,205	3,062	4,808	2,156
1945	11.2	14,782	10,754	4,028	3,718	3,301	5,321	2,442
1946	11.5	16,152	12,074	4,078	3,859	3,599	6,276	2,418
1947	11.5	16,538	12,560	3,978	3,690	3,750	6,691	2,407
1948	11.2	16,354	12,505	3,849	3,830	3,577	6,660	2,287
1949	11.4	16,993	13,209	3,784	3,834	3,641	7,215	2,303

Notes appear at end of table

(continued)

TABLE Ec182–189 Reported suicides and suicide rates, by sex and mode of death: 1900–1997 *Continued*

					Reported suicides			
						Suicides by		
	Crude suicide rates	Total	Male	Female	Poisoning	Hanging or strangulation	Firearms and explosives	Unstated means
	Ec182	Ec183	Ec184	Ec185	Ec186	Ec187	Ec188	Ec189
Year	Per 100,000	Number	Number	Number	Number	Number	Number	Number
1950	11.4	17,145	13,297	3,848	3,969	3,592	7,377	2,207
1951	10.4	15,909	12,300	3,609	3,664	3,360	6,873	2,012
1952	10.0	15,567	12,115	3,452	3,187	3,358	7,013	2,009
1953	10.1	15,947	12,534	3,413	3,269	3,397	7,293	1,988
1954	10.1	16,356	12,964	3,392	3,516	3,370	7,539	1,931
1955	10.2	16,760	12,961	3,799	3,429	3,591	7,763	1,977
1956	10.0	16,727	12,968	3,759	3,367	3,638	7,817	1,905
1957	9.8	16,632	12,951	3,681	3,347	3,559	7,841	1,885
1958	10.7	18,519	14,366	4,153	3,958	3,562	8,871	2,128
1959	10.6	18,633	14,441	4,192	4,048	3,525	8,788	2,272
1960	10.6	19,041	14,539	4,502	4,330	3,366	9,017	2,328
1961	10.4	18,999	14,460	4,539	4,501	3,157	9,037	2,304
1962	10.9	20,207	15,062	5,145	5,126	3,154	9,487	2,440
1963	11.0	20,825	15,276	5,549	5,785	3,057	9,595	2,388
1964	10.8	20,588	15,092	5,496	5,541	3,005	9,806	2,236
1965	11.1	21,507	15,490	6,017	5,995	3,197	9,898	2,417
1966	10.9	21,281	15,416	5,865	5,588	2,863	10,407	2,423
1967	10.8	21,325	15,187	6,138	5,695	2,778	10,550	2,302
1968	10.7	21,372	15,379	5,993	5,684	3,099	10,911	1,678
1969	11.1	22,364	15,857	6,507	6,118	3,158	11,304	1,784
1970	11.6	23,480	16,629	6,851	6,584	3,253	11,772	1,871
1971	11.7	24,092	16,860	7,232	6,490	3,461	12,288	1,853
1972	12.0	25,004	17,768	7,236	6,450	3,300	13,348	1,906
1973	11.9	25,118	18,108	7,010	6,256	3,548	13,317	1,997
1974	12.1	25,683	18,595	7,088	5,993	3,477	14,345	1,868
1975	12.6	27,063	19,622	7,441	6,426	3,661	14,873	2,103
1976	12.3	26,832	19,493	7,339	6,144	3,689	14,728	2,271
1977	13.0	28,681	21,109	7,572	6,487	3,830	16,084	2,280
1978	12.3	27,294	20,188	7,106	6,017	3,512	15,387	2,378
1979	12.1	27,206	20,256	6,950	5,728	3,525	15,543	2,410
1980	11.8	26,869	20,505	6,364	5,453	3,691	15,396	2,329
1981	12.0	27,596	20,809	6,787	5,431	3,755	16,139	2,271
1982	12.2	28,242	21,625	6,617	5,359	4,061	16,560	2,262
1983	12.1	28,295	21,786	6,509	5,617	3,931	16,600	2,147
1984	12.4	29,286	22,689	6,597	5,609	4,341	17,113	2,223
1985	12.4	29,453	23,145	6,308	5,704	4,264	17,363	2,122
1986	12.9	30,904	24,226	6,678	6,036	4,606	18,153	2,109
1987	12.7	30,796	24,272	6,524	6,321	4,235	18,136	2,104
1988	12.4	30,407	24,078	6,329	5,825	4,375	18,169	2,038
1989	12.2	30,232	24,102	6,130	5,443	4,484	18,178	2,127
1990	12.4	30,906	24,724	6,182	5,424	4,444	18,885	2,153
1991	12.2	30,810	24,769	6,041	5,544	4,561	18,526	2,179
1992	12.0	30,484	24,457	6,027	5,495	4,678	18,169	2,142
1993	12.1	31,102	25,007	6,095	—	—	—	—
1994	12.0	31,142	25,174	5,968	—	—	—	—
1995	11.9	31,284	25,369	5,915	—	—	—	—
1996	11.6	30,903	24,998	5,905	—	—	—	—
1997	11.4	30,535	24,492	6,043	—	—	—	—

[1] Before 1933, data are from only U.S. death registration states. For 1933–1999, data are from the entire United States.

[2] 1907 is the first year for which the registration states accurately counted deaths by suicide.

[3] North Carolina data are excluded.

[4] Totals include deaths by suicide of military personnel within the registration states that were not published in the original volume. See text.

[5] Includes twenty-eight suicides received late or omitted by oversight. Breakdown of the mode of suicide is not available.

Sources

1900–1936, U.S. Bureau of the Census, *Mortality Statistics* (annual reports); 1937–1992, U.S Bureau of the Census (originally; agency varies), *Vital Statis-tics of the United States* (annual reports); National Center for Health Statistics, "Advance Report of Final Mortality Statistics, 1993," *Monthly Vital Statistics Report* 44, number 7, Supplement (February 29, 1996), Tables 20 and 21; National Center for Health Statistics, "Advance Report of Final Mortality Statistics, 1994," *Monthly Vital Statistics Report* 45, number 3, Supplement (September 30, 1996), Tables 10 and 11; National Center for Health Statistics, "Report of Final Mortality Statistics, 1995," *Monthly Vital Statistics Report*, 45, number 11, Supplement 2 (June 12, 1997), Tables 10 and 11; National Center for Health Statistics, "Deaths: Final Data for 1996," *National Vital Statistics Reports* 47, number 9 (November 10, 1998), Tables 12 and 13; National Center for Health Statistics, "Deaths: Final Data for 1997," *National Vital Statistics Reports* 47, number 19 (June 30, 1999), Tables 12 and 13.

TABLE Ec182–189   Reported suicides and suicide rates, by sex and mode of death: 1900–1997   *Continued*

Documentation

See the text for Table Ec190–198 for a description of the data source and for the composition of the Death Registration States and Death Registration Area.

Totals for 1917 include 104 deaths by suicide of military personnel within the registration states that were not published in the original volume. Totals for 1918 include 287 such deaths.

Series Ec182. Suicide rates for 1949–1992 are calculated using population figures from U.S. decennial censuses. All other rates in the series are provided in death registration (vital statistics) reports.

TABLE Ec190–198   Reported homicides and homicide rates, by sex and mode of death: 1900–1997[1,2,3]

Contributed by Douglas Eckberg

			Reported homicides						
						Homicides by			
Year	Crude homicide rate (Census)	Crude homicide rates (Eckberg)	Total	Males	Females	Guns and explosives	Cutting and piercing instruments	Police	Unstated means
	Ec190	Ec191	Ec192	Ec193	Ec194	Ec195 [4,5]	Ec196	Ec197	Ec198 [5,6]
	Per 100,000	Per 100,000	Number	Number	Number	Number	Number	Number	Number
1900	1.2	6.4	230	167	63	—	—	—	—
1901	1.2	7.7	233	150	83	—	—	—	—
1902	1.2	6.5	255	168	87	—	—	—	—
1903	1.1	7.7	236	175	61	—	—	—	—
1904	1.3	8.3	283	193	90	—	—	—	—
1905	2.1	8.1	463	339	124	—	—	—	—
1906	3.9	8.4	1,310	1,013	297	—	—	—	—
1907	4.9	7.9	1,701	1,334	367	—	—	—	—
1908	4.8	7.9	1,858	1,421	437	—	—	—	—
1909	4.2	7.1	1,857	1,400	457	—	—	—	—
1910 [7]	4.6	7.9	2,161	1,670	491	1,174	289	—	698
1911 [7]	5.5	8.7	2,978	2,385	593	1,743	478	—	757
1912 [7]	5.4	8.4	2,938	2,305	633	1,775	417	—	746
1913 [7]	6.1	9.1	3,521	2,818	703	2,123	492	—	906
1914 [7]	6.2	9.4	3,776	3,000	776	2,366	511	—	899
1915 [7]	5.9	8.9	3,633	2,829	804	2,213	483	—	937
1916	6.3	8.9	4,237	3,419	818	2,708	546	—	983
1917 [8]	6.9	9.1	4,864	3,904	960	3,205	621	—	1,038
1918 [8,9]	6.5	7.9	5,113	4,107	1,006	3,475	603	—	1,035
1919	7.2	8.2	5,973	4,820	1,153	4,247	632	—	1,094
1920	6.8	7.8	5,815	4,661	1,154	4,178	587	—	1,050
1921	8.1	9.3	7,090	5,682	1,408	5,178	687	—	1,225
1922	8.0	8.7	7,381	5,996	1,385	5,430	763	—	1,188
1923	7.8	8.8	7,557	6,096	1,461	5,422	884	—	1,251
1924	8.1	9.1	8,014	6,408	1,606	5,736	920	—	1,358
1925	8.3	9.3	8,440	6,823	1,617	5,908	1,130	—	1,402
1926	8.4	9.4	8,740	7,057	1,683	6,035	1,239	—	1,466
1927	8.4	9.2	8,997	7,168	1,829	6,004	1,376	—	1,617
1928	8.6	9.1	9,780	7,889	1,891	6,668	1,409	—	1,703
1929	8.4	8.8	9,637	7,644	1,993	6,362	1,539	—	1,736
1930	8.8	9.2	10,331	8,233	2,098	6,995	1,553	—	1,783
1931	9.2	9.7	10,862	8,761	2,101	7,335	1,662	—	1,865
1932	9.0	9.5	10,722	8,646	2,076	7,252	1,578	—	1,892
1933	9.7	—	12,124	9,874	2,250	7,863	2,065	—	2,196
1934	9.5	—	12,055	9,850	2,205	7,702	2,122	—	2,231
1935	8.3	—	10,587	8,554	2,033	6,506	2,018	—	2,063
1936	8.0	—	10,232	8,134	2,098	6,016	2,151	—	2,065
1937	7.6	—	9,811	7,731	2,080	5,701	2,192	—	1,918
1938	6.8	—	8,799	6,935	1,864	5,055	2,018	—	1,726
1939	6.4	—	8,394	6,657	1,737	4,799	2,048	—	1,547
1940	6.2	—	8,208	6,526	1,682	4,655	2,064	—	1,489
1941	5.9	—	7,929	6,290	1,639	4,525	2,034	—	1,370
1942	5.7	—	7,743	6,120	1,623	4,204	2,120	—	1,419
1943	4.9	—	6,690	5,233	1,457	3,444	1,849	—	1,397
1944	4.7	—	6,553	5,132	1,421	3,449	1,741	—	1,363

Notes appear at end of table

(continued)

TABLE Ec190–198   Reported homicides and homicide rates, by sex and mode of death: 1900–1997 *Continued*

| | | | | | Reported homicides | | | |
| | | | | | | Homicides by | | |
Year	Crude homicide rate (Census) Ec190 Per 100,000	Crude homicide rates (Eckberg) Ec191 Per 100,000	Total Ec192 Number	Males Ec193 Number	Females Ec194 Number	Guns and explosives Ec195 [4,5] Number	Cutting and piercing instruments Ec196 Number	Police Ec197 Number	Unstated means Ec198 [5,6] Number
1945	5.2	—	7,412	5,835	1,577	4,029	1,837	—	1,546
1946	6.1	—	8,784	6,885	1,899	4,966	2,159	—	1,659
1947	5.9	—	8,555	6,707	1,848	4,922	1,981	—	1,652
1948	5.8	—	8,536	6,651	1,885	4,894	2,074	—	1,568
1949	5.3	—	7,915	6,096	1,819	4,235	1,869	277	1,534
1950	5.2	—	7,861	6,008	1,853	4,179	1,879	282	1,521
1951	4.8	—	7,390	5,565	1,825	3,898	1,787	227	1,478
1952	5.1	—	7,971	6,119	1,852	4,244	1,986	256	1,485
1953	4.7	—	7,578	5,769	1,809	4,013	1,837	255	1,473
1954	4.7	—	7,653	5,806	1,847	4,115	1,793	244	1,501
1955	4.4	—	7,339	5,552	1,787	3,807	1,826	227	1,479
1956	4.5	—	7,565	5,641	1,924	4,039	1,854	226	1,446
1957	4.4	—	7,577	5,676	1,901	4,010	1,867	228	1,472
1958	4.5	—	7,765	5,754	2,011	4,230	1,765	229	1,541
1959	4.6	—	8,110	6,019	2,091	4,457	1,804	227	1,622
1960	4.7	—	8,408	6,213	2,195	4,627	1,836	245	1,700
1961	4.7	—	8,537	6,305	2,232	4,753	1,819	237	1,728
1962	4.9	—	8,966	6,661	2,305	4,954	1,978	187	1,847
1963	4.9	—	9,204	6,900	2,304	5,126	1,990	246	1,842
1964	5.2	—	9,799	7,352	2,447	5,474	2,108	278	1,939
1965	5.6	—	10,705	8,141	2,564	6,158	2,292	271	1,984
1966	6.0	—	11,605	8,728	2,877	6,855	2,330	298	2,122
1967	6.8	—	13,423	10,234	3,189	8,332	2,467	387	2,237
1968	7.4	—	14,686	11,523	3,163	9,425	2,626	350	2,285
1969	7.7	—	15,477	12,166	3,311	10,174	2,726	354	2,223
1970	8.3	—	16,848	13,278	3,570	11,213	2,780	333	2,522
1971	9.1	—	18,787	14,812	3,975	12,423	3,237	412	2,715
1972	9.4	—	19,638	15,642	3,996	13,382	3,196	300	2,760
1973	9.7	—	20,465	15,840	4,625	13,752	3,254	376	3,083
1974	10.1	—	21,465	16,747	4,718	14,737	3,366	375	2,987
1975	9.9	—	21,310	16,553	4,757	14,295	3,362	336	3,317
1976	9.0	—	19,554	15,142	4,412	12,766	3,304	294	3,190
1977	9.1	—	19,967	15,354	4,613	12,874	3,542	268	3,283
1978	9.2	—	20,431	15,837	4,594	13,386	3,512	265	3,268
1979	10.0	—	22,547	17,625	4,992	14,491	4,077	345	3,634
1980	10.7	—	24,278	19,088	5,190	15,500	4,354	311	4,113
1981	10.3	—	23,645	18,571	5,074	15,089	4,312	284	3,960
1982	9.7	—	22,356	17,313	5,043	13,830	4,365	283	3,878
1983	8.6	—	20,187	15,510	4,677	12,040	4,173	265	3,709
1984	8.4	—	19,775	15,018	4,757	11,815	4,015	265	3,680
1985	8.3	—	19,876	15,049	4,827	11,836	3,994	248	3,798
1986	9.0	—	21,714	16,578	5,136	13,029	4,342	252	4,091
1987	8.7	—	21,077	15,829	5,248	12,657	4,099	265	4,056
1988	9.0	—	22,021	16,701	5,320	13,645	3,939	237	4,200
1989	9.3	—	22,893	17,670	5,223	14,464	3,980	315	4,134
1990	10.0	—	24,911	19,583	5,328	16,218	4,101	297	4,295
1991	10.5	—	26,500	20,755	5,745	17,746	4,030	246	4,478
1992	10.0	—	25,458	20,085	5,373	17,488	3,528	314	4,128
1993 [10]	10.1	—	26,009	20,290	5,719	—	—	—	—
1994 [10]	9.6	—	24,926	19,707	5,219	—	—	—	—
1995 [10]	8.7	—	22,895	17,740	5,155	—	—	—	—
1996 [10]	7.9	—	20,971	16,269	4,702	—	—	—	—
1997 [10]	—	—	19,846	15,449	4,397	—	—	—	—

[1] Before 1933, data are from U.S. death registration states only. For 1933–1999, data are from the entire United States.

[2] 1907 is the first year for which registration states accurately reported deaths by homicide.

[3] Starting in 1940, figures vary slightly from the previous edition of *Historical Statistics of the United States*, which included legal executions as homicides by "unstated means." They have been removed here to maintain comparability over time.

[4] In 1949, homicides by explosives were first added to homicides by firearms. They were not separately enumerated previously.

[5] In 1979, homicides by explosives were transferred from "homicides by firearms" to homicides by unstated ("other") means. The small difference can be determined by inspecting vital statistics tables of deaths by "all causes."

TABLE Ec190–198   Reported homicides and homicide rates, by sex and mode of death: 1900–1997   *Continued*

[6] Starting in 1949, legal executions became included in vital statistics publications as homicides by unstated ("other") means. They have been removed here for comparability.

[7] North Carolina data are excluded.

[8] Totals include deaths by homicide of military personnel within the registration states that were not published in the original volume. See text.

[9] Excludes an unknown number of homicides among 3,402 transcripts of death certificates received late or omitted by oversight.

[10] Includes executions.

Sources

All series except series Ec191. 1900–1936, U.S. Bureau of the Census, *Mortality Statistics* (annual reports); 1937–1992, U.S. Bureau of the Census (originally; agency varies), *Vital Statistics of the United States* (annual reports); National Center for Health Statistics, "Advance Report of Final Mortality Statistics, 1993," *Monthly Vital Statistics Report* 44, number 7, Supplement (February 29, 1996), Tables 20 and 21; National Center for Health Statistics, "Advance Report of Final Mortality Statistics, 1994," *Monthly Vital Statistics Report* 45, number 3, Supplement (September 30, 1996), Tables 10 and 11; National Center for Health Statistics, "Report of Final Mortality Statistics, 1995," *Monthly Vital Statistics Report* 45, number 11, Supplement 2 (June 12, 1997), Tables 10 and 11; National Center for Health Statistics, "Deaths: Final Data for 1996," *National Vital Statistics Reports* 47, number 9 (November 10, 1998), Tables 12 and 13; National Center for Health Statistics, "Deaths: Final Data for 1997," *National Vital Statistics Reports* 47, number 19 (June 30, 1999), Tables 12 and 13.

Series Ec191. Douglas Eckberg, "Estimates of Early Twentieth-Century U.S. Homicide Rates: An Econometric Forecasting Approach," *Demography* 32 (February 1995): 1–16.

Documentation

The data reported in this table are gathered from descriptive information on all death certificates filed in all the states in the United States and the District of Columbia. It is believed that more than 99 percent of deaths in the United States are reported. Data for the years before 1933 are known to be incomplete for three reasons. First, they are based on death certificates only from states in the U.S. Death Registration Area. The first six years of published data (1900–1905) represent only ten states and the District of Columbia. Texas was the last state to enter the registration area in 1933. Second, admission to the registration area required initially only that at least 90 percent of deaths be recorded. Third, prior to 1907 deaths by homicide were seriously underreported within the death registration states themselves, often recorded incorrectly as accidental deaths. Series Ec191 provides crude homicide rate estimates for the entire United States through 1932.

Homicide counts included here will vary somewhat from those reported in the Uniform Crime Reports of the Federal Bureau of Investigation (FBI). FBI data are, first, based on police records rather than death certificates. Occasionally a different agency will categorize a death differently. Second, FBI data exclude justifiable homicides by police or others, as well as executions. Justifiable homicides are included in vital statistics totals; executions have been included inconsistently, though they are removed from the totals in this table to maintain comparability of data over time. Third, FBI data are estimates of crime totals based on incomplete data from reporting agencies, whereas vital statistics data are based on 100 percent tabulations from death certificates.

The composition of the death registration states is as follows: 1900–1905, Connecticut, District of Columbia, Indiana, Massachusetts, Maine, Michigan, New Hampshire, New Jersey, New York, Rhode Island, and Vermont; 1906, add California, Colorado, Maryland, Pennsylvania, and South Dakota; 1908, add Washington and Wisconsin; 1909, add Ohio; 1910, remove South Dakota and add Minnesota, Montana, and Utah; 1911, add Kentucky and Missouri; 1913, add Virginia; 1914, add Kansas; 1916, add North Carolina and South Carolina; 1917, add Tennessee; 1918, add Illinois, Louisiana, and Oregon; 1919, add Delaware, Florida, and Mississippi; 1920, add Nebraska; 1922, add Georgia, Idaho, and Wyoming; 1923, add Iowa; 1924, add North Dakota; 1925, remove Georgia and add Alabama and West Virginia; 1926, add Arizona; 1927, add Arkansas; 1928, add Georgia and Oklahoma; 1929, add New Mexico and Nevada; 1930, add South Dakota; 1933, add Texas; 1959, add Alaska; 1960, add Hawai'i.

From 1910 through 1915, North Carolina was included as a registration state although only cities and towns over 1,000 population provided data. For those years, North Carolina data are excluded from Tables Ec182–236.

1900 through 1933 data also are available for the Death Registration Area, which consisted of the registration states plus a shifting group of registration cities that lay in nonregistration states. Since 1910, homicide has been defined according to the *International Classification of Diseases*, presently in its ninth revision, and available online from the Web site of the National Center for Health Statistics. Accessed June 23, 2004.

Totals for 1917 include twenty-two deaths by homicide of military personnel within the registration states that were not published in the original volume. Totals for 1918 include forty-five such deaths.

Series Ec190. Homicide rates for 1940–1992 are calculated using population figures from U.S. decennial censuses. All other rates in the series are provided in death registration (vital statistics) reports.

TABLE Ec199–236 Suicides and homicides, by race and ethnicity: 1910–1997[1]

Contributed by Douglas Eckberg

					Suicides							
	U.S. Death Registration Area			U.S. death registration states								
						All death registration states						
								Nonwhites				
	Total	Whites	Nonwhites	Total	Whites	Total	Blacks	American Indians	Chinese	Japanese	Hawaiians	Filipinos
	Ec199	Ec200	Ec201	Ec202	Ec203	Ec204	Ec205	Ec206	Ec207	Ec208	Ec209	Ec210
Year	Number	Number	Number	Number	Number	Number	Number	Number	Number	Number	Number	Number
1910 [2]	8,590	8,378	212	7,283	7,134	149	—	—	—	—	—	—
1911 [2]	9,622	9,363	259	8,612	8,394	218	—	—	—	—	—	—
1912 [2]	9,656	9,427	229	8,549	8,378	171	—	—	—	—	—	—
1913 [2]	9,988	9,712	276	8,932	8,711	221	—	—	—	—	—	—
1914 [2]	10,933	10,620	313	9,802	9,548	254	—	—	—	—	—	—
1915 [2]	11,216	10,909	307	10,011	9,765	246	—	—	—	—	—	—
1916	10,162	9,905	257	9,181	8,966	215	—	—	—	—	—	—
1917 [3]	10,056	9,656	286	9,157	8,820	233	—	—	—	—	—	—
1918 [3]	9,965	9,321	324	9,685	9,091	307	—	—	—	—	—	—
1919	9,732	9,438	294	9,543	9,262	281	—	—	—	—	—	—
1920	8,959	8,681	278	8,790	8,529	261	—	—	—	—	—	—
1921	11,136	10,786	350	10,906	10,569	337	253	12	34	34	—	—
1922	11,053	10,676	377	10,876	10,509	367	289	12	23	40	—	—
1923	11,287	10,942	345	11,096	10,766	330	257	6	35	31	—	—
1924	12,061	11,660	401	11,846	11,461	385	282	16	46	37	—	—
1925	12,495	12,118	377	12,209	11,846	363	299	7	29	22	—	—
1926	13,410	12,997	413	13,082	12,680	402	328	7	30	36	—	—
1927	14,356	13,880	476	14,096	13,635	461	373	13	44	30	—	—
1928	15,566	15,006	560	15,390	14,844	546	445	21	36	40	—	—
1929	16,260	15,681	579	16,045	15,476	569	447	33	40	37	—	—
1930	18,551	17,936	615	18,323	17,723	600	458	32	47	40	—	—
1931	20,088	19,410	678	19,807	19,156	651	509	17	31	46	—	—
1932	20,927	20,213	714	20,646	19,957	689	523	21	34	59	—	—
1933	—	—	—	19,993	19,306	687	519	21	34	40	—	—
1934	—	—	—	18,828	18,156	672	480	29	45	46	—	—
1935	—	—	—	18,214	17,559	655	549	25	26	39	—	—
1936	—	—	—	18,294	17,686	608	502	25	33	36	—	—
1937	—	—	—	19,294	18,651	643	541	25	29	35	—	—
1938	—	—	—	19,802	19,150	652	549	31	27	38	—	—
1939	—	—	—	18,511	17,949	562	454	24	32	34	—	—
1940	—	—	—	18,907	18,284	623	517	28	35	33	—	—
1941	—	—	—	17,102	16,536	566	461	22	33	38	—	—
1942	—	—	—	16,117	15,572	545	446	32	28	32	—	—
1943	—	—	—	13,725	13,306	419	345	23	33	13	—	—
1944	—	—	—	13,231	12,808	423	345	24	37	13	—	—
1945	—	—	—	14,782	14,294	488	404	18	27	32	—	—
1946	—	—	—	16,152	15,573	579	484	33	33	23	—	—
1947	—	—	—	16,538	15,929	609	507	33	32	28	—	—
1948	—	—	—	16,354	15,720	634	538	25	42	20	—	—
1949	—	—	—	16,993	16,330	663	549	36	35	31	—	—
1950	—	—	—	17,145	16,468	677	577	35	39	16	—	—
1951	—	—	—	15,909	15,252	657	558	35	33	22	—	—
1952	—	—	—	15,567	14,963	604	507	35	33	24	—	—
1953	—	—	—	15,947	15,307	640	515	41	45	26	—	—
1954	—	—	—	16,356	15,652	704	602	39	29	23	—	—
1955	—	—	—	16,760	16,092	668	557	39	32	23	—	—
1956	—	—	—	16,727	16,034	693	568	45	41	25	—	—
1957	—	—	—	16,632	15,878	754	619	58	37	26	—	—
1958	—	—	—	18,519	17,684	835	686	61	47	24	—	—
1959	—	—	—	18,633	17,719	914	779	60	31	32	—	—
1960	—	—	—	19,041	18,121	920	741	59	53	45	—	—
1961	—	—	—	18,999	18,012	987	781	60	49	55	—	—
1962 [4]	—	—	—	20,207	18,677	981	786	59	44	47	—	—
1963 [5]	—	—	—	20,825	19,168	1,073	844	67	51	70	—	—
1964	—	—	—	20,588	19,545	1,043	880	61	36	39	—	—

Notes appear at end of table

TABLE Ec199–236   Suicides and homicides, by race and ethnicity: 1910–1997   *Continued*

	Suicides											
	U.S. Death Registration Area			U.S. death registration states								
						All death registration states						
								Nonwhites				
	Total	Whites	Nonwhites	Total	Whites	Total	Blacks	American Indians	Chinese	Japanese	Hawaiians	Filipinos
	Ec199	Ec200	Ec201	Ec202	Ec203	Ec204	Ec205	Ec206	Ec207	Ec208	Ec209	Ec210
Year	Number	Number	Number	Number	Number	Number	Number	Number	Number	Number	Number	Number
1965	—	—	—	21,507	20,342	1,165	958	72	57	54	—	—
1966	—	—	—	21,281	20,100	1,181	956	70	43	64	—	—
1967	—	—	—	21,325	20,116	1,209	982	97	33	59	—	—
1968	—	—	—	21,372	20,212	1,160	954	101	34	37	—	—
1969	—	—	—	22,364	21,038	1,326	1,090	98	49	51	—	—
1970	—	—	—	23,480	22,059	1,421	1,167	112	45	55	—	—
1971	—	—	—	24,092	22,577	1,515	1,220	140	47	57	—	—
1972	—	—	—	25,004	23,264	1,740	1,412	154	52	62	—	—
1973	—	—	—	25,118	23,412	1,706	1,383	160	53	67	—	—
1974	—	—	—	25,683	23,923	1,760	1,442	163	41	57	—	—
1975	—	—	—	27,063	25,173	1,890	1,512	193	44	63	—	—
1976	—	—	—	26,832	24,854	1,978	1,614	175	55	56	—	—
1977	—	—	—	28,681	26,579	2,102	1,673	202	55	63	—	—
1978	—	—	—	27,294	25,250	2,044	1,677	156	49	66	—	—
1979	—	—	—	27,206	24,945	2,261	1,812	198	67	63	—	32
1980	—	—	—	26,869	24,829	2,040	1,607	181	66	58	—	27
1981	—	—	—	27,596	25,452	2,144	1,658	199	67	70	—	25
1982	—	—	—	28,242	26,141	2,101	1,639	182	63	65	—	26
1983	—	—	—	28,295	26,157	2,138	1,623	202	63	46	—	32
1984	—	—	—	29,286	27,002	2,284	1,760	188	60	51	—	30
1985	—	—	—	29,453	27,087	2,366	1,795	210	66	69	—	42
1986	—	—	—	30,904	28,437	2,467	1,892	218	65	81	—	36
1987	—	—	—	30,796	28,217	2,579	1,963	225	82	66	—	35
1988	—	—	—	30,407	27,790	2,617	2,022	228	90	53	—	40
1989	—	—	—	30,232	27,424	2,808	2,153	232	85	66	16	54
1990	—	—	—	30,906	28,086	2,820	2,111	252	91	70	24	63
1991	—	—	—	30,810	27,996	2,814	2,097	231	98	72	20	63
1992	—	—	—	30,484	27,611	2,873	2,143	228	111	63	31	63
1993 [6]	—	—	—	31,102	28,035	3,067	2,259	—	—	—	—	—
1994 [6]	—	—	—	31,142	27,976	3,166	2,271	—	—	—	—	—
1995 [6]	—	—	—	31,284	28,187	3,097	2,231	—	—	—	—	—
1996 [6]	—	—	—	30,903	27,856	3,047	2,164	—	—	—	—	—
1997 [6]	—	—	—	30,535	27,513	3,022	2,103	—	—	—	—	—

	Suicides							Homicides				
	U.S. death registration states							U.S. Death Registration Area			U.S. death registration states	
	All death registration states		Hispanic, from states reporting such ancestry								All death registration states	
	Nonwhites											
	Unspecified Asian or Pacific island	Unspecified nonwhite	Total	Mexicans	Puerto Ricans	Cubans	Unspecified Hispanic	Total	Whites	Nonwhites	Total	Whites
	Ec211	Ec212	Ec213	Ec214	Ec215	Ec216	Ec217	Ec218	Ec219	Ec220	Ec221	Ec222
Year	Number	Number	Number	Number	Number	Number	Number	Number	Number	Number	Number	Number
1910 [2]	—	—	—	—	—	—	—	3,190	—	—	2,161	—
1911 [2]	—	—	—	—	—	—	—	3,907	—	—	2,978	—
1912 [2]	—	—	—	—	—	—	—	3,954	—	—	2,938	—
1913 [2]	—	—	—	—	—	—	—	4,567	—	—	3,521	—
1914 [2]	—	—	—	—	—	—	—	4,847	3,470	1,377	3,776	—
1915 [2]	—	—	—	—	—	—	—	4,670	3,341	1,329	3,633	—
1916	—	—	—	—	—	—	—	5,050	3,522	1,528	4,237	—
1917 [3]	—	—	—	—	—	—	—	5,781	3,958	1,796	4,864	—
1918 [3]	—	—	—	—	—	—	—	5,508	3,589	1,867	5,113	—
1919	—	—	—	—	—	—	—	6,386	4,114	2,272	5,973	—

Notes appear at end of table

(continued)

TABLE Ec199–236   Suicides and homicides, by race and ethnicity: 1910–1997   *Continued*

	Suicides							Homicides				
	U.S. death registration states							U.S. Death Registration Area			U.S. death registration states	
	All death registration states		Hispanic, from states reporting such ancestry								All death registration states	
	Nonwhites											
	Unspecified Asian or Pacific island	Unspecified nonwhite	Total	Mexicans	Puerto Ricans	Cubans	Unspecified Hispanic	Total	Whites	Nonwhites	Total	Whites
	Ec211	Ec212	Ec213	Ec214	Ec215	Ec216	Ec217	Ec218	Ec219	Ec220	Ec221	Ec222
Year	Number	Number	Number	Number	Number	Number	Number	Number	Number	Number	Number	Number
1920	—	—	—	—	—	—	—	6,205	3,978 [7]	2,227 [7]	5,815	3,844
1921	—	4	—	—	—	—	—	7,545	4,990	2,555	7,090	4,797
1922	—	3	—	—	—	—	—	7,788	4,751	3,037	7,381	4,557
1923	—	1	—	—	—	—	—	7,878	4,481	3,397	7,557	4,348
1924	—	4	—	—	—	—	—	8,420	4,820	3,600	8,014	4,642
1925	—	6	—	—	—	—	—	8,893	5,040	3,853	8,440	4,843
1926	—	1	—	—	—	—	—	9,210	5,028	4,182	8,740	4,845
1927	—	1	—	—	—	—	—	9,470	5,184	4,286	8,997	5,001
1928	—	4	—	—	—	—	—	10,050	5,445	4,605	9,780	5,307
1929	—	12	—	—	—	—	—	9,909	5,463	4,446	9,637	5,308
1930	—	23	—	—	—	—	—	10,617	5,974	4,643	10,331	5,841
1931	—	9	—	39	—	—	—	11,160	6,198	4,962	10,862	6,064
1932	—	12	—	40	—	—	—	11,035	6,202	4,833	10,722	6,060
1933	—	13	—	60	—	—	—	—	—	—	12,124	6,617
1934	—	8	—	64	—	—	—	—	—	—	12,055	6,271
1935	—	16	—	—	—	—	—	—	—	—	10,587	5,434
1936	—	12	—	—	—	—	—	—	—	—	10,232	4,998
1937	—	13	—	—	—	—	—	—	—	—	9,811	4,861
1938	—	7	—	—	—	—	—	—	—	—	8,799	4,321
1939	—	18	—	—	—	—	—	—	—	—	8,394	3,850
1940	—	10	—	—	—	—	—	—	—	—	8,208	3,723
1941	—	12	—	—	—	—	—	—	—	—	7,929	3,417
1942	—	7	—	—	—	—	—	—	—	—	7,743	3,341
1943	—	5	—	—	—	—	—	—	—	—	6,690	3,163
1944	—	4	—	—	—	—	—	—	—	—	6,553	2,973
1945	—	7	—	—	—	—	—	—	—	—	7,412	3,494
1946	—	6	—	—	—	—	—	—	—	—	8,784	3,998
1947	—	9	—	—	—	—	—	—	—	—	8,555	3,953
1948	—	9	—	—	—	—	—	—	—	—	8,536	3,880
1949	—	12	—	—	—	—	—	—	—	—	7,915	3,593
1950	—	10	—	—	—	—	—	—	—	—	7,861	3,499
1951	—	9	—	—	—	—	—	—	—	—	7,390	3,307
1952	—	5	—	—	—	—	—	—	—	—	7,971	3,467
1953	—	13	—	—	—	—	—	—	—	—	7,578	3,395
1954	—	11	—	—	—	—	—	—	—	—	7,653	3,440
1955	—	17	—	—	—	—	—	—	—	—	7,339	3,316
1956	—	14	—	—	—	—	—	—	—	—	7,565	3,362
1957	—	14	—	—	—	—	—	—	—	—	7,577	3,412
1958	—	17	—	—	—	—	—	—	—	—	7,765	3,632
1959	—	12	—	—	—	—	—	—	—	—	8,110	3,840
1960	—	22	—	—	—	—	—	—	—	—	8,408	3,965
1961	—	42	—	—	—	—	—	—	—	—	8,537	4,154
1962 [4]	—	45	—	—	—	—	—	—	—	—	8,966	4,201
1963 [5]	—	41	—	—	—	—	—	—	—	—	9,204	4,287
1964	—	27	—	—	—	—	—	—	—	—	9,799	4,626
1965	—	24	—	—	—	—	—	—	—	—	10,705	5,033
1966	—	48	—	—	—	—	—	—	—	—	11,605	5,381
1967	—	38	—	—	—	—	—	—	—	—	13,423	6,211
1968	—	34	—	—	—	—	—	—	—	—	14,686	6,806
1969	—	38	—	—	—	—	—	—	—	—	15,477	7,016
1970	—	42	—	—	—	—	—	—	—	—	16,848	7,803
1971	—	51	—	—	—	—	—	—	—	—	18,787	8,561
1972	—	60	—	—	—	—	—	—	—	—	19,638	8,976
1973	—	43	—	—	—	—	—	—	—	—	20,465	9,986
1974	—	57	—	—	—	—	—	—	—	—	21,465	10,648

Notes appear at end of table

TABLE Ec199–236   Suicides and homicides, by race and ethnicity: 1910–1997 *Continued*

	Suicides							Homicides				
	U.S. death registration states							U.S. Death Registration Area			U.S. death registration states	
	All death registration states		Hispanic, from states reporting such ancestry								All death registration states	
	Nonwhites											
	Unspecified Asian or Pacific island	Unspecified nonwhite	Total	Mexicans	Puerto Ricans	Cubans	Unspecified Hispanic	Total	Whites	Nonwhites	Total	Whites
	Ec211	Ec212	Ec213	Ec214	Ec215	Ec216	Ec217	Ec218	Ec219	Ec220	Ec221	Ec222
Year	Number	Number	Number	Number	Number	Number	Number	Number	Number	Number	Number	Number
1975	—	78	—	—	—	—	—	—	—	—	21,310	10,973
1976	—	78	—	—	—	—	—	—	—	—	19,554	10,115
1977	—	109	—	—	—	—	—	—	—	—	19,967	10,737
1978	—	96	—	—	—	—	—	—	—	—	20,431	11,199
1979	85	4	—	—	—	—	—	—	—	—	22,547	12,332
1980	98	3	—	—	—	—	—	—	—	—	24,278	13,558
1981	123	2		—	—	—	—	—	—	—	23,645	13,065
1982	124	2	—	—	—	—	—	—	—	—	22,356	12,438
1983	169	3	—	—	—	—	—	—	—	—	20,187	11,232
1984	192	3	471	310	54	14	93	—	—	—	19,775	11,114
1985	176	8	808	554	57	32	165	—	—	—	19,876	11,153
1986	173	2	943	575	93	35	240	—	—	—	21,714	11,680
1987	200	8	947	610	82	27	228	—	—	—	21,077	11,115
1988	181	3	1,029	660	81	29	259	—	—	—	22,021	11,060
1989	192	10	1,550	772	190	151	437	—	—	—	22,893	11,300
1990	201	8	1,403	775	121	123	384	—	—	—	24,911	12,139
1991	226	7	1,518	831	130	161	396	—	—	—	26,500	12,775
1992	234	0	1,632	865	167	134	466	—	—	—	25,458	12,449
1993 [6]	—	—	—	—	—	—	—	—	—	—	26,009	12,286
1994 [6]	—	—	—	—	—	—	—	—	—	—	24,926	11,976
1995 [6]	—	—	—	—	—	—	—	—	—	—	22,895	11,364
1996 [6]	—	—	—	—	—	—	—	—	—	—	20,971	10,317
1997 [6]	—	—	—	—	—	—	—	—	—	—	19,846	9,913

	Homicides													
	U.S. death registration states													
	All death registration states									Hispanic, from states reporting such ancestry				
	Nonwhites													
	Total	Blacks	American Indians	Chinese	Japanese	Hawaiians	Filipinos	Unspecified Asian or Pacific island	Unspecified nonwhite	Total	Mexicans	Puerto Ricans	Cubans	Unspecified Hispanic
	Ec223	Ec224	Ec225	Ec226	Ec227	Ec228	Ec229	Ec230	Ec231	Ec232	Ec233	Ec234	Ec235	Ec236
Year	Number	Number	Number	Number	Number	Number	Number	Number	Number	Number	Number	Number	Number	Number
1910 [2]	—	—	—	—	—	—	—	—	—	—	—	—	—	—
1911 [2]	—	—	—	—	—	—	—	—	—	—	—	—	—	—
1912 [2]	—	—	—	—	—	—	—	—	—	—	—	—	—	—
1913 [2]	—	—	—	—	—	—	—	—	—	—	—	—	—	—
1914 [2]	—	—	—	—	—	—	—	—	—	—	—	—	—	—
1915 [2]	—	—	—	—	—	—	—	—	—	—	—	—	—	—
1916	—	—	—	—	—	—	—	—	—	—	—	—	—	—
1917 [3]	—	—	—	—	—	—	—	—	—	—	—	—	—	—
1918 [3]	—	—	—	—	—	—	—	—	—	—	—	—	—	—
1919	—	—	—	—	—	—	—	—	—	—	—	—	—	—
1920	1,971	—	—	—	—	—	—	—	—	—	—	—	—	—
1921	2,293	2,160	18	86	24	—	—	—	5	—	—	—	—	—
1922	2,824	2,741	16	48	15	—	—	—	4	—	—	—	—	—
1923	3,209	3,163	13	10	22	—	—	—	1	—	—	—	—	—
1924	3,372	3,270	24	47	28	—	—	—	3	—	—	—	—	—

Notes appear at end of table

(continued)

TABLE Ec199–236 Suicides and homicides, by race and ethnicity: 1910–1997 *Continued*

	Homicides													
	U.S. death registration states													
	All death registration states									Hispanic, from states reporting such ancestry				
		Nonwhites												
	Total	Blacks	American Indians	Chinese	Japanese	Hawaiians	Filipinos	Unspecified Asian or Pacific island	Unspecified nonwhite	Total	Mexicans	Puerto Ricans	Cubans	Unspecified Hispanic
	Ec223	Ec224	Ec225	Ec226	Ec227	Ec228	Ec229	Ec230	Ec231	Ec232	Ec233	Ec234	Ec235	Ec236
Year	Number	Number	Number	Number	Number	Number	Number	Number	Number	Number	Number	Number	Number	Number
1925	3,597	3,527	20	39	10	—	—	—	1	—	—	—	—	—
1926	3,895	3,822	22	34	16	—	—	—	1	—	—	—	—	—
1927	3,996	3,917	25	37	14	—	—	—	3	—	—	—	—	—
1928	4,473	4,374	40	34	17	—	—	—	8	—	—	—	—	—
1929	4,329	4,235	45	28	11	—	—	—	10	—	—	—	—	—
1930	4,490	4,306	43	44	17	—	—	—	80	—	—	—	—	—
1931	4,798	4,573	42	27	14	—	—	—	18	—	124	—	—	—
1932	4,662	4,428	63	32	21	—	—	—	25	—	93	—	—	—
1933	5,507	5,218	55	25	10	—	—	—	22	—	177	—	—	—
1934	5,784	5,487	59	21	10	—	—	—	21	—	186	—	—	—
1935	5,153	5,059	52	12	7	—	—	—	23	—	—	—	—	—
1936	5,234	5,130	60	10	9	—	—	—	25	—	—	—	—	—
1937	4,950	4,842	50	19	15	—	—	—	24	—	—	—	—	—
1938	4,478	4,394	51	10	6	—	—	—	17	—	—	—	—	—
1939	4,544	4,482	37	7	6	—	—	—	12	—	—	—	—	—
1940	4,485	4,412	47	10	4	—	—	—	12	—	—	—	—	—
1941	4,512	4,436	37	7	16	—	—	—	16	—	—	—	—	—
1942	4,402	4,317	46	10	13	—	—	—	16	—	—	—	—	—
1943	3,527	3,471	40	2	4	—	—	—	10	—	—	—	—	—
1944	3,580	3,516	40	9	6	—	—	—	9	—	—	—	—	—
1945	3,918	3,842	47	12	4	—	—	—	13	—	—	—	—	—
1946	4,786	4,703	54	14	2	—	—	—	13	—	—	—	—	—
1947	4,602	4,527	55	6	2	—	—	—	12	—	—	—	—	—
1948	4,656	4,584	59	3	3	—	—	—	7	—	—	—	—	—
1949	4,322	4,247	50	7	1	—	—	—	17	—	—	—	—	—
1950	4,362	4,298	46	10	1	—	—	—	7	—	—	—	—	—
1951	4,083	4,015	56	7	1	—	—	—	4	—	—	—	—	—
1952	4,504	4,407	79	8	1	—	—	—	9	—	—	—	—	—
1953	4,183	4,093	74	6	4	—	—	—	6	—	—	—	—	—
1954	4,213	4,140	57	7	6	—	—	—	3	—	—	—	—	—
1955	4,023	3,938	73	4	3	—	—	—	5	—	—	—	—	—
1956	4,203	4,116	73	5	2	—	—	—	7	—	—	—	—	—
1957	4,165	4,074	73	5	3	—	—	—	10	—	—	—	—	—
1958	4,133	4,044	69	8	2	—	—	—	10	—	—	—	—	—
1959	4,270	4,181	67	7	4	—	—	—	11	—	—	—	—	—
1960	4,443	4,323	80	6	9	—	—	—	25	—	—	—	—	—
1961	4,383	4,287	65	8	5	—	—	—	18	—	—	—	—	—
1962 [4]	4,575	4,457	80	9	6	—	—	—	23	—	—	—	—	—
1963 [5]	4,725	4,607	90	2	6	—	—	—	20	—	—	—	—	—
1964	5,173	5,067	85	3	5	—	—	—	13	—	—	—	—	—
1965	5,672	5,522	108	10	9	—	—	—	23	—	—	—	—	—
1966	6,224	6,091	86	6	7	—	—	—	34	—	—	—	—	—
1967	7,212	7,036	119	7	14	—	—	—	36	—	—	—	—	—
1968	7,880	7,701	128	11	9	—	—	—	31	—	—	—	—	—
1969	8,461	8,233	142	17	9	—	—	—	60	—	—	—	—	—
1970	9,045	8,834	131	15	11	—	—	—	54	—	—	—	—	—
1971	10,226	9,964	163	30	11	—	—	—	58	—	—	—	—	—
1972	10,662	10,362	192	28	26	—	—	—	54	—	—	—	—	—
1973	10,479	10,181	208	23	17	—	—	—	50	—	—	—	—	—
1974	10,817	10,458	218	39	18	—	—	—	84	—	—	—	—	—
1975	10,337	10,021	194	27	17	—	—	—	78	—	—	—	—	—
1976	9,439	9,094	207	27	12	—	—	—	99	—	—	—	—	—
1977	9,230	8,869	210	49	15	—	—	—	87	—	—	—	—	—
1978	9,232	8,857	234	28	19	—	—	—	94	—	—	—	—	—
1979	10,215	9,811	219	46	22	—	31	82	4	—	—	—	—	—

Notes appear at end of table

TABLE Ec199–236   Suicides and homicides, by race and ethnicity: 1910–1997   *Continued*

Homicides

U.S. death registration states

	All death registration states									Hispanic, from states reporting such ancestry				
	Nonwhites													
	Total	Blacks	American Indians	Chinese	Japanese	Hawaiians	Filipinos	Unspecified Asian or Pacific island	Unspecified nonwhite	Total	Mexicans	Puerto Ricans	Cubans	Unspecified Hispanic
	Ec223	Ec224	Ec225	Ec226	Ec227	Ec228	Ec229	Ec230	Ec231	Ec232	Ec233	Ec234	Ec235	Ec236
Year	Number	Number	Number	Number	Number	Number	Number	Number	Number	Number	Number	Number	Number	Number
1980	10,720	10,283	219	46	25	—	35	105	7	—	—	—	—	—
1981	10,580	10,137	215	49	14	—	39	122	4	—	—	—	—	—
1982	9,918	9,472	194	55	18	—	30	138	11	—	—	—	—	—
1983	8,955	8,493	226	53	13	—	19	147	4	—	—	—	—	—
1984	8,661	8,232	198	46	10	—	23	147	5	1,519	774	358	84	302
1985	8,723	8,275	200	30	20	—	34	159	5	2,260	1,454	313	76	417
1986	10,034	9,488	249	56	20	—	47	169	5	2,512	1,510	356	89	557
1987	9,962	9,474	209	55	15	—	41	158	10	2,301	1,347	348	67	539
1988	10,961	10,398	228	67	18	—	47	198	5	2,511	1,372	300	49	790
1989	11,593	10,954	249	66	19	14	55	227	9	3,436	1,701	461	158	1,116
1990	12,772	12,137	228	64	22	6	40	264	11	3,259	2,238	222	149	650
1991	13,725	12,952	256	75	22	9	60	332	19	3,602	2,517	250	144	691
1992	13,009	12,307	225	55	20	16	69	317	0	4,338	2,638	420	115	1,165
1993 [6]	13,723	12,937	—	—	—	—	—	—	—	—	—	—	—	—
1994 [6]	12,950	12,207	—	—	—	—	—	—	—	—	—	—	—	—
1995 [6]	11,531	10,783	—	—	—	—	—	—	—	—	—	—	—	—
1996 [6]	10,654	9,983	—	—	—	—	—	—	—	—	—	—	—	—
1997 [6]	9,933	9,253	—	—	—	—	—	—	—	—	—	—	—	—

[1] See text for discussion of the limitations and coverage of the Hispanic data.

[2] North Carolina data are excluded.

[3] Totals include deaths of military personnel within the registration area that were not published in the original volume, as described in the text.

[4] New Jersey did not record racial data on death certificates; consequently, 549 deaths by suicide and 170 deaths by homicide lack racial identification.

[5] New Jersey did not record racial data on death certificates; consequently, 584 deaths by suicide and 192 deaths by homicide lack racial identification.

[6] Includes executions.

[7] Absolute figure is not available; see text.

Sources

1900–1936, U.S. Bureau of the Census, *Mortality Statistics* (annual reports); 1937–1992, U.S. Bureau of the Census (originally; agency varies), *Vital Statistics of the United States* (annual reports); National Center for Health Statistics, "Advance Report of Final Mortality Statistics, 1993," *Monthly Vital Statistics Report* 44, number 7, Supplement (February 29, 1996), Tables 20 and 21; National Center for Health Statistics, "Advance Report of Final Mortality Statistics, 1994," *Monthly Vital Statistics Report* 45, number 3, Supplement (September 30, 1996), Tables 10 and 11; National Center for Health Statistics, "Report of Final Mortality Statistics, 1995," *Monthly Vital Statistics Report* 45, number 11, Supplement 2 (June 12, 1997), Tables 10 and 11; National Center for Health Statistics, "Deaths: Final Data for 1996," *National Vital Statistics Reports* 47, number 9 (November 10, 1998), Tables 12 and 13; National Center for Health Statistics, "Deaths: Final Data for 1997," *National Vital Statistics Reports* 47, number 19 (June 30, 1999), Tables 12 and 13.

Documentation

See the text for Table Ec190–198 for a discussion of the source and the composition of the Death Registration States and the Death Registration Area. The registration states encompass the entire United States beginning in 1933.

Homicide counts included here will vary somewhat from those reported in the Federal Bureau of Investigation's Uniform Crime Reports, as explained in the text for Table Ec190–198. Differences in local counts are further affected by the fact that crime data are tabulated according to jurisdiction of the crime, whereas since the late 1930s vital statistics counts have been tabulated according to the place of residence of the deceased.

Beginning in 1949, legal executions were included among homicides in vital statistics publications. They are removed from this table to maintain continuity but may be found in Table Ec343–357.

Totals for 1917 include 114 suicides and 27 homicides of military personnel within the registration area, of which 104 suicides and 22 homicides were in the registration states, none of which were included in the original volume. The racial breakdown of the decedents is not available. Totals for 1918 include 292 suicides and 52 homicides of military personnel in the registration area, of which 287 suicides and 45 homicides were in the death registration states, none of which were included in the original volume. The suicide total also includes 28 deaths received late or left out of the original volume by oversight. The number of homicides so excluded is not available, and the racial breakdown of the decedents is not available.

Series Ec213–217 and Ec232–236. Both total and subcategorized counts of homicides and suicides of Hispanics suffer three limitations: (1) Hispanics may be of any racial category and so will be found in other columns as well; (2) the counts may include some executions; and (3) states reporting Hispanic ancestry by cause of death do not encompass the entire United States. In 1984, only fifteen states reported cause of death by Hispanic ancestry. By 1992, forty-eight states and the District of Columbia reported those data. An additional qualification deals with persons of Mexican ancestry, series Ec214 and Ec233: for 1931–1932, the data are from the U.S. death registration states; for 1933–1934, the data are from the entire United States.

Series Ec214 and Ec232. Homicide and suicide counts of people of Mexican ancestry, 1931–1934, were known to be incomplete.

Series Ec219–220. Absolute figures were not available for 1920. A rate table shows a white homicide rate of 5.0 per 100,000 and a nonwhite homicide rate of 29.6 per 100,000. Variation caused by rounding error of the rate cannot be more than plus or minus three homicides from the provided figure. The sum of the figures from series Ec219–220 must equal the figure for series Ec218.

TABLE Ec237–241   Homicides in New York City and Philadelphia – number, indictments, and rates: 1797–1999

Contributed by Douglas Eckberg

Year	Homicides, New York City Ec237 [1,2] Number	Philadelphia Homicide indictments, seven-year total Ec238 [3] Number	Philadelphia Arrest rate Murder and manslaughter Ec239 Per 100,000	Philadelphia Arrest rate Murder Ec240 Per 100,000	Philadelphia Murders and nonnegligent manslaughters Ec241 Number
1797	4	—	—	—	—
1798	4	—	—	—	—
1799	4	—	—	—	—
1800	3	—	—	—	—
1801	2	—	—	—	—
1802	5	—	—	—	—
1803	1	—	—	—	—
1804	3	—	—	—	—
1805	6	—	—	—	—
1806	6	—	—	—	—
1807	2	—	—	—	—
1808	4	—	—	—	—
1809	3	—	—	—	—
1810	8	—	—	—	—
1811	11	—	—	—	—
1812	1	—	—	—	—
1813	2	—	—	—	—
1814	7	—	—	—	—
1815	4	—	—	—	—
1816	6	—	—	—	—
1817	2	—	—	—	—
1818	8	—	—	—	—
1819	9	—	—	—	—
1820	4	—	—	—	—
1821	6	—	—	—	—
1822	3	—	—	—	—
1823	4	—	—	—	—
1824	3	—	—	—	—
1825	11	—	—	—	—
1826	6	—	—	—	—
1827	8	—	—	—	—
1828	4	—	—	—	—
1829	3	—	—	—	—
1830	5	—	—	—	—
1831	8	—	—	—	—
1832	6	—	—	—	—
1833	11	—	—	—	—
1834	4	—	—	—	—
1835	12	—	—	—	—
1836	17	—	—	—	—
1837	12	—	—	—	—
1838	18	—	—	—	—
1839	17	73	—	—	—
1840	15	—	—	—	—
1841	11	—	—	—	—
1842	11	—	—	—	—
1843	14	—	—	—	—
1844	26	—	—	—	—
1845	14	—	—	—	—
1846	10	85	—	—	—
1847	16	—	—	—	—
1848	27	—	—	—	—
1849	34	—	—	—	—
1850	28	—	—	—	—
1851	28	—	—	—	—
1852	27	—	—	—	—
1853	57	138	—	—	—
1854	46	—	—	—	—
1855	39	—	—	—	—
1856	41	—	—	—	—
1857	94	—	—	—	—
1858	53	—	—	—	—
1859	71	—	—	—	—
1860	69	100	—	—	—
1861	66	—	—	—	—
1862	52	—	—	—	—
1863	127 [4]	—	—	—	—
1864	114	—	—	—	—
1865	67	—	—	—	—
1866	39	—	—	—	—
1867	59	156	—	—	—
1868	50	—	—	—	—
1869	73	—	—	—	—
1870	38	—	—	—	—
1871	55	—	—	—	—
1872	73	—	—	—	—
1873	65	—	—	—	—
1874	56	205	—	—	—
1875	59	—	—	—	—
1876	53	—	—	—	—
1877	53	—	—	—	—
1878	57	—	—	—	—
1879	46	—	—	—	—
1880	52	—	—	—	—
1881	61	159	—	—	—
1882	70	—	—	—	—
1883	56	—	—	—	—
1884	51	—	—	—	—
1885	54	—	—	—	—
1886	62	—	—	—	—
1887	68	—	—	—	—
1888	54	167	—	—	—
1889	65	—	—	—	—
1890	56	—	—	—	—
1891	49	—	—	—	—
1892	38	—	—	—	—
1893	44	—	—	—	—
1894	57	—	—	—	—
1895	68	231	—	—	—
1896	64	—	—	—	—
1897	61	—	—	—	—
1898	108	—	—	—	—
1899	130	—	5.0	3.2	—
1900	132	—	2.1	1.7	—
1901	101	—	4.1	4.1	—
1902	120	—	4.3	3.2	—
1903	123	—	5.0	4.0	—
1904	166	—	5.3	4.8	—
1905	161	—	4.6	3.3	—
1906	243	—	7.1	5.1	—
1907	273	—	8.3	6.2	—
1908	222	—	8.2	6.0	—
1909	177	—	8.0	4.0	—

Notes appear at end of table

TABLE Ec237–241　Homicides in New York City and Philadelphia – number, indictments, and rates: 1797–1999
Continued

		Philadelphia			
	Homicides, New York City	Homicide indictments, seven-year total	Arrest rate Murder and manslaughter	Murder	Murders and nonnegligent manslaughters
	Ec237 [1,2]	Ec238 [3]	Ec239	Ec240	Ec241
Year	Number	Number	Per 100,000	Per 100,000	Number
1910	259	—	14.6	7.0	—
1911	253	—	7.8	3.8	—
1912	265	—	10.7	3.8	—
1913	280	—	9.6	4.4	—
1914	289	—	10.0	4.1	—
1915	227	—	9.6	6.8	—
1916	230	—	12.5	4.6	—
1917	209	—	14.4	4.7	—
1918	229	—	22.4	6.5	—
1919	270	—	20.4	3.6	—
1920	308	—	19.5	5.0	—
1921	284	—	16.4	4.6	—
1922	319	—	21.8	5.2	—
1923	290	—	25.6	7.3	—
1924	364	—	—	—	—
1925	328	—	—	6.3	—
1926	329	—	—	6.0	—
1927	340	—	—	6.7	—
1928	386	—	—	6.6	—
1929	410	—	—	5.3	—
1930	478	—	—	6.9	—
1931	562	—	—	—	119
1932	557	—	—	5.8	
1933	513	—	—	5.1	—
1934	448	—	—	4.1	—
1935	431	—	—	—	115
1936	362	—	—	—	112
1937	354	—	—	—	112
1938	287	—	—	—	106
1939	295	—	—	—	129
1940	279	—	—	—	110
1941	271	—	—	—	105
1942	249	—	—	—	109
1943	208	—	—	—	90
1944	216	—	—	—	85
1945	302	—	—	—	100
1946	350	—	—	—	152
1947	349	—	—	—	118
1948	323	—	—	—	117
1949	307	—	—	—	122
1950	294	—	—	—	122
1951	284	—	—	—	118
1952	318	—	—	—	—
1953	314	—	—	—	125
1954	342	—	—	—	134
1955	306	—	—	—	126
1956	315	—	—	—	129
1957	304	—	—	—	135
1958	354	—	—	—	117
1959	390	—	—	—	119
1960	390	—	—	—	150
1961	483	—	—	—	144
1962	508	—	—	—	124
1963	549	—	—	—	125
1964	537	—	—	—	188
1965	634	—	—	—	205
1966	654	—	—	—	178
1967	746	—	—	—	234
1968	986	—	—	—	262
1969	1,043	—	—	—	271
1970	1,117	—	—	—	352
1971	1,466	—	—	—	435
1972	1,691	—	—	—	413
1973	1,680	—	—	—	430
1974	1,554	—	—	—	444
1975	1,645	—	—	—	434
1976	1,622	—	—	—	338
1977	1,557	—	—	—	323
1978	1,504	—	—	—	351
1979	1,733	—	—	—	385
1980	1,814	—	—	—	436
1981	1,826	—	—	—	362
1982	1,668	—	—	—	332
1983	1,622	—	—	—	311
1984	1,450	—	—	—	264
1985	1,384	—	—	—	273
1986	1,582	—	—	—	343
1987	1,672	—	—	—	338
1988	1,896	—	—	—	371
1989	1,905	—	—	—	475
1990	2,245	—	—	—	503
1991	2,154	—	—	—	440
1992	1,995	—	—	—	425
1993	1,946	—	—	—	439
1994	1,561	—	—	—	404
1995	1,177	—	—	—	—
1996	984	—	—	—	414
1997	770	—	—	—	—
1998	633	—	—	—	—
1999	671	—	—	—	—

[1]　New York City included only Manhattan prior to 1898.

[2]　Homicides exclude infant deaths, accidental deaths, and deaths caused by abortion.

[3]　Values reported for the first year of each seven-year period.

[4]　Excludes deaths caused directly by the 1863 Draft Riot.

Sources
Series Ec237. Eric Monkkonen, *Murder in New York City* (University of California Press, 2001).

Series Ec238. Roger Lane, *Violent Death in the City: Suicide, Accident and Murder in Nineteenth-Century Philadelphia*, 2nd edition (Ohio State University Press, 1999).

Series Ec239–240. Roger Lane, "On the Social Meaning of Homicide Trends in America," in Ted Robert Gurr, editor, *Violence in America*, volume 1, *The History of Crime* (Sage Publications, 1989).

Series Ec241. Annual editions of Federal Bureau of Investigation, Uniform Crime Reports (title varies).

TABLE Ec242–250   Police officers feloniously killed, by weapon: 1968–1997

Contributed by Douglas Eckberg

Year	Total	Firearms	Handguns	Rifles	Shotguns	Knives	Bombs	Personal weapons	Weapons not elsewhere specified
	Ec242	Ec243	Ec244	Ec245	Ec246	Ec247	Ec248	Ec249	Ec250
	Number	Number	Number	Number	Number	Number	Number	Number	Number
1968	64	61	46	9	6	0	0	1	2
1969	86	83	67	6	10	0	0	0	3
1970	100	93	73	8	12	3	2	1	1
1971	129	124	97	16	11	2	0	2	1
1972	117	112	78	16	18	3	1	0	1
1973	134	127	93	21	13	2	0	0	5
1974	132	128	95	12	21	1	0	0	3
1975	129	127	93	21	13	0	0	0	2
1976	112	95	67	12	16	5	4	0	8
1977	93	83	59	13	11	0	0	1	9
1978	93	91	67	13	11	0	0	1	1
1979	106	100	76	18	6	4	1	0	1
1980	104	95	69	13	13	3	0	0	6
1981	91	86	67	14	5	1	0	0	4
1982	92	82	60	17	5	3	0	2	5
1983	80	74	54	12	8	2	0	0	4
1984	72	66	46	9	11	2	0	2	2
1985	78	70	58	3	9	1	0	0	7
1986	66	62	51	8	3	0	0	0	4
1987	74	67	49	9	9	3	0	0	4
1988	78	76	63	11	2	0	0	0	2
1989	66	57	40	10	7	2	0	1	6
1990	66	57	48	8	1	3	0	2	4
1991	71	68	50	14	4	0	1	0	2
1992	63	54	43	9	2	1	1	1	6
1993	70	67	50	14	3	0	0	0	3
1994	79	78	66	8	4	0	0	0	1
1995	74	62	43	14	5	2	8	0	2
1996	56	52	45	6	1	1	1	0	2
1997	65	62	44	12	6	2	0	1	0

Source

U.S. Federal Bureau of Investigation, *Law Enforcement Officers Killed* (subsequently *Law Enforcement Officers Killed and Assaulted*) (annual reports), and data supplied by the FBI.

Documentation

Felonious killings of sworn federal, state, and local law enforcement officers are tabulated as part of the Uniform Crime Reporting program of the Federal Bureau of Investigation (FBI). In 1970, a new program was developed to tabulate the killings of law enforcement officers. Starting in 1971, deaths of officers in Puerto Rico were included, and, starting in 1975, killings of U.S. law enforcement officers in all U.S. territories and other countries were included.

Some data on killings of law enforcement officers are available from as early as 1945, but data published prior to the start of the new program are not considered reliable and so are not presented here. The FBI "Police employees" data file, which contains information on police killings, begins with 1960 data, but felonious killings are not separately enumerated before 1972. In this table, figures published in annual issues of *Law Enforcement Officers Killed* or its successor are reprinted, including some figures from the late 1960s. Counts have been updated and may differ from those published previously.

Series Ec249. "Personal weapons" refers to the use of parts of one's body, such as hands, fists, or feet, as weapons.

TABLE Ec251–253   Reported victims of lynching, by race: 1882–1964

Contributed by Douglas Eckberg

	Total	Whites	Blacks		Total	Whites	Blacks		Total	Whites	Blacks
	Ec251	Ec252	Ec253		Ec251	Ec252	Ec253		Ec251	Ec252	Ec253
Year	Number	Number	Number	Year	Number	Number	Number	Year	Number	Number	Number
1882	113	64	49	1915	69	13	56	1945	1	0	1
1883	130	77	53	1916	54	4	50	1946	6	0	6
1884	211	160	51	1917	38	2	36	1947	1	0	1
1885	184	110	74	1918	64	4	60	1948	2	1	1
1886	138	64	74	1919	83	7	76	1949	3	0	3
1887	120	50	70	1920	61	8	53	1950	2	1	1
1888	137	68	69	1921	64	5	59	1951	1	0	1
1889	170	76	94	1922	57	6	51	1952	0	0	0
1890	96	11	85	1923	33	4	29	1953	0	0	0
1891	184	71	113	1924	16	0	16	1954	0	0	0
1892	230	69	161	1925	17	0	17	1955	8	0	8
1893	152	34	118	1926	30	7	23	1956	0	0	0
1894	192	58	134	1927	16	0	16	1957	1	1	0
1895	179	66	113	1928	11	1	10	1958	0	0	0
1896	123	45	78	1929	10	3	7	1959	1	0	1
1897	158	35	123	1930	21	1	20	1960	0	0	0
1898	120	19	101	1931	13	1	12	1961	1	0	1
1899	106	21	85	1932	8	2	6	1962	0	0	0
1900	115	9	106	1933	28	4	24	1963	1	0	1
1901	130	25	105	1934	15	0	15	1964	3	2	1
1902	92	7	85	1935	20	2	18				
1903	99	15	84	1936	8	0	8				
1904	83	7	76	1937	8	0	8				
1905	62	5	57	1938	6	0	6				
1906	65	3	62	1939	3	1	2				
1907	60	2	58	1940	5	1	4				
1908	97	8	89	1941	4	0	4				
1909	82	13	69	1942	6	0	6				
1910	76	9	67	1943	3	0	3				
1911	67	7	60	1944	2	0	2				
1912	63	2	61								
1913	52	1	51								
1914	33	4	51								

Sources

1882–1951, *The 1952 Negro Year Book* (William Wise, 1952), p. 278; 1952–1964, unpublished estimates from Tuskegee Institute, Alabama, Department of Records and Research; compiled in U.S. Bureau of the Census, *Historical Statistics of the United States: From Colonial Times to the Present* (1975), series H1168–1170, p. 422.

Documentation

The table follows the definition of the term "lynching" endorsed by anti-lynching activists in 1940, that (1) there is legal evidence that a person was killed, (2) the action was illegal, (3) it was performed by a group of three or more people, and (4) the group acted under the pretense of service to justice, race, or tradition.

The National Association for the Advancement of Colored People, the *Chicago Tribune,* and the Department of Records and Archives at Tuskegee University all collected statistics on lynchings, drawing heavily on newspaper accounts.

The figures in the table are known to be inaccurate. Recent scholarship has shown earlier lists of lynchings to overlook some lynchings, include non-lynchings, and place lynchings in incorrect locations, among other problems. Unfortunately, there has as yet been no comprehensive review of the data. However, Table Ec254–289 presents recent tabulations of lynchings in eleven Southern states. For a discussion, see the text for Table Ec254–289, as well as the essay on crime and victimization in this chapter.

The table presents data on lynchings only for whites and blacks; however, James E. Cutler's *Lynch Law: An Investigation into the History of Lynching in the United States* (Longmans-Green, 1905) presents lynchings of forty-five Native Americans, twelve Chinese persons, one Japanese person, and twenty persons of Mexican ancestry between 1882 and 1903.

TABLE Ec254–289   Known victims of lynching in eleven Southern states, by race: 1882–1930

Contributed by Douglas Eckberg

						All races						
	Total	Alabama	Arkansas	Florida	Georgia	Kentucky	Louisiana	Mississippi	North Carolina	South Carolina	Tennessee	Virginia
	Ec254	Ec255	Ec256	Ec257	Ec258	Ec259	Ec260	Ec261	Ec262	Ec263	Ec264	Ec265
Year	Number	Number	Number	Number	Number	Number	Number	Number	Number	Number	Number	Number
1882	45	6	4	3	3	8	9	3	0	6	2	1
1883	56	5	7	2	6	5	3	16	4	2	5	1
1884	62	3	3	5	6	9	9	16	4	1	3	3
1885	66	4	5	2	7	3	3	18	8	1	11	4
1886	73	6	3	9	9	6	4	23	1	4	6	2
1887	63	4	8	4	4	4	12	13	2	6	5	1
1888	70	9	2	1	12	7	7	12	10	1	6	3
1889	88	5	6	0	11	8	9	20	4	11	7	7
1890	65	8	4	3	12	4	8	13	2	5	5	1
1891	127	18	10	9	12	9	26	24	2	2	9	6
1892	138	18	17	11	12	9	25	12	5	3	17	9
1893	128	23	10	6	13	6	14	14	1	12	17	12
1894	118	11	13	8	17	16	18	13	4	4	13	1
1895	89	9	7	15	10	15	5	13	0	5	10	0
1896	80	12	2	5	7	9	22	9	1	3	10	0
1897	81	13	6	7	9	6	12	19	0	5	2	2
1898	84	10	12	1	10	5	7	13	2	17	4	3
1899	83	7	8	6	25	3	12	15	2	0	4	1
1900	81	13	4	9	10	1	11	18	3	1	6	5
1901	96	13	5	8	11	7	14	17	3	4	12	2
1902	65	4	5	4	7	6	11	11	4	4	6	3
1903	73	2	8	9	11	2	11	18	1	6	5	0
1904	64	6	15	3	12	2	2	13	1	6	1	3
1905	43	2	3	0	10	2	4	14	1	3	3	1
1906	49	4	3	6	7	1	9	9	4	5	1	0
1907	48	10	2	0	8	0	12	12	0	1	3	0
1908	77	3	1	7	14	14	7	20	1	1	9	0
1909	56	6	4	8	10	3	9	11	0	3	1	1
1910	55	9	10	14	10	1	2	5	1	1	2	0
1911	52	4	4	7	22	4	2	5	0	1	3	0
1912	54	9	3	4	15	0	8	6	0	7	2	0
1913	43	3	1	4	10	1	5	14	1	2	2	0
1914	38	2	1	4	2	1	12	10	1	4	1	0
1915	58	9	7	5	16	5	2	8	2	2	2	0
1916	40	1	4	8	14	2	2	2	3	1	3	0
1917	28	5	4	1	7	1	3	1	0	1	3	2
1918	40	3	1	1	12	1	8	7	2	1	3	1
1919	63	8	8	5	21	0	7	9	3	1	1	0
1920	37	7	1	8	8	1	0	7	3	1	0	1
1921	52	3	6	6	9	1	3	13	4	5	1	1
1922	37	1	5	3	11	0	5	8	1	1	2	0
1923	26	1	2	11	2	0	1	8	0	0	0	1
1924	14	0	0	4	4	1	0	3	0	1	1	0
1925	14	0	1	2	2	0	1	6	0	0	1	1
1926	25	0	3	7	3	1	1	3	2	3	1	1
1927	13	0	3	0	0	0	1	5	1	0	2	1
1928	7	0	0	0	0	0	2	5	0	0	0	0
1929	9	0	0	4	0	1	0	1	2	0	1	0
1930	13	1	0	1	5	0	0	3	1	2	0	0

TABLE Ec254–289   Known victims of lynching in eleven Southern states, by race: 1882–1930   *Continued*

									Blacks			
	Total	Alabama	Arkansas	Florida	Georgia	Kentucky	Louisiana	Mississippi	North Carolina	South Carolina	Tennessee	Virginia
	Ec266	Ec267	Ec268	Ec269	Ec270	Ec271	Ec272	Ec273	Ec274	Ec275	Ec276	Ec277
Year	Number	Number	Number	Number	Number	Number	Number	Number	Number	Number	Number	Number
1882	34	5	3	2	3	3	8	3	0	5	2	0
1883	47	5	4	2	5	4	2	15	4	2	4	0
1884	45	3	2	4	4	5	4	14	4	1	2	2
1885	50	4	2	2	6	0	3	15	7	0	8	3
1886	58	5	1	3	8	6	3	20	0	4	6	2
1887	50	4	1	4	4	2	11	11	2	5	5	1
1888	61	7	1	1	12	6	6	11	8	1	5	3
1889	65	4	2	0	11	4	8	17	2	10	0	7
1890	54	7	3	3	11	3	6	11	1	3	5	1
1891	95	11	7	7	11	4	14	23	2	2	8	6
1892	111	15	13	9	12	5	22	11	3	3	13	5
1893	114	19	10	6	13	4	14	13	1	11	12	11
1894	95	11	7	8	16	8	15	12	1	4	12	1
1895	74	8	6	14	7	8	4	13	0	5	9	0
1896	63	11	1	4	7	5	17	9	1	3	5	0
1897	73	13	4	7	7	3	12	19	0	5	2	1
1898	78	10	11	1	9	4	7	12	2	17	4	1
1899	71	7	6	6	24	3	5	14	2	0	3	1
1900	77	13	3	9	10	1	10	18	3	1	6	3
1901	88	13	3	8	11	7	14	14	2	4	10	2
1902	62	4	5	4	7	5	10	11	4	4	5	3
1903	68	2	7	6	11	1	11	18	1	6	5	0
1904	61	6	13	3	12	2	2	13	1	5	1	3
1905	41	2	3	0	9	2	3	14	1	3	3	1
1906	47	4	3	6	7	1	8	9	3	5	1	0
1907	45	10	2	0	7	0	10	12	0	1	3	0
1908	73	3	1	6	14	13	7	20	1	1	7	0
1909	54	6	4	8	10	3	8	11	0	3	1	0
1910	50	9	9	12	10	0	1	5	1	1	2	0
1911	50	4	3	7	21	4	2	5	0	1	3	0
1912	53	9	3	4	14	0	8	6	0	7	2	0
1913	43	3	1	4	10	1	5	14	1	2	2	0
1914	37	2	1	4	2	0	12	10	1	4	1	0
1915	50	9	4	4	15	3	2	7	2	2	2	0
1916	39	1	4	7	14	2	2	2	3	1	3	0
1917	28	5	4	1	7	1	3	1	0	1	3	2
1918	39	3	1	1	11	1	8	7	2	1	3	1
1919	60	7	6	5	21	0	7	9	3	1	1	0
1920	36	6	1	8	8	1	0	7	3	1	0	1
1921	46	1	6	5	9	1	2	12	4	5	0	1
1922	32	1	5	3	11	0	2	8	1	1	0	0
1923	24	0	1	11	2	0	1	8	0	0	0	1
1924	14	0	0	4	4	1	0	3	0	1	1	0
1925	14	0	1	2	2	0	1	6	0	0	1	1
1926	21	0	3	6	1	1	1	2	2	3	1	1
1927	13	0	3	0	0	0	1	5	1	0	2	1
1928	7	0	0	0	0	0	2	5	0	0	0	0
1929	6	0	0	3	0	0	0	1	1	0	1	0
1930	12	1	0	0	5	0	0	3	1	2	0	0

(continued)

TABLE Ec254–289   Known victims of lynching in eleven Southern states, by race: 1882–1930   *Continued*

						Whites						
	Total	Alabama	Arkansas	Florida	Georgia	Kentucky	Louisiana	Mississippi	North Carolina	South Carolina	Tennessee	Virginia
	Ec278	Ec279	Ec280	Ec281	Ec282	Ec283	Ec284	Ec285	Ec286	Ec287	Ec288	Ec289
Year	Number	Number	Number	Number	Number	Number	Number	Number	Number	Number	Number	Number
1882	10	1	1	1	0	5	1	0	0	0	0	1
1883	9	0	3	0	1	1	1	1	0	0	1	1
1884	16	0	1	1	2	4	4	2	0	0	1	1
1885	16	0	3	0	1	3	0	3	1	1	3	1
1886	9	1	1	2	1	0	1	2	1	0	0	0
1887	10	0	6	0	0	1	1	1	0	1	0	0
1888	7	1	1	0	0	1	1	0	2	0	1	0
1889	20	1	4	0	0	4	0	2	2	0	7	0
1890	11	1	1	0	1	1	2	2	1	2	0	0
1891	28	7	3	2	1	3	12	0	0	0	0	0
1892	20	1	4	0	0	1	3	1	2	0	4	4
1893	12	4	0	0	0	1	0	0	0	1	5	1
1894	11	0	4	0	1	1	2	0	3	0	0	0
1895	14	1	1	1	3	6	1	0	0	0	1	0
1896	15	1	1	0	0	3	5	0	0	0	5	0
1897	3	0	0	0	1	1	0	0	0	0	0	1
1898	6	0	1	0	1	1	0	1	0	0	0	2
1899	12	0	2	0	1	0	7	1	0	0	1	0
1900	4	0	1	0	0	0	1	0	0	0	0	2
1901	8	0	2	0	0	0	0	3	1	0	2	0
1902	3	0	0	0	0	1	1	0	0	0	1	0
1903	5	0	1	3	0	1	0	0	0	0	0	0
1904	3	0	2	0	0	0	0	0	0	1	0	0
1905	2	0	0	0	1	0	1	0	0	0	0	0
1906	2	0	0	0	0	0	1	0	1	0	0	0
1907	3	0	0	0	1	0	2	0	0	0	0	0
1908	4	0	0	1	0	1	0	0	0	0	2	0
1909	2	0	0	0	0	0	1	0	0	0	0	1
1910	4	0	1	2	0	0	1	0	0	0	0	0
1911	2	0	1	0	1	0	0	0	0	0	0	0
1912	1	0	0	0	1	0	0	0	0	0	0	0
1913	0	0	0	0	0	0	0	0	0	0	0	0
1914	0	0	0	0	0	0	0	0	0	0	0	0
1915	6	0	1	1	1	2	0	1	0	0	0	0
1916	1	0	0	1	0	0	0	0	0	0	0	0
1917	0	0	0	0	0	0	0	0	0	0	0	0
1918	0	0	0	0	0	0	0	0	0	0	0	0
1919	2	1	1	0	0	0	0	0	0	0	0	0
1920	1	1	0	0	0	0	0	0	0	0	0	0
1921	6	2	0	1	0	0	1	1	0	0	1	0
1922	5	0	0	0	0	0	3	0	0	0	2	0
1923	2	1	1	0	0	0	0	0	0	0	0	0
1924	0	0	0	0	0	0	0	0	0	0	0	0
1925	0	0	0	0	0	0	0	0	0	0	0	0
1926	4	0	0	1	2	0	0	1	0	0	0	0
1927	0	0	0	0	0	0	0	0	0	0	0	0
1928	0	0	0	0	0	0	0	0	0	0	0	0
1929	3	0	0	1	0	1	0	0	1	0	0	0
1930	1	0	0	1	0	0	0	0	0	0	0	0

Source

All data except Virginia: Stewart E. Tolnay and E. M. Beck, *A Festival of Violence: An Analysis of Southern Lynchings, 1882–1930* (University of Illinois Press, 1995), Table C-3, pp. 271–2, and data provided by E. M. Beck; Virginia data: W. Fitzhugh Brundage, *Lynching in the New South: Georgia and Virginia, 1880–1930* (University of Illinois Press, 1993).

Documentation

See the text for Table Ec251–253 for a definition of lynching.

The data reflect the most recent scholarship on lynching. Data originally were collected by the National Association for the Advancement of Colored People, the *Chicago Tribune*, and the Office of Archives and Records of Tuskegee University. They are, however, known to be inaccurate as to both the number and location of incidents. Although there has yet to be a comprehensive reconstruction of lynching figures for the nation, several scholars have approached the topic on a state-by-state basis. Even here there is not unanimity on totals because of problems of categorizing the events reported in some accounts. Lynching was usually a very public event; nevertheless, some incidents undoubtedly have not been identified, and scholars disagree on the likely number of untabulated lynchings.

The major source of data is newspaper accounts, from both major papers and local papers. Even though some accounts can be extracted from coroner's reports, for example, relatively few of these exist from the period in question for several Southern states. Stewart Tolnay and E. M. Beck have undertaken the most geographically comprehensive analysis and provide the

TABLE Ec254–289 Known victims of lynching in eleven Southern states, by race: 1882–1930 *Continued*

figures for ten Southern states. W. Fitzhugh Brundage provides counts for Virginia and has, in addition, constructed a lynching series for Georgia that is very similar to that of Tolnay and Beck. George C. Wright has developed a data series for Kentucky that counts twenty more lynchings than reported by Tolnay and Beck. See *Racial Violence in Kentucky, 1865–1940: Lynchings, Mob Rule, and 'Legal Lynchings'* (Louisiana State University Press, 1990). The state of Texas is conspicuous by its absence.

Detailed figures in the table are provided only for black and white victims of lynching. However, series Ec254–265 include victims of other races as well.

Most analyses of lynching begin with the post-Reconstruction period, specifically the early 1880s. They end, usually with 1930, because of the rapid decrease in the annual number of lynchings at that time. Table Ec251–253, however, shows sporadic lynchings as late as 1964.

TABLE Ec290–297 Bombing incidents known to police, and resulting property damage, injuries, and deaths, by type of device: 1972–1996

Contributed by Douglas Eckberg

		Detonations		Attempted detonations				
	Total incidents	Explosive devices	Incendiary devices	Explosive devices	Incendiary devices	Property damage	Persons injured	Deaths
	Ec290	Ec291	Ec292	Ec293	Ec294	Ec295	Ec296	Ec297
Year	Number	Number	Number	Number	Number	Dollars	Number	Number
1972	1,962	714	793	237	218	7,991,815	176	25
1973	1,955	742	787	253	173	7,261,832	187	22
1974	2,044	893	758	236	157	9,886,563	207	24
1975	2,074	1,088	613	238	135	27,003,981	326	69
1976	1,570	852	405	188	125	11,265,426	212	50
1977	1,318	867	248	118	85	8,943,300	162	22
1978	1,301	768	349	105	79	9,161,485	135	18
1979	1,220	728	305	104	83	9,273,024	173	22
1980	1,249	742	336	99	72	12,562,257	160	34
1981	1,142	637	315	92	98	67,082,456	133	30
1982	795	485	194	77	39	7,202,848	99	16
1983	687	442	127	77	41	6,342,652	100	12
1984	803	518	127	118	40	5,618,581	112	6
1985	847	575	102	113	57	6,352,000	144	28
1986	858	580	129	101	48	3,405,000	185	14
1987	848	600	104	102	42	4,201,000	107	21
1988	977 [1]	593	156	161	40	2,257,000	145	20
1989	1,208 [2]	641	203	243	91	5,000,000	202	11
1990	1,582	931	267	254	130	9,600,000	222	27
1991	2,499	1,551	423	395	130	6,440,000	230	29
1992	2,989	1,911	582	384	112	12,500,000	349	26
1993	2,980	1,880	538	375	187	518,000,000	1,323	49
1994	3,163	1,916	545	522	180	7,500,000	308	31
1995	2,577	1,562	406	417	192	105,100,000	744	193
1996	2,573	1,457	427	504	185	5,000,000	336	23

[1] Totals include twenty-seven incidents involving combination devices.

[2] Totals include thirty incidents involving combination devices.

Source

Compiled in U.S. Bureau of Justice Statistics, *Sourcebook of Criminal Justice Statistics 1998* (1999), Table 3.179; from U.S. Federal Bureau of Investigation (FBI), *Bomb Summary 1980* (1981), Table 1; FBI, *Bomb Summary 1982* (1983), Table 1; FBI, *Bomb Summary 1993* (1984), p. 15; U.S. Department of Justice, *1994 Bombing Incidents*, FBI Explosives Unit–Bomb Center General Information Bulletin 95-2 (1995), p. 3; U.S. Department of Justice, *1996 Bomb Summary*, FBI Explosives Unit–Bomb Center General Information Bulletin 96-1 (1998), p. 6.

Documentation

Bombing incidents refer to actual or attempted detonations of explosive or incendiary devices in violation of local, state, or federal law. Prior to 1990, these excluded hoax bomb devices, accidental explosions, and recoveries of explosive or incendiary devices. Bomb threats and misdemeanor offenses such as illegal use of fireworks are excluded.

Data were gathered via the FBI Uniform Crime Reporting program until 1988, when collection was taken over by the FBI Bomb Data Center. Incident reports are gathered from state and local public safety agencies, the U.S. Postal Inspection Service, Military Ordnance Disposal units, and the Bureau of Alcohol, Tobacco and Firearms.

INCARCERATION AND EXECUTION

Douglas Eckberg

TABLE Ec298–308   Sentenced prisoners and prisoners entering state and federal institutions, by sex: 1925–1998[1]

Contributed by Douglas Eckberg

	Sentenced prisoners					Prisoners received from the courts			Conditionally released prisoners returned to prison		
	State and federal institutions			Federal institutions	State institutions	State and federal institutions	Federal institutions	State institutions	State and federal institutions	Federal institutions	State institutions
	Total	Male	Female								
	Ec298	Ec299	Ec300	Ec301	Ec302	Ec303	Ec304	Ec305	Ec306	Ec307	Ec308
Year	Number	Number	Number	Number	Number	Number	Number	Number	Number	Number	Number
1925	91,669	88,231	3,438	6,430	85,239	—	—	—	—	—	—
1926	97,991	94,287	3,704	6,803	91,188	47,000	5,010	41,990	2,228	26	2,202
1927	109,983 [2]	104,983	4,363	7,722	102,261	51,936	5,021	46,915	2,393	36	2,357
1928	116,390	111,836	4,554	8,204	108,186	55,746	5,570	50,176	2,750	63	2,687
1929	120,496	115,876	4,620	12,964	107,532	58,906	9,734	49,172	2,820	42	2,778
1930	129,453	124,785	4,668	12,181	117,272	66,013	9,800	56,213	3,158	79	3,079
1931	137,082	132,638	4,444	12,964	124,118	71,520	10,615	60,905	3,658	120	3,538
1932	137,997	133,573	4,424	12,282	125,715	67,477	9,652	57,825	4,257	172	4,085
1933	136,810	132,520	4,290	10,851	125,959	62,801	8,333	54,468	4,073	177	3,896
1934	138,316	133,769	4,547	12,080	126,236	62,251	9,275	52,976	4,154	161	3,993
1935	144,180	139,278	4,902	14,777	129,403	65,723	11,837	53,886	4,795	292	4,503
1936	145,038	139,990	5,048	15,373	129,665	60,925	11,459	49,466	4,575	348	4,227
1937	152,741	147,375	5,366	15,309	137,432	63,552	11,171	52,381	5,928	437	5,491
1938	160,285	154,826	5,459	17,083	143,202	68,326	12,538	55,788	5,964	558	5,406
1939	179,818	173,143	6,675	19,730	160,088	66,024	12,027	53,997	5,900	645	5,255
1940	173,706	167,345	6,361	19,260	154,446	81,193	15,109	66,084	6,658	834	5,824
1941	165,439	159,228	6,211	18,465	146,974	77,219	15,350	61,869	7,254	898	6,356
1942	150,384	144,167	6,217	16,623	133,761	66,329	13,725	52,604	7,007	742	6,265
1943	137,220	131,054	6,166	16,113	121,107	54,236	12,203	42,033	6,728	708	6,020
1944	132,456	126,350	6,106	18,139	114,317	53,984	14,047	39,937	7,088	599	6,489
1945	133,649	127,609	6,040	18,638	115,011	56,444	14,171	42,273	6,792	632	6,160
1946	140,079	134,075	6,004	17,622	122,457	64,044	14,950	49,094	7,324	688	6,636
1947	151,304	144,961	6,343	17,146	134,158	68,281	12,948	55,333	8,263	946	7,317
1948	155,977	149,739	6,238	16,328	139,649	70,825	12,430	58,395	8,226	1,099	7,127
1949	163,749	157,663	6,086	16,868	146,881	71,703	13,130	58,573	9,079	1,529	7,550
1950	166,123	160,309	5,814	17,134	148,989	69,473	14,237	55,236	8,692	1,371	7,321
1951	165,680	159,610	6,070	17,395	148,285	66,380	14,120	52,260	9,124	1,226	7,898
1952	168,233	161,994	6,239	18,014	150,219	69,986	15,305	54,681	9,465	995	8,470
1953	173,579	166,909	6,670	19,363	154,216	73,299	16,376	56,923	10,036	956	9,080
1954	182,901	175,907	6,994	20,003	162,898	79,946	16,685	63,261	10,355	902	9,453
1955	185,780	178,655	7,125	20,088	165,692	78,479	15,286	63,193	10,872	980	9,892
1956	189,565	182,190	7,375	20,134	169,431	77,988	13,454	64,534	11,591	1,032	10,559
1957	195,414	188,113	7,301	20,420	174,994	80,557	13,305	67,252	11,948	1,092	10,856
1958	205,643	198,208	7,435	21,549	184,094	88,725	13,803	74,922	12,815	1,275	11,540
1959	208,105	200,469	7,636	22,492	185,613	87,266	13,872	73,394	13,418	1,362	12,056
1960	212,953	205,265	7,688	23,218	189,735	88,575	13,723	74,852	15,042	1,456	13,586
1961	220,149	212,268	7,881	23,696	196,453	93,590	13,517	80,073	16,409	1,587	14,822
1962	218,830	210,823	8,007	23,944	194,886	89,082	13,514	75,568	17,236	1,643	15,593
1963	217,283	209,538	7,745	23,128	194,155	87,826	12,882	74,944	18,906	1,650	17,256
1964	214,336	206,632	7,704	21,709	192,627	87,578	12,482	75,096	19,558	1,691	17,867
1965	210,895	203,327	7,568	21,040	189,855	87,505	12,781	74,724	19,393	1,823	17,570
1966	199,654	192,703	6,951	19,245	180,409	77,857	11,508	66,349	17,662	1,746	15,916
1967	194,896	188,661	6,235	19,579	175,317	77,850	11,447	66,403	17,583	1,774	15,809
1968	187,914	182,102	5,812	19,703	168,211	72,058	11,120	60,938	17,680	1,855	15,825
1969	196,007	189,413	6,594	19,623	176,384	75,277	11,589	63,688	15,844	1,607	14,237
1970	196,429	190,794	5,635	20,038	176,391	79,351	12,047	67,304	17,294	1,530	15,764
1971	198,061	191,732	6,329	20,948	177,113	—	—	84,099	—	—	14,821
1972	196,092	189,823	6,269	21,713	174,379	—	—	—	—	—	—
1973	204,211 [2]	197,523	6,004	22,815	181,396	—	—	—	—	—	—
1974	218,466	211,077	7,389	22,361	196,105	103,754	14,511	89,243	16,917	1,033	15,884

Notes appear at end of table

TABLE Ec298–308   Sentenced prisoners and prisoners entering state and federal institutions, by sex: 1925–1998
Continued

	Sentenced prisoners					Prisoners received from the courts			Conditionally released prisoners returned to prison		
	State and federal institutions			Federal institutions	State institutions	State and federal institutions	Federal institutions	State institutions	State and federal institutions	Federal institutions	State institutions
	Total	Male	Female								
	Ec298	Ec299	Ec300	Ec301	Ec302	Ec303	Ec304	Ec305	Ec306	Ec307	Ec308
Year	Number	Number	Number	Number	Number	Number	Number	Number	Number	Number	Number
1975	240,593	231,918	8,675	24,131	216,462	129,573	16,770	112,803	18,956	1,281	17,675
1976	262,833	252,794	10,039	26,980	235,853	129,482	17,437	112,045	22,792	1,754	21,038
1977	285,456	274,244	11,212	28,650	256,806	128,050	13,820	114,230	21,746	2,129	19,617
1978	294,396	282,813	11,583	26,391	268,005	126,121	13,247	112,874	23,844	1,429	22,415
1979	301,470	289,465	12,005	22,588	278,882	131,047	12,619	118,428	25,668	1,454	24,214
1980	315,974	303,643	12,331	20,611	295,363	142,122	10,907	131,215	28,817	1,640	27,177
1981	353,167	338,940	14,227	22,169	330,998	160,272	11,086	149,186	35,674	1,709	33,965
1982	394,374	378,045	16,329	23,652	370,722	177,109	12,461	164,648	39,003	2,317	36,686
1983	419,820	402,391	17,429	26,331	393,489	187,408	14,119	173,289	45,568	2,583	42,985
1984	443,398	424,193	19,205	27,602	415,796	180,418	13,491	166,927	52,007	2,475	49,532
1985	480,568 [2]	458,972	21,296	32,695	447,873	198,499	15,368	183,131	58,694	2,502	56,192
1986	522,084	497,540	24,544	36,531	485,553	219,382	16,067	203,315	71,184	2,401	68,783
1987	560,812	533,990	26,822	39,523	521,289	241,887	16,260	225,627	82,959	2,435	80,524
1988	603,732	573,587	30,145	42,738	560,994	261,242	15,932	245,310	101,354	2,744	98,610
1989	680,907	643,643	37,264	47,168	633,739	316,215	18,388	297,827	122,156	1,611	120,545
1990	739,980	699,416	40,564	50,403	689,577	341,545	18,476	323,069	—	—	133,870
1991	789,610	745,808	43,802	56,696	732,914	337,478	20,241	317,237	—	—	142,100
1992	846,277	799,776	46,501	65,706	780,571	356,498	22,197	334,301	—	—	141,961
1993	932,074	878,037	54,037	74,399	857,675	341,722	23,653	318,069	147,712	1,346	146,366
1994	1,016,691	956,566	60,125	79,795	936,896	346,097	23,956	322,141	170,974	3,146	167,828
1995	1,085,022	1,021,059	63,963	83,663	1,001,359	361,464	23,972	337,492	178,641	2,915	175,726
1996	1,137,722	1,068,123	69,599	88,815	1,048,004	353,893	27,346	326,547	175,305	2,672	172,633
1997	1,195,498	1,121,663	73,835	—	—	—	—	334,525	—	—	186,659
1998	1,220,474	1,145,078	75,396	—	—	—	—	—	—	—	—

[1] In 1977, the criterion of imprisonment changes from the "custody" to the "jurisdiction" criterion.

[2] The total of all prisoners is larger than the sum of male and female prisoners.

Sources

U.S. Bureau of Justice Statistics, *Prisoners 1925–1981*, NCJ-85861 (1983), p. 2; U.S. Department of Justice, *Prisoners in State and Federal Institutions on December 31st*, National Prisoner Statistics Bulletins (1982–1984 annual issues); U.S. Bureau of Justice Statistics, *Correctional Populations in the United States* (1985–1996 annual issues); U.S. Bureau of Justice Statistics, *Sourcebook of Criminal Justice Statistics 1998* (1999), Table 6.36; U.S. Bureau of Justice Statistics, *Prisoners in 1998*, NCJ-175687 (1999); U.S. Bureau of Justice Statistics, *Probation and Parole Violators in State Prison, 1991*, Special Report, NCJ-149076 (1995), Appendix Table 2.

Documentation

National Prisoner Statistics (NPS), a voluntary reporting program begun by the federal government in 1926, is the principal source of historical statistics on U.S. prison populations. In the program, prison officials are asked to complete a series of forms. Responsibility for NPS has rested with four different entities, the Bureau of the Census (1926–1949), the Federal Bureau of Prisons (1950–1970), the Law Enforcement Assistance Administration (1971–1979), and the Bureau of Justice Statistics (1980–present).

The data presented here are for sentenced prisoners only, not all prisoners held in state and federal institutions. The composition of prisoners has changed several times. From 1926 to 1936 and 1980 to 1982, data are for all newly sentenced prisoners. From 1937 to 1960, they are for newly sentenced "felons," generally defined as prisoners serving sentences of six months or longer. From 1964 to 1970, they are for "felons," meaning prisoners with sentences of at least one year, and after 1970 they indicate prisoners with sentences longer than a year.

In 1977, the criterion for imprisonment changed from being in "custody" to being under the "jurisdiction" of prison authorities. In 1977 the population "under jurisdiction" was 2.6 percent higher than the population "in custody." Custody figures for 1977, which are not reported in this table, included 267,097 males and 11,044 females. Admissions are for new commitments from the courts and parole or other conditional release violators returned to prison for violating the conditions of their release. They do not include prisoners returned to prison after escaping or going absent without leave, returns from appeals or bond, transfers from other jurisdictions, or a small number of other admissions. Not all states return data every year, and some data are estimated. Figures are revised following initial publication as additional data are received and may be revised several times, with most revisions representing changes in counts of prisoners in state institutions. The present data will differ somewhat from those in earlier publications. The most recent years' figures are preliminary and may be revised.

Series Ec298–302. The population of sentenced prisoners is obtained on December 31 of the stated year.

TABLE Ec309–327 Sentenced prisoners admitted to state and federal institutions, by race: 1926–1996[1]

Contributed by Douglas Eckberg

For whom racial data are available (applies to the Federal institutions and State institutions groups)

		State and federal institutions						Federal institutions						State institutions					
	Total	Total	Whites	Blacks	Nonwhite–nonblack	Nonwhites	Unreported race	Total	Whites	Blacks	Nonwhite–nonblack	Nonwhites	Unreported race	Total	Whites	Blacks	Nonwhite–nonblack	Nonwhites	Unreported race
Year	Ec309	Ec310	Ec311	Ec312	Ec313	Ec314	Ec315	Ec316	Ec317	Ec318	Ec319	Ec320	Ec321	Ec322	Ec323	Ec324	Ec325	Ec326	Ec327
1926[2]	48,108	43,328	33,559	9,274	409	9,683	86	5,010	4,042	641	323	964	4	38,318	28,701	8,633	902	9,535	82
1927	51,936	44,062	34,131	9,290	464	9,754	177	5,021	4,093	668	105	773	155	39,041	30,038	8,622	359	8,981	22
1928	56,746	48,212	37,724	9,959	518	10,477	11	5,570	—	—	—	—	—	42,642	—	—	—	11,547	—
1929	58,906	58,906	45,979	12,362	555	12,917	10	9,734	8,364	1,206	164	1,370	0	49,172	37,615	11,156	391	—	10
1930	66,013	66,013	50,663	14,771	568	15,339	11	9,800	8,471	1,211	117	1,328	1	56,213	42,192	13,560	451	14,011	10
1931	71,520	71,520	55,434	15,441	645	16,086	0	10,615	9,298	1,140	177	1,317	0	60,905	46,136	14,301	468[6]	14,769	0
1932	67,477	67,477	52,200	14,613	664	15,277	0	9,652	8,469	997	186	1,183	0	57,825	43,731[6]	13,616	478	14,094	0
1933	62,801	62,801	47,717	14,368	716	15,084	0	8,333	7,334	799	200	999	0	54,468	40,383[6]	13,569	516	14,085	0
1934	62,251	62,251	46,744	14,853	654	15,507	0	9,275	8,076	1,001	198	1,199	0	52,976	38,668	13,852	456	14,308	0
1935	65,723	65,723	48,582	16,362	779	17,141	0	11,837	9,867	1,693	277	1,970	0	53,886	38,715	14,669	502	15,171	0
1936	60,925	60,925	44,708	15,478	739	16,217	0	11,459	9,217	1,986	256	2,242	0	49,466	35,491	13,492	483	13,975	0
1937[3]	63,552	59,073	42,940	15,384	749	16,133	0	10,342	8,277	1,811	254	2,065	0	46,412	33,244	12,696	472	13,168	0
1938[3]	68,326	64,265	46,655	16,875	735	17,610	0	11,664	9,081	2,306	277	2,583	0	50,169	36,059	13,671	439	14,110	0
1939[3]	66,024	62,000	44,990	16,309	701	17,010	0	11,108	8,432	2,390	286	2,676	0	48,324	34,985	12,950	389	13,339	0
1940[3]	73,104	62,692	44,258	17,677	757	18,434	0	12,621	9,440	2,878	303	3,181	0	47,462	33,212	13,828	422	14,250	0
1941[3]	68,700	56,023	38,927	16,355	741	17,096	0	12,586	9,356	2,938	292	3,230	0	41,202	28,307	12,479	416	12,895	0
1942	58,858	47,761	32,482	14,660	619	15,279	0	12,112	9,221	2,664	227	2,891	0	35,649	23,261	11,996	392	12,388	0
1943	50,082	40,273	27,616	12,131	526	12,657	0	10,736	8,404	2,097	235	2,332	0	29,537	19,212	10,034	291	10,325	0
1944	50,162	41,058	28,280	12,165	613	12,778	0	12,417	9,455	2,571	391	2,962	0	28,641	18,825	9,594	222	9,816	0
1945	53,212	43,281	29,539	13,207	535	13,742	0	11,831	8,699	2,877	255	3,132	0	31,450	20,840	10,330	280	10,610	0
1946	61,338	56,432	37,146	18,655	631	19,286	0	12,753	9,279	3,237	237	3,474	0	43,679	27,867	15,418	394	15,812	0
1947[4]	64,804	51,016	35,265	15,139	612	15,751	0	10,415	7,812	2,401	202	2,603	0	40,601	27,453	12,738	410	13,148	0
1948[4]	63,777	49,834	34,658	14,549	627	15,176	0	9,935	7,553	2,184	198	2,382	0	39,899	27,105	12,365	429	12,794	0
1949[4]	68,925	54,370	38,155	15,640	575	16,215	0	10,429	7,764	2,465	200	2,665	0	43,941	30,391	13,175	375	13,550	0
1950	69,473	57,988	40,057	17,211	720	17,931	0	11,492	8,090	3,214	188	3,402	0	46,496	31,967	13,997	532	14,529	0
1960[5]	88,575	84,068	55,253	27,089	1,726	28,815	0	14,833	10,487	3,692	654	4,346	0	69,235	44,766	23,397	1,072	24,469	0
1964[5]	87,578	81,099	52,458	27,191	1,450	28,641	0	13,220	9,680	3,281	259	3,540	0	67,879	42,778	23,910	1,191	25,101	0
1970[5]	79,351	48,497	29,354	—	—	19,143	0	11,060	8,078	—	—	2,982	0	37,437	21,276	—	—	16,161	0
1974[5]	103,754	52,245	30,045	—	—	20,957	1,243	15,181	9,874	—	—	4,064	1,243	37,064	20,171	15,134	1,759	16,893	0
1975[5]	129,573	42,351	26,375	—	—	14,793	1,183	16,555	10,753	—	—	4,619	1,183	25,796	15,622	9,761	413	10,174	0
1976[5]	129,482	69,746	41,841	—	—	26,767	1,138	18,711	12,460	—	—	5,113	1,138	51,035	29,381	19,053	2,601	21,654	0
1977[5]	128,050	72,183	42,955	—	—	26,939	2,289	18,160	11,081	—	—	4,855	2,224	54,023	31,874	21,329	755	22,084	65
1978[5]	126,121	95,502	52,548	—	—	38,484	4,470	18,485	10,430	—	—	4,610	3,445	77,017	42,118	33,088	786	33,874	1,025
1979[5]	131,047	94,828	55,807	—	—	36,934	2,087	15,293	10,136	—	—	3,727	1,430	79,535	45,671	32,277	930	33,207	657
1980[5]	182,617	134,634	76,382	—	—	54,465	3,787	17,383	10,483	—	—	3,919	2,981	117,251	65,899	49,144	1,402	50,546	806
1981[5]	195,946	135,611	75,836	—	—	57,855	1,920	14,400	9,182	—	—	3,298	1,920	121,211	66,654	52,727	1,830	54,557	0
1982[5]	216,112	131,617	70,638	—	—	57,160	3,819	17,226	10,552	—	—	3,535	3,139	114,391	60,086	52,634	991	53,625	680
1983[5]	187,408	122,575	69,381	—	—	49,806	3,388	18,987	13,054	—	—	4,187	1,746	103,588	56,327	44,795	824	45,619	1,642
1984[5]	180,418	137,583	76,936	—	—	55,302	5,345	18,541	13,772	—	—	4,075	694	119,042	63,164	50,402	825	51,227	4,651
1985	198,499	—	109,900	—	—	88,600	0	15,368	11,700	—	—	3,700	0	183,131	98,200	83,000	1,800	—	0
1986	219,382	—	121,100	97,800	2,600	—	0	16,067	12,300	3,400	300	—	0	203,315	108,800	94,300	2,200	—	0
1987	241,887	—	129,200	110,000	2,600	—	0	16,260	11,900	4,000	400	—	0	225,627	117,300	106,000	2,300	—	0
1988	261,242	—	129,000	130,100	2,100	—	0	15,932	11,300	4,300	400	—	0	245,310	117,700	125,800	1,700	—	0
1989	316,215	—	148,200	165,300	2,800	—	0	18,388	12,400	5,700	400	—	0	297,827	135,800	159,600	2,400	—	0

For whom racial data are available

	State and federal institutions							Federal institutions						State institutions					
Year	Total	Total	Whites	Blacks	Nonwhite–nonblack	Nonwhites	Unreported race	Total	Whites	Blacks	Nonwhite–nonblack	Nonwhites	Unreported race	Total	Whites	Blacks	Nonwhite–nonblack	Nonwhites	Unreported race
	Ec309	Ec310	Ec311	Ec312	Ec313	Ec314	Ec315	Ec316	Ec317	Ec318	Ec319	Ec320	Ec321	Ec322	Ec323	Ec324	Ec325	Ec326	Ec327
	Number	Number	Number	Number	Number	Number	Number	Number	Number	Number	Number	Number	Number	Number	Number	Number	Number	Number	Number
1990	341,545	—	169,300	169,500	2,800	—	0	18,476	12,200	5,900	400	—	0	323,069	157,100	163,600	2,400	—	0
1991	337,478	—	163,200	170,700	3,600	—	0	20,241	13,300	6,400	500	—	0	317,237	149,900	164,300	3,100	—	0
1992	356,498	—	175,700	177,400	3,500	—	0	22,197	14,400	7,300	600	—	0	334,301	161,300	170,100	2,900	—	0
1993	341,722	—	168,700	169,500	3,600	—	0	23,653	15,000	8,100	600	—	0	318,069	153,700	161,400	3,000	—	0
1994	346,097	—	172,800	169,200	4,100	—	0	23,956	14,800	8,500	700	—	0	322,141	158,000	160,700	3,400	—	0
1995	361,464	—	186,700	170,800	4,000	—	0	23,972	15,900	7,300	800	—	0	337,492	170,800	163,500	3,200	—	0
1996	353,893	—	185,700	163,900	4,300	—	0	27,346	17,100	9,400	900	—	0	326,547	168,600	154,500	3,400	—	0

1 Beginning in 1985 counts by race from the "admission" data series are replaced by estimates, to the nearest 100, from the more complete "movement" data series.

2 Included with whites are 816 prisoners of Mexican ancestry for the U.S. total, but these same prisoners are included with nonwhite-nonblack prisoners for state and federal totals.

3 State data include male prisoners only, but U.S. totals include females.

4 Includes male prisoners only.

5 Federal figures are based on fiscal year, rather than calendar year, and are incomplete.

6 Corrected from the original published figures based on internal evidence in the table.

Sources

U.S. Bureau of Justice Statistics, *Race of Prisoners Admitted to State and Federal Institutions, 1926–86*, NCJ-125618 (May 1991); U.S. Bureau of Justice Statistics, *Correctional Populations in the United States* (annual issues).

Documentation

See the text for Table Ec298–308 for a description of the source and a discussion of the changing composition of the prison population.

The data presented here are from two National Prisoner Statistics (NPS) forms. The "movement series" consists of aggregate data on the numbers and categories of prisoners admitted and released during the year as well as a count of all inmates on December 31st of the year. Before 1978, the series collected no information on race; since then, it has compiled year-end counts of prisoners of each race. The "admission series" obtains information on each individual prisoner, giving information on such things as age, sex, race, offense, and sentence length.

There are significant gaps in the data. In some years, the federal government did not collect admissions series data. There are also major lapses in compliance by prison officials and by states. Even though the movement series often includes data from all states and never has lacked data from more than five states, the admissions series is often very incomplete. Data are incomplete because some states – as many as thirty-four in 1975 – submitted no data, submitted data with missing records, or, rarely, submitted records that did not identify the race of the prisoners. The compilers attempted to generate data on newly sentenced felons.

TABLE Ec328–342 Prisoners released from state and federal institutions, by type of release: 1926–1996

Contributed by Douglas Eckberg

Year	All prisoners Ec328	Federal institutions							State institutions						
		All prisoners Ec329	Released conditionally Ec330	Paroled Ec331	Granted a conditional release besides parole Ec332	Released unconditionally Ec333	Released at the expiration of sentence Ec334	Released unconditionally, but not from the expiration of sentence Ec335	All prisoners Ec336	Released conditionally Ec337	Paroled Ec338	Granted a conditional release besides parole Ec339	Released unconditionally Ec340	Released at the expiration of sentence Ec341	Released unconditionally, but not from the expiration of sentence Ec342
1926	39,044	4,248	834	834	0	3,414	3,413	1	34,796	19,083	19,083	0	15,713	14,418	1,295
1927	41,356	4,179	688	688	0	3,491	3,491	0	37,177	20,964	20,964	0	16,213	14,964	1,249
1928	45,124	4,983	1,082	1,082	0	3,901	3,900	1	40,141	22,887	22,887	0	17,254	16,575	679
1929	45,986	5,610	1,347	1,347	0	4,263	4,261	2	40,376	22,791	22,791	0	17,585	16,931	654
1930	54,925	8,926	4,145	4,157	0	4,769	4,764	5	45,999	25,352	25,352	0	20,647	20,112	535
1931	60,930	9,749	4,643	4,643	0	5,106	5,105	1	51,181	30,339	30,339	0	20,842	20,321	521
1932	66,863	10,394	5,050	5,050	0	5,344	5,314	30	56,469	32,087	32,087	0	24,382	20,530	3,852
1933	63,640	10,206	5,445	4,242	1,203	4,761	4,756	5	53,434	30,597	30,597	0	22,837	21,194	1,643
1934	60,732	8,310	5,596	2,709	2,887	2,714	2,709	5	52,422	29,931	29,747	184	22,491	20,761	1,730
1935	60,475	9,010	6,663	2,369	4,294	2,347	2,345	2	51,465	28,430	28,039	391	23,035	20,990	2,045
1936	62,750	10,965	8,701	2,445	6,256	2,264	2,263	1	51,785	29,093	28,686	407	22,692	21,778	914
1937	60,462	11,477	9,510	2,944	6,566	1,967	1,950	17	48,985	27,852	24,331	3,521	21,133	20,766	367
1938	62,771	11,102	9,211	2,416	6,795	1,891	1,876	15	51,669	29,520	25,220	4,300	22,149	21,754	395
1939	66,303	11,794	9,247	2,315	6,932	2,547	2,538	9	54,509	31,122	25,568	5,554	23,387	22,898	489
1940	88,640	16,280	10,560	2,572	7,988	5,720	5,702	18	72,360	38,441	30,360	8,081	33,919	32,092	1,827
1941	86,887	16,998	10,306	2,723	7,583	6,692	6,669	23	69,889	38,618	32,246	6,372	31,271	30,500	771
1942	81,630	16,032	10,241	3,079	7,162	5,791	5,776	15	65,598	38,829	30,980	7,849	26,769	26,143	626
1943	69,723	13,190	8,954	3,101	5,853	4,236	4,223	13	56,533	35,857	30,526	5,331	20,676	20,426	250
1944	59,860	12,457	8,056	3,272	4,784	4,401	4,263	138	47,403	30,603	26,029	4,574	16,800	16,520	280
1945	57,500	13,598	8,343	3,101	5,242	5,255	5,229	26	43,902	28,400	24,255	4,145	15,502	14,935	567
1946	59,289	15,544	10,553	5,362	5,191	4,991	4,869	122	43,745	28,212	24,571	3,641	15,533	14,959	574
1947	60,080	14,246	8,913	4,020	4,893	5,333	5,317	16	45,834	27,873	25,107	2,766	17,961	17,107	854
1948	65,978	14,243	8,946	3,822	5,124	5,297	5,146	151	51,735	30,268	27,062	3,206	21,467	19,798	1,669
1949	69,051	13,999	8,647	3,051	5,596	5,352	5,317	35	55,052	30,857	28,267	2,590	24,195	22,368	1,827
1950	72,179	15,187	9,466	3,294	6,172	5,721	5,710	11	56,992	32,770	31,428	1,342	24,222	22,147	2,075
1951	73,937	14,974	7,544	3,495	4,049	7,430	7,422	8	58,963	34,402	32,936	1,466	24,561	22,064	2,497
1952	74,268	15,524	5,763	3,642	2,121	9,761	9,761	0	58,744	34,099	32,712	1,387	24,645	22,037	2,608
1953	75,125	15,813	6,154	3,793	2,361	9,659	9,659	0	59,312	34,033	32,525	1,508	25,279	22,693	2,586
1954	78,184	16,743	6,917	4,410	2,507	9,826	9,825	1	61,441	35,330	33,551	1,779	26,111	23,276	2,835
1955	82,924	15,776	6,440	3,823	2,617	9,336	9,328	8	67,148	39,473	37,631	1,842	27,675	24,678	2,997
1956	83,099	14,285	7,062	3,975	3,087	7,223	7,209	14	68,814	40,176	38,288	1,888	28,638	25,489	3,149
1957	85,356	14,029	7,080	3,822	3,258	6,949	6,941	8	71,327	41,682	39,535	2,147	29,645	26,467	3,178
1958	88,679	13,970	6,895	3,587	3,308	7,075	7,072	3	74,709	44,813	42,320	2,493	29,896	26,682	3,214
1959	96,530	14,215	7,309	4,220	3,089	6,906	6,906	0	82,315	51,227	48,278	2,949	31,088	27,552	3,536
1960	96,362	14,196	7,712	4,344	3,368	6,484	6,484	0	82,166	51,686	48,457	3,229	30,480	27,144	3,336
1961	100,724	14,519	8,235	4,380	3,855	6,284	6,284	0	86,205	54,848	51,445	3,403	31,357	27,859	3,498
1962	106,143	14,814	8,518	4,915	3,603	6,296	6,296	0	91,329	58,269	54,420	3,849	33,060	29,159	3,901
1963	105,050	15,181	8,874	5,127	3,747	6,307	6,307	0	89,869	57,592	53,934	3,658	32,277	28,599	3,678
1964	106,633	15,100	8,920	5,178	3,742	6,180	—	—	91,533	59,032	55,024	4,008	32,501	—	—

	Federal institutions								State institutions						
	All prisoners	All prisoners	Released conditionally	Paroled	Granted a conditional release besides parole	Released unconditionally	Released at the expiration of sentence	Released unconditionally, but not from the expiration of sentence	All prisoners	Released conditionally	Paroled	Granted a conditional release besides parole	Released unconditionally	Released at the expiration of sentence	Released unconditionally, but not from the expiration of sentence
	Ec328	Ec329	Ec330	Ec331	Ec332	Ec333	Ec334	Ec335	Ec336	Ec337	Ec338	Ec339	Ec340	Ec341	Ec342
Year	Number	Number	Number	Number	Number	Number	Number	Number	Number	Number	Number	Number	Number	Number	Number
1965	106,161	14,874	8,696	5,109	3,587	6,178	—	—	51,287	59,348	55,606	3,742	31,939	—	—
1966	102,335	14,695	9,273	6,029	3,244	5,422	—	—	87,640	57,635	53,678	3,957	30,005	—	—
1967	96,377	12,361	8,037	5,297	2,740	4,324	—	—	84,016	56,793	52,424	4,369	27,223	—	—
1968	85,968	12,175	4,400	—	—	7,775	—	—	73,793	50,309	—	—	23,484	—	—
1969	89,060	11,406	6,881	—	—	4,525	—	—	77,654	52,030	—	—	25,624	—	—
1970	91,732	11,689	5,696	—	—	5,993	—	—	80,043	56,181	—	—	23,862	—	—
1972	107,514	12,794	7,397	—	—	5,397	—	—	94,720	71,652	—	—	23,068	—	—
1973	105,044	12,280	6,974	—	—	5,306	—	—	92,764	71,288	—	—	21,476	—	—
1974	102,147	12,957	7,270	5,310	1,960	5,687	5,687	0	89,190	69,768	63,652	9,116	19,422	17,620	1,802
1975	120,502	13,760	7,485	5,783	1,702	6,275	6,275	0	106,742	82,323	72,941	9,382	24,419	20,365	4,054
1976	119,191	12,263	5,028	3,457	1,571	7,235	7,235	0	105,928	84,225	73,724	10,501	22,703	20,535	2,168
1977	124,282	9,069	5,248	3,214	2,034	3,821	3,658	163	115,213	94,982	82,797	12,185	20,231	18,535	1,696
1978	133,593	13,797	9,651	6,267	3,384	4,146	4,009	137	113,796	98,040	84,317	13,723	21,756	20,396	1,360
1979	143,889	14,935	10,442	6,682	3,760	4,493	4,295	198	123,954	106,693	77,605	29,088	22,261	21,001	1,260
1980	148,867	11,899	8,252	5,215	3,037	3,647	3,439	208	135,968	114,700	78,602	36,098	22,268	20,460	1,808
1981	152,316	9,827	6,431	4,055	2,376	3,396	3,228	168	142,489	117,984	77,839	40,145	24,505	19,755	4,750
1982	169,092	11,948	7,086	5,059	2,027	4,862	4,689	173	157,144	133,093	81,548	51,545	24,051	22,584	1,467
1983	204,652	13,415	8,151	5,916	2,235	5,264	5,106	158	191,237	158,194	92,043	66,151	33,043	30,807	2,236
1984	205,609	14,110	8,933	6,362	2,571	5,177	4,939	238	191,499	157,484	88,000	69,484	34,015	31,194	2,821
1985	216,831	12,936	8,748	5,836	2,912	4,188	3,969	219	203,895	166,168	88,069	78,099	37,727	34,489	3,238
1986	245,362	14,690	10,118	6,466	3,652	4,572	4,280	292	230,672	192,412	99,665	92,747	38,260	34,236	4,024
1987	286,124	15,618	11,358	6,851	4,507	4,260	4,034	226	270,506	221,513	109,852	111,661	48,993	43,878	5,115
1988	316,326	14,948	9,511	6,352	3,159	5,437	5,181	256	310,378	244,140	120,471	122,669	57,238	50,587	6,651
1989	364,434	18,000	13,136	7,982	5,154	4,864	4,623	241	346,434	289,191	134,582	154,609	57,243	53,513	3,730
1990	—	—	—	—	—	—	—	—	394,682	339,439	159,731	179,708	55,243	51,288	3,955
1991	—	—	—	—	—	—	—	—	409,353	353,774	167,487	186,287	55,579	45,661	9,918
1992	—	—	—	—	—	—	—	—	416,156	357,731	170,095	187,636	58,425	48,971	9,454
1993	425,409	18,543	5,742	3,009	2,733	12,801	12,416	385	406,866	350,031	162,185	187,846	56,835	49,622	7,213
1994	425,856	20,776	4,790	2,621	2,169	15,986	15,623	363	405,080	348,230	146,383	201,847	56,850	52,164	4,686
1995	462,564	21,801	3,747	2,185	1,562	18,054	17,728	326	440,763	370,736	147,139	223,597	70,027	66,017	4,010
1996	473,243	22,875	3,176	1,873	1,303	19,699	19,223	476	450,368	366,632	141,808	224,824	83,736	78,192	5,544

Sources

1926–1970 data are from U.S. Bureau of the Census, *Historical Statistics of the United States: From Colonial Times to the Present* (1975), series H1144–1154. Original data, 1926–1946, U.S. Bureau of Prisons, *Prisoners in State and Federal Prisons and Reformatories* (annual issues); 1947–1948, U.S. Bureau of Prisons unpublished data; 1949–1970, U.S. Department of Justice, *National Prisoner Statistics* (annual issues); 1971–1984, U.S. Department of Justice, National Prisoner Statistics, *Prisoners in State and Federal Institutions on December 31st* (annual bulletins); 1985–present, U.S. Bureau of Justice Statistics, *Correctional Populations in the United States* (annual issues).

Documentation

See the text for Tables Ec298–327 for a description of the source and discussions of the changing composition of prisoners and changes in the criteria for imprisonment.

Not all states return data every year, and some data are estimated. Figures are revised following initial publication as additional data are received and may be revised several times, with most revisions representing changes in counts of prisoners in state institutions. The present data will differ somewhat from those in earlier publications. The most recent years' figures are preliminary and may be revised.

Conditional releases include prisoners paroled, on probation, or undergoing supervised mandatory release, and a few unnamed "other" conditional releases. Unconditional releases include prisoners released at the expiration of sentences, commutations of sentences, full pardons, and a few unnamed "other" unconditional releases. Releases do not include escaped prisoners, prisoners who have gone absent without leave, prisoners released during appeal or out on bond, prisoners transferred to other jurisdictions, prisoners who have died, or a few unnamed "other" releases.

TABLE Ec343–357   Prisoners executed under civil authority, by race and offense: 1930–1998

Contributed by Douglas Eckberg

					Murder				Rape				Offenses other than murder and rape		
	Total	Whites	Blacks	Other races	Total	Whites	Blacks	Other races	Total	Whites	Blacks	Other races	Total	Whites	Blacks
	Ec343	Ec344	Ec345	Ec346	Ec347	Ec348	Ec349	Ec350	Ec351	Ec352	Ec353	Ec354	Ec355	Ec356	Ec357
Year	Number	Number	Number	Number	Number	Number	Number	Number	Number	Number	Number	Number	Number	Number	Number
1930	155	90	65	0	147	90	57	0	6	0	6	0	2	0	2
1931	153	77	72	4	137	76	57	4	15	1	14	0	1	0	1
1932	140	62	75	3	128	62	63	3	10	0	10	0	2	0	2
1933	160	77	81	2	151	75	74	2	7	1	6	0	2	1	1
1934	168	65	102	1	154	64	89	1	14	1	13	0	0	0	0
1935	199	119	77	3	184	115	66	3	13	2	11	0	2	2	0
1936	195	92	101	2	181	86	93	2	10	2	8	0	4	4	0
1937	147	69	74	4	133	67	62	4	13	2	11	0	1	0	1
1938	190	96	92	2	154	89	63	2	25	1	24	0	11	6	5
1939	160	80	77	3	145	79	63	3	12	0	12	0	3	1	2
1940	124	49	75	0	105	44	61	0	15	2	13	0	4	3	1
1941	123	59	63	1	102	55	46	1	20	4	16	0	1	0	1
1942	147	67	80	0	115	57	58	0	25	4	21	0	7	6	1
1943	131	54	74	3	118	54	63	1	13	0	11	2	0	0	0
1944	120	47	70	3	96	45	48	3	24	2	22	0	0	0	0
1945	117	41	75	1	90	37	52	1	26	4	22	0	1	0	1
1946	131	46	84	1	107	45	61	1	22	0	22	0	2	1	1
1947	153	42	111	0	129	40	89	0	23	2	21	0	1	0	1
1948	119	35	82	2	95	32	61	2	22	1	21	0	2	2	0
1949	119	50	67	2	107	49	56	2	10	0	10	0	2	1	1
1950	82	40	42	0	68	36	32	0	13	4	9	0	1	0	1
1951	105	57	47	1	87	55	31	1	17	2	15	0	1	0	1
1952	83	36	47	0	71	35	36	0	12	1	11	0	0	0	0
1953	62	30	31	1	51	25	25	1	7	1	6	0	4	4	0
1954	81	38	42	1	71	37	33	1	9	1	8	0	1	0	1
1955	76	44	32	0	65	41	24	0	7	1	6	0	4	2	2
1956	65	21	43	1	52	20	31	1	12	0	12	0	1	1	0
1957	65	34	31	0	54	32	22	0	10	2	8	0	1	0	1
1958	49	20	28	1	41	20	20	1	7	0	7	0	1	0	1
1959	49	16	33	0	41	15	26	0	8	1	7	0	0	0	0
1960	56	21	35	0	44	18	26	0	8	0	8	0	4	3	1
1961	42	20	22	0	33	18	15	0	8	1	7	0	1	1	0
1962	47	28	19	0	41	26	15	0	4	2	2	0	2	0	2
1963	21	13	8	0	18	12	6	0	2	0	2	0	1	1	0
1964	15	8	7	0	9	5	4	0	6	3	3	0	0	0	0
1965	7	6	1	0	7	6	1	0	0	0	0	0	0	0	0
1966	1	1	0	0	1	1	0	0	0	0	0	0	0	0	0
1967	2	1	1	0	2	1	1	0	0	0	0	0	0	0	0
1968	0	0	0	0	0	0	0	0	0	0	0	0	0	0	0
1969	0	0	0	0	0	0	0	0	0	0	0	0	0	0	0
1970	0	0	0	0	0	0	0	0	0	0	0	0	0	0	0
1971	0	0	0	0	0	0	0	0	0	0	0	0	0	0	0
1972	0	0	0	0	0	0	0	0	0	0	0	0	0	0	0
1973	0	0	0	0	0	0	0	0	0	0	0	0	0	0	0
1974	0	0	0	0	0	0	0	0	0	0	0	0	0	0	0
1975	0	0	0	0	0	0	0	0	0	0	0	0	0	0	0
1976	0	0	0	0	0	0	0	0	0	0	0	0	0	0	0
1977	1	1	0	0	1	1	0	0	0	0	0	0	0	0	0
1978	0	0	0	0	0	0	0	0	0	0	0	0	0	0	0
1979	2	2	0	0	2	2	0	0	0	0	0	0	0	0	0
1980	0	0	0	0	0	0	0	0	0	0	0	0	0	0	0
1981	1	1	0	0	1	1	0	0	0	0	0	0	0	0	0
1982	2	1	1	0	2	1	1	0	0	0	0	0	0	0	0
1983	5	4	1	0	5	4	1	0	0	0	0	0	0	0	0
1984	21	13	8	0	21	13	8	0	0	0	0	0	0	0	0
1985	18	11	7	0	18	11	7	0	0	0	0	0	0	0	0
1986	18	11	7	0	18	11	7	0	0	0	0	0	0	0	0
1987	25	13	12	0	25	13	12	0	0	0	0	0	0	0	0
1988	11	6	5	0	11	6	5	0	0	0	0	0	0	0	0
1989	16	8	8	0	16	8	8	0	0	0	0	0	0	0	0

TABLE Ec343–357   Prisoners executed under civil authority, by race and offense: 1930–1998   *Continued*

					Murder				Rape				Offenses other than murder and rape		
	Total	Whites	Blacks	Other races	Total	Whites	Blacks	Other races	Total	Whites	Blacks	Other races	Total	Whites	Blacks
	Ec343	Ec344	Ec345	Ec346	Ec347	Ec348	Ec349	Ec350	Ec351	Ec352	Ec353	Ec354	Ec355	Ec356	Ec357
Year	Number	Number	Number	Number	Number	Number	Number	Number	Number	Number	Number	Number	Number	Number	Number
1990	23	16	7	0	23	16	7	0	0	0	0	0	0	0	0
1991	14	7	7	0	14	7	7	0	0	0	0	0	0	0	0
1992	31	19	11	1	31	19	11	1	0	0	0	0	0	0	0
1993	38	23	14	1	38	23	14	1	0	0	0	0	0	0	0
1994	31	20	11	0	31	20	11	0	0	0	0	0	0	0	0
1995	56	33	22	1	56	33	22	1	0	0	0	0	0	0	0
1996	45	31	14	0	45	31	14	0	0	0	0	0	0	0	0
1997	74	46	26	2	—	—	—	—	—	—	—	—	—	—	—
1998	68	48	18	2	—	—	—	—	—	—	—	—	—	—	—

Source

1930–1995, U.S. Bureau of Justice Statistics, *Correctional Populations in the United States, 1995* (1998), Table 7.26; 1996, U.S. Bureau of Justice Statistics, *Correctional Populations in the United States, 1996*, Table 7.26; 1997–1998, U.S. Bureau of Justice Statistics, *Capital Punishment 1997*, NCJ-172881 (1998). Recent editions of both publications are available online from the Bureau of Justice Statistics Web site.

Documentation

In 1926, the Bureau of the Census began the annual collection of prisoner statistics. The first annual report, published that year, included information on prisoners under sentence of death. In 1950, the program was transferred to the Bureau of Prisons in the Department of Justice. In 1971, it was transferred to the Law Enforcement Assistance Administration, predecessor to the present Bureau of Justice Statistics.

Figures represent federal executions and all executions occurring within the states whether they were carried out by state institutions or local agencies. Executions by military authorities are excluded. The Army (including the Air Force) carried out 160 executions, 148 between 1942 and 1950, three each in 1954, 1955, and 1957, and one each in 1958, 1959, and 1961. One hundred six of the Army's executions were for murder (including twenty-one involving rape), fifty-three for rape, and one for desertion. Prior to 1960, executions in Alaska and Hawai'i are excluded, except for single federal executions in Alaska in 1939, 1948, and 1950.

Totals include twenty white females and twelve black females executed for murder, and two white females executed for other offenses.

Series Ec355–357. Offenses other than murder or rape include armed robbery (twenty-five executions), kidnapping (twenty executions), burglary (eleven executions), sabotage (six executions), aggravated assault (six executions), and espionage (two executions).

TABLE 358–401 Persons in custody in training schools for juvenile delinquents and in detention centers, by sex, race, ethnicity, and age: 1950–1990

Contributed by Douglas Eckberg

Persons in training schools for juvenile delinquents

	Total	Male	Female	White	Nonwhite	Hispanic	Younger than 10	10–13	14	15–19	Older than 19
									Age		
	Ec358	Ec359	Ec360	Ec361	Ec362	Ec363 [1]	Ec364	Ec365	Ec366	Ec367	Ec368
Year	Number	Number	Number	Number	Number	Number	Number	Number	Number	Number	Number
1950	36,986	23,968	13,018	28,578	8,408	—	735	5,170	4,859	23,978	2,244
1960 [2]	45,695	33,765	11,930	31,294	14,401	—	476	6,131	6,078	31,316	1,694
1970 [3]	66,457	52,769	13,688	39,757	26,700	5,287	1,006	7,291	8,272	42,767	7,121
1980 [3]	41,945	34,184	7,761	23,876	18,069	4,499	485	2,870	4,388	28,811	5,391
1990 [4]	49,991	42,478	7,513	24,278	25,713	12,873	460	3,857	5,079	37,815	2,780

Persons in public training schools for juvenile delinquents

	Total	Male	Female	White	Nonwhite	Hispanic	Younger than 10	10–13	14	15–19	Older than 19
						Age					
	Ec369	Ec370	Ec371	Ec372	Ec373	Ec374 [1]	Ec375	Ec376	Ec377	Ec378	Ec379
Year	Number	Number	Number	Number	Number	Number	Number	Number	Number	Number	Number
1950	29,042	21,679	7,363	21,342	7,700	—	507	3,908	3,825	19,360	1,442
1960 [2]	38,359	29,681	8,678	24,900	13,459	—	327	4,858	5,067	26,676	1,431
1970 [3]	57,691	46,867	10,824	33,428	24,263	5,006	647	5,581	6,873	37,929	6,661
1980 [3]	33,184	27,704	5,480	17,685	15,499	3,939	398	1,886	3,153	23,379	4,368
1990 [4]	34,553	30,699	3,854	14,435	20,118	9,230	82	1,846	3,039	27,542	2,044

Persons in private training schools for juvenile delinquents

	Total	Male	Female	White	Nonwhite	Hispanic	Younger than 10	10–13	14	15–19	Older than 19
									Age		
	Ec380	Ec381	Ec382	Ec383	Ec384	Ec385 [1]	Ec386	Ec387	Ec388	Ec389	Ec390
Year	Number	Number	Number	Number	Number	Number	Number	Number	Number	Number	Number
1950	7,944	2,289	5,655	7,236	708	—	228	1,262	1,034	4,618	802
1960 [2]	7,336	4,084	3,252	6,394	942	—	149	1,273	1,011	4,640	263
1970 [3]	8,766	5,902	2,864	6,329	2,437	281	359	1,710	1,399	4,838	460
1980 [3]	8,761	6,480	2,281	6,191	2,570	560	87	984	1,235	5,432	1,023
1990 [4]	14,196	10,836	3,360	9,207	4,989	3,243	320	1,859	1,879	9,476	662

Persons in detention centers

	Total	Male	Female	White	Nonwhite	Hispanic	Younger than 10	10–13	14	15–19	Older than 19
									Age		
	Ec391	Ec392	Ec393	Ec394	Ec395	Ec396 [1]	Ec397	Ec398	Ec399	Ec400	Ec401
Year	Number	Number	Number	Number	Number	Number	Number	Number	Number	Number	Number
1950	3,894	3,018	876	2,847	1,047	—	334	527	342	1,244	1,447
1960 [2]	10,821	7,680	3,141	7,342	3,479	—	785	2,468	1,625	4,988	955
1970 [3]	10,272	6,590	3,682	6,754	3,518	765	481	1,986	1,656	5,937	212
1980 [3]	17,469	14,045	3,424	10,234	7,235	2,217	555	1,793	2,238	12,194	689
1990 [4]	9,730	8,207	1,523	4,704	5,023	2,954	84	1,045	1,343	7,128	130

[1] Hispanics may be of any race.

[2] Data are estimates based on a 25 percent sample.

[3] Data are estimates based on a 20 percent sample.

[4] The training school total is greater than the sum of public and private training school totals because some juveniles were housed in training schools of unknown ownership.

Sources

U.S. Bureau of the Census, *U.S. Census of Population: 1950*, volume 4, part 2, *Institutional Population*; U.S. Bureau of the Census, *U.S. Census of Population: 1960*, *Final Report PC (2)-8A, Inmates of Institutions*; U.S. Bureau of the Census, *U.S. Census of Population: 1970, Final Report PC (2)-4E, Persons in Institutions and Other Group Quarters*; U.S. Bureau of the Census, *U.S. Census of Population: 1980*, volume 2, *Subject Reports, PC80-2-4D, Persons in Institutions and Other Group Quarters*; 1990 data were previously unpublished and have been provided by the U.S. Bureau of the Census.

Documentation

Public training schools for juvenile delinquents are readily identifiable institutions. Most are state institutions operated by state agencies such as departments of welfare or corrections, or youth authorities. Some are operated by county or city governments. These are specialized institutions serving delinquent children, generally between the ages of 10 and 17, though younger children and even some adults may be held there. Generally, residents are committed to the institutions by the courts.

Private training schools are operated under private auspices. Some children held there are committed to them by the courts as delinquents, but others are referred by parents or social agencies for delinquent behavior. A distinguishing factor between private and public training schools is that, by their administrative policy, the former can control their selection and intake.

Detention centers are institutions that provide temporary care for delinquent children pending disposition of their cases and for neglected or abandoned children pending court disposition.

TABLE Ec402–425   Juveniles in public or private facilities for juvenile delinquents, by sex, race, and ethnicity: 1956–1993[1,2]

Contributed by Douglas Eckberg

	All facilities							
	Total	Male	Female	White	Black	Nonwhite	Unreported ethnicity	Hispanic
	Ec402	Ec403	Ec404	Ec405	Ec406	Ec407	Ec408	Ec409 [3]
Year	Number	Number	Number	Number	Number	Number	Number	Number
1956	—	—	—	—	—	—	—	—
1958	—	—	—	—	—	—	—	—
1962	—	—	—	—	—	—	—	—
1963	—	—	—	—	—	—	—	—
1964	—	—	—	—	—	—	—	—
1966	—	—	—	—	—	—	—	—
1968	—	—	—	—	—	—	—	—
1969	—	—	—	—	—	—	—	—
1970	—	—	—	—	—	—	—	—
1971	—	—	—	—	—	—	—	—
1973	—	—	—	—	—	—	—	—
1974	—	—	—	—	—	—	—	—
1975	76,671	56,887	19,784	—	—	—	—	—
1977	73,166	57,308	15,858	49,880	20,870	23,063	223	6,105
1979	71,922	57,679	14,243	47,707	19,595	21,736	2,479	6,301
1983	80,091	64,424	15,667	50,182	25,842	27,862	1,772	7,844
1985	83,402	66,393	17,009	53,968	27,473	29,434	0	9,061
1987	91,646	72,611	19,035	57,942	31,414	33,704	0	10,699
1989	93,945	76,045	17,900	56,401	35,079	37,544	0	11,753
1991	93,732	77,015	16,717	53,233	37,624	40,499	0	13,507
1993	99,646	81,922	17,724	56,325	40,004	43,321	0	16,288

	Public facilities							
	Total	Male	Female	White	Black	Nonwhite	Unreported ethnicity	Hispanic
	Ec410	Ec411	Ec412	Ec413	Ec414	Ec415	Ec416	Ec417 [3]
Year	Number	Number	Number	Number	Number	Number	Number	Number
1956	32,968	24,628	8,340	20,182	—	10,509	2,277	—
1958	35,913	27,110	8,803	—	—	—	—	—
1962	38,725	30,288	8,437	—	—	—	—	—
1963	38,468	29,996	8,472	—	—	—	—	—
1964	44,136	34,881	9,255	—	—	—	—	—
1966	50,749	39,963	10,786	—	—	—	—	—
1968	53,735	35,773 [4]	9,427 [4]	—	—	—	—	—
1969	50,783	—	—	—	—	—	—	—
1970	49,811	— [5]	— [5]	—	—	—	—	—
1971	54,729	41,781	12,948	—	—	—	—	—
1973	45,694	35,057	10,637	—	—	—	—	—
1974	44,922	34,783	10,139	—	—	—	—	—
1975	46,980	37,926	9,054	—	—	—	—	—
1977	44,096	36,921	7,175	27,963	14,865	15,910	223	4,009
1979	43,234	37,167	6,067	26,053	13,752	14,702	2,479	4,395
1983	48,701	42,182	6,519	27,805	18,020	19,124	1,772	5,727
1985	49,322	42,549	6,773	29,969	18,269	19,353	0	6,551
1987	53,503	46,272	7,231	31,103	21,057	22,400	0	7,887
1989	56,123	49,443	6,680	30,705	24,003	25,418	0	8,671
1991	57,542	51,214	6,328	29,869	25,773	27,673	0	10,371
1993	60,406	53,932	6,474	31,547	26,644	28,859	0	12,569

Notes appear at end of table

(continued)

TABLE Ec402–425   Juveniles in public or private facilities for juvenile delinquents, by sex, race, and ethnicity: 1956–1993   Continued

	Private facilities							
	Total	Male	Female	White	Black	Nonwhite	Unreported ethnicity	Hispanic
	Ec418	Ec419	Ec420	Ec421	Ec422	Ec423	Ec424	Ec425 [3]
Year	Number	Number	Number	Number	Number	Number	Number	Number
1956	—	—	—	—	—	—	—	—
1958	—	—	—	—	—	—	—	—
1962	—	—	—	—	—	—	—	—
1963	—	—	—	—	—	—	—	—
1964	—	—	—	—	—	—	—	—
1966	—	—	—	—	—	—	—	—
1968	—	—	—	—	—	—	—	—
1969	—	—	—	—	—	—	—	—
1970	—	—	—	—	—	—	—	—
1971	—	—	—	—	—	—	—	—
1973	—	—	—	—	—	—	—	—
1974	31,749	22,104	9,645	—	—	—	—	—
1975	27,290	19,152	8,138	—	—	—	—	—
1977	29,070	20,387	8,683	21,917	—	7,153	0	2,096
1979	28,688	20,512	8,176	21,654	5,843	7,034	0	1,906
1983	31,390	22,242	9,148	22,377	7,822	8,738	275	2,117
1985	34,080	23,844	10,236	23,999	9,204	10,081	0	2,510
1987	38,143	26,339	11,804	26,839	10,357	11,304	0	2,812
1989	37,822	26,602	11,220	25,696	11,076	12,126	0	3,082
1991	36,190	25,801	10,389	23,364	11,851	12,826	0	3,136
1993	39,240	27,990	11,250	24,778	13,360	14,462	0	3,719

[1] In 1971, coverage was extended to include public facilities that served children awaiting court action, as well as those already adjudicated, thereby including detention centers and shelters.

[2] In 1973, coverage was extended to private facilities.

[3] Hispanics may be of any race.

[4] The gender breakdown is limited to residents of training schools; males comprised approximately 65 percent of the 3,720 residents of diagnostic centers and 99 percent of the 4,815 residents of forestry camps.

[5] The gender breakdown is limited to percentage distributions; males comprised 77 percent of the 42,371 children in public training schools, 73 percent of the 2,316 children in reception and diagnostic centers, and 88 percent of the 5,124 in forestry camps.

Sources

U.S. Department of Health, Education, and Welfare, "Statistics on Public Institutions for Delinquent Children: 1956," Children's Bureau Statistical Series, number 48 (1958); U.S. Department of Health, Education, and Welfare, "Statistics on Public Institutions for Delinquent Children: 1958," Children's Bureau Statistical Series, number 59 (1960); U.S. Department of Health, Education, and Welfare, "Statistics on Public Institutions for Delinquent Children: 1962," Children's Bureau Statistical Series, number 70 (1963); U.S. Department of Health, Education, and Welfare, "Statistics on Public Institutions for Delinquent Children: 1963," Children's Bureau Statistical Series, number 78 (1964); U.S. Department of Health, Education, and Welfare, "Statistics on Public Institutions for Delinquent Children: 1966," Children's Bureau Statistical Series, number 89 (1967); U.S. Department of Health, Education, and Welfare, Office of Juvenile Delinquency and Youth Development, "Statistics on Public Institutions for Delinquent Children: 1968," Statistical Series number 96 (1970); U.S. Department of Health, Education, and Welfare, National Center for Social Statistics, "Statistics on Public Institutions for Delinquent Children: 1970," NCSS Report PIDC-1970 (1971); National Criminal Justice Information and Statistics Service, "Children in Custody: A Report of the Juvenile Detention and Correctional Facility Census of 1971" (1975); National Criminal Justice Information and Statistics Service, "Children in Custody: A Report of the Juvenile Detention and Correctional Facility Census of 1973," number SD-JD-2F (1977); U.S. Bureau of Justice Statistics, "Children in Custody, 1975–85: Census of Public and Private Juvenile Detention, Correctional, and Shelter Facilities, 1975, 1977,

1979, 1983, and 1985," NCJ-114065 (1989); 1987–1993 data were compiled by the editor from data and codebooks available online at the National Archive of Criminal Justice Data, at the Inter-university Consortium for Political and Social Research.

Documentation

Following a preliminary study in 1953 (U.S. Department of Health, Education, and Welfare, "Some Facts about Public State Training Schools for Juvenile Delinquents," Children's Bureau Statistical Series, number 33, 1956), the Children's Bureau of the U.S. Department of Health, Education, and Welfare began a series of quasi-annual surveys of public facilities for adjudicated delinquent children. This was taken over by the Law Enforcement Assistance Administration (later, the Bureau of Justice Statistics) in 1971, as a census of public juvenile detention, correctional, and shelter facilities, with data collection carried out by the Bureau of the Census. This was called the "children in custody" series. In 1974, private juvenile facilities were added. The series became biennial in 1975.

Institutions for delinquent children, also known as training schools, are defined as a specialized children's institution. Public institutions operate under public auspices, serving delinquent children committed to them by juvenile courts, and are intended to provide primarily long-term treatment. They include forestry camps and diagnostic and reception centers, but until 1971 they excluded detention homes that provide short-term care for juveniles pending court disposition. They exclude institutions or camps used primarily for young adult offenders; however, public state-run facilities with greater than 1 percent juvenile offenders, or who indicated authority to hold juvenile offenders, are included in the children in custody series. Private facilities are operated under private auspices. Some children held there are committed to them by the courts as delinquents, but others are referred by parents or social agencies for delinquent behavior. A distinguishing factor between private and public training schools is that, by their administrative policy, the former can control their selection and intake.

The survey or census effective date has varied. The first survey's count was as of December 31, 1956. Thereafter, through 1975, the date was June 30. The 1977 and 1979 Censuses reverted to the December 31 date. The 1983 and 1985 Censuses were dated February 1. The dates for the 1987, 1989, 1991, and 1993 Censuses were February 2, February 15 (twice), and February 16.

VICTIMIZATION AND DELINQUENCY OF HIGH SCHOOL SENIORS

Douglas Eckberg

TABLE Ec426–445 Percentage of high school seniors experiencing violent victimization in the past year: 1976–1998

Contributed by Douglas Eckberg

	Injured with a weapon					Threatened with (but not injured by) a weapon				
	Zero times	Once	Twice	Three or four times	Five or more times	Zero times	Once	Twice	Three or four times	Five or more times
	Ec426	Ec427	Ec428	Ec429	Ec430	Ec431	Ec432	Ec433	Ec434	Ec435
Year	Percent	Percent	Percent	Percent	Percent	Percent	Percent	Percent	Percent	Percent
1976	95.0	3.4	0.9	0.2	0.4	84.0	9.9	3.2	1.6	1.2
1977	95.5	3.2	0.8	0.3	0.3	84.2	9.7	3.0	1.7	1.4
1978	95.4	3.1	0.7	0.6	0.2	83.7	10.0	3.6	1.8	1.0
1979	95.1	3.7	0.8	0.3	0.1	83.7	11.1	2.7	1.6	0.9
1980	95.4	3.5	0.5	0.3	0.2	83.4	10.6	3.2	1.6	1.2
1981	95.1	3.7	0.7	0.3	0.2	82.1	12.1	3.3	1.4	1.1
1982	95.2	3.5	0.8	0.3	0.2	83.7	10.5	3.3	1.5	1.0
1983	94.8	3.2	1.3	0.4	0.3	82.7	10.8	3.2	1.9	1.4
1984	94.8	3.7	1.0	0.3	0.3	83.4	10.3	3.2	1.7	1.4
1985	95.2	3.1	1.1	0.3	0.3	83.8	10.0	3.7	1.4	1.1
1986	95.3	3.3	0.9	0.3	0.2	84.2	10.4	3.3	1.1	1.0
1987	95.0	3.8	0.7	0.2	0.2	83.2	10.6	3.2	1.6	1.4
1988	95.5	3.0	0.9	0.4	0.2	82.8	10.8	3.5	1.7	1.3
1989	94.7	3.9	0.8	0.3	0.3	81.3	12.2	3.1	1.7	1.7
1990	94.4	3.7	1.1	0.4	0.4	81.9	10.4	3.9	2.0	1.8
1991	94.5	4.1	0.7	0.4	0.3	81.4	11.1	3.9	2.0	1.6
1992	94.3	4.0	1.4	0.1	0.2	80.7	10.9	4.0	2.4	2.1
1993	93.9	3.6	1.4	0.7	0.4	79.6	11.5	3.8	2.8	2.3
1994	94.9	3.5	1.1	0.3	0.2	80.9	11.3	3.7	2.4	1.7
1995	95.0	3.0	1.1	0.5	0.3	82.1	9.3	4.5	2.2	1.8
1996	95.0	2.9	0.9	0.5	0.6	81.0	10.7	4.6	1.9	1.9
1997	94.9	2.8	1.1	0.8	0.4	81.8	11.1	3.3	2.3	1.5
1998	95.0	3.0	1.0	0.6	0.4	82.3	9.8	4.2	1.7	2.0

	Injured on purpose, without use of a weapon					Threatened with injury (but not injured) by an unarmed person				
	Zero times	Once	Twice	Three or four times	Five or more times	Zero times	Once	Twice	Three or four times	Five or more times
	Ec436	Ec437	Ec438	Ec439	Ec440	Ec441	Ec442	Ec443	Ec444	Ec445
Year	Percent	Percent	Percent	Percent	Percent	Percent	Percent	Percent	Percent	Percent
1976	85.2	8.7	3.2	1.7	1.2	72.9	14.3	4.7	3.9	4.3
1977	85.8	7.9	3.8	1.2	1.3	75.0	11.3	5.6	3.7	4.3
1978	84.6	9.5	2.8	1.8	1.3	72.9	12.5	5.8	4.4	4.3
1979	86.2	8.3	3.0	1.2	1.2	71.9	14.3	5.4	4.1	4.2
1980	84.8	8.7	3.3	2.0	1.3	72.3	12.7	6.5	3.7	4.9
1981	85.7	8.9	2.8	1.5	1.1	72.4	13.0	6.5	4.0	4.2
1982	84.9	9.2	3.1	1.5	1.3	71.7	14.5	5.5	3.7	4.6
1983	83.6	9.5	3.8	1.7	1.3	70.8	14.5	5.4	4.2	5.1
1984	83.4	9.6	3.4	2.2	1.4	72.4	13.3	5.3	4.5	4.4
1985	83.6	9.4	3.5	2.0	1.6	71.8	13.3	6.2	4.0	4.7
1986	84.4	10.1	2.9	1.6	1.1	71.7	15.2	5.8	4.0	3.3
1987	82.8	10.5	3.5	2.0	1.3	70.3	14.1	6.3	4.6	4.7
1988	84.1	9.2	3.2	1.3	2.1	69.3	14.7	7.1	4.8	4.1
1989	84.2	9.6	3.0	1.8	1.4	69.6	14.2	6.2	4.4	5.5
1990	83.3	10.1	3.3	2.0	1.3	66.8	15.3	8.0	4.7	5.2
1991	83.8	9.6	3.1	1.9	1.6	69.1	13.5	6.8	4.9	5.7
1992	84.0	9.3	3.1	2.1	1.5	69.3	13.7	6.2	5.3	5.4
1993	83.6	9.2	3.4	2.0	1.8	69.0	13.1	7.6	4.2	6.1
1994	84.9	9.3	2.7	1.7	1.4	70.1	13.2	6.8	4.5	5.5
1995	84.1	9.0	3.7	1.8	1.4	70.2	12.8	6.4	4.5	6.1
1996	84.4	7.9	3.2	2.6	1.9	69.9	13.4	6.2	4.0	6.5
1997	85.4	7.8	2.7	2.1	2.0	71.7	13.5	5.3	3.8	5.8
1998	85.3	8.6	2.6	2.2	1.3	71.5	12.4	6.4	4.1	5.5

(continued)

TABLE Ec426–445   Percentage of high school seniors experiencing violent victimization in the past year: 1976–1998
Continued

Sources

1976–1984: U.S. Bureau of Justice Statistics, *Sourcebook of Criminal Justice Statistics 1985* (1987), Table 3.57; 1985–1996: U.S. Bureau of Justice Statistics, *Sourcebook of Criminal Justice Statistics 1996* (1997), Table 3.35; 1997–1998: U.S. Bureau of Justice Statistics, *Sourcebook of Criminal Justice Statistics, 1998* (1999), Table 3.41; originally from Lloyd D. Johnson, Jerald G. Bachman, and Patrick M. O'Malley, *Monitoring the Future* (1975 through 1998 annual reports), and data supplied by the Monitoring the Future Project (Institute for Social Research, University of Michigan).

Documentation

Data are gathered via surveys of multistage, random samples of high school seniors in public and private schools throughout the continental United States. Sample sizes vary, averaging between 2,500 and 3,000. The percentages reported are based on weighted cases.

Because of small sample sizes, results for racial and ethnic groups other than blacks and whites are not shown in tables that provide such breakdowns.

The wording of the measures used in Tables Ec426–950 is shown here.

Tables Ec426–445 and Ec461–540, violent victimization. (1) "During the last twelve months, how often has someone injured you with a weapon (like a knife, gun, or club)?" (2) "During the last twelve months, how often has someone threatened you with a weapon, but not actually injured you?" (3) "During the last twelve months, how often has someone injured you on purpose, without using a weapon?" (4) "During the last twelve months, how often has an unarmed person threatened you with injury, but not actually injured you?"

Tables Ec446–460 and Ec541–600, property crime victimization. (1) "During the last twelve months, how often has something of yours (worth under $50) been stolen?" (2) "During the last twelve months, how often has something of yours (worth over $50) been stolen?" (3) "During the last twelve months, how often has someone deliberately damaged your property (your car, clothing, etc.)?"

Tables Ec601–625 and Ec671–770, violent delinquency. (1) "During the last twelve months, how often have you hit an instructor or supervisor?" (2) "During the last twelve months, how often have you gotten into a serious fight in school or at work?" (3) "During the last twelve months, how often have you taken part in a fight where a group of your friends were against another group?" (4) "During the last twelve months, how often have you hurt someone badly enough to need bandages or a doctor?" (5) "During the last twelve months, how often have you used a knife or gun or some other thing (like a club) to get something from a person?"

Tables Ec626–650 and Ec771–870, involvement in property crime. (1) "During the last twelve months, how often have you taken something not belonging to you (worth under $50)?" (2) "During the last twelve months, how often have you taken something not belonging to you (worth over $50)?" (3) "During the last twelve months, how often have you taken something from a store without paying for it?" (4) "During the last twelve months, how often have you taken a car that didn't belong to someone in your family without permission of the owner?" (5) "During the last twelve months, how often have you taken part of a car without permission of the owner?"

Tables Ec651–670 and Ec871–950, involvement in trespassing and vandalism. (1) "During the last twelve months, how often have you gone into some house or building when you weren't supposed to be there?" (2) "During the last twelve months, how often have you set fire to someone's property on purpose?" (3) "During the last twelve months, how often have damaged school property on purpose?" (4) "During the last twelve months, how often have you damaged property at work on purpose?"

TABLE Ec446–460   Percentage of high school seniors experiencing property crime victimization in the past year: 1976–1998

Contributed by Douglas Eckberg

	Experienced a theft of less than fifty dollars					Experienced a theft of more than fifty dollars					Experienced vandalism of property				
	Zero times	Once	Twice	Three or four times	Five or more times	Zero times	Once	Twice	Three or four times	Five or more times	Zero times	Once	Twice	Three or four times	Five or more times
	Ec446	Ec447	Ec448	Ec449	Ec450	Ec451	Ec452	Ec453	Ec454	Ec455	Ec456	Ec457	Ec458	Ec459	Ec460
Year	Percent	Percent	Percent	Percent	Percent	Percent	Percent	Percent	Percent	Percent	Percent	Percent	Percent	Percent	Percent
1976	55.4	25.8	10.8	6.3	1.7	87.8	9.3	2.2	0.4	0.2	69.2	19.0	7.6	3.4	0.9
1977	58.6	23.7	10.5	4.9	2.4	87.7	9.8	1.4	0.7	0.4	70.1	18.2	7.2	3.3	1.2
1978	57.1	24.4	11.4	5.2	1.9	86.7	10.5	2.1	0.6	0.1	67.9	19.1	8.3	3.7	1.1
1979	55.6	24.8	11.4	5.8	2.3	84.8	11.6	2.5	0.8	0.4	65.1	21.4	8.6	3.5	1.4
1980	56.1	24.4	11.9	5.3	2.4	84.7	12.0	2.4	0.6	0.3	64.7	20.9	9.6	3.3	1.5
1981	56.3	24.9	11.5	5.1	2.2	83.3	12.6	2.8	1.0	0.3	65.8	21.2	8.7	2.8	1.5
1982	54.8	27.4	11.2	4.5	2.1	83.8	12.7	2.1	1.1	0.4	66.4	21.1	7.8	3.5	1.3
1983	52.4	27.2	12.2	6.4	1.8	83.7	12.2	2.9	0.9	0.3	66.9	19.9	8.8	3.1	1.2
1984	56.0	25.8	10.9	5.4	2.0	83.6	12.0	2.8	1.2	0.4	69.1	18.7	6.8	3.6	1.7
1985	55.6	26.9	10.6	5.0	1.9	85.1	10.7	3.1	0.9	0.3	68.9	19.4	7.6	3.0	1.1
1986	52.7	28.6	11.2	5.4	2.1	82.5	13.5	2.6	1.0	0.3	67.9	21.7	7.0	2.5	0.9
1987	52.2	28.4	11.5	5.2	2.6	79.7	15.2	3.2	1.3	0.7	66.2	21.5	8.4	3.0	0.9
1988	52.5	28.5	11.5	5.3	2.3	78.0	15.9	3.8	1.5	0.7	65.7	21.1	8.6	3.5	1.1
1989	56.3	26.2	10.6	4.7	2.2	79.4	15.6	3.0	1.3	0.6	66.7	21.3	7.8	2.9	1.3
1990	54.6	24.8	12.2	6.0	2.4	77.9	15.2	4.1	2.0	0.9	66.3	19.5	8.9	4.0	1.3
1991	55.4	26.2	10.9	5.2	2.3	77.2	15.7	4.8	1.7	0.6	65.8	21.6	7.7	3.6	1.3
1992	55.4	27.0	10.6	5.0	2.0	77.5	15.3	4.6	1.9	0.7	66.4	19.8	9.4	3.4	0.9
1993	55.3	25.6	11.0	5.7	2.4	75.1	17.2	4.0	2.6	1.0	66.1	19.1	9.2	4.2	1.4
1994	56.6	25.3	11.0	5.1	2.1	76.8	16.8	4.1	1.6	0.7	67.0	19.6	8.5	3.8	1.2
1995	55.4	25.7	10.7	5.2	3.0	76.0	16.4	4.7	2.1	0.7	66.4	19.5	8.6	3.7	1.8
1996	52.5	27.0	11.0	6.4	3.1	73.3	17.0	5.7	2.5	1.5	65.6	20.9	8.8	3.0	1.6
1997	54.0	26.8	11.0	5.3	3.0	74.2	17.2	5.5	2.3	0.8	67.4	19.9	8.2	3.4	1.1
1998	54.7	25.6	11.1	5.9	2.6	73.4	17.3	5.5	2.3	1.5	67.5	19.3	7.6	3.8	1.8

Sources

1976–1984: U.S. Bureau of Justice Statistics, *Sourcebook of Criminal Justice Statistics 1985* (1987), Table 3.57; 1985–1996: U.S. Bureau of Justice Statistics, *Sourcebook of Criminal Justice Statistics, 1996* (1997), Table 3.35; 1997–1998: U.S. Bureau of Justice Statistics, *Sourcebook of Criminal Justice Statistics 1998* (1999), Table 3.41; originally from Lloyd D. Johnson, Jerald G. Bachman, and Patrick M. O'Malley, *Monitoring the Future* (1975 through 1998 annual reports), and data supplied by the Monitoring the Future Project (Institute for Social Research, University of Michigan).

Documentation

See the text for Table Ec426–445 for a description of the source and the wording of the measures.

TABLE Ec461–540 Percentage of high school seniors experiencing violent victimization in the past year, by race and sex: 1976–1998

Contributed by Douglas Eckberg

	Whites									
	Injured with a weapon					Threatened with (but not injured by) a weapon				
	Zero times	Once	Twice	Three or four times	Five or more times	Zero times	Once	Twice	Three or four times	Five or more times
	Ec461	Ec462	Ec463	Ec464	Ec465	Ec466	Ec467	Ec468	Ec469	Ec470
Year	Percent	Percent	Percent	Percent	Percent	Percent	Percent	Percent	Percent	Percent
1976	96.3	2.7	0.5	0.2	0.3	85.6	8.8	3.1	1.3	1.2
1977	96.8	2.4	0.5	0.2	0.2	85.5	9.0	2.6	1.8	1.1
1978	96.0	2.9	0.4	0.6	0.2	84.6	9.1	3.9	1.7	0.7
1979	95.5	3.4	0.7	0.3	0.1	84.8	10.2	2.6	1.6	0.9
1980	96.0	3.2	0.4	0.2	0.2	83.9	10.1	3.2	1.8	1.0
1981	95.6	3.5	0.5	0.3	0.1	83.8	10.6	3.0	1.5	1.1
1982	95.8	3.0	0.7	0.3	0.2	85.2	9.4	2.9	1.6	0.9
1983	95.3	2.8	1.3	0.3	0.2	84.1	10.2	2.9	1.8	1.0
1984	95.6	3.3	0.6	0.3	0.2	84.8	9.5	3.2	1.5	1.0
1985	95.4	3.0	1.1	0.3	0.2	85.7	8.7	3.2	1.2	1.2
1986	96.1	2.6	0.9	0.2	0.2	85.8	9.8	2.8	0.7	0.9
1987	95.8	3.4	0.5	0.2	0.2	84.4	9.8	3.2	1.6	1.0
1988	96.3	2.7	0.7	0.4	(Z)	84.0	10.7	3.2	1.2	0.9
1989	95.3	3.6	0.7	0.2	0.3	82.6	11.5	2.7	1.8	1.4
1990	95.3	3.1	1.0	0.3	0.4	82.6	10.1	3.7	2.1	1.6
1991	95.1	3.7	0.4	0.3	0.4	83.5	10.3	3.3	1.3	1.6
1992	96.0	3.0	0.8	0.1	0.1	83.1	9.9	3.5	2.0	1.5
1993	95.0	3.1	1.4	0.4	0.2	81.0	11.0	3.4	2.5	2.2
1994	96.7	2.5	0.6	0.2	0.1	82.6	10.4	3.5	2.2	1.3
1995	96.1	2.4	0.9	0.4	0.2	84.6	8.5	3.8	1.8	1.3
1996	95.8	2.9	0.7	0.3	0.3	82.9	9.8	4.8	1.5	1.1
1997	96.3	2.2	0.8	0.6	0.1	83.9	9.8	2.5	2.3	1.5
1998	96.1	2.4	0.8	0.5	0.2	83.6	8.9	4.1	1.6	1.8

	Whites									
	Injured on purpose, without use of a weapon					Threatened with injury (but not injured) by an unarmed person				
	Zero times	Once	Twice	Three or four times	Five or more times	Zero times	Once	Twice	Three or four times	Five or more times
	Ec471	Ec472	Ec473	Ec474	Ec475	Ec476	Ec477	Ec478	Ec479	Ec480
Year	Percent	Percent	Percent	Percent	Percent	Percent	Percent	Percent	Percent	Percent
1976	85.5	8.7	3.2	1.4	1.2	72.2	14.2	4.9	4.2	4.5
1977	86.2	7.5	3.9	1.3	1.2	74.9	11.0	5.6	4.0	4.5
1978	84.8	9.2	2.7	1.9	1.4	72.6	12.3	5.9	4.9	4.4
1979	86.2	8.2	3.2	1.2	1.2	71.7	14.4	5.6	4.2	4.1
1980	84.2	8.9	3.3	2.2	1.4	71.5	12.6	6.6	4.1	5.2
1981	85.8	8.7	2.8	1.5	1.2	71.0	13.1	7.1	4.3	4.5
1982	85.2	8.8	3.2	1.5	1.2	70.7	14.4	5.9	4.1	4.8
1983	83.0	9.9	3.9	1.8	1.3	70.2	14.6	5.5	4.5	5.1
1984	83.4	9.7	3.4	2.3	1.2	72.4	13.3	5.1	4.7	4.4
1985	83.6	9.3	3.6	1.9	1.6	71.1	13.3	6.6	4.2	4.8
1986	83.9	10.7	3.1	1.3	1.0	71.3	15.4	5.9	4.1	3.3
1987	81.9	11.0	3.8	2.0	1.2	69.4	14.3	6.6	4.9	4.8
1988	84.1	9.4	3.2	1.3	1.9	68.9	14.8	7.4	4.8	4.1
1989	83.7	10.5	2.6	1.9	1.4	68.8	14.8	6.1	5.0	5.4
1990	83.0	10.2	3.5	2.1	1.2	65.1	15.6	8.6	5.1	5.6
1991	83.7	9.7	3.2	1.9	1.5	68.6	12.7	7.0	5.2	6.4
1992	83.9	9.8	3.2	1.9	1.2	68.0	13.5	7.2	5.6	5.7
1993	83.5	10.0	3.4	1.3	1.8	67.5	13.7	8.4	4.4	6.1
1994	85.5	9.0	2.7	1.6	1.2	69.2	14.2	6.3	5.0	5.3
1995	85.3	8.1	3.6	1.6	1.4	70.4	13.0	6.9	3.7	6.0
1996	86.0	6.7	3.4	2.4	1.6	69.0	14.6	6.5	3.7	6.1
1997	85.5	8.0	2.7	2.0	1.7	70.5	14.0	5.1	3.7	6.7
1998	86.0	7.8	2.8	2.3	1.2	70.3	12.3	7.3	4.4	5.7

TABLE Ec461–540   Percentage of high school seniors experiencing violent victimization in the past year, by race and sex: 1976–1998 *Continued*

Blacks

	Injured with a weapon					Threatened with (but not injured by) a weapon				
	Zero times	Once	Twice	Three or four times	Five or more times	Zero times	Once	Twice	Three or four times	Five or more times
	Ec481	Ec482	Ec483	Ec484	Ec485	Ec486	Ec487	Ec488	Ec489	Ec490
Year	Percent	Percent	Percent	Percent	Percent	Percent	Percent	Percent	Percent	Percent
1976	91.5	6.6	1.5	0.3	0.0	77.6	13.9	4.2	2.7	1.5
1977	92.6	5.9	0.7	0.2	0.5	80.9	13.7	3.7	1.2	0.5
1978	94.2	3.6	1.7	0.7	0.0	80.0	13.2	2.9	1.7	1.9
1979	94.8	4.3	1.1	0.0	0.0	80.8	14.0	2.9	1.7	0.6
1980	94.7	4.2	0.5	0.5	0.2	82.7	11.8	3.0	0.9	1.6
1981	93.9	3.9	2.0	0.2	0.0	75.6	16.8	5.4	1.1	1.1
1982	94.8	4.1	0.7	0.3	0.2	76.6	16.1	5.3	0.6	1.4
1983	93.2	4.4	1.4	0.5	0.5	76.5	15.1	4.7	1.5	2.2
1984	94.3	4.2	1.3	0.2	0.0	77.9	14.7	4.2	1.8	1.5
1985	94.0	4.9	0.7	0.5	0.0	74.9	16.5	5.9	2.3	0.4
1986	94.8	4.1	0.8	0.4	0.0	78.4	12.9	4.8	2.1	1.7
1987	91.8	7.1	0.5	0.4	0.2	75.0	16.8	3.8	1.2	3.2
1988	92.7	4.7	1.8	0.6	0.1	78.0	12.6	4.7	2.6	2.0
1989	94.0	4.9	0.3	0.6	0.2	73.9	16.5	5.8	0.7	3.0
1990	94.4	4.3	0.8	0.3	0.2	79.7	11.4	4.1	2.4	2.4
1991	92.1	5.7	1.8	0.0	0.4	71.2	15.7	6.9	3.8	2.4
1992	93.3	4.9	1.6	0.2	0.1	74.1	14.0	4.5	3.7	3.7
1993	93.6	3.9	0.7	1.4	0.4	76.0	14.6	5.0	2.8	1.6
1994	87.6	8.4	2.6	1.3	0.1	71.9	14.3	5.0	4.6	4.2
1995	93.2	4.7	1.8	0.0	0.3	73.2	12.2	5.6	4.7	4.3
1996	92.1	3.8	2.2	1.2	0.7	79.3	10.8	3.1	5.0	1.9
1997	91.5	4.8	2.4	0.5	0.9	74.9	15.0	6.4	2.0	1.7
1998	94.2	3.9	1.5	0.3	0.1	79.2	10.9	5.4	3.0	1.4

Blacks

	Injured on purpose, without use of a weapon					Threatened with injury (but not injured) by an unarmed person				
	Zero times	Once	Twice	Three or four times	Five or more times	Zero times	Once	Twice	Three or four times	Five or more times
	Ec491	Ec492	Ec493	Ec494	Ec495	Ec496	Ec497	Ec498	Ec499	Ec500
Year	Percent	Percent	Percent	Percent	Percent	Percent	Percent	Percent	Percent	Percent
1976	84.8	9.1	3.0	1.8	1.2	74.9	14.1	4.9	3.1	3.4
1977	86.0	8.6	3.2	1.0	1.0	77.3	11.3	6.2	3.0	2.2
1978	84.9	9.6	3.1	1.2	1.0	75.8	14.1	6.2	1.9	1.9
1979	87.6	9.8	1.4	0.9	0.3	76.8	13.2	3.4	3.7	3.2
1980	89.1	6.7	2.3	1.4	0.5	77.6	11.3	6.0	1.4	3.5
1981	87.4	8.7	3.1	0.9	0.2	75.8	13.5	3.9	3.1	3.7
1982	85.7	10.1	2.3	0.6	1.3	74.2	14.8	6.1	0.9	3.9
1983	86.1	8.2	3.6	1.0	1.1	71.8	17.5	4.5	1.9	4.3
1984	86.0	9.5	2.5	0.6	1.5	74.1	13.5	6.2	3.1	3.0
1985	86.5	7.5	3.4	0.8	1.8	75.5	12.0	3.9	4.5	4.1
1986	88.7	8.3	1.5	1.3	0.3	72.4	15.2	5.1	3.7	3.7
1987	88.3	9.4	0.5	1.0	0.8	71.9	14.9	5.0	4.5	3.7
1988	87.3	6.7	3.6	1.0	1.3	73.3	14.2	5.4	2.8	4.3
1989	89.5	6.0	2.8	0.8	1.0	70.1	14.2	5.5	3.8	6.4
1990	83.9	11.4	1.8	0.8	2.2	69.4	17.2	7.6	3.4	2.4
1991	83.1	9.3	2.3	2.6	2.7	65.7	16.1	6.7	5.7	5.7
1992	87.3	6.6	2.5	1.2	2.3	73.8	12.6	3.0	4.2	6.4
1993	85.6	6.9	2.8	3.2	1.6	72.3	11.3	6.6	5.2	4.6
1994	80.7	11.4	3.0	3.4	1.6	69.0	8.6	9.3	3.7	9.6
1995	81.4	9.6	5.0	3.4	0.6	68.4	13.6	5.6	7.6	4.8
1996	79.3	12.8	2.3	4.6	1.1	67.6	13.7	9.0	3.9	5.8
1997	85.7	6.4	2.9	2.8	2.2	75.7	10.6	6.9	3.2	3.7
1998	88.5	7.4	2.3	1.6	0.2	76.4	10.4	6.8	2.6	3.8

(continued)

TABLE Ec461–540   Percentage of high school seniors experiencing violent victimization in the past year, by race and sex: 1976–1998 *Continued*

Males

	Injured with a weapon					Threatened with (but not injured by) a weapon				
	Zero times	Once	Twice	Three or four times	Five or more times	Zero times	Once	Twice	Three or four times	Five or more times
	Ec501	Ec502	Ec503	Ec504	Ec505	Ec506	Ec507	Ec508	Ec509	Ec510
Year	Percent	Percent	Percent	Percent	Percent	Percent	Percent	Percent	Percent	Percent
1976	92.5	5.5	1.3	0.4	0.3	78.3	12.3	4.9	2.3	2.1
1977	93.5	4.3	1.4	0.4	0.5	78.9	12.3	4.0	2.6	2.2
1978	92.4	4.9	1.2	1.0	0.3	77.4	12.8	5.8	2.0	2.0
1979	92.1	5.9	1.2	0.6	0.2	77.5	14.9	3.8	2.6	1.1
1980	92.9	5.5	0.8	0.4	0.4	76.8	14.1	4.7	2.3	2.1
1981	92.8	5.5	0.9	0.6	0.2	74.8	16.5	4.8	2.1	1.8
1982	93.0	5.1	1.1	0.3	0.4	78.5	13.4	4.9	1.5	1.7
1983	92.2	4.8	1.9	0.6	0.6	77.1	14.0	4.2	2.8	1.9
1984	92.4	5.3	1.5	0.4	0.4	77.2	13.9	4.8	2.3	1.7
1985	93.3	4.2	1.7	0.5	0.4	78.9	12.6	4.5	2.2	1.8
1986	93.3	4.6	1.2	0.5	0.4	79.4	12.6	4.9	1.7	1.4
1987	92.5	5.6	1.3	0.4	0.3	76.7	14.4	4.7	2.2	2.0
1988	92.7	5.0	1.3	0.7	0.4	76.7	14.1	5.0	2.1	2.1
1989	91.8	5.6	1.4	0.6	0.6	74.8	16.2	4.5	2.2	2.3
1990	91.2	5.9	1.8	0.6	0.5	76.1	13.6	5.3	3.0	2.0
1991	92.0	5.9	1.0	0.7	0.5	75.2	14.0	5.4	2.9	2.6
1992	90.8	6.2	2.4	0.3	0.3	73.8	13.3	6.3	3.7	2.9
1993	91.3	4.6	2.6	0.9	0.6	72.7	14.0	4.8	4.8	3.7
1994	93.1	5.1	1.4	0.3	(Z)	74.3	13.4	6.2	3.7	2.4
1995	93.0	4.2	1.8	0.6	0.4	74.4	12.7	6.4	3.4	3.1
1996	92.0	4.8	1.4	1.1	0.8	74.6	12.6	7.3	2.9	2.6
1997	92.4	3.8	1.8	1.4	0.5	74.0	14.7	5.1	3.8	2.4
1998	92.7	4.1	1.4	1.1	0.7	75.6	12.5	6.0	2.6	3.3

Males

	Injured on purpose, without use of a weapon					Threatened with injury (but not injured) by an unarmed person				
	Zero times	Once	Twice	Three or four times	Five or more times	Zero times	Once	Twice	Three or four times	Five or more times
	Ec511	Ec512	Ec513	Ec514	Ec515	Ec516	Ec517	Ec518	Ec519	Ec520
Year	Percent	Percent	Percent	Percent	Percent	Percent	Percent	Percent	Percent	Percent
1976	83.1	10.1	3.7	1.9	1.3	64.6	17.2	6.7	5.8	5.7
1977	84.6	9.2	3.8	1.0	1.4	69.1	13.5	6.5	4.7	6.2
1978	83.6	10.5	3.5	1.3	1.1	65.4	14.1	7.8	6.2	6.4
1979	84.6	9.9	3.1	1.4	1.1	63.9	17.3	6.6	5.8	6.4
1980	83.0	10.1	4.0	1.5	1.4	63.4	15.6	9.1	4.8	7.0
1981	84.4	9.9	3.3	1.4	1.0	64.8	14.9	8.8	5.3	6.3
1982	82.7	10.8	3.6	1.6	1.3	63.9	17.3	7.3	5.1	6.5
1983	82.5	10.6	3.6	2.1	1.2	63.4	17.1	7.5	5.1	7.0
1984	81.8	9.9	4.0	2.5	1.7	65.4	14.6	6.9	6.1	6.9
1985	82.9	9.5	3.5	2.2	1.8	65.1	15.2	8.1	5.4	6.2
1986	83.8	10.4	3.2	1.3	1.3	65.6	16.9	7.4	5.3	4.8
1987	81.2	11.9	4.0	1.9	0.9	65.2	14.9	7.4	6.5	6.0
1988	83.4	9.5	3.8	1.2	2.1	62.1	17.8	8.8	5.9	5.4
1989	84.6	10.0	2.9	1.7	0.9	63.1	16.3	7.7	5.4	7.5
1990	83.3	10.9	3.3	1.5	1.0	60.9	16.7	9.9	5.7	6.8
1991	83.2	10.3	3.3	1.7	1.6	62.3	14.5	8.8	5.7	8.7
1992	82.8	10.8	2.8	2.5	1.2	63.4	14.8	8.2	5.7	7.9
1993	82.7	10.6	3.2	1.8	1.7	63.5	14.4	8.7	4.4	9.0
1994	84.1	10.9	2.5	1.5	1.0	63.4	14.7	7.8	6.3	7.7
1995	82.7	9.8	4.1	1.9	1.6	61.9	14.4	8.4	6.2	9.1
1996	82.3	9.7	3.7	2.7	1.6	63.9	15.6	6.0	5.8	8.7
1997	84.7	8.2	3.1	1.9	2.1	64.3	16.6	6.6	4.7	7.8
1998	82.1	11.2	2.7	2.2	1.8	63.1	15.2	7.6	5.6	8.5

TABLE Ec461–540   Percentage of high school seniors experiencing violent victimization in the past year, by race and sex: 1976–1998   *Continued*

	Females									
	Injured with a weapon					Threatened with (but not injured by) a weapon				
	Zero times	Once	Twice	Three or four times	Five or more times	Zero times	Once	Twice	Three or four times	Five or more times
	Ec521	Ec522	Ec523	Ec524	Ec525	Ec526	Ec527	Ec528	Ec529	Ec530
Year	Percent	Percent	Percent	Percent	Percent	Percent	Percent	Percent	Percent	Percent
1976	97.9	1.3	0.4	0.1	0.3	90.2	7.1	1.5	0.8	0.4
1977	98.0	1.5	0.2	0.2	0.1	89.9	6.9	1.9	1.0	0.4
1978	98.5	1.2	0.2	0.1	0.0	89.8	7.0	1.5	1.5	0.2
1979	98.3	1.5	0.1	0.0	0.1	90.3	7.0	1.6	0.6	0.6
1980	98.3	1.3	0.2	0.1	0.1	90.5	6.6	1.8	0.9	0.3
1981	97.6	1.8	0.4	0.1	0.2	89.9	7.2	1.8	0.6	0.5
1982	97.8	1.6	0.5	0.2	0.0	89.1	7.3	1.8	1.4	0.4
1983	97.8	1.2	0.8	0.2	0.1	89.4	7.5	2.0	0.6	0.6
1984	97.7	1.9	0.2	0.2	0.0	90.7	6.2	1.5	0.9	0.6
1985	97.3	2.0	0.5	0.1	0.1	89.2	7.2	2.7	0.5	0.4
1986	97.4	1.9	0.6	0.1	(Z)	89.2	8.1	1.6	0.4	0.7
1987	97.6	2.1	(Z)	0.1	0.2	89.6	6.8	1.9	0.9	0.8
1988	98.2	1.2	0.5	0.1	(Z)	88.9	7.8	1.9	0.9	0.4
1989	97.4	2.2	0.4	(Z)	(Z)	87.4	8.6	1.8	1.1	1.1
1990	98.3	1.3	0.2	0.1	0.2	88.7	7.0	2.1	0.8	1.4
1991	97.2	2.3	0.4	0.1	0.1	87.9	8.2	2.4	1.1	0.5
1992	98.4	1.3	0.3	0.0	0.1	88.3	8.6	1.3	1.0	0.7
1993	97.1	2.1	0.1	0.4	0.3	86.5	8.6	2.9	1.1	0.9
1994	96.9	1.8	0.9	0.2	0.2	87.8	8.6	1.5	1.3	0.9
1995	97.3	1.7	0.4	0.3	0.3	90.4	5.6	2.3	1.0	0.6
1996	98.6	1.1	0.2	0.1	0.1	88.5	8.1	1.7	0.9	0.8
1997	97.8	1.7	0.3	0.1	0.1	89.0	7.9	1.7	0.8	0.7
1998	97.3	1.9	0.6	(Z)	0.2	88.7	7.1	2.6	0.9	0.7

	Females									
	Injured on purpose, without use of a weapon					Threatened with injury (but not injured) by an unarmed person				
	Zero times	Once	Twice	Three or four times	Five or more times	Zero times	Once	Twice	Three or four times	Five or more times
	Ec531	Ec532	Ec533	Ec534	Ec535	Ec536	Ec537	Ec538	Ec539	Ec540
Year	Percent	Percent	Percent	Percent	Percent	Percent	Percent	Percent	Percent	Percent
1976	87.7	6.9	2.8	1.3	1.1	81.3	11.3	2.7	1.9	2.9
1977	87.2	6.4	3.8	1.3	1.3	80.9	8.9	4.6	2.9	2.6
1978	85.8	8.3	2.0	2.3	1.6	80.0	11.0	3.9	2.9	2.1
1979	87.7	6.8	3.0	1.1	1.5	80.2	11.2	4.2	2.3	2.2
1980	86.6	7.2	2.6	2.5	1.1	81.2	9.8	3.7	2.5	2.9
1981	87.1	7.6	2.5	1.5	1.3	79.7	11.2	4.2	2.7	2.2
1982	87.4	7.4	2.6	1.3	1.3	79.4	11.5	3.8	2.3	2.9
1983	85.3	8.2	3.8	1.4	1.3	78.6	12.0	3.4	3.1	2.9
1984	85.7	9.0	2.8	1.6	1.0	80.0	11.7	3.7	2.8	1.8
1985	84.9	8.8	3.3	1.5	1.5	79.1	10.9	4.4	2.6	3.1
1986	85.4	9.5	2.5	1.6	0.9	77.8	13.3	4.4	2.6	1.8
1987	84.5	8.7	3.1	2.2	1.5	75.0	13.2	5.3	3.0	3.4
1988	84.9	8.8	2.6	1.5	2.3	76.7	11.5	5.3	3.6	2.9
1989	84.2	9.1	3.0	1.8	1.8	75.9	12.4	4.9	3.5	3.3
1990	83.1	9.5	3.5	2.5	1.4	73.3	14.1	6.2	3.7	2.8
1991	84.6	8.7	3.0	2.1	1.7	75.9	12.7	4.8	4.0	2.5
1992	86.3	7.5	3.2	1.5	1.6	75.6	12.9	4.5	4.5	2.6
1993	84.9	7.3	3.8	2.0	1.9	74.7	11.6	6.6	3.9	3.1
1994	85.6	8.1	2.7	2.0	1.8	76.5	11.7	5.4	2.9	3.5
1995	85.7	7.7	3.4	1.8	1.3	77.9	11.2	4.9	2.9	3.1
1996	87.0	6.3	2.7	2.3	1.7	76.3	11.7	6.3	2.0	3.7
1997	86.6	7.3	2.2	2.1	1.8	79.0	10.5	4.2	2.7	3.6
1998	88.7	5.9	2.3	2.2	0.9	79.8	9.5	5.4	2.5	2.8

(Z) Less than 0.05 percent.

Sources

1976–1984: U.S Bureau of Justice Statistics, *Sourcebook of Criminal Justice Statistics 1985* (1987), Tables 3.58 and 3.59; 1985–1996: U.S. Bureau of Justice Statistics, *Sourcebook of Criminal Justice Statistics 1996* (1997), Tables 3.36 and 3.37; 1997–1998: U.S. Bureau of Justice Statistics, *Sourcebook of Criminal Justice Statistics 1998* (1999), Tables 3.42 and 3.43; originally from Lloyd D. Johnson, Jerald G. Bachman, and Patrick M. O'Malley, *Monitoring the Future* (1975 through 1998 annual reports), and data supplied by the Monitoring the Future Project (Institute for Social Research, University of Michigan).

Documentation

See the text for Table Ec426–445 for a description of the source and the wording of the measures.

TABLE Ec541–600   Percentage of high school seniors experiencing property crime victimization in the past year, by race and sex: 1976–1998

Contributed by Douglas Eckberg

Whites

	Experiencing a theft of under fifty dollars					Experiencing a theft of over fifty dollars					Experiencing vandalism of property				
	Zero times	Once	Twice	Three or four times	Five or more times	Zero times	Once	Twice	Three or four times	Five or more times	Zero times	Once	Twice	Three or four times	Five or more times
	Ec541	Ec542	Ec543	Ec544	Ec545	Ec546	Ec547	Ec548	Ec549	Ec550	Ec551	Ec552	Ec553	Ec554	Ec555
Year	Percent	Percent	Percent	Percent	Percent	Percent	Percent	Percent	Percent	Percent	Percent	Percent	Percent	Percent	Percent
1976	55.2	26.0	10.8	6.5	1.5	89.1	8.3	2.1	0.4	0.2	69.4	19.2	7.2	3.2	0.9
1977	58.0	24.7	10.5	4.6	2.2	88.4	9.5	1.3	0.5	0.2	69.8	18.5	7.8	2.9	1.0
1978	56.6	24.9	11.5	5.2	1.8	87.6	10.0	1.8	0.5	0.1	67.5	19.5	8.0	4.0	1.0
1979	56.3	24.5	11.4	5.5	2.3	85.8	11.3	2.2	0.5	0.1	64.3	21.9	8.7	3.8	1.4
1980	55.8	24.4	12.4	5.1	2.2	86.1	11.2	2.1	0.5	0.1	65.1	21.0	9.6	3.1	1.3
1981	56.2	25.1	11.3	5.3	2.2	85.1	11.2	2.6	0.9	0.2	65.4	21.5	8.7	2.8	1.5
1982	55.1	26.9	11.9	4.2	1.8	85.7	11.4	1.9	0.9	0.1	66.2	21.5	7.7	3.5	1.1
1983	52.2	27.5	12.2	6.5	1.5	85.3	11.1	2.4	0.9	0.2	66.0	20.7	9.1	3.1	1.1
1984	57.6	24.8	10.5	5.2	1.8	86.2	10.3	2.0	1.1	0.3	69.6	18.7	6.8	3.5	1.4
1985	56.8	26.3	10.4	4.7	1.8	86.2	10.3	2.7	0.7	0.2	68.8	19.9	7.8	2.6	0.9
1986	53.0	28.2	11.1	5.5	2.1	84.2	12.6	2.3	0.7	0.2	67.8	22.1	7.3	2.3	0.6
1987	52.1	28.1	12.1	5.1	2.6	80.8	14.5	3.1	1.1	0.5	66.0	22.1	8.2	2.9	0.9
1988	53.7	27.9	11.2	5.1	2.2	81.3	13.7	3.0	1.5	0.4	66.3	21.6	8.3	2.8	1.0
1989	57.9	24.9	11.1	4.3	1.8	81.5	14.6	2.1	1.4	0.4	67.2	21.1	7.5	2.9	1.3
1990	54.1	25.4	12.5	5.7	2.3	79.9	14.3	3.9	1.4	0.5	67.3	19.7	8.7	3.2	1.1
1991	57.9	25.4	10.2	4.4	2.1	80.4	14.3	4.0	1.0	0.3	66.3	21.3	7.8	3.5	1.1
1992	58.2	26.2	9.7	4.6	1.4	80.6	14.1	3.4	1.6	0.2	67.3	20.7	8.5	3.1	0.4
1993	55.6	25.6	11.1	5.6	2.2	77.5	16.5	3.2	2.1	0.8	66.4	19.7	8.4	4.2	1.4
1994	59.0	23.8	10.5	5.2	1.5	79.8	15.5	3.3	1.1	0.3	66.9	21.3	7.6	3.3	0.9
1995	57.7	25.4	8.9	5.2	2.7	79.2	14.9	4.1	1.5	0.4	67.0	19.7	8.4	3.7	1.2
1996	53.9	26.0	11.5	6.0	2.6	75.1	16.2	7.5	1.9	1.0	65.6	21.7	8.5	3.0	1.3
1997	54.8	27.6	10.6	4.6	2.4	76.4	16.6	5.2	1.3	0.5	66.9	20.5	8.8	2.8	1.0
1998	57.2	25.1	10.0	5.4	2.2	76.2	16.4	4.6	1.8	1.1	68.3	20.1	7.1	3.4	1.1

Blacks

	Experiencing a theft of under fifty dollars					Experiencing a theft of over fifty dollars					Experiencing vandalism of property				
	Zero times	Once	Twice	Three or four times	Five or more times	Zero times	Once	Twice	Three or four times	Five or more times	Zero times	Once	Twice	Three or four times	Five or more times
	Ec556	Ec557	Ec558	Ec559	Ec560	Ec561	Ec562	Ec563	Ec564	Ec565	Ec566	Ec567	Ec568	Ec569	Ec570
Year	Percent	Percent	Percent	Percent	Percent	Percent	Percent	Percent	Percent	Percent	Percent	Percent	Percent	Percent	Percent
1976	52.9	27.7	9.7	6.7	3.0	82.8	15.0	1.9	0.0	0.3	71.1	16.7	7.9	4.0	0.6
1977	64.0	17.6	9.3	6.4	2.9	88.9	8.4	1.0	0.5	1.0	74.5	16.7	4.2	3.9	0.7
1978	60.2	21.3	11.3	5.3	1.9	83.6	11.4	3.6	1.2	0.0	72.2	18.4	6.7	1.7	0.7
1979	54.2	26.4	10.9	7.4	1.1	83.4	10.0	2.9	2.9	0.6	74.5	16.9	5.7	2.0	0.9
1980	58.7	22.6	10.4	5.3	3.0	80.8	14.8	2.8	0.9	0.5	65.9	18.8	7.4	4.9	3.0
1981	55.4	26.0	11.3	5.0	2.4	76.6	18.6	3.3	1.1	0.4	68.7	17.8	8.9	2.8	2.0
1982	53.9	27.8	8.4	5.8	4.0	79.3	15.7	2.8	1.7	0.6	68.5	19.7	7.7	3.3	0.8
1983	51.9	25.0	13.1	6.8	3.1	78.1	15.0	5.2	1.0	0.6	71.3	16.0	7.4	3.3	2.0
1984	47.5	30.6	13.1	7.0	1.9	75.6	18.2	5.1	1.0	0.0	69.7	18.3	6.7	3.4	1.8
1985	52.6	29.3	8.5	6.6	3.0	79.5	14.0	3.5	2.6	0.4	72.5	16.7	5.3	4.1	1.4
1986	53.8	27.8	10.7	5.2	2.5	79.8	15.2	2.3	1.7	0.9	72.6	18.5	5.5	2.2	1.2
1987	54.8	31.5	8.2	4.6	1.0	79.2	14.5	3.5	1.5	1.3	71.4	17.4	8.1	2.0	1.1
1988	47.8	29.7	11.8	6.2	4.6	67.1	22.6	6.8	1.3	2.2	67.5	18.0	7.9	5.8	0.7
1989	51.1	29.7	11.0	5.3	2.8	71.1	20.3	5.7	1.1	1.8	70.5	18.7	6.1	2.8	1.9
1990	54.0	24.6	11.7	8.4	1.3	71.4	19.9	5.6	2.3	0.8	69.4	15.3	9.6	4.6	1.0
1991	47.3	25.3	15.6	7.8	3.9	68.8	20.5	5.7	3.4	1.6	67.3	22.8	4.7	3.6	1.6
1992	52.0	25.0	11.5	7.6	3.8	71.3	18.3	6.4	2.4	1.7	73.4	14.8	8.0	2.5	1.3
1993	54.2	23.0	10.3	8.1	4.3	67.5	19.9	5.3	5.6	1.7	70.9	17.1	7.3	3.5	1.2
1994	48.7	29.5	11.2	5.7	4.9	65.8	21.8	7.4	2.5	2.5	68.9	12.8	9.3	6.1	2.9
1995	49.9	26.4	13.1	7.2	3.4	65.9	23.0	5.0	5.3	0.8	68.9	15.8	8.0	4.3	3.0
1996	46.4	27.1	11.7	10.1	4.6	66.2	19.9	8.0	3.5	2.4	71.1	13.6	9.1	3.6	2.7
1997	53.3	22.2	12.8	8.3	3.3	67.7	17.3	6.4	6.5	2.1	73.2	15.7	5.8	3.6	1.7
1998	48.6	24.2	15.1	10.0	2.0	67.0	19.2	8.3	4.1	1.4	67.9	17.0	7.3	3.6	4.1

TABLE Ec541–600   Percentage of high school seniors experiencing property crime victimization in the past year, by race and sex: 1976–1998 *Continued*

Males

	Experiencing a theft of under fifty dollars					Experiencing a theft of over fifty dollars					Experiencing vandalism of property				
	Zero times	Once	Twice	Three or four times	Five or more times	Zero times	Once	Twice	Three or four times	Five or more times	Zero times	Once	Twice	Three or four times	Five or more times
	Ec571	Ec572	Ec573	Ec574	Ec575	Ec576	Ec577	Ec578	Ec579	Ec580	Ec581	Ec582	Ec583	Ec584	Ec585
Year	Percent	Percent	Percent	Percent	Percent	Percent	Percent	Percent	Percent	Percent	Percent	Percent	Percent	Percent	Percent
1976	49.5	26.6	12.9	8.6	2.4	84.0	12.0	3.2	0.5	0.4	61.0	24.0	9.5	4.1	1.3
1977	53.5	24.9	12.3	5.8	3.4	83.3	12.8	2.1	1.2	0.7	61.9	22.2	10.0	4.4	1.6
1978	52.5	26.5	13.1	5.6	2.3	83.3	12.8	2.6	1.1	0.2	58.8	24.0	10.2	5.4	1.6
1979	51.4	24.9	13.4	6.9	3.3	79.9	15.3	3.7	0.7	0.5	56.4	25.4	11.0	5.6	1.5
1980	49.6	26.7	13.5	6.5	3.5	80.6	15.2	2.9	0.9	0.4	57.3	23.4	12.7	4.7	1.9
1981	50.4	26.8	13.3	6.4	3.0	80.3	14.0	4.2	1.1	0.3	57.9	26.6	10.5	3.0	2.0
1982	50.8	28.3	13.4	4.8	2.7	80.5	14.8	2.8	1.5	0.4	59.3	25.0	9.8	4.2	1.8
1983	47.9	27.3	14.4	8.1	2.2	79.8	14.9	3.5	1.4	0.4	58.1	24.9	11.6	4.2	1.3
1984	51.7	25.9	12.5	7.1	2.8	79.5	14.6	3.8	1.6	0.5	62.1	22.0	8.7	4.9	2.3
1985	50.7	28.2	12.6	6.2	2.3	81.9	12.7	4.4	0.7	0.3	62.5	23.3	9.6	3.4	1.2
1986	47.7	29.8	12.3	7.1	3.1	77.9	16.8	3.5	1.3	0.5	61.1	25.2	8.8	3.8	1.0
1987	47.0	30.4	12.9	6.1	3.6	75.1	18.5	4.2	1.4	0.8	62.0	23.6	9.9	3.5	1.0
1988	46.5	30.3	13.1	6.7	3.4	72.4	19.6	4.7	2.2	1.1	59.7	24.8	9.7	4.3	1.5
1989	53.2	27.0	12.0	5.4	2.4	76.8	16.7	3.6	2.1	0.8	60.9	25.4	9.6	2.5	1.6
1990	52.8	24.8	12.5	6.6	3.5	75.6	16.5	4.9	2.0	1.1	60.8	21.9	10.5	4.9	1.9
1991	50.4	28.1	12.1	6.1	3.2	73.2	18.5	5.6	1.9	0.7	59.7	24.5	10.0	3.9	1.9
1992	49.9	28.8	12.7	5.7	2.9	73.3	17.5	6.0	2.4	0.8	61.3	21.5	11.9	4.2	1.1
1993	50.9	25.9	13.1	6.6	3.5	69.0	20.8	5.3	3.3	1.6	61.6	21.7	9.8	4.8	2.2
1994	53.8	24.1	12.9	6.4	2.8	73.6	19.0	4.6	2.2	0.6	61.8	22.0	10.9	4.4	0.9
1995	50.7	26.2	12.1	6.7	4.3	70.8	19.6	6.2	2.9	0.5	61.2	22.1	10.1	4.8	1.8
1996	48.4	26.0	13.1	8.1	4.4	68.8	18.0	7.9	3.2	2.1	59.6	24.6	9.8	3.7	2.3
1997	49.3	26.6	13.7	6.1	4.3	69.0	20.3	7.1	2.4	1.1	59.3	24.3	10.4	4.6	1.3
1998	49.5	27.4	12.0	7.7	3.4	68.8	20.7	5.9	2.4	2.2	61.4	21.9	9.1	4.9	2.6

Females

	Experiencing a theft of under fifty dollars					Experiencing a theft of over fifty dollars					Experiencing vandalism of property				
	Zero times	Once	Twice	Three or four times	Five or more times	Zero times	Once	Twice	Three or four times	Five or more times	Zero times	Once	Twice	Three or four times	Five or more times
	Ec586	Ec587	Ec588	Ec589	Ec590	Ec591	Ec592	Ec593	Ec594	Ec595	Ec596	Ec597	Ec598	Ec599	Ec600
Year	Percent	Percent	Percent	Percent	Percent	Percent	Percent	Percent	Percent	Percent	Percent	Percent	Percent	Percent	Percent
1976	61.0	25.7	8.4	3.9	1.1	91.8	6.7	1.1	0.2	0.1	77.5	14.0	5.6	2.3	0.6
1977	63.9	22.2	8.8	3.8	1.3	92.2	6.7	0.8	0.1	0.2	78.1	14.5	4.6	2.2	0.6
1978	61.8	22.8	9.6	4.4	1.4	90.8	7.6	1.5	0.2	0.1	76.6	14.7	6.2	2.2	0.3
1979	60.0	24.7	9.4	4.6	1.2	90.5	7.3	1.2	0.8	0.2	73.6	17.8	6.1	1.4	1.1
1980	62.6	21.7	10.5	4.1	1.3	89.2	8.9	1.5	0.3	0.2	72.3	18.4	6.5	1.6	1.2
1981	62.0	23.3	9.5	3.9	1.3	87.1	10.3	1.5	0.9	0.2	73.5	16.0	6.9	2.7	0.9
1982	59.1	26.3	9.0	4.1	1.5	87.5	10.4	1.3	0.6	0.2	73.5	17.0	5.8	2.7	0.8
1983	56.8	27.1	10.1	4.6	1.4	88.0	9.5	2.0	0.3	0.2	76.1	14.9	6.0	1.9	1.1
1984	61.0	25.2	9.3	3.5	1.0	88.5	9.2	1.5	0.7	0.1	76.4	15.0	5.2	2.4	1.0
1985	60.7	25.3	8.7	3.8	1.6	88.3	8.8	1.6	1.0	0.3	75.3	15.7	5.5	2.5	1.1
1986	57.4	27.7	9.8	3.8	1.3	86.9	10.5	1.8	0.7	0.1	74.0	18.5	5.5	1.3	0.7
1987	57.1	26.4	10.2	4.5	1.8	84.2	12.0	2.1	1.1	0.6	70.6	19.6	6.6	2.3	0.9
1988	58.8	26.2	10.0	3.9	1.1	84.0	11.9	3.0	0.9	0.1	72.1	17.7	7.2	2.4	0.6
1989	59.8	25.4	9.3	3.9	1.6	81.8	15.1	2.3	0.5	0.3	72.6	17.6	5.9	3.0	1.0
1990	57.3	24.9	11.5	5.1	1.2	81.2	13.6	2.9	2.0	0.3	73.2	16.1	7.3	2.8	0.6
1991	60.9	23.9	9.8	4.0	1.4	81.6	13.1	3.7	1.2	0.4	72.3	18.8	5.1	3.1	0.7
1992	60.8	25.5	8.3	4.2	1.2	82.7	12.2	3.1	1.4	0.6	71.8	18.4	6.8	2.3	0.7
1993	60.3	24.4	9.0	5.0	1.3	81.3	13.9	2.6	1.9	0.3	71.1	16.2	8.6	3.5	0.6
1994	59.5	26.5	9.1	3.6	1.2	81.0	14.4	3.2	0.9	0.5	72.1	17.2	6.0	3.3	1.4
1995	60.3	24.8	9.3	4.1	1.6	82.3	12.9	2.9	1.4	0.6	71.1	17.5	7.2	2.6	1.6
1996	57.1	27.9	9.0	4.4	1.6	78.2	15.9	3.6	1.8	0.5	71.9	17.3	7.9	2.4	0.5
1997	57.9	27.4	8.6	4.4	1.7	78.6	14.7	4.2	2.1	0.4	74.6	16.3	6.1	2.3	0.8
1998	59.4	23.9	10.5	4.4	1.8	78.2	14.2	4.8	2.2	0.7	73.3	17.1	5.7	2.8	1.1

Sources

1976–1984: U.S. Bureau of Justice Statistics, *Sourcebook of Criminal Justice Statistics 1985* (1987), Table 3.58 and 3.59; 1985–1996: U.S. Bureau of Justice Statistics, *Sourcebook of Criminal Justice Statistics 1996* (1997), Tables 3.36 and 3.37; 1997–1998: U.S. Bureau of Justice Statistics, *Sourcebook of Criminal Justice Statistics 1998* (1999), Tables 3.42 and 3.43; originally from Lloyd D. Johnson, Jerald G. Bachman, and Patrick M. O'Malley, *Monitoring the Future* (1975 through 1998 annual reports), and data supplied by the Monitoring the Future Project (Institute for Social Research, University of Michigan).

Documentation

See the text for Table Ec426–445 for a description of the source and the wording of the measures.

TABLE Ec601–625   Percentage of high school seniors involved in violent delinquency in the past year: 1975–1998

Contributed by Douglas Eckberg

	Hit an instructor or supervisor					Got into a serious fight at school or work					Took part in a gang fight		
	Zero times	Once	Twice	Three or four times	Five or more times	Zero times	Once	Twice	Three or four times	Five or more times	Zero times	Once	Twice
	Ec601	Ec602	Ec603	Ec604	Ec605	Ec606	Ec607	Ec608	Ec609	Ec610	Ec611	Ec612	Ec613
Year	Percent	Percent	Percent	Percent	Percent	Percent	Percent	Percent	Percent	Percent	Percent	Percent	Percent
1975	96.9	2.1	0.4	0.4	0.2	85.4	9.1	3.3	1.7	0.6	82.6	10.8	3.6
1976	96.7	1.9	0.8	0.1	0.4	85.8	8.2	3.0	1.8	1.0	85.0	8.9	2.8
1977	96.7	2.2	0.5	0.3	0.3	86.0	8.2	3.5	1.6	0.8	85.5	8.4	2.7
1978	96.9	2.0	0.7	0.2	0.2	85.9	8.8	2.8	1.8	0.7	85.0	9.2	2.9
1979	96.9	1.9	0.6	0.2	0.4	84.8	9.0	3.4	2.1	0.7	82.8	10.3	3.9
1980	96.8	2.0	0.6	0.2	0.5	84.2	9.3	3.9	1.7	0.9	82.4	10.5	3.7
1981	97.0	2.0	0.6	0.2	0.3	84.6	9.5	3.1	1.8	1.0	83.2	9.5	3.6
1982	97.3	1.6	0.5	0.1	0.4	82.7	11.2	3.0	1.8	1.3	81.9	10.0	4.2
1983	96.6	1.9	0.7	0.5	0.3	82.4	10.7	3.4	2.6	0.9	82.1	10.1	4.2
1984	96.6	2.4	0.5	0.2	0.3	82.6	10.1	3.5	2.4	1.4	82.1	10.1	4.0
1985	96.9	2.0	0.3	0.4	0.3	81.8	11.2	3.6	2.2	1.1	79.4	12.0	4.8
1986	96.9	1.9	0.6	0.4	0.2	82.8	11.3	3.4	1.7	0.9	80.5	11.3	4.4
1987	97.6	1.5	0.5	0.2	0.2	82.1	10.4	4.6	1.9	1.0	80.4	11.3	4.4
1988	97.3	1.4	0.7	0.3	0.4	81.8	10.6	4.2	2.0	1.3	80.5	11.1	4.4
1989	96.7	2.0	0.3	0.6	0.5	80.3	11.6	4.9	1.9	1.3	79.7	12.1	3.9
1990	97.4	1.5	0.7	0.2	0.3	81.1	11.4	4.4	1.9	1.2	78.8	11.4	4.4
1991	97.0	1.6	0.7	0.2	0.6	82.1	10.3	4.0	2.0	1.6	79.6	11.2	5.0
1992	96.7	1.9	0.5	0.3	0.6	81.1	11.5	4.0	1.8	1.7	78.7	11.5	4.4
1993	96.2	2.2	0.6	0.4	0.6	82.3	10.3	3.6	2.4	1.3	77.8	11.2	5.8
1994	97.0	1.5	0.9	0.2	0.4	83.8	9.1	3.9	2.0	1.1	80.7	10.2	4.0
1995	96.9	1.6	0.6	0.3	0.6	85.2	8.2	3.4	2.2	1.0	81.4	10.1	3.6
1996	96.3	2.0	0.7	0.4	0.6	83.3	9.3	3.9	1.6	1.8	79.8	10.8	4.3
1997	96.4	1.8	0.8	0.3	0.8	82.6	10.1	3.8	1.8	1.7	78.5	11.0	5.1
1998	96.7	1.6	0.8	0.3	0.6	83.4	9.8	3.7	1.6	1.6	79.4	10.3	5.1

	Took part in a gang fight		Injured someone badly enough to need bandages or a doctor					Used a knife, gun, or other weapon to get something from a person				
	Three or four times	Five or more times	Zero times	Once	Twice	Three or four times	Five or more times	Zero times	Once	Twice	Three or four times	Five or more times
	Ec614	Ec615	Ec616	Ec617	Ec618	Ec619	Ec620	Ec621	Ec622	Ec623	Ec624	Ec625
Year	Percent	Percent	Percent	Percent	Percent	Percent	Percent	Percent	Percent	Percent	Percent	Percent
1975	1.8	1.2	90.5	6.1	2.0	0.8	0.5	97.3	1.3	0.6	0.4	0.4
1976	2.1	1.2	90.2	6.5	1.5	0.9	0.9	97.5	1.2	0.5	0.4	0.4
1977	2.0	1.3	91.3	5.8	1.5	0.7	0.7	97.2	1.4	0.6	0.4	0.4
1978	1.9	1.0	90.3	6.1	1.8	1.0	0.7	97.2	1.4	0.8	0.3	0.3
1979	1.9	1.1	90.3	6.2	2.0	1.0	0.5	97.4	1.8	0.4	0.3	0.2
1980	1.9	1.5	88.3	7.6	2.4	1.1	0.5	97.1	1.7	0.6	0.4	0.2
1981	2.3	1.4	90.4	6.0	2.2	0.8	0.6	97.5	1.4	0.4	0.4	0.2
1982	2.4	1.5	88.6	7.5	2.1	0.8	0.9	97.7	1.6	0.3	0.2	0.2
1983	2.2	1.3	88.9	7.2	1.7	1.3	0.9	97.0	1.5	0.6	0.3	0.6
1984	2.4	1.4	89.4	6.3	2.2	1.1	1.1	96.8	1.7	0.5	0.5	0.6
1985	2.3	1.5	88.5	6.9	2.2	1.4	0.9	96.5	1.8	0.7	0.3	0.6
1986	2.4	1.3	88.9	7.0	2.3	0.9	0.8	96.6	1.8	0.6	0.6	0.4
1987	2.6	1.4	88.3	7.6	2.6	0.8	0.7	96.7	1.8	0.7	0.3	0.5
1988	2.4	1.6	89.6	6.2	1.8	1.4	1.0	97.2	1.4	0.5	0.3	0.5
1989	2.4	1.8	87.7	8.0	1.8	1.5	1.0	96.3	1.7	0.7	0.4	0.9
1990	3.3	2.1	87.1	7.6	3.0	1.3	1.1	96.5	1.9	0.8	0.3	0.5
1991	2.5	1.7	87.1	8.2	2.3	1.1	1.3	96.6	1.6	0.6	0.3	0.9
1992	3.2	2.2	87.2	7.3	2.9	1.6	1.1	95.7	2.2	1.0	0.5	0.5
1993	2.9	2.3	86.6	7.1	2.7	1.7	1.8	95.4	1.8	0.9	1.2	0.8
1994	2.8	2.3	86.6	7.5	2.5	2.1	1.4	95.2	2.4	0.9	0.7	0.8
1995	2.9	2.0	87.7	6.5	2.7	2.0	1.2	96.5	1.9	0.7	0.4	0.6
1996	2.3	2.8	85.7	8.4	2.9	1.7	1.4	96.3	1.5	0.7	0.6	1.0
1997	3.4	2.0	85.4	8.9	2.7	1.6	1.6	95.5	1.5	1.2	1.0	0.8
1998	3.0	2.2	85.6	7.9	3.1	1.7	1.7	95.7	2.2	0.8	0.5	0.9

TABLE Ec601–625 Percentage of high school seniors involved in violent delinquency in the past year: 1975–1998
Continued

Sources

1976–1984: U.S. Bureau of Justice Statistics, *Sourcebook of Criminal Justice Statistics 1985* (1987), Table 3.60; 1985–1996: U.S. Bureau of Justice Statistics, *Sourcebook of Criminal Justice Statistics 1996* (1997), Table 3.38; 1997–1998: U.S. Bureau of Justice Statistics, *Sourcebook of Criminal Justice Statistics 1998* (1999), Table 3.47; originally from Lloyd D. Johnson, Jerald G. Bachman, and Patrick M. O'Malley, *Monitoring the Future* (1975 through 1998 annual reports), and data supplied by the Monitoring the Future Project (Institute for Social Research, University of Michigan).

Documentation

See the text for Table Ec426–445 for a description of the source and the wording of the measures.

TABLE Ec626–650   Percentage of high school seniors involved in property crime in the past year: 1975–1998

Contributed by Douglas Eckberg

	Stole something worth less than fifty dollars					Stole something worth more than fifty dollars					Took something from a store without paying		
	Zero times	Once	Twice	Three or four times	Five or more times	Zero times	Once	Twice	Three or four times	Five or more times	Zero times	Once	Twice
	Ec626	Ec627	Ec628	Ec629	Ec630	Ec631	Ec632	Ec633	Ec634	Ec635	Ec636	Ec637	Ec638
Year	Percent	Percent	Percent	Percent	Percent	Percent	Percent	Percent	Percent	Percent	Percent	Percent	Percent
1975	67.6	13.2	7.3	5.6	6.3	94.4	2.7	1.0	0.8	1.2	64.9	13.7	7.1
1976	69.0	13.5	6.5	5.3	5.7	93.9	3.0	0.9	0.9	1.2	67.7	13.5	7.2
1977	69.4	12.6	7.0	5.2	5.8	95.2	2.4	0.9	0.6	0.9	69.8	12.7	6.0
1978	69.2	13.5	7.0	5.2	5.2	94.4	2.6	1.0	0.8	1.2	69.9	12.0	6.6
1979	66.6	14.5	8.0	5.6	5.4	93.1	4.1	1.1	0.8	0.9	68.2	13.5	6.6
1980	66.9	14.6	7.4	5.5	5.6	93.4	3.7	1.1	0.5	1.3	69.2	13.0	6.2
1981	69.0	14.6	6.0	5.3	5.2	92.9	3.9	1.5	0.7	1.0	71.4	12.8	6.1
1982	68.7	13.9	6.9	5.4	5.2	93.1	3.7	1.1	0.9	1.2	71.2	12.5	5.8
1983	69.3	14.8	6.6	4.6	4.6	93.6	3.5	1.3	0.9	0.8	73.9	12.7	5.2
1984	69.7	13.3	7.2	5.1	4.8	93.3	4.0	0.9	0.9	1.0	73.2	12.4	5.0
1985	69.9	14.2	6.6	4.5	4.8	93.0	3.4	1.3	0.9	1.4	73.5	11.7	6.1
1986	68.0	16.2	6.9	4.5	4.4	93.4	3.5	1.2	1.0	0.9	72.1	12.8	6.1
1987	66.1	15.9	6.9	5.3	5.9	91.5	4.0	1.7	1.5	1.3	70.3	13.5	4.5
1988	66.6	15.1	7.2	5.3	5.9	91.5	4.1	2.0	0.9	1.5	69.6	12.9	6.4
1989	68.4	13.7	6.9	4.7	6.4	91.9	3.7	1.5	1.3	1.6	70.8	12.8	5.4
1990	67.7	13.5	6.8	5.7	6.3	89.9	4.8	1.9	1.2	2.1	68.1	13.2	6.6
1991	68.1	13.7	7.7	4.1	6.5	89.9	4.6	2.1	1.7	1.8	68.9	11.9	7.4
1992	67.4	14.2	7.5	5.6	5.2	89.5	5.5	1.7	1.5	1.7	69.6	12.6	6.7
1993	67.9	13.8	7.3	4.5	6.5	88.7	5.0	2.1	1.5	2.8	69.3	13.4	5.8
1994	69.3	13.1	6.6	5.7	5.3	89.0	5.1	2.1	1.4	2.3	69.7	11.5	6.9
1995	68.6	14.0	7.2	4.6	5.6	90.7	3.7	2.0	1.8	1.9	70.1	12.0	6.0
1996	67.6	14.2	6.9	4.7	6.6	87.7	5.3	2.6	1.8	2.6	67.8	12.9	6.5
1997	65.8	12.5	9.3	5.9	6.4	87.2	6.3	2.6	1.6	2.3	66.6	11.4	7.3
1998	68.8	13.2	7.4	4.9	5.7	88.4	5.3	2.6	1.4	2.3	70.3	12.5	6.5

	Took something from a store without paying		Took a car belonging to someone outside the family without permission					Took part of a car without permission of the owner				
	Three or four times	Five or more times	Zero times	Once	Twice	Three or four times	Five or more times	Zero times	Once	Twice	Three or four times	Five or more times
	Ec639	Ec640	Ec641	Ec642	Ec643	Ec644	Ec645	Ec646	Ec647	Ec648	Ec649	Ec650
Year	Percent	Percent	Percent	Percent	Percent	Percent	Percent	Percent	Percent	Percent	Percent	Percent
1975	6.7	7.6	96.1	2.2	0.6	0.4	0.6	94.4	3.2	1.2	0.6	0.6
1976	4.9	6.7	95.8	2.1	1.1	0.3	0.7	94.1	3.2	1.2	0.8	0.8
1977	5.7	5.8	95.9	2.0	0.7	0.8	0.5	93.7	3.7	1.4	0.7	0.6
1978	6.1	5.4	95.7	2.4	0.9	0.6	0.3	94.0	3.3	1.5	0.7	0.5
1979	6.0	5.7	95.7	2.3	1.1	0.5	0.4	93.2	3.6	1.7	0.7	0.8
1980	5.3	6.4	95.2	2.3	1.1	0.9	0.5	92.9	3.9	1.7	1.0	0.6
1981	4.6	5.1	96.1	2.5	0.7	0.3	0.4	94.7	3.0	1.2	0.7	0.4
1982	4.6	5.9	95.9	2.4	0.6	0.5	0.7	94.3	3.4	1.2	0.4	0.7
1983	4.2	4.0	94.5	3.1	1.1	0.6	0.7	94.3	2.9	1.5	0.7	0.6
1984	5.0	4.4	94.2	3.5	1.3	0.5	0.5	93.6	3.7	1.1	0.8	0.9
1985	4.2	4.5	94.4	3.1	1.0	0.6	0.9	93.3	3.4	1.8	0.5	1.0
1986	4.4	4.5	94.9	3.1	1.1	0.4	0.4	94.4	3.2	1.2	0.6	0.6
1987	4.7	6.9	94.4	3.0	1.3	0.6	0.7	93.3	3.6	1.5	0.8	0.7
1988	4.9	6.1	94.4	3.6	0.9	0.5	0.6	94.1	3.3	1.1	0.6	0.8
1989	4.1	6.9	94.6	3.0	1.1	0.5	0.9	93.2	3.8	1.3	0.9	0.8
1990	5.2	6.9	93.4	3.4	1.6	0.7	0.9	93.1	3.8	1.6	0.6	1.0
1991	5.3	6.5	93.8	3.3	1.2	1.0	0.7	93.7	3.3	1.3	0.6	1.0
1992	5.2	5.9	94.0	3.1	1.4	0.7	0.9	93.9	3.2	1.2	1.0	0.8
1993	4.9	6.5	93.6	3.0	1.4	1.0	1.0	92.7	3.2	1.5	1.2	1.3
1994	5.2	6.7	94.1	3.0	1.3	0.8	0.7	94.3	2.9	1.0	0.8	1.0
1995	5.5	6.4	95.2	2.7	1.0	0.6	0.6	94.9	2.6	1.2	0.6	0.7
1996	5.2	7.6	94.8	2.4	1.3	0.8	0.8	94.7	2.7	1.5	0.3	0.8
1997	7.4	7.2	93.9	3.4	1.2	0.6	0.9	94.6	2.2	1.4	0.9	0.9
1998	4.1	6.4	95.2	2.7	0.9	0.6	0.7	94.9	2.5	1.2	0.6	0.8

TABLE Ec626–650   **Percentage of high school seniors involved in property crime in the past year: 1975–1998**
Continued

Sources
1976–1984: U.S. Bureau of Justice Statistics, *Sourcebook of Criminal Justice Statistics 1985* (1987), Table 3.60; 1985–1996: U.S. Bureau of Justice Statistics, *Sourcebook of Criminal Justice Statistics 1996* (1997), Table 3.38; 1997–1998: U.S. Bureau of Justice Statistics, *Sourcebook of Criminal Justice Statistics 1998* (1999), Table 3.47; originally from Lloyd D. Johnson, Jerald

G. Bachman, and Patrick M. O'Malley, *Monitoring the Future* (1975 through 1998 annual reports), and data supplied by the Monitoring the Future Project (Institute for Social Research, University of Michigan).

Documentation
See the text for Table Ec426–445 for a description of the source and the wording of the measures.

TABLE Ec651–670   **Percentage of high school seniors involved in trespassing and vandalism in the past year: 1975–1998**
Contributed by Douglas Eckberg

	Went into a house or building when they were not supposed to be there					Deliberately set fire to someone's property				
	Zero times	Once	Twice	Three or four times	Five or more times	Zero times	Once	Twice	Three or four times	Five or more times
	Ec651	Ec652	Ec653	Ec654	Ec655	Ec656	Ec657	Ec658	Ec659	Ec660
Year	Percent	Percent	Percent	Percent	Percent	Percent	Percent	Percent	Percent	Percent
1975	71.9	13.2	7.5	3.8	3.6	98.3	1.0	0.4	0.2	0.2
1976	76.7	11.5	5.6	3.3	2.9	98.3	0.8	0.5	0.1	0.3
1977	77.9	10.1	5.9	3.3	2.8	98.3	0.9	0.2	0.2	0.3
1978	75.9	11.8	5.9	3.2	3.2	98.3	1.0	0.4	0.1	0.2
1979	75.9	11.8	6.7	3.0	2.6	98.8	0.7	0.2	0.2	0.2
1980	74.9	12.1	5.5	4.7	2.8	98.5	1.2	0.1	0.1	0.1
1981	77.1	11.4	6.2	2.7	2.5	98.3	1.2	0.2	0.1	0.2
1982	75.5	12.6	6.5	3.0	2.4	98.8	0.7	0.2	0.1	0.2
1983	76.6	11.5	6.8	3.0	2.1	98.7	0.7	0.2	0.1	0.2
1984	74.8	12.3	6.1	3.9	2.9	98.1	1.1	0.4	0.1	0.4
1985	73.8	13.4	6.5	3.2	3.1	98.1	1.1	0.3	0.2	0.3
1986	75.5	12.1	6.3	3.1	3.0	98.0	1.1	0.3	0.3	0.4
1987	73.0	12.4	7.9	4.0	2.7	98.4	1.0	0.3	0.1	0.2
1988	72.7	12.7	6.9	4.0	3.8	98.3	1.0	0.3	0.1	0.3
1989	74.4	11.9	7.1	3.4	3.2	97.5	1.5	0.4	0.2	0.4
1990	74.4	10.6	7.8	4.3	2.9	97.8	1.2	0.5	0.2	0.3
1991	75.7	10.8	6.7	3.4	3.6	97.9	1.1	0.4	0.1	0.5
1992	74.0	12.1	6.9	3.9	3.2	97.2	1.6	0.4	0.4	0.4
1993	73.7	12.1	7.0	3.4	3.8	96.6	1.5	0.7	0.6	0.6
1994	75.2	11.2	6.5	4.1	3.0	96.8	1.7	0.5	0.5	0.5
1995	76.5	10.9	6.1	3.1	3.3	97.5	1.5	0.4	0.3	0.4
1996	76.0	10.6	7.1	3.5	2.9	97.0	1.5	0.6	0.2	0.7
1997	75.3	10.5	7.0	3.8	3.5	96.9	1.7	0.4	0.2	0.7
1998	75.4	10.6	6.5	3.6	3.9	97.1	1.1	0.8	0.2	0.8

(continued)

TABLE Ec651–670   Percentage of high school seniors involved in trespassing and vandalism in the past year: 1975–1998   *Continued*

Year	Deliberately damaged any school property					Deliberately damaged any property at work				
	Zero times	Once	Twice	Three or four times	Five or more times	Zero times	Once	Twice	Three or four times	Five or more times
	Ec661	Ec662	Ec663	Ec664	Ec665	Ec666	Ec667	Ec668	Ec669	Ec670
	Percent	Percent	Percent	Percent	Percent	Percent	Percent	Percent	Percent	Percent
1975	87.2	6.3	3.6	1.5	1.5	94.9	2.3	1.4	0.7	0.8
1976	88.1	6.7	2.7	1.4	1.1	94.2	3.1	1.3	0.6	0.7
1977	87.6	6.4	3.0	1.6	1.4	94.5	2.4	1.4	1.1	0.7
1978	87.7	6.9	2.4	1.5	1.4	93.8	2.9	1.6	0.9	0.8
1979	85.8	8.0	3.4	1.5	1.2	91.9	4.1	1.8	1.1	1.1
1980	86.8	7.4	2.8	1.8	1.3	93.0	3.5	1.6	1.0	0.9
1981	86.7	7.3	3.5	1.2	1.3	93.5	3.1	1.6	1.1	0.6
1982	87.6	6.9	3.2	1.2	1.2	94.2	3.1	1.5	0.6	0.7
1983	85.9	7.0	3.2	2.3	1.6	94.5	2.6	1.4	0.9	0.6
1984	85.9	7.3	3.1	1.8	1.9	95.0	2.4	1.2	0.7	0.7
1985	86.2	6.7	3.7	1.8	1.6	94.5	2.7	1.5	0.7	0.6
1986	86.8	6.8	3.0	1.9	1.4	94.8	2.7	1.2	0.8	0.6
1987	84.9	8.2	3.2	2.0	1.7	94.7	2.5	1.5	0.7	0.6
1988	85.8	7.8	3.2	1.6	1.6	94.0	3.3	1.4	0.6	0.8
1989	86.8	6.3	3.1	1.7	2.2	93.6	2.9	1.7	1.0	0.9
1990	86.6	6.4	3.8	1.7	1.6	93.4	3.0	1.9	0.7	1.0
1991	87.2	6.5	3.0	1.3	2.0	93.4	3.2	1.3	0.8	1.3
1992	85.3	7.9	3.5	1.2	2.1	94.0	2.7	1.3	1.0	1.0
1993	85.3	6.4	4.0	2.0	2.2	93.6	2.9	1.5	0.8	1.1
1994	86.2	6.5	3.5	2.0	1.9	94.4	2.3	1.5	0.9	1.0
1995	86.0	6.5	3.2	2.6	1.7	93.8	3.3	1.2	0.7	1.0
1996	85.7	7.2	3.1	2.0	2.0	93.7	3.3	0.8	0.7	1.4
1997	84.8	7.7	3.1	2.2	2.2	93.3	2.8	1.7	1.0	1.1
1998	85.7	7.5	2.6	2.0	2.3	92.7	3.3	1.6	0.9	1.6

Sources

1976–1984: U.S. Bureau of Justice Statistics, *Sourcebook of Criminal Justice Statistics 1985* (1987), Table 3.60; 1985–1996: U.S. Bureau of Justice Statistics, *Sourcebook of Criminal Justice Statistics 1996* (1997), Table 3.38; 1997–1998: U.S. Bureau of Justice Statistics, *Sourcebook of Criminal Justice Statistics 1998* (1999), Table 3.47; originally from Lloyd D. Johnson, Jerald G. Bachman, and Patrick M. O'Malley, *Monitoring the Future* (1975 through

1998 annual reports), and data supplied by the Monitoring the Future Project (Institute for Social Research, University of Michigan).

Documentation

See the text for Table Ec426–445 for a description of the source and the wording of the measures.

TABLE Ec671–770　Percentage of high school seniors involved in violent delinquency in the past year, by race and sex: 1975–1998

Contributed by Douglas Eckberg

Whites

	Hit an instructor or supervisor					Got into a serious fight at school or work				
	Zero times	Once	Twice	Three or four times	Five or more times	Zero times	Once	Twice	Three or four times	Five or more times
	Ec671	Ec672	Ec673	Ec674	Ec675	Ec676	Ec677	Ec678	Ec679	Ec680
Year	Percent	Percent	Percent	Percent	Percent	Percent	Percent	Percent	Percent	Percent
1975	—	—	—	—	—	—	—	—	—	—
1976	96.8	2.0	0.8	0.1	0.3	86.7	7.8	3.0	1.6	0.9
1977	97.4	1.9	0.5	0.2	0.1	86.7	7.7	3.4	1.6	0.7
1978	97.1	2.0	0.6	0.1	0.1	86.2	8.7	2.7	1.8	0.6
1979	97.3	1.7	0.6	0.1	0.3	85.0	9.1	3.3	2.1	0.5
1980	96.8	2.0	0.6	0.1	0.6	84.2	9.0	4.1	1.9	0.9
1981	97.5	1.5	0.5	0.2	0.2	84.8	9.2	3.2	1.8	1.0
1982	97.5	1.5	0.5	0.1	0.4	83.6	10.6	3.0	1.6	1.1
1983	96.9	1.6	0.8	0.3	0.3	82.3	10.4	3.8	2.8	0.7
1984	96.7	2.3	0.4	0.3	0.3	82.4	10.5	3.6	2.3	1.2
1985	96.9	2.1	0.3	0.5	0.3	81.5	11.5	3.7	2.2	1.1
1986	97.3	1.7	0.6	0.2	0.2	83.3	10.9	3.7	1.5	0.6
1987	97.6	1.6	0.3	0.2	0.2	83.2	9.8	4.3	1.8	0.9
1988	97.8	1.4	0.3	0.2	0.3	82.5	10.7	3.8	1.9	1.1
1989	97.0	2.1	0.2	0.5	0.2	79.8	12.5	4.7	2.0	1.0
1990	97.7	1.1	0.8	0.2	0.2	80.4	11.8	5.0	2.0	0.9
1991	97.3	1.5	0.5	0.1	0.5	83.1	9.7	4.0	1.7	1.6
1992	97.2	1.8	0.5	0.2	0.4	82.1	10.8	4.3	1.7	1.2
1993	96.9	1.9	0.6	0.3	0.3	82.8	10.3	3.6	2.3	1.0
1994	97.5	1.1	0.8	0.2	0.4	85.3	8.3	3.5	1.8	1.1
1995	97.7	1.0	0.6	0.1	0.6	86.4	7.3	3.2	2.1	1.1
1996	97.1	1.7	0.4	0.4	0.3	84.9	9.0	3.3	1.4	1.4
1997	96.9	1.7	0.6	0.2	0.5	84.9	8.6	3.5	1.8	1.2
1998	97.5	1.2	0.9	0.1	0.4	85.5	9.0	2.9	1.7	0.9

Whites

	Took part in a gang fight					Injured a person badly enough to need bandages or a doctor				
	Zero times	Once	Twice	Three or four times	Five or more times	Zero times	Once	Twice	Three or four times	Five or more times
	Ec681	Ec682	Ec683	Ec684	Ec685	Ec686	Ec687	Ec688	Ec689	Ec690
Year	Percent	Percent	Percent	Percent	Percent	Percent	Percent	Percent	Percent	Percent
1975	—	—	—	—	—	—	—	—	—	—
1976	85.4	8.8	2.6	2.2	1.1	90.9	6.4	1.3	0.8	0.5
1977	85.8	8.6	2.8	1.7	1.1	92.2	5.5	1.2	0.6	0.4
1978	85.3	9.0	2.9	1.9	0.9	91.0	5.6	1.8	1.0	0.6
1979	82.7	10.4	4.0	1.8	1.0	91.3	5.4	1.9	1.1	0.4
1980	82.3	10.8	3.8	1.8	1.3	88.2	7.4	2.7	1.3	0.4
1981	83.0	9.6	3.6	2.4	1.3	90.7	6.1	2.0	0.8	0.4
1982	82.4	9.9	4.4	2.0	1.3	89.8	6.8	1.9	0.9	0.7
1983	82.2	10.0	4.0	2.6	1.2	89.1	7.0	1.8	1.2	0.8
1984	83.1	9.8	3.4	2.4	1.3	90.0	6.0	2.3	0.8	0.9
1985	79.5	11.9	4.6	2.6	1.4	88.9	6.6	2.2	1.5	0.8
1986	81.3	11.3	3.8	2.4	1.1	89.8	6.4	2.2	0.9	0.7
1987	80.8	11.7	4.0	2.5	1.0	89.2	7.5	2.0	0.6	0.6
1988	81.6	10.8	3.9	2.5	1.2	90.3	5.9	1.6	1.4	0.8
1989	80.3	12.6	3.5	2.5	1.2	88.2	8.0	1.7	1.6	0.5
1990	78.4	12.0	4.8	3.2	1.7	87.7	7.6	2.6	1.2	0.9
1991	80.8	11.3	4.6	2.2	1.2	88.2	7.7	2.0	1.1	0.9
1992	79.3	11.6	4.1	2.8	2.2	87.9	7.3	2.9	1.3	0.6
1993	78.7	11.1	6.0	2.5	1.8	87.5	7.2	2.9	1.4	1.0
1994	81.7	10.1	4.1	2.5	1.5	88.0	6.9	2.1	1.8	1.2
1995	82.3	10.2	3.1	2.4	1.9	88.9	5.7	2.7	1.7	1.0
1996	81.1	11.1	3.5	2.1	2.2	87.3	7.8	2.6	1.6	0.7
1997	80.0	10.2	5.0	3.4	1.4	87.9	7.5	2.3	1.2	1.1
1998	79.9	10.6	5.2	2.8	1.5	86.8	7.4	3.1	1.7	1.0

(continued)

TABLE Ec671–770   Percentage of high school seniors involved in violent delinquency in the past year, by race and sex: 1975–1998   Continued

	Whites						Blacks				
	Used a knife, gun, or other weapon to get something from a person						Hit an instructor or supervisor				
	Zero times	Once	Twice	Three or four times	Five or more times		Zero times	Once	Twice	Three or four times	Five or more times
	Ec691	Ec692	Ec693	Ec694	Ec695		Ec696	Ec697	Ec698	Ec699	Ec700
Year	Percent	Percent	Percent	Percent	Percent		Percent	Percent	Percent	Percent	Percent
1975	—	—	—	—	—		—	—	—	—	—
1976	98.2	1.0	0.2	0.3	0.2		97.6	1.2	1.2	0.0	0.3
1977	98.1	0.9	0.4	0.4	0.2		96.1	2.9	0.2	0.2	0.5
1978	97.5	1.2	0.9	0.2	0.2		96.4	2.2	0.7	0.2	0.7
1979	97.4	1.6	0.4	0.3	0.2		98.0	1.4	0.0	0.6	0.0
1980	97.3	1.6	0.5	0.4	0.2		97.9	1.4	0.0	0.5	0.0
1981	98.1	1.2	0.3	0.4	0.1		97.0	2.4	0.0	0.2	0.4
1982	98.2	1.3	0.2	0.1	0.2		96.9	1.8	1.0	0.0	0.2
1983	97.9	1.0	0.5	0.2	0.4		97.2	1.9	0.5	0.4	0.0
1984	97.3	1.2	0.5	0.4	0.6		98.1	1.4	0.3	0.0	0.2
1985	97.1	1.4	0.6	0.3	0.6		98.4	1.2	0.2	0.2	0.0
1986	96.9	1.8	0.5	0.5	0.3		97.1	2.4	0.0	0.3	0.2
1987	97.5	1.5	0.5	0.3	0.3		98.4	0.4	1.2	0.0	0.0
1988	97.9	1.2	0.4	0.3	0.3		96.5	1.9	1.0	0.5	0.1
1989	97.0	1.5	0.9	0.2	0.4		97.5	0.4	0.2	1.7	0.2
1990	97.2	1.6	0.6	0.1	0.4		95.9	2.7	0.4	0.2	0.8
1991	97.4	1.4	0.3	0.1	0.8		95.9	1.9	0.8	0.5	0.8
1992	97.1	1.5	0.9	0.3	0.2		96.4	2.2	0.8	0.5	0.1
1993	96.0	1.2	1.0	1.0	0.8		96.1	1.7	0.3	1.0	1.0
1994	96.4	1.8	0.7	0.5	0.6		95.2	2.9	1.0	0.3	0.7
1995	97.5	1.5	0.3	0.3	0.4		95.2	3.2	0.6	0.9	0.1
1996	97.5	1.4	0.4	0.3	0.4		94.0	2.9	2.4	0.4	0.4
1997	96.6	1.1	1.0	0.7	0.6		94.6	1.9	2.1	(Z)	1.3
1998	97.1	1.3	0.6	0.5	0.5		97.3	1.8	0.4	0.5	(Z)

	Blacks										
	Got into a serious fight at school or work						Took part in a gang fight				
	Zero times	Once	Twice	Three or four times	Five or more times		Zero times	Once	Twice	Three or four times	Five or more times
	Ec701	Ec702	Ec703	Ec704	Ec705		Ec706	Ec707	Ec708	Ec709	Ec710
Year	Percent	Percent	Percent	Percent	Percent		Percent	Percent	Percent	Percent	Percent
1975	—	—	—	—	—		—	—	—	—	—
1976	85.9	8.1	2.7	2.7	0.9		84.7	9.3	4.2	0.6	1.2
1977	88.7	7.6	2.0	1.0	0.7		87.5	7.6	2.0	1.7	1.5
1978	87.4	8.5	2.6	0.9	0.5		86.6	9.3	2.6	1.0	0.7
1979	88.7	6.2	2.5	1.1	1.1		89.8	7.6	1.4	0.8	0.3
1980	87.1	9.2	2.3	0.7	0.5		87.5	7.2	3.0	1.4	1.2
1981	86.2	10.1	2.2	0.9	0.6		87.1	7.1	3.0	1.5	1.3
1982	83.8	10.2	2.1	1.8	2.0		82.0	10.2	2.5	2.9	2.4
1983	82.5	12.0	1.9	3.1	0.5		85.9	7.0	4.1	1.5	1.5
1984	87.4	7.8	2.8	1.1	0.8		81.9	9.8	4.9	2.2	1.2
1985	83.4	11.5	3.4	0.9	0.9		80.8	10.7	4.9	2.1	1.5
1986	83.1	10.3	2.9	2.2	1.5		82.1	10.4	4.3	2.3	0.9
1987	83.0	10.7	2.9	1.2	2.2		79.2	9.2	5.9	1.8	4.0
1988	84.2	8.3	4.7	1.9	1.0		78.6	11.4	5.7	1.8	2.5
1989	84.3	9.0	5.4	0.8	0.6		79.1	11.6	5.6	1.5	2.3
1990	82.2	12.4	2.2	1.3	1.9		80.1	8.8	3.8	3.7	3.6
1991	76.8	13.6	5.3	2.1	2.2		76.5	9.7	6.6	3.9	3.3
1992	80.6	12.7	2.7	1.9	2.1		76.3	12.8	4.4	3.7	2.8
1993	83.5	9.2	4.2	1.7	1.4		75.4	9.0	8.5	2.4	4.6
1994	77.5	11.7	6.5	3.0	1.4		74.0	10.8	3.6	6.5	5.1
1995	82.0	11.4	3.5	2.4	0.7		76.7	9.4	7.0	5.2	1.7
1996	81.4	11.3	3.7	1.4	2.2		79.7	9.5	6.0	2.4	2.4
1997	79.3	12.6	4.0	2.0	2.1		76.8	11.9	4.1	3.6	3.7
1998	79.0	13.7	4.6	0.8	1.8		79.2	9.5	6.3	2.4	2.6

Note appears at end of table

TABLE Ec671–770   Percentage of high school seniors involved in violent delinquency in the past year, by race and sex: 1975–1998   *Continued*

Blacks

	Injured a person badly enough to need bandages or a doctor					Used a knife, gun, or other weapon to get something from a person				
	Zero times	Once	Twice	Three or four times	Five or more times	Zero times	Once	Twice	Three or four times	Five or more times
	Ec711	Ec712	Ec713	Ec714	Ec715	Ec716	Ec717	Ec718	Ec719	Ec720
Year	Percent	Percent	Percent	Percent	Percent	Percent	Percent	Percent	Percent	Percent
1975	—	—	—	—	—	—	—	—	—	—
1976	91.0	6.0	0.3	0.9	1.8	95.2	2.1	0.9	0.9	0.6
1977	89.7	7.4	1.7	0.2	0.7	95.3	3.2	0.7	0.5	0.5
1978	90.2	6.9	1.9	0.2	0.7	95.9	2.4	1.2	0.5	0.0
1979	89.8	8.8	1.1	0.3	0.0	97.2	2.5	0.0	0.0	0.3
1980	90.5	7.4	0.7	0.2	1.2	97.5	1.6	0.2	0.5	0.5
1981	90.3	5.0	3.0	0.6	1.1	95.9	2.2	0.6	0.4	0.9
1982	86.8	9.0	2.6	0.4	1.2	97.8	1.6	0.3	0.1	0.2
1983	88.3	7.9	1.5	1.8	0.5	94.9	3.3	0.7	0.5	0.5
1984	91.2	6.0	0.8	1.1	0.9	96.1	3.0	0.5	0.4	0.0
1985	88.4	8.3	2.0	0.8	0.5	95.4	3.0	0.8	0.9	0.0
1986	88.8	8.4	1.5	0.9	0.4	96.5	2.2	0.3	0.8	0.2
1987	87.3	6.2	3.8	1.2	1.6	92.1	4.0	1.8	0.3	1.9
1988	89.3	6.1	2.4	1.0	1.3	96.0	2.5	0.8	0.1	0.7
1989	89.2	5.9	2.3	1.0	1.6	96.3	0.6	0.1	0.8	2.1
1990	85.3	9.3	3.6	1.0	0.9	94.0	3.0	1.7	0.4	0.9
1991	84.4	10.0	1.7	0.7	3.2	94.1	1.7	2.1	0.5	1.6
1992	84.7	7.8	2.9	1.9	2.8	93.2	2.9	1.5	1.3	1.0
1993	85.5	6.2	2.0	2.0	4.3	94.2	3.1	0.6	1.3	0.9
1994	77.0	12.2	5.6	2.7	2.5	90.2	5.0	1.4	0.9	2.6
1995	83.9	7.6	2.8	4.3	1.3	92.8	3.4	2.2	0.8	0.7
1996	84.4	8.1	3.5	2.1	1.8	93.1	2.7	1.4	2.2	0.6
1997	83.2	7.8	4.2	2.7	2.1	91.7	2.3	3.0	1.4	1.6
1998	82.7	10.4	3.7	1.5	1.7	92.6	4.9	2.0	0.4	0.2

Males

	Hit an instructor or supervisor					Got into a serious fight at school or work				
	Zero times	Once	Twice	Three or four times	Five or more times	Zero times	Once	Twice	Three or four times	Five or more times
	Ec721	Ec722	Ec723	Ec724	Ec725	Ec726	Ec727	Ec728	Ec729	Ec730
Year	Percent	Percent	Percent	Percent	Percent	Percent	Percent	Percent	Percent	Percent
1975	94.5	3.6	0.7	0.7	0.4	80.0	11.6	5.0	2.3	1.1
1976	95.2	2.8	1.2	0.2	0.5	80.6	10.9	4.1	2.6	1.7
1977	95.2	3.3	0.5	0.5	0.4	81.5	9.9	5.1	2.3	1.2
1978	94.6	3.5	1.0	0.3	0.4	80.6	11.6	3.9	2.7	1.2
1979	95.5	2.6	0.8	0.4	0.7	80.6	10.8	4.1	3.3	1.2
1980	94.5	3.4	1.0	0.3	0.9	78.9	11.0	6.1	2.4	1.6
1981	95.1	3.3	0.7	0.3	0.6	79.1	12.6	4.2	2.6	1.5
1982	95.6	2.8	0.8	0.2	0.7	79.2	13.0	3.6	2.2	2.0
1983	94.6	2.9	1.1	0.9	0.5	75.3	14.0	5.1	4.1	1.4
1984	94.7	3.5	0.8	0.5	0.6	78.3	11.9	4.4	3.2	2.1
1985	94.9	3.1	0.5	0.8	0.7	76.3	13.8	4.5	3.3	2.1
1986	95.5	2.7	1.0	0.4	0.4	79.5	12.6	4.6	2.1	1.2
1987	96.1	2.5	0.7	0.4	0.3	78.2	12.4	5.3	2.6	1.5
1988	95.8	2.2	1.0	0.3	0.6	77.6	12.0	5.8	2.9	1.7
1989	94.3	3.4	0.3	1.2	0.8	76.3	12.7	6.5	2.3	2.2
1990	96.6	1.6	1.1	0.3	0.4	75.9	13.1	6.2	2.7	2.1
1991	95.3	2.4	0.9	0.4	1.0	76.6	12.4	5.5	2.8	2.7
1992	94.8	2.6	1.0	0.6	0.9	76.9	12.7	5.4	2.4	2.6
1993	94.3	3.3	1.0	0.4	1.0	78.4	11.2	5.2	3.1	2.1
1994	95.0	2.4	1.5	0.3	0.7	80.3	10.3	4.9	2.8	1.8
1995	95.8	1.7	0.8	0.6	1.0	82.1	9.3	4.1	2.8	1.7
1996	94.2	3.3	0.9	0.7	0.8	77.4	11.8	6.1	1.9	2.9
1997	94.5	2.9	1.0	0.3	1.2	78.5	11.8	4.9	2.3	2.5
1998	95.3	2.2	1.4	0.3	0.8	78.6	12.0	4.4	2.5	2.5

(continued)

TABLE Ec671–770   Percentage of high school seniors involved in violent delinquency in the past year, by race and sex: 1975–1998 *Continued*

	Males									
	Took part in a gang fight					Injured a person badly enough to need bandages or a doctor				
	Zero times	Once	Twice	Three or four times	Five or more times	Zero times	Once	Twice	Three or four times	Five or more times
	Ec731	Ec732	Ec733	Ec734	Ec735	Ec736	Ec737	Ec738	Ec739	Ec740
Year	Percent	Percent	Percent	Percent	Percent	Percent	Percent	Percent	Percent	Percent
1975	76.8	13.6	5.1	2.6	1.9	82.5	11.1	3.8	1.7	1.0
1976	81.0	10.2	3.9	2.8	2.1	83.6	10.6	2.5	1.6	1.6
1977	81.2	10.1	4.0	2.8	1.9	85.4	9.5	2.5	1.4	1.2
1978	82.0	10.3	3.7	2.2	1.8	83.3	10.4	3.1	1.7	1.3
1979	78.1	11.3	5.6	3.2	1.7	83.8	10.3	3.3	1.8	0.7
1980	75.8	13.4	5.4	3.0	2.5	79.4	13.3	4.1	2.2	1.0
1981	77.9	11.6	4.8	3.3	2.3	83.6	10.0	3.9	1.4	1.1
1982	77.6	12.0	4.9	3.1	2.4	82.1	11.0	3.9	1.7	1.3
1983	78.5	11.1	5.3	3.0	2.2	81.4	11.7	2.9	2.5	1.5
1984	76.5	12.7	4.6	3.6	2.5	82.9	9.8	3.4	2.0	1.9
1985	73.9	13.2	6.5	3.8	2.6	81.0	11.1	3.7	2.4	1.8
1986	76.5	12.4	6.1	3.2	1.7	81.0	11.7	4.3	1.5	1.5
1987	76.3	12.7	5.5	3.4	2.2	79.9	12.8	4.5	1.4	1.4
1988	75.6	12.8	5.4	3.6	2.5	82.5	10.2	3.0	2.7	1.6
1989	72.2	15.8	5.6	3.4	3.0	79.0	13.4	3.2	2.8	1.7
1990	73.2	12.4	6.0	4.7	3.8	79.8	11.2	4.9	2.3	1.9
1991	73.8	13.4	6.8	3.5	2.5	79.1	13.4	3.7	1.9	2.0
1992	73.0	12.9	6.0	4.7	3.4	78.5	11.9	5.2	2.5	1.9
1993	71.0	13.8	7.2	4.1	3.9	78.6	11.1	4.1	2.9	3.3
1994	75.4	10.8	5.9	3.8	4.1	79.1	10.8	4.3	3.6	2.3
1995	76.7	11.3	4.5	4.1	3.4	79.6	10.1	4.2	3.9	2.2
1996	73.0	13.3	5.7	3.4	4.6	77.5	12.2	4.9	3.1	2.3
1997	73.1	12.5	6.0	5.0	3.4	77.0	12.9	4.7	3.0	2.4
1998	74.2	12.3	6.0	3.8	3.7	77.2	12.6	5.1	2.8	2.3

	Males					Females				
	Used a knife, gun, or other weapon to get something from a person					Hit an instructor or supervisor				
	Zero times	Once	Twice	Three or four times	Five or more times	Zero times	Once	Twice	Three or four times	Five or more times
	Ec741	Ec742	Ec743	Ec744	Ec745	Ec746	Ec747	Ec748	Ec749	Ec750
Year	Percent	Percent	Percent	Percent	Percent	Percent	Percent	Percent	Percent	Percent
1975	95.2	2.4	1.2	0.7	0.5	99.1	0.8	0.1	0.1	0.0
1976	96.1	1.7	0.7	0.8	0.8	98.7	0.8	0.4	0.0	0.1
1977	95.2	2.3	0.9	0.7	0.8	98.4	0.9	0.4	0.1	0.1
1978	95.7	2.1	1.2	0.5	0.5	99.1	0.5	0.2	0.0	0.1
1979	95.6	2.8	0.7	0.5	0.4	98.6	1.1	0.1	0.1	0.0
1980	94.8	2.8	1.1	0.8	0.5	99.0	0.6	0.1	0.2	0.1
1981	96.2	2.1	0.6	0.7	0.4	99.0	0.6	0.3	0.1	0.0
1982	96.8	2.0	0.4	0.4	0.4	99.1	0.5	0.2	0.1	0.1
1983	95.2	2.2	1.0	0.6	1.0	98.7	0.7	0.4	0.1	0.1
1984	95.2	2.4	0.6	0.8	1.0	98.8	1.1	0.1	(Z)	0.0
1985	94.7	2.1	1.2	0.7	1.3	99.0	0.8	0.2	0.1	0.0
1986	95.1	2.8	0.8	0.9	0.5	98.3	1.3	(Z)	0.3	0.1
1987	94.9	2.6	1.1	0.5	0.9	98.9	0.6	0.3	0.1	0.1
1988	95.6	2.4	0.6	0.5	0.9	99.0	0.6	0.3	0.1	0.0
1989	93.5	2.9	1.5	0.9	1.3	99.1	0.6	0.1	0.0	0.2
1990	94.6	3.1	1.4	0.4	0.6	98.6	1.2	0.1	0.0	(Z)
1991	94.7	2.5	0.9	0.5	1.4	98.9	0.8	0.1	(Z)	0.2
1992	93.3	3.2	1.9	0.9	0.8	98.9	0.8	0.1	(Z)	0.2
1993	91.9	2.6	1.7	2.2	1.6	98.3	1.1	0.1	0.3	0.1
1994	92.5	3.7	1.4	1.0	1.4	99.3	0.5	0.2	0.0	(Z)
1995	94.6	2.8	1.1	0.6	1.0	98.3	1.0	0.3	0.1	0.3
1996	94.1	2.5	0.9	0.9	1.6	98.9	0.7	0.2	0.1	0.1
1997	93.6	1.6	2.1	1.8	0.9	98.4	0.7	0.5	0.2	0.3
1998	93.2	3.2	1.4	0.8	1.3	98.6	0.5	0.3	0.3	0.3

TABLE Ec671-770   Percentage of high school seniors involved in violent delinquency in the past year, by race and sex: 1975-1998 *Continued*

Females

	Got into a serious fight at school or work					Took part in a gang fight				
	Zero times	Once	Twice	Three or four times	Five or more times	Zero times	Once	Twice	Three or four times	Five or more times
	Ec751	Ec752	Ec753	Ec754	Ec755	Ec756	Ec757	Ec758	Ec759	Ec760
Year	Percent	Percent	Percent	Percent	Percent	Percent	Percent	Percent	Percent	Percent
1975	90.5	6.3	2.0	1.0	0.1	87.6	8.6	2.2	1.2	0.4
1976	91.8	5.3	1.9	1.0	0.1	89.5	7.4	1.5	1.5	0.3
1977	90.9	6.3	1.8	0.8	0.3	89.6	6.9	1.5	1.3	0.8
1978	91.3	5.7	1.7	1.0	0.3	88.1	8.0	2.1	1.7	0.2
1979	89.1	7.1	2.7	0.9	0.1	87.4	9.5	2.1	0.5	0.4
1980	89.5	7.6	1.8	1.0	0.1	89.4	7.4	1.8	0.9	0.5
1981	90.1	6.5	2.2	1.0	0.3	88.7	7.3	2.5	1.1	0.4
1982	87.0	8.9	2.2	1.3	0.6	86.5	8.2	3.2	1.6	0.5
1983	89.6	7.2	1.6	1.3	0.4	86.1	9.0	3.1	1.3	0.5
1984	88.0	8.1	2.3	1.2	0.3	88.7	7.0	3.0	1.0	0.3
1985	87.3	8.6	2.8	1.2	0.2	85.1	10.5	3.0	1.0	0.5
1986	86.6	9.4	2.2	1.4	0.4	84.6	10.2	2.7	1.7	0.8
1987	86.1	8.0	4.0	1.3	0.5	84.3	9.9	3.5	1.8	0.5
1988	86.6	9.1	2.5	1.2	0.7	85.5	9.7	3.4	1.0	0.4
1989	84.3	10.9	3.1	1.3	0.4	87.4	8.4	2.2	1.3	0.6
1990	86.9	9.6	2.4	1.0	0.1	85.0	10.5	2.7	1.6	0.1
1991	88.1	8.2	2.4	1.0	0.3	86.4	8.7	2.8	1.2	0.9
1992	85.8	10.2	2.5	0.9	0.6	85.3	9.3	2.8	1.9	0.8
1993	87.0	8.5	2.3	1.9	0.4	85.5	8.2	4.3	1.4	0.6
1994	87.9	7.6	2.9	1.0	0.6	86.0	9.6	2.2	1.7	0.5
1995	88.6	7.0	2.5	1.6	0.3	86.1	9.1	2.6	1.8	0.6
1996	90.0	6.3	1.9	1.3	0.5	86.9	8.2	3.0	1.1	0.7
1997	87.3	7.8	2.9	1.2	0.8	84.2	9.6	3.6	1.9	0.8
1998	88.6	7.6	2.6	0.7	0.5	84.7	8.3	4.5	1.8	0.7

Females

	Injured a person badly enough to need bandages or a doctor					Used a knife, gun, or other weapon to get something from a person				
	Zero times	Once	Twice	Three or four times	Five or more times	Zero times	Once	Twice	Three or four times	Five or more times
	Ec761	Ec762	Ec763	Ec764	Ec765	Ec766	Ec767	Ec768	Ec769	Ec770
Year	Percent	Percent	Percent	Percent	Percent	Percent	Percent	Percent	Percent	Percent
1975	97.8	1.5	0.5	0.1	0.0	99.2	0.3	0.1	0.1	0.4
1976	97.6	1.8	0.3	0.1	0.1	99.3	0.6	0.1	0.1	0.0
1977	97.3	2.1	0.4	0.0	0.2	99.3	0.4	0.1	0.1	0.1
1978	97.6	1.6	0.7	0.1	0.0	99.1	0.4	0.5	0.1	0.0
1979	97.3	1.6	0.6	0.3	0.1	99.2	0.6	0.1	0.1	0.1
1980	97.2	2.1	0.6	0.1	0.0	99.1	0.8	0.1	0.0	0.0
1981	97.4	2.0	0.5	0.1	0.1	99.1	0.7	0.0	0.1	0.1
1982	95.8	3.4	0.4	(Z)	0.4	98.7	1.1	(Z)	0.0	0.1
1983	96.7	2.5	0.5	(Z)	0.2	99.0	0.7	0.2	0.0	0.1
1984	96.7	2.3	0.8	0.1	0.1	98.7	0.7	0.4	0.2	0.0
1985	96.3	2.7	0.7	0.3	0.0	98.7	1.2	0.1	0.0	0.0
1986	97.0	2.2	0.4	0.4	0.1	98.5	0.8	0.3	0.2	0.1
1987	96.4	2.7	0.5	0.3	0.2	98.5	1.1	0.2	0.1	0.1
1988	96.6	2.2	0.8	0.3	0.1	99.0	0.6	0.3	(Z)	0.2
1989	96.6	2.5	0.3	0.2	0.4	99.0	0.5	0.1	(Z)	0.5
1990	95.9	3.3	0.7	0.1	(Z)	99.2	0.5	(Z)	0.1	0.1
1991	96.0	2.9	0.5	0.4	0.2	98.8	0.6	0.4	0.2	0.1
1992	96.0	2.8	0.6	0.4	0.2	98.6	0.9	0.2	0.2	0.2
1993	95.0	3.0	1.4	0.5	0.1	99.0	0.7	0.1	0.2	0.0
1994	94.5	4.1	0.8	0.3	0.3	98.3	1.1	0.5	0.1	(Z)
1995	95.9	2.8	0.7	0.3	0.3	98.6	0.6	0.3	0.3	0.2
1996	94.6	4.1	0.9	0.3	0.1	98.9	0.4	0.5	0.2	0.0
1997	93.9	4.6	0.9	0.2	0.4	97.8	1.2	0.5	(Z)	0.5
1998	93.9	3.2	1.0	0.9	1.0	98.2	1.2	0.2	0.2	0.3

Notes appear on next page

(continued)

TABLE Ec671–770   Percentage of high school seniors involved in violent delinquency in the past year, by race and sex: 1975–1998   *Continued*

(Z) Less than 0.05 percent.

Sources

1976–1984: U.S. Bureau of Justice Statistics, *Sourcebook of Criminal Justice Statistics 1985* (1987), Tables 3.61 and 3.62; 1985–1996: U.S. Bureau of Justice Statistics, *Sourcebook of Criminal Justice Statistics 1996* (1997), Tables 3.39 and 3.40; 1997–1998: U.S. Bureau of Justice Statistics, *Sourcebook of Criminal Justice Statistics 1998* (1999), Tables 3.48 and 3.49; originally from Lloyd D.

Johnson, Jerald G. Bachman, and Patrick M. O'Malley, *Monitoring the Future* (1975 through 1998 annual reports), and data supplied by the Monitoring the Future Project (Institute for Social Research, University of Michigan).

Documentation

See the text for Table Ec426–445 for a description of the source and the wording of the measures.

TABLE Ec771–870   Percentage of high school seniors involved in property crime in the past year, by race and sex: 1975–1998

Contributed by Douglas Eckberg

	Whites									
	Stole something worth less than fifty dollars					Stole something worth more than fifty dollars				
	Zero times	Once	Twice	Three or four times	Five or more times	Zero times	Once	Twice	Three or four times	Five or more times
	Ec771	Ec772	Ec773	Ec774	Ec775	Ec776	Ec777	Ec778	Ec779	Ec780
Year	Percent	Percent	Percent	Percent	Percent	Percent	Percent	Percent	Percent	Percent
1975	—	—	—	—	—	—	—	—	—	—
1976	68.1	13.7	6.9	5.5	5.9	94.7	2.7	0.8	0.9	0.9
1977	68.7	12.6	7.2	5.5	6.0	96.0	2.1	0.9	0.3	0.6
1978	68.1	13.9	7.4	5.3	5.2	94.8	2.5	1.0	0.7	1.0
1979	65.8	14.4	8.5	5.6	5.8	93.4	3.8	1.1	0.5	1.3
1980	64.8	15.4	8.0	5.8	5.9	93.4	3.8	1.1	0.5	1.3
1981	67.1	15.1	6.5	5.8	5.5	93.0	3.9	1.5	0.7	1.0
1982	67.7	14.6	7.1	5.5	5.2	94.1	3.3	1.1	0.8	0.7
1983	67.2	15.4	7.4	5.0	4.9	94.3	3.2	1.1	0.7	0.7
1984	67.9	13.5	8.2	5.6	4.8	93.3	3.9	0.9	0.9	0.9
1985	68.8	14.5	7.1	4.7	4.9	93.4	3.3	1.0	0.9	1.4
1986	65.2	17.5	7.7	5.0	4.6	93.7	3.2	1.2	0.8	1.1
1987	64.1	16.9	6.7	6.0	6.3	91.7	3.8	1.7	1.6	1.3
1988	65.3	15.3	8.0	5.6	5.8	92.6	3.6	1.8	0.9	1.1
1989	65.5	14.5	7.5	5.2	7.3	91.8	4.1	1.4	1.3	1.5
1990	64.8	14.4	7.2	6.8	6.8	89.6	4.8	2.2	1.4	2.0
1991	67.2	13.9	7.9	3.8	7.2	90.5	4.4	2.1	1.3	1.7
1992	65.3	14.9	9.2	5.7	5.0	89.9	5.2	1.7	1.4	1.8
1993	66.1	15.4	7.2	5.0	6.3	89.2	5.4	1.8	1.2	2.4
1994	69.4	13.1	6.7	5.3	5.6	90.2	4.5	1.6	1.3	2.4
1995	69.4	14.2	6.9	4.6	4.9	91.6	3.5	1.8	1.5	1.7
1996	67.8	14.4	7.0	4.5	6.3	90.0	4.7	1.8	1.5	2.0
1997	66.0	12.8	9.5	6.0	5.7	89.2	5.4	2.2	1.2	2.0
1998	69.3	13.3	7.3	5.1	5.0	90.8	4.3	2.0	1.5	1.6

TABLE Ec771–870   Percentage of high school seniors involved in property crime in the past year, by race and sex: 1975–1998 *Continued*

	Whites									
	Took something from a store without paying					Took a car belonging to someone outside the family without permission				
	Zero times	Once	Twice	Three or four times	Five or more times	Zero times	Once	Twice	Three or four times	Five or more times
	Ec781	Ec782	Ec783	Ec784	Ec785	Ec786	Ec787	Ec788	Ec789	Ec790
Year	Percent	Percent	Percent	Percent	Percent	Percent	Percent	Percent	Percent	Percent
1975	—	—	—	—	—	—	—	—	—	—
1976	68.6	13.0	6.9	5.3	6.2	96.1	1.9	1.1	0.1	0.7
1977	71.3	11.9	5.8	5.5	5.6	96.3	1.8	0.6	0.8	0.4
1978	70.5	11.2	6.8	6.1	5.5	95.8	2.2	1.1	0.5	0.4
1979	68.8	12.7	6.5	6.0	5.9	96.0	2.1	1.0	0.5	0.3
1980	68.4	13.1	6.8	5.3	6.4	95.5	2.1	1.1	0.9	0.4
1981	72.1	12.1	6.0	4.6	5.2	96.3	2.3	0.7	0.4	0.4
1982	71.5	12.4	5.9	4.5	5.7	96.3	2.2	0.6	0.4	0.5
1983	73.7	12.7	5.4	4.4	3.9	94.8	3.1	1.1	0.6	0.4
1984	74.2	11.3	5.1	4.8	4.6	94.5	3.4	1.4	0.3	0.4
1985	73.5	11.8	6.3	3.9	4.5	94.9	3.0	0.8	0.6	0.7
1986	71.2	12.7	6.6	4.7	4.7	95.0	3.2	1.0	0.4	0.4
1987	70.1	13.1	4.5	5.2	7.2	95.1	2.7	1.1	0.6	0.6
1988	69.1	13.3	6.5	5.0	6.2	94.9	3.3	0.9	0.5	0.4
1989	69.5	13.0	5.4	4.4	7.7	94.9	2.6	1.2	0.5	0.8
1990	66.9	14.1	6.2	5.5	7.3	93.5	3.3	1.7	0.7	0.7
1991	68.3	12.1	7.1	5.3	7.1	94.4	3.2	1.1	0.9	0.5
1992	70.0	12.3	6.6	5.5	5.6	95.1	2.3	1.4	0.5	0.8
1993	69.4	13.6	5.6	5.5	5.9	94.7	2.9	1.1	0.7	0.6
1994	71.0	10.8	7.4	4.6	6.1	95.4	2.6	1.0	0.3	0.7
1995	72.1	11.7	5.2	5.5	5.5	96.1	2.3	0.6	0.6	0.3
1996	69.1	12.3	7.2	5.0	6.4	95.6	2.3	0.9	0.7	0.4
1997	67.6	11.7	7.3	7.0	6.4	95.6	2.3	0.9	0.5	0.6
1998	72.6	12.4	6.3	3.5	5.3	96.6	2.2	0.5	0.3	0.4

	Whites					Blacks				
	Took part of a car without permission of the owner					Stole something worth less than fifty dollars				
	Zero times	Once	Twice	Three or four times	Five or more times	Zero times	Once	Twice	Three or four times	Five or more times
	Ec791	Ec792	Ec793	Ec794	Ec795	Ec796	Ec797	Ec798	Ec799	Ec800
Year	Percent	Percent	Percent	Percent	Percent	Percent	Percent	Percent	Percent	Percent
1975	—	—	—	—	—	—	—	—	—	—
1976	93.9	3.3	1.4	0.6	0.9	76.4	11.8	4.2	4.5	3.6
1977	94.5	3.2	1.2	0.6	0.5	77.5	11.1	3.0	4.4	3.7
1978	93.7	3.4	1.5	0.8	0.5	77.3	13.2	3.3	3.3	2.9
1979	93.1	3.8	1.5	0.7	0.9	76.3	12.9	5.4	4.0	1.7
1980	92.6	4.2	1.7	1.0	0.5	76.9	10.7	4.7	3.3	4.7
1981	94.2	3.4	1.2	0.8	0.4	80.4	9.5	4.1	2.6	3.4
1982	94.5	3.6	1.0	0.4	0.5	77.2	11.2	4.1	4.3	3.2
1983	94.3	3.1	1.3	0.7	0.5	80.0	11.1	3.7	2.5	2.7
1984	93.2	4.1	1.0	0.9	0.8	80.8	9.5	3.5	2.7	3.4
1985	93.4	3.2	1.9	0.5	0.9	78.3	9.8	4.8	3.2	3.9
1986	94.2	3.3	1.3	0.5	0.6	83.6	8.0	4.3	1.3	2.8
1987	93.3	3.9	1.4	0.7	0.7	72.4	13.1	6.1	2.9	5.6
1988	94.5	3.3	1.0	0.6	0.6	73.3	12.2	5.2	4.0	5.3
1989	94.0	3.4	1.2	0.7	0.7	81.4	9.0	3.9	1.8	3.9
1990	92.6	4.1	1.7	0.7	0.8	78.7	8.8	5.7	2.5	4.5
1991	94.6	3.1	1.0	0.5	0.9	74.9	11.2	6.5	3.0	4.5
1992	94.7	2.7	0.9	1.2	0.5	79.0	7.8	3.9	5.3	4.0
1993	93.3	3.1	1.3	1.1	1.1	78.3	8.4	3.4	2.8	7.0
1994	95.3	2.2	1.0	0.6	0.8	65.7	13.9	5.5	7.8	7.1
1995	95.8	2.1	1.0	0.4	0.6	69.9	8.4	8.5	5.2	7.9
1996	95.8	2.5	1.0	0.2	0.4	68.1	10.2	8.2	7.8	5.8
1997	95.2	1.9	1.4	0.9	0.6	69.0	9.4	8.3	4.7	8.7
1998	95.8	2.2	1.2	0.4	0.4	74.3	11.7	6.3	4.1	3.6

(continued)

TABLE Ec771–870   Percentage of high school seniors involved in property crime in the past year, by race and sex: 1975–1998   *Continued*

Blacks

	Stole something worth more than fifty dollars					Took something from a store without paying				
	Zero times	Once	Twice	Three or four times	Five or more times	Zero times	Once	Twice	Three or four times	Five or more times
	Ec801	Ec802	Ec803	Ec804	Ec805	Ec806	Ec807	Ec808	Ec809	Ec810
Year	Percent	Percent	Percent	Percent	Percent	Percent	Percent	Percent	Percent	Percent
1975	—	—	—	—	—	—	—	—	—	—
1976	93.7	3.3	0.3	0.9	1.5	63.4	15.9	9.8	3.0	7.9
1977	93.8	2.7	0.7	1.2	1.5	64.9	16.0	6.4	6.6	5.9
1978	94.2	3.1	1.2	0.7	0.7	70.4	14.7	6.0	4.8	4.1
1979	94.2	4.0	0.9	0.0	0.9	69.5	14.5	7.4	5.1	3.1
1980	96.0	1.4	0.5	0.5	1.6	74.9	11.1	4.4	5.1	4.4
1981	93.9	3.0	1.7	0.4	0.6	74.0	12.9	5.0	3.7	4.4
1982	92.7	5.0	0.3	0.9	1.1	74.7	12.7	4.7	2.1	5.8
1983	92.7	4.0	0.9	1.7	0.7	75.8	13.9	4.3	2.7	3.3
1984	95.2	3.5	0.3	0.5	0.5	74.3	14.4	3.7	5.0	2.6
1985	93.8	2.7	1.6	1.0	0.8	79.2	9.7	3.2	3.9	4.1
1986	95.0	2.7	1.2	0.9	0.2	80.8	10.6	3.6	2.9	2.2
1987	91.3	4.7	2.0	1.5	0.6	76.8	11.9	3.0	2.2	6.1
1988	90.6	5.6	2.1	0.4	1.2	75.3	9.7	5.1	4.8	5.1
1989	95.7	1.0	1.5	0.3	1.5	80.2	10.2	3.2	2.0	4.4
1990	91.4	4.7	0.8	1.3	1.9	74.3	10.0	6.9	3.6	5.2
1991	93.2	3.0	1.4	1.6	0.8	74.5	9.4	6.8	4.1	5.2
1992	92.2	3.4	1.6	1.7	1.2	74.0	10.6	5.8	5.0	4.6
1993	90.6	2.1	1.8	1.4	4.1	73.4	8.9	5.5	3.9	8.3
1994	84.1	7.8	3.4	1.8	3.0	65.1	12.0	7.4	5.5	10.0
1995	87.6	4.0	3.7	2.1	2.6	62.2	13.6	6.3	5.7	12.2
1996	82.1	7.3	5.6	2.6	2.4	64.5	12.8	6.3	6.9	9.6
1997	83.2	6.6	3.6	3.5	3.1	65.7	9.6	9.3	7.5	7.9
1998	87.2	5.7	3.9	1.2	2.0	70.5	10.7	6.6	5.9	6.3

Blacks

	Took a car belonging to someone outside the family without permission					Took part of a car without permission of the owner				
	Zero times	Once	Twice	Three or four times	Five or more times	Zero times	Once	Twice	Three or four times	Five or more times
	Ec811	Ec812	Ec813	Ec814	Ec815	Ec816	Ec817	Ec818	Ec819	Ec820
Year	Percent	Percent	Percent	Percent	Percent	Percent	Percent	Percent	Percent	Percent
1975	—	—	—	—	—	—	—	—	—	—
1976	94.3	3.0	0.6	1.2	0.9	97.3	1.8	0.0	0.3	0.3
1977	96.3	2.0	0.5	0.5	0.5	94.4	4.4	0.7	0.5	0.2
1978	95.7	3.3	0.2	0.7	0.2	96.2	2.4	1.2	0.2	0.0
1979	95.5	2.5	1.1	0.6	0.3	96.5	1.7	1.4	0.3	0.3
1980	94.9	2.8	0.7	1.2	0.7	94.5	3.2	1.4	0.2	0.5
1981	95.9	3.0	0.6	0.2	0.0	97.2	1.5	0.9	0.6	0.0
1982	95.2	3.1	0.4	0.5	0.7	94.8	2.9	1.3	0.7	0.3
1983	95.6	3.0	0.4	0.5	0.6	94.8	2.1	1.8	0.6	0.7
1984	95.8	2.5	0.3	0.9	0.5	96.0	2.3	0.6	0.3	0.8
1985	94.7	3.9	0.0	1.0	0.4	96.1	1.8	1.0	0.8	0.3
1986	96.1	2.3	1.2	0.0	0.4	98.0	0.8	0.7	0.1	0.4
1987	92.9	3.7	2.8	0.2	0.4	92.9	3.6	2.5	0.5	0.5
1988	95.0	3.0	1.3	0.1	0.5	95.0	2.7	0.8	0.6	0.9
1989	96.2	1.6	1.1	0.2	0.8	92.6	4.6	1.7	0.7	0.4
1990	93.7	2.4	2.4	0.1	1.4	94.8	2.0	1.3	0.5	1.4
1991	92.2	4.2	1.2	1.4	1.1	91.8	4.6	1.8	0.5	1.2
1992	91.9	4.6	1.0	1.4	1.1	95.0	3.2	0.8	0.6	0.4
1993	93.4	1.1	1.7	1.3	2.5	92.7	2.6	2.1	1.2	1.4
1994	89.7	4.1	2.6	2.2	1.4	88.5	6.9	1.2	1.5	2.0
1995	90.7	3.2	3.4	1.1	1.5	90.4	4.9	2.0	1.3	1.3
1996	94.0	2.2	2.9	0.7	0.3	94.5	2.1	2.2	0.8	0.3
1997	88.2	5.8	2.3	2.2	1.5	92.8	2.1	2.5	1.4	1.2
1998	94.5	3.1	1.5	0.9	(Z)	95.0	2.4	0.8	1.5	0.2

TABLE Ec771–870   Percentage of high school seniors involved in property crime in the past year, by race and sex: 1975–1998   *Continued*

Males

	Stole something worth less than fifty dollars					Stole something worth more than fifty dollars				
	Zero times	Once	Twice	Three or four times	Five or more times	Zero times	Once	Twice	Three or four times	Five or more times
	Ec821	Ec822	Ec823	Ec824	Ec825	Ec826	Ec827	Ec828	Ec829	Ec830
Year	Percent	Percent	Percent	Percent	Percent	Percent	Percent	Percent	Percent	Percent
1975	56.9	15.6	9.8	7.5	10.1	89.3	5.1	2.0	1.4	2.2
1976	59.9	16.0	8.2	6.5	9.4	89.7	5.2	1.3	1.7	2.0
1977	61.2	14.6	9.6	6.8	7.7	92.1	3.9	1.4	1.0	1.6
1978	60.6	16.2	9.3	6.6	7.2	90.4	4.4	1.9	1.3	1.9
1979	58.1	17.3	10.3	6.4	7.8	89.2	6.3	1.7	1.1	1.6
1980	57.5	17.8	9.4	6.7	8.5	88.3	6.3	2.1	0.9	2.4
1981	60.2	17.0	7.3	7.1	8.3	88.8	6.0	2.5	1.1	1.7
1982	60.4	15.7	9.2	6.7	8.1	89.3	5.4	2.0	1.6	1.7
1983	61.5	16.6	8.8	6.3	6.8	89.9	5.7	2.0	1.3	1.1
1984	62.0	15.6	9.1	6.7	6.6	89.2	6.4	1.4	1.3	1.6
1985	61.4	16.7	8.9	6.3	6.7	88.1	5.7	1.9	1.7	2.7
1986	62.3	18.5	7.2	5.0	6.9	90.6	4.6	1.9	1.7	1.3
1987	59.2	17.8	7.8	6.9	8.2	86.4	6.0	2.7	2.5	2.4
1988	57.8	17.8	9.8	6.6	8.0	86.9	6.3	3.0	1.3	2.4
1989	61.3	16.0	8.2	5.7	8.9	87.5	5.6	2.6	2.0	2.3
1990	60.3	15.4	8.0	7.7	8.6	84.9	6.6	2.7	2.2	3.5
1991	58.2	16.5	9.5	5.9	9.9	85.0	6.2	3.5	2.8	2.5
1992	59.7	16.6	9.8	6.4	7.5	84.8	8.2	2.3	2.2	2.5
1993	59.9	15.8	7.7	5.7	11.0	82.5	7.6	3.4	2.1	4.5
1994	60.6	14.9	8.4	8.2	7.9	82.6	8.2	3.2	2.2	3.8
1995	59.6	16.5	9.3	6.1	8.5	85.6	5.3	3.5	2.6	3.1
1996	61.3	16.1	6.9	6.1	9.6	82.2	6.7	4.2	2.8	4.1
1997	58.4	14.2	12.0	7.2	8.1	82.3	8.2	4.1	2.2	3.1
1998	61.5	14.8	9.3	6.9	7.5	83.3	7.7	4.0	1.7	3.3

Males

	Took something from a store without paying					Took a car belonging to someone outside the family without permission				
	Zero times	Once	Twice	Three or four times	Five or more times	Zero times	Once	Twice	Three or four times	Five or more times
	Ec831	Ec832	Ec833	Ec834	Ec835	Ec836	Ec837	Ec838	Ec839	Ec840
Year	Percent	Percent	Percent	Percent	Percent	Percent	Percent	Percent	Percent	Percent
1975	55.3	16.0	9.2	7.5	12.0	94.1	3.0	0.9	0.8	1.3
1976	62.2	13.1	9.0	5.7	9.9	93.9	3.0	1.7	0.1	1.3
1977	64.0	14.5	7.9	6.2	7.3	93.8	2.8	1.1	1.4	0.9
1978	65.2	11.9	7.3	7.3	8.2	93.8	3.5	1.0	1.0	0.6
1979	62.7	14.3	7.8	7.7	7.5	94.2	3.1	1.4	0.9	0.4
1980	61.8	14.6	7.6	7.2	8.8	92.7	3.4	1.9	1.2	0.8
1981	64.6	14.7	7.0	5.4	8.3	94.5	3.1	1.3	0.5	0.7
1982	65.2	13.4	7.1	6.2	8.1	94.6	3.1	0.9	0.6	0.9
1983	68.4	13.9	6.7	5.6	5.3	92.3	3.9	1.6	1.1	1.1
1984	69.3	12.8	5.8	5.9	6.3	92.4	4.0	2.0	0.8	0.9
1985	68.2	12.6	7.5	5.4	6.2	92.2	3.9	1.4	1.1	1.4
1986	67.2	13.5	7.5	4.9	6.9	93.3	4.1	1.2	0.7	0.7
1987	64.0	15.5	4.8	5.8	9.9	91.9	4.0	2.2	0.8	1.1
1988	63.2	13.8	8.5	6.2	8.4	92.9	4.1	1.3	0.7	0.9
1989	65.3	13.8	6.8	4.5	9.7	93.0	3.4	1.7	0.6	1.3
1990	63.1	14.3	6.9	6.3	9.4	91.5	4.4	1.6	1.1	1.4
1991	60.4	14.7	7.6	7.7	9.7	91.7	3.8	1.8	1.5	1.2
1992	62.5	14.2	8.6	6.6	8.1	91.5	4.0	1.9	1.1	1.4
1993	62.4	15.1	6.1	7.1	9.4	91.2	4.3	1.7	1.4	1.4
1994	63.9	12.7	8.2	6.2	9.0	91.6	3.7	2.3	1.2	1.2
1995	64.3	12.8	6.7	7.0	9.2	93.4	3.6	1.5	0.6	0.9
1996	63.1	14.3	6.8	5.1	10.7	92.6	3.1	1.6	1.7	1.0
1997	62.4	12.3	8.7	7.9	8.7	91.6	4.0	2.0	1.2	1.2
1998	66.5	12.7	7.3	4.8	8.7	93.5	3.5	1.4	0.9	0.7

(continued)

TABLE Ec771–870   Percentage of high school seniors involved in property crime in the past year, by race and sex: 1975–1998   *Continued*

	Males						Females				
	Took part of a car without permission of the owner						Stole something worth less than fifty dollars				
	Zero times	Once	Twice	Three or four times	Five or more times		Zero times	Once	Twice	Three or four times	Five or more times
	Ec841	Ec842	Ec843	Ec844	Ec845		Ec846	Ec847	Ec848	Ec849	Ec850
Year	Percent	Percent	Percent	Percent	Percent		Percent	Percent	Percent	Percent	Percent
1975	89.4	6.1	2.3	0.9	1.3		76.7	11.1	5.2	4.0	2.9
1976	89.4	5.4	2.4	1.4	1.5		78.6	10.8	4.6	3.9	2.0
1977	89.8	5.6	2.3	1.1	1.2		77.7	10.2	4.6	3.6	3.8
1978	89.4	5.6	2.4	1.5	1.0		77.7	10.9	4.8	3.5	3.1
1979	88.6	5.9	2.9	1.2	1.4		74.9	11.5	5.9	4.6	3.0
1980	87.3	6.9	2.8	1.9	1.0		75.6	11.8	5.3	4.3	2.9
1981	90.3	5.2	2.2	1.3	0.9		77.7	11.7	4.8	3.5	2.2
1982	90.6	5.5	2.2	0.7	1.0		77.0	12.1	4.5	4.1	2.3
1983	90.9	4.7	2.2	1.1	1.1		77.2	13.3	4.3	2.9	2.3
1984	89.4	6.2	1.7	1.3	1.4		78.4	10.2	5.2	3.6	2.7
1985	88.9	5.1	3.2	0.8	1.9		78.5	11.4	4.5	2.8	2.9
1986	90.6	5.2	2.2	0.9	1.1		72.8	14.4	6.7	4.0	2.2
1987	88.8	5.8	3.1	1.2	1.1		72.1	14.2	5.9	3.9	3.8
1988	91.6	4.3	1.5	1.2	1.4		74.7	12.7	5.0	3.9	3.6
1989	89.5	5.9	1.8	1.5	1.2		75.5	11.3	5.9	3.6	3.7
1990	88.7	6.4	2.4	1.0	1.5		75.0	11.5	5.9	3.8	3.8
1991	89.4	5.6	2.0	1.1	1.9		78.3	10.8	5.7	2.2	3.0
1992	90.4	4.6	1.9	1.7	1.4		75.3	11.9	5.5	4.6	2.7
1993	87.5	5.9	2.1	2.3	2.2		76.5	11.9	6.2	3.1	2.3
1994	90.3	4.5	2.0	1.3	1.8		77.0	11.4	5.0	3.6	3.0
1995	91.1	4.1	1.9	1.0	1.1		76.9	11.8	4.9	3.4	3.1
1996	90.6	4.6	2.9	0.5	1.4		73.3	12.9	7.2	3.1	3.6
1997	90.9	3.6	2.6	1.7	1.2		72.5	11.1	7.0	4.9	4.5
1998	92.1	4.1	1.6	1.1	1.1		75.5	11.8	6.0	2.8	4.0

	Females										
	Stole something worth more than fifty dollars						Took something from a store without paying				
	Zero times	Once	Twice	Three or four times	Five or more times		Zero times	Once	Twice	Three or four times	Five or more times
	Ec851	Ec852	Ec853	Ec854	Ec855		Ec856	Ec857	Ec858	Ec859	Ec860
Year	Percent	Percent	Percent	Percent	Percent		Percent	Percent	Percent	Percent	Percent
1975	99.0	0.6	0.1	0.1	0.3		72.9	11.8	5.3	6.2	3.9
1976	98.7	0.6	0.2	0.2	0.2		74.0	13.3	5.2	4.2	3.3
1977	98.3	0.8	0.3	0.3	0.4		75.3	11.2	4.3	5.1	4.1
1978	98.5	0.7	0.2	0.2	0.4		74.5	11.9	5.9	5.0	2.7
1979	97.3	1.6	0.3	0.4	0.3		73.8	12.3	5.4	4.6	3.9
1980	98.3	1.2	0.1	0.1	0.2		76.6	11.1	4.9	3.5	3.8
1981	97.2	1.7	0.6	0.3	0.2		78.7	10.5	5.1	3.7	2.1
1982	97.2	1.9	0.1	0.2	0.6		77.2	11.5	4.5	3.1	3.7
1983	97.8	1.0	0.5	0.4	0.2		79.5	11.9	3.4	2.6	2.6
1984	97.9	1.3	0.2	0.5	0.2		78.6	11.3	4.0	3.8	2.4
1985	97.9	1.1	0.5	0.2	0.3		79.2	10.5	4.3	3.2	2.8
1986	96.0	2.5	0.7	0.2	0.6		76.8	12.0	4.6	4.0	2.6
1987	96.2	2.1	0.7	0.6	0.4		76.4	11.6	4.1	3.8	4.0
1988	96.3	1.8	1.0	0.4	0.4		76.2	11.9	4.5	3.5	3.9
1989	96.6	1.9	0.3	0.7	0.5		76.8	11.7	3.9	3.7	3.9
1990	95.8	2.6	1.0	0.2	0.5		73.9	11.9	6.1	4.1	3.9
1991	95.6	2.7	0.4	0.3	0.9		78.0	8.7	7.2	2.9	3.3
1992	94.9	2.7	0.9	0.5	0.9		76.5	11.3	5.0	3.8	3.4
1993	95.6	2.3	0.6	0.7	0.9		76.7	11.5	5.1	3.0	3.6
1994	95.3	2.2	1.2	0.6	0.8		74.8	10.4	6.0	4.1	4.7
1995	95.5	2.1	0.6	1.1	0.8		76.0	10.8	5.0	4.4	3.9
1996	93.5	3.7	1.2	0.7	1.0		72.3	11.4	6.7	5.3	4.3
1997	92.0	4.3	1.1	1.2	1.4		70.1	10.7	6.5	7.1	5.7
1998	93.3	3.1	1.0	1.3	1.3		73.9	12.1	5.9	3.7	4.4

TABLE Ec771–870   Percentage of high school seniors involved in property crime in the past year, by race and sex: 1975–1998   *Continued*

	Females									
	Took a car belonging to someone outside the family without permission					Took part of a car without permission of the owner				
	Zero times	Once	Twice	Three or four times	Five or more times	Zero times	Once	Twice	Three or four times	Five or more times
	Ec861	Ec862	Ec863	Ec864	Ec865	Ec866	Ec867	Ec868	Ec869	Ec870
Year	Percent	Percent	Percent	Percent	Percent	Percent	Percent	Percent	Percent	Percent
1975	97.9	1.5	0.4	0.1	0.1	98.8	0.7	0.1	0.3	0.1
1976	97.9	1.2	0.6	0.4	0.1	98.7	1.0	0.2	0.1	0.1
1977	98.0	1.1	0.4	0.3	0.1	98.2	1.3	0.4	0.2	0.1
1978	97.5	1.5	0.7	0.2	0.1	98.2	1.2	0.5	0.1	0.1
1979	97.5	1.3	0.7	0.3	0.3	98.0	1.3	0.4	0.2	0.1
1980	97.9	1.1	0.1	0.7	0.2	98.6	0.7	0.6	0.0	0.1
1981	97.8	1.8	0.2	0.2	0.0	99.0	0.8	0.1	0.1	0.1
1982	97.2	1.8	0.4	0.3	0.3	98.2	1.3	0.2	0.1	0.3
1983	97.0	2.3	0.5	0.1	0.1	98.0	1.2	0.6	0.2	(Z)
1984	96.3	2.9	0.5	0.1	0.1	98.3	1.1	0.2	0.2	0.2
1985	96.6	2.3	0.5	0.2	0.4	97.7	1.5	0.4	0.2	0.1
1986	96.6	2.1	1.0	0.2	0.1	98.0	1.3	0.3	0.4	0.1
1987	96.9	2.1	0.4	0.3	0.2	97.6	1.6	0.2	0.4	0.2
1988	96.2	2.7	0.5	0.2	0.2	96.7	2.4	0.6	0.1	0.2
1989	96.3	2.3	0.6	0.4	0.4	97.0	1.9	0.6	0.3	0.2
1990	95.6	2.3	1.8	0.1	0.2	98.3	1.0	0.4	0.1	0.2
1991	96.1	2.9	0.4	0.4	0.3	98.3	1.1	0.4	0.1	0.1
1992	96.6	2.0	0.8	0.3	0.2	98.0	1.4	0.2	0.3	0.1
1993	96.2	1.7	1.3	0.4	0.4	97.9	0.7	1.0	0.1	0.3
1994	97.3	2.1	0.4	0.1	0.1	98.3	1.2	0.1	0.3	(Z)
1995	97.0	1.7	0.5	0.5	0.3	97.7	1.3	0.5	0.2	0.3
1996	97.4	1.5	0.8	(Z)	0.3	99.1	0.8	0.0	0.0	0.0
1997	96.2	3.0	0.3	0.1	0.5	98.1	0.8	0.3	0.2	0.6
1998	97.1	1.7	0.4	0.2	0.6	98.2	0.7	0.5	0.1	0.5

(Z) Less than 0.05 percent.

Sources

1976–1984: U.S. Bureau of Justice Statistics, *Sourcebook of Criminal Justice Statistics 1985* (1987), Tables 3.61 and 3.62; 1985–1996: U.S. Bureau of Justice Statistics, *Sourcebook of Criminal Justice Statistics 1996* (1997), Tables 3.39 and 3.40; 1997–1998: U.S. Bureau of Justice Statistics, *Sourcebook of Criminal Justice Statistics 1998* (1999), Tables 3.48 and 3.49; originally from Lloyd D. Johnson, Jerald G. Bachman, and Patrick M. O'Malley, *Monitoring the Future* (1975 through 1998 annual reports), and data supplied by the Monitoring the Future Project (Institute for Social Research, University of Michigan).

Documentation

See the text for Table Ec426–445 for a description of the source and the wording of the measures.

TABLE Ec871–950   Percentage of high school seniors involved in trespassing and vandalism in the past year, by race and sex: 1975–1998

Contributed by Douglas Eckberg

	Whites									
	Went into a house or building when they were not supposed to be there					Deliberately set fire to someone's property				
	Zero times	Once	Twice	Three or four times	Five or more times	Zero times	Once	Twice	Three or four times	Five or more times
	Ec871	Ec872	Ec873	Ec874	Ec875	Ec876	Ec877	Ec878	Ec879	Ec880
Year	Percent	Percent	Percent	Percent	Percent	Percent	Percent	Percent	Percent	Percent
1975	—	—	—	—	—	—	—	—	—	—
1976	76.5	11.7	5.8	3.3	2.8	98.7	0.6	0.5	(Z)	0.2
1977	77.2	10.4	6.3	3.3	2.7	98.8	0.8	0.1	0.2	0.1
1978	75.0	12.4	6.4	3.3	3.0	98.5	0.9	0.5	0.1	0.2
1979	75.4	11.8	7.2	2.9	2.6	98.9	0.7	0.2	0.1	0.1
1980	73.5	12.5	5.8	5.3	2.8	98.6	1.2	0.1	0.1	0.1
1981	76.1	11.9	6.5	2.8	2.7	98.3	1.1	0.2	0.2	0.2
1982	75.1	12.7	6.6	3.1	2.5	99.0	0.6	0.2	(Z)	0.1
1983	75.3	11.8	7.9	3.1	1.9	99.1	0.5	0.1	0.1	0.2
1984	73.8	12.6	6.3	4.5	2.8	98.4	0.8	0.4	(Z)	0.3
1985	72.9	13.9	6.8	3.2	3.1	98.3	1.0	0.2	0.2	0.0
1986	74.2	13.0	6.5	3.3	3.0	98.4	0.9	0.1	0.2	0.3
1987	71.7	13.0	8.4	4.1	2.7	98.7	0.9	0.2	0.2	(Z)
1988	71.3	13.2	7.2	4.5	3.8	98.8	0.7	0.2	0.1	0.2
1989	72.5	12.6	7.9	4.0	3.0	98.0	1.4	0.2	0.2	0.1
1990	72.3	11.5	8.5	4.6	3.0	98.1	1.0	0.5	0.2	0.2
1991	75.0	11.6	6.8	3.2	3.4	98.1	1.0	0.3	(Z)	0.5
1992	71.7	13.1	8.1	4.1	2.9	97.3	1.8	0.4	0.3	0.2
1993	72.8	12.5	7.1	3.7	4.0	96.8	1.4	0.7	0.6	0.6
1994	75.5	11.0	6.6	4.3	2.5	97.1	1.7	0.6	0.4	0.2
1995	77.5	10.8	5.9	3.3	2.5	97.8	1.3	0.3	0.3	0.3
1996	75.5	11.5	6.9	3.9	2.1	97.5	1.2	0.6	0.2	0.5
1997	74.1	11.9	7.2	3.8	2.9	97.6	1.1	0.1	0.3	0.8
1998	75.1	11.0	6.8	4.0	3.2	98.3	0.9	0.3	0.1	0.4

	Whites									
	Deliberately damaged any school property					Deliberately damaged any property at work				
	Zero times	Once	Twice	Three or four times	Five or more times	Zero times	Once	Twice	Three or four times	Five or more times
	Ec881	Ec882	Ec883	Ec884	Ec885	Ec886	Ec887	Ec888	Ec889	Ec890
Year	Percent	Percent	Percent	Percent	Percent	Percent	Percent	Percent	Percent	Percent
1975	—	—	—	—	—	—	—	—	—	—
1976	88.0	6.8	2.8	1.4	1.1	94.1	3.3	1.2	0.7	0.7
1977	87.4	6.7	3.1	1.6	1.2	94.8	2.3	1.4	1.0	0.5
1978	87.0	7.4	2.6	1.5	1.6	93.5	2.9	1.7	1.1	0.8
1979	85.3	8.4	3.6	1.7	1.1	91.5	4.3	1.8	1.3	1.1
1980	85.8	7.8	3.1	1.8	1.5	92.8	3.5	1.9	0.9	0.9
1981	86.0	7.3	4.0	1.2	1.4	92.8	3.5	1.8	1.4	0.5
1982	87.4	7.1	3.4	1.1	1.0	94.0	3.3	1.6	0.6	0.5
1983	85.3	7.4	3.5	2.5	1.3	94.5	2.3	1.5	0.9	0.7
1984	85.4	7.1	3.4	2.1	1.9	94.9	2.4	1.2	0.8	0.7
1985	86.0	6.8	3.8	1.8	1.6	94.4	2.8	1.5	0.6	0.7
1986	86.7	6.8	3.2	2.0	1.2	94.7	2.6	1.4	0.8	0.5
1987	85.0	8.4	3.1	2.0	1.6	94.9	2.6	1.4	0.5	0.6
1988	84.1	9.0	3.5	1.8	1.5	93.7	3.4	1.5	0.5	0.9
1989	86.6	6.7	3.4	1.4	1.9	93.4	3.1	1.9	1.1	0.5
1990	86.0	6.6	4.3	1.9	1.2	93.1	3.1	2.2	0.8	0.9
1991	87.4	6.9	2.4	1.1	2.1	93.4	3.1	1.2	0.9	1.4
1992	85.8	8.1	3.0	1.0	2.0	93.8	2.8	1.4	1.2	0.8
1993	84.7	6.6	4.1	2.0	2.5	93.7	3.1	1.5	0.7	1.0
1994	86.6	6.2	3.6	2.1	1.4	94.5	2.5	1.6	0.7	0.7
1995	85.7	6.7	3.4	2.7	1.5	93.8	3.5	1.3	0.5	0.8
1996	86.1	7.1	2.9	2.4	1.6	94.5	3.1	0.7	0.8	1.0
1997	84.7	8.3	3.3	2.1	1.5	93.2	2.8	1.8	1.1	1.2
1998	86.1	7.8	2.7	2.0	1.4	92.5	3.8	1.7	0.7	1.3

Note appears at end of table

TABLE Ec871–950   Percentage of high school seniors involved in trespassing and vandalism in the past year, by race and sex: 1975–1998   Continued

Blacks

	Went into a house or building when they were not supposed to be there					Deliberately set fire to someone's property				
	Zero times	Once	Twice	Three or four times	Five or more times	Zero times	Once	Twice	Three or four times	Five or more times
	Ec891	Ec892	Ec893	Ec894	Ec895	Ec896	Ec897	Ec898	Ec899	Ec900
Year	Percent	Percent	Percent	Percent	Percent	Percent	Percent	Percent	Percent	Percent
1975	—	—	—	—	—	—	—	—	—	—
1976	78.1	12.0	3.6	4.2	2.1	98.5	0.9	0.3	0.0	0.3
1977	83.8	8.4	3.9	2.9	1.2	97.3	1.5	0.7	0.2	0.5
1978	82.0	9.1	3.4	2.2	3.4	98.1	1.2	0.2	0.7	0.0
1979	84.1	8.8	2.3	2.0	2.8	98.6	0.0	0.0	0.8	0.6
1980	81.9	10.2	3.0	2.3	2.6	98.1	1.2	0.0	0.2	0.2
1981	84.0	9.1	3.9	2.2	0.9	98.9	0.6	0.2	0.0	0.2
1982	80.3	9.3	6.7	1.3	2.4	98.7	0.4	0.3	0.4	0.2
1983	83.1	10.0	2.7	2.7	1.5	98.2	1.2	0.6	0.0	0.0
1984	81.1	9.5	5.0	1.5	2.9	97.8	1.6	0.3	0.0	0.2
1985	80.7	9.8	5.3	1.9	2.3	98.6	1.2	0.0	0.0	0.2
1986	82.6	7.3	5.5	1.7	2.9	96.2	2.4	1.1	0.1	0.1
1987	77.7	9.3	7.0	4.1	1.9	97.9	0.6	0.5	0.1	0.8
1988	75.8	13.4	6.1	2.7	1.9	96.9	2.0	0.7	0.4	0.0
1989	83.1	9.7	2.6	1.3	3.3	96.8	1.7	0.8	0.0	0.7
1990	80.7	6.1	7.3	3.1	2.8	97.2	1.3	0.4	0.3	0.8
1991	78.6	8.0	5.2	3.6	4.6	98.3	0.8	0.6	0.3	0.0
1992	81.1	8.0	3.6	4.1	3.2	98.2	0.7	0.3	0.3	0.6
1993	80.5	9.0	3.4	3.2	3.9	96.6	2.1	0.9	0.2	0.3
1994	72.4	9.7	6.2	5.7	6.0	95.6	2.3	0.0	1.3	0.8
1995	74.9	11.3	5.2	2.0	6.7	96.7	2.1	0.2	0.2	0.8
1996	79.8	6.7	8.3	2.4	2.8	96.0	2.6	0.9	(Z)	0.5
1997	79.8	6.5	7.8	3.1	2.8	97.3	2.2	0.1	0.1	0.3
1998	77.7	11.9	5.3	3.3	1.7	98.4	0.9	0.2	0.5	(Z)

Blacks

	Deliberately damaged any school property					Deliberately damaged any property at work				
	Zero times	Once	Twice	Three or four times	Five or more times	Zero times	Once	Twice	Three or four times	Five or more times
	Ec901	Ec902	Ec903	Ec904	Ec905	Ec906	Ec907	Ec908	Ec909	Ec910
Year	Percent	Percent	Percent	Percent	Percent	Percent	Percent	Percent	Percent	Percent
1975	—	—	—	—	—	—	—	—	—	—
1976	89.2	6.6	1.8	1.5	0.9	96.1	1.8	1.2	0.0	0.6
1977	88.7	6.1	2.7	1.2	1.2	95.1	2.0	1.2	1.2	0.5
1978	92.5	4.1	1.4	1.7	0.0	97.1	1.9	0.7	0.0	0.0
1979	91.7	4.0	2.3	0.6	1.1	94.9	3.1	1.1	0.3	0.9
1980	91.4	4.4	1.6	1.9	0.9	94.4	2.5	0.5	1.2	1.4
1981	90.3	5.4	2.4	1.3	0.9	96.1	1.3	1.5	0.7	0.7
1982	89.5	7.1	1.7	0.5	1.1	95.9	2.4	0.6	0.4	0.6
1983	89.3	6.6	1.5	1.3	1.3	95.6	2.7	0.9	0.8	0.1
1984	89.2	7.3	2.1	0.3	1.1	97.5	1.6	0.7	0.0	0.2
1985	91.7	5.3	1.6	0.9	0.4	96.5	2.2	1.1	0.2	0.0
1986	90.2	5.4	3.0	0.6	0.7	95.9	1.9	0.6	0.8	0.7
1987	86.0	6.5	3.2	2.3	2.0	96.4	1.5	0.6	0.6	0.9
1988	93.0	3.0	2.0	1.0	1.0	97.0	1.2	1.0	0.5	0.3
1989	88.9	5.2	0.9	0.9	4.1	95.6	1.1	0.3	0.9	2.0
1990	87.9	5.7	2.7	1.2	2.6	95.1	2.2	1.3	0.0	1.4
1991	88.0	4.0	4.3	2.0	1.6	95.7	2.1	1.7	0.0	0.5
1992	88.2	5.6	3.9	1.4	0.9	96.3	1.7	0.5	0.9	0.6
1993	89.2	4.5	2.6	2.2	1.5	94.1	2.8	1.0	1.1	0.9
1994	81.5	8.3	4.3	3.5	2.4	90.5	3.2	1.3	2.9	2.1
1995	87.0	6.2	2.6	2.0	2.1	93.9	2.7	0.2	1.4	1.8
1996	85.8	7.9	3.6	1.7	0.9	91.4	4.9	1.4	0.7	1.6
1997	88.3	6.0	1.8	1.5	2.4	93.7	3.5	1.3	1.3	0.3
1998	86.0	7.2	2.5	1.8	2.4	96.4	1.0	0.4	0.9	1.3

(continued)

TABLE Ec871–950   Percentage of high school seniors involved in trespassing and vandalism in the past year, by race and sex: 1975–1998   *Continued*

	Males									
	Went into a house or building when they were not supposed to be there					Deliberately set fire to someone's property				
	Zero times	Once	Twice	Three or four times	Five or more times	Zero times	Once	Twice	Three or four times	Five or more times
	Ec911	Ec912	Ec913	Ec914	Ec915	Ec916	Ec917	Ec918	Ec919	Ec920
Year	Percent	Percent	Percent	Percent	Percent	Percent	Percent	Percent	Percent	Percent
1975	60.5	16.6	11.8	5.5	5.5	96.7	1.8	0.8	0.3	0.3
1976	69.8	14.1	8.3	4.0	4.0	97.1	1.5	0.9	0.1	0.4
1977	71.0	12.5	7.9	4.1	4.5	97.0	1.7	0.4	0.3	0.6
1978	68.3	14.6	8.0	4.7	4.4	96.9	1.7	0.8	0.2	0.5
1979	69.0	14.6	8.9	4.1	3.5	98.1	1.0	0.3	0.3	0.3
1980	66.5	14.8	7.4	6.8	4.5	97.3	2.2	0.1	0.2	0.2
1981	69.7	13.4	8.8	4.2	3.9	96.9	2.1	0.5	0.3	0.3
1982	69.4	14.2	8.7	4.2	3.5	98.3	1.1	0.3	0.1	0.2
1983	69.3	13.6	9.5	4.5	3.1	97.7	1.2	0.4	0.3	0.4
1984	68.5	13.6	8.5	5.4	4.0	96.7	1.8	0.7	0.2	0.5
1985	65.5	17.5	8.3	3.7	4.9	97.1	1.5	0.6	0.3	0.5
1986	70.6	12.2	8.4	4.3	4.4	96.7	1.9	0.3	0.4	0.7
1987	66.9	13.9	9.9	5.6	3.7	97.3	1.6	0.5	0.3	0.4
1988	67.1	15.0	8.2	5.4	4.2	97.3	1.5	0.5	0.2	0.4
1989	69.4	12.9	9.6	4.3	3.8	95.7	2.6	0.8	0.4	0.5
1990	68.3	13.0	8.2	6.0	4.4	96.5	1.9	1.0	0.3	0.4
1991	69.3	12.8	7.5	4.9	5.6	96.4	1.6	0.7	0.3	1.0
1992	68.7	12.4	9.4	5.0	4.5	95.3	2.6	0.7	0.6	0.8
1993	65.9	13.9	8.2	5.2	6.8	94.1	2.4	1.1	1.0	1.3
1994	67.8	13.0	9.5	5.4	4.3	94.7	2.6	1.1	1.0	0.5
1995	70.4	12.4	8.2	4.4	4.6	96.3	2.4	0.5	0.4	0.4
1996	71.0	12.1	8.7	4.4	3.8	95.1	2.6	1.0	0.3	0.9
1997	69.4	12.2	8.6	5.2	4.7	95.2	2.7	0.5	0.4	1.1
1998	69.4	10.7	8.5	6.3	5.1	95.8	1.5	0.9	0.5	1.3

	Males									
	Deliberately damaged any school property					Deliberately damaged any property at work				
	Zero times	Once	Twice	Three or four times	Five or more times	Zero times	Once	Twice	Three or four times	Five or more times
	Ec921	Ec922	Ec923	Ec924	Ec925	Ec926	Ec927	Ec928	Ec929	Ec930
Year	Percent	Percent	Percent	Percent	Percent	Percent	Percent	Percent	Percent	Percent
1975	79.0	10.2	6.1	2.1	2.7	90.4	4.2	2.6	1.3	1.6
1976	82.0	10.1	3.9	2.1	2.0	90.1	5.2	2.0	1.3	1.3
1977	81.6	8.5	4.8	2.4	2.6	91.0	3.9	2.2	1.8	1.2
1978	82.5	9.5	3.5	2.2	2.4	89.2	4.9	2.9	1.6	1.5
1979	78.8	11.3	5.2	2.6	2.1	86.4	6.4	3.3	2.1	1.9
1980	81.1	9.5	4.4	2.9	2.2	87.8	5.8	3.2	1.5	1.7
1981	79.7	10.8	5.2	2.0	2.2	89.1	4.9	2.9	1.9	1.1
1982	82.3	9.9	4.1	1.9	1.8	90.6	4.6	2.6	1.0	1.2
1983	78.5	9.9	4.8	4.1	2.7	90.1	4.3	2.6	1.8	1.2
1984	79.9	9.8	4.3	2.7	3.2	91.4	3.8	2.3	1.1	1.4
1985	81.1	8.5	5.2	2.5	2.6	90.1	4.8	2.7	1.1	1.3
1986	81.3	9.0	4.6	3.2	1.9	91.0	4.2	2.2	1.5	1.1
1987	78.6	11.2	5.0	2.5	2.7	90.7	4.3	2.8	1.0	1.2
1988	79.8	10.6	4.6	2.4	2.6	89.6	5.4	2.6	0.8	1.6
1989	80.7	7.9	5.3	2.7	3.4	89.7	4.0	3.3	1.7	1.4
1990	81.7	7.8	5.5	2.6	2.4	89.2	5.0	2.9	1.2	1.6
1991	81.2	8.7	4.5	2.0	3.6	89.2	4.9	2.1	1.4	2.4
1992	79.7	10.0	5.1	1.4	3.7	90.5	4.0	1.9	1.7	1.9
1993	77.7	8.6	6.2	3.3	4.2	89.5	4.4	2.6	1.4	2.1
1994	78.9	8.8	5.6	3.3	3.4	90.7	3.7	2.6	1.4	1.6
1995	78.6	9.1	4.8	4.3	3.2	89.8	5.6	1.9	1.0	1.7
1996	79.4	9.6	4.5	3.1	3.3	89.6	5.1	1.3	1.5	2.4
1997	78.8	10.3	4.3	3.0	3.6	90.0	3.9	2.6	1.8	1.7
1998	79.5	9.6	3.7	3.4	3.8	87.4	5.8	2.9	1.4	2.6

TABLE Ec871–950   Percentage of high school seniors involved in trespassing and vandalism in the past year, by race and sex: 1975–1998   *Continued*

	Females									
	Went into a house or building when they were not supposed to be there					Deliberately set fire to someone's property				
	Zero times	Once	Twice	Three or four times	Five or more times	Zero times	Once	Twice	Three or four times	Five or more times
	Ec931	Ec932	Ec933	Ec934	Ec935	Ec936	Ec937	Ec938	Ec939	Ec940
Year	Percent	Percent	Percent	Percent	Percent	Percent	Percent	Percent	Percent	Percent
1975	81.7	10.3	3.7	2.1	2.1	99.7	0.1	0.0	0.1	0.0
1976	83.6	9.3	3.1	2.4	1.5	99.5	0.2	0.1	0.0	0.1
1977	84.2	8.0	4.2	2.2	1.3	99.8	0.1	0.1	0.0	0.1
1978	83.1	9.0	4.2	1.7	2.1	99.6	0.4	0.1	0.0	0.0
1979	82.6	9.3	4.4	1.8	1.9	99.6	0.2	0.1	0.1	0.1
1980	83.1	9.7	3.6	2.4	1.2	99.7	0.2	0.0	0.0	0.1
1981	84.6	9.5	3.6	1.2	1.1	99.7	0.3	0.0	0.0	0.0
1982	81.9	10.9	4.3	1.5	1.4	99.3	0.4	0.2	0.0	0.1
1983	84.2	9.1	4.2	1.6	0.9	99.9	0.1	0.0	0.0	(Z)
1984	81.7	10.7	3.6	2.5	1.5	99.8	0.1	0.0	0.0	(Z)
1985	82.0	9.2	4.8	2.4	1.5	99.4	0.5	0.1	(Z)	(Z)
1986	80.1	11.8	4.4	1.9	1.8	99.4	0.2	0.2	0.1	0.1
1987	78.8	10.8	6.2	2.5	1.7	99.5	0.4	(Z)	0.0	(Z)
1988	78.2	10.4	5.4	2.8	3.2	99.4	0.5	0.1	(Z)	(Z)
1989	79.2	11.2	4.7	2.6	2.3	99.3	0.4	(Z)	0.0	0.2
1990	81.8	7.8	7.1	2.3	1.0	99.3	0.5	0.0	0.1	0.1
1991	82.7	8.7	6.0	1.3	1.3	99.4	0.5	0.0	0.0	0.1
1992	79.6	11.8	4.4	2.4	1.8	99.1	0.6	0.2	0.1	(Z)
1993	82.5	9.4	5.4	1.7	0.9	99.1	0.4	0.4	0.1	0.0
1994	82.6	8.9	4.0	2.8	1.6	99.2	0.5	(Z)	0.1	0.2
1995	82.9	9.1	4.0	1.9	2.1	98.8	0.6	0.1	0.2	0.3
1996	81.6	9.1	5.2	2.6	1.5	99.1	0.6	0.2	(Z)	0.1
1997	81.2	8.5	5.6	2.5	2.2	98.7	0.8	(Z)	0.0	0.4
1998	81.0	10.1	4.8	1.4	2.7	98.9	0.4	0.3	(Z)	0.3

	Females									
	Deliberately damaged any school property					Deliberately damaged any property at work				
	Zero times	Once	Twice	Three or four times	Five or more times	Zero times	Once	Twice	Three or four times	Five or more times
	Ec941	Ec942	Ec943	Ec944	Ec945	Ec946	Ec947	Ec948	Ec949	Ec950
Year	Percent	Percent	Percent	Percent	Percent	Percent	Percent	Percent	Percent	Percent
1975	94.2	3.1	1.5	0.9	0.3	98.9	0.5	0.4	0.1	0.2
1976	94.4	3.2	1.4	0.6	0.3	98.6	0.9	0.4	0.0	0.1
1977	93.7	4.0	1.2	0.8	0.4	98.2	0.8	0.4	0.4	0.1
1978	92.9	4.5	1.4	0.8	0.4	98.5	0.8	0.4	0.1	0.1
1979	93.1	4.8	1.3	0.6	0.3	97.7	1.6	0.2	0.3	0.2
1980	92.4	5.3	1.4	0.4	0.4	98.4	1.1	0.1	0.3	0.1
1981	93.6	3.7	1.9	0.5	0.4	97.9	1.1	0.5	0.4	0.1
1982	93.0	3.7	2.3	0.5	0.5	98.1	1.3	0.3	(Z)	0.2
1983	93.3	4.2	1.6	0.5	0.5	98.9	0.8	0.3	0.0	(Z)
1984	92.4	4.6	1.8	0.8	0.4	99.0	0.7	0.2	(Z)	0.0
1985	91.5	4.8	2.0	1.1	0.6	99.0	0.7	0.1	0.2	0.0
1986	92.4	4.8	1.6	0.7	0.6	98.3	1.2	0.3	0.1	(Z)
1987	90.8	5.4	1.6	1.5	0.7	98.3	0.9	0.2	0.4	0.2
1988	91.8	5.3	1.6	0.8	0.5	98.4	1.1	0.3	0.1	0.1
1989	92.5	4.6	1.2	0.7	1.0	97.1	1.9	0.4	0.3	0.3
1990	92.3	4.6	2.0	0.6	0.5	98.1	0.7	0.7	0.1	0.3
1991	93.5	4.1	1.4	0.4	0.5	98.2	1.1	0.2	0.2	0.3
1992	91.5	5.2	2.0	0.8	0.5	97.8	1.2	0.6	0.3	0.1
1993	92.8	4.3	1.9	0.7	0.3	98.0	1.2	0.4	0.3	0.1
1994	92.6	4.5	1.5	0.9	0.5	98.0	0.9	0.5	0.4	0.3
1995	92.6	4.1	1.7	1.1	0.5	97.6	1.0	0.6	0.3	0.4
1996	92.5	4.8	1.4	1.0	0.3	98.2	1.4	0.3	0.1	0.1
1997	90.4	5.7	1.8	1.4	0.6	96.7	1.7	0.8	0.3	0.4
1998	91.8	5.2	1.6	0.7	0.8	97.6	1.1	0.2	0.3	0.8

Note appears on next page

(continued)

TABLE Ec871–950   Percentage of high school seniors involved in trespassing and vandalism in the past year, by race and sex: 1975–1998   *Continued*

(Z) Less than 0.05 percent.

Sources

1976–1984: U.S. Bureau of Justice Statistics, *Sourcebook of Criminal Justice Statistics 1985* (1987), Tables 3.61 and 3.62; 1985–1996: U.S. Bureau of Justice Statistics, *Sourcebook of Criminal Justice Statistics 1996* (1997), Tables 3.39 and 3.40; 1997–1998: U.S. Bureau of Justice Statistics, *Sourcebook of Criminal Justice Statistics 1998* (1999), Tables 3.48 and 3.49; originally from Lloyd D. Johnson, Jerald G. Bachman, and Patrick M. O'Malley, *Monitoring the Future* (1975 through 1998 annual reports), and data supplied by the Monitoring the Future Project (Institute for Social Research, University of Michigan).

Documentation

See the text for Table Ec426–445 for a description of the source and the wording of the measures.

DRUG AND ALCOHOL ABUSE

Douglas Eckberg

TABLE Ec951–962   Percentage of survey respondents and estimated number of persons using selected drugs in the past year, by drug: 1979–1998

Contributed by Douglas Eckberg

	Estimated population using drug in past year (age 12 and older)						Percentage of survey respondents reporting using drug in past year					
	Any illicit drug	Marijuana and hashish	Cocaine	Any hallucinogens	Heroin	Alcohol	Any illicit drug	Marijuana and hashish	Cocaine	Any hallucinogens	Heroin	Alcohol
	Ec951	Ec952	Ec953	Ec954	Ec955	Ec956	Ec957	Ec958	Ec959	Ec960	Ec961	Ec962
Year	Thousand	Thousand	Thousand	Thousand	Thousand	Thousand	Percent	Percent	Percent	Percent	Percent	Percent
1979	31,485	29,869	8,608	5,260	427	131,443	17.5	16.6	4.8	2.9	0.2	72.9
1982	—	29,685	10,458	4,149	323	126,534	—	15.9	5.6	2.2	0.2	67.9
1985	31,488	26,145	9,839	3,198	347	140,394	16.3	13.6	5.1	1.7	0.2	72.9
1988	24,577	19,492	7,151	3,200	508	135,044	12.4	9.8	3.6	1.6	0.3	68.1
1990	23,449	18,931	5,442	2,350	443	132,859	11.7	9.4	2.7	1.2	0.2	66.0
1991	22,612	18,067	5,284	2,562	359	138,113	11.1	8.9	2.6	1.3	0.2	68.1
1992	20,046	16,322	4,332	2,530	304	133,090	9.7	7.9	2.1	1.2	0.1	64.7
1993	21,402	17,510	3,947	2,479	230	137,771	10.3	8.5	1.9	1.2	0.1	66.5
1994	22,663	17,813	3,664	2,725	281	140,121	10.8	8.5	1.7	1.3	0.1	66.9
1995	22,662	17,755	3,664	3,416	428	138,314	10.7	8.4	1.7	1.6	0.2	65.4
1996	23,182	18,398	4,033	3,602	455	138,912	10.8	8.6	1.9	1.7	0.2	64.9
1997	24,189	19,446	4,169	4,063	597	138,500	11.2	9.0	1.9	1.9	0.3	64.1
1998	23,115	18,710	3,811	3,565	253	139,807	10.6	8.6	1.7	1.6	0.1	64.0

Sources

U.S. Substance Abuse and Mental Health Services Administration (SAMHSA), *Preliminary Results from the 1996 National Household Survey on Drug Abuse* DHHS Publication number [SMA] 97-3149 (1997), Tables 4A and 4B. SAMHSA, *Summary Findings from the 1998 National Household Survey on Drug Abuse*, Tables 4A and 4B (accessed on SAMHSA's Internet site, August 1999).

Documentation

The National Household Survey on Drug Abuse (NHSDA) sample is representative of the general U.S. population age 12 and older and always has oversampled youths and young adults. The 1997 NHSDA employed a multistage area probability sample of 24,505 persons. The surveys cover residents of households and noninstitutional group quarters (for example, shelters, rooming houses, dormitories) and civilians living on military bases. They exclude homeless people who do not use shelters, active military personnel, and residents of institutional group quarters (for example, jails, hospitals). The earliest surveys date from 1971, but pre-1979 data are not comparable with later data and are not reported here.

Pre-1994 estimates provided here differ from those published previously. Improvements to the questionnaire and estimation procedures were instituted in 1994, leading to data that were not directly comparable to 1979–1993 data. To maintain comparability, pre-1994 data have been adjusted using comparisons of results from 1993, in which both the old and the new methodologies were used. Most 1979–1993 data were adjusted using a simple ratio correction factor. Prevalence of use of alcohol, marijuana, cigarettes, and "any illicit drug" were adjusted by means of formal models. A detailed discussion of the revised methodology can be found in SAMHSA, *Development and Implementation of a New Data Collection Instrument for the 1994 National Household Survey on Drug Abuse*, DHHS Publication number [SMA] 96-3084 (1996). For a discussion of the approaches to adjustment, see SAMHSA, *Preliminary Results from the 1997 National Household Survey on Drug Abuse*, DHHS Publication number [SMA] 98-3251 (1998), pp. 43–5.

TABLE Ec963–974 Percentage of survey respondents and estimated number of persons using selected drugs in the past month, by drug: 1979–1998

Contributed by Douglas Eckberg

	Estimated population using drug in past month (age 12 and older)						Survey respondents reporting using drug in past month					
	Any illicit drug	Marijuana and hashish	Cocaine	Hallucinogens	Heroin	Alcohol	Any illicit drug	Marijuana and hashish	Cocaine	Hallucinogens	Heroin	Alcohol
	Ec963	Ec964	Ec965	Ec966	Ec967	Ec968	Ec969	Ec970	Ec971	Ec972	Ec973	Ec974
Year	Thousand	Thousand	Thousand	Thousand	Thousand	Thousand	Percent	Percent	Percent	Percent	Percent	Percent
1979	25,399	23,790	4,743	3,382	128	114,065	14.1	13.2	2.6	1.9	0.1	63.2
1982	—	21,507	4,491	1,608	162	105,613	—	11.5	2.4	0.9	0.1	56.6
1985	23,272	18,641	5,686	2,257	137	115,984	12.1	9.7	3.0	1.2	0.1	60.2
1988	15,192	12,353	3,140	1,245	79	108,882	7.7	6.2	1.6	0.6	(Z)	54.9
1990	13,526	10,913	1,720	887	41	105,869	6.7	5.4	0.9	0.4	(Z)	52.6
1991	13,368	10,366	2,032	1,115	71	105,938	6.6	5.1	1.0	0.5	(Z)	52.2
1992	12,033	9,676	1,402	842	92	100,789	5.8	4.7	0.7	0.4	(Z)	49.0
1993	12,256	9,610	1,404	826	68	105,351	5.9	4.6	0.7	0.4	(Z)	50.8
1994	12,553	10,112	1,382	960	117	112,804	6.0	4.8	0.7	0.5	0.1	53.9
1995	12,823	9,842	1,453	1,469	196	110,501	6.1	4.7	0.7	0.7	0.1	52.2
1996	13,035	10,095	1,749	1,316	216	109,149	6.1	4.7	0.8	0.6	0.1	51.0
1997	13,904	11,109	1,505	1,632	325	111,071	6.4	5.1	0.7	0.8	0.2	51.4
1998	13,615	11,016	1,750	1,514	130	112,850	6.2	5.0	0.8	0.7	0.1	51.7

(Z) Less than 0.05 percent.

Sources

U.S. Substance Abuse and Mental Health Services Administration (SAMHSA), *Preliminary Results from the 1996 National Household Survey on Drug Abuse*, DHHS Publication number [SMA] 97-3149 (1997), Tables 5A and 5B. SAMHSA, *Summary Findings from the 1998 National Household Survey on Drug Abuse*, Tables 5A and 5B (accessed on SAMHSA's Internet site, August 1999).

Documentation

See the text for Table Ec951–962 for a description of the data source and methodology.

TABLE Ec975–1014 Percentage of survey respondents reporting use of selected drugs in the past month, by drug, age, race, ethnicity, and sex: 1979–1998

Contributed by Douglas Eckberg

	Any illicit drug									
	Age				Race and ethnicity				Sex	
	12–17	18–25	26–34	35 and older	White	Black	Hispanic	Nonwhite, nonblack, non-Hispanic	Male	Female
	Ec975	Ec976	Ec977	Ec978	Ec979	Ec980	Ec981	Ec982	Ec983	Ec984
Year	Percent	Percent	Percent	Percent	Percent	Percent	Percent	Percent	Percent	Percent
1979	16.3	38.0	20.8	2.8	14.2	13.3	12.9	15.1	19.2	9.4
1982	—	—	—	—	—	—	—	—	—	—
1985	13.2	25.3	23.1	3.9	12.3	12.7	8.9	10.7	14.9	9.5
1988	8.1	17.9	14.7	2.3	7.7	6.6	6.9	—	9.4	6.0
1990	7.1	15.0	10.9	3.1	6.9	7.3	5.6	3.4	8.2	5.3
1991	5.8	15.4	10.0	3.4	6.5	8.1	5.3	6.0	7.9	5.4
1992	5.3	13.1	11.4	2.5	6.1	5.6	4.4	3.9	7.6	4.2
1993	5.7	13.6	9.5	3.0	6.1	5.8	5.2	4.3	7.7	4.3
1994	8.2	13.3	8.5	3.2	6.0	7.3	5.4	3.1	7.9	4.3
1995	10.9	14.2	8.3	2.8	6.0	7.9	5.1	4.0	7.8	4.5
1996	9.0	15.6	8.4	2.9	6.1	7.5	5.2	4.8	8.1	4.2
1997	11.4	14.7	7.4	3.6	6.4	7.5	5.9	5.4	8.5	4.5
1998	9.9	16.1	7.0	3.3	6.1	8.2	6.1	3.8	8.1	4.5

TABLE Ec975–1014   Percentage of survey respondents reporting use of selected drugs in the past month, by drug, age, race, ethnicity, and sex: 1979–1998   *Continued*

Marijuana

	Age				Race and ethnicity				Sex	
	12–17	18–25	26–34	35 and older	White	Black	Hispanic	Nonwhite, nonblack, non-Hispanic	Male	Female
	Ec985	Ec986	Ec987	Ec988	Ec989	Ec990	Ec991	Ec992	Ec993	Ec994
Year	Percent	Percent	Percent	Percent	Percent	Percent	Percent	Percent	Percent	Percent
1979	14.2	35.6	19.7	2.9	13.6	11.0	11.4	12.2	18.1	8.7
1982	9.9	27.2	19.0	3.9	11.9	11.5	8.6	—	16.4	7.1
1985	10.2	21.7	19.0	2.6	10.0	9.9	6.4	7.6	12.6	7.1
1988	5.4	15.3	12.3	1.8	6.3	4.7	4.9	—	8.4	4.2
1990	4.4	12.7	9.5	2.4	5.7	5.1	3.9	—	6.8	4.2
1991	3.6	12.9	7.7	2.6	5.2	5.5	3.6	4.2	6.8	3.6
1992	3.4	10.9	9.3	2.0	5.1	3.9	3.0	2.6	6.4	3.1
1993	4.0	11.1	7.5	2.4	4.9	4.2	3.9	3.2	6.4	3.0
1994	6.0	12.1	6.9	2.3	4.8	5.9	4.1	3.0	6.7	3.1
1995	8.2	12.0	6.7	1.8	4.7	5.9	3.9	2.8	6.2	3.3
1996	7.1	13.2	6.3	2.0	4.6	6.6	3.7	3.7	6.5	3.1
1997	9.4	12.8	6.0	2.6	5.2	6.1	4.0	4.6	7.0	3.5
1998	8.3	13.8	5.5	2.5	5.0	6.6	4.5	3.4	6.7	3.5

Cocaine

	Age				Race and ethnicity				Sex	
	12–17	18–25	26–34	35 and older	White	Black	Hispanic	Nonwhite, nonblack, non-Hispanic	Male	Female
	Ec995	Ec996	Ec997	Ec998	Ec999	Ec1000	Ec1001	Ec1002	Ec1003	Ec1004
Year	Percent	Percent	Percent	Percent	Percent	Percent	Percent	Percent	Percent	Percent
1979	1.5	9.9	3.0	0.2	2.4	2.8	4.8	3.5	3.5	1.8
1982	1.9	7.0	3.5	0.5	2.5	2.4	1.5	—	3.4	1.5
1985	1.5	8.1	6.3	0.5	3.0	3.4	2.5	—	3.9	2.1
1988	1.2	4.8	2.8	0.4	1.4	2.2	2.8	1.7	2.2	1.0
1990	0.6	2.3	1.9	0.2	0.6	1.8	2.0	—	1.2	0.6
1991	0.4	2.2	1.9	0.5	0.7	1.9	1.7	2.1	1.4	0.6
1992	0.3	2.0	1.5	0.2	0.6	1.0	1.3	0.1	1.0	0.4
1993	0.4	1.6	1.0	0.4	0.5	1.4	1.2	—	1.0	0.4
1994	0.3	1.2	1.3	0.4	0.5	1.3	1.1	—	0.9	0.4
1995	0.8	1.3	1.2	0.4	0.6	1.1	0.7	0.3	1.0	0.4
1996	0.6	2.0	1.5	0.4	0.8	1.0	1.1	0.5	1.1	0.5
1997	1.0	1.2	0.9	0.5	0.6	1.4	0.8	0.5	0.9	0.5
1998	0.8	2.0	1.2	0.5	0.7	1.3	1.3	0.3	1.1	0.5

Alcohol

	Age				Race and ethnicity				Sex	
	12–17	18–25	26–34	35 and older	White	Black	Hispanic	Nonwhite, nonblack, non-Hispanic	Male	Female
	Ec1005	Ec1006	Ec1007	Ec1008	Ec1009	Ec1010	Ec1011	Ec1012	Ec1013	Ec1014
Year	Percent	Percent	Percent	Percent	Percent	Percent	Percent	Percent	Percent	Percent
1979	49.6	75.1	71.6	59.7	64.4	58.8	58.6	50.9	72.4	54.9
1982	34.9	66.6	71.5	53.0	58.4	49.4	53.1	—	66.8	47.4
1985	41.2	70.1	70.6	57.5	62.8	50.6	49.3	—	69.2	52.0
1988	33.4	64.7	65.3	52.6	56.7	47.8	48.1	—	62.3	48.1
1990	32.5	62.8	64.4	49.5	54.6	47.0	45.8	37.7	60.5	45.4
1991	27.0	63.1	62.7	50.4	54.0	47.2	46.3	42.4	59.6	45.4
1992	20.9	58.6	62.3	47.4	50.9	42.8	43.7	39.2	57.2	41.4
1993	23.9	58.7	63.8	49.8	54.0	40.5	44.3	33.0	58.7	43.6
1994	21.6	63.1	65.3	54.1	56.7	43.8	47.7	42.0	60.3	47.9
1995	21.1	61.3	63.0	52.6	55.6	40.8	45.2	36.9	60.1	45.0
1996	18.8	60.0	61.6	51.7	54.2	41.9	43.1	35.6	58.9	43.6
1997	20.5	58.4	60.2	52.8	55.1	40.4	42.4	37.0	58.2	45.1
1998	19.1	60.0	60.9	53.1	55.3	39.8	45.4	35.8	58.7	45.1

Sources

U.S. Substance Abuse and Mental Health Services Administration (SAMHSA), *Preliminary Results from the 1996 National Household Survey on Drug Abuse*, DHHS Publication number [SMA] 97-3149 (1997), Tables 11 through 15. SAMHSA, *Summary Findings from the 1998 National Household Survey on Drug Abuse*, Tables 11 through 14 (accessed on SAMHSA's Internet site, August 1999).

Documentation

See the text for Table Ec951–962 for a description of the data source and methodology.

TABLE Ec1015–1028 Percentage of high school seniors reporting use of selected drugs in the past twelve months, by drug; 1975–1999
Contributed by Douglas Eckberg

Year	Any illicit drug	Any illicit drug other than marijuana	Marijuana or hashish	Inhalants	LSD	PCP	Cocaine	Heroin	Narcotics besides heroin	Amphetamines [1]	Barbiturates	Methaqualone	Tranquilizers	Alcohol [2]
	Ec1015	Ec1016	Ec1017	Ec1018	Ec1019	Ec1020	Ec1021	Ec1022	Ec1023	Ec1024	Ec1025	Ec1026	Ec1027	Ec1028
	Percent	Percent	Percent	Percent	Percent	Percent	Percent	Percent	Percent	Percent	Percent	Percent	Percent	Percent
1975	45.0	26.2	40.0	—	7.2	—	5.6	1.0	5.7	16.2	10.7	5.1	10.6	84.8
1976	48.1	25.4	44.5	—	6.4	—	6.0	0.8	5.7	15.8	9.6	4.7	10.3	85.7
1977	51.1	26.0	47.6	—	5.5	—	7.2	0.8	6.4	16.3	9.3	5.2	10.8	87.0
1978	53.8	27.1	50.2	—	6.3	—	9.0	0.8	6.0	17.1	8.1	4.9	9.9	87.7
1979	54.2	28.2	50.8	8.9	6.6	7.0	12.0	0.5	6.2	18.3	7.5	5.9	9.6	88.1
1980	53.1	30.4	48.8	7.9	6.5	4.4	12.3	0.5	6.3	20.8	6.8	7.2	8.7	87.9
1981	52.1	34.0	46.1	6.1	6.5	3.2	12.4	0.5	5.9	26.0	6.6	7.6	8.0	87.0
1982	49.4	30.1	44.3	6.6	6.1	2.2	11.5	0.6	5.3	20.3	5.5	6.8	7.0	86.8
1983	47.4	28.4	42.3	6.2	5.4	2.6	11.4	0.6	5.1	17.9	5.2	5.4	6.9	87.3
1984	45.8	28.0	40.0	7.2	4.7	2.3	11.6	0.5	5.2	17.7	4.9	3.8	6.1	86.0
1985	46.3	27.4	40.6	7.5	4.4	2.9	13.1	0.6	5.9	15.8	4.6	2.8	6.1	85.6
1986	44.3	25.9	38.8	8.9	4.5	2.4	12.7	0.5	5.2	13.4	4.2	2.1	5.8	84.5
1987	41.7	24.1	36.3	8.1	5.2	1.3	10.3	0.5	5.3	12.2	3.6	1.5	5.5	85.7
1988	38.5	21.1	33.1	7.1	4.8	1.2	7.9	0.5	4.6	10.9	3.2	1.3	4.8	85.3
1989	35.4	20.0	29.6	6.9	4.9	2.4	6.5	0.6	4.4	10.8	3.3	1.3	3.8	82.7
1990	32.5	17.9	27.0	7.5	5.4	1.2	5.3	0.5	4.5	9.1	3.4	0.7	3.5	80.6
1991	29.4	16.2	23.9	6.9	5.2	1.4	3.5	0.4	3.5	8.2	3.4	0.5	3.6	77.7
1992	27.1	14.9	21.9	6.4	5.6	1.4	3.1	0.6	3.3	7.1	2.8	0.6	2.8	76.8
1993	31.0	17.1	26.0	7.4	6.8	1.4	3.3	0.5	3.6	8.4	3.4	0.2	3.5	72.7
1994	35.8	18.0	30.7	8.2	6.9	1.6	3.6	0.6	3.8	9.4	4.1	0.8	3.7	73.0
1995	39.0	19.4	34.7	8.4	8.4	1.8	4.0	1.1	4.7	9.3	4.7	0.7	4.4	73.7
1996	40.2	19.8	35.8	8.5	8.8	2.6	4.9	1.0	5.4	9.5	4.9	1.1	4.6	72.5
1997	42.4	20.7	38.5	7.3	8.4	2.3	5.5	1.2	6.2	10.2	5.1	1.0	4.7	74.8
1998	41.4	20.2	37.5	7.1	7.6	2.1	5.7	1.0	6.3	10.1	5.5	1.1	5.5	74.3
1999	42.1	20.7	37.8	6.0	8.1	1.8	6.2	1.1	6.7	10.2	—	1.1	5.5	74.3

Ec1016 — Any illicit drug other than marijuana. See text.
Ec1017 — See text.

[1] Question wording changed in 1982. See text.

[2] Question wording changed in 1993. See text.

Sources

Lloyd D. Johnson, Patrick M. O'Malley, and Jerald G. Bachman, *National Survey Results on Drug Use from the Monitoring the Future Study, 1975–1998*, volume 1, *Secondary School Students*, NIH Publication number 99-4660 (National Institute on Drug Abuse, 1999), Table 5-2. "Drug Trends in 1999 among American Teens Are Mixed" (University of Michigan News and Information Services, December 17, 1999), Table 3.

Data are available from the Substance Abuse and Mental Health Data Archive at the Internet site of the Inter-University Consortium for Political and Social Research.

Documentation

Beginning in 1975, the Monitoring the Future study has surveyed high school seniors in approximately 125 to 145 public and private high schools per year, chosen to represent high schools in the conterminous United States, using a multistage, random sampling procedure. Surveying takes place in the spring. Surveys of eighth and tenth graders, and of young adults, began substantially later and their results are not reported here. Several questionnaire forms are used, and most drug-use questions are on the "core" form. Weighted sample size for the drug-use questions varies from approximately 9,400 to approximately 17,800. In most cases, questions are identical across the surveys.

Series Ec1018. Findings concerning inhalants before 1979 are not comparable to those after because of confusion on the part of some participants concerning whether amyl and butyl nitrites were inhalants. The earlier findings are excluded.

Series Ec1024–1025 and Ec1027. The questions on amphetamines, barbiturates, and tranquilizers refer only to nonprescription use of the drugs.

Series Ec1024. Beginning in 1982, the question about amphetamine use was revised to get respondents to exclude the inappropriate reporting of nonprescription amphetamines. The original table states that the "prevalence rate dropped slightly as a result of this methodological change."

Series Ec1028. In 1993, the alcohol question text was changed in three of six forms to indicate that a "drink" meant "more than a few sips." This produced a 3.3 percent drop in annual prevalence. The revised figure is shown in the table. Beginning in 1994, data are based on all six forms.

TABLE Ec1029–1043 Percentage of high school seniors reporting use of selected drugs in the past thirty days, by drug: 1975–1999

Contributed by Douglas Eckberg

Year	Any illicit drug Ec1029 Percent	Any illicit drug other than marijuana Ec1030 Percent	Marijuana or hashish Ec1031 Percent	Inhalants Ec1032 Percent	LSD Ec1033 Percent	PCP Ec1034 Percent	Cocaine Ec1035 Percent	Heroin Ec1036 Percent	Narcotics besides heroin Ec1037 Percent	Amphetamines Ec1038 [1] Percent	Barbiturates Ec1039 Percent	Methaqualone Ec1040 Percent	Tranquilizers Ec1041 Percent	Alcohol Ec1042 [2] Percent	Cigarettes Ec1043 Percent
1975	30.7	15.4	27.1	—	2.3	—	1.9	0.4	2.1	8.5	4.7	2.1	4.1	68.2	36.7
1976	34.2	13.9	32.2	—	1.9	—	2.0	0.2	2.0	7.7	3.9	1.6	4.0	68.3	38.8
1977	37.6	15.2	35.4	—	2.1	—	2.5	0.3	2.8	8.8	4.3	2.3	4.6	71.2	38.4
1978	38.9	15.1	37.1	—	2.1	—	3.9	0.3	2.1	8.7	3.2	1.9	3.4	72.1	36.7
1979	38.9	16.8	36.5	3.2	2.4	2.4	5.7	0.2	2.4	9.9	3.2	2.3	3.7	71.8	34.4
1980	37.2	18.4	33.7	2.7	2.3	1.4	5.2	0.2	2.4	12.1	2.9	3.3	3.1	72.0	30.5
1981	36.9	21.7	31.6	2.5	2.5	1.4	5.8	0.2	2.1	15.8	2.6	3.1	2.7	70.7	29.4
1982	32.5	17.0	28.5	2.5	2.4	1.0	5.0	0.2	1.8	10.7	2.0	2.4	2.4	69.7	30.0
1983	30.5	15.4	27.0	2.5	1.9	1.3	4.9	0.2	1.8	8.9	2.1	1.8	2.5	69.4	30.3
1984	29.2	15.1	25.2	2.6	1.5	1.0	5.8	0.3	1.8	8.3	1.7	1.1	2.1	67.2	29.3
1985	29.7	14.9	25.7	3.0	1.6	1.6	6.7	0.3	2.3	6.8	2.0	1.0	2.1	65.9	30.1
1986	27.1	13.2	23.4	3.2	1.7	1.3	6.2	0.2	2.0	5.5	1.8	0.8	2.1	65.3	29.6
1987	24.7	11.6	21.0	3.5	1.8	0.6	4.3	0.2	1.8	5.2	1.4	0.6	2.0	66.4	29.4
1988	21.3	10.0	18.0	3.0	1.8	0.3	3.4	0.2	1.6	4.6	1.2	0.5	1.5	63.9	28.7
1989	19.7	9.1	16.7	2.7	1.8	1.4	2.8	0.3	1.6	4.2	1.4	0.6	1.3	60.0	28.6
1990	17.2	8.0	14.0	2.9	1.9	0.4	1.9	0.2	1.5	3.7	1.3	0.2	1.2	57.1	29.4
1991	16.4	7.1	13.8	2.6	1.9	0.5	1.4	0.2	1.1	3.2	1.4	0.2	1.4	54.0	28.3
1992	14.4	6.3	11.9	2.5	2.0	0.6	1.3	0.3	1.2	2.8	1.1	0.4	1.0	51.3	27.8
1993	18.3	7.9	15.5	2.8	2.4	1.0	1.3	0.2	1.3	3.7	1.3	0.1	1.2	48.6	29.9
1994	21.9	8.8	19.0	2.9	2.6	0.7	1.5	0.3	1.5	4.0	1.7	0.4	1.4	50.1	31.2
1995	23.8	10.0	21.2	3.5	4.0	0.6	1.8	0.6	1.8	4.0	2.2	0.4	1.8	51.3	33.5
1996	24.6	9.5	21.9	2.9	2.5	1.3	2.0	0.5	2.0	4.1	2.1	0.6	2.0	50.8	34.0
1997	26.2	10.7	23.7	2.9	3.1	0.7	2.3	0.5	2.3	4.8	2.1	0.3	1.8	52.7	36.5
1998	25.6	10.7	22.8	3.1	3.2	1.0	2.4	0.5	2.4	4.6	2.6	0.6	2.4	52.0	35.1
1999	25.9	10.4	23.1	2.4	2.7	0.8	2.6	0.5	2.6	4.5	—	—	—	—	—

[1] Question wording changed in 1982. See text.
[2] Question wording changed in 1993. See text.

Sources

Lloyd D. Johnson, Patrick M. O'Malley, and Jerald G. Bachman, *National Survey Results on Drug Use from the Monitoring the Future Study, 1975–1998,* volume 1, *Secondary School Students,* NIH Publication number 99-4660 (National Institute on Drug Abuse, 1999), Table 5-3. "Drug Trends in 1999 among American Teens Are Mixed" (University of Michigan News and Information Services, December 17, 1999), Table 4.

Data are available from the Substance Abuse and Mental Health Data Archive at the Internet site of the Inter-University Consortium for Political and Social Research.

Documentation

See the text for Table Ec1015–1028 for a description of the data source.

Series Ec1038. Beginning in 1982 the question about amphetamine use was revised to get respondents to exclude the inappropriate reporting of nonprescription amphetamines. The original table states that the "prevalence rate dropped slightly as a result of this methodological change."

Series Ec1042. In 1993, the alcohol question text was changed in three of six forms to indicate that a "drink" meant "more than a few sips." This produced a 2.4 percent drop in monthly prevalence. The revised figure is shown in the table. Beginning in 1994, data are based on all six forms.

TABLE Ec1044–1056   Percentage of high school seniors reporting "daily" use of selected drugs in the past thirty days, by drug: 1975–1999[1]

Contributed by Douglas Eckberg

Year	Marijuana or hashish	Inhalants	LSD	PCP	Cocaine	Heroin	Narcotics besides heroin	Amphetamines [2]	Barbiturates	Methaqualone	Tranquilizers	Alcohol [3]	Cigarettes
	Ec1044	Ec1045	Ec1046	Ec1047	Ec1048	Ec1049	Ec1050	Ec1051	Ec1052	Ec1053	Ec1054	Ec1055	Ec1056
	Percent	Percent	Percent	Percent	Percent	Percent	Percent	Percent	Percent	Percent	Percent	Percent	Percent
1975	6.0	—	(Z)	—	0.1	0.1	0.1	0.5	0.1	(Z)	0.1	5.7	26.9
1976	8.2	(Z)	(Z)	—	0.1	(Z)	0.1	0.4	0.1	(Z)	0.2	5.6	28.8
1977	9.1	(Z)	(Z)	—	0.1	(Z)	0.2	0.5	0.2	(Z)	0.3	6.1	28.8
1978	10.7	0.1	(Z)	—	0.1	(Z)	0.1	0.5	0.1	(Z)	0.1	5.7	27.5
1979	10.3	(Z)	(Z)	0.1	0.2	(Z)	(Z)	0.6	(Z)	(Z)	0.1	6.9	25.4
1980	9.1	0.1	(Z)	0.1	0.2	(Z)	0.1	0.7	0.1	0.1	0.1	6.0	21.3
1981	7.0	0.1	0.1	0.1	0.3	(Z)	0.1	1.2	0.1	0.1	0.1	6.0	20.3
1982	6.3	0.1	(Z)	0.1	0.2	(Z)	0.1	0.7	0.1	0.1	0.1	5.7	21.1
1983	5.5	0.1	0.1	0.1	0.2	0.1	0.1	0.8	0.1	(Z)	0.1	5.5	21.2
1984	5.0	0.1	0.1	0.1	0.2	(Z)	0.1	0.6	(Z)	(Z)	0.1	4.8	18.7
1985	4.9	0.2	0.1	0.3	0.4	(Z)	0.1	0.4	0.1	(Z)	(Z)	5.0	19.5
1986	4.0	0.2	(Z)	0.2	0.4	(Z)	0.1	0.3	0.1	(Z)	(Z)	4.8	18.7
1987	3.3	0.1	0.1	0.3	0.3	(Z)	0.1	0.3	0.1	(Z)	0.1	4.8	18.7
1988	2.7	0.2	(Z)	0.1	0.2	(Z)	0.1	0.3	(Z)	0.1	(Z)	4.2	18.1
1989	2.9	0.2	(Z)	0.2	0.3	0.1	0.2	0.3	0.1	(Z)	0.1	4.2	18.9
1990	2.2	0.3	0.1	0.1	0.1	(Z)	0.1	0.2	0.1	(Z)	0.1	3.7	19.1
1991	2.0	0.2	0.1	0.1	0.1	(Z)	0.1	0.2	0.1	(Z)	0.1	3.6	18.5
1992	1.9	0.1	0.1	0.1	0.1	(Z)	(Z)	0.2	(Z)	0.1	(Z)	3.4	17.2
1993	2.4	0.1	0.1	0.1	0.1	(Z)	(Z)	0.2	0.1	0.0	(Z)	3.4	19.0
1994	3.6	0.1	0.1	0.3	0.1	(Z)	0.1	0.2	(Z)	0.1	0.1	2.9	19.4
1995	4.6	0.1	0.1	0.3	0.2	0.1	0.1	0.3	0.1	0.1	(Z)	3.5	21.6
1996	4.9	0.2	(Z)	0.3	0.2	0.1	0.2	0.3	0.1	0.0	0.2	3.7	22.2
1997	5.8	0.1	0.2	0.1	0.2	0.1	0.2	0.3	0.1	0.1	0.1	3.9	24.6
1998	5.6	0.2	0.1	0.3	0.2	0.1	0.1	0.3	0.1	0.0	0.1	3.9	22.4
1999	6.0	0.2	0.1	0.2	0.2	0.1	0.2	0.3	0.2	0.0	0.1	3.4	23.1

(Z) Less than 0.05 percent.

[1] "Daily" means use on at least twenty occasions in the past thirty days, except in the case of cigarettes, where actual daily use is measured.

[2] Question wording changed in 1982. See text.

[3] Question wording changed in 1993. See text.

Sources

Lloyd D. Johnson, Patrick M. O'Malley, and Jerald G. Bachman, *National Survey Results on Drug Use from the Monitoring the Future Study, 1975–1998*, volume 1, *Secondary School Students*, NIH Publication number 99-4660 (National Institute on Drug Abuse, 1999), Table 5-4; "Drug Trends in 1999 among American Teens Are Mixed" (University of Michigan News and Information Services, December 17, 1999), Table 5.

Data are available from the Substance Abuse and Mental Health Data Archive at the Internet site of the Inter-University Consortium for Political and Social Research.

Documentation

See text for Table Ec1015–1028 for a description of the data source.

Series Ec1051. Beginning in 1982, the question about amphetamine use was revised to get respondents to exclude the inappropriate reporting of nonprescription amphetamines. The original table states that the "prevalence rate dropped slightly as a result of this methodological change."

Series Ec1055. In 1993, the alcohol question text was changed in three of six forms to indicate that a "drink" meant "more than a few sips." This produced a 0.9 percent increase in daily use. The revised figure is shown in the table. Beginning in 1994, data are based on all six forms.

TABLE Ec1057–1106   Percentage of high school seniors reporting use of selected drugs in the past twelve months, by drug, sex, race, and ethnicity: 1975–1998[1]

Contributed by Douglas Eckberg

	Marijuana or hashish					Inhalants				
	Male	Female	White	Black	Hispanic	Male	Female	White	Black	Hispanic
	Ec1057	Ec1058	Ec1059	Ec1060	Ec1061	Ec1062	Ec1063	Ec1064	Ec1065	Ec1066
Year	Percent	Percent	Percent	Percent	Percent	Percent	Percent	Percent	Percent	Percent
1975	45.8	34.9	—	—	—	—	—	—	—	—
1976	50.6	37.8	—	—	—	3.8	2.0	—	—	—
1977	53.2	42.0	46.8	37.9	45.8	5.1	2.4	3.6	1.5	2.7
1978	55.9	44.3	50.1	39.6	43.4	5.6	2.8	4.3	1.3	3.0
1979	55.8	45.7	51.8	38.4	42.1	6.7	4.2	5.1	2.1	2.9
1980	53.4	44.1	51.2	37.5	44.1	5.9	3.5	5.3	2.2	2.9
1981	49.2	42.5	49.1	36.1	41.2	5.1	3.2	4.7	2.1	3.5
1982	47.2	40.8	47.1	35.5	38.8	5.8	3.1	4.7	1.9	4.1
1983	45.7	38.4	44.6	37.4	38.3	5.8	2.8	4.8	1.8	3.4
1984	43.2	36.0	42.0	36.4	38.8	6.5	3.8	5.1	2.2	4.6
1985	43.1	37.8	41.6	33.4	37.8	6.9	4.5	5.9	2.0	6.5
1986	41.2	36.0	41.4	30.6	36.7	7.8	4.7	6.5	2.1	5.5
1987	38.6	33.8	39.7	25.7	33.3	8.3	5.6	7.3	3.0	4.6
1988	35.8	30.3	37.6	21.2	29.6	8.2	4.9	7.6	3.1	4.1
1989	32.8	26.3	34.5	17.8	25.0	7.8	4.0	7.0	2.2	4.7
1990	29.4	24.2	31.6	13.7	21.6	8.8	4.9	7.2	2.1	4.8
1991	27.2	20.1	28.2	11.4	23.6	8.2	5.0	7.6	2.7	5.4
1992	24.4	18.9	24.9	11.5	24.7	8.0	4.5	7.2	2.5	6.0
1993	29.0	22.4	25.9	14.2	23.5	9.2	4.8	7.6	2.2	5.7
1994	35.1	26.4	30.2	20.7	25.7	9.6	6.0	8.6	2.4	5.5
1995	38.1	30.6	34.2	26.8	29.7	9.9	6.2	9.1	2.6	5.8
1996	39.4	31.6	36.4	30.2	32.3	9.1	6.1	9.0	2.2	5.9
1997	40.9	35.5	38.7	30.4	36.4	8.3	5.2	8.6	1.9	4.7
1998	41.7	33.0	39.9	30.0	37.2	7.5	5.1	7.9	1.7	4.5

	Hallucinogens					LSD				
	Male	Female	White	Black	Hispanic	Male	Female	White	Black	Hispanic
	Ec1067	Ec1068	Ec1069	Ec1070	Ec1071	Ec1072	Ec1073	Ec1074	Ec1075	Ec1076
Year	Percent	Percent	Percent	Percent	Percent	Percent	Percent	Percent	Percent	Percent
1975	13.7	9.0	—	—	—	9.6	5.6	—	—	—
1976	11.6	6.9	—	—	—	7.9	4.6	—	—	—
1977	10.8	6.5	9.8	2.4	7.9	7.1	3.9	6.3	1.3	6.1
1978	11.6	7.3	9.9	2.3	7.2	7.8	4.5	6.3	1.3	5.0
1979	11.8	7.6	10.5	2.0	7.0	8.0	4.8	6.8	1.2	4.9
1980	11.7	6.7	10.3	1.9	7.1	8.1	4.8	7.0	1.1	5.2
1981	10.9	6.8	10.0	1.9	7.0	8.0	4.7	7.2	1.0	4.5
1982	9.6	6.1	9.3	1.8	7.7	7.4	4.3	6.9	0.9	5.2
1983	8.6	5.5	8.3	2.2	6.6	6.7	3.8	6.2	0.9	5.0
1984	7.9	4.7	7.5	1.7	5.2	5.8	3.1	5.5	0.7	4.1
1985	8.1	4.4	7.0	1.2	5.7	5.9	2.8	5.0	0.7	3.9
1986	7.2	4.7	6.7	1.6	5.7	5.5	3.4	4.9	1.0	3.9
1987	7.5	5.2	6.8	1.5	5.0	6.4	3.9	5.4	0.8	4.0
1988	7.2	3.7	6.8	1.0	4.0	6.5	3.0	5.8	0.6	3.1
1989	7.4	3.6	6.4	0.9	3.2	6.5	3.2	5.7	0.7	2.3
1990	7.7	3.8	6.7	0.8	3.3	7.1	3.6	6.1	0.6	2.7
1991	7.5	3.9	6.8	0.6	4.4	6.8	3.4	6.3	0.6	3.6
1992	7.1	4.7	6.9	0.7	4.6	6.7	4.4	6.4	0.6	4.1
1993	8.9	5.6	7.9	0.8	5.3	8.4	5.1	7.4	0.6	5.1
1994	9.2	5.8	8.6	1.2	5.8	8.4	5.3	8.0	0.9	5.4
1995	11.9	6.3	9.5	1.2	7.1	10.7	5.8	8.6	1.0	6.4
1996	12.4	7.3	10.8	1.7	8.3	10.9	6.5	9.7	1.3	7.4
1997	12.0	7.4	11.6	1.9	7.3	10.3	6.2	10.1	1.6	6.3
1998	11.0	6.8	11.3	1.4	6.8	9.3	5.7	9.5	1.1	5.9

Notes appear at end of table   (continued)

TABLE Ec1057–1106   Percentage of high school seniors reporting use of selected drugs in the past twelve months, by drug, sex, race, and ethnicity: 1975–1998   *Continued*

	Cocaine					Heroin				
	Male	Female	White	Black	Hispanic	Male	Female	White	Black	Hispanic
	Ec1077	Ec1078	Ec1079	Ec1080	Ec1081	Ec1082	Ec1083	Ec1084	Ec1085	Ec1086
Year	Percent	Percent	Percent	Percent	Percent	Percent	Percent	Percent	Percent	Percent
1975	7.5	3.9	—	—	—	1.2	0.8	—	—	—
1976	7.5	4.4	—	—	—	1.0	0.5	—	—	—
1977	9.3	4.9	6.5	4.8	7.2	1.2	0.4	0.8	0.6	1.2
1978	11.4	6.5	8.3	4.6	7.5	1.1	0.6	0.8	0.6	2.0
1979	14.6	9.3	10.9	4.6	8.9	0.6	0.3	0.6	0.5	1.7
1980	14.8	9.8	12.8	5.2	11.2	0.6	0.4	0.5	0.5	0.4
1981	13.8	10.4	13.0	4.8	12.4	0.6	0.3	0.4	0.6	0.3
1982	13.1	9.6	12.6	5.2	12.1	0.8	0.4	0.5	0.7	0.4
1983	13.2	9.3	11.8	7.2	11.4	0.7	0.4	0.5	0.6	0.6
1984	13.8	9.1	11.9	6.3	13.3	0.7	0.3	0.5	0.4	1.1
1985	14.8	11.2	13.0	5.3	16.3	0.8	0.3	0.5	0.5	1.0
1986	14.3	10.9	13.5	5.8	16.7	0.7	0.2	0.5	0.5	0.9
1987	11.3	9.2	12.0	4.8	14.0	0.7	0.3	0.4	0.5	0.9
1988	9.1	6.5	9.6	3.8	9.9	0.7	0.3	0.4	0.7	0.5
1989	8.1	4.9	7.6	2.9	7.8	0.9	0.4	0.5	0.6	0.5
1990	6.6	3.8	6.3	1.7	7.4	0.6	0.3	0.6	0.3	0.6
1991	4.1	2.6	4.6	1.5	6.1	0.6	0.3	0.5	0.2	0.6
1992	3.7	2.4	3.3	1.2	5.2	0.8	0.3	0.5	0.5	0.9
1993	4.0	2.3	3.1	0.8	5.8	0.7	0.3	0.5	0.4	0.7
1994	4.5	2.8	3.5	0.9	5.4	0.8	0.4	0.5	0.3	0.5
1995	4.8	3.1	4.0	1.0	5.5	1.4	0.8	0.8	0.4	1.2
1996	6.0	3.5	4.5	0.8	7.3	1.3	0.7	1.0	0.5	1.5
1997	6.6	4.2	5.5	0.9	7.6	1.5	0.9	1.2	0.5	1.1
1998	6.8	4.5	6.3	0.9	6.7	1.4	0.7	1.2	0.4	0.8

	Narcotics other than heroin					Amphetamines				
	Male	Female	White	Black	Hispanic	Male	Female	White	Black	Hispanic
	Ec1087	Ec1088	Ec1089	Ec1090	Ec1091	Ec1092 [2]	Ec1093 [2]	Ec1094 [2]	Ec1095 [2]	Ec1096 [2]
Year	Percent	Percent	Percent	Percent	Percent	Percent	Percent	Percent	Percent	Percent
1975	6.6	4.8	—	—	—	15.6	16.5	—	—	—
1976	6.8	4.7	—	—	—	15.8	15.4	—	—	—
1977	7.3	5.4	6.6	2.2	3.8	16.0	16.4	17.3	5.3	12.3
1978	6.9	5.1	6.7	2.0	3.5	16.9	17.1	18.2	4.7	12.2
1979	7.3	5.1	6.6	1.8	3.5	18.4	17.8	19.2	4.2	12.8
1980	7.1	5.4	6.8	1.7	3.7	19.7	21.8	21.3	5.3	14.5
1981	6.5	5.3	6.7	1.9	4.3	24.8	26.9	26.4	5.8	17.5
1982	6.0	4.6	6.2	1.8	4.1	19.6	20.3	23.6	6.0	12.3
1983	6.0	4.2	5.8	1.7	4.0	17.2	17.9	22.3	5.7	11.5
1984	6.2	4.2	5.7	1.6	4.2	16.8	18.2	20.5	4.7	13.2
1985	6.8	5.1	6.3	1.6	3.6	14.9	16.4	18.9	4.3	14.6
1986	5.9	4.6	6.3	1.7	3.0	12.7	13.8	16.4	4.0	10.8
1987	5.6	4.9	6.0	1.6	2.4	11.8	12.4	14.3	3.8	8.7
1988	5.1	4.1	5.8	1.5	2.2	10.8	10.9	13.0	3.9	9.6
1989	4.9	3.8	5.3	1.5	2.5	11.1	10.5	12.4	3.6	9.0
1990	5.0	3.9	5.2	1.4	2.4	9.4	8.6	11.4	3.1	7.0
1991	3.9	3.1	4.7	1.1	2.3	8.3	7.9	9.8	2.7	6.1
1992	3.3	3.3	4.1	0.9	2.1	7.2	6.9	8.8	2.2	6.0
1993	3.6	3.3	4.1	1.0	2.3	8.2	8.5	9.0	2.3	6.2
1994	4.3	3.4	4.3	1.5	2.2	9.2	9.4	10.4	3.4	6.4
1995	5.6	3.8	5.0	1.4	2.5	9.5	8.9	10.7	3.4	7.1
1996	6.4	4.4	5.9	1.2	3.7	9.6	8.8	10.5	2.9	7.8
1997	7.1	5.4	7.1	1.8	3.1	10.1	10.2	11.4	2.8	7.3
1998	7.4	5.1	7.6	2.4	2.8	10.3	9.8	12.1	2.8	7.0

Notes appear at end of table

TABLE Ec1057–1106   Percentage of high school seniors reporting use of selected drugs in the past twelve months, by drug, sex, race, and ethnicity: 1975–1998 *Continued*

	Barbiturates					Tranquilizers				
	Male	Female	White	Black	Hispanic	Male	Female	White	Black	Hispanic
	Ec1097	Ec1098	Ec1099	Ec1100	Ec1101	Ec1102	Ec1103	Ec1104	Ec1105	Ec1106
Year	Percent	Percent	Percent	Percent	Percent	Percent	Percent	Percent	Percent	Percent
1975	12.3	9.9	—	—	—	10.0	11.1	—	—	—
1976	9.9	9.2	—	—	—	9.4	11.0	—	—	—
1977	10.2	8.4	10.2	3.3	7.4	10.2	11.4	11.4	4.3	8.4
1978	8.4	7.7	9.3	3.2	5.8	9.7	10.1	11.1	4.2	8.2
1979	7.6	7.0	8.2	2.6	5.8	9.9	9.3	10.5	3.6	7.4
1980	7.3	6.0	7.5	2.5	5.8	9.0	8.5	9.9	3.1	6.4
1981	7.2	5.8	7.2	2.4	5.7	8.0	7.7	9.1	3.0	5.7
1982	5.9	5.0	6.5	2.0	5.1	6.9	7.1	8.3	2.5	5.8
1983	5.9	4.2	5.8	1.7	4.1	7.0	6.7	7.8	2.3	5.1
1984	5.5	4.0	5.5	1.6	4.4	6.3	5.8	7.3	2.1	5.3
1985	5.2	3.9	5.1	1.6	4.6	6.4	5.7	6.8	1.7	5.0
1986	4.7	3.8	4.7	1.6	3.6	5.9	5.8	6.6	1.7	4.4
1987	4.0	3.2	4.2	1.7	2.8	5.2	5.8	6.3	2.0	3.7
1988	3.4	3.0	3.7	1.5	2.8	4.7	4.8	5.9	2.0	2.5
1989	3.5	3.0	3.5	1.1	3.2	4.0	3.5	5.0	1.2	1.6
1990	3.8	3.0	3.7	1.1	2.8	3.5	3.5	4.2	0.7	1.9
1991	3.4	3.2	3.8	1.2	2.4	3.5	3.6	4.1	0.9	2.7
1992	2.9	2.6	3.5	1.1	2.2	2.7	3.0	3.7	1.3	2.4
1993	3.4	3.3	3.6	1.0	1.9	3.5	3.3	3.7	1.0	2.0
1994	4.3	3.8	4.3	1.5	2.6	4.0	3.5	4.2	1.1	2.4
1995	5.1	4.2	4.9	1.6	3.5	4.7	4.1	4.6	1.2	3.5
1996	5.2	4.4	5.4	1.1	4.0	5.0	4.0	5.1	0.9	4.3
1997	5.3	4.8	5.9	1.0	3.7	5.4	3.9	5.5	0.8	3.8
1998	6.3	4.8	6.5	1.4	3.3	6.3	4.7	6.2	1.0	3.3

[1] For racial/ethnic subgroups, percentages are two-year moving averages (including the previous year's data).

[2] Question wording changed in 1982. See text.

Sources

Lloyd D. Johnson, Patrick M. O'Malley, and Jerald G. Bachman, *National Survey Results on Drug Use from the Monitoring the Future Study, 1975–1998*, volume 1, *Secondary School Students*, NIH Publication number 99-4660 (National Institute on Drug Abuse, 1999), Tables D-6, D-8, D-10, D-12, D-14, D-20, D-21, D-23, D-24, and D-26.

Data are available from the Substance Abuse and Mental Health Data Archive at the Internet site of the Inter-University Consortium for Political and Social Research.

Documentation

See the text for Table Ec1015–1028 for a description of the Monitoring the Future study.

Series Ec1062–1066. Findings for inhalants are not adjusted for underreporting of amyl and butyl nitrite use.

Series Ec1067–1071. Findings for hallucinogens are not adjusted for underreporting of PCP (the drug phencyclidine) use.

Series Ec1087–1106. The questions on narcotics other than heroin, amphetamines, barbiturates, and tranquilizers refer only to nonmedical use of the drugs.

Series Ec1092–1096. Findings for amphetamines are adjusted to exclude the inappropriate reporting of nonprescription amphetamines. Beginning in 1982, the question about amphetamine use was revised to get respondents to exclude the inappropriate reporting of nonprescription amphetamines. The original table states that the "prevalence rate dropped slightly as a result of this methodological change."

TABLE Ec1107–1126 Percentage of high school seniors reporting recent use of alcohol and cigarettes, by usage, sex, race, and ethnicity: 1975–1999[1,2]

Contributed by Douglas Eckberg

	Use of alcohol in the past thirty days					Having had at least five drinks in a row in past two weeks				
	Male	Female	White	Black	Hispanic	Male	Female	White	Black	Hispanic
	Ec1107	Ec1108	Ec1109	Ec1110	Ec1111	Ec1112	Ec1113	Ec1114	Ec1115	Ec1116
Year	Percent	Percent	Percent	Percent	Percent	Percent	Percent	Percent	Percent	Percent
1975	75.0	62.2	—	—	—	49.0	26.4	—	—	—
1976	74.5	61.8	—	—	—	47.9	25.9	—	—	—
1977	77.8	65.0	72.8	49.5	63.0	50.0	29.3	40.5	19.0	36.4
1978	77.5	67.1	75.0	48.7	64.5	51.4	29.6	42.4	19.3	37.2
1979	76.7	67.0	75.3	47.2	63.8	51.9	30.9	43.5	18.9	33.6
1980	77.4	66.8	75.4	47.6	63.6	52.1	30.5	44.3	17.7	33.1
1981	75.7	65.7	75.4	46.7	62.0	51.6	30.8	44.9	17.1	34.8
1982	74.1	65.4	74.6	46.0	60.3	49.8	31.1	44.9	17.1	32.9
1983	74.4	64.3	73.9	47.7	59.1	50.4	31.0	44.5	18.3	32.5
1984	71.4	62.8	72.8	45.5	59.7	47.5	29.6	43.6	17.2	33.0
1985	69.8	62.1	71.2	42.8	58.1	45.3	28.2	41.5	15.7	31.7
1986	69.0	61.9	70.2	42.1	56.3	46.1	28.1	40.3	16.4	30.8
1987	69.9	63.1	71.0	39.4	57.2	46.1	29.2	40.9	15.8	33.0
1988	68.0	59.9	70.6	39.8	57.8	43.0	26.5	40.0	15.2	33.7
1989	65.1	54.9	67.3	39.5	52.9	41.2	24.9	37.9	15.7	28.8
1990	61.3	52.3	63.8	35.8	49.1	39.1	24.4	36.6	14.4	25.6
1991	58.4	49.0	60.0	33.7	51.5	37.8	21.2	34.6	11.7	27.9
1992	55.8	46.8	56.8	31.7	53.8	35.6	20.3	32.1	11.3	31.1
1993	54.2	43.4	55.6	32.4	50.5	34.6	20.7	31.3	12.6	27.2
1994	55.5	45.2	54.0	33.8	45.9	37.0	20.2	31.5	14.4	24.3
1995	55.7	47.0	54.5	35.2	48.7	36.9	23.0	32.3	14.9	26.6
1996	54.8	46.9	54.8	36.5	47.5	37.0	32.5	33.4	15.3	27.1
1997	56.2	48.9	56.4	34.3	48.2	37.9	24.4	35.1	13.4	27.6
1998	57.3	46.9	57.7	33.3	49.8	39.2	24.0	36.4	12.3	28.1
1999	—	—	—	—	—	—	—	—	—	—

	Having smoked a cigarette in past thirty days					Having smoked cigarettes daily in the past thirty days				
	Male	Female	White	Black	Hispanic	Male	Female	White	Black	Hispanic
	Ec1117	Ec1118	Ec1119	Ec1120	Ec1121	Ec1122	Ec1123	Ec1124	Ec1125	Ec1126
Year	Percent	Percent	Percent	Percent	Percent	Percent	Percent	Percent	Percent	Percent
1975	37.2	35.9	—	—	—	26.9	26.4	—	—	—
1976	37.7	39.1	—	—	—	28.0	28.8	—	—	—
1977	36.6	39.6	38.3	36.7	35.7	27.1	30.0	28.9	24.9	22.6
1978	34.5	38.1	37.6	32.7	32.8	26.0	28.3	28.3	22.7	20.4
1979	31.2	37.1	36.0	30.2	26.8	22.3	27.8	26.9	20.9	15.8
1980	26.8	33.4	33.0	26.8	22.6	18.5	23.5	23.9	17.4	12.8
1981	26.5	31.6	30.5	23.7	23.2	18.1	21.7	21.4	14.6	13.6
1982	26.8	32.6	30.7	21.8	24.7	18.2	23.2	21.6	13.1	14.3
1983	28.0	31.6	31.3	21.2	24.7	19.2	22.2	22.1	12.5	14.9
1984	25.9	31.9	31.2	19.3	25.3	16.0	20.5	21.0	10.7	13.9
1985	28.2	31.4	31.3	18.1	25.5	17.8	20.6	20.4	9.9	11.8
1986	27.9	30.6	31.9	16.9	23.7	16.9	19.8	20.6	9.4	11.3
1987	27.0	31.4	32.1	14.2	22.7	16.4	20.6	20.5	7.9	11.0
1988	28.0	28.9	32.2	13.3	21.9	17.4	18.1	20.6	7.3	10.9
1989	27.7	29.0	32.2	12.6	20.6	17.9	19.4	21.1	6.4	10.8
1990	29.1	29.2	32.3	12.2	21.7	18.6	19.3	21.8	5.8	10.9
1991	29.0	27.5	32.2	10.6	24.0	18.8	17.9	21.5	5.1	11.5
1992	29.2	26.1	31.8	8.7	25.0	17.2	16.7	20.5	4.2	12.5
1993	30.7	28.7	33.2	9.5	24.2	19.4	18.2	21.4	4.1	11.8
1994	32.9	29.2	35.2	10.9	23.6	20.4	18.1	22.9	4.9	10.6
1995	34.5	32.0	36.6	12.9	25.1	21.7	20.8	23.9	6.1	11.6
1996	34.9	32.4	38.1	14.2	25.4	22.2	21.8	25.4	7.0	12.9
1997	37.3	35.2	40.7	14.3	25.9	24.8	23.6	27.8	7.2	14.0
1998	36.3	33.3	41.7	14.9	26.6	22.7	21.5	28.3	7.4	13.6
1999	35.4	33.5	40.1	14.9	27.3	—	—	—	—	—

TABLE Ec1107–1126   Percentage of high school seniors reporting recent use of alcohol and cigarettes, by usage, sex, race, and ethnicity: 1975–1999   *Continued*

[1] For racial and ethnic subgroups, percentages are two-year moving averages (including the previous year's data).

[2] Alcohol question wording changed in 1993. See text.

Sources

Lloyd D. Johnson, Patrick M. O'Malley, and Jerald G. Bachman, *National Survey Results on Drug Use from the Monitoring the Future Study, 1975–1998*, volume 1, *Secondary School Students*, NIH Publication number 99-4660 (National Institute on Drug Abuse, 1999), Tables D-28, D-32, D-34, and D-36; "Cigarette Smoking among American Teens Continues Gradual Decline" (University of Michigan News and Information Services, December 17, 1999), Table 3.

Data are available from the Substance Abuse and Mental Health Data Archive at the Internet site of the Inter-University Consortium for Political and Social Research.

Documentation

See the text for Table Ec1015–1028 for a description of the Monitoring the Future study.

Series Ec1107–1116. Beginning in 1993, the question text for alcohol use was changed slightly in three of the six forms used, to indicate that a "drink" meant "more than a few sips." For males, those forms yielded a rate of alcohol use 0.7 percent below that gained via the original wording; for females, the reduction was 3.3 percent. For racial and ethic subgroups, because data are based on two-year moving averages, revised figures are unavailable for 1993. In this table, the original percentages are shown for 1993. Beginning in 1994, the data are based on all six forms.

FIREARM POSSESSION

Douglas Eckberg

TABLE Ec1127–1134   Estimated size of the civilian gun stock, by gun type: 1945–1995
Contributed by Douglas Eckberg

Year	Guns added to stock			Gun stock			Estimated guns per 1,000 population	
	Total	Handguns	Long guns	Total	Handguns	Long guns	Total	Handguns
	Ec1127	Ec1128	Ec1129	Ec1130	Ec1131	Ec1132	Ec1133	Ec1134
	Number	Number	Number	Number	Number	Number	Per 1,000	Per 1,000
1945	—	—	—	46,909,183	12,657,618	34,251,565	351.6	94.9
1946	1,533,365	176,745	1,356,620	48,442,548	12,834,363	35,608,185	344.3	91.2
1947	2,100,925	264,256	1,836,669	50,543,473	13,098,619	37,444,854	350.8	91.3
1948	2,659,558	444,034	2,215,524	53,203,031	13,542,653	39,660,378	362.6	92.7
1949	2,203,429	262,504	1,940,925	55,406,460	13,805,157	41,601,303	371.1	92.9
1950	2,495,621	278,038	2,217,583	57,902,081	14,083,195	43,818,886	381.3	93.5
1951	2,086,583	348,373	1,738,210	59,988,664	14,431,568	45,557,096	389.6	94.1
1952	1,957,651	454,229	1,503,422	61,946,315	14,885,797	47,060,518	396.1	95.6
1953	1,998,920	415,857	1,583,063	63,945,235	15,301,654	48,643,581	402.3	96.7
1954	1,612,817	376,455	1,236,362	65,558,052	15,678,109	49,879,943	405.0	97.3
1955	1,829,083	429,237	1,399,846	67,387,135	16,107,346	51,279,789	408.2	98.0
1956	2,048,798	534,964	1,513,834	69,435,933	16,642,310	52,793,623	413.1	99.5
1957	1,980,576	538,032	1,442,544	71,416,509	17,180,342	54,236,167	417.2	100.8
1958	1,746,941	519,362	1,227,579	73,163,450	17,699,704	55,463,746	420.1	102.1
1959	2,174,738	648,672	1,526,066	75,338,188	18,348,376	56,989,812	425.3	103.9
1960	2,162,877	602,843	1,560,034	77,501,065	18,951,219	58,549,846	430.6	105.4
1961	2,035,551	561,742	1,473,809	79,536,616	19,512,961	60,023,655	434.6	106.6
1962	2,066,368	598,649	1,467,719	81,602,984	20,111,610	61,491,374	439.3	108.3
1963	2,231,824	676,062	1,555,762	83,834,808	20,787,672	63,047,136	444.8	110.3
1964	2,522,893	744,273	1,778,620	86,357,701	21,531,945	64,825,756	451.8	112.6
1965	3,121,221	1,013,300	2,107,921	89,478,922	22,545,245	66,933,677	462.4	116.5
1966	3,522,067	1,212,817	2,309,250	93,000,989	23,758,062	69,242,927	475.5	121.5
1967	4,086,762	1,673,417	2,413,345	97,087,751	25,431,479	71,656,272	491.7	128.8
1968	5,214,500	2,414,724	2,799,776	102,302,251	27,846,203	74,456,048	513.1	139.7
1969	4,809,569	1,725,383	3,084,186	107,111,820	29,571,586	77,540,234	532.0	146.8
1970	4,805,913	1,673,227	3,132,686	111,917,733	31,244,813	80,672,920	548.7	153.2
1971	5,011,048	1,777,862	3,233,186	116,928,781	33,022,675	83,906,106	567.3	160.1
1972	5,376,199	2,106,883	3,269,316	122,304,980	35,129,558	87,175,422	587.7	168.7
1973	5,711,693	1,781,261	3,930,432	128,016,673	36,910,819	91,105,854	610.3	175.9
1974	6,570,608	2,175,818	4,394,790	134,587,281	39,086,637	95,500,644	627.0	184.9
1975	5,327,844	1,995,077	3,332,767	139,915,125	41,081,714	98,833,411	657.1	192.8
1976	5,735,664	2,026,689	3,708,975	145,650,789	43,108,403	102,542,386	678.5	200.8
1977	5,097,211	1,914,050	3,183,161	150,748,000	45,022,453	105,725,547	696.7	208.1
1978	5,416,518	1,972,498	3,444,020	156,164,518	46,994,951	109,169,567	715.6	215.3
1979	5,724,343	2,231,088	3,493,255	161,888,861	49,226,039	112,662,822	720.9	219.2
1980	5,792,726	2,481,230	3,311,496	167,681,587	51,707,269	115,974,318	737.9	227.5
1981	5,581,168	2,712,200	2,868,968	173,262,755	54,419,469	118,843,286	755.1	237.2
1982	4,956,135	2,469,671	2,486,464	178,218,890	56,889,140	121,329,750	769.3	245.6
1983	4,054,373	1,943,069	2,111,304	182,273,263	58,832,209	123,441,054	779.6	251.6
1984	4,410,604	1,904,029	2,506,575	186,683,867	60,736,238	125,947,629	791.6	257.5
1985	3,974,269	1,684,754	2,289,515	190,658,136	62,420,992	128,237,144	801.3	262.4
1986	3,523,936	1,538,080	1,985,856	194,182,072	63,959,072	130,223,000	808.6	266.3
1987	4,344,436	1,842,145	2,502,291	198,526,508	65,801,217	132,725,291	819.4	271.6
1988	4,840,313	2,235,483	2,604,830	203,366,821	68,036,700	135,330,121	831.5	278.3
1989	5,122,788	2,353,087	2,769,701	208,489,609	70,389,787	138,099,822	844.7	285.2
1990	4,333,938	2,109,394	2,224,544	212,823,547	72,499,181	140,324,366	853.3	290.7
1991	3,872,399	1,941,977	1,930,422	216,695,946	74,441,158	142,254,788	859.4	295.2
1992	5,371,397	2,803,330	2,568,067	222,067,343	77,244,488	144,822,855	870.7	302.9
1993	6,593,623	3,668,945	2,924,678	228,660,966	80,913,433	147,747,533	887.0	313.9
1994	6,943,035	3,752,257	3,190,778	235,604,001	84,665,690	150,938,311	905.0	325.2
1995	5,197,207	2,359,153	2,838,054	240,801,208	87,024,843	153,776,365	916.0	331.0

TABLE Ec1127–1134   Estimated size of the civilian gun stock, by gun type: 1945–1995   *Continued*

Sources

Compiled by Gary Kleck, *Targeting Guns: Firearms and Their Control* (Aldine de Gruyter, 1997), pp. 96–7; 1995 data provided by Gary Kleck. No single official source provides the full data set. Relevant sources for different years are as follows: 1945–1968: George D. Newton and Franklin E. Zimring, *Firearms and Violence in American Life: A Staff Report to the National Commission on the Causes and Prevention of Violence* (U.S. Government Printing Office, 1969), p. 174; 1969–1972: Franklin E. Zimring, "Firearms and Federal Law: The Gun Control Act of 1968," *Journal of Legal Studies* 4 (1) (1975): 168–9, Bureau of Alcohol, Tobacco and Firearms (BATF) column and Table 5; U.S. Bureau of the Census, *Statistical Abstract of the United States 1976* (1976), p. 156; BATF, *ATF Ready Reference* (annual issues); 1973–1981: BATF, *ATF Ready Reference* (annual issues); 1982–1983: BATF data reported in Walter Howe, "Firearms Production by U.S. Manufacturers, 1973–1985," *Shooting Industry* (Shot Show Issue, 1988) (1987): 101–12; BATF letter to Gary Kleck dated June 29, 1989, detailing 1984–1987 gun production figures; 1984–1991: BATF, *ATF Ready Reference* (1994); 1992–1994: Ann Y. Smith, "Shooting Industry Market Trend Analysis," *Shooting Industry* 38 (12) (1993): 144ff; Russ Thurman, "Firearms Business Analysis," *Shooting Industry* 39 (1994): 107–12, 118; Russ Thurman, "Firearms Business Analysis," *Shooting Industry* 41 (6) (1996): 54ff; 1995: Russ Thurman, "Firearms Business Analysis," *Shooting Industry* 42 (7) (1997): 30–45.

Documentation

Additions to the stock are the sum of domestically manufactured guns, minus exported guns, plus imported guns, within each gun type category. Shipments to the military are excluded. The 1982–1991 import figures for the federal fiscal year were used for the corresponding calendar years. Kleck argues persuasively that pre-1945 figures understate the true amount of increase. He does not offer comprehensive figures for reductions from the gun stock, and he argues that firm figures are unavailable. Therefore, the table actually reports documentable additions to the gun stock, not the size of the stock itself. See the discussion in Gary Kleck, *Point Blank: Guns and Violence in America* (Aldine de Gruyter, 1991), Appendix 1.

TABLE Ec1135–1138   Survey estimates of the rate of household firearm possession: 1959–1998

Contributed by Douglas Eckberg

Year	Gallup poll Ec1135 Percent	General Social Survey Ec1136 Percent	Harris poll Ec1137 Percent	CBS poll Ec1138 Percent	Year	Gallup poll Ec1135 Percent	General Social Survey Ec1136 Percent	Harris poll Ec1137 Percent	CBS poll Ec1138 Percent
1959	49	—	—	—	1985	44	45	—	—
1965	48	—	—	—	1986	42	—	—	—
1966	48	—	—	—	1987	—	43	—	—
1968	50	—	50 [2]	44	1988	—	41	—	—
1971	—	—	51	—	1989	47	46	45	52
1972	43	—	—	—	1990	47	43	—	—
1973	—	48	—	—	1991	47 [1]	40	—	49
1974	—	47	—	—	1992	—	—	—	49
1975	46 [1]	—	47	—	1993	49 [1]	42	—	49
1976	—	47	—	—	1994	—	41	—	53
1977	—	51	—	—	1995	—	—	—	45
1978	—	—	—	51	1996	40 [1]	40	40	—
1980	45	48	—	—	1998	—	35	—	—
1982	—	44	—	—					
1983	40	—	—	—					
1984	—	45	—	—					

[1] The average of two to three surveys conducted by Gallup in that year. The individual survey results are all within 2 percentage points of the average.

[2] The average of two surveys, which yielded figures of 51 and 49 percent.

Sources

The collection appears in Gary Kleck, *Targeting Guns* (Aldine de Gruyter, 1997), pp. 98–100, except for 1996 General Social Survey data and 1997 Gallup data, which are published in U.S. Bureau of Justice Statistics, *Sourcebook of Criminal Justice Statistics* (annual issues). Most of the surveys across the past two decades are available online on the DIALOG databank's Public Opinion files. Gallup organization data are published in the *Gallup Poll Monthly*.

Documentation

There are no centralized data on firearm possession. Gary Kleck has compiled data from a variety of survey sources. Reported here are findings from the four survey organizations whose data series cover over a quarter century span: the Gallup polls, the General Social Surveys (National Opinion Research Center), the Harris polls, and CBS polls. The surveys inquire about household possession, using for the most part probability samples of American adults, but the details of sample selection and item wording vary across organizations and over time.

TABLE Ec1139–1158   Percentage of adults reporting possession of firearms, by sex, race, education, region, and metropolitan residence: 1973–1998

Contributed by Douglas Eckberg

	All persons	Male	Female	White	Black	Less than a high school degree	High school degree	Associate degree	Bachelor's degree	Graduate degree
	Ec1139	Ec1140	Ec1141	Ec1142	Ec1143	Ec1144	Ec1145	Ec1146	Ec1147	Ec1148
Year	Percent	Percent	Percent	Percent	Percent	Percent	Percent	Percent	Percent	Percent
1973	47.8	53.3	42.9	49.2	39.9	44.9	52.8	35.0	46.2	40.6
1974	46.8	51.8	42.0	48.6	32.5	46.4	47.4	36.0	44.5	45.8
1976	47.2	52.2	43.2	48.2	37.5	45.3	49.7	37.5	49.0	35.0
1977	50.8	55.3	47.0	53.1	34.3	49.5	54.8	50.0	38.4	46.0
1980	47.8	55.9	41.4	49.8	29.5	47.0	51.8	57.8	32.3	36.2
1982	44.3	53.5	37.6	48.2	34.9	42.9	47.2	45.2	36.7	33.3
1984	45.4	53.6	39.8	48.2	27.0	44.3	49.5	35.2	41.0	29.9
1985	44.6	54.7	36.4	46.8	29.3	41.8	49.3	36.7	37.0	36.0
1987	42.7	49.6	37.6	48.9	28.6	39.6	46.3	53.2	31.3	43.7
1988	40.5	50.5	33.6	43.2	25.0	36.7	44.4	38.6	40.6	26.6
1989	46.1	54.9	39.4	49.8	25.5	42.2	51.7	45.0	33.9	36.6
1990	42.7	53.2	34.6	45.1	24.7	44.4	45.4	42.6	34.7	29.1
1991	40.3	50.9	32.1	42.4	33.3	41.2	42.5	43.9	32.4	30.9
1993	42.4	52.8	34.5	45.6	28.0	42.6	47.1	50.0	27.8	33.8
1994	41.1	50.9	33.5	44.8	25.9	37.4	43.2	49.6	38.4	32.8
1996	40.3	47.5	34.6	44.4	26.7	37.9	43.6	36.3	37.2	34.4
1998	35.0	42.7	29.3	39.8	19.4	31.2	38.7	43.2	27.2	27.2

	Region				Metropolitan residence				Counties outside the 100 largest SMSAs	
					100 largest SMSAs					
					Central cities		Suburbs			
	Northeast	Midwest	South	West	Twelve largest SMSAs	Other SMSAs	Twelve largest SMSAs	Other SMSAs	With towns of 10,000 population	Rural
	Ec1149	Ec1150	Ec1151	Ec1152	Ec1153	Ec1154	Ec1155	Ec1156	Ec1157	Ec1158
Year	Percent	Percent	Percent	Percent	Percent	Percent	Percent	Percent	Percent	Percent
1973	22.3	51.7	62.7	47.6	21.0	40.7	28.8	43.5	57.0	66.9
1974	26.8	49.7	59.6	42.1	14.9	43.9	25.6	42.6	53.6	69.1
1976	28.7	48.3	60.7	45.0	20.1	41.2	26.0	40.0	53.4	68.2
1977	32.4	53.2	61.9	46.0	21.2	36.5	37.6	42.6	57.6	71.8
1980	27.2	51.5	59.2	43.7	12.2	33.9	22.7	47.0	57.4	68.8
1982	31.2	44.9	51.1	44.9	19.9	38.0	28.4	45.1	49.4	63.6
1984	32.4	43.7	52.4	49.8	21.4	31.6	26.4	44.2	55.7	69.0
1985	28.1	47.9	53.7	40.2	22.0	33.8	22.8	39.9	49.5	68.5
1987	27.9	43.0	48.3	46.7	23.1	32.7	24.5	41.9	52.4	61.2
1988	24.6	41.5	47.3	43.4	14.1	24.5	30.9	40.1	48.5	58.5
1989	32.0	45.7	53.4	47.8	19.4	29.7	31.5	41.0	55.9	65.0
1990	29.5	44.4	51.6	39.2	9.3	29.1	31.9	44.6	49.2	63.6
1991	28.0	42.0	50.3	32.0	18.2	26.0	19.2	25.7	53.2	61.5
1993	28.8	41.4	52.3	39.1	11.8	31.2	35.3	41.1	47.9	65.9
1994	25.7	46.2	48.8	35.8	22.5	31.2	29.6	36.4	49.3	65.7
1996	24.1	42.2	48.8	39.6	11.6	32.2	32.8	34.7	47.3	67.2
1998	22.3	37.2	42.1	32.2	9.9	19.2	25.5	28.9	44.0	70.0

Source

Series entries are computed by the editor from data in the *General Social Surveys, 1972–1998* [machine-readable data file]. Principal Investigator, James A. Davis; Director and Co-Principal Investigator, Tom W. Smith, National Opinion Research Center, University of Chicago.

Documentation

The General Social Surveys are surveys of the non-institutionalized, English-speaking, adult population (age 18 and older). They have been conducted annually in February, March, and April of 1972 through 1993, with the exceptions of 1979, 1981, and 1992. Beginning in 1994, they have been conducted biannually. Block quota sampling was used in the 1972, 1973, and 1974 surveys and in half the 1975 and 1976 surveys. All other surveys have used full-probability sampling. The 1982 and 1987 surveys included black oversamples.

The wording of the firearm question is: "Do you happen to have in your home or garage any guns or revolvers?" A very small number of respondents who refused to answer or indicated that they were unsure are deleted from the calculations.

Series Ec1149–1152. See Table Ap-G in Appendix 2 regarding the composition of census regions and divisions.

COURTS AND CRIMINAL JUSTICE

Richard Sutch

TABLE Ec1159–1178   Criminal justice expenditures, by level of government: 1902–1996

Contributed by Richard Sutch

	All governments					Federal				
			Judicial and legal activities					Judicial and legal activities		
	Total	Police protection	Total	Judicial activities	Corrections	Total	Police protection	Total	Judicial activities	Corrections
	Ec1159	Ec1160	Ec1161	Ec1162	Ec1163	Ec1164	Ec1165	Ec1166	Ec1167	Ec1168
Fiscal year	Million dollars	Million dollars	Million dollars	Million dollars	Million dollars	Million dollars	Million dollars	Million dollars	Million dollars	Million dollars
1902	—	50	—	—	—	—	—	—	—	—
1913	—	92	—	—	—	—	3	—	—	—
1922	—	204	—	—	—	—	14	—	—	—
1927	—	290	—	—	—	—	20	—	—	—
1932	—	349	—	—	—	—	31	—	—	—
1936	—	331	—	—	—	—	17	—	—	—
1938	—	378	—	—	—	—	19	—	—	—
1940	—	386	—	—	—	—	21	—	—	—
1942	—	444	—	—	—	—	50	—	—	—
1944	—	497	—	—	—	—	83	—	—	—
1945	—	—	—	—	—	—	—	—	—	—
1946	—	549	—	—	—	—	70	—	—	—
1947	—	—	—	—	—	—	—	—	—	—
1948	—	724	—	—	—	—	80	—	—	—
1950	—	864	—	—	—	—	88	—	—	—
1951	—	—	—	—	—	—	104	—	—	—
1952	—	1,080	—	—	365	—	141	—	—	28
1953	—	1,160	—	—	—	—	122	—	—	—
1954	2,080	1,254	—	399	427	210	124	—	56	30
1955	2,231	1,359	—	409	463	206	129	—	49	28
1956	2,434	1,487	—	447	500	250	156	—	61	33
1957	2,655	1,624	—	481	550	252	155	—	62	35
1958	2,861	1,769	—	519	573	261	159	—	63	39
1959	3,149	1,880	—	561	708	275	170	—	68	37
1960	3,349	2,030	—	597	722	291	173	—	74	44
1961	3,613	2,210	—	593	810	298	193	—	58	47
1962	3,795	2,326	—	628	841	304	196	—	57	51
1963	4,009	2,440	—	693	876	358	209	—	94	55
1964	4,222	2,586	—	697	939	342	220	—	66	56
1965	4,573	2,792	—	748	1,033	377	243	—	75	59
1966	4,903	3,033	—	793	1,077	393	257	—	79	57
1967	5,424	3,331	—	894	1,199	429	282	—	87	60
1968	6,070	3,725	—	976	1,369	445	290	—	90	65
1969	7,340	4,430	1,449	1,002	1,462	800	492	238	106	71
1970	8,571	5,080	1,734	1,190	1,706	978	589	287	129	83
1971	10,513	6,165	1,978	1,358	2,291	1,211	804	284	134	111
1972	11,725	6,903	2,239	1,491	2,422	1,496	962	366	179	133
1973	13,051	7,624	2,450	1,579	2,740	1,695	1,089	331	118	171
1974	14,954	8,512	2,814	1,798	3,240	1,961	1,222	346	136	215
1975	17,249	9,786	3,281	2,068	3,843	2,189	1,461	429	165	217
1976	19,681	11,028	3,807	2,428	4,386	2,450	1,612	472	219	256
1977	21,574	11,865	4,267	2,638	4,934	2,779	1,795	616	290	299
1978	24,132	13,120	5,051	3,067	5,523	3,122	1,952	746	321	337
1979	25,871	13,812	5,634	3,389	5,986	3,269	1,948	876	370	354
1980	—	15,163	—	—	6,901	—	1,739	—	—	387
1981	—	16,822	—	—	7,869	—	1,904	—	—	413
1982	35,842	19,022	7,771	—	9,049	4,269	2,366	1,390	—	513
1983	39,680	20,648	8,621	—	10,411	4,844	2,745	1,523	—	576
1984	43,943	22,686	9,463	—	11,794	5,787	3,355	1,785	—	647

(continued)

TABLE Ec1159–1178   Criminal justice expenditures, by level of government: 1902–1996   *Continued*

	All governments					Federal				
			Judicial and legal activities					Judicial and legal activities		
	Total	Police protection	Total	Judicial activities	Corrections	Total	Police protection	Total	Judicial activities	Corrections
	Ec1159	Ec1160	Ec1161	Ec1162	Ec1163	Ec1164	Ec1165	Ec1166	Ec1167	Ec1168
Fiscal year	Million dollars	Million dollars	Million dollars	Million dollars	Million dollars	Million dollars	Million dollars	Million dollars	Million dollars	Million dollars
1985	48,563	24,399	10,629	—	13,535	6,279	3,430	2,129	—	720
1986	53,500	26,255	11,485	—	15,759	6,430	3,542	2,090	—	798
1987	58,871	28,768	12,555	—	17,549	7,231	4,036	2,271	—	924
1988	65,231	30,961	13,971	—	20,299	8,464	4,657	2,639	—	1,168
1989	70,949	32,794	15,589	—	22,567	9,204	4,952	2,949	—	1,303
1990	79,434	35,923	17,357	—	26,154	10,219	5,344	3,281	—	1,594
1991	87,567	38,971	19,298	—	29,297	12,106	6,170	3,995	—	1,941
1992	93,777	41,327	20,989	—	31,461	13,529	6,703	4,415	—	2,411
1993	97,542	44,037	21,558	—	31,947	14,429	7,345	4,662	—	2,422
1994	103,471	46,005	22,602	—	34,864	14,626	7,318	4,721	—	2,587
1995	112,868	48,645	24,472	—	39,752	16,741	7,548	5,309	—	3,884
1996	120,194	53,007	26,158	—	41,029	17,480	8,281	5,693	—	3,506

	State					Local				
			Judicial and legal activities					Judicial and legal activities		
	Total	Police protection	Total	Judicial activities	Corrections	Total	Police protection	Total	Judicial activities	Corrections
	Ec1169	Ec1170	Ec1171	Ec1172	Ec1173	Ec1174	Ec1175	Ec1176	Ec1177	Ec1178
Fiscal year	Million dollars	Million dollars	Million dollars	Million dollars	Million dollars	Million dollars	Million dollars	Million dollars	Million dollars	Million dollars
1902	—	—	—	—	14	—	50	—	—	—
1913	—	1	—	—	28	—	88	—	—	—
1922	—	4	—	—	64	—	186	—	—	—
1927	—	7	—	—	64	—	263	—	—	—
1932	—	15	—	—	87	—	303	—	—	—
1936	—	19	—	—	73	—	295	—	—	—
1938	—	30	—	—	85	—	329	—	—	—
1940	—	34	—	—	86	—	331	—	—	—
1942	—	40	—	—	80	—	354	—	—	—
1944	159	41	—	35	83	—	373	—	—	—
1945	—	—	—	—	82	—	—	—	—	—
1946	—	45	—	—	97	—	434	—	—	—
1947	—	—	—	—	107	—	—	—	—	—
1948	—	65	—	—	153	—	579	—	—	—
1950	332	85	—	49	198	—	691	—	—	—
1951	365	97	—	53	215	—	—	—	—	—
1952	386	106	—	57	223	—	833	—	—	114
1953	418	119	—	61	238	—	919	—	—	—
1954	446	130	—	66	250	1,424	1,000	—	277	147
1955	475	139	—	68	268	1,550	1,091	—	292	167
1956	526	159	—	72	295	1,658	1,172	—	314	172
1957	584	179	—	77	328	1,819	1,290	—	342	187
1958	671	214	—	87	370	1,929	1,396	—	369	164
1959	733	228	—	92	413	2,141	1,482	—	401	258
1960	769	245	—	99	425	2,289	1,612	—	424	253
1961	849	261	—	109	479	2,466	1,756	—	426	284
1962	902	276	—	118	508	2,589	1,854	—	453	282
1963	960	297	—	127	536	2,691	1,934	—	472	285
1964	1,042	315	—	141	586	2,838	2,051	—	490	297
1965	1,135	348	—	155	632	3,062	2,201	—	518	343
1966	1,224	385	—	175	664	3,286	2,391	—	539	356
1967	1,381	441	—	193	747	3,615	2,609	—	614	392
1968	1,622	541	—	209	872	4,003	2,894	—	677	432
1969	1,849	621	—	236	914	4,691	3,317	—	660	477

TABLE Ec1159–1178 Criminal justice expenditures, by level of government: 1902–1996 *Continued*

	State					Local				
			Judicial and legal activities					Judicial and legal activities		
	Total	Police protection	Total	Judicial activities	Corrections	Total	Police protection	Total	Judicial activities	Corrections
	Ec1169	Ec1170	Ec1171	Ec1172	Ec1173	Ec1174	Ec1175	Ec1176	Ec1177	Ec1178
Fiscal year	Million dollars	Million dollars	Million dollars	Million dollars	Million dollars	Million dollars	Million dollars	Million dollars	Million dollars	Million dollars
1970	2,134	689	—	282	1,051	5,454	3,803	—	779	572
1971	2,681	873	438	314	1,323	6,621	4,488	1,257	911	857
1972	2,948	993	495	346	1,378	7,281	4,948	1,376	965	911
1973	3,304	1,132	566	386	1,534	8,052	5,403	1,551	1,075	1,035
1974	3,900	1,308	669	439	1,813	9,092	5,982	1,799	1,223	1,213
1975	4,612	1,512	779	498	2,193	10,449	6,813	2,073	1,405	1,434
1976	5,204	1,696	903	585	2,475	12,027	7,720	2,432	1,624	1,654
1977	5,812	1,800	1,026	651	2,847	12,983	8,300	2,626	1,698	1,788
1978	6,688	1,892	1,497	1,013	3,177	14,322	9,276	2,809	1,733	2,009
1979	7,346	1,988	1,754	1,207	3,478	15,256	9,876	3,004	1,812	2,154
1980	8,323	2,027	1,925	—	4,258	—	11,397	—	—	2,256
1981	9,375	2,241	2,189	—	4,844	—	12,677	—	—	2,612
1982	10,651	2,486	2,606	—	5,560	20,922	14,170	3,775	—	2,976
1983	11,709	2,630	2,756	—	6,323	23,127	15,273	4,342	—	3,512
1984	13,081	2,817	3,085	—	7,178	25,075	16,513	4,593	—	3,969
1985	14,903	3,126	3,442	—	8,336	27,381	17,843	5,058	—	4,479
1986	16,978	3,364	3,737	—	9,878	30,092	19,349	5,659	—	5,084
1987	18,465	3,647	4,085	—	10,733	33,175	21,085	6,199	—	5,892
1988	20,880	3,937	4,539	—	12,404	35,887	22,367	6,792	—	6,728
1989	23,009	4,173	4,982	—	13,854	38,736	23,669	7,637	—	7,409
1990	25,764	4,484	5,438	—	15,842	43,451	26,095	8,638	—	8,718
1991	28,493	4,786	5,917	—	17,790	46,968	28,015	9,386	—	9,367
1992	30,271	4,967	6,553	—	18,751	49,977	29,656	10,021	—	10,300
1993	30,696	4,961	6,644	—	19,091	52,417	31,731	10,252	—	10,433
1994	33,495	5,325	6,904	—	21,266	55,349	33,362	10,976	—	11,011
1995	37,360	5,735	7,534	—	24,091	58,768	35,362	11,629	—	11,777
1996	39,903	6,499	8,110	—	25,294	62,811	38,227	12,355	—	12,229

Sources

U.S. Bureau of the Census, *Governmental Finances* (annual issues); *State Government Finances* (annual issues); *U.S. Census of Governments: Historical Statistics on Governmental Finances and Employment, 1957, 1962, and 1967; Criminal Justice Expenditure and Employment for Selected Large Governmental Units, 1967–1968*. U.S. Law Enforcement Assistance Administration, *Expenditure and Employment Data for the Criminal Justice System* (annual issues). U.S. Bureau of Justice Statistics, *Expenditure and Employment Data for the Criminal Justice System* (annual issues); *Justice Expenditure and Employment in the U.S.* (annual issues); *Criminal Justice Expenditure and Employment Extracts* (annual issues). U.S. Bureau of the Census, *Statistical Abstract of the United States* (1973, 1976, 1981, 1984, 1990).

Documentation

Expenditures include all amounts of money paid out (net of recoveries and any correcting transactions) other than for retirement of debt (including interest), investment in securities, extensions of loans, or agency transactions. It includes only external cash payments and excludes noncash transactions, such as the provision of meals or housing of employees. The data include direct expenditures only and exclude intergovernmental transfers. Between 1969 and 1981 inclusive, the totals include a residual category of "other expenditures" not shown separately.

The federal government expenditure data are for the fiscal year, which since 1976 ended on September 30 of the year indicated. The state expenditure data presented cover fiscal years ending June 30 for all states except four whose fiscal years ended as follows: New York, March 31; Texas, August 31; and Alabama and Michigan, September 30. For local governments, the fiscal years reported are those that closed between July 1 and June 30. Most municipalities and counties end their fiscal years on December 31 or June 30. Thus, some local jurisdictions that ended their fiscal year on December 31 are included for the following year. The fiscal years reported for Washington, D.C., ended on September 30 of the year indicated.

These statistics are the products of the Census Bureau's governmental statistics program, which consisted of a quinquennial census, recurrent surveys, and special studies done either as in-house research or on a contractual basis. Those Census Bureau surveys traditionally have provided limited data on the justice sectors of police protection (from 1902) and corrections (from 1954), with slightly more data being collected for state governments and the largest local governments. The data were obtained through a combination of field compilation, office compilation, and mail canvass. Field compilation was used for states and for large counties and cities; mail canvass and office compilation for the federal government, counties under 100,000 population, and cities under 50,000 population.

The Bureau of Justice Statistics (BJS) began the collection of justice expenditure and employment data with fiscal 1971, using a special sample drawn by the U.S. Bureau of the Census especially for this purpose. The annual Criminal Justice Expenditure and Employment (CJEE) Survey provided comparable trend data from 1971 to 1979. In 1980, BJS discontinued the CJEE Survey for budgetary reasons following the collection of 1979 data. The cancellation of the CJEE Survey left a gap in national criminal justice statistics, which the CJEE Extracts series is designed to fill, albeit on a limited basis. Instead of presenting data based on a separate survey, the CJEE Extracts contains justice expenditure and employment data from the Census Bureau's annual sample surveys of government finances and public employment. Beginning with 1982, these surveys began collecting "judicial and legal services" data as a separate category, allowing estimation of total justice expenditure and employment from the Census Bureau surveys. The CJEE Extracts data are assembled from data collected through the Census Bureau's annual surveys of government finances and public employment. The samples of local governments for those surveys are drawn from the most recent available quinquennial Census of Governments. The samples consist

(continued)

TABLE Ec1159–1178   Criminal justice expenditures, by level of government: 1902–1996   *Continued*

of all large local general-purpose governments above a certain population threshold (certainty units) plus a sample below the certainty level.

Federal government financial data were obtained from actual data presented in *The Budget of the United States Government* for each fiscal year displayed. Certain adjustments were made in federal data to arrive at Census Bureau "expenditure" amounts. State finance statistics as well as those for large counties and cities were compiled by Census Bureau representatives from official reports and records, with the advice of state and local officers and employees. The data were compiled from state government audits, budgets, and other financial reports, either in printed or electronic format. The compilation generally involved recasting the state financial records into the classification categories used for reporting by the Census Bureau. The initial local government data collection phase used two methods to obtain data: mail canvass and central collection from state sources. In about thirty states, all or part of the data for local governments was obtained from cooperative arrangements between the Census Bureau and a state government agency. These usually involved a data collection effort carried out to meet the needs of both agencies – the state agency for purposes of audit, oversight, or information and the Census Bureau for statistical purposes. Data for the balance of local governments in the annual surveys were obtained via mail questionnaires sent directly to county, municipal, township, special district, and school district governments.

Series Ec1159–1163. Equals the total of the federal, state, and local governments in each category.

Series Ec1164–1168. The term "federal" encompasses all activities of the U.S. government other than employment of the armed forces. District of Columbia data are excluded from this category and included with data for municipalities.

Series Ec1169–1173. Data refer to the governments of the fifty states that constitute the United States.

Series Ec1174–1178. The Bureau of the Census classifies local governments by five major types: county, municipality, township, independent school district, and special district. No justice statistics are collected from school or special districts. Expenditures on college campus police and justice are excluded.

Series Ec1159, Ec1164, Ec1169, and Ec1174. Criminal justice includes the combined functions of police protection, judicial and legal services, and corrections as defined later. For 1902–1968 and 1980–1982, there are no data for legal services. The totals given for the period before 1969 are not comparable with those reported for 1969 through 1996. However, the older, narrower definition can be calculated for the components for 1969 through 1981. Note that the total will to some degree include civil justice functions as well as criminal justice functions where criminal functions cannot be segregated in available source documents.

Series Ec1160, Ec1165, Ec1170, and Ec1175. Police protection is the function of enforcing the law, preserving order and traffic safety, and apprehending those who violate the law, whether these activities are performed by a police department, a sheriffs' department, or a special police force that is maintained by an agency whose prime responsibility is outside the justice system but that has a police force to perform these activities in its specialized area (geographic or functional). This category includes regular police services; police patrols and communications; crime prevention activities; temporary lockups and "holding tanks"; traffic safety and engineering (but not highway planning and engineering); vehicular inspection and licensing; buildings used exclusively for police purposes; the maintenance of buildings used for police purposes; medical examiners and coroners; law enforcement activities of sheriffs' offices; and unsworn school crossing guards, parking meter readers, and animal wardens, if employed by a police agency. Private security police are outside the scope of the survey. The special police forces included in the data are only those that are part of a general-purpose

government. Those special police forces that are part of independent school districts or special districts are not included in the data. Short-term custody and detention are considered part of the police protection function. Data for lockups or "tanks" holding prisoners less than forty-eight hours are included in the police protection category. Data for institutions with authority to hold prisoners forty-eight hours or more are included in the corrections category.

Series Ec1161, Ec1166, Ec1171, and Ec1176. Judicial and legal services covers all civil and criminal activities associated with courts, including prosecution and public defense. Activities associated with courts include the maintenance and support of law libraries, grand juries, and petit juries; medical and social service activities (except probation, which is classified as corrections where separately identifiable); provision of court reporters, judicial councils, bailiffs, and "register of wills" and similar probate functions; and court ("civil") activities of sheriffs' offices in some jurisdictions. This category excludes monetary judgments and claims or other payments of a government as a defendant in judicial or administrative proceedings, as well as legal units of noncriminal justice agencies, whose functions may be performed by a legal service department in other jurisdictions (such as a county counsel).

Series Ec1162, Ec1167, Ec1172, and Ec1177. Judicial activities encompass all courts and activities associated with courts such as law libraries, grand juries, petit juries, and the like. Judicial activities exclude legal services and public-supported indigent defense. Indigent defense includes activities associated with the right of persons to have legal counsel and representation, the office of the public defender, and other government programs that pay the fees of court-appointed counsel. These include court-paid fees to individually retained counsel, fees paid by the court to court-appointed counsel, government contributions to private legal aid societies and bar association-sponsored programs, and the activities of an established public defender office or program.

Series Ec1163, Ec1168, Ec1173, and Ec1178. Corrections is that function of government involving the confinement and rehabilitation of adults and juveniles convicted of offenses against the law and the confinement of persons suspected of a crime and awaiting adjudication. Correctional institutions include prisons and penitentiaries; reformatories; jails; houses of correction; other variously named correctional institutions, such as correctional farms, workhouses, industrial schools, and training schools; institutions and facilities exclusively for the confinement of the criminally insane; institutions and facilities for the examination, evaluation, classification, and assignment of inmates; and facilities for the confinement, treatment, and rehabilitation of drug addicts and alcoholics, if the institution is administered by a correctional agency. When an institution maintains a prison industry or agricultural program, data on the cost of production or the value of prison labor used by agencies of the same government, if identifiable, are excluded (and classed as expenditure for the function using the product or services). Expenditure for the manufacture, production, sale, and distribution of goods produced for sale or use outside the government is included under this heading. It excludes the cost of maintaining prisoners in institutions of other governments, which are classified as an intergovernmental expenditure for which the "institutions" versus "other corrections" distinctions are not applied. The category "corrections" consists of all noninstitutional correctional activities including parole boards and programs; pardon boards; nonresidential resettlement or halfway houses for those not in need of institutionalization; probation activities and programs, even if administered by a court; and correctional administration not directly connectable to institutions. Payments to another government for boarding prisoners are classified as "intergovernmental expenditure" for which the institutions and other corrections distinctions discussed previously are not applied. In practice, intergovernmental payments of this type are difficult to detect for insignificant amounts between local government and for miscellaneous items that cannot be directly related to institutional care.

TABLE Ec1179   U.S. Supreme Court cases – number: 1880–1939

Contributed by Richard Sutch

Year	New cases filed Ec1179 Number	Year	New cases filed Ec1179 Number	Year	New cases filed Ec1179 Number
1880	417	1900	406	1920	565
1881	411	1901	386	1921	673
1882	434	1902	391	1922	720
1883	439	1903	430	1923	631
1884	477	1904	403	1924	909
1885	493	1905	502	1925	790
1886	499	1906	484	1926	718
1887	489	1907	480	1927	751
1888	556	1908	494	1928	776
1889	500	1909	514	1929	838
1890	636	1910	516	1930	845
1891	383	1911	532	1931	877
1892	290	1912	521	1932	897
1893	280	1913	526	1933	1,005
1894	341	1914	530	1934	937
1895	386	1915	557	1935	983
1896	295	1916	658	1936	950
1897	307	1917	590	1937	981
1898	523	1918	593	1938	942
1899	384	1919	587	1939	981

Sources

Lee Epstein, Jeffrey A. Segal, et al., editors, *The Supreme Court Compendium: Data, Decisions, and Developments,* second edition (Congressional Quarterly, 1996), pp. 71–6, Table 2 2. The underlying source for this data is Gerhard Casper and Richard A. Posner, *The Workload of the Supreme Court* (American Bar Foundation, 1976), p. 3.

Documentation

See series Ec1180 for more recent data.

TABLE Ec1180–1195 U.S. Supreme Court cases – number and disposition: 1940–1969
Contributed by Richard Sutch

	Total cases							Petitions for review			Pauper petitions for review			Motions for leave to file various writs		
	Filed	Disposed of		Remaining on docket	Original cases filed	Appeals filed	Pauper appeals filed	Filed	Granted	Denied or dismissed	Filed	Granted	Denied or dismissed	Filed	Granted	Denied or dismissed
		Total	Opinions													
Year	Ec1180	Ec1181	Ec1182	Ec1183	Ec1184	Ec1185	Ec1186	Ec1187	Ec1188	Ec1189	Ec1190	Ec1191	Ec1192	Ec1193	Ec1194	Ec1195
	Number	Number	Number	Number	Number	Number	Number	Number	Number	Number	Number	Number	Number	Number	Number	Number
1940	977	985	281	124	4	84	—	769	174	592	120	19	101	—	—	—
1941	1,178	1,168	376	134	3	213	—	784	150	623	178	16	162	—	—	—
1942	984	997	259	121	5	105	—	727	158	592	147	8	139	—	—	—
1943	997	962	210	156	1	82	—	700	127	547	214	12	202	—	—	—
1944	1,237	1,249	274	144	2	93	—	803	176	642	339	10	329	—	—	—
1945	1,316	1,292	215	168	1	64	—	727	155	565	393	15	378	131	—	131
1946	1,510	1,520	256	158	0	97	—	731	148	586	528	8	520	154	—	154
1947	1,295	1,322	208	131	0	69	—	647	97	555	426	17	400	153	—	150
1948	1,465	1,425	238	171	2	86	—	687	144	523	447	18	425	243	2	241
1949	1,270	1,301	202	140	0	85	—	633	85	556	441	7	436	111	0	108
1950	1,181	1,202	191	119	0	77	—	582	89	495	404	17	386	118	0	121
1951	1,234	1,207	197	146	1	104	—	612	94	518	413	19	386	104	1	102
1952	1,283	1,278	193	151	2	87	—	655	104	541	434	11	429	105	0	104
1953	1,302	1,293	170	160	0	81	—	603	78	522	528	10	507	90	0	92
1954	1,397	1,352	196	205	0	87	8	626	108	532	543	12	494	133	0	126
1955	1,644	1,630	246	219	4	104	17	787	123	643	583	16	579	149	2	155
1956	1,802	1,670	266	351	3	123	24	851	139	664	639	38	584	162	0	153
1957	1,639	1,765	323	225	2	110	17	716	110	670	680	34	648	114	0	119
1958	1,819	1,763	275	281	3	126	25	760	108	641	772	24	716	133	1	123
1959	1,862	1,787	249	356	0	90	22	767	122	645	836	55	743	147	0	146
1960	1,940	1,911	282	385	0	124	28	718	87	628	950	22	871	120	0	125
1961	2,185	2,142	264	428	2	110	36	778	103	665	1,138	38	1,093	121	1	120
1962	2,373	2,327	388	474	2	134	36	823	115	690	1,213	88	1,086	165	7	156
1963	2,294	2,401	393	367	1	147	28	870	118	733	1,069	69	1,093	179	1	180
1964	2,288	2,173	275	482	4	118	29	920	116	791	1,025	21	927	192	1	178
1965	2,774	2,665	338	591	8	158	42	1,030	124	900	1,388	43	1,271	148	1	147
1966	2,752	2,890	402	453	5	144	48	1,058	121	922	1,319	56	1,371	178	2	188
1967	3,106	2,946	462	613	2	162	36	1,114	166	979	1,610	84	1,337	182	5	166
1968	3,271	3,117	346	767	1	192	40	1,131	101	983	1,744	62	1,603	163	2	168
1969	3,405	3,379	347	793	6	204	51	1,253	108	1,121	1,772	38	1,759	119	3	121

Series Ec1180. See series Ec1179 for earlier data.

Source
U.S. Administrative Office of the United States Courts, *Annual Report of the Director* (various issues).

Documentation
Data are for years beginning in June. The statutory term of the Court begins the first Monday in October, but, for statistical purposes, the new term begins upon adjournment of preceding term, usually in June.

TABLE Ec1196–1220 U.S. Supreme Court cases – number and disposition: 1969–1997

Contributed by Richard Sutch

		Appellate cases on docket								Pauper cases on docket		
	Total cases on docket	Total	From prior term	Docketed during present term	Acted upon				Not acted upon	Total	Acted upon	
					Total	Granted review	Denied, dismissed, or withdrawn	Summarily decided			Total	Granted review
	Ec1196	Ec1197	Ec1198	Ec1199	Ec1200	Ec1201	Ec1202	Ec1203	Ec1204	Ec1205	Ec1206 [1]	Ec1207
Year	Number	Number	Number	Number	Number	Number	Number	Number	Number	Number	Number	Number
1969	4,202	1,758	271	1,487	1,529	222	1,219	88	229	2,429	1,971	30
1970	4,212	1,903	325	1,578	1,613	214	1,285	114	290	2,289	1,802	41
1971	4,533	2,070	362	1,708	1,752	238	1,409	105	318	2,445	2,023	61
1972	4,640	2,183	442	1,741	1,834	217	1,397	220	349	2,436	1,982	35
1973	5,079	2,480	412	2,068	1,948	229	1,572	147	532	2,585	2,013	30
1974	4,668	2,308	540	1,768	1,967	235	1,594	138	341	2,348	1,976	28
1975	4,761	2,352	431	1,921	1,900	244	1,538	118	452	2,395	1,997	28
1976	4,731	2,324	452	1,872	2,019	237	1,620	162	305	2,398	2,083	30
1977	4,704	2,341	472	1,869	1,979	224	1,676	79	362	2,349	1,960	24
1978	4,731	2,383	434	1,949	2,023	210	1,734	79	360	2,331	1,996	27
1979	4,781	2,509	425	2,084	2,050	199	1,776	75	459	2,249	1,838	32
1980	5,144	2,749	527	2,222	2,324	167	1,999	90	425	2,371	2,027	17
1981	5,311	2,935	522	2,413	2,513	203	2,100	114	422	2,354	2,039	7
1982	5,079	2,710	545	2,165	2,279	169	1,892	113	413	2,352	2,013	10
1983	5,100	2,688	520	2,168	2,220	140	1,902	71	468	2,394	1,992	9
1984	5,006	2,575	539	2,036	2,253	167	1,953	59	322	2,416	2,087	18
1985	5,158	2,571	400	2,171	2,185	166	1,863	78	386	2,577	2,189	20
1986	5,123	2,547	476	2,071	2,189	152	1,876	71	358	2,564	2,250	15
1987	5,268	2,577	440	2,137	2,224	157	1,919	66	353	2,675	2,263	23
1988	5,657	2,587	446	2,141	2,271	130	1,973	75	316	3,056	2,638	17
1989	5,746	2,416	384	2,032	2,096	103	1,881	44	320	3,316	2,891	19
1990	6,316	2,351	365	1,986	2,042	114	1,802	81	309	3,951	3,436	27
1991	6,770	2,451	365	2,086	2,125	103	1,914	52	326	4,307	3,768	17
1992	7,245	2,441	379	2,062	2,140	83	1,920	84	301	4,792	4,261	14
1993	7,786	2,442	342	2,100	2,099	78	1,947	34	343	5,332	4,621	21
1994	8,100	2,515	377	2,138	2,185	83	2,016	52	330	5,574	4,983	10
1995	7,565	2,456	361	2,095	2,130	92	1,945	62	326	5,098	4,514	13
1996	7,602	2,430	375	2,055	2,124	74	1,955	66	306	5,165	4,613	13
1997	7,692	2,432	347	2,085	2,142	75	1,990	36	290	5,253	4,616	14

TABLE Ec1196–1220   U.S. Supreme Court cases – number and disposition: 1969–1997   *Continued*

	Pauper cases on docket			Original cases on docket			Cases disposed of						
	Acted upon												
Year	Denied, dismissed, or withdrawn	Summarily decided	Not acted upon	Total	Disposed of during term	Total cases available for argument	Total	Argued	Dismissed or remanded without argument	Cases remaining	Cases decided by signed opinion	Cases decided by per curiam opinion	Signed opinions
	Ec1208	Ec1209	Ec1210	Ec1211	Ec1212	Ec1213	Ec1214	Ec1215	Ec1216	Ec1217	Ec1218	Ec1219	Ec1220
	Number	Number	Number	Number	Number	Number	Number	Number	Number	Number	Number	Number	Number
1969	1,916	25	458	15	5	241	147	144	3	94	105	21	88
1970	1,683	78	487	20	7	267	160	151	9	107	126	22	109
1971	1,781	181	422	18	8	280	181	176	5	99	143	24	129
1972	1,902	45	454	21	8	256	180	177	3	76	159	18	140
1973	1,942	41	572	14	4	261	172	170	2	89	161	8	140
1974	1,914	34	372	12	4	278	178	175	3	100	144	20	123
1975	1,903	66	398	14	7	280	181	179	2	99	160	16	138
1976	2,013	40	315	8	2	269	181	176	5	88	154	22	126
1977	1,899	37	389	14	3	260	185	172	13	75	153	8	129
1978	1,938	31	335	17	0	249	170	168	2	79	153	8	130
1979	1,757	49	411	23	1	238	160	156	4	78	143	12	130
1980	1,968	32	344	24	7	264	162	154	8	102	144	8	123
1981	2,014	12	315	22	6	318	192	184	8	126	170	10	141
1982	1,995	6	339	17	3	312	199	183	16	113	174	6	151
1983	1,968	10	402	18	7	269	189	184	5	80	174	6	151
1984	2,050	14	329	15	8	271	184	175	9	87	159	11	139
1985	2,136	24	388	10	2	276	175	171	4	101	161	10	146
1986	2,186	38	314	12	1	270	179	175	4	91	164	10	145
1987	2,210	21	412	16	5	280	175	167	8	105	151	9	139
1988	2,577	32	418	14	2	254	173	170	3	81	156	12	133
1989	2,824	35	425	14	2	204	147	146	1	57	143	3	129
1990	3,369	28	515	14	3	201	131	125	6	70	121	4	112
1991	3,716	22	539	12	1	196	130	127	3	66	120	3	107
1992	4,209	25	531	12	1	166	120	116	4	46	111	4	107
1993	4,566	30	711	12	1	145	105	99	6	40	93	6	84
1994	4,955	14	591	11	2	136	97	94	3	39	91	3	82
1995	4,439	55	584	11	5	145	93	90	3	52	87	3	75
1996	4,582	15	552	7	2	140	92	90	2	48	87	3	80
1997	4,581	14	637	7	1	138	97	96	1	41	93	1	91

[1] Beginning 1980, includes cases granted review and carried over to next term, not shown separately.

Documentation

The statutory term of the court begins the first Monday in October.

Source

U.S. Bureau of the Census, *Statistical Abstract of the United States* (1975, 1980, 1999).

TABLE Ec1221–1234 Courts of appeals cases docketed and disposed, by type of case: 1893–1995

Contributed by Eric W. Rise

			Docketed								Disposed			
			Civil								Civil			
	Total	Criminal	Total	United States	Private	Administrative	Other	Total	Criminal	Total	United States	Private	Administrative	Other
	Ec1221	Ec1222	Ec1223	Ec1224	Ec1225	Ec1226	Ec1227	Ec1228	Ec1229	Ec1230	Ec1231	Ec1232	Ec1233	Ec1234
Fiscal year	Number	Number	Number	Number	Number	Number	Number	Number	Number	Number	Number	Number	Number	Number
1893	841	8	833	—	—	—	—	403	2	401	—	—	—	—
1894	902	10	756	—	—	—	—	958	5	679	—	—	—	—
1895	929	2	813	—	—	—	—	955	6	818	—	—	—	—
1897	917	9	766	—	—	—	—	863	3	726	—	—	—	—
1898	948	29	777	—	—	—	—	975	22	811	—	—	—	—
1899	1,026	18	839	—	—	—	—	989	16	840	—	—	—	—
1900	1,093	27	925	—	—	—	—	1,023	21	896	—	—	—	—
1901	1,157	39	964	—	—	—	—	1,056	37	870	—	—	—	—
1902	1,157	39	964	—	—	—	—	1,056	37	870	—	—	—	—
1903	1,099	26	939	—	—	—	—	1,132	22	979	—	—	—	—
1904	1,160	55	966	—	—	—	—	1,140	48	961	—	—	—	—
1905	1,293	51	1,075	—	—	—	—	1,211	37	999	—	—	—	—
1906	1,418	55	1,180	—	—	—	—	1,325	45	1,140	—	—	—	—
1907	1,371	80	1,113	—	—	—	—	1,412	67	1,176	—	—	—	—
1908	1,482	91	1,186	—	—	—	—	1,404	62	1,147	—	—	—	—
1909	1,467	73	1,210	—	—	—	—	1,452	94	1,160	—	—	—	—
1910	1,672	77	1,371	—	—	—	—	1,514	78	1,236	—	—	—	—
1911	1,442	104	1,141	—	—	—	—	1,609	92	1,296	—	—	—	—
1912	1,438	71	1,170	—	—	—	—	1,402	87	1,132	—	—	—	—
1913	1,465	71	1,191	—	—	—	—	1,515	66	1,253	—	—	—	—
1914	1,586	97	1,283	—	—	—	—	1,448	88	1,155	—	—	—	—
1915	1,629	144	1,308	—	—	—	—	1,685	113	1,369	—	—	—	—
1916	1,740	109	1,409	—	—	—	—	1,658	116	1,343	—	—	—	—
1917	1,627	111	1,336	—	—	—	—	1,657	117	1,370	—	—	—	—
1918	1,510	184	1,136	—	—	—	—	1,644	138	1,339	—	—	—	—
1919	1,506	261	1,063	—	—	—	—	1,508	245	1,093	—	—	—	—
1920	1,523	198	1,110	—	—	—	—	1,458	226	1,046	—	—	—	—
1921	1,838	280	1,191	—	—	—	—	1,672	230	1,142	—	—	—	—
1922	1,826	261	1,360	—	—	—	—	1,864	277	1,310	—	—	—	—
1923	1,956	365	1,339	—	—	—	—	1,988	323	1,408	—	—	—	—
1924	2,471	491	1,631	—	—	—	—	2,181	407	1,491	—	—	—	—
1925	2,525	521	1,640	—	—	—	—	2,509	544	1,631	—	—	—	—
1926	2,588	584	1,694	—	—	—	—	2,558	582	1,626	—	—	—	—
1927	2,525	401	1,811	—	—	—	—	2,601	487	1,806	—	—	—	—
1928	2,610	327	1,877	—	—	—	—	2,495	362	1,797	—	—	—	—
1929	2,926	351	2,150	—	—	—	—	2,826	309	1,987	—	—	—	—
1930	2,874	399	2,150	—	—	—	—	2,898	430	2,216	—	—	—	—
1931	2,893	411	2,238	—	—	—	—	2,992	425	2,285	—	—	—	—
1932	3,305	424	2,526	—	—	—	—	3,198	404	2,434	—	—	—	—
1933	3,105	284	2,487	—	—	—	—	3,177	349	2,475	—	—	—	—
1934	3,406	321	2,755	—	—	—	—	3,261	338	2,548	—	—	—	—
1935	3,514	329	3,193	—	—	—	—	3,452	259	3,193	—	—	—	—
1936	3,521	314	3,207	—	—	—	—	3,526	326	3,200	—	—	—	—
1937	3,231	303	2,928	—	—	—	—	3,215	267	2,948	—	—	—	—
1938	3,218	339	1,879	—	—	—	—	3,113	306	2,807	—	—	—	—
1939	3,318	274	3,044	—	—	—	—	3,442	353	3,089	—	—	—	—
1940	3,446	260	3,186	—	—	—	—	3,434	256	3,178	—	—	—	—
1941	3,213	249	2,964	—	—	—	—	3,448	272	3,176	—	—	—	—
1942	3,228	339	2,890	510	1	835	1,544	2,999	287	2,713	486	1	830	1,396
1943	3,093	363	2,730	581	950	826	373	3,197	319	2,878	529	1,089	841	419
1944	3,072	437	2,635	621	954	717	343	3,039	395	2,644	599	967	738	340
1945	2,730	486	2,244	651	758	511	324	2,848	469	2,379	633	836	566	344
1946	2,627	400	2,227	690	894	418	225	2,621	418	2,203	640	829	503	231
1947	2,615	370	2,245	770	861	400	214	2,654	383	2,271	780	853	412	226
1948	2,758	359	2,399	677	1,118	381	223	2,577	356	2,221	702	925	359	235
1949	2,989	309	2,680	791	1,171	491	227	2,753	318	2,435	665	1,132	418	220
1950	2,830	308	2,522	708	1,114	485	215	3,064	342	2,722	783	1,184	541	214
1951	2,982	298	2,684	677	1,172	566	269	2,829	291	2,538	688	1,119	481	250
1952	3,079	391	2,688	724	1,133	610	221	3,048	362	2,686	687	1,141	598	260
1953	3,226	454	2,772	815	1,106	639	212	3,043	398	2,645	700	1,124	621	200
1954	3,481	550	2,931	875	1,124	659	273	3,192	460	2,732	809	986	689	248

(continued)

TABLE Ec1221-1234   Courts of appeals cases docketed and disposed, by type of case: 1893-1995   *Continued*

			Docketed							Disposed				
			Civil							Civil				
Fiscal year	Total	Criminal	Total	United States	Private	Administrative	Other	Total	Criminal	Total	United States	Private	Administrative	Other
	Ec1221	Ec1222	Ec1223	Ec1224	Ec1225	Ec1226	Ec1227	Ec1228	Ec1229	Ec1230	Ec1231	Ec1232	Ec1233	Ec1234
	Number	Number	Number	Number	Number	Number	Number	Number	Number	Number	Number	Number	Number	Number
1955	3,695	677	3,018	811	1,363	576	268	3,654	670	2,984	893	1,289	523	279
1956	3,588	557	3,031	872	1,361	609	189	3,734	573	3,161	865	1,445	626	225
1957	3,701	535	3,166	895	1,464	618	189	3,687	544	3,143	905	1,388	666	184
1958	3,694	599	3,095	836	1,447	625	187	3,704	596	3,108	878	1,482	567	181
1959	3,754	616	3,138	802	1,501	606	229	3,753	633	3,120	831	1,473	601	215
1960	3,899	623	3,276	788	1,534	737	217	3,713	580	3,133	750	1,517	660	206
1961	4,204	616	3,588	903	1,617	846	222	4,049	628	3,421	881	1,483	825	232
1962	4,823	773	4,050	1,066	1,692	1,024	268	4,167	622	3,545	936	1,508	855	246
1963	5,437	965	4,472	1,054	2,030	1,141	247	5,011	862	4,149	1,049	1,894	962	244
1964	6,023	1,043	4,980	1,309	2,299	983	389	5,700	917	4,783	1,183	2,159	1,105	336
1965	6,766	1,223	5,543	1,387	2,677	1,106	373	5,771	1,014	4,757	1,229	2,183	1,004	341
1966	7,183	1,458	5,725	1,338	2,809	1,254	324	6,571	1,214	5,357	1,309	2,552	1,141	355
1967	7,903	1,665	6,238	1,372	3,101	1,385	380	7,527	1,524	6,003	1,378	2,968	1,257	400
1968	9,116	2,098	7,018	1,500	3,569	1,545	404	8,264	1,754	6,510	1,356	3,268	1,512	374
1969	10,248	2,508	7,740	1,823	4,197	1,345	375	9,014	2,022	6,992	1,559	3,679	1,394	360
1970	11,662	2,660	9,002	2,167	4,834	1,522	479	10,699	2,581	8,118	1,912	4,367	1,407	432
1971	12,788	3,197	9,591	2,367	5,234	1,383	607	12,368	3,047	9,321	2,258	5,065	1,503	495
1972	14,535	3,980	10,555	2,604	5,795	1,509	647	13,828	3,799	10,029	2,512	5,399	1,448	670
1973	15,629	4,453	11,176	2,704	6,172	1,616	684	15,112	4,210	10,902	2,722	6,030	1,493	657
1974	16,436	4,067	12,669	3,267	6,157	2,505	740	15,422	4,299	11,123	2,791	5,847	1,734	751
1975	16,658	4,187	11,782	2,981	6,511	2,290	—	16,000	4,005	11,255	3,094	6,252	1,909	—
1976	18,408	4,650	12,919	3,327	7,077	2,515	—	16,426	4,238	11,460	2,853	6,248	2,359	—
1977	19,118	4,738	13,544	3,622	7,358	2,564	—	17,784	4,554	12,388	3,198	6,680	2,510	—
1978	18,918	4,487	13,544	3,928	7,234	2,382	—	17,714	4,461	12,506	3,437	6,813	2,256	—
1979	20,219	4,102	15,142	3,983	8,237	2,922	—	18,928	4,320	13,634	3,857	7,175	2,602	—
1980	23,200	4,405	17,804	4,654	10,200	2,950	—	20,887	3,993	15,931	4,346	8,942	2,643	—
1981	26,362	4,377	20,814	4,940	12,074	3,800	—	25,066	4,192	19,651	5,021	11,327	3,303	—
1982	27,946	4,767	21,902	5,517	13,267	3,118	—	27,984	4,522	22,172	5,508	13,115	3,549	—
1983	29,630	4,790	23,318	5,820	14,429	3,069	—	28,660	4,777	22,555	5,585	13,710	3,260	—
1984	31,490	4,881	24,770	6,259	15,466	3,045	—	31,185	4,876	24,595	6,074	15,309	3,212	—
1985	33,360	4,989	26,750	6,744	16,827	3,179	—	31,387	4,892	24,866	6,363	15,743	2,760	—
1986	34,292	5,134	29,478	6,415	19,876	3,187	—	33,774	5,134	27,046	6,535	17,276	3,235	—
1987	35,176	5,260	28,261	6,292	19,246	2,723	—	34,444	5,039	27,802	6,227	18,338	3,237	—
1988	37,524	6,012	29,717	6,210	20,464	3,043	—	35,888	5,284	28,809	6,386	19,798	2,625	—
1989	39,734	8,020	29,940	6,349	20,626	2,965	—	37,372	6,297	29,354	6,127	20,313	2,914	—
1990	40,898	9,493	29,694	6,626	20,490	2,578	—	38,520	7,509	29,330	6,379	20,369	2,582	—
1991	42,033	9,949	30,216	6,663	20,789	2,764	—	41,414	9,198	30,425	6,579	20,698	3,148	—
1992	46,032	10,956	33,027	7,113	22,862	3,052	—	42,933	9,830	30,226	6,797	20,628	2,801	—
1993	49,770	11,885	35,612	7,758	24,030	3,824	—	47,466	11,043	34,363	7,462	23,437	3,464	—
1994	48,815	11,052	35,859	7,518	24,781	3,560	—	48,546	11,519	35,060	7,637	23,943	3,480	—
1995	49,671	10,171	36,998	7,761	26,992	2,245	—	50,085	11,320	36,538	7,710	25,574	3,254	—

Source

Annual Reports of the Attorney General of the United States (through 1939); *Annual Reports of the Administrative Office of United States Courts* (1940 to the present). The method of collecting and compiling these statistics is discussed in the Administrative Office of United States Courts' *Guide to Judiciary Policies and Procedures*, volumes 11 and 11-A.

Documentation

In 1891, Congress created the circuit courts of appeals to relieve the Supreme Court of its growing appellate caseload. In 1948, these were renamed the courts of appeal for the [First, Second, etc.] Circuit. Each circuit hears appeals from the federal district courts in a specific geographic region. For instance, the Third Circuit consists of Pennsylvania, New Jersey, Delaware, and the Virgin Islands. Originally comprised of nine circuits, there are presently eleven numbered circuits and a court of appeal for the District of Columbia Circuit. The courts of appeal function as the intermediate appellate courts in the federal system.

Data are for fiscal years ending June 30 (through 1992) and September 30 thereafter.

Series Ec1221. Data represent the total number of cases filed in the U.S. circuit courts of appeal in the given statistical reporting year.

Series Ec1222. Data represent the total number of criminal appeals filed in the U.S. circuit courts of appeal in the given statistical reporting year. This in-

cludes only direct appeals from the federal district courts. Collateral attacks on the constitutionality of a conviction (for example, petitions for writs of habeas corpus) and civil rights cases involving prisoners are considered part of the civil docket.

Series Ec1223-1227. Data represent the number of civil cases filed in the U.S. circuit courts of appeal in the given statistical reporting year. Civil appeals involve cases in which the U.S. government was a party. Private civil appeals are cases involving lawsuits between individuals or organizations. Administrative civil appeals involve cases appealed directly to the circuit courts from federal administrative agencies such as the National Labor Relations Board. Other civil appeals include cases in which the circuit court had original jurisdiction, bankruptcy appeals, and appeals from territorial supreme courts and municipal courts in the District of Columbia.

Series Ec1228-1234. Data represent cases disposed of by the U.S. courts of appeal corresponding to the categories defined above. Not every case is disposed of after a full hearing. Sometimes the appellant abandons the appeal, and in other cases the court dismisses the appeal for technical or procedural reasons, such as lack of jurisdiction. Judge Richard Posner estimates that nearly half of federal civil appeals are terminated for procedural reasons rather than disposed of on the merits. See Posner, *The Federal Courts: Challenge and Reform* (Harvard University Press, 1996), p. 67.

TABLE Ec1235–1251 U.S. district courts – civil and criminal cases, by disposition: 1941–1999[1]

Contributed by Susan B. Carter and Richard Sutch

	Civil cases		Criminal cases															
	Cases commenced	Cases terminated	Cases commenced	Defendants disposed of														
				Total	Not convicted		Acquitted		Total	Convicted								
					Total	Dismissed	Court	Jury		By guilty plea or nolo contendere	By nolo contendere	By court or jury	By jury	Imprisonment	Probation	Fine	Other
Year	Ec1235	Ec1236[2]	Ec1237[3]	Ec1238[4]	Ec1239	Ec1240	Ec1241	Ec1242	Ec1243	Ec1244	Ec1245	Ec1246	Ec1247	Ec1248	Ec1249[5]	Ec1250[6]	Ec1251
	Number	Number	Number	Number	Number	Number	Number	Number	Number	Number	Number	Number	Number	Number	Number	Number	Number
1941	38,477	38,561	31,823	—	—	—	—	—	—	—	—	—	—	—	—	—	—
1942	38,140	38,352	33,294	—	—	—	—	—	—	—	—	—	—	—	—	—	—
1943	36,789	36,044	36,588	—	—	—	—	—	—	—	—	—	—	—	—	—	—
1944	38,499	37,086	39,621	—	—	—	—	—	—	—	—	—	—	—	—	—	—
1945	60,965	52,300	39,429	41,653	7,536	6,369	319	848	34,117	30,817	—	3,300	—	16,311	13,153	4,653	—
1946	67,835	61,000	33,203	36,482	6,597	5,519	243	835	29,885	27,385	—	2,500	—	14,353	11,446	4,086	—
1947	58,956	54,515	33,652	36,635	5,527	4,452	274	801	31,108	29,138	—	1,970	—	14,375	12,612	4,121	—
1948	46,725	48,791	32,097	34,242	4,862	3,948	218	696	29,380	27,833	—	1,547	—	12,961	13,422	2,997	—
1949	53,421	48,396	34,432	36,264	4,190	3,280	295	615	32,074	30,447	—	1,627	—	14,204	14,690	3,180	—
1950	54,622	53,259	36,383	37,675	4,173	3,237	270	666	33,502	31,739	—	1,763	—	14,435	16,046	3,021	—
1951	51,600	52,119	38,670	41,066	4,066	3,180	303	583	37,000	35,271	—	1,729	—	14,963	19,271	2,766	—
1952	58,428	53,150	37,950	38,622	3,834	2,891	282	661	34,788	32,734	—	2,054	—	15,379	17,018	2,391	—
1953	64,001	57,490	37,291	37,762	4,289	3,167	402	720	33,473	31,336	—	2,137	—	15,637	15,118	2,718	—
1954	59,461	57,903	41,808	42,989	4,848	3,571	492	785	38,141	35,560	—	2,581	—	18,483	16,856	2,802	—
1955	59,375	58,974	35,310	38,990	5,135	3,792	441	902	33,855	31,148	—	2,707	—	16,889	14,021	2,945	—
1956	62,394	67,700	28,739	31,811	4,244	3,068	406	770	27,567	25,029	—	2,538	—	12,854	11,759	2,954	—
1957	62,380	63,568	28,120	29,725	3,471	2,366	335	770	26,254	23,867	—	2,387	—	12,986	10,760	2,508	—
1958	67,115	61,285	28,897	30,469	3,661	2,571	357	733	26,808	24,256	—	2,552	—	13,288	10,903	2,617	—
1959	57,800	62,172	28,729	30,729	3,696	2,638	310	748	27,033	24,793	—	2,240	—	13,648	10,726	2,659	—
1960	59,284	61,829	28,137	30,512	3,784	2,596	329	859	26,728	24,245	—	2,483	—	13,433	10,391	2,904	—
1961	58,293	55,416	28,460	32,671	4,046	2,887	291	868	28,625	24,830	—	3,795	—	14,462	10,714	2,772	677
1962	61,836	57,996	37,665	33,110	4,599	3,374	390	835	28,511	24,639	—	3,872	—	14,042	11,071	2,618	780
1963	63,630	62,379	39,920	34,845	5,042	3,735	544	763	29,803	25,924	—	3,879	—	13,639	12,047	2,847	1,270
1964	66,930	63,954	30,268	33,381	4,211	2,936	559	716	29,170	26,273	—	2,897	—	13,273	11,634	2,689	1,574
1965	67,678	65,478	33,334	33,718	4,961	3,789	463	709	28,757	25,923	—	2,834	—	13,668	10,779	2,477	1,833
1966	70,906	66,184	31,494	31,975	4,661	3,570	397	694	27,314	24,127	—	3,187	—	13,282	10,256	2,356	1,420
1967	70,961	70,172	32,207	31,535	5,191	4,196	409	586	26,344	23,131	—	3,213	—	13,085	9,435	2,293	1,531
1968	71,449	68,873	32,571	31,843	6,169	4,981	484	704	25,674	22,055	—	3,619	—	12,610	9,820	1,816	1,428
1969	77,193	73,354	35,413	32,796	5,993	4,867	483	643	26,803	23,138	—	3,665	—	12,847	9,991	1,682	2,283
1970	87,321	80,435	39,959	36,356	8,178	6,608	703	867	28,178	24,111	—	4,067	—	12,415	11,387	1,935	2,441
1971	93,396	85,638	41,290	44,615	12,512	10,655	1,857[9]	—	32,103	27,544	—	4,559	—	14,378	13,243	4,482	—
1972	96,173	94,256	47,043	49,516	12,296	10,219	2,077[9]	—	37,220	31,714	—	5,506	—	16,832	15,395	4,993	—
1973	98,560	97,402	38,449	46,724	11,741	9,757	1,984[9]	—	34,983	29,009	—	5,974	—	17,540	15,026	2,417	—
1974	130,500	96,700	37,700	48,000	11,800	10,000	1,800	—	41,500	35,300	—	6,100	—	19,600	16,100	5,800	—
1975	117,300	103,800	41,100	49,200	11,800	10,300	1,500[9]	—	37,400	31,800	—	5,600	—	17,300	17,900	2,200	—
1976	130,600	108,300	39,100	51,600	11,500	9,800	1,700[9]	—	40,100	34,000	—	6,100	—	18,500	18,200	3,400	—
1977	130,600	115,500	39,800	53,200	11,700	10,000	1,800	—	41,500	35,300	—	6,100	—	19,600	16,100	5,800	—
1978	138,800	123,200	34,600	45,900	9,400	7,800	1,600	—	36,500	31,100	—	5,400	—	17,400	14,500	4,600	—
1979	154,700	140,000	31,500	41,200	8,300	6,800	1,500	—	32,900	27,300	—	5,600	—	14,600	13,500	4,900	—

Notes appear at end of table

(continued)

U.S. district courts – civil and criminal cases, by disposition: 1941–1999 Continued

	Civil cases			Criminal cases												
				Defendants disposed of												
					Not convicted				Convicted							
							Acquitted									
	Cases commenced	Cases terminated	Cases commenced	Total	Total	Dismissed	Court	Jury	Total	By guilty plea or nolo contendere	By nolo contendere	By court or jury	By jury	Imprisonment	Probation	Fine	Other
Year	Ec1235	Ec1236 [2]	Ec1237 [3]	Ec1238 [4]	Ec1239	Ec1240	Ec1241	Ec1242	Ec1243	Ec1244	Ec1245	Ec1246	Ec1247	Ec1248	Ec1249 [5]	Ec1250 [6]	Ec1251
	Number	Number	Number	Number	Number	Number	Number	Number	Number	Number	Number	Number	Number	Number	Number	Number	Number
1980	168,800	155,000	28,000	36,600 [8]	8,000	6,600	1,300	—	28,600	23,100	—	5,500	—	13,200	11,100	4,400	—
1981	180,600	172,900	30,400	38,100 [8]	8,300	7,000	1,300	—	29,900	24,300	—	5,500	—	13,700	12,200	4,000	—
1982	206,200	185,500	31,600	40,500 [8]	8,200	7,100	1,200	—	32,300	27,400	—	4,900	—	15,900	12,700	3,600	—
1983	241,800	213,600	34,900	43,300	7,700	6,600	1,200	—	35,600	30,500	—	5,100	—	17,900	14,100	3,700	—
1984	261,500	241,800	35,900	44,500	8,400	7,000	1,400	—	36,100	31,500	—	4,600	—	17,700	13,900	4,500	—
1985	273,700	268,600	38,500	47,400	8,800	—	—	—	38,500	—	—	—	—	18,700	14,400	5,400	—
1986	254,800	265,800	40,400	50,000	9,300	—	—	—	40,700	—	—	—	—	20,600	15,200	4,900	—
1987	239,000	237,500	42,200	54,200	10,200	—	—	—	43,900	—	—	—	—	23,300	16,000	4,600	—
1988	239,600	238,100	43,500	52,800	9,900	—	—	—	42,900	—	—	—	—	22,500	16,100	4,400	—
1989	233,500	234,600	44,900	54,600	10,100	—	—	—	44,500	—	—	—	—	24,900	15,000	4,700	—
1990	217,900	213,400	46,500	56,500	9,800	—	—	—	—	—	—	—	—	27,800	14,200	4,700	—
1991	207,700	211,700	45,100	56,700	10,000	—	—	—	—	—	—	—	—	29,200	13,800	3,800	—
1992	226,900	239,600	47,500	58,400	10,000	—	—	—	—	—	—	—	—	31,100	13,100	4,300	—
1993	228,600	225,200	45,700	59,500	9,200	—	—	—	—	—	—	—	—	34,200	12,600	3,700	—
1994	236,000	228,900	44,900	61,200	10,000	—	—	—	—	—	—	—	—	34,500	12,800	3,900	—
1995	239,000	226,100	44,200	55,300	9,000	—	—	—	—	—	—	—	—	31,700	11,500	3,200	—
1996	272,700	246,400	47,100	59,500	8,500	—	—	—	—	—	—	—	—	36,500	11,600	2,900	—
1997 [7]	272,027	272,602	50,363	63,148	7,500	6,607	400	493	55,648	51,647 [10]	271	499 [11]	3,231	41,105	—	2,672	—
1998 [7]	256,787	262,301	57,691	67,934	8,049	6,968	594	487	59,885	55,913 [10]	343	601 [11]	3,028	45,166	—	2,732	—
1999	260,271	272,526	59,923	73,481	8,666	7,649	553	464	64,815	61,239 [10]	387	487 [11]	2,702	50,076	—	2,496	—

1 Data are for years ending June 30, unless otherwise specified.
2 Excludes land condemnation cases, 1971–1996.
3 Excludes transfers.
4 Includes District of Columbia beginning with 1975. Includes Guam, Virgin Islands, and Northern Mariana Islands beginning with 1980.
5 Includes probation and suspended sentence.
6 Beginning with 1971, series Ec1251 included under series Ec1250.
7 Figures are for twelve-month period ending September 30 of specified year.
8 Includes the Canal Zone.
9 By court and jury.
10 Only guilty pleas.
11 By court only.

Sources

1941–1970: U.S. Administrative Office of the United States Courts, Annual Report of the Director (various issues). 1971–1996: U.S. Bureau of the Census, Statistical Abstract of the United States (various issues).

Documentation

U.S. district courts try federal crimes and a limited number of civil cases in which the U.S. Constitution and Acts of Congress specifically confer jurisdiction upon them. Federal crimes are defined by Acts of Congress in connection with enforcing laws relating primarily to customs, taxation, and interstate matters. Crimes such as murder, robbery, burglary, larceny, rape, and arson may also be federal crimes if they are committed within a federal reservation or facility.

In civil matters, federal courts generally have jurisdiction over the following types of cases: suits or proceedings by or against the United States; civil actions between private parties arising under the Constitution, laws, or treaties of the United States; civil actions between private litigants who are citizens of different states; civil cases involving admiralty, maritime, or prize jurisdiction; and all matters and proceedings in bankruptcy.

Whether a state court or a federal court has jurisdiction over a particular action is often difficult to determine.

U.S. district courts are the federal courts of original jurisdiction for federal crimes. One or more federal court is established in every state, and one each is set up in Puerto Rico, the Virgin Islands, the Canal Zone, and Guam. Appeals from the U.S. district courts are taken to intermediate appellate courts, of which there are eleven, known as U.S. courts of appeal. The Supreme Court of the United States is the final and highest appellate court in the federal system.

Comprehensive information on the business of the federal courts is collected by the Administrative Office of the U.S. Courts and is published in the Annual Report of the Director and in Operations Branch, Division of Information Systems, Administrative Office of the United States Courts, Juror Utilization in United States District Courts.

TABLE Ec1252–1258   U.S. district courts – civil and criminal trials: 1944–1999[1]

Contributed by Richard Sutch

		Civil trials			Criminal trials		
	Total	Total	Nonjury	Jury	Total	Nonjury	Jury
	Ec1252	Ec1253	Ec1254	Ec1255	Ec1256	Ec1257	Ec1258
Year	Number	Number	Number	Number	Number	Number	Number
1944	9,951	5,025	2,702	2,323	4,926	1,819	3,107
1945	9,779	5,265	3,561	1,704	4,514	1,503	3,011
1946	9,030	5,220	3,633	1,587	3,810	1,250	2,560
1947	8,818	5,850	3,989	1,861	2,968	1,112	1,856
1948	8,905	6,156	4,204	1,952	2,749	892	1,857
1949	9,282	6,426	4,149	2,277	2,856	997	1,859
1950	9,572	6,539	4,276	2,263	3,033	961	2,072
1951	9,878	6,962	4,492	2,470	2,916	1,035	1,881
1952	10,073	6,668	4,179	2,489	3,405	1,167	2,238
1953	10,768	6,861	4,272	2,589	3,907	1,361	2,546
1954	11,275	6,958	4,182	2,776	4,317	1,493	2,824
1955	11,138	7,049	4,110	2,939	4,089	1,351	2,738
1956	11,198	7,341	3,811	3,530	3,857	1,319	2,538
1957	10,443	6,884	3,595	3,289	3,559	1,214	2,345
1958	10,888	7,057	3,666	3,391	3,831	1,326	2,505
1959	10,293	6,896	3,566	3,330	3,397	1,033	2,364
1960	9,998	6,488	3,453	3,035	3,510	1,008	2,502
1961	9,594	6,156	3,245	2,911	3,438	982	2,456
1962	10,048	6,260	3,335	2,925	3,788	1,090	2,698
1963	10,960	7,095	3,925	3,170	3,865	1,159	2,706
1964	11,079	7,155	4,063	3,092	3,924	1,076	2,848
1965	11,485	7,613	4,459	3,154	3,872	1,143	2,729
1966	12,193	7,783	4,607	3,176	4,410	1,239	3,171
1967	12,500	8,095	4,742	3,353	4,405	1,345	3,060
1968	11,221	8,688	3,478	3,210	5,533	1,800	3,733
1969	11,397	8,834	5,619	3,215	5,563	1,883	3,680
1970	16,032	9,449	6,078	3,371	6,583	2,357	4,226
1971	17,549	10,093	6,600	3,493	7,456	2,923	4,533
1972	18,780	10,962	7,285	3,677	7,818	2,968	4,850
1973	19,467	10,896	7,289	3,607	8,571	2,927	5,644
1974	18,572	10,972	7,403	3,569	7,600	2,753	4,847
1975	19,236	11,603	7,903	3,700	7,633	2,726	4,907
1976	19,580	11,656	8,098	3,558	7,924	2,773	5,151
1977	18,827	11,605	7,792	3,813	7,222	2,661	4,561
1978	18,851	11,515	8,326	3,189	7,336	3,344	3,992
1979	18,563	11,764	8,348	3,416	6,799	3,132	3,667
1980	19,825	13,191	9,254	3,937	6,634	3,216	3,418
1981	21,239	14,697	10,047	4,650	6,542	2,962	3,580
1982	21,397	14,753	10,074	4,679	6,644	3,076	3,568
1983	21,345	14,689	9,712	4,977	6,656	3,003	3,653
1984	20,830	14,374	9,037	5,337	6,456	2,823	3,633
1985	20,729	14,254	8,817	5,437	6,475	2,778	3,697
1986	20,242	13,276	8,054	5,222	6,966	3,066	3,900
1987	19,985	13,162	7,597	5,565	6,823	2,912	3,911
1988	19,901	12,536	7,088	5,448	7,365	3,215	4,150
1989	20,102	12,085	6,878	5,207	8,017	3,553	4,464
1990	20,433	11,502	6,737	4,765	8,931	3,870	5,061
1991	19,949	11,024	6,507	4,517	8,925	3,678	5,247
1992	19,992	10,527	6,289	4,238	9,465	3,832	5,633
1997 [2]	16,969	10,155 [3]	5,664 [3]	4,491 [3]	6,814	2,882	3,932
1998 [2]	16,196	9,349 [3]	5,224 [3]	4,125 [3]	6,847	3,036	3,811
1999 [2]	14,993	8,532 [3]	4,737 [3]	3,795 [3]	6,461	2,775	3,686

[1] Through 1960, data are for trials commenced; thereafter, trials completed.

[2] During the twelve-month period ending September 30 of specified year.

[3] Includes trials of miscellaneous cases.

Sources

1944–1970: U.S. Administrative Office of the United States Courts, *Annual Report of the Director* (various issues).

1971–1996: U.S. Bureau of the Census, *Statistical Abstract of the United States* (various issues).

Documentation

Data are for years ending June 30 unless otherwise noted.

See the text for Table Ec1235–1251.

Series Ec1256–1258. Data on criminal cases exclude the Juvenile Delinquency Act.

TABLE Ec1259–1312 U.S. district courts – offenders convicted, offenders sentenced to prison, and average length of sentence, by type of offense: 1980–1997[1]

Contributed by Richard Sutch

Offenders convicted

	Total	Violent offenses Total	Property offenses							Drug offenses			Public order offenses					
			Total	Fraudulent offenses				Counterfeiting and other offenses Total	Larceny	Total	Possession	Trafficking and manufacturing	Total	Regulatory offenses	Other offenses			
				Total	Embezzlement	Fraud	Forgery								Total	Weapons	Immigration	Tax law violations
Year	Ec1259 [2]	Ec1260	Ec1261	Ec1262	Ec1263	Ec1264 [3]	Ec1265	Ec1266	Ec1267	Ec1268	Ec1269	Ec1270	Ec1271	Ec1272	Ec1273	Ec1274	Ec1275	Ec1276 [3]
	Number	Number	Number	Number	Number	Number	Number	Number	Number	Number	Number	Number	Number	Number	Number	Number	Number	Number
1980	29,943	2,134	10,780	6,733	1,605	3,307	1,180	4,047	3,026	5,135	502	4,633	11,893	1,828	10,065	980	2,200	1,407
1987	44,518	2,241	14,349	10,443	1,918	6,588	1,348	3,906	3,057	13,423	2,199	11,224	14,500	1,847	12,653	1,730	2,138	1,374
1988	43,550	2,139	13,436	9,583	1,775	6,193	1,007	3,853	2,964	13,376	1,815	11,561	14,593	1,965	12,628	1,803	1,851	1,429
1989	46,805	2,180	13,552	9,918	1,796	6,533	1,019	3,634	2,810	15,799	1,776	14,023	15,246	2,024	13,222	2,151	2,446	1,160
1990	47,494	2,331	13,593	10,127	1,833	6,881	907	3,466	2,709	16,311	1,301	15,010	15,259	2,054	13,205	2,440	2,569	1,165
1991	48,946	2,513	13,178	9,473	1,759	6,412	749	3,705	2,917	17,349	1,163	16,186	15,906	2,337	13,569	3,136	2,306	1,048
1992	52,348	2,942	14,330	10,334	1,757	7,272	732	3,995	3,110	18,846	1,129	17,717	16,229	2,196	14,032	4,017	2,383	1,070
1993	53,435	3,077	14,758	10,764	1,713	7,824	627	3,994	2,929	20,458	1,230	19,228	15,134	2,040	13,094	3,178	2,583	1,036
1994	48,678	2,927	13,201	9,466	1,311	6,909	536	3,735	2,728	17,722	1,308	16,414	14,825	1,905	12,920	2,879	2,588	901
1995	47,556	2,658	13,488	9,847	1,212	7,500	330	3,641	2,396	16,728	1,428	15,270	14,657	1,629	13,028	3,180	3,533	787
1996	53,076	2,849	14,027	10,506	1,157	8,222	300	3,521	2,609	18,557	1,974	16,532	17,613	1,974	15,639	3,111	5,501	871
1997	56,570	3,097	15,054	11,616	1,092	9,302	265	3,438	2,547	20,093	1,937	18,121	18,180	1,950	16,230	2,916	6,523	876

Convicted offenders sent to prison

	Total	Violent offenses Total	Property offenses							Drug offenses			Public order offenses					
			Total	Fraudulent offenses				Counterfeiting and other offenses Total	Larceny	Total	Possession	Trafficking and manufacturing	Total	Regulatory offenses	Other offenses			
				Total	Embezzlement	Fraud	Forgery								Total	Weapons	Immigration	Tax law violations
Year	Ec1277 [1]	Ec1278	Ec1279	Ec1280	Ec1281	Ec1282 [3]	Ec1283	Ec1284	Ec1285	Ec1286	Ec1287	Ec1288	Ec1289	Ec1290	Ec1291	Ec1292	Ec1293	Ec1294 [3]
	Number	Number	Number	Number	Number	Number	Number	Number	Number	Number	Number	Number	Number	Number	Number	Number	Number	Number
1980	13,766	1,770	4,630	2,825	460	1,384	610	1,805	1,180	3,675	115	3,560	3,690	484	3,206	578	1,017	487
1987	23,579	1,837	6,234	4,610	551	3,097	606	1,624	1,125	10,196	612	9,584	5,312	601	4,711	1,188	1,355	640
1988	23,450	1,733	5,723	4,182	490	2,915	459	1,541	978	10,599	402	10,197	5,395	640	4,755	1,262	1,287	629
1989	27,377	1,892	5,974	4,400	510	3,028	518	1,574	1,036	13,306	474	12,832	6,194	746	5,448	1,647	1,658	543
1990	28,659	2,032	5,885	4,464	520	3,230	397	1,421	940	14,092	452	13,640	6,650	799	5,851	1,894	1,876	507
1991	30,555	2,260	6,033	4,542	614	3,251	361	1,491	951	15,012	454	14,558	7,250	884	6,366	2,632	1,742	434
1992	34,352	2,675	6,699	5,148	734	3,749	343	1,551	921	16,757	423	16,334	8,220	875	7,345	3,500	1,779	445
1993	34,844	2,679	6,980	5,378	650	4,154	262	1,602	929	17,343	676	16,667	7,833	912	6,921	2,910	2,099	370
1994	31,586	2,443	6,466	4,967	519	3,855	197	1,499	851	14,835	563	14,272	7,838	876	6,962	2,812	2,243	329
1995	31,805	2,250	6,746	5,258	521	4,183	123	1,488	754	14,067	900	13,167	8,735	748	7,987	2,813	3,169	306
1996	36,373	2,475	7,192	5,751	521	4,597	136	1,441	805	16,492	1,209	15,283	10,206	737	9,469	2,785	4,492	339
1997	39,431	2,696	7,709	6,282	513	5,086	116	1,427	850	17,964	1,180	16,764	11,057	782	10,275	2,668	5,502	346

Average length of sentence

Year	All offenses [1] Ec1295	Violent offenses Ec1296	Property offenses — All Ec1297	Fraudulent offenses — All Ec1298	Embezzlement Ec1299	Fraud Ec1300 [3]	Forgery Ec1301	Counterfeiting and other offenses — All Ec1302	Larceny Ec1303	Drug offenses — All Ec1304	Possession Ec1305	Trafficking and manufacturing Ec1306	Public order offenses — All Ec1307	Regulatory offenses Ec1308	All Ec1309	Other offenses — Weapons Ec1310	Immigration Ec1311	Tax law violations Ec1312 [3]
	Months	Months	Months	Months	Months	Months	Months	Months	Months	Months	Months	Months	Months	Months	Months	Months	Months	Months
1980	—	—	—	—	—	—	—	—	—	—	—	—	—	—	—	—	—	—
1987	55.2	126.2	32.5	31.1	22.1	32.1	30.6	36.5	33.8	67.8	48.1	69.1	35.5	42.1	32.2	53.3	15.2	21.1
1988	55.1	110.7	31.5	31.0	19.6	32.9	32.1	32.7	27.5	71.3	13.6	73.6	30.7	30.4	30.7	52.3	11.7	22.8
1989	54.5	90.6	26.0	26.1	16.5	29.8	18.3	25.7	22.7	74.9	8.1	77.3	27.6	24.0	28.1	47.1	9.3	25.2
1990	57.2	89.2	22.0	21.9	17.5	23.4	16.9	22.4	18.8	80.9	14.9	83.1	28.3	26.7	28.5	47.3	10.5	24.3
1991	61.9	90.7	22.2	20.1	15.5	21.6	16.6	24.6	17.5	85.7	21.7	87.4	37.8	26.5	39.3	63.0	12.5	24.9
1992	62.6	94.8	21.8	20.3	16.3	21.1	18.7	27.6	18.6	82.9	22.1	84.3	28.8	8.6	40.9	64.6	15.0	22.2
1993	60.6	88.8	23.7	19.2	12.3	20.6	14.9	38.8	22.2	79.7	18.0	82.2	42.1	26.8	44.1	66.6	18.8	21.1
1994	60.9	88.2	25.1	20.7	14.3	22.1	16.8	39.9	25.0	80.1	22.0	82.5	46.0	31.7	47.8	81.2	19.9	15.7
1995	60.9	93.8	24.9	20.2	15.4	20.9	16.4	41.9	20.5	82.5	34.0	85.9	46.6	28.0	48.4	50.9	21.0	17.6
1996	61.2	90.7	22.5	19.7	15.8	20.5	13.4	33.6	22.2	82.4	51.3	84.8	47.5	25.8	49.1	99.4	22.1	30.3
1997	58.9	83.4	22.8	20.8	14.3	21.1	13.1	31.8	21.5	79.5	62.6	80.8	45.2	26.6	46.6	101.9	22.3	20.0

[1] Totals may include offenses not shown separately.

[2] May include offenders for whom offense category could not be determined.

[3] Tax fraud included under tax law violations.

Source

U.S. Bureau of Justice Statistics, *Compendium of Federal Justice Statistics* (annual).

Documentation

The data are derived from the Bureau of Justice Statistics (BJS) Federal Justice Statistics data base. The data base is constructed from source files provided by the Executive Office for U.S. Attorneys, the Administrative Office of the U. S. Courts (AO), the Pretrial Services Agency, the U.S. Sentencing Commission, and the Federal Bureau of Prisons.

The unit of analysis is a combination of a person (or corporation) and a matter or case. For example, if a single person is involved in three different cases during the time period specified in the table, that person is counted three times in the tabulation.

Where more than one offense is charged or adjudicated, the most serious offense, the one that may or did result in the most severe sentence, is used in the classification. Prisoners are classified according to the offense that bears the longest incarceration sentence. The offense description may change as a case goes through the criminal justice process.

Data from the Federal Criminal Case Processing report describing the number and rate of prosecutions and the results of magistrate proceedings include only those cases handled by U.S. attorneys and those matters in which U.S. attorneys provide local assistance to Department of Justice attorneys in the litigating divisions. Data describing the number and rate of convictions, sentencing patterns, incarceration rates, and lengths of sentences imposed and served, include all cases regardless of the prosecuting agency.

In 1991, the Department of Justice provided U.S. attorneys with lists of cases shown in the data as having remained inactive for long periods of time and directed that resolutions be reported to the docket and reporting system, if possible. As a result, many cases that had been shown as pending were reported to be declined for prosecution, or were shown as resolved by U.S. magistrates. Statistics for 1991 were substantially affected by these record-keeping activities.

Sentencing figures differ from statistics published by the AO for the average "regular" sentence imposed. Regular sentences exclude two categories of offenders included in the BJS calculations: offenders receiving a "split" sentence (five days through six months followed by probation) and offenders sentenced under 18 U.S.C. 4205(b)(1) and (b)(2) (where a maximum term is set accompanied by no or a small minimum).

TABLE Ec1313–1318   State court cases filed, by type of case: 1984–1998

Contributed by Richard Sutch

Year	Total Ec1313 Number	Juvenile Ec1314 Number	Traffic Ec1315 Number	Domestic Ec1316 Number	Criminal Ec1317 Number	Civil Ec1318 Number
1984	86,597,518	1,209,975	61,253,218	2,878,399	9,769,414	11,486,512
1985	89,328,265	1,228,754	62,796,183	3,093,975	10,165,406	12,043,947
1986	92,252,606	1,294,384	64,450,893	3,182,859	10,718,247	12,606,223
1987	93,986,346	1,364,029	65,248,766	3,284,511	11,171,382	12,917,658
1988	97,303,808	1,435,857	67,234,854	3,536,241	11,691,329	13,405,527
1989	97,945,721	1,463,410	66,877,743	3,669,358	12,182,596	13,752,614
1990	96,895,184	1,532,957	64,284,000	3,963,798	12,679,774	14,434,655
1991	94,328,632	1,639,910	60,886,306	4,135,915	12,595,542	15,070,959
1992	92,496,118	1,683,635	58,260,430	4,422,112	12,889,305	15,240,636
1993	88,855,411	1,730,473	55,253,428	4,542,410	12,662,878	14,666,222
1994	84,894,731	1,823,636	50,757,220	4,719,648	13,081,088	14,513,139
1995	86,091,501	1,915,648	51,028,411	4,922,240	13,485,615	14,739,587
1996	87,792,486	1,985,585	51,882,563	5,046,650	13,802,959	15,074,729
1997	89,409,300	2,037,608	52,742,117	5,106,756	14,136,752	15,386,067
1998	91,486,547	2,097,025	54,325,712	5,023,831	14,623,330	15,416,649

Source

Internet site of the National Center for State Courts, Court Statistics Project. Accessed June 23, 2004.

TABLE Ec1319–1340   Juvenile court cases disposed, by type of offense: 1940–1997

Contributed by Richard Sutch

	All offenses						Violent offenses				
	Including traffic violations (Children's Bureau)		Excluding traffic violations								
			U.S. Social and Rehabilitation Service		National Center for Juvenile Justice						
	Number	Rate per 1,000 youth	Number	Rate per 1,000 youth	Number	Rate per 1,000 youth	Total	Homicide	Forcible rape	Robbery	Aggravated assault
	Ec1319	Ec1320	Ec1321	Ec1322	Ec1323	Ec1324	Ec1325	Ec1326	Ec1327	Ec1328	Ec1329
Year	Thousand	Per 1000	Thousand	Per 1000	Thousand	Per 1000	Thousand	Thousand	Thousand	Thousand	Thousand
1940	200	10.5	—	—	—	—	—	—	—	—	—
1941	224	11.8	—	—	—	—	—	—	—	—	—
1942	250	13.4	—	—	—	—	—	—	—	—	—
1943	344	18.8	—	—	—	—	—	—	—	—	—
1944	330	18.6	—	—	—	—	—	—	—	—	—
1945	344	19.6	—	—	—	—	—	—	—	—	—
1946	295	16.9	—	—	—	—	—	—	—	—	—
1947	262	15.1	—	—	—	—	—	—	—	—	—
1948	254	14.7	—	—	—	—	—	—	—	—	—
1949	272	15.7	—	—	—	—	—	—	—	—	—
1950	280	16.1	—	—	—	—	—	—	—	—	—
1951	298	16.8	—	—	—	—	—	—	—	—	—
1952	332	18.2	—	—	—	—	—	—	—	—	—
1953	374	19.7	—	—	—	—	—	—	—	—	—
1954	395	20.2	—	—	—	—	—	—	—	—	—
1955	431	21.4	—	—	—	—	—	—	—	—	—
1956	520	25.2	—	—	—	—	—	—	—	—	—
1957	—	—	440	19.8	—	—	—	—	—	—	—
1958	—	—	470	20.0	—	—	—	—	—	—	—
1959	—	—	483	19.6	—	—	—	—	—	—	—
1960	—	—	510	20.1	—	—	—	—	—	—	—
1961	—	—	503	19.3	—	—	—	—	—	—	—
1962	—	—	555	20.6	—	—	—	—	—	—	—
1963	—	—	601	21.4	—	—	—	—	—	—	—
1964	—	—	686	23.5	—	—	—	—	—	—	—

TABLE Ec1319–1340   Juvenile court cases disposed, by type of offense: 1940–1997   *Continued*

	All offenses						Violent offenses				
	Including traffic violations (Children's Bureau)		Excluding traffic violations								
			U.S. Social and Rehabilitation Service		National Center for Juvenile Justice						
	Number	Rate per 1,000 youth	Number	Rate per 1,000 youth	Number	Rate per 1,000 youth	Total	Homicide	Forcible rape	Robbery	Aggravated assault
	Ec1319	Ec1320	Ec1321	Ec1322	Ec1323	Ec1324	Ec1325	Ec1326	Ec1327	Ec1328	Ec1329
Year	Thousand	Per 1000	Thousand	Per 1000	Thousand	Per 1000	Thousand	Thousand	Thousand	Thousand	Thousand
1965	—	—	697	23.6	—	—	—	—	—	—	—
1966	—	—	745	24.7	—	—	—	—	—	—	—
1967	—	—	811	26.3	—	—	—	—	—	—	—
1968	—	—	900	28.5	—	—	—	—	—	—	—
1969	—	—	989	30.8	—	—	—	—	—	—	—
1970	—	—	1,052	32.3	—	—	—	—	—	—	—
1971	—	—	1,125	34.1	—	—	—	—	—	—	—
1972	—	—	1,112	33.6	—	—	—	—	—	—	—
1973	—	—	1,143	34.2	—	—	—	—	—	—	—
1974	—	—	1,252	37.5	—	—	—	—	—	—	—
1975	—	—	1,317	38.8	1,050	33.8	—	—	—	—	—
1976	—	—	1,237	38.1	1,077	35.1	—	—	—	—	—
1977	—	—	1,389	42.2	1,076	35.8	—	—	—	—	—
1978	—	—	1,359	42.1	1,023	34.6	—	—	—	—	—
1979	—	—	1,374	43.4	1,048	36.2	—	—	—	—	—
1980	—	—	1,445	46.4	1,093	38.3	—	—	—	—	—
1981	—	—	1,350	43.9	1,100	39.1	—	—	—	—	—
1982	—	—	1,292	43.2	1,073	39.1	57	2	3	26	27
1983	—	—	1,276	43.5	1,030	38.3	55	1	3	24	27
1984	—	—	1,304	45.8	1,034	38.7	61	1	3	22	35
1985	—	—	—		1,112	42.2	67	1	4	26	36
1986	—	—	—		1,180	45.5	71	2	5	26	39
1987	—	—	—	—	1,181	46.2	66	1	4	22	38
1988	—	—	—	—	1,190	47.0	70	2	4	22	43
1989	—	—	—	—	1,236	49.1	80	2	5	23	51
1990	—	—	—	—	1,320	51.7	97	2	5	28	62
1991	—	—	—	—	1,413	54.4	109	2	6	31	70
1992	—	—	—	—	1,484	55.8	121	2	6	33	79
1993	—	—	—	—	1,515	55.8	124	3	7	35	80
1994	—	—	—	—	1,605	58.2	135	3	6	37	88
1995	—	—	—	—	1,703	60.7	141	3	7	39	93
1996	—	—	—	—	1,758	61.8	137	2	7	37	90
1997	—	—	—	—	1,755	—	—	—	—	—	—

	Property offenses					Other delinquency offenses					
	Total	Burglary	Larceny	Motor vehicle theft	Arson	Total	Simple assault	Vandalism	Drug law violations	Obstruction of justice	Miscellaneous
	Ec1330	Ec1331	Ec1332	Ec1333	Ec1334	Ec1335	Ec1336	Ec1337	Ec1338	Ec1339	Ec1340
Year	Thousand	Thousand	Thousand	Thousand	Thousand	Thousand	Thousand	Thousand	Thousand	Thousand	Thousand
1940	—	—	—	—	—	—	—	—	—	—	—
1941	—	—	—	—	—	—	—	—	—	—	—
1942	—	—	—	—	—	—	—	—	—	—	—
1943	—	—	—	—	—	—	—	—	—	—	—
1944	—	—	—	—	—	—	—	—	—	—	—
1945	—	—	—	—	—	—	—	—	—	—	—
1946	—	—	—	—	—	—	—	—	—	—	—
1947	—	—	—	—	—	—	—	—	—	—	—
1948	—	—	—	—	—	—	—	—	—	—	—
1949	—	—	—	—	—	—	—	—	—	—	—
1950	—	—	—	—	—	—	—	—	—	—	—
1951	—	—	—	—	—	—	—	—	—	—	—
1952	—	—	—	—	—	—	—	—	—	—	—
1953	—	—	—	—	—	—	—	—	—	—	—
1954	—	—	—	—	—	—	—	—	—	—	—

(continued)

TABLE Ec1319–1340   Juvenile court cases disposed, by type of offense: 1940–1997 *Continued*

	Property offenses					Other delinquency offenses					
	Total	Burglary	Larceny	Motor vehicle theft	Arson	Total	Simple assault	Vandalism	Drug law violations	Obstruction of justice	Miscellaneous
	Ec1330	Ec1331	Ec1332	Ec1333	Ec1334	Ec1335	Ec1336	Ec1337	Ec1338	Ec1339	Ec1340
Year	Thousand	Thousand	Thousand	Thousand	Thousand	Thousand	Thousand	Thousand	Thousand	Thousand	Thousand
1955	—	—	—	—	—	—	—	—	—	—	—
1956	—	—	—	—	—	—	—	—	—	—	—
1957	—	—	—	—	—	—	—	—	—	—	—
1958	—	—	—	—	—	—	—	—	—	—	—
1959	—	—	—	—	—	—	—	—	—	—	—
1960	—	—	—	—	—	—	—	—	—	—	—
1961	—	—	—	—	—	—	—	—	—	—	—
1962	—	—	—	—	—	—	—	—	—	—	—
1963	—	—	—	—	—	—	—	—	—	—	—
1964	—	—	—	—	—	—	—	—	—	—	—
1965	—	—	—	—	—	—	—	—	—	—	—
1966	—	—	—	—	—	—	—	—	—	—	—
1967	—	—	—	—	—	—	—	—	—	—	—
1968	—	—	—	—	—	—	—	—	—	—	—
1969	—	—	—	—	—	—	—	—	—	—	—
1970	—	—	—	—	—	—	—	—	—	—	—
1971	—	—	—	—	—	—	—	—	—	—	—
1972	—	—	—	—	—	—	—	—	—	—	—
1973	—	—	—	—	—	—	—	—	—	—	—
1974	—	—	—	—	—	—	—	—	—	—	—
1975	—	—	—	—	—	—	—	—	—	—	—
1976	—	—	—	—	—	—	—	—	—	—	—
1977	—	—	—	—	—	—	—	—	—	—	—
1978	—	—	—	—	—	—	—	—	—	—	—
1979	—	—	—	—	—	—	—	—	—	—	—
1980	—	—	—	—	—	—	—	—	—	—	—
1981	—	—	—	—	—	—	—	—	—	—	—
1982	475	158	278	34	5	541	86	64	62	47	282
1983	451	145	270	31	5	524	81	64	57	55	268
1984	442	129	276	31	6	530	73	69	65	63	260
1985	489	139	307	36	7	555	92	84	76	68	235
1986	518	142	327	43	6	590	101	87	72	72	258
1987	519	134	331	48	6	595	105	86	72	74	258
1988	518	132	325	55	7	601	109	84	81	75	253
1989	545	136	334	68	7	611	114	85	78	77	256
1990	564	146	341	71	7	658	128	100	71	80	278
1991	613	154	381	72	7	690	139	112	65	76	298
1992	617	158	381	71	8	746	155	118	73	80	320
1993	593	149	374	63	8	798	171	119	91	90	328
1994	594	142	381	61	9	877	184	124	125	102	343
1995	619	139	416	53	11	943	204	120	159	109	351
1996	623	141	422	52	9	998	217	120	176	126	359
1997	—	—	—	—	—	—	—	—	—	—	—

Sources

U.S. Social and Rehabilitation Service, *Juvenile Court Statistics* (1969 and 1970). National Center for Juvenile Justice, *Juvenile Court Statistics* (1997 and earlier annual editions).

Documentation

Since its inception, the *Juvenile Court Statistics* series has been the primary source of information on juvenile court activities in the United States. The first *Juvenile Court Statistics* report was published in 1929 and described cases handled during 1927 by forty-two courts. At that time, few courts kept statistics or statistical records on the cases they handled. At the request of the Children's Bureau in the U.S. Department of Labor, courts volunteered to complete a statistical reporting card on each delinquency case they handled. Reliable statistics begin in 1940.

In the mid-1940s, this case-level reporting was determined to be impractical. The primary focus of the reporting system then became aggregate counts of the number of delinquency cases handled by courts with juvenile jurisdiction. Each year, courts were asked to complete a single form that recorded the number of various case types they processed during the previous year.

In 1957, the Children's Bureau (by then within the U.S. Department of Health, Education, and Welfare) initiated a new data-collection program that for the first time enabled the development of national estimates of juvenile court activity. A stratified probability sample of more than 500 courts was constructed. Each court was asked to provide annual aggregate counts of the number of delinquency cases it handled.

The statistical integrity of the Children's Bureau sample was difficult to maintain. After a decade, the project adopted a policy of collecting annual case counts from any court that could provide them. National estimates were then generated from this nonprobability sample.

Following the passage of the Juvenile Justice and Delinquency Prevention Act of 1974, the primary responsibility for juvenile delinquency activities at the federal level was delegated to the Office of Juvenile Justice and Delinquency Prevention (OJJDP) within the U.S. Department of Justice, and OJJDP assumed responsibility for the reporting series. In 1975, the National Center for Juvenile Justice (NCJJ) was awarded a grant by OJJDP to continue the Juvenile Court Statistics series. NCJJ agreed to continue the data collection and reporting procedures established by the Children's Bureau.

TABLE Ec1319–1340   Juvenile court cases disposed, by type of offense: 1940–1997   *Continued*

A critical innovation in the *Juvenile Court Statistics* series occurred with the proliferation of computers in state and local governments during the mid-1970s. Many juvenile courts began to develop automated record-keeping and statistical-reporting systems. The data files they generated contained detailed, case-level data on each case disposed. Although the design and structure of the courts' automated information systems varied, the information they collected on juvenile cases was similar. Through careful processing, automated records from many jurisdictions were combined to produce a detailed national portrait of juvenile-court activity.

Today, the National Juvenile Court Data Archive, maintained at NCJJ, collects these data and prepares the annual *Juvenile Court Statistics* reports.

Courts with juvenile jurisdiction may handle a variety of matters, including status offenses, child abuse and neglect, traffic violations, child support, and adoptions. This table presents data only on the "delinquency" cases processed by the courts. The unit of count used in *Juvenile Court Statistics* is the number of cases disposed.

A case represents a youth processed by a juvenile court on a new referral regardless of the number of law violations contained in the referral. A youth charged with four burglaries in a single referral would be represented by a single case. A youth referred for three burglaries and referred again the following week on another burglary charge would contribute two cases, even if the court eventually merged the two referrals for more efficient processing.

The fact that a case is disposed means that a definite action was taken as the result of the referral (that is, a plan of treatment was selected or initiated). It does not mean that a case was necessarily closed or terminated in the sense that all contact between the court and the youth ceased. For example, a case is considered to be disposed when the court orders probation, not when the term of probation supervision is completed.

Series Ec1319–1320. Prior to 1957, data were estimated by the Children's Bureau, based on reports from a comparable group of courts. Juvenile cases

are those that involved children or youth of juvenile court age (generally under the age of 18) including traffic offenses. Cases would be referred to juvenile court for acts defined in the statutes of the state as a violation of a state law or municipal ordinance or for conduct so seriously antisocial as to interfere with the rights of others or to menace the welfare of the youth or of the community. This broad definition of delinquency includes conduct that violates the law only when committed by children (for example, truancy, ungovernable behavior, and running away).

Series Ec1320, Ec1322, and Ec1324. The number of cases disposed (series Ec1319, Ec1321, and Ec1323, respectively) per one thousand youths between the ages of 10 and 17.

Series Ec1321–1322. From 1957 through 1975, national estimates on the number of cases disposed of by juvenile courts were based on data derived from a national sample of juvenile courts that was considered to be representative of the country as a whole. These data exclude traffic violations but are otherwise comparable to series Ec1319.

Series Ec1323–1324. A *delinquency* offense is an act committed by a juvenile for which an adult could be prosecuted. It excludes traffic offenses and antisocial acts such as truancy, running away, and ungovernable behavior. Series Ec1323 is the sum of series Ec1325, Ec1330, and Ec1335.

Series Ec1325. Equals the sum of series Ec1326–1329.

Series Ec1330. Equals the sum of series Ec1331–1334.

Series Ec1335. Equals the sum of series Ec1336–1340.

Series Ec1340. Includes such offenses as stolen property offenses, trespassing, weapons offenses, sex offenses other that forcible rape, liquor law violations, disorderly conduct, and other miscellaneous offenses.

TABLE Ec1341–1352   Lawyers, by sex and employment setting: 1948–1995

Contributed by Susan B. Carter

		Sex		Employment setting								
					Judicial		Other government		Salaried			
Year	All lawyers	Male	Female	Private practice	Federal	State and local	Federal	State and local	Private industry	Educational institutions	Other private employment	Retired or inactive
	Ec1341	Ec1342	Ec1343	Ec1344	Ec1345	Ec1346	Ec1347	Ec1348	Ec1349	Ec1350	Ec1351	Ec1352
	Number	Number	Number	Number	Number	Number	Number	Number	Number	Number	Number	Number
1948	—	168,113	2,997	152,649	—	—	—	—	—	—	—	6,043
1951	221,605	199,052	5,059	176,995	675	6,796	8,314	11,596	11,274	1,213	510	6,974
1954	241,514	216,564	5,036	189,423	621	7,282	9,040	12,239	15,063	1,351	234	6,581
1957	262,320	229,433	6,350	188,955	769	7,141	12,458	11,787	18,911	1,504	639	7,661
1960	285,933	245,897	6,488	192,353	599	7,581	13,045	12,576	22,533	1,798	867	10,887
1963	296,069	261,639	7,143	200,586	707	8,041	15,113	14,201	26,492	2,100	918	12,024
1966	316,656	281,336	8,068	212,662	800	8,912	16,284	14,996	29,405	2,717	1,100	14,881
1971	355,242	315,715	9,103	236,085	878	9,471	18,710	17,093	33,593	3,732	3,161	16,812
1980	542,205	498,019	44,185	370,111	2,611	16,549	20,132	30,358	54,626	6,606	12,630	28,582
1985	655,191	569,649	85,542	460,206	3,003	18,674	19,989	33,046	63,622	7,254	12,967	36,430
1988	723,189	606,768	116,421	519,941	2,551	16,520	23,042	34,700	66,627	7,575	11,469	40,762
1991	805,872	646,495	159,377	587,289	3,119	18,417	27,985	38,242	71,022	8,177	14,651	36,971
1995	857,931	655,623	202,308	634,475	2,937	18,690	26,805	38,823	71,349	8,186	13,992	42,673

Sources

1948–1970: American Bar Foundation, *The 1971 Lawyer Statistical Report* (American Bar Foundation, 1971), Tables 1–6.

1971–1991: Barbara A. Curran and Clara N. Carson, *The Lawyer Statistical Report: The U.S. Legal Profession in the 1990s* (American Bar Foundation, 1994), Tables 1–6.

1995: Clara N. Carson. *The Lawyer Statistical Report: The U.S. Legal Profession in 1995* (American Bar Foundation, 1999), Tables 1, 2, and 4.

Documentation

These statistics are from data provided to the American Bar Foundation by Martindale-Hubbell of New Providence, New Jersey, publishers of the *Martindale-Hubbell Law Directory*.

Martindale-Hubbell acquires its data in a variety of ways. The principal source of information is the questionnaire completed by thousands of members of the legal profession. In addition to the questionnaire, Martindale-Hubbell relies upon reports by its traveling field representatives,

(continued)

TABLE Ec1341-1352   Lawyers, by sex and employment setting: 1948-1995   Continued

newspaper clippings, bar association rosters and publications, correspondence, and reports by the National Conference of Bar Examiners to maintain current information.

For an alternative estimate of the number of lawyers and judges from the U.S. Census of Occupations see Table Ba1159-1395.

A lawyer is defined as any individual (1) who is licensed to practice law in any of the fifty states or the District of Columbia, and (2) whose place of employment or, if not employed, whose residence is in one of the fifty states or the District.

In some cases, if more than one subentry for employment setting was applicable, the person was counted in each.

Series Ec1344. A lawyer is classified as a private practitioner unless the individual reported being retired or inactive or employed by the judiciary, government, private industry, legal aid, public defender program, educational institution, or other private or public association or organization. All lawyers practicing solo or in law firm settings are considered to be in private practice. Lawyers employed in law firms, in whatever capacity, are considered to be private practitioners.

Series Ec1345-1346. A lawyer is classified as employed in the judiciary if employed as a judge or support staff by the judicial branch of the federal government or by judicial department of any state or a subdivision thereof, or by a local court. Administrative law judges are classified as employed in government and not the judiciary.

Series Ec1349. Private industry includes any organization engaged in providing goods or services for profit. This classification excludes law firms.

Series Ec1350. Employment in education includes employment in any capacity by public or private elementary or secondary educational institutions, trade schools, colleges, or universities.

Series Ec1351. Includes private associations, legal aid, and public defenders. A private association is any nongovernmental organization that does not qualify under private industry. Examples of private associations are trade associations, unions, special interest groups, public interest groups, and charitable and religious organizations. The legal aid and public defender categories include nonprofit programs providing legal services to indigents in civil or criminal matters whether supported by government or private funds or both. Clinics affiliated with law schools that provide such services are included in this group.

Series Ec1352. A lawyer is recorded as retired or inactive if he or she so reports. Senior judges are not classified as retired.

TABLE Ec1353-1355   Law enforcement officers: 1975-1999

Contributed by Richard Sutch

	Population covered by UCR agencies	Law enforcement officers				Population covered by UCR agencies	Law enforcement officers	
		Number	Per 100,000 inhabitants				Number	Per 100,000 inhabitants
	Ec1353	Ec1354	Ec1355			Ec1353	Ec1354	Ec1355
Year	Thousand	Number	Per 100,000		Year	Thousand	Number	Per 100,000
1975	194,260	411,000	212		1990	233,212	523,262	224
1976	198,351	418,000	211		1991	238,056	535,629	225
1977	201,390	437,000	217		1992	241,519	544,309	225
1978	203,023	431,000	212		1993	244,320	553,773	227
1979	207,136	437,000	211		1994	244,517	561,543	230
1980	210,846	438,442	208		1995	245,846	586,756	239
1981	217,844	444,240	204		1996	248,724	595,170	239
1982	219,521	448,927	205		1997	251,315	618,127	246
1983	222,333	449,370	202		1998	259,549	641,208	247
1984	224,720	467,117	208		1999	253,242	637,551	252
1985	224,328	470,678	210					
1986	224,842	475,853	212					
1987	226,796	480,383	212					
1988	230,905	485,566	210					
1989	229,678	496,353	216					

Source

Federal Bureau of Investigation, *Crime in the United States* (annual issues).

Documentation

The data are from the Uniform Crime Reporting (UCR) program of the Federal Bureau of Investigation (FBI). The UCR program is a nationwide, cooperative statistical effort of over 17,000 city, county, and state law enforcement agencies voluntarily reporting data on crimes brought to their attention. However, only 13,313 city, county, and state policy agencies reported for 1999. During 1999, law enforcement agencies that were active in the UCR program and that reported the data on law enforcement officers represented 253 million inhab-itants, or 93 percent of the total population as established by the Census Bureau. During the period covered by the statistics, the coverage has varied between 90.2 percent of the resident population (in 1975) to 96 percent (in 1998).

Series Ec1353. Figures are the population represented by the FBI's UCR agencies.

Series Ec1354. Figures are the number of sworn law enforcement personnel on full-time duty during the pay period that includes October 31 of the given year.

Series Ec1355. Equals 100,000 multiplied by series Ec1354 divided by series Ec1353.

TABLE Ec1356–1370 Federal prosecutions of public corruption: 1970–1996

Contributed by Richard Sutch

	Total			Federal officials			State officials			Local officials			Nonpublic officials		
	Indicted	Convicted	Awaiting trial	Indicted	Convicted	Awaiting trial	Indicted	Convicted	Awaiting trial	Indicted	Convicted	Awaiting trial	Indicted	Convicted	Awaiting trial
	Ec1356	Ec1357	Ec1358	Ec1359 [1]	Ec1360 [1]	Ec1361	Ec1362	Ec1363	Ec1364	Ec1365	Ec1366	Ec1367	Ec1368	Ec1369	Ec1370
Year	Number	Number	Number	Number	Number	Number	Number	Number	Number	Number	Number	Number	Number	Number	Number
1970	63	44	0	9	9	0	10	7	0	26	16	0	18	12	0
1971	160	108	0	58	40	0	21	16	0	46	28	0	35	24	0
1972	208	142	5	58	42	4	17	10	0	106	75	0	27	15	1
1973	191	144	18	60	48	2	19	17	0	85	64	2	27	15	14
1974	305	213	5	59	51	1	36	23	0	130	87	4	80	52	0
1975	294	211	27	53	43	5	36	18	5	139	94	15	66	56	2
1976	391	260	199	111	101	1	59	35	30	194	100	98	27	24	70
1977	535	440	210	129	94	32	50	38	33	157	164	62	199	144	83
1978	530	418	205	133	91	42	55	56	20	171	127	72	171	144	71
1979	579	419	178	114	102	21	56	31	29	211	151	63	198	135	65
1980	727	602	213	123	131	16	72	51	28	247	168	82	285	252	87
1981	808	730	231	198	159	23	87	66	36	244	211	102	279	294	70
1982	813	671	186	158	147	38	49	43	18	257	232	58	349	249	72
1983	1,076	972	222	460	424	58	81	65	26	270	226	61	265	257	77
1984	931	934	269	408	429	77	58	52	21	203	196	74	262	257	97
1985	1,157	997	256	563	470	90	79	66	20	248	221	49	267	240	97
1986	1,208	1,026	246	596	523	83	88	71	24	232	207	55	292	225	84
1987	1,276	1,081	368	651	545	118	102	76	26	246	204	89	277	256	135
1988	1,274	1,067	288	629	529	86	66	69	14	276	229	79	303	240	109
1989	1,348	1,149	375	695	610	126	71	54	18	269	201	122	313	284	109
1990	1,176	1,084	300	615	583	103	96	79	28	257	225	98	208	197	71
1991	1,452	1,194	346	803	665	149	115	77	42	242	180	88	292	272	67
1992	1,189	1,081	380	624	532	139	84	92	24	232	211	91	252	246	126
1993	1,371	1,362	403	627	595	133	113	133	39	309	272	132	322	362	99
1994	1,165	969	332	571	488	124	99	97	17	248	202	96	247	182	95
1995	1,051	878	323	527	438	120	61	61	23	236	191	89	227	188	91
1996	984	902	244	456	459	64	109	83	40	219	190	60	200	170	80

[1] The sharp increase between 1982 and 1983 in the number of federal officials indicted and convicted reflects both an increased enforcement effort and a better accounting of lower-level officials indicted and convicted.

Sources

U.S. Department of Justice, Public Integrity Section, *Federal Prosecution of Corrupt Public Officials 1970–1980*, and U.S. Department of Justice, Public Integrity Section, *Report to Congress on the Activities and Operations of the Public Integrity Section* (annual publication).

Documentation

The Public Integrity Section of the U.S. Department of Justice oversees the federal effort to combat corruption through the prosecution of elected and appointed public officials at all levels of government. The Section has exclusive jurisdiction over allegations of criminal misconduct on the part of federal judges and also monitors the investigation and prosecution of election and conflict of interest crimes. Since 1978, the Section has supervised the administration of the Independent Counsel provisions of the Ethics in Government Act.

The data for those awaiting trial is as of December 31 of the year indicated. Included are prosecution of persons who have corrupted public office in violation of federal criminal statutes including individuals who are neither public officials nor employees but who were involved with public officials or employees in violating the law (series Ec1368–1370).

CHAPTER Ed

National Defense, Wars, Armed Forces, and Veterans

Editor: Scott Sigmund Gartner

Associate editor: Hugh Rockoff

NATIONAL DEFENSE, WARS, AND ARMED FORCES

Scott Sigmund Gartner

War and military power have always been central to American political, economic, and social development. Indeed, elements of the U.S. military predate the creation of the nation. Yet, the government and people of the United States historically have expressed ambivalence about a standing army, foreign commitments, and defense spending. Despite being former generals, Presidents George Washington and Dwight Eisenhower used their presidential farewell addresses to warn of the potential dangers of military excess: Washington admonished against international alliances, and Eisenhower warned about the dangers of the military–industrial complex.

The armed forces represent one of America's most important continuous institutions, yet the role of the military and its relationship with the nation has varied considerably across time (Weigley 1977; Millet and Maslowski 1994). Quantitative data provide an excellent way to examine and understand these dynamic changes. Similar to other government agencies, the armed forces have budgets and personnel, but only the military prepares for and fights wars. This chapter, as a consequence, contains series common to other chapters, such as budget outlays and personnel, but it also contains data unique to the armed forces and national defense, such as a chronology of arms control treaties, lists of battles and campaigns, and a variety of series on military casualties.

Branches of the U.S. Armed Forces

Today the military forces of the United States are divided into three separate branches: the Army, the Navy (including the Marine

Corps and, in time of war, the Coast Guard), and the Air Force. The military forces that would become the American Army and Navy were developed at the end of the eighteenth century and were critical to ending British rule over the Colonies. During the Revolutionary War, General George Washington maintained that the American Army *was* the nation and that, as long as the Army existed, so too would the dream of an independent America (Ellis 2002, pp. 130–1). Figure Ed A shows armed personnel strength for the military, relative to the U.S. population, from 1794 to 1995. The U.S. armed forces grew rapidly from fewer than 1,000 in 1789 to a peacetime force of more than 10,000 by 1809. Five years later, after war with England broke out, U.S. forces increased to more than 45,000. The ability to mobilize rapidly has been a characteristic of the American military throughout its long history as evidenced by the sharp spikes in the figure coinciding with each of the major wars.

The nation's physical isolation from Europe and Asia has greatly influenced the development of the U.S. armed forces, especially the Navy. Although the Atlantic and Pacific Oceans protected the young nation from potential adversaries abroad, they also required the Navy to defend two extensive coastlines and to be ready to project force over great distances when needed (Beach 1986; Howarth 1991). Table Ed198–199, which lists overseas naval engagements from the Revolutionary War on, shows that the American Navy acquired this ability early in its history.

The Marine Corps began as naval troops who boarded enemy ships and attacked foreign ports and other distant shore targets. The Marine Corps fought during the Revolution and was active in some of the earliest battles the United States fought after the Revolutionary War, such as the fights with Barbary Pirates between 1801 and 1805. At the beginning of the twentieth century, as the Army fought more battles abroad, some of the differences between the Army and the Marine Corps began to blur. The Marine Corps, fearful for its organizational independence, created a culture and mission different from their traditional naval role and distinct from the regular Army. Most significantly, the Corps developed methods

Acknowledgments

Scott Gartner acknowledges the research assistance of Bethany Barratt, Michael Koch, and Patricia Sullivan, as well as the research support of the Institute of Governmental Affairs at the University of California, Davis. He also thanks the Division of Social Science and the Department of Political Science at the University of California, Davis; the Department of Political Science at the University of Iowa; and the Department of Political Science at the University of Canterbury, New Zealand, for helping to provide the time and resources to complete this project.

Hugh Rockoff thanks Henry Caplan, Annette Hamilton, and Michael Wells, of the U.S. Department of Veterans Affairs, and David J. Fleck of the

Census Bureau, who provided help with preparing the statistics for the veterans tables. Neither they nor the Department of Veterans Affairs nor the Bureau of the Census are responsible for any of the opinions expressed here, or the use made of their work. In addition, James W. Chamberlin, Stanley Engerman, Scott Gartner, and Sam Williamson read previous drafts of this chapter and made valuable suggestions. Rockoff also thanks Deepa Bhat, a graduate student at Rutgers University, for her help in preparing the tables. The Department of Economics of Rutgers University provided the research assistance that made this work possible.

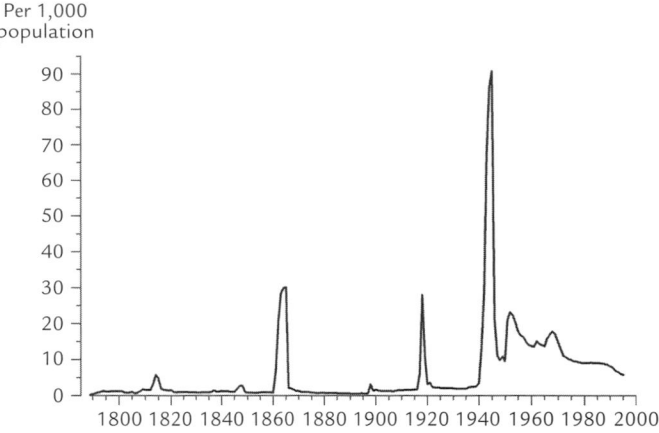

FIGURE Ed-A   Military personnel on active duty, per 1,000 population: 1794–1995

Sources
Series Aa7 and Ed26.

Documentation
Note that only Union army personnel are included during the Civil War, whereas the population series used in the denominator covers all states, both Union and Confederate. As a result, this graph significantly understates the extent of military mobilization during the war.

for fighting small conflicts, frequently against adversaries employing guerrilla tactics (Bickel 2000).

Although many associate the Marines with amphibious landings, the Army actually made more amphibious landings in World War II than the Marine Corps. And, even though the Marines fought many large-scale battles during World War II, such as Iwo Jima and Okinawa, they retained much of their small-war focus. This long-time distinction was largely terminated during the Vietnam War when the Army encouraged the Corps to convert into a large-scale attack force similar to that of the Army (Gartner 1997).

Today, the key distinguishing feature of the Marine Corps is its integrated fighting units. Marine Corps units contain their own artillery, tank, air, and infantry capabilities. This makes them comparatively self-contained and facilitates their rapid global deployment. Some records on the Marine Corps are aggregated with Navy data; however, separate information on the Marine Corps can be found in Tables Ed26–119.

A major organizational change that followed the Second World War was the creation, by the National Security Act of 1947, of an independent Air Force from what had previously been the Army Air Force (Sherry 1987). Table Ed26–47 identifies Air Force enlisted and officer strength (see also Table Ed82–119). Table Ed48–81 provides information on the Air National Guard. Air Force casualties are described in Table Ed1–5, and Air Force and Army Air Force major air battles can be found in Table Ed200–201.

Mission and Governance

The U.S. military conducts a variety of activities, from education of military dependents to hurricane relief; however, the armed forces' singular mission is to prepare for and fight wars. But what is a war? Scholars, politicians, and military officers often disagree. The most common definition among scholars of international conflict comes from the *Correlates of War Project*, which defines war as the use of force by a country that results in at least 1,000 battle deaths from all

combatants (Small and Singer 1982). Using this definition, smaller military operations, such as the air strikes against Libya in 1986, the invasion of Panama in 1989, and conflicts with nonnational actors like Al Qaeda in 2001 and 2002, would not qualify as wars.

Politically, a president's use of force does not require a Congressional declaration of war. Yet most major U.S. military incursions began with either formal, legislative declarations of war (such as World Wars I and II) or informal votes (such as the Gulf of Tonkin Resolution in Vietnam). Nonetheless, the use of force without a Congressional declaration is neither a recent nor a rare phenomenon (Keynes 1991). Furthermore, even when made, formal and informal legislative declarations of war have not always been unanimously supported, and some have passed by comparatively small margins (for example, World War I and the Persian Gulf War).

Declarations of war represent visible signs of civilian control of the military, but there are many other aspects of civilian oversight. That elected officials direct, supervise, and command the military is not a given in any society – not even in democracies. In the United States, however, the historical record suggests that civilian oversight, though not perfect, does work. Examples of civilian–military disagreements that show the power of civilian oversight include the disputes between Lincoln and McClellan during the Civil War and between Truman and McArthur during the Korean Conflict. It is important to keep in mind that most of the behavior described by data presented here is the result of complicated political processes involving civilian and military interests as well as the constraints and pressures imposed by the country's foreign relations.

Territorial Expansion

An important mission of the military dating from the nation's beginning and lasting for most of the nineteenth century was to effect the political expansion of the United States across the continent, parts of which were claimed at various times by Spain, France, England, Russia, Mexico, and, for brief periods, independent states in Texas, Utah (Commonwealth of Deseret), and California (Bauer 1969, 1974; Meinig 1988). The war with Mexico (1846–1848) not only brought Texas into the Union but also culminated in the Mexican cession of its claims to Alta California and much of the territory to the west and north of Texas. In addition, western expansion inevitably brought the United States into conflict with a succession of Indian nations (Dillon 1983; Afton, Halaas, and Maisch 1997). The duration, cost, and activity of the U.S. government's war with the various Native American nations from 1866 to 1891 are portrayed in Tables Ed202–222. These tables provide the location of critical battles between the U.S. armed forces and Native Americans and include casualty figures for non-Indian military, non-Indian civilians, and Indians. Army battles against Mexico are shown in Table Ed196–197, and their corresponding casualties and financial costs are listed in Tables Ed1–5, Ed82–119, and Ed168–179.

American military expansion in the late nineteenth and early twentieth centuries led to the Spanish-American War (1898), with military attacks on Cuba and the Philippines and the American accession of Puerto Rico, Guam, the Philippines, and a protectorate over Cuba (Cosmas 1971). The military was also called upon to suppress the Insurrection in the Philippines against the United States, and American military rule of the islands lasted until 1901.

The military's contribution to territorial expansion extends beyond conflict with Mexico, the Native American nations, and Spain in many ways that are not captured by the data. For example, the Army was largely responsible for exploring and surveying the West; frontier posts and army fortifications provided protection and assistance to pioneers and trappers. Moreover, the potential might of the U.S. armed forces likely influenced negotiations with other European claimants that eventually determined the nation's final boundary.

Major Wars and Battles

It is traditional to list ten major wars in U.S. history: the Revolutionary War (1775–1783), the War of 1812 (1812–1815), the Mexican War (1846–1848), the Civil War (1861–1865), the Spanish–American War (1898), World War I (1917–1918), World War II (1941–1946), the Korean Conflict (1950–1953), the Vietnam War (1964–1973), and the Persian Gulf War (1990–1991). Dates shown here refer to U.S. involvement, not necessarily to the time span of the entire war. There is a large scholarly literature that explores these wars from different perspectives.[1]

Major wars, such as World War II, are frequently described by their battles (for example, the Battle of the Bulge, Iwo Jima, the Battle of Britain, and the Battle of the Atlantic). Major World War II battles are shown in Tables Ed196–201. Identifying a campaign and battle is necessary not just for political and historical reasons but also for such organizational routines as awarding battle pins recognizing hazardous service – a status that has financial consequences for military personnel.

There is great variation both across and within services on what constitutes a battle. In general, Army battles are the shortest and most intense. Even here, there is variation (Young 1959; Weigley 1984). For example, among Army battles, the Revolutionary War Battle of Lexington lasted less than one day (April 19, 1775), whereas the World War II Battle of Guadalcanal lasted from August 7, 1942 to February 21, 1943 (see Table Ed196–197). Likewise, although the famous Navy Battle of Mobile Bay lasted just one day during the Civil War (August 5, 1864), many other Navy operations are more akin to patrols than battles (Sims 1921; Beach 1986; Howarth 1991). Some of these campaigns and operations lasted for years, such as the U.S. patrol around the islands of Quemoy and Matsu that protected Taiwan from a possible Chinese attack, conducted from August 23, 1958, to June 1, 1963. Some naval battles, such as the Battle of the Atlantic in World War II, span an entire war and have no definitive dates (see Table Ed198–199). In the Air Force, there are a few short air operations, such as the U.S. Air Force's expeditionary service in the Congo from November 23 to 27, 1964 (Sherry 1987). Most Air Force actions are much longer, such as the antisubmarine mission in the Atlantic Ocean conducted by the Army Air Forces during the entire duration of the Second World War, from December 7, 1941, to September 2, 1945 (see Table Ed200–201).

Casualties

Battles may be the chronological markers of war, but casualties are their metric. Members of the armed forces become casualties when they are killed in action (KIA), missing in action (MIA), wounded in action (WIA), or taken as prisoners of war (POW). Twentieth-century American casualty data represent one of the most reliable types of military information (Adams 1991). More suspect are casualty figures from the nineteenth century. Although military personnel die or are injured in peacetime, war leads to dramatic increases in the human and economic costs paid by a nation for its national defense. Casualties represent the most costly aspect of national defense, although these costs are not usually quantified in dollars and cents. They are also the most critical factor in determining the domestic political consequences of war. The number of U.S. military personnel killed in action has been shown to be the main influence on American attitudes toward a conflict (Mueller 1973, 1994; Gartner and Segura 1998, 2000).

The human costs of major U.S. conflicts are shown in Table Ed1–5, which includes personnel killed in action and wounded in action. The series on casualties to active-duty forces from all hostile actions includes more information but covers far fewer years (Table Ed6–25). Casualties from wars with Native Americans are presented in Tables Ed202–222, which includes data on both U.S. military and Native American casualties, as well as non-Indian civilians (it is rare to have data on civilian casualties, even if just for one side).

The Cold War and Nuclear Weapons

In 1945 the United States and the Soviet Union (USSR) began a competition for global superiority called the Cold War, which the Department of Defense defines as spanning the period between September 2, 1945 (the surrender of Japan and the end of World War II) and December 26, 1991 (the founding of the Russian Federation and the dissolution of the Soviet Union). Cold War stakes were high, with most of the world divided into two camps. Each side possessed nuclear weapons that could destroy the other. During the Cold War, security expenditures in both the United States and the USSR were enormous. The Cold War led to a significant expansion in the size of U.S. forces and the use of force abroad compared to what had hitherto been the norm in peacetime. In addition to fighting major wars in Korea and Vietnam, U.S. armed forces fought smaller conflicts in Panama, the Dominican Republic, and Grenada. For decades, thousands of U.S. forces were stationed in Korea and Japan, and hundreds of thousands were stationed in Europe to support the North Atlantic Treaty Organization (NATO). Data on defense spending (Tables Ed146–167 and Ed180–195) and the number of military personnel (Table Ed26–47) provide a picture of some of the economic costs of peacetime mobilization during the Cold War.[2]

America initiated atomic warfare with the bombings of Hiroshima and Nagasaki, Japan, in August 1945. Atomic weapons represented a fundamental change in deliverable explosive power. They were initially difficult to manufacture, and the United States had comparatively few of them immediately following the Second World War. This changed rapidly as the Cold War escalated. By 1952, the United States was able to produce atomic weapons

---

[1] For good overviews of individual wars see the following: Colonial conflicts (Dederer 1990; Ferling 1993), Revolutionary War (Ellis 2002; Wood 1990); War of 1812 (Hickey 1995); Mexican-American War (Bauer 1974); Civil War (Livermore 1957; McPherson 1988; McWhiney and Jamieson 1982); Spanish–American War (Cosmas 1971; Trask 1981); World War I (Gilbert 1994; Sims 1921; Terraine 1981; Young 1959); World War II (Davis 1965; MacDonald 1986; Morison 1963; Perret 1991; Weinberg 1994); Korean Conflict (Hastings 1987; Gartner and Myers 1995); the Vietnam War (Clodfelter 1995; Gartner 1998; Karnow 1991; Thayer 1985), and the Gulf War (Gordon and Trainor 1995).

[2] Good sources for the Cold War are Gaddis (1982, 1987); and LaFeber (1997).

Number

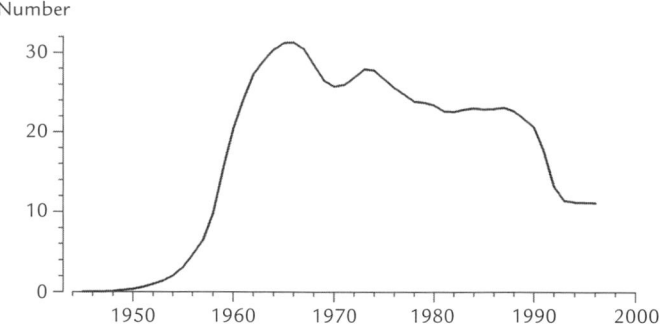

FIGURE Ed-B   U.S. stockpiled strategic nuclear weapons: 1945–1996

Source
Series Ed227.

in considerably greater quantity and developed the first hydrogen bomb, a weapon ten times more powerful than previous atomic devices.

With the Soviet Union's successful test of its atomic bomb in August 1949 and its development of bombers, missiles, and submarines capable of attacking the United States, the defensive advantage of the physical distance from Europe and Asia diminished. Thus, the United States faced a serious threat to its continental homeland for the first time since the British burned Washington D.C., in the War of 1812. This helped to fuel American hysteria at home (McCarthyism), a rapid expansion of alliances, and a nuclear arms race between the super-powers.

Figure Ed-B shows the number of U.S. nuclear warheads stockpiled from 1945 to 1995. The figure shows the dramatic rise in nuclear weapons during the Cold War. It is important to remember, however, that these data do not control for weapon type (all the weapons before 1952 are atomic weapons, whereas later figures include hydrogen weapons) or weapon size (the 1945 weapons, such as that dropped on Hiroshima, were the equivalent of about 12.5 kilotons of TNT; later ones represent many megatons). The United States divides its nuclear forces into land-, air-, and water-based systems, called the Triad, represented by land-based, intercontinental ballistic missiles (ICBMs), long-range bombers, and submarine-launched ballistic missiles (SLBMs). Table Ed223–227 provides data on warheads for each component of the Triad. Finally, Table Ed155–167 provides data on atomic energy spending by the military.

The destructive power of missiles with nuclear warheads, which could not be called back or destroyed after being launched, created an incentive to negotiate meaningful arms control agreements. International arms control efforts had begun in the late nineteenth century but, with a few exceptions, had minimal impact on the growth and development of weapons systems. Table Ed228 shows these and all other arms control agreements signed by the United States. Many of the arms control treaties deal primarily with nuclear weapons and are bilateral between the United States and the USSR. The number of treaties signed increased dramatically after the 1962 Cuban Missile Crisis.

Recent Minor Wars and Terrorism

The Cold War ended when the USSR dissolved in 1991. Counter to many hopeful expectations, this led to only a slight decrease in

the size of the U.S. military (Table Ed26–47). The end of the Cold War was followed by an increase in a range of American military activity around the globe (Tables Ed6–25 and Ed196–201). U.S. troops became involved in humanitarian missions (for example, Somalia), peacekeeping missions (for example, Bosnia), and long-term military operations (for example, patrolling the no-fly zones in Iraq).

The 1991 Gulf War to repel the Iraqi invasion of neighboring Kuwait ("Desert Storm") showed the effectiveness of high-tech weapons and modern logistics (Pagonis and Cruikshank 1992; Murray 1995). Politically, the Gulf War demonstrated the consensus approach that many U.S. leaders saw as critical if the world's lone remaining superpower wanted to avoid engendering international resentment. The end of the Cold War eliminated hostile nations that were likely to threaten the U.S. homeland and dramatically reduced concerns about U.S. nuclear vulnerability. Instead, the threat would come from nonnational sources.

The attacks of September 11, 2001, and the U.S. response in Afghanistan and war in Iraq suggest that the United States will continue to maintain active and powerful armed forces, and that unilateral actions, small wars, and counterterrorist actions will become increasingly central to the mission of the U.S. armed forces. Casualty figures for 1980–1998 include American military deaths caused by terrorist actions, broken down by service (see Table Ed6–25). Other data relevant to the study of terrorism include military sales to foreign countries, found in Table Ed180–195.

The Military Draft and Military Personnel

Throughout most of the nation's history, the armed forces depended exclusively on volunteers. The United States initiated compulsory service (the draft) during the Civil War. It was reintroduced for World War I and World War II. In 1951, during the Korean War, President Truman reinstituted the draft and, since it was not repealed at the end of the hostilities in Korea, this action became the genesis of the peacetime draft that continued until 1973. Since then, the United States has had an all-volunteer military.

During conscription, not all military draftees report for duty. Tables Ed120–145 provide the annual number of registered conscientious objectors, convictions for Selective Service violations, and civilians inducted into military service, and the amount of time served in prison by convicted Selective Service violators.

Personnel are the key to the military, and the demographics of those serving have altered dramatically over time. Perhaps the most important recent change has been the introduction of women into the military. Women served in the military in the First World War and many more served in a larger variety of roles in the Second World War (Braybon and Summerfield 1987). Nevertheless, women began to be a significant part of the peacetime military only during the Cold War. Table Ed26–47 shows the number of women in the U.S. armed forces. There are separate series for officer and enlisted women broken down by each service.

The percentage of women dramatically increased with the end of conscription and the introduction of the all-volunteer force. Figure Ed-C shows active-duty women in the U.S. military as a proportion of all active-duty forces from World War II to the present. The absolute number of women in the U.S. armed forces decreased after the Cold War ended, but the proportion represented by women has continued to increase. One reason for this is that the roles for women have steadily increased. Today, women can participate in almost all aspects of military service, including most combat duties.

Officers, from lieutenants to generals, form the military chain of command, but most military personnel are enlisted (for example, privates and sergeants). Although the basic distinction between officer and enlisted personnel has remained constant throughout America's history, the number and percentage of officers in the U.S. military are not fixed and has fluctuated. As the U.S. military introduced technology into all aspects of military service, it required more highly skilled personnel to operate and maintain these new systems. For example, the introduction of nuclear power onto Navy ships (aircraft carriers) and boats (submarines) requires naval nuclear engineer officers. At the same time, while the primary purpose of the U.S. armed forces is to prepare for and fight wars, the military routinely conducts a variety of other noncombat-related operations. For example, the U.S. military operates one of the largest primary and secondary educational systems in the world. More direct to its missions, each service operates a variety of schools that teach subjects from parachute jumping to coffee purchasing. Many of these functions have also increased over time, especially with the end of conscription in the 1970s and the need for the volunteer force to compete with the private sector for employees.

Although civilians handle much of the noncombat-related supervision, and new technology has made it easier to conduct some critical military functions, many of these new tasks and operations require additional technically skilled military leaders and administrators. This need resulted in a systematic expansion of the officer corps during the Cold War that was much greater, comparatively, than that of enlisted personnel. Figure Ed-C displays the number of military officers as a percentage of total forces from 1801 to 1995 (excluding the Civil War, for which the data are not clear). Since the end of World War II, there has been a significant and rather steady expansion of the officer corps in relation to the changes in total armed forces personnel. Historically, the Air Force and Navy have had a much higher percentage of officers than the Army. Given the rapid rise in enlisted personnel during wartime mobilization discussed earlier, it is not surprising that the ratio of officers to enlisted personnel falls in wartime.

Officers and enlisted military personnel serve either in active service (their full-time job is to be in the armed forces) or in the reserves, in which case the military is mostly a part-time proposition for them unless they are "called up" to active duty. The U.S. reserves combine state-level forces that can be federalized and national reserve forces. In war, when called up, both types of units support the active troops by providing additional personnel to fight or to provide logistical support. After the Vietnam War, the military incorporated the reserves more tightly into the military organization through the use of Round-Out Brigades for each of its active divisions. This change was intended to make it harder to deploy a large number of forces without mobilizing the reserve – as Presidents Johnson and Nixon had done throughout most of the Vietnam War. During both the war against Iraq and its occupation, considerable numbers of reserves were called up and deployed to the Middle East.

The use of reserve troops to fight in shorter wars, however, has had mixed results. In the Gulf War, most Army reserve Round Out Brigades intended for the ground war were unable to finish their battle training in time to contribute to combat. Navy and Air Force air units and personnel, however, found it easier to make the transition from civilian to active-duty. The easiest transition of all was among the many support units and personnel, such as stevedores, who essentially do the same job when mobilized as they do in peacetime. The Army, Navy, Marines, Coast Guard, and Air Force all have reserve units. These forces create the Army National Guard, Army Reserve, Naval Reserve, Marine Corps Reserve, Air National Guard, Air Force Reserve, and Coast Guard Reserve (see Table Ed48–81).

The racial composition of U.S. reserve and active troops has changed significantly over time. In the nineteenth century, African Americans fought in the Civil War and in frontier battles with Native Americans (the Buffalo Soldiers). African Americans served primarily as service support troops in the First and Second World Wars. Although most black troops were restricted from combat, this did not mean that they did not face risks and sometime death. During World War II, more than 200 African Americans died while loading an ammunition ship that exploded at Port Chicago in the San Francisco Bay.

Starting with Truman's 1948 executive order to end segregation in the military, the U.S. armed forces were in the vanguard of civil rights advances. The military began to integrate blacks into regular combat service first as segregated units (as in the Korean War) and then as individuals (as occurred in the Vietnam War). After the integration of African Americans into the U.S. military, there has been a concern that blacks began to represent a disproportionate percentage of those drafted into the military and subsequently killed in war – especially during the Vietnam War (Gartner and Segura 2000).

Other minority groups, such as Japanese Americans, Filipinos, Latinos, and Native Americans, also played important roles in the armed forces. Unfortunately, the available data do not effectively capture their roles.

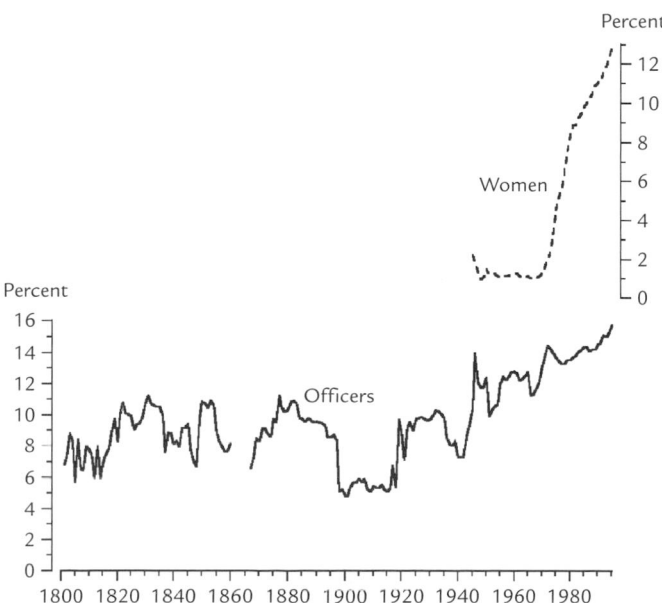

FIGURE Ed-C Officers and women as a percentage of all military personnel on active duty: 1801–1995

Sources

Series Ed26–27, Ed29, Ed34, Ed39, and Ed44.

Military Data

The selection of series for this chapter illustrates the nature and transformation of the U.S. armed forces and its conflicts over the last two centuries. There has been an effort to identify as many important military variables as possible from "peacetime" periods, such as the size of the reserves and the defense budget. New categories have been added to traditionally important series, such as the inclusion of gender in the series on active military personnel. Also, when possible, the data are broken down by military department (Army, Navy, and Air Force) or military service (Army, Navy, Marines, Air Force, and Coast Guard). Perhaps more importantly, compared with past compilations, the scope of the topics covered has been expanded, including series on U.S. conflicts with Native Americans, battles and campaigns fought, and expanded casualty figures. Also included are data on the arms race between the United States and the Soviet Union, such as information on U.S. nuclear warheads, arms control treaties, and reserve levels.

A word of caution is in order because there are systematic reasons why some of these data are likely to contain errors. To begin with, on issues of national security, the government is often disinclined to release accurate or timely data. As a result, data on weapons, such as the number of nuclear warheads or delivery vehicles in the nuclear Triad, were retrospectively revised as perceptions of the Communist threat, and thus security procedures, changed throughout the Cold War.

Even more fundamentally, the destructive nature of war itself often destroys wartime data. As a result, data from the Revolutionary and Civil Wars – especially, in the latter case, those that deal with the Confederacy – tend to be incomplete. Many of the U.S. battles fought, and forts and other military construction efforts undertaken, were on the American frontier or overseas – conditions that decrease the likelihood of obtaining complete and accurate data.

Military organizations, like all organizations, have incentives to exaggerate or downplay particular data. The Department of Defense tended to minimize the amount it was spending on defense. This is particularly true in the Cold War when massive amounts of defense spending and research development were channeled through the Department of Energy and other agencies such as the National Science Foundation. Prior to the Cold War, the government frequently allocated some defense spending through the Departments of Interior or Indian Affairs. In almost all cases, military data tend to be predominantly produced by the military itself. Only recently have external auditors, such as Congress, regularly exercised oversight over the creation and dissemination of U.S. military information, increasing the confidence we can have in these data. Finally, the data do not paint a complete picture of all critical factors in the U.S. armed forces or its conflicts. Some critical issues, such as race, are largely missing from the data. On the other hand, the range of the data extends beyond the topics discussed in this essay and include subjects such as the proportion of KIA to WIA over time (Tables Ed1–25), spending on research and development (Table Ed155–167), and the effectiveness of wartime medical care (Table Ed82–119).

The U.S. military represents one of the largest and most complex organizations in the world. The data in this chapter provide a dynamic, motion picture-like window into what is today, clearly, the most powerful military in the world.

Appendix: Glossary (United States, Joint Chiefs of Staff, 1988)

Personnel Status

Active duty. Full-time duty in the active service of a uniformed service, including duty on the active list, full-time training duty, and attendance while in the active service at a school designated as a service school.

Enlisted member. A person enlisted, enrolled, or conscripted into the military service. Also includes enlisted personnel currently enrolled in an officer training program.

Enlistment. (1) A voluntary entrance into military service under enlisted status, as distinguished from induction through Selective Service. (2) A period of time, contractual or prescribed by law, which enlisted members serve between enrollment and discharge.

Officer. A commissioned or warrant officer.

Casualties

Casualty. Any person who is lost to the organization by reasons of having been declared dead, missing, captured, interned, wounded, injured, or seriously ill.

Captured or interned. Active-duty military personnel who have been detained as the result of action of an unfriendly military or paramilitary force in a foreign country.

Died of wounds received in action. A battle casualty who dies of wounds or other injuries received in action, after having reached a medical treatment facility.

Friendly fire. Being accidentally attacked by one's own military (for example, U.S. soldier injured or killed by U.S. forces).

Hostilities, hostile conditions, or hostile actions. A battle casualty is any casualty incurred in action. "In action" characterizes the casualty status as having been the direct result of hostile action; sustained in combat or relating thereto; or sustained going to or returning from a combat mission, provided that the occurrence was directly related to hostile action. Included are persons killed or wounded mistakenly or accidentally by friendly fire. However, injuries resulting from the elements or self-inflicted wounds are not to be considered as sustained in action.

Killed in action. A battle casualty who is killed outright or who dies as a result of wounds or other injuries before reaching a medical treatment facility.

Missing. Active-duty military personnel who are not present at their duty station owing to apparent involuntary reasons and whose location is not known.

Wounded in action. A battle casualty who incurs an injury as a result of an external agent or cause. The term encompasses all kinds of wounds and other injuries incurred in action whether there is a piercing of the body, as in a penetrating or perforated wound, or none, as in the contused wound.

Branches of the U.S. Armed Forces

Air Force. The department consists of the Office of the Secretary of the Air Force; the chief of staff of the Air Force; the Air Staff, which provides assistance to the secretary and the chief of staff; and the field organization, which, in the late 1990s, consisted of eight major commands, thirty-seven field operating agencies, and several other units. The eight major commands of the Air Force are the Air Combat Command, which is responsible for all combat aircraft based in the continental United States; Air Force Materiel Command; Air Education and Training Command; Air Force Space Command; Air Mobility Command; Air Force Special Operations Command; Pacific Air Forces; and U.S. Air Forces in Europe.

Army. The Army furnishes most of the ground forces in the U.S. military organization. The major Army field commands are: Forces Command, which is responsible for all Army forces in the continental United States, the Army Reserve, and the Army National Guard; Training and Doctrine Command; Materiel Command, which is responsible for supply logistics and research, development, and evaluation of new materiel; Intelligence and Security Command; Medical Command; Criminal Investigation Command; Corps of Engineers, which oversees a variety of military and civil development projects; Special Operations Command; Military Traffic Management Command; Military District of Washington, which is charged with defense of the national capital; U.S. Army Europe; U.S. Army Pacific; Eighth Army (stationed in South Korea); and U.S. Army South. The Army also administers the U.S. Military Academy at West Point, New York.

Coast Guard. The Coast Guard is the military service within the U.S. armed forces that is charged with the enforcement of maritime laws. It consists of approximately 30,000 officers and enlisted personnel, in addition to civilians. During peacetime, it is under the jurisdiction of the Department of Transportation; in time of war, it is within the Department of the Navy and under the direction of the president. The Coast Guard was established in 1790 by Secretary of the Treasury Alexander Hamilton as the Revenue Marine Service. It later became the Revenue Cutter Service and, in 1915, was combined with the U.S. Lifesaving Service (formed 1878) to become the Coast Guard. It was under the (peacetime) jurisdiction of the Treasury Department until 1967. The Coast Guard enforces all applicable federal laws on the high seas and waters within the territorial jurisdiction of the United States. It administers laws and promulgates and enforces regulations for the promotion of safety of life and property along the entire U.S. coast (including Alaska and Hawai'i). It develops and operates aids to navigation to maintain the safety of ports and vessels in U.S. territorial waters.

Marine Corps. The Marine Corps, within the Department of the Navy, provides fleet marine forces of combined arms, together with supporting air components, for service with the fleet in the seizure or defense of advanced naval bases and for the conduct of such land operations as may be essential to the prosecution of a naval campaign. In addition, the Marine Corps provides detachments and organizations for service on armed vessels of the Navy as well as security detachments for the protection of naval property at naval stations and bases.

Navy. The Navy's four operating forces are the Pacific Fleet, which operates in the Pacific and Indian Oceans; the Atlantic Fleet, which operates in the Atlantic Ocean and the Mediterranean Sea; the Naval Forces, Europe; and the Military Sealift Command, which provides ocean transport on government or commercial vessels for the Department of Defense and other federal agencies, provides at-sea logistic support to the armed forces, and conducts scientific and other projects for federal agencies.

Composition of the Reserve Components

There are seven Reserve components: the Army National Guard, Army Reserve, Naval Reserve, Marine Corps Reserve, Air National Guard, Air Force Reserve, and Coast Guard Reserve. Within the Reserve components, personnel serve in one of three manpower management categories: Ready Reserve, Standby Reserve, and Retired Reserve. There is no Standby Reserve in the Army National Guard or Air National Guard. The Ready Reserve is made up of three subgroups: the Selected Reserve, the Individual Ready Reserve (IRR), and the Inactive National Guard (ING). The Selected Reserve train regularly and are paid for their participation in unit or individual programs. IRR members have a service obligation but do not train and are not paid. In time of war or national emergency, the president may recall Ready Reserve personnel from all Department of Defense components for up to 270 days if necessary.

Weaponry and Arms Control

Arms Control. (1) Any plan, arrangement, or process, resting upon explicit or implicit international agreement, governing any aspect of the following: the numbers, type, and performance characteristics of weapon systems; and the numerical strength, organization, equipment, deployment, or employment of the armed forces retained by the parties (it encompasses "disarmament"). (2) On some occasions, those measures taken for the purpose of reducing instability in the military environment.

Bombers. Manned airplanes, such as the B-2 and B-1, that either penetrate enemy airspace and drop nuclear bombs or approach enemy airspace and launch nuclear air-launched cruise missiles (ALCMs).

Intercontinental ballistic missile (ICBM). A land-based ballistic missile housed in a hardened, concrete silo with a range capability of about 3,000 to 8,000 nautical miles.

Submarine-launched ballistic missile (SLBM). A ballistic missile housed in a nuclear submarine.

Triad. The Triad represents the three types of delivery platforms relied on by the United States for its strategic, long-range nuclear forces. The forces each operate primarily on land, in the water, and in air and include intercontinental ballistic missiles, submarine launched ballistic missiles, and bombers.

References

Adams, Margaret O. 1991. "Electronic Records." *Prologue: Quarterly of the National Archives* 23 (1): 76–84.

Afton, Jean, David Halaas, and Andrew Maisch. 1997. *Cheyenne Dog Soldiers: A Ledgerbook History of Coups and Combat.* University of Colorado Press.

Bauer, K. J. 1969. *Surfboats and Horse Marines.* U.S. Naval Institute Press.

Bauer, K. J. 1974. *The Mexican War.* Macmillan.

Beach, Edward L. 1986. *The United States Navy: A 200 Year History.* Houghton Mifflin.

Bickel, Keith B. 2000. *Mars Learning: The Marine Corps' Development of Small Wars Doctrine, 1915–1940*. Westview Press.

Braybon, Gail, and Penny Summerfield. 1987. *Out of the Cage: Women's Experiences in Two World Wars*. Routledge & Kegan Paul.

Clodfelter, Micheal. 1995. *Vietnam in Military Statistics: A History of the Indochina Wars, 1772–1991*. McFarland.

Cosmas, Graham. 1971. *An Army for Empire: The United States Army in the Spanish-American War*. University of Missouri Press.

Davis, Kenneth S. 1965. *Experience of War: The United States in World War II*. Doubleday.

Dederer, John M. 1990. *War in America to 1775: Before Yankee Doodle*. New York University Press.

Dillon, Richard H. 1983. *North American Indian War*. Facts On File.

Ellis, Joseph J. 2002. *Founding Brothers: The Revolutionary Generation*. Vintage Books.

Ferling, John. 1993. *Struggle for a Continent: The Wars of Early America*. Harlan Davidson.

Gaddis, John L. 1982. *Strategies of Containment: A Critical Appraisal of Postwar American National Security Policy*. Oxford University Press.

Gaddis, John L. 1987. *The Long Peace: Inquiries into the History of the Cold War*. Oxford University Press.

Gartner, Scott S. 1997. *Strategic Assessment in War*. Yale University Press.

Gartner, Scott S. 1998. "Differing Evaluations of Vietnamization." *Journal of Interdisciplinary History* 29: 243–62.

Gartner, Scott S., and Marissa E. Myers. 1995. "Body Counts and 'Success' in the Vietnam and Korean Wars." *Journal of Interdisciplinary History* 25 (3): 377–95.

Gartner, Scott S., and Gary M. Segura. 1998. "War, Casualties and Public Opinion." *Journal of Conflict Resolution* 42 (3): 278–300.

Gartner, Scott S., and Gary M. Segura. 2000. "Race, Opinion, and Casualties in the Vietnam War." *Journal of Politics* 62 (1): 115–46.

Gilbert, Martin. 1994. *The First World War: A Complete History*. Henry Holt.

Gordon, Michael, and Bernard Trainor. 1995. *The General's War*. Little, Brown.

Hastings, Max. 1987. *The Korean War*. Simon and Schuster.

Hickey, Donald R. 1995. *The War of 1812: A Short History*. University of Illinois.

Howarth, Stephen. 1991. *To Shining Sea: A History of the United States Navy, 1775–1991*. Random House.

Karnow, Stanley. 1991. *Vietnam: A History*. Penguin Press.

Keynes, Edward. 1991. *Undeclared War: Twilight Zone of Constitutional Power*. Pennsylvania State University Press.

LaFeber, Walter. 1997. *America, Russia, and the Cold War, 1945–1996*. 8th edition. McGraw-Hill.

Livermore, Thomas. 1957. *Numbers and Losses in the Civil War in America: 1861–1865*. Indiana University Press.

MacDonald, Charles. 1986. *The Mighty Endeavor: The American War in Europe*. William Morrow.

McPherson, James M. 1988. *Battle Cry of Freedom: The Civil War Era*. Oxford University Press.

McWhiney, Grady, and Perry D. Jamieson. 1982. *Attack and Die: Civil War Military Tactics and the Southern Heritage*. University of Alabama Press.

Meinig, D. W. 1988. *The Shaping of America: A Geographical Perspective of 500 Years of History*, volume 2, *Continental America, 1800–1867*. Yale University Press.

Millett, Allan R., and Peter Maslowski. 1994. *For the Common Defense: A Military History of the United States of America*. Revised and expanded edition. Free Press.

Morison, Samuel Eliot. 1963. *The Two-Ocean War: A Short History of the United States Navy in the Second World War*. Little, Brown.

Mueller, John. 1994. *Policy and Opinion in the Gulf War*. University of Chicago Press.

Mueller, John E. 1973. *War, Presidents, and Public Opinion*. John Wiley.

Murray, Williamson. 1995. *Air War in the Persian Gulf*. Nautical & Aviation Publishing Company of America.

Pagonis, William G., and Jeffrey L. Cruikshank. 1992. *Moving Mountains: Lessons in Leadership and Logistics from the Gulf War*. Harvard Business School Press.

Perret, Geoffrey, 1991. *There's a War to Be Won: The United States Army in World War II*. Random House.

Sherry, Michael S. 1987. *The Rise of American Air Power: The Creation of Armageddon*. Yale University Press.

Sims, William Sowden. 1921. *The Victory at Sea*. Doubleday, Page & Co.

Small, Melvin, and J. David Singer. 1982. *Resort to Arms: International and Civil Wars 1816–1980*. Sage Publications.

Terraine, John. 1981. *To Win a War: 1918, The Year of Victory*. Doubleday & Co.

Thayer, Thomas C. 1985. *War without Fronts: The American Experience in Vietnam*. Westview Press.

Trask, David. 1981. *The War with Spain*. Macmillan.

U.S. Joint Chiefs of Staff. 1988. *A Dictionary of United States Military Terms, Prepared for Joint Usage of the Armed Services*. Public Affairs Press.

Weigley, Russell. 1984. *The History of the United States Army*. Indiana University Press.

Weigley, Russell F. 1977. *The American Way of War: A History of United States Military Strategy and Policy*. Indiana University Press.

Weinberg, Gerhard L. 1994. *A World at Arms: A Global History of World War II*. Cambridge University Press.

Wood, W. J. 1990. *Battles of the Revolutionary War*. Algonquin Books.

Young, Gordon R. 1959. *Army Almanac*. Stackpole.

Veterans

Hugh Rockoff

Veterans have played an important role in the political and economic life of the United States throughout its history. Politicians and interest groups continue to seek the support of veterans and their organizations. Women and minority veterans have become assertive symbols of competence and patriotism. And the institutions created for veterans, such as pensions and the hospital system, have been the testing grounds for the welfare state. This chapter provides background for understanding these issues and the historical statistics they generated.

In general terms, veterans are simply former members of the armed forces – "those who served." Traditionally, in times of peace, the United States relies on a small professional force; however, that force is augmented during major wars by large numbers of volunteers or draftees. When a major war is over, the programs and facilities designed to care for disabled and retired professional soldiers cannot be expanded easily to take care of the needs of citizen soldiers. Instead, to meet these needs, Congress creates new programs and facilities that are run by special veterans' agencies. Most of the statistics shown here refer to programs originally created for these temporary members of the armed forces rather than for the professionals.

Two types of data on veterans are presented: (1) data on the number of veterans by age and by period of service; and (2) data on the benefits that have been awarded to veterans, whether in cash or in kind. Examples of in-kind benefits are medical care and domiciliary care. The nature and limitations of the data will emerge from the historical narrative, but a few general remarks on the quality of the data will be useful to have in mind from the start. As is often the case, the amount and quality of the data improve as one moves forward in time. Considerable information about veterans from the colonial and antebellum periods can be found in government documents, but this information has only rarely been assembled by scholars. (Table Ed-D documents some of the important events in the history of veterans.) Some of the unique problems associated with these periods – the important role of land grants, for

TABLE Ed-D   Important events in the history of veterans: 1636–1989

1636	To encourage service in the Pequot War, the Plymouth colony provides for the maintenance of disabled soldiers, the first veteran's benefits in an English-speaking colony.
1776	The Continental Congress promises pensions to officers and soldiers disabled in the course of service.
1778	The Continental Congress promises half pay for seven years for officers who serve until the end of the war.
1780	The Continental Congress promises half pay for seven years for the widows and orphans of officers who die in service. This is the nation's first provision for widows and orphans.
1783	Washington addresses his officers at Newburgh, New York, counseling patience in pursuing demands for past pay and pensions. The Commutation Act is passed. The Society of Cincinnati, the nation's first veterans' organization, is founded.
1828	Full pay for life is granted to surviving officers, noncommissioned officers, and soldiers who had served until the end of the war.
1865	National Home for Disabled Volunteer Soldiers is established.
1879	The Arrears of Pension Act is passed.
1890	Disability Pension Act is passed.
1913	The Veterans of Foreign Wars is formed from the merger of smaller organizations of veterans of the Spanish–American War and the Philippine Insurrection.
1917	Legislation authorizes the issuance of life insurance policies to members of the armed services.
1921	The Veterans Bureau is established to consolidate veterans' services into one agency.
1936	Congress passes legislation (over President Roosevelt's veto) providing for immediate payment of the World War I bonus.
1944	President Roosevelt signs the "Servicemen's Readjustment Act of 1944," commonly known as the GI Bill of Rights (Public Law 346, passed unanimously by the 78th Congress), offering home loan and education benefits to veterans.
1965	Servicemembers' Group Life Insurance – subsidized term life insurance purchased from private insurers – is made available.
1973	The United States institutes an all-volunteer armed force. Veteran's benefits become an important incentive for recruitment.
1977	Rosalyn Yalow and Andrew Schally, scientists at the Veterans Administration, receive the Nobel Prize in Medicine.
1989	The Department of Veterans Affairs (VA) is established.

example – will be discussed here. The Civil War also presents problems for the chronicler of America's veterans primarily because of the incomplete information about the number of people serving in the Confederate forces, their subsequent histories, and the scattered records of the Southern states concerning aid to Confederate veterans.

Beginning with the Union veterans of the Civil War, however, the records of the Commissioner of Pensions (founded in 1833, it became the Veterans Administration in 1930 after consolidations with other agencies), combined with data collected by the military services and, in more recent decades, by the Bureau of the Census and other government agencies, provide an accurate record of how the federal government has rewarded its veterans. Inevitably, many things remain uncounted. Many laws, for example, gave veterans preferences in hiring, and many employers have acted on this principle even when not compelled to do so. Comprehensive estimates of the value of these preferences have not been made. In addition, certain categories of aid to veterans have been subject to manipulation. Often the amount of benefits received by a veteran depended on whether a disability suffered by the veteran was found to be service-connected or non-service-connected. For this reason, the breakdown in the tables based on this distinction, although highly accurate with respect to ex-post decisions, may not reflect the division that would be made by an impartial observer. Nevertheless, the data presented here, especially the broad totals, provide an accurate record of how the United States has rewarded, or in some cases failed to reward, its veterans.

From Colonial Times to the Civil War

The colonial system of veterans' benefits was derived from the British system. Legislation passed during the Elizabethan era (the 1592–1593 session of parliament) provided relief for the crown's soldiers and sailors who had become sick or disabled while serving.

In the English North American colonies, legislation passed in Virginia in 1624 would have provided for medical care and maintenance of disabled soldiers, but this legislation was not ratified in London. Plymouth colony in New England was the first to pass veterans' legislation that went into effect. This law, passed in 1636 to encourage service in the Pequot War, provided for the public maintenance of disabled soldiers. Similar legislation was passed in other colonies throughout the colonial era. A Maryland law of 1678 is notable because it provided pensions for the widows and dependent children of soldiers killed in military service, as well as relief for disabled soldiers.

Given the colonial tradition, it was naturally assumed that the new state governments and the Continental Congress would provide benefits for soldiers and sailors disabled during the Revolutionary War and for their widows and orphans. In August 1776, Congress adopted the first national pension law. It provided half pay for life for soldiers and sailors incapable of earning a living as a result of wounds suffered in the War for Independence. After the war, considerable pressure was brought to bear to increase the pensions and liberalize eligibility. In 1818 a service pension (a pension that required military service but not a service-connected disability) was finally signed for Revolutionary officers and men "in need of assistance." This law was revised repeatedly. In 1820, concerns about the federal budget led to the striking of many pensioners from the rolls. But the law of 1823, passed in more prosperous circumstances, restored many pensioners.

The demand made by Continental Army officers for annual half pay for life contingent solely on service until the end of the war, a demand based on the policy in the British army, generated far more controversy than did the demand for pensions for soldiers who were suffering from disabling injuries or in need of financial assistance. George Washington, although dubious at first, became a strong advocate of half pay when resignations at Valley Forge threatened the very existence of the Army. In 1778, Congress promised seven years' half pay. And in 1780, this allowance was extended to the widows and orphans of officers who died during the war. As the end of the war neared, the officers became increasingly concerned about the willingness and ability of Congress and the states to finance their pensions. At Newburgh, New York, the site of the so-called Newburgh Conspiracy, Washington himself was forced to address his officers on March 12, 1783, when the idea that the army should not be disbanded until Congress addressed its financial needs gained headway. Congress responded by passing the Commutation Act. In lieu of half pay for life, the officers were offered five years' full pay in government securities bearing 6 percent interest. There was considerable opposition to the Act, based partly on fiscal considerations and partly on the distinction between the officers and the enlisted men, who were offered only one year's pay.

As many of the officers had feared, the Confederation failed to pay even the interest on the Commutation Bonds. The Society of Cincinnati, formed in 1783 by ex-officers after the end of the war and before the Army disbanded, was the first American veterans' organization. Its goals were to continue the ties formed during the war and to pressure the government to fulfill the pledges made to the officers. Although the Society was initially feared as a threat to democracy, the decrease in the number of surviving officers and the requirement that membership pass through the eldest son led to a gradual decrease in the influence wielded by the Society in the postwar era.

In 1791, under the new federal government, provision was made for paying the Commutation Bonds as part of the general funding of the debt. In the meantime, many officers had parted with their bonds at bargain prices and so began a long campaign for relief. Success did not come until 1828 when full pay for life was granted to surviving officers, noncommissioned officers, and soldiers who had served until the end of the war. In 1832, pensions were authorized on the basis of two years of service. The eligibility of widows and orphans continued to be an issue. The Widows Pension Act of 1836 pensioned widows who were married at the time of the Revolution to men who would have been eligible for a service pension under the Act of 1832. In subsequent years, the requirement that the marriage date from the Revolution was gradually eased and eventually eliminated.

In addition to the pensions paid in cash, veterans of the Revolution received warrants for western public land ranging from 100 acres for a private to 1,100 acres for a major general. This was a standard policy of British and colonial governments. During the Revolution, the government had even offered land to Hessian soldiers who deserted from the British forces. In all, warrants for more than 9.5 million acres were awarded to veterans of the Revolution. Warrants were also issued to veterans of the War of 1812, the Indian Wars, and the Mexican War. During the Revolution, the warrants were for land in certain designated western tracts (perhaps to provide protection for the frontier), but during the Mexican War transferable warrants to 160 acres of any part of the public domain were offered to men volunteering for service. Because the land could be sold, these land grants were essentially cash grants.

Warrants for almost 73.5 million acres had been issued by 1860. The value of the land transferred through veteran warrants has not been determined. Valued at $1.10 per acre (a small discount from $1.25, the price at which much of the public domain was sold), the total would be about $81 million, about $1.8 billion today. The settlement of these claims became a major political issue in a number of states, Tennessee in particular. Close to 40 percent of the arable land in Iowa (the state with the highest percentage) was transferred on the basis of veteran warrants. Many of the warrants, once they were made transferable, were sold to speculators. This practice led to considerable criticism of the warrant system and was another reason, along with the declining amount of suitable land, for its abandonment. Nevertheless, the cash-like system adopted in the Mexican War provided an important precedent for the use of land grants to finance the land grant college system and the transcontinental railroads.[1]

Although land grants were by far the most important form of in-kind aid provided to veterans, there were also attempts to provide more direct forms of aid. In 1798, a tax was levied on seamen to provide funds for hospital care and, in the event of a surplus, for the construction of hospitals. This system was extended to the Navy the following year. Eventually, a system of naval hospitals was constructed including facilities on the East Coast and the Mississippi River. In 1834, a home was established for old and disabled naval personnel, and in 1851, a home for old and disabled soldiers was created.

In some important respects, the evolution of monetary pensions for veterans of the War of 1812, the Mexican War, and the Indian Wars was similar to that of the Revolutionary War. Initially pensions were established only for invalids, or their widows and orphans. Then pressure gradually mounted for pensions based on service alone. Eventually, service pensions were granted, but they were established so many years after the conflict that they were, in effect, old-age pensions. The service pension for the War of 1812 was established in 1871. The rules were liberalized in 1878: the required service was reduced to 14 days, and for widows the requirement that the marriage date from the war was eliminated. Service pensions for veterans of the Mexican War were first granted in 1887. Service pensions for veterans of some of the Indian Wars – such as the Black Hawk War and the Seminole Wars – were not granted until 1892. Subsequent legislation liberalized the requirements, increased the benefits, and pensioned veterans of other campaigns against Native Americans.

From the Civil War to World War I

The sheer magnitude of the Civil War and prosperity in the postwar North meant that the veterans of this conflict would play a far different role in postbellum America than had the veterans of earlier conflicts. About 9.6 percent of Americans (North and South) participated, which is similar to the Revolution in which about 10.4 percent of all Americans served. The percentage serving was much smaller in other wars in the nineteenth and twentieth centuries, with the exception of World War II, in which 11.8 percent served. Perhaps equally important in creating pressure for veterans' benefits was the sanguinary nature of the conflict. Of those serving in the Union forces, 16.5 percent died in battle or from other causes, and 12.7 percent were wounded. No other war really compares. In the Mexican War, although the death rate was similar (16.9 percent), the proportion wounded was much lower (5.3 percent).[2]

Figure Ed-E shows the number of veterans as a percentage of total population, beginning in 1865 and continuing to 1999. The

---

[1] O'Callaghan (1954) and Oberly (1990) provide details on the land grants.
[2] Military personnel: Chambers (1999), p. 849; total population: U.S. Bureau of the Census (1975), series A6, A7, and Z1.

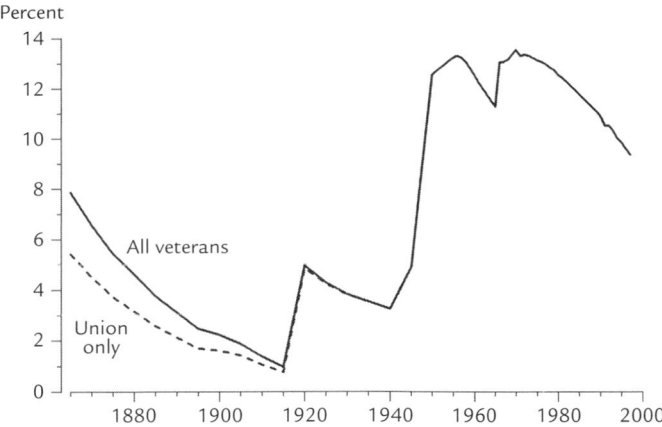

FIGURE Ed-E   Veterans as a percentage of the total population: 1865–1999

Sources

Veterans: series Ed229 and Ed248. Resident population: series Aa7.

Documentation

Confederate veterans were estimated by multiplying the number of Union veterans, series Ed248, by 0.4685, an estimate of the ratio of Confederate to Union forces.

lower line includes only Union veterans of the Civil War. The upper line includes a makeshift estimate of the number of Confederate veterans. Estimates of the number of soldiers and sailors who served in the Confederate forces are subject to a wide margin of error, and there are no estimates of the number of surviving Confederate veterans in the postbellum era. Here the ratio of Confederate survivors of the war to Union survivors (0.4685) was applied to the number of Union veterans in subsequent years (series Ed248) to get an estimate of the number of Confederate veterans. Most likely mortality at younger ages would have been higher for Confederate veterans than for Union veterans because of lower standards of living in the South, lower payments to veterans, and a less favorable disease environment. So this procedure probably overestimates the number of Confederate veterans. Nevertheless, the main point is evident – the important political and economic role played by veterans of the Civil War. Veterans were close to 8 percent of the American population at the end of the Civil War, a share not surpassed until World War II.

In 1862, soon after the outbreak of the Civil War, Congress passed legislation providing pensions for disabilities caused by the war, as well as pensions for widows, orphans, and, in some cases – a new feature – dependent mothers and sisters. This was the basic law in force until 1890. In addition, in 1865, Congress authorized the establishment of a "National Asylum" for Disabled Veterans.[3] Facilities had been established earlier for soldiers and sailors in the regular armed forces, but they had been relatively small affairs supported by contributions from the soldiers and sailors and from naval prizes. The scale of the Civil War recommended a new agency.

To receive a pension, veterans had to be able to demonstrate some disability that could be traced to the war. Inevitably, pressure grew to liberalize the rules and their administration. The Grand Army of the Republic (GAR), an association of Union army

veterans formed in 1866, became a formidable lobbying force on behalf of larger pensions. On other issues, the GAR tended to avoid controversy. Although some 216,000 black soldiers had served with great distinction with the Union forces, almost 10 percent of the total (Chambers 1999, p. 8), the GAR generally avoided racial issues. White veterans typically viewed the war as a fight over union and states rights. And the organization of local units was left to the localities, which in practice meant that they were segregated.

Success in increasing benefits varied with the state of the federal budget (surpluses were good for the veterans), with the party in power (Republican Congresses and administrations were good for the veterans), and with the proximity to elections. Lawyers who specialized in winning pensions for their clients, it must be admitted, also became effective lobbyists for more generous pensions. The amount of money transferred to veterans and their families, mainly Union veterans until World War I, is shown in Figure Ed-F, which traces the total amount spent by the Department of Veterans Affairs and its predecessor agencies, and the amount spent on compensation and pensions, per thousand dollars of gross domestic product (GDP) from 1869 to 1998. In the 1870s, spending on Union veterans amounted to about $3.50 per $1,000 of GDP, almost all in the form of compensation for death or disabilities caused by the war.

The Arrears Act of 1879 was an important victory for advocates of more generous pensions. Prior to this law, a veteran's pension began when he was added to the roles, no matter how long after the original disability was incurred. Under the Arrears Act, pensioners could have their cases reopened and be awarded the amount of pension due from the time they incurred their disability to the

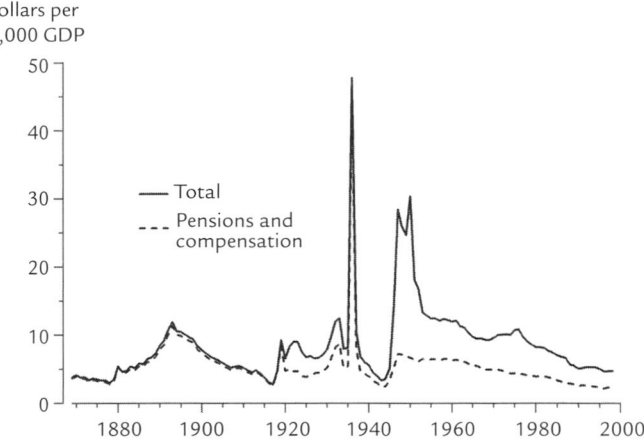

FIGURE Ed-F   Veterans benefits relative to gross domestic product: 1869–1998

Sources

Total expenditures of the Veterans Administration and predecessor agencies: through 1959, series Ed297; thereafter, series Ed311.

Expenditures on pensions and compensation: through 1959, series Ed298 plus series Ed305; thereafter, series Ed318.

Gross domestic product or gross national product: through 1928, gross national product (GNP), Christina D. Romer, "Prewar Estimates of GNP Reconsidered: New Estimates of Gross National Product, 1869–1908," *Journal of Political Economy* 97 (February 1987): 22–3; thereafter, gross domestic product (GDP), series Ca1.

Documentation

For display purposes, the GNP/GDP data were converted to five-year moving averages in order to abstract from sharp cyclical fluctuations.

The peak during the 1930s is the Veteran's bonus (see the essay text).

---

[3] The Asylum in Washington, D.C., was renamed the National Home for Disabled Volunteer Soldiers in 1873; colloquially it became known as the Old Soldiers Home.

time they were placed on the rolls. The law also covered veterans whose eligibility for a pension would be recognized in the future. Substantial amounts were awarded under the Arrears Act, and the incentive to apply for a pension was increased substantially.

The effect of the Arrears Act on the level of pension payments can be observed in Figure Ed-F, which indicates that Civil War pensions and benefits reached a peak relative to a five-year moving average of GNP in the early 1890s at a figure of more than $10.00 per $1,000 of GNP. This was nearly thirty years after the end of the fighting, when many of the surviving veterans were in their fifties. The contrast with World War II, when spending relative to GDP reached its peak in the immediate aftermath of the war and then trended downward, is evident.

Despite lobbying by the Civil War veterans and their allies, the ultimate goal of many of the veterans – a service pension – was long in coming, as it was for veterans of earlier wars. In 1887, while signing legislation granting service pensions for Mexican War veterans, President Grover Cleveland, a Democrat, vetoed a similar measure for veterans of the Civil War on the grounds that they were still too young. Three years later, however, Congress passed the Disability Pension Act of 1890, understandably signed by Republican President Benjamin Harrison. This Act, although nominally a disability law, came very close to meeting the demand for a pure service pension. Under the Act of 1890, the mere existence of a disability limiting the veteran's ability to earn a living was sufficient for a pension (as long as the disability didn't arise from "vicious habits"): it wasn't necessary to show that the disability had resulted from military service. Eligibility was not limited to the poor, and the service requirement was simply ninety days and honorable discharge. Because the commissioner of pensions was given some discretion under the law when it came to fixing individual pensions, the policy of the commissioner became a major political issue. Pressure for more liberal pension benefits continued, and in 1904 Republican President Roosevelt issued Executive Order 78, which defined age itself to be a disability, creating an authentic service pension. Thus, the service pension came thirty-nine years after the end of the Civil War, the same period that veterans of the Mexican War had to wait, and a bit shorter than the forty-four-year wait of veterans of the Revolution and the fifty-six-year wait of veterans of the War of 1812. Between 1865 and 1905, the number of Northern veterans of the Civil War, to put the figure in a somewhat different perspective, declined from 1,830,000 to 821,000 (series Ed248).

Under the 1904 executive order, pensions started at age 62, and the amount awarded increased at ages 65, 68, and 70. Subsequent legislation broadened and codified the idea behind Executive Order 78. The law of 1912, for example, included a schedule of pensions ranging from $13 per month for a man aged 62, who had served only ninety days, to a maximum of $30 per month for a man aged 75, who had served for three years. The rules with respect to widows were also gradually eased, so in the end it became possible for a young woman to marry an aged veteran of the Civil War and thus to secure a pension throughout her adult life.

The liberalization of the pension system in 1890 was the result of a number of important factors: precedent established by earlier wars (a factor often neglected by historians), lobbying by the Grand Army of the Republic, lobbying by the pension lawyers, increasing sympathy for the veterans as they entered middle age, and the bitter political struggles between the Democrats and the Republicans (the Republicans who controlled both houses and the

presidency in 1890 relied on the overwhelming support of the veterans). But the state of the federal budget also played a role. The federal budget had been in surplus for a number of years prior to 1890. Taxes could be cut, but this would have meant cutting the tariff, which would offend powerful business interests, or cutting the alcohol and tobacco taxes, which would offend anti-drinking and anti-tobacco activists. The close association between the surplus, the tariff, and pensions for veterans of the Civil War was a reprise of events in the 1820s involving veterans of the Revolutionary War. Various schemes for increased spending were floated, but liberalizing the pension emerged as the plan with the greatest political payoff (Skocpol 1992, 1993; Holcombe 1999).

The liberalization of the Civil War pension system helped to offset the decrease in the number of veterans and their widows. The dollar amount paid out in Civil War pensions actually peaked in 1921, fifty-six years after the end of the war. The Union pension system eventually covered a substantial fraction of native-born Northern men and their survivors. By 1900, according to Dora L. Costa, a leading authority on the Civil War pensions, "21 percent of all white males over the age of 55, were on the pension roles," and "the average pension paid to Union Army veterans from 1866 to 1912 replaced about 30 percent of the income of an unskilled laborer, making the Union army pension program as generous as Social Security retirement benefits today" (Costa 1998, p. 197).

The Civil War pension system, as a number of prominent scholars have argued, was America's first national welfare system (Skocpol 1992). At the turn of the twentieth century, liberal reformers, such as Isaac Max Rubinow, hoped that as the number of veterans and their survivors declined, "room" would be created in the federal budget for a general old-age pension and other welfare-state benefits (Rubinow 1913). As a share of the federal budget, veterans spending reached its peak, 43 percent, in 1893. In 1914, on the eve of World War I, payments to veterans accounted for 25 percent of the budget. Conservatives, on the other hand, hoped that the unsavory reputation of the Civil War pension would discourage welfare experiments. The pension system was often perceived, with some justice, as a system rampant with abuses (such as the "pension marriages" mentioned earlier) and as a system that debased national political life, as both parties sought to buy the votes of the pension recipients. A number of states created welfare benefits for women and children prior to 1929, but a national social security system was not established until the 1930s. Although the establishment of a national system was mainly a product of the Great Depression, it also owed a great deal to the Civil War pension. As Baack and Ray showed, the Civil War pension educated congressmen about the political benefits of old-age pensions and was a focal point for the development of special interests that could lobby effectively for benefits (Baack and Ray 1988).

Civil War veterans were not awarded warrants for land. But their military service was counted toward the residence requirement of the Homestead Act. Civil War veterans were also given preference in hiring by the federal civil service and by many states. Military service, moreover, was a valuable help, although not a requirement, for those seeking political office. No estimate of the monetary value of these privileges is available.

Federal benefits were paid only to veterans of the Union forces.[4] The Southern states, however, provided pensions and benefits in

---

[4] There was one exception: in 1958, Congress pardoned and provided a pension for the last surviving Confederate veteran.

kind for Confederate veterans, such as soldiers' homes. Prosthetic devices were a major item in several state budgets after the war, illustrating both the severity of the war and the poverty of Southern states. Like their Northern counterparts, the Confederate veterans organized effectively. Local veterans associations formed soon after the war ended, and in 1889 a national organization, the United Confederate Veterans, was formed from these separate associations. The relative poverty of the South and the lack of certain fiscal resources (such as the tariff) meant, however, that the amount of resources that veterans could expect from Southern legislatures was limited. Exact figures on the amount of benefits paid to Confederate veterans are not available, but these benefits were clearly meager compared with the benefits paid to Union veterans and their survivors. One estimate places the total amount spent by the Southern states on Confederate pensions at $350 million to $400 million, perhaps 4.1 to 4.7 percent of what was spent on Union veterans (or 9.0 to 10.3 percent on a per capita basis). Veterans of the Confederacy were also accorded preferences in hiring and political life in the South because of their veteran status.

Overall, the statistics that we do have, mainly on the amount of pensions paid to Union veterans, appear to be highly accurate. The problem areas are the lack of statistics for the Confederate veterans, and the amount of nonfinancial benefits, such as preferences for jobs in civilian life.

The Civil War pensions left behind an enormous quantity of medical records because a medical disability attested to by a pension office surgeon was a requirement for a pension. Modern computers make encoding and manipulating this mass of data possible. As a result, scholars have used these records in recent years to analyze the effects of income, wartime stress, and other factors on the health and economic behavior of the veterans. Robert Fogel has been the leader of the effort to use these data. Research based on these data has led to a number of important academic papers and monographs. At the time of writing, considerable information on the project, and data created by it, was available at the Internet site of the Center for Population Economics, at the University of Chicago Graduate School of Business.

After the Spanish–American War (1898) and the Philippine Insurrection (1899–1902), a number of veterans' organizations were founded to provide mutual support, to affirm the values shared by the veterans, and to lobby for benefits. In 1913, the merger of two of these organizations (which had grown through earlier mergers) produced the Veterans of Foreign Wars, an organization that would continue to play a major role in veterans' affairs for the remainder of the century. In truth, however, the veterans of these two wars had an easier time winning recognition for their services in part because of the previous work done by the Civil War veterans. Because the total number of men and women engaged was relatively small, these two wars made a relatively small impact on the number of veterans in civilian life, and on the overall level of federal spending on veterans, as can be seen in Figures Ed-E and Ed-F.

The World Wars

Although America's relatively brief (1917–1918) involvement in World War I would not leave as large an imprint on the structure of the nation's population as the Civil War or World War II, the impact – as shown in Figure Ed-E – was nonetheless significant. In the immediate aftermath of the war, close to 5 percent of Americans

were veterans, a level not seen in the United States for decades. Even though the number of veterans was reminiscent of the Civil War era, the structure of benefits created to aid them was very different. Insurance and medical care, rather than pensions, became the immediate priorities.

The origins of the current programs for insuring members of the armed forces and veterans can be traced to World War I. Shortly after the war began, companies shipping goods to Europe found it hard to get marine insurance at what seemed like reasonable rates. The risks for commercial insurers were very great and very difficult to calculate on the basis of past experience. Under the War Risk Insurance Act (September 2, 1914), the U.S. government supplied marine insurance. When the United States entered the war in April 1917, the opportunity to buy insurance was extended to merchant marine personnel. A more comprehensive measure, the War Insurance Act (Soldiers and Sailor's Insurance Law), was passed a few months later, in October 1917. This law provided compulsory pay allotments for the families of service personnel during the war, compensation for death or disability, medical and rehabilitation services, as well as subsidized term life insurance. The idea was that a soldier would have the peacetime cost of the insurance deducted from his pay, but the government would pay the additional costs of insuring the higher risks caused by the war. The Bureau of War Risk Insurance was created within the Treasury to administer the new system. More than four million policies were issued during the war.

The insurance program that emerged from World War I was continued after the war but modified in response to subsequent wars and changing economic conditions. The National Service Life Insurance program was established in 1940 in response to World War II. This legislation was replaced in 1951 by the Servicemen's Indemnity Insurance program. Another program, the Veterans' Special Life Insurance, was established a short time later to meet the needs of members of the armed forces serving during the Korean Conflict.

In the early 1950s, private insurers began to complain that competition from the Veterans Administration was unfair, and the industry began to lobby Congress for a new approach. The result was the Servicemembers' Group Life Insurance program (1965) for members of the armed forces serving during the Vietnam Conflict and in subsequent periods, and the Veterans' Group Life Insurance (1974) for veterans after separation from the armed forces. Under these programs, term life insurance is provided under group plans issued by private insurers, but the government defrays the costs. As a matter of accounting, and following earlier traditions, the member of the armed forces is said to pay for the ordinary cost of insurance through deductions from pay, and the government is said to pay for the extra part of the premium that reflects the additional risks of service in the armed forces. Over time, these popular programs have been expanded. The maximum amount of insurance per individual has been raised in a series of steps from $10,000 to $200,000 in 1992, and coverage has been extended to members of the National Guard. A program was created in 1971 to provide mortgage protection life insurance to disabled veterans who had received grants for the purchase of specially adapted housing (see Table Ed400–403).

A hospital system was also created to provide medical care for World War I veterans (see Table Ed404–414). Insurance and the government-provided hospital system were new departures in the government's approach to veterans. Previously, veterans had been aided mostly by writing checks based on disabilities or death resulting from service during a war. There had been some expenditure for homes for aged veterans, but quantitatively they were of minor importance. Now, however, more emphasis was placed on in-kind services and payments earmarked for education.

Part of the explanation for the emphasis on in-kind aid after World War I was the widespread perception, not always an accurate one, that the Civil War pension had been abused – for example, by encouraging pension marriages or by encouraging shirking by able-bodied men – and the hope that in-kind benefits would be harder to exploit (Blanck 2001). Another factor was the new view about the appropriate role of the government in the economy that had evolved during the Progressive Era. Historically, most Americans had been skeptical about the ability of government bureaucracies to perform efficiently. Now many Americans were convinced that government could provide high-quality services at a reasonable cost. The new view of government was especially relevant in the case of medical care because it was believed that veterans would face unique medical problems, "shell shock" for example, that physicians in the private sector would lack the experience to handle properly.

After World War I, as after previous wars, pressure began to build to reward veterans more generously and to include those who had not suffered disabilities as a result of their service. The American Legion, founded by members of the American Expeditionary Forces in 1919, was especially effective in lobbying for a "bonus" for veterans. The point was made that the enlisted men, who had served for a dollar a day during the war, had suffered from wartime inflation and deserved additional compensation. Congress finally agreed, and in 1924 a "bonus" was awarded, but it was not scheduled for payment with interest until 1945. The amount of the "adjusted service certificate" was calculated on the basis of $1.00 per day of service in the United States up to $500, and $1.25 per day overseas up to $625, plus an additional 25 percent (U.S. Veterans Administration 1936, pp. 21–2).

Although veterans could and did borrow against the security of their adjusted service compensation certificates, many veterans joined a campaign in the early 1930s for an early payment of the bonus in order to alleviate the distress caused by the Depression. In 1932, thousands of veterans (estimates run from fifteen thousand to forty thousand) converged on Washington to demand immediate payment of the bonus. Most of the veterans returned home after the Senate failed to pass a measure providing for immediate payment, but a small group remained. President Herbert Hoover ordered the police to clear out the remainder of the Bonus Army that was occupying some abandoned federal buildings. In the ensuing melee, two veterans and two policemen were killed. Hoover then asked the Army to assist the police, and federal forces commanded by General Douglas MacArthur drove the veterans from the city and forced them to burn their encampment. More than one hundred veterans were injured in the Bonus March. The use of what appeared to many to be excessive force further undermined Hoover's reputation. A second Bonus Army came to Washington in 1933, after Democrat Franklin Roosevelt replaced Hoover, but again no legislation was passed.

In 1936, however, Congress finally passed legislation, over a presidential veto, providing for immediate payment. The amount of the bonus was substantial given the depressed incomes of the day. The bonus averaged about $550 per veteran, about one third of mean family personal income at the time (U.S. Bureau of the Census 1975, series G308). Altogether, certificates worth $1.893 billion (after deductions for loans) were approved. About 80 percent were cashed in 1936 and 1937, a two-year total of $1.5 billion, equal to 23 percent of federal outlays in 1935 (U.S. Veterans Administration 1936, p. 24; U.S. Bureau of the Census 1975, series Y466). The bonus can be seen as the sharp peak in Figure Ed-F. From a Keynesian perspective, this is just what the economy needed. In his classic study of fiscal policy in the 1930s, E. Cary Brown concluded that there were only two years, 1931 and 1936, in which fiscal policy (combining all levels of government) was markedly more expansionary than it was in 1929, and that in both cases it was the result of payments to veterans (Brown 1956, p. 863).

In some ways, World War II gave veterans more prominence in American society than they had ever had before. As can be seen in Figure Ed-E, the number of veterans as a percentage of the population rose to a height that exceeded even the level reached immediately after the Civil War. Overall, the military participation rate during World War II reached 11.8 percent, compared with 9.6 percent in the Civil War. The difference between the wars was the death rate. Deaths from combat, disease, and other service-related causes during the Civil War amounted to 1.4 percent of the 1865 population. The comparable figure for World War II was 0.3 percent of the 1945 population.[5]

The unity of the nation, the clear-cut victory over the Axis, and the return to prosperity ensured that the United States would do well by the veterans of World War II. The result was a large number of innovative programs. Planning for World War II veterans began during the war. The Postwar Manpower Committee reported to President Roosevelt in June 1943 proposing a number of benefits for veterans. The report was influenced by the perception that demobilization had gone badly after World War I, by the Wisconsin Educational Bonus Law of 1919 (which had provided tuition, a subsistence allowance, and other benefits for disabled veterans attending vocational schools, high schools, or colleges), and by recently passed Canadian legislation. These examples were brought home to the Congress through the lobbying efforts of the veterans' organizations, the Veterans of Foreign Wars, and the American Legion. The landmark legislation that finally passed Congress in 1944, the Servicemen's Readjustment Act, has been known ever since by its popular name, the GI Bill of Rights or GI Bill for short.

The GI Bill provided a wide range of benefits including health care; mustering out pay; job placement; unemployment insurance; loans to buy a home, farm, or business; reemployment rights and other employment preferences; and educational benefits (see Tables Ed453–482). The bill reflected a variety of concerns, but the fear that the veterans would return to find the depressed economic conditions of the 1930s, that they would go from battle lines to bread lines, gave special urgency to the bill, and there was little opposition.

The revolutionary education title provided tuition, fees, and subsistence support. The Veterans Administration determined who was eligible, the veteran chose the school, and the school determined whether the veteran would be admitted. The schools had to be accredited, but the Act specifically denied the federal government any control over the schools that were accepting veterans. For white

---

[5] Military personnel: Chambers (1999), p. 849; population: U.S. Bureau of the Census (1975), series A6 and A7.

veterans, this system provided about as much freedom of choice as a veteran could reasonably expect. For African-American veterans, especially in the South, access was still severely restricted by segregation.

College enrollments boomed after the war, partly as a result of the GI Bill. The peak year in GI-Bill-financed education, when measured as a percentage of total college enrollment, was 1947 when 1.7 million veterans were enrolled in higher education, making up about 71 percent of the student body. The impact of the student loan program on the structure of federal spending on veterans can be seen in Figure Ed-F. A large gap opened up between total spending and spending on compensation and pensions: while the total reached unprecedented levels, the latter remained at levels comparable to those reached after the Civil War.

As Figure Ed-G shows, enrollment in colleges and universities remained high and continued to grow long after students supported by the GI Bill and its extensions ceased to be a major factor in total enrollment. Note that even though the number of veterans enrolled skyrocketed again during the Vietnam period, they never constituted more than 18 percent of a much larger total enrollment. Evidently, the often-made claim that the GI Bill was the major cause of the vast expansion of higher education in the United States after World War II cannot be taken at face value (Stanley 2000). The decision to stress education in the GI Bill simply reflected a widely shared underlying faith in education, a faith that earlier in the century had led to the expansion of America's high schools. Nevertheless, the GI Bill deserves some of the credit for the postwar expansion of higher education. There were effects on attitudes and institutions that don't show up in the numbers. Despite complaints that some veterans were just in college for a good time, most veterans acquitted themselves well, overcoming fears that the expansion of higher education would reduce quality. The

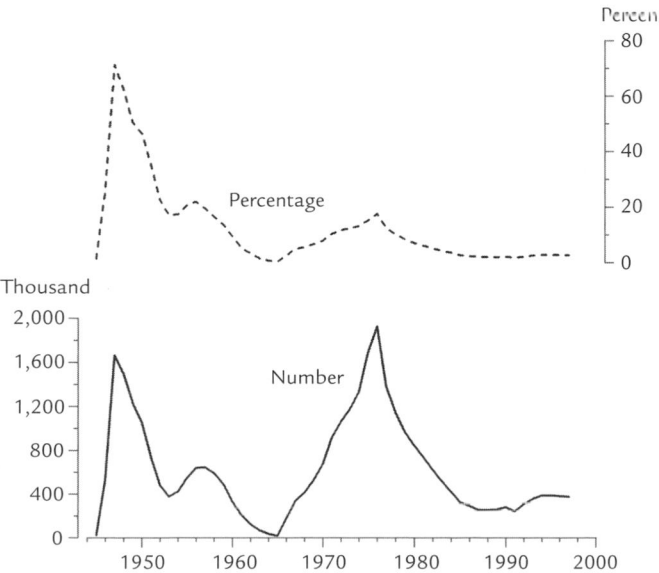

FIGURE Ed-G Veterans enrolled in institutions of higher education under GI Bills – number and as a percentage of total enrollment: 1945–1997

Sources

Veteran enrollment: the sum of series Ed468, Ed472, Ed476, and Ed481–482.

Total enrollment: through 1995, series Bc523; thereafter, U.S. Bureau of the Census, *Statistical Abstract of the United States* (annual issues).

training programs introduced during the war, especially on the East Coast, and the large number of veterans who entered immediately afterward, forced once genteel liberal arts colleges to learn how to provide higher education for a mass constituency. There would have been more resistance to the postwar expansion of higher education had the way not been paved by the veterans.

The Postwar Era

In terms of sheer numbers, World War II gave the veteran an unprecedented prominence in American life. As Figure Ed-E shows, veterans represented more than 13 percent of the American population as a result of World War II. As this percentage declined, it was reinforced subsequently by veterans of the conflicts in Korea, Vietnam, the Persian Gulf, and elsewhere. As a result, the number of veterans as a share of the U.S. population was still higher at the end of the twentieth century than it had been in the immediate aftermath of the Civil War.

The Korean War GI Bill – the Veterans' Readjustment Assistance Act of 1952 – was similar in many ways to the World War II legislation. The education title of the Korean War bill was, however, somewhat less generous than that of the World War II bill. The 1952 Act, for example, limited educational or vocational training to thirty-six months, whereas the 1944 Act permitted training for up to forty-eight months. Reduced fears of widespread unemployment and a perception that some veterans had unfairly exploited the original GI Bill may account for the difference.

The Vietnam GI Bill was passed in 1966, and in some respects its education title was less generous again than the education title in the 1952 GI Bill. One would certainly reach this conclusion if one compared education benefits with current wages. The Vietnam Bill, however, did provide benefits for those who served between the Korean and Vietnam Conflicts. Initially, the number of veterans taking advantage of the Vietnam-era provisions was disappointing. But within a few years, partly in response to an increase in benefits, utilization of the education provisions increased so that usage was comparable to that of World War II benefits. Although educational benefits were substantial, subsequent research showed that serving in Vietnam was an economic disadvantage in the long run (Angrist 1990). Draftees who served in the Vietnam Conflict ended up earning 15 percent less in civilian life, other things being equal, than men who did not serve. The reason may simply be that the men who served lost time in the private sector that they would have spent developing their skills and advancing their careers. It is not known whether the experience of the Vietnam veterans in this respect was better or worse than that of the veterans of other wars, and research would be helpful.

In 1973, the United States ended the draft and established an all-volunteer armed force. The movement toward an all-volunteer force was driven partly by the desire to implement libertarian political principles, and partly by the hope that ending the draft would reduce antiwar activities and domestic dissension. Although changes had been in the works for some time, the establishment of an all-volunteer force significantly altered the role of veterans' benefits. Historically veterans' benefits, although occasionally legislated with an eye toward current recruitment, had mainly been a reward granted ex-post by a grateful nation for service performed during a war (and by politicians anxious to curry favor with a powerful interest group). But with a volunteer army, veterans' benefits became a recruiting tool designed to help fill the ranks.

Beginning in the 1970s, the general pressure from the women's rights movements for equality in all lines of work, and the need from the all-volunteer armed forces to recruit from as large a pool as possible, led to a gradual easing of the restrictions imposed on women in the military, and to an increase in their numbers. To be sure, women had served in all of America's wars, but until World War II, they had served in very small numbers and with little official recognition for women veterans. About 34,000 women served in World War I, mainly in the Army and Navy Nurse Corps and in clerical positions. More than 350,000 women served in World War II – about 2.2 percent of the veteran population (Chambers 1999, p. 808) – primarily in medical and administrative jobs, but also as pilots, truck drivers, electricians, among many other jobs. Many served in the Women's Army Corps created in 1942. The Veterans Preference Act of 1944, which gave veterans a preference in federal employment, explicitly included women veterans and their husbands and widowers. This law may have been the first official recognition of women veterans. In 1948, Congress passed the Women's Armed Services Integration Act, which provided a legal framework defining and limiting the role of women in the armed forces. Under this Act, the number of women in the armed forces was capped at 2 percent of active duty personnel, and women were excluded from combat. The latter limitation remained in effect (with an exception for pilots) into the late 1990s. As more women have served in the armed forces, the number of women veterans in civilian life has increased. About 41,000 women took part in the Persian Gulf War, about 7 percent of the total. In March 1994, the Veterans Administration established the Women Veterans Program Office to improve the delivery of services to women veterans and to increase recognition for their contributions. This legislation was followed in 1995 by the establishment of a number of health care centers dedicated to dealing with the unique health care problems of women veterans.

In the late 1970s, as soaring inflation cut the purchasing power of the wages of the average enlisted person's income, it became increasingly clear that significant financial incentives would be needed to fill the ranks with higher quality personnel. In 1977, Congress passed the Post-Vietnam Era Veterans' Educational Assistance Act. The Act instituted a system of federal matching funds for personal expenditures for education, but it was not utilized as much as had been hoped. In 1984, Congress passed a new measure, the All-Volunteer Force Educational Assistance Program, to provide a permanent system of benefits and to make service in the armed forces more attractive. The title was later changed to the Montgomery GI Bill – Active Duty Educational Assistance Program, in honor of G.V. "Sonny" Montgomery, Democrat of Mississippi, who served on the House Veterans Affairs and Armed Services Committees. It provides cash grants for education based on service and financial contributions made while on active duty and continues to be the basis for educational aid for veterans. Most of the veterans who make use of this program attend colleges or universities. Research by Joshua Angrist showed that these programs did encourage veterans to attend school and did increase their long-run income, although whether this effect offset the loss of experience in the civilian labor market is an open question (Angrist 1993).

Increased understanding of the physiological and psychological problems faced by veterans has repeatedly produced additions to the list of benefits and services provided veterans. In 1979, responding to the concern that Vietnam veterans were not receiving sufficient help adjusting to civilian life, the Veterans Administration set up a group of centers specially designed to help Vietnam veterans with post-traumatic stress disorder, alcohol and drug dependency, and similar problems. In 1988, in response to disclosures about service people's exposure to nuclear testing during the early Cold War era, Congress passed the Radiation-Exposed Veterans Compensation Act that provided for veterans suffering from disabilities caused by atomic radiation. A long-drawn-out battle, one that involved considerable criticism of the Veterans Administration, concerned the payment of compensation and provision of medical care for health problems caused by the use of Agent Orange as a defoliant in Vietnam. The Veterans Administration responded by gradually adding to the list of disabilities that it considered to have been caused by Agent Orange. Finally, in 1991, Congress passed the Agent Orange Act creating the presumption that a range of disabilities were linked to the use of herbicides in Vietnam and should be treated as service-related disabilities.

Prompted by these and related concerns, the Department of Veterans Affairs has continually devoted resources to basic medical research. Although a small part of total spending on medical programs (less than 3 percent in recent years), this area has become a source of pride for the Department of Veterans Affairs, especially in 1977 when two scientists from the Department, Rosalyn Yalow and Andrew Schally, shared the Nobel Prize in Medicine with Roger Guillemin for their work on peptide hormones.

Although veterans' benefits have long been one of the major items in the federal budget and the Veterans Administration has been one of the largest federal employers, the agency did not become a cabinet-level department until 1989. A year later in fall 1990, the United States launched operation Desert Shield to block further expansion of Saddam Hussein's Iraq. In January 1991, Operation Desert Storm was launched, marking the beginning of the Persian Gulf War, which drove Iraqi forces out of Kuwait. In the following month, Congress passed the Persian Gulf Conflict Supplemental Authorization and Personnel Benefits Act, which declared the military action in the Persian Gulf to be a war for the purposes of determining eligibility for veterans' benefits.

At the time of this writing, the current rules and regulations governing the payment of veterans benefits, and recent statistics on the number of veterans in civil life by age and period of service, expenditures of the Department of Veterans Affairs, and so on could be found at the Internet site of the U.S. Department of Veterans Affairs.

Conclusion

After America's wars, especially the Civil War, World War I, and World War II, America's veterans were at the center of the national stage. Politicians from both major parties listened intently to the millions of veterans and vied for their support. Veterans' organizations, such as the Grand Army of the Republic for Union Army veterans of the Civil War, the Veterans of Foreign Wars, and the American Legion, played important roles in focusing and maintaining the influence of veterans. But these organizations were not the source of the veterans' influence. Ultimately, this influence grew out of both the moral debt that Americans believed they owed the veterans, those former citizen soldiers, and the sheer numerical weight of veterans in the polity. The result was a series of laws establishing veterans' benefits, laws that created major precedents for the welfare state: the Civil War pension for Union veterans, insurance and hospital care for World War I veterans, and the famous GI Bill of Rights, which provided educational, housing, and other benefits for World War II veterans. Liberals have cited the Civil War pensions as a form of old-age pension and wondered why it took the United States so long to enact social security; conservatives have cited the educational benefits provided to GIs after World War II as a successful example of educational vouchers, and wondered why educational vouchers provoke so much opposition. Supporters and opponents of socialized health care point to the Veterans Hospital and Medical care system, the nation's largest, as an example of what could or would happen if health care were socialized.

In the post–World War II era, however, the role of veterans changed. The smaller scale of the wars between 1950 and 1991, the deep divisions over the Vietnam Conflict, and the establishment of the all-volunteer armed forces meant that there were fewer young veterans in society, and that they spoke with distinct voices, and in the long run that meant that veterans would have less weight in political deliberations. A more mundane consideration, the need to provide an attractive package of benefits to men and women planning a career in the armed forces, will determine the type of benefits won by veterans.

References

Angrist, Joshua D. 1990. "Lifetime Earnings and the Vietnam Era Draft Lottery: Evidence from Social Security Administrative Records." *American Economic Review* 80 (3): 313–36.

Angrist, Joshua D. 1993. "The Effect of Veterans Benefits on Education and Earnings." *Industrial and Labor Relations Review* 46 (July): 637–52.

Baack, Ben, and Edward John Ray. 1988. "Federal Transfer Payments in America: Veterans' Pensions and the Rise of Social Security." *Economic Inquiry* 26: 687–702.

Blanck, Peter. 2001. "Civil War Pensions and Disabilities." *Ohio State Law Journal* 62 (1): 109–238.

Brown, E. Cary. 1956. "Fiscal Policy in the Thirties: A Reappraisal." *American Economic Review* 46 (5): 857–79.

Chambers, John Whiteclay, II, editor in chief. 1999. *The Oxford Companion to American Military History*. Oxford University Press.

Costa, Dora L. 1998. *The Evolution of Retirement: An American Economic History, 1880–1990*. University of Chicago Press.

Holcombe, Randall G. 1999. "Veterans Interests and the Transition to Government Growth: 1870–1915." *Public Choice* 99 (3–4): 311–26.

Oberly, James W. 1990. *Sixty Million Acres: American Veterans and the Public Lands before the Civil War*. Kent State University Press.

O'Callaghan, Jerry. 1954. "The War Veteran and the Public Lands." *Agricultural History* 28: 163–68.

Rubinow, Isaac Max. 1913. *Social Insurance: With Special Reference to American Conditions*. H. Holt.

Skocpol, Theda. 1992. *Protecting Soldiers and Mothers: The Political Origins of Social Policy in the United States*. Belknap Press of Harvard University Press.

Skocpol, Theda. 1993. "America's First Social Security System: The Expansion of Benefits for Civil War Veterans." *Political Science Quarterly* 108 (1): 85–116.

Stanley, Marcus Magnus. 2000. "Essays in Program Evaluation." Ph.D. dissertation, Harvard University.

U.S. Bureau of the Census. 1975. *Historical Statistics of the United States*.

U.S. Veterans Administration. 1936. *Annual Report*.

MILITARY PERSONNEL AND CASUALTIES

Scott Sigmund Gartner

TABLE Ed1-5   Military personnel and casualties, by war and branch of service: 1775–1991

Contributed by Scott Sigmund Gartner

Period, war, and branch of service	Personnel serving worldwide	Casualties [7]			Wounds (not mortal)
		Deaths			
		Total	Battle	Other	
	Ed1	Ed2	Ed3	Ed4	Ed5
	Number	Number	Number	Number	Number
1775–1783: Revolutionary War					
Total	— [4]	4,435	4,435	—	6,188
Army	—	4,044	4,044	—	6,004
Navy	—	342	342	—	114
Marines	—	49	49	—	70
1812–1815: War of 1812					
Total	286,730 [5]	2,260	2,260	—	4,505
Army	—	1,950	1,950	—	4,000
Navy	—	265	265	—	439
Marines	—	45	45	—	66
1846–1848: Mexican War					
Total	78,718 [5]	13,283	1,733	11,550	4,152
Army	—	13,271	1,721	11,550	4,102
Navy	—	1	1	—	3
Marines	—	11	11	—	47
1861–1865: Civil War (Union)					
Total	2,213,363	364,511	140,414	224,097	281,881
Army	2,128,948 [5]	359,528	138,154	221,374	280,040
Navy	84,415 [6]	4,523	2,112	2,411	1,710
Marines	— [6]	460	148	312	131
1898–1898: Spanish–American War					
Total	306,760	2,446	385	2,061	1,662
Army	280,564	2,430	369	2,061	1,594
Navy	22,875	10	10	—	47
Marines	3,321	6	6	—	21
1917–1918: World War I					
Total	4,734,991	116,516	53,402	63,114	204,002
Army [1]	4,057,101	106,378	50,510	55,868	193,663
Navy	599,051	7,287	431	6,856	819
Marines	78,839	2,851	2,461	390	9,520
1941–1946: World War II					
Total	16,112,566	405,399	291,557	113,842	671,846
Army [2]	11,260,000	318,274	234,874	83,400	565,861
Navy [3]	4,183,466	62,614	36,950	25,664	37,778
Marines	669,100	24,511	19,733	4,778	68,207
1950–1953: Korean Conflict [7]					
Total	5,720,000	36,576	33,741	2,835	103,284
Army	2,834,000	29,856	27,731	2,125	77,596
Navy	1,177,000	660	506	154	1,576
Marines	424,000	4,508	4,266	242	23,744
Air Force	1,285,000	1,552	1,238	314	368
1964–1973: Vietnam Conflict [7]					
Total	8,744,000	58,200	47,415	10,785	153,303
Army	4,368,000	38,213	30,952	7,261	96,802
Navy	1,842,000	2,562	1,628	934	4,178
Marines	794,000	14,840	13,091	1,749	51,392
Air Force	1,740,000	2,585	1,744	841	931
1990–1991: Persian Gulf War [7]					
Total	2,225,000	382	147	235	467
Army	782,000	224	98	126	354
Navy	669,000	55	5	50	12
Marines	213,000	68	24	44	92
Air Force	561,000	35	20	15	9

TABLE Ed1–5   Military personnel and casualties, by war and branch of service: 1775–1991   *Continued*

[1] Includes air service. Battle deaths and wounds not mortal include casualties suffered by American forces in northern Russia to August 25, 1919, and in Siberia to April 1, 1920. Other deaths cover the period April 1, 1917, to December 31, 1918.

[2] Includes Army air forces.

[3] Battle deaths and wounds not mortal include casualties incurred in October 1941 as a result of hostile action.

[4] Not known, but official U.S. Department of Defense estimates range from 184,000 to 250,000.

[5] As reported by the U.S. Commissioner of Pensions in his annual report for fiscal year 1903.

[6] The Civil War Navy figure includes both Union Naval and Marine Corps personnel.

[7] Starting with the Korean Conflict, casualties listed occurred in the combat zone, whereas earlier conflicts' casualties are worldwide.

Sources

U.S. Department of Defense, Directorate for Information, Operations, and Reports Internet site, "Principal Wars in Which the United States Participated, U.S. Military Personnel Serving and Casualties," "Deaths by Casualty Type within Service," and "Worldwide U.S. Active Duty Military Deaths, Selected Military Operations," accessed April 15 and June 2, 2004.

Documentation

This table contains a listing of the principal wars the United States has engaged in from the Revolutionary War to the Persian Gulf War. The U.S. Department of Defense (DOD) determines whether or not a conflict classifies as a "principal war."

Air Force data for World War I and World War II are included in Army figures. The status of Coast Guard casualties is unclear.

All data are from the DOD estimates as of October 8, 2002. Dates of entry and exit pertain solely to the United States, and some conflicts, such as World War I and World War II, were ongoing when the United States joined.

For a list of battles and campaigns conducted during these conflicts as well as those from more minor engagements, see Tables Ed196–201.

Data prior to World War I are based on incomplete records in many cases. Casualty data are confined to dead and wounded and, therefore, exclude personnel captured or missing in action who were subsequently returned to military control.

As of 2002, official DOD sources state that "Authoritative statistics for the Confederate forces [during the Civil War] are not available. Estimates of the number who served range from 600,000 to 1,500,000. The final report of the Provost Marshal General, 1863–1866, indicated 133,821 Confederate deaths (74,524 battle and 59,297 other) based upon incomplete returns. In addition, an estimated 26,000 to 31,000 Confederate personnel died in Union prisons"(U.S Department of Defense, Directorate for Information, Operations, and Reports, Internet site, "Historical Background Notes" for the table: "Principal Wars in Which the United States Participated, U.S. Military Personnel Serving and Casualties," accessed October 8, 2002).

Dates for the Spanish–American War were missing from the source and were added by the editor. Number serving covers the period April 21 to August 13, 1898, whereas dead and wounded data are for the period May 1 to August 31, 1898. Active hostilities ceased on August 13, 1898, but ratifications of the Treaty of Peace were not exchanged between the United States and Spain until April 11, 1899.

Data for World War II are for the period December 1, 1941, through December 31, 1946, when hostilities were officially terminated by Presidential Proclamation, but a few battle deaths or wounds not mortal were incurred after the Japanese acceptance of the Allied peace terms on August 14, 1945. Numbers serving worldwide from December 1, 1941, through August 31, 1945, were as follows: 14,903,213 total; 10,420,000 Army; 3,883,520 Navy; and 599,693 Marine Corps.

Casualty figures for the Korean Conflict are as of June 1, 2000. Review of Korean Conflict casualty records is ongoing. Slight adjustments to some of the numbers are expected as the review is finalized. American military deaths worldwide during the time the Korean Conflict was fought, including the 36,576 in theater, totaled 54,246. This number will not change.

Number serving during the Vietnam Conflict covers the period August 4, 1964, through January 27, 1973 (date of cease-fire). Data on nonmortal wounds exclude 150,332 persons not requiring hospital care. Known status of casualties is as of June 1, 2000 (casualty record information is updated each year).

Figures for the Persian Gulf War include Desert Shield (August 7, 1990, start date, 84 deaths) and Desert Storm (January 17, 1991, start date, 299 deaths). Data are updated annually and are current as of September 2001. Coast Guard numbers are included with the Navy. The total for Desert Shield and Desert Storm includes one death of a prisoner of war not reported in the table.

Series Ed5. Marine Corps data for World War II, the Spanish-American War, and prior wars represent the number of individuals wounded, whereas all other data in this series represent the total number (incidence) of wounds.

TABLE Ed6–25   Active-duty military deaths resulting from hostile action, by branch of service: 1980–1998

Contributed by Scott Sigmund Gartner and Richard Sutch

	Total				Army				Navy	
	Killed in action	Died from wounds	Died while missing or captured	Died in terrorist action	Killed in action	Died from wounds	Died while missing or captured	Died in terrorist action	Killed in action	Died from wounds
	Ed6	Ed7	Ed8	Ed9	Ed10	Ed11	Ed12	Ed13	Ed14	Ed15
Fiscal year	Number	Number	Number	Number	Number	Number	Number	Number	Number	Number
1980	1	0	0	0	1	0	0	0	0	0
1981	0	0	0	0	0	0	0	0	0	0
1982	0	0	0	0	0	0	0	0	0	0
1983	5	1	0	0	0	0	0	0	1	0
1984	273	3	0	0	16	1	0	0	25	0
1985	4	0	1	0	0	0	0	0	0	0
1986	2	0	0	0	0	0	0	0	0	0
1987	38	0	0	0	1	0	0	0	37	0
1988	2	1	0	0	0	0	0	0	2	1
1989	0	0	0	0	0	0	0	0	0	0
1990	20	3	1	0	15	3	0	0	4	0
1991	144	4	0	0	96	2	0	0	6	0
1992	1	0	0	0	1	0	0	0	0	0
1993	0	0	0	10	0	0	0	8	0	0
1994	0	0	0	19	0	0	0	19	0	0
1995	0	0	0	6	0	0	0	2	0	0
1996	1	0	0	20	1	0	0	1	0	0
1997	0	0	0	0	0	0	0	0	0	0
1998	0	0	0	3	0	0	0	1	0	0

	Navy		Air Force				Marine Corps			
	Died while missing or captured	Died in terrorist action	Killed in action	Died from wounds	Died while missing or captured	Died in terrorist action	Killed in action	Died from wounds	Died while missing or captured	Died in terrorist action
	Ed16	Ed17	Ed18	Ed19	Ed20	Ed21	Ed22	Ed23	Ed24	Ed25
Fiscal year	Number	Number	Number	Number	Number	Number	Number	Number	Number	Number
1980	0	0	0	0	0	0	0	0	0	0
1981	0	0	0	0	0	0	0	0	0	0
1982	0	0	0	0	0	0	0	0	0	0
1983	0	0	0	0	0	0	4	1	0	0
1984	0	0	0	0	0	0	232	2	0	0
1985	1	0	0	0	0	0	4	0	0	0
1986	0	0	2	0	0	0	0	0	0	0
1987	0	0	0	0	0	0	0	0	0	0
1988	0	0	0	0	0	0	0	0	0	0
1989	0	0	0	0	0	0	0	0	0	0
1990	0	0	0	0	0	0	1	0	1	0
1991	0	0	20	0	0	0	22	2	0	0
1992	0	0	0	0	0	0	0	0	0	0
1993	0	0	0	0	0	0	0	0	0	2
1994	0	0	0	0	0	0	0	0	0	0
1995	0	0	0	0	0	2	0	0	0	2
1996	0	0	0	0	0	19	0	0	0	0
1997	0	0	0	0	0	0	0	0	0	0
1998	0	0	0	0	0	1	0	0	0	1

Source

U.S. Department of Defense, Secretary of Defense, Internet site, Table 12, "Worldwide U.S. Active Duty Military Deaths Resulting from Hostile Action," accessed August 31, 2000, Table 13, "Worldwide U.S. Active Duty Military Deaths, Selected Military Operations," accessed June 2, 2004.

Documentation

These series include all active military personnel deaths from hostile action (not just those from major battles). Casualties can occur worldwide. Killed in action refers to those who died immediately as a result of a hostile action and does not include those who later died of wounds, while in captivity, or from terrorist acts.

The total deaths by military operation or incident include the Iranian Hostage Rescue Mission (April 25, 1980), 8 deaths; the Lebanon Peacekeeping Mission (August 25, 1982 to February 26, 1984), 265 deaths; Operation Urgent Fury, Grenada (1983), 19 deaths; Operation Just Cause, Panama (1989), 23 deaths; Operation Restore Hope, Somalia (1992–1994), 43 deaths; and Operation Uphold Democracy, Haiti (1994–1996), 4 deaths.

TABLE Ed26–47 Military personnel on active duty, by branch of service and sex: 1789–1995[1]

Contributed by Scott Sigmund Gartner

	Total		Army						Air Force				
	Total	Female	Total	Officers		Enlisted			Officers		Enlisted		
				Total	Female	Total	Female	Total	Total	Female	Total	Female
	Ed26 [2]	Ed27 [2,3]	Ed28 [4]	Ed29 [4,5]	Ed30 [4,5]	Ed31 [4,5]	Ed32 [4,5]	Ed33 [3]	Ed34 [3]	Ed35 [3]	Ed36 [3]	Ed37 [3]
Year	Number	Number	Number	Number	Number	Number	Number	Number	Number	Number	Number	Number
1789	718	—	718	46	—	672	—	—	—	—	—	—
1794	5,669	—	3,813	235	—	3,578	—	—	—	—	—	—
1795	5,296	—	3,440	212	—	3,228	—	—	—	—	—	—
1798	—	—	—	—	—	—	—	—	—	—	—	—
1799	—	—	—	—	—	—	—	—	—	—	—	—
1800	—	—	—	—	—	—	—	—	—	—	—	—
1801	7,108	—	4,051	248	—	3,803	—	—	—	—	—	—
1802	5,432	—	2,873	175	—	2,698	—	—	—	—	—	—
1803	4,528	—	2,486	174	—	2,312	—	—	—	—	—	—
1804	5,323	—	2,734	216	—	2,518	—	—	—	—	—	—
1805	6,498	—	2,729	159	—	2,570	—	—	—	—	—	—
1806	4,076	—	2,653	142	—	2,511	—	—	—	—	—	—
1807	5,323	—	2,775	146	—	2,629	—	—	—	—	—	—
1808	8,200	—	5,712	327	—	5,385	—	—	—	—	—	—
1809	12,375	—	6,977	533	—	6,444	—	—	—	—	—	—
1810	11,554	—	5,956	441	—	5,515	—	—	—	—	—	—
1811	11,528	—	5,608	396	—	5,212	—	—	—	—	—	—
1812	12,631	—	6,686	299	—	6,387	—	—	—	—	—	—
1813	25,152	—	19,036	1,476	—	17,560	—	—	—	—	—	—
1814	46,858	—	38,186	2,271	—	35,915	—	—	—	—	—	—
1815	40,885	—	33,424	2,272	—	31,152	—	—	—	—	—	—
1816	16,743	—	10,231	735	—	9,496	—	—	—	—	—	—
1817	14,606	—	8,446	647	—	7,799	—	—	—	—	—	—
1818	14,260	—	8,155	697	—	7,458	—	—	—	—	—	—
1819	13,259	—	8,506	705	—	7,801	—	—	—	—	—	—
1820	15,113	—	10,554	696	—	9,858	—	—	—	—	—	—
1821	10,587	—	5,773	547	—	5,226	—	—	—	—	—	—
1822	9,863	—	5,358	512	—	4,846	—	—	—	—	—	—
1823	10,871	—	6,117	525	—	5,592	—	—	—	—	—	—
1824	11,008	—	5,973	532	—	5,441	—	—	—	—	—	—
1825	11,089	—	5,903	562	—	5,341	—	—	—	—	—	—
1826	11,586	—	5,989	540	—	5,449	—	—	—	—	—	—
1827	11,627	—	5,885	546	—	5,339	—	—	—	—	—	—
1828	11,431	—	5,702	540	—	5,162	—	—	—	—	—	—
1829	12,096	—	6,332	608	—	5,724	—	—	—	—	—	—
1830	11,942	—	6,122	627	—	5,495	—	—	—	—	—	—
1831	11,173	—	6,055	613	—	5,442	—	—	—	—	—	—
1832	12,478	—	6,268	659	—	5,609	—	—	—	—	—	—
1833	12,895	—	6,579	666	—	5,913	—	—	—	—	—	—
1834	13,396	—	7,030	669	—	6,361	—	—	—	—	—	—
1835	14,311	—	7,337	680	—	6,657	—	—	—	—	—	—
1836	16,874	—	9,945	857	—	9,088	—	—	—	—	—	—
1837	22,462	—	12,449	873	—	11,576	—	—	—	—	—	—
1838	17,948	—	9,197	717	—	8,480	—	—	—	—	—	—
1839	19,317	—	10,691	749	—	9,942	—	—	—	—	—	—
1840	21,616	—	12,330	789	—	11,541	—	—	—	—	—	—
1841	20,793	—	11,319	754	—	10,565	—	—	—	—	—	—
1842	22,851	—	10,780	781	—	9,999	—	—	—	—	—	—
1843	20,741	—	9,102	805	—	8,297	—	—	—	—	—	—
1844	20,919	—	8,730	813	—	7,917	—	—	—	—	—	—
1845	20,726	—	8,509	826	—	7,683	—	—	—	—	—	—
1846	39,165	—	27,867	2,003	—	25,864	—	—	—	—	—	—
1847	57,761	—	44,736	2,863	—	41,873	—	—	—	—	—	—
1848	60,308	—	47,319	2,865	—	44,454	—	—	—	—	—	—
1849	23,165	—	10,744	945	—	9,799	—	—	—	—	—	—
1850	20,824	—	10,929	948	—	9,981	—	—	—	—	—	—
1851	20,699	—	10,714	944	—	9,770	—	—	—	—	—	—
1852	21,349	—	11,376	957	—	10,419	—	—	—	—	—	—
1853	20,667	—	10,572	961	—	9,611	—	—	—	—	—	—
1854	21,134	—	10,894	956	—	9,938	—	—	—	—	—	—

Notes appear at end of table

(continued)

TABLE Ed26–47   Military personnel on active duty, by branch of service and sex: 1789–1995   *Continued*

	Total		Army					Air Force				
				Officers		Enlisted			Officers		Enlisted	
	Total	Female	Total	Total	Female	Total	Female	Total	Total	Female	Total	Female
	Ed26 [2]	Ed27 [2, 3]	Ed28 [4]	Ed29 [4, 5]	Ed30 [4, 5]	Ed31 [4, 5]	Ed32 [4, 5]	Ed33 [3]	Ed34 [3]	Ed35 [3]	Ed36 [3]	Ed37 [3]
Year	Number	Number	Number	Number	Number	Number	Number	Number	Number	Number	Number	Number
1855	26,402	—	15,911	1,042	—	14,869	—	—	—	—	—	—
1856	25,867	—	15,715	1,072	—	14,643	—	—	—	—	—	—
1857	27,345	—	15,918	1,097	—	14,821	—	—	—	—	—	—
1858	29,014	—	17,678	1,099	—	16,579	—	—	—	—	—	—
1859	28,978	—	17,243	1,070	—	16,173	—	—	—	—	—	—
1860	27,958	—	16,215	1,080	—	15,135	—	—	—	—	—	—
1861	217,112	—	186,845	—	—	—	—	—	—	—	—	—
1862	673,124	—	637,264	—	—	—	—	—	—	—	—	—
1863	960,061	—	918,354	—	—	—	—	—	—	—	—	—
1864	1,031,724	—	970,905	—	—	—	—	—	—	—	—	—
1865	1,062,848	—	1,000,692	—	—	—	—	—	—	—	—	—
1866	76,749	—	57,072	—	—	—	—	—	—	—	—	—
1867	74,786	—	57,194	3,056	—	54,138	—	—	—	—	—	—
1868	66,412	—	51,066	2,835	—	48,231	—	—	—	—	—	—
1869	51,632	—	36,953	2,700	—	34,253	—	—	—	—	—	—
1870	50,348	—	37,240	2,541	—	34,699	—	—	—	—	—	—
1871	42,238	—	29,115	2,105	—	27,010	—	—	—	—	—	—
1872	42,205	—	28,322	2,104	—	26,218	—	—	—	—	—	—
1873	43,228	—	28,812	2,076	—	26,736	—	—	—	—	—	—
1874	43,609	—	28,640	2,081	—	26,559	—	—	—	—	—	—
1875	38,105	—	25,513	2,068	—	23,445	—	—	—	—	—	—
1876	40,591	—	28,565	2,151	—	26,414	—	—	—	—	—	—
1877	34,094	—	24,140	2,177	—	21,963	—	—	—	—	—	—
1878	36,444	—	26,023	2,153	—	23,870	—	—	—	—	—	—
1879	38,022	—	26,601	2,127	—	24,474	—	—	—	—	—	—
1880	37,894	—	26,594	2,152	—	24,442	—	—	—	—	—	—
1881	37,845	—	25,842	2,181	—	23,661	—	—	—	—	—	—
1882	37,850	—	25,811	2,162	—	23,649	—	—	—	—	—	—
1883	37,278	—	25,652	2,143	—	23,509	—	—	—	—	—	—
1884	39,400	—	26,666	2,147	—	24,519	—	—	—	—	—	—
1885	39,098	—	27,157	2,154	—	25,003	—	—	—	—	—	—
1886	38,636	—	26,727	2,102	—	24,625	—	—	—	—	—	—
1887	38,763	—	26,719	2,200	—	24,519	—	—	—	—	—	—
1888	39,035	—	27,019	2,189	—	24,830	—	—	—	—	—	—
1889	39,452	—	27,759	2,177	—	25,582	—	—	—	—	—	—
1890	38,666	—	27,373	2,168	—	25,205	—	—	—	—	—	—
1891	37,868	—	26,463	2,052	—	24,411	—	—	—	—	—	—
1892	38,677	—	27,190	2,140	—	25,050	—	—	—	—	—	—
1893	39,492	—	27,830	2,158	—	25,672	—	—	—	—	—	—
1894	42,101	—	28,265	2,146	—	26,119	—	—	—	—	—	—
1895	42,226	—	27,495	2,154	—	25,341	—	—	—	—	—	—
1896	41,680	—	27,375	2,169	—	25,206	—	—	—	—	—	—
1897	43,656	—	27,865	2,179	—	25,686	—	—	—	—	—	—
1898	235,785	—	209,714	10,516	—	199,198	—	—	—	—	—	—
1899	100,166	—	80,670	3,581	—	77,089	—	—	—	—	—	—
1900	125,923	—	101,713	4,227	—	97,486	—	—	—	—	—	—
1901	112,322	—	85,557	3,468	—	82,089	—	—	—	—	—	—
1902	111,145	—	81,275	4,049	—	77,226	—	—	—	—	—	—
1903	106,043	—	69,595	3,927	—	65,668	—	—	—	—	—	—
1904	110,129	—	70,387	3,971	—	66,416	—	—	—	—	—	—
1905	108,301	—	67,526	4,034	—	63,492	—	—	—	—	—	—
1906	112,216	—	68,945	3,989	—	64,956	—	—	—	—	—	—
1907	108,375	—	64,170	3,896	—	60,274	—	—	—	—	—	—
1908	128,500	—	76,942	4,047	—	72,895	—	—	—	—	—	—
1909	142,200	—	84,971	4,299	—	80,672	—	—	—	—	—	—
1910	139,344	—	81,251	4,535	—	76,716	—	—	—	—	—	—
1911	144,846	—	84,006	4,585	—	79,421	—	—	—	—	—	—
1912	153,174	—	92,121	4,775	—	87,346	—	—	—	—	—	—
1913	154,914	—	92,756	4,970	—	87,786	—	—	—	—	—	—
1914	165,919	—	98,544	5,033	—	93,511	—	—	—	—	—	—

Notes appear at end of table

TABLE Ed26–47   Military personnel on active duty, by branch of service and sex: 1789–1995   *Continued*

	Total		Army						Air Force				
				Officers		Enlisted				Officers		Enlisted	
	Total	Female	Total	Total	Female	Total	Female	Total	Total	Female	Total	Female
	Ed26 [2]	Ed27 [2, 3]	Ed28 [4]	Ed29 [4, 5]	Ed30 [4, 5]	Ed31 [4, 5]	Ed32 [4, 5]	Ed33 [3]	Ed34 [3]	Ed35 [3]	Ed36 [3]	Ed37 [3]
Year	Number	Number	Number	Number	Number	Number	Number	Number	Number	Number	Number	Number
1915	174,112	—	106,754	4,948	—	101,806	—	—	—	—	—	—
1916	179,376	—	108,399	5,175	—	103,224	—	—	—	—	—	—
1917	643,833	—	421,467	34,224	—	387,243	—	—	—	—	—	—
1918	2,897,167	—	2,395,742	130,485	—	2,265,257	—	—	—	—	—	—
1919	1,172,602	—	851,624	91,975	—	759,649	—	—	—	—	—	—
1920	343,302	—	204,292	18,999	—	185,293	—	—	—	—	—	—
1921	386,542	—	230,725	16,501	—	214,224	—	—	—	—	—	—
1922	270,207	—	148,763	15,667	—	133,096	—	—	—	—	—	—
1923	247,011	—	133,243	14,021	—	119,222	—	—	—	—	—	—
1924	261,189	—	142,673	13,784	—	128,889	—	—	—	—	—	—
1925	251,756	—	137,048	14,594	—	122,454	—	—	—	—	—	—
1926	247,396	—	134,938	14,143	—	120,795	—	—	—	—	—	—
1927	248,943	—	134,829	14,020	—	120,809	—	—	—	—	—	—
1928	250,907	—	136,084	14,019	—	122,065	—	—	—	—	—	—
1929	255,031	—	139,118	14,047	—	125,071	—	—	—	—	—	—
1930	255,648	—	139,378	14,151	—	125,227	—	—	—	—	—	—
1931	252,605	—	140,516	14,159	—	126,357	—	—	—	—	—	—
1932	244,902	—	134,957	14,111	—	120,846	—	—	—	—	—	—
1933	243,845	—	136,547	13,896	—	122,651	—	—	—	—	—	—
1934	247,137	—	138,464	13,761	—	124,703	—	—	—	—	—	—
1935	251,799	—	139,486	13,471	—	126,015	—	—	—	—	—	—
1936	291,356	—	167,816	13,512	—	154,304	—	—	—	—	—	—
1937	311,808	—	179,968	13,740	—	166,228	—	—	—	—	—	—
1938	322,932	—	185,488	13,975	—	171,513	—	—	—	—	—	—
1939	334,473	—	189,839	14,486	—	175,353	—	—	—	—	—	—
1940	458,365	—	269,023	18,326	—	250,697	—	—	—	—	—	—
1941	1,801,101	—	1,462,315	99,536	—	1,362,779	—	—	—	—	—	—
1942	3,858,791	—	3,075,608	206,422	—	2,869,186	—	—	—	—	—	—
1943	9,044,745	—	6,994,472	579,576	—	6,414,896	—	—	—	—	—	—
1944	11,451,719	—	7,994,750	776,980	—	7,217,770	—	—	—	—	—	—
1945	12,055,884	266,256	8,266,373	891,663	62,775	7,374,710	93,095	—	—	—	—	—
1946	3,024,893	—	1,435,496	185,411	—	1,248,764	—	455,515	81,733	—	373,782	—
1947	1,582,111	—	685,458	89,759	—	594,078	—	305,827	42,745	—	263,082	—
1948	1,444,283	14,458	554,030	68,178	4,829	484,061	3,266	387,730	48,957	733	338,773	1,433
1949	1,613,686	18,081	660,473	77,272	5,021	581,422	4,256	419,347	57,851	973	361,496	2,347
1950	1,459,462	22,069	593,167	72,566	4,431	518,921	6,551	411,277	57,006	1,532	354,271	3,782
1951	3,249,371	39,625	1,531,774	130,540	6,970	1,399,362	10,883	788,381	107,099	2,735	681,282	7,514
1952	3,635,912	45,934	1,596,419	148,427	7,206	1,446,266	10,228	983,261	128,742	3,827	854,519	10,943
1953	3,555,067	45,485	1,533,815	145,633	6,501	1,386,500	8,760	977,593	130,769	4,139	846,824	11,779
1954	3,302,104	38,600	1,404,598	128,208	5,807	1,274,803	6,787	947,918	129,752	3,558	818,166	9,728
1955	2,935,107	35,191	1,109,296	121,947	5,222	985,659	7,716	959,946	137,149	3,080	822,797	8,282
1956	2,806,441	33,646	1,025,778	118,364	4,876	905,711	7,770	909,958	142,093	3,334	767,602	7,853
1957	2,794,761	32,173	997,994	111,187	4,574	885,056	7,156	919,835	140,563	3,700	778,768	7,458
1958	2,599,518	31,176	898,925	104,716	4,390	792,508	7,074	871,156	132,939	3,608	737,048	7,212
1959	2,503,631	31,718	861,964	101,690	4,331	758,458	7,837	840,435	131,602	3,630	707,219	6,371
1960	2,475,438	31,550	873,078	101,236	4,263	770,112	8,279	814,752	129,689	3,675	683,114	5,651
1961	2,482,905	32,071	858,622	99,921	4,251	756,932	8,560	821,151	128,793	3,680	690,091	5,296
1962	2,805,603	32,213	1,066,404	116,050	4,353	948,597	8,721	884,025	134,908	3,954	746,597	4,822
1963	2,698,927	30,771	975,916	108,302	3,852	865,768	8,292	869,431	133,763	3,909	733,008	4,804
1964	2,685,782	29,795	973,238	110,870	3,772	860,514	7,958	856,798	133,389	4,031	720,571	4,845
1965	2,653,926	30,610	969,066	112,120	3,806	854,929	8,520	824,662	131,578	4,100	690,177	4,741
1966	3,092,175	32,589	1,199,784	117,786	4,143	1,079,682	9,179	887,353	130,724	4,189	753,477	5,050
1967	3,375,485	35,173	1,442,498	143,517	4,742	1,296,603	9,741	897,494	135,485	4,670	758,648	5,188
1968	3,546,071	38,397	1,570,343	166,173	5,096	1,401,727	10,711	904,850	139,691	4,991	761,507	6,123
1969	3,458,072	39,506	1,512,169	172,590	5,157	1,337,047	10,721	862,353	135,476	4,858	722,936	7,407
1970	3,064,760	41,479	1,322,548	166,721	5,248	1,153,013	11,476	791,349	129,803	4,667	657,402	8,987
1971	2,713,044	42,775	1,123,810	148,950	5,040	971,872	11,825	755,300	125,919	4,718	624,980	10,132
1972	2,321,959	45,033	810,960	121,290	4,422	686,695	12,349	725,838	121,674	4,766	599,774	11,725
1973	2,251,936	55,402	800,973	116,205	4,279	681,972	16,457	691,182	115,036	4,727	571,790	15,023
1974	2,162,005	74,715	783,330	105,998	4,388	674,466	26,327	643,970	110,491	4,767	529,067	19,465

Notes appear at end of table

(continued)

TABLE Ed26–47   Military personnel on active duty, by branch of service and sex: 1789–1995   Continued

	Total		Army						Air Force				
				Officers		Enlisted				Officers		Enlisted	
	Total	Female	Total	Total	Female	Total	Female	Total	Total	Female	Total	Female
	Ed26 [2]	Ed27 [2,3]	Ed28 [4]	Ed29 [4,5]	Ed30 [4,5]	Ed31 [4,5]	Ed32 [4,5]	Ed33 [3]	Ed34 [3]	Ed35 [3]	Ed36 [3]	Ed37 [3]
Year	Number	Number	Number	Number	Number	Number	Number	Number	Number	Number	Number	Number
1975	2,128,120	96,868	784,333	102,992	4,594	678,324	37,701	612,751	105,161	4,981	503,176	25,232
1976	2,081,910	109,133	779,417	98,647	4,844	677,725	43,806	585,416	99,787	4,967	481,214	29,235
1977	2,074,543	118,966	782,246	97,738	5,696	680,062	46,094	570,695	96,256	5,383	469,878	34,610
1978	2,061,708	134,312	771,624	97,785	6,292	669,515	50,549	569,712	95,463	6,010	469,862	41,084
1979	2,026,892	151,082	758,852	97,381	6,866	657,184	55,151	559,455	96,135	7,276	458,953	46,427
1980	2,050,627	171,418	777,036	98,717	7,609	673,944	61,729	557,969	97,649	8,493	455,909	51,901
1981	2,082,560	184,651	781,419	101,850	8,349	675,087	65,304	570,302	99,367	9,106	466,520	54,372
1982	2,108,612	189,048	780,391	103,109	9,033	672,699	64,071	582,845	101,890	9,942	476,472	54,506
1983	2,123,349	197,878	779,643	105,674	9,490	669,364	66,535	592,044	104,556	10,560	483,022	55,305
1984	2,138,157	202,830	780,180	107,883	10,230	667,711	67,126	597,125	106,239	11,234	486,410	55,882
1985	2,151,032	211,606	780,787	109,687	10,828	666,557	68,419	601,515	108,400	11,927	488,603	58,134
1986	2,169,112	218,889	780,980	109,757	11,263	666,668	69,669	608,199	109,048	12,377	494,666	61,227
1987	2,174,217	223,805	780,815	107,964	11,569	668,410	71,608	607,035	107,338	12,642	495,244	63,239
1988	2,138,213	224,836	771,847	106,963	11,750	660,445	72,018	576,446	105,126	12,899	466,856	61,549
1989	2,130,229	232,823	769,741	106,877	12,197	658,321	74,297	570,880	103,697	13,403	462,831	63,700
1990	2,043,705	227,018	732,403	104,498	12,204	623,519	71,217	535,233	100,045	13,331	430,818	60,803
1991	1,985,555	221,138	710,821	103,703	12,532	602,777	67,774	510,432	96,599	13,323	409,425	59,113
1992	1,807,177	210,048	610,450	94,845	11,738	511,335	61,692	470,315	90,376	12,683	375,684	56,106
1993	1,705,103	203,506	572,423	87,845	11,140	480,379	60,188	444,351	84,073	12,251	356,126	54,481
1994	1,610,490	199,688	541,343	84,807	10,884	452,513	58,994	426,327	81,003	12,332	341,317	53,992
1995 [6]	1,547,185	198,057	524,897	85,010	10,995	435,803	58,478	408,657	79,800	12,129	324,645	52,816

	Navy					Marines				
		Officers		Enlisted			Officers		Enlisted	
	Total	Total	Female	Total	Female	Total	Total	Female	Total	Female
	Ed38 [4]	Ed39 [4]	Ed40 [4]	Ed41 [4]	Ed42 [4]	Ed43 [4]	Ed44 [4]	Ed45 [4]	Ed46 [4]	Ed47 [4]
Year	Number	Number	Number	Number	Number	Number	Number	Number	Number	Number
1789	—	—	—	—	—	—	—	—	—	—
1794	1,856	150	—	1,706	—	—	—	—	—	—
1795	1,856	150	—	1,706	—	—	—	—	—	—
1798	1,856	150	—	1,706	—	83	25	—	58	—
1799	2,200	200	—	2,000	—	368	25	—	343	—
1800	5,400	400	—	5,000	—	525	38	—	487	—
1801	2,700	200	—	2,500	—	357	38	—	319	—
1802	2,200	200	—	2,000	—	359	29	—	330	—
1803	1,700	200	—	1,500	—	342	25	—	317	—
1804	2,200	200	—	2,000	—	389	25	—	364	—
1805	3,191	191	—	3,000	—	578	22	—	556	—
1806	1,105	191	—	914	—	318	11	—	307	—
1807	2,145	191	—	1,954	—	403	11	—	392	—
1808	1,616	191	—	1,425	—	872	11	—	861	—
1809	4,875	450	—	4,425	—	523	10	—	513	—
1810	5,149	450	—	4,699	—	449	9	—	440	—
1811	5,364	454	—	4,910	—	556	14	—	542	—
1812	5,452	442	—	5,010	—	493	10	—	483	—
1813	5,525	525	—	5,000	—	591	12	—	579	—
1814	8,024	524	—	7,500	—	648	11	—	637	—
1815	6,773	531	—	6,242	—	688	8	—	680	—
1816	6,040	500	—	5,540	—	472	21	—	451	—
1817	5,494	494	—	5,000	—	666	14	—	652	—
1818	5,545	545	—	5,000	—	560	24	—	536	—
1819	4,068	568	—	3,500	—	685	21	—	664	—
1820	3,988	537	—	3,451	—	571	19	—	552	—
1821	3,935	484	—	3,451	—	879	35	—	844	—
1822	3,774	534	—	3,240	—	731	23	—	708	—
1823	4,053	553	—	3,500	—	701	20	—	681	—
1824	4,095	531	—	3,564	—	940	50	—	890	—

Notes appear at end of table

TABLE Ed26–47   Military personnel on active duty, by branch of service and sex: 1789–1995   *Continued*

	Navy					Marines				
	Officers		Enlisted			Officers		Enlisted		
	Total	Total	Female	Total	Female	Total	Total	Female	Total	Female
	Ed38 [4]	Ed39 [4]	Ed40 [4]	Ed41 [4]	Ed42 [4]	Ed43 [4]	Ed44 [4]	Ed45 [4]	Ed46 [4]	Ed47 [4]
Year	Number	Number	Number	Number	Number	Number	Number	Number	Number	Number
1825	4,405	505	—	3,900	—	781	35	—	746	—
1826	4,762	471	—	4,291	—	835	39	—	796	—
1827	4,796	505	—	4,291	—	946	43	—	903	—
1828	4,797	506	—	4,291	—	932	40	—	892	—
1829	4,869	555	—	4,314	—	895	43	—	852	—
1830	4,929	615	—	4,314	—	891	37	—	854	—
1831	4,303	612	—	3,691	—	815	35	—	780	—
1832	5,312	642	—	4,670	—	898	38	—	860	—
1833	5,420	664	—	4,756	—	896	43	—	853	—
1834	5,451	695	—	4,756	—	915	46	—	869	—
1835	5,557	756	—	4,801	—	1,417	68	—	1,349	—
1836	5,588	787	—	4,801	—	1,341	43	—	1,298	—
1837	8,452	801	—	7,651	—	1,561	37	—	1,524	—
1838	7,656	847	—	6,809	—	1,095	28	—	1,067	—
1839	7,676	922	—	6,754	—	950	34	—	916	—
1840	8,017	932	—	7,085	—	1,269	46	—	1,223	—
1841	8,274	940	—	7,334	—	1,200	44	—	1,156	—
1842	10,782	998	—	9,784	—	1,289	46	—	1,243	—
1843	10,555	1,055	—	9,500	—	1,084	43	—	1,041	—
1844	11,103	1,063	—	10,040	—	1,086	40	—	1,046	—
1845	11,189	1,095	—	10,094	—	1,028	42	—	986	—
1846	10,131	1,053	—	9,078	—	1,167	41	—	1,126	—
1847	11,193	1,126	—	10,067	—	1,832	75	—	1,757	—
1848	11,238	1,141	—	10,097	—	1,751	42	—	1,709	—
1849	11,345	1,282	—	10,063	—	1,076	46	—	1,030	—
1850	8,794	1,273	—	7,521	—	1,101	46	—	1,055	—
1851	8,792	1,246	—	7,546	—	1,193	43	—	1,150	—
1852	8,805	1,232	—	7,573	—	1,168	47	—	1,121	—
1853	8,841	1,250	—	7,591	—	1,254	49	—	1,205	—
1854	8,879	1,254	—	7,625	—	1,361	49	—	1,312	—
1855	8,887	1,236	—	7,651	—	1,604	52	—	1,552	—
1856	8,681	1,027	—	7,654	—	1,471	57	—	1,414	—
1857	9,676	1,031	—	8,645	—	1,751	57	—	1,694	—
1858	9,729	1,068	—	8,661	—	1,607	52	—	1,555	—
1859	9,884	1,117	—	8,767	—	1,851	47	—	1,804	—
1860	9,942	1,150	—	8,792	—	1,801	46	—	1,755	—
1861	27,881	1,114	—	26,767	—	2,386	48	—	2,338	—
1862	33,454	3,224	—	30,230	—	2,406	51	—	2,355	—
1863	38,707	4,209	—	34,498	—	3,000	69	—	2,931	—
1864	57,680	5,679	—	52,001	—	3,139	64	—	3,075	—
1865	58,296	6,759	—	51,537	—	3,860	87	—	3,773	—
1866	16,340	2,297	—	14,043	—	3,337	79	—	3,258	—
1867	14,081	1,801	—	12,280	—	3,511	73	—	3,438	—
1868	12,268	1,976	—	10,292	—	3,078	81	—	2,997	—
1869	12,295	1,649	—	10,646	—	2,384	70	—	2,314	—
1870	10,562	1,551	—	9,011	—	2,546	77	—	2,469	—
1871	10,610	1,702	—	8,908	—	2,513	74	—	2,439	—
1872	11,680	1,699	—	9,981	—	2,203	77	—	2,126	—
1873	11,654	1,655	—	9,999	—	2,762	87	—	2,675	—
1874	12,700	1,595	—	11,105	—	2,269	85	—	2,184	—
1875	10,479	1,571	—	8,908	—	2,113	76	—	2,037	—
1876	10,046	1,646	—	8,400	—	1,980	76	—	1,904	—
1877	8,057	1,591	—	6,466	—	1,897	73	—	1,824	—
1878	8,087	1,582	—	6,505	—	2,334	77	—	2,257	—
1879	9,453	1,695	—	7,758	—	1,968	62	—	1,906	—
1880	9,361	1,713	—	7,648	—	1,939	69	—	1,870	—
1881	10,101	1,866	—	8,235	—	1,902	70	—	1,832	—
1882	10,170	1,911	—	8,259	—	1,869	63	—	1,806	—
1883	9,842	1,819	—	8,023	—	1,784	60	—	1,724	—
1884	10,846	1,660	—	9,186	—	1,888	66	—	1,822	—

Notes appear at end of table

(continued)

TABLE Ed26–47 Military personnel on active duty, by branch of service and sex: 1789–1995 *Continued*

	Navy					Marines				
		Officers		Enlisted			Officers		Enlisted	
	Total	Total	Female	Total	Female	Total	Total	Female	Total	Female
	Ed38 [4]	Ed39 [4]	Ed40 [4]	Ed41 [4]	Ed42 [4]	Ed43 [4]	Ed44 [4]	Ed45 [4]	Ed46 [4]	Ed47 [4]
Year	Number	Number	Number	Number	Number	Number	Number	Number	Number	Number
1885	10,057	1,611	—	8,446	—	1,884	65	—	1,819	—
1886	9,909	1,549	—	8,360	—	2,000	66	—	1,934	—
1887	10,113	1,542	—	8,571	—	1,931	61	—	1,870	—
1888	10,115	1,528	—	8,587	—	1,901	72	—	1,829	—
1889	9,921	1,530	—	8,391	—	1,772	54	—	1,718	—
1890	9,246	1,489	—	7,757	—	2,047	61	—	1,986	—
1891	9,247	1,510	—	7,737	—	2,158	66	—	2,092	—
1892	9,448	1,468	—	7,980	—	2,039	66	—	1,973	—
1893	9,529	1,486	—	8,043	—	2,133	63	—	2,070	—
1894	11,460	1,405	—	10,055	—	2,376	67	—	2,309	—
1895	11,846	1,412	—	10,434	—	2,885	71	—	2,814	—
1896	12,088	1,425	—	10,663	—	2,217	72	—	2,145	—
1897	11,985	1,399	—	10,586	—	3,806	71	—	3,735	—
1898	22,492	1,432	—	21,060	—	3,579	98	—	3,481	—
1899	16,354	1,588	—	14,766	—	3,142	76	—	3,066	—
1900	18,796	1,683	—	17,113	—	5,414	174	—	5,240	—
1901	20,900	1,742	—	19,158	—	5,865	171	—	5,694	—
1902	23,648	1,822	—	21,826	—	6,222	191	—	6,031	—
1903	29,790	1,893	—	27,897	—	6,658	213	—	6,445	—
1904	32,158	2,014	—	30,144	—	7,584	255	—	7,329	—
1905	33,764	2,079	—	31,685	—	7,011	270	—	6,741	—
1906	35,053	2,133	—	32,920	—	8,218	278	—	7,940	—
1907	36,119	2,238	—	33,881	—	8,086	279	—	7,807	—
1908	42,322	2,463	—	39,859	—	9,236	283	—	8,953	—
1909	47,533	2,630	—	44,903	—	9,696	328	—	9,368	—
1910	48,533	2,699	—	45,834	—	9,560	328	—	9,232	—
1911	51,230	2,886	—	48,344	—	9,610	328	—	9,282	—
1912	51,357	3,074	—	48,283	—	9,696	337	—	9,359	—
1913	52,202	3,273	—	48,929	—	9,956	331	—	9,625	—
1914	56,989	3,406	—	53,583	—	10,386	336	—	10,050	—
1915	57,072	3,593	—	53,479	—	10,286	338	—	9,948	—
1916	60,376	4,022	—	56,354	—	10,601	348	—	10,253	—
1917	194,617	8,383	—	186,234	—	27,749	776	—	26,973	—
1918	448,606	23,631	—	424,975	—	52,819	1,503	—	51,316	—
1919	272,144	19,357	—	252,787	—	48,834	2,270	—	46,564	—
1920	121,845	10,642	—	111,203	—	17,165	1,104	—	16,061	—
1921	132,827	9,979	—	122,848	—	22,990	1,087	—	21,903	—
1922	100,211	8,334	—	91,877	—	21,233	1,135	—	20,098	—
1923	94,094	8,410	—	85,684	—	19,674	1,141	—	18,533	—
1924	98,184	8,651	—	89,533	—	20,332	1,157	—	19,175	—
1925	95,230	8,918	—	86,312	—	19,478	1,168	—	18,310	—
1926	93,304	9,091	—	84,213	—	19,154	1,178	—	17,976	—
1927	94,916	9,440	—	85,476	—	19,198	1,198	—	18,000	—
1928	95,803	9,401	—	86,402	—	19,020	1,198	—	17,822	—
1929	97,117	9,434	—	87,683	—	18,796	1,181	—	17,615	—
1930	96,890	9,540	—	87,350	—	19,380	1,208	—	18,172	—
1931	93,307	9,849	—	83,458	—	18,782	1,196	—	17,586	—
1932	93,384	9,967	—	83,417	—	16,561	1,196	—	15,365	—
1933	91,230	9,947	—	81,283	—	16,068	1,192	—	14,876	—
1934	92,312	9,972	—	82,340	—	16,361	1,187	—	15,174	—
1935	95,053	10,115	—	84,938	—	17,260	1,163	—	16,097	—
1936	106,292	10,247	—	96,045	—	17,248	1,208	—	16,040	—
1937	113,617	10,367	—	103,250	—	18,223	1,312	—	16,911	—
1938	119,088	10,739	—	108,349	—	18,356	1,359	—	16,997	—
1939	125,202	12,023	—	113,179	—	19,432	1,380	—	18,052	—
1940	160,997	13,604	—	147,393	—	28,345	1,800	—	26,545	—
1941	284,427	29,092	—	255,335	—	54,359	3,339	—	51,020	—
1942	640,570	69,564	—	571,006	—	142,613	7,138	—	135,475	—
1943	1,741,750	179,676	—	1,562,074	—	308,523	21,384	—	287,139	—
1944	2,981,365	276,153	—	2,705,212	—	475,604	32,788	—	442,816	—

Notes appear at end of table

TABLE Ed26-47   Military personnel on active duty, by branch of service and sex: 1789-1995   *Continued*

	Navy					Marines				
		Officers		Enlisted			Officers		Enlisted	
	Total	Total	Female	Total	Female	Total	Total	Female	Total	Female
	Ed38 [4]	Ed39 [4]	Ed40 [4]	Ed41 [4]	Ed42 [4]	Ed43 [4]	Ed44 [4]	Ed45 [4]	Ed46 [4]	Ed47 [4]
Year	Number	Number	Number	Number	Number	Number	Number	Number	Number	Number
1945	3,319,586	331,379	19,188	2,988,207	72,833	469,925	37,067	809	432,858	17,556
1946	978,203	141,161	—	834,722	—	155,679	14,208	—	141,471	—
1947	497,773	52,434	—	442,729	—	93,053	7,506	—	85,547	—
1948	417,535	45,416	2,412	369,136	1,618	84,988	6,907	8	78,081	159
1949	447,901	47,975	2,511	396,895	2,620	85,965	7,250	31	78,715	322
1950	380,739	44,641	2,447	332,905	2,746	74,279	7,254	45	67,025	535
1951	736,596	70,513	4,190	663,326	5,268	192,620	15,150	63	177,470	2,002
1952	824,265	82,247	4,026	738,451	7,242	231,967	16,413	115	215,554	2,347
1953	794,440	81,731	3,636	709,254	8,008	249,219	18,731	160	230,488	2,502
1954	725,720	77,280	3,273	644,965	6,945	223,868	18,593	163	205,275	2,339
1955	660,695	74,527	2,936	582,675	5,707	205,170	18,417	135	186,753	2,113
1956	669,925	71,770	2,852	594,509	5,214	200,780	17,809	113	182,971	1,634
1957	676,071	73,703	2,831	599,733	4,837	200,861	17,434	107	183,427	1,510
1958	639,942	71,560	2,696	564,899	4,551	189,495	16,741	115	172,754	1,530
1959	625,661	69,795	2,738	553,332	4,985	175,571	16,065	123	159,506	1,703
1960	616,987	69,559	2,711	544,770	5,360	170,621	16,203	123	154,418	1,488
1961	626,223	69,981	2,736	552,262	5,936	176,909	16,132	117	160,777	1,495
1962	664,212	75,302	2,740	584,773	5,926	190,962	16,861	121	174,101	1,576
1963	663,897	75,549	2,660	584,235	5,556	189,683	16,737	135	172,946	1,563
1964	665,969	76,400	2,678	585,419	5,063	189,777	16,843	128	172,934	1,320
1965	669,985	77,866	2,601	587,940	5,261	190,213	17,258	140	172,955	1,441
1966	743,322	79,805	2,808	659,186	5,388	261,716	20,512	153	241,204	1,679
1967	750,224	81,902	3,018	663,923	5,503	285,269	23,592	189	261,677	2,122
1968	763,626	85,425	3,032	673,610	5,664	307,252	24,555	225	282,697	2,555
1969	773,779	85,199	2,884	684,145	5,752	309,771	25,698	284	284,073	2,443
1970	691,126	80,761	2,888	605,899	5,795	259,737	24,941	299	234,796	2,119
1971	621,565	74,782	2,871	542,298	5,930	212,369	21,765	278	190,604	1,981
1972	586,923	73,155	3,185	510,669	6,257	198,238	19,843	263	178,395	2,066
1973	563,683	70,566	3,454	490,009	9,174	196,098	19,282	315	176,816	1,973
1974	545,903	67,227	3,649	475,479	13,381	188,802	18,740	336	170,062	2,402
1975	535,085	65,680	3,676	466,121	17,498	195,951	18,591	345	177,360	2,841
1976	524,678	63,718	3,544	457,692	19,288	192,399	18,882	386	173,517	3,063
1977	529,895	63,312	3,791	462,176	19,464	191,707	18,650	422	173,057	3,506
1978	529,557	62,639	3,980	463,217	21,312	190,815	18,388	433	172,427	4,652
1979	523,335	62,384	4,358	457,102	25,044	185,250	18,229	459	167,021	5,501
1980	527,153	63,058	4,877	459,569	30,103	188,469	18,198	487	170,271	6,219
1981	540,219	65,462	5,345	470,184	34,558	190,620	18,363	526	172,257	7,091
1982	552,996	67,273	5,740	481,186	37,321	192,380	18,975	560	173,405	7,875
1983	557,573	68,494	6,300	484,568	40,792	194,089	19,983	623	174,106	8,273
1984	564,638	68,856	6,553	491,288	42,580	196,214	20,366	648	175,848	8,577
1985	570,705	70,657	6,913	495,444	45,690	198,025	20,175	654	177,850	9,041
1986	581,119	72,051	7,260	504,389	47,204	198,814	20,199	643	178,615	9,246
1987	586,842	72,038	7,223	510,208	47,735	199,525	20,047	649	179,478	9,140
1988	592,570	72,427	7,335	515,548	49,672	197,350	20,079	653	177,271	8,960
1989	592,652	72,153	7,453	515,898	52,065	196,956	20,099	696	176,857	9,012
1990	579,417	72,090	7,808	502,804	52,099	196,652	19,958	677	176,694	8,679
1991	570,262	70,824	7,981	495,103	51,410	194,040	19,753	685	174,287	8,320
1992	541,883	69,099	8,294	468,412	51,011	184,529	19,132	649	165,397	7,875
1993	509,950	66,346	8,265	439,461	49,336	178,379	18,430	639	159,949	7,206
1994	468,662	61,750	7,966	402,635	47,859	174,158	17,823	643	156,335	7,028
1995 [6]	441,685	60,498	7,912	378,069	47,722	171,946	17,871	655	153,449	7,350

[1] Beginning in 1878 for the Army, 1900 for the Navy, and 1798 for the Marine Corps, data are based on totals as of June 30. For prior years, the month for which the most complete records were available was used.

[2] Excludes Coast Guard. Beginning 1980, excludes Naval Reserve personnel on active duty for Training and Administration of Reserves (TARS).

[3] As of June 30 for years 1976 and prior; as of September 30 for years after 1976.

[4] Includes Army personnel assigned to other commands.

[5] Represents command strength prior to June 30, 1956.

[6] As of June 30.

Sources

U.S. Office of the Assistant Secretary of Defense (Comptroller), *Selected Manpower Statistics*, U.S. Department of Defense (DOD), Directorate for Infor-

mation, Operations and Reports (various years); and unpublished DOD data.

Recent data in some categories are available at the Directorate for Information, Operations, and Reports.

Documentation

Data include cadets as well as reserve and retired regular personnel on extended or continuous active duty.

Data for the Air Force are included with the Army prior to 1946. For 1946 and 1947, the Air Force series includes Army Air Force figures. See the essay on national defense, wars, and armed forces in this chapter for a discussion of the creation of the Air Force.

TABLE Ed48–81   Military reserve personnel, by branch of service and reserve status: 1946–1996[1]

Contributed by Scott Sigmund Gartner

	All military									
	Total Reserve	Total Ready and Standby Reserve	Active Duty Reserve	Selected Reserve	Reserve not on active duty	Individual Ready Reserve, Inactive National Guard, and Standby Reserve	Officers		Enlisted	
							Total Reserve	Active Reserve	Total Reserve	Active Reserve
	Ed48	Ed49	Ed50	Ed51	Ed52	Ed53	Ed54	Ed55	Ed56	Ed57
Year	Number	Number	Number	Number	Number	Number	Number	Number	Number	Number
1946	—	—	—	—	—	—	—	—	—	—
1947	—	—	—	—	2,026,537	—	—	—	—	—
1948	2,685,126	—	87,875	—	2,597,251	—	939,099	70,020	1,746,027	17,855
1949	2,597,647	—	111,868	—	2,485,779	—	973,470	94,165	1,624,177	17,703
1950	2,730,915	—	100,351	—	2,630,564	—	1,006,633	84,261	1,724,282	16,090
1951	2,733,655	—	731,175	—	2,002,480	—	1,050,444	215,497	1,683,211	515,678
1952	2,446,507	—	507,797	—	1,938,710	—	1,066,984	256,237	1,379,523	251,560
1953	2,474,299	—	377,901	—	2,096,398	—	953,526	255,727	1,520,773	122,174
1954	2,821,436	—	334,076	—	2,487,360	—	916,429	236,489	1,905,007	97,587
1955	3,305,888	—	320,592	—	2,985,296	—	866,139	238,186	2,439,749	82,406
1956	3,916,177	—	334,944	—	3,581,173	—	850,504	233,938	3,065,613	101,006
1957	4,010,870	—	379,199	—	3,631,671	—	840,604	225,499	3,170,266	153,700
1958	4,335,515	—	313,454	—	4,022,061	—	808,645	186,278	3,526,870	127,176
1959	4,600,633	—	246,628	—	4,354,005	—	804,860	171,734	3,795,773	74,894
1960	4,367,059	—	219,765	—	4,147,294	—	803,518	163,757	3,563,541	56,008
1961	3,965,507	—	209,261	—	3,756,246	—	804,778	159,375	3,160,729	49,886
1962	3,359,548	—	364,915	—	2,994,633	—	796,140	182,052	2,563,408	182,863
1963	2,669,144	—	233,612	—	2,435,532	—	799,374	173,036	1,869,770	60,576
1964	2,781,067	—	230,351	—	2,550,716	—	798,797	172,388	1,982,270	57,963
1965	2,808,250	—	231,845	—	2,576,405	—	809,977	169,591	1,998,273	62,254
1966	3,026,042	—	257,414	—	2,768,628	—	822,638	175,641	2,203,404	81,773
1967	3,061,055	—	303,441	—	2,757,614	—	865,026	209,215	2,196,029	94,226
1968	3,194,731	—	349,997	—	2,884,734	—	879,107	236,828	2,315,624	113,169
1969	3,570,393	—	310,926	—	3,259,467	—	889,615	239,787	2,680,778	71,139
1970	3,914,876	—	275,398	—	3,639,478	—	913,069	226,604	3,001,807	48,794
1971	4,149,913	—	245,851	—	3,904,062	—	915,901	197,883	3,234,012	47,968
1972	3,916,835	—	205,614	—	3,711,221	—	912,172	160,152	3,004,663	45,462
1973	3,598,844	—	186,507	—	3,412,337	—	873,988	145,963	2,724,856	40,544
1974	3,232,953	—	168,387	—	3,064,566	—	844,557	128,862	2,388,396	39,525
1975	2,816,447	—	160,631	—	2,655,816	—	823,963	121,837	1,992,484	38,794
1976	2,573,950	—	155,169	—	2,418,781	—	809,939	113,220	1,764,011	41,949
1977	2,400,295	1,457,196	151,266	807,549	2,249,029	649,647	804,298	109,731	1,595,997	41,535
1978	2,277,551	1,326,902	159,157	787,767	2,118,394	539,135	790,246	109,742	1,487,305	49,415
1979	2,273,929	1,306,063	165,089	807,136	2,108,840	498,927	—	—	—	—
1980	2,337,022	1,360,035	167,537	868,717	2,169,485	491,318	—	—	—	—
1981	—	1,392,088	—	917,189	—	474,899	—	—	—	—
1982	—	1,422,454	—	974,578	—	447,876	—	—	—	—
1983	—	1,464,497	—	1,004,547	—	459,950	—	—	—	—
1984	—	1,534,107	—	1,045,828	—	488,279	—	—	—	—
1985	—	1,610,082	—	1,088,062	—	522,020	—	—	—	—
1986	—	1,653,258	—	1,130,100	—	523,158	—	—	—	—
1987	—	1,657,399	—	1,150,855	—	506,544	—	—	—	—
1988	—	1,676,920	—	1,158,357	—	518,563	—	—	—	—
1989	—	1,660,810	—	1,170,560	—	490,250	—	—	—	—
1990	—	1,670,847	—	1,153,213	—	517,634	—	—	—	—
1991	—	1,786,328	—	1,154,570	—	631,758	—	—	—	—
1992	—	1,882,659	—	1,114,905	—	767,754	—	—	—	—
1993	—	1,866,904	—	1,057,676	—	809,228	—	—	—	—
1994	—	1,804,936	—	998,330	—	806,606	—	—	—	—
1995	—	1,659,001	—	945,852	—	713,149	—	—	—	—
1996	—	1,550,077	—	920,438	—	629,639	—	—	—	—

Note appears at end of table

TABLE Ed48–81   Military reserve personnel, by branch of service and reserve status: 1946–1996   *Continued*

	Army National Guard				Army				Navy			
	Active Duty Reserve	Ready and Standby Reserve	Reserve not on active duty	Individual Ready Reserve and Inactive National Guard	Active Duty Reserve	Ready and Standby Reserve	Reserve not on active duty	Individual Ready Reserve and Inactive National Guard	Active Duty Reserve	Ready and Standby Reserve	Reserve not on active duty	Individual Ready Reserve and Inactive National Guard
	Ed58	Ed59	Ed60	Ed61	Ed62	Ed63	Ed64	Ed65	Ed66	Ed67	Ed68	Ed69
Year	Number	Number	Number	Number	Number	Number	Number	Number	Number	Number	Number	Number
1946	—	—	—	—	—	—	—	—	462,009	—	222,130	—
1947	—	—	78,241	—	—	—	710,094	—	27,976	—	763,385	—
1948	309	—	289,531	—	39,090	—	752,271	—	20,503	—	987,319	—
1949	575	—	313,805	—	54,149	—	588,972	—	21,638	—	1,027,595	—
1950	489	—	352,883	—	44,107	—	613,526	—	18,454	—	1,115,285	—
1951	96,076	—	241,547	—	205,338	—	465,484	—	183,680	—	919,726	—
1952	53,810	—	234,206	—	118,444	—	520,376	—	159,940	—	770,837	—
1953	15,150	—	278,164	—	115,119	—	798,026	—	120,173	—	665,571	—
1954	10,656	—	338,669	—	107,791	—	1,108,967	—	82,843	—	595,359	—
1955	8,334	—	378,046	—	102,688	—	1,648,626	—	75,122	—	466,067	—
1956	5,551	—	420,535	—	106,016	—	1,975,559	—	86,072	—	547,640	—
1957	5,354	—	441,798	—	124,779	—	1,839,474	—	94,986	—	583,733	—
1958	3,775	—	442,369	—	104,773	—	2,034,598	—	84,543	—	674,763	—
1959	2,035	—	404,036	—	74,976	—	2,282,550	—	75,059	—	727,727	—
1960	1,624	—	407,549	—	63,018	—	2,217,472	—	69,901	—	672,227	—
1961	1,401	—	400,455	—	58,762	—	1,893,747	—	67,599	—	648,446	—
1962	43,599	—	366,517	—	128,884	—	1,445,901	—	84,861	—	539,185	—
1963	1,977	—	368,017	—	64,897	—	1,092,834	—	83,775	—	446,712	—
1964	1,543	—	389,067	—	67,976	—	1,131,782	—	82,791	—	471,451	—
1965	1,477	—	385,981	—	68,808	—	1,128,566	—	88,051	—	467,681	—
1966	1,436	—	426,258	—	74,373	—	1,222,165	—	96,608	—	479,830	—
1967	1,524	—	420,565	—	100,115	—	1,217,984	—	108,960	—	479,213	—
1968	12,780	—	390,798	—	127,513	—	1,335,230	—	108,535	—	458,249	—
1969	12,142	—	389,862	—	134,025	—	1,605,906	—	79,996	—	509,222	—
1970	1,721	—	409,872	—	121,575	—	1,811,235	—	73,804	—	573,705	—
1971	1,480	—	403,457	—	102,592	—	2,033,269	—	69,498	—	568,330	—
1972	1,248	—	388,384	—	71,905	—	2,003,660	—	65,904	—	503,628	—
1973	1,304	—	386,633	—	66,057	—	1,752,989	—	57,048	—	503,622	—
1974	1,042	—	411,603	—	55,798	—	1,465,513	—	53,185	—	456,956	—
1975	1,082	—	403,057	—	53,373	—	1,228,341	—	51,687	—	387,173	—
1976	1,145	—	377,097	—	51,432	—	1,011,576	226,380	53,099	—	373,146	—
1977	1,170	365,406	365,406	10,700	51,636	491,631	877,999	149,427	52,358	244,998	366,671	106,087
1978	1,531	349,615	349,615	8,619	52,307	437,037	828,341	168,607	59,959	212,656	337,395	93,207
1979	1,617	350,041	350,041	4,513	52,924	422,337	823,162	201,803	63,836	199,828	326,527	85,521
1980	1,482	373,788	373,788	7,203	53,078	431,329	843,784	198,737	65,011	217,495	335,612	96,973
1981	—	399,530	—	10,521	—	442,942	—	205,897	—	217,584	—	99,251
1982	—	418,570	—	10,969	—	476,007	—	218,991	—	200,246	—	77,738
1983	—	427,239	—	10,061	—	512,810	—	246,361	—	191,894	—	70,270
1984	—	443,739	—	9,480	—	551,957	—	276,651	—	201,215	—	69,173
1985	—	450,696	—	10,744	—	594,171	—	301,825	—	214,265	—	71,462
1986	—	455,716	—	9,522	—	610,845	—	300,818	—	227,747	—	73,824
1987	—	462,143	—	10,285	—	601,488	—	287,459	—	237,748	—	78,429
1988	—	464,154	—	8,972	—	606,112	—	292,857	—	244,225	—	83,969
1989	—	467,086	—	10,126	—	594,464	—	274,588	—	248,040	—	86,556
1990	—	455,260	—	11,036	—	595,107	—	284,248	—	252,019	—	87,439
1991	—	454,194	—	8,073	—	669,944	—	359,074	—	270,961	—	107,345
1992	—	433,764	—	7,236	—	722,489	—	418,592	—	296,765	—	144,681
1993	—	416,813	—	6,894	—	714,857	—	438,036	—	302,387	—	156,257
1994	—	403,698	—	6,770	—	673,236	—	412,235	—	317,435	—	195,614
1995	—	381,372	—	6,442	—	619,218	—	376,790	—	280,063	—	166,759
1996	—	375,267	—	5,292	—	545,478	—	318,229	—	262,452	—	152,451

(continued)

TABLE Ed48–81   Military reserve personnel, by branch of service and reserve status: 1946–1996 *Continued*

	Marines				Air National Guard				Air Force Reserve			
	Active Duty Reserve	Ready and Standby Reserve	Reserve not on active duty	Individual Ready Reserve and Inactive National Guard	Active Duty Reserve	Ready and Standby Reserve	Reserve not on active duty	Individual Ready Reserve and Inactive National Guard	Active Duty Reserve	Ready and Standby Reserve	Reserve not on active duty	Individual Ready Reserve and Inactive National Guard
	Ed70	Ed71	Ed72	Ed73	Ed74	Ed75	Ed76	Ed77	Ed78	Ed79	Ed80	Ed81
Year	Number	Number	Number	Number	Number	Number	Number	Number	Number	Number	Number	Number
1946	53,039	—	22,807	—	—	—	—	—	—	—	—	—
1947	2,507	—	45,536	—	—	—	10,087	—	—	—	419,194	—
1948	1,623	—	111,122	—	13	—	29,048	—	26,337	—	427,960	—
1949	1,694	—	123,817	—	24	—	41,418	—	33,788	—	390,172	—
1950	2,398	—	128,839	—	14	—	45,084	—	34,889	—	374,947	—
1951	82,381	—	40,367	—	36,500	—	20,114	—	127,200	—	315,242	—
1952	19,347	—	81,435	—	33,358	—	15,006	—	122,898	—	316,850	—
1953	19,165	—	78,455	—	4,719	—	35,556	—	103,575	—	240,626	—
1954	29,019	—	138,846	—	1,746	—	49,845	—	102,021	—	255,674	—
1955	24,974	—	185,677	—	1,019	—	61,306	—	108,455	—	245,574	—
1956	22,816	—	229,641	—	3,679	—	63,534	—	110,810	—	344,264	—
1957	40,356	—	270,300	—	887	—	67,950	—	112,837	—	428,416	—
1958	31,295	—	301,376	—	346	—	69,995	—	88,722	—	498,960	—
1959	12,360	—	315,930	—	257	—	70,994	—	81,941	—	552,768	—
1960	8,369	—	258,477	—	277	—	70,820	—	76,576	—	520,749	—
1961	7,275	—	242,691	—	225	—	70,895	—	73,999	—	500,102	—
1962	9,016	—	177,581	—	21,028	—	50,319	—	77,527	—	415,130	—
1963	8,211	—	134,336	—	390	—	74,325	—	74,362	—	319,308	—
1964	7,344	—	136,001	—	361	—	73,217	—	70,336	—	349,198	—
1965	6,923	—	134,002	—	299	—	76,410	—	66,287	—	383,765	—
1966	18,026	—	148,977	—	225	—	79,883	—	66,746	—	411,515	—
1967	20,090	—	144,288	—	154	—	83,758	—	72,598	—	411,806	—
1968	12,424	—	167,910	—	10,336	—	75,261	—	78,409	—	417,286	—
1969	12,899	—	202,578	—	879	—	83,414	—	70,985	—	468,485	—
1970	11,618	—	234,418	—	387	—	89,847	—	66,293	—	520,401	—
1971	9,343	—	270,657	—	403	—	85,689	—	62,535	—	542,660	—
1972	7,695	—	246,193	—	236	—	89,237	—	58,626	—	480,119	—
1973	8,199	—	221,100	—	229	—	90,371	—	53,670	—	457,622	—
1974	8,234	—	182,872	—	209	—	94,892	—	49,919	—	452,730	—
1975	7,908	—	133,728	—	224	—	95,759	—	46,357	—	407,758	—
1976	7,082	—	116,210	—	220	—	91,459	—	42,191	—	449,293	—
1977	6,223	105,024	108,843	45,277	189	92,092	92,092	252	39,690	158,045	438,018	63,422
1978	5,548	93,082	97,531	39,614	256	91,901	91,901	227	39,556	142,611	413,611	45,795
1979	5,060	95,209	100,378	59,207	299	93,599	93,599	220	41,353	145,049	415,133	44,242
1980	5,152	94,183	102,370	56,592	270	96,595	96,572	312	42,544	146,645	417,359	45,469
1981	—	90,496	—	51,411	—	98,418	—	125	—	143,118	—	43,744
1982	—	86,508	—	44,574	—	100,777	—	120	—	140,346	—	43,389
1983	—	91,340	—	46,537	—	102,189	—	19	—	139,025	—	42,865
1984	—	91,669	—	48,429	—	105,037	—	25	—	140,490	—	40,966
1985	—	91,941	—	47,855	—	109,490	—	92	—	149,519	—	45,983
1986	—	93,140	—	49,340	—	112,759	—	167	—	153,051	—	48,709
1987	—	88,243	—	44,580	—	114,595	—	0	—	153,182	—	48,288
1988	—	87,406	—	42,389	—	115,221	—	0	—	159,802	—	55,914
1989	—	81,529	—	36,552	—	116,061	—	0	—	153,630	—	53,117
1990	—	82,779	—	36,825	—	117,786	—	0	—	167,896	—	68,714
1991	—	95,989	—	50,401	—	117,786	—	0	—	177,454	—	78,681
1992	—	106,924	—	64,200	—	119,083	—	0	—	203,634	—	108,187
1993	—	111,604	—	69,539	—	117,162	—	0	—	204,081	—	112,248
1994	—	108,585	—	67,639	—	113,587	—	0	—	188,395	—	98,848
1995	—	103,884	—	62,735	—	109,825	—	0	—	164,639	—	74,919
1996	—	101,534	—	59,281	—	110,484	—	0	—	154,862	—	66,827

[1] Data after 1976 are based on September totals; data prior to 1977 are based on June totals.

Sources

U.S. Office of the Assistant Secretary of Defense (Comptroller), *Selected Manpower Statistics*, U.S. Department of Defense, Directorate for Information, Operations and Reports (various years).

Data after 1986 available from the Directorate for Information, Operations, and Reports Internet site, accessed June 1, 2000.

Documentation

There are seven Reserve components: the Army National Guard, Army Reserve, Naval Reserve, Marine Corps Reserve, Air National Guard, Air Force Reserve, and Coast Guard Reserve. Within the Reserve components, personnel serve in one of three manpower management categories: Ready Reserve, Standby Reserve, and Retired Reserve. There is no Standby Reserve in the Army National Guard or Air National Guard. The Ready Reserve is made up of three subgroups: the Selected Reserve, the Individual Ready Reserve (IRR),

TABLE Ed48-81   Military reserve personnel, by branch of service and reserve status: 1946-1996   Continued

and the Inactive National Guard (ING). There is no IRR or ING in the Air National Guard. The Selected Reserve consists of Reserve unit members, to include those in training, Individual Mobilization Augmentee (IMA) members, as well as Full-Time Support (FTS) personnel.

For definitions of terms see the glossary in the essay on national defense, wars, and armed forces, in this chapter.

In 1970, in response to the forthcoming end of the Selective Service and cutbacks likely associated with withdrawal from Vietnam, Secretary of Defense Melvin Laird introduced the concept of "Total Force" to the military. The policy's basic tenet was that the Guard and Reserve should constitute the primary augmentation for the active component in a military emergency; prior to this it was performed by the Selective Service. The United States would henceforth rely on the Guard and Reserve to sustain active military operations. Therefore, in the 1970s the data reflect a tremendous shift in manpower associated with the creation of an all-volunteer army, the end of the Selective Service and the Vietnam War, and the new policy of reliance on Guard and Reserve troops for active missions.

Series Ed48-49. The largest change in accounting between these series is the exclusion of the Retired Reserve, which represented a significant portion of total Reserve personnel.

Series Ed50-51. Series Ed50 indicates all Reserve personnel called into service. The highest point of the active Reserve force was during the Korean Conflict, in which Reserve units were used instead of draftees, whereas the

lowest point was during the Vietnam Conflict. Series Ed51 refers predominantly to the Selected Reserve, which after the structural changes associated with Total Force became a much larger portion of military manpower.

Series Ed52-53. Series Ed52 refers to all military personnel who are categorized as "reserve" but are not active. This group includes Retired Reserves as well as most Guard and Reserve units. Series Ed53 refers to all inactive Ready Reserves, which would include a large number of IRRs. Note that this does not include the Retired Reserve.

Series Ed58-59, Ed62-63, Ed66-67, Ed70-71, Ed74-75, and Ed78-79. The series covering the 1948-1980 period roughly account for Reserve personnel who most closely resemble the Selected Reserve personnel. The other series, those beginning in 1977, include Ready Reserve, which comprises the Selected Reserve, the IRR, and the Standby Reserve. Initially the IRR was the larger of the two branches of the Ready Reserve force but Total Force policy has made the Selected Reserve the larger portion of Reserve personnel.

Series Ed60-61, Ed64-65, Ed68-69, Ed72-73, Ed76-77, and Ed80-81. The series covering the 1948-1980 period account for Reserve strength before Total Force was implemented. These figures include all nonactive personnel, including retired personnel. The other series represent Reserve personnel numbers under Total Force and exclude retired personnel. However, nonactive IRR personnel are included; hence, there is some overlap with the figures presented in series Ed58-59, Ed62-63, Ed66-67, Ed70-71, Ed74-75, and Ed78-79.

TABLE Ed82-119   Selected characteristics of the armed forces – personnel, draftees, medical care, and military pay, by war: 1861-1975

Contributed by Scott Sigmund Gartner

War	Military personnel						Draftees			
	Total	Army	Air Force	Navy	Marines	Coast Guard	Classified	Examined	Rejected	Inducted
	Ed82	Ed83	Ed84	Ed85	Ed86	Ed87	Ed88	Ed89	Ed90	Ed91
	Thousand	Thousand	Thousand	Thousand	Thousand	Thousand	Thousand	Thousand	Thousand	Thousand
Civil War (Union only)	2,213	2,129	—	84 [5]	— [5]	—	777	522	160	46
Spanish–American War	307	281	—	23	3	—	—	—	—	—
World War I	4,735	4,057	—	599	79	9	24,234	3,764	803	2,820
World War II	16,354	11,260	—	4,183	669	241	36,677	17,955	6,420	10,022
Korean Conflict	5,764	2,834	1,285	1,177	424	44	9,123	3,685	1,189	1,560
Vietnam Conflict [4]	—	—	—	—	—	—	75,717	8,611	3,880	1,759

War	Average duration of service			Overseas service		Occupations of enlisted personnel – percentage distribution						
	All personnel	Officers	Enlisted	Percentage of total military personnel	Average months served	Technical and scientific	Administrative and clerical	Mechanics and repairmen	Craftsmen	Service workers	Operators and laborers	Military-type occupations, not elsewhere classified
	Ed92	Ed93	Ed94	Ed95	Ed96 [1,2]	Ed97	Ed98	Ed99	Ed100	Ed101	Ed102	Ed103
	Thousand	Per 1,000	Months	Months	Months	Percent	Months	Percent	Percent	Percent	Percent	Percent
Civil War (Union only)	20	—	—	—	—	0.2 [7]	0.7 [7]	0.1 [7]	0.5 [7]	2.4 [7]	2.9 [7]	93.2 [7]
Spanish–American War	8	8	8	29 [1]	1.5	0.5 [7]	3.1 [7]	1.0 [7]	0.1 [7]	6.5 [7]	2.2 [7]	86.6 [7]
World War I	12	14	12	53	5.5	3.7 [7]	8.0 [7]	8.5 [7]	13.0 [7]	12.5 [7]	20.2 [7]	34.1 [7]
World War II	33	39	33	73 [6]	16.2	10.4	12.6	16.6	5.9	9.6	6.1	38.8
Korean Conflict	19	24	18	56	13.4	12.7	18.1	15.3	4.7	12.4	6.5	30.3
Vietnam Conflict [4]	23	—	—	—	—	—	—	—	—	—	—	—

Notes appear at end of table

(continued)

TABLE Ed82–119   Selected characteristics of the armed forces – personnel, draftees, medical care, and military pay, by war: 1861–1975 *Continued*

	Medical care									
	Army					Navy and Marine Corps				
	Admissions for care, all causes		Noneffectiveness, total			Admissions for care, all causes		Noneffectiveness, total		
	Total	Annual rate per 1,000 average strength	Man-days lost	Daily rate per 1,000 average strength	Wounded who died subsequently	Total	Annual rate per 1,000 average strength	Man-days lost	Daily rate per 1,000 average strength	Percentage of wounded who died subsequently
	Ed104	Ed105	Ed106	Ed107	Ed108	Ed109	Ed110	Ed111	Ed112	Ed113
War	Percent	Percent	Thousand	Per 1,000	Percent	Thousand	Per 1,000	Thousand	Per 1,000	Percent
Civil War (Union only)	6,455	2,478	—	—	13.3	—	—	—	—	—
Spanish–American War	317	2,146	4,355	80.7	6.3	25	1,038	248	28.3	5.9
World War I	4,039	978	86,947	57.7	8.1	1,073	1,024	12,705	33.2	9.0
World War II	17,919	704	413,393	44.5	4.5	5,514	553	115,700	31.8	3.2
Korean Conflict	2,717	511	49,810	25.7	2.6	1,200	337	23,998	18.5	2.2
Vietnam Conflict [4]	—	—	—	—	—	—	—	—	—	—

	Military pay, annual					
	Basic pay			Pay and allowances		
	All personnel	Officers	Enlisted personnel	All personnel	Officers	Enlisted personnel
	Ed114	Ed115	Ed116	Ed117	Ed118	Ed119
War	Dollars	Dollars	Dollars	Dollars	Dollars	Dollars
Civil War (Union only)	231	717	202	510	1,912	427
Spanish–American War	282	2,101	205	528	2,489	444
World War I	510	2,141	417	968	2,698	870
World War II	1,017	2,442	856	1,811	3,777	1,587
Korean Conflict	1,776	4,453	1,473	2,940	6,234	2,584
Vietnam Conflict [4]	5,715	11,876	4,690	6,811	14,043	5,607

[1] Excludes Navy.

[2] During hostilities only.

[3] "Pay and allowances" interpreted as "regular military compensation (RMC)."

[4] For military pay, 1972 outlays used as representative of Vietnam Conflict.

[5] Navy and Marines combined.

[6] Army and Marines only.

[7] Army personnel only.

Sources

The President's Commission on Veterans Pensions, *Veterans' Benefits in the United States*, volume 1; Staff Report number 4, "Veterans in our Society,"

House Committee Print 261, 84th Congress, 2d session; and revised estimates prepared by the U.S. Department of Defense (DOD).

Vietnam Conflict: DOD unpublished data.

Documentation

For the Revolutionary War, the number of personnel serving is not known, but estimates range from 184,000 to 250,000; for the War of 1812, 286,730 served; and for the Mexican War, 78,710 served.

TABLE Ed120–129   Selective Service registrants, by classification: 1940–1970[1]

Contributed by Scott Sigmund Gartner

	Classification status of registrants, 18 1/2 to 26 years old									
	Total	Class I: available for military service	Class IV: conscientious objectors	Class I: fulfilling military obligation	Class IV: completed military obligation	Class II and III: deferred	Class IV: exempted	Class IV: disqualified for military service	Unclassified	Inducted
	Ed120	Ed121	Ed122	Ed123	Ed124	Ed125	Ed126	Ed127	Ed128	Ed129
Year	Thousand	Thousand	Thousand	Thousand	Thousand	Thousand	Thousand	Thousand	Thousand	Thousand
1940 [2]	16,317	—	—	—	—	—	—	—	—	19
1941 [3]	14,690	982	6	974	99	10,760	213	1,098	558	924
1942 [4]	28,477	1,572	11	5,778	—	15,690	190	2,418	2,820	3,033
1943 [5]	22,138	1,090	—	8,970	—	8,560	—	3,353	—	3,324
1944 [6]	8,654	480	—	5,803	117	841	—	1,364	—	1,592
1945 [6]	8,817	444	—	6,228	—	809	—	1,288	—	946
1946 [7]	3,459	268	9	—	—	305	—	2,261	—	184
1947 [8]	3,690	268	8	—	—	278	—	2,217	—	—
1948	8,946	501	5	47	213	212	17	234	7,718	20
1949	8,924	1,233	9	271	2,719	882	34	523	3,253	10
1950	9,239	1,402	12	870	2,699	1,236	50	907	2,063	220
1951	8,638	1,154	8	2,375	1,995	1,288	67	1,283	468	552
1952	8,993	1,117	5	3,364	1,253	1,483	75	1,532	164	438
1953	9,727	1,116	3	4,052	578	1,529	72	1,818	559	472
1954	10,157	1,564	5	4,219	255	1,439	70	1,992	612	253
1955	10,609	1,736	5	4,221	113	1,419	67	2,122	926	153
1956	11,087	1,904	6	1,903	2,281	1,361	63	2,293	1,275	152
1957	11,674	2,105	7	1,969	2,275	1,372	64	2,574	1,309	139
1958	12,376	2,132	8	2,037	2,231	1,607	67	2,936	1,359	142
1959	13,179	2,295	9	2,069	2,211	1,804	68	3,145	1,578	96
1960	14,057	2,287	9	2,180	2,191	2,014	70	3,315	1,992	87
1961	14,868	2,329	10	2,448	2,132	2,302	76	3,421	2,152	119
1962	15,410	2,298	10	2,543	2,175	2,534	79	3,598	2,174	82
1963	16,027	1,743	8	2,645	2,243	3,613	82	3,593	2,101	119
1964	16,835	2,006	11	2,856	2,304	4,899	95	4,149	514	112
1965	17,968	1,485	10	3,167	2,399	5,830	103	4,640	334	231
1966	18,971	1,165	9	3,733	2,521	6,091	115	4,988	350	382
1967	19,901	1,412	11	3,802	2,672	6,578	121	4,909	396	228
1968	20,829	1,446	13	3,887	2,946	6,798	126	5,189	424	296
1969	21,785	1,469	16	3,885	3,308	6,971	130	5,583	425	284
1970	22,705	2,596	28	3,504	3,801	6,151	130	5,959	537	163

[1] Data for 1940–1947 are for varying dates and age groups, as noted, and refer to conterminous United States; totals include classes not shown separately. Data for 1948–1970 are as of December 31 and include Puerto Rico and outlying areas.

[2] As of October 20, ages 21–35.

[3] As of September 30, ages 21–35.

[4] As of December 31, ages 18–37.

[5] As of December 1, ages 18–37.

[6] As of December 1, ages 18–25.

[7] As of December 2, ages 18–29. Excludes classes I-C (already in armed forces) and III-A (registrants having dependents).

[8] As of April 1, ages 18–29. Excludes classes I-C (already in armed forces) and III-A (registrants having dependents).

Sources

U. S. Selective Service System.

U.S. Bureau of the Census, *Historical Statistics of the United States, Colonial Times to 1970, Bicentennial Edition* (1975), Series Y 917–926, p. 1136.

TABLE Ed130-145 Defendants charged with violation of Selective Service Act, by disposition of case: 1945–1970

Contributed by Scott Sigmund Gartner

	Total	Not convicted				Convicted and sentenced				Type of sentence						
		Total	Dismissed	Acquitted by		Total	Plea of guilty or nolo contendre	Convicted by		Total	Imprisonment				Probation, fine, and other	Average sentence of imprisonment
				Court	Jury			Court	Jury		1 year and 1 day and under	Over 1 year and 1 day to 3 years	3 to 5 years	5 years and over		
	Ed130	Ed131	Ed132	Ed133	Ed134	Ed135	Ed136	Ed137	Ed138	Ed139	Ed140	Ed141	Ed142	Ed143	Ed144	Ed145
Year	Number	Number	Number	Number	Number	Number	Number	Number	Number	Number	Number	Number	Number	Number	Number	Months
1945	4,287	1,449	1,399	25	25	2,838	1,823	319	696	2,368	438	775	744	411	470	32
1946	2,651	999	953	26	20	1,652	1,130	222	300	1,339	547	501	244	47	313	21
1947	2,074	937	908	18	11	1,137	898	178	61	775	394	317	61	3	362	14
1948	833	529	511	7	11	304	264	11	29	212	133	69	9	1	92	14
1949	506	214	202	3	9	292	263	20	9	213	134	62	17	0	79	15
1950	449	274	272	1	1	175	156	6	13	109	78	24	6	1	66	13
1951	368	212	202	6	4	156	105	24	27	123	35	37	29	22	33	30
1952	561	248	222	16	10	313	160	97	56	272	58	77	97	40	41	31
1953	630	285	236	39	10	345	185	129	31	280	61	101	84	34	65	29
1954	822	398	278	116	4	424	194	185	45	356	78	137	126	15	68	26
1955	719	430	367	57	6	289	157	106	26	217	54	105	47	11	72	25
1956	371	185	167	16	2	186	109	67	10	123	35	50	35	3	63	24
1957	357	95	75	17	3	262	183	70	9	194	60	85	41	8	68	24
1958	325	96	66	26	4	229	154	66	9	190	66	81	42	1	39	22
1959	258	56	44	11	1	202	159	39	4	152	46	63	39	4	50	23
1960	239	73	65	7	1	166	131	31	4	126	47	48	28	3	40	22
1961	244	45	37	8	0	199	160	33	6	141	45	59	35	2	58	23
1962	274	49	46	2	1	225	182	31	12	164	58	75	28	3	61	22
1963	338	73	66	7	0	265	212	46	7	189	79	65	36	9	76	22
1964	276	70	63	6	1	206	161	32	13	146	46	77	22	1	60	21
1965	341	99	88	8	3	242	197	28	17	189	64	90	30	5	53	21
1966	516	145	132	11	2	371	265	74	32	301	61	128	95	17	70	26
1967	996	248	224	22	2	748	538	141	69	666	47	270	291	58	82	32
1968	1,192	408	353	49	6	784	520	196	68	580	44	131	301	104	204	37
1969	1,744	844	747	88	9	900	511	252	137	544	40	155	261	88	356	36
1970	2,833	1,806	1,570	222	14	1,027	570	321	136	450	53	144	208	45	577	33

Source

U.S. Administrative Office of the U.S. Courts, *Federal Offenders in the U.S. District Courts* (1970), Table H10.

Documentation

Series Ed139–143. Includes sentences of more than six months that are to be followed by a term of probation (mixed sentences).

Series Ed140. Includes split sentences where a defendant receives a sentence on a one-count indictment of six months or less in a jail-type institution, followed by a term of probation. Included in the figures are mixed sentences involving confinement for six months or less on one count, to be followed by a term of probation on one or more other counts.

MILITARY EXPENDITURES

Scott Sigmund Gartner

TABLE Ed146–154   National defense outlays and veterans' benefits: 1915–1995

Contributed by Scott Sigmund Gartner

	Defense and veterans' benefits outlays				Annual percentage change, defense and veterans' benefits			Defense as a percentage of	
		Defense							
	Total	Current dollars	Constant dollars	Veterans' benefits	Total	Defense	Veterans' benefits	Total federal outlays	Gross domestic product
	Ed146	Ed147	Ed148	Ed149	Ed150 [1]	Ed151 [1]	Ed152 [1]	Ed153	Ed154
Fiscal year	Billion dollars	Billion dollars	Billion 1995 dollars	Billion dollars	Percent	Percent	Percent	Percent	Percent
1915	0.5	0.3	4.5	0.2	—	—	—	—	—
1916	0.5	0.3	4.1	0.2	—	—	—	—	—
1917	0.8	0.6	7.1	0.2	—	—	—	—	—
1918	7.3	7.1	71.6	0.2	—	—	—	—	—
1919	13.9	13.5	118.9	0.3	—	—	—	—	—
1920	4.3	4.0	30.4	0.3	—	—	—	—	—
1921	3.2	2.6	22.1	0.6	—	—	—	—	—
1922	1.6	0.9	8.1	0.7	—	—	—	—	—
1923	1.4	0.7	6.2	0.7	—	—	—	—	—
1924	1.3	0.6	5.3	0.7	—	—	—	—	—
1925	1.3	0.6	5.2	0.7	—	—	—	—	—
1926	1.4	0.6	5.1	0.8	—	—	—	—	—
1927	1.4	0.6	5.2	0.8	—	—	—	—	—
1928	1.5	0.7	6.2	0.8	—	—	—	—	—
1929	1.5	0.7	6.2	0.8	—	—	—	—	—
1930	1.6	0.7	6.3	0.8	—		—	—	—
1931	1.8	0.7	7.0	1.0	—		—	—	—
1932	1.7	0.7	7.7	1.0	—	—	—	—	—
1933	1.5	0.6	7.0	0.9	—	—	—	—	—
1934	1.1	0.5	5.6	0.6	—	—	—	—	—
1935	1.3	0.7	7.7	0.6	—	—	—	—	—
1936	3.3	0.9	9.8	2.4	—	—	—	—	—
1937	2.1	0.9	9.5	1.1	—	—	—	—	—
1938	1.6	1.0	10.8	0.6	—	—	—	—	—
1939	1.6	1.1	12.0	0.6	—	—	—	—	—
1940	2.1	1.5	16.3	0.6	—	—	—	16.5	1.4
1941	6.6	6.0	62.2	0.6	—	—	—	45.7	4.7
1942	24.5	23.9	223.4	0.6	—	—	—	70.4	14.7
1943	63.8	63.2	556.7	0.6	—	—	—	79.6	31.8
1944	77.4	76.7	664.1	0.7	—	—	—	80.8	34.9
1945	83.3	81.2	687.4	2.1	—	—	—	82.7	36.4
1946	47.6	43.2	337.6	4.4	—	—	—	71.7	19.4
1947	21.7	14.4	98.4	7.4	—	—	—	37.0	5.8
1948	18.4	11.8	74.6	6.7	—	—	—	35.7	4.3
1949	19.6	12.9	82.6	6.7	—	—	—	32.7	4.8
1950	19.7	13.0	82.2	6.6	—	—	—	32.9	4.4
1951	27.8	22.4	131.2	5.3	—	—	—	51.1	6.5
1952	48.8	44.0	253.0	4.9	—	—	—	67.4	12.2
1953	54.7	50.4	287.6	4.3	—	—	—	68.1	13.2
1954	51.2	46.9	265.7	4.3	—	—	—	69.6	12.3
1955	45.1	40.6	230.8	4.5	—	—	—	63.2	9.7
1956	45.4	40.7	228.0	4.8	—	—	—	61.5	9.2
1957	48.1	43.3	234.8	4.8	—	—	—	62.9	9.3
1958	49.2	44.2	233.0	5.0	—	—	—	62.0	9.4
1959	51.5	46.4	243.0	5.2	—	—	—	57.9	9.1
1960	53.5	48.1	247.6	5.4	2.5	2.4	3.1	52.2	9.1
1961	52.3	46.6	237.5	5.7	−2.5	−3.1	5.6	47.6	8.5
1962	56.0	50.5	254.8	5.6	7.1	8.2	−3.1	47.2	8.6
1963	57.0	51.5	256.4	5.5	1.8	2.2	−1.8	46.3	8.3
1964	58.4	52.7	259.0	5.7	2.5	2.3	3.6	44.4	7.9

Note appears at end of table   (continued)

TABLE Ed146–154   National defense outlays and veterans' benefits: 1915–1995 *Continued*

	Defense and veterans' benefits outlays				Annual percentage change, defense and veterans' benefits			Defense as a percentage of	
		Defense							
	Total	Current dollars	Constant dollars	Veterans' benefits	Total	Defense	Veterans' benefits	Total federal outlays	Gross domestic product
	Ed146	Ed147	Ed148	Ed149	Ed150 [1]	Ed151 [1]	Ed152 [1]	Ed153	Ed154
Fiscal year	Billion dollars	Billion dollars	Billion 1995 dollars	Billion dollars	Percent	Percent	Percent	Percent	Percent
1965	56.3	50.6	244.8	5.7	−6.8	−7.6	0.7	42.8	7.0
1966	64.0	58.1	273.2	5.9	13.7	14.8	3.5	43.2	7.3
1967	78.1	71.4	325.7	6.7	22.1	22.9	13.8	45.4	8.5
1968	88.9	81.9	358.6	7.0	13.8	14.7	4.4	46.0	8.9
1969	90.1	82.5	342.5	7.6	1.3	0.7	8.5	44.9	8.3
1970	90.4	81.7	320.9	8.7	0.3	−1.0	13.6	41.8	7.8
1971	88.7	78.9	296.8	9.8	−1.9	−3.5	12.7	37.5	6.9
1972	89.9	79.2	288.7	10.7	1.4	0.4	9.8	34.3	6.3
1973	88.7	76.7	263.2	12.0	1.3	−3.1	12.0	31.2	5.5
1974	92.7	79.3	245.1	13.4	4.6	3.5	11.4	29.5	5.2
1975	103.1	86.5	245.0	16.6	11.2	9.0	24.0	26.0	5.2
1976	108.1	89.6	239.9	18.4	4.8	3.6	11.0	24.1	4.9
(TQ)	26.2	22.3	59.7	4.0	—	—	—	23.2	—
1977	115.2	97.2	244.4	18.0	6.7	8.5	−2.1	23.8	4.7
1978	123.5	104.5	244.2	19.0	7.1	7.5	5.2	22.8	4.5
1979	136.2	116.3	244.1	19.9	10.4	11.3	5.0	23.1	4.5
1980	155.2	134.0	247.8	21.2	13.9	15.2	6.3	22.7	4.7
1981	180.5	157.5	264.0	23.0	16.3	17.6	8.5	23.2	5.0
1982	209.3	185.3	292.6	24.0	15.9	17.6	4.2	24.8	5.6
1983	234.7	209.9	321.1	24.8	12.1	13.3	3.3	26.0	5.9
1984	253.0	227.4	333.5	25.6	7.8	8.3	3.2	26.7	5.7
1985	279.0	252.7	357.9	26.3	10.3	11.1	2.7	26.7	5.9
1986	299.8	273.4	380.1	26.4	7.4	8.2	0.4	27.6	6.1
1987	308.8	282.0	378.3	26.8	3.0	3.1	1.5	28.1	5.9
1988	319.8	290.4	374.1	29.4	3.6	3.0	9.7	27.3	5.6
1989	333.7	303.6	373.1	30.1	4.3	4.5	2.4	26.6	5.5
1990	328.4	299.3	348.9	29.1	−1.6	−1.4	−3.3	23.9	5.1
1991	304.6	273.3	305.8	31.3	−7.2	−8.7	7.6	20.7	4.5
1992	332.5	298.4	324.1	34.1	12.0	12.4	8.0	21.6	4.7
1993	326.1	291.1	307.0	35.7	−1.9	−2.4	4.6	20.7	4.3
1994	319.2	281.6	289.5	37.6	−2.3	−3.3	5.3	19.3	3.9
1995	310.0	271.6	271.6	38.4	−2.9	−3.6	2.1	17.6	3.6

(TQ) Transition quarter.

[1] Change from prior year shown; for 1960, change from 1955.

Sources

U.S. Office of Management and Budget, *Historical Tables* (annual).

U.S. Census Bureau, *Statistical Abstract of the United States* (various years; primarily 1999, 1993, 1975, 1970, 1965, 1960, 1955).

Documentation

Figures include outlays of Department of Defense, Department of Veterans Affairs, and other agencies for activities primarily related to national defense and veterans programs. Minus sign indicates decline. See U.S. Bureau of the Census, *U.S. Historical Statistics, Colonial Times to 1970* (1975), series Y 472, 473 and Y 476, for related data.

Series Ed148. Constant dollars obtained using series Cc1.

Series Ed154. Calculated by dividing series Ed147 by series Ca1.

TABLE Ed155–167   Federal budget outlays for national defense: 1967–1996

Contributed by Scott Sigmund Gartner

			Defense Department, military										
				Personnel								Atomic	Defense-
		Percentage change from prior year	Total	Outlays	As a percentage of total Defense Department expenditures	Operation and maintenance	Procurement	Research and development	Military construction	Family housing	Other	energy activities	related activities
	Total												
	Ed155	Ed156	Ed157	Ed158	Ed159	Ed160	Ed161	Ed162	Ed163	Ed164	Ed165	Ed166	Ed167
Year	Billion dollars	Percent	Billion dollars	Billion dollars	Percent	Billion dollars	Billion dollars	Billion dollars	Billion dollars	Billion dollars	Billion dollars	Billion dollars	Billion dollars
1967	70.0	—	67.5	18.0	26.6	12.3	19.0	7.2	1.5	0.5	0.4	2.3	(Z)
1968	80.5	15.0	77.4	19.9	25.7	19.0	23.3	7.7	1.3	0.5	1.9	2.5	0.1
1969	81.2	0.9	77.9	21.4	27.4	20.6	24.0	7.5	1.4	0.6	−1.7	2.5	0.3
1970	80.2	−1.2	77.1	23.0	29.9	22.2	21.6	7.2	1.2	0.6	−0.9	2.5	0.1
1971	77.7	−3.1	74.5	22.6	30.4	21.6	18.9	7.3	1.1	0.6	−0.3	2.3	−0.1
1972	78.3	0.8	75.1	23.0	30.7	20.9	17.1	7.9	1.1	0.7	−0.3	2.4	0.1
1973	76.0	−2.9	73.2	23.2	31.7	21.7	15.7	8.2	1.1	0.7	−1.1	2.4	0.2
1974	79.3	4.3	79.1	30.4	38.4	22.5	15.2	8.6	1.4	0.9	0.1	1.5	−1.2
1975	86.5	9.1	85.9	32.2	37.5	26.3	16.0	8.9	1.5	1.1	−0.1	1.5	0.9
1976	89.6	3.6	88.1	32.5	36.9	27.8	16.0	8.9	2.0	1.2	−0.4	1.6	(Z)
1977	97.2	8.5	95.3	33.7	35.4	30.6	18.2	9.8	1.9	1.4	−0.2	1.9	(Z)
1978	104.5	7.5	102.3	35.6	34.8	33.6	20.0	10.5	1.9	1.4	−0.6	2.1	0.1
1979	116.3	11.3	113.6	37.3	32.9	36.4	25.4	11.2	2.1	1.5	−0.3	2.5	0.2
1980	134.0	15.2	130.9	40.9	31.2	44.8	29.0	13.1	2.5	1.7	−1.1	2.9	0.2
1981	157.5	17.5	153.9	47.9	31.2	51.9	35.2	15.3	2.5	1.7	−0.6	3.4	0.2
1982	185.3	17.7	180.7	55.2	30.5	59.7	43.3	17.7	2.9	2.0	−0.1	4.3	0.3
1983	209.9	13.3	204.4	60.9	29.8	64.9	53.6	20.6	3.5	2.1	−1.2	5.2	0.3
1984	227.4	8.3	220.9	64.2	29.0	67.4	61.9	23.1	3.7	2.4	−1.7	6.1	0.4
1985	252.7	11.1	245.2	67.8	27.7	72.4	70.4	27.1	4.3	2.6	0.6	7.1	0.5
1986	273.4	8.2	265.5	71.5	26.9	75.3	76.5	32.3	5.1	2.8	2.0	7.4	0.5
1987	282.0	3.2	274.0	72.0	26.3	76.2	80.3	33.8	5.9	2.9	2.8	7.5	0.6
1988	290.4	3.0	281.9	76.3	27.1	84.5	77.2	34.8	5.9	3.1	0.2	7.9	0.5
1989	303.6	4.5	294.9	80.7	27.0	87.0	81.6	37.0	5.3	3.3	0.1	8.1	0.6
1990	299.3	−1.4	289.8	75.6	26.1	88.3	81.0	37.5	5.1	3.5	−1.2	9.0	0.6
1991	273.3	−8.7	262.4	83.4	31.8	101.8	82.0	34.6	3.5	3.3	−46.2	10.0	0.9
1992	298.4	9.2	286.9	81.2	28.3	92.0	74.9	34.6	4.3	3.3	−3.3	10.6	0.8
1993	291.1	−2.4	278.6	75.9	27.2	94.1	69.6	37.0	4.8	3.3	−6.4	11.0	1.5
1994	281.6	3.3	268.6	73.1	27.2	87.9	61.8	34.8	5.0	3.3	2.8	11.9	1.1
1995	272.1	−3.4	259.4	70.8	27.3	90.9	55.0	34.6	6.8	3.6	−2.2	11.8	0.8
1996	265.6	−2.4	254.3	67.4	26.5	91.7	48.1	34.4	6.5	4.0	2.0	10.2	1.1

(Z) Greater than –$500 million and less than zero.

Source

U.S. Office of Management and Budget, *The Budget of the United States Government* (annual reports).

Documentation

Series Ed165. Includes revolving and management funds, trust funds, special foreign currency program allowances, and offsetting receipts.

Series Ed166. Includes defense activities only.

Series Ed167. Includes Civil Defense activities.

TABLE Ed168-179 Estimated costs of U.S. wars: 1775-1992

Contributed by Scott Sigmund Gartner

War	Estimated total war costs	Original war costs	Original incremental direct costs			Veterans' benefits				Estimated interest payments on war loans		
			Current dollars	Constant dollars	As a percentage of 1 year's GNP	Total costs under present law	As a percentage of original war costs	Total costs to 1970	Service-connected benefits to 1992	Amount	As a percentage of original war costs	Current costs to 1992
	Ed168	Ed169	Ed170	Ed171	Ed172	Ed173	Ed174	Ed175	Ed176	Ed177	Ed178	Ed179 [1]
	Million dollars	Million dollars	Million dollars	Million 1967 dollars	Percent	Million dollars	Percent	Million dollars	Million dollars	Million dollars	Percent	Million dollars
American Revolution	190	100	—	—	104	70	70	70	28	20 [4]	20	170
War of 1812	158	93	89	170	14	49	53	49	20	16	17	120
Mexican War	147	73	82	300	4	64	88	64	26	10	14	120
Civil War (Confederate only)	—	—	1,000	3,700	123	—	—	—	—	—	—	—
Civil War (Union only)	12,952	3,200	2,300	8,500	74	8,580	260	8,570	3,290	1,172	37	6,790
Spanish-American War	6,460	400	270	1,100	2	6,000	1,505	5,436	2,111	60	15	2,441
World War I	112,000	26,000	32,700	100,000	43	75,000	290	45,585	19,630	11,000	42	63,000
World War II	664,000	288,000	360,000	816,300	188	290,000	100	87,445	107,500	86,000	30	468,000
Korean Conflict	164,000	54,000	50,000	69,300	15	99,000	184	15,016	22,700	11,000	20	73,000
Vietnam Conflict [2]	352,000	110,000	140,600	148,800	14	220,000 [3]	200 [3]	2,461	35,400	22,000 [5]	20 [5]	176,000

[1] Figures are rounded estimates.

[2] Estimates based on assumption that war would end by June 30, 1970 (except for veterans' benefit costs to 1970). Occupation costs not included.

[3] Total cost to 1992. See text.

[4] Medium-level estimate of 20 percent (high, 30; low, 10) based on figures expressing relationship of veterans' benefits to original costs of other major U.S. wars.

[5] Medium-level estimate of 200 percent (high, 300; low, 100) based on figures expressing relationship of veterans' benefits to original costs of other major U.S. wars.

Sources

Series Ed168-169 and Ed173-179. U.S. Congress, Joint Economic Committee, "The Military Budget and National Economic Priorities," part 1, pp. 149 and 150, 91st Congress, 1st session (statement of James L. Clayton, University of Utah, at Hearings before the Subcommittee on Economy in Government); and for series Ed175, U.S. Veterans Administration, "Annual Report of Administrator of Veterans Affairs." For the Vietnam conflict the original war costs through 1970 were estimated to be $108.5 billion for "Major national security expenditures for Vietnam Conflict, 1965-1970" (fiscal years), plus $1.5 billion for "supporting American personnel in South Vietnam, 1954-1964 at $25,000 per man-year."

Series Ed170-172. Claudia D. Goldin, *Encyclopedia of American Economic History* (Scribner, 1980), p.938. Figures are rounded from source.

Documentation

Series Ed168-169. Information on the 1990-1991 Persian Gulf War can be found in Tables Ed1-25 and Ed196-201.

Series Ed168. Represents the estimated costs of the war in total.

Series Ed169. Based on expenditures of Departments of the Army and Navy to World War I and major national security expenditures thereafter. Usually the figures begin with the year the war began and extend one year beyond the end of the actual conflict.

Series Ed170-172. Incremental direct costs are those incurred over the duration of the war only. This means that elements, such as pension costs and other delayed costs such as veteran's benefits or interest on war bonds, debt, and so on, are omitted. Damages to the national infrastructure during those wars waged on American soil are omitted.

Series Ed172. Appears to be based on an average "year" of the years spanning the wars.

Series Ed173-174. For the Vietnam Conflict, interest payments are a very rough approximation based on the percentage of the original costs of the war financed by money creation and debt, the difference between the level of public debt at the beginning of the war and at its end, and the approximate time required to pay off the war debts.

Series Ed173. To World War I, estimates are based on Veterans Administration data. For World War I, World War II, and the Korean Conflict, estimates are those of the 1956 report of the President's Commission on Veterans' Pensions (U.S. Government Printing Office), plus 25 percent (the increase in the average value of benefits since the Commission made its report).

Series Ed176. Total cost to October 1, 1992. For World War I, and later wars, benefits are actual service-connected figures from *Annual Report* of Veterans Affairs (U.S. Government Printing Office, various years). For earlier wars, service-connected veterans' benefits are estimated at 40 percent of total, the approximate ratio of service-connected to total benefits since World War I.

Series Ed179. Represents war costs actually paid up to 1992.

TABLE Ed180–195 World military expenditures – developing and developed countries, the United States, and NATO: 1965–1993

Contributed by Scott Sigmund Gartner

	Current dollars						Constant dollars					Percentage of total GNP				
	Total	United States	United States as a percentage of total	Developed countries	Developing countries	NATO countries	Total	United States	Developed countries	Developing countries	NATO countries	Worldwide	United States	Developed countries	Developing countries	NATO countries
	Ed180	Ed181	Ed182	Ed183	Ed184	Ed185	Ed186	Ed187	Ed188	Ed189	Ed190	Ed191	Ed192	Ed193	Ed194	Ed195
Year	Billion dollars	Billion dollars	Percent	Billion dollars	Billion dollars	Billion dollars	Billion 1995 dollars	Billion 1995 dollars	Billion 1995 dollars	Billion 1995 dollars	Billion 1995 dollars	Percent	Percent	Percent	Percent	Percent
1965	143.0	51.6	36.1	127.0	16.0	90.0	690.8	251.2	613.5	77.3	434.8	6.8	7.6	7.3	4.4	6.4
1966	160.0	63.2	39.5	143.0	17.0	102.0	751.2	295.8	671.4	79.8	478.9	6.9	8.5	7.6	4.6	6.8
1967	181.0	75.7	41.8	161.0	20.0	115.0	826.5	347.0	735.2	91.3	525.0	7.2	9.5	7.9	4.6	7.4
1968	221.8	80.7	38.0	188.6	33.3	179.6	973.7	355.3	829.0	144.7	739.5	7.2	9.3	7.4	6.1	6.8
1969	235.0	81.4	36.0	197.6	37.5	174.1	975.1	336.1	821.6	157.7	722.0	6.9	8.7	7.1	6.1	6.3
1970	245.8	77.9	33.0	202.2	43.6	163.0	964.7	305.9	792.2	172.5	635.2	6.5	7.6	6.6	6.1	5.8
1971	258.0	74.9	30.0	209.6	49.3	155.5	969.9	282.0	789.5	184.2	582.5	6.3	7.0	6.3	6.2	5.3
1972	277.0	77.6	29.0	222.9	54.2	157.7	1,010.9	284.7	813.9	197.1	576.6	6.1	6.6	6.1	6.2	5.1
1973	299.0	78.4	27.0	238.0	61.1	154.0	1,027.5	268.0	817.9	209.6	529.2	5.9	6.0	5.8	6.1	4.7
1974	334.0	85.9	27.0	266.4	68.0	156.2	1,061.3	266.3	823.5	210.5	483.0	5.9	6.1	5.9	5.8	4.8
1975	378.0	90.9	25.0	292.7	85.4	153.3	1,070.8	257.8	830.0	240.8	433.4	6.0	5.9	5.9	6.3	4.8
1976	403.1	91.0	23.0	310.3	92.8	150.0	1,080.4	244.0	831.1	249.3	402.0	5.8	5.4	5.7	6.2	4.4
1977	433.9	100.9	24.0	337.0	96.9	156.1	1,090.5	253.8	846.7	243.7	418.0	5.7	5.4	5.6	6.8	4.5
1978	502.8	109.2	21.7	391.3	111.6	187.0	1,175.2	254.7	913.5	261.7	457.0	5.4	4.9	5.1	7.0	4.1
1979	550.9	122.3	22.2	435.4	115.6	208.7	1,157.6	256.3	913.9	243.7	459.0	5.2	4.9	5.0	6.3	4.1
1980	627.4	144.0	23.0	495.9	131.5	241.1	1,159.0	266.2	916.8	244.0	445.5	5.4	5.3	5.2	6.2	4.3
1981	710.3	169.9	23.9	559.5	150.8	278.3	1,191.3	285.2	939.6	253.4	466.4	5.5	5.6	5.3	6.4	4.5
1982	792.0	196.0	24.8	627.0	165.0	330.0	1,251.2	309.6	990.5	260.7	521.3	5.7	6.2	5.5	6.2	4.7
1983	852.0	218.0	25.6	676.0	176.0	361.0	1,302.8	333.0	1,033.6	269.1	552.0	5.7	6.3	5.6	6.2	4.8
1984	903.0	237.0	26.3	719.0	183.0	388.0	1,324.0	347.5	1,054.3	268.3	568.9	5.6	6.2	5.5	5.9	4.7
1985	943.0	258.0	27.4	756.0	188.0	405.0	1,335.7	365.4	1,070.8	266.2	573.7	5.4	6.4	5.4	5.4	4.8
1986	988.0	281.0	28.4	797.0	191.0	432.0	1,374.1	390.8	1,108.5	265.6	601.0	5.4	6.6	5.4	5.2	4.9
1987	1,020.0	288.0	28.2	833.0	188.0	448.0	1,369.1	386.6	1,118.2	252.3	601.3	5.2	6.3	5.4	4.7	4.8
1988	1,047.0	293.0	28.0	860.0	187.0	456.0	1,349.2	377.6	1,108.2	241.0	587.6	4.9	6.0	5.1	4.3	4.5
1989	1,059.0	304.0	28.7	867.0	192.0	475.0	1,301.0	373.5	1,065.0	235.9	583.5	4.6	5.8	4.8	4.0	4.3
1990	1,073.0	306.0	28.5	849.0	224.0	486.0	1,250.6	356.6	989.5	261.1	566.4	4.4	5.5	4.5	4.4	4.2
1991	1,021.0	280.0	27.5	787.0	234.0	467.0	1,142.1	313.2	880.3	261.7	522.4	4.1	4.9	4.0	4.2	3.8
1992	932.0	305.0	32.7	689.0	244.0	489.0	1,011.9	331.2	748.1	264.9	530.9	3.7	5.1	3.7	3.7	3.8
1993	869.0	298.0	34.2	648.0	221.0	480.0	916.6	314.3	683.5	233.1	506.3	3.3	4.7	3.4	3.1	3.6

Source

U.S. Arms Control and Disarmament Agency, *World Military Expenditures and Arms Transfers* (U.S. Government Printing Office, annual).

Documentation

There are twenty-eight developed countries for the purposes of this table. For a complete list see source. NATO is the North Atlantic Treaty Organization.

BATTLE CAMPAIGNS

Scott Sigmund Gartner

TABLE Ed196–197   U.S. Army battle campaigns: 1775–1995

Contributed by Scott Sigmund Gartner

		War and theater	Battle or campaign
		Ed196	Ed197
Date began	Date ended	—	—
Apr 19, 1775	Apr 19, 1775	Revolutionary War	Lexington
May 10, 1775	May 10, 1775	Revolutionary War	Ticonderoga
June 17, 1775	Mar 17, 1776	Revolutionary War	Boston
Aug 28, 1775	July 3, 1776	Revolutionary War	Quebec
June 28, 1776	June 29, 1776	Revolutionary War	Charleston
Aug 26, 1776	Aug 29, 1776	Revolutionary War	Long Island
Dec 26, 1776	Dec 26, 1776	Revolutionary War	Trenton
Jan 3, 1777	Jan 3, 1777	Revolutionary War	Princeton
July 2, 1777	Oct 17, 1777	Revolutionary War	Saratoga
Sept 11, 1777	Sept 11, 1777	Revolutionary War	Brandywine
Oct 4, 1777	Oct 4, 1777	Revolutionary War	Germantown
June 28, 1778	June 28, 1778	Revolutionary War	Monmouth
Dec 29, 1778	Dec 29, 1778	Revolutionary War	Savannah
Sept 16, 1779	Oct 10, 1779	Revolutionary War	Savannah
Mar 29, 1780	Mar 29, 1780	Revolutionary War	Charleston
Jan 17, 1781	Jan 17, 1781	Revolutionary War	Cowpens
Mar 15, 1781	Mar 15, 1781	Revolutionary War	Guilford Court House
Sept 28, 1781	Oct 19, 1781	Revolutionary War	Yorktown
Jan 1790	Aug 1795	Indian Wars	Miami
Sept 21, 1811	Nov 18, 1811	Indian Wars	Tippecanoe
June 18, 1812	Feb 17, 1815	War of 1812	Canada
July 27, 1813	Aug 1814	Indian Wars	Creek
July 5, 1814	July 5, 1814	War of 1812	Chippewa
July 25, 1814	July 25, 1814	War of 1812	Lundy's Lane
Aug 17, 1814	Aug 29, 1814	War of 1812	Bladensburg
Sept 13, 1814	Sept 13, 1814	War of 1812	McHenry
Sept 23, 1814	Jan 8, 1815	War of 1812	New Orleans
Nov 20, 1817	Oct 31, 1818	Indian Wars	Seminole
Apr 26, 1832	Sept 20, 1832	Indian Wars	Black Hawk
Dec 28, 1835	Aug 14, 1842	Indian Wars	Seminole
Feb 1836	July 1837	Indian Wars	Creek
May 8, 1846	May 8, 1846	Mexican War	Palo Alto
May 9, 1846	May 9, 1846	Mexican War	Resaca de la Palma
Sept 21, 1846	Sept 21, 1846	Mexican War	Monterey
Feb 22, 1847	Feb 23, 1847	Mexican War	Buena Vista
Mar 9, 1847	Mar 29, 1847	Mexican War	Vera Cruz
Apr 17, 1847	Apr 17, 1847	Mexican War	Cerro Gordo
Aug 18, 1847	Aug 20, 1847	Mexican War	Contreras
Aug 20, 1847	Aug 20, 1847	Mexican War	Churubusco
Sept 8, 1847	Sept 8, 1847	Mexican War	Molino del Rey
Sept 13, 1847	Sept 13, 1847	Mexican War	Chapultepec
Dec 15, 1855	May 1858	Indian Wars	Seminole
Apr 12, 1861	Apr 13, 1861	Civil War	Sumter
July 16, 1861	July 22, 1861	Civil War	Bull Run
Feb 6, 1862	Feb 16, 1862	Civil War	Henry and Donelson
Feb 6, 1862	July 9, 1863	Civil War	Mississippi River
Mar 17, 1862	Aug 3, 1862	Civil War	Peninsula
Apr 6, 1862	Apr 7, 1862	Civil War	Shiloh
May 15, 1862	June 17, 1862	Civil War	Valley
Aug 7, 1862	Sept 2, 1862	Civil War	Manassas
Sep 3, 1862	Sept 17, 1862	Civil War	Antietam
Nov 9, 1862	Dec 15, 1862	Civil War	Fredericksburg
Dec 26, 1862	Jan 4, 1863	Civil War	Murfreesboro
Mar 29, 1863	July 4, 1863	Civil War	Vicksburg
Apr 27, 1863	May 6, 1863	Civil War	Chancellorsville

TABLE Ed196–197   U.S. Army battle campaigns: 1775–1995   *Continued*

Date began	Date ended	War and theater	Battle or campaign
		Ed196	Ed197
		—	—
June 29, 1863	July 3, 1863	Civil War	Gettysburg
Aug 16, 1863	Sept 22, 1863	Civil War	Chickamauga
Nov 23, 1863	Nov 27, 1863	Civil War	Chattanooga
May 4, 1864	May 7, 1864	Civil War	Wilderness
May 7, 1864	Sept 2, 1864	Civil War	Atlanta
May 8, 1864	May 21, 1864	Civil War	Spotsylvania
May 22, 1864	June 3, 1864	Civil War	Cold Harbor
June 4, 1864	Apr 2, 1865	Civil War	Petersburg
Aug 7, 1864	Nov 28, 1864	Civil War	Shenandoah
Nov 17, 1864	Nov 30, 1864	Civil War	Franklin
Dec 1, 1864	Dec 16, 1864	Civil War	Nashville
Apr 3, 1865	Apr 9, 1865	Civil War	Appomattox
1867	1875	Indian Wars [1]	Comanches
1872	1873	Indian Wars [1]	Modocs
1873	1873	Indian Wars [1]	Apaches
1876	1877	Indian Wars [1]	Little Big Horn
1877	1877	Indian Wars [1]	Nez Perces
1878	1878	Indian Wars [1]	Bannocks
1878	1879	Indian Wars [1]	Cheyennes
Sept 1879	Nov 1880	Indian Wars [1]	Utes
1885	1886	Indian Wars [1]	Apaches
Nov 1890	Jan 1891	Indian Wars [1]	Pine Ridge
June 22, 1898	July 11, 1898	War with Spain	Santiago
July 25, 1898	Aug 13, 1898	War with Spain	Puerto Rico
July 31, 1898	Aug 13, 1898	War with Spain	Manila
Feb 4, 1899	Mar 17, 1899	Philippine Insurrection [1]	Manila
Feb 8, 1899	Feb 12, 1899	Philippine Insurrection [1]	Iloilo
Mar 24, 1899	Aug 16, 1899	Philippine Insurrection [1]	Malolos
Apr 8, 1899	Apr 17, 1899	Philippine Insurrection [1]	Laguna de Bay
Apr 12, 1899	May 30, 1899	Philippine Insurrection [1]	San Isidro
June 13, 1899	June 13, 1899	Philippine Insurrection [1]	Zapote River
Oct 7, 1899	Oct 13, 1899	Philippine Insurrection [1]	Cavite
Oct 15, 1899	Nov 19, 1899	Philippine Insurrection [1]	San Isidro
Nov 5, 1899	Nov 20, 1899	Philippine Insurrection [1]	Tarlac
Nov 6, 1899	Nov 19, 1899	Philippine Insurrection [1]	San Fabian
Jan 4, 1900	Feb 9, 1900	Philippine Insurrection [1]	Cavite
July 13, 1900	July 13, 1900	China Relief Expedition [1]	Tientsin
Aug 6, 1900	Aug 6, 1900	China Relief Expedition [1]	Yang-tsun
Aug 14, 1900	Aug 15, 1900	China Relief Expedition [1]	Peking
July 4, 1902	Dec 31, 1904	Philippine Insurrection [1]	Mindanao
May 1, 1905	May 24, 1905	Philippine Insurrection [1]	Jolo
Oct 22, 1905	Oct 22, 1905	Philippine Insurrection [1]	Mindanao
Mar 6, 1906	Mar 8, 1906	Philippine Insurrection [1]	Jolo
June 11, 1913	June 15, 1913	Philippine Insurrection [1]	Jolo
Mar 14, 1916	Feb 17, 1917	Mexican Expedition [1]	Mexico
Nov 20, 1917	Dec 4, 1917	World War I	Cambrai
Mar 21, 1918	Apr 6, 1918	World War I	Somme Defensive
Apr 9, 1918	Apr 27, 1918	World War I	Lys
May 27, 1918	June 5, 1918	World War I	Aisne
June 9, 1918	June 13, 1918	World War I	Montdidier–Noyon
July 15, 1918	July 18, 1918	World War I	Champagne–Marne
July 18, 1918	Aug 6, 1918	World War I	Aisne–Marne
Aug 8, 1918	Nov 11, 1918	World War I	Somme Offensive
Aug 18, 1918	Nov 11, 1918	World War I	Oise–Aisne
Aug 19, 1918	Nov 11, 1918	World War I	Ypres–Lys
Sept 12, 1918	Sept 16, 1918	World War I	St. Mihiel
Sept 26, 1918	Nov 11, 1918	World War I	Meuse–Argonne
Oct 24, 1918	Nov 4, 1918	World War I	Vittorio Veneto
Dec 7, 1941	May 10, 1942	World War II: Asia–Pacific	Philippine Island
Dec 7, 1941	May 26, 1942	World War II: Asia–Pacific	Burma
Dec 7, 1941	Dec 6, 1943	World War II: Asia–Pacific	Central Pacific
Dec 7, 1941	Sept 2, 1945	World War II: Europe–Africa–Middle East	Antisubmarine Campaign
Jan 1, 1942	July 22, 1942	World War II: Asia–Pacific	East Indies
Apr 2, 1942	Jan 28, 1945	World War II: Asia–Pacific	India–Burma
Apr 17, 1942	Sept 2, 1945	World War II: Asia–Pacific	Air Offensive, Japan

Note appears at end of table

(continued)

TABLE Ed196–197   U.S. Army battle campaigns: 1775–1995   *Continued*

		War and theater	Battle or campaign
		Ed196	**Ed197**
Date began	**Date ended**	—	—
June 3, 1942	Aug 24, 1943	World War II: Asia–Pacific	Aleutian Islands
June 11, 1942	Feb 12, 1943	World War II: Europe–Africa–Middle East	Egypt–Libya
July 4, 1942	June 5, 1944	World War II: Europe–Africa–Middle East	Air Offensive, European
July 4, 1942	May 4, 1945	World War II: Asia–Pacific	China Defensive
July 23, 1942	Jan 23, 1943	World War II: Asia–Pacific	Papua
Aug 7, 1942	Feb 21, 1943	World War II: Asia–Pacific	Guadalcanal
Nov 8, 1942	Nov 11, 1942	World War II: Europe–Africa–Middle East	Algeria–French Morocco
Nov 17, 1942	May 13, 1943	World War II: Europe–Africa–Middle East	Tunisia
Jan 24, 1943	Dec 31, 1944	World War II: Asia–Pacific	New Guinea
Feb 22, 1943	Nov 21, 1944	World War II: Asia–Pacific	Northern Solomons
July 9, 1943	Aug 17, 1943	World War II: Europe–Africa–Middle East	Sicily
Aug 18, 1943	Jan 21, 1944	World War II: Europe–Africa–Middle East	Naples–Foggia
Sept 9, 1943	Jan 21, 1944	World War II: Europe–Africa–Middle East	Naples–Foggia
Dec 15, 1943	Nov 27, 1944	World War II: Asia–Pacific	Bismarck Archipelago
Jan 22, 1944	May 24, 1944	World War II: Europe–Africa–Middle East	Anzio
Jan 22, 1944	Sept 9, 1944	World War II: Europe–Africa–Middle East	Rome–Arno
Jan 31, 1944	June 14, 1944	World War II: Asia–Pacific	Eastern Mandates
June 6, 1944	July 24, 1944	World War II: Europe–Africa–Middle East	Normandy
June 15, 1944	Sept 2, 1945	World War II: Asia–Pacific	Western Pacific
July 25, 1944	Sept 14, 1944	World War II: Europe–Africa–Middle East	Northern France
Aug 15, 1944	Sept 14, 1944	World War II: Europe–Africa–Middle East	Southern France
Oct 17, 1944	July 1, 1945	World War II: Asia–Pacific	Leyte
Dec 15, 1944	July 4, 1945	World War II: Asia–Pacific	Luzon
Jan 29, 1945	July 15, 1945	World War II: Asia–Pacific	Central Burma
Feb 27, 1945	July 4, 1945	World War II: Asia–Pacific	Southern Philippines
Mar 22, 1945	May 11, 1945	World War II: Europe–Africa–Middle East	Central Europe
Mar 26, 1945	July 2, 1945	World War II: Asia–Pacific	Ryukyus
Apr 5, 1945	May 8, 1945	World War II: Europe–Africa–Middle East	Po Valley
May 5, 1945	Sept 2, 1945	World War II: Asia–Pacific	China Offensive
Sept 10, 1944	Apr 4, 1945	World War II: Europe–Africa–Middle East	North Apennines
Sept 15, 1944	Mar 21, 1945	World War II: Europe–Africa–Middle East	Rhineland
Dec 16, 1944	Jan 25, 1945	World War II: Europe–Africa–Middle East	Ardennes–Alsace
June 27, 1950	Sept 15, 1950	Korean War	United Nations Defensive
Sept 16, 1950	Nov 2, 1950	Korean War	United Nations Offensive
Nov 3, 1950	Jan 24, 1951	Korean War	Chinese Communist Forces Intervention
Jan 25, 1951	Apr 21, 1951	Korean War	First United Nations Counteroffensive
Apr 22, 1951	July 8, 1951	Korean War	Chinese Communist Forces Spring Offensive
July 9, 1951	Nov 27, 1951	Korean War	United Nations Summer–Fall Offensive
Nov 28, 1951	Apr 30, 1952	Korean War	Second Korean Winter
May 1, 1952	Nov 30, 1952	Korean War	Korea, Summer–Fall 1952
Dec 1, 1952	Apr 30, 1953	Korean War	Third Korean Winter
May 1, 1953	July 27, 1953	Korean War	Korea, Summer 1953
Mar 15, 1962	Mar 7, 1965	Vietnam War	Advisory
Mar 8, 1965	Dec 24, 1965	Vietnam War	Defense
Apr 28, 1965	Sept 21, 1966	—[1]	Dominican Republic
Dec 25, 1965	June 30, 1966	Vietnam War	Counteroffensive
July 1, 1966	May 31, 1967	Vietnam War	Counteroffensive, Phase II
June 1, 1967	Jan 29, 1968	Vietnam War	Counteroffensive, Phase III
Jan 30, 1968	Apr 1, 1968	Vietnam War	Tet Counteroffensive
Apr 2, 1968	June 30, 1968	Vietnam War	Counteroffensive, Phase IV
July 1, 1968	Nov 1, 1968	Vietnam War	Counteroffensive Phase V
Nov 2, 1968	Feb 22, 1969	Vietnam War	Counteroffensive, Phase VI
Feb 23, 1969	June 8, 1969	Vietnam War	Tet 69/Counteroffensive
June 9, 1969	Oct 31, 1969	Vietnam War	Summer–Fall 1969
Nov 1, 1969	Apr 30, 1970	Vietnam War	Winter–Spring 1970
May 1, 1970	June 30, 1970	Vietnam War	Sanctuary Counteroffensive
July 1, 1970	June 30, 1971	Vietnam War	Counteroffensive, Phase VII
July 1, 1971	Nov 30, 1971	Vietnam War	Consolidation I
Dec 1, 1971	Mar 29, 1972	Vietnam War	Consolidation II
Mar 30, 1972	Jan 28, 1973	Vietnam War	Cease-Fire
Oct 23, 1983	Nov 21, 1983	—[1]	Grenada
Dec 20, 1989	Jan 31, 1990	—[1]	Panama
Aug 2, 1990	Jan 16, 1991	Gulf War: Southwest Asia	Defense of Saudi Arabia
Jan 17, 1991	Apr 11, 1991	Gulf War: Southwest Asia	Liberation and Defense of Kuwait
Apr 12, 1991	Nov 30, 1995	Gulf War: Southwest Asia	Cease-Fire

TABLE Ed196–197 U.S. Army battle campaigns: 1775–1995 *Continued*

[1] Denotes action less than war.

Sources

U.S. Army Center for Military History Internet site, CMH Publication 30-1: American Military History: Combat Medals, Streamers, and Campaigns, accessed May 20, 2000.

Documentation

Battle campaigns are denoted by official military medals and streamers.

TABLE Ed198–199 U.S. Navy battle campaigns: 1776–1995

Contributed by Scott Sigmund Gartner

		War and theater	Battle or campaign
		Ed198	Ed199
Date began	Date ended	–	–
Mar 3, 1776	Mar 3, 1776	Revolutionary War	New Providence, Bahamas
—	—	Revolutionary War	Inland waters and amphibious assault [2]
—	—	Revolutionary War	West Indies and European Convoy [2]
—	—	Revolutionary War	Operations in European waters [2]
—	—	Revolutionary War	Commerce raiding operations [2]
Mar 7, 1778	Mar 7, 1778	Revolutionary War	*Randolph–Yarmouth*
Apr 24, 1778	Apr 24, 1778	Revolutionary War	*Ranger–Drake*
Sept 23, 1779	Sept 23, 1779	Revolutionary War	*Bonhomme Richard–Serapis*
—	—	Revolutionary War	Other single-ship actions [2]
—	—	Revolutionary War	Transport and packet operations [2]
1798	1801	Quasi War with France	—
Feb 9, 1799	Feb 9, 1799	Quasi War with France	*Constellation–L'Insurgente*
Feb 1, 1800	Feb 2, 1800	Quasi War with France	*Constellation–La Vengeance*
—	—	Quasi War with France	Anti-privateering [2]
1801	1805	Barbary Wars [1]	—
—	—	Barbary Wars [1]	Actions in Tripoli harbor [2]
—	—	Barbary Wars [1]	Blockade of Tripolitan coast [2]
Feb 16, 1804	Feb 16, 1804	Barbary Wars [1]	Destruction of the captured USS *Philadelphia*
Aug 19, 1812	Aug 19, 1812	War of 1812	*Constitution–Guerriere*
Oct 28, 1812	Oct 28, 1812	War of 1812	*United States–Macedonia*
Dec 29, 1812	Dec 29, 1812	War of 1812	*Constitution–Java*
June 1, 1813	June 1, 1813	War of 1812	*Chesapeake–Shannon*
Sept 10, 1813	Sept 10, 1813	War of 1812	Battle of Lake Erie
Mar 28, 1814	Mar 28, 1814	War of 1812	*Essex–Phoebe* and *Cherub*
—	—	War of 1812	Sloop-of-war and brig single-ship actions [2]
—	—	War of 1812	Commerce raiding in the Atlantic [2]
—	—	War of 1812	Operations against whaling fleets in the Pacific [2]
July 1814	Aug 1814	War of 1812	Defense of Washington
Sept 11, 1814	Sept 11, 1814	War of 1812	Battle of Lake Champlain
Sept 1814	Sept 1814	War of 1812	Defense of Baltimore
Dec 1814	Jan 1815	War of 1812	Battle of New Orleans
Feb 20, 1815	Feb 20, 1815	War of 1812	*Constitution–Cyane* and *Levant*
1815	1815	Barbary Wars II	Operations against Algiers (1815)
1820	1861	— [1]	African slave trade patrol
1822	1830s	— [1]	Operations against West Indian pirates
1835	1842	The Indian Wars [1]	—
Mar 9, 1847	Mar 9, 1847	Mexican War	Veracruz landing
—	—	Mexican War	Riverine operations [2]
—	—	Mexican War	East Coast blockade [2]
—	—	Mexican War	West Coast blockade and operations in California [2]
1861	1865	Civil War	Blockade operations
Aug 29, 1861	Aug 29, 1861	Civil War	Capture of Hatteras Inlet, North Carolina
Nov 7, 1861	Nov 7, 1861	Civil War	Capture of Port Royal Sound, South Carolina
Feb 6, 1862	Feb 6, 1862	Civil War	Capture of Fort McHenry, Tennessee River
Feb 7, 1862	Feb 8, 1862	Civil War	Capture of Roanoke Island-key to Albemarle Sound
Mar 9, 1862	Mar 9, 1862	Civil War	USS *Monitor*–CSS *Virginia* (*Merrimack*)
Apr 24, 1862	Apr 24, 1862	Civil War	Battle of New Orleans
July 4, 1863	July 4, 1863	Civil War	Capture of Vicksburg
June 19, 1864	June 19, 1864	Civil War	USS *Kearsarge*–CSS *Alabama*
Aug 5, 1864	Aug 5, 1864	Civil War	Battle of Mobile Bay

Notes appear at end of table

(continued)

TABLE Ed198–199   U.S. Navy battle campaigns: 1776–1995   *Continued*

		War and theater	Battle or campaign
		Ed198	Ed199
Date began	Date ended	—	—
Oct 27, 1864	Oct 28, 1864	Civil War	Destruction of CSS *Albemarle*
Jan 13, 1865	Jan 15, 1865	Civil War	Capture of Fort Fisher, Wilmington, North Carolina
—	—	Civil War	Operations on the Mississippi and tributaries [2]
—	—	Civil War	Campaigns in the Chesapeake and tributaries [2]
—	—	Civil War	Atlantic operations against commerce raiders and blockade runners [2]
May 1, 1898	May 1, 1898	Spanish–American War	Battle of Manila Bay
1898	1898	Spanish–American War	Pacific Ocean operation
July 3, 1898	July 3, 1898	Spanish–American War	Battle of Santiago
1898	1898	Spanish–American War	Atlantic/Caribbean operations
1899	1902	— [1]	Philippine Insurrection Campaign
1900	1901	— [1]	China Relief Expedition
1906	1909	Latin American Campaigns [1]	Cuban Pacification Campaign
1912	1912	Latin American Campaigns [1]	First Nicaraguan Campaign
1914	1914	Latin American Campaigns [1]	Mexican Service Campaign
1915	1915	Latin American Campaigns [1]	Haitian Campaign
1916	1916	Latin American Campaigns [1]	Dominican Campaign
1919	1920	Latin American Campaigns [1]	Haitian Campaign
—	—	World War I	Atlantic convoy operations [2]
—	—	World War I	Western Atlantic operation [2]
—	—	World War I	Operations in Northern European waters [2]
—	—	World War I	Mediterranean operations [2]
—	—	World War I	Operations on the European continent [2]
1926	1933	Latin American Campaigns [1]	Second Nicaraguan Campaign
1926	1927	— [1]	Yangtze Service
1930	1932	— [1]	Yangtze Service
1937	1939	— [1]	China Service
1941	1946	World War II: America	Escort, antisubmarine, armed guard, and special operations
Dec 7, 1941	—	World War II: Asia–Pacific	Pearl Harbor–Midway
—	—	World War II: Asia–Pacific	Wake Island [2]
—	—	World War II: Asia–Pacific	Philippine Island operation [2]
—	—	World War II: Asia–Pacific	Netherlands East Indies engagements [2]
1942	1942	World War II: Asia–Pacific	Pacific raids [2]
—	—	World War II: Asia–Pacific	Coral Sea [2]
—	—	World War II: Asia–Pacific	Midway [2]
—	—	World War II: Asia–Pacific	Guadalcanal–Tulagi landings [2]
—	—	World War II: Asia–Pacific	Capture and defense of Guadalcanal [2]
—	—	World War II: Asia–Pacific	Makin raid [2]
—	—	World War II: Asia–Pacific	Eastern Solomons [2]
—	—	World War II: Asia–Pacific	Buin–Faisi–Tonolai raid [2]
—	—	World War II: Asia–Pacific	Cape Esperance [2]
—	—	World War II: Asia–Pacific	Santa Cruz Islands [2]
—	—	World War II: Asia–Pacific	Guadalcanal (Third Savo) [2]
—	—	World War II: Asia–Pacific	Tassafaronga [2]
—	—	World War II: Asia–Pacific	Eastern New Guinea operation [2]
—	—	World War II: Asia–Pacific	Rennel Island [2]
—	—	World War II: Asia–Pacific	Consolidation of Solomon Islands [2]
—	—	World War II: Asia–Pacific	Aleutians operation [2]
—	—	World War II: Asia–Pacific	New Georgia Group operation [2]
—	—	World War II: Asia–Pacific	Bismarck Archipelago operation [2]
1943	1943	World War II: Asia–Pacific	Pacific Raids [2]
—	—	World War II: Asia–Pacific	Treasury–Bougainville operations [2]
—	—	World War II: Asia–Pacific	Gilbert Islands operation [2]
—	—	World War II: Asia–Pacific	Marshall Island operations [2]
1944	1944	World War II: Asia–Pacific	Asia–Pacific raids [2]
—	—	World War II: Asia–Pacific	Western New Guinea operation [2]
—	—	World War II: Asia–Pacific	Marianas operation [2]
—	—	World War II: Asia–Pacific	Western Caroline Island operation [2]
—	—	World War II: Asia–Pacific	Leyte operation [2]
—	—	World War II: Asia–Pacific	Luzon operation [2]
—	—	World War II: Asia–Pacific	Iwo Jima operation [2]

Notes appear at end of table

TABLE Ed198–199   U.S. Navy battle campaigns: 1776–1995   *Continued*

		War and theater	Battle or campaign
		Ed198	Ed199
Date began	Date ended	—	—
—	—	World War II: Asia–Pacific	Okinawa Gunto operation [2]
—	—	World War II: Asia–Pacific	Third Fleet operations against Japan [2]
—	—	World War II: Asia–Pacific	Kurile Islands operation [2]
—	—	World War II: Asia–Pacific	Borneo operation [2]
—	—	World War II: Asia–Pacific	Tinian capture and consolidation [2]
—	—	World War II: Asia–Pacific	Consolidation of the Southern Philippines [2]
—	—	World War II: Asia–Pacific	Hollandia operation [2]
—	—	World War II: Asia–Pacific	Manila Bay–Bicol operation [2]
—	—	World War II: Asia–Pacific	Escort, antisubmarine, armed guard and special operations [2]
—	—	World War II: Asia–Pacific	Submarine war patrols (Pacific) [2]
—	—	World War II: Europe–Africa–Middle East	North African occupation [2]
—	—	World War II: Europe–Africa–Middle East	Sicilian occupation [2]
—	—	World War II: Europe–Africa–Middle East	Salerno landings [2]
1944	1944	World War II: Europe–Africa–Middle East	West Coast of Italy operation (1944) [2]
—	—	World War II: Europe–Africa–Middle East	Invasion of Normandy [2]
—	—	World War II: Europe–Africa–Middle East	Northeast Greenland operation [2]
—	—	World War II: Europe–Africa–Middle East	Invasion of Southern France [2]
—	—	World War II: Europe–Africa–Middle East	Reinforcement of Malta [2]
—	—	World War II: Europe–Africa–Middle East	Escort, antisubmarine, armed guard and special operations [2]
1945	1957	— [1]	China Service
—	—	Korean Service	North Korean aggression [2]
—	—	Korean Service	Communist China aggression [2]
—	—	Korean Service	Inchon landing [2]
—	—	Korean Service	First UN counteroffensive [2]
—	—	Korean Service	Communist China, Spring Offensive [2]
—	—	Korean Service	United Nations Summer–Fall offensive [2]
—	—	Korean Service	Second Korean Winter [2]
1952	1952	Korean Service	Korean defense, Summer–Fall
—	—	Korean Service	Third Korean Winter
1953	1953	Korean Service	Korean Summer–Fall
July 1, 1958	Nov 1, 1958	Armed Forces Expeditionary Service [1]	Lebanon
July 1, 1958	July 3, 1965	Armed Forces Expeditionary Service [1]	Vietnam
Aug 23, 1958	Jan 1, 1959	Armed Forces Expeditionary Service [1]	Taiwan Straits
Aug 23, 1958	June 1, 1963	Armed Forces Expeditionary Service [1]	Quemoy and Matsu Islands
July 14, 1960	Sept 1, 1962	Armed Forces Expeditionary Service [1]	Congo
Apr 19, 1961	Oct 7, 1962	Armed Forces Expeditionary Service [1]	Laos
Aug 14, 1961	June 1, 1963	Armed Forces Expeditionary Service [1]	Berlin
Mar 15, 1962	Mar 7, 1965	Vietnam Service [1]	Advisory Campaign
Oct 24, 1962	June 1, 1963	Armed Forces Expeditionary Service [1]	Cuba
Nov 23, 1964	Nov 27, 1964	Armed Forces Expeditionary Service [1]	Congo II
1965	Sept 21, 1966	Armed Forces Expeditionary Service [1]	Dominican Republic
Mar 8, 1965	Dec 24, 1965	Vietnam War	Defense Campaign
Dec 25, 1965	June 30, 1966	Vietnam War	Counteroffensive
July 1, 1966	May 31, 1967	Vietnam War	Counteroffensive, Phase II
Oct 1, 1966	June 30, 1974	Armed Forces Expeditionary Service [1]	Korea
June 1, 1967	Jan 29, 1968	Vietnam War	Counteroffensive, Phase III
Jan 30, 1968	Apr 1, 1968	Vietnam War	Tet Counteroffensive
Apr 2, 1968	June 30, 1968	Vietnam War	Counteroffensive, Phase IV
July 1, 1968	Nov 1, 1969	Vietnam War	Counteroffensive Phase V
Nov 2, 1968	Feb 22, 1969	Vietnam War	Counteroffensive, Phase VI
Feb 23, 1969	June 8, 1969	Vietnam War	Tet 69/Counteroffensive
June 9, 1969	Oct 31, 1969	Vietnam War	Summer–Fall 1969
Nov 1, 1969	Apr 30, 1970	Vietnam War	Winter–Spring 1970
May 1, 1970	June 30, 1970	Vietnam War	Sanctuary Counteroffensive
July 1, 1970	June 30, 1971	Vietnam War	Counteroffensive, Phase VII
July 1, 1971	Nov 30, 1971	Vietnam War	Consolidation I
Dec 1, 1971	Mar 29, 1972	Vietnam War	Consolidation II
Mar 30, 1972	Jan 28, 1973	Vietnam War	Cease-Fire
Mar 29, 1973	Aug 15, 1973	Armed Forces Expeditionary Service [1]	Cambodia
Mar 29, 1973	Aug 15, 1973	Armed Forces Expeditionary Service [1]	Thailand

Notes appear at end of table

(continued)

TABLE Ed198–199   U.S. Navy battle campaigns: 1776–1995   *Continued*

Date began	Date ended	War and theater	Battle or campaign
		Ed198	Ed199
		—	—
Apr 11, 1975	Apr 13, 1975	Armed Forces Expeditionary Service [1]	Cambodia Evacuation (Operation Eagle Pull)
Apr 29, 1975	Apr 30, 1975	Armed Forces Expeditionary Service [1]	Vietnam Evacuation (Operation Frequent Wind)
May 15, 1975	May 15, 1975	Armed Forces Expeditionary Service [1]	Mayaguez
Jan 1, 1981	Feb 1, 1992	Armed Forces Expeditionary Service [1]	El Salvador
June 1, 1983	Dec 1, 1987	Armed Forces Expeditionary Service [1]	Lebanon
Oct 23, 1983	Nov 21, 1983	Armed Forces Expeditionary Service [1]	Grenada (Operation Urgent Fury)
Apr 12, 1986	Apr 17, 1986	Armed Forces Expeditionary Service [1]	Libya (Operation El Dorado Canyon)
July 24, 1987	Aug 1, 1990	Armed Forces Expeditionary Service [1]	Persian Gulf (Operation Earnest Will)
Dec 20, 1989	Jan 31, 1990	Armed Forces Expeditionary Service [1]	Panama (Operation Just Cause)
Aug 2, 1990	Jan 16, 1991	Gulf War	Defense of Saudi Arabia
Jan 17, 1991	Apr 11, 1991	Gulf War	Liberation and Defense of Kuwait
Apr 12, 1991	Nov 30, 1995	Gulf War	Southwest Asia Cease-Fire Campaign
Dec 3, 1992	Mar 31, 1995	Armed Forces Expeditionary Service [1]	Somalia (Operation Restore Hope)
Dec 1, 1993	—	Armed Forces Expeditionary Service [1]	Persian Gulf/Iraq (Operation Southern Watch)
Sept 16, 1994	Mar 31, 1995	Armed Forces Expeditionary Service [1]	Haiti (Operation Uphold Democracy)

[1] Denotes action less than war.

[2] No specific start and end dates are used by the Navy; the action began and ended during the denoted war.

Source

U.S. Naval History Center Internet site, U.S. Navy Combat Medals, Streamers, and Campaigns, accessed May 15, 2000.

Documentation

Battle campaigns are those denoted by official military medals and streamers. Marine Corps actions are included with the Navy.

TABLE Ed200–201   U.S. Air Force and Army Air Force battle campaigns: 1916–1991

Contributed by Scott Sigmund Gartner

Date began	Date ended	War and theater	Battle or campaign
		Ed200	Ed201
		—	—
Mar 14, 1916	Feb 7, 1917	—	Mexican Expedition
Mar 21, 1918	Apr 6, 1918	World War I	Somme Defensive
Apr 9, 1918	Apr 27, 1918	World War I	Lys
July 15, 1918	July 18, 1918	World War I	Champagne-Marne
July 18, 1918	Aug 6, 1918	World War I	Aisne–Marne
Aug 8, 1918	Nov 11, 1918	World War I	Somme Offensive
Aug 18, 1918	Nov 11, 1918	World War I	Oise–Aisne
Sept 12, 1918	Sept 16, 1918	World War I	St. Mihiel
Sept 26, 1918	Nov 11, 1918	World War I	Meuse–Argonne
Dec 7, 1941	May 10, 1942	World War II: Asia–Pacific	Philippine Islands
Dec 7, 1941	May 26, 1942	World War II: Asia–Pacific	Burma: 1942
Dec 7, 1941	Dec 6, 1943	World War II: Asia–Pacific	Central Pacific
Dec 7, 1941	Sept 2, 1945	World War II: America	Antisubmarine
Dec 7, 1941	Sept 2, 1945	World War II: Asia–Pacific	Antisubmarine
Dec 7, 1941	Sept 2, 1945	World War II: Asia–Pacific	Air Combat
Dec 7, 1941	Sept 2, 1945	World War II: Europe–Atlantic–Middle East	Air Combat
Dec 7, 1941	Sept 2, 1945	World War II: Europe–Atlantic–Middle East	Antisubmarine
Jan 1, 1942	July 22, 1942	World War II: Asia–Pacific	East Indies
Apr 2, 1942	Jan 28, 1945	World War II: Asia–Pacific	India–Burma
Apr 17, 1942	Sept 2, 1945	World War II: Asia–Pacific	Air Offensive Japan
June 3, 1942	Aug 24, 1943	World War II: Asia–Pacific	Aleutian Islands
June 11, 1942	Feb 12, 1943	World War II: Europe–Atlantic–Middle East	Egypt–Libya
July 4, 1942	June 5, 1944	World War II: Europe–Atlantic–Middle East	Air Offensive Europe
July 4, 1942	May 4, 1945	World War II: Asia–Pacific	China Defensive
July 23, 1942	Jan 23, 1943	World War II: Asia–Pacific	Papua
Aug 7, 1942	Feb 21, 1943	World War II: Asia–Pacific	Guadalcanal
Nov 8, 1942	Nov 11, 1942	World War II: Europe–Atlantic–Middle East	Algeria–French Morocco
Nov 12, 1942	May 13, 1943	World War II: Europe–Atlantic–Middle East	Tunisia
Jan 24, 1943	Dec 31, 1944	World War II: Asia–Pacific	New Guinea
Feb 22, 1943	Nov 21, 1944	World War II: Asia–Pacific	Northern Solomons

TABLE Ed200–201   U.S. Air Force and Army Air Force battle campaigns: 1916–1991
Continued

		War and theater	Battle or campaign
		Ed200	Ed201
Date began	Date ended	–	–
May 14, 1943	Aug 17, 1943	World War II: Europe–Atlantic–Middle East	Sicily
Aug 18, 1943	Jan 21, 1944	World War II: Europe–Atlantic–Middle East	Naples–Foggia
Dec 7, 1943	Apr 16, 1944	World War II: Asia–Pacific	Eastern Mandates
Dec 15, 1943	Nov 27, 1944	World War II: Asia–Pacific	Bismarck Archipelago
Jan 22, 1944	May 24, 1944	World War II: Europe–Atlantic–Middle East	Anzio
Jan 22, 1944	Sept 9, 1944	World War II: Europe–Atlantic–Middle East	Rome–Arno
Apr 17, 1944	Sept 2, 1945	World War II: Asia–Pacific	Western Pacific
June 6, 1944	July 24, 1944	World War II: Europe–Atlantic–Middle East	Normandy
July 25, 1944	Sept 14, 1944	World War II: Europe–Atlantic–Middle East	Northern France
Aug 15, 1944	Sept 14, 1944	World War II: Europe–Atlantic–Middle East	Southern France
Sept 10, 1944	Apr 4, 1945	World War II: Europe–Atlantic–Middle East	North Apennines
Sept 15, 1944	Mar 21, 1945	World War II: Europe–Atlantic–Middle East	Rhineland
Oct 17, 1944	July 1, 1945	World War II: Asia–Pacific	Leyte
Dec 15, 1944	July 4, 1945	World War II: Asia–Pacific	Luzon
Dec 16, 1944	Jan 25, 1945	World War II: Europe–Atlantic–Middle East	Ardennes–Alsace
Jan 29, 1945	July 15, 1945	World War II: Asia–Pacific	Central Burma
Feb 27, 1945	July 4, 1945	World War II: Asia–Pacific	Southern Philippines
Mar 22, 1945	May 11, 1945	World War II: Europe–Atlantic–Middle East	Central Europe
Mar 26, 1945	July 2, 1945	World War II: Asia–Pacific	Ryukus
Apr 5, 1945	May 8, 1945	World War II: Europe–Atlantic–Middle East	Po Valley
May 5, 1945	Sept 2, 1945	World War II: Asia–Pacific	China Offensive
June 27, 1950	Sept 15, 1950	Korean Service	United Nations Defensive
Sept 16, 1950	Nov 2, 1950	Korean Service	United Nations Offensive
Nov 3, 1950	Jan 24, 1951	Korean Service	Chinese Communist Forces Invasion
Jan 25, 1951	Apr 21, 1951	Korean Service	First United Nations Counteroffensive
Apr 22, 1951	July 8, 1951	Korean Service	Chinese Communist Forces Spring Offensive
July 9, 1951	Nov 27, 1951	Korean Service	United Nations Summer–Fall Offensive
Nov 28, 1951	Apr 30, 1952	Korean Service	Second Korean Winter
May 1, 1952	Nov 30, 1952	Korean Service	Korea Summer–Fall 1952
Dec 1, 1952	Apr 30, 1953	Korean Service	Third Korean Winter
May 1, 1953	July 27, 1953	Korean Service	Korea Summer 1953
July 1, 1958	Nov 1, 1958	Armed Forces Expeditionary Service	Lebanon
July 1, 1958	July 3, 1965	Armed Forces Expeditionary Service	Vietnam
Aug 23, 1958	Jan 1, 1959	Armed Forces Expeditionary Service	Taiwan Straits
Aug 23, 1958	June 1, 1963	Armed Forces Expeditionary Service	Quemoy and Matsu Islands
July 14, 1960	Sept 1, 1962	Armed Forces Expeditionary Service	Congo
Apr 19, 1961	Oct 7, 1962	Armed Forces Expeditionary Service	Laos
Aug 14, 1961	June 1, 1963	Armed Forces Expeditionary Service	Berlin
Nov 15, 1961	Mar 1, 1965	Vietnam Service	Vietnam Advisory
Oct 24, 1962	June 1, 1963	Armed Forces Expeditionary Service	Cuba
Nov 23, 1964	Nov 27, 1964	Armed Forces Expeditionary Service	Congo
Mar 2, 1965	Jan 30, 1966	Vietnam Service	Vietnam Defensive
Apr 28, 1965	Sept 21, 1966	Armed Forces Expeditionary Service	Dominican Republic
Jan 31, 1966	June 28, 1966	Vietnam Service	Vietnam Air
June 29, 1966	Mar 8, 1967	Vietnam Service	Vietnam Air Offensive
Oct 1, 1966	June 30, 1974	Armed Forces Expeditionary Service	Korea
Mar 9, 1967	Mar 31, 1968	Vietnam Service	Vietnam Air Offensive Phase II
Jan 22, 1968	July 7, 1968	Vietnam Service	Vietnam Air/Ground
Apr 1, 1968	Oct 31, 1968	Vietnam Service	Vietnam Air Offensive Phase III
Nov 1, 1968	Feb 22, 1969	Vietnam Service	Vietnam Air Offensive Phase IV
Feb 23, 1969	June 8, 1969	Vietnam Service	Tet 69/Counteroffensive
June 9, 1969	Oct 31, 1969	Vietnam Service	Vietnam Summer/Fall 1969
Nov 1, 1969	Apr 30, 1970	Vietnam Service	Vietnam Winter/Spring 1970
May 1, 1970	June 30, 1970	Vietnam Service	Sanctuary Counteroffensive
July 1, 1970	Nov 30, 1970	Vietnam Service	Southwest Monsoon

(continued)

TABLE Ed200–201 U.S. Air Force and Army Air Force battle campaigns: 1916–1991
Continued

		War and theater	Battle or campaign
		Ed200	Ed201
Date began	Date ended	—	—
Dec 1, 1970	May 14, 1971	Vietnam Service	Commando Hunt V
May 15, 1971	Oct 31, 1971	Vietnam Service	Commando Hunt VI
Nov 1, 1971	Mar 29, 1972	Vietnam Service	Commando Hunt VII
Mar 30, 1972	Jan 28, 1973	Vietnam Service	Vietnam Cease-Fire
Mar 29, 1973	Aug 15, 1973	Armed Forces Expeditionary Service	Cambodia
Mar 29, 1973	Aug 15, 1973	Armed Forces Expeditionary Service	Thailand (in support of Cambodia)
Apr 11, 1975	Apr 13, 1975	Armed Forces Expeditionary Service	Cambodia (Operation Eagle Pull)
Apr 29, 1975	Apr 30, 1975	Armed Forces Expeditionary Service	Vietnam (Operation Frequent Wind)
May 15, 1975	May 15, 1975	Armed Forces Expeditionary Service	Mayaguez
June 1, 1983	Oct 1, 1987	Armed Forces Expeditionary Service	Lebanon
Oct 23, 1983	Nov 21, 1983	Armed Forces Expeditionary Service	Grenada
Apr 14, 1986	Apr 17, 1986	Armed Forces Expeditionary Service	Libya (El Dorado Canyon)
July 24, 1987	Nov 30, 1990	Armed Forces Expeditionary Service	Persian Gulf (Earnest Will)
Dec 20, 1989	Jan 31, 1990	Armed Forces Expeditionary Service	Panama (Operation Just Cause)

Source

Timothy Warnock, *Air Force Combat Medals, Streamers, and Campaigns* (1990).

Documentation

Battle campaigns are those denoted by official military medals and streamers.

Series Ed200. Denotes action less than war when no value is given or when Armed Forces Expeditionary Service is listed.

TABLE Ed202–211   Hostile engagements with Indians – military, civilian, and Indian casualties: 1866–1891

Contributed by Scott Sigmund Gartner

		Non-Indians						Indians		
		Killed			Wounded					
	Engagements	Officers	Enlisted men	Civilians	Officers	Enlisted men	Civilians	Killed	Wounded	Captured
	Ed202	Ed203	Ed204	Ed205	Ed206	Ed207	Ed208	Ed209	Ed210	Ed211
Year	Number	Number	Number	Number	Number	Number	Number	Number	Number	Number
1866	51	7	97	0	1	40	0	475	166	106
1867	124	5	77	10	6	117	12	683	190	174
1868	139	4	48	160	9	78	32	556	182	188
1869	112	0	28	48	3	67	9	362	119	66
1870	51	1	8	30	2	13	5	315	98	204
1871	39	1	5	49	1	13	3	123	40	76
1872	54	4	23	23	1	25	3	240	29	163
1873	51	6	40	1	7	77	3	250	27	350
1874	49	1	9	1	3	24	2	211	52	638
1875	18	0	5	0	0	21	0	93	2	155
1876	38	16	260	13	5	117	8	101	6	2,447
1877	45	6	113	30	14	135	12	244	111	2,844
1878	37	1	9	33	0	13	7	34	13	127
1879	39	2	48	37	3	70	6	117	6	251
1880	48	1	16	43	2	30	3	105	9	317
1881	21	1	8	9	1	4	1	21	5	1,458
1882	10	0	8	0	3	16	1	30	1	0
1883	7	0	0	11	0	0	0	11	0	74
1884	1	0	0	2	0	0	0	0	0	0
1885	11	1	11	0	1	7	0	11	2	30
1886	6	0	3	0	1	3	0	2	1	47
1887	3	0	1	0	1	2	0	7	10	9
1888	2	0	0	0	0	2	0	1	1	0
1889	2	0	0	0	0	9	0	0	0	34
1890	9	1	30	0	9	44	0	140	33	403
1891	2	1	0	0	0	0	0	1	1	0

Source

U.S. Army War College Internet site, Carlisle Barracks, "Chronological List of Actions, &C., with Indians, From January 1, 1866, to January, 1891," with corrections by the editors made from the original document, accessed March 30, 2004.

Documentation

The source used for this table, "Chronological List of Actions, &C., with Indians, From January 1, 1866, to January, 1891," was published as an office memo (unknown date – probably in the 1890s) by the U.S. War Department Adjutant-General's Office. Only engagements that involved troops of the U.S. Army are included; thus, hostilities between Indians and civilians that resulted in casualties are excluded. This is the standard "official" source on engagements with Indians for the protracted series of battles, skirmishes, and other hostilities known as the Indian Wars, which began at the end of the Civil War and ended with the last engagement at Wounded Knee, South Dakota, on January 1 and 3, 1891. The original provides detailed casualty counts for each one of the 969 separate engagements (see Table Ed212–222). However, historians of many of the individual battles report differing figures for casualties – particularly of Indian and civilian – often citing contemporary newspaper accounts, letters and diaries of individuals, and the like. When several engagements took place in the same region and were closely separated in time, there is often uncertainty as to which of the engagements a particular casualty should be assigned. This table summarizes the data by presenting annual totals. In general, the annual totals are more accurate than the numbers for any given engagement because of the uncertainty to which battle a casualty should be ascribed. For an overview of the Indian Wars see Richard H. Dillon, *North American Indian Wars* (Facts On File, 1983).

TABLE Ed212–222 Hostile engagements with Indians – military, civilian, and Indian casualties, by place of action: 1866–1891
Contributed by Scott Sigmund Gartner

			Non-Indians						Indians		
			Killed			Wounded					
Date	Place	State or territory	Officers	Enlisted men	Civilians	Officers	Enlisted men	Civilians	Killed	Wounded	Captured
	Ed212	Ed213	Ed214	Ed215	Ed216	Ed217	Ed218	Ed219	Ed220	Ed221	Ed222
	—	—	Number	Number	Number	Number	Number	Number	Number	Number	Number
Jan 12, 1866	Fish Creek	Nevada	0	0	0	0	5	0	34	0	0
Jan 21, 1866	Fort Grant	Arizona	0	0	0	0	0	0	13	0	6
Feb 15, 1866	Rock Canyon	Nevada	0	1	0	1	6	0	96	15	19
Feb 16, 1866	Jordan Creek	Oregon	0	0	0	0	1	0	1	0	0
Feb 22, 1866	Jordan Creek	Oregon	0	1	0	0	1	0	18	2	0
Mar 6–9, 1866	Palos Biancos (Ft MacDowell)	Arizona	0	0	0	0	0	0	20	7	0
Mar 20–25, 1866	Salt River	Arizona	0	0	0	0	0	0	22	7	2
Mar 22, 1866	Round Valley	Arizona	2	2	0	0	0	0	0	0	0
Mar 28, 1866	Rita Mangas	New Mexico	0	0	0	0	0	0	1	6	0
Mar 31, 1866	Pimos Village	Arizona	0	1	0	0	2	0	25	0	16
Apr 11, 1866	Forts Lincoln and Whipple	Arizona	0	0	0	0	0	0	16	0	0
Apr 22, 1866	Canon De Chelly	New Mexico	0	0	0	0	0	0	26	30	9
May 27, 1866	Owyhee River	Idaho	0	1	0	0	0	0	7	12	0
July 17, 1866	Steins Mountain	Oregon	0	0	0	0	1	0	3	5	0
July 17, 1866	Reno Creek	Dakota	0	1	0	0	4	0	0	0	0
July 18, 1866	Malheur River	Oregon	0	1	0	0	0	0	11	0	0
July 21, 1866	Crazy Woman's Fork	Dakota	1	1	0	0	0	0	0	0	0
July 29, 1866	Camp Cady	California	0	3	0	0	1	0	0	0	0
July 31, 1866	Fort Rice	Dakota	0	1	0	0	0	0	0	0	0
Aug 13, 1866	Grape Vine Springs	Arizona	0	1	0	0	0	0	33	40	0
Aug 17, 1866	Salt River	Arizona	0	0	0	0	0	0	1	0	1
Aug 24, 1866	San Francisco Mts.	Arizona	0	0	0	0	0	0	0	1	2
Aug 29, 1866	Owyhee River	Idaho	0	0	0	0	0	0	7	0	0
Sept 10–16, 1866	Fort Phil Kearney	Dakota	0	2	0	0	2	0	0	0	1
Sept 14, 1866	Camp Watson	Oregon	0	0	0	0	0	0	1	0	0
Sept 20, 1866	Fort C.F. Smith	Montana	0	2	0	0	0	0	0	0	0
Sept 21, 1866	Tongue River	Dakota	0	0	0	0	2	0	0	0	0
Sept 28, 1866	Dunder and Blitzen Creek	Idaho	0	0	0	0	1	0	0	0	0
Sept 28, 1866	La Bonte Creek	Montana	0	0	0	0	1	0	0	0	0
Sept 29, 1866	Fort Phil Kearney	Dakota	0	1	0	0	0	0	0	0	0
Oct 3, 1866	Cedar Valley	Arizona	0	0	0	0	0	0	15	0	10
Oct 3, 1866	Trinidad	Colorado	0	1	0	0	3	0	13	0	0
Oct 3, 1866	Long Valley	Nevada	0	0	0	0	0	0	8	0	0
Oct 5, 1866	Fort Klammath	Oregon	0	0	0	0	0	0	4	0	0
Oct 14, 1866	Harney Lake Valley	Oregon	0	0	0	0	1	0	3	0	8
Oct 15, 1866	Fort Klammath	Oregon	0	0	0	0	2	0	14	20	0
Oct 23, 1866	North Fork Platte River	Colorado	0	0	0	0	2	0	4	7	0
Oct 26, 1866	Lake Albert	Oregon	0	0	0	0	2	0	14	0	7
Oct 30, 1866	Malheur Country	Oregon	0	0	0	0	0	0	2	3	8
Nov 1, 1866	Trout Creek Canyon	Oregon	0	0	0	0	0	0	4	8	0

			Non-Indians						Indians		
			Killed			Wounded					
Date	Place	State or territory	Officers	Enlisted men	Civilians	Officers	Enlisted men	Civilians	Killed	Wounded	Captured
	Ed212	Ed213	Ed214	Ed215	Ed216	Ed217	Ed218	Ed219	Ed220	Ed221	Ed222
	–	–	Number	Number	Number	Number	Number	Number	Number	Number	Number
Nov 17, 1866	Sierra Ancha	Arizona	0	0	0	0	0	0	6	0	5
Nov 18, 1866	John Day's River	Oregon	0	0	0	0	0	0	3	1	0
Dec 3, 1866	Camp Watson	Oregon	0	0	0	0	0	0	14	0	5
Dec 5, 1866	Surprise Valley	California	0	0	0	0	0	0	0	0	0
Dec 6, 1866	Goose Creek	Dakota	1	1	0	0	2	0	0	0	0
Dec 11, 1866	Grief Hill	Arizona	0	1	0	0	0	0	0	0	0
Dec 14, 1866	Pinal Mountains	Arizona	0	0	0	0	0	0	3	0	0
Dec 21, 1866	Fort Phil Kearney	Dakota	3	74	0	0	0	0	0	0	0
Dec 24, 1866	Mud Creek	Texas	0	0	0	0	0	0	0	2	0
Dec 24–25, 1866	Fort Buford	Dakota	0	0	0	0	0	0	3	0	0
Dec 26, 1866	Owyhee Creek	Idaho	0	1	0	0	1	0	30	0	7
Jan 1, 1867	Fort Stanton	New Mexico	0	0	0	0	1	0	5	0	0
Jan 6, 1867	Crooked River	Oregon	0	0	0	0	1	0	26	0	8
Jan 8, 1867	Owyhee River	Idaho	0	0	0	0	0	0	0	0	0
Jan 9, 1867	Malheur River	Oregon	0	0	0	0	0	0	0	0	30
Jan 18, 1867	Eden Valley	Nevada	0	0	0	0	1	0	2	0	0
Jan 19, 1867	Nueces River	Texas	0	0	0	0	0	0	2	0	0
Jan 29, 1867	Owyhee River	Idaho	0	0	0	0	3	1	60	0	27
Jan 29, 1867	Camp MacDowell	Arizona	0	0	0	0	0	0	0	0	1
Feb 7, 1867	Vicksburg Mines	Nevada	0	0	0	0	1	0	0	0	0
Feb 15, 1867	Black Slate Mountain	Nevada	0	0	0	0	0	0	6	0	0
Feb 16, 1867	Surprise Valley	California	0	0	0	0	0	0	5	0	2
Feb 18, 1867	Warm Springs	Idaho	0	0	0	0	0	0	2	0	5
Feb 23, 1867	Meadow Valley	Arizona	0	0	0	0	1	0	0	0	0
Feb 27, 1867	Fort Reno	Dakota	0	3	0	0	0	0	0	0	0
Mar 11, 1867	Arab Canyon	California	0	0	0	0	0	0	12	0	0
Mar 12, 1867	Pecos River	Texas	0	1	1	0	2	0	25	0	0
Mar 28, 1867	Murderers' Creek	Oregon	0	0	0	0	0	0	0	0	0
Apr 3, 1867	Tonto Valley	Arizona	0	0	0	0	0	0	3	0	1
Apr 10, 1867	Black Mountains	Arizona	0	0	0	0	0	0	3	0	0
Apr 15, 1867	Fort Lyon	Colorado	0	0	0	0	1	0	0	0	0
Apr 16, 1867	Black Mountains	Arizona	0	0	0	0	0	0	20	0	0
Apr 18, 1867	Rio Verde	Arizona	0	1	0	0	1	0	30	0	0
Apr 19, 1867	Cimarron Crossing	Kansas	0	0	0	0	1	0	6	0	0
Apr 21, 1867	Fort Mojave	Arizona	0	0	0	0	0	0	5	5	0
Apr 26, 1867	Fort Reno	Dakota	0	1	0	0	0	0	0	0	0
Apr 27, 1867	Sivie's Creek	Oregon	0	0	0	0	0	0	6	0	0
May 1, 1867	La Prelle Creek	Dakota	0	1	0	0	0	0	0	0	0
May 5, 1867	Camp Watson	Oregon	0	0	0	0	0	0	1	0	0
May 6, 1867	Mazatzal Mountains	Arizona	0	0	0	0	1	0	2	0	0
May 6, 1867	Four Peaks	Arizona	0	0	0	0	0	0	0	0	0
May 23, 1867	Bridger's Ferry	Dakota	0	2	0	0	0	0	0	0	0
May 23, 1867	Big Timbers	Kansas	0	0	0	0	1	0	0	0	0
May 27, 1867	Pond Creek Station	Kansas	0	0	0	0	0	0	1	0	0
May 30, 1867	Fort Reno	Dakota	0	1	0	0	0	0	2	0	0

(continued)

TABLE Ed212–222   Hostile engagements with Indians – military, civilian, and Indian casualties, by place of action: 1866–1891 *Continued*

			Non-Indians						Indians		
			Killed			Wounded					
Date	Place	State or territory	Officers	Enlisted men	Civilians	Officers	Enlisted men	Civilians	Killed	Wounded	Captured
	Ed212	Ed213	Ed214	Ed215	Ed216	Ed217	Ed218	Ed219	Ed220	Ed221	Ed222
	—	—	Number	Number	Number	Number	Number	Number	Number	Number	Number
May 30, 1867	Beale Station	Arizona	0	0	0	0	0	0	5	0	0
May 31, 1867	Bluff Ranch	Kansas	0	2	0	0	0	0	0	0	0
June 1, 1867	Fairview	Colorado	0	1	0	0	0	0	0	0	0
June 8, 1867	Chalk Bluffs	Kansas	0	0	0	0	0	0	0	0	0
June 11, 1867	Big Timbers	Kansas	0	1	0	0	0	0	0	0	0
June 12, 1867	Fort Dodge	Kansas	0	0	0	0	1	0	0	0	0
June 12, 1867	Fort Phil Kearney	Dakota	0	1	0	0	0	0	0	0	0
June 14, 1867	Grinnell Springs	Kansas	0	1	0	0	0	0	0	0	0
June 14, 1867	Yampai Valley	Arizona	0	2	0	0	0	0	20	0	9
June 15, 1867	Big Timbers	Kansas	0	2	1	0	1	2	0	0	0
June 16, 1867	Gallinas Mountains	New Mexico	0	0	0	0	0	0	1	0	2
June 19, 1867	Steins Mountain	Oregon	0	0	0	0	0	0	12	1	2
June 20, 1867	Black Hills	Nebraska	0	0	0	0	0	0	2	0	0
June 21, 1867	Fort Wallace	Kansas	0	2	0	0	2	0	0	0	0
June 21, 1867	Calabases	Arizona	0	0	0	0	0	0	3	1	6
June 22, 1867	Goose Creek Station	Colorado	0	0	0	0	2	0	0	0	0
June 22, 1867	Fort Wallace	Kansas	0	0	0	0	0	0	0	0	0
June 24, 1867	Republican River	Kansas	0	0	0	0	1	0	0	0	0
June 26, 1867	Wilson's Creek	Kansas	0	0	0	0	0	0	5	0	0
June 26, 1867	Republican River	Kansas	0	0	0	0	2	0	5	0	0
June 26, 1867	Fort Wallace	Kansas	0	6	0	0	6	0	0	0	0
June 30, 1867	Fort Phil Kearney	Dakota	0	0	0	0	0	0	0	0	0
July 3, 1867	Goose Creek Station	Colorado	0	0	0	0	1	0	0	0	0
July 5, 1867	Dunder and Blitzen	Oregon	0	0	0	0	0	0	5	0	3
July 7, 1867	Beale's Spring	Arizona	0	1	0	0	0	0	0	0	0
July 8, 1867	Malheur River	Oregon	0	0	0	0	0	0	2	0	14
July 9, 1867	Truxton's Springs	Arizona	0	0	0	1	1	0	3	0	0
July 9, 1867	Fort Sumner	New Mexico	0	3	1	0	4	0	0	0	0
July 13, 1867	Malheur River	Oregon	0	1	0	0	0	0	5	0	2
July 19, 1867	Malheur County	Oregon	0	0	0	0	0	0	2	0	8
July 21, 1867	Buffalo Springs	Texas	0	0	0	0	0	0	1	0	0
July 22, 1867	Beaver Creeek	Kansas	1	10	2	0	0	0	0	0	0
July 27, 1867	Camps Smith and Harney	Oregon	0	0	0	0	0	0	0	0	0
July 29, 1867	Willows	Arizona	0	0	0	0	0	0	0	0	0
Aug 1, 1867	Fort Smith	Montana	1	1	1	0	1	0	8	30	0
Aug 2, 1867	Fort Phil Kearney	Dakota	1	5	0	1	2	0	60	120	0
Aug 2, 1867	Saline River	Kansas	0	1	1	1	0	0	0	0	0
Aug 8, 1867	Fort Stevenson	Dakota	0	0	1	0	0	0	0	0	0
Aug 13, 1867	O'Connor's Springs	Dakota	0	0	0	0	3	0	0	0	0
Aug 14, 1867	Fort Reno	Dakota	0	0	0	0	0	0	0	0	0
Aug 14, 1867	Chalk Springs	Dakota	0	1	0	0	0	0	0	0	0
Aug 16, 1867	Fort Reno	Dakota	0	0	2	0	0	0	0	0	0
Aug 17, 1867	Plum Creek	Nebraska	0	0	0	0	0	0	15	0	2
Aug 21–22, 1867	Prairie Dog Creek	Kansas	0	3	0	0	35	0	150	0	0
Aug 22, 1867	Fort Chadbourne	Texas	0	2	0	0	0	0	0	0	0

Date	Place	State or territory	Non-Indians — Killed Officers	Killed Enlisted men	Killed Civilians	Wounded Officers	Wounded Enlisted men	Wounded Civilians	Indians Killed	Indians Wounded	Indians Captured
	Ed212	Ed213	Ed214	Ed215	Ed216	Ed217	Ed218	Ed219	Ed220	Ed221	Ed222
	—	—	Number	Number	Number	Number	Number	Number	Number	Number	Number
Aug 22, 1867	Surprise Valley	California	0	0	0	0	0	0	2	7	0
Aug 23, 1867	Fort Concho	Texas	0	1	0	0	0	0	0	0	0
Aug 28, 1867	Camp Goodwin	Arizona	0	0	0	0	0	1	0	0	0
Aug 30, 1867	Fort Belknap	Texas	0	2	0	0	0	0	0	0	0
Sept 6, 1867	Silver River	Oregon	0	2	0	0	0	0	1	0	5
Sept 8, 1867	—	—	0	0	0	0	2	0	23	0	14
Sept 10, 1867	Live Oak Creek	Texas	0	0	0	0	0	0	0	0	0
Sept 16, 1867	Fort Inge	Texas	0	0	0	0	0	0	0	0	0
Sept 16, 1867	Saline River	Kansas	0	0	2	0	1	0	0	0	0
Sept 19, 1867	Walker's Creek	Kansas	0	1	0	0	3	0	2	0	0
Sept 20, 1867	Devil's River	Texas	0	0	0	0	0	0	1	0	0
Sept 23, 1867	Arkansas River	Kansas	0	1	1	1	0	0	0	0	0
Sept 24, 1867	Nine Mile Ridge	Kansas	0	0	0	0	1	0	0	0	0
Sept 26–28, 1867	Infernal Caverns	California	1	6	1	0	11	0	20	12	2
Sept 29, 1867	Fort Garland	Colorado	0	2	0	0	0	0	0	0	0
Oct 1, 1867	Howard's Well	Texas	0	2	0	0	0	0	1	0	0
Oct 6, 1867	Trout Creek	Arizona	0	0	0	0	0	0	7	0	0
Oct 10, 1867	Camp Lincoln	Arizona	0	0	0	0	0	0	1	0	0
Oct 10, 1867	Fort Stevenson	Dakota	0	0	0	0	1	0	0	0	0
Oct 17, 1867	Deep Creek	Texas	0	0	0	0	0	0	3	0	1
Oct 18, 1867	Sierra Diablo	New Mexico	0	1	0	0	6	0	0	0	0
Oct 20, 1867	Crazy Woman's Fork	Dakota	0	0	0	0	0	0	1	0	0
Oct 25, 1867	Truxell Springs	Arizona	0	0	0	0	0	0	1	0	0
Oct 26, 1867	Shell Creek	Dakota	0	0	0	0	0	0	0	0	0
Oct 26, 1867	Camp Winfield Scott	Nevada	0	0	0	0	0	0	3	0	4
Nov 3, 1867	Willow Grove	Arizona	0	1	0	0	0	0	32	0	0
Nov 4, 1867	Goose Creek	Dakota	0	1	0	1	3	0	0	0	0
Nov 5, 1867	Camp Bowie	Arizona	1	0	0	0	0	1	0	0	0
Nov 7, 1867	Toll Gate	Arizona	0	0	0	0	0	0	3	0	0
Nov 7, 1867	Willows	Arizona	0	0	0	1	5	0	19	0	17
Nov 11, 1867	Camp Lincoln	Arizona	0	0	0	0	3	0	0	0	0
Nov 13, 1867	Aqua Frio Springs	Arizona	0	0	0	1	2	0	0	0	0
Nov 15, 1867	Tonto Creek	Arizona	0	0	0	0	0	0	4	0	9
Nov 17, 1867	Fort Sumner	New Mexico	0	1	0	0	0	0	0	0	0
Nov 20, 1867	Fort Selden	New Mexico	0	0	0	0	0	0	2	0	0
Nov 22, 1867	De Schmidt Lake	Dakota	0	0	0	0	0	0	1	3	0
Nov 29, 1867	Shell Creek	Dakota	0	1	0	0	0	0	4	0	0
Dec 2, 1867	Crazy Woman's Creek	Dakota	0	1	0	0	3	4	0	0	0
Dec 5, 1867	Eagle Springs	Texas	0	1	0	0	0	0	0	0	0
Dec 12, 1867	Owyhee River	Oregon	0	0	0	0	0	0	7	0	0
Dec 14, 1867	Fort Phil Kearney	Dakota	0	0	0	0	0	2	0	0	0
Dec 19, 1867	Camp Wallen	Arizona	0	0	0	0	0	0	1	0	0
Dec 26, 1867	Fort Lancaster	Texas	0	3	0	0	0	0	20	11	0
Jan 4, 1868	Owyhee River	Idaho	0	0	0	0	0	0	1	0	15
Jan 14, 1868	Difficult Canyon	Arizona	0	0	0	0	2	0	16	6	0

(continued)

TABLE Ed212–222   Hostile engagements with Indians – military, civilian, and Indian casualties, by place of action: 1866–1891   Continued

			Non-Indians						Indians		
			Killed			Wounded					
Date	Place	State or territory	Officers	Enlisted men	Civilians	Officers	Enlisted men	Civilians	Killed	Wounded	Captured
	Ed212	Ed213	Ed214	Ed215	Ed216	Ed217	Ed218	Ed219	Ed220	Ed221	Ed222
	—	—	Number	Number	Number	Number	Number	Number	Number	Number	Number
Jan 14, 1868	Beale Springs	Arizona	0	0	0	1	0	0	5	0	0
Jan 16, 1868	Malheur River	Oregon	0	0	0	0	0	0	0	0	0
Mar 6, 1868	Paint Creek	Texas	0	0	0	0	2	0	7	0	0
Mar 10, 1868	Colorado River	Texas	0	0	0	0	0	0	1	0	0
Mar 11, 1868	Tularosa	New Mexico	0	0	13	0	0	0	0	0	0
Mar 14, 1868	Dunder and Blitzen Creek	Oregon	0	0	0	1	2	0	12	0	2
Mar 18, 1868	Fort Fetterman	Dakota	0	1	0	0	0	0	0	0	0
Mar 20, 1868	Horseshoe Ranch	Dakota	0	0	3	0	0	0	0	0	0
Mar 21, 1868	Camp Willow Grove	Arizona	0	2	0	0	0	0	0	0	0
Mar 25, 1868	Cottonwood Spings	Arizona	0	0	0	0	1	1	1	2	0
Mar 25, 1868	Bluff Creek	Kansas	0	0	0	0	0	0	0	0	0
Mar 26, 1868	Owyhee River	Oregon	0	0	0	0	0	0	1	0	0
Apr 1, 1868	Pinal Mountains	Arizona	0	0	0	0	0	0	0	0	0
Apr 3, 1868	Rock Creek	Wyoming	0	0	0	0	0	0	1	0	0
Apr 5, 1868	Malheur River	Oregon	0	0	0	0	0	0	32	0	2
Apr 17, 1868	Owyhee River	Idaho	0	0	0	0	0	0	5	0	3
Apr 17, 1868	Nesmith's Mills	New Mexico	0	0	0	0	1	5	10	25	0
Apr 21, 1868	Camp Grant	Arizona	0	0	0	0	0	0	2	0	0
Apr 21, 1868	Upper Yellowstone River	Montana	0	0	1	0	0	0	2	0	0
Apr 22, 1868	Fort McPherson	Nebraska	0	0	6	0	0	0	0	0	0
Apr 23, 1868	Camp Harney	Oregon	0	0	0	0	0	0	1	0	0
Apr 23, 1868	Fort Ellis	Montana	0	0	1	0	0	0	0	0	0
Apr 29, 1868	Camp Winfield Scott	Nevada	0	0	0	1	2	0	0	0	0
Apr 29, 1868	Warner Mountains	Oregon	0	0	0	0	2	0	0	0	0
May 1, 1868	Camp Crittenden	Arizona	0	0	0	0	1	0	0	0	0
May 1, 1868	San Pedro River	Arizona	0	0	0	0	0	0	3	0	0
May 1, 1868	Gila River	Arizona	0	0	0	0	0	0	6	4	0
May 1, 1868	Hoag's Bluff	Oregon	0	0	1	0	1	0	0	0	0
May 13, 1868	Fort Buford	Dakota	0	0	2	0	0	0	0	0	0
May 15, 1868	Fort Totten	Dakota	0	0	2	0	0	0	0	0	0
May 18, 1868	Rio Salinas	Arizona	0	0	0	0	0	0	6	0	0
May 19, 1868	Musselshell River	Dakota	0	2	0	0	0	0	0	10	0
May 24, 1868	—	—	0	0	0	0	0	0	0	0	0
May 24, 1868	Yellowstone River	Montana	0	0	0	0	0	0	0	0	0
May 29, 1868	Owyhee River	Idaho	0	0	0	0	0	0	34	0	0
May 30, 1868	Tonto Basin	Arizona	0	0	1	0	1	0	0	0	0
May 31, 1868	Castle Rock	Oregon	0	0	0	0	1	0	0	0	0
June 8–13, 1868	Apache Springs	New Mexico	0	0	0	0	0	0	3	0	0
June 9, 1868	Snake Canyon	Idaho	0	0	0	0	0	0	3	0	0
June 13, 1868	Tewnty Five Yard Creek	Montana	0	0	0	0	0	0	0	0	0
June 16, 1868	Toddy Mountain	Arizona	0	4	0	0	0	0	1	0	0
June 24, 1868	Battle Creek	Idaho	0	0	0	0	0	0	3	0	3
July 8, 1868	Verde and Salt Rivers	Arizona	0	0	0	0	0	0	1	0	0
July 11, 1868	Niobrara River	Mexico	0	0	1	0	0	2	0	0	0
July 19, 1868	Fort Reno	Dakota	0	1	0	0	1	0	0	0	0

Date	Place Ed212	State or territory Ed213	Non-Indians Killed — Officers Ed214	Non-Indians Killed — Enlisted men Ed215	Non-Indians Killed — Civilians Ed216	Non-Indians Wounded — Officers Ed217	Non-Indians Wounded — Enlisted men Ed218	Non-Indians Wounded — Civilians Ed219	Indians Killed Ed220	Indians Wounded Ed221	Indians Captured Ed222
			Number	Number	Number	Number	Number	Number	Number	Number	Number
July 26, 1868	Big Salmon River	Idaho	0	0	0	0	0	0	0	0	41
July 26, 1868	Juniper Canyon	Idaho	0	0	0	0	0	0	5	0	4
July 28, 1868	Sully's Old Camp	Dakota	0	0	0	0	0	0	0	0	0
July 30, 1868	Tonto Valley	Arizona	0	0	0	0	1	0	0	0	0
Aug 2, 1868	Cimarron River	Kansas	0	0	0	0	0	0	0	0	0
Aug 6, 1868	Fort Quitman	Texas	0	0	0	0	0	0	0	0	0
Aug 8–Sept 5, 1868	Juniper Mountains	Idaho	0	0	0	0	0	0	0	0	16
Aug 10, 1868	Saline River	Kansas	0	0	0	0	0	0	0	0	0
Aug 12, 1868	Republican River	Kansas	0	0	2	0	0	0	0	0	0
Aug 12, 1868	Cimmaron River	Kansas	0	2	0	0	3	0	12	15	0
Aug 13, 1868	Solomon River	Kansas	0	0	17	0	0	4	0	0	0
Aug 13, 1868	Walnut Grove	Arizona	0	0	0	0	0	0	3	0	0
Aug 13, 1868	Saline River	Kansas	0	0	0	0	0	0	3	10	0
Aug 19, 1868	Twin Butte Creek	Kansas	0	0	3	0	0	0	0	0	0
Aug 20, 1868	Fort Bufort	Dakota	0	3	0	1	3	0	0	0	0
Aug 20, 1868	Comstock's Ranch	Kansas	0	0	2	0	0	1	0	0	0
Aug 22, 1868	Santa Maria River	Arizona	0	0	0	0	0	0	2	0	1
Aug 23, 1868	Pond Creek and Lake Station	Colorado	0	0	8	0	0	0	0	0	0
Aug 23, 1868	Fort Totten	Dakota	0	3	0	0	0	0	0	0	0
Aug 25, 1868	Fort Dodge	Kansas	0	0	1	0	0	0	0	0	0
Aug 27, 1868	Forts Lyon and Sheridan	Colorado and Kansas	0	0	1	0	0	0	0	0	0
Aug 27, 1868	Hatchet Mountains	New Mexico	0	0	0	0	0	0	3	0	0
Aug 28, 1868	Kiowa Station	Kansas	0	0	3	0	0	0	0	0	0
Aug 28, 1868	Platte River	Nebraska	0	0	0	0	0	0	0	0	0
Aug 30, 1868	Republican River	Nebraska	0	0	0	0	0	0	0	0	0
Sept 1, 1868	Lake Station	Colorado	0	0	2	0	0	0	0	0	0
Sept 1, 1868	Reed's Springs	Colorado	0	0	3	0	0	3	0	0	0
Sept 1, 1868	Spanish Fort	Texas	0	0	9	0	0	0	0	0	0
Sept 2, 1868	Little Coon Creek	Kansas	0	0	0	0	3	0	3	1	0
Sept 3, 1868	Hugo Springs	Colorado	0	0	0	0	0	0	0	0	0
Sept 3, 1868	Colorado City	Colorado	0	0	4	0	0	0	0	0	0
Sept 4, 1868	Tonto Creek	Arizona	0	0	0	0	0	0	1	0	1
Sept 5, 1868	Willow Springs Station	Colorado	0	0	0	0	0	0	0	0	0
Sept 6–7, 1868	Colorado Territory	Colorado	0	0	25	0	0	0	0	0	0
Sept 8, 1868	Turkey Creek	Kansas	0	0	0	0	0	0	0	0	0
Sept 8, 1868	Cimarron Crossing	Kansas	0	0	17	0	0	0	0	0	0
Sept 8, 1868	Sheridan	Kansas	0	0	2	0	0	0	0	0	0
Sept 9, 1868	Forts Sheridan and Wallace	Kansas	0	0	6	0	0	0	0	0	0
Sept 9, 1868	Tonto Plateau	Arizona	0	0	0	0	0	0	2	0	4
Sept 10, 1868	Rule Creek	Colorado	0	2	0	0	1	0	4	0	0
Sept 10, 1868	Lake Station	Colorado	0	0	0	0	0	0	0	0	0
Sept 10, 1868	Lower Aqua Fria	Arizona	0	0	0	0	0	0	4	0	3
Sept 11, 1868	Rio Verde	Arizona	0	0	0	0	0	0	5	0	0
Sept 11–15, 1868	Sand Hills	Indian Territory	0	3	0	0	5	0	22	12	0
Sept 12, 1868	Fort Reynolds	Colorado	0	0	0	0	0	0	0	0	0

(continued)

TABLE Ed212–222   Hostile engagements with Indians – military, civilian, and Indian casualties, by place of action: 1866–1891 *Continued*

			Non-Indians						Indians		
			Killed			Wounded			Killed	Wounded	Captured
Date	Place	State or territory	Officers	Enlisted men	Civilians	Officers	Enlisted men	Civilians			
	Ed212	Ed213	Ed214	Ed215	Ed216	Ed217	Ed218	Ed219	Ed220	Ed221	Ed222
	—	—	Number	Number	Number	Number	Number	Number	Number	Number	Number
Sept 13, 1868	Dragoon Fork	Arizona	0	0	0	0	1	0	2	0	0
Sept 14, 1868	Horse Head Hills	Texas	0	0	0	0	1	0	25	25	0
Sept 15, 1868	Big Sandy Creek	Colorado	0	0	0	0	7	0	11	14	0
Sept 17, 1868	Ellis Station	Kansas	0	0	1	0	0	0	0	0	0
Sept 17, 1868	Fort Bascom	New Mexico	0	0	1	0	0	1	0	0	0
Sept 17–25, 1868	Arickaree Fork	Kansas	2	0	4	1	0	15	35	0	0
Sept 17, 1868	Saline River	Kansas	0	0	0	0	0	0	3	5	0
Sept 26, 1868	Fort Rice	Dakota	0	1	0	0	0	0	0	0	0
Sept 29, 1868	Sharp's Creek	Kansas	0	0	1	0	0	0	0	0	0
Oct 2, 1868	Fort Zarah	Kansas	0	0	0	0	0	0	0	0	0
Oct 3, 1868	Membres Mounatains	New Mexico	0	0	0	0	1	0	0	0	0
Oct 4, 1868	Fort Dodge	Kansas	0	0	2	0	0	1	0	0	0
Oct 7, 1868	Purgatory River	Colorado	0	0	1	0	0	0	0	0	0
Oct 9, 1868	Salt River and Cherry Creek	Arizona	0	0	0	0	0	0	13	0	0
Oct 10, 1868	Fort Zarah	Kansas	0	0	0	0	0	0	0	0	0
Oct 12, 1868	Ellsworth	Kansas	0	0	1	0	0	0	0	0	0
Oct 12, 1868	Arkansas River	Kansas	0	0	0	0	0	0	2	0	0
Oct 13–30, 1868	White Woman's Fork	Kansas	0	0	0	0	0	0	2	3	0
Oct 14, 1868	Sand Creek	Colorado	0	0	0	0	0	0	0	0	0
Oct 14, 1868	Prairie Dog Creek	Kansas	0	1	0	0	1	0	2	0	0
Oct 15, 1868	Fisher and Yocucy Creeks	Kansas	0	0	4	0	1	0	30	0	0
Oct 18, 1868	Beaver Creek	Kansas	0	0	0	0	8	0	10	0	0
Oct 19, 1868	Dragoon Fork	Arizona	0	0	0	0	1	0	7	0	0
Oct 21, 1868	Forts Verde and Whipple	Arizona	0	0	0	0	1	0	0	0	0
Oct 23, 1868	Fort Zarah	Kansas	0	0	2	0	0	0	2	0	0
Oct 25–26, 1868	Beaver and Prairie Dog Creeks	Kansas	0	0	0	1	1	0	30	0	0
Oct 26, 1868	Central City	New Mexico	0	0	3	0	0	0	0	0	0
Oct 30, 1868	Grinnell Station	Kansas	0	0	0	0	0	0	0	1	0
Nov 2, 1868	Wickenberg and Prescott	Arizona	0	1	0	0	0	0	0	0	0
Nov 3, 1868	Big Coon Creek	Kansas	0	0	0	0	0	0	0	0	0
Nov 7, 1868	Coon Creek	Kansas	0	0	0	0	0	0	2	0	0
Nov 7, 1868	Willow Grove	Arizona	0	0	0	0	0	0	11	2	20
Nov 11, 1868	Tonto Plateau	Arizona	0	0	0	0	2	0	15	40	0
Nov 18, 1868	Fort Hays	Kansas	0	2	0	0	0	0	2	0	0
Nov 19, 1868	Fort Dodge	Kansas	0	0	0	0	0	0	5	0	0
Nov 19, 1868	Little Coon Creek	Kansas	0	0	1	0	0	0	2	0	0
Nov 19, 1868	Fort Dodge	Kansas	0	0	0	0	0	0	4	0	0
Nov 19, 1868	—	—	0	0	0	0	3	0	4	6	0
Nov 20, 1868	Mulberry Creek	Kansas	0	0	2	0	0	0	0	0	0
Nov 23, 1868	Bill Williams Mountain	Arizona	0	0	0	0	0	0	2	1	0
Nov 25–27, 1868	Camp McDowell	Arizona	0	0	0	0	1	0	2	0	0
Nov 27, 1868	Black Kettle Villages	Indian Territory	2	19	0	3	13	0	103	0	53
Dec 10, 1868	Walker Springs	Arizona	0	0	0	0	0	0	3	0	6
Dec 11, 1868	Willow Grove	Arizona	0	1	0	0	0	0	8	0	0
Dec 13, 1868	Walker Springs	Arizona	0	0	0	0	0	0	8	0	14

| Date | Place | State or territory | Non-Indians Killed Officers | Non-Indians Killed Enlisted men | Non-Indians Killed Civilians | Non-Indians Wounded Officers | Non-Indians Wounded Enlisted men | Non-Indians Wounded Civilians | Indians Killed | Indians Wounded | Indians Captured |
| | Ed212 | Ed213 | Ed214 | Ed215 | Ed216 | Ed217 | Ed218 | Ed219 | Ed220 | Ed221 | Ed222 |
			Number	Number	Number	Number	Number	Number	Number	Number	Number
Dec 25, 1868	Elm Creek	Indian Territory	0	0	0	0	3	0	25	0	0
Jan 8, 1869	Lake Station	Colorado	0	0	2	0	0	0	0	0	0
Jan 8–15, 1869	Bill Williams Mountain	Arizona	0	0	0	0	0	0	1	0	0
Jan 13, 1869	Mount Turnbull	Arizona	0	0	0	0	0	0	1	1	0
Jan 29, 1869	Mulberry Creek	Kansas	0	0	0	0	2	0	6	0	0
Jan 30, 1869	Saline River	Kansas	0	0	2	0	0	0	0	0	0
Feb 4, 1869	Arivaypa Mountains	Arizona	0	0	0	0	0	0	8	0	8
Feb 5, 1869	Black Meza	Arizona	0	0	0	0	0	0	1	0	0
Feb 27, 1869	Camp Grant	Arizona	0	0	2	0	1	0	0	0	0
Mar 3, 1869	Oak Grove	Arizona	0	0	0	0	0	0	1	0	0
Mar 9, 1869	Fort Harker	Kansas	0	0	0	0	0	0	0	0	5
Mar 13, 1869	Shields River	Montana	0	0	2	0	0	0	4	0	0
Mar 16, 1869	Fort Randall	Dakota	0	1	0	0	0	0	0	0	0
Mar 17, 1869	Fort Bayard	New Mexico	0	0	0	0	0	0	0	5	0
Mar 17–30, 1869	Camp Goodwin	Arizona	0	0	0	0	0	0	2	0	0
Mar 22, 1869	Fort Fred Steele	Wyoming	0	0	0	0	0	0	5	0	0
Mar 23, 1869	Camp Grant	Arizona	0	0	1	0	2	0	0	0	0
Apr 6, 1869	La Bonte Creek	Wyoming	0	2	0	0	0	0	0	0	0
Apr 7, 1869	Musselshell River	Montana	0	1	0	0	2	0	9	0	0
Apr 14, 1869	Cienega	Arizona	0	0	0	0	2	0	0	0	0
Apr 16, 1869	Fort Wallace	Kansas	0	1	0	0	0	0	0	0	0
Apr 20, 1869	Crittenden	Arizona	0	0	0	0	0	0	0	0	0
Apr 22, 1869	Sangre Canyon	New Mexico	0	0	0	0	0	0	0	5	0
Apr 29, 1869	Turnbull Mountain	Arizona	0	0	0	0	0	0	28	0	8
May 2, 1869	San Augustine	New Mexico	0	2	0	0	4	0	5	10	0
May 2–9, 1869	Val de Chino Valley	Arizona	0	0	0	0	0	0	2	0	0
May 6, 1869	Grief Hill	Arizona	0	0	0	0	5	0	0	0	0
May 7, 1869	San Augustine Pass	New Mexico	0	1	0	0	1	1	0	0	0
May 7, 1869	Paint Creek	Texas	0	0	0	0	0	0	14	0	0
May 10, 1869	Fort Hays	Kansas	0	1	0	0	0	0	0	0	0
May 13, 1869	Beaver Creek or Elephant Rock	Kansas	0	4	0	0	3	0	25	20	0
May 15, 1869	Fort Lowell	Arizona	0	0	0	0	1	0	0	0	0
May 16, 1869	Spring Creek	Nebraska	0	0	0	0	3	0	0	0	0
May 18, 1869	Fort Bayard	New Mexico	0	0	0	0	0	0	0	0	0
May 18–26, 1869	Black Range	New Mexico	0	0	0	0	0	0	0	0	0
May 21, 1869	Fort Fred Steele	Wyoming	0	0	0	0	0	0	0	0	0
May 22–28, 1869	Mineral Springs	Arizona	0	0	0	0	0	0	4	0	4
May 25, 1869	Jewell County	Kansas	0	0	6	0	0	0	0	0	0
May 26, 1869	Sheridan	Kansas	0	0	0	0	0	2	0	0	0
May 29, 1869	Fossil Station	Kansas	0	0	2	0	0	4	0	0	0

(continued)

TABLE Ed212–222   Hostile engagements with Indians – military, civilian, and Indian casualties, by place of action: 1866–1891   Continued

Date	Place	State or territory	Non-Indians Killed			Non-Indians Wounded			Indians Killed	Indians Wounded	Indians Captured
			Officers	Enlisted men	Civilians	Officers	Enlisted men	Civilians			
	Ed212	Ed213	Ed214	Ed215	Ed216	Ed217	Ed218	Ed219	Ed220	Ed221	Ed222
			Number	Number	Number	Number	Number	Number	Number	Number	Number
May 30, 1869	Salt Creek	Kansas	0	0	1	0	0	0	0	0	0
May 30–June 3, 1869	Toll Gate	Arizona	0	0	0	0	0	0	4	0	0
May 30, 1869	Fort Hays	Kansas	0	0	0	0	0	0	0	0	0
May 31, 1869	Rose Creek	Kansas	0	0	0	0	2	0	0	5	0
June 1, 1869	Solomon River	Kansas	0	0	13	0	1	0	0	1	0
June 7, 1869	Pecos River	Texas	0	1	0	0	0	0	2	0	0
June 11, 1869	Solomon River	Kansas	0	0	0	0	0	0	0	0	0
June 16, 1869	Toll Gate	Arizona	0	1	0	0	1	0	3	0	0
June 19, 1869	Fort Wallace	Kansas	0	0	0	0	0	0	0	0	0
June 19, 1869	Sheridan	Kansas	0	0	0	0	2	0	4	12	0
June 20, 1869	Scandinavia	Kansas	0	0	0	0	0	0	1	0	0
June 30–July 5, 1869	Red Rock Country	Arizona	0	0	0	0	0	0	7	0	1
June 26, 1869	Santa Maria River	Arizona	0	0	0	0	0	0	4	0	0
June 26, 1869	Sheridan	Kansas	0	1	0	0	0	0	0	0	0
June 27, 1869	Great Mouth Canyon	Arizona	0	0	0	0	0	0	3	0	0
June 30, 1869	Burro Mountains	New Mexico	0	0	0	0	0	0	0	4	0
July 3, 1869	Hell Canyon	Arizona	0	0	0	0	0	0	4	0	0
July 6, 1869	Hac Qua-Halla Water	Arizona	0	0	0	0	1	0	9	10	0
July 6, 1869	Frenchman's Fork	Nebraska	0	0	0	0	0	0	3	3	0
July 8, 1869	Republican River	Kansas	0	0	0	0	1	0	0	2	0
July 10–17, 1869	—	New Mexico	0	0	10	0	0	0	0	0	0
July 11, 1869	Summit Springs	Colorado	0	0	0	0	1	0	52	0	15
July 13–19, 1869	White Mountains	Arizona	0	0	0	0	0	0	11	2	13
July 22–23, 1869	North Platte	Nebraska	0	0	0	0	1	0	0	0	0
July 27, 1869	New Mexico	New Mexico	0	0	0	0	0	0	0	3	0
Aug 3, 1869	Fort Stevenson	Dakota	0	0	0	0	0	0	0	0	0
Aug 10, 1869	Fort Buford	Dakota	0	0	4	0	0	0	0	0	0
Aug 15, 1869	San Augustine Pass	New Mexico	0	0	0	0	0	0	0	0	0
Aug 19, 1869	Eagle Creek	Montana	0	0	1	0	0	0	4	2	0
Aug 19, 1869	Helena	Montana	0	0	1	0	0	1	0	0	0
Aug 21, 1869	Cayote Station	Kansas	0	0	0	0	0	0	0	0	0
Aug 25, 1869	Santa Maria River	Arizona	0	0	0	0	0	0	9	7	0
Aug 25, 1869	Tonto Station	Arizona	0	0	0	0	2	0	6	7	1
Aug 26, 1869	Tonto Plateau	Arizona	0	1	0	0	0	0	0	0	0
Sept 5, 1869	Fort Stanton	New Mexico	0	0	0	0	2	0	3	7	0
Sept 5, 1869	Camp Date Creek	Arizona	0	0	0	0	0	0	3	0	0
Sept 12, 1869	Laramie Peak	Wyoming	0	1	0	0	1	0	9	0	0
Sept 14, 1869	Popo Agie	Wyoming	0	0	0	0	2	0	2	7	0
Sept 14, 1869	Little Wind River	Wyoming	0	1	0	0	0	0	0	0	0
Sept 15, 1869	Whiskey Gap	Wyoming	0	1	0	0	0	0	0	0	0
Sept 16, 1869	Brazos River	Texas	0	0	0	0	3	0	0	0	0
Sept 17, 1869	Fort Stanton	New Mexico	0	0	0	0	0	0	0	3	0
Sept 17, 1869	Point of Rocks	Wyoming	0	0	1	0	0	0	2	7	0
Sept 17, 1869	Twin Creek	Wyoming	0	0	0	0	0	0	0	0	0
Sept 20–21, 1869	Brazos River	Texas	0	0	0	0	1	0	0	0	0

			Non-Indians						Indians		
			Killed			Wounded			Killed	Wounded	Captured
	Place	State or territory	Officers	Enlisted men	Civilians	Officers	Enlisted men	Civilians	Number	Number	Number
	Ed212	Ed213	Ed214	Ed215	Ed216	Ed217	Ed218	Ed219	Ed220	Ed221	Ed222
Date	—		Number	Number	Number	Number	Number	Number	Number	Number	Number
Sept 23, 1869	Red Creek	Arizona	0	0	0	0	0	0	0	0	0
Sept 24, 1869	Fort Bayard	New Mexico	0	0	0	0	0	0	0	3	0
Sept 26, 1869	San Francisco Mountains	New Mexico	0	0	0	0	0	0	2	0	0
Sept 26, 1869	Prairie Dog Creek	Kansas	0	0	0	0	0	0	1	0	1
Sept 29, 1869	Fort Bayard	New Mexico	0	0	0	0	1	0	3	3	0
Oct 5, 1869	Dragoon Springs	Arizona	0	4	0	0	0	0	0	0	0
Oct 8, 1869	Chiricahua Mountains	Arizona	0	0	0	0	2	0	12	0	0
Oct 12, 1869	Red Rock	Arizona	0	0	0	0	0	0	2	0	0
Oct 20, 1869	Chiricahua Mountains	Arizona	0	2	0	1	2	0	18	0	0
Oct 23, 1869	Miembres Mountains	New Mexico	0	0	0	0	1	0	3	3	0
Oct 28–29, 1869	Brazos River	Texas	0	0	0	0	8	0	50	0	7
Oct 31, 1869	Chiricahua Mountains	Arizona	0	0	0	0	0	0	2	0	0
Nov 6, 1869	Garde	Arizona	0	0	0	0	0	0	0	0	2
Nov 6, 1869	Forts Fetterman and Laramie	Wyoming	0	2	0	0	0	0	0	0	0
Nov 10, 1869	Tompkins Valley	Arizona	0	0	0	0	0	0	4	0	0
Nov 16–28, 1869	Santa Maria River	Arizona	0	0	0	0	2	0	2	0	0
Nov 18, 1869	Guadaloupe Mountains	New Mexico	0	0	0	1	2	0	1	0	1
Nov 24, 1869	Llano River	Texas	0	0	0	0	0	0	1	0	0
Dec 1, 1869	Horseshoe	Wyoming	0	0	0	0	3	0	0	0	0
Dec 10, 1869	Mount Buford	Arizona	0	0	0	0	1	0	11	0	0
Dec 25, 1869	Johnson's Mail Station	Texas	0	0	0	0	0	0	0	0	0
Dec 26, 1869	Sanguinara Canyon	Texas	0	0	0	1	0	0	0	0	0
Dec 26, 1869	Fort Wrangel	Alaska	0	0	0	0	0	1	1	1	0
Dec 30, 1869	Delaware Creek	Texas	0	0	0	0	0	0	0	0	0
Jan 3–8, 1870	Rio Grande	Texas	0	0	0	0	0	0	0	0	0
Jan 6, 1870	Guadaloupe Mountains	Texas	0	0	0	0	0	0	0	0	0
Jan 11, 1870	Pecos River	Texas	0	0	0	0	0	0	1	0	0
Jan 20, 1870	Delaware Creek	Texas	0	0	0	0	2	0	0	0	0
Jan 23, 1870	Marias River	Montana	0	1	0	0	0	0	175	40	140
Jan 28, 1870	Dragoon Mountains	Arizona	0	0	0	0	0	0	13	0	2
Mar 9, 1870	Reno Road	Arizona	0	0	0	0	1	1	4	0	0
Mar 15–16, 1870	Sol's Wash	Arizona	0	0	0	0	0	0	2	0	0
Apr 2, 1870	Sweetwater	Wyoming	0	0	6	0	0	0	0	0	0
Apr 3, 1870	San Martine Springs	Texas	0	0	0	0	0	0	1	0	0
Apr 3, 1870	North Hubbard	Texas	0	0	0	0	0	0	2	4	0
Apr 6, 1870	Bluff Creek	Kansas	0	0	0	0	0	0	0	3	0
Apr 6, 1870	Clear Creek	Texas	0	0	0	0	0	0	1	0	10
Apr 25, 1870	Crow Springs	Texas	0	0	0	0	0	0	0	0	0
Apr 30, 1870	Pinal Mountains	Arizona	0	0	0	0	0	0	11	0	4
May 4, 1870	Miner's Delight	Wyoming	1	0	0	0	1	0	7	1	0
May 16, 1870	Kansas Pacific Railroad	Kansas	0	0	10	0	0	0	0	0	0
May 17, 1870	Springs Creek	Nebraska	0	0	0	0	1	0	1	7	0
May 15–20, 1870	Kickapoo Springs	Texas	0	0	0	0	0	0	0	4	0
May 25, 1870	Tonto Valley	Arizona	0	0	0	0	0	0	21	0	12
May 28, 1870	Camp Supply	Indian Territory	0	0	2	0	0	0	0	0	0

(continued)

TABLE Ed212–222 Hostile engagements with Indians – military, civilian, and Indian casualties, by place of action: 1866–1891 *Continued*

			Non-Indians						Indians		
			Killed			Wounded					
Date	Place	State or territory	Officers	Enlisted men	Civilians	Officers	Enlisted men	Civilians	Killed	Wounded	Captured
	Ed212	Ed213	Ed214	Ed215	Ed216	Ed217	Ed218	Ed219	Ed220	Ed221	Ed222
	—	—	Number	Number	Number	Number	Number	Number	Number	Number	Number
May 29, 1870	Bass Canyon	Texas	0	1	0	0	0	0	0	0	0
May 29–June 3, 1870	Camp Apache	Arizona	0	0	0	0	0	0	0	1	6
May 30, 1870	Holiday Creek	Texas	0	1	2	0	0	0	0	0	0
May 31, 1870	Carlyle Station	Kansas	0	0	0	2	0	0	0	3	0
May 31, 1870	Bear Creek	Kansas	0	2	0	0	0	0	5	0	10
June 1, 1870	Solomon River	Kansas	0	0	0	0	0	0	0	4	0
June 2, 1870	Copper Canyon	Arizona	0	1	0	0	0	0	1	0	0
June 3, 1870	Fort Whipple	Arizona	0	0	0	0	0	0	2	0	0
June 5, 1870	Apache Mountains	Arizona	0	0	0	0	0	0	30	0	0
June 5, 1870	Black Canyon	Arizona	0	0	0	0	0	0	2	0	0
June 8, 1870	Fort Dodge	Kansas	0	0	0	0	2	0	3	0	0
June 8, 1870	Red Willow Creek	Nebraska	0	0	0	0	0	0	3	0	0
June 10, 1870	Snake Creek	Indian Territory	0	0	0	0	0	0	0	0	0
June 11, 1870	Camp Supply	Indian Territory	0	0	0	0	0	0	6	10	0
June 13, 1870	Fort Buford	Dakota	0	0	0	0	0	4	1	0	0
June 13, 1870	Grinnell Station	Kansas	0	0	0	0	0	0	3	10	0
June 15, 1870	Fort Bascom	New Mexico	0	0	1	0	0	0	0	0	0
June 15, 1870	Rio Verde	Arizona	0	0	0	0	0	0	0	0	0
June 16, 1870	Mulberry Creek	Kansas	0	0	3	0	0	0	0	0	0
June 18, 1870	North Platte	Nebraska	0	0	0	0	0	0	0	1	0
June 21, 1870	Carlson	Colorado	0	0	5	0	0	0	0	0	8
June 25, 1870	Medicine Bow	Wyoming	0	0	0	0	0	0	0	0	3
June 27, 1870	Pine Grove Meadow	Wyoming	0	0	0	0	1	0	15	0	0
Aug 1, 1870	Washita River	Indian Territory	0	2	0	0	5	0	3	10	9
Oct 6, 1870	Looking Glass Creek	Nebraska	0	0	0	0	0	0	1	0	0
Oct 16, 1870	Guadaloupe Mountains	New Mexico	0	0	0	0	0	0	1	0	0
Oct 30, 1870	Fort Stanton	New Mexico	0	0	0	0	0	0	0	0	0
Nov 10, 1870	Carson	Colorado	0	0	0	0	0	0	0	0	0
Nov 18, 1870	Lowell Station	Kansas	0	0	1	0	0	0	0	0	0
Nov, 1870	Guadaloupe Mountains	New Mexico	0	0	0	0	0	0	0	0	0
Feb 17, 1871	Fort Bayard	New Mexico	0	1	0	0	2	0	14	20	0
Feb 26, 1871	Grinnell	Kansas	0	0	0	0	0	0	0	0	0
Mar 18, 1871	Fort Dodge	Kansas	0	0	3	0	0	0	0	5	0
Apr 30, 1871	—	Colorado	0	0	20	0	0	0	0	0	0
May 2, 1871	Fort Selden	New Mexico	0	0	0	0	0	0	0	0	0
May 3, 1871	Cimmaron	New Mexico	0	0	3	0	0	0	0	0	22
May 5, 1871	Whetstone Mountains	Arizona	1	1	0	0	1	0	13	0	0
May 12, 1871	Red River	Texas	0	0	7	0	0	0	3	4	0
May 17, 1871	Fort Sill	Indian Territory	0	0	0	0	1	0	1	0	2
May 20, 1871	Brazos and Big Wishita	Texas	0	0	0	0	1	0	1	0	0
May 21, 1871	Camp Melvin Station	Texas	0	0	0	0	2	0	0	0	0
May 24, 1871	Birdwood Creek	Nebraska	0	0	0	0	0	0	0	0	6
May 28, 1871	Canadian Mountains	Texas	0	0	0	0	0	0	0	0	12
May 29, 1871	Kiowa Springs	New Mexico	0	0	0	0	0	0	0	0	22
June 1, 1871	Huachuca Mountains	Arizona	0	0	0	0	0	0	3	0	0

Date	Place	State or territory	Non-Indians						Indians		
			Killed			Wounded			Killed	Wounded	Captured
			Officers	Enlisted men	Civilians	Officers	Enlisted men	Civilians			
	Ed212	Ed213	Ed214	Ed215	Ed216	Ed217	Ed218	Ed219	Ed220	Ed221	Ed222
	—	—	Number	Number	Number	Number	Number	Number	Number	Number	Number
June 8–9, 1871	Verde River	Arizona	0	0	0	0	0	0	56	8	0
June 10, 1871	Huachuca Mountains	Arizona	0	0	0	0	0	0	0	0	0
June 26, 1871	Camp Brown	Wyoming	0	0	0	0	0	0	0	0	0
June 28, 1871	Pawnee Fork	Kansas	0	0	0	0	0	0	0	0	0
June 30, 1871	Staked Plains	Texas	0	0	0	0	0	0	0	0	1
July 1871	Forts Apache and McDowell	Arizona	0	0	0	0	0	0	7	0	11
July 2, 1871	Fort Larned	Kansas	0	0	0	0	0	0	0	0	0
July 13, 1871	Cienega de Los Pinos	Arizona	0	1	0	0	3	0	15	0	0
July 15, 1871	Double Mountain Fork	Texas	0	0	0	0	0	0	0	0	0
July 19, 1871	Bear Springs	Arizona	0	0	2	0	1	0	0	0	0
July 22, 1871	Concho River	Texas	0	0	1	0	1	0	0	0	0
July 31, 1871	McKavett	Texas	0	0	0	0	0	0	1	0	0
Aug 18, 1871	Fort Stanton	New Mexico	0	0	1	0	0	0	0	0	0
Aug 25, 1871	Arivaypa Canyon	Arizona	0	0	0	0	0	0	5	0	0
Sept 1, 1871	McKavett	Texas	0	0	0	0	0	0	0	0	0
Sept 5, 1871	Chino Valley	Arizona	0	0	1	0	1	0	0	0	0
Sept 13, 1871	Tucson	Arizona	0	0	2	0	0	0	1	0	0
Sept 19, 1871	Foster Springs	Indian Territory	0	1	0	0	0	0	2	3	0
Sept 22, 1871	Fort Sill	Indian Territory	0	0	2	0	0	0	0	0	0
Oct 11, 1871	Brazos River	Texas	0	1	0	0	0	0	0	0	0
Oct 14, 1871	Cienega Sauz	Arizona	0	0	1	0	0	1	0	0	0
Oct 19, 1871	Brazos River	Texas	0	0	0	1	0	0	2	0	0
Oct 24, 1871	Horseshoe Canyon	Arizona	0	0	1	0	1	0	0	0	0
Nov 5, 1871	Wickenburgh	Arizona	0	0	6	0	0	2	0	0	0
Jan 20, 1872	Tucson and Camp Bowie	Arizona	0	0	3	0	0	1	0	0	0
Feb 9, 1872	North Concho Station	Texas	0	0	0	0	0	0	0	0	0
Feb 22, 1872	Cullumber's Station	Arizona	0	0	2	0	0	0	6	0	0
Feb 26, 1872	Camp Bowie	Arizona	0	0	1	0	0	0	0	0	0
Mar 17, 1872	Camp Verde	Arizona	0	0	1	0	1	0	1	1	0
Mar 27–28, 1872	Fort Concho	Texas	0	0	0	0	1	0	2	3	1
Apr 17, 1872	Camp Apache	Arizona	0	1	1	0	0	0	0	2	0
Apr 20, 1872	Howard's Wells	Texas	1	0	0	0	0	0	6	0	0
Apr 26, 1872	South Fork Loup River	Nebraska	0	0	0	0	0	0	0	0	0
May 6, 1872	Tierra Amarilla	New Mexico	0	1	0	0	1	0	1	1	0
May 12, 1872	Big and Little Wichita Rivers	Texas	0	0	0	0	1	0	2	2	0
May 19, 1872	Fort Belknap	Texas	0	0	1	0	0	0	2	2	0
May 20, 1872	La Pendencia	Texas	0	0	0	0	0	0	0	0	0
May 22, 1872	Fort Dodge	Kansas	0	1	0	0	1	0	1	0	0
May 22, 1872	Sonoita Valley	Arizona	0	0	1	0	0	0	0	0	0
May 23, 1872	Sycamore Canyon	Arizona	0	0	0	0	0	0	0	0	0
May 24, 1872	Lost Creek	Texas	0	1	0	0	1	0	0	0	0
June 10, 1872	Bill Williams Mountain	Arizona	0	0	0	0	0	0	1	1	0
June 13, 1872	Prescott	Arizona	0	0	1	0	0	0	1	0	0
June 14, 1872	Ponca Agency	Dakota	0	0	0	0	0	0	0	0	0
June 15, 1872	Granite Mountains	Arizona	0	0	0	0	0	2	2	0	0

(continued)

TABLE Ed212–222 Hostile engagements with Indians – military, civilian, and Indian casualties, by place of action: 1866–1891 Continued

			Non-Indians						Indians		
			Killed			Wounded					
Date	Place	State or territory	Officers	Enlisted men	Civilians	Officers	Enlisted men	Civilians	Killed	Wounded	Captured
	Ed212	Ed213	Ed214	Ed215	Ed216	Ed217	Ed218	Ed219	Ed220	Ed221	Ed222
	—	—	Number	Number	Number	Number	Number	Number	Number	Number	Number
June 15, 1872	Johnson's Station	Texas	0	0	0	0	0	0	2	0	0
July 12, 1872	Deep River	Indian Territory	0	0	0	0	0	0	0	0	0
July 13, 1872	Whetstone Mountains	Arizona	0	0	0	0	2	0	4	0	0
July 22, 1872	Otter Creek	Indian Territory	0	0	0	0	0	0	0	1	0
July 26–Oct 15, 1872	Yellowstone Expedition	Montana	1	0	1	1	0	0	0	0	0
July 27, 1872	Mount Graham	Arizona	0	0	0	0	0	0	1	0	0
July 28, 1872	Central Station	Texas	0	0	0	0	0	0	0	0	0
Aug 6, 1872	Chiricahua Mountains	Arizona	0	0	0	0	0	0	2	0	0
Aug 14, 1872	Prior's Fork	Montana	0	1	1	0	5	0	2	10	0
Aug 15, 1872	Palo Duro	New Mexico	0	0	0	0	1	0	4	8	0
Aug 26, 1872	Fort McKeen	Dakota	1	6	2	0	0	0	0	0	0
Aug 27, 1872	Santa Cruz	Arizona	0	0	4	0	0	0	0	0	0
Aug 27, 1872	Davidson's Canyon	Arizona	1	1	2	0	0	0	0	0	0
Sept 4, 1872	Camp Mojave	Arizona	0	0	1	0	0	0	0	1	0
Sept 10–13, 1872	Beaver Creek and Sweetwater	Wyoming	0	0	0	0	0	0	0	0	0
Sept 25, 1872	Muchos Canyon	Arizona	0	0	0	0	0	0	40	0	0
Sept 29, 1872	Red River	Texas	0	1	0	0	3	0	23	1	120
Sept 30, 1872	Squaw Peak	Arizona	0	0	0	0	0	0	17	0	1
Sept 30, 1872	Camp Crittenden	Arizona	0	4	0	0	0	0	0	0	0
Oct 2, 1872	Fort McKeen	Dakota	0	3	0	0	1	0	0	0	0
Oct 14, 1872	—	Dakota	0	0	2	0	0	0	3	0	0
Oct 25–Nov 3, 1872	Santa Maria Mountains	Arizona	0	0	0	0	0	0	9	0	4
Nov 25, 1872	Red Rocks	Arizona	0	1	0	0	0	0	11	0	0
Nov 29, 1872	Lost River	Oregon	0	1	0	0	7	0	8	0	0
Nov 29, 1872	Modoc Campaign	—	0	0	0	0	0	0	0	0	0
Dec 2, 1872	Land's Ranch	California	0	1	0	0	1	0	0	0	0
Dec 7–8, 1872	Red Rock Country	Arizona	0	0	0	0	0	0	12	0	0
Dec 11, 1872	Bad Rock Mountain	Arizona	0	0	0	0	0	0	14	0	6
Dec 13, 1872	Mazatzal Mountains	Arizona	0	0	0	0	0	0	11	0	9
Dec 14, 1872	Indian Run	Arizona	0	0	0	0	0	0	0	0	0
Dec 28, 1872	Salt River	Arizona	0	1	0	0	1	0	57	0	20
Dec 30, 1872	Baby Canyon	Arizona	0	0	0	0	0	0	6	1	2
Jan 2, 1873	Clear Creek	Arizona	0	0	0	0	1	0	0	0	0
Jan 12, 1873	Tule Lake	California	0	0	0	0	1	0	0	0	0
Jan 16, 1873	Superstition Mountain	Arizona	0	0	0	0	0	0	4	0	12
Jan 17, 1873	Modoc Caves	California	0	9	0	3	27	0	0	0	0
Jan 19, 1873	Verde River	Arizona	0	0	0	0	0	0	5	0	0
Jan 20, 1873	Miembres	New Mexico	0	0	0	0	0	0	1	0	0
Jan 22, 1873	Tonto Creek	Arizona	0	1	0	0	0	0	17	0	0
Feb 6, 1873	Hell Canyon	Arizona	0	0	0	0	0	0	2	0	1
Feb 20, 1873	Fossil Creek	Arizona	0	0	0	0	0	0	5	0	4
Feb 26, 1873	Angostura	New Mexico	0	0	0	0	0	0	5	7	5
Mar 19, 1873	Mazatzal Mountains	Arizona	0	0	0	0	0	0	8	0	5
Mar 25, 1873	Turret Mountains	Arizona	0	0	0	0	0	0	10	0	3
Mar 27, 1873	Turret Mountains	Arizona	0	0	0	0	0	0	23	0	10

Date	Place	State or territory	Non-Indians						Indians		
			Killed			Wounded			Killed	Wounded	Captured
			Officers	Enlisted men	Civilians	Officers	Enlisted men	Civilians			
	Ed212	Ed213	Ed214	Ed215	Ed216	Ed217	Ed218	Ed219	Ed220	Ed221	Ed222
	—	—	Number	Number	Number	Number	Number	Number	Number	Number	Number
Apr 11–20, 1873	Lava Beds	California	1	6	1	2	13	2	0	0	0
Apr 25, 1873	Canyon Creek	Arizona	0	0	0	0	0	1	0	0	0
Apr 26, 1873	Lava Beds	California	4	18	0	1	16	1	0	0	0
Apr 27, 1873	Eagle Springs	Texas	0	0	0	0	0	0	0	0	0
May, 1873	Barilla Springs	Texas	0	0	0	0	0	0	0	0	0
May 6, 1873	Santa Maria River	Arizona	0	0	0	0	0	0	4	0	0
May 7, 1873	Lava Beds	California	0	0	0	0	1	0	0	0	0
May 7, 1873	—	Oregon	0	0	0	0	2	0	0	0	0
May 7, 1873	Fort Lincoln	Dakota	0	0	0	0	0	0	1	3	0
May 10, 1873	Soras Lake	California	0	2	0	0	7	0	1	2	0
May 17, 1873	Butte Creek	Oregon	0	0	0	0	0	0	2	0	0
May 18, 1873	Remolina	Mexico	0	0	0	0	3	0	19	2	42
May 22, 1873	Fairchild's Ranch	California	0	0	0	0	0	0	0	0	150
May 27, 1873	San Carlos Agency	Arizona	1	0	0	0	0	0	0	0	0
May 30, 1873	Langell's Valley	California	0	0	0	0	0	0	0	0	33
June 1, 1873	Willow Creek	California	0	0	0	0	0	0	0	0	7
June 15–17, 1873	Fort Lincoln	Dakota	0	0	0	0	1	0	4	8	0
June 16, 1873	Tonto Creek	Arizona	0	0	0	0	1	0	14	0	5
July 13, 1873	Canada Alamosa	New Mexico	0	1	0	0	0	0	3	0	0
Aug 11, 1873	Yellostone River	Montana	0	3	0	1	3	0	0	0	0
Aug 19, 1873	Barrilla Springs	Texas	0	0	0	0	0	0	1	0	0
Aug 31, 1873	Pease River	Texas	0	0	0	0	0	0	4	1	0
Sept 1, 1873	Sierra San Matar	New Mexico	0	0	0	0	0	0	2	0	0
Sept 20, 1873	Fort Fetterman	Wyoming	0	0	0	0	0	0	0	0	0
Sept 23, 1873	Hardscrabble Creek	Arizona	0	0	0	0	0	0	14	0	5
Sept 29, 1873	Sierra Ancha	Arizona	0	0	0	0	0	0	2	0	4
Oct 1, 1873	Central Station	Texas	0	0	0	0	0	0	0	0	0
Oct 1, 1873	Guadaloupe Mountains	New Mexico	0	0	0	0	0	0	3	1	0
Oct 8, 1873	Chiricahua Mountains	Arizona	0	0	0	0	0	0	0	0	0
Sept 28–30, 1873	Mazatzal Mountains	Arizona	0	0	0	0	0	0	25	0	6
Sept 30, 1873	Pajarita Springs	New Mexico	0	0	0	0	0	0	0	0	18
Dec 4, 1873	Verde River	Arizona	0	0	0	0	0	0	15	0	0
Dec 5, 1873	Elm Creek	Texas	0	0	0	0	0	0	4	0	16
Dec 8, 1873	San Carlos Agency	Arizona	0	0	0	0	0	0	25	0	17
Dec 10, 1873	Kickapoo Springs	Texas	0	0	0	0	1	0	9	0	0
Dec 21, 1873	Ehrenberg	Arizona	0	0	0	0	0	0	6	0	1
Dec 23, 1873	Cave Creek	Arizona	0	0	0	0	0	0	9	3	0
Dec 31, 1873	Sunflower Valley	Arizona	0	0	0	0	0	0	7	0	11
Jan 4, 1874	Wild Rye Creek	Arizona	0	0	0	0	0	0	4	0	0
Jan 8, 1874	Pleasant Valley	Arizona	0	0	0	0	0	0	2	0	0
Jan 10, 1874	Canyon Creek	Arizona	0	0	0	0	0	0	4	3	3
Feb 2, 1874	Home Creek	Texas	0	0	0	0	0	0	0	0	0
Feb 5, 1874	Double Mountain Fork	Texas	0	1	0	0	1	0	10	0	0
Feb 9, 1874	Cottonwood Creek	Wyoming	1	0	0	0	0	0	0	0	0
Feb 2–April 21, 1874	Bill Williams Mountain	Arizona	0	0	0	0	0	0	3	0	0

(continued)

TABLE Ed212–222 Hostile engagements with Indians – military, civilian, and Indian casualties, by place of action: 1866–1891 *Continued*

Column groups: Ed214–Ed216 = Non-Indians Killed (Officers, Enlisted men, Civilians); Ed217–Ed219 = Non-Indians Wounded (Officers, Enlisted men, Civilians); Ed220 = Indians Killed; Ed221 = Indians Wounded; Ed222 = Indians Captured. All values are Number.

Date	Place (Ed212)	State or territory (Ed213)	Officers (Ed214)	Enlisted men (Ed215)	Civilians (Ed216)	Officers (Ed217)	Enlisted men (Ed218)	Civilians (Ed219)	Killed (Ed220)	Wounded (Ed221)	Captured (Ed222)
Mar 8, 1874	Pinal Mountain	Arizona	0	0	0	0	0	0	12	0	25
Mar 15, 1874	—	Arizona	0	0	0	0	2	0	0	0	0
Mar 25–26, 1874	Superstition Mountains	Arizona	0	0	0	0	0	0	12	0	2
Apr, 1874	China Tree Creek	Texas	0	0	0	0	0	0	0	1	0
Apr 2, 1874	Pinal Creek	Arizona	0	0	0	0	0	0	31	0	50
Apr 3–14, 1874	Pinal Mountains	Indian Territory	0	0	0	0	0	0	14	0	28
Apr 11, 1874	Bull Bear Creek	Indian Territory	0	0	0	0	0	0	0	0	0
Apr 23, 1874	Fort Lincoln	Dakota	0	0	0	0	0	0	0	1	0
Apr 28, 1874	Arivaypa Mountains	Arizona	0	0	0	0	0	0	23	0	12
May 2, 1874	Red River and Big Wichita	Texas	0	0	0	0	0	0	0	0	0
May 18, 1874	Western Texas	Texas	0	0	0	0	0	0	0	0	0
June 21, 1874	Buffalo Creek	Indian Territory	0	0	0	0	1	1	0	0	0
June 24, 1874	Bear Creek	Indian Territory	0	0	0	0	0	0	4	—[1]	0
July 4, 1874	Bad Water branch of Wind River	Wyoming	0	4	0	1	5	0	26	21	0
July 13, 1874	Sweetwater	Wyoming	0	0	0	0	0	0	1	0	0
July 20, 1874	Palo Pinto County	Texas	0	0	0	0	0	0	0	0	0
Aug 22, 1874	Wichita Agency	Indian Territory	0	0	0	0	4	0	8	8	0
Aug 30, 1874	Salt Fork of the Red River	Texas	0	0	1	0	1	1	3	0	0
Sept 9, 1874	Washita River	Texas	0	1	1	1	1	0	0	0	1
Sept 11–12, 1874	Washita River	Texas	0	1	0	0	4	0	0	0	0
Sept 12, 1874	Between Sweetwater and Dry Fork of Washita River	Texas	0	0	0	0	0	0	2	6	0
Sept 26–29, 1874	Red River Canyon	Texas	0	0	0	0	1	0	4	0	0
Oct, 1874	Canadian River	Texas	0	0	0	0	0	0	1	0	0
Oct 4–31, 1874	Fort Sill	Indian Territory	0	0	0	0	0	0	1	0	0
Oct 9, 1874	Red River	Texas	0	0	0	0	0	0	0	0	0
Oct 13, 1874	Gageby Creek	Indian Territory	0	0	0	0	0	0	0	0	0
Oct 17, 1874	Washita River	Indian Territory	0	0	0	0	0	0	0	0	0
Oct 23, 1874	Old Pueblo Fork	Arizona	0	0	0	0	0	0	16	0	1
Oct 28–Nov 8, 1874	Fort Sill	Indian Territory	0	0	0	0	0	0	0	0	391
Oct 29, 1874	Cave Creek	Arizona	0	0	0	0	0	0	8	0	5
Nov 1, 1874	Little Colorado River	Arizona	0	0	0	1	0	0	1	0	0
Nov 3, 1874	Laguna Curato	Texas	0	0	0	0	0	0	2	0	19
Nov 6, 1874	McClellan Creek	Texas	0	2	0	0	4	0	4	10	0
Nov 6, 1874	Laguna Tahoka	Texas	0	0	0	0	0	0	2	0	0
Nov 8, 1874	McClellan Creek	Texas	0	0	0	0	0	0	0	0	0
Nov 25, 1874	Snow Lake	Arizona	0	0	0	0	0	0	3	0	9
Dec 1, 1874	Canyon Creek, Tonto Basin	Arizona	0	0	0	0	0	0	8	2	14
Dec 2, 1874	Gageby Creek	Indian Territory	0	0	0	0	0	0	0	0	0
Dec 7, 1874	Kingfisher Creek	Indian Territory	0	0	0	0	0	0	0	0	26
Dec 8, 1874	Muchague Valley	Texas	0	0	0	0	0	0	2	0	1
Dec 12, 1874	Standing Rock Agency	Dakota	0	0	0	0	0	0	0	0	0
Dec 28, 1874	Canadian River	Indian Territory	0	0	0	0	0	0	0	0	52
Jan 2–23, 1875	Camp Apache	Arizona	0	0	0	0	0	0	15	0	122
Jan 3–6, 1875	Hackberry Creek	Indian Territory	0	0	0	0	0	0	0	0	4
Jan 9, 1875	Camp Apache	Arizona	0	0	0	0	0	0	0	0	0

			Non-Indians						Indians		
			Killed			Wounded					
Date	Place	State or territory	Officers	Enlisted men	Civilians	Officers	Enlisted men	Civilians	Killed	Wounded	Captured
	Ed212	Ed213	Ed214	Ed215	Ed216	Ed217	Ed218	Ed219	Ed220	Ed221	Ed222
	—	—	Number	Number	Number	Number	Number	Number	Number	Number	Number
Apr 6, 1875	Cheyenne Agency	Texas	0	0	0	0	19	0	11	0	0
Apr 23, 1875	Sappa Creek	Kansas	0	2	0	0	0	0	27	0	0
Apr 25, 1875	Eagle Nest Crossing	Texas	0	0	0	0	0	0	3	1	0
Apr 30, 1875	La Luz Canyon	New Mexico	0	0	0	0	0	0	0	0	9
May 5, 1875	Battle Point	Texas	0	0	0	0	0	0	0	1	0
June 3, 1875	Hackberry Creek	Indian Territory	0	0	0	0	0	0	1	0	0
June 27, 1875	Tonto Basin	Arizona	0	0	0	0	1	0	30	0	15
June 29, 1875	Reynold's Ranch	Texas	0	0	0	0	0	0	1	0	0
July 1, 1875	Little Popo Agie River	Wyoming	0	0	0	0	0	0	2	0	0
July 6, 1875	Ponca Agency	Dakota	0	0	0	0	0	0	0	0	0
July 7, 1875	Camp Lewis	Montana	0	3	0	0	0	0	0	0	0
Aug 28–Sept 2, 1875	North Platte River	Nebraska	0	0	0	0	0	0	0	0	0
Oct 27, 1875	Buffalo Station	Kansas	0	0	0	0	1	0	2	0	0
Nov 2, 1875	Pecos River	Texas	0	0	0	0	0	0	1	0	5
Nov 20, 1875	Antelope Station	Nebraska	0	0	0	0	0	0	0	0	0
Jan 9, 1876	Camp Apache	Arizona	0	0	0	0	0	0	1	0	5
Jan 22, 1876	Cimarron River	Indian Territory	0	0	0	0	0	0	3	0	4
Feb 1, 1876	Chevelous Fork	Arizona	0	0	0	0	0	0	4	0	6
Feb 18, 1876	Carrizo Mountains	Texas	0	0	0	0	0	0	0	0	0
Feb 22–17, 1876	Fort Pease	Montana	0	0	6	0	0	8	0	0	0
Mar 5, 1876	Powder River	Wyoming	0	0	0	0	1	0	0	0	0
Mar 17, 1876	Little Powder River	Montana	0	4	0	1	5	0	0	0	0
Mar 27–28, 1876	Tonto Basin	Arizona	0	0	0	0	0	0	16	0	0
Apr., 1876	Central Station	Texas	0	0	1	0	0	0	0	0	0
Apr 10, 1876	San Jose Mountains	Arizona	0	0	0	0	0	0	0	0	0
Apr 13, 1876	Fort Sill	Indian Territory	0	0	0	0	0	0	0	0	6
June 9, 1876	Tongue River	Wyoming	0	0	0	0	1	0	0	5	0
June 17, 1876	Rose Bud River	Montana	0	9	0	1	20	0	11	1	0
June 22, 1876	Elkhorn River	Nebraska	0	0	1	0	0	0	1	0	0
June 25, 1876	Little Big Horn River	Montana	13	189	4	0	0	0	0	0	0
June 25–26, 1876	Little Big Horn River	Montana	2	46	1	2	44	0	0	0	0
July 7, 1876	Tongue River	Montana	0	0	0	0	0	0	0	5	0
July 17, 1876	Hat Creek	Wyoming	0	0	0	0	0	0	1	1	0
July 29, 1876	Powder River	Montana	0	0	0	0	1	0	0	0	0
July 30, 1876	Saragossa	Mexico	0	0	0	0	0	0	12	0	4
Aug 1, 1876	Red Canyon	Montana	0	0	0	0	0	0	0	0	0
Aug 2, 1876	Rosebud River	Montana	0	1	0	0	0	0	1	0	0
Aug 14, 1876	Fort Buford	Dakota	0	0	0	0	0	0	0	0	0
Aug 15, 1876	Red Rock Country	Arizona	0	0	0	0	1	0	7	0	7
Aug 23, 1876	Yellowstone River	Montana	0	1	0	0	0	0	0	0	0
Sept 9, 1876	Slim Buttes	Dakota	0	3	0	1	13	0	0	0	0
Sept 14, 1876	Owl Creek	Dakota	0	1	0	0	0	0	0	0	0
Sept 15, 1876	Florida Mountains	New Mexico	0	0	0	0	1	0	1	1	0
Sept 18, 1876	Caves	Arizona	0	0	0	0	0	0	5	0	13
Oct 4, 1876	Tonto Basin	Arizona	0	0	0	0	0	0	8	0	2

(continued)

TABLE Ed212–222 Hostile engagements with Indians – military, civilian, and Indian casualties, by place of action: 1866–1891 Continued

Date	Place	State or territory	Non-Indians Killed Officers	Enlisted men	Civilians	Non-Indians Wounded Officers	Enlisted men	Civilians	Indians Killed	Indians Wounded	Indians Captured
	Ed212	Ed213	Ed214	Ed215	Ed216	Ed217	Ed218	Ed219	Ed220	Ed221	Ed222
	—	—	Number	Number	Number	Number	Number	Number	Number	Number	Number
Oct 9, 1876	Eagle Springs	Texas	0	0	1	0	0	0	0	0	0
Oct 11, 1876	Spring Creek	Montana	0	0	0	0	0	0	0	0	0
Oct 14, 1876	Richard Creek	Wyoming	0	1	0	0	0	0	0	0	0
Oct 15, 1876	Clear Creek	Montana	0	0	0	0	3	0	0	0	0
Oct 21, 1876	Big Dry River	Montana	0	0	0	0	2	0	5	0	0
Oct 23, 1876	Camp Robinson	Nebraska	0	0	0	0	0	0	0	0	400
Oct 27, 1876	Big Dry River	Montana	0	0	0	0	0	0	0	0	2,000
Nov 25–26, 1876	Powder River	Montana	1	5	0	0	25	0	25	0	0
Jan 8, 1877	Wolf Mountains	Montana	0	3	0	0	8	0	0	0	0
Jan 9–Feb 5, 1877	Tonto Basin	Arizona	0	0	0	0	0	0	18	0	20
Jan 9, 1877	Leidendorf Range	New Mexico	0	0	0	0	1	0	10	0	1
Jan 12, 1877	Elkhorn Creek	Wyoming	0	0	0	0	3	0	0	0	0
Jan 23, 1877	Florida Mountains	New Mexico	0	0	0	0	0	0	0	0	0
Jan 28, 1877	Siena Boca	Mexico	0	0	0	0	0	0	0	0	0
Feb 22, 1877	Staked Plains	Texas	0	0	1	0	0	0	0	0	0
Feb 23, 1877	Deadwood	Dakota	0	0	0	0	0	0	1	0	0
Mar 7, 1877	Fort Davis	Texas	0	0	2	0	0	0	0	0	0
Apr 1, 1877	Rio Grande	Texas	0	0	0	0	0	0	0	0	0
April–May, 1877	Red Cloud and Spotted Trail	Indian Territory	0	0	0	0	0	0	0	0	2,300
April 20–22, 1877	Fort Clark	Texas	0	0	3	0	0	0	0	0	0
May 4, 1877	Lake Quemado	Texas	0	1	0	0	0	0	4	0	6
May 7, 1877	Little Muddy Creek	Montana	0	4	0	1	7	0	30	20	40
May 29, 1877	Camp Bowie	Arizona	0	0	0	0	0	0	0	0	0
May 30, 1877	Fort Davis	Texas	0	0	1	0	0	0	0	0	0
June 15–Oct 5, 1877	Nez Perces Campaign	—	0	0	0	0	0	0	0	0	0
June 15, 1877	John Day's Creek	Idaho	0	0	4	0	0	0	0	0	0
June 17, 1877	White Bird Canyon	Idaho	1	33	0	0	2	0	0	0	0
June 28, 1877	White Bird River	Idaho	0	0	0	0	0	0	0	0	0
July 1–3, 1877	Cottonwood Ranch	Idaho	1	10	2	0	0	0	0	0	0
July 4–5, 1877	Cottonwood Ranch	Idaho	0	0	0	0	2	0	0	0	0
July 4, 1877	Norton's Ranch	Idaho	0	0	0	0	0	0	0	0	0
July 11–12, 1877	Clearwater	Idaho	0	13	0	2	25	0	23	46	40
July 13, 1877	Kamiah	Idaho	0	0	1	0	0	0	0	0	0
July 17, 1877	Weippe	Idaho	1	1	0	0	1	0	1	0	0
July 21, 1877	Belle Fourche	Dakota	0	0	0	0	0	0	0	0	0
Aug 1, 1877	El Muerto	Texas	0	0	2	0	0	0	0	0	0
Aug 9–10, 1877	Big Hole Basin	Montana	2	21	6	5	31	4	89	0	0
Aug 20, 1877	Camas Meadows	Idaho	0	1	0	1	6	0	0	0	0
Sept 8–10, 1877	San Francisco River	New Mexico	0	0	0	0	0	0	12	0	13
Sept 13, 1877	Canyon Creek	Montana	0	3	0	1	10	0	21	0	0
Sept 23, 1877	Cow Island	Montana	0	1	2	0	0	0	0	0	0
Sept 25, 1877	Cow Creek	Montana	0	0	1	0	0	0	0	2	0
Sept 26, 1877	Saragossa	Mexico	0	0	0	0	0	0	0	0	5
Sept 30, 1877	Snake or Eagle Creek	Montana	2	22	0	4	38	8	17	40	0
Oct 4–5, 1877	Bear Paw Mountains	Montana	0	0	0	0	0	0	0	0	418

Date	Place	State or territory	Non-Indians						Indians		
			Killed			Wounded			Killed	Wounded	Captured
			Officers	Enlisted men	Civilians	Officers	Enlisted men	Civilians	Killed	Wounded	Captured
	Ed212	Ed213	Ed214	Ed215	Ed216	Ed217	Ed218	Ed219	Ed220	Ed221	Ed222
	—	—	Number	Number	Number	Number	Number	Number	Number	Number	Number
Oct 22, 1877	Flat Rocks	Texas	0	0	1	0	0	0	0	0	0
Nov 1, 1877	Rio Grande	Texas	0	0	0	0	0	0	0	0	0
Nov 16, 1877	Indian Creek	Texas	0	0	1	0	0	0	0	0	0
Nov 18, 1877	Sauz Ranch	Texas	0	0	2	0	0	0	0	3	0
Nov 29–30, 1877	Sierra Carmel Ranch	Mexico	0	0	0	0	1	0	2	3	0
Dec 13, 1877	Ralston Flat	New Mexico	0	0	0	0	0	0	1	0	0
Dec 18, 1877	Las Animas Mountains	Mexico	0	0	0	0	0	0	15	0	1
Dec 23, 1877	Bass Canyon	Texas	0	0	2	0	0	0	0	0	0
Jan 5, 1878	Presidio Del Norte	Texas	0	0	6	0	0	0	0	0	0
Jan 7, 1878	Tonto Creek	Arizona	0	0	0	0	0	3	0	0	0
Jan 16, 1878	Mason County	Texas	0	0	2	0	0	0	0	0	0
Jan 16, 1878	Brady City	Texas	0	0	1	0	0	0	0	0	0
Feb 16, 1878	Limpia Canyon	Texas	0	0	2	0	0	0	0	0	0
Feb 23, 1878	Fort Duncan	Texas	0	0	2	0	0	0	0	0	0
Apr 15, 1878	Carrizo Mountains	Texas	0	0	0	0	0	0	0	0	0
Apr 17, 1878	Brown's Ranch, Steele's Ranch, San Ygnacio and McMullen County	Texas	0	0	5	0	0	0	0	0	0
Apr 18, 1878	Rancho Soledad and Charco Escondido, Duval County	Texas	0	0	2	0	0	2	0	0	0
Apr 19, 1878	Charco Escondido and Quijoto Gordo	Texas	0	0	1	0	0	1	0	0	0
Apr 20, 1878	Point of Rocks	Texas	0	0	3	0	0	0	0	0	0
May 20, 1878	White's Gulch	Montana	0	0	0	0	0	0	1	2	0
May 30–Sept 10, 1878	Bannock Campaign	—	0	0	0	0	0	0	0	0	0
June 1, 1878	Camp Wood	Texas	0	0	2	0	0	0	0	0	0
June 28, 1878	Silver River	Oregon	0	3	0	0	2	0	5	2	0
June 28, 1878	Fort Sill	Indian Territory	0	0	0	0	0	0	2	1	0
July 8, 1878	Birch Creek	Oregon	0	1	0	0	4	0	0	0	0
July 12, 1878	Ladd's Canyon	Oregon	0	0	0	0	0	0	0	0	21
July 13, 1878	Umatilla Agency	Oregon	0	0	0	0	2	0	0	0	0
July 20, 1878	John Day's River	Oregon	0	0	1	0	1	1	0	0	0
July 21, 1878	Clearwater River	Montana	0	0	0	0	0	0	6	3	31
July 26, 1878	Baker City	Idaho	0	0	0	0	0	0	0	0	0
July 29, 1878	Sacramento Mountains	Arizona	0	0	0	0	0	0	3	3	1
Aug 5, 1878	Dog Canyon	New Mexico	0	0	0	0	0	0	3	2	1
Aug 9, 1878	Bennett Creek	Idaho	0	0	0	0	1	0	0	0	0
Aug 20, 1878	Big Creek	Idaho	0	1	0	0	0	0	0	0	0
Aug 20, 1878	Salmon River	Idaho	0	0	0	0	0	0	0	0	0
Aug 27, 1878	Henry's Lake	Idaho	0	0	0	0	0	0	0	0	0
May 29–30, 1878	Index Peak	Wyoming	0	0	1	0	0	0	0	0	0
Sept 4, 1878	Clark's Fort	Montana	1	0	0	0	2	0	11	0	31
Sept 12, 1878	Big Wind	Wyoming	0	0	0	0	1	0	1	0	0
Sept 13, 1878	Turkey Springs	Indian Territory	0	2	0	0	1	0	0	0	0
Sept 14, 1878	Red Hill	Indian Territory	0	1	0	0	0	0	0	0	0
Sept 17, 1878	Bear Creek	New Mexico	0	1	0	0	0	0	2	0	0
Oct 5, 1878	Johnson's Fork	Texas	0	0	4	0	0	0	0	0	35
Oct 22, 1878	Fort Benton	Texas	0	0	1	0	0	0	0	0	7
Nov 27, 1878	Fort Ellis	Montana	0	0	0	0	0	0	0	0	

(continued)

TABLE Ed212–222 Hostile engagements with Indians – military, civilian, and Indian casualties, by place of action: 1866–1891 *Continued*

			Non-Indians						Indians		
			Killed			Wounded			Killed	Wounded	Captured
Date	Place	State or territory	Officers	Enlisted men	Civilians	Officers	Enlisted men	Civilians			
	Ed212	Ed213	Ed214	Ed215	Ed216	Ed217	Ed218	Ed219	Ed220	Ed221	Ed222
	—	—	Number	Number	Number	Number	Number	Number	Number	Number	Number
Jan 10, 1879	Fort Robinson	—	0	5	0	0	7	0	32	0	71
Jan 20, 1879	Hat Creek	Wyoming	0	3	0	1	2	0	23	3	9
Feb 13, 1879	Ojo Caliente	New Mexico	0	0	0	0	0	0	0	0	0
Mar 28, 1879	Big Horn River	Montana	0	0	1	0	0	2	0	0	0
Mar 25, 1879	Fort Keogh	Montana	0	0	0	0	0	0	0	0	114
Apr 6, 1879	Powder River	Montana	0	0	1	0	0	1	0	0	0
Apr 17, 1879	Musselshell River	Montana	0	2	0	0	1	0	8	0	0
Apr 22, 1879	Countryman's Ranch	Montana	0	0	0	0	0	0	1	0	0
Apr 30, 1879	Ojo Caliente	New Mexico	0	1	0	0	0	0	0	0	0
May 1, 1879	Between Fort Ewell and Corpus Christi	Texas	0	0	1	0	0	0	0	0	0
May 1, 1879	Fort Mcintosh	Texas	0	0	1	0	0	0	0	0	0
May 29, 1879	Black Range of Miembres Mountains	New Mexico	0	1	0	0	2	0	0	0	0
June 1, 1879	Camp Wood	Texas	0	0	3	0	0	0	0	0	0
June 25, 1879	Tonto Basin	Arizona	0	0	0	0	0	0	6	0	0
June 29, 1879	Alkali Creek	Montana	0	1	0	0	4	0	4	0	0
June 30, 1879	North Concho River	Texas	0	0	1	0	0	1	0	0	0
July 17, 1879	Milk River	Montana	0	3	0	0	3	0	0	0	0
July 19, 1879	Camp Loder	Montana	0	0	0	0	0	0	1	0	0
July 25, 1879	Salt Lake or Sulpher Springs	Texas	0	0	0	0	2	0	0	3	0
July 29, 1879	Big Creek	Idaho	0	0	0	0	2	0	0	0	0
Aug 10, 1879	Missouri River	Montana	0	1	0	0	0	0	0	0	57
Aug 20, 1879	Salmon River	Idaho	0	0	0	0	0	0	0	0	0
Sept 4, 1879	Ojo Caliente	New Mexico	0	5	3	0	2	0	0	0	0
Sept 10, 1879	Mcever's Ranch	New Mexico	0	0	7	0	0	0	0	0	0
Sept 10, 1879	Arroyo Seco	New Mexico	0	0	2	0	0	0	0	0	0
Sept 16, 1879	Van Horn Mopuntains	Texas	0	0	0	0	0	0	0	0	0
Sept 17, 1879	Black Range	New Mexico	0	0	2	0	0	0	0	0	0
Sept 18, 1879	Las Animas	New Mexico	0	4	1	0	2	0	0	0	0
Sept 19, 1879	Miembres Mountains	New Mexico	0	2	0	0	0	0	0	0	0
Sept 26–30, 1879	Ojo Caliente	New Mexico	0	1	0	0	0	0	3	0	0
Sept 29–Oct 1, 1879	Milk River	Colorado	1	9	3	2	43	3	37	0	0
Sept 29–30, 1879	Cuchillo Negro River	New Mexico	0	2	0	0	0	0	0	0	0
Oct 2–4, 1879	Milk River	Colorado	0	0	0	0	0	0	0	0	0
Oct 10, 1879	White River	Colorado	0	0	0	0	0	0	0	0	0
Oct 13, 1879	Lloyd's Ranch	New Mexico	0	6	0	0	0	0	0	0	0
Oct 13, 1879	Slocum's Ranch	New Mexico	0	0	11	0	0	0	0	0	0
Oct 20, 1879	White River	Colorado	1	1	0	0	0	0	2	0	0
Oct 27, 1879	Guzman Mounatin	Mexico	0	1	0	0	2	0	0	0	0
Jan 12, 1880	Rio Puerco	New Mexico	0	2	0	0	1	0	0	0	0
Jan 17, 1880	San Mateo Mountains	New Mexico	1	0	0	0	2	0	0	0	0
Jan 30, 1880	Cabello Mountains	New Mexico	0	0	0	0	3	0	1	0	0
Jan 12, 1880	Pumpkin Creek	New Mexico	0	1	0	0	1	0	1	2	3
Jan 28, 1880	Sacramento Mountains	New Mexico	0	0	0	0	0	0	0	0	0
Mar 1, 1880	La Luz	New Mexico	0	0	3	0	0	0	0	0	0
Mar 8, 1880	Porcupine Creek	Montana	0	0	0	0	0	0	0	0	0

			Non-Indians						Indians		
			Killed			Wounded			Killed	Wounded	Captured
Date	Place	State or territory	Officers	Enlisted men	Civilians	Officers	Enlisted men	Civilians	Number	Number	Number
	Ed212	Ed213	Ed214	Ed215	Ed216	Ed217	Ed218	Ed219	Ed220	Ed221	Ed222
		—	Number	Number	Number	Number	Number	Number	Number	Number	Number
Mar 8, 1880	Rosebud Creek	Montana	0	2	0	0	1	0	3	3	0
Mar 13, 1880	Russell's Ranch	Texas	0	0	1	0	0	0	0	0	0
Mar 15, 1880	Blazer's Mill	New Mexico	0	0	1	0	0	0	0	0	0
Apr 1, 1880	O'Fallon's Creek	Montana	0	1	0	0	0	0	0	0	5
Apr 3, 1880	Pecos Falls	Texas	0	0	0	0	0	0	1	0	0
Apr 5, 1880	San Andres Mountains	New Mexico	0	0	0	0	1	1	0	0	0
Apr 6–9, 1880	—	—	0	0	0	1	7	0	0	0	0
Apr 9, 1880	San Andres Springs	New Mexico	0	0	0	0	0	0	1	0	0
Apr 9, 1880	Shakehand Springs	Texas	0	0	0	0	0	0	1	0	5
Apr 15, 1880	Pato Springs	New Mexico	0	0	1	0	0	0	0	0	0
Apr 16, 1880	South Fork	New Mexico	0	0	0	0	0	0	1	0	300
Apr 16, 1880	Mescalero Agency	New Mexico	0	0	0	0	0	0	10	0	0
Apr 17, 1880	Dog Canyon	New Mexico	0	0	0	0	0	0	3	0	0
Apr 20, 1880	Sacramento Mountains	New Mexico	0	0	0	0	0	0	1	0	0
Apr 27, 1880	Ojo Caliente	New Mexico	0	0	3	0	0	0	0	0	0
Apr 28, 1880	Rio Gilitfe	New Mexico	0	0	6	0	0	0	0	0	0
Apr 29, 1880	Mogollon	New Mexico	0	0	3	0	0	0	0	0	0
May 2, 1880	San Francisco River	New Mexico	0	0	7	0	0	0	0	0	0
May 4, 1880	Las Lentes	New Mexico	0	0	6	0	0	0	0	0	0
May 7, 1880	Ash Creek Valley	Arizona	0	1	0	0	1	0	0	0	0
May 13, 1880	Bass Canyon	Texas	0	0	2	0	0	2	0	0	0
May 14, 1880	Tularosa	New Mexico	0	0	0	1	0	0	0	0	0
May 15, 1880	Kelly's Ranch	New Mexico	0	0	3	0	0	0	0	0	0
May 24, 1880	Polomas River	New Mexico	0	0	0	0	0	0	55	0	0
May 29, 1880	Cook's Canyon	New Mexico	0	0	5	0	0	0	0	0	0
June 5, 1880	—	—	0	0	0	0	0	0	10	3	0
June 11, 1880	Ojo Viejo	Texas	0	1	0	1	2	0	1	2	0
July 30, 1880	Rocky Ridge	Texas	0	1	0	1	3	0	7	0	0
July 31, 1880	Eagle Springs	Texas	0	0	2	0	0	0	0	0	0
Aug 3, 1880	Sierra Diablo	Texas	0	0	0	0	0	0	0	0	0
Aug 3, 1880	Alamo Springs	Texas	0	0	0	0	1	0	0	0	0
Aug 4, 1880	Guadaloupe Mountains	Texas	0	1	0	0	0	0	0	0	0
Aug 6, 1880	Guadaloupe Mountains	Texas	0	0	0	0	0	0	2	0	0
Aug 6, 1880	Rattlesnake Spring	Texas	0	0	0	0	0	0	1	0	0
Aug 6, 1880	Rattlesnake Canyon	Texas	0	0	0	0	0	0	4	0	0
Aug 17, 1880	Little Missouri River	Montana	0	0	0	0	0	0	2	1	0
Sept 1, 1880	Aqua Chiquita	New Mexico	0	0	0	0	2	0	0	0	0
Sept 7, 1880	Fort Cummings	New Mexico	0	1	0	0	3	0	0	0	0
Oct 28, 1880	Ojo Caliente	Texas	0	5	0	0	0	0	0	0	0
Nov 11, 1880	Musselshell River	Montana	0	0	0	0	0	0	1	0	0
Dec 2, 1880	South Fork in White Mountains	New Mexico	0	0	0	0	2	2	0	1	4
Jan 2, 1881	Poplar River	Montana	0	0	0	0	0	0	8	0	324
Jan 24, 1881	Canada Alamosa	New Mexico	0	0	0	0	1	0	0	0	0
Jan 29, 1881	Poplar River	Montana	0	0	0	0	0	0	0	0	64
Feb 5, 1881	Candelaria Mountains	Mexico	0	0	0	0	0	0	0	0	0

(continued)

TABLE Ed212–222   Hostile engagements with Indians – military, civilian, and Indian casualties, by place of action: 1866–1891   Continued

			Non-Indians						Indians		
			Killed			Wounded			Killed	Wounded	Captured
Date	Place	State or territory	Officers	Enlisted men	Civilians	Officers	Enlisted men	Civilians	Number	Number	Number
	Ed212	Ed213	Ed214	Ed215	Ed216	Ed217	Ed218	Ed219	Ed220	Ed221	Ed222
	—	—	Number	Number	Number	Number	Number	Number	Number	Number	Number
Feb 12, 1881	Redwater	Montana	0	0	0	0	0	0	0	0	185
Feb 26, 1881	Fort Buford	Dakota	0	0	0	0	0	0	0	0	325
Apr 11, 1881	Fort Buford	Dakota	0	0	0	0	0	0	0	0	135
Apr 18, 1881	Fort Keogh	Montana	0	0	0	0	0	0	0	0	156
Apr 29, 1881	Mexican Line	Mexico	0	1	0	0	0	0	0	0	0
May 3, 1881	Sierra Burras Mountains	Mexico	0	0	0	0	0	0	4	0	2
May 24, 1881	Poplar River	Montana	0	0	0	0	0	0	0	0	50
May 26, 1881	Fort Buford	Dakota	0	0	0	0	0	0	0	0	32
July 17, 1881	Alamo Canyon	New Mexico	0	0	0	0	0	1	0	0	0
July 19, 1881	Arena Blanca	New Mexico	0	0	3	0	0	0	0	0	0
July 20, 1881	Fort Buford	Dakota	0	0	0	0	0	0	0	0	185
July 25, 1881	San Andres Mountains	New Mexico	0	0	0	0	0	0	3	2	0
July 25, 1881	White Sands	New Mexico	0	0	1	0	0	0	0	0	0
July 30, 1881	San Mateo Mountains	Mexico	0	0	4	0	0	1	0	0	0
Aug 12, 1881	Sabinal	New Mexico	0	1	0	0	3	0	1	3	0
Aug 16, 1881	Cuehillo Negro	New Mexico	0	2	0	1	0	0	5	0	0
Aug 18, 1881	Mcever's Ranch	New Mexico	0	4	1	0	0	0	0	0	0
Apr 20, 1882	Fort Thomas	Arizona	0	0	0	0	0	0	0	1	0
Apr 23, 1882	Stein's Pass	Arizona	0	4	0	0	0	0	0	0	0
Apr 23, 1882	Horseshoe Canyon	New Mexico	0	1	0	1	6	0	0	0	0
Apr 28, 1882	Hatchet Mountains	New Mexico	0	1	0	0	2	0	6	0	0
Apr 29, 1882	Shoshone Agency	Wyoming	0	1	0	0	0	0	1	0	0
June 1, 1882	Cloverdale	New Mexico	0	0	0	0	0	0	2	0	0
July 9, 1882	Medicine Lodge	Montana	0	0	0	0	0	0	0	0	0
July 17, 1882	Big Dry Wash	Arizona	0	1	0	2	7	0	16	0	0
July 23, 1882	Fort Stanton	New Mexico	0	0	0	0	0	1	3	0	0
Nov 8, 1882	Tullock's Fork	Montana	0	0	0	0	1	0	2	0	0
Mar 21, 1883	Fort Huachuca	Arizona	0	0	4	0	0	0	0	0	0
Mar 22, 1883	Total Wreck Mine	Arizona	0	0	3	0	0	0	0	0	0
Mar 23, 1883	Point of Mountain	Arizona	0	0	2	0	0	0	0	0	0
Mar 28, 1883	Silver City and Lordsburg	New Mexico	0	0	2	0	0	0	0	0	0
Apr 14, 1883	Beaver Creek	Montana	0	0	0	0	0	0	0	0	69
Apr 19, 1883	Wild Horse Lake	Montana	0	0	0	0	0	0	2	0	0
May 15, 1883	Babispe River	Mexico	0	0	0	0	0	0	9	0	5
July 15, 1884	Wormington Canyon	Colorado	0	0	2	0	0	0	0	0	0
May 22, 1885	Devil's Creek, Mogollon Mountains	New Mexico	0	0	0	0	4	0	0	0	0
June 8, 1885	Guadaloupe Canyon	Sonora Mexico	0	3	0	0	0	0	0	0	0
June 21, 1885	Oputo	Sonora Mexico	0	1	0	0	0	0	0	0	0
June 23, 1885	Babispe Mountains	Sonora Mexico	0	0	0	0	0	0	1	0	15
July 28, 1885	Sierra Madre	Sonora Mexico	0	0	0	0	0	0	2	0	0
Aug 7, 1885	—	Mexico	0	0	0	0	0	0	5	0	15
Sept 22, 1885	Teres Mountains	New Mexico	0	1	0	0	1	0	1	2	0
Oct 10, 1885	Lang's Ranch	New Mexico	0	1	0	0	0	0	0	0	0
Nov 7, 1885	Florida Mountains	New Mexico	0	1	0	0	1	0	0	0	0
Dec 9, 1885	Lillie's Ranch	New Mexico	0	0	0	0	0	0	2	0	0

Date	Place	State or territory	Non-Indians						Indians		
			Killed			Wounded			Killed	Wounded	Captured
			Officers	Enlisted men	Civilians	Officers	Enlisted men	Civilians			
	Ed212	Ed213	Ed214	Ed215	Ed216	Ed217	Ed218	Ed219	Ed220	Ed221	Ed222
	—	—	Number	Number	Number	Number	Number	Number	Number	Number	Number
Dec 19, 1885	Little Dry Creek	New Mexico	1	4	0	1	1	0	0	0	0
Jan 10–11, 1886	Aros River	Sonora Mexico	0	0	0	0	0	0	0	0	0
May 3, 1886	Penito Mountains	Sonora Mexico	0	1	0	0	1	0	2	1	0
May 15, 1886	Pinto Mountains	Mexico	0	2	0	0	2	0	0	0	0
June 6, 1886	Patagonia Mountains	Arizona	0	0	0	0	0	0	0	0	0
Sept 4, 1886	Skeleton Canyon	Arizona	0	0	0	0	0	0	0	0	39
Oct 18, 1886	Black River Mountains	Arizona	0	0	0	0	0	0	0	0	8
Mar 10, 1887	San Carlos Agency	Arizona	0	0	0	1	0	0	0	0	0
June 11, 1887	Rincon Mountains	Arizona	0	0	0	0	0	0	0	0	0
Nov 5, 1887	Crow Agency	Montana	0	1	0	0	2	0	7	10	9
June 16, 1888	Pompey's Pillar on Yellowstone River	Montana	0	0	0	0	0	0	1	1	0
July 28, 1888	San Carlos Agency	Arizona	0	0	0	0	2	0	0	0	0
May 11, 1889	Cedar Springs	Arizona	0	0	0	0	9	0	0	0	0
June 2, 1889	Missouri River	North Dakota	0	0	0	0	0	0	0	0	34
Mar 11, 1890	Salt River	Arizona	0	0	0	0	0	0	2	0	3
Sept 13, 1890	Tongue River	Montana	0	0	0	0	0	0	2	0	0
Dec 15, 1890	Grand River	Montana	0	4	0	0	3	0	8	0	0
Dec 22, 1890	Cherry Creek	South Dakota	0	0	0	0	0	0	0	0	294
Dec 28, 1890	Porcupine Creek	South Dakota	0	0	0	0	0	0	0	0	106
Dec 29, 1890	Pine Ridge Agency	South Dakota	0	0	0	0	3	0	0	0	0
Dec 29, 1890	Wounded Knee Creek	South Dakota	1	24	0	8	32	0	128	33	0
Dec 30, 1890	Pine Ridge Agency	South Dakota	0	1	0	0	0	0	0	0	0
Dec 30, 1890	White Clay Creek	South Dakota	0	1	0	1	6	0	1	0	0
Jan 1, 1891	Wounded Knee Creek	South Dakota	0	0	0	0	0	0	1	1	0
Jan 3, 1891	Pine Ridge Agency	South Dakota	1	0	0	0	0	0	0	0	0

[1] Several.

Documentation

See the text for Table Ed202–211.

When the place, state, or territory of the action is not available, this denotes an encounter with a regiment or troop outside of the assignment, commonly a run-in while returning from a prior engagement.

Source

U.S. Army War College Internet site, Carlisle Barracks, "Chronological List of Actions, &C., with Indians, From January 1, 1866, to January, 1891," with corrections by the editors made from the original document, accessed March 30, 2004.

NUCLEAR WEAPONS AND ARMS CONTROL

Scott Sigmund Gartner

TABLE Ed223–227   U.S. strategic nuclear weapons: 1945–1996
Contributed by Scott Sigmund Gartner

	Ballistic missiles		Strategic warheads deliverable by bomber	Strategic nuclear weapons			Ballistic missiles		Strategic warheads deliverable by bomber	Strategic nuclear weapons	
	Intercontinental	Submarine-launched		Active	Stockpiled		Intercontinental	Submarine-launched		Active	Stockpiled
	Ed223	Ed224	Ed225	Ed226	Ed227		Ed223	Ed224	Ed225	Ed226	Ed227
Year	Number	Number	Number	Number	Number	Year	Number	Number	Number	Number	Number
1945	—	—	6	6	6	1975	2,251	4,771	6,911	13,933	26,675
1946	—	—	11	11	11	1976	2,251	5,359	6,647	14,257	25,579
1947	—	—	32	32	32	1977	2,251	5,477	6,592	14,320	24,722
1948	—	—	110	110	110	1978	2,251	5,712	6,264	14,227	23,866
1949	—	—	235	235	235	1979	2,251	5,645	6,252	14,148	23,730
1950	—	—	369	369	369	1980	2,251	5,309	6,239	13,799	23,387
1951	—	—	549	549	640	1981	2,251	4,990	6,244	13,485	22,654
1952	—	—	800	800	1,005	1982	2,246	5,006	5,820	13,072	22,585
1953	—	—	1,000	1,000	1,436	1983	2,237	5,208	5,663	13,108	22,902
1954	—	—	1,500	1,500	2,063	1984	2,226	5,611	6,118	13,955	23,051
1955	—	—	2,200	2,200	3,057	1985	2,216	5,645	6,180	14,040	22,941
1956	—	—	3,000	3,000	4,618	1986	2,273	5,712	6,493	14,478	22,995
1957	—	—	4,200	4,200	6,444	1987	2,415	5,914	6,624	14,953	23,167
1958	—	—	5,700	5,700	9,822	1988	2,562	5,578	6,624	14,764	22,705
1959	6	—	7,000	7,006	15,468	1989	2,562	5,410	5,965	13,937	21,767
1960	13	34	6,954	7,000	20,434	1990	2,562	5,480	5,330	13,372	20,684
1961	60	84	6,730	6,874	24,156	1991	2,200	5,480	3,400	11,080	17,734
1962	213	151	6,847	7,211	27,305	1992	2,200	3,630	3,510	9,340	13,259
1963	627	168	6,303	7,098	29,049	1993	2,200	3,630	3,410	9,240	11,476
1964	952	403	6,471	7,827	30,400	1994	2,200	3,630	3,410	9,240	11,288
1965	897	773	6,567	8,237	31,265	1995	2,180	3,630	3,410	9,220	11,226
1966	1,054	1,327	6,633	9,014	31,323	1996	2,180	3,630	3,360	9,170	11,155
1967	1,096	1,630	6,861	9,587	30,516						
1968	1,096	1,630	6,590	9,316	28,507						
1969	1,096	1,630	6,421	9,147	26,533						
1970	1,306	1,630	6,465	9,401	25,742						
1971	1,516	2,587	6,252	10,355	25,988						
1972	1,726	3,276	7,360	13,363	26,919						
1973	1,936	4,318	6,991	13,244	27,958						
1974	2,041	4,654	6,788	13,483	27,793						

Sources

Thomas Cochran, William M. Arkin, and Milton Hoenig, *Nuclear Weapons Databook* (Ballinger, 1984, 1994).

Thomas Cochran, William M. Arkin, and Milton Hoenig, *Nuclear Warhead Production* (Ballinger, 1987).

Thomas Cochran, William M. Arkin, and Milton Hoenig, *Nuclear Weapons Databook, Working Paper* (Natural Resources Defense Council, 1997).

Robert S. Norris and Thomas Cochran, *US and USSR/Russian Strategic Offensive Nuclear Forces 1945–1996* (Natural Resources Defense Council, 1997).

Natural Resources Defense Council Internet site, Archive of Nuclear Data, accessed May 20, 2000.

Documentation

An active nuclear weapon is one that is completely assembled (that is, implosion type, gun type, or thermonuclear type), in its intended ultimate configuration, which is mounted with the appropriate delivery vehicle and can be immediately sent to target. A stockpiled nuclear weapon is one that requires any or all of the following: removing from storage, assembling, testing, or transporting to its delivery vehicle.

TABLE Ed228 U.S. arms control and weapons treaties and agreements: 1922–1996[1]

Contributed by Scott Sigmund Gartner

| | | Treaty name |
Date signed	Date entered into force	Ed228
Feb 6, 1922	June 9, 1923	Conference on the limitation of armament (Washington Naval Treaty)
June 17, 1925	Feb 8, 1928	Protocol for the prohibition of the use in war of asphyxiating, poisonous, or other gases and of bacteriological methods of warfare
Dec 1, 1959	June 23, 1961	The Antarctic Treaty
June 20, 1963	June 20, 1963	Memorandum of understanding between the United States of America and the Union of Soviet Socialist Republics regarding the establishment of a direct communications link
Aug 5, 1963	Oct 10, 1963	Treaty banning nuclear weapons tests in the atmosphere, in outer space, and under water
Jan 27, 1967	Oct 10, 1967	Treaty on principles governing the activities of states in the exploration and use of outer space, including the moon and other celestial bodies
Feb 14, 1967	Dec 11, 1969	Treaty for the prohibition of nuclear weapons in Latin America
July 1, 1968	Mar 5, 1970	Treaty on the nonproliferation of nuclear weapons
Sept 30, 1971	Sept 30, 1971	The agreement on measures to reduce the risk of outbreak of nuclear war between the United States of America and the Union of Soviet Socialist Republics
Feb 11, 1971	May 18, 1972	Treaty on the prohibition of the emplacement of nuclear weapons and other weapons of mass destruction on the seabed and the ocean floor and in the subsoil thereof
May 26, 1972	May 26, 1972	Strategic arms limitations talks (SALT I)
May 26, 1972	Oct 3, 1972	Interim agreement between the United States of America and the Union of Soviet Socialist Republics on certain measures with respect to the limitation of strategic offensive arms
June 1, 1973	June 1, 1973	Agreement between the United States of America and the Union of Soviet Socialist Republics on the prevention of nuclear war
Apr 10, 1972	Mar 26, 1975	Convention on the prohibition of the development, production, and stockpiling of bacteriological (biological) and toxin weapons and on their destruction
May 18, 1977	Oct 5, 1978	Convention on the prohibition of military or any other hostile use of environmental modification techniques
June 18, 1979	June 18, 1979	Treaty between the United States of America and the Union of Soviet Socialist Republics on the limitation of strategic offensive arms, together with agreed statements and common understandings regarding the treaty (SALT II)
Nov 18, 1977	Dec 9, 1980	Agreement between the United States of America and the International Atomic Energy Agency for the application of safeguards in the United States
Sept 22, 1986	—	Conference on confidence- and security-building measures and disarmament in Europe
Aug 8, 1986	Dec 11, 1986	South Pacific Nuclear Free Zone Treaty/Treaty of Raratonga
Mar 3, 1980	Feb 8, 1987	Convention on the physical protection of nuclear material
May 31, 1988	May 31, 1988	Agreement between the United States of America and the Union of Soviet Socialist Republics on notifications of launches of intercontinental ballistic missiles and submarine-launched ballistic missiles
Dec 8, 1987	June 1, 1988	Treaty between the United States of America and the Union of Soviet Socialist Republics on the elimination of their intermediate-range and shorter-range missiles
Nov 21, 1990	Nov 21, 1990	Charter of Paris for a New Europe: A new era of democracy, peace, and unity
May 28, 1976	Dec 11, 1990	Treaty between the United States of America and the Union of Soviet Socialist Republics on underground nuclear explosions for peaceful purposes
July 3, 1974	Dec 11, 1990	Treaty between the United States of America and the Union of Soviet Socialist Republics on the limitation of underground nuclear weapons tests
Nov 19, 1990	Nov 9, 1992	Treaty on conventional armed forces in Europe
July 31, 1991	July 31, 1991	Treaty between the United States of America and the Union of Soviet Socialist Republics on the reduction and limitation of strategic offensive arms
Jan 3, 1993	Jan 3, 1993	Treaty between the United States of America and the Russian Federation on further reduction and limitation of strategic offensive arms
Jan 15, 1993	Apr 29, 1997	Convention on the development, stockpiling, and use of chemical weapons and their destruction
Apr 11, 1996	—	African Nuclear-Weapons-Free Zone Treaty
Sept 24, 1996	—	Comprehensive Nuclear Test-Ban treaty signatories/ratifiers

[1] When no date is given, treaty never went or has not yet gone into force.

Sources

Blacker D. Coit and Gloria Duffy, editors, *International Arms Control Issues and Agreements, by the Stanford Arms Control Group* (Stanford University Press, 1984); Council for a Liveable World, Coalition to Reduce Nuclear Dangers, Internet site, "Treaty Documents on Arms Control and Non-Proliferation," accessed April 4, 2000; Robert A. Divine, editor, *American Foreign Policy: Current Documents* (Meridian Books, various years); Chalmers Hardenbergh, editor, *The Arms Control Reporter: A Chronicle of Treaties, Negotiations, Proposals* (Institute for Defense and Disarmament Studies, 1984); Stockholm International Peace Research Institute Internet site, accessed June 14, 2000; United States, *United States Treaties, Conventions, International Acts, Protocols, and Agreements between the United States of America and Other Powers* (U.S. Government Printing Office, 1938); United States, *United States Treaties, Conventions, International Acts, Protocols, and Agreements between the United States of America and Other Powers* (Greenwood Press, 1968); Hunter Miller, editor, *Treaties and Other International Acts of the United States of America* (U.S. Government Printing Office, various years); U.S. Arms Control and Disarmament Agency, *Arms Control and Disarmament Agreements: Texts and Histories of the Negotiations* (U.S. Government Printing Office, 1996); U.S. Department of State, *Treaties in Force: A List of Treaties and Other International Acts of the US in Force . . .* (U.S. Government Printing Office, various years); U.S. Department of State Internet site, accessed June 14, 2000.

VETERANS

Hugh Rockoff

TABLE Ed229–244   Veterans living in the United States and Puerto Rico, by age: 1865–1999[1]

Contributed by Scott Sigmund Gartner and Hugh Rockoff

Fiscal year	Total (all ages) Ed229	Under 20 Ed230	Under 30 Ed231	20 to 24 Ed232	25 to 29 Ed233	30 to 34 Ed234	35 to 39 Ed235	40 to 44 Ed236	45 to 49 Ed237	50 to 54 Ed238	55 to 59 Ed239	60 to 64 Ed240	65 to 69 Ed241	65 and older Ed242	70 and older Ed243	Unknown age Ed244
	Thousand	Thousand	Thousand	Thousand	Thousand	Thousand	Thousand	Thousand	Thousand	Thousand	Thousand	Thousand	Thousand	Thousand	Thousand	Thousand
1865	1,908	18	1,268	820	430	239	159	116	70	9	1	(Z)	9	46	37	0
1870	1,802	0	801	17	784	411	228	152	109	65	8	(Z)	(Z)	28	28	0
1875	1,698	0	17	0	17	748	390	216	142	103	59	7	(Z)	16	16	0
1880	1,593	0	0	0	0	16	710	370	203	133	93	53	5	15	10	0
1885	1,475	0	0	0	0	0	15	670	347	189	121	82	44	51	7	0
1890	1,341	0	0	0	0	0	0	14	628	321	171	105	67	102	35	0
1895	1,187	0	0	0	0	0	0	0	13	578	289	148	85	156	71	3
1900	1,224	12	167	91	64	26	11	5	3	14	521	251	121	225	104	1
1905	1,192	(Z)	177	21	156	109	44	18	9	4	13	458	208	358	150	2
1910	977	0	20	(Z)	20	150	105	42	17	8	4	11	380	618	238	2
1915	773	(Z)	(Z)	0	(Z)	19	145	100	40	16	8	3	8	425	417	17
1920	5,146	17	3,508	1,416	2,075	903	107	180	112	44	18	7	3	248	245	19
1925	4,894	0	1,403	17	1,386	2,026	877	103	172	105	41	15	6	136	130	16
1930	4,680	0	17	0	17	1,356	1,974	849	98	162	97	37	13	69	56	21
1935	4,494	0	0	0	0	16	1,323	1,917	815	93	149	86	31	59	28	36
1940	4,286	0	0	0	0	0	16	1,287	1,848	773	86	131	72	107	35	38
1945	6,498	28	1,405	637	740	497	380	130	1,295	1,764	718	77	111	188	77	44
1950	19,077	1	7,220	2,196	5,023	4,064	2,154	1,280	458	1,390	1,653	650	72	208	136	0
1955	21,861	26	5,290	1,398	3,866	5,143	4,095	2,155	1,265	445	1,288	1,482	555	698	143	0
1956	22,372	17	4,989	1,446	3,526	5,008	4,528	2,469	1,380	563	866	1,720	691	849	158	0
1957	22,634	4	4,528	989	3,535	4,810	4,854	2,803	1,513	720	624	1,743	816	1,039	223	0
1958	22,727	(Z)	4,052	857	3,195	4,498	5,023	3,227	1,665	889	503	1,617	944	1,253	309	0
1959	22,666	(Z)	3,411	521	2,890	4,222	5,139	3,624	1,873	1,054	418	1,423	1,091	1,502	411	0
1960	22,534	(Z)	2,706	281	2,425	3,962	5,127	4,060	2,115	1,219	426	1,138	1,260	1,781	521	0
1961	22,403	(Z)	2,074	98	1,976	3,715	4,955	4,494	2,429	1,333	530	772	1,461	2,101	640	0
1962	22,275	(Z)	1,446	20	1,426	3,502	4,773	4,839	2,765	1,461	676	555	1,478	2,258	780	0
1963	22,166	(Z)	919	13	906	3,316	4,508	5,025	3,189	1,614	835	451	1,365	2,309	944	0
1964	22,013	0	593	13	580	2,930	4,222	5,148	3,596	1,823	996	378	1,200	2,327	1,127	0
1965	21,834	(Z)	327	13	314	2,458	3,967	5,137	4,036	2,059	1,152	387	958	2,311	1,353	0
1966	25,534	39	3,217	1,100	2,078	2,799	3,759	4,977	4,451	2,360	1,253	476	646	2,242	1,596	0
1967	25,805	31	3,275	1,095	2,149	2,541	3,580	4,791	4,785	2,680	1,374	610	466	2,169	1,703	0
1968	26,273	24	3,499	1,282	2,193	2,382	3,482	4,511	4,958	3,082	1,514	752	376	2,093	1,717	0
1969	26,925	18	3,906	1,527	2,361	2,318	3,291	4,243	5,071	3,469	1,709	894	315	2,024	1,709	0
1970	27,647	24	4,345	1,693	2,628	2,321	3,039	4,017	5,066	3,895	1,934	1,034	326	1,996	1,670	0
1971	27,523	35	4,538	1,899	2,604	2,292	2,971	3,794	4,567	3,834	2,110	1,212	572	2,205	1,633	0
1972	27,956	41	4,749	1,790	2,918	2,305	2,771	3,635	4,476	4,123	2,363	1,309	654	2,229	1,575	0
1973	28,125	46	4,657	1,458	3,153	2,359	2,591	3,531	4,326	4,320	2,654	1,415	750	2,272	1,522	0
1974	28,218	55	4,483	1,145	3,283	2,435	2,463	3,430	4,130	4,428	2,974	1,543	851	2,330	1,479	0

Fiscal year	Total (all ages) Ed229 Thousand	Under 20 Ed230 Thousand	Under 30 Ed231 Thousand	20 to 24 Ed232 Thousand	25 to 29 Ed233 Thousand	30 to 34 Ed234 Thousand	35 to 39 Ed235 Thousand	40 to 44 Ed236 Thousand	45 to 49 Ed237 Thousand	50 to 54 Ed238 Thousand	55 to 59 Ed239 Thousand	60 to 64 Ed240 Thousand	65 to 69 Ed241 Thousand	65 and older Ed242 Thousand	70 and older Ed243 Thousand	Unknown age Ed244 Thousand
1975	28,281	63	4,264	932	3,269	2,546	2,384	3,270	3,947	4,458	3,298	1,708	951	2,407	1,456	0
1976	28,405	105	3,943	860	2,978	2,837	2,332	3,023	3,734	4,401	3,691	1,964	1,065	2,523	1,458	0
(TQ)	28,447	100	4,003	858	3,045	2,771	2,341	3,073	3,776	4,416	3,613	1,911	1,043	2,499	1,456	0
1977	28,526	96	3,516	873	2,547	3,154	2,360	2,822	3,585	4,303	3,949	2,203	1,149	2,635	1,486	0
1978	28,546	74	3,099	868	2,157	3,370	2,425	2,649	3,496	4,142	4,111	2,480	1,246	2,774	1,528	0
1979	28,605	66	2,824	891	1,867	3,481	2,509	2,532	3,392	3,945	4,193	2,781	1,365	2,946	1,581	0
1980	28,500	54	2,693	877	1,762	3,496	2,551	2,475	3,300	3,836	4,203	2,920	1,424	3,027	1,603	0
1981	28,505	56	2,526	841	1,629	3,381	2,689	2,409	3,102	3,693	4,184	3,227	1,620	3,295	1,675	0
1982	28,407	36	2,377	754	1,587	2,924	3,049	2,381	2,912	3,526	4,116	3,524	1,836	3,598	1,762	0
1983	28,277	10	2,203	671	1,522	2,501	3,294	2,439	2,713	3,419	4,026	3,736	2,080	3,947	1,867	0
1984	28,154	7	2,099	599	1,493	2,117	3,451	2,487	2,579	3,364	3,838	3,857	2,365	4,363	1,998	0
1985	28,007	8	1,976	529	1,439	1,845	3,486	2,577	2,485	3,225	3,677	3,923	2,655	4,815	2,160	0
1986	27,864	9	1,855	474	1,372	1,692	3,377	2,707	2,429	3,036	3,548	3,913	2,937	5,308	2,371	0
1987	27,708	11	1,737	439	1,287	1,639	2,930	3,061	2,411	2,855	3,398	3,857	3,212	5,821	2,609	0
1988	27,541	12	1,625	405	1,208	1,574	2,518	3,303	2,478	2,665	3,304	3,780	3,410	6,294	2,884	0
1989	27,374	13	1,540	402	1,125	1,540	2,146	3,465	2,537	2,539	3,259	3,611	3,528	6,738	3,210	0
1990	27,184	16	1,470	401	1,053	1,478	1,883	3,506	2,636	2,451	3,133	3,468	3,596	7,159	3,563	0
1991	26,629	—	1,132	—	—	1,458	1,787	3,268	2,952	2,378	2,815	3,194	—	7,646	—	0
1992	26,992	—	1,394	—	—	1,389	1,691	2,892	3,205	2,403	2,732	3,198	—	8,088	—	0
1993	26,789	—	1,334	—	—	1,367	1,644	2,503	3,431	2,465	2,557	3,104	—	8,000	—	0
1994	26,365	1	1,233	311	921	1,322	1,602	2,184	3,515	2,531	2,419	3,018	3,233	8,542	5,309	0
1995	26,198	1	1,133	—	—	1,277	1,587	1,969	3,535	2,646	2,362	2,899	—	8,791	—	0
1996	25,881	1	1,079	207	872	1,229	1,521	1,849	3,355	2,815	2,318	2,720	3,002	8,994	5,992	0
1997	25,551	1	1,000	192	808	1,192	1,470	1,799	2,922	3,152	2,312	2,555	2,886	9,149	6,263	0
1998	25,188	1	914	184	730	1,150	1,427	1,740	2,537	3,369	2,373	2,396	2,808	9,280	6,472	0
1999	24,803	1	833	181	652	1,107	1,387	1,700	2,236	3,467	2,451	2,285	2,751	9,336	6,585	0

(TQ) Transition quarter.

(Z) Fewer than 500.

[1] Veterans who served in two or more wars prior to the Korean Conflict are included two or more times; see text.

Sources

1865–1970: U.S. Bureau of the Census, *Historical Statistics of the United States, Colonial Times to 1970* (1975), part 2, series Y943–Y956.

1971–1999: U.S. Department of Veterans Affairs, *Annual Reports* (various years), and unpublished data provided by the Department of Veterans Affairs.

Documentation

A veteran appears to have been defined, typically, as anyone who served in the armed forces during a designated period and received a discharge other than dishonorable. For World War I and earlier wars, the Department of Veterans Affairs made the estimates by applying appropriate survival rates to the number of veterans on the pension roles at certain dates. Those dates, often occurring long after the wars, were chosen on the assumption that changes in the law assured that a large proportion of the surviving veterans were then on the roles. Estimates for the pre–Civil War era are not available.

Only Union veterans of the Civil War are counted. Adequate statistics on the number of Confederate veterans are not available. The estimates for World War II and later wars were based, in part, on data provided by the military services on discharged veterans and on surveys taken by the Department of Veterans Affairs. The Censuses of 1980 and 1990 provided additional information that was used to center estimates of the number of veterans. More detailed discussions for years before World War II can be found in U.S. Bureau of the Census (1975), p. 1136.

Prior to the Korean Conflict, veterans who served in two or more wars are counted two or more times. Veterans who served only in the Korean Conflict or subsequent wars, however, are counted only once even if they served in more than one war. Prior to 1966, peacetime veterans were included only if they were drawing veterans benefits. This change in the statistics reflects Public Law 89-358, adopted on March 3, 1966, which conferred veteran status on all persons serving on active duty in the armed forces after January 31, 1955. Data that break down veterans into more advanced age groups (70–74, 75–79, 80–84, and 85 and older) are available in the U.S. Department of Veterans Affairs, *Annual Reports*.

Data are as of June 30 for 1940–1976, and September 30 for other years.

TABLE Ed245–261   Veterans in civil life, by period of service: 1865–1999[1]

Contributed by Scott Sigmund Gartner and Hugh Rockoff

Year	Total	War of 1812	Mexican War	Civil War	Indian Wars[2]	Spanish-American War	World War I	World War II[3]	Korean Conflict Total[3]	Korean Conflict No prior wartime service	Vietnam era Total[4]	Vietnam era No prior wartime service	Service between Vietnam era and Persian Gulf	Regular establishment	Persian Gulf Total	Persian Gulf No prior wartime service	Other peacetime service
	Ed245	Ed246	Ed247	Ed248	Ed249	Ed250	Ed251	Ed252	Ed253	Ed254	Ed255	Ed256	Ed257	Ed258	Ed259	Ed260	Ed261
	Thousand	Thousand	Thousand	Thousand	Thousand	Thousand	Thousand	Thousand	Thousand	Thousand	Thousand	Thousand	Thousand	Thousand	Thousand	Thousand	Thousand
1865	1,908	46	32	1,830	—	—	—	—	—	—	—	—	—	—	—	—	—
1870	1,802	28	30	1,744	—	—	—	—	—	—	—	—	—	—	—	—	—
1875	1,698	16	28	1,654	—	—	—	—	—	—	—	—	—	—	—	—	—
1880	1,593	10	26	1,557	—	—	—	—	—	—	—	—	—	—	—	—	—
1885	1,475	3	23	1,449	—	—	—	—	—	—	—	—	—	—	—	—	—
1890	1,341	(Z)	19	1,322	3	—	—	—	—	—	—	—	—	—	—	—	—
1895	1,187	(Z)	14	1,170	1	—	—	—	—	—	—	—	—	—	—	—	—
1900	1,224	(Z)	9	1,000	1	214	—	—	—	—	—	—	—	—	—	—	—
1905	1,192	—	5	821	2	364	—	—	—	—	—	—	—	—	—	—	—
1910	977	—	2	624	2	349	—	—	—	—	—	—	—	—	—	—	—
1915	773	—	1	424	1	332	—	—	—	—	—	—	—	15	—	—	—
1920	5,146	—	(Z)	244	4	317	4,566	—	—	—	—	—	—	15	—	—	—
1925	4,894	—	(Z)	127	4	298	4,453	—	—	—	—	—	—	12	—	—	—
1930	4,680	—	—	49	5	274	4,336	—	—	—	—	—	—	16	—	—	—
1935	4,494	—	—	13	4	244	4,201	—	—	—	—	—	—	32	—	—	—
1940	4,286	—	—	2	2	206	4,040	—	—	—	—	—	—	36	—	—	—
1941	4,337	—	—	2	2	198	4,002	95	—	—	—	—	—	38	—	—	—
1942	4,485	—	—	1	2	190	3,961	289	—	—	—	—	—	42	—	—	—
1943	5,002	—	—	1	1	182	3,917	858	—	—	—	—	—	43	—	—	—
1944	5,689	—	—	(Z)	1	173	3,871	1,601	—	—	—	—	—	43	—	—	—
1945	6,498	—	—	(Z)	1	164	3,821	2,469	—	—	—	—	—	43	—	—	—
1946	16,655	—	—	(Z)	1	155	3,768	12,687	—	—	—	—	—	44	—	—	—
1947	18,262	—	—	—	1	146	3,711	14,361	—	—	—	—	—	43	—	—	—
1948	18,745	—	—	—	1	136	3,651	14,914	—	—	—	—	—	43	—	—	—
1949	18,945	—	—	—	1	127	3,587	15,182	—	—	—	—	—	48	—	—	—
1950	19,077	—	—	(Z)	1	118	3,518	15,386	—	(Z)	—	—	—	54	—	—	—
1951	18,919	—	—	(Z)	(Z)	108	3,452	15,200	211	100	—	—	—	59	—	—	—
1952	19,338	—	—	(Z)	(Z)	99	3,382	15,369	867	428	—	—	—	60	—	—	—
1953	20,196	—	—	(Z)	(Z)	89	3,308	15,440	1,955	1,297	—	—	—	62	—	—	—
1954	20,951	—	—	(Z)	(Z)	80	3,230	15,425	2,912	2,153	—	—	—	63	—	—	—
1955	21,861	—	—	(Z)	(Z)	72	3,150	15,405	3,999	3,171	—	—	—	63	—	—	4
1956	22,372	—	—	(Z)	(Z)	63	3,061	15,370	4,686	3,812	—	—	—	66	—	—	30
1957	22,634	—	—	—	(Z)	55	2,971	15,332	5,105	4,202	—	—	—	74	—	—	186
1958	22,727	—	—	—	(Z)	48	2,876	15,288	5,353	4,431	—	—	—	84	—	—	569
1959	22,666	—	—	—	(Z)	43	2,778	15,243	5,448	4,507	—	—	—	95	—	—	967
1960	22,534	—	—	—	(Z)	36	2,673	15,202	5,482	4,520	—	—	—	103	—	—	1,380
1961	22,403	—	—	—	(Z)	31	2,565	15,156	5,531	4,538	—	—	—	113	—	—	1,760
1962	22,275	—	—	—	(Z)	26	2,455	15,126	5,586	4,546	—	—	—	122	—	—	2,156
1963	22,166	—	—	—	(Z)	22	2,343	15,100	5,663	4,567	—	—	—	134	—	—	2,617
1964	22,013	—	—	—	(Z)	18	2,226	15,048	5,708	4,574	—	—	—	147	—	—	3,119

Year	Total Ed245 Thousand	War of 1812 Ed246 Thousand	Mexican War Ed247 Thousand	Civil War Ed248 Thousand	Indian Wars Ed249 [2] Thousand	Spanish-American War Ed250 Thousand	World War I Ed251 Thousand	World War II Ed252 [3] Thousand	Korean Conflict Total Ed253 [3] Thousand	Korean Conflict No prior wartime service Ed254 Thousand	Vietnam era Total Ed255 [4] Thousand	Vietnam era No prior wartime service Ed256 Thousand	Service between Vietnam era and Persian Gulf Ed257 Thousand	Regular establishment Ed258 Thousand	Persian Gulf Total Ed259 Thousand	Persian Gulf No prior wartime service Ed260 Thousand	Other peacetime service Ed261 Thousand
1965	21,834	—	—	—	(Z)	15	2,121	14,969	5,718	4,568	456	434	—	161	—	—	3,152
1966	25,534	—	—	—	(Z)	12	2,007	14,916	5,770	4,568	962	884	—	175	—	—	3,147
1967	25,805	—	—	—	(Z)	10	1,888	14,832	5,797	4,563	1,493	1,370	—	195	—	—	3,142
1968	26,273	—	—	—	(Z)	8	1,766	14,718	5,814	4,567	2,234	2,070	—	180	—	—	3,139
1969	26,925	—	—	—	(Z)	6	1,647	14,592	5,847	4,590	3,169	2,956	—	183	—	—	3,134
1970	27,647	—	—	—	(Z)	5	1,536	14,458	5,867	4,605	4,173	3,918	—	185	—	—	3,125
1971	27,523	—	—	—	(Z)	4	1,302	13,713	5,485	4,225	4,948	4,488	—	—	—	—	3,791
1972	27,956	—	—	—	(Z)	3	1,189	13,532	5,520	4,275	5,694	5,192	—	—	—	—	3,766
1973	28,125	—	—	—	(Z)	2	1,082	13,343	5,555	4,324	6,182	5,634	—	—	—	—	3,741
1974	28,218	—	—	—	—	1	980	13,147	5,581	4,365	6,602	6,009	—	—	—	—	3,716
1975	28,281	—	—	—	—	1	883	12,943	5,592	4,392	6,999	6,370	—	—	—	—	3,692
1976	28,405	—	—	—	—	(Z)	793	12,733	5,578	4,395	7,386	6,740	77	—	—	—	3,667
(TQ)	28,447	—	—	—	—	(Z)	772	12,678	5,573	4,394	7,481	6,832	111	—	—	—	3,661
1977	28,526	—	—	—	—	(Z)	686	12,451	5,547	4,385	7,736	7,078	292	—	—	—	3,635
1978	28,546	—	—	—	—	(Z)	605	12,216	5,514	4,371	7,908	7,245	500	—	—	—	3,609
1979	28,605	—	—	—	—	(Z)	530	11,972	5,476	4,352	8,032	7,367	801	—	—	—	3,582
1980	28,640	—	—	—	—	(Z)	493	11,841	5,454	4,340	8,073	7,409	989	—	—	—	3,568
1981	28,519	—	—	—	—	(Z)	426	11,628	5,425	4,330	8,135	7,472	1,247	—	—	—	3,416
1982	28,432	—	—	—	—	(Z)	365	11,404	5,390	4,315	8,172	7,513	1,444	—	—	—	3,390
1983	28,316	—	—	—	—	(Z)	310	11,171	5,352	4,298	8,196	7,542	1,631	—	—	—	3,364
1984	28,207	—	—	—	—	(Z)	261	10,927	5,310	4,277	8,216	7,568	1,835	—	—	—	3,338
1985	28,075	—	—	—	—	(Z)	217	10,673	5,264	4,254	8,230	7,590	2,029	—	—	—	3,312
1986	27,946	—	—	—	—	(Z)	178	10,410	5,214	4,226	8,244	7,612	2,235	—	—	—	3,284
1987	27,803	—	—	—	—	(Z)	144	10,137	5,159	4,196	8,249	7,628	2,444	—	—	—	3,254
1988	27,650	—	—	—	—	(Z)	113	9,854	5,100	4,162	8,255	7,645	2,651	—	—	—	3,225
1989	27,497	—	—	—	—	(Z)	86	9,561	5,036	4,125	8,264	7,666	2,866	—	—	—	3,194
1990	27,320	—	—	—	—	(Z)	63	9,258	4,969	4,084	8,268	7,681	3,072	—	—	—	3,162
1991	27,152	—	—	—	—	(Z)	45	8,841	4,867	4,016	8,269	7,697	3,067	—	425	363	3,124
1992	26,980	—	—	—	—	—	34	8,499	4,782	3,958	8,278	7,718	3,060	—	730	618	3,092
1993	26,789	—	—	—	—	—	25	8,150	4,692	3,897	8,287	7,740	3,054	—	1,027	863	3,059
1994	26,503	—	—	—	—	—	19	7,795	4,597	3,832	8,284	7,750	3,048	—	1,242	1,035	3,025
1995	26,198	—	—	—	—	—	13	7,433	4,499	3,764	8,273	7,753	3,041	—	1,450	1,206	2,988
1996	25,881	—	—	—	—	—	10	7,066	4,396	3,692	8,248	7,742	3,034	—	1,658	1,388	2,950
1997	25,551	—	—	—	—	—	7	6,695	4,290	3,617	8,212	7,722	3,027	—	1,864	1,575	2,911
1998	25,188	—	—	—	—	—	5	6,319	4,179	3,538	8,166	7,690	3,018	—	2,048	1,748	2,870
1999	24,803	—	—	—	—	—	3	5,940	4,064	3,456	8,113	7,653	3,010	—	2,223	1,915	2,825

(TQ) Transition quarter.

(Z) Fewer than 500.

[1] Veterans who served in two or more wars prior to the Korean Conflict are included two or more times; see text.

[2] Includes only veterans on the benefit rolls of the U.S. Department of Veterans Affairs or predecessor agencies. Last known survivor died June 1973.

[3] Includes veterans who served in both World War II and the Korean Conflict.

[4] Includes veterans who served in both the Vietnam era and the Korean Conflict or World War II.

Sources

1865–1970: U.S. Bureau of the Census, *Historical Statistics of the United States, Colonial Times to 1970* (1975), series Y957–Y970.

1971–1995: U.S. Department of Veterans Affairs (VA), *Trend Data – 1971–1995*, p. 1, VA Internet site, accessed June 30, 2001. These data were originally compiled from the *Annual Reports* of the VA and its predecessor agencies and from data produced by other government agencies.

1996–1999: VA, *Annual Reports* (various years), and unpublished data provided by the VA.

Documentation

The methods by which the VA constructed the data underlying this table are described in the text for Table Ed229–244.

(continued)

TABLE Ed245–261   Veterans in civil life, by period of service: 1865–1999   *Continued*

Veterans who served only in the Korean Conflict or subsequent wars are counted only once even if they served in more than one war. Prior to the Korean Conflict, however, veterans who served in two or more wars are counted two or more times. Therefore series Ed245 – which is the sum of series Ed246–252, Ed254, Ed256–258, and Ed260–261 – is not measured consistently over the pre- and post–World War II eras.

The estimates for 1970–1980 are consistent with information drawn from the Census of 1980. Estimates for 1990–1995 are based on the Census of 1990.

Data are as of June 30.

The dates of America's wars, for the purpose of determining veteran status, are defined as follows.

War of 1812: June 18, 1812, through February 17, 1815.

Mexican War: April 25, 1846, through May 30, 1848.

Civil War: April 12, 1861, through April 13, 1865.

Indian Wars: 1817 through 1898 (approximately).

Spanish–American War: April 21, 1898, through July 4, 1902. Includes the war with Spain, the Boxer Rebellion, and the Philippine Insurrection. For persons serving in the Moro Province of the Philippines, hostilities ended July 15, 1903.

World War I: April 6, 1917, through November 11, 1918. For persons serving in Russia, the war ended April 1, 1920.

World War II: September 16, 1940, through July 25, 1947.

Korean Conflict: June 27, 1950, through January 31, 1955.

Vietnam era: August 4, 1964, through May 7, 1975.

Service between Vietnam era and the Persian Gulf War: between May 7, 1975 and August 1, 1990.

Persian Gulf War: August 1, 1990 (ending date yet to be determined).

Series Ed250. Last known survivor died September 1973.

Series Ed258. Covers former members of Regular Establishment (peacetime) receiving disability compensation from the VA or predecessor agencies. Beginning June 1966, Regular Establishment veterans are excluded from total veterans because they are, for the most part, included as veterans with service between the Korean Conflict and Vietnam era or as veterans of a war period.

Series Ed261. Includes peacetime veterans whose service was either between World War I and World War II only or between World War II and the Korean Conflict only and peacetime veterans whose only service was between January 31, 1955, and August 5, 1964. Public Law 89-358, March 3, 1966, conferred veteran status on all persons serving on active duty in the armed forces after January 31, 1955. Veterans with service between the Korean Conflict and the Vietnam era (February 1, 1955–August 4, 1964) and Vietnam-era veterans (service after August 4, 1964) were included in the total veteran count beginning June 1966. Prior to 1966, peacetime veterans were included only if they were receiving VA disability compensation.

TABLE Ed262-272   Female veterans in civil life, by period of service: 1970-1997

Contributed by Hugh Rockoff

Year	Total	World War I	World War II	Korean Conflict Total	Korean Conflict No prior wartime service	Vietnam era Total	Vietnam era No prior wartime service	Persian Gulf War Total	Persian Gulf War No prior wartime service	Peacetime veterans Post-Vietnam era	Peacetime veterans Other
	Ed262	Ed263	Ed264	Ed265	Ed266	Ed267	Ed268	Ed269	Ed270	Ed271	Ed272
	Thousand	Thousand	Thousand	Thousand	Thousand	Thousand	Thousand	Thousand	Thousand	Thousand	Thousand
1970	959.4	31.5	444.0	124.5	97.7	126.2	115.3	—	—	—	270.8
1971	964.2	29.6	440.3	124.6	98.1	140.2	129.0	—	—	—	267.2
1972	968.0	27.8	436.5	124.7	98.4	153.3	141.8	—	—	—	263.5
1973	971.0	26.0	432.5	124.6	98.7	166.0	154.1	—	—	—	259.8
1974	977.1	24.3	428.4	124.4	98.7	181.8	169.6	—	—	—	256.1
1975	985.9	22.6	424.2	124.1	98.8	200.4	188.0	—	—	—	252.3
1976	1,001.7	21.0	419.8	123.6	98.5	215.7	203.2	—	—	10.5	248.6
(TQ)	1,007.6	20.6	418.6	123.4	98.5	220.7	208.2	—	—	14.0	247.7
1977	1,030.4	19.0	413.9	122.7	98.1	235.3	222.9	—	—	33.0	243.6
1978	1,057.0	17.4	408.9	122.0	97.8	245.0	232.7	—	—	60.6	239.6
1979	1,088.0	15.9	403.7	121.2	97.3	251.1	238.9	—	—	96.4	235.8
1980	1,111.3	15.1	400.9	120.8	97.1	253.3	241.1	—	—	123.4	233.7
1981	1,003.2	13.5	395.2	119.3	96.3	253.7	241.9	—	—	151.9	104.4
1982	1,015.6	12.1	389.3	117.7	95.4	252.9	241.4	—	—	174.5	102.9
1983	1,025.5	10.6	383.0	116.1	94.4	251.3	240.1	—	—	195.8	101.5
1984	1,036.6	9.3	376.5	114.4	93.4	249.6	238.8	—	—	218.6	100.0
1985	1,047.4	8.0	369.5	112.7	92.4	247.6	237.2	—	—	241.7	98.5
1986	1,059.1	6.8	362.3	110.9	91.3	245.5	235.5	—	—	266.3	97.0
1987	1,069.4	5.7	354.7	109.0	90.2	242.6	233.0	—	—	290.4	95.4
1988	1,081.4	4.7	346.7	107.1	89.1	240.1	230.9	—	—	316.2	93.8
1989	1,094.4	3.7	338.5	105.0	87.9	237.7	228.9	—	—	343.3	92.2
1990	1,098.4	2.8	329.9	103.0	86.6	226.9	218.5	—	—	370.0	90.5
1991	1,140.3	2.2	319.4	101.3	85.4	227.3	219.2	59.6	56.4	368.2	89.6
1992	1,139.7	1.8	310.5	99.9	84.6	228.3	220.3	91.0	86.3	367.8	88.5
1993	1,180.1	1.4	301.3	98.5	83.6	229.8	221.9	123.7	117.0	367.5	87.5
1994	1,191.5	1.1	291.7	97.0	82.6	231.7	224.0	147.9	138.5	367.1	86.4
1995	1,204.3	(Z)	281.8	95.4	81.5	233.5	226.1	174.0	162.0	366.8	85.3
1996	1,215.0	(Z)	272.0	94.0	80.0	235.0	227.0	198.0	184.0	366.0	84.0
1997	1,225.0	(Z)	261.0	92.0	79.0	235.0	228.0	223.0	208.0	366.0	83.0

(TQ) Transition quarter.

(Z) Fewer than 1,000.

Source

U.S. Department of Veterans Affairs (VA), *Annual Reports* (annual issues), and unpublished data provided by the VA.

Documentation

Little attention was paid to female veterans until comparatively recent years; consequently, data were not collected. The Census of 1980 was the first that asked women whether they were veterans, and about 1.2 million women answered affirmatively. Soon after, Congress granted veteran status to women who had served in the Women's Army Auxiliary Corps (WACS) during World War II, inaugurating a series of actions to provide services for women veterans. In response to the new awareness of the role of women veterans, the Department of Veterans Affairs (VA) compiled estimates of the number of women veterans back to 1970 based on the information uncovered by the Census of 1980. Estimates for 1990 and subsequent years were based on information uncovered by the Census of 1990.

Veterans who served in more than one wartime period are counted only once. Therefore series Ed262 is the sum of series Ed263-264, Ed266, Ed268, and Ed270-272.

The dates of America's wars, for the purpose of delineating veteran status, are described in the text for Table Ed245-261.

Data are as of June 30.

Series Ed272. Includes peacetime veterans whose only service was either between World War I and World War II or between World War II and the Korean Conflict, and peacetime veterans whose only service was between January 31, 1955, and August 5, 1964. Prior to 1966, peacetime veterans were included only if they were receiving VA disability compensation.

TABLE Ed273–296 Veterans, by age, sex, race, and Hispanic origin: 1990
Contributed by Hugh Rockoff

	Total			White			African-American			American Indian, Aleut and Eskimo		
	Total	Male	Female	Total	Male	Female	Total	Male	Female	Total	Male	Female
	Ed273	Ed274	Ed275	Ed276	Ed277	Ed278	Ed279	Ed280	Ed281	Ed282	Ed283	Ed284
Age	Number	Number	Number	Number	Number	Number	Number	Number	Number	Number	Number	Number
Total	27,183,662	26,089,741	1,093,921	24,107,579	23,186,148	921,431	2,330,229	2,195,849	134,380	189,788	178,516	11,272
16–19	15,548	13,121	2,427	11,400	9,807	1,593	2,879	2,352	527	246	196	50
20–24	401,400	356,606	44,794	315,497	283,469	32,028	64,219	54,254	9,965	3,952	3,421	531
25–29	1,052,824	929,273	123,551	821,551	731,716	89,835	175,025	147,921	27,104	11,890	10,307	1,583
30–34	1,478,154	1,321,445	156,709	1,153,867	1,032,351	121,516	248,142	220,035	28,107	17,031	15,199	1,832
35–39	1,883,264	1,761,411	121,853	1,540,219	1,444,022	96,197	254,992	235,286	19,706	22,218	20,513	1,705
40–44	3,505,998	3,421,122	84,876	3,073,214	3,003,540	69,674	314,449	303,008	11,441	31,433	30,195	1,238
45–49	2,636,304	2,575,450	60,854	2,345,478	2,293,994	51,484	213,188	206,313	6,875	22,051	21,142	909
50–54	2,450,939	2,396,481	54,458	2,191,938	2,145,261	46,677	192,753	187,122	5,631	18,980	18,294	686
55–59	3,132,620	3,070,003	62,617	2,843,868	2,789,623	54,245	219,344	213,015	6,329	18,664	17,835	829
60–64	3,467,957	3,415,097	52,860	3,178,491	3,132,158	46,333	223,482	218,516	4,966	16,285	15,819	466
65–69	5,595,997	5,427,328	168,669	4,326,614	4,165,866	160,748	214,449	208,199	6,250	14,317	13,570	747
70–74	213,657	126,071	87,586	1,060,034	977,196	82,838	124,385	120,656	3,729	7,985	7,540	445
75–79	874,702	833,135	41,567	807,888	768,898	38,990	54,596	52,399	2,197	3,074	2,907	167
80–84	320,562	302,048	18,514	295,245	277,805	17,440	19,476	18,572	904	1,110	1,046	64
85–89	81,307	73,393	7,914	74,779	67,303	7,476	4,681	4,290	391	358	338	20
90–94	54,540	51,191	3,349	51,408	48,251	3,157	2,535	2,391	144	127	127	0
95+	17,889	16,566	1,323	16,088	14,888	1,200	1,634	1,520	114	67	67	0

(continued)

	Asian or Pacific Islander			Other race			Hispanic			Non-Hispanic white		
	Total	Male	Female	Total	Male	Female	Total	Male	Female	Total	Male	Female
	Ed285	Ed286	Ed287	Ed288	Ed289	Ed290	Ed291	Ed292	Ed293	Ed294	Ed295	Ed296
Age	Number	Number	Number	Number	Number	Number	Number	Number	Number	Number	Number	Number
Total	246,242	233,580	12,662	309,824	295,648	14,176	925,349	884,898	40,451	23,527,720	22,629,933	897,787
16–19	382	281	101	641	485	156	1,473	1,186	287	10,657	9,175	1,482
20–24	6,151	5,182	969	11,581	10,280	1,301	27,269	24,224	3,045	301,197	270,690	30,507
25–29	13,651	11,747	1,904	30,707	27,582	3,125	71,591	64,207	7,384	784,216	698,163	86,053
30–34	18,202	16,144	2,058	40,912	37,716	3,196	95,837	88,044	7,793	1,103,982	986,644	117,338
35–39	22,493	20,575	1,918	43,342	41,015	2,327	104,262	98,246	6,016	1,484,295	1,391,475	92,820
40–44	33,437	32,208	1,229	53,465	52,171	1,294	146,606	142,719	3,887	2,985,527	2,918,111	67,416
45–49	26,366	25,393	973	29,221	28,608	613	91,217	89,043	2,174	2,287,066	2,236,951	50,115
50–54	23,888	22,885	1,003	23,380	22,919	461	79,853	77,938	1,915	2,138,270	2,092,902	45,368
55–59	26,818	26,041	777	23,926	23,489	437	89,673	87,804	1,869	2,781,018	2,728,135	52,883
60–64	28,337	27,733	604	21,362	20,871	491	84,499	82,749	1,750	3,117,546	3,072,346	45,200
65–69	23,656	23,084	572	16,961	16,609	352	71,877	69,754	2,123	4,273,417	4,114,288	159,129
70–74	12,489	12,150	339	8,764	8,529	235	38,254	37,134	1,120	1,031,521	949,530	81,991
75–79	5,551	5,415	136	3,593	3,516	77	14,740	14,184	556	797,291	758,693	38,598
80–84	3,365	3,316	49	1,366	1,309	57	5,677	5,398	279	291,243	274,012	17,231
85–89	1,115	1,109	6	374	353	21	1,605	1,470	135	73,631	66,265	7,366
90–94	298	283	15	172	139	33	629	541	88	50,980	47,872	3,108
95+	43	34	9	57	57	0	287	257	30	15,863	14,681	1,182

Source
Unpublished data provided by the U.S. Department of Veterans Affairs.

Documentation
These estimates were prepared by the Department of Veterans Affairs using data from the Census of 1990. Similar estimates based on the Census of 1980, and similar estimates for more recent years based on the Current Population Survey (CPS), can be obtained from the Department of Veterans Affairs, although the categories available vary. The estimates based on the CPS may be less accurate because they are based on a sample. The definitions of race follow the standard census practice.

TABLE Ed297–310 Expenditures of the Veterans Administration, by function: 1790–1970[1,2]

Contributed by Scott Sigmund Gartner and Hugh Rockoff

Fiscal year	Total	Compensation and pensions	Insurance and servicemen's indemnities[3]	Readjustment benefits					Miscellaneous benefit payments	Medical, hospital, and domiciliary services	Hospital and domiciliary facilities	Administration and other benefits	From general and special fund appropriations	Transfers to insurance trust funds
				Education and training	Vocational and rehabilitation	Unemployment and self-employment allowances	Loan guaranty	Direct loans					Total	
	Ed297	Ed298	Ed299	Ed300	Ed301	Ed302	Ed303	Ed304	Ed305	Ed306	Ed307	Ed308	Ed309	Ed310
	Thousand dollars	Thousand dollars	Thousand dollars	Thousand dollars	Thousand dollars	Thousand dollars	Thousand dollars	Thousand dollars	Thousand dollars	Thousand dollars	Thousand dollars	Thousand dollars	Thousand dollars	Thousand dollars
1790–1865	96,445	96,445	—	—	—	—	—	—	—	—	—	—	96,445	—
1866	15,858	15,451	—	—	—	—	—	—	—	—	—	407	15,858	—
1867	21,276	20,785	—	—	—	—	—	—	—	—	—	491	21,276	—
1868	24,164	23,102	—	—	—	—	—	—	—	509	—	553	24,164	—
1869	29,658	28,513	—	—	—	—	—	—	—	580	—	565	29,658	—
1870	30,543	29,351	—	—	—	—	—	—	—	591	—	601	30,543	—
1871	30,081	28,519	—	—	—	—	—	—	—	699	—	863	30,081	—
1872	31,454	29,753	—	—	—	—	—	—	—	750	—	951	31,454	—
1873	28,681	26,982	—	—	—	—	—	—	—	695	—	1,004	28,681	—
1874	31,908	30,207	—	—	—	—	—	—	—	734	—	967	31,908	—
1875	31,106	29,270	—	—	—	—	—	—	—	853	—	983	31,106	—
1876	29,887	27,936	—	—	—	—	—	—	—	936	—	1,015	29,887	—
1877	30,145	28,183	—	—	—	—	—	—	—	928	—	1,034	30,145	—
1878	28,764	26,786	—	—	—	—	—	—	—	945	—	1,033	28,764	—
1879	35,526	33,664	—	—	—	—	—	—	—	1,024	—	838	35,526	—
1880	58,585	56,689	—	—	—	—	—	—	—	961	—	935	58,585	—
1881	52,771	50,583	—	—	—	—	—	—	—	1,116	—	1,072	52,771	—
1882	56,882	54,313	—	—	—	—	—	—	—	1,103	—	1,466	56,882	—
1883	64,361	60,428	—	—	—	—	—	—	—	1,341	—	2,592	64,361	—
1884	62,184	57,912	—	—	—	—	—	—	—	1,437	—	2,835	62,184	—
1885	70,196	65,172	—	—	—	—	—	—	—	1,631	—	3,393	70,196	—
1886	68,931	64,091	—	—	—	—	—	—	—	1,595	—	3,245	68,931	—
1887	79,451	73,753	—	—	—	—	—	—	—	1,945	—	3,753	79,451	—
1888	84,512	78,951	—	—	—	—	—	—	—	2,046	—	3,515	84,512	—
1889	95,066	88,843	—	—	—	—	—	—	—	2,756	—	3,467	95,066	—
1890	112,647	106,094	—	—	—	—	—	—	—	3,027	—	3,525	112,647	—
1891	125,351	117,313	—	—	—	—	—	—	—	3,338	—	4,700	125,351	—
1892	147,784	139,394	—	—	—	—	—	—	—	3,491	—	4,899	147,784	—
1893	165,315	156,907	—	—	—	—	—	—	—	3,540	—	4,868	165,315	—
1894	147,408	139,987	—	—	—	—	—	—	—	3,457	—	3,964	147,408	—
1895	147,606	139,812	—	—	—	—	—	—	—	3,456	—	4,333	147,606	—
1896	145,789	138,221	—	—	—	—	—	—	—	3,577	—	3,991	145,789	—
1897	147,903	139,950	—	—	—	—	—	—	—	3,965	—	3,988	147,903	—
1898	152,814	144,652	—	—	—	—	—	—	—	4,048	—	4,114	152,814	—
1899	146,822	138,355	—	—	—	—	—	—	—	4,320	—	4,147	146,822	—
1900	146,887	138,462	—	—	—	—	—	—	—	4,583	—	3,842	146,887	—
1901	147,275	138,531	—	—	—	—	—	—	—	4,875	—	3,869	147,275	—
1902	146,575	137,504	—	—	—	—	—	—	—	5,240	—	3,831	146,575	—
1903	147,079	137,760	—	—	—	—	—	—	—	5,326	—	3,993	147,079	—
1904	150,716	141,094	—	—	—	—	—	—	—	5,773	—	3,849	150,716	—

Notes appear at end of table

(continued)

TABLE Ed297–310 Expenditures of the Veterans Administration, by function: 1790–1970 Continued

| Fiscal year | Total Ed297 | Compensation and pensions Ed298 | Insurance and servicemen's indemnities Ed299 [3] | Readjustment benefits | | | | | Miscellaneous benefit payments Ed305 | Medical, hospital, and domiciliary services Ed306 | Hospital and domiciliary facilities Ed307 | Administration and other benefits Ed308 | From general and special fund appropriations | |
| | | | | Education and training Ed300 | Vocational and rehabilitation Ed301 | Unemployment and self-employment allowances Ed302 | Loan guaranty Ed303 | Direct loans Ed304 | | | | | Total Ed309 | Transfers to insurance trust funds Ed310 |
	Thousand dollars	Thousand dollars	Thousand dollars	Thousand dollars	Thousand dollars	Thousand dollars	Thousand dollars	Thousand dollars	Thousand dollars	Thousand dollars	Thousand dollars	Thousand dollars	Thousand dollars	Thousand dollars
1905	150,851	141,143	—	—	—	—	—	—	—	5,986	—	3,722	150,851	—
1906	148,421	139,000	—	—	—	—	—	—	—	5,897	—	3,524	148,421	—
1907	147,482	138,155	—	—	—	—	—	—	—	6,018	—	3,309	147,482	—
1908	162,398	153,093	—	—	—	—	—	—	—	6,504	—	2,801	162,398	—
1909	171,458	161,974	—	—	—	—	—	—	—	6,632	—	2,852	171,458	—
1910	169,492	159,974	—	—	—	—	—	—	—	6,860	—	2,658	169,492	—
1911	166,448	157,325	—	—	—	—	—	—	—	6,606	—	2,517	166,448	—
1912	162,125	152,986	—	—	—	—	—	—	—	6,690	—	2,449	162,125	—
1913	183,138	174,172	—	—	—	—	—	—	—	6,423	—	2,543	183,138	—
1914	180,866	172,418	—	—	—	—	—	—	—	6,382	—	2,066	180,866	—
1915	173,729	165,518	—	—	—	—	—	—	—	6,431	—	1,780	173,729	—
1916	167,393	159,155	—	—	—	—	—	—	—	6,581	—	1,657	167,393	—
1917	169,264	160,895	—	—	—	—	—	—	—	6,806	—	1,563	169,264	—
1918	327,100	180,177	840	—	—	—	—	—	134,806	6,920	—	4,357	260,898	—
1919	701,131	233,461	43,798	—	67	—	—	—	400,589	5,512	—	17,704	499,311	—
1920	514,980	316,418	85,974	—	34,652	—	—	—	54,084	5,829	—	18,023	494,183	—
1921	664,538	380,026	96,961	—	99,065	—	—	—	23,831	53,128	—	11,527	652,157	—
1922	740,624	377,158	104,801	—	166,051	—	—	—	5,231	77,062	917	9,404	736,731	4,273
1923	740,783	388,607	103,334	—	149,433	—	—	—	−264	59,262	2,644	37,767	737,000	2,785
1924	652,101	345,490	106,036	—	106,962	—	—	—	17	48,422	9,215	35,959	647,283	2,685
1925	617,486	346,748	109,762	—	60,486	—	—	—	7,657	55,024	3,895	33,914	607,246	3,336
1926	649,143	372,281	142,507	—	25,840	—	—	—	20,927	53,113	4,511	29,964	628,271	4,350
1927	640,549	403,630	128,415	—	2,206	—	—	—	24,180	53,235	4,599	24,284	618,791	4,413
1928	652,712	410,765	131,277	—	234	—	—	—	27,189	53,121	5,222	24,904	625,144	7,158
1929	665,342	418,821	135,704	—	−3	—	—	—	26,191	54,682	4,044	25,903	631,248	7,946
1930	675,788	418,433	139,212	—	−20	—	—	—	23,263	60,426	8,241	26,233	639,213	8,235
1931	752,816	488,389	137,325	—	−22	—	—	—	21,862	68,591	9,040	27,631	714,022	6,551
1932	835,357	545,777	146,397	—	−17	—	—	—	25,958	75,020	12,876	29,346	789,251	6,080
1933	827,825	550,559	145,426	—	−16	—	—	—	27,034	65,435	13,517	25,870	780,758	5,674
1934	540,991	321,377	124,494	—	−7	—	—	—	28,065	45,962	3,170	17,930	496,215	4,847
1935	605,686	374,407	123,297	—	−9	—	—	—	29,802	57,047	2,903	18,239	556,857	4,230
1936	3,835,661 [4]	398,992	118,862	—	−6	—	—	—	3,234,247 [4]	62,481	2,938	18,147	580,249	3,459
1937	891,426	396,030	114,880	—	−9	—	—	—	289,957	64,154	8,964	17,450	579,352	2,568
1938	627,399	402,769	111,727	—	−1	—	—	—	20,757	66,626	9,347	16,174	581,923	2,431
1939	597,461	416,704	70,965	—	−2	—	—	—	14,045	69,651	10,958	15,140	555,175	2,760
1940	637,611	429,138	87,899	—	−3	—	—	—	15,690	74,497	13,638	16,752	557,690	1,516
1941	612,721	433,114	69,588	—	−4	—	—	—	9,626	78,458	4,541	17,398	553,013	1,636
1942	642,917	431,284	56,516	—	−4	—	—	—	49,974	81,973	4,046	19,128	556,198	4,813
1943	619,764	442,360	55,508	—	−3	—	—	—	8,063	86,623	2,720	24,493	605,693	36,492
1944	723,445	494,364	86,392	—	659	—	—	—	10,077	98,041	4,851	29,061	743,596	104,947

Fiscal year	Total	Compensation and pensions	Insurance and servicemen's indemnities [3]	Readjustment benefits						Medical, hospital, and domiciliary services	Hospital and domiciliary facilities	Administration and other benefits	From general and special fund appropriations	
				Education and training	Vocational rehabilitation	Unemployment and self-employment allowances	Loan guaranty	Direct loans	Miscellaneous benefit payments				Total	Transfers to insurance trust funds
	Ed297	Ed298	Ed299 [3]	Ed300	Ed301	Ed302	Ed303	Ed304	Ed305	Ed306	Ed307	Ed308	Ed309	Ed310
	Thousand dollars	Thousand dollars	Thousand dollars	Thousand dollars	Thousand dollars	Thousand dollars	Thousand dollars	Thousand dollars	Thousand dollars	Thousand dollars	Thousand dollars	Thousand dollars	Thousand dollars	Thousand dollars
1945	1,140,829	732,535	175,935	8,693	8,348	23,512	—	—	21,744	101,611	15,801	52,650	2,084,668	1,130,490
1946	3,382,777	1,215,688	340,594	350,561	45,087	1,000,909	5,225	—	18,007	213,816	34,313	158,573	4,425,001	1,389,296
1947	6,972,077	1,731,973	328,211	2,122,292	221,147	1,447,916	75,493	—	44,409	415,813	153,880	430,943	7,470,600	833,278
1948	6,744,852	1,820,685	381,281	2,498,884	333,313	677,256	64,354	—	39,780	519,722	16,980	392,597	6,497,681	144,458
1949	6,987,596	1,891,283	401,454	2,703,862	335,200	509,592	40,038	—	40,700	574,178	124,025	367,264	6,660,350	89,154
1950	9,278,335	2,009,462	3,108,957	2,595,728	272,292	138,191	58,671	—	41,222	592,082	151,532	310,198	6,627,657	474,648
1951	5,953,879	2,035,988	607,104	1,943,341	176,875	8,378	90,108	60,932	62,530	594,084	103,878	270,661	5,356,639	44,555
1952	5,869,841	2,105,973	1,110,193	1,325,403	97,902	76	78,355	87,276	53,267	662,683	113,011	235,702	4,944,187	204,644
1953	5,013,733	2,376,307	737,575	667,802	57,768	-516	65,843	92,760	63,809	662,858	88,183	201,244	4,354,220	84,725
1954	5,075,185	2,450,518	869,579	544,119	41,294	-245	44,640	117,709	51,537	712,828	51,043	192,163	4,282,592	73,477
1955	5,170,768	2,634,293	724,069	664,514	40,770	-200	28,831	125,126	51,000	696,750	32,510	173,105	4,483,137	31,160
1956	5,402,035 [5]	2,748,989	686,013	766,900	38,134	-2	40,062	103,118	55,726	760,409	26,882	176,944	4,801,885	79,041
1957	5,553,871 [5]	2,828,516	696,646	776,277	30,598	5	60,125	130,219	58,915	768,076	36,342	168,799	4,884,506	19,993
1958	5,948,131 [5]	3,062,211	761,075	698,415	26,095	2	80,039	228,868	63,189	823,963	32,904	171,627	5,205,941	15,570
1959	6,129,139 [5]	3,225,527	796,315	574,029	22,307	1	120,933	203,971	81,232	880,787	45,145	178,838	5,343,711	12,426
1960	6,215,378 [5]	3,314,761	831,760	382,861	17,910	(Z)	121,829	312,777	89,088	912,967	56,854	174,768	5,389,378	11,120
1961	6,636,402 [5]	3,568,396	1,068,544	237,264	11,837	(Z)	159,885	286,271	96,241	978,048	51,428	178,917	5,567,531	9,829
1962	6,529,104 [5]	3,652,598	882,269	142,557	10,336	(Z)	234,993	252,827	102,998	1,022,323	53,008	175,330	5,636,630	8,351
1963	6,816,023 [5]	3,814,749	930,873	88,209	9,243	(Z)	309,520	246,332	104,737	1,071,790	66,170	174,640	5,866,233	8,053
1964	6,866,474	3,900,203	827,763	58,566	11,757	(Z)	355,314	237,280	113,536	1,119,811	68,576	173,656	6,008,129	8,527
1965	6,967,530 [5]	4,042,144	783,139	37,443	14,533	(Z)	363,926	171,394	118,376	1,181,512	76,996	178,125	6,150,021	8,910
1966	7,325,325	4,305,368	867,999	30,988	17,426	0	378,028	92,432	141,686	1,229,254	83,464	178,689	6,410,840	8,256
1967	8,003,404	4,392,834	1,039,099	286,597	19,186	0	368,873	161,660	155,364	1,325,705	60,035	194,051	6,913,666	9,066
1968	8,425,437	4,519,304	1,083,335	446,490	22,755	0	328,090	208,382	144,238	1,418,953	49,883	204,007	7,290,882	6,968
1969	9,025,846	4,848,852	1,068,437	661,095	29,965	0	282,955	208,546	139,825	1,515,851	47,872	222,448	7,907,776	9,790
1970	10,122,477 [5]	5,253,840	1,169,451	991,443	41,643	0	248,961	180,403	153,926	1,748,432	74,605	262,605	8,905,065	11,381

(Z) Less than $500.

[1] Data for 1970 are on an accrued expenditures basis; prior data based on nonaccrual basis.

[2] Credits (inflows instead of outflows) are shown as negative numbers.

[3] Largely consists of payments from trust accounts. Through 1948, the figures are on a net basis; thereafter, they are on a gross basis.

[4] Includes total payments to veterans and beneficiaries on adjusted service certificates – the World War I "bonus."

[5] Detail does not add to total because of adjustments for overpayments collected and items written off as uncollectible under the readjustment benefits program.

Source

U.S. Bureau of the Census, *Historical Statistics of the United States, Colonial Times to 1970* (1975), series Y984–Y997.

Documentation

The data were originally compiled from the *Annual Reports* of the predecessor agencies of the U.S. Department of Veterans Affairs and their unpublished data. Series Ed297–310 are series Y984 to Y997 from U.S. Bureau of the Census (1975) and are described fully on pp. 1137–8. The expenditure data

were based on checks paid through December 31, 1947, and on vouchers issued thereafter. Receipts from various funds were not deducted, and so the figures differed from those reported by the Treasury or the Bureau of the Budget.

Series Ed297. Equals the sum of series Ed298–308. In some cases, the separate columns do not add to the total because of rounding or for other reasons described in the text.

Series Ed298. Figures are total payments made to living veterans or to the dependents of deceased veterans as a reward for service in the armed forces and to compensate for disabilities or death, whether or not service-connected.

Series Ed299. Figures are payments made to living veterans or to the dependents of deceased veterans on the basis of insurance policies purchased by veterans. This program was launched in World War I. From 1949, the series is on a gross basis. Cash dividends paid by the insurance trust funds are included, but premiums paid are not deducted. Prior to 1949, the series was on a net basis. In 1948, the cumulative difference for prior years between the net figures and what they would have been on a gross basis was $295,651,000. Transfers to the insurance trust funds are shown in series Ed310.

(continued)

TABLE Ed297–310   Expenditures of the Veterans Administration, by function: 1790–1970   *Continued*

Series Ed300. Figures are expenditures for education and training provided to living veterans and to the dependents of deceased veterans. These programs date from World War II.

Series Ed301. Figures are expenditures for education and training provided to veterans for vocational rehabilitation. These programs date from World War I.

Series Ed302. Figures are expenditures for unemployment compensation and self-employment allowances to veterans of World War II. Similar allowances paid to veterans of the Korean and Vietnam Conflicts through the Department of Labor are excluded.

Series Ed303. Figures are amounts paid on defaulted loans guaranteed by the Veterans Administration and related costs. Recoveries are not shown. They amounted to a cumulative total of $2.9 billion through June 30, 1970.

Series Ed304. Figures are expenses incurred in the programs that provide direct loans to veterans.

Series Ed305. Covers a wide range of relatively small programs including conveyances and adapted homes for disabled veterans, payments to participants in yellow fever experiments, and so on. The World War I bonus is included in this series.

Series Ed306. Figures are the sum of expenditures for medical and domiciliary services such as medical and dental treatment, domiciliary care, and nursing bed care.

Series Ed307. Figures are expenditures for constructing and equipping hospitals and residential facilities and for major alterations and repairs.

Series Ed308. Figures are expenditures for general administration and certain benefits including vocational counseling, travel to attend programs, and reporting allowances paid schools for certifying the attendance of veteran trainees.

Series Ed309. Figures are expenditures made by the Veterans Administration and predecessor agencies from appropriations made by Congress to finance general operations. After 1917, expenditures made from trust funds are excluded.

TABLE Ed311–323   Expenditures of the U.S. Department of Veterans Affairs, by function: 1960–1998[1]
Contributed by Hugh Rockoff

		Medical programs						Compensation and pensions	Vocational rehabilitation and education				All other expenditures
	Total	Total	Administration and miscellaneous operating expenditures	Medical care	Medical and prosthetic research	Construction of hospitals and other facilities	General operating expenditures		Total	Vocational rehabilitation	Veterans' educational assistance	Dependents' educational assistance	
	Ed311	Ed312	Ed313	Ed314	Ed315	Ed316	Ed317	Ed318	Ed319	Ed320	Ed321	Ed322	Ed323
Fiscal year	Thousand dollars	Thousand dollars	Thousand dollars	Thousand dollars	Thousand dollars	Thousand dollars	Thousand dollars	Thousand dollars	Thousand dollars	Thousand dollars	Thousand dollars	Thousand dollars	Thousand dollars
1960	6,333,440	919,440	29,220	890,220	—[2]	56,854	164,081	3,311,652	400,771	17,910	371,404	11,457	1,480,642
1961	6,758,006	987,218	34,481	952,736	—[2]	51,428	165,367	3,565,537	249,101	11,837	220,971	16,293	1,739,355
1962	6,660,112	1,034,891	40,854	994,037	—[2]	53,008	161,001	3,649,786	152,893	10,336	121,191	21,366	1,608,533
1963	6,953,174	1,087,197	15,984	1,043,762	27,451	66,170	158,933	3,811,991	97,452	9,243	62,505	25,704	1,731,431
1964	6,997,526	1,133,848	14,295	1,087,848	31,704	68,576	157,845	3,897,543	70,509	11,757	33,947	24,805	1,669,205
1965	7,085,500	1,195,287	14,137	1,144,011	37,139	76,996	162,764	4,039,618	51,974	14,533	11,870	25,570	1,558,861
1966	7,416,770	1,242,070	13,142	1,190,451	38,477	83,464	164,339	4,302,936	48,554	17,426	16	31,113	1,575,407
1967	8,061,740	1,339,259	14,000	1,281,232	44,027	59,957	178,940	4,390,582	305,160	19,186	251,652	34,322	1,787,842
1968	8,494,740	1,430,406	12,762	1,372,301	45,343	47,993	189,641	4,522,437	466,907	22,755	407,047	37,105	1,837,356
1969	9,099,968	1,528,804	14,322	1,464,104	50,378	46,103	206,239	4,848,972	685,023	29,965	614,737	40,320	1,784,827
1970	10,201,210	1,764,759	17,781	1,687,623	59,355	74,605	243,025	5,251,902	1,032,346	41,643	938,775	51,928	1,834,573
1971	11,565,102	1,996,833	20,186	1,913,509	63,139	85,087	260,147	5,724,573	1,651,073	58,729	1,521,700	70,644	1,847,389
1972	12,723,327	2,360,467	22,322	2,269,186	68,959	109,889	290,516	6,043,457	1,954,055	64,989	1,812,434	76,632	1,964,943
1973	13,973,825	2,649,133	25,044	2,545,677	78,412	95,083	317,105	6,424,975	2,685,050	71,956	2,513,215	99,879	1,802,479
1974	15,281,999	2,946,238	31,034	2,833,622	81,582	109,213	343,916	6,614,009	3,189,038	67,745	3,005,746	115,546	2,039,586
1975	18,002,861	3,480,597	36,663	3,348,139	95,795	122,733	438,660	7,383,479	4,401,118	73,066	4,164,775	163,278	2,176,273
1976	20,167,675	3,967,552	34,479	3,831,943	101,130	197,187	479,214	8,074,489	5,300,006	85,580	5,028,844	185,583	2,149,226
(TQ)	4,524,307	1,072,126	11,249	1,033,503	27,374	51,261	123,645	2,040,463	716,392	20,256	667,906	28,230	520,420
1977	20,284,739	4,550,932	39,435	4,402,752	108,745	228,217	522,061	8,874,720	3,870,101	100,696	3,567,244	202,161	2,238,708
1978	20,937,106	5,108,597	42,737	4,948,297	117,563	250,113	575,214	9,455,752	3,343,971	100,053	3,026,936	216,982	2,203,459
1979	22,178,871	5,580,201	46,372	5,408,252	125,577	254,496	625,741	10,322,184	2,750,621	96,405	2,450,155	204,061	2,645,628

		Medical programs							Vocational rehabilitation and education				
Fiscal year	Total	Total	Administration and miscellaneous operating expenditures	Medical care	Medical and prosthetic research	Construction of hospitals and other facilities	General operating expenditures	Compensation and pensions	Total	Vocational rehabilitation	Veterans' educational assistance	Dependents' educational assistance	All other expenditures
	Ed311	Ed312	Ed313	Ed314	Ed315	Ed316	Ed317	Ed318	Ed319	Ed320	Ed321	Ed322	Ed323
	Thousand dollars	Thousand dollars	Thousand dollars	Thousand dollars	Thousand dollars	Thousand dollars	Thousand dollars	Thousand dollars	Thousand dollars	Thousand dollars	Thousand dollars	Thousand dollars	Thousand dollars
1980	23,186,845	6,041,536	47,047	5,857,450	137,039	300,318	605,217	11,044,453	2,349,632	87,980	2,067,505	194,147	2,845,689
1981	25,203,252	6,571,641	51,047	6,378,209	142,385	408,756	627,612	12,225,027	2,291,101	113,876	1,972,446	204,779	3,079,115
1982	26,937,379	7,348,276	55,099	7,155,117	138,060	450,727	661,553	13,132,666	1,771,399	116,284	1,477,973	177,142	3,573,758
1983	27,802,852	8,030,759	56,306	7,813,302	161,151	441,780	691,690	13,697,939	1,683,239	117,598	1,394,067	171,574	3,257,445
1984	28,854,489	8,426,915	65,576	8,171,039	190,300	482,899	695,457	13,747,920	1,411,666	110,187	1,147,836	153,643	4,088,632
1985	29,359,223	9,226,965	65,798	8,936,261	224,906	556,683	765,036	14,037,218	1,161,291	107,480	912,073	144,738	3,609,130
1986	30,549,808	9,344,793	53,826	9,106,124	184,843	567,165	736,406	14,219,157	1,075,328	103,159	849,467	122,702	4,606,959
1987	31,812,228	9,876,427	41,991	9,628,996	205,440	588,877	764,887	14,241,298	846,778	105,086	625,300	116,392	5,493,961
1988	29,270,886	10,283,103	40,463	10,045,310	197,330	649,456	780,581	14,710,218	717,364	111,120	497,627	108,617	2,130,164
1989	30,040,682	10,744,573	45,094	10,514,539	184,940	703,018	766,461	15,009,042	585,270	118,749	367,297	103,224	2,228,318
1990	28,998,299	11,582,196	45,566	11,330,062	206,568	661,084	810,725	14,674,411	451,833	139,571	206,045	106,217	818,050
1991	31,214,023	12,472,066	47,951	12,210,722	213,393	608,377	885,518	16,079,780	541,294	166,053	264,153	111,088	628,988
1992	33,900,284	13,814,634	45,942	13,566,532	202,160	639,040	926,464	16,281,864	694,822	191,416	392,335	111,071	1,549,460
1993	35,460,005	14,602,952	61,412	14,295,510	246,030	621,775	905,171	16,881,938	863,181	222,246	532,397	108,538	1,585,988
1994	37,401,009	15,430,403	73,634	15,115,924	240,845	694,879	906,056	17,188,447	1,119,338	274,540	742,457	102,341	2,061,886
1995	37,775,408	16,255,135	70,837	15,933,197	251,101	640,531	951,896	17,765,045	1,126,937	305,639	718,937	102,361	1,033,864
1996	36,915,281	16,336,777	56,697	16,047,971	232,109	697,851	960,643	17,055,809	1,212,385	354,600	756,181	101,604	651,816
1997	39,277,066	16,899,995	63,489	16,601,655	234,851	596,586	1,063,232	19,284,287	1,287,479	401,467	781,296	104,716	145,487
1998	41,775,743	17,575,433	57,426	17,271,136	246,871	514,566	876,830	20,168,906	1,310,475	—	—	—	1,329,533

(TQ) Transition quarter.

[1] Beginning 1988, data are for outlays.

[2] Medical and prosthetic research included under series Ed313.

Sources

1960–1970: U.S. Department of Veterans Affairs (VA), *Annual Reports* (various years). VA, *Trend Data* – *1960–1984* (U.S. Office of Information Management and Statistics, 1985), pp. 7–14.

1971–1995: VA, *Trend Data – 1971–1995*, pp. 4–12, VA Internet site, accessed June 30, 2001.

1996–1998: data provided by the VA.

Documentation

The VA and its predecessor agencies originally compiled the data. The data exclude expenditures made on behalf of veterans from their personal funds. Over time, modifications in the accounting procedures used by the VA have altered the meaning of the totals they compute. For this reason, series that are conceptually identical to the series presented in Table Ed297–310 are not available for recent years. This table is based on the procedures currently employed by the VA.

Series Ed311. Intended to be the continuation of series Ed297, this series is somewhat higher during the years 1960–1970 when both series are available.

Series Ed312. Extends series Ed306.

Series Ed314. Figures are expenditures for medical care including the services of nurses and physicians.

Series Ed316. Figures are expenditures for constructing and equipping hospitals and other facilities. It extends series Ed307.

Series Ed318. Extends series Ed298.

Series Ed319. Figures are moneys paid to veterans for tuition, supplies, and subsistence allowances related to education and training. It extends series Ed300–301.

Series Ed321. Figures are expenditures for schooling, including higher education under various GI Bills.

Series Ed322. Figures are expenditures for the schooling of the dependents of veterans.

Series Ed323. Covers all other expenditures, including insurance and indemnities.

TABLE Ed324–336   Expenditures of the Veterans Administration, by period of service: 1790–1970[1]

Contributed by Scott Sigmund Gartner and Hugh Rockoff

Year(s)	Total (all wars)	War of 1812	Mexican War	Civil War	Indian War	Spanish-American War	World War I	World War II	Korean Conflict	Between Korean Conflict and Vietnam	Vietnam era	Regular establishment	Undistributed, and other periods of service
	Ed324	Ed325	Ed326	Ed327	Ed328	Ed329	Ed330	Ed331	Ed332	Ed333	Ed334	Ed335	Ed336
	Thousand dollars	Thousand dollars	Thousand dollars	Thousand dollars	Thousand dollars	Thousand dollars	Thousand dollars	Thousand dollars	Thousand dollars	Thousand dollars	Thousand dollars	Thousand dollars	Thousand dollars
1790–1865	96,445	—	—	—	—	—	—	—	—	—	—	—	—
1866	15,859	—	—	—	—	—	—	—	—	—	—	—	—
1867	21,276	—	—	—	—	—	—	—	—	—	—	—	—
1868	24,164	—	—	—	—	—	—	—	—	—	—	—	—
1869	29,658	—	—	—	—	—	—	—	—	—	—	—	—
1870	30,543	—	—	—	—	—	—	—	—	—	—	—	—
1871	30,081	—	—	—	—	—	—	—	—	—	—	—	—
1872	31,454	2,411	—	—	—	—	—	—	—	—	—	—	—
1873	28,681	2,875	—	—	—	—	—	—	—	—	—	—	—
1874	31,908	2,305	—	—	—	—	—	—	—	—	—	—	—
1875	31,106	1,981	—	—	—	—	—	—	—	—	—	—	—
1876	29,887	1,622	—	—	—	—	—	—	—	—	—	—	—
1877	30,145	1,373	—	—	—	—	—	—	—	—	—	—	—
1878	28,764	1,128	—	—	—	—	—	—	—	—	—	—	—
1879	35,526	3,317	—	—	—	—	—	—	—	—	—	—	—
1880	58,585	3,573	—	—	—	—	—	—	—	—	—	—	—
1881	52,771	3,135	—	—	—	—	—	—	—	—	—	—	—
1882	56,882	2,656	—	—	—	—	—	—	—	—	—	—	—
1883	64,361	2,448	—	—	—	—	—	—	—	—	—	—	—
1884	62,184	2,157	—	—	—	—	—	—	—	—	—	—	—
1885	70,196	1,911	—	—	—	—	—	—	—	—	—	—	—
1886	68,931	1,727	—	—	—	—	—	—	—	—	—	—	—
1887	79,451	1,984	142	—	—	—	—	—	—	—	—	—	—
1888	84,512	1,755	2,624	—	—	—	—	—	—	—	—	—	—
1889	95,066	1,521	2,672	—	—	—	—	—	—	—	—	—	—
1890	112,647	1,359	2,598	—	—	—	—	—	—	—	—	—	—
1891	125,351	1,115	2,499	121,284	—	—	—	—	—	—	—	—	—
1892	147,784	876	2,254	144,295	—	—	—	—	—	—	—	—	—
1893	165,315	758	2,257	161,783	251	—	—	—	—	—	—	—	—
1894	147,408	668	2,291	143,366	871	—	—	—	—	—	—	—	—
1895	147,606	561	2,340	143,821	820	—	—	—	—	—	—	—	—
1896	145,789	471	2,277	142,093	777	—	—	—	—	—	—	—	—
1897	147,903	400	2,190	144,455	707	—	—	—	—	—	—	—	—
1898	152,814	357	2,150	149,559	644	—	—	—	—	—	—	—	—
1899	146,822	301	2,014	143,775	601	31	—	—	—	—	—	—	—
1900	146,887	255	1,893	143,726	545	344	—	—	—	—	—	—	—
1901	147,275	216	1,788	143,409	488	1,247	—	—	—	—	—	(Z)	—
1902	146,575	188	1,729	142,253	435	1,865	—	—	—	—	—	2	—
1903	147,079	165	1,687	142,295	447	2,369	—	—	—	—	—	3	—
1904	150,716	144	1,739	142,248	778	3,318	—	—	—	—	—	2,376	—

Years(s)	Total (all wars) Ed324	War of 1812 Ed325	Mexican War Ed326	Civil War Ed327	Indian War Ed328	Spanish-American War Ed329	World War I Ed330	World War II Ed331	Korean Conflict Ed332	Between Korean Conflict and Vietnam Ed333	Vietnam era Ed334	Regular establishment Ed335	Undistributed, and other periods of service Ed336
	Thousand dollars	Thousand dollars	Thousand dollars	Thousand dollars	Thousand dollars	Thousand dollars	Thousand dollars	Thousand dollars	Thousand dollars	Thousand dollars	Thousand dollars	Thousand dollars	Thousand dollars
1905	150,851	117	1,572	142,191	686	3,667	—	—	—	—	—	2,512	—
1906	148,421	103	1,423	139,767	650	3,726	—	—	—	—	—	2,614	—
1907	147,482	86	1,381	138,808	587	3,770	—	—	—	—	—	2,727	—
1908	162,398	70	1,512	153,267	553	4,009	—	—	—	—	—	2,853	—
1909	171,458	64	1,647	161,747	659	4,279	—	—	—	—	—	2,972	—
1910	169,492	52	1,492	159,861	640	4,343	—	—	—	—	—	3,102	—
1911	166,448	45	1,348	156,651	592	4,508	—	—	—	—	—	3,302	2
1912	162,125	38	1,191	152,355	538	4,585	—	—	—	—	—	3,418	—
1913	183,138	33	1,207	173,038	545	4,735	—	—	—	—	—	3,569	11
1914	180,866	28	1,077	170,928	575	4,663	—	—	—	—	—	3,586	9
1915	173,729	23	939	163,778	526	4,821	—	—	—	—	—	3,642	—
1916	167,393	19	815	157,447	488	4,887	—	—	—	—	—	3,737	—
1917	169,264	19	852	159,237	428	4,948	—	—	—	—	—	3,780	—
1918	260,898	21	892	176,653	971	5,379	72,622	—	—	—	—	4,360	—
1919	499,311	18	765	217,640	1,594	4,813	270,256	—	—	—	—	4,245	—
1920	494,183	21	683	207,948	1,784	5,748	273,806	—	—	—	—	4,193	—
1921	652,157	24	894	252,792	1,614	8,046	384,582	—	—	—	—	4,205	—
1922	736,731	20	781	241,662	1,844	13,933	474,415	—	—	—	—	4,076	—
1923	737,000	18	724	243,965	1,964	21,071	465,051	—	—	—	—	4,207	—
1924	647,283	15	585	207,148	1,970	25,197	408,400	—	—	—	—	3,970	—
1925	607,246	9	511	190,003	2,011	29,929	380,780	—	—	—	—	4,003	—
1926	628,271	7	438	174,645	1,951	35,806	411,083	—	—	—	—	4,336	—
1927	618,791	10	572	169,124	2,141	63,338	379,084	—	—	—	—	4,522	—
1928	625,144	9	547	151,718	4,123	77,476	386,452	—	—	—	—	4,819	—
1929	631,248	7	475	145,301	4,646	84,230	391,305	—	—	—	—	5,284	—
1930	639,213	6	397	127,458	4,786	91,700	409,307	—	—	—	—	5,559	—
1931	714,022	5	347	123,400	4,797	110,375	468,926	—	—	—	—	6,172	—
1932	789,251	4	327	109,315	4,865	122,829	544,910	—	—	—	—	6,977	24
1933	780,758	4	286	99,204	5,039	131,328	537,434	—	—	—	—	7,437	26
1934	496,215	3	199	70,797	3,887	61,415	350,201	—	—	—	—	9,695	18
1935	556,857	3	181	64,400	4,013	83,413	393,314	—	—	—	—	11,515	18
1936	580,249	1	155	56,340	3,911	116,189	391,916	—	—	—	—	11,720	17
1937	579,352	1	133	47,292	3,664	121,591	392,615	—	—	—	—	14,036	16
1938	581,923	1	117	39,791	3,671	125,160	398,395	—	—	—	—	14,273	15
1939	555,175	(Z)	103	33,615	3,554	131,774	371,627	—	—	—	—	14,487	15
1940	557,690	(Z)	85	28,255	3,313	134,166	372,522	—	—	—	—	19,334	15
1941	553,013	(Z)	66	23,504	3,025	133,744	366,260	5,244	—	—	—	21,155	15
1942	556,198	(Z)	55	19,791	2,782	132,593	370,162	7,851	—	—	—	22,949	15
1943	605,693	(Z)	50	16,776	2,517	130,189	375,435	54,327	—	—	—	26,385	14
1944	743,596	(Z)	39	14,070	2,324	132,116	355,691	213,346	—	—	—	25,999	11
1945	2,084,668	(Z)	31	12,007	2,348	148,109	400,440	1,494,977	—	—	—	26,747	9
1946	4,425,001	(Z)	27	10,513	2,169	145,783	444,965	3,794,869	—	—	—	26,667	8
1947	7,470,600	0	26	9,104	2,008	153,191	573,034	6,696,915	—	—	—	36,316	6
1948	6,497,681	0	23	9,081	1,971	175,716	647,393	5,624,766	—	—	—	38,725	6
1949	6,660,350	0	17	7,938	1,920	174,787	717,947	5,705,569	—	—	—	52,166	6

Notes appear at end of table

(continued)

TABLE Ed324–336 Expenditures of the Veterans Administration, by period of service: 1790–1970 Continued

Year	Total (all wars) Ed324	War of 1812 Ed325	Mexican War Ed326	Civil War Ed327	Indian War Ed328	Spanish-American War Ed329	World War I Ed330	World War II Ed331	Korean Conflict Ed332	Between Korean Conflict and Vietnam Ed333	Vietnam era Ed334	Regular establishment Ed335	Undistributed, and other periods of service Ed336
	Thousand dollars	Thousand dollars	Thousand dollars	Thousand dollars	Thousand dollars	Thousand dollars	Thousand dollars	Thousand dollars	Thousand dollars	Thousand dollars	Thousand dollars	Thousand dollars	Thousand dollars
1950	6,627,657	0	14	6,864	1,719	168,449	793,337	5,593,899	—	—	—	63,369	6
1951	5,356,639	0	13	6,974	1,532	164,525	851,288	4,255,015	4,003	—	—	73,284	5
1952	4,944,187	0	11	5,168	1,348	160,434	903,432	3,747,014	53,706	—	—	73,070	4
1953	4,354,220	0	8	4,739	1,326	163,000	1,019,190	2,869,785	216,054	—	—	80,116	2
1954	4,282,592	0	5	4,112	1,192	164,889	1,067,701	2,416,000	548,801	—	—	79,891	1
1955	4,483,137	0	5	3,697	1,101	152,663	1,188,768	2,137,246	914,123	—	—	85,532	2
1956	4,801,885	0	4	3,257	983	145,738	1,284,202	2,135,904	1,140,840	—	—	90,955	2
1957	4,884,506	0	3	2,839	863	137,279	1,349,830	2,059,223	1,231,723	—	—	102,742	4
1958	5,205,941	0	3	2,458	724	129,569	1,445,443	2,270,189	1,234,720	—	—	122,831	4
1959	5,343,711	0	3	3,428	712	130,155	1,564,592	2,354,010	1,151,933	—	—	138,873	5
1960	5,389,378	0	2	3,130	632	123,733	1,693,360	2,398,350	1,008,037	—	—	162,129	5
1961	5,567,531	0	1	2,740	547	113,160	1,870,473	2,447,984	956,369	—	—	176,253	4
1962	5,636,630	0	2	2,533	468	103,872	1,907,004	2,661,322	767,487	—	—	193,940	2
1963	5,866,233	0	1	2,052	400	96,909	1,947,434	2,856,483	746,745	—	—	216,209	—
1964	6,008,129	0	0	1,774	362	89,899	1,946,465	3,058,185	664,094	—	—	247,350	—
1955	6,150,021	0	0	1,522	297	78,947	1,962,712	3,108,782	720,802	—	—	276,959	—
1966	6,410,840	0	0	1,309	243	70,390	1,980,136	3,323,174	707,581	—	—	328,007	—
1967	6,913,666	0	0	1,132	205	65,413	1,891,630	3,483,144	794,651	189,796	200,576	287,119	—
1968	7,290,882	0	0	1,090	206	58,999	1,901,226	3,295,979	755,536	535,088	464,537	278,221	—
1969	7,907,776	0	0	945	190	60,948	1,910,450	3,521,688	675,500	844,240	624,258	269,557	—
1970	8,905,065	0	0	1,014	167	54,475	1,943,366	3,880,834	898,251	480,794	1,327,690	318,474	—

(Z) Less than $500.

¹ Some expenditures are not shown annually by war; see text.

Source

U.S. Bureau of the Census, *Historical Statistics of the United States, Colonial Times to 1970* (1975), series Y971–Y983, pp. 1145–6.

Documentation

Expenditures are from appropriated funds. Data cover the Veterans Administration and its predecessor agencies.

The U.S. Veterans Administration compiled the estimates for *Historical Statistics* based on data in *Annual Reports* of the Administrator of Veterans Affairs, Veterans Bureau, Bureau of Pensions, National

Home for Disabled Volunteer Soldiers, and records of the Veterans Administration. Although pension expenditures could be easily allocated by period of service, the distribution of other expenditures had to be estimated with what the agency referred to as "a varying and unknown degree of error." Further details are available in U.S. Bureau of the Census (1975), p. 1137. Table Ed337–350 shows the pension expenditures only, by period of service from 1960 to 1997.

Some expenditures are not shown annually by war but are distributed by year under series Ed324.

Also, series Ed324 includes $70,045,000 for the Revolutionary War spent prior to 1911. The expenditures not shown annually by war are as follows: $132,000 spent prior to 1872 (War of 1812); $78,000 spent prior to 1877 (Mexican War); $1,168,119,000 spent prior to 1891 (Civil War); and $16,487,000 spent prior to 1911 (other, series Ed336).

Data are for years ending June 30.

TABLE Ed337–350   Compensation and pensions for veterans – expenditures and number of veterans receiving benefits: 1866–1998[1,2,3]

Contributed by Scott Sigmund Gartner and Hugh Rockoff

	Veterans							Expenditures						
	Pensions					Compensation		Total			Pensions		Compensation	
	Total			Non-service death	Non-service disability	Service death	Service disability	Total	Death	Disability	Death	Disability	Death	Disability
	Total	Death	Disability											
	Ed337	Ed338	Ed339	Ed340	Ed341	Ed342	Ed343	Ed344	Ed345	Ed346	Ed347	Ed348	Ed349	Ed350
Fiscal year	Thousand	Thousand	Thousand	Thousand	Thousand	Thousand	Thousand	Million dollars	Million dollars	Million dollars	Million dollars	Million dollars	Million dollars	Million dollars
1866	127	—	—	—	—	—	—	15	—	—	—	—	—	—
1867	155	—	—	—	—	—	—	21	—	—	—	—	—	—
1868	170	—	—	—	—	—	—	23	—	—	—	—	—	—
1869	188	—	—	—	—	—	—	29	—	—	—	—	—	—
1870	199	—	—	—	—	—	—	29	—	—	—	—	—	—
1871	207	—	—	—	—	—	—	29	—	—	—	—	—	—
1872	232	—	—	—	—	—	—	30	—	—	—	—	—	—
1873	238	—	—	—	—	—	—	27	—	—	—	—	—	—
1874	236	—	—	—	—	—	—	30	—	—	—	—	—	—
1875	235	—	—	—	—	—	—	29	—	—	—	—	—	—
1876	232	—	—	—	—	—	—	28	—	—	—	—	—	—
1877	232	—	—	—	—	—	—	28	—	—	—	—	—	—
1878	224	—	—	—	—	—	—	27	—	—	—	—	—	—
1879	243	—	—	—	—	—	—	34	—	—	—	—	—	—
1880	251	—	—	—	—	—	—	57	—	—	—	—	—	—
1881	269	—	—	—	—	—	—	51	—	—	—	—	—	—
1882	286	—	—	—	—	—	—	54	—	—	—	—	—	—
1883	304	—	—	—	—	—	—	50	—	—	—	—	—	—
1884	323	—	—	—	—	—	—	58	—	—	—	—	—	—
1885	345	—	—	—	—	—	—	65	—	—	—	—	—	—
1886	366	—	—	—	—	—	—	64	—	—	—	—	—	—
1887	406	—	—	—	—	—	—	74	—	—	—	—	—	—
1888	453	—	—	—	—	—	—	79	—	—	—	—	—	—
1889	490	—	—	—	—	—	—	89	—	—	—	—	—	—
1890	538	—	—	—	—	—	—	106	—	—	—	—	—	—
1891	676	139	537	—	—	—	—	117	31	86	—	—	—	—
1892	876	173	703	—	—	—	—	140	31	109	—	—	—	—
1893	966	206	760	—	—	—	—	157	37	120	—	—	—	—
1894	969	215	754	—	—	—	—	140	33	107	—	—	—	—
1895	970	219	751	—	—	—	—	140	32	108	—	—	—	—
1896	971	222	749	—	—	—	—	138	32	106	—	—	—	—
1897	976	229	747	—	—	—	—	140	34	106	—	—	—	—
1898	994	235	759	—	—	—	—	145	35	110	—	—	—	—
1899	991	237	754	—	—	—	—	139	32	107	—	—	—	—
1900	994	241	753	—	—	—	—	138	31	107	—	—	—	—
1901	998	249	749	—	—	—	—	138	32	106	—	—	—	—
1902	999	260	739	—	—	—	—	137	33	104	—	—	—	—
1903	996	267	729	—	—	—	—	138	34	104	—	—	—	—
1904	995	274	721	271	711	3	10	141	35	106	34	104	1	2
1905	999	281	718	277	708	3	10	141	35	106	34	104	1	2
1906	985	284	701	281	691	4	11	139	35	104	34	103	1	2
1907	967	287	680	283	669	4	11	139	35	104	34	102	1	2
1908	952	293	659	289	647	4	12	153	35	118	34	116	1	2
1909	947	314	633	310	620	4	12	162	47	115	46	113	1	2

(continued)

Notes appear at end of table

TABLE Ed337–350 Compensation and pensions for veterans – expenditures and number of veterans receiving benefits: 1866–1998 Continued

	Veterans							Expenditures						
	Total			Pensions		Compensation		Total			Pensions		Compensation	
Fiscal year	Total	Death	Disability	Non-service death	Non-service disability	Service death	Service disability	Total	Death	Disability	Death	Disability	Death	Disability
	Ed337	Ed338	Ed339	Ed340	Ed341	Ed342	Ed343	Ed344	Ed345	Ed346	Ed347	Ed348	Ed349	Ed350
	Thousand	Thousand	Thousand	Thousand	Thousand	Thousand	Thousand	Million dollars	Million dollars	Million dollars	Million dollars	Million dollars	Million dollars	Million dollars
1910	921	318	603	314	589	4	13	160	48	112	47	110	1	2
1911	892	322	570	317	557	4	14	157	48	109	47	107	1	2
1912	860	322	538	318	524	4	14	153	48	105	47	103	1	2
1913	821	317	504	312	489	4	15	174	47	127	46	124	1	3
1914	786	315	471	310	456	4	15	172	47	125	46	123	1	3
1915	748	310	438	306	422	4	15	166	47	119	46	116	1	3
1916	709	306	403	302	388	5	16	159	46	113	45	110	1	3
1917	673	303	370	298	354	5	16	161	55	106	54	103	1	3
1918	650	308	342	302	325	6	16	180	81	99	80	97	1	3
1919	674	336	338	307	299	29	40	234	101	133	95	124	6	9
1920	770	350	420	302	271	47	149	316	115	201	93	117	22	85
1921	769	346	423	294	254	52	169	380	127	253	108	147	19	106
1922	772	341	431	286	244	55	187	377	124	253	106	144	17	109
1923	778	341	437	282	241	59	196	389	133	256	113	146	20	110
1924	762	335	427	274	236	62	191	345	122	223	102	125	20	99
1925	791	334	457	264	232	70	224	347	124	223	97	117	26	107
1926	807	334	473	252	233	83	240	372	125	247	93	111	32	136
1927	817	327	490	240	233	86	257	404	126	278	96	131	30	147
1928	835	318	517	229	245	89	271	411	124	287	92	132	32	154
1929	832	306	526	215	245	91	281	419	132	287	100	126	32	162
1930	841	298	543	203	241	95	301	418	128	290	94	120	34	170
1931	1,080	289	791	192	468	97	323	489	124	365	91	168	32	197
1932	1,278	284	994	182	641	102	354	545	124	421	87	215	38	206
1933	1,271	273	998	169	636	103	362	550	122	428	85	228	37	200
1934	839	258	581	153	218	105	363	322	94	228	59	80	34	148
1935	839	253	586	146	215	107	371	374	96	278	61	96	35	182
1936	852	251	601	144	230	107	371	399	100	299	63	119	37	180
1937	842	243	599	136	227	107	371	396	96	300	60	121	37	179
1938	837	236	601	132	225	104	375	402	101	301	56	126	45	176
1939	843	240	603	130	225	109	378	417	109	308	55	129	54	179
1940	849	239	610	130	224	110	386	429	115	314	55	130	60	184
1941	857	238	619	130	229	108	390	433	113	320	54	132	59	188
1942	860	236	624	129	231	107	392	431	111	320	53	132	58	188
1943	861	239	622	127	227	112	395	443	113	330	52	139	61	190
1944	1,066	253	813	124	221	129	593	494	126	368	50	80	76	288
1945	1,513	369	1,144	177	220	193	924	732	185	547	69	166	116	381
1946	2,632	502	2,130	227	219	275	1,911	1,215	305	910	108	167	198	744
1947	2,920	566	2,354	253	233	314	2,121	1,732	367	1,365	138	194	229	1,171
1948	2,918	603	2,315	279	249	324	2,066	1,821	385	1,436	152	234	233	1,201
1949	2,950	636	2,314	302	290	334	2,024	1,891	457	1,434	171	253	286	1,181
1950	3,026	658	2,368	322	345	336	2,023	2,009	485	1,524	181	295	304	1,229
1951	3,057	683	2,374	339	394	343	1,980	2,036	501	1,535	190	330	311	1,205
1952	3,125	707	2,418	353	437	353	1,981	2,106	538	1,568	195	364	343	1,204
1953	3,254	748	2,506	379	485	369	2,021	2,376	608	1,768	231	431	377	1,337
1954	3,368	778	2,590	403	533	375	2,057	2,450	612	1,838	243	475	369	1,364

	Veterans							Expenditures						
	Total		Pensions			Compensation		Total			Pensions		Compensation	
	Total	Death	Disability	Non-service death	Non-service disability	Service death	Service disability	Total	Death	Disability	Death	Disability	Death	Disability
	Ed337	Ed338	Ed339	Ed340	Ed341	Ed342	Ed343	Ed344	Ed345	Ed346	Ed347	Ed348	Ed349	Ed350
Fiscal year	Thousand	Thousand	Thousand	Thousand	Thousand	Thousand	Thousand	Million dollars	Million dollars	Million dollars	Million dollars	Million dollars	Million dollars	Million dollars
1955	3,477	808	2,669	426	832	382	1,837	2,634	664	1,970	265	538	400	1,432
1956	3,576	837	2,739	454	654	383	2,085	2,749	694	2,055	281	604	413	1,451
1957	3,660	863	2,797	478	720	385	2,076	2,829	729	2,100	295	657	434	1,443
1958	3,734	884	2,850	497	785	387	2,065	3,062	776	2,286	309	729	467	1,557
1959	3,850	916	2,934	528	880	388	2,054	3,225	811	2,414	339	815	472	1,599
1960	3,960	951	3,009	559	981	392	2,028	3,315	824	2,491	354	911	470	1,580
1961	4,174	1,067	3,107	683	1,106	384	2,001	3,568	926	2,642	461	1,072	465	1,570
1962	4,272	1,122	3,150	745	1,162	377	1,988	3,653	965	2,688	510	1,124	455	1,564
1963	4,364	1,183	3,181	810	1,191	373	1,990	3,815	995	2,820	547	1,151	448	1,669
1964	4,436	1,239	3,197	872	1,203	367	1,994	3,900	1,047	2,853	585	1,155	462	1,698
1965	4,511	1,294	3,217	929	1,224	365	1,993	4,042	1,111	2,931	640	1,224	471	1,707
1966	4,540	1,339	3,201	974	1,207	365	1,994	4,305	1,172	3,133	689	1,300	483	1,833
1967	4,570	1,388	3,182	1,025	1,182	363	2,000	4,393	1,210	3,183	713	1,263	497	1,920
1968	4,607	1,443	3,164	1,075	1,152	368	2,011	4,524	1,296	3,228	779	1,272	517	1,954
1969	4,657	1,497	3,160	1,125	1,120	372	2,039	4,851	1,385	3,466	849	1,318	536	2,146
1970	4,722	1,541	3,181	1,169	1,089	372	2,091	5,254	1,502	3,752	907	1,357	595	2,393
1971	4,806	1,584	3,222	1,211	1,076	373	2,146	5,724	1,609	4,115	964	1,386	645	2,729
1972	4,909	1,641	3,268	1,266	1,086	375	2,182	6,015	1,736	4,279	1,066	1,477	670	2,802
1973	4,911	1,655	3,256	1,281	1,053	374	2,203	6,425	1,835	4,590	1,098	1,477	737	3,113
1974	4,868	1,627	3,241	1,256	1,030	371	2,211	6,614	1,853	4,761	1,093	1,476	760	3,285
1975	4,854	1,628	3,226	1,259	1,006	369	2,220	7,383	2,013	5,370	1,153	1,573	860	3,797
1976	4,866	1,631	3,235	1,263	1,003	368	2,232	8,074	2,182	5,892	1,226	1,654	956	4,238
(TQ)	4,880	1,629	3,251	1,262	1,016	367	2,235	2,041	547	1,494	304	415	243	1,079
1977	4,911	1,633	3,278	1,268	1,031	365	2,247	8,874	2,334	6,540	1,288	1,838	1,046	4,702
1978	4,905	1,622	3,283	1,260	1,024	362	2,259	9,455	2,451	7,004	1,331	1,927	1,120	5,077
1979	4,769	1,529	3,240	1,168	974	361	2,266	10,322	2,618	7,704	1,402	2,150	1,216	5,554
1980	4,647	1,451	3,196	1,093	922	358	2,274	11,045	2,714	8,331	1,369	2,227	1,345	6,104
1981	4,535	1,381	3,154	1,026	875	355	2,279	12,225	2,906	9,319	1,371	2,380	1,535	6,939
1982	4,406	1,307	3,099	957	824	350	2,275	13,133	3,081	10,052	1,379	2,458	1,702	7,594
1983	4,286	1,242	3,044	896	781	346	2,263	13,698	3,198	10,500	1,372	2,493	1,826	8,007
1984	4,124	1,143	2,981	801	730	342	2,251	13,748	3,215	10,533	1,346	2,492	1,869	8,041
1985	4,005	1,075	2,930	739	690	336	2,240	14,037	3,295	10,742	1,337	2,472	1,958	8,270
1986	3,899	1,016	2,883	685	658	331	2,225	14,219	3,369	10,850	1,348	2,471	2,021	8,379
1987	3,807	964	2,843	636	631	328	2,212	14,240	3,376	10,864	1,314	2,440	2,062	8,424
1988	3,725	920	2,805	595	606	325	2,199	14,711	3,486	11,225	1,324	2,503	2,162	8,722
1989	3,654	878	2,776	555	584	323	2,192	15,009	3,556	11,453	1,309	2,516	2,247	8,937
1990	3,583	837	2,746	517	562	320	2,184	14,674	3,670	11,004	1,318	2,667	2,352	8,337
1991	3,509	800	2,709	482	530	318	2,179	16,080	3,807	12,273	1,325	2,661	2,482	9,612
1992	3,428	754	2,674	440	493	314	2,181	16,282	3,822	12,460	1,237	2,428	2,585	10,031
1993	3,374	714	2,660	404	462	310	2,198	16,882	3,928	12,954	1,119	2,409	2,809	10,545
1994	3,342	683	2,659	376	441	308	2,218	17,188	3,845	13,343	871	2,287	2,974	11,056
1995	3,331	662	2,669	355	432	307	2,236	17,765	3,914	13,851	811	2,207	3,103	11,644
1996	3,308	637	2,671	332	418	306	2,253	17,056	3,952	13,104	803	2,032	3,149	11,072
1997	3,281	614	2,667	309	404	305	2,263	19,284	4,003	15,280	768	2,276	3,235	13,004
1998	3,263	595	2,668	291	391	303	2,277	20,169	4,082	16,087	762	2,292	3,320	13,795

Notes appear on next page

(continued)

TABLE Ed337–350 Compensation and pensions for veterans – expenditures and number of veterans receiving benefits: 1866–1998 *Continued*

(TQ) Transition quarter.

[1] Excludes World War I Emergency Officers and World War II Retired Reserve Officers.

[2] Separate data are not available prior to 1890 for living veterans receiving disability pensions and deceased veterans whose dependents were receiving benefits. Separate data are not available prior to 1904 on pensions and compensation.

[3] Beginning 1988, expenditure data are for outlays.

Sources

1866–1970: U.S. Bureau of the Census, *Historical Statistics of the United States, Colonial Times to 1970* (1975), series Y998–Y1009.

1971–1995: U.S. Department of Veterans Affairs (VA), *Trend Data – 1971–1995*, pp. 8–11, 21–4, VA Internet site, accessed June 30, 2001. These data were originally compiled from the *Annual Reports* of the VA and its predecessor agencies.

1996–1998: compiled from VA, *Annual Reports* (various years) and data provided by the VA.

Documentation

The payment of pecuniary benefits has always been a major function of the VA and its predecessor agencies.

The term "compensation" is used when benefits are paid to veterans or their survivors as a result of death or disabilities that were the result of mili-

tary service. The term "pension" is used when the money is paid because of a death or disability that was not the result of military service; it is simply a reward for service.

Data are for years ending June 30 (through 1975) and September 30 (thereafter).

Series Ed337. Figures are the number of living veterans receiving pensions and the number of deceased veterans whose dependents were receiving pensions.

Series Ed338. Figures are the number of deceased veterans whose dependents were receiving benefits. Note that this series does not show the number of dependents receiving the benefits, which was larger. Series Ed338 equals the sum of series Ed340 and Ed342, the number of deceased veterans whose dependents were being paid benefits for non-service-connected and service-connected deaths.

Series Ed339. Figures are the number of living veterans receiving benefits. Series Ed339 equals the sum of series Ed341 and Ed343, the number of living veterans to whom benefits were being paid for non-service-connected and service-connected disabilities.

Series Ed344–350. Figures are the benefits paid to the veterans counted in the parallel series Ed337–343.

TABLE Ed351–371 Compensation and pensions for veterans – expenditures, by period of service: 1960–1997[1]

Contributed by Hugh Rockoff

	Total compensation and pensions	Payments to veterans for disability									
		Compensation					Pensions				
		Vietnam era	Korean Conflict	World War II	World War I	All other	Vietnam era	Korean Conflict	World War II	World War I	All other
	Ed351	Ed352	Ed353	Ed354 [2]	Ed355 [3]	Ed356	Ed357	Ed358	Ed359	Ed360	Ed361
Fiscal year	Thousand dollars	Thousand dollars	Thousand dollars	Thousand dollars	Thousand dollars	Thousand dollars	Thousand dollars	Thousand dollars	Thousand dollars	Thousand dollars	Thousand dollars
1960	3,311,653	—	179,447	1,119,742	204,704	73,580	—	5,756	79,513	780,033	45,090
1961	3,565,539	—	182,258	1,112,860	192,304	79,773	—	7,388	100,483	924,711	39,199
1962	3,649,786	—	184,021	1,109,232	181,376	86,463	—	9,054	119,591	961,576	33,707
1963	3,811,993	—	200,764	1,180,216	184,263	100,655	—	10,465	140,362	971,797	28,499
1964	3,897,542	—	208,560	1,199,030	174,967	113,279	—	12,438	167,773	950,507	23,863
1965	4,039,618	—	214,080	1,201,241	165,221	124,255	—	16,019	219,347	968,030	20,535
1966	4,302,934	—	235,392	1,282,981	166,579	145,504	—	19,873	282,229	980,621	17,850
1967	4,390,584	—	251,006	1,331,920	163,464	171,451	—	22,139	312,462	914,304	14,288
1968	4,522,439	38,974	257,515	1,334,886	152,850	169,655	287	25,735	358,458	876,131	11,835
1969	4,848,973	118,021	281,248	1,419,159	154,561	173,094	1,062	30,359	418,715	858,141	9,643
1970	5,251,902	227,233	308,306	1,511,210	154,955	191,034	2,100	36,143	483,978	827,316	7,576
1971	5,724,573	355,347	344,843	1,657,282	157,055	214,727	3,416	42,671	555,299	778,880	6,078
1972	6,043,457	434,438	351,577	1,654,273	142,697	218,586	5,507	53,543	665,388	746,828	5,359
1973	6,424,975	535,324	388,596	1,806,160	140,503	242,550	7,644	62,936	732,359	669,524	4,188
1974	6,614,009	591,581	404,745	1,844,036	130,349	314,701	9,708	71,412	791,952	599,331	3,145
1975	7,383,479	739,926	463,762	2,094,047	133,262	366,333	13,447	88,731	912,194	555,819	2,694
1976	8,074,489	881,685	514,895	2,296,677	132,886	411,974	17,239	108,244	1,025,064	501,639	2,128
(TQ)	2,040,463	232,983	130,242	577,984	31,256	106,610	5,057	29,593	264,199	115,611	447
1977	8,874,720	1,046,174	566,829	2,488,563	124,329	476,007	24,186	134,936	1,163,146	514,451	1,742
1978	9,455,752	1,171,343	606,227	2,637,895	117,134	544,741	29,750	154,119	1,244,048	497,629	1,452
1979	10,322,184	1,320,729	660,947	2,830,670	109,545	632,208	37,486	192,521	1,440,778	478,194	1,332
1980	11,044,453	1,495,831	717,772	3,047,037	103,788	739,215	51,085	230,476	1,511,355	433,300	863
1981	12,225,027	1,748,185	804,521	3,392,715	100,985	892,615	66,175	274,660	1,634,358	404,267	726
1982	13,132,666	1,961,241	873,933	3,638,997	93,093	1,026,378	82,502	313,087	1,694,386	367,859	548
1983	13,697,939	2,120,410	913,501	3,761,227	82,418	1,129,439	97,500	343,726	1,727,177	323,704	434
1984	13,747,920	2,178,438	910,471	3,702,793	68,001	1,181,475	110,050	370,157	1,730,943	280,449	376
1985	14,037,118	2,292,011	928,320	3,727,176	57,362	1,265,211	118,116	387,489	1,720,970	245,240	362
1986	14,219,157	2,380,493	936,330	3,688,868	47,105	1,326,323	128,890	409,257	1,720,403	212,579	325
1987	14,241,298	2,473,735	940,540	3,611,755	37,954	1,360,230	140,553	430,346	1,687,950	181,086	353
1988	14,710,218	2,632,871	961,511	3,659,437	30,230	1,437,902	160,739	466,447	1,720,864	153,938	537
1989	15,009,042	2,790,531	985,560	3,596,365	23,879	1,540,285	179,974	499,688	1,707,365	128,726	500

Notes appear at end of table

TABLE Ed351–371 Compensation and pensions for veterans – expenditures, by period of service: 1960–1997
Continued

	Total compensation and pensions	Payments to veterans for disability									
		Compensation					Pensions				
		Vietnam era	Korean Conflict	World War II	World War I	All other	Vietnam era	Korean Conflict	World War II	World War I	All other
	Ed351	Ed352	Ed353	Ed354 [2]	Ed355 [3]	Ed356	Ed357	Ed358	Ed359	Ed360	Ed361
Fiscal year	Thousand dollars	Thousand dollars	Thousand dollars	Thousand dollars	Thousand dollars	Thousand dollars	Thousand dollars	Thousand dollars	Thousand dollars	Thousand dollars	Thousand dollars
1990	14,674,411	2,988,079	1,016,016	2,667,916	18,502	1,646,883	208,939	541,097	1,809,741	106,436	741
1991	16,079,780	3,202,536	1,031,311	3,590,606	14,076	1,773,641	241,808	576,090	1,760,110	81,622	1,086
1992	16,281,864	3,452,206	1,051,333	3,614,860	10,335	1,902,470	269,218	605,831	1,492,584	59,983	707
1993	16,881,938	3,584,138	1,099,304	3,710,848	8,164	2,142,482	307,713	558,050	1,472,838	35,614	34,514
1994	17,188,447	4,008,176	1,116,235	3,535,756	5,961	2,390,095	372,794	567,913	1,282,617	23,592	40,383
1995	17,765,046	4,370,143	1,139,984	3,478,034	4,182	2,651,907	462,066	572,411	1,132,704	15,607	24,226
1996	17,284,208	4,721,831	1,160,377	3,420,678	2,955	1,765,774	531,791 [4]	557,159 [4]	1,158,029 [4]	10,239 [4]	2,898 [4]
1997	19,284,287	5,146,708	1,190,139	3,356,826	2,299	3,308,105	627,227	536,722	1,100,600	6,624	5,053

	Payments to survivors									
	Dependency and indemnity or death compensation					Death pensions				
	Vietnam era	Korean Conflict	World War II	World War I	All other	Vietnam era	Korean Conflict	World War II	World War I	All other
	Ed362	Ed363	Ed364	Ed365	Ed366	Ed367	Ed368	Ed369	Ed370	Ed371
Fiscal year	Thousand dollars	Thousand dollars	Thousand dollars	Thousand dollars	Thousand dollars	Thousand dollars	Thousand dollars	Thousand dollars	Thousand dollars	Thousand dollars
1960	—	48,437	310,886	63,606	48,170	—	1,528	36,226	250,250	64,685
1961	—	49,710	301,041	63,197	52,947	—	7,282	110,578	279,581	62,227
1962	—	50,228	287,019	61,751	57,343	—	11,446	149,416	287,804	59,759
1963	—	50,971	273,588	60,932	62,771	—	14,819	176,853	298,088	56,930
1964	—	53,513	272,038	63,286	72,944	—	18,766	205,757	307,154	53,667
1965	—	55,129	271,058	64,089	81,084	—	23,845	240,194	325,367	50,124
1966	—	56,468	271,519	64,913	90,140	—	28,990	270,642	342,044	47,189
1967	—	57,278	273,701	64,423	101,817	—	33,979	290,847	343,978	43,527
1968	19,458	58,117	276,410	64,049	98,660	309	41,464	325,084	368,455	44,107
1969	49,745	59,083	275,265	63,885	87,776	944	48,921	356,334	400,314	42,703
1970	71,499	63,303	289,972	72,568	97,275	2,182	56,877	385,277	423,188	39,910
1971	89,943	66,856	305,231	78,296	104,993	4,480	64,947	409,686	447,477	37,066
1972	104,188	72,011	326,593	83,741	113,145	7,262	76,524	455,841	491,450	34,506
1973	116,786	75,408	340,017	86,485	118,650	10,096	85,462	478,348	491,533	32,406
1974	127,252	78,005	346,176	87,336	121,291	12,979	92,518	488,776	469,097	29,619
1975	153,129	88,392	383,777	97,462	137,407	17,302	105,329	530,500	472,564	27,402
1976	179,556	98,544	420,409	106,371	151,077	23,446	120,192	581,380	475,536	25,547
(TQ)	46,393	25,155	106,573	26,405	38,037	6,745	31,113	144,759	115,272	6,029
1977	205,585	108,254	454,739	111,894	165,768	31,586	135,447	627,882	470,295	22,907
1978	225,434	116,698	482,326	115,307	180,291	38,737	145,970	656,487	469,105	21,059
1979	247,151	127,137	521,698	121,220	198,470	41,311	140,180	683,067	517,997	19,543
1980	276,498	141,292	574,742	129,329	222,782	38,845	127,550	672,289	511,505	18,899
1981	322,344	162,774	651,066	141,160	257,598	36,906	118,500	685,393	512,536	17,543
1982	362,832	182,156	718,493	148,690	289,422	36,228	114,075	693,235	519,138	16,373
1983	395,607	197,114	769,299	150,725	313,251	35,759	111,805	698,863	511,118	14,862
1984	410,826	203,857	785,428	143,805	324,831	33,482	108,875	693,574	496,509	13,580
1985	437,990	216,188	821,884	139,866	342,057	32,918	110,418	686,546	494,787	12,207
1986	462,646	227,167	846,108	132,654	352,105	31,788	117,832	691,744	495,118	11,422
1987	485,876	235,332	859,619	123,436	358,041	30,641	120,698	664,965	487,709	10,479
1988	519,946	249,693	905,664	116,401	370,103	30,886	130,672	675,067	477,234	10,076
1989	555,947	265,100	933,750	108,738	383,873	31,650	139,523	664,170	463,719	9,699
1990	597,521	281,283	973,753	101,827	397,315	34,319	151,578	669,967	453,017	9,481
1991	654,453	297,897	1,022,795	95,011	412,138	37,847	161,867	674,260	441,194	9,432
1992	698,079	313,388	1,060,506	86,247	426,911	39,781	156,735	629,795	401,545	9,350
1993	740,643	339,834	1,193,963	88,692	446,274	44,300	152,137	605,064	310,166	7,200
1994	814,559	359,430	1,246,330	83,055	470,374	48,968	149,662	491,878	175,951	4,718
1995	903,347	371,898	1,265,988	73,268	488,729	53,952	148,329	456,143	147,999	4,129
1996	928,389	381,622	1,279,339	63,082	497,467	59,849	141,959	465,201	131,752	3,816
1997	990,835	392,834	1,288,250	54,698	508,765	66,442	135,240	451,770	111,558	3,592

Notes appear on next page

TABLE Ed351–371   Compensation and pensions for veterans – expenditures, by period of service: 1960–1997
Continued

(TQ) Transition quarter.

[1] Beginning 1988 data are for outlays.

[2] Excludes expenditures for World War II Retired Reserve.

[3] Excludes expenditures for World War I Emergency Officers.

[4] Estimated from the monthly value for September 1996 provided by the U.S. Department of Veterans Affairs.

Sources

1960–1970: U.S. Department of Veterans Affairs (VA), *Trend Data – 1960–1984* (U.S. Office of Information Management and Statistics, 1985), pp. 10–13.

1971–1995: VA, *Trend Data – 1971–1995*, pp. 8–11, VA Internet site, accessed June 30, 2001.

1996–1997: data provided by the VA.

Documentation

See the text for Table Ed337–350 for definitions of compensation and pension.

Series Ed356, Ed361, Ed366, and Ed371. Includes veterans of the Spanish-American War, Mexican Border Service, and peacetime periods.

TABLE Ed372–399   Compensation and pensions for veterans – number of veterans receiving benefits, by period of service: 1960–1995[1]

Contributed by Hugh Rockoff

	Living veterans receiving compensation or pensions													
	Service-connected disability							Non-service-connected disability						
Fiscal year ending	Total	Persian Gulf War	Vietnam era	Korean Conflict	World War II	World War I	All other	Total	Persian Gulf War	Vietnam era	Korean Conflict	World War II	World War I	All other
	Ed372	Ed373	Ed374	Ed375	Ed376	Ed377	Ed378	Ed379	Ed380	Ed381	Ed382	Ed383	Ed384	Ed385
	Number	Number	Number	Number	Number	Number	Number	Number	Number	Number	Number	Number	Number	Number
1960	2,026,821	—	—	206,388	1,543,920	173,084	103,429	980,720	—	—	6,469	89,526	851,257	33,468
1961	1,999,531	—	—	208,084	1,520,875	157,517	113,055	1,106,160	—	—	7,622	105,415	964,084	29,039
1962	1,987,028	—	—	211,737	1,506,465	146,676	122,150	1,161,976	—	—	8,937	121,990	1,006,535	24,514
1963	1,988,668	—	—	216,309	1,501,107	137,688	133,564	1,190,945	—	—	10,401	144,023	1,014,108	22,413
1964	1,993,550	—	—	221,091	1,495,870	129,347	147,242	1,202,664	—	—	12,470	173,280	999,797	17,117
1965	1,992,234	—	—	225,334	1,486,365	119,692	160,843	1,223,692	—	—	14,824	211,166	983,545	14,157
1966	1,993,162	—	—	229,115	1,476,894	112,629	174,524	1,206,803	—	—	16,676	245,061	933,609	11,457
1967	1,999,279	—	—	232,809	1,465,913	105,655	194,902	1,182,028	—	—	18,800	277,202	876,806	9,220
1968	2,011,323	—	46,774	235,115	1,450,754	98,287	180,393	1,151,927	—	327	21,152	308,299	814,917	7,232
1969	2,039,219	—	95,124	237,069	1,433,223	91,181	182,622	1,120,087	—	802	23,365	338,688	751,740	5,492
1970	2,091,469	—	167,350	238,646	1,415,577	84,595	185,301	1,088,994	—	1,423	26,204	371,065	685,890	4,412
1971	2,146,085	—	244,567	239,606	1,395,911	78,261	187,740	1,075,729	—	2,298	30,446	415,718	623,762	3,505
1972	2,182,209	—	308,812	240,325	1,372,083	71,151	189,838	1,086,103	—	3,563	36,122	474,559	568,793	3,066
1973	2,203,041	—	354,062	240,756	1,351,425	65,163	191,635	1,053,242	—	4,760	41,111	508,664	496,357	2,350
1974	2,210,756	—	388,851	240,406	1,329,774	59,148	192,577	1,030,097	—	5,885	45,587	536,614	440,185	1,826
1975	2,220,169	—	422,536	240,038	1,308,914	54,679	194,002	1,006,168	—	7,299	51,660	571,093	374,715	1,401
1976	2,232,213	—	458,111	239,780	1,288,457	49,934	195,931	1,003,248	—	8,954	59,258	609,362	324,629	1,045
(TQ)	2,235,227	—	466,996	239,654	1,282,531	48,624	197,422	1,015,658	—	9,707	62,021	626,939	315,999	992
1977	2,247,315	—	496,815	239,204	1,261,159	43,131	207,006	1,031,179	—	12,138	70,942	669,904	277,452	743
1978	2,258,790	—	519,142	238,464	1,240,788	38,166	222,230	1,024,064	—	14,141	77,817	691,045	240,509	552
1979	2,266,243	—	537,208	237,102	1,217,522	34,217	240,194	973,813	—	15,210	80,266	681,495	196,423	419
1980	2,273,589	—	553,326	235,654	1,193,196	29,720	261,693	921,626	—	16,049	81,018	656,401	167,808	350
1981	2,279,070	—	568,234	233,820	1,167,481	25,417	284,118	874,799	—	17,411	82,938	633,279	140,920	251
1982	2,274,634	—	579,451	231,475	1,140,144	21,556	302,008	824,341	—	18,727	83,882	604,718	116,820	194
1983	2,263,335	—	587,032	228,651	1,110,971	18,078	318,603	780,515	—	19,966	84,601	579,898	95,914	136
1984	2,250,782	—	594,938	225,542	1,080,364	15,078	334,860	729,520	—	21,262	85,391	550,828	71,939	100
1985	2,240,277	—	603,889	222,630	1,048,976	12,293	352,489	690,391	—	22,336	86,230	525,715	56,027	83
1986	2,225,289	—	612,937	220,155	1,015,380	9,870	366,947	658,106	—	23,772	88,023	502,770	43,478	63
1987	2,212,303	—	623,430	217,743	981,534	7,894	381,702	631,306	—	25,456	89,870	481,989	33,922	69
1988	2,198,857	—	633,068	214,981	946,767	6,106	397,935	605,527	—	27,563	91,557	460,449	25,899	59
1989	2,191,549	—	642,642	211,804	911,791	4,631	420,681	584,037	—	29,989	94,296	440,137	19,550	65
1990	2,184,262	—	651,756	208,517	876,359	3,444	444,186	562,040	—	32,748	96,647	417,979	14,603	63
1991	2,179,122	—	661,884	205,384	841,143	2,620	468,091	530,356	—	35,927	98,574	385,193	10,611	51
1992	2,180,936	337	671,480	201,961	805,212	1,928	500,018	492,884	1	39,687	98,280	347,539	7,343	34
1993	2,197,635	76,062	682,352	198,492	768,618	1,372	470,739	462,384	38	45,134	97,871	314,324	4,985	32
1994	2,217,908	105,616	693,811	194,577	730,724	927	492,253	440,787	104	51,924	97,850	287,534	3,353	22
1995	2,235,675	134,160	704,785	190,531	691,942	602	513,655	432,895	216	61,608	99,849	268,968	2,236	18

Note appears at end of table

TABLE Ed372–399   Compensation and pensions for veterans – number of veterans receiving benefits, by period of service: 1960–1995   *Continued*

Deceased veterans with survivors receiving compensation or pensions

	Dependency and indemnity or death compensation							Death pension						
	Total	Persian Gulf War	Vietnam era	Korean Conflict	World War II	World War I	All other	Total	Persian Gulf War	Vietnam era	Korean Conflict	World War II	World War I	All other
Fiscal year ending	Ed386	Ed387	Ed388	Ed389	Ed390	Ed391	Ed392	Ed393	Ed394	Ed395	Ed396	Ed397	Ed398	Ed399
	Number	Number	Number	Number	Number	Number	Number	Number	Number	Number	Number	Number	Number	Number
1960	391,439	—	—	37,662	274,974	45,841	32,962	559,363	—	—	2,375	55,956	418,998	82,034
1961	383,987	—	—	38,355	266,015	44,235	35,382	682,949	—	—	9,563	148,230	446,655	78,501
1962	376,640	—	—	38,926	256,545	42,975	38,194	745,408	—	—	14,153	191,786	464,964	74,505
1963	372,543	—	—	39,620	249,281	42,074	41,568	810,444	—	—	18,688	232,688	487,610	71,458
1964	367,341	—	—	39,592	241,599	41,202	44,948	871,894	—	—	23,701	273,124	507,459	67,610
1965	365,422	—	—	40,152	236,316	40,562	48,392	929,024	—	—	28,879	308,749	527,819	63,577
1966	364,790	—	—	40,367	232,276	39,961	52,186	974,419	—	—	33,909	340,524	541,202	58,784
1967	362,937	—	—	40,126	225,436	39,252	58,123	1,024,882	—	—	40,204	375,813	554,490	54,375
1968	367,905	—	19,511	40,176	221,558	38,713	47,947	1,074,962	—	581	46,819	407,993	569,460	50,109
1969	372,480	—	28,181	40,083	217,534	38,239	48,443	1,124,578	—	1,634	53,861	436,792	585,412	46,897
1970	371,623	—	34,918	39,591	211,054	37,461	48,599	1,169,226	—	3,310	61,743	465,028	596,380	42,765
1971	372,729	—	39,972	39,471	207,252	37,068	48,966	1,211,438	—	5,556	69,983	493,014	604,557	38,328
1972	375,354	—	44,078	39,627	205,058	37,067	49,524	1,266,016	—	8,437	78,852	523,352	620,261	35,114
1973	373,643	—	47,528	39,401	200,639	36,553	49,522	1,280,644	—	11,098	86,086	535,015	616,754	31,691
1974	371,202	—	50,616	39,246	196,462	35,802	49,076	1,256,280	—	13,483	90,958	530,408	592,726	28,705
1975	368,955	—	53,985	39,350	191,898	35,015	48,707	1,259,191	—	16,480	96,526	539,926	580,802	25,457
1976	367,601	—	57,420	39,322	188,185	34,351	48,323	1,263,229	—	20,460	102,550	553,278	564,173	22,768
(TQ)	366,873	—	58,176	39,309	187,142	34,145	48,101	1,261,753	—	21,669	103,202	552,372	562,374	22,136
1977	364,881	—	60,750	39,280	183,371	33,141	48,339	1,267,694	—	25,906	107,728	564,548	549,869	19,643
1978	362,189	—	62,734	39,235	179,397	31,949	48,874	1,260,060	—	29,774	109,890	568,579	534,288	17,529
1979	360,688	—	64,076	39,237	176,742	31,284	49,349	1,168,499	—	28,891	99,113	531,716	493,171	15,608
1980	357,971	—	65,284	39,186	173,286	30,128	50,087	1,092,814	—	27,861	89,753	497,073	464,327	13,800
1981	355,011	—	66,815	39,192	169,791	28,731	50,182	1,026,245	—	26,034	81,914	471,151	434,320	12,026
1982	350,357	—	67,601	38,809	165,890	27,247	50,810	957,353	—	25,824	73,864	442,562	404,566	10,537
1983	346,291	—	68,341	38,609	162,432	25,696	51,213	895,516	—	25,020	66,738	419,732	374,811	9,215
1984	341,702	—	68,905	38,302	158,607	24,027	51,861	801,305	—	22,161	57,518	389,900	323,742	7,984
1985	335,612	—	69,669	37,812	153,814	22,298	52,019	739,160	—	20,567	52,553	368,598	290,545	6,897
1986	331,394	—	70,512	37,594	151,099	20,419	51,770	684,992	—	18,656	49,656	350,476	260,142	6,062
1987	327,689	—	71,770	37,814	147,821	18,661	51,623	636,193	—	17,022	48,056	331,396	234,397	5,322
1988	325,246	—	73,176	37,920	145,588	17,162	51,400	595,363	—	15,619	47,104	316,433	211,379	4,828
1989	322,969	—	74,919	38,035	143,441	15,399	51,175	555,101	—	14,398	46,709	301,236	188,434	4,324
1990	320,095	—	76,354	38,026	141,326	13,740	50,649	517,499	—	13,512	46,668	287,314	166,103	3,902
1991	317,694	—	78,389	37,841	138,998	12,182	50,284	481,982	—	12,900	46,063	272,952	146,617	3,450
1992	313,689	31	79,958	37,640	135,610	10,666	49,784	440,291	—	12,484	44,515	254,181	126,057	3,054
1993	309,967	1,681	81,382	37,796	132,228	9,271	47,609	403,791	11	12,344	42,446	238,076	108,246	2,668
1994	307,522	2,417	83,783	37,539	129,248	8,047	46,488	375,678	28	12,611	40,896	227,294	92,545	2,304
1995	307,097	3,189	88,043	37,393	126,236	6,825	45,411	354,582	50	13,544	39,933	220,089	78,942	2,024

(TQ) Transition quarter.

[1] Excludes World War I Emergency Officers and World War II Retired Reserve Officers.

Sources

1960–1970: U.S. Department of Veterans Affairs (VA), *Trend Data – 1960– 1984* (U.S. Office of Information Management and Statistics, 1985), pp. 24–8; 1971–1995: VA, *Trend Data – 1971–1995*, pp. 21–4, VA Internet site, accessed June 30, 2001.

Documentation

See the text for Table Ed337–350 for definitions of compensation and pension.

Series Ed378, Ed385, Ed392, and Ed399. Cover veterans of the Spanish American War and Mexican Border Service. In addition, series Ed378 and Ed392 cover veterans of all peacetime periods; series Ed392 and Ed399 cover veterans of the Civil War; and series Ed399 covers veterans of Indian Wars.

Series Ed386–399. Values are the number of veterans whose deaths gave rise to payments to survivors. The number of survivors receiving these benefits is not available.

TABLE Ed400–403　Life insurance for veterans: 1921–1999

Contributed by Scott Sigmund Gartner and Hugh Rockoff

	Individual		Group				Individual		Group	
	Policies in force	Benefits and dividends paid	Persons insured	Amount of insurance			Policies in force	Benefits and dividends paid	Persons insured	Amount of insurance
	Ed400	Ed401	Ed402	Ed403			Ed400	Ed401	Ed402	Ed403
Year	Number	Thousand dollars	Number	Million dollars		Year	Number	Thousand dollars	Number	Million dollars
1921	651,054	101,410	—	—		1965	5,823,981	767,035	—	—
1922	581,778	104,363	—	—		1966	5,879,886	783,573	3,334,000	33,264
1923	560,065	105,218	—	—		1967	5,817,697	885,118	3,571,272	35,356
1924	562,000	109,103	—	—		1968	5,713,489	850,941	3,729,233	37,107
						1969	5,623,206	870,809	3,782,590	37,711
1925	552,340	127,005	—	—						
1926	553,660	136,784	—	—		1970	5,540,553	930,053	3,716,561	37,369
1927	587,980	130,536	—	—		1971	5,449,796	900,421	4,353,807	49,939
1928	660,374	136,978	—	—		1972	5,360,111	890,500	3,958,722	44,510
1929	650,066	141,523	—	—		1973	5,275,399	924,993	3,725,486	40,206
						1974	5,191,211	933,866	3,494,728	41,626
1930	648,248	142,870	—	—						
1931	646,055	148,982	—	—		1975	5,098,381	983,419	3,477,897	68,328
1932	641,247	158,712	—	—		1976	5,002,586	1,068,916	3,430,118	67,753
1933	616,069	149,112	—	—		(TQ)	4,979,837	250,813	3,470,404	68,434
1934	598,266	141,810	—	—		1977	4,881,336	1,125,066	3,512,812	69,381
						1978	4,787,545	1,161,488	3,538,107	69,992
1935	590,865	130,670	—	—		1979	4,676,657	1,267,349	3,588,107	71,296
1936	593,213	123,785	—	—						
1937	596,982	120,396	—	—		1980	4,564,252	1,410,975	3,649,793	72,603
1938	602,963	99,481	—	—		1981	4,445,939	1,489,545	3,656,261	72,769
1939	606,071	97,397	—	—		1982	4,314,535	1,552,847	3,685,830	110,661
						1983	4,183,498	1,561,903	3,754,703	125,871
1940	609,094	91,989	—	—		1984	3,989,302	1,668,753	3,712,343	125,727
1941	972,860	71,816	—	—						
1942	3,217,499	66,176	—	—		1985	3,866,616	1,829,851	3,689,713	126,172
1943	9,394,598	76,414	—	—		1986	3,739,853	1,908,817	3,680,853	165,496
1944	15,068,150	124,864	—	—		1987	3,613,214	1,904,857	3,782,748	184,959
						1988	3,506,877	1,967,349	3,800,789	186,797
1945	16,512,099	287,219	—	—		1989	3,388,516	2,013,484	3,787,341	186,668
1946	9,814,873	369,715	—	—						
1947	6,380,103	383,374	—	—		1990	3,293,257	2,084,750	3,807,778	188,100
1948	6,291,263	376,281	—	—		1991	3,195,047	2,132,399	3,705,565	267,645
1949	6,038,865	450,525	—	—		1992	3,090,950	2,246,649	3,577,993	340,515
						1993	2,994,350	1,864,320	3,439,307	421,265
1950	6,113,308	3,144,507	—	—		1994	2,889,057	1,986,628	3,309,516	487,384
1951	7,625,694	1,026,661	—	—						
1952	7,538,729	822,818	—	—		1995	2,781,361	2,000,634	3,081,000	465,723
1953	7,003,942	804,819	—	—		1996	2,664,000	2,032,071	2,992,000	535,648
1954	6,530,816	755,058	—	—		1997	2,540,000	2,057,096	2,878,000	505,100
						1998	2,416,000	2,042,118	2,766,000	480,674
1955	6,449,437	662,750	—	—		1999	2,295,000	1,977,631	2,692,000	461,881
1956	6,442,956	649,903	—	—						
1957	6,565,985	656,207	—	—						
1958	6,485,256	720,567	—	—						
1959	6,401,240	759,440	—	—						
1960	6,319,847	791,640	—	—						
1961	6,214,879	1,032,072	—	—						
1962	5,999,125	853,299	—	—						
1963	5,935,798	903,286	—	—						
1964	5,885,857	809,444	—	—						

(TQ) Transition quarter.

Sources

Series Ed400–401. 1921–1970: U.S. Bureau of the Census, *Historical Statistics of the United States, Colonial Times to 1970* (1975), series Y1028 and series Y1031, p.1152. 1971–1994: U.S. Department of Veterans Affairs (VA), *Trend Data – 1971–1995*, pp. 33, 34, VA Internet site, accessed June 30, 2001. 1995–1999: VA, *Annual Reports,* (various years) and data provided by the Department of Veterans Affairs.

Series Ed402–403. 1966–1970: VA, *Trend Data – 1960–1984* (U.S. Office of Information Management and Statistics, 1985), pp. 39, 41. 1971–1994: VA, *Trend Data – 1971–1995*, pp. 35–36, VA Internet site, accessed June 30, 2001. 1995–1999: VA, *Annual Reports* (various years) and data provided by the Department of Veterans Affairs.

Documentation

The VA administers a number of important insurance programs. In the year 2000, it was the fifth largest insurer in the United States in terms of the amount of insurance in force. For additional information on these programs, see the essay on veterans in this chapter. Additional data on policies by legislation and more detailed information on the sources and uses of funds are available in the sources listed for this table.

Data are as of June 30.

Series Ed400. Figures are the total number of policies in force under various programs under which the VA or its predecessor agencies acted directly as the issuer of insurance policies for individual members of the armed services.

Series Ed401. Figures are the amount of benefits or dividends paid under the policies in series Ed400.

Series Ed402. Figures are yearly averages of the number of people insured under group life insurance policies purchased by the VA from private firms for active-duty personnel, reservists, and veterans.

Series Ed403. Figures are yearly averages of the amount of insurance in force under the policies in series Ed402.

TABLE Ed404–414 Hospital and domiciliary care authorized by the U.S. Department of Veterans Affairs – patients, operating expenses, and daily costs: 1921–1995

Contributed by Scott Sigmund Gartner and Hugh Rockoff

	Patients per day						Residents per day – veterans receiving domiciliary care			Operating expenses of VA hospitals	Cost per patient day in VA hospitals
		VA medical centers				Non-VA hospitals	Total	Veterans Administration	State homes		
	Total	General medical	Surgical	Psychiatric	Tuberculosis						
	Ed404 [1]	Ed405 [2]	Ed406 [2]	Ed407 [2]	Ed408 [2]	Ed409	Ed410	Ed411	Ed412	Ed413	Ed414
Fiscal year	Number	Number	Number	Number	Number	Number	Number	Number	Number	Million dollars	Dollars
1921	26,237	8,401	—	7,499	10,337	—	—	—	—	—	—
1922	27,240	7,160	—	9,231	10,849	—	—	—	—	23.5	4.74
1923	23,805	4,516	—	9,403	9,886	—	—	—	—	21.7	4.99
1924	22,978	4,272	—	9,875	8,831	—	—	—	—	19.2	4.55
1925	27,218	5,202	—	12,224	9,792	—	—	—	—	23.4	4.04
1926	25,965	5,200	—	12,902	7,863	—	—	—	—	25.3	4.19
1927	25,440	5,736	—	12,748	6,956	—	—	—	—	25.3	4.00
1928	26,257	6,658	—	13,057	6,542	—	—	—	—	26.1	4.00
1929	27,897	7,569	—	13,781	6,547	—	—	—	—	28.2	4.01
1930	30,556	8,788	—	15,035	6,733	—	—	—	—	28.5	3.86
1931	35,145	11,649	—	16,936	6,560	—	—	—	—	30.4	3.72
1932	43,469	16,956	—	19,528	6,985	—	—	—	—	32.0	3.44
1933	33,844	8,249	—	19,791	5,804	—	—	—	—	33.4	2.99
1934	38,733	11,975	—	21,475	5,283	—	—	—	—	32.6	2.51
1935	41,728	13,664	—	22,781	5,283	—	14,566	10,406	4,160	39.9	2.78
1936	41,251	12,673	—	24,025	4,553	—	16,741	12,008	4,733	42.4	2.82
1937	46,235	15,002	—	26,246	4,987	—	15,296	10,364	4,932	43.3	2.81
1938	50,640	16,279	—	29,299	5,062	—	19,136	13,514	5,622	44.2	2.65
1939	53,745	17,624	—	31,080	5,041	—	21,687	15,709	5,978	48.0	2.68
1940	56,450	18,720	—	32,882	4,848	—	22,926	16,708	6,218	49.9	2.60
1941	58,241	19,226	—	34,257	4,758	—	22,662	16,696	5,966	55.4	2.78
1942	56,103	16,417	—	34,596	5,090	—	20,101	14,371	5,730	59.1	2.96
1943	56,850	15,356	—	36,345	5,149	—	15,328	10,430	4,898	65.7	3.37
1944	63,890	17,500	—	40,076	6,314	—	13,852	9,447	4,405	72.1	3.38
1945	70,246	19,304	—	44,078	6,864	—	13,161	9,002	4,159	80.3	3.42
1946	87,257	30,095	—	48,687	8,475	—	15,190	10,547	4,643	136.2	5.22
1947	104,443	38,094	—	53,913	12,436	—	18,637	13,113	5,524	271.1	8.67
1948	103,576	35,741	—	54,790	13,045	—	20,552	14,402	6,150	307.7	9.05
1949	107,073	37,113	—	55,150	14,810	—	22,000	15,288	6,712	353.4	10.24
1950	102,303	33,523	—	54,419	14,361	—	24,307	16,870	7,437	384.6	10.90
1951	100,517	32,705	—	52,987	14,825	—	24,564	16,790	7,774	409.8	11.66
1952	103,774	34,842	—	53,570	15,362	—	24,792	16,892	7,900	474.9	13.24
1953	102,323	34,472	—	52,559	15,292	—	25,035	16,919	8,116	486.2	13.61
1954	108,357	37,805	—	54,916	15,636	—	25,291	16,945	8,346	530.6	14.05
1955	110,257	36,072	—	59,349	14,836	—	25,774	16,972	8,802	542.2	13.93
1956	112,660	37,362	—	61,703	13,595	—	25,786	17,047	8,739	602.9	15.22
1957	110,715	36,941	—	61,550	12,224	—	25,846	16,908	8,938	617.7	15.45
1958	110,721	38,405	—	61,638	10,678	—	25,991	16,673	9,318	676.2	16.81
1959	111,380	39,556	—	61,953	9,871	—	26,518 [3]	16,840	9,678	732.6	17.82
1960	114,356	40,935	—	61,436	9,037	2,948	26,274 [3]	16,856 [5]	9,418	763.0	18.44
1961	114,321	41,757	—	61,441	8,153	2,970	26,197 [3]	16,812	9,385	822.5	19.93
1962	113,764	42,271	—	61,240	7,373	2,880	25,435 [3,4]	16,373	9,062	858.3	20.87
1963	113,016	37,389	17,250	55,555	—	2,822	25,173 [3,4]	16,012	9,161	873.3	21.56
1964	112,881	36,707	17,429	56,023	—	2,722	24,575 [4]	15,229	9,346	904.5	22.43
1965	111,782	36,424	17,328	55,431	—	2,599	23,526 [4]	14,380	9,146	946.4	23.75
1966	109,882	35,949	17,183	54,256	—	2,493	21,319 [4]	13,091	8,228	976.1	24.90
1967	105,807	35,033	16,693	51,667	—	2,413	20,382 [4]	12,694	7,688	1,034.4	27.41
1968	99,450	33,255	16,287	47,883	—	2,025	20,058 [4]	12,592	7,466	1,088.6	30.53
1969	93,547	32,060	15,956	43,861	—	1,669	19,552 [4]	12,412	7,140	1,145.4	34.16
1970	87,042	30,448	15,615	39,483	—	1,495	18,680 [4]	11,998	6,682	1,278.8	38.42
1971	85,253	30,570	15,755	37,677	—	1,251	17,888 [4]	12,008	5,880	1,333.5	38.42
1972	82,125	34,208	15,340	31,422	—	1,154	17,324 [4]	11,355	5,969	1,569.3	43.41
1973	83,510	38,753	15,691	28,036	—	1,031	16,286	10,261	6,025	1,745.9	62.61
1974	82,506	38,988	15,629	26,836	—	1,053	15,584	9,723	5,861	2,070.4	57.92

Notes appear at end of table

TABLE Ed404–414   Hospital and domiciliary care authorized by the U.S. Department of Veterans Affairs – patients, operating expenses, and daily costs: 1921–1995   *Continued*

	Patients per day						Residents per day – veterans receiving domiciliary care				
		VA medical centers									
	Total	General medical	Surgical	Psychiatric	Tuberculosis	Non-VA hospitals	Total	Veterans Administration	State homes	Operating expenses of VA hospitals	Cost per patient day in VA hospitals
	Ed404 [1]	Ed405 [2]	Ed406 [2]	Ed407 [2]	Ed408 [2]	Ed409	Ed410	Ed411	Ed412	Ed413	Ed414
Fiscal year	Number	Number	Number	Number	Number	Number	Number	Number	Number	Million dollars	Dollars
1975	81,240	38,280	15,634	26,059	—	1,267	15,030	9,181	5,849	2,370.6	65.08
1976	79,497	37,985	15,440	24,839	—	1,233	14,652	9,090	5,562	2,703.4	76.71
(TQ)	77,978	37,178	15,312	24,163	—	1,325	14,194	9,044	5,177	—	87.86
1977	76,629	36,802	15,000	23,483	—	1,344	14,214	8,933	5,281	3,052.4	103.27
1978	74,386	35,798	14,374	22,836	—	1,378	13,957	8,721	5,236	3,421.6	119.10
1979	71,003	34,363	13,825	21,633	—	1,182	13,744	8,448	5,296	3,917.6	133.82
1980	69,322	33,712	13,379	21,018	—	1,213	12,786	7,894	4,892	4,404.9	164.00
1981	67,598	32,963	12,923	20,490	—	1,222	11,925	7,353	4,572	4,702.9	166.05
1982	66,002	32,176	12,323	20,395	—	1,108	11,580	7,087	4,493	5,072.3	190.36
1983	66,093	32,412	12,355	20,225	—	1,101	11,341	6,852	4,489	5,627.9	206.89
1984	64,080	31,603	11,848	19,643	—	986	10,637	6,236	4,401	5,916.2	220.49
1985	60,258	30,462	10,756	18,092	—	948	10,313	5,979	4,334	6,229.7	249.02
1986	57,716	30,108	9,703	17,129	—	776	10,089	5,767	4,322	6,239.3	255.16
1987	55,198	29,455	8,620	16,489	—	634	10,022	5,837	4,185	6,368.6	272.95
1988	52,682	28,351	7,769	15,991	—	571	10,087	6,061	4,026	5,912.6	289.27
1989	49,515	26,792	7,018	15,231	—	475	10,148	6,315	3,833	7,024.0	356.30
1990	47,169	25,564	6,638	14,526	—	441	10,258	6,526	3,732	7,193.8	387.84
1991	44,490	24,077	6,307	13,689	—	417	10,231	6,575	3,656	7,964.3	438.29
1992	43,568	22,562	6,093	14,161	—	752	9,883	6,441	3,442	8,605.7	489.76
1993	42,419	21,529	5,790	14,386	—	714	9,523	6,197	3,326	9,081.1	526.73
1994	40,647	20,515	5,317	14,121	—	694	9,359	6,051	3,308	—	—
1995	37,630	18,906	4,777	13,320	—	627	9,191	5,711	3,480	—	—

(TQ) Transition quarter. Reflects status as of September 30, 1976.

[1] Total may not add to the sum of the other columns owing to rounding.

[2] Through 1962, surgical patients included under series Ed405 and neurological patients included under series Ed407. Beginning with 1963, neurological and tuberculosis patients included under series Ed405.

[3] Includes member employees located in Veterans Administration (VA) hospitals.

[4] Includes residents of VA restoration centers. This program was discontinued in 1972.

[5] Includes residents of VA restoration centers.

Sources

1921–1959: U.S. Bureau of the Census, *Historical Statistics of the United States, Colonial Times to 1970* (1975), series Y1013–Y1018 and Y1023–Y1027, p. 1150. 1960–1970: U.S. Department of Veterans Affairs (VA), *Trend Data – 1960–1984* (U.S. Office of Information Management and Statistics, November 1985), p. 46; 1971–1995: VA, *Trend Data – 1971–1995*, p. 42, VA Internet site, accessed June 30, 2001.

Documentation

The system of veterans' hospitals was organized in World War I and has become one of the largest suppliers of medical care in the United States. The data in this table show the number of patients in the system at a particular date, or on average throughout the year. Table Ed415–418 shows the total number of patients treated during the year.

For 1921–1954, the figures are the number of patients as of June 30; for 1955–1959, they represent the number of patients as of May 31. Beginning

in 1960, the figures are the average daily census defined as the number of total patient-days accumulated during the year divided by the days in the year. Estimates as of May 31 for 1960–1970 are available in U.S. Bureau of the Census (1975), p. 1150. Those estimates differ from, but are generally within 1 or 2 percent of, the estimates shown here.

Series Ed404–409. Through 1959, series Ed406–408 refer only to veterans, but series Ed404–405 include small numbers of nonveterans treated in veterans hospitals, generally for charitable reasons. Beginning in 1960, series Ed406–408 refer only to patients treated in veterans hospitals, and patients treated in non-VA hospitals are then shown separately as series Ed409 and included in series Ed404. Patients treated in state home hospitals are excluded. Additional information on specific conditions, and on whether the condition was service connected, is available in U.S. Bureau of the Census (1975) and the *Annual Reports* of the VA, although coverage varies from year to year.

Series Ed410–412. Figures in series Ed410 are the number of residents of VA domiciliary facilities. Homeless veterans cared for in VA hospitals are excluded. Residents of state homes who receive a subsidy from the VA because they qualify for a VA facility are shown separately in series Ed411–412.

Series Ed413–414. These series were estimated by the VA; they update series Y1026 and Y1027 in U.S. Bureau of the Census (1975).

TABLE Ed415–418 Patients treated by the U.S. Department of Veterans Affairs, by type of facility: 1963–1999

Contributed by Hugh Rockoff

Fiscal year	Total Ed415 [1] Number	Hospitals Ed416 Number	Residential care facilities Ed417 Number	Nursing homes Ed418 Number	Fiscal year	Total Ed415 [1] Number	Hospitals Ed416 Number	Residential care facilities Ed417 Number	Nursing homes Ed418 Number
1963	794,478	737,910	56,568	—	1985	1,435,455	1,341,000	21,566	72,889
1964	816,944	763,035	53,909	—	1986	1,461,523	1,361,023	21,522	78,978
					1987	1,465,703	1,362,142	21,953	81,608
1965	804,973	754,876	48,436	1,661	1988	1,224,375	1,116,681	24,018	83,676
1966	825,252	766,946	46,269	12,037	1989	1,152,643	1,053,942	24,825	73,876
1967	846,396	781,994	46,126	18,276					
1968	854,483	787,871	46,098	20,514	1990	1,113,126	1,016,430	25,670	71,026
1969	868,340	800,012	45,334	22,994	1991	1,071,945	974,065	25,735	72,145
					1992	1,085,126	988,203	25,501	71,422
1970	879,049	813,062	41,243	24,744	1993	1,075,111	974,102	25,374	75,635
1971	912,342	847,475	39,262	25,605	1994	1,066,534	962,531	24,666	79,337
1972	944,189	876,274	38,322	29,593					
1973	1,081,965	1,014,383	34,793	32,789	1995	1,034,945	930,078	25,074	79,793
1974	1,140,750	1,072,125	32,374	36,251	1996	960,524	850,098	28,036	82,390
					1997	826,851	699,544	38,650	88,657
1975	1,220,107	1,149,444	30,550	40,113	1998	778,136	631,581	49,987	96,568
1976	1,287,125	1,214,981	29,952	42,192	1999	751,791	612,800	49,774	89,217
(TQ)	413,352	370,094	18,950	24,308					
1977	1,322,773	1,249,011	28,455	45,307					
1978	1,342,164	1,266,651	27,772	47,741					
1979	1,342,161	1,265,712	27,077	49,372					
1980	1,359,269	1,282,966	24,966	51,337					
1981	1,360,256	1,284,196	24,179	51,881					
1982	1,357,547	1,276,383	23,318	57,846					
1983	1,401,018	1,315,244	22,981	62,793					
1984	1,411,834	1,324,628	21,579	65,627					

(TQ) Transition quarter.

[1] "One-day" dialysis patients counted as outpatients, except for 1973–1987, when they were counted as inpatients.

Sources

1963–1970: U.S. Department of Veterans Affairs (VA), *Trend Data – 1960–1984,* p. 43 (U.S. Office of Information Management and Statistics, 1985).

1971–1991: VA, *Trend Data – 1971–1995,* p. 37, VA Internet site, accessed June 30, 2001.

1992–1999: Data provided by the VA.

Documentation

In recent years the VA has stressed "patients treated" – defined as "the sum of discharges and deaths during the period plus patients remaining as bed occupants or absent bed occupants at the end of the period" – as a basic measure of its workload. This statistic has the merit of being straightforward, and of being admirably neutral on the question of whether the treatment was successful or unsuccessful.

Series Ed415. Figures are the number of patients treated in all facilities, whether VA or non-VA.

Series Ed416. Figures are the number of patients treated in hospitals, whether VA or non-VA. The percentage treated in non-VA hospitals has been low – on average about 2 percent of the total in the early 1990s. In recent years, the *Annual Reports* of the VA have provided data on patients treated by condition (psychiatric care, rehabilitative care, and so on).

Series Ed417. Figures are the number of patients treated in residential facilities, including VA homes, state homes, and VA restoration centers (a program that ended in 1972).

Series Ed418. Figures are the number of patients receiving nursing bed care in VA facilities, state homes, and other nursing homes. In the early 1990s, around 40 percent of medical treatments in nursing care facilities occurred in VA facilities.

TABLE Ed419–430   Outpatient medical care authorized by the U.S. Department of Veterans Affairs – visits and outpatients, by purpose of visit: 1948–1999

Contributed by Hugh Rockoff

	Total			Service-connected medical treatments		Compensation and pension examinations		Examinations to determine need for care		Nonveteran and miscellaneous		
	Visits									Non-service-connected medical treatments – visits		
	Total	Fee-basis physicians	Outpatients	Visits	Outpatients	Visits	Outpatients	Visits	Outpatients		Visits	Outpatients
	Ed419 [1,2]	Ed420	Ed421	Ed422 [3]	Ed423	Ed424	Ed425	Ed426 [4]	Ed427	Ed428 [3]	Ed429 [3]	Ed430
Fiscal year	Number	Number	Number	Number	Number	Number	Number	Number	Number	Number	Number	Number
1948	—	—	3,998,786	—	2,131,475	—	1,223,108	—	303,680	—	—	340,523
1949	—	—	3,606,429	—	1,891,162	—	1,006,598	—	331,307	—	—	377,362
1950	—	—	3,508,471	—	2,037,752	—	747,859	—	323,075	—	—	399,785
1951	—	—	3,072,753	—	1,901,102	—	569,588	—	238,701	—	—	363,362
1952	—	—	2,492,361	—	1,601,645	—	460,698	—	204,773	—	—	225,245
1953	—	—	2,359,453	—	1,631,213	—	415,262	—	173,110	—	—	139,868
1954	—	—	2,270,330	—	1,590,929	—	426,420	—	140,441	—	—	112,540
1955	—	—	2,267,168	—	1,598,385	—	429,174	—	136,338	—	—	103,271
1956	—	—	2,199,667	—	1,561,047	—	410,453	—	130,908	—	—	97,259
1957	—	—	2,122,072	—	1,516,868	—	385,740	—	132,662	—	—	86,802
1958	—	—	2,148,264	—	1,524,406	—	377,159	—	141,191	—	—	105,508
1959	3,436,619	—	2,207,301	2,699,755	1,529,387	425,927	406,807	171,700	153,045	—	139,237	118,062
1960	3,511,279	—	2,364,758	2,681,588	1,598,500	499,127	478,789	172,859	154,408	—	157,705	133,061
1961	3,567,193	—	2,376,354	2,776,668	1,653,852	427,464	409,205	192,881	172,000	—	170,180	141,297
1962	3,656,104	—	—	2,932,203	—	368,930	—	176,903	—	—	178,068	—
1963	5,900,554	—	—	3,102,740	—	323,904	—	1,008,046	—	762,262	703,602	—
1964	6,178,633	—	—	3,201,786	—	313,345	—	1,051,393	—	855,676	756,433	—
1965	5,987,225	—	—	3,271,824	—	321,293	—	1,047,550	—	889,642	456,916	—
1966	6,181,678	—	—	3,314,610	—	303,817	—	1,059,415	—	997,256	506,580	—
1967	6,268,056	—	—	3,293,114	—	289,251	—	1,038,174	—	1,170,324	477,193	—
1968	6,563,787	—	—	3,352,693	—	302,865	—	1,090,904	—	1,314,588	502,737	—
1969	6,947,074	—	—	3,458,673	—	345,408	—	1,173,117	—	1,459,848	510,028	—
1970	7,311,894	—	—	3,573,133	—	390,100	—	1,222,591	—	1,616,242	509,828	—
1971	8,064,092	—	—	3,857,659	—	456,302	—	1,373,368	—	1,873,801	502,962	—
1972	9,526,881	—	—	4,258,093	—	406,065	—	1,494,491	—	2,836,997	531,235	—
1973	10,858,491	—	—	4,355,368	—	339,557	—	1,577,282	—	4,034,009	552,275	—
1974	12,266,476	—	—	4,465,156	—	316,359	—	1,692,876	—	4,966,868	825,217	—
1975	14,629,517	—	—	4,895,716	—	353,590	—	1,951,618	—	6,526,989	901,604	—
1976	16,409,850	—	—	5,284,220	—	388,674	—	2,126,614	—	7,709,368	900,974	—
1977	17,045,079	—	—	5,811,207	—	421,425	—	2,205,165	—	7,790,633	816,649	—
1978	17,416,275	—	—	6,022,072	—	405,301	—	2,244,929	—	7,814,548	929,425	—
1979	17,262,408	—	—	6,735,356	—	372,077	—	2,239,313	—	7,023,288	892,374	—
1980	17,971,407	—	—	7,284,333	—	373,300	—	2,435,856	—	6,940,318	937,600	—
1981	17,929,550	—	—	7,310,554	—	377,559	—	2,463,349	—	6,870,678	907,410	—
1982	17,808,977	—	—	7,428,408	—	365,218	—	2,402,135	—	6,537,701	1,075,515	—
1983	18,509,552	—	—	7,725,734	—	370,552	—	2,581,957	—	6,919,907	911,402	—
1984	18,616,073	—	—	7,670,978	—	364,840	—	2,626,087	—	6,881,822	1,072,346	—
1985	19,600,849	—	—	8,108,273	—	385,837	—	2,510,342	—	7,540,486	1,055,911	—
1986	20,188,132	—	—	8,272,497	—	378,595	—	2,510,824	—	8,195,934	830,282	—
1987	21,634,757	1,797,333	—	8,759,011	—	390,064	—	2,552,303	—	10,104,380	974,033	—
1988	23,232,895	1,759,492	—	9,396,760	—	420,843	—	2,691,584	—	10,805,912	1,270,731	—
1989	22,629,343	1,603,456	—	9,590,760	—	442,503	—	2,726,888	—	10,623,025	812,102	—
1990	22,602,540	1,203,198	—	9,885,926	—	420,887	—	2,806,549	—	10,683,641	829,775	—
1991	23,034,516	1,102,090	—	10,109,392	—	443,996	—	2,713,776	—	10,985,504	837,530	—
1992	23,901,825	1,113,394	—	10,433,307	—	575,968	—	2,757,353	—	11,428,714	926,410	—
1993	24,236,095	1,091,699	—	10,516,758	—	448,082	—	2,721,349	—	11,611,791	1,015,847	—
1994	25,157,983	1,023,144	—	10,916,062	—	575,408	—	2,692,937	—	12,184,438	1,034,339	—
1995	27,565,000	1,064,167	—	12,026,845	—	596,227	—	2,429,675	—	13,429,571	1,044,584	—
1996	29,294,620	934,967	—	12,926,578	—	—	—	—	—	13,793,318	1,639,757	—
1997	31,919,001	1,482,706	—	13,900,526	—	—	—	—	—	15,543,822	991,947	—
1998	34,972,000	1,555,000	—	—	—	—	—	—	—	—	—	—
1999	36,928,000	1,692,000	—	—	—	—	—	—	—	—	—	—

[1] "One-day" dialysis patients counted as outpatients, except for 1973–1987, when they were counted as inpatients.

[2] Beginning 1987, total does not include series Ed424 and Ed426.

[3] Beginning 1987, includes only visits to U.S. Department of Veterans Affairs (VA) staff.

[4] Through 1962, examinations to determine the need for inpatient care were reported only by VA facilities with outpatient clinics.

TABLE Ed419–430   Outpatient medical care authorized by the U.S. Department of Veterans Affairs – visits and outpatients, by purpose of visit: 1948–1999   *Continued*

Sources

1960–1970: U.S. Department of Veterans Affairs (VA), *Trend Data – 1960– 1984*, p. 52 (U.S. Office of Information Management and Statistics, 1985).

1971–1986: VA, *Trend Data – 1971–1995*, p. 47, VA Internet site, accessed June 30, 2001.

1987–1999: Compiled from the *Annual Reports* of the VA and data provided by the VA.

Documentation

Outpatient care has become an increasingly important part of medical care at the VA, as in the rest of the U.S. medical system. An "outpatient visit" is defined as the presence of a patient on one day in a VA outpatient clinic or in the office of a fee-basis physician. An "outpatient" is defined as a person who receives outpatient medical care one or more times during a month. The series measuring number of outpatients, although not available for recent years, provide a useful way to judge the amount of outpatient care available in earlier years.

Series Ed424–425. Cover visits to determine eligibility for benefits.

Series Ed428. Prior to 1963, pre-bed and post-hospital cares are not reported separately and are excluded from the total.

Series Ed429–430. Include visits for vocational rehabilitation, insurance examinations, and medical treatments performed for the beneficiaries of other federal agencies or for humanitarian purposes, and other miscellaneous cases.

TABLE Ed431–436   Operating beds in medical centers of the U.S. Department of Veterans Affairs, by type of bed: 1936–1997[1, 2]

Contributed by Hugh Rockoff

	Total					
	End of fiscal year	Monthly average	General medical	Surgical	Psychiatric	Tuberculosis
	Ed431	Ed432	Ed433	Ed434	Ed435	Ed436
Fiscal year	Number	Number	Number	Number	Number	Number
1936	44,846	—	14,885	—	24,069	5,892
1937	47,406	—	15,611	—	26,269	5,526
1938	51,460	—	16,336	—	29,988	5,136
1939	54,280	—	17,844		31,115	5,321
1940	58,834	—	19,042	—	34,594	5,198
1941	61,405	—	20,445	—	35,864	5,096
1942	60,666	—	19,537	—	35,605	5,524
1943	61,717	—	19,409	—	36,799	5,509
1944	70,598	—	20,793	—	42,281	7,524
1945	77,727	—	21,399	—	48,525	7,803
1946	87,379	—	25,951	—	52,806	8,622
1947	101,273	96,451	34,786	—	55,513	10,974
1948	102,219	102,383	34,604	—	56,101	11,514
1949	105,412	103,854	36,259	—	55,142	14,011
1950	106,287	106,012	38,086	—	54,084	14,117
1951	108,231	107,568	40,602	—	53,302	14,327
1952	110,243	109,790	41,371	—	53,795	15,077
1953	109,035	108,967	46,117	—	48,651	14,267
1954	117,032	114,244	49,094	—	50,128	15,022
1955	118,608	117,643	45,224	—	55,667	16,752
1956	—	120,649	46,085	—	58,817	15,747
1957	—	121,144	47,640	—	59,174	14,330
1958	—	121,201	48,969	—	59,337	12,895
1959	—	120,489	51,304	—	57,942	11,243
1960	—	120,257	51,507	—	58,503	10,247
1961	—	120,380	52,314	—	58,793	9,273
1962	—	120,946	53,187	—	59,257	8,502
1963	—	120,304	41,160	20,124	59,020	—
1964	—	119,902	40,561	20,098	59,243	—
1965	—	119,118	40,238	20,044	58,835	—
1966	—	116,975	39,339	19,735	57,902	—
1967	—	115,193	39,098	19,893	56,203	—
1968	—	112,394	38,790	19,856	53,748	—
1969	—	107,013	37,412	19,472	50,129	—
1970	—	102,633	36,166	19,386	47,082	—
1971	—	98,956	35,733	19,366	43,857	—
1972	—	96,352	40,003	19,212	37,137	—
1973	—	97,689	45,261	19,640	32,788	—
1974	—	96,106	45,331	19,597	31,178	—

Notes appear at end of table

TABLE Ed431–436   Operating beds in medical centers of the U.S. Department of Veterans Affairs, by type of bed: 1936–1997   *Continued*

	Total					
	End of fiscal year	Monthly average	General medical	Surgical	Psychiatric	Tuberculosis
	Ed431	Ed432	Ed433	Ed434	Ed435	Ed436
Fiscal year	Number	Number	Number	Number	Number	Number
1975	—	94,801	44,893	19,725	30,183	—
1976	—	94,075	44,941	19,854	29,279	—
(TQ)	—	93,296	44,856	19,839	28,601	—
1977	—	92,401	44,583	19,618	28,200	—
1978	—	91,215	44,372	19,175	27,669	—
1979	—	87,713	42,772	18,542	26,402	—
1980	—	84,129	41,203	18,040	24,886	—
1981	—	82,079	40,501	17,533	24,045	—
1982	—	80,154	39,539	16,866	23,748	—
1983	—	79,859	39,578	16,517	23,764	—
1984	—	79,222	39,241	16,292	23,689	—
1985	—	78,357	39,339	15,952	23,066	—
1986	—	77,548	39,575	15,356	22,617	—
1987	—	76,213	39,317	14,414	22,482	—
1988	—	73,913	38,124	13,630	22,159	—
1989	—	71,311	37,310	12,614	21,388	—
1990	—	69,746	36,585	12,167	20,994	—
1991	—	66,664	34,934	11,681	20,049	—
1992	—	56,139	29,097	9,479	17,563	—
1993	—	54,110	27,743	8,978	17,389	—
1994	—	53,082	27,191	8,552	17,339	—
1995	—	50,787	25,957	7,820	17,010	—
1996	—	45,739	23,238	6,827	15,674	—
1997	—	35,717	18,255	5,070	12,392	—

(TQ) Transition quarter. Reflects status as of September 30, 1976.

[1] Effective date and table total changes over time; see text.

[2] Surgical beds (through 1962) and tuberculosis beds (beginning in 1963) included under series Ed433.

Sources
1936–1959 and 1996–1997: Compiled from the *Annual Reports* of the U.S. Department of Veterans Affairs (VA).

1960–1970: VA, *Trend Data – 1960–1984* (U.S. Office of Information Management and Statistics, 1985), p. 44.

1971–1995: VA, *Trend Data – 1971–1995*, p. 39, VA Internet site, accessed June 30, 2001.

Documentation
The number of operating beds is a commonly used measure of the capacity of a hospital or system of hospitals. The data shown here divide the total number of beds available into broad categories. More detailed data (for example, on neurological beds) is available in the *Annual Reports* of the VA and its predecessor agencies, although at scattered dates.

Through 1952, the data in series Ed433–436 are for the last month of the fiscal year, and the series sums to the total in series Ed431. For 1953–1976, averages were based on the number of operating beds at the end of each month for thirteen consecutive months, beginning with June of the prior fiscal year and ending with June of the indicated fiscal year. Beginning in 1977, averages are based on the number of operating beds at the end of each month for thirteen consecutive months, starting with September of the prior year and ending with September of the indicated fiscal year. Beginning in 1953, the amounts shown in series Ed433–436 sum to the amount shown in series Ed432.

TABLE Ed437–452   Nursing home care authorized by the U.S. Department of Veterans Affairs – patients, by type of facility: 1965–1995

Contributed by Hugh Rockoff

Fiscal year	Total – all facilities				VA medical centers				State nursing homes				Community nursing homes			
	Average daily census	Admissions	Discharges	Patients treated	Average daily census	Admissions	Discharges	Patients treated	Average daily census	Admissions	Discharges	Patients treated	Average daily census	Admissions	Discharges	Patients treated
	Ed437	Ed438	Ed439	Ed440	Ed441	Ed442	Ed443	Ed444	Ed445	Ed446	Ed447	Ed448	Ed449	Ed450	Ed451	Ed452
	Number	Number	Number	Number	Number	Number	Number	Number	Number	Number	Number	Number	Number	Number	Number	Number
1965	324	1,968	598	1,968	150	950	264	950	156	753	295	753	18	265	39	265
1966	3,854	12,223	7,815	13,593	1,245	3,214	2,088	3,900	972	2,213	1,327	2,671	1,637	6,796	4,400	7,022
1967	6,694	15,968	13,588	18,276	2,484	4,316	2,728	5,150	1,423	2,187	1,996	2,474	2,787	9,465	8,864	10,652
1968	8,067	16,734	16,048	20,514	3,468	4,381	4,170	6,074	1,795	2,885	2,508	3,022	2,804	9,468	9,370	11,418
1969	9,030	19,312	17,589	22,994	3,700	3,929	3,800	5,803	2,153	3,937	3,588	3,851	3,177	11,446	10,201	13,340
1970	9,773	22,889	23,203	24,744	3,760	3,989	3,986	5,844	2,432	4,444	4,114	4,325	3,581	14,456	15,103	14,575
1971	10,874	21,432	19,924	25,605	4,599	5,875	4,843	7,389	2,898	5,286	4,730	5,413	3,377	10,271	10,351	12,803
1972	12,765	24,779	22,890	29,593	5,440	6,571	5,961	8,586	3,335	5,805	5,423	6,218	3,990	12,403	11,506	14,789
1973	14,328	27,204	26,120	32,789	6,094	7,474	6,607	9,535	3,662	6,395	6,122	6,967	4,572	13,335	13,391	16,287
1974	15,308	28,563	26,469	36,251	6,418	6,070	5,786	10,324	4,005	7,083	6,772	7,790	4,885	15,410	13,911	18,137
1975	17,101	31,431	30,591	40,113	6,739	6,074	5,837	10,532	4,123	6,857	6,871	7,832	6,239	18,500	17,883	21,749
1976	17,883	33,187	32,188	42,192	6,992	6,686	6,323	10,979	4,245	7,254	6,917	8,215	6,646	19,247	18,948	22,998
(TQ)	18,222	7,604	8,137	24,308	7,166	1,675	1,687	8,364	4,472	1,772	1,673	5,395	6,584	4,157	4,777	10,549
1977	19,279	27,468	24,593	45,307	7,166	3,966	3,714	11,317	4,606	4,162	3,831	8,632	7,507	19,340	17,048	25,358
1978	20,422	28,397	26,353	47,741	7,480	4,157	3,778	11,671	4,945	4,352	3,915	9,074	7,997	19,888	18,660	26,996
1979	21,089	28,540	27,095	49,372	7,760	4,428	4,190	12,283	5,203	4,187	3,934	9,282	8,126	19,925	18,971	27,807
1980	22,048	29,073	29,011	51,337	7,933	4,666	4,461	12,750	5,586	4,797	4,344	10,051	8,529	19,610	20,206	28,536
1981	22,347	30,165	27,674	51,881	8,145	5,368	4,913	13,554	5,855	4,531	4,011	10,085	8,348	20,265	18,750	28,242
1982	24,439	34,049	31,595	57,846	8,486	6,530	6,003	15,072	6,428	4,884	4,516	11,116	9,525	22,635	21,076	31,658
1983	25,980	37,130	35,578	62,793	8,849	7,520	7,213	16,473	6,919	5,687	4,836	12,228	10,212	23,923	23,529	34,092
1984	27,136	39,247	37,127	65,627	9,060	8,056	7,601	17,187	7,467	5,577	5,155	12,889	10,609	25,614	24,371	35,551
1985	28,846	45,193	42,020	72,889	9,556	10,844	9,808	20,442	7,846	5,862	5,562	13,540	11,444	28,487	26,650	38,907
1986	30,538	49,289	46,773	78,978	10,482	13,536	12,682	23,940	8,030	6,000	5,577	13,914	12,026	29,753	28,514	41,124
1987	31,727	50,178	48,314	81,608	10,945	14,422	13,919	25,567	8,531	5,770	5,452	14,116	12,251	29,986	28,943	41,925
1988	32,415	50,908	51,280	83,676	11,344	15,932	15,240	27,220	8,666	5,626	5,473	14,224	12,405	29,350	30,567	42,232
1989	29,769	41,333	42,955	73,081	11,468	15,008	14,582	26,561	8,996	5,716	5,198	14,311	9,305	20,606	23,175	32,209
1990	29,660	41,401	39,924	71,026	11,787	15,495	14,529	27,067	9,438	6,009	5,341	15,108	8,435	19,897	20,054	28,851
1991	30,474	42,578	40,584	72,145	12,295	16,873	15,475	28,376	9,832	5,668	5,341	15,319	8,347	20,037	19,768	28,450
1992	31,077	40,197	39,545	71,422	13,111	17,755	16,571	30,404	10,145	5,842	5,460	15,956	7,821	16,600	17,514	25,062
1993	32,495	44,540	40,867	75,404	13,476	17,985	17,274	31,668	10,601	6,543	6,375	16,849	8,418	20,012	17,518	26,887
1994	33,405	44,919	43,791	77,895	13,502	17,491	16,974	30,926	10,922	7,396	6,487	17,873	8,981	20,032	20,330	29,096
1995	33,764	46,412	40,799	79,373	13,569	19,713	18,914	33,061	11,869	7,757	7,132	19,341	8,326	18,942	14,753	26,971

(TQ) Transition quarter. Reflects status as of September 30, 1976.

Sources

1965–1970: U.S. Department of Veterans Affairs (VA), *Trend Data – 1960–1984* (U.S. Office of Information Management and Statistics, 1985), pp. 50–1. 1971–1995: VA, *Trend Data – 1971–1995*, p. 44; VA Internet site, accessed June 30, 2001.

Documentation

The growth of nursing home care in society at large has been paralleled by the growth of nursing home care provided through the VA.

Additional data on the type of extended care provided in VA medical centers or on behalf of the VA is available in the VA's *Annual Reports*. Recent data are also available at the VA Internet site.

Series Ed437. Figures are the average daily census in all facilities, whether the care is provided by or on behalf of the VA.

Series Ed440. Figures are the total number of patients treated, defined as the number of discharges and deaths during the year plus the number remaining on the rolls at the end of the year.

TABLE Ed453–462   Guaranteed or insured loans for veterans – number and amount, by purpose of loan: 1944–1999
Contributed by Hugh Rockoff

	Total		Home		Manufactured (mobile) home		Farm		Business	
	Number	Amount	Number	Amount	Number	Amount	Number	Amount	Number	Amount
	Ed453	Ed454	Ed455	Ed456	Ed457	Ed458	Ed459	Ed460	Ed461	Ed462
Fiscal year	Number	Thousand dollars	Number	Thousand dollars	Number	Thousand dollars	Number	Thousand dollars	Number	Thousand dollars
1944–1946 [1]	183,250	8,846,421	161,405	8,781,712	—	—	6,296	18,986	15,549	45,723
1947	640,298	3,611,614	562,985	3,346,387	—	—	24,690	97,844	52,623	167,383
1948	520,094	2,962,836	479,337	2,817,335	—	—	14,474	59,174	26,283	86,327
1949	279,231	1,352,643	260,380	1,292,711	—	—	6,062	21,736	12,789	38,196
1950	397,784	2,162,517	380,360	2,112,708	—	—	4,972	17,826	12,452	31,983
1951	538,010	3,692,156	516,136	3,631,688	—	—	4,354	18,904	17,520	41,564
1952	424,654	3,312,965	367,886	3,198,615	—	—	2,837	10,461	53,931	103,889
1953	316,682	2,779,673	300,433	2,734,985	—	—	1,566	6,730	14,683	37,958
1954	332,569	3,224,429	322,156	3,193,273	—	—	1,319	5,836	9,094	25,320
1955	571,150	6,053,163	562,892	6,023,019	—	—	1,788	9,105	6,470	21,039
1956	606,957	6,800,959	600,507	6,773,924	—	—	1,559	7,950	4,891	19,085
1957	441,350	5,206,968	436,791	5,187,546	—	—	1,007	4,807	3,552	14,615
1958	173,307	1,148,145	170,366	1,145,972	—	—	421	430	2,520	1,743
1959	206,967	2,633,284	204,958	2,623,807	—	—	226	1,461	1,783	8,016
1960	178,809	2,376,281	177,208	2,369,326	—	—	128	798	1,473	6,157
1961	125,541	1,701,797	124,291	1,696,127	—	—	70	398	1,180	5,272
1962	166,178	2,285,963	165,127	2,280,567	—	—	52	343	999	5,053
1963	203,065	2,878,588	202,399	2,874,651	—	—	37	343	629	3,594
1964	199,156	2,949,071	198,764	2,947,024	—	—	7	108	385	1,939
1965	176,317	2,764,808	175,963	2,762,564	—	—	28	335	326	1,909
1966	152,280	2,522,984	152,113	2,521,993	—	—	21	294	146	697
1967	167,836	2,766,330	167,722	2,765,493	—	—	26	304	88	533
1968	220,294	3,827,386	220,212	3,826,790	—	—	10	192	72	404
1969	219,334	4,017,558	219,278	4,017,042	—	—	21	286	35	230
1970	186,209	3,682,644	186,187	3,682,340	—	—	14	206	8	98
1971	197,915	4,112,014	197,606	4,109,367	278	2,211	19	334	12	102
1972	359,010	7,860,828	354,571	7,822,580	4,430	38,118	4	88	5	47
1973	365,132	8,357,618	359,266	8,306,047	5,856	51,459	7	70	3	42
1974	311,260	7,709,564	306,188	7,663,716	5,062	45,725	8	102	2	21
1975	290,195	8,091,382	288,163	8,072,101	2,028	19,264	2	11	2	6
1976	326,727	9,951,196	324,968	9,930,076	1,759	21,120	—	—	—	—
(TQ)	81,022	2,620,700	80,744	2,617,251	278	3,449	—	—	—	—
1977	382,586	13,135,825	379,793	13,099,441	2,793	36,384	—	—	—	—
1978	380,869	14,658,657	376,561	14,598,972	4,308	59,685	—	—	—	—
1979	364,578	16,071,991	357,850	15,955,333	6,728	116,658	—	—	—	—
1980	297,447	14,815,266	289,164	14,653,112	8,283	162,154	—	—	—	—
1981	187,628	10,008,945	178,239	9,821,789	9,389	187,156	—	—	—	—
1982	103,439	5,541,915	92,930	5,331,522	10,509	210,393	—	—	—	—
1983	245,122	14,670,261	231,620	14,389,968	13,502	280,293	—	—	—	—
1984	251,588	15,611,818	238,478	15,332,916	13,110	278,902	—	—	—	—
1985	178,931	11,451,748	170,015	11,262,756	8,916	188,992	—	—	—	—
1986	313,769	21,965,777	307,747	21,832,718	6,022	133,059	—	—	—	—
1987	479,491	34,900,051	474,391	34,783,518	5,100	116,533	—	—	—	—
1988	234,709	17,302,354	232,638	17,254,292	2,071	48,062	—	—	—	—
1989	189,705	14,416,164	188,871	14,396,350	834	19,814	—	—	—	—
1990	196,600	15,779,002	196,166	15,768,431	434	10,571	—	—	—	—
1991	181,165	15,454,126	180,852	15,446,037	313	8,089	—	—	—	—
1992	266,021	22,959,806	265,895	22,956,501	126	3,305	—	—	—	—
1993	383,303	34,634,878	383,236	34,632,993	67	1,885	—	—	—	—
1994	602,244	55,141,335	602,220	55,140,529	24	806	—	—	—	—
1995	263,130	25,340,889	263,102	25,340,157	28	732	—	—	—	—
1996	320,776	32,609,380	320,767	32,609,037	9	343	—	—	—	—
1997	258,775	27,042,262	258,766	27,042,078	9	184	—	—	—	—
1998	343,954	37,906,134	343,954	37,906,134	0	0	—	—	—	—
1999	485,610	54,087,681	485,610	54,087,681	0	0	—	—	—	—

(TQ) Transition quarter.

[1] Total estimated for 1944–1946.

Sources

1944–1959 and 1996–1999: data provided by the U.S. Department of Veterans Affairs (VA).

1960–1970: VA, *Trend Data – 1960–1984* (U.S. Office of Information Management and Statistics, 1985), pp. 35, 37.

1971–1995: VA, *Trend Data – 1971–1995*, pp. 29, 30, VA Internet site, accessed June 30, 2001.

TABLE Ed453–462 Guaranteed or insured loans for veterans – number and amount, by purpose of loan: 1944–1999
Continued

Documentation

The Servicemen's Readjustment Act of 1944 provided guarantees or insurance for loans to veterans. The main purpose of this provision was to make it easier for a veteran to purchase a home by reducing the risk to the lender and hence the interest rate or down payment required from the veteran.

These series include direct loans sold with a guaranty, as well as loans for condominiums, refinancing, and alterations and repairs. The figures are the number and dollar amount of loans closed in each fiscal year. The government guarantee or insurance applied only to a portion of the amount shown here.

Series Ed455–458. Loans to buy traditional mobile homes were authorized in 1970. These are shown separately in series Ed457–458. Modular homes are included in series Ed455–456.

Series Ed459–462. Although the main purpose of the program was to encourage home ownership, some loans for the purchase of farms and small businesses were also included in the original legislation. This part of the program was discontinued December 31, 1974. Additional information on the loans (for example, the average rate of interest) is available in the *Annual Reports* of the VA, although coverage varies from year to year.

TABLE Ed463–466 Defaults on guaranteed or insured loans under the Veterans Loan Program: 1960–1999
Contributed by Hugh Rockoff

Fiscal year	Loans outstanding Ed463 [1] Number	Defaults reported Ed464 Number	Defaults cured or withdrawn Ed465 Number	Loans in default Ed466 Number	Fiscal year	Loans outstanding Ed463 [1] Number	Defaults reported Ed464 Number	Defaults cured or withdrawn Ed465 Number	Loans in default Ed466 Number
1960	3,955,478	89,776	79,431	45,488	1980	4,100,165	138,323	115,349	60,080
1961	3,842,026	110,259	88,746	53,889	1981	4,103,071	146,455	126,800	67,089
1962	3,724,408	107,192	86,393	55,534	1982	4,082,200	158,808	125,650	84,257
1963	3,729,886	107,935	84,798	55,545	1983	4,170,475	162,765	127,917	96,796
1964	3,612,626	111,599	88,393	54,432	1984	4,227,982	158,633	126,181	102,022
1965	3,579,468	108,469	84,777	53,810	1985	4,201,596	170,385	127,635	115,282
1966	3,454,516	105,336	83,731	52,869	1986	4,177,382	182,323	136,725	127,678
1967	3,465,814	95,444	83,535	43,561	1987	4,115,803	182,044	132,653	136,682
1968	3,462,974	84,292	74,166	36,978	1988	4,025,856	176,503	126,927	133,600
1969	3,520,986	79,115	70,264	33,342	1989	3,937,986	171,295	132,214	126,877
1970	3,549,944	82,659	71,991	33,589	1990	3,856,173	163,854	132,346	115,392
1971	3,597,757	83,023	69,950	36,266	1991	3,773,005	166,945	120,789	118,716
1972	3,743,938	88,868	75,049	38,247	1992	3,683,388	153,389	124,131	113,654
1973	3,659,977	92,204	78,377	37,211	1993	3,512,394	142,196	115,568	110,792
1974	3,764,819	103,433	85,947	39,118	1994	3,428,939	125,463	103,732	106,717
1975	3,856,154	118,653	97,571	47,310	1995	3,375,830	120,910	101,301	102,137
1976	3,953,468	110,623	94,624	46,193	1996	3,355,391	123,236	91,390	113,799
(TQ)	3,898,817	25,238	18,278	49,401	1997	3,302,150	132,534	92,344	132,245
1977	3,956,751	112,461	97,248	48,343	1998	3,229,524	132,147	103,712	133,573
1978	4,001,721	117,204	101,487	49,448	1999	3,171,862	118,426	102,367	121,997
1979	4,040,006	120,284	108,268	48,141					

(TQ) Transition quarter. Reflects status as of September 30, 1976.

[1] Includes refinancing and condominium loans.

Sources

Series Ed463. 1960–1970 and 1996–1999: Data provided by the U.S. Department of Veterans Affairs (VA). 1971–1995: VA, *Trend Data – 1971–1995*, p. 31, VA Internet site, accessed June 30, 2001.

Series Ed464–466. 1960–1970: VA, *Trend Data – 1960–1984* (U.S. Office of Information Management and Statistics, 1985), p. 38. 1971–1995: VA, *Trend Data – 1971–1995*, p. 31. 1996–1999: Data provided by the VA.

Documentation

This table provides information on the size and default record of the Veterans Loan Program. The information here is in terms of the number of loans.

Additional information, including the amount of loans and amount in default is available in the *Annual Reports* of the VA, although the information provided varies from year to year.

Series Ed463. Figures are the number of loans outstanding at the end of the fiscal year.

Series Ed464–465. Series Ed464 is the number of defaults reported during the fiscal year, and series Ed465 is the number of defaults that were cured or withdrawn. The difference between the series is, therefore, the number of loans for which the VA became responsible in some measure for repaying.

Series Ed466. Figures are the number of loans that remained in default at the end of the fiscal year because they had still not been cured, withdrawn, or repaid.

TABLE Ed467–482 Veterans participating in training programs under GI Bills, by legislation and type of training: 1945–1997
Contributed by Hugh Rockoff

	Total, all GI Bills	WWII GI Bill				Korean Conflict GI Bill				Post-Korean and Vietnam-era GI Bills					Montgomery GI Bill	
		College	Other schools	On-the-job training	Farm training	College	Other schools	On-the-job training	Farm training	College	Other schools	On-the-job training	Other training	Post-Vietnam-era GI Bill, total	Active duty personnel	Reserve personnel
Fiscal year	Ed467	Ed468	Ed469	Ed470	Ed471	Ed472	Ed473	Ed474	Ed475	Ed476	Ed477	Ed478	Ed479	Ed480	Ed481	Ed482
	Number	Number	Number	Number	Number	Number	Number	Number	Number	Number	Number	Number	Number	Number	Number	Number
1945	35,000	24,000	8,000	2,000	—	—	—	—	—	—	—	—	—	—	—	—
1946	1,180,000	535,000	265,000	352,000	29,000	—	—	—	—	—	—	—	—	—	—	—
1947	3,639,000	1,664,000	815,000	915,000	245,000	—	—	—	—	—	—	—	—	—	—	—
1948	3,579,000	1,492,000	1,090,000	702,000	294,000	—	—	—	—	—	—	—	—	—	—	—
1949	3,223,000	1,232,000	1,106,000	542,000	343,000	—	—	—	—	—	—	—	—	—	—	—
1950	3,098,000	1,056,000	1,302,000	374,000	367,000	—	—	—	—	—	—	—	—	—	—	—
1951	2,500,000	732,000	1,160,000	226,000	383,000	—	—	—	—	—	—	—	—	—	—	—
1952	1,743,000	478,000	859,000	123,000	282,000	—	—	—	—	—	—	—	—	—	—	—
1953	1,121,000	283,000	429,000	60,000	160,000	96,000	57,000	28,000	6,000	—	—	—	—	—	—	—
1954	956,000	164,000	186,000	21,000	74,000	260,000	163,000	64,000	24,000	—	—	—	—	—	—	—
1955	1,078,000	93,000	95,000	6,000	27,000	454,000	280,000	81,000	41,000	—	—	—	—	—	—	—
1956	1,128,000	50,000	50,000	1,000	2,000	587,000	301,000	88,000	48,000	—	—	—	—	—	—	—
1957	1,059,000	1,000	1,000	—	—	643,000	286,000	77,000	49,000	—	—	—	—	—	—	—
1958	952,000	—	—	—	—	590,000	268,000	53,000	40,000	—	—	—	—	—	—	—
1959	755,000	—	—	—	—	493,000	205,000	28,000	29,000	—	—	—	—	—	—	—
1960	502,000	—	—	—	—	332,000	140,000	13,000	17,000	—	—	—	—	—	—	—
1961	306,000	—	—	—	—	210,000	83,000	6,000	8,000	—	—	—	—	—	—	—
1962	172,000	—	—	—	—	123,000	44,000	2,000	3,000	—	—	—	—	—	—	—
1963	93,000	—	—	—	—	69,000	23,000	1,000	1,000	—	—	—	—	—	—	—
1964	48,000	—	—	—	—	36,000	11,000	—	—	—	—	—	—	—	—	—
1965	22,000	—	—	—	—	16,000	5,000	—	—	—	—	—	—	—	—	—
1966	0	—	—	—	—	—	—	—	—	—	—	—	—	—	—	—
1967	468,000	—	—	—	—	—	—	—	—	339,000	129,000	—	—	—	—	—
1968	687,000	—	—	—	—	—	—	—	—	414,000	255,000	19,000	—	—	—	—
1969	925,000	—	—	—	—	—	—	—	—	529,000	330,000	66,000	—	—	—	—
1970	1,211,000	—	—	—	—	—	—	—	—	677,000	417,000	117,000	—	—	—	—
1971	1,585,000	—	—	—	—	—	—	—	—	917,000	522,000	146,000	—	—	—	—
1972	1,864,000	—	—	—	—	—	—	—	—	1,065,000	638,000	162,000	—	—	—	—
1973	2,126,000	—	—	—	—	—	—	—	—	1,181,000	756,000	189,000	—	—	—	—
1974	2,359,000	—	—	—	—	—	—	—	—	1,337,000	810,000	212,000	—	—	—	—
1975	2,692,000	—	—	—	—	—	—	—	—	1,696,000	804,000	192,000	—	—	—	—
1976	2,822,000	—	—	—	—	—	—	—	—	1,925,000	750,000	146,000	—	—	—	—
1977	1,938,000	—	—	—	—	—	—	—	—	1,381,000	444,000	112,000	—	—	—	—
1978	1,522,037	—	—	—	—	—	—	—	—	1,145,000	283,000	94,000	—	37	—	—
1979	1,278,456	—	—	—	—	—	—	—	—	968,000	226,000	84,000	—	456	—	—
1980	1,108,947	—	—	—	—	—	—	—	—	843,000	190,000	74,000	—	1,947	—	—
1981	957,324	—	—	—	—	—	—	—	—	736,000	157,000	55,000	—	8,324	—	—
1982	801,517	—	—	—	—	—	—	—	—	621,000	119,000	38,000	—	23,517	—	—
1983	673,508	—	—	—	—	—	—	—	—	518,000	101,000	25,000	—	29,508	—	—
1984	566,310	—	—	—	—	—	—	—	—	421,280	78,013	19,499	9,676	38,310	—	—

Fiscal year	Total, all GI Bills	WWII GI Bill				Korean Conflict GI Bill				Post-Korean and Vietnam-era GI Bills					Montgomery GI Bill	
		College	Other schools	On-the-job training	Farm training	College	Other schools	On-the-job training	Farm training	College	Other schools	On-the-job training	Other training	Post-Vietnam-era GI Bill, total	Active duty personnel	Reserve personnel
	Ed467	Ed468	Ed469	Ed470	Ed471	Ed472	Ed473	Ed474	Ed475	Ed476	Ed477	Ed478	Ed479	Ed480	Ed481	Ed482
	Number	Number	Number	Number	Number	Number	Number	Number	Number	Number	Number	Number	Number	Number	Number	Number
1985	450,110	—	—	—	—	—	—	—	—	326,012	53,634	15,197	7,438	48,110	—	—
1986	402,537	—	—	—	—	—	—	—	—	257,437	35,197	9,473	5,530	63,221	1	31,678
1987	368,159	—	—	—	—	—	—	—	—	202,508	25,526	6,558	4,206	76,772	130	52,459
1988	368,700	—	—	—	—	—	—	—	—	176,177	18,586	4,467	3,539	87,486	5,599	72,846
1989	362,113	—	—	—	—	—	—	—	—	144,163	13,288	3,275	3,186	83,787	23,830	90,584
1990	361,109	—	—	—	—	—	—	—	—	76,533	6,045	1,933	1,714	70,870	101,781	102,233
1991	299,589	—	—	—	—	—	—	—	—	—	—	—	—	56,186	141,080	102,323
1992	354,118	—	—	—	—	—	—	—	—	—	—	—	—	44,901	194,948	114,269
1993	391,632	—	—	—	—	—	—	—	—	—	—	—	—	35,118	246,057	110,457
1994	412,698	—	—	—	—	—	—	—	—	—	—	—	—	25,529	284,108	103,061
1995	408,131	—	—	—	—	—	—	—	—	—	—	—	—	18,927	291,958	97,246
1996	396,734	—	—	—	—	—	—	—	—	—	—	—	—	14,185	296,353	86,196
1997	384,898	—	—	—	—	—	—	—	—	—	—	—	—	9,868	297,030	78,000

Source

Data provided by the U.S. Department of Veterans Affairs.

Documentation

Under the original World War II GI Bill (Servicemen's Readjustment Act of 1944) and subsequent legislation, a veteran was eligible for educational assistance in the form of tuition, fees, and subsistence support, even when the veteran was not disabled. The amount of aid varied from program to program. The Korean Conflict and Vietnam-era GI Bills were somewhat less generous than the World War II Bill. Under the Vietnam-era Veteran's Educational Assistance Program and subsequent programs,

members of the armed forces were required to set aside for their education part of the pay earned while on active duty. The government then provided additional funds. Most of the veterans receiving educational benefits under the post-Vietnam-era and Montgomery GI Bills were enrolled in colleges and universities.

The estimates in the table refer only to veterans who were currently receiving training. Estimates of the cumulative number trained are available in the *Annual Reports* of the Department of Veterans Affairs. The Veterans Administration also administers programs, not shown here, that provide funds for vocational rehabilitation for disabled veterans and for the spouses and children of totally disabled or deceased veterans.

CHAPTER Ee

International Trade and Exchange Rates

Editors: Michael Edelstein, Douglas A. Irwin, and Lawrence H. Officer

INTERNATIONAL TRANSACTIONS AND FOREIGN COMMERCE

Michael Edelstein

Throughout the history of the United States, the balance of trade, the overall balance of payments, the foreign purchase of American assets, the American purchase of foreign assets, and the exchange value of the dollar have been major political concerns. The statistics presented in this chapter describe the international economic relations of the United States and help to provide a context for evaluating these historical and modern controversies. These statistics are presented in three separate sections. The first section presents summary information on U.S. international transactions (Tables Ee1–361). Included are data on the balance of international payments, the international investment position of the United States, and the U.S. government foreign grants and credits. The second section offers detailed statistics on the type and location of U.S. trade in goods and services (Tables Ee362–611). Exchange rate data are presented in the final section (Tables Ee612–683).

Colonial Era

From its first years as a region of European exploration, settlement, and colonization, the Atlantic coastal area of the North American continent engaged in a relatively high level of trade in goods and services. Although not the source of the gold, silver, and spices that filled the imaginations of the early European explorers, the region's tobacco, shipping services, bread and flour, rice, fish, ships, and other exports proved highly salable in Great Britain and the West Indies (Walton and Shepherd 1998, pp. 101, 194–5), placing the thirteen British colonies among the world's leading exporters, more than twice as trade-oriented as Europe itself (Lipsey 2000, p. 685). As a rough estimate, exports were 15–20 percent of colonial gross national product (GNP) in 1770. Colonial exports reflected the relative abundance of natural resources of the region's land, forests, and seas. Imports, on the other hand, were largely manufactured goods from Great Britain. On average, the overall balance on current account of the thirteen colonies from 1768 to 1772 produced a small deficit, perhaps 0.15–0.20 percent of GNP (Walton and Shepherd 1998, p. 87). The substantial goods deficit, made larger by payments for indentured servants and slaves, was almost offset

Acknowledgments

Michael Edelstein is most thankful for suggestions and encouragement from Christopher Bach, Douglas A. Irwin, Robert E. Lipsey, Lawrence H. Officer, and an anonymous referee.

by colonial ship sales, shipping and mercantile service earnings, and British military and civil expenditures.

The Republic's First Century

With the American revolution and independence, the new nation lost its special place in the British empire. Trading volumes and partners were further disordered from 1791 to 1815 by trade embargoes and other disruptions associated with the French revolution and the long European war. Yet, even before the Napoleonic Wars ended in 1815, the structure of U.S. international transactions for most of the nineteenth century had emerged.

Trade as a share of the American economy in the nineteenth century was lower than in the colonial era. Table Ee-A presents the trends in annual U.S. international transactions, averaged by decade. As in the standard international accounting framework, the net balances on goods, services, investment income, and unilateral transfers are summed into the overall balance on current account. The balance on current account is conceptually very similar to the net export component of GNP. When the balance on current account is positive, it represents American savings flowing into the purchase of foreign assets; when it is negative, it represents foreign savings flowing into the purchase of American assets. Figure Ee-B displays the annual balance on current account as a percentage of GDP from 1840 to the present. Longer-term trends in the balance on current account as a percentage of GDP are indicated with decadal averages in Table Ee-A.

From the 1810s to the 1870s, the average decadal share of goods exports in GNP varied from 5.3 percent to 6.3 percent, while the average decadal share of goods imports ranged a bit higher, 5.6 percent to 6.7 percent. Through the 1870s, the United States tended to import goods more than it exported goods, thus producing a deficit on the net goods account. The net service account was positive, dominated by earnings from American shipping services, sometimes nearly covering the net deficit on the goods trade. The early negative balance on investment income was the consequence of the new federal government's decision to pay the debts of its thirteen states from the revolutionary period and the willingness of foreign investors to buy a portion of the new nation's debt instruments.

Summing the net goods, net service, net investment income, and infrequent unilateral transfers accounts, the current account for the first seven decades of the republic showed an average tendency to deficit. The deficit tended to grow larger from the 1820s onward as the trade in goods began to rely on foreign shippers more heavily. In addition, from the 1830s onward, interest payments to foreign lenders began to rise as American state governments and private enterprises raised a portion of their finance for financial and social overhead capital formation abroad. The annual rate of

TABLE Ee-A   U.S. international transactions – annual averages by decade: 1790–1998

	Balance on goods account	Balance on service account	Balance on investment income account	Unilateral transfers	Balance on current account	
					Amount	As a percentage of GDP
Decade	Million dollars	Million dollars	Million dollars	Million dollars	Million dollars	Percent
1790–1799	−10	12	−5	—	−2	—
1800–1809	−19	24	−5	—	−1	—
1810–1819	−23	18	−5	—	−10	—
1820–1829	−4	8	−5	—	0	—
1830–1839	−25	7	−7	5	−21	—
1840–1849	2	8	−9	8	8	0.4
1850–1859	−9	−5	−17	13	−19	−0.5
1860–1869	−19	−16	−43	2	−77	−1.0
1870–1879	93	−29	−89	−5	−30	−0.4
1880–1889	103	−59	−93	−23	−71	−0.5
1890–1899	263	−71	−129	−50	13	0.0
1900–1909	569	−178	−74	−139	177	0.8
1910–1919	1,952	−390	104	−283	1,382	2.6
1920–1929	1,117	−339	656	−415	1,019	1.2
1930–1939	449	−263	395	−226	355	0.4
1940–1949	6,658	75	645	−5,838	1,540	0.7
1950–1959	2,934	202	2,547	−5,081	602	0.1
1960–1969	4,082	−897	4,877	−4,729	3,333	0.5
1970–1979	−10,383	2,170	14,762	−6,863	−315	0.0
1980–1989	−93,862	9,066	26,280	−20,051	−78,567	−1.7
1990–1998	−154,065	66,771	15,709	−32,806	−104,392	−1.4

Sources

Balance on goods account: series Ee3. Balance on service account: series Ee7 minus series Ee3. Balance on investment income account: series Ee10. Unilateral transfers: series Ee11. Balance on current account: series Ee12. Gross domestic product: series Ca10.

Documentation

The balance on current account equals the sum of the first four columns shown in this table – that is, the sum of series Ee7 and Ee10–11.

U.S. borrowing was not very large in these decades. Robert Lipsey found that net foreign claims as a percentage of the domestic capital stock fell from 12.9 percent in 1774 to 6.2 percent in 1840, dropping further in the 1840s and 1850s but rising with the Civil War to 6.9 percent (Lipsey 2000, p. 695).

Late Nineteenth Century to the Mid-Twentieth Century

A somewhat different configuration of U.S. international transactions began to emerge in the 1870s, which eventually shifted the nation to a net surplus on current account in the 1890s, a circumstance that lasted until the 1970s. Starting in the 1870s, the United States exhibited an increasingly positive net goods account, driven most strongly by the manufactured products of America's industrialization (see Tables Ee416–417 and Ee446–457). Semimanufactured and manufactured goods were around 15 percent of U.S. exports in 1860; by 1910, they were around 50 percent. In 1860, almost 60 percent of imported goods were in the semimanufactured and manufactured categories; by 1920, such imports had fallen to around 30 percent.

At first in the 1870s and 1880s, the positive balance on the merchandise account was offset by increased deficits in the net service and net investment income accounts. The net service account deficit grew with the larger trade volumes carried by foreign ships and as American tourism became significant. The net investment income account also moved more strongly into deficit as, first, the federal government borrowed abroad during the Civil War, and then, after the Civil War, American railroad companies utilized European capital markets to finance a portion of their renewed capital formation.

However, by the late 1890s, the rising tide of American exports produced substantial overall surpluses on current account. This, in turn, meant that in most years through 1913 the United States lent more abroad than foreign investors lent to the United States. The United States's investment strategy was unique among the nations that invested abroad in the late nineteenth century in that the bulk of U.S. investment abroad took the form of direct investment rather than portfolio investment. Cleona Lewis estimates that in 1897, when the stock of U.S. investment abroad totaled $684.5 million, $634.4 million were direct investments; by 1914, of the $3,513.8 million invested abroad, $2,562.3 million were

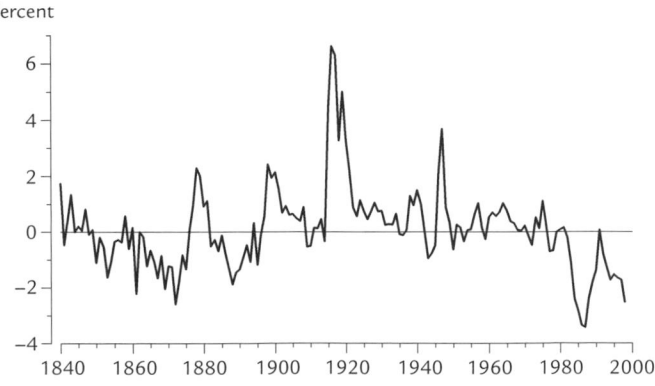

FIGURE Ee-B   U.S. balance on current account as a percentage of gross domestic product: 1840–1998

Sources

Balance on current account: series Ee12. Gross domestic product: series Ca10.

direct investments (Lewis 1938, p. 605). Soon after the Civil War, certain American businesses began to launch overseas subsidiaries or branches. Often these firms had first established national markets in the United States, selling unique products that were produced with the "American system of manufacturing" (Wilkins 1970, p. 35; Lewis 1938, pp. 300–1).

Yet, as of 1914, the United States remained a net debtor – that is, the accumulated stock of foreign-owed American assets, $7,200 million, still exceeded the accumulated stock of U.S.-owned foreign assets, $3,513.8 million (Table Ee23–36). Then, the huge cost of World War I to the European belligerents catapulted the United States into net creditor status. The goods demands of the European belligerents drove up American net exports immediately. The net surplus was covered by American stocks and bonds commandeered by European governments and sold to U.S. residents, by new borrowing in U.S. capital markets, and, after 1917 when the United States entered the war, with loans from the U.S. government. Lewis estimates that by the close of 1919, the negative $3,686 million net investment position of 1914 had become a positive net investment position of $12,562 million, $9,591 million of which was the net owed to the U.S. government (Lewis 1938, p. 447). Coinciding with the turn of the United States from net debtor to net creditor, the annual net investment income account also turned positive in the 1910s.

For the next five decades through 1970, the annual overall balance on current account was typically positive. At first the net goods account provided the dominant weight. As in the period from 1860 to World War I, the strength of American manufacturing exports sales was the major force determining the goods account surplus (Table Ee416–417). Then, in the 1950s and 1960s, the surplus on the net goods account was joined by a large jump in the net surplus in investment income account. Moving in the opposite direction, however, was a very substantial negative net annual outward flow in unilateral transfers, which first appeared during World War II, dominated by military and civilian aid (Table Ee166–361).

The overall surplus on current account took the form of a strong net outward movement of American capital. In the 1920s, both direct and portfolio American investment abroad expanded, moving most heavily to Europe, Canada, and the Americas. The Great Depression in the 1930s saw a sharp reversal of these trends, with a substantial fraction of the overseas portfolio investment of the 1920s liquidated or defaulted by 1935. Indeed, in the late 1930s, the United States saw a surge of flight capital from a riskier and more uncertain Europe.

After World War II, the overall surplus on current account reemerged, which meant the dominant movement of the capital account was again toward net investment abroad. Yet, it is also the case that the *gross* movements of both American investment abroad and foreign investment in the United States were large. From 1945 to 1970, U.S. residents acquired an additional $130 billion in assets abroad, 54 percent in direct investments, 17 percent in long-term securities, 11 percent in private short-term assets, and the rest in U.S. government–owned assets. Over the same period, foreign residents acquired an additional $80 billion in U.S. assets: 13.4 percent in direct investments, 37 percent in long-term securities, 28 percent in private short-term assets, and the rest in foreign government–owned assets. Clearly, Americans tended to own longer-term investments, particularly direct investments, while foreigners tended to hold long- and short-term paper assets (Branson 1980, pp. 236–48).

1970s to the 1990s

The 1970s were a turbulent decade for U.S. international transactions. The average annual balance on current account for the decade was negative, but this average is based on years of both negative (1971–1972, 1976–1979) and positive (1970, 1973–1976) overall balances. Again the overall balance was briefly positive (1980–1981), but thereafter to the present, excepting only 1991, the annual balance on current account was in deficit. The exceptional surplus in 1991 was partly the result of a large spike in unilateral transfers from the Gulf States and others for American military services and equipment during the Gulf War.

The tendency toward overall deficit in the 1970s had its origins in the net goods account. The net goods deficit, in turn, was dominated by a sharp rise in goods imports, largely a result of the rising cost of petroleum imports (Tables Ee418–423 and Ee590–611). Total goods exports contracted sharply in the 1980s, dropping from 8.1 percent of GDP in 1980 to 5.1 percent in 1986, and then rebounded slowly in the late 1980s and 1990s (series Ca10 and Ee419). U.S. manufacturing exports were a significant element in both the contraction and the slow rebound. Nevertheless, in the 1990s, the net goods account deficit increased, the dominant movement stemming from a broad-based increase in manufactured goods imports (Table Ee418–423).

In the 1970s, economists became less certain that the U.S. Department of Commerce distinction between short-term and long-term financial assets in the U.S. balance of payments accounting was meaningful. With the increasing globalization of financial markets, it was no longer clear that long-term financial assets (for example, bonds of one or more year's maturity) were being held for long periods. Indeed, the Commerce Department began a reform of its accounts that ended the distinction between short-term and long-term financial assets and focused more on which types of institutions held foreign assets.

The Commerce Department also began to invest considerably more resources in improving the evaluation of both U.S.-owned assets abroad and foreign-owned assets in the United States. Through 1924, the Commerce Department's estimates of foreign-owned U.S. assets and U.S.-owned foreign assets relied on Lewis, who evaluated equity shares at market value and direct investments and bonds at book or par value (Lewis 1938). For the data after 1924, the Commerce Department itself evaluated financial assets at market value but direct investment at book value (Eichengreen 2000). The reforms and revisions beginning in the mid-1970s led to a more comprehensive and rigorous accounting of the nation's net investment position for the years 1976 to the present, with separate market and current-cost estimates of the investment position (Table Ee72–131).

The movement to annual overall deficits on current account that started in the 1970s meant that foreign residents were annually acquiring more U.S. assets than American residents were annually purchasing abroad. By 1986 on a current-cost basis, or by 1989 on a market-cost basis, the stock of foreign-owned U.S. assets exceeded the stock of U.S.-owned foreign assets, making the United States a debtor in its net investment position. Another consequence was that by the late 1990s, the net balance on investment income turned negative for the first time since 1914.

The period since 1970 has also seen shifts in the types of international investment, both inflows and outflows (Table Ee37–71). From more than 50 percent of U.S. overseas assets in 1970, direct investment fell to around a quarter by the end of the 1990s, with foreign security holdings and deposits in overseas branches of U.S. banks rising sharply. Foreign-owned investments in the United States also altered in character, acquiring relatively less direct investments and private U.S. securities and more U.S. government obligations, currency, and bank deposits.

In the first decades of the post–World War II era, U.S. direct investment abroad focused on petroleum and manufacturing facilities, amounting to almost 70 percent of U.S. total direct investments abroad (Table Ee72–131) (see also Lipsey 1988). Thereafter, both declined so that by 1998 these two sectors represented around 50 percent of U.S. direct investments abroad while finance and banking accounted for 39 percent. Foreign direct investment in the United States shifted in similar directions, in the period up to 1970 toward petroleum and manufacturing and afterward away from these sectors and toward finance and insurance (Table Ee132–165) (see also Lipsey 1993).

Throughout the 1950s and 1960s, Canada remained a target for around 30 percent of U.S. direct investment, while Europe rose from around 15 percent in 1950 to 34 percent in 1970. In the same years, Latin America dropped from 39 percent to 17 percent, while the Middle East rose from 6 percent to 12 percent. Since 1970, Canada has become a much smaller recipient of U.S. direct investment, falling to 11 percent of the total in 1998. Europe is now the host of 50 percent of U.S. direct investment. With shifts in the ownership of petroleum resources in the 1970s, the Middle East and Africa have dropped to 3 percent, their place taken by a significant increase to 17 percent in the share of Asia and the Pacific.

The countries dominating direct investment in the United States in the 1950s and 1960s were the United Kingdom, Canada, Switzerland, and the Netherlands, making up 80–85 percent of all foreign direct investment in the United States. In the decades since 1970, however, these countries' combined share fell to 46 percent in 1998. The major new direct investors in the United States in 1998 were Germany (12 percent) and Japan (16 percent).

For most of the nineteenth century, the value of the U.S. dollar was fixed in terms of gold, as were the currencies of its major trading and investing partners (Tables Ee612–620). The terms of trade of goods and services, of course, fluctuated owing to changes in productivity, factor prices, tariffs, and the like (Table Ee431–445). Only in the "greenback era" (1862–1879) did the U.S. dollar float freely against the currencies of its major trading and investment partners. From 1879 to 1971, the U.S. dollar operated under a gold standard in some form (except for the paper standards, yielding floating exchange rates, during 1917–1922 and 1933–1934), the only change in its gold value occurring in 1934. Still, the currency disruptions for many countries stemming from World War I and its aftermath, the Great Depression of the 1930s, and World War II meant that bilateral exchange rates with major and minor trading and investment partners were subject to substantial fluctuations and shifts (Table Ee621–636). In separate steps in 1971 and 1973, the United States moved to a floating exchange regime with major consequences for its bilateral exchange values (Tables Ee621–678) and its overall average trading values (Table Ee679–683). Broad indexes of the foreign exchange value of the dollar show a fairly steady appreciation trend since the beginning of the floating exchange era in 1973.

The switch from fixed to floating exchange rates in the early 1970s meant that the overall balance on current account conveys different kinds of information about the state of the nation's international transactions. Under the fixed exchange rate regime that widely prevailed before the early 1970s, changes in the international economy were reflected in the overall balance on current account and its subcomponents, that is, in the dollar balances. With the move to flexible exchange rates in the early 1970s, changes in the international economy became reflected in shifts in exchange rates as well as shifts in the dollar balances of the international accounts. For example, under fixed exchange rates, the extent of an overall surplus or deficit balance of payments can signal whether the currency is "undervalued" or "overvalued." Under a relatively unmanaged floating exchange rate regime, a deficit may not communicate anything about competitiveness of U.S. trade and the like, particularly because the dollar has been highly valued as a world currency since the late twentieth century. When a currency becomes more rigidly managed by a government or monetary authority (that is, floats less freely), the definition and interpretation of the overall balance of payments becomes more difficult (Eichengreen 2000). What is clear is that study of the patterns of international economic problems and the pressures under the current flexible exchange rate regime should combine examination and analysis of the patterns of both international transactions and exchange rates.

References

Branson, William H. 1980. "Trends in United States International Trade and Investment since World War II." In Martin S. Feldstein, editor. *The American Economy in Transition*. University of Chicago Press.

Eichengreen, Barry. 2000. "U.S. Foreign Financial Relations in the Twentieth Century." In Stanley L. Engerman and Robert E. Gallman, editors. *The Cambridge Economic History of the United States,* volume 3, *The Twentieth Century*. Cambridge University Press.

Lewis, Cleona. 1938. *America's Stake in International Investment*. Brookings Institution Press.

Lipsey, Robert E. 1988. "Changing Patterns of International Investment in and by the United States." In Martin S. Feldstein, editor. *The United States in the World Economy*. University of Chicago Press.

Lipsey, Robert E. 1993. *Foreign Direct Investment in the United States: Changes over Three Decades*. University of Chicago Press.

Lipsey, Robert E. 2000. "U.S. Foreign Trade and the Balance of Payments, 1800–1913." In Stanley L. Engerman and Robert E. Gallman, editors. *The Cambridge Economic History of the United States,* volume 2, *The Long Nineteenth Century*. Cambridge University Press.

Walton, Gary M., and James F. Shepherd. 1998. *History of the American Economy*. 8th edition. Dryden Press.

Wilkins, Mira. 1970. *The Emergence of Multinational Enterprise*. Harvard University Press.

INTERNATIONAL TRADE IN GOODS AND SERVICES

Douglas A. Irwin

Statistics on U.S. international trade in goods and services are presented in Tables Ee362–611. Separate tables show the value of U.S. trade (exports and imports) in goods and services, the value of that trade in relation to gross domestic product, different breakdowns of that trade in terms of class of good being exchanged, price and quantity indicators of trade, and the primary trading partners of the United States.

The character of U.S. international trade has changed considerably over the course of the nation's history. For most of the nineteenth century, America's exports consisted largely of

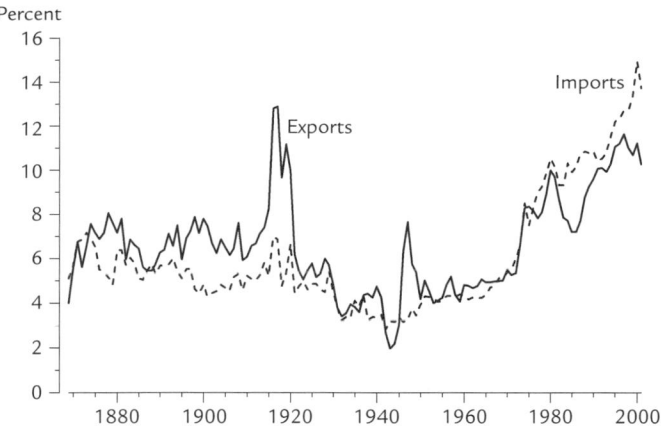

FIGURE Ee-C Trade in goods and services as a percentage of gross domestic product: 1869–2001

Sources

Series Ca10, Ee416–418, and Ee421.

Documentation

Through 1928, the data cover goods only; thereafter, goods and services are included.

agricultural-based commodities, particularly cotton, tobacco, and, later in the century, wheat. Cotton was the country's dominant export for most of the century. U.S. imports consisted of a widely diverse bundle of goods, however, ranging from manufactured goods (such as textiles and iron goods) to consumer items (such as coffee, tea, fruits, wine, and spirits). Around 1900 exports of manufactured goods began to rise rapidly, and by World War I manufactured goods accounted for a majority of U.S. exports. Many of these exports were natural-resource- or mineral-based manufactured goods, such as iron and steel products (using iron ore and coal resources), copper goods, and petroleum products. By World War II, the United States had an advantage in exporting technological and skill-intensive products and services. Exports of shipping services had been an important source of export earnings after independence, but they were relatively unimportant until the post–World War II rise in trade in services.

Throughout most of U.S. history, merchandise trade has fluctuated between 5 and 10 percent of GDP. However, there have been some exceptional periods. During World Wars I and II, exports surged as the United States supplied food and manufactured goods to Western Europe. During the Great Depression of the 1930s, by contrast, the ratio of trade to gross domestic product (GDP) fell to about 2 percent, a historic low. By the year 2000, the value of trade as a share of GDP reached the highest levels seen in a century (see Tables Ee416–423 and Figure Ee-C).

Data Collection

International trade data are subject to a variety of special statistical problems relating to compilation, publication, coverage, valuation, and classification.[1] The first Congress of the United States provided for the compilation of statistics on foreign trade, and the U.S. Treasury Department, through its customhouses, began keeping a record of foreign trade beginning August 1, 1789. Compared with currently compiled statistics, these earliest records left a great

deal to be desired. J. Edward Ely, writing on the historical development of foreign trade statistics, observes that:

> The United States may be said to have had an adequate set of import and export statistics only since about 1821. Prior to that time no information was compiled on the amount of imports of articles which were free of duty upon importation into the United States. No value figures were compiled on imports subject to specific rates of duty and the dollar value for imports subject to ad valorem rates of duty, although apparently accurate, was compiled only as a total with no information on how much of each commodity was imported. Existing figures on the total dollar value of imports during the years 1795 to 1801 were apparently estimated at the time by the Secretary of the Treasury, and the figures for 1790–1794 and from 1802–1820 were apparently estimated many years later. (Ely 1953, p. 269)

Douglass North observes that the 1789–1820 figures were "officially overhauled and published in the Report of the Secretary of the Treasury on Finances for 1835" (North 1960). In employing the early records, North found a number of deficiencies, and users of figures for 1790–1820 should note his revised figures and consider the criticisms in the appendix to his paper. The adequacy of the early records, of course, depends on the use made of them. Some of the earliest records were not published officially, and scholars have had to depend on information from contemporary sources, such as Tench Coxe, *A View of the United States of America* (1794); Samuel Blodget Jr., *Economica: A Statistical Manual for the United States of America* (1806); Timothy Pitkin, *A Statistical View of Commerce of the United States of America* (1816), which presents many tables obtained directly from the Treasury books; and Adam Seybert, *Statistical Annuals* (1818), covering the period 1789–1818, and giving statistics of population, commerce, public land, and the like. Such data as were published annually for 1790–1820 were brought together later in *American State Papers*, Class 4, "Commerce and Navigation" (U.S. Congress 1832, 1834).

In 1820, Congress passed a law to provide for obtaining accurate statements of the foreign commerce of the United States and, at the same time, established the Division of Commerce and Navigation in the office of the Register of the Treasury. It required collectors of customs to compile and transmit annual reports to that office showing the detailed trade with foreign countries and the navigation employed therein. Beginning with 1821, these reports were consolidated and published annually in *Commerce and Navigation of United States*. Foreign trade statistics published by the federal government after 1820 are regarded as superior to those for the earlier period but are still subject to some deficiencies, notably with respect to valuation imports. Their coverage of overland exports also suffered (see North 1960, Appendix II; and Ely 1953, pp. 270–1).

The Civil War introduced two special difficulties. For the last three quarters of fiscal year ending June 30, 1861, certain ports of the Southern states failed to make reports, and it was necessary for the Treasury Department to introduce estimates of the exports of cotton by the Southern states during the war based on records of the main recipient countries in Europe (see U.S. Treasury Department 1864, p. 39).

The second difficulty was introduced in 1862 when the United States abandoned the specie backing for its money. The dollar fluctuated against foreign currencies and gold with each reverse or success of the Northern forces. Imports and reexports continued to be valued in specie (dollars of a fixed parity to gold) because these goods were initially expressed in foreign currencies, but domestic exports were recorded in "mixed values" – partly gold dollars and

---

[1] This section is taken largely from *Historical Statistics of the United States* (1975).

partly dollars of a fluctuating value – from 1862 until the resumption of specie payment in 1879. These deficiencies were recognized at the time both officially by the Director of the Bureau of Statistics (established in the Treasury Department in 1866) and by private observers.[2] Treasury statisticians sought to adjust mixed currency values to specie values of total imports and exports and some other broad aggregates. The adjustments, however, were not carried through completely to country and commodity detail, and only a limited number of domestic export series are available for 1862–1879 in terms of "specie values," while the domestic export figures for countries and individual commodities are available only in mixed currency values.

When Congress established the Bureau of Statistics in 1866, it also specified that the kinds, quantities, and values of all articles exported and imported should be distinctly set forth in the statistical accounts, by countries of destination or of shipment, and that the exports of articles produced or manufactured in the United States should be shown separately from the reexports of foreign articles imported into the United States. Prior to 1866, only annual statistics of the foreign commerce of the United States were published; since then, monthly statistics have also been published. Since the first appearance of the *Statistical Abstract of the United States* in 1878, official time series on foreign trade have been presented in that publication; therefore, it is cited here as a primary source for certain of the foreign trade data shown.

The first report of the Director of the Bureau of Statistics in 1867 contains several pointed criticisms of the previous statistics, and the subsequent annual reports of *Foreign Commerce and Navigation* emphasized the shortcomings of the figures presented, especially the difficulty, which became important in the post–Civil War period, of reporting on trade with Canada in the absence of any mandatory reporting requirement of the railroads.[3] An Act of March 3, 1893, provided for obtaining information on exports by rail and apparently eliminated this deficiency in the subsequent figures, but prior to that time trade totals and figures on trade with Canada suffer from lack of coverage in varying degrees.[4]

In 1923, the function of compiling foreign trade statistics was transferred to the Department of Commerce; the release and publication of the annual figures had been done by that department since 1903. In 1941, the compilation function was transferred from the Bureau of Foreign and Domestic Commerce to the Bureau of the Census.

A problem affecting comparability of value statistics arose between January 31, 1934, and March 10, 1953, when the foreign exchange value of the dollar was permitted to depreciate as a result of the restriction placed on gold shipments to foreign countries. For this period, unless otherwise noted, values stated are in U.S. dollars without reference to changes in the gold parity value of the dollar.

Import data compiled by the Department of Commerce are from import entries (various Customs forms) that importers are required to file with Customs officials for each shipment arriving. Import values are, in general, based on market or selling price and are free on board (f.o.b.) the exporting country. Values do not include import duties. The country of origin is defined as the country in which the merchandise was grown, mined, or manufactured. If the importer cannot obtain the information as to the country of origin, the merchandise is credited (for statistical purposes) to the country of shipment.

Imports are classified as either general imports or imports for consumption. General imports represent total arrivals of imported goods (except for in-transit shipments), that is, merchandise released from Customs custody immediately upon arrival plus merchandise entered into a Customs-bonded storage, manufacturing, or refining warehouse immediately upon arrival. Imports for consumption comprise merchandise entered into the U.S. consumption channels, that is, merchandise released from Customs custody immediately upon arrival, merchandise entered into a Customs-bonded manufacturing warehouse (other than smelting or refining warehouse), merchandise withdrawn from a Customs-bonded storage warehouse for release into domestic consumption channels, and imported ores and crude metals that have been processed in a Customs-bonded smelting warehouse and then withdrawn for consumption and export. During past periods, data for some low-valued imports have been fully compiled while data for others have been estimated.[5]

Export data are from shippers' export declarations, which exporters are required to file with Customs officials for each shipment leaving the United States. Export data include shipments made after World War II under the Department of the Army Civilian Supply Program only for 1948 and subsequent years. In addition, export data include U.S. exports under the Lend-Lease, United Nations Relief and Rehabilitation Administration, Economic Cooperation Administration, Mutual Defense Assistance, and other mutual security programs. Shipments to U.S. armed forces for their own use are not included in export statistics for any period.

Export value figures are based on the selling price (or on the cost, if not sold) of the commodity shipped and include inland freight, insurance, and other charges to the U.S. place of export. Transportation and other costs beyond the U.S. port of exportation are excluded. The country of destination is defined as the country of ultimate destination or country where the merchandise is to be consumed, further processed, or manufactured. In the event the exporter does not have definite information as to the country of ultimate destination for a shipment, it is credited (for statistical purposes) to the country to which it is consigned.

Certain export commodity classifications were grouped for security reasons into special categories beginning with May 1949, with periodic amendments to include additional commodities. With the adoption of new security regulations, effective July 1950, the publication of the country of destination and customs district detail for the special category commodities and groups was discontinued. Effective January 1965, some changes were made in the security

[2] See, for example, Louis Blodgett (1864) for criticism and evaluation of U.S. foreign trade statistics in the early 1860s.

[3] See, for example, U.S. Bureau of Statistics (1878), pp. xii–xiii, table showing "the imports into Ontario, Quebec, and Manitoba, from the United States in excess of the domestic exports from the United States to Canada, as returned to the Bureau of Statistics by U.S. collectors of customs during the fiscal year ended June 30, 1877."

[4] For additional analysis of foreign trade data for 1861–1900, see U.S. Treasury Department (1893), Simon (1960).

[5] Some indication of the undercounting in the detailed commodity statistics for imports is presented in the appendixes to the annual issues, from 1954 to 1965, of U.S. Bureau of the Census, Report FT 110, *United States Imports of Merchandise for Consumption,* and beginning in 1967, U.S. Bureau of the Census, Report FT 135, *Imports, Commodity by Country.* Explanations of the sampling procedures are given in Report FT 110 for 1956; monthly issues of Report FT 135, *Foreign Commerce and Navigation of the United States, 1965;* and annual issues of *Guide to Foreign Trade Statistics,* all by the U.S. Bureau of the Census.

restrictions primarily because of revisions in export commodity classifications. Permission was granted to release data on exports of some commodities, which were previously classified as special category commodities with the result that security restrictions were applied to considerably fewer commodities than before. In addition, permission was granted to release some commodity data for 1964 and prior years, which was withheld when statistics for those years were initially released. Data for special category commodities are included, however, in all total export statistics and in the category of finished manufactures (except automobiles and parts, from which machinery and vehicles manufactured to military specifications have been excluded beginning in July 1949).[6]

The geographic area covered by these statistics, except as noted, is the U.S. customs area, which includes Alaska, Hawai'i, and Puerto Rico, and, for 1935–1939, the Virgin Islands.

Recent Changes in the Compilation of Trade Statistics

A thorough overview of the compilation of U.S. trade statistics (as of 1985) is Victor Bailey and Sara Bowden's *Understanding United States Foreign Trade Data* (1985). In 1989, however, the implementation of the Harmonized System (HS) radically changed the U.S. international trade classification system. The HS is an internationally standardized method of reporting international trade transactions with all signatory countries adopting the same definitions and assumptions. Most if not all pre-HS trade series stopped in 1987 or 1988, and the new HS series began in 1988 or 1989. Pre-HS commodity data may not be accurately linked with the replacement data. For such a link that uses a concordance of the pre- and post-HS systems, however, see Feenstra (1996, 1997).

The Omnibus Trade and Competitiveness Act of 1988 required the United States to implement the HS of commodity classification as of January 1, 1989. The change to HS sharply increased the number of commodity classifications at the most detailed level from 10,500 to 14,000 for imports, and from 4,500 to 8,000 for exports. The United States now collects data on the basis of the HS and reports it in the Standard International Trade Classification Revision 3 format (SITC Rev. 3). The world trade community moved toward standardized presentation of international trade data in the 1950s when the United States developed the Standard International Trade Classification (SITC) system.

Before the implementation of the HS, there were six major international trade data classifications unique to the United States: Tariff Schedule of the United States, Annotated (TSUSA); Schedule B; Schedule A; Schedule E; End-Use; and Standard Industrial Classification–based (SIC-based). Prior to the HS, TSUSA and Schedule B were the detailed classification systems in which U.S. import and export data, respectively, were originally recorded. All other U.S. import and export data classification systems were transformations of TSUSA and Schedule B. Schedules A and E were rearrangements of the TSUSA import data and the Schedule B export data in a form closely resembling the SITC format.

The implementation of the HS reduced the number of schedules to five: HTSUSA; HS-based Schedule B; SITC Rev. 3; End-Use; and SIC-based. The U.S. Bureau of Economic Analysis (BEA) reclassifies data from the original census categories based on the characteristics of the goods themselves into categories associated with the principal users of the goods to create the End-Use data. The SIC data facilitate the linkage of foreign and domestic commerce and are a data system unique to the United States.[7] The 1987 SIC revision, however, made SIC more closely fit the HS-based trade data classifications.

Appendix: Terminology

C.i.f. import value. The c.i.f. (cost, insurance, and freight) value represents the value at the first port of arrival. It is import charges plus customs value and, therefore, excludes U.S. import duties.

Calculated duties. The calculated duty represents the estimated import duties collected. Estimated duties are calculated based on the applicable rate(s) as shown in the Harmonized Tariff Schedule.

Customs value. The customs value is the value of imports as appraised by the Customs Service. This value is defined as the price actually paid for merchandise, excluding U.S. import duties, freight, insurance, and other charges.

Domestic exports. Domestic exports include commodities that are grown, produced, or manufactured in the United States and commodities of foreign origin that have been changed in the United States (including U.S. Foreign Trade Zones) or have been enhanced in value.

Dutiable customs value. The dutiable value represents, in general, the customs value of foreign merchandise imported into the United States that is subject to duty.

F.a.s. export value. The f.a.s. (free alongside ship) value is the value of exports at the U.S. port, based on the transaction price, including inland freight, insurance, and other charges. The value excludes the cost of loading the merchandise and also excludes further cost.

Foreign exports. Foreign exports (reexports) are commodities of foreign origin that have entered the United States for consumption or that are in Customs-bonded warehouses or U.S. Foreign Trade Zones, and that are in substantially the same condition as when they were imported.

General c.i.f. value. The general c.i.f. (cost, insurance, and freight) value represents the landed value of the merchandise. It is computed by adding import charges to the customs value and excludes U.S. import duties.

General customs value. The general customs value is the value of general imports as appraised by the U.S. Customs Service. This is the price actually paid or payable for merchandise, excluding U.S. import duties, freight, insurance, and other charges.

General imports. General imports are the total merchandise physically arriving from foreign countries, whether such merchandise enters consumption channels immediately or

---

[6] Shipments individually valued, prior to October 1969, at less than $100 and, thereafter, at $250 and less, are not classified by commodity but are reported in a single separate category. Details concerning sampling error and procedures are given in U.S. Bureau of the Census, *Quarterly Summary of Foreign Commerce of the United States*, January–December 1956; *Foreign Commerce and Navigation of the United States, 1965*; monthly issues of Report FT 410, *Exports, Schedule B Commodity by Country*; and annual issues of *Guide to Foreign Trade Statistics*.

[7] The SIC system has been replaced by the new North American Industrial Classification System (NAICS). See the Introduction to Part D for a discussion of industrial classification and the SIC and NAICS systems.

is entered into bonded warehouses or Foreign Trade Zones under Customs custody.

Imports for consumption. Imports for consumption are the merchandise that has physically cleared Customs either entering consumption channels immediately or entering after withdrawal from bonded warehouses under Customs custody or from Foreign Trade Zones.

Total exports. Total exports are domestic exports plus foreign exports.

Total f.a.s. export value. The total f.a.s. value is the value of exports at the U.S. port, based on the transaction price, including inland freight, insurance, and other charges. This excludes the cost of loading the merchandise or further costs.

References

Bailey, Victor, and Sara Bowden. 1985. *Understanding United States Foreign Trade Data.* U.S. Department of Commerce, International Trade Administration.

Blodget, Samuel, Jr. 1806. *Economica: A Statistical Manual for the United States of America.* Printed for the author.

Blodgett, Louis. 1864. *The Commercial Financial Strength of the United States as Shown in the Balances of Foreign Trade and the Increased Production of Staple Articles.* King and Baird.

Coxe, Tench. 1794. *A View of the United States of America.* William Hall.

Ely, J. Edward. 1953. "United States." In R. D. G. Allen and J. Edward Ely, editors. *International Trade Statistics.* Wiley.

Feenstra, Robert C. 1996. "U.S. Imports, 1972–1994: Data and Concordances." NBER working paper number 5515.

Feenstra, Robert C. 1997. "U.S. Exports, 1972–1994: With State Exports and Other U.S. Data." NBER working paper number 5990.

North, Douglass C. 1960. "United States Balance of Payments, 1790–1860." In *Trends in the American Economy in the Nineteenth Century: A Report of the National Bureau of Economic Research.* Studies in Income and Wealth, volume 24. Princeton University Press.

Pitkin, Timothy. 1816. *A Statistical View of Commerce of the United States of America.* Charles Hosmer.

Seybert, Adam. 1818. *Statistical Annuals.* Thomas Dobson.

Simon, Mathew. 1960. "Statistical Estimates of the Balance of International Payments and the International Capital Movements of the United States, 1861–1900." In *Trends in the American Economy in the Nineteenth Century: A Report of the National Bureau of Economic Research.* Studies in Income and Wealth, volume 24. Princeton University Press.

U.S. Bureau of Statistics. 1878. *Annual Report of the Chief of the Bureau of Statistics on the Commerce and Navigation of the United States for the Fiscal Year Ended June 30, 1877.*

U.S. Congress. 1832. *American State Papers,* Class 4, "Commerce and Navigation," volume 1. Gales and Seaton.

U.S. Congress. 1834. *American State Papers,* Class 4, "Commerce and Navigation," volume 2. Gales and Seaton.

U.S. Treasury Department. 1864. *Statistics of the Foreign and Domestic Commerce of the United States.*

U.S. Treasury Department. 1893. *Statistical Tables Exhibiting the Commerce of the United States with European Countries from 1790 to 1890.*

EXCHANGE RATES

Lawrence H. Officer

Definition of Exchange Rate

An exchange rate is the price of one currency in terms of another, that is, the number of units of the second currency per unit of the first currency. The currency roles can be reversed. Thus the price of the dollar in terms of a foreign currency (for example, the number of yen per dollar) is the inverse of the price of the foreign currency in terms of the dollar (the number of dollars per yen). If 200 is the price of the dollar in terms of the yen (200 yen per dollar, the exchange value of the dollar), then $\frac{1}{200} = 0.005$ is the price of the yen in terms of the dollar (0.005 dollar per yen, the exchange value of the yen). The exchange rate can also be written as an equation: 200 yen = \$1, or \$0.005 = 1 yen.

Almost all the series in Tables Ee612–683 follow the standard convention in expressing the exchange rate as the number of units of foreign currency per dollar, that is, they show the exchange value of the dollar. Expressing the exchange rate in this way, as the exchange rate increases (decreases), the dollar appreciates (depreciates) in the foreign-exchange market. In other words, the dollar becomes "stronger" ("weaker") – is worth more (less) compared to the foreign currency.

There are three exceptions to the rule that exchange rates be the exchange value of the dollar. These exceptions involve the U.K. pound, the Irish pound, and special drawing rights (SDR). The exchange rate involving the U.K. pound is expressed as the number of dollars per pound (rather than the number of pounds per dollar) both in the tables and in the data source. The proximate explanation for this definition of the exchange rate is tradition. The ultimate explanation is threefold. First, in the nineteenth century, among currencies traded against the dollar in the United States, the British pound was the only unit "larger than the dollar" (worth more than one dollar). Thus, to avoid an exchange rate below unity, the number of dollars per pound rather than its inverse was the exchange-rate expression.[1] Second, the pound sterling (British pound) was of overwhelming importance in the U.S. foreign-exchange market. Third, the pound was the dominant currency in world trade and payments.

Because of its close connection to the U.K. pound, the Irish pound is also expressed as the number of dollars per pound, both in the tables and in the data source. The final exception is the SDR. Because of its role in the international monetary system, this basket of currencies is of special interest. Therefore the pertinent exchange rate is the number of dollars per SDR rather than the inverse, even though the data source presents both the direct and the inverse exchange rate.

When the exchange rate is defined as for the exceptions (number of dollars per unit of foreign currency), a higher (lower) exchange rate now means a weaker (stronger) dollar: the dollar depreciates (appreciates); it is worth less (more) in terms of foreign currency.

Use of Exchange Rate

The primary importance of exchange rates lies in conversion of a price or value from one currency to another. The product of a dollar price or value and the foreign-currency–dollar exchange rate yields the equivalent foreign-currency price or value. The division of a foreign-currency price or value by the foreign-currency–dollar exchange rate yields the equivalent dollar price or value. Such computations are essential to international trade and payments.

The implication of a higher exchange value of the dollar (higher foreign-currency–dollar exchange rate) is that foreign

---

[1] This is the explanation offered in Myers (1931), p. 347.

goods, services, and capital assets are cheaper for Americans, while American goods, services, and capital assets are more expensive for foreigners. The implication of a lower exchange value of the dollar (lower foreign-currency–dollar exchange rate) is that foreign goods, services, and capital assets are more expensive for Americans, while American goods, services, and capital assets are cheaper for foreigners.

Either the current exchange rate or exchange-rate parity can be used for the purpose of converting prices or values between a dollar denomination and a foreign-currency expression (in either direction).

Exchange-Rate Parity

Exchange-rate parity in the form of dollar–sterling parity (number of dollars per pound sterling) is the subject of Table Ee612–614. Parity is a hypothetical rather than actual or quoted exchange rate. It is a norm value of the exchange rate. Traditionally, there are two types of parity. The first is mint parity, which implies gold (or silver) coinage in the countries. Mint parity is the ratio of the gold (or silver) content of the pound to the gold (or silver) content of the dollar; it is the number of grains of gold (or silver) coined per pound divided by the number of grains of gold (or silver) coined per dollar.[2] The result is the gold (or silver) parity. The second concept of parity is legal parity, involving government or central-bank declaration of a parity value and not requiring gold or silver coinage.

Dollar-sterling parity has a long history, going back to 1704, when Queen Anne declared that the Spanish dollar had a "just Proportion" to British coin of 4 shillings and 6 pence (see Officer 1996, p. 50). With 12 shillings per pence and 20 shillings per pound, the pound is equivalent to $\frac{240}{54} = 4.44\frac{4}{9}$ Spanish dollars. Because this parity emanated from a royal proclamation, it was a legal parity. However, the proclaimed value of the Spanish dollar in terms of British coin was based on the relative silver content of the Spanish dollar and British coin, implying that the parity was also mint (silver) parity. Indeed, from colonial times to the mid-1790s, there was no U.S. mint that produced coined money, and the dominant coin in the United States was the Spanish silver dollar. The country was on a silver standard.

Because the Spanish dollar is the forerunner of the American dollar – and indeed, when the U.S. dollar was created in 1792, it was declared equal in value to the Spanish dollar – the parity of $4.44\frac{4}{9}$ per pound was the original dollar–sterling exchange-rate parity and was the parity of custom until 1873. Termed "nominal par" in the nineteenth century, this original mint and legal parity was succeeded by the values listed in series Ee612 as mint parity and by the figures in series Ee613–614 as legal parity. Deviations of the U.S. legal and mint parities from nominal par occurred from their inception, as the series show. Yet, remarkably, until Congressional legislation of 1873, exchange-rate quotations were expressed as a percentage deviation or index number with respect to nominal par as the base (see Officer 1996, p. 59). The use of nominal par was a legal fiction; it was known to contemporaries that it was not the true or applicable parity.

The longevity of nominal par gave rise to the equivalent terminology "technical par" and "customary par." Gold parity was called "real par" and computable even when the United States was on an effective silver standard, that is, prior to July 31, 1834 (see the discussion that follows). Until that date, gold par, at $4.5657, was itself expressed as 2.73 percent above nominal par. From July 31, 1834, gold par was identical to true mint parity. From July 31, 1834, to January 17, 1837, gold par was 9.50 percent over nominal par. From January 18, 1837, to January 30, 1934, it was 9.59 percent over nominal par.

Dollar–Sterling Exchange Rate, 1791–1914

Two features of the dollar–sterling exchange rate from colonial times to World War I are indisputable. First, the British pound was the overwhelmingly important foreign currency in the American foreign-exchange market; therefore, dollar–sterling was the dominant exchange rate. Second, the dollar–sterling foreign-exchange market was located not in London but rather in various American cities, with the dominant location originally Boston, then Philadelphia, possibly Baltimore at the turn of the nineteenth century, and then New York by the early 1820s. So in a fundamental sense the American dollar–sterling exchange market represented not only the American foreign-exchange market but also the dollar–sterling world market (Cole 1929)

Other elements of the dollar–sterling exchange rate are controversial or have been subject to changing views over time. (1) The transatlantic cable was laid in 1866, but there was a half-century delay before the cable transfer became the dominant foreign-exchange instrument, succeeding the sight bill of exchange. Some observers claim in effect that the delay was shorter (Perkins 1975). (2) Traditional exchange-rate series are quoted or advertised rates. Some modern authors consider such series unreliable and insist on series that represent market rates, that is, prices at which actual transactions occur. (3) An exchange-rate series can refer to one exchange-market instrument throughout (for example, sixty-day bill of exchange, sight bill, or cable transfer – these three instruments involve immediate dollar payment but differ on the time at which pounds are received), or it can pertain to the dominant instrument at the time (for example, switching from sixty-day to sight when the latter replaced the former as the primary medium). (4) If time bills of exchange are to be converted to a sight-equivalent basis, it is controversial whether the rate of discount (that is, the rate of interest) should pertain to the drawer city (for example, Philadelphia or New York, where bills are created) or the drawee city (for example, London, where bills are payable). Most modern authors opt for the latter. (5) Exchange rates are generally expressed as the price at which foreign exchange is purchasable; a superior alternative is the midpoint of the buying and selling price, with broker's commission constituting the difference in the prices. (6) An exchange-rate series can be left in pristine form, thereby reflecting whatever monetary standard or exchange-rate system is in existence. Alternatively, the series can be corrected for the depreciation of the dollar (pound) in terms of the metallic standard of Britain (United States) when a gold or silver standard is temporarily relinquished by the United States (Britain) in favor of a paper standard – what is today called a "floating exchange rate." The resulting exchange-rate series permits mint parity to serve as the norm value about which "gold points" are expected to contain the exchange rate.

---

[2] A grain is one 480th of a Troy ounce, or one 437.5th of an avoirdupois ounce. Precious metals are measured in Troy weight; other substances are measured in avoirdupois weight (in the United States) or in metric weight (in most other countries and in international trade).

Table Ee615–620 exhibits six pre–World War I dollar–sterling series, each of which involves a stance on some or all of these issues. The period 1791–1914 encompassed by these series covers a variety of monetary standards for the United States. The monetary standard is important because it affects the range of exchange-rate fluctuations. One must distinguish between the legal and the effective monetary standard (Nussbaum 1950). Legally, the Mint Act of 1786 provided for a bimetallic (both gold and silver) standard, but the Act was not put into effect. The Mint Act of 1792 again established legal bimetallism, which reigned until the legislation of February 12, 1873, which ended coinage of the silver dollar, and June 22, 1874, which limited the legal-tender property of existing silver coin to $5 in any payment. These Acts demonetized silver, thus replacing the legal bimetallic standard with a gold standard, which was confirmed by the Gold Standard Act of March 14, 1900.

The effective monetary standard of the United States was somewhat different from the legal stipulation. The 1792 Act undervalued gold and overvalued silver compared to world markets, and so the country remained on an effective silver standard. The Act of June 28, 1834, did the opposite, placing the United States on an effective gold standard.

Metallic (gold or silver) standards generally confine a country's exchange rate to the neighborhood of mint parity, the range delimited by "gold points." So the exchange rate is fairly stable during these standards, indeed becoming more stable over time as gold points become closer to mint parity (reflecting decreased costs of shipping gold internationally). However, the U.S. metallic standards of 1791–1913 were occasionally disrupted by "paper standards," during which gold points became inoperative and the exchange rate could undergo considerable fluctuation. These periods were August 30, 1814–February 19, 1817; May 10, 1837–March 17, 1842; October 14–December 13, 1857; and the famous "greenback period" of December 30, 1861–December 31, 1878.

Bilateral Exchange Rates, 1913–1999

With World War I, the American foreign-exchange market became diffused in terms of currencies, and the dominance of sterling ended. The market also was to become diffused in location, with the dollar traded actively not only in New York but also often in the foreign country's financial center. Tables Ee621–661 present dollar exchange rates for all foreign currencies for which Federal Reserve publications provide at least one annual exchange-rate observation in the post–World War II period. Presumably, these are the currencies deemed to trade most actively against the dollar.

The period 1913–1999 witnessed a paper standard from April 6, 1917, to March 17, 1922, and again from March 6, 1933, to January 30, 1934. Indeed, the U.S. gold standard was legally terminated by the Act of January 30, 1934, and gold coin could no longer circulate as money. From January 31, 1934, to February 12, 1973, the United States was on a limited international (but no longer domestic) gold standard, with the exchange rate restricted within "parity points" (except for bilateral exchange cases when the other country elected to have a floating exchange rate – for example, Canada in 1950–1962). After World War II, this standard was formalized in the "Bretton Woods," or International Monetary Fund (IMF), system, which broke down temporarily from August 15 to December 17, 1971, and then permanently beginning February 13, 1973. The floating exchange rates that began on that date in 1973 continued to the end of the twentieth century and beyond.

The six issues concerning the pre–World War I dollar–sterling exchange rate, the subject of Table Ee615–620, may be revisited from the perspective of post–World War I dollar exchange rates. (1) With rare exceptions, exchange rates are for cable transfer, that being the dominant exchange-market instrument after World War I. (2) Whenever possible, the series pertain to market rates. Sometimes official rates are used, where data on market rates are unavailable. (3) The cable transfer was dominant through 1999. (4) Time-bill data are not used, and so the issue is not applicable. (5) The primary data source, Federal Reserve publications, provides buying rates for foreign exchange. The secondary data source, the IMF, generates exchange rates that are the midpoints of buying and selling prices of the dollar. Although this treatment is inconsistent, the practices of the respective sources are followed because information on buy–sell spreads is unavailable. Certainly, spreads are much lower in the twentieth century than they were in the nineteenth century, and they exhibit a trend decline over time (see Officer 1996, p. 75). So the inconsistency is of lesser importance in Tables Ee621–661 than it is in Table Ee615–620. (6) The exchange rates are in pristine form; that is, they reflect the current monetary standard or exchange-rate system. There is no correction for depreciation or appreciation of the dollar or foreign currencies with respect to gold. The reason is that the gold standard no longer serves as the norm. Its abandonment by all countries in the 1920s and 1930s marked the termination of the gold standard (Eichengreen 1992).[3]

A seventh issue concerns the expression of the exchange rate when there is a change in the currency unit of a country. This situation does not apply to dollar–sterling exchange rates (Table Ee615–620) because the United States has not experienced a change in its currency unit since the dollar was adopted as the unit of account in 1792, and Britain's pound has remained its primary currency unit.

However, many currencies presented in Tables Ee621–661 have undergone changes in their currency unit since 1913, sometimes multiple changes. Two examples may be considered: France and Germany. In 1960, the new franc replaced the old franc as the monetary unit of France, at the rate 1 new franc = 100 old francs. In 1924, the reichsmark succeeded the mark as the German currency unit, at the rate 1 reichsmark = 1,000,000,000,000 marks; in 1948 the reichsmark was superseded by the deutsche mark, at the rate 1 deutsche mark = 10 reichsmarks. Generally, as in the French and German cases, a new currency unit is worth a multiple of the former currency unit – which might be termed a domestic (as distinct from exchange-market) appreciation of the currency because a lesser amount of the currency is now needed to purchase a given commodity or asset. Exceptional situations are Australia, New Zealand, and South Africa in the 1960s, when the Australian, New Zealand, and South African pound were replaced by the Australian dollar, New Zealand dollar, and South African rand, at the rate 1 dollar or 1 rand = 2 pounds.

How should an exchange-rate series be expressed under such changes in currency unit? There are two sensible choices, and both are selected, each being alternative to the other. One possibility is to adopt the standpoint of contemporaries and accept whatever currency unit is in place at a given time. This is the focus of

---

[3] For a complete list of countries on the gold standard and the periods during which they were on it, see Officer (2001), Tables 1–2.

Tables Ee621–661. For example, in Table Ee621–636, the French-currency–dollar exchange rate is the number of old francs per dollar for 1913–1959 and the number of new francs per dollar for 1960–1999. Another example: the German-currency–dollar exchange rate is the number of marks per dollar for 1913–1924, the number of reichsmarks per dollar for 1925–1941, and the number of deutsche marks per dollar for 1950–1999 (there are gaps in the series). In leaving undisturbed the part of the exchange-rate series prior to alteration of the currency unit, the entire series reflects the perspective of the contemporary observer: it is how the exchange rate was actually measured at the time. Certainly, this is a useful characteristic of an exchange-rate series. To the layperson who wants to know the actual foreign-currency–dollar exchange rate in a given year or to the historian who is interested in a time period that does not span beyond an unchanged currency unit, exchange-rate series in contemporary currency units are necessary; hence Tables Ee621–661.

However, these tables have the disadvantage that the exchange-rate series is not a consistent series: observations are not comparable over a change in currency unit. When multiple changes in currency unit occur, the series becomes more akin to a collection of subseries rather than a true time series. The analyst who is interested in calculating changes in exchange rates over time (for example, in comparison with price-index movements: "purchasing-power-parity" computations) requires exchange-rate series that are consistent over the time period of interest (as, of course, the price indexes should be). Therefore, the alternative is to express an entire exchange-rate series in terms of a given currency unit. Logically, this would be the most recent currency unit. A consistent series is thereby achieved. This is the basis of Table Ee662–678, which provides exchange rates in consistent currency units for those countries (in Tables Ee621–661) that experienced one or more changes in currency unit. In Table Ee662–678, for example, the French-currency–dollar exchange rate is the number of new francs per dollar and the German-currency–dollar exchange rate is the number of deutsche marks – throughout 1913–1999. This uniformity is achieved by converting the contemporary exchange rates into the most recent currency-unit expression.

Consider the French-currency–dollar exchange rate in 1959. In terms of the contemporary currency unit, the old franc, the exchange rate is 490.6771 old francs per dollar (series Ee625). In terms of the most recent currency unit, the new franc, the exchange rate is 4.9068 new francs per dollar (series Ee665); the equivalence 1 new franc = 100 old francs implies that the new-franc–dollar exchange rate is 490.6771/100 = 4.9068 (except for rounding).

The German case is more complex, but it is just as logical. Consider the German-currency–dollar exchange rate in 1920. The contemporary exchange rate is 57.1102 marks per dollar (series Ee626), the mark being the currency unit then in effect. To obtain the corresponding exchange rate in deutsche marks per dollar, the equivalence between the mark and deutsche mark must be obtained. For this purpose, and also to express the exchange rate, scientific notation is convenient.[4] Then: 1 reichsmark = 1,000,000,000,000 marks = 1.0E + 12 marks and 1 deutsche mark = 10 reichsmarks, implying that 1 deutsche mark = 1.0E + 13 marks. Therefore, 57.1102 marks per dollar is equivalent to $57.1102/(1.0E + 13) =$

$57.1102E{-}13 = 5.711E{-}12$ deutsche marks per dollar (series Ee666).

Often, a country changes its currency unit (undertakes a domestic appreciation of its currency) because it has undergone massive inflation that greatly reduces the exchange value of its currency or, equivalently, that greatly increases the exchange value of the dollar versus its currency. Before the inflation occurred, the former currency unit was much stronger against the dollar (the dollar was much weaker against it); and so the consistent (as distinct from contemporary) exchange rate (exchange value of the dollar) is very low prior to the inflation. The preceding example of the German-currency–dollar exchange rate in 1920 illustrates this point: 5.7110E–12 deutsche marks per dollar (the deutsche mark is very strong against the dollar) but only 57.1102 marks per dollar (the contemporary currency unit, the mark, is much weaker against the dollar). The Latin American changes in currency unit are generally of this nature (compare the pertinent series in Tables Ee637–645 and Ee662–678), as is some European experience. Conspicuous cases in which a change in currency unit occurred in the absence of massive inflation are France in 1960 (discussed earlier), South Africa in 1961, Australia in 1966, and New Zealand in 1967.

Multilateral Exchange Rates, 1967–1999

Bilateral exchange rates are the rates observed in the foreign-exchange market, but they relate the dollar to only one foreign currency at a time. If the dollar appreciates against some currencies and depreciates against others, it is logical to inquire whether it appreciates or depreciates in total. Even if the dollar moves in the same direction against a collection of foreign currencies, the magnitudes of the changes may differ, and an average amount of dollar depreciation or appreciation is of interest. Multilateral exchange rates, which are combinations or averages of bilateral rates, provide the series that deal with these issues. In Table Ee679–683, five multilateral exchange rates for the dollar, representing two different methodologies, are presented: a basket of currencies (SDR) and effective exchange rates. They are arbitrary constructs, in the sense that the weights of the currencies composing the basket or effective rate are determined by the creator of the multilateral rate (the IMF and Board of Governors of the Federal Reserve Board, respectively). For more institutional detail, see the annual IMF report, *Exchange Arrangements and Exchange Restrictions*.

References

Cole, Arthur H. 1929. "Evolution of the Foreign-Exchange Market of the United States." *Journal of Economic and Business History* 1 (May): 384–421.

Eichengreen, Barry. 1992. *Golden Fetters: The Gold Standard and the Great Depression, 1919–1939*. Oxford University Press.

International Monetary Fund. *Exchange Arrangements and Exchange Restrictions*. Annual Reports.

Myers, Margaret G. 1931. *The New York Money Market*, volume 1, *Origins and Development*. Columbia University Press.

Nussbaum, Arthur. 1950. *Money in the Law: National and International*. Foundation Press.

Officer, Lawrence H. 1996. *Between the Dollar–Sterling Gold Points: Exchange Rates, Parity, and Market Behavior*. Cambridge University Press.

Officer, Lawrence H. 2001. "Gold Standard." In Robert Whaples, editor. EH.Net Encyclopedia. Available at the EH.Net Internet site.

Perkins, Edwin J. 1975. *Financing Anglo-American Trade: The House of Brown, 1800–1880*. Harvard University Press.

---

[4] In scientific notation, "E + x" following a number means "move the decimal point x places to the right," while "E–y" following a number means "move the decimal place y places to the left."

BALANCE OF PAYMENTS

Michael Edelstein

TABLE Ee1–21 Balance of international payments: 1790–1998[1,2,3]

Contributed by Michael Edelstein

Year	Goods			Services			Balance of goods and services	Investment income, receipts of U.S. assets abroad	Payments on foreign assets in the United States	Investment income, net	Unilateral transfers, net
	Exports	Imports	Net balance	Net military transactions	Net travel and transportation receipts	Other services, net					
	Ee1[4]	Ee2	Ee3	Ee4[5]	Ee5[6]	Ee6[7,8,9,10,11]	Ee7	Ee8[10,12,13,14,15,16]	Ee9[10,13,16,17,18]	Ee10	Ee11[14,19,20]
	Million dollars	Million dollars	Million dollars	Million dollars	Million dollars	Million dollars	Million dollars	Million dollars	Million dollars	Million dollars	Million dollars
1790	21	−24	−3	—	5	−1	1	—	−4	−4	—
1791	21	−31	−10	—	6	−1	−5	—	−4	−4	—
1792	23	−33	−10	—	7	−1	−4	—	−4	−4	—
1793	28	−33	−5	—	12	−1	6	—	−5	−5	−1
1794	36	−36	0	—	15	−1	14	—	−5	−5	—
1795	48	−73	−25	—	19	−3	−9	—	−4	−4	−1
1796	67	−84	−17	—	22	−3	2	—	−5	−5	−1
1797	57	−77	−20	—	17	−3	−6	—	−5	−5	—
1798	62	−72	−10	—	17	−3	4	—	−6	−6	—
1799	80	−81	−1	—	24	−3	20	—	−6	−6	—
1800	74	−93	−19	—	26	−4	3	—	−5	−5	—
1801	95	−114	−19	—	31	−5	7	—	−5	−5	—
1802	75	−78	−3	—	18	−3	12	—	−5	−5	—
1803	59	−67	−8	—	24	−3	13	—	−4	−4	—
1804	81	−87	−6	—	27	−4	17	—	−5	−5	−11
1805	97	−128	−31	—	30	−5	−6	—	−4	−4	—
1806	105	−137	−32	—	34	−6	−4	—	−4	−4	—
1807	109	−146	−37	—	42	−6	−1	—	−5	−5	—
1808	26	−58	−32	—	23	−2	−11	—	−5	−5	—
1809	55	−61	−6	—	26	−2	18	—	−6	−6	—
1810	68	−91	−23	—	39	−4	12	—	−6	−6	—
1811	63	−61	2	—	41	−2	41	—	−5	−5	—
1812	39	−83	−44	—	29	−3	−18	—	−3	−3	—
1813	32	−22	10	—	10	—	20	—	−4	−4	—
1814	8	−16	−8	—	2	—	−6	—	−3	−3	—
1815	55	−85	−30	—	21	−2	−11	—	−4	−4	—
1816	84	−151	−67	—	17	−3	−53	—	−5	−5	—
1817	89	−102	−13	—	11	−2	−4	—	−7	−7	—
1818	95	−128	−33	—	16	−3	−20	—	−6	−6	—
1819	72	−94	−22	—	15	−2	−9	—	−6	−6	—
1820	70	−75	−5	—	9	−2	4	—	−5	−5	1
1821	66	−63	3	—	6	−3	9	—	−5	−5	1
1822	73	−83	−10	—	6	−2	−4	—	−5	−5	—
1823	75	−78	−3	—	10	—	7	—	−5	−5	—
1824	77	−81	−4	—	10	—	6	—	−5	−5	1

	Goods			Services			Balance of goods and services	Investment income, receipts of U.S. assets abroad	Payments on foreign assets in the United States	Investment income, net	Unilateral transfers, net
	Exports	Imports	Net balance	Net military transactions	Net travel and transportation receipts	Other services, net					
	Ee1 [4]	Ee2	Ee3	Ee4 [5]	Ee5 [6]	Ee6 [7,8,9,10,11]	Ee7	Ee8 [10,12,13,14,15,16]	Ee9 [10,13,16,17,18]	Ee10	Ee11 [14,19,20]
Year	Million dollars	Million dollars	Million dollars	Million dollars	Million dollars	Million dollars	Million dollars	Million dollars	Million dollars	Million dollars	Million dollars
1825	100	−96	4	—	7	—	11	—	−5	−5	1
1826	78	−85	−7	—	8	—	1	—	−5	−5	1
1827	83	−80	3	—	9	—	12	—	−5	−5	2
1828	73	−89	−16	—	6	—	−10	—	−4	−4	2
1829	73	−75	−2	—	5	—	3	—	−5	−5	2
1830	74	−71	3	—	8	—	11	—	−5	−5	2
1831	82	−103	−21	—	10	—	−11	—	−4	−4	1
1832	88	−103	−15	—	8	—	−7	—	−5	−5	5
1833	90	−110	−20	—	6	—	−14	—	−5	−5	5
1834	105	−129	−24	—	6	—	−18	—	−6	−6	6
1835	122	−153	−31	—	4	—	−27	—	−7	−7	3
1836	129	−194	−65	—	5	—	−60	—	−9	−9	10
1837	118	−144	−26	—	7	—	−19	—	−9	−9	7
1838	109	−116	−7	—	10	—	3	—	−10	−10	3
1839	121	−165	−44	—	4	—	−40	—	−14	−14	4
1840	133	−109	24	—	15	—	39	—	−12	−12	4
1841	122	−130	−8	—	4	—	−4	—	−8	−8	4
1842	105	−102	3	—	5	—	8	—	−8	−8	6
1843	85	−66	19	—	7	—	26	—	−7	−7	2
1844	112	−111	1	—	6	—	7	—	−7	−7	4
1845	115	−120	−5	—	11	—	6	—	−9	−9	6
1846	114	−126	−12	—	11	—	−1	—	−9	−9	11
1847	160	−151	9	—	10	−8 [27]	11	—	−9	−9	16
1848	155	−161	−6	—	11	−8 [27]	−3	—	−12	−12	13
1849	146	−154	−8	—	11	—	3	—	−12	−12	10
1850	153	−185	−32	—	0	—	−32	—	−12	−12	16
1851	219	−225	−6	—	−1	—	−7	—	−13	−13	15
1852	211	−221	−10	—	−8	—	−18	—	−15	−15	17
1853	231	−279	−48	—	−11	—	−59	—	−16	−16	19
1854	281	−316	−35	—	−8	—	−43	—	−20	−20	21
1855	279	−272	7	—	−7	—	0	—	−22	−22	8
1856	329	−327	2	—	1	—	3	—	−23	−23	8
1857	366	−375	−9	—	−6	—	−15	—	−15	−15	14
1858	326	−293	33	—	0	—	33	—	−15	−15	7
1859	358	−352	6	—	−14	—	−8	—	−23	−23	6
1860	401	−376	25	—	0	—	25	—	−25	−25	8
1861	261	−344	−83	—	5	−1	−79	—	−24	−24	−1
1862	248	−211	37	—	−4	−1	32	—	−30	−30	—
1863	287	−260	27	—	−8	−2	17	—	−31	−31	3
1864	288	−339	−51	—	−24	−5	−80	—	−34	−34	3
1865	261	−256	5	—	−21	−3	−19	—	−45	−45	5
1866	446	−459	−13	—	−22	−5	−40	—	−51	−51	−4
1867	369	−430	−61	—	−26	−5	−92	—	−58	−58	4
1868	395	−382	13	—	−18	−4	−9	—	−67	−67	4
1869	365	−450	−85	—	−14	−6	−105	—	−69	−69	−3

Notes appear at end of table

(continued)

TABLE Ee1–21 Balance of international payments: 1790–1998 *Continued*

	Goods			Services			Balance of goods and services	Investment income, receipts of U.S. assets abroad	Payments on foreign assets in the United States	Investment income, net	Unilateral transfers, net
	Exports	Imports	Net balance	Net military transactions	Net travel and transportation receipts	Other services, net					
	Ee1 [4]	Ee2	Ee3	Ee4 [5]	Ee5 [6]	Ee6 [7,8,9,10,11]	Ee7	Ee8 [10,12,13,14,15,16]	Ee9 [10,13,16,17,18]	Ee10	Ee11 [14,19,20]
Year	Million dollars	Million dollars	Million dollars	Million dollars	Million dollars	Million dollars	Million dollars	Million dollars	Million dollars	Million dollars	Million dollars
1870	473	−475	−2	—	−14	−5	−21	—	−80	−80	1
1871	564	−557	7	—	−17	−7	−17	—	−84	−84	—
1872	539	−662	−123	—	−27	−9	−159	—	−86	−86	4
1873	631	−683	−52	—	−20	−9	−81	—	−99	−99	14
1874	669	−593	76	—	−27	−8	41	—	−102	−102	−11
1875	590	−556	34	—	−27	−8	−1	—	−99	−99	−14
1876	620	−478	142	—	−22	−5	115	—	−96	−96	−11
1877	687	−475	212	—	−17	−6	189	—	−86	−86	−13
1878	780	−462	318	—	−19	−5	294	—	−76	−76	−11
1879	784	−469	315	—	−29	−6	280	—	−78	−78	−8
1880	929	−694	235	—	−31	−11	193	—	−79	−79	−4
1881	936	−672	264	—	−29	−10	225	—	−88	−88	−5
1882	824	−747	77	—	−36	−12	29	—	−84	−84	−13
1883	875	−748	127	—	−38	−12	77	—	−89	−89	−22
1884	822	−730	92	—	−49	−12	31	—	−90	−90	−24
1885	792	−635	157	—	−49	−10	98	—	−86	−86	−27
1886	781	−698	83	—	−55	−12	16	—	−93	−93	−28
1887	774	−759	15	—	−61	−13	−59	—	−98	−98	−28
1888	750	−791	−41	—	−65	−13	−119	—	−107	−107	−30
1889	841	−817	24	—	−60	−13	−49	—	−118	−118	−44
1890	921	−866	55	—	−66	−14	−25	—	−125	−125	−45
1891	997	−875	122	—	−63	−14	45	—	−134	−134	−50
1892	1,084	−888	196	—	−60	−13	123	—	−143	−143	−54
1893	974	−898	76	—	−42	−14	20	—	−139	−139	−44
1894	943	−692	251	—	−30	−9	212	—	−113	−113	−54
1895	855	−774	81	—	−71	−11	−1	—	−126	−126	−55
1896	1,048	−816	232	—	−64	−12	156	—	−122	−122	−49
1897	1,136	−803	333	—	−63	−11	259	—	−127	−127	−41
1898	1,304	−653	651	—	−66	−9	576	—	−133	−133	−44
1899	1,363	−735	628	—	−67	−10	551	—	−124	−124	−68
1900 [26]	1,534	−894	640	—	−86	−12	542	—	−114	−114	−54
1900 [26]	1,623	−869	754	—	−148	—	606	38	−137	−99	−95
1901	1,585	−912	673	—	−147	—	526	47	−135	−88	−104
1902	1,473	−996	477	—	−139	—	338	57	−137	−80	−105
1903	1,575	−1,019	556	—	−144	—	412	67	−139	−72	−115
1904	1,563	−1,062	501	—	−151	—	350	70	−141	−71	−137
1905	1,751	−1,215	536	—	−169	—	367	76	−145	−69	−133
1906	1,921	−1,365	556	—	−198	—	358	86	−148	−62	−147
1907	2,051	−1,469	582	—	−220	—	362	87	−153	−66	−177
1908	1,880	−1,159	721	—	−223	—	498	89	−160	−71	−192
1909	1,857	−1,522	335	—	−245	—	90	100	−164	−64	−187

Year	Goods			Services			Balance of goods and services	Investment income, receipts of U.S. assets abroad	Payments on foreign assets in the United States	Investment income, net	Unilateral transfers, net
	Exports	Imports	Net balance	Net military transactions	Net travel and transportation receipts	Other services, net					
	Ee1 [4]	Ee2	Ee3	Ee4 [5]	Ee5 [6]	Ee6 [7, 8, 9, 10, 11]	Ee7	Ee8 [10, 12, 13, 14, 15, 16]	Ee9 [10, 13, 16, 17, 18]	Ee10	Ee11 [14, 19, 20]
	Million dollars	Million dollars	Million dollars	Million dollars	Million dollars	Million dollars	Million dollars	Million dollars	Million dollars	Million dollars	Million dollars
1910	1,995	−1,609	386	—	−276	—	110	108	−172	−64	−204
1911	2,228	−1,576	652	—	−302	—	350	114	−190	−76	−224
1912	2,532	−1,866	666	—	−335	—	331	123	−197	−74	−212
1913	2,600	−1,829	771	—	−324	—	447	137	−210	−73	−207
1914	2,230	−1,815	415	—	−304	—	111	145	−200	−55	−170
1915	3,686	−1,813	1,873	—	−189	—	1,684	200	−136	64	−150
1916	5,560	−2,423	3,137	—	−167	—	2,970	250	−118	132	−150
1917	6,398	−3,006	3,392	—	−167	—	3,225	350	−100	250	−205
1918	6,432	−3,103	3,329	−1,018	−203	—	2,108	450	−100	350	−268
1919	8,891	−3,995	4,896	−757	224	−84	4,279	719	−130	589	−1,044
1920	8,481	−5,384	3,097	−123	148	−75	3,047	596	−120	476	−679
1921	4,586	−2,572	2,014	−65	−64	−103	1,782	445	−105	340	−509
1922	3,929	−3,184	745	−42	−237	−34	432	670	−105	555	−352
1923	4,266	−3,866	400	−33	−219	−16	132	840	−130	710	−365
1924	4,741	−3,684	1,057	−36	−272	−20	729	762	−140	622	−364
1925	5,011	−4,291	720	−39	−337	1	345	912	−170	742	−403
1926	4,922	−4,500	422	−43	−307	1	73	953	−200	753	−381
1927	4,982	−4,240	742	−38	−343	−29	332	981	−240	741	−357
1928	5,249	−4,159	1,090	−44	−415	−59	572	1,080	−275	805	−365
1929	5,347	−4,463	884	−50	−463	−32	339	1,139	−330	809	−377
1930	3,929	−3,104	825	−49	−486	−3	287	1,040	−295	745	−342
1931	2,494	−2,120	374	−48	−366	10	−30	766	−220	546	−319
1932	1,667	−1,343	324	−47	−278	16	15	527	−135	392	−238
1933	1,736	−1,510	226	−41	−179	30	36	437	−115	322	−208
1934	2,238	−1,763	475	−34	−200	58	299	437	−135	302	−172
1935	2,404	−2,462	−58	−41	−211	72	−238	521	−155	366	−182
1936	2,590	−2,546	44	−38	−269	79	−184	569	−270	299	−208
1937	3,451	−3,181	270	−41	−343	129	15	577	−295	282	−235
1938	3,243	−2,173	1,070	−41	−209	86	906	585	−200	385	−182
1939	3,347	−2,409	938	−46	−219	82	755	541	−230	311	−178
1940	4,124	−2,698	1,426	−61	−27	27	1,365	564	−210	354	−210
1941	5,343	−3,416	1,927	−162	77	211	2,053	544	−187	357	−1,136
1942	9,187	−3,499	5,688	−953	353	969	6,057	514	−158	356	−6,336
1943	15,115	−4,599	10,516	−1,763	678	1,253	10,684	509	−155	354	−12,907
1944	16,969	−5,043	11,926	−1,982	799	1,297	12,040	573	−161	412	−14,142
1945	12,473	−5,245	7,228	−2,434	741	148	5,683	589	−231	358	−7,113
1946	11,764	−5,067	6,697	−424	733	310	7,316	772	−212	560	−2,991
1947	16,097	−5,973	10,124	−358	946	145	10,857	1,102	−245	857	−2,722
1948	13,265	−7,557	5,708	−351	374	175	5,906	1,921	−437	1,484	−4,973
1949	12,213	−6,881	5,339	−410	230	208	5,367	1,831	−476	1,355	−5,849
1950	10,203	−9,081	1,122	−56	−120	242	1,188	2,068	−559	1,509	−4,537
1951	14,243	−11,176	3,067	169	298	254	3,788	2,633	−583	2,050	−4,954
1952	13,449	−10,838	2,611	528	83	309	3,531	2,751	−555	2,196	−5,113
1953	12,412	−10,975	1,437	1,753	−238	307	3,259	2,736	−624	2,112	−6,657
1954	12,929	−10,353	2,576	902	−269	305	3,514	2,929	−582	2,347	−5,642

Notes appear at end of table

(continued)

TABLE Ee1–21   Balance of international payments: 1790–1998   Continued

	Goods				Services						
	Exports	Imports	Net balance	Net military transactions	Net travel and transportation receipts	Other services, net	Balance of goods and services	Investment income, receipts of U.S. assets abroad	Payments on foreign assets in the United States	Investment income, net	Unilateral transfers, net
Year	Ee1 [4]	Ee2	Ee3	Ee4 [5]	Ee5 [6]	Ee6 [7, 8, 9, 10, 11]	Ee7	Ee8 [10, 12, 13, 14, 15, 16]	Ee9 [10, 13, 16, 17, 18]	Ee10	Ee11 [14, 19, 20]
	Million dollars	Million dollars	Million dollars	Million dollars	Million dollars	Million dollars	Million dollars	Million dollars	Million dollars	Million dollars	Million dollars
1955	14,424	−11,527	2,897	−113	−297	299	2,786	3,406	−676	2,730	−5,086
1956	17,556	−12,803	4,753	−221	−361	447	4,618	3,837	−735	3,102	−4,990
1957	19,562	−13,291	6,271	−423	−189	482	6,141	4,180	−796	3,384	−4,763
1958	16,414	−12,952	3,462	−849	−633	486	2,466	3,790	−825	2,965	−4,647
1959	16,458	−15,310	1,148	−831	−821	573	69	4,132	−1,061	3,071	−4,422
1960	19,650	−14,758	4,892	−1,057	−964	639	3,508	4,616	−1,238	3,379	−4,062
1961	20,108	−14,537	5,571	−1,131	−978	732	4,195	4,999	−1,245	3,755	−4,127
1962	20,781	−16,260	4,521	−912	−1,152	912	3,370	5,618	−1,324	4,294	−4,277
1963	22,272	−17,048	5,224	−742	−1,309	1,036	4,210	6,157	−1,560	4,596	−4,392
1964	25,501	−18,700	6,801	−794	−1,146	1,161	6,022	6,824	−1,783	5,041	−4,240
1965	26,461	−21,510	4,951	−487	−1,280	1,480	4,664	7,437	−2,088	5,350	−4,583
1966	29,310	−25,493	3,817	−1,043	−1,331	1,497	2,940	7,528	−2,481	5,047	−4,955
1967	30,666	−26,866	3,800	−1,187	−1,750	1,742	2,604	8,021	−2,747	5,274	−5,294
1968	33,626	−32,991	635	−596	−1,548	1,759	250	9,367	−3,378	5,990	−5,629
1969	36,414	−35,807	607	−718	−1,763	1,964	91	10,913	−4,869	6,044	−5,735
1970	42,469	−39,866	2,603	−641	−2,038	2,330	2,254	11,746	−5,515	6,233	−6,156
1971	43,319	−45,579	−2,260	653	−2,345	2,649	−1,303	12,707	−5,435	7,272	−7,402
1972	49,381	−55,797	−6,416	1,072	−3,063	2,965	−5,443	14,765	−6,572	8,192	−8,544
1973	71,410	−70,499	911	740	−3,158	3,406	1,900	21,808	−9,655	12,153	−6,913
1974	98,306	−103,811	−5,505	165	−3,184	4,231	−4,292	27,587	−12,084	15,503	−9,249 [28]
1975	107,088	−98,185	8,903	1,461	−2,812	4,854	12,404	25,351	−12,564	12,787	−7,075
1976	114,745	−124,228	−9,483	931	−2,558	5,027	−6,082	29,375	−13,311	16,063	−5,686
1977	120,816	−151,907	−31,091	1,731	−3,565	5,680	−27,246	32,354	−14,217	18,137	−5,226
1978	142,075	−176,002	−33,927	857	−3,573	6,879	−29,763	42,088	−21,680	20,408	−5,788
1979	184,439	−212,007	−27,568	−1,313	−2,935	7,251	−24,565	63,834	−32,961	30,873	−6,593
1980	224,250	−249,750	−25,500	−1,822	−997	8,912	−19,407	72,606	−42,532	30,074	−8,349
1981	237,044	−265,067	−28,023	−844	144	12,552	−16,172	86,529	−53,626	32,903	−11,702
1982	211,157	−247,642	−36,485	112	−992	13,209	−24,156	91,690	−56,572	35,118	−17,139
1983	201,799	−268,901	−67,102	−563	−4,227	14,124	−57,767	90,050	−53,703	36,347	−17,778
1984	219,926	−332,418	−112,492	−2,547	−8,438	14,404	−109,073	108,958	−73,977	34,981	−20,661
1985	215,915	−338,088	−122,173	−4,390	−9,798	14,483	−121,880	98,736	−73,156	25,580	−22,762
1986	223,344	−368,425	−145,081	−5,181	−8,779	17,484	−139,786	96,366	−79,229	15,368	−24,818
1987	250,208	−409,765	−159,557	−3,844	−8,010	17,314	−152,753	107,434	−91,935	14,155	−24,047
1988	320,230	−447,189	−126,959	−6,320	−3,013	19,984	−115,455	136,005	−116,605	18,548	−26,139
1989	362,120	−477,365	−115,245	−6,749	3,551	25,665	−91,509	160,549	−139,556	19,724	−27,116
1990	389,307	−498,337	−109,030	−7,599	7,501	26,897	−79,939	170,906	−140,185	28,429	−27,821
1991	416,913	−490,981	−74,068	−5,274	16,561	30,563	−29,484	148,268	−121,582	23,950	9,819
1992	440,352	−536,458	−96,106	−1,448	19,969	37,232	−37,025	131,098	−105,501	22,269	−35,873
1993	456,832	−589,441	−132,609	1,385	19,714	37,873	−69,940	133,187	−106,313	23,176	−38,522
1994	502,398	−668,590	−166,192	2,570	16,305	44,513	−98,395	164,425	−144,109	15,907	−39,192
1995	575,845	−749,574	−173,729	4,600	21,772	45,316	−97,539	210,472	−186,560	19,410	−35,437
1996	612,057	−803,327	−191,270	4,707	24,969	52,732	−104,318	222,863	−201,109	17,210	−42,187
1997	679,715	−876,366	−196,651	5,863	21,948	59,156	−104,730	256,861	−248,676	3,231	−41,966
1998	670,246	−917,178	−246,932	4,314	10,405	62,682	−164,282	256,467	−263,423	−12,205	−44,075

		U.S. assets abroad, net				Foreign assets in the United States, net				
	Balance on current account	Total	U.S. official reserves assets, net [21]	Other U.S. government assets	U.S. private assets [10, 15, 16, 22, 23]	Total [21, 24]	Foreign official assets	Other foreign assets [16, 22, 23, 25]	Allocations of special drawing rights (SDRs)	Statistical discrepancy
	Ee12	Ee13	Ee14	Ee15	Ee16	Ee17	Ee18	Ee19	Ee20	Ee21
Year	Million dollars	Million dollars	Million dollars	Million dollars	Million dollars	Million dollars	Million dollars	Million dollars	Million dollars	Million dollars
1790	−1	—	—	—	—	1	—	—	—	—
1791	−8	—	—	—	—	8	—	—	—	—
1792	−8	—	—	—	—	8	—	—	—	—
1793	2	—	—	—	—	−2	—	—	—	—
1794	9	—	—	—	—	−9	—	—	—	—
1795	−13	—	—	—	—	13	—	—	—	—
1796	−4	—	—	—	—	4	—	—	—	—
1797	−11	—	—	—	—	11	—	—	—	—
1798	−2	—	—	—	—	2	—	—	—	—
1799	15	—	—	—	—	−15	—	—	—	—
1800	−2	—	—	—	—	2	—	—	—	—
1801	2	—	—	—	—	−2	—	—	—	—
1802	7	—	—	—	—	−7	—	—	—	—
1803	−3	—	—	—	—	3	—	—	—	—
1804	12	—	—	—	—	−12	—	—	—	—
1805	−10	—	—	—	—	10	—	—	—	—
1806	−7	—	—	—	—	7	—	—	—	—
1807	−5	—	—	—	—	5	—	—	—	—
1808	−17	—	—	—	—	17	—	—	—	—
1809	12	—	—	—	—	−12	—	—	—	—
1810	7	—	—	—	—	−7	—	—	—	—
1811	35	—	—	—	—	−35	—	—	—	—
1812	−21	—	—	—	—	21	—	—	—	—
1813	15	—	—	—	—	−15	—	—	—	—
1814	−9	—	—	—	—	9	—	—	—	—
1815	−15	—	—	—	—	15	—	—	—	—
1816	−58	—	—	—	—	58	—	—	—	—
1817	−11	—	—	—	—	11	—	—	—	—
1818	−25	—	—	—	—	25	—	—	—	—
1819	−15	—	—	—	—	15	—	—	—	—
1820	2	—	—	—	—	−1	—	—	—	—
1821	5	—	—	—	—	−5	—	—	—	—
1822	−9	—	—	—	—	8	—	—	—	—
1823	2	—	—	—	—	−2	—	—	—	—
1824	—	—	—	—	—	−1	—	—	—	—
1825	7	—	—	—	—	−7	—	—	—	—
1826	−3	—	—	—	—	3	—	—	—	—
1827	10	—	—	—	—	−10	—	—	—	—
1828	−12	—	—	—	—	11	—	—	—	—
1829	—	—	—	—	—	−2	—	—	—	—
1830	8	—	—	—	—	−8	—	—	—	—
1831	−14	—	—	—	—	14	—	—	—	—
1832	−7	—	—	—	—	7	—	—	—	—
1833	−14	—	—	—	—	14	—	—	—	—
1834	−18	—	—	—	—	19	—	—	—	—

Notes appear at end of table

(continued)

TABLE Ee1–21   Balance of international payments: 1790–1998   *Continued*

	Balance on current account	U.S. assets abroad, net				Foreign assets in the United States, net			Allocations of special drawing rights (SDRs)	Statistical discrepancy
		Total	U.S. official reserves assets, net	Other U.S. government assets	U.S. private assets	Total	Foreign official assets	Other foreign assets		
Year	Ee12	Ee13	Ee14 [21]	Ee15	Ee16 [10, 15, 16, 22, 23]	Ee17 [21, 24]	Ee18	Ee19 [16, 22, 23, 25]	Ee20	Ee21
	Million dollars	Million dollars	Million dollars	Million dollars	Million dollars	Million dollars	Million dollars	Million dollars	Million dollars	Million dollars
1835	−30	—	—	—	—	30	—	—	—	—
1836	−58	—	—	—	—	59	—	—	—	—
1837	−21	—	—	—	—	22	—	—	—	—
1838	−4	—	—	—	—	3	—	—	—	—
1839	−49	—	—	—	—	49	—	—	—	—
1840	30	—	—	—	—	−31	—	—	—	—
1841	−8	—	—	—	—	8	—	—	—	—
1842	7	—	—	—	—	−6	—	—	—	—
1843	22	—	—	—	—	−22	—	—	—	—
1844	—	—	—	—	—	−4	—	—	—	—
1845	4	—	—	—	—	−4	—	—	—	—
1846	1	—	—	—	—	−1	—	—	—	—
1847	19	—	—	—	—	−19	—	—	—	—
1848	−2	—	—	—	—	2	—	—	—	—
1849	2	—	—	—	—	−3	—	—	—	—
1850	−28	—	—	—	—	29	—	—	—	—
1851	−5	—	—	—	—	6	—	—	—	—
1852	−16	—	—	—	—	16	—	—	—	—
1853	−56	—	—	—	—	56	—	—	—	—
1854	−42	—	—	—	—	42	—	—	—	—
1855	−14	—	—	—	—	15	—	—	—	—
1856	−12	—	—	—	—	12	—	—	—	—
1857	−16	—	—	—	—	17	—	—	—	—
1858	24	—	—	—	—	−23	—	—	—	—
1859	−26	—	—	—	—	26	—	—	—	—
1860	7	—	—	—	—	−7	—	—	—	—
1861	−104	—	—	—	—	103	—	—	—	—
1862	—	—	—	—	—	—	—	—	—	—
1863	−12	—	—	—	—	13	—	—	—	—
1864	−111	—	—	—	—	111	—	—	—	—
1865	−59	—	—	—	—	59	—	—	—	—
1866	−95	—	—	—	—	95	—	—	—	—
1867	−145	—	—	—	—	145	—	—	—	—
1868	−73	—	—	—	—	73	—	—	—	—
1869	−175	—	—	—	—	176	—	—	—	—
1870	−100	—	—	—	—	100	—	—	—	—
1871	−101	—	—	—	—	101	—	—	—	—
1872	−242	—	—	—	—	242	—	—	—	—
1873	−167	—	—	—	—	167	—	—	—	—
1874	−72	—	−11	—	—	82	—	—	—	—
1875	−113	—	27	—	—	87	—	—	—	—
1876	9	—	−10	—	—	2	—	—	—	—
1877	89	—	−33	—	—	−57	—	—	—	—
1878	207	—	−44	—	—	−162	—	—	—	—
1879	194	—	−34	—	—	−160	—	—	—	—

Year	Balance on current account	U.S. assets abroad, net				Foreign assets in the United States, net			Allocations of special drawing rights (SDRs)	Statistical discrepancy
		Total	U.S. official reserves assets, net	Other U.S. government assets	U.S. private assets	Total	Foreign official assets	Other foreign assets		
	Ee12	Ee13	Ee14 [21]	Ee15	Ee16 [10, 15, 16, 22, 23]	Ee17 [21, 24]	Ee18	Ee19 [16, 22, 23, 25]	Ee20	Ee21
	Million dollars	Million dollars	Million dollars	Million dollars	Million dollars	Million dollars	Million dollars	Million dollars	Million dollars	Million dollars
1880	110	—	-140	—	—	30	—	—	—	—
1881	132	—	-91	—	—	-41	—	—	—	—
1882	-68	—	-42	—	—	110	—	—	—	—
1883	-34	—	-17	—	—	51	—	—	—	—
1884	-83	—	-23	—	—	105	—	—	—	—
1885	-15	—	-19	—	—	34	—	—	—	—
1886	-105	—	-32	—	—	137	—	—	—	—
1887	-185	—	-46	—	—	231	—	—	—	—
1888	-256	—	-30	—	—	287	—	—	—	—
1889	-210	—	8	—	—	202	—	—	—	—
1890	-195	—	1	—	—	194	—	—	—	—
1891	-140	—	4	—	—	136	—	—	—	—
1892	-74	—	33	—	—	41	—	—	—	—
1893	-163	—	17	—	—	146	—	—	—	—
1894	44	—	22	—	—	-66	—	—	—	—
1895	-182	—	44	—	—	137	—	—	—	—
1896	-15	—	-25	—	—	40	—	—	—	—
1897	91	—	-68	—	—	-23	—	—	—	—
1898	400	—	-121	—	—	-279	—	—	—	—
1899	359	—	-130	—	—	-229	—	—	—	—
1900 [26]	375	—	-78	—	—	-296	—	—	—	—
1900 [26]	412	-234	-91	—	-143	-75	—	—	—	-103
1901	334	-273	-61	—	-212	-33	—	—	—	-28
1902	153	-176	-71	—	-105	-30	—	—	—	53
1903	225	-112	-71	—	-41	20	—	—	—	-133
1904	142	-134	-25	-40 [29]	-69	59	—	—	—	-67
1905	165	-210	-71	—	-139	56	—	—	—	-11
1906	149	-217	-171	—	-46	114	—	—	—	-46
1907	119	-219	-154	—	-65	136	—	—	—	-36
1908	235	17	-44	—	61	89	—	—	—	-145
1909	-161	-94	18	—	-112	171	—	—	—	84
1910	-158	-161	-71	—	-90	345	—	—	—	-26
1911	50	-213	-90	—	-123	171	—	—	—	-8
1912	45	-290	-81	—	-209	232	—	—	—	13
1913	167	-190	-25	—	-165	252	—	—	—	-229
1914	-114	460	100	450	-90	18	—	—	—	86
1915	1,598	-839	-499	450	-790	-339	—	—	—	30
1916	2,952	-2,495	-531	-900	-1,064	-1,291	—	—	—	-66
1917	3,270	-4,562	-312	-3,656	-594	364	—	—	—	928
1918	2,190	-4,429	-5	-4,028	-396	422	—	—	—	1,817
1919	3,824	-2,331	166	-2,328	-169	-215	—	—	—	-1,278
1920	2,844	-661	68	-175	-554	-278	—	—	—	-1,905
1921	1,613	-1,293	-735	30	-588	-4	—	—	—	-316
1922	645	-1,060	-269	31	-822	7	—	—	—	408
1923	477	-689	-315	91	-465	387 [30]	—	—	—	-175
1924	987	-1,222	-256	28	-994	413 [30]	—	—	—	-178

(continued)

Notes appear at end of table

TABLE Ee1–21 Balance of international payments: 1790–1998 Continued

Year	Balance on current account	U.S. assets abroad, net				Foreign assets in the United States, net				Statistical discrepancy
		Total	U.S. official reserves assets, net	Other U.S. government assets	U.S. private assets	Total	Foreign official assets	Other foreign assets	Allocations of special drawing rights (SDRs)	
	Ee12	Ee13	Ee14 [21]	Ee15	Ee16 [10, 15, 16, 22, 23]	Ee17 [21, 24]	Ee18	Ee19 [16, 22, 23, 25]	Ee20	Ee21
	Million dollars	Million dollars	Million dollars	Million dollars	Million dollars	Million dollars	Million dollars	Million dollars	Million dollars	Million dollars
1925	684	−790	100	27	−917	241 [30]	—	—	—	−135
1926	445	−920	−93	30	−857	550	—	—	—	−75
1927	716	−1,177	113	46	−1,336	884	—	—	—	−423
1928	1,012	−1,254	238	49	−1,541	346	—	—	—	−104
1929	771	−941	−143	38	−836	554	—	—	—	−384
1930	690	−788	−310	77	−555	−222	—	—	—	320
1931	197	1,203	133	14	1,056	−1,199	—	—	—	99
1932	169	451	−53	26	478	−699	—	—	—	79
1933	150	118	131	−7	−6	−329 [31]	—	—	—	61
1934	429	−982	−1,266	−5	289	141 [31]	—	—	—	412
1935	−54	−1,268	−1,822	1	553	968	—	—	—	364
1936	−93	−1,040	−1,272	3	229	976	—	—	—	157
1937	62	−1,043	−1,364	2	319	556	—	—	—	425
1938	1,109	−1,732	−1,799	−9	76	374	—	—	—	249
1939	888	−2,849	−3,174	−14	339	1,173	—	—	—	788
1940	1,509	−4,049	−4,243	−51	245	1,263	—	—	—	1,277
1941	1,274	−1,023	−719	−391	87	−727	—	—	—	476
1942	77	−167	23	−221	31	98	—	—	—	−8
1943	−1,869	676	757	−109	28	1,159	—	—	—	34
1944	−1,690	1,043	1,350	−231	−76	684	—	—	—	−37
1945	−1,072	−1,021	548	−1,019	−550	2,085	—	—	—	8
1946	4,885	−4,060	−623	−3,024	−413	−985	—	—	—	160
1947	8,992	−8,481	−3,315	−4,224	−942	−1,327	—	—	—	816
1948	2,417	−3,666	−1,736	−1,024	−906	558	—	—	—	691
1949	873	−1,471	−266	−652	−553	174	—	—	—	424
1950	−1,840	337	1,758	−156	−1,265	1,912	—	—	—	−409
1951	884	−1,237	−33	−156	−1,048	581	—	—	—	−228
1952	614	−1,995	−415	−420	−1,160	1,673	—	—	—	−292
1953	−1,286	655	1,256	−218	−383	1,074	—	—	—	−443
1954	219	−1,049	480	93	−1,622	1,310	—	—	—	−480
1955	430	−1,383	182	−310	−1,255	1,357	—	—	—	−404
1956	2,730	−4,569	−869	−629	−3,071	2,457	—	—	—	−618
1957	4,762	−5,700	−1,165	−958	−3,577	1,132	—	—	—	−194
1958	784	−1,615	2,292	−971	−2,936	1,259	—	—	—	−428
1959	−1,282	−1,693	1,035	−353	−2,375	3,571	—	—	—	−596
1960	2,825	−4,099	2,145	−1,100	−5,144	2,294	1,473	821	—	−1,019
1961	3,822	−5,538	607	−910	−5,235	2,705	765	1,939	—	−989
1962	3,387	−4,174	1,535	−1,085	−4,623	1,911	1,270	641	—	−1,124
1963	4,414	−7,270	378	−1,662	−5,986	3,217	1,986	1,231	—	−360
1964	6,823	−9,560	171	−1,680	−8,050	3,643	1,660	1,983	—	−907
1965	5,431	−5,716	1,225	−1,605	−5,336	742	134	607	—	−457
1966	3,031	−7,321	570	−1,543	−6,347	3,661	−672	4,333	—	629
1967	2,583	−9,757	53	−2,423	−7,386	7,379	3,451	3,928	—	−205
1968	611	−10,977	−870	−2,274	−7,833	9,928	−774	10,703	—	438
1969	399	−11,585	−1,179	−2,200	−8,206	12,702	−1,301	14,002	—	−1,516

	Balance on current account	U.S. assets abroad, net				Foreign assets in the United States, net			Allocations of special drawing rights (SDRs)	Statistical discrepancy
		Total	U.S. official reserves assets, net	Other U.S. government assets	U.S. private assets	Total	Foreign official assets	Other foreign assets		
	Ee12	Ee13	Ee14 21	Ee15	Ee16 10, 15, 16, 22, 23	Ee17 21, 24	Ee18	Ee19 16, 22, 23, 25	Ee20	Ee21
Year	Million dollars	Million dollars	Million dollars	Million dollars	Million dollars	Million dollars	Million dollars	Million dollars	Million dollars	Million dollars
1970	2,331	−9,337	2,481	−1,589	−10,229	6,359	6,908	−550	867	−219
1971	−1,433	−12,475	2,349	−1,884	−12,940	22,970	26,879	−3,909	717	−9,779
1972	−5,795	−14,497	−4	−1,568	−12,925	21,461	10,475	10,986	710	−1,879
1973	7,140	−22,874	158	−2,644	−20,388	18,388	6,026	12,362	0	−2,654
1974	1,962	−34,745	−1,467	366	−33,643	35,341	10,546	24,796	0	−2,558
1975	18,116	−39,703	−849	−3,474	−35,380	17,170	7,027	10,143	0	4,417
1976	4,295	−51,269	−2,558	−4,214	−44,498	38,018	17,693	20,326	0	8,955
1977	−14,335	−34,785	−375	−3,693	−30,717	53,219	36,816	16,403	0	−4,099
1978	−15,143	−61,130	732	−4,660	−57,202	67,036	33,678	33,358 32	0	9,236
1979	−285	−64,915	−1,133	−3,746	−61,176	40,852	−13,665	54,516 32	0	24,349
1980	2,317	−85,815	−8,155	−5,162	−73,651	62,612	15,497	47,115 32	1,152	20,886
1981	5,030	−113,054	−5,175	−5,097	−103,875	86,232	4,960	81,272 32	1,093	21,792
1982	−6,177	−127,825	−4,965	−6,131	−116,729	96,578	3,593	92,986 32	0	37,224
1983	−39,198	−66,423	−1,196	−5,006	−60,222	88,783	5,845	82,938 32	0	16,630
1984	−94,753	−40,515	−3,131	−5,489	−31,896	117,973	3,140	114,833	0	17,059
1985	−119,062	−44,946	−3,858	−2,821	−38,268	146,452	−1,119	147,570	0	17,242
1986	−149,236	−111,933	312	−2,022	−110,224	230,345	35,648	194,696	0	30,524
1987	−162,645	−79,540	9,149	1,006	−89,694	249,016	45,387	203,629	0	−7,196
1988	−123,046	−106,860	−3,912	2,967	−105,915	246,948	39,758	207,190	0	−17,535
1989	−98,900	−175,662	−25,293	1,233	−151,602	225,307	8,503	216,804	0	48,920
1990	−79,332	−81,570	−2,158	2,317	−81,729	142,028	33,910	108,118	0	25,454
1991	4,284	−64,732	5,763	2,924	−73,419	111,332	17,389	93,944	0	−46,405
1992	−50,629	−74,877	3,901	−1,667	−77,111	171,815	40,477	131,338	0	−46,921
1993	−85,286	−201,014	−1,379	−351	−199,284	283,230	71,753	211,477	0	3,157
1994	−121,680	−176,586	5,346	−390	−181,542	307,306	39,583	267,723	0	−8,571
1995	−113,566	−330,675	−9,742	−984	−319,949	467,552	109,880	357,672	0	−23,683
1996	−129,295	−380,762	6,668	−989	−386,441	574,847	127,390	447,457	0	−65,462
1997	−143,465	−465,296	−1,010	68	−464,354	751,661	18,119	733,542	0	−143,192
1998	−220,562	−292,818	−6,784	−429	−285,605	502,637	−21,684	524,321	0	10,126

1 Credits (+); debits (−).

2 Beginning in 1983, revised estimates of merchandise exports, merchandise imports, other transportation receipts, and other transport payments reflecting improvements in the arrival dates of merchandise imports. *Survey of Current Business (SCB)*, October 1985, p. 3; *SCB*, June 1986, p. 41.

3 Data before and after 1900 are not fully compatible. Two sets of data are provided for 1900. See text.

4 Prior to 1946, military grants and receipts for military cash and credit transactions are included in merchandise exports. Military grants are also included in unilateral transfers, net.

5 Prior to 1946, includes only overseas military expenditures. For 1790–1945, military grants and receipts for military cash and credit transactions are included in merchandise exports. For 1946–1999, this series includes military grants, military cash and credit transactions, and overseas military expenditures. Military grants are also included in unilateral transfers, net.

6 Revised or new estimates starting in 1984 and 1986. See text.

7 For 1919–1939, includes certain adjustments to merchandise transactions.

8 Beginning in 1982, data are presented on a gross basis. The definition of exports was revised to exclude U.S. parents' payments to foreign affiliates and to include U.S. affiliates' receipts from foreign parents.

9 Beginning in 1981, change in data coverage and estimates. See text.

10 New estimates of financial services that expand coverage and revise previous coverage starting in 1992. The expanded coverage includes financial management services, financial advisory and custody services, credit card services, securities lending services, foreign exchange brokerage services, and other services that recently became significant elements in service exports and imports. *SCB*, July 1996, pp. 57–9.

11 Beginning in 1986, revised estimates of receipts and payments for financial services, insurance services, and business, professional, and technical services (*SCB*, June 1989, p. 57); new estimates and updated source data for exports of financial services (*SCB*, June 1996, pp. 57–9); new estimates and expanded coverage of earnings and expenditures of foreign residents employed temporarily in the United States (*SCB*, July 1997, pp. 52–3).

12 Beginning in 1946, income on investments includes direct investment fees and royalties.

13 Revised estimates beginning in 1982. See text.

14 Beginning in 1982, new estimates of nonresident taxes (*SCB*, June 1992, pp. 74–5).

15 Beginning in 1988, new estimates of foreign commercial paper issued in the United States and associated income receipts and U.S. bank holdings of foreign certificates of deposit and associated portfolio income estimates (*SCB*, June 1993, p. 61).

16 Beginning in 1991, new source data on new issues of foreign bonds placed in the U.S. market (*SCB*, June 1995, pp. 72–3, 75).

(continued)

TABLE Ee1–21   Balance of international payments: 1790–1998   *Continued*

[17] Net of receipts and payments of investment income, 1790–1900. See text.

[18] Beginning in 1979, includes a new series covering payments on foreign private holdings of U.S. government agency obligations, previously excluded (*SCB*, June 1985, p. 39).

[19] Beginning in 1982, the "other transfers" component includes taxes paid by U.S. private residents to foreign governments and taxes paid by private nonresidents to the U.S. government.

[20] New or revised estimates starting in 1981 and 1986. See text.

[21] For 1874–1900, data in series Ee14 included in net capital movement figure in series Ee17.

[22] Beginning in 1992, new measures of U.S. banks' own claims and liabilities denominated in foreign currencies, the most important being the removal of unrealized currency translation gains and losses from U.S. banks' capital flows (*SCB*, July 1997, p. 53).

[23] Beginning in 1982, revised estimates include the removal of capital gains and losses from direct investment flows (*SCB*, June 1992, p. 73); the shift to measuring direct investment on a current-cost (replacement-cost) basis (*SCB*, June 1992, pp. 72–3); and the removal of the currency translation adjustment (*SCB*, June 1990, pp. 72–3).

[24] U.S. net capital flow, 1900–1970.

[25] Beginning in 1974, new series introduced for foreign-held U.S. currency flows (*SCB*, July 1997, pp. 48–50).

[26] Two sets of data are shown for this year, the first comparable with earlier years, the second with later years. See text for additional information.

[27] Military expenditures in Mexico.

[28] Includes extraordinary U.S. government transactions with India (*SCB*, June 1974, p. 27).

[29] Includes the payment by the U.S. government of $40 million for the original Panama Canal Company. This transaction was not included in Goldsmith's *Study of Saving in the United States*.

[30] Includes transactions in securities that cannot be separated between domestic and foreign.

[31] In 1933, includes a net outflow of $40 million; in 1934, includes a net inflow of $30 million of funds through arbitrage operation in securities, which cannot be divided between domestic and foreign securities.

[32] Includes foreign-currency-denominated notes sold to private residents abroad.

Sources

1790–1918 (except series Ee14, 1874–1900), U.S. Office of Business Economics, unpublished data.

1874–1900, series Ee14, U.S. Department of the Treasury, *Annual Report, Director of the Mint* (1921), p. 130.

1919–1945, U.S. Bureau of Economic Analysis (formerly Office of Business Economics), *Balance of Payments Statistical Supplement* (1958), pp. 10–13.

1946–1964 (except series Ee13 and Ee15–17, 1946–1959), Council of Economic Advisors, *Economic Report of the President* (1997), pp. 414–15.

1946–1959, series Ee13 and Ee15–17, *Survey of Current Business* 50 (6) (June 1970): 34, as revised for 1946 and 1947 in U.S. Bureau of the Census, *Historical Statistics of the United States* (1975), p. 866.

1965–1981, U.S. Bureau of Economic Analysis, *Survey of Current Business* 78 (7) (July 1998): 68–9, 89.

1982–1999, U.S. Bureau of Economic Analysis, *Survey of Current Business* 79 (7) (July 1999): 84–5, 105.

Documentation

The figures for 1790–1918 are from publications by private authors. In preparation for *Historical Statistics of the United States* (1975), the figures, as shown by these authors, were rearranged and adjusted, and in some cases supplemented, by the former U.S. Office of Business Economics (OBE). The reclassified figures fit into the concepts and framework then used in the official balance of payments statements by the OBE, and they continue to be utilized by its successor, the Balance of Payments Division of the Bureau of Economic Analysis.

The original figures are from the following private publications: 1790–1860, Douglass C. North, "The United States Balance of Payments, 1790–1860," in *Trends in the American Economy in the Nineteenth Century: A Report of the National Bureau of Economic Research*, Studies in Income and Wealth, volume 24 (Princeton University Press, 1960); 1861–1900, Matthew Simon, "The United States Balance of Payments, 1861–1900," in *Trends in the American Economy in the Nineteenth Century: A Report of the National Bureau of Economic*

Research, Studies in Income and Wealth, volume 24 (Princeton University Press, 1960); and 1901–1918 (with the exception of exports and imports of merchandise trade and silver), Paul D. Dickens, "The Transitional Period of American International Financing, 1897–1914" (Ph.D. dissertation, George Washington University, 1933), and C. J. Bullock, John H. Williams, and Rufus S. Tucker, "The Balance of Trade of the United States," *Review of Economic Statistics* (1) (July 1919): 215–54. Data on merchandise trade and silver for 1901–1918 were taken from U.S. Department of Commerce, *Monthly Summary of Foreign Commerce* (various issues).

The estimates for 1900–1918 were revised primarily to make them consistent with, and to link them to, data prepared for subsequent years. The revised estimates were published by Raymond W. Goldsmith in *Study of Savings in the United States*, volume 1 (Princeton University Press, 1956), pp. 1078, 1080, 1081, 1084, 1086.

The Department of Commerce began its series in 1922, later extending the data backward to cover 1919–1921. Data for quarterly U.S. international transactions, total and with individual regions of the rest of the world, are available currently in the January, April, July, and October issues of the *Survey of Current Business* (*SCB*). The Balance of Payments Division presents revised and updated historical balance of payments data with a full discussion of its revision methodology annually in the July issue of *SCB*.

The procedure generally followed by North and Simon in their studies was to estimate receipts and payments on account of merchandise trade, transportation, travel, interest, dividends, and remittances. The authors then assumed that the balance indicated net flows of U.S. and foreign capital. This estimate of the net flows of U.S. and foreign capital, 1790–1900, is presented in series Ee13. This balance, of course, includes any errors and omissions in their estimates of international transactions in goods, services, income, and unilateral transfers.

Data on exports and imports of merchandise used in the study by North (1960) are reported to include gold and silver prior to 1821 (see *Statistical Abstract of the United States*, 1957, p. 890). A separate estimate, however, was made by North for net movements of gold because he concluded on the basis of his research that specie movements were in fact not included in the merchandise trade figures prior to 1821. (See North 1960, pp. 24–5.) This estimate is included in series Ee1–2. Although the annual amounts are small, varying from net exports of $1 million to $2.5 million to net imports of $1 million to $4 million, the residual item, or net movement of capital, may be in error by the same amount.

North indicates that the reliability of the data on exports prior to 1820 is doubtful and that data on imports are incomplete. The paucity of information also makes the estimates for other transactions for this period considerably less satisfactory than for subsequent years. Consequently, North suggests that five-year averages may be more reliable than the annual data. Such averages are included in his study.

For the classification and contents of all series in this table for 1900–1918, see Goldsmith (1956). Three transactions that did not appear in Goldsmith's study have been entered. See the text for series Ee11 and Ee15.

For methods of estimating the data for 1919–1945, see Office of Business Economics, *Balance of Payments of the United States, 1949–1951*, a supplement to *SCB*. For 1946–1999, the detailed methodology of the Balance of Payments Division of the Department of Commerce's detailed methodologies is set out in *The Balance of Payments of the United States: Concepts, Data Sources, and Estimating Procedures* (National Technical Information Service, 1990). Changes and improvements in the methods of collecting data have been continuous, and the figures have become progressively more reliable over time, with the latest revisions of current and historical data discussed annually in the July issue of *SCB*.

With the increased complexity and breadth of international transactions, as well as the several changes in the international monetary system, Commerce Department specialists in international transactions statistics and others have regularly evaluated the department's data collection systems, statistical methodologies, and table organization. Important post–World War II evaluations have been: Report of the Review Committee for Balance of Payments Statistics to the Bureau of the Budget, *The Balance of Payments Statistics of the United States: A Review and Appraisal* (April 1965); Advisory Committee on the Presentation of the Balance of Payments, "Report of the Advisory Committee on the Presentation of the Balance of Payments," *SCB* 56 (6)

TABLE Ee1–21 Balance of international payments: 1790–1998 *Continued*

(June 1976): 18–27; R. M. Stern, C. F. Schwartz, et al., "The Presentation of the U. S. Balance of Payments: A Symposium," *Essays in International Finance*, number 123 (August 1977); P. Hooper and J. D. Richardson, editors, *International Economic Transactions: Issues in Measurement and Empirical Research* (University of Chicago Press, 1991); and National Research Council, *Behind the Numbers: U.S. Trade in the World Economy* (National Academy Press, 1992).

Since its origins in 1922, the presentation of the summary balances of international transactions in *SCB* has, with a variable lag, reflected major changes in the international monetary system. Starting in the late 1970s, the summary balances have been separately reported as memoranda at the bottom of the Bureau of Economic Analysis's international transactions table. This change was, in part, a reaction to the termination of the Bretton Woods system of fixed exchange values and the arrival of flexible exchange rates in 1971 and 1973. With flexible exchange rates, changes in the international economy were reflected in shifts in exchange rates, as well as shifts in certain dollar balances.

The presentation of the balances followed here derives from the international transaction table found in the current issues of the annual report of the Council of Economic Advisors. This table puts the sub- and summary balances in the heart of the table. Such a presentation has the advantage that it makes clear the types of transactions that comprise the sub- and summary balances. Under the fixed exchange-rate regimes that were dominant in the United States and the world from 1790 to 1971, the prominence of these balances has some justification. However, it is clear that under the current flexible exchange system of international monetary affairs, there is a danger in treating these balances as the only important indicators of international economic problems and pressures. It therefore should be emphasized that study of the patterns of international economic problems and pressures under the current flexible exchange-rate regime should combine examination and analysis of the patterns of both international transactions and exchange rates.

Series Ee1–3, goods. The estimates for ship sales for 1790–1900 are included in series Ee1. For 1790–1819, the net export and net import of specie are included in series Ee1 and series Ee2, respectively. The gross movements of specie were not available. For 1820–1860, exports of specie are included in series Ee1, and imports are in series Ee2. Exports and imports of gold for 1861–1873, of nonmonetary gold for 1874–1900, and of silver for 1861–1900 are included in series Ee1–2, respectively. The data for 1901–1918 include merchandise trade proper, silver, and nonmonetary gold. The basic data on merchandise trade for 1919–1970 are the official trade statistics published until 1965 in *Foreign Commerce and Navigation* and since then in the foreign trade reports of the Bureau of the Census. For 1919–1999, adjustments in both exports and imports have been made to correct for known overvaluation or undervaluation, to exclude noncommercial items, to include an estimate for unrecorded trade, and to adjust for certain differences in territorial coverage (for example, to exclude the trade with the Panama Canal Zone from 1940 through 1979). For World War II and early postwar years, data on government purchases were substituted for certain import data. For government-financed transfers of merchandise, the figures based on fiscal records were used instead of the figures appearing in the recorded export statistics. For the years after World War I and World War II, sales and other transfers of surplus property located abroad were added to recorded export statistics. Prior to 1946, series Ee1 also includes the transfers with or without compensation to Allied countries of military equipment, including that purchased abroad under the Mutual Defense Assistance Program. A small amount of services connected with these transfers was also included. Series Ee1–2 include nonmonetary movements of gold. For the treatment of monetary gold, see the text for series Ee14.

Series Ee3. The sum of series Ee1–2.

Series Ee4, net military transactions. There are three major types of international military transactions: military grants, transfers under U.S. military sales contracts, and direct overseas defense expenditures. *Prior to 1946, only direct military expenditures are included.* Military grants and transfers of U.S. military sales for cash or credit are included in series Ee1, goods exports. Military grants are also summed in series Ee11, net unilateral transfers. From 1946 onward, all three types of international military transactions (military grants, transfers of U.S. military agency sales, and direct military expenditures) are included in net military transactions. Military grants are also summed in net unilateral transfers.

Series Ee5, net travel and transportation. For 1790–1819, transportation payments represent gross earnings on freight carried in U.S. ships. Some adjustment was made to eliminate earnings from ships carrying U.S. imports.

Series Ee5. For 1820–1860, credits include earnings by U.S. ships from carrying U.S. exports and from carrying freight between foreign ports. They also include American port charges paid by foreign ships. Debits include transportation payments consisting of freight payments to foreign ships for carrying U.S. imports, and expenditures of American ships in foreign ports. Port expenditures and receipts are estimated as a percentage of freight earnings by American and foreign ships, respectively. (Fare payments to American ships by immigrants are included in the estimate for immigrant funds. See the text for series Ee11.) For 1861–1900, transportation payments (debits) include ocean freight earnings from carrying U.S. exports and from carrying freight between foreign ports, and port expenditures in the United States of the foreign merchant marine and of passenger steamships. The estimates for the years 1871–1900 also include earnings from carrying overland freight. Payments for transportation include ocean freight payments on U.S. imports, and expenditures in foreign ports by the U.S. merchant marine. Passenger fares are included in the underlying travel account. The data for 1900–1918 include receipts (credits) and payments (debits) on account of ocean freight, and port charges. For 1916–1918, payments (debits) for charter hire were added.

Series Ee5. For 1919–1999, the transportation category includes international freight, fares and shipboard expenses of travelers, revenues and expenditures resulting from the charter of vessels and the rental of freight cars, and the expenses of U.S. transportation companies abroad and foreign transportation companies in the United States. The data cover air and surface transportation.

Series Ee5. For 1790–1819, no estimate was made for international travel expenditures. For 1820–1860, the net travel data include tourist expenditures (credits) in the United States and their fare payments to American ships but debit American tourist expenditures abroad. North assumed that American tourists going abroad and, for the most part, foreigners coming to the United States traveled on American ships during this period. The method employed in the source study for estimating tourism precludes the transfer-of-fare payments to the transportation account. For 1861–1900, series Ee5 includes outlays of foreign travelers in the United States. It was assumed that alien travelers came to the United States on foreign lines and, therefore, no estimate was made for receipt of fares. Series Ee5 includes payments abroad (debits) by American tourists for maintenance and for ocean fares. Simon (1960) assumed that the bulk of the travel during 1861–1900 was on foreign ships and was thus a debit item. The outlays for procurement of sundry items and luxury consumption goods were not included in his estimate for expenditures abroad by American tourists.

Series Ee5. The data for 1900–1918 include fares paid to U.S. ships by foreign tourists (credits) and to foreign ships by U.S. tourists (debits).

Series Ee5. For 1919–1999, all expenditures made in the United States by foreign residents, except those of diplomats and other official personnel stationed here, are included in the travel receipts. Expenditures made in foreign countries by U.S. travelers for food, lodging, amusements, gifts, and other personal purchases constitute travel payments (debits).

Series Ee5. From 1984, data represent revised estimates of passenger fares and other travel expenditures of U.S. residents abroad and passenger fares and other travel expenditures of foreign travelers in the United States. New surveys and other sources were utilized to increase coverage and refine travel expenditure data, including U.S. travelers in Mexico and Mexican travelers in the United States (*SCB*, June 1989, p. 59; June 1990, p. 73; June 1992, pp. 71–2; June 1993, pp. 58–9). Starting in 1986, revised and new estimates of other transport service exports and imports including revised estimates of receipts from U.S. railway transportation of foreign goods in transit in the United States (*SCB*, June 1992, p. 72) and new coverage of transportation services by truck between the United States and Canada (*SCB*, June 1995, pp. 70–1).

(continued)

TABLE Ee1–21   Balance of international payments: 1790–1998   *Continued*

Series Ee6, other services, net. Marine insurance and brokers' commissions constitute the series for 1790–1819. No estimate was made for these transactions between 1820 and 1860. For 1861–1900, series Ee6 consists of receipts on marine insurance (credits) and payments for marine insurance and net payments for brokers' commissions (debits). For 1900–1918, no estimates were made. For 1919–1999, the coverage of miscellaneous service items has expanded and now includes receipts (credits) and payments (debits) from insurance transactions, communications, management services, and motion picture and other royalties; receipts (credits) from fees of American engineering, construction, and consulting firms, from foreign contracts, and from foreign governments in the United States; and expenditures of U.S. government agencies abroad, except expenditures by the Department of Defense. For the treatment of international military transactions, see the text for series Ee4.

Series Ee6. Starting in 1981, data include new financial services series covering receipts and payments from commissions and other transactions associated with the purchase or sale of securities. Previously these financial payments and receipts were implicit in various capital accounts; they are now excluded from the capital account series (*SCB*, June 1987, p. 52). From 1981, figures reflect revised estimates of U.S. student spending abroad and foreign student spending in the United States (*SCB*, June 1989, pp. 58–9).

Series Ee7, balance of goods and services. The sum of series Ee1–2 and Ee4–6.

Series Ee8, investment income, receipts of U.S. assets abroad. For 1915–1918, includes income on private and government war loans (see Goldsmith 1956, p. 1078). For 1919–1999, investment income from overseas assets includes all interest, dividends, and branch profits effectively paid or credited during the period, after payment of all taxes in the country in which the payer of income resides. Beginning in 1919, the series includes interest received by the U.S. government on long- and short-term loans and other investments.

Series Ee8. Includes private income in the form of interest, dividends, and branch profits from direct investments, and interest and dividends received from holdings of foreign bonds by residents in the United States; from stocks issued by foreign corporations that are not U.S. direct investments; from loans by banks and other financial or commercial organizations; and from miscellaneous assets such as commercial real estate, insurance policies, commercial claims of various kinds, trusts and estates, and mortgages. Reinvested earnings, or the parent company's equity in the undistributed earnings on common stock of foreign subsidiary companies, are included.

Series Ee8–9. Beginning in 1982, data reflect revised estimates of direct investment receipts to U.S. residents on U.S. assets abroad, and direct investment payments to nonresidents on foreign assets held in the United States. Revisions include removal of capital gains and losses from the reinvestment earnings component of direct investment income (*SCB*, June 1992, p. 73); a shift to measuring direct investment income on a current-cost (replacement-cost) basis after adjustment to reported depreciation, depletion, and expensed exploration and development costs (*SCB*, June 1992, pp. 72–3); increased coverage of nonresident taxes (*SCB*, June 1992, p 73); and the removal of the currency translation adjustment (*SCB*, June 1990, pp. 72–3; June 1991, pp. 41–2). In addition, the current-cost adjustment to direct investment income reflects improved estimates of economic depreciation and improved estimates of charges taken by direct investment affiliates for depreciation, depletion, and expensed exploration and development expenditures (*SCB*, July 1999, pp. 65–7).

Series Ee9, payments on foreign assets in the United States. For 1790–1900, represents *net* payments of income on investments by the United States. The income was computed by applying an assumed yield rate to the net indebtedness of the United States. From 1900 onward, separate estimates were made of investment income receipts and payments (see series Ee8). For 1919–1999, the series includes payments of interest, dividends, and branch profits (including reinvested earnings) by foreign direct investment companies in the United States, interest and dividend payments to foreign holders of other American bonds and stocks (including U.S. government securities), and payments of income on various miscellaneous assets such as estates and trusts.

Series Ee10, balance on investment income, net. The sum of series Ee8–9.

Series Ee11, unilateral transfers, net. No estimate was made prior to 1820. For 1820–1860, the series includes the excess of funds brought into the United States by immigrants and their fare payments to American shipping companies over the amounts remitted abroad after their arrival in this country. For 1861–1916, the data include the immigrant remittances and funds carried by immigrants into the country (credits) and out (debits). The estimate for immigrant remittances includes remittances through banks and an estimate for outlays by U.S. residents for prepayment of passage for friends and relatives planning to emigrate to the United States. For 1917 and subsequent years, remittances in cash and kind by religious, educational, and charitable institutions are also included.

Series Ee11. Includes transfers of goods and services under military grant programs. Also included in the series is $0.6 million for 1794–1796, representing annual payments to Barbary pirates and the payment of $11.2 million in 1803 to France for the purchase of the Louisiana Territory. The United States acquired sovereignty over this territory in 1803 and issued bonds for the amount of the purchase. These 860 bonds carried an interest rate of 6 percent per year and were redeemed between 1812 and 1823. The interest during this period amounted to $8.2 million, $5.6 million of which was paid in the first ten years. See E. M. Douglas, *Boundaries, Areas, Geographic Centers and Altitudes of the United States and the Several States* (U.S. Government Printing Office, 1930). Presumably the interest is included in the estimate for income payments, series Ee9. The entries of $5.5 million for 1836–1838 represent receipts by the U.S. government from France on behalf of American citizens in satisfaction of claims for indemnities arising from the Napoleonic Wars. See J. T. Adams, editor, *Dictionary of American History* (Scribner's, 1940), volume 2, p. 348. Interest of $0.5 million ($0.3 million, $0.1 million, and $0.1 million for 1836–1838, respectively) is included. In 1848, at the end of the Mexican War, the United States and Mexico signed the treaty of Guadelupe-Hidalgo, which gave to the United States the present states of Arizona, New Mexico, California, Nevada, Utah, and Colorado west of the Rockies. The payment by the United States of $15 million for this territory, plus interest of $1.4 million, is represented by the entries for 1849–1852. These entries were referred to by North (1960) as indemnity payments and entered in the capital account. The entries for 1854–1856, aggregating $10 million, represent the Gadsden Purchase. In March 1867, Russia agreed to sell Alaska to the United States for $7.2 million in gold. The United States took possession in fiscal year 1868, but payment was not made until fiscal year 1869. During the Civil War, Great Britain sold to the Confederate states ships that were used as privateers to sink Union ships. An international tribunal in 1873 held Great Britain liable to the extent of $15.5 million. Payment was made to the United States in 1873, as indemnity on behalf of its citizens. The treaty of peace with Spain in 1898, as a result of which the Philippines, Guam, and Puerto Rico were ceded to the United States, stipulated a payment to Spain of $20 million.

Series Ee11. The figures include two transactions that are not included in Goldsmith (1956) for the 1900–1918 period. In 1904, the U.S. government paid $10 million to the Republic of Panama for lease of the Panama Canal, and in 1917, the United States bought the Virgin Islands from Denmark for $25 million.

Series Ee11. For 1919–1970, includes government transfers of goods, services, or cash, in both dollars and foreign currencies, for which payment by the foreign country has not been made, is not expected, or has not been specified, less reverse lend-lease, counterpart funds in certain foreign-aid programs, and other receipts. Also included are government payments of pensions and receipts or payments for indemnities, intangible rights, or other considerations.

Series Ee11. Starting with 1981, data include new estimates of personal remittances of the foreign-born population in the United States (*SCB*, June 1992, p. 75). Starting in 1986, figures reflect revised estimates of personal remittances of the foreign-born population of the United States as a result of new and updated census and Immigration and Naturalization Service (INS) source materials (*SCB*, July 1996, p. 60).

TABLE Ee1–21   Balance of international payments: 1790–1998 *Continued*

Series Ee12, balance on current account. The sum of series Ee7 and Ee10–11. This table follows current practice and includes unilateral transfers in the balance on current account. Conceptually, the sum of the balance on current account and allocations of special drawing rights is equal to "net foreign investment" in the national income and product accounts (hereafter, NIPAs). However, the foreign transactions account in the NIPAs includes (a) adjustments to the international transactions accounts for the treatment of gold, (b) adjustments for the different geographical treatment of transactions with U.S. territories and Puerto Rico, and (c) services furnished without payment by financial pension plans except life insurance carriers and private noninsured pension plans. A reconciliation of the balance of goods and services from the international accounts and the NIPA net exports appears annually in the *SCB* July issue, which presents the latest revisions of U.S. international transactions. A reconciliation of the other foreign transactions in the two sets of accounts appears in the same edition of *SCB*.

Series Ee13, U.S. assets abroad, net, total. The sum of series Ee14–16. For 1790–1900, the outflow of U.S. investment abroad is included in the net inflow estimate found in series Ee17. From 1900 onward, series Ee13 represents the changes in U.S. net assets abroad, that is, the annual outflow of U.S. investment abroad. For 1900–1918, see Goldsmith (1956), pp. 1080–1.

Series Ee13–16. For 1919–1945, see U.S. Bureau of Economic Analysis (formerly Office of Business Economics), *Balance of Payments Statistical Supplement* (1958), pp. 10–13. For 1946–1959, see *SCB* 50 (6) (June 1970): 34, as revised for 1946 and 1947 in *Historical Statistics of the United States* (1975), p. 866.

Series Ee13–16. For 1919–1999, the data represent changes in assets or investments of the United States abroad. No distinction is made between short- and long-term transactions. The Department of Commerce and many outside observers decided in the late 1970s that the stated maturities of assets were not a good guide to the holding patterns of asset owners. The Department of Commerce ceased to publish data categorized by maturity in 1978. See Advisory Committee on the Presentation of the Balance of Payments (1976); and Stern, Schwartz, et al. (1977).

Series Ee14, transactions in U.S. official reserve assets, net. This entry measures net changes in the official reserve assets of the United States, which consist of U.S. holdings of monetary gold, special drawing rights, convertible foreign currencies, and reserve position (formerly called gold trance) in the International Monetary Fund (IMF).

Series Ee14. Monetary gold includes the U.S. gold stock held by the U.S. Treasury and the Exchange Stabilization Fund. (On December 9, 1974, the Treasury acquired all gold held by the Exchange Stabilization Fund.) This includes gold sold to the United States by the IMF with the right to repurchase and gold deposited by the IMF to mitigate the impact on the U.S. gold stock of foreign purchases for gold subscription to the IMF under quota increases. Convertible foreign currencies represent Treasury and Federal Reserve System holdings of convertible foreign currencies in U.S. dollar equivalents. The U.S. reserve position in the IMF represents the amount that the United States could purchase in foreign currencies automatically if needed; if positive, it is equivalent to the U.S. quota in the IMF minus the Fund's holdings of U.S. dollars.

Series Ee14. For all areas, amounts outstanding March 31, 1998, were as follows in millions of dollars: U.S. official reserve assets, net, 69,353; gold, 11,049; special drawing rights, 10,108; reserve position in the IMF, 17,976; foreign currencies, 30,220.

Series Ee15, other U.S. government assets. Includes sales of foreign obligations to foreigners. For 1919–1999, includes disbursements of foreign loans, net of repayments, by all U.S. government agencies, whether made in dollars or in foreign currencies. Also included are movements of capital related to the operation by the U.S. government of productive facilities abroad, and U.S. capital contributions to international organizations such as the IMF, the International Bank for Reconstruction and Development, and the International Finance Corporation. Loan operations between these organizations and foreign countries are not included because such organizations are regarded as

foreign entities in the U.S. balance of payments. Loans made by private banks and guaranteed by the Export-Import Bank are included in series Ee16, U.S. private assets. Real property purchased by the government for administrative purposes is included in series Ee6, other service transactions, while all expenditures of religious, educational, and charitable institutions are included in series Ee11, unilateral transfers, even if they involve the purchase of fixed assets. For 1919–1999, series Ee15 also includes changes in the U.S. government short-term claims arising from holdings of foreign currencies (received as a counterpart to foreign grants or through sales of agricultural and other surplus products), deposits abroad, and various advances.

Series Ee16, U.S. private assets. For 1919–1999, the changes in capital claims refer not only to securities (stocks, bonds, mortgages, and so forth) but also to real property (farms, branch factories, and real estate). The series consists of net purchases of stocks in, and of changes in, net claims by U.S. parent companies against foreign incorporated companies in the management of which U.S. companies have an important voice, and net changes in the equity in foreign branches of U.S. companies. Series Ee16 also consists of U.S. purchases of newly issued foreign securities, amortizations of foreign bonds, net transactions in outstanding foreign securities, and net changes in long-term claims reported by U.S. banks (including loans made by private banks and guaranteed by the Export-Import Bank) and other commercial enterprises. Also included are changes in bank deposits, brokerage and commercial balances, and uncollected bills.

Series Ee17, foreign assets in the United States, net, total. The sum of series Ee18–19. For 1790–1900, the data for series Ee17 represent the net flow of U.S. and foreign capital and were estimated as residuals to balance the other items in the balance of payments. Consequently, they also reflect errors and omissions in the estimates of the other items. For some of these years, particularly 1861–1900, the data shown here differ from those in the source studies because of adjustments in some of the other series. From 1900 onward, series Ee17 is the net total changes in foreign assets in the United States held by foreign official and nonofficial asset holders.

Series Ee18, foreign official assets. This series is estimated by the Bureau of Economic Analysis for 1960–1999. Confidentiality of certain data sets and lack of other data prevent the Bureau of Economic Analysis from constructing a series before 1960. Foreign official assets were probably quite small before World War II. Series Ee18 consists of any public or private assets held by foreign governments. This would include foreign official claims on the U.S. government, deposits with the Treasury and other government agencies, and changes in official foreign holdings of U.S. government securities of all maturities. Official foreign short-term claims on private Americans include foreign deposits in U.S. banks by foreign official agencies, changes in foreign official holdings of privately issued securities, and other commercial liabilities of all maturities. The data also include an estimate of movements in foreign official holdings of U.S. currency and coins.

Series Ee19, other foreign assets. For 1960–1999, the data represent changes in liabilities of the United States to residents of foreign countries, or changes in assets held in the United States by residents of foreign countries, other than foreign official holdings. Series Ee19 includes shifts in foreign claims on the United States, including changes in the investments of foreign corporations in their branches and subsidiaries in the United States. Also included are net foreign purchases by nonofficial foreigners of U.S. public and private securities, including U.S. Treasury securities.

Series Ee20, allocations of special drawing rights. Special drawing rights are international reserve assets created through amendments to the Articles of Agreement of the IMF to provide orderly and adequate growth in international liquidity.

Series Ee21, statistical discrepancy. The negative value of the sum of series Ee12–13, Ee17, and Ee20. As indicated previously, this is the residual item necessary to make the statement balance. It compensates for missing data, possible errors in the estimates, as well as seasonal and other leads and lags in the reporting of the debit and credit phases of transactions that are compensating over a period of time.

TABLE Ee22   International investment position of the United States – net liabilities: 1789–1900

Contributed by Michael Edelstein

Year	Net liabilities Ee22 Million dollars	Year	Net liabilities Ee22 Million dollars	Year	Net liabilities Ee22 Million dollars	Year	Net liabilities Ee22 Million dollars
1789	60	1820	88	1850	217	1880	1,584
1790	61	1821	83	1851	223	1881	1,543
1791	69	1822	91	1852	239	1882	1,653
1792	77	1823	89	1853	295	1883	1,704
1793	75	1824	88	1854	337	1884	1,809
1794	66	1825	81	1855	352	1885	1,843
1795	79	1826	84	1856	364	1886	1,980
1796	83	1827	74	1857	381	1887	2,211
1797	94	1828	85	1858	358	1888	2,498
1798	96	1829	83	1859	384	1889	2,700
1799	81	1830	75	1860	377	1890	2,894
1800	83	1831	89	1861	480	1891	3,030
1801	81	1832	96	1862	480	1892	3,071
1802	74	1833	110	1863	493	1893	3,217
1803	77	1834	129	1864	604	1894	3,151
1804	65	1835	159	1865	663	1895	3,288
1805	75	1836	218	1866	758	1896	3,328
1806	82	1837	240	1867	903	1897	3,305
1807	87	1838	243	1868	976	1898	3,026
1808	104	1839	292	1869	1,152	1899	2,797
1809	92	1840	261	1870	1,252	1900	2,501
1810	85	1841	257 [1]	1871	1,353		
1811	50	1842	239 [1]	1872	1,595		
1812	71	1843	217	1873	1,762		
1813	56	1844	213	1874	1,844		
1814	65	1845	209	1875	1,931		
1815	80	1846	208	1876	1,933		
1816	118 [1]	1847	189	1877	1,876		
1817	109 [1]	1848	191	1878	1,714		
1818	104 [1]	1849	188	1879	1,554		
1819	89 [1]						

[1] Includes defaults totaling $20 million in 1816 and 1817; a total of $30 million in 1818 and 1819; and a total of $12 million in 1841 and 1842.

Sources

1790–1860, Douglass C. North, "The United States Balance of Payments, 1790–1860," in *Trends in the American Economy in the Nineteenth Century: A Report of the National Bureau of Economic Research,* Studies in Income and Wealth, volume 24 (Princeton University Press, 1960); 1861–1900, Matthew Simon, "The United States Balance of Payments, 1861–1900," in *Trends in the American Economy in the Nineteenth Century: A Report of the National Bureau of Economic Research,* Studies in Income and Wealth, volume 24 (Princeton University Press, 1960).

Documentation

In the source studies, a net liability of $60 million was estimated for 1789. For the subsequent years, the changes were computed by adding the annual net international flow of capital, series Ee17. For 1789–1900, series Ee17 is the balancing item for the sum of exports and imports of goods, services, and unilateral transactions. For certain years, adjustments were made for defaults. Differences between the accumulating "net indebtedness" in the source studies and the data in series Ee22 are attributable to adjustments incorporated in the series in Table Ee1–21, as explained in the text for those series.

TABLE Ee23–36 International investment position of the United States: 1843–1977

Contributed by Michael Edelstein

	U.S. investments abroad							Foreign investments in the United States						
	Total	Private					U.S. government	Total	Long-term			Short-term		
		Total	Long-term			Short-term			Total	Direct	Other	Total	Private obligations	U.S. government obligations
			Total	Direct	Other									
Year	Ee23 [1]	Ee24	Ee25	Ee26 [2]	Ee27	Ee28	Ee29 [1]	Ee30	Ee31	Ee32	Ee33	Ee34	Ee35	Ee36
	Billion dollars	Billion dollars	Billion dollars	Billion dollars	Billion dollars	Billion dollars	Billion dollars	Billion dollars	Billion dollars	Billion dollars	Billion dollars	Billion dollars	Billion dollars	Billion dollars
1843	(Z)	—	—	—	—	—	—	0.2	—	—	—	—	—	—
1869	0.1	0.1	—	—	—	—	—	1.5	1.4	—	—	0.2	—	—
1897	0.7	0.7	0.7	0.6	0.1	—	—	3.4	3.1	—	—	0.3	—	—
1908	2.5	2.5	2.5	1.6	0.9	—	—	6.4	6.4	—	—	—	—	—
1914 [3]	5.0	3.5	3.5	2.7	0.8	—	1.5	7.2	6.7	1.3	5.4	0.5	0.5	—
1919	9.7	7.0	6.5	3.9	2.6	0.5	2.7	3.3	2.5	0.9	1.6	0.8	0.8	—
1924	15.1	10.9	10.0	5.4	4.6	0.8	4.2	3.9	2.9	1.0	1.9	1.0	1.0	—
1927	17.9	13.8	12.5	6.6	5.9	1.3	4.1	6.6	3.7	—	—	2.9	2.7	—
1930	21.5	17.2	15.2	8.0	7.2	2.0	4.3	8.4	5.7 [5]	1.4 [5]	4.3 [5]	2.7	—	—
1931	20.1	15.9	14.6	8.1	6.5	1.3	4.2	3.8	2.3	—	—	1.5	—	—
1935	23.6	13.5	12.6	7.8	4.8	0.9	10.1	6.4	5.1	1.6	3.5	1.2	1.2	—
1940	34.3	12.2	11.3	7.3	4.0	0.9	22.1	13.5	8.1	2.9	5.2	5.4	5.1	0.3
1945	36.9	14.7	13.7	8.4	5.3	1.0	22.2	17.0	8.0	2.5	5.5	9.0	5.3	3.7
1946	39.4	13.5	12.3	7.2 [4]	5.0	1.3	25.9	15.2	7.0	2.5	4.5	8.3	5.3	3.0
1947	48.3	14.9	13.4	8.4	5.1	1.5	33.4	13.8	6.8	2.6	4.2	7.0	5.0	2.0
1948	52.5	16.3	14.7	9.6	5.1	1.6	36.2	14.4	6.8	2.8	4.0	7.7	5.5	2.1
1949	53.9	16.9	15.6	10.7	4.9	1.3	37.0	14.8	7.1	2.9	4.2	7.7	5.7	2.0
1950	54.4	19.0	17.5	11.8	5.7	1.5	35.4	17.6	8.0	3.4	4.6	9.6	6.6	3.1
1951	56.4	20.8	19.2	13.0	6.2	1.7	35.6	18.7	8.8	3.7	5.1	10.0	6.6	3.3
1952	59.1	22.7	21.0	14.7	6.3	1.7	36.4	20.8	9.4	3.9	5.4	11.5	7.2	4.2
1953	60.2	23.8	22.2	16.3	5.9	1.6	36.4	21.9	9.6	4.3	5.4	12.2	7.6	4.6
1954	62.4	26.6	24.4	17.6	6.7	2.2	35.8	25.0	11.6	4.6	7.0	13.5	8.5	5.0
1955	65.1	29.1	26.7	19.4	7.4	2.4	35.9	27.8	13.4	5.1	8.3	14.4	8.4	6.0
1956	70.8	33.4	30.4	22.5	7.9	2.9	37.4	30.5	14.3	5.5	8.8	16.3	9.4	6.8
1957	76.4	36.9	33.7	25.4	8.4	3.2	39.5	30.7	13.8	5.7	8.1	17.0	9.9	7.1
1958	79.2	41.1	37.6	27.4	10.2	3.5	38.1	34.4	16.4	6.1	10.3	18.0	10.9	7.1
1959	82.2	44.8	41.2	29.8	11.4	3.6	37.4	39.1	18.0	6.5	11.4	21.1	10.8	10.2
1960	85.6	49.3	44.5	31.9	12.6	4.8	36.3	40.9	18.4	6.9	11.5	22.4	11.7	10.8
1961	92.0	55.6	49.1	34.7	14.3	6.5	36.4	46.0	21.4	7.4	14.1	24.5	13.4	11.2
1962	96.5	60.1	52.8	37.3	15.5	7.3	36.4	46.3	20.2	7.6	12.6	26.1	13.3	12.7
1963	103.9	66.6	58.4	40.7	17.6	8.2	37.4	51.5	22.8	7.9	14.8	28.7	14.9	13.8
1964	114.7	75.9	65.0	44.5	20.5	10.9	38.8	56.9	25.0	8.4	16.6	31.9	17.5	14.4
1965	120.4	81.5	71.4	49.5	21.9	10.2	38.8	58.8	26.4	8.8	17.6	32.4	18.2	14.2
1966	125.2	86.4	75.8	54.8	21.0	10.6	38.8	60.4	27.0	9.1	18.0	33.4	20.8	12.6
1967	134.7	93.6	81.7	59.5	22.2	11.9	41.1	69.7	32.0	9.9	22.1	37.7	23.0	14.8
1968	146.8	102.5	89.5	65.0	24.5	13.0	44.3	81.2	40.4	10.8	29.5	40.9	22.6	18.3
1969	158.1	110.4	96.3	71.0	25.3	14.1	47.7	90.8	41.1	11.8	29.3	49.7	37.9	11.9

Notes appear at end of table

(continued)

TABLE Ee23–36 International investment position of the United States: 1843–1977 Continued

	U.S. investments abroad							Foreign investments in the United States						
		Private							Long-term			Short-term		
	Total	Total	Long-term			Short-term	U.S. government	Total	Total	Direct	Other	Total	Private obligations	U.S. government obligations
			Total	Direct	Other									
Year	Ee23 [1]	Ee24	Ee25	Ee26 [2]	Ee27	Ee28	Ee29 [1]	Ee30	Ee31	Ee32	Ee33	Ee34	Ee35	Ee36
	Billion dollars	Billion dollars	Billion dollars	Billion dollars	Billion dollars	Billion dollars	Billion dollars	Billion dollars	Billion dollars	Billion dollars	Billion dollars	Billion dollars	Billion dollars	Billion dollars
1970	166.9	120.2	105.0	78.2	26.8	15.2	46.7	97.7	48.7	13.3	35.4	49.0	28.1	20.9
1971	179.5	133.1	114.5	83.0	31.5	18.6	46.3	123.3	54.0	13.9	40.1	69.3	22.5	46.8
1972	199.0	149.7	127.2	89.9	37.4	22.4	49.3	161.8	72.6	14.8	57.8	89.2	33.5	55.7
1973	222.5	169.2	139.8	101.3	38.5	29.4	53.2	174.9	72.1	18.3	53.8	102.8	45.3	57.5
1974	255.7	201.5	151.0	110.1	40.9	50.5	54.2	196.9	67.6	25.1	42.5	129.3	66.9	62.4
1975	295.1	237.1	174.4	124.1	50.3	62.7	58.0	220.5	80.7	27.7	53.1	139.8	67.8	72.0
1976	347.2	282.4	198.8	136.8	62.0	83.6	64.8	264.6	92.5	30.8	61.8	172.0	82.4	89.7
1977	383.0	314.1	218.0	149.8	68.1	96.1	68.9	310.6	94.3	34.6	59.7	216.3	92.1	124.2

(Z) Less than $50 million.

[1] Beginning 1914, includes U.S. monetary gold stock.

[2] Beginning 1960, excludes Cuba.

[3] As of June 30.

[4] Beginning in 1946, new annual series for direct investment utilizes better survey data; not compatible with earlier years.

[5] For 1929.

Source

Figures are as of the end of the year.

1843–1914, Cleona Lewis, *America's Stake in International Investments* (Brookings Institution Press, 1938). 1919–1945, U.S. Office of Business Economics, various publications. 1946–1970, U.S. Bureau of Economic Analysis (formerly Office of Business Economics), *Balance of Payments Statistical Supplement, Revised Edition* (various issues); U.S. Office of Business Economics, *Investments of the United States* (1953); and *Survey of Current Business (SCB)* (August 1963): 22; (August 1964): 24; (September 1965): 32; (September 1966): 40; (October 1968): 20; (October 1969): 24; (October 1970): 23; (October 1971): 23; (October 1972): 21. 1971, *SCB* (October 1975): 32. 1972, *SCB* (October 1977): 23. 1973, *SCB* (August 1978): 57. 1974–1977, *SCB* (August 1979): 56.

Documentation

Figures are as of the end of the year.

The estimates for 1919–1945 are based on the following publications: (1) U.S. Office of Business Economics, *The United States in the World Economy*, Economic Series number 23 (1943), p. 123; (2) U.S. Bureau of Foreign and Domestic Commerce, *The Balance of International Payments of the United States in 1931*, Trade Information Bulletin number 803 (1932), pp. 44, 48, and 62; (3) U.S. Bureau of Foreign and Domestic Commerce, *Foreign Investments in the United States* (1937), p. 5; (4) Cleona Lewis, *America's Stake in International Investments* (Brookings Institution Press, 1938); (5) U.S. Office of Business Economics, *International Transactions of the United States during the War 1940–45* (as revised), Economic Series number 65 (1948), p. 110.

In *America's Stake in International Investments*, direct investments are based on book value wherever possible; portfolio investments are calculated at par value for bonds and preferred stocks and at market value for common stocks. Similar practices were followed in the estimates of the Department of Commerce for 1930, 1931, and 1935; miscellaneous portfolio investments for the same years were calculated at market values wherever possible. For 1940, 1945, and 1946–1977, the values of bonds and preferred stocks as well as of common stocks were calculated at market prices wherever possible.

The estimates for these series prior to 1919 were prepared by compilers who used different valuation methods and whose data varied in completeness. While the estimates are therefore not homogeneous, they do present rough indications of the magnitudes involved.

The last year for which the Department of Commerce published the U.S. international investment position where it distinguished between short- and long-term assets and liabilities was 1977. Accumulating evidence convinced the Department of Commerce and many outside observers that the stated maturities of assets were not a good guide to the holding patterns of asset owners. See Advisory Committee on the Presentation of the Balance of Payments, "Report of the . . . ," *SCB* 56 (6) (June 1976): 18–27; R. M. Stern, C. F. Schwartz, et al., "The Presentation of the U. S. Balance of Payments: A Symposium," *Essays in International Finance*, number 123 (August 1977).

Series Ee26. Through 1961, U.S. direct investments in foreign countries include all foreign enterprises whose voting stock is owned to the extent of at least 25 percent by U.S. organizations or individuals, or in the management of which Americans have an important voice. Starting with 1962, direct investments include voting stock owned to the extent of at least 10 percent by U.S. organizations or individuals, or in the management of which Americans have an important voice. In addition, they include unincorporated foreign branches or other direct foreign operations of U.S. interests, including mining claims, oil concessions, and other property held for business purposes such as real estate. U.S. direct investment abroad is valued at book cost, also known as historical cost.

Series Ee27. Other private long-term investment abroad include U.S.-held foreign bonds and corporate stocks, long-term U.S. claims on unaffiliated foreigners reported by U.S. nonbanking concerns, and long-term U.S. claims reported by U.S. banks, not reported elsewhere.

Series Ee28. Total private short-term investment abroad include short-term U.S. claims on unaffiliated foreigners reported by U.S. nonbanking concerns, and short-term U.S. claims reported by U.S. banks, not reported elsewhere.

Series Ee29. Total U.S. government investment abroad includes U.S. official reserve assets (gold, special drawing rights, reserve position in the International Monetary Fund, foreign currencies) and other U.S. government assets (U.S. loans and other long-term assets).

Series Ee32. Through 1973, foreign direct investments in the United States cover U.S. business enterprises, including real estate investments, in which there is a foreign interest or ownership of 25 percent or more. Starting in 1974, foreign direct investments in the United States cover U.S. business enterprises, including real estate investments, in which there is a foreign interest or ownership of

25 percent or more. Starting in 1974, foreign direct investments in the United States cover U.S. business enterprises, including real estate investments, in which there is a foreign interest or ownership of 10 percent or more. Foreign direct investment in the United States is valued at book cost, also known as historical cost.

Series Ee33. Other long-term foreign investments in the United States include U.S. securities other than U.S. Treasuries (corporate and other bonds, corporate stock), U.S. long-term liabilities to unaffiliated foreigners reported by U.S. nonbanking concerns, and long-term U.S. liabilities reported by U.S. banks.

Series Ee35. Foreign-owned short-term private obligations include liquid liabilities to private foreigners and other readily marketable and nonliquid liabilities to foreign official agencies.

Series Ee36. Foreign-owned U.S. government obligations include U.S. government securities held as foreign official assets in the United States, other U.S. government liabilities held as foreign official assets in the United States, and U.S. Treasury securities held as foreign private assets in the United States reported by U.S. banks. The series includes long-term and short-term obligations.

TABLE Ee37-71 International investment position of the United States: 1970–1998

Contributed by Michael Edelstein

	Net international investment position		U.S. assets abroad		U.S. official reserve assets					U.S. government assets, other		
	Current cost	Market cost	Current cost	Market cost	Total	Gold	Special drawing rights	Reserve position in IMF	Foreign currencies	Total	U.S. loans and other long-term assets	U.S. foreign currency holdings and short-term assets
	Ee37	Ee38	Ee39	Ee40	Ee41	Ee42	Ee43	Ee44	Ee45	Ee46	Ee47	Ee48
Year	Billion dollars	Billion dollars	Billion dollars	Billion dollars	Billion dollars	Billion dollars	Billion dollars	Billion dollars	Billion dollars	Billion dollars	Billion dollars	Billion dollars
1970	—	—	—	—	14.5	11.1	0.9	1.9	0.6	31.4	29.7	1.7
1971	—	—	—	—	12.2	10.2	1.1	0.6	0.3	33.3	31.8	1.5
1972	—	—	—	—	13.2	10.5	2.0	0.5	0.2	35.3	34.1	1.2
1973	—	—	—	—	14.4	11.7	2.2	0.6	(Z)	38.0	36.2	1.8
1974	—	—	—	—	15.9	11.7	2.4	1.9	(Z)	37.2	36.3	0.9
1975	—	—	—	—	16.2	11.6	2.3	2.2	0.1	40.7	39.8	0.9
1976	168.1	—	462.5	—	44.1	36.9	2.4	4.4	0.3	45.0	44.1	0.9
1977	176.9	—	519.0	—	53.4	45.8	2.6	4.9	(Z)	48.6	47.7	0.8
1978	211.9	—	627.3	—	69.5	62.5	1.6	1.0	4.4	53.2	52.3	0.9
1979	323.4	—	792.9	—	143.3	135.5	2.7	1.3	3.8	57.4	56.5	0.9
1980	368.5	—	936.3	—	171.4	155.8	2.6	2.9	10.1	63.9	62.0	1.8
1981	347.0	—	1,004.2	—	124.6	105.6	4.1	5.1	9.8	68.8	67.2	1.6
1982	331.6	233.7	1,100.7	958.8	143.4	120.6	5.3	7.3	10.2	74.7	72.9	1.8
1983	299.4	255.3	1,199.4	1,127.6	123.1	100.5	5.0	11.3	6.3	79.6	77.8	1.8
1984	162.9	132.1	1,191.9	1,125.2	105.0	81.2	5.6	11.5	6.7	85.0	82.9	2.1
1985	57.4	94.8	1,272.8	1,300.7	117.9	85.8	7.3	11.9	12.9	87.8	85.8	1.9
1986	-32.8	98.6	1,452.5	1,592.4	139.9	102.4	8.4	11.7	17.3	89.6	88.7	0.9
1987	-76.8	48.7	1,626.6	1,756.9	162.4	127.6	10.3	11.3	13.1	88.9	88.1	0.8
1988	-175.4	8.7	1,806.4	2,006.6	144.2	107.4	9.6	9.7	17.4	86.1	85.4	0.7
1989	-254.9	-49.1	2,045.5	2,348.1	168.7	105.2	10.0	9.0	44.6	84.5	83.9	0.6
1990	-240.6	-166.8	2,150.0	2,291.7	174.7	102.4	11.0	9.1	52.2	82.0	81.4	0.6
1991	-301.6	-263.1	2,254.5	2,468.4	159.2	92.6	11.2	9.5	45.9	79.1	77.5	1.6
1992	-421.1	-454.6	2,298.6	2,464.2	147.4	87.2	8.5	11.8	40.0	80.7	79.1	1.6
1993	-295.3	-180.4	2,718.4	3,055.3	164.9	102.6	9.0	11.8	41.5	81.0	79.1	1.9
1994	-300.5	-174.3	2,956.8	3,276.1	163.4	100.1	10.0	12.0	41.2	80.1	77.8	2.3
1995	-500.2	-422.6	3,405.8	3,869.7	176.1	101.3	11.0	14.6	49.1	81.1	78.5	2.5
1996	-578.7	-547.5	3,958.5	4,544.5	160.7	96.7	10.3	15.4	38.3	82.0	79.6	2.4
1997	-968.2	-1,066.3	4,508.6	5,288.9	134.8	75.9	10.0	18.1	30.8	82.0	79.6	2.4
1998	-1,239.2	-1,537.5	4,930.9	5,948.0	146.0	75.3	10.6	24.1	36.0	82.4	80.2	2.2

(continued)

TABLE Ee37–71 International investment position of the United States: 1970–1998 *Continued*

All values in billion dollars.

Year	U.S. private assets — Current cost (Ee49)	U.S. private assets — Market cost (Ee50)	Direct investment abroad — Current cost (Ee51) [1,2]	Direct investment abroad — Market cost (Ee52) [1]	Foreign securities (Ee53) [3]	U.S. claims — On unaffiliated foreigners (Ee54) [4]	U.S. claims — Reported by U.S. banks (Ee55) [5]	Foreign assets in the United States — Current cost (Ee56)	Foreign assets in the United States — Market cost (Ee57)	Foreign official assets — Total (Ee58)	Foreign official assets — U.S. government securities (Ee59) [6]	Foreign official assets — Other U.S. government liabilities (Ee60)
1970	—	—	—	—	20.9	8.5	13.8	—	—	26.2	17.7	1.8
1971	—	—	—	—	23.4	9.6	16.9	—	—	52.5	44.4	1.3
1972	—	—	—	—	27.4	11.4	20.7	—	—	63.0	52.9	1.4
1973	—	—	—	—	27.4	13.8	26.7	—	—	69.3	53.8	2.4
1974	—	—	—	—	28.2	17.0	46.2	—	—	79.9	58.1	2.7
1975	—	—	—	—	34.9	18.3	59.8	—	—	86.9	63.6	4.2
1976	373.4	—	227.8	—	44.2	20.3	81.1	294.4	—	104.4	72.6	9.0
1977	417.1	—	252.8	—	49.4	22.3	92.6	342.1	—	140.9	105.4	10.3
1978	504.6	—	291.0	—	53.4	29.4	130.8	415.4	—	173.1	128.5	12.7
1979	592.2	—	343.9	—	56.8	34.4	157.0	469.5	—	159.9	106.6	12.7
1980	701.0	—	396.2	—	62.5	38.4	203.9	567.8	—	176.1	118.2	13.4
1981	810.8	—	412.4	—	62.1	42.8	293.5	657.2	—	180.4	125.1	13.0
1982	882.5	740.7	368.5	226.6	74.0	35.4	404.6	769.1	725.1	189.1	132.6	13.6
1983	996.6	924.9	346.1	274.3	84.7	131.3	434.5	900.2	872.3	194.5	137.0	14.2
1984	1,001.9	935.1	337.6	270.6	88.8	130.1	445.6	1,029.0	993.0	199.7	144.7	15.0
1985	1,067.1	1,095.0	358.5	386.4	119.4	141.9	447.4	1,215.4	1,205.8	202.5	145.1	15.8
1986	1,223.0	1,362.9	390.1	530.1	158.1	167.4	507.3	1,485.3	1,493.9	241.2	178.9	18.0
1987	1,375.4	1,505.7	460.0	590.2	188.6	177.4	549.5	1,703.5	1,708.2	283.1	220.5	15.7
1988	1,576.1	1,776.3	492.3	692.5	232.8	197.8	653.2	1,981.8	1,997.9	322.0	260.9	15.2
1989	1,792.3	2,094.9	529.9	832.5	314.3	234.3	713.8	2,300.4	2,397.2	341.7	263.6	15.4
1990	1,893.3	2,035.1	590.0	731.8	342.3	265.3	695.7	2,390.5	2,458.6	373.3	291.2	17.2
1991	2,016.1	2,230.0	613.7	827.5	455.8	256.3	690.4	2,556.1	2,731.4	398.5	311.2	18.6
1992	2,070.5	2,236.0	633.1	798.6	515.1	254.3	668.0	2,719.7	2,918.8	437.3	329.3	20.8
1993	2,472.5	2,809.3	690.7	1,027.5	853.5	242.0	686.2	3,013.7	3,235.7	509.4	381.7	22.1
1994	2,713.3	3,032.6	748.5	1,067.8	948.7	323.0	693.1	3,257.3	3,450.4	535.2	407.2	23.7
1995	3,148.6	3,612.5	843.3	1,307.2	1,169.6	367.6	768.1	3,905.9	4,292.3	671.7	497.8	23.6
1996	3,715.7	4,301.7	940.2	1,526.2	1,468.0	450.0	857.5	4,537.2	5,092.0	799.0	610.5	23.3
1997	4,291.8	5,072.1	1,004.2	1,784.5	1,739.4	562.4	985.8	5,476.8	6,355.2	835.7	614.5	21.5
1998	4,702.5	5,719.6	1,123.4	2,140.5	1,969.0	596.2	1,013.9	6,170.1	7,485.4	836.1	620.2	18.3

Year	Foreign official assets in the U.S. — U.S. liabilities reported by U.S. banks — Ee61 (Billion dollars)	Foreign official assets in the U.S. — Other foreign official assets — Ee62 [6] (Billion dollars)	Direct investments — Current cost — Ee63 (Billion dollars)	Direct investments — Market cost — Ee64 (Billion dollars)	Direct investments — Current cost — Ee65 [7] (Billion dollars)	Direct investments — Market cost — Ee66 [7] (Billion dollars)	U.S. Treasury securities — Ee67 [6] (Billion dollars)	U.S. currency — Ee68 (Billion dollars)	U.S. securities other than U.S. Treasury securities — Ee69 [6] (Billion dollars)	U.S. liabilities — To unaffiliated foreigners — Ee70 [1] (Billion dollars)	U.S. liabilities — Reported by U.S. banks — Ee71 (Billion dollars)
1970	6.7	(Z)	—	—	—	—	1.2	5.7	34.8	8.8	22.7
1971	6.8	(Z)	—	—	—	—	1.2	6.5	40.2	9.2	16.5
1972	8.5	0.2	—	—	—	—	1.2	7.1	50.7	10.7	21.2
1973	12.6	0.5	—	—	—	—	1.0	7.7	46.1	11.7	25.9
1974	18.4	0.6	—	—	—	—	1.7	8.9	34.9	13.6	41.8
1975	16.3	2.9	—	—	—	—	4.2	10.2	45.7	13.9	42.5
1976	17.2	5.8	189.9	—	49.8	—	7.0	11.8	54.9	12.9	53.5
1977	18.0	7.2	201.3	—	56.7	—	7.6	13.7	51.2	11.9	60.2
1978	23.3	8.5	242.5	—	69.6	—	8.9	16.6	53.6	16.0	77.7
1979	30.5	9.9	309.7	—	88.3	—	14.2	19.6	58.6	18.7	110.3
1980	30.4	14.1	391.7	—	125.9	—	16.1	24.1	74.1	30.4	121.1
1981	26.7	15.5	476.8	—	159.9	—	18.5	27.3	75.1	30.6	165.4
1982	25.0	17.9	580.0	536.0	174.5	130.4	25.8	31.3	93.0	27.5	228.0
1983	25.5	17.7	705.7	677.8	181.2	153.3	33.8	36.8	113.8	61.7	278.3
1984	26.1	14.0	829.3	793.4	208.4	172.4	62.1	40.8	128.5	77.4	312.2
1985	26.7	14.9	1,012.9	1,003.3	229.5	220.0	88.0	46.0	207.9	87.0	354.5
1986	27.9	16.4	1,244.1	1,252.6	264.4	273.0	96.1	50.1	309.8	90.7	433.0
1987	31.8	15.0	1,420.4	1,425.1	311.5	316.2	82.6	55.6	341.7	110.2	518.8
1988	31.5	14.3	1,659.8	1,675.9	375.4	391.5	100.9	61.3	392.3	144.5	585.4
1989	36.5	26.3	1,958.7	2,055.5	437.9	534.7	166.5	67.1	482.9	167.1	637.1
1990	39.9	24.9	2,017.2	2,085.3	471.6	539.5	152.5	85.9	460.6	213.4	633.3
1991	38.4	30.3	2,157.5	2,332.9	493.7	669.1	170.3	101.3	546.0	208.9	637.2
1992	55.0	32.2	2,282.5	2,481.5	497.1	696.2	197.7	114.8	599.4	220.7	652.7
1993	69.7	35.9	2,504.3	2,726.3	546.4	768.4	221.5	133.7	696.4	229.0	677.1
1994	73.4	31.0	2,722.1	2,915.2	564.7	757.9	235.7	157.2	739.7	239.8	784.9
1995	107.4	43.0	3,234.2	3,620.6	619.4	1,005.7	358.5	169.5	971.4	300.4	815.0
1996	113.1	52.2	3,738.2	4,293.0	674.3	1,229.1	502.6	186.8	1,199.5	346.7	828.2
1997	135.4	64.3	4,641.1	5,519.4	764.0	1,642.4	662.2	211.6	1,578.7	453.6	971.0
1998	123.9	73.5	5,334.0	6,649.4	878.7	2,194.1	727.3	228.3	2,021.8	460.8	1,017.1

(Z) Less than $50 million.

[1] Break in series in 1994. See text.

[2] Improved estimation procedures beginning in 1982. See text.

[3] Estimates include new survey results starting in 1994 and 1997. See text.

[4] There are several breaks in the series. See text.

[5] A break in series in 1988 reflects the introduction of data on holdings of foreign commercial paper.

[6] Estimates include results of 1978, 1984, 1989, and 1994 portfolio benchmark surveys conducted by the U.S. Department of the Treasury.

[7] Improved estimation procedures beginning in 1982. See text.

Sources

1970–1982, U.S. Bureau of Economic Analysis, Balance of Payments Division, unpublished data; 1983–1999, Survey of Current Business (SCB), 79 (7) (July 1999): 46, 74.

Documentation

The U.S. international investment position shows the stock of U.S. assets abroad (claims on foreigners) and of foreign assets in the United States (liabilities to foreigners) at year end. It is analogous to a balance sheet in that it measures stocks. The U.S. Bureau of Economic Analysis (BEA) uses either reports of currently held stocks (outstanding) or reports of outstandings from some time in the past (a benchmark) in combination with cumulated changes. The changes reflect capital flows and changes in the valuation of the outstandings.

On the recommendation of the Working Group on Economic Statistics (see "Improving the Quality of Economic Statistics," SCB, February 1990), the BEA introduced current-cost and market-cost valuations of the U.S. international investment position in its annual update and revision of international transactions in the June 1992 SCB. In published and unpublished sources cited previously, the BEA has provided estimates of the total stocks in current cost from 1976 and market cost from 1982.

The difference between the current-cost and market-cost total stock estimates depends on the method used to value U.S. direct investment abroad and foreign direct investment in the United States.

(continued)

TABLE Ee37-71   International investment position of the United States: 1970-1998   *Continued*

Current-cost valuation of direct investment reflects changes in the average price of the capital stock, as well as gains or losses on foreign-currency-denominated assets owing to their revaluation at current exchange rates. Market-cost valuation of direct investment reflects changes in stock market prices (after removing the effects of reinvested earnings) and gains or losses on foreign-currency-denominated assets resulting from their revaluation at current exchange rates. All other components of the international investment position are evaluated at market cost with one exception; the claims and liabilities reported by U.S. bank and nonbanks are estimated at book or historical cost.

For explanations of the series, see the text and sources for Table Ee1-21.

Series Ee51 and Ee65. Measured on a current-cost (replacement-cost) basis after adjustment to reported depreciation, depletion, and expensed exploration and development costs; the current-cost adjustment, which is the sum of these three items, is classified as a valuation adjustment. Also capital gains and losses are removed from the capital flow data and classified as a valuation adjustment. The current-cost valuation reflects changes in the average price of the capital stock, as well as gains or losses on foreign-currency-denominated assets resulting from their revaluation at current exchange rates.

Series Ee42. U.S. official gold evaluated at market price.

Series Ee47. Also includes paid-in capital subscriptions to international financial institutions and outstanding amounts of miscellaneous claims that have been settled through international agreements to be payable to the U.S. government over periods in excess of one year. Excludes World War I debts that are not being serviced. Includes indebtedness that the borrower may contractually, or at its option, repay with its currency, with a third country's currency, or by delivery of materials or transfer of services.

Series Ee51. Starting in 1982, the current-cost adjustment to direct investment capital reflects improved estimates of economic depreciation and improved estimates of charges taken by direct investment affiliates for depreciation, depletion, and expensed exploration and development expenditures (*SCB*, July 1999, pp. 65-7). Estimates for 1983 forward reflect 1982 base-year price indexes for tangible assets, which replace 1987 base-year price indexes previously used in the national income and product accounts.

Series Ee51-52. A break in the series in 1994 reflects the incorporation of results of the 1994 benchmark survey of U.S. direct investment abroad and the reclassification from the direct investment capital accounts to the nonbank investment accounts of intercompany debt transactions between parent companies and affiliates that are not depository institutions and that are primarily engaged in financial intermediation. Estimates for 1983-1993

are linked to the 1982 and 1989 benchmark surveys of U.S. direct investment abroad.

Series Ee53. Estimates include results of the Benchmark Survey of U.S. Ownership of Foreign Long-Term Securities as of March 31, 1994, conducted by the U.S. Department of the Treasury, and as of December 31, 1997, also conducted by the U.S. Department of the Treasury (*SCB*, July 1999, pp. 67-8).

Series Ee54. Breaks in the series reflect the following: in 1983, the introduction of data from the United Kingdom and from the Bank of International Settlements for Austria, Belgium, Denmark, Finland, Germany, Ireland, Luxembourg, Norway, Spain, Sweden, Switzerland, Caribbean banking centers, and Asian banking centers. Bank of International Settlements data were introduced for the Netherlands in 1986 and for France and Italy in 1989. Bank of International Settlements data for Switzerland were improved in 1989. Bank of International Settlements coverage for Austria, Switzerland, and Asian banking centers was also improved in 1989. BEA methodology for estimating positions vis-à-vis Canada and Germany was adjusted beginning in 1993 and vis-à-vis Asian banking centers in 1994. In 1994, intercompany debt transactions between parent companies and affiliates that are not depository institutions and that are primarily engaged in financial intermediation are reclassified from direct investment accounts to nonbank investment accounts.

Series Ee60. Primarily U.S. government liabilities associated with military sales contracts and other transactions arranged with or through foreign official agencies.

Series Ee65-66. Starting in 1982, the current-cost adjustment to direct investment capital reflects improved estimates of economic depreciation and improved estimates of charges taken by direct investment affiliates for depreciation, depletion, and expensed exploration and development expenditures (*SCB*, July 1999, pp. 65-7). Estimates for 1983 forward are linked to the 1987 and 1992 benchmark surveys of foreign direct investment in the United States.

Series Ee70. A break in the series in 1994 reflects the reclassification of intercompany debt transactions between parent companies and affiliates that are not depository institutions and that are primarily engaged in financial intermediation from direct investment accounts to nonbank investment accounts.

Series Ee52 and Ee66. Measured at market-cost valuation, which reflects changes in stock market prices (after removing the effects of reinvested earnings), and the gains or losses on foreign-currency-denominated assets resulting from their revaluation at current exchange rates.

TABLE Ee72–131   U.S. direct investment in foreign countries, by region and industry: 1929–1998[1, 2]

Contributed by Michael Edelstein

	Total						Mining and smelting					
	Total	Canada	Europe	Latin American and Caribbean	Asia and Pacific	Africa, Middle East, and international	Total	Canada	Europe	Latin America and Caribbean	Asia and Pacific	Africa, Middle East, and international
	Ee72	Ee73	Ee74 [3]	Ee75	Ee76	Ee77 [4]	Ee78	Ee79	Ee80 [3]	Ee81	Ee82	Ee83 [4]
Year	Million dollars	Million dollars	Million dollars	Million dollars	Million dollars	Million dollars	Million dollars	Million dollars	Million dollars	Million dollars	Million dollars	Million dollars
1929 [7]	7,528	2,010	1,353	3,519	—	646	1,185	400	— [9]	732	—	53 [9]
1936 [7]	6,691	1,952	1,245	2,847	—	647 [8]	1,032	239	43	708	—	42
1940 [7]	7,000	2,103	1,420	2,771	—	706	782	187	53	512	—	30
1950	11,788	3,579	1,733	4,577	566	1,332	1,129	334	31	667	23	74
1951	12,979	3,969	1,989	4,949	691	1,384	1,292	406	32	750	24	81
1952	14,721	4,641	2,153	5,514	825	1,586	1,622	564	34	900	27	98
1953	16,253	5,349	2,375	5,774	901	1,854	1,920	698	36	1,037	29	120
1954	17,631	6,043	2,643	5,929	1,022	1,994	2,066	822	40	1,031	36	137
1955	19,395	6,761	3,002	6,242	1,193	2,198	2,197	904	45	1,048	43	158
1956	22,505	7,795	3,561	7,298	1,359	2,492	2,419	1,002	51	1,143	48	173
1957	25,394	8,769	4,151	8,052	1,577	2,843	2,361	856	55	1,232	38	181
1958	27,409	9,470	4,573	8,469	1,740	3,158	2,558	938	52	1,316	40	212
1959	29,827	10,310	5,323	8,887	1,905	3,402	2,848	1,089	50	1,412	47	249
1960	31,865	11,179	6,691	8,366	2,147	3,482	2,997	1,325	49	1,318	57	246
1961	34,717	11,602	7,742	9,239	2,344	3,789	3,094	1,367	48	1,332	61	284
1962	37,276	12,133	8,930	9,524	2,571	4,118	3,244	1,489	50	1,321	73	309
1963	40,736	13,044	10,340	9,941	2,976	5,036	3,419	1,549	55	1,352	112	351
1964	44,480	13,855	12,129	10,255	3,384	4,856	3,665	1,713	56	1,404	131	361
1965	49,474	15,318	13,985	10,885	3,846	5,439	3,931	1,851	54	1,474	196	356
1966	51,792	15,713	16,390	9,752	4,004	5,931	3,983	1,976	19	1,340	287	320
1967	56,560	16,703	18,231	10,298	4,735	6,601	4,449	2,216	26	1,458	362	386
1968	61,907	17,952	19,851	11,342	5,369	7,392	4,837	2,370	26	1,623	415	404
1969	68,093	19,578	22,246	12,039	6,135	8,095	4,998	2,443	35	1,604	481	435
1970	75,480	21,015	25,255	12,961	7,030	9,219	5,405	2,574	36	1,712	607	473
1971	82,760	21,818	28,654	14,013	8,376	9,899	5,787	2,707	44	1,724	698	614
1972	89,878	22,985	31,696	14,897	9,654	10,645	5,667	2,408	46	1,689	943	580
1973	101,313	25,541	38,255	16,484	11,068	9,965	6,038	2,666	56	1,682	1,016	619
1974	110,078	28,404	44,652	19,527	12,893	4,599	5,790	2,794	38	1,131	1,163	665
1975	124,050	31,038	49,305	22,167	15,316	7,023	6,548	3,053	41	1,476	1,236	743
1976	136,809	33,838	55,139	23,934	15,563	8,334	7,060	3,200	34	1,601	1,405	820
1977	145,990	35,052	62,552	27,514	16,329	4,544	5,996	2,923	21	1,317	1,142	594
1978	162,727	36,396	70,647	31,770	18,550	5,364	5,733	2,724	16	1,177	1,224	592
1979	107,858	40,662	83,056	35,220	21,281	7,639	6,006	2,887	38	1,219	1,277	584
1980	215,375	45,119	96,287	38,761	22,963	12,246	6,754	3,051	35	1,624	1,422	622
1981	228,348	47,073	101,601	38,838	27,264	13,573	7,227	3,180	29	1,950	1,439	629
1982	207,752	43,511	92,449	28,161	28,282	15,351	—	—	—	—	—	—
1983	212,150	44,779	94,400	25,631	30,916	16,424	—	—	—	—	—	—
1984	218,093	47,498	94,388	26,549	33,405	16,253	—	—	—	—	—	—
1985	238,369	47,934	108,664	30,417	35,294	16,062	—	—	—	—	—	—
1986	270,472	52,006	125,613	39,318	38,472	15,064	—	—	—	—	—	—
1987	326,253	59,145	156,003	50,147	46,925	14,033	—	—	—	—	—	—
1988	347,179	63,900	163,138	55,411	52,206	12,524	—	—	—	—	—	—
1989	381,781	63,948	189,467	62,145	55,805	10,416	—	—	—	—	—	—
1990	430,521	69,508	214,739	71,413	64,718	10,144	—	—	—	—	—	—
1991	467,844	70,711	235,163	77,677	72,219	12,074	—	—	—	—	—	—
1992	502,063	68,690	248,744	91,307	79,962	13,359	—	—	—	—	—	—
1993	564,283	69,922	285,735	100,482	92,671	15,473	—	—	—	—	—	—
1994	612,893	74,221	297,133	116,478	108,528	16,533	—	—	—	—	—	—
1995	699,015	83,498	344,596	131,377	122,711	16,833	—	—	—	—	—	—
1996	795,195	89,592	389,378	155,925	139,548	20,751	—	—	—	—	—	—
1997	865,531	96,031	420,108	178,505	146,610	24,277	—	—	—	—	—	—
1998	980,565	105,905	489,539	196,655	161,797	28,668	—	—	—	—	—	—

Notes appear at end of table

(continued)

TABLE Ee72–131   U.S. direct investment in foreign countries, by region and industry: 1929–1998 *Continued*

	Petroleum						Manufacturing					
	Total	Canada	Europe	Latin America and Caribbean	Asia and Pacific	Africa, Middle East, and international	Total	Canada	Europe	Latin America and Caribbean	Asia and Pacific	Africa, Middle East, and international
	Ee84	Ee85	Ee86 [3]	Ee87	Ee88	Ee89 [4]	Ee90	Ee91	Ee92 [3]	Ee93	Ee94	Ee95 [4]
Year	Million dollars	Million dollars	Million dollars	Million dollars	Million dollars	Million dollars	Million dollars	Million dollars	Million dollars	Million dollars	Million dollars	Million dollars
1929 [7]	1,117	55	231	617	—	214	1,813	820	629	231	—	134
1936 [7]	1,074	108	275	453	—	238	1,710	799	611	192	—	108
1940 [7]	1,278	120	306	572	—	280	1,926	943	639	210	—	133
1950	3,390	418	426	1,303	258	985	3,831	1,897	932	781	166	56
1951	3,687	563	512	1,294	318	1,001	4,348	2,009	1,074	982	210	73
1952	4,273	719	532	1,455	417	1,147	4,967	2,303	1,194	1,153	243	74
1953	4,914	941	609	1,554	447	1,363	5,340	2,540	1,310	1,134	275	82
1954	5,297	1,165	668	1,539	466	1,460	5,899	2,777	1,478	1,223	325	96
1955	5,899	1,381	762	1,622	564	1,570	6,623	3,093	1,685	1,353	381	111
1956	7,355	1,759	990	2,197	643	1,764	7,561	3,526	1,952	1,531	429	124
1957	9,055	2,016	1,253	2,997	833	1,956	8,009	3,924	2,195	1,280	490	120
1958	9,822	2,293	1,320	3,152	899	2,158	8,673	4,164	2,475	1,334	565	135
1959	10,324	2,467	1,452	3,208	931	2,265	9,707	4,565	2,947	1,417	634	143
1960	10,810	2,664	1,763	3,122	994	2,267	11,051	4,827	3,804	1,521	753	144
1961	12,190	2,828	2,152	3,674	982	2,554	11,997	5,076	4,255	1,707	808	153
1962	12,725	2,875	2,385	3,642	1,079	2,745	13,250	5,312	4,883	1,944	934	177
1963	13,652	3,134	2,776	3,636	1,210	2,895	14,937	5,761	5,634	2,212	917	211
1964	14,328	3,196	3,122	3,589	1,279	3,142	16,935	6,198	6,587	2,507	1,377	267
1965	15,298	3,356	3,427	3,546	1,408	3,564	19,339	6,872	7,606	2,944	1,579	338
1966	13,893	3,171	3,627	2,456	1,223	3,415	20,740	6,697	8,906	2,973	1,762	381
1967	15,166	3,372	4,158	2,391	1,394	3,851	22,803	7,059	9,867	3,238	2,222	417
1968	16,574	3,625	4,434	2,551	1,605	4,367	25,160	7,535	10,940	3,723	2,511	451
1969	17,612	3,881	4,756	2,533	1,810	4,632	28,332	8,404	12,372	4,202	2,850	504
1970	19,754	4,337	5,481	2,703	2,103	5,131	31,049	8,971	13,819	4,541	3,155	562
1971	21,794	4,643	6,247	2,939	2,617	5,348	34,359	9,504	15,628	4,995	3,590	641
1972	23,385	4,764	6,872	2,979	3,033	5,736	38,325	10,491	17,529	5,620	4,026	659
1973	24,951	5,320	8,524	3,043	3,375	4,689	44,370	11,755	20,777	6,456	4,626	755
1974	21,418	5,731	9,830	3,564	3,882	−1,589	51,172	13,450	23,990	7,541	5,250	938
1975	25,972	6,220	11,145	3,324	5,082	176	55,886	14,691	26,013	8,562	5,525	1,093
1976	28,775	7,119	12,726	2,932	5,010	985	61,161	15,965	28,788	9,275	5,975	1,161
1977	28,030	7,015	13,629	2,786	4,595	5	62,019	14,795	30,470	9,614	5,969	1,172
1978	30,532	7,686	14,326	3,088	4,733	699	69,669	15,736	34,655	11,153	6,879	1,247
1979	39,128	8,964	17,748	4,026	5,510	2,879	79,023	17,531	39,629	12,440	7,997	1,426
1980	47,591	10,800	20,101	4,380	5,611	6,699	89,290	19,028	45,287	14,590	8,628	1,756
1981	53,244	10,677	22,681	4,831	7,386	7,670	92,388	19,818	45,270	15,809	9,629	1,863
1982	57,817	10,421	21,230	7,626	8,255	10,286	83,452	18,825	37,820	15,789	9,200	1,819
1983	58,524	10,392	20,891	7,518	9,027	10,697	83,768	19,453	38,231	14,082	10,215	1,787
1984	59,110	11,149	20,918	6,058	10,324	10,661	87,331	21,391	38,200	14,698	11,377	1,666
1985	58,724	10,443	22,039	5,042	10,540	10,660	96,741	22,306	46,248	14,944	11,981	1,262
1986	59,625	10,659	21,080	7,336	10,173	10,376	108,107	24,205	53,643	15,084	13,895	1,280
1987	60,807	11,042	22,675	6,094	11,445	9,551	135,271	27,886	71,613	16,416	17,987	1,368
1988	58,444	11,302	21,885	5,078	11,914	8,265	142,598	29,763	72,368	18,733	20,393	1,340
1989	48,325	10,455	17,698	3,883	10,968	5,321	147,944	30,154	71,578	21,438	23,382	1,393
1990	52,826	10,494	21,326	4,196	12,214	4,597	170,164	33,274	85,030	23,655	26,391	1,815
1991	57,742	10,050	23,895	4,050	13,824	5,923	179,230	32,042	92,302	24,618	28,105	2,163
1992	58,537	8,133	24,300	5,247	15,065	5,794	186,285	32,740	94,013	26,710	30,100	2,722
1993	64,175	8,688	25,290	6,057	17,734	6,408	192,244	33,371	94,886	27,333	33,518	3,136
1994	67,592	10,398	23,855	6,039	18,742	8,558	200,996	33,994	99,259	28,322	37,195	2,225
1995	68,639	9,875	23,603	6,063	20,792	8,305	243,954	39,754	122,521	36,273	42,848	2,558
1996	75,232	10,131	25,558	6,981	22,291	10,271	270,288	42,637	136,009	40,927	47,553	3,091
1997	82,215	11,018	28,001	9,917	21,228	12,052	290,332	44,464	136,593	46,124	49,529	3,621
1998	91,113	12,559	30,640	9,711	23,228	14,975	304,690	46,428	154,864	48,008	51,065	4,322

Notes appear at end of table

TABLE Ee72–131   U.S. direct investment in foreign countries, by region and industry: 1929–1998   *Continued*

	Transportation, communication, and public utilities						Trade					
	Total	Canada	Europe	Latin America and Caribbean	Asia and Pacific	Africa, Middle East, and international	Total	Canada	Europe	Latin America and Caribbean	Asia and Pacific	Africa, Middle East, and international
	Ee96	Ee97	Ee98	Ee99	Ee100	Ee101 [5]	Ee102	Ee103	Ee104 [3]	Ee105	Ee106	Ee107 [4]
Year	Million dollars	Million dollars	Million dollars	Million dollars	Million dollars	Million dollars	Million dollars	Million dollars	Million dollars	Million dollars	Million dollars	Million dollars
1929 [7]	1,610	542	145	887	—	36	368	38	139	119	—	72
1936 [7]	1,640	520	91	937	—	92	391	79	144	100	—	68
1940 [7]	1,514	407	74	962	—	71	523	112	245	82	—	84
1950	1,425	284	27	942	51	121	762	240	186	245	64	27
1951	1,432	287	28	941	53	124	876	262	207	301	75	32
1952	1,477	290	29	967	55	136	963	289	218	341	81	35
1953	1,516	303	30	976	57	151	1,047	342	234	352	82	38
1954	1,566	304	31	992	62	176	1,170	377	256	401	92	44
1955	1,647	329	32	1,013	66	205	1,296	411	297	433	105	51
1956	1,778	353	41	1,065	70	249	1,483	464	326	513	125	56
1957	2,145	581	38	1,049	76	399	1,668	499	433	571	117	48
1958	2,270	601	41	1,097	85	444	1,786	524	480	604	125	53
1959	2,445	633	44	1,152	92	522	2,039	564	586	683	155	52
1960	2,215	626	45	869	97	575	2,353	630	736	738	188	60
1961	1,988	471	47	750	112	627	2,670	646	893	855	211	65
1962	1,989	473	50	739	35	691	2,985	699	1,084	889	234	78
1963	2,061	457	44	763	38	760	3,307	747	1,237	964	269	90
1964	2,020	471	53	616	52	827	3,688	805	1,446	1,034	302	103
1965	2,136	486	60	640	60	890	4,219	882	1,730	1,132	349	127
1966	2,260	441	76	542	87	1,114	4,331	859	1,932	851	282	408
1967	2,383	470	85	546	79	1,205	4,640	926	2,059	905	313	435
1968	2,586	519	99	562	93	1,314	4,872	1,010	2,113	944	337	467
1969	2,637	565	91	567	112	1,302	5,452	1,093	2,456	987	421	496
1970	2,759	598	113	469	147	1,429	6,201	1,162	2,872	1,135	469	562
1971	2,807	616	129	493	162	1,408	6,871	1,261	3,229	1,229	578	574
1972	2,844	623	130	471	183	1,439	7,799	1,447	3,686	1,343	718	604
1973	2,837	665	136	454	193	1,389	9,313	1,606	4,519	1,563	919	705
1974	3,105	702	156	473	189	1,584	11,331	1,844	5,473	2,003	1,161	851
1975	3,184	761	153	354	216	1,782	12,505	2,006	6,084	2,321	1,266	824
1976	3,229	771	154	286	199	1,817	13,577	2,112	6,690	2,417	1,435	924
1977	—	—	—	—	—	—	16,836	2,990	8,773	2,359	2,171	542
1978	—	—	—	—	—	—	19,517	3,169	10,303	2,687	2,751	607
1979	—	—	—	—	—	—	22,670	3,588	12,135	3,211	3,037	699
1980	—	—	—	—	—	—	25,913	3,894	14,116	3,881	3,236	785
1981	—	—	—	—	—	—	28,336	4,162	15,316	4,198	3,894	765
1982	—	—	—	—	—	—	20,788	2,754	10,975	2,780	3,500	779
1983	—	—	—	—	—	—	21,661	2,630	11,129	2,782	4,269	851
1984	—	—	—	—	—	—	21,849	2,574	11,411	2,666	4,451	747
1985	—	—	—	—	—	—	23,894	2,597	12,459	2,929	4,926	982
1986	—	—	—	—	—	—	27,841	2,791	16,034	2,650	5,836	529
1987	—	—	—	—	—	—	33,836	3,448	20,032	2,768	7,204	385
1988	—	—	—	—	—	—	36,359	3,819	20,744	3,135	8,185	477
1989	—	—	—	—	—	—	38,454	4,854	21,832	2,807	8,604	357
1990	—	—	—	—	—	—	43,681	5,368	25,815	2,816	9,275	407
1991	—	—	—	—	—	—	49,927	6,848	27,553	4,462	10,761	303
1992	—	—	—	—	—	—	52,694	6,076	29,452	4,582	12,262	321
1993	—	—	—	—	—	—	57,534	6,982	30,933	4,956	14,312	351
1994	—	—	—	—	—	—	59,030	6,865	30,040	6,151	15,528	446
1995	—	—	—	—	—	—	68,102	7,390	34,237	9,677	16,184	613
1996	—	—	—	—	—	—	67,125	7,091	36,068	6,347	17,160	460
1997	—	—	—	—	—	—	64,432	7,146	32,759	6,897	17,135	496
1998	—	—	—	—	—	—	75,188	7,265	40,750	7,997	18,692	484

Notes appear at end of table

(continued)

TABLE Ee72–131   U.S. direct investment in foreign countries, by region and industry: 1929–1998   *Continued*

	Finance						Banking					
	Total	Canada	Europe	Latin American and Caribbean	Asia and Pacific	Africa, Middle East, and international	Total	Canada	Europe	Latin America and Caribbean	Asia and Pacific	Africa, Middle East, and international
	Ee108	Ee109	Ee110	Ee111	Ee112	Ee113	Ee114	Ee115	Ee116	Ee117	Ee118	Ee119
Year	Million dollars	Million dollars	Million dollars	Million dollars	Million dollars	Million dollars	Million dollars	Million dollars	Million dollars	Million dollars	Million dollars	Million dollars
1929 [7]	—	—	—	—	—	—	—	—	—	—	—	—
1936 [7]	—	—	—	—	—	—	—	—	—	—	—	—
1940 [7]	—	—	—	—	—	—	—	—	—	—	—	—
1950	—	—	—	—	—	—	—	—	—	—	—	—
1951	—	—	—	—	—	—	—	—	—	—	—	—
1952	—	—	—	—	—	—	—	—	—	—	—	—
1953	—	—	—	—	—	—	—	—	—	—	—	—
1954	—	—	—	—	—	—	—	—	—	—	—	—
1955	—	—	—	—	—	—	—	—	—	—	—	—
1956	—	—	—	—	—	—	—	—	—	—	—	—
1957	—	—	—	—	—	—	—	—	—	—	—	—
1958	—	—	—	—	—	—	—	—	—	—	—	—
1959	—	—	—	—	—	—	—	—	—	—	—	—
1960	—	—	—	—	—	—	—	—	—	—	—	—
1961	—	—	—	—	—	—	—	—	—	—	—	—
1962	—	—	—	—	—	—	—	—	—	—	—	—
1963	—	—	—	—	—	—	—	—	—	—	—	—
1964	—	—	—	—	—	—	—	—	—	—	—	—
1965	—	—	—	—	—	—	—	—	—	—	—	—
1966	4,540	2,198	1,237	957	75	17	—	—	—	—	—	—
1967	4,864	2,242	1,412	1,052	87	71	—	—	—	—	—	—
1968	5,387	2,446	1,564	1,138	108	132	—	—	—	—	—	—
1969	6,331	2,678	1,818	1,249	124	462	—	—	—	—	—	—
1970	7,190	2,728	2,106	1,411	168	774	—	—	—	—	—	—
1971	7,784	2,386	2,469	1,615	208	1,044	—	—	—	—	—	—
1972	8,169	2,496	2,397	1,743	307	1,226	—	—	—	—	—	—
1973	9,726	2,752	3,065	2,108	381	1,419	—	—	—	—	—	—
1974	12,631	3,160	3,793	3,459	508	1,712	—	—	—	—	—	—
1975	14,619	3,490	4,160	4,649	586	1,735	—	—	—	—	—	—
1976	16,793	3,785	4,688	5,825	722	1,772	—	—	—	—	—	—
1977	21,248	5,412	5,674	8,787	840	534	4,370	117	2,021	1,367	675	189
1978	23,339	5,419	6,315	10,358	1,042	203	5,622	—	2,506	1,926	—	—
1979	25,129	5,774	7,393	10,490	1,219	255	6,501	—	3,033	2,194	—	—
1980	27,506	6,104	9,866	9,760	1,444	332	7,264	—	3,218	2,501	—	—
1981	26,561	6,541	11,217	6,556	1,901	345	8,513	380	3,294	3,180	—	—
1982	18,018	5,644	14,264	−4,499	2,374	235	10,317	439	4,107	3,412	1,782	578
1983	17,327	6,012	14,925	−6,094	2,234	250	12,482	496	4,910	4,311	2,071	694
1984	18,272	6,186	14,765	−5,368	2,434	254	13,673	521	5,025	5,353	2,085	690
1985	25,301	5,824	16,894	−893	3,134	341	14,734	549	6,326	5,484	1,889	488
1986	39,742	7,387	21,901	5,590	3,838	1,025	14,910	574	7,213	4,934	1,852	338
1987	56,408	10,067	27,275	13,139	4,570	1,357	18,400	594	7,814	7,471	2,584	−64
1988	66,071	11,012	32,308	16,581	4,909	1,261	19,337	782	8,168	7,290	3,187	−90
1989	101,086	10,512	60,136	24,581	4,548	1,307	19,378	985	8,276	6,125	3,679	312
1990	109,657	11,661	60,636	30,424	5,770	1,167	20,670	1,076	9,119	6,028	4,129	318
1991	120,552	12,040	66,420	32,599	8,013	1,480	21,283	1,078	9,136	6,417	4,291	362
1992	137,186	12,781	72,666	41,144	9,091	1,503	24,653	874	10,735	7,539	5,103	402
1993	174,684	11,511	102,387	47,483	11,574	1,731	27,074	840	12,146	7,496	6,055	536
1994	195,879	13,029	105,811	58,037	16,903	2,099	27,444	904	11,891	6,770	7,209	671
1995	218,313	14,994	118,430	62,615	20,033	2,241	29,181	918	13,300	5,685	8,519	759
1996	254,739	17,465	133,056	78,546	23,247	2,423	36,807	1,013	18,972	5,681	11,247	958
1997	293,116	20,186	154,513	87,472	28,224	2,771	40,169	1,041	23,342	4,685	10,020	1,037
1998	337,600	22,057	178,179	98,845	36,714	2,806	42,029	1,203	25,614	3,198	—	1,152

Notes appear at end of table

TABLE Ee72–131   U.S. direct investment in foreign countries, by region and industry: 1929–1998 *Continued*

	Services						Other					
	Total	Canada	Europe	Latin America and Caribbean	Asia and Pacific	Africa, Middle East, and international	Total	Canada	Europe	Latin America and Caribbean	Asia and Pacific	Africa, Middle East, and international
	Ee120	Ee121	Ee122	Ee123	Ee124	Ee125	Ee126 [6]	Ee127 [6]	Ee128 [3,6]	Ee129 [6]	Ee130 [6]	Ee131 [4,6]
Year	Million dollars	Million dollars	Million dollars	Million dollars	Million dollars	Million dollars	Million dollars	Million dollars	Million dollars	Million dollars	Million dollars	Million dollars
1929 [7]	—	—	—	—	—	—	1,435	157	209	933	—	137
1936 [7]	—	—	—	—	—	—	844	207	80	457	—	99
1940 [7]	—	—	—	—	—	—	979	333	104	433	—	109
1950	—	—	—	—	—	—	1,251	406	130	639	49	27
1951	—	—	—	—	—	—	1,343	443	137	681	60	24
1952	—	—	—	—	—	—	1,419	476	146	698	73	25
1953	—	—	—	—	—	—	1,514	526	157	720	89	28
1954	—	—	—	—	—	—	1,632	599	170	742	91	30
1955	—	—	—	—	—	—	1,733	643	180	772	103	34
1956	—	—	—	—	—	—	1,909	693	200	848	122	47
1957	—	—	—	—	—	—	2,157	894	177	923	118	44
1958	—	—	—	—	—	—	2,300	950	205	965	123	56
1959	—	—	—	—	—	—	2,463	993	244	1,016	139	71
1960	—	—	—	—	—	—	2,438	1,107	293	798	154	86
1961	—	—	—	—	—	—	2,778	1,215	347	940	168	107
1962	—	—	—	—	—	—	3,083	1,285	477	989	215	117
1963	—	—	—	—	—	—	3,359	1,396	594	1,014	228	127
1964	—	—	—	—	—	—	3,844	1,473	864	1,103	254	158
1965	—	—	—	—	—	—	4,550	1,871	1,107	1,148	263	159
1966	—	—	—	—	—	—	2,046	371	595	633	238	207
1967	—	—	—	—	—	—	2,256	419	625	700	227	286
1968	—	—	—	—	—	—	2,491	447	677	801	247	319
1969	—	—	—	—	—	—	2,731	515	718	897	287	314
1970	—	—	—	—	—	—	3,123	645	824	991	336	327
1971	—	—	—	—	—	—	3,357	701	906	1,014	363	369
1972	—	—	—	—	—	—	3,688	756	1,036	1,052	405	439
1973	—	—	—	—	—	—	4,079	778	1,178	1,177	468	478
1974	—	—	—	—	—	—	4,630	723	1,373	1,356	610	567
1975	—	—	—	—	—	—	5,335	814	1,690	1,482	587	763
1976	—	—	—	—	—	—	6,213	865	2,059	1,598	658	1,033
1977	—	—	—	—	—	—	7,489	1,800	1,963	1,283	687	1,756
1978	—	—	—	—	—	—	8,315	—	2,525	1,382	—	—
1979	—	—	—	—	—	—	9,406	—	3,080	1,640	—	—
1980	—	—	—	—	—	—	11,056	—	3,664	2,024	—	—
1981	—	—	—	—	—	—	12,080	2,315	3,793	2,314	—	—
1982	4,615	814	2,477	626	539	159	12,745	4,614	1,575	2,428	2,633	1,495
1983	4,903	758	2,735	492	506	411	13,484	5,038	1,579	2,540	2,593	1,736
1984	4,795	765	2,758	405	519	348	13,063	4,912	1,311	2,737	2,214	1,888
1985	5,201	848	2,978	507	520	346	13,775	5,366	1,720	2,405	2,303	1,980
1986	5,770	948	3,781	545	540	−44	14,478	5,441	1,961	3,180	2,338	1,559
1987	7,635	1,009	4,295	1,265	729	337	13,897	5,101	2,299	2,994	2,405	1,098
1988	8,831	1,283	4,949	1,568	875	157	15,538	5,938	2,716	3,028	2,743	1,113
1989	11,736	—	7,288	876	1,332	—	14,859	—	2,658	2,435	3,291	—
1990	13,446	2,185	8,707	967	1,399	188	20,077	5,450	4,108	3,328	5,540	1,650
1991	15,781	3,038	9,663	1,190	1,608	281	23,330	5,615	6,193	4,341	5,617	1,563
1992	17,208	2,857	11,362	1,095	1,543	351	25,500	5,229	6,216	4,991	6,799	2,267
1993	19,489	3,164	12,984	702	2,290	348	29,083	5,366	7,109	6,456	7,189	2,963
1994	26,993	3,250	15,564	2,922	4,821	437	34,960	5,780	10,713	8,238	8,132	2,097
1995	29,721	3,633	19,138	2,289	4,284	378	41,105	6,933	13,367	8,774	10,051	1,979
1996	37,850	3,973	23,614	4,615	5,274	375	53,155	7,283	16,031	12,827	13,840	3,175
1997	42,342	4,307	26,039	5,921	5,560	515	62,925	7,868	18,863	17,539	14,870	3,786
1998	52,514	4,578	33,810	6,910	6,436	759	77,432	9,799	25,682	21,986	15,798	4,166

[1] Series Ee96–101 included with "other" beginning with 1977; series Ee78–83 included with "other" beginning with 1982.

[2] All figures are book value at year end.

[3] Includes Eastern Europe in 1929, 1936, and 1940, amounting to $89 million, $93 million, and $259 million, respectively. Excludes Turkey for 1936 and 1940.

[4] Includes Turkey for 1936 and 1940, and Western European dependencies for 1929, 1936, and 1940.

[5] Beginning 1982, includes "Mining and smelting."

[6] Excludes insurance in 1929; beginning with 1950, includes "Agriculture"; beginning with 1977, includes "Transportation, communication, and public utilities"; beginning with 1982, includes "Mining and smelting."

[7] Caribbean combined with "Africa, Middle East, and international."

[8] Includes $26 million reported as "international."

[9] Europe combined with "Africa, Middle East and international."

(continued)

TABLE Ee72–131   U.S. direct investment in foreign countries, by region and industry: 1929–1998   *Continued*

Sources

1929–1949, U.S. Office of Business Economics, *The United States in the World Economy*, Economic Series number 23 (1943), p. 123; U.S. Bureau of Foreign and Domestic Commerce, *The Balance of International Payments of the United States in 1931*, Trade Information Bulletin number 803 (1932), pp. 44, 48, 62; U.S. Bureau of Foreign and Domestic Commerce, *Foreign Investments in the United States* (1937), p. 5; Cleona Lewis, *America's Stake in International Investments* (Brookings Institution Press, 1938); U.S. Office of Business Economics, *International Transactions of the United States during the War 1940–45* (as revised), Economic Series number 65 (1948), p. 110.

1950–1976, U.S. Bureau of Economic Analysis, *Selected Data on U.S. Direct Investment Abroad, 1950–76*, PB87121869 (U.S. Department of Commerce/National Technical Information Service, February 1982).

1977–1981: U.S. Bureau of Economic Analysis, *U.S. Direct Investment Abroad: Balance of Payments and Direct Investment Position Estimates, 1977–81*, PB87-178265 (U.S. Department of Commerce/National Technical Information Service, November 1986).

1982–1998, U.S. Bureau of Economic Analysis, *U.S. Direct Investment Abroad: Balance of Payments and Direct Investment Position Estimates, 1982–1998*, IID (BE-50), IDN-0241 (U.S. Bureau of Economic Analysis, August 5, 1999).

Documentation

U.S. direct investment abroad is valued at book cost at year end, also known as historical cost. The U.S. Bureau of Economic Analysis (BEA) uses either reports of currently held stocks (outstandings) or reports of outstandings from some time in the past (a benchmark) in combination with cumulated changes. The changes reflect capital flows and changes in the valuation of the outstandings.

In these tables, industry classification is by the industry of the foreign affiliate. The country classification "international," grouped with Africa and the Middle East, consists of affiliates that have operations spanning more than one country and that are engaged in petroleum shipping, other water transportation, or offshore oil and gas shipping. Some data have been suppressed by the BEA to avoid disclosure of data on individual companies.

Through 1961, U.S. direct investments in foreign countries include all foreign enterprises whose voting stock is owned to the extent of at least 25 percent by U.S. organizations or individuals, or in the management of which Americans have an important voice. Starting with 1962, direct investments abroad include voting stock owned to the extent of at least 10 percent by U.S. organizations or individuals, or in the management of which Americans have an important voice. In addition, they include unincorporated foreign branches or other direct foreign operations of U.S. interests, including mining claims, oil concessions, and other property held for business purposes, such as real estate.

TABLE Ee132–165   Foreign direct investment in the United States, by country and industry: 1937–1998[1,2]

Contributed by Michael Edelstein

	All areas				Canada				Europe			
									Total			
Year	Total	Petroleum	Manufacturing	Finance and insurance	Total	Petroleum	Manufacturing	Finance and insurance	Total	Petroleum	Manufacturing	Finance and insurance
	Ee132	Ee133	Ee134	Ee135	Ee136	Ee137	Ee138	Ee139	Ee140	Ee141	Ee142	Ee143
	Million dollars	Million dollars	Million dollars	Million dollars	Million dollars	Million dollars	Million dollars	Million dollars	Million dollars	Million dollars	Million dollars	Million dollars
1937	1,882	283	729	412	463	—	—	—	1,337	—	—	—
1941	2,312	222	714	521	530	—	—	—	1,569	—	—	—
1950	3,391	405	1,138	1,065	1,029	56	468	153	2,228	349	669	870
1951	3,658	466	1,274	1,105	1,109	62	525	150	2,410	404	747	912
1952	3,945	552	1,377	1,170	1,218	90	592	149	2,575	462	782	977
1953	4,251	706	1,451	1,219	1,350	168	611	162	2,751	538	836	1,014
1954	4,633	776	1,582	1,371	1,427	192	651	168	3,049	584	925	1,158
1955	5,076	853	1,759	1,499	1,542	196	711	179	3,369	657	1,040	1,272
1956	5,459	937	1,940	1,534	1,690	200	775	196	3,598	737	1,155	1,289
1957	5,710	1,043	2,083	1,496	1,773	211	816	208	3,753	832	1,248	1,238
1958	6,115	1,099	2,232	1,660	1,835	214	863	222	4,070	885	1,332	1,384
1959	6,604	1,184	2,471	1,734	1,896	207	907	227	4,452	972	1,501	1,451
1960	6,910	1,238	2,611	1,810	1,934	203	932	246	4,707	1,028	1,611	1,504
1961	7,392	1,325	2,754	2,025	1,989	194	975	274	5,129	1,125	1,708	1,690
1962	7,612	1,419	2,885	1,943	2,064	212	1,015	269	5,245	1,203	1,797	1,611
1963	7,944	1,513	3,018	2,045	2,183	213	1,063	337	5,491	1,306	1,881	1,640
1964	8,363	1,612	3,213	2,181	2,284	205	1,129	382	5,819	1,404	2,005	1,723
1965	8,797	1,710	3,478	2,169	2,388	208	1,219	370	6,076	1,481	2,167	1,724
1966	9,054	1,740	3,789	2,072	2,439	98	1,342	386	6,273	1,620	2,335	1,611
1967	9,923	1,885	4,181	2,193	2,575	99	1,397	354	7,005	1,772	2,669	1,758
1968	10,815	2,261	4,475	2,305	2,659	100	1,413	376	7,750	2,146	2,941	1,855
1969	11,818	2,493	5,344	2,189	2,834	132	1,644	325	8,510	2,322	3,530	1,766
1970	13,270	2,992	6,140	2,256	3,117	190	1,836	324	9,554	2,777	4,091	1,805
1971	13,914	3,139	6,722	2,553	3,335	207	2,013	330	10,336	2,893	4,455	2,048
1972	14,868	3,272	7,262	2,911	3,466	243	2,201	353	11,087	3,012	4,836	2,336
1973	20,556	4,792	8,231	3,415	4,203	426	2,319	376	13,937	4,079	4,790	2,174
1974	25,144	5,614	10,387	3,530	5,136	547	2,905	425	16,756	4,714	6,109	1,954
1975	27,662	6,213	11,386	3,928	5,352	596	3,061	451	18,584	5,478	6,673	2,218
1976	30,770	5,921	12,620	4,741	5,907	676	3,386	541	20,162	4,999	7,426	2,815
1977	34,595	6,573	14,030	5,398	5,650	710	3,077	464	23,754	5,523	9,267	3,273
1978	42,471	7,762	17,202	6,392	6,180	734	3,213	540	29,180	6,569	11,717	3,905
1979	54,462	9,906	20,876	9,395	7,154	943	3,615	839	37,403	8,010	13,952	6,080
1980	83,046	12,200	33,011	18,147	12,162	1,817	5,227	2,770	54,688	10,137	21,972	10,927
1981	108,714	15,246	40,533	23,712	12,116	1,801	3,376	3,551	72,377	12,854	30,897	13,805
1982	124,677	17,660	44,065	29,453	11,708	1,550	3,500	3,682	83,193	15,071	33,032	17,720
1983	137,061	18,209	47,665	34,267	11,434	1,391	3,313	3,827	92,936	16,326	36,866	20,862
1984	164,583	25,400	51,802	42,642	15,286	1,544	4,115	6,089	108,211	23,142	39,083	24,200
1985	184,615	28,270	59,584	79,831	17,131	1,589	4,607	6,758	121,413	25,636	45,841	25,943
1986	220,414	29,094	71,963	57,490	20,318	1,432	6,108	7,603	144,181	26,139	56,016	31,608
1987	263,394	37,815	93,865	61,480	24,684	1,088	8,085	9,645	181,006	35,700	74,300	35,494
1988	314,754	36,006	122,582	69,877	26,566	1,181	9,730	9,237	208,942	33,499	95,641	36,360
1989	368,924	40,345	150,949	89,983	30,370	1,141	9,766	12,240	239,190	32,649	118,129	43,197
1990	394,911	42,882	152,805	88,863	29,544	1,373	9,201	12,356	247,320	34,284	115,831	39,959
1991	419,108	40,051	157,115	103,201	36,834	2,468	15,716	13,462	256,053	31,436	114,248	49,621
1992	423,131	34,746	160,360	103,897	37,515	2,404	15,757	12,401	249,904	25,458	116,132	48,197
1993	467,412	32,214	168,147	135,161	40,373	2,846	16,030	12,743	285,004	23,697	124,675	73,428
1994	480,667	32,290	189,459	122,712	41,219	3,097	17,439	11,478	294,035	23,947	138,751	65,175
1995	535,553	34,907	214,504	149,503	45,618	3,241	20,320	13,128	332,374	24,039	156,543	80,000
1996	598,021	43,483	245,662	160,088	54,836	3,220	23,096	17,031	370,843	29,194	176,309	84,963
1997	693,201	42,085	273,122	192,083	69,866	3,177	27,811	22,943	432,622	29,750	197,819	104,150
1998	811,756	53,254	329,346	220,457	74,840	2,633	26,152	26,643	539,906	42,771	252,893	125,687

Notes appear at end of table   (continued)

TABLE Ee132–165   Foreign direct investment in the United States, by country and industry: 1937–1998   *Continued*

	Europe										
	United Kingdom				Netherlands				Switzerland		
	Total	Petroleum	Manufacturing	Finance and insurance	Total	Petroleum	Manufacturing	Finance and insurance	Total	Manufacturing	Finance and insurance
	Ee144	Ee145	Ee146	Ee147	Ee148	Ee149	Ee150	Ee151	Ee152	Ee153	Ee154
Year	Million dollars	Million dollars	Million dollars	Million dollars	Million dollars	Million dollars	Million dollars	Million dollars	Million dollars	Million dollars	Million dollars
1937	833	—	—	—	179	—	—	—	74	—	—
1941	712	—	—	—	336	—	—	—	138	—	—
1950	1,168	95	337	554	334	226	44	34	348	204	147
1951	1,273	118	388	583	376	257	54	34	369	215	155
1952	1,345	137	395	626	423	289	68	34	390	224	165
1953	1,422	163	419	647	480	333	80	35	415	237	176
1954	1,590	180	460	751	533	364	98	36	466	257	201
1955	1,749	204	510	836	613	411	127	37	522	282	223
1956	1,833	227	566	841	681	461	142	38	557	304	230
1957	1,881	271	611	794	747	512	155	39	576	324	223
1958	2,024	283	640	889	816	553	176	41	636	344	261
1959	2,167	316	698	927	892	607	197	42	716	395	280
1960	2,248	339	722	953	947	639	213	42	773	427	300
1961	2,484	381	750	1,091	1,023	693	231	43	830	433	345
1962	2,474	416	762	1,023	1,082	736	248	43	836	454	339
1963	2,665	480	779	1,085	1,134	772	275	36	825	477	307
1964	2,796	498	812	1,154	1,231	842	296	39	896	530	321
1965	2,852	511	839	1,176	1,304	887	328	36	940	590	303
1966	2,864	558	906	1,075	1,402	953	356	39	949	615	287
1967	3,156	612	1,009	1,189	1,508	1,021	388	41	1,096	744	309
1968	3,409	749	1,076	1,239	1,750	1,215	426	54	1,238	863	331
1969	3,496	829	1,176	1,143	1,966	1,275	535	55	1,395	1,026	323
1970	4,127	1,220	1,391	1,141	2,151	1,311	652	58	1,545	1,147	351
1971	4,583	1,270	1,615	1,326	2,224	1,353	697	41	1,576	1,124	394
1972	4,987	1,297	1,719	1,567	2,357	1,407	769	46	1,675	1,194	416
1973	5,403	1,212	1,551	1,236	4,017	—	997	153	1,420	922	321
1974	5,744	1,502	1,792	898	4,698	—	1,213	—	1,949	1,222	273
1975	6,331	—	1,833	—	5,347	—	1,345	—	2,138	1,308	375
1976	5,802	602	1,963	—	6,255	—	1,501	491	2,295	1,357	—
1977	6,397	486	2,305	1,506	7,830	—	2,237	—	2,651	1,769	493
1978	7,638	492	3,014	1,691	10,078	5,041	3,058	848	2,879	1,949	527
1979	9,796	199	3,547	2,620	12,672	6,478	3,492	1,328	3,449	2,281	604
1980	14,105	−257	4,166	—	19,140	9,265	4,777	2,848	5,070	3,116	1,113
1981	18,585	−124	7,602	—	26,824	11,547	9,018	4,125	5,474	3,278	—
1982	28,447	5,444	8,504	7,721	26,191	8,098	9,901	5,433	6,378	3,584	—
1983	32,152	5,955	9,221	9,363	29,182	8,646	11,222	6,126	7,464	4,165	—
1984	38,387	10,991	9,719	9,620	33,728	9,981	12,497	7,313	8,146	4,774	—
1985	43,555	12,155	11,687	11,247	37,056	11,481	13,351	7,637	10,568	6,881	2,503
1986	55,935	11,758	16,500	15,374	40,717	—	13,293	9,110	12,058	7,520	—
1987	75,519	17,950	30,372	13,834	46,636	—	15,615	11,334	13,772	6,921	3,405
1988	95,698	16,522	41,708	15,459	48,128	9,045	17,843	12,748	14,372	7,613	3,687
1989	103,458	16,666	50,166	17,277	56,734	10,061	23,090	13,961	18,746	11,798	4,635
1990	98,676	15,900	42,365	16,714	64,671	13,267	24,734	12,352	17,674	10,651	5,095
1991	100,085	14,068	41,924	18,835	63,113	12,444	19,540	16,323	18,482	10,222	6,467
1992	86,587	10,999	40,195	16,586	69,107	11,349	21,480	18,631	19,646	9,954	6,417
1993	98,739	9,651	43,151	25,513	72,893	11,855	22,130	22,957	21,681	11,773	6,426
1994	98,732	9,489	47,334	17,461	66,600	11,444	19,782	21,077	24,936	13,212	7,890
1995	116,272	9,275	56,703	24,547	65,116	11,588	19,130	22,083	27,258	13,506	10,044
1996	121,582	11,060	58,675	20,381	73,349	12,142	27,437	22,637	30,363	16,203	9,703
1997	131,315	11,068	58,342	24,429	89,570	12,949	31,565	28,966	38,281	21,187	12,693
1998	151,335	26,277	64,022	21,233	96,904	11,505	35,109	34,230	54,011	26,310	19,801

TABLE Ee132–165   Foreign direct investment in the United States, by country and industry: 1937–1998   *Continued*

	Europe							Japan			
	Germany			Other Europe							Other areas
Year	Total	Manufacturing	Finance and insurance	Total	Petroleum	Manufacturing	Finance and insurance	Total	Manufacturing	Finance and insurance	Other areas
	Ee155 [3]	Ee156 [3]	Ee157 [3]	Ee158 [3]	Ee159 [3]	Ee160 [3]	Ee161 [3]	Ee162	Ee163	Ee164	Ee165
	Million dollars	Million dollars	Million dollars	Million dollars	Million dollars	Million dollars	Million dollars	Million dollars	Million dollars	Million dollars	Million dollars
1937	—	—	—	—	—	—	—	—	—	—	82
1941	—	—	—	—	—	—	—	—	—	—	213
1950	—	—	—	377	28	84	135	—	—	—	134
1951	—	—	—	392	29	90	140	—	—	—	139
1952	—	—	—	417	36	95	152	—	—	—	152
1953	—	—	—	434	42	100	156	—	—	—	150
1954	—	—	—	460	40	110	170	—	—	—	157
1955	—	—	—	485	42	121	176	—	—	—	165
1956	—	—	—	527	49	143	180	—	—	—	171
1957	—	—	—	549	49	158	182	—	—	—	184
1958	—	—	—	594	49	172	193	—	—	—	210
1959	—	—	—	677	49	211	201	80	—	16	176
1960	—	—	—	739	50	249	209	88	50	19	181
1961	—	—	—	791	51	294	211	92	51	18	182
1962	—	—	—	855	51	333	207	112	51	19	190
1963	—	—	—	867	54	350	212	104	55	20	165
1964	—	—	—	897	64	367	209	72	54	22	187
1965	—	—	—	980	83	410	209	118	56	22	214
1966	—	—	—	1,059	109	458	210	103	60	22	238
1967	—	—	—	1,245	139	528	219	108	64	25	235
1968	—	—	—	1,353	182	576	231	181	65	33	225
1969	—	—	—	1,653	218	793	245	176	67	39	298
1970	—	—	—	1,731	246	901	255	229	70	43	370
1971	—	—	—	1,953	270	1,019	287	−227	76	50	471
1972	—	—	—	2,068	308	1,154	307	−154	72	57	468
1973	965	593	—	3,097	—	727	—	152	141	282	2,264
1974	1,535	852	—	4,368	—	1,030	—	345	330	404	2,907
1975	1,408	894	—	4,768	494	1,293	—	591	325	—	3,135
1976	2,097	1,173	—	5,810	661	1,432	—	1,178	304	—	3,523
1977	2,529	1,301	217	6,875	—	1,655	—	1,755	332	583	3,436
1978	3,654	1,920	315	8,585	1,028	1,776	524	2,749	474	—	4,362
1979	5,665	2,665	899	11,487	1,314	1,967	629	3,493	696	768	6,412
1980	7,596	2,291	2,044	8,777	1,129	7,622	4,922	4,723	1,033	—	11,473
1981	5,876	4,199	—	15,618	1,431	6,800	9,680	7,697	1,321	—	16,524
1982	9,850	4,239	2,204	12,327	1,529	6,804	2,362	9,677	1,624	1,320	20,099
1983	10,845	4,487	2,568	13,293	1,725	7,771	2,805	11,336	1,605	—	21,355
1984	12,330	4,389	2,868	15,620	2,170	7,704	4,399	16,044	2,460	3,248	25,042
1985	14,816	6,015	—	15,418	2,000	7,907	4,556	19,313	2,738	3,863	26,758
1986	17,250	7,426	3,095	18,221	—	11,277	4,029	26,824	3,578	—	29,091
1987	21,905	10,298	4,482	23,174	—	11,094	2,439	34,421	4,970	11,223	23,283
1988	25,250	13,980	3,756	25,494	7,932	14,497	710	51,126	11,065	18,489	28,120
1989	28,386	15,560	4,321	31,866	5,922	17,515	3,003	67,268	15,601	25,287	32,096
1990	28,232	15,718	3,737	38,067	5,117	22,363	2,061	83,091	17,145	30,476	34,956
1991	29,335	15,659	3,546	45,038	4,924	26,903	4,450	95,142	18,177	32,398	31,079
1992	29,419	16,537	2,814	45,145	3,110	27,966	3,749	97,769	18,781	31,300	37,943
1993	34,987	18,119	6,559	56,704	2,191	29,502	11,973	100,721	18,375	31,389	41,314
1994	39,630	22,380	7,377	64,137	3,014	36,043	11,370	98,513	20,636	27,566	46,900
1995	46,017	24,989	9,495	77,711	3,176	42,215	13,831	104,997	25,535	34,175	52,564
1996	61,096	29,596	13,030	84,453	5,992	44,398	19,212	116,144	35,521	33,904	56,198
1997	71,289	34,522	17,388	102,167	5,733	52,203	20,674	125,131	37,356	35,504	65,582
1998	95,045	51,018	20,657	142,611	4,989	76,434	29,766	132,569	39,918	38,221	64,441

[1] All figures are book value at year end.

[2] Through 1979, banking included in "other." Thereafter, banking included in finance and insurance.

[3] Prior to 1973, Germany included in "Other Europe."

Sources

1937–1961, U.S. Office of Business Economics, *Foreign Business Investments in the United States, 1962;* 1950–1979, U.S. Bureau of Economic Analysis

(BEA), *Selected Data on Foreign Investment in the United States, 1950–79,* IPN0064 (BEA, December 1984). 1980–1986, BEA, *Foreign Investment in the United States: Balance of Payments and Direct Investment Position Estimates, 1980–1986,* IID (BE-50), IDN0066 (BEA, 1990). 1987–1998, BEA, *Foreign Investment in the United States: Balance of Payments and Direct Investment Position Estimates 1987–1997,* IID (BE-50), IDN-0242 (U.S. Bureau of Economic Analysis, September 3, 1999).

(continued)

TABLE Ee132–165   Foreign direct investment in the United States, by country and industry: 1937–1998 *Continued*

Documentation

The basic data for these series were derived from reports filed with the Department of Commerce by enterprises in the United States. Reports were required by law under section 8 of the Bretton Woods Agreements Act (59 Stat. 515, 22 U.S.C. 286f). Forms and instructions were mailed directly to lists of companies developed from tax records, news reports, previous census studies, and records of the Office of Business Economics. Some data have been suppressed by the Department of Commerce to avoid disclosure of data on individual companies.

Through 1973, direct foreign investments in the United States included the following U.S. business enterprises for which reports were required: (1) A U.S. corporation in which 25 percent or more of the voting stock was owned directly or indirectly by a foreign person or organization; (2) branches of foreign corporations resident in the United States; (3) partnerships and proprietorships resident in the United States in which 25 percent or more ownership was held by a foreign person or organization; (4) U.S. enterprises held as part of an estate or trust created under the laws of the United States in which foreign beneficial owners held an interest of 25 percent or more; and (5) real estate and other real property, including leaseholds, acquired for commercial purposes, in which an interest of 25 percent or more was held by a foreign person or organization. Starting in 1974, foreign direct investments in the United States cover U.S. business enterprises, including real estate investments, in which there is a foreign interest or ownership of 10 percent or more. Foreign direct investment in the United States is valued at book cost, also known as historical cost.

There were certain exemptions from filing a report, as follows: (1) If the value of total assets was less than $50,000, a report was required only for information identifying the reporter; (2) reports were not required from religious bodies, charitable organizations, or other nonprofit organizations in the United States; and (3) reports were not required in connection with real or personal property acquired for personal use or occupancy.

The coverage is believed to be quite complete for substantial industrial investments. However, there are probably many small trading organizations and holdings of real estate not covered. The extent of these investments is not believed to be significant.

This survey does not cover portfolio foreign holdings of U.S. corporate securities, or other miscellaneous investments here.

These series cover the fifty states, the District of Columbia, the Commonwealth of Puerto Rico, outlying areas of the United States, and the Panama Canal Zone from 1940 through 1979.

Each reporter or foreign-owned U.S. company is classified by the country of the foreign parent organization. Secondary reporters or subsidiaries of the primary organization are given the same country classification as the primary.

The major areas for classification were Canada, United Kingdom, other Western Europe, Latin American Republics, Asia, Africa, and Australia. The investment was generally quite small for countries in Asia, Africa, or Latin America.

The Standard Industrial Classification (SIC) issued by the then Bureau of the Budget was the basic guide used for classifying reporters by industry. See the Introduction to Part D for a discussion of SIC codes. However, certain departures were made in connection with grouping certain industries into major divisions. This change in grouping consisted, for the most part, in shifting certain industries to major divisions on the basis of their relationship or integration of operations. For example, reporters engaged in petroleum production and others engaged in petroleum refining were classified under petroleum as a major industrial division. The SIC had no such classification, and production is included under mining (not shown separately here) and refining under manufacturing. Similarly, other integrated operations of oil companies were included under petroleum.

Frequently a reporter was engaged in more than one business activity, especially in those cases where the report furnished was a consolidation of several companies in different lines of business. Such a report was classified according to the basic activity involved. Reporters who were primarily holding companies of U.S. operating companies were classified according to the industry of the operating companies.

Series Ee132, Ee136, Ee140, Ee144, Ee148, Ee152, Ee155, Ee158, and Ee162. Includes industries not shown separately: mining and smelting, transportation and utilities, trade, and miscellaneous.

Series Ee165. Includes balance of North America, and South America, Africa, Asia, and Oceania.

TABLE Ee166–361   U.S. government foreign grants and credits, by country: 1945–1998

Contributed by Michael Edelstein

	Net total U.S. government foreign grants and credits	U.S. government investments in international financial agencies	Net U.S. government foreign grants and credits under assistance programs	U.S. government new foreign military grants								
				Net	Gross	Gross, less reverse grants and returns	To Western Europe excluding Greece and Turkey	To the Near East including Greece, Turkey, UAR, and South Asia	To Africa, excluding UAR	To the Far East and Pacific	To the Western Hemisphere	To unspecified areas
	Ee166 [1]	Ee167 [2]	Ee168	Ee169	Ee170	Ee171	Ee172	Ee173	Ee174	Ee175	Ee176	Ee177
Year	Million dollars	Million dollars	Million dollars	Million dollars	Million dollars	Million dollars	Million dollars	Million dollars	Million dollars	Million dollars	Million dollars	Million dollars
1945	1,987	(Z)	1,987	610	610	—	—	—	—	610	—	—
1946	5,710	317	5,392	69	69	—	—	—	—	69	—	—
1947	6,080	318	5,763	97	97	—	—	43	—	54	—	—
1948	5,480	0	5,480	473	540	67	—	250	—	224	—	—
1949	5,673	0	5,673	213	213	0	—	171	—	42	—	—
1950	4,180	0	4,180	519	523	4	324	118	—	63	—	15
1951	4,621	0	4,621	1,440	1,456	16	859	185	—	292	67	37
1952	5,043	0	5,043	2,656	2,722	66	1,888	289	—	382	60	36
1953	6,352	0	6,352	4,266	4,329	63	3,102	329	2	769	31	33
1954	5,095	0	5,095	3,431	3,439	8	1,984	342	2	1,037	47	20
1955	4,909	0	4,909	2,672	2,681	9	1,423	335	3	862	30	19
1956	4,986	35	4,951	2,634	2,649	16	1,570	337	2	643	56	25
1957	5,070	0	5,070	2,483	2,496	12	1,059	511	9	814	66	25
1958	4,926	0	4,926	2,368	2,379	11	726	648	9	885	71	28
1959	3,924	(Z)	3,923	2,031	2,052	21	823	445	7	669	59	28
1960	4,590	153	4,437	1,812	1,822	11	623	332	12	743	77	24
1961	4,236	172	4,064	1,515	1,523	8	412	241	18	689	133	22
1962	4,528	122	4,406	1,622	1,758	136	363	337	30	789	74	28
1963	5,055	62	4,993	1,628	1,637	9	447	383	30	685	56	27
1964	4,923	112	4,811	1,394	1,403	8	289	309	25	687	59	26
1965	5,052	0	5,052	1,673	1,682	9	243	330	24	1,014	59	3
1966	5,505	−101	5,606	2,112	2,118	5	137	255	34	1,609	72	5
1967	6,673	194	6,479	2,506	2,511	4	148	345	29	1,915	64	5
1968	6,787	127	6,660	2,923	2,927	4	133	283	34	2,405	64	4
1969	6,697	184	6,513	2,954	2,958	4	62	266	26	2,561	36	4
1970	5,895	234	5,661	2,748	2,751	3	66	200	19	2,235	25	4
1971	7,468	246	7,221	3,580	3,582	2	—	—	—	—	—	—
1972	8,242	271	7,971	4,527	4,529	2	—	—	—	—	—	—
1973	6,804	373	6,431	2,852	2,862	10	—	—	—	—	—	—
1974	7,323	537	6,785	2,842	2,850	7	—	—	—	—	—	—
1975	8,671	654	8,017	2,891	2,895	4	3	601	71	1,391	157	266
1976	7,930	1,102	6,828	1,339	1,342	3	3	1,796	93	562	140	273
1977	6,741	870	5,871	766	769	3	171	1,439	115	402	49	228
1978	7,998	867	7,131	817	821	4	—	—	—	—	—	—
1979	7,901	551	7,350	1,070	1,073	3	—	—	—	—	—	—
1980	10,988	796	10,192	1,652	1,656	4	—	—	—	—	—	—
1981	10,558	1,142	9,416	1,159	1,163	4	—	—	—	—	—	—
1982	11,928	1,007	10,920	1,369	1,373	4	—	—	—	—	—	—
1983	11,614	1,369	10,245	1,317	1,321	4	—	—	—	—	—	—
1984	13,987	1,427	12,560	2,320	2,326	6	—	—	—	—	—	—
1985	14,322	1,302	13,020	3,130	3,133	3	—	—	—	—	—	—
1986	15,030	1,481	13,549	4,133	4,136	3	—	—	—	—	—	—
1987	9,428	1,212	8,216	3,135	3,140	5	—	—	—	—	—	—
1988	8,129	1,314	6,816	3,561	3,563	2	—	—	—	—	—	—
1989	10,247	1,173	9,074	3,733	3,736	3	—	—	—	—	—	—
1990	14,396	1,304	13,092	3,598	6,603	5	—	—	—	—	—	—
1991	−31,939	1,503	−33,442	4,124	4,125	1	—	—	—	—	—	—
1992	18,281	1,427	16,854	7,129	7,140	11	—	—	—	—	—	—
1993	18,002	1,143	16,859	5,756	5,759	1	—	—	—	—	—	—
1994	16,426	1,430	14,996	4,246	4,247	1	—	—	—	—	—	—
1995	12,668	1,517	11,151	2,069	2,065	—	—	—	—	—	—	—
1996	16,645	1,833	14,812	4,983	4,983	—	—	—	—	—	—	—
1997	12,749	1,588	11,160	3,452	3,452	—	—	—	—	—	—	—
1998	13,820	1,580	12,240	3,513	3,512	—	—	—	—	—	—	—

Notes appear at end of table

(continued)

TABLE Ee166–361   U.S. government foreign grants and credits, by country: 1945–1998

Contributed by Michael Edelstein

	U.S. government new economic and technical aid grants					U.S. government new credits				
	Net				Less: reverse grants and returns	Net				Less: principal collections
Year	Total	To developed countries	To developing countries	Gross		Total	To developed countries	To developing countries	Gross	
	Ee178 [3]	Ee179	Ee180	Ee181	Ee182	Ee183 [3,4]	Ee184	Ee185	Ee186	Ee187
	Million dollars	Million dollars	Million dollars	Million dollars	Million dollars	Million dollars	Million dollars	Million dollars	Million dollars	Million dollars
1945	1,340	867	473	1,453	113	37	19	17	81	44
1946	2,830	1,956	874	2,954	124	2,494	2,192	301	2,562	69
1947	1,887	1,241	646	2,126	239	3,779	3,57 2	208	4,061	282
1948	3,864	3,127	736	3,928	65	1,143	1,058	85	1,561	418
1949	4,984	4,327	657	5,227	243	476	382	94	669	193
1950	3,506	2,909	597	3,658	153	155	−53	208	443	288
1951	3,040	2,320	721	3,164	123	141	−167	308	446	305
1952	1,980	1,189	791	2,065	85	408	147	261	828	420
1953	1,845	919	925	1,947	103	233	−138	371	710	477
1954	1,661	848	813	1,726	65	−201	−236	36	290	491
1955	1,933	601	1,331	1,974	42	−26	−135	109	384	410
1956	1,741	286	1,455	1,796	55	18	−161	179	484	466
1957	1,603	149	1,454	1,676	72	363	187	177	1,001	638
1958	1,643	107	1,535	1,682	39	646	−137	783	1,180	534
1959	1,633	67	1,565	1,667	34	5	−609	614	1,030	1,025
1960	1,671	50	1,622	1,705	34	430	−168	597	1,039	609
1961	1,855	44	1,812	1,882	27	489	−818	1,306	1,757	1,268
1962	1,916	40	1,877	1,934	17	727	−802	1,529	2,006	1,279
1963	1,917	28	1,889	1,937	19	1,162	−401	1,563	2,142	980
1964	1,888	21	1,867	1,901	14	1,559	−3	1,562	2,270	711
1965	1,808	21	1,787	1,814	6	1,598	−255	1,853	2,463	865
1966	1,910	12	1,898	1,914	4	1,388	−283	1,671	2,613	1,225
1967	1,805	10	1,795	1,808	3	2,445	367	2,078	3,443	998
1968	1,709	19	1,690	1,712	3	2,208	121	2,087	3,587	1,378
1969	1,649	6	1,643	1,651	2	2,111	206	1,905	3,300	1,190
1970	1,736	10	1,726	1,737	1	1,278	−284	1,561	2,991	1,713
1971	2,043	5	2,038	2,043	1	1,845	−145	1,991	3,935	2,090
1972	2,173	−113	2,286	2,290	118	1,484	7	1,477	3,534	2,050
1973	1,938	−119	2,057	2,059	120	1,690	198	1,492	4,252	2,562
1974	4,538	−1	4,539	4,540	2	−348	13	−360	4,468	4,816
1975	2,247	−1	2,248	2,249	2	2,849	138	2,711	5,293	2,444
1976	2,266	(Z)	2,266	2,272	6	3,275	181	3,093	5,838	2,563
1977	2,283	2	2,281	2,283	0	2,861	−157	3,018	5,546	2,685
1978	2,676	12	2,663	2,676	0	3,691	89	3,602	6,599	2,908
1979	3,050	19	3,031	3,050	0	3,299	−217	3,516	7,071	3,772
1980	3,971	8	3,963	3,971	0	4,638	78	4,559	8,730	4,093
1981	4,149	24	4,125	4,149	0	4,122	270	3,852	8,102	3,980
1982	4,746	94	4,652	4,746	0	4,801	−387	5,188	8,594	3,792
1983	5,354	100	5,254	5,354	0	3,579	−54	3,633	8,176	4,597
1984	6,519	120	6,399	6,519	0	3,714	−176	3,891	7,775	4,061
1985	8,258	84	8,174	8,258	0	1,623	−730	2,353	5,914	4,290
1986	7,906	100	7,805	7,957	52	1,506	557	948	7,155	5,649
1987	7,442	72	7,370	7,442	0	−2,333	−1,098	−1,236	4,835	7,169
1988	7,282	72	7,210	7,282	0	−3,993	−481	−3,511	5,913	9,906
1989	7,653	59	7,594	7,653	0	−2,310	−294	−2,016	3,968	3,278
1990	10,239	−602	10,840	15,755	0	−3,712	238	−3,964	6,636	10,347
1991	−32,193	−15,395	−16,798	14,683	0	−5,396	−376	−5,020	10,870	16,267
1992	9,544	131	9,412	10,903	0	182	−371	552	5,468	5,286
1993	12,180	216	11,963	12,182	0	−1,073	−377	−696	4,650	5,723
1994	11,872	107	11,764	11,872	0	−1,108	−6	−1,102	3,402	4,511
1995	9,850	184	9,666	9,850	0	−743	−19	−724	2,747	3,490
1996	10,545	217	10,329	10,545	0	−722	−259	−463	2,556	3,278
1997	9,279	197	9,082	9,279	0	−1,592	−399	−1,193	3,159	4,751
1998	9,652	100	9,553	9,692	0	−926	−428	−498	2,429	3,354

Notes appear at end of table

TABLE Ee166–361   U.S. government foreign grants and credits, by country: 1945–1998   *Continued*

Year	Other U.S. government assistance through net accumulation of foreign currency claims			Gross U.S. government currency claims		Other U.S. government grants, credits, and other assistance through net accumulation of foreign currency claims		
	Total	To developed countries	To developing countries	Acquired	Disbursed	Total	To developed countries	To developing countries
	Ee188	Ee189	Ee190	Ee191	Ee192	Ee193	Ee194	Ee195
	Million dollars	Million dollars	Million dollars	Million dollars	Million dollars	Million dollars	Million dollars	Million dollars
1945	—	—	—	—	—	1,377	886	491
1946	—	—	—	—	—	5,323	4,148	1,175
1947	—	—	—	—	—	5,666	4,813	853
1948	—	—	—	—	—	5,006	4,185	821
1949	—	—	—	—	—	5,460	5,709	751
1950	—	—	—	—	—	3,661	2,856	805
1951	—	—	—	—	—	3,182	2,153	1,029
1952	—	—	—	—	—	2,388	1,336	1,051
1953	8	8	—	8	—	2,086	789	1,297
1954	203	102	101	248	46	1,664	714	950
1955	330	80	250	556	226	2,237	546	1,691
1956	558	104	454	1,079	520	2,318	229	2,089
1957	620	46	573	1,233	614	2,587	382	2,205
1958	270	31	239	1,023	753	2,559	1	2,558
1959	254	1	254	934	679	1,892	−541	2,433
1960	524	85	439	1,186	662	2,625	−32	2,657
1961	206	31	175	1,147	941	2,550	−743	3,293
1962	141	9	132	1,140	998	2,785	−753	3,537
1963	285	35	250	1,284	999	3,365	−337	3,702
1964	−30	17	−46	1,394	1,424	3,417	34	3,383
1965	−27	−29	2	1,079	1,106	3,379	−263	3,642
1966	195	−14	210	953	757	3,493	−285	3,779
1967	−278	−15	−263	851	1,128	3,972	363	3,610
1968	−179	−17	−162	700	879	3,738	123	3,614
1969	−201	−17	−184	486	687	3,559	194	3,364
1970	−101	−20	−80	451	552	2,913	−295	3,208
1971	−246	−23	−224	339	585	3,642	−163	3,805
1972	−213	−30	−183	345	558	3,444	−136	3,580
1973	−49	−17	−32	361	410	3,579	45	3,533
1974	−247	−21	−226	2,214	2,461	3,943	−9	3,952
1975	30	−28	58	189	159	5,126	109	5,017
1976	−53	−23	−30	129	182	5,488	159	5,330
1977	−39	−33	−6	175	214	5,105	−188	5,293
1978	−52	−23	−29	124	177	6,315	78	6,237
1979	−69	−24	−45	127	196	6,279	−223	6,502
1980	−69	−18	−51	101	170	8,540	69	8,471
1981	−15	46	−60	176	191	8,257	340	7,916
1982	3	28	−25	126	123	9,551	−264	9,815
1983	−5	−1	−4	93	98	8,928	45	8,883
1984	7	−1	8	79	72	10,240	−58	10,298
1985	9	−7	15	97	89	9,890	−652	10,542
1986	5	−3	8	134	129	9,416	655	8,761
1987	−27	−38	11	84	111	5,081	−1,064	6,145
1988	−35	−26	−10	80	116	3,254	−435	3,689
1989	−2	−17	15	64	66	5,341	−252	5,593
1990	−33	−7	−25	76	108	6,494	−372	6,866
1991	23	1	22	100	76	−37,566	−15,770	−21,796
1992	(Z)	(Z)	0	31	31	9,726	−240	9,965
1993	−5	(Z)	−6	35	40	11,101	−161	11,262
1994	−13	−1	−12	23	35	10,751	100	10,651
1995	−20	(Z)	−21	26	46	9,056	165	8,891
1996	6	6	—	28	22	9,829	−42	9,871
1997	21	17	2	16	−6	7,709	−199	7,907
1998	(Z)	(Z)	1	22	21	8,726	−329	9,055

Notes appear at end of table

(continued)

TABLE Ee166–361   U.S. government foreign grants and credits, by country: 1945–1998   *Continued*

Net U.S. government foreign claims and credits to

Western Europe

Year	Total	Austria	Belgium and Luxembourg	Bosnia and Herzegovina	Croatia	Denmark	Finland	France	Federal Republic of Germany	Iceland	Ireland	Italy	Macedonia	Malta	Netherlands
	Ee196	Ee197	Ee198	Ee199	Ee200	Ee201	Ee202	Ee203	Ee204	Ee205	Ee206	Ee207	Ee208	Ee209	Ee210
	Million dollars	Million dollars	Million dollars	Million dollars	Million dollars	Million dollars	Million dollars	Million dollars	Million dollars	Million dollars	Million dollars	Million dollars	Million dollars	Million dollars	Million dollars
1945	713	18	36	—	—	—	—	149	26	—	—	136	—	—	63
1946	3,275	73	153	—	—	(Z)	—	1,158	300	—	(Z)	500	—	—	133
1947	4,291	146	−2	—	—	1	—	588	417	—	—	313	—	—	85
1948	3,799	197	80	—	—	39	—	781	1,130	—	—	422	—	—	123
1949	4,202	194	240	—	—	102	—	765	948	—	67	445	—	—	286
1950	2,676	101	176	—	—	52	—	460	467	—	55	269	—	—	224
1951	2,064	147	42	—	—	75	—	416	361	—	24	268	—	—	102
1952	1,378	82	13	—	—	8	—	343	103	—	(Z)	175	—	—	44
1953	867	36	−2	—	—	7	—	263	35	—	(Z)	109	—	—	10
1954	810	15	−4	—	—	−1	—	268	83	—	0	101	—	—	2
1955	692	9	−6	—	—	2	—	286	37	—	0	57	—	—	−19
1956	351	24	−6	—	—	−1	—	46	25	—	−1	71	—	—	−25
1957	503	25	−7	—	—	−2	—	−49	−11	—	−1	100	—	—	−15
1958	157	17	−2	—	—	−3	—	−16	−23	—	−1	30	—	—	−19
1959	−438	3	−11	—	—	−2	—	−76	−205	—	−1	−4	—	—	−14
1960	−16	9	4	—	—	−2	—	−48	−28	—	−1	12	—	—	−11
1961	−594	4	−8	—	—	−2	—	−68	−587	—	−2	−27	—	—	−52
1962	−690	−12	−18	—	—	−2	—	−541	−3	—	−2	−176	—	—	−12
1963	−249	5	−6	—	—	−2	—	−244	−14	—	−2	5	—	—	−72
1964	126	8	−8	—	—	−2	—	−38	−5	—	−2	78	—	—	−1
1965	−100	4	−8	—	—	−2	—	−205	(Z)	—	−3	32	—	—	−2
1966	−243	−2	−6	—	—	−2	—	−96	−207	—	−3	−122	—	—	(Z)
1967	284	−1	12	—	—	−1	—	−2	13	—	−2	41	—	—	(Z)
1968	152	(Z)	−8	—	—	−1	—	12	8	—	−6	−22	—	—	−66
1969	142	−12	−8	—	—	−1	—	−3	−4	—	4	224	—	—	(Z)
1970	−278	−6	5	—	—	−1	−8	−27	−16	−2	23	−8	—	—	(Z)
1971	−140	9	−9	—	—	−5	(Z)	7	6	−2	−20	−7	—	—	2
1972	−160	(Z)	−6	—	—	−1	−2	32	3	−2	−5	−15	—	—	38
1973	−20	−2	3	—	—	24	−6	12	8	−3	−10	11	—	—	52
1974	131	−3	15	—	—	10	(Z)	−11	46	−3	−15	−8	—	—	34
1975	271	−2	18	—	—	15	7	−15	33	3	−18	−13	—	—	56
1976	182	2	−2	—	—	−4	10	−41	−22	−3	−6	−13	—	14	14
1977	−51	−4	−8	—	—	(Z)	—	−27	−14	−3	—	1	—	11	−10
1978	334	−5	−7	—	—	−9	—	−45	−14	−2	—	−8	—	10	−25
1979	−118	−5	−7	—	—	−3	—	−48	−14	−5	—	−17	—	0	−29
1980	395	14	52	—	—	15	—	−31	−14	0	(Z)	184	—	0	−27
1981	148	12	−11	—	—	2	17	34	−13	−1	44	122	—	0	−33
1982	−172	8	−15	—	—	−4	−6	−5	−9	−1	8	−28	—	0	−26
1983	154	(Z)	−17	—	—	−13	19	6	−6	−1	−7	−25	—	0	−20
1984	253	3	−17	—	—	−12	−11	−17	−6	−1	−4	−12	—	0	−14
1985	−203	10	−15	—	—	−30	−2	−47	−2	−1	(Z)	−84	—	(Z)	−9
1986	−6	−9	−9	—	—	−7	−47	−26	0	−2	2	−107	—	(Z)	−1
1987	−169	−9	−9	—	—	−6	8	−13	−3	−2	−2	−21	—	(Z)	−1
1988	122	−9	−9	—	—	0	6	−14	0	−4	−6	−32	—	—	0
1989	−243	−11	−9	—	—	0	7	−14	−1	(Z)	−7	−29	—	—	0
1990	−103	−10	−9	—	—	0	−8	−15	−338	(Z)	2	−30	—	—	0
1991	−6,040	−19	−3	—	—	0	−5	−8	−6,117	0	−6	−14	—	—	0
1992	328	−1	0	—	—	0	−5	−2	0	0	−6	0	—	—	0
1993	349	−1	0	51	63	0	−26	−2	−1	0	−8	(Z)	63	—	0
1994	174	−1	0	84	52	0	−1	−1	0	0	36	0	52	—	0
1995	177	−1	0	92	9	0	−1	1	(Z)	0	0	(Z)	9	—	0
1996	270	−1	0	235	−10	0	−1	0	(Z)	0	11	0	−10	—	0
1997	319	−1	0	252	−7	0	0	0	0	0	39	—	−7	—	0
1998	258	−1	0	220	−12	0	0	0	0	0	0	0	−12	—	0

Notes appear at end of table

TABLE Ee166–361   U.S. government foreign grants and credits, by country: 1945–1998   *Continued*

Net U.S. government foreign claims and credits to

	Western Europe								Eastern Europe						
Year	Norway	Portugal	Slovenia	Spain	Sweden	United Kingdom	Yugoslavia	Other and unspecified countries	Total	Albania	Armenia	Azerbaijan	Belarus	Bulgaria	Czechoslovakia
	Ee211	Ee212	Ee213	Ee214	Ee215	Ee216	Ee217	Ee218	Ee219	Ee220	Ee221	Ee222	Ee223	Ee224	Ee225
	Million dollars	Million dollars	Million dollars	Million dollars	Million dollars	Million dollars	Million dollars	Million dollars	Million dollars	Million dollars	Million dollars	Million dollars	Million dollars	Million dollars	Million dollars
1945	(Z)	—	—	—	1	34	115	—	274	—	—	—	—	—	54
1946	8	—	—	—	(Z)	750	150	—	663	—	—	—	—	—	106
1947	24	(Z)	—	—	0	2,662	34	—	178	—	—	—	—	—	31
1948	61	(Z)	—	—	3	937	0	—	13	—	—	—	—	—	3
1949	64	0	—	—	39	1,009	0	—	−13	—	—	—	—	—	−6
1950	61	18	—	(Z)	43	624	36	—	−9	—	—	—	—	—	(Z)
1951	41	20	—	17	27	118	120	—	−15	—	—	—	—	—	(Z)
1952	26	8	—	24	−4	398	80	—	−4	—	—	—	—	—	(Z)
1953	15	5	—	21	−1	229	98	—	4	—	—	—	—	—	0
1954	12	12	—	44	(Z)	102	97	—	7	—	—	—	—	—	1
1955	−1	3	—	89	(Z)	58	130	—	−1	—	—	—	—	—	2
1956	−9	9	—	157	−1	−43	94	—	−3	—	—	—	—	—	0
1957	−12	(Z)	—	88	−1	242	133	—	63	—	—	—	—	—	0
1958	−11	1	—	131	−1	−52	100	—	98	—	—	—	—	—	0
1959	−9	2	—	88	−1	−323	111	—	61	—	—	—	—	—	0
1960	−7	2	—	90	(Z)	−89	49	—	123	—	—	—	—	—	0
1961	−6	1	—	110	−1	−83	123	—	53	—	—	—	—	—	0
1962	−4	20	—	12	−16	−77	143	—	54	—	—	—	—	—	0
1963	−4	17	—	1	(Z)	−75	131	—	43	—	—	—	—	—	0
1964	−5	30	—	−10	−1	−14	87	—	46	—	—	—	—	—	0
1965	−4	12	—	19	(Z)	−20	72	—	−12	—	—	—	—	—	0
1966	−3	5	—	31	0	57	94	—	−13	—	—	—	—	—	0
1967	−1	−4	—	69	6	126	7	—	−13	—	—	—	—	—	0
1968	−2	6	—	45	2	185	(Z)	—	2	—	—	—	—	—	0
1969	−2	−2	—	15	3	−42	−28	—	−29	—	—	—	—	—	0
1970	−2	−34	—	1	2	−143	−36	7	5	—	—	—	—	—	0
1971	6	−6	—	−17	−1	−138	26	16	−2	—	—	—	—	—	0
1972	42	16	—	−16	−3	−208	55	30	70	—	—	—	—	—	0
1973	38	11	—	106	−1	−132	−44	38	369	—	—	—	—	—	0
1974	95	7	—	91	6	−162	−27	67	−102	—	—	—	—	—	0
1975	92	15	—	94	4	−89	39	44	−58	—	—	—	—	—	0
1976	30	113	—	18	11	−18	78	26	174	—	—	—	—	—	0
1977	−36	166	—	33	4	−152	23	−40	219	—	—	—	—	—	0
1978	−46	476	—	157	1	−142	39	−37	415	—	—	—	—	—	0
1979	−44	94	—	134	−3	−123	−25	−23	200	—	—	—	—	—	0
1980	−52	−99	—	159	5	178	22	−10	−285	—	—	—	—	—	0
1981	−36	−100	—	79	−1	−125	12	144	174	—	—	—	—	—	0
1982	−26	(Z)	—	27	−4	−208	−31	147	55	—	—	—	—	—	(Z)
1983	−12	55	—	101	−5	−119	20	178	54	—	—	—	—	—	−2
1984	−4	129	—	222	−3	−134	17	116	5	—	—	—	—	—	−3
1985	−31	101	—	−85	−6	−121	18	102	15	—	—	—	—	—	0
1986	−16	178	—	66	−6	−202	−21	202	1,249	—	—	—	—	—	0
1987	−4	8	—	−11	−5	−347	−41	295	−161	—	—	—	—	—	0
1988	0	69	—	−113	−3	−105	−2	343	−121	—	—	—	—	—	0
1989	0	71	—	−474	−2	−109	11	324	421	—	—	—	—	—	0
1990	0	56	—	−122	0	−111	−39	520	973	—	—	—	—	—	(Z)
1991	−1	44	—	−76	0	−113	−55	335	833	13	—	—	—	56	1
1992	−15	159	—	−54	0	−115	−7	375	913	81	28	(Z)	30	1	1
1993	4	112	−6	31	0	−118	9	241	3,372	43	96	0	120	22	15
1994	0	115	−17	−55	0	−120	−1	82	2,910	16	127	24	37	8	1
1995	0	−16	−24	−59	0	−118	(Z)	293	1,963	15	102	19	49	6	−2
1996	0	−3	−27	−48	0	−125	(Z)	236	1,953	58	80	14	31	13	3
1997	0	−12	−16	−37	0	−127	−8	220	1,413	11	26	4	19	14	−11
1998	0	−15	−16	−37	0	−130	6	228	1,785	16	38	5	4	13	0

Notes appear at end of table

(continued)

TABLE Ee166–361   U.S. government foreign grants and credits, by country: 1945–1998   *Continued*

Net U.S. government foreign claims and credits to

Eastern Europe

Year	Czech Republic Ee226 Million dollars	Estonia Ee227 Million dollars	Georgia Ee228 Million dollars	Hungary Ee229 Million dollars	Kazakhstan Ee230 Million dollars	Kyrgyzstan Ee231 Million dollars	Latvia Ee232 Million dollars	Lithuania Ee233 Million dollars	Moldova Ee234 Million dollars	Poland Ee235 Million dollars	Romania Ee236 Million dollars	Russia Ee237 Million dollars	Slovakia Ee238 Million dollars	Tajikistan Ee239 Million dollars	Turkmenistan Ee240 Million dollars
1945	—	—	—	—	—	—	—	—	—	75	—	—	—	—	—
1946	—	—	—	—	—	—	—	—	—	251	—	—	—	—	—
1947	—	—	—	—	—	—	—	—	—	96	—	—	—	—	—
1948	—	—	—	—	—	—	—	—	—	19	—	—	—	—	—
1949	—	—	—	—	—	—	—	—	—	1	—	—	—	—	—
1950	—	—	—	—	—	—	—	—	—	(Z)	—	—	—	—	—
1951	—	—	—	—	—	—	—	—	—	−1	—	—	—	—	—
1952	—	—	—	—	—	—	—	—	—	−3	—	—	—	—	—
1953	—	—	—	—	—	—	—	—	—	−4	—	—	—	—	—
1954	—	—	—	—	—	—	—	—	—	−4	—	—	—	—	—
1955	—	—	—	—	—	—	—	—	—	−5	—	—	—	—	—
1956	—	—	—	—	—	—	—	—	—	−6	—	—	—	—	—
1957	—	—	—	—	—	—	—	—	—	56	—	—	—	—	—
1958	—	—	—	—	—	—	—	—	—	99	—	—	—	—	—
1959	—	—	—	—	—	—	—	—	—	66	—	—	—	—	—
1960	—	—	—	—	—	—	—	—	—	127	—	—	—	—	—
1961	—	—	—	—	—	—	—	—	—	57	—	—	—	—	—
1962	—	—	—	—	—	—	—	—	—	61	—	—	—	—	—
1963	—	—	—	—	—	—	—	—	—	48	—	—	—	—	—
1964	—	—	—	—	—	—	—	—	—	52	—	—	—	—	—
1965	—	—	—	—	—	—	—	—	—	−5	—	—	—	—	—
1966	—	—	—	—	—	—	—	—	—	−5	—	—	—	—	—
1967	—	—	—	—	—	—	—	—	—	−3	—	—	—	—	—
1968	—	—	—	—	—	—	—	—	—	10	—	—	—	—	—
1969	—	—	—	—	—	—	—	—	—	−19	—	—	—	—	—
1970	—	—	—	(Z)	—	—	—	—	—	−19	33	—	—	—	—
1971	—	—	—	−1	—	—	—	—	—	−13	23	—	—	—	—
1972	—	—	—	(Z)	—	—	—	—	—	−22	−10	—	—	—	—
1973	—	—	—	1	—	—	—	—	—	11	−1	—	—	—	—
1974	—	—	—	−1	—	—	—	—	—	−24	27	—	—	—	—
1975	—	—	—	−1	—	—	—	—	—	9	20	—	—	—	—
1976	—	—	—	(Z)	—	—	—	—	—	142	22	—	—	—	—
1977	—	—	—	—	—	—	—	—	—	135	−21	—	—	—	—
1978	—	—	—	—	—	—	—	—	—	343	45	—	—	—	—
1979	—	—	—	—	—	—	—	—	—	129	76	—	—	—	—
1980	—	—	—	—	—	—	—	—	—	−243	−23	—	—	—	—
1981	—	—	—	—	—	—	—	—	—	236	−49	—	—	—	—
1982	—	—	—	—	—	—	—	—	—	86	−16	—	—	—	—
1983	—	—	—	—	—	—	—	—	—	74	5	—	—	—	—
1984	—	—	—	—	—	—	—	—	—	67	−18	—	—	—	—
1985	—	—	—	—	—	—	—	—	—	45	35	—	—	—	—
1986	—	—	—	−6	—	—	—	—	—	1,348	−26	—	—	—	—
1987	—	—	—	0	—	—	—	—	—	−44	−50	—	—	—	—
1988	—	—	—	0	—	—	—	—	—	−53	−1	—	—	—	—
1989	—	—	—	0	—	—	—	—	—	526	−59	—	—	—	—
1990	—	—	—	1	—	—	—	—	—	912	79	—	—	—	—
1991	—	—	—	3	—	—	—	—	—	646	50	—	—	—	—
1992	—	28	6	2	23	1	28	28	9	110	10	186	—	10	11
1993	2	1	103	3	17	105	1	24	35	33	15	2,164	1	19	34
1994	2	(Z)	86	4	17	36	3	15	22	8	10	1,184	1	30	13
1995	3	2	89	35	16	33	2	28	19	5	8	455	2	34	16
1996	9	7	79	15	59	38	10	17	15	49	29	421	12	32	19
1997	5	4	38	−16	52	26	4	23	8	28	3	356	11	27	1
1998	4	5	27	12	67	30	8	14	5	36	26	435	6	27	3

Notes appear at end of table

TABLE Ee166–361   U.S. government foreign grants and credits, by country: 1945–1998   *Continued*

	Eastern Europe				Near East and South Asia										
	Ukraine	U.S.S.R	Uzbekistan	Other	Total	Afghanistan	Bangladesh	Cyprus	Egypt	Greece	India	Iran	Iraq	Israel	Jordan
	Ee241	Ee242	Ee243	Ee244	Ee245	Ee246	Ee247	Ee248	Ee249	Ee250	Ee251	Ee252	Ee253	Ee254	Ee255
Year	Million dollars	Million dollars	Million dollars	Million dollars	Million dollars	Million dollars	Million dollars	Million dollars	Million dollars	Million dollars	Million dollars	Million dollars	Million dollars	Million dollars	Million dollars
1945	—	133	—	—	148	—	—	—	(Z)	121	29	1	—	—	—
1946	—	285	—	—	182	—	—	—	9	168	−9	3	1	—	—
1947	—	45	—	—	150	—	—	—	(Z)	156	−3	−3	(Z)	—	—
1948	—	−8	—	—	157	—	—	—	−5	164	−4	−3	−1	—	—
1949	—	−8	—	—	183	(Z)	—	—	4	108	(Z)	15	0	7	—
1950	—	−9	—	—	221	(Z)	—	—	(Z)	108	1	4	(Z)	50	—
1951	—	−13	—	—	468	11	—	—	1	189	108	4	(Z)	66	1
1952	—	0	—	—	442	6	—	—	(Z)	123	94	11	(Z)	109	1
1953	—	0	—	—	362	4	—	—	2	66	37	52	2	49	4
1954	—	(Z)	—	—	302	4	—	—	3	47	29	65	2	62	7
1955	—	(Z)	—	—	551	6	—	—	27	74	118	64	3	46	14
1956	—	0	—	—	687	13	—	—	47	69	119	61	3	57	5
1957	—	0	—	—	642	13	—	—	7	31	187	47	3	35	20
1958	—	0	—	—	800	19	—	—	2	23	243	50	4	51	57
1959	—	−4	—	—	983	19	—	—	75	37	320	91	2	56	60
1960	—	−4	—	—	1,227	13	—	—	108	28	523	33	1	42	62
1961	—	−4	—	—	1,238	30	—	—	110	31	373	129	1	41	61
1962	—	−6	—	—	1,499	13	—	—	185	21	534	46	1	58	53
1963	—	−5	—	—	1,741	33	—	—	184	30	740	20	5	49	55
1964	—	−5	—	—	1,789	37	—	—	194	35	864	−6	12	34	45
1965	—	−5	—	—	1,673	34	—	—	97	27	854	8	7	61	38
1966	—	−7	—	—	1,461	28	—	—	60	5	761	31	4	61	58
1967	—	−9	—	—	1,462	24	—	—	5	11	841	18	2	26	19
1968	—	−8	—	—	1,202	15	—	—	7	−2	576	70	−1	35	13
1969	—	−9	—	—	1,107	13	—	—	4	6	466	107	−1	105	13
1970	—	−10	—	—	991	2	—	3	(Z)	(Z)	434	58	−2	84	14
1971	—	−10	—	—	1,610	20	—	1	106	−10	469	196	(Z)	377	48
1972	—	102	—	—	1,104	22	79	1	−6	−9	112	72	−2	249	107
1973	—	359	—	—	1,027	30	137	−1	−20	43	67	221	−2	238	64
1974	—	−104	—	—	623	9	105	1	27	65	−182	37	−2	199	57
1975	—	−86	—	—	1,936	18	380	14	87	112	243	−103	−2	803	63
1976	—	2	—	(Z)	2,407	20	78	21	231	121	120	−109	−2	1,405	100
1977	—	99	—	0	2,661	13	97	47	417	172	46	−105	—	1,476	139
1978	—	32	—	5	2,633	12	168	24	619	162	81	−170	—	1,306	72
1979	—	−7	—	8	3,276	38	161	14	890	24	94	−158	—	1,563	85
1980	—	−14	—	−4	4,618	4	175	17	1,470	−52	168	(Z)	—	1,858	160
1981	—	−17	—	3	5,210	−5	130	−1	1,397	−49	215	(Z)	−1	2,441	315
1982	—	−11	—	−4	6,036	−1	202	−2	2,344	−52	89	0	−1	2,181	170
1983	—	−21	—	−2	5,968	−2	219	(Z)	2,060	19	74	−306	32	2,660	67
1984	—	−39	—	−2	6,458	−4	265	1	1,925	−14	83	0	−8	3,094	−15
1985	—	−68	—	3	7,436	−21	175	17	2,231	−21	42	0	−12	3,807	−1
1986	—	−66	—	0	7,928	−3	178	21	2,729	72	36	0	−5	4,030	6
1987	—	−66	—	0	6,279	29	150	17	1,614	304	66	0	21	3,115	109
1988	—	−66	—	0	2,131	30	170	14	3,490	488	139	−19	29	−1,826	−231
1989	—	−46	—	(Z)	4,506	86	138	19	2,085	306	101	0	−16	1,903	171
1990	—	−30	—	11	6,656	57	181	16	4,976	282	13	0	−7	4,380	155
1991	—	3	—	60	−24,646	59	179	18	2,500	−179	103	−23	365	2,002	74
1992	8	124	(Z)	187	8,230	74	181	10	2,537	665	124	(Z)	125	4,692	117
1993	70	240	1	207	8,019	51	123	14	2,766	313	92	0	116	3,295	125
1994	105	735	6	413	7,042	9	202	16	2,258	262	45	0	135	3,106	98
1995	170	617	1	241	3,022	10	87	6	1,637	261	48	0	128	420	129
1996	232	584	4	124	7,552	14	48	11	1,320	12	55	−21	119	5,294	168
1997	95	595	2	85	4,723	17	42	10	1,377	−211	237	0	4	2,896	232
1998	140	659	6	200	4,979	0	27	14	2,014	−240	160	0	(Z)	2,840	160

Notes appear at end of table

(continued)

TABLE Ee166–361   U.S. government foreign grants and credits, by country: 1945–1998 *Continued*

Net U.S. government foreign claims and credits to

Near East and South Asia

Year	Kuwait Ee256 Million dollars	Lebanon Ee257 Million dollars	Nepal Ee258 Million dollars	Oman Ee259 Million dollars	Pakistan Ee260 Million dollars	Saudi Arabia Ee261 Million dollars	Sri Lanka (Ceylon) Ee262 Million dollars	Syria Ee263 Million dollars	Turkey Ee264 Million dollars	United Arab Emirates Ee265 Million dollars	Yemen (Sanaa) Ee266 Million dollars	Yemen Ee267 Million dollars	UNRWA Ee268 Million dollars	West Bank Ee269 Million dollars	Other and unspecified Ee270 Million dollars
1945	—	—	—	—	—	1	—	—	—	—	—	—	—	—	—
1946	—	2	—	—	—	10	—	—	−1	—	—	—	—	—	—
1947	—	(Z)	—	—	—	5	—	—	9	—	—	—	—	—	—
1948	—	−1	—	—	(Z)	−3	—	—	10	—	—	—	—	—	—
1949	—	(Z)	—	—	(Z)	−1	(Z)	—	34	—	—	—	15	—	—
1950	—	(Z)	—	—	(Z)	(Z)	(Z)	—	39	—	—	—	20	—	—
1951	—	(Z)	(Z)	—	(Z)	2	(Z)	—	52	—	—	—	24	—	—
1952	—	1	(Z)	—	8	(Z)	(Z)	—	59	—	—	—	22	—	—
1953	—	3	(Z)	—	91	(Z)	(Z)	—	40	—	—	—	9	—	—
1954	—	4	1	—	12	(Z)	0	—	47	—	—	—	18	—	—
1955	—	7	2	—	67	−1	(Z)	—	97	—	—	—	23	—	—
1956	—	5	2	—	154	−1	2	—	123	—	—	—	27	—	—
1957	—	4	2	—	100	21	8	—	141	—	—	—	23	—	—
1958	—	28	6	—	145	12	20	—	122	—	—	—	16	—	—
1959	—	10	3	—	142	1	19	—	111	—	—	—	27	—	—
1960	—	10	8	—	229	2	8	—	101	—	—	—	22	—	—
1961	—	8	10	—	218	−7	10	—	153	—	—	—	34	—	—
1962	—	4	9	—	323	−26	9	—	203	—	—	—	31	—	—
1963	—	3	14	—	380	−2	5	—	175	—	—	—	35	—	—
1964	—	−2	17	—	377	3	4	—	132	—	—	—	32	—	—
1965	—	(Z)	16	—	349	1	4	—	140	—	—	—	28	—	—
1966	—	1	12	—	221	54	6	—	125	—	—	—	27	—	—
1967	—	1	11	—	331	3	14	—	104	—	—	—	27	—	—
1968	—	4	8	—	282	8	18	—	94	—	—	—	28	—	—
1969	—	4	9	—	209	27	21	—	84	—	—	—	32	—	—
1970	—	7	11	—	242	−16	11	(Z)	88	—	3	—	32	—	20
1971	—	−1	9	—	216	−13	14	(Z)	109	—	(Z)	—	37	—	34
1972	−10	5	13	—	154	−4	20	−1	164	—	(Z)	—	34	—	104
1973	−10	4	12	—	134	−17	24	(Z)	65	—	2	—	20	—	16
1974	−10	22	10	—	122	−21	2	(Z)	121	—	8	—	33	—	21
1975	−5	37	8	—	134	−11	20	18	73	—	6	—	28	—	12
1976	0	7	16	—	253	−12	21	23	57	—	8	—	39	—	8
1977	—	32	12	—	84	—	38	48	83	—	7	—	55	—	0
1978	—	13	6	—	44	—	41	19	175	—	7	—	52	—	2
1979	—	10	8	—	18	—	39	80	337	—	9	—	50	—	14
1980	—	18	17	—	67	—	55	23	538	—	16	—	54	—	29
1981	—	30	19	30	94	6	32	17	393	—	26	—	65	—	56
1982	—	−2	22	22	167	−1	49	27	695	—	30	—	69	—	26
1983	—	57	28	3	348	−2	63	25	490	—	37	—	71	—	26
1984	—	32	24	14	415	−2	83	1	442	—	33	—	67	—	22
1985	—	34	26	−4	481	−1	90	(Z)	479	—	41	—	75	—	−3
1986	0	−12	20	12	347	0	65	(Z)	298	—	0	39	67	(Z)	28
1987	0	−4	22	−33	235	0	40	(Z)	449	—	0	47	61	1	36
1988	0	−7	19	9	389	0	43	(Z)	−721	(Z)	0	33	54	1	28
1989	0	2	15	8	−387	0	45	0	−91	0	0	42	39	2	30
1990	−2,506	9	20	4	531	−1,614	72	(Z)	367	−361	0	43	7	1	29
1991	−13,550	4	16	3	354	−13,913	112	0	798	−3,709	0	19	76	5	41
1992	−2	12	20	13	126	−1,328	64	0	673	0	0	15	69	12	31
1993	0	7	21	20	−35	0	88	3	813	0	0	22	140	19	27
1994	0	5	20	1	−158	0	41	0	224	0	0	1	7	64	705
1995	0	5	19	4	−187	0	26	0	147	0	0	3	103	58	118
1996	0	11	21	12	−164	0	6	0	−61	0	0	5	72	33	298
1997	0	3	24	25	−62	0	7	0	−19	0	0	12	59	53	20
1998	0	1	20	20	−82	0	1	0	−162	0	0	4	78	80	44

Notes appear at end of table

TABLE Ee166–361   U.S. government foreign grants and credits, by country: 1945–1998   *Continued*

Net U.S. government foreign claims and credits to

Africa

Year	Total	Algeria	Angola	Benin (Dahomey)	Botswana	Burkina Faso (Upper Volta)	Burundi	Cameroon	Cape Verde	Chad	Eritrea	Ethiopia	Ghana	Guinea	The Ivory Coast
	Ee271	Ee272	Ee273	Ee274	Ee275	Ee276	Ee277	Ee278	Ee279	Ee280	Ee281	Ee282	Ee283	Ee284	Ee285
	Million dollars	Million dollars	Million dollars	Million dollars	Million dollars	Million dollars	Million dollars	Million dollars	Million dollars	Million dollars	Million dollars	Million dollars	Million dollars	Million dollars	Million dollars
1945	1	(Z)	—	—	—	—	—	—	—	—	—	—	—	—	—
1946	4	(Z)	—	—	—	—	—	—	—	—	—	(Z)	—	—	—
1947	−87	(Z)	—	—	—	—	—	—	—	—	—	1	—	—	—
1948	2	0	—	—	—	—	—	—	—	—	—	(Z)	—	—	—
1949	4	0	—	—	—	—	—	—	—	—	—	(Z)	—	—	—
1950	9	0	—	—	—	—	—	—	—	—	—	1	(Z)	—	—
1951	8	0	—	—	—	—	—	—	—	—	—	−1	0	—	—
1952	56	0	—	—	—	—	—	—	—	—	—	1	0	—	—
1953	40	1	—	—	—	—	—	—	—	—	—	1	(Z)	—	—
1954	46	(Z)	—	—	—	—	—	—	—	—	—	1	0	—	—
1955	59	(Z)	—	—	—	—	—	—	—	—	—	4	(Z)	—	—
1956	45	(Z)	—	—	—	—	—	—	—	—	—	3	(Z)	—	—
1957	44	1	—	—	—	—	—	—	—	—	—	7	(Z)	—	—
1958	69	(Z)	—	—	—	—	—	—	—	—	—	6	1	—	—
1959	125	1	—	—	—	—	—	—	—	—	—	10	1	—	—
1960	180	1	—	—	—	—	—	—	—	—	—	7	2	—	—
1961	296	2	—	—	—	—	—	—	—	—	—	14	2	—	—
1962	365	42	—	—	—	—	—	—	—	—	—	24	3	—	—
1963	308	40	—	—	—	—	—	—	—	—	—	18	13	—	—
1964	288	39	—	—	—	—	—	—	—	—	—	8	8	—	—
1965	376	8	—	—	—	—	—	—	—	—	—	11	33	—	—
1966	412	27	—	—	—	—	—	—	—	—	—	19	62	—	—
1967	337	11	—	—	—	—	—	—	—	—	—	11	35	—	—
1968	276	(Z)	—	—	—	—	—	—	—	—	—	15	26	—	—
1969	279	3	—	—	—	—	—	—	—	—	—	14	34	—	—
1970	275	1	—	1	—	1	—	10	—	—	—	9	2	4	12
1971	348	12	—	1	—	4	—	6	—	—	—	21	15	7	6
1972	259	2	—	1	—	4	—	12	—	—	—	14	15	3	8
1973	298	50	—	(Z)	—	7	—	3	—	1	—	18	6	8	16
1974	465	115	—	3	—	11	—	1	—	8	—	26	1	6	3
1975	409	41	—	2	—	6	—	5	—	5	—	30	6	9	1
1976	509	67	—	7	—	8	—	5	—	6	—	34	16	9	(Z)
1977	578	40	—	9	5	15	—	9	—	11	—	14	19	9	8
1978	620	113	—	4	13	21	—	3	—	13	—	11	9	10	5
1979	750	150	1	4	11	24	3	14	4	12	—	13	20	4	1
1980	1,109	125	8	2	16	31	5	25	6	6	—	20	16	7	27
1981	1,239	172	45	4	20	40	9	52	8	2	—	3	19	17	9
1982	1,192	(Z)	37	4	20	30	8	14	12	6	—	2	7	1	−5
1983	1,224	−83	−8	2	18	30	8	3	12	23	—	6	8	2	−3
1984	1,803	−108	−5	4	28	40	13	20	6	29	—	30	20	4	2
1985	2,004	−131	38	5	29	49	9	5	5	41	—	157	18	11	12
1986	1,303	−128	27	3	20	30	5	11	9	25	—	88	13	16	5
1987	1,125	−98	24	3	28	24	5	13	7	48	—	13	10	24	1
1988	1,243	−58	2	5	20	18	5	24	6	27	—	71	17	19	20
1989	1,073	−77	−13	13	15	15	3	18	4	13	—	49	48	5	14
1990	1,883	59	−15	5	17	15	18	42	8	24	—	57	14	16	18
1991	1,518	−42	−4	10	11	35	6	57	8	30	—	115	32	25	59
1992	1,855	−14	−12	18	9	21	16	42	11	26	—	102	46	27	47
1993	1,989	−11	16	13	15	26	19	23	7	22	4	179	60	41	23
1994	2,031	28	58	17	15	14	55	13	7	10	28	168	65	38	38
1995	2,213	755	37	14	18	23	39	4	11	14	8	127	63	28	16
1996	1,945	644	42	13	9	11	2	4	10	8	18	104	34	29	22
1997	1,339	93	41	23	9	15	4	(Z)	11	6	17	77	55	28	16
1998	1,277	45	35	14	4	17	6	9	7	3	16	116	40	18	8

Notes appear at end of table

(continued)

TABLE Ee166–361   U.S. government foreign grants and credits, by country: 1945–1998 *Continued*

Net U.S. government foreign claims and credits to

Africa

Year	Kenya	Lesotho	Liberia	Libya	Madagascar	Malawi	Mali	Mauritania	Morocco	Mozambique	Niger	Nigeria	Rwanda	Senegal	Sierra Leone
	Ee286	Ee287	Ee288	Ee289	Ee290	Ee291	Ee292	Ee293	Ee294	Ee295	Ee296	Ee297	Ee298	Ee299	Ee300
	Million dollars	Million dollars	Million dollars	Million dollars	Million dollars	Million dollars	Million dollars	Million dollars	Million dollars	Million dollars	Million dollars	Million dollars	Million dollars	Million dollars	Million dollars
1945	—	—	1	—	—	—	—	—	—	—	—	—	—	—	—
1946	—	—	4	—	—	—	—	—	—	—	—	—	—	—	—
1947	—	—	3	—	—	—	—	—	—	—	—	—	—	—	—
1948	—	—	2	—	—	—	—	—	—	—	—	—	—	—	—
1949	—	—	4	—	—	—	—	—	1	—	—	—	—	—	—
1950	—	—	4	(Z)	—	—	—	—	4	—	—	—	—	—	—
1951	—	—	2	(Z)	—	—	—	—	3	—	—	—	—	—	—
1952	—	—	3	2	—	—	—	—	9	—	—	—	—	—	—
1953	—	—	−2	1	—	—	—	—	−3	—	—	(Z)	—	—	—
1954	—	—	2	4	—	—	—	—	−4	—	—	(Z)	—	—	—
1955	—	—	2	17	—	—	—	—	−2	—	—	(Z)	—	—	—
1956	—	—	3	13	—	—	—	—	−1	—	—	(Z)	—	—	—
1957	—	—	5	17	—	—	—	—	18	—	—	(Z)	—	—	—
1958	—	—	8	18	—	—	—	—	26	—	—	(Z)	—	—	—
1959	—	—	9	33	—	—	—	—	45	—	—	1	—	—	—
1960	—	—	8	34	—	—	—	—	61	—	—	3	—	—	—
1961	—	—	19	23	—	—	—	—	98	—	—	6	—	—	—
1962	—	—	35	20	—	—	—	—	50	—	—	11	—	—	—
1963	—	—	11	16	—	—	—	—	56	—	—	15	—	—	—
1964	—	—	12	6	—	—	—	—	39	—	—	25	—	—	—
1965	—	—	25	3	—	—	—	—	51	—	—	26	—	—	—
1966	—	—	23	(Z)	—	—	—	—	50	—	—	31	—	—	—
1967	—	—	37	−6	—	—	—	—	34	—	—	35	—	—	—
1968	—	—	13	3	—	—	—	—	53	—	—	30	—	—	—
1969	—	—	7	1	—	—	—	—	38	—	—	33	—	—	—
1970	6	4	(Z)	(Z)	2	4	2	—	64	—	2	36	—	1	2
1971	19	4	5	(Z)	2	3	4	—	70	—	1	48	—	4	4
1972	6	3	2	(Z)	1	2	3	—	20	—	2	29	—	2	3
1973	6	3	−3	(Z)	(Z)	1	8	—	13	—	10	24	—	8	2
1974	9	5	−2	0	1	4	22	—	30	—	29	10	—	7	3
1975	9	4	(Z)	0	2	5	11	—	8	—	11	8	—	8	4
1976	18	6	15	0	1	5	5	—	105	—	9	3	—	8	7
1977	58	6	−1	0	1	5	6	3	37	8	8	−7	—	14	10
1978	21	7	10	0	2	4	16	5	57	10	10	−6	—	23	9
1979	27	11	9	0	2	4	15	6	36	24	17	−3	5	32	5
1980	50	20	30	0	(Z)	4	25	17	40	17	10	−3	7	38	9
1981	87	32	76	0	10	5	18	21	52	17	12	7	11	37	6
1982	54	27	72	0	15	3	15	13	56	5	22	−5	12	33	8
1983	81	28	68	0	10	7	16	22	117	11	18	80	11	50	11
1984	68	37	107	0	20	10	32	26	313	21	25	49	19	75	9
1985	82	23	71	0	24	8	51	38	138	51	93	151	16	51	11
1986	40	23	52	0	21	11	45	19	177	34	39	1	24	45	12
1987	46	24	23	0	17	19	34	12	83	69	43	1	16	49	12
1988	47	23	27	0	21	34	50	11	185	56	25	169	16	45	8
1989	58	19	13	0	7	48	29	16	2	71	34	44	9	47	14
1990	115	16	32	0	34	34	31	13	96	83	34	156	13	61	2
1991	91	13	56	0	30	55	48	7	100	103	51	34	27	43	10
1992	97	18	57	0	25	48	31	3	28	107	38	31	10	52	18
1993	99	9	46	0	28	50	39	10	12	94	30	18	39	58	13
1994	54	8	66	0	23	37	30	2	27	82	16	52	220	33	10
1995	35	13	67	0	33	64	31	2	−48	114	31	1	138	24	11
1996	6	4	58	0	42	36	12	2	−4	53	15	−4	93	38	28
1997	27	5	28	0	35	30	11	5	−42	78	11	−10	87	36	18
1998	36	3	16	0	44	22	36	4	−49	74	13	−4	28	18	13

Notes appear at end of table

TABLE Ee166–361   U.S. government foreign grants and credits, by country: 1945–1998 *Continued*

Net U.S. government foreign claims and credits to

					Africa									Far East and Pacific	
	Somalia	South Africa	Sudan	Swaziland	Tanzania	Togo	Tunisia	Uganda	Zaire	Zambia	Zimbabwe	Other and unspecified	Total	Australia	Brunei
	Ee301	Ee302	Ee303	Ee304	Ee305	Ee306	Ee307	Ee308	Ee309	Ee310	Ee311	Ee312	Ee313	Ee314	Ee315
Year	Million dollars	Million dollars	Million dollars	Million dollars	Million dollars	Million dollars	Million dollars	Million dollars	Million dollars	Million dollars	Million dollars	Million dollars	Million dollars	Million dollars	Million dollars
1945	—	—	—	—	—	—	—	—	—	—	—	—	178	10	—
1946	—	—	—	—	—	—	—	—	—	—	—	—	832	−11	—
1947	—	—	—	—	—	—	—	—	—	—	—	—	914	(Z)	—
1948	—	(Z)	—	—	—	—	—	—	—	—	—	—	857	1	—
1949	—	0	—	—	—	—	—	—	—	—	—	—	902	−1	—
1950	—	−1	—	—	—	—	(Z)	—	(Z)	—	—	—	608	−1	—
1951	—	(Z)	—	—	—	—	(Z)	—	0	—	—	—	506	(Z)	—
1952	—	26	—	—	—	—	(Z)	—	(Z)	—	—	—	383	(Z)	—
1953	—	35	—	—	—	—	(Z)	—	−1	—	—	—	397	1	—
1954	—	31	—	—	—	—	(Z)	—	(Z)	—	—	—	390	4	—
1955	—	21	—	—	—	—	1	—	(Z)	—	—	—	784	−1	—
1956	—	11	—	—	—	—	3	—	(Z)	—	—	—	1,004	−8	—
1957	—	−5	—	—	—	—	6	—	(Z)	—	—	—	977	−2	—
1958	—	−14	—	—	—	—	26	—	(Z)	—	—	—	785	−2	—
1959	—	−13	—	—	—	—	33	—	(Z)	—	—	—	716	2	—
1960	—	−13	—	—	—	—	55	—	11	—	—	—	786	−3	—
1961	—	−13	—	—	—	—	77	—	30	—	—	—	748	18	—
1962	—	−13	—	—	—	—	54	—	73	—	—	—	775	−6	—
1963	—	−16	—	—	—	—	38	—	43	—	—	—	776	−14	—
1964	—	−11	—	—	—	—	44	—	40	—	—	—	573	3	—
1965	—	−13	—	—	—	—	55	—	51	—	—	—	648	12	—
1966	—	−4	—	—	—	—	39	—	38	—	—	—	974	33	—
1967	—	−2	—	—	—	—	49	—	35	—	—	—	1,001	153	—
1968	—	−2	—	—	—	—	44	—	21	—	—	—	1,033	159	—
1969	—	−2	—	—	—	—	49	—	12	—	—	—	1,144	26	—
1970	5	−2	−2	—	9	1	49	5	11	(Z)	—	34	985	−17	0
1971	7	(Z)	−1	—	11	2	37	5	13	6	—	36	982	26	12
1972	3	0	10	—	8	1	36	4	20	1	—	39	1,217	39	3
1973	1	0	16	—	8	2	12	2	11	8	—	58	948	−59	4
1974	(Z)	0	7	—	11	3	17	1	63	9	—	58	1,370	−62	(Z)
1975	6	(Z)	13	—	37	3	12	(Z)	97	5	—	65	1,161	−23	0
1976	3	(Z)	−4	—	37	3	13	(Z)	37	8	—	76	1,081	−46	−20
1977	3	(Z)	9	—	30	4	33	(Z)	117	31	—	64	720	−50	0
1978	14	(Z)	11	—	15	2	30	(Z)	61	35	—	82	1,240	−36	0
1979	22	(Z)	25	3	24	7	10	(Z)	100	40	—	69	973	−29	(Z)
1980	70	—	73	11	30	6	50	15	148	42	26	77	834	(Z)	—
1981	70	—	104	7	31	5	25	10	65	29	28	75	932	81	—
1982	77	—	261	7	28	7	118	2	85	15	27	97	814	37	—
1983	91	—	212	11	20	8	125	4	44	25	62	75	1,193	75	—
1984	115	—	223	7	22	8	113	3	208	53	74	87	658	−5	—
1985	117	—	443	8	21	9	40	5	66	51	54	130	220	−39	—
1986	111	2	164	9	10	10	7	4	105	77	22	115	−63	−118	—
1987	69	6	101	16	30	13	−7	17	112	36	33	148	−2,594	−30	—
1988	62	10	110	12	16	9	−175	21	142	18	6	123	377	−26	—
1989	42	18	128	11	16	16	60	20	72	21	12	140	483	−18	—
1990	80	20	150	14	51	10	44	43	242	63	10	157	39	−34	—
1991	11	28	105	13	42	19	5	43	50	50	27	114	−8,968	−26	—
1992	356	44	55	13	27	12	16	30	33	132	67	168	806	−18	—
1993	522	66	53	15	28	9	−4	65	9	52	29	164	25	−2	—
1994	34	71	60	10	24	8	2	57	1	21	34	492	751	−1	—
1995	26	112	11	13	19	3	−5	56	1	27	29	245	749	0	—
1996	10	99	16	21	16	1	−24	41	(Z)	21	22	393	780	0	—
1997	9	111	24	12	18	1	−9	56	(Z)	47	20	336	130	0	—
1998	3	89	23	14	26	2	−22	17	1	14	46	473	735	0	—

Notes appear at end of table

(continued)

TABLE Ee166–361   U.S. government foreign grants and credits, by country: 1945–1998   *Continued*

Net U.S. government foreign claims and credits to

Far East and Pacific

Year	Burma	Cambodia (Kampuchea)	China, Mainland	China, Taiwan	Hong Kong	Indonesia	Japan and the Ryukyu Islands	Korea, Republic of	Laos	Malaysia	Mongolia	New Zealand	The Trust Territory of the Pacific Islands	Papua New Guinea	The Philippines
	Ee316	Ee317	Ee318	Ee319	Ee320	Ee321	Ee322	Ee323	Ee324	Ee325	Ee326	Ee327	Ee328	Ee329	Ee330
	Million dollars	Million dollars	Million dollars	Million dollars	Million dollars	Million dollars	Million dollars	Million dollars	Million dollars	Million dollars	Million dollars	Million dollars	Million dollars	Million dollars	Million dollars
1945	—	—	—	121	—	4	9	1	—	—	—	—	—	—	29
1946	—	—	—	315	—	62	380	33	—	—	—	—	—	—	42
1947	5	—	—	187	—	—	488	84	—	—	—	—	—	—	150
1948	(Z)	—	—	151	—	20	418	134	—	—	—	—	—	—	131
1949	(Z)	—	—	33	—	41	550	77	—	—	—	—	—	—	203
1950	−1	—	—	18	—	36	252	102	—	—	—	—	—	—	200
1951	5	—	—	65	—	(Z)	279	118	—	—	—	—	—	—	13
1952	7	—	—	80	—	34	65	155	—	—	—	—	—	—	10
1953	5	—	—	90	—	17	6	206	—	—	—	—	—	—	24
1954	1	(Z)	—	89	—	23	10	169	(Z)	—	—	—	—	—	9
1955	(Z)	28	—	109	—	9	67	279	37	—	—	—	—	—	21
1956	3	41	—	112	—	51	125	307	52	—	—	—	—	—	28
1957	18	32	—	98	—	51	52	373	38	—	—	—	—	—	39
1958	3	37	—	84	—	24	−1	311	30	—	—	—	—	—	42
1959	14	21	—	86	—	17	51	232	35	—	—	—	—	—	24
1960	13	25	—	109	—	45	28	261	33	—	—	—	—	—	24
1961	4	24	—	119	—	54	31	230	51	—	—	—	—	—	12
1962	3	20	—	82	—	89	68	238	30	—	—	—	—	—	26
1963	10	20	—	76	—	78	40	240	32	—	—	—	—	—	11
1964	5	7	—	45	—	32	−27	158	39	—	—	—	—	—	49
1965	3	2	—	49	—	−3	−38	167	58	—	—	—	—	—	46
1966	2	(Z)	—	30	—	27	59	168	56	—	—	—	—	—	22
1967	1	(Z)	—	38	—	52	7	193	58	—	—	—	—	—	33
1968	1	(Z)	—	32	—	125	−111	191	44	—	—	—	—	—	34
1969	5	(Z)	—	12	—	153	41	260	51	—	—	—	—	—	29
1970	1	(Z)	—	14	(Z)	189	−40	198	53	−2	—	—	48	13	63
1971	3	24	—	14	(Z)	135	−59	194	56	−1	—	—	53	10	55
1972	3	72	—	26	3	159	−60	221	48	15	—	—	57	5	70
1973	1	128	—	39	(Z)	160	−230	214	54	−5	—	8	64	3	71
1974	(Z)	288	—	119	13	125	2	63	36	19	—	16	73	(Z)	43
1975	−1	74	—	191	19	165	10	314	16	3	—	30	79	(Z)	77
1976	−1	0	—	145	6	333	58	344	0	15	—	13	90	−12	109
1977	8	0	—	69	−4	163	−48	250	0	24	—	3	92	−18	151
1978	2	0	—	52	−3	178	46	698	0	5	—	−1	100	(Z)	120
1979	5	0	—	171	−5	214	−69	228	0	−16	—	−3	125	(Z)	141
1980	44	0	—	388	10	137	−49	101	0	−10	—	−4	108	—	33
1981	(Z)	0	1	191	32	19	68	300	0	−17	—	−18	133	—	58
1982	6	0	12	35	11	21	−84	475	0	−5	—	−19	188	—	61
1983	3	0	9	−44	−9	259	−16	449	0	61	—	−15	127	—	239
1984	7	0	20	−144	−14	224	−99	208	0	−6	—	−13	143	—	141
1985	7	0	6	−255	−14	37	−87	58	0	−11	—	−11	154	—	334
1986	7	5	−8	−262	−11	13	−88	−146	(Z)	−15	—	−10	210	—	449
1987	10	2	9	−970	−8	−12	−319	−1,717	0	−12	—	−4	175	—	332
1988	9	4	48	−8	−9	−3	−4	−383	2	−9	—	−4	220	—	428
1989	1	5	35	−7	−9	37	−1	−132	0	−36	—	−4	217	—	341
1990	1	5	71	−7	−8	46	−635	−192	(Z)	−1	—	−2	220	—	557
1991	−3	6	55	−8	0	22	−9,377	−331	(Z)	−2	17	−2	179	—	389
1992	(Z)	14	31	−7	0	82	−30	−133	1	(Z)	2	−1	204	—	547
1993	−2	29	14	−9	1	−64	−2	−431	1	(Z)	47	0	152	—	131
1994	−2	16	6	−8	1	24	−1	−55	2	1	18	0	317	—	−52
1995	−2	39	136	−5	73	25	(Z)	−50	3	(Z)	11	0	209	—	55
1996	−2	36	113	−3	133	44	(Z)	−62	4	1	7	0	215	—	64
1997	−2	27	227	−1	44	−48	0	−52	3	1	14	0	140	—	−46
1998	−2	33	249	−1	17	19	0	−52	3	1	19	0	175	—	296

Notes appear at end of table

TABLE Ee166–361   U.S. government foreign grants and credits, by country: 1945–1998   *Continued*

	Far East and Pacific			Western Hemisphere										
					Net U.S. government foreign claims and credits to									
	Singapore	South Vietnam	Thailand	Other and unspecified	Total	Argentina	Bolivia	Brazil	Canada	The Cayman Islands	Chile	Colombia	Costa Rica	The Dominican Republic	Ecuador
	Ee331	Ee332	Ee333	Ee334	Ee335	Ee336	Ee337	Ee338	Ee339	Ee340	Ee341	Ee342	Ee343	Ee344	Ee345
Year	Million dollars	Million dollars	Million dollars	Million dollars	Million dollars	Million dollars	Million dollars	Million dollars	Million dollars	Million dollars	Million dollars	Million dollars	Million dollars	Million dollars	Million dollars
1945	—	—	—	—	10	(Z)	(Z)	2	—	—	2	1	1	(Z)	2
1946	—	—	5	—	84	(Z)	6	28	—	—	5	1	2	(Z)	1
1947	—	—	(Z)	—	111	(Z)	9	30	—	—	6	2	(Z)	(Z)	1
1948	—	—	1	—	58	(Z)	2	9	—	—	18	4	(Z)	−1	3
1949	—	—	(Z)	—	73	(Z)	3	5	—	—	28	3	(Z)	(Z)	2
1950	—	—	(Z)	—	64	(Z)	3	(Z)	—	—	33	6	(Z)	(Z)	2
1951	—	—	5	—	114	92	7	4	—	—	−2	4	1	(Z)	2
1952	—	—	4	—	91	5	5	4	—	—	(Z)	10	2	(Z)	4
1953	—	—	5	—	375	3	3	328	—	—	(Z)	−5	2	(Z)	1
1954	—	41	4	—	68	−9	17	24	—	—	−3	2	2	(Z)	4
1955	—	203	16	—	102	−5	21	37	—	—	−1	2	5	1	6
1956	—	229	39	—	151	12	31	28	—	—	10	10	3	(7)	8
1957	—	236	33	—	253	−6	25	16	—	—	32	19	9	(Z)	4
1958	—	218	30	—	568	48	22	145	—	—	47	92	10	(Z)	3
1959	—	177	48	—	338	73	22	35	—	—	33	32	8	(Z)	2
1960	—	186	42	—	194	47	13	42	—	—	10	−7	4	(Z)	7
1961	—	151	29	—	711	41	24	270	—	—	122	53	7	(Z)	11
1962	—	157	31	—	587	66	29	159	—	—	88	45	9	22	12
1963	—	212	29	—	576	11	45	139	—	—	111	69	7	48	14
1964	—	221	18	—	448	5	34	213	—	—	97	38	10	22	17
1965	—	301	25	—	644	−3	30	153	—	—	102	35	14	79	17
1966	—	503	20	—	739	−3	21	236	—	—	88	59	10	54	21
1967	—	401	39	—	655	−20	24	143	—	—	50	86	12	60	27
1968	—	437	30	—	806	−14	38	199	—	—	151	108	11	46	15
1969	—	446	38	—	605	5	28	99	—	—	106	101	13	37	11
1970	—	418	34	2	541	20	24	93	9	—	56	118	8	33	8
1971	—	427	29	4	407	22	18	98	28	—	−16	83	10	21	10
1972	—	539	19	5	461	5	38	53	28	—	16	65	11	25	9
1973	—	437	21	37	530	−11	10	82	65	—	28	95	10	19	11
1974	—	585	19	29	799	−4	26	263	87	10	84	45	9	10	7
1975	—	164	11	29	826	−4	12	193	45	2	128	36	10	36	7
1976	—	0	7	42	518	20	30	145	13	−1	−71	21	7	29	15
1977	−3	0	72	11	433	6	32	41	−19	1	12	1	5	1	5
1978	39	0	24	13	293	−8	61	−36	−8	−7	−32	7	7	−3	16
1979	93	0	107	11	361	−29	36	−17	−9	−2	−184	−6	8	59	8
1980	25	0	31	21	687	−30	29	−28	95	—	−68	6	3	30	16
1981	−14	0	35	61	588	−25	19	−83	47	—	−86	−4	11	23	−1
1982	−15	0	49	42	1,862	31	33	−127	91	—	−51	−7	46	73	−4
1983	−34	0	60	29	832	26	52	40	97	—	−47	83	202	38	10
1984	56	0	110	31	2,078	16	39	90	98	—	−28	104	183	141	46
1985	−53	0	68	26	2,142	14	71	368	−87	—	−7	93	213	154	50
1986	−184	1	62	31	1,820	85	111	7	−61	—	56	63	136	230	59
1987	1	1	−77	25	2,096	27	124	34	−158	—	25	22	162	78	60
1988	−1	1	72	42	1,453	16	85	(Z)	−50	—	9	−23	107	52	47
1989	(Z)	1	12	41	1,189	−6	134	−202	−30	—	−46	−32	143	53	26
1990	(Z)	1	−19	38	2,025	64	114	261	−41	—	−32	−30	108	28	61
1991	(Z)	1	49	63	2,011	87	202	−21	−50	—	−40	7	63	25	29
1992	(Z)	1	44	70	2,533	92	193	410	−38	—	−55	−78	23	3	32
1993	(Z)	1	85	73	807	86	151	−187	−41	—	−36	−220	14	161	15
1994	(Z)	0	247	238	1,005	33	156	−59	−120	—	−33	20	−5	(Z)	18
1995	1	(Z)	203	51	476	−27	101	−204	0	—	−25	4	−30	−15	5
1996	(Z)	(Z)	196	34	491	−52	100	−191	0	—	−3	27	−44	−19	6
1997	0	48	−288	64	592	−84	122	−33	0	—	−6	25	−30	−29	6
1998	0	−10	−68	57	987	−88	96	88	0	—	−8	42	−28	−14	2

Notes appear at end of table

(continued)

TABLE Ee166–361   U.S. government foreign grants and credits, by country: 1945–1998   *Continued*

Net U.S. government foreign claims and credits to

Western Hemisphere

Year	El Salvador	Guatemala	Guyana	Haiti	Honduras	Jamaica	Mexico	Nicaragua	Panama	Paraguay	Peru	Trinidad and Tobago	Uruguay	Venezuela	Other and unspecified	Other international organizations and unspecified areas
	Ee346	Ee347	Ee348	Ee349	Ee350	Ee351	Ee352	Ee353	Ee354	Ee355	Ee356	Ee357	Ee358	Ee359	Ee360	Ee361
	Million dollars	Million dollars	Million dollars	Million dollars	Million dollars	Million dollars	Million dollars	Million dollars	Million dollars	Million dollars	Million dollars	Million dollars	Million dollars	Million dollars	Million dollars	Million dollars
1945	1	(Z)	—	(Z)	(Z)	—	2	1	(Z)	(Z)	(Z)	—	(Z)	(Z)	—	53
1946	(Z)	2	—	(Z)	(Z)	(Z)	35	2	(Z)	1	1	—	1	(Z)	—	283
1947	(Z)	1	—	(Z)	1	0	58	(Z)	(Z)	(Z)	5	—	(Z)	1	—	108
1948	(Z)	2	—	(Z)	(Z)	0	20	(Z)	(Z)	(Z)	(Z)	—	2	2	—	119
1949	(Z)	2	—	−1	(Z)	0	33	(Z)	1	(Z)	(Z)	—	(Z)	1	—	108
1950	(Z)	1	—	(Z)	(Z)	4	19	(Z)	1	(Z)	1	—	(Z)	(Z)	—	93
1951	(Z)	(Z)	—	(Z)	(Z)	11	−5	(Z)	1	−1	1	—	(Z)	1	—	37
1952	(Z)	1	—	1	1	5	29	1	3	1	7	—	2	4	—	42
1953	1	(Z)	—	3	1	−1	18	1	1	1	11	—	(Z)	(Z)	—	40
1954	1	(Z)	—	10	1	−3	27	1	−1	1	2	—	(Z)	−3	—	41
1955	1	11	—	14	2	(Z)	−10	2	3	1	13	—	2	(Z)	—	51
1956	1	20	—	9	2	(Z)	−8	2	3	5	24	—	(Z)	−3	—	82
1957	1	23	—	4	3	−1	23	3	5	8	53	—	4	−1	—	105
1958	1	12	—	5	5	−8	78	5	7	4	60	—	−1	7	—	80
1959	1	9	—	13	6	−3	14	4	6	7	52	—	13	−3	—	108
1960	1	16	—	5	4	1	21	8	12	6	−16	—	20	6	—	131
1961	8	14	—	14	8	1	83	9	9	10	−20	—	3	32	—	98
1962	6	9	—	10	4	2	3	7	11	4	5	—	4	64	—	194
1963	11	10	—	3	5	3	−18	7	19	9	4	—	8	43	—	170
1964	10	9	—	4	4	3	−55	7	10	7	17	—	(Z)	−40	—	148
1965	11	11	—	5	10	4	38	7	21	5	33	—	2	40	—	149
1966	17	8	—	3	7	6	54	11	22	4	30	—	4	41	—	163
1967	11	15	—	3	6	10	50	9	17	3	24	—	4	48	—	247
1968	7	17	—	4	7	6	53	10	10	8	24	—	23	33	—	266
1969	7	10	—	3	9	3	16	17	12	9	10	—	16	33	—	311
1970	10	10	5	4	10	8	−1	21	15	6	13	−2	9	16	—	396
1971	7	11	9	3	8	14	−18	13	13	12	16	−1	8	−19	59	437
1972	9	17	6	6	10	7	−10	6	20	7	48	3	19	3	63	492
1973	9	15	4	4	10	18	−4	20	39	5	43	1	5	−16	72	427
1974	4	17	5	3	13	22	95	18	29	7	−19	6	1	−13	75	657
1975	7	21	16	11	24	25	70	13	24	7	50	(Z)	(Z)	−19	111	581
1976	9	43	7	18	18	8	34	17	36	3	43	−4	5	−22	94	626
1977	14	24	6	28	18	7	75	21	10	4	96	−1	(Z)	−19	64	550
1978	11	16	4	29	16	19	17	25	6	2	71	−2	−4	−3	92	769
1979	10	17	3	29	28	19	103	29	5	2	95	29	−3	13	116	830
1980	49	15	3	37	20	12	180	78	13	−1	−2	89	−3	18	125	1,108
1981	121	18	7	40	45	58	160	15	4	(Z)	−10	51	−4	40	142	1,125
1982	240	23	5	46	85	106	1,084	6	13	2	(Z)	11	10	−1	147	1,133
1983	329	33	2	42	112	114	−549	3	15	3	68	−19	−5	6	177	820
1984	446	25	−1	44	210	152	97	1	54	(Z)	213	19	−3	−37	169	1,304
1985	448	52	(Z)	56	243	151	−40	−2	43	1	181	−21	−4	−30	195	1,405
1986	376	91	2	87	236	121	−29	(Z)	24	(Z)	98	−32	11	−31	180	1,319
1987	418	159	8	94	201	92	543	(Z)	10	(Z)	74	−33	−3	−38	197	1,640
1988	405	142	5	41	193	95	62	(Z)	13	(Z)	67	−11	9	−28	218	1,611
1989	408	162	8	80	134	141	−98	(Z)	8	1	39	16	−6	−21	276	1,645
1990	303	98	42	54	226	108	140	105	102	(Z)	93	5	−3	−18	236	1,619
1991	309	80	11	70	192	106	22	396	152	1	142	5	−5	−14	242	1,852
1992	281	110	9	59	131	85	−109	213	195	(Z)	706	−10	2	−2	280	2,191
1993	217	76	9	67	101	37	−147	43	49	1	145	−11	2	2	274	2,299
1994	92	57	11	125	54	99	−229	46	8	3	157	−9	2	2	579	1,084
1995	119	39	10	156	77	30	−199	41	8	1	150	−14	1	−3	250	2,551
1996	79	4	11	82	31	−13	−127	37	−4	2	75	−15	3	1	502	1,821
1997	92	37	12	92	29	−30	−91	43	−15	3	133	5	2	1	309	2,646
1998	44	35	12	87	47	−22	−126	70	−20	2	88	204	1	4	473	2,218

TABLE Ee166-361 U.S. government foreign grants and credits, by country: 1945-1998 *Continued*

(Z) Greater than -$500,000 and less than $500,000.

[1] All World War II lend-lease credits and conversions of prior grants to credits are from V-J Day (September 2, 1945).

[2] Organizations included changes over time. See text.

[3] Some grants and credits included for some years. See text.

[4] Outstanding credits on December 31, 1992, totaled $54,754 million. See text for details.

Sources

1945-1969, U.S. Bureau of Economic Analysis, unpublished summary of data published in more detail in "Foreign Aid by the United States Government, 1940-1951," a 1952 supplement to the *Survey of Current Business*, and in the periodic report *Foreign Grants and Credits by the United States Government*. 1970-1999, U.S. Bureau of the Census, *Statistical Abstract of the United States* (1975, 1978, 1981, 1984, 1986, 1988, 2000).

Documentation

These series are compiled by the U.S. Bureau of Economic Analysis from information made available by agencies operating the grant, credit, and other assistance programs and include some estimates for transactions not yet recorded on the operating agencies' books. Items based on estimates are adjusted or qualified on the basis of information received to the date of preparation of these series, but in some instances they are subject to future adjustments. The series, revised with the latest information, are annually published by the Bureau of the Census in the *Statistical Abstract of the United States*.

The data on credits are comparable, with minor exceptions, to those appearing in *Foreign Credits by the United States Government*, a semiannual publication of the U.S. Department of the Treasury, in which a detailed enumeration of every active foreign credit of the U.S. government, showing its current status, is presented.

The data are divided into three categories: grants, credits, and other assistance through net accumulation of foreign currency claims under programs for the sale of agricultural commodities. The government's capital investments in, or contributions to, the international financial institutions constitute an additional measure taken by this government to promote foreign economic recovery and development. Payments to these institutions do not result in immediate equivalent aid to foreign countries. Use of available dollar funds is largely determined by the managements of the institutions, in some instances subject to certain controls that can be exercised by the U.S. government. Changes in the procedures for disbursing the contributions of the U.S. government, initiated in 1965, have retarded such actual government payments to agree more closely with the actual disbursement of assistance by the international institution to the foreign country.

Grants are transfers for which no payment is expected, or which at most involve an obligation on the part of the receiver to extend aid to the United States or other countries to achieve a common objective. *Credits* are loan disbursements or transfers under other agreements that give rise to specific obligations to repay, over a period of years, usually with interest. *Other assistance* represents the transfer of U.S. farm products in exchange for foreign currencies (plus - since the enactment of Public Law 87-128 - principal and interest collections in foreign currencies for credits extended under the farm products sales program) less the government's disbursements of the currencies as grants, credits, or for purchases. The net acquisition of currencies represents net transfers of resources to foreign countries under the agricultural programs, in addition to those classified as grants or credits.

Occasionally, assistance has been given under indeterminate conditions, subject to future settlement. Indeterminate aid on this basis is included with grants, in the period rendered. When settlement for such indeterminate aid is agreed upon, the terms may call for a cash settlement or may establish a long-term credit. Cash settlements are included in returned grants. Amounts of the newly established credits are added to outstanding indebtedness.

The U.S. government receives some returns on its gross grants and credits. The returns that are deducted from gross grants and credits to arrive at net grants and credits include (1) reverse lend-lease; (2) the dollar value of the portion of grant counterpart funds paid to the United States for its use; (3) returned lend-lease and civilian supply ships; (4) returns of military equipment "loaned"; (5) cash received in war-account settlements for lend-lease and other aid; and (6) principal repaid on credits, but not interest. The government's disbursements of currencies are deducted from the accumulation of currency claims in calculating net other assistance.

The measure of foreign grants and credits generally is in terms of (1) dollars disbursed by the U.S. government to or for the account of a foreign government or other foreign entity or individual, and (2) dollar equivalents of goods delivered or shipped, services rendered, or foreign currencies disbursed to or for such foreign account. Correspondingly, returns are measured in terms of the dollars received by the U.S. government, or the dollar equivalents of goods, services, and foreign currencies received. Dollar equivalents are, of necessity, frequently estimated.

Assistance is shown by country or general area where possible. In certain instances (particularly in the earlier post-World War II period), data for parent countries include those for their dependent area. For example, although goods have been shipped to a then dependent area, Tunisia, such aid was reported as rendered to the parent country, France.

Transactions shown for a country are not necessarily with the government of such country but are often with individuals, relief organizations, international organizations, or other private entities located in the designated country and considered being within its economy. Information is made available by agencies operating the grant, credit, and other assistance programs and includes some estimates for transactions not yet recorded on the operating agencies' books. Items based on estimates have been adjusted or qualified on the basis of information received to the date of preparation of these series, but in some instances they are subject to future adjustments.

"Developed countries" include Australia, Canada, Japan, New Zealand, Republic of South Africa, and countries of Western Europe except Spain, Yugoslavia, and Malta. "Developing countries" include all other nations.

Series Ee167. Included from 1945 onward is the Asian Development Bank, Inter-American Development Bank, International Bank for Reconstruction and Development, International Development Association, and International Finance Corporation. Included from 1976 is the African Development Fund and from 1983 the African Development Bank; from 1988 the Special Facility for Sub-Sahara Africa, the Multilateral Guarantee Agency, and the Inter-American Investment Corporation; and from 1991 the European Bank for Reconstruction and Development.

Series Ee178 and Ee183. Net new grants are not adjusted for settlements for postwar relief and other grants under agreements, and net new credits exclude prior grants converted into credits, which were as follows: July 1944-December 1955, $2,198 million; 1956-1966, $491 million; 1972, $994 million. Repayment on these settlements is included in net new credits.

Series Ee183. Outstanding credits on December 31, 1992, totaled $54,754 million, representing net credits extended since the organization of the Export-Import Bank, February 12, 1934, less charge-offs and net adjustments owing to exchange rates ($2,083 million), and excluding World War I debts. The amount repayable in dollars at U.S. government option was $53,659 million; the remainder was repayable in foreign currencies, commodities, or services at the option of the borrowers.

Series Ee188. Equivalent value of currencies still available to be used, including some funds advanced from foreign governments and after loss by exchange rate fluctuations ($1,618 million), was $56 million on December 31, 1992.

Series Ee218. Includes European Atomic Energy Commission, European Coal and Steel Community, European Payments Union, European Productivity Agency, North Atlantic Treaty Organization, and Organization for European Economic Co-operation.

Series Ee268. United Nations Relief and Works Agency for Palestine refugees.

Series Ee328. Includes transactions with Federated States of Micronesia, Republic of the Marshall Islands, and Republic of Palau. Prior to October 1986, includes transactions with Commonwealth of the Northern Mariana Islands.

Series Ee360. Includes Andean Development Corporation, Eastern Caribbean Central Bank, Inter-American Institute of Agricultural Services, Organization of American States, and Pan American Health Organization.

EXPORTS AND IMPORTS

Douglas A. Irwin

TABLE Ee362–375 Exports and imports of merchandise, gold, and silver: 1790–2002[1]

Contributed by Douglas A. Irwin

	Merchandise, gold, and silver			Merchandise							Gold		Silver	
	Exports	Imports	Excess of exports or imports	Exports and reexports			General imports				Exports	Imports	Exports	Imports
				Total	Exports of U.S. merchandise	Reexports	Total	For immediate consumption	For warehouse	Excess of exports or imports				
Year	Ee362[2]	Ee363	Ee364	Ee365	Ee366	Ee367	Ee368	Ee369	Ee370	Ee371	Ee372[3]	Ee373	Ee374[3,4]	Ee375[4]
	Million dollars	Million dollars	Million dollars	Million dollars	Million dollars	Million dollars	Million dollars	Million dollars	Million dollars	Million dollars	Million dollars	Million dollars	Million dollars	Million dollars
1790	—	—	—	20	—	—	23	—	—	−3	—	—	—	—
1791	—	—	—	19	19	1	29	—	—	−10	—	—	—	—
1792	—	—	—	21	19	2	32	—	—	−11	—	—	—	—
1793	—	—	—	26	24	2	31	—	—	−5	—	—	—	—
1794	—	—	—	33	27	7	35	—	—	−2	—	—	—	—
1795	—	—	—	48	40	8	70	—	—	−22	—	—	—	—
1796	—	—	—	59	32	26	81	—	—	−23	—	—	—	—
1797	—	—	—	51	24	27	75	—	—	−24	—	—	—	—
1798	—	—	—	61	28	33	69	—	—	−7	—	—	—	—
1799	—	—	—	79	33	46	79	—	—	(Z)	—	—	—	—
1800	—	—	—	71	32	39	91	—	—	−20	—	—	—	—
1801	—	—	—	93	46	47	111	—	—	−18	—	—	—	—
1802	—	—	—	72	36	36	76	—	—	−4	—	—	—	—
1803	—	—	—	56	42	14	65	—	—	−9	—	—	—	—
1804	—	—	—	78	41	36	85	—	—	−7	—	—	—	—
1805	—	—	—	96	42	53	121	—	—	−25	—	—	—	—
1806	—	—	—	102	41	60	129	—	—	−28	—	—	—	—
1807	—	—	—	108	49	60	139	—	—	−30	—	—	—	—
1808	—	—	—	22	9	13	57	—	—	−35	—	—	—	—
1809	—	—	—	52	31	21	59	—	—	−7	—	—	—	—
1810	—	—	—	67	42	24	85	—	—	−19	—	—	—	—
1811	—	—	—	61	45	16	53	—	—	8	—	—	—	—
1812	—	—	—	39	30	8	77	—	—	−39	—	—	—	—
1813	—	—	—	28	25	3	22	—	—	6	—	—	—	—
1814	—	—	—	7	7	(Z)	13	—	—	−6	—	—	—	—
1815	—	—	—	53	46	7	113	—	—	−60	—	—	—	—
1816	—	—	—	82	65	17	147	—	—	−65	—	—	—	—
1817	—	—	—	88	68	19	99	—	—	−12	—	—	—	—
1818	—	—	—	93	74	19	122	—	—	−28	—	—	—	—
1819	—	—	—	70	51	19	87	—	—	−17	—	—	—	—
1820	—	—	—	70	52	18	74	—	—	−5	—	—	—	—
1821	65	63	2	55	41	11	55	44	11	(Z)	—[7]	—[7]	10[7]	8[7]
1822	72	83	−11	61	50	11	80	68	11	−19	—[7]	—[7]	11[7]	3[7]
1823	75	78	−3	68	47	21	72	51	21	−4	—[7]	—[7]	6[7]	5[7]
1824	76	81	−5	69	51	18	72	54	18	−3	—[7]	—[7]	7[7]	8[7]

	Merchandise, gold, and silver			Merchandise							Gold		Silver	
				Exports and reexports			General imports							
Year	Exports	Imports	Excess of exports or imports	Total	Exports of U.S. merchandise	Reexports	Total	For immediate consumption	For warehouse	Excess of exports or imports	Exports	Imports	Exports	Imports
	Ee362 [2]	Ee363	Ee364	Ee365	Ee366	Ee367	Ee368	Ee369	Ee370	Ee371	Ee372 [3]	Ee373	Ee374 [3,4]	Ee375 [4]
	Million dollars	Million dollars	Million dollars	Million dollars	Million dollars	Million dollars	Million dollars	Million dollars	Million dollars	Million dollars	Million dollars	Million dollars	Million dollars	Million dollars
1825	100	96	3	91	67	24	90	66	24	1	(Z)	1	8	6
1826	78	85	−7	73	52	20	78	58	20	−5	1	1	4	6
1827	82	79	3	74	58	16	71	55	16	3	2	1	6	7
1828	72	89	−16	64	50	14	81	67	14	−17	2	1	7	7
1829	72	74	−2	67	55	12	67	55	12	(Z)	2	1	3	7
1830	74	71	3	72	59	13	63	50	13	9	1	1	1	7
1831	81	103	−22	72	59	13	96	83	13	−24	3	1	6	6
1832	87	101	−14	82	62	20	95	75	20	−14	2	1	4	5
1833	90	108	−18	88	70	18	101	83	18	−14	1	1	2	6
1834	104	127	−22	102	81	22	109	87	22	−6	1	4	1	14
1835	122	150	−28	115	100	15	137	122	15	−22	1	2	5	11
1836	129	190	−61	124	107	18	177	159	18	−52	1	7	4	6
1837	117	141	−24	111	94	17	130	113	17	−19	3	2	3	8
1838	108	114	−5	105	96	9	96	87	9	9	1	12	2	6
1839	121	162	−41	112	102	11	156	146	11	−44	5	1	4	4
1840	132	107	25	124	112	12	98	86	12	25	4	3	5	6
1841	122	128	−6	112	104	8	123	115	8	−11	4	1	6	4
1842	105	100	5	100	92	8	96	88	8	4	2	1	3	3
1843 [5]	84	65	20	83	78	5	42	37	5	40	(Z)	17	1	5
1844	111	108	3	106	100	6	103	96	6	3	1	2	4	4
1845	115	117	−3	106	98	8	113	106	8	−7	3	1	6	3
1846	113	122	−8	110	102	8	118	110	8	−8	2	1	2	3
1847	159	147	12	157	151	6	122	116	6	34	1	22	1	3
1848	154	155	−1	138	130	8	149	141	8	−10	11	3	5	3
1849	146	148	−2	140	132	9	141	133	9	−1	2	4	3	3
1850	152	178	−26	144	135	9	174	164	9	−29	5	2	3	3
1851	218	216	2	189	179	10	211	200	10	−22	23	4	7	2
1852	210	213	−3	167	155	12	207	195	12	−40	40	4	3	3
1853	231	268	−37	203	190	14	264	250	14	−60	25	2	2	2
1854	278	305	−26	237	215	22	298	276	22	−61	40	3	1	4
1855	275	261	14	219	193	26	258	232	26	−39	55	1	1	3
1856	327	315	12	281	266	15	310	296	15	−29	45	1	1	3
1857	363	361	2	294	279	15	348	334	15	−55	65	7	4	6
1858	325	283	42	272	251	21	263	243	21	9	50	12	3	8
1859	357	339	18	293	278	15	331	317	15	−38	61	2	3	5
1860	400	362	38	334	316	17	354	336	17	−20	58	3	8	6
1861	249	336	−86	220	205	15	289	275	15	−70	27	42	2	4
1862	228	206	22	191	180	11	189	178	11	1	35	14	1	3
1863	268	253	15	204	186	18	243	225	18	−39	62	6	2	4
1864	264	330	−65	159	144	15	316	301	15	−158	101	11	5	2
1865	234	249	−15	166	137	29	239	210	29	−73	58	6	9	3
1866	435	446	−11	349	338	11	435	423	11	−86	71	8	15	3
1867	355	418	−62	295	280	15	396	378	18	−101	39	17	22	5
1868	376	372	4	282	269	13	357	345	13	−75	72	9	21	5
1869	343	437	−94	286	275	11	418	394	23	−131	36	14	21	6

(continued)

Notes appear at end of table

TABLE Ee362–375   Exports and imports of merchandise, gold, and silver: 1790–2002   Continued

Year	Merchandise, gold, and silver			Merchandise							Gold		Silver	
				Exports and reexports			General imports							
	Exports	Imports	Excess of exports or imports	Total	Exports of U.S. merchandise	Reexports	Total	For immediate consumption	For warehouse	Excess of exports or imports	Exports	Imports	Exports	Imports
	Ee362 [2]	Ee363	Ee364	Ee365	Ee366	Ee367	Ee368	Ee369	Ee370	Ee371	Ee372 [3]	Ee373	Ee374 [3,4]	Ee375 [4]
	Million dollars	Million dollars	Million dollars	Million dollars	Million dollars	Million dollars	Million dollars	Million dollars	Million dollars	Million dollars	Million dollars	Million dollars	Million dollars	Million dollars
1870	451	462	−11	393	377	16	436	426	10	−43	34	12	25	14
1871	541	541	(Z)	443	428	14	520	500	20	−77	67	7	32	14
1872	524	640	−116	444	428	16	627	560	67	−182	50	9	30	5
1873	607	664	−57	522	505	17	642	663	−21	−120	45	9	40	13
1874	653	596	57	586	569	17	567	568	(Z)	19	34	120	33	9
1875	606	554	52	513	499	14	533	526	7	−20	67	14	25	7
1876	597	477	120	540	526	15	461	465	−4	80	31	8	25	8
1877	659	492	167	602	590	13	451	440	11	151	27	26	30	15
1878	729	467	262	695	681	14	437	439	−2	258	9	13	25	16
1879	735	466	269	710	698	12	446	440	6	265	5	6	20	15
1880	853	761	92	836	824	12	668	628	40	168	4	81	14	12
1881	922	753	169	902	884	18	643	651	−8	260	3	100	17	11
1882	800	767	33	751	733	17	725	717	8	26	33	34	17	8
1883	856	752	104	824	804	20	723	701	22	101	12	18	20	11
1884	808	705	103	741	725	16	668	668	(Z)	73	41	23	26	15
1885	784	621	164	742	727	16	578	579	−2	165	8	27	34	17
1886	752	674	78	680	666	14	635	624	11	44	43	21	30	18
1887	752	752	(Z)	716	703	13	692	680	13	24	10	43	26	17
1888	742	783	−41	696	684	12	724	707	17	−28	18	44	28	15
1889	839	774	65	742	730	12	745	735	10	−3	60	10	37	19
1890	910	823	87	858	845	13	789	766	24	69	17	13	35	21
1891	993	881	112	884	872	12	845	845	1	40	86	18	23	18
1892	1,113	897	216	1,030	1,016	15	827	804	23	203	50	50	33	20
1893	997	911	86	848	831	17	866	833	34	−19	109	21	41	23
1894	1,020	741	279	892	869	23	655	630	25	237	77	72	50	13
1895	921	789	133	808	793	14	732	731	1	76	66	36	47	20
1896	1,056	842	214	883	863	19	780	760	20	103	112	34	61	29
1897	1,153	880	273	1,051	1,032	19	765	789	−25	286	40	85	62	31
1898	1,302	767	535	1,231	1,210	21	616	587	29	615	15	120	55	31
1899	1,321	817	504	1,227	1,204	23	697	685	12	530	38	89	56	31
1900	1,499	930	570	1,394	1,371	24	850	831	19	545	48	45	57	35
1901	1,605	926	680	1,488	1,460	27	823	808	15	665	53	66	64	36
1902	1,480	984	496	1,382	1,355	26	903	900	4	478	49	52	50	28
1903	1,511	1,095	417	1,420	1,392	28	1,026	1,008	18	394	47	45	44	24
1904	1,592	1,118	474	1,461	1,435	26	991	982	9	470	81	99	49	28
1905	1,660	1,199	461	1,519	1,492	27	1,118	1,087	30	401	93	54	49	27
1906	1,848	1,367	481	1,744	1,718	26	1,227	1,213	13	517	39	96	66	44
1907	1,989	1,592	397	1,881	1,854	27	1,434	1,415	19	446	51	115	57	43
1908	1,991	1,387	604	1,861	1,835	26	1,194	1,183	11	666	72	148	58	45
1909	1,810	1,400	410	1,663	1,638	25	1,312	1,282	30	351	92	44	56	44
1910	1,919	1,646	273	1,745	1,710	35	1,557	1,547	10	188	119	43	55	45
1911	2,137	1,647	490	2,049	2,014	36	1,527	1,528	−1	522	23	74	65	46
1912	2,327	1,749	577	2,204	2,170	34	1,653	1,641	13	551	57	49	65	47
1913	2,615	1,923	692	2,466	2,429	37	1,813	1,767	46	653	78	69	72	41
1914	2,532	1,991	541	2,365	2,330	35	1,894	1,906	−12	471	112	67	55	30

	Merchandise, gold, and silver			Merchandise							Gold		Silver	
	Exports	Imports	Excess of exports or imports	Exports and reexports			General imports			Excess of exports or imports	Exports	Imports	Exports	Imports
				Total	Exports of U.S. merchandise	Reexports	Total	For immediate consumption	For warehouse					
	Ee362 [2]	Ee363	Ee364	Ee365	Ee366	Ee367	Ee368	Ee369	Ee370	Ee371	Ee372 [3]	Ee373	Ee374 [3,4]	Ee375 [4]
Year	Million dollars	Million dollars	Million dollars	Million dollars	Million dollars	Million dollars	Million dollars	Million dollars	Million dollars	Million dollars	Million dollars	Million dollars	Million dollars	Million dollars
1915	2,966	1,875	1,091	2,769	2,716	52	1,674	1,648	26	1,094	146	172	51	29
1916	5,709	3,110	2,599	5,483	5,423	60	2,392	2,179	213	3,091	156	686	71	32
1917	6,690	3,558	3,131	6,234	6,170	64	2,952	2,667	285	3,281	372	552	84	53
1918	6,443	3,165	3,278	6,149	6,048	101	3,031	2,865	166	3,118	41	62	253	71
1919	8,528	4,070	4,457	7,920	7,750	171	3,904	3,828	76	4,016	368	77	239	89
1920	8,664	5,784	2,880	8,228	8,080	148	5,278	4,789	490	2,950	322	417	114	88
1921	4,560	3,264	1,297	4,485	4,379	106	2,509	2,280	230	1,976	24	691	52	63
1922	3,931	3,459	473	3,832	3,765	67	3,113	2,776	337	719	37	275	63	71
1923	4,269	4,189	79	4,167	4,091	77	3,792	3,341	451	375	29	323	72	74
1924	4,763	4,004	759	4,591	4,498	93	3,610	3,153	457	981	62	320	110	74
1925	5,272	4,419	852	4,910	4,819	91	4,227	3,702	524	683	263	128	99	65
1926	5,017	4,714	303	4,809	4,712	97	4,431	3,949	482	378	116	214	92	70
1927	5,142	4,447	695	4,865	4,759	107	4,185	3,720	465	681	201	208	76	55
1928	5,776	4,328	1,448	5,128	5,030	98	4,091	3,655	436	1,037	561	169	87	68
1929	5,441	4,755	686	5,241	5,157	84	4,399	3,925	474	842	117	292	83	64
1930	4,013	3,500	514	3,843	3,781	62	3,061	2,765	296	782	116	396	54	43
1931	2,918	2,731	186	2,424	2,378	46	2,091	1,881	210	334	467	612	26	29
1932	2,434	1,706	729	1,611	1,576	35	1,323	1,198	125	288	810	363	14	20
1933	2,061	1,703	358	1,675	1,647	28	1,450	1,254	196	225	367	193	19	60
1934	2,202	2,944	−742	2,133	2,100	33	1,655	1,388	267	478	53	1,187	17	103
1935	2,304	4,143	−1,839	2,283	2,243	40	2,047	1,762	285	235	2	1,741	19	355
1936	2,495	3,750	−1,254	2,456	2,419	37	2,423	2,095	328	33	28	1,144	12	183
1937	3,407	4,807	−1,400	3,349	3,299	50	3,084	2,614	470	265	46	1,632	12	92
1938	3,107	4,170	−1,063	3,094	3,057	37	1,960	1,666	294	1,134	6	1,979	7	231
1939	3,192	5,978	−2,786	3,177	3,123	54	2,318	1,918	400	859	1	3,575	15	85
1940	4,030	7,433	−3,403	4,021	3,934	87	2,625	2,170	455	1,396	5	4,749	4	58
1941	5,153	4,375	778	5,147	5,020	127	3,345	2,716	629	1,802	(Z)	982	6	47
1942	8,081	3,113	4,968	8,079	8,003	76	2,756 [6]	2,286	459	5,323	(Z)	316	2	41
1943	13,028	3,511	9,517	12,965	12,842	123	3,381	3,034	347	9,583	33	102	31	28
1944	15,345	4,066	11,279	14,259	14,162	97	3,929 [6]	3,515	404	10,330	959	114	127	23
1945	10,097	4,280	5,816	9,806	9,585	221	4,159 [6]	3,689	458	5,646	200	94	91	27
1946	9,996	5,533	4,464	9,738	9,500	238	4,942	4,285	657	4,796	221	533	36	58
1947	14,674	7,904	6,770	14,430	14,252	177	5,756	5,074	682	8,673	213	2,080	31	68
1948	12,967	9,176	3,791	12,653	12,532	121	7,124	6,361	763	5,529	301	1,981	13	71
1949	12,160	7,467	4,693	12,051	11,936	115	6,622	5,942	680	5,429	85	771	24	74
1950	10,816	9,125	1,691	10,275	10,142	133	8,852	7,815	1,037	1,423	534	163	7	110
1951	15,672	11,152	4,520	15,032	14,879	153	10,967	9,600	1,367	4,065	631	81	9	103
1952	15,262	11,525	3,737	15,201	15,049	152	10,717	9,768	949	4,483	56	740	5	67
1953	15,827	11,015	4,812	15,774	15,652	122	10,873	9,972	902	4,900	45	47	9	95
1954	15,136	10,333	4,803	15,110	14,981	129	10,215	9,442	773	4,894	22	38	5	80
1955	15,563	11,562	4,001	15,547	15,419	128	11,384	10,467	917	4,163	7	105	8	73
1956	19,124	12,877	6,247	19,090	18,940	150	12,615	11,591	1,024	6,475	27	133	7	129
1957	21,029	13,413	7,617	20,850	20,671	180	12,982	11,894	1,088	7,868	168	273	11	158
1958	17,945	13,215	4,730	17,910	17,745	165	12,792	11,780	1,012	5,118	31	291	4	132
1959	17,646	15,574	2,072	17,634	17,451	183	15,207	13,908	1,299	2,427	2	304	10	63

Notes appear at end of table

(continued)

TABLE Ee362–375 Exports and imports of merchandise, gold, and silver: 1790–2002 *Continued*

	Merchandise, gold, and silver			Merchandise							Gold		Silver	
				Exports and reexports			General imports							
	Exports	Imports	Excess of exports or imports	Total	Exports of U.S. merchandise	Reexports	Total	For immediate consumption	For warehouse	Excess of exports or imports	Exports	Imports	Exports	Imports
	Ee362 [2]	Ee363	Ee364	Ee365	Ee366	Ee367	Ee368	Ee369	Ee370	Ee371	Ee372 [3]	Ee373	Ee374 [3,4]	Ee375 [4]
Year	Million dollars	Million dollars	Million dollars	Million dollars	Million dollars	Million dollars	Million dollars	Million dollars	Million dollars	Million dollars	Million dollars	Million dollars	Million dollars	Million dollars
1960	20,603	15,046	5,557	20,575	20,375	200	14,654	13,282	1,372	5,922	2	335	26	57
1961	21,812	14,815	6,997	20,999	20,755	245	14,714	13,361	1,353	6,286	775	56	38	45
1962	22,096	16,606	5,491	21,700	21,431	269	16,380	14,928	1,451	5,320	381	151	15	75
1963	23,593	17,253	6,339	23,347	23,062	285	17,138	15,644	1,493	6,209	204	44	42	71
1964	27,075	18,791	8,284	26,508	26,156	352	18,684	17,087	1,597	7,824	423	41	144	66
1965	28,809	21,533	7,276	27,470	27,127	343	21,364	19,661	1,705	6,105	1,285	102	54	65
1966	30,891	25,663	5,229	30,320	29,884	436	25,542	23,870	1,673	4,777	457	42	114	78
1967	32,632	26,925	5,708	31,526	31,142	384	26,812	25,330	1,483	4,714	1,005	33	101	80
1968	35,475	33,452	2,023	34,636	34,199	437	33,226	31,439	1,787	1,410	839	226	—	—
1969	38,018	36,279	1,739	38,006	37,462	544	36,043	34,238	1,805	1,964	12	237	—	—
1970	43,265	40,189	3,076	43,224	42,590	634	39,952	38,064	1,888	3,272	41	237	—	—
1971	44,181	45,847	−1,666	44,130	43,492	638	45,563	43,488	2,075	−1,433	51	284	—	—
1972	49,822	55,940	−6,118	49,759	48,979	780	55,582	53,080	2,502	−5,823	63	358	—	—
1973	71,485	69,831	1,654	71,339	70,246	1,093	69,475	66,513	2,962	1,864	146	356	—	—
1974	98,736	101,394	−2,658	98,507	97,144	1,363	100,997	97,342	3,655	−2,490	229	397	—	—
1975	108,509	97,359	11,150	108,050	106,561	1,489	96,902	96,447	455	11,148	459	457	—	—
1976	115,688	122,457	−6,770	115,340	113,666	1,674	122,126	121,452	674	−6,786	348	331	—	—
1977	122,255	149,393	−27,138	121,212	119,006	2,206	148,719	147,976	743	−27,507	1,043	674	—	—
1978	143,663	173,250	−29,587	143,663	141,126	2,537	173,250	172,912	338	−29,587	—	—	—	—
1979	181,816	207,058	−25,242	181,816	178,591	3,225	207,058	205,840	1,218	−25,242	—	—	—	—
1980	220,783	245,262	−24,479	220,783	216,668	4,115	245,262	244,007	1,255	−24,479	—	—	—	—
1981	233,739	260,982	−27,243	233,739	228,961	4,778	260,982	259,012	1,970	−27,243	—	—	—	—
1982	212,275	243,953	−31,678	212,275	207,158	5,117	243,953	242,340	1,613	−31,678	—	—	—	—
1983	200,538	258,048	−57,510	200,538	195,969	4,569	258,048	256,680	1,368	−57,510	—	—	—	—
1984	217,888	325,726	−107,838	217,888	212,057	5,831	325,726	322,990	2,736	−107,838	—	—	—	—
1985	213,146	345,275	−132,129	213,146	206,925	6,221	345,275	343,522	1,753	−132,129	—	—	—	—
1986	227,159	365,438	−138,279	227,159	206,376	10,928	365,438	368,657	−3,219	−138,279	—	—	—	—
1987	254,122	406,241	−152,119	254,122	243,859	9,007	406,241	402,066	4,175	−152,119	—	—	—	—
1988	322,426	440,952	−118,526	322,426	308,024	14,402	440,952	436,799	4,153	−118,526	—	—	—	—
1989	363,766	473,397	−109,631	363,766	349,433	14,333	473,397	468,012	5,385	−109,631	—	—	—	—
1990	392,976	496,028	−103,052	392,976	374,537	18,439	496,028	491,322	4,706	−103,052	—	—	—	—
1991	421,854	488,832	−66,978	421,854	400,842	21,012	488,832	483,737	5,095	−66,978	—	—	—	—
1992	447,471	532,053	−84,582	447,471	424,971	22,500	532,053	525,127	6,926	−84,582	—	—	—	—
1993	464,858	580,469	−115,611	464,858	439,295	25,563	580,469	574,862	5,607	−115,611	—	—	—	—
1994	512,416	663,830	−151,414	512,416	481,887	30,529	663,830	657,885	5,945	−151,414	—	—	—	—
1995	583,031	743,505	−160,474	583,031	546,465	36,566	743,505	739,660	3,845	−160,474	—	—	—	—
1996	622,827	791,316	−168,489	622,827	582,137	40,690	791,316	790,479	837	−168,489	—	—	—	—
1997	687,598	870,213	−182,615	687,598	643,222	44,376	870,213	862,426	7,787	−182,615	—	—	—	—
1998	680,474	913,885	−233,411	680,474	634,705	45,769	913,885	907,647	6,238	−272,942	—	—	—	—
1999	692,821	1,024,766	−331,945	692,821	642,189	50,632	1,024,766	1,017,435	7,331	−375,253	—	—	—	—
2000	780,419	1,216,888	−436,469	780,419	712,287	68,132	1,216,888	1,205,339	11,549	−436,469	—	—	—	—
2001	731,026	1,141,959	−410,933	731,026	666,021	65,005	1,141,959	1,132,635	9,324	−410,933	—	—	—	—
2002	693,257	1,163,549	−470,292	693,257	629,599	63,658	1,163,549	1,154,810	8,739	−470,292	—	—	—	—

TABLE Ee362-375   Exports and imports of merchandise, gold, and silver: 1790-2002   *Continued*

(Z) Greater than –$500,000 and less than $500,000.

[1] Year-ending date varies over time. See text.

[2] Includes gold and silver prior to 1821. Beginning in 1861, includes exports and imports of uranium, thorium, and related products. Beginning in 1968, includes silver ore and bullion.

[3] Prior to 1864, domestic exports of silver are included with gold.

[4] Beginning in 1968, silver ore and bullion are included in merchandise exports and imports.

[5] Period beginning October 1, 1842, and ending June 30, 1843.

[6] Does not sum owing to revisions that were not carried to detail.

[7] Data shown under silver are for gold and silver.

Sources

Series Ee362-364 are summary measures of the following documented series.

Series Ee365-366 and Ee370-371. 1790, U.S. Bureau of Foreign and Domestic Commerce, *Foreign Commerce and Navigation of the United States* (1912), p. 43. 1791-1880, U.S. Bureau of Statistics, *Monthly Summary of Imports and Exports of the United States for the Fiscal Year* (1896), pp. 622-3. 1881-1903, U.S. Bureau of the Census, *Statistical Abstract of the United States* (1924), pp. 420, 421, 424. 1904-1941, *Statistical Abstract of the United States* (1948), pp. 902-3. 1942-1946, U.S. Bureau of the Census, *Summary of Foreign Commerce of the United States* (annual issues). 1947-1965, U.S. Bureau of the Census, *Foreign Commerce and Navigation of the United States* (1964, 1965). 1966-1987, U.S. Bureau of Foreign and Domestic Commerce, *Highlights of Exports and Imports*, FT 990 (December issues). 1989-2002, data base from the U.S. International Trade Commission's Internet site.

Series Ee367-369. 1821-1880, U.S. Bureau of Foreign and Domestic Commerce, *Foreign Commerce and Navigation of the United States* (1912), p. 50. 1881-1915, *Foreign Commerce and Navigation of the United States* (1924), p. lxvii. 1916-1941, U.S. Bureau of the Census, *Statistical Abstract of the United States* (1948), p. 939. 1942-1946, *Statistical Abstract of the United States* (1951), p. 854. 1947-1965, U.S. Bureau of Foreign and Domestic Commerce, *Foreign Commerce and Navigation of the United States* (1964, 1965). 1966-1988, U.S. Bureau of the Census, *Highlights of Exports and Imports*, FT 990 (December issues). 1989-1996, data base from the U.S. International Trade Commission's Internet site.

Series Ee372-375. 1821-1864, U.S. Bureau of Foreign and Domestic Commerce, *Foreign Commerce and Navigation of the United States* (1912), p. 43. 1865-1880, U.S. Department of the Treasury, *Statistical Abstract of the United States* (1887), pp. 41, 42. 1881-1903, U.S. Bureau of the Census, *Statistical Abstract of the United States* (1924), pp. 420, 421. 1904-1941, *Statistical Abstract of the United States* (1948), p. 903. 1942-1946, U.S. Bureau of the Census, *Summary of Foreign Commerce of the United States* (annual issues). 1947-1965, U.S. Bureau of Foreign and Domestic Commerce, *Foreign Commerce and Navigation of the United States* (1964, 1965). 1966-1974, U.S. Bureau of the Census, *U.S. Foreign Trade, Gold Movements*, FT 2402 (December issues). 1975-1977, U.S. Bureau of the Census, *Highlights of Exports and Imports*, FT 990 (December issues).

Documentation

Merchandise export statistics include data on all shipments of commodities and merchandise leaving the U.S. Customs area except: (1) gold (prior to 1977) and silver (prior to 1968) and evidences of debt; (2) in-transit merchandise; (3) bunker fuel, stores, supplies, and equipment for vessels and planes; (4) temporary exports; (5) merchandise having small value or no commercial value; (6) shipments of military and naval supplies and equipment to the U.S. armed forces; and (7) shipments of office equipment and related items to U.S. government agencies or establishments.

Merchandise import statistics include data on all commodities and merchandise reaching the United States except: (1) merchandise not entering the U.S. Customs area, such as articles excluded from the United States by law; (2) bunker fuel and ships' stores; (3) in-transit merchandise; (4) certain domestic merchandise returned from foreign countries; (5) gold and silver (prior to 1968) and evidences of debt; (6) merchandise having small value or no commercial value; and (7) commodities entered under special provisions, such as articles consigned to diplomatic officers.

The data are for the year ending September 30 (1790-1842) and June 30 (1843-1915), and for calendar years thereafter. For the six-month transition period in 1915 (July 1 to December 31), the values for series Ee362-369 and Ee372-375 are as follows: 1,905, 1,239, +667, 1,853, 1,820, 33, 913, +940, 24, 307, 29, and 19, respectively (in millions of dollars).

Series Ee364 and Ee371. Excess of exports are shown as a positive number; excess of imports as a negative number.

Series Ee365. For 1944-1947, series values that include estimates of civilian supplies shipped to occupied areas through U.S. armed forces and other relief agencies are as follows: 14,414, 10,530, 10,184, and 15,338, respectively (in millions of dollars).

Series Ee366. Exports of U.S. merchandise consist of commodities grown, produced, or manufactured in the United States, and commodities of foreign origin that have been changed in the United States from the form in which they were imported or that have been enhanced in value by further manufacture in the United States.

Series Ee367. Reexports comprise withdrawals from Customs-bonded storage warehouses for exportation and exports of foreign merchandise (principally duty-free articles) that have previously been formally entered through Customs. Exports of foreign merchandise consist of commodities of foreign origin that have entered the United States as imports and that, at the time of exportation, are in the same condition as when imported.

Series Ee368. General imports consist of entries for immediate consumption and entries into bonded warehouses, and, therefore, they comprise the total arrivals of merchandise, whether they enter consumption channels immediately or are entered into warehouses under Customs custody to be subsequently withdrawn for consumption or withdrawn for exportation. Imports for consumption are the total of the entries for immediate consumption and the withdrawals from warehouse for consumption. The terms "entered for immediate consumption" and "withdrawn from warehouse for consumption" are taken from the language used in handling the transactions through Customs and are sometimes misleading in their implication that the merchandise is immediately assimilated by being processed, merchandised, or consumed. Although all Customs barriers to such assimilation have been removed, merchandise for "immediate consumption" may, in fact, be warehoused by the importer outside of Customs custody. In the case of withdrawal for "consumption," although duties have been paid and the goods released from Customs control, they may remain in storage for a further period of time. Any of this "for consumption" merchandise could conceivably be exported subsequent to its release from Customs custody and thus never enter actual U.S. consumption channels.

Series Ee372-375. Prior to 1895, figures for gold and silver relate to coin and bullion only; subsequently, they include ore also. Domestic exports of gold and silver cannot be separately stated prior to 1864, but it is probable that the greater portion of the exports was gold. In the series shown here, the data on exports of gold prior to 1864 include domestic exports of silver. The exports of silver for years prior to 1864, therefore, consist of only foreign exports or reexports.

TABLE Ee376–384   Exports and imports of goods and services: 1929–2002

Contributed by Douglas A. Irwin

	Exports			Imports			Trade balance		
	Total	Goods	Services	Total	Goods	Services	Total	Goods	Services
	Ee376	Ee377	Ee378	Ee379	Ee380	Ee381	Ee382	Ee383	Ee384
Year	Billion dollars	Billion dollars	Billion dollars	Billion dollars	Billion dollars	Billion dollars	Billion dollars	Billion dollars	Billion dollars
1929	5.900	5.300	0.600	5.600	4.500	1.100	0.400	0.800	−0.500
1930	4.400	3.900	0.500	4.100	3.100	1.000	0.300	0.800	−0.500
1931	2.900	2.500	0.400	2.900	2.100	0.800	0.000	0.400	−0.400
1932	2.000	1.700	0.300	1.900	1.300	0.600	0.000	0.400	−0.300
1933	2.000	1.700	0.300	1.900	1.500	0.400	0.100	0.200	−0.100
1934	2.600	2.200	0.300	2.200	1.800	0.500	0.300	0.400	−0.200
1935	2.800	2.400	0.400	3.000	2.500	0.500	−0.200	−0.100	−0.100
1936	3.000	2.600	0.400	3.200	2.500	0.600	−0.200	0.100	−0.200
1937	4.000	3.500	0.600	4.000	3.200	0.800	0.000	0.300	−0.200
1938	3.800	3.200	0.500	2.800	2.200	0.700	0.900	1.000	−0.200
1939	3.900	3.300	0.600	3.100	2.400	0.700	0.800	0.900	−0.100
1940	4.800	4.100	0.700	3.400	2.700	0.700	1.400	1.400	0.000
1941	5.400	4.500	0.900	4.400	3.400	1.000	1.000	1.100	−0.100
1942	4.300	3.400	0.900	4.600	2.700	1.900	−0.300	0.700	−1.000
1943	3.900	2.900	1.000	6.300	3.400	2.800	−2.400	−0.500	−1.800
1944	4.800	3.600	1.200	6.900	3.800	3.100	−2.200	−0.200	−1.900
1945	6.700	5.400	1.300	7.500	3.900	3.700	−0.900	1.500	−2.400
1946	14.100	11.800	2.300	7.000	5.100	1.900	7.100	6.700	0.400
1947	18.700	16.100	2.600	7.900	6.000	2.000	10.800	10.100	0.600
1948	15.500	13.300	2.200	10.100	7.600	2.500	5.400	5.700	−0.300
1949	14.400	12.200	2.200	9.200	6.900	2.400	5.200	5.300	−0.200
1950	12.300	10.200	2.100	11.600	9.100	2.500	0.700	1.100	−0.400
1951	17.000	14.200	2.800	14.600	11.200	3.400	2.400	3.000	−0.600
1952	16.300	13.400	2.900	15.300	10.800	4.500	1.000	2.600	−1.600
1953	15.200	12.400	2.800	16.000	11.000	5.000	−0.800	1.400	−2.200
1954	15.700	12.900	2.800	15.400	10.400	5.100	0.300	2.500	−2.300
1955	17.600	14.400	3.200	17.200	11.500	5.700	0.400	2.900	−2.500
1956	21.200	17.600	3.600	18.900	12.800	6.100	2.300	4.800	−2.500
1957	23.900	19.600	4.300	19.900	13.300	6.700	4.000	6.300	−2.400
1958	20.400	16.400	4.000	20.000	13.000	7.100	0.400	3.400	−3.100
1959	20.600	16.500	4.200	22.300	15.300	7.000	−1.700	1.200	−2.800
1960	25.300	19.650	6.290	22.432	14.758	7.674	2.868	4.892	−1.384
1961	26.000	20.108	6.295	22.208	14.537	7.671	3.792	5.571	−1.376
1962	27.400	20.781	6.941	24.352	16.260	8.092	3.048	4.521	−1.151
1963	29.400	22.272	7.348	25.410	17.048	8.362	3.990	5.224	−1.014
1964	33.600	25.501	7.840	27.319	18.700	8.619	6.281	6.801	−0.779
1965	35.400	26.461	8.824	30.621	21.510	9.111	4.779	4.951	−0.287
1966	38.900	29.310	9.616	35.987	25.493	10.494	2.913	3.817	−0.878
1967	41.333	30.666	10.667	38.729	26.866	11.863	2.604	3.800	−1.196
1968	45.543	33.626	11.917	45.293	32.991	12.302	0.250	0.635	−0.385
1969	49.220	36.414	12.806	49.129	35.807	13.322	0.091	0.607	−0.516
1970	56.640	42.469	14.171	54.386	39.866	14.520	2.254	2.603	−0.349
1971	59.677	43.319	16.358	60.979	45.579	15.400	−1.302	−2.260	0.958
1972	67.222	49.381	17.841	72.665	55.797	16.868	−5.443	−6.416	0.973
1973	91.242	71.410	19.832	89.342	70.499	18.843	1.900	0.911	0.989
1974	120.897	98.306	22.591	125.190	103.811	21.379	−4.293	−5.505	1.212
1975	132.585	107.088	25.497	120.181	98.185	21.996	12.404	8.903	3.501
1976	142.716	114.745	27.971	148.798	124.228	24.570	−6.082	−9.483	3.401
1977	152.301	120.816	31.485	179.547	151.907	27.640	−27.246	−31.091	3.845
1978	178.428	142.075	36.353	208.191	176.002	32.189	−29.763	−33.927	4.164
1979	224.131	184.439	39.692	248.696	212.007	36.689	−24.565	−27.568	3.003
1980	271.834	224.250	47.584	291.241	249.750	41.491	−19.407	−25.500	6.093
1981	294.398	237.044	57.354	310.570	265.067	45.503	−16.172	−28.023	11.851
1982	275.236	211.157	64.079	299.391	247.642	51.749	−24.155	−36.485	12.330
1983	266.106	201.799	64.307	323.874	268.901	54.973	−57.768	−67.102	9.334
1984	291.094	219.926	71.168	400.166	332.418	67.748	−109.072	−112.492	3.420
1985	289.070	215.915	73.155	410.950	338.088	72.862	−121.880	−122.173	0.293
1986	308.786	223.344	86.689	448.572	368.425	80.147	−139.786	−145.081	5.295
1987	347.799	250.208	98.661	500.552	409.765	90.787	−152.753	−159.557	6.804
1988	430.260	320.230	110.919	545.715	447.189	98.526	−115.455	−126.959	11.504
1989	487.003	359.916	127.087	579.844	477.665	102.479	−92.841	−117.749	23.737

TABLE Ee376–384   Exports and imports of goods and services: 1929–2002   *Continued*

	Exports			Imports			Trade balance		
	Total	Goods	Services	Total	Goods	Services	Total	Goods	Services
	Ee376	Ee377	Ee378	Ee379	Ee380	Ee381	Ee382	Ee383	Ee384
Year	Billion dollars	Billion dollars	Billion dollars	Billion dollars	Billion dollars	Billion dollars	Billion dollars	Billion dollars	Billion dollars
1990	535.233	387.401	147.832	615.996	498.435	117.659	−80.763	−111.034	29.092
1991	578.344	414.083	164.261	609.440	491.020	118.459	−31.096	−76.937	44.584
1992	616.547	439.631	176.916	652.934	536.528	116.476	−36.387	−96.897	59.081
1993	642.884	456.943	185.941	711.675	589.394	122.281	−68.791	−132.451	63.660
1994	703.890	502.859	201.031	800.568	668.690	131.878	−96.678	−165.831	69.153
1995	794.433	575.204	219.229	890.821	749.374	141.447	−96.388	−174.170	77.782
1996	852.120	612.113	240.007	953.963	803.113	150.850	−101.843	−191.000	89.157
1997	934.980	678.366	256.614	1,042.745	876.485	166.260	−107.765	−198.119	90.354
1998	932.679	670.416	262.263	1,099.612	917.112	182.500	−166.933	−246.696	79.763
1999	957.146	683.965	273.181	1,219.383	1,029.987	189.396	−262.237	−346.022	83.785
2000	1,064.239	771.994	292.245	1,442.920	1,224.417	218.503	−378.681	−452.423	73.742
2001	998.022	718.762	279.260	1,356.312	1,145.927	210.385	−358.290	−427.165	68.875
2002	972.995	682.586	290.409	1,408.211	1,166.939	241.272	−435.216	−484.353	49.137

Source

1929–1997, U.S. Bureau of Economic Analysis (BEA), *Survey of Current Business* (August 1998, with updates from March 2003). Later updates available at the BEA Internet site.

Documentation

All series are presented on a balance of payments (BOP) basis. The BOP basis for goods reflects adjustments for timing, coverage, and valuation to the data provided by the Census Bureau. These adjustments include military trade of U.S. defense agencies, additional nonmonetary gold transactions, and inland freight in Canada and Mexico. Goods valuation are free alongside ship (f.a.s.) for exports and customs value for imports.

TABLE Ee385–399 Exports and imports of goods: 1970–2002

Contributed by Douglas A. Irwin

	Total			Manufactured goods			Agricultural goods			Mineral fuels			Other goods		
	Exports	Imports	Trade balance	Exports	Imports	Trade balance	Exports	Imports	Trade balance	Exports	Imports	Trade balance	Exports	Imports	Trade balance
	Ee385	Ee386	Ee387	Ee388	Ee389	Ee390	Ee391	Ee392	Ee393	Ee394	Ee395	Ee396	Ee397	Ee398	Ee399
Year	Billion dollars	Billion dollars	Billion dollars	Billion dollars	Billion dollars	Billion dollars	Billion dollars	Billion dollars	Billion dollars	Billion dollars	Billion dollars	Billion dollars	Billion dollars	Billion dollars	Billion dollars
1970	43.8	40.4	3.4	31.7	27.3	4.4	7.3	5.8	1.6	1.6	3.1	−1.5	3.1	4.2	−1.1
1971	44.7	46.2	−1.5	32.9	32.1	0.8	7.8	5.8	2.0	1.5	3.7	−2.2	2.5	4.6	−2.1
1972	50.5	56.4	−5.9	36.5	39.7	−3.2	9.5	6.5	3.0	1.6	4.8	−3.2	2.9	5.3	−2.4
1973	72.5	70.5	2.0	48.5	47.1	1.3	17.9	8.5	9.4	1.7	8.2	−6.5	4.5	6.7	−2.2
1974	100.0	102.6	−2.5	68.5	57.8	10.7	22.3	10.4	11.9	3.4	25.5	−22.0	5.8	8.9	−3.1
1975	109.3	98.5	10.8	76.9	54.0	22.9	22.1	9.5	12.6	4.5	26.5	−22.0	5.9	8.6	−2.7
1976	117.0	123.5	−6.5	83.1	67.6	15.5	23.3	11.2	12.1	4.2	34.0	−29.8	6.4	10.7	−4.3
1977	123.2	151.0	−27.8	88.9	80.5	8.4	24.2	13.6	10.6	4.2	47.2	−43.0	5.9	9.8	−3.9
1978	145.9	174.8	−28.8	103.6	104.3	−0.7	29.8	15.0	14.8	3.9	42.0	−38.1	8.6	13.4	−4.8
1979	186.5	209.5	−22.9	132.7	117.1	15.6	35.2	16.9	18.3	5.7	59.9	−54.2	12.9	15.5	−2.7
1980	225.7	245.3	−19.5	160.7	133.0	27.7	41.8	17.4	24.3	8.2	78.9	−70.7	15.1	15.9	−0.8
1981	238.7	261.0	−22.3	171.7	149.8	22.0	43.8	17.2	26.6	10.3	81.2	−70.9	12.8	12.8	0.0
1982	216.4	244.0	−27.5	155.3	151.7	3.6	37.0	15.7	21.3	12.8	65.3	−52.5	11.3	11.3	0.1
1983	205.6	258.0	−52.4	148.5	171.2	−22.7	36.5	16.5	19.9	9.8	57.8	−48.0	10.9	12.5	−1.6
1983[1]	205.6	258.0	−52.4	148.7	170.9	−22.2	36.1	16.0	20.2	9.8	57.8	−48.0	11.0	13.4	−2.4
1984	224.0	330.7	−106.7	164.1	230.9	−66.8	37.9	19.3	18.6	9.7	60.8	−51.1	12.3	19.6	−7.3
1985	218.8	336.5	−117.7	168.0	257.5	−89.5	29.3	19.5	9.8	10.3	53.7	−43.4	11.2	5.9	5.3
1986	227.2	365.4	−138.3	179.8	296.7	−116.8	26.3	20.9	5.4	8.4	37.2	−28.8	12.6	10.7	1.9
1987	254.1	406.2	−152.1	199.9	324.4	−124.6	28.7	20.3	8.4	8.0	44.1	−36.1	17.5	17.4	0.1
1988	322.4	441.0	−118.5	255.6	361.4	−105.7	37.1	20.7	16.4	8.5	41.0	−32.5	21.2	17.8	3.3
1989	363.8	473.2	−109.4	287.0	379.4	−92.4	41.6	21.1	20.5	9.9	52.6	−42.7	25.3	20.0	5.2
1990	393.6	495.3	−101.7	315.4	388.8	−73.5	39.6	22.3	17.2	12.4	64.7	−52.3	26.3	19.5	6.8
1991	421.7	488.5	−66.7	345.1	392.4	−47.3	39.4	22.1	17.2	12.3	54.1	−41.8	24.9	19.8	5.1
1992	448.2	532.7	−84.5	368.5	434.3	−65.9	43.1	23.4	19.8	11.3	55.3	−43.9	25.2	19.7	5.5
1993	465.1	580.7	−115.6	388.7	479.9	−91.2	42.8	23.6	19.2	9.9	55.9	−46.0	23.7	21.2	2.5
1994	512.6	663.3	−150.6	431.1	557.3	−126.3	45.9	26.0	20.0	9.0	56.4	−47.4	26.7	23.6	3.1
1995	584.7	743.4	−158.7	486.7	629.7	−143.0	56.0	29.3	26.8	10.5	59.1	−48.6	31.6	25.4	6.2
1996	625.1	795.3	−170.2	524.7	658.8	−134.1	60.6	32.6	28.1	12.4	78.1	−65.7	27.4	25.8	1.5
1997	689.2	870.7	−181.5	592.5	728.9	−136.4	57.1	35.2	21.9	13.0	78.3	−65.3	26.7	28.3	−1.7
1998	682.1	911.9	−299.8	596.6	790.8	−194.2	52.0	35.7	16.3	10.4	57.3	−47.0	23.2	28.1	−4.9
1999	695.8	1,025.6	−328.8	611.6	882.7	−271.1	48.2	36.7	11.5	9.9	75.2	−65.3	26.1	30.0	−3.9
2000	781.9	1,218.0	−436.1	691.5	1,012.9	−321.3	53.0	39.2	13.8	13.4	135.4	−122.0	26.9	30.6	−3.7
2001	729.1	1,414.0	−411.9	640.2	950.7	−310.4	55.2	39.5	15.7	12.7	121.9	−109.2	20.9	28.9	−7.9
2002	693.5	1,163.6	−470.1	606.6	975.4	−368.8	54.7	42.0	12.7	11.7	117.1	−105.4	20.5	20.5	−8.6

1 Based on the old (non-Harmonized System) of commodity classification. See text.

Sources

1970–1996, U.S. International Trade Administration, Office of Trade and Economic Analysis (OTEA), U.S. Foreign Trade Highlights, 1997 (August 1998). 1997–2002, available at the OTEA Internet site.

Documentation

These series are presented both on a census basis and on the basis of the Harmonized System of commodity classification. Data for 1983–1988 are estimated, based on the Harmonized System of commodity classification. Data before 1983 are on a Schedule A/E basis and have been adjusted to match the latest trade definitions as closely as possible. Census data concordances link the 1980–1992 trade figures into time series that are as consistent as possible. Data for 1970–1979 are not linked and are from published sources.

Total goods include nonmonetary gold, military grant aid, special category shipments, trade between the U.S. Virgin Islands and foreign countries, and undocumented exports to Canada. Adjustments were also made for carryover. Import values are based on transaction prices whenever possible (free alongside ship for 1974–1979 and Customs value thereafter). Import data before 1974 do not exist on a transaction price valuation basis. Data for 1970–1980 exclude trade between the U.S. Virgin Islands and foreign countries.

Series Ee388–390, manufactured goods. Includes commodity sections 5–9 under Schedules A and E for 1970–1982 and Standard International Trade Classification (SITC) Revision 3 for 1983 forward. Manufactures include undocumented exports to Canada, nonmonetary gold (excluding gold ore, scrap, and base bullion), and special category shipments.

Series Ee391–393, agricultural goods. Beginning in 1983, utilizes the latest census definition, which excludes manufactured goods that were previously classified as manufactured agricultural products.

Series Ee394–396, mineral fuels. Includes commodity section 3 under SITC Revision 1 for 1970–1976, SITC Revision 2 for 1977–1982, and SITC Revision 3 for 1983 forward.

TABLE Ee400–415 Exports and imports of services: 1970–2002

Contributed by Douglas A. Irwin

	Total		Private										Government			
			Travel		Passenger fares		Other transportation		Royalties and license fees		Other private services		Military-defense transfers and expenditures		U.S. government miscellaneous services	
	Exports	Imports	Exports	Imports	Exports	Imports	Exports	Imports	Exports	Imports	Exports	Imports	Exports	Imports	Exports	Imports
	Ee400	Ee401	Ee402	Ee403	Ee404	Ee405	Ee406	Ee407	Ee408	Ee409	Ee410	Ee411	Ee412	Ee413	Ee414	Ee415
Year	Billion dollars	Billion dollars	Billion dollars	Billion dollars	Billion dollars	Billion dollars	Billion dollars	Billion dollars	Billion dollars	Billion dollars	Billion dollars	Billion dollars	Billion dollars	Billion dollars	Billion dollars	Billion dollars
1970	14.2	14.5	2.3	4.0	0.5	1.2	3.1	2.8	2.3	0.2	1.3	0.8	4.2	4.9	0.3	0.6
1971	16.4	15.4	2.5	4.4	0.6	1.3	3.3	3.1	2.5	0.2	1.5	1.0	5.5	4.8	0.3	0.6
1972	17.8	16.9	2.8	5.0	0.7	1.6	3.6	3.5	2.8	0.3	1.8	1.0	5.9	4.8	0.4	0.6
1973	19.8	18.8	3.4	5.5	1.0	1.8	4.5	4.7	3.2	0.4	2.0	1.2	5.4	4.6	0.4	0.6
1974	22.6	21.4	4.0	6.0	1.1	2.1	5.7	5.9	3.8	0.3	2.3	1.3	5.2	5.0	0.4	0.7
1975	25.5	22.0	4.7	6.4	1.0	2.3	5.8	5.7	4.3	0.5	2.9	1.6	6.3	4.8	0.4	0.8
1976	28.0	24.6	5.7	6.9	1.2	2.6	6.7	6.9	4.4	0.5	3.6	2.0	5.8	4.9	0.5	0.9
1977	31.5	27.6	6.2	7.5	1.4	2.7	7.1	8.0	4.9	0.5	3.8	2.2	7.6	5.8	0.6	1.0
1978	36.4	32.2	7.2	8.5	1.6	2.9	8.1	9.1	5.9	0.7	4.7	2.6	8.2	7.4	0.6	1.1
1979	39.7	36.7	8.4	9.4	2.2	3.2	10.0	10.9	6.2	0.8	5.4	2.8	7.0	8.3	0.5	1.2
1980	47.6	41.5	10.6	10.4	2.6	3.6	11.6	11.8	7.1	0.7	6.3	2.9	9.0	10.9	0.4	1.2
1981	57.4	45.5	12.9	11.5	3.1	4.5	12.6	12.5	7.3	0.7	10.3	3.6	10.7	11.6	0.5	1.3
1982	64.1	51.7	12.4	12.4	3.2	4.8	12.3	11.7	5.6	0.8	17.4	8.2	12.6	12.5	0.6	1.5
1983	64.2	54.9	10.9	13.1	3.6	6.0	12.6	12.2	5.7	0.9	18.1	7.9	12.5	13.1	0.7	1.6
1984	71.0	67.7	17.2	22.9	4.1	5.7	13.8	14.8	6.1	1.2	19.1	9.0	10.0	12.5	0.7	1.5
1985	72.9	72.8	17.8	24.6	4.4	6.4	14.7	15.6	6.6	1.2	19.9	10.2	8.7	13.1	0.9	1.7
1986	86.4	81.8	20.4	25.9	5.6	6.5	15.8	16.7	7.9	1.4	27.7	14.8	8.5	13.7	0.6	1.7
1987	98.6	92.3	23.6	29.3	7.0	7.3	17.3	17.8	9.9	1.8	29.2	18.0	11.1	15.0	0.5	1.9
1988	111.1	100.0	29.4	32.1	9.0	7.7	19.5	19.5	11.8	2.6	31.3	19.1	9.3	15.6	0.7	1.9
1989	127.2	104.2	36.3	33.4	10.6	8.2	20.5	20.7	13.8	2.5	36.9	20.6	8.6	15.3	0.6	1.9
1990	147.9	120.0	43.0	37.3	15.3	10.5	22.0	23.4	17.1	3.2	40.3	24.6	9.7	17.5	0.7	1.9
1991	164.3	121.2	48.4	35.3	15.9	10.0	22.3	23.3	18.5	4.2	47.8	22.3	10.5	16.4	0.7	2.1
1992	176.9	116.5	54.7	38.6	16.6	10.6	21.5	23.8	20.8	5.2	50.0	26.3	12.4	13.8	0.8	2.3
1993	185.9	122.3	57.9	40.7	16.5	11.4	22.0	24.5	21.7	5.0	53.5	30.4	13.5	12.1	0.9	2.3
1994	201.0	131.9	58.4	43.8	17.0	13.1	23.8	26.0	26.7	5.9	61.5	35.2	12.8	10.2	0.9	2.6
1995	219.2	141.4	63.4	44.9	18.9	14.7	26.1	27.0	30.3	6.9	65.1	38.0	14.6	10.0	0.8	2.6
1996	240.0	150.9	69.8	48.1	20.4	15.8	26.1	27.4	32.5	7.8	73.9	43.5	16.4	11.1	0.9	2.7
1997	256.6	166.3	73.4	52.1	20.9	18.1	27.0	29.0	33.2	9.2	84.5	49.4	16.7	11.7	1.0	2.8
1998	262.3	182.5	71.3	56.5	20.1	20.0	25.6	30.4	35.6	11.2	91.3	46.3	17.4	12.2	0.9	2.8
1999	273.2	189.4	74.7	58.9	19.8	21.3	26.9	34.1	36.9	12.6	98.2	55.3	15.8	13.3	0.9	2.8
2000	292.2	218.5	82.3	64.8	20.8	24.3	30.1	41.6	39.6	16.1	104.7	55.3	14.0	13.6	0.8	2.9
2001	279.3	210.4	73.1	60.1	18.0	22.4	28.3	38.8	38.7	16.4	108.1	54.6	12.2	15.2	0.8	2.9
2002	290.4	241.3	70.6	59.5	17.4	21.0	28.3	38.6	43.2	20.4	118.1	79.4	12.0	19.4	0.8	2.9

Sources

1970–1996, U.S. International Trade Administration, Office of Trade and Economic Analysis (OTEA), *U.S. Foreign Trade Highlights, 1997* (August 1998). 1997–2002, updates from the OTEA Internet site.

Documentation

These series are on a balance of payments basis.

Series Ee412–413, military-defense transfers and expenditures. Defined as transfers under U.S. military sales contracts for exports and direct defense expenditures for imports.

TABLE Ee416–417   Exports and imports of goods: 1869–1928

Contributed by Douglas A. Irwin

	Exports	Imports		Exports	Imports		Exports	Imports
	Ee416	Ee417		Ee416	Ee417		Ee416	Ee417
Year	Million dollars	Million dollars	Year	Million dollars	Million dollars	Year	Million dollars	Million dollars
1869	343	437	1890	910	823	1910	1,919	1,646
1870	451	462	1891	993	881	1911	2,137	1,647
1871	541	541	1892	1,113	897	1912	2,327	1,749
1872	524	640	1893	997	911	1913	2,615	1,923
1873	607	664	1894	1,020	741	1914	2,532	1,991
1874	653	596	1895	921	789	1915	2,966	1,875
1875	606	554	1896	1,056	842	1916	5,709	3,110
1876	597	477	1897	1,153	880	1917	6,690	3,558
1877	659	492	1898	1,302	767	1918	6,443	3,165
1878	729	467	1899	1,321	817	1919	8,528	4,070
1879	735	466	1900	1,499	930	1920	8,664	5,784
1880	853	761	1901	1,605	926	1921	4,560	3,264
1881	922	753	1902	1,480	984	1922	3,931	3,459
1882	800	767	1903	1,511	1,095	1923	4,269	4,189
1883	856	752	1904	1,592	1,118	1924	4,763	4,004
1884	808	705	1905	1,660	1,199	1925	5,272	4,419
1885	784	621	1906	1,848	1,367	1926	5,017	4,714
1886	752	674	1907	1,989	1,592	1927	5,142	4,447
1887	752	752	1908	1,991	1,387	1928	5,776	4,328
1888	742	783	1909	1,810	1,400			
1889	839	774						

Sources

1869–1880, U.S. Bureau of Statistics, *Monthly Summary of Imports and Exports of the United States for the Fiscal Year* (1896), pp. 622–3. 1881–1903, U.S. Bureau

of the Census, *Statistical Abstract of the United States* (1924), pp. 420, 421, 424; 1904–1928, *Statistical Abstract of the United States* (1948), pp. 902–3.

TABLE Ee418–423   Exports and imports of goods and services: 1929–2001

Contributed by Douglas A. Irwin

	Exports			Imports		
	Total	Goods	Services	Total	Goods	Services
	Ee418	Ee419	Ee420	Ee421	Ee422	Ee423
Year	Billion dollars	Billion dollars	Billion dollars	Billion dollars	Billion dollars	Billion dollars
1929	5.9	5.3	0.6	5.6	4.5	1.1
1930	4.4	3.9	0.5	4.1	3.1	1.0
1931	2.9	2.5	0.4	2.9	2.1	0.8
1932	2.0	1.7	0.3	1.9	1.3	0.6
1933	2.0	1.7	0.3	1.9	1.5	0.4
1934	2.6	2.2	0.3	2.2	1.8	0.5
1935	2.8	2.4	0.4	3.0	2.5	0.5
1936	3.0	2.6	0.4	3.2	2.5	0.6
1937	4.0	3.5	0.6	4.0	3.2	0.8
1938	3.8	3.2	0.5	2.8	2.2	0.7
1939	3.9	3.3	0.6	3.1	2.4	0.7
1940	4.8	4.1	0.7	3.4	2.7	0.7
1941	5.4	4.5	0.9	4.4	3.4	1.0
1942	4.3	3.4	0.9	4.6	2.7	1.9
1943	3.9	2.9	1.0	6.3	3.4	2.8
1944	4.8	3.6	1.2	6.9	3.8	3.1
1945	6.7	5.4	1.3	7.5	3.9	3.7
1946	14.1	11.8	2.3	7.0	5.1	1.9
1947	18.7	16.1	2.6	7.9	6.0	2.0
1948	15.5	13.3	2.2	10.1	7.6	2.5
1949	14.4	12.2	2.2	9.2	6.9	2.4

TABLE Ee418–423   Exports and imports of goods and services: 1929–2001   Continued

	Exports			Imports		
	Total	Goods	Services	Total	Goods	Services
	Ee418	Ee419	Ee420	Ee421	Ee422	Ee423
Year	Billion dollars	Billion dollars	Billion dollars	Billion dollars	Billion dollars	Billion dollars
1950	12.3	10.2	2.1	11.6	9.1	2.5
1951	17.0	14.2	2.8	14.6	11.2	3.4
1952	16.3	13.4	2.9	15.3	10.8	4.5
1953	15.2	12.4	2.8	16.0	11.0	5.0
1954	15.7	12.9	2.8	15.4	10.4	5.1
1955	17.6	14.4	3.2	17.2	11.5	5.7
1956	21.2	17.6	3.6	18.9	12.8	6.1
1957	23.9	19.6	4.3	19.9	13.3	6.7
1958	20.4	16.4	4.0	20.0	13.0	7.1
1959	20.6	16.5	4.2	22.3	15.3	7.0
1960	25.3	20.5	4.8	22.8	15.2	7.6
1961	26.0	20.9	5.1	22.7	15.1	7.6
1962	27.4	21.7	5.7	25.0	16.9	8.1
1963	29.4	23.3	6.1	26.1	17.7	8.4
1964	33.6	26.7	6.9	28.1	19.4	8.7
1965	35.4	27.8	7.6	31.5	22.2	9.3
1966	38.9	30.7	8.2	37.1	26.3	10.7
1967	41.4	32.2	9.2	39.9	27.8	12.2
1968	45.3	35.3	10.0	46.6	33.9	12.6
1969	49.3	38.3	11.0	50.5	36.8	13.7
1970	57.0	44.5	12.4	55.8	40.9	14.9
1971	59.3	45.6	13.8	62.3	46.6	15.8
1972	66.2	51.8	14.4	74.2	56.9	17.3
1973	91.8	73.9	17.8	91.2	71.8	19.3
1974	124.3	101.0	23.3	127.5	104.5	22.9
1975	136.3	109.6	26.7	122.7	99.0	23.7
1976	148.9	117.8	31.1	151.1	124.6	26.5
1977	158.8	123.7	35.1	182.4	152.6	29.8
1978	186.1	145.4	40.7	212.3	177.4	34.8
1979	228.7	184.0	44.7	252.7	212.8	39.9
1980	278.9	225.8	53.2	293.8	248.6	45.3
1981	302.8	239.1	63.7	317.8	267.8	49.9
1982	282.6	215.0	67.6	303.2	250.5	52.6
1983	277.0	207.3	69.7	328.6	272.7	56.0
1984	303.1	225.6	77.5	405.1	336.3	68.8
1985	303.0	222.2	80.8	417.2	343.3	73.9
1986	320.3	226.0	94.7	452.2	370.0	82.2
1987	365.6	257.5	108.1	507.9	414.8	93.1
1988	446.9	325.8	121.1	553.2	452.1	101.1
1989	509.0	371.7	137.3	589.7	484.5	105.2
1990	557.2	398.5	158.6	628.6	508.0	120.6
1991	601.6	426.4	175.2	622.3	500.7	121.6
1992	636.8	448.7	188.1	664.6	544.9	119.8
1993	658.0	459.7	198.3	718.5	592.8	125.7
1994	725.1	509.6	215.5	812.1	676.8	135.4
1995	818.6	583.8	234.7	902.8	757.6	145.2
1996	874.2	618.4	255.8	963.1	808.3	154.8
1997	966.4	688.9	277.5	1,055.8	885.1	170.7
1998	964.9	681.3	283.6	1,116.8	930.0	186.7
1999	989.3	697.3	292.0	1,239.2	1,045.3	193.9
2000	1,101.1	785.0	316.1	1,466.6	1,243.1	223.5
2001	1,034.1	733.5	300.6	1,383.0	1,167.2	215.8

Sources

1929–1997, U.S. Bureau of Economic Analysis (BEA), *Survey of Current Business* (August 1998, with revisions from March 2003). Updates available from the BEA Internet site.

TABLE Ee424–430   Merchandise imports and duties: 1790–2000[1]

Contributed by Douglas A. Irwin

Year	Imports Total	For consumption Total	Free	Dutiable	Duties calculated Total	As a percentage of Total imports	Dutiable imports
	Ee424	Ee425	Ee426	Ee427	Ee428	Ee429	Ee430
	Million dollars	Million dollars	Million dollars	Million dollars	Million dollars	Percent	Percent
1790	24.0	24	—	—	3	12.50	—
1791	31.0	30	—	—	3	10.00	—
1792	33.0	32	—	—	5	15.63	—
1793	33.0	31	—	—	7	22.58	—
1794	36.0	30	—	—	9	30.00	—
1795	71.0	63	—	—	11	17.46	—
1796	83.0	57	—	—	13	22.81	—
1797	77.0	50	—	—	12	24.00	—
1798	71.0	38	—	—	12	31.58	—
1799	81.0	36	—	—	16	44.44	—
1800	93.0	54	—	—	16	29.63	—
1801	113.0	67	—	—	20	29.85	—
1802	78.0	43	—	—	15	34.88	—
1803	66.0	52	—	—	14	26.92	—
1804	87.0	51	—	—	21	41.18	—
1805	126.0	72	—	—	24	33.33	—
1806	137.0	76	—	—	26	34.21	—
1807	145.0	85	—	—	27	31.76	—
1808	58.0	45	—	—	11	24.44	—
1809	61.0	40	—	—	12	30.00	—
1810	89.0	65	—	—	17	26.15	—
1811	58.0	42	—	—	10	23.81	—
1812	79.0	70	—	—	15	21.43	—
1813	22.0	19	—	—	7	36.84	—
1814	13.0	13	—	—	4	30.77	—
1815	85.0	79	—	—	38	48.10	—
1816	152.0	134	—	—	33	24.63	—
1817	102.0	82	—	—	22	26.83	—
1818	127.0	108	—	—	26	24.07	—
1819	94.0	74	—	—	21	28.38	—
1820	75.0	57	—	—	17	29.82	—
1821	55.0	44	2	42	19	43.21	45.00
1822	80.0	68	4	65	24	35.23	37.16
1823	72.0	51	3	49	22	43.69	46.04
1824	72.0	54	3	51	26	47.39	50.26
1825	90.0	66	4	63	32	47.72	50.54
1826	78.0	58	5	53	26	45.28	49.26
1827	71.0	55	3	52	28	50.93	53.76
1828	81.0	67	4	63	30	44.74	47.59
1829	67.0	55	3	51	28	50.73	54.17
1830	63.0	50	4	46	28	57.32	61.69
1831	96.0	83	6	77	37	44.23	47.38
1832	95.0	75	7	68	29	38.97	42.96
1833	101.0	83	20	63	24	28.99	38.25
1834	109.0	87	40	47	19	21.83	40.19
1835	137.0	122	58	64	26	21.25	40.38
1836	177.0	159	70	89	31	19.51	34.94
1837	130.0	113	51	62	18	16.05	29.19
1838	96.0	87	38	48	20	23.11	41.33
1839	156.0	146	65	81	26	17.57	31.77
1840	98.0	86	42	44	15	17.60	34.39
1841	123.0	115	57	58	20	17.37	34.56
1842	96.0	88	23	65	17	18.96	25.81
1843 [2]	42.0	37	12	26	8	20.13	29.19
1844	103.0	96	17	80	29	30.50	36.88
1845	113.0	106	16	90	31	29.34	34.45
1846	118.0	110	19	91	30	27.70	33.35
1847	122.0	116	16	100	28	24.20	28.02
1848	149.0	141	15	126	33	23.49	26.28
1849	141.0	133	14	119	31	23.41	26.11

Notes appear at end of table

TABLE Ee424–430 Merchandise imports and duties: 1790–2000 *Continued*

	Imports				Duties calculated		
	Total	For consumption			Total	As a percentage of	
		Total	Free	Dutiable		Total imports	Dutiable imports
	Ee424	Ee425	Ee426	Ee427	Ee428	Ee429	Ee430
Year	Million dollars	Million dollars	Million dollars	Million dollars	Million dollars	Percent	Percent
1850	174.0	164	16	148	40	24.50	27.14
1851	211.0	200	18	183	49	24.26	26.63
1852	207.0	195	22	174	48	24.35	27.38
1853	264.0	250	25	225	58	23.37	25.94
1854	298.0	276	23	254	65	23.52	25.61
1855	258.0	232	30	202	54	23.36	26.83
1856	310.0	296	50	246	64	21.68	26.05
1857	348.0	334	50	284	64	19.09	22.45
1858	263.0	243	55	187	42	17.33	22.44
1859	331.0	317	67	250	49	15.43	19.56
1860	354.0	336	68	268	53	15.67	19.67
1861	289.0	275	67	207	39	14.21	18.84
1862	189.0	178	50	128	47	26.08	36.20
1863	243.0	225	30	195	64	28.28	32.62
1864	316.0	301	38	263	96	32.04	36.69
1865	239.0	210	40	170	81	38.46	47.56
1866	435.0	423	57	366	177	41.81	48.33
1867	396.0	378	17	361	169	44.56	46.66
1868	357.0	345	15	330	161	46.56	48.70
1869	418.0	394	22	373	177	44.76	47.37
1870	436.0	426	20	406	192	44.89	47.13
1871	520.0	500	40	460	202	40.51	44.04
1872	627.0	560	47	513	213	37.99	41.46
1873	642.0	663	178	485	185	27.90	38.12
1874	567.0	568	151	416	161	28.29	38.58
1875	533.0	526	146	380	155	29.36	40.66
1876	461.0	465	140	324	145	31.25	44.76
1877	451.0	440	140	299	128	29.20	42.91
1878	437.0	439	141	297	127	29.00	42.77
1879	446.0	440	143	297	133	30.33	44.90
1880	668.0	628	208	420	183	29.12	43.54
1881	643.0	651	202	448	194	29.79	43.23
1882	725.0	717	211	506	216	30.16	42.71
1883	723.0	701	207	494	211	30.04	42.61
1884	668.0	668	211	457	190	28.50	41.67
1885	578.0	579	192	387	178	30.75	46.05
1886	635.0	624	210	414	189	30.35	45.78
1887	692.0	680	229	450	214	31.52	47.57
1888	724.0	707	239	468	216	30.55	46.15
1889	745.0	735	250	485	221	30.02	45.49
1890	789.0	766	258	508	227	29.59	44.63
1891	845.0	845	379	466	217	25.65	46.50
1892	827.0	804	449	356	174	21.65	48.98
1893	866.0	833	432	400	199	23.91	49.75
1894	655.0	630	372	258	130	20.56	50.29
1895	732.0	731	377	354	149	20.44	42.19
1896	780.0	760	369	391	157	20.67	40.18
1897	765.0	789	382	407	173	21.89	42.41
1898	616.0	587	292	296	145	24.77	49.20
1899	697.0	685	300	386	202	29.48	52.38
1900	850.0	831	367	464	229	27.62	49.46
1901	823.0	808	339	469	234	28.91	49.83
1902	903.0	900	397	503	251	27.95	49.97
1903	1,026.0	1,008	437	571	281	27.85	49.20
1904	991.0	982	454	528	258	26.29	48.92
1905	1,118.0	1,087	517	570	258	23.77	45.33
1906	1,227.0	1,213	549	665	294	24.22	44.22
1907	1,434.0	1,415	642	773	329	23.28	42.60
1908	1,194.0	1,183	526	657	283	23.88	42.98
1909 [3]	1,312.0	1,282	509	682	295	22.99	43.19

Notes appear at end of table

(continued)

TABLE Ee424–430 Merchandise imports and duties: 1790–2000 *Continued*

	Imports				Duties calculated		
		For consumption				As a percentage of	
	Total	Total	Free	Dutiable	Total	Total imports	Dutiable imports
	Ee424	Ee425	Ee426	Ee427	Ee428	Ee429	Ee430
Year	Million dollars	Million dollars	Million dollars	Million dollars	Million dollars	Percent	Percent
1910	1,557.0	1,547	761	786	327	21.11	41.56
1911	1,527.0	1,528	777	751	310	20.29	41.27
1912	1,653.0	1,641	882	759	305	18.58	40.16
1913	1,813.0	1,767	987	780	313	17.69	40.08
1914	1,894.0	1,906	1,152	754	284	14.88	37.63
1915	1,674.0	1,648	1,033	616	206	12.49	33.46
1916	2,392.0	2,359	1,615	744	214	9.08	28.80
1917	2,952.0	2,919	2,141	778	205	7.01	26.28
1918	3,031.0	2,952	2,229	723	171	5.79	23.65
1919	3,904.0	3,828	2,711	1,116	237	6.20	21.27
1920	5,278.0	5,102	3,116	1,986	326	6.38	16.40
1921	2,509.0	2,557	1,564	993	292	11.44	29.46
1922	3,113.0	3,074	1,888	1,186	451	14.68	38.07
1923	3,792.0	3,732	2,165	1,567	567	15.18	36.17
1924	3,610.0	3,575	2,118	1,457	532	14.89	36.53
1925	4,227.0	4,176	2,709	1,467	552	13.21	37.61
1926	4,431.0	4,408	2,908	1,500	590	13.39	39.34
1927	4,185.0	4,163	2,680	1,483	575	13.81	38.76
1928	4,091.0	4,078	2,679	1,399	542	13.30	38.76
1929	4,399.0	4,339	2,880	1,458	585	13.48	40.10
1930	3,061.0	3,114	2,081	1,033	462	14.83	44.71
1931	2,091.0	2,088	1,392	697	371	17.75	53.21
1932	1,323.0	1,325	886	440	260	19.59	59.06
1933	1,450.0	1,433	904	529	284	19.80	53.58
1934	1,655.0	1,636	991	645	301	18.41	46.70
1935	2,047.0	2,039	1,206	833	357	17.52	42.88
1936	2,423.0	2,424	1,385	1,039	408	16.84	39.28
1937	3,084.0	3,010	1,765	1,245	471	15.63	37.80
1938	1,960.0	1,950	1,183	767	301	15.46	39.30
1939	2,318.0	2,276	1,397	879	328	14.41	37.33
1940	2,625.0	2,541	1,649	892	318	12.51	35.63
1941	3,345.0	3,222	2,031	1,191	438	13.59	36.75
1942	2,756.0	2,780	1,779	1,002	320	11.51	31.96
1943	3,381.0	3,390	2,193	1,197	393	11.57	32.79
1944	3,929.0	3,887	2,718	1,170	367	9.45	31.41
1945	4,159.0	4,098	2,749	1,349	381	9.29	28.24
1946	4,942.0	4,825	2,935	1,890	478	9.90	25.28
1947	5,756.0	5,666	3,455	2,212	428	7.55	19.34
1948	7,124.0	7,092	4,175	2,918	405	5.71	13.87
1949	6,622.0	6,592	3,883	2,708	365	5.53	13.46
1950	8,852.0	8,743	4,767	3,976	522	5.97	13.14
1951	10,967.0	10,817	5,993	4,824	591	5.47	12.26
1952	10,717.0	10,747	6,257	4,491	570	5.30	12.69
1953	10,873.0	10,779	5,920	4,859	584	5.42	12.02
1954	10,215.0	10,240	5,668	4,572	529	5.17	11.58
1955	11,384.0	11,337	6,037	5,300	633	5.59	11.95
1956	12,615.0	12,516	6,235	6,281	710	5.67	11.30
1957	12,982.0	12,951	6,036	6,914	746	5.76	10.79
1958	12,792.0	12,739	5,342	7,398	821	6.44	11.09
1959	15,207.0	14,994	5,823	9,170	1,052	7.02	11.53
1960	14,654.0	14,650	5,780	8,870	1,084	7.40	12.22
1961	14,714.0	14,658	5,923	8,735	1,057	7.21	12.10
1962	16,380.0	16,242	6,216	10,026	1,220	7.50	12.17
1963	17,138.0	17,001	6,258	10,743	1,240	7.29	11.54
1964	18,684.0	18,601	7,029	11,572	1,340	7.20	11.58
1965	21,364.0	21,282	7,434	13,848	1,643	7.72	11.86
1966	25,542.0	25,360	9,344	16,016	1,920	7.57	11.99
1967	26,812.0	26,733	10,215	16,518	2,016	7.54	12.20
1968	33,226.0	33,066	12,342	20,724	2,341	7.08	11.30
1969	36,043.0	35,863	13,057	22,805	2,551	7.11	11.19

TABLE Ee424–430   Merchandise imports and duties: 1790–2000   *Continued*

	Imports				Duties calculated		
	Total	For consumption			Total	As a percentage of	
		Total	Free	Dutiable		Total imports	Dutiable imports
	Ee424	Ee425	Ee426	Ee427	Ee428	Ee429	Ee430
Year	Million dollars	Million dollars	Million dollars	Million dollars	Million dollars	Percent	Percent
1970	39,952.0	39,756	13,870	25,886	2,584	6.50	9.98
1971	45,563.0	45,516	15,286	30,230	2,767	6.08	9.15
1972	55,582.0	55,290	18,915	36,375	3,124	5.65	8.59
1973	69,475.0	69,024	28,258	40,766	3,620	5.24	8.88
1974	100,997.0	100,140	52,052	48,088	3,771	3.77	7.84
1975	96,902.0	96,516	31,030	65,486	3,780	3.92	5.77
1976	122,126.0	121,121	37,190	83,931	4,675	3.86	5.57
1977	148,719.0	147,075	43,633	103,442	5,485	3.73	5.30
1978	173,250.0	172,952	51,827	121,125	7,162	4.14	5.91
1979	207,058.0	205,922	103,278	102,645	7,202	3.50	7.02
1980	245,262.0	239,943	107,092	132,851	7,535	3.09	5.67
1981	260,982.0	259,012	76,338	182,674	8,893	3.43	4.87
1982	243,953.0	242,340	64,745	177,594	8,688	3.59	5.22
1983	258,048.0	256,679	83,397	173,283	9,430	3.67	5.44
1984	325,726.0	322,989	102,977	220,012	12,042	3.73	5.47
1985	345,275.0	343,553	106,035	237,518	13,067	3.80	5.50
1986	365,438.0	368,657	121,742	246,915	13,312	3.61	5.39
1987	406,241.0	402,066	132,152	269,914	13,923	3.46	5.16
1988	440,952.0	437,140	151,693	285,447	15,054	3.44	5.27
1989	473,397.0	468,012	156,365	311,647	16,096	3.44	5.16
1990	496,028.0	490,554	161,108	329,446	16,339	3.33	4.96
1991	488,832.0	483,028	167,641	315,386	16,197	3.35	5.14
1992	532,053.0	525,091	194,583	330,508	17,164	3.27	5.19
1993	580,469.0	574,863	236,007	338,856	18,334	3.19	5.41
1994	663,830.0	657,885	292,257	365,628	19,846	3.02	5.43
1995	743,505.0	739,660	373,948	365,713	18,597	2.51	5.09
1996	791,316.0	790,468	406,640	383,829	18,005	2.28	4.69
1997	870,213.0	862,426	458,169	404,257	18,428	2.14	4.56
1998	913,885.0	907,647	521,132	386,514	18,270	2.01	4.73
1999	1,024,766.0	1,017,435	652,936	364,498	18,464	1.81	5.07
2000	1,216,888.0	1,205,339	797,605	407,734	19,754	1.64	4.84

[1] Year-ending date varies over time. See text.

[2] Period beginning October 1, 1842, and ending June 30, 1843.

[3] Agrees with source; however, figures for components do not add to imports total shown.

Sources

Series Ee424. 1790, U.S. Bureau of Foreign and Domestic Commerce, *Foreign Commerce and Navigation of the United States* (1912), p. 43. 1791–1821, U.S. Department of the Treasury, Bureau of Statistics, *Monthly Summary of Imports and Exports of the United States for the Fiscal Year* (1896), pp. 622–3. Early years revised by Douglass North, "Balance of Payments, 1790–1860," in *Trends in the American Economy in the Nineteenth Century: A Report of the National Bureau of Economic Research,* Studies in Income and Wealth, volume 24 (Princeton University Press, 1960).

Series Ee425–427. 1790–1820, Douglass C. North, *The Economic Growth of the United States, 1790–1860* (Prentice Hall, 1961), p. 228. 1821–1880, U.S. Bureau of Foreign and Domestic Commerce, *Foreign Commerce and Navigation of the United States* (1912), p. 50. 1881–1915, *Foreign Commerce and Navigation of the United States* (1924), p. lxvii. 1916–1941, U.S. Bureau of the Census, *Statistical Abstract of the United States* (1948), p. 939. 1942–1946, *Statistical Abstract of the United States* (1951), p. 854. 1947–1965, U.S. Bureau of Foreign and Domestic Commerce, *Foreign Commerce and Navigation of the United States* (1964, 1965).1966–2000, U.S. Bureau of the Census, *Highlights of Exports and Imports,* FT 990 (December issues). 1989–1996, data from the Internet site of the U.S. International Trade Commission (USITC).

Series Ee428–430. 1790–1820, *Report from the Secretary of the Treasury on Duties Received, Outstanding Bonds, etc.,* House Document number 85, 20th

Congress, 2nd Session, p. 2. 1821–1970, see source for series Ee424. 1971–2000, USITC, Statistical and Editorial Services Division, *Value of U.S. Imports for Consumption, Duties Collected, and Ratio of Duties to Values, 1891–2000* (March 2001), also available at the USITC Internet site.

Documentation

From May 1, 1900, to July 25, 1901, merchandise brought from Puerto Rico was dutiable at 15 percent of regular rates. The duties collected thereon were as follows: May 1, 1900–June 30, 1900, $134,593; July 1, 1900–July 25, 1901, $448,193.

The data are for the year ending September 30 (1790–1842) and June 30 (1843–1915), and for calendar years thereafter. For the six-month transition period in 1915 (July 1 to December 31), the values for series Ee425–430 are as follows: 935, 631, 303, 96, 10.26 percent, and 31.61 percent, respectively (in millions of dollars unless percent is indicated).

Series Ee424 and Ee428. For the period 1790–1821, series Ee424 is not imports for consumption, but total value of imports, and series Ee428 is not duties calculated but actual duties collected on merchandise imports. For data on imports for consumption, see North (1961), p. 228, and Douglas A. Irwin, "New Estimates of the Average Tariff of the United States, 1790–1820," *Journal of Economic History* 63 (2003): 506–13. Duties collected do not include remissions resulting from drawbacks; see Irwin for details on this important consideration. The figures for this period are not directly comparable to those after 1821.

Series Ee425. Beginning in 1961, imports for consumption include uranium, thorium, and related products. Beginning in 1968, silver ore and bullion are included.

(continued)

TABLE Ee424–430   Merchandise imports and duties: 1790–2000   *Continued*

Series Ee425–427. For 1821–1866, the figures for import values represent net general imports (total imports less reexports), the amount of duty collected (calculated) being the annual amounts collected on merchandise only. For 1867–2000, the figures of import values represent imports entered for consumption. Imports for consumption consist of entries for immediate consumption and withdrawals from warehouses for consumption. The term "entry for consumption" is the technical name of the import entry made at the customhouse and implies that the goods have been delivered into the custody of the importer and that the duties have been paid on the dutiable portion. Some of them may be exported afterward.

Series Ee428. Labeled here as "duties calculated," the series is identified in annual volumes of *Foreign Commerce and Navigation* ..., through the 1925 issue, as "duties collected"; subsequent issues label it as "duties calculated." In spite of its label, it was a computed figure at least back to 1876. The evidence indicates that data from the earlier years, at least in part, were on a duties-collected basis. This series should not be confused with the modern series called "duties collected" (not shown here), which represents the total amount of duties actually collected (on individual shipments) as reported to the Treasury Department by Customs officials, subject in certain cases to subsequent refund as well as drawback. In contrast, duties calculated is a statistical measure derived by applying the appropriate rates to totals for all imports of the given commodity received at all ports of entry; it does not reflect drawbacks or refunds and is subject to some time lag in reporting.

Series Ee429–430. These series are similar to, but not identical with, the series labeled "ratios of duties to total" shown in annual issues of *Foreign Commerce and Navigation* ..., 1925–1946, and as "average ad valorem rates" in earlier issues. These series have been computed as shown here because of conflicts in source volumes with respect to early years.

TABLE Ee431–445 Exports and imports of merchandise – price indexes and terms of trade: 1790–2002

Contributed by Douglas A. Irwin

Year	North (1790 base)			North (1830 base)			Simon			Lipsey			Survey of Current Business		
	Price index		Terms of trade	Price index		Terms of trade	Price index		Terms of trade	Price index		Terms of trade	Price index		Terms of trade
	Exports	Imports		Exports	Imports		Exports	Imports		Exports	Imports		Exports	Imports	
	Ee431	Ee432	Ee433	Ee434	Ee435	Ee436	Ee437	Ee438	Ee439	Ee440	Ee441	Ee442	Ee443	Ee444	Ee445
	Index 1790 = 100	Index 1790 = 100	Index 1790 = 100	Index 1830 = 100	Index 1830 = 100	Index 1830 = 100	Index 1860 = 100	Index 1860 = 100	Index 1860 = 100	Index 1913 = 100	Index 1913 = 100	Index 1913 = 100	Index 1996 = 100	Index 1996 = 100	Index 1996 = 100
1790	100.0	100.0	100.0	—	—	—	—	—	—	—	—	—	—	—	—
1791	85.8	109.8	78.1	—	—	—	—	—	—	—	—	—	—	—	—
1792	81.7	118.8	68.8	—	—	—	—	—	—	—	—	—	—	—	—
1793	97.8	108.4	90.2	—	—	—	—	—	—	—	—	—	—	—	—
1794	103.6	129.2	80.2	—	—	—	—	—	—	—	—	—	—	—	—
1795	153.6	124.3	123.6	—	—	—	—	—	—	—	—	—	—	—	—
1796	172.6	132.8	130.0	—	—	—	—	—	—	—	—	—	—	—	—
1797	174.8	139.9	124.9	—	—	—	—	—	—	—	—	—	—	—	—
1798	207.4	127.6	162.5	—	—	—	—	—	—	—	—	—	—	—	—
1799	220.3	135.5	162.6	—	—	—	—	—	—	—	—	—	—	—	—
1800	145.9	124.6	117.1	—	—	—	—	—	—	—	—	—	—	—	—
1801	154.1	119.9	128.5	—	—	—	—	—	—	—	—	—	—	—	—
1802	131.6	111.8	117.7	—	—	—	—	—	—	—	—	—	—	—	—
1803	132.8	118.0	112.5	—	—	—	—	—	—	—	—	—	—	—	—
1804	147.7	134.7	109.7	—	—	—	—	—	—	—	—	—	—	—	—
1805	156.4	139.5	112.1	—	—	—	—	—	—	—	—	—	—	—	—
1806	142.0	129.5	109.4	—	—	—	—	—	—	—	—	—	—	—	—
1807	136.2	124.7	109.2	—	—	—	—	—	—	—	—	—	—	—	—
1808	115.3	124.3	92.8	—	—	—	—	—	—	—	—	—	—	—	—
1809	116.2	129.1	90.0	—	—	—	—	—	—	—	—	—	—	—	—
1810	128.6	129.8	99.1	—	—	—	—	—	—	—	—	—	—	—	—
1811	128.6	121.1	106.2	—	—	—	—	—	—	—	—	—	—	—	—
1812	127.1	131.7	96.5	—	—	—	—	—	—	—	—	—	—	—	—
1813	126.5	179.7	70.4	—	—	—	—	—	—	—	—	—	—	—	—
1814	127.3	232.3	54.8	—	—	—	—	—	—	—	—	—	—	—	—
1815	182.9	191.3	95.6	182.9	222.7	82.1	—	—	—	—	—	—	—	—	—
1816	—	—	—	248.2	194.9	127.3	—	—	—	—	—	—	—	—	—
1817	—	—	—	240.3	176.8	135.9	—	—	—	—	—	—	—	—	—
1818	—	—	—	245.5	189.7	129.4	—	—	—	—	—	—	—	—	—
1819	—	—	—	194.7	171.9	113.3	—	—	—	—	—	—	—	—	—
1820	—	—	—	144.2	151.2	95.4	—	—	—	—	—	—	—	—	—
1821	—	—	—	127.9	134.0	95.4	—	—	—	—	—	—	—	—	—
1822	—	—	—	136.3	133.6	102.0	—	—	—	—	—	—	—	—	—
1823	—	—	—	114.4	127.7	89.6	—	—	—	—	—	—	—	—	—
1824	—	—	—	126.2	119.8	105.3	—	—	—	—	—	—	—	—	—
1825	—	—	—	152.5	127.1	120.0	—	—	—	—	—	—	—	—	—
1826	—	—	—	114.8	121.6	94.4	—	—	—	—	—	—	—	—	—
1827	—	—	—	102.5	111.1	92.3	—	—	—	—	—	—	—	—	—
1828	—	—	—	102.1	112.3	90.9	—	—	—	—	—	—	—	—	—
1829	—	—	—	107.1	105.9	101.1	—	—	—	—	—	—	—	—	—

(continued)

TABLE Ee431–445   Exports and imports of merchandise – price indexes and terms of trade: 1790–2002   *Continued*

	North (1790 base)			North (1830 base)			Simon			Lipsey			Survey of Current Business		
	Price index			Price index			Price index			Price index			Price index		
	Exports	Imports	Terms of trade	Exports	Imports	Terms of trade	Exports	Imports	Terms of trade	Exports	Imports	Terms of trade	Exports	Imports	Terms of trade
	Ee431	Ee432	Ee433	Ee434	Ee435	Ee436	Ee437	Ee438	Ee439	Ee440	Ee441	Ee442	Ee443	Ee444	Ee445
	Index	Index	Index	Index	Index	Index	Index	Index	Index	Index	Index	Index	Index	Index	Index
Year	1790 = 100	1790 = 100	1790 = 100	1830 = 100	1830 = 100	1830 = 100	1860 = 100	1860 = 100	1860 = 100	1913 = 100	1913 = 100	1913 = 100	1996 = 100	1996 = 100	1996 = 100
1830	—	—	—	100.0	100.0	100.0	—	—	—	—	—	—	—	—	—
1831	—	—	—	98.8	95.8	103.1	—	—	—	—	—	—	—	—	—
1832	—	—	—	104.6	93.6	111.8	—	—	—	—	—	—	—	—	—
1833	—	—	—	115.1	100.0	115.1	—	—	—	—	—	—	—	—	—
1834	—	—	—	127.0	103.3	122.9	—	—	—	—	—	—	—	—	—
1835	—	—	—	149.8	101.3	147.9	—	—	—	—	—	—	—	—	—
1836	—	—	—	155.4	109.6	141.8	—	—	—	—	—	—	—	—	—
1837	—	—	—	142.6	104.1	137.0	—	—	—	—	—	—	—	—	—
1838	—	—	—	115.9	90.8	127.6	—	—	—	—	—	—	—	—	—
1839	—	—	—	155.9	97.8	159.4	—	—	—	—	—	—	—	—	—
1840	—	—	—	99.7	94.0	106.1	—	—	—	—	—	—	—	—	—
1841	—	—	—	110.2	91.3	120.7	—	—	—	—	—	—	—	—	—
1842	—	—	—	93.8	82.8	113.3	—	—	—	—	—	—	—	—	—
1843	—	—	—	75.8	79.4	95.5	—	—	—	—	—	—	—	—	—
1844	—	—	—	89.2	78.2	114.1	—	—	—	—	—	—	—	—	—
1845	—	—	—	78.3	80.9	96.8	—	—	—	—	—	—	—	—	—
1846	—	—	—	92.8	81.6	113.7	—	—	—	—	—	—	—	—	—
1847	—	—	—	112.8	82.3	137.1	—	—	—	—	—	—	—	—	—
1848	—	—	—	94.3	74.1	127.3	—	—	—	—	—	—	—	—	—
1849	—	—	—	84.2	72.0	116.9	—	—	—	—	—	—	—	—	—
1850	—	—	—	120.7	74.2	162.7	—	—	—	—	—	—	—	—	—
1851	—	—	—	123.7	78.8	157.0	—	—	—	—	—	—	—	—	—
1852	—	—	—	96.3	75.5	127.5	—	—	—	—	—	—	—	—	—
1853	—	—	—	93.5	83.3	112.2	—	—	—	—	—	—	—	—	—
1854	—	—	—	116.7	83.2	140.3	—	—	—	—	—	—	—	—	—
1855	—	—	—	119.0	84.7	140.5	—	—	—	—	—	—	—	—	—
1856	—	—	—	124.4	89.8	138.5	—	—	—	—	—	—	—	—	—
1857	—	—	—	141.9	95.8	148.1	—	—	—	—	—	—	—	—	—
1858	—	—	—	128.3	91.7	139.9	—	—	—	—	—	—	—	—	—
1859	—	—	—	126.5	90.2	140.2	—	—	—	—	—	—	—	—	—
1860	—	—	—	119.8	92.2	129.9	100	100	100	—	—	—	—	—	—
1861	—	—	—	—	—	—	99	96	103	—	—	—	—	—	—
1862	—	—	—	—	—	—	102	95	107	—	—	—	—	—	—
1863	—	—	—	—	—	—	86	96	90	—	—	—	—	—	—
1864	—	—	—	—	—	—	88	109	81	—	—	—	—	—	—
1865	—	—	—	—	—	—	91	114	80	—	—	—	—	—	—
1866	—	—	—	—	—	—	106	139	76	—	—	—	—	—	—
1867	—	—	—	—	—	—	123	119	103	—	—	—	—	—	—
1868	—	—	—	—	—	—	118	114	104	—	—	—	—	—	—
1869	—	—	—	—	—	—	121	116	104	—	—	—	—	—	—
1870	—	—	—	—	—	—	122	125	98	—	—	—	—	—	—
1871	—	—	—	—	—	—	123	129	95	—	—	—	—	—	—
1872	—	—	—	—	—	—	122	120	102	—	—	—	—	—	—
1873	—	—	—	—	—	—	118	119	99	—	—	—	—	—	—
1874	—	—	—	—	—	—	120	113	106	—	—	—	—	—	—

	North (1790 base)			North (1830 base)			Simon			Lipsey			Survey of Current Business		
	Price index		Terms of trade	Price index		Terms of trade	Price index		Terms of trade	Price index		Terms of trade	Price index		Terms of trade
	Exports	Imports		Exports	Imports		Exports	Imports		Exports	Imports		Exports	Imports	
	Ee431	Ee432	Ee433	Ee434	Ee435	Ee436	Ee437	Ee438	Ee439	Ee440	Ee441	Ee442	Ee443	Ee444	Ee445
Year	Index 1790 = 100	Index 1790 = 100	Index 1790 = 100	Index 1830 = 100	Index 1830 = 100	Index 1830 = 100	Index 1860 = 100	Index 1860 = 100	Index 1860 = 100	Index 1913 = 100	Index 1913 = 100	Index 1913 = 100	Index 1996 = 100	Index 1996 = 100	Index 1996 = 100
1875	—	—	—	—	—	—	126	110	115	—	—	—	—	—	—
1876	—	—	—	—	—	—	114	99	115	—	—	—	—	—	—
1877	—	—	—	—	—	—	110	109	101	—	—	—	—	—	—
1878	—	—	—	—	—	—	107	110	97	—	—	—	—	—	—
1879	—	—	—	—	—	—	113	108	105	92.5	102.4	90.3	—	—	—
1880	—	—	—	—	—	—	—	—	—	101.5	113.1	89.7	—	—	—
1881	—	—	—	—	—	—	—	—	—	103.8	107.7	96.4	—	—	—
1882	—	—	—	—	—	—	—	—	—	107.0	108.3	98.8	—	—	—
1883	—	—	—	—	—	—	—	—	—	101.4	101.8	99.6	—	—	—
1884	—	—	—	—	—	—	—	—	—	97.6	95.4	102.3	—	—	—
1885	—	—	—	—	—	—	—	—	—	91.0	87.7	103.8	—	—	—
1886	—	—	—	—	—	—	—	—	—	85.7	87.5	97.9	—	—	—
1887	—	—	—	—	—	—	—	—	—	85.5	90.9	94.1	—	—	—
1888	—	—	—	—	—	—	—	—	—	89.7	88.8	101.0	—	—	—
1889	—	—	—	—	—	—	—	—	—	86.0	93.9	91.6	—	—	—
1890	—	—	—	—	—	—	—	—	—	85.0	93.2	91.2	—	—	—
1891	—	—	—	—	—	—	—	—	—	87.9	92.0	95.5	—	—	—
1892	—	—	—	—	—	—	—	—	—	81.9	88.4	92.6	—	—	—
1893	—	—	—	—	—	—	—	—	—	80.2	92.0	87.2	—	—	—
1894	—	—	—	—	—	—	—	—	—	70.5	83.5	84.4	—	—	—
1895	—	—	—	—	—	—	—	—	—	71.8	79.5	90.3	—	—	—
1896	—	—	—	—	—	—	—	—	—	71.0	80.7	88.0	—	—	—
1897	—	—	—	—	—	—	—	—	—	69.1	75.9	91.0	—	—	—
1898	—	—	—	—	—	—	—	—	—	68.4	75.7	90.4	—	—	—
1899	—	—	—	—	—	—	—	—	—	72.3	81.5	88.7	—	—	—
1900	—	—	—	—	—	—	—	—	—	81.0	86.7	93.4	—	—	—
1901	—	—	—	—	—	—	—	—	—	79.4	82.6	96.1	—	—	—
1902	—	—	—	—	—	—	—	—	—	81.4	80.8	100.7	—	—	—
1903	—	—	—	—	—	—	—	—	—	86.6	84.0	103.1	—	—	—
1904	—	—	—	—	—	—	—	—	—	86.9	85.8	101.3	—	—	—
1905	—	—	—	—	—	—	—	—	—	83.7	90.6	92.4	—	—	—
1906	—	—	—	—	—	—	—	—	—	89.9	94.7	94.9	—	—	—
1907	—	—	—	—	—	—	—	—	—	95.2	99.2	96.0	—	—	—
1908	—	—	—	—	—	—	—	—	—	90.1	88.0	102.4	—	—	—
1909	—	—	—	—	—	—	—	—	—	94.3	88.0	107.2	—	—	—
1910	—	—	—	—	—	—	—	—	—	102.1	94.6	107.9	—	—	—
1911	—	—	—	—	—	—	—	—	—	93.5	96.1	97.3	—	—	—
1912	—	—	—	—	—	—	—	—	—	95.5	101.0	94.6	—	—	—
1913	—	—	—	—	—	—	—	—	—	100.0	100.0	100.0	—	—	—
1914	—	—	—	—	—	—	—	—	—	97.7	93.7	104.3	—	—	—
1915	—	—	—	—	—	—	—	—	—	105.1	97.2	108.1	—	—	—
1916	—	—	—	—	—	—	—	—	—	135.5	120.2	112.7	—	—	—
1917	—	—	—	—	—	—	—	—	—	177.0	145.3	121.8	—	—	—
1918	—	—	—	—	—	—	—	—	—	206.1	161.3	127.8	—	—	—
1919	—	—	—	—	—	—	—	—	—	215.7	181.0	119.2	—	—	—

(continued)

TABLE Ee431–445 Exports and imports of merchandise – price indexes and terms of trade: 1790–2002 Continued

	North (1790 base)			North (1830 base)			Simon			Lipsey			Survey of Current Business		
	Price index		Terms of trade	Price index		Terms of trade	Price index		Terms of trade	Price index		Terms of trade	Price index		Terms of trade
	Exports	Imports		Exports	Imports		Exports	Imports		Exports	Imports		Exports	Imports	
	Ee431	Ee432	Ee433	Ee434	Ee435	Ee436	Ee437	Ee438	Ee439	Ee440	Ee441	Ee442	Ee443	Ee444	Ee445
Year	Index 1790 = 100	Index 1790 = 100	Index 1790 = 100	Index 1830 = 100	Index 1830 = 100	Index 1830 = 100	Index 1860 = 100	Index 1860 = 100	Index 1860 = 100	Index 1913 = 100	Index 1913 = 100	Index 1913 = 100	Index 1996 = 100	Index 1996 = 100	Index 1996 = 100
1920	—	—	—	—	—	—	—	—	—	232.5	219.1	106.1	—	—	—
1921	—	—	—	—	—	—	—	—	—	157.5	125.2	125.8	—	—	—
1922	—	—	—	—	—	—	—	—	—	143.8	119.6	120.2	—	—	—
1923	—	—	—	—	—	—	—	—	—	154.2	136.6	112.9	—	—	—
1924	—	—	—	—	—	—	—	—	—	151.1	133.5	113.2	—	—	—
1925	—	—	—	—	—	—	—	—	—	153.2	145.1	105.6	—	—	—
1926	—	—	—	—	—	—	—	—	—	140.8	142.0	99.2	—	—	—
1927	—	—	—	—	—	—	—	—	—	131.6	131.9	99.8	—	—	—
1928	—	—	—	—	—	—	—	—	—	134.7	128.1	105.2	—	—	—
1929	—	—	—	—	—	—	—	—	—	133.6	119.5	111.8	19.05	11.88	160.35
1930	—	—	—	—	—	—	—	—	—	—	—	—	17.04	9.80	173.88
1931	—	—	—	—	—	—	—	—	—	—	—	—	13.08	7.67	170.53
1932	—	—	—	—	—	—	—	—	—	—	—	—	11.28	6.01	187.69
1933	—	—	—	—	—	—	—	—	—	—	—	—	11.80	6.01	196.34
1934	—	—	—	—	—	—	—	—	—	—	—	—	13.80	6.87	200.87
1935	—	—	—	—	—	—	—	—	—	—	—	—	14.14	6.98	202.58
1936	—	—	—	—	—	—	—	—	—	—	—	—	14.48	7.49	193.32
1937	—	—	—	—	—	—	—	—	—	—	—	—	15.35	8.37	183.39
1938	—	—	—	—	—	—	—	—	—	—	—	—	14.20	7.50	189.33
1939	—	—	—	—	—	—	—	—	—	—	—	—	13.89	7.64	181.81
1940	—	—	—	—	—	—	—	—	—	—	—	—	14.89	8.15	182.70
1941	—	—	—	—	—	—	—	—	—	—	—	—	15.96	8.74	182.61
1942	—	—	—	—	—	—	—	—	—	—	—	—	19.43	10.13	191.81
1943	—	—	—	—	—	—	—	—	—	—	—	—	21.43	10.98	195.17
1944	—	—	—	—	—	—	—	—	—	—	—	—	24.54	11.73	209.21
1945	—	—	—	—	—	—	—	—	—	—	—	—	24.44	12.02	203.33
1946	—	—	—	—	—	—	—	—	—	—	—	—	23.19	13.54	171.27
1947	—	—	—	—	—	—	—	—	—	—	—	—	27.60	16.62	166.06
1948	—	—	—	—	—	—	—	—	—	—	—	—	29.38	18.36	160.02
1949	—	—	—	—	—	—	—	—	—	—	—	—	27.22	17.38	156.62
1950	—	—	—	—	—	—	—	—	—	—	—	—	26.31	18.80	139.95
1951	—	—	—	—	—	—	—	—	—	—	—	—	30.16	23.60	127.80
1952	—	—	—	—	—	—	—	—	—	—	—	—	30.03	22.43	133.88
1953	—	—	—	—	—	—	—	—	—	—	—	—	29.73	21.47	138.47
1954	—	—	—	—	—	—	—	—	—	—	—	—	29.30	21.93	133.61
1955	—	—	—	—	—	—	—	—	—	—	—	—	29.58	21.87	135.25
1956	—	—	—	—	—	—	—	—	—	—	—	—	30.70	22.30	137.67
1957	—	—	—	—	—	—	—	—	—	—	—	—	31.70	22.50	140.89
1958	—	—	—	—	—	—	—	—	—	—	—	—	31.36	21.33	147.02
1959	—	—	—	—	—	—	—	—	—	—	—	—	31.66	21.48	147.39
1960	—	—	—	—	—	—	—	—	—	—	—	—	31.87	21.71	146.80
1961	—	—	—	—	—	—	—	—	—	—	—	—	32.48	21.50	151.07
1962	—	—	—	—	—	—	—	—	—	—	—	—	32.23	20.99	153.55
1963	—	—	—	—	—	—	—	—	—	—	—	—	32.12	21.18	151.65
1964	—	—	—	—	—	—	—	—	—	—	—	—	32.34	21.76	148.62

	North (1790 base)			North (1830 base)			Simon			Lipsey			Survey of Current Business		
	Price index		Terms of trade	Price index		Terms of trade	Price index		Terms of trade	Price index		Terms of trade	Price index		Terms of trade
	Exports	Imports		Exports	Imports		Exports	Imports		Exports	Imports		Exports	Imports	
	Ee431	Ee432	Ee433	Ee434	Ee435	Ee436	Ee437	Ee438	Ee439	Ee440	Ee441	Ee442	Ee443	Ee444	Ee445
	Index	Index	Index	Index	Index	Index	Index	Index	Index	Index	Index	Index	Index	Index	Index
Year	1790 = 100	1790 = 100	1790 = 100	1830 = 100	1830 = 100	1830 = 100	1860 = 100	1860 = 100	1860 = 100	1913 = 100	1913 = 100	1913 = 100	1996 = 100	1996 = 100	1996 = 100
1965	—	—	—	—	—	—	—	—	—	—	—	—	33.46	21.86	153.06
1966	—	—	—	—	—	—	—	—	—	—	—	—	34.61	22.36	154.79
1967	—	—	—	—	—	—	—	—	—	—	—	—	36.06	22.39	161.05
1968	—	—	—	—	—	—	—	—	—	—	—	—	36.62	22.69	161.39
1969	—	—	—	—	—	—	—	—	—	—	—	—	37.75	23.33	161.81
1970	—	—	—	—	—	—	—	—	—	—	—	—	39.46	24.91	158.41
1971	—	—	—	—	—	—	—	—	—	—	—	—	40.51	26.19	154.68
1972	—	—	—	—	—	—	—	—	—	—	—	—	41.59	28.20	147.48
1973	—	—	—	—	—	—	—	—	—	—	—	—	48.27	33.23	145.26
1974	—	—	—	—	—	—	—	—	—	—	—	—	61.08	49.73	122.82
1975	—	—	—	—	—	—	—	—	—	—	—	—	67.89	53.90	125.96
1976	—	—	—	—	—	—	—	—	—	—	—	—	69.63	55.34	125.82
1977	—	—	—	—	—	—	—	—	—	—	—	—	72.16	60.42	119.43
1978	—	—	—	—	—	—	—	—	—	—	—	—	76.32	64.45	118.42
1979	—	—	—	—	—	—	—	—	—	—	—	—	86.40	76.00	113.68
1980	—	—	—	—	—	—	—	—	—	—	—	—	94.71	95.90	98.76
1981	—	—	—	—	—	—	—	—	—	—	—	—	101.38	101.25	100.13
1982	—	—	—	—	—	—	—	—	—	—	—	—	100.21	97.16	103.14
1983	—	—	—	—	—	—	—	—	—	—	—	—	99.48	93.10	106.85
1984	—	—	—	—	—	—	—	—	—	—	—	—	100.34	92.46	108.52
1985	—	—	—	—	—	—	—	—	—	—	—	—	95.62	88.84	107.63
1986	—	—	—	—	—	—	—	—	—	—	—	—	92.49	86.85	106.49
1987	—	—	—	—	—	—	—	—	—	—	—	—	94.89	93.04	101.99
1988	—	—	—	—	—	—	—	—	—	—	—	—	101.00	97.47	103.62
1989	—	—	—	—	—	—	—	—	—	—	—	—	102.33	100.23	102.10
1990	—	—	—	—	—	—	—	—	—	—	—	—	101.36	102.02	99.35
1991	—	—	—	—	—	—	—	—	—	—	—	—	101.26	100.62	100.64
1992	—	—	—	—	—	—	—	—	—	—	—	—	99.75	100.21	99.54
1993	—	—	—	—	—	—	—	—	—	—	—	—	99.21	99.06	100.15
1994	—	—	—	—	—	—	—	—	—	—	—	—	100.27	99.83	100.44
1995	—	—	—	—	—	—	—	—	—	—	—	—	102.65	102.51	100.14
1996	—	—	—	—	—	—	—	—	—	—	—	—	100.00	100.00	100.00
1997	—	—	—	—	—	—	—	—	—	—	—	—	97.29	95.88	101.47
1998	—	—	—	—	—	—	—	—	—	—	—	—	94.25	90.17	104.52
1999	—	—	—	—	—	—	—	—	—	—	—	—	92.98	90.31	102.96
2000	—	—	—	—	—	—	—	—	—	—	—	—	94.05	94.63	99.39
2001	—	—	—	—	—	—	—	—	—	—	—	—	93.42	91.87	101.69
2002	—	—	—	—	—	—	—	—	—	—	—	—	92.98	90.32	102.95

Sources

Series Ee431–436: Douglass C. North, *The Economic Growth of the United States, 1790–1860* (Prentice Hall, 1961), Appendix I. Series Ee437–439: Matthew Simon, "The United States Balance of Payments, 1861–1900," in *Trends in the American Economy in the Nineteenth Century: A Report of the National Bureau of Economic Research*, Studies in Income and Wealth, volume 24 (Princeton University Press, 1960). Series Ee440–442: Robert E. Lipsey, *Price and Quantity Trends in the Foreign Trade of the United States* (Princeton University Press, 1963), Table A-1, A-3. Series Ee443–445: *Survey of Current Business* (August 1998), 1998–2002, based on data available at the Internet site of the U.S. Bureau of Economic Analysis (BEA).

Documentation

The 1929–2002 data is based on a chain index of prices of goods exports and imports. The BEA also produces a chain index of prices of service exports and imports for this period.

TABLE Ee446–457   Exports and imports of merchandise – crude and manufactured goods: 1821–1984[1,2,3]
Contributed by Douglas A. Irwin

	Domestic exports						General imports					
	Total	Crude materials	Crude foods	Manufactured foods	Semimanufactured	Finished manufactured	Total	Crude materials	Crude foods	Manufactured foods	Semimanufactured	Finished manufactured
	Ee446	Ee447	Ee448	Ee449	Ee450	Ee451	Ee452	Ee453	Ee454	Ee455	Ee456	Ee457
Year	Million dollars	Million dollars	Million dollars	Million dollars	Million dollars	Million dollars	Million dollars	Million dollars	Million dollars	Million dollars	Million dollars	Million dollars
1821	52	31	2	10	5	3	55	3	6	11	4	31
1830	59	37	3	10	4	5	63	5	7	10	5	36
1840	112	76	5	16	5	11	98	12	15	15	11	44
1850	135	84	8	20	6	17	174	13	18	21	26	95
1851	179	125	5	20	6	23	211	17	20	29	27	118
1852	155	101	7	20	6	21	207	14	24	29	21	120
1853	190	124	8	27	6	24	264	18	26	33	42	144
1854	214 [4]	108	22	47	11	27	298	23	25	33	45	173
1855	193	109	11	33	11	29	258	27	33	34	35	129
1856	266	145	29	53	8	31	310	27	39	46	41	157
1857	279	158	31	49	11	30	348	34	41	72	39	163
1858	251	155	18	39	10	30	263	34	36	46	31	116
1859	278	190	10	32	11	35	331	39	44	57	40	151
1860	316	217	12	39	13	36	354	40	46	60	35	172
1861	205	58	49	54	8	36	289	31	40	54	33	132
1862	180	18	56	70	8	27	189	33	32	35	24	66
1863	186	30	45	66	11	33	243	48	30	35	35	95
1864	144	29	25	55	10	25	316	40	44	52	52	128
1865	137	34	14	48	11	30	239	30	35	48	30	96
1866	338	228	17	41	12	39	435	48	61	72	56	198
1867	280	167	21	34	15	44	396	43	51	65	56	181
1868	269	133	35	42	17	43	357	41	52	78	53	133
1869	275	145	25	44	14	47	418	50	53	95	63	157
1870	377	214	42	51	14	56	436	57	54	96	56	174
1871	428	224	49	67	14	76	520	78	64	103	72	203
1872	428	198	59	84	21	65	627	103	77	122	88	238
1873	505	233	70	101	25	76	642	108	83	122	97	232
1874	569	229	119	114	26	81	567	89	94	120	72	192
1875	499	208	79	110	27	75	533	89	90	113	63	178
1876	526	204	94	122	31	74	461	78	94	92	51	146
1877	590	205	91	150	32	113	451	76	86	115	49	126
1878	681	216	155	170	29	110	437	79	84	102	47	125
1879	698	202	189	174	30	103	446	81	82	103	50	130
1880	824	243	266	193	29	93	668	142	100	118	111	197
1881	884	281	242	226	33	102	643	125	102	123	88	204
1882	733	238	155	178	37	125	725	143	105	139	99	239
1883	804	294	163	186	38	122	723	146	93	142	99	243
1884	725	244	130	195	38	118	668	131	103	131	95	208
1885	727	251	123	202	39	111	578	120	93	103	78	183
1886	666	257	101	163	34	112	635	145	92	113	92	195
1887	703	253	125	176	37	112	692	151	106	112	120	203
1888	684	274	86	170	40	114	724	164	116	111	122	211
1889	730	291	99	175	43	123	745	172	123	122	115	212
1890	845	309	132	225	46	133	789	180	128	133	117	231
1891	872	351	106	226	48	140	845	193	151	148	136	218
1892	1,016	320	262	250	50	133	827	195	176	140	113	205
1893	831	252	153	247	49	130	866	217	132	154	136	229
1894	869	283	133	250	67	136	655	135	133	155	83	149
1895	793	269	99	219	62	144	732	188	141	107	96	200
1896	863	257	129	219	76	182	780	203	130	119	101	227
1897	1,032	304	181	235	98	213	765	201	128	129	88	218
1898	1,210	296	305	285	102	223	616	194	104	86	79	153
1899	1,204	286	233	305	118	263	697	213	99	123	92	170
1900	1,371	340	226	320	153	332	850	282	98	133	134	203
1901	1,460	411	246	337	148	318	823	254	110	126	128	206
1902	1,355	388	185	329	132	322	903	309	120	95	148	231
1903	1,392	416	185	323	141	327	1,026	336	119	117	196	258
1904	1,435	467	136	309	175	349	991	328	132	118	160	253

Notes appear at end of table

TABLE Ee446–457   Exports and imports of merchandise – crude and manufactured goods: 1821–1984 *Continued*

	Domestic exports						General imports					
Year	Total	Crude materials	Crude foods	Manufactured foods	Semimanufactured	Finished manufactured	Total	Crude materials	Crude foods	Manufactured foods	Semimanufactured	Finished manufactured
	Ee446	Ee447	Ee448	Ee449	Ee450	Ee451	Ee452	Ee453	Ee454	Ee455	Ee456	Ee457
	Million dollars	Million dollars	Million dollars	Million dollars	Million dollars	Million dollars	Million dollars	Million dollars	Million dollars	Million dollars	Million dollars	Million dollars
1905	1,492	479	118	283	210	402	1,118	396	146	145	178	252
1906	1,718	507	177	347	226	460	1,227	424	134	140	220	308
1907	1,854	601	167	346	259	481	1,434	488	150	159	274	364
1908	1,835	563	189	332	261	489	1,194	374	146	147	196	332
1909	1,638	529	136	303	231	440	1,312	461	164	166	222	299
1910	1,710	574	110	259	268	499	1,557	578	145	182	285	368
1911	2,014	721	103	282	309	598	1,527	525	181	172	288	361
1912	2,170	731	100	319	348	672	1,653	573	230	196	294	360
1913	2,429	740	182	321	409	776	1,813	649	212	194	349	408
1914	2,330	800	137	293	374	725	1,894	650	248	228	319	449
1915	2,716	591	507	455	356	807	1,674	591	224	286	237	336
1916	5,423	816	421	648	912	2,625	2,392	1,029	260	339	419	346
1917	6,170	833	509	807	1,315	2,706	2,952	1,286	386	352	537	392
1918	6,048	972	547	1,406	1,053	2,069	3,031	1,234	346	397	650	405
1919	7,750	1,623	678	1,963	922	2,564	3,904	1,701	545	556	609	493
1920	8,080	1,883	918	1,117	958	3,205	5,278	1,784	578	1,238	802	877
1921	4,379	984	673	685	410	1,627	2,509	859	300	368	362	620
1922	3,765	988	459	588	438	1,292	3,113	1,180	330	387	553	663
1923	4,091	1,208	257	583	564	1,478	3,792	1,407	363	530	721	771
1924	4,498	1,333	393	573	611	1,588	3,610	1,258	425	522	656	749
1925	4,819	1,422	318	574	662	1,843	4,227	1,748	495	433	755	796
1926	4,712	1,261	335	503	656	1,957	4,431	1,792	540	418	804	877
1927	4,759	1,193	421	463	700	1,982	4,185	1,601	505	451	750	879
1928	5,030	1,293	295	466	716	2,260	4,091	1,467	550	406	763	906
1929	5,157	1,142	270	484	729	2,532	4,399	1,559	539	424	885	994
1930	3,781	829	179	363	513	1,898	3,061	1,002	400	293	608	757
1931	2,378	567	127	247	318	1,120	2,091	642	305	222	372	549
1932	1,576	514	89	152	197	624	1,323	358	233	174	217	341
1933	1,647	591	48	155	237	617	1,450	418	216	201	292	322
1934	2,100	653	59	168	342	879	1,636	461	254	264	307	350
1935	2,243	683	59	157	350	994	2,039	582	322	319	410	406
1936	2,419	670	58	144	393	1,154	2,424	733	349	386	490	466
1937	3,299	731	105	178	669	1,617	3,010	971	413	440	634	551
1938	3,057	607	249	184	494	1,523	1,950	576	260	311	385	418
1939	3,123	545	111	202	599	1,667	2,276	745	291	313	487	440
1940	3,934	464	74	167	900	2,330	2,541	1,011	285	277	559	409
1941	5,020	362	84	418	771	3,385	3,222	1,376	376	322	724	423
1942	8,003	418	68	926	920	5,672	2,780	1,061	349	275	640	457
1943	12,842	662	109	1,551	1,089	9,431	3,390	1,037	584	421	678	670
1944	14,162	554	134	1,633	1,097	10,744	3,887	1,078	841	521	706	741
1945	9,585	871	432	1,246	780	6,257	4,098	1,183	693	462	928	832
1946	9,500	1,416	648	1,522	895	5,019	4,825	1,729	814	504	931	847
1947	14,274	1,579	849	1,528	1,734	8,583	5,743	1,770	1,017	656	1,279	1,022
1948	12,533	1,488	1,266	1,367	1,371	7,042	7,178	2,150	1,272	731	1,679	1,346
1949	11,938	1,780	1,342	908	1,356	6,553	6,679	1,857	1,333	741	1,457	1,292
1950	9,864	1,886	760	634	1,121	5,463	8,845	2,466	1,750	898	2,172	1,558
1951	13,820	2,471	1,401	881	1,668	7,399	10,919	3,365	2,077	1,022	2,514	1,942
1952	13,053	1,982	1,369	736	1,622	7,344	10,847	2,937	2,068	1,083	2,627	2,132
1953	12,142	1,626	962	759	1,424	7,371	10,889	2,613	2,185	1,108	2,752	2,232
1954	12,728	1,899	741	832	1,820	7,437	10,396	2,413	2,200	1,117	2,433	2,232
1955	14,172	1,907	930	1,012	2,311	8,011	11,519	2,845	1,998	1,118	2,933	2,624
1956	17,193	2,515	1,333	1,264	2,782	9,300	12,805	3,087	2,036	1,167	3,219	3,296
1957	19,337	3,110	1,332	1,163	3,255	10,476	13,387	3,211	2,020	1,272	3,277	3,607
1958	16,211	2,139	1,280	1,102	2,285	9,405	13,344	2,749	1,942	1,517	3,191	3,946
1959	16,243	1,913	1,448	1,078	2,478	9,327	15,476	3,097	1,824	1,599	3,763	5,194
1960	19,459	2,588	1,645	1,117	3,535	10,574	15,068	3,012	1,720	1,566	3,493	5,276
1961	19,981	2,545	1,898	1,151	3,287	11,102	14,703	2,875	1,717	1,602	3,415	5,094
1962	20,717	2,234	2,010	1,366	3,042	12,065	16,326	3,086	1,776	1,792	3,677	5,995
1963	22,183	2,577	2,273	1,496	3,348	12,488	17,068	3,141	1,725	1,998	3,810	6,393
1964	25,479	2,896	2,540	1,687	4,090	14,265	18,749	3,474	2,034	1,819	4,045	7,377

(continued)

TABLE Ee446–457   Exports and imports of merchandise – crude and manufactured goods: 1821–1984   *Continued*

	Domestic exports						General imports					
	Total	Crude materials	Crude foods	Manufactured foods	Semimanufactured	Finished manufactured	Total	Crude materials	Crude foods	Manufactured foods	Semimanufactured	Finished manufactured
	Ee446	Ee447	Ee448	Ee449	Ee450	Ee451	Ee452	Ee453	Ee454	Ee455	Ee456	Ee457
Year	Million dollars	Million dollars	Million dollars	Million dollars	Million dollars	Million dollars	Million dollars	Million dollars	Million dollars	Million dollars	Million dollars	Million dollars
1965	26,399	2,888	2,587	1,590	4,114	15,220	21,427	3,653	2,008	1,877	5,013	8,876
1966	29,054	3,143	3,198	1,582	4,368	16,763	25,618	3,851	2,117	2,309	5,631	11,710
1967	30,646	3,293	2,595	1,596	4,489	18,673	26,889	3,707	1,981	2,518	5,592	13,091
1968	33,626	3,467	2,334	1,671	5,117	21,036	33,226	4,012	2,294	2,882	7,141	16,897
1969	36,788	3,475	2,085	1,782	5,774	23,671	36,043	4,124	2,141	3,043	6,768	19,967
1970	42,029	4,492	2,748	1,921	6,866	26,001	39,963	4,129	2,580	3,523	7,268	22,463
1971	42,916	4,562	2,676	2,020	5,680	27,979	45,602	4,375	2,616	3,696	8,561	26,354
1972	48,421	5,242	3,737	2,325	6,163	30,941	55,553	5,345	2,868	4,321	10,261	32,754
1973	69,720	5,519	3,361	3,522	9,247	40,334	69,481	7,833	3,562	5,517	13,130	39,443
1974	96,535	5,532	3,002	4,196	14,194	56,617	100,968	19,996	3,720	6,265	22,066	48,371
1975	105,637	7,151	3,957	4,221	12,816	65,916	96,908	23,484	3,641	5,953	17,324	46,408
1976	113,084	7,263	3,853	4,766	13,970	71,237	121,753	32,014	5,224	6,275	20,489	57,744
1977	117,987	8,346	5,381	5,363	13,983	75,065	145,738	40,740	7,072	6,748	25,052	66,110
1978	140,972	8,787	4,840	6,655	18,899	87,203	173,165	40,110	7,250	8,133	29,190	88,626
1979	178,360	8,807	4,323	7,581	30,974	104,009	207,045	56,013	7,686	9,619	34,279	99,492
1980	216,220	10,435	6,496	9,520	37,616	126,132	241,177	73,336	7,671	10,363	37,807	111,788
1981	228,585	10,202	7,069	10,248	34,581	139,705	260,996	73,011	7,211	10,821	40,414	129,307
1982	206,798	9,864	5,530	8,545	30,798	128,682	243,946	55,581	7,240	9,824	36,102	134,992
1983	195,728	8,557	5,540	8,555	29,457	121,858	258,081	46,440	7,579	10,545	41,593	151,783
1984	211,745	8,876	5,917	7,934	33,155	133,031	325,698	46,683	8,689	12,282	51,370	206,587

[1] General imports through 1933; thereafter, imports for consumption. See text for 1933 data on imports for consumption.

[2] Excludes trade in silver prior to 1947 and military grant-aid beginning in 1950.

[3] Year-ending date varies over time. See text.

[4] Excludes exports from San Francisco valued at $1,343,064.

Sources

1820–1881, U.S. Bureau of the Census, *Statistical Abstract of the United States* (1907), pp. 698–701. 1882–1903, *Statistical Abstract of the United States* (1926), pp. 448, 449. 1904–1918, *Statistical Abstract of the United States* (1947), pp. 896, 897. 1919–1971, U.S. Bureau of the Census, *Indexes of U.S. Exports and Imports by Economic Class: 1919 to 1971* (1972), Tables 1 and 5. 1972–1984, U.S. Bureau of the Census, *Statistical Abstract of the United States* (various years).

Documentation

For additional information, see the text for series Ee365–371 and Ee424–428.

This long-standing group of data series was terminated in the mid-1980s after the classification scheme was superseded by the Harmonized System of commodity classification.

The economic classes shown here are broad categories based on groupings of more than 2,000 individual commodities listed in the Census Bureau's *Schedule B: Statistical Classification of Domestic and Foreign Commodities Exported from the United States.* Some of the important and typical commodities in each of the economic classes include: Crude Materials Exports: crude petroleum, coal, raw cotton; Crude Materials Imports: crude rubber, raw silk, hides and skins; Crude Foodstuffs Exports: grains, fruits, vegetables; Crude Foodstuffs Imports: coffee, tea, fruits; Manufactured Foodstuffs Exports: meat, lard, prepared foods; Manufactured Foodstuffs Imports: sugar, meat, wheat flour; Semimanufactures Exports: iron and steel plates, lumber, refined copper; Semimanufactured Imports: wood pulp, copper and tin in bars; Finished Manufactures Exports: aircraft, cigarettes, radio and television sets; and Finished Manufactured Imports: wool manufactures, newsprint, automobiles and parts.

In a report on *Exports of Manufactures from the United States and Their Distribution by Articles and Countries, 1800–1906* (1907), the U.S. Department of Commerce and Labor presented trade figures by economic classes annually back to 1850 and for selected years back to 1820. This study provided a different grouping of commodities than the Bureau of Statistics of the Treasury Department had previously employed for exports. In "Exports of Domestic Manufactures and Their Distribution" (*Monthly Summary of Commerce and Finance of the United States*, April 1903, p. 3239 ff.), the Treasury tabulated domestic exports for 1800–1850 by decade years and for 1851–1902 annually according to economic sector ("sources of production") as follows (p. 3249): agriculture, manufactures, mining, forest, fisheries, and miscellaneous. But it tabulated imports "according to degree of manufacture and uses" for 1821, 1830, 1840, 1850, and 1851–1902 as follows (pp. 3279–80): food and live animals, crude articles for domestic industries, articles manufactured wholly or partially for use as material in the mechanic arts, articles manufactured ready for consumption, and articles of voluntary use, luxuries, and so on. This report noted that values for exports were in fluctuating currency for 1862–1879 and gave specie values both for total exports and for exports of manufactures (p. 3315).

Trade in agricultural and forest products has been of special concern to the Department of Agriculture. Bulletin number 51 of the Bureau of Statistics of the Department of Agriculture (1909) provides the "only compilation . . . ever to be completed [to that time]" of the "Foreign Trade of the United States in Forest Products, 1851–1908." Bulletin numbers 74 and 75 in the same series, published in 1910, reviewed the "Imports of Farm Products into the United States, 1851–1908" and "Exports of Farm Products from the United States, 1851–1908," respectively.

The data are for the year ending September 30 (1821–1840) and June 30 (1850–1915), and for calendar years thereafter. For the six-month transition period in 1915 (July 1 to December 31), the values for series Ee446–457 are as follows: 1,820, 303, 158, 293, 268, 799, 913, 378, 130, 113, 144, and 147, respectively (in millions of dollars).

Series Ee449 and Ee455. Includes beverages.

Series Ee450–451. Beginning in 1950, for security reasons, a small amount of semimanufactured exports are included with finished manufactures.

Series Ee452–457. Imports for consumption were as follows in 1933: 1,433, 420, 215, 191, 290, and 317, respectively (in millions of dollars).

TABLE Ee458–505   Indexes of quantity and unit value of exports and imports – crude and manufactured goods: 1879–1986[1, 2]

Contributed by Douglas A. Irwin

						Lipsey						
						Domestic exports						
			Crude materials		Crude foods		Manufactured food		Semimanufactured		Finished manufactured	
	Quantity	Unit value	Quantity	Unit value	Quantity	Unit value	Quantity	Unit value	Quantity	Unit value	Quantity	Unit value
	Ee458 [3]	Ee459 [3]	Ee460 [3]	Ee461 [3]	Ee462 [3]	Ee463 [3]	Ee464 [3]	Ee465 [3]	Ee466 [3]	Ee467 [3]	Ee468 [3]	Ee469 [3]
	Index	Index	Index	Index	Index	Index	Index	Index	Index	Index	Index	Index
Year	1913 = 100	1913 = 100	1913 = 100	1913 = 100	1913 = 100	1913 = 100	1913 = 100	1913 = 100	1913 = 100	1913 = 100	1913 = 100	1913 = 100
1879	33.1	92.5	37.0	80.1	134.1	93.6	74.4	76.7	10.1	79.3	9.7	119.3
1880	35.0	101.5	41.1	89.4	146.5	96.3	80.1	86.6	9.5	87.5	8.7	132.4
1881	31.8	103.8	39.8	86.8	106.3	102.9	67.2	97.6	10.4	92.1	11.6	124.8
1882	28.4	107.0	40.4	88.3	73.5	109.2	51.7	106.8	11.7	93.0	12.1	123.3
1883	31.1	101.4	43.7	82.1	74.7	104.2	64.1	99.7	12.1	90.8	12.6	121.8
1884	30.5	97.6	43.4	83.3	69.7	91.6	64.8	92.2	12.3	86.4	11.8	122.3
1885	30.0	91.0	39.0	80.2	64.0	85.6	73.8	80.9	12.1	83.7	12.1	115.5
1886	33.1	85.7	46.6	74.9	80.4	80.6	70.6	76.3	12.0	80.5	12.8	109.0
1887	33.4	85.5	46.6	74.5	77.0	81.8	72.4	76.3	12.8	82.2	13.1	106.1
1888	30.7	89.7	46.7	78.1	51.2	86.2	63.6	81.3	13.7	84.7	13.0	110.9
1889	38.4	86.0	55.4	77.5	77.6	75.5	82.9	76.7	15.8	81.9	15.6	106.7
1890	40.4	85.0	52.3	78.5	87.2	76.8	97.1	73.6	16.1	82.5	16.3	104.4
1891	44.2	87.9	60.1	74.1	107.6	100.3	94.5	76.7	18.3	81.7	17.1	100.3
1892	45.8	81.9	53.8	67.8	127.1	86.8	108.6	77.7	17.2	78.7	17.5	91.8
1893	43.3	80.2	54.7	66.4	97.3	77.9	89.6	85.6	23.1	71.8	19.7	87.0
1894	46.5	70.5	62.8	55.3	87.7	67.8	100.8	74.2	25.6	67.7	20.7	82.0
1895	45.7	71.8	59.0	56.7	83.1	69.5	100.5	69.5	25.5	71.7	22.2	91.4
1896	56.4	71.0	65.6	61.0	141.4	63.6	114.3	63.5	34.5	70.1	25.6	96.8
1897	63.4	69.1	67.2	54.3	178.6	71.5	121.8	64.8	39.6	69.6	30.6	88.1
1898	73.2	68.4	82.0	48.9	197.1	76.9	139.8	68.0	41.8	70.4	36.3	82.6
1899	70.3	72.3	66.8	55.1	183.9	73.2	148.2	66.9	41.8	84.9	41.4	90.3
1900	72.8	81.0	75.7	72.2	168.4	74.4	142.9	71.3	48.6	89.5	42.2	98.9
1901	74.0	79.4	77.0	67.9	182.7	77.4	143.4	76.0	40.0	86.0	42.9	94.2
1902	66.9	81.4	73.8	69.1	112.1	82.0	120.6	83.8	44.4	83.5	43.6	94.0
1903	68.8	86.6	77.2	81.0	123.1	81.4	123.1	81.8	46.0	87.3	43.2	98.9
1904	67.0	86.9	73.1	84.3	73.2	80.3	113.4	77.8	60.2	85.9	48.4	98.8
1905	78.0	83.7	84.7	75.6	108.8	82.4	129.8	75.7	58.4	93.6	58.5	94.5
1906	80.5	89.9	84.2	83.8	126.1	81.7	131.8	80.7	60.0	105.9	61.8	97.5
1907	81.3	95.2	89.3	87.4	118.2	95.0	121.8	86.5	62.6	109.9	62.5	102.2
1908	78.4	90.1	91.3	79.8	98.3	99.8	114.6	87.9	64.5	92.4	56.4	100.5
1909	73.7	94.3	83.5	91.4	65.1	104.2	94.3	93.7	69.8	91.0	60.7	97.4
1910	73.1	102.1	79.4	108.4	55.1	98.7	73.6	107.3	77.0	93.4	69.0	93.7
1911	90.0	93.5	96.2	90.9	68.5	97.9	103.2	93.3	89.7	93.2	84.0	95.5
1912	101.1	95.5	115.3	89.3	79.4	104.2	97.8	97.0	97.9	100.3	95.5	97.2
1913	100.0	100.0	100.0	100.0	100.0	100.0	100.0	100.0	100.0	100.0	100.0	100.0
1914	86.6	97.7	74.9	87.9	140.0	114.5	93.0	103.3	87.4	97.6	86.0	94.3
1915	135.7	105.1	103.1	86.0	200.6	133.8	160.5	106.5	111.7	113.2	163.6	100.9
1916	163.3	135.5	90.9	115.5	168.6	144.2	164.8	118.4	155.8	156.5	252.0	130.6
1917	142.2	177.0	64.4	166.8	134.4	214.8	147.0	170.5	168.5	198.4	225.0	150.4
1918	119.7	206.1	57.0	219.0	132.8	234.6	203.9	214.2	129.5	202.8	153.4	169.7
1919	146.6	215.7	86.7	241.3	156.3	241.7	257.6	237.4	126.4	199.5	179.9	174.4
1920	141.8	232.5	84.8	285.3	192.2	268.2	161.2	217.2	120.8	210.5	202.2	197.7
1921	113.4	157.5	81.3	156.4	252.8	155.7	153.9	136.2	72.2	143.5	125.6	163.9

Notes appear at end of table

(continued)

TABLE Ee458–505   Indexes of quantity and unit value of exports and imports – crude and manufactured goods: 1879–1986   *Continued*

			Lipsey									
			General imports									
			Crude materials		Crude foods		Manufactured food		Semimanufactured		Finished manufactured	
	Quantity	Unit value	Quantity	Unit value	Quantity	Unit value	Quantity	Unit value	Quantity	Unit value	Quantity	Unit value
	Ee470 [3]	Ee471 [3]	Ee472 [3]	Ee473 [3]	Ee474 [3]	Ee475 [3]	Ee476 [3]	Ee477 [3]	Ee478 [3]	Ee479 [3]	Ee480 [3]	Ee481 [3]
	Index	Index	Index	Index	Index	Index	Index	Index	Index	Index	Index	Index
Year	1913 = 100	1913 = 100	1913 = 100	1913 = 100	1913 = 100	1913 = 100	1913 = 100	1913 = 100	1913 = 100	1913 = 100	1913 = 100	1913 = 100
1879	26.7	102.4	17.9	95.0	38.8	114.3	28.4	132.4	28.9	78.0	37.4	102.8
1880	32.8	113.1	22.9	104.2	36.8	123.3	31.5	158.7	41.4	91.1	52.8	105.4
1881	33.1	107.7	21.5	99.3	42.9	112.4	32.4	157.6	38.4	83.8	51.3	103.2
1882	37.0	108.3	23.0	104.5	46.1	105.2	37.7	159.6	43.8	84.9	59.1	103.6
1883	35.9	101.8	23.1	96.9	45.0	94.6	38.9	145.8	41.0	80.8	54.0	101.6
1884	35.1	95.4	23.4	91.9	46.1	95.5	42.4	116.6	36.0	80.1	51.5	96.1
1885	35.6	87.7	25.3	84.6	46.9	88.3	43.8	105.0	37.0	71.8	48.0	90.7
1886	40.3	87.5	29.7	84.5	48.2	87.3	45.7	107.4	43.7	73.1	57.9	87.4
1887	41.4	90.9	29.7	85.8	43.9	118.9	44.8	97.6	50.5	71.8	61.7	87.5
1888	43.4	88.8	32.2	81.3	49.4	108.4	45.8	110.1	47.6	69.5	64.8	85.1
1889	43.6	93.9	35.2	83.0	48.4	112.4	43.1	131.6	47.3	72.5	64.7	87.6
1890	46.9	93.2	36.4	82.2	49.0	123.7	49.6	113.3	49.7	75.3	71.6	86.4
1891	47.7	92.0	38.6	77.6	49.9	122.8	63.7	116.1	50.7	74.3	58.8	86.1
1892	50.4	88.4	42.9	74.9	52.1	113.7	54.4	112.7	50.3	72.4	64.0	84.8
1893	44.7	92.0	37.1	75.6	48.2	123.9	54.6	122.4	45.4	73.7	59.5	84.6
1894	44.4	83.5	37.6	68.5	52.5	114.8	58.2	101.7	40.9	65.2	48.2	80.4
1895	55.7	79.5	50.6	70.0	55.8	111.6	53.2	80.7	50.8	63.4	75.8	80.3
1896	46.6	80.7	35.7	71.0	53.2	99.5	56.6	94.3	40.7	64.9	60.4	81.2
1897	54.0	75.9	51.9	71.4	64.9	81.8	56.4	84.7	44.1	63.4	62.3	79.4
1898	46.3	75.7	40.7	76.2	59.3	68.4	49.3	92.6	43.6	60.8	50.9	79.4
1899	54.1	81.5	48.6	83.2	67.5	66.4	61.4	99.1	50.6	73.4	56.0	82.8
1900	53.2	86.7	47.7	87.7	64.2	72.9	58.8	101.4	48.8	82.7	58.8	87.4
1901	59.4	82.6	56.6	82.0	77.5	66.1	64.0	96.0	52.0	82.4	60.8	88.6
1902	67.0	80.8	61.8	83.0	79.0	67.9	67.6	80.5	66.2	80.0	71.5	86.0
1903	66.1	84.0	58.6	88.5	78.8	67.3	63.1	88.2	66.6	82.9	73.7	87.6
1904	67.3	85.8	62.4	89.2	89.9	73.0	73.6	93.7	60.3	83.4	68.3	87.7
1905	72.6	90.6	70.0	93.5	81.6	74.2	70.9	113.2	70.5	85.4	76.9	90.1
1906	77.8	94.7	71.0	100.7	79.6	75.9	75.0	97.1	78.8	97.4	90.2	93.2
1907	80.0	99.2	70.7	106.2	86.7	78.2	78.7	101.8	77.0	103.1	96.1	97.1
1908	70.7	88.0	65.6	89.7	87.0	72.8	74.8	105.8	64.2	83.9	74.5	90.4
1909	93.5	88.0	90.4	95.3	106.4	71.1	82.7	104.3	94.6	81.2	96.9	86.3
1910	92.2	94.6	85.1	104.8	85.6	80.9	86.0	113.8	102.4	85.7	99.7	86.5
1911	89.0	96.1	83.2	99.9	90.8	94.5	83.5	109.7	95.8	90.4	92.7	90.2
1912	100.4	101.0	104.6	100.4	103.2	104.0	87.8	119.0	97.0	96.9	103.0	95.4
1913	100.0	100.0	100.0	100.0	100.0	100.0	100.0	100.0	100.0	100.0	100.0	100.0
1914	106.5	93.7	106.0	92.8	117.5	91.1	117.1	110.7	87.1	93.3	110.2	90.7
1915	102.1	97.2	126.6	89.7	120.6	89.9	96.6	142.9	77.3	99.8	79.3	90.3
1916	111.0	120.2	144.9	113.1	117.0	98.7	98.1	172.3	96.8	128.1	75.2	112.2
1917	113.4	145.3	149.1	139.8	154.9	106.7	89.5	196.9	96.1	160.4	69.7	136.1
1918	104.9	161.3	137.2	147.3	132.4	110.5	92.9	216.5	92.3	180.4	63.4	180.1
1919	120.4	181.0	171.7	161.6	150.6	159.4	112.4	255.7	86.5	183.1	63.0	195.2
1920	134.4	219.1	159.9	179.1	155.7	166.4	133.8	472.4	112.7	204.2	89.9	223.5
1921	111.8	125.2	140.3	99.8	135.8	101.1	100.7	179.0	75.8	135.0	86.6	164.6

Notes appear at end of table

TABLE Ee458–505　Indexes of quantity and unit value of exports and imports – crude and manufactured goods: 1879–1986　*Continued*

			Bureau of the Census										
			Domestic exports										
			Crude materials		Crude foods		Manufactured food		Semimanufactured		Finished manufactured	
	Quantity	Unit value	Quantity	Unit value	Quantity	Unit value	Quantity	Unit value	Quantity	Unit value	Quantity	Unit value
	Ee482 [4]	Ee483 [4]	Ee484 [4]	Ee485 [4]	Ee486 [4]	Ee487 [4]	Ee488 [4]	Ee489 [4]	Ee490 [4]	Ee491 [4]	Ee492 [4]	Ee493 [4]
Year	Index 1967 = 100	Index 1967 = 100	Index 1967 = 100	Index 1967 = 100	Index 1967 = 100	Index 1967 = 100	Index 1967 = 100	Index 1967 = 100	Index 1967 = 100	Index 1967 = 100	Index 1967 = 100	Index 1967 = 100
1913	18.3	40.3	61.6	38.3	11.4	57.3	35.0	58.1	20.4	43.5	9.2	40.1
1914	—	—	—	—	—	—	—	—	—	—	—	—
1915	—	—	—	—	—	—	—	—	—	—	—	—
1916	—	—	—	—	—	—	—	—	—	—	—	—
1917	—	—	—	—	—	—	—	—	—	—	—	—
1918	—	—	—	—	—	—	—	—	—	—	—	—
1919	28.5	88.6	52.1	94.6	18.8	138.6	87.5	140.6	24.2	86.4	17.5	78.4
1920	27.5	95.9	53.2	107.4	23.0	153.9	54.3	129.0	23.6	92.5	19.2	89.5
1921	22.9	62.5	54.0	55.3	29.1	89.1	54.3	79.1	14.5	64.1	12.3	70.8
1922	21.2	58.0	43.7	68.6	23.5	75.3	62.6	70.1	17.5	56.8	12.0	57.8
1923	21.5	66.2	42.0	87.3	13.1	75.4	51.2	71.4	20.8	61.6	14.3	55.2
1924	24.1	61.0	49.5	81.7	17.1	88.4	50.2	71.6	23.5	59.0	15.6	54.5
1925	25.4	61.8	58.5	73.8	12.0	101.9	42.1	85.5	24.2	62.1	17.9	55.1
1926	27.2	56.6	67.2	57.0	14.7	88.0	38.5	81.9	24.4	61.2	19.0	55.3
1927	29.2	53.2	65.3	55.5	18.5	87.6	38.6	75.2	27.6	57.6	21.2	50.1
1928	30.3	54.1	62.0	63.3	13.8	82.3	40.8	73.0	28.4	57.4	24.4	49.5
1929	31.3	53.7	56.6	61.3	13.2	78.7	41.5	73.2	27.3	60.7	27.8	48.7
1930	25.8	47.9	52.9	47.6	9.7	70.7	34.0	66.9	22.2	52.6	21.8	46.6
1931	21.0	36.9	53.7	32.1	10.0	49.0	29.6	52.3	16.8	43.1	16.0	37.6
1932	16.1	31.9	57.4	27.2	8.3	41.6	23.8	40.0	12.6	35.6	9.8	34.2
1933	16.2	33.2	56.4	31.8	4.5	41.5	23.3	41.5	14.6	36.8	10.1	32.8
1934	17.5	39.1	47.2	42.0	4.7	48.2	22.2	47.3	18.5	41.9	13.4	35.2
1935	18.4	39.8	48.6	42.7	4.6	48.9	17.9	55.0	19.1	41.6	14.8	35.9
1936	19.4	40.7	46.5	43.6	4.3	52.7	16.0	56.4	20.2	44.4	17.1	36.2
1937	24.8	43.3	51.3	42.7	7.1	56.5	18.5	60.3	28.7	53.8	22.8	37.9
1938	24.9	40.1	48.7	37.8	20.8	46.2	22.3	51.8	23.7	47.5	21.9	37.2
1939	26.0	39.2	44.6	37.1	11.0	38.9	26.3	48.8	28.7	47.4	24.2	36.9
1940	30.6	42.0	35.7	39.4	6.3	45.1	21.3	49.2	40.8	50.2	31.8	39.9
1941	36.2	45.2	24.1	45.6	6.1	52.5	45.4	58.7	31.8	55.2	43.7	41.4
1942	47.6	54.8	24.1	52.7	4.1	63.0	72.2	80.8	35.0	59.8	59.6	50.9
1943	69.4	60.4	34.4	58.5	5.3	79.5	114.1	86.3	40.1	61.8	88.7	56.8
1944	66.8	69.2	27.6	60.9	5.8	89.6	107.3	97.5	39.0	64.0	86.5	66.3
1945	45.3	69.0	43.1	61.3	17.0	97.9	83.9	96.0	28.2	62.8	50.4	66.0
1946	47.5	65.3	62.1	69.2	23.3	107.1	98.5	99.0	31.5	64.7	46.3	57.7
1947	59.8	77.9	59.5	80.6	26.5	123.5	78.2	122.5	46.2	83.7	68.1	67.5
1948	49.4	82.8	48.9	92.5	38.4	127.0	68.4	125.2	33.6	90.8	52.8	71.4
1949	50.6	77.0	61.6	87.7	46.2	111.9	57.2	99.5	35.1	86.1	51.6	68.0
1950	42.9	75.0	63.0	90.9	30.4	96.2	46.9	84.7	29.7	84.0	44.1	66.4
1951	52.4	86.0	69.6	107.8	50.3	107.8	52.0	106.1	36.0	103.2	53.8	73.7
1952	49.8	85.6	59.4	101.3	45.3	116.4	46.3	99.7	35.5	101.7	53.1	74.1
1953	46.8	84.7	51.7	95.5	33.9	109.3	45.3	102.7	32.0	99.0	52.8	74.8
1954	49.7	83.6	59.3	97.1	29.2	97.6	50.8	102.7	41.2	98.3	54.0	73.8
1955	54.7	84.5	59.8	96.9	38.0	94.4	67.8	93.6	49.2	104.7	57.3	74.9
1956	64.0	87.6	79.4	96.2	54.0	95.1	86.4	91.7	53.4	116.1	63.8	78.0
1957	69.7	90.5	97.5	96.9	54.4	94.3	76.5	95.2	63.7	113.8	67.8	82.8
1958	59.1	89.5	68.2	95.2	53.1	92.9	71.6	96.5	49.9	102.0	59.9	84.1
1959	59.1	89.7	63.3	91.7	60.5	92.2	76.0	88.8	52.8	104.6	58.2	85.8
1960	70.2	90.4	86.5	90.8	69.1	91.8	80.3	87.2	75.1	104.8	64.8	87.4
1961	70.8	92.1	81.1	95.3	77.5	94.4	81.3	88.7	70.9	103.2	66.6	89.3
1962	73.9	91.5	70.9	95.7	80.3	96.5	98.2	87.2	69.0	98.2	72.4	89.3
1963	79.3	91.3	82.2	95.2	88.6	98.9	106.5	88.0	78.2	95.4	75.1	89.1
1964	90.2	92.2	93.1	95.2	98.5	99.4	117.3	90.1	94.9	96.0	84.8	90.1
1965	90.5	95.2	88.7	98.9	103.8	96.0	104.9	95.0	90.3	101.5	87.3	93.4
1966	96.6	98.1	92.8	102.8	124.6	98.9	98.0	101.2	94.5	103.0	93.3	96.2
1967	100.0	100.0	100.0	100.0	100.0	100.0	100.0	100.0	100.0	100.0	100.0	100.0
1968	108.2	101.4	107.5	97.9	94.0	95.7	104.0	100.7	119.2	95.6	108.0	104.3
1969	114.7	104.7	105.9	99.6	83.2	96.6	109.9	101.6	133.7	96.2	116.1	109.2

Notes appear at end of table

(continued)

TABLE Ee458–505   Indexes of quantity and unit value of exports and imports – crude and manufactured goods: 1879–1986 *Continued*

Bureau of the Census

Domestic exports

	Crude materials		Crude foods		Manufactured food		Semimanufactured		Finished manufactured	
	Quantity	Unit value	Quantity	Unit value	Quantity	Unit value	Quantity	Unit value	Quantity	Unit value	Quantity	Unit value
	Ee482 [4]	Ee483 [4]	Ee484 [4]	Ee485 [4]	Ee486 [4]	Ee487 [4]	Ee488 [4]	Ee489 [4]	Ee490 [4]	Ee491 [4]	Ee492 [4]	Ee493 [4]
	Index	Index	Index	Index	Index	Index	Index	Index	Index	Index	Index	Index
Year	1967 = 100	1967 = 100	1967 = 100	1967 = 100	1967 = 100	1967 = 100	1967 = 100	1967 = 100	1967 = 100	1967 = 100	1967 = 100	1967 = 100
1970	123.9	110.7	127.1	107.3	106.9	99.0	114.2	105.4	150.8	101.4	120.4	115.6
1971	122.4	114.4	119.0	116.4	98.3	104.9	115.4	109.7	125.4	100.9	125.7	119.2
1972	134.3	117.6	124.5	127.9	136.9	105.2	122.0	119.4	137.8	99.6	135.8	122.0
1973	165.6	137.4	146.4	162.4	211.9	160.1	121.7	181.4	161.3	127.7	167.6	128.9
1974	180.5	174.5	148.8	227.5	164.9	242.7	125.6	209.4	161.6	195.6	203.0	149.3
1975	176.7	195.1	131.8	250.7	187.5	242.5	131.9	200.5	143.7	198.7	200.3	176.4
1976	183.0	202.0	140.0	251.0	201.0	219.0	162.0	184.0	165.0	188.0	199.0	192.0
1977	183.0	210.0	150.0	256.0	192.0	189.0	167.0	201.0	160.0	197.0	199.0	202.0
1978	205.0	225.0	167.0	284.0	239.0	205.0	191.0	218.0	201.0	210.0	214.0	218.0
1979	228.0	256.0	186.0	285.0	256.0	238.0	199.0	239.0	262.0	263.0	231.0	241.0
1980	243.0	274.0	208.0	328.0	282.0	265.0	244.0	244.0	254.0	330.0	248.0	272.0
1981	236.0	300.0	199.0	346.0	293.0	277.0	251.0	256.0	235.0	327.0	241.0	311.0
1982	211.0	303.0	206.0	354.0	267.0	242.0	226.0	237.0	225.0	305.0	206.0	334.0
1983	197.0	306.0	178.0	331.0	249.0	255.0	227.0	236.0	221.0	296.0	192.0	340.0
1984	211.0	310.0	178.0	332.0	264.0	257.0	205.0	243.0	242.0	305.0	208.0	342.0
1985	207.0	308.0	172.0	345.0	215.0	232.0	204.0	227.0	246.0	285.0	208.0	353.0
1986	206.0	309.0	170.0	311.0	184.0	207.0	235.0	223.0	259.0	268.0	205.0	367.0

Bureau of the Census

General imports

	Crude materials		Crude foods		Manufactured food		Semimanufactured		Finished manufactured	
	Quantity	Unit value	Quantity	Unit value	Quantity	Unit value	Quantity	Unit value	Quantity	Unit value	Quantity	Unit value
	Ee494 [4]	Ee495 [4]	Ee496 [4]	Ee497 [4]	Ee498 [4]	Ee499 [4]	Ee500 [4]	Ee501 [4]	Ee502 [4]	Ee503 [4]	Ee504 [4]	Ee505 [4]
	Index	Index	Index	Index	Index	Index	Index	Index	Index	Index	Index	Index
Year	1967 = 100	1967 = 100	1967 = 100	1967 = 100	1967 = 100	1967 = 100	1967 = 100	1967 = 100	1967 = 100	1967 = 100	1967 = 100	1967 = 100
1913	15.4	43.7	24.0	63.0	39.6	28.0	18.8	41.2	16.1	42.9	8.5	37.0
1914	—	—	—	—	—	—	—	—	—	—	—	—
1915	—	—	—	—	—	—	—	—	—	—	—	—
1916	—	—	—	—	—	—	—	—	—	—	—	—
1917	—	—	—	—	—	—	—	—	—	—	—	—
1918	—	—	—	—	—	—	—	—	—	—	—	—
1919	18.8	77.6	45.0	102.8	62.9	43.8	20.8	106.0	14.8	74.1	5.3	70.5
1920	20.4	96.7	42.8	113.4	64.8	45.0	22.3	220.5	17.0	85.0	8.3	80.7
1921	17.1	54.6	37.0	63.2	56.3	26.9	19.2	76.2	11.3	57.5	7.7	61.7
1922	22.1	52.4	46.2	69.5	55.9	29.8	28.6	53.8	19.0	52.4	9.2	55.3
1923	23.0	61.4	46.4	82.6	61.3	29.9	23.3	90.3	22.4	58.1	10.2	57.5
1924	22.4	60.1	42.8	80.1	60.6	35.4	25.6	81.0	21.2	55.8	10.3	55.5
1925	24.1	65.3	48.2	98.7	57.4	43.5	30.5	56.3	23.5	57.8	10.1	60.4
1926	25.9	63.7	50.1	97.3	63.4	43.0	31.5	52.6	25.0	58.0	11.7	57.4
1927	26.3	59.4	53.3	81.7	62.6	40.2	28.8	62.2	23.5	57.6	12.2	55.1
1928	26.6	57.4	53.5	74.6	63.9	43.4	29.2	55.2	25.1	54.7	12.1	57.4
1929	30.4	53.9	61.1	69.4	66.3	41.0	35.5	47.4	28.3	56.3	14.5	52.5
1930	25.8	44.2	49.7	54.9	66.8	30.3	29.8	39.1	22.7	48.3	12.3	46.9
1931	22.6	34.5	46.7	37.4	65.2	23.6	25.2	35.1	17.5	38.3	10.5	40.0
1932	18.3	26.9	36.9	26.4	58.8	20.0	23.9	28.9	12.8	30.6	8.0	32.6
1933	20.1	26.9	41.5	27.4	59.5	18.3	26.6	30.1	16.2	32.5	8.1	30.5
1934	19.9	30.7	38.3	32.7	61.4	20.9	30.9	33.8	14.4	38.4	8.3	32.4
1935	24.3	31.3	46.1	34.4	83.4	19.5	33.9	37.3	19.4	38.0	9.7	31.9
1936	26.9	33.6	48.8	40.9	86.3	20.4	38.2	40.2	22.7	39.0	11.4	31.2
1937	29.9	37.6	54.5	48.5	85.8	24.3	42.4	41.2	26.2	43.6	13.0	32.3
1938	21.6	33.6	38.6	40.7	67.0	19.6	34.2	36.1	17.5	39.7	9.2	34.5
1939	24.9	34.1	45.6	44.5	76.0	19.3	35.4	35.1	22.3	39.4	9.8	34.3

Notes appear at end of table

TABLE Ee458–505   Indexes of quantity and unit value of exports and imports – crude and manufactured goods: 1879–1986 *Continued*

Bureau of the Census

General imports

			Crude materials		Crude foods		Manufactured food		Semimanufactured		Finished manufactured	
	Quantity	Unit value	Quantity	Unit value	Quantity	Unit value	Quantity	Unit value	Quantity	Unit value	Quantity	Unit value
	Ee494 [4]	Ee495 [4]	Ee496 [4]	Ee497 [4]	Ee498 [4]	Ee499 [4]	Ee500 [4]	Ee501 [4]	Ee502 [4]	Ee503 [4]	Ee504 [4]	Ee505 [4]
	Index	Index	Index	Index	Index	Index	Index	Index	Index	Index	Index	Index
Year	1967 = 100	1967 = 100	1967 = 100	1967 = 100	1967 = 100	1967 = 100	1967 = 100	1967 = 100	1967 = 100	1967 = 100	1967 = 100	1967 = 100
1940	26.0	36.4	56.5	48.7	78.2	18.4	32.6	33.8	23.0	43.7	8.3	37.7
1941	30.8	39.0	73.9	50.7	83.7	22.7	34.7	36.9	28.4	46.0	8.1	39.9
1942	22.9	45.3	50.6	57.1	58.1	30.3	21.9	49.7	22.9	50.6	7.9	44.0
1943	25.7	49.2	44.5	63.4	89.9	32.8	31.2	53.6	23.2	52.7	10.5	48.6
1944	27.6	52.6	43.5	67.5	117.0	36.3	37.8	54.8	23.6	54.2	10.5	53.8
1945	28.2	54.2	46.1	69.8	93.3	37.5	31.8	57.7	30.6	54.8	11.4	55.5
1946	30.3	60.2	66.9	70.4	86.9	47.3	30.3	66.0	28.3	61.4	10.4	64.2
1947	28.8	74.1	61.2	78.1	77.2	66.5	32.0	81.4	29.3	77.9	9.7	80.4
1948	32.6	81.9	66.0	87.9	87.3	73.5	35.1	82.8	33.9	88.5	11.7	87.5
1949	31.8	78.0	59.4	84.3	95.2	70.7	37.1	79.2	32.3	80.6	11.7	84.7
1950	38.8	84.7	71.8	92.6	90.9	97.2	45.0	79.3	49.3	78.8	14.4	82.7
1951	38.2	106.2	67.1	135.2	95.6	109.6	46.8	86.6	45.2	99.4	15.3	96.9
1952	40.1	100.6	71.1	111.5	94.6	110.4	49.4	87.0	46.5	101.0	17.0	95.8
1953	42.0	96.5	70.1	100.5	99.2	111.2	50.9	86.5	51.4	95.7	18.1	94.1
1954	39.2	98.5	66.8	97.5	83.4	133.2	51.9	85.5	46.8	92.9	18.1	94.0
1955	43.6	98.3	74.4	103.2	88.5	114.0	52.6	84.3	52.2	100.5	21.7	92.5
1956	48.0	99.3	79.1	105.3	93.4	110.1	54.7	84.7	53.9	106.9	26.7	94.3
1957	49.2	101.2	79.4	109.1	94.5	107.9	56.9	88.7	55.8	105.0	28.7	95.9
1958	51.6	96.2	72.8	101.8	96.2	101.9	68.7	87.6	59.4	96.1	32.0	94.3
1959	60.9	94.5	81.5	102.5	101.8	90.4	72.7	87.4	69.9	96.2	42.1	94.2
1960	58.4	96.0	77.0	105.5	97.7	88.9	72.4	85.9	63.6	98.2	41.9	96.1
1961	57.8	94.6	76.6	101.3	102.1	84.9	73.7	86.3	63.3	96.5	40.2	96.8
1962	65.7	92.4	83.8	99.4	107.9	83.1	82.8	85.9	71.4	92.1	48.3	94.9
1963	68.1	93.2	84.7	100.0	104.8	83.1	84.9	93.4	74.6	91.3	51.4	95.0
1964	73.0	95.5	93.4	100.3	102.2	100.5	78.9	91.5	76.8	94.2	59.4	94.9
1965	82.6	96.5	98.2	100.4	101.4	100.0	81.4	91.6	91.4	98.1	71.2	95.2
1966	96.0	99.2	100.6	103.3	103.7	103.1	93.8	97.8	102.0	98.7	91.6	97.7
1967	100.0	100.0	100.0	100.0	100.0	100.0	100.0	100.0	100.0	100.0	100.0	100.0
1968	122.3	101.0	107.9	100.3	114.5	101.1	113.0	101.3	124.1	102.9	128.7	100.3
1969	128.6	104.2	106.1	104.9	103.0	104.9	113.3	106.6	116.3	104.1	147.1	103.7
1970	133.2	111.6	105.8	105.3	106.4	122.4	124.4	112.5	118.0	110.1	152.9	112.2
1971	144.2	117.6	110.7	106.6	113.2	116.7	125.3	117.1	134.3	114.0	166.1	121.2
1972	163.8	126.1	130.0	111.1	116.3	124.5	136.5	125.7	151.8	120.9	190.8	131.1
1973	174.0	148.5	153.6	137.5	117.8	152.7	142.5	153.7	157.6	149.0	201.5	149.5
1974	168.1	223.3	154.5	349.1	108.6	173.0	132.2	204.5	143.3	275.4	198.6	186.1
1975	149.4	241.2	174.3	364.8	109.4	168.0	109.0	216.2	110.7	280.0	167.7	211.4
1976	182.0	249.0	219.0	394.0	115.0	230.0	115.0	187.0	133.0	276.0	205.0	216.0
1977	201.0	270.0	259.0	424.0	98.0	365.0	98.0	177.0	147.0	305.0	221.0	228.0
1978	221.0	291.0	248.0	436.0	107.0	341.0	107.0	198.0	161.0	325.0	264.0	256.0
1979	222.0	347.0	259.0	584.0	110.0	353.0	110.0	237.0	142.0	433.0	271.0	281.0
1980	206.0	435.0	208.0	951.0	102.0	378.0	153.0	300.0	130.0	522.0	278.0	307.0
1981	211.0	459.0	187.0	1,056.0	103.0	354.0	148.0	291.0	137.0	526.0	303.0	324.0
1982	201.0	452.0	153.0	986.0	109.0	336.0	135.0	265.0	134.0	481.0	306.0	336.0
1983	221.0	433.0	141.0	892.0	118.0	324.0	137.0	269.0	160.0	466.0	354.0	327.0
1984	275.0	441.0	145.0	870.0	126.0	347.0	134.0	265.0	201.0	457.0	464.0	340.0
1985	298.0	430.0	140.0	814.0	136.0	341.0	128.0	252.0	201.0	419.0	527.0	339.0
1986	331.0	415.0	171.0	489.0	143.0	388.0	132.0	259.0	231.0	365.0	576.0	355.0

[1] Based on imports for consumption, 1934–1963.

[2] Data on the 1967 base exclude trade in silver prior to 1947 and military grant-aid beginning in 1950.

[3] Series has no data after 1921.

[4] Series has no data before 1913.

Sources

Series Ee458–481. Robert E. Lipsey, *Price and Quantity Trends in the Foreign Trade of the United States* (Princeton University Press, 1963). Series Ee482–505. 1913: U.S. Bureau of International Commerce, unpublished data. 1919–1971: U.S. Bureau of the Census, *Indexes of U.S. Exports and Imports by Economic Class* (1919–1971); 1972–1986, U.S. Bureau of the Census, *Statistical Abstract of the United States* (various years).

Documentation

Publication of this index ceased with the adoption of the Harmonized System of commodity classification. Descriptions of methods used for the two sets of indexes are available in the sources. The U.S. Bureau of International Commerce indexes are computed by the Fisher formula, chained annually so that weights are taken from the given and preceding years. Commodities not directly entering into the calculations are taken into account in the weighting within the economic classes on the basis of certain assumptions regarding

(continued)

TABLE Ee458–505 Indexes of quantity and unit value of exports and imports – crude and manufactured goods: 1879–1986 *Continued*

similarity of their price movements to price changes of commodities specifically covered.

The National Bureau of Economic Research (NBER) indexes for the years 1879–1921 also used the Fisher formula linked from four time segments, within each of which weights are taken from the given year and the latest year of the segment. The NBER supplemented the U.S. foreign trade data with price information from other sources.

All commodities in U.S. export and import trade have been grouped into five economic classes as follows: (1) crude foods – products for edible use (by man or animals) that have not been substantially processed after sale by the farmer, fisherman, rancher, or other primary producer; (2) manufactured foods – processed forms of crude foods, edible and refined oils, and oilcake and meal; (3) crude materials – products of farms, forests, fisheries, and mines for nonfood use that are unprocessed by manufacturing; (4) semimanufactures – manufactured materials in the early stages of processing; and (5) finished manufactures – highly processed bulk materials and products manufactured from semimanufactures or other finished products.

TABLE Ee506–520 Exports and imports, by broad end-use class: 1923–2001

Contributed by Douglas A. Irwin

	Exports								Imports						
	Total	Foods, feeds, and beverages	Industrial supplies and materials	Capital goods, except automotive	Automotive vehicles, parts, and engines	Consumer goods (nonfood), except automotive	Special category (military-type goods)	Not elsewhere classified, and reexports	Total	Foods, feeds, and beverages	Industrial supplies and materials	Capital goods, except automotive	Automotive vehicles, parts, and engines	Consumer goods (nonfood), except automotive	Not elsewhere classified, and reexports
	Ee506	Ee507	Ee508	Ee509	Ee510	Ee511	Ee512	Ee513	Ee514	Ee515	Ee516	Ee517	Ee518	Ee519	Ee520
Year	Million dollars	Million dollars	Million dollars	Million dollars	Million dollars	Million dollars	Million dollars	Million dollars	Million dollars	Million dollars	Million dollars	Million dollars	Million dollars	Million dollars	Million dollars
1923	—	—	—	—	—	—	—	—	3,792.0	891.0	2,468.0	17.0	1.0	364.0	51.0
1924	—	—	—	—	—	—	—	—	3,610.0	942.0	2,245.0	14.0	1.0	369.0	39.0
1925	4,910	890	2,854	415	324	287	5	135.0	4,227.0	918.0	2,855.0	16.0	1.0	394.0	43.0
1926	4,809	835	2,784	445	328	289	6	122.0	4,431.0	953.0	2,979.0	23.0	1.0	433.0	41.0
1927	4,865	883	2,685	478	397	287	5	130.0	4,185.0	950.0	2,727.0	24.0	2.0	439.0	43.0
1928	5,128	762	2,879	543	509	308	6	122.0	4,091.0	951.0	2,618.0	27.0	3.0	446.0	46.0
1929	5,240	753	2,827	657	547	343	8	104.0	4,399.0	955.0	2,837.0	39.0	3.0	516.0	49.0
1930	3,843	542	2,111	547	284	255	7	96.0	3,061.0	684.0	1,943.0	29.0	2.0	347.0	56.0
1931	2,424	374	1,321	326	152	176	5	71.0	2,091.0	523.0	1,268.0	14.0	1.0	239.0	46.0
1932	1,611	243	996	131	78	102	5	55.0	1,333.0	404.0	742.0	8.0	(Z)	142.0	37.0
1933	1,674	204	1,105	134	92	96	6	38.0	1,450.0	403.0	861.0	7.0	(Z)	141.0	38.0
1934	2,133	224	1,308	218	192	127	12	53.0	1,655.0	514.0	933.0	11.0	(Z)	155.0	42.0
1935	2,283	216	1,372	265	232	145	10	44.0	2,047.0	535.0	1,183.0	14.0	(Z)	182.0	33.0
1936	2,456	203	1,424	342	246	182	14	45.0	2,423.0	728.0	1,443.0	17.0	1.0	215.0	19.0
1937	3,349	283	1,899	509	354	217	22	66.0	3,084.0	844.0	1,856.0	23.0	1.0	255.0	105.0
1938	3,094	433	1,560	528	277	202	37	58.0	1,960.0	566.0	1,150.0	16.0	2.0	186.0	40.0
1939	3,177	321	1,670	583	260	219	54	70.0	2,318.0	500.0	1,431.0	13.0	1.0	198.0	75.0
1940	4,021	246	2,045	954	259	234	169	114.0	2,625.0	556.0	1,778.0	9.0	1.0	166.0	115.0
1946	9,770	2,206	3,864	1,660	556	1,084	99	301.0	5,003.0	1,328.0	3,065.0	32.0	5.0	492.0	82.0
1947	15,359	3,178	5,997	3,199	1,153	1,333	175	324.0	5,829.0	1,573.0	3,626.0	55.0	6.0	375.0	94.0
1948	12,654	2,659	4,865	2,626	939	1,033	254	278.0	7,207.0	1,986.0	4,508.0	103.0	35.0	434.0	141.0
1949	12,053	2,335	4,877	2,562	772	923	311	274.0	6,706.0	2,068.0	4,011.0	106.0	13.0	404.0	104.0
1950	10,277	1,482	4,358	2,144	746	850	445	255.0	8,954.0	2,642.0	5,493.0	111.0	23.0	540.0	145.0
1951	15,038	2,433	6,190	2,526	1,218	1,111	1,269	291.0	11,068.0	3,087.0	6,952.0	170.0	38.0	666.0	156.0
1952	15,203	2,201	5,553	2,812	1,024	1,015	2,274	323.0	10,817.0	3,156.0	6,537.0	227.0	56.0	663.0	178.0
1953	15,775	1,838	4,826	2,929	998	1,086	3,801	299.0	10,983.0	3,282.0	6,456.0	224.0	53.0	757.0	211.0
1954	15,112	1,713	5,479	2,919	1,072	1,097	2,549	282.0	10,369.0	3,317.0	5,754.0	220.0	53.0	787.0	228.0
1955	15,553	2,119	6,065	3,071	1,276	1,134	1,592	297.0	11,562.0	3,108.0	6,843.0	254.0	85.0	991.0	280.0
1956	19,096	2,807	7,383	3,834	1,395	1,246	2,074	357.0	12,902.0	3,190.0	7,674.0	364.0	145.0	1,133.0	396.0
1957	20,859	2,781	8,669	4,487	1,349	1,336	1,861	377.0	13,412.0	3,306.0	7,595.0	400.0	339.0	1,210.0	562.0
1958	17,912	2,590	6,436	4,752	1,123	1,314	1,149	548.0	13,419.0	3,472.0	6,944.0	460.0	555.0	1,195.0	793.0
1959	17,642	2,871	6,146	4,617	1,187	1,371	967	484.0	15,688.0	3,445.0	8,343.0	591.0	844.0	1,632.0	834.0
1960	20,600	3,170	7,924	5,511	1,266	1,396	840	492.0	15,072.0	3,286.0	7,837.0	562.0	633.0	1,901.0	802.0
1961	21,037	3,418	7,705	5,910	1,188	1,441	826	549.0	14,759.0	3,331.0	7,714.0	693.0	383.0	1,889.0	749.0
1962	21,714	3,829	7,132	6,443	1,301	1,455	971	583.0	16,453.0	3,573.0	8,573.0	758.0	521.0	2,276.0	752.0
1963	23,387	4,282	7,822	6,604	1,468	1,558	1,025	625.0	17,205.0	3,753.0	8,874.0	823.0	586.0	2,389.0	781.0
1964	26,650	4,849	9,185	7,463	1,729	1,751	951	723.0	18,749.0	3,915.0	9,553.0	1,039.0	767.0	2,694.0	771.0
1965	27,521	4,928	8,917	8,039	1,929	1,799	1,229	680.0	21,520.0	3,946.0	11,024.0	1,458.0	939.0	3,305.0	849.0
1966	30,430	5,489	9,613	8,892	2,354	2,035	1,249	798.0	25,618.0	4,499.0	12,152.0	2,136.0	1,910.0	3,912.0	1,000.0
1967	31,622	4,998	9,971	9,913	2,784	2,111	1,103	743.0	26,889.0	4,586.0	11,856.0	2,382.0	2,634.0	4,213.0	1,219.0
1968	34,636	4,813	11,006	11,072	3,453	2,334	1,110	849.0	33,226.0	5,271.0	14,159.0	2,825.0	4,295.0	5,330.0	1,347.0
1969	37,988	4,687	11,758	12,322	3,888	2,596	1,650	1,085.0	36,052.0	5,239.0	14,163.0	3,331.0	5,346.0	6,503.0	1,469.0

Note appears at end of table

(continued)

TABLE Ee506–520   Exports and imports, by broad end-use class: 1923–2001   Continued

	Exports								Imports						
	Total	Foods, feeds, and beverages	Industrial supplies and materials	Capital goods, except automotive	Automotive vehicles, parts, and engines	Consumer goods (nonfood), except automotive	Special category (military-type goods)	Not elsewhere classified, and reexports	Total	Foods, feeds, and beverages	Industrial supplies and materials	Capital goods, except automotive	Automotive vehicles, parts, and engines	Consumer goods (nonfood), except automotive	Not elsewhere classified, and reexports
	Ee506	Ee507	Ee508	Ee509	Ee510	Ee511	Ee512	Ee513	Ee514	Ee515	Ee516	Ee517	Ee518	Ee519	Ee520
Year	Million dollars	Million dollars	Million dollars	Million dollars	Million dollars	Million dollars	Million dollars	Million dollars	Million dollars	Million dollars	Million dollars	Million dollars	Million dollars	Million dollars	Million dollars
1970	42,469	5,874	13,795	14,659	3,870	2,798	1,359	1,473.0	39,866.0	6,147.0	15,343.0	3,978.0	5,515.0	7,403.0	1,480.0
1971	43,319	6,110	12,703	15,372	4,698	2,913	—	1,523.0	45,579.0	6,364.0	17,444.0	4,334.0	7,358.0	8,388.0	1,691.0
1972	49,381	7,504	13,966	16,914	5,484	3,583	—	1,929.0	55,797.0	7,258.0	20,958.0	5,919.0	8,685.0	11,104.0	1,873.0
1973	71,410	15,199	19,862	21,999	6,878	4,800	—	2,672.0	70,499.0	9,119.0	28,049.0	8,263.0	10,257.0	12,892.0	1,919.0
1974	98,306	18,638	30,129	30,878	8,678	6,399	—	3,637.0	103,649.0	10,568.0	54,428.0	9,819.0	12,028.0	14,380.0	2,426.0
1975	107,088	19,234	29,945	36,639	8,625	6,560	—	4,079.0	98,041.0	9,642.0	51,030.0	10,166.0	11,693.0	13,211.0	2,299.0
1976	114,745	19,830	32,116	39,112	10,631	8,022	—	3,565.0	124,051.0	11,546.0	64,332.0	12,282.0	16,169.0	17,165.0	2,557.0
1977	120,816	19,723	34,477	39,767	12,100	8,932	—	4,553.0	151,689.0	13,981.0	80,653.0	13,985.0	18,641.0	21,796.0	2,633.0
1978	145,800	25,600	39,000	46,900	14,600	11,100	—	8,600.0	173,300.0	15,800.0	79,200.0	19,700.0	25,900.0	29,600.0	3,100.0
1979	186,300	30,300	57,300	58,800	16,600	13,400	—	9,900.0	207,100.0	18,000.0	102,600.0	24,900.0	26,900.0	31,300.0	3,400.0
1980	225,700	36,000	70,600	74,800	16,000	17,200	—	11,100.0	241,400.0	18,500.0	124,700.0	31,100.0	28,200.0	34,300.0	4,600.0
1981	238,600	38,600	67,700	82,500	18,300	17,100	—	14,400.0	261,000.0	18,500.0	130,700.0	37,000.0	30,700.0	38,400.0	5,700.0
1982	216,500	32,000	62,100	75,100	16,000	15,700	—	15,600.0	244,000.0	17,500.0	107,700.0	38,400.0	34,300.0	39,600.0	6,500.0
1983	205,600	30,700	57,400	70,600	15,400	16,200	—	15,300.0	258,100.0	18,500.0	105,300.0	39,400.0	42,100.0	46,300.0	6,500.0
1984	223,200	31,300	62,600	76,400	18,600	16,400	—	17,900.0	325,700.0	21,500.0	121,600.0	58,000.0	55,100.0	61,400.0	8,100.0
1985	219,300	24,100	59,200	78,900	20,600	15,800	—	20,700.0	345,300.0	22,300.0	114,100.0	62,400.0	66,600.0	69,900.0	10,000.0
1986	227,600	22,500	62,000	81,800	19,900	17,800	—	23,600.0	370,000.0	24,500.0	102,900.0	72,600.0	78,500.0	80,300.0	11,200.0
1987	254,100	24,300	66,700	86,200	24,600	17,700	—	34,600.0	424,400.0	26,800.0	117,300.0	87,000.0	87,500.0	93,600.0	12,200.0
1988	322,400	32,300	85,100	109,200	29,300	23,100	—	43,400.0	440,900.0	24,800.0	118,300.0	101,400.0	87,700.0	95,900.0	12,800.0
1989	363,700	37,200	99,300	138,800	34,800	36,400	—	17,200.0	473,300.0	25,100.0	132,300.0	113,300.0	86,100.0	102,900.0	13,600.0
1990	393,600	35,100	104,400	152,700	37,400	43,300	—	20,700.0	495,300.0	26,600.0	143,200.0	116,400.0	87,300.0	105,700.0	16,100.0
1991	421,700	35,700	109,700	166,700	40,000	45,900	—	23,700.0	488,400.0	26,500.0	131,600.0	120,700.0	85,700.0	108,000.0	15,900.0
1992	448,100	40,300	109,100	175,900	47,000	51,400	—	24,400.0	532,700.0	27,600.0	138,600.0	134,300.0	91,800.0	122,700.0	17,700.0
1993	465,100	40,600	111,800	181,700	52,400	54,700	—	23,900.0	580,700.0	27,900.0	145,600.0	152,400.0	102,400.0	134,000.0	18,400.0
1994	512,700	42,000	121,400	205,000	57,800	60,000	—	26,500.0	663,400.0	31,000.0	162,100.0	184,400.0	118,300.0	146,300.0	21,300.0
1995	584,600	50,500	146,200	233,000	61,800	64,400	—	28,700.0	743,500.0	33,200.0	181,800.0	221,400.0	123,800.0	159,900.0	23,400.0
1996	625,000	55,500	147,700	252,900	65,000	70,100	—	33,800.0	795,300.0	35,700.0	204,500.0	229,100.0	128,900.0	171,000.0	26,100.0
1997	689,000	51,400	158,200	294,500	74,000	77,400	—	33,500.0	869,700.0	39,700.0	213,800.0	253,300.0	139,800.0	193,800.0	29,300.0
1998	683,000	46,400	148,300	299,600	73,700	79,300	—	35,400.0	911,000.0	41,200.0	200,100.0	269,600.0	149,100.0	216,500.0	34,500.0
1999	696,000	46,000	147,500	311,000	75,300	80,900	—	35,300.0	1,024,600.0	43,600.0	221,400.0	295,700.0	179,000.0	241,900.0	43,000.0
2000	782,000	47,900	172,600	356,900	80,400	89,400	—	34,800.0	1,219,000.0	46,000.0	300,000.0	347,000.0	195,900.0	281,800.0	48,300.0
2001	729,000	49,400	160,100	321,700	75,400	88,300	—	34,100.0	1,141,000.0	46,600.0	273,900.0	298,000.0	189,800.0	284,300.0	48,400.0

(Z) Less than $500,000.

Sources

1923–1967 (excluding World War II years), U.S. Office of Business Economics, *U.S. Exports and Imports Classified by OBE End-Use Commodity Categories, 1923–1968* (1971), Tables 1 and 2. 1968–1977, U.S. Bureau of Economic Analysis, *Survey of Current Business*, March issues. 1978–1996, U.S. International Trade Administration, *U.S. Foreign Trade Highlights 1996* (August 1997), Table 4. 1997–2001, available at the Internet site of the International Trade Administration. Compiled from official statistics of the U.S. Bureau of the Census publication FT-900 on a census basis (domestic and foreign exports, free alongside ship or f.a.s.; general imports, customs).

Documentation

The Bureau of Economic Analysis's (BEA) end-use categories classification scheme was designed to fill a gap in the presentation of foreign trade statistics by regrouping commodity exports and imports as compiled by the Bureau of the Census into new, broad commodity categories based on a concept of end-use demand. The data have customarily been classified in terms of the physical nature of commodities and their stage of processing, or in terms of the principal industries *producing the* commodities. The end-use classification is associated with the principal sectors of the economy *using or consuming* the commodities.

It should be noted that inasmuch as the BEA end-use categories are constructed from the Census Bureau's Schedule B (export) and Tariff Schedule of the United States, Annotated (TSUSA) (import) classifications, prior to 1988, and later the Harmonized System (HS), the validity of the assignments of individual commodities to end-use categories is subject to the limitations of the census classifications systems. The "individual" commodities classified in HS very frequently represent not a single commodity but rather a number of different items not separately classified. These items are related by their material content or general function, but not necessarily by their end-use. This is especially true of "basket" classifications. For example, "rubber products not elsewhere classified" may include erasers and soap dishes for consumer use, as well as rubber flanges, rings, and valves for industrial use. In such cases, the products deemed to comprise most of the value of the "basket" commodity – based on advice of foreign trade commodity specialists – determine the end-use assignment it will receive. As another example, the commodity "ball bearings" is a machinery part that has been assigned to the export end-use category "capital goods, except automotive" even though it includes ball bearings for autos and trucks that would be assigned, if they were separately identifiable, to the end-use category "automotive vehicles, parts, and engines."

Foods, Feeds, and Beverages
Series Ee507 and Ee515. Comprised of food for human consumption and animal feeds and includes edible animals. It excludes work animals and animals for breeding, which are included in "materials associated with nondurable goods and farm output," a grouping within the industrial supplies and materials category. Tobacco is not included in the foods category: cigarettes and the like are in the consumer goods (nonfood) category, whereas unmanufactured tobacco is considered to be an industrial material (used in the manufacture of cigarettes and other tobacco products). A distinction is made in the foods category between *agricultural* and *nonagricultural* commodities in exports, but not in imports. This category, unlike the other principal end-use categories, does not distinguish between *manufactured* and *unmanufactured* commodity classes in either exports or imports.

Industrial Supplies and Materials
Series Ee508 and Ee516. Encompasses crude and processed materials and supplies primarily associated with, or used in, the producing sectors of the economy – manufacturing, farming, and construction. Both the export and the import sides are set up so as to separate *manufactured* from *unmanufactured* goods. *Agricultural* and *nonagricultural* aggregates can be obtained for exports but not for imports.

The industrial supplies and materials end-use category is subdivided on the import side into five major intermediate groupings as follows: (1) fuels and lubricants; (2) paper and paper-base stocks; (3) materials associated with nondurable goods and farm output; (4) selected building materials, except metals; and (5) materials associated with durable goods output. These aggregates were established in order to facilitate analysis of the relationships between domestic economic conditions and imports of industrial supplies and materials. For example, shifts in imports of materials associated with durable goods output can be examined for their relationship to changes in the Federal Reserve Board's production index of durable manufactures, and imports of selected building materials can be related to domestic construction and housing indicators.

On the export side, the industrial supplies and materials category is broken down between agricultural and nonagricultural goods; intermediate groupings similar to (3), (4), and (5), listed in the preceding paragraph, are not constructed.

(1) *Fuels and lubricants* comprise coal, oil, and gas. This grouping excludes petrochemicals, which are included with chemicals in another grouping within the industrial supplies and materials category. Although fuels and lubricants are partly associated with consumer goods as well as industrial supplies, it was not considered feasible to try to distinguish between fuel for home heating, for example, and fuel for industrial heating and energy. Fuels and lubricants have been established as an independent major subcomponent of the industrial supplies and materials category on both the export and the import sides because of their magnitude in our international trade, and because of the difficulty of associating them with the output of nondurable as distinguished from durable goods.

(2) *Paper and paper-base stocks* consist of pulpwood, woodpulp, and scrap materials for making paper; also paper products, mainly newsprint, but including also kraft paper, paperboard, and similar products. Excluded are paper products such as stationery, which are allocated to the consumer goods end-use category. The precominance of newsprint imports in the paper grouping, and the unique nature of this product, led to the establishment of paper, like the fuels and lubricants grouping, as a separate major subcomponent of industrial supplies and materials for both exports and imports.

(3) *Materials associated with nondurable goods and farm output* consist of supplies and materials related to the manufacture of products considered to be nondurables. The category includes goods such as crude and processed textiles, but not those manufactured into final products such as apparel and household furnishings. The latter are in the consumer goods category. Also included are unmanufactured tobacco, chemicals (except medicinals), hides and skins, undressed furs, and soap and perfumery ingredients, among others. Seeds, fertilizers, farm work animals and breeding animals, and eggs for hatching are included as materials associated with farm output. This grouping is constructed only for imports.

(4) *Selected building materials, except metals* consist of major (nonmetal) building materials such as lumber, plywood and veneers, stone, sand, cement, lime, glass (except automotive), asbestos, gypsum, mil work, molding, and prefabricated structures. The category excludes metals used in building (such as steel beams, copper tubing, wire, pipe, and latches and locks). This grouping is constructed only for imports.

(5) *Materials associated with durable goods output* consist of supplies and materials related to the manufacture of products defined to be durables. The category includes primary metals and metal shapes, anc fabricated metal manufactures for further assembly or incorporaticn in other goods (door hinges, latches, locks, and parts components not included elsewhere). This grouping is constructed only for imports.

It should be noted that the allocation of individual commodities to the various subcomponents outlined previously is based on end-use demand and not on the nature of the commodities from a production (supply) viewpoint. To Illustrate, imports of primary rubber, a "nondurable" commodity, is classified under "materials associated with durable goods output" because its major end-use – as a tire-making material – is associated with the production of durable goods such as motor vehicles, tractors, and aircraft.

Capital Goods, Except Automotive
Series Ee509 and Ee517. Defined to include all (nonmilitary) machinery, equipment, apparatus, and instruments and their parts, components, accessories, and attachments. These products are associated with investment outlays for industrial and agricultural plant and equipment; for commercial, scientific, professional, and service-industry capital goods; for natural resource development (petroleum and mining); and for construction. Also included is transportation equipment such as civilian aircraft and parts, railway rolling stock, and, for exports only, commercial cargo and passenger-carrying vessels. Automotive products are excluded from the capital goods end-use category as are other transportation items classifiable as consumer goods (such as yachts and other pleasure craft and motorcycles).

Automotive Vehicles, Parts, and Engines
Series Ee510 and Ee518. Contains commodities that might have qualified for assignment to two other end-use categories; passenger cars and parts to consumer goods (nonfood), and trucks and buses and parts to capital goods. However, because it has not been possible to distinguish parts for passenger cars from parts for trucks and buses, and because of the overall magnitude and importance of U.S. automotive trade, a separate automotive category was established. There are groupings within the category for passenger cars, trucks and buses, and automotive parts and engines (including engine parts).

(continued)

TABLE Ee506–520   Exports and imports, by broad end-use class: 1923–2001   *Continued*

Consumer Goods (Nonfood), Except Automotive

Series Ee511 and Ee519. Covers products used by the final consumer. This category has been subdivided into *durables* and *nondurables*, as well as *manufactured* and *unmanufactured*. The overall category encompasses a broad variety of products: consumer-type transportation equipment other than automotive-pleasure craft, motorcycles, and so on; furniture, rugs, appliances, radios and TVs, clocks and watches, precious stones, and other *durables*; and apparel and household softgoods, leather, rubber and plastic articles, notions and toiletries, medicinal preparations, and other *nondurables*. In general, consumer goods have been classified as *durables* or *nondurables* on the basis of whether they are, respectively, *hardgoods* or *softgoods*. Rugs are an exception; they can be classified as durable goods because of their long life and relatively high cost, but they can be characterized as consumer "capital goods," along with furniture and appliances. The consumer goods category consists predominantly of manufactured products, but it also includes unmanufactured items such as gem stones, Christmas trees, nursery stock, and pet birds.

Special Category, Domestic (Military-Type Goods)

Series Ee512. An export category only. It includes military aircraft, engines, turbines, missiles and rockets, military trucks, warships, ordnance, and other military material classified confidential by the U.S. Department of Defense as to country of destination. (Prior to 1965, the Department of Defense classified many military items confidential as to their identity as well as their destination.) A few other

military items currently of minor value, not classified as special category – military cars and buses – are included in the category "exports not elsewhere classified." From 1958 on, parts for aircraft (exports) are not separately identifiable as being for military or civilian aircraft, and therefore all aircraft parts have been included, along with civilian aircraft, in the capital goods category. Imports of military aircraft and parts are included in the category "imports not elsewhere shown." Other military imports are either minimal in value or are unidentifiable, and they are included, as appropriate, in other end-use categories.

Exports N.e.c. and Imports N.e.c.

Series Ee514 and Ee520. Includes transactions and commodities not elsewhere classified (n.e.c.) or shown. "Exports n.e.c." include reexports (exports of foreign merchandise imported into the United States and then reexported with no significant change in form or content), low-value shipments (commodity detail unavailable), a few military items not classified as special category, and special transactions such as goods imported for repair and exported. "Imports n.e.c." include low-value shipments, U.S. goods returned (after having been exported), and U.S. government purchases of uranium ores and oxides and of military aircraft and parts; the category also includes movies, exhibits, and laboratory, zoo, and show animals. (Exports of uranium and nongovernment imports of uranium are included in the industrial supplies and materials category.)

TABLE Ee521–532 Export and import price indexes, by broad end-use class: 1977–1999

Contributed by Douglas A. Irwin

	Export prices						Import prices					
	Total	Foods, feeds, and beverages	Industrial supplies and materials	Capital goods, except automotive	Automotive vehicles, parts, and engines	Consumer goods (nonfood), except automotive	Total	Foods, feeds, and beverages	Industrial supplies and materials	Capital goods, except automotive	Automotive vehicles, parts, and engines	Consumer goods (nonfood), except automotive
	Ee521	Ee522	Ee523	Ee524	Ee525	Ee526	Ee527	Ee528	Ee529	Ee530	Ee531	Ee532
Year	Index 1995 = 100	Index 1995 = 100	Index 1995 = 100	Index 1995 = 100	Index 1995 = 100	Index 1995 = 100	Index 1995 = 100	Index 1995 = 100	Index 1995 = 100	Index 1995 = 100	Index 1995 = 100	Index 1995 = 100
1977	—	—	—	—	—	—	—	71.9	—	—	—	—
1978	—	—	—	60.9	—	—	—	69.5	—	—	—	—
1979	—	—	—	65.0	—	—	—	76.9	—	68.1	—	—
1980	—	—	—	71.0	65.4	—	—	78.4	—	72.2	—	—
1981	—	—	—	78.1	72.6	—	—	72.2	—	72.8	63.0	—
1982	—	—	—	80.9	76.8	—	79.4	72.6	—	70.8	62.6	69.5
1983	82.1	98.8	75.0	82.6	79.8	75.1	77.5	75.5	—	71.7	64.9	69.8
1984	81.0	86.3	73.8	85.5	81.2	76.0	76.6	73.9	96.9	69.2	65.8	70.2
1985	80.7	82.1	71.6	86.0	83.4	76.2	77.4	77.0	92.9	71.8	69.6	70.8
1986	80.2	74.9	69.7	87.0	85.5	80.2	77.2	79.9	76.2	79.1	76.8	76.7
1987	84.9	80.2	80.9	87.8	86.4	82.3	85.1	82.6	87.5	87.7	80.8	84.2
1988	90.3	97.4	85.9	90.9	89.0	86.0	88.8	84.1	90.0	91.6	86.5	88.4
1989	90.8	89.8	85.9	93.6	91.5	89.2	91.1	80.3	95.9	91.1	87.1	90.8
1990	92.7	84.1	89.3	96.2	93.7	92.5	97.8	85.7	110.9	96.5	89.3	94.1
1991	92.1	87.9	82.2	99.2	95.9	95.3	93.7	87.7	93.3	96.2	91.7	94.9
1992	92.7	86.1	82.7	99.9	97.3	97.7	93.9	85.3	91.9	97.1	92.1	97.0
1993	93.7	94.2	82.9	99.8	98.0	98.3	93.0	87.9	84.2	97.8	95.7	97.9
1994	97.2	91.6	95.9	98.7	99.4	98.8	97.9	100.3	95.1	98.8	98.6	99.0
1995	100.5	109.9	97.3	100.4	101.0	100.3	100.4	98.1	100.9	99.9	100.8	100.7
1996	99.3	102.7	95.0	100.5	101.5	101.8	101.9	96.8	110.1	96.1	100.8	100.1
1997	98.2	99.3	93.7	98.9	102.3	102.7	96.6	98.1	98.6	89.0	101.3	99.2
1998	94.8	91.2	87.1	97.1	102.8	101.9	90.5	95.1	81.9	84.5	101.3	97.9
1999	95.3	86.0	91.7	96.1	104.0	102.4	96.8	94.7	109.5	81.6	102.0	97.4

Source

Available through the U.S. Bureau of Labor Statistics (BLS) Internet site.

Documentation

Figures are for December of each year.

The BLS's International Price Program (IPP) was established in 1971 to produce export and import price indexes. These price indexes utilize the end-use classification system used by the Bureau of Economic Analysis (BEA) to categorize items by use or consumption rather than by the more traditional stage of production. The end-use system is also useful in demand analysis and is characterized by more equal weighting of major groups. Among its disadvantages are that its titles do not clearly indicate what products are included in its product categories and also that the system is unfamiliar to many users.

The BLS also produces export and import price indexes based on the Harmonized Commodity Based International System. The IPP uses the Harmonized System for sampling the export and import universe as well as for weighting and collecting its price data. The Harmonized System has limited historical value because it was not formally adopted by the United States until January 1989. In addition, price indexes are produced using the Standard International Trade Classification System (SITC) created by the United Nations, which was the first classification system used by the IPP to publish its price indexes. The IPP indexes contain historical data of export and import prices going back as far

as 1974 for some categories. It is compatible with the Harmonized System; however, it is unfamiliar to most reporters who provide export and import price data. It cannot be used for sampling, and at aggregate levels it gives unequal weighting to major commodity groups.

Export and import price indexes are very sensitive to the changing composition of world trade. The IPP reweights its index aggregation structures every five years at the stratum level. Below the stratum level, the weights used in aggregation are based on the sample design. These weights are primarily based on the value of exports (or imports) for a given company in a specific product category. The IPP resamples each quarter of the export/import universe every two years.

The history of petroleum imports serves as a good example of the impact of changes in trade composition on the movement of price indexes. The relative importance of petroleum imports to the U.S. economy has shifted considerably. In 1980, following the price increases induced by the Organization of Petroleum Exporting Countries, the value of U.S. petroleum imports was $75.5 billion. At that time, petroleum imports accounted for approximately 31.3 percent of the nation's total imports. Five years later, petroleum imports, valued at $51.3 billion, had dropped to 14.9 percent of imports. When the annual change in the all-imports price index from December 1985 to December 1986 was first published using 1980 weights, the index fell 8.7 percent. However, when the series was recalculated based on 1985 weights, the index covering the same twelve-month period increased 0.3 percent, primarily as a result of the change in the relative importance of petroleum imports.

TABLE Ee533–550 Exports, by country of destination: 1790–2001[1]

Contributed by Douglas A. Irwin

Year	Total Ee533	The Americas Total Ee534	Canada Ee535[2]	Cuba Ee536	Mexico Ee537	Brazil Ee538	Other countries Ee539	Europe Total Ee540	United Kingdom Ee541	France Ee542	Germany Ee543[3]	Other countries Ee544	Asia Total Ee545	China Ee546[4]	Japan Ee547[5]	Other countries Ee548	Australia and Oceania Ee549[6]	Africa Ee550[6]
	Million dollars	Million dollars	Million dollars	Million dollars	Million dollars	Million dollars	Million dollars	Million dollars	Million dollars	Million dollars	Million dollars	Million dollars	Million dollars	Million dollars	Million dollars	Million dollars	Million dollars	Million dollars
1790	20	—	—	—	—	—	—	13	7	1	(Z)	5	—	—	—	—	—	—
1791	19	—	—	—	—	—	—	10	6	1	(Z)	3	—	—	—	—	—	—
1792	21	—	—	—	—	—	—	12	5	2	1	4	—	—	—	—	—	—
1793	26	—	—	—	—	—	—	15	6	2	2	5	—	—	—	—	—	—
1794	33	—	—	—	—	—	—	21	6	1	5	9	—	—	—	—	—	—
1795	48	—	—	—	—	—	—	31	6	8	10	7	—	—	—	—	—	—
1796	59	—	—	—	—	—	—	39	17	3	10	9	—	—	—	—	—	—
1797	51	—	—	—	—	—	—	29	6	4	10	9	—	—	—	—	—	—
1798	61	—	—	—	—	—	—	39	12	1	15	11	—	—	—	—	—	—
1799	79	—	—	—	—	—	—	45	19	—	18	8	—	—	—	—	—	—
1800	71	—	—	—	—	—	—	41	19	(Z)	8	14	—	—	—	—	—	—
1801	93	—	—	—	—	—	—	59	31	4	11	13	—	—	—	—	—	—
1802	72	—	—	—	—	—	—	44	16	8	6	14	—	—	—	—	—	—
1803	56	—	—	—	—	—	—	37	18	4	4	11	—	—	—	—	—	—
1804	78	—	—	—	—	—	—	51	13	9	6	23	—	—	—	—	—	—
1805	96	—	—	—	—	—	—	61	15	13	4	29	—	—	—	—	—	—
1806	102	—	—	—	—	—	—	65	16	11	6	32	—	—	—	—	—	—
1807	108	—	—	—	—	—	—	71	23	13	3	32	—	—	—	—	—	—
1808	22	—	—	—	—	—	—	7	3	3	(Z)	1	—	—	—	—	—	—
1809	52	—	—	—	—	—	—	34	6	—	2	26	—	—	—	—	—	—
1810	67	—	—	—	—	—	—	47	12	(Z)	2	33	—	—	—	—	—	—
1811	61	—	—	—	—	—	—	40	14	2	(Z)	24	—	—	—	—	—	—
1812	39	—	—	—	—	—	—	27	6	3	—	18	—	—	—	—	—	—
1813	28	—	—	—	—	—	—	22	—	4	—	18	—	—	—	—	—	—
1814	7	—	—	—	—	—	—	1	—	(Z)	—	1	—	—	—	—	—	—
1815	53	—	—	—	—	—	—	38	18	7	2	11	—	—	—	—	—	—
1816	82	—	—	—	—	—	—	59	30	10	4	15	—	—	—	—	—	—
1817	88	—	—	—	—	—	—	58	33	9	3	13	—	—	—	—	—	—
1818	93	—	—	—	—	—	—	68	38	12	3	15	—	—	—	—	—	—
1819	70	—	—	—	—	—	—	47	24	9	4	10	—	—	—	—	—	—
1820	70	—	—	—	—	—	—	48	24	8	3	13	—	—	—	—	—	—
1821	55	15	2	4	—	1	8	36	19	6	2	9	2	4	—	—	—	—
1822	61	20	2	3	—	1	14	40	24	6	3	7	1	6	—	—	—	—
1823	68	22	2	5	—	1	14	44	22	9	3	10	2	5	—	—	—	—
1824	69	28	2	6	—	2	18	40	21	10	2	7	1	5	—	—	—	—
1825	91	30	3	5	6	2	14	59	37	10	3	9	2	6	—	—	—	—
1826	73	30	2	6	6	2	14	42	21	11	2	8	1	3	—	—	—	—
1827	74	21	2	6	4	2	7	49	26	11	3	9	2	4	—	—	—	—
1828	64	23	2	6	3	2	10	39	20	9	3	7	2	1	—	—	—	—
1829	67	21	2	5	2	2	10	45	24	10	3	8	1	1	—	—	—	—
1830	72	23	3	5	5	2	8	48	26	11	2	9	1	1	—	—	—	—
1831	72	26	3	5	6	2	10	45	31	6	5	5	2	1	—	—	—	—
1832	82	26	3	5	3	2	13	55	29	12	4	10	1	1	—	—	—	—
1833	88	29	4	5	5	3	12	57	32	14	3	8	2	1	—	—	—	—
1834	102	27	3	5	5	2	12	74	44	15	5	10	1	1	—	—	—	—

	The Americas							Europe					Asia				Australia and Oceania	Africa
	Total	Total	Canada[2]	Cuba	Mexico	Brazil	Other countries	Total	United Kingdom	France	Germany[3]	Other countries	Total	China[4]	Japan[5]	Other countries	[6]	[6]
Year	Ee533	Ee534	Ee535	Ee536	Ee537	Ee538	Ee539	Ee540	Ee541	Ee542	Ee543	Ee544	Ee545	Ee546	Ee547	Ee548	Ee549	Ee550
	Million dollars	Million dollars	Million dollars	Million dollars	Million dollars	Million dollars	Million dollars	Million dollars	Million dollars	Million dollars	Million dollars	Million dollars	Million dollars	Million dollars	Million dollars	Million dollars	Million dollars	Million dollars
1835	115	30	3	5	9	2	11	83	52	19	4	8	1	2	—	—	—	1
1836	124	26	3	6	6	2	9	96	58	21	4	13	2	1	—	—	—	1
1837	111	24	3	6	4	2	9	86	52	19	4	11	1	1	—	—	—	—
1838	105	23	2	6	2	2	11	80	52	15	3	10	1	2	—	—	—	1
1839	112	24	4	6	3	2	9	86	57	18	3	8	1	2	—	—	—	1
1840	124	30	6	6	3	2	13	92	55	20	4	13	1	1	—	—	—	1
1841	112	30	6	6	2	3	13	80	47	18	5	10	2	1	—	—	—	1
1842	100	27	6	5	2	3	11	72	40	17	5	10	2	1	—	—	—	—
1843[7]	83	16	3	3	1	2	7	63	41	12	4	6	3	2	—	—	—	1
1844	106	28	6	5	2	3	12	76	49	13	4	10	2	2	—	—	—	1
1845	106	29	6	6	1	3	13	73	45	12	6	10	3	2	—	—	—	1
1846	110	31	7	5	2	3	14	76	46	14	5	11	2	1	—	—	—	1
1847	157	31	7	6	1	3	14	123	87	19	5	12	2	2	—	—	—	1
1848	138	35	8	7	4	3	13	99	67	15	4	13	3	2	—	—	—	1
1849	140	29	8	5	2	3	11	107	78	13	3	13	3	2	—	—	—	1
1850	144	30	10	5	2	3	10	109	71	18	5	15	3	2	—	—	—	2
1851	189	39	12	5	2	3	17	146	101	21	6	18	2	2	—	—	—	2
1852	167	34	10	6	2	3	13	124	81	19	6	18	3	3	—	—	—	6
1853	203	43	12	6	4	4	17	151	103	22	7	19	4	4	—	—	—	5
1854	237	60	24	8	3	4	21	170	117	25	9	19	2	1	—	—	—	5
1855	219	62	28	8	3	4	19	148	92	29	9	18	3	2	(Z)	—	—	6
1856	281	66	29	7	4	5	21	204	128	35	13	28	3	3	(Z)	(Z)	—	8
1857	294	64	24	9	4	5	22	218	135	32	15	36	4	4	(Z)	(Z)	—	8
1858	272	62	24	11	3	5	19	199	129	28	12	30	5	6	(Z)	(Z)	—	6
1859	293	70	28	12	3	6	21	210	133	30	15	32	6	7	(Z)	(Z)	—	7
1860	334	69	23	12	5	6	23	249	169	39	15	26	8	9	(Z)	(Z)	—	8
1861	220	61	23	10	2	5	21	147	108	15	11	13	6	7	(Z)	(Z)	—	6
1862	193	57	21	9[8]	2	4	21	127	86	20	10	11	3	5	(Z)	(Z)	—	6
1863	268	83	28	14[8]	9	5	27	173	128	14	14	17	5	6	(Z)	(Z)	—	7
1864	235	92	27	13[8]	9	5	40	138	97	13	13	15	4	9	(Z)	(Z)	—	1
1865	281	110	29	19	16	6	40	158	103	11	20	24	4	3	(Z)	1	7	2
1866	479	80	24	15	5	6	30	386	288	51	22	25	5	3	1	2	7	2
1867	398	77	21	14	5	5	32	307	225	34	22	26	5	4	1	—	6	3
1868	383	81	24	15	6	6	30	287	198	26	31	32	6	4	1	1	6	3
1869	382	74	23	12	5	6	28	291	185	33	38	35	7	5	1	1	6	3
1870	471	79	25	14	6	6	28	381	248	46	42	45	4	3	1	—	5	2
1871	493	89	32	15	8	6	28	394	273	27	35	59	3	2	1	1	4	3
1872	492	89	29	14	6	6	34	393	265	31	41	56	4	3	1	—	4	2
1873	594	102	33	16	6	7	40	479	317	34	62	66	5	1	1	3	5	3
1874	651	110	42	17	6	8	37	528	345	43	63	77	5	1	1	3	5	3
1875	574	100	35	15	6	8	36	459	317	34	50	58	7	1	2	4	5	3
1876	610	96	33	13	6	7	37	497	336	40	51	70	8	1	1	6	5	4
1877	645	99	37	13	6	8	35	525	346	45	58	76	10	2	1	7	8	3
1878	710	100	37	12	7	9	35	584	387	55	55	87	12	4	2	6	9	4
1879	712	91	30	13	7	8	33	594	349	90	57	98	12	3	3	6	10	5

Notes appear at end of table

(continued)

TABLE Ee533–550   Exports, by country of destination: 1790–2001   Continued

	Total	The Americas						Europe					Asia				Australia and Oceania	Africa
		Total	Canada [2]	Cuba	Mexico	Brazil	Other countries	Total	United Kingdom	France	Germany [3]	Other countries	Total	China [4]	Japan [5]	Other countries	[6]	[6]
Year	Ee533	Ee534	Ee535	Ee536	Ee537	Ee538	Ee539	Ee540	Ee541	Ee542	Ee543	Ee544	Ee545	Ee546	Ee547	Ee548	Ee549	Ee550
	Million dollars	Million dollars	Million dollars	Million dollars	Million dollars	Million dollars	Million dollars	Million dollars	Million dollars	Million dollars	Million dollars	Million dollars	Million dollars	Million dollars	Million dollars	Million dollars	Million dollars	Million dollars
1880	836	93	29	11	8	9	36	719	454	100	57	108	12	1	3	8	7	5
1881	902	108	38	11	11	9	39	766	481	94	70	121	13	5	1	7	10	5
1882	751	113	37	12	15	9	40	600	408	50	54	88	19	6	3	10	13	6
1883	824	129	44	15	17	9	44	660	425	59	66	110	17	4	3	10	14	4
1884	741	123	44	11	13	9	46	584	386	51	61	86	17	5	3	9	13	3
1885	742	104	38	9	8	7	42	599	398	47	62	92	21	6	3	12	14	4
1886	680	98	33	10	8	7	40	541	348	42	62	89	23	8	3	12	15	3
1887	716	104	35	11	8	8	42	575	366	57	59	93	20	6	3	11	14	3
1888	696	110	36	10	10	7	47	549	362	39	56	92	20	5	4	11	15	3
1889	742	125	41	12	11	9	52	579	383	46	68	82	19	6	5	8	16	4
1890	858	133	40	13	13	12	55	684	448	50	86	100	20	3	5	12	16	5
1891	884	131	38	12	15	14	52	705	445	61	93	106	26	9	5	12	18	5
1892	1,030	139	43	18	14	14	50	851	499	99	106	147	20	7	3	10	16	5
1893	848	152	47	24	20	12	49	662	421	47	84	110	17	4	3	10	11	5
1894	892	153	57	20	13	14	49	701	431	55	92	123	22	6	4	12	12	5
1895	808	143	53	13	15	15	47	628	387	45	92	104	18	4	5	9	13	6
1896	883	153	60	8	19	14	52	673	406	47	98	122	26	7	8	11	17	14
1897	1,051	159	65	8	23	12	51	813	483	58	125	147	39	12	13	14	23	17
1898	1,231	174	84	10	21	13	46	974	541	95	155	183	45	10	20	15	22	18
1899	1,227	194	88	19	25	12	50	937	512	61	156	208	49	14	17	18	29	19
1900	1,394	227	95	26	35	12	59	1,040	534	83	187	236	68	15	29	24	41	19
1901	1,488	241	106	26	36	12	61	1,137	631	79	192	235	53	10	19	24	31	26
1902	1,382	242	110	27	40	10	55	1,008	549	72	173	214	69	25	21	23	29	33
1903	1,420	256	123	22	42	11	58	1,029	524	77	194	234	62	19	21	22	33	38
1904	1,461	286	131	27	46	11	71	1,058	537	84	215	222	65	13	25	27	28	24
1905	1,519	318	141	38	46	11	82	1,021	523	76	194	228	135	53	52	30	27	19
1906	1,744	383	157	48	58	15	105	1,200	583	98	235	284	111	44	38	29	30	24
1907	1,881	432	183	49	66	19	115	1,298	608	114	257	319	101	26	39	36	33	17
1908	1,861	409	167	47	56	19	120	1,284	581	116	277	310	113	22	41	50	35	20
1909	1,663	387	163	44	50	18	112	1,147	515	109	235	288	83	19	27	37	30	17
1910	1,745	479	216	53	58	23	129	1,136	506	118	250	262	78	16	22	40	34	19
1911	2,049	566	270	61	61	27	147	1,308	577	135	287	309	105	19	37	49	46	24
1912	2,204	648	329	62	53	35	169	1,342	564	135	307	336	141	24	53	64	48	24
1913	2,466	763	415	71	54	43	180	1,479	597	146	332	404	140	21	58	61	54	29
1914	2,365	654	345	69	39	30	171	1,486	594	160	345	387	141	25	51	65	56	28
1915	2,769	576	301	76	34	26	139	1,971	912	369	29	661	139	16	41	82	53	29
1916	5,483	1,145	605	165	54	48	273	3,813	1,887	861	2	1,063	388	32	109	247	83	54
1917	6,234	1,573	829	196	111	66	371	4,062	2,009	941	(Z)	1,112	469	40	186	243	77	51
1918	6,149	1,628	887	227	98	57	359	3,859	2,061	931	—	867	498	53	274	171	105	59
1919	7,920	1,738	734	278	131	115	480	5,188	2,279	893	93	1,923	772	106	366	300	126	98
1920	8,228	2,553	972	515	208	157	701	4,466	1,825	676	311	1,654	872	146	378	348	172	166
1921	4,485	1,403	594	188	222	58	341	2,364	942	225	372	825	533	108	238	187	113	73
1922	3,832	1,142	577	128	110	43	284	2,083	856	267	316	644	449	100	222	127	102	56
1923	4,167	1,355	652	192	120	46	345	2,093	882	272	317	622	511	109	267	135	146	61
1924	4,591	1,404	624	200	135	65	380	2,445	983	282	440	740	515	109	253	153	157	70

		The Americas							Europe				Asia					
	Total	Total	Canada[2]	Cuba	Mexico	Brazil	Other countries	Total	United Kingdom	France	Germany[3]	Other countries	Total	China[4]	Japan[5]	Other countries	Australia and Oceania[6]	Africa[6]
Year	Ee533	Ee534	Ee535	Ee536	Ee537	Ee538	Ee539	Ee540	Ee541	Ee542	Ee543	Ee544	Ee545	Ee546	Ee547	Ee548	Ee549	Ee550
	Million dollars	Million dollars	Million dollars	Million dollars	Million dollars	Million dollars	Million dollars	Million dollars	Million dollars	Million dollars	Million dollars	Million dollars	Million dollars	Million dollars	Million dollars	Million dollars	Million dollars	Million dollars
1925	4,910	1,541	649	199	145	87	461	2,604	1,034	280	470	820	487	94	230	163	189	89
1926	4,809	1,620	739	160	135	95	491	2,310	973	264	364	709	565	110	261	194	213	101
1927	4,865	1,691	837	155	109	89	501	2,314	840	229	482	763	560	83	258	219	194	107
1928	5,128	1,802	915	128	116	100	543	2,375	847	241	467	820	655	138	288	229	180	117
1929	5,241	1,934	948	129	134	109	614	2,341	848	266	410	817	643	124	259	260	192	131
1930	3,843	1,357	659	94	116	54	434	1,838	678	224	278	658	448	90	165	193	108	92
1931	2,424	750	396	47	52	29	226	1,187	456	122	166	443	386	98	156	132	42	60
1932	1,611	462	241	29	32	29	131	784	288	112	134	250	292	56	135	101	37	36
1933	1,675	455	211	25	38	30	151	850	312	122	140	276	292	52	143	97	35	43
1934	2,133	648	302	45	55	40	206	950	383	116	109	342	401	69	210	122	57	77
1935	2,283	706	323	60	66	44	213	1,029	433	117	92	387	378	38	203	137	74	96
1936	2,456	821	384	67	76	49	245	1,043	440	129	102	372	399	47	204	148	79	114
1937	3,349	1,158	509	92	109	69	379	1,360	536	165	126	533	580	50	289	241	99	152
1938	3,094	1,040	468	76	62	62	372	1,326	521	134	107	564	517	35	240	242	94	118
1939	3,177	1,131	489	82	83	80	397	1,290	505	132	46	557	562	56	232	274	80	115
1940	4,021	1,501	713	85	97	111	495	1,645	1,011	252	(Z)	382	619	78	227	314	94	161
1941	5,147	2,047	994	126	159	148	620	1,847	1,637	2	(Z)	208	625	95	60	470	123	504
1942	8,079	2,205	1,334	133	148	105	485	4,009	2,529	1	—	1,479	688	80	—	608	361	816
1943	12,965	2,418	1,444	134	187	156	497	7,633	4,505	—	—	3,128	838	53	2	783	569	1,507
1944	14,259	2,627	1,441	167	264	218	537	9,364	5,243	18	(Z)	4,103	996	52	—	944	410	861
1945	9,806	2,564	1,178	196	307	219	664	5,515	2,193	472	2	2,848	849	108	1	740	354	524
1946	9,738	3,684	1,442	272	505	356	1,109	4,122	855	709	83	2,475	1,327	465	102	760	117	489
1947	14,430	6,183	2,114	492	630	643	2,304	5,269	1,103	817	128	3,221	1,835	353	60	1,422	320	821
1948	12,653	5,307	1,944	441	522	497	1,903	4,380	644	591	863	2,282	2,029	273	325	1,431	153	785
1949	12,051	4,861	1,959	380	468	383	1,671	4,239	700	497	822	2,220	2,135	83	468	1,584	195	622
1950	10,275	4,902	2,039	464	526	365	1,508	3,306	548	455	441	1,842	1,539	37	418	1,084	151	376
1951	15,032	6,607	2,693	548	730	739	1,897	5,121	1,000	843	523	2,755	2,410	(Z)	601	1,809	270	624
1952	15,201	6,682	3,003	525	683	597	1,874	5,089	787	1,013	450	2,839	2,541	—	633	1,908	267	621
1953	15,774	6,514	3,197	436	663	379	1,839	5,711	826	1,256	363	3,286	2,783	—	686	2,097	203	563
1954	15,110	6,520	2,966	439	649	507	1,959	5,118	808	783	505	3,022	2,577	6	693	1,878	264	630
1955	15,547	6,903	3,404	463	719	273	2,044	5,126	1,006	536	607	2,977	2,581	3	683	1,895	295	642
1956	19,090	8,243	4,149	528	860	326	2,380	6,434	982	829	943	3,680	3,417	—	998	2,419	265	731
1957	20,850	9,001	4,041	628	917	512	2,903	6,838	1,162	708	1,330	3,638	3,961	9	1,319	2,633	295	755
1958	17,910	7,999	3,539	553	904	567	2,436	5,566	905	570	887	3,204	3,411	5	987	2,419	282	652
1959	17,634	7,692	3,825	442	755	435	2,235	5,554	1,097	483	878	3,096	3,284	3	1,079	2,202	376	728
1960	20,575	7,684	3,810	225	831	464	2,354	7,398	1,487	699	1,272	3,940	4,186	—	1,447	2,739	514	793
1961	20,999	7,673	3,826	14	828	545	2,460	7,370	1,206	704	1,343	4,117	4,652	7	1,837	2,808	445	859
1962	21,700	7,724	4,045	13	821	449	2,396	7,758	1,128	735	1,581	4,314	4,676	23	1,574	3,079	519	1,023
1963	23,347	7,944	4,251	36	873	405	2,379	8,338	1,213	813	1,582	4,730	5,448	4	1,844	3,600	565	1,054
1964	26,508	9,207	4,915	(Z)	1,107	402	2,783	9,436	1,532	990	1,606	5,308	5,802	3	2,009	3,790	803	1,259
1965	27,470	9,908	5,642	(Z)	1,104	341	2,821	9,364	1,615	971	1,649	5,129	6,012	(Z)	2,080	3,932	956	1,229
1966	30,320	11,429	6,661	(Z)	1,180	575	3,013	10,003	1,737	1,007	1,674	5,585	6,733	(Z)	2,364	4,369	805	1,349
1967	31,526	11,883	7,165	(Z)	1,222	547	2,949	10,297	1,960	1,025	1,706	5,606	7,146	(Z)	2,695	4,451	1,017	1,182
1968	34,636	13,411	8,072	(Z)	1,378	705	3,257	11,347	2,289	1,095	1,709	6,254	7,582	(Z)	2,954	4,628	1,026	1,269
1969	38,006	14,713	9,137	(Z)	1,450	672	3,454	12,641	2,335	1,195	2,142	6,969	8,261	—	3,490	4,771	998	1,392

Notes appear at end of table

(continued)

TABLE Ee533–550   Exports, by country of destination: 1790–2001   Continued

	Total	The Americas						Europe					Asia				Australia and Oceania[6]	Africa[6]
		Total	Canada[2]	Cuba	Mexico	Brazil	Other countries	Total	United Kingdom	France	Germany[3]	Other countries	Total	China[4]	Japan[5]	Other countries		
Year	Ee533	Ee534	Ee535	Ee536	Ee537	Ee538	Ee539	Ee540	Ee541	Ee542	Ee543	Ee544	Ee545	Ee546	Ee547	Ee548	Ee549	Ee550
	Million dollars	Million dollars	Million dollars	Million dollars	Million dollars	Million dollars	Million dollars	Million dollars	Million dollars	Million dollars	Million dollars	Million dollars	Million dollars	Million dollars	Million dollars	Million dollars	Million dollars	Million dollars
1970	43,224	15,612	9,079	(Z)	1,704	840	3,989	14,817	2,536	1,483	2,741	8,057	10,027	—	4,652	5,375	1,189	1,580
1971	44,130	16,850	10,365	(Z)	1,620	966	3,899	14,562	2,369	1,373	2,831	7,989	9,588	—	4,055	5,533	1,168	1,694
1972	49,779	19,690	12,415	(Z)	1,982	1,243	4,050	16,180	2,658	1,609	2,808	9,105	11,297	—	4,963	6,334	1,034	1,577
1973	71,339	25,033	15,104	(Z)	2,937	1,916	5,076	23,161	3,564	2,263	3,756	13,578	18,416	—	8,313	10,106	1,744	2,306
1974	98,507	35,745	19,936	(Z)	4,855	3,088	7,866	30,070	4,574	2,942	4,985	17,569	25,785	—	10,697	15,088	2,697	3,659
1975	107,592	38,843	21,744	(Z)	5,141	3,056	8,902	32,732	4,527	3,031	5,194	19,980	28,223	—	9,563	18,660	2,340	4,949
1976	114,992	41,074	24,106	(Z)	4,990	2,809	9,169	35,900	4,801	3,446	5,731	21,922	29,729	—	10,145	19,584	2,690	5,206
1977	121,212	43,751	25,788	(Z)	4,822	2,490	10,651	37,304	5,951	3,503	5,989	21,861	31,436	—	10,529	20,907	2,877	5,546
1978	143,663	50,394	28,374	(Z)	6,680	2,981	12,359	43,608	7,116	4,166	6,957	25,369	39,630	—	12,885	26,745	3,464	5,887
1979	181,816	61,555	33,096	(Z)	9,847	3,442	15,170	60,026	10,635	5,587	8,478	35,326	48,771	—	17,581	31,190	4,319	6,299
1980	220,783	74,114	35,395	(Z)	15,145	4,343	19,231	71,371	12,694	7,485	10,960	40,232	60,168	—	20,790	39,378	4,876	9,060
1981	233,739	81,667	39,564	(Z)	17,789	3,798	20,516	69,715	12,439	7,341	10,277	39,658	63,849	—	21,823	42,026	6,436	11,448
1982	212,275	67,312	33,720	(Z)	11,817	3,423	18,352	63,664	10,645	7,110	9,291	36,618	64,822	—	20,966	43,856	5,700	10,271
1983	200,538	63,970	38,244	(Z)	9,082	2,557	14,087	58,871	10,621	5,961	8,787	33,552	63,813	—	21,894	41,919	4,827	8,768
1984	217,888	76,209	46,524	(Z)	11,992	2,640	15,053	59,207	12,210	6,037	9,084	31,876	64,533	—	23,575	40,958	5,745	8,827
1985	218,828	84,307	53,287	1	13,635	3,140	17,384	59,979	11,273	6,096	9,123	33,487	60,747	3,856	22,631	34,260	6,399	7,388
1986	227,159	86,591	55,512	2	12,392	3,885	18,685	63,632	11,418	7,216	10,628	34,370	64,534	3,106	26,882	34,546	6,658	5,978
1987	254,122	94,794	59,814	1	14,582	4,040	20,397	71,918	14,114	7,943	11,802	38,059	73,268	3,497	28,249	41,522	6,527	6,283
1988	322,426	115,484	71,622	3	20,628	4,266	23,231	91,507	18,364	9,970	14,457	48,716	99,570	5,021	37,725	56,824	8,242	7,398
1989	363,812	127,892	78,809	3	24,982	4,804	24,098	105,473	20,837	11,579	16,956	56,101	112,537	5,755	44,494	62,288	9,817	7,703
1990	393,592	137,605	83,674	1	28,279	5,048	25,651	117,271	23,049	13,664	18,760	61,798	120,271	4,806	48,580	66,885	9,969	7,956
1991	421,730	148,592	85,150	1	33,277	6,148	24,016	123,469	22,046	15,345	21,302	64,776	130,629	6,278	48,125	76,226	9,797	8,820
1992	448,164	166,395	90,594	1	40,592	5,751	29,457	122,617	22,800	14,593	21,249	63,975	138,262	7,418	47,813	83,031	10,682	9,907
1993	465,091	178,870	100,444	2	41,581	6,058	30,785	119,785	26,438	13,267	18,932	61,148	146,726	8,763	47,891	90,072	9,938	9,428
1994	512,627	206,994	114,439	5	50,844	8,102	33,604	123,479	26,900	13,619	19,229	63,731	160,995	9,282	53,488	98,225	11,687	9,219
1995	584,742	223,470	127,226	6	46,292	11,439	38,507	140,564	28,857	14,245	22,394	75,068	197,402	11,754	64,343	121,305	12,794	9,904
1996	625,075	243,567	134,210	6	56,792	12,718	39,841	148,810	30,963	14,456	23,495	79,896	207,328	11,993	67,607	127,728	14,087	10,615
1997	689,182	286,183	151,767	10	71,388	15,915	47,103	163,273	36,425	15,965	24,458	86,425	213,547	12,862	65,549	135,136	14,450	11,390
1998	682,138	298,781	156,603	4	78,773	15,142	48,258	170,008	39,058	17,729	26,657	86,564	187,566	14,241	57,831	115,494	14,216	11,167
1999	695,797	308,668	166,600	5	86,909	13,203	41,951	171,834	38,407	18,877	26,800	87,750	190,881	13,111	57,466	120,304	14,163	9,880
2000	781,918	349,576	178,941	7	111,349	15,321	43,958	187,448	41,570	20,362	29,448	96,068	218,796	16,185	64,924	137,687	14,825	10,966
2001	729,100	322,992	163,424	7	101,296	15,879	42,386	181,529	40,714	19,864	29,995	90,956	198,929	19,182	57,452	122,295	13,379	12,119

(Z) Less than $500,000.

1 For years ending September 30 (1790–1842) and June 30 (1843–1915), and for calendar years thereafter.
2 Series composition changes over time. See text.
3 Only West Germany, 1952–1990.
4 Through 1864, includes gold and silver.
5 Beginning with 1954, excludes Ryukyu Islands.
6 Through 1864, Australia and Oceania are included under series Ee550.
7 For nine months.
8 Includes Puerto Rico.

Sources

1790–1820, series Ee533, the sum of series Ee534, Ee540, Ee545, and Ee549–550; series Ee534–549, U.S. Department of the Treasury, Bureau of Statistics, *Statistical Tables Exhibiting the Commerce of the U.S. with European Countries, 1790–1890* (1893), pp. xiii, xiv, xviii, xix.

1821–1881, series Ee533, U.S. Statistics Bureau, *Monthly Summary of Commerce and Finance* (MSCF) (April 1898), p. 1632; series Ee535 1821–1872, MSCF (June 1898), p. 2091; 1873–1881, U.S. Department of Commerce and Labor, *Statistical Abstract of the United States* (1907), p. 317; series Ee536–538, MSCF (August 1901), pp. 618, 626–7, 632–3; series Ee540–544, MSCF (October 1896), pp. 718, 730–2, 745–6; series Ee545–548, MSCF (April 1898), pp. 1632, 1637, 1638 (except for China, 1865–1881, *Statistical Abstract of the United States* (1907), p. 350); series Ee549–550, 1821–1864, MSCF (June 1896), pp. 1612, 1621, 1622; 1865–1881, *Statistical Abstract of the United States* (1907), pp. 366, 376. (Data for series Ee534 and Ee539 were obtained as residuals for 1821–1881.)

1882–1946 and 1966–1970, the following editions of *Statistical Abstract of the United States*: 1882–1889, (1907), pp. 284, 288–369; 1890–1906, (1910), pp. 328–376; 1907–1915, (1916), pp. 347–81; 1916–1920, (1920), pp. 398–425; 1921–1923, (1926), pp. 452, 458–63; 1924–1928, (1930), pp. 482, 492–7; 1929–1932, (1934), pp. 418, 424–9; 1933–1936, (1938), pp. 456, 460–4; 1937–1940, (1943), pp. 530, 534–8; 1941–1945, (1948), pp. 922, 926–30; 1946, (1952), pp. 856, 858–60; 1966–1968, (1969), pp. 808–11; 1969–1970, (1972), pp. 778–81.

1947–1965, U.S. Bureau of the Census, *Foreign Commerce and Navigation of the United States* (1964, 1965).

1971–1990, U.S. International Trade Administration, *U.S. Foreign Trade Highlights, 1991* (August 1991), pp. 30–1.

1991–2001, available at the Internet site for the International Trade Administration.

Documentation

Imports are shown according to country of origin; exports according to ultimate destination. When the final destination is not known, the shipment is credited statistically to the country to which it is consigned. Accurate information on country of origin is difficult to obtain; consequently, the directional breakdown of foreign trade is at best approximate.

Trade with Canada and the United Kingdom is especially difficult to measure. Considerable U.S. merchandise normally moves to foreign destinations via Canada and some moves across Canada to destinations in the United States, notably from ports in Michigan to ports in New York. At times, such movements have been counted as trade with Canada. Also, considerable Canadian trade with other countries moves through the United States. A good deal of U.S. merchandise has been consigned to the United Kingdom and reexported to other markets by the United Kingdom, as can be observed by the difference between general imports and retained imports in the United Kingdom's record of trade with the United States.

Special studies of U.S.–Canadian trade have been made from time to time. In this connection, see U.S. Bureau of Foreign and Domestic Commerce, *Commerce Yearbook* (1931), volume 2, the headnote on p. 295, as well as *MSCF* (June and July 1898), pp. 2084–9, and p. 2075, where it is also noted that "exports to Canada are incomplete prior to April 1, 1893, the date on which the law requiring exporters to clear their goods exported by railways went into effect." For an effort at adjusting the U.S. trade record for this deficiency and the similar lack of coverage in the report of trade with Mexico, see Tables 2 and 3 of Matthew Simon's "The United States Balance of Payments, 1861–1900," in *Trends in the American Economy in the Nineteenth Century: A Report of the National Bureau of Economic Research, Studies in Income and Wealth,* volume 24 (Princeton University Press, 1960). For a discussion of shortcomings in the U.S. record of trade with the United Kingdom in the early years of the Civil War, see the Treasury's report in 1864 to Congress, *Statistics of the Foreign and Domestic Commerce of the United States,* pp. 37 ff.

For certain periods, such as the Civil War and the greenback era, partners' records of trade with the United States are more reliable than the U.S. record and in some ways more revealing of certain aspects of the trade.

For 1862–1879, exports of domestic merchandise are mixed gold and currency values. Imports and reexports, however, are specie values.

Asia includes the Philippines in all years and the portion of Turkey in Europe for 1926–1951. Oceania includes Hawai'i prior to 1901. Europe includes the portion of the Soviet Republic in Asia since 1923 and Iceland in all years.

Series Ee535 and Ee553. Prior to 1873, trade figures for Canada are actually trade figures for all of the British North American Provinces, a somewhat larger area than the Dominion of Canada. In the year ending June 30, 1873, the United States traded with the British North American Provinces in the following amounts: exports, $34.6 million; imports, $37.6 million. The figures include Newfoundland and Labrador beginning with 1950 for series Ee535, and 1947 for series Ee553. Since 1990, U.S exports to Canada are derived from import data compiled by Canada.

TABLE Ee551–568   Imports, by country of origin: 1790–2001[1]
Contributed by Douglas A. Irwin

Year	Total	The Americas						Europe					Asia				Australia and Oceania	Africa
	Ee551[2]	Total Ee552	Canada Ee553[3]	Cuba Ee554	Mexico Ee555	Brazil Ee556	Other countries Ee557	Total Ee558	United Kingdom Ee559	France Ee560	Germany Ee561[4]	Other countries Ee562	Total Ee563	China Ee564[5]	Japan Ee565[6]	Other countries Ee566	Ee567[7]	Ee568[7]
	Million dollars	Million dollars	Million dollars	Million dollars	Million dollars	Million dollars	Million dollars	Million dollars	Million dollars	Million dollars	Million dollars	Million dollars	Million dollars	Million dollars	Million dollars	Million dollars	Million dollars	Million dollars
1790	23	—	—	—	—	—	—	—	—	—	—	—	—	—	—	—	—	—
1791	29	—	—	—	—	—	—	—	—	—	—	—	—	—	—	—	—	—
1792	32	—	—	—	—	—	—	—	—	—	—	—	—	—	—	—	—	—
1793	31	—	—	—	—	—	—	—	—	—	—	—	—	—	—	—	—	—
1794	35	—	—	—	—	—	—	—	—	—	—	—	—	—	—	—	—	—
1795	70	—	—	—	—	—	—	—	—	—	—	—	—	—	—	—	—	—
1796	81	—	—	—	—	—	—	—	—	—	—	—	—	—	—	—	—	—
1797	75	—	—	—	—	—	—	—	—	—	—	—	—	—	—	—	—	—
1798	69	—	—	—	—	—	—	—	—	—	—	—	—	—	—	—	—	—
1799	79	—	—	—	—	—	—	—	—	—	—	—	—	—	—	—	—	—
1800	91	—	—	—	—	—	—	—	—	—	—	—	—	—	—	—	—	—
1801	111	—	—	—	—	—	—	—	—	—	—	—	—	—	—	—	—	—
1802	76	—	—	—	—	—	—	—	—	—	—	—	—	—	—	—	—	—
1803	65	—	—	—	—	—	—	—	—	—	—	—	—	—	—	—	—	—
1804	85	—	—	—	—	—	—	—	—	—	—	—	—	—	—	—	—	—
1805	121	—	—	—	—	—	—	—	—	—	—	—	—	—	—	—	—	—
1806	129	—	—	—	—	—	—	—	—	—	—	—	—	—	—	—	—	—
1807	139	—	—	—	—	—	—	—	—	—	—	—	—	—	—	—	—	—
1808	57	—	—	—	—	—	—	—	—	—	—	—	—	—	—	—	—	—
1809	59	—	—	—	—	—	—	—	—	—	—	—	—	—	—	—	—	—
1810	85	—	—	—	—	—	—	—	—	—	—	—	—	—	—	—	—	—
1811	53	—	—	—	—	—	—	—	—	—	—	—	—	—	—	—	—	—
1812	77	—	—	—	—	—	—	—	—	—	—	—	—	—	—	—	—	—
1813	22	—	—	—	—	—	—	—	—	—	—	—	—	—	—	—	—	—
1814	13	—	—	—	—	—	—	—	—	—	—	—	—	—	—	—	—	—
1815	113	—	—	—	—	—	—	—	—	—	—	—	—	—	—	—	—	—
1816	147	—	—	—	—	—	—	—	—	—	—	—	—	—	—	—	—	—
1817	99	—	—	—	—	—	—	—	—	—	—	—	—	—	—	—	—	—
1818	122	—	—	—	—	—	—	—	—	—	—	—	—	—	—	—	—	—
1819	87	—	—	—	—	—	—	—	—	—	—	—	—	—	—	—	—	—
1820	74	—	—	—	—	—	—	—	—	—	—	—	—	—	—	—	—	—
1821	55	15	(Z)	5	—	1	9	35	24	4	1	6	5	3	—	—	—	(Z)
1822	80	19	(Z)	7	—	1	11	51	35	6	2	8	9	5	—	—	—	1
1823	72	18	(Z)	7	—	1	10	43	28	6	2	7	11	7	—	—	—	(Z)
1824	72	22	(Z)	7	1	2	13	44	28	7	2	7	6	6	—	—	—	(Z)
1825	90	21	(Z)	7	1	2	11	59	37	11	3	8	10	8	—	—	—	(Z)
1826	78	20	(Z)	7	1	2	10	46	26	8	3	9	11	7	—	—	—	1
1827	71	19	(Z)	7	1	2	9	48	30	8	2	8	4	4	—	—	—	(Z)
1828	81	20	(Z)	6	1	3	10	54	33	9	3	9	7	5	—	—	—	(Z)
1829	67	17	(Z)	5	1	2	9	44	25	9	2	8	6	5	—	—	—	(Z)

Year	Total Ee551 [2]	The Americas Total Ee552	Canada Ee553 [3]	Cuba Ee554	Mexico Ee555	Brazil Ee556	Other countries Ee557	Europe Total Ee558	United Kingdom Ee559	France Ee560	Germany Ee561 [4]	Other countries Ee562	Asia Total Ee563	China Ee564 [5]	Japan Ee565 [6]	Other countries Ee566	Australia and Oceania Ee567 [7]	Africa Ee568 [7]
	Million dollars	Million dollars	Million dollars	Million dollars	Million dollars	Million dollars	Million dollars	Million dollars	Million dollars	Million dollars	Million dollars	Million dollars	Million dollars	Million dollars	Million dollars	Million dollars	Million dollars	Million dollars
1830	63	17	(Z)	5	1	2	9	40	24	8	2	6	5	4	—	—	—	1
1831	96	22	1	8	1	2	10	68	44	14	4	6	5	3	—	—	—	1
1832	95	22	1	7	1	4	9	63	37	12	3	11	9	5	—	—	—	1
1833	101	27	1	10	1	5	10	63	38	13	2	10	11	8	—	—	—	(Z)
1834	109	26	1	8	1	5	11	71	41	15	3	12	11	8	—	—	—	1
1835	137	28	1	11	1	6	9	99	60	22	4	13	9	6	—	—	—	1
1836	177	35	2	13	1	7	12	128	76	32	5	15	13	7	—	—	—	1
1837	130	23	2	11	1	5	9	86	45	21	6	14	14	9	—	—	—	2
1838	96	26	1	11	1	3	10	62	36	16	3	7	7	5	—	—	—	1
1839	156	35	2	12	1	5	15	114	65	32	5	12	6	4	—	—	—	1
1840	98	25	1	9	1	5	9	62	33	15	3	10	10	7	—	—	—	1
1841	123	33	1	11	1	6	14	83	46	24	2	11	7	4	—	—	—	(Z)
1842	96	26	(Z)	7	1	6	11	61	34	17	2	8	9	5	—	—	—	(Z)
1843 [8]	42	16	(Z)	4	1	4	7	20	12	5	1	2	6	4	—	—	—	1
1844	103	28	1	10	1	7	9	67	41	17	2	7	8	5	—	—	—	(Z)
1845	113	25	1	6	1	6	11	78	45	21	3	9	10	7	—	—	—	(Z)
1846	118	27	1	8	1	7	10	80	45	24	3	8	10	7	—	—	—	1
1847	122	30	1	12	(Z)	7	10	83	48	24	4	7	8	6	—	—	—	1
1848	149	33	3	12	1	8	9	103	60	25	6	9	12	8	—	—	—	1
1849	141	31	2	10	1	8	10	100	58	24	8	10	9	6	—	—	—	1
1850	174	38	5	10	1	9	13	124	75	27	9	13	11	7	—	—	—	1
1851	211	49	5	17	1	12	14	148	93	31	10	14	12	7	—	—	—	2
1852	207	54	5	18	1	12	18	134	89	25	8	12	18	11	—	—	—	1
1853	264	55	7	19	1	15	13	190	130	35	14	13	17	11	—	—	—	2
1854	298	72	9	17	1	14	31	204	146	36	17	5	20	11	—	—	—	2
1855	258	70	15	18	1	15	21	165	106	32	13	14	21	11	(Z)	10	—	2
1856	310	86	21	24	1	19	21	199	122	45	15	13	23	10	(Z)	13	—	2
1857	348	116	22	45	1	21	27	205	127	46	15	17	25	8	(Z)	17	—	2
1858	263	79	16	23	2	17	22	153	89	33	14	17	28	11	(Z)	17	—	3
1859	331	102	19	33	2	22	27	201	126	41	18	16	25	11	(Z)	14	—	3
1860	354	104	24	32	2	21	25	217	138	43	19	17	29	14	(Z)	15	—	4
1861	289	94	23	31	2	18	21	166	105	32	15	14	26	11	(Z)	15	—	3
1862	189	69	19	21	1	13	15	105	75	8	14	8	13	7	(Z)	6	—	2
1863	243	71	17	21	3	11	19	148	113	11	13	11	20	11	(Z)	9	—	4
1864	316	112	30	33	6	14	29	179	142	11	14	12	19	10	(Z)	9	—	6
1865	239 [9]	100	33	30	6	10	21	109	85	7	10	7	13	5	(Z)	8	1	3
1866	435 [9]	132	49	38	2	17	26	266	202	23	26	15	23	10	2	11	4	3
1867	396	111	25	38	1	19	28	245	172	29	27	17	30	12	3	15	7	3
1868	357	130	26	50	2	24	28	196	132	25	22	17	28	11	2	15	1	2
1869	418	147	29	57	2	25	34	235	159	30	25	21	31	13	3	15	2	3
1870	436	153	36	54	3	25	35	241	152	43	27	19	37	15	3	19	2	3
1871	520	170	33	58	3	31	45	297	221	28	25	23	48	20	5	23	1	4
1872	627	191	36	67	4	30	54	365	249	43	46	27	60	27	7	26	5	6
1873	642	204	37	77	4	39	47	361	237	34	61	29	66	26	8	33	5	6
1874	567	209	34	85	4	44	42	302	180	52	44	26	50	18	6	26	3	3

Notes appear at end of table

(continued)

TABLE Ee551–568 Imports, by country of origin: 1790–2001 *Continued*

Year	Total Ee551 [2]	The Americas Total Ee552	Canada Ee553 [3]	Cuba Ee554	Mexico Ee555	Brazil Ee556	Other countries Ee557	Europe Total Ee558	United Kingdom Ee559	France Ee560	Germany Ee561 [4]	Other countries Ee562	Asia Total Ee563	China Ee564 [5]	Japan Ee565 [6]	Other countries Ee566	Australia and Oceania Ee567 [7]	Africa Ee568 [7]
	Million dollars	Million dollars	Million dollars	Million dollars	Million dollars	Million dollars	Million dollars	Million dollars	Million dollars	Million dollars	Million dollars	Million dollars	Million dollars	Million dollars	Million dollars	Million dollars	Million dollars	Million dollars
1875	533	191	28	65	5	42	51	281	155	60	40	26	52	13	8	31	5	3
1876	461	170	29	56	5	45	35	232	123	51	35	23	53	12	15	26	3	2
1877	451	182	24	66	5	43	44	214	114	48	33	19	49	11	14	24	4	2
1878	437	176	25	60	5	43	43	204	107	43	35	19	51	16	7	28	4	2
1879	446	172	26	64	5	39	38	216	109	51	36	20	52	16	10	26	4	2
1880	668	212	33	65	7	52	55	371	211	69	52	39	74	22	15	37	7	4
1881	643	215	38	63	8	53	53	341	174	70	53	44	74	22	14	38	8	5
1882	725	238	51	70	8	49	60	398	196	89	56	57	73	20	14	39	12	5
1883	723	222	44	66	8	44	60	410	189	98	57	66	73	20	15	38	13	5
1884	668	212	38	57	9	50	58	371	163	71	65	72	68	16	11	41	13	4
1885	578	183	37	42	9	45	50	319	137	57	63	62	61	16	12	33	12	3
1886	635	191	37	51	11	42	50	358	154	63	69	72	69	19	15	35	14	3
1887	692	211	38	50	15	53	55	391	165	68	81	77	72	19	17	36	15	4
1888	724	224	43	49	17	54	61	407	178	71	78	80	73	17	19	37	16	3
1889	745	243	43	52	21	60	67	403	178	70	82	73	76	17	17	42	19	4
1890	789	238	39	54	23	59	63	450	186	78	99	87	81	16	21	44	17	3
1891	845	282	39	62	27	83	71	459	195	77	97	90	79	19	19	41	20	4
1892	827	325	35	78	28	119	65	392	156	69	83	84	89	20	24	45	17	5
1893	866	286	38	79	34	76	59	458	183	76	96	103	99	21	27	51	17	6
1894	655	267	31	76	29	79	52	295	107	48	69	71	75	17	19	39	14	3
1895	732	246	37	53	16	79	61	384	159	62	81	82	84	21	24	39	13	6
1896	780	236	41	40	17	71	67	419	170	66	94	89	95	22	26	47	20	11
1897	765	213	40	18	19	69	67	430	168	68	111	83	92	20	24	48	20	10
1898	616	183	32	15	19	62	55	306	109	53	70	74	96	20	25	51	23	7
1899	697	199	31	25	23	58	62	354	118	62	84	90	112	19	27	66	23	10
1900	850	224	39	31	29	58	67	441	160	73	97	111	146	27	33	86	29	11
1901	823	255	42	43	29	71	70	430	143	75	100	112	122	18	29	75	7	9
1902	903	271	48	35	40	79	69	475	166	83	102	124	136	21	38	77	8	13
1903	1,026	297	55	63	41	67	71	547	190	90	120	147	159	27	44	88	10	13
1904	991	319	52	77	44	76	70	499	166	81	109	143	156	29	47	80	8	9
1905	1,118	378	62	86	46	100	84	541	176	90	118	157	175	28	52	95	13	11
1906	1,227	375	68	85	51	80	91	633	210	108	135	180	192	29	53	110	12	13
1907	1,434	424	73	97	57	98	99	747	246	128	162	211	224	33	69	122	18	21
1908	1,194	364	75	83	47	75	84	608	190	102	143	173	191	26	68	97	15	16
1909	1,312	418	79	97	48	98	96	654	209	108	144	193	207	29	70	108	18	15
1910	1,557	503	95	123	59	108	118	806	271	132	169	234	210	30	66	114	20	17
1911	1,527	488	101	110	57	101	119	768	261	115	163	229	231	34	79	118	13	27
1912	1,653	549	109	120	66	124	130	820	273	125	171	251	249	30	81	138	13	23
1913	1,813	580	121	126	78	120	135	893	296	137	189	271	298	39	92	167	17	26
1914	1,894	650	161	131	93	101	164	896	294	141	190	271	305	39	107	159	24	19
1915	1,674	734	160	186	78	99	211	614	256	77	91	190	272	40	99	133	29	25
1916	2,392	1,086	237	244	105	132	368	633	305	109	6	213	551	80	182	289	60	62
1917	2,952	1,471	414	249	130	145	533	551	280	99	(Z)	172	821	125	254	442	37	73
1918	3,031	1,585	452	279	159	98	597	318	149	60	(Z)	109	939	111	302	526	103	86
1919	3,904	1,844	495	419	149	234	547	751	309	124	11	307	1,108	154	410	544	89	112

	Total	The Americas						Europe					Asia				Australia and Oceania	Africa
		Total	Canada	Cuba	Mexico	Brazil	Other countries	Total	United Kingdom	France	Germany	Other countries	Total	China	Japan	Other countries		
	Ee551 [2]	Ee552	Ee553 [3]	Ee554	Ee555	Ee556	Ee557	Ee558	Ee559	Ee560	Ee561 [4]	Ee562	Ee563	Ee564 [5]	Ee565 [6]	Ee566	Ee567 [7]	Ee568 [7]
Year	Million dollars	Million dollars	Million dollars	Million dollars	Million dollars	Million dollars	Million dollars	Million dollars	Million dollars	Million dollars	Million dollars	Million dollars	Million dollars	Million dollars	Million dollars	Million dollars	Million dollars	Million dollars
1920	5,278	2,424	612	722	179	228	683	1,228	514	166	89	459	1,397	193	415	789	80	150
1921	2,509	1,051	335	230	119	96	271	765	239	142	80	304	618	101	251	266	35	40
1922	3,113	1,181	364	268	132	120	297	991	357	143	117	374	827	135	354	338	49	65
1923	3,792	1,469	416	376	140	143	394	1,157	404	150	161	442	1,020	188	347	485	59	87
1924	3,610	1,461	399	362	167	179	354	1,096	366	148	139	443	931	118	340	473	49	73
1925	4,227	1,499	454	262	179	222	382	1,239	413	157	164	505	1,319	169	384	766	78	92
1926	4,431	1,580	476	251	169	235	449	1,278	383	152	198	545	1,409	143	401	865	68	96
1927	4,185	1,504	475	257	138	203	431	1,265	358	168	201	538	1,268	152	402	714	55	93
1928	4,091	1,530	489	203	125	221	492	1,249	349	159	222	519	1,169	140	384	645	53	90
1929	4,399	1,621	503	207	118	208	585	1,334	330	171	255	578	1,279	166	432	681	57	109
1930	3,061	1,195	402	122	80	131	460	911	210	114	177	410	854	101	279	474	33	68
1931	2,091	824	266	90	48	110	310	641	135	79	127	300	574	67	206	301	19	33
1932	1,323	539	174	58	37	82	188	390	75	45	74	196	362	26	134	202	8	24
1933	1,450	520	185	58	31	83	163	463	111	50	78	224	425	38	128	259	13	28
1934	1,655	628	232	79	36	91	190	490	115	61	69	245	489	44	119	326	15	33
1935	2,047	776	286	104	42	100	244	599	155	58	78	308	605	64	153	388	26	42
1936	2,423	910	376	127	49	102	256	718	200	65	80	373	708	74	172	462	36	51
1937	3,084	1,113	398	148	60	121	386	843	203	76	92	472	967	104	204	659	68	92
1938	1,960	753	260	106	49	98	240	567	118	54	65	330	570	47	127	396	16	55
1939	2,318	898	340	105	56	107	290	617	149	62	52	354	700	62	161	477	27	77
1940	2,625	1,089	424	105	76	105	379	390	155	37	5	193	981	93	158	730	35	131
1941	3,345	1,657	554	181	98	184	640	281	136	5	3	137	1,088	87	78	923	159	161
1942	2,756	1,762	717	161	124	165	595	220	134	1	(Z)	85	340	16	(Z)	324	231	204
1943	3,381	2,458	1,024	292	192	228	722	240	105	(Z)	(Z)	135	235	12	(Z)	223	245	204
1944	3,929	2,965	1,260	387	204	293	821	289	84	(Z)	(Z)	205	322	11	(Z)	311	130	222
1945	4,159	2,874	1,125	337	231	311	870	409	90	13	1	305	407	6	(Z)	401	171	297
1946	4,942	2,762	883	324	232	408	915	804	158	63	3	580	887	93	81	713	183	306
1947	5,756	3,398	1,127	510	247	446	1,068	877	205	47	6	619	998	117	35	846	156	327
1948	7,124	4,099	1,593	375	246	514	1,371	1,171	290	73	32	776	1,296	120	63	1,113	164	394
1949	6,622	3,995	1,551	388	243	552	1,261	981	228	51	45	647	1,184	106	82	996	125	338
1950	8,852	5,063	1,960	406	315	715	1,667	1,449	335	132	104	878	1,638	146	182	1,310	208	494
1951	10,967	5,826	2,275	418	326	911	1,896	2,119	466	253	233	1,157	1,983	45	205	1,733	451	589
1952	10,717	6,025	2,386	440	410	808	1,981	2,029	485	157	212	1,165	1,813	28	229	1,556	243	607
1953	10,873	6,117	2,462	431	355	768	2,101	2,335	546	136	277	1,326	1,626	1	262	1,363	201	593
1954	10,215	5,896	2,377	401	328	682	2,108	2,083	501	157	278	1,147	1,467	(Z)	279	1,188	165	605
1955	11,384	6,262	2,653	422	397	633	2,157	2,453	616	202	366	1,269	1,876	(Z)	432	1,444	174	619
1956	12,615	6,856	2,894	457	401	745	2,359	2,963	726	236	494	1,507	1,996	(Z)	558	1,438	203	597
1957	12,982	7,048	2,907	482	430	700	2,529	3,147	766	256	607	1,518	1,985	(Z)	601	1,384	216	587
1958	12,792	6,703	2,674	524	454	565	2,486	3,340	864	308	629	1,539	1,983	(Z)	666	1,317	208	557
1959	15,207	7,071	3,042	475	435	628	2,491	4,607	1,137	462	920	2,088	2,603	(Z)	1,029	1,574	338	589
1960	14,654	6,864	2,901	357	443	570	2,593	4,268	993	396	897	1,982	2,721	(Z)	1,149	1,572	266	534
1961	14,714	6,995	3,270	35	538	562	2,590	4,141	898	455	856	1,952	2,583	(Z)	1,055	1,528	320	672
1962	16,380	7,591	3,660	7	578	541	2,805	4,621	1,005	428	962	2,226	2,960	(Z)	1,358	1,602	440	754
1963	17,138	7,850	3,829	(Z)	594	562	2,865	4,811	1,079	431	1,003	2,298	3,192	(Z)	1,498	1,694	502	777
1964	18,684	8,390	4,239	(Z)	643	535	2,973	5,307	1,143	455	1,171	2,498	3,620	(Z)	1,768	1,852	440	917

Notes appear at end of table

(continued)

TABLE Ee551–568   Imports, by country of origin: 1790–2001   *Continued*

	Total	The Americas						Europe					Asia				Australia and Oceania [7]	Africa [7]
		Total	Canada [3]	Cuba	Mexico	Brazil	Other countries	Total	United Kingdom	France	Germany [4]	Other countries	Total	China [5]	Japan [6]	Other countries		
	Ee551 [2]	Ee552	Ee553	Ee554	Ee555	Ee556	Ee557	Ee558	Ee559	Ee560	Ee561	Ee562	Ee563	Ee564	Ee565	Ee566	Ee567	Ee568
Year	Million dollars	Million dollars	Million dollars	Million dollars	Million dollars	Million dollars	Million dollars	Million dollars	Million dollars	Million dollars	Million dollars	Million dollars	Million dollars	Million dollars	Million dollars	Million dollars	Million dollars	Million dollars
1965	21,364	9,203	4,833	(Z)	638	512	3,220	6,292	1,405	615	1,341	2,931	4,528	(Z)	2,414	2,114	453	878
1966	25,542	10,829	6,125	(Z)	750	600	3,354	7,857	1,786	698	1,796	3,577	5,276	(Z)	2,963	2,313	593	979
1967	26,812	11,741	7,107	(Z)	749	559	3,326	8,227	1,710	690	1,955	3,872	5,348	(Z)	2,999	2,349	581	906
1968	33,226	14,148	9,005	(Z)	910	670	3,563	10,337	2,058	842	2,721	4,716	6,911	(Z)	4,054	2,857	696	1,122
1969	36,043	15,547	10,384	(Z)	1,029	617	3,517	10,334	2,120	842	2,603	4,769	8,274	(Z)	4,888	3,386	828	1,046
1970	39,952	16,928	11,092	(Z)	1,219	670	3,947	11,395	2,194	942	3,127	5,132	9,621	(Z)	5,875	3,746	871	1,113
1971	45,563	18,730	12,692	(Z)	1,262	762	4,014	12,881	2,499	1,088	3,651	5,643	11,780	—	7,259	4,521	895	1,236
1972	55,563	21,911	14,907	(Z)	1,632	942	4,430	15,744	2,987	1,369	4,250	7,138	15,117	—	9,064	6,053	1,145	1,595
1973	69,476	27,322	17,715	(Z)	2,306	1,189	6,112	19,812	3,657	1,732	5,345	9,078	18,157	—	9,676	8,481	1,562	2,583
1974	100,997	40,710	22,286	(Z)	3,386	1,705	13,333	24,625	4,023	2,305	6,429	11,868	27,522	—	12,456	15,066	1,505	6,621
1975	96,902	38,209	22,151	(Z)	3,066	1,467	11,525	20,892	3,773	2,164	5,410	10,276	27,252	—	11,425	15,827	1,508	8,299
1976	120,678	43,356	26,237	(Z)	3,598	1,737	11,784	22,789	4,254	2,509	5,592	11,290	39,367	—	15,504	23,863	1,671	12,644
1977	147,671	50,697	29,599	(Z)	4,694	2,241	14,163	27,669	5,141	3,032	7,238	13,390	49,312	—	18,550	30,762	1,728	17,121
1978	171,978	56,473	33,525	(Z)	6,094	2,826	14,028	36,483	6,514	4,051	9,962	17,458	58,264	—	24,458	33,806	2,350	16,898
1979	206,256	68,509	38,046	(Z)	8,800	3,118	18,545	41,681	8,028	4,768	10,955	19,796	66,739	—	26,248	40,491	3,072	24,382
1980	244,871	78,489	41,459	(Z)	12,519	3,715	15,841	46,602	9,842	5,265	11,693	21,235	80,299	—	30,714	49,585	3,392	34,410
1981	261,305	85,436	46,414	(Z)	13,765	4,475	20,719	51,855	12,835	5,851	11,379	23,345	92,033	—	37,612	54,421	3,353	27,071
1982	243,952	84,436	46,477	(Z)	15,566	4,285	12,455	52,346	13,095	5,545	11,975	22,798	85,170	—	37,744	47,426	3,131	17,770
1983	258,048	93,873	52,130	(Z)	16,776	4,946	5,673	53,884	12,470	6,025	12,695	24,053	91,464	—	41,183	50,281	3,044	14,250
1984	325,726	114,373	66,478	(Z)	18,020	7,621	19,726	71,153	14,492	8,113	16,996	32,985	120,132	—	57,135	62,997	3,558	14,355
1985	336,536	115,915	69,006	0	19,132	7,526	20,251	81,693	14,937	9,482	20,331	36,943	131,884	3,862	68,783	59,239	3,819	11,964
1986	365,438	110,202	68,253	0	17,302	6,813	17,834	91,825	15,396	10,129	25,210	41,090	153,869	4,771	81,911	67,187	3,717	10,348
1987	406,241	117,954	71,085	0	20,271	7,865	18,733	97,420	17,341	10,730	27,155	42,194	174,453	6,293	84,575	83,585	4,137	11,939
1988	440,952	132,540	81,398	0	23,260	9,294	18,588	102,605	17,976	12,508	26,472	45,649	190,166	8,511	89,519	92,136	4,826	10,815
1989	473,211	145,285	87,953	0	27,162	8,410	21,760	103,827	18,319	13,014	24,971	47,523	204,683	11,990	93,553	99,140	5,258	14,157
1990	495,311	155,234	91,380	0	30,157	7,898	25,799	111,221	20,188	13,153	28,162	49,718	207,304	15,237	89,684	102,383	5,760	15,775
1991	488,453	153,521	91,064	0	31,130	6,717	24,610	104,062	18,413	13,333	26,137	46,179	210,207	18,969	91,511	99,727	5,337	14,002
1992	532,665	167,385	98,630	0	35,211	7,609	25,935	112,707	20,093	14,797	28,820	48,997	233,130	25,728	97,414	109,988	5,097	14,346
1993	580,659	185,603	111,216	0	39,917	7,479	26,991	119,082	21,730	15,279	28,562	53,511	256,424	31,540	107,246	117,638	4,752	14,798
1994	663,256	216,371	128,406	0	49,494	8,683	29,788	136,562	25,058	16,699	31,744	63,061	291,318	38,787	119,156	133,375	4,914	14,091
1995	743,445	248,930	144,370	0	62,101	8,833	33,626	152,376	26,930	17,209	36,844	71,393	321,647	45,543	123,479	152,625	5,085	15,481
1996	795,289	279,721	155,893	0	74,297	8,773	40,758	164,587	28,979	18,646	38,945	78,017	326,611	51,513	115,187	159,911	5,601	18,744
1997	870,671	279,721	168,201	0	85,938	9,626	44,080	181,440	32,659	20,636	43,122	85,023	354,997	62,558	121,663	170,776	6,465	19,925
1998	911,896	318,163	173,256	0	94,629	10,102	40,176	202,874	34,838	24,016	49,842	94,178	367,661	71,169	121,845	174,647	7,373	15,825
1999	1,024,618	366,915	198,711	1	109,721	11,314	47,168	224,790	39,237	25,709	55,228	104,616	408,542	81,788	130,864	195,890	7,381	16,991
2000	1,218,022	440,136	230,838	0	135,926	13,853	59,519	256,756	43,345	29,800	58,513	125,098	484,650	100,018	146,479	238,153	8,831	27,642
2001	1,140,999	415,008	216,268	0	131,338	14,466	52,936	253,767	41,369	30,408	59,077	122,913	437,749	102,278	126,473	208,998	9,034	25,436

TABLE Ee551–568   Imports, by country of origin: 1790–2001   *Continued*

(Z) Less than $500,000.

[1] For years ending September 30 (1790–1842) and June 30 (1843–1915), and for calendar years thereafter.

[2] Beginning with 1962, includes data on imports from countries that could not be identified because of illegible reporting on import entries for low-valued shipments not included in the detail figures.

[3] Series composition changes over time. See text.

[4] Only West Germany, 1952–1990.

[5] Through 1865, includes gold and silver.

[6] Beginning with 1954, excludes Ryukyu Islands.

[7] Through 1864, Australia and Oceania are included under series Ee568.

[8] For nine months.

[9] Agrees with source; however, figures for components do not add to total shown.

Sources

1790–1820, series Ee551, the sum of series Ee552, Ee558, Ee563, and Ee567–568; series Ee552–567, U.S. Department of the Treasury, Bureau of Statistics, *Statistical Tables Exhibiting the Commerce of the U.S. with European Countries, 1790–1890* (1893), pp. xiii, xiv, xviii, xix.

1821–1881, series Ee551, U.S. Statistics Bureau, *Monthly Summary of Commerce and Finance (MSCF)* (April 1898), p. 1632; series Ee553 1821–1872, *MSCF* (June 1898), p. 2091; 1873–1881, U.S. Department of Commerce and Labor, *Statistical Abstract of the United States* (1907), p. 317; series Ee554–556, *MSCF* (August 1901), pp. 618, 626–7, 632–3; series Ee558–562, *MSCF* (October 1896), pp. 718, 730–2, 745–6; series Ee563–566, *MSCF* (April 1898), pp. 1632, 1637, 1638 (except for China, 1865–1881, *Statistical Abstract of the United States* (1907), p. 350); series Ee567–568, 1821–1864, *MSCF* (June 1896), pp. 1612, 1621, 1622; 1865–81, *Statistical Abstract of the United States* (1907), pp. 366, 376. (Data for series Ee552 and Ee557 were obtained as residuals for 1821–1881.)

1882–1946 and 1966–1970, the following editions of *Statistical Abstract of the United States:* 1882–1889, (1907), pp. 284, 288–369; 1890–1906, (1910), pp. 328–76; 1907–1915, (1916), pp. 347–81; 1916–1920, (1920), pp. 398–425; 1921–1923, (1926), pp. 452, 458–63; 1924–1928, (1930), pp. 482, 492–7; 1929–1932, (1934), pp. 418, 424–9; 1933–1936, (1938), pp. 456, 460–4; 1937–1940, (1943), pp. 530, 534–8; 1941–1945, (1948), pp. 922, 926–30; 1946, (1952), pp. 856, 858–60; 1966–1968, (1969), pp. 808–11; 1969–1970, (1972), pp. 778–81.

1947–1965, U.S. Bureau of the Census, *Foreign Commerce and Navigation of the United States* (1964, 1965).

1971–1990, U.S. International Trade Administration, *U.S. Foreign Trade Highlights, 1991* (August 1991), pp. 30–1.

1991–2001, available at the Internet site for the International Trade Administration.

Documentation

See the text for Table Ee533–550.

TABLE Ee569–589   Exports of selected commodities: 1790–1989[1]

Contributed by Douglas A. Irwin

Year	Total value, selected commodities Ee569 Million dollars	Cotton, unmanufactured Quantity Ee570 Million pounds	Cotton, unmanufactured Value Ee571 Million dollars	Leaf tobacco Quantity Ee572 [2] Million pounds	Leaf tobacco Value Ee573 Million dollars	Wheat Quantity Ee574 Million 60-pound bushels	Wheat Value Ee575 Million dollars	Value Wheat and wheat flour Ee576 Million dollars	Value Cotton manufactures Ee577 Million dollars	Value Animal fats and oils Ee578 [3] Million dollars	Value Fruits and nuts Ee579 [4] Million dollars
1790	—	—	—	118	4	1	1	—	—	—	—
1791	—	(Z)	—	101	3	1	1	—	—	—	—
1792	—	(Z)	—	112	—	1	—	—	—	—	—
1793	—	(Z)	—	60	—	1	—	—	—	—	—
1794	—	6	—	77	—	1	—	—	—	—	—
1795	—	6	—	61	—	(Z)	—	—	—	—	—
1796	—	6	—	69	—	(Z)	—	—	—	—	—
1797	—	4	—	58	—	(Z)	—	—	—	—	—
1798	—	9	—	69	—	(Z)	—	—	—	—	—
1799	—	10	—	96	—	(Z)	—	—	—	—	—
1800	—	18	—	79	—	(Z)	—	—	—	—	—
1801	—	21	—	104	—	(Z)	—	—	—	—	—
1802	11	28	5	78	6	(Z)	—	—	—	—	—
1803	14	41	8	86	6	1	—	—	—	—	—
1804	14	38	8	83	6	(Z)	—	—	—	—	—
1805	15	38	9	71	6	(Z)	—	—	—	—	—
1806	15	36	8	83	7	(Z)	—	—	—	—	—
1807	19	64	14	62	5	1	—	—	—	—	—
1808	3	11	2	10	1	(Z)	—	—	—	—	—
1809	13	51	9	54	4	(Z)	—	—	—	—	—
1810	27	93	15	84	5	(Z)	—	7	—	—	—
1811	12	62	10	36	2	(Z)	—	—	—	—	—
1812	5	29	3	26	2	(Z)	—	—	—	—	—
1813	2	19	2	5	(Z)	(Z)	—	—	—	—	—
1814	3	18	3	3	(Z)	—	—	—	—	—	—
1815	26	83	18	85	8	(Z)	—	—	—	—	—
1816	37	82	24	69	13	(Z)	—	—	—	—	—
1817	32	86	23	62	9	(Z)	(Z)	—	—	—	—
1818	41	94	31	84	10	(Z)	(Z)	—	—	—	—
1819	29	88	21	69	8	(Z)	(Z)	—	—	—	—
1820	39	128	22	84	8	(Z)	(Z)	5	—	—	—
1821	26	125	20	67	6	(Z)	(Z)	—	—	—	—
1822	30	145	24	83	6	(Z)	(Z)	—	—	—	—
1823	26	174	20	99	6	(Z)	(Z)	—	—	—	—
1824	27	142	22	78	5	(Z)	(Z)	—	—	—	—
1825	43	176	37	76	6	(Z)	(Z)	—	—	—	—
1826	30	205	25	64	5	(Z)	(Z)	—	—	—	—
1827	36	294	29	100	7	(Z)	(Z)	—	—	—	—
1828	27	211	22	96	5	(Z)	(Z)	—	—	—	—
1829	32	265	27	77	5	(Z)	(Z)	—	—	—	—
1830	45	298	30	84	6	(Z)	(Z)	6	1	—	—
1831	31	277	25	87	5	(Z)	(Z)	—	—	—	—
1832	38	322	32	107	6	(Z)	(Z)	—	—	—	—
1833	42	325	36	83	6	(Z)	(Z)	—	—	—	—
1834	56	385	49	88	7	(Z)	(Z)	—	—	—	—
1835	73	387	65	94	8	(Z)	(Z)	—	—	—	—
1836	81	424	71	109	10	(Z)	(Z)	—	—	—	—
1837	69	444	63	100	6	(Z)	(Z)	—	—	—	—
1838	69	596	62	111	7	(Z)	(Z)	—	—	—	—
1839	71	414	61	79	10	(Z)	(Z)	—	—	—	—
1840	94	744	64	119	10	2	2	12	4	—	—
1841	68	530	54	148	13	1	1	—	—	—	—
1842	59	585	48	159	10	1	1	—	—	—	—
1843 [10]	54	792	49	94	5	(Z)	(Z)	—	—	—	—
1844	63	664	54	163	8	1	1	—	—	—	—
1845	59	873	52	147	7	(Z)	(Z)	—	—	—	—
1846	53	548	43	150	8	2	2	—	—	—	—
1847	66	527	53	136	7	4	6	—	—	—	—
1848	73	814	62	131	8	2	3	—	—	—	—
1849	74	1,027	66	102	6	2	2	—	—	—	—

Notes appear at end of table

TABLE Ee569–589   Exports of selected commodities: 1790–1989   *Continued*

Year	Total value, selected commodities Ee569 Million dollars	Cotton, unmanufactured Quantity Ee570 Million pounds	Cotton, unmanufactured Value Ee571 Million dollars	Leaf tobacco Quantity Ee572 [2] Million pounds	Leaf tobacco Value Ee573 Million dollars	Wheat Quantity Ee574 Million 60-pound bushels	Wheat Value Ee575 Million dollars	Value Wheat and wheat flour Ee576 Million dollars	Value Cotton manufactures Ee577 Million dollars	Value Animal fats and oils Ee578 [3] Million dollars	Value Fruits and nuts Ee579 [4] Million dollars
1850	101	635	72	146	10	1	1	8	5	—	—
1851	122	927	112	96	9	1	1	—	—	—	—
1852	101	1,093	88	137	10	3	3	—	—	—	—
1853	124	1,112	109	160	11	4	4	—	—	—	—
1854	116	988	94	126	10	8	12	—	—	—	—
1855	151	1,008	88	150	15	1	1	12	6	—	—
1856	155	1,351	128	117	12	8	15	—	—	—	—
1857	174	1,048	132	157	20	15	22	—	—	—	—
1858	157	1,119	131	128	17	9	9	—	—	—	—
1859	185	1,386	161	199	21	3	3	—	—	—	—
1860	270	1,768	192	167	16	4	4	20	11	—	—
1861	86	308	34	161	14	31	38	—	—	—	—
1862	56	5 [11]	1 [11]	107	12	37	43	—	—	—	—
1863	74	11 [11]	7 [11]	112	20	36	47	—	—	—	—
1864	64	12 [11]	10 [11]	110	23	24	31	—	—	—	—
1865	154	9 [11]	7 [11]	149	42	10	19	47	3	—	—
1866	318	651	281	191	29	6	8	—	—	—	—
1867	229	661	201	185	20	6	8	—	—	—	—
1868	206	785	153	206	23	16	30	—	—	—	—
1869	208	644	163	182	21	18	24	—	—	—	—
1870	359	959	227	186	21	37	47	68	4	—	—
1871	358	1,463	218	216	20	34	45	69	4	—	—
1872	341	934	181	235	24	26	39	57	2	—	—
1873	421	1,200	227	214	23	39	51	71	3	—	
1874	475	1,359	211	318	30	71	101	131	3	—	
1875	395	1,260	191	224	25	53	60	83	4		—
1876	421	1,491	193	218	23	55	68	93	8		—
1877	409	1,445	171	282	29	40	47	69	10		—
1878	471	1,608	180	284	25	72	97	122	11		—
1879	483	1,628	162	322	25	122	131	160	11		—
1880	600	1,822	212	216	16	153	191	226	10	—	—
1881	654	2,191	248	227	19	151	168	213	14	—	—
1882	593	1,740	200	224	19	95	113	149	13	37	2
1883	659	2,288	247	236	19	106	120	175	13	35	3
1884	564	1,863	197	207	18	70	75	126	12	36	2
1885	565	1,892	202	219	22	85	73	125	12	32	4
1886	518	2,058	205	282	27	58	50	89	14	27	3
1887	575	2,169	206	294	26	102	91	143	15	32	3
1888	564	2,264	223	249	22	66	56	111	13	32	4
1889	576	2,385	238	212	19	46	42	87	10	36	5
1890	645	2,472	251	244	21	54	45	102	10	48	4
1891	703	2,907	291	237	21	55	51	106	14	51	2
1892	797	2,935	258	241	20	157	161	237	13	49	7
1893	651	2,212	189	248	22	117	94	169	12	51	4
1894	655	2,683	211	269	23	88	59	129	14	57	2
1895	586	3,517	205	—	—	76	44	95	14	48	5
1896	610	2,335	190	—	—	61	40	92	17	47	6
1897	725	3,104	231	—	—	80	60	116	21	43	8
1898	874	3,850	230	252	22	148	146	215	17	55	9
1899	875	3,773	210	272	25	139	104	177	24	61	8
1900	973	3,101	242	335	29	102	73	141	24	62	12
1901	1,058	3,331	314	307	27	132	97	166	20	68	11
1902	1,030	3,501	291	291	27	155	113	179	32	73	9
1903	1,044	3,543	316	357	35	114	88	162	32	72	18
1904	1,089	3,063	371	305	29	44	36	105	22	71	21
1905	1,102	4,305	380	328	30	4	4	44	50	70	16
1906	1,247	3,634	401	302	29	35	29	88	53	92	15
1907	1,404	4,518	481	332	33	77	60	122	32	94	18
1908	1,413	3,817	438	323	34	100	100	164	25	92	14
1909	1,255	4,448	417	283	31	67	68	119	32	87	17

Notes appear at end of table

(continued)

TABLE Ee569–589   Exports of selected commodities: 1790–1989 *Continued*

Year	Total value, selected commodities	Cotton, unmanufactured Quantity	Value	Leaf tobacco Quantity	Value	Wheat Quantity	Value	Wheat and wheat flour	Cotton manufactures	Animal fats and oils	Fruits and nuts
	Ee569	Ee570	Ee571	Ee572 [2]	Ee573	Ee574	Ee575	Ee576	Ee577	Ee578 [3]	Ee579 [4]
	Million dollars	Million pounds	Million dollars	Million pounds	Million dollars	Million 60-pound bushels	Million dollars	Million dollars	Million dollars	Million dollars	Million dollars
1910	1,290	3,207	450	353	38	47	48	95	33	72	19
1911	1,528	4,034	585	352	39	24	22	71	41	86	24
1912	1,633	5,535	566	375	43	30	28	79	51	86	31
1913	1,831	4,562	547	414	49	92	89	142	52	89	37
1914	1,822	4,761	610	447	54	92	88	142	49	81	32
1915	1,804	4,404	376	348	44	260	334	428	70	79	35
1916	2,746	3,645	545	477	63	154	227	313	127	85	37
1917	3,534	2,476	575	251	46	106	246	384	157	100	35
1918	4,155	2,118	674	404	123	111	261	505	179	181	32
1919	5,229	3,368	1,137	766	260	148	357	650	270	326	126
1920	5,848	3,179	1,136	468	245	218	597	821	398	192	84
1921	3,263	3,339	534	515	205	280	433	551	116	140	70
1922	2,711	3,153	673	431	146	165	206	292	137	116	76
1923	3,124	2,743	807	475	152	99	116	205	136	158	69
1924	3,496	3,483	951	547	163	166	237	328	131	158	98
1925	3,707	4,384	1,060	468	153	87	149	234	146	148	102
1926	3,683	4,692	814	479	137	138	202	285	129	135	112
1927	3,641	4,897	826	506	139	168	240	325	133	116	122
1928	3,861	4,579	920	575	154	96	120	194	135	119	129
1929	3,963	3,982	771	555	146	90	112	192	135	124	137
1930	2,905	3,492	497	561	145	88	88	157	89	88	111
1931	1,782	3,667	326	504	110	80	50	84	60	60	109
1932	1,200	4,803	345	388	65	55	33	51	46	38	77
1933	1,268	4,523	398	420	82	8	5	19	39	40	70
1934	1,612	3,149	373	419	125	17	10	27	43	31	74
1935	1,719	3,234	391	381	134	—	—	15	39	15	93
1936	1,821	2,974	361	407	137	2	2	19	44	16	81
1937	2,513	3,223	369	418	134	35	39	64	60	18	82
1938	2,226	2,442	229	473	155	87	78	101	57	20	99
1939	2,198	2,562	243	327	77	63	37	61	68	23	83
1940	2,456	2,046	213	217	44	14	11	33	76	14	36
1941	2,608	625	83	363	65	13	11	95	135	41	52
1942	3,266	539	99	237	68	7	7	28	131	95	51
1943	4,407	842	184	393	170	12	16	56	192	144	80
1944	5,398	531	115	280	146	10	16	76	232	163	126
1945	4,949	1,282	279	470	239	129	240	330	236	103	128
1946	5,747	1,999	536	642	350	187	391	610	375	95	171
1947	8,789	1,380	423	493	270	167	429	868	852	111	199
1948	8,188	1,474	511	415	214	328	909	1,393	499	89	194
1949	7,750	2,708	874	493	252	340	835	1,002	366	135	140
1950	6,491	2,963	1,024	471	250	206	405	489	263	112	100
1951	9,415	2,618	1,146	518	325	423	887	997	478	214	108
1952	8,825	2,141	874	391	245	369	841	942	370	147	125
1953	7,845	1,497	521	513	339	236	506	590	329	130	129
1954	7,982	2,231	788	450	303	192	350	427	317	181	171
1955	8,667	1,415	477	535	355	222	386	483	293	190	161
1956	10,880	2,511	729	506	333	409	694	798	293	207	230
1957	12,285	3,648	1,059	492	359	415	732	848	314	198	214
1958	9,223	2,368	661	381	279	330	570	686	280	151	367
1959	8,800	2,013	452	459	346	357	613	719	274	176	210
1960	10,614	3,909	988	495	370	504	852	971	284	176	229
1961	10,798	3,376	884	494	390	629	1,114	1,227	272	181	238
1962	10,704	2,050	537	459	371	517	934	1,060	262	148	259
1960	—	3,766	980	488	379	535	967	1,029	—	295	265
1961	—	3,196	875	494	390	659	1,227	1,300	—	272	280
1962	—	1,925	528	459	372	548	1,058	1,136	—	301	300
1963	—	2,170	577	489	401	642	1,148	1,331	—	303	295
1964	—	2,621	682	495	409	756	1,362	1,532	—	414	307

Notes appear at end of table

TABLE Ee569–589   Exports of selected commodities: 1790–1989 *Continued*

Year	Total value, selected commodities	Cotton, unmanufactured Quantity	Cotton, unmanufactured Value	Leaf tobacco Quantity	Leaf tobacco Value	Wheat Quantity	Wheat Value	Value Wheat and wheat flour	Value Cotton manufactures	Value Animal fats and oils	Value Fruits and nuts
	Ee569	Ee570	Ee571	Ee572 [2]	Ee573	Ee574	Ee575	Ee576	Ee577	Ee578 [3]	Ee579 [4]
	Million dollars	Million pounds	Million dollars	Million pounds	Million dollars	Million 60-pound bushels	Million dollars	Million dollars	Million dollars	Million dollars	Million dollars
1965	—	1,898	486	447	378	640	1,064	1,184	—	472	339
1966	—	1,799	432	516	472	826	1,396	1,536	—	357	340
1967	—	1,987	464	527	487	642	1,120	1,207	—	338	338
1968	—	1,935	459	537	511	592	993	1,101	—	274	303
1969	—	1,199	280	523	529	444	726	831	—	308	370
1970	—	1,491	372	452	481	641	1,012	1,112	—	493	406
1971	—	—	583	—	454	—	—	1,090	—	615	430
1972	—	—	503	—	639	—	—	1,452	—	508	526
1973	—	—	929	—	681	—	—	4,152	—	684	662
1974	—	—	1,335	—	832	—	—	4,589	—	1,423	757
1975	—	—	991	—	852	—	—	5,293	—	944	871
1976	—	—	1,049	—	922	—	—	4,040	—	978	976
1977	—	—	1,530	—	1,094	—	—	2,883	—	1,309	1,080
1978	—	—	1,740	—	1,358	—	—	4,532	—	1,521	1,335
1979	—	—	2,198	—	1,184	—	—	5,491	—	1,845	1,525
1980	—	—	2,864	—	1,334	—	—	6,586	—	1,946	1,938
1981	—	—	2,260	—	1,457	—	—	8,073	—	1,750	1,983
1982	—	—	1,955	—	1,547	—	—	6,869	—	1,541	1,778
1983	—	—	1,817	—	1,462	—	—	6,509	—	1,459	1,701
1984	—	—	2,441	—	1,511	—	—	6,698	—	1,922	1,676
1985	—	—	1,633	—	1,521	—	—	3,780	—	1,434	1,710
1986	—	—	773	—	1,209	—	—	3,217	—	1,015	1,876
1987	—	—	1,631	—	1,090	—	—	3,248	—	981	2,144
1988	—	—	1,975	—	1,252	—	—	5,080	—	1,522	2,540
1989	—	—	2,250	—	1,341	—	—	6,187	—	1,350	2,283

Year	Value Meat products	Naval stores, gums, and resins	Automobiles, including engines and parts	Saw mill products	Other wood manufactures	Coal and related fuels	Petroleum and products	Iron and steel mill products	Machinery	Copper and manufactures
	Ee580 [5]	Ee581	Ee582 [6]	Ee583 [7, 8]	Ee584 [7, 8]	Ee585 [9]	Ee586	Ee587	Ee588	Ee589
	Million dollars	Million dollars	Million dollars	Million dollars	Million dollars	Million dollars	Million dollars	Million dollars	Million dollars	Million dollars
1790	—	—	—	—	—	—	—	—	—	—
1791	—	—	—	—	—	—	—	—	—	—
1792	—	—	—	—	—	—	—	—	—	—
1793	—	—	—	—	—	—	—	—	—	—
1794	—	—	—	—	—	—	—	—	—	—
1795	—	—	—	—	—	—	—	—	—	—
1796	—	—	—	—	—	—	—	—	—	—
1797	—	—	—	—	—	—	—	—	—	—
1798	—	—	—	—	—	—	—	—	—	—
1799	—	—	—	—	—	—	—	—	—	—
1800	—	—	—	—	—	—	—	—	—	—
1801	—	—	—	—	—	—	—	—	—	—
1802	—	—	—	—	—	—	—	—	—	—
1803	—	—	—	—	—	—	—	—	—	—
1804	—	—	—	—	—	—	—	—	—	—
1805	—	—	—	—	—	—	—	—	—	—
1806	—	—	—	—	—	—	—	—	—	—
1807	—	—	—	—	—	—	—	—	—	—
1808	—	—	—	—	—	—	—	—	—	—
1809	—	—	—	—	—	—	—	—	—	—
1810	—	—	(Z)	—	—	—	—	—	—	(Z)
1811	—	—	—	—	—	—	—	—	—	—
1812	—	—	—	—	—	—	—	—	—	—
1813	—	—	—	—	—	—	—	—	—	—
1814	—	—	—	—	—	—	—	—	—	—

Notes appear at end of table

(continued)

TABLE Ee569–589   Exports of selected commodities: 1790–1989 *Continued*

	Value									
Year	Meat products	Naval stores, gums, and resins	Automobiles, including engines and parts	Saw mill products	Other wood manufactures	Coal and related fuels	Petroleum and products	Iron and steel mill products	Machinery	Copper and manufactures
	Ee580 [5]	Ee581	Ee582 [6]	Ee583 [7,8]	Ee584 [7,8]	Ee585 [9]	Ee586	Ee587	Ee588	Ee589
	Million dollars	Million dollars	Million dollars	Million dollars	Million dollars	Million dollars	Million dollars	Million dollars	Million dollars	Million dollars
1815	—	—	—	—	—	—	—	—	—	—
1816	—	—	—	—	—	—	—	—	—	—
1817	—	—	—	—	—	—	—	—	—	—
1818	—	—	—	—	—	—	—	—	—	—
1819	—	—	—	—	—	—	—	—	—	—
1820	—	—	(Z)	—	4	—	—	—	—	(Z)
1821	—	—	—	—	—	—	—	—	—	—
1822	—	—	—	—	—	—	—	—	—	—
1823	—	—	—	—	—	—	—	—	—	—
1824	—	—	—	—	—	—	—	—	—	—
1825	—	—	—	—	—	—	—	—	—	—
1826	—	—	—	—	—	—	—	—	—	—
1827	—	—	—	—	—	—	—	—	—	—
1828	—	—	—	—	—	—	—	—	—	—
1829	—	—	—	—	—	—	—	—	—	—
1830	—	(Z)	(Z)	—	2	—	—	—	—	(Z)
1831	—	—	—	—	—	—	—	—	—	—
1832	—	—	—	—	—	—	—	—	—	—
1833	—	—	—	—	—	—	—	—	—	—
1834	—	—	—	—	—	—	—	—	—	—
1835	—	—	—	—	—	—	—	—	—	—
1836	—	—	—	—	—	—	—	—	—	—
1837	—	—	—	—	—	—	—	—	—	—
1838	—	—	—	—	—	—	—	—	—	—
1839	—	—	—	—	—	—	—	—	—	—
1840	—	1	(Z)	—	3	—	—	—	—	(Z)
1841	—	—	—	—	—	—	—	—	—	—
1842	—	—	—	—	—	—	—	—	—	—
1843 [10]	—	—	—	—	—	—	—	—	—	—
1844	—	—	—	—	—	—	—	—	—	—
1845	—	—	—	—	—	—	—	—	—	—
1846	—	—	—	—	—	—	—	—	—	—
1847	—	—	—	—	—	—	—	—	—	—
1848	—	—	—	—	—	—	—	—	—	—
1849	—	—	—	—	—	—	—	—	—	—
1850	—	1	(Z)	—	5	—	—	—	—	(Z)
1851	—	—	—	—	—	—	—	—	—	—
1852	—	—	—	—	—	—	—	—	—	—
1853	—	—	—	—	—	—	—	—	—	—
1854	—	—	—	—	—	—	—	—	—	—
1855	16	3	(Z)	—	10	—	—	—	—	1
1856	—	—	—	—	—	—	—	—	—	—
1857	—	—	—	—	—	—	—	—	—	—
1858	—	—	—	—	—	—	—	—	—	—
1859	—	—	—	—	—	—	—	—	—	—
1860	14	4	1	—	10	—	—	—	—	2
1861	—	—	—	—	—	—	—	—	—	—
1862	—	—	—	—	—	—	—	—	—	—
1863	—	—	—	—	—	—	—	—	—	—
1864	—	—	—	—	—	—	—	—	—	—
1865	35	(Z)	1	—	18	—	—	—	—	1
1866	—	—	—	—	—	—	—	—	—	—
1867	—	—	—	—	—	—	—	—	—	—
1868	—	—	—	—	—	—	—	—	—	—
1869	—	—	—	—	—	—	—	—	—	—
1870	21	3	1	—	13	—	—	—	—	1
1871	30	3	1	—	13	—	—	—	—	(Z)
1872	55	6	1	—	15	—	—	—	—	(Z)
1873	71	6	2	—	18	—	—	—	—	(Z)
1874	71	6	2	—	21	—	—	—	—	(Z)

Notes appear at end of table

TABLE Ee569–589   Exports of selected commodities: 1790–1989   *Continued*

	Value								
	Meat products	Naval stores, gums, and resins	Automobiles, including engines and parts	Saw mill products	Other wood manufactures	Coal and related fuels	Petroleum and products	Iron and steel mill products	Machinery	Copper and manufactures
	Ee580 [5]	Ee581	Ee582 [6]	Ee583 [7,8]	Ee584 [7,8]	Ee585 [9]	Ee586	Ee587	Ee588	Ee589
Year	Million dollars	Million dollars	Million dollars	Million dollars	Million dollars	Million dollars	Million dollars	Million dollars	Million dollars	Million dollars
1875	68	5	1	—	17	—	—	—	—	1
1876	79	4	1	—	17	—	—	—	—	3
1877	101	5	1	—	20	—	—	—	—	3
1878	107	5	2	—	17	—	—	—	—	2
1879	102	4	1	—	15	—	—	—	—	3
1880	114	5	1	—	15	—	—	—	—	1
1881	134	5	2	18	18	—	—	—	—	1
1882	69	7	3	12	10	4	52	1	14	1
1883	61	8	4	13	11	4	46	1	17	2
1884	64	7	3	12	10	5	48	2	16	6
1885	63	5	2	11	8	5	52	1	11	10
1886	54	5	2	11	8	4	52	1	10	6
1887	53	6	2	11	8	5	49	1	11	4
1888	52	6	2	13	8	6	49	2	12	9
1889	59	6	3	16	10	7	52	2	16	10
1890	78	7	5	17	10	7	54	3	20	8
1891	81	8	5	15	9	8	56	3	21	12
1892	83	8	3	15	9	9	49	3	21	13
1893	79	7	3	15	9	10	47	3	22	9
1894	80	7	3	14	11	12	45	3	22	22
1895	81	7	2	15	10	11	50	3	24	16
1896	81	9	5	17	12	11	67	5	29	22
1897	88	9	10	22	14	12	68	11	38	34
1898	104	9	10	20	13	12	62	19	44	33
1899	109	10	10	24	14	14	63	29	61	36
1900	114	12	10	29	17	21	84	39	78	59
1901	121	13	11	32	15	24	78	40	73	45
1902	121	12	1	28	16	22	81	26	68	44
1903	104	13	1	34	19	23	77	21	76	41
1904	101	16	2	42	18	30	88	31	84	58
1905	99	16	2	37	17	31	88	45	89	88
1906	115	20	3	45	20	31	93	51	108	83
1907	108	22	6	59	20	38	94	55	125	97
1908	102	22	5	55	22	42	113	58	121	106
1909	82	15	6	45	19	40	112	47	99	87
1910	62	19	11	54	20	44	107	60	117	89
1911	66	25	16	64	23	48	105	79	151	105
1912	72	27	26	68	25	56	123	102	161	117
1913	68	26	33	78	30	68	150	124	195	143
1914	68	20	35	71	25	63	162	91	168	151
1915	132	11	70	31	15	58	148	85	120	102
1916	198	16	123	35	19	73	221	376	278	237
1917	274	14	124	42	25	119	275	645	356	363
1918	668	10	101	57	25	120	371	632	270	207
1919	698	31	156	80	49	126	377	450	362	131
1920	279	35	303	114	60	360	593	498	588	142
1921	157	11	84	55	26	171	401	236	408	98
1922	140	19	103	70	23	96	346	136	234	104
1923	154	25	171	107	30	166	367	167	281	129
1924	121	25	210	106	28	116	444	150	310	157
1925	127	32	318	103	32	107	474	144	366	161
1926	107	37	320	102	33	204	555	174	398	141
1927	71	34	389	111	34	110	487	161	433	150
1928	68	26	502	113	33	100	527	180	491	170
1929	79	31	541	115	37	106	562	200	604	183
1930	66	23	279	82	26	90	495	189	513	105
1931	36	15	148	47	17	65	271	63	316	55
1932	19	12	76	27	9	45	209	29	131	21
1933	26	15	91	33	11	40	201	46	132	25
1934	35	15	190	44	13	57	228	89	218	50

Notes appear at end of table

(continued)

TABLE Ee569–589   Exports of selected commodities: 1790–1989 *Continued*

					Value				
Year	Meat products	Naval stores, gums, and resins	Automobiles, including engines and parts	Saw mill products	Other wood manufactures	Coal and related fuels	Petroleum and products	Iron and steel mill products	Machinery	Copper and manufactures
	Ee580 [5]	Ee581	Ee582 [6]	Ee583 [7, 8]	Ee584 [7, 8]	Ee585 [9]	Ee586	Ee587	Ee588	Ee589
	Million dollars	Million dollars	Million dollars	Million dollars	Million dollars	Million dollars	Million dollars	Million dollars	Million dollars	Million dollars
1935	28	17	227	42	13	52	251	88	265	49
1936	25	19	240	45	14	57	265	112	335	51
1937	25	22	347	56	18	67	378	300	479	94
1938	28	12	270	38	14	56	390	184	486	87
1939	32	15	254	41	14	67	385	236	502	97
1940	22	12	254	37	21	87	310	516	671	110
1941	99	15	339	30	21	119	285	501	740	48
1942	353	13	433	27	24	152	350	592	763	82
1943	617	14	279	26	38	172	517	615	1,194	109
1944	535	14	643	31	43	182	960	551	1,478	103
1945	290	13	588	34	55	198	753	457	1,191	55
1946	341	27	549	50	36	316	436	447	1,369	39
1947	129	48	1,149	121	68	632	641	824	2,352	102
1948	57	30	930	64	36	492	657	649	2,259	114
1949	51	32	753	60	31	308	562	732	2,355	97
1950	43	42	723	48	25	278	499	472	2,035	88
1951	60	48	1,191	96	37	605	783	611	2,615	101
1952	52	25	987	77	33	510	793	621 [12]	2,868	156
1953	60	27	963	65	29	346	692	495 [12]	3,013	117
1954	61	38	1,036	70	30	312	658	516 [12]	2,875	199
1955	70	39	1,238	89	33	495	646	818 [12]	3,057	218
1956	99	39	1,357	88	42	745	766	1,075 [12]	3,813	266
1957	113	42	1,309	89	46	846	994	1,377	4,178	299
1958	83	36	1,087	78	44	534	462	563	3,682	230
1959	106	45	1,258	90	53	388	480	372	3,706	125
1960	125	68	1,298	104	51	362	479	610	4,121	378
1961	148	53	1,201	87	56	349	445	429	4,497	341
1962	152	48	1,362	91	53	385	443	438	4,851	244
1960	115	—	1,270	104	—	354	468	635	4,476	291
1961	133	—	1,188	87	—	340	432	454	4,968	271
1962	138	—	1,365	91	—	376	430	455	5,447	222
1963	144	—	1,518	108	—	474	479	505	5,702	208
1964	177	—	1,749	120	—	463	461	664	6,525	228
1965	162	—	1,744	119	—	477	418	607	6,935	293
1966	159	—	2,154	132	—	468	434	537	7,678	307
1967	151	—	2,503	135	—	483	539	539	8,280	209
1968	162	—	3,123	151	—	503	454	583	8,844	282
1969	199	—	3,514	175	—	594	433	941	10,137	282
1970	175	—	3,245	193	—	962	488	1,188	11,685	358
1971	192	—	3,879	178	—	902	479	760	11,839	265
1972	252	—	4,473	285	—	984	444	800	13,562	248
1973	444	—	5,573	473	—	1,014	518	1,258	17,588	384
1974	371	—	7,248	468	—	2,437	792	2,500	24,318	415
1975	528	—	9,290	413	—	3,259	908	2,382	29,215	333
1976	798	—	10,132	563	—	2,910	998	1,833	32,113	282
1977	797	—	10,887	551	—	2,655	1,280	1,608	32,630	196
1978	958	—	12,150	618	—	2,046	1,564	1,646	38,105	310
1979	1,127	—	13,904	1,015	—	3,328	1,914	2,227	45,914	425
1980	1,293	—	13,117	1,060	—	4,621	2,833	2,998	57,263	434
1981	1,482	—	14,733	933	—	5,909	3,696	2,801	64,426	388
1982	1,285	—	12,751	811	—	5,987	5,947	2,101	59,821	322
1983	1,191	—	13,492	914	—	4,051	4,557	1,415	54,695	386
1984	1,208	—	17,651	841	—	4,132	4,470	1,248	61,464	395
1985	1,153	—	19,445	760	—	4,464	4,707	1,152	60,573	299
1986	1,424	—	17,695	994	—	3,928	3,639	1,020	60,809	682
1987	1,768	—	19,952	1,349	—	3,366	3,922	1,223	70,080	345
1988	2,430	—	23,972	1,825	—	4,009	3,679	2,017	88,531	707
1989	2,819	—	24,089	2,130	—	4,286	4,828	3,167	109,786	889

TABLE Ee569–589   Exports of selected commodities: 1790–1989   *Continued*

(Z) Series Ee570, less than 500,000 pounds. Series Ee573, Ee575, Ee581–582, and Ee589, less than $500,000. Series Ee574, less than 500,000 bushels.

[1] Table uses two classification systems: first Schedule B and then Schedule B-SITC. Two sets of values are shown for 1960–1962, the first based on Schedule B, the second on Schedule B-SITC.

[2] Prior to 1865, quantity in hogsheads. Includes some leaf tobacco that had been partly processed.

[3] Includes margarine of vegetable origin since 1948. Excludes inedible fish oils. Excludes lard compounds since 1921; now classified as vegetable cooking fats.

[4] Includes fruit and nut preparations since 1946.

[5] 1855–1881, "Meats and meat products"; 1882–1904, "Meats."

[6] "Cars, carriages, automobiles, etc.," prior to 1902. Excludes machinery and vehicles manufactured to military specifications beginning with July 1949.

[7] Includes box, crate, and package shooks (except fruit and vegetables) beginning with 1949; classified as "sawmill products" in prior years.

[8] Prior to 1881, sawmill products included under series Ee584.

[9] "Coal and coke" prior to 1946.

[10] For nine months.

[11] No record of cotton exports for Southern ports.

[12] Includes a small amount of nonferrous metal articles.

Sources

Series Ee569, summary data. See text for other series.

Series Ee570–571. 1791–1889, U.S. Department of the Treasury, Bureau of Statistics, *Monthly Summary of Commerce and Finance (MSCF)* (1895–1896), p. 290; 1890–1897, *MSCF* (March 1900), p. 2561; 1898–1940, the following editions of *Statistical Abstract of the United States:* 1898–1905, (1907), pp. 417–77; 1906–1915, (1916), pp. 392–438; 1916–1919, (1920), pp. 435–511; 1920–1922, (1924), pp. 448–536; 1923–1925, (1928), pp. 480–552; 1926–1929, (1931), pp. 528–609; 1930–1932, (1934), pp. 440–521; 1933–1935, (1937), pp. 467–554; 1936–1940, (1942), pp. 575–669; 1941–1962, U.S. Bureau of the Census, *Summary of Foreign Commerce* (various issues). 1960–1989, Standard International Trade Classification (SITC), U.S. Bureau of the Census, *U.S. Foreign Trade – Highlights of Exports and Imports,* FT 990 (December issues); and unpublished data.

Series Ee572–573. 1690–1894, U.S. Department of the Treasury, Bureau of Statistics, *MSCF* (June 1895), pp. 1418–21; 1898–1970, see the source for series Ee570–571.

Series Ee574–575. 1790–1897, see the source for series Ee572–573; 1898–1940, the following editions of *Statistical Abstract of the United States:*

1898–1905, (1907), pp. 417–77; 1906–1915, (1916), pp. 392–438; 1916–1919, (1920), pp. 435–511; 1920–1922, (1924), pp. 448–536; 1923–1925 (1928), pp. 480–552; 1926–1929, (1931), pp. 528–609; 1930–1932, (1934), pp. 440–521; 1933–1935, (1937), pp. 467–554; 1936–1940, (1942), pp. 575–669; 1941–1962, U.S. Bureau of the Census, *Summary of Foreign Commerce* (various issues); 1963–1989 (SITC), U.S. Bureau of the Census, *U.S. Foreign Trade – Highlights of Exports and Imports,* FT 990 (December issues); and unpublished data.

Series Ee576–589. 1810–1961, the following editions of *Statistical Abstract of the United States* except as noted below for series Ee582 and Ee589: 1810–1881, (1924), pp. 446–7; 1882–1904 (1882–1907 for imports), (1926), pp. 470–3; 1905–1945 (1908–1945 for imports), (1948), pp. 916–19; 1946–1949, (1954), pp. 910–11; 1950–1954, (1958), pp. 885–6; 1955–1961, (1962), pp. 887; series Ee582, 1860–1900, *Statistical Abstract of the United States* (1924), p. 447. Series Ee589, 1903–1907, *Statistical Abstract of the United States* (1947), p. 905; 1962, unpublished data. 1963–1989 (SITC), U.S. Bureau of the Census, *U.S. Foreign Trade – Highlights of Exports and Imports,* FT 990 (December issues); and unpublished data.

Series Ee574–575. 1790–1897, see the source for series Ee572–573; 1898–1970, see the source for series Ee570–571.

Series Ee574–589. 1810–1961, the following editions of *Statistical Abstract of the United States* except as noted below for series Ee582 and Ee589: 1810–1881, (1924), pp. 446–7; 1882–1904 (1882–1907 for imports), (1926), pp. 470–3; 1905–1945 (1908–1945 for imports), (1948), pp. 916–19; 1946–1949, (1954), pp. 910–11; 1950–1954, (1958), pp. 885–6; 1955–1961, (1962), pp. 887; series Ee582, 1860–1900, *Statistical Abstract of the United States* (1924), p. 447. Series Ee589, 1903–1907, *Statistical Abstract of the United States* (1947), p. 905; 1962, unpublished data. 1960–1970 (SITC), see the source for series Ee570–571.

Documentation

The data are for years ending September 30 (1790–1842) and June 30 (1843–1915), and for calendar years thereafter. The last six months of 1915 are omitted.

Series Ee569. Where both are available, total includes "wheat and wheat flour, value" but not "wheat."

Series Ee577. Includes semimanufactures.

TABLE Ee590–611   Imports of selected commodities: 1790–1989[1, 2]

Contributed by Douglas A. Irwin

Year	Total value, selected commodities	Coffee		Tea		Sugar		Rubber, crude		Raw silk	
		Quantity	Value	Quantity	Value	Quantity	Value	Quantity	Value	Quantity	Value
	Ee590	Ee591	Ee592	Ee593	Ee594	Ee595	Ee596	Ee597	Ee598	Ee599	Ee600
	Million dollars	Million pounds	Million dollars	Million pounds	Million dollars	Million pounds	Million dollars	Million pounds	Million dollars	Million pounds	Million dollars
1790	—	4	—	3	—	18	—	—	—	—	—
1791	—	4	—	1	—	25	—	—	—	—	—
1792	—	9	—	3	—	24	—	—	—	—	—
1793	—	34	—	3	—	48	—	—	—	—	—
1794	—	37	—	3	—	49	—	—	—	—	—
1795	—	54	—	3	—	64	—	—	—	—	—
1796	—	61	—	2	—	60	—	—	—	—	—
1797	—	49	—	2	—	73	—	—	—	—	—
1798	—	58	—	2	—	88	—	—	—	—	—
1799	—	30	—	5	—	104	—	—	—	—	—

Notes appear at end of table

(continued)

TABLE Ee590-611   Imports of selected commodities: 1790-1989 *Continued*

	Total value, selected commodities	Coffee		Tea		Sugar		Rubber, crude		Raw silk	
		Quantity	Value	Quantity	Value	Quantity	Value	Quantity	Value	Quantity	Value
	Ee590	Ee591	Ee592	Ee593	Ee594	Ee595	Ee596	Ee597	Ee598	Ee599	Ee600
Year	Million dollars	Million pounds	Million dollars	Million pounds	Million dollars	Million pounds	Million dollars	Million pounds	Million dollars	Million pounds	Million dollars
1800	—	47	—	5	—	113	—	—	—	—	—
1801	—	57	—	4	—	137	—	—	—	—	—
1802	—	41	—	4	—	99	—	—	—	—	—
1803	—	17	—	6	—	74	—	—	—	—	—
1804	—	53	—	3	—	128	—	—	—	—	—
1805	—	56	—	5	—	187	—	—	—	—	—
1806	—	56	—	7	—	199	—	—	—	—	—
1807	—	59	—	8	—	221	—	—	—	—	—
1808	—	37	—	5	—	104	—	—	—	—	—
1809	—	36	—	1	—	77	—	—	—	—	—
1810	—	31	—	8	—	55	—	—	—	—	—
1811	—	30	—	3	—	77	—	—	—	—	—
1812	—	28	—	3	—	83	—	—	—	—	—
1813	—	12	—	1	—	33	—	—	—	—	—
1814	—	8	—	(Z)	—	30	—	—	—	—	—
1815	—	20	—	2	—	45	—	—	—	—	—
1816	—	26	—	3	—	55	—	—	—	—	—
1817	—	31	—	7	—	93	—	—	—	—	—
1818	—	29	—	6	—	68	—	—	—	—	—
1819	—	23	—	7	—	74	—	—	—	—	—
1820	—	—	—	—	—	—	—	—	—	—	—
1821	9	21	4	5	1	60	4	—	—	—	—
1822	13	26	6	7	2	88	5	—	—	—	—
1823	12	37	7	8	2	61	3	—	—	—	—
1824	13	39	5	9	3	94	5	—	—	—	—
1825	13	45	5	10	4	72	4	—	—	—	—
1826	13	37	4	10	4	85	5	—	—	—	—
1827	11	50	4	6	2	77	5	—	—	—	—
1828	11	55	5	8	2	57	4	—	—	—	—
1829	11	51	5	7	2	63	4	—	—	—	—
1830	29	51	4	9	2	86	5	—	—	—	—
1831	12	82	6	5	1	109	5	—	—	—	—
1832	15	92	9	10	3	66	3	—	—	—	—
1833	21	100	11	15	5	98	5	—	—	—	—
1834	21	80	9	16	6	115	6	—	—	—	—
1835	23	103	11	14	5	126	7	—	—	—	—
1836	28	94	10	16	5	191	13	—	—	—	—
1837	22	88	9	17	6	136	7	—	—	—	—
1838	19	88	8	14	3	154	8	—	—	—	—
1839	22	107	10	9	2	195	10	—	—	—	—
1840	47	95	9	20	5	121	6	—	—	—	—
1841	22	115	10	12	3	184	9	—	—	—	—
1842	20	113	9	16	5	172	6	—	—	—	—
1843 [5]	12	93	6	14	4	71	2	—	—	—	—
1844	21	161	10	16	4	185	7	—	—	—	—
1845	17	108	6	20	6	114	5	—	—	—	—
1846	18	133	8	20	5	128	5	—	—	—	—
1847	23	157	9	17	4	236	10	—	—	—	—
1848	23	151	8	24	6	255	9	—	—	—	—
1849	21	165	9	16	4	259	8	—	—	—	—
1850	87	145	11	30	5	218	8	—	—	—	—
1851	31	153	13	17	5	368	13	—	—	—	—
1852	36	194	14	29	7	457	15	—	—	—	—
1853	39	199	16	23	8	464	15	—	—	—	—
1854	36	162	15	24	7	455	14	—	—	—	—
1855	118	191	17	25	7	474	15	—	2	—	—
1856	53	236	22	23	7	544	24	—	—	—	—
1857	71	241	22	20	6	776	43	—	—	—	—
1858	48	189	18	33	7	519	23	—	—	—	—
1859	63	264	25	29	7	656	31	—	—	—	—

Notes appear at end of table

TABLE Ee590–611   Imports of selected commodities: 1790–1989   *Continued*

Year	Total value, selected commodities	Coffee		Tea		Sugar		Rubber, crude		Raw silk	
		Quantity	Value	Quantity	Value	Quantity	Value	Quantity	Value	Quantity	Value
	Ee590	Ee591	Ee592	Ee593	Ee594	Ee595	Ee596	Ee597	Ee598	Ee599	Ee600
	Million dollars	Million pounds	Million dollars	Million pounds	Million dollars	Million pounds	Million dollars	Million pounds	Million dollars	Million pounds	Million dollars
1860	170	202	22	32	9	694	31	—	1	—	—
1861	59	184	21	26	7	809	31	—	—	—	—
1862	41	123	14	25	7	557	20	—	—	—	—
1863	37	80	10	30	8	517	19	—	—	—	—
1864	57	132	16	37	11	632	30	—	—	—	—
1865	101	106	11	20	5	651	27	—	1	—	1
1866	73	181	21	43	11	998	41	—	—	—	—
1867	69	187	21	40	12	849	36	—	—	—	—
1868	85	249	25	38	11	1,121	49	—	—	—	—
1869	99	254	25	44	14	1,247	60	—	—	—	—
1870	205	235	24	47	14	1,197	57	—	3	—	3
1871	260	318	31	51	17	1,276	65	—	4	—	6
1872	334	299	38	64	23	1,509	81	—	5	—	6
1873	344	293	44	65	24	1,568	83	—	7	—	6
1874	298	285	55	56	21	1,701	82	—	6	—	4
1875	272	318	51	65	23	1,797	73	—	5	—	5
1876	231	340	57	63	20	1,494	58	—	4	—	5
1877	239	332	54	58	16	1,654	85	—	6	—	7
1878	222	310	52	65	16	1,538	73	—	5	—	5
1879	217	378	47	60	15	1,834	72	—	6	—	8
1880	341	447	60	72	20	1,830	80	—	10	—	12
1881	320	455	57	82	21	1,947	87	—	11	—	11
1882	403	460	46	79	19	1,990	90	—	14	—	13
1883	403	516	42	73	17	2,138	92	—	16	—	14
1884	376	535	50	68	14	2,756	98	—	14	—	12
1885	317	573	47	72	14	2,718	73	—	9	—	12
1886	362	565	43	82	16	2,690	81	—	12	—	17
1887	392	526	56	90	17	3,136	78	—	14	—	19
1888	397	424	61	85	13	2,700	74	—	16	—	19
1889	418	578	75	80	13	2,762	89	—	12	—	19
1890	440	499	78	84	12	2,934	96	—	15	—	23
1891	483	520	96	83	14	3,479	106	—	18	—	18
1892	485	633	127	90	14	3,542	104	—	20	—	24
1893	475	541	77	89	14	3,733	115	—	18	—	29
1894	386	532	87	94	14	4,286	125	—	15	—	16
1895	416	646	95	97	13	3,516	75	—	18	—	22
1896	449	581	85	94	13	3,709	84	—	17	—	26
1897	355	—	—	—	—	4,720	94	—	17	—	18
1898	343	871	65	72	10	2,589	58	46	25	10	31
1899	387	832	55	74	9	3,917	93	51	32	10	32
1900	475	788	52	85	11	4,007	100	49	31	11	45
1901	438	855	63	90	11	3,865	88	55	28	9	29
1902	463	1,091	71	76	9	2,941	53	50	25	13	42
1903	535	915	59	109	16	4,163	71	55	30	14	49
1904	516	995	70	113	18	3,684	71	59	40	13	44
1905	626	1,048	85	103	16	3,658	97	67	50	18	60
1906	654	852	73	94	15	3,970	85	58	45	15	53
1907	755	985	78	86	14	4,384	93	77	59	17	70
1908	603	891	68	94	16	3,365	80	62	37	15	64
1909	711	1,050	79	115	19	4,184	96	88	62	23	79
1910	823	871	69	86	14	3,913	102	101	101	20	65
1911	749	876	91	103	18	3,703	90	72	76	22	73
1912	844	885	118	101	18	3,663	104	110	93	22	67
1913	913	863	119	95	17	4,533	99	113	90	26	82
1914	934	1,002	111	91	17	4,948	99	132	71	29	98
1915	908	1,119	107	97	18	5,093	166	172	83	26	81
1916	1,373	1,167	119	105	19	5,530	227	270	160	32	145
1917	1,692	1,287	123	127	26	4,941	222	406	233	37	184
1918	1,608	1,052	99	134	30	5,167	241	326	146	33	180
1919	2,309	1,334	261	81	20	7,020	393	536	216	45	329

(continued)

TABLE Ee590–611   Imports of selected commodities: 1790–1989 *Continued*

Year	Total value, selected commodities	Coffee		Tea		Sugar		Rubber, crude		Raw silk	
		Quantity	Value	Quantity	Value	Quantity	Value	Quantity	Value	Quantity	Value
	Ee590	Ee591	Ee592	Ee593	Ee594	Ee595	Ee596	Ee597	Ee598	Ee599	Ee600
	Million dollars	Million pounds	Million dollars	Million pounds	Million dollars	Million pounds	Million dollars	Million pounds	Million dollars	Million pounds	Million dollars
1920	3,212	1,297	252	90	24	8,065	1,115	567	243	30	285
1921	1,429	1,341	143	76	14	5,967	235	415	74	45	259
1922	1,831	1,246	161	97	24	9,722	252	674	102	51	366
1923	2,302	1,410	190	105	30	7,709	380	692	185	49	392
1924	2,190	1,421	249	93	27	8,272	364	735	174	51	328
1925	2,534	1,284	286	101	31	8,920	246	888	430	64	396
1926	2,653	1,493	323	96	31	9,420	233	926	506	66	393
1927	2,430	1,433	264	89	28	8,431	258	955	340	74	390
1928	2,346	1,457	310	90	27	7,737	207	978	245	75	368
1929	2,477	1,482	302	89	26	9,777	209	1,263	241	87	427
1930	1,695	1,599	209	85	23	6,990	130	1,090	141	74	263
1931	1,207	1,742	175	87	19	6,353	113	1,124	74	84	191
1932	784	1,501	137	95	12	5,943	97	929	33	74	114
1933	820	1,586	124	97	14	5,669	105	938	46	67	103
1934	894	1,524	133	76	16	5,994	118	1,036	102	56	72
1935	1,063	1,756	137	86	17	5,910	133	1,045	119	68	96
1936	1,255	1,739	134	82	18	5,939	158	1,091	159	60	102
1937	1,560	1,697	151	95	21	6,395	166	1,339	248	58	107
1938	1,034	1,987	138	81	18	5,949	130	917	130	55	89
1939	1,243	2,014	140	98	21	5,807	125	1,114	178	52	121
1940	1,529	2,055	127	99	23	5,829	113	1,825	318	45	125
1941	1,974	2,255	177	107	29	5,807	117	2,294	418	23	62
1942	1,499	1,715	205	50	18	3,968	107	620	118	—	—
1943	1,577	2,200	273	89	29	6,684	184	117	33	—	—
1944	1,722	2,608	326	90	30	7,728	212	239	76	—	—
1945	2,005	2,717	346	84	29	6,574	202	312	99	—	1
1946	2,673	2,738	472	94	34	5,284	196	840	228	13	128
1947	3,233	2,501	600	68	28	8,330	411	1,587	317	2	16
1948	3,911	2,774	698	91	45	6,397	313	1,646	309	6	15
1949	3,796	2,924	796	95	46	7,457	372	1,480	240	3	7
1950	5,040	2,442	1,092	113	53	7,349	381	1,800	458	8	21
1951	6,143	2,693	1,361	87	41	7,278	387	1,642	807	5	19
1952	5,895	2,681	1,376	93	39	7,667	415	1,804	619	8	34
1953	5,747	2,786	1,468	108	48	7,613	426	1,450	331	5	26
1954	5,503	2,260	1,486	115	62	7,485	409	284	262	7	31
1955	6,142	2,602	1,357	104	64	7,806	414	1,423	442	8	34
1956	6,619	2,810	1,439	101	51	8,287	437	1,297	398	8	32
1957	6,431	2,761	1,376	102	51	8,273	459	1,243	349	6	25
1958	6,311	2,668	1,171	103	48	9,464	520	1,063	248	4	16
1959	6,880	3,076	1,097	110	52	9,082	496	1,285	383	7	25
1960	6,886	2,917	1,003	115	56	9,367	507	920	322	6	27
1961	6,570	2,962	964	109	54	8,447	458	876	216	6	27
1962	7,099	3,248	989	130	60	9,143	505	943	228	5	27
1963	—	3,152	955	126	58	—	611	—	197	—	—
1964	—	3,019	1,197	134	60	7,182	458	1,004	206	—	—
1965	—	2,816	1,058	130	57	7,703	442	1,015	188	—	—
1966	—	2,919	1,067	133	57	8,453	501	974	181	—	—
1967	—	2,819	963	143	58	9,430	588	1,026	174	—	—
1968	—	3,357	1,140	156	61	9,944	640	1,223	192	—	—
1969	—	2,676	894	140	53	9,528	638	1,321	279	—	—
1970	—	2,609	1,160	137	53	10,490	725	1,246	231	—	—
1971	—	—	1,167	—	71	—	764	—	211	—	—
1972	—	—	1,182	—	63	—	832	—	190	—	—
1973	—	—	1,570	—	70	—	925	—	340	—	—
1974	—	—	1,505	—	80	—	2,247	—	507	—	—
1975	—	—	1,561	—	88	—	1,865	—	353	—	—
1976	—	—	2,632	—	96	—	1,154	—	513	—	—
1977	—	—	3,910	—	176	—	1,076	—	642	—	—
1978	—	—	3,728	—	115	—	723	—	840	—	—
1979	—	—	3,820	—	126	—	974	—	1,058	—	—

TABLE Ee590–611   Imports of selected commodities: 1790–1989 *Continued*

	Total value, selected commodities	Coffee		Tea		Sugar		Rubber, crude		Raw silk	
		Quantity	Value	Quantity	Value	Quantity	Value	Quantity	Value	Quantity	Value
	Ee590	Ee591	Ee592	Ee593	Ee594	Ee595	Ee596	Ee597	Ee598	Ee599	Ee600
Year	Million dollars	Million pounds	Million dollars	Million pounds	Million dollars	Million pounds	Million dollars	Million pounds	Million dollars	Million pounds	Million dollars
1980	—	—	3,872	—	131	—	1,987	—	980	—	—
1981	—	—	2,622	—	133	—	2,142	—	980	—	—
1982	—	—	2,730	—	129	—	863	—	735	—	—
1983	—	—	2,590	—	132	—	1,046	—	909	—	—
1984	—	—	3,064	—	203	—	1,258	—	1,132	—	—
1985	—	—	3,130	—	166	—	936	—	654	—	—
1986	—	—	4,293	—	133	—	670	—	921	—	—
1987	—	—	2,706	—	106	—	438	—	1,125	—	—
1988	—	—	2,030	—	129	—	436	—	1,445	—	—
1989	—	—	2,272	—	127	—	611	—	1,459	—	—

	Value										
	Wool and mohair	Wool manufactures	Iron and steel manufactures	Tin (including ores)	Cotton manufactures	Copper and manufactures	Hides and skins	Furs and manufactures	Fruits and nuts	Forest products	Petroleum and products
	Ee601	Ee602	Ee603	Ee604	Ee605	Ee606 [3]	Ee607	Ee608 [4]	Ee609	Ee610	Ee611
Year	Million dollars	Million dollars	Million dollars	Million dollars	Million dollars	Million dollars	Million dollars	Million dollars	Million dollars	Million dollars	Million dollars
1790	—	—	—	—	—	—	—	—	—	—	—
1791	—	—	—	—	—	—	—	—	—	—	—
1792	—	—	—	—	—	—	—	—	—	—	—
1793	—	—	—	—	—	—	—	—	—	—	—
1794	—	—	—	—	—	—	—	—	—	—	—
1795	—	—	—	—	—	—	—	—	—	—	—
1796	—	—	—	—	—	—	—	—	—	—	—
1797	—	—	—	—	—	—	—	—	—	—	—
1798	—	—	—	—	—	—	—	—	—	—	—
1799	—	—	—	—	—	—	—	—	—	—	—
1800	—	—	—	—	—	—	—	—	—	—	—
1801	—	—	—	—	—	—	—	—	—	—	—
1802	—	—	—	—	—	—	—	—	—	—	—
1803	—	—	—	—	—	—	—	—	—	—	—
1804	—	—	—	—	—	—	—	—	—	—	—
1805	—	—	—	—	—	—	—	—	—	—	—
1806	—	—	—	—	—	—	—	—	—	—	—
1807	—	—	—	—	—	—	—	—	—	—	—
1808	—	—	—	—	—	—	—	—	—	—	—
1809	—	—	—	—	—	—	—	—	—	—	—
1810	—	—	—	—	—	—	—	—	—	—	—
1811	—	—	—	—	—	—	—	—	—	—	—
1812	—	—	—	—	—	—	—	—	—	—	—
1813	—	—	—	—	—	—	—	—	—	—	—
1814	—	—	—	—	—	—	—	—	—	—	—
1815	—	—	—	—	—	—	—	—	—	—	—
1816	—	—	—	—	—	—	—	—	—	—	—
1817	—	—	—	—	—	—	—	—	—	—	—
1818	—	—	—	—	—	—	—	—	—	—	—
1819	—	—	—	—	—	—	—	—	—	—	—
1820	—	6	—	—	8	—	—	—	—	—	—
1821	—	—	—	—	—	—	—	—	—	—	—
1822	—	—	—	—	—	—	—	—	—	—	—
1823	—	—	—	—	—	—	—	—	—	—	—
1824	—	—	—	—	—	—	—	—	—	—	—
1825	—	—	—	—	—	—	—	—	—	—	—
1826	—	—	—	—	—	—	—	—	—	—	—
1827	—	—	—	—	—	—	—	—	—	—	—
1828	—	—	—	—	—	—	—	—	—	—	—
1829	—	—	—	—	—	—	—	—	—	—	—

Notes appear at end of table

(continued)

TABLE Ee590–611   Imports of selected commodities: 1790–1989   *Continued*

					Value						
	Wool and mohair	Wool manufactures	Iron and steel manufactures	Tin (including ores)	Cotton manufactures	Copper and manufactures	Hides and skins	Furs and manufactures	Fruits and nuts	Forest products	Petroleum and products
	Ee601	Ee602	Ee603	Ee604	Ee605	Ee606 [3]	Ee607	Ee608 [4]	Ee609	Ee610	Ee611
Year	Million dollars	Million dollars	Million dollars	Million dollars	Million dollars	Million dollars	Million dollars	Million dollars	Million dollars	Million dollars	Million dollars
1830	—	6	6	—	6	—	—	—	—	—	—
1831	—	—	—	—	—	—	—	—	—	—	—
1832	—	—	—	—	—	—	—	—	—	—	—
1833	—	—	—	—	—	—	—	—	—	—	—
1834	—	—	—	—	—	—	—	—	—	—	—
1835	—	—	—	—	—	—	—	—	—	—	—
1836	—	—	—	—	—	—	—	—	—	—	—
1837	—	—	—	—	—	—	—	—	—	—	—
1838	—	—	—	—	—	—	—	—	—	—	—
1839	—	—	—	—	—	—	—	—	—	—	—
1840	1	11	8	—	7	—	—	—	—	—	—
1841	—	—	—	—	—	—	—	—	—	—	—
1842	—	—	—	—	—	—	—	—	—	—	—
1843 [5]	—	—	—	—	—	—	—	—	—	—	—
1844	—	—	—	—	—	—	—	—	—	—	—
1845	—	—	—	—	—	—	—	—	—	—	—
1846	—	—	—	—	—	—	—	—	—	—	—
1847	—	—	—	—	—	—	—	—	—	—	—
1848	—	—	—	—	—	—	—	—	—	—	—
1849	—	—	—	—	—	—	—	—	—	—	—
1850	2	20	20	—	21	—	—	—	—	—	—
1851	—	—	—	—	—	—	—	—	—	—	—
1852	—	—	—	—	—	—	—	—	—	—	—
1853	—	—	—	—	—	—	—	—	—	—	—
1854	—	—	—	—	—	—	—	—	—	—	—
1855	2	28	29	—	18	—	—	—	—	—	—
1856	—	—	—	—	—	—	—	—	—	—	—
1857	—	—	—	—	—	—	—	—	—	—	—
1858	—	—	—	—	—	—	—	—	—	—	—
1859	—	—	—	—	—	—	—	—	—	—	—
1860	5	43	26	—	33	—	—	—	—	—	—
1861	—	—	—	—	—	—	—	—	—	—	—
1862	—	—	—	—	—	—	—	—	—	—	—
1863	—	—	—	—	—	—	—	—	—	—	—
1864	—	—	—	—	—	—	—	—	—	—	—
1865	8	22	17	—	9	—	—	—	—	—	—
1866	—	—	—	—	—	—	—	—	—	—	—
1867	—	—	—	—	—	—	—	—	—	—	—
1868	—	—	—	—	—	—	—	—	—	—	—
1869	—	—	—	—	—	—	—	—	—	—	—
1870	7	34	40	—	23	—	—	—	—	—	—
1871	10	44	53	—	30	—	—	—	—	—	—
1872	26	52	68	—	35	—	—	—	—	—	—
1873	20	51	74	—	35	—	—	—	—	—	—
1874	8	47	47	—	28	—	—	—	—	—	—
1875	11	45	31	—	28	—	—	—	—	—	—
1876	8	33	23	—	23	—	—	—	—	—	—
1877	7	26	19	—	19	—	—	—	—	—	—
1878	8	25	19	—	19	—	—	—	—	—	—
1879	5	24	20	—	20	—	—	—	—	—	—
1880	24	34	71	—	30	—	—	—	—	—	—
1881	10	31	61	—	31	—	—	—	—	—	—
1882	11	37	68	5	34	1	28	8	19	10	—
1883	11	44	58	6	37	(Z)	28	8	20	10	—
1884	12	41	40	5	29	1	22	8	20	10	—
1885	9	36	34	4	27	(Z)	21	5	17	9	—
1886	17	41	38	6	30	1	27	7	17	9	—
1887	16	45	49	7	29	(Z)	24	7	21	10	—
1888	16	48	49	9	29	(Z)	24	7	21	11	—
1889	18	53	42	7	27	(Z)	25	7	19	12	—

Notes appear at end of table

TABLE Ee590–611   Imports of selected commodities: 1790–1989   *Continued*

	Value										
Year	Wool and mohair	Wool manufactures	Iron and steel manufactures	Tin (including ores)	Cotton manufactures	Copper and manufactures	Hides and skins	Furs and manufactures	Fruits and nuts	Forest products	Petroleum and products
	Ee601	Ee602	Ee603	Ee604	Ee605	Ee606 [3]	Ee607	Ee608 [4]	Ee609	Ee610	Ee611
	Million dollars	Million dollars	Million dollars	Million dollars	Million dollars	Million dollars	Million dollars	Million dollars	Million dollars	Million dollars	Million dollars
1890	15	57	42	7	30	1	22	8	21	13	
1891	18	41	54	8	30	1	28	10	26	15	—
1892	20	36	29	9	28	1	27	10	21	15	—
1893	21	38	35	12	34	1	28	11	24	18	—
1894	6	19	21	3	22	1	17	8	19	13	—
1895	26	39	23	7	33	1	26	10	17	11	—
1896	32	53	25	7	33	2	31	9	19	13	—
1897	53	49	16	7	35	2	28	6	17	13	—
1898	17	15	13	9	27	4	37	8	15	9	—
1899	9	14	12	12	32	7	42	11	18	9	—
1900	20	16	20	19	42	15	58	12	19	15	—
1901	13	15	18	20	40	21	48	11	20	13	—
1902	18	17	27	19	45	25	58	16	21	17	—
1903	22	20	52	24	53	21	58	15	24	21	—
1904	25	18	27	21	50	22	52	15	24	19	—
1905	46	18	24	23	50	25	65	18	26	23	—
1906	39	23	29	31	64	33	84	22	29	29	—
1907	42	22	41	38	75	48	83	22	36	34	—
1908	24	19	28	25	69	32	55	16	37	32	1
1909	45	18	22	26	63	38	78	21	30	34	1
1910	51	24	40	31	68	40	112	27	37	40	2
1911	23	19	36	38	67	40	71	24	40	40	3
1912	33	15	27	46	65	45	102	25	43	38	5
1913	36	16	34	53	66	60	117	24	41	48	11
1914	53	34	32	39	71	55	120	14	51	54	15
1915	68	30	23	31	46	32	104	10	41	57	11
1916	126	16	24	56	55	95	173	21	45	77	15
1917	172	23	28	68	56	138	210	29	45	113	22
1918	252	23	25	105	41	134	108	34	49	114	27
1919	217	19	27	63	53	86	307	76	79	130	33
1920	127	58	50	93	138	90	244	92	102	231	68
1921	60	51	29	22	75	46	68	41	74	159	79
1922	87	59	48	46	87	67	107	69	72	195	89
1923	130	69	54	63	100	96	119	89	70	255	80
1924	93	69	44	69	91	96	75	88	72	248	103
1925	142	74	—	95	79	84	97	117	89	259	109
1926	107	71	—	105	67	100	97	120	88	286	126
1927	83	79	—	101	66	85	113	138	85	285	115
1928	80	78	—	87	69	98	151	122	90	280	134
1929	87	79	—	92	69	154	137	126	87	296	145
1930	37	40	—	60	46	105	92	69	75	259	146
1931	22	23	—	37	41	49	50	56	60	204	93
1932	6	13	—	16	28	24	22	28	44	149	61
1933	21	16	—	51	32	18	46	38	37	143	26
1934	17	15	—	45	32	28	35	41	46	157	37
1935	30	20	—	70	41	33	46	53	55	175	38
1936	53	30	—	76	49	30	55	82	58	210	41
1937	96	32	—	104	57	53	71	86	67	256	45
1938	23	18	—	45	35	38	30	46	55	200	39
1939	50	26	—	71	40	44	47	55	58	223	44
1940	85	25	—	131	31	73	50	80	61	217	70
1941	205	28	—	177	23	142	83	109	62	260	82
1942	311	27	—	51	10	165	78	69	35	268	37
1943	296	16	—	38	12	157	66	91	41	256	85
1944	186	17	—	47	12	166	61	126	68	282	113
1945	241	25	—	42	38	195	50	144	110	331	152
1946	289	41	—	69	45	86	77	238	143	468	159
1947	209	40	—	86	31	176	86	126	136	721	250
1948	308	79	—	176	53	203	108	165	161	862	416
1949	222	72	—	212	50	224	73	109	147	748	478

Notes appear at end of table

(continued)

TABLE Ee590–611   Imports of selected commodities: 1790–1989   *Continued*

Value

Year	Wool and mohair	Wool manufactures	Iron and steel manufactures	Tin (including ores)	Cotton manufactures	Copper and manufactures	Hides and skins	Furs and manufactures	Fruits and nuts	Forest products	Petroleum and products
	Ee601	Ee602	Ee603	Ee604	Ee605	Ee606 [3]	Ee607	Ee608 [4]	Ee609	Ee610	Ee611
	Million dollars	Million dollars	Million dollars	Million dollars	Million dollars	Million dollars	Million dollars	Million dollars	Million dollars	Million dollars	Million dollars
1950	428	114	—	202	81	243	119	109	169	978	592
1951	714	152	—	159	81	280	133	114	169	1,125	601
1952	382	165	—	298	67	411	60	79	164	1,094	692
1953	296	140	—	271	80	433	74	73	188	1,131	762
1954	223	128	—	184	83	363	53	72	177	1,141	829
1955	260	168	—	179	132	455	57	88	201	1,266	1,026
1956	242	196	—	178	161	502	66	86	192	1,354	1,286
1957	211	191	—	130	143	384	49	87	194	1,234	1,548
1958	164	175	77	102	155	246	54	88	195	1,427	1,625
1959	224	234	111	127	209	298	87	108	218	1,676	1,535
1960	197	266	125	119	265	401	71	109	230	1,644	1,544
1961	198	251	122	120	217	279	64	101	220	1,636	1,643
1962	209	308	149	117	303	273	66	117	220	1,763	1,765
1963	280	—	598	109	—	331	65	114	235	—	1,814
1964	263	—	715	104	—	400	82	102	301	—	1,907
1965	282	—	1,140	167	—	425	80	113	339	—	2,092
1966	277	—	1,183	154	—	611	89	126	369	—	2,127
1967	168	—	1,289	167	—	656	61	92	360	—	2,086
1968	199	—	1,962	184	—	855	78	103	437	—	2,343
1969	155	—	1,724	189	—	486	62	94	429	—	2,560
1970	116	—	1,952	190	—	532	51	59	447	—	2,764
1971	72	—	2,615	167	—	463	52	53	460	—	3,323
1972	95	—	2,743	200	—	516	65	52	496	—	4,300
1973	123	—	2,775	199	—	678	85	78	578	—	7,614
1974	74	—	4,756	295	—	1,189	78	79	627	—	24,293
1975	73	—	4,037	315	—	419	78	79	637	—	24,814
1976	89	—	3,809	329	—	777	89	101	760	—	31,794
1977	117	—	5,302	458	—	855	97	122	957	—	41,756
1978	147	—	6,681	598	—	1,069	106	142	1,126	—	39,104
1979	134	—	6,764	720	—	984	139	183	1,324	—	56,046
1980	146	—	6,692	776	—	1,470	88	143	1,245	—	77,637
1981	210	—	10,347	644	—	1,279	101	168	1,604	—	75,577
1982	152	—	9,184	378	—	988	71	127	1,774	—	59,396
1983	176	—	6,338	453	—	1,341	64	126	1,855	—	52,325
1984	211	—	10,208	513	—	1,512	70	160	2,673	—	55,906
1985	166	—	10,266	426	—	1,146	74	173	2,717	—	49,607
1986	186	—	8,168	243	—	1,377	65	145	2,781	—	34,140
1987	251	—	8,493	270	—	1,551	82	218	3,098	—	41,529
1988	331	—	10,274	316	—	2,098	102	154	3,244	—	38,175
1989	341	—	9,401	338	—	2,196	—	—	2,319	—	49,141

(Z) Series Ee593, less than 500,000 pounds. Series Ee606, less than $500,000.

[1] Schedule A classification through 1962 and the Tariff Schedules of the United States Annotated, Standard International Trade Classification, Revised (TSUSA-SITC) thereafter.

[2] For years ending September 30 (1790–1842) and June 30 (1843–1915), and for calendar years thereafter. The last six months of 1915 omitted.

[3] Includes ore and manufactures since 1946.

[4] Includes fur hats beginning in 1921; formerly classified as miscellaneous textile products.

[5] For nine months.

Sources

Series Ee590–610, 1790–1889, U.S. Department of the Treasury, Bureau of Statistics, *Monthly Summary of Commerce and Finance (MSCF)* (1895–1896), p. 290; 1890–1897, *MSCF* (March 1900), p. 2561; 1898–1940, the following editions of *Statistical Abstract of the United States*: 1898–1905 (1907), pp. 417–77; 1906–1915 (1916), pp. 392–438; 1916–1919 (1920), pp. 435–511;

1920–1922 (1924), pp. 448–536; 1923–1925 (1928), pp. 480–552; 1926–1929 (1931), pp. 528–609; 1930–1932 (1934), pp. 440–521; 1933–1935 (1937), pp. 467–554; 1936–1940 (1942), pp. 575–669; 1941–1962, U.S. Bureau of the Census, *Summary of Foreign Commerce*, various issues. 1963–1989, Standard International Trade Classification (SITC), U.S. Bureau of the Census, *U.S. Foreign Trade – Highlights of Exports and Imports*, FT 990, December issues; and unpublished data.

Documentation

Imports for consumption values for 1933 are as follows: series Ee597, 19; series Ee598, 16; series Ee602, 51; series Ee603, 31; series Ee604, 15; series Ee605, 45; series Ee608, 37; series Ee609, 37; series Ee610, 144; series Ee611, 26 (in millions of dollars).

Series Ee605. Includes semimanufactures.

Series Ee610. Includes sawmill products, woodpulp, and paper and manufactures.

EXCHANGE RATES

Lawrence H. Officer

TABLE Ee612–614 Dollar–sterling parity: 1789–1978

Contributed by Lawrence H. Officer

Year	Dollar–sterling par value Ee612 [1] Dollars per pound	Legal parity Appraisal of British merchandise for tariffs Ee613 [2] Dollars per pound	Legal parity Rating of British coin Ee614 [2] Dollars per pound	Year	Dollar–sterling par value Ee612 [1] Dollars per pound	Legal parity Appraisal of British merchandise for tariffs Ee613 [2] Dollars per pound	Legal parity Rating of British coin Ee614 [2] Dollars per pound	Year	Dollar–sterling par value Ee612 [1] Dollars per pound	Legal parity Appraisal of British merchandise for tariffs Ee613 [2] Dollars per pound	Legal parity Rating of British coin Ee614 [2] Dollars per pound
1789	—	4.4400 [2]	4.5714 [2]	1840	4.8666	4.8000	4.8693	1890	4.8666	4.8665	—
1790	—	4.4400	4.5714	1841	4.8666	4.8000	4.8693	1891	4.8666	4.8665	—
1791	4.5840	4.4400	4.5714	1842	4.8666	4.8183 [2]	4.8693	1892	4.8666	4.8665	—
1792	4.6206	4.4400	4.5714	1843	4.8666	4.8400	4.8693	1893	4.8666	4.8665	—
1793	4.5688	4.4400	4.5663 [2]	1844	4.8666	4.8400	4.8693	1894	4.8666	4.8665	—
1794	4.6705	4.4400	4.5657	1845	4.8666	4.8400	4.8693	1895	4.8666	4.8665	—
1795	4.7002	4.4400	4.5657	1846	4.8666	4.8400	4.8693	1896	4.8666	4.8665	—
1796	4.7636	4.4400	4.5657	1847	4.8666	4.8400	4.8693	1897	4.8666	4.8665	—
1797	4.6905	4.4400	4.5657	1848	4.8666	4.8400	4.8693	1898	4.8666	4.8665	—
1798	4.7453	4.4400	4.5657	1849	4.8666	4.8400	4.8693	1899	4.8666	4.8665	—
1799	4.7910	4.4400	4.5657	1850	4.8666	4.8400	4.8693	1900	4.8666	4.8665	—
1800	4.7727	4.4400	4.5657	1851	4.8666	4.8400	4.8693	1901	4.8666	4.8665	—
1801	4.7057	4.4400	4.5657	1852	4.8666	4.8400	4.8693	1902	4.8666	4.8665	—
1802	4.6449	4.4400	4.5657	1853	4.8666	4.8400	4.8693	1903	4.8666	4.8665	—
1803	4.6903	4.4400	4.5657	1854	4.8666	4.8400	4.8693	1904	4.8666	4.8665	—
1804	4.6905	4.4400	4.5657	1855	4.8666	4.8400	4.8693	1905	4.8666	4.8665	—
1805	4.8062	4.4400	4.5657	1856	4.8666	4.8400	4.8693	1906	4.8666	4.8665	—
1806	4.7240	4.4400	4.5657	1857	4.8666	4.8400	4.8693 [2]	1907	4.8666	4.8665	—
1807	4.6966	4.4400	4.5657	1858	4.8666	4.8400	—	1908	4.8666	4.8665	—
1808	4.8945	4.4400	4.5657	1859	4.8666	4.8400	—	1909	4.8666	4.8665	—
1809	4.8579	4.4400	4.5657	1860	4.8666	4.8400	—	1910	4.8666	4.8665	—
1810	4.8001	4.4400	4.5657	1861	4.8666	4.8400	—	1911	4.8666	4.8665	—
1811	4.7270	4.4400	4.5657	1862	4.8666	4.8400	—	1912	4.8666	4.8665	—
1812	4.9036	4.4400	4.5657	1863	4.8666	4.8400	—	1913	4.8666	4.8665	—
1813	4.9462	4.4400	4.5657	1864	4.8666	4.8400	—	1914	4.8666	4.8665	—
1814	4.5779	4.4400	4.5657	1865	4.8666	4.8400	—	1915	4.8666	4.8665	—
1815	4.6449	4.4400	4.5657	1866	4.8666	4.8400	—	1916	4.8666	4.8665	—
1816	4.6509	4.4400	4.5657	1867	4.8666	4.8400	—	1917	4.8666	4.8665	—
1817	4.5992	4.4400	4.5657	1868	4.8666	4.8400	—	1918	4.8666	4.8665	—
1818	4.6723	4.4400	4.5657	1869	4.8666	4.8400	—	1919	4.8666	4.8665	—
1819	4.6662	4.4400	4.5657	1870	4.8666	4.8400	—	1920	4.8666	4.8665	—
1820	4.7544	4.4400	4.5657	1871	4.8666	4.8400	—	1921	4.8666	4.8665 [2]	—
1821	4.8549	4.4400	4.5657	1872	4.8666	4.8400	—	1922	4.8666	—	—
1822	4.8092	4.4400	4.5657	1873	4.8666	4.8619 [2]	—	1923	4.8666	—	—
1823	4.8214	4.4400	4.5657	1874	4.8666	4.8665	—	1924	4.8666	—	—
1824	4.8153	4.4400	4.5657	1875	4.8666	4.8665	—	1925	4.8666	—	—
1825	4.7788	4.4400	4.5657	1876	4.8666	4.8665	—	1926	4.8666	—	—
1826	4.7971	4.4400	4.5657	1877	4.8666	4.8665	—	1927	4.8666	—	—
1827	4.7910	4.4400	4.5657	1878	4.8666	4.8665	—	1928	4.8666	—	—
1828	4.8031	4.4400	4.5657	1879	4.8666	4.8665	—	1929	4.8666	—	—
1829	4.8031	4.4400	4.5657	1880	4.8666	4.8665	—	1930	4.8666	—	—
1830	4.8153	4.4400	4.5657	1881	4.8666	4.8665	—	1931	4.8666	—	—
1831	4.7849	4.4400	4.5657	1882	4.8666	4.8665	—	1932	4.8666	—	—
1832	4.7879	4.4400	4.5657	1883	4.8666	4.8665	—	1933	4.8666	—	—
1833	4.8488	4.7381 [2]	4.5657	1884	4.8666	4.8665	—	1934	4.8666 [1]	—	—
1834	4.8225 [1]	4.8000	4.7201 [2]	1885	4.8666	4.8665	—	1939	4.0308 [1]	—	—
1835	4.8708	4.8000	4.8693	1886	4.8666	4.8665	—	1940	4.0300	—	—
1836	4.8708	4.8000	4.8693	1887	4.8666	4.8665	—	1941	4.0300	—	—
1837	4.8668 [1]	4.8000	4.8693	1888	4.8666	4.8665	—	1942	4.0300	—	—
1838	4.8666	4.8000	4.8693	1889	4.8666	4.8665	—	1943	4.0300	—	—
1839	4.8666	4.8000	4.8693					1944	4.0300	—	—

Notes appear at end of table

(continued)

TABLE Ee612–614   Dollar–sterling parity: 1789–1978 *Continued*

	Legal parity					Legal parity					Legal parity		
	Dollar–sterling par value	Appraisal of British merchandise for tariffs	Rating of British coin			Dollar–sterling par value	Appraisal of British merchandise for tariffs	Rating of British coin			Dollar–sterling par value	Appraisal of British merchandise for tariffs	Rating of British coin
	Ee612 [1]	Ee613 [2]	Ee614 [2]			Ee612 [1]	Ee613 [2]	Ee614 [2]			Ee612 [1]	Ee613 [2]	Ee614 [2]
Year	Dollars per pound	Dollars per pound	Dollars per pound	Year		Dollars per pound	Dollars per pound	Dollars per pound	Year		Dollars per pound	Dollars per pound	Dollars per pound
1945	4.0300	—	—	1960		2.8000	—	—	1975		2.6057	—	—
1946	4.0300 [1]	—	—	1961		2.8000	—	—	1976		2.6057	—	—
1947	4.0300	—	—	1962		2.8000	—	—	1977		2.6057	—	—
1948	4.0300	—	—	1963		2.8000	—	—	1978		2.6057 [1]	—	—
1949	3.6781 [1]	—	—	1964		2.8000	—	—					
1950	2.8000	—	—	1965		2.8000	—	—					
1951	2.8000	—	—	1966		2.8000	—	—					
1952	2.8000	—	—	1967		2.7522 [1]	—	—					
1953	2.8000	—	—	1968		2.4000	—	—					
1954	2.8000	—	—	1969		2.4000	—	—					
1955	2.8000	—	—	1970		2.4000	—	—					
1956	2.8000	—	—	1971		2.4077 [1]	—	—					
1957	2.8000	—	—	1972		2.6057 [1]	—	—					
1958	2.8000	—	—	1973		2.6057	—	—					
1959	2.8000	—	—	1974		2.6057	—	—					

[1] Mint parity, 1791–1934; U.K. official exchange rate, 1939–1946; par value of pound, 1946–1978. See text for further information on various historical developments affecting the series.

[2] See text for discussion of various parity changes and other historical developments affecting the series.

Sources

Series Ee612. Lawrence H. Officer, *Between the Dollar–Sterling Gold Points: Exchange Rates, Parity, and Market Behavior* (Cambridge University Press, 1996), Table 5.2, pp. 54–5, and Officer's unpublished quarterly series underlying Table 5.2; *The Economist* (September 9, 1939): 509; (September 16, 1939): 548; and (January 13, 1940): 80; Margaret G. de Vries and J. Keith Horsefield, *The International Monetary Fund, 1945–1965*, volume 2, *Analysis* (International Monetary Fund, 1969), pp. 84, 116; and Margaret Garritsen de Vries, *The International Monetary Fund, 1966–1971: The System under Stress*, volume 1, *Narrative* (International Monetary Fund, 1976), pp. 438, 554–5.

Series Ee613–614. Officer (1996), pp. 52–3, 58.

Documentation

Series Ee612 has three components, corresponding to three concepts of exchange-rate parity, as one concept evolved into the other over time. Mint parity (1791–1934) is based conceptually on Table 5.2 in Officer (1996); however, this component is the annual average of Officer's unpublished quarterly series underlying Table 5.2, which series has more significant digits than the table shows. The U.K. official exchange rate (1939–1946) is the midpoint of Bank of England fixed buying and selling rates, found in *The Economist*. The par value of the pound (1946–1978) established with the International Monetary Fund (IMF) is taken from de Vries and Horsefield (1969) and de Vries (1976).

Unlike the usual concept of an exchange rate, parity is neither an exchange-rate quotation nor a market rate; rather, it is a norm value of the exchange rate. Parity has several uses. In series Ee612 form, it is the exchange rate about which specie or parity points (bounds to the exchange rate under a metallic or other fixed monetary standard) can be constructed. Under this circumstance, parity may be used as an approximation of the market exchange rate. Indeed, percentage values of the exchange rate are often computed as deviations from this parity. Series Ee613 enabled conversion of pound-denominated merchandise into dollars, for the computation of ad valorem tariffs, and (from July 17, 1842) applied to all payments by or to the U.S. Treasury involving computation of the dollar value of the pound. The parity concept underlying series Ee614 was useful when foreign coin circulated as legal tender in the United States.

Mint parity is the specie content of the pound relative to the dollar (ratio of number of grains of specie per pound to number of grains of specie

per dollar). If both the United States and the United Kingdom are on the same metallic (either gold or silver) standard, then the computation of parity is straightforward, and either a gold or silver parity is calculated. When the countries are on different standards, the relative market price of gold in terms of silver is used to achieve comparability. This situation (the United States on an effective silver, Britain on a gold, standard) existed until 1834.

Determination of parity under the other concepts of exchange-rate parity (all under the legal-parity rubric) emanates directly from government or central-bank policy of one of the countries. For the U.K. official exchange rate and the par value of the pound, it is generally only U.K. or Bank of England policy that is relevant. (For a situation in which U.S. policy was also pertinent, see de Vries 1976, pp. 553–5.) Legal parities for the appraisal of British merchandise and for the rating of British coin were entirely a matter of U.S. policy, determined by Act of Congress.

Noteworthy in series Ee612 is the almost full century (1837–1934) for which mint parity was unchanged at $4.8665635. The decline in parity from 1939 means that the dollar is strengthening against the pound, at least in a parity sense. In fact, the behavior of this series is broadly reflective of the dollar–sterling exchange rate, shown in Table Ee615–620 and series Ee636.

For further reading on exchange-rate parity in general and dollar–sterling parity in particular, see Arthur Nussbaum, *Money in the Law: National and International* (Foundation Press, 1950), pp. 332–9; Officer (1996), Chapter 5; de Vries and Horsefield (1969), Chapters 4–5; and de Vries (1976), Chapters 21, 26–7. For the underlying monetary standards and exchange-rate policy in the two countries, see Officer (1996), Chapters 3–4.

Series Ee612. Effective July 31, 1834, the United States switched from an effective silver to an effective gold standard, to which Britain had adhered since the early eighteenth century. Therefore – for the first time in U.S. history, and to endure for a century – gold parity became the relevant mint parity. This parity was $4.8707588 – computed as $(113 + 1/623)/(23.2)$ – where the numerator (denominator) is the number of grains of pure gold in the pound (dollar).

Series Ee612. Effective January 18, 1837, gold parity changed to $4.8665635 (to eight significant digits), with the pure gold content of the dollar increasing to 23.22 grains. The 1837 value is the average of the two gold parities weighted by the respective number of days for which they are applicable.

Series Ee612. The 1934 figure is applicable only through January 30. After that date, mint parity became inoperative. On January 31, 1934, the dollar was devalued to $13\frac{5}{7}$ grains of pure gold (equivalent to $35 per ounce), implying a mint parity of $8.2397004. In fact, the mint parity of $4.8665635

TABLE Ee612–614   Dollar–sterling parity: 1789–1978   *Continued*

continued in use by custom, but without legitimacy. Further, the United States had abandoned the gold standard on March 6, 1933, and the United Kingdom had done the same on September 20, 1931.

Series Ee612. The 1939 figure is applicable beginning September 5. The midpoint of Bank of England fixed buying and selling rates for the pound was $4.04 September 5–13 and $4.03 thereafter. The 1939 figure is the average of the two midpoints, weighted by the number of days for which they are applicable.

Series Ee612. On December 18, 1946, the United Kingdom established an initial par value of $4.03 with the IMF. This replaced, at the same value, the midpoint of Bank of England fixed buying and selling rates previously in force.

Series Ee612. On September 18, 1949, the par value of the pound was changed to $2.80. The value given for that year is the average of $4.03 and $2.80, weighted by the number of days for which they are applicable.

Series Ee612. On November 18, 1967, the par value of the pound was changed to $2.40. The value given for that year is the average of $2.80 and $2.40, weighted by the number of days for which they are applicable.

Series Ee612. On December 18, 1971, the devaluation of the dollar from $35 to $38 per ounce of gold, combined with the decision of the United Kingdom to retain the existing par value of the pound in terms of gold, yielded a par value of $2.6057143 – computed as $(\frac{38}{35})(2.40)$. The value given for that year is the average of $2.40 and $2.6057143, weighted by the number of days for which they are applicable.

Series Ee612. On June 23, 1972, the United Kingdom ceased to maintain the exchange value of the pound within announced limits around the par value, but the par value itself was retained.

Series Ee612. The figure for 1978 is applicable only through March 31. Effective April 1, the par value system was formally terminated by the IMF.

Series Ee613. The first value given for the series is applicable July 31, 1789 (Act of Congress of that date). Parity was changed as follows: to $4.80 effective March 3, 1833 (Act of Congress of July 14, 1832); to $4.84 effective July 17, 1842 (Act of Congress of that date); and to $4.8665 effective March 3, 1873 (Act of Congress of that date). For the years during which parity was changed, the value given in the series is an average of the two parity values during the year, weighted by the number of days each was applicable. The last value given for the series is applicable through May 26, as the Act of Congress of May 27, 1921, effectively made this concept of legal parity inoperative.

Series Ee614. The first value given for the series is applicable July 31, 1789 (Act of Congress of that date). Parity was changed as follows: to $4.56572 effective February 9, 1793 (Act of Congress of that date); and to $4.86934 effective June 28, 1834 (Act of Congress of that date). For the years during which parity was changed, the value given in the series is an average of the two parity values during the year, weighted by the number of days each was applicable. The last value given for the series is applicable through February 20, as the Act of February 21, 1857, terminated the legal-tender status of foreign coin.

TABLE Ee615–620   Dollar–sterling exchange rates: 1791–1914

Contributed by Lawrence H. Officer

	Bill of exchange			Bill of exchange		
					Sterling premium	
Year	60-day exchange rate	Sight exchange rate	Cable-transfer exchange rate	Sight-equivalent exchange rate	Sight-equivalent exchange rate	Sight-equivalent exchange rate corrected for paper-currency depreciation
	Ee615 [1,2]	Ee616 [1,2,3]	Ee617	Ee618 [4]	Ee619 [4]	Ee620 [5]
	Dollars per pound	Dollars per pound	Dollars per pound	Dollars per pound	Percent	Percent
1791	—	—	—	4.5554	−0.63	−0.63
1792	—	—	—	4.4663	−3.34	−3.34
1793	—	—	—	4.5089	−1.31	−1.31
1794	4.7631	—	—	4.7484	1.67	1.67
1795	4.5496	—	—	4.5257	−3.71	−3.71
1796	4.3521	—	—	4.2862	−10.02	−10.02
1797	4.3938	—	—	4.4366	−5.41	−2.69
1798	4.3956	—	—	4.3883	−7.52	−6.40
1799	4.1006	—	—	4.1321	−13.75	−7.46
1800	4.4724	—	—	4.5479	−4.71	6.93
1801	4.3096	—	—	4.3809	−6.90	7.96
1802	4.3873	—	—	4.4848	−3.45	6.41
1803	4.5279	—	—	4.5405	−3.20	5.15
1804	4.5621	—	—	4.5516	−2.96	4.21
1805	4.3614	—	—	4.3475	−9.54	−2.49
1806	4.4095	—	—	4.4328	−6.16	3.40
1807	4.3614	—	—	4.4254	−5.77	3.29
1808	4.6898	—	—	4.6259	−5.49	1.28
1809	4.5723	—	—	4.5739	−5.85	3.48
1810	4.2421	—	—	4.2992	−10.44	1.88
1811	3.8388	—	—	3.8165	−19.26	−2.27
1812	3.5789	—	—	3.6161	−26.26	−5.14
1813	3.7463	—	—	3.7497	−24.19	2.73
1814	4.0830	—	—	4.2398	−7.39	7.06

Notes appear at end of table

(continued)

TABLE Ee615–620   Dollar–sterling exchange rates: 1791–1914   *Continued*

	Bill of exchange			Bill of exchange		
					Sterling premium	
Year	60-day exchange rate	Sight exchange rate	Cable-transfer exchange rate	Sight-equivalent exchange rate	Sight-equivalent exchange rate	Sight-equivalent exchange rate corrected for paper-currency depreciation
	Ee615 [1,2]	Ee616 [1,2,3]	Ee617	Ee618 [4]	Ee619 [4]	Ee620 [5]
	Dollars per pound	Dollars per pound	Dollars per pound	Dollars per pound	Percent	Percent
1815	4.5381	—	—	4.9043	5.59	4.29
1816	4.7411	—	—	5.2236	12.31	−1.19
1817	4.5103	—	—	4.6018	0.06	3.05
1818	4.4428	—	—	4.4997	−3.69	5.19
1819	4.4679	—	—	4.5127	−3.29	1.57
1820	4.4928	—	—	4.5219	−4.89	−5.61
1821	4.7855	—	—	4.8208	−0.70	−1.21
1822	4.9206	—	—	4.9777	3.50	3.50
1823	4.7770	—	—	4.7995	−0.46	−0.46
1824	4.8406	—	—	4.8673	1.08	1.08
1825	4.8003	—	—	4.8295	1.06	1.06
1826	4.8885	—	—	4.9204	2.57	2.57
1827	4.9145	—	—	4.9358	3.02	3.02
1828	4.9075	—	—	4.9284	2.61	2.61
1829	4.8331	—	—	4.8620	1.23	1.23
1830	4.7590	—	—	4.7616	−1.12	−1.12
1831	4.8288	—	—	4.8601	1.57	1.57
1832	4.8438	—	—	4.8577	1.46	1.46
1833	4.7859	—	—	4.7872	−1.27	−1.27
1834	4.6126	—	—	4.6382	−3.83	−3.83
1835	4.8234	—	—	4.8498	−0.43	−0.43
1836	4.7874	—	—	4.8173	−1.10	−1.10
1837	5.0644	—	—	5.0985	4.76	−0.38
1838	4.8140	—	—	4.8863	0.41	−1.48
1839	4.8513	—	—	4.9845	2.42	−0.20
1840	4.7885	—	—	5.0003	2.75	−1.51
1841	4.8188	—	—	4.9893	2.52	−0.10
1842	4.7603	—	—	4.7972	−1.43	−1.98
1843	4.7781	—	—	4.7878	−1.62	−1.62
1844	4.8503	—	—	4.8595	−0.14	−0.14
1845	4.8646	—	—	4.8713	0.10	0.10
1846	4.8087	—	—	4.8159	−1.04	−1.04
1847	4.7471	—	—	4.7934	−1.50	−1.50
1848	4.8700	—	—	4.8685	0.04	0.04
1849	4.8262	—	—	4.8139	−1.08	−1.08
1850	4.8336	—	—	4.8702	0.08	0.08
1851	4.8970	—	—	4.9127	0.95	0.95
1852	4.8914	—	—	4.9018	0.72	0.72
1853	4.8622	—	—	4.8877	0.43	0.43
1854	4.8498	—	—	4.8826	0.33	0.33
1855	4.8558	—	—	4.8862	0.40	0.40
1856	4.8623	—	—	4.9089	0.87	0.87
1857	4.8255	4.9354 [6]	—	4.8886	0.45	0.34
1858	4.8636	—	—	4.8575	−0.19	−0.19
1859	4.8791	—	—	4.8992	0.67	0.67
1860	4.8170	—	—	4.8493	−0.35	−0.35
1861	4.7393	—	—	4.7735	−1.91	−1.91
1862	5.4885	—	—	5.5582	14.21	0.91
1863	7.1151	—	—	7.0750	45.38	0.18
1864	9.3490	—	—	9.9743	104.96	1.66
1865	4.8428	4.8864 [6]	—	7.6918	58.05	0.73
1866	4.7624	4.8087	—	6.8769	41.31	0.38
1867	4.8602	4.8843	—	6.7514	38.73	0.51
1868	4.8753	4.8820	—	6.8278	40.30	0.60
1869	4.8475	4.8598	—	6.4833	33.22	0.17

Notes appear at end of table

TABLE Ee615–620 Dollar–sterling exchange rates: 1791–1914 *Continued*

	Bill of exchange				Bill of exchange	
					Sterling premium	
	60-day exchange rate	Sight exchange rate	Cable-transfer exchange rate	Sight-equivalent exchange rate	Sight-equivalent exchange rate	Sight-equivalent exchange rate corrected for paper-currency depreciation
	Ee615 [1,2]	Ee616 [1,2,3]	Ee617	Ee618 [4]	Ee619 [4]	Ee620 [5]
Year	Dollars per pound	Dollars per pound	Dollars per pound	Dollars per pound	Percent	Percent
1870	4.8463	4.8776	—	5.5882	14.83	−0.05
1871	4.8584	4.8887	—	5.4603	12.20	0.22
1872	4.8420	4.8822	—	5.4447	11.88	−0.52
1873	4.8167	4.8618	—	5.5473	13.99	0.19
1874	4.8574	4.8904	—	5.4203	11.38	0.13
1875	4.8497	4.8833	—	5.5898	14.86	−0.09
1876	4.8570	4.8798	—	5.4232	11.44	−0.09
1877	4.8435	4.8701	—	5.0772	4.33	−0.40
1878	4.8330	4.8655	—	4.8900	0.48	−0.32
1879	4.8424	4.8667	4.8500 [6]	4.8535	−0.27	−0.27
1880	4.8315	4.8571	4.8485	4.8445	−0.15	−0.45
1881	4.8344	4.8604	4.8625	4.8295	−0.76	−0.76
1882	4.8482	4.8884	4.8897	4.8698	0.07	0.07
1883	4.8285	4.8601	4.8646	4.8490	−0.36	−0.36
1884	4.8472	4.8726	4.8710	4.8538	−0.26	−0.26
1885	4.8471	4.8696	4.8654	4.8560	−0.22	−0.22
1886	4.8561	4.8785	4.8774	4.8614	−0.11	−0.11
1887	4.8359	4.8662	4.8640	4.8518	−0.30	−0.30
1888	4.8573	4.8844	4.8814	4.8703	0.08	0.08
1889	4.8565	4.8846	4.8827	4.8687	0.04	0.04
1890	4.8355	4.8713	4.8682	4.8605	−0.13	−0.13
1891	4.8415	4.8771	4.8672	4.8611	0.11	−0.11
1892	4.8642	4.8823	4.8768	4.8731	0.13	0.13
1893	4.8492	4.8761	4.8718	4.8639	−0.06	−0.06
1894	4.8725	4.8873	4.8805	4.8769	0.21	0.21
1895	4.8874	4.8960	4.8932	4.8883	0.45	0.45
1896	4.8664	4.8825	4.8774	4.8712	0.09	0.09
1897	4.8542	4.8742	4.8680	4.8633	−0.07	−0.07
1898	4.8330	4.8596	4.8537	4.8477	−0.39	−0.39
1899	4.8434	4.8730	4.8702	4.8638	−0.06	−0.06
1900	4.8394	4.8750	4.8728	4.8652	−0.03	−0.03
1901	4.8494	4.8800	4.8789	4.8727	0.13	0.13
1902	4.8520	4.8796	4.8779	4.8719	0.11	0.11
1903	4.8320	4.8642	4.8685	4.8631	−0.07	−0.07
1904	4.8414	4.8659	4.8692	4.8676	0.02	0.02
1905	4.8420	4.8652	4.8693	4.8652	−0.03	−0.03
1906	4.8166	4.8506	4.8568	4.8508	−0.32	−0.32
1907	4.8166	4.8572	4.8658	4.8579	−0.18	−0.18
1908	4.8415	4.8641	4.8679	4.8656	−0.02	−0.02
1909	4.8521	4.8726	4.8759	4.8729	0.13	0.13
1910	4.8373	4.8631	4.8670	4.8639	−0.06	−0.06
1911	4.8370	4.8621	4.8656	4.8623	−0.09	−0.09
1912	4.8342	4.8660	4.8700	4.8658	−0.02	−0.02
1913	4.8264	4.8653	4.8701	4.8637	−0.06	−0.06
1914 [6]	4.8426	4.8670	4.8707	4.8696	0.06	0.06

[1] Bankers' bills (bills drawn on British banks) from 1867, with prime bills selected over second-class bills.

[2] For 1902–1909, basic data are weekly averages of high and low rate.

[3] Prior to 1880, bills are "three days to sight."

[4] Not comparable to series Ee616 in several respects. See text.

[5] Fundamentally different from series Ee615–619. See text.

[6] Average based on only a portion of the year. See text.

Sources

Series Ee615–617. Jürgen Schneider, Oskar Schwarzer, and Friedrich Zellfelder, *Währunger der Welt I: Europäische und Nordamerikanische Devisenkurse, 1777–1914*, volume 1 (Franz Steiner, 1991), pp. 320–5, 329–31, and 334–5, respectively.

Series Ee618–619. Previously unpublished, developed by Lawrence H. Officer.

Series Ee620. Tables 6.8, 6.10, 6.11, and 6.13 in Lawrence H. Officer, *Between the Dollar–Sterling Gold Points: Exchange Rates, Parity, and Market Behavior* (Cambridge University Press, 1996), pp. 82–6, 88–90, 97; and unpublished quarterly series underlying those tables.

Documentation

Until World War I the dollar–sterling, meaning dollar–(British) pound, exchange rate was of overwhelming importance in the American foreign-exchange market. There were three main exchange-market instruments: (1) the sixty-day bill of exchange, (2) the sight (or demand) bill of exchange, and (3) the cable (or telegraphic) transfer, each with its associated exchange rate. The purchaser of sterling made dollar payment immediately but received

(continued)

TABLE Ee615–620   Dollar–sterling exchange rates: 1791–1914   *Continued*

pounds at a later time, varying with the exchange-market instrument: (1) the period used up by oceanic shipment across the Atlantic and presentation of the bill in London plus an additional sixty-three days (three of which constituted "days of grace"), (2) the period used up by oceanic shipment across the Atlantic and presentation of the bill in London, and (3) generally on the same business day. The dominant exchange-market instrument was the sixty-day bill until the Civil War, the demand bill beginning in 1879, and the cable transfer after World War I. It may be noted that a *t*-day bill with $t > 0$ was called a time bill, whereas $t = 0$ characterized a sight bill.

Ideally, for maximum representativeness given annual frequency, exchange-rate series should be annual averages of daily values. Series Ee615–617 are averages of monthly values; the nature and frequency of the intra-monthly observations underlying the monthly values are not stated by the authors. Series Ee618–620 are averages of quarterly values, the quarterly values themselves averages of all intraquarterly observations for 1791–1833 (third quarter) and 1835–1869, monthly rates (one day per month) for 1833 (fourth quarter)–1834, and daily rates for 1870–1914.

Reliable exchange-rate data emanate from actual foreign-exchange market transactions, as in series Ee617 (cable transfer). However, recorded prices of bills of exchange, the source of exchange-rate data for this instrument (with the exchange rate computed as the bill's dollar market-price/pound face-value ratio), do not necessarily pertain to actual transactions but alternatively could reflect merely quotations of brokers, dealers, or even commodity traders or could apply only to small transactions (so-called posted rates). Series Ee618–620 pertain to actual transactions, except for 1833 (fourth quarter)–1834. This is because Officer (1996, pp. 64–8, 74) deliberately selected data sources that recorded actual-transaction prices and corrected posted rates so that they were converted to actual (large-transaction) rates. In contrast, the data sources listed by Schneider, Schwarzer, and Zellfelder (1991, pp. xxxv–xxxvi) suggest that the actual-transactions property for series Ee615–617 is applicable only to 1896–1914 (see Officer 1996, pp. 64–6).

However, the Schneider, Schwarzer, and Zellfelder series have the advantage that they pertain to one place of quotation, New York, for the entire period – and New York became the dominant American foreign-exchange market early in the nineteenth century. The Officer series have New York as the city of quotation only from 1870, with Baltimore 1791–1829 (third quarter) and Philadelphia 1829 (fourth quarter)–1869. This is the trade-off for actual transactions as the data-source criterion.

All recorded exchange-rate data are the price at which foreign exchange (pounds) can be purchased, the selling rate of brokers or dealers. Schneider, Schwarzer, and Zellfelder retain this property in their series. Officer adopts the principle that the "true" exchange rate is the midpoint of the buying and selling rates (with broker's commission constituting the difference between the two rates).

The Schneider, Schwarzer, and Zellfelder series are each internally consistent and enable comparison of the three main exchange rates (sixty-day bills, sight bills, and cable transfers) for periods when data exist for more than one series. In contrast, Officer adopts the principle that long-term pre–World War I exchange rate series should *both* pertain to the dominant exchange-rate instrument, even as this changed over time, *and* have the property of internal consistency. Because (1) the cable transfer became dominant only after World War I, (2) the sight bill succeeded the time bill as the principal instrument thirty-five years prior to the war, and (3) the sight bill provides the bill exchange rate closest to the cable rate, the time-bill exchange-rate series (dominant 1791–1878) is converted to a sight-bill basis by factoring out the interest component of the time-bill exchange rate with respect to a hypothetical sight-bill rate. The corrected series is then joined to the sight-bill exchange-rate series for the period when the sight bill was dominant (1879–1914).

The Officer series all have the conceptual bases described previously, but they differ in other respects. Series Ee620 corrects the exchange rate for the depreciation of the paper-currency pound or dollar during periods when Britain or the United States, respectively, was on a paper rather than specie (gold or silver) standard. It is a series with the counterfactual basis that both countries remained on a specie standard throughout 1791–1914. The series

is expressed as the percentage deviation from mint parity; so a positive (negative) value means a sterling premium (discount), a higher (lower) exchange value for the pound than that given by parity. Series Ee619 removes the correction for paper-currency depreciations, so that the exchange rate is factual in nature, and it is the annual average of a computation involving quarterly series. Series Ee618 differs from series Ee619 in the unit of measurement – dollars per pound, comparable to series Ee615–617 – rather than percentage deviation from parity. For detailed discussion of the methodology of the Officer series, see Officer (1996), Chapter 6.

The difference between series Ee615–619 and series Ee620 may be stated in another way. The first five series provide the exchange rate between U.S. and British *paper currency*. For Britain, that currency is Bank of England notes; for the United States, it is either commercial-bank notes, or, from 1861, U.S. Treasury paper currency (Treasury demand notes, U.S. notes (popularly called greenbacks), gold certificates, and Treasury notes of 1890). Series Ee620 presents the exchange rate between U.S. and British *gold and/or silver coin*: gold coin when the country is on an effective or virtual gold standard (Britain, 1791–1914; the United States, July 31, 1834–1914); silver coin when the country is on an effective or virtual silver standard (the United States, 1791–July 30, 1834). As long as both countries were on effective gold or silver standards, whether the exchange rate pertains to paper currency or to coin is insignificant because paper currency was convertible into coin on demand. However, when at least one country was on a paper standard, then its paper currency was not convertible into coin, and the difference between series Ee615–619 and series Ee620 becomes important. The first five series then reflect depreciation of the paper currency in terms of coin, whereas series Ee620 does not do so. The years including a paper standard were 1797–1821 for Britain; 1814–1817, 1837–1842, 1857, and 1861–1878 for the United States.

Returning to the Schneider-Schwarzer-Zellfelder series, the ranking of sixty-day bill, sight bill, cable transfer in order of delay of pound receipt (longer delay first) suggests that, for consistent data, the sixty-day, sight, and cable rate have the same ordering (lower exchange rate first): the purchaser of pounds would pay a higher dollar price for a shorter delay of pound receipt. Although series Ee616 uniformly exceeds series Ee615, series Ee617 exceeds series Ee616 only in 1881–1883 and 1903–1914. This anomaly in 1880 and 1884–1902 may be explainable in terms of inconsistent data, market imperfection, or objectives (such as "window dressing") beyond cost minimization or profit maximization. (Comparison for 1879 is inappropriate because series Ee617 is for December only.)

Interesting is the absence of trend in the dollars-per-pound series, notwithstanding the instability during periods of paper standard (series Ee615–618). Series Ee620 corrects for paper-currency depreciation and is expressed as the percentage deviation from mint parity; the downward trend in the magnitude of this series to an absolute value so low that it permanently falls below 1 percent of parity after 1864 and below one tenth of 1 percent from 1910, illustrates the integration of the American foreign-exchange market over time and the remarkable stability of the dollar–sterling exchange rate as World War I approached.

The literature on the pre–World War I dollar–sterling exchange rate is highlighted by the following works: Arthur H. Cole, "Evolution of the Foreign-Exchange Market of the United States," *Journal of Economic and Business History* 1 (May 1929): 384–421; Arthur H. Cole, "Seasonal Variation of Sterling Exchange," *Journal of Economic and Business History* 2 (November 1929): 203–18; Lance E. Davis and Jonathan R. T. Hughes, "A Dollar-Sterling Exchange, 1803–1895," *Economic History Review* 13 (August 1960): 52–78; Edwin J. Perkins, *Financing Anglo-American Trade: The House of Brown, 1800–1880* (Harvard University Press, 1975); and Officer (1996).

In some cases averages were calculated from data for only a portion of the year. Series Ee616: 1857, November and December; 1865, June to December. Series Ee617: 1879, December. Series Ee615–620: 1914, January to June.

Series Ee620. Based conceptually on tables in Officer (1996); however, series Ee620 is the annual average of Officer's unpublished quarterly series underlying those tables – series that have more significant digits than the tables show.

TABLE Ee621–636 Bilateral exchange rates – Europe: 1913–1999 [Contemporary currency units]

Contributed by Lawrence H. Officer

Year	Austria Ee621 [1] Currency per dollar	Belgium Ee622 [1,2] Currency per dollar	Denmark Ee623 Kroner per dollar	Finland Ee624 [1] Currency per dollar	France Ee625 [1,3] Currency per dollar	Germany Ee626 [1] Currency per dollar	Greece Ee627 [1] Currency per dollar	Ireland Ee628 Dollars per pound
1913	4.95549961	5.21536865	3.73767502	—	5.18411380	4.20281084	—	—
1914	5.08432351 [7]	5.17804715 [7]	3.75575570 [7]	—	5.09489237	4.22988584	—	—
1915	6.50474196	—	3.87650990	—	5.56929315	4.84733324	5.23938762 [8]	—
1916	7.95272898	—	3.53148495	—	5.88650812	5.49547173	5.12043257 [8]	—
1917	8.89766792 [8]	—	3.32937138	—	5.7643647	5.77317207 [8]	5.05466622	—
1918	—	—	3.30651748	—	5.61639989	—	5.14946317	—
1919	—	7.83269366 [7]	4.29461026	—	7.30887297	32.85151117 [8]	—	—
1920	—	13.55013550	6.33914422	—	14.20454545	57.11022273	—	—
1921	994.03578529 [8]	13.43020991	5.61920870	60.38647343 [8]	13.41309655	83.02200083	19.89614214 [8]	—
1922	10,309.27835052	13.01591847	4.77395331	46.22353703	12.19318888	430.47783039	30.24894885	—
1923	71,428.57142857	19.16075877	5.44534777	37.27032164	16.44439328	50,000.00000000	58.33965346	—
1924	71,428.57142857	21.53408846	5.97985983	39.87876854	19.09563092	4,329,004,329,004.33000000 [9]	55.86592179	—
1925	7.11769102 [9]	21.01723413	4.73238370	39.65421524	20.97711397	4.20145118	64.04508774	—
1926	7.10530055	30.62505742 [9]	3.81305361	39.66837241	30.83849878	4.20175129	79.49757532	—
1927	7.10408911	7.18612790	3.74180078	39.68726436	25.48419980	4.20808120	75.91285205	—
1928	7.10514910	7.17973019	3.73935219	39.72510229	25.50369804	4.19086893	76.66360012	—
1929	7.11364041	7.18783244	3.74809784	39.74562798	25.53560941	4.20016297	77.31560229	—
1930	7.09768544	7.16722571	3.73622268	39.31141563	25.47835614	4.19215145	77.16544803	—
1931	7.13129426	7.17952400	3.99072555	41.84481675	25.51020408	4.23187277	77.36345350	—
1932	7.16337510	7.18716086	5.31019504	64.22109089	25.46084123	4.21066815	120.19230769	—
1933	6.47341369	5.58671702	5.24359102	53.45306821	19.87557888	3.27676544	138.25521913	—
1934	5.32113021	4.29429674	4.44448395	44.88934776	15.22348070	2.53967609	106.36034886	—
1935	5.31042064	5.42767354	4.56967382	46.23849817	15.14853135	2.48400919	106.54165779	—
1936	5.32147000	5.91135335	4.50667664	45.65584623	16.35563697	2.48156815	107.65421466	—
1937	5.32770727	5.92553967	4.53122239	45.84842511	24.71576866	2.48733326	110.43622308	—
1938	5.28664171 [8]	5.91919120	4.58200646	46.36713497	34.74514437	2.48979805	111.63206073	—
1939	—	5.93404898	4.91487438	50.13033888	39.83587619	2.49618707	122.65423770	—
1940	—	5.92406533 [8]	5.17911986 [8]	53.44735436	48.01459644 [8]	2.49869443	148.92032762 [8]	—
1941	—	—	—	49.74876872 [8]	—	2.50202664 [8]	—	—
1942	—	—	—	—	—	—	—	—
1943	—	—	—	—	—	—	—	—
1944	—	—	—	—	—	—	—	—
1945	—	43.74453193 [8]	4.79023558 [8]	—	50.73309320 [8]	—	—	—
1946	—	43.80393359	4.79301370	—	118.92020454	—	—	—
1947	—	43.82697112	4.79448443	—	118.94849530	—	—	—
1948	—	43.82889201	5.23100100	—	308.64197531 [7]	—	—	—
1949	—	45.43595802	—	—	331.45508784	—	—	—
1950	—	50.23106289	6.89950186	—	349.89503149	4.19500040 [8]	—	—
1951	—	50.35500277	6.90078738	—	350.14005602	4.19500040	—	2.803750 [8]
1952	—	50.30687192	6.90054928	—	350.14005602	4.19500040	—	2.796761
1953	25.92016589 [8]	49.97751012	6.89954946	—	350.14005602	4.19500040	—	2.812655
1954	25.92016589	50.06257822	6.90421779	—	350.14005602	4.19500040	—	2.808686

Notes appear at end of table

(continued)

TABLE Ee621–636   Bilateral exchange rates – Europe: 1913–1999   [Contemporary currency units]   _Continued_

Year	Austria Ee621 [1] Currency per dollar	Belgium Ee622 [1,2] Currency per dollar	Denmark Ee623 Kroner per dollar	Finland Ee624 [1] Currency per dollar	France Ee625 [1,3] Currency per dollar	Germany Ee626 [1] Currency per dollar	Greece Ee627 [1] Currency per dollar	Ireland Ee628 Dollars per pound
1955	25.92016589	50.23863351	6.90502824	—	350.14005602	4.20788642	—	2.791288
1956	25.92016589	49.92511233	6.90502824	—	350.26269702	4.20413603	—	2.795681
1957	25.94774125	50.23610972	6.90502824	—	420.87542088 [8]	4.20196316	—	2.793246
1958	25.94976126	49.89024147	6.90498056	—	421.22999158	4.19320617	—	2.809753
1959	25.89399000	49.97001799	6.89270132	—	490.67713445	4.17950122	—	2.808807
1960	26.00036401	49.86785020	6.89407936	—	4.90455731	4.17076792	—	2.807564
1961	25.98685065	49.87033712	6.90512360	—	4.90580848	4.01558045	—	2.802200
1962	25.84981259	49.76857612	6.90131125	—	4.90075962	3.99792108	—	2.807800
1963	25.84647196	49.87033712	6.90417012	—	4.90099980	3.98660501	—	2.800000
1964	25.84112874	49.75371909	6.91562932	—	4.90099980	3.97503677	—	2.792100
1965	25.83712278	49.64257347	6.91562932	—	4.90172050	3.99424828	—	2.795900
1966	25.84914439	49.83305925	6.90846287	—	4.91352201	3.99888031	—	2.793000
1967	25.84780811	49.68944099	6.98080279	—	4.92053339	3.98660501	—	2.750400
1968	25.85649644	49.93508439	7.48390959	—	4.95270170	3.99233472	—	2.393500
1969	25.87054380	50.14542172	7.51936236	—	5.18081028	3.92295320	—	2.390100
1970	25.86719781	49.65489846	7.49962502	—	5.52883286	3.64644107	—	2.395900
1971	24.99437627	48.54840276	7.40302043	4.20964008	5.51024906	3.47608454	—	2.444200
1972	23.13315444	44.02183483	6.95216908	4.15644873	5.04413619	3.18836883	—	2.500800
1973	19.36145908	38.81836885	6.02300789	3.81213785	4.43734469	2.64844536	—	2.451000
1974	18.66925547	38.89083343	6.08198516	3.76435159	4.80653689	2.58244454	—	2.340300
1975	17.40129118	36.69320809	5.73493147	3.66501741	4.28192173	2.45525301	—	2.221600
1976	17.93915040	38.57875854	6.04375680	3.85534737	4.77509311	2.51654629	—	1.804800
1977	16.53056501	35.82816811	6.00312162	4.01396861	4.91545419	2.32131665	—	1.744900
1978	14.50158067	31.43764343	5.50782111	4.10896988	4.50085516	2.00533419	—	1.918400
1979	13.38700000	29.34200000	5.26220000	3.88860000	4.25660000	1.83420000	—	2.046500
1980	12.94500000	29.23700000	5.63450000	3.72060000	4.22500000	1.81750000	—	2.057700
1981	15.94800000	37.19400000	7.13500000	4.31280000	5.43960000	2.26310000	—	1.613200
1982	17.06000000	45.78000000	8.34430000	4.80860000	6.57930000	2.42800000	66.87200000	1.420500
1983	17.96800000	51.12100000	9.14830000	5.56360000	7.62030000	2.55390000	87.89500000	1.248100
1984	20.00500000	57.74900000	10.35400000	6.00070000	8.73550000	2.84540000	112.73000000	1.086400
1985	20.67600000	59.33600000	10.59800000	6.19710000	8.97990000	2.94190000	138.40000000	1.066200
1986	15.26000000	44.66400000	8.09550000	5.07220000	6.92570000	2.17050000	139.93000000	1.341400
1987	12.64900000	37.35800000	6.84780000	4.40370000	6.01220000	1.79810000	135.47000000	1.487900
1988	12.35700000	36.78500000	6.74120000	4.19330000	5.95950000	1.75700000	142.00000000	1.524900
1989	13.23600000	39.40900000	7.32100000	4.29630000	6.38020000	1.88080000	162.60000000	1.418000
1990	11.33100000	33.42400000	6.18900000	3.83000000	5.44670000	1.61660000	158.59000000	1.657600
1991	11.68600000	34.19500000	6.40380000	4.04810000	5.64680000	1.66100000	182.63000000	1.613900
1992	10.99200000	32.14800000	6.03720000	4.48650000	5.29350000	1.56180000	190.81000000	1.704200
1993	11.63900000	34.58100000	6.48630000	5.72510000	5.66690000	1.65450000	229.64000000	1.464700
1994	11.40900000	33.42600000	6.35610000	5.23400000	5.54590000	1.62160000	242.50000000	1.496900
1995	10.07600000	29.47200000	5.59990000	4.37630000	4.98640000	1.43210000	231.68000000	1.603500
1996	10.58900000	30.97000000	5.80030000	4.59480000	5.11580000	1.50490000	240.82000000	1.599500
1997	12.20600000	35.80700000	6.60920000	5.19560000	5.83930000	1.73480000	273.28000000	1.516300
1998	12.37900000	36.31000000	6.70300000	5.34730000	5.89950000	1.75970000	295.70000000	1.424800
1999	14.65900000	42.97400000	6.99000000	6.33400000	6.98790000	2.08350000	306.30000000	0.839000

Year	Italy Ee629 [4] Lire per dollar	Netherlands Ee630 Guilders per dollar	Norway Ee631 Kroner per dollar	Portugal Ee632 Escudos per dollar	Spain Ee633 [1,5] Pesetas per dollar	Sweden Ee634 Kronor per dollar	Switzerland Ee635 Francs per dollar	United Kingdom Ee636 [6] Dollars per pound
1913	5.26379509	2.49253486	—	—	—	—	5.19896457	4.868917
1914	5.19494013	2.46216878	—	—	—	—	5.13299592 [7]	4.929646
1915	6.05008258	2.46962973	3.86407722	—	5.26537489	3.86186868	5.32739506	4.756961
1916	6.54990372	2.39150919	3.49313250	1.45963667 [8]	5.00317702	3.45550860	5.22018751	4.766011
1917	7.50857855	2.38254642	3.27141633	1.50668895	4.42286088	3.05763645	4.76869447	4.764430
1918	7.86188245	2.12561537	3.24228983	1.57440149	4.05873806	3.02720244	4.37929993	4.765051
1919	8.79584836	2.55447416	4.06901042	—	5.04464511	3.91512019	5.26787125	4.425800
1920	20.12072435	2.90537203	6.04960678	10.02305302 [8]	6.27431296	4.87947692	5.91610957	3.664270
1921	23.29047885	2.97203317	6.70834787	14.99250375	7.39010908	4.36092783	5.76242567	3.849023
1922	21.02651443	2.59757127	5.71376331	23.51447316	6.45878007	3.82173881	5.24515872	4.429165
1923	21.73157163	2.55751205	5.99844041	29.54209749	6.91902663	3.76579752	5.53709856	4.574825
1924	22.94630564	2.61705430	7.17344677	19.84245094	7.49765698	3.77041207	5.48763088	4.417064
1925	25.14078842	2.49003364	5.59171531	19.51067234	6.97141025	3.72468610	5.17416230	4.828944
1926	25.71090657	2.49386509	4.47733795	19.88466892	6.71325667	3.73627852	5.17785947	4.858235
1927	19.39487975	2.49336143	3.83911055	22.38388360	5.86193960	3.72928383	5.19162280	4.861024
1928	19.02189420	2.48609032	3.74705856	22.36436016	6.02620193	3.73131544	5.19221583	4.866223
1929	19.10803684	2.48990344	3.74774667	22.25189141	6.81045814	3.73358622	5.18693722	4.856879
1930	19.09344331	2.48600998	3.73694871	23.56545305	8.57118368	3.72379842	5.15942627	4.862126
1931	19.20749861	2.48571954	3.99128304	31.28911139	10.47636009	3.95976875	5.15440005	4.534990
1932	19.51105301	2.48170364	5.55435211	25.53300140	12.43193516	5.41389205	5.15333756	3.506067
1933	14.90446240	1.93345437	4.66652978	21.69715116	9.32931551	4.53877017	4.02649433	4.236821
1934	11.67992338	1.48405164	3.95005550	22.43409983	7.34484025	3.84889248	3.08963335	5.039302
1935	12.12547441	1.47678421	4.06061689	22.15820962	7.31085003	3.95710498	3.07718819	4.901761
1936	13.71441110	1.55085165	4.00419640	22.32541525	8.12096997	3.90222583	3.31250870	4.970943
1937	19.00887715	1.81671193	4.02582972	22.59019134	16.52182533	3.92363046	4.35961601	4.944022
1938	19.00959985	1.81789096	4.07069992	24.76780186	17.85714286	3.96874219	4.37229191	4.889375
1939	19.24594392	1.87494141	4.30546406	26.94691458	9.40724923 [7,8]	4.16826450	4.43961020	4.435385
1940	19.83851449	1.88225374 [8]	4.40354045 [8]	24.98563326 [8]	10.72765697	4.20130997	4.40994884	3.830003
1941	19.72269885 [8]	—	—	—	10.95290252 [8]	4.19654960 [8]	4.30858054 [8]	4.031832
1942	—	—	—	—	—	—	—	4.034977
1943	—	—	—	—	—	—	—	4.035000 [10]
1944	—	2.63624788 [8]	—	—	—	—	—	4.035000
1945	225.52999549	—	4.95633469 [8]	—	—	—	—	4.030178 [8]
1946	269.17900404	2.64459313	4.96034207	24.69074838 [8]	10.95002409 [8]	3.86709566 [8]	4.28032719 [8]	4.032843
1947	574.71264368	2.64829807	4.96066195	24.83053162	10.95002409	3.59403247	4.28030887	4.028572
1948	588.58151854	2.65476623	5.41110901	24.88614588	10.95002409 [8]	3.59396788	4.28030887	4.031317
1949	624.60961899	2.89620857	—	25.77319588	—	3.92470839	4.28934184	3.687222
1950	625.00000000	3.80919005	7.13500863	28.81512218	—	5.17274378	4.32219360	2.800666
1951	625.00000000	3.80747865	7.13500863	28.78609056	—	5.17413553	4.33343822	2.799644
1952	625.00000000	3.80017177	7.13500863	28.69193470	—	5.17429617	4.32310230	2.792598
1953	625.00000000	3.79649280	7.13500863	28.66397225	—	5.17509949	4.28882675	2.812655
1954	625.00000000	3.79067872	7.13877784	28.65329513	—	5.17250297	4.28785209	2.808688
1955	625.00000000	3.81239945	7.13877784	28.65329513	—	5.17250297	4.28616127	2.791280
1956	625.00000000	3.82952487	7.13877784	28.65329513	—	5.17250297	4.28553674	2.795685
1957	625.00000000	3.82114008	7.13877784	28.65329513	—	5.17301137	4.28627150	2.793244
1958	624.60961899	3.78524059	7.13872688	28.65329513	41.99916002	5.17373399	4.28671248	2.809753
1959	621.11801242	3.77471020	7.12880322	28.59839277	48.59322610	5.17504593	4.32116637	2.808807

Notes appear at end of table

(continued)

TABLE Ee621–636   Bilateral exchange rates – Europe: 1913 – 1999   [Contemporary currency units]   Continued

Year	Italy Ee629 [4] Lire per dollar	Netherlands Ee630 Guilders per dollar	Norway Ee631 Kroner per dollar	Portugal Ee632 Escudos per dollar	Spain Ee633 [1] [5] Pesetas per dollar	Sweden Ee634 Kronor per dollar	Switzerland Ee635 Francs per dollar	United Kingdom Ee636 [6] Dollars per pound
1960	621.11801242	3.77180575	7.13368526	28.62294988	60.11421701	5.16827917	4.31933724	2.807564
1961	621.11801242	3.62910543	7.14285714	28.64590793	60.08532116	5.16715755	4.31946784	2.802200
1962	620.84807848	3.60295442	7.13775874	28.58286172	60.04563468	5.15543641	4.32451133	2.807800
1963	621.61994157	3.60100828	7.14949596	28.66068614	60.00960154	5.18887505	4.32170794	2.800000
1964	624.45360310	3.60698312	7.15717149	28.73563218	60.01320290	5.15092202	4.31928127	2.792100
1965	624.84378905	3.60048967	7.15051841	28.71170576	60.01680471	5.15836170	4.32788020	2.795900
1966	624.45360310	3.61925443	7.15102975	28.71500359	60.05645307	5.16582292	4.32638228	2.793000
1967	624.14180502	3.60243525	7.15051841	28.74885065	61.03888177	5.16182316	4.32825485	2.750400
1968	623.36367037	3.61977847	7.14285714	28.68288206	70.06726457	5.16822575	4.31611205	2.393500
1969	627.35257215	3.62423891	7.14438808	28.56082027	70.09673349	5.17009616	4.31294747	2.390100
1970	627.15584823	3.61650573	7.1494111	28.58939905	70.02801120	5.18618401	4.31053063	2.395900
1971	618.27624583	3.49040140	7.03977473	28.20397112	69.52652437	5.10412413	4.11099692	2.444200
1972	583.70301191	3.20996373	6.58761528	27.01023688	64.27148274	4.75692132	3.81781392	2.500800
1973	581.66589111	2.77955360	5.74514535	24.34274586	58.21399464	4.35350457	3.15457413	2.451000
1974	650.53343742	2.68333915	5.51906838	25.31261074	57.68010613	4.43203475	2.96841605	2.340300
1975	652.40083507	2.52321356	5.21376434	25.45436033	57.39210285	4.14233048	2.58111143	2.221600
1976	830.28894055	2.64228716	5.45643040	30.15772490	66.85385747	4.35596986	2.49918776	1.804800
1977	882.76836158	2.45386729	5.32226303	38.11847221	75.26153383	4.46676636	2.39727669	1.744900
1978	848.75233407	2.16057385	5.24136485	43.89430252	76.49353630	4.51691585	1.77673543	1.918400
1979	831.10000000	2.00720000	5.06500000	48.95300000	67.15800000	4.28920000	1.66430000	2.122400
1980	856.20000000	1.98750000	4.93810000	50.08200000	71.75800000	4.23090000	1.67720000	2.325800
1981	1,138.60000000	2.49980000	5.74300000	61.73900000	92.39600000	5.06590000	1.96740000	2.024300
1982	1,354.00000000	2.67190000	6.45670000	80.10100000	110.09000000	6.28380000	2.03270000	1.748000
1983	1,519.30000000	2.85430000	7.30120000	111.61000000	143.50000000	7.67170000	2.10060000	1.515900
1984	1,756.10000000	3.20830000	8.15960000	147.70000000	160.78000000	8.27060000	2.35000000	1.336600
1985	1,908.90000000	3.31840000	8.59330000	172.07000000	169.98000000	8.60310000	2.45510000	1.297400
1986	1,491.16000000	2.44850000	7.39850000	149.80000000	140.04000000	7.12730000	1.79790000	1.467700
1987	1,297.03000000	2.02640000	6.74090000	141.20000000	123.54000000	6.34690000	1.49180000	1.639800
1988	1,302.39000000	1.97780000	6.52430000	144.27000000	116.53000000	6.13700000	1.46430000	1.781300
1989	1,372.28000000	2.12190000	6.91310000	157.53000000	118.44000000	6.45590000	1.63690000	1.638200
1990	1,198.27000000	1.82150000	6.25410000	142.70000000	101.96000000	5.92310000	1.39010000	1.784100
1991	1,241.28000000	1.87200000	6.49120000	144.77000000	104.01000000	6.05210000	1.43560000	1.767400
1992	1,232.17000000	1.75870000	6.21420000	135.07000000	102.38000000	5.82580000	1.40640000	1.766300
1993	1,573.41000000	1.85850000	7.10090000	161.08000000	127.48000000	7.79560000	1.47810000	1.501600
1994	1,611.49000000	1.81900000	7.05530000	165.93000000	133.88000000	7.71610000	1.36670000	1.531900
1995	1,629.45000000	1.60440000	6.33550000	149.88000000	124.64000000	7.14060000	1.18120000	1.578500
1996	1,542.76000000	1.68630000	6.45940000	154.28000000	126.68000000	6.70820000	1.23610000	1.560700
1997	1,703.81000000	1.95250000	7.08570000	175.44000000	146.53000000	7.64460000	1.45140000	1.637600
1998	1,736.85000000	1.98370000	7.55210000	180.25000000	149.41000000	7.95220000	1.45060000	1.657300
1999	2,062.71000000	2.34760000	7.80710000	213.57000000	177.25000000	8.27400000	1.50450000	1.617200

[1] Monetary unit changes. See text.

[2] Official exchange rate rather than bank-notes-account rate, 1949–1951.

[3] Free exchange rate rather than official exchange rate, 1948–1949 and 1957.

[4] Official exchange rate rather than free exchange rate, 1946–1947.

[5] The series prior to 1939 is not compatible with series from 1939.

[6] Free exchange rate rather than official exchange rate, 1940–1942 and 1945; free rate (equal to official rate) in 1943; official rate in 1944.

[7] Quotations not available for part of the year. See text.

[8] Average based on only a portion of the year. See text.

[9] Change in monetary units during year. Figure is a weighted average. See text.

[10] Free exchange rate through February 1; official rate throughout year.

Sources

Publications of the Board of Governors of the Federal Reserve System. 1913–1941, *Banking and Monetary Statistics 1914–1941 (1943)*; 1941–1970, *Banking and Monetary Statistics 1941–1970 (1976)*; 1970–1978,

Annual Statistical Digest 1970–1979 (1981); 1979–1999, *Federal Reserve Bulletin* (various issues). Information on changes in currency units is taken from these Federal Reserve publications; William F. Spalding, *Dictionary of the World's Currencies and Foreign Exchanges* (Pitman, 1928); and B. R. Mitchell, *European Historical Statistics 1750–1988* (Stockton Press, 1992), p. vii.

Documentation

Until World War I, the most important instrument in the U.S. foreign-exchange market was the sterling bill of exchange – hence the specificity of Tables Ee612–620 to dollar-sterling exchange. Subsequently, the market became broader in traded currencies, and the cable transfer replaced the bill as the dominant exchange-market instrument. Table Ee621–636 includes dollar exchange rates for all European currencies for which the Federal Reserve publications listed as sources provide at least one annual exchange-rate observation in the post-World War II period. The series are annual averages of daily exchange rates in the New York market, and they are the prices at which foreign exchange can be purchased. The rates pertain to cable transfers, with the following exceptions: (1) 1913–1914: bankers' sight bills for all countries except France, Germany, and the United Kingdom; (2) 1915: bankers' sight bills for Austria and Norway; bankers' checks for Denmark, Spain, and Sweden.

Expression of the exchange rate has several dimensions or degrees of freedom. First, an exchange rate is traditionally represented either in pristine form (number of units of one currency per unit of the other currency) or as the percentage deviation of this form from parity. Consistent with the format of the Federal Reserve data, the pristine form is shown in the table.

Second, given this choice, the exchange rate can be expressed either as the number of domestic-currency units per foreign-currency unit or the number of foreign-currency units per domestic-currency unit. The Federal Reserve data have the former expression for 1913–1978 and the latter expression thereafter (except for Ireland and the United Kingdom, for which the former is used throughout). It is reasonable to adopt the more recent Federal Reserve usage, including the inverse expression for Ireland and the United Kingdom (providing consistency with Tables Ee612–620).

Third, either cents or dollars can be the U.S. currency unit. The Federal Reserve publications express exchange rates as the number of cents per unit of foreign currency for all series until 1978 and for Ireland and the United Kingdom thereafter as well; subsequently (except for the latter two countries), the measure is the number of units of foreign currency per dollar. It is appropriate to use the dollar, which is the basic U.S. currency unit, for all exchange rates throughout the time period. Therefore series Ee628 and Ee636 are measured as the *number of dollars per (Irish or U.K.) pound* and the remaining series as the *number of units of foreign currency per dollar.*

Fourth, of the sixteen countries in the table, seven – Austria, Belgium, Finland, France, Germany, Greece, and Spain – experienced one or more changes in currency unit during the period spanning the observations for the country. In this situation, the standpoint of either the contemporary observer or the time-series analyst may be adopted, with different implication for exchange-rate expression. The contemporary standpoint is that the currency unit for the exchange rate should be that in existence at the time; the time-series view is that the exchange rate should be expressed in a uniform currency unit throughout the period of observations. The contemporary position is accepted here. The result is that series Ee621–622, Ee624–627, and Ee633 reflect the actual currency unit in effect at any time, but they are not internally consistent because they lack a uniform currency unit for their period of observation. The time-series analyst is not neglected: the corresponding consistent series, data permitting, are presented in Table Ee662–678.

When a new currency unit is instituted at any time other than January 1, the exchange rate is expressed in the unit ruling during the greater part of the year; the full-year exchange-rate experience is incorporated (data permitting), via conversion of the unit pertaining to the lesser part of the year. For example, the German monetary unit switched from the mark to the reichsmark on October 11, 1924. For most of 1924, the mark was the monetary unit; therefore, the exchange rate is expressed as the number of marks per dollar.

The inflation-induced currency depreciation that frequently precedes a change in currency unit is seen in the experiences of Austria in 1921–1924 and Germany in 1919–1924.

At the beginning of 1999, the Federal Reserve began to report the European Monetary Union's euro-dollar exchange rate in place of the bilateral dollar exchange rates of the individual currencies of the euro-area countries (Austria, Belgium–Luxembourg, Finland, France, Germany, Ireland, Italy, Netherlands, Portugal, and Spain). The latter rates (number of units of individual currency per dollar) are readily derived as the product of the euro-dollar exchange rate (number of euros per dollar) and the fixed individual-currency euro-conversion rate (number of units of individual currency per euro).

Detailed information on the source data is in Board of Governors of the Federal Reserve System (1943), pp. 572–3; (1976), p. 931. The literature on exchange rates is voluminous. The International Monetary Fund's *Exchange Arrangements and Exchange Restrictions: Annual Report* (1950–) is invaluable for information on institutional arrangements of individual countries' foreign-exchange markets. The following studies may be mentioned by virtue of their long-run historical bent: Paul Einzig, *The History of Foreign Exchange,* 2nd edition (Macmillan, 1970), parts 5–6; Leland B. Yeager, *International Monetary Relations: Theory, History and Policy,* 2nd edition (Harper & Row, 1976), part 2; Barry Eichengreen, *Golden Fetters: The Gold Standard and the Great Depression, 1919–1939* (Oxford University Press, 1992); and Lawrence H. Officer, *Between the Dollar–Sterling Gold Points: Exchange Rates, Parity, and Market Behavior* (Cambridge University Press, 1996).

In some cases, averages were calculated from data for only a portion of the year. Series Ee621: 1917, through April 10; 1921, from June 1; 1938, through March 12; 1953, from November 30. Series Ee622: 1940, through May 9; 1945, from September 24. Series Ee623: 1940, through April 8; 1946, from February 5. Series Ee624: 1921, from June 1; 1941, through June 14. Series Ee625: 1940, through June 15; 1945, from August 1; 1957, through August 12. Series Ee626: 1917, through April 10; 1919, from September 15; 1941, through June 14; 1950, from June 22. Series Ee627: 1915, from April 1; 1916, from October 6; 1921, from June 1; 1940, through October 26. Series Ee628: 1951, from October 29. Series Ee629: 1941, through June 14. Series Ee630: 1940, through May 9; 1945, from November 2. Series Ee631: 1940: through April 8; 1946, from February 5. Series Ee632: 1916, from January 12; 1921, from June 1; 1941, through June 14; 1946, from February 5. Series Ee633: 1939, from April 1; 1941, through June 14; 1946, from February 5; 1948, through December 17. Series Ee634: 1941, through June 14; 1946, from February 5. Series Ee635: 1941, through June 14; 1946, from February 5. Series Ee636: 1945, from July 2.

In some cases, quotations were not available for part of the year. Series Ee621: 1914, September. Series Ee622: 1914, August and October–December; 1919, January 1–April 25 and August 1–September 25. Series Ee623: 1914, September–October. Series Ee625: 1948, January 1–February 9 and October 16–31. Series Ee633: 1939, January 25–March 31. Series Ee635: 1914, August.

Changes in Monetary Units

Series Ee621. On December 20, 1924, the monetary unit of Austria was changed from the krone to the schilling, where 1 schilling = 10,000 kronen. Federal Reserve quotations switched from the krone to the schilling on March 13, 1925. In 1947–1948 a new schilling was issued, where 1 new schilling = 3 old schillings. The exchange rate is expressed as kronen per dollar in 1913–1924, old schillings per dollar in 1925–1938, and (new) schillings per dollar in 1953–1999.

Series Ee621. Original 1925 data in cents per krone January 1–March 12 and in cents per (old) schilling March 13–December 31, converted to annual figure in cents per schilling by taking weighted average of average for krone (converted to schilling) January 1–March 12 and average for schilling March 13–December 31, with the number of foreign-exchange market days as weights. Figure in cents per schilling then converted to schillings per dollar.

Series Ee622. On October 25, 1926, Belgium adopted a new monetary unit, the belga, for foreign-exchange transactions, with 1 belga = 5 francs. Foreign-exchange transactions in terms of the belga ceased in 1940. After World War II, the belga was not restored. The exchange rate is expressed as francs per dollar in 1913–1926 and 1945–1999, belgas per dollar in 1927–1940.

Series Ee622. Original 1926 data in cents per franc January 1–October 25 and in cents per belga October 26–December 31, converted to annual figure in cents per franc by taking weighted average of average for franc January 1–October 25 and average for belga (converted to franc) October 26–December 31, with the number of foreign-exchange market days as weights. Figure in cents per franc then converted to francs per dollar.

(continued)

TABLE Ee621–636 Bilateral exchange rates – Europe: 1913 – 1999 [Contemporary currency units] *Continued*

Series Ee624. On January 1, 1963, the new markkaa replaced the old markkaa as the monetary unit of Finland, where 1 new markkaa = 100 old markkaa. The exchange rate is expressed as old markkaa per dollar in 1921–1941 and (new) markkaa per dollar in 1971–1999.

Series Ee625. On January 1, 1960, the new franc replaced the (old) franc as the monetary unit of France, where 1 new franc = 100 old francs. On January 1, 1963, the franc replaced the new franc as the monetary unit, where 1 franc = 1 new franc. The exchange rate is expressed as old francs per dollar in 1913–1959 and francs per dollar in 1960–1999.

Series Ee626. On October 11, 1924, the monetary unit of Germany was changed from the mark to the reichsmark, where 1 reichsmark = 1,000,000,000,000 marks. Federal Reserve quotations switched from the mark to the reichsmark on October 29, 1924. In June 1948, the monetary unit was changed to the deutsche mark, where 1 deutsche mark = 10 reichsmarks. The exchange rate is expressed in marks per dollar in 1913–1924, reichsmarks per dollar in 1925–1941, and deutsch marks per dollar in 1950–1999.

Series Ee626. Original 1924 data in cents per billion marks October 29–December 31, converted to annual figure in cents per billion marks by taking weighted average of average for billion marks January 1–October 28 and average for reichsmark (converted to billion marks) October 29–December 31, with the number of foreign-exchange market days as weights. Figure in cents per billion marks then converted to marks per dollar.

Series Ee627. In November 1944, the "new" drachma replaced the old drachma at the rate 1 "new" drachma = 50,000 million old drachmas. In May 1954, an again new drachma became the monetary unit of Greece, where 1 (again new) drachma =1,000 "new" drachmas. The exchange rate is expressed in old drachmas per dollar in 1915–1940 and drachmas per dollar in 1982–1999.

Series Ee633. Federal Reserve quotations for the Loyalist peseta discontinued on January 25, 1939; quotations for the National peseta began on April 1, 1939. For January 1–24, the exchange rate averages 21.6769 Loyalist pesetas per dollar. The exchange rate is expressed in Loyalist pesetas per dollar prior to 1939 and National pesetas per dollar thereafter.

TABLE Ee637–645 Bilateral exchange rates – Americas: 1913–1999 [Contemporary currency units]
Contributed by Lawrence H. Officer

Year	Argentina Ee637 [1,2] Currency per dollar	Brazil Ee638 [1,3] Currency per dollar	Canada Ee639 [4] Canadian dollars per dollar	Chile Ee640 [1,5] Currency per dollar	Colombia Ee641 Pesos per dollar	Mexico, at New York Ee642 [1,6] Currency per dollar	Mexico Ee643 [1] Currency per dollar	Peru Ee644 [1] Currency per dollar	Venezuela Ee645 Bolivares per dollar
1913	—	—	1.0009801	—	—	—	—	—	—
1914	—	—	0.99923858	—	—	—	—	—	—
1915	—	—	1.00403723	—	—	—	—	—	—
1916	0.96663187	4.20995908	1.00235654	—	—	—	—	—	—
1917	0.99862689	3.99568466	1.00189458	3.56600315 [9]	—	—	—	—	—
1918	0.99845639	3.95049243	1.01654322	3.37859525	—	—	—	—	—
1919	1.00991739	3.74041519	1.04605793	4.43360674	—	—	—	—	—
1920	1.10248721	4.44187803	1.12012187	5.41887938	—	—	—	—	—
1921	1.36981423	7.62200931	1.11678313	8.32688000	—	2.05752850 [9]	—	—	—
1922	1.22224585	7.72284262	1.01545214	8.18310516	—	2.05275582	—	—	—
1923	1.27270668	9.77660459	1.02004178	8.16839973	—	2.05988073	—	—	—
1924	1.27990498	9.14051717	1.01284080	9.48334724	—	2.06124792	—	—	—
1925	1.09430502	8.19927518	1.00038515	8.61838647	—	2.02459478	—	—	—
1926	1.08519073	6.92727059	1.00011101	8.28047629	1.01569554	2.07002051	—	—	—
1927	1.03847552	8.44715880	1.00028008	8.28830024	1.02366823	2.11842415	—	—	—
1928	1.03648317	8.35163734	1.00090682	8.23377329	1.02360746	2.07871253	—	—	—
1929	1.05122184	8.46940850	1.00758510	8.29180521	1.03571991	2.07542079	—	—	—
1930	1.19753308	9.33393070 [8]	1.00157849	8.27917374	1.03634461	2.12165124	—	—	—
1931	1.49840794	14.22677479	1.03814347	8.28713257	1.03552149	2.09859184 [9]	—	—	—
1932	1.71106012	14.04040830	1.13520779	12.64558227	1.04959328	3.13971743	—	—	—
1933	1.37083950 [7]	12.55808113	1.08744469	13.02303775	1.22404115	3.55840228	—	—	—
1934	2.97802515	11.86690084	0.99004020	9.85687813	1.61864943	3.60460380	—	—	—
1935	3.06198999	12.05589111	1.00509281	19.67226015	1.78536359	3.59998416	—	—	—
1936	3.01782023	11.67119898	1.00086976	19.51600312	1.75185039	3.60235738	—	—	—
1937	3.03411866	11.56911971 [8]	0.99996300	19.34348221	1.76286939	3.60357763	—	—	—
1938	3.06774815	17.11215305	1.00584699	19.33637559	1.78721107	4.52044825	—	—	—
1939	3.24144906 [8]	16.65917004	1.04146705	19.33226361	1.75251661	5.18054188	—	—	—

Year	Argentina Ee637 [1,2] Currency per dollar	Brazil Ee638 [1,3] Currency per dollar	Canada Ee639 [4] Canadian dollars per dollar	Chile Ee640 [1,5] Currency per dollar	Colombia Ee641 Pesos per dollar	Mexico, at New York Ee642 [1,6] Currency per dollar	Mexico Ee643 [1] Currency per dollar	Peru Ee644 [1] Currency per dollar	Venezuela Ee645 Bolivares per dollar
1940	3.35872530	16.51200423	1.17451950	19.35433924	1.75176446	5.39202735	—	—	—
1941	3.35871402	16.50846059	1.14488916	19.35583772 [9]	1.75427825	4.86895215	—	—	—
1942	—	—	1.13149435	—	—	4.86161415	—	—	—
1943	—	—	1.11138649	—	—	4.85979492	—	—	—
1944	—	—	1.11292394	—	—	4.85880318	—	—	—
1945	—	—	1.10515677	—	—	4.85892122	—	—	—
1946	—	—	1.07195498	—	—	4.85892122	—	—	—
1947	—	—	1.08696834	—	—	4.85974768	—	—	—
1948	4.81000000	18.99061643	1.09062077	32.99903600	1.76000000	5.30236751 [8]	4.8550000	16.1000000	3.7500000
1949	9.02000000	18.99061643	1.07665226	35.99894800	1.96000000	7.92386748	8.6500000	14.8100000	3.3540000
1950	14.02000000	18.99061643	1.09321279	47.99859900	1.96000000	8.64334117	8.6500000	14.9500000	3.7540000
1951	14.46000000	18.99061643	1.05330791	55.99836400	2.40000000	8.64760159	8.6500000	15.2800000	3.3410000
1952	13.98000000	18.99061643	0.97896594	61.99818900	2.51000000	8.62976579	8.6500000	15.5000000	3.3010000
1953	13.98000000	42.97876275	0.98376590	70.99792600	2.51000000	8.61541643	8.6500000	19.3900000	3.2040000
1954	13.98000000	50.96987325	0.97348045	91.99731300	2.51000000	11.04789261	12.5000000	19.0000000	3.6680000
1955	36.10000000	70.96493525	0.98618746	161.99527000	2.51000000	12.49125612	12.5000000	19.0000000	3.2270000
1956	37.45000000	69.96542850	0.98424712	335.99019000	2.51000000	12.49125612	12.5000000	19.0000000	3.2410000
1957	37.00000000	75.96246350	0.95885827	521.31811000	3.79750000	12.49125612	12.5000000	19.0000000	3.3503333
1958	70.00000000	128.93628825	0.97063631	704.64609000	6.40000000	12.49125612	12.5000000	23.8600000	3.3500000
1959	79.92083300	150.92542575	0.95907438	944.30576000	6.40000000	12.49125612	12.5000000	27.9000000	3.3496667
1960	82.89000000	186.90764400	0.96972706	1.04896940	6.63500000	12.49125612	12.5000000	27.2991670	3.3495833
1961	82.85583300	269.86665475	1.01255569	1.05013600	6.70000000	12.49125612	12.5000000	26.8166670	3.3498333
1962	116.22833000	387.80838250	1.06882141	1.05763580	6.90120830	12.49125612	12.5000000	26.8200000	3.3496667
1963	138.71667000	574.71601000	1.07876029	1.62178600	9.00000000	12.49125612	12.5000000	26.8200000	3.3496667
1964	140.39167000	1,252.38118500	1.07887667	2.30743260	9.00000000	12.49125612	12.5000000	26.8200000	4.3987500
1965	169.56667000	1,898.06212750	1.07824849	3.15665780	10.47500000	12.49125612	12.5000000	26.8200000	4.4500000
1966	209.15000000	2,218.90361000	1.07745849	3.85113760	13.50000000	12.49125612	12.5000000	26.8200000	4.4500000
1967	333.42500000	2.66268434	1.07887667	5.06826870	14.50639200	12.49125612	12.5000000	30.2483330	4.4500000
1968	350.00000000	3.39432280	1.07757460	6.87646590	16.29066700	12.49125612	12.5000000	38.7000000	4.4500000
1969	350.00000000	4.07298760	1.07694793	8.61758170	17.52014200	12.49125612	12.5000000	38.7000000	4.4500000
1970	3.79166670	4.59073175	1.04381954	11.27750400	18.44310000	12.49125612	12.5000000	38.7000000	4.4500000
1971	4.52166700	5.28538835	1.00988679	12.20864400	19.53193300	12.49125612	12.5000000	38.7000000	4.4467392
1972	5.00000000	5.93106938	0.99071698	20.83522500	21.86564200	12.50000000	12.5000000	38.7000000	4.4000000
1973	5.00000000	6.12297455	1.00023005	71.64190800	23.63698300	12.50000000	12.4999520	38.7000000	4.3045000
1974	5.00000000	6.78664663	0.97792816	592.82626000	26.06412500	12.50000000	12.4999690	38.7000000	4.2850000
1975	36.57500000	8.12298630	1.01732505	4,910.41670000	30.52894200	12.50000000	12.5000000	40.3708330	4.2850000
1976	139.98333000	10.66772878	0.98609605	13.05416700	34.69392500	14.45901592	15.4258500	55.7558330	4.2898908
1977	407.63333000	14.13701465	1.06256375	21.53583300	36.77486700	22.60448925	22.5728670	84.2348330	4.2925000
1978	795.75000000	18.06107573	1.13987393	31.65583300	39.05464200	22.78111901	22.7672830	156.3488300	4.2925000
1979	1,316.96670000	26.93269205	1.16030000	37.24583300	42.54977500	22.81600000	22.8053830	224.7189200	4.2925000
1980	1,837.15830000	52.68796500	1.16930000	39.00000000	47.28030800	22.96800000	22.9510080	288.8552500	4.2925000
1981	4,402.69170000	93.07884300	1.19900000	39.00000000	54.49055000	24.54700000	24.5146000	422.3180000	4.2925000
1982	25,922.53300000	179.42559250	1.23440000	50.90833300	64.08471700	72.99000000	56.4017000	697.5667500	4.2925000
1983	10.52995700	576.75967250	1.23250000	78.78833300	78.85430000	155.01000000	120.0935800	1,628.6342000	4.2974717
1984	67.64911700	1,847.11648000	1.29530000	98.47750000	100.81724000	192.31000000	167.8275800	3,466.8542000	7.0174600
1985	0.60180900	6,197.33647500	1.36580000	160.86000000	142.31176000	—	256.8715800	10.9749420	7.5000000
1986	0.94303167	13.64928428	1.38960000	192.93000000	194.25142000	—	611.7725800	13.9475000	8.0833333
1987	2.14429830	39.20920025	1.32590000	219.40667000	242.60750000	—	1,378.1825000	16.8358330	14.5000000
1988	8.75260420	261.99867375	1.23060000	245.01167000	299.17383000	—	2,273.1050000	128.8316700	14.5000000
1989	423.30000000	2.83390223	1.18420000	266.95417000	382.56808000	—	2,461.4725000	2,666.1875000	34.6814920

Notes appear at end of table

(continued)

TABLE Ee637–645 Bilateral exchange rates – Americas: 1913–1999 [Contemporary currency units] Continued

Year	Argentina Ee637 [1,2] Currency per dollar	Brazil Ee638 [1,3] Currency per dollar	Canada Ee639 [4] Canadian dollars per dollar	Chile Ee640 [1,5] Currency per dollar	Colombia Ee641 Pesos per dollar	Mexico, at New York Ee642 [1,6] Currency per dollar	Mexico Ee643 [1] Currency per dollar	Peru Ee644 [1] Currency per dollar	Venezuela Ee645 Bolivares per dollar
1990	4,875.90000000	68.30012200	1.1668000	304.90333000	502.25925000	—	2,812.5992000	187,885.580000000	46.9004670
1991	9,535.50000000	406.60686000	1.14600000	349.21583000	633.04517000	—	3,018.4300000	0.7725000	56.8160830
1992	0.9906400	4,512.98815000	1.2085000	362.57583000	759.28200000	—	3,094.8983000	1.2458333	68.3763250
1993	0.99895000	88,440.00000000	1.29020000	404.16583000	863.06468000	3.12370000	3.1156167	1.9883189	90.8260500
1994	0.99901000	1,758.01700000	1.36640000	420.17667000	844.83589000	3.38530000	3.3751167	2.1950000	148.5026600
1995	0.99975000	0.91767000	1.37250000	396.77333000	912.82642000	6.44670000	6.4194250	2.2533333	176.8425000
1996	0.99996000	1.00510000	1.36380000	412.26667000	1,036.68640000	7.60040000	7.5994484	2.4533333	417.3325000
1997	0.99950000	1.07800000	1.38490000	419.29500000	1,140.96000000	7.91770000	7.9185000	2.6642000	488.6350000
1998	0.99950000	1.16100000	1.48360000	460.29000000	1,426.04000000	9.15200000	9.1360000	2.9300000	547.5560000
1999	0.99950000	1.81500000	1.48580000	508.78000000	1,756.23000000	9.55300000	9.5604000	3.3830000	605.7170000

[1] Monetary unit changes. See text.

[2] Official exchange rate rather than special export rate in 1941.

[3] Official exchange rate rather than free rate, 1936–1937 and 1939–1941.

[4] Free exchange rate rather than official rate, 1940–1950.

[5] Official exchange rate rather than export rate, 1937–1941.

[6] The series prior to 1932 is not compatible with series from 1932.

[7] Change in monetary units during year. Figure is a weighted average. See text.

[8] Quotations not available for part of the year. See text.

[9] Average based on only a portion of the year. See text.

Sources

1913–1941. Board of Governors of the Federal Reserve System, *Banking and Monetary Statistics 1914–1941* (1943).

1941–1999, series Ee639 and Ee642. Board of Governors of the Federal Reserve System, *Banking and Monetary Statistics 1941–1970* (1976), *Annual Statistical Digest 1970–1979* (1981), *Federal Reserve Bulletin* (various issues), and *Federal Reserve Statistical Release G.5A* (January 7, 1997).

1948–1999, series Ee637–638, Ee640–641, and Ee643–645. International Monetary Fund, *International Financial Statistics, Yearbook* (monthly) and CD-ROM (various issues).

Information on changes in currency units is taken from these Federal Reserve publications; International Monetary Fund, *International Financial Statistics* (various *Yearbook* and monthly issues); B. R. Mitchell, *International Historical Statistics: The Americas 1750–1988* (Stockton Press, 1993), p. xiii; and Harold Edwin Peters, *The Foreign Debt of the Argentine Republic* (Johns Hopkins University Press, 1934), pp. 53–5.

Documentation

Five of the eight countries in the table – Argentina, Brazil, Chile, Mexico, and Peru – experienced one or more changes in currency unit during the period spanning the observations for the country. As with Table Ee621–636, the contemporary exchange rate is shown, notwithstanding that the resulting series are inconsistent over time. For corresponding series that are consistent (with the same currency unit throughout the period of observations), data permitting, see Table Ee662–678. See the text for Table Ee621–636 for additional information.

Table Ee637–645 includes dollar exchange rates for all North, Central, and South American currencies for which the source Federal Reserve publications provide at least one annual exchange-rate observation in the post–World War II period. No Central American currency fulfills the criterion. Federal Reserve publications are the primary data source, but their coverage is insufficient. Therefore, the International Monetary Fund (IMF) is used as a secondary source. In the case of Mexico, Federal Reserve

data are not available for 1985–1992. For completeness, two series of maximum length are shown: series Ee642–643, from the Federal Reserve and IMF, respectively.

Three features of the IMF exchange-rate data that differ from those of the Federal Reserve data should be noted.

First, the market of quotation is not New York but rather the major financial center of the domestic country (for example, Mexico City for series Ee643). This is a limitation of the IMF data.

Second, the entire exchange-rate series for a given country is expressed in terms of the most recent currency unit rather than leaving the series segmented in terms of contemporary currency units (the Federal Reserve practice). Therefore the IMF data, for periods for which a country was on a former currency unit, require conversion from the most recent currency unit to the currency unit applicable for the period in question. When a currency unit changes at a date other than January 1, the exchange rate is expressed in the unit ruling during the greater part of the year – with the full-year experience, data permitting (the practice in Table Ee621–636). Thus, a contemporary series is inherent in the Federal Reserve data but requires external construction for the IMF data.

Third, even though the Federal Reserve data are always market rates, the IMF data are unambiguously market rates only since 1974. Prior to that year, the data are the fixed exchange rate (par value or central rate), if such a rate has been agreed with the IMF, and a market exchange rate otherwise. The IMF provides many alternative exchange-rate series for a given country; the series designated by the code *rf*, which has this property, is selected. This series expresses the exchange rate in terms of the number of units of domestic currency per dollar and is the annual average of daily exchange rates. For further information on the exchange-rate data, see IMF, *International Financial Statistics: Supplement on Exchange Rates*, Supplement Series number 9 (1985).

All the currency changes in Table Ee637–645 pertain to the postwar period (since 1948) and, except for Mexico, are preceded by inflation-induced currency depreciation: Argentina and Brazil, several occurrences each; Chile and Peru, two each.

In some cases, averages were calculated from data for only a portion of the year. Series Ee640: 1917, from November 17; 1941, through May 20. Series Ee642: 1921, from June 1; 1931, through July 29.

In some cases, quotations were not available for part of the year. Series Ee637: 1939, August 28–October 16. Series Ee638: 1930, October 7–December 1; 1937, November 18–December 23. Series Ee642: 1948, July 22–October 12.

Changes in Monetary Units

Series Ee637. Federal Reserve quotations switched from the gold peso to the paper peso (peso moneda nacional) on December 13, 1933, where 1 peso moneda nacional = 0.44 gold peso. On January 1, 1970, the monetary unit of Argentina was changed from the peso moneda nacional to the (old) peso, where 1 peso = 100 pesos moneda nacional. On June 1, 1983, the monetary unit became the (old) peso argentino, where 1 peso argentino = 10,000 pesos. On June 14, 1985, the monetary unit became the austral, where 1 austral = 1,000 pesos argentino. On January 1, 1992, the austral was replaced by the (new) peso argentino, where 1 peso argentino = 10,000 australes. The exchange rate is expressed as gold pesos per dollar in 1916–1933, pesos moneda nacional per dollar in 1934–1969, pesos per dollar in 1970–1982, old pesos argentino per dollar in 1983–1984, australes per dollar in 1985–1991, and (new) pesos argentino per dollar in 1992–1999.

Series Ee637. Original 1933 data in cents per gold peso January 1–December 10 and in cents per peso moneda nacional December 13–31 converted to annual figure in cents per gold peso by taking weighted average of average for gold peso January 1–December 10 and average for peso moneda nacional (converted to gold peso) December 13–31, with the number of foreign-exchange market days as weights. Figure in cents per gold peso then converted to gold pesos per dollar.

Series Ee638. In 1942, the name of the monetary unit of Brazil was changed from the milreis to the cruzeiro. On February 13, 1967, the monetary unit became the new cruzeiro, where 1 new cruzeiro = 1,000 old cruzeiros; and on May 15, 1970, the new cruzeiro was renamed the cruzeiro. On February 28, 1986, the monetary unit was changed to the cruzado, where 1 cruzado = 1,000 cruzeiros. On January 15, 1989, the new cruzado was established, where 1 new cruzado = 1,000 old cruzados. On March 16, 1990, the (again new) cruzeiro replaced the cruzado, where 1 cruzeiro = 1 cruzado. On August 1, 1993, the monetary unit became the cruzeiro real, where 1 cruzeiro real = 1,000 cruzeiros. On July 1, 1994, the monetary unit was changed to the real, where 1 real = 2,750 cruzeiros reais. The exchange rate is expressed as milreis per dollar in 1916–1941, old cruzeiros per dollar in 1948–1966,

(new) cruzeiros per dollar in 1967–1985, cruzados per dollar in 1986–1988, new cruzados per dollar in 1989, (again new) cruzeiros per dollar in 1990–1993, cruzeiros reais per dollar in 1994, and reais per dollar in 1995–1999.

Series Ee640. On January 1, 1960, the monetary unit of Chile was changed from the (old) peso to the escudo, where 1 escudo = 1,000 (old) pesos. On September 29, 1975, the peso replaced the escudo, where 1 peso = 1,000 escudos. The exchange rate is expressed as old pesos per dollar in 1917–1959, escudos per dollar in 1960–1975, and pesos per dollar in 1976–1999.

Series Ee642. Federal Reserve quotations switched from the gold to the silver peso on July 30, 1931. Average for silver peso July 30–December 31 is 2.8175 old pesos per dollar. Series prior to 1932 pertains to gold peso, not compatible with series from 1932. On January 1, 1993, the monetary unit of Mexico was changed from the old peso to the (new) peso, where 1 peso = 1,000 old pesos. The exchange rate is expressed as old pesos per dollar in 1921–1984 and pesos per dollar in 1993–1999.

Series Ee643. On January 1, 1993, the monetary unit of Mexico was changed from the old peso to the (new) peso, where 1 peso = 1,000 old pesos. The exchange rate is expressed as old pesos per dollar in 1948–1992 and pesos per dollar in 1993–1999.

Series Ee644. On February 1, 1985, the monetary unit of Peru was changed from the sol to the inti, where 1 inti = 1,000 soles. On July 1, 1991, the new sol replaced the inti, where 1 new sol = 1,000,000 intis. The exchange rate is expressed as soles per dollar in 1948–1984, intis per dollar in 1985–1990, and new soles per dollar in 1991–1999.

TABLE Ee646–661 Bilateral exchange rates – Africa, Asia, Australasia: 1916–1999 [Contemporary currency units]
Contributed by Lawrence H. Officer

Year	Australia Ee646[1,2] Currency per dollar	China Ee647[1] Currency per dollar	Hong Kong Ee648 Hong Kong dollars per dollar	India Ee649 Rupees per dollar	Indonesia Ee650 Rupiah per dollar	Israel Ee651[1] Currency per dollar	Japan Ee652 Yen per dollar	Korea Ee653 Won per dollar	Malaysia Ee654[1] Currency per dollar	New Zealand Ee655[1] Currency per dollar	Philippines Ee656 Pesos per dollar	Singapore Ee657 Singapore dollars per dollar	South Africa Ee658[1] Currency per dollar	Sri Lanka Ee659 Rupees per dollar	Taiwan Ee660 Taiwanese dollars per dollar	Thailand Ee661 Baht per dollar
1916	—	—	1.95301438	3.04279694	—	—	1.97409981	—	—	—	—	—	—	—	—	—
1917	—	—	1.56041538	2.92041575	—	—	1.94771932	—	—	—	—	—	—	—	—	—
1918	—	—	1.27327710	2.72121431	—	—	1.88465532	—	—	—	—	—	—	—	—	—
1919	—	—	—	2.48169748	—	—	1.95373554	—	—	—	—	—	—	—	—	—
1920	—	—	—	2.57208262	—	—	1.98538755	—	—	—	—	—	—	—	—	—
1921	—	1.79745875	1.91257980 [3]	3.81418802	—	—	2.07268921	—	2.28101669 [3]	—	—	—	—	—	—	—
1922	—	1.90033503	1.79492610	3.47936216	—	—	2.09188828	—	.96946153	—	—	—	—	—	—	—
1923	—	1.89041277	1.89041277	3.21436952	—	—	2.05826961	—	.86921478	—	—	—	—	—	—	—
1924	—	1.89763043	1.90588365	3.14628660	—	—	2.42802720	—	.95113195	—	—	—	—	—	—	—
1925	—	1.75726541	1.76928834	2.75754049	—	—	2.43687281	—	.78079801	—	—	—	—	—	—	—
1926	—	2.00077230	1.87515236	2.75279615	—	—	2.12240774	—	.77713011	—	—	—	—	—	—	—
1927	—	2.27575817	2.03216924	2.75393331	—	—	2.10920181	—	.78419772	—	—	—	—	—	—	—
1928	0.20694508	2.16742021	1.99713611	2.74225792	—	—	2.15472661	—	.77671017	0.20638557	—	—	0.20652623	—	—	—
1929	0.20797371	2.38659497	2.12013085	2.76227833	—	—	2.16921151	—	.78534128	0.20694936	—	—	0.20692367	—	—	—
1930	0.21805495	3.34262583	2.95394795	2.77260225	—	—	2.02470956	—	1.78686618	0.21357482	—	—	0.20670125	—	—	—
1931	0.28449502	4.45694370	4.11006761	2.96828389	—	—	2.04704519	—	1.90675583	0.24079559	—	—	0.20800399	—	—	—
1932	0.35723217	4.60072599	4.26250192	3.79552735	—	—	3.55730100	—	2.47543134	0.31231456	—	—	0.20983717	—	—	—
1933	0.29667173	3.49676025 [3]	3.39540127 [3]	3.14308255	—	—	3.89928916	—	2.03119922	0.29411531	—	—	0.24097529	—	—	—
1934	0.24940834	2.93309321	2.58293814	2.63996431	—	—	3.36526974	—	1.69476589	0.24846980	—	—	0.20068494	—	—	—

Notes appear at end of table

(continued)

TABLE Ee646–661   Bilateral exchange rates – Africa, Asia, Australasia: 1916–1999   [Contemporary currency units]   *Continued*

Year	Australia Ee646 [1,2] Currency per dollar	China Ee647 [1] Currency per dollar	Hong Kong Ee648 Hong Kong dollars per dollar	India Ee649 Rupees per dollar	Indonesia Ee650 Rupiah per dollar	Israel Ee651 [1] Currency per dollar	Japan Ee652 Yen per dollar	Korea Ee653 Won per dollar	Malaysia Ee654 [1] Currency per dollar	New Zealand Ee655 [1] Currency per dollar	Philippines Ee656 Pesos per dollar	Singapore Ee657 Singapore dollars per dollar	South Africa Ee658 [1] Currency per dollar	Sri Lanka Ee659 Rupees per dollar	Taiwan Ee660 Taiwanese dollars per dollar	Thailand Ee661 Baht per dollar
1935	0.25716269	2.73442947	2.07394441	2.70533492	—	—	3.48350733	—	1.74906818	0.25558152	—	—	0.20633068	—	—	—
1936	0.25256135	3.36127675	3.15352959	2.66503211	—	—	3.44566191	—	1.71649067	0.25067387	—	—	0.20339735	—	—	—
1937	0.25384641	3.37764808	3.25792327	2.67913357	—	—	3.47334382	—	1.72494687	0.25194432	—	—	0.20424144	—	—	—
1938	0.25670336	4.68173561	3.28327434	2.73286018	—	—	3.51481494	—	1.75693815	0.25487369	—	—	0.20654427	—	—	—
1939	0.28298293	8.41800443	3.64244321	3.00488895	—	—	3.85164985	—	1.93290874	0.28183638	—	—	0.22718330	—	—	—
1940	0.32769297	16.66722224	4.35570423	3.31619964	—	—	4.26688513	—	2.12861519	0.32639281	—	—	0.25126379	—	—	—
1941	0.31126176	18.82069524 [3]	4.06631344 [3]	3.31821334	—	—	4.26644822 [3]	—	2.12163773	0.31004349	—	—	0.25125628	—	—	—
1942	0.31103880	—	—	3.31987677	—	—	—	—	2.13135544 [3]	0.30980518	—	—	0.25125628	—	—	—
1943	0.31103880 [3]	—	—	3.31986574	—	—	—	—	—	0.30844824	—	—	0.25125628	—	—	—
1944	0.30978934	—	—	3.31988779	—	—	—	—	—	0.30824212	—	—	0.25125628	—	—	—
1945	0.31135683 [3]	—	—	3.31988779	—	—	—	—	—	0.30916173	—	—	0.25059215	—	—	—
1946	0.31119241	—	—	3.31625462	—	—	—	—	—	0.30994950	—	—	0.24968789	—	—	—
1947	0.31152192	—	—	3.31518820	—	—	—	—	—	0.31027725	—	—	0.24953923	—	—	—
1948	0.31131574	—	—	3.31469371	—	0.24973046	—	—	—	0.28532090 [3]	2.0000000	—	0.24953213	—	—	—
1949	0.34036725	—	—	3.60930045	—	0.35961186	—	—	2.32702090 [3]	0.27392090	2.0000000	—	0.27276087	—	—	—
1950	0.44812324	—	—	4.79154388	—	0.35961186	—	—	3.04986840	0.36064095	2.0000000	—	0.35922766	—	—	—
1951	0.44828817	—	—	4.79175052	—	0.35961186	—	—	3.04426977	0.36076168	2.0000000	—	0.35928858	—	—	—
1952	0.44918242	—	—	4.77954355	—	0.35961186	—	—	3.06734353	0.36167582	2.0000000	—	0.35945789	—	—	—
1953	0.44619750	—	—	4.75079695	—	0.99892183	—	—	3.06800227	0.35909105	2.0000000	—	0.35686896	—	—	—
1954	0.44682732	—	—	4.75730603	—	1.79999610	—	—	3.06361286	0.35959801	2.0000000	—	0.35737272	—	—	—
1955	0.44961441	—	—	4.78597136	—	1.79999610	—	—	3.06518108	0.36184097	2.0000000	—	0.35960189	—	—	—
1956	0.44890617	—	—	4.77689511	—	1.79999511	359.84166967 [3]	—	3.06918872	0.36127115	2.0000000	—	0.35903562	—	—	—
1957	0.44929806	—	—	4.78230928	—	1.79999610	359.84166967	—	3.07436899	0.36158637	2.0000000	—	0.35934887	—	—	—
1958	0.44665848	—	—	4.75097751	—	1.79999610	359.84166967	—	3.05183232	0.35946216	2.0000000	—	0.35723778	—	—	—
1959	0.44680896	—	—	4.75495347	—	1.79999610	359.97120230	—	3.04348223	0.35958327	2.0000000	—	0.35735817	—	—	—
1960	0.44700669	—	—	4.76914933	—	.79999610	359.97120230	—	3.04721043	0.35974251	2.0149985	—	0.35751633	—	—	—
1961	0.44786815	—	—	4.76644423	—	1.79999610	361.14120621	—	3.06194311	0.36042530	2.0199980	—	0.71638370 [4]	—	—	—
1962	0.44696733	—	—	4.75601636	—	2.89999360	360.85450346	—	3.05278261	0.35971223	3.7278516	—	0.71494960	—	—	—
1963	0.44822949	—	—	4.76962702	—	2.99999340	361.49369194	—	3.06147441	0.36072433	3.9104231	—	0.71694867	—	—	—
1964	0.44947860	—	—	4.77942934	—	2.99999340	361.99095023	—	3.07068722	0.36172906	3.9100073	—	0.71895895	—	—	—
1965	0.44887333	—	—	4.77600535	—	2.99999340	361.50676018	—	3.06663804	0.36124557	3.9091733	—	0.71802973	—	—	—
1966	0.89863408 [4]	—	—	6.02554832	149.58000	2.99999340	362.34509747	—	3.07332965	0.36161134	3.9000000	—	0.71875225	—	—	—
1967	0.89887640	—	—	7.54432290	296.29167	3.08332660	362.14826350	—	3.07512531	0.36963111 [4]	3.9000000	—	0.71895895	—	—	—
1968	0.89887640	—	—	7.53636295	326.00000	3.49999230	360.55525509	—	3.06833175	0.89790787	3.9000000	—	0.71890726	—	—	—
1969	0.90009001	—	—	7.55857899	362.83333	3.49999230	358.38440311	—	3.06532201	0.89919971	3.9000000	—	0.71994240	—	—	—
1970	0.89798851	—	—	7.55686541	391.87500	3.49999230	358.15336127	—	3.08680084	0.89702189	5.9043500	—	0.71818443	—	—	—
1971	0.88020421	—	—	7.49737592	415.00000	4.19999480	347.47558984	—	3.03131347	0.87943013	6.4317083	—	0.71280918	5.54692700	—	—
1972	0.83871509	—	—	7.54944889	415.00000	4.17979670	303.07622367	—	2.80819994	0.83787181	6.6748417	—	0.77261840	6.22665006	—	—
1973	0.70452304	—	—	8.28431779	415.00000	4.19469230	270.89259109	—	2.43973846	0.73507792	6.7562833	—	0.69502363	6.36415707	—	—
1974	0.69497533	—	—	8.02568218	415.00000	4.45153400	291.52819078	—	2.39117112	0.66657779	6.7878750	—	0.68036468	6.67645881	—	—
1975	0.76470138	—	—	8.38504109	415.00000	6.33614930	296.69188548	—	2.39503748	0.82535490	7.2479000	—	0.73276178	6.95168578	—	—
1976	0.81866558	—	—	8.97021887	415.00000	7.92557150	296.37532972	—	2.54194204	1.00892902	7.4402583	—	0.87070091	8.39771582	—	—
1977	0.90236419	—	—	8.76731545	415.00000	10.44545800	267.79497617	—	2.46184146	1.03206630	7.4028250	—	0.86964084	8.35840856	—	—
1978	0.87404947	—	—	8.19202097	442.04542	17.43537200	208.41583127	—	2.31427910	0.96487843	7.3657583	—	0.86948961	15.66661444	—	—
1979	0.89469446	—	—	8.15550000	623.05550	25.40636900	219.02000000	—	2.17210000	0.97818644	7.3775500	—	0.84231806	15.57000000	—	—

Year	Australia Ee646 [1,2] Currency per dollar	China Ee647 [1] Currency per dollar	Hong Kong Ee648 Hong Kong dollars per dollar	India Ee649 Rupees per dollar	Indonesia Ee650 Rupiah per dollar	Israel Ee651 [1] Currency per dollar	Japan Ee652 Yen per dollar	Korea Ee653 Won per dollar	Malaysia Ee654 [1] Currency per dollar	New Zealand Ee655 [1] Currency per dollar	Philippines Ee656 Pesos per dollar	Singapore Ee657 Singapore dollars per dollar	South Africa Ee658 [1] Currency per dollar	Sri Lanka Ee659 Rupees per dollar	Taiwan Ee660 Taiwanese dollars per dollar	Thailand Ee661 Baht per dollar
1980	0.87719298	—	—	7.86660000	626.99400	5.12429170	226.63000000	—	2.17670000	1.02732690	7.5114333	—	0.77796795	16.16700000	—	—
1981	0.86994345	1.70310000	5.56780000	8.68070000	631.75667	11.43057500	220.63000000	—	2.30480000	1.15143699	7.8996500	2.1053	0.87130783	18.96700000	—	21.731
1982	0.98376783	1.89780000	6.06970000	9.48460000	661.42075	24.26700000	249.06000000	731.93	2.33950000	1.33154019	8.5400000	2.1406	1.08345883	20.75600000	—	23.014
1983	1.10938540	1.98090000	7.26900000	10.10400000	909.27000	56.21449200	237.55000000	776.04	2.32040000	1.49723012	11.1127170	2.1136	1.11296605	23.51000000	—	22.991
1984	1.13717775	2.33080000	7.81880000	11.34800000	1,025.94480	293.20967000	237.45000000	807.51	2.34480000	1.72899701	16.6987080	2.1325	1.43814537	25.42800000	39.633	23.582
1985	1.42804101	2.94340000	7.79110000	12.33200000	1,110.58000	1,178.84930000	238.47000000	861.89	2.48060000	2.00996945	18.6073420	2.2008	2.23430000	27.18700000	39.889	27.193
1986	1.49042403	3.46160000	7.80380000	12.59760000	1,282.56000	1.48784170	168.35000000	884.63	2.58310000	1.90632327	20.3856830	2.1783	2.29190000	27.93400000	37.839	26.315
1987	1.42578097	3.73140000	7.79860000	12.94300000	1,643.84830	1.59464170	144.60000000	825.94	2.51860000	1.68554477	20.5576750	2.1059	2.03850000	29.47200000	31.753	25.775
1988	1.27536380	3.73140000	7.80720000	13.90000000	1,685.70420	1.59893330	128.17000000	734.52	2.61900000	1.52532032	21.0946750	2.0133	2.27700000	31.82000000	28.636	25.312
1989	1.26284949	3.76730000	7.80080000	16.21300000	1,770.05920	1.91641670	138.07000000	674.29	2.70790000	1.67243657	21.7366830	1.9511	2.62140000	35.94700000	26.407	25.725
1990	1.28091816	4.79210000	7.78990000	17.49200000	1,842.81330	2.01617500	145.00000000	710.64	2.70570000	1.67731763	24.3105000	1.8134	2.58850000	40.07800000	26.918	25.609
1991	1.28415862	5.33370000	7.77120000	22.71200000	1,950.31750	2.27910830	134.59000000	736.73	2.75030000	1.72914649	27.4786330	1.7283	2.76330000	41.20000000	26.759	25.528
1992	1.36015560	5.52060000	7.74020000	28.15600000	2,029.92080	2.45908330	126.78000000	784.66	2.54630000	1.85901249	25.5124920	1.6294	2.85240000	44.01300000	25.160	25.411
1993	1.47073963	5.77950000	7.73570000	31.29100000	2,087.10390	2.83008330	111.08000000	805.75	2.57380000	1.84750679	27.1198420	1.6158	3.27290000	48.21100000	26.416	25.333
1994	1.36684846	8.63970000	7.72900000	31.39400000	2,160.75370	3.01105520	102.18000000	806.93	2.62370000	1.68469288	26.4171670	1.5275	3.55260000	49.17000000	26.465	25.161
1995	1.35001958	8.37000000	7.73570000	32.41800000	2,248.60800	3.01129170	93.96000000	772.69	2.50730000	1.52380952	25.7144670	1.4171	3.62840000	51.04700000	26.495	24.921
1996	1.27741655	8.33890000	7.73450000	35.50600000	2,342.29630	3.19165000	108.78000000	805.00	2.51540000	1.45422817	26.2161000	1.4100	4.30110000	55.28900000	27.468	25.359
1997	1.34466427	8.31930000	7.74310000	36.36500000	2,909.38000	3.44940000	121.06000000	947.65	2.81730000	1.50950232	29.4707000	1.4857	4.60720000	59.02600000	28.775	31.072
1998	1.58957200	8.30080000	7.74670000	41.36000000	10,013.60000	3.80010000	130.90000000	1,400.40	3.92540000	1.86532400	40.8930000	1.6722	5.54170000	65.30500000	33.547	41.262
1999	1.54942700	8.27810000	7.59400000	43.13000000	7,855.20000	4.13970000	113.73000000	1,189.84	3.80000000	1.88893100	39.0890000	1.6951	6.11910000	70.86800000	32.322	37.887

[1] Monetary unit changes. See text.

[2] Free exchange rate rather than official rate, 1940–1943 and 1945.

[3] Average based on data for only a portion of the year. See text.

[4] Change in monetary units during year. Figure is a weighted average. See text.

Sources

Series Ee650–651 and Ee656. International Monetary Fund, International Financial Statistics, Yearbook (monthly) and CD-ROM (various issues).

All other series. Publications of the Board of Governors of the Federal Reserve System. 1913–1941, Banking and Monetary Statistics 1914–1941 (1943); 1941–1970, Banking and Monetary Statistics 1941–1970 (1976); 1970–1978, Annual Statistical Digest 1970–1979 (1981); 1979–1999, Federal Reserve Bulletin (various issues).

Information on changes in currency units is taken from these Federal Reserve publications; International Monetary Fund, International Financial Statistics (various Yearbook and monthly issues), and Twenty-Seventh Annual Report on Exchange Restrictions (1976), p. 305; B. R. Mitchell, International Historical Statistics: Africa and Asia (New York University Press, 1982), p. xv; and Tadao Miyashita, The Currency and Financial System of Mainland China (University of Washington Press, 1966), pp. 57, 65–8.

Documentation

The majority of the text for Tables Ee621–645 applies to the present table. Table Ee646–661 includes dollar exchange rates for all African, Asian, and Australasian currencies for which the Federal Reserve publications cited in the source section provide at least one annual exchange-rate observation in the post-World War II period, except that Iran is excluded. Five of the sixteen countries in the table –

Australia, China, Israel, New Zealand, and South Africa – underwent substantive changes in currency unit during the period spanning the observations for the country (the changes for Malaysia were purely nominal). As for Tables Ee621–645, the contemporary exchange rate is shown, notwithstanding that the resulting series is inconsistent over time. Data permitting, consistent series (with the same currency unit throughout the period of observation) are in Table Ee662–678. Of the five cases of substantive change in currency unit, only Israel involved preceding inflation-induced currency depreciation, shown in series Ee651 in 1971–1985 (for two changes in currency unit).

In some cases, averages were calculated from data for only a portion of the year. Series Ee646: 1943, through February 1; 1945, from July 7. Series Ee647: 1933, from April 10; 1941, through July 25. Series Ee648: 1921, from June 1; 1941, through December 24. Series Ee652: 1941, through July 25; 1956, from November 26. Series Ee654: 1921, from June 1; 1942, through February 14; 1949, from January 24.

Changes in Monetary Units

Series Ee646. On February 14, 1966, the Australian dollar replaced the Australian pound as the monetary unit, where 1 dollar = 2 pounds. The exchange rate is expressed as pounds per dollar in 1928–1965 and Australian dollars per U.S. dollar in 1966–1999.

Series Ee646. Original 1966 data in cents per pound January 1–February 11 and in cents per Australian dollar February 14–December 31 converted to annual figure in cents per Australian dollar by taking weighted average of average for pound (converted to Australian dollar) January 1–February 11 and average for Australian dollar February 14–December 31, with the number of foreign-exchange market days as weights. Figure in cents per Australian dollar then converted to Australian dollars per U.S. dollar.

(continued)

TABLE Ee646–661   Bilateral exchange rates – Africa, Asia, Australasia: 1916–1999   [Contemporary currency units]
Continued

Series Ee647. Federal Reserve quotations for old yuan ended on April 8, 1933; quotations for "new" yuan began on April 10, 1933. For January 1–April 8, 1933, exchange rate averages 4.9480 old yuan per dollar. On August 19, 1948, the Kuomintang government changed its currency unit to the new gold yuan, at the rate 1 new gold yuan = 3,000,000 "new" yuan. As the communists captured cities from the Kuomintang in 1949, they offered to convert gold yuan notes to People's Currency for limited periods. The most important conversion was in Shanghai, May 30–June 5, during which probably more than half the total gold yuan notes outstanding were exchanged for People's Currency, at the rate 1 yuan People's Currency = 100,000 new gold yuan. On March 1, 1955, the new People's Currency succeeded the (old) People's Currency as the currency unit of China at the rate 1 yuan new People's Currency = 10,000 yuan (old) People's Currency. The exchange rate is expressed as old yuan per dollar in 1922–1932, "new" yuan per dollar in 1933–1941, and (new People's Currency) yuan per dollar in 1981–1999.

Series Ee651. On February 22, 1980, the sheqel replaced the Israel pound as the monetary unit, where 1 sheqel = 10 pounds. On September 4, 1985, the (old) sheqel was succeeded by the new sheqel, where 1 new sheqel = 1,000 old sheqalim. The exchange rate is expressed as pounds per dollar in 1948–1979, old sheqalim per dollar in 1980–1985, and new sheqalim per dollar in 1986–1999.

Series Ee654. On August 27, 1951, quotations switched from the Straits Settlements dollar to the Malayan dollar, where 1 Malayan dollar = 1 Straits Settlements dollar. On June 12, 1967, the name of the Malaysian currency

was changed to the Malaysian dollar, and on August 21, 1975, to the ringgit. The exchange rate is expressed as Straits Settlements dollars per U.S. dollar in 1921–1951, Malayan dollars per U.S. dollar in 1952–1966, Malaysian dollars per U.S. dollar in 1967–1975, and ringgit per dollar in 1976–1999.

Series Ee655. On July 10, 1967, the New Zealand dollar replaced the New Zealand pound as the monetary unit, where 1 dollar = 2 pounds. The exchange rate is expressed as pounds per dollar in 1928–1967 and New Zealand dollars per U.S. dollar in 1968–1999.

Series Ee655. Original 1967 data in cents per pound January 1–July 7 and in cents per New Zealand dollar July 10–December 31 converted to annual figure in cents per pound by taking weighted average of average for pound January 1–July 7 and average for New Zealand dollar (converted to pound) July 10–December 31, with the number of foreign-exchange market days as weights. Figure in cents per pound then converted to pounds per dollar.

Series Ee658. On February 14, 1961, the rand replaced the South African pound as the South African monetary unit, where 1 rand = 2 pounds. The exchange rate is expressed as pounds per dollar in 1928–1960 and rand per dollar in 1961–1999.

Series Ee658. Original 1961 data in cents per pound January 1–February 10 and in cents per rand February 14–December 31, converted to annual figure in cents per rand by taking weighted average of average for South African pound (converted to rand) January 1–February 10 and average for rand February 14–December 31, with the number of foreign-exchange market days as weights. Figure in cents per rand then converted to rand per dollar.

TABLE Ee662–678   Bilateral exchange rates: 1913–1999   [Consistent currency units]
Contributed by Lawrence H. Officer

Year	Austria	Belgium	Finland	France	Germany	Greece	Argentina	Brazil	Chile
	Ee662 [1]	Ee663 [1,2]	Ee664 [1]	Ee665 [1,3]	Ee666 [1]	Ee667 [1]	Ee668 [1,4]	Ee669 [1,5]	Ee670 [1,6]
	Schillings per dollar	Francs per dollar	Markkaa per dollar	Francs per dollar	Deutsche marks per dollar	Drachmas per dollar	Pesos argentino per dollar	Reais per dollar	Pesos per dollar
1913	0.00016518	5.21536865	—	0.05184114	(Z)	—	—	—	—
1914	0.00016948 [8]	5.17804715 [8]	—	0.05094892	(Z)	—	—	—	—
1915	0.00021682	—	—	0.05569293	(Z)	(Z) [9]	—	—	—
1916	0.00026509	—	—	0.05886508	(Z)	(Z) [9]	(Z)	(Z)	—
1917	0.00029659 [9]	—	—	0.05764386	(Z) [9]	(Z)	(Z)	(Z)	0.00000357 [9]
1918	—	—	—	0.05616400	—	(Z)	(Z)	(Z)	0.00000338
1919	—	7.83269366 [8]	—	0.07308873	(Z) [9]	—	(Z)	(Z)	0.00000443
1920	—	13.55013550	—	0.14204545	(Z)	—	(Z)	(Z)	0.00000542
1921	0.03313453 [9]	13.43020991	0.60386473 [9]	0.13413097	(Z)	(Z) [9]	(Z)	(Z)	0.00000833
1922	0.34364261	13.01591847	0.46223537	0.12193189	(Z)	(Z)	(Z)	(Z)	0.00000818
1923	2.38095238	19.16075877	0.37270322	0.16444393	0.00000001	(Z)	(Z)	(Z)	0.00000817
1924	2.38095238	21.53408846	0.39878769	0.19095631	0.43290043 [10]	(Z)	(Z)	(Z)	0.00000948
1925	2.37256367 [10]	21.01723413	0.39654215	0.20977114	0.42014512	(Z)	(Z)	(Z)	0.00000862
1926	2.36843352	30.62505742 [10]	0.39668372	0.30838499	0.42017513	(Z)	(Z)	(Z)	0.00000828
1927	2.36802970	35.93063949	0.39687264	0.25484200	0.42080812	(Z)	(Z)	(Z)	0.00000829
1928	2.36838303	35.89865093	0.39725102	0.25503698	0.41908689	(Z)	(Z)	(Z)	0.00000823
1929	2.37121347	35.93916219	0.39745628	0.25535609	0.42001630	(Z)	(Z)	(Z)	0.00000829
1930	2.36589515	35.83612855	0.39731416	0.25478356	0.41921515	(Z)	(Z)	(Z) [8]	0.00000828
1931	2.37709809	35.89761999	0.41884817	0.25510204	0.42318728	(Z)	(Z)	(Z)	0.00000829
1932	2.38779170	35.93580428	0.64321091	0.25460841	0.42106681	(Z)	(Z)	(Z)	0.00001265
1933	2.15780456	27.93358511	0.53453068	0.19875579	0.32767654	(Z)	(Z) [10]	(Z)	0.00001302
1934	1.77371007	21.47148372	0.44889348	0.15223481	0.25396761	(Z)	(Z)	(Z)	0.00000986
1935	1.77014021	27.13836768	0.46238498	0.15148531	0.24840092	(Z)	(Z)	(Z)	0.00001967
1936	1.77382333	29.55676673	0.45655846	0.16355637	0.24815682	(Z)	(Z)	(Z)	0.00001952
1937	1.77590242	29.62769834	0.45848425	0.24715769	0.24873333	(Z)	(Z)	(Z) [8]	0.00001934
1938	1.76221390 [9]	29.59595601	0.46367135	0.34745144	0.24897981	(Z)	(Z)	(Z)	0.00001934
1939	—	29.67024490	0.50130339	0.39835876	0.24961871	(Z)	(Z) [8]	(Z)	0.00001933

Notes appear at end of table

TABLE Ee662–678   Bilateral exchange rates: 1913–1999   [Consistent currency units]   *Continued*

	Austria	Belgium	Finland	France	Germany	Greece	Argentina	Brazil	Chile
	Ee662 [1]	Ee663 [1,2]	Ee664 [1]	Ee665 [1,3]	Ee666 [1]	Ee667 [1]	Ee668 [1,4]	Ee669 [1,5]	Ee670 [1,6]
Year	Schillings per dollar	Francs per dollar	Markkaa per dollar	Francs per dollar	Deutsche marks per dollar	Drachmas per dollar	Pesos argentino per dollar	Reais per dollar	Pesos per dollar
1940	—	29.62032665 [9]	0.53447354	0.48014596 [9]	0.24986944	(Z) [9]	(Z)	(Z)	0.00001935
1941	—	—	0.49748769 [9]	—	0.25020266 [9]	—	(Z)	(Z)	0.00001936 [9]
1942	—	—	—	—	—	—	—	—	—
1943	—	—	—	—	—	—	—	—	—
1944	—	—	—	—	—	—	—	—	—
1945	—	43.74453193 [9]	—	0.50733093 [9]	—	—	—	—	—
1946	—	43.80393359	—	1.18920205	—	—	—	—	—
1947	—	43.82697112	—	1.18948495	—	—	—	—	—
1948	—	43.82889201	—	3.08641975 [8]	—	—	(Z)	(Z)	0.00003300
1949	—	45.43595802	—	3.31455088	—	—	(Z)	(Z)	0.00003600
1950	—	50.23106289	—	3.49895031	4.19500040 [9]	—	(Z)	(Z)	0.00004800
1951	—	50.35500277	—	3.50140056	4.19500040	—	(Z)	(Z)	0.00005600
1952	—	50.30687192	—	3.50140056	4.19500040	—	(Z)	(Z)	0.00006200
1953	25.92016589 [9]	49.97751012	—	3.50140056	4.19500040	—	(Z)	(Z)	0.00007100
1954	25.92016589	50.06257822	—	3.50140056	4.19500040	—	(Z)	(Z)	0.00009200
1955	25.92016589	50.23863351	—	3.50140056	4.20788642	—	(Z)	(Z)	0.00016200
1956	25.92016589	49.92511233	—	3.50262697	4.20413603	—	(Z)	(Z)	0.00033599
1957	25.94774125	50.23610972	—	4.20875421 [9]	4.20196316	—	(Z)	(Z)	0.00052132
1958	25.94976126	49.89024147	—	4.21229992	4.19320617	—	(Z)	(Z)	0.00070465
1959	25.89399000	49.97001799	—	4.90677134	4.17950122	—	(Z)	(Z)	0.00094431
1960	26.00036401	49.86785020	—	4.90455731	4.17076792	—	(Z)	(Z)	0.00104900
1961	25.98685065	49.87033712	—	4.90580848	4.01558045	—	(Z)	(Z)	0.00105010
1962	25.84981259	49.76857612	—	4.90075962	3.99792108	—	(Z)	(Z)	0.00105760
1963	25.84647196	49.87033712	—	4.90099980	3.98660501	—	(Z)	(Z)	0.00162180
1964	25.84112874	49.75371909	—	4.90099980	3.97503677	—	(Z)	(Z)	0.00230740
1965	25.83712278	49.64257347	—	4.90172050	3.99424828	—	(Z)	(Z)	0.00315670
1966	25.84914439	49.83305925	—	4.91352201	3.99888031	—	(Z)	(Z)	0.00385110
1967	25.84780811	49.68944099	—	4.92053339	3.98660501	—	(Z)	(Z)	0.00506830
1968	25.85649644	49.93508439	—	4.95270170	3.99233472	—	(Z)	(Z)	0.00687650
1969	25.87054380	50.14542172	—	5.18081028	3.92295320	—	(Z)	(Z)	0.00861760
1970	25.86719781	49.65489846	—	5.52883286	3.64644107	—	(Z)	(Z)	0.01130000
1971	24.99437627	48.54840276	4.20964008	5.51024906	3.47608454	—	(Z)	(Z)	0.01220000
1972	23.13315444	44.02183483	4.15644873	5.04413619	3.18836883	—	(Z)	(Z)	0.02080000
1973	19.36145908	38.81836885	3.81213785	4.43734469	2.64844536	—	(Z)	(Z)	0.07160000
1974	18.66925547	38.89083343	3.76435159	4.80653689	2.58244454	—	(Z)	(Z)	0.59280000
1975	17.40129118	36.69320809	3.66501741	4.28192173	2.45525301	—	(Z)	(Z)	4.91040000
1976	17.93915040	38.57875854	3.85534737	4.77509311	2.51654629	—	(Z)	(Z)	13.05420000
1977	16.53056501	35.82816811	4.01396861	4.91545419	2.32131665	—	(Z)	(Z)	21.53580000
1978	14.50158067	31.43764343	4.10896988	4.50085516	2.00533419	—	0.00000001	(Z)	31.65580000
1979	13.38700000	29.34200000	3.88860000	4.25660000	1.83420000	—	0.00000001	(Z)	37.24580000
1980	12.94500000	29.23700000	3.72060000	4.22500000	1.81750000	—	0.00000002	(Z)	39.00000000
1981	15.94800000	37.19400000	4.31280000	5.43960000	2.26310000	—	0.00000004	(Z)	39.00000000
1982	17.06000000	45.78000000	4.80860000	6.57930000	2.42800000	66.87200000	0.00000026	(Z)	50.90830000
1983	17.96800000	51.12100000	5.56360000	7.62030000	2.55390000	87.89500000	0.00000105	(Z)	78.78830000
1984	20.00500000	57.74900000	6.00070000	8.73550000	2.84540000	112.73000000	0.00000676	(Z)	98.47750000
1985	20.67600000	59.33600000	6.19710000	8.97990000	2.94190000	138.40000000	0.00006018	(Z)	160.86000000
1986	15.26000000	44.66400000	5.07220000	6.92570000	2.17050000	139.93000000	0.00009430	(Z)	192.93000000
1987	12.64900000	37.35800000	4.40370000	6.01220000	1.79810000	135.47000000	0.00021443	0.00000001	219.40670000
1988	12.35700000	36.78500000	4.19330000	5.95950000	1.75700000	142.00000000	0.00087526	0.00000010	245.01170000
1989	13.23600000	39.40900000	4.29630000	6.38020000	1.88080000	162.60000000	0.04233000	0.00000103	266.95420000
1990	11.33100000	33.42400000	3.83000000	5.44670000	1.61660000	158.59000000	0.48759000	0.00002484	304.90330000
1991	11.68600000	34.19500000	4.04810000	5.64680000	1.66100000	182.63000000	0.95355000	0.00014786	349.21580000
1992	10.99200000	32.14800000	4.48650000	5.29350000	1.56180000	190.81000000	0.99064000	0.00164110	362.57580000
1993	11.63900000	34.58100000	5.72510000	5.66690000	1.65450000	229.64000000	0.99895000	0.03220000	404.16580000
1994	11.40900000	33.42600000	5.23400000	5.54590000	1.62160000	242.50000000	0.99901000	0.63930000	420.17670000
1995	10.07600000	29.47200000	4.37630000	4.98640000	1.43210000	231.68000000	0.99975000	0.91770000	396.77330000
1996	10.58900000	30.97000000	4.59480000	5.11580000	1.50490000	240.82000000	0.99966000	1.00510000	412.26670000
1997	12.20600000	35.80700000	5.19560000	5.83930000	1.73480000	273.28000000	0.99950000	1.07800000	419.29500000
1998	12.37900000	36.31000000	5.34730000	5.89950000	1.75970000	295.70000000	0.99950000	1.16100000	460.29000000
1999	14.65900000	42.97400000	6.33400000	6.98790000	2.08350000	306.30000000	0.99950000	1.81500000	508.78000000

Notes appear at end of table

(continued)

TABLE Ee662–678   Bilateral exchange rates: 1913–1999   [Consistent currency units]   *Continued*

	Mexico							
	At New York	At Mexico City	Peru	Australia	China	Israel	New Zealand	South Africa
	Ee671 [1]	Ee672 [1]	Ee673 [1]	Ee674 [1,7]	Ee675 [1]	Ee676 [1]	Ee677 [1]	Ee678 [1]
Year	Pesos per dollar	Pesos per dollar	New soles per dollar	Australian dollars per dollar	(New People's Currency) yuan per dollar	New sheqalim per dollar	New Zealand dollars per dollar	Rand per dollar
1913	—	—	—	—	—	—	—	—
1914	—	—	—	—	—	—	—	—
1915	—	—	—	—	—	—	—	—
1916	—	—	—	—	—	—	—	—
1917	—	—	—	—	—	—	—	—
1918	—	—	—	—	—	—	—	—
1919	—	—	—	—	—	—	—	—
1920	—	—	—	—	—	—	—	—
1921	0.0020575 [9]	—	—	—	—	—	—	—
1922	0.0020528	—	—	—	(Z)	—	—	—
1923	0.0020599	—	—	—	(Z)	—	—	—
1924	0.0020612	—	—	—	(Z)	—	—	—
1925	0.0020246	—	—	—	(Z)	—	—	—
1926	0.0020700	—	—	—	(Z)	—	—	—
1927	0.0021184	—	—	—	(Z)	—	—	—
1928	0.0020787	—	—	0.413890	(Z)	—	0.412771	0.413052
1929	0.0020754	—	—	0.415947	(Z)	—	0.413899	0.413847
1930	0.0021217	—	—	0.436110	(Z)	—	0.427150	0.413403
1931	0.0020986 [9]	—	—	0.568990	(Z)	—	0.481591	0.416008
1932	0.0031397	—	—	0.714464	(Z)	—	0.624629	0.419674
1933	0.0035584	—	—	0.593343	(Z) [9]	—	0.588231	0.481951
1934	0.0036046	—	—	0.498817	(Z)	—	0.496940	0.401370
1935	0.0036000	—	—	0.514325	(Z)	—	0.511163	0.412661
1936	0.0036024	—	—	0.505123	(Z)	—	0.501348	0.406795
1937	0.0036036	—	—	0.507693	(Z)	—	0.503889	0.408483
1938	0.0045204	—	—	0.513407	(Z)	—	0.509747	0.413089
1939	0.0051805	—	—	0.565966	(Z)	—	0.563673	0.454367
1940	0.0053920	—	—	0.655386	(Z)	—	0.652786	0.502528
1941	0.0048690	—	—	0.622524	(Z) [9]	—	0.620087	0.502513
1942	0.0048616	—	—	0.622078	—	—	0.619610	0.502513
1943	0.0048598	—	—	0.622078 [9]	—	—	0.616896	0.502513
1944	0.0048588	—	—	0.619579	—	—	0.616484	0.502513
1945	0.0048589	—	—	0.622714 [9]	—	—	0.618323	0.501184
1946	0.0048589	—	—	0.622385	—	—	0.619899	0.499376
1947	0.0048597	—	—	0.623044	—	—	0.620555	0.499078
1948	0.0053024 [8]	0.004855	0.00000002	0.622631	—	0.00002497	0.570642	0.499064
1949	0.0079239	0.008650	0.00000001	0.680734	—	0.00003596	0.547842	0.545522
1950	0.0086433	0.008650	0.00000001	0.896246	—	0.00003596	0.721282	0.718455
1951	0.0086476	0.008650	0.00000002	0.896576	—	0.00003596	0.721523	0.718577
1952	0.0086298	0.008650	0.00000002	0.898365	—	0.00003596	0.723352	0.718916
1953	0.0086154	0.008650	0.00000002	0.892395	—	0.00009989	0.718182	0.713738
1954	0.0110000	0.012500	0.00000002	0.893655	—	0.00018000	0.719196	0.714745
1955	0.0125000	0.012500	0.00000002	0.899229	—	0.00018000	0.723682	0.719204
1956	0.0125000	0.012500	0.00000002	0.897812	—	0.00018000	0.722542	0.718071
1957	0.0125000	0.012500	0.00000002	0.898596	—	0.00018000	0.723173	0.718698
1958	0.0125000	0.012500	0.00000002	0.893317	—	0.00018000	0.718924	0.714476
1959	0.0125000	0.012500	0.00000003	0.893618	—	0.00018000	0.719167	0.714716
1960	0.0125000	0.012500	0.00000003	0.894013	—	0.00018000	0.719485	0.715033
1961	0.0125000	0.012500	0.00000003	0.895736	—	0.00018000	0.720851	0.716384 [10]
1962	0.0125000	0.012500	0.00000003	0.893935	—	0.00029000	0.719424	0.714950
1963	0.0125000	0.012500	0.00000003	0.896459	—	0.00030000	0.721449	0.716949
1964	0.0125000	0.012500	0.00000003	0.898957	—	0.00030000	0.723458	0.718959
1965	0.0125000	0.012500	0.00000003	0.897747	—	0.00030000	0.722491	0.718030
1966	0.0125000	0.012500	0.00000003	0.898634 [10]	—	0.00030000	0.723223	0.718752
1967	0.0125000	0.012500	0.00000003	0.898876	—	0.00030833	0.739262 [10]	0.718959
1968	0.0125000	0.012500	0.00000004	0.898876	—	0.00035000	0.897908	0.718907
1969	0.0125000	0.012500	0.00000004	0.900090	—	0.00035000	0.899200	0.719942
1970	0.0125000	0.012500	0.00000004	0.897989	—	0.00035000	0.897022	0.718184
1971	0.0125000	0.012500	0.00000004	0.880204	—	0.00042000	0.879430	0.712809
1972	0.0125000	0.012500	0.00000004	0.838715	—	0.00041798	0.837872	0.772618
1973	0.0125000	0.012500	0.00000004	0.704523	—	0.00041947	0.735078	0.695024
1974	0.0125000	0.012500	0.00000004	0.694975	—	0.00044515	0.666578	0.680365

Notes appear at end of table

TABLE Ee662–678   Bilateral exchange rates: 1913–1999   [Consistent currency units]   *Continued*

	Mexico		Peru	Australia	China	Israel	New Zealand	South Africa
	At New York	At Mexico City						
	Ee671 [1]	Ee672 [1]	Ee673 [1]	Ee674 [1,7]	Ee675 [1]	Ee676 [1]	Ee677 [1]	Ee678 [1]
Year	Pesos per dollar	Pesos per dollar	New soles per dollar	Australian dollars per dollar	(New People's Currency) yuan per dollar	New sheqalim per dollar	New Zealand dollars per dollar	Rand per dollar
1975	0.0125000	0.012500	0.00000004	0.764701	—	0.00063361	0.825355	0.732762
1976	0.0145000	0.015400	0.00000006	0.818666	—	0.00079256	1.008929	0.870701
1977	0.0226000	0.022600	0.00000008	0.902364	—	0.00104450	1.032066	0.869641
1978	0.0228000	0.022800	0.00000016	0.874049	—	0.00174350	0.964878	0.869490
1979	0.0228000	0.022800	0.00000022	0.894694	—	0.00254060	0.978186	0.842318
1980	0.0230000	0.023000	0.00000029	0.877193	—	0.00512430	1.027327	0.777968
1981	0.0245000	0.024500	0.00000042	0.869943	1.70310000	0.01140000	1.151437	0.871308
1982	0.0730000	0.056400	0.00000070	0.983768	1.89780000	0.02430000	1.331540	1.083459
1983	0.1550000	0.120100	0.00000163	1.109385	1.98090000	0.05620000	1.497230	1.112966
1984	0.1923000	0.167800	0.00000347	1.137178	2.33080000	0.29320000	1.728997	1.438145
1985	—	0.256900	0.00001098	1.428041	2.94340000	1.17880000	2.009969	2.234300
1986	—	0.611800	0.00001395	1.490424	3.46160000	1.48780000	1.906323	2.291900
1987	—	1.378200	0.00001684	1.425781	3.73140000	1.59460000	1.685545	2.038500
1988	—	2.273100	0.00012883	1.275364	3.73140000	1.59890000	1.525320	2.277000
1989	—	2.461500	0.00266620	1.262849	3.76730000	1.91640000	1.672437	2.621400
1990	—	2.812600	0.18790000	1.280918	4.79210000	2.01620000	1.677318	2.588500
1991	—	3.018400	0.77250000	1.284159	5.33370000	2.27910000	1.729146	2.763300
1992	—	3.094900	1.24580000	1.360156	5.52060000	2.45910000	1.859012	2.852400
1993	3.1237000	3.115600	1.98830000	1.470740	5.77950000	2.83010000	1.847507	3.272900
1994	3.3853000	3.375100	2.19500000	1.366848	8.63970000	3.01110000	1.684693	3.552600
1995	6.4467000	6.419400	2.25330000	1.350020	8.37000000	3.01130000	1.523810	3.628400
1996	7.6004000	7.599400	2.45330000	1.277417	8.33890000	3.19170000	1.454228	4.301100
1997	7.9177000	7.918500	2.66420000	1.344664	8.31930000	3.44940000	1.509502	4.607200
1998	9.1520000	9.136000	2.93000000	1.589572	8.30080000	3.80010000	1.865324	5.541700
1999	9.5530000	9.560400	3.38300000	1.549427	8.27810000	4.13970000	1.888931	6.119100

(Z) Less than 0.000000005 foreign currency unit per dollar.

[1] Monetary unit changes. See text.

[2] Official exchange rate rather than bank-notes-account rate, 1949–1951.

[3] Free exchange rate rather than official exchange rate, 1948–1949 and 1957.

[4] Official exchange rate rather than special export rate in 1941.

[5] Official exchange rate rather than free rate, 1936–1937 and 1939–1941.

[6] Official exchange rate rather than export rate, 1937–1941.

[7] Free exchange rate rather than official rate, 1940–1943 and 1945.

[8] Quotations not available for part of the year. See text.

[9] Average based on data for only a portion of the year. See text.

[10] Change in monetary units during year. Figure is a weighted average. See text.

Sources

Series Ee668–670, Ee672–673, and Ee676, 1948–1999: International Monetary Fund, *International Financial Statistics, Yearbook* (monthly) and CD-ROM (various issues). All other series: publications of the Board of Governors of the Federal Reserve System: *Banking and Monetary Statistics 1914–1941* (1943); *Banking and Monetary Statistics 1941–1970* (1976); *Annual Statistical Digest 1970–1979* (1981); *Federal Reserve Bulletin* (various issues); *Federal Reserve Statistical Release G.5A* (January 7, 1997).

Information on changes in currency units is taken from these Federal Reserve publications; International Monetary Fund, *International Financial Statistics* (various *Yearbook* and monthly issues), and *Twenty-Seventh Annual Report on Exchange Restrictions* (1976), p. 305; B. R. Mitchell, *European Historical Statistics, 1750–1988* (Stockton Press, 1992), p. vii, *International Historical Statistics: Africa and Asia* (New York University Press, 1982), p. xv, and *International Historical Statistics: The Americas, 1750–1988* (Stockton Press, 1993), p. xiii; Tadao Miyashita, *The Currency and Financial System of Mainland China* (University of Washington Press, 1966), pp. 57, 65–8; William F. Spalding, *Dictionary of the World's Currencies and Foreign Exchanges* (Pitman, 1928); and Harold Edwin Peters, *The Foreign Debt of the Argentine Republic* (Johns Hopkins University Press, 1934), pp. 53–5.

Documentation

This table provides exchange-rate series that are consistent over time for those countries in Tables Ee621–661 that experienced one or more changes in currency unit during the period spanning the observations for the coun-

try. The technique is to express the exchange rate in a uniform currency throughout the period of observations, and logically this would be the most recent currency unit. Therefore, in spite of changes in currency units, the series in Table Ee662–678 are consistent series, via conversion of contemporary exchange rates into the most recent currency-unit expression. The corresponding contemporary exchange-rate series, which retain the currency unit in existence at the time and thus become inconsistent with a change in currency unit, are presented in Tables Ee621–661.

For three countries, a change in currency unit could not be corrected to obtain consistency. For Spain, series Ee633 for 1915–1938 is inconsistent with 1939–1999 because of lack of information to convert the Loyalist to the National peseta (see text and notes for the series). The switch in exchange-rate expression from Loyalist to National pesetas per dollar was a consequence of the Nationalist victory in the Spanish Civil War. The inconsistency is not serious for the examination of long-term exchange-rate behavior because the segments of the series are of the same order of magnitude.

For Mexico, series Ee671 for 1921–1931 pertains to the gold, rather than silver, peso – not compatible with the series from 1932 because of lack of a conversion factor between the gold and silver peso (see text and notes for the series). Again, the inconsistency is not serious from a long-term perspective.

For China, series Ee675 for 1922–1932 is inconsistent with 1933–1999 because there is no conversion factor to transform old yuan into "new" yuan (see further text for the series and series Ee647). The reason is that the legislation of March 8, 1933, which authorized the "new" yuan, provided that old yuan coin not conforming with the weight and fineness originally fixed could be converted into "new" yuan not on a one-to-one basis but rather only into the actual amount of pure silver contained plus a minting charge of 2.25 percent (see L. Y. Shen, *China's Currency Reform: A Historical Survey* (Mercury, 1941), pp. 145–7). Therefore, there is no factor to convert the 1922–1932 contemporary exchange rate (expressed in old yuan per dollar in series Ee647) into "new" yuan per dollar (the expression of the 1933–1941 contemporary exchange rate in series Ee647). However, these segments of series Ee675, the consistent exchange rate for China, again are of the same order of magnitude.

In sum, there are sixteen countries with currency-unit changes corrected for consistent exchange-rate expression in this table, of which two (Mexico

(continued)

TABLE Ee662–678   Bilateral exchange rates: 1913–1999   [Consistent currency units]   *Continued*

and China) retain a slight inconsistency for long-term exchange rate behavior. Only series Ee671 – and not series Ee672 – for Mexico involves the inconsistency because series Ee672 does not begin until 1948. Also there is one country (Spain) that experienced a currency-unit change not correctable but again involving only a minor inconsistency. For all other countries in Tables Ee621–661, the contemporary exchange-rate expression provides a consistent time series because, except for Malaysia, there were no changes in currency unit. Although the contemporary exchange-rate series for Malaysia (series Ee654) involves several currency units, the changes are purely nominal – so the series is consistent.

Therefore (1) the seventeen exchange-rate series in this table and (2) the twenty-four series that remain in Tables Ee621–661 after deletion of the contemporary series corresponding to these seventeen series constitute a set of exchange-rate series that are consistent – or, in the cases of Spain, Mexico, and China, nearly consistent – over time. The reader is reminded that *for Ireland and the United Kingdom* (series Ee628 and Ee636), *a lower exchange rate implies a stronger dollar (fewer dollars per pound)*, whereas *for the other countries, a higher exchange rate means a stronger dollar (more units of foreign currency per dollar)*.

When a country changes its currency unit (domestically appreciates its currency) subsequent to a severe inflation that greatly reduces the exchange value of its currency, the contemporary exchange value of its currency is greatly increased. Equivalently, the exchange value of the dollar is much reduced. Therefore, prior to the inflation, the former currency unit was stronger against the dollar by an order of magnitude (the dollar weaker against it by an order of magnitude), and so the consistent (as distinct from contemporary) exchange rate (exchange value of the dollar) was very low. This means that over time the dollar greatly appreciates against such a currency (in consistent units). This pattern is followed in the currency changes of Austria, Finland, Germany, Greece, Peru, China, and Israel and for some of the currency changes of Argentina, Brazil, and Chile.

In contrast, some changes in currency unit do not give rise to a discontinuity in the consistent series at the time of the change. There are two alternative reasons for this scenario. First, the change in currency unit is purely nominal, without significant inflation around the time of the currency change. This is the case for Belgium, France, Mexico (in 1993), Australia, New Zealand, and South Africa. Second, the inflation and currency depreciation that precedes a domestic currency appreciation (change in currency unit) is gradual rather than abrupt. Some of the currency changes of Argentina, Brazil, and Chile are of this mode.

The longest available exchange-rate information is for the United Kingdom. The dollar–pound exchange rate, series Ee677, can be extended back to 1879, series Ee617. These series are conceptually consistent in that both pertain to cable transfers but are inconsistent in timing and/or frequency of intra-annual observations, as evidenced by the differing values of the series in 1913. (Comparisons of Table Ee615–620 with series Ee677 for 1914 are inappropriate because the former series are for January–June, whereas series Ee636 pertains to the full year.) Series Ee618 carries the dollar–pound exchange rate back to 1791, but it is on a sight-equivalent basis. The close correspondence of series Ee618 and Ee677 for 1913 (4.8637 and 4.8689) is not indicative of earlier years, when oceanic transportation took much longer than in the late steamship era (see the text for Table Ee615–620 and also Lawrence H. Officer, *Between the Dollar–Sterling Gold Points: Exchange Rates, Parity, and Market Behavior* (Cambridge University Press, 1996), p. 166).

In some cases, averages were calculated from data for only a portion of the year. Series Ee662: 1917, through April 10; 1921, from June 1; 1938, through March 12; 1953, from November 30. Series Ee663: 1940, through May 9; 1945, from September 24. Series Ee664: 1921, from June 1; 1941, through June 14. Series Ee665: 1940, through June 15; 1945, from August 1; 1957, from August 12. Series Ee666: 1917, through April 10; 1919, from September 15; 1941, through June 14; 1950, from June 22. Series Ee667: 1915, from April 1; 1916, from October 6; 1921, from June 1; 1940, through October 26. Series Ee670: 1917, from November 17; 1941, through May 20. Series Ee671: 1921, from June 1; 1931, through July 29. Series Ee674: 1943, through February 1; 1945, from July 7. Series Ee675: 1933, from April 10; 1941, through July 25.

In some cases, quotations were not available for part of the year. Series Ee662: 1914, September. Series Ee663: 1914, August and October–

December; 1919, January 1–April 25 and August 1–September 25. Series Ee665: 1948, January 1–February 9 and October 16–31. Series Ee668: 1939, August 28–October 16. Series Ee669: 1930, October 7–December 1; 1937, November 18–December 23. Series Ee671: 1948, July 22–October 12.

Changes in Monetary Units

Series Ee662. On December 20, 1924, the monetary unit of Austria was changed from the krone to the schilling, where 1 schilling = 10,000 kronen. Federal Reserve quotations switched from the krone to the schilling on March 13, 1925. In 1947–1948, a new schilling was issued, where 1 new schilling = 3 old schillings. The exchange rate is expressed as (new) schillings per dollar throughout.

Series Ee662. Original 1925 data in cents per krone January 1–March 12 and in cents per old schilling March 13–December 31 converted to annual figure in cents per schilling by taking weighted average of average for krone (converted to old schilling) January 1–March 12 and average for old schilling March 13–December 31, with the number of foreign-exchange market days as weights. Figure in cents per old schilling then converted to (new) schillings per dollar.

Series Ee663. On October 25, 1926, Belgium adopted a new monetary unit, the belga, for foreign-exchange transactions, with 1 belga = 5 francs. Foreign-exchange transactions in terms of the belga ceased in 1940. After World War II, the belga was not restored. The exchange rate is expressed as francs per dollar throughout.

Series Ee663. Original 1926 data in cents per franc January 1–October 25 and in cents per belga October 26–December 31 converted to annual figure in cents per franc by taking weighted average of average for franc January 1–October 25 and average for belga (converted to franc) October 26–December 31, with the number of foreign-exchange market days as weights. Figure in cents per franc then converted to francs per dollar.

Series Ee664. On January 1, 1963, the new markkaa replaced the old markkaa as the monetary unit of Finland, where 1 new markkaa = 100 old markkaa. The exchange rate is expressed as (new) markkaa per dollar throughout.

Series Ee665. On January 1, 1960, the new franc replaced the (old) franc as the monetary unit of France, where 1 new franc = 100 old francs. On January 1, 1963, the franc replaced the new franc as the monetary unit, where 1 franc = 1 new franc. The exchange rate is expressed as (new) francs per dollar throughout.

Series Ee666. On October 11, 1924, the monetary unit of Germany was changed from the mark to the reichsmark, where 1 reichsmark = 1,000,000,000,000 marks. Federal Reserve quotations switched from the mark to the reichsmark on October 29, 1924. In June 1948, the monetary unit was changed to the deutsche mark, where 1 deutsche mark = 10 reichsmarks. The exchange rate is expressed as deutsche marks per dollar throughout.

Series Ee666. Original 1924 data in cents per billion marks January 1–October 28 and in cents per reichsmark October 29–December 31 converted to annual figure in cents per billion marks by taking weighted average of average for billion marks January 1–October 28 and average for reichsmark (converted to billion mark) October 29–December 31, with the number of foreign-exchange market days as weights. Figure in cents per billion marks then converted to deutsche marks per dollar.

Series Ee667. In November 1944, the "new" drachma replaced the old drachma at the rate 1 "new" drachma = 50,000 million old drachmas. In May 1954, an again new drachma became the monetary unit of Greece, where 1 (again new) drachma = 1,000 "new" drachmas. The exchange rate is expressed in (again new) drachmas per dollar throughout.

Series Ee668. Federal Reserve quotations switched from the gold peso to the paper peso (peso moneda nacional) on December 13, 1933, where 1 peso moneda nacional = 0.44 gold peso. On January 1, 1970, the monetary unit of Argentina was changed from the peso moneda nacional to the peso, where 1 peso = 100 pesos moneda nacional. On June 1, 1983, the monetary unit became the (old) peso argentino, where 1 peso argentino = 10,000 pesos. On June 14, 1985, the monetary unit became the austral, where 1 austral =

TABLE Ee662–678   Bilateral exchange rates: 1913–1999   [Consistent currency units]   *Continued*

1,000 pesos argentino. On January 1, 1992, the austral was replaced by the (new) peso argentino, where 1 peso argentino = 10,000 australes. The exchange rate is expressed as (new) pesos argentino per dollar throughout.

Series Ee668. Original 1933 data in cents per gold peso January 1–December 10 and in cents per peso moneda nacional December 13–31 converted to annual figure in cents per gold peso by taking weighted average of average for gold peso January 1–December 10 and average for peso moneda nacional (converted to gold peso) December 13–31, with the number of foreign-exchange market days as weights. Figure in cents per gold peso then converted to (new) pesos argentino per dollar.

Series Ee669. In 1942, the name of the monetary unit of Brazil was changed from the milreis to the cruzeiro. On February 13, 1967, the monetary unit became the new cruzeiro, where 1 new cruzeiro = 1,000 old cruzeiros; and on May 15, 1970, the new cruzeiro was renamed the cruzeiro. On February 28, 1986, the monetary unit was changed to the cruzado, where 1 cruzado = 1,000 cruzeiros. On January 15, 1989, the new cruzado was established, where 1 new cruzado = 1,000 old cruzados. On March 16, 1990, the (again new) cruzeiro replaced the cruzado, where 1 cruzeiro = 1 cruzado. On August 1, 1993, the monetary unit became the cruzeiro real, where 1 cruzeiro real = 1,000 cruzeiros. On July 1, 1994, the monetary unit was changed to the real, where 1 real = 2750 cruzeiros reais. The exchange rate is expressed as reais per dollar throughout.

Series Ee670. On January 1, 1960, the monetary unit of Chile was changed from the (old) peso to the escudo, where 1 escudo = 1,000 (old) pesos. On September 29, 1975, the peso replaced the escudo, where 1 peso = 1,000 escudos. The exchange rate is expressed as pesos per dollar throughout.

Series Ee671. Federal Reserve quotations switched from the gold to the silver peso on July 30, 1931. The average for silver peso July 30–December 31, 1931, is 2.8175E–03 new pesos per dollar. The series prior to 1932 pertains to the gold peso, not compatible with the series from 1932. On January 1, 1993, the monetary unit of Mexico was changed from the old peso to the (new) peso, where 1 peso = 1,000 old pesos. The exchange rate is expressed as (new) pesos per dollar throughout.

Series Ee672. On January 1, 1993, the monetary unit of Mexico was changed from the old peso to the (new) peso, where 1 peso = 1,000 old pesos. The exchange rate is expressed as (new) pesos per dollar throughout.

Series Ee673. On February 1, 1985, the monetary unit of Peru was changed from the sol to the inti, where 1 inti = 1,000 soles. On July 1, 1991, the new sol replaced the inti, where 1 new sol = 1,000,000 intis. The exchange rate is expressed as new soles per dollar throughout.

Series Ee674. On February 14, 1966, the Australian dollar replaced the Australian pound as the monetary unit, where 1 dollar = 2 pounds. The exchange rate is expressed as Australian dollars per U.S. dollar throughout.

Series Ee674. Original 1966 data in cents per pound January 1–February 11 and in cents per Australian dollar February 14–December 31 converted to annual figure in cents per Australian dollar by taking weighted average of average for pound (converted to Australian dollar) January 1–February 11 and average for Australian dollar February 14–December 31, with the number of foreign-exchange market days as weights. Figure in cents per Australian dollar then converted to Australian dollars per U.S. dollar.

Series Ee675. Federal Reserve quotations for old yuan ended on April 8, 1933; quotations for "new" yuan began on April 10, 1933. The exchange rate is "new" yuan per dollar, 1933–1941. For January 1–April 8, 1933, the exchange rate averages 1.6490E–15 with old yuan per dollar as the exchange rate. On August 19, 1948, the Kuomintang government changed its currency unit to the new gold yuan, at the rate 1 new gold yuan = 3,000,000 "new" yuan. As the communists captured cities from the Kuomintang in 1949, they offered to convert gold yuan notes to People's Currency for limited periods. The most important conversion was in Shanghai May 30–June 5, during which time probably more than half the total gold yuan notes outstanding were exchanged for People's Currency, at the rate 1 yuan People's Currency = 100,000 new gold yuan. On March 1, 1955, the new People's Currency succeeded the (old) People's Currency as the currency unit of China at the rate 1 yuan new People's Currency = 10,000 yuan (old) People's Currency. The exchange rate is expressed as (new People's Currency) yuan per dollar throughout.

Series Ee676. On February 22, 1980, the sheqel replaced the Israel pound as the monetary unit, where 1 sheqel = 10 pounds. On September 4, 1985, the (old) sheqel was succeeded by the new sheqel, where 1 new sheqel = 1,000 old sheqalim. The exchange rate is expressed as new sheqalim per dollar throughout.

Series Ee677. On July 10, 1967, the New Zealand dollar replaced the New Zealand pound as the monetary unit, where 1 dollar = 2 pounds. The exchange rate is expressed as New Zealand dollars per U.S. dollar throughout.

Series Ee677. Original 1967 data in cents per pound January 1–July 7 and in cents per New Zealand dollar July 10–December 31 converted to annual figure in cents per New Zealand dollar by taking weighted average of average for pound (converted to New Zealand dollar) January 1–July 7 and average for New Zealand dollar July 10–December 31, with the number of foreign-exchange market days as weights. Figure in cents per New Zealand dollar then converted to New Zealand dollars per U.S. dollar.

Series Ee678. On February 14, 1961, the rand replaced the South African pound as the South African monetary unit, where 1 rand = 2 pounds. The exchange rate is expressed as rand per dollar throughout.

Series Ee678. Original 1961 data in cents per pound January 1–February 10 and in cents per rand February 14–December 31 converted to annual figure in cents per rand by taking weighted average of average for South African pound (converted to rand) January 1–February 10 and average for rand February 14–December 31, with the number of foreign-exchange market days as weights. Figure in cents per rand then converted to rand per dollar.

TABLE Ee679–683   Multilateral exchange rates: 1967–1999

Contributed by Lawrence H. Officer

	Special drawing rights	Effective exchange rate: exchange-rate indexes, per dollar			
		Group-of-Ten currencies	Broad group of currencies	Major currencies	Other important trading partners' currencies
	Ee679	Ee680	Ee681	Ee682	Ee683
Year	Dollars per Special Drawing Rights	Foreign currencies per dollar, March 1973 = 100	Foreign currencies per dollar, January 1997 = 100	Foreign currencies per dollar, March 1973 = 100	Foreign currencies per dollar, January 1997 = 100
1967	1.00000	119.95500	—	—	—
1968	1.00000	122.05830	—	—	—
1969	1.00000	122.39420	—	—	—
1970	1.00000	121.06500	—	—	—
1971	1.00298	117.80830	—	—	—
1972	1.08571	109.06830	—	—	—
1973	1.19213	99.13667	29.94	100.28	2.30
1974	1.20264	101.41500	30.75	102.06	2.41
1975	1.21415	98.34000	31.83	102.35	2.67
1976	1.15452	105.57000	33.77	105.95	2.98
1977	1.16752	103.31000	34.74	105.48	3.29
1978	1.25200	92.39000	33.11	96.33	3.44
1979	1.29200	88.09000	33.49	94.94	3.68
1980	1.30153	87.39000	34.56	94.85	4.05
1981	1.17916	102.94000	38.22	103.55	4.59
1982	1.10401	116.57000	44.30	114.21	5.83
1983	1.06900	125.34000	49.76	118.12	7.68
1984	1.02501	138.19000	56.75	125.85	10.03
1985	1.01534	143.01000	63.82	130.58	13.43
1986	1.17317	112.22000	59.66	107.26	16.64
1987	1.29307	96.94000	58.08	94.86	19.88
1988	1.34392	92.72000	58.76	88.17	23.86
1989	1.28176	98.60000	64.78	91.81	29.41
1990	1.35675	89.09000	70.03	87.82	40.03
1991	1.36816	89.84000	73.20	86.37	46.67
1992	1.40838	86.61000	76.01	84.89	53.13
1993	1.39633	93.18000	82.89	87.15	63.58
1994	1.43170	91.32000	90.53	85.63	81.06
1995	1.51695	84.25000	92.50	80.80	92.59
1996	1.45176	87.34000	97.40	84.60	98.26
1997	1.37600	96.38000	104.44	91.24	104.67
1998	1.35650	98.85000	116.48	95.79	126.03
1999	1.36730	—	116.87	94.06	129.94

Sources

Series Ee679. International Monetary Fund, *International Financial Statistics* (various issues).

Series Ee680. Board of Governors of the Federal Reserve System, *Federal Reserve Bulletin* (August 1978 for 1967–1974, various issues beginning December 1978 for 1975–1999).

Series Ee681–683. Internet site of Federal Reserve Board and *Federal Reserve Bulletin* (various issues).

Documentation

The series are annual averages of daily rates, except that series Ee680 for 1967–1974 and series Ee681–683 for 1973–1995 are computed as the annual average of monthly averages of daily rates. The technique of determining valuation of the special drawing rights (SDR) in terms of the dollar, underlying series Ee679, has evolved over time, whereas the method of computation of the effective exchange rate, series Ee680, has remained unchanged since that series was revised in 1978 and recomputed on that basis back to 1967. The method of calculating series Ee681–683 was established in 1998.

When the SDR came into existence with establishment of the Special Drawing Account of the International Monetary Fund (IMF) on August 6, 1969 (consequent upon the amendment to the Articles of Agreement of the IMF effective July 28, 1969), the SDR was given a fixed gold value, that of the dollar on July 1, 1944, namely, $35 per ounce. Through December 17,

1971, the dollar continued to have that gold value; therefore, $1 = SDR 1. On December 18, 1971, the dollar was devalued to $38 per ounce of gold, implying an SDR value of $38/35 = $1.085714. On February 12, 1973, the dollar was further devalued to $42.2222 per ounce, with the SDR value thereby changing to $42.2222/35 = $1.206349.

On July 1, 1974, the method of valuation of the SDR changed radically. The SDR became a basket of currencies, that is, fixed amounts of each currency in a predetermined set of currencies. Through December 31, 1980, the set of currencies was determined by the rule that all countries with a share in world exports of goods and services in excess of 1 percent would have their currencies included, and sixteen countries fulfilled the criterion. For July 1, 1974, to June 30, 1978, exports were averaged over the five-year period 1968–1972, and the currencies included in the basket were the U.S. dollar, German deutsche mark, Japanese yen, French franc, U.K. pound, Canadian dollar, Italian lira, Netherlands guilder, Belgian franc, Swedish krone, Australian dollar, Danish krone, Norwegian krone, Spanish peseta, Austrian schilling, and South African rand. For July 1, 1978, to December 31, 1980, a new basket was in effect, with exports averaged over 1972–1976, and the Iranian rial and Saudi Arabian riyal replaced the Danish krone and South African rand. On January 1 of 1981, 1986, 1991, and 1996, new baskets were established, but only five currencies were included (U.S. dollar, deutsche mark, yen, French franc, U.K. pound) – these being the currencies of the countries with the largest value of exports of goods and services over the periods 1975–1979,

TABLE Ee679–683   Multilateral exchange rates: 1967–1999   *Continued*

1980–1984, 1985–1989, and 1990–1994. A new SDR basket came into existence on January 1, 2001, for the period 2001–2005, and will in turn be replaced every five years thereafter, on the same basis. On January 1, 1999, the deutsche mark and French franc were replaced with equivalent amounts of the euro, based on the fixed conversion rates between the euro and these currencies.

The IMF computes daily values of the SDR in terms of the dollar by summing the dollar equivalents of each currency in the SDR basket, where a currency's dollar equivalent is the ratio of the currency amount to the currency–dollar exchange rate. A currency's weight in the SDR is the ratio of its dollar equivalent to the SDR value. Even for a given SDR basket, this weight changes as the currency–dollar exchange rates change. A country's currency amount in a new SDR basket is determined by making initial weights (using exchange rates averaged over the three months ending on the last day of the previous basket) broadly proportional to average exports of goods and services over the corresponding five-year period but enhanced for the United States in view of its commercial and financial importance in international transactions (sixteen-currency baskets) or based on these exports and the balances of the country's currency held as reserves by IMF members (five-currency basket). In the six SDR baskets covered here, the amount of the dollar included is 0.40, 0.40, 0.54, 0.452, 0.572, and 0.582; and the initial percentage weight of the dollar is 33, 33, 42, 42, 40, and 39. To ensure a consistent SDR valuation series, the IMF adjusts the currency amounts in a new basket to equate the new and old values of the SDR on the last day in which the former basket was in effect.

In contrast to series Ee679, which has meaning as the value of an exchange rate (number of dollars per SDR), series Ee680–683 can be measured only as index numbers because each is an effective exchange rate, that is, a weighted average of indexes of bilateral exchange rates for a set of currencies versus the dollar. The base period (for which the series is set at value 100) is March 1973 for series Ee680 and Ee682 and January 1997 for series Ee681 and Ee683. For series Ee680, the currencies involved are those of the non-U.S. members of the Group of Ten, the countries that negotiated the Smithsonian Agreement in 1971: Belgium, Canada, France, Germany, Italy, Japan, Netherlands, Sweden, Switzerland, and the United Kingdom. The broad index, series Ee681, incorporates currencies of thirty-five foreign countries, the criterion of selection of which is a share of at least 0.5 percent of U.S. non-oil imports or of U.S. nonagricultural exports. The number of currencies was reduced to twenty-six in 1999, with the euro replacing the currencies of the euro-area countries; see the text of Table Ee621–636.

The remaining series are subsets of series Ee681. The major-currencies series (series Ee682) comprises the currencies of sixteen foreign countries (collapsing to seven currencies in 1999, with the advent of the euro): the euro area, Australia, Canada, Japan, Sweden, Switzerland, and the United Kingdom. These currencies are distinguished by their financial importance in the global economy. The other-important-trading-partners index, series Ee683, involves the remaining currencies in the broad index, those of important U.S. trading partners in Latin America (Argentina, Brazil, Chile, Colombia, Mexico, and Venezuela), Asia (China, Hong Kong, India, Indonesia, Korea, Malaysia, Philippines, Singapore, Taiwan, and Thailand), the Middle East (Israel and Saudi Arabia), and Eastern Europe (Russia).

The Group-of-Ten series (series Ee680) has fixed weights, proportionate to the average global trade (exports plus imports) of the countries for 1972–1976. The other Federal Reserve series (series Ee681–683) have more sophisticated weights: the average of a country's share in U.S. non-oil imports and an export-share indicator. The latter is (1) the average of the country's share as a destination of U.S. nonagricultural, nonmilitary exports, and (2) the average, over third countries, of the country's share in third-country imports weighted by the third-country share in U.S. exports. These weights vary over time; the weights used were established on November 1, 1999.

In addition to the unit of measurement and internal weighting pattern, series Ee679 differs from series Ee680–683 in other respects. The Federal Reserve effective exchange rates use exchange rates at New York; but the SDR basket takes exchange rates at London, resorting to New York only if the London market is closed. For each index, the Federal Reserve annual or monthly series is an arithmetic average of daily values, while the IMF annual, quarterly, or monthly dollar–SDR series is a geometric average of daily values. Ironically, the SDR basket is the sum of dollar equivalents of the component currencies (arithmetic in nature), whereas each Federal Reserve index is a geometric weighted average of the component exchange-rate indexes.

Also, the Federal Reserve series have no significance beyond multilateral measurement of the exchange value of the dollar. In contrast, the SDR has a number of substantive roles. It is an official reserve asset lodged in the IMF and the unit of account of the IMF. It is also the unit of account, or the basis of the unit of account, of some fifteen other international or regional organizations and of several international conventions. In principle, a reform of the international monetary system could involve an "SDR standard," in which countries peg their currencies to the SDR or manage their floating currencies with reference to their SDR value. In practice, a few countries do peg their currencies to the SDR. "Private SDRs," assets or liabilities denominated in SDRs, have as yet experienced only a limited development.

A higher value of series Ee679 implies a lower value of the dollar versus the SDR. A higher value of the Federal Reserve indexes, series Ee680–683, means a higher value of the dollar relative to foreign currencies. Series Ee682 tracks series Ee680 very well, and indeed it was designed to replace it. Series Ee683 exhibits an incredible appreciation of the dollar over a quarter century, reflecting massive currency depreciation (in consistent currency units) in the currencies of countries experiencing severe inflation. This phenomenon is analogous to the behavior of a number of series in Table Ee662–678.

Literature on the SDR and its valuation includes IMF, *Annual Report* (various issues); *IMF Survey* (various issues); and *Financial Organization and Operations of the IMF,* Pamphlet Series number 45, 4th edition (1995), pp. 103–19. Additional readings on the topic are: Margaret Garritsen de Vries, *The International Monetary Fund, 1966–1971: The System under Stress,* volume 1, *Narrative* (IMF, 1976), pp. 11–250; Margaret Garritsen de Vries, *The International Monetary Fund, 1972–1978: Cooperation on Trial,* volume 1, (IMF, 1985), pp. 281–96; volume 2 (IMF, 1985), pp. 871–900; and George M. von Furstenberg, "SDR," in Peter Newman, Murray Milgate, and John Eatwell, editors, *The New Palgrave Dictionary of Money and Finance* (Macmillan, 1992), volume 3, pp. 402–4.

On effective exchange rates, see S. H. Thomas, "Effective Exchange Rates," in Peter Newman, Murray Milgate, and John Eatwell, editors, *The New Palgrave Dictionary of Money and Finance* (Macmillan, 1992), volume 1, pp. 733–5. The Federal Reserve effective exchange rates are discussed in "Index of the Weighted-Average Exchange Value of the U.S. Dollar: Revision," *Federal Reserve Bulletin* (August 1978): 700; Peter Hooper and John Morton, "Summary Measures of the Dollar's Foreign Exchange Value," *Federal Reserve Bulletin* (October 1978): 783–9; B. Dianne Pauls, "Measuring the Foreign-Exchange Value of the Dollar," *Federal Reserve Bulletin* (June 1987): 411–22; and Michael P. Leahy, "New Summary Measures of the Foreign Exchange Value of the Dollar," *Federal Reserve Bulletin* (October 1998): 811–18.

Series Ee680. The 1975 annual average of monthly values of daily rates is 98.50, versus 98.34 for the series, implying that the 1967–1974 and 1975–1999 segments of the series are closely comparable (see preceding text).

Series Ee681–683. The 1996 annual average of monthly values of daily data has the identical value as the series Ee681–683 (to two decimal places), implying that the 1973–1995 and 1996–1999 segments of these series are closely comparable (see preceding text).

CHAPTER Ef

Outlying Areas

Editor: Sumner J. La Croix

OUTLYING AREAS

Sumner J. La Croix

Outlying areas are geographical areas over which the U.S. government exercises jurisdiction, control, or sovereignty and are not U.S. states.[1] They typically have been treated in an anomalous fashion in censuses and other governmental data collection efforts. Despite being geographically peripheral by definition, they are important for understanding various aspects of American history, in particular the American imperialism of the late nineteenth century that was often the reason behind their acquisition and retention. Outlying areas receive separate treatment in *Historical Statistics* because of their unique histories, distinct data sources, and typical exclusion from the other historical data series in the volume. Despite the fragmentary nature of many of the series, a broad-sweeping analysis of major trends reveals dramatic changes in the economic, political, and social life of people in outlying areas since the acquisition of these areas by the United States.

Twelve outlying areas were selected for inclusion. Two of them were U.S. territories for approximately 60 years (Hawai'i) and 90 years (Alaska) before becoming states.[2] The territories of

Hawai'i and Alaska are included in the group of outlying areas for two reasons: they were important U.S. territories that were not part of the contiguous landmass of the 48 states, and they were both U.S. territories for a particularly long time before becoming states. That said, historical data from other U.S. territories that went on to become states (for example, the territory of Arizona) are not included.

Five of the twelve areas included in this discussion are currently U.S. territories or commonwealths: American Samoa, Guam, Commonwealth of Northern Mariana Islands, Commonwealth of Puerto Rico, and the U.S. Virgin Islands.[3] These areas are included because of the significant size of their populations (Puerto Rico and Guam) and their organized, elected governments (all of the above). We do not have historical data from Midway Island, Johnston Island, Navassa Island, Palmyra Island, Kingman Reef, Howland and Baker Islands, Wake Island, and other islands under U.S. sovereignty without elected governments or indigenous populations (all are currently uninhabited except for a small military base on Johnston Island). These territories may, nonetheless, remain strategically important possessions.

The remaining five outlying areas were formerly under U.S. sovereignty or held in trust by the United States: the Panama Canal Zone, the Philippines, and three sovereign states carved from a portion of the Trust Territory of the Pacific – the Federated States of Micronesia, the Republic of the Marshall Islands, and the Republic of Palau. These outlying areas are included because of the significant size of their populations (the Philippines), their historical significance for the United States as a world power (Canal Zone and Trust Territory of the Pacific) or their unique status as a United Nations trust (Trust Territory of the Pacific). This chapter does not include historical data from countries occupied in the aftermath of war (for example, Germany and Japan after World War II) or U.S. military action (for example, Vera Cruz, Mexico, in 1914; Nicaragua for most of the period 1912–1933; or Panama after the U.S. invasion in 1989). The chapter also excludes military protectorates of the United States, such as Cuba 1898–1934,

Acknowledgments

Sumner J. La Croix would like to acknowledge assistance from staff at the Barnard College Library, Columbia University libraries, the University of Hawai'i libraries, the Bancroft Library at the University of California, Berkeley, the University of Washington Library, the Bank of Hawai'i, the New York Public Library, the New York University Library, the National Archives, the Library of Congress, the U.S. Bureau of Labor Statistics, the Virgin Islands Department of Economic Development, the Puerto Rico Planning Board, the Puerto Rico Office of Management and Budget, the Puerto Rico Department of Labor, the Hawai'i State Department of Business, Economic Development, and Tourism, the American Samoa Development Planning Office, the Palau Office of Planning and Statistics, the Marshall Islands Department of Commerce, the Federated States of Micronesia Bureau of Economic Research, the Guam Department of Commerce, the Northern Mariana Islands Departments of Commerce and Labor, the Office of the Governor of the Northern Mariana Islands, and the Institute of Social and Economic Research at the University of Alaska–Anchorage. The librarians in the Government Documents Collection at the University of Hawai'i's Hamilton Library went the extra mile in helping to track down obscure sources and locate obvious ones. Special thanks are also due to Linda Barrington, Susan Carter, Alan Dye, Chris Grandy, Monty Hindman, Matthew Sobek, Richard Sutch, Peter Xenos, and many others who provided support and data over the course of the project. Most important, the project could not have been completed without research assistance from Stephen James Noll, Jian Zhang, Randi Kirtman, Manu Gayatrinath, Mishuku Matsuda, and Min Min Thaw.

[1] The U.S. Census Bureau now refers to these areas as "insular areas." The federal government oversees them through the Office of Insular Affairs, U.S. Department of Interior. For additional information on the territorial history of the United States, see the essay on natural resources and the environment in Chapter Cf.

[2] A U.S. territory is a partially self-governing geographical area of the United States that has not been granted statehood. The District of Columbia is a U.S. territory but is not included here.

[3] A U.S. commonwealth is a self-governing autonomous political unit in political union with the United States as well as under the sovereignty of the United States.

Panama 1903–1939, Dominican Republic 1905–1941, and Haiti 1915–1936.

The twelve outlying areas considered here are extremely heterogeneous in their geography, economic development, political status, languages, and cultures (see Table Ef-A). They are geographically far flung, from the Marshall Islands in the Northwest Pacific to American Samoa in the South Pacific to the U.S. Virgin Islands in the Caribbean Sea. Their level of economic development varies tremendously, from the high per capita income of Hawai'i residents to the low per capita income of citizens of the Federated States of Micronesia. Most outlying areas are, however, very poor by U.S. standards, with per capita incomes in 1970 typically far less than those observed in the poorest U.S. state. English is or was used as at least a secondary language in all outlying areas, but numerous other languages are also spoken, including Hawaiian, Samoan, Spanish, and Tagalog. Some outlying areas are populated primarily by native peoples (for example, American Samoa), while others are primarily populated by immigrant peoples (for example, Hawai'i). The heterogeneity of the twelve outlying areas establishes a basis for providing separate historical series for each outlying area.

One feature common to many of the outlying areas is that their acquisition was a consequence of U.S. involvement in war (see Table Ef-B). After its defeat in the Spanish-American War, Spain ceded Puerto Rico, Guam, and the Philippines to the United States in 1898. The annexation of Hawai'i by the United States in 1898 was also a byproduct of the Spanish-American War, as Congress had repeatedly rejected measures to annex the Republic of Hawai'i, despite the fact that the U.S. military was involved in the 1893 overthrow of the Hawaiian monarchy, until battles in the Philippines during the spring and summer of 1898 increased the strategic importance of Hawai'i.

The United States purchased the U.S. Virgin Islands from Denmark during World War I to prevent them from falling into the hands of Germany. The United States obtained the Trust Territories of the Pacific – Palau, the Federated States of Micronesia, Northern Mariana Islands, and the Marshall Islands – after Japan's defeat in World War II and the forfeiture of its mandate from the League of Nations over these islands. Only Alaska and the Canal Zone are exceptions to the rule of wartime acquisition. Alaska was purchased from Russia in 1867 and the Canal Zone's perpetual lease was negotiated by treaty in 1903, albeit only after the U.S. military supported the Panamanian Rebellion against Colombia.

Selection of the Historical Series

The selection of historical series for the volume was guided by two main principles: the series should be important indicators of a wide spectrum of demographic, economic, and social characteristics; and they should be available for most outlying areas. Table Aa93–109 presents the basic census population counts for the period 1880–2000. Tables Ef1–45 provide the core demographic data series. More detailed information on the native and immigrant populations of Hawai'i and Alaska is presented because of their ethnic diversity as well as their later transition to statehood. Estimated annual population is reported to facilitate calculation of per capita measures from aggregate data series. The reader is cautioned that the estimated population series are often provisional and sometimes based on simple interpolations between census data. Infant

mortality is an important demographic variable in its own right, and is much more readily available in the outlying areas than another critical demographic variable, life expectancy. The relatively long series on infant mortality assume a heightened importance as an indicator of development for outlying areas, as the historical series on real per capita income are often problematic.[4]

Four other tables provide a more complex portrait of each area's human resources. Tables Ef46–66 cover school enrollment and thus provide at least a rough measure of investment in human capital. Historical series on public and private employment (Table Ef75–84) and unemployment (Table Ef85–92) are somewhat fragmentary for many of the developing areas. In many cases, the only reliable employment and unemployment data come from the U.S. Census of Outlying Areas. Due to the limited availability and reliability of the unemployment series in particular, Table Ef85–92 does not report annual data; instead it reports measures of unemployment only for years in which the Census of Outlying Areas was taken.

Five historical tables provide information on particular sectors of the economy. Series on the value of exports and value of imports are particularly important, because in the absence of reliable national income data they are often the "best available" indicators of trends and cycles in the domestic economy (Tables Ef100–121). Such series should be used for this purpose with a great degree of caution, as their long-run trends and short-run variation may also be driven by changing trade policies, the growth or decline of the tradable good sectors of the economy, changing terms of trade, and changing usage of intermediate products. Two additional historical tables chart the traditional industry of most outlying areas, agriculture, and the newly dominant industry, tourism. Table Ef93–99 presents data on the value of the major crops of selected outlying areas, while Table Ef122–130 presents surprisingly complete data on visitor arrivals. Table Ef131–140 reports data on the number of telephone lines or telephones in use, a measure of the development of public infrastructure as well as another indicator of the degree of economic development.

Aggregate data on gross territorial product (GTP) are provided in Table Ef67–74, and consumer price indexes (CPI) for outlying areas may be found in Table Ef141–148.[5] With the exceptions of Hawai'i and Puerto Rico, most outlying areas only began to calculate national income and consumer price indexes in the 1970s. These series are, therefore, relatively short, and early values were often produced by outside consultants. The inexperience of most outlying area governments in constructing these measures should alone be adequate warning concerning the reliability of GTP and CPI estimates.

The chapter also contains two tables related to government activity: total government revenues and expenditures (Tables Ef149–172). A table on government employment would nicely complement these series, as it would provide a better measure of government consumption of resources than government expenditures. It was not reported, however, due to fragmentary data in numerous outlying areas.

---

[4] Infant mortality was clearly underreported in rural parts of outlying areas, particularly prior to the 1950s when more comprehensive tracking of vital statistics was instituted.

[5] GTP is also known as gross island product, gross domestic product, and gross commonwealth product.

TABLE Ef-A Vital facts of the outlying areas

Outlying area	Location	Land area (square miles)	Notable geographic characteristics	Capital	Major languages	Political status as outlying area	Political status in 2000	U.S. citizenship rights in 2000	Currency in 2000
Alaska	Northwest extreme of North American continent	570,374	Three major geographic regions; 150 Aleutian islands; Alexander Archipelago	Juneau	English, numerous Native Alaskan languages	Incorporated, organized territory, 1912–1959	49th U.S. state since 1959	Citizens	U.S. dollar
Hawai'i	North Pacific Ocean	6,423	Hawai'i, Kauai, Maui, Oahu, and Molokai are largest islands; active volcanoes; in hurricane path	Honolulu	English and Hawaiian	Incorporated, organized territory, 1900–1959	50th U.S. state since 1959	Citizens	U.S. dollar
American Samoa	South Pacific Ocean	77	Tutuila is largest of seven islands; Pago Pago Harbor; in hurricane path	Pago Pago	Samoan and English	Unincorporated, unorganized territory since 1951	Unincorporated, unorganized territory	Nationals	U.S. dollar
Guam	Northwest Pacific Ocean	210	One major island; Apra Harbor; in hurricane path	Agana	English and Chamorro	Unincorporated, organized territory since 1950	Unincorporated, organized territory	Citizens	U.S. dollar
Commonwealth of Northern Mariana Islands	Northwest Pacific Ocean; 125 miles north of Guam	179	Saipan, Tinian, Rota are the largest of fourteen islands; in hurricane path	Saipan	English, Chamorro, and Carolinian	United Nations trust territory, 1946–1986	U.S. commonwealth since 1986	Citizens	U.S. dollar
Commonwealth of Puerto Rico	West Indies	3,427	One major island; several smaller islands; in hurricane path	San Juan	Spanish and English	U.S. commonwealth since 1952	U.S. commonwealth	Citizens	U.S. dollar
Virgin Islands	Group of islands in the Lesser Antilles chain in the West Indies	134	Three main islands are St. Croix, St. John, and St. Thomas; fifty islets; in hurricane path	Charlotte Amalie	English	Unincorporated, organized territory since 1936	Unincorporated organized territory	Citizens	U.S. dollar
Canal Zone	Panamanian isthmus of Central America	362	Five-mile-wide strip of land on each side of the Panama Canal	Balboa Heights	Spanish and English	Leased land under U.S. control, 1904–1979	Part of sovereign state of Panama since 1999	None	U.S. dollar
Federated States of Micronesia	Northwest Pacific Ocean	271	607 islands and atolls; four FSM states span 1,700 miles	Palikir, Pohnpei	English and eight major Micronesian languages	United Nations trust territory, 1946–1986	Sovereign state in compact of free association with U.S. since 1986	None	U.S. dollar
Republic of Marshall Islands	Northwest Pacific Ocean	70	Thirty-four coral islands; 870 reefs; average elevation above sea level is seven feet	Majuro	English and Marshallese dialects	United Nations trust territory, 1946–1986	Sovereign state in compact of free association with U.S. since 1986	None	U.S. dollar
Republic of Palau	Northwest Pacific Ocean	177	343 islands, with main group encircled by 100-mile reef; Rock Islands	Koror	English, Palauan, Sonsorolese-Tobian	United Nations trust territory, 1946–1994	Sovereign state in compact of free association with U.S. since 1994	None	U.S. dollar
Republic of the Philippines	Western Pacific Ocean, east of Vietnam; part of the Malay Archipelago	115,124 [1]	7,100 islands with eleven major islands; active volcanoes	Manila	Tagalog, English, and ten major regional languages	U.S. commonwealth, 1935–1946	Sovereign state since 1946	None	Philippine peso

[1] Also includes water area.

TABLE Ef–B Acquisition and political status of outlying areas

U.S. States

Alaska. On the initiative of U.S. Secretary of State William H. Seward, the United States paid Russia $7,200,000 for Alaska on October 18, 1867. The U.S. Congress provided Alaska with a simple civil government in 1884. In 1912, Congress passed the 2nd Alaska Organic Act, providing Alaska with an elected bicameral legislature and an appointed governor. After several failed statehood petitions, the U.S. Congress approved the Alaska Statehood Act on May 26, 1958, and Alaska officially became the forty-ninth state on January 3, 1959.

Hawai'i. U.S. Marines assisted a successful overthrow of Hawai'i's monarchy by the Caucasian minority on January 17, 1893. After several failed annexation measures, President McKinley signed a joint resolution of Congress to annex Hawai'i on July 7, 1898. The United States assumed sovereignty on August 12, 1898, and Hawai'i became a U.S. territory on June 14, 1900. The Organic Act of 1900 established territorial government with an appointed governor and an elected bicameral legislature. After several failed statehood petitions, the Hawai'i Statehood Act was signed into law on March 18, 1959, and Hawai'i officially became the fiftieth state on August 21, 1959.

U.S. Territories and Commonwealths

American Samoa. By the Treaty of Berlin, signed December 2, 1899, and ratified February 16, 1900, the United States acquired rights to the Samoan islands east of longitude 171 degrees. Samoan chiefs then ceded Tutuila and Aunuu to the United States in 1900 and the Manua group in 1904. The United States annexed Swains Island in 1925 and placed it in the American Samoan territory. On February 20, 1929, Congress formally accepted sovereignty over these Islands. The U.S. Navy administered American Samoa from 1900 to 1951, when jurisdiction was transferred to the Department of the Interior. The Constitution of 1960 established Samoa as a territory with an appointed governor and an elected bicameral legislature. The revised constitution of 1966 has allowed for an elected governor since 1977. American Samoa is an unorganized unincorporated territory of the United States under the jurisdiction of the Department of the Interior.

Guam. The United States acquired Guam from Spain at the end of the Spanish–American War under the Treaty of Paris on December 10, 1898. The island was placed under U.S. Navy rule. The Japanese invaded Guam on December 8, 1941, and held it until July 21, 1944. The Organic Act of August 1, 1950, established a civilian government, with an appointed governor and an elected unicameral legislature. Guam's governor became popularly elected in 1970. Guam's official status is as an organized unincorporated territory of the United States under the jurisdiction of the Department of the Interior.

Northern Mariana Islands. On July 18, 1947, the Northern Marianas were included in the United Nations' Trust Territory of the Pacific. The United States administered the Trust Territory until its dissolution. In 1975, residents of the Northern Marianas approved commonwealth status for the island group, which effectively gave the islands political union with the United States. The U.S. Congress approved commonwealth status in 1976. In 1978, self-government was established, and on November 3, 1986, the commonwealth was fully implemented. The Northern Marianas have an elected governor and an elected bicameral legislature.

Puerto Rico. Spain ceded Puerto Rico to the United States under the Treaty of Paris on December 10, 1898. The United States established a civil territorial government in 1900, with an appointed governor and an elected legislature. The Constitution of 1952 established Puerto Rico as a commonwealth, with an elected governor and a bicameral legislature.

Virgin Islands. The United States acquired the American Virgin Islands from Denmark on March 31, 1917, for $25 million in gold as a naval base to protect against German attacks on Panama Canal Zone shipping. The U.S. Navy ran the island government from 1917 to 1931. U.S. citizenship was granted to native Virgin Islanders in 1927. The Organic Act of 1931 established a government under the U.S. Department of the Interior, with an appointed governor and elected municipal councils. The Second Organic Act of 1954 mandated an elected senate. The Virgin Islands Elective Governor Act of August 1968 allowed for a governor and lieutenant governor to be elected to four-year terms beginning with the November 1970 election. The Virgin Islands are an organized unincorporated U.S. territory under the jurisdiction of the Department of the Interior.

U.S. Sovereignty Ended

Canal Zone. The Hay–Bunau–Varilla Treaty of 1903 between Panama and the United States was ratified by the United States on November 18, 1903, and by Panama on February 23, 1904. This treaty created the Canal Zone, a strip of land across Panama. The United States was given the right to build and operate the Panama Canal and to control the Canal Zone as if it were U.S. territory. The U.S. Army appointed the governor of the Canal Zone. On September 7, 1977, the U.S. and Panama governments signed a treaty ending U.S. control over the Canal Zone on October 1, 1979. The United States turned over the Canal Zone to Panama on December 31, 1999.

Federated States of Micronesia. On July 18, 1947, the Micronesian islands were included in the United Nations' Trust Territory of the Pacific. The United States administered the Trust Territory until its dissolution. Following a constitutional convention, the people of Truk, Yap, Pohnpei, and Kosrae voted to form a federation on July 12, 1978. The government of the Federated States of Micronesia (FSM) was established on May 10, 1979. In 1983 FSM voters approved the compact of Free Association with the United States. The Compact grants sovereignty to FSM and provides for U.S. aid and defense of the islands. After ratification of the Compact by the U.S. Congress, FSM became an independent state on November 3, 1986.

Republic of the Marshall Islands. On July 18, 1947, the Marshall Islands were included in the United Nations' Trust Territory of the Pacific. The United States administered the Trust Territory until its dissolution. In 1978 the Marshall Islands Constitutional Convention adopted a constitution, and the government of the Republic of the Marshall Islands (RMI) was established in 1979. In 1983 RMI voters approved the compact of free association with the United States. The compact grants sovereignty to RMI and provides for U.S. aid and defense of the islands in exchange for continued U.S. use of the missile testing range at Kwajalein Atoll. After ratification of the compact by the U.S. Congress, RMI became an independent state on October 21, 1986.

Palau. On July 18, 1947, Palau was included in the United Nations' Trust Territory of the Pacific. The United States administered the Trust Territory until its dissolution. In 1980 voters adopted a constitution, effective January 1, 1981. In 1986 the U.S. Congress approved a compact of free association agreed to by U.S. and Palauan negotiators. After rejecting the compact seven times, Palauan voters approved the compact on November 9, 1993, after the Palau Constitution was amended to reduce the majority vote required for approval. On October 1, 1994, Palau became an independent state.

Philippines. The United States acquired the Philippine Islands from Spain at the end of the Spanish–American War under the Treaty of Paris on December 10, 1898. Guerilla warfare between Filipino nationalists and U.S. forces continued into 1902. The Philippine Bill of 1902 established an appointed governor and a bicameral legislature, one house of which was elected. The Jones Act established an elected upper house in 1916 and pledged future independence. The Tydings–McDuffie Bill of 1934 promised independence by 1946 and established an interim commonwealth with a popularly elected Philippine president. The Republic of the Philippines was formally proclaimed on July 4, 1946.

TABLE Ef–B   Acquisition and political status of outlying areas *Continued*

Trust Territory of the Pacific. During World War I, Japan captured the Marshall Islands, the Northern Mariana Islands, Palau, the Federated States of Micronesia, and the Caroline Islands from Germany. The League of Nations subsequently granted a mandate to Japan to administer the islands. The United States occupied these islands during the last two years of World War II and was designated in 1947 by the United Nations as the trustee of the Trust Territory of the Pacific Islands (TTPI). The U.S. Navy administered the TTPI until 1951, when the U.S. Department of the Interior became the administrative authority. The President of the United States appointed a High Commissioner of the TTPI, who appointed administrators for four districts within the TTPI. In 1965, the Congress of Micronesia was formed, with representatives from all TTPI islands. During the 1970s the various component parts of the TTPI began the process of deciding the future status of their islands. The United Nations Security Council voted in December 1990 to dissolve the trusteeship with the exception of Palau. The trust territory was dissolved in 1994 after Palau's voters approved a compact of free association with the United States.

Major Data Sources and Their Limitations

Data feasts, famines, and fragments – the usual lot of the quantitative historian – are writ large in the historical data series for outlying areas. Hawai'i provides relatively ample data, for the researcher Robert C. Schmitt has compiled a magisterial volume, *Historical Statistics of Hawaii*, containing thousands of important historical series and virtually every series required for this work. In contrast to Hawai'i, Alaska has few historical series covering even medium-length portions of the 1868–1958 pre-statehood period. The *Annual Report*s from the governor of Alaska to the U.S. Secretary of the Interior contain some relevant data, but reporting of important series is typically sporadic and many series end after just a few years. Before Alaska became a state, the territorial government did not appear to calculate a consumer price index or gross territorial product, or keep statistics on total employment or unemployment.

American Samoa, the Canal Zone, Guam, Puerto Rico, and the Virgin Islands are all rich in unorganized, unanalyzed historical data. The *Annual Report*s of the territorial governors to the Secretary of the Interior or to the Secretary of the Navy often contain important data series (for example, school enrollment), but in most cases only fragments of these series have been assembled. Many of the series presented here represent the first systematic effort to assemble these data into long historical series. Data were combined from the *Annual Report*s with data gathered by the area's statistical abstract or digest and with data supplied by each area's economic development and planning agencies. Some of the annual series pieced together from these multiple data sources are complete, while others remain fragmentary due to the irregular coverage in the underlying sources.

Data for the four main districts of the Trust Territory of the Pacific are very fragmentary for the first five to eight years after the United States assumed the United Nations trust in 1946. *Annual Report*s by the U.S. Secretary of State to the United Nations improve dramatically in the early 1950s, allowing relatively detailed data for each of the four trust districts to be identified from the early 1950s through the mid-1970s. After 1976, the data provided in the *Annual Report*s become less detailed, as the Trust Territory government turned its data collection responsibilities over to newly established regional governments. The four separate governments regularly published some data series previously reported in the *Annual Report*s, but other data series (for example, government revenues and expenditures) were only sporadically reported and are often hard to interpret.

An impressive array of historical series for the Philippines during the U.S. colonial period is reported in the 1940 and 1946 editions of the *Yearbook of Philippine Statistics*. While there are numerous underutilized series covering internal and international migration, labor stoppages, and agricultural output by province, some aggregate series required for this project (for example, employment, unemployment, consumer price index, and gross commonwealth product) were either never assembled by the commonwealth government or only initiated in the mid-1930s.

Data for the Pacific territories during World War II are typically unavailable, with the significant exception of Hawai'i. Pre–World War II data for many areas are particularly erratic in quality. Consider, for example, infant mortality rates. Pre–World War II infant mortality series are available for the Philippines and Puerto Rico but are of poor quality due to serious underreporting of birthrates. Given the problems with both data series, they have not been reported here.

Major Trends

Several outlying areas share common trends for a number of important series. First, population grew more rapidly in the outlying areas than in the contiguous forty-eight states (Tables Aa93–109 and Ef1–45). Exceptions were Alaska and the Virgin Islands in the 1920s and 1930s, both of which suffered from declines in staple industries; the Canal Zone, with its temporary bulge in population during canal construction and World War II; and Hawai'i, with its huge influx of military personnel during World War II and their ensuing exodus.

Infant mortality rates were at high levels in each outlying area when it was acquired by the United States (Table Ef36–45). In all outlying areas, infant mortality rates decline rapidly after World War II. The rate of decline has been sufficiently large to ensure that all outlying areas have been converging to, albeit not yet reaching, the moving target set by the slowly declining infant mortality rates in the U.S. states.

Enrollment in public schools displayed impressive increases throughout the twentieth century, with the proportion of the population attending primary school increasing substantially and the proportion attending secondary school also increasing but with significant delays (Tables Ef46–66). The raw enrollment numbers are nonetheless difficult to interpret, as the percentage of young people in most outlying areas has also been increasing due to high population growth rates. Yet in most outlying areas, the increase in enrollment has so outstripped population growth that it is obvious that both public primary and secondary enrollment rates among school-age children have increased dramatically.

Nominal merchandise imports have increased rapidly over long time periods in all outlying areas, but the trends with respect to nominal merchandise exports have varied more substantially across areas (Tables Ef100–121).[6] Alaska, Puerto Rico, American Samoa, and Hawai'i saw steady in increases in both imports and exports, and had overall merchandise trade surpluses for long periods. The Northern Mariana Islands, the Federated States of Micronesia, the Marshall Islands, Palau, and Guam all experienced large increases in imports after 1950 that were not matched by similar increases in exports. The ensuing large trade deficits were indirectly financed in the 1970s and 1980s by grants from the U.S. government and in the 1990s in the Marshall Islands, Palau, and the Federated States of Micronesia by revenues from the compacts of free association with the United States.[7]

Since 1960 many outlying areas have made a rapid transition from an agriculture-based economy to a service-based economy, in which tourism services have become the main output.[8] The steep decline in the Puerto Rican sugar crop since the 1960s, the end of sugar cultivation in the U.S. Virgin Islands in 1967, and the general decline of agriculture in the territories of the Northwest Pacific Ocean have been offset by even more rapid growth in these areas' tourism industries (Tables Ef93–99 and Ef122–130). Hawai'i, Puerto Rico, the U.S. Virgin Islands, the Northern Mariana Islands, Guam, and Palau all experienced sustained growth in visitor arrivals after World War II, with the beginning of sustained growth varying within the group. American Samoa, however, has not shared in the tourism boom, and the 1970s booms in visitor arrivals to the Federated States of Micronesia and the Marshall Islands turned out to be short-lived.

The historical series on telephone lines provides a more tangible indicator of delayed development for some outlying areas (Table Ef131–140). A few areas, in particular Puerto Rico and Hawai'i, had relatively large numbers of telephones in use prior to World War II. Other areas, in particular the U.S. Virgin Islands and Guam, experienced rapid advances only after World War II. By contrast, some trust territories had no nonmilitary phone lines in place as late as 1960. However, during the 1970s and 1980s, Palau, the Federated States of Micronesia, the Northern Mariana Islands, and American Samoa all experienced dramatic increases in telephone lines and service availability.

The historical series on gross territorial product (GTP) show rapid increases in the national output of many outlying areas (Table Ef67–74). An immediate warning should be noted, as the figures are not deflated and are not expressed in per capita terms. Thus, growth in nominal GTP could be due to inflation and population growth and may not indicate increases in the real output available to each resident. Rapid increases in GTP have been observed in several outlying areas. Guam saw a doubling of its nominal GTP within a span of three years, from 1985 to 1988. Puerto Rico and the U.S. Virgin Islands have seen steady increases in their nominal GDP since the early 1960s. Nominal GTP doubled in Hawai'i between 1940 and 1950. In the Northern Mariana Islands, nominal GDP increased from $50 million to over $250 million in just ten

years. These rapid growth rates have typically meant that nominal per capita GDP has been converging, in fits and starts, with the level observed in the U.S. states. Nominal GDP series from the former trust territories are only available since the late 1970s and early 1980s. Per capita nominal GDP levels remain relatively low in the three independent countries carved from the Trust Territory, and there is little if any indication of a trend in these three areas of convergence with nominal per capita GDP levels in the U.S. states.

Constructing real GTP series is problematic, as only a few outlying areas have maintained reliable GTP deflators. Most outlying areas have focused instead on constructing a consumer price index (CPI) using well-established methodologies of data collection and index construction (Table Ef141–148). Many of these CPI series, however, are relatively short, as efforts to construct and maintain such complex series as consumer price indexes, gross territorial product, and personal income only commenced in some outlying areas during the 1960s or 1970s. In addition, the base weights in most CPI series are derived from consumer expenditure surveys that have been undertaken only sporadically. This is particularly problematic for fast-growing economies with rapidly changing consumer expenditure patterns. In these economies, as the benchmark survey year recedes into the past, the more likely it becomes that the measured consumer price index contains more substantial errors.

Finally, nominal government expenditures and revenues have grown rapidly in most outlying areas since World War II (Tables Ef149–172). Revenue and expenditure series are, however, extremely difficult to compare across outlying areas due to substantial differences in revenue and expenditure definitions.

Conclusion

The historical statistics of outlying areas are clearly still a work in progress. Many series contain rounded data due to government reporting of series in this form. Other series have missing data points, even for relatively recent years. Some series are somewhat vague as to their exact coverage or the methodology by which they were collected. And government bureaucrats maintaining some series have declined to release them even after numerous inquiries.

There is, however, reason to expect that some of these deficiencies can be remedied in the future. Many government agencies maintain records with unrounded data but have been unwilling to make them available. Some "missing" data may be contained in records maintained at government agencies that have not yet been published. Archives in outlying areas are also likely to contain data that could be used to construct relevant series. These sources are more likely to be exploited as the outlying areas become more affluent and interest in their history increases concomitantly. It would not be surprising, following the precedent of Hawai'i, to see historical statistics assembled and published in specialized volumes for the larger outlying areas (Alaska, Guam, and Puerto Rico) or for outlying areas with relatively abundant unorganized data (the Canal Zone, the Marshall Islands, Palau, the Federated States of Micronesia, and the Northern Mariana Islands). Researchers in the Philippines may decide to undertake a similar project as interest in the U.S. colonial era revives.[9] I hope that the few tables assembled here will provide a solid foundation for those future endeavors.

---

[6] Merchandise exports are a poor measure of overall export earnings in economies specializing in selling domestic tourism services to visitors.

[7] Under the compacts of free association, the Republic of Palau, the Republic of the Marshall Islands, and the Federated States of Micronesia granted exclusive military access to the United States for fifteen years in exchange for monetary assistance with economic and social development.

[8] Beginning in the 1940s, Puerto Rico accumulated a substantial manufacturing base, and several major oil refineries and alumina processing plants located in the Virgin Islands.

---

[9] See the Internet site of the Asian Historical Statistics Project at Hitotsubashi University in Tokyo, Japan.

References

American Samoa Office of Development and Planning. Various years. *American Samoa Statistical Digest*. Pago Pago, American Samoa.

Federated States of Micronesia Office of Planning and Statistics. Various years. *FSM Statistical Yearbook*. Department of Economic Affairs, Federated States of Micronesia.

Governor of Alaska. Various years. *Annual Report to the Secretary of the Interior*. U.S. Government Printing Office.

Governor of American Samoa. Various years. *Annual Report to the Secretary of the Interior*. U.S. Government Printing Office.

Governor of Guam. Various years. *Annual Report to the Secretary of the Interior*. U.S. Government Printing Office.

Governor of the Panama Canal. Various years. *Annual Report*. U.S. Government Printing Office.

Governor of Puerto Rico. Various years. *Annual Report to the Secretary of the Interior*. U.S. Government Printing Office.

Governor of the Virgin Islands. Various years. *Annual Report to the Secretary of the Interior*. U.S. Government Printing Office.

Guam Department of Commerce. Various years. *Guam Annual Economic Review*. Department of Commerce, Government of Guam. Agana.

Marshall Islands Office of Planning and Development. Various years. *Statistical Abstract*. Economic Policy, Planning and Statistics Office, Marshall Islands.

N. Mariana Islands Department of Commerce. *Commonwealth of the Northern Mariana Islands Statistical Yearbook*. Various years. Department of Commerce, Mariana Islands.

Palau Office of Planning and Statistics. Various years. *Statistical Yearbook*. Office of Planning and Statistics, Republic of Palau.

Republic of Philippines, Bureau of the Census and Statistics. 1947. *Yearbook of Philippine Statistics 1946*. Bureau of Printing.

Schmitt, Robert C. 1977. *Historical Statistics of Hawaii*. University Press of Hawai'i.

U.S. Secretary of State. Various years. *Trust Territory of the Pacific, Annual Report*. U.S. Government Printing Office.

POPULATION AND SOCIAL STATISTICS

Sumner J. La Croix

TABLE Ef1-12   Population of outlying areas: 1898-1999   [Annual estimates]

Contributed by Sumner J. La Croix

Year	Alaska	Hawai'i	American Samoa	Guam	Northern Mariana Islands	Puerto Rico	Virgin Islands	Canal Zone	Federated States of Micronesia	Marshall Islands	Palau	Philippines
	Ef1	Ef2	Ef3	Ef4 [1]	Ef5	Ef6	Ef7	Ef8	Ef9	Ef10	Ef11	Ef12
	Number	Number	Number	Number	Number	Number	Number	Number	Number	Number	Number	Number
1898	—	120,600	—	—	—	—	—	—	—	—	—	—
1899	—	137,300	—	—	—	—	—	—	—	—	—	—
1900	—	154,193	—	—	—	963,335	—	—	—	—	—	—
1901	—	155,547	—	9,676	—	979,131	—	—	—	—	—	—
1902	—	157,436	—	—	—	994,927	—	—	—	—	—	—
1903	—	162,634	—	—	—	1,010,724	—	—	—	—	—	7,691,824
1904	—	167,976	—	—	—	1,026,521	—	—	—	—	—	7,861,016
1905	—	166,728	—	—	—	1,042,318	—	—	—	—	—	8,030,208
1906	—	166,895	—	—	—	1,058,115	—	—	—	—	—	8,199,400
1907	—	174,740	—	11,227	—	1,073,912	—	—	—	—	—	8,368,592
1908	—	182,662	—	11,490	—	1,089,709	—	—	—	—	—	8,537,784
1909	64,294	188,316	—	11,760	—	1,105,506	—	—	—	—	—	8,706,977
1910	64,156	193,225	—	11,973	—	1,121,913	—	—	—	—	—	8,876,170
1911	63,196	196,735	—	—	—	1,140,638	—	—	—	—	—	9,045,363
1912	62,236	207,276	—	12,517	—	1,159,364	—	61,279	—	—	—	9,214,556
1913	61,276	218,417	—	12,963	—	1,178,090	—	57,400	—	—	—	9,383,749
1914	60,316	226,868	—	13,380	—	1,196,816	—	37,706	—	—	—	9,552,942
1915	59,356	231,515	—	13,689	—	1,215,542	—	29,926	—	—	—	9,722,135
1916	58,396	237,538	—	14,142	—	1,234,268	—	31,048	—	—	—	9,891,328
1917	57,436	250,138	—	14,532	—	1,252,994	—	23,295	—	—	—	10,060,521
1918	56,476	254,465	—	14,969	—	1,271,720	—	21,707	—	—	—	10,229,714
1919	55,516	260,408	—	14,635	—	1,290,446	—	21,759	—	—	—	10,398,503
1920	55,243	260,726	—	14,824	—	1,311,717	—	21,650	—	—	—	10,566,889
1921	55,656	271,790	—	—	—	1,335,532	—	23,757	—	—	—	10,735,275
1922	56,070	284,290	—	—	—	1,359,347	—	23,671	—	—	—	10,903,661
1923	56,484	299,507	—	16,224	—	1,383,162	—	23,671	—	—	—	11,072,047
1924	56,898	308,912	—	16,524	—	1,406,977	—	27,143	—	—	—	11,240,433
1925	57,312	325,960	—	16,648	—	1,430,792	—	27,151	—	—	—	11,408,819
1926	57,726	331,126	—	16,938	—	1,454,607	—	27,692	—	—	—	11,577,205
1927	58,140	337,294	—	17,018	—	1,478,422	—	27,624	—	—	—	11,745,591
1928	58,554	351,382	—	17,654	—	1,502,237	—	28,002	—	—	—	11,913,978
1929	58,968	360,406	—	18,620	—	1,526,052	—	30,300	—	—	—	12,082,366
1930	60,271	367,880	—	19,139	—	1,549,868	—	39,467	—	—	—	13,583,756
1931	61,596	377,530	—	20,857	—	1,573,700	—	41,500	—	—	—	13,868,056
1932	62,921	385,013	—	19,673	—	1,597,500	—	43,100	—	—	—	14,152,355
1933	64,245	383,973	—	19,800	—	1,621,300	—	44,700	—	—	—	14,436,655
1934	65,570	384,331	—	20,391	—	1,645,100	—	46,400	—	—	—	14,720,955
1935	66,894	389,562	—	20,899	—	1,710,000	—	—	—	—	—	15,005,255
1936	68,219	396,072	—	21,496	—	1,743,000	—	—	—	—	—	15,289,554
1937	69,544	400,816	—	22,132	—	1,777,000	—	—	—	—	—	15,573,854
1938	70,868	409,960	—	23,314	—	1,810,000	—	—	—	—	—	15,858,154
1939	72,193	415,705	—	22,843	—	1,844,000	—	—	—	—	—	16,142,453
1940	75,000	427,884	—	23,067 [1]	—	1,880,000	25,000	57,000	—	—	—	16,426,752
1941	88,000	459,335	—	23,394	—	1,935,000	25,800	83,800	—	—	—	16,711,052
1942	141,000	582,026	—	—	—	1,987,000	26,100	121,500	—	—	—	—
1943	233,000	649,650	—	—	—	2,033,000	27,400	126,200	—	—	—	—
1944	185,000	858,945	—	—	—	2,062,000	27,100	98,900	—	—	—	—
1945	139,000	814,601	—	—	—	2,099,000	26,700	87,800	—	—	—	—
1946	99,000	545,439	—	—	—	2,141,000	27,100	66,800	—	—	—	—
1947	108,000	526,238	—	—	4,827	2,162,000	27,200	64,600	28,746	7,838	6,023	—
1948	120,000	517,013	—	—	5,991	2,187,000	26,900	63,800	28,632	10,495	6,357	—
1949	130,000	511,039	—	—	6,071	2,197,000	26,700	61,100	—	10,802	—	—
1950	135,000	497,980	19,100	59,900	6,286	2,218,000	26,900	53,200	30,715	10,904	7,251	—
1951	158,000	514,256	19,500	63,400	6,507	2,235,000	27,700	55,500	31,674	11,266	7,448	—
1952	189,000	517,378	19,300	63,600	6,736	2,227,000	27,900	58,100	32,664	11,640	7,651	—
1953	205,000	509,947	19,200	68,700	6,973	2,204,000	26,900	57,000	33,684	12,027	7,859	—
1954	215,000	505,461	19,500	67,100	7,219	2,214,000	27,200	55,300	34,736	12,427	8,073	—

Note appears at end of table

TABLE Ef1–12   Population of outlying areas: 1898–1999   [Annual estimates]   *Continued*

Year	Alaska	Hawai'i	American Samoa	Guam	Northern Mariana Islands	Puerto Rico	Virgin Islands	Canal Zone	Federated States of Micronesia	Marshall Islands	Palau	Philippines
	Ef1	Ef2	Ef3	Ef4 [1]	Ef5	Ef6	Ef7	Ef8	Ef9	Ef10	Ef11	Ef12
	Number	Number	Number	Number	Number	Number	Number	Number	Number	Number	Number	Number
1955	222,000	539,292	19,800	68,700	7,473	2,250,000	27,600	54,900	35,821	12,840	8,292	—
1956	224,000	558,575	20,100	69,200	7,736	2,249,000	28,400	53,400	36,940	13,267	8,518	—
1957	231,000	584,466	20,300	66,500	8,008	2,260,000	29,400	51,600	38,094	13,707	8,749	—
1958	224,000	605,356	20,500	66,700	8,290	2,299,000	30,000	43,300	39,284	14,163	8,987	—
1959	—	—	20,400	67,800	8,571	2,322,000	31,000	42,000	40,511	14,634	9,231	—
1960	—	—	20,000	66,900	8,861	2,358,000	32,500	42,300	41,777	15,120	9,482	—
1961	—	—	19,900	66,400	9,160	2,402,514	34,300	43,200	43,081	15,622	9,740	—
1962	—	—	21,000	69,100	9,470	2,448,046	35,000	44,800	44,427	16,142	10,005	—
1963	—	—	23,100	72,000	9,791	2,496,601	39,800	50,000	45,815	16,678	10,277	—
1964	—	—	23,200	72,500	10,122	2,552,181	40,800	53,900	47,246	17,232	10,557	—
1965	—	—	24,600	74,100	10,465	2,596,774	43,500	54,100	48,722	17,805	10,844	—
1966	—	—	26,700	79,200	10,819	2,627,368	46,200	56,800	50,244	18,397	11,138	—
1967	—	—	25,100	81,400	11,185	2,648,961	49,100	55,600	51,813	19,008	11,413	—
1968	—	—	28,100	83,800	11,563	2,673,568	55,700	—	53,432	19,870	11,607	—
1969	—	—	30,400	83,700	11,954	2,722,232	60,300	—	55,101	20,772	11,804	—
1970	—	—	27,267	86,470	12,359	2,721,754	63,476	43,800	56,822	21,714	12,005	—
1971	—	—	27,731	92,287	12,972	2,766,299	70,937	42,300	58,597	22,699	12,208	—
1972	—	—	28,202	96,755	13,572	2,847,132	76,319	41,600	60,427	23,729	12,416	—
1973	—	—	28,612	105,550	14,200	2,863,420	84,121	41,000	62,731	24,806	12,627	—
1974	—	—	29,057	101,302	14,596	2,886,600	89,941	40,800	64,241	25,645	12,745	—
1975	—	—	29,640	102,110	14,938	2,935,124	94,484	40,500	66,222	26,423	12,838	—
1976	—	—	30,272	102,478	15,316	3,026,125	96,166	40,000	68,263	27,224	12,931	—
1977	—	—	30,839	101,167	15,710	3,080,828	93,203	—	70,368	28,050	13,025	—
1978	—	—	31,411	101,960	16,118	3,117,884	95,929	—	72,538	28,901	13,120	—
1979	—	—	31,964	103,941	16,497	3,168,446	96,183	—	74,774	29,778	13,215	—
1980	—	—	32,418	106,869	16,890	3,209,648	99,636		77,080	30,681	13,311	—
1981	—	—	33,595	109,166	17,576	3,238,968	99,853	—	79,581	31,996	13,408	—
1982	—	—	34,706	109,275	18,301	3,279,001	100,068	—	82,188	33,058	13,507	—
1983	—	—	35,838	114,080	19,139	3,316,031	100,348	—	84,942	34,243	13,605	—
1984	—	—	37,092	117,296	20,109	3,350,037	100,600	—	87,784	35,431	13,705	—
1985	—	—	38,633	120,615	21,386	3,382,106	100,760	—	90,631	36,660	13,804	—
1986	—	—	40,164	122,880	23,026	3,413,303	100,842	—	—	—	13,963	—
1987	—	—	41,876	125,724	25,400	3,444,468	100,901	—	—	—	14,264	—
1988	—	—	43,623	127,545	29,053	3,474,992	100,952	—	—	—	14,572	—
1989	—	—	45,384	130,947	35,294	3,505,600	101,041	—	—	—	14,886	—
1990	—	—	47,199	134,110	44,037	3,536,910	104,235	—	—	—	15,207	—
1991	—	—	49,099	138,083	46,700	3,571,328	106,185	—	—	—	15,549	—
1992	—	—	51,049	142,185	49,519	3,603,755	108,226	—	—	—	15,916	—
1993	—	—	53,082	143,619	52,425	3,643,638	110,258	—	—	—	16,285	—
1994	—	—	55,072	142,889	55,298	3,687,158	112,190	—	—	—	—	—
1995	—	—	56,911	143,856	58,128	3,731,006	113,896	—	—	—	—	—
1996	—	—	58,656	144,924	60,951	3,782,862	115,387	—	—	—	—	—
1997	—	—	60,383	146,330	63,764	3,828,061	116,882	—	—	—	—	—
1998	—	—	62,092	149,180	66,527	3,860,091	118,305	—	—	—	—	—
1999	—	—	63,781	151,968	69,216	3,889,507	119,615	—	—	—	—	—

[1] Through 1941, based on fiscal year from July 1 to June 30.

Sources

Alaska. 1909–1949: U.S. Bureau of the Census, *Statistical Abstract of the United States*: 1936, p. 10; 1948, p. 9; and 1957, p. 920. 1950–1958: U.S. Bureau of the Census, *Current Population Survey*, Series P-25, number 304, p. 10.

Hawai'i. Robert C. Schmitt, *Historical Statistics of Hawaii* (University Press of Hawai'i, 1977). The underlying source is Hawai'i State Department of Health, "Vital Statistics and Population of Hawaii, 1900–1973," R&S Report number 5 (June 1974), Tables 1 and 2.

American Samoa. U.S. Bureau of the Census, International Data Base, available at the Census Bureau's Internet site.

Canal Zone. 1912–1967: U.S. Bureau of the Census, *Statistical Abstract of the United States*, 1934, p. 10; 1954, p. 940; 1958, p. 908; 1962, p. 898; 1967, p. 846. 1970–1976: U.S. Bureau of the Census, *Population Estimates and Projections: Estimates of the Population of Puerto Rico and the Outlying Areas: 1970–1976*, Series P-25, number 731 (September 1978).

Guam. 1901–1941: U.S. Navy, *Annual Reports of the Governor of Guam*. 1950–1999: U.S. Bureau of the Census, International Data Base, available at the Census Bureau's Internet site.

Northern Mariana Islands, Federated States of Micronesia, Marshall Islands, and Palau. 1947–1949: U.S. Department of State, *Trust Territory of the Pacific, Annual Report*. 1950–1999: U.S. Bureau of the Census, International Data Base, available at the Census Bureau's Internet site.

Puerto Rico, Virgin Islands, and Philippines. 1902–1949: U.S. Bureau of the Census, *Statistical Abstract of the United States*; the underlying data source is U.S. Bureau of the Census, *Current Population Reports*, Series P-25, Population Estimates, various years. 1950–1999: U.S. Bureau of the Census, International Data Base, available at the Census Bureau's Internet site.

Documentation

For decennial population data covering the United States and outlying areas, see Table Aa93–109.

TABLE Ef13–23   Population of Alaska, by sex and ethnic group: 1880–1950

Contributed by Sumner J. La Croix

	Total	Sex		Ethnic group							
		Male	Female	Caucasian	Native	Western Eskimo	Aleut	Northern Athapascan Indian	Northwest Coast Indian	Unclassified native	Unclassified
	Ef13	Ef14	Ef15	Ef16	Ef17	Ef18	Ef19	Ef20	Ef21	Ef22	Ef23
Year	Number	Number	Number	Number	Number	Number	Number	Number	Number	Number	Number
1880	33,426	—	—	430	32,996	17,617	2,628	8,510	4,057	184	—
1890	32,052	19,248	12,804	4,298	25,354	13,871	1,679	5,463	3,520	821	2,400
1900	63,592	45,872	17,720	30,493	29,536	—	—	—	—	—	3,563
1910	64,356	45,857	18,499	36,400	25,331 [2]	15,279	1,451	5,685	3,916	0	2,625
1920	55,036	34,539	20,497	27,883	26,558	14,990	1,650	5,261	4,657	0	595
1929 [1]	59,278	35,764	23,514	28,640	29,983	17,171	1,857	5,895	4,935	125	655
1939 [1]	72,524	43,003	29,521	39,170	32,458	19,169	2,006	6,179	4,671	433	896
1950	128,643	79,472	49,171	92,808	33,863	19,320	2,180	7,300	5,100	0	1,972

[1] Census taken in the summer due to weather considerations.

[2] Includes 88 Native Alaskans enumerated in the continental United States.

Sources

1880: Ivan Petroff, "Alaska: Its Population, Industries, and Resources." (U.S. Government Printing Office, 1884).

1890: *Eleventh Census of the United States: 1890*, "Report on Population and Resources of Alaska," p. 3 and Tables 1–8.

1900 and 1910: *Thirteenth Census of the United States*, volume 3, Tables 9–10. *Twelfth Census of the United States, Population*, volume 2, pp. ccxv–ccxvi.

1920: *Fifteenth Census of the United States: 1930*, "Outlying Territories and Possessions," p. 15, Table 2.

1929: *Fifteenth Census of the United States: 1930*, "Outlying Territories and Possessions," Tables 2, 13.

1939–1950: *Census of Population: 1950*, volume 2, part 51, Table 6. *Census of Population: 1960*, volume 1, part 3, Table 15.

Classification of native populations: David T. Kresge, Thomas A. Morehouse, and George W. Rogers, *Issues in Alaska Development* (University of Washington Press, 1977), Table 2.1.

Documentation

Series Ef17. Native population includes people classified as "Creole" or "mixed" in census.

TABLE Ef24–35   Population of Hawai'i, by sex and ethnic group: 1900–1950

Contributed by Sumner J. La Croix

	Total	Sex		Ethnic group								
		Male	Female	Hawaiian	Part-Hawaiian	Caucasian	Puerto Rican	Portuguese	Chinese	Filipino	Japanese	Other groups
	Ef24 [1]	Ef25	Ef26	Ef27	Ef28	Ef29	Ef30	Ef31	Ef32	Ef33	Ef34	Ef35
Year	Number	Number	Number	Number	Number	Number	Number	Number	Number	Number	Number	Number
1900	154,001	106,369	47,632	29,799	9,857	8,547	0	18,272	25,767	0	61,111	648
1910	191,909	123,099	68,810	26,041	12,506	16,857	4,890	22,301	21,674	2,361	79,675	5,604
1920	255,912	151,146	104,766	23,723	18,027	22,138	5,602	27,002	23,507	21,031	109,274	5,608
1930	368,336	222,640	145,896	22,636	28,224	46,114	6,671	27,588	27,179	63,052	139,631	7,241
1940	423,330	245,135	178,195	14,375	49,935	103,791 [2]	8,296	—	28,774	52,569	157,905	7,685
1950	499,769	273,895	225,899	12,205	73,885	114,793 [2]	9,551	—	32,376	61,062	184,598	11,299

[1] Includes persons on Midway Island (1910–1940) and other small outlying islands, not legally part of the territory of Hawai'i (1940).

[2] Includes Portuguese.

Sources

Ethnic classification: Robert C. Schmitt, *Historical Statistics of Hawaii* (University Press of Hawai'i, 1977), Table 1.12, p. 25; Andrew Lind, *Hawaii's People*, 3rd edition (University of Hawai'i Press, 1967). 1900–1910: *Thirteenth Census of the United States: 1910*, volume 3, Table 8. 1920–1930: *Fifteenth Census of the United States: 1930*, Outlying Territories and Possessions, Table 4. 1940: *Sixteenth Census of the United States: 1940*, Population (second series), p. 1. 1950: U.S. Census of Population, Reports, P-C52, Table A; P-B52, Table 9.

Documentation

Persons with multiethnic backgrounds, other than part-Hawaiians, were classified by race of non-Caucasian parent if part-Caucasian, or by race of father if non-Caucasian. Ethnic classifications for 1900 are based on estimates by Romanzo Adams and Andrew W. Lind from census tabulations on country of birth.

TABLE Ef36–45   Infant mortality in outlying areas: 1902–1999

Contributed by Sumner J. La Croix

Year	Alaska	Hawai'i	American Samoa	Guam	Northern Mariana Islands	Puerto Rico	Virgin Islands	Federated States of Micronesia	Marshall Islands	Palau
	Ef36	Ef37	Ef38 [1]	Ef39	Ef40	Ef41	Ef42	Ef43	Ef44	Ef45
	Per 1,000	Per 1,000	Per 1,000	Per 1,000	Per 1,000	Per 1,000	Per 1,000	Per 1,000	Per 1,000	Per 1,000
1902	—	269.4	—	—	—	—	—	—	—	—
1903	—	174.2	—	—	—	—	—	—	—	—
1904	—	106.8	—	—	—	—	—	—	—	—
1905	—	198.5	—	—	—	—	—	—	—	—
1906	—	280.2	—	—	—	—	—	—	—	—
1907	—	234.8	—	—	—	—	—	—	—	—
1908	—	158.0 [3]	—	—	—	—	—	—	—	—
1909	—	174.2 [3]	—	—	—	—	—	—	—	—
1910	—	226.5	—	—	—	—	—	—	—	—
1911	—	205.8	—	—	—	—	—	—	—	—
1912	—	190.6	—	—	—	—	—	—	—	—
1913	—	181.3	—	—	—	—	—	—	—	—
1914	—	178.5	—	—	—	—	—	—	—	—
1915	—	156.8	—	—	—	—	—	—	—	—
1916	—	157.6	—	—	—	—	—	—	—	—
1917	—	137.4	—	—	—	—	328.9	—	—	—
1918	—	138.8	—	—	—	—	—	—	—	—
1919	—	105.8	—	—	—	—	—	—	—	—
1920	—	108.8	—	—	—	—	—	—	—	—
1921	—	119.7	—	—	—	—	—	—	—	—
1922	—	134.3	—	—	—	—	—	—	—	—
1923	—	135.4	—	—	—	—	193.2	—	—	—
1924	—	100.4	—	—	—	—	178.2	—	—	—
1925	—	112.2	—	—	—	—	140.4	—	—	—
1926	—	94.2	—	—	—	—	120.9	—	—	—
1927	—	97.3	—	—	—	—	208.0	—	—	—
1928	—	83.4	—	—	—	—	213.8	—	—	—
1929	—	101.0	—	—	—	—	145.5	—	—	—
1930	—	82.3	—	—	—	—	119.9	—	—	—
1931	—	76.3	—	—	—	—	119.2	—	—	—
1932	—	76.1	—	—	—	—	133.8	—	—	—
1933	—	72.1	—	—	—	—	157.2	—	—	—
1934	—	75.1	—	—	—	—	97.6	—	—	—
1935	—	67.4	—	—	—	—	170.5	—	—	—
1936	—	73.0	—	—	—	—	106.8	—	—	—
1937	—	68.7	—	—	—	—	124.3	—	—	—
1938	—	58.5	—	—	—	—	131.9	—	—	—
1939	—	52.7	—	—	—	—	101.7	—	—	—
1940	—	43.7	—	—	—	—	136.2	—	—	—
1941	—	40.3	—	—	—	—	112.2	—	—	—
1942	—	39.0	—	—	—	—	101.2	—	—	—
1943	—	38.2	—	—	—	—	83.8	—	—	—
1944	—	30.6	—	—	—	—	101.0	—	—	—
1945	75.5 [2]	27.6	—	—	—	—	124.0	—	—	—
1946	70.9	30.7	—	—	—	83.8	91.6	—	—	—
1947	63.7	30.8	—	—	—	71.5	89.0	—	—	—
1948	47.1	28.7	—	—	—	78.5	88.4	—	—	—
1949	47.6	25.1	—	—	—	67.6	90.3	—	—	—
1950	51.8	23.8	—	—	—	68.3	57.0	—	—	—
1951	52.9	23.7	—	—	—	67.1	57.7	—	—	—
1952	39.8	21.2	76.1	—	—	66.6	53.4	—	—	—
1953	41.2	21.0	87.8	—	—	63.3	41.3	—	—	—
1954	35.1	22.4	—	—	—	57.8	38.7	—	—	—
1955	37.4	20.6	—	—	—	55.1	44.9	—	—	—
1956	41.2	22.4	50.5	—	—	55.4	66.5	—	—	—
1957	38.0	23.9	69.3	—	—	50.6	50.1	—	—	—
1958	38.7	23.0	55.8	—	—	53.7	44.3	—	—	—
1959	—	—	33.6	—	—	48.1	43.3	—	—	—

Notes appear at end of table

(continued)

TABLE Ef36–45   Infant mortality in outlying areas: 1902–1999   *Continued*

Year	Alaska Ef36 Per 1,000	Hawai'i Ef37 Per 1,000	American Samoa Ef38 [1] Per 1,000	Guam Ef39 Per 1,000	Northern Mariana Islands Ef40 Per 1,000	Puerto Rico Ef41 Per 1,000	Virgin Islands Ef42 Per 1,000	Federated States of Micronesia Ef43 Per 1,000	Marshall Islands Ef44 Per 1,000	Palau Ef45 Per 1,000
1960	—	—	31.5	—	—	43.7	35.6	—	—	—
1961	—	—	23.7	—	—	41.3	41.9	—	—	—
1962	—	—	45.6	—	—	41.6	29.1	—	—	—
1963	—	—	35.9	—	52.1	44.8	31.7	27.6	—	—
1964	—	—	32.6	—	—	51.7	31.8	27.6	65.9	—
1965	—	—	33.6	32.5	65.7	43.0	30.0	32.4	34.7	80.5
1966	—	—	36.1	20.4	42.5	37.6	30.7	18.3	20.4	31.5
1967	—	—	28.6	22.7	37.7	32.8	30.8	31.5	27.1	52.5
1968	—	—	15.0	20.3	41.3	29.2	33.2	27.3	36.7	37.2
1969	—	—	23.5	27.7	52.7	29.7	27.7	32.5	22.0	50.1
1970	—	—	26.7	21.8	37.3	28.6	24.8	16.1	24.2	47.6
1971	—	—	24.8	20.0	53.9	27.5	26.8	34.9	34.4	30.7
1972	—	—	33.4	—	32.8	27.1	24.6	32.1	28.0	32.4
1973	—	—	29.0	22.7	27.0	24.2	29.9	24.3	48.6	42.8
1974	—	—	16.5	23.3	45.1	23.0	24.9	27.2	17.9	56.2
1975	—	—	23.1	20.2	25.8	20.9	26.1	23.4	33.4	53.4
1976	—	—	19.7	18.0	19.2	20.2	29.0	22.2	17.4	24.0
1977	—	—	16.5	15.3	34.8	20.1	21.9	34.4	44.6	26.2
1978	—	—	19.0	15.9	14.2	18.5	22.5	20.1	45.9	32.7
1979	—	—	15.8	11.2	39.5	19.9	21.8	26.3	24.7	46.4
1980	—	—	16.4	16.3	26.1	19.0	24.4	37.9	16.4	26.4
1981	—	—	14.7	11.0	12.9	18.6	22.5	—	29.1	11.5
1982	—	—	19.8	—	25.1	17.2	19.5	19.8	22.2	22.2
1983	—	—	6.8	7.5	15.6	17.3	20.9	13.0	25.6	23.0
1984	—	—	4.4	—	23.8	15.7	22.6	8.8	33.0	32.7
1985	—	—	11.1	12.2	20.1	14.9	17.7	—	43.0	27.0
1986	—	—	9.9	—	—	13.7	13.1	—	—	26.0
1987	—	—	10.4	11.9	—	14.2	—	—	—	19.0
1988	—	—	10.5	—	—	12.6	—	—	—	27.0
1989	—	—	8.1	15.2	—	14.3	12.5	—	—	16.0
1990	—	—	14.0	9.1	10.5	13.4	14.8	—	—	25.0
1991	—	—	10.9	9.2	8.4	13.0	21.1	—	—	19.8
1992	—	—	6.9	10.5	11.1	12.7	13.7	—	—	19.8
1993	—	—	11.6	8.7	11.1	13.4	12.1	—	—	19.8
1994	—	—	12.9	9.6	7.2	11.5	9.6	—	—	19.8
1995	—	—	11.3	8.9	8.1	12.7	12.5	—	—	—
1996	—	—	11.0	9.1	8.7	10.5	10.1	—	—	—
1997	—	—	10.8	8.4	5.8	11.5	10.7	—	—	—
1998	—	—	10.5	7.9	6.0	10.2	10.1	—	—	—
1999	—	—	10.6	7.0	5.9	10.0	9.9	—	—	—

[1] Through 1967, data for fiscal year ending June 30 of year shown.

[2] Civilian population only.

[3] Calendar year data interpolated from fiscal year data.

Sources

Alaska (1945–1958) and Virgin Islands (1943–1976). U.S. Bureau of the Census, *Statistical Abstract of the United States*, various issues.

Hawai'i. Robert C. Schmitt, *Historical Statistics of Hawaii* (University Press of Hawai'i, 1977), Table 2.5. Underlying data source is Hawai'i State Department of Health, "Vital Statistics and Population of Hawaii, 1900–1973," R&S Report number 5 (June 1974), Tables 1 and 2.

American Samoa. 1952–1967: Governor of American Samoa to the Secretary of the Interior, *Annual Report*, various years. 1968–1989: American Samoa Government (ASG) Development Planning Office, *American Samoa Statistical Digest*, various years. Underlying source is ASG Health Planning and Development Planning Agency Annual Reports (unpublished).

American Samoa (1990–1999), Guam (1974–1999), Northern Mariana Islands (1975–1999), Puerto Rico (1996–1999), Virgin Islands (1977–1999), and Palau (1991–1994). U.S. Bureau of the Census, International Data Base, available at the Census Bureau's Internet site.

Guam (1965–1973). Office of Vital Statistics, Department of Public Health and Social Services, Government of Guam.

Northern Mariana Islands (1963–1974), Federated States of Micronesia (1963–1984), Marshall Islands (1964–1975), and Palau (1964–1979). U.S. Department of State, Trust Territory of the Pacific, *Annual Report*, various years, in particular 1985.

Puerto Rico (1946–1995). Puerto Rico Departamento de Salud, *Informe Anual de Estadísticas Vitales*, various years.

Virgin Islands (1917–1942). Governor of the Virgin Islands, *Annual Report to the Secretary of the Interior*, various issues.

Marshall Islands (1976–1985). Office of Planning and Statistics, Republic of Marshall Islands, *Marshall Islands Statistical Abstract 1988*.

Palau (1980–1990). Office of Planning and Statistics, Republic of Palau, 1990 Census Monograph, Population and Housing Characteristics, February 1993.

Documentation

Data in this table are deaths of infants younger than 1 year of age per 1,000 births.

TABLE Ef46–57   Enrollment in primary schools in outlying areas: 1899–2000[1]

Contributed by Sumner J. La Croix

School year ending	Alaska	Hawai'i	American Samoa	Guam	Northern Mariana Islands	Puerto Rico	Virgin Islands	Canal Zone	Federated States of Micronesia	Marshall Islands	Palau	Philippines
	Ef46	Ef47	Ef48	Ef49	Ef50	Ef51	Ef52	Ef53	Ef54	Ef55	Ef56	Ef57
	Number	Number	Number	Number	Number	Number	Number	Number	Number	Number	Number	Number
1899	—	14,997	—	—	—	—	—	—	—	—	—	
1900	1,753	15,490	—	—	—	—	—	—	—	—	—	6,900
1901	—	15,537	—	—	—	—	—	—	—	—	—	150,000
1902	—	17,518	—	—	—	—	—	—	—	—	—	201,500
1903	—	18,415	—	—	—	—	—	—	—	—	—	227,600
1904	—	19,299	—	—	—	—	—	—	—	—	—	263,974
1905	—	20,406	—	—	—	—	—	—	—	—	—	311,439
1906	2,136	21,358	—	1,592	—	—	—	—	—	—	—	375,246
1907	2,639	22,458	—	1,417	—	—	—	—	—	—	—	479,454
1908	3,068	23,445	—	1,588	—	—	—	—	—	—	—	485,033
1909	3,809	24,889	—	1,605	—	—	—	—	—	—	—	568,109
1910	3,964	25,537	—	1,790	—	94,706	—	1,812	—	—	—	584,234
1911	3,841	26,122	—	1,637	—	113,125	—	1,837	—	—	—	607,089
1912	4,018	29,909	—	1,560	—	123,738	—	2,105	—	—	—	525,556
1913	3,563	32,938	—	—	—	130,637	—	2,199	—	—	—	434,824
1914	3,666	33,288	—	—	—	180,478	—	2,762	—	—	—	614,592
1915	3,436	36,529	—	—	—	157,394	—	2,576	—	—	—	602,943
1916	3,666	37,946	—	2,090	—	146,775	3,771	2,149	—	—	—	629,444
1917	—	39,028	—	1,863	—	142,892	—	2,373	—	—	—	666,540
1918	—	41,644	—	2,106	—	134,630	—	2,774	—	—	—	656,909
1919	—	43,271	—	1,735	—	153,068	—	3,006	—	—	—	665,160
1920	3,610	45,701	—	2,239	—	174,253	—	3,485	—	—	—	774,422
1921	—	48,724	—	1,964	—	182,041	3,987	3,536	—	—	—	924,410
1922	—	52,461	—	2,080	—	208,937	4,309	3,706	—	—	—	1,053,180
1923	4,000	57,200	—	2,507	—	206,181	4,396	3,776	—	—	—	1,069,148
1924	—	61,114	—	2,817	—	205,314	4,418	4,005	—	—	—	1,091,421
1925	—	64,916	—	—	—	207,526	4,410	4,588	—	—	—	1,080,619
1926	—	68,511	1,800	2,837	—	205,177	4,269	4,728	—	—	—	1,053,799
1927	3,616	72,524	—	—	—	204,753	4,247	4,909	—	—	—	1,013,033
1928	3,832	75,931	1,800	3,442	—	214,013	4,050	5,615	—	—	—	1,047,161
1929	—	81,307	—	3,647	—	213,096	4,040	5,865	—	—	—	1,050,072
1930	3,899	85,015	1,952	3,683	—	214,135	4,138	—	—	—	—	1,097,978
1931	4,206	88,708	—	3,491	—	219,235	4,238	6,838	—	—	—	1,143,708
1932	4,386	91,280	2,102	3,676	—	221,979	4,420	7,082	—	—	—	1,135,221
1933	4,229	92,750	—	3,817	—	226,162	4,649	7,110	—	—	—	1,135,658
1934	4,356	93,052	2,165	4,015	—	231,729	4,721	6,758	—	—	—	1,121,028
1935	4,299	96,449	—	—	—	237,827	4,692	6,661	—	—	—	1,150,199
1936	4,464	99,447	—	4,424	—	245,780	4,576	6,317	—	—	—	1,181,228
1937	5,477	101,332	—	4,528	—	235,550	4,642	6,252	—	—	—	1,208,788
1938	4,723	105,329	—	4,130	—	249,931	4,773	6,160	—	—	—	1,423,918
1939	4,996	109,422	—	4,271	—	265,525	4,819	6,128	—	—	—	1,666,012
1940	6,623	110,029	3,000	4,694	—	270,000	4,947	6,353	—	—	—	1,850,213
1941	6,900	112,260	—	5,084	—	—	—	7,213	—	—	—	—
1942	—	110,933	—	—	—	—	—	7,264	—	—	—	—
1943	6,497	99,773	—	—	—	—	—	5,937	—	—	—	—
1944	6,670	100,401	—	—	—	—	—	6,007	—	—	—	—
1945	5,839	—	—	—	—	330,870	—	—	—	—	—	2,182,209
1946	5,489	98,962	—	—	—	—	6,141	—	—	—	—	2,386,800
1947	—	104,764	—	—	—	—	6,111	6,793	—	—	—	—
1948	3,718	108,248	2,485	—	—	377,349	6,337	7,192	—	—	—	—
1949	4,082	111,595	—	—	1,077	386,229	6,667	7,786	4,537	1,461	—	—
1950	5,407	114,986	3,000	—	1,083	408,128	7,202	7,923	4,272	1,590	—	—
1951	—	118,099	—	8,583	—	—	7,687	7,960	—	—	—	—
1952	5,000	121,821	—	8,296	1,006	394,125	7,650	8,395	4,572	1,615	1,462	—
1953	5,000	127,241	—	8,886	979	—	—	8,920	4,744	1,731	1,286	—
1954	639	132,361	—	9,304	—	—	7,846	10,673	—	—	—	—
1955	—	139,162	—	9,389	—	—	—	10,797	—	—	—	—
1956	—	145,794	—	9,721	—	471,355	8,604	10,865	—	—	—	—
1957	—	152,444	—	10,136	1,273	474,358	8,756	11,207	6,197	2,482	1,697	—
1958	—	157,571	—	10,911	1,373	—	8,821	—	6,855	2,653	1,885	—
1959	—	163,787	—	11,555	1,472	—	9,565	11,230	7,615	3,057	2,038	—

Note appears at end of table

(continued)

TABLE Ef46–57 Enrollment in primary schools in outlying areas: 1899–2000 *Continued*

School year ending	Alaska	Hawai'i	American Samoa	Guam	Northern Mariana Islands	Puerto Rico	Virgin Islands	Canal Zone	Federated States of Micronesia	Marshall Islands	Palau	Philippines
	Ef46	Ef47	Ef48	Ef49	Ef50	Ef51	Ef52	Ef53	Ef54	Ef55	Ef56	Ef57
	Number	Number	Number	Number	Number	Number	Number	Number	Number	Number	Number	Number
1960	—	—	—	12,033	1,577	480,233	10,045	11,733	7,805	3,209	2,105	—
1961	—	—	—	12,054	1,605	478,470	10,764	12,343	8,266	3,572	2,262	—
1962	—	—	4,560	12,229	1,687	480,958	11,417	12,940	8,857	4,536	2,311	—
1963	—	—	—	12,554	1,733	483,431	12,141	13,964	10,364	4,985	2,598	—
1964	—	—	5,376	12,321	2,001	488,224	13,269	13,813	11,869	5,668	2,778	—
1965	—	—	5,690	13,030	1,749	498,141	14,247	14,791	11,747	5,301	2,661	—
1966	—	—	6,000	13,653	2,189	507,312	15,140	13,254	12,247	5,193	3,036	—
1967	—	—	—	14,618	2,315	526,086	16,562	13,646	14,038	5,930	3,082	—
1968	—	—	6,115	15,557	2,485	531,952	19,061	13,454	15,094	5,691	3,311	—
1969	—	—	—	16,551	2,535	539,304	21,037	13,813	15,685	5,817	3,376	—
1970	—	—	6,957	17,839	3,218	537,335	23,001	13,206	16,019	5,690	3,433	—
1971	—	—	6,000	20,674	3,235	543,313	24,568	12,875	16,134	6,186	3,493	—
1972	—	—	6,013	—	3,495	547,801	26,561	12,270	16,199	6,313	3,487	—
1973	—	—	—	22,504	3,085	556,207	28,066	11,644	17,120	6,724	3,515	—
1974	—	—	5,981	22,786	3,135	554,371	30,518	11,128	17,049	6,711	3,535	—
1975	—	—	—	23,303	3,221	542,410	30,876	10,785	17,351	6,657	3,409	—
1976	—	—	—	23,075	3,320	538,537	31,730	9,892	16,705	6,651	3,259	—
1977	—	—	—	22,030	3,322	543,096	32,240	9,104	16,786	7,122	3,177	—
1978	—	—	—	22,034	3,344	545,392	31,923	—	17,140	7,169	2,990	—
1979	—	—	—	21,784	—	539,796	32,721	—	—	7,246	3,037	—
1980	—	—	—	21,884	3,357	532,996	32,365	—	17,563	7,628	2,967	—
1981	—	—	5,467	21,733	—	529,381	32,475	—	17,221	7,717	2,945	—
1982	—	—	5,575	21,165	2,811	526,607	32,880	—	—	7,962	2,926	—
1983	—	—	5,586	20,949	2,935	524,930	33,092	—	—	8,110	3,011	—
1984	—	—	5,916	21,423	2,877	521,963	33,040	—	23,345	8,876	2,907	—
1985	—	—	6,101	21,359	2,895	515,502	31,943	—	23,636	9,379	2,893	—
1986	—	—	6,296	21,090	3,077	510,987	30,809	—	—	9,513	2,842	—
1987	—	—	6,882	21,030	3,207	506,287	30,460	—	—	—	2,784	—
1988	—	—	6,663	20,901	3,456	502,200	29,874	—	—	—	2,723	—
1989	—	—	7,163	—	3,662	495,082	27,296	—	—	—	2,627	—
1990	—	—	7,395	19,009	3,761	489,189	28,691	—	—	—	2,511	—
1991	—	—	8,233	21,408	3,779	483,047	29,336	—	—	—	2,468	—
1992	—	—	8,616	22,912	4,105	477,230	29,560	—	—	—	2,531	—
1993	—	—	10,143	21,769	4,411	472,107	29,880	—	—	—	2,498	—
1994	—	—	9,317	22,665	4,666	464,196	29,943	—	—	—	2,505	—
1995	—	—	9,485	23,722	4,915	455,231	28,749	—	—	—	—	—
1996	—	—	9,727	23,915	4,965	459,624	28,633	—	—	—	—	—
1997	—	—	9,852	24,756	5,263	455,862	28,303	—	—	—	—	—
1998	—	—	10,292	23,976	5,355	455,440	27,420	—	—	—	—	—
1999	—	—	10,405	23,307	5,591	450,171	—	—	—	—	—	—
2000	—	—	10,506	—	5,651	444,383	—	—	—	—	—	—

[1] Enrollment coverage and timing varies by series; see text.

Sources

Alaska. U.S. Bureau of the Census, *Statistical Abstract of the United States*, various issues. Governor of Alaska, *Annual Report to the Secretary of the Interior*, various issues.

Hawai'i. Robert C. Schmitt, *Historical Statistics of Hawaii* (University Press of Hawai'i, 1977), Tables 9.3 and 9.4.

American Samoa. U.S. Bureau of the Census, *Statistical Abstract of the United States*, various issues. Governor of American Samoa, *Annual Report,* various issues. Economic Development and Planning Office, *American Samoa Government, American Samoa Statistical Digest 1986*, Table 8. Data for 1987–2000 supplied by Department of Education, American Samoa Government.

Guam. Governor of Guam, *Annual Report to the Secretary of the Interior*, various issues. U.S. Bureau of the Census, *Statistical Abstract of the United States*, various issues. Department of Education, Government of Guam, *Statistical Tables: Department of Education, 1950–1971*, Table 3. Guam Department of Commerce, *1998–1999 Guam Annual Economic Review*, Table ED2; *Guam Annual Economic Review 1988*, Table 22; *Guam Annual Economic Review 1983*, Table 19.

Northern Mariana Islands. Data through 1980 from U.S. Department of State, *Trust Territory of the Pacific, Annual Report*, various years. 1981–2000

data supplied by the Office of the Governor of the Commonwealth of the Northern Mariana Islands.

Puerto Rico. 1910–1939: Blanton Winship, *Thirty-Ninth Annual Report of the Governor of Puerto Rico* (Bureau of Supplies, Printing and Transportation, 1939), Exhibit number 61. 1940–1950: *Statistical Abstract of the United States*, various issues. 1952–2000: Data supplied by Area for Planning and Educational Development, Department of Education, Puerto Rico.

Virgin Islands. Governor of the Virgin Islands, *Annual Report to the Secretary of the Interior*, various issues, in particular 1940, Appendix 7. Bureau of Economic Research, U.S. Virgin Islands Government Development Bank, *U.S. Virgin Islands Annual Economic Indicators*, various issues.

Canal Zone. Governor of the Panama Canal, *Annual Report*, various years. Panama Canal Company and Canal Zone Government, *Annual Report*, various years.

Federated States of Micronesia. U.S. Department of State, *Trust Territory of the Pacific, Annual Report*, various years. Office of Planning and Statistics, Federated States of Micronesia National Government, *National Yearbook of Statistics 1981*, Table 10.1.

Marshall Islands. U.S. Department of State, *Trust Territory of the Pacific, Annual Report*, various years. Office of Planning and Statistics, Republic of the

TABLE Ef46–57   Enrollment in primary schools in outlying areas: 1899–2000   *Continued*

Marshall Islands, *Marshall Islands Statistical Abstract 1985,* Table 9.3; *Marshall Islands Statistical Abstract 1990–1991*, Tables 4.8 and 4.10.

Palau. Palau Office of Planning and Statistics, *Statistical Yearbook 1998*, Table 11.1; *Statistical Yearbook 1992,* Table 9.1. U.S. Department of State, *Trust Territory of the Pacific, Annual Report,* various years.

Philippines. Republic of Philippines, Bureau of the Census and Statistics, *Yearbook of Philippine Statistics 1946* (Bureau of Printing, 1947), Table 16.

Documentation

Series Ef46. Public enrollment, primary and secondary, in native schools. Most native schools transferred to territorial system beginning 1954.

Series Ef47. Public enrollment, primary and secondary.

Series Ef48. Public enrollment, primary.

Series Ef49. Public enrollment; K–9 through 1988; K–8 thereafter.

Series Ef50. Public enrollment, primary; K–6 beginning 1982.

Series Ef51. Public day schools only, 1910–1939; thereafter, public enrollment, primary, K–8. Beginning 1952, enrollment is for first school month.

Series Ef52. Public and private enrollment, primary and secondary.

Series Ef53. Public enrollment, primary and secondary. October enrollment (1910 1912, 1931–1953); February enrollment (1954–1977).

Series Ef54–56. Public and private enrollment; K–9 through 1965; K–8 thereafter.

Series Ef57. Public primary enrollment. March enrollment, except for 1945 (September).

TABLE Ef58–66   Enrollment in secondary schools in outlying areas: 1905–2000[1]

Contributed by Sumner J. La Croix

School year ending	American Samoa	Guam	Northern Mariana Islands	Puerto Rico	Canal Zone	Federated States of Micronesia	Marshall Islands	Palau	Philippines
	Ef58	Ef59	Ef60	Ef61	Ef62	Ef63	Ef64	Ef65	Ef66
	Number	Number	Number	Number	Number	Number	Number	Number	Number
1905	—	—	—	—	—	—	—	—	404
1906	—	—	—	—	—	—	—	—	308
1907	—	—	—	—	—	—	—	—	924
1908	—	—	—	—	—	—	—	—	1,643
1909	—	—	—	—	—	—	—	—	2,393
1910	—	—	—	608	—	—	—	—	3,083
1911	—	—	—	793	—	—	—	—	3,404
1912	—	—	—	1,135	—	—	—	—	4,109
1913	—	—	—	1,436	—	—	—	—	5,226
1914	—	—	—	2,288	—	—	—	—	6,438
1915	—	—	—	2,960	—	—	—	—	7,576
1916	—	—	—	3,211	—	—	—	—	9,099
1917	—	—	—	3,294	—	—	—	—	11,432
1918	—	—	—	3,346	—	—	—	—	14,539
1919	—	—	—	3,467	—	—	—	—	16,899
1920	—	—	—	3,782	—	—	—	—	17,023
1921	—	—	—	4,364	—	—	—	—	18,813
1922	—	27	—	5,481	—	—	—	—	24,685
1923	—	—	—	6,850	—	—	—	—	32,999
1924	—	—	—	7,422	—	—	—	—	40,942
1925	—	—	—	7,686	—	—	—	—	49,145
1926	—	76	—	7,962	—	—	—	—	54,486
1927	—	—	—	7,055	—	—	—	—	58,411
1928	—	75	—	6,790	—	—	—	—	63,361
1929	—	—	—	6,878	—	—	—	—	69,990
1930	—	34	—	7,054	—	—	—	—	75,538
1931	—	—	—	6,980	—	—	—	—	79,054
1932	—	70	—	7,190	—	—	—	—	76,355
1933	—	—	—	7,295	—	—	—	—	66,860
1934	21	70	—	7,766	—	—	—	—	56,255
1935	—	—	—	8,587	—	—	—	—	52,689
1936	43	108	—	10,548	—	—	—	—	53,485
1937	—	—	—	11,318	—	—	—	—	58,830
1938	—	—	—	12,329	—	—	—	—	68,084
1939	—	—	—	15,834	—	—	—	—	76,758
1940	—	—	—	16,000	—	—	—	—	90,579
1945	—	—	—	—	—	—	—	—	98,286
1946	—	—	0	16,976	—	—	0	0	112,951
1947	—	—	0	27,463	—	—	0	0	—
1948	655	—	0	28,229	—	—	0	0	—
1949	—	—	0	29,115	—	—	0	0	—
1950	1,000	—	0	—	—	—	0	0	—
1951	—	642	0	—	—	—	0	0	—
1952	—	729	0	50,132	—	—	0	0	—
1953	—	875	0	—	—	—	0	0	—
1954	—	1,225	0	—	—	—	0	0	—
1955	—	1,499	0	—	—	—	0	0	—
1956	—	1,544	0	66,690	—	—	0	0	—
1957	—	1,437	0	70,535	—	218	0	0	—
1958	—	1,458	0	—	—	236	0	0	—
1959	—	1,432	0	—	—	187	0	0	—
1960	—	1,556	0	86,929	—	249	0	0	—
1961	—	1,592	0	92,017	—	258	0	42	—
1962	889	1,896	0	101,674	—	275	0	36	—
1963	—	2,344	29	108,578	—	310	23	67	—
1964	1,493	2,712	97	114,858	—	442	58	155	—
1965	1,609	3,110	—	119,780	—	1,806	—	301	—
1966	2,000	3,286	350	123,121	2,531	—	376	451	—
1967	—	3,407	485	124,772	2,567	1,522	299	718	—
1968	1,884	3,396	514	126,281	2,570	1,872	800	857	—
1969	—	3,721	552	129,641	2,623	2,011	879	982	—

Note appears at end of table

TABLE Ef58–66   Enrollment in secondary schools in outlying areas: 1905–2000   *Continued*

School year ending	American Samoa	Guam	Northern Mariana Islands	Puerto Rico	Canal Zone	Federated States of Micronesia	Marshall Islands	Palau	Philippines
	Ef58	Ef59	Ef60	Ef61	Ef62	Ef63	Ef64	Ef65	Ef66
	Number	Number	Number	Number	Number	Number	Number	Number	Number
1970	1,822	3,942	708	133,900	2,564	2,179	1,072	1,063	—
1971	2,000	4,083	816	142,746	2,493	2,453	1,215	1,039	—
1972	2,005	—	1,149	149,609	2,445	2,879	1,207	1,212	—
1973	—	4,418	1,120	155,031	2,373	2,303	1,380	1,280	—
1974	2,184	4,545	1,067	158,795	2,310	3,452	1,398	1,258	—
1975	—	4,881	1,169	161,696	2,199	4,080	1,234	1,295	—
1976	2,097	5,131	1,075	171,037	2,062	3,939	1,336	1,374	—
1977	2,204	5,242	893	178,747	1,911	3,935	1,443	1,354	—
1978	2,269	5,346	1,075	182,326	1,778	3,916	1,465	1,310	—
1979	—	4,277	—	181,623	—	—	1,388	1,296	—
1980	—	5,342	1,193	183,142	—	3,801	1,393	1,156	—
1981	2,476	4,323	—	183,499	—	3,832	1,371	1,169	—
1982	2,456	4,165	1,639	185,141	—	—	1,402	1,221	—
1983	2,526	4,406	1,596	183,743	—	—	1,483	1,177	—
1984	2,676	4,472	1,644	179,962	—	4,159	1,516	1,191	—
1985	2,715	4,304	1,637	177,421	—	4,780	1,603	1,062	—
1986	—	4,244	1,894	175,927	—	—	1,717	962	—
1987	2,875	4,111	1,752	173,202	—	—	—	1,009	—
1988	2,862	4,511	1,889	170,637	—	—	—	1,045	—
1989	2,791	—	1,801	166,494	—	—	—	1,035	—
1990	2,942	7,121	1,929	162,036	—	—	—	1,006	—
1991	3,038	4,534	2,373	161,687	—	—	—	983	—
1992	3,272	4,926	2,532	164,511	—	—	—	981	—
1993	3,380	7,631	2,897	163,972	—	—	—	965	—
1994	3,362	7,752	3,044	163,964	—	—	—	812	—
1995	3,317	7,989	3,140	161,801	—	—	—	—	—
1996	3,402	8,083	3,288	162,654	—	—	—	—	—
1997	3,417	8,176	3,201	162,048	—	—	—	—	—
1998	3,664	8,468	3,303	161,359	—	—	—	—	—
1999	2,991	8,364	3,381	158,347	—	—	—	—	—
2000	3,526	—	3,492	161,742	—	—	—	—	—

[1] Enrollment coverage and timing varies by series; see text.

Sources

American Samoa. U.S. Bureau of the Census, *Statistical Abstract of the United States*, various issues. Governor of American Samoa, *Annual Report to the Secretary of the Interior*, various issues. Economic Development and Planning Office, American Samoa Government, *American Samoa Statistical Digest 1986*, Table 8. Data for 1987–2000 school years supplied by Department of Education, American Samoa Government.

Guam. Governor of Guam, *Annual Report to the Secretary of the Interior*, various issues. U.S. Bureau of the Census, *Statistical Abstract of the United States*, various issues. Department of Education, Government of Guam, *Statistical Tables: Department of Education, 1950–1971*, Table 3. Guam Department of Commerce, *1998–1999 Guam Annual Economic Review*, Table ED2; *Guam Annual Economic Review 1988*, Table 22; *1983 Guam Annual Economic Review*, Table 19.

Northern Mariana Islands. 1981–2000 data supplied by the Office of the Governor of the Commonwealth of the Northern Mariana Islands. U.S. Department of State, *Trust Territory of the Pacific, Annual Report*, various years.

Puerto Rico. 1910–1939: Blanton Winship, *Thirty-Ninth Annual Report of the Governor of Puerto Rico* (Bureau of Supplies, Printing and Transportation, 1939), Exhibit number 61. 1940–1950: *Statistical Abstract of the United States*, various issues. 1952–2000: Data supplied by Area for Planning and Educational Development, Department of Education, Puerto Rico.

Canal Zone. Governor of the Panama Canal, *Annual Report*, various years. Panama Canal Company and Canal Zone Government, *Annual Report*, various years.

Federated States of Micronesia. U.S. Department of State, *Trust Territory of the Pacific, Annual Report*, various years. Office of Planning and Statistics,

Federated States of Micronesia National Government, *National Yearbook of Statistics 1981*, Table 10.1.

Marshall Islands. U.S. Department of State, *Trust Territory of the Pacific, Annual Report*, various years. Office of Planning and Statistics, Republic of the Marshall Islands, *Marshall Islands Statistical Abstract 1986*, Tables 9.1 and 9.2; *Marshall Islands Statistical Abstract 1990–1991*, Tables 4.8 and 4.10.

Palau. U.S. Department of State, *Trust Territory of the Pacific, Annual Report*, various years. Palau Office of Planning and Statistics, *Statistical Yearbook 1992*, Table 9.1; *Statistical Yearbook 1998*, Table 11.1.

Philippines. Republic of Philippines, Bureau of the Census and Statistics, *Yearbook of Philippine Statistics 1946* (Bureau of Printing, 1947), Table 16.

Documentation

Series Ef58. Grades 9–12. Beginning 1987, figures are for March enrollment.

Series Ef58–60. Enrollment in public schools.

Series Ef59. Grades 10–12 through 1988; grades 9–12 thereafter. Beginning 1990, June enrollment.

Series Ef60. Grades 10–12 through 1965; grades 9–12 after 1965. Beginning 1982, includes intermediate schools.

Series Ef61. Enrollment in public day schools only, grades 9–12 (1910–1939). Beginning 1952, first school month enrollment.

Series Ef62. Grades 10–12, October enrollment.

Series Ef63–65. Enrollment in public and private schools. Grades 10–12 through 1965; grades 9–12 thereafter.

Series Ef66. All enrollments are for March except for 1945 (September).

ECONOMIC STATISTICS

Sumner J. La Croix

TABLE Ef67–74   Gross domestic product of outlying areas: 1939–1999

Contributed by Sumner J. La Croix

Year	Hawai'i	Guam	Northern Mariana Islands	Puerto Rico	Virgin Islands	Federated States of Micronesia	Marshall Islands	Palau
	Ef67	Ef68	Ef69	Ef70	Ef71	Ef72	Ef73	Ef74
	Million dollars	Million dollars	Million dollars	Million dollars	Million dollars	Million dollars	Million dollars	Million dollars
1939	270.0	—	—	—	—	—	—	—
1940	309.0	—	—	—	—	—	—	—
1941	438.0	—	—	—	—	—	—	—
1942	742.9	—	—	—	—	—	—	—
1943	944.4	—	—	—	—	—	—	—
1944	1,247.9	—	—	—	—	—	—	—
1945	1,224.8	—	—	—	—	—	—	—
1946	872.8	—	—	—	—	—	—	—
1947	875.2	—	—	572.3	—	—	—	—
1948	880.0	—	—	614.2	—	—	—	—
1949	831.5	—	—	681.1	—	—	—	—
1950	839.9	—	—	723.9	—	—	—	—
1951	1,010.0	—	—	767.8	—	—	—	—
1952	1,050.0	—	—	877.5	—	—	—	—
1953	1,087.6	—	—	933.7	—	—	—	—
1954	1,102.1	—	—	1,006.4	—	—	—	—
1955	1,179.8	—	—	1,062.3	—	—	—	—
1956	1,263.5	—	—	1,147.8	—	—	—	—
1957	1,352.2	—	—	1,234.9	—	—	—	—
1958	1,424.8	—	—	1,337.2	—	—	—	—
1959	1,609.5	—	—	1,495.9	—	—	—	—
1960	—	—	—	1,691.9	21.8	—	—	—
1961	—	—	—	1,865.1	25.5	—	—	—
1962	—	—	—	2,094.4	33.5	—	—	—
1963	—	—	—	2,333.6	38.9	—	—	—
1964	—	—	—	2,570.5	53.8	—	—	—
1965	—	—	—	2,881.5	63.1	—	—	—
1966	—	—	—	3,170.5	89.8	—	—	—
1967	—	—	—	3,532.7	119.0	—	—	—
1968	—	—	—	3,941.7	193.1	—	—	—
1969	—	—	—	4,460.7	231.5	—	—	—
1970	—	—	—	5,034.7	252.9	—	—	—
1971	—	—	—	5,646.8	303.0	—	—	—
1972	—	358.3	—	6,328.9	376.5	—	—	—
1973	—	471.7	—	7,002.4	389.9	—	—	—
1974	—	452.9	—	7,684.8	438.6	—	—	—
1975	—	498.8	40.6	8,198.3	475.8	—	—	14.5
1976	—	455.4	—	8,968.6	488.0	—	23.5	—
1977	—	—	—	9,910.9	512.0	48.8	24.1	—
1978	—	—	—	11,165.0	542.7	—	—	—
1979	—	—	—	12,750.0	—	—	—	17.4
1980	—	—	137.0	14,436.1	727.8	—	—	—
1981	—	—	—	15,955.7	821.8	—	31.9	—
1982	—	—	165.0	16,764.2	832.6	—	36.1	—
1983	—	—	179.0	17,276.6	916.9	106.5	42.2	31.6
1984	—	—	195.1	19,162.6	985.4	—	45.3	34.0
1985	—	—	256.3	20,289.2	990.4	—	45.2	33.2
1986	—	1,301.5	—	21,969.4	1,035.6	—	—	—
1987	—	—	—	23,878.0	1,147.8	—	—	—
1988	—	1,729.4	—	26,178.4	1,204.6	—	—	—
1989	—	1,897.5	—	28,266.8	1,343.9	—	—	—

TABLE Ef67–74 Gross domestic product of outlying areas: 1939–1999 *Continued*

Year	Hawai'i Ef67 Million dollars	Guam Ef68 Million dollars	Northern Mariana Islands Ef69 Million dollars	Puerto Rico Ef70 Million dollars	Virgin Islands Ef71 Million dollars	Federated States of Micronesia Ef72 Million dollars	Marshall Islands Ef73 Million dollars	Palau Ef74 Million dollars
1990	—	2,312.5	—	30,603.9	1,564.7	—	—	76.9
1991	—	2,667.4	—	32,287.0	1,671.2	—	—	83.9
1992	—	2,902.1	—	34,630.4	1,770.9	—	—	82.5
1993	—	2,916.8	846.8	36,922.5	1,996.0	—	—	75.9
1994	—	3,013.7	962.3	39,690.6	—	—	—	88.9
1995	—	2,998.6	1,490.7	42,647.3	—	—	—	—
1996	—	2,992.5	1,761.1	45,340.8	—	—	—	—
1997	—	3,108.6	1,988.2	48,187.0	—	—	—	—
1998	—	3,302.7	1,912.5	53,875.4	—	—	—	—
1999	—	—	—	59,946.3	—	—	—	—

Sources

Hawai'i. Robert C. Schmitt, *Historical Statistics of Hawaii* (University Press of Hawai'i, 1977), Table 6.1.

Guam. Guam Department of Commerce, *Guam Annual Economic Review 1997–1998*, Table GI2. 1986-1998 data supplied by Guam Department of Commerce. Russell C. Krueger, *The Gross Island Product of Guam* (Department of Commerce, Government of Guam, 1978).

Northern Mariana Islands. Commonwealth of the Northern Mariana Islands, *Capital Improvement Strategy: Fiscal Years 1986–1992*, p. 5. 1993–1998 data supplied by Office of the Governor, Commonwealth of the Northern Mariana Islands.

Puerto Rico. Data supplied by Puerto Rico Planning Board.

Virgin Islands. U.S. Virgin Islands Bureau of Economic Research, Government Development Bank, *U.S. Virgin Islands Annual Economic Indicators*, various issues.

Federated States of Micronesia. U.S. State Department, *1983 Trust Territory of the Pacific Islands*, Table 94; *1979 Trust Territory of the Pacific Islands*, Table 35.a.

Marshall Islands. Republic of the Marshall Islands, Office of Planning and Statistics, *Statistical Abstract 1990–1991*, Table 11.1; *Marshall Islands Statistical Abstract 1986*, Table 4.1.

Palau. U.S. State Department, *1979 Trust Territory of the Pacific Islands*, Table 35.a; *1987 Trust Territory of the Pacific Islands*, Table 7. Republic of Palau, Office of Planning and Statistics, *First National Development Plan 1987–1991*, Table 3.4. 1990–1994 data supplied by Office of Planning and Statistics, Republic of Palau.

Documentation

"Gross territorial product" and "gross island product" are the names assigned by some governments of outlying areas to gross domestic product.

Series Ef70. Data are for fiscal year ending June 30.

Series Ef73. Data are for fiscal year ending September 30.

TABLE Ef75–84 Employment in outlying areas: 1900–1998

Contributed by Sumner J. La Croix

Year	Hawai'i Ef75 [1] Number	American Samoa Ef76 Number	Guam Ef77 [2] Number	Northern Mariana Islands Ef78 [3] Number	Puerto Rico Ef79 [4] Number	Virgin Islands Ef80 Number	Canal Zone Ef81 [5] Number	Federated States of Micronesia Ef82 Number	Marshall Islands Ef83 [6] Number	Palau Ef84 [7] Number
1900	90,172	—	—	—	314,695	—	—	—	—	—
1910	101,194	—	—	—	393,027	—	—	—	—	—
1917	—	—	—	—	—	14,590	24,146	—	—	—
1920	111,882	—	—	—	407,324	—	22,536	—	—	—
1930	154,262	—	—	—	502,759	9,920	15,124	—	—	—
1940	155,531	—	—	—	512,214 [8]	7,133 [9]	24,149	—	—	—
1941	173,068	—	—	—	—	—	33,254	—	—	—
1942	213,455	—	—	—	—	—	37,236	—	—	—
1943	216,615	—	—	—	—	—	34,650	—	—	—
1944	212,922	—	—	—	—	—	30,014	—	—	—
1945	208,868	—	—	—	—	—	31,032	—	—	—
1946	188,165	—	—	—	579,900 [8]	—	27,862	—	—	—
1947	188,742	—	—	—	—	—	24,694	—	—	—
1948	184,020	—	—	—	589,000	—	31,439	—	—	—
1949	173,340	—	—	—	585,000	—	29,662	—	—	—
1950	170,075	5,650	18,671	—	596,000	8,269	18,792	—	—	—
1951	183,129	—	—	—	604,000	—	18,735	—	—	—
1952	185,639	—	—	—	571,000	—	18,239	—	—	—
1953	186,437	—	—	—	550,000	—	16,828	—	—	—
1954	185,514	—	—	—	540,000	—	15,275	—	—	—

Notes appear at end of table   (continued)

TABLE Ef75–84   Employment in outlying areas: 1900–1998   *Continued*

Year	Hawai'i Ef75 [1] Number	American Samoa Ef76 Number	Guam Ef77 [2] Number	Northern Mariana Islands Ef78 [3] Number	Puerto Rico Ef79 [4] Number	Virgin Islands Ef80 Number	Canal Zone Ef81 [5] Number	Federated States of Micronesia Ef82 Number	Marshall Islands Ef83 [6] Number	Palau Ef84 [7] Number
1955	189,291	—	—	—	539,000	—	14,353	—	—	—
1956	195,075	—	—	—	558,000	—	13,781	—	—	—
1957	199,831	—	—	—	552,000	—	13,160	—	—	—
1958	199,793	—	—	—	555,000	—	14,032	—	—	—
1959	—	—	—	—	546,000	—	12,662	—	—	—
1960	—	5,833	17,208	—	542,000	11,639	13,048	—	—	—
1961	—	4,618	—	—	565,000	12,881	13,417	—	—	—
1962	—	4,762	—	—	568,000	14,289	13,717	—	—	—
1963	—	4,893	—	—	561,000	16,210	14,129	—	—	—
1964	—	6,126	—	—	586,000	19,585	13,941	—	—	—
1965	—	9,927	—	—	605,000	22,700	14,103	—	—	—
1966	—	—	—	—	634,000	26,220	14,194	—	—	—
1967	—	—	21,257	—	643,000	29,400	15,282	—	—	—
1968	—	—	23,000	—	654,000	30,940	15,893	—	—	—
1969	—	—	—	—	675,000	32,490	15,870	—	—	—
1970	—	7,000	25,340	2,180	681,000	35,118	15,734	4,641	4,858	1,875
1971	—	7,400	26,753	—	695,000	36,400	15,242	—	—	—
1972	—	7,800	30,365	—	733,000	36,683	15,035	—	—	—
1973	—	8,200	37,779	—	741,000	37,420	14,877	—	3,468	—
1974	—	7,994	38,500	—	741,000	38,910	14,991	—	—	—
1975	—	7,878	34,900	—	696,000	39,921	14,898	—	—	—
1976	—	7,297	31,000	—	675,000	38,330	13,721	—	3,809	—
1977	—	7,815	32,700	—	691,000	38,160	14,095	—	4,203	—
1978	—	9,302	32,800	—	732,000	36,980	14,295	—	—	—
1979	—	8,812	33,800	—	735,000	39,310	12,885	12,191	5,665	—
1980	—	8,106	32,700	5,941	753,000	40,503	—	—	3,560	2,745
1981	—	8,443	33,600	—	759,000	40,820	—	—	—	—
1982	—	8,780	30,610	—	721,000	40,320	—	—	4,980	—
1983	—	9,116	31,600	—	709,000	40,370	—	—	4,298	—
1984	—	9,453	34,480	—	754,000	40,380	—	—	—	—
1985	—	9,790	37,910	—	774,000	40,960	—	—	5,487	—
1986	—	10,127	41,140	—	798,000	41,910	—	—	6,971	—
1987	—	10,464	44,150	—	863,000	43,600	—	—	—	—
1988	—	11,582	48,323	—	909,000	45,000	—	—	—	—
1989	—	12,396	51,888	—	948,000	44,360	—	—	—	—
1990	—	12,593	56,080	25,965	963,000	46,930	—	—	—	5,599
1991	—	13,810	61,750	—	977,000	47,580	—	—	—	—
1992	—	13,627	69,569	—	978,000	48,210	—	—	—	—
1993	—	13,543	68,420	—	999,000	51,650	—	—	—	—
1994	—	12,971	66,570	—	1,011,000	47,550	—	—	—	—
1995	—	13,455	65,220	34,812	1,051,000	45,070	—	—	—	—
1996	—	13,949	68,440	—	1,092,000	43,230	—	—	—	—
1997	—	—	66,800	—	1,128,000	43,453	—	—	—	—
1998	—	—	64,230	48,142	—	43,507	—	—	—	—

[1] Annual averages from 1940. Gainful workers, through 1930. Figure for 1900 includes workers 10–13 years old. Beginning 1940, data measure jobs; persons holding more than one job are counted more than once.

[2] From 1974 to 1987, data are employed civilian labor force in March.

[3] Employment figures (with exception of 1998) are for census dates. Value for 1970 includes workers 14–15 years old; other values are for workers 16 years and older.

[4] First value is for the year 1899. For 1910–1946, the values are for the following dates: 1910, April 15; 1920, January 1; and 1930–1940, April 1. Beginning 1948, data are annual averages for the fiscal year ending June 30.

[5] Through 1975, employment at end of fiscal year ending June 30; thereafter, September 30.

[6] Employment figures are for particular census and survey dates.

[7] Employment figures are for census dates.

[8] Figures for 1940 and 1946 include an additional 24,100 and 12,648 "unemployed" workers, respectively, who were on emergency employment by the government.

[9] An additional 2,000 workers on emergency employment by the government are not included.

Sources

Hawai'i. Robert C. Schmitt, *Historical Statistics of Hawaii* (University Press of Hawai'i, 1977), Tables 4.1 and 4.3.

American Samoa. Economic Development and Planning Office, *Statistical Bulletin 1978*, labor force section; *Statistical Bulletin 1980*, Table 11; *American Samoa Statistical Digest 1986*, Table 37; *American Samoa Statistical Digest 1992*, Table 10.1; *Statistical Yearbook 1996*, Table 10.1; Governor of American Samoa, *1965 Annual Report to the Secretary of the Interior*, Appendix 3, Table 6 and Appendix 6, Table 4; and U.S. Bureau of the Census, *Statistical Abstract of the United States, 1953*.

Guam. Data from 1990–1998 supplied by Guam Department of Labor. Economic Research Center, Guam Department of Commerce, *Annual Economic Review and Statistical Abstract 1987*, Table 1; Department of Commerce, Government of Guam, *Guam 1970: An Economy in Transition* (February 1971), p. 6. U.S. Bureau of the Census, *Statistical Abstract of the United States, 1953*.

TABLE Ef75–84   Employment in outlying areas: 1900–1998   *Continued*

Northern Mariana Islands. Department of Commerce, Central Statistics Division, *1995 Commonwealth of the Northern Mariana Islands Statistical Yearbook*, Table 4.1. 1998 data supplied by Commonwealth of the Northern Mariana Islands Department of Commerce. U.S. Bureau of the Census, *Characteristics of the Population, 1970 Census of Population*, Table 12.

Puerto Rico. Data for fiscal years 1947–1997 supplied by Puerto Rican Department of Labor and Human Resources. Earlier data from Harvey S. Perloff, *Puerto Rico's Economic Future: A Study in Planned Development* (University of Chicago Press, 1950), Appendix B.

Virgin Islands. Governor of the Virgin Islands, *Annual Report to the Secretary of the Interior*, various issues; U.S. Virgin Islands Bureau of Economic Research, *U.S. Virgin Islands Economic Indicators*, various issues; Jannette Olivia Domingo, "The Role of Imported Labor in Virgin Islands Economic History" (Ph.D. dissertation, Columbia University, 1986), Table IV-7.

Canal Zone. Governor of the Panama Canal, *Annual Report*, various issues.

Federated States of Micronesia. Federated States of Micronesia National Government, Office of Planning and Statistics, *National Yearbook of Statistics 1981*, February 1982, Table 3.1; U.S. Bureau of the Census, *1970 Census of Population, Characteristics of the Population*, Outlying Areas, Table 12.

Marshall Islands. Republic of Marshall Islands, Office of Planning and Statistics, *Marshall Islands Statistical Abstract 1986*, Table 6.4; *Statistical Abstract 1993 and 1994*, Table 6.9; U.S. Bureau of the Census, *1970 Census of Population, Characteristics of the Population*, Outlying Areas, Table 12.

Palau. Republic of Palau, Office of Planning and Statistics, *Statistical Yearbook 1998*, Table 5.3. Bureau of the Census, *1970 Census of Population, Characteristics of the Population*, Outlying Areas, Table 12.

TABLE Ef85–92   Unemployment in outlying areas: 1930–1995

Contributed by Sumner J. La Croix

Year	Hawai'i	American Samoa	Guam	Northern Mariana Islands	Puerto Rico	Virgin Islands	Marshall Islands	Palau
	Ef85	Ef86	Ef87	Ef88	Ef89	Ef90	Ef91	Ef92
	Number	Number	Number	Number	Number	Number	Number	Number
1930	—	—	—	—	—	343		—
1940	7,232	—	—	—	89,776		—	—
1950	17,698	—	—	—	31,638	—	—	—
1960	—	51	391		33,968	383	—	—
1970	—	1,486	384	65	37,454	1,191	130	142
1980	—	1,149	3,505	148	131,797	2,346	711	143
1990	—	1,811	1,263	616	239,940	3,176	—	471
1995	—	837	3,855	2,728	—	—	—	—

Sources

Hawai'i. Robert C. Schmitt, *Historical Statistics of Hawaii* (University Press of Hawai'i, 1977), Table 4.3.

American Samoa. 1995 data supplied by Statistics Division, Department of Commerce, American Samoa Government. Economic Development and Planning Office, American Samoa Government, *American Samoa Statistical Digest 1987*, Table 10.8; *American Samoa Statistical Digest 1993*, Table 10.1; *Statistical Bulletin 1978*, labor force section. U.S. Bureau of the Census, *Statistical Abstract of the United States, 1965*.

Guam. Guam Department of Commerce, *Guam Annual Economic Review 1996/1997*, Table EM4; *Guam Annual Economic Review 1992*, Table 37; *Guam Annual Economic Review 1983*, Table 33. U.S. Bureau of the Census, *Statistical Abstract of the United States*, various years.

Northern Mariana Islands. General Statistics Division, Department of Commerce, *1995 Commonwealth of the Northern Mariana Islands Statistical Yearbook*, Table 4.1. *1997 Commonwealth of the Northern Mariana Islands Statistical Yearbook*, Table 4.1. U.S. Bureau of the Census, *Characteristics of the Population, 1970 Census of Population*, volume 1, part 58, Table 12.

Puerto Rico. U.S. Department of Commerce, Bureau of the Census, *Census of Population 1960*, volume 1, *Characteristics of the Population*, part 53, Puerto Rico,

Table 48; *Census of Population 1970*, volume 1, *Characteristics of the Population*, part 53, Puerto Rico, Table 48; *Census of Population 1980*, Detailed Population Characteristics, Puerto Rico, Table 95(a); *Census of Population 1990*, Social and Economic Characteristics, Puerto Rico, Table 11.

Virgin Islands. U.S. Bureau of the Census, *Fifteenth Census of the United States 1930*, Outlying Territories and Possessions, Table 22; *Census of Population 1960*, volume 1, *Characteristics of the Population*, parts 54–57, Outlying Areas, Table 383; *Census of Population 1970*, volume 1, *Characteristics of the Population*, parts 54–58, Outlying Areas, Table 12; *Census of Population* 1980, Detailed Population Characteristics, Virgin Islands, Table 71; *Census of Population 1990*, Social and Economic Characteristics, Virgin Islands of the United States, Table 18.

Marshall Islands. Republic of the Marshall Islands, *Census of Population and Housing 1988: Final Report*, Table 7.6. U.S. Bureau of the Census, *Census of Population 1970*, volume 1, *Characteristics of the Population*, part 58, Table 12.

Palau. 1970: U.S. Bureau of the Census, *Census of Population 1970*, volume 1, *Characteristics of the Population*, part 58, Table 12. 1980: Republic of Palau, *1980 Census of Population and Housing*, Table 37. 1990: Republic of Palau, *1990 Census Monograph: Population and Housing Characteristics*, Table 11.1.

TABLE Ef93–99   Major crop production of outlying areas: 1898–1999

Contributed by Sumner J. La Croix

	Hawai'i		Puerto Rico, sugar	Virgin Islands, sugar	Marshall Islands, copra	Philippines	
	Raw sugar	Canned pineapple				Copra	Sugar
	Ef93	Ef94 [1,2]	Ef95	Ef96	Ef97	Ef98	Ef99
Year	Tons	Thousand cases	Short tons	Short tons	Tons	Thousand metric tons	Thousand short tons
1898	229,414	—	60,285	—	—	—	—
1899	282,807	—	39,200	—	—	—	—
1900	289,544	—	81,526	—	—	—	—
1901	360,038	—	103,152	—	—	—	—
1902	355,611	—	100,576	—	—	43	—
1903	437,991	2	139,096	—	—	—	—
1904	367,475	10	151,088	—	—	—	—
1905	426,248	45	214,480	—	—	—	—
1906	429,213	74	206,864	—	—	—	—
1907	440,017	168	230,095	—	—	—	—
1908	521,123	344	277,093	—	—	—	—
1909	545,738	402	346,786	—	—	—	—
1910	529,940	465	349,840	—	—	125	168
1911	582,196	726	371,070	—	—	118	269
1912	607,863	1,313	398,004	—	—	174	281
1913	556,654	1,667	351,666	—	—	117	345
1914	624,165	2,269	346,490	—	—	107	408
1915	650,970	2,670	345,490	—	—	172	421
1916	596,703	2,609	483,589	—	—	142	412
1917	654,388	2,607	503,081	7,725	—	186	425
1918	582,192	3,847	453,793	5,841	—	365	474
1919	607,174	5,072	406,002	9,723	—	349	453
1920	560,379	5,987	485,077	13,329	—	362	466
1921	546,273	5,263	491,000	—	—	375	589
1922	618,457	4,770	405,000	6,345	—	367	533
1923	554,199	5,896	379,000	1,948	—	368	476
1924	715,918	6,826	447,000	2,385	—	387	529
1925	781,000	8,729	660,003	10,653	—	362	779
1926	804,644	8,940	603,187	6,343	—	366	608
1927	831,648	8,879	629,133	6,860	—	410	767
1928	920,887	8,663	748,677	11,275	—	433	808
1929	925,140	9,210	586,760	2,825	—	480	934
1930	939,287	12,672	866,109	—	—	460	984
1931	1,018,047	12,808	783,163	—	—	420	958
1932	1,057,303	407	922,335	4,288	—	406	1,175
1933	1,063,605	4,678	816,337	4,125	—	472	1,343
1934	959,337	8,733	1,103,822	4,088	—	475	1,652
1935	986,849	9,201	773,021	1,670	—	540	754
1936	1,042,316	11,428	926,344	3,730	—	651	1,043
1937	944,382	12,071	1,077,149	6,811	—	522	1,186
1938	941,293	12,599	851,969	4,062	—	698	1,116
1939	994,173	11,142	1,016,803	4,956	—	—	1,149
1940	976,677	12,924	932,000	2,672	—	—	1,142
1941	947,190	10,947	1,147,591	2,052	—	—	—
1942	870,099	12,086	1,039,239	1,441	—	—	617
1943	885,640	11,943	723,612	3,689	—	—	—
1944	874,947	11,127	963,775	2,644	—	—	—
1945	821,216	10,164	909,085	4,046	—	—	—
1946	680,073	9,051	1,088,000	4,968	—	—	115
1947	872,187	10,237	1,108,000	2,973	—	—	—
1948	835,107	11,400	1,277,000	4,531	—	—	—
1949	955,890	13,697	1,286,000	4,609	—	—	—
1950	960,961	14,073	1,228,000	10,853	—	—	—
1951	955,759	15,098	1,360,000	7,568	4,980	—	—
1952	1,020,450	14,690	1,170,000	11,714	4,565	—	—
1953	1,099,316	16,915	1,190,000	13,523	4,580	—	—
1954	1,077,347	16,581	1,204,000	9,845	3,896	—	—
1955	1,140,112	16,399	1,165,000	10,220	4,434	—	—
1956	1,099,543	18,613	1,152,000	12,885	5,480	—	—
1957	1,084,646	17,992	990,000	15,101	6,034	—	—
1958	764,953	16,798	934,000	5,984	5,701	—	—
1959	974,632	17,677	1,087,000	12,470	3,700	—	—

Notes appear at end of table

TABLE Ef93–99   Major crop production of outlying areas: 1898–1999   *Continued*

Year	Hawai'i Raw sugar Ef93 Tons	Hawai'i Canned pineapple Ef94 [1,2] Thousand cases	Puerto Rico, sugar Ef95 Short tons	Virgin Islands, sugar Ef96 Short tons	Marshall Islands, copra Ef97 Tons	Philippines Copra Ef98 Thousand metric tons	Philippines Sugar Ef99 Thousand short tons
1960	—	—	—	6,972	4,436	—	—
1961	—	—	1,096,850	16,643	6,060	—	—
1962	—	—	996,824	10,752	4,521	—	—
1963	—	—	978,501	15,527	4,975	—	—
1964	—	—	978,320	15,336	5,742	—	—
1965	—	—	886,851	4,283	5,807	—	—
1966	—	—	886,851	5,406	5,554	—	—
1967	—	—	808,279	0	6,272	—	—
1968	—	—	637,767	0	6,311	—	—
1969	—	—	478,395	0	6,401	—	—
1970	—	—	455,193	0	7,348	—	—
1971	—	—	320,648	0	5,344	—	—
1972	—	—	295,305	0	5,715	—	—
1973	—	—	252,272	0	4,574	—	—
1974	—	—	283,539	0	6,336	—	—
1975	—	—	299,095	0	6,482	—	—
1976	—	—	307,970	0	5,685	—	—
1977	—	—	263,764	0	6,075	—	—
1978	—	—	201,216	0	5,876	—	—
1979	—	—	191,507	0	6,488	—	—
1980	—	—	174,741	0	6,257	—	—
1981	—	—	150,895	0	6,288	—	—
1982	—	—	111,970	0	5,774	—	—
1983	—	—	99,206	0	6,490	—	—
1984	—	—	95,766	0	4,483	—	—
1985	—	—	107,630	0	4,301	—	—
1986	—	—	95,760	0	6,921	—	—
1987	—	—	96,438	0	—	—	—
1988	—	—	102,330	0	—	—	—
1989	—	—	91,290	0	—	—	—
1990	—	—	68,100	0	—	—	—
1991	—	—	73,951	0	—	—	—
1992	—	—	67,452	0	—	—	—
1993	—	—	64,228	0	—	—	—
1994	—	—	49,721	0	—	—	—
1995	—	—	45,397	0	—	—	—
1996	—	—	33,491	0	—	—	—
1997	—	—	27,105	0	—	—	—
1998	—	—	—	0	—	—	—
1999	—	—	—	0	—	—	—

[1] January through May only (1932); thereafter, June 1 to May 31 pack year.

[2] Cases are not standardized.

Sources

Hawai'i, sugar. U.S. Commissioner of Labor, *Report of the U.S. Commissioner of Labor on Hawai'i, 1905* (1906). U.S. Commissioner of Labor, *Report of the U.S. Commissioner of Labor on Hawaii 1910* (1911). Unpublished data from 1912 supplied by Hawai'i State Department of Business, Economic Development, and Tourism.

Hawai'i, pineapple. Robert C. Schmitt, *Historical Statistics of Hawaii* (University Press of Hawai'i, 1977), Table 16.4.

Puerto Rico. 1901–1935: Blanton Winship, *Thirty-Fifth Annual Report of the Governor of Puerto Rico, 1935,* Exhibit number 38. 1936–1959: 57th Congress, 1st Session, *Special Study on Sugar: A Report of the Special Study Group on Sugar of the U.S. Department of Agriculture* (February 14, 1961), Table 9. Data since 1960 from Internet site of the Food and Agriculture Organization of the United Nations.

Virgin Islands. U.S. Department of Interior, *General Information Regarding the Virgin Islands of the United States* (1932). U.S. Department of Agriculture,

Commodity Stabilization Service, Sugar Division, *Agricultural, Manufacturing and Income Statistics for the Domestic Sugar Area*, 1954, volume 2, Table 92. U.S. Department of Labor, *Wage and Hour and Public Contract Divisions, Economic Report on Industries in the Virgin Islands* (August 1963), Table 4. International Sugar Council/Organization (ISCO), *Sugar Yearbook* (ISCO, various years).

Marshall Islands. Office of Planning and Statistics, Republic of the Marshall Islands, *Statistical Abstract 1988/89,* Table 6.6.

Philippines, copra. Nyle Ray Spoelstra. "Export Growth and Change in the Philippine Sugar and Coconut Products Industries, 1900–1940" (Ph.D dissertation, University of Wisconsin, 1969), Table 12.

Philippines, sugar. U.S. House of Representatives Committee on Agriculture, *Special Study on Sugar: A Report of the Special Study Group on Sugar of the U.S. Department of Agriculture* (1961). United States Cuban Sugar Council, *Sugar: Facts and Figures . . . , 1948,* Table 6.

Documentation

Series Ef93, Ef95–96, and Ef99. Values given in terms of raw value.

Series Ef96. Fiscal year ending June 30.

TABLE Ef100-110   Merchandise exports of outlying areas: 1879-1998
Contributed by Sumner J. La Croix

Year	Alaska Ef100 [1] Dollars	Hawai'i Ef101 Dollars	American Samoa Ef102 [2] Dollars	Guam Ef103 Dollars	Northern Mariana Islands Ef104 Dollars	Puerto Rico Ef105 Dollars	Virgin Islands Ef106 Dollars	Federated States of Micronesia Ef107 Dollars	Marshall Islands Ef108 Dollars	Palau Ef109 Dollars	Philippines Ef110 [3] Thousand pesos
1879	50,378	—	—	—	—	—	—	—	—	—	—
1880	31,543	—	—	—	—	—	—	—	—	—	—
1881	69,183	—	—	—	—	—	—	—	—	—	—
1882	38,520	—	—	—	—	—	—	—	—	—	—
1883	28,393	—	—	—	—	—	—	—	—	—	—
1884	8,438	—	—	—	—	—	—	—	—	—	—
1885	24,468	—	—	—	—	—	—	—	—	—	—
1886	8,022	—	—	—	—	—	—	—	—	—	—
1887	7,336	—	—	—	—	—	—	—	—	—	—
1888	23,499	—	—	—	—	—	—	—	—	—	—
1889	200	—	—	—	—	—	—	—	—	—	—
1890	4,682	—	—	—	—	—	—	—	—	—	—
1891	39,073	—	—	—	—	—	—	—	—	—	—
1892	14,165	—	—	—	—	—	—	—	—	—	—
1893	10,211	—	—	—	—	—	—	—	—	—	—
1894	2,663	—	—	—	—	—	—	—	—	—	—
1895	11,520	—	—	—	—	—	—	—	—	—	—
1896	5,358	—	—	—	—	—	—	—	—	—	—
1897	27,206	—	—	—	—	—	—	—	—	—	—
1898	30,705	17,346,745	—	4,070 [5,6]	—	1,505,946 [5]	—	—	—	—	10,331
1899	45,729	22,628,742	—	6,883 [5]	—	2,685,848 [5]	—	—	—	—	29,693
1900	566,347	14,404,496 [4]	—	13,247 [5]	—	4,640,449 [5]	—	—	—	—	45,981
1901	2,534,318	28,023,269	—	34,691	—	8,583,967	—	—	—	—	49,007
1902	2,612,021	24,793,607	—	18,746	—	12,433,956	—	—	—	—	57,344
1903	11,840,697	26,275,438	43,143	2,794	—	15,089,079	—	—	—	—	64,793
1904	11,730,830	25,204,875	33,729	14,735	—	16,265,903	—	—	—	—	58,299
1905	11,889,611	36,171,596	47,453	16,711	—	18,709,565	—	—	—	—	66,910
1906	10,649,735	26,938,512	53,245	26,891	—	23,257,530	—	—	—	—	65,286
1907	13,644,884	29,301,727	42,935	19,237 [7]	—	26,996,300	—	—	—	—	66,196
1908	12,825,682	42,238,145	67,155	31,595 [7]	—	30,644,470	—	—	—	—	65,202
1909	14,072,011	40,517,097	—	43,442 [7]	—	30,391,225	—	—	—	—	69,849
1910	13,608,394	46,490,028	—	33,611 [7]	—	37,960,220	—	—	—	—	81,257
1911	15,192,074	41,938,293	99,040	51,049 [7]	—	39,918,377	—	—	—	—	89,674
1912	22,788,136	55,449,343	146,275	65,456 [7]	—	49,705,413	—	—	—	—	109,847
1913	26,112,978	43,471,830	132,645	37,373 [7]	—	49,103,565	—	—	—	—	95,546
1914	22,941,647	41,593,825	71,417	51,093 [7]	—	43,102,769	—	—	—	—	97,379
1915	28,443,724	62,464,759	121,125	22,458 [7]	—	49,356,907	—	—	—	—	107,626
1916	50,894,548	64,665,044	62,062	62,313	—	66,587,695	—	—	—	—	139,874
1917	63,248,753	74,098,090	198,496	80,435	—	80,970,904	1,259,607 [5]	—	—	—	191,209
1918	74,057,884	80,946,626	118,520	131,758	—	74,269,100	1,249,346	—	—	—	270,389
1919	62,021,797	102,613,918	90,421	64,552	—	89,395,805	1,919,525	—	—	—	226,236
1920	62,469,096	195,820,884	98,213	50,498	—	174,668,780	4,749,319	—	—	—	302,248
1921	38,361,966	73,019,598	117,446	40,342	—	78,741,706	883,735	—	—	—	176,231
1922	52,454,485	74,688,569	98,216	62,931	—	65,117,447	835,505	—	—	—	191,167
1923	55,087,267	102,666,806	95,164	94,086	—	86,071,995	514,042	—	—	—	241,506
1924	56,325,548	109,889,203	150,280	66,095	—	84,728,540	461,556	—	—	—	270,689
1925	57,820,289	104,625,291	150,333	99,954	—	99,733,049	1,020,748 [5]	—	—	—	297,754
1926	73,822,387	100,145,020	78,033	119,028	—	97,746,450	810,410 [5]	—	—	—	273,769
1927	51,832,367	111,504,035	40,852	154,271	—	104,459,765	968,463 [5]	—	—	—	311,148
1928	68,209,945	119,479,835	179,068	242,532	—	103,666,994	1,195,314 [5]	—	—	—	310,109
1929	64,174,694	108,439,103	166,756	348,369	—	83,244,375	603,323 [5]	—	—	—	328,894
1930	49,344,153	100,915,783	140,422	197,560	—	103,948,871	768,342 [5]	—	—	—	266,335
1931	43,591,272	102,737,835	60,287	81,910	—	91,084,185	408,932 [5]	—	—	—	207,944
1932	30,418,883	83,448,296	29,077	49,684	—	76,418,077	405,163 [5]	—	—	—	190,676
1933	33,297,742	92,952,801	20,966	62,449	—	78,661,083	516,846 [5]	—	—	—	211,542
1934	45,381,462	95,830,059	24,927	31,376	—	83,907,747	575,052 [5]	—	—	—	220,807
1935	37,130,832	100,033,996	83,254	124,188	—	89,641,421	553,842	—	—	—	188,492
1936	61,259,807	127,176,805	56,717	136,934	—	105,900,934	793,651	—	—	—	272,896
1937	62,763,444	132,239,814	115,075	228,229	—	105,505,241	1,319,895	—	—	—	302,533
1938	56,650,028	98,086,121	110,657	118,122	—	86,531,138	1,541,472	—	—	—	231,591
1939	42,765,802	115,095,809	84,852	112,104	—	90,527,565	1,664,933	—	—	—	136,030

Notes appear at end of table

TABLE Ef100–110   Merchandise exports of outlying areas: 1879–1998   *Continued*

Year	Alaska Ef100 [1] Dollars	Hawai'i Ef101 Dollars	American Samoa Ef102 [2] Dollars	Guam Ef103 Dollars	Northern Mariana Islands Ef104 Dollars	Puerto Rico Ef105 Dollars	Virgin Islands Ef106 Dollars	Federated States of Micronesia Ef107 Dollars	Marshall Islands Ef108 Dollars	Palau Ef109 Dollars	Philippines Ef110 [3] Thousand pesos
1940	40,585,267	103,067,965	72,396	103,094	—	85,041,449	1,527,709	—	—	—	226,824
1941	68,471,531	133,653,066	103,129	50,175	—	101,580,919	2,564,856	—	—	—	—
1942	59,018,262	96,903,545	5,664	—	—	105,477,270	1,846,267	—	—	—	—
1943	287,899,094	103,391,087	—	—	—	115,946,349	3,622,139	—	—	—	—
1944	343,470,611	85,140,644	—	—	—	125,604,083	6,839,921	—	—	—	—
1945	238,922,661	88,046,893	31,975	—	—	148,407,331	4,356,431	—	—	—	—
1946	69,892,767	140,042,662	190,925	3,433,354	—	168,190,917	4,138,205	—	—	—	—
1947	125,548,863	236,432,720	261,297	3,639,977	—	199,383,482	2,300,915	—	—	—	—
1948	—	—	259,648	5,980,079	—	194,533,110	1,796,308	—	—	—	—
1949	—	—	394,238	2,358,142	—	222,365,733	—	—	—	—	—
1950	—	—	306,758	771,098	—	246,946,731	3,857,168	—	—	—	—
1951	—	—	282,863	4,881,399	—	264,527,351	2,715,901	—	—	—	—
1952	—	—	315,865	4,095,564	—	292,331,241	3,385,419	—	—	—	—
1953	—	—	219,651	3,644,194	—	343,854,727	3,256,990	—	—	—	—
1954	—	—	788,977	4,466,447	74,717	347,214,000	4,261,158	668,445	459,672	2,139,956	—
1955	—	—	3,712,250	5,129,356	102,644	382,173,000	4,294,036	866,111	465,884	2,866,943	—
1956	—	—	4,448,579	6,545,636	197,587	433,281,000	5,804,703	793,559	578,713	162,735	—
1957	—	—	5,171,000	5,522,039	154,347	458,207,000	5,006,873	697,100	719,023	79,434	—
1958	—	—	7,824,000	3,927,211	153,542	473,417,000	3,534,805	712,559	633,640	153,234	—
1959	—	—	7,573,000	5,911,496	125,487	576,775,000	6,536,285	528,183	450,705	140,459	—
1960	—	—	7,571,000	2,733,359	216,124	604,279,000	8,355,000	901,637	624,944	148,595	—
1961	—	—	—	8,120,906	323,271	711,150,000	9,133,124	897,550	738,282	171,282	—
1962	—	—	—	6,352,606	421,779	809,805,000	20,064,920	831,031	702,028	170,426	—
1963	—	—	12,707,373	7,259,662	162,716	854,872,000	24,931,000	1,053,511	759,524	185,722	—
1964	—	—	10,429,649	9,106,011	274,577	935,573,000	27,168,000	1,213,048	974,914	201,566	—
1965	—	—	11,063,057	9,323,356	320,835	1,005,565,000	36,256,000	1,285,494	1,082,438	463,692	—
1966	—	—	20,866,677	6,741,683	346,388	1,135,462,000	—	1,349,527	1,032,407	280,840	—
1967	—	—	27,180,000	7,616,788	320,182	1,313,167,000	56,144,017	1,011,737	660,494	329,258	—
1968	—	—	28,015,859	8,589,287	128,899	1,465,615,000	153,892,000	1,222,369	1,251,907	422,396	—
1969	—	—	—	1,076,352 [7]	113,928	1,535,473,000	—	1,207,310	1,021,037	514,498	—
1970	—	—	36,735,384	5,832,316	254,635	1,680,000,000	261,981,506	1,442,406	1,321,253	1,157,709	—
1971	—	—	41,396,235	10,494,743	281,324	1,735,000,000	—	879,007	876,942	963,411	—
1972	—	—	53,738,997	16,403,416	263,468	2,241,000,000	325,838,320	683,634	753,843	935,790	—
1973	—	—	66,576,005	10,939,062	222,789	2,727,000,000	400,892,057	676,987	549,239	436,520	—
1974	—	—	82,988,726	19,992,624	389,611	3,275,000,000	1,658,922,610	2,175,837	2,278,867	3,193,380	—
1975	—	—	55,897,558	24,380,479	401,999	3,000,000,000	1,933,333,000	1,444,395	1,829,279	3,150,041	—
1976	—	—	64,892,749	21,531,042	—	3,735,000,000	2,010,165,000	683,331	995,229	3,130,329	—
1977	—	—	81,232,067	18,735,196 [8]	755,900	4,516,000,000	2,606,980,000	857,000	994,600	8,093,600	—
1978	—	—	104,155,656	49,346,443 [8]	—	5,123,000,000	2,542,300,000	1,612,000	—	—	—
1979	—	—	125,220,561	44,408,558 [8]	—	6,539,000,000	3,092,675,000	3,478,000	3,397,000	—	—
1980	—	—	127,148,018	61,043,487 [8]	—	6,576,000,000	4,315,112,000	3,219,000	2,577,000	—	—
1981	—	—	199,075,687	—	—	7,047,000,000	5,066,700,000	2,427,000	2,968,000	—	—
1982	—	—	186,800,000	—	—	8,888,000,000	4,961,100,000	2,088,000	2,225,000	—	—
1983	—	—	177,200,000	39,224,728 [8]	—	8,242,000,000	3,649,300,000	1,632,000	3,143,000	308,000	—
1984	—	—	212,000,000	—	—	9,426,000,000	3,974,600,000	2,202,000 [9]	5,522,000	464,000	—
1985	—	—	202,300,000	—	—	11,087,000,000	3,357,000,000	2,562,000 [9]	2,691,000	—	—
1986	—	—	253,600,000	—	—	11,854,000,000	2,118,900,000	—	1,159,000	—	—
1987	—	—	288,140,584	—	—	12,508,000,000	2,195,500,000	—	—	—	—
1988	—	—	367,793,266	—	—	14,436,000,000	—	—	—	—	—
1989	—	—	307,497,386	—	—	17,455,000,000	2,402,800,000	—	—	556,024	—
1990	—	—	310,500,000	—	—	20,402,000,000	2,820,700,000	—	—	—	—
1991	—	—	326,800,000	84,543,162	—	21,128,000,000	2,518,400,000	—	—	17,100,000	—
1992	—	—	317,700,000	86,076,253	—	20,455,000,000	2,303,500,000	—	—	26,900,000	—
1993	—	—	488,200,000	112,794,634	—	20,351,000,000	2,191,400,000	—	—	17,700,000	—
1994	—	—	252,200,000	92,543,142	—	22,711,000,000	2,847,700,000	—	—	12,600,000	—
1995	—	—	271,700,000	89,648,738	—	23,573,000,000	3,026,300,000	—	—	—	—
1996	—	—	312,800,000	81,067,643	—	22,379,000,000	3,651,500,000	—	—	—	—
1997	—	—	423,900,000	88,712,171	—	26,653,000,000	3,453,500,000	—	—	—	—
1998	—	—	—	86,451,932	—	28,109,000,000	—	—	—	—	—

[1] Through 1902, exports only to foreign countries.

[2] Exports only to United States (1905–1907, 1916–1923, and 1926–1968).

[3] 1898 is August to December only; 1939 is January to June only; 1940 is July 1939 to June 1940.

[4] January 1 to June 14.

[5] Exports only to United States.

[6] Includes Northern Mariana Islands.

[7] Exports only to foreign countries.

(continued)

TABLE Ef100–110   Merchandise exports of outlying areas: 1879–1998   *Continued*

[8] Includes re-exports and transshipments.

[9] Includes estimated purchases of handicrafts, souvenirs, and gifts.

Sources

Alaska and Hawai'i. U.S. Bureau of the Census, *Statistical Abstract of the United States*, various years.

American Samoa. 1916–1969: U.S. Bureau of the Census, *Statistical Abstract of the United States, 1943, 1953, 1957, 1963, 1966, 1971*. 1970–1981: Economic Development and Planning Office, American Samoa Government, *Statistical Bulletin 1978, 1982*. 1982–1996: Economic Development and Planning Office, American Samoa Government, *American Samoa Statistical Digest*, various issues. 1997: American Samoa Government.

Guam. 1898–1951: U.S. Bureau of the Census, *Statistical Abstract of the United States*, various years. 1952–1976: Guam Department of Commerce, *Statistical Abstract 1971*, Table 91, and *Statistical Abstract 1977*, Table 83. 1977–1998: Guam Department of Commerce, *Guam Annual Economic Review 1994*, Tables T11 and T12, and *Guam Annual Economic Review*, various issues.

Northern Mariana Islands. 1954–1977: U.S. State Department, *Annual Report to the United Nations on the Administration of the Trust Territory of the Pacific Islands*, various issues.

Puerto Rico. U.S. Bureau of the Census, *Statistical Abstract of the United States*, various issues.

Virgin Islands. U.S. Bureau of the Census, *Statistical Abstract of the United States*, various issues. Governor of the Virgin Islands, *Annual Report to the Secretary of the Interior*, various issues. U.S. Virgin Islands Bureau of Economic Research, *U.S. Virgin Islands Annual Economic Indicators*, various issues.

Federated States of Micronesia. 1954–1976: U.S. State Department, *Annual Report to the United Nations on the Administration of the Trust Territory of the Pacific Islands*, various issues. 1977–1985: Asian Development Bank, *Key Indicators of Developing Asian and Pacific Countries* (Oxford University Press, 1995), pp. 202–3.

Marshall Islands. 1954–1977: U.S. State Department, *Annual Report to the United Nations on the Administration of the Trust Territory of the Pacific Islands*, various issues. 1979–1986: Office of Planning and Statistics, *Marshall Islands Statistical Abstract, 1988/89*, Table 7.1.

Palau. 1954–1989: U.S. State Department, *Annual Report to the United Nations on the Administration of the Trust Territory of the Pacific Islands*, various issues. 1991–1994: Data supplied by Palau Office of Planning and Statistics.

Philippines. Yoshiko Nagano, "Intra-Asian Trade at the Turn of the Twentieth Century," in Florentino Rodao and Felice Noelle Rodriguez, editors, *The Philippine Revolution of 1896: Ordinary Lives in Extraordinary Times* (Ateneo de Manila University Press, 2001), Table 2.

Documentation

The following values are for fiscal year ending June 30: series Ef100, through 1918; series Ef101, 1901–1918; series Ef102, 1916–1918 and 1970–1997; series Ef103, through 1918 and 1957–1976; series Ef105, through 1918; series Ef106, 1917, 1967, and 1970; and all values for series Ef104 and Ef107–109.

TABLE Ef111–121   Merchandise imports of outlying areas: 1879–1998[1]

Contributed by Sumner J. La Croix

Year	Alaska	Hawai'i	American Samoa	Guam	Northern Mariana Islands	Puerto Rico	Virgin Islands	Federated States of Micronesia	Marshall Islands	Palau	Philippines
	Ef111 [2]	Ef112	Ef113 [3]	Ef114	Ef115	Ef116	Ef117	Ef118	Ef119 [4]	Ef120 [5]	Ef121 [6]
	Dollars	Dollars	Dollars	Dollars	Dollars	Dollars	Dollars	Dollars	Dollars	Dollars	Thousand pesos
1879	321,791	—	—	—	—	—	—	—	—	—	—
1880	466,032	—	—	—	—	—	—	—	—	—	—
1881	558,966	—	—	—	—	—	—	—	—	—	—
1882	593,484	—	—	—	—	—	—	—	—	—	—
1883	682,945	—	—	—	—	—	—	—	—	—	—
1884	619,420	—	—	—	—	—	—	—	—	—	—
1885	861,944	—	—	—	—	—	—	—	—	—	—
1886	888,252	—	—	—	—	—	—	—	—	—	—
1887	1,352,636	—	—	—	—	—	—	—	—	—	—
1888	1,515,211	—	—	—	—	—	—	—	—	—	—
1889	1,718,809	—	—	—	—	—	—	—	—	—	—
1890	1,921,577	—	—	—	—	—	—	—	—	—	—
1891	1,996,302	—	—	—	—	—	—	—	—	—	—
1892	2,027,691	—	—	—	—	—	—	—	—	—	—
1893	2,354,362	—	—	—	—	—	—	—	—	—	—
1894	2,874,490	—	—	—	—	—	—	—	—	—	—
1895	3,072,850	—	—	—	—	—	—	—	—	—	—
1896	3,574,414	—	—	—	—	—	—	—	—	—	—
1897	4,020,694	—	—	—	—	—	—	—	—	—	—
1898	13,857,235	10,368,815	—	8,811 [10]	—	—	1,404,004 [9]	—	—	—	10,762
1899	9,840,251	16,069,577	—	10,649	—	—	9,805,916	—	—	—	38,386
1900	18,848,317	10,231,198 [8]	—	1,320	—	—	5,251,457 [12]	—	—	—	49,728
1901	14,014,992	2,835,278 [7]	—	1,044	—	—	8,918,136	—	—	—	60,325
1902	511,830 [7]	3,036,583 [7]	—	—	—	—	13,209,610	—	—	—	66,684
1903	9,987,164	14,085,074	117,386	65,575	—	—	14,449,286	—	—	—	67,623
1904	10,772,465	15,481,034	76,245	196,293	—	—	13,169,029	—	—	—	59,155
1905	12,955,165	14,768,144	93,690	74,649	—	—	16,536,259	—	—	—	60,101
1906	15,715,118	15,311,917	98,212	116,262	—	—	21,827,665	—	—	—	52,808
1907	19,536,956	18,587,434	93,932	94,621	—	—	29,267,172	—	—	—	60,908
1908	17,354,877	19,720,554	79,002	117,627	—	—	25,825,665	—	—	—	58,372
1909	18,409,931	21,814,352	—	86,819	—	—	26,544,326	—	—	—	62,169

Notes appear at end of table

TABLE Ef111–121   **Merchandise imports of outlying areas: 1879–1998** *Continued*

Year	Alaska Ef111 [2] Dollars	Hawai'i Ef112 Dollars	American Samoa Ef113 [3] Dollars	Guam Ef114 Dollars	Northern Mariana Islands Ef115 Dollars	Puerto Rico Ef116 Dollars	Virgin Islands Ef117 Dollars	Federated States of Micronesia Ef118 Dollars	Marshall Islands Ef119 [4] Dollars	Palau Ef120 [5] Dollars	Philippines Ef121 [6] Thousand pesos
1910	19,289,687	25,166,435	—	94,667	—	—	30,634,855	—	—	—	99,439
1911	16,911,901	27,115,626	85,224	140,316	—	—	38,786,997	—	—	—	96,049
1912	19,980,730	30,251,349	110,249	129,466	—	—	42,972,891	—	—	—	123,336
1913	21,809,533	37,519,620	133,399	160,249	—	—	36,900,062	—	—	—	106,626
1914	23,029,122	32,055,970	100,824	165,250	—	—	36,406,787	—	—	—	97,177
1915	21,900,928	30,720,787	111,069	245,284	—	—	33,884,296	—	—	—	98,624
1916	28,152,900	37,196,106	118,294	256,948	—	—	38,950,915	—	—	—	90,993
1917	40,461,573	50,813,426	110,314	286,652	—	—	53,545,224	1,438,904 [9]	—	—	131,594
1918	45,247,607	50,453,563	145,899	358,147	—	—	63,389,282	1,892,429	—	—	197,198
1919	38,925,594	58,964,573	182,959	447,181	—	—	73,060,593	2,276,512	—	—	237,278
1920	38,388,973	86,337,045	225,295	355,652	—	—	129,073,978	4,856,097	—	—	298,877
1921	20,209,228	73,975,928	222,487	483,684	—	—	68,354,363	3,038,750	—	—	231,677
1922	27,648,733	61,082,653	196,903	596,120	—	—	64,817,210	2,009,951	—	—	160,395
1923	31,145,832	75,106,197	198,860	674,556	—	—	84,467,120	1,940,767	—	—	174,999
1924	32,575,891	78,651,916	194,362	632,721	—	—	87,749,447	2,028,718	—	—	216,022
1925	33,199,511	83,753,918	192,412	585,835	—	—	89,120,682	1,915,277 [9]	—	—	239,466
1926	32,131,020	86,517,189	318,140	493,355	—	—	97,401,601	1,799,444 [9]	—	—	238,598
1927	36,370,410	88,801,904	203,368	404,277	—	—	97,590,929	2,053,340 [9]	—	—	231,703
1928	32,618,238	88,124,233	204,750	661,264	—	—	95,265,911	2,277,030 [9]	—	—	269,314
1929	34,174,857	92,703,456	201,971	812,815	—	—	87,708,510	2,298,269 [9]	—	—	294,321
1930	33,012,927	91,126,049	206,060	668,419	—	—	84,537,868	1,672,903 [9]	—	—	246,186
1931	23,036,493	86,956,866	183,447	579,287	—	—	68,511,042	1,250,406 [9]	—	—	198,357
1932	19,875,556	63,630,077	157,600	456,861	—	—	56,036,476	929,980 [9]	—	—	158,790
1933	20,816,867	63,127,969	168,514	378,991	—	—	57,843,575	1,075,512 [9]	—	—	134,723
1934	30,269,608	69,233,683	201,612	439,207	—	—	66,239,329	1,544,424 [9]	—	—	167,214
1935	32,261,832	84,552,884	281,414	638,220	—	—	76,647,739	2,503,027	—	—	171,048
1936	39,325,725	92,443,911	341,873	779,500	—	—	93,159,305	3,599,617	—	—	202,252
1937	43,083,995	113,975,459	374,187	857,904	—	—	99,188,310	4,148,593	—	—	218,051
1938	42,851,647	109,659,721	355,731	698,433	—	—	88,683,766	3,346,563	—	—	265,215
1939	44,414,093	109,251,672	277,318	735,906	—	—	92,920,704	3,456,895	—	—	99,946
1940	48,189,293	135,446,957	332,718	859,624	—	—	110,629,960	4,164,428	—	—	289,171
1941	82,206,605	192,855,457	714,589	1,060,980	—	—	153,259,895	6,307,730	—	—	—
1942	91,524,276	143,377,345	896,495	—	—	—	102,378,764	4,862,986	—	—	—
1943	76,007,574	185,766,176	1,081,442	—	—	—	109,066,388	4,847,655	—	—	—
1944	62,638,819	198,509,464	1,009,574	656,777 [9]	—	—	136,445,478	4,750,640	—	—	—
1945	67,088,955	267,045,937	689,782	—	—	—	181,912,120	5,332,105	—	—	—
1946	75,576,054	236,306,962	678,344	1,096,858 [9]	—	—	298,697,281	8,540,350	—	—	—
1947	117,311,766	349,627,410	892,027	9,368,182 [9]	—	—	341,842,882	8,990,646	—	—	—
1948	—	—	1,043,171	9,530,325 [9]	—	—	360,403,762	9,465,562	—	—	—
1949	—	—	1,194,287	11,296,852 [9]	—	—	333,672,371	9,967,225	—	—	—
1950	—	—	917,208	13,702,182	—	—	390,945,172	11,046,282	—	—	—
1951	—	—	963,190	12,504,191	—	—	442,900,808	11,686,154	—	—	—
1952	—	—	1,065,772	17,257,151	—	—	468,749,423	13,870,399	—	—	—
1953	—	—	1,076,018	19,649,655	—	—	526,233,633	16,015,290	—	—	—
1954	—	—	1,397,552	20,518,699	1,050,230	187,202	532,044,225	15,696,811	648,501	406,693	—
1955	—	—	2,009,022	23,131,130	1,221,436	—	603,023,871	16,255,575	631,099	426,366	—
1956	—	—	2,661,640	21,842,442	1,423,182	385,656	667,085,098	18,947,426	829,560	556,679	—
1957	—	—	2,816,000	24,354,700	1,847,330	761,083	734,965,000	21,239,242	939,253	609,883	—
1958	—	—	4,048,000	21,200,478	1,846,761	934,906	756,563,000	23,622,093	846,728	706,843	—
1959	—	—	4,778,000	28,318,811	1,474,982	1,097,685	862,124,000	33,634,692	835,349	601,020	—
1960	—	—	5,042,000	25,357,680	1,565,076	782,350	1,022,142,000	42,257,000	800,029	599,279	—
1961	—	—	3,871,000 [9]	24,667,985	1,596,296	1,109,850	1,124,908,000	50,219,000	1,285,523	568,446	—
1962	—	—	8,217,000 [9]	20,717,274	1,565,085	1,064,276	1,202,536,000	61,738,000	963,264	545,995	—
1963	—	—	14,358,000 [9]	30,366,528	1,886,683	1,339,135	1,476,557,000	76,043,000	1,195,474	607,916	—
1964	—	—	9,849,000 [9]	41,978,958	1,936,063	1,464,037	—	96,002,000	1,455,279	830,206	—
1965	—	—	13,536,000 [9]	41,414,027	3,173,401	2,085,954	1,542,663,000	118,675,918	827,263	1,004,298	—
1966	—	—	—	40,422,177	3,576,754	2,240,614	—	137,700,000	1,887,958	1,211,291	—
1967	—	—	—	63,688,219	3,593,602	2,400,647	1,845,796,000	172,155,000	2,571,402	1,253,829	—
1968	—	—	—	63,099,961	4,071,049	4,561,400	2,118,970,000	260,160,000	2,805,121	2,134,482	—
1969	—	—	—	55,594,080	4,303,777	4,413,604	2,338,000,000	—	2,929,800	2,294,976	—

Notes appear at end of table

(continued)

TABLE Ef111–121 Merchandise imports of outlying areas: 1879–1998 *Continued*

Year	Alaska Ef111 [2] Dollars	Hawai'i Ef112 Dollars	American Samoa Ef113 [3] Dollars	Guam Ef114 Dollars	Northern Mariana Islands Ef115 Dollars	Puerto Rico Ef116 Dollars	Virgin Islands Ef117 Dollars	Federated States of Micronesia Ef118 Dollars	Marshall Islands Ef119 [4] Dollars	Palau Ef120 [5] Dollars	Philippines Ef121 [6] Thousand pesos
1970	—	—	15,713,339	96,402,314	7,806,529	5,290,223	2,681,000,000	400,615,068	5,630,200	2,193,366	—
1971	—	—	19,556,873	115,029,876	7,909,875	8,637,312	2,884,000,000	551,649,665	7,416,800	2,202,966	—
1972	—	—	24,114,332	166,767,662	8,743,883	6,638,644	3,324,000,000	596,241,872	7,986,460	2,965,075	—
1973	—	—	35,952,859	211,130,608	6,546,183	8,270,833	3,593,000,000	850,627,626	8,495,620	2,714,991	—
1974	—	—	46,549,418	259,089,275	9,788,745	9,151,229	4,961,000,000	2,220,424,517	6,347,122	3,962,476	—
1975	—	—	49,893,544	266,249,576	14,303,492	11,619,834	4,885,000,000	2,196,290,000	6,307,079	5,981,348	—
1976	—	—	50,690,638	267,592,589	12,209,437	12,552,452	5,928,000,000	2,685,348,000	6,906,004	6,727,587	—
1977	—	—	54,941,048	293,447,496	21,183,000	—	6,200,000,000	2,976,687,000	9,581,500	9,102,100	—
1978	—	—	73,339,727	368,179,562	22,352,000	—	6,918,000,000	3,171,140,000	10,763,033	8,311,414	—
1979	—	—	90,286,132	445,792,921	25,772,000	31,100,000	7,834,000,000	3,773,465,000	14,238,000	8,364,187	—
1980	—	—	95,235,650	544,183,553	28,729,000	—	9,018,000,000	4,919,483,000	17,155,000	—	—
1981	—	—	115,038,968	—	38,569,000	—	9,329,000,000	4,889,500,000	22,208,000	—	—
1982	—	—	119,416,900	—	43,404,000	—	8,167,000,000	5,234,300,000	18,777,000	—	—
1983	—	—	112,201,353	636,081,997	48,877,000	65,200,000	8,708,000,000	4,663,700,000	17,503,000	13,551,500	—
1984	—	—	166,790,298	—	38,155,000 [11]	98,000,000	10,116,000,000	4,761,000,000	22,608,000	23,025,800	—
1985	—	—	163,711,819	—	41,415,000 [11]	82,900,000	10,162,000,000	3,710,600,000	29,176,000	—	—
1986	—	—	140,952,814	—	—	105,100,000	10,321,000,000	2,642,800,000	30,571,000	—	—
1987	—	—	139,307,600	—	—	149,300,000	11,308,000,000	3,370,400,000	—	—	—
1988	—	—	148,441,764	—	—	219,600,000	13,096,000,000	2,314,500,000	—	—	—
1989	—	—	168,724,669	—	—	313,700,000	15,010,000,000	3,169,700,000	—	24,563,000	—
1990	—	—	166,782,108	—	—	342,100,000	16,200,000,000	3,294,700,000	—	—	—
1991	—	—	182,222,958	—	—	392,600,000	15,079,000,000	3,118,000,000	—	32,300,000	—
1992	—	—	183,000,000	—	—	493,900,000	16,476,000,000	3,550,800,000	—	38,100,000	—
1993	—	—	204,400,000	—	—	513,000,000	16,124,000,000	2,625,600,000	—	42,200,000	—
1994	—	—	215,100,000	—	—	513,700,000	17,152,000,000	3,154,000,000	—	44,200,000	—
1995	—	—	229,900,000	—	—	528,000,000	18,969,000,000	3,166,000,000	—	—	—
1996	—	—	228,300,000	—	—	551,200,000	19,422,000,000	3,594,900,000	—	—	—
1997	—	—	—	—	—	836,200,000	21,928,000,000	3,825,800,000	—	—	—
1998	—	—	—	—	—	—	21,706,000,000	—	—	—	—

[1] Imports after 1933 are for consumption only.

[2] Through 1901, covers estimated value of merchandise shipped from Pacific Coast ports to Alaska.

[3] Beginning 1970, government imports not included.

[4] Beginning 1979, government imports and duty-free imports not included.

[5] Calendar-year basis beginning 1983.

[6] 1898 is August to December only; 1939 is January to June only; 1940 is July 1939 to June 1940.

[7] Imports only from foreign countries.

[8] January 1 to June 14.

[9] Imports only from United States.

[10] Includes Northern Mariana Islands.

[11] Petroleum products imported through Mobil Oil Micronesia not included.

[12] January 1 to June 30.

Sources
Alaska and Hawai'i. U.S. Bureau of the Census, *Statistical Abstract of the United States*, various years.

American Samoa. 1916–1971: U.S. Bureau of the Census, *Statistical Abstract of the United States, 1943, 1953, 1957, 1963, 1966, 1971*. 1970–1981: Economic Development and Planning Office, American Samoa Government, *Statistical Bulletin 1978, 1982*. 1982–1996: Economic Development and Planning Office, American Samoa Government, *American Samoa Statistical Digest*, various issues. 1997: American Samoa Government.

Guam. 1898–1951: U.S. Bureau of the Census, *Statistical Abstract of the United States*, various years. 1952–1976: Guam Department of Commerce, *Statistical Abstract 1971*, Table 91, and *Statistical Abstract 1977*, Table 83. 1978–1998: Guam Department of Commerce, *Guam Annual Economic Review 1994*, Table T11, and *Guam Annual Economic Review*, various years.

Northern Mariana Islands. 1954–1977: U.S. State Department, *Annual Report to the United Nations on the Administration of the Trust Territory of the Pacific Islands*, various issues.

Puerto Rico. U.S. Bureau of the Census, *Statistical Abstract of the United States*, various years.

Virgin Islands. U.S. Bureau of the Census, *Statistical Abstract of the United States*, various years. Governor of the Virgin Islands, *Annual Report to the Secretary of the Interior*, various issues. U.S. Virgin Islands Bureau of Economic Research, *U.S. Virgin Islands Annual Economic Indicators*, various issues.

Federated States of Micronesia. 1954–1976: U.S. State Department, *Annual Report to the United Nations on the Administration of the Trust Territory of the Pacific Islands*, various issues. 1977–1985: Asian Development Bank, *Key Indicators of Developing Asian and Pacific Countries* (Oxford University Press, 1995), pp. 202–3.

Marshall Islands. 1954–1977: U.S. State Department, *Annual Report to the United Nations on the Administration of the Trust Territory of the Pacific Islands*, various issues. 1979–1986: Office of Planning and Statistics, *Marshall Islands Statistical Abstract, 1988/89*, Table 7.1.

Palau. 1954–1989: U.S. State Department, *Annual Report to the United Nations on the Administration of the Trust Territory of the Pacific Islands*, various issues. 1992–1994: Data supplied by Palau Office of Planning and Statistics.

Philippines. Yoshiko Nagano, "Intra-Asian Trade at the Turn of the Twentieth Century," Table 2, in Florentino Rodao and Felice Noelle Rodriguez, editors, *The Philippine Revolution of 1896: Ordinary Lives in Extraordinary Times* (Ateneo de Manila University Press, 2001), Table 3.

Documentation
The following values are for fiscal year ending June 30: series Ef111, though 1918; series Ef112, 1901–1918; series Ef113, 1903–1917 and 1977–1996; series Ef114, through 1918 and 1951–1976; series Ef117, 1901–1918; series Ef118, 1917; and all values for series Ef115–116 and Ef119–120.

TABLE Ef122–130   Visitor arrivals in outlying areas: 1922–1998

Contributed by Sumner J. La Croix

Year	Hawai'i Ef122 [1] Number	American Samoa Ef123 Number	Guam Ef124 Number	Northern Mariana Islands Ef125 [2] Number	Puerto Rico Ef126 [3] Number	Virgin Islands Ef127 [4] Number	Federated States of Micronesia Ef128 Number	Marshall Islands Ef129 [5,6] Number	Palau Ef130 [5] Number
1922	9,676	—	—	—	—	—	—	—	—
1923	12,021	—	—	—	—	—	—	—	—
1924	12,468	—	—	—	—	—	—	—	—
1925	15,193	—	—	—	—	—	—	—	—
1926	16,762	—	—	—	—	—	—	—	—
1927	17,451	—	—	—	—	—	—	—	—
1928	19,980	—	—	—	—	—	—	—	—
1929	22,190	—	—	—	—	—	—	—	—
1930	18,651	—	—	—	—	—	—	—	—
1931	15,780	—	—	—	—	—	—	—	—
1932	10,370	—	—	—	—	—	—	—	—
1933	10,111	—	—	—	—	—	—	—	—
1934	16,161	—	—	—	—	—	—	—	—
1935	19,933	—	—	—	—	—	—	—	—
1936	22,199	—	—	—	—	—	—	—	—
1937	21,987	—	—	—	—	—	—	—	—
1938	23,043	—	—	—	—	—	—	—	—
1939	24,390	—	—	—	—	—	—	—	—
1940	25,373	—	—	—	—	—	—	—	—
1941	31,846	—	—	—	—	—	—	—	—
1946	15,000	—	—	—	—	21,058	—	—	—
1947	25,000	—	—	—	40,380	31,150	—	—	—
1948	36,397	—	—	—	49,401	—	—	—	—
1949	34,386	—	—	—	59,039	—	—	—	—
1950	46,593	—	—	—	64,507	23,800	—	—	—
1951	51,565	—	—	—	78,367	57,700	—	—	—
1952	60,539	—	—	—	99,871	109,800	—	—	—
1953	80,346	—	—	—	118,401	61,500	—	—	—
1954	91,289	—	—	—	125,710	70,100	—	—	—
1955	109,798	—	—	—	134,625	86,800	—	—	—
1956	133,815	—	—	—	162,522	99,400	—	—	—
1957	168,829	—	—	—	187,321	108,400	—	—	—
1958	171,588	—	—	—	218,840	117,000	—	—	—
1959	243,216	—	—	—	274,767	148,500	—	—	—
1960	—	—	—	—	347,425	184,000	—	—	—
1961	—	—	—	—	354,963	234,100	—	—	—
1962	—	—	—	—	396,675	266,300	—	—	—
1963	—	—	198 [7]	—	461,857	307,800	—	—	—
1964	—	—	300 [7]	—	526,641	459,200	—	—	—
1965	—	—	500 [7]	—	606,093	508,500	—	—	—
1966	—	4,401	1,500 [7]	—	723,543	608,700	—	—	—
1967	—	9,617	4,284 [7]	—	815,505	693,800	—	—	—
1968	—	11,786	18,000	—	910,903	1,012,200	—	—	—
1969	—	13,940	58,265	16,224	1,067,511	1,073,500	2,052	905	1,519
1970	—	16,182	73,723	19,428	1,088,379	1,016,500	4,114	1,246	1,950
1971	—	22,439	119,174	—	1,088,965	1,076,400	7,180	1,862	2,230
1972	—	26,025	185,399	24,676	1,201,609	1,211,600	7,513	1,359	2,768
1973	—	—	241,146	32,467	1,377,884	1,243,400	10,148	3,153	4,095
1974	—	34,752	260,568	44,438	1,396,409	1,062,800	9,094	2,705	3,712
1975	—	—	239,695	49,130	1,300,234	1,000,600	10,476	3,347	5,404
1976	—	—	201,344	51,600	1,275,922	1,041,800	9,408	2,919	5,386
1977	—	—	240,467	52,180	1,343,096	1,151,300	12,691	3,801	5,768
1978	—	51,190	231,975	86,718	1,466,846	1,202,700	14,397	3,799	4,915
1979	—	49,893	264,326	100,357	1,636,806	1,321,700	17,917	2,833	5,876
1980		48,093	291,129	117,149	1,638,779	1,217,400	10,922	—	5,640
1981	—	46,403	312,862	117,572	1,567,981	1,170,200	10,304	1,242	5,057
1982	—	40,480	316,746	111,173	1,617,092	1,056,100	9,708	2,258	5,330
1983	—	37,150	345,805	124,024	1,594,868	1,108,700	10,340	3,630	6,388
1984	—	42,773	361,423	131,823	1,582,659	1,159,300	9,463	3,913	9,014

Notes appear at end of table

(continued)

TABLE Ef122–130 Visitor arrivals in outlying areas: 1922–1998 *Continued*

Year	Hawai'i Ef122 [1] Number	American Samoa Ef123 Number	Guam Ef124 Number	Northern Mariana Islands Ef125 [2] Number	Puerto Rico Ef126 [3] Number	Virgin Islands Ef127 [4] Number	Federated States of Micronesia Ef128 Number	Marshall Islands Ef129 [5,6] Number	Palau Ef130 [5] Number
1985	—	47,125	364,938	142,284	1,642,307	1,220,600	11,855	2,914	13,410
1986	—	39,762	407,070	157,207	1,695,626	1,559,400	—	—	13,653
1987	—	45,127	477,491	186,203	2,034,854	1,822,800	—	—	16,695
1988	—	46,524	576,170	233,291	2,280,512	1,846,900	—	—	22,675
1989	—	43,785	658,883	301,818	2,443,785	1,738,300	—	—	26,005
1990	—	51,721	769,876	435,454	2,559,737	1,811,500	—	—	32,846
1991	—	44,923	728,722	429,864	2,612,991	1,899,500	—	—	32,700
1992	—	40,433	863,074	505,295	2,656,628	1,929,700	—	—	36,117
1993	—	34,154	775,115	545,803	2,854,468	1,923,100	—	—	40,497
1994	—	39,803	1,076,437	596,033	3,042,375	1,921,400	—	—	—
1995	—	39,749	1,350,476	676,161	3,130,662	1,741,300	—	—	—
1996	—	41,201	1,352,361	736,117	3,065,056	1,778,700	—	—	—
1997	—	—	—	—	3,241,774	2,128,000	—	—	—
1998	—	—	—	—	3,396,115	2,138,900	—	—	—

[1] Visitors staying overnight or longer.

[2] Data are reported by fiscal year ending June 30, except 1969, 1970, and 1995–1999, which are reported by calendar year.

[3] Includes all visitors staying in hotels and elsewhere, regardless of their length of stay or purpose of trip. Data reported by fiscal year ending June 30. Through 1971, cruise ship visitors who stayed in Puerto Rico for less than a day and U.S. servicemen on leave after maneuvers are not included.

[4] Only tourist arrivals are reported. Prior to 1980, data are reported by fiscal year ending June 30. Beginning 1950, data reported to nearest hundred.

[5] Passport holders from Federated States of Micronesia and Palau are excluded from the count.

[6] Only visitors to Majuro are reported.

[7] Only tourist arrivals are reported.

Sources

Hawai'i. Robert C. Schmitt, *Historical Statistics of Hawaii* (University Press of Hawai'i, 1977), Table 11.7.

American Samoa. Economic Development and Planning Office, *American Samoa Statistical Digest*, various years. Economic Development and Planning Office, *American Samoa Statistical Yearbook*, various years.

Guam. Economic Research Center, Guam Department of Commerce, *Guam Annual Economic Review*, various years.

Northern Mariana Islands. U.S. State Department, *Annual Report to the United Nations on the Administration of the Trust Territory of the Pacific Islands*, various issues. Department of Commerce, Commonwealth of the Northern Mariana Islands, *1995 Commonwealth of the Northern Mariana Islands Statistical Yearbook*. Marianas Visitor Bureau, *Annual Report*, various years.

Puerto Rico. Data supplied by Office of Statistics, Puerto Rico Tourism Company.

Virgin Islands. Governor of the Virgin Islands, *Annual Report to the Secretary of the Interior*, various issues. U.S. Virgin Islands Bureau of Economic Research, *U.S. Virgin Islands Annual Tourism Indicators*, various issues. Jannette Olivia Domingo, "The Role of Imported Labor in Virgin Islands Economic History" (Ph.D. dissertation, Columbia University, 1969), Table IV-14.

Federated States of Micronesia. U.S. State Department, *Annual Report to the United Nations on the Administration of the Trust Territory of the Pacific Islands*, various issues. Federated States of Micronesia (FSM) Office of Planning and Statistics, *National Yearbook of Statistics: 1981*, Table 4.5. FSM Office of Planning and Statistics, *Information Handbook: June 1992*, Table 7.

Marshall Islands. U.S. State Department, *Annual Report to the United Nations on the Administration of the Trust Territory of the Pacific Islands*, various issues. Office of Planning and Statistics, *Marshall Islands Statistical Abstract: 1993 and 1994*, 8th edition, Table 9.1.

Palau. U.S. State Department, *Annual Report to the United Nations on the Administration of the Trust Territory of the Pacific Islands*, various issues. Palau Office of Planning and Statistics, *Statistical Yearbook*, 1992, 1998 issues.

TABLE Ef131–140   Telephones in outlying areas: 1898–1998

Contributed by Sumner J. La Croix

Year	Hawai'i Ef131 [1] Number	American Samoa Ef132 Number	Guam Ef133 Number	Northern Mariana Islands Ef134 Number	Puerto Rico Ef135 Number	Virgin Islands Ef136 [2] Number	Canal Zone Ef137 Number	Federated States of Micronesia Ef138 Number	Marshall Islands Ef139 Number	Palau Ef140 Number
1898	1,340	—	—	—	—	—	—	—	—	—
1899	1,459	—	—	—	—	—	—	—	—	—
1900	1,393	—	—	—	—	—	—	—	—	—
1901	1,586	—	—	—	—	—	—	—	—	—
1902	1,607	—	—	—	—	—	—	—	—	—
1903	1,629	—	—	—	—	—	—	—	—	—
1904	1,652	—	—	—	—	—	—	—	—	—
1905	1,800	—	—	—	—	—	—	—	—	—
1906	2,070	—	—	—	—	—	—	—	—	—
1907	2,105	—	—	—	—	—	—	—	—	—
1908	2,164	—	—	—	—	—	—	—	—	—
1909	2,508	—	—	—	—	—	—	—	—	—
1910	2,657	—	—	—	—	—	—	—	—	—
1911	3,512	—	—	—	—	—	—	—	—	—
1912	3,870	—	—	—	—	—	—	—	—	—
1913	5,000	—	—	—	—	—	—	—	—	—
1914	5,800	—	—	—	—	—	—	—	—	—
1915	6,527	—	—	—	—	—	1,609	—	—	—
1916	6,965	—	—	—	—	—	—	—	—	—
1917	7,775	—	—	—	—	—	2,154	—	—	—
1918	7,928	—	—	—	—	—	2,523	—	—	—
1919	9,279	—	—	—	—	—	2,967	—	—	—
1920	10,761	—	—	—	—	—	3,330	—	—	—
1921	11,090	—	—	—	—	—	2,992	—	—	—
1922	14,805	—	—	—	549	—	2,417	—	—	—
1923	16,651	—	—	—	615	—	2,554	—	—	—
1924	17,222	—	—	—	—	—	2,717	—	—	—
1925	18,332	—	—	—	—	—	2,836	—	—	—
1926	19,076	—	—	—	—	—	2,888	—	—	—
1927	20,867	—	—	—	—	—	2,665	—	—	—
1928	22,666	—	—	—	—	—	2,674	—	—	—
1929	23,605	—	—	—	—	—	—	—	—	—
1930	24,319	—	—	—	—	—	2,936	—	—	—
1931	24,983	—	—	—	—	—	2,999	—	—	—
1932	23,390	—	—	—	—	—	2,949	—	—	—
1933	22,337	—	—	—	—	—	2,766	—	—	—
1934	23,074	—	—	—	—	—	2,709	—	—	—
1935	24,664	—	—	—	—	—	2,811	—	—	—
1936	26,693	—	—	—	—	—	2,865	—	—	—
1937	29,519	—	—	—	—	—	3,015	—	—	—
1938	32,205	—	—	—	—	—	3,049	—	—	—
1939	35,107	—	—	—	—	—	3,268	—	—	—
1940	39,179	—	—	—	—	—	—	—	—	—
1941	45,501	—	—	—	17,738	—	—	—	—	—
1942	51,264	—	—	—	19,279	—	4,973	—	—	—
1943	53,387	—	—	—	—	—	5,482	—	—	—
1944	55,271	—	—	—	—	—	5,502	—	—	—
1945	54,734	—	—	—	—	—	5,674	—	—	—
1946	61,373	—	—	—	—	—	5,267	—	—	—
1947	70,564	—	—	—	—	—	5,594	—	—	—
1948	78,847	—	—	—	29,898	—	5,926	—	—	—
1949	89,204	—	—	—	—	—	—	—	—	—
1950	99,310	—	—	—	—	—	6,112	—	—	—
1951	109,329	—	—	—	—	—	6,184	—	—	—
1952	119,146	—	—	—	—	—	6,514	—	—	—
1953	125,077	—	—	—	—	—	6,965	—	—	—
1954	132,822	—	—	—	—	1,500	7,132	134	—	54

Notes appear at end of table

(continued)

TABLE Ef131–140 Telephones in outlying areas: 1898–1998 *Continued*

Year	Hawai'i Ef131 [1] Number	American Samoa Ef132 Number	Guam Ef133 Number	Northern Mariana Islands Ef134 Number	Puerto Rico Ef135 Number	Virgin Islands Ef136 [2] Number	Canal Zone Ef137 Number	Federated States of Micronesia Ef138 Number	Marshall Islands Ef139 Number	Palau Ef140 Number
1955	143,063	212 [2]	632	—	—	1,850	7,371	—	—	—
1956	154,212	222 [2]	844	175	—	1,700	7,551	139	—	57
1957	166,385	226 [2]	1,355	—	—	2,825	7,530	—	—	54
1958	176,750	227 [2]	1,534	—	—	2,379	7,670	—	—	—
1959	191,373	246 [2]	2,224	—	—	3,112	7,803	—	—	—
1960	—	277 [2]	2,644	—	—	3,905	8,005	—	—	—
1961	—	285 [2]	3,225	—	—	—	8,113	—	—	—
1962	—	349 [2]	3,656	—	—	—	8,972	—	—	—
1963	—	—	—	—	—	—	8,943	—	—	—
1964	—	—	4,067	—	—	—	9,400	—	—	—
1965	—	—	4,992	—	—	8,824	9,820	—	—	—
1966	—	—	5,663	—	—	—	9,999	—	—	—
1967	—	—	6,055	—	—	—	10,259	—	—	—
1968	—	—	6,223	—	—	—	—	—	—	—
1969	—	—	6,153	—	—	—	—	—	—	—
1970	—	—	6,785	—	—	22,506	—	—	—	—
1971	—	—	7,685	—	—	26,820	—	—	—	—
1972	—	—	8,836	—	—	30,885	—	—	—	—
1973	—	—	11,180	—	—	32,000	—	—	—	—
1974	—	—	11,795	—	—	35,100	—	—	—	—
1975	—	—	15,028	—	242,900	35,796	—	—	—	—
1976	—	—	13,691	—	276,200	35,097	—	789	168	352
1977	—	—	10,919	—	306,800	33,500	—	1,000	191	380
1978	—	—	12,332	—	340,200	35,768	—	—	—	—
1979	—	—	14,056	—	377,400	37,667	—	—	—	—
1980	—	—	17,540	—	413,200	41,175	—	1,070	—	—
1981	—	5,210	19,177	—	451,600	44,285	—	—	—	—
1982	—	5,550	21,713	1,603	473,792	48,226	—	—	—	—
1983	—	5,608	23,442	1,829	501,400	51,509	—	1,000	—	—
1984	—	5,692	23,354	2,245	547,462	53,469	—	1,100	—	—
1985	—	5,880	23,527	2,389	593,500	52,314	—	1,270	—	—
1986	—	7,305	24,481	4,576	639,368	54,474	—	—	—	—
1987	—	7,806	25,496	5,022	696,100	55,400	—	—	—	—
1988	—	8,015	28,350	5,634	763,584	57,932	—	—	—	2,481
1989	—	8,276	32,068	7,232	812,998	58,880	—	—	—	3,026
1990	—	8,399	37,787	9,773	982,187	58,931	—	—	—	1,595
1991	—	8,600	41,782	12,240	1,032,758	63,291	—	—	—	1,801
1992	—	8,800	49,507	12,971	1,096,225	65,638	—	—	—	2,231
1993	—	8,900	54,529	13,618	1,095,446	68,122	—	—	—	2,528
1994	—	8,950	69,464	14,358	1,130,238	70,571	—	—	—	—
1995	—	9,000	75,595	15,460	1,195,921	69,953	—	—	—	—
1996	—	9,500	83,799	14,567	1,254,088	70,725	—	—	—	—
1997	—	—	82,669	16,306	1,322,499	62,140	—	—	—	—
1998	—	—	84,134	19,610	—	63,798	—	—	—	—

[1] Through 1912, data only for Oahu.

[2] Fiscal year ending June 30.

Sources

Hawai'i. Robert C. Schmitt, *Historical Statistics of Hawaii* (University Press of Hawai'i, 1977), Table 18.1.

American Samoa. Department of Commerce, Statistics Division, *American Samoa Statistical Digest 1986*, Table 42; *American Samoa Statistical Digest 1993*, Table 12.1; *American Samoa Statistical Yearbook 1996*, Table 12.1. Governor of American Samoa, *Annual Report to the Secretary of the Interior*, various years.

Guam. Guam Department of Commerce, *Guam Annual Economic Review 1998–1998*, Table PH8; *Guam Annual Economic Review 1994*, Table PH8; *Guam Annual Economic Review 1985*, Table 68; *Statistical Abstract Guam 1970*, Table 45; *Statistical Abstract Guam 1977*, Table 48; Governor of Guam, *Report to the Secretary of the Interior*, various issues.

Northern Mariana Islands. Department of Commerce, *1997 Commonwealth of the Northern Mariana Islands Statistical Yearbook*, Table 10.9. U.S. State Department, *Annual Report to the United Nations on the Administration of the Trust Territory of the Pacific Islands*, various issues.

Puerto Rico. International Telecommunication Union, *World Telecommunication Indicators Database*, March 1998. Governor of Puerto Rico, *Annual Report to the Secretary of the Interior*, various years.

Virgin Islands. Governor of the Virgin Islands, *Annual Report to the Secretary of the Interior*, various issues. U.S. Virgin Islands Bureau of Economic Research, *U.S. Virgin Islands Annual Economic Indicators*, various issues.

Canal Zone. *Annual Report of the Governor of the Panama Canal*, various issues.

Federated States of Micronesia and Marshall Islands. U.S. State Department, *Annual Report to the United Nations on the Administration of the Trust Territory of the Pacific Islands*, various issues. Federated States of Micronesia National Government, Office of Planning and Statistics, *National Yearbook of Statistics 1981*, February 1982, Table 6.3.

Palau. Republic of Palau, Office of Planning and Statistics, *Statistical Yearbook 1998*, Table 13.1a. U.S. State Department, *Annual Report to the United Nations on the Administration of the Trust Territory of the Pacific Islands*, various issues.

Documentation

Series Ef131. In service on December 31.

TABLE Ef141–148   Consumer price indexes for outlying areas: 1935–1999

Contributed by Sumner J. La Croix

	Hawai'i	American Samoa	Guam	Northern Mariana Islands	Puerto Rico		Marshall Islands	Philippines
					All families	Wage earners' families		
	Ef141 [1]	Ef142 [2]	Ef143 [3]	Ef144 [4]	Ef145	Ef146	Ef147 [5]	Ef148 [6]
Year	Index 1967 = 100	Index	Index	Index 1977 = 100	Index 1967 = 100	Index 1984 = 100	Index	Index 1941 = 100
1935	—	—	—	—	—	—	—	90.2
1936	—	—	—	—	—	—	—	88.2
1937	—	—	—	—	—	—	—	89.2
1938	—	—	—	—	—	—	—	92.4
1939	—	—	—	—	—	—	—	93.9
1940	40.5	—	—	—	—	—	—	97.7
1941	42.9	—	—	—	—	—	—	100.0
1942	48.5	—	—	—	—	—	—	—
1943	52.2	—	—	—	52.7	21.1	—	—
1944	53.2	—	—	—	53.8	21.5	—	—
1945	54.4	—	—	—	55.0	22.0	—	691.1
1946	58.3	—	—	—	59.5	23.8	—	521.6
1947	67.3	—	—	—	67.6	27.1	—	—
1948	70.9	—	—	—	67.1	26.9	—	—
1949	69.7	—	—	—	61.4	24.6	—	—
1950	66.9	—	—	—	60.3	24.1	—	—
1951	71.0	—	—	—	66.5	26.6	—	—
1952	73.1	—	—	—	70.1	28.1	—	—
1953	73.7	—	—	—	72.2	28.9	—	—
1954	74.4	—	—	—	74.2	29.7	—	—
1955	75.4	—	—	—	73.5	29.4	—	—
1956	76.4	—	—	—	74.4	29.8	—	—
1957	79.0	—	—	—	77.4	31.0	—	—
1958	82.8	—	—	—	79.3	31.7	—	—
1959	—	—	—	—	81.2	32.5	—	—
1960	—	—	—	—	83.4	33.4	—	—
1961	—	—	—	—	85.4	34.2	—	—
1962	—	—	—	—	86.9	34.8	—	—
1963	—	—	—	—	89.0	35.6	—	—
1964	—	—	—	—	91.0	36.4	—	—
1965	—	—	—	—	93.2	37.3	—	—
1966	—	—	—	—	96.0	38.4	—	—
1967	—	—	—	—	100.0	40.0	—	—
1968	—	—	—	—	102.8	41.2	—	—
1969	—	—	—	—	106.0	42.4	—	—
1970	—	—	—	—	109.6	43.9	—	—
1971	—	—	—	—	114.4	45.8	—	—
1972	—	—	101.3	—	117.9	47.2	—	—
1973	—	—	110.3	—	126.6	50.7	—	—
1974	—	105.0	127.0	—	151.7	60.7	—	—
1975	—	125.1	139.3	—	164.7	65.9	—	—
1976	—	125.9	142.7	—	168.0	67.3	—	—
1977	—	132.0	147.4	100.0	175.3	70.2	101.9	—
1978	—	139.5	100.0	—	183.9	73.6	109.6	—
1979	—	164.0	112.1	—	195.8	78.4	115.7	—
1980	—	191.7	134.0	—	216.2	85.6	—	—
1981	—	207.6	161.4	—	236.6	94.0	—	—
1982	—	220.0	169.7	—	244.3	97.5	100.0	—
1983	—	100.8	175.6	—	245.1	98.1	102.8	—
1984	—	102.7	190.9	—	249.8	100.0	108.2	—
1985	—	103.9	198.3	—	250.3	100.4	108.0	—
1986	—	107.1	205.5	—	249.1	100.2	112.5	—
1987	—	111.8	212.7	—	255.2	102.9	—	—
1988	—	119.8	223.8	179.5	262.2	105.9	—	—
1989	—	124.7	248.2	190.2	272.1	109.8	—	—

Notes appear at end of table

(continued)

TABLE Ef141–148   Consumer price indexes for outlying areas: 1935–1999 *Continued*

	Hawai'i	American Samoa	Guam	Northern Mariana Islands	Puerto Rico All families	Puerto Rico Wage earners' families	Marshall Islands	Philippines
	Ef141 [1]	Ef142 [2]	Ef143 [3]	Ef144 [4]	Ef145	Ef146	Ef147 [5]	Ef148 [6]
Year	Index 1967 = 100	Index	Index	Index 1977 = 100	Index 1967 = 100	Index 1984 = 100	Index	Index 1941 = 100
1990	—	134.0	283.5	199.3	286.6	116.1	—	—
1991	—	140.5	312.5	214.9	292.9	119.8	—	—
1992	—	146.1	344.2	232.8	299.9	123.3	—	—
1993	—	147.7	372.9	243.2	308.6	126.7	—	—
1994	—	150.9	436.0	250.0	322.5	131.2	—	—
1995	—	155.0	459.2	254.5	337.7	137.0	—	—
1996	—	161.7	99.6	261.9	356.1	144.5	—	—
1997	—	—	101.3	264.9	—	152.4	—	—
1998	—	—	100.8	—	—	160.5	—	—
1999	—	—	100.5	—	—	169.6	—	—

[1] Consumer price index for Honolulu.

[2] Price index changes: 1974–1982, March 1974 = 100; 1983–1996, November 1982 = 100.

[3] Price index changes: 1972–1977, third quarter 1972 = 100; 1978–1995, 1978 = 100; 1996–1999, third quarter 1996 = 100.

[4] Index is based on 1977 third quarter prices.

[5] Price index changes: 1977–1979, retail price index for Majuro, June 1978 = 100; 1982–1986, consumer price index for Majuro, fourth quarter 1982 = 100.

[6] Cost of living index for a family of 4.9 people. 1941 = 100.

Sources

Hawai'i. Robert C. Schmitt, *Historical Statistics of Hawaii* (University Press of Hawai'i, 1977), Table 5.1.

American Samoa. Economic Development and Planning Office, *American Samoa Statistical Digest 1996*, Table 11.2; *American Samoa Statistical Digest 1992*, Table 11.2; *American Samoa Statistical Digest 1987*, Table 11.4. Economic Development and Planning Office, *Statistical Bulletin 1983*, Table 28.

Guam. Guam Department of Commerce, *Guam Annual Economic Review 1979*, Table 41; *Guam Annual Economic Review 1985*, Table 43; *Guam Annual Economic Review 1994*, Table PR3; Guam Department of Commerce's Internet site for price index statistics.

Northern Mariana Islands. Department of Commerce, *1997 Commonwealth of the Northern Mariana Islands Statistical Yearbook*, Table 14.1.

Puerto Rico. Data supplied by the Government of Puerto Rico, Department of Labor and Human Resources.

Marshall Islands. Office of Planning and Statistics, *Marshall Islands Statistical Abstract, 1988/89*. U.S. Department of State, *Trust Territory of the Pacific, Annual Report 1980*, Table 15.a.

Philippines. Bureau of the Census and Statistics, Republic of the Philippines, *Yearbook of Philippine Statistics 1946* (Bureau of Printing, 1947).

Documentation

Series Ef145 is a consumer price index for all families, while series Ef146 is a consumer price index for families with at least one wage or salary earner.

GOVERNMENT

Sumner J. La Croix

TABLE Ef149–160 Government revenues and expenditures of outlying areas: 1898–1999
[Alaska, Hawai'i, American Samoa, Guam, Puerto Rico, and the Philippines]

Contributed by Sumner J. La Croix

	Alaska		Hawai'i		American Samoa		Guam		Puerto Rico		Philippines	
	Receipts	Disbursements	Receipts	Expenditures	Revenues	Expenditures	Revenues	Expenditures	Net revenues	Consolidated expenses	Revenues	Expenditures
	Ef149	Ef150	Ef151 [1]	Ef152 [2]	Ef153 [3,4]	Ef154 [3,5]	Ef155 [6,7]	Ef156 [7]	Ef157 [8]	Ef158 [9]	Ef159 [10]	Ef160 [11]
Year	Dollars	Dollars	Thousand dollars	Thousand dollars	Dollars	Dollars	Dollars	Dollars	Million dollars	Million dollars	Million pesos	Million pesos
1898	—	—	2,568 [12]	2,186 [12]	—	—	—	—	—	—	—	—
1899	—	—	3,345	2,394 [12]	—	—	—	—	—	—	—	—
1900	—	—	2,773	3,005 [12]	—	—	—	—	—	—	—	—
1901	—	—	2,140	2,577	—	—	53,357 [13]	41,772 [13]	—	—	21	12
1902	—	—	2,473	2,383	—	—	44,652 [13]	57,777 [13]	—	—	23	18
1903	—	—	2,388	2,603	—	—	—	—	—	—	26	25
1904	—	—	2,415	2,844	—	—	—	—	—	—	37	41
1905	—	—	2,355	2,241	—	—	—	—	—	—	40	40
1906	—	—	3,321	2,513	—	—	—	—	—	—	40	36
1907	—	—	2,717	2,666	—	—	—	—	—	—	39	37
1908	—	—	2,552	2,698	—	—	—	—	—	—	43	40
1909	—	—	2,938	2,820	—	—	—	—	—	—	47	49
1910	—	—	2,975	2,558	—	—	45,945	50,247	—	—	54	52
1911	—	—	2,822	2,861	—	—	48,422	34,222	—	—	63	59
1912	—	—	3,964	4,002	—	—	44,223	40,805	—	—	68	65
1913	—	—	4,301	4,261	—	—	45,865	46,600	—	—	66	69
1914			3,925	4,264	—	—	67,166	49,483	—	—	59	62
1915	—	—	4,539	4,446	—	—	76,728	72,162	—	—	81	78
1916	—	—	5,627	5,554	—	—	91,816	87,059	—	—	85	80
1917	—	—	5,945	5,638	—	—	94,183	94,630	—	—	93	80
1918	—	—	7,208	7,441	—	—	109,528	110,360	—	—	109	103
1919	—	—	4,121	4,307	—	—	128,814	131,346	—	—	125	135
1920	—	—	6,696	6,129	—	—	155,209	137,206	—	—	148	134
1921	—	—	6,789	8,054	—	—	112,852	66,278	—	—	111	118
1922	—	—	7,151	7,487	—	—	104,179	74,863	—	—	61	76
1923	—	—	6,952	8,901	—	—	106,719	106,874	—	—	67	68
1924	—	—	8,048	8,859	—	—	137,805	152,781	—	—	76	67
1925	—	—	9,106	10,260	—	—	149,748	153,737	—	—	83	69
1926	—	—	9,553	10,126	—	—	154,514	149,156	—	—	80	76
1927	—	—	10,291	11,990	—	—	154,163	123,483	—	—	80	78
1928	—	—	11,706	12,479	—	—	168,773	149,592	—	—	88	84
1929	1,287,284	1,224,413	12,478	12,266	—	—	167,776	155,703	—	—	94	84
1930	1,153,238	1,282,605	12,609	13,367	—	—	193,696	165,443	—	—	69	79
1931	904,169	1,196,731	13,638	13,292	—	—	197,344	194,577	—	—	60	66
1932	994,530	1,022,017	13,235	13,279	—	—	170,850	145,445	—	—	75	80
1933	1,151,175	1,041,083	11,083	11,579	—	—	168,833	154,798	—	—	70	70
1934	1,935,184	1,800,310	10,936	10,832	—	—	170,920	159,381	—	—	79	71
1935	2,088,415	1,907,257	13,129	11,715	—	—	186,563	161,258	—	—	83 [12]	76 [12]
1936	2,351,175	2,580,315	15,987	12,534	—	—	188,623	163,413	—	—	104 [12]	92 [12]
1937	2,710,973	2,503,216	17,617	14,953	—	—	311,073	289,588	—	—	231 [12]	114 [12]
1938	2,986,786	2,726,289	20,944	16,903	—	—	283,297	268,160	—	—	131 [12]	139 [12]
1939	2,986,786	2,726,289	20,791	19,877	—	—	274,004	257,911	—	—	158	184
1940	2,845,454	3,065,881	22,518	18,869	—	—	283,619	259,626	18.2	15.4	159	168
1941	3,739,191	3,758,439	23,632	18,000	—	—	328,718	318,600	25.3	21.7	—	—
1942	3,797,863	3,648,433	26,413	19,235	—	—	—	—	42.0	27.5	—	—
1943	2,773,608	2,737,055	35,477	20,936	—	—	—	—	47.1	43.2	—	—
1944	3,142,045	2,735,579	40,240	25,339	—	—	—	—	108.3	50.7	—	—
1945	2,969,042	3,314,233	42,584	28,455	—	—	—	—	84.2	61.7	127	213
1946	3,512,533	3,999,008	45,454	34,595	—	—	—	—	129.1	108.1	264	381
1947	6,828,337	7,175,463	48,535	41,034	—	—	—	—	83.0	116.9	—	—
1948	8,835,283	8,230,729	61,057	53,815	—	—	—	—	91.1	95.3	—	—
1949	8,765,805	8,922,673	68,991	66,885	—	—	—	—	83.4	76.2	—	—

Notes appear at end of table

(continued)

TABLE Ef149–160   Government revenues and expenditures of outlying areas: 1898–1999
[Alaska, Hawai'i, American Samoa, Guam, Puerto Rico, and the Philippines]   *Continued*

	Alaska		Hawai'i		American Samoa		Guam		Puerto Rico		Philippines	
	Receipts	Disbursements	Receipts	Expenditures	Revenues	Expenditures	Revenues	Expenditures	Net revenues	Consolidated expenses	Revenues	Expenditures
	Ef149	Ef150	Ef151 [1]	Ef152 [2]	Ef153 [3,4]	Ef154 [3,5]	Ef155 [6,7]	Ef156 [7]	Ef157 [8]	Ef158 [9]	Ef159 [10]	Ef160 [11]
Year	Dollars	Dollars	Thousand dollars	Thousand dollars	Dollars	Dollars	Dollars	Dollars	Million dollars	Million dollars	Million pesos	Million pesos
1950	15,108,415	13,204,620	70,335	78,287	—	—	—	—	114.5	113.7	—	—
1951	18,009,456	16,154,161	75,140	79,187	—	—	4,168,867	5,144,405	157.3	118.7	—	—
1952	24,996,111	20,769,638	74,045	75,272	119,174	1,324,327	9,492,600	7,735,600	180.7	149.6	—	—
1953	24,159,240	21,153,351	79,776	81,855	453,632	1,704,502	9,996,700	9,571,700	204.9	174.7	—	—
1954	26,302,545	26,769,488	84,995	89,054	—	—	11,801,400	10,957,600	196.2	169.9	—	—
1955	26,210,442	28,484,917	85,183	92,257	591,362	1,565,101	10,189,700	9,872,600	214.4	179.5	—	—
1956	31,948,530	30,047,461	92,386	94,668	670,206	1,579,043	10,575,090	—	198.7	193.1	—	—
1957	47,122,153	44,976,733	100,388	102,278	792,904	1,709,543	10,016,505	11,306,736	240.5	230.4	—	—
1958	—	—	119,235	110,748	767,002	1,721,279	12,504,886	12,728,532	253.2	245.5	—	—
1959	—	—	—	—	911,818	1,750,528	13,751,727	13,097,644	272.0	269.8	—	—
1960	—	—	—	—	1,003,923	1,891,071	16,151,174	14,152,414	296.4	278.6	—	—
1961	—	—	—	—	1,068,415	2,059,474	15,820,000	15,530,000	339.6	313.2	—	—
1962	—	—	—	—	1,321,336	3,312,040	13,500,000	14,550,000	322.6	317.4	—	—
1963	—	—	—	—	1,685,209	—	15,250,000	17,230,000	382.4	379.1	—	—
1964	—	—	—	—	2,478,330	—	17,340,000	17,130,000	468.9	449.3	—	—
1965	—	—	—	—	2,416,000	—	18,530,000	18,910,000	534.3	525.9	—	—
1966	—	—	—	—	3,563,000	—	20,810,000	20,480,000	560.0	549.5	—	—
1967	—	—	—	—	—	—	28,620,000	22,720,000	712.0	685.3	—	—
1968	—	—	—	—	—	—	37,140,000	33,010,000	745.4	723.8	—	—
1969	—	—	—	—	—	—	47,210,000	37,420,000	865.9	814.1	—	—
1970	—	—	—	—	—	—	57,690,000	48,940,000	1,029.9	970.0	—	—
1971	—	—	—	—	18,896,000	—	59,633,999	65,207,045	1,172.5	1,103.8	—	—
1972	—	—	—	—	26,052,000	—	65,416,753	71,926,611	1,331.1	1,246.6	—	—
1973	—	—	—	—	33,921,000	—	86,034,571	80,135,011	1,572.9	1,543.5	—	—
1974	—	—	—	—	43,672,000	—	100,957,366	91,242,491	1,639.6	1,623.1	—	—
1975	—	—	—	—	37,566,000	—	102,467,000	118,581,380	1,969.2	1,983.4	—	—
1976	—	—	—	—	55,809,000	—	84,292,000	—	2,112.0	1,980.7	—	—
1977	—	—	—	—	62,381,000	—	—	—	2,134.9	2,080.7	—	—
1978	—	—	—	—	48,750,000	—	—	—	5,434.3	5,306.4	—	—
1979	—	—	—	—	65,919,500	—	—	—	5,629.7	5,574.5	—	—
1980	—	—	—	—	60,618,500	—	—	—	6,282.9	6,243.6	—	—
1981	—	—	—	—	72,515,900	—	—	—	7,355.3	6,728.5	—	—
1982	—	—	—	—	75,096,000	—	—	—	7,079.6	6,481.0	—	—
1983	—	—	—	—	90,532,956	—	—	—	7,234.9	6,597.3	—	—
1984	—	—	—	—	76,566,083	—	—	—	7,586.9	7,027.0	—	—
1985	—	—	—	—	88,345,000	90,024,000	—	—	8,444.5	8,346.2	—	—
1986	—	—	—	—	87,463,000	92,635,000	—	—	9,295.2	8,914.2	—	—
1987	—	—	—	—	108,835,000	102,622,000	—	—	9,089.7	8,924.8	—	—
1988	—	—	—	—	90,320,000	93,157,000	287,202,236	193,281,860	10,525.7	10,115.4	—	—
1989	—	—	—	—	88,456,000	97,533,000	372,405,747	202,298,083	10,832.3	10,594.5	—	—
1990	—	—	—	—	128,094,000	127,312,000	458,000,000	418,700,000	11,262.0	10,909.0	—	—
1991	—	—	—	—	103,503,000	108,555,000	539,100,000	604,900,000	11,985.2	11,460.2	—	—
1992	—	—	—	—	146,387,000	165,951,000	562,300,000	595,200,000	12,009.7	12,848.0	—	—
1993	—	—	—	—	94,083,000	97,286,000	562,400,000	659,500,000	14,431.1	13,532.8	—	—
1994	—	—	—	—	106,253,000	114,216,000	575,100,000	616,800,000	14,294.9	13,424.1	—	—
1995	—	—	—	—	111,311,000	114,635,000	679,400,000	576,200,000	15,640.8	15,161.8	—	—
1996	—	—	—	—	119,949,000	126,559,000	591,700,000	542,600,000	16,913.3	16,385.2	—	—
1997	—	—	—	—	—	—	583,700,000	549,900,000	18,100.4	17,610.5	—	—
1998	—	—	—	—	—	—	592,300,000	554,000,000	18,835.7	18,395.6	—	—
1999	—	—	—	—	—	—	—	—	19,715.2	19,154.2	—	—

[1] 1898–1900, current receipts, exclusive of postal savings bank and loan fund receipts; 1899, 1921–1925, territorial revenues from all funds; 1900–1920, 1926–1951, territorial revenue receipts; 1952–1958, territorial receipts from general and special funds.

[2] 1898–1900, current expenditures, excluding debt redemption; 1901–1925, total disbursements from all funds; 1926–1951, government cost payments; 1952–1958, territorial operating expenditures.

[3] Fiscal year ending September 30.

[4] Beginning 1987, revenues for all governmental funds.

[5] Beginning 1987, functional expenditures for all governmental funds.

[6] Through 1941, territorial revenue receipts.

[7] Beginning 1988, fiscal year ending September 30.

[8] Beginning 1978, includes revenues of public corporations.

[9] Beginning 1978, includes expenses of public corporations.

[10] Through 1920, revenues of provincial governments and central government.

[11] Through 1920, expenditures of provincial governments and central government.

[12] Calendar year.

[13] Mexican dollars.

TABLE Ef149–160   Government revenues and expenditures of outlying areas: 1898–1999
[Alaska, Hawai'i, American Samoa, Guam, Puerto Rico, and the Philippines]   *Continued*

Sources

Alaska. Governor of Alaska, *Annual Report to the Secretary of the Interior*, various issues.

Hawai'i. Robert C. Schmitt, *Historical Statistics of Hawaii* (University Press of Hawai'i, 1977), Table 25.3.

American Samoa. Governor of American Samoa, *Annual Report to the Secretary of the Interior*, various issues. Economic Development and Planning Office, *Statistical Bulletin 1984*, Table 12; *American Samoa Statistical Digest 1986*, Tables 28 and 29; *American Samoa Statistical Digest 1992*, Tables 9.2 and 9.3; *American Samoa Statistical Digest 1996*, Tables 9.5 and 9.6. American Samoa Government, *Comprehensive Annual Financial Report for the Fiscal Year Ended September 30, 1989.*

Guam. Governor of Guam, *Annual Report to the Secretary of the Interior*, various issues. Department of Commerce, Government of Guam, *Guam 1970: An Economy in Transition*, p. 43. Governor of Guam, *Annual Report to the Secretary of the Interior*, various issues. Department of Commerce, *Guam 1973: Facing the*

Issues, Tables VII-2, VII-3. Department of Commerce, *Guam Annual Economic Review 1974*, Table 13; *Guam Annual Economic Review 1976*, Tables IV and V; *Annual Economic Review and Statistical Abstract 1987*, Table 1; *1990 Guam Annual Economic Review*, Table 55. Government of Guam, Internet site, Department of Commerce, Guam Economic Overview, Table GG7.

Puerto Rico. Data from 1910–1939 from Governor of Puerto Rico, *Annual Report to the Secretary of the Interior*, various issues. Data from 1940–1999 supplied by the Office of Management and Budget, Government of Puerto Rico.

Philippines. B. R. Mitchell, *International Historical Statistics: Africa, Asia and Oceania, 1750–1993* (Stockton Press, 1995), Tables G5 and G6.

Documentation

Data are for fiscal year ending June 30, except where otherwise indicated.

Data are for territorial governments for Alaska, Hawai'i, and Samoa; territorial government general fund for Guam; Commonwealth government for Puerto Rico; and the central government for the Philippines.

TABLE Ef161–172 Government revenues and expenditures of outlying areas: 1940–1998 [Northern Mariana Islands, Virgin Islands, Federated States of Micronesia, Marshall Islands, Palau, and Trust Territory of the Pacific]

Contributed by Sumner J. La Croix

	Northern Mariana Islands		Virgin Islands		Federated States of Micronesia		Marshall Islands		Palau		Trust Territory of the Pacific	
Fiscal year	Revenues Ef161[1]	Expenditures Ef162[1]	Net revenues Ef163	Expenditures Ef164	Revenues Ef165[2]	Expenditures Ef166[2]	Revenues Ef167[3]	Expenditures Ef168[4]	Revenues Ef169[5]	Expenditures Ef170[6]	Local revenues Ef171	Obligations Ef172
	Dollars	Dollars	Dollars	Dollars	Dollars	Dollars	Dollars	Dollars	Dollars	Dollars	Dollars	Dollars
1940	—	—	408,861	547,239	—	—	—	—	—	—	—	—
1948	—	—	—	—	—	—	—	—	—	—	162,574	950,137
1949	—	—	—	—	—	—	—	—	—	—	367,952	1,384,455
1950	—	—	—	—	—	—	—	—	—	—	336,728	1,242,083
1951	—	—	—	—	—	—	—	—	—	—	346,327	7,557,109
1952	—	—	2,313,543	—	—	—	—	—	—	—	1,717,836	5,504,663
1953	—	—	2,692,278	—	—	—	—	—	—	—	1,523,002	7,554,520
1954	—	—	3,157,429	—	—	—	—	—	—	—	1,764,672	6,982,396
1955	75,097	74,979	6,678,196	—	47,476	33,913	19,564	15,119	35,861	33,496	1,615,378	7,073,420
1956	184,588	173,051	—	—	62,489	45,376	21,369	12,278	35,565	32,040	1,724,797	7,695,153
1957	185,636	174,427	7,628,751	4,738,210	77,764	48,495	24,151	16,628	56,763	46,453	1,845,647	7,355,492
1958	197,872	220,772	9,219,712	6,299,167	107,815	71,652	25,492	21,118	65,258	51,745	1,620,305	7,701,594
1959	219,349	218,232	—	7,977,214	145,218	126,473	34,608	50,630	64,229	54,119	1,298,138	8,169,303
1960	236,939	235,222	12,280,931	10,000,108	153,370	115,889	72,953	39,010	69,448	55,797	1,407,148	8,224,897
1961	240,536	247,426	15,478,235	13,154,996	194,917	142,043	67,712	62,748	70,041	63,541	1,296,956	7,430,324
1962	318,628	314,021	17,443,685	14,891,083	216,364	148,555	149,654	95,770	70,083	55,907	1,673,633	7,954,356
1963	295,981	265,501	19,948,780	18,463,562	236,438	168,130	182,866	143,430	83,541	74,094	1,744,888	16,744,888
1964	332,926	302,375	24,803,519	22,590,852	347,336	238,607	211,449	168,397	88,372	86,573	799,206	22,078,769
1965	281,987	232,632	28,935,903	27,723,949	365,835	169,274	180,189	104,419	63,379	45,774	2,053,473	23,507,736
1966	291,168	203,418	—	—	419,877	233,163	188,669	154,271	69,886	54,478	1,090,104	23,755,638
1967	191,371	190,315	61,504,681	61,197,859	467,993	311,626	187,078	139,653	88,430	70,658	1,090,877	26,436,205
1968	217,231	134,177	71,894,766	80,856,031	547,582	380,284	191,406	143,675	108,864	86,600	1,442,459	37,997,947
1969	329,251	270,504	—	—	680,061	570,805	289,421	196,206	156,370	144,619	1,298,114	41,252,410
1970	433,334	275,807	64,000,000	64,856,000	765,117	678,691	410,017	305,707	218,820	212,640	1,434,800	52,894,456
1971	596,205	528,542	—	—	1,050,377	928,219	621,268	422,766	247,830	225,344	1,489,384	62,916,093
1972	545,860	532,383	—	—	1,049,201	923,963	740,842	575,450	322,371	290,714	4,085,404	73,569,796
1973	383,147	313,773	—	—	1,129,285	1,094,364	570,196	565,283	333,849	304,319	5,702,183	79,605,496
1974	772,207	745,222	—	—	1,052,403	1,002,493	632,395	590,746	355,762	347,088	—	—
1975	—	—	—	122,123,000	1,434,354	1,277,683	669,058	663,127	333,825	331,050	—	—
1976	1,115,613	437,237	—	120,681,000	1,843,389	1,679,080	80,994	80,994	463,703	392,992	—	—
1977	—	—	—	128,974,000	2,662,276	2,562,619	1,398,989	1,277,989	575,031	550,823	—	—
1978	14,900,000	14,900,000	—	110,117,000	—	—	—	—	—	—	—	—
1979	19,400,000	19,300,000	—	174,224,000	—	—	4,033,800	8,731,000	2,075,300	—	—	—
1980	23,200,000	23,000,000	144,600,000	174,076,000	—	—	20,822,000	24,665,000	—	—	—	—
1981	25,200,000	25,800,000	176,900,000	223,800,000	—	—	23,004,000	24,677,000	3,575,300	18,617,000	—	—
1982	29,400,000	29,800,000	182,200,000	226,400,000	—	—	25,838,000	25,220,000	3,535,100	20,459,000	—	—
1983	37,600,000	38,000,000	190,100,000	252,400,000	—	—	24,477,000	23,621,000	4,028,300	23,670,000	—	—
1984	40,700,000	44,700,000	200,300,000	267,700,000	—	—	28,639,000	22,233,000	3,749,500	23,177,000	—	—

Fiscal year	Northern Mariana Islands		Virgin Islands		Federated States of Micronesia		Marshall Islands		Palau		Trust Territory of the Pacific	
	Revenues	Expenditures	Net revenues	Expenditures	Revenues	Expenditures	Revenues	Expenditures	Revenues	Expenditures	Local revenues	Obligations
	Ef161 [1]	Ef162 [1]	Ef163	Ef164	Ef165 [2]	Ef166 [2]	Ef167 [3]	Ef168 [4]	Ef169 [5]	Ef170 [6]	Ef171	Ef172
	Dollars	Dollars	Dollars	Dollars	Dollars	Dollars	Dollars	Dollars	Dollars	Dollars	Dollars	Dollars
1985	49,300,000	51,000,000	211,700,000	263,300,000	—	—	33,617,000	24,460,000	5,591,400	24,254,000	—	—
1986	61,000,000	58,500,000	239,000,000	260,300,000	—	—	28,691,000 [7]	25,687,000 [7]	—	—	—	—
1987	69,800,000	68,500,000	312,500,000	306,400,000	—	—	—	—	—	—	—	—
1988	87,301,000	73,368,000	278,000,000	321,000,000	—	—	—	—	—	—	—	—
1989	96,750,000	81,217,000	316,000,000	359,600,000	—	—	—	—	—	—	—	—
1990	116,749,000	108,632,000	327,700,000	381,400,000	—	—	—	—	10,620,000	25,308,000	—	—
1991	151,019,000	156,319,000	327,500,000	443,100,000	—	—	—	—	12,808,000	26,689,000	—	—
1992	159,479,000	156,939,000	344,500,000	447,300,000	—	—	—	—	15,187,000	27,297,000	—	—
1993	138,649,000	154,063,000	375,800,000	414,000,000	—	—	—	—	17,040,000	—	—	—
1994	152,962,000	181,501,000	343,200,000	422,500,000	—	—	—	—	—	—	—	—
1995	203,650,000	191,446,000	332,300,000	475,000,000	—	—	—	—	—	—	—	—
1996	226,701,000	221,715,000	335,800,000	490,300,000	—	—	—	—	—	—	—	—
1997	248,036,000	268,122,000	374,400,000	459,500,000	—	—	—	—	—	—	—	—
1998	233,684,000	244,502,000	460,200,000	560,200,000	—	—	—	—	—	—	—	—

[1] Through 1976, district and municipal governments only; thereafter, total for commonwealth government.

[2] District and municipal governments only.

[3] Through 1977, district and municipal governments only; thereafter, recurrent government revenues.

[4] Through 1977, district and municipal governments only; thereafter, recurrent government expenditures.

[5] Through 1977, district and municipal governments; thereafter, locally generated revenues.

[6] Through 1977, district and municipal governments; thereafter, recurrent expenditures/obligations of the national government.

[7] Nine months.

Sources

Northern Mariana Islands. U.S. State Department, *Annual Report to the United Nations on the Administration of the Trust Territory of the Pacific Islands*, various issues. Office of Planning and Budget, Executive Office of the Governor, Commonwealth of the Northern Mariana Islands (CNMI), *Economic Development Strategy: A Prospectus for Guiding Growth*, 2nd revised edition (1993), pp. 155, 157. Data for 1988–1998 supplied by CNMI Department of Finance.

Virgin Islands. Governor of the Virgin Islands, *Annual Report to the Secretary of the Interior*, various issues. Bureau of Economic Research, Virgin Islands Government Development Bank, *U.S. Virgin Islands Annual Economic Indicators*, various issues.

Federated States of Micronesia. U.S. State Department, *Annual Report to the United Nations on the Administration of the Trust Territory of the Pacific Islands*, various issues.

Marshall Islands. U.S. State Department, *Annual Report to the United Nations on the Administration of the Trust Territory of the Pacific Islands*, various issues. Republic of the Marshall Islands, Office of Planning and Statistics, *Marshall Islands Statistical Abstract 1988/89*, Tables 5.1, 5.2, 5.5, 5.6, and 5.7.

Palau. U.S. State Department, *Annual Report to the United Nations on the Administration of the Trust Territory of the Pacific Islands*, various issues. Data from 1981 to 1993 supplied by Palau Office of Planning and Statistics.

Trust Territory of the Pacific. U.S. State Department, *Annual Report to the United Nations on the Administration of the Trust Territory of the Pacific Islands*, various issues.

Documentation

Data are for fiscal year ending June 30.

Series Ef161–162. Northern Mariana Islands Commonwealth Government.

Series Ef163–164. Virgin Islands General Fund.

CHAPTER Eg
Colonial Statistics

Editor: John J. McCusker

COLONIAL STATISTICS

John J. McCusker

This chapter tells a story in numbers. The data in the tables that follow were derived from and depict a polity, society, and economy that functioned well enough over the period from the early seventeenth century to nearly the end of the eighteenth century that its economy grew at the fastest rate of all known contemporary economies and that, by the end of that period, afforded its citizens on average the highest standard of living in the world. It is a story of success – a successful establishment of a new nation, a new life by European settlers on the eastern fringe of the continent of North America, and a new economy that was strong and grew stronger over time. What unfolds here is the first half of the history of a country that in the following two centuries went on to become the nation it is today, the United States of America.[1]

Yet all was not perfect. The history of the Thirteen Continental Colonies and the early United States partly recounted by the data presented here is not one of continuing, unmitigated triumphs. Even though polity, society, and economy surely progressed over these two centuries, they did so only very slowly, very haltingly.

Government had its flaws and failings – and then there was a revolution. Periods of advance in the economy alternated with periods of decline. Among the settlers of European origin, some fared better, some worse, and some not at all. The European Americans who prospered most did so at the expense, economically and humanly, of their African brothers and sisters whom they kidnapped, enslaved, denigrated, and exploited. Nevertheless, for most inhabitants of the Thirteen Continental Colonies, life was better there than it was elsewhere, better later than it was earlier, and as full of promise for them then as it is for Americans today. Three and four centuries ago, the Thirteen Continental Colonies were, just as the modern United States is now, the land of hope, a magnet attracting immigrants. The tale told in this chapter's tables is one of good people struggling, achieving some success, and making

---

[1] For much that follows, there is a fuller exposition of the basic elements in McCusker and Menard (1991). References found there are generally not repeated here. See also the papers presented at the conference on "The Economy of Early British America: The Domestic Sector" held at the Huntington Library, San Marino, California, in October 1995 and published as a special issue of the *William and Mary Quarterly*, 3rd series, 56 (January 1999), and McCusker (2001b) and Menard (2001).

Acknowledgments

John McCusker thanks all who responded with advice and data as this chapter developed. He undertook this task while serving as a member of and, later, as the chair of the Standing Committee for Research, Archives and Data Bases of the Economic History Association. The support of other members of the committee was critical to the success of this effort. He is particularly grateful to the two authors of the earlier versions of this chapter in previous editions of *Historical Statistics of the United States*, Lawrence A. Harper and Jacob M. Price. In addition, he wishes to thank the following individuals: Dauril Alden, Bernard Bailyn, Robert A. Becker, Stephen D. Behrendt, Ira Berlin, Richard Buel Jr., Trevor G. Burnard, Lois Green Carr, Cary Carson, Joyce E. Chaplin, Paul G. E. Clemens, Converse D. Clowse, Peter A. Coclanis, Nicholas F. R. Crafts, François M. Crouzet, Louis Cullen, Paul A. David, K. G. Davies, Lance E. Davis, Thomas M. Doerflinger, Carville V. Earle, Christopher R. Eck, Marc M. Egnal, David Eltis, Stanley L. Engerman, Joseph A. Ernst, Robert William Fogel, David W. Galenson, Robert E. Gallman, Henry A. Gemery, Jack P. Greene, Farley Grubb, Michael R. Haines, Gewndolyn Midlo Hall, David J. Hancock, Stephen G. Hardy, Charles Knick. Harley, Lawrence A. Harper, P. M. G. Harris, William J. Hausman, John M. Hemphill, II, Ruth Wallis Herndon, Barry W. Higman, Ronald Hoffman, Stephen Innes, Michael J. Jarvis, Rupert C. Jarvis, Alice Hanson Jones, Dwyryd W. Jones, Laura Croghan Kamoie, John Komlos, Allan L. Kulikoff, William Letwin, Gloria L. Main, Jackson T. Main, Peter C. Mancall, Peter Mathias, Cathy D. Matson, Russell R. Menard, Ronald W. Michener, Annie M. Millard, Alexander Moore, Kenneth J. Morgan, Philip D. Morgan, Gary B. Nash, Robert C. Nash, Margaret Ellen Newell, Eric P. Newman, Douglass C. North, Patrick K. O'Brien, Paul F. Paskoff, Edwin J. Perkins, Jacob M. Price, David Richardson, James C. Riley, Donna J. Rilling, Joshua L. Rosenbloom, Winifred B. Rothenberg, Peter L. Rousseau, Jean Elliott Russo, Anita H. Rutman, Darrett B. Rutman, Neal Salisbury, Jürgen Schneider, Stuart Schwartz, Mary McKinney Schweitzer, Carole Shammas, James F. Shepherd, Billy G. Smith, Bruce Smith, Daniel S. Smith, Simon D. Smith, T. C. Smout, Richard H. Steckel, Richard Sutch, Richard E. Sylla, Thomas M. Truxes, Daniel F. Vickers, , John Joseph Wallis, Lorena S. Walsh, Gary M. Walton, Thomas J. Weiss, Elmus Wicker, Robert E. Wright, and Nuala B. Zahedieh.

McCusker is also very grateful for all of the financial and institutional support he has received: Trinity University; Mr. Gilbert M. Denman Jr. and the Ewing Halsell Foundation, Mr. and Mrs. A. Baker Duncan, and Mr. and Mrs. A. Randy Townsend for research support; the University of Cambridge for an appointment as a Visiting Senior Mellon Scholar in American History; the Institute of United States Studies, University of London, for a John Adams Fellowship; the British Library for a fellowship at the Eccles Centre for American Studies; the Leverhulme Trust of Great Britain for an appointment as a Leverhulme Trust Visiting Fellow at the University of Cambridge; Girton College, University of Cambridge, for a Helen Cam Fellowship; the Fulbright Foundation for an appointment as a Fulbright Senior Scholar to Great Britain; the Rockefeller Center, Bellagio, Italy, for a period as a Scholar in Residence; the Bibliographical Society of America and the Bibliographical Society of Great Britain for a Fredson Bowers Grant; the Bibliographical Society of America for a Reese Fellowship; the American Philosophical Society for a Franklin Research Grant; the Royal Flemish Academy of Belgium for Science and the Arts, Brussels, for the offer of a fellowship.

some mistakes to fashion out of their constrained circumstances lives of dignity and worth for themselves and their progeny.[2]

Contemporary observers and modern scholars almost universally concur that those who inhabited early British America benefited from the efforts of their predecessors. In each successive age, their lives were better in almost every way than the lives of those who preceded them. Such blanket pronouncements beg for definition, for nuance, for explanation, but the general proposition holds nonetheless: The generation that joined the American Revolution was considerably better off than the generation that had established the colonies of Virginia and Massachusetts. The data in the tables that follow this introductory summary support these propositions, but such notions gain from confirmation from other sources, additional evidence that rests less on "hard" data and more on anecdote and inference. Much more so than the second half of the history of the United States, the history of the first two centuries of the nation is in the hands of those who, like historians of medieval Europe, work with insight and imagination as well as documents and data. As Jacob Price (1976, p. 701) reminds us: "Little quantitative evidence from the seventeenth or eighteenth century comes down to us in the form we would wish. We must, for all that, build our historical edifices with the bricks at hand."

The people about whom all of our evidence speaks were residents of the Thirteen Continental Colonies, entities that shared many important similarities and a common destiny. For the most part, the settlers came from Great Britain, although they included a significant sprinkling of others from Northern and Western Europe.[3] All quickly took on the garb and gait of English women and men. Thus, the English language, law, religion, fashions, and manners, as well as English attitudes early and rapidly became the norm, even as everything began to take on a certain local, American flavor. The largest exception to this rule was found among those of African origin, although they, too, educated themselves in the ways of their masters, sometimes all too smartly for the taste of those who believed they controlled them body and soul. Sharing a thin but rapidly expanding sliver of settlement in the Atlantic coastal plain of the middle portion of the continent of North America, the colonists cherished their common characteristics even as they differentiated themselves from others in the neighboring colonies – and, to a much larger extent, from others on the continent immediately to their north, south, and west (see Map Eg-A).[4] They were English – not French, not Spanish, certainly not Native American – just as those people knew they were not English and did not want to be. This was especially the case for the Native Americans who were forced by the ever-advancing march of colonial expansion to keep moving westward and die.[5]

The polities, societies, and economies created in each of the Thirteen Continental Colonies that later became the United States of America were founded in ideas and attitudes that tied them together much more than separated them. The residents of Massachusetts and Virginia may have wished to maintain their distance, even their distinctiveness, from each other, but they quickly identified their considerable strength in a recognizable commonality that in time of severe trial coalesced into a political unity. Their mutual ideas and attitudes, having in fact given rise to remarkably similar governments, economies, and societies, allowed them to create a new nation based on those commonly shared notions. The collective threads that helped bind these people together aid historians who seek to explain aspects of their economic and social history. However many individual parts there may have been, even in the colonial period, they can be treated in many ways as one society, one economy. E pluribus unum is not a hollow motto.

None of this denies the differences among them any more than the history of the United States after the American Revolution is diminished by attention to the parts as well as to the whole. Historians have regularly and profitably talked about regional differences that separate out New England, the Middle Colonies, the Upper South, and the Lower South based on political groupings and geographical borders. By the end of the colonial period, the colonists themselves were well aware of a division within most colonies between the coastal plain and the piedmont or "back country," marked in each of them by where eastward running rivers broke over rapids and waterfalls as they tumbled down to the plain and ran to the sea. This "fall line," above which seagoing vessels could not sail, also

---

[2] One is reminded of the words of Karl Marx (1869, p. 1): "Die Menschen machen ihre eigene Geschichte, aber sie machen sie nicht aus freien Stücken, nicht unter selbstgewählten, sondern unter unmittelbar vorgefundenen, gegebenen und überlieferten Umständen" – "Humans make their own histories, yet they do not choose freely, entirely on their own, but constrained by circumstances that are powerfully determining, pervasive, and freighted with tradition" [translation by the author].

The history of colonies advancing from strength to strength is contrary to an older, now discarded account of a people held under constant check by a British government intent on holding them subservient for its own purposes. The latter recounted a teleological saga of a repressed people who struggled against all odds from their earliest days of settlement to overcome a politically and economically tyrannical and usurping mother country, a struggle for freedom at its most thrilling, a triumph of good over evil. The best exemplar of this outmoded version of U.S. history is Bancroft (1876).

[3] Writing in the pre–Revolutionary War period, Crèvecœur remarked on the fusion in the colonies of diverse European national groups into the American type: "I could point out to you a family whose grandfather was an Englishman, whose wife was Dutch, whose son married a French woman, and whose present four sons have now four wives of different nations. He is an American." St. John [de Crèvecœur] (1782), p. 51 (emphasis as in the original); compare p. 48. For the composition of the population of the United States in 1790, see Table Eg65–84.

[4] Accurate comparisons with other times and places require careful definitions of the limits of one's study. For present purposes, the unit of analysis over the period before 1775 is "the colonies that became the United States" and, after 1775, those United States. Gallman (1999), pp. 23–4 (quotation on p. 24). Compare Engerman and Gallman (1983). Note especially Gallman's reference to Kuznets (1951), which establishes the absolute necessity of such distinctions. Compare, generally, the principles set out in Kuznets (1953). Allen (2003) is a recent and persuasive demonstration of the value for comparative analysis within countries and among countries over time of the nation as a unit of analysis.

[5] As has just been said, this chapter focuses on the Thirteen Continental Colonies, "the colonies that became the United States." Limiting this chapter to the Thirteen Continental Colonies in no way suggests that other peoples or other places are not worthy of study. There can be no argument that the economies of the Native American Indians deserve careful analysis. Such a study is simply not part of a discussion of the economy of the Thirteen Continental Colonies because the Native American Indians were not part of the Thirteen Continental Colonies – and clearly did not want to be. Anyone interested in pursuing the subject must begin with Salisbury's superb essay (1996). Other recent works of particular interest to economic historians include Murphy (1999). See the very positive comments on this work by Weiss (1999). An example of a very insightful approach that offers an explanation of American Indian economic behavior carefully grounded in the context of Indian institutions is Mann (1999). By contrast, see Mancall, Rosenbloom, and Weiss (2002). They equate "British North America" with the entirety of the eastern half of the Continent from New Orleans to Newfoundland, and include in their study all Indians living in that territory, all lumped together.

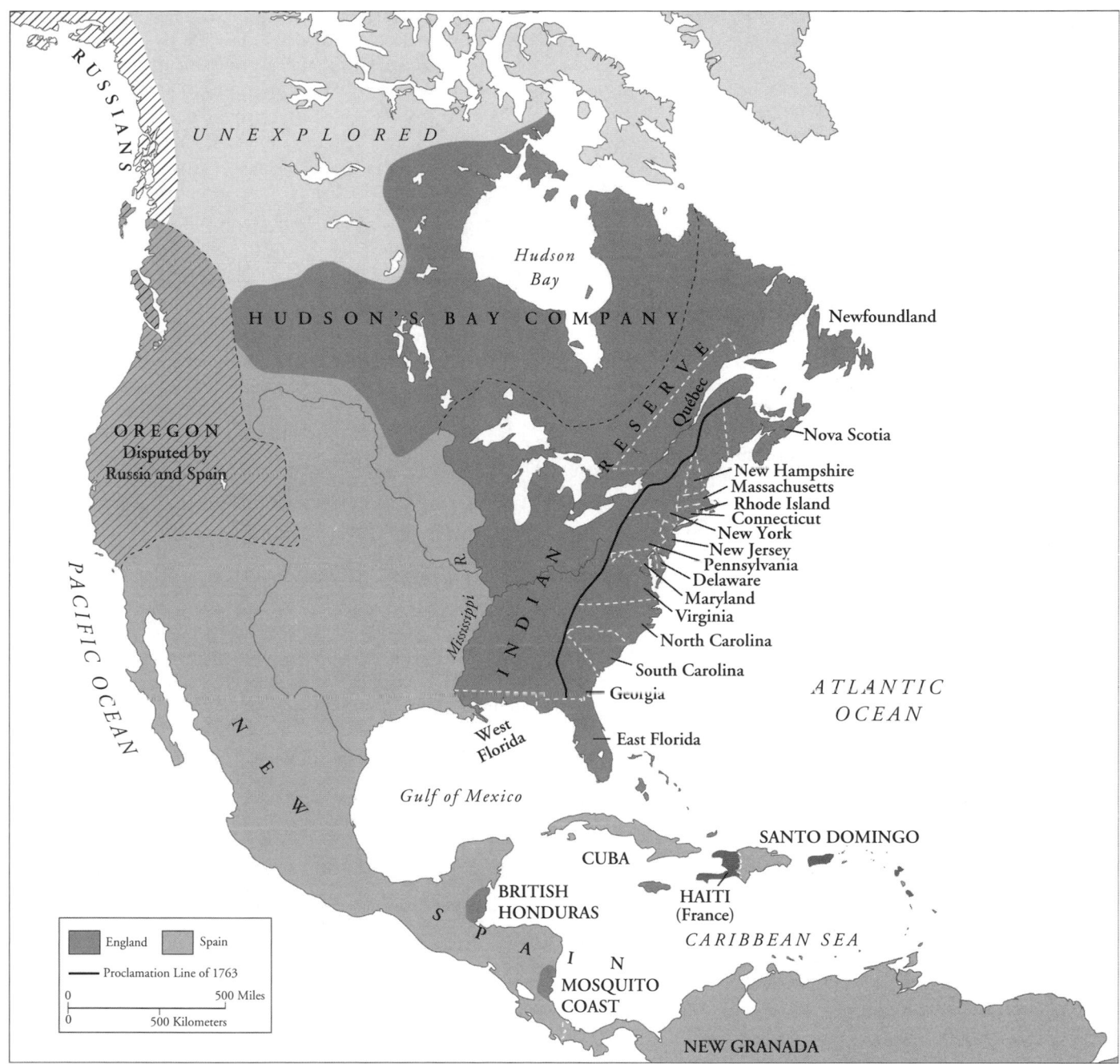

MAP Eg-A Map of North America: 1763

Source

Neal Salisbury, "The History of Native Americans from before the Arrival of the Europeans and Africans until the American Civil War," in Stanley L. Engerman and Robert E. Gallman, editors, *The Cambridge Economic History of the United States* (Cambridge University Press, 1996–2001), volume 1, p. xi.

created an opportunity recurrent across the colonies where enterprising settlers established ports, mills, and mill towns, the mills relying on the waterpower generated at the falls. Pawtucket, Rhode Island; Wilmington, Delaware; Georgetown, Maryland (later part of the District of Columbia); and Richmond, Virginia, are only four in a string of such places all with similar early histories – and the same evocative resonance to their names (Semple 1903).

More recently, encouraged again by historical geographers, economic historians have learned to group settlements by social and economic characteristics that were shared across rivers and bays, appreciating what the colonists themselves knew, that bodies of

water served more to link people than separate them. Historians have undertaken to redraw their mental maps and to talk fruitfully, for instance, about the economy and society of the Piscataqua River basin – and thereby avoid many of the difficulties of pointlessly trying to sort out what people who lived in the area all knew they held in common even if they belonged politically to New Hampshire or Massachusetts (the part that later came to be Maine). Long Island Sound, the Hudson River valley, the Delaware River valley, and famously the Chesapeake Bay, all connected people of similar economic concerns and social attitudes much more than they separated them – just as did the notion "American" when times turned tough and revolution moved from broadsides and boycotts to bayonets and bullets.

Founded mostly in the seventeenth century, the English colonies created parallel political structures out of the same set of shared ideas and attitudes that forged similar societies and economies. Even though there were certain differences, they all had local and colonial governments that individual voters had some voice in determining. The franchise was limited to adult, free, white males who had a stake in society measured largely by the property they owned and the taxes they paid. The prosperous few spoke for the many dependent on them in ways fully compatible with the ideas of John Locke, no matter how different they may have been from voting and office holding practices in more enlightened, later times. The number of participants in the society and the economy was certainly greater than that of those who practiced politics. For many, indeed, their entrée into the practice of politics was success in the economy and a place in society. Upward economic and social mobility offered a means to advancement, if not for oneself, then for one's children. Many identified instantly a threat to property as a threat to the established order and thus a threat to their liberty and their ability to lead the good life, to pursue happiness.

The data presented in the tables of this chapter attest to the advances in society and economy, under the aegis of government – local, colonial, and imperial – that were the results of such pursuits and that provoked those who, discovering the status quo threatened, rose to defend it. We can find evidence of this advancement in many things, some of it testified to in the data series presented herein, some of it apparent only from other, related materials gathered in the works of historians whose emphasis is more the society than the economy. Nevertheless, data and narrative, analysis and description unite to testify to that good and happy life, attained, shared, enjoyed, and defended.

Economic Growth

There seems general agreement on several aspects of the economy of early British America:[6]

The economy of the Thirteen Continental Colonies developed as it grew between 1607 and 1775 – and grew as it developed.

Over the seventeenth and eighteenth centuries, the long-term rate of growth exceeded, perhaps even doubled, the rate of growth of Great Britain.

Growth was not constant. The usual, shorter sequential cycles of expansion and contraction resolved themselves into five longer periods of advance and retreat.

The dominant sector of the economy was agriculture, and the driving force of the colonial economy was its overseas trade, a trade grounded in the export of surplus agricultural commodities.

The colonists learned over time to diversify their economy both by exploring new sectors outside agriculture (commerce; industry) and by exploring variations within sectors (new agricultural crops; new ways to conduct trade).

Over the eighteenth century, the expanding demand for foodstuffs in the Atlantic World tended to drive upward the prices

of agricultural produce, while increasing industrialization in the Atlantic World tended to push downward the prices of manufactured goods. The result was a shift in the commodity terms of trade in favor of the Thirteen Continental Colonies.

On the eve of the American Revolution, real per capita gross domestic product in the Thirteen Continental Colonies was

- higher by far than it had been a century or a century and a half earlier,
- higher than that of any other nation in the world at the time, and
- higher than it would be again in the United States for a while.

Surely the most significant thing to say about the economy of early British America is that it continued to grow over time to the benefit of almost all, rich and poor. By just about every measure we can determine, the economic performance of the colonies was far better at the end of the colonial era than it had been at the beginning. There is no question that it grew extensively. Table Eg1–59 shows that the population of the colonies grew at an annual average compound rate of 5.6 percent between 1610 and 1770 or at a rate of 3.2 percent between 1650 and 1770.[7]

More significant – and harder to measure – is the rate at which the economy grew intensively.[8] The usual measure of intensive economic performance is the gross domestic product (GDP), the total value of goods and services produced by an economy. To allow for comparisons, it is usually expressed per person and adjusted for inflation or deflation; this is called real per capita GDP.[9] In a survey of recent contributions to the subject, Lance Davis and Stanley Engerman (1999, p. 21) concluded that there was "slow, but positive, growth in per capita income and wealth in most parts of the colonies between original settlement and the time of the American Revolution. Slow as it was, growth was probably higher

---

[6] As discussed in McCusker and Menard (1991), pp. 51–70, and McCusker (2000b). See Table Eg217–222.

[7] For some details of colonial population growth, see Tables Eg85–109 and Eg117–193. See also Table Eg194–200. In comparison, between 1651 and 1771 the population of England grew by only 0.17 percent annually (Wrigley and Schofield 1981, pp. 528–9).

[8] See the prescient comments on "the rate of growth of 'national' income" during the colonial period and the reasons for it offered by Somers and Williamson (1951), pp. 83–4.

[9] In 1991, the U.S. Department of Commerce switched from gross national product (GNP) to gross domestic product as its preferred measure of aggregate economic activity. GNP is the total value of final goods and services produced during a given period of time by the citizens of a nation no matter where they are resident. GDP is the total value of final goods and services produced within a nation's borders during a given period of time regardless of the nationality or residence of the owners of productive resources. GDP estimates stretching back to 1790 are available in Chapter Ca on national income and product; see the discussion there for more details. Colonial economic historians have begun to address the issue. Some, while noting that "for most of American history" the difference between GDP and GNP "has not been very large," "for the colonial era the differences are likely to have been larger" (Mancall, Rosenbloom, and Weiss, 2004, pp. 414–15 n. 15). As a point of reference the difference between GNP and GDP is negligible for the modern United States – less than three tenths of 1 percent at the end of the twentieth century. See U.S. Department of Commerce, Bureau of Economic Analysis (1998), volume 1, pp. M-1/M-2, 38 (see especially Table 1.9 [1990–1994], pp. 37–44). See also Inter-Secretariat Working Group on National Accounts (1993), p. 41 and elsewhere. Given that it may well prove impossible to measure for earlier times, the distinction will be ignored in what follows.

than in most of the world at that time."[10] The estimates in Table Eg217–222 indicate that, by 1774, per capita GDP in the Thirteen Continental Colonies averaged approximately $1,430 (in 2003 dollars; compare Table Eg223–246). That figure is about twice the GDP of France and Great Britain for 1775 as estimated by Patrick O'Brien and Peter Mathias (1976, pp. 611–12).[11] Projected back in time at an annual average compound rate of 0.6 percent, the data in Table Eg217–222 track an economy that between 1650 and 1774 grew at a rate twice that of the mother country itself and, it should be noted, higher than it was to be again in the United States for the next two decades. Recent work by Angus Maddison supports all these propositions.[12]

However fast or slow, the rate of growth in the colonial economy was not steady across the years. Just as in the nineteenth and twentieth centuries, there were cycles in the performance of the colonial economy. Good times, periods of expansion, alternated with bad times, periods of contraction. Between 1668 and 1789, the economy of early British America experienced thirty short-term cycles of contraction and expansion. The length of an entire cycle

FIGURE Eg-B   Commodity price indexes, United States and Great Britain: 1665–1860

Source

John J. McCusker, *How Much Is That in Real Money? A Historical Commodity Price Index for Use as a Deflator of Money Values in the Economy of the United States*, 2nd edition (American Antiquarian Society, 2001), p. 30.

Documentation

The values for the United States can be found in series Cc1 and Eg247.

---

[10] Compare Galenson (1996), pp. 189–207; Engerman (2000), especially pp. 245–6. See also Egnal (1975); Egnal (1996), pp. 3–7. See also Egnal (1998), p. vi and elsewhere, where he proclaims as the "central argument" of his book that "the pace of economic development in the colonies reflected the rate of growth in the mother country." Walton and Shepherd (1969), p. 141, thought that "growth rates in the colonies were probably roughly similar to those in England," that is, 0.3 percent.

Casting their study more broadly, Mancall and Weiss (1999) came to a determination different from everyone else's. One reason why is that they account as the territory occupied by the "denizens of the British mainland colonies" (p. 19) the entirety of the North American continent east of the Mississippi River from the Gulf of Mexico to well into modern Canada from Ontario through to Newfoundland, and thus include French and Spanish territories as well as all the lands and peoples of the Native American Indians. Compare Mancall, Rosenbloom, and Weiss (2004).

[11] According to their estimates, in 1775 French GDP was $780 per capita and British GDP was $890 per capita (in 2003 dollars). Compare Braudel (1979), volume 3, pp. 328–30. Data developed by Clark (2001a), pp. 403–36, with reference to Clark (2001b), suggest a much higher figure for Great Britain, about twice the O'Brien and Mathias estimate.

[12] See his estimates of real, per capita GDP for the United States in 1600, 1700, and 1820 in Maddison (2001), p. 264. According to Maddison's data, the annual average compound rate of growth for the seventeenth century was 0.28 percent and for the extended eighteenth century, 0.73 percent. One can argue that 1650 would be a better date than 1600 for his first estimate; then the rate for the seventeenth century is 0.55 percent. Over the years 1650–1829, the rate is 0.68 percent. Note, too, that for the whole period 1500–1820 (Maddison 2001, p. 265), the rate of growth for the United States is the highest in the world.

For the origins of such estimates for Great Britain, see Deane and Cole (1967). Compare Crouzet (1990), pp. 12–43. Deane and Cole's estimates have been revised downwards by Harley (1982); Crafts (1985); and Crafts and Harley (1992). Maddison (2001), pp. 264–5, shows the British economy growing at an annual average compound rate of 0.27 percent between 1500 and 1820. Compare Bairoch (1976), p. 277.

For estimates for England for an earlier period, see Mayhew (1995). Compare Eltis (1995). Not only does Eltis provide estimates of total and per capita product for this one English colony for the mid-1660s and the end of the seventeenth century, but he also establishes comparisons with the Thirteen Continental Colonies and with the Mother Country. In real terms (1700–1702 = 100), he estimates "Barbados income ... at £16.0 in 1665 and 1666, and £21.3 in the years 1699 to 1701" (p. 330). This suggests an annual average rate of increase in real, per capita GDP of something more than eight tenths of 1 percent (0.845 percent). This is well above the long-term estimates for either England or the Thirteen Continental Colonies at any time before the end of the eighteenth century. See also Eltis (1997).

including both phases varied considerably but averaged about four years (McCusker 2001a, pp. 107–10).[13] As Figure Eg-B suggests, one could argue that the entire British-American economy shared these cycles.

The short-term ups and downs in the business cycle resolved themselves into somewhat longer periods of expansion and contraction. Between the early years of the seventeenth century and the American Revolution, there were five such long-term periods of growth and decline:

Period One: An expansion that lasted into the 1660s.

Period Two: A contraction, into the 1690s.

Period Three: A slower expansion, until about 1720.

Period Four: A contraction, until the late 1730s–early 1740s.

Period Five: A long, powerful expansion that persisted until the beginning of the American Revolutionary War.

A chart of the last four parts of this five-part periodization resembles the letter "W" in its configuration, with the peak at the center lower than the two arms. The expansion that ended about 1720 was weak enough that Periods Two through Four can simply be viewed as one long decline. Thus, the time from 1660 through 1775 can be portrayed graphically as a "V" with the nadir near 1740. Once again, it appears as if the course of these periods of expansion and contraction found parallels in the other Atlantic economies.[14]

The years of the Revolutionary War and after were a near disaster for the new national economy. We are only beginning to appreciate the dimensions of that disaster; our data are still somewhat

---

[13] Between 1668 and November 2001, the economy of the United States experienced seventy-three cycles that averaged, peak to peak, about fifty-five months in duration.

[14] See McCusker and Menard (1991), pp. 66–8. Compare Gibson and Smout (1995), pp. 164–7.

uncertain, and our analyses are therefore subject to revision.[15] Be all that as it may, current estimates of GDP show a decline between 1774 and 1781 of nearly 15 percent. In other words, during the American Revolutionary War, the economy of the country declined at an annual average compound rate of 2.2 percent per year. Even in 1793, a decade after the war had ended, the economy still had not been restored to its pre-Revolutionary vigor (Shepherd 1980). Brought down on one knee during the Revolutionary War, if not onto both as happened during the Great Depression (when it declined 32.6 percent), the American economy took twice as long to rise again after 1774 as it did after 1929 – with the help of a world war both times (McCusker 2000b, pp. 158–9).

Income and Wealth Distribution

Just as economic growth was not spread evenly across the years, so also were the benefits of that growth not spread evenly across the society. Some people benefited more, others much less. One fifth of the population of early British America in 1770, slave labor subservient to the other four fifths, benefited hardly at all from economic growth. In the seventeenth and eighteenth centuries, just as in the Cotton South of the nineteenth-century United States, no higher rates of return on average were possible than those to be earned from slave-based plantation agriculture.[16] But none of that return accrued to enslaved workers. Under the law and in any contemporary accounting of the economy, slaves occupied a status similar to that of horses and cattle. They were categorized as property owned by their masters. As a consequence, economic historians regularly treat them as part of the wealth of their owners, as in Table Eg-C (compare Table Eg223–246). Their labor was expropriated by their owners, and their income credited as the income of the owners; the data presented herein reflect that sad reality.[17] Slaves shared little if at all in the economic growth that they helped produce.[18]

Even among just the white population of the British colonies, income and wealth were unevenly distributed both by region and by rank in society. There were considerable regional differences. As Table Eg-C shows, on the eve of the American Revolutionary War, residents in the southern colonies had higher levels of income

TABLE Eg-C Private physical wealth in the British Empire: 1774

| Location | Physical wealth (in £ sterling) | | |
| | | Per free white | |
	Total	person	Per capita
Thirteen Continental Colonies	109,570,000	60.20	46.50
New England Colonies	22,238,000	38.20	36.60
Middle Colonies	26,814,000	45.80	41.90
Southern Colonies	60,518,000	92.70	54.70
British West Indies	51,926,000	1,042.50	114.10
British America	161,496,000	89.60	57.50
England and Wales	278,000,000	42.10	42.30

Source

T[revor] G. Burnard, " 'Prodigious Riches': The Wealth of Jamaica before the American Revolution," *Economic History Review*, 2nd series, 54 (August 2001): 506–24.

and wealth than those farther north (Burnard 2001, p. 506–24).[19] Free whites in the southern Continental Colonies were twice as wealthy as their cousins in the Middle Colonies and almost three times richer than those in the New England colonies. People of European origin living in British America held twice the wealth of residents of the British Isles.

In a similar way, within each of those areas there were also differences in wealth, income, and spending among the white population. Those differences appear to have grown over time as increasingly larger percentages of both income and wealth went to families and individuals in the upper ranks. Among the white colonists, it seems that while the rich got richer, the poor prospered, too, but at a slower rate.[20] Obviously this does not mean that those at the bottom failed completely to benefit from the advancing economy. They did so, but to a lesser degree than those at the top. The colonies experienced little if any of the abject poverty found in contemporary Europe or in the United States during the nineteenth century.[21] The "predicament of poverty," in Hannah Arendt's phrase, "was absent from the American scene" (Arendt 1965, p. 62). Or, perhaps more precisely, "what were absent from the American scene were misery and want rather than poverty" (Arendt 1965, p. 63).[22]

---

[15] See Buel (1998). Compare McCusker and Menard (1991), pp. 365–7. See also Doerflinger (1986), pp. 197–250.

[16] "Investments in new cotton lands and slaves brought higher returns than any of the possible alternatives." Kenneth M. Stampp in Blum, McFeely, et al. (1993), p. 215.

[17] For the sake of continuity in comparisons with GDP estimates for later periods, the data in Table Eg217–222 include black Americans as part of the producing population. Compare Weiss (1992). Had GDP been measured only against the free population, the annual average rate in increase of GDP, 1650–1774, would be reported at 0.8 percent.

[18] Despite their deplorable treatment, there is a hint of some benefit from economic growth for the enslaved people of the Thirteen Continental Colonies in their attainment of increasingly faster rates of natural increase through reproduction. Perhaps this was a consequence of marginally better food, perhaps better housing or better clothing, perhaps better medical care: we are only guessing. See McCusker and Menard (1991), pp. 230–4. Compare Higman (1984), pp. 307–14. Walsh (1997), p. 200, identifies some "small improvements in livings standards" for slaves across the eighteenth century but credits such improvements to "their own initiative." Perhaps the developing, growing colonial economy simply permitted even slaves some opportunity, some incentive, some examples for them, too, to be innovative in dealing with their circumstances.

[19] For earlier estimates, see McCusker and Menard (1991), p. 61, and Coclanis (1990).

[20] McCusker (1972b), as revised and updated in McCusker (1997), pp. 245–57, especially p. 256 n. 34. Compare Main (2001), p. 210: the "rich got a good deal richer, but the poor of rural New England were not becoming poorer. The growing economy, like the incoming tide, was lifting all boats."

[21] Stephen Innes has recently put such work into better perspective: "early Americanists [who] are ... preoccupied with oppression" fixate on "inequality in colonial and revolutionary America without once acknowledging this society as the only one of its time to afford work-based mobility to the mass of its free inhabitants." After all, as he points out, "two-thirds of its householders owned and worked their own land by the mid-eighteenth century." Innes (2001), pp. 468–9. Compare Bushman (1998).

[22] One reason for the relative absence of misery and want was that citizens of various colonial communities taxed themselves for poor relief. On the eve of the American Revolution, Philadelphians and New Yorkers did so at a rate of approximately 2s. 6d. sterling each; Bostonians 3s. each. Jacob Price notes that this was not simply a reflection of the increase in the numbers of the poor "but also ... the growth of wealth and civic consciousness that made communities more willing to take care of the unfortunate" (Price 1976, p. 708). His observation was provoked by Nash (1976), especially p. 557, who looked at the same evidence and spied oppression. Price cautioned: "I only want to suggest that ... [Nash's] evidence is not as clear as his rhetoric" (p. 706).

In 1751, the governor of South Carolina, James Glen, sought to sort out what these differences meant for his colony in response to an inquiry from the Board of Trade.[23] He divided the white population of the colony into four groups and then estimated what each group spent per day and per year "for Food and Raiment and all other Necessarys whatsoever." Although initially he suggested that such expenditures totaled £500,000 sterling per year, he decided to use a more conservative figure, £400,000, for his detailed estimates. In the first group, five thousand people, he placed those "who have plenty of the good things of Life, and spend at the rate of two Shillings per day, [which] is £182500 a year." The second group, five thousand people more, were those "who have some of the Conveniencys of Life, and spend at the rate of one Shilling per day, [which] is £91250." The largest group was the third one, ten thousand people, "who have the Necessarys of Life, and spend at the rate of Six pence per day" to a total of £91,250 per year. At the bottom of Glen's ranking were five thousand more people "who have a bare subsistence and spend about a Groat per day which is £35000 a Year" (a groat was four pennies).[24] One is tempted to apply modern, conventional labels to his categories – upper class, upper middle class, lower middle class, lower class – though Glen did not use those terms. He did share Arendt's sense about the least well-to-do of these groups: "our poor or middling sort of people, if there are any who may be called so, live better than those in England."[25] The top 20 percent of South Carolinians accounted for 46 percent of consumption; the bottom 20 percent, less than 9 percent; these percentages sound quite familiar to twenty-first-century ears.[26] At whatever level, all were producers and consumers in a thriving economy, even if, as a group, those at the bottom produced and consumed at a rate only one sixth of their much better-off neighbors. The point here is that – just as Glen observed – rich and poor prospered in the economy, varying only in the level of their participation, even as it changed over time.

A widening gap between the rich and the poor suggests an explanation for the growth of domestic capital in the Thirteen Continental Colonies. Economists recognize that the well-to-do regularly have a higher propensity to save marginal income than to spend it.[27] This means that the better off people are, the more likely they are to put aside any increase in income rather than to use it to buy something. Just the opposite is also true: Those relatively less well off are more likely to spend any additional income than to save it. Although poorer colonists most likely spent that extra dollar on more food, more clothing, and better shelter, richer colonists were more likely to have saved it than to have spent it just because they already had enough food, clothing, and shelter. One consequence of this for the increasingly prosperous colonial economy was that the better off among the white colonists, in saving their marginal dollars, added to the supply of domestically generated investment capital. It grew at a rate faster than the economy itself (McCusker (1972b), as revised and updated in McCusker (1997), pp. 245–57).[28] Domestic savings mobilized became money capital available for investment purposes. Such locally generated investment capital was extremely important to the growing economy of early British America; it helped to fuel colonial economic development, a topic that we will return to later.

A leading role in the realization of the social and economic benefits of the developing, prosperous economy for the lives of ordinary people, most particularly farm families, was taken by the farm wife. It has always been clear that the entire farm family contributed its energy to the successful operation of the enterprise. But the questions of what special place, if any, the farm wife occupied, and how, if at all, her role changed under the circumstances of an expanding economy and generally higher levels of income and wealth can now be answered more completely given much recent research (see, for instance, Carr and Walsh 1977, pp. 542–71).

Significant in all such discussions of changing living standards in the Thirteen Continental Colonies are the ideas connected with the ethic of gentility (Bushman 1992). Genteel ideals and standards are most properly ascribed to the English gentry of the eighteenth century, but, by the middle of the eighteenth century, the ethic of gentility had come to be fashionable in the colonies. As Governor James Glen put it in 1751, concerning the people of Charleston, "in proportion as they thrive they delight to have good things from England."[29] Genteel ideals began to influence the lifestyles of many colonists, in their homes and in their dress, in what they ate and how they behaved, from the richest to the poorest. In their material aspect at least, the attitudes of gentility reached down into even the lowest orders of society; certainly they reached into the homes of farmers. Perhaps poorer people were not fully able to act out the

---

For taxation in the colonies, see Tables Eg420–428. Compare estimates of taxes collected in Boston, 1692–1775, in Warden (1976), p. 591.

[23] "An Attempt towards an Estimate of the Value of So. Carolina," March 1750/51, enclosure in Governor James Glen, at Charleston, to Board of Trade, June 24, 1751, Colonial Office Records, CO 5/373, folio 139r–v, Public Record Office, National Archives, London (PRO/TNA).

[24] Glen wrote "five or six thousand more." Five thousand makes his total population 25,000 but his total spending only £30,417; six thousand makes his total population 26,000 and his total spending £36,500. "An Attempt towards an Estimate of the Value of So. Carolina," CO 5/373, folio 139v. Compare Glen's distinctions with Benjamin Franklin's sorting of the colonists' imports from Great Britain into "necessaries, mere conveniences, or superfluities." Great Britain, Parliament, 1766, House of Commons 1767, p. 23.

[25] "An Attempt towards an Estimate of the Value of So. Carolina," CO 5/373, folio 140r, PRO/TNA.

[26] According to the estimates assembled by Massie (1760) as recompiled by Mathias (1957), in the year 1759, the top 25.7 percent of the families of Great Britain in terms of "annual income or expenses" accounted for 47.5 percent of the total, but the bottom 15 percent of families account for 4.8 percent of the total. More recently, the revisionist calculations of per capita expenditure distribution for 1990–1995 calculated by Slesnick (2001), p. 136, indicate that the bottom one fifth of people accounted for about 7 percent of expenditures while the top one fifth accounted for about 42 percent of expenditures. Compare Table Be1–18.

[27] This is a corollary of "Engel's Law," propounded by Ernst Engel, which says simply that the proportion of income spent on food declines as income rises. He based his conclusions on a statistical analysis of the household budgets of some two hundred Belgian workers. (Engel 1857; revised and expanded as Engel 1895). See also Houthakker (1987).

[28] Data developed there indicate an increase in capital formation at 1.6 percent annually between 1730 and 1770. Table Eg217–222 shows GDP growing during the same period at 0.6 percent.

[29] The full quotation reads: "There are besides in other parts of the Town many Houses that cost a thousand and twelve hundred pounds Sterling. The Furniture in these Houses must be very considerable and Plate begins to shine upon their side Boards, and in proportion as they thrive they delight to have good things from England." "An Attempt towards an Estimate of the Value of So. Carolina," in Governor Glen to Board of Trade, 24 June 1751, CO 5/373, folio 131r–v, PRO/TNA. As far as influences on colonial consumption were concerned, "London was the metropolitan center" (Carr and Walsh 1988, p. 139).

genteel ideal, but they as well as the rich shaped their lives by it. All the colonists wanted both to drink tea and to do so properly! (Carr and Walsh 1978, 1994).

Gloria Main has suggested that women not only introduced genteel notions into rural households but also worked, quite literally, to facilitate their realization. Main has written of the farm wife as one who, given higher levels of income and wealth, could now afford to remain seated and participate in a conversation while serving her guests because her house had enough chairs. She could now afford to serve her guests properly because she owned the proper tea service. Even more riveting is Main's suggestion that "perhaps it was her [own] money, earned by selling butter and eggs or spun yarn and knitted stocking, which purchased the packets of tea and the pretty new dishes" with which to serve the tea properly (Main 1988, p. 129).[30] This is certainly what one might have expected in the midst of a prospering economy that expanded opportunities for all, rich and poor, farmer and city dweller.

An Agricultural Economy

The second most significant thing to say about the economy of early British America is that, although it was primarily agricultural, it sidestepped what Mark Elvin (1973, pp. 298–319) has called the "high level equilibrium trap." Obviously, of the three sectors of the colonial economy that contributed to GDP, agriculture was by far the largest throughout the pre–Revolutionary War period.[31] The trap for a closed agricultural economy is that, when everyone or almost everyone is a farmer, once farm families raise sufficient food to feed themselves adequately, producing more fails to accomplish anything. A farmer and his family can only eat so much and, with everyone else a farmer, too, there is no one with whom to exchange any surplus for nonagricultural goods or services. With no one producing more, an economy stops growing or grows only very, very slowly. Any intraregional or interregional exchange of different food crops would equally quickly reach stasis, and the economy would stagnate.

We see the colonists in early British America avoiding this trap in three ways: by developing an export sector as a "vent" for their surplus agricultural produce, by developing their agricultural sector's potential for growth through crop diversification and agricultural innovation, and by developing their economy more broadly by branching out into commerce and industry. Although neither the commercial nor the industrial sectors of the economy were anywhere near fully articulated by 1775, they had come a long way toward supplementing the well-developed agricultural sector. The combination of a dominant agricultural sector producing a surplus for export with a burgeoning commercial sector and a small but dynamic industrial sector animated real growth in the colonial economy. As John Shepard, the author of *The Artist and Tradesman's Guide*, suggested in 1829: "Agriculture, never arrives at any considerable, much less at its highest degree of perfection, where it is not connected with trade" (Shepard 1829, p. 257). The colonies' existence as part of a closed empire that diminished foreign competition afforded them considerable opportunities within the bounds of the Navigation Acts that contributed to that growth (McCusker forthcoming).

Agriculture developed through diversification and innovation – whence came greater productivity.[32] Roughly speaking, there were two themes in the history of colonial agriculture, one associated with New England and a second associated with the Middle Atlantic and Southern Colonies. Agriculture in New England advanced slowly but steadily across the decades but changed not much if at all. While it did not develop, its growth helped the New England economy to expand "at a healthy long-term rate, that showed little sign of slowing as the American Revolution approached" (Main and Main 1999).[33] The colonies south of New England lived a different experience, usually described in terms of several regions each devoted to the growing of one particular crop: grains (wheat and corn) in the Hudson River and Delaware River valleys; tobacco in the Chesapeake Bay region; rice (and, later, indigo), in the Carolinas and Georgia. Even though all this is true enough in crude outline, it leaves out a transformation of considerable importance that applies to greater or lesser degrees in all these regions but was particularly important for the Chesapeake.

Agriculture in Maryland and Virginia can be seen to have evolved through three developmental stages, again roughly speaking. In the first stage, planters, having discovered tobacco, committed all of their resources to growing and processing it for export to the exclusion of anything else. Regularly quoted in this regard from the parallel circumstance in Barbados is the declaration of the Barbadian planter Richard Vines in a 1647 letter to John Winthrop: "Men are so intent upon planting sugar that they had rather buy foode at very deare rates than produce it by labour, soe infinite is the profitt of sugar workes."[34] Such were the returns from Chesapeake tobacco in its earliest years that planters could afford to buy from off the plantation everything else they required.[35] As yields and profits diminished after the initial rush subsided, some

---

[30] Concerning the importance of "the tea" as a social event, see Shand (1927), pp. 39–43, and Roth (1961). Compare Mintz (1985), pp. 141–2. Women carried the idea, the ceremony, and the equipment with them as settlement drove westward in the early Republic. See Perkins (1991), p. 489. For tea shipped to the colonies, see Table Eg1152–1159.

[31] In 1787, Benjamin Franklin wrote: "The great business of the continent is agriculture. For every artisan, or merchant, I suppose we have at least a hundred farmers." Franklin (1787), p. 6. One is loath ever to argue with Benjamin Franklin, but McCusker and Menard (1991, p. 248) estimate that the share of the workforce in agriculture on the eve of the American Revolution was more like 80 percent. The occupational distribution of colonial cities in the 1780s and 1790s, based on Boston, New York, and Philadelphia, was 50 percent employed in internal service functions, 24 percent in industrial production, 23 percent in maritime commerce, and 4 percent in administration (civil and ecclesiastical) (Price 1974, pp. 128–37, 177–85).

[32] For a summary of developments in colonial agriculture, see McCusker and Menard (1991), pp. 295–308 and elsewhere (see index, under "Agriculture"). See also Vickers (1996); and Menard (1996). Less useful conceptually but with a valuable bibliography is Kulikoff (2000). Chaplin (1993) notes the success Southern agriculture achieved in its pursuit of greater productivity. Coclanis (1989) is less sanguine. See also Carr, Menard, and Walsh (1991).

[33] Main (2001) argues that even New Englanders were able to farm more productively over time, partly through more efficient modes of farming, partly through greater engagement with markets. See also Table Eg325–328. Compare Rothenberg (1992), who also emphasizes the importance for the New England economy of productivity gains in agriculture. For other recent work that stresses the entrepreneurial character of the New England economy, see Innes (1995) and Newell (1998).

[34] Letter from Vines, at Barbados, to Winthrop, at Boston, July 19, 1647, in Forbes (1947), p. 172. Vines (fl. 1616–1651), a long-time resident of Maine, had only recently emigrated to Barbados. For him, see Noyes, Libby, and Davis (1928–1939), volume 5, pp. 705–6.

[35] For the tobacco trade, see Tables Eg1038–1151. For the cost of shipping tobacco, see Table Eg686–687.

planters began to devote some of their resources to producing on the plantation a few of the things they had been importing from elsewhere. A local trade grew up in goods and services within which planters exchanged small surpluses of one thing or another with planters who had reciprocal needs and surpluses. We can see signs of this activity as early as the 1630s in Virginia.[36] Cost savings and the consequent added profits redounded to all involved and encouraged economic growth. Out of this growth came further incentives to development and the capital to do so. An important element in this transition was the shift away from white indentured servants to enslaved black Africans as the primary source of bound labor. The key was capital (see Rutman and Rutman 1984).[37]

Over the next century, this local trade grew even while settlement in the colony began to move inland from the tidewater and beyond the fall line. By the beginning of the second third of the eighteenth century, Chesapeake planters in the region's backcountry had found their best advantage in producing only foodstuffs – again, corn and wheat, plus some livestock – for sale in the tidewater port towns (Walsh 2000; see also Walsh, Martin, and Bowen 1997; Clemens 1980). Some of the surplus ended up in the hands of merchants recently established there who were prepared to act as middlemen in the sale of such produce, at first locally, then regionally, later up and down the Atlantic coast, and still later across the ocean to feed the growing demand for American grains in a hungry Europe. New York City, Philadelphia, later Baltimore and Norfolk, and in a somewhat different way Charleston: by the late 1760s all had become major export centers for the shipment of foods from the Thirteen Continental Colonies to a transatlantic market.[38] South Carolina marched to a different drummer, yet just as entrepreneurially in its own way, by developing new crops, first rice and then indigo (see Nash 2001, especially p. 97; compare Coclanis 1989 and Chaplin 1993). The increased level of demand internationally for foodstuffs produced in the colonies tended over the long term to push up the prices for grains and other commodities to the benefit of colonial producers and shippers.[39] In the development of colonial agriculture, venting its surplus to export markets became the first and most significant escape from the "high level equilibrium trap."[40]

Commerce developed through diversification and innovation – whence came greater productivity.[41] Merchants in the ports of the Thirteen Continental Colonies were active in the pursuit of the "carrying trade" from the founding of the colonies. For many, the route to success was simply expanding the business available to them in the traditional coastwise trade, the trade with the neighboring colonies that extended from Newfoundland in the north to Barbados in the south. There were many such opportunities, and the growing population in all of the colonies promised that more of the same would always be the case. An important consequence of the ever-expanding coastwise trade was the increasing integration of the colonial economies. This also contributed to advances in productivity by diminishing transaction costs.[42]

Of particular importance was the extraordinarily rapid growth of the trade with the West Indies, a commerce that supplied to the voracious sugar industry the timber products, draft animals, foodstuffs, and almost everything else it required as it expanded mightily from the 1640s onward (McCusker and Menard 2004). Just as Richard Vines suggested in 1647, the "very deare rates" the planters were willing to pay for all they required meant very high returns for all willing to provide them. The Caribbean sugar industry drove much of the Atlantic economy (see McCusker and Menard 1991, pp. 144–68; McCusker 1989). Early in the eighteenth century, in a mere extension of what had been the case before, merchants in the ports of the Thirteen Continental Colonies began to pursue direct trade with the French, the Dutch, and, later, the Danish West Indies. Yet this was nothing really new, only a rerouting of a commerce that had up until then gone by way of British West Indian ports such a Bridgetown, Barbados, and Port Royal, Jamaica. (The best business with the Spanish Main continued to be either through the Dutch West Indian merchants based at St. Eustatius, Curaçao, or Suriname, or through Jamaican merchants located in Kingston

---

[36] See, for example, the testimony by Governor John Harvey that "Virginia is become (like another Sicily to home) the Granary of all his Majesties northerne Collonies." Letter from Harvey, at Virginia, to [Secretary of State Francis Windebank], at London, July 14, 1634, CO 1/8, folio 74r, PRO/TNA. Compare Earle (1975).

[37] Three important studies that include much information about the African contribution to the economic development of the Thirteen Continental Colonies are Walsh (1997), Berlin (1998), and Morgan (1998).

[38] For the Chesapeake's participation in these developments, see Hardy (1999), pp. 96–135. For the exportation of rice and other commodities from the Lower South, see Tables Eg1027–1037 and Eg1160–1170.

[39] See the analysis of price trends in the colonies by Harris (1996). Given the countervailing tendency for prices of manufactured goods in the Atlantic World to decline, thanks to increasing industrialization, the terms of trade shifted decidedly in favor of the colonists. Compare Egnal (1975), pp. 199–205, and Menard (2001), p. 10 n. 32. This development was all the more potent because agricultural productivity increases made colonial farming ever more profitable (see the discussion that follows).

[40] In addition to agriculture, other forms of colonial extractive enterprise also grew over time. For whaling and fishing, see Tables Eg329–355; for coal, Tables Eg755–810; for furs, Table Eg1013–1026; and for the timber industry, Tables Eg1171–1179.

[41] For a summary of developments in colonial commerce, see McCusker and Menard (1991), pp. 71–88, 277–94, and elsewhere. For the value of colonial trade with England and Scotland, see Tables Eg429–460.

[42] Rothenberg (1992) chronicles the last stages of the growing synchroneity and congruence, even convergence among colonial markets. It had its beginnings in the earliest days of colonial settlement, as soon as businessmen learned that there were sellers and buyers up and down the North American coast for nearly everything they had to buy and sell. For the development of the coastwise trade in the eighteenth century, see Klingaman (1989). Some of the best evidence we have of these developments is the close parallels to be found in the movements of the prices of goods in the different colonial ports. Intercolonial trade, even more powerfully when more limited colonial economies were linked by waterborne commerce than later when states were connected by road, canal, and railroad, served to facilitate commercial arbitrage and thereby to maintain a certain commonality in the pricing of goods, even over the short haul. Not only would we expect this to have been the case, but it proves to have been so upon investigation. Reductions in the costs of information and transportation go far to explain the increasing integration of markets and the diminution in the difference of prices across such markets. Compare the conclusions drawn from the several studies conducted under the aegis of the International Scientific Committee on Price History as summarized by Cole (1938), volume 1, pp. 94–114 (quotation, pp. 95–6): "All the results . . . indicate increasing agreement among such movements [of the general price indexes] . . . as the decades pass." This is even more obvious when we reduce prices to their equivalence in sterling. Compare Harris (1996). For prices of the major colonial staples, see Tables Eg248–270 and Eg299–301. Note that some of these are "farm prices" and some are "market prices." Compare these price series with Table Cc205–266. Table Eg247 compiles a commodity price index for the Thirteen Continental Colonies and the United States, 1665–1790. Compare the discussions in Bushman (1998), p. 355, and McCusker (2001a), pp. 47–8 n. 18.

TABLE Eg-D Export trade of Philadelphia – clearances from Philadelphia to five trading areas: 1750–1774

Destination	1750–1754			1770–1774		
	Average number of vessels per year	Registered tonnage		Average number of vessels per year	Registered tonnage	
		Average per vessel	Total		Average per vessel	Total
Great Britain	16	71.0	1,136	26	116.7	3,034
Ireland	36	69.2	2,491	28	103.6	2,901
Southern Europe	36	48.3	1,739	101	88.7	8,959
West Indies	191	66.4	12,682	340	57.5	19,550
Coastwise	166	43.4	7,204	262	42.1	11,030
Total clearances	445	—	25,252	757	—	45,474

Sources

Vessels clearing Philadelphia. Taken from the weekly shipping reports in the *Pennsylvania Gazette* (Philadelphia) as compiled in Arthur L. Jensen, *The Maritime Commerce of Colonial Philadelphia* (State Historical Society of Wisconsin for the Department of History, University of Wisconsin, 1963), p. 290.

Registered tonnage. Calculated from two sets of sources. For 1750–1754, they are obtained from the Naval Office Shipping Lists (NOSL), Port of Entry (POE) Philadelphia, 1741–1742, which are catalogued as the Register of

Ships Entering Port of Philadelphia, 1741–1742, Collection number 542, and the Ships' Register [of Vessels Clearing Outward from the Port of Philadelphia], 1742, Collection number 1321, Historical Society of Pennsylvania, Philadelphia. Note that, despite the names given to these collections, these two items are not records of the registry of ships at the port but are NOSL showing the ships and their cargoes as they cleared inwards and outwards. For 1770–1774, the average tonnages are from the Ledger of Imports and Exports, British North America, 1768–1772, pp. 3–4, 39–40, 101–2, 167–8, 227–8, Customs 16/1, PRO/TNA.

or, much later, that island's outports.) All earned good profits for the merchants who owned the vessels and organized the trade. All earned the colonial economy credits in the current account of its balance of payments. To quote Thomas Willing, the foremost merchant of pre–Revolutionary War Philadelphia: "Carriage is an amazing Revenue."[43]

Yet the most lucrative trades, the transatlantic trades in the major staple exports, were effectively denied merchants based in the Continental Colonies because such trades were controlled from the first by the dominant tobacco and sugar merchant firms of London, Bristol, and Glasgow. Only with the growing demand in Europe for North American grains did the Atlantic Ocean and its opportunities for a real diversification of the colonial carrying trade become possible – and colonial merchants rushed to take advantage of them, especially merchants based in Philadelphia (see McCusker 1972a). Shipowners in colonial ports instructed colonial shipbuilders to build them larger vessels patterned on a Dutch model – the fluijt – designed to maximize their ability to carry bulk cargoes and to minimize their costs, especially in the size of the crew, thereby increasing productivity (McCusker 1981, as revised and updated in McCusker 1997, pp. 60–1). Over the fifty years between 1720 and 1770, the proportion of the ships clearing Philadelphia that were owned in that port expanded steadily, the type and size of these vessels grew from smaller craft fitted to the coastwise trade to larger ocean-going bulk carriers, and their destinations shifted more and more to ports on the other side of the Atlantic Ocean (see Table Eg-D).[44]

We have known for some time that the middle third of the eighteenth century was the period during which Philadelphia merchants began to expand their ownership of the vessels that cleared the Delaware, increasingly for transatlantic destinations. What we have learned more recently is that merchants in the Chesapeake

were doing something similar. They encouraged others in the same locale to support such ventures, organizing voyages based on capital invested by people of all sorts, including the large planters. The Chesapeake story has a second parallel with their neighbors to the north in that such investment in shipping ventures rapidly became an investment in ships, one of which was George Washington's brig, which he named *The Farmer* (Hardy 1999, pp. 136–74).[45] Colonial investment in transatlantic ships and cargoes altered the essential posture of colonial commerce. Soon colonial business owners were opening branch offices in London the better to monitor and expand their European affairs (Johnson 1979, p. xii). Colonial commerce grew through diversification more than it would have otherwise and with linkages to the other sectors of the colonial economy, one of which was manufacturing.

Manufacturing developed through diversification and innovation – whence came greater productivity. The most important manufacturing industries in the Thirteen Continental Colonies were associated with commerce.[46] Business owners engaged in colonial manufacturing were well connected with developments abroad and could utilize their contacts to remain up-to-date with the latest revolutionary breakthroughs in manufacturing happening in Great Britain, the scene of much industrial innovation in the seventeenth and eighteenth centuries.[47]

---

[43] Willing made the comment in a committee meeting during the Second Continental Congress, October 4, 1775. See John Adams's notes on the debate in Adams (1961), volume 1, pp. 188–92 (quotation on p. 190). For Willing, see Slaski (1971).

[44] Compare the shipping data in Tables Eg461–685.

---

[45] For Chesapeake planter investment in shipping, see Kamoie (1999), pp. 240–71. Both Virginia and Georgia undertook to promote local investment in shipping by giving tax breaks to ships owned by their citizens. See McCusker (1981), as revised and updated in McCusker (1997), pp. 43–75 (note especially pp. 56–7); and the "Fees taken by His Majestys Searcher at the Port of Savannah in Georgia . . . ," signed by William Brown and enclosed "In Govr Wrights Lre," of April 13, 1771, T 1/482, folio 280r, with reference to the fees set by the Council, January 2, 1757, and extended by it, November 3, 1767, CO 5/693, folio 76v–77v, and CO 5/701, folio 251v, PRO/TNA.

[46] For a summary of developments in colonial manufacturing, see McCusker and Menard (1991), pp. 307–30, and elsewhere (see index, under "Manufacturing"). For several different types of businesses, see Table Eg404–419; for the iron industry, see Tables Eg811–1012.

[47] The evidence of the colonists' participation in the early stages of Great Britain's Industrial Revolution is considerable even if sometimes unsystematic.

One developing industry was distilling. It is a classic example of import substitution manufacturing. The colonists early discovered the joys of rum and soon learned that, rather than merely profiting by importing the finished product from the West Indies, they could make even more money by distilling their own rum from Caribbean molasses and domestically available syrup, the latter itself a by-product from the mainland colonists' own sugar refining industry. Begun on a small scale with equipment imported from England, the colonial industry grew in extent and in scale. By the time of the American Revolution, there were some 140 distilleries in cities up and down the coast operating in ways very similar to those in the Mother Country (McCusker 2000a).[48] Much the same thing can be said about another colonial industry that produced locally a commodity that had previously been imported: sugar refining. Colonial-owned and -operated sugar refineries relied heavily on London equipment manufacturers and sugar refiners not only for their physical plants but also for their personnel.

The "spread" effects of the growing colonial export trade also encouraged colonial industry. One industry that was also closely connected with merchants was milling. The needs to control quality and to ensure supplies were powerful motives for colonial merchants to establish flour mills, merchant-owned flour mills, "merchant mills." The additional profits from the vertical integration of their entire enterprise made the proposition an obvious winner. The availability of waterpower along fast-moving streams and at the falls of the many eastward-flowing rivers provided the energy source, and the towns established at these points provided the ports for shipping. The extension and articulation of milling into the lower Delaware River basin and the concentration there of millers encouraged experimentation and innovation that greatly increased productivity in this major colonial manufacturing industry, initially sawing wood for building and processing grain for export and later much more – including, in the early nineteenth century, gunpowder mills (Welsh 1956, 1957).

There is reason to believe that the large grain mills established by colonial merchants were technically in advance of those back home. The best millstones were thought to be those made in Europe, but the colonists' mode of siting, constructing, organizing, and operating the mills were the subjects of so much curiosity from visiting Englishmen that something must have been going on.[49] Victor S. Clark (1929, volume 1, p. 180) concluded that "techni-

cally colonial mills were abreast of the English, and probably in advance of them." It was only a matter of time before the new technology moved into the Chesapeake, but, well before the American Revolution, upriver ports such as Alexandria, Virginia, and its environs had become places where merchants established flour mills to process grain for export based, almost exclusively, on local investment capital (Kamoie 1999).

The building of ships was the most complex of colonial manufacturing industries, a large-scale enterprise that employed capital and labor and management in the fabrication of the biggest manufactured objects produced in the colonies.[50] Earlier writers have noted the importance of this industry to the New England and Middle Atlantic colonies, but its development in the Chesapeake Bay area, some of it centered at and near Norfolk, has only recently become better known and is still not fully explored (Kelso 1971–1972; Kamoie 1999).[51] Its expansion into Maryland and Virginia contributed to the development of these colonial economies. Much like other colonial industries, shipbuilding patterned itself on European models – like the fluijt mentioned previously – but built ships that were recognized universally as distinctively American and preferred. The Bristol merchant Richard Champion (1784, p. 50) wrote that "the most beautiful [ships] are those built in Philadelphia, where this art has attained to the greatest perfection, equal, perhaps superior, to any other ports of the world." About the same time, the Portuguese political economist Manoel Ferreira da Camara (1789, p. 348) urged his countrymen to resist the temptation of buying "os carvalhos da Pensilvania" and build their own, so pervasive was the product of the shipbuilders of the Delaware River (McCusker 1972).

Important innovations in all three sectors contributed to the developing economy by introducing notable productivity gains. Lorena Walsh has demonstrated the extent of productivity gains in colonial agriculture with her work on farming in the Chesapeake Bay region. Between the 1730s and the 1810s, output per worker in corn went up 200 percent; it advanced by 50 percent in the three decades from the 1730s to the 1760s. Both translate into annual average compound rates of growth of more than 1.3 percent. The increases were even greater in wheat production (Walsh 1989, pp. 398–9).[52] A similar argument has been made for rice (Hardy 2001, pp. 112–44; Nash 1992). Total factor productivity gains in shipping between 1675 and 1775 have been estimated to have increased by at least 0.8 percent annually, which one study has argued is much too low because it fails to take into account improvements

---

Witness, for instance, the apprehensive tone of the report in *Lloyd's Evening Post* (London), August 10, 1764, p. 2. First was the account of the recent importation from Pennsylvania of "some beautiful samples" of cotton goods made in Philadelphia; then the report that "divers artificers in other branches have lately gone over to Pennsylvania." Finally the editor drew his lesson: "by which it would seem, that our American colonies intend to shake off, by degrees, what they have long called a slavish dependence on the mother country." Compare Hood (1972). See also n. 69 in this essay.

[48] Eventually some colonial coppersmiths began manufacturing distilling equipment (Eck 1993).

[49] The royal governor of Virginia, John Murray, Earl of Dunmore, was so taken with the mill owned by James Parker of Norfolk that he asked Parker to oversee the building of a similar one on his own country estate, Porto Bello. Parker ordered some of the materials from London. Letter from Parker, at Norfolk, to Charles Steuart, at London, June 1 and 2, 1773, Charles Steuart Papers, 1758–1798, MS 5028, folios 79–83, National Library of Scotland, Edinburgh. In his memorial to the Loyalist Claims Commission, London, February 25, 1784, Dunmore valued the grist mill at £800 sterling. He also listed a "Saw Mill newly erected" worth £400. AO 13/28, no. 550, PRO/TNA.

---

[50] For shipbuilding in the Thirteen Continental Colonies, see Tables Eg356–403. For the price of ships built at Philadelphia, 1715–1790, see Table Eg271–274.

[51] When scholars seek to expand on our current understanding of this subject, they will find useful as a source the Henry Fleming Letterbook, 1772–1775, Cumbria Record Office, The Castle, Carlisle, England.

[52] Compare Weiss (1993), where he argues that between 1800 and 1860 the output per worker in agriculture rose at an annual rate 0.30 percent, and between 1860 and 1900 at 0.77 percent.

"Learning by doing," the acquisition and perfection of skills through experience on the job, was – and is – an important means of increasing human capital in agriculture, one that helped expand colonial agricultural productivity. See Foster and Rosenzweig (1995). Russell R. Menard determined that labor productivity in tobacco growing doubled between the 1630s and the 1650s. Menard (1976), p. 404. It seems quite certain that this stemmed from experience gained in the field. Compare Cateau (1995), pp. 1–36.

in shipping technology (McCusker and Menard 1991, p. 266).[53] To the extent that colonial distillers patterned themselves on their London counterparts, which they clearly did, they enjoyed a doubling of output per input between 1705 and 1783, an annual average rate of increase in productivity of 0.9 percent. Improvements in technology, organization, and management were the reasons for this increase.[54] Future research will add to these examples for all sectors of the colonial economy. Such productivity gains fueled the considerable increase in GDP discussed previously.

Capital

Diversification and newer technologies in all these sectors required investment capital, ideally mobilized locally and therefore more cheaply than that imported from abroad. A third significant theme in the development of the economy of the Thirteen Continental Colonies and one that has become increasingly better articulated over the past several decades is the emergence of colonial capital markets as a complement to and component of the British imperial capital market centered in London.[55] We know very little about how colonial capital markets worked, but we see evidence everywhere that they did work – based, in part, on the growing disparity in the distribution of wealth discussed earlier. Such locally generated investment capital was critical to the developing economy of early British America.[56] Overseas investment capital continued to be important – and its cost dropped over the seventeenth and eighteenth centuries – but domestic capital was even cheaper than imported capital. This meant that those colonists who undertook to start a new business, be it a farm or a store, could do so more easily than if they had had to borrow from abroad. With interest rates falling across the empire, colonial venture capital seems to have sought and found profitable uses increasingly in activities close to home.[57] Investment in "western" lands clearly became more

common and better organized. Land companies were formed and appealed to investors on both sides of the Atlantic. Their activities obviously had great geopolitical consequences.

That is an old story.[58] More recently attention has focused on the mobilization of domestic savings, and we have been able to read about developing investment markets funding agricultural pursuits in New England, South Carolina, and the West Indies (Rothenberg 1988; Menard 1994; Hancock 1994, pp. 61–84; Woods 1998; Pruden 2001; and Flynn 2001). Less clear is the way in which investors sought – and were sought out for – investment opportunities in commerce and manufacturing. As the optimum size of sailing vessels, trading voyages, and industrial enterprises grew, their startup costs expanded beyond the resources of one individual (McCusker 1972b, as revised and updated in McCusker 1997, pp. 245–57). The mobilization of colonial investment capital became something of a business itself.[59] Related to this was the functioning of particular coffeehouses in the colonial ports that operated as mercantile exchanges or bourses, obviously following the example of the likes of Jonathan's Coffee House in 'Change Alley in London, out of which was soon to emerge the London Stock Exchange. We know more about the results of such activity than the activity itself but we are learning.[60] For Maryland and Virginia, the quarterly meetings of the colonies' merchants at Williamsburg and the business at the tobacco warehouses served similar functions (Thomson 1955, pp. 287–98).[61] Tobacco warehouses had been in operation in Virginia (since 1730) and Maryland (since 1747) for a long time when William Tatham proclaimed them "the best banks in the state, and a respectable treasury of the American nation" (Tatham 1800, p. 86; Schweitzer 1980). All

---

[53] Also see McCusker (1972b), as revised and updated in McCusker (1997), pp. 245–57; Rosenberg (1972); Hardy (1999), pp. 43–95; and Hardy (2001). McCusker and Menard (1991), p. 266, suggest that there may have been even greater improvements in the productivity of shipping — stemming from the adoption of technological improvements — than others have credited. "It was not necessary that colonial shipbuilders invent improvements in order for them to have had an impact; it was only necessary that shipbuilders incorporate such improvements of whatever origin into their designs."

[54] McCusker (2000a), p. 200, with reference to the "Report, by the Commissioners of Excise in Scotland, to the Committee of the House of Commons, Appointed in the Year 1783, to Enquire into the Illicit Practices Then Used in Defrauding the Revenue . . . ," as printed in Great Britain, Parliament, House of Commons (1798), p. 401.

[55] See the summary of the literature on this subject in McCusker and Menard (1991), pp. 334–7.

[56] As was an adequate supply of money. See McCusker and Menard (1991), pp. 337–1, for an argument that the supply of money in the Thirteen Continental Colonies was adequate. For the colonial money supply, see Table Eg302–314.

[57] A seventeenth-century example of this process is at the root of the explanation offered for the shift from indentured servants to slaves by middling planters who had accumulated capital sufficient to make such an economically rational choice – however humanly horrid in its consequences (Rutman and Rutman 1984). For the growth of the slave trade, see Tables Eg201–216. For prices paid for slaves, see Table Eg300–301. Nearly a century later, Charles Carroll of Annapolis, one of the richest men of his era, pointedly chose to lend money locally rather than invest in England (Hoffman 2000), pp. 114, 122–3, 263–4. See the letter of Carroll to Clement Hill, December 24, 1761, Charles Carroll of Annapolis Letterbook, 1757–1761, p. 98, MS 214, Maryland Historical Society,

Baltimore: "I knew . . . Money kept at Interest here would be more beneficial" than invested "in the Funds in England" – and so it proved to be, under his careful management. The Annapolis firm of Wallace, Davidson, and Johnson raised money in Maryland to fund the opening of its London office. See Johnson (1979), pp. xi, xiv, and elsewhere.

For Carroll's fortune and that of other well-to-do colonists, see Price (1980), pp. 169–70 n. 30. See also Price (1980), pp. 28–43; Doerflinger (1986), pp. 126–34; and Burnard (2002), pp. 245–7. The Marquis de Chastellux's comment upon meeting Robert Morris in Philadelphia in December 1780 that he "possede une fortune de 8 million [livres tournois]" put him in another league altogether given that such a sum, the equivalent of some £340,000 sterling, made him the equal of the very richest of London merchants and West Indian nabobs. Chastellux (1786), volume 1, pp. 166–7. Nearly two decades later, Alexander Baring, the London banker, estimated the worth of William Bingham, Morris's contemporary, at between £400,000 and £500,000 sterling. Alberts (1969), p. 283.

[58] See Raymond De Roover's (1954) summary of the history of banking in Europe and the Atlantic World, 1300–1800, including several insightful comments on banking in the Thirteen Continental Colonies.

[59] The emergence of businessmen who specialized in brokerage is a sign of this development. See, for example, Philip Henry's advertisement of his services in a variety of financial capacities in the *South-Carolina and American General Gazette*, March 25, 1774, p. 1, col. 3. Compare Table Eg404–419.

[60] For an example of the mobilization of and uses for locally generated business capital, see Johnson (1979). Compare Price (1980). For the role of colonial coffeehouses, see McCusker (2000c).

[61] Also see Soltow (1965). The meetings of merchants at Williamsburg every three months resembled in their purpose, organization, and operation nothing so much as the European financial fairs like those held at Piacenza (the Besançon fairs), Frankfurt am Main, and Lyons. The literature on this subject is broad and deep. Two useful starting points are Gioffrè (1960) and Schneider (1991). An important part of such meetings on both sides of the Atlantic was the negotiation of bills of exchange. See McCusker (1992). Compare McCusker and Gravesteijn (1991). For colonial exchange rate data, see Table Eg315–324.

of the recent investigations link neatly with work being done on the American financial sector in the 1780s and after, allowing us, once again, to see more clearly the colonial origins of economic structures and institutions that were more fully realized in the early national period, in a United States now further distanced from Great Britain and its financial sector (Wright 1996, 2001; Rousseau and Sylla 1999).[62]

Expansion

The consequences of the developing, increasingly prosperous economy exhibited themselves in many ways; their implications were enormous and sweeping, reaching all across the society and the polity. Consider something as basic as the decision about whether and when to get married and to start a family, perhaps the most elemental of human decisions. As the Registrar-General of Great Britain, George Graham, commented from his survey of the variations in the numbers of people married in England between 1756 and 1845: "the fluctuation in the marriages of a country expresses the views which the great body of the people take of their prospects in the world."[63] At least in developing societies, given good prospects, people married earlier and had larger families. Conversely, when people's prospects seemed bleaker, they delayed getting married, thereby limiting their number of children when it seemed less likely that they could provide for them adequately. We are discovering evidence that the state of the economy in early British America and age at first marriage and size of family are highly correlated.

There are two related observations in this regard. Mentioned previously were the longer-term periods of expansion and contraction in the colonial economy that climaxed in the later 1730s to early 1740s with the ending of a long period of contraction and the start of a major expansionary period. This expansion continued across the next several decades until the start of the Revolutionary War. Gloria Main has worked out the rates of population growth in colonial New England, almost all of which was through natural increase if only because, after the middle of the seventeenth century, few immigrants chose to settle in that region. She has established a two-phase pattern in the growth of population over time. She makes the point, first, that, after the initially very large family sizes associated with the founding generation of settlers in the early and middle seventeenth century, there was a decline in family size that started before the end of that century. She then tells us that, by the middle of the next century, the decrease in family size had been reversed and population growth in New England took off again (Main 1988, p. 124). The growing population sought opportunity farther to the west of the older, already established areas. The rate at which new towns were being founded in New England tripled in the years after the end of the French and Indian War (Main 1988, p. 124, citing Bailyn 1986, p. 133).[64] In other words, demographic and economic cycles coincided.[65]

Gloria Main goes on to develop some intriguing inferences from her evidence. Westward migration, which some have seen as an act of desperation, as the "safety valve" releasing the pressures of overpopulation in the East, seems more accurately characterized in these decades at least as the pursuit of still better opportunities during a period of a rapidly expanding economy. Intriguingly, Main (1988, p. 127 n. 7) has found evidence that the residents of the older towns used their increasing incomes and wealth to help finance the movement westward of the settlers, many of whom were, after all, their own children.[66]

The implications of such insights need to be highlighted. Wealth levels grew during periods of population increase; population increased during periods of rising levels of wealth. Or, to say this yet another way, people chose to marry earlier and have more children when times seemed more prosperous, when their incomes were growing larger, when their prospects seemed brighter. Lest this seem obvious, contrast it with the older, opposing view that linked population growth with deepening destitution and suggested that the more children that families had, the greater the burden, the thinner they had to stretch scarce resources, and the poorer everyone became as a result – all of which may well have been true if income had remained static or declined. But it is evident now that this notion needs correction. To state the point as clearly as possible, the colonists of early British America, poor and rich, enjoyed an improving standard of living over the colonial era, increasingly so after the beginning of the second third of the eighteenth century. Now that prospects seemed more promising, they chose to respond to these changing circumstances in the most human of ways, not only buying more consumer goods but also by marrying earlier, starting families, and having more children (Main and Main 1988, 1999). As an earlier observer of the American economy and society, Benjamin Franklin, put it:

> When Families can be easily supported, more Persons marry and earlier in Life . . . .
>
> Land being thus plenty in America, and so cheap that a labouring Man, that understands Husbandry, can in a short Time save Money enough to purchase a Piece of new Land sufficient for a Plantation, whereon he may subsist a Family; such are not afraid to marry; for if they even look far enough forward to consider how their Children when grown up are to be provided for, they see that more Land is to be had at Rates equally easy, all Circumstances considered.
>
> Hence Marriages in America are more general, and more generally early, than in Europe.

---

[62] Compare Perkins (1994). Although I have serious reservations about this book, the simple fact is that there is nothing else of such scope.

[63] Great Britain, General Register Office (1849): *Eighth Annual Report*, p. 6. See also Southall and Gilbert (1996).

[64] See Table Eg194–200.

[65] Anthropomorphic evidence seems to substantiate these settlement patterns. For native-born white males born between 1700 and 1740, the average adult height either stayed flat or dropped a bit, depending on the study. After 1740

average adult height began to rise, suggesting better nutrition and better health care generally, thanks to the improving economy. See Steckel (1999).

[66] Compare Carr and Walsh (1994). See also Russo (1999, 2003). The latter is cited with the author's permission.

Marc Egnal (1996, pp. 7–12), offers, in effect, two case studies of what Main has described in his analysis of the ways in which two different farm families were provided with land by parents who had produced surpluses for sale in the market to purchase that land, just as, presumably, they themselves were saving some of the profits from the sale of their own surpluses to provide for their own children. The one family resided in Chester County, Pennsylvania, the other in the parish of St. Ours in French Canada. Egnal estimates (pp. 8, 209–10) that the two farm families shipped for sale outside their communities about one fifth of the value of their produce, a proportion strikingly similar to the 17–19 percent of total GDP generated for the Thirteen Continental Colonies by their export sector. McCusker and Menard (1991), pp. 85–6.

It was no coincidence that Franklin wrote this in 1751, well into that several-decades-long period of economic expansion, during a time of increasing prosperity.[67] Note, especially, his premise: "a labouring Man . . . can in a short Time save Money enough to purchase a Piece of new Land."

Recall in this context the point made earlier about people in the older settled eastern towns saving their surplus income and then using the accumulated savings for subsequent investment. Some employed their savings to invest in land, thereby helping their children get a start farther west, just as Benjamin Franklin argued. Choosing as their fortunes rose to save their marginal dollars rather than to spend them, they accumulated enough thereby to grub-stake their children.[68] People who bought lands in the West as an investment, on a large scale or a small one, had accumulated the money that they invested by consciously deciding not to spend their next dollar but to save it and to invest it. That they had such extra dollars and such discretion in their allocation was one of the fruits of the growing, developing, prospering colonial economy.[69]

Appendix A: General Discussion of the Tables, Data Sources, and Related Issues

The tables in this chapter present a variety of statistics for the United States during its colonial and pre-Federal periods through 1790. These tables describe statistically many characteristics of the life of the people who inhabited that part of early British America that afterward became the United States of America. They aim to cover all of the Thirteen Continental Colonies from Maine through Georgia across the entire period but, given the immense problems caused by incomplete data, rarely does any table come close to being complete either chronologically or geographically. Nevertheless, the data, for all their defects, do give us glimpses of the world that preceded the era of even more rapid development and,

of course, of considerably richer data, the subject of the other chapters in this book. It would have been possible to distribute these series grouped here among the other topical chapters, but all involved believe that a separate chapter especially organized to cover the earlier period would be more valuable in itself and would also provide a more suitable context for the statistics, many of which – though not all – are by their very nature less refined than those developed for the years after 1790.

Just as these considerations suggest, in the presentation and interpretation of the data for this chapter, there are many issues and concerns that involve more than one of the sets of tables presented in this chapter and that are, consequently, better discussed more fully here in this general introductory note (to which reference will be made, as appropriate, in the specific notes to each table). Gathering such thoughts here will also serve to diminish repeated references to a variety of primary and secondary sources.

In the past, statistics for the colonial and pre-Federal period were largely dependent on compilations made during the seventeenth and eighteenth centuries by writers such as Charles Whitworth (1776) and David Macpherson (1805) (see Palmer 1977 for an introduction). Even though Whitworth, Macpherson, and others like them are still a presence in what follows, current scholarship no longer relies solely on such authors. Increasingly over the last half century, economic historians have ferreted out statistical information and constructed statistical series from original records found in archives around the world.[70] Several of the series appear here for the first time; others represent substantial revision of earlier efforts. The compilers of each series are identified in the source citations. The two most important twentieth-century practitioners of this art were Lawrence A. Harper and Jacob M. Price, who were also, successively, the authors of this chapter in the two prior editions.[71]

The repository of documents drawn on most frequently for this chapter is the Public Record Office, The National Archives of the United Kingdom, in London (hereafter abbreviated PRO/TNA).[72] The PRO/TNA contains many collections that throw light on every aspect of the relationship between Great Britain and its colonies (and the newly established United States), but most particularly on the economic ties (commerce, agriculture, manufacturing) between them, especially when considered with reference to the mercantilist laws passed by the British Parliament.[73] Every archive has its own reference scheme, and the collections in the PRO/TNA

---

[67] Franklin (1961), as quoted in McCusker and Menard (1991), p. 212. The Swedish botanist Pehr Kalm (1937, volume 1, p. 211), who visited the colonies in 1750, expressed strikingly similar sentiments: "It does not seem difficult to find out the reason why the people multiply faster here than in Europe. As soon as a person is old enough he may marry in these provinces without any fear of poverty. There is such an amount of good land yet uncultivated that a newly married man can, without difficulty, get a spot of ground where he may comfortably subsist with his wife and children. The taxes are very low, and he need not be under any concern on their account. The liberties he enjoys are so great that he considers himself a prince in his possessions."

[68] Pruden (2001) makes the point that, at least in South Carolina, many of the investors in mortgages were women.

[69] Contemporaries far and wide seem to have appreciated these developments, at least to the degree that they identified the Thirteen Continental Colonies as the future seat of the British empire. See the advice offered by Colonel Samuel Martin, the doyen of Antigua sugar planters, to his son: "As it is highly probable that N[orth] America will be the seat of [the] British Empire in half a century, so I think it would be prudent in your eldest brother [Samuel], yourself, and me to make our [homes (?)] there." Colonel Samuel Martin to Captain Henry Martin, September 22, 1767, Letter Book of Samuel Martin, 1765–1774, folio 56, Martin Papers, Add. MS 41350, BL. Josiah Martin, the last royal governor of North Carolina was also a son of Colonel Martin.

Compare the exchange between two sophisticated Europeans in the middle of the next decade. Ferdinando Galiani wrote from Naples: "We are seeing the total collapse of Europe: the time for emigration to America has come." "Buy one [a house] in Philadelphia," not Paris, was the essence of his recommendation. Louise Florence Pétronille Tardieu d'Esclavelles, marquise d'Épinay, replied from Paris: "I think you're right." As quoted in Steegmuller (1991), pp. 213–4.

---

[70] For a discussion of these archives and libraries and the means of their use, see McCusker (1984), as revised and updated in McCusker (1997), pp. 1–21.

[71] *Historical Statistics of the United States* (1960); *Historical Statistics of the United States* (1975). Just as with tables in the other chapters in these volumes, those in this chapter accord "primary emphasis . . . [to] absolute rather than derived data." *Historical Statistics of the United States* (1975), volume 1, p. xiii. Most attention has been given to the collection, evaluation, and compilation of contemporary data; only rarely does material in the tables attempt more than that and then only when we have tried to answer questions with these data that contemporaries never asked. Two exceptions are the tables that deal with estimates of GDP (Table Eg217–222) and estimates of private wealth (Table Eg223–246).

[72] Quotations from and reproductions of unpublished crown-copyright materials in the Public Record Office, The National Archives, London, appear with the permission of the Controller of Her Majesty's Stationery Office.

[73] These laws are cited at various points in the text and footnotes by reference to the reigning monarch, the regnal year, and the chapter number– for example, Act of 5 Geo. II c. 22 (the fifth year of the reign of King George II, Chapter 22). For the text of these laws, see Great Britain, Laws and Statutes (1804–1869,

provide an apposite example of the mechanics of such references. Collections within the PRO/TNA are identified by title.[74] Chief among the collections used for this chapter are the Board of Trade Records (hereinafter abbreviated BT), the Colonial Office Records (CO), the Board of Customs and Excise Records (CUST), and the Treasury Office Records (T).[75] Citations to PRO/TNA materials involve several elements: first is a class code (for example, CO 5); within the class, volumes or boxes are specified by a piece number (for example, CO 5/65); internal references within pieces can be by page number, by folio number, or by date (for example, CO 5/65, folio 53r). There are, of course, numerous variations on this scheme.

Of special significance in detailing commercial contacts between the colonies and Great Britain are the compilations of trade data collected and organized under the direction of the Inspectors General of Imports and Exports responsible for Great Britain and for North America. These records of colonial trade are utilized throughout this chapter and contain enough traps for the unwary to require extra attention in this introduction. Given that much

of British trade was with the colonies and vice versa, they are frequently two sides of the same coin: The Customs records of sailing vessels clearing inward and outward at ports of entry (hereinafter abbreviated POE) in Great Britain; and the Customs records of vessels clearing inward and outward at POE in British America.

The annually compiled English and Scottish Inspector's General ledgers are reasonably conveniently arranged for statistical purposes, but they are so voluminous that the process of drawing data from them is immensely laborious.[76] Helping with that task are innumerable contemporary extracts from them and commentaries on them available in a wide range of other government documents. The volumes of data for England and Wales, compiled into the annual series of Ledgers of Imports and Exports of England, 1696–1780, are known as CUST 2/1–10, CUST 3/1–82, PRO/TNA; the Ledgers of Imports and Exports, Scotland, 1755–1827, are CUST 14, PRO/TNA. Many of the tables in this chapter draw heavily on these accounts. See especially Tables Eg429–460.

It is crucial to an adequately informed use of the trade data presented in these tables to understand how, why, and by what agency they were prepared. The data in the ledgers of imports and exports of England, Wales, and Scotland were gathered day by day from the clearances inward and outward of vessels and cargoes at each of the POE of Great Britain.[77] These data were then transferred to the office of the Inspector General of Imports and Exports of England and Wales, in London, and Inspector General of Imports and Exports of Scotland, in Edinburgh, where they were tabulated, assigned a valuation, and transcribed into the annual ledgers. It should be emphasized that the yearly volumes record the quantities and values of goods imported into and exported from Great Britain and therefore not the quantities and values of goods exported from any given overseas point of origin or imported into any given overseas destination. However transparent this may seem in the abstract, all too frequently writers have reported the amount of tobacco or sugar imported into Great Britain from the Chesapeake Bay colonies or, say, Barbados, as the amount of these commodities exported from them – or, even worse, produced by them. The distinction is fundamental because it is obvious that Barbados produced more sugar than it exported and that it exported sugar, quite legally, to places other than Great Britain – notably to the other British colonies on the North American continent.

Probably no more confusing statement can be made about these volumes than that they do not record the actual, current value of the trade of England and Wales (and Scotland). As was stated earlier, as part of their tabulation of the data, the clerks in the Inspector General's office multiplied the quantities imported and exported by a price to arrive at the values of each commodity transcribed into the ledgers. Summed up for imports and for exports for each of the nation's trading partners, the totals were meant to indicate England's balance of trade. In doing the calculations, the

---

1810–1828, 1911, 1804–1869). Note that acts passed in a particular regnal year frequently came into force only in a subsequent year and that the popular name for an act more often than not referred to the year in which it became operational. See, for example, Table Eg420–424.

[74] For this and much else, including "the Catalogue" (formerly "PROCAT"), see the National Archives Internet site (accessed May 25, 2005).

[75] For the early Colonial Office Records there exists a relatively easy mode of access in an ongoing calendaring of that collection: Great Britain, Public Record Office (1860 to date). Up till now, 45 volumes (in 46 parts) have appeared. The newest volume, for the year 1739, appeared in 1994. Similar calendars have been prepared for the Treasury Records: Great Britain, Public Record Office (1868–1889, 1898–1903, 1904 to date). Equally helpful are the projects that transcribed or made photographic copies of documents for the study of colonial history organized on a state or local basis, sometimes with the help of government funds. The Virginia Colonial Records Project is a good example. Its "Survey Reports" are guides to the copies collected over the years. They can be used at the John D. Rockefeller Jr. Library, Colonial Williamsburg Foundation, Williamsburg, Virginia; the Library of Virginia, Richmond; and the Alderman Library, University of Virginia, Charlottesville. See Boyd (1958) and Virginia Committee on Colonial Records (1960). A similar project copied many documents having to do with South Carolina. The original thirty-six volumes of transcripts have been indexed and microfilmed. See Carson (1973). Historians of early British America need to be cautious and careful in their use of both resources. Just as the compilers of calendars and indexes have had to be selective, so those who organized the copying of documents were forced to make compromises that can affect the ability of other historians to use what they have done. These calendars and collections cannot be approached uncritically. By definition, calendars are only synopses of documents, synopses that may not mention topics of concern to a particular researcher; they are aids to research, not substitutes for the documents themselves. Collections of transcripts of documents are selective and have not exhausted an archive. Even though the results are still very helpful, these projects left out a great deal by definition.

The careful historian, having found something in a calendar or a collection of transcripts, must check it in the original – and sometimes cite both sources. The careful historian, failing to find something in a calendar or a collection of copies, cannot assume that what he or she is seeking is not in the original document or elsewhere in the repository. Indeed, early printed calendars – and copying projects based on them – systematically omitted materials now considered significant to historians, especially economic historians (tabular and statistical material, for instance). See McCusker (1992), pp. 119–20 n 13. See also Andrews (1934–1938), volume 4, pp. 18 n. 2, and 139 n. 6; Carson (1973), pp. 6–7; and Smith (1981). Rupert Jarvis (1958, p. 215) found "the indexing...the fullness and [the] adequacy" of the various PRO calendars "most uneven."

[76] To extract and compile the data in John J. McCusker (1989), volume 2, pp. 879–997, took fifteen weeks during the winter and spring of 1966–1967 and then several weeks more cross-checking the resulting tables against various contemporary and modern compilations.

[77] For these ledgers and their creation, see Price (1975); McCusker (1985), pp. 15–16; and McCusker (1971), as revised and updated in McCusker (1997), pp. 222–44. In addition to the works already cited (and the sources cited in them), one should consult Clark (1938), which provides a valuable history and analysis of the basic statistics and a useful appendix that has a chronological list of statistical material for 1663–1783 and specifies where the data may be found. Compare Palmer (1977).

clerks did not use current commodity prices, however, but instead resorted to a set price for each commodity that had been established for this purpose early in the eighteenth century. Thus, the numbers to be found in the ledgers are not the actual values of the goods traded but their nominal value – not a current value series but a constant value series. The situation continued to exist and to cause considerable confusion well into the nineteenth century. However aware or not contemporaries were of this anomaly, historians have come to terms with it less than perfectly.[78]

There are other difficulties with these records (in addition to those mentioned in individual tables in this chapter). The accounts in the Inspector General's ledgers are divided into two categories, London and the "Outports" – that is, all of the other English and Welsh POE combined, an unfortunate grouping for those interested in, say, the sugar trade with Bristol or the slave trade of Liverpool. The listing of places to and from which goods were traded, which no doubt reflected the reporting of clearances inward and outward as recorded by the Customs officials in the various POE, is far from optimal for historians of the Thirteen Continental Colonies. Thus, for instance, "New England" combines British trade with many colonies, which economic historians find unfortunate because they would prefer to distinguish the trade of each colony. Even more problematic is the omission of New Jersey as a separate entry – a matter that causes more than one conundrum. The imports and exports of eastern New Jersey passed through POE New York just as those of western New Jersey passed through POE Philadelphia – at least as recorded in the Ledgers of Imports and Exports of England. As a consequence, not only do we have no record of New Jersey's trade with England, but we are also saddled with an overstatement of the trade figures of New York and Pennsylvania. Even more significant, because it involved the extremely important tobacco trade, is the failure of the English ledgers to separate Virginia and Maryland – although the annual ledgers produced in the office of the Inspector General of Scotland did so (see Table Eg443–460).

The parallel accounts – the other side of the bureaucratic coin – are the records created in each of the colonial POE by the chief administrative clerk of the port. Called somewhat confusingly the "naval officer" – there was no connection with the Royal Navy – he was essentially the port's chief statistical officer, a position the origins of which can be traced to as early as the mid-1630s (see Beer 1908, p. 207 n. 2). Although the naval officers functioned originally as part of the local, colonial bureaucracy, they eventually became one component of the Royal Customs administration.[79] The articulation of these offices and the establishment of their jurisdictions evolved into a settled system of POE and port officials. By the time of the American Revolution, there were more than 60 POE in British America, 44 of them in British North America, 35 of which were in colonies that joined the revolt and eventually became the United States. Those 35 divided up the coastline from Maine (still then politically part of Massachusetts) to Georgia. One can best visualize the limits of the POE by consulting the excellent maps in Cappon, Petchenik, and Long (1976), pp. 40, 119–20. These maps illustrate nicely a key point: Just as in Great Britain, colonial POE were not harbors but jurisdictions. For instance, the entirety of the colony of New York was served by POE New York in the same way

that POE Philadelphia was coterminus with the whole colony of Pennsylvania. Nor were such boundaries inviolable. As indicated earlier, much of the shipping and trade of western New Jersey cleared by happenstance through POE Philadelphia and much of the shipping and trade of eastern New Jersey cleared through POE New York–New Jersey, the keg tapped at both ends.[80] Note, too, that a goodly portion of the trade of northern Massachusetts cleared officially through POE Piscataqua (New Hampshire). (See Table Eg674–685.)

The reports the naval officers produced are referred to as the colonial naval office shipping lists (hereinafter abbreviated NOSL). The NOSL recorded the clearances inward and outward for every vessel that visited each colonial port, stating the full particulars of the vessel and the details of its cargo. They naval officers submitted their returns quarterly, but frustrating for the modern economic historian is the near-random pattern to their survival. The NOSL can be found only incompletely for each POE, and there is not one year for which we have all the NOSL for all POE. Returns for less than a full four quarters have some value but are far less useful because of the seasonal nature of what they include and what they omit. Obviously one cannot simply assume that returns for three quarters of a year contain a record of three quarters of the trade and shipping that cleared the port.

Nevertheless, all such trade did clear port. Certainly in the eighteenth century, even in the seventeenth century, vessels and their cargoes clearing inward and outward were regularly and consistently recorded in the books of the naval officers. Although there are flaws in the NOSL, the accounts are as internally complete and reliable as we can expect them to be. The singular, indeed notorious, anomaly involved the import trade in sugar, molasses, and rum from the mid-1730s onward. But everyone knew about the problem, and both contemporary officials and modern writers have taken it into account when discussing issues affected by that trade.[81] Lawrence A. Harper (1939, p. 263), the leading twentieth-century authority on such matters, settled the issue once and for all: "Although the lurid accounts of frauds contained in administrative reports and court records make interesting reading, they must not be allowed to confuse us as to the extent of illegal activities"; "illicit trade constituted only a small fraction of the legitimate commerce" of the Thirteen Continental Colonies (see also Dickerson 1951; McCusker forthcoming). The point is that the NOSL and contemporary accounts based on them afford us a reasonably accurate picture of the shipping and trade of the Thirteen Continental Colonies. As a consequence, eighteenth-century writers and later historians have found in the NOSL a rich and reliable store of data with which to interpret the overseas shipping and trade of the colonies.

That rich store of data gathered by the naval officers survives in three forms. Scattered extant NOSL can be found in many repositories, but the largest collection is, again, in the PRO/TNA. Extracts from them abound, made by contemporaries, organized for this or that port, drawn for longer and shorter periods. Some of these accounts were published in colonial newspapers such as the *Pennsylvania Gazette* and the *South-Carolina Gazette* (see, for example, Table Eg674–685). The only complete contemporary

---

[78] McCusker (1971), as revised and updated in McCusker (1997), attempts to construct a current value series using these data.

[79] The discussion of all this by Andrews (1934–1938, volume 4, pp. 178–221) may be considered definitive.

---

[80] There are some naval office shipping lists from the three New Jersey POE. See Levitt (1981).

[81] This is a constant theme in McCusker (1989).

compilation from the NOSL is the Ledger of Imports and Exports, British North America, 1768–1772, CUST 16/1, PRO/TNA. A modern attempt to gather and assemble as much of the extant NOSL data as possible was established in the 1930s under the supervision of Lawrence A. Harper. He did this as part of a New Deal Works Progress Administration project conducted at the University of California, Berkeley, titled "Trade and Commerce of the English Colonies in America."[82] The work of Harper and his associates formed the basis of many of the tables presented in the prior editions of *Historical Statistics of the United States*, most especially the 1975 edition.[83] Other, later authors have attempted similar projects on a smaller scale.[84] Insofar as was possible, all such compilations used for this chapter, both eighteenth-century and twentieth-century, have been rechecked and many revised and corrected.

The extensive, pervasive use in this chapter of the Customs Ledger of Imports and Exports, British North America, 1768–1772, the volume referred to earlier (CUST 16/1, PRO/TNA), underscores just how rich the NOSL are as a source for historians of colonial shipping and trade. The one-volume ledger is, in effect, a (nearly) complete compilation of the shipping lists for what were, arguably, the five most important years in pre–Revolutionary War American commerce. Organized by Thomas Irving, Inspector General of Imports and Exports of North America and Register of Shipping, this immensely valuable resource is the exception that proves some of the rules just enunciated. In May 1768, newly arrived as part of the American Board of Customs, operating out of his office in the Custom House, Boston, Irving ordered the Customs officials in each POE of British North America to send him their quarterly accounts rather than post them to London as they had done in the past.[85] He and his clerks then checked and rechecked every entry before assembling the annual accounts and, eventually, gathering them into a single volume that survives. Despite some flaws, the ledger presents a summation of all of the quarterly reports from all colonial POE. It constitutes a point of departure and a point of comparison for all discussions of colonial shipping and colonial trade and is the basis of many of the tables in this chapter. Irving, who had probably honed his skills as a minor functionary in the Office of the Scottish Inspector General before being posted to Boston, later went on to become the Inspector General of Import and Export of Great Britain in London. His son, William Irving, held that office after his father's death in 1800 until his own demise in 1855, a remarkable longevity and continuity in a key governmental position, the history of which has yet to be written.[86]

What follows are discussions of several other general points about the information found in these records and the data generated from them that are presented in the tables in this chapter: units of time; varieties of money; forms of weights and measures generally;

the measurement of a ship's tonnage; modes of calculation; and designations of place. The theme of all such discussions may well be that nothing about this early modern period can be assumed to be as simple as it seems.

Time

Reference was made earlier to the four quarters of the year. The British government worked with an administrative year divided into four parts that corresponded, roughly, to the four seasons. In principle, all governmental accounts – including the NOSL – were kept according to these quarters. The starting and ending dates of the quarters were set but Great Britain's latter-day adoption of calendar reform in 1752, which eliminated eleven days from that year, shifted the dates to accommodate the change and to make up for the "lost" days. The beginning dates of the four quarters, before and after the calendar reform, were as follows:[87]

Quarter Day	Prior to 1752 reform	After 1752 reform
Christmas	December 25	January 5
Ladyday	March 25	April 5
Midsummer	June 24	July 5
Michaelmas	September 29	October 9

In practice, although initially there was some confusion, matters quickly sorted themselves out. Thus, sometimes despite appearances, quarterly accounts such as the colonial NOSL and annual accounts, such as the CUST 3 ledgers, conformed reasonably quickly to the new dating. The confusion arises largely with regard to the CUST 3 ledgers because the clerks who prepared the annual volumes retained the old wording even though the Customs officers who gathered the raw data were using the new system (see McCusker 1971, pp. 226–7). Thus, with exceptions specified in individual tables in this chapter, before 1752 the reporting years for the Customs accounts on both sides of the Atlantic Ocean ran from December 25 through December 24; for 1752 and after, they ran from January 5 through January 4.

In conformity with the convention adopted by most historians of the early modern period, dates are reproduced herein as they were recorded by each individual with two exceptions: The new year is considered to have begun on January 1; and documents through 1752 that were dated between January 1 and March 24 are set down here with the double dating of the year to reflect both the "Old Style" Julian Calendar and the "New Style" Gregorian Calendar (for example, February 22, 1731/32).

Money

All of the British empire shared the same twelve-based notational scheme for money – 1 pound equaled 20 shillings; 1 shilling equaled 12 pence (abbreviated £, s, d; for example, £3 6s 11d) – but every part of the British empire valued its money of account differently. Thus, the British pound sterling was worth more than the Irish pound, which differed in worth from the Massachusetts pound, the New York pound, the Barbados pound, and so forth. (The modern

[82] Records of the project constitute part of the Lawrence A. Harper Papers, Accession number D-271, General Library, Department of Special Collections, University of California, Davis. For some early evidence of the project, see Cox (1939) and Harper and Cox (1942).

[83] *Historical Statistics of the United States* (1975), volume 2, pp. 1152–1200 (series Z1–615). Compare *Historical Statistics of the United States* (1960), pp. 743–74.

[84] The most recent and most impressive of such ventures is Hardy (1999).

[85] Irving's jurisdiction, and thus the coverage of the ledger, extended from Newfoundland to Florida and included Bermuda and the Bahama Islands.

[86] For Irving, the collection of these data, and the compiling of the ledger, see McCusker (1979), as revised and updated in McCusker (1997), pp. 190–221.

[87] For these calendar changes generally, see McCusker and Gravesteijn (1991), pp. 445–9. Compare McCusker (1997), pp. xix–xx. For a discussion of the impact of these changes in Great Britain and, most particularly, on the Customs and Excise, see Jarvis (1964). See also Smith (1998).

analogue is the dollar, which has a different worth in the United States, Canada, Australia, Hong Kong, and so forth.) The tables in this chapter usually report values in the original money of account. The series in Table Eg315–324 offer the ability to reduce one money of account to another. In many of the tables presented later, amounts originally stated in pounds, shillings, and pence have been converted to a decimalized format in order to make them easier to use in calculations (for example £3.35).

By the end of the colonial period, the dollar had been introduced into more that one colony as a parallel money of account. By the 1780s, use of the dollar as a money of account had become much more widespread. Although some citizens of the United States continued to price goods and services in older money units, before the end of the Revolutionary War, the relationships between pound local currency and the dollar had become fixed and unvarying – as the Euro has to the former national currencies of the participating member states of the European Union. At par, one pound sterling (£1) equaled $4.44 (McCusker 2001a).

Weights and Measures

Although most of the issues created by the many different units of weight and measure employed in the period are sorted through in specific tables, one or two generic points can be made. In general, the British Americans employed the same systems used in Great Britain. Thus, for instance, the foot as a unit of length, the acre as the unit of area, and the avoirdupois pound (abbreviated "lb") as a unit of weight were standard across the British empire. The liquid gallon (abbreviated "gal") was the one then common to both Great Britain and the colonies ("Queen Anne's gallon," 231 cubic inches); it continues to be used in the United States today but as of May 1, 1825, it was replaced in Great Britain and the British empire (including Canada and the British West Indies) by the imperial gallon (277.42 cubic inches) (Act of 5 George IV, c. 74, 1824).[88] In most instances, the original units have been retained in the following tables. The only conversions made here have been the contraction of different subsets of a measure to one larger unit (thus, pounds, quarters, hundredweight, and tons are added together and expressed as tons). Frequently, such totals have been converted to the largest unit and a decimalized expression of the fraction (for example, 18.5 long tons). Once again, this has been done to make subsequent calculations easier.

A fair example of the considerable potential for confusion caused by the various schemes of weights and measures in use in the Thirteen Continental Colonies is to be found in Tables Eg329–355. The size of the fleet of fishing vessels was measured by the ships' tonnage, stated in tons (for which see the following discussion). The size of the fleets' catch of cod was measured in terms of hundredweight of fish, the hundredweight measuring 100 pounds avoirdupois, twenty of which equaled a short ton (2,000 pounds).[89] Whale oil was sold by the barrel measuring 31.5 gallons, eight of which equaled a tun (252 gallons), usually spelled "ton." All three were fundamentally different units of measure even though all three bore the same name.

Obviously, then, great difficulty occurs when seemingly the same "measure" was used for different commodities or in separate places to mean different amounts, even different things altogether. The chief offender was, of course, the hundredweight (abbreviated "cwt.," otherwise known as the quintal, which itself was spelled in a variety of ways) and the ton, equal to twenty hundredweight. The hundredweight weighed 100 pounds (the short hundredweight) in some circumstances and 112 pounds (the long hundredweight) in others – and it is not always obvious just which was the case. The only real way to know is to consult merchant accounts and the records of trade. In each particular instance in the tables in this chapter, the one that applied will be specified but mentioning the matter in advance serves to point out that caution is necessary when confronting colonial counting.[90]

A parallel concern involves the capacity of containers, which frequently served as surrogate measures of quantity. People bought, sold, and shipped commodities one barrel or one hogshead at a time. Not only did the wooden cask (the only generic word for such things) differ in size by commodity, but some of them, in some trades, changed in size over time. Thus, the hogshead – despite what statute law and mercantile treatises might otherwise imply – was not a standard-sized unit.[91] The text for Tables Eg275–284 and Eg299 discusses this issue particularly with regard to rice and tobacco; for sugar casks, see McCusker (1989), volume 2, pp. 768–878.

All who attempt to compare commodity prices from this early period with later periods and other places need to be alert to anomalies such as the following. In 1789, the state of Pennsylvania legislated a change in the size of the barrel of beef or pork. The law set November 1 as the effective date of this change, but in practice merchants adopted it in March of that year. Some wines that were shipped in casks that ranged in size from 110 to 140 gallons were priced per nominal cask of 60 gallons. As of July 13, 1824, by mutual agreement among the merchants of Pennsylvania, the long hundredweight of 112 pounds replaced the short hundredweight of 100 pounds (Bezanson, Gray, and Hussey 1936–1937, volume 1, pp. 336–8).

Tonnage

The shipping industry of the period referred to a vessel's capacity in three different ways. The first of these was *measured tonnage*, which, just as its name implies, was computed by a set formula known and applied reasonably consistently in the British empire during the seventeenth and eighteenth centuries down into the mid-1780s. Alternatively, when referring to the quantity of goods a vessel could carry, people talked about the vessel's *cargo tonnage*. The tonnage recorded for purposes of registration with colonial and imperial governments – analogous to modern motor vehicle registration – was called its *registered tonnage*. All three were different; they existed in roughly the ratio of 2:3:4, that is, two tons registered tonnage to three tons measured tonnage to four tons

---

[88] Most of this is addressed in Klopfer (1936); in McCusker (1989), volume 2, pp. 768–878; and in McCusker (1973), as revised and updated in McCusker (1997), pp. 76–101. See also McCusker (1981), as revised and updated in McCusker (1997), Table 3.5, pp. 70–5.

[89] McCusker (1973), as revised and updated in McCusker (1997), p. 86 n. 12. The long hundredweight measured 112 pounds and the long ton, 2,240 pounds.

[90] The work that has sorted these issues out most carefully for the colonial period is Klopfer (1936). For a discussion of these issues with references to the wider literature on the subject, see McCusker (1973), as revised and updated in McCusker (1997), pp. 76–101.

[91] Therein lies the fatal flaw in much of the otherwise admirable work of Zupko (1968, 1977, 1985). As Klopfer (1936) demonstrates, the only way to know the capacity of a cask in lieu of weighing or measuring its contents ourselves is to examine the ledgers and accounts of merchants engaged in the trades.

cargo tonnage. This means that any given vessel was registered at roughly two thirds its measured tonnage and that the cargo it carried, in terms of cargo tonnage, was roughly twice its registered tonnage (see, for example, Table Eg634–673). None of this necessarily involved subterfuge or deception; there were simply three different ways of referring to the size of the same vessel – all, again frightfully confusingly, employing the same words (see McCusker 1981, as revised and updated in McCusker 1997, pp. 43–75).

It is worth noting also that both Great Britain and the United States changed the legal mode of calculating measured tonnage during the 1780s, making comparisons spanning this decade more difficult (McCusker 1981, as revised and updated in McCusker 1997, p. 58).

Calculations

Given the incomplete data from this early period, some procedures have been adopted to minimize potential distortions introduced by what has simply chanced to survive. Of special note is one that applies to all tables that deal with prices. Monthly averages were calculated as the mean of the averages for each third of the month (days 1–10, 11–20, and 21–31). The annual averages were then calculated by first computing the average of each quarter, and then averaging each of the four quarters. In some instances, short-term gaps in the data have been filled by estimates calculated as straight-line interpolations based on neighboring data. Such estimates have been indicated in the text for the relevant tables (see McCusker 1992, pp. 23–4). As mentioned earlier, the subunits of the pound and weights and measures have been decimalized in aid of calculations. In addition, numbers are frequently rounded one or more places to the left of the decimal point to avoid any implication of precision in data that are far from precise (for example, £5,000 rather than £5,027); compare Table Eg60–64.

Places

For the geographical parameters of the Thirteen Continental Colonies and the immediate post-Revolutionary United States, see Map Eg-A (also consult the maps in Cappon, Petchenik, and Long 1976). Although references to the Thirteen Continental Colonies are understandable enough, it should be made explicit that "British America" in the era before the American Revolution included many more than thirteen colonies in a long string extending from Newfoundland in the north to Barbados in the south. As the map makes clear, this chapter covers much less territory than Great Britain laid claim to, especially after 1763, simply because such territory was not part of either what was then the Continental Colonies or what was later to be the United States. (Florida is an exception, having been part of British North America from 1763 to 1783 and becoming part of the United States after 1819.) The tables in this chapter can be presumed to account for the Thirteen Continental Colonies and the subsequent United States in the limited form that they were known prior to 1790. Exceptions to that coverage will be made explicit in the titles or text accompanying the tables. None of these discussions include territory under the jurisdiction of other powers (for example, France, Spain, or the Native American Indians).

One source used repeatedly in the following tables involved particular geographical issues. The Ledger of Imports and Exports, British North America, 1768–1772, the volume referred to earlier (CUST 16/1, PRO/TNA), a product of the Royal Customs

administration, gathered data from ports of entry throughout its jurisdiction. What constituted a "port of entry" was discussed earlier. The jurisdiction of the American Board of Customs, just like its predecessors, extended all along the coast from Newfoundland through to Georgia and, after 1763, included East Florida and West Florida. It also included the Bermuda and Bahama Islands. When data from the ledger are used in this chapter, care is taken to distinguish among potentially confusing territorial limits.

It is usual when dealing in sequence with all of the Thirteen Continental Colonies to do so in geographical order, north to south. On occasion, one also groups them by region. The four conventional regions have reference to political (rather than geographical) boundaries: New England consisted of the colonies and later states of Maine (part of Massachusetts until 1820), New Hampshire, Massachusetts, Rhode Island, and Connecticut; the Middle Atlantic region consisted of New York, New Jersey, Pennsylvania, and Delaware; the Upper South was Maryland and Virginia; and the Lower South consisted of North Carolina, South Carolina, and Georgia.[92]

Appendix B: Abbreviations Used in This Chapter

Act of...	in Great Britain, Laws and Statutes, *The Statutes of the Realm* (for the years prior to 1714, with the exception of 1642–1660); *Acts and Ordinances of the Interregnum,* (for 1642–1660); *The Statutes at Large ... of Great Britain* (for the period from 1714 to 1806); or *The Statutes of the United Kingdom of Great Britain and Ireland* (for the years after 1806)[93]
Add. MSS	Additional Manuscripts, in the British Library (BL)
AO	Audit Department Records, in the Public Record Office (PRO/TNA)
BL	British Library (formerly British Museum Library), London
BT	Board of Trade Records, in the Public Record Office (PRO/TNA)
CO	Colonial Office Records, in the Public Record Office (PRO/TNA)
CUST	Board of Customs and Excise Records, in the Public Record Office (PRO/TNA)
HLRO	House of Lords Record Office, London
LC	Library of Congress, Washington, D.C.
NOSL	Naval Office Shipping List(s)
POE	Port(s) of Entry
PRO/TNA	Public Record Office, The National Archives, London
T	Treasury Office Records, in the Public Record Office (PRO/TNA)

References

Adams, John. 1961. *Diary and Autobiography of John Adams,* edited by L[yman] H. Butterfield. 4 volumes. The Adams Papers, series 1. Harvard University Press.

Alberts, Robert C. 1969. *The Golden Voyage: The Life and Times of William Bingham, 1752–1804.* Houghton-Mifflin.

Allen, Robert C. 2003. "Progress and Poverty in Early Modern Europe," *Economic History Review,* 2nd series, 56 (August): 403–43.

Andrews, Charles M. 1934–1938. *The Colonial Period of American History.* 4 volumes. Yale University Press.

Arendt, Hannah. 1965. *On Revolution.* 2nd edition, revised. Viking Press.

Bailyn, Bernard. 1986. *The Peopling of British North America: An Introduction.* Knopf.

---

[92] For a discussion of the strengths and weaknesses of these divisions, see McCusker and Menard (1991), pp. 86–8.

[93] See Great Britain, Laws and Statutes (1762–1807, 1804–1869, 1810–1828, and 1911).

Bairoch, Paul. 1976. "Europe's Gross National Product, 1800–1975." *Journal of European Economic History* 5 (Fall): 273–340.

Bancroft, George. 1876. *History of the United States of America from the Discovery of the Continent*. Revised, centenary edition. 6 volumes. Little, Brown.

Beer, George Louis. 1908. *The Origins of the British Colonial System, 1578–1660*. Macmillan.

Berlin, Ira. 1998. *Many Thousands Gone: The First Two Centuries of Slavery in North America*. Harvard University Press.

Bezanson, Anne, Robert D. Gray, and Miriam Hussey. 1936–1937. *Wholesale Prices in Philadelphia, 1784–1861*. University of Pennsylvania, Wharton School of Finance and Commerce, Industrial Research Department, Research Studies, volumes 29–30. University of Pennsylvania Press.

Blum, John M., William S. McFeely, et al. 1993. *The National Experience: A History of the United States*. 8th edition. Harcourt Brace Jovanovich.

Boyd, Julian P. 1958. "A New Guide to the Indispensable Sources of Virginia History." *William and Mary Quarterly*, 3rd series, 15 (January): 3–13.

Braudel, Fernand [P.]. 1979. *Civilisation matérielle, économie et capitalisme, XVe–XVIIIe siècle*. Armand Colin.

Buel, Richard, Jr. 1998. *In Irons: Britain's Naval Supremacy and the American Revolutionary Economy*. Yale University Press.

Burnard, T[revor] G. 2001. "'Prodigious Riches': The Wealth of Jamaica before the American Revolution." *Economic History Review*, 2nd series, 54 (August): 506–24.

Burnard, Trevor [G.]. 2002. *Creole Gentlemen: The Maryland Elite, 1691–1776*. Routledge.

Bushman, Richard L[yman]. 1992. *The Refinement of America: Persons, Houses, Cities*. Knopf.

Bushman, Richard Lyman. 1998. "Markets and Composite Farms in Early America." *William and Mary Quarterly*, 3rd series, 55 (July): 351–74.

Caley, Percy Burdelle. 1939. "Dunmore, Colonial Governor of New York and Virginia, 1770–1782." Ph.D. dissertation, University of Pittsburgh.

Cappon, Lester J., Barbara Bartz Petchenik, and John Hamilton Long, editors. 1976. *Atlas of Early American History: The Revolutionary Era, 1760–1790*. Princeton University Press.

Carr, Lois Green, and Lorena S. Walsh. 1977. "The Planter's Wife: The Experience of White Women in Seventeenth-Century Maryland." *William and Mary Quarterly*, 3rd series, 34 (October): 542–71.

Carr, Lois Green, and Lorena S. Walsh. 1978. "Changing Life Styles in Colonial St. Mary's County." *Working Papers from the Regional Economic History Research Center* 1 (3): 73–118.

Carr, Lois Green, and Lorena S. Walsh. 1988. "The Standard of Living in Colonial Chesapeake." *William and Mary Quarterly*, 3rd series, 45 (January): 135–59.

Carr, Lois Green, and Lorena S. Walsh. 1994. "Changing Lifestyles and Consumer Behavior in the Colonial Chesapeake." In Cary Carson, Ronald Hoffman, and Peter J. Albert, editors. *Of Consuming Interests: The Style of Life in the Eighteenth Century*. University Press of Virginia.

Carr, Lois Green, Russell R. Menard, and Lorena S. Walsh. 1991. *Robert Cole's World: Agriculture and Society in Early Maryland*. University of North Carolina Press.

Carson, Helen Craig. 1973. *Records in the British Public Record Office Relating to South Carolina, 1663–1782*. Pamphlet Accompanying South Carolina Archives Microcopy, number 1. South Carolina Department of Archives and History.

Cateau, Heather. 1995. "Conservation and Change: Implementation in the British West Indian Sugar Industry, 1750–1810." *Journal of Caribbean History* 29 (2): 1–36.

[Champion, Richard]. 1784. *Considerations on the Present Situation of Great Britain and the United States of North America, with a View to Their Future Commercial Connections*. 1st edition. John Stockdale.

Chaplin, Joyce E. 1993. *An Anxious Pursuit: Agricultural Innovation and Modernity in the Lower South, 1730–1815*. University of North Carolina Press.

[Chastellux, François Jean de Beauvoir de]. 1786. *Voyages de M. le marquis de Chastellux dans l'Amérique septentrionale dans les années 1780, 1781 et 1782*. 2 volumes. Prault.

Clark, G[eorge] N. 1938. "Guide to English Commercial Statistics, 1696–1782." *Royal Historical Society Guides and Handbooks*, number 1. Royal Historical Society.

Clark, Gregory. 2001a. "Debt, Deficits, and Crowding Out: England, 1727–1840." *European Review of Economic History* 5 (December): 403–36.

Clark, Gregory. 2001b. "The Secret History of the Industrial Revolution." Paper, University of California, Davis, October. Accessed via the Internet, May 25, 2005.

Clark, Victor S. 1929. *History of Manufactures in the United States*. Carnegie Institution of Washington, Publication number 215B. 2nd edition. 3 volumes. Carnegie Institution of Washington.

Clemens, Paul G. E. 1980. *The Atlantic Economy and Colonial Maryland's Eastern Shore: From Tobacco to Grain*. Cornell University Press.

Coclanis, Peter A. 1989. *The Shadow of a Dream: Economic Life and Death in the South Carolina Low Country, 1670–1720*. Oxford University Press.

Coclanis, Peter A. 1990. "The Wealth of British America on the Eve of the Revolution." *Journal of Interdisciplinary History* 21 (Autumn): 245–60.

Cole, Arthur Harrison. 1938. *Wholesale Commodity Prices in the United States, 1700–1861*. 2 volumes. Harvard University Press.

Cox, John H. 1939. "Compilations of Colonial Imports and Exports on Film." *Journal of Documentary Reproduction* 2 (September): 198–201.

Crafts, N[icholas] F. R. 1985. *British Economic Growth during the Industrial Revolution*. Clarendon Press.

Crafts, N[icholas] F. R., and C[harles] K. Harley. 1992. "Output Growth and the British Industrial Revolution: A Restatement of the Crafts-Harley View." *Economic History Review*, 2nd series, 45 (November): 703–30.

Crouzet, François [M.]. 1990. *Britain Ascendant: Comparative Studies in Franco-British Economic History*. Translated by Martin Thom. Cambridge University Press; Éditions de la Maison des Sciences de l'Homme.

Davis, Lance [E.], and Stanley [L.] Engerman. 1999. "The Economy of British North America: Miles Traveled, Miles Still to Go." *William and Mary Quarterly*, 3rd series, 56 (January): 9–22.

Deane, Phyllis, and William A. Cole. 1967. *British Economic Growth, 1688–1959: Trends and Structure*. 2nd edition. Cambridge University Press.

De Roover, Raymond [A.]. 1954. "New Interpretations in the History of Banking." *Cahiers d'Histoire Mondiale* 2 (July): 38–76.

Dickerson, Oliver M. 1951. *The Navigation Acts and the American Revolution*. University of Pennsylvania Press.

Doerflinger, Thomas M. 1986. *A Vigorous Spirit of Enterprise: Merchants and Economic Development in Revolutionary Philadelphia*. University of North Carolina Press.

Earle, Carville V. 1975. *The Evolution of a Tidewater Settlement System: All Hallow's Parish, Maryland, 1650–1783*. University of Chicago, Department of Geography, Research Paper number 170.

Eck, Christopher R. 1993. "The Spirits of Massachusetts: Distillers and Distilling in Seventeenth- and Eighteenth-Century Boston." M.A. thesis, University of Massachusetts at Boston.

Egnal, Marc [M.]. 1975. "The Economic Development of the Thirteen Continental Colonies, 1720 to 1775." *William and Mary Quarterly*, 3rd series, 32 (April): 191–222.

Egnal, Marc [M.]. 1996. *Divergent Paths: How Culture and Institutions Have Shaped North American Growth*. Oxford University Press.

Egnal, Marc [M.]. 1998. *New World Economies: The Growth of the Thirteen Colonies and Early Canada*. Oxford University Press.

Eltis, David. 1995. "The Total Product of Barbados, 1664–1701." *Journal of Economic History* 55 (June): 321–38.

Eltis, David. 1997. "The Slave Economies of the Caribbean: Structure, Performance, Evolution and Significance." In Franklin W. Knight, editor. *The Slave Societies of the Caribbean*. Macmillan.

Elvin, Mark. 1973. *The Pattern of the Chinese Past: A Social and Economic Interpretation*. Eyre Methuen/Stanford University Press.

Engel, Ernst. 1857. "Die Productions- und Consumtionsverhältnisse des Königreichs Sachsen." *Zeitschrift des Statistischen Bureaus des Königlich Sächsischen Ministeriums des Innern* 8–9 (November).

Engel, Ernst. 1895. *Die Lebenskosten belgischer Arbeiter-Familien früher und jetzt: Ermittelt aus Familien-Haushaltsrechnungen und vergleichend zusammengestellt*. Heinrich.

Engerman, Stanley L. 2000. "France, Britain and the Economic Growth of Colonial North America," In John J. McCusker and Kenneth [J.] Morgan, editors. *The Early Modern Atlantic Economy*. Cambridge University Press.

Engerman, Stanley L., and Robert E. Gallman. 1983. "U.S. Economic Growth, 1783–1860." *Research in Economic History* 8: 1–46.

Ferreira da Camara, Manoel. 1789. "Ensaio de Descrição Fizica, e Economica da Comarca dos Ilheos na America." *Memórias Económicas da Academia Real das Sciencias de Lisboa* 1: 304–50.

Flynn, David T. 2001. "Credit and the Economy of Colonial New England." Ph.D. dissertation, Indiana University.

Forbes, Allyn Bailey, editor. 1947. *Winthrop Papers, volume 5, 1645–1649*. Massachusetts Historical Society.

Foster, Andrew D., and Mark R. Rosenzweig. 1995. "Learning by Doing and Learning from Others: Human Capital and Technical Change in Agriculture." *Journal of Political Economy* 103 (December): 1176–1209.

Franklin, Benjamin. 1787. "Comfort for America, or Remarks on Her Real Situation, Interests, and Policy." *American Museum, or Universal Magazine* 1 (January): 5–9.

Franklin, Benjamin. 1961. "Observations Concerning the Increase of Mankind, Peopling of Countries, etc." [1751]. In Leonard W. Labaree, Whitfield J. Bell Jr., et al., editors. *The Papers of Benjamin Franklin*, volume 4. Yale University Press.

Galenson, David W. 1996. "The Settlement and Growth of the Colonies: Population, Labor, and Economic Development." In Stanley L. Engerman and Robert E. Gallman, editors. *The Cambridge Economic History of the United States*, volume 1. Cambridge University Press.

Gallman, Robert E. 1999. "Can We Build National Accounts for the Colonial Period of American History?" *William and Mary Quarterly*, 3rd series, 56 (January): 23–30.

Gibson, A[lex] J. S., and T[homas] C. Smout. 1995. *Prices, Food and Wages in Scotland, 1550–1780*. Cambridge University Press.

Gioffrè, Domenico. 1960. *Gênes et les foires de change de Lyon à Besançon*. École Pratique des Hautes Études, VIe Section, Centre de Recherches Historiques, Affaires et Gens d'Affaires, numéro 21. S.E.V.P.E.N.

Great Britain. General Register Office. 1837–1973. *Annual Report of the Registrar-General of Births, Deaths and Marriages, in England*. Longman/Orme/Brown/Green/Longmans.

Great Britain. Laws and Statutes. 1762-1807. *The Statutes at Large . . . of Great Britain [1225-1806]*. [Edited by Danby Pickering.]. 46 volumes in 56 parts. Cambridge University Press.

Great Britain. Laws and Statutes. 1804–1869. *The Statutes of the United Kingdom of Great Britain and Ireland [1801–1869]*. Edited by T[homas] E. Tomlins, John Raithby, et al. 29 volumes George Eyre and Andrew Strahan.

Great Britain. Laws and Statutes. 1810–1828. *The Statutes of the Realm. Printed . . . from Original Records and Authentic Manuscripts [1225–1713]*. Edited by Alexander Luders, T[homas] E. Tomlins, et al. 11 volumes in 12 parts. George Eyre and Andrew Strahan.

Great Britain. Laws and Statutes. 1911. *Acts and Ordinances of the Interregnum, 1642–1660*. Edited by C[harles] H. Firth and R[obert] S. Rait. 3 volumes. H. M. Stationery Office.

Great Britain. Parliament. 1766. House of Commons. 1767. *The Examination of Doctor Benjamin Franklin Relative to the Repeal of the American Stamp Act, in MDCCLXVI*. J. Almon.

Great Britain. Parliament. House of Commons. 1798. *Report Respecting the Scotch Distillery Duties*. [House of Commons, Sessional Papers to 1801, volume 51: Reports, volume 21 (1797–1798), number 144]. House of Commons.

Great Britain. Public Record Office. 1860. *Calendar of State Papers, Colonial Series, America and West Indies [1574–1739]*. Edited by W[illiam] Noel Sainsbury, J[ohn] W. Fortescue, et al. Longman and Green.

Great Britain. Public Record Office. 1868–1889. *Calendar of Treasury Papers Preserved in Her Majesty's Public Record Office, 1556/57–1728*. Edited by Joseph Redington. 6 volumes. Longman and Green.

Great Britain. Public Record Office. 1898–1909. *Calendar of Treasury Books and Papers Preserved in Her Majesty's Public Record Office, 1729–1745*. Edited by William A. Shaw. H. M. Stationery; Eyre and Spottiswoode.

Great Britain. Public Record Office. 1904 to date. *Calendar of Treasury Books Preserved in Her Majesty's Public Record Office*. Edited by William A. Shaw. H. M. Stationery Office.

Hancock, David [J.]. 1994. "'Capital and Credit with Approved Security': Financial Markets in Montserrat and South Carolina, 1748–1775." *Business and Economic History*, 2nd series, 23 (Winter): 61–84.

Hardy, Stephen Gregg. 1999. "Trade and Economic Growth in the Eighteenth-Century Chesapeake." Ph.D. dissertation, University of Maryland.

Hardy, Stephen G[regg]. 2001. "Colonial South Carolina's Rice Industry and the Atlantic Economy: Patterns of Trade, Shipping, and Growth." In Jack P. Greene, Rosemary Brana-Shute, and Randy J. Sparks, editors. *Money, Trade, and Power: The Evolution of Colonial South Carolina's Plantation Society*. University of South Carolina Press.

Harley, C[harles] Knick. 1982. "British Industrialization before 1841: Evidence of Slower Growth during the Industrial Revolution." *Journal of Economic History* 42 (1982): 267–89.

Harper, Lawrence A. 1939. *The English Navigation Laws: A Seventeenth Century Experiment in Social Engineering*. Columbia University Press.

Harper, Lawrence A., and John H. Cox. 1942. *A Commodity Analysis of the Imports and Exports of the Port of New York, 1715–1764*. N.p.

Harris, P[eter] M. G. 1996. "Inflation and Deflation in Early America, 1634–1860: Patterns of Change in the British-American Economy." *Social Science History* 20 (Winter): 469–505.

Higman, B[arry] W. 1984. *Slave Populations of the British Caribbean, 1807–1834*. Johns Hopkins University Press.

Hoffman, Ronald. 2000. *Princes of Ireland, Planters of Maryland: A Carroll Saga, 1500–1782*. University of North Carolina Press.

Hood, Graham. 1972. *Bonnin and Morris of Philadelphia: The First American Porcelain Factory, 1770–1772*. University of North Carolina Press.

Houthakker, H[endrik] S. 1987. "Engel's Law." In *The New Palgrave: A Dictionary of Economics*, edited by John Eatwell, Murray Milgate, and Peter Newman, volume 2. Macmillan.

Innes, Stephen. 1995. *Creating the Commonwealth: The Economic Culture of Puritan New England*. Norton.

Innes, Stephen. 2001. "Review of *Inequality in Early America* edited by Carla Gardina Pestana and Sharon V. Salinger." *Journal of Interdisciplinary History* 31 (Winter): 468–9.

Inter-Secretariat Working Group on National Accounts. 1993. *System of National Accounts, 1993*. Revised edition. Commission of the European Communities – Eurostat.

Jarvis, Rupert C. 1958. "The Sources of Transport History: Sources for the History of Ships and Shipping." *Journal of Transport History* 3 (November): 212–34.

Jarvis, Rupert C. 1964. "Office Trade and Revenue Statistics." *Economic History Review*, 2nd series, 17 (August): 43–62.

Johnson, Joshua. 1979. *Joshua Johnson's Letterbook, 1771–1774: Letters from a Merchant in London to His Partners in Maryland*. Edited by Jacob M. Price. London Record Society, Publications, volume 15. London Record Society.

Kalm, Pehr. 1937. *The America of 1750: Peter Kalm's Travels in North America – The English Version of 1770*. [Translated by John Reinhold Forster and Edith M. L. Carlborg.] Edited by Adolph B. Benson. 2 volumes. Wilson-Erickson.

Kamoie, Laura Croghan. 1999. "Three Generations of Planter-Businessmen: The Tayloes, Slave Labor, and Entrepreneurialism in Virginia, 1710–1830." Ph.D. dissertation, College of William and Mary.

Kelso, William M. 1971–1972. "Shipbuilding in Virginia, 1763–1774." *Records of the Columbia Historical Society of Washington, D.C.* 48: 1–13.

Klingaman, David C. 1989. "Colonial Virginia's Coastwise and Grain Trade." Ph.D. dissertation, University of Virginia, 1967. Reprinted, Arno Press.

Klopfer, Helen Louise. 1936. "Statistics of the Foreign Trade of Philadelphia, 1700–1860." Ph.D. dissertation, University of Pennsylvania.

Kulikoff, Allan [L.]. 2000. *From British Peasants to Colonial American Farmers*. University of North Carolina Press.

Kuznets, Simon [S.] 1951. "The State as a Unit in Study of Economic Growth." *Journal of Economic History* 11 (Winter): 25–41.

Kuznets, Simon [S.]. 1953. *Economic Change: Selected Essays in Business Cycles, National Income, and Economic Growth*. Norton.

Levitt, James H. 1981. *For Want of Trade: Shipping and the New Jersey Ports, 1680–1783*, Collections of the New Jersey Historical Society, volume 17. New Jersey Historical Society.

Macpherson, David. 1805. *Annals of Commerce, Manufactures, Fisheries and Navigation . . . of the British Empire and Other Countries, from the Earliest Accounts to . . . 1801.* 4 volumes. Nichols.

Maddison, Angus. 2001. *The World Economy: A Millennial Perspective.* Development Centre of the Organisation for Economic Co-Operation and Development.

Main, Gloria L. 1988. "The Standard of Living in Southern New England, 1640–1773." *William and Mary Quarterly*, 3rd series, 45 (January): 124–34.

Main, Gloria L. 2001. *Peoples of a Spacious Land: Families and Cultures in Colonial New England.* Harvard University Press.

Main, Gloria L., and Jackson T. Main. 1988. "Economic Growth and the Standard of Living in Southern New England, 1640–1774." *Journal of Economic History* 47 (March): 27–46.

Main, Gloria L., and Jackson T. Main. 1999. "The Red Queen in New England?" *William and Mary Quarterly*, 3rd series, 56 (January): 121–50.

Mancall, Peter C., and Thomas [J.] Weiss. 1999. "Was Economic Growth Likely in Colonial British North America." *Journal of Economic History* 59 (March): 17–40.

Mancall, Peter C., Joshua L. Rosenbloom, and Thomas [J.] Weiss. 2002. "The Economic Activity of Native Americans in British North America." Paper presented at Session 56 of the *XIIIth International Economic History Congress*, July 26, 2002. Available at the EH.Net Internet site, Economic History Services. Accessed May 25, 2005.

Mancall, Peter C., Joshua L. Rosenbloom, and Thomas [J.] Weiss. 2004. "Conjectural Estimates of Economic Growth in the Lower South, 1720 to 1800." In Timothy Guinnane, William A. Sundstrom, and Warren C. Whatley, editors. *History Matters: Essays on Economic Growth, Technology, and Demographic Change.* Stanford University Press.

Mann, Barbara A. 1999. "Haudenosaunee (Iroquois) Economy." In Bruce E. Johansen, editor. *The Encyclopedia of Native American Economic History.* Greenwood Press.

Marx, Karl. 1869. *Der achtzehnte Brumaire des Louis Bonaparte.* 2nd edition, revised. Otto Meißner.

Massie, J[oseph]. 1760. *A Computation of the Money That Hath Been Exorbitantly Raised upon the People of Great Britain by the Sugar-Planters . . .* N.p.

Mathias, Peter. 1957. "The Social Structure in the Eighteenth Century: A Calculation by Joseph Massie." *Economic History Review*, 2nd series, 10 (1): 30–45.

Mayhew, N. J. 1995. "Population, Money Supply, and the Velocity of Circulation in England, 1300–1700." *Economic History Review* 47 (May): 238–57.

McCusker, John J. 1971. "The Current Value of English Exports, 1697 to 1800." *William and Mary Quarterly*, 3rd series, 28 (October): 607–28.

McCusker, John J. 1972a. "The Pennsylvania Shipping Industry in the Eighteenth Century." Typescript. Copy on deposit as Collection number 1880, Historical Society of Pennsylvania

McCusker, John J. 1972b. "Sources of Investment Capital in the Colonial Philadelphia Shipping Industry." *Journal of Economic History* 32 (March): 146–57.

McCusker, John J. 1973. "Weights and Measures in the Colonial Sugar Trade: The Gallon and the Pound and Their International Equivalents." *William and Mary Quarterly*, 3rd series, 30 (October 1973), 599–624.

McCusker, John J. 1979. "Colonial Civil Servant and Counter-Revolutionary: Thomas Irving (1738?–1800) in Boston, Charleston, and London." *Perspectives in American History* 12: 314–50.

McCusker, John J. 1981. "The Tonnage of Ships Engaged in British Colonial Trade during the Eighteenth Century." *Research in Economic History* 6: 73–105.

McCusker, John J. 1984. "New Guides to Primary Sources for the History of Early British America." *William and Mary Quarterly*, 3rd series, 41 (April): 277–95.

McCusker, John J. 1985. *European Bills of Entry and Marine Lists: Early Commercial Publications and the Origins of the Business Press.* Harvard University Library.

McCusker, John J. 1989. "Rum and the American Revolution: The Rum Trade and the Balance of Payments of the Thirteen Continental Colonies, 1650–1775." 2 volumes. Ph.D. dissertation, University of Pittsburgh, 1970. Reprinted Garland.

McCusker, John J. 1992. *Money and Exchange in Europe and America, 1600–1775: A Handbook.* 2nd edition. University of North Carolina Press.

McCusker, John J. 1997. *Essays in the Economic History of the Atlantic World.* Routledge.

McCusker, John J. 2000a. "The Business of Distilling in the Old World and the New World during the Seventeenth and Eighteenth Centuries: The Rise of a New Enterprise and Its Connection with Colonial America." In John J. McCusker and Kenneth [J.] Morgan, editors. *The Early Modern Atlantic Economy.* Cambridge University Press.

McCusker, John J. 2000b. "Estimating Early American Gross Domestic Product." *Historical Methods: A Journal of Quantitative and Interdisciplinary History* 33 (Summer): 155–62.

McCusker, John J. 2000c. "'The Freshest Advices': The Emergence of Robert Morris's Philadelphia as the Early Center of Trade and Commerce in Post-Revolutionary United States and the Development of an Indigenous American Commercial and Financial Press." Paper presented at "Re-Examining the Economic and Political History of the Confederation through the Papers of Robert Morris" – A Conference in Celebration of the Completion of *The Papers of Robert Morris, 1781–1784*, New York, April 7.

McCusker, John J. 2001a. *How Much Is That in Real Money? A Historical Commodity Price Index for Use as a Deflator of Money Values in the Economy of the United States.* 2nd edition. American Antiquarian Society.

McCusker, John J. 2001b. "Rethinking the Economy of Early British America." Paper presented at the Library Company of Philadelphia, Conference on "The Past and Future of Early American Economic History," Philadelphia, Pennsylvania, April 20.

McCusker, John J. Forthcoming. *Mercantilism and the Economic History of the Early Modern Atlantic World.* Cambridge University Press.

McCusker, John J., and Cora Gravesteijn. 1991. *The Beginnings of Commercial and Financial Journalism: The Commodity Price Currents, Exchange Rate Currents, and Money Currents of Early Modern Europe.* Nederlandsch Economisch-Historisch Archief, series 3, number 11. Nederlandsch Economisch-Historisch Archief.

McCusker, John J., and Russell R. Menard. 1991. *The Economy of British America, 1607–1789.* 2nd edition. University of North Carolina Press.

McCusker, John J., and Russell R. Menard. 2004. "The Sugar Industry in the Seventeenth Century: A New Perspective on the Barbadian 'Sugar Revolution.'" In Stuart B. Schwartz, editor. *Tropical Babylons: Sugar and the Making of the Atlantic World before the "Sugar Revolution."* University of North Carolina Press.

Menard, Russell R. 1976. "A Note on Chesapeake Tobacco Prices, 1618–1660." *Virginia Magazine of History and Biography* 84 (October): 401–10.

Menard, Russell R. 1994. "Financing the Lowcountry Export Boom: Capital and Growth in Early South Carolina." *William and Mary Quarterly*, 3rd series, 51 (October): 659–76.

Menard, Russell R. 1996. "Economic and Social Development of the South." In Stanley L. Engerman and Robert E. Gallman, editors. *The Cambridge Economic History of the United States*, volume 1. Cambridge University Press.

Menard, Russell R. 2001. "New Directions in Early American Agricultural History." Paper presented at the Library Company of Philadelphia, Program in Early American Economy and Society. Conference on "The Past and Future of Early American Economic History," Philadelphia, Pennsylvania, April 20.

Mintz, Sidney Wilfred. 1985. *Sweetness and Power: The Place of Sugar in Modern History.* Viking.

Morgan, Philip D. 1998. *Slave Counterpoint: Black Culture in the Eighteenth-Century Chesapeake and Lowcountry.* University of North Carolina Press.

Murphy, Edward. 1999. "The Eighteenth-Century Southeastern American Indian Economy: Subsistence versus Trade and Growth." In Linda Barrington, editor. *The Other Side of the Frontier: Economic Explorations into Native American History.* Westview Press.

Nash, Gary B. 1976. "Urban Wealth and Poverty in Pre-Revolutionary America." *Journal of Interdisciplinary History* 6 (Spring): 545–84.

Nash, R[obert] C. 1992. "South Carolina and the Atlantic Economy in the Late Seventeenth and Eighteenth Centuries." *Economic History Review*, 2nd series, 45 (November): 677–702.

Nash, R[obert] C. 2001. "The Organization of Trade and Finance in the Atlantic Economy: Britain and South Carolina, 1670–1775." In Jack P. Greene, Rosemary Brana-Shute, and Randy J. Sparks, editors. *Money, Trade, and Power: The Evolution of Colonial South Carolina's Plantation Society*. University of South Carolina Press.

Newell, Margaret Ellen. 1998. *From Dependency to Independence: Economic Revolution in Colonial New England*. Cornell University Press.

Noyes, Sybil, Charles Thornton Libby, and Walter Goodwin Davis, compilers. 1928–1939. *Genealogical Dictionary of Maine and New Hampshire*. 5 volumes. Southworth-Anthoensen Press.

O'Brien, Patrick [K.], and Peter Mathias. 1976. "Taxation in Britain and France, 1750–1810: A Comparison of the Social and Economic Incidence of Taxes Collected for the Central Governments." *Journal of European Economic History* 5 (Winter): 601–50.

Palmer, Stanley H. 1977. *Economic Arithmetic: A Guide to the Statistical Sources of English Commerce, Industry, and Finance, 1700–1850*. Garland Reference Library of Social Science, volume 26. Garland.

Perkins, Edwin J. 1994. *American Public Finance and Financial Services, 1700–1815*. Ohio State University Press.

Perkins, Elizabeth A. 1991. "The Consumer Frontier: Household Consumption in Early Kentucky." *Journal of American History* 78 (September): 486–510.

Price, Jacob M. 1974. "Economic Function and the Growth of American Port Towns in the Eighteenth Century." *Perspectives in American History*, 1st series, 8: 123–86.

Price, Jacob M. 1975. "New Time Series for Scotland's and Britain's Trade with the Thirteen Colonies and States, 1740 to 1791." *William and Mary Quarterly*, 3rd series, 32 (April): 307–25.

Price, Jacob M. 1976. "Quantifying Colonial America: A Comment on Nash ['Urban Wealth and Poverty in Pre-Revolutionary America'] and Warden ['Inequality and Instability in Eighteenth Century Boston. A Reappraisal']." *Journal of Interdisciplinary History* 6 (Spring): 701–9.

Price, Jacob M. 1980. *Capital and Credit in British Overseas Trade: The View from the Chesapeake, 1700–1776*. Harvard University Press.

Pruden, Elizabeth M. 2001. "Investing Widows: Autonomy in a Nascent Capitalist Society." In Jack P. Greene, Rosemary Brana-Shute, and Randy J. Sparks, editors. *Money, Trade, and Power: The Evolution of Colonial South Carolina's Plantation Society*. University of South Carolina Press.

Rosenberg, Nathan. 1972. "Factors Affecting the Diffusion of Technology." *Explorations in Economic History* 10 (Fall): 3–33.

Roth, Rodris. 1961. *Tea Drinking in 18th-Century America: Its Etiquette and Equipage*. United States National Museum, Bulletin number 225: Contributions from the Museum of History and Technology, Paper number 14. Smithsonian Institution.

Rothenberg, Winifred B[arr]. 1988. "The Emergence of a Capital Market in Rural Massachusetts, 1730–1838." In Ronald Hoffman, John J. McCusker, et al., editors. *The Economy of Early America: The Revolutionary Period, 1763–1790*. University Press of Virginia.

Rothenberg, Winifred Barr. 1992. *From Market-Places to a Market Economy: The Transformation of Rural Massachusetts, 1750–1850*. University of Chicago Press.

Rousseau, Peter L., and Richard [E.] Sylla. 1999. *Emerging Financial Markets and Early U.S. Growth*. National Bureau of Economic Research, Working Paper, number 7448. National Bureau of Economic Research.

Russo, Jean Elliott. 1999. "'The Interest of the County': Population, Economy, and Society in Eighteenth-Century Somerset County, Maryland." Ph.D. dissertation, University of Minnesota.

Russo, Jean Elliott. 2003. "'At Present Possessed of a Negroe Man': Patterns of Slave Acquisition in Eighteenth-Century Somerset County, Maryland." Paper presented at the Washington Area Seminar on Early American History, University of Maryland, College Park, Maryland, February 20.

Rutman, Darrett B., and Anita H. Rutman. 1984. *A Place in Time: Middlesex County, Virginia, 1650–1750*. 2 volumes. Norton.

St. John [de Crèvecœur], J. Hector. 1782. *Letters from an American Farmer: Describing Certain Provincial Situations, Manners, and Customs, not Generally Known; and Conveying Some Idea of the Late and Present Interior Circumstances of the British Colonies in North America. Written for the Information of a Friend in England*. T. Davies and Lockyer Davis.

Salisbury, Neal. 1996. "The History of Native Americans from before the Arrival of the Europeans and Africans until the American Civil War." In Stanley L. Engerman and Robert E. Gallman, editors. *The Cambridge Economic History of the United States*, volume 1. Cambridge University Press.

Schneider, Jürgen. 1991. "Frankreichs Messeplätze und das europäische Messesystem in der frühen Neuzeit." In Hans Pohl, editor. *Frankfurt im Messenetz Europas – Erträge der Forschung*, volume 1, *Brücke zwischen der Völkern: Zur Geschichte der Frankfurter Messe*, edited by Rainer Koch. [Frankfurt am Main] Historisches Museum.

Schweitzer, Mary McKinney. 1980. "Economic Regulation and the Colonial Economy: The Maryland Tobacco Inspection Act of 1747." *Journal of Economic History* 40 (September): 551–69.

Semple, Ellen Churchill. 1903. *American History and Its Geographic Conditions*. Houghton, Mifflin.

Shand, P[hilip] Morton. 1927. *A Book of Food*. Jonathan Cape.

Shepherd, James F. 1980. "Economy from the Revolution to 1815." In [Patrick] Glenn Porter, editor. *Encyclopedia of American Economic History: Studies of the Principal Movements and Ideas*, volume 1. Charles Scribner's Sons.

[Shepard, John]. 1829. *The Artist and Tradesman's Guide; Embracing Some Leading Facts and Principles of Science, and a Variety of Matter Adapted to the Wants of the Artist, Mechanic, Manufacturer, and Mercantile Community: To Which Is Annexed an Abstract of Tonnage, Duties, Custom-House Tares, Allowances, and Useful Mensuration Tables*. 3rd edition. J. C. Johnson.

Slaski, Eugene R. 1971. "Thomas Willing: Moderation during the American Revolution." Ph.D. dissertation, Florida State University.

Slesnick, Daniel T. 2001. *Consumption and Social Welfare: Living Standards and Their Distribution in the United States*. Cambridge University Press.

Smith, Mark M. 1998. "Culture, Commerce, and Calendar Reform in Colonial America." *William and Mary Quarterly*, 3rd series, 55 (October): 557–84.

Smith, Paul H. 1981. "Review of *Documents of the American Revolution, 1770–1783, Colonial Office Series*, Edited by K[enneth] G. Davies." *American Historical Review* 86 (December): 1146–7.

Soltow, James H. 1965. *The Economic Role of Williamsburg*. Williamsburg Research Studies. Colonial Williamsburg Foundation.

Somers, Harold M., and Harold F. Williamson. 1951. "The Performance of the American Economy to 1789." In Harold F. Williamson, editor. *The Growth of the American Economy*. 2nd edition. Prentice Hall.

Southall, Humphrey, and David Gilbert. 1996. "A Good Time to Wed?: Marriage and Economic Distress in England and Wales, 1839–1914." *Economic History Review*, 2nd series, 49 (February): 35–57.

Steckel, Richard H. 1999. "Nutritional Status in the Colonial American Economy." *William and Mary Quarterly*, 3rd series, 56 (January): 31–52.

Steegmuller, Francis. 1991. *A Woman, a Man, and Two Kingdoms: The Story of Madame d'Épinay and the Abbé Galiani*. Knopf.

Tatham, William. 1800. *An Historical and Practical Essay on the Culture and Commerce of Tobacco*. Vernor and Hood.

Thomson, Robert Polk. 1955. "The Merchant in Virginia, 1700–1775." Ph.D. dissertation, University of Wisconsin.

U.S. Department of Commerce, Bureau of Economic Analysis. 1998. *National Income and Product Accounts of the United States, 1929–94*. 2 volumes. U.S. Government Printing Office.

Vickers, Daniel [F.]. 1996. "The Northern Colonies: Economy and Society, 1600–1775." In Stanley L. Engerman and Robert E. Gallman, editors. *The Cambridge Economic History of the United States*, volume 1. Cambridge University Press.

Virginia. Committee on Colonial Records. 1960. *The British Public Record Office: History, Description, Record Groups, Finding Aids, and Materials for American History, with Special Reference to Virginia*. Special Reports 25, 26, 27, and 28 of the Virginia Colonial Records Project. Virginia State Library Publications, number 12. Virginia State Library.

Walsh, Lorena S. 1989. "Plantation Management in the Chesapeake, 1620–1820." *Journal of Economic History* 49 (June): 393–406.

Walsh, Lorena S. 1997. *From Calabar to Carter's Grove: The History of a Virginia Slave Community*. University Press of Virginia.

Walsh, Lorena S. 2000. "Provisioning Tidewater Towns." *Explorations in Early American Culture* 4: 46–80.

Walsh, Lorena S., Ann Smart Martin, and Joanne Bowen. 1997. *Provisioning Early American Towns. The Chesapeake: A Multidisciplinary Case Study – Final Performance Report*. Colonial Williamsburg Foundation.

Walton, Gary M., and James F. Shepherd. 1969. *The Economic Rise of Early America*. Cambridge University Press.

Warden, G[erard] B. 1976. "Inequality and Instability in Eighteenth-Century Boston: A Reappraisal." *Journal of Interdisciplinary History* 6 (Spring): 585–620.

Weiss, Thomas [J.]. 1992. "U.S. Labor Force Estimates and Economic Growth, 1800–1860." In Robert E. Gallman and John Joseph Wallis, editors. *American Economic Growth and Standards of Living before the Civil War*. National Bureau of Economic Research Conference Report. University of Chicago Press.

Weiss, Thomas [J.]. 1993. "Long-Term Changes in US Agricultural Output per Worker, 1800–1900." *Economic History Review* 46 (May): 324–41.

Weiss, Thomas [J.]. 1999. "Review of *The Other Side of the Frontier: Economic Explorations into Native American History* Edited by Linda Barrington" (January). Available at the EH.net Internet site, Economic History Services. Accessed May 25, 2005.

Welsh, Peter C. 1956. "The Brandywine Mills: A Chronicle of an Industry, 1762–1816." *Delaware History* 7 (March): 17–36.

Welsh, Peter C. 1957. "Merchants, Millers, and Ocean Ships: The Components of an Early American Industrial Town." *Delaware History* 7 (September): 319–36.

Whitworth, Charles. 1776. *State of the Trade of Great Britain in Its Imports and Exports, Progressively from the Year 1697 [to 1773]: Also of the Trade to Each Particular Country, during the above Period, Distinguishing Each Year . . . .* G. Robinson, J. Robson, J. Walter, T. Cadell, and J. Sewell.

Woods, [Thomas] Michael. 1998. "The Culture of Credit in Colonial Charleston." *South Carolina Historical Magazine* 99 (October): 358–80.

Wright, Robert E. 1996. "Banking and Politics in New York, 1784–1829." Ph.D. dissertation, State University of New York at Buffalo.

Wright, Robert E. 2001. *The Origins of Commercial Banking in America, 1750–1800*. Rowman and Littlefield.

Wrigley, E[dward] A., and R[oger] S. Schofield. 1981. *The Population History of England, 1541–1871: A Reconstruction*. Harvard University Press.

Zupko, Ronald Edward. 1968. *A Dictionary of English Weights and Measures from Anglo-Saxon Times to the Nineteenth Century*. University of Wisconsin Press.

Zupko, Ronald Edward. 1977. *British Weights and Measures: A History from Antiquity to the Seventeenth Century*. University of Wisconsin Press.

Zupko, Ronald Edward. 1985. *A Dictionary of Weights and Measurers for the British Isles: The Middle Ages to the Twentieth Century*. Memoirs of the American Philosophical Society, volume 168. American Philosophical Society.

POPULATION

John J. McCusker

TABLE Eg1–59   Population, by race and by colony or locality: 1610–1780

Contributed by John J. McCusker

	Total									
	Total	Maine	New Hampshire	Vermont	Plymouth	Massachusetts	Rhode Island	Connecticut	New York	New Jersey
	Eg1	Eg2 [1]	Eg3	Eg4	Eg5 [2]	Eg6 [1,2]	Fg7	Eg8	Eg9	Eg10
Year	Number	Number	Number	Number	Number	Number	Number	Number	Number	Number
1610	350	—	—	—	—	—	—	—	—	—
1620	2,302	—	—	—	102	—	—	—	—	—
1630	4,646	400	500	—	390	506	—	—	350	—
1640	26,634	900	1,055	—	1,020	8,932	300	1,472	1,930	—
1650	50,368	1,000	1,305	—	1,566	14,037	785	4,139	4,116	—
1660	75,058	—	1,555	—	1,980	20,082	1,539	7,980	4,936	—
1670	111,935	—	1,805	—	5,333	30,000	2,155	12,603	5,754	1,000
1680	151,507	—	2,047	—	6,400	39,752	3,017	17,246	9,830	3,400
1690	210,372	—	4,164	—	7,424	49,504	4,224	21,645	13,909	8,000
1700	251,444	—	4,958	—	—	55,941	5,894	25,970	19,107	14,010
1710	327,360	—	5,681	—	—	62,390	7,573	39,450	21,625	19,872
1720	467,465	—	9,375	—	—	91,008	11,680	58,830	36,919	29,818
1730	636,045	—	10,755	—	—	114,116	16,950	75,530	48,594	37,510
1740	912,742	—	23,256	—	—	151,613	25,255	89,580	63,665	51,373
1750	1,186,408	—	27,505	—	—	188,000	33,226	111,280	76,696	71,393
1760	1,593,625	20,000	39,093	—	—	202,600	45,471	142,470	117,138	93,813
1770	2,165,076	31,257	62,396	10,000	—	235,308	58,196	183,881	162,920	117,431
1780	2,797,854	49,133	87,802	47,620	—	268,627	52,946	206,701	210,541	139,627

	Total									
	Pennsylvania	Delaware	Maryland	Virginia	North Carolina	South Carolina	Georgia	Florida	Kentucky	Tennessee
	Eg11	Eg12	Eg13	Eg14	Eg15	Eg16	Eg17	Eg18	Eg19	Eg20
Year	Number	Number	Number	Number	Number	Number	Number	Number	Number	Number
1610	—	—	—	350	—	—	—	—	—	—
1620	—	—	—	2,200	—	—	—	—	—	—
1630	—	—	—	2,500	—	—	—	—	—	—
1640	—	—	583	10,442	—	—	—	—	—	—
1650	—	185	4,504	18,731	—	—	—	—	—	—
1660	—	540	8,426	27,020	1,000	—	—	—	—	—
1670	—	700	13,226	35,309	3,850	200	—	—	—	—
1680	680	1,005	17,904	43,596	5,430	1,200	—	—	—	—
1690	11,450	1,482	24,024	53,046	7,600	3,900	—	—	—	—
1700	17,950	2,470	29,604	58,560	10,720	6,260	—	—	—	—
1710	24,450	3,645	42,741	74,513	15,120	10,300	—	—	—	—
1720	30,962	5,385	66,133	87,757	21,270	18,328	—	—	—	—
1730	51,707	9,170	91,113	120,600	30,000	30,000	—	—	—	—
1740	85,637	19,870	116,093	180,440	51,760	54,200	—	—	—	—
1750	119,666	28,704	141,073	236,681	72,984	74,000	5,200	—	—	—
1760	183,703	33,250	162,267	339,726	110,442	94,074	9,578	—	—	—
1770	240,057	35,496	202,599	447,016	197,200	124,244	23,375	17,000	15,700	1,000
1780	327,305	45,385	247,959	538,004	270,133	180,000	56,071	15,000	45,000	10,000

Notes appear at end of table

(continued)

TABLE Eg1–59 Population, by race and by colony or locality: 1610–1780 *Continued*

					White					
	Total	Maine	New Hampshire	Vermont	Plymouth	Massachusetts	Rhode Island	Connecticut	New York	New Jersey
	Eg21	Eg22 [1]	Eg23	Eg24	Eg25 [2]	Eg26 [1,2]	Eg27	Eg28	Eg29	Eg30
Year	Number	Number	Number	Number	Number	Number	Number	Number	Number	Number
1610	350	—	—	—	—	—	—	—	—	—
1620	2,282	—	—	—	102	—	—	—	—	—
1630	4,586	400	500	—	390	506	—	—	340	—
1640	26,037	900	1,025	—	1,020	8,782	300	1,457	1,698	—
1650	48,768	1,000	1,265	—	1,566	13,742	760	4,119	3,616	—
1660	72,138	—	1,505	—	1,980	19,660	1,474	7,955	4,336	—
1670	107,400	—	1,740	—	5,333	29,840	2,040	12,568	5,064	940
1680	144,536	—	1,972	—	6,400	39,582	2,842	17,196	8,630	3,200
1690	193,643	—	4,064	—	7,424	49,104	3,974	21,445	12,239	7,550
1700	223,071	—	4,828	—	—	55,141	5,594	25,520	16,851	13,170
1710	284,662	—	5,531	—	—	61,080	7,198	38,700	18,814	18,540
1720	398,798	—	9,205	—	—	88,858	11,137	57,737	31,179	27,433
1730	538,424	—	10,555	—	—	111,336	15,302	74,040	41,638	34,502
1740	755,539	—	22,756	—	—	148,578	22,847	86,982	54,669	47,007
1750	934,340	—	26,955	—	—	183,925	29,879	108,270	65,682	66,039
1760	1,267,819	19,700	38,493	—	—	198,034	42,003	138,687	100,798	87,246
1770	1,696,254	30,782	61,742	9,975	—	230,554	54,435	178,183	143,808	109,211
1780	2,209,949	48,675	87,261	47,570	—	263,805	50,275	200,816	189,487	129,167

					White					
	Pennsylvania	Delaware	Maryland	Virginia	North Carolina	South Carolina	Georgia	Florida	Kentucky	Tennessee
	Eg31	Eg32	Eg33	Eg34	Eg35	Eg36	Eg37	Eg38	Eg39	Eg40
Year	Number	Number	Number	Number	Number	Number	Number	Number	Number	Number
1610	—	—	—	350	—	—	—	—	—	—
1620	—	—	—	2,180	—	—	—	—	—	—
1630	—	—	—	2,450	—	—	—	—	—	—
1640	—	—	563	10,292	—	—	—	—	—	—
1650	—	170	4,204	18,326	—	—	—	—	—	—
1660	—	510	7,668	26,070	980	—	—	—	—	—
1670	—	660	12,036	33,309	3,700	170	—	—	—	—
1680	655	950	16,293	40,596	5,220	1,000	—	—	—	—
1690	11,180	1,400	21,862	43,701	7,300	2,400	—	—	—	—
1700	17,520	2,335	26,377	42,170	10,305	3,260	—	—	—	—
1710	22,875	3,145	34,796	55,163	14,220	4,600	—	—	—	—
1720	28,962	4,685	53,634	61,198	18,270	6,500	—	—	—	—
1730	50,466	8,692	73,893	84,000	24,000	10,000	—	—	—	—
1740	83,582	18,835	92,062	120,440	40,760	15,000	2,021	—	—	—
1750	116,794	27,208	97,623	129,581	53,184	25,000	4,200	—	—	—
1760	179,294	31,517	113,263	199,156	76,888	36,740	6,000	—	—	—
1770	234,296	33,660	138,781	259,411	127,600	49,066	12,750	8,000	13,200	800
1780	319,450	42,389	164,959	317,422	179,133	83,000	35,240	5,000	37,800	8,500

Notes appear at end of table

TABLE Eg1–59   Population, by race and by colony or locality: 1610–1780   *Continued*

					Black					
	Total	Maine	New Hampshire	Vermont	Massachusetts	Rhode Island	Connecticut	New York	New Jersey	Pennsylvania
	Eg41	Eg42 [1]	Eg43	Eg44	Eg45 [1,2]	Eg46	Eg47	Eg48	Eg49	Eg50
Year	Number	Number	Number	Number	Number	Number	Number	Number	Number	Number
1610	0	—	—	—	—	—	—	—	—	—
1620	20	—	—	—	—	—	—	—	—	—
1630	60	—	—	—	—	—	—	10	—	—
1640	597	—	30	—	150	—	15	232	—	—
1650	1,600	—	40	—	295	25	20	500	—	—
1660	2,920	—	50	—	422	65	25	600	—	—
1670	4,535	—	65	—	160	115	35	690	60	—
1680	6,971	—	75	—	170	175	50	1,200	200	25
1690	16,729	—	100	—	400	250	200	1,670	450	270
1700	28,373	—	130	—	800	300	450	2,256	840	430
1710	42,698	—	150	—	1,310	375	750	2,811	1,332	1,575
1720	68,667	—	170	—	2,150	543	1,093	5,740	2,385	2,000
1730	97,621	—	200	—	2,780	1,648	1,490	6,956	3,008	1,241
1740	159,224	—	500	—	3,035	2,408	2,598	8,996	4,366	2,055
1750	252,068	—	550	—	4,075	3,347	3,010	11,014	5,354	2,872
1760	325,806	300	600	—	4,566	3,468	3,783	16,340	6,567	4,409
1770	468,822	475	654	25	4,754	3,761	5,698	19,112	8,220	5,761
1780	587,905	458	541	50	4,822	2,671	5,885	21,054	10,460	7,855

				Black					
	Delaware	Maryland	Virginia	North Carolina	South Carolina	Georgia	Florida	Kentucky	Tennessee
	Eg51	Eg52	Eg53	Eg54	Eg55	Eg56	Eg57	Eg58	Eg59
Year	Number	Number	Number	Number	Number	Number	Number	Number	Number
1610	—	—	0	—	—	—	—	—	—
1620	—	—	20	—	—	—	—	—	—
1630	—	—	50	—	—	—	—	—	—
1640	—	20	150	—	—	—	—	—	—
1650	15	300	405	—	—	—	—	—	—
1660	30	758	950	20	—	—	—	—	—
1670	40	1,190	2,000	150	30	—	—	—	—
1680	55	1,611	3,000	210	200	—	—	—	—
1690	82	2,162	9,345	300	1,500	—	—	—	—
1700	135	3,227	16,390	415	3,000	—	—	—	—
1710	500	7,945	19,350	900	5,700	—	—	—	—
1720	700	12,499	26,559	3,000	11,828	—	—	—	—
1730	478	17,220	36,600	6,000	20,000	—	—	—	—
1740	1,035	24,031	60,000	11,000	39,200	—	—	—	—
1750	1,496	43,450	107,100	19,800	49,000	1,000	—	—	—
1760	1,733	49,004	140,570	33,554	57,334	3,578	—	—	—
1770	1,836	63,818	187,605	69,600	75,178	10,625	9,000	2,500	200
1780	2,996	83,000	220,582	91,000	97,000	20,831	10,000	7,200	1,500

Notes appear on next page   (continued)

TABLE Eg1–59   Population, by race and by colony or locality: 1610–1780   *Continued*

[1] For 1660–1750, Maine counties are included with Massachusetts. Maine was a part of Massachusetts until it became a separate state in 1820.

[2] Plymouth became a part of the Province of Massachusetts in 1691. After 1690, data for Plymouth are included with Massachusetts.

Source

John J. McCusker and Russell R. Menard, *The Economy of British America, 1607–1789*, 2nd edition (University of North Carolina Press, 1991), Tables 5.1, 6.4, 8.1, and 9.4, pp. 103, 136, 172, 203, as revised, updated, and augmented by ongoing research detailed below.

Documentation

See the Appendixes to the essay in this chapter for a general discussion of the tables and the sources of the data, along with a key to abbreviations used in this chapter and general information on matters such as regional definitions, calendar differences, money, and weights and measures. Note that Florida is included here as part of British North America but it was not one of the Thirteen Continental Colonies. The settlements in what later became the states of Kentucky and Tennessee were considered as simply western extensions of Virginia and North Carolina but are entered separately in this table. See the map "De Facto Government, 1785" in Lester J. Cappon, Barbara Bartz Petchenik, and John Hamilton Long, editors, *Atlas of Early American History: The Revolutionary Era, 1760–1790* (Princeton University Press, 1976), p. 17.

These data were originally compiled by Stella H. Sutherland, chiefly from the following sources: B. J. Brawley, *A Short History of the American Negro* (Macmillan, 1913); Elizabeth Donnan, editor, *Documents Illustrative of the History of the Slave Trade to America* (Carnegie Institution, 1930–1935); Evarts B. Greene and Virginia D. Harrington, *American Population before the Federal Census of 1790* (Columbia University Press, 1932); Stella H. Sutherland, *Population Distribution in Colonial America* (Columbia University Press, 1936); Edward R. Turner, *The Negro in Pennsylvania: Slavery – Servitude – Freedom, 1639–1851* (American Historical Association, 1911); U.S. Bureau of the Census, *A Century of Population Growth: From the First Census of the United States to the Twelfth, 1790–1900*, compiled by William Sidney Rossiter (1909); Thomas J. Wertenbaker, *The Planters of Colonial Virginia* (Princeton University Press, 1922); and George W. Williams, *The History of the Negro Race in America from 1619 to 1880* (Putnam's, 1883).

Although largely dependent on the original Sutherland compilation, the data presented by McCusker and Menard were checked and corrected, as discussed in McCusker and Menard (1991). Additional corrections and additions newly offered here are based on unpublished research and on Peter H. Wood, *Black Majority: Negroes in Colonial South Carolina from 1670 through the Stono Rebellion* (Knopf, 1974), p. 152 and elsewhere; Allan [L.] Kulikoff, "A 'Prolifick' People: Black Population Growth in the Chesapeake Colonies, 1700–1790," *Southern Studies* 14 (Winter 1977): 415–6; Charles Loch Mowat, *East Florida as a British Province, 1763–1784*, University of California Publications in History (University of California Press, 1943), volume 32, pp. 64, 126, 188 n. 63; J[ames] Leitch Wright Jr., *Florida in the American Revolution* (University Presses of Florida, 1975), pp. 11–3, 155 n. 18; Peter A. Coclanis, *The Shadow of a Dream: Economic Life and Death in the South Carolina Low Country, 1670–1720* (Oxford University Press, 1989), p. 64; and Philip D. Morgan, *Slave Counterpoint: Black Culture in the Eighteenth-Century Chesapeake and Lowcountry* (Omohundro Institute of Early American History and Culture, 1998), p. 61. See also Sutherland, "Colonial Statistics," *Explorations in Economic History*, 2nd series, 5 (Fall 1967): 58–107; Robert V. Wells, *The Population of the British Colonies in America before 1776: A Survey of Census Data* (Princeton University Press, 1975).

Much of the original data were obtained from communications of a variety of kinds – censuses, population counts, and estimates of population – sent by many different colonial officials to the Commissioners of Trade and Plantations in London. These officials reported on elements of the population within their jurisdiction with varying degrees of completeness and accuracy.

The bounds to such jurisdictions shifted over time as the colonies expanded but can generally be seen to have been limited to the areas of each colony then organized into settlements. Population counts ordinarily attempted to enumerate all of the residents of the inhabited areas. Thus, the Native American Indians who lived within the settled areas of the colonies were usually included as part of the population, sometimes as part of the white population, but more frequently as part of the black population. See, for example, Tables Eg117–131 and Eg141–154. Native American Indian residents of the region who lived outside the areas settled by the British are not included in these (or subsequent) population estimates. For a crude, preliminary attempt to estimate the Indian populations within the territories contiguous to British settlement and with whom, therefore, the British maintained commercial contact, see John J. McCusker, *Rum and the American Revolution: The Rum Trade and the Balance of Payments of the Thirteen Continental Colonies, 1650–1775* (Garland, 1989), volume 2, pp. 713–6. For estimates of the size of the entire population of Native Americans in the whole of North America between 1500 and 1970, see Douglas H. Ubelaker, "North American Indian Population Size: Changing Perspectives," in John W. Verano and Douglas H. Ubelaker, editors, *Disease and Demography in the Americas* (Smithsonian Institution Press, 1992), pp. 169–76. Compare Peter H. Wood, "The Changing Population of the Colonial South: An Overview by Race and Region, 1685–1790," in Peter H. Wood, Gregory A. Waselkov, and M. Thomas Hatley, editors, *Powhatan's Mantle: Indians in the Colonial Southeast* (University of Nebraska Press, 1989), pp. 35–103. Note that for purposes of this essay he defines the "colonial south" as "Southeastern North America," "the entire domain east of the Great Plains and south of the Ohio and Potomac rivers" (pp. 35, 36). See also the maps in Neal Salisbury, "Native People and European Settlers in Eastern North America, 1600–1783," in Bruce G. Trigger and Wilcomb E. Washburn, editors, *The Cambridge History of the Native Peoples of the Americas* (Cambridge University Press, 1996), volume 1, part 1, pp. 399–460.

Not infrequently, a census or head count sent to London supplied evidence of the total number of inhabitants; for other reports, the militia rolls or the tax lists or both were used, accompanied by an estimate of the whole population based on such rolls or lists. Estimates made by colonial officials and by other informed contemporaries, who did not disclose the figures on which their conclusions were based, have occasionally been included in these series. However, such estimates were selected in accordance with the general pattern of population growth. Nevertheless, such counts – and thus the tables based on them – should in no way be thought similar to modern censuses. Population estimates for blacks, both enslaved and free, are thought to be especially prone to inaccuracy.

Estimates of total colonial populations sometimes rest on partial data extrapolated to some total using ratios derived from other, contemporary data. Some ratios come from militia records and some from tax records. The ratio of the militia to the whole population was generally $1:5\frac{1}{3}$, but there were many exceptions. In Massachusetts, it was 1:6 in 1751 and 1:4 in 1763; in Connecticut, it was 1:6 in 1722 and 1756 and 1:7 in 1749, 1761, and 1774; it was 1:6 in Virginia and 1:7 in South Carolina at various times. No generalization can safely be made as to the ratio borne by the northern polls and ratables and by the southern taxables and tithables to the whole population of the colonies. In every province, the figure was different. In the North, it ranged from 1:4 to $1:5\frac{1}{2}$; in Pennsylvania, it was 1:7 in the 1750s, but 1:5.8 was the more common figure; in Maryland and Virginia, where both male and female slaves appeared on the tax lists, the ratio was 1:3 or 3.5 in the seventeenth century and 1:2.4 or 2.6 in the eighteenth century. The North Carolina white taxables were multiplied by 4 and the black taxables by 2. See the works cited earlier for a thorough discussion of this subject.

Two chapters in Michael R. Haines and Richard H. Steckel, editors, *A Population History of North America* (Cambridge University Press, 2000), add impressive analyses to our developing understanding of the colonial population data: Lorena S. Walsh, "The African American Population of the

TABLE Eg1–59　Population, by race and by colony or locality: 1610–1780　*Continued*

Colonial United States," pp. 191–239; and Henry A. Gemery, "The White Population of the Colonial United States, 1607–1790," pp. 143–90.

In addition to the total colonial population, the estimated populations of colonial towns and cities are worth recording. See Table Eg60–64.

Also of interest, for purposes of comparison, are data on the white and black population of the British West Indies. They are as originally presented in McCusker (1989), volume 2, pp. 548–767, corrected by additional, ongoing research, some of which was reported in John J. McCusker, "The Economy of the British West Indies, 1763–1790: Growth, Stagnation, or Decline?" as revised and updated in McCusker, *Essays in the Economic History of the Atlantic World* (Routledge, 1997), pp. 310–30. Note that the figures for 1760 given here differ from those offered in the latter source, which, for purposes of the argument developed there, included some islands that were not part of the British empire at the time (but were soon to be, as a consequence of the Seven Years' War and the Treaty of Paris, 1763). See also Stanley L. Engerman, "A Population History of the Caribbean," in Haines and Steckel (2000), pp. 483–528.

Year	Total	White	Black
1650	55	40	15
1660	76	44	32
1670	99	45	54
1680	117	42	75
1690	135	37	98
1700	147	32	115
1710	166	29	137
1720	219	36	184
1730	249	36	213
1740	282	35	247
1750	328	35	293
1760	377	37	340
1770	479	45	434
1780	539	48	491
1790	570	51	518

See Appendix 2, on states and census regions, for the dates when Vermont (1791), Kentucky (1792), and Tennessee (1796) were admitted to the union.

TABLE Eg60–64　Population of cities – Boston, Newport, New York, Philadelphia, and Charleston: 1630–1790

Contributed by John J. McCusker

	Boston	Newport	New York	Philadelphia	Charleston
	Eg60	Eg61	Eg62	Eg63	Eg64
Year	Number	Number	Number	Number	Number
1630	—	—	300	—	—
1640	1,200	100	400	—	—
1650	2,000	300	1,000	—	—
1660	3,000	700	2,400	—	—
1680	4,500	2,500	3,200	—	700
1685	—	—	—	2,500	900
1690	7,000	2,600	3,900	4,000	1,100
1700	6,700	2,600	5,000	5,000	2,000
1710	9,000	2,800	5,700	6,500	3,000
1720	12,000	3,800	7,000	10,000	3,500

	Boston	Newport	New York	Philadelphia	Charleston
	Eg60	Eg61	Eg62	Eg63	Eg64
Year	Number	Number	Number	Number	Number
1730	13,000	4,600	8,600	11,500	4,500
1740	17,000	—	—	—	—
1742	16,300	6,200	11,000	13,000	6,800
1760	15,600	7,500	18,000	23,800	8,000
1775	16,000	11,000	25,000	33,500	12,000
1790	18,000	6,700	32,300	42,500	16,400

Sources

Carl Bridenbaugh, *Cities in the Wilderness: The First Century of Urban Life in America, 1625–1742* (Ronald Press, 1938), pp. 6 n. 5, 143 n. 1, and 303 n. 1; Bridenbaugh, *Cities in Revolt: Urban Life in America, 1743–1776* (Knopf, 1955), pp. 5, 216–7, as revised by ongoing research detailed later; and Lester J. Cappon, Barbara Bartz Petchenik, and John Hamilton Long, *Atlas of Early American History: The Revolutionary Era, 1760–1790* (Princeton University Press, 1976), p. 97, as revised by ongoing research detailed later.

Documentation

See the Appendixes to the essay in this chapter for a general discussion of the tables and the sources of the data, along with a key to abbreviations used in this chapter and general information on matters such as regional definitions,

calendar differences, money, and weights and measures. See also the text for Table Eg1–59.

This table shows the changing population of the five largest cities in the Thirteen Continental Colonies in 1775. As presented here, the figures are rounded to the nearest significant digit and the 1775 estimate for Philadelphia and its suburbs has been lowered to the figure suggested by John K. Alexander, "The Philadelphia Numbers Game: An Analysis of Philadelphia's Eighteenth-Century Population," *Pennsylvania Magazine of History and Biography* 98 (July 1974): 314–24. By 1790, Baltimore, with a population of 13,500, had supplanted Newport as the fifth largest city in the country. See also U.S. Bureau of the Census, *A Century of Population Growth: From the First Census of the United States to the Twelfth, 1790–1900*, compiled by William S. Rossiter (1909), pp. 78–9.

TABLE Eg65–84   Nationality of the white population, by state or locality – percentage distribution: 1790

Contributed by John J. McCusker

Nationality	American states									
	Overall	Maine	New Hampshire	Vermont	Massachusetts	Rhode Island	Connecticut	New York	New Jersey	Pennsylvania
	Eg65	Eg66 [1]	Eg67	Eg68	Eg69 [1]	Eg70	Eg71	Eg72	Eg73	Eg74
	Percentage	Percentage	Percentage	Percentage	Percentage	Percentage	Percentage	Percentage	Percentage	Percentage
English	60.9	60.0	61.0	76.0	82.0	71.0	67.0	52.0	47.0	35.3
Scottish	8.3	4.5	6.2	5.1	4.4	5.8	2.2	7.0	7.7	8.6
Irish: Northern Ireland	6.0	8.0	4.6	3.2	2.6	2.0	1.8	5.1	6.3	11.0
Irish: Republic of Ireland	3.7	3.7	2.9	1.9	1.3	0.8	1.1	3.0	3.2	3.5
German	8.7	1.3	0.4	0.2	0.3	0.5	0.3	8.2	9.2	33.3
Dutch	3.4	0.1	0.1	0.6	0.2	0.4	0.3	17.5	16.6	1.8
French	1.7	1.3	0.7	0.4	0.8	0.8	0.9	3.8	2.4	1.8
Swedish	0.7	—	—	—	—	0.1	—	0.5	3.9	0.8
Spanish	—	—	—	—	—	—	—	—	—	—
Unassigned	6.6	21.1	24.1	12.6	8.4	18.6	26.4	2.9	3.7	3.9

Nationality	American states								Other areas		
	Delaware	Maryland	Virginia	North Carolina	South Carolina	Georgia	Kentucky and Tennessee		Northwest Territory	Spanish United States	French United States
	Eg75	Eg76	Eg77	Eg78	Eg79	Eg80	Eg81		Eg82	Eg83	Eg84
	Percentage	Percentage	Percentage	Percentage	Percentage	Percentage	Percentage		Percentage	Percentage	Percentage
English	60.0	64.5	68.5	66.0	60.2	57.4	57.9		29.8	2.5	11.2
Scottish	8.0	7.6	10.2	14.8	15.1	15.5	10.0		4.1	0.3	1.6
Irish: Northern Ireland	6.3	5.8	6.2	5.7	9.4	11.5	7.0		2.9	0.2	1.1
Irish: Republic of Ireland	5.4	6.5	5.5	5.4	4.4	3.8	5.2		1.8	0.1	0.7
German	1.1	11.7	6.3	4.7	5.0	7.6	14.0		4.3	0.4	8.7
Dutch	4.3	0.5	0.3	0.3	0.4	0.2	1.3		—	—	—
French	1.6	1.2	1.5	1.7	3.9	2.3	2.2		57.1	—	64.2
Swedish	8.9	0.5	0.6	0.2	0.2	0.6	0.5		—	—	—
Spanish	—	—	—	—	—	—	—		—	96.5	12.5
Unassigned	4.4 [2]	1.7	0.9	1.2	1.4	1.1	1.9		—	—	—

[1] Maine was a part of Massachusetts until it became a separate state in 1820.

[2] Corrected figure; does not agree with source.

Source

American Council of Learned Societies, Committee on Linguistic and National Stocks in the Population of the United States, "Report of Committee on Linguistic and National Stocks in the Population of the United States," in *Annual Report of the American Historical Association . . . for the Year 1931* (U.S. Government Printing Office, 1932), volume 1, p. 124. See especially the appended segments prepared by Howard F. Barker (Annex A) and Marcus L. Hansen (Annexes B and C). This report was later reprinted with a new title: *Surnames in the United States Census of 1790: An Analysis of National Origins of the Population* (Genealogical Publishing, 1969).

Documentation

See the Appendixes to the essay in this chapter for a general discussion of the tables and the sources of the data, along with a key to abbreviations used in this chapter and general information on matters such as regional definitions, calendar differences, money, and weights and measures.

The distribution was made primarily on the basis of family names. See the source for an explanation of the methods used.

Series Eg76. Includes the District of Columbia.

Series Eg77. Includes West Virginia.

Series Eg83–84. In an exception for this chapter, these series include data from areas of North America that were only later to become part of the United States. For a description of these regions, see the source.

TABLE Eg85–96   Population of Maine, by age, sex, race, and ethnicity: 1764–1784

Contributed by John J. McCusker

			Population									
				White			Black and mulatto			French neutral		
	Houses	Families	Total	Total	Male	Female	Total	Male	Female	Total	Male	Female
	Eg85	Eg86	Eg87	Eg88	Eg89	Eg90	Eg91	Eg92	Eg93	Eg94	Eg95	Eg96
Year and age	Number	Number	Number	Number	Number	Number	Number	Number	Number	Number	Number	Number
1764–1765												
Total [1]	2,486	3,481	21,857	21,451	10,870	10,581	344	192	152	62	27	35
Younger than 16 years	—	—	—	10,709	5,532	5,177	—	—	—	36	16	20
16 years and older	—	—	—	10,742	5,338	5,404	—	—	—	26	11	15
1776	—	—	47,767	47,279	—	—	488	—	—	—	—	—
1784	—	—	50,493	—	—	—	—	—	—	—	—	—

[1] William D. Williamson, *The History of the State of Maine: From Its First Discovery, A.D. 1602, to the Separation, A.D. 1820, Inclusive* (Glazier, Masters, 1832), volume 2, p. 373, has somewhat higher numbers: 2,789 houses, 3,572 families, 23,685 whites, 332 blacks, and a total population of 24,020.

Sources

Tables Eg85–193 were originally compiled by Robert C. Klove, U.S. Bureau of the Census, with the advice and assistance of Stella Sutherland, chiefly from the following secondary sources: Evarts B. Greene and Virginia D. Harrington, *American Population before the Federal Census of 1790* (Columbia University Press, 1932), and U.S. Bureau of the Census, *A Century of Population Growth: From the First Census of the United States to the Twelfth, 1790-1900*, compiled by William S. Rossiter (1909). Some minor changes have been made to correct for errors in transcription.

Documentation

Orginal data were obtained as follows.

1764-1765: J[osiah] H. Benton Jr., *Early Census Making in Massachusetts, 1643-1765, with a Reproduction of the Lost Census of 1765 (Recently Found) and Documents Relating Thereto* (Goodspeed, 1905). Corrected in U.S. Bureau of the Census (1909), p. 162. For Massachusetts and Maine, Benton used the Crane MS, which was discovered about 1900. Greene and Harrington (1932, pp. 21-2 n. a) also preferred the Crane MS as published by Benton. The table in U.S. Bureau of the Census (1909), p. 162, is reproduced here because it gives more detail. Joseph B. Felt, *Population of Massachusetts*, Collections of the American Statistical Association (American Statistical Association, 1845), volume 1, part 2, pp. 146-57, 211-3, published data based on a manuscript that Judge Samuel Dana printed in *The Columbian Centinel* (Boston), August 17, 1822. Williamson (1832, volume 2, p. 373) reported population data for the three counties in Maine as well as estimates for the areas that were omitted in the enumeration. His source is also the Dana MS as printed in *The Columbian Centinel*, August 17, 1832. See also the text for Table Eg117-131.

TABLE Eg97–109   Population of New Hampshire, by age, sex, race, slave status, and marital status: 1767–1786

Contributed by John J. McCusker

			Free white								Slave			
			Male				Female							
	Total	Total	Total	Single	Married	Total	Single	Married	Widowed	Total	Male	Female	Other
	Eg97	Eg98	Eg99	Eg100	Eg101	Eg102	Eg103	Eg104	Eg105	Eg106	Eg107	Eg108	Eg109
Year and age	Number	Number	Number	Number	Number	Number	Number	Number	Number	Number	Number	Number	Number
1767													
Total	52,720	52,087	26,264	—	—	25,823	15,992	8,467	1,364	633	384	249	—
Under 16	—	—	12,924	12,924	0	—	—	—	—	—	—	—	—
16–60	—	—	12,180	4,510	7,670	—	—	—	—	—	—	—	—
60 and older	—	—	1,160	—	—	—	—	—	—	—	—	—	—
1773													
Total	73,097	72,423	36,739	—	—	35,684	22,228	11,887	1,569	674	379	295	—
Under 16	—	—	18,334	18,334	0	—	—	—	—	—	—	—	—
16–60	—	—	16,867	6,236	10,604	—	—	—	—	—	—	—	—
60 and older	—	—	1,538	—	—	—	—	—	—	—	—	—	—
1775													
Total	81,300	80,644	41,016	—	—	39,628	—	—	—	656 [2]	—	—	—
Under 16	—	—	20,863	—	—	—	—	—	—	—	—	—	—
16–50	—	—	14,231 [1]	—	—	—	—	—	—	—	—	—	—
50 and older	—	—	3,436	—	—	—	—	—	—	—	—	—	—
In Army	—	—	2,486	—	—	—	—	—	—	—	—	—	—
1786													
Total	95,849	95,452	—	—	—	—	—	—	—	46	—	—	351

[1] Reported as "Males from 16 to 50 not in the army."

[2] Reported as "Negroes and slaves for life."

Sources

See the sources for Table Eg85–96.

Documentation

The ambiguous age groupings are artifacts of the original data. Original data were obtained as follows.

1767: Nathaniel Bouton, Isaac Weare Hammond, et al., editors, *Provincial and State Papers: Documents and Records Relating to New Hampshire* (G. E. Jenks et al., 1867–1943), volume 7, pp. 168–70, as corrected in U.S. Bureau of the Census (1909), pp. 149–50.

1773: Bouton, Hammond, et al. (1867–1943), volume 10, pp. 621–36, as corrected in U.S. Bureau of the Census (1909), pp. 150–1.

1775: "Census of 1775. Return of the Number of Inhabitants in the Several Towns and Places in New-Hampshire, Taken by Order of the Convention, with the Number of Fire-Arms, Powder, &c.," *Collections of the New-Hampshire Historical Society* 1 (1824): 231–5. See also U.S. Bureau of the Census (1909), pp. 152–4, which did not total the figures, which are given by towns. The census was incomplete, with data not reported for several towns. The town figures in Greene and Harrington (1932), pp. 74–9, which are town totals only, differ in a few instances from those given by U.S. Bureau of the Census (1909). See also Bouton, Hammond, et al. (1867–1943), volume 7, pp. 724–81.

1786: Bouton, Hammond, et al. (1867–1943), volume 10, pp. 637–89, as corrected in U.S. Bureau of the Census (1909), pp. 154–6, and Greene and Harrington (1932), p. 74. Although some towns distinguished among various elements in their population, many did not.

TABLE Eg110–116   Population of Vermont, by age, sex, and race: 1771

Contributed by John J. McCusker

		White			Black		
	Total	Total	Male	Female	Total	Male	Female
	Eg110	Eg111	Eg112	Eg113	Eg114	Eg115	Eg116
Year and age	Number	Number	Number	Number	Number	Number	Number
1771							
Total	4,669	4,650	2,503	2,147	19	13	6
Under 16	2,389	2,383	1,249	1,134	6	2	4
16–60	—	—	1,187	—	—	10	—
16 and over	2,280	2,267	—	1,013	13	—	2
Over 60	—	—	67	—	—	1	—

Sources

See the sources for Table Eg85–96.

Documentation

Original data were obtained as follows.

These figures are for Cumberland and Gloucester counties, which in 1771 were part of the colony of New York. From the mid-1770s, the territory that was to be detached from New York and admitted to the union as a separate state in 1791 operated increasingly independently. Compare Table Eg404–419.

London Documents, volume 44, p. 144; as quoted in E[dmund] B. O'Callaghan, editor, *The Documentary History of the State of New York* (Weed, Parsons; Van Benthuysen, 1849–1851), volume 1, pp. 474, 697; New York [State], Secretary of State, *Census of the State of New York, for 1855: Taken in Pursuance of Article Third of the Constitution of the State, and of Chapter Sixty-Four of the Laws of 1855*, edited by Franklin B. Hough (Van Benthuysen, 1857), p. vii, as quoted and corrected in U.S. Bureau of the Census (1909), p. 183, and Greene and Harrington (1932), pp. 86, 102.

TABLE Eg117–131   Population of Massachusetts, by age, sex, race, and ethnicity: 1764–1784

Contributed by John J. McCusker

				Population											
			White			Black and mulatto			Indian			French neutral			
	Houses	Families	Total	Total	Male	Female	Total	Male	Female	Total	Male	Female	Total	Male	Female
	Eg117	Eg118	Eg119	Eg120	Eg121	Eg122	Eg123	Eg124	Eg125	Eg126	Eg127	Eg128	Eg129	Eg130	Eg131
Year and age	Number	Number	Number	Number	Number	Number	Number	Number	Number	Number	Number	Number	Number	Number	Number
1764–1765															
Total	31,707	43,483	223,841	216,700	106,611	110,089	4,891	2,824	2,067	1,681	728	953	569	274	295
Younger than 16	—	—	—	103,477	52,859	50,588	—	—	—	—	—	—	261	133	128
16 and older	—	—	—	113,253	53,752	59,501	—	—	—	—	—	—	308	141	167
1776	—	—	290,900	286,139	—	—	4,761	—	—	—	—	—	—	—	—
1784	—	—	307,018	—	—	—	—	—	—	—	—	—	—	—	—

Sources
See the sources for Table Eg85–96.

Documentation
Original data were obtained as follows.

1764–1765: Benton (1905), corrected in U.S. Bureau of the Census (1909), p. 161. See the text for Table Eg85–96 and the discussion there of the similarities and differences of the several surviving versions of that census. Note that Benton's reprinting of the tabulation retains the distinction present in the original between blacks and Indians; in earlier versions their numbers were "combined under the general head of 'Negroes'" (Benton 1905, p. 69).

1776: Jesse Chickering, *A Statistical View of the Population of Massachusetts, from 1765 to 1840* (Little and Brown, 1846), p. 9. See also Greene and Harrington (1932), p. 17.

1784: Jedidiah Morse, *The American Geography; or, A View of the Present Situation of the United States of America . . .* (Published by the author, 1789), p. 172. See also Greene and Harrington (1932), p. 46.

TABLE Eg132–140   Population of Rhode Island, by age, sex, and race: 1708–1783

Contributed by John J. McCusker

				Population						
			White			Black				
	Families	Total	Total	Male	Female	Total	Male	Female	Indian
	Eg132	Eg133	Eg134	Eg135	Eg136	Eg137	Eg138	Eg139	Eg140
Year and age	Number	Number	Number	Number	Number	Number	Number	Number	Number
1708	—	7,181	—	2,432 [1]	—	426	—	—	—
1730	—	17,935	15,302	—	—	1,648	—	—	985
1748	—	34,128	29,755	—	—	3,101	—	—	1,272
1755									
Total	—	40,636	35,939	17,960	17,979	4,697 [2]	2,387	2,310	—
Adults	—	20,663	18,121	9,177	8,944	2,542	1,277	1,265	—
Children	—	19,973	17,818	8,783	9,035	2,155	1,110	1,045	—
1774									
Total	9,450	59,607	54,460	26,763	27,697	3,668	—	—	1,479
Under 16	—	—	25,079	12,731	12,348	—	—	—	—
16 and over	—	—	29,381	14,032	15,349	—	—	—	—
1783	—	51,887	48,556	—	—	2,806 [3]	—	—	525

[1] Including 1,015 freemen, 1,362 militia, and 55 white servants.

[2] Combines blacks and Indians.

[3] Including 464 mulattos.

Sources
See the sources for Table Eg85–96.

Documentation
Original data were obtained as follows.

1708: John Russell Bartlett, editor, *Records of the Colony of Rhode Island and Providence Plantations, in New England* (Crawford Greene, 1856–1865), volume 4, p. 59, as quoted and corrected in U.S. Bureau of the Census (1909), pp. 162, 163, and Greene and Harrington (1932), p. 65.

1730: "Number of Inhabitants of Rhode Island [1730–1791]," *Collections of the Massachusetts Historical Society*, 2nd series, 7 (1818): 113. See also U.S. Bureau of the Census (1909), p. 163.

1748: "Number of Inhabitants of Rhode Island [1730–1791]," *Collections of the Massachusetts Historical Society*, 2nd series, 7 (1818): 113. Compare U.S. Bureau of the Census (1909), p. 162.

1755: "Account of the People in the Colony of Rhode Island . . . ," enclosure in letter from Governor Stephen Hopkins, at Rhode Island, to the Commissioners for Trade and Plantations, December 24, 1755, CO 5/1274, folios 118v–119r, PRO/TNA. Governor Hopkins described this as an account of "the Number of People [which] . . . we have caused to be exactly taken" (folio 116v). He went on to compare this census with two earlier counts. See U.S. Bureau of the Census (1909), p. 163; Greene and Harrington (1932), p. 67.

1774: Rhode Island, General Assembly, *Census of the Inhabitants of the Colony of Rhode Island and Providence Plantations [1774]*, edited by John Russell Bartlett (Knowles, Anthony, 1858), p. 239, as quoted and corrected in U.S. Bureau of the Census (1909), pp. 162–3.

1783: Bartlett (1856–1865), volume 7, p. 299, as cited and corrected in Greene and Harrington (1932), pp. 69–70. See also Morse (1789), p. 201; U.S. Bureau of the Census (1909), p. 163.

TABLE Eg141–154 Population of Connecticut, by age, sex, race, and marital status: 1756–1782

Contributed by John J. McCusker

	Total	White							Black			Indian		
		Total	Male			Female			Total	Male	Female	Total	Male	Female
			Total	Married	Single	Total	Married	Single						
	Eg141	Eg142	Eg143	Eg144	Eg145	Eg146	Eg147	Eg148	Eg149	Eg150	Eg151	Eg152	Eg153	Eg154
Year and age	Number	Number	Number	Number	Number	Number	Number	Number	Number	Number	Number	Number	Number	Number
1756	130,612	126,976	—	—	—	—	—	—	3,019	—	—	617	—	—
1774	197,842	191,378 [1]	96,182	30,524	65,658	94,296	30,636	63,660	5,101	2,883	2,218	1,363	635	728
Under 20 years	—	—	—	—	—	—	—	—	2,471	1,306	1,165	746	391	355
Over 20 years	—	—	—	—	—	—	—	—	2,630	1,577	1,053	617	244	373
Under 10 years	—	61,164	31,114	0	31,114	30,050	0	30,050	—	—	—	—	—	—
10–20 years	—	46,828	24,271	222	24,049	22,557	697	21,860	—	—	—	—	—	—
20–70 years	—	78,310	38,807	28,866	9,941	39,503	29,017	10,486	—	—	—	—	—	—
Over 70 years	—	4,176	1,990	1,436	554	2,186	922	1,264	—	—	—	—	—	—
1782	209,177	202,904 [2]	—	—	—	—	—	—	6,273 [3]	—	—	—	—	—

[1] Includes 900 people not distributed by sex.

[2] Equals the sum of the components and disagrees with the source. See also Evarts B. Greene and Virginia D. Harrington, *American Population before the Federal Census of 1790* (Columbia University Press, 1932), p. 61. Jedidiah Morse, *American Geography* (Published by the author, 1789), p. 218, also indicated that the population included 39,388 males between the ages of 16 and 50 and 103,735 females.

[3] Blacks and Indians.

Sources
See the sources for Table Eg85–96.

Documentation
The ambiguous demarcations of age groupings are an artifact of the original data. Original data were obtained as follows.

1756: James Hammond Trumbull and Charles Jeremy Hoadly, editors, *The Public Records of the Colony of Connecticut* (Case, Lockwood, and Brainard, 1850–1890), volume 11, p. 630; volume 14, p. 492. Note the corrected total in U.S. Bureau of the Census (1909), p. 164. Greene and Harrington (1932), pp. 58–61, accept Rossiter's correction.

1774: Trumbull and Hoadly (1850–1890), volume 14, pp. 485–91, as reprinted in U.S. Bureau of the Census (1909), pp. 166–9, with some corrected totals. Greene and Harrington (1932), pp. 58–61, used the same source and give approximately the same figures, but not in as much detail.

1782: Morse (1789), p. 218. See also Greene and Harrington (1932), pp. 46 n. a, 61 n. r.

TABLE Eg155–161 Population of New York, by age, sex, and race: 1698–1786

Contributed by John J. McCusker

	Total	White			Black		
		Total	Male	Female	Total	Male	Female
	Eg155	Eg156	Eg157	Eg158	Eg159	Eg160	Eg161
Year and age	Number	Number	Number	Number	Number	Number	Number
1698							
Total	18,067	15,897	—	—	2,170	—	—
Adults	—	9,743	5,066	4,677	—	—	—
Children	—	6,154	—	—	—	—	—
1703							
Total	20,665	18,282	9,197	9,085	2,258	1,174	1,084
Under 16	10,483	9,634	4,710	4,924	849	467	382
16 and over [1]	10,182	8,648	4,487	4,161	1,409	707	702
1712–1714							
Total [2]	22,608	16,979	8,601	8,378	2,425	1,334	1,091
Under 16	9,294	8,450	4,389	4,061	844	434	410
16–60	—	7,853	3,850	4,003	—	—	—
16 and over	10,110	—	—	—	1,581	900	681
Over 60	—	676	362	314	—	—	—
1723							
Total	40,564	34,393	17,583	16,810	6,171	3,364	2,807
Adults	21,842	17,846	9,083	8,763	3,996	2,186	1,810
Children	18,722	16,547	8,500	8,047	2,175	1,178	997
1731							
Total	50,286	43,055	24,853	18,202	7,231	4,334	2,897
Under 10	19,362	16,916	10,243	6,673	2,446	1,402	1,044
10 and over	30,924	26,139	14,610	11,529	4,785	2,932	1,853

Notes appear at end of table

TABLE Eg155–161   Population of New York, by age, sex, and race: 1698–1786   *Continued*

	Total	White			Black		
		Total	Male	Female	Total	Male	Female
	Eg155	Eg156	Eg157	Eg158	Eg159	Eg160	Eg161
Year and age	Number	Number	Number	Number	Number	Number	Number
1737							
Total	60,437	51,496	25,740	25,756	8,941	4,948	3,993
Under 10	19,261	16,585	8,347	8,238	2,676	1,397	1,279
10 and over	41,176	34,911	17,393	17,518	6,265	3,551	2,714
1746							
Total	61,589	52,482	26,860	25,622	9,107	4,857	4,250
Under 16	29,924	25,744	12,938	12,806	4,180	1,964	2,216
16–60	—	—	12,522	—	—	2,529	—
16 and over	31,665	26,738	—	12,816	4,927	—	2,034
Over 60	—	—	1,400	—	—	364	—
1749							
Total	73,348	62,756	32,355	30,401	10,592	5,696	4,896
Under 16	34,688	30,069	15,457	14,612	4,619	2,379	2,240
16–60	—	—	15,332	—	—	2,950	—
16 and over	38,660	32,687	—	15,789	5,973	—	2,656
Over 60	—	—	1,566	—	—	367	—
1756							
Total	96,790	83,242	43,261	39,981	13,548	7,570	5,978
Under 16	45,713	39,653	20,669	18,984	6,060	3,280	2,780
16–60	—	—	19,825	—	—	3,797	—
16 and over	51,077	43,589	—	20,997	7,488	—	3,198
Over 60	—	—	2,767	—	—	493	—
1771							
Total	163,348	143,474	73,990	69,484	19,874	10,623	9,251
Under 16	74,456	65,986	33,628	32,358	8,470	4,414	4,056
16–60	—	—	36,115	—	—	5,362	—
16 and over	88,892	77,488	—	37,126	11,404	—	5,195
Over 60	—	—	4,247	—	—	847	—
1786							
Total [3]	238,897	219,996	112,465	107,531	18,889	9,521	9,368
Under 16	—	106,573	54,807	51,766	—	—	—
16–60	—	—	52,927	—	—	—	—
16 and over	—	113,423	—	55,765	—	—	—
Over 60	—	—	4,731	—	—	—	—

[1] Total includes 125 persons more than 60 years of age not distributed by sex or race.

[2] Includes 3,204 persons in Kings and Richmond counties not returned in detail. An "imperfect" census, according to *Century of Population Growth*, compiled by William S. Rossiter (U.S. Government Printing Office, 1909), p. 181.

[3] Total includes twelve Indians who paid taxes.

Sources
See the sources for Table Eg85–96.

Documentation
Original data were obtained as follows.

1698: Account of the population of New York, enclosure in Governor Richard Coote, Earl of Bellomont, at New York, to the Commissioners of Trade and Plantations, November 7, 1698, CO 5/1041, 20, vi, PRO/TNA. See also U.S. Bureau of the Census (1909), p. 170; and Greene and Harrington (1932), p. 92.

1703: New York [State], Secretary of State (1857) p. iv. See also U.S. Bureau of the Census (1909), p. 170; and Greene and Harrington (1932), p. 95.

1712–1714: New York Colonial Manuscripts, LVII, Manuscripts and Special Collections, New York State Library, Albany, New York, as quoted in U.S. Bureau of the Census (1909), p. 181. See also New York [State], Secretary of State (1857), p. v, where Hough noted that the figures he reported were obtained from a partial census, rendered imperfect on account of "the people being deterred by a simple superstition, and observation that the sickness followed upon the last numbering of the people."

1723: O'Callaghan (1849–1851), volume 1, p. 693. See also U.S. Bureau of the Census (1909), p. 181; and Greene and Harrington (1932), p. 96. See also New York [State], Secretary of State (1857), p. v.

1731–1771: O'Callaghan (1849–1851), volume 1, pp. 694–7, omitting Albany County in 1746. See also U.S. Bureau of the Census (1909), pp. 181–3, with corrections; and Greene and Harrington (1932), pp. 97–102. See also New York [State], Secretary of State (1857), pp. v–vii.

1786: New York [State], Secretary of State (1857), p. viii. See also Morse (1789), p. 248; U.S. Bureau of the Census (1909), p. 183; and Greene and Harrington (1932), p. 104.

TABLE Eg162-168   Population of New Jersey, by age, sex, and race: 1726-1784

Contributed by John J. McCusker

Year and age	Total	White			Black		
		Total	Male	Female	Total	Male	Female
	Eg162	Eg163	Eg164	Eg165	Eg166 [1]	Eg167	Eg168
	Number	Number	Number	Number	Number	Number	Number
1726							
Total	32,442	29,861	15,737	14,124	2,581	1,435	1,146
Under 16	15,585	14,506	7,558	6,948	1,079	563	516
16 and over	16,857	15,355	8,179	7,176	1,502	872	630
1738							
Total	46,676	42,695	22,270	20,425	3,981	2,208	1,773
Under 16	21,963	20,339	10,639	9,700	1,624	849	775
16 and over	24,713	22,356	11,631	10,725	2,357	1,359	998
1745							
Total	61,403	56,797 [2]	29,339	27,458	4,606	2,588	2,018
Under 16	—	28,007	14,253	13,754	—	—	—
16 and over	—	28,790	15,086	13,704	—	—	—
1772	122,003	—	—	—	—	—	—
1784	149,435	138,934	—	—	10,501 [3]	—	—

[1] The 1738 count reported "Negroes and other slaves," and the 1745 count reported "slaves."

[2] 9,736 persons were reported as Quakers.

[3] 1,959 persons were reported as slaves.

Sources

See the sources for Table Eg85-96.

Documentation

Original data were obtained as follows.

1726: William A. Whitehead, Frederick William Ricord, and William Nelson, editors, *Documents Relating to the Colonial History of the State of New Jersey*, Archives of the State of New Jersey, 1st series (State of New Jersey, 1880-1886), volume 5, p. 164, as printed and corrected in U.S. Bureau of the Census (1909), p. 184; and Greene and Harrington (1832), p. 109. See also S[amuel] D. Dickinson, editor, *Compendium of Censuses 1726-1905: Together with the Tabulated Returns of 1905* (Census Bureau, Department of State, State of New Jersey, 1906), p. 41.

1738-1745: Whitehead, Ricord, and Nelson (1880-1886), volume 6, pp. 242-4. See also the returns as corrected in U.S. Bureau of the Census (1909), p. 184, and Greene and Harrington (1932), pp. 110-1. See also Dickinson (1906), p. 41.

1772: Whitehead, Ricord, and Nelson (1880-1886), volume 10, pp. 452-3; see also p. 445. See also Stella H. Sutherland, *Population Distribution in Colonial America* (Columbia University Press, 1936), pp. 98-9. Separate figures for whites and blacks are indicated for only eight out of fourteen counties.

1784: Dickinson (1906), p. 41; and Morse (1789), p. 284.

TABLE Eg169–181   Population of Maryland, by age, sex, race, slave or servant status, and taxable status: 1704–1782

Contributed by John J. McCusker

		White						Mulatto			Black		
	Total	Total	Free	Servant	Masters and taxable men	Women	Children	Total	Free	Slave	Total	Free	Slave
	Eg169	Eg170	Eg171	Eg172	Eg173	Eg174	Eg175	Eg176	Eg177	Eg178	Eg179	Eg180	Eg181
Year, age, taxable status, and sex	Number	Number	Number	Number	Number	Number	Number	Number	Number	Number	Number	Number	Number
1704	34,912	30,437	—	—	11,026 [9]	7,163 [10]	12,248	—	—	—	4,475 [11]	—	—
1710	42,741	34,796	—	—	11,091	8,294	15,411	—	—	—	7,945	—	—
1712	46,151	37,743	—	—	11,029	9,081	17,633	—	—	—	8,408	—	—
1755													
Total	153,505 [1]	108,193	99,352	8,841	—	—	—	3,608	1,460	2,148	41,704	357	41,347
Younger than 16	77,444	53,321	51,773	1,548	—	—	—	2,026	811	1,215	22,097	111	21,986
Male	39,802	27,752	26,637	1,115 [5]	—	—	—	996	419	577	11,054	71	10,983
Female	37,642	25,569	25,136 [3]	433 [6]	—	—	—	1,030	392	638	11,043	40	11,003
16 and older, taxable	48,811	28,469	23,386	5,083	—	—	—	1,388	554	834	18,954	188	18,766
Male	40,165	28,469	23,386	5,083 [7]	—	—	—	749	307	442	10,947	119	10,828
Female	8,646	0	0	0	—	—	—	639	247	392	8,007 [12]	69	7,938
16 and older, not taxable	27,250	26,403	24,193	2,210	—	—	—	194	95	99	653	58 [14]	595 [14]
Male	—	672	672 [4]	0	—	—	—	—	—	—	—	—	—
Female	—	25,731	23,521	2,210 [8]	—	—	—	—	—	—	—	—	—
1782	254,050	170,688 [2]	—	—	—	—	—	—	—	—	83,362 [13]	—	—

[1] 153,565 persons according to Evarts B. Greene and Virginia D. Harrington, *American Population* (Columbia University Press, 1932), p. 126.

[2] Including 35,268 free males older than 18 years of age.

[3] 24,141 persons according to Greene and Harrington (1932), p. 126.

[4] Includes 35 clergy and 637 poor men.

[5] Including 1,048 hired or indentured and 67 convicts.

[6] Including 412 hired or indentured and 21 convicts.

[7] Including 3,576 hired or indentured and 1,507 convicts.

[8] Including 1,824 hired or indentured and 386 convicts.

[9] Masters, freemen, and servants.

[10] Free women and servants.

[11] Slaves.

[12] 9,007 persons according to Greene and Harrington (1932), p. 126.

[13] Including 27,626 blacks younger than 8 years of age; 13,399 males and females 8 to 14 years of age; 16,246 males 14 to 45 years of age; 13,832 females 14 to 36 years of age; and 12,259 males older than 45 years of age and females older than 36 years of age.

[14] Past labor or cripples.

Sources
See the sources for Table Eg85–96.

Documentation
Original data were obtained as follows.

1704: William Hand Browne, Clayton Colman Hall, et al., editors, *Archives of Maryland* (Maryland Historical Society, 1883–1972), volume 25, p. 256, as cited in Greene and Harrington (1932), p. 129.

1710–1712: Browne, Hall, et al. (1883–1972), volume 25, pp. 258–9, as cited in Greene and Harrington (1932), p. 129.

1755: *Gentleman's Magazine* 34 (1764): 261, as cited and corrected in U.S. Bureau of the Census (1909), p. 185, which offers more detail than Greene and Harrington (1932), pp. 125–6. Although Greene and Harrington have some figures that vary considerably from those given in U.S. Bureau of the Census (1909), the difference in total population is only sixty. Greene and Harrington take their figures from a different source: Maryland Records, Miscellaneous, 1755–1775, number 11, Peter Force Transcripts, Manuscript Division, LC, Washington, D.C. This was copied from Ezra Stiles's Papers.

1782: Morse (1789), p. 350. Also in Greene and Harrington (1932), p. 127. Morse stated that the count of the black population – and, presumably, the white population – was "taken by several assessors, in March 1782."

TABLE Eg182–193   Population of Virginia, by age, sex, race, and free status: 1624–1701

Contributed by John J. McCusker

		White							Black				
		Total	Free		Servants				Total	Male	Female	Children	Indian
	Total	Total	Male	Female	Male	Female	Children	Total					
	Eg182	Eg183	Eg184	Eg185	Eg186	Eg187	Eg188	Eg189	Eg190	Eg191	Eg192	Eg193
Year(s)	Number	Number	Number	Number	Number	Number	Number	Number	Number	Number	Number	Number
1624–1625	1,227	1,202	432	176	441	46	107	23	11	10	2	2
1634	4,909	—	—	—	—	—	—	—	—	—	—	—
1699	58,040 [1]	—	—	—	—	—	—	—	—	—	—	—
1701	57,596 [1]	—	—	—	—	—	—	—	—	—	—	—

[1] Includes the following numbers of tithables and untithables: 21,606 and 36,434 in 1699; and 21,712 and 35,884 in 1701.

Sources

See the sources for Table Eg85–96.

Documentation

Original data were obtained as follows.

1624–1625: Alexander Brown, *The First Republic in America: An Account of the Origin of This Nation, Written from the Records Then (1624) Concealed by the Council, Rather than from the Histories Then Licensed by the Crown* (Houghton Mifflin, 1898), pp. 617–27; and "The Virginia Census, 1624–25," *Virginia Magazine of History and Biography* 7 (April 1900): 364–7. See also Greene and Harrington (1932), p. 144. Irene W. D. Hecht, "The Virginia Muster of 1624/5 as a Source for Demographic History," *William and Mary Quarterly*, 3rd series, 30 (January 1973): 65–92, offered a detailed analysis of the data and stated the total as 1,218.

1634: "A List of the number of men, women, and children Inhabitinge in the severall Counties within the colony of Virginia . . . 1634," in [Thomas H. Wynne, editor], *Colonial Records of Virginia* (Virginia General Assembly, Joint Committee on the State Library 1874), p. 91. "After this list was brought in there arrived a ship of Holland with 145 persons from Bermudas. And since that 60 more in an English shipp which likewise came from the Bermudas." See also Papers Relating to Virginia, volume 1, p. 18, George Chalmers Papers, 1606–1812, Manuscripts and Archives Section, New York Public Library. See also Greene and Harrington (1932), p. 145.

1699: Enclosure in Gov. Francis Nicholson to the Commissioners of Trade and Plantations, December 2, 1701, CO 5/1312, number 19 (xi), PRO/TNA, as cited by Greene and Harrington (1932), p. 137.

1701: Enclosure in Nicholson to the Commissioners of Trade and Plantations, December 2, 1701, CO 5/1312, number 19 (x), PRO/TNA, as cited by Greene and Harrington (1932), pp. 147–8.

John J. McCusker

TABLE Eg194–200   Towns settled and incorporated in New England, by colony or locality: 1620–1799

Contributed by John J. McCusker

	Maine		New Hamphsire, incorporated	Vermont, settled	Massachusetts		Connecticut, settled
	Settled	Incorporated			Settled	Incorporated	
	Eg194	Eg195	Eg196	Eg197	Eg198	Eg199	Eg200
Year	Number	Number	Number	Number	Number	Number	Number
1620	—	—	—	—	2	1	—
1621	—	—	—	—	0	0	—
1622	1	—	—	—	0	0	—
1623	2	—	—	—	2	0	—
1624	1	—	—	—	3	0	—
1625	4	—	—	—	2	0	—
1626	1	—	—	—	4	0	—
1627	1	—	—	—	0	0	—
1628	3	—	—	—	0	0	—
1629	1	—	—	—	4	0	—
1630	8	—	—	—	12	4	—
1631	1	—	—	—	0	0	—
1632	0	—	—	—	3	0	—
1633	1	—	—	—	3	0	—
1634	0	—	—	—	5	1	—
1635	0	—	—	—	11	6	—
1636	0	—	—	—	6	2	—
1637	0	—			3	1	3
1638	1	—		—	12	2	0
1639	0	—	—	—	8	4	1
1640	2	—	—	—	9	3	2
1641	0	—	—	—	3	2	0
1642	0	—	—	—	6	2	1
1643	1	—	—	—	1	1	2
1644	0	—	—	—	3	2	0
1645	0	—	—	—	2	2	1
1646	0	—	—	—	0	1	0
1647	0	—	—	—	1	0	0
1648	0	—	—	—	0	0	0
1649	0	—	—	—	3	2	0
1650	1	—	—	—	8	1	0
1651	0	—	—	—	3	1	1
1652	0	2	—	—	3	0	0
1653	0	3	—	—	2	1	2
1654	0	0	—	—	3	0	0
1655	0	0	—	—	2	3	0
1656	0	0	—	—	3	2	0
1657	0	0	—	—	3	0	0
1658	0	8	—	—	0	0	1
1659	0	0	—	—	7	0	0
1660	0	0	—	—	11	1	0
1661	0	0	—	—	3	1	0
1662	0	0	—	—	5	1	0
1663	3	3	—	—	0	0	0
1664	1	1	—	—	7	1	0
1665	0	0	—	—	2	0	1
1666	0	0	—	—	1	0	0
1667	0	0	—	—	2	0	1
1668	0	0	—	—	2	1	1
1669	0	0	—	—	5	2	0
1670	0	0	—	—	5	1	1
1671	0	0	—	—	1	2	0
1672	0	0	—	—	2	0	0
1673	0	0	—	—	4	2	0
1674	0	0	—	—	0	1	2

(continued)

TABLE Eg194–200   Towns settled and incorporated in New England, by colony or locality: 1620–1799 *Continued*

Year	Maine Settled	Maine Incorporated	New Hamphsire, incorporated	Vermont, settled	Massachusetts Settled	Massachusetts Incorporated	Connecticut, settled
	Eg194	Eg195	Eg196	Eg197	Eg198	Eg199	Eg200
	Number	Number	Number	Number	Number	Number	Number
1675	0	0	—	—	2	0	1
1676	0	0	—	—	2	0	0
1677	0	0	—	—	1	1	0
1678	0	0	—	—	3	0	0
1679	0	0	—	—	1	0	0
1680	3	3	—	—	3	0	0
1681	0	0	—	—	1	0	0
1682	0	0	—	—	1	0	0
1683	0	0	—	—	0	2	1
1684	0	0	—	—	0	1	0
1685	0	0	—	—	0	0	0
1686	0	0	—	—	2	1	2
1687	0	0	—	—	1	0	2
1688	0	0	—	—	0	0	0
1689	0	0	—	—	0	0	0
1690	0	0	—	—	0	0	2
1691	0	0	—	—	0	1	0
1692	0	0	—	—	1	0	1
1693	0	0	—	—	1	1	0
1694	0	0	—	—	1	4	0
1695	0	0	—	—	0	0	0
1696	0	0	—	—	0	0	0
1697	0	0	—	—	0	0	1
1698	0	0	—	—	0	2	0
1699	0	0	—	—	1	0	0
1700	0	0	—	—	4	1	1
1701	0	0	—	—	0	0	0
1702	0	0	—	—	0	1	1
1703	0	0	—	—	1	0	1
1704	0	0	—	—	4	0	0
1705	0	0	—	—	1	1	1
1706	0	0	—	—	1	0	0
1707	0	0	—	—	0	1	2
1708	0	0	—	—	0	0	2
1709	0	0	—	—	1	1	1
1710	0	0	—	—	2	0	1
1711	0	0	—	—	0	2	1
1712	0	0	—	—	0	4	2
1713	0	1	—	—	6	4	1
1714	0	0	—	—	2	6	0
1715	0	0	—	—	3	1	1
1716	0	1	—	—	2	0	0
1717	0	0	—	—	2	1	0
1718	0	0	—	—	2	1	0
1719	3	0	—	—	0	1	2
1720	1	0	—	—	4	0	1
1721	0	0	—	—	3	0	2
1722	0	0	—	—	1	1	0
1723	0	0	—	—	1	0	0
1724	0	0	—	—	1	2	1
1725	4	0	—	—	1	3	1
1726	0	0	—	—	3	2	1
1727	0	0	—	—	2	5	0
1728	0	0	—	—	1	2	1
1729	0	0	—	—	1	2	0
1730	1	0	—	—	4	1	0
1731	0	0	—	—	1	2	1
1732	0	0	—	—	1	3	2
1733	1	0	—	—	1	1	0
1734	0	0	—	—	2	2	3

TABLE Eg194–200   Towns settled and incorporated in New England, by colony or locality: 1620–1799   *Continued*

Year	Maine		New Hamphsire, incorporated	Vermont, settled	Massachusetts		Connecticut, settled
	Settled	Incorporated			Settled	Incorporated	
	Eg194	Eg195	Eg196	Eg197	Eg198	Eg199	Eg200
	Number	Number	Number	Number	Number	Number	Number
1735	2	0	—	—	8	4	1
1736	2	0	—	—	2	0	0
1737	0	1	—	—	4	0	0
1738	0	0	—	—	4	3	4
1739	0	0	—	—	2	4	3
1740	3	0	—	—	3	1	2
1741	0	0	—	—	1	2	2
1742	0	0	—	—	1	1	0
1743	1	0	—	—	2	1	1
1744	0	0	—	—	0	0	1
1745	0	0	—	—	1	0	0
1746	0	0	—	—	1	0	0
1747	0	0	—	—	0	0	0
1748	1	0	—	—	0	0	0
1749	0	0	—	—	3	0	0
1750	4	0	—	0	5	0	0
1751	1	0	—	1	3	0	0
1752	0	0	—	1	1	1	0
1753	2	1	—	1	2	0	0
1754	1	0	—	1	1	2	0
1755	0	0	—	0	1	0	0
1756	0	0	—	0	1	0	0
1757	1	0	—	0	0	0	0
1758	0	1	—	0	0	0	1
1759	5	1	—	0	0	0	1
1760	11	1	—	0	6	0	0
1761	1	0	—	7	1	5	1
1762	7	4	—	2	7	6	1
1763	11	0	—	7	1	2	0
1764	10	2	—	8	3	3	0
1765	7	2	—	4	1	9	0
1766	0	0	—	7	2	0	0
1767	2	1	—	0	4	1	3
1768	2	1	—	7	0	2	1
1769	6	0	—	6	1	0	0
1770	14	0	—	5	2	1	0
1771	3	4	—	5	0	4	1
1772	6	1	—	2	0	0	0
1773	7	1	—	4	0	2	0
1774	16	2	—	7	0	3	0
1775	10	0	—	11	0	36	0
1776	6	1	2	5	1	1	0
1777	2	3	3	1	1	2	1
1778	2	1	5	1	0	5	0
1779	6	1	5	4	1	3	3
1780	16	0	0	9	1	4	1
1781	2	0	2	7	0	4	0
1782	7	0	2	3	1	0	0
1783	3	0	0	11	1	2	0
1784	7	1	3	12	0	2	2
1785	2	2	1	9	0	3	2
1786	6	4	0	5	0	2	9
1787	2	4	3	7	0	2	2
1788	2	9	1	7	0	0	1
1789	2	11	0	9	0	0	1

(continued)

TABLE Eg194–200   Towns settled and incorporated in New England, by colony or locality: 1620–1799 *Continued*

Year	Maine		New Hamphsire, incorporated	Vermont, settled	Massachusetts		Connecticut, settled
	Settled	Incorporated			Settled	Incorporated	
	Eg194	Eg195	Eg196	Eg197	Eg198	Eg199	Eg200
	Number	Number	Number	Number	Number	Number	Number
1790	6	1	1	6	0	2	1
1791	4	2	3	3	0	0	0
1792	4	6	0	4	0	3	0
1793	3	2	—	4	0	5	0
1794	4	10	—	6	0	0	1
1795	4	9	—	4	1	0	1
1796	1	7	—	1	0	0	1
1797	1	5	—	4	0	3	0
1798	3	8	—	3	0	1	0
1799	2	1	—	2	0	1	0

Sources

Data were originally compiled by Paul F. Paskoff for an unpublished study of the formation and incorporation of towns in seventeen colonies/states through the mid-nineteenth century. He used the following sources, which vary from state to state as to their nature and comprehensiveness: Arthur H. Hughes and Morse S. Allen, *Connecticut Place Names* (Connecticut Historical Society, 1976); Stanley Bearce Attwood, *The Length and Breadth of Maine*, Maine Studies, number 96 (University of Maine at Orono Press, 1973), pp. 20-2; Ava Harriet Chadbourne, *Maine Place Names and the Peopling of Its Towns* (Bond Wheelwright, 1955); Richard W. Wilkie and Jack Tager, editors, *Historical Atlas of Massachusetts* (University of Massachusetts Press, 1991), pp. 140-4 ("Statistical Appendix"); New Hampshire, Laws and Statutes, *Laws of New Hampshire, Including Public and Private Acts and Resolves and the Royal Commissions and Instructions, with Historical and Descriptive Notes and an Appendix*, edited by A[lbert] S. Batchellor, Henry Harrison Metcalf, et al., (J. B. Clarke et al., 1904-1922), volumes 4-5 (see the index under "Towns, incorporated"); and David Maunsell, Lawton V. Crocker, and Dorman B. E. Kent, *Gazetteer of Vermont Heritage: A Concise Account of the Discovery Settlement, and Progress of Interesting and Remarkable Events in the Green Mountain Country, Embellished with Pictures of Manners, Customs, etc.* (National Survey, 1966), pp. 31-92.

Documentation

See the Appendixes to the essay in this chapter for a general discussion of the tables and the sources of the data, along with a key to abbreviations used in this chapter and general information on matters such as regional definitions, calendar differences, money, and weights and measures.

New England was established and settled one town (township) at a time. The date of incorporation generally followed the date of settlement.

These data allow us to get a sense of the pace and pattern of settlement across the region. In New England, the township was not an urban place (as it was in England and as it came to be elsewhere in the Thirteen Continental Colonies) but a combination of a central small village and the associated farms of the inhabitants radiating from that village, sometimes as much as fifteen or twenty miles distant. The township was the organizational mode of settlement, the later system of local government – justly celebrated for its feisty unwillingness to yield to higher authority – and the hive from which those who wished moved off to found their own, new town. As such, it is the ideal unit by which to measure the changing pace of advancing settlement, northward and westward from the coast. See Roy H. Akagi, *The Town Proprietors of the New England Colonies: A Study of Their Development, Organization, Activities, and Controversies, 1620-1770* (Press of the University of Pennsylvania, 1924). See also Bruce C. Daniels, *The Connecticut Town: Growth and Development, 1635-1790* (Wesleyan University Press, 1979).

As more than one author has argued, the long-term cycles in the movement of peoples westward can be seen to parallel the periods of expansion and contraction in the economy, rising in periods of good times, declining in periods of bad times. It is a persistent theme in John J. McCusker and Russell R. Menard, *The Economy of British America, 1607-1789*, 2nd edition (University of North Carolina Press, 1991). For a sophisticated articulation of the argument, see Carville V. Earle, "The Rate of Frontier Expansion in American History, 1650-1890," in John J. McCusker, Russell R. Menard, et al., editors, *Lois Green Carr: The Chesapeake and Beyond – A Celebration* (Maryland Historical and Cultural Publications, 1992), pp. 183-204.

Additional insights into the subject of colonial expansion can be gained from a careful analysis of the settlement patterns established in the series of maps presented in Herman R. Friis, *A Series of Population Maps of the Colonies and the United States, 1625-1790*, American Geographical Society, Mimeographed Publication number 3 (American Geographical Society, 1940). See also the set of maps in B[onnie] Barton, *The Comparability of Geographic Methodologies: A Study of New England Settlement*, Michigan Geographical Publications, number 20 (University of Michigan, Department of Geography, 1977), Appendix II: Expansion of Settlement, pp. 145-54.

TABLE Eg201–213 Slaves imported and exported, by colony and by origin or destination: 1768–1772

Contributed by John J. McCusker

Year and origin or destination	Total Eg201	New Hampshire Eg202	Massachusetts Eg203	Rhode Island Eg204	Connecticut Eg205	New York Eg206	Pennsylvania Eg207	Maryland Eg208	Virginia Eg209	North Carolina Eg210	South Carolina Eg211	Georgia Eg212	Florida Eg213
	Number	Number	Number	Number	Number	Number	Number	Number	Number	Number	Number	Number	Number
1768													
Imported, total	2,496	12	0	70	14	19	0	301	354	198	249	1,001	278
West Indies and Africa	2,204	12	0	59	14	19	0	288	354	170	187	971	130
Other continental colonies	292	0	0	11	0	0	0	13	0	28	62	30	148
Exported, total	282	1	0	34	0	0	0	14	0	14	39	61	119
West Indies and Africa	107	0	0	8	0	0	0	1	0	1	0	5	92
Other continental colonies	175	1	0	26	0	0	0	13	0	13	39	56	27
1768													
Imported, total	6,736	4	0	6	0	0	10	203	493	169	4,888	687	276
Africa	5,161	0	0	6	0	0	0	180	234	36	4,138	448	119
West Indies	1,222	4	0	0	0	0	10	23	258	79	675	91	82
Other continental colonies	353	0	0	0	0	0	0	0	1	54	75	148	75
Exported, total	336	0	0	4	0	0	0	1	0	5	298	28	0
West Indies	9	0	0	0	0	0	0	1	0	5	3	0	0
Other continental colonies	327	0	0	4	0	0	0	0	0	0	295	28	0
1770													
Imported, total	3,069	0	0	0	0	69	0	532	905	115	123	1,144	181
Africa	2,266	0	0	0	0	67	0	517	631	0	0	875	176
West Indies	600	0	0	0	0	2	0	14	274	103	81	126	0
Other continental colonies	203	0	0	0	0	0	0	1	0	12	42	143	5
Exported, total	144	0	1	13	0	0	0	1	0	19	88	22	0
West Indies	27	0	0	0	0	0	0	1	0	14	5	7	0
Other continental colonies	117	0	1	13	0	0	0	0	0	5	83	15	0
1771													
Imported, total [1]	4,970	0	0	12	0	3	0	227	762	82	3,100	758	20
Africa	2,754	0	0	0	0	3	0	194	13	7	2,051	489	0
West Indies	2,020	0	0	7	0	3	0	27	744	68	998	148	20
Other continental colonies	196	0	0	5	0	1	0	6	5	7	51	121	0
Exported, total	341	0	1	6	1	0	1	2	0	0	297	5	28
West Indies	3	0	0	0	0	0	0	2	0	0	1	0	0
Other continental colonies	338	0	1	6	1	0	1	0	0	0	296	5	28
1772													
Imported, total	10,165	4	4	2	0	25	0	175	2,104	155	7,201	328	169
Africa	6,638	0	0	0	0	19	0	86	1,271	0	5,145	117	0
West Indies	3,146	4	0	2	0	2	0	82	794	145	2,027	69	19
Other continental colonies	381	0	4	0	0	0	0	7	39	10	29	142	150
Exported, total	495	4	0	0	0	2	20	0	0	5	463	1	1
West Indies	3	0	0	0	0	2	0	0	0	0	0	0	0
Other continental colonies	492	4	0	0	0	0	20	0	0	5	463	0	0

[1] The import data for 1771 for POE Philadelphia are defective in the source.

Source

Originally compiled by Lawrence A. Harper from the Ledger of Imports and Exports of North America, 1768–1772, CUST 16/1, PRO/TNA.

Documentation

See the Appendixes to the essay in this chapter for a general discussion of the tables and the sources of the data, along with a key to abbreviations used in this chapter and general information on matters such as regional definitions, calendar differences, money, and weights and measures. Note that Florida is included here as part of British North America but that it was not one of the Thirteen Continental Colonies.

The black population of the colonies grew through natural increase and through immigration, just as did the white population. The key difference, obviously, was that blacks were enslaved and forcibly carried to the colonies in the slave trade. Thus the two basic sources for the demographic study of the colonial black population are population statistics (see Tables Eg1–193) and commercial statistics concerning slave imports.

(continued)

TABLE Eg201–213 Slaves imported and exported, by colony and by origin or destination: 1768–1772 *Continued*

Little is known about the operation of natural increase in building the colonies' black population, but what is available suggests that it was of considerable importance. One study has argued that the black population of the colonies began to expand through reproduction in the 1720s in Maryland and Virginia and in the 1770s in South Carolina – but, by contrast, not until about 1810 in Barbados and 1840 in Jamaica. See John J. McCusker and Russell R. Menard, *The Economy of British America, 1607–1789*, 2nd edition (University of North Carolina Press, 1991), pp. 231–4.

Nevertheless, the slave trade was – and continued to be for most of the period – the major source of additional black slaves for the British colonies. Even though the last half-century witnessed much work on the slave trade, and indeed on slavery in general, it has not yet resulted in a settled series of numbers imported, either for individual colonies or for the colonies as a whole. Older estimates have been largely cast into question (one of the casualties of these developments has been the tables in the earlier editions of *Historical Statistics of the United States* (1975) volume 2, pp. 1172–4); and newer estimates have yet to be developed, one significant exception being series Eg215. When they are, they will be based on two lines of research: the large-scale collective effort done under the sponsorship of the W. E. B. Du Bois Institute for African and African American Research at Harvard University that produced David Eltis, Stephen D. Behrendt, et al., compilers, *The Trans-Atlantic Slave Trade: A Database on CD-ROM* (Cambridge University Press, 1999); and a careful review of all available contemporary records in repositories such as the Public Record Office, London. An initial summation of the latter can be found in John J. McCusker, *Rum and the American Revolution: The Rum Trade and the Balance of Payments of the Thirteen Continental Colonies, 1650–1775* (Garland, 1989), volume 2, pp. 548–767.

An example of one such contemporary compilation – and as close to a definitive count of the slave trade as can be found – is the import and export figures for the five years 1768–1772, in the Ledger of Imports and Exports, British North America, 1768–1772, CUST 16/1, PRO/TNA. See the discussion of this source in Appendix A to the essay in this chapter.

One warning about even these data, as carefully and completely compiled as they were: they are totals by colony of the data from each of the colonial ports of entry (POE). The limits of those jurisdictions were not always precisely defined nor were they fully observed. As one example, the colony of Virginia had six POEs, the most northerly of which was "South Potomac." That POE shared the traffic of the Potomac River with the colony of Maryland, one of whose POE was North Potomac. Donald M. Sweig, "The Importation of African Slaves to the Potomac River, 1732–1772," *William and Mary Quarterly*, 3rd series, 42 (October 1985): 507–24, has argued convincingly that the very few slaves recorded as imported into Virginia's POE North Potomac can best be explained by the resort by Virginia planters to purchasing slaves landed on the Maryland side of the river where the import duties were lower than in Virginia. Obviously the intercolonial trade in slaves should have been recorded in these records but was not. Some of the Africans accounted as imported into Maryland were, in fact, enslaved in Virginia. As a consequence, the net totals of imports and exports into the Thirteen Continental Colonies can be relied on a bit more than the numbers for the individual colonies.

TABLE Eg214–216 Slaves imported into Virginia and Maryland: 1698–1774

Contributed by John J. McCusker

	Total	Virginia	Maryland
	Eg214	Eg215	Eg216
Years	Number	Number	Number
1698–1703	4,512	1,882	2,630
1704–1718	13,610	11,295	2,315
1719–1730	17,619	15,467	2,152
1731–1745	25,259	22,586	2,673
1746–1760	18,446	15,211	3,235
1761–1774	16,943	11,632	5,311

Sources
Lorena S. Walsh, "The Chesapeake Slave Trade: Regional Patterns, African Origins, and Some Implications," *William and Mary Quarterly*, 3rd series, 58 (January 2001): 139–70, with important supplementary material available at the Internet site of the *William and Mary Quarterly* (accessed March 5, 2005).

Documentation
See the Appendixes to the essay in this chapter for a general discussion of the tables and the sources of the data, along with a key to abbreviations used in this chapter and general information on matters such as regional definitions, calendar differences, money, and weights and measures.

The singular exception that proves the rule set out in the text for Table Eg201–213 is Lorena S. Walsh's intensive investigation into the slave trade of Virginia and Maryland. It is based on two sets of sources: David Eltis, Stephen D. Behrendt, et al., compilers, *The Trans-Atlantic Slave Trade: A Database on CD-ROM* (Cambridge University Press, 1999); and Walsh's own careful review of all available contemporary records, most particularly the colonial NOSL (discussed in Appendix A to the essay in this chapter), as well as a variety of other materials detailed in her study. She compiled all of her evidence into her "Chesapeake Slave Trade Database."

Walsh's Table II (pp. 168–9) includes slaves imported coastwise from other British colonies and indicates that, especially for the earliest of her periods, the data represent an undercounting of unknown size.

Among the work superseded by Walsh's are the table published in *Historical Statistics of the United States* (1975), volume 2, p. 1172 (series Z146–149); Darold D. Wax, "Black Immigrants: The Slave Trade in Colonial Maryland," *Maryland Historical Magazine* 73 (Spring 1978): 30–45; Walter [E.] Minchinton, Celia King, and Peter Waite, editors, *Virginia Slave-Trade Statistics, 1698–1775* (Virginia State Library, 1984); and David W. Galenson, "The Settlement and Growth of the Colonies: Population, Labor, and Economic Development," in Stanley L. Engerman and Robert E. Gallman, editors, *The Cambridge Economic History of the United States* (Cambridge University Press, 1996), volume 1, p. 180.

GROSS DOMESTIC PRODUCT AND WEALTH

John J. McCusker

TABLE Eg217–222   Gross domestic product: 1650–1800

Contributed by John J. McCusker

			Gross domestic product			
			Aggregate		Per capita	
Year	Commodity price index	Population	Constant dollars	Current dollars	Constant dollars	Annual average growth rate
	Eg217	Eg218	Eg219	Eg220	Eg221	Eg222
	Index 1840 = 100	Thousand	Thousand 1840 dollars	Thousand dollars	1840 dollars	Percent
1650	130	50	1,500	1,900	30	—
1720	73	467	21,300	15,500	46	0.6
1774	93	2,420	152,000	142,000	63	0.6
1781	128	2,895	155,000	198,000	54	−2.3
1793	114	4,343	252,000	288,000	58	0.7
1800	145	5,308	350,000	508,000	66	1.9

Source

John J. McCusker, "Estimating Early American Gross Domestic Product," *Historical Methods* 33 (Summer 2000): 155-62, as revised, updated, and augmented by ongoing research detailed below. Underlying data are detailed in the source.

Documentation

See the Appendixes to the essay in this chapter for a general discussion of the tables and the sources of the data, along with a key to abbreviations used in this chapter and general information on matters such as regional definitions, calendar differences, money, and weights and measures.

The general state of the economy of the Continental Colonies and the early United States has concerned both contemporaries and later writers. These data repeat and attempt to reconcile several twentieth-century estimates of either the gross domestic product (GDP) at some point during the seventeenth or eighteenth centuries or the rate of growth of GDP between two or more points over the period. GDP measures the total output of goods and services in the economy, valued at market prices. As presented here, these data offer estimates of GDP in current dollars and in constant or real (1840) dollars. They differ only slightly from the numbers given in the source reflecting the revised population estimates presented herein (Table Eg1–59). Although these series provide only the crudest of estimates, they do support the proposition that the economy grew intensively over a century and a half, albeit very slowly by modern standards.

For the sake of continuity in comparisons with GDP estimates for later periods, the data in this table include black Americans as part of the producing population even though the fruits of their labor, as enslaved people, were expropriated by their owners. Compare Thomas [J.] Weiss, "U.S. Labor Force Estimates and Economic Growth, 1800–1860," in Robert E.

Gallman and John Joseph Wallis, editors, *American Economic Growth and Standards of Living before the Civil War*, National Bureau of Economic Research Conference Report (University of Chicago Press, 1992), pp. 19–75. Had GDP (series Eg219) been measured against only the free population, the annual average rate in increase of GDP, 1650–1774, would be reported at 0.8 percent.

Another discussion of early American GDP can be found in John J. McCusker and Russell R. Menard, *The Economy of British America, 1607–1789*, 2nd edition (University of North Carolina Press, 1991), pp. 51–70. See also David W. Galenson, "The Settlement and Growth of the Colonies: Population, Labor, and Economic Development," in Stanley L. Engerman and Robert E. Gallman, editors, *The Cambridge Economic History of the United States* (Cambridge University Press, 1996), volume 1, pp. 189–207. More recently, the topic was the focus of a special issue of the *William and Mary Quarterly*, 3rd series, 56 (January 1999). See especially the introductory essay by the two editors of the issue, Lance Davis and Stanley Engerman, "The Economy of British North America: Miles Traveled, Miles Still to Go" (pp. 9–22).

Angus Maddison, *The World Economy: A Millennial Perspective* (Development Centre of the Organisation for Economic Co-Operation and Development, 2001), p. 264, presented estimates of real, per capita GDP for the United States in 1600, 1700, and 1820 that support the figures in this table. According to his data, the annual average compound rate of growth for the seventeenth century was 0.28 percent and for the extended eighteenth century, 0.73 percent. One can argue that 1650 would be a better date than 1600 for the first estimate; then the rate for the seventeenth century is 0.55 percent. Over the years 1650–1829, the rate is 0.68 percent. Note, too, that for the whole period 1500–1820 (p. 265), the rate of growth for the United States is the highest in the world.

TABLE Eg223–246   Private wealth per free person, by region and type of wealth: 1774

Contributed by John J. McCusker

		Physical wealth											
		Portable physical wealth											
							Producer durables				Producer perishables		
Area	Net worth	Total	Land	Total	Servants and slaves	Total	Livestock	Farm tools and household equipment	Equipment of clearly separable nonfarm business	Materials	Total	Crops	Other
	Eg223	Eg224	Eg225	Eg226	Eg227	Eg228	Eg229	Eg230	Eg231	Eg232	Eg233	Eg234	Eg235
	Dollars	Dollars	Dollars	Dollars	Dollars	Dollars	Dollars	Dollars	Dollars	Dollars	Dollars	Dollars	Dollars
Thirteen Colonies	329	338	168	170	95	36	26	8	1	(Z)	11	10	1
New England	145	170	121	48	1	20	13	6	2	(Z)	3	1	2
Middle Colonies	228	204	124	81	8	32	23	6	1	(Z)	11	11	(Z)
South	586	608	246	361	256	54	40	12	(Z)	1	18	17	(Z)

	Physical wealth						Financial assets				
	Portable physical wealth							Other assets			
	Consumer durables										
Area	Total	Apparel	Other	Consumer perishables	Separable nonfarm business inventories	Nonseparable items	Total	Cash	Collectable debts	Not collectable debts	Financial liabilities
	Eg236	Eg237	Eg238	Eg239	Eg240	Eg241	Eg242	Eg243	Eg244	Eg245	Eg246
	Dollars	Dollars	Dollars	Dollars	Dollars	Dollars	Dollars	Dollars	Dollars	Dollars	Dollars
Thirteen Colonies	22	4	18	2	4	1	55	7	46	3	63
New England	19	4	15	1	4	1	30	2	28	0	54
Middle Colonies	17	5	12	1	8	3	71	9	62	0	47
South	28	4	25	3	1	0	62	8	48	6	84

(Z) Less than $0.49.

Sources

Originally calculated by Alice Hanson Jones, based on her dissertation and published works: "Wealth Estimates for the American Middle Colonies, 1774" (Ph.D. dissertation, University of Chicago, 1968); "Wealth Estimates for the American Middle Colonies, 1774," *Economic Development and Cultural Change* 18 (July 1970): part 2, pp. 1–172; "La fortune privée en Pennsylvanie, New Jersey, Delaware (1774)," *Annales: Économies, Sociétés, Civilisations* 24 (March–April 1969): 235–49; "Wealth Estimates for the New England Colonies about 1770," *Journal of Economic History* 32 (March 1972): 98–127; *American Colonial Wealth: Documents and Methods*, 2nd edition (Arno Press, 1978); and *Wealth of a Nation to Be: The American Colonies on the Eve of the Revolution* (Columbia University Press, 1980).

Documentation

See the Appendixes to the essay in this chapter for a general discussion of the tables and the sources of the data, along with a key to abbreviations used in this chapter and general information on matters such as regional definitions, calendar differences, money, and weights and measures.

Jones's wealth estimates were based on a sample drawn from all estates probated in the Thirteen Continental Colonies in 1774. To select the sample, every county then in existence was given a chance to be drawn proportionate to its total wealthholding population in 1774. Each county, or cluster of counties, drawn for the sample represented an equal stratum of living wealthholders. Wealthholders are defined to include all free adult males aged 21 and older, white and black, and 10 percent of all free adult females, chiefly widows, omitting black females in the South. Enslaved and indentured servants were not counted as wealthholders. Because of the sample design and weighting procedures followed, the combination of data from sample counties within a region yielded an unbiased regional estimate of wealth of probated estates, and the regional estimates combined, except for the weakness of the New York data, yielded an unbiased estimate for all the Thirteen Continental Colonies. The data for probated decedents were adjusted, through the weighting procedure, to represent the age structure of the living and to include an allowance for wealth of persons not probated, and hence to represent the larger statistical population of living wealthholders. The figures

are in dollars and give the average per capita, excluding slaves and indentured servants.

The counties included in the sample and numbers of probate cases for each are indicated here. In addition, twenty-three probate inventories from nine counties in New York, together with regional data for New England and Middle Colonies, served to form an estimate for New York, which, although part of the total for the Thirteen Continental Colonies, was not shown separately.

Number of probate cases for counties included in the sample

New England		South	
Connecticut		Maryland	
Litchfield	31	Queen Anne	38
New Haven	37	Anne Arundel	27
Massachusetts		Virginia	
Essex	102	Charlotte-Halifax	25
Hampshire	27	Southampton-Brunswick-	
Plymouth	35	Mecklenburg	23
Suffolk	100	Charlotte-Spotsylvania-Fairfax	30
Worcester	49	North Carolina	
Total	381	Halifax	39
Middle Colonies		Orange	32
Pennsylvania		South Carolina	
Northampton	21	Charles Town District	87
Westmoreland	7	Total	301
Philadelphia	135		
New Jersey			
Burlington	25		
Delaware			
Kent	29		
Total	217		

All the inventories probated in 1774 within the sampled counties or county-clusters were included, with a few exceptions. In Essex County, Massachusetts, there was a cut-off at 102 cases, taking all surnames alphabetically from A to part way through the Ps. In several counties or

TABLE Eg223–246   Private wealth per free person, by region and type of wealth: 1774   *Continued*

county-clusters, some cases randomly drawn from 1773 or 1775 were added to provide an adequate number of cases. In the then-frontier county of Westmoreland, Pennsylvania, three cases for 1774, two for 1773, and two for 1775 are all that exist for those dates. For New York, the twenty-three cases used represent all the cases located that were probated in any year from 1772 through 1775, not only in the two sample counties of Suffolk and Albany but also in any county in the province.

Data from each county or county-cluster received equal weight in its regional average, inasmuch as each was considered to represent an equal stratum of living wealthholders. The procedure meant that the counties with larger numbers of cases did not dominate or bias their respective regional averages, yet that full use could be made of all the available cases. For the New York estimate, the twenty-three cases received 10 percent weight, the New England averaged 30 percent, and the Middle Colonies averaged 60 percent. The assumption was that if more cases for New York could be found, they would have shown wealth resembling that found in the adjoining New England and Middle Colonies, somewhat more like the latter than the former. The total for the Thirteen Continental Colonies gave each component regional average an importance in proportion to its 1774 living wealthholder population, including the estimate for New York.

For all regions, data on portable physical wealth and on financial assets came from the probate inventories with occasional adjustments for data found in estate accounts. For New England, the inventories are also the source of data on land. In the other regions, land was usually not shown in the inventories. For the Middle Colonies, original data on land came from tax lists and, for the South, from deeds and land grants. Data on financial liabilities for New England came from documents filed with probate inventories or from accounts of estate administrators or executors; in the other regions, they came from the estate accounts.

The average wealth of the "non-probate-type living" (meaning persons who, upon death, would probably not have their estates probated) was assumed to equal one fourth the average wealth of the age-adjusted "probate-type living" (that is, people whose estates were entered into probate) in New York, the Middle Colonies, and the South, but one half in New England. The larger figure was used for New England because a higher proportion of the wealthholders in those colonies was not probated. The numbers of living wealthholders, and the percentage of these wealthholders of non-probate-type are estimated as shown here. Also shown is the population of free people used to construct the table, along with the percentage that these population figures constitute of the total population, free and nonfree.

	Living wealthholders	Percentage nonprobate	Free population	Free population as a percentage of total population
New England	137,934	66	582,285	95.8
New York	45,128	40	180,116	88.8
Middle Colonies	98,448	36	405,033	92.5
South	153,325	27	652,585	59.0
Thirteen Continental Colonies	434,835		1,820,019	77.3

The total population figures were interpolated to 1774 on the basis of compound annual rates of population growth between the decennial estimates in Table Eg1–59, separately for whites and for blacks. The proportions of indentured whites and of free blacks that underlay the figures on free population were estimated from secondary sources. The underlying age structure of the living population, used for age adjustment from decedent to 1774 living wealthholders, was based on proportions of free whites in the 1800 Census, modified slightly in the proportions of children. A fuller discussion of these methods and fuller tables can be found in Jones (1980), pp. 28–43.

Wealth figures in the original documents were always stated in the local currency of each colony. Because each of these currencies was of different value, to make comparisons possible Jones reduced them all to the equivalent value in British pounds sterling, using exchange rates similar to those in Table Eg315–324. At the time, £100 sterling equaled, at par, $444.44 and Jones's original estimates in pounds sterling have been converted to 1774 dollars at that rate. When adjusted for inflation, $329 in 1774 is the equivalent of roughly $7,500 in dollars of the year 2003. For the basis of these admittedly very crude calculations, see John J. McCusker, *How Much Is That in Real Money? A Historical Commodity Price Index for Use as a Deflator of Money Values in the Economy of the United States*, 2nd edition (American Antiquarian Society, 2001).

There have been some strenuous objections to Jones's work but they focus less on the care with which she derived her data and more on the extrapolation of her conclusions to the wider economy. In other words, there are troubling issues with her data, but they become great faults only if we rely on them too heavily for providing us with anything more than a very cloudy view of what they purport to reveal – which, unfortunately, can be said of all too many of the "statistics" from the seventeenth and eighteenth centuries. Jones's estimates deserve a place here, nonetheless, if only to show what can be done and to encourage others to do it better. For such objections – and encouragement – see Gloria L. Main, "Review of *American Colonial Wealth: Documents and Methods*, by Alice Hanson Jones," *Business History Review* 52 (Autumn 1978): 408–10; Linda Auwers, "History from the Mean – Up, Down, and Around: A Review Essay [of *American Colonial Wealth: Documents and Methods*, by Alice Hanson Jones]," *Historical Methods* 12 (Winter 1979): 39–45; John J. McCusker, "Review of *Wealth of a Nation to Be: The American Colonies on the Eve of the Revolution*, by Alice Hanson Jones," *Journal of American History* 68 (June 1981): 113; John J. McCusker and Russell R. Menard, *The Economy of British America, 1607–1789*, 2nd edition (University of North Carolina Press, 1991), pp. 51–70; and Peter A. Coclanis, "The Wealth of British America on the Eve of the Revolution," *Journal of Interdisciplinary History* 21 (Fall 1990): 245–60.

For definitions of the terms and distinctions used in the table, see the original source.

Series Eg241. Supplementary information in estate accounts allowed for the occasional adjustment to a wealth category. When information was sufficiently specific, a sum was added to or subtracted from the affected subcategory. For instance, when there was no breakdown of such an adjustment as "what the goods sold for more than appraised," in the Middle Colonies, the value is added to series Eg241. In the same way, this series also includes, for New England, several cases where no subdivision of "personal estate" was shown on the probate inventory.

Series Eg244–245. In the original sources, collectible debts are frequently described as "good" and uncollectible ones categorized as "doubtful," "bad," or "desperate."

PRICES AND COMMODITY PRICE INDEX

John J. McCusker

TABLE Eg247   Commodity price index: 1665–1790

Contributed by John J. McCusker

Year	Commodity price index Eg247 1860 = 100	Year	Commodity price index Eg247 1860 = 100	Year	Commodity price index Eg247 1860 = 100	Year	Commodity price index Eg247 1860 = 100
1665	105.5	1700	92.8	1735	68.4	1765	89.2
1666	105.9	1701	97.6	1736	65.4	1766	97.3
1667	114.3	1702	90.4	1737	66.8	1767	95.5
1668	118.1	1703	89.4	1738	69.9	1768	90.3
1669	109.9	1704	100.8	1739	62.6	1769	92.7
1670	107.7	1705	91.2	1740	65.8	1770	99.8
1671	110.5	1706	97.7	1741	91.0	1771	96.1
1672	109.2	1707	94.5	1742	81.5	1772	109.4
1673	104.0	1708	74.4	1743	70.7	1773	101.6
1674	111.9	1709	89.2	1744	66.6	1774	97.0
1675	96.9	1710	80.5	1745	64.5	1775	92.0
1676	98.0	1711	78.6	1746	65.3	1776	105.0
1677	98.7	1712	74.9	1747	71.4	1777	128.0
1678	96.7	1713	79.6	1748	82.2	1778	166.0
1679	96.0	1714	73.3	1749	83.7	1779	147.0
1680	110.3	1715	82.1	1750	84.1	1780	165.0
1681	112.9	1716	77.4	1751	85.0	1781	133.0
1682	92.1	1717	82.5	1752	86.4	1782	146.0
1683	91.9	1718	77.5	1753	84.2	1783	128.0
1684	92.1	1719	82.2	1754	81.3	1784	123.0
1685	99.0	1720	75.7	1755	79.1	1785	117.0
1686	93.3	1721	71.2	1756	77.4	1786	114.0
1687	92.8	1722	75.0	1757	81.2	1787	112.0
1688	84.8	1723	76.0	1758	86.6	1788	107.0
1689	87.3	1724	79.4	1759	99.2	1789	106.0
1690	88.7	1725	90.3	1760	96.3	1790	110.0
1691	92.9	1726	86.4	1761	88.0		
1692	88.5	1727	86.2	1762	95.2		
1693	82.8	1728	80.6	1763	95.0		
1694	87.9	1729	79.6	1764	87.8		
1695	80.9	1730	80.1				
1696	95.5	1731	71.2				
1697	92.8	1732	66.5				
1698	88.3	1733	67.6				
1699	96.2	1734	66.2				

Sources

John J. McCusker, *How Much Is That in Real Money? A Historical Commodity Price Index for Use as a Deflator of Money Values in the Economy of the United States*, 2nd edition (American Antiquarian Society, 2001). See also McCusker, "How Much Is That Worth Today? Purchasing Power of the Dollar, 1665–Present," October 2000, Economic History Services, available at the EH.net Internet site (accessed July 23, 2003).

Documentation

See the Appendixes to the essay in this chapter for a general discussion of the tables and the sources of the data, along with a key to abbreviations used in this chapter and general information on matters such as regional definitions, calendar differences, money, and weights and measures.

This index of commodity prices was estimated by splicing comparably calculated series from different periods and linking them into one, longer series reduced to the same base period. In the source, the series is extended from 1774 into the twenty-first century, grounded in the same data that are the basis of series Cc2, Paul A. David and Pete Solar, "A Bicentenary Contribution to the History of the Cost of Living in America," *Research in Economic History*

2 (1977): 1–80, and the monthly and annual data produced by the United States, Department of Labor, Bureau of Labor Statistics (available at the BLS Internet site). For the earlier period, it draws upon Anne Bezanson, Robert D. Gray, and Miriam Hussey, *Prices in Colonial Pennsylvania*, University of Pennsylvania, Wharton School of Finance and Commerce, Industrial Research Department, Research Studies, volume 26 (University of Pennsylvania Press, 1935); P. M. G. Harris, "Inflation and Deflation in Early America, 1634–1860: Patterns of Change in the British-American Economy," *Social Science History* 20 (Winter 1996): 469–505; and Stephen Gregg Hardy, "Trade and Economic Growth in the Eighteenth-Century Chesapeake" (Ph.D. dissertation, University of Maryland, 1999), pp. 405–9 (Table 29, second column). Some of the price data that Bezanson and her colleagues used to compile her index numbers are presented in Table Eg251–270 and continued in Table Cc205–266.

Note also the estimated commodity price index number for 1650 developed in John J. McCusker, "Estimating Early American Gross Domestic Product," *Historical Methods* 33 (Summer 2000): 155–62, and reported in series Eg217 (130 on base 1840 = 100; 135 on base 1860 - 100).

TABLE Eg248–250   Wholesale price of codfish in New England, by grade: 1634–1775[1]   [Massachusetts currency]
Contributed by John J. McCusker

Year	Merchantable Eg248 Shillings per hundredweight	Jamaica Eg249 Shillings per hundredweight	Refuse Eg250 Shillings per hundredweight	Year	Merchantable Eg248 Shillings per hundredweight	Jamaica Eg249 Shillings per hundredweight	Refuse Eg250 Shillings per hundredweight
1634	10.50	—	4.00	1715	25.59	—	15.45
1638	18.90	—	—	1716	24.21	—	14.95
1639	20.16	—	—	1717	—	—	12.07
1640	20.00	—	—	1719	25.93	—	11.88
1641	18.90	—	—	1720	—	—	12.58
1642	18.27	—	8.00	1721	—	—	12.96
1643	—	—	10.08	1722	29.70	—	16.03
1645	22.40	—	—	1723	29.93	—	17.86
1647	18.90	—	—	1724	33.97	—	—
1649	—	—	9.97	1725	34.24	—	—
1650	15.46	—	10.98	1726	40.06	—	24.97
1653	16.02	—	10.53	1727	34.95	—	18.64
1658	—	—	10.98	1728	37.48	—	19.34
1659	14.34	—	—	1729	37.16	—	17.95
1660	16.06	—	10.00	1730	39.71	—	18.17
1661	—	—	10.77	1731	40.12	—	19.39
1662	15.70	—	10.31	1732	39.28	—	20.14
1663	15.57	—	8.96	1733	39.54	—	22.20
1664	16.39	—	9.83	1734	41.81	—	19.98
1665	15.80	—	9.92	1735	47.88	—	19.08
1666	13.65	—	9.95	1736	55.01	—	24.96
1667	14.96	—	9.16	1737	55.85	—	24.15
1668	17.83	—	9.95	1738	48.29	—	21.35
1669	16.01	—	9.98	1739	51.31	—	20.52
1670	15.06	—	9.64	1740	39.47	—	20.25
1671	15.13	—	9.75	1741	—	—	28.02
1672	14.88	—	9.60	1742	50.08	—	30.82
1673	15.75	—	10.00	1743	53.31	—	33.67
1674	16.93	—	9.89	1744	49.25	—	34.18
1675	18.70	—	—	1745	53.25	—	38.84
1676	14.26	—	—	1746	—	—	56.28
1677	15.91	—	—	1747	103.38	—	70.37
1678	14.40	—	9.36	1748	128.15	—	96.11
1679	14.62	—	—	1749	133.74	—	66.87
1680	14.35	—	10.01	1750	16.51	6.67	5.93
1681	13.97	—	10.16	1751	15.33	7.50	6.27
1682	13.10	—	9.07	1752	14.93	9.00	6.80
1683	13.25	—	9.50	1753	15.34	9.00	—
1684	13.26	—	8.80	1754	15.33	9.48	—
1685	13.40	—	9.24	1755	15.27	9.11	—
1686	12.88	—	—	1756	16.00	9.72	7.33
1687	12.81	—	—	1757	14.47	10.84	—
1688	13.02	—	—	1758	15.79	12.63	—
1689	15.86	—	—	1759	—	13.50	—
1693	12.48	—	—	1760	—	14.48	—
1695	17.41	—	13.49	1761	—	15.33	—
1696	—	—	13.38	1762	18.44	13.94	10.14
1697	18.36	—	14.01	1763	17.83	13.69	10.13
1698	17.32	—	10.31	1764	19.79	13.15	9.63
1699	15.84	—	11.67	1765	19.76	13.14	9.48
1701	12.29	—	8.46	1766	19.97	13.45	9.98
1704	—	—	15.35	1767	20.00	11.92	8.67
1705	16.82	—	—	1768	20.14	12.67	8.50
1708	18.57	—	16.83	1769	19.05	13.22	10.31
1709	23.42	—	—	1770	18.12	13.58	10.64
1710	20.76	—	16.30	1771	18.67	13.54	10.67
1711	21.09	—	16.18	1772	19.71	13.21	—
1712	20.55	—	16.05	1773	19.07	11.21	10.99
1713	22.50	—	13.95	1774	17.81	9.82	—
1714	25.27	—	14.73	1775	18.17	11.50	13.42

Note appears on next page   (continued)

TABLE Eg248–250   Wholesale price of codfish in New England, by grade: 1634–1775   [Massachusetts currency]
Continued

[1] Figures are expressed in Massachusetts currency: through 1749, "Old Tenor," and thereafter, "Lawful Money." The ratio between the two currencies was 7.5:1.

Sources

Series Eg248 and Eg250. Daniel [F.]. Vickers, "'A knowen and staple commoditie': Codfish Prices in Essex County, Massachusetts, 1640–1775," *Essex Institute Historical Collections* 124 (July 1988): 186–203. See also Vickers, "The Price of Fish: A Price Index for Cod, 1505–1892," *Acadiensis: Journal of the History of the Atlantic Region/Revue d'Histoire de la Région Atlantique* 25 (Spring 1996): 92–104. Vickers supplied additional price data for these series from ongoing research and helped cull several earlier prices from the *Trelawny Papers*, edited by James Phinney Baxter, *Collections of the Maine Historical Society*, 2nd series, *Documentary History of the State of Maine* (Hoyt, Fogg, and Donham, 1844), volume 3, pp. 43, 135, 162, 163, 195, 199, 259, 321, 335, 349.

Series Eg249. Ruth Crandall, "Wholesale Commodity Prices in Boston during the Eighteenth Century," *Review of Economic Statistics* 16 (June, September 1934): 182, as published in Arthur Harrison Cole, *Wholesale Commodity Prices in the United States, 1700–1861* (Harvard University Press, 1938), volume 2, pp. 35–68.

Documentation

See the Appendixes to the essay in this chapter for a general discussion of the tables and the sources of the data, along with a key to abbreviations used in this chapter and general information on matters such as regional definitions, calendar differences, money, and weights and measures.

These data give average annual wholesale prices in Massachusetts currency for three grades of codfish for sale at the fishing ports of New England, mostly Massachusetts, more frequently than not, Boston, Salem, or Marblehead. To compare prices quoted in Massachusetts currency with prices in other colonies or in England, one can use the exchange rate data in Table Eg315–324.

As Vickers makes clear in the sources cited previously, the pricing of codfish became more complex over time as the market matured. What had at first been sold in two grades – "spring merchantable cod" and "refuse cod" – later came to be sold in six grades or more, the distinctions among which seem less than clear at this distance in time. He strove to avoid confusion "by concentrating on those grades of fish whose value is clearest: the best and the worst of the New England fishery" (Vickers 1988, p. 188). Spring merchantable codfish was the best grade; it applied to fish landed in season before July 1. As a testament to the potential for confusion, Crandall consistently referred to "Jamaica or 'refuse' codfish," but the price data she presented indicated that such fish, exported to feed slaves in the West Indies, were nevertheless a cut above the absolute worst fish available in the New England market, a conclusion with which Vickers concurs. "Jamaica" was "a middling grade – unfit for European markets and sometimes sent southward, but not spoiled" (private communication, July 5, 2001).

The wholesale price for codfish in the New England market was customarily quoted in terms of shillings Massachusetts currency per hundredweight (or quintal) of 100 pounds. See John J. McCusker, "Weights and Measures in the Colonial Sugar Trade: The Gallon and the Pound and Their International Equivalents," *William and Mary Quarterly*, 3rd series, 30 (October 1973) – as revised and updated in McCusker, *Essays in the Economic History of the Atlantic World* (Routledge, 1997), p. 86 n. 15. Compare Cole (1938), volume 2, p. x n. 80. Vickers (and others) have been misled by the complexities of European and North American weights and assumed that the hundredweight for fish was the long hundredweight (112 pounds) as it was in Great Britain. He (like others) also translated the Spanish *libra* into its English-language equivalent, the pound, but neglected to account for their different weights. The *libra* equals 0.4601 kg; the pound, 0.4536 kg. The appropriate adjustments have been made in the data for this and for subsequent tables in this chapter.

Because of the method employed in this chapter for computing annual averages from fragmented data, the series offered here differs slightly from that presented by Crandall (1934), p. 182. See Appendix A to the essay in this chapter. See also the text for Table Eg275–284, as well as the prices for codfish referred to in the text for Table Eg329–338.

As indicated in the preceding, the data as collected were usually quoted in Massachusetts currency, the New England money of account. The only exception to this rule is the series of prices from the *Trelawny Papers*, which were frequently quoted in "rialls [reales]" per quintal. The "real" was, of course, the eighth part of the Spanish *peso de ocho reales*, the piece of eight or dollar. This practice probably reflected both a traditional usage founded in the ultimate market for much New England cod fish, Spain, and the circulation of Spanish silver coin in New England and the other colonies. Prices in reales were reduced to sterling at the par value of the two monies; one piece of eight equaled 4s 6d sterling. Vickers converted his series to pounds sterling of Great Britain using John J. McCusker, *Money and Exchange in Europe and America, 1600–1775: A Handbook*, 2nd edition (University of North Carolina Press, 1992), pp. 138–42. Those same exchange rates have been used to reconvert all prices from sterling to Massachusetts currency. Crandall presented her data in Massachusetts currency.

The earliest of these quotations – in 1634 – can be compared to prices the same year in England of 12s sterling per quintal (hundredweight) for "merchantable" cod and 5s 6d for "refuse" cod (*Trelawny Papers*, edited by Baxter, pp. 37, 39).

The project that studied Massachusetts prices was one of many sponsored by the International Scientific Committee on Price History. See Arthur H. Cole and Ruth Crandall, "The International Scientific Committee on Price History," *Journal of Economic History* 24 (September 1964): 381–8. The results of several of those studies were drawn together in Cole, *Wholesale Commodity Prices in the United States*. See also G[eorge] F. Warren, F[rank] A. Pearson, and Herman M. Stoker, *Wholesale Prices for 213 Years, 1720 to 1932*, Cornell University, Agricultural Experiment Station, Memoir 412 (Cornell University, 1932). There are important archival collections associated with these studies, each containing a great deal of additional material: Records of the International Scientific Committee on Price History, 1928–1939, Manuscript and Archives Division, Baker Library, Graduate School of Business Administration, Harvard University; the Frank Ashmore Pearson Papers, Albert R. Mann Library, Cornell University; and the "Industrial Research Department, Wholesale Prices" Collection, Wharton School of Finance and Commerce, University of Pennsylvania.

TABLE Eg251–270   Wholesale prices of selected commodities in Philadelphia: 1700–1775   [Pennsylvania currency]
Contributed by John J. McCusker

	Corn	Wheat	Tobacco	Rice	Bread Middling	Bread Ship	Flour	Beef	Pork	Salt Coarse	Salt Fine
	Eg251	Eg252	Eg253	Eg254	Eg255	Eg256	Eg257	Eg258	Eg259	Eg260	Eg261
Year	Shillings per bushel	Shillings per bushel	Shillings per hundredweight	Shillings per hundredweight	Shillings per hundredweight	Shillings per hundredweight	Shillings per hundredweight	Shillings per barrel	Shillings per barrel	Shillings per bushel	Shillings per bushel
1700	—	5.00	—	—	—	—	20.67	—	—	—	2.19
1701	—	4.69	—	—	—	—	21.83	—	—	—	3.09
1702	—	4.39	—	—	—	—	19.56	—	—	—	3.98
1703	—	4.08	—	—	—	—	15.88	—	—	—	4.88
1704	—	3.94	—	—	—	—	14.79	—	—	—	4.17
1705	—	3.77	—	—	—	—	14.83	—	—	—	4.30
1706	—	4.09	—	—	—	—	16.39	—	—	—	3.95
1707	—	4.82	—	—	—	—	17.94	—	—	—	4.85
1708	—	5.31	—	—	—	—	19.50	—	—	—	3.57
1709	—	3.85	—	—	—	—	13.30	—	—	—	3.06
1710	—	3.42	—	—	—	—	11.86	—	—	—	3.14
1711	—	3.34	—	—	—	—	11.31	—	—	—	3.74
1712	—	3.41	—	—	—	—	11.94	—	—	—	5.45
1713	—	4.48	—	—	—	—	16.32	—	—	—	3.33
1714	—	4.03	—	—	—	—	17.01	—	—	—	3.76
1715	—	2.74	—	—	—	—	10.40	—	—	—	2.92
1716	—	2.52	—	—	—	—	7.59	—	—	—	2.41
1717	—	2.71	—	—	—	—	8.39	—	—	—	2.66
1718	—	2.33	—	—	—	—	11.31	—	—	—	2.60
1719	—	3.22	—	—	—	—	11.31	—	—	—	2.58
1720	1.73	3.08	13.79	16.92	13.31	—	9.25	30.00	46.46	2.31	2.31
1721	1.76	3.05	10.04	15.44	13.00	—	8.83	30.00	45.00	1.46	1.85
1722	1.73	2.97	10.25	13.92	12.54	—	8.93	30.67	45.00	1.19	1.65
1723	1.86	2.73	—	14.13	11.67	—	8.80	30.58	40.48	2.05	2.81
1724	2.12	3.36	—	14.56	11.92	—	10.95	30.65	36.00	2.23	3.14
1725	2.13	3.87	33.46	19.98	12.79	—	12.12	30.17	39.29	2.51	2.83
1726	2.13	3.82	17.22	—	14.08	—	12.51	—	48.58	—	1.85
1727	2.02	3.27	17.87	—	13.46	—	11.46	—	47.79	—	2.07
1728	2.26	3.39	16.06	—	13.72	—	10.02	36.72	59.17	—	1.85
1729	2.15	3.70	15.08	18.74	14.00	—	10.65	—	51.65	—	2.15
1730	1.93	3.68	—	—	14.88	—	11.56	—	59.24	—	3.09
1731	1.65	2.47	13.45	15.04	11.72	—	8.02	36.31	55.97	1.88	3.14
1732	1.81	2.70	15.53	—	11.91	—	8.17	—	49.41	1.95	2.40
1733	2.10	3.06	—	—	12.85	10.39	8.84	—	47.54	—	2.36
1734	2.02	3.55	—	—	13.75	10.90	10.51	30.56	43.58	—	2.04
1735	1.58	3.85	15.65	18.50	14.58	12.33	11.47	30.61	37.59	1.56	2.08
1736	1.89	3.24	15.08	17.15	12.77	10.94	9.61	33.50	41.72	1.36	1.92
1737	2.08	3.88	17.41	17.44	15.21	11.78	11.71	36.06	54.44	1.22	2.24
1738	2.10	3.48	17.00	20.67	16.75	12.58	11.16	36.67	59.58	1.35	2.19
1739	1.41	2.82	15.63	17.08	13.01	9.60	8.03	35.75	54.88	1.24	2.16
1740	1.50	3.25	13.92	12.75	13.56	10.31	8.72	35.63	46.04	1.67	2.20
1741	2.74	4.47	14.83	16.58	19.58	15.83	13.66	40.63	49.83	2.47	2.19
1742	2.69	3.58	17.65	16.17	15.96	11.77	10.98	36.63	54.17	2.90	2.67
1743	2.14	2.84	16.25	11.96	14.31	9.06	8.69	44.75	68.52	1.94	2.20
1744	1.53	2.49	12.65	11.03	13.32	8.47	7.68	41.94	60.49	2.05	2.23
1745	1.69	2.60	13.05	10.00	13.06	8.81	8.01	36.88	53.02	2.63	2.56
1746	1.82	2.87	13.93	6.99	14.95	10.15	9.07	41.13	53.79	3.76	3.75
1747	1.92	3.29	16.38	11.40	16.48	11.53	10.01	40.55	57.66	3.58	3.84
1748	2.28	5.04	18.00	15.83	19.67	13.89	15.41	44.29	61.04	3.17	3.07
1749	2.63	5.66	17.10	18.98	26.30	17.60	16.59	37.31	60.16	2.18	2.51
1750	2.56	4.51	19.98	20.63	23.82	15.23	13.10	38.17	63.99	1.41	1.69
1751	2.79	4.28	20.19	17.29	22.37	14.20	12.34	48.44	69.97	1.16	1.30
1752	2.56	4.38	19.90	16.32	21.94	13.17	13.13	51.01	72.35	1.26	1.53
1753	2.91	4.48	19.47	20.97	21.52	13.87	12.80	45.70	63.20	1.43	1.85
1754	2.34	4.46	17.77	17.06	21.64	15.89	14.11	45.13	61.19	1.47	1.63
1755	2.16	4.49	15.08	16.50	21.42	14.50	13.76	47.85	65.94	1.49	1.54
1756	2.50	4.34	15.88	14.50	21.21	13.65	12.76	48.96	61.42	2.15	2.39
1757	1.72	3.79	17.74	14.84	21.24	14.16	11.31	46.43	60.94	2.83	2.56
1758	1.94	3.89	18.33	—	21.84	13.98	12.27	48.18	59.49	2.36	2.41
1759	2.99	4.96	20.42	—	22.14	14.33	14.59	48.66	69.19	2.13	2.40

(continued)

TABLE Eg251–270   Wholesale prices of selected commodities in Philadelphia: 1700–1775   [Pennsylvania currency]
Continued

	Corn	Wheat	Tobacco	Rice	Bread		Flour	Beef	Pork	Salt	
					Middling	Ship				Coarse	Fine
	Eg251	Eg252	Eg253	Eg254	Eg255	Eg256	Eg257	Eg258	Eg259	Eg260	Eg261
Year	Shillings per bushel	Shillings per bushel	Shillings per hundredweight	Shillings per hundredweight	Shillings per hundredweight	Shillings per hundredweight	Shillings per hundredweight	Shillings per barrel	Shillings per barrel	Shillings per bushel	Shillings per bushel
1760	2.96	5.11	20.43	19.00	24.36	13.40	14.96	53.72	69.30	2.14	2.97
1761	2.42	5.03	21.52	16.58	25.18	12.67	14.82	54.91	73.92	1.98	2.86
1762	3.48	5.66	21.42	13.90	28.88	17.49	16.82	58.04	85.63	2.86	—
1763	3.75	6.06	19.48	15.50	30.18	17.82	16.94	60.29	86.95	2.21	—
1764	2.74	4.60	17.71	14.52	23.84	12.95	12.81	60.00	98.26	1.92	—
1765	3.01	4.70	18.13	14.34	24.92	13.88	13.50	58.75	74.36	1.70	—
1766	3.29	5.73	20.42	16.69	24.54	15.44	14.81	55.21	76.88	1.70	—
1767	2.93	6.25	21.89	17.54	27.47	16.80	17.16	55.35	71.76	1.64	1.76
1768	2.57	6.31	21.83	17.74	26.38	15.91	16.89	52.41	73.43	1.61	1.53
1769	2.80	5.48	25.12	17.71	25.45	13.65	15.04	55.21	80.29	1.43	1.81
1770	3.60	5.92	28.73	16.29	28.53	14.11	15.71	51.39	77.04	1.63	1.89
1771	3.50	6.78	32.50	16.86	28.93	15.68	17.50	51.48	80.31	1.65	1.55
1772	3.69	7.74	32.29	23.39	31.23	19.95	20.26	57.05	93.46	1.85	1.85
1773	3.14	7.42	—	18.34	30.93	17.30	18.92	54.58	83.97	1.69	2.22
1774	2.83	6.93	—	16.92	31.08	14.57	18.12	54.31	69.50	1.38	2.05
1775	2.90	5.68	—	17.38	—	—	15.36	57.00	64.88	2.13	3.71

	Molasses	Muscovado sugar	Rum		Madeira wine	Barrel staves	Pitch	Tar	Cotton
			New England	West Indian					
	Eg262	Eg263	Eg264	Eg265	Eg266	Eg267	Eg268	Eg269	Eg270
Year	Shillings per gallon	Shillings per hundredweight	Shillings per gallon	Shillings per gallon	Pounds (£) per pipe	Shillings per thousand	Shillings per barrel	Shillings per barrel	Shillings per pound
1700	2.60	60.21	—	5.27	—	—	—	—	—
1701	2.65	71.15	—	4.82	—	—	—	—	—
1702	2.61	81.25	—	5.90	—	—	—	—	—
1703	2.41	56.78	—	4.47	—	—	—	—	—
1704	2.21	57.30	—	3.52	—	—	—	—	—
1705	2.00	48.17	—	2.96	—	—	—	—	—
1706	2.21	—	—	3.07	—	—	—	—	—
1707	1.98	33.00	—	2.83	—	—	—	—	—
1708	2.39	—	—	3.86	—	—	—	—	—
1709	2.20	44.72	—	2.55	—	—	—	—	—
1710	2.23	39.92	—	2.26	—	—	—	—	—
1711	2.24	42.28	—	3.36	—	—	—	—	—
1712	2.32	44.00	—	4.23	—	—	—	—	—
1713	2.31	63.53	—	3.34	—	—	—	—	—
1714	1.79	52.18	—	3.48	—	—	—	—	—
1715	1.62	41.83	—	2.68	—	—	—	—	—
1716	1.53	44.43	—	3.00	—	—	—	—	—
1717	1.33	45.31	—	3.04	—	—	—	—	—
1718	1.62	46.70	—	2.94	—	—	—	—	—
1719	1.51	36.61	—	3.46	—	—	—	—	—
1720	1.34	35.52	—	2.66	17.99	22.50	14.17	9.83	—
1721	1.16	33.13	—	2.31	19.08	22.50	12.00	8.33	—
1722	1.24	31.88	—	2.94	20.50	22.50	13.50	10.25	—
1723	1.31	36.88	—	2.57	—	22.50	12.63	11.38	—
1724	1.49	29.42	—	2.35	—	—	15.50	10.67	—
1725	1.70	38.44	—	2.85	—	—	18.42	—	—
1726	1.45	36.35	—	3.19	—	—	19.19	—	—
1727	1.43	32.63	—	2.87	—	—	18.40	—	—
1728	1.51	35.17	—	2.61	—	—	13.11	11.92	—
1729	1.53	35.00	—	2.60	—	—	12.08	11.00	—
1730	1.54	32.13	—	2.51	—	—	15.00	11.04	—
1731	1.37	33.88	—	2.64	—	—	14.31	11.10	1.13
1732	1.37	33.35	—	2.50	—	—	13.75	10.10	0.97
1733	1.39	28.93	—	2.30	—	—	17.17	12.25	1.08
1734	1.50	29.20	—	2.63	—	—	12.92	10.14	1.01

TABLE Eg251–270   Wholesale prices of selected commodities in Philadelphia: 1700–1775   [Pennsylvania currency]
Continued

Year	Molasses	Muscovado sugar	Rum New England	Rum West Indian	Madeira wine	Barrel staves	Pitch	Tar	Cotton
	Eg262	Eg263	Eg264	Eg265	Eg266	Eg267	Eg268	Eg269	Eg270
	Shillings per gallon	Shillings per hundredweight	Shillings per gallon	Shillings per gallon	Pounds (£) per pipe	Shillings per thousand	Shillings per barrel	Shillings per barrel	Shillings per pound
1735	1.65	35.64	—	2.36	21.47	36.37	12.83	9.63	1.07
1736	1.68	32.83	—	2.24	21.58	35.21	12.25	8.98	1.09
1737	1.58	35.64	—	2.65	20.88	45.36	10.85	8.56	1.17
1738	1.60	38.98	—	2.29	22.00	47.56	11.33	8.63	1.22
1739	1.59	38.08	—	2.33	21.58	44.58	11.42	9.42	1.33
1740	1.65	37.88	1.81	2.53	20.17	39.42	14.29	10.88	1.29
1741	1.82	36.39	2.46	2.96	21.83	49.17	17.54	14.08	1.16
1742	2.28	40.94	2.84	3.64	24.35	47.81	16.21	12.75	1.01
1743	1.87	38.93	2.36	3.16	27.38	40.85	14.25	10.40	0.99
1744	1.80	49.97	2.52	3.20	27.85	40.00	13.90	10.92	1.19
1745	2.34	43.03	2.65	3.25	27.50	39.79	13.50	10.38	1.33
1746	2.50	47.15	2.69	3.03	22.90	40.63	11.42	9.11	1.83
1747	2.63	55.02	3.62	4.46	24.42	56.03	13.19	10.30	1.94
1748	2.82	51.63	3.60	4.63	25.60	61.06	14.76	11.06	1.77
1749	2.08	46.83	2.72	3.77	28.77	68.79	15.41	10.49	1.65
1750	1.69	51.98	2.53	3.46	29.74	68.36	18.91	12.89	1.89
1751	1.86	47.05	2.51	3.49	30.07	51.50	21.56	11.07	2.18
1752	1.94	48.00	2.39	3.22	30.10	53.28	20.06	10.08	1.90
1753	2.03	51.70	2.47	3.08	30.70	56.87	16.05	9.76	1.65
1754	2.00	50.85	2.44	3.22	28.96	55.94	15.71	10.67	1.58
1755	1.89	48.47	2.27	2.84	29.56	51.54	14.92	11.54	1.40
1756	2.04	48.84	1.93	2.73	32.78	41.63	13.93	11.42	1.49
1757	2.45	47.99	1.60	3.17	39.46	50.82	15.19	9.85	1.52
1758	2.51	47.71	2.37	3.72	41.77	60.73	15.11	9.75	1.40
1759	2.87	45.18	3.94	4.99	43.26	60.69	16.07	10.68	1.51
1760	2.70	47.84	3.54	4.73	50.31	68.82	14.47	10.82	1.32
1761	2.42	49.13	3.04	3.93	48.83	86.91	14.06	11.25	1.45
1762	2.29	52.14	2.79	3.94	50.79	90.85	13.47	10.04	2.04
1763	1.99	49.78	2.59	3.72	49.34	66.04	14.93	12.30	1.87
1764	1.63	48.73	2.05	3.26	50.56	64.90	15.28	12.36	—
1765	1.76	52.94	2.04	3.02	47.29	70.63	17.33	12.40	—
1766	1.93	55.74	2.23	3.02	48.92	67.71	17.25	11.90	—
1767	1.74	49.61	2.08	3.00	50.97	79.60	16.16	11.69	1.93
1768	1.81	46.26	2.23	3.34	47.73	65.47	14.34	11.01	1.71
1769	1.78	52.74	2.16	3.29	48.02	61.32	11.93	10.17	1.37
1770	2.00	56.30	2.19	3.01	49.58	68.68	11.54	11.33	1.32
1771	1.77	50.86	2.18	3.35	50.00	75.15	12.19	12.41	1.24
1772	1.75	49.17	2.19	3.44	54.03	71.85	14.54	14.32	1.27
1773	1.74	50.02	2.20	3.25	56.75	63.49	14.70	13.79	1.44
1774	1.79	55.57	2.17	3.03	55.17	72.54	15.13	13.81	1.48
1775	1.75	52.94	1.64	3.05	64.06	—	—	—	—

Sources

Anne Bezanson, Robert D. Gray, and Miriam Hussey, *Prices in Colonial Pennsylvania*, University of Pennsylvania, Wharton School of Finance and Commerce, Industrial Research Department, Research Studies, volume 26 (University of Philadelphia Press, 1935), pp. 422–4 and elsewhere; and Arthur Harrison Cole, *Wholesale Commodity Prices in the United States, 1700–1861* (Harvard University Press, 1938), volume 2, pp. 1–70. Additions and changes to the prices for sugar, molasses, and rum are from John J. McCusker, *Rum and the American Revolution: The Rum Trade and the Balance of Payments of the Thirteen Continental Colonies, 1650–1775* (Garland, 1989), volume 2, pp. 1061–140, as revised, updated, and augmented by ongoing research.

Documentation

See the Appendixes to the essay in this chapter for a general discussion of the tables and the sources of the data, along with a key to abbreviations used in this chapter and general information on matters such as regional definitions, calendar differences, money, and weights and measures.

The primary sources of the original data were a variety of mercantile records, such as merchants' account books and letter books, along with the occasional lists of "prices current" that were printed in colonial newspapers such as *The American Mercury* (Philadelphia). All prices were expressed in Pennsylvania currency, the local money of account, and were for commodities in specific, customary units of measure. Corn (shelled Indian corn or maize) and wheat were priced per bushel, conventionally fifty-six pounds. Flour also weighed fifty-six pounds per bushel. (Compare Tables Eg285–298.) Tobacco and other commodities were sold by the hundredweight. At Philadelphia, for everything but tobacco, this was the equivalent of 112 pounds. The tobacco hundredweight measured 100 pounds. Barrels, in the case of beef and pork, weighed 220 pounds; in the case of pitch and tar, barrels contained 31.5 gallons. The bushel of fine salt weighed sixty-two pounds; the bushel of coarse salt weighed eighty pounds or more (Bezanson, Gray, and Hussey 1935, p. 240). The unit of measure of Madeira wine, the pipe, contained 110 gallons. Staves were sold by the "thousand," which meant in practice 1,200 staves. Most of this is addressed in Helen Louise Klopfer, "Statistics of the Foreign Trade of Philadelphia, 1700–1860" (Ph.D. dissertation, University of Pennsylvania, 1936). See also the text for Table Eg1174–1179. In the source for this table, the price of salt between

(continued)

TABLE Eg251–270   Wholesale prices of selected commodities in Philadelphia: 1700–1775   [Pennsylvania currency]
Continued

1700 and 1719 was for an "unspecified" grade presumed here to have been "fine."

To compare prices quoted in Pennsylvania currency with prices in other colonies or in England, one can use the exchange rate data in Table Eg315–324.

The project that studied Philadelphia prices was one of many sponsored by the International Scientific Committee in Price History. See Arthur H. Cole and Ruth Crandall, "The International Scientific Committee on Price History," *Journal of Economic History* 24 (September 1964): 381–8. The results of several of those studies were drawn together in Cole (1938). In addition to discussions and analyses of prices, Cole's book offered a statistical supplement of monthly prices for the principal commercial centers. The tables in it, however, rest primarily on the Philadelphia prices until the 1750s – and presented additional data collected and compiled after the Bezanson volume was published. Prior to 1750, Boston has only two series, wheat and molasses, which begin in 1720. Although there are gaps in the data, Charleston has series for bread, corn, rice, rum, wine, molasses, and staves beginning in 1732; sugar beginning in 1744; beef, pork, and indigo beginning in 1747; and coffee, leather, and lumber beginning in 1749. New York has series for flour, bread, rice, sugar, salt, rum, and molasses beginning in 1748; and for wheat, beef, and pork beginning in 1749.

Price series for the other Philadelphia commodities are presented in the source volumes: for example, brown bread, white bread, London loaf sugar, Pennsylvania loaf sugar, indigo, bar iron, pig iron, hogshead staves, pipe staves, turpentine, and gunpowder. In addition to the annual averages, the source contains average monthly prices and monthly and annual indexes (both arithmetic and geometric) of twenty commodities in Philadelphia.

Some of the original studies continued their coverage beyond the colonial period, notably the Philadelphia project and the New York project. They form the basis of price data presented in Table Cc205–266. See also G[eorge] F. Warren, F[rank] A. Pearson, and Herman M. Stoker, *Wholesale Prices for 213 Years, 1720 to 1932*, Cornell University, Agricultural Experiment Station, Memoir number 412 (Cornell University, 1932). There are important archival collections associated with these studies, each containing a great deal of additional material: Records of the International Scientific Committee on Price History, 1928–1939, Manuscript and Archives Division, Baker Library, Graduate School of Business Administration, Harvard University; the Frank Ashmore Pearson Papers, Albert R. Mann Library, Cornell University; and the "Industrial Research Department – Wholesale Prices" Collection, Wharton School of Finance and Commerce, University of Pennsylvania.

TABLE Eg271–274   Price of ships at Philadelphia, by vessel type: 1715–1790   [Pennsylvania currency]

Contributed by John J. McCusker

	Fore-and-aft rigged		Square-rigged	
	Hull only	Completed vessel	Hull only	Completed vessel
	Eg271	Eg272	Eg273	Eg274
Year(s)	Pounds (£) per ton	Pounds (£) per ton	Pounds (£) per ton	Pounds (£) per ton
1715–1738	3.00	7.60	4.00	9.90
1739–1748	3.50	8.80	4.70	11.40
1749–1753	3.80	9.40	5.00	13.50
1754–1763	3.40	8.50	4.50	13.90
1764–1774	4.60	11.70	6.20	15.90
1775–1783	6.30	15.90	8.20	20.60
1784–1790	5.30	13.20	7.00	19.40

Source

John J. McCusker, "The Price of a Ship at Philadelphia in the Eighteenth Century" (manuscript).

Documentation

See the Appendixes to the essay in this chapter for a general discussion of the tables and the sources of the data, along with a key to abbreviations used in this chapter and general information on matters such as regional definitions, calendar differences, money, and weights and measures.

This table presents the average price of ships sold at Philadelphia, expressed in pounds Pennsylvania currency per ton. The unit of measure for the pricing of vessels was the measured ton, one of three kinds of tons associated with ships and the shipping industry during the period. To compare prices quoted in Pennsylvania currency with prices in other colonies or in England, one can use the exchange rate data in Table Eg315–324.

The wooden ocean-going vessel was the largest and most complex manufactured item fabricated for sale in the colonies. It was produced in a variety of forms, under a variety of names but of two general types based on the arrangement of its sails. Vessels rigged with sails that ran parallel to the line of motion of the vessel – fore-and-aft rigged vessels – were the smaller of the two types. Vessels with at least some of their sails set perpendicular to the vessel's line of motion – square-rigged or "topsail" vessels – were the larger of the two. In the eighteenth century, depending on just how they were rigged,

the former were known as sloops, schooners, and hoys; the latter were known as brigantines, snows, and ships. For illustrations of these six types of vessels, see the drawings by Henry Rusk in Howard I. Chapelle, *The History of American Sailing Ships* (Norton, 1935), pp. 11, 12, 14, 16, 17. (Note that, except in such comparative contexts, the word "ship" is usually employed herein as a generic term, the equivalent of the phrase "seagoing vessel.") Of the vessels registered at POE Philadelphia between 1720 and 1775, 54.6 percent by count and 80.8 percent by tonnage were square-rigged. Over the period, as Philadelphia-based merchant ship owners extended the reach of their trade, more and more of these ships were ocean-going vessels of larger and larger capacity. See John J. McCusker, "The Pennsylvania Shipping Industry in the Eighteenth Century" (1972), unpublished typescript, copy on deposit, Collection number 1880, Historical Society of Pennsylvania, Philadelphia.

Prices of vessels were initially discussed among builders and buyers in terms of the cost per measured ton of the basic structure (hull only); thereafter, all were more interested in the cost of the finished vessel. The total cost of a vessel increased as the vessel acquired its iron work, its rope and rigging, its anchors, its sails, and all of the other things that made it ready to set sail. In general, a vessel ready for sea cost two-and-half times the price of the hull only. Not included in the price of the completed vessel – essentially its capital cost – were the additional costs of actually setting off on a voyage.

TABLE Eg271–274   Price of ships at Philadelphia, by vessel type: 1715–1790   [Pennsylvania currency]   *Continued*

The continuing, repeated costs of outfitting a vessel for its next venture were accounted as its operating costs.

The prices presented in the table were collected from a variety of mercantile letters and accounts almost all of which are in the Historical Society of Pennsylvania, Philadelphia. They supersede similar tables presented in John J. McCusker, "Sources of Investment Capital in the Colonial Philadelphia Shipping Industry," *Journal of Economic History* 32 (March 1972): 146–57, as revised and updated in McCusker, *Essays in the Economic History of the Atlantic World* (Routledge, 1997), pp. 245–57. Rarely in such sources can the price be found for both states of the same vessel; ratios were developed to help estimate the completed cost if the price of just the hull was found and vice

versa. All of this is explained in the source. Earlier forms of this table discussed the price of vessels in terms of the hull only. See, for example, Thomas M. Doerflinger, *A Vigorous Spirit of Enterprise: Merchants and Economic Development in Revolutionary Philadelphia* (University of North Carolina Press, 1986).

The compiled data are grouped into seven periods that distinguish times of peace and times of war. Prices generally are thought to have been heavily influenced by the ongoing, repeated phases of the Second Hundred Years' War between Great Britain and France. See also John J. McCusker, *How Much Is That in Real Money? A Historical Commodity Price Index for Use as a Deflator of Money Values in the Economy of the United States*, 2nd edition (American Antiquarian Society, 2001), pp. 33–5 n. 35.

TABLE Eg275–284   Wholesale tobacco prices in Virginia and Maryland, by region: 1647–1820   [Virginia currency]

Contributed by John J. McCusker

	Virginia								Maryland	
	York River Basin	New Kent and King William counties	James River Basin	Rappahannock River Basin	Potomac River Basin	Hanover and Louisa counties	Virginia Piedmont	All sweet-scented	Western Shore	Eastern Shore
	Eg275	Eg276	Eg277	Eg278	Eg279	Eg280	Eg281	Eg282	Eg283	Eg284
Year	Pence per pound	Pence per pound	Pence per pound	Pence per pound	Pence per pound	Pence per pound	Pence per pound	Pence per pound	Pence per pound	Pence per pound
1647	—	—	—	—	—	—	—	2.80	—	—
1648	2.80	—	—	—	—	—	—	2.80	—	—
1658	2.00	—	—	—	—	—	—	2.00	—	—
1659	2.15	—	—	—	—	—	—	2.15	—	—
1660	2.50	—	—	—	—	—	—	2.50	—	—
1661	2.20	—	—	—	—	—	—	2.20	—	—
1664	1.60	—	—	—	—	—	—	1.60	—	—
1665	1.20	—	—	—	—	—	—	1.20	—	—
1666	1.20	—	—	—	—	—	—	1.20	—	—
1667	1.20	—	—	—	—	—	—	1.20	—	—
1668	2.40	—	—	—	—	—	—	2.40	—	—
1669	2.00	—	—	—	—	—	—	2.00	—	—
1670	—	—	—	1.34	—	—	—	—	—	—
1671	2.00	—	—	1.34	—	—	—	2.00	—	—
1672	—	—	—	1.34	—	—	—	—	—	—
1673	—	—	—	1.34	—	—	—	—	—	—
1674	—	—	—	1.34	—	—	—	1.30	—	—
1675	1.20	—	—	1.34	—	—	—	1.27	—	—
1676	—	—	—	1.34	—	—	—	1.27	—	—
1677	—	—	—	1.34	—	—	—	1.27	—	—
1678	—	—	—	1.34	—	—	—	1.35	—	—
1679	1.50	—	—	1.34	—	—	—	1.42	—	—
1680	1.30	—	—	1.32	—	—	—	1.31	—	—
1681	1.20	—	—	1.32	—	—	—	1.26	—	—
1682	1.20	—	—	1.32	—	—	—	1.26	—	—
1683	1.44	—	—	1.32	—	—	—	1.38	—	—
1684	1.20	—	—	1.32	—	—	—	1.26	—	—
1685	—	—	—	1.32	—	—	—	1.27	—	—
1686	1.63	—	—	1.32	—	—	—	1.28	—	—
1687	1.20	—	—	1.32	—	—	—	1.26	—	—
1688	1.20	—	—	1.32	—	—	—	1.26	—	—
1689	1.20	—	—	1.32	—	—	—	1.26	—	—
1690	1.20	—	—	1.30	—	—	—	1.25	—	—
1691	1.20	—	—	1.30	—	—	—	1.25	—	—
1692	1.20	—	—	1.30	—	—	—	1.25	—	—
1693	—	—	—	1.30	—	—	—	1.30	—	—
1694	1.20	—	—	1.30	—	—	—	1.25	—	—
1695	1.20	—	—	1.30	—	—	—	1.25	—	—
1696	1.20	—	—	1.30	—	—	—	1.25	—	—
1697	1.20	—	—	1.30	—	—	—	1.25	—	—
1698	—	—	—	1.30	—	—	—	1.30	—	—
1699	—	—	—	1.30	—	—	—	1.30	—	—

(continued)

TABLE Eg275–284   Wholesale tobacco prices in Virginia and Maryland, by region: 1647–1820   [Virginia currency]
Continued

	Virginia								Maryland	
	York River Basin	New Kent and King William counties	James River Basin	Rappahannock River Basin	Potomac River Basin	Hanover and Louisa counties	Virginia Piedmont	All sweet-scented	Western Shore	Eastern Shore
	Eg275	Eg276	Eg277	Eg278	Eg279	Eg280	Eg281	Eg282	Eg283	Eg284
Year	Pence per pound	Pence per pound	Pence per pound	Pence per pound	Pence per pound	Pence per pound	Pence per pound	Pence per pound	Pence per pound	Pence per pound
1700	—	—	—	1.68	—	—	—	1.68	—	—
1701	—	—	—	1.42	—	—	—	1.42	—	—
1702	1.35	—	—	—	—	—	—	1.49	—	—
1703	1.60	—	—	1.42	—	—	—	1.48	—	—
1704	1.87	—	—	1.57	—	—	—	1.67	—	—
1705	—	—	—	1.63	—	—	—	1.63	—	—
1706	1.21	—	—	1.84	—	—	—	1.69	—	—
1707	1.50	—	—	1.63	—	—	—	1.57	—	—
1708	2.00	—	—	1.71	1.20	—	—	1.81	—	—
1709	1.10	—	—	1.81	—	—	—	1.57	—	—
1710	—	—	—	1.75	1.00	—	—	1.75	—	—
1711	1.20	—	—	1.70	—	—	—	1.45	—	—
1712	1.05	—	—	2.05	—	—	—	1.72	—	—
1713	1.36	—	—	1.70	—	—	—	1.53	—	—
1714	1.00	—	—	1.70	—	—	—	1.35	—	—
1715	—	—	—	2.05	—	—	—	2.05	—	—
1716	2.45	—	—	2.05	—	—	—	2.18	—	—
1717	2.20	—	—	1.95	—	—	—	2.03	—	—
1718	2.40	—	—	2.05	—	—	—	2.16	—	—
1719	2.26	—	—	2.09	—	—	—	2.14	—	—
1720	2.06	—	—	1.90	—	—	—	1.95	—	—
1721	1.57	—	—	1.74	1.33	—	—	1.68	—	—
1722	1.65	—	—	1.71	—	—	—	1.69	—	—
1723	1.64	—	—	1.56	—	—	—	1.69	—	—
1724	2.06	—	—	1.56	—	—	—	1.81	—	—
1725	1.67	—	—	1.56	—	—	—	1.67	—	—
1726	1.69	—	—	1.56	—	—	—	1.69	—	—
1727	1.57	—	—	1.78	—	2.23	—	1.84	—	—
1728	1.34	—	—	1.33	—	2.33	—	1.58	—	—
1729	1.50	—	—	1.51	—	1.20	—	1.43	—	—
1730	1.50	—	—	1.57	—	1.35	—	1.50	—	—
1731	1.38	1.32	—	1.57	1.61	—	—	1.46	—	—
1732	1.50	1.97	—	1.99	1.80	—	—	1.86	—	—
1733	2.27	2.03	—	1.81	—	—	—	1.98	—	—
1734	2.13	2.08	—	1.82	—	2.40	—	2.11	—	—
1735	2.12	2.16	—	1.82	2.37	2.26	—	2.06	—	—
1736	1.84	1.75	—	1.96	—	2.68	—	2.07	—	—
1737	1.66	1.88	1.68	1.85	—	2.37	—	1.97	—	—
1738	2.19	2.08	—	1.94	—	2.47	—	2.13	—	—
1739	2.02	2.70	—	1.82	—	2.32	—	2.17	—	—
1740	1.84	1.93	—	1.73	1.20	2.09	—	1.89	—	—
1741	1.60	1.84	—	1.83	—	2.40	—	1.88	—	—
1742	1.77	1.68	—	1.72	—	—	1.71	1.74	—	—
1743	1.76	1.80	—	1.74	1.55	—	1.77	1.76	—	—
1744	1.81	1.80	—	1.75	—	2.20	1.82	1.84	—	—
1745	1.56	1.40	—	1.84	1.08	1.93	—	1.75	—	—
1746	1.66	1.74	—	1.85	1.20	—	—	1.76	—	—
1747	1.77	1.90	—	1.67	1.20	—	1.59	1.72	—	—
1748	1.74	1.91	2.00	1.89	1.47	2.02	1.90	1.87	—	—
1749	1.85	1.86	1.86	2.30	1.20	—	2.00	2.04	—	—
1750	1.89	—	1.98	1.87	1.48	2.20	—	1.96	—	—
1751	2.01	—	2.16	1.87	—	2.40	—	2.09	—	—
1752	2.01	—	—	1.87	—	—	—	1.97	—	—
1753	1.86	—	—	1.87	—	—	—	1.86	—	—
1754	1.79	—	1.65	1.87	—	1.97	—	1.87	—	—
1755	1.87	—	—	1.87	2.16	2.14	—	1.97	—	—
1756	2.08	—	2.19	1.87	1.68	2.39	—	2.29	—	—
1757	2.19	—	2.43	2.21	—	2.34	—	2.13	—	—
1758	3.34	6.00	2.00	2.51	3.12	1.87	—	3.57	—	—
1759	2.00	—	—	1.87	3.67	2.16	2.82	2.77	—	—

TABLE Eg275–284   Wholesale tobacco prices in Virginia and Maryland, by region: 1647–1820   [Virginia currency]
Continued

				Virginia					Maryland	
	York River Basin	New Kent and King William counties	James River Basin	Rappahannock River Basin	Potomac River Basin	Hanover and Louisa counties	Virginia Piedmont	All sweet-scented	Western Shore	Eastern Shore
	Eg275	Eg276	Eg277	Eg278	Eg279	Eg280	Eg281	Eg282	Eg283	Eg284
Year	Pence per pound	Pence per pound	Pence per pound	Pence per pound	Pence per pound	Pence per pound	Pence per pound	Pence per pound	Pence per pound	Pence per pound
1760	2.20	—	—	—	2.25	2.42	2.55	2.33	—	—
1761	2.08	2.52	—	2.28	2.13	2.64	—	2.42	—	—
1762	2.20	—	—	2.40	1.94	3.14	—	2.54	—	—
1763	—	—	—	2.43	2.23	2.28	—	2.27	—	—
1764	—	—	—	1.65	—	2.86	—	2.10	—	—
1765	—	—	—	2.00	1.80	2.34	—	2.15	—	—
1766	—	—	—	2.40	—	2.73	—	2.51	—	—
1767	1.90	—	2.28	—	2.02	2.62	—	2.33	—	—
1768	2.49	2.20	—	—	—	2.76	—	2.53	—	—
1769	2.17	2.00	3.03	2.00	—	2.84	—	2.37	—	—
1770	2.80	—	2.75	—	2.70	2.89	—	2.71	2.76	2.32
1771	2.52	—	—	2.40	2.16	2.40	—	2.49	2.46	1.90
1772	2.45	2.20	—	—	—	2.78	2.23	2.45	2.35	2.04
1773	2.01	1.84	1.96	1.56	—	2.04	2.29	2.01	2.28	1.56
1774	2.37	2.40	—	—	1.59	2.58	2.70	2.37	2.09	1.50
1775	2.26	—	3.00	—	—	2.58	3.06	2.26	2.06	2.14
1776	3.66	—	—	2.21	2.12	2.08	4.80	3.66	2.02	1.80
1777	1.59	—	2.80	2.40	2.57	2.95	3.90	1.54	2.86	4.15
1778	3.00	—	5.76	—	4.65	3.96	—	3.00	4.68	—
1779	1.87	—	—	2.70	1.80	3.50	—	1.87	3.96	1.99
1780	3.24	—	—	—	1.44	3.75	1.20	3.24	1.97	2.40
1781	2.58	—	1.80	—	1.80	1.88	1.80	2.58	1.90	1.90
1782	2.84	—	2.94	1.93	1.80	2.43	2.51	2.84	1.56	1.97
1783	3.01	3.48	2.87	—	2.19	3.24	3.45	3.01	2.50	2.52
1784	3.64	3.38	4.32	4.56	3.84	4.04	3.49	3.64	2.62	2.57
1785	3.67	3.00	3.96	3.72	2.70	4.12	2.73	3.67	2.93	2.52
1786	4.43	2.68	2.98	2.40	2.57	2.94	2.76	4.43	2.69	1.92
1787	2.86	2.70	2.83	2.31	2.43	3.07	2.59	4.78	3.14	1.94
1788	2.76	2.52	2.56	2.41	2.47	2.87	2.43	2.76	2.45	1.92
1789	2.70	—	2.45	2.16	1.94	3.16	2.34	2.00	3.34	1.78
1790	2.70	—	2.62	2.28	2.18	2.80	2.31	2.70	2.21	1.90
1791	2.32	—	2.25	2.16	1.69	2.27	1.84	2.32	2.38	1.46
1792	2.58	—	2.66	1.92	1.64	2.51	2.15	2.58	2.28	1.44
1793	3.25	—	2.47	2.54	1.96	2.25	2.42	3.25	2.42	1.78
1794	2.88	—	1.51	2.40	1.87	2.33	2.95	—	2.42	1.32
1795	1.98	—	—	2.40	1.98	2.16	2.94	—	2.11	1.58
1796	3.24	—	3.09	—	2.40	3.84	5.40	—	3.17	1.90
1797	5.04	—	6.00	3.84	—	6.09	—	—	4.01	1.78
1798	6.72	—	6.48	5.22	—	6.72	4.81	—	4.54	3.84
1799	4.68	—	3.24	4.32	3.24	4.90	2.37	—	5.38	2.74
1800	3.54	—	3.14	3.06	2.25	3.60	3.05	—	2.45	2.62
1801	3.65	—	3.94	3.28	3.02	3.90	4.01	—	2.74	3.25
1802	3.25	—	4.11	—	2.88	3.29	3.55	—	3.22	—
1803	3.59	—	4.11	—	—	4.20	4.10	—	4.27	—
1804	4.20	—	4.25	—	—	4.26	4.15	—	4.61	—
1805	3.04	—	3.93	—	—	3.96	3.42	—	4.25	—
1806	3.24	—	3.73	—	—	3.14	3.33	—	4.39	—
1807	4.44	—	3.86	3.78	—	4.44	3.80	—	4.15	—
1808	3.00	—	2.71	2.89	—	3.00	3.15	—	3.65	—
1809	3.84	—	3.48	—	—	3.00	3.38	—	3.53	—
1810	3.54	—	3.95	5.22	—	3.75	4.75	—	2.57	—
1811	3.69	—	4.51	4.50	—	2.16	5.04	—	1.92	—
1812	2.16	—	3.11	2.88	—	1.92	4.18	—	1.51	—
1813	—	—	3.86	—	—	—	2.70	—	1.92	—
1814	—	—	4.98	—	—	—	3.79	—	3.36	—
1815	—	—	10.06	—	—	—	8.44	—	5.78	—
1816	—	—	12.20	—	—	—	7.13	—	9.05	—
1817	—	—	7.24	—	—	—	5.84	—	6.53	—
1818	—	—	8.86	—	—	—	8.09	—	9.60	—
1819	8.64	—	5.46	—	—	—	5.94	—	7.46	7.32
1820	—	—	5.28	—	—	—	5.28	—	6.10	3.98

(continued)

TABLE Eg275–284   Wholesale tobacco prices in Virginia and Maryland, by region: 1647–1820   [Virginia currency]
Continued

Sources

Compiled by Lorena S. Walsh from the following sources.

Virginia. Compiled from planter and merchant account and letter books, probate inventories, and, for the 1800s, newspapers, with some shorter series compiled by Peter Bergstrom (seventeenth-century tobacco), Harold Gill (eighteenth-century tobacco), Darrett Rutman and Anita Rutman (Middlesex County to 1750), Ransom True (Louisa County), Arthur Peterson (1801–1820), and Historic St. Mary's City.

Maryland. Compiled from planter and merchant account books, by Historic St. Mary's City from probate inventories, and shorter series compiled by Paul Clemens (Eastern Shore) and Bayly Marks (St. Mary's County).

Documentation

See the Appendixes to the essay in this chapter for a general discussion of the tables and the sources of the data, along with a key to abbreviations used in this chapter and general information on matters such as regional definitions, calendar differences, money, and weights and measures.

These figures are the average wholesale farm prices (producer prices) for the two most widely grown strains of tobacco in the Chesapeake Bay: sweet-scented and oronoco. As a rule, sweet-scented was the finer, milder tobacco and oronoco was a coarser and stronger-flavored tobacco. Generally, sweet-scented tobacco was grown in the lower Chesapeake Bay (the York and Rappahannock River basins and the northern shore of the James River basin) – series Eg275–278. Oronoco tobacco was produced in the upper Chesapeake Bay (the Potomac River basin shared by Maryland and Virginia, on both the Western and Eastern Shores), the southern shore of the upper James River basin, and the "back country" or piedmont – series Eg279–281. See the discussion and the map (Figure 1) in Lorena S. Walsh, "Summing the Parts: Implications for Estimating Chesapeake Output and Income Subregionally," *William and Mary Quarterly*, 3rd series, 56 (January 1999): 53–94, especially pp. 87–94. See also one of her sources for the map: "An Account of the Quantity of Tobacco Planted and Tended in Virginia in the Year 1724," an enclosure in the letter of Governor Hugh Drysdale, at Williamsburg, to the Commissioners of Trade and Plantations, January 29, 1724/25, CO 5/1319, folio 220r, PRO/TNA. The Drysdale account listed (county by county) the nature and amount of each type of tobacco produced. As time went on, these distinctions became less definitive, so much so that, by the end of the eighteenth century, the inspectors in Virginia's tobacco warehouses were classifying all tobacco as oronoco. See [George] Melvin Herndon, *Tobacco in Colonial Virginia: "The Sovereign Remedy,"* Jamestown 350th Anniversary Historical Booklet, number 20 (Virginia 350th Anniversary Celebration Corporation, 1957), p. 22. In the present table, the data are organized by district or region within the Chesapeake Bay, just as they are in the source.

All prices in these series are stated in pence Virginia currency. In Virginia, tobacco, corn, and wheat were bought and sold in Virginia currency, the local money of account; in Maryland, the money of account was Maryland hard currency. Each colony established the worth of its own currency with reference to Spanish silver coin, specifically the *peso de ocho reales* or piece of eight, which was later adopted as the currency of the United States, the dollar. In law Virginia currency was rated at 6s per dollar and Maryland hard currency was rated at 7s 6d per dollar. Thus, at legal par, the two currencies were at the ratio of 6:7.5 or 1:1.25. To create a consistent series that allows for easier comparisons, Walsh expressed prices for both colonies in pence Virginia currency. The conversion of Maryland prices was more simply accomplished than it might have been because the value of the dollar in Virginia currency, 6s each, was also the value of the dollar in Maryland current money, the pre-Revolutionary Maryland paper money, the valuation of which was later retained as a notational currency, the currency in which inventories were taken through 1781. Any Maryland prices expressed in Maryland hard currency (at dollars valued at 7s 6d) were reduced to Maryland current money at 1:1.25. Virginia prices for the years 1770–1779, when the dollar was valued at 6s 8d, were reduced at 1:1.033. Prices from the early national period expressed in dollars and cents were reduced at 6:3.333 or 1:0.556. See John J. McCusker, *Money and Exchange in Europe and America, 1600–1775: A Handbook*, 2nd edition (University of North Carolina Press, 1992), pp. 189–214;

and McCusker, *How Much Is That in Real Money? A Historical Commodity Price Index for Use as a Deflator of Money Values in the Economy of the United States*, 2nd edition (American Antiquarian Society, 2001), pp. 71–88. To compare prices quoted in Virginia currency with prices in other colonies or in England, one can use the exchange rate data in Table Eg315–324.

For the context of the collection and compilation of these data, see Lorena S. Walsh, Ann Smart Martin, and Joanne Bowen, *Provisioning Early American Towns. The Chesapeake: A Multidisciplinary Case Study – Final Performance Report* (Colonial Williamsburg Foundation, 1997). See also Lorena S. Walsh, "Chesapeake Planters and the International Market, 1770–1820," in John J. McCusker, editor, *Lois Green Carr: The Chesapeake and Beyond – A Celebration* (Maryland Historical and Cultural Publications, 1992), pp. 205–27; and Walsh, "Slave Life, Slave Society, and Tobacco Production in the Tidewater Chesapeake, 1620–1820," in Ira Berlin and Philip D. Morgan, editors, *Cultivation and Culture: Labor and the Shaping of Slave Life in the Americas* (University Press of Virginia, 1993), pp. 170–99.

These price data largely supersede other, earlier such series, most particularly the tables in *Historical Statistics of the United States* (1975), volume 2, p. 1198 (series Z 578–582 and series Z 583–584). Still of some value are the limited series for oronoco tobacco and tobacco grown in outlying (peripheral) areas found in Russell R. Menard, "The Tobacco Industry in the Chesapeake Colonies, 1617–1730: An Interpretation," *Research in Economic History* 5 (1980): 109–77, and recently recapitulated in Walsh (1999), pp. 87–91.

An issue of considerable significance in deriving these data is the size of the tobacco hogshead, which differed by colony and grew in capacity over time. It is an issue because tobacco prices were frequently stated in terms of so much currency per hogshead. From the same sources that Walsh consulted for price quotations, she collected and compiled data on the weight in pounds of the Maryland and Virginia tobacco hogshead, namely:

	Virginia				Maryland			
			Range				Range	
Years	Number	Mean	Low	High	Number	Mean	Low	High
1627–1639	268	144	141	300	–	–	–	–
1640–1649	179	324	220	419	–	–	–	–
1650–1659	677	398	223	624	–	–	–	–
1660–1669	761	463	332	670	–	–	–	–
1670–1679	222	306	358	701	–	–	–	–
1680–1688	116	486	351	700	–	–	–	–
1689–1701	203	613	284	707	–	–	–	–
1697–1701	147	621	300	677	–	–	–	–
1702–1713	680	863	420	1,219	228	604	493	800
1714–1720	554	604	277	937	463	618	450	824
1721–1729	92	760	429	1,350	243	780	400	990
1730–1738	162	822	358	1,020	101	856	455	1,178
1739–1743	122	941	834	1,123	127	990	645	1,242
1744–1748	463	983	769	1,191	84	1,048	946	1,226
1749–1752	148	1,006	836	1,112	191	1,050	853	1,293
1754–1763	1,045	1,145	827	1,409	358	993	814	1,864
1764–1769	849	1,104	793	1,513	101	1,143	1,020	1,361
1770–1774	804	1,074	803	1,321	95	1,020	826	1,209
1775–1781	633	1,027	686	1,216	123	1,086	928	1,282
1782–1789	877	1,063	685	1,322	316	1,020	943	1,116
1790–1799	812	1,157	800	1,660	550	988	601	1,195
1800–1807	1,474	1,363	886	1,613	324	984	800	1,188
1808–1815	1,086	1,407	1,009	1,686	41	926	434	1,023
1816–1820	382	1,351	1,135	1,589	29	975	916	1,085

The differences in size had much less to do with the colony of origin than with the nature of the tobacco and the way in which it was packed in the cask. See the testimony of several London tobacco merchants on this subject before the Board of Trade, May 3, 1711, in Great Britain, Board of Trade, *Journal of the Commissioners for Trade and Plantations, 1704–1782* (H. M. Stationery Office,

TABLE Eg275–284   Wholesale tobacco prices in Virginia and Maryland, by region: 1647–1820   [Virginia currency]
Continued

1920–1938), volume 2, pp. 267–8: "'tis true that sweet scented Virginia tobacco will bear pressing better than the Maryland [oronoco] tobacco, and so by consequence a hogshead of Virginia will weigh considerably more than a hogshead of Maryland." In the first two decades of the eighteenth century (1702–1720), the former averaged 20 percent heavier than the latter. Over the subsequent century, the difference was closer to 10 percent. Compare Walsh's data with those assembled by Stephen Gregg Hardy, "Trade and

Economic Growth in the Eighteenth-Century Chesapeake" (Ph.D. dissertation, University of Maryland, 1999), pp. 457–61.

The progressive increase in the weight of tobacco casks was a phenomenon shared with rice casks and sugar casks. For rice casks, see the text for series Eg299. For sugar casks, see John J. McCusker, *Rum and the American Revolution: The Rum Trade and the Balance of Payments of the Thirteen Continental Colonies, 1650–1775* (Garland, 1989), volume 2, pp. 768–878.

TABLE Eg285–291   Wholesale corn prices in Virginia and Maryland, by region: 1750–1820 [Virginia currency]

Contributed by John J. McCusker

	Virginia					Maryland	
	James River Basin	York River Basin	Rappahannock River Basin	Potomac River Basin	Virginia Piedmont	Western Shore	Eastern Shore
	Eg285	Eg286	Eg287	Eg288	Eg289	Eg290	Eg291
Year	Pounds (£) per barrel	Pounds (£) per barrel	Pounds (£) per barrel	Pounds (£) per barrel	Pounds (£) per barrel	Pounds (£) per barrel	Pounds (£) per barrel
1750	—	0.39	—	—	—	—	—
1751	—	0.42	—	—	—	—	—
1752	—	0.46	—	—	—	—	—
1753	—	0.43	—	—	—	—	—
1754	—	0.39	—	—	—	—	—
1755	—	0.44	—	—	—	—	—
1756	—	0.33	—	—	—	—	—
1757	—	0.36	—	—	—	—	—
1758	—	0.37	—	—	—	—	—
1759	—	0.43	—	—	—	—	—
1760	—	0.44	—	—	—	—	—
1761	—	0.47	—	—	—	—	—
1762	—	0.41	—	—	—	—	—
1763	—	0.50	—	—	—	—	—
1764	—	0.47	—	—	—	—	—
1765	—	0.50	—	—	—	—	—
1766	—	0.52	—	—	—	—	—
1767	—	0.48	—	—	—	—	—
1768	—	0.47	—	—	—	—	—
1769	—	0.50	—	—	—	—	—
1770	—	0.50	—	—	—	0.49	0.52
1771	—	0.52	—	—	—	0.52	0.49
1772	—	0.55	0.61	—	0.51	0.58	0.54
1773	—	0.61	0.61	—	—	0.51	0.46
1774	—	0.47	—	—	0.37	0.42	0.43
1775	—	0.47	0.48	—	0.40	0.45	0.50
1776	—	0.46	0.80	0.44	0.34	0.48	0.44
1777	0.61	0.75	0.48	0.75	0.60	0.56	0.44
1778	1.34	0.75	—	0.88	0.81	0.69	—
1779	—	0.99	—	0.73	0.48	0.65	0.44
1780	—	0.91	—	—	0.52	0.48	0.58
1781	—	0.61	—	0.45	—	0.37	0.50
1782	—	0.56	0.45	0.71	0.37	0.39	0.38
1783	1.13	0.69	0.58	0.80	0.75	0.50	0.53
1784	1.00	0.97	—	0.68	0.70	0.44	0.52
1785	0.75	0.74	—	0.50	0.70	0.51	0.59
1786	—	0.79	0.69	0.88	0.66	0.58	0.63
1787	—	0.76	0.75	0.75	0.66	0.53	0.48
1788	—	0.69	—	0.83	0.69	0.61	0.49
1789	0.45	0.52	—	0.62	0.51	0.41	0.47
1790	0.62	0.59	0.75	0.80	0.59	0.51	0.62
1791	0.48	0.53	—	0.53	—	0.45	0.42
1792	0.75	0.64	—	0.70	0.60	0.56	0.52
1793	0.80	0.73	0.50	0.61	0.69	0.69	0.62
1794	0.74	0.61	0.71	0.73	1.00	0.72	0.65

(continued)

TABLE Eg285–291   Wholesale corn prices in Virginia and Maryland, by region: 1750–1820 [Virginia currency] *Continued*

	Virginia					Maryland	
	James River Basin	York River Basin	Rappahannock River Basin	Potomac River Basin	Virginia Piedmont	Western Shore	Eastern Shore
	Eg285	Eg286	Eg287	Eg288	Eg289	Eg290	Eg291
Year	Pounds (£) per barrel	Pounds (£) per barrel	Pounds (£) per barrel	Pounds (£) per barrel	Pounds (£) per barrel	Pounds (£) per barrel	Pounds (£) per barrel
1795	1.03	0.65	0.63	0.75	0.64	0.64	0.66
1796	1.24	0.90	0.80	—	1.20	0.83	0.75
1797	—	1.09	0.83	—	0.56	0.75	0.79
1798	0.75	0.79	0.90	0.81	0.78	0.70	0.54
1799	0.88	0.71	0.90	—	1.10	0.69	0.60
1800	1.09	0.73	1.06	0.98	1.20	0.73	1.01
1801	1.11	1.06	1.35	1.20	0.75	0.93	—
1802	0.80	0.71	0.87	—	0.76	0.66	—
1803	0.72	0.76	0.88	—	0.63	0.68	—
1804	1.34	1.13	—	—	0.75	1.08	0.60
1805	1.49	0.97	—	0.86	0.97	1.15	0.83
1806	0.92	0.94	—	—	0.50	0.81	0.93
1807	1.22	1.20	1.02	—	—	1.11	0.71
1808	0.67	0.60	—	—	—	0.75	0.84
1809	0.79	0.76	—	—	0.75	0.78	1.13
1810	1.08	0.94	1.10	—	0.68	0.91	1.05
1811	1.17	0.92	—	—	0.80	0.94	0.93
1812	0.99	0.91	1.02	—	0.76	0.84	1.55
1813	0.96	1.13	0.86	—	0.81	0.80	—
1814	0.98	1.05	0.78	0.75	0.70	0.87	1.61
1815	1.33	1.05	0.90	—	1.05	1.16	—
1816	1.69	1.70	—	—	0.88	1.40	—
1817	2.68	1.91	—	—	0.75	1.55	1.17
1818	1.18	1.16	—	—	0.75	1.19	0.73
1819	1.12	1.75	—	—	0.98	1.01	0.73
1820	0.70	0.81	0.68	0.90	1.10	0.81	0.77

Sources

See the sources for Table Eg275–284.

Documentation

See the Appendixes to the essay in this chapter for a general discussion of the tables and the sources of the data, along with a key to abbreviations used in this chapter and general information on matters such as regional definitions, calendar differences, money, and weights and measures. See also the text for Table Eg275–284.

These figures are the average wholesale farm prices (producer prices) for corn (Indian corn; maize) in the several regions of Maryland and Virginia. To facilitate comparisons, the prices in both colonies are quoted in pounds (£) Virginia currency. See the text for Table Eg275–284. To compare prices quoted in Virginia currency with prices in other colonies or in England, one can use the exchange rate data in Table Eg315–324.

Corn in the Chesapeake was sold as shelled corn; the barrel of corn was

the equivalent of five bushels. See Arthur G. Peterson, *Historical Study of Prices Received by Producers of Farm Products in Virginia, 1801–1927*, Virginia Agricultural Experiment Station, Technical Bulletin number 37 (Virginia Agricultural Experiment Station, 1929), p. 51: "Throughout the nineteenth century the common practice in Virginia was to sell corn by the barrel of five bushels and this is still practiced by many farmers, especially in the older sections east of the Blue Ridge. In the Shenandoah Valley and west of the Blue Ridge, corn has often been sold as ear corn (husked) in barrels of 105 pounds or the equivalent of one and one half bushels of shelled corn." In almost every state that enacted statutory equivalents, by law the bushel of shelled corn weighed fifty-six pounds. See, for instance, J[ames] L. Nichols, *The Business Guide or Safe Methods of Business* (Nichols, 1912), p. 362. Compare U.S. Department of Commerce, National Bureau of Standards, *Legal Weights (in Pounds) per Bushel of Various Commodities*, Circular of the Bureau of Standards number 10, 1st edition (1905).

TABLE Eg292–298   Wholesale wheat prices in Virginia and Maryland, by region: 1750–1820
[Virginia currency]

Contributed by John J. McCusker

	Virginia					Maryland	
	James River Basin	York River Basin	Rappahannock River Basin	Potomac River Basin	Virginia Piedmont	Western Shore	Eastern Shore
	Eg292	Eg293	Eg294	Eg295	Eg296	Eg297	Eg298
Year	Pounds (£) per bushel	Pounds (£) per bushel	Pounds (£) per bushel	Pounds (£) per bushel	Pounds (£) per bushel	Pounds (£) per bushel	Pounds (£) per bushel
1750	0.19	—	—	—	—	—	—
1751	0.18	—	—	—	—	—	—
1752	0.18	—	—	—	—	—	—
1753	0.22	—	—	—	—	—	—
1754	0.20	—	—	—	—	—	—
1755	0.18	—	—	—	—	—	—
1756	0.16	—	—	—	—	—	—
1757	0.16	—	—	—	—	—	—
1758	0.15	—	—	—	—	—	—
1759	0.20	—	—	—	—	—	—
1760	0.20	—	—	—	—	—	—
1761	0.18	—	—	—	—	—	—
1762	0.23	—	—	—	—	—	—
1763	0.23	—	—	—	—	—	—
1764	0.22	—	—	—	—	—	—
1765	0.22	—	—	—	—	—	—
1766	0.18	—	—	—	—	—	—
1767	0.18	—	—	—	—	—	—
1768	0.22	—	—	—	—	—	—
1769	0.20	—	—	—	—	—	—
1770	0.20	—	—	0.17	0.19	—	—
1771	0.21	—	—	0.18	0.21	—	—
1772	0.21	—	0.15	0.21	0.23	—	—
1773	0.22	—	0.17	0.22	0.26	—	—
1774	0.24	0.24	0.19	0.22	0.24	—	—
1775	0.17	—	0.17	0.19	0.18	—	—
1776	0.16	0.15	0.13	0.14	0.20	—	—
1777	0.29	0.21	0.23	0.21	0.22	0.18	—
1778	0.58	0.41	0.27	0.29	0.26	—	—
1779	0.36	0.29	0.19	0.36	0.21	—	—
1780	0.43	0.23	0.20	0.16	0.26	—	—
1781	0.20	0.26	—	0.26	0.23	0.21	0.24
1782	0.23	0.25	0.20	0.16	0.19	0.25	0.19
1783	—	0.27	—	0.23	0.21	0.25	0.24
1784	—	0.26	0.22	0.26	0.21	0.27	0.29
1785	—	0.30	0.23	0.30	0.23	0.22	0.26
1786	—	0.30	0.30	0.25	0.22	0.25	0.25
1787	0.20	0.26	0.30	0.25	0.20	0.22	0.25
1788	0.23	0.23	0.25	0.26	0.19	0.24	0.22
1789	0.23	0.23	—	0.26	0.26	0.23	0.24
1790	0.25	0.26	0.28	0.32	0.24	0.31	0.30
1791	0.23	0.24	—	0.26	0.20	0.26	0.27
1792	0.26	0.24	0.25	0.20	0.23	0.25	0.28
1793	0.27	0.28	0.38	0.24	0.22	0.29	0.29
1794	0.28	0.24	0.23	0.27	0.27	0.27	0.34
1795	0.45	0.35	0.43	0.44	0.43	0.43	0.45
1796	0.50	0.53	0.50	—	0.50	0.47	0.59
1797	0.35	0.33	0.44	0.40	0.31	0.42	0.42
1798	0.30	0.33	0.43	0.43	0.45	0.39	0.34
1799	0.42	0.45	0.49	0.49	0.45	0.38	0.41
1800	0.47	0.46	—	—	0.45	0.42	0.54
1801	0.50	0.36	0.52	—	0.49	0.38	0.53
1802	0.30	0.29	—	0.34	0.26	0.32	0.32
1803	0.29	0.25	0.40	—	0.35	0.36	0.28
1804	0.37	0.42	0.40	—	—	0.33	0.46
1805	0.46	0.45	0.37	—	0.31	0.42	0.41
1806	0.34	0.36	—	—	0.32	0.34	0.38
1807	0.32	0.30	0.30	—	0.29	0.35	0.28
1808	0.23	0.24	0.25	—	0.22	0.24	0.24
1809	0.31	0.30	0.30	—	0.29	0.29	0.35

(continued)

**TABLE Eg292–298   Wholesale wheat prices in Virginia and Maryland, by region: 1750–1820
[Virginia currency]   *Continued***

	Virginia					Maryland	
	James River Basin	York River Basin	Rappahannock River Basin	Potomac River Basin	Virginia Piedmont	Western Shore	Eastern Shore
	Eg292	Eg293	Eg294	Eg295	Eg296	Eg297	Eg298
Year	Pounds (£) per bushel	Pounds (£) per bushel	Pounds (£) per bushel	Pounds (£) per bushel	Pounds (£) per bushel	Pounds (£) per bushel	Pounds (£) per bushel
1810	0.48	0.30	0.41	—	0.28	0.46	0.49
1811	0.46	0.40	0.40	0.40	0.45	0.50	0.48
1812	0.45	0.45	0.39	0.45	0.41	0.45	0.44
1813	0.54	0.55	0.29	—	0.45	0.27	0.40
1814	0.31	0.23	0.30	0.18	0.22	0.30	0.37
1815	0.46	0.42	0.25	—	0.35	0.32	0.50
1816	0.46	0.48	0.52	—	0.53	0.40	0.74
1817	0.57	0.55	—	—	0.53	0.43	0.69
1818	0.53	0.50	0.48	0.49	0.56	—	—
1819	0.36	0.31	0.43	0.43	0.41	—	—
1820	0.26	0.25	0.25	0.23	0.23	0.22	—

Sources
See the sources for Table Eg275–284.

Documentation
See the Appendixes to the essay in this chapter for a general discussion of the tables and the sources of the data, along with a key to abbreviations used in this chapter and general information on matters such as regional definitions, calendar differences, money, and weights and measures. See also the text for Table Eg275–284.

These figures are the average wholesale farm prices (producer prices) for wheat in several regions of Maryland and Virginia. To facilitate comparisons, the prices in both colonies are quoted in pounds (£) Virginia currency. See the text for Table Eg275–284. To compare prices quoted in Virginia currency with prices in other colonies or in England, one can use the exchange rate data in Table Eg315–324.

The standard bushel of wheat measured fifty-six pounds at Philadelphia. Helen Louise Klopfer, "Statistics of the Foreign Trade of Philadelphia, 1700–1860" (Ph.D. dissertation, University of Pennsylvania, 1936), p. 71. Given

that much Chesapeake wheat was sold through Philadelphia, we can reasonably expect this to have been the weight per bushel in Maryland and Virginia, too, and so it appears to have been, more or less. See John J. McCusker, "The Tonnage of Ships Engaged in British Colonial Trade during the Eighteenth Century," *Research in Economic History* 6 (1981): 73–105, as revised and updated in McCusker, *Essays in the Economic History of the Atlantic World* (Routledge, 1997), pp. 43–75. But see McCusker, "Weights and Measures in the Colonial Sugar Trade: The Gallon and the Pound and Their International Equivalents," *William and Mary Quarterly*, 3rd series, 30 (October 1973), as revised and updated in McCusker (1997), p. 92 n. 24; and Thomas Ringgold, at Chestertown, Maryland, to Samuel Galloway, at West River, Maryland, September 4, 1774, and October 31, 1774, in Galloway Correspondence, XIII, numbers 10247, 10267, Galloway–Maxcy–Markoe Family Papers, Manuscript Division, LC. See also U.S. Department of Commerce, National Bureau of Standards, *Legal Weights (in Pounds) per Bushel of Various Commodities*, Circular of the Bureau of Standards number 10, 1st edition (1905).

TABLE Eg299   Wholesale price of rice in Charleston: 1701–1775   [South Carolina currency]

Contributed by John J. McCusker

| | Price | | | Price | | | Price | | | Price |
| | Eg299 | | | Eg299 | | | Eg299 | | | Eg299 |
Year	Shillings per hundredweight		Year	Shillings per hundredweight		Year	Shillings per hundredweight		Year	Shillings per hundredweight
1701	12.50		1730	40.69		1745	16.04		1765	45.00
1702	17.50		1731	37.23		1746	15.67		1766	56.93
1703	20.00		1732	42.12		1747	33.29		1767	56.04
1704	15.00		1733	40.03		1748	49.06		1768	64.85
1705	15.00		1734	60.51		1749	60.00		1769	60.32
1706	15.00		1735	57.79		1750	63.02		1770	48.44
1707	15.00		1736	50.93		1751	45.71		1771	55.47
1722	30.00		1737	66.90		1752	55.52		1772	81.67
1723	40.56		1738	69.93		1753	66.85		1773	65.83
1724	40.03		1739	43.33		1754	43.38		1774	51.56
1725	37.78		1740	37.46		1755	40.73		1775	50.00
1726	46.00		1741	51.46		1756	34.52			
1727	56.18		1742	44.00		1757	33.75			
1728	46.36		1743	37.21		1758	43.13			
1729	44.69		1744	30.42		1759	65.83			
						1760	51.46			
						1761	38.54			
						1762	33.33			
						1763	45.21			
						1764	43.02			

TABLE Eg299   Wholesale price of rice in Charleston: 1701–1775   [South Carolina currency]   *Continued*

Sources

1701–1707. Daniel Axtell Account Book, 1699–1772, Massachusetts Historical Society, as transcribed in Alexander Moore, editor, "An Edition of Daniel Axtell's Account Book, 1699–1707," pp. 38, 39, 69, 70, 74, 106, 113-4, Manuscript 43/2103, South Carolina Historical Society, Charleston, South Carolina. See also Moore, "Daniel Axtell's Account Book and the Economy of Early South Carolina," *South Carolina Historical Magazine* 95 (October 1994): 280-301.

1722–1731. Peter A. Coclanis, "Rice Prices in the 1720's and the Evolution of the South Carolina Economy," *Journal of Southern History* 48 (November 1982): 531-44.

1732–1775. George Rogers Taylor, "Wholesale Commodity Prices at Charleston, South Carolina, 1732-1861," *Journal of Economic and Business History* 4 (February, August 1932): 356-77, 848-[876], but as published in Arthur Harrison Cole, *Wholesale Commodity Prices in the United States, 1700–1861* (Harvard University Press, 1938), volume 2, pp. 15-69. For some of the months for which Taylor had no data, figures have been supplied from Walter B. Edgar, editor, *The Letterbook of Robert Pringle, 1737–1745* (University of South Carolina Press, 1972); and Philip M. Hamer, George C. Rogers Jr., et al., editors, *The Papers of Henry Laurens* (University of South Carolina Press, 1968 to date)

Documentation

See the Appendixes to the essay in this chapter for a general discussion of the tables and the sources of the data, along with a key to abbreviations used in this chapter and general information on matters such as regional definitions, calendar differences, money, and weights and measures.

The prices presented in the table are the annual average wholesale price for "clean," "merchantable" rice (not "rough" rice) at the Charleston market in terms of shillings South Carolina currency per hundredweight of 100 pounds. To compare prices quoted in South Carolina currency with prices in other colonies or in England, one can use the exchange rate data in Table Eg315–324.

There are three sources for this series. Over the years 1699–1707, Daniel Axtell recorded in his account book (cited earlier) transactions for the sawmill, tannery, tar kiln, and plantation, Newington, that he managed near the town of Dorchester, on the Ashley River some thirty miles from Charleston, South Carolina. They are the prices Axtell set down in his annual summary accounting done in January or February. Note that the depreciation in the value of South Carolina currency across the subsequent two decades – traced with reference to the exchange rate on pounds sterling (Table Eg315–324) – effectively disguises the fact that Axtell sold his rice for much more than what rice sold for in the 1720s. Peter A. Coclanis extracted and compiled prices from early South Carolina probate records for the years 1722–1731. These are estimated farm prices that he argues to have been "probably a bit lower than the wholesale price of rice, perhaps two or three shillings currency per hundredweight" (Coclanis 1982, p. 536 n. 13). The longer series, 1732–1775, is part of the data collected by George Rogers Taylor, largely from the lists of "prices current" printed in colonial newspapers such as *The South-Carolina Gazette* (Charleston). The figures shown here are as published by Cole, because Taylor's presentation of the data in "South Carolina sterling" is flawed. For more about all of this, see Taylor (1932), p. 372; and Cole (1938), volume 2, pp. 15-69. See also John J. McCusker, "The Tonnage of Ships Engaged in British Colonial Trade during the Eighteenth Century," *Research in Economic History* 6 (1981): 73-105, as revised and updated in McCusker, *Essays in the Economic History of the Atlantic World* (Routledge, 1997), pp. 70-5. For South Carolina currency, see also McCusker, *Money and Exchange in Europe and America, 1600–1775: A Handbook*, 2nd edition (University of North Carolina Press, 1992), pp. 220-6; and McCusker, *How Much Is That in Real Money? A Historical Commodity Price Index for Use as a Deflator of Money Values in the Economy of the United States*, 2nd edition (American Antiquarian Society, 2001), pp. 71-88.

A continuing conundrum is the quantity of rice in a barrel because the size of the rice barrel grew larger over time. It is an issue because prices were sometimes quoted per barrel and sometimes per hundredweight; because quantities exported and imported were also stated in terms of barrels, other containers, and hundredweight; and because freight rates were charged per barrel. In the previous edition of *Historical Statistics of the United States* (1975), volume 2, p. 1164, Lawrence A. Harper established a crude but workable set of estimates for the changing size of the South Carolina rice barrel. He determined that, up to 1720, the barrel held on average 350 pounds of rice; across the next decade, it gained in size ten pounds per year; it contained 450 pounds from 1730 through 1740; and over the next fifteen years it increased once again, this time at a rate of five pounds per year until it reached a peak of 525 pounds in 1755. It seems to have maintained roughly this size through until at least 1775.

Not only does more recently discovered evidence support these estimates but almost everyone working in the field has accepted them; they are employed in this table and also in Table Eg1160–1165. Thus, for instance, between 1702 and 1707, Daniel Axtell used barrels that contained, on average, 352 pounds of rice (Moore, editor, "Axtell Account Book," pp. 38, 39, 70, 106, 113-4). Francis Yonge, South Carolina's London agent, used a 400-pound barrel for his estimate of crop size and amount exported in 1719 and 1721 as presented in his letter to the Board of Trade, London, February 5, 1722/23, CO 5/358, folios 272-9, PRO/TNA; see also [Yonge], *A View of the Trade of South-Carolina, with Proposals Humbly Offer'd for Improving the Same* (N.p., 1723), p. 10. Compare letter of Robert Pringle, at Charleston, to Richard Thompson, at Hull, September 2, 1738, in Edgar (1972), volume 1, p. 32: "rice...sold...[in] barrels of about 500 lb. Each"; the export data, implicitly based on a barrel weighing 500 pounds, in Governor James Glen's report on South Carolina enclosed in his letter to the Board of Trade, Charleston, May 31, 1749, CO 5/461, folio 45v, PRO/TNA; and the average barrel of rice as exported from Charleston in 1767–1771 weighing 527 pounds (Ledger of Imports and Exports, British North America, 1768–1772, pp. 54, 142, 198, 201, CUST 16/1, PRO/TNA). See also the evidence that the barrel of rice weighed 333 pounds during the decade 1720-1729, 400 pounds during the decade 1730-1739, and 475 pounds during the decade 1740-1749, in [James Glen], *A Description of South Carolina; Containing, Many Curious and Interesting Particulars Relating to the Civil, Natural and Commercial History of That Colony, viz. The Succession of European Settlers There; . . . The Nature of the Climate; . . . The Culture and Produce of Rice, Indian Corn, and Indigo; . . . The State of Their Maritime Trade in the Years 1710, 1723, 1740 and 1748, with the Number or Tonnage of Shipping employed . . . To Which is Added, A Very Particular Account of Their Rice-Trade for Twenty Years, with Their Exports of Raw Silk and Imports of British Silk Manufactures for Twenty-Five Years* (Dodsley, 1761), p. 88. The weight of the rice barrel seems to have begun growing again after the American Revolution. Witness the account of the exports from Charleston for 1785 that identified the average weight of the 63,713 barrels of rice exported as 570 pounds net, as printed in *The Pennsylvania Packet, and Daily Advertiser* (Philadelphia), March 20, 1786; and the statement that, for the years 1792–1796, "Tierces of [rice weighed] 600 lbs." in François-Alexandre-Frédéric La Rochefoucauld-Liancourt, *Travels through the United States of North America, the Country of the Iroquois, and Upper Canada, in the Years 1795, 1796, and 1797; With an Authentic Account of Lower Canada*, translated by H[enry] Neuman (Phillips, 1799), volume 2, p. 589.

Most economic historians of the rice trade have adopted Harper's schema. See Converse Dilworth Clowse, "The Charleston Export Trade 1717–1737" (Ph.D. dissertation, Northwestern University, 1963), pp. 27-8, 188–90; Clowse, *Measuring Charleston's Overseas Commerce, 1717–1767: Statistics from the Port's Naval Lists* (University Press of America, 1981), pp. 57-8. The most recent study of the subject tests Harper's proposition against a wide range of contemporary observations and finds it quite satisfactory, even if, perhaps, a slight understatement of the actual capacity. See Stephen G. Hardy, "Colonial South Carolina's Rice Industry and the Atlantic Economy: Patterns of Trade, Shipping, and Growth," in Jack P. Greene, Rosemary Brana-Shute, and Randy J. Sparks, editors, *Money, Trade, and Power: The Evolution of Colonial South Carolina's Plantation Society* (University of South Carolina Press, 2001), pp. 121-3, 143-4.

In similar ways and for similar reasons, tobacco casks and sugar casks also increased in size over the seventeenth and eighteenth centuries. For Virginia and Maryland tobacco hogsheads, see Lorena S. Walsh's data presented in the text for Table Eg275–284. For sugar casks, see John J. McCusker, *Rum and the American Revolution: The Rum Trade and the Balance of Payments of the Thirteen*

(continued)

TABLE Eg299   Wholesale price of rice in Charleston: 1701–1775   [South Carolina currency]   *Continued*

Continental Colonies, 1650–1775 (Garland, 1989), volume 2, pp. 768–878. See also the situation at Philadelphia as explored in Helen Louise Klopfer, "Statistics of the Foreign Trade of Philadelphia, 1700-1860" (Ph.D. dissertation, University of Pennsylvania, 1936). Note that rice was bought and sold at Philadelphia by the long hundredweight of 112 pounds.

Other, miscellaneous containers used in the sale and shipment of rice at South Carolina have been converted to barrels. The term "cask" has been considered synonymous with "barrel," following the usage in the Ledger of Imports and Exports, British North America, 1768-1772, p. 54, CUST 16/1, PRO/TNA. The remaining equivalents are rough approximations suggested by the weights of other commodities as given in Malachy Postlethwayt, *The Universal Dictionary of Trade and Commerce*, 4th edition (W. Strahan et al., 1774); J[ohn] H. Alexander, *Universal Dictionary of Weights and Measures, Ancient and Modern; Reduced to the Standards of the United States of America* (Minifie, 1850); and James A. H. Murray, R. W. Burchfield, et al., editors, *The Oxford English Dictionary: Being a Corrected Re-Issue . . . of A New English Dictionary on Historical Principles* (Oxford University Press, 1933). See George K. Holmes, *Rice Crop of the United States, 1712–1911*, U.S. Department of Agriculture, Bureau of Statistics, Circular number 34 (1912), p. 4. A tierce has been considered to equal $1\frac{1}{3}$ barrels; a hogshead, 2 barrels; a puncheon, $2\frac{2}{3}$ barrels; a butt, 4 barrels; half-barrels, small barrels, and small casks, $\frac{1}{2}$ of a barrel; seroons, boxes, and bags, $\frac{2}{5}$ of a barrel; kegs, $\frac{1}{5}$ of a barrel; and bushels, $\frac{1}{8}$ of a barrel. These random and extremely infrequently used colonial containers varied so greatly in size that these estimates can be considered only the crudest

of approximations. Moreover, container sizes varied by commodity and the relationships employed here may not apply in other trades. For present purposes, these maverick units constitute such a negligible part of the whole that errors in estimating their weight seem unlikely to exceed differences resulting from rounding.

The project that studied Charleston prices was one of many sponsored by the International Scientific Committee in Price History. See Arthur H. Cole and Ruth Crandall, "The International Scientific Committee on Price History," *Journal of Economic History* 24 (September 1964): 381–8. The results of several of those studies were drawn together in Cole (1938). Like Taylor's, others of the original studies continued their coverage beyond the colonial period, most notably the Philadelphia project and the New York project. The Philadelphia studies form the basis of price data presented in Table Eg251–270. See G[eorge] F. Warren, F[rank] A. Pearson, and Herman M. Stoker, *Wholesale Prices for 213 Years, 1720 to 1932*, Cornell University, Agricultural Experiment Station, Memoir number 412 (Cornell University, 1932). There are important archival collections associated with these studies, each containing a great deal of additional material: Records of the International Scientific Committee on Price History, 1928-1939, Manuscript and Archives Division, Baker Library, Graduate School of Business Administration, Harvard University; the Frank Ashmore Pearson Papers, Albert R. Mann Library, Cornell University; and the "Industrial Research Department – Wholesale Prices" Collection, Wharton School of Finance and Commerce, University of Pennsylvania.

TABLE Eg300–301   Price of slaves in the Western Hemisphere: 1673–1807

Contributed by John J. McCusker

	Mean	Standard deviation
	Eg300	Eg301
Year(s)	Pounds (£) sterling	Pounds (£) sterling
1673–1674	23.57	0.84
1675–1688	20.85	3.58
1689–1713	31.25	7.68
1714–1738	28.27	7.27
1739–1748	30.42	8.18
1749–1753	32.45	8.56
1754–1763	33.61	7.08
1764–1774	44.40	7.95
1775–1783	44.43	7.83
1784–1792	60.58	13.16
1793–1807	72.33	14.35

Sources

Originally compiled by David Eltis and David Richardson from a subset of the same data that they used in their large-scale collective effort done under the sponsorship of the W. E. B. Du Bois Institute for African and African American Research at Harvard University and that they published as David Eltis, Stephen D. Behrendt, et al., compilers, *The Trans-Atlantic Slave Trade: A Database on CD-ROM* (Cambridge University Press, 1999). See also David Eltis and [Peter] David Richardson, "Prices of African Slaves Newly Arrived in the Americas, 1673-1865: New Evidence on Long-Run Trends and Regional Differentials," in *Slavery in the Development of the Americas*, edited by David Eltis, Frank D. Lewis, and Kenneth L. Sokoloff (Cambridge University Press, 2004), pp. 181–218.

Documentation

See the Appendixes to the essay in this chapter for a general discussion of the tables and the sources of the data, along with a key to abbreviations used in this chapter and general information on matters such as regional definitions, calendar differences, money, and weights and measures.

This table presents the average price in pounds (£) sterling of a nominal "prime field hand" at Jamaica. To derive a series that adequately presents

estimates of the prices paid for enslaved African Americans is an exercise fraught with significant problems, many more than the usual issues encountered in establishing an historical price series. Difficult as it is to establish a consistent series for the price of sugar or tobacco, it is much harder to collect and compile the price of "a slave." The issues are obvious: consistency of "commodity" (people came in all kinds, places of origin, ages, conditions, etc.); place of sale (enslaved individuals were traded in every colony of the Americas); units of measure (people were bought and sold singly and in various multiples, for example, the "*pieza de Indias*"); terms and conditions of sale (deals were done for cash or for credit, for money, and for goods); and currency (each colony had its own money of account and some traders preferred to use the money of account of the metropolis for negotiations of this kind; all used a variety of real moneys). Eltis and Richardson attempted to deal with these issues as best they could by taking each of them into account in ways that are significantly more sensitive to all of these nuances than previous studies – including most especially the one drawn on for *Historical Statistics of the United States* (1975), volume 2, p. 1174 (series Z 165–168). They adjusted and corrected all of the transactions to a uniform standard: the cash price in pounds sterling at Jamaica of a young adult male slave in

TABLE Eg300-301   Price of slaves in the Western Hemisphere: 1673-1807   *Continued*

good health newly arrived from Africa. The result was a price series showing 1,030 separate average prices from the sale of an estimated 240,000 slaves listed by year over 134 years, nearly eight average prices per year, each sale involving on average about 230 slaves. To compare prices quoted in pounds sterling with prices in the other colonies, one can use the exchange rate data in Table Eg315-324.

The data derive from the records of voyages of vessels that carried slaves to the mainland and island British, Dutch, and French colonies (there were also a few records of deliveries to mainland Spanish colonies). Roughly two thirds of the voyages were British. The largest delivery point for enslaved Africans in the British colonies between 1673 and 1807 was Jamaica. Fitting prices generated elsewhere to a standard price for prime-age male slaves at Jamaica required converting credit prices to cash prices; adjusting prices for mixed groups of slaves to prime-age male equivalent; and equating slave prices from other markets to their sterling value at Jamaica. The methods of adjustment are set out in Eltis and Richardson (2004). Reducing values in various currencies depended on exchange rate data from John J. McCusker, *Money and Exchange in Europe and America, 1600–1775: A Handbook*, 2nd edition (University of North Carolina Press, 1992). As presented in the table, the compiled data are grouped into seven periods that distinguish between times of peace and times of war. Prices generally are thought to have been heavily influenced by the successive phases of the Second Hundred Years' War between Great Britain and France. See in this regard John J. McCusker, *How Much Is That in Real Money? A Historical Commodity Price Index for Use as a Deflator of Money Values in the Economy of the United States*, 2nd edition (American Antiquarian Society, 2001), pp. 33–5 n. 35. Compare J[ohn] R. Ward, *British West Indian Slavery, 1750–1834: The Process of Amelioration* (Clarendon Press, 1988), p. 210.

For a series of prices for "a fine man slave" on the African coast at the Danish fort of Christiansborg, see Per O. Hernæs, *Slaves, Danes, and the African Coast Society: The Danish Slave Trade from West Africa and Afro-Danish Relations on the Eighteenth-Century Gold Coast*, Trondheim Studies in History number 6 (Department of History, University of Trondheim, Norway, 1995), pp. 318–20, 391–3. Compare [Peter] David Richardson, "Prices of Slaves in West and West-Central Africa: Toward an Annual Series, 1698-1807," *Bulletin of Economic Research* 43 (1) (1991): 21–56.

Note that the data presented here avoid the one major failing of many alternative series. These prices were generated by actual market transactions. They are not estimated valuations of slaves done for purposes of settling a decedent's estate. Although probate estimates can be assumed to have had some passing relationship to the market price and a series derived from them serves many good purposes – such as tracking change over time and allowing for the differentiation among the many variables set out previously – they were not meant to be and cannot be conceived of as market prices. Of course, any valid tracking of change over time presumes that the valuations are for comparable slaves, a requirement rarely met in such series. Rendered completely useless by these failings are series based on valuations (not prices) published in such efforts as Peter C. Mancall, Joshua L. Rosenbloom, and Thomas Weiss, "Slave Prices and the South Carolina Economy, 1722-1809," *Journal of Economic History* 51 (September 2001): 616–39.

As an illustration of many of the issues raised previously – especially the problem with estimated probate valuations – see the "Inventory & Valuation" of the estate on the island of Grenada owned by Alexander Johnstone, dated December 1, 1770, item 41/32, Records of the Westerhall Estate, West Indian Documents, University Library, University of Bristol. The values were stated in Grenada currency, which was then exchanged at the rate of £160 currency per £100 sterling. Included in the list were 266 slaves:

3 drivers	2 at £200, 1 at £150
5 coopers	3 at £150, 2 £100
3 carpenters	at £150
3 masons	at £150

2 boilers	at £150
82 field men	at £85
62 field women	at £75
20 field boys	at £55
15 field girls	at £50
31 children	at £30
8 servants	at £80
6 cattle keepers and sick nurses	at £63 6s 8d
16 infirm and superannuated	at £10
10 "new negroes"	at £37 sterling, a total of £370 sterling, which, with the exchange at £160, equals £592
266 slaves in total	£18,572 in total

Clearly in evidence is the large difference between the cost of the newly landed African and the estimated value of the prime field hand, the latter worth well in excess of the former (£85 versus £59). Also see the range of prices for slaves in Rio de Janeiro in 1775 compiled by Dauril Alden, *Royal Government in Colonial Brazil: With Special Reference to the Administration of the Marquis of Lavradio, Viceroy, 1769–1779* (University of California Press, 1968), pp. 510-1.

The standard deviations from the mean of the averages generated for each of the seven periods are also listed in the table. The standard deviation is a measure of the variation from the mean value in any set of data. The standard deviations reported – large and growing over time – tell us that the means here compiled by period contain an increasingly large variance, that the central tendencies indicated by the successive mean fell within an increasingly large range. Nevertheless, even though the Eltis–Richardson series is far from meeting the qualitative standards that apply to all other series offered in this chapter, they will have to do for the moment. They are thought to serve reasonably well as an indicator of the "market price" in the non Hispanic parts of the New World, with the caveat that, for any given slave, on any given day, in any given colony, there will have been some variation around that market price. They provide a crude basis for many purposes and offer a benchmark against which others may measure their own progress as they develop other, better series.

As a guide to what a better series might look like – with the luxury of more and better data – see Lawrence J. Kotlikoff, "Quantitative Description of the New Orleans Market, 1804 to 1862," in Robert William Fogel and Stanley L. Engerman, editors, *Without Consent or Contract: The Rise and Fall of American Slavery . . . Technical Papers* (Norton, 1992), volume 1, pp. 31–53. Kotlikoff addresses many of the same questions that Eltis and Richardson deal with but is better able to answer them.

Although what Eltis and Richardson have accomplished easily supersedes earlier "global" efforts, there are some particular compilations that supplement what they have done. One is especially notable. Even though using much the same data as Eltis and Richardson (albeit adjusted by them, as earlier), the chapter "Slave Prices in the Barbados Market, 1673-1723," in David W. Galenson, *Traders, Planters, and Slaves: Market Behavior in Early British America* (Cambridge University Press, 1986), pp. 53–69, compiles data, estimates prices, and explores the subject in much more complex ways to considerably greater depth – and, obviously, sets the stage on a different Caribbean island. Eltis and Richardson used methods suggested by the Galenson study to convert cash prices for mixed groups of slaves into prime-age male equivalent prices.

There is a good, contemporary definition of the *pieza de Indias* in I[rene] A. Wright, "The Coymans Asiento (1685-1689)," *Bijdragen voor Vaderlandsche Geschiedenis en Oudheidkunde*, 6th series, 1 (1 and 2) (1924): 50 n. 1. This unit of measure was widely used outside of the Spanish colonies, and it varied in practice, of course. See also Waldemar [C.] Westergaard, *The Danish West Indies under Company Rule (1671–1754), with a Supplementary Chapter, 1755–1917* (Macmillan, 1917), p. 149.

FINANCE

John J. McCusker

TABLE Eg302–314   Paper money in circulation, by colony: 1703–1775[1]   [Local colonial currencies]

Contributed by John J. McCusker

	Massachusetts	Connecticut	New Hampshire	Rhode Island	New York	Pennsylvania	New Jersey	Maryland	Delaware	Virginia	North Carolina	South Carolina	Georgia
	Eg302	Eg303	Eg304	Eg305	Eg306	Eg307	Eg308	Eg309	Eg310	Eg311	Eg312	Eg313	Eg314
Year	Thousand pounds (£)	Thousand pounds (£)	Thousand pounds (£)	Thousand pounds (£)	Thousand pounds (£)	Thousand pounds (£)	Thousand pounds (£)	Thousand pounds (£)	Thousand pounds (£)	Thousand pounds (£)	Thousand pounds (£)	Thousand pounds (£)	Thousand pounds (£)
1703	6.4	—	—	—	—	—	—	—	—	—	—	—	—
1704	17.7	—	—	—	—	—	—	—	—	—	—	—	—
1705	29.5	—	—	—	—	—	—	—	—	—	—	—	—
1706	31.1	—	—	—	—	—	—	—	—	—	—	—	—
1707	40.8	—	—	—	—	—	—	—	—	—	—	—	—
1708	57.0	—	—	—	—	—	—	—	—	—	—	—	—
1709	66.4	—	3.0	—	13.0	—	—	—	—	—	—	—	—
1710	86.6	13.7	5.5	7.0	10.0	—	—	—	—	—	—	—	—
1711	103.4	18.7	7.5	13.3	—	—	—	—	—	—	—	—	—
1712	169.0	23.6	8.0	13.3	—	—	—	—	—	—	—	—	—
1713	174.0	24.2	8.0	13.3	—	—	—	—	—	—	—	—	—
1714	152.1	22.9	9.2	12.2	27.7	—	—	—	—	—	—	—	—
1715	171.8	22.5	8.3	51.9	6.0	—	—	—	—	—	—	—	—
1716	157.1	23.7	8.3	51.9	—	—	—	—	—	—	—	—	—
1717	231.9	20.4	8.3	50.2	16.6	—	—	—	—	—	—	—	—
1718	217.5	20.1	22.4	48.8	—	—	—	—	—	—	—	—	—
1719	200.7	19.8	22.3	47.7	—	—	—	—	—	—	—	—	—
1720	189.9	17.8	22.3	46.8	2.0	—	—	—	—	—	—	—	—
1721	182.2	17.5	21.4	86.5	—	—	—	—	—	—	—	—	—
1722	235.1	17.5	25.0	85.9	—	—	—	—	—	—	—	—	—
1723	260.1	16.8	24.6	85.2	2.1	15.0	—	—	11.0	—	—	—	—
1724	290.0	14.7	26.3	84.7	9.6	44.9	40.0	—	—	—	—	—	—
1725	325.2	12.2	24.6	84.4	—	38.9	35.9	—	—	—	—	—	—
1726	358.1	8.0	27.6	84.2	3.0	38.9	30.9	—	—	—	—	—	—
1727	338.7	10.3	28.4	82.4	—	38.9	27.8	—	8.3	—	—	—	—
1728	356.4	9.2	27.4	129.4	—	38.9	23.8	—	—	—	—	—	—
1729	344.4	6.7	27.3	128.9	—	68.9	20.7	—	—	—	—	—	—
1730	335.3	4.4	27.2	128.1	4.8	68.9	17.6	—	—	—	—	—	—
1731	327.8	4.7	27.2	186.1	—	68.9	14.6	—	—	—	—	—	—
1732	310.5	2.6	26.2	192.7	—	68.9	11.5	—	—	—	—	—	—
1733	290.6	52.0	25.2	292.2	—	68.9	28.5	—	—	—	—	—	—
1734	462.6	52.5	24.8	289.7	12.0	68.9	25.4	—	20.3	—	—	—	—
1735	449.1	52.8	22.8	287.6	—	68.9	22.7	56.5	—	—	—	—	—
1736	469.2	51.2	21.8	285.0	—	68.9	20.0	57.9	—	—	—	—	—
1737	437.0	55.7	27.3	281.0	48.4	68.9	60.0	69.9	—	—	—	—	—
1738	452.8	54.2	25.0	281.0	—	68.9	60.0	74.8 [2]	—	—	—	—	—
1739	442.2	50.9	23.0	376.2	10.0	80.0	60.0	79.8	17.3	—	—	—	—

Year	Massachusetts Eg302 Thousand pounds (£)	Connecticut Eg303 Thousand pounds (£)	New Hampshire Eg304 Thousand pounds (£)	Rhode Island Eg305 Thousand pounds (£)	New York Eg306 Thousand pounds (£)	Pennsylvania Eg307 Thousand pounds (£)	New Jersey Eg308 Thousand pounds (£)	Maryland Eg309 Thousand pounds (£)	Delaware Eg310 Thousand pounds (£)	Virginia Eg311 Thousand pounds (£)	North Carolina Eg312 Thousand pounds (£)	South Carolina Eg313 Thousand pounds (£)	Georgia Eg314 Thousand pounds (£)
1740	370.4	168.1	23.7	370.0	—	80.0	62.0	78.5	—	—	—	—	—
1741	403.9	153.1	23.7	466.1	—	80.0	61.0	83.4	—	—	—	—	—
1742	427.1	149.5	38.8	455.4	—	80.0	57.5	82.1	—	—	—	—	—
1743	491.6	146.4	43.9	454.8	—	80.0	55.0	82.2 [2]	—	—	—	—	—
1744	456.4	204.4	142.3	609.1	—	80.0	52.5	82.3	—	—	—	—	—
1745	818.1	322.6	250.3	642.3	53.0	80.0	50.0	83.1	—	—	—	—	—
1746	1,581.9	511.9	488.9	684.3	189.5	85.0	57.4	84.2 [2]	20.0	—	—	—	—
1747	2,142.7	507.9	480.4	723.1	172.0	85.0	50.9	85.3	—	—	—	—	—
1748	2,323.2	500.1	475.5	736.0	163.0	85.0	43.4	86.0	—	—	21.4	—	—
1749	2,456.7	480.9	475.5	620.6	—	85.0	37.9	—	—	—	21.2	—	—
1750	2,442.4	476.7	475.5	579.9	153.9	84.5	32.9	—	—	—	20.6	—	—
1751	187.5	379.8	475.5	795.8	148.2	84.0	27.9	—	—	—	20.1	—	—
1752	46.0	—	—	605.1	141.0	83.5	22.9	—	—	—	19.0	—	—
1753	22.1	—	—	577.1	132.5	82.5	15.3	—	3.0	—	18.3	152.3	—
1754	17.5	—	—	559.1	126.1	81.5	13.8	—	—	—	58.0	156.2	—
1755	48.9	62.0	30.0	765.1	179.1	96.0	52.2	—	—	60.0	56.1	221.4	3.0
1756	156.0	—	52.6	937.1	230.8	147.5	58.2	—	2.0	100.0	58.0	311.8	3.0
1757	226.0	—	—	714.9	219.3	247.0	106.7	—	—	180.0	68.3	542.8	0.6
1758	212.5	30.0	45.0	782.6	307.2	312.9	155.2	—	12.0	261.5	70.3	595.6	—
1759	285.0	70.0	55.8	950.6	481.2	422.9	193.6	—	27.0	308.8	69.5	521.4	0.8
1760	451.5	70.0	—	1,421.6	410.4	446.2	222.1	—	4.0	325.0	75.8	863.8	—
1761	505.3	45.0	9.0	1,398.6	366.2	409.0	233.1	—	—	303.4	95.3	867.7	4.0
1762	481.3	65.0	13.0	1,680.1	330.8	320.7	246.5	96.0	—	291.1	85.3	726.3	7.4
1763	490.2	10.0	15.0	1,244.7 [2]	287.2	264.5	240.0	62.0	—	238.4 [2]	85.0	584.9	—
1764	387.0	7.0	20.0	809.3	243.9	316.1	252.5	41.3	—	219.5 [2]	75.0	585.2	8.2
1765	336.4	85.0	10.0	—	166.5	305.1	240.0	—	—	216.6 [2]	75.0	472.4	0.7
1766	261.0	—	—	—	134.0	281.4	227.5	—	—	213.8	68.0	446.7	1.8
1767	211.0	—	33.2	—	109.8	258.4	215.0	173.7	—	170.4	68.0	344.1	—
1768	164.9	—	—	—	87.3	233.9	202.5	173.7	—	151.4	98.0	482.0	6.4
1769	129.7	—	—	—	82.8	220.9	190.0	173.7	—	129.9	—	497.7	2.2
1770	100.3	10.0	—	—	81.6	201.2	177.5	491.7	—	125.4	75.0	424.2	3.4
1771	85.9	12.0	—	—	198.5	171.9	165.0	491.7	—	135.3 [2]	60.0	413.2 [2]	—
1772	76.3	—	—	—	194.4	149.1	152.5	491.7	—	98.3	—	402.3 [2]	—
1773	77.2	12.0	—	—	190.4	135.0	140.0	491.7	—	70.7	—	391.4	11.0
1774	56.2	—	—	—	187.7	217.6	125.0	971.7	—	43.4	—	259.0	—
1775	129.8	162.0	40.1	60.0	235.2	318.6	110.0	1,773.5	—	420.0	125.0	1,379.0	10.0

[1] Figures are expressed in the currency of the relevant colony. Colonial currencies differed in value among the colonies and changed in value over time. See Appendix A in the essay to the chapter.

[2] Interpolated value.

Sources

These estimates are derived from Leslie Van Horn Brock, "The Currency of the American Colonies, 1700–1764: A Study in Colonial Finance and Imperial Relations" (Ph.D. dissertation, University of Michigan, 1941). Reference is also made to Eric P. Newman, *The Early Paper Money of America: An Illustrated, Historical and Descriptive Compilation of Data Relating to American Paper Currency from Its Inception in 1686 to the Year 1800 . . .*, 3rd edition, expanded (Krause Publications, 1990).

Documentation

See the Appendixes to the essay in this chapter for a general discussion of the tables and the sources of the data, along with a key to abbreviations used in this chapter and general information on matters such as regional definitions, calendar differences, money, and weights and measures.

These series offer estimates of the amount of paper money in circulation near the end of each year – unless otherwise indicated – in terms of the money of account of that colony in use at the end of that year (with some exceptions, as noted in this discussion). To compare amounts quoted in one colonial currency with amounts in other colonies or in England, one can use the exchange rate data in Table Eg315-324.

(continued)

TABLE Eg302–314   Paper money in circulation, by colony: 1703–1775   [Local colonial currencies]   *Continued*

The estimates are based on the Ph.D. dissertation of Leslie Van Horn Brock (1903–1985), completed in 1941 and later reprinted virtually unchanged as *The Currency of the American Colonies, 1700–1764: A Study in Colonial Finance and Imperial Relations* (Arno, 1975). It is immensely important to appreciate that this work was originally researched and composed in the late 1930s and that everything written on the subject after its completion needs otherwise to be taken into account. The reprinted version of Brock's dissertation included both an introductory preface and an appendix that revised a few of the tables to a minor extent but in no way adequately addressed the literature on the subject published since 1940. Moreover, the 1975 version omitted some pages of the original dissertation (Brock did not number the pages on which his tables appeared in the dissertation; as a consequence some were not reproduced in the reprinted version), and there are other differences in pagination. Some added material can be found in a posthumously published article, edited by Ronald W. Michener: Brock, "The Colonial Currency, Prices, and Exchange Rates," *Essays in History* 34 (1992): 70–132, which is available at the Internet site of the Electronic Text Center at the University of Virginia Library. Some of Michener's editorial interventions are less acceptable than others, especially when they change Brock's data (rather than simply correcting a mistake in copying from a source) or alter his interpretations, somehow "knowing [what] Brock would have used" or what he meant to say (p. 74). Mention should also be made of the extensive collection of notes to and copies of original source materials in the Papers of Leslie Van Horn Brock, 1600–1986, University of Virginia Library.

Underlying data are detailed in the source, but, unfortunately, Brock's citations to his sources are frequently not full, specific, or adequate. In a few instances, his transcriptions were not completely accurate. As editor of Brock's posthumously published article, Michener corrected some of Brock's errors in transcription; others remain, largely because, as Michener notes, it has proven almost impossible to check and verify some of Brock's citations to his sources. Thus, his data need to be treated with some care. Despite all these cautions, his work is monumental and the starting point not only for this table but also for any subsequent studies of the subject.

Another source used for this table is the equally impressive and substantial book by Eric P. Newman (1990). It is much to be lamented that Newman chose to indicate his sources only in the crudest fashion, making it impossible to trace whence comes much of his information.

These estimates presented here replace those in *Historical Statistics of the United States* (1975), volume 2, pp. 1199–200 (series Z587–598 and Z599–610), which were based on B[enjamin] U. Ratchford, *American State Debts* (Duke University Press, 1941), as discussed on pp. 9–29 and summarized in his Tables 1 and 2 (pp. 26–8). Ratchford's discussion of government debt is still useful.

The subject of the size – and, therefore, the adequacy (at least quantitatively) – of the money supply of the Thirteen Continental Colonies is of considerable importance to our understanding of the colonial economy and has occasioned significant discussion and debate among economists and historians. There were several components to the total money supply. The real money that the colonists used consisted of the following: paper currency; gold, silver and, copper coin; commodity money and commodity notes; circulating financial instruments (such as bills of exchange); and bookkeeping barter arrangements organized through local merchants (that had something of the character of modern credit card accounts, though usually without interest charges against outstanding balances). See W[illiam] T. Baxter, *The House of Hancock: Business in Boston, 1724–1775*, Harvard Studies in British History, volume 10 (Harvard University Press, 1945), pp. 11–38 and elsewhere, as well as John J. McCusker, "Colonial Paper Money," in Eric P. Newman and Richard G. Doty, editors, *Studies on Money in Early America* (American Numismatic Society, 1976), pp. 94–104.

Although attempts to estimate the full extent of all of these have yet to be undertaken, one key component that can be grasped a bit more firmly is the subject of this table: paper money or, more precisely, the welter of bills and notes issued in the several colonies. Like commodities and coin, however, colonial paper currencies circulated outside the borders of the issuing colonies. The subject is, then, not the size of each individual colony's paper money supply but the money supply of the Thirteen Continental Colonies in toto.

To the extent that his sources allowed him to do so, Brock estimated, year by year, the amounts of every currency issue that was in circulation – or, at least, had not officially been withdrawn from circulation by the issuing authority. Sometimes he was able to compile his data into tables; sometimes the data reside only in his text and footnotes. Moreover, he twice revised at least some of his estimates, once when his dissertation was published (1975), and once for the article published posthumously (1992). His work was more thorough for the period up to the early 1750s, as his title suggests; although there is some information in his dissertation on the period from the early 1760s to 1775, it is much less complete. The series presented here rely on Newman to fill some of that gap and Newman states only how much each colony issued in any given year and not how much was in circulation, although it is possible to use his information to derive reasonable inferences. The amount issued in any given year can be assumed to provide a lower-bound estimate of what was outstanding at the end of any year. Note that these series omit years for which we have no data. Nevertheless, it would be wrong to infer that the paper money supply dropped to zero in years for which there is no estimate given. In one or two instances, to underscore this point, estimates have been inserted into this table based on straight-line interpolations. Much more needs to be done to fill in the remaining gaps before we can say we have more than just a preliminary understanding of the nature and size of the colonial paper money supply.

As this table makes clear, each colony had its own currency, its own money of account. Over time, individual colonies changed from one currency to another, most notoriously in the instance of Massachusetts which went from "Old Tenor" to "Lawful Money" as of March 30, 1750 (at a ratio of 7.5:1). Given that each colony's money of account was of different value, to make comparisons possible, they must all be reduced to some common denominator. A convenient common point of reference is the currency equivalent in British pounds sterling, the reduction accomplished using exchange rates such as those in Table Eg315–324. For more on this subject, see John J. McCusker, *Money and Exchange in Europe and America, 1600–1775: A Handbook*, 2nd edition (University of North Carolina Press, 1992).

For a discussion of these issues and an argument that the colonial money supply was in fact adequate quantitatively and qualitatively, see John J. McCusker and Russell R. Menard, *The Economy of British America, 1607–1789*, 2nd edition (University of North Carolina Press, 1991), pp. 337–41, 356.

During the 1980s and 1990s, a vigorous debate raged among economists over whether the experiences of the colonists undermined or supported the quantity theory of money. Central to that debate was the size and components of the money supply and the relationship between any changes in that supply and changing levels of prices. A sample of the arguments can be found in the writings of Robert Craig West, Bruce Smith, Elmus Wicker, and Charles W. Calomiris, who adduced evidence denying the relevance of the quantity theory; on the other side of the debate are scholars such as Ronald W. Michener, Michael D. Bordo, Ivan A. Marcotte, and Bennett T. McCallum. Before the impact of changes in the quantity of money can be reasonably argued, we will need to establish the quantity of money as it changed over time. The perfection of the series in this table will be a good first step in that direction. See West, "Money in the Colonial American Economy," *Economic Inquiry* 16 (January 1978): 1–15; Smith, "Money and Inflation in Colonial Massachusetts," *Federal Reserve Bank of Minnesota Quarterly Review* 8 (Summer 1984): 1–14; Smith, "American Colonial Monetary Regimes: The Failure of the Quantity Theory and Some Evidence in Favour of an Alternative View," *Canadian Journal of Economics/Revue canadienne d'économique* 18 (August 1985): 531–65; Smith, "Some Colonial Evidence on Two Theories of Money: Maryland and the Carolinas," *Quarterly Journal of Economics*, 93 (January 1985): 1178–211; Smith, *Money and Inflation in the American Colonies: Further Evidence on the Failure of the Quantity Theory*, University of Western Ontario, Centre for the Study of International Economic Relations, Working Paper number 8715C (1987); Smith, "The Relationship between Money and Prices: Some Historical Evidence Reconsidered," *Federal Reserve Bank of Minnesota Quarterly Review* 12 (Summer 1988): 18–32; Calomiris, "Institutional Failure, Monetary Scarcity, and the Depreciation of the Continental," *Journal of Economic History* 48 (March 1988): 47–68; Wicker, "Colonial Monetary Standards Contrasts: Evidence from the Seven Years' War," *Journal of Economic History* 45 (December 1985): 869–84; Michener, "Fixed Exchange Rates and the

TABLE Eg302–314   Paper money in circulation, by colony: 1703–1775   [Local colonial currencies]   *Continued*

Quantity Theory in Colonial America," *Carnegie–Rochester Conference Series on Public Policy* 27 (1987): 233–307; Michener, "Backing Theories and the Currencies of Eighteenth-Century America: A Comment," *Journal of Economic History* 48 (September 1988): 682–92; Bordo and Marcotte, "Purchasing Power Parity in Colonial America: Some Evidence for South Carolina, 1732–1774," *Carnegie–Rochester Conference Series on Public Policy*, 27 (1987): 311–24; Marcotte, "Colonial South Carolina: A Quantity Theoretic Perspective" (Ph.D. dissertation, University of South Carolina, 1989); and McCallum, "Money and Prices in Colonial America: A New Test of Competing Theories," *Journal of Political Economy* 100 (February 1992): 143–61. See also William Letwin, "Monetary Practice and Theory of the North American Colonies during the 17th and 18th Centuries," in Vera Barbagli Bagnoli, editor, *La Moneta nell'Economia Europea, Secoli XIII–XVIII*, Istituto Internazionale di Storia Economica "F. Datini," Pubblicazioni, Serie 2: Atti delle Settimane di Studi e Altri Convegni, volume 7 (Le Monnier, 1981), pp. 439–69; and Edwin J. Perkins, "Conflicting Views on Fiat Currency: Britain and Its North American Colonies in the Eighteenth Century," *Business History* 33 (July 1991): 8–30.

Series Eg302, Massachusetts. Omits the bills issued before 1702. The annual figures specify the amount in circulation at the end of each May. They are in Old Tenor terms through 1750 and in Massachusetts Lawful Money thereafter. The figures for 1734–1743 include Boston merchants' notes; the figures for 1750 and 1751 include Massachusetts treasurer's certificates. See Brock (1941), pp. 17–36, 53–4, 244–91; Brock (1975), pp. 591–[7]; and Brock (1992), pp. 106–7. See also Newman, *Early Paper Money of America*, pp. 157–83. The sum for 1775 includes the amount issued that year.

Series Eg303, Connecticut. See Brock (1941), pp. 43–9, 50–2, 306–24; Brock (1975), pp. 591–3, 598; Brock (1992), pp. 106–7; and Newman, *Early Paper Money of America*, pp. 65–87. Connecticut officially shifted from Old Tenor to Connecticut Lawful Money as of November 1, 1756, but Lawful Money was in common use at least a year before and the colony's bills of credit issued in 1755 and after are recorded here in terms of Connecticut Lawful Money. The amounts entered for 1755–1764 are the sums issued in those years, as are the amounts for 1770–1775. For the former period, see also *The Public Records of the Colony of Connecticut*, edited by James Hammond Trumbull and Charles Jeremy Hoadly (Case, Lockwood and Brainard, 1850–1890), volume 12, p. 339. The amount entered for 1765 is the amount of the prior decade's issuance still outstanding.

Series Eg304, New Hampshire. See Brock (1941), pp. 49–50, 291–306; Brock (1975), pp. 591–3; and Brock (1992), pp. 106–7; and Newman, *Early Paper Money of America*, pp. 197–215. After 1751, New Hampshire used at first two and later three currencies concurrently. New Hampshire Old Tenor and New Hampshire New Tenor coexisted at a ratio of 4:1; New Hampshire "sterling" bills were rated against Old Tenor at 1:25, against New Tenor at a ratio of 1:6.25, though both ratios began to shift as time went on. The colony did away with this multiplicity of currencies in 1763 when it adopted New Hampshire Lawful Money. Bills of credit issued in 1755 and 1756 were denominated in New Tenor. Those issued between 1758 and 1762 were in New Hampshire "sterling." The figures in the table for these years are the value of the bills issued in those years, as is the sum for 1775. The figure for 1764 is the amount of the total issued between 1758 and 1762 still outstanding.

Series Eg305, Rhode Island. See Brock (1941), pp. 36–43, 54–7, 325–33; Brock (1975), pp. 591–3; Brock (1992), pp. 106–7; and Newman, *Early Paper Money of America*, pp. 365–89. The source for Brock's revised series is John Blanchard MacInnes, "Rhode Island Bills of Public Credit, 1710–1755" (Ph.D. dissertation, Brown University, 1952). Rhode Island continued to use Old Tenor as one mode of currency after 1751 but it also used, concurrently, Rhode Island Lawful Money. These dual currencies continued in use until the late 1760s; by 1769 Rhode Island Old Tenor and Rhode Island Lawful Money were in the ratio of 26.67:1. McCusker (1992), p. 136; Ruth Wallis Herndon, "Governing the Affairs of the Town: Continuity and Change in Rhode Island, 1750–1800" (Ph.D. dissertation, American University, 1992), pp. 352–70. The figures in the table are all the sums outstanding at the end of the year expressed in Rhode Island Old Tenor except for the one for 1775, which is the amount on Rhode Island Lawful money issued that year.

Series Eg306, New York. See Brock (1941), pp. 66–74, 336–53; and Newman (1990), pp. 243–60; and compare to Joseph Albert Ernst, *Money and*

Politics in America, 1755–1775: A Study in the Currency Act of 1764 and the Political Economy of Revolution (University of North Carolina Press, 1973), pp. 365–6. For 1709–1747, the figures are for the amounts issued each year. Of the total issued, £246,228, the amount outstanding at the end of 1747 was £189,601. From 1747 onward, the figures in the table are the amounts outstanding at the end of the year (November). For 1714–1760, see "An Account of the Several Emissions of Paper Currency in the Colony of New-York, together with what hath and what ought to have been cancelled . . . ," March 11, 1762, in New York (Colony), General Assembly, *Journal of the Votes and Proceedings of the General Assembly of the Colony of New-York. Begun the 9th day of April, 1691; And Ended . . . the 23d of December, 1765* (Gaine, 1764–1766), volume 2, p. 696 – incorporating references to the folio numbers of the original ledgers. The total for 1775 includes the amount issued that year. Contrast Cathy [D.] Matson, *Merchants and Empire: Trading in Colonial New York* (Johns Hopkins University Press, 1998), p. 325.

Series Eg307, Pennsylvania. Brock (1992), p. 113, supersedes Brock (1941), p. [386c]. Otherwise, see Brock (1941), pp. 74–84, 353–91. See also Newman (1990), pp. 325–47, and compare to Ernst, *Money and Politics*, p. 368. Pennsylvania's fiscal year ended on September 30. See also Paton [W.] Yoder, "Paper Currency in Colonial Pennsylvania" (Ph.D. dissertation, Indiana University, 1941).

Series Eg308, New Jersey. See Brock (1941), pp. 84–95, 393–410; and Newman, *Early Paper Money of America*, pp. 221–33; and compare to Ernst, *Money and Politics*, p. 367. See also Donald L. Kemmerer, "A History of Paper Money in Colonial New Jersey, 1668–1775," *Proceedings of the New Jersey Historical Society* 74 (April 1956): 107–44.

Series Eg309, Maryland. See Brock (1941), pp. 99–106, 412–28 (especially pp. 421–2); and Newman, *Early Paper Money of America*, pp. 141–9; and compare to Ernst (1973), p. 369. The figures for 1766–1775 are the cumulative amounts issued in those years. Prior to 1763, Maryland's paper money was denominated in pounds currency; beginning with the issue of $173,733 authorized on November 1, 1766, the colony's paper money was denominated in dollars, marking it is the equivalent of the Spanish silver dollar, the *peso de ocho reales*. ("An Act for the Payment of the Publick Claims for Emitting Bills of Credit," 1766, chapter 25 in William Hand Browne, editor, *Archives of Maryland* (Maryland Historical Society, 1883–1972), volume 61, pp. 264–75.) These two paper currencies represented two different currency regimes; they were not of equal value. At par, the older paper currency was at the ratio of £133.33 per £100 sterling; the newer, paper currency was at the ratio of £166.67 per £100 sterling. The newer paper money was the paper version of what had existed for decades as Maryland "hard currency." This was the continuing money of account in which goods were regularly priced, and commodities and labor were bought and sold. See McCusker (1990), pp. 189–204. For the introduction of the paper dollar, see Eric P. Newman, "The Earliest Money Using the Dollar as an Official Unit of Value," *The Numismatist* 98 (November 1985): 2181–7.

Series Eg310, Delaware. See Brock (1941), pp. 95–9 (especially p. 98 n. 78), pp. 391–3; and Newman, *Early Paper Money of America*, pp. 95–101. The sums for the years 1746–1760 are the totals issued in the years indicated.

Series Eg311, Virginia. See Brock (1992), p. 115; Ernst (1973), p. 370; and Newman (1990), pp. 431–40; and compare to Brock (1941), pp. 465–527. The amounts outstanding are for December 1760–1774. The figure for 1775 is the amount issued that year plus the amount stated as outstanding from earlier years. Brock (1992), p. 115, seems to have interpolated some of his data but this is not made explicit.

Series Eg312, North Carolina. See Brock (1941), pp. 106–13, 428–46; Newman (1990), pp. 287–95; and compare to Ernst (1973), p. 371. The figures for 1763–1771 are from Ernst. The data for 1771 and 1775 are the amounts issued in those years. All the earlier sums are in North Carolina pounds currency; the figure for 1775 is in dollars.

Series Eg313, South Carolina. See Brock (1941), pp. 114–27, 446–62; and Newman (1990), pp. 399–414; and compare to Ernst (1973), p. 372. The amount for 1775 includes £1,120,000 issued that year. See also Ivan Allen Marcotte, "Colonial South Carolina: A Quantity Theoretic Perspective"

(continued)

TABLE Eg302–314   Paper money in circulation, by colony: 1703–1775   [Local colonial currencies]   *Continued*

(Ph.D. dissertation, University of South Carolina, 1989), especially pp. 50– [73d]; and the discussion of Georgia, next.

Series Eg314, Georgia. See Brock (1941), pp. 127–9, 462–464a; B[enjamin] U. Ratchford, *American State Debts* (Duke University Press, 1941), p. 19; Ernst (1973), p. 372; Newman (1990), pp. 107–17. The figures for 1761, 1764, and 1773 are the totals outstanding in those years. The data for other years are the sums issued in those years. In a way that is misleading and confusing, Georgia denominated its paper currency, both the early "sola" bills and its later issue of paper, in "sterling." This was not pounds sterling as in Great Britain, however, but Georgia's own currency, Georgia's money of account, "Georgia sterling." Georgians did not use the same money of account that the Mother Country did, no matter what they called it. The simple fact of the matter is that, like all other colonies, when Georgians drew bills of exchange on the metropolis, they paid a premium in Georgia currency. By the 1760s, the rate of exchange between Georgia currency and British pounds sterling averaged about 8 percent, that is, it cost £108 Georgia currency per £100 sterling. Sometime after 1764, the par of exchange at Georgia, based, as usual, on the comparable values of the piece of eight at home and in Great Britain (5s versus 4s 6d), was £111 per £100 sterling. At the end of the American Revolution, South Carolinians did something similar, in effect adopting Georgia's money of account as their own. For all of this, see McCusker (1992), pp. 227–9; and McCusker, *How Much Is That in Real Money? A Historical Commodity Price Index for Use as a Deflator of Money Values in the Economy of the United States*, 2nd edition (American Antiquarian Society, 2001), pp. 71–88.

TABLE Eg 315–324   Rates of exchange on London, by colony or state: 1649–1790   [Local colonial currencies]

Contributed by John J. McCusker

125	Massachusetts	New York	New Jersey	Pennsylvania	Maryland		Virginia	North Carolina	South Carolina	Georgia
					Hard currency	Paper currency				
	Eg315	Eg316	Eg317	Eg318	Eg319	Eg320	Eg321	Eg322	Eg323	Eg324
	Pounds (£) local currency per £100 sterling	Pounds (£) local currency per £100 sterling	Pounds (£) local currency per £100 sterling	Pounds (£) local currency per £100 sterling	Pounds (£) local currency per £100 sterling	Pounds (£) local currency per £100 sterling	Pounds (£) local currency per £100 sterling	Pounds (£) local currency per £100 sterling	Pounds (£) local currency per £100 sterling	Pounds (£) local currency per £100 sterling
1649	112.00	—	—	—	—	—	—	—	—	—
1660	112.33	—	—	—	—	—	—	—	—	—
1661	114.92 [1]	—	—	—	—	—	—	—	—	—
1662	117.50 [1]	—	—	—	—	—	—	—	—	—
1663	112.00	—	—	—	—	—	—	—	—	—
1664	113.00	—	—	—	—	—	—	—	—	—
1665	115.33	—	—	—	—	—	—	—	—	—
1666	115.67 [1]	—	—	—	—	—	—	—	—	—
1667	116.00	—	—	—	—	—	—	—	—	—
1668	115.75	—	—	—	—	—	—	—	—	—
1669	116.00	—	—	—	—	—	—	—	—	—
1670	120.50 [1]	—	—	—	—	—	—	—	—	—
1671	125.00	—	—	—	—	—	—	—	—	—
1672	120.00	—	—	—	—	—	—	—	—	—
1673	125.00	—	—	—	—	—	—	—	—	—
1674	123.61 [1]	—	—	—	—	—	—	—	—	—
1675	122.22	—	—	—	—	—	—	—	—	—
1676	122.92	—	—	—	—	—	—	—	—	—
1677	127.28	—	—	—	—	—	—	—	—	—
1678	120.00	—	—	—	—	—	—	—	—	—
1679	124.93	—	—	—	—	—	—	—	—	—
1680	120.63	125.00	—	—	—	—	—	—	—	—
1681	127.01	126.00 [1]	—	—	—	—	—	—	—	—
1682	126.01 [1]	127.00 [1]	—	—	—	—	—	—	—	—
1683	125.00	128.00 [1]	—	125.00	—	—	—	—	—	—
1684	127.50	129.00 [1]	—	125.00	—	—	—	—	—	—
1685	130.13	130.00	—	126.00	—	—	—	—	—	—
1686	125.00	128.33 [1]	—	127.00	—	—	—	—	—	—
1687	121.96	126.67 [1]	—	128.00	—	—	—	—	—	—
1688	140.00	125.00	—	129.00	—	—	—	—	—	—
1689	137.08 [1]	130.00	—	130.00	—	—	—	—	—	—
1690	134.17 [1]	129.83 [1]	—	131.17	—	—	—	—	—	—
1691	131.25	129.67 [1]	—	132.34	—	—	110.00	—	—	—
1692	130.00	129.50 [1]	—	133.52	—	—	—	—	—	—
1693	130.00	129.33 [1]	—	134.69	—	—	—	—	—	—
1694	130.48	129.17	—	135.86	—	—	—	—	—	—
1695	134.93	130.01	—	142.93	—	—	—	—	—	—
1696	132.50	130.00	—	150.00	—	—	—	—	—	—
1697	135.99	130.00 [1]	—	150.00	—	—	—	—	—	—
1698	138.11 [1]	130.00	—	150.00	—	—	—	—	—	—
1699	140.24	142.86	—	149.31	—	—	—	—	111.75	—
1700	139.42	132.72	—	148.61	—	—	—	—	131.13	—
1701	136.33	132.50	—	147.92	—	—	—	—	137.42 [1]	—
1702	135.00	133.33	—	150.70	111.11	—	—	—	143.71 [1]	—
1703	135.50	135.00	166.67	150.84	—	—	—	—	150.00	—
1704	140.50	130.00	—	150.00	—	—	—	—	150.00 [1]	—
1705	142.78	134.42 [1]	—	150.05	—	—	—	—	150.00 [1]	—
1706	148.33	138.83 [1]	—	150.09	—	—	—	—	150.00 [1]	—
1707	140.00	143.25 [1]	—	152.92	—	—	—	—	150.00	—
1708	153.75	147.67 [1]	—	153.65	—	—	110.00	—	150.00	—
1709	158.75	152.08	—	120.02 [2]	133.33	—	110.00	—	150.10 [1]	—
1710	153.15	146.69	—	127.99	—	—	109.75 [1]	—	150 00	—
1711	144.44	150.63	—	128.99 [1]	—	—	109.50	—	162.50	—
1712	150.00	154.38	—	129.98	—	—	110.00	—	150.00	—
1713	150.00	153.75	—	131.68	—	—	110.00 [1]	—	150.00	—
1714	155.00	154.85	—	131.85	—	—	110.00	—	200.00	—

Notes appear at end of table

(continued)

TABLE Eg 315–324 Rates of exchange on London, by colony or state: 1649–1790 [Local colonial currencies]
Continued

	Massachusetts	New York	New Jersey	Pennsylvania	Maryland		Virginia	North Carolina	South Carolina	Georgia
					Hard currency	Paper currency				
125	Eg315	Eg316	Eg317	Eg318	Eg319	Eg320	Eg321	Eg322	Eg323	Eg324
	Pounds (£) local currency per £100 sterling	Pounds (£) local currency per £100 sterling	Pounds (£) local currency per £100 sterling	Pounds (£) local currency per £100 sterling	Pounds (£) local currency per £100 sterling	Pounds (£) local currency per £100 sterling	Pounds (£) local currency per £100 sterling	Pounds (£) local currency per £100 sterling	Pounds (£) local currency per £100 sterling	Pounds (£) local currency per £100 sterling
1715	162.04	153.19	—	130.31	132.34	—	108.50 [1]	150.00	300.00	—
1716	163.75	155.00	142.86	133.68	133.32	—	107.00 [1]	—	300.00	—
1717	186.25	160.00	146.97 [1]	134.83	134.97	—	105.50	—	443.75	—
1718	200.00	157.73 [1]	151.07 [1]	132.22	127.49	—	107.76 [1]	—	562.50	—
1719	218.28	155.46	155.18	135.42	130.84	—	110.02	—	454.68	—
1720	220.51	162.92	155.37 [1]	138.75	133.30	—	111.60	—	521.64	—
1721	231.73	162.50	155.55	137.50	127.53	—	113.17	—	546.11	—
1722	235.80	165.00	—	134.98	129.20	—	115.00	500.00	526.43	—
1723	242.68	164.59	—	140.38	131.06	—	115.25	500.00 [1]	650.00	—
1724	270.00	165.00	—	144.43	133.32	—	115.22	500.00	675.00	—
1725	290.13	165.00	—	146.33	132.48	—	114.00	500.00	670.49	—
1726	290.34	165.00	—	153.34	133.28	—	113.85	500.00	700.00	—
1727	291.25	165.00	—	149.59	134.26	—	115.83	500.00	700.00	—
1728	299.03	165.00	—	150.63	136.25	—	115.42	500.00	700.00	—
1729	313.81	165.00	—	149.03	133.33	—	119.39	500.00	700.00	—
1730	336.87	166.25	—	152.03	133.52	—	119.92	—	691.67	—
1731	334.38	165.00	—	153.42	133.37	—	118.67	650.00	700.00	—
1732	335.10	165.00	—	161.68	133.33	—	120.00	—	700.00 [1]	—
1733	372.89	165.00	—	163.75	133.33	—	120.00 [1]	—	700.00	—
1734	447.78	165.00	—	171.67	133.89	160.00	120.00	—	700.00	—
1735	486.67	165.00	—	166.11	133.33	140.00	120.00	860.00	705.56	—
1736	500.62	165.00	—	165.72	133.47	230.00	122.71	850.00	739.66	—
1737	509.38	165.63	170.00	169.42	137.77	250.00	121.63	883.33	770.53	—
1738	509.77	165.83	169.17 [1]	162.92	135.42	233.33	123.75	1,000.00	785.00	—
1739	508.95	166.94	168.33	169.79	133.34	226.10	122.50	1,000.00	788.82	—
1740	518.96	169.06	160.62	165.45	143.36	231.14	123.54	1,077.78	796.67	—
1741	549.48	159.44	142.50	146.47	138.82	244.79	123.88	1,000.00	709.08	—
1742	550.28	170.74	150.00	159.13	138.95	277.50	121.25	—	698.96	—
1743	560.69	174.67	160.00	160.35	137.78	258.42	121.25	—	700.00	—
1744	579.02	175.42	167.50 [1]	165.51	139.44	206.00	121.88	—	700.00	—
1745	626.53	183.33	175.00 [1]	172.45	140.00	200.00	127.64	1,000.00	700.00	—
1746	721.53	185.83	182.50	179.74	137.78	206.67	133.82	1,000.00	750.00	—
1747	868.75	191.46	178.33 [1]	183.34	140.82	216.83	135.72	1,025.01 [1]	761.02	—
1748	970.83	180.08	174.17 [1]	174.07	140.97	201.41	132.29	140.00 [2]	758.33	—
1749	1,077.08	178.96	170.00	171.74	135.49 [1]	185.00	123.33	133.33	724.98	—
1750	142.51 [2]	179.14	173.75	170.65	130.00	177.60	125.63	133.33	702.35	—
1751	133.33	181.39	172.50	170.06	140.00	166.83	128.86	—	700.00	—
1752	133.33	179.63	166.25	167.38	150.00	157.50	129.67	—	700.00	—
1753	130.00	179.25	167.50	167.49	152.78	152.33	129.33	—	700.00	—
1754	133.33	179.90	168.17	168.25	156.88	157.50	126.95	166.67	700.00	—
1755	132.78	178.64	170.00	168.90	157.38	162.92	128.75	175.00	700.00	—
1756	133.33	181.94	165.92	172.62	151.19 [1]	163.89	127.69	179.80	708.87	—
1757	132.72	178.44	166.10	165.62	145.00	164.43	136.53	179.90 [1]	700.28	—
1758	129.45	172.74	161.25	159.26	157.50	157.46	138.96	180.00	700.00	—
1759	132.78	168.04	156.25	153.60	165.00	150.00	139.30	185.12	700.00	—
1760	130.99	167.09	153.30	159.14	158.62	147.50	141.69	190.00	700.00	—
1761	137.99	182.74	171.25	173.02	169.10	148.75	143.04	195.00	700.00	—
1762	140.77	189.42	176.88	175.92	172.50	145.00	152.84	200.00	700.00	—
1763	136.61	184.31	169.83	172.95	167.28	140.00	160.13	200.00	716.61	—
1764	133.75	184.72	172.02	172.88	166.57	140.00	160.57	191.00	724.55	—
1765	133.53	183.13	166.01 [1]	170.02	166.56	—	161.01	200.00	709.33	108.50
1766	133.11	177.96	160.00	163.57	163.65	—	128.62	189.81 [1]	702.33	—
1767	133.33	178.72	—	165.85	163.97	—	125.50	179.63	700.00	—
1768	130.75	179.50	—	166.79	164.94	—	125.02	180.00	699.91	108.93
1769	130.48	170.94	—	157.39	161.30	—	121.70	174.67 [1]	700.39	—
1770	126.57	166.05	—	153.86	151.04	—	118.15	169.35 [1]	691.23	—
1771	133.33	178.31	—	165.67	159.48	—	121.75	164.02	694.46	—
1772	131.42	173.30	—	160.82	151.88	—	123.29	172.02	685.81	108.76
1773	132.46	177.75	—	166.45	164.68	—	130.30	173.51 [1]	711.84	—
1774	133.90	180.48	169.50	169.72	167.15	—	131.08	175.00	726.38	—

TABLE Eg 315–324   Rates of exchange on London, by colony or state: 1649–1790   [Local colonial currencies]
Continued

125	Massachusetts Eg315 Pounds (£) local currency per £100 sterling	New York Eg316 Pounds (£) local currency per £100 sterling	New Jersey Eg317 Pounds (£) local currency per £100 sterling	Pennsylvania Eg318 Pounds (£) local currency per £100 sterling	Maryland Hard currency Eg319 Pounds (£) local currency per £100 sterling	Maryland Paper currency Eg320 Pounds (£) local currency per £100 sterling	Virginia Eg321 Pounds (£) local currency per £100 sterling	North Carolina Eg322 Pounds (£) local currency per £100 sterling	South Carolina Eg323 Pounds (£) local currency per £100 sterling	Georgia Eg324 Pounds (£) local currency per £100 sterling
1775	118.73	171.75	—	161.18	156.81	—	122.85	177.77	742.89	108.00
1776	132.06	175.93 [1]	—	192.72	170.00	—	131.53	—	—	—
1777	—	180.11	—	250.00	—	—	128.75	—	850.00	—
1778	—	177.77	—	437.50	—	—	133.88	—	—	—
1779	—	168.40	—	—	—	—	—	—	—	—
1780	—	160.37	—	155.00	—	—	—	—	—	—
1781	—	168.91	—	147.50	—	—	—	—	—	—
1782	—	175.29	—	159.80	—	—	133.33	—	—	—
1783	—	171.84	—	168.25	—	—	—	—	—	—
1784	—	—	—	173.35	170.00	—	133.33	—	100.00 [2]	—
1785	—	—	—	177.74	—	—	—	—	107.04	—
1786	—	—	—	177.58	—	—	130.00	—	110.17	—
1787	—	—	—	175.84	170.00	—	140.00	—	120.00	—
1788	—	—	—	173.95	—	—	125.00	—	—	—
1789	139.86	—	—	171.75	—	—	—	—	—	—
1790	—	—	—	163.47	—	—	—	—	—	—

[1] Interpolated value.

[2] Change in money of account; see text.

Source

John J. McCusker, *Money and Exchange in Europe and America, 1600–1775: A Handbook,* 2nd edition (University of North Carolina Press, 1992), pp. 315-7, as revised and updated by ongoing research.

Documentation

See the Appendixes to the essay in this chapter for a general discussion of the tables and the sources of the data, along with a key to abbreviations used in this chapter and general information on matters such as regional definitions, calendar differences, money, and weights and measures.

The figures indicate year by year the average number of pounds in each colonial or state currency equal to £100 sterling. In the source, the rates are presented month by month. In some instances (see footnotes), short-term gaps in the data have been filled by estimates calculated as straight-line interpolations based on neighboring data.

Rather than rely on data published in secondary sources, great care has been taken to check every rate against the original source of the quotation in order to avoid distortions introduced by counting the same datum twice. Thus, these series may sometimes not agree in detail with other, similar tables. The effort to perfect these series is ongoing. See also the discussion in John J. McCusker, *How Much Is That in Real Money? A Historical Commodity Price Index for Use as a Deflator of Money Values in the Economy of the United States,* 2nd edition (American Antiquarian Society, 2001), pp. 61–70 and elsewhere.

In ways similar to the introduction of the euro into the member nations of the European Union, important changes occurred with the moneys of account of the Thirteen Continental Colonies and the early United States, several of which are reflected in these series. Most notable is the Massachusetts replacement, effective March 31, 1750, of Old Tenor by Lawful Money. The ratio between the two was set in law at £7.50 Old Tenor to £1.00 Lawful

Money. Although the former ceased to exist in law, people continued for a while to refer to it as a money of account, largely in the pricing of traditional goods and services, sometimes even in the drafting of bills of exchange. Note that the considerable difference in the exchange rates for Massachusetts for 1749 and 1750 is a consequence of this devaluation. To strike an annual average for the latter year, exchange rate quotations for the first three months of 1750, originally expressed in Old Tenor, were converted to Lawful Money. In Old Tenor terms, the average rate for 1750 was £1,058.10 Massachusetts currency per £100 sterling. See McCusker (1992), pp. 131–4. A similar change occurred in North Carolina a couple of years before. As of May 1, 1709, Pennsylvania adopted a new money of account and, as a consequence, the par of exchange dropped by one quarter. From that date forward, the old money and the "new money" existed in a ratio of £1.33 to £1.00. To calculate the annual average for 1709, exchange rate quotations from the first five months of the year are converted to "new money." In terms of the old currency, the average rate for 1709 was £160.03 Pennsylvania currency per £100 sterling. See McCusker (1992), pp. 175–6. See, too, the introduction of South Carolina "sterling" after the American Revolution. Most notable of all was the change from pounds colonial currency to the dollar at the very end of the period. See the text for Table Eg302–314; and McCusker (2001), pp. 71–88.

The source volume argues throughout that, in lieu of quotations of the actual rate of exchange, one can fall back to the par of exchange as a reasonable surrogate. Thus, for Virginia, for the years 1655–1718, the par of exchange at £111.11 Virginia currency per £100 sterling is thought to approximate the commercial rate of exchange.

The source volume contains analogous data series for many of the other colonies in the Western Hemisphere and for the six related European metropoles. For a similar, complementary, but much larger effort that spans the world and covers much more time, see Jürgen Schneider, Oskar Schwarzer, et al., *Währungen der Welt,* Beiträge zur Wirtschafts- und Sozialgeschichte, volumes 44–50, 57, 59, 61, 87 (Franz Steiner, 1991–1999).

AGRICULTURE AND FISHERIES

John J. McCusker

TABLE Eg325–328   Acreage and livestock in Maine, Massachusetts, and New Jersey: 1784

Contributed by John J. McCusker

	Acreage		Livestock	
	Improved land	Unimproved land	Horses	Horned cattle
	Eg325	Eg326	Eg327	Eg328
State	Acres	Acres	Number	Number
Maine	165,810	1,325,594	5,448	49,006
Massachusetts	921,563	1,860,263	43,969	237,993
New Jersey	2,032,587	484,954	52,488	102,221

Source

Jedidiah Morse, *The American Geography; or, A View of the Present Situation of the United States of America . . .* (Published by the author, 1789), pp. 172, 284.

Documentation

See the Appendixes to the essay in this chapter for a general discussion of the tables and the sources of the data, along with a key to abbreviations used in this chapter and general information on matters such as regional definitions, calendar differences, money, and weights and measures.

These very limited data stem from the earliest of what later came to be called "agricultural censuses." It may be assumed that both the population and the agricultural information in the two states were collected at the same time in the year, 1784. Morse (1789), p. 172, noted that the numbers of horses and cattle were "taken in 1784, and supposed to be less than the reality," that is, the "reality" in 1789.

Other agricultural statistics of this type, except for a few estimates for parts of colonies, do not appear to exist for the colonial and pre-Federal period.

Maine was a part of Massachusetts until it became a state in 1820.

TABLE Eg329–338   Cod fishery of Massachusetts – vessels, tonnage, seamen, and codfish exports, by port: 1765–1790

Contributed by John J. McCusker

	Annual averages for 1765–1775					Annual averages for 1786–1790				
				Codfish exported					Codfish exported	
	Vessels	Tonnage	Seamen	To Europe	To the West Indies	Vessels	Tonnage	Seamen	To Europe	To the West Indies
	Eg329	Eg330	Eg331	Eg332	Eg333	Eg334	Eg335	Eg336	Eg337	Fg338
Fishing port	Number	Tons	Number	Hundredweight	Hundredweight	Number	Tons	Number	Hundredweight	Hundredweight
Total	665	25,630	4,405	178,800	172,500	539	19,185	3,287	108,600	142,050
Marblehead	150	7,500	1,200	80,000	40,000	90	5,400	720	50,000	25,000
Gloucester	146	5,530	888	35,000	42,500	160	3,600	680	19,500	28,500
Manchester	25	1,500	200	10,000	10,000	15	900	120	3,000	7,500
Beverly	15	750	120	6,000	6,000	19	1,235	152	5,200	10,000
Salem	30	1,500	240	12,000	12,000	20	1,300	160	6,000	10,000
Newburyport	10	400	60	2,000	2,000	10	460	80	1,000	5,000
Ipswich	50	900	190	8,000	5,500	56	860	248	3,000	6,000
Plymouth	60	2,400	420	8,000	16,000	36	1,440	252	6,000	12,000
Cohasset	6	240	42	800	1,600	5	200	35	1,000	1,500
Hingham	6	240	42	800	1,600	4	180	32	800	1,200
Scituate	10	400	70	1,000	3,000	2	90	16	400	600
Duxborough	4	160	28	400	1,200	9	360	72	1,500	3,000
Kingston	6	240	42	800	1,600	4	160	28	700	1,300
Yarmouth	30	900	180	3,000	6,000	30	900	180	2,000	10,000
Wellfleet	3	90	21	300	600	0	0	0	0	0
Truro	10	400	80	1,000	3,000	0	0	0	0	0
Provincetown	4	160	32	500	1,100	11	550	88	3,000	5,200
Chatham	30	900	240	4,000	8,000	30	900	240	3,000	9,000
Nantucket	8	320	64	1,000	2,200	5	200	40	500	1,500
Maine	60	1,000	230	4,000	8,000	30	300	120	1,000	3,500
Weymouth	2	100	16	200	600	3	150	24	1,000	1,250

Sources

Report enclosed in a letter from Governor John Hancock, at Boston, to Secretary of State Thomas Jefferson, at Philadelphia, October 25, 1789, Massachusetts Archives Collection, volume 289: Letters, 1786–1792, Massachusetts Archives, Boston, Massachusetts. See also Thomas Jefferson Papers, series I: General Correspondence, 1651–1827, volume 60, folio 375, item number 10433, Manuscript Division, LC.

Documentation

See the Appendixes to the essay in this chapter for a general discussion of the tables and the sources of the data, along with a key to abbreviations used in this chapter and general information on matters such as regional definitions, calendar differences, money, and weights and measures. In this table, the unit of measure for vessels is the registered ton, one of three kinds of tons associated with ships and the shipping industry of the period. Codfish were priced and exported per hundredweight (or "quintal") of 100 pounds. See the text for Table Eg248–250.

The table indicates for two periods, before and after the Revolutionary War, fishing port by fishing port, the average annual numbers of vessels employed in the Massachusetts cod fishery, their tonnage and their crews, and the average annual exports of codfish to the two major markets, Europe and the West Indies. The report was prepared by a committee of the Massachusetts legislature chaired by Peleg Coffin Jr., at the request of Governor John Hancock in response to the letter sent to him by Secretary of State Thomas Jefferson, August 24, 1789. Jefferson reproduced the table in his own report on American fisheries that he sent to the U.S. House of Representatives on February 1, 1791. Jefferson had his report published, and this table appears in it. For the original table, Jefferson's report, the origins of both, and associated materials, see Julian P. Boyd, Lyman H. Butterfield, et al., editors, *The Papers of Thomas Jefferson* (Princeton University Press, 1950 to date), volume 19, pp. 140–237. The table is on p. 223. See also U.S. Department of State, *Report of the Secretary of State, on the Subject of the Cod and Whale Fisheries, Made Conformably to an Order of the House of Representatives of the United States, Referring to Him the Representation of the General Court of the*

Commonwealth of Massachusetts on Those Subjects; February 1, 1791, by Thomas Jefferson (Francis Childs and John Swaine, 1791), p. 14. The original manuscript table is available online in "The Papers of Thomas Jefferson," Online Collections, Manuscript Division, LC.

The table as originally compiled concerned the average annual catch of fish but see the comment appended to the table as sent by Hancock to Jefferson, October 25, 1790: "N.B. The quantity of fish consumed in the United States being inconsiderable the Committee have made no allowance for that consumption, but have considered the whole quantity taken as Exported" (Boyd, Butterfield, et al. (1950 to date), volume 19, p. 223 n).

For 1765–1775, the committee valued exports to Europe at $3.50 per hundredweight and to the West Indies at $2.60; for 1786–1790, the prices were $3.00 and $2.00, respectively. From Table Eg248–250, the average price for merchantable codfish, 1765–1775, was $3.30 per hundredweight; for Jamaican codfish, $2.15; and for refuse codfish, $1.79.

The table has been reproduced in many places, sometimes with minor inaccuracies. See, for example, Timothy Pitkin, *A Statistical View of the Commerce of the United States of America: Its Connections with Agriculture and Manufactures: and An Account of the Public Debt, Revenues, and Expenditures of the United States. With a Brief Review of the Trade, Agriculture, and Manufactures of the Colonies, Previous to Their Independence. Accompanied with Tables, Illustrative of the Principles and Objects of the Work*, 1st edition (Charles Hosmer, 1816), p. 74.

One may compare these data with "A Calculation of the State of the Cod and Whale Fishery, Belonging to Massachusetts in 1763: Copied from a Paper Published in 1764," *Collections of the Massachusetts Historical Society* [1st series], 8 (1802): 202–3. In that year, there were 300 Massachusetts vessels engaged in the cod fishery (and ninety in the mackerel fishery). The cod fishermen caught 102,265 hundredweight of merchantable fish and 137,794 hundredweight of "West-India fish," the former worth £61,359 sterling, the latter, £62,007 6s 0d. Added to that were 3,600 barrels of cod oil valued at £5,400 sterling for a total of nearly £139,000 sterling.

Note that Maine was a part of Massachusetts until it became a separate state in 1820.

TABLE Eg339–342   Whaling at Nantucket – vessels, tonnage, and oil taken: 1715–1789

Contributed by John J. McCusker

Year(s)	Vessels Eg339 Number	Tonnage per vessel Eg340 [1] Tons	Oil taken Quantity Eg341 Barrels	Oil taken Value Eg342 Pounds (£) sterling	Year(s)	Vessels Eg339 Number	Tonnage per vessel Eg340 [1] Tons	Oil taken Quantity Eg341 Barrels	Oil taken Value Eg342 Pounds (£) sterling
1715	6	38	600	1,100 [4]	1768	125 [2]	75	15,439 [2]	—
1730	25	44	3,700	3,238 [5]	1769	119	—	19,140	—
1748	60	63	11,250	19,648 [5]	1770	125 [2]	93	14,331 [2]	—
1756	80	75	12,000	27,000 [5]	1771	115	—	12,754	—
1762	78	—	9,440	—	1772	98	—	7,825	—
1763	60	—	9,238	—	1772–1775	150	135	30,000	137,875
1764	72	—	11,983	—	1783	19	—	2,260	16,280
1765	101	—	11,512	—	1784	28	—	5,400	14,500
1766	118	—	11,969	—	1785	15	—	— [3]	— [3]
1767	108	—	16,561	—	1787–1789	36	113	12,060	22,303

[1] Some values are the midpoint of a range as given in the source; see text.

[2] There are different figures in "Progress of the Whale Fishery at Nantucket," p. 161.

[3] Ships were still at sea at time of reporting.

[4] Includes the value of 11,000 pounds of whale bone.

[5] Small calculation errors in the original table are corrected here.

Sources

1715–1785, except as noted later. "Progress of the Whale Fishery at Nantucket," *Collections of the Massachusetts Historical Society* [1st series], 3 (1794): 161.

1762–1772. Obed Macy, *The History of Nantucket, Being a Compendious Account of the First Settlement of the Island by the English, Together with the Rise and Progress of the Whale Fishery; and Other Historical Facts Relative to Said Island and Its Inhabitants*, 2nd edition (Macy and Pratt, 1880), p. 65.

1772–1775 and 1787–1789. Enclosure number 5 in a letter from Governor John Hancock, at Boston, to Secretary of State Thomas Jefferson, at Philadelphia, October 25, 1789, Massachusetts Archives Collection, volume 289: Letters, 1786–1792, Massachusetts Archives, Boston, Massachusetts. See also Thomas Jefferson Papers, series I: General Correspondence, 1651–1827, volume 60, folio 396, item number 10456, Manuscript Division, LC.

Documentation

The unit of measure for vessels is the registered ton, one of three kinds of tons associated with ships and the shipping industry of the period. In the original sources, the tonnage data for three years were stated as ranges, which have been converted here to their midpoint values: 1730, 38–50 tons; 1748, 50–75 tons; and 1770, 75–110 tons. Whale oil was sold and exported by the tun/ton of 252 gallons; there were eight barrels per ton (31.5 gallons each).

The table indicates for two periods, before and after the Revolutionary War, fishing port by fishing port, the average annual numbers of vessels employed in the Massachusetts whale fishery, their tonnage and their crews, and the average take of spermaceti oil and whale oil. The report was prepared by a committee of the Massachusetts legislature chaired by Peleg Coffin Jr. at the request of Governor John Hancock in response to a letter sent to him by Secretary of State Thomas Jefferson, August 24, 1789. Jefferson reproduced the table in his own report on American fisheries that he sent to the U.S. House of Representatives on February 1, 1791. Jefferson had his report published, and this table appears in it. For the original table, Jefferson's report, the origins of both, and associated materials, see Julian P. Boyd, Lyman H. Butterfield, et al., editors, *The Papers of Thomas Jefferson* (Princeton University Press, 1950 to date), volume 19, pp. 140–237. The table is on pp. 230–1. See also U.S. Department of State, *Report of the Secretary of State, on the Subject of the Cod and Whale Fisheries, Made Conformably to an Order of the House of Representatives of the United States, Referring to Him the Representation of the General Court of the Commonwealth of Massachusetts on Those Subjects; February 1, 1791* (Francis Childs and John Swaine, 1791), p. 25, which has a mistake or two in the printing. The original manuscript table is available online in "The Papers of Thomas Jefferson," Online Collections, Manuscript Division, LC.

The development of whaling in Nantucket, Massachusetts, followed the same pattern as other colonies. See Alexander Starbuck, *History of the American Whale Fishery from Its Earliest Inception to the Year 1876*, U.S. Commission on Fish and Fisheries, Report, 1875–1876, part 4. U.S. Congress, Senate, 44th

Congress, 1st Session, Senate Miscellaneous Documents, number 107 (U.S. Government Printing Office, 1878); Macy (1880); and Walter S. Tower, *A History of the American Whale Fishery*, Publications of the University of Pennsylvania, Series in Political Economy and Public Law, number 20 (University of Pennsylvania, 1907). The early settlers first processed drift whales; then they engaged in the offshore fisheries, which probably reached its culmination at Nantucket in 1726 when eighty-six whales were taken (Alexander Starbuck, *The History of Nantucket, County, Island, and Town, Including Genealogies of First Inhabitants* (Goodspeed, 1924), p. 356). The first deep-sea venture seems to have occurred about 1712, when a strong wind blew an offshore vessel to sea where it caught a spermaceti whale. By 1746, Nantucket whalers were making their way to Davis Straits, and by 1774, they were sailing as far away as the coast of Brazil (Macy 1880, pp. 48 and 54).

The figures for Nantucket may be seen in better perspective by noting that about 1730 the New England whaling fleet totaled 1,300 tons, roughly 85 percent of which was based at Nantucket; and in 1763 that of Massachusetts consisted of 180 sailing vessels, of which one third were based at Nantucket. For the 1730 figure, see Fayrer Hall, *The Importance of the British Plantations in America to This Kingdom; with the State of Their Trade, and Methods for Improving It; Also a Description of the Several Colonies There* (Peele, 1731), p. 103. For the 1763 figure, see "A Calculation of the State of the Cod and Whale Fishery, belonging to Massachusetts in 1763: Copied from a Paper Published in 1764," *Collections of the Massachusetts Historical Society* [1st series], 8 (1802): 203; and compare to Raymond McFarland, *A History of the New England Fisheries* (University of Pennsylvania, 1911), pp. 86, 99. On the eve of the Revolutionary War (1771–1775), New England had 304 whalers, totaling 27,840 tons, out of an estimated American fleet of 360 vessels. The New Englanders harvested 47,040 barrels of whale oil. Of those totals, Nantucket accounted for 150 vessels, 15,075 tons of shipping, and 30,000 barrels of oil. For 1787–1789, New England had 122 whalers, totaling 10,210 tons of shipping. The New Englanders harvested 21,110 barrels of whale oil. Of those totals, Nantucket accounted for 36 vessels, 4,050 tons of shipping, and 12,060 barrels of oil. See Boyd, Butterfield, et al. (1950 to date), volume 19, pp. 230–1. See also Macy (1880), p. 80; Starbuck (1924), p. 176 n.; and, especially, Timothy Pitkin, *A Statistical View of the Commerce of the United States of America: Its Connections with Agriculture and Manufactures: and an Account of the Public Debt, Revenues, and Expenditures of the United States. With a Brief Review of the Trade, Agriculture, and Manufactures of the Colonies, Previous to Their Independence. Accompanied with Tables, Illustrative of the Principles and Objects of the Work*, 1st edition (Charles Hosmer, 1816), pp. 42–7, 79.

According to the 1790 report of the committee of the Massachusetts legislature, on average during 1771–1775, sixty-five Nantucket vessels were fitted out for the northern fishery (totaling 4,875 tons) and eighty-five for the southern fishery (10,200 tons). They took an annual average of 26,000 barrels of spermaceti oil (worth £40 sterling a ton) and 8,260 barrels of whale oil ($70/£15.75 a ton). For the three years, 1787–1789, on average, 18 Nantucket vessels were fitted out for the northern fishery (totaling 1,350 tons) and 18 for the southern fishery (2,700 tons). They took an annual average of 3,800 barrels of spermaceti oil (worth $100 a ton) and 8,260 barrels of whale oil ($50 a ton) (Boyd, Butterfield, et al. (1950 to date), volume 19, pp. 230–1). At par, £100 sterling equaled $444.44.

TABLE Eg343–355 Fishing industry exports, by commodity and destination: 1790

Contributed by John J. McCusker

	Quantity						Value						
Class and destination	Dried fish Eg343 Hundredweight	Pickled fish Eg344 Barrels	Whale oil Eg345 Barrels	Spermaceti oil Eg346 Barrels	Whale bone Eg347 Pounds	Spermaceti candles Eg348 Pounds	Total Eg349 Dollars	Dried fish Eg350 Dollars	Pickled fish Eg351 Dollars	Whale oil Eg352 Dollars	Spermaceti oil Eg353 Dollars	Whale bone Eg354 Dollars	Spermaceti candles Eg355 Dollars
Both, total	378,721	36,804	15,765	5,431	121,281	70,379	1,194,287	828,531	113,165	124,908	79,542	20,417	27,724
First, total	251,659	29,306	11,670	1,483	108,807	39,954	749,497	519,374	90,838	87,452	18,552	17,917	15,364
France	543	12	9,914	1,403	108,807	1,200	110,793	1,086	20	73,767	17,523	17,917	480
French West Indies	251,116	29,294	1,756	80	0	38,754	638,704	518,288	90,818	13,685	1,029	0	14,884
Second, total	127,062	7,498	4,095	3,948	12,474	30,425	444,790	309,157	22,327	37,456	60,990	2,500	12,360
Spain	72,300	280	593	0	0	2,896	200,700	194,457	813	4,174	0	0	1,256
Spanish West Indies and Florida	824	300	5	3,840	0	1,685	62,576	978	886	38	60,000	0	674
Great Britain	5	0	1,738	0	1,075	0	21,273	10	0	21,048	0	215	0
British West Indies	1,970	795	15	0	0	756	7,666	4,114	3,075	124	0	0	353
Nova Scotia	0	13	1	0	0	0	50	0	40	10	0	0	0
Holland	0	15	807	100	5,220	0	7,648	0	45	5,683	870	1,050	0
Dutch West Indies	23,822	4,778	179	0	0	23,162	72,626	48,631	13,404	1,317	0	0	9,274
Portugal	18,594	69	4	0	0	0	41,608	41,306	242	60	0	0	0
Portuguese Islands	5,432	292	139	8	0	148	13,529	11,307	801	1,243	120	0	58
Germany	0	0	470	0	6,150	0	4,220	0	0	2,990	0	1,230	0
Danish West Indies	1,180	803	3	0	0	0	4,834	2,386	2,421	27	0	0	0
African Islands and Coast of Africa	613	147	6	0	0	165	1,996	1,324	564	42	0	0	66
Mediterranean	2,314	6	135	0	29	328	5,519	4,628	36	700	0	5	150
Sweden	8	0	0	0	0	0	16	16	0	0	0	0	0
East Indies	0	0	0	0	0	1,285	529	0	0	0	0	0	529

Source

See the Appendixes to the essay in this chapter for a general discussion of the tables and the sources of the data, along with a key to abbreviations used in this chapter and general information on matters such as regional definitions, calendar differences, money, and weights and measures.

Codfish were priced and exported per hundredweight (cwt., or "quintal") of 100 pounds. See the text for Table Eg248–250. The barrel of pickled fish usually measured "30 @ 32 Gallons" and weighed, net, "About 2 Cwt." Enclosure in a letter from Joseph Anthony, at Philadelphia, to Tench Coxe at Philadelphia, November 27, 1790, in Julian P. Boyd, Lyman H. Butterfield, et al., editors, The Papers of Thomas Jefferson (Princeton University Press, 1950 to date), volume 19, p. 199. Whale oil was usually sold and exported by the tun/ton of 252 gallons; there were eight barrels per ton (31.5 gallons each). Jefferson had the report published, and this table appears in it. For the original table, Jefferson's report, their origins, and associated materials, see Boyd, Butterfield, et al. (1950 to date), volume 19, pp. 140–237. The table is on p. 224. See also U.S. Department of State, Report of the Secretary of State, on the Subject of the Cod and Whale Fisheries, Made Conformably to an Order of the House of Representatives of the United States, Referring to Him the Representation of the General Court of the Commonwealth of Massachusetts on Those Subjects; February 1, 1791, by Thomas Jefferson (Francis Childs and John Swaine, 1791), p. 15. The original manuscript table is available online in "The Papers of Thomas Jefferson," Online Collections, Manuscript Division, LC.

Documentation

For, presumably, the shipping season for the catch of the year 1789 that stretched "from about August 20th, 1789, to September 30th, 1790," the table exhibits the export of all commodities related to the fishing industry, including whale bone and spermaceti candles. This appears to have been part of the materials assembled for Jefferson by Assistant Secretary of the Treasury, Tench Coxe, and referred to by him in his "Miscellaneous Notes on the Fisheries" that he sent to Jefferson on November 23, 1790. Boyd, Butterfield, et al. (1950 to date), volume 19, pp. 158–9, 169, 182–95. In those notes, he discusses "the return of exports now making up at the Treasury" and suggests the necessity of adding to those data "an estimate of that portion of them, which is never entered in the United States being carried immediately from the Scenes of the fisheries to foreign Markets; and a further estimate of the value of the commodities, which being consumed in our families, manufactures and public establishments, cannot appear in our list of exports" (Boyd, Butterfield, et al. 1950 to date, pp. 182–3).

The division into "1st Class" and "2nd Class" apparently had more to do with Jefferson's argument that France and her colonies were the most important consumers of U.S. exports of fish and whale products than with the quality of the commodities exported.

MANUFACTURING

John J. McCusker

TABLE Eg356–361   Vessels built in British North America – number and tonnage, by vessel type: 1768–1773

Contributed by John J. McCusker

	Total		Square-rigged		Fore-and-aft-rigged	
	Number	Tonnage	Number	Tonnage	Number	Tonnage
	Eg356	Eg357	Eg358	Eg359	Eg360	Eg361
Year	Number	Tons	Number	Tons	Number	Tons
1768	486	29,452	157	19,098	329	10,354
1769	450	21,460	114	11,247	336	10,213
1770	515	24,198	130	11,216	385	12,982
1771	478	25,275	131	14,695	347	10,580
1772	557	32,423	184	19,854	373	12,569
1773	638	38,029	212	24,500	426	13,529

Sources

George Chalmers, *Opinions on Interesting Subjects of Public Law and Commercial Policy; Arising from American Independence*, new edition, corrected (Debrett, 1785), p. 110. See also an earlier, detailed version of this table (with slightly variant data), for the three years 1769–1771 only, in John [Baker Holroyd], Lord Sheffield, *Observations on the Commerce of the American States*, 6th edition, enlarged (Debrett, 1784), p. 96.

Documentation

See the Appendix to the essay in this chapter for a general discussion of the tables and the sources of the data, along with a key to abbreviations used in this chapter and general information on matters such as regional definitions, calendar differences, money, and weights and measures. In this table, the unit of measure for vessels is the registered ton, one of three kinds of tons associated with ships and the shipping industry of the period. For a discussion of the different types of vessels built in the colonies, see Table Eg271–274. In the source, the table distinguished between the two types of

vessels using the designations "topsails" and "sloops and schooners." For the sake of continuity with other tables in this chapter, the former has been changed to "square-rigged" and the latter to "fore-and-aft-rigged."

Chalmers's data recorded the number and tonnage of vessels built and registered in all of British North America, from Newfoundland through Florida, as well as the Bahamas and Bermuda. The figures were originally compiled in the office of the Inspector General of Import and Exports and Register of Shipping, Boston, from the duplicate copies of ship registry certificates submitted by the colonial governments. For that office and its operation, see John J. McCusker, "Colonial Civil Servant and Counter-Revolutionary: Thomas Irving (1738?–1800) in Boston, Charleston, and London," *Perspectives in American History* 12 (1979): 314–50, as revised and updated in McCusker, *Essays in the Economic History of the Atlantic World* (Routledge, 1997), pp. 190–221. See also Chalmers (1785), p. 111 n. The earlier table, reproduced by Sheffield, is signed by Irving and dated "Custom House, Boston" (Sheffield 1784, p. 96).

TABLE Eg362–403 Vessels built – number and tonnage, by colony and vessel type: 1769–1771

Contributed by John J. McCusker

	Total			New Hampshire			Massachusetts			Rhode Island			Connecticut			New York			New Jersey		
	Square-rigged	Fore-and-aft-rigged	Tonnage	Square-rigged	Fore-and-aft-rigged	Tonnage	Square-rigged	Fore-and-aft-rigged	Tonnage	Square-rigged	Fore-and-aft-rigged	Tonnage	Square-rigged	Fore-and-aft-rigged	Tonnage	Square-rigged	Fore-and-aft-rigged	Tonnage	Square-rigged	Fore-and-aft-rigged	Tonnage
	Eg362	Eg363	Eg364	Eg365	Eg366	Eg367	Eg368	Eg369	Eg370	Eg371	Eg372	Eg373	Eg374	Eg375	Eg376	Eg377	Eg378	Eg379	Eg380	Eg381	Eg382
Year	Number	Number	Tons	Number	Number	Tons	Number	Number	Tons	Number	Number	Tons	Number	Number	Tons	Number	Number	Tons	Number	Number	Tons
1769	114	276	20,081	16	29	2,452	40	97	8,013	8	31	1,428	7	43	1,542	5	14	955	1	3	83
1770	118	283	20,620	27	20	3,581	31	118	7,274	16	49	2,035	5	41	1,522	8	10	960	0	0	0
1771	128	293	24,092	15	40	4,991	42	83	7,704	15	60	2,148	7	39	1,483	9	28	1,698	0	2	70

	Pennsylvania			Maryland			Virginia			North Carolina			South Carolina			Georgia			West Florida		
	Square-rigged	Fore-and-aft-rigged	Tonnage	Square-rigged	Fore-and-aft-rigged	Tonnage	Square-rigged	Fore-and-aft-rigged	Tonnage	Square-rigged	Fore-and-aft-rigged	Tonnage	Square-rigged	Fore-and-aft-rigged	Tonnage	Square-rigged	Fore-and-aft-rigged	Tonnage	Square-rigged	Fore-and-aft-rigged	Tonnage
	Eg383	Eg384	Eg385	Eg386	Eg387	Eg388	Eg389	Eg390	Eg391	Eg392	Eg393	Eg394	Eg395	Eg396	Eg397	Eg398	Eg399	Eg400	Eg401	Eg402	Eg403
Year	Number	Number	Tons	Number	Number	Tons	Number	Number	Tons	Number	Number	Tons	Number	Number	Tons	Number	Number	Tons	Number	Number	Tons
1769	14	8	1,469	9	11	1,344	6	21	1,269	3	9	607	4	8	789	0	2	50	1	0	80
1770	18	8	2,354	7	10	1,545	6	15	1,105	0	5	125	0	3	52	0	3	57	0	1	10
1771	15	6	1,307	10	8	1,645	10	9	1,678	0	8	241	3	4	560	2	4	543	0	2	24

Sources

John [Baker Holroyd], Lord Sheffield, *Observations on the Commerce of the American States*, 6th edition, enlarged (Debrett, 1784), p. 96. Sheffield printed a table prepared under the direction of, and signed by, Thomas Irving, "Inspector General of Imports and Exports of North America, and Register of Shipping," dated at the Custom House, Boston. David Macpherson, *Annals of Commerce, Manufactures, Fisheries and Navigation . . . the British Empire and Other Countries, from the Earliest Accounts to . . . 1801* (Nichols and Son et al., 1805), volume 3, p. 570, printed the same table, saying that it was "copied from [one] . . . in the custom-house [London]" (p. 569), presumably among the papers carried there from Irving's office in Boston.

Documentation

See the Appendix to the essay in this chapter for a general discussion of the tables and the sources of the data, along with a key to abbreviations used in this chapter and general information on matters such as regional differences, calendar differences, money, and weights and measures. In this table, the unit of measure for vessels is the registered ton, one of three kinds of tons associated with ships and the shipping industry of the period. For a discussion of the different types of vessels built in the colonies, see Table Eg271–274. In the source, the table distinguished between the two types of vessels using the designations "topsails" and "sloops and schooners." For the sake of continuity with other tables in this chapter, the former has been changed to "square-rigged" and the latter to "fore-and-aft-rigged." Note that Florida is included here as part of British North America but that it was not one of the Thirteen Continental Colonies.

Lord Sheffield's data recorded the number, type, and tonnage of vessels built and registered in all of British North America over the three-year period. The figures were originally compiled in the office of the Inspector General of Import and Exports and Register of Shipping, Boston, from the duplicate copies of ship registry certificates submitted by the colonial governments. For that office and its operation, see John J. McCusker, "Colonial Civil Servant and Counter-Revolutionary: Thomas Irving (1738?–1800) in Boston, Charleston, and London," *Perspectives in American History* 12 (1979): 314–50, as revised and updated in McCusker, *Essays in the Economic History of the Atlantic World* (Routledge, 1997), pp. 190–221.

Present in the original table but omitted here are the data for the remaining British colonies in North America: Newfoundland, "Island St. John's" (modern Prince Edward Island), Canada (Quebec), Nova Scotia (which included modern New Brunswick), the Bahamas, and Bermuda. While shipbuilding was unimportant in most of the rest of these colonies, that was not the case for Bermuda, which built two topsail vessels and 143 sloops and schooners measuring 3,249 tons during these three years, thus accounting for one out of every seven of the fore-and-aft rigged vessels built in British North America. At Bermuda, these vessels were, of course, the famous Bermuda sloops, large numbers of which were exported and sold to buyers in the Thirteen Continental Colonies. See Michael J. Jarvis, "'In the Eye of All Trade': Maritime Revolution and the Transformation of Bermudian Society, 1612–1800" (Ph.D. dissertation, College of William and Mary, 1998).

TABLE Eg404–419 Business establishments, by region and type of establishment: 1760–1790

Contributed by John J. McCusker

Region	Marine insurance offices, ca. 1763	Sugar refineries, ca. 1770	Rum distilleries, ca. 1770	Potteries 1760–1775	Potteries 1776–1790	Paper mills 1760–1775	Paper mills 1776–1790	Silversmiths 1775	Silversmiths 1790	Ironworks 1760–1775	Ironworks Ca. 1790	Glassworks 1760–1790	Saltworks 1760–1790	Textile manufactories, 1760–1790	Chartered business corporations, 1760–1790	Societies promoting useful knowledge, 1760–1790
	Eg404	Eg405	Eg406	Eg407	Eg408	Eg409	Eg410	Eg411	Eg412	Eg413	Eg414	Eg415	Eg416	Eg417	Eg418	Eg419
	Number	Number	Number	Number	Number	Number	Number	Number	Number	Number	Number	Number	Number	Number	Number	Number
Total	14	26	143	36	60	34	62	117	174	168	130	13	47	36	31	22
New England	8	13	96	12	25	10	19	68	104	13	15	2	10	21	12	2
Middle Atlantic	6	11	36	19	29	22	40	23	30	113	84	9	15	11	4	12
Upper South	0	0	7	0	3	2	2	16	26	38	28	2	19	2	9	5
Lower South	0	2	4	5	3	0	1	10	14	4	3	0	3	2	6	3

Source

William H. Bedford, Lester J. Cappon, et al., "Economic Activity," in Lester J. Cappon, Barbara Bartz Petchenik, and John Hamilton Long, editors, *Atlas of Early American History: The Revolutionary Era, 1760–1790* (Princeton University Press, 1976), pp. 26–30, 103–7.

Documentation

See the Appendixes to the essay in this chapter for a general discussion of the tables and the sources of the data, along with a key to abbreviations used in this chapter and general information on matters such as regional definitions, calendar differences, money, and weights and measures.

A large variety of businesses are known to have been in operation in the Thirteen Continental Colonies and the United States in the period 1760–1790. The source listed and mapped the location of many such establishments. There is no pretense to having identified all such enterprises, nor is there any suggestion that all of them were in existence over the entire period; indeed, it is known that many that were in operation before the American Revolutionary War did not outlast the war years.

Series Eg411–412. For silversmiths, the count is the number of places at which a silversmith was known to be working rather than the number of silversmiths at work. In 1790, there were also silversmiths in three towns in Ohio and one town in Kentucky. They are included in the total for the Upper South.

Series Eg413–414. The four ironworks located circa 1790 in towns near the border of New York, in what was to become the state of Vermont, are included with New England. Compare Table Eg110–116.

Series Eg416. Between 1760 and 1790, there were twelve saltworks in what are today the states of Kentucky and Illinois. They are included in the total for the Upper South.

Series Eg417. "The total number of [textile manufacturing] establishments before 1776 was thirteen, only one of which survived the war . . . . During 1780–1790 twenty-four new factories, most of them dating from 1788, were established" (Bedford, Cappon, et al., 1976, p. 107). One of the latter was in Kentucky, here included with the total for the Upper South.

GOVERNMENT

John J. McCusker

TABLE Eg420–424 Imperial taxes collected under selected British revenue laws: 1765–1774

Contributed by John J. McCusker

| | | New Revenue Acts | | | |
Year	Total	Sugar Act (1764, 1766)	Stamp Act (1765)	Townshend Revenue Act (1767)	Plantation Duty Act (1673)
	Eg420	Eg421	Eg422	Eg423	Eg424
	Pounds (£) sterling	Pounds (£) sterling	Pounds (£) sterling	Pounds (£) sterling	Pounds (£) sterling
1765	17,383	14,091	3,292	—	2,954
1766	26,696	26,696	—	—	7,373
1767	34,041	33,844	—	197	3,905
1768	37,861	24,659	—	13,202	1,160
1769	45,499	39,938	—	5,561	1,294
1770	33,637	30,910	—	2,727	1,828
1771	31,761	27,086	—	4,675	1,446
1772	45,870	42,570	—	3,300	1,490
1773	42,103	39,531	—	2,572	2,517
1774	27,995	27,074	—	921	672

Source

Oliver M. Dickerson, *The Navigation Acts and the American Revolution* (University of Pennsylvania Press, 1951), p. 201, Table 13: "Total Collections in America under the Different Revenue Laws, Exclusive of Seizures. . . . "

Documentation

See the Appendixes to the essay in this chapter for a general discussion of the tables and the sources of the data, along with a key to abbreviations used in this chapter and general information on matters such as regional definitions, calendar differences, money, and weights and measures.

This table gives the total revenues in pounds sterling collected in the Thirteen Continental Colonies as reported to the British government. These data are the net payments made into the Exchequer. They come, directly and indirectly, from the accounts presented to the British Treasury. Some of the accounts are in the Treasury Office Records; others are in the Exchequer and Audit Department Records in the PRO/TNA. The revenues were collected under the authority of several different statutes, both the older "Navigation Acts" and the newer revenue acts passed after the Seven Years' War: Act of 25 Charles II, c. 7 (commonly know as the "Plantation Duty Act," 1673); Act of 6 George III, c. 13 (the "Molasses Act," 1733); Act of 4 George III, c. 15, 1763 (the "Sugar Act," of 1764); Act of 5 George III, c. 12 (the "Stamp Act," 1765); the Revenue Act of 1766, Act of 6 George III, c. 52 (1766); and the

Revenue Act of 1767, Act of 7 George III, c. 46 (the "Townshend Act" 1766). For the rationale behind these acts, see John J. McCusker, *Mercantilism and the Economic History of the Early Modern Atlantic World* (Cambridge University Press, forthcoming). For a contemporary discussion of the workings of these acts, see John Reeves, *A History of the Law of Shipping and Navigation*, 1st edition (E. Lynch, P. Wogan, P. Byrne, J. Moore, W. Jones, R. M'Allister, H. Watts, and J. Rice, 1792).

Dickerson (1951, p. 202) estimated that, between 1768 and 1774, seizures (often highly technical) under the new *revenue* program cost the residents of the Thirteen Continental Colonies not less than £60,956 sterling, "which, added to the direct collections," totaled £403,802 "as the direct takings of the customs officers exclusive of fees, direct plunder, and costs of defending suits in the admiralty courts." This is an annual average, 1765–1774, of roughly £40,400 sterling. As a point of reference, in 1763 the government told Parliament that it expected to spend about £350,000 sterling a year to maintain the civil and military establishment in the colonies. Three quarters of that was required for a standing army of ten thousand men. See Great Britain, Parliament, House of Commons, *Journals of the House of Commons* (House of Commons, 1742 to date), volume 29, pp. 681, 686-7. See also George Louis Beer, *British Colonial Policy, 1754–1765* (Macmillan, 1907), pp. 274-86.

TABLE Eg425–426   South Carolina tax revenues: 1736–1772

Contributed by John J. McCusker

	Quitrent revenues	Provincial tax revenues		Quitrent revenues	Provincial tax revenues		Quitrent revenues	Provincial tax revenues
	Eg425	Eg426		Eg425	Eg426		Eg425	Eg426
Year	Pounds (£) sterling	Pounds (£) sterling	Year	Pounds (£) sterling	Pounds (£) sterling	Year	Pounds (£) sterling	Pounds (£) sterling
1736	705	4,102	1750	1,029	8,594	1765	1,333	15,920
1737	1,026	4,530	1751	—	5,634	1766	1,825	6,694
1738	677	1,065	1753	—	6,157	1767	1,779	14,544
1739	1,189	4,543	1754	—	5,414	1768	2,012	13,348
1740	1,153	5,031	1755	—	8,876	1769	1,883	8,705
1741	1,046	6,337	1756	—	12,859	1770	1,813	0
1742	—	5,573	1757	—	14,342	1771	2,282	0
1743	—	7,314	1758	—	23,777	1772	3,855	0
1744	—	7,315	1759	—	13,909			
1745	893	6,485	1760	1,250	23,387			
1746	1,380	6,683	1761	1,918	37,692			
1747	1,626	6,942	1762	1,769	23,079			
1748	1,046	7,733	1763	1,731	16,931			
1749	1,497	6,680	1764	1,959	16,903			

Source

Alan D. Watson, "The Quitrent System in Royal South Carolina," *William and Mary Quarterly*, 3rd series, 33 (April 1976): 183–211.

Documentation

See the Appendixes to the essay in this chapter for a general discussion of the tables and the sources of the data, along with a key to abbreviations used in this chapter and general information on such matters as regional definitions, calendar differences, money, and weights and measures.

This table gives the total revenues in pounds sterling from the taxes collected in South Carolina. Quitrents were a continuing tax on land paid to a colonial government. In South Carolina, the rate set in 1731 was four shillings "proclamation money" (three shillings sterling) per hundred acres. Colonial governments also raised revenues taxing a variety of other things (for example, imports, exports, property, income). The rate between proclamation money and sterling was fixed and unvarying, meaning that the taxes were effectively set in pounds sterling rather than in pounds South Carolina currency. For colonial taxes in general, see Jackson Turner Main and Jerome [R.] Reich, "Taxation: The British Colonies," in Jacob Ernest Cooke, W[illiam] J. Eccles, et al., editors, *Encyclopedia of the North American Colonies* (Charles Scribner's Sons, 1993), volume 1, pp. 373–81. In addition to Watson (1976), see also Maurice A. Crouse, *The Public Treasury of Colonial South Carolina*, South Carolina Tricentennial Commission, Tricentennial Studies, number 10 (University of South Carolina Press, 1977), and Robert K. Ackerman, *South Carolina Colonial Land Policies*, South Carolina Tricentennial Commission, Tricentennial Studies, number 9 (University of South Carolina Press, 1977). Compare Beverley W. Bond Jr., *The Quit-Rent System in the American Colonies* (Yale University Press, 1919).

Watson drew his data for his Table 1 (1976, pp. 192–3) from three sources: (1) Accounts of Quit Rents Paid, 1733–1742, 1735–1742, 1760–1768, Parts I and II, and 1768–1774, Records of the Receiver General, South Carolina Department of Archives and History, Columbia; (2) "The Account of His Majesty's Quitrents at South Carolina," March 26, 1745, to March 26, 1751, T 1/347, number 84, PRO/TNA; and (3) Thomas Cooper and David J. McCord, editors, *The Statutes at Large of South Carolina* (A. S. Johnson, 1836–1841), volume 3, pp. 438–48, 472–84, 502–13, 527–41, 592, 593, 597, 629, 647, 678, 714, 729, 727, 738; volume 4, pp. 6, 10, 19, 34, 45, 53, 103, 128.

Because the actual provincial tax revenues survive in the records only for the years 1761–1769, Watson substituted the legislature's projected tax yields for the remaining years (1976, p. 206). Crouse (1977, p. 83), using different sources, compared both the expected revenues and the revenues actually collected, 1761–1769. For 1761–1764, his data for the actual receipts are the same as Watson's; for 1765–1769, there are some small differences. More important are the differences between projected and actual revenues, with some years in surplus and others in deficit. On balance over the decade, revenue collected exceeded projected revenues by about 4 percent, lending credibility to Watson's method of estimation. Both Watson and Crouse divide in half the total collected in the two years 1763–1764 and assign one half to each of the two years.

Watson's data on the revenues from the quitrents, which were expressed in "proclamation money," have been converted to sterling at the fixed rate of £133 $\frac{1}{3}$ currency to £100 sterling. For his own purposes, Watson reduced the values for provincial tax revenues that were originally stated in South Carolina currency to proclamation money at a ratio of 5:1. For this table, these data were first reconverted to South Carolina currency at that same ratio and then reduced to sterling using the exchange rates in series Eg323.

The annual average total of provincial taxes paid between 1760 and 1769 amounted to just under £20,000 sterling. While the quitrents diminished over time from about 20 percent of the total tax revenues of the colony in 1736–1741 to just over 10 percent in 1760–1769, they assumed greater importance during the years from 1769 through 1775 because a major and continuing disagreement between the Commons House and the governor prevented the enactment of any revenue bills after 1769. Calculating the white population at the midpoint of the decade 1760–1769 at about 43,000 people (series Eg36), a total of £20,000 per year equaled about nine shillings sterling per taxpayer or roughly $2.00 each annually.

Newton B. Jones, *Records of the Treasurers of South Carolina, 1725–1776*, Pamphlet Accompanying South Carolina Archives Microcopy, number 3 (South Carolina Department of Archives and History, 1969), pp. 7–19, presented very detailed accounts of both income and expenditures from the public treasurers' ledgers and journals. Apparently unknown to both Watson and Crouse, these accounts have yet to be integrated into the discussions of the colony's finances. One thing that Jones's figures make clear is that, contrary to the impression created by Watson and Crouse, the colony continued to earn some revenues during the post-1769 period from tax laws already on the books, that is: in 1770, £9,318 sterling; in 1771, £10,734; in 1772, £15,583; in 1773, £18.349; in 1774, £15,008; and in 1775, £4,812.

TABLE Eg427-428   Annual taxes paid in Massachusetts and Virginia per free person: 1765-1796

Contributed by John J. McCusker

Years and nature of tax	Massachusetts Eg427 Dollars	Virginia Eg428 Dollars
1765-1773 (Provincial)	0.94	0.98
1795-1796 (Total)	3.63	3.22
Federal	1.57	2.26
State	0.35	0.35
Local	1.71	0.61

Source

H[erbert] James Henderson, "Taxation and Political Culture: Massachusetts and Virginia, 1760-1800," *William and Mary Quarterly*, 3rd series, 47 (January 1990): 90-114.

Documentation

See the Appendixes to the essay in this chapter for a general discussion of the tables and the sources of the data, along with a key to abbreviations used in this chapter and general information on matters such as regional definitions, calendar differences, money, and weights and measures.

This table calculates the per capita taxes paid by citizens of Massachusetts and Virginia before and after the American Revolution. For an explanation of the sources Henderson used and the methods he employed, see the source, Tables I and VI. He calculated the taxes paid in 1765-1773 in colonial currency. For purposes of comparison with his second period, his figures have been converted first to sterling using the exchange rates in series Eg315 and Eg321 and thence to dollars. At par, £100 sterling equaled $444.44. See John J. McCusker, *How Much Is That in Real Money? A Historical Commodity Price Index for Use as a Deflator of Money Values in the Economy of the United States*, 2nd edition (American Antiquarian Society, 2001). In his Table VI, Henderson reported the subtotals in per capita terms and the total in both per person and per free person. The figures for the components per free person have been adjusted accordingly. From Table Eg425-426, we see that in the decade 1760-1769, South Carolinians paid annually about $2.00 each in provincial taxes.

The better to make the data for 1765-1773 comparable with those for 1794-1796, we can add in Oliver M. Dickerson's estimate of the amounts paid for imperial taxes and other assessments (Table Eg420-424). The £40,400 sterling annually paid by the Continental Colonies to Great Britain works out to $0.11 per free white person making the total of provincial and imperial taxes paid by the free citizens of Massachusetts $1.05, by Virginians, $1.09, and by South Carolinians, $2.11.

In the decade prior to the American Revolution, the average person in Great Britain paid about $6.10 annually in taxes. The net receipts of all public revenues for Great Britain averaged £10,682,600 annually between 1765 and 1774. B[rian] R. Mitchell, *British Historical Statistics* (Cambridge University Press, 1988), p. 576. The estimated population of England, Wales, and Scotland in 1770 is 7,782,000. E[dward] A. Wrigley and R[oger] S. Schofield, *The Population History of England, 1541-1871: A Reconstruction* (Harvard University Press, 1981), p. 534; John J. McCusker, *Rum and the American Revolution: The Rum Trade and the Balance of Payments of the Thirteen Continental Colonies, 1650-1775* (Garland, 1989), p. 552. Compare Patrick K. O'Brien, "The Political Economy of British Taxation, 1660-1815," *Economic History Review*, 2nd series, 41 (February 1988): 3, where the data he presented suggests a somewhat lower figure, $5.54 per person (1768-1772).

In the dramatic debate in Parliament on February 2, 1775, the British Prime Minister, Lord North, argued that the average inhabitant of Great Britain "paid at least 25 shillings" in taxes annually, $5.56, and the average American, six pence, $0.11. William Cobbett, editor, *The Parliamentary History of England from the Earliest Period to the Year 1803* (T. C. Hansard, 1806-1820), volume 18, p. 222. North was spot on with his estimate of how much the Continental Colonies paid in imperial revenues and not so very far off in his estimate of how much his fellow countrymen paid in taxes to his government (he erred because he overestimated the size of the population), but his essential point was completely off the mark because he failed to account for taxes the colonists paid to colonial governments. The ratio between the two was closer to 5:1 than 50:1. For South Carolinians, the ratio was somewhat less than 3:1.

Compare the discussions of comparative levels of taxation in Lawrence Henry Gipson, *The Coming of the Revolution, 1763-1775*, New American Nation Series (Harper and Row, 1954), pp. 116-61; R[obert] R. Palmer, *The Age of the Democratic Revolution: A Political History of Europe and America, 1760-1800* (Princeton University Press, 1959-1964), volume 1, pp. 153-8; Robert A. Becker, *Revolution, Reform, and the Politics of American Taxation, 1763-1783* (Louisiana State University Press, 1980); and Lance E. Davis and Robert A. Huttenback, "The Cost of Empire," in Roger L. Ransom, Richard Sutch, and Gary M. Walton, editors, *Explorations in the New Economic History: Essays in Honor of Douglass C. North* (Academic Press, 1982), pp. 41-9. See also J[oseph] Massie, *Calculations of the Present Taxes Yearly Paid by a Family of Each Rank, Degree, or Class*, 2nd edition (T. Payne, W. Owen, and C. Henderson, 1761).

INTERNATIONAL TRANSACTIONS AND FOREIGN COMMERCE

John J. McCusker

TABLE Eg429–442 Value of imports into and exports from England, by colony or locality: 1693–1791[1]
Contributed by John J. McCusker

Imports to England from the colonies

Year	Total Eg429	New England[2] Eg430	New York[2] Eg431	Pennsylvania Eg432	Virginia and Maryland Eg433	Carolina Eg434	Georgia Eg435
	Pounds (£) sterling (constant value)	Pounds (£) sterling (constant value)	Pounds (£) sterling (constant value)	Pounds (£) sterling (constant value)	Pounds (£) sterling (constant value)	Pounds (£) sterling (constant value)	Pounds (£) sterling (constant value)
1693	113,600	35,662	—	1,572	76,366	0	—
1694	293,069	29,422	—	1,828	257,050	4,769	—
1695	482,883	30,255	—	1,198	446,066	5,364	—
1697	279,852	26,282	10,093	3,347	227,756	12,374	—
1698	226,055	31,254	8,763	2,720	174,053	9,265	—
1699	255,397	26,660	16,818	1,477	198,115	12,327	—
1700	395,021	41,486	17,567	4,608	317,302	14,058	—
1701	309,134	32,656	18,547	5,220	235,738	16,973	—
1702	335,788	37,026	7,965	4,145	274,782	11,870	—
1703	204,295	33,539	7,471	5,160	144,928	13,197	—
1704	321,972	30,823	10,540	2,430	264,112	14,067	—
1705	150,961	22,793	7,393	1,309	116,768	2,698	—
1706	187,073	22,210	2,849	4,210	149,152	8,652	—
1707	284,798	38,793	14,283	786	207,625	23,311	—
1708	286,435	49,635	10,847	2,120	213,493	10,340	—
1709	324,534	29,559	12,259	617	261,668	20,431	—
1710	249,814	31,112	8,203	1,277	188,429	20,793	—
1711	324,698	26,415	12,193	38	273,181	12,871	—
1712	365,971	24,699	12,466	1,471	297,941	29,394	—
1713	303,222	49,904	14,428	178	206,263	32,449	—
1714	395,774	51,541	29,810	2,663	280,470	31,290	—
1715	297,246	66,555	21,316	5,461	174,756	29,158	—
1716	424,389	69,595	21,971	5,193	281,343	46,287	—
1717	426,090	58,898	24,534	4,499	296,884	41,275	—
1718	457,471	61,591	27,331	5,588	316,576	46,385	—
1719	463,054	54,452	19,596	6,564	332,069	50,373	—
1720	468,188	49,206	16,836	7,928	331,482	62,736	—
1721	493,871	50,483	15,681	8,037	357,812	61,858	—
1722	437,696	47,955	20,118	6,882	283,091	79,650	—
1723	461,761	59,337	27,992	8,332	287,997	78,103	—
1724	462,681	69,585	21,191	4,057	277,344	90,504	—
1725	415,650	72,021	24,976	11,981	214,730	91,942	—
1726	526,303	63,816	38,307	5,960	324,767	93,453	—
1727	637,135	75,052	31,617	12,823	421,588	96,055	—
1728	605,324	64,689	21,141	15,230	413,089	91,175	—
1729	575,282	52,512	15,833	7,434	386,174	113,329	—

Exports from England to the colonies

Year	Total Eg436	New England[2] Eg437	New York[2] Eg438	Pennsylvania Eg439	Virginia and Maryland Eg440	Carolina Eg441	Georgia Eg442
	Pounds (£) sterling (constant value)	Pounds (£) sterling (constant value)	Pounds (£) sterling (constant value)	Pounds (£) sterling (constant value)	Pounds (£) sterling (constant value)	Pounds (£) sterling (constant value)	Pounds (£) sterling (constant value)
1693	169,381	66,492	—	12,153	83,474[3]	7,262	—
1694	268,186	121,639	—	1,929	139,878	4,740	—
1695	222,693	62,733	—	14,709	137,438	7,813	—
1697	140,129	68,468	4,579	2,997	58,796	5,289	—
1698	458,097	93,517	25,279	10,704	310,135	18,462	—
1699	403,614	127,279	42,792	17,064	205,078	11,401	—
1700	344,341	91,918	49,410	18,529	173,481	11,003	—
1701	343,826	86,322	31,910	12,003	199,683	13,908	—
1702	186,809	64,625	29,991	9,342	72,391	10,460	—
1703	296,210	59,608	17,562	9,899	196,713	12,428	—
1704	176,088	74,896	22,294	11,819	60,458	6,621	—
1705	291,722	62,504	27,902	7,206	174,322	19,788	—
1706	161,691	57,050	31,588	11,037	58,015	4,001	—
1707	413,244	120,631	29,855	14,365	237,901	10,492	—
1708	240,183	115,505	26,899	6,722	79,061	11,996	—
1709	269,596	120,349	34,577	5,881	80,268	28,521	—
1710	293,659	106,338	31,475	8,594	127,639	19,613	—
1711	297,626	137,421	28,856	19,408	91,535	20,406	—
1712	309,691	128,105	18,524	8,464	134,583	20,015	—
1713	284,556	120,778	46,470	17,037	76,304	23,967	—
1714	333,443	121,288	44,643	14,927	128,873	23,712	—
1715	451,366	164,650	54,629	16,182	199,274	16,631	—
1716	402,042	121,156	52,173	21,842	179,599	27,272	—
1717	439,666	132,001	44,140	22,505	215,962	25,058	—
1718	425,333	131,885	62,966	22,716	191,925	15,841	—
1719	393,000	125,317	56,355	27,068	164,630	19,630	—
1720	319,702	128,767	37,397	24,531	110,717	18,290	—
1721	331,905	114,524	50,754	21,548	127,376	17,703	—
1722	424,725	133,722	57,478	26,397	172,754	34,374	—
1723	411,590	176,486	53,013	15,992	123,853	42,246	—
1724	461,584	168,507	63,020	30,324	161,894	37,839	—
1725	549,693	201,768	70,650	42,209	195,884	39,182	—
1726	553,297	200,882	84,866	37,634	185,981	43,934	—
1727	502,927	187,277	67,452	31,979	192,965	23,254	—
1728	517,861	194,590	81,634	37,478	171,092	33,067	—
1729	422,958	161,102	64,760	29,799	108,931	58,366	—

Imports to England from the colonies (Eg429–435) — Exports from England to the colonies (Eg436–442). All figures: Pounds (£) sterling (constant value).

Year	Total Eg429	New England Eg430	New York Eg431	Pennsylvania Eg432	Virginia and Maryland Eg433	Carolina Eg434	Georgia Eg435	Total Eg436	New England Eg437	New York Eg438	Pennsylvania Eg439	Virginia and Maryland Eg440	Carolina Eg441	Georgia Eg442
1730	572,585	54,701	8,740	10,582	346,823	151,739	—	536,860	208,196	64,356	48,592	150,931	64,785	—
1731	650,863	49,048	20,756	12,786	408,502	159,771	—	536,266	183,467	66,116	44,260	171,278	71,145	—
1732	519,036	64,095	9,411	8,524	310,799	126,207	0	531,253	216,600	65,540	41,698	148,289	58,298	828
1733	669,633	61,983	11,626	14,776	403,198	177,845	203	548,890	184,570	65,417	40,565	186,177	70,466	1,695
1734	611,350	82,252	15,307	20,217	373,090	120,466	18	556,275	146,460	81,758	54,392	172,086	99,658	1,921
1735	652,326	72,899	14,155	21,919	394,995	145,348	3,010	668,664	189,125	80,405	48,804	220,381	117,837	12,112
1736	699,764	66,788	17,944	20,786	380,163	214,083	0	677,624	222,158	86,000	61,513	204,794	101,147	2,012
1737	775,382	63,347	16,833	15,198	492,246	187,758	0	682,434	223,923	125,833	56,690	211,301	58,986	5,701
1738	620,212	59,116	16,228	11,918	391,814	141,119	17	751,270	203,233	133,438	61,450	258,860	87,793	6,496
1739	754,276	46,604	18,459	8,134	444,654	236,192	233	695,869	220,378	106,070	54,452	217,200	94,445	3,324
1740	718,416	72,389	21,498	15,048	341,997	266,560	924	813,382	171,081	158,777	56,751	281,428	181,821	3,524
1741	912,291	60,052	21,142	17,158	577,109	236,830	0	885,492	198,147	140,430	91,010	248,582	204,770	2,553
1742	659,227	53,166	13,536	8,527	427,769	154,607	1,622	800,052	148,899	167,591	75,295	264,186	127,063	17,018
1743	880,807	63,185	15,067	9,596	557,821	235,136	2	829,273	172,461	135,487	79,340	328,195	111,499	2,291
1744	667,524	50,248	14,527	7,446	402,709	192,594	0	640,881	143,982	119,920	62,214	234,855	79,141	769
1745	554,431	38,948	14,083	10,130	399,423	91,847	0	535,253	140,463	54,957	54,280	197,799	86,815	939
1746	559,500	38,612	8,841	15,779	419,371	76,897	0	755,926	209,177	86,712	73,699	282,545	102,809	984
1747	660,715	41,771	14,992	3,832	492,619	107,500	0	726,669	210,640	137,984	82,404	200,088	95,529	24
1748	716,626	29,748	12,358	12,363	494,852	167,305	0	830,433	197,682	143,311	75,330	252,624	160,172	1,314
1749	663,524	39,999	23,413	14,944	434,618	150,499	51	1,230,386	238,286	265,773	238,637	323,600	164,085	5
1750	814,768	48,455	35,634	28,191	508,939	191,607	1,942	1,313,083	343,659	267,130	217,713	349,419	133,037	2,125
1751	835,651	63,287	42,363	23,870	460,085	245,491	555	1,233,168	305,974	248,941	190,917	347,027	138,244	2,065
1752	1,004,182	74,313	40,648	29,978	569,453	288,264	1,526	1,148,127	273,340	194,030	201,666	325,151	150,777	3,163
1753	972,740	83,395	50,553	38,527	632,574	164,634	3,057	1,452,944	345,523	277,864	245,644	356,776	213,009	14,128
1754	1,007,759	66,538	26,663	30,649	573,435	307,238	3,236	1,176,279	329,433	127,497	244,647	323,513	149,215	1,974
1755	939,553	59,533	28,054	32,336	489,668	325,525	4,437	1,112,997	341,796	151,071	144,456	285,157	187,887	2,630
1756	659,356	47,359	24,073	20,095	337,759	222,915	7,155	1,352,178	384,371	250,425	200,169	334,897	181,780	536
1757	610,684	27,556	19,168	14,190	418,881	130,889	0	1,628,348	363,404	353,311	268,426	426,687	213,949	2,571
1758	670,720	30,204	14,260	21,383	454,362	150,511	0	1,712,887	465,694	356,555	260,953	438,471	181,002	10,212
1759	639,909	25,985	21,684	22,404	357,228	206,534	6,074	2,345,453	527,067	630,785	498,161	459,007	215,255	15,178
1760	761,099	37,802	21,125	22,754	504,451	162,769	12,198	2,611,764	599,647	480,106	707,998	605,882	218,131	0
1761	847,892	46,225	48,648	39,170	455,083	253,002	5,764	1,652,078	334,225	289,570	204,067	545,350	254,587	24,279
1762	742,632	41,733	58,882	38,091	415,709	181,695	6,522	1,377,160	247,385	288,046	206,199	417,599	194,170	23,761
1763	1,106,161	74,815	53,989	38,228	642,294	282,366	14,469	1,631,997	258,854	238,560	284,152	555,391	250,132	44,908
1764	1,110,572	88,157	53,697	36,258	559,408	341,727	31,325	2,249,710	459,765	515,416	435,191	515,192	305,808	18,338
1765	1,151,698	145,819	54,959	25,148	505,671	385,918	34,183	1,944,114	451,299	382,349	363,368	333,224	334,709	29,165
1766	1,043,958	141,733	67,020	26,851	461,693	293,587	53,074	1,804,333	409,642	330,829	327,314	372,548	296,732	67,268
1767	1,096,079	128,207	61,422	37,641	437,926	395,027	35,856	1,900,923	406,081	417,957	371,830	437,628	244,093	23,334
1768	1,251,454	148,375	87,115	59,406	406,048	508,108	42,402	2,157,218	419,797	482,930	432,107	475,954	289,868	56,562
1769	1,060,206	129,353	73,466	26,111	361,892	387,114	82,270	1,336,122	207,993	74,918	199,909	488,362	306,600	58,340
1770	1,015,535	148,011	69,882	28,109	435,094	278,907	55,532	1,925,571	394,451	475,991	134,881	717,782	146,273	56,193
1771	1,339,840	150,381	95,875	31,615	577,848	420,311	63,810	4,202,472	1,420,119	653,621	728,744	920,326	409,169	70,493
1772	1,258,515	126,265	82,707	29,133	528,404	425,923	66,083	2,012,635	824,830	343,970	507,909	793,910	449,610	92,406
1773	1,369,229	124,624	76,246	36,652	589,803	456,513	85,391	2,079,412	527,055	289,214	426,448	428,904	344,859	62,932
1774	1,373,846	112,248	80,008	69,611	612,030	432,302	67,647	2,590,437	562,476	437,937	625,652	528,738	378,116	57,518

Notes appear at end of table

(continued)

TABLE Eg429–442 Value of imports into and exports from England, by colony or locality: 1693–1791

Contributed by John J. McCusker

Imports to England from the colonies

Year	Total Eg429	New England Eg430 [2]	New York Eg431 [2]	Pennsylvania Eg432	Virginia and Maryland Eg433	Carolina Eg434	Georgia Eg435
	Pounds (£) sterling (constant value)	Pounds (£) sterling (constant value)	Pounds (£) sterling (constant value)	Pounds (£) sterling (constant value)	Pounds (£) sterling (constant value)	Pounds (£) sterling (constant value)	Pounds (£) sterling (constant value)
1775	1,920,950	116,588	187,018	175,962	758,356	579,549	103,477
1776	103,964	762	2,318	1,421	73,226	13,668	12,569
1777	12,619	1,880	8,430	17	58	2,234	0
1778	17,694	372	16,192	56	0	1,074	0
1779	20,579	808	14,862	570	0	3,732	607
1780	18,560	32	15,532	37	0	708	2,251
1781	99,847	2,068	2,905	0	0	94,368	506
1782	28,676	0	7,690	0	0	14,182	6,804
1783	314,058	26,350	83,413	30,053	93,888	74,589	5,765
1784	701,190	49,831	43,360	68,828	352,742	163,540	22,889
1785	775,892	56,648	56,844	55,984	350,122	212,229	44,065
1786	743,644	45,303	69,397	22,834	376,027	198,454	31,629
1787	780,444	67,399	80,731	34,796	344,217	229,086	24,215
1788	883,618	66,306	97,607	30,489	406,422	258,029	24,765
1789	893,296	88,488	80,769	36,050	446,543	215,890	25,556
1790	1,043,389	98,383	97,607	50,540	483,962	253,022	59,875
1791	1,011,313	75,750	151,605	54,141	447,358	230,879	51,580

Exports from England to the colonies

Year	Total Eg436	New England Eg437 [2]	New York Eg438 [2]	Pennsylvania Eg439	Virginia and Maryland Eg440	Carolina Eg441	Georgia Eg442
	Pounds (£) sterling (constant value)	Pounds (£) sterling (constant value)	Pounds (£) sterling (constant value)	Pounds (£) sterling (constant value)	Pounds (£) sterling (constant value)	Pounds (£) sterling (constant value)	Pounds (£) sterling (constant value)
1775	196,162	71,625	1,228	1,366	1,921	6,245	113,777
1776	55,415	55,050	0	365	0	0	0
1777	57,295	0	57,295	0	0	0	0
1778	33,986	0	26,449	7,537	0	0	0
1779	349,797	0	349,712	0	0	0	85
1780	825,431	0	496,602	0	0	236,941	91,888
1781	847,883	0	502,977	0	0	330,847	14,059
1782	256,325	0	186,242	0	0	69,743	340
1783	1,435,229	199,558	547,132	239,462	199,657	226,737	22,683
1784	3,418,407	521,743	653,508	653,678	1,099,782	442,465	47,231
1785	2,078,744	162,939	390,965	344,986	857,069	278,389	44,396
1786	1,431,255	125,128	204,285	203,870	701,834	181,410	14,728
1787	1,794,214	200,693	339,444	206,213	744,143	281,647	22,074
1788	1,709,928	232,744	301,932	203,394	656,678	291,429	23,751
1789	2,306,529	347,624	400,693	349,691	803,043	359,214	46,264
1790	3,258,238	338,784	497,699	728,439	1,292,207	359,592	41,517
1791	4,014,416	580,737	772,187	697,132	1,440,194	431,880	92,286

[1] The year of record ended December 24 for 1693–1695; September 28 for 1697–1698; December 24 for 1699–1751;

[2] For 1693–1695, New York was included as part of New England.

[3] Value is defective in the source.

Source

For 1693–1695, the data are drawn from the "Account of Exports and Imports, London and the Outports," 1693–1695, Parchment Collection, Sessional Papers, House of Lords, HLRO. See especially the covering letter from the Commissioners of the Customs to the Lords Committee Appointed to Consider the State of Trade, February, 16, 1696/97. For 1697–1791, the data are drawn from the Ledgers of Imports and Exports of England, CUST 3/1-82, PRO/TNA, contemporary accounts extracted from them, and related documents as discussed in the documentation for this table. The earlier data have been compiled by D. W. Jones; the series for 1697–1791 were originally compiled by Jacob M. Price. Some corrections to earlier presentations of theses data have been made (for example, New York, 1763; Virginia and Maryland, 1773), as discussed in John J. McCusker, "The Current Value of English Exports, 1697 to 1800," *William and Mary Quarterly*, 3rd series, 28 (October 1971): 607–28, as revised and updated in McCusker, *Essays in the Economic History of the Atlantic World* (Routledge, 1997), pp. 222–44.

Documentation

See the Appendixes to the essay in this chapter for a general discussion of the tables and the sources of the data, along with a key to abbreviations used in this chapter and general information on matters such as regional definitions, calendar differences, money, and weights and measures. Note especially the discussion of the time periods used for compiling these records.

Presented here are the annual total values in pounds sterling of the goods imported into all English and Welsh ports of entry (POE) – London and "the Outports" – from the Thirteen Continental Colonies (later, the United States) and exported from those same POE to the colonies. These are decidedly *not*, therefore, the records of the good exported or imported at American POE and thus provide only a limited view of the trade of the colonies. For the imports and exports of the colonies, compare the data for 1768–1772 in CUST 16/1, PRO/TNA. See also Tables Eg461–473 and Eg688–754. The original accounts list each commodity, distinguish between English-made goods being exported and foreign-made goods being reexported, and, reflecting their origins in the British Customs administration, further distinguish between reexported goods shipped "in time" to qualify for the rebate of duties paid upon importation and goods that did not quality for a rebate ("out-of-time").

The data presented here were initially collected by the Customs officers in the POE of England and Wales and were then transmitted to London where they were compiled into annual totals under the direction of the Commissioners of the Customs, after 1697 in the office of the Inspector General of Imports and Exports located in the Custom House. The accounts for 1693–1695 were assembled pursuant to orders of the House of Lords, December 30, 1695, and January 8, 1695/96. The Commissioners of the Customs presented the accounts and summaries based on them to the House of Lords just over a year later, on February 16, 1696/97. They exist as a set of thin folio volumes, numbered Liber 1–Liber 12, Parchment Collection, Sessional Papers, House of Lords, HLRO. For their origin, see Great Britain, Parliament, House of Lords, *The Manuscripts of the House of Lords* (Royal Commission on Historical Manuscripts; H. M. Stationery Office, 1871 to date), new series, volume 2, pp. 411 et seq. See also CO 323/2, folio 169v, PRO/TNA. The Welsh scholar Dwyryd Jones identified these materials and computed the value of imports and exports based on the quantities of goods recorded in them and the fixed valuations employed in the later ledgers for the years 1699–1791. His data are reproduced

TABLE Eg429–442   Value of imports into and exports from England, by colony or locality: 1693–1791   *Continued*

here. See also D. W. Jones, *War and Economy in the Age of William III and Marlborough* (Basil Blackwell, 1988), pp. 136, 323, and elsewhere. Those earlier accounts obviously became the incentive for and the prototype of the preparation of the later, long series of annual ledgers. Almost all of the large post-1697 volumes survive in CUST 2 and CUST 3, PRO/TNA, but some do not. Two volumes from early in the eighteenth century, for 1705 and 1712, and all volumes from late in that same century and early in the nineteenth century are missing, presumably destroyed in the 1715 or 1814 Custom House fires. T[homas]. F. Reddaway, "The London Custom House, 1666–1740," *London Topographical Record* 21 (1958): 17, 25; Rupert C. Jarvis, "The Archival History of the Customs Records," *Journal of the Society of Archivists* 1 (April 1959): 244–5. The series in this table are complemented by those for Scotland in Table Eg443–460.

On numerous occasions throughout the eighteenth and early nineteenth centuries, extracts were drawn from these volumes, and they have been preserved in various places; some were published. Chief among these was Charles Whitworth, *State of the Trade of Great Britain in Its Imports and Exports, Progressively from the Year 1697 [to 1773]: Also of the Trade to Each Particular Country, during the Above Period, Distinguishing Each Year . . .* (G. Robinson, J. Robson, J. Walter, T. Cadell, and J. Sewell, 1776). Despite his title, Whitworth included data only for England and Wales. A contemporary carefully added in manuscript to two copies of this book all of the data for the remaining years of the century down though 1801. One copy of this corrected, annotated, and extended volume is in the Public Record Office, London (BT 6/185, PRO/TNA); the other copy, a duplicate of the first, is in the George Chalmers Collection, Peter Force Papers, Manuscript Division, LC. The provenance of the latter volume may suggest something about its origins. George Chalmers (1742–1825) was the Scottish-born antiquary and one-time Maryland lawyer who, having returned to London in 1775, held the position of Chief Clerk of the Board of Trade from 1785 to his death in 1825. Over his life he amassed an immense collection of books and papers dealing with the United States. See Grace Amelia Cockroft, *The Public Life of George Chalmers*, Columbia University, Studies in History, Economics and Public Law, number 454 (Columbia University Press, 1939). A volume that appears to be this one was among the many in his library sold at auction after his death. See *Catalogue of the Very Curious, Valuable and Extensive Library of the Late George Chalmers . . .* (Evans, 1841–1842), volume 2, p. 93 (item number 1409). It sold for four shillings and is described as "Whitworth's (Sir C.) State of the Trade . . ., Folio, with a Continuation in Manuscript by Mr. Chalmers." Thus, it seems that Chalmers himself was re-

sponsible for copying out the additional data. However that may be, these volumes allow us to continue the data in this table down to 1791. In addition to Whitworth, David Macpherson, *Annals of Commerce, Manufactures, Fisheries and Navigation . . . of the British Empire and Other Countries, from the Earliest Accounts to . . . 1801* (Nichols and Son et al., 1805), volumes 3–4, printed the annual summaries of English trade from 1760 to 1800. Other contemporary reports of these data appear to have followed Macpherson. See, for example, Timothy Pitkin, *A Statistical View of the Commerce of the United States of America: Its Connections with Agriculture and Manufactures: and an Account of the Public Debt, Revenues, and Expenditures of the United States. With a Brief Review of the Trade, Agriculture, and Manufactures of the Colonies, Previous to Their Independence. Accompanied with Tables, Illustrative of the Principles and Objects of the Work*, 1st edition (Charles Hosmer, 1816), p. 30; Adam Seybert, *Statistical Annals . . . of the United States of America: Founded on Official Documents* (Thomas Dobson and Son, 1818), p. 286.

In one very important way, the original data themselves are as misleading as the title of Whitworth's book: they do not record the current value of the trade of England and Wales. The Customs clerks in the various POE sent to London the quantities of goods imported and exported. The clerks in the Inspector General's office carefully copied these data and then multiplied quantity times price to arrive at the value of the import or export. In doing so, they did not use current prices, however, but had to resort to a set price for each commodity that was established for this purpose early in the eighteenth century. Thus, the series presented here are a measure by nominal value of the changing volume – the constant value – of the imports and exports of England and Wales (or of Scotland, in the case of Table Eg443–460). For a discussion of these issues – and the establishment and compilation of a current value series based on these data – see McCusker (1971).

One should also note that there is little argument that the quantities were essentially correct. As Lawrence A. Harper stated – and Jacob M. Price repeated – in the prior editions of this chapter: "Smuggling . . . does not constitute a material factor during the years under consideration" (*Historical Statistics of the United States* [1975], p. 1157). For an intelligent and persuasive review of the issues, see "The Reliability of Eighteenth-Century Customs Accounts" in S[imon] D. Smith, "British Exports to Continental North America, 1690–1776" (Ph.D. dissertation, University of Cambridge, 1992), pp. 334–71. See also the discussion in John J. McCusker, *Mercantilism and the Economic History of the Early Modern Atlantic World* (Cambridge University Press, forthcoming).

TABLE Eg443–460 Value of imports into and exports from Scotland, by colony or locality: 1740–1791[1]

Contributed by John J. McCusker

	Imports to Scotland from the colonies								
	Total	New England	New York	Pennsylvania	Maryland	Virginia	North Carolina	South Carolina	Georgia
	Eg443	Eg444	Eg445	Eg446	Eg447	Eg448	Eg449	Eg450	Eg451
Year	Pounds (£) sterling (constant value)	Pounds (£) sterling (constant value)	Pounds (£) sterling (constant value)	Pounds (£) sterling (constant value)	Pounds (£) sterling (constant value)	Pounds (£) sterling (constant value)	Pounds (£) sterling (constant value)	Pounds (£) sterling (constant value)	Pounds (£) sterling (constant value)
1740	52,146	2,301	0	595	9,910	38,125	1,215	0	0
1741	86,118	3,978	0	778	19,029	62,330	0	3	0
1742	101,725	1,988	0	564	15,611	79,575	1,710	2,277	0
1743	119,799	1,615	0	0	22,947	93,253	1,694	290	0
1744	103,494	2,419	0	0	16,186	77,392	789	6,708	0
1745	124,140	979	0	1,269	17,734	103,563	595	0	0
1746	99,981	2,477	0	0	10,924	75,734	0	10,846	0
1747	117,192	5,545	0	1,148	6,234	91,285	0	12,980	0
1748	162,677	2,703	0	0	18,105	128,049	0	13,820	0
1749	178,582	4,629	0	0	31,387	137,895	365	4,306	0
1750	160,797	3,205	0	896	26,246	128,804	349	1,297	0
1751	199,521	6,402	0	5	27,123	163,488	430	2,073	0
1752	187,011	5,975	2,019	1,217	20,928	154,814	281	1,777	0
1753	215,217	6,319	936	0	27,003	177,324	0	3,635	0
1754	167,481	7,055	1,357	1,395	25,414	130,237	1,473	550	0
1755	185,480	6,243	1,121	4,852	23,853	145,659	1,716	2,036	0
1756	162,151	14,418	1,630	2,390	40,239	95,006	0	8,468	0
1757	209,431	4,513	303	1,176	35,523	156,956	812	10,148	0
1758	315,970	71	286	0	68,485	221,320	4,343	20,449	1,016
1759	209,858	755	6,224	1,584	45,883	124,179	7,253	21,512	2,468
1760	389,394	2,006	13,241	92	84,288	270,299	1,938	17,530	0
1761	312,713	5,627	811	1,038	92,270	196,992	3,382	11,268	1,325
1762	326,347	9,403	2,981	616	59,535	242,057	1,086	10,669	0
1763	353,811	4,282	0	250	71,846	272,251	1,822	3,360	0
1764	337,962	9,104	8,197	6,440	56,625	244,723	6,849	6,024	0
1765	421,944	29,754	4,932	3,963	84,543	288,860	4,342	4,954	596
1766	393,591	15,809	315	1,292	78,859	255,481	12,467	19,319	10,049
1767	376,810	19,309	3,072	5,022	94,908	237,156	12,247	5,096	0
1768	405,128	9,429	4,694	2,265	97,242	273,364	8,708	9,426	0
1769	471,307	13,422	39,916	2,001	98,353	299,715	11,312	6,588	0
1770	482,206	9,432	29,115	2,956	97,667	315,236	16,911	10,363	526
1771	606,464	12,542	19	20,042	125,424	423,105	16,458	8,874	0
1772	541,896	12,775	0	70	122,517	385,556	16,716	4,262	0
1773	517,954	7,454	2,304	0	91,232	374,243	24,586	3,563	14,572
1774	473,070	11,550	3,472	0	84,235	341,407	32,380	0	26
1775	536,112	11,587	9,204	758	140,644	348,041	25,878	0	0
1776	81,852	0	0	0	13,606	68,172	74	0	0
1777	3,991	0	3,161	0	0	830	0	0	0
1778	24,834	0	21,303	0	1,177	0	0	2,354	0
1779	33,815	0	33,599	216	0	0	0	0	0
1780	79,687	2,200	52,308	8,662	0	15,296	0	1,221	0
1781	44,310	0	32,866	0	0	0	0	11,057	387
1782	106,827	0	106,827	0	0	0	0	0	0
1783	34,670	176	19,366	801	0	11,175	991	2,161	0
1784	48,140	1,248	3,943	1,435	4,789	32,720	2,210	1,795	0
1785	117,705	0	4,828	1,722	5,362	88,097	7,283	8,559	1,854
1786	99,476	89	5,896	0	96	75,548	10,024	7,811	12
1787	113,191	297	6,429	0	2,976	76,142	7,200	17,186	2,961
1788	140,171	840	14,241	2,318	2,258	95,992	15,505	8,725	292
1789	156,894	1,904	19,030	0	293	92,519	19,984	23,087	77
1790	147,682	2,481	22,364	1,191	12,532	70,280	14,952	18,358	5,524
1791	182,866	3,464	12,901	0	20,070	104,846	19,606	18,362	3,617

TABLE Eg443–460   Value of imports into and exports from Scotland, by colony or locality: 1740–1791   *Continued*

	Total	New England	New York	Pennsylvania	Maryland	Virginia	North Carolina	South Carolina	Georgia
	Eg452	Eg453	Eg454	Eg455	Eg456	Eg457	Eg458	Eg459	Eg460
Year	Pounds (£) sterling (constant value)	Pounds (£) sterling (constant value)	Pounds (£) sterling (constant value)	Pounds (£) sterling (constant value)	Pounds (£) sterling (constant value)	Pounds (£) sterling (constant value)	Pounds (£) sterling (constant value)	Pounds (£) sterling (constant value)	Pounds (£) sterling (constant value)
1740	82,090	5,714	0	936	528	74,724	0	188	0
1741	78,951	4,380	0	735	2,449	70,204	838	345	0
1742	108,654	13,022	0	2,634	11,272	81,726	0	0	0
1743	130,460	7,003	0	0	8,237	112,550	460	2,210	0
1744	89,656	7,112	0	2,800	555	77,905	0	1,284	0
1745	97,207	5,601	0	1,658	4,640	82,033	0	3,275	0
1746	174,954	22,827	0	407	6,000	142,361	0	3,359	0
1747	190,560	18,259	2,787	5,157	16,211	146,337	0	1,809	0
1748	191,634	25,961	0	61	19,231	146,381	0	0	0
1749	114,819	11,370	1,466	1,521	9,109	85,144	576	5,633	0
1750	127,196	14,385	1,944	500	14,341	94,529	0	1,497	0
1751	164,205	21,242	1,417	2,214	17,550	113,449	2,713	5,620	0
1752	155,090	13,754	1,555	1,309	7,609	124,991	2,070	3,802	0
1753	157,542	12,386	3,767	2,547	6,046	120,901	173	11,722	0
1754	121,313	7,976	666	1,079	9,877	96,288	1,046	4,381	0
1755	110,086	6,218	1,024	2,001	8,493	91,002	431	917	0
1756	111,665	9,957	8,063	106	14,097	74,399	0	5,043	0
1757	123,794	7,841	10,174	641	16,615	85,676	1,484	1,363	0
1758	135,235	11,723	7,360	1,984	19,147	89,296	305	5,420	0
1759	160,544	22,715	13,789	4,626	15,858	96,381	460	6,715	0
1760	186,014	12,132	10,959	1,597	43,044	112,021	3,141	3,120	0
1761	144,520	4,245	3,774	0	45,664	86,514	400	3,923	0
1762	169,961	14,258	22,563	0	19,579	104,976	2,557	6,028	0
1763	260,943	20,405	17,698	11,913	20,923	175,112	4,843	10,049	0
1764	224,949	28,792	8,894	3,096	18,234	155,266	4,437	6,230	0
1765	175,811	17,404	4,996	5,653	27,012	108,642	7,408	4,696	0
1766	177,666	9,773	2,088	6,854	37,790	109,391	7,063	4,707	0
1767	267,187	10,105	6,022	11,291	30,538	184,506	14,884	9,694	147
1768	233,101	11,010	7,743	9,722	40,774	152,795	6,330	4,727	0
1769	268,849	15,701	1,013	5,070	51,512	175,069	11,847	8,637	0
1770	335,964	22,243	4,229	4,753	54,458	224,917	17,968	4,259	3,137
1771	374,472	15,718	1,529	18,725	52,999	250,401	14,033	19,765	1,302
1772	298,088	19,592	5,494	18,032	50,747	170,913	18,562	11,481	3,267
1773	233,053	16,110	6,739	9,492	15,887	144,636	19,653	16,366	4,170
1774	253,032	14,175	21,701	19,973	24,454	136,874	28,491	5,859	1,505
1775	24,193	13,489	241	0	0	0	395	140	9,928
1776	905	905	0	0	0	0	0	0	0
1777	35,553	0	35,553	0	0	0	0	0	0
1778	35,210	0	28,693	6,517	0	0	0	0	0
1779	62,626	0	62,505	0	0	0	0	0	121
1780	171,317	0	73,705	0	0	0	0	69,519	28,093
1781	147,568	0	101,219	0	0	0	0	46,349	0
1782	44,324	0	44,324	0	0	0	0	0	0
1783	108,636	2,998	56,020	5,796	2,458	17,719	7,656	15,989	0
1784	319,604	4,818	56,040	35,813	11,521	161,043	30,611	19,758	0
1785	229,282	410	14,798	24,230	4,387	153,647	12,444	19,366	0
1786	172,211	1,705	22,008	7,722	7,919	115,068	6,643	11,146	0
1787	219,898	682	21,585	3,484	26,142	135,479	13,350	17,570	1,606
1788	176,224	946	28,743	9,109	30,241	79,363	9,668	17,560	594
1789	188,893	2,494	29,252	5,021	13,588	95,837	19,643	22,025	1,033
1790	173,542	1,189	34,428	3,383	11,302	85,748	15,665	21,009	818
1791	209,033	8,002	51,979	7,602	22,182	85,844	11,758	21,666	0

[1] The year of record ended January 4.

Source

Jacob M. Price, "New Time Series for Scotland's and Britain's Trade with the Thirteen Colonies and States, 1740 to 1791," *William and Mary Quarterly*, 3rd series, 32 (April 1975): 307–25.

Documentation

See the Appendixes to the essay in this chapter for a general discussion of the tables and the sources of the data, along with a key to abbreviations used in this chapter and general information on matters such as regional definitions, calendar differences, money, and weights and measures. Note especially the discussion of the time periods used for compiling these records.

Presented here are the annual total values in pounds sterling of the goods imported into all Scottish ports of entry (POE) from the Thirteen Continental Colonies (later, the United States) and exported from those same POE to the colonies. These are decidedly *not*, therefore, the records of good exported at or imported at American posts and thus provide only a limited view of the trade of the colonies and the United States. For the imports and exports of

(continued)

TABLE Eg443–460   Value of imports into and exports from Scotland, by colony or locality: 1740–1791   *Continued*

the colonies, compare the data for 1768–1772 in CUST 16/1, PRO/TNA. See also Tables Eg461–473 and Eg688–754.

The series in this table complement those for England and Wales in Table Eg429–442. Even after the Act of Union, Act of 6 Anne, c. 40 (1707), Scotland maintained its own Customs administration, which, of course, compiled its own records. Although the central government introduced some standardization, the differences in the records are greater than the similarities until well into the second half of the eighteenth century. Thus, for instance, Ledgers of Imports and Exports of Scotland exist only from 1755 on (CUST 14/1-39, PRO/TNA). Prior to mid-century, Parliament's demands for trade data were met on an ad hoc basis and explain the variety of fragmented, specific accounts of Scotland's trade that live on in a variety of archives. See Price (1975), and compare to John J. McCusker, "The Current Value of English Exports, 1697 to 1800," *William and Mary Quarterly*, 3rd series, 33 (October 1971): 607-28, as revised and updated in McCusker, *Essays in the Economic History of the Atlantic World* (Routledge, 1997), pp. 222-44.

The two chief sources that Price drew on for the series compiled for this table are examples of the two phases of these developments. For the years 1740-1773, he used the account ordered by the House of Lords on February 7, 1775, and presented to it the following November. See House of Lords, Main Papers, November 20, 1775, HLRO; Great Britain, Parliament, House of Lords, *Journals of the House of Lords* (House of Lords, 1767 to date), volume

35, pp. 308, 512. For the years 1774–1791, he used a contemporary compilation based on the Ledgers of Imports and Exports of Scotland (CUST 14, PRO/TNA). See BT 6/185, folios 188v-204r, PRO/TNA. David Macpherson, *Annals of Commerce, Manufactures, Fisheries and Navigation . . . of the British Empire and Other Countries, from the Earliest Accounts to . . . 1801* (Nichols and Son et al., 1805), volume 4, printed the annual summaries of Scottish trade from 1784 to 1800.

As with the contemporary compilation of the English ledgers of trade, these accounts of Scottish trade are potentially misleading because they do not record the current value of the trade. Also, as with the English trade data, there is little argument that the quantities were essentially correct. See the text for Table Eg429-442 for additional details on both of these issues.

Note that *Historical Statistics of the United States* (1975), volume 2, pp. 1177-8 (series Z227-244), made a significant mistake in the presentation of these data, which has been corrected here. The columns of imports and exports were mislabeled. A loose "Correction Sheet" was distributed with later printings of the volume by the U.S. Government Printing Office but had no impact on the publishers of a commercial edition of the book. See Ben J. Wattenberg, editor, *The Statistical History of the United States, from Colonial Times to the Present* (Basic Books, 1976), which duplicated the mistake and omitted the errata sheet. See also Jacob M. Price, "Letter to the Editor," *William and Mary Quarterly*, 3rd series, 34 (July 1977): [517].

TABLE Eg461–473 Shipping tonnage and value of cargoes clearing colonial ports of entry, by colony and by origin or destination: 1769–1770[1]

Contributed by John J. McCusker

Year; tonnage or value; direction of trade; and destination or origin	Total	New Hampshire	Massachusetts	Rhode Island	Connecticut	New York	New Jersey	Pennsylvania	Maryland	Virginia	North Carolina	South Carolina	Georgia
	Eg461	Eg462	Eg463	Eg464	Eg465	Eg466	Eg467	Eg468	Eg469	Eg470	Eg471	Eg472	Eg473
	Number	Number	Number	Number	Number	Number	Number	Number	Number	Number	Number	Number	Number
1769													
Tonnage													
Outward-bound, total	339,302	19,744	63,666	17,775	17,966	26,859	1,093	42,986	30,996	52,008	23,113	33,855	9,241
Great Britain and Ireland	99,121	2,822	14,044	540	580	6,470	0	7,219	16,116	24,594	7,805	15,902	3,029
Southern Europe and Africa	42,601	170	5,102	863	200	3,483	0	12,070	6,224	7,486	1,030	5,773	200
British and foreign West Indies	96,382	12,878	17,532	6,060	9,201	5,466	555	11,959	3,358	11,397	6,945	6,377	4,654
America, Bermuda, and Bahamas	101,198	3,874	26,988	10,312	7,985	11,440	538	11,738	5,298	8,531	7,333	5,803	1,358
Inward-bound, total	332,146	16,446	66,451	16,836	18,016	26,632	936	45,028	30,688	47,237	23,076	31,107	9,693
Great Britain and Ireland	90,710	915	14,340	415	150	5,224	0	9,369	15,486	20,652	6,415	15,281	2,523
Southern Europe and Africa	34,151	480	6,595	226	105	2,730	25	10,745	4,095	4,600	700	3,325	525
British and foreign West Indies	94,916	9,500	17,898	5,958	7,790	6,964	257	12,521	4,533	11,612	6,702	6,893	4,288
America, Bermuda, and Bahamas	112,369	5,551	27,618	10,237	9,971	11,714	654	12,453	6,574	10,373	9,259	5,608	2,357
Value – pounds (£) sterling													
Exports, total	2,852,441	550,090[3]	—[3]	—[3]	—[3]	231,906	2,532	410,757	991,402[4]	—[4]	569,585[5]	—[5]	96,170
Great Britain	1,531,516	142,776[3]	—[3]	—[3]	—[3]	113,382	0	28,112	759,961[4]	—[4]	405,015[5]	—[5]	82,270
Southern Europe and Africa	573,015	561	86,503	9,255	2,567	52,199	0	204,313	66,556	73,635	3,310	73,501	614
West Indies	747,910	40,431	123,394	65,207	79,395	66,325	2,532	178,331	22,303	68,946	27,944	59,815	13,286
Imports, total	2,623,412	564,034[3]	—[3]	—[3]	—[3]	188,976	1,991	399,821	851,140[4]	—[4]	535,714[5]	—[5]	81,736
Great Britain	1,604,976	223,696[3]	—[3]	—[3]	—[3]	75,931	0	204,980	714,944[4]	—[4]	327,084[5]	—[5]	58,341
Southern Europe and Africa	228,682	652	21,908	2,761	267	15,625	327	14,249	10,083	16,462	2,013	130,347	13,987
West Indies	789,754	48,529	155,387	56,840	53,994	97,420	1,664	180,592	32,198	77,454	10,604	65,666	9,408
1770													
Tonnage													
Outward-bound, total	351,664	20,192	70,282	20,661	20,263	26,653	1,181	49,654	33,474	45,179	21,490	32,031	10,604
Great Britain and Ireland	98,825[2]	1,910	13,778	955	426	7,357	0	7,999	17,967	25,123	7,393	12,457	3,460
Southern Europe and Africa	37,237	185	5,419	755	180	3,018	0	11,395	5,337	3,682	655	6,291	320
British and foreign West Indies	108,050[2]	12,419	20,957	6,779	9,923	7,005	648	14,839	5,118	10,096	6,893	8,194	5,179
America, Bermuda, and Bahamas	107,552	5,678	30,128	12,172	9,734	9,273	533	15,421	5,052	6,278	6,549	5,089	1,645
Inward-bound, total	331,942	15,362	65,271	18,667	19,223	25,539	1,018	50,901	30,477	44,803	20,963	29,804	9,914
Great Britain and Ireland	82,934	1,200	13,916	400	20	5,722	0	7,917	13,693	21,236	6,202	10,163	2,275
Southern Europe and Africa	37,717	—	6,213	101	—	3,354	140	15,010	5,005	4,403	440	2,256	795
British and foreign West Indies	106,713	10,300	19,917	7,121	8,656	8,695	365	15,883	5,093	9,547	5,930	10,588	4,618
America, Bermuda, and Bahamas	104,578	3,862	25,225	11,045	10,357	7,768	513	12,091	6,686	9,617	8,391	6,797	2,226

1 Values are expressed in pounds sterling; shipping tonnages are expressed in tons.

2 Figures disagree with source; they have been corrected to agree with the sum of components and with original data (CUST 16/1, pp. 101–2, PRO/TNA). See the text.

3 Massachusetts, Rhode Island, and Connecticut are included under New Hampshire.

4 Virginia is included under Maryland.

5 South Carolina is included under North Carolina.

Source

David Macpherson, *Annals of Commerce, Manufactures, Fisheries and Navigation ... of the British Empire and Other Countries, from the Earliest Accounts to ... 1801* (Nichols and Son et al., 1805), volume 3, pp. 571–2. Macpherson stated that these "accounts [were] copied from those in the custom-house [London]" (p. 569).

Documentation

See the Appendixes to the essay in this chapter for a general discussion of the tables and the sources of the data, along with a key to abbreviations used in this chapter and general information on matters such as regional definitions, calendar differences, money, and weights and measures. The year of record ended January 4.

Presented are two ways of measuring the foreign commerce of the several Continental Colonies with their various trading overseas partners: by volume and by value. The measure of the volume of trade is the size in tons of ships registered as they cleared inward and outward with the Customs authorities based in the colonial ports of entry (POE). The measure of the value of trade in pounds sterling is an estimate of the cost of the quantities of imported and exported commodities reported to these same authorities. Note that the original tables from which Macpherson has extracted these data included the other British North America colonies. Omitted from the table produced here is the shipping and trade of – or with – Newfoundland, "Island St. John's" (modern Prince Edward Island), Canada (Quebec), Nova Scotia (which included modern New Brunswick), the Bahamas, and Bermuda.

In this table, the unit of measure for vessels is the registered ton, one of three kinds of tons associated with ships and the shipping industry of the period. Note David Macpherson's (1805, p. 571) statement concerning this matter citing Thomas Irving as his authority. In addition to being the Inspector

(continued)

TABLE Eg461–473 Shipping tonnage and value of cargoes clearing colonial ports of entry, by colony and by origin or destination: 1769–1770 *Continued*

General of Imports and Exports, Irving also served as the Register of Shipping of North America, 1767–1774, before moving on to become the Inspector General of Imports and Exports of Great Britain. See John J. McCusker, "Colonial Civil Servant and Counter-Revolutionary: Thomas Irving (1738?–1800) in Boston, Charleston, and London," *Perspectives in American History* 12 (1979): 314–50, as revised and updated in McCusker, *Essays in the Economic History of the Atlantic World* (Routledge, 1997), pp. 190–221.

Macpherson's mistake in putting the 1769 inward-bound tonnage data for Southern Europe in the West Indies column (and vice versa) has been corrected here. Other minor mistakes in his transcription have also been corrected. Macpherson's data on ships and tonnage for 1770 were earlier published in John [Baker Holroyd], Lord Sheffield, *Observations on the Commerce of the American States*, 6th edition, enlarged (J. Debrett, 1784), Table VII. He stated that the table was prepared under the direction of, and signed by, Thomas Irving, "Inspector General of Imports and Exports of North America, and Register of Shipping," dated at the Custom House, Boston, October 1, 1771. The source of Irving's data was the Ledger of Imports and Exports, British North America, 1768–1772, CUST 16/1, PRO/TNA.

Macpherson gives no indication how the value of colonial exports and imports for 1769 was determined other than to say that everything was all expressed in pounds sterling. Nevertheless, he does reproduce a related table for the next year, 1770: "An account of the principal articles exported . . . and their official value at the ports of exportation, during the year 1770" (Macpherson 1805, volume 3, pp. 572–3). It is a truncated version of

the table published in Sheffield (1784), Tables V–VI. Sheffield cited the table as prepared under the direction of and signed by, Thomas Irving, "Inspector General of Imports and Exports of North America, and Register of Shipping," dated at the Custom House, Boston, October 1, 1771. See Table Eg688–754. Irving's table set down in elaborate detail the quantities of "all the goods and produce exported" from the entirety of British North America, assigned to each one of them a unit value, and then worked out the sums both by commodity and by destination. Where it is possible to check, the unit values are the prices that applied in the colonies in the late 1760s and early 1770s reduced to sterling. See the text for Table Eg688–754. Except for collapsing categories and miscopying some numbers, Macpherson reproduced 1770 Irving's table in detail down to its final totals. It is a fair assumption that Macpherson's account for 1769 also reproduced a table produced under the direction of Thomas Irving, one that was compiled in the same way. Given the tradition out of which Irving operated, it is also quite likely that he used the same unit values for both years. Given the sophisticated manner in which he consistently worked, it is equally likely that the unit prices for imported goods were FOB values at the point of export. See in John J. McCusker, "The Current Value of English Exports, 1697 to 1800," *William and Mary Quarterly*, 3rd series, 28 (October 1971): 607–28, as revised and updated in McCusker, *Essays in the Economic History of the Atlantic World* (Routledge, 1997), pp. 230, 237. The source of Irving's data for both 1769 and 1770 was, again, the Ledger of Imports and Exports, British North America, 1768–1772, CUST 16/1, PRO/TNA.

TABLE Eg474–513 Vessels clearing Boston – number and tonnage, by origin or destination: 1714–1772

Contributed by John J. McCusker

	Vessels									
	Outward									
	Total	Great Britain	Ireland	Europe	Africa	Bahama Islands	Bermuda Islands	Caribbean	Thirteen Continental Colonies	Other American colonies
	Eg474	Eg475	Eg476	Eg477	Eg478	Eg479	Eg480	Eg481	Eg482	Eg483
Year(s)	Number	Number	Number	Number	Number	Number	Number	Number	Number	Number
1714–1717	416	48	—	19	—	4	5	191	130	19 [1]
1754	447	26	3	31	1	5	0	149	156	76
1755	406	35	2	29	0	1	3	133	122	81
1766	585	59	—	22	—	—	—	125	—	379
1767	591	62	—	11	—	—	—	128	—	390
1768	612	67	2	22	0	0	0	147	281	93
1769	828	66	1	20	4	6	1	143	457	130
1770	800	56	0	15	6	5	0	131	464	123
1771	794	55	0	22	4	12	1	136	439	125
1772	845	57	1	11	5	8	1	178	443	141

	Vessels									
	Inward									
	Total	Great Britain	Ireland	Europe	Africa	Bahama Islands	Bermuda Islands	Caribbean	Thirteen Continental Colonies	Other American colonies
	Eg484	Eg485	Eg486	Eg487	Eg488	Eg489	Eg490	Eg491	Eg492	Eg493
Year(s)	Number	Number	Number	Number	Number	Number	Number	Number	Number	Number
1714–1717	—	—	—	—	—	—	—	—	—	—
1754	303	43	2	37	0	7	0	71	139	11
1755	287	32	2	27	0	0	2	48	149	28
1766	637	74	—	28	—	—	—	110	—	425
1767	601	59	—	19	—	—	—	162	—	361
1768	549	69	3	22	0	0	0	160	204	91
1769	879	75	1	31	0	5	1	172	430	164
1770	819	74	0	23	0	4	1	188	422	107
1771	821	72	0	17	0	9	2	196	382	143
1772	852	93	0	20	0	11	1	204	427	96

Note appears at end of table

TABLE Eg474–513   Vessels clearing Boston – number and tonnage, by origin or destination: 1714–1772   *Continued*

Tonnage

Outward

Year(s)	Total	Great Britain	Ireland	Europe	Africa	Bahama Islands	Bermuda Islands	Caribbean	Thirteen Continental Colonies	Other American colonies
	Eg494	Eg495	Eg496	Eg497	Eg498	Eg499	Eg500	Eg501	Eg502	Eg503
	Tons	Tons	Tons	Tons	Tons	Tons	Tons	Tons	Tons	Tons
1714–1717	20,929	3,985	—	1,185	—	124	124	10,898	3,863	750 [1]
1754	26,669	2,510	165	2,465	75	260	0	10,521	7,052	3,621
1755	21,295	2,975	100	1,853	0	50	80	7,945	4,854	3,438
1766	31,214	5,822	—	1,350	—	—	—	7,806	—	16,236
1767	33,205	6,257	—	754	—	—	—	9,079	—	17,115
1768	33,695	6,428	170	1,333	0	0	0	10,095	11,451	4,218
1769	37,045	6,707	60	1,081	495	175	20	8,995	16,132	3,380
1770	36,965	5,819	0	813	415	100	—	8,248	16,638	4,932
1771	38,995	5,750	0	1,113	267	320	40	9,171	16,764	5,570
1772	42,506	6,178	170	555	420	215	70	10,703	17,528	6,667

Tonnage

Inward

Year(s)	Total	Great Britain	Ireland	Europe	Africa	Bahama Islands	Bermuda Islands	Caribbean	Thirteen Continental Colonies	Other American colonies
	Eg504	Eg505	Eg506	Eg507	Eg508	Eg509	Eg510	Eg511	Eg512	Eg513
	Tons	Tons	Tons	Tons	Tons	Tons	Tons	Tons	Tons	Tons
1714–1717	—	—	—	—	—	—	—	—	—	—
1754	17,575	4,448	110	2,763	0	345	0	4,432	5,347	445
1755	14,585	3,040	85	1,963	0	0	60	2,391	5,651	1,475
1766	33,855	7,312	—	2,018	—	—	—	6,295	—	18,230
1767	31,752	6,190	—	1,699	—	—	—	8,584	—	15,279
1768	31,983	6,946	220	1,871	0	0	0	10,811	8,266	3,869
1769	40,483	7,333	100	2,129	0	160	20	10,495	14,200	6,046
1770	38,360	6,830	0	1,640	0	110	45	11,088	14,118	4,529
1771	39,420	7,502	0	1,055	0	215	85	12,155	12,827	5,581
1772	43,633	9,325	0	1,343	0	340	70	12,469	14,713	5,373

[1] Included in the number and tonnage cleared outward to other American colonies are four vessels and 138 tons "to ports unknown."

Sources

The sources of these data are the records kept in each of the colonial ports of entry (POE) by the administrative clerk of the port, the colonial naval officer. The original quarterly reports of the naval officers – the naval officer shipping lists (NOSL) – and various accounts based on them survive in many places, in many forms. The most important contemporary compilation of these reports was made under the direction of Thomas Irving, the Boston-based Inspector General of Imports and Exports of North America, and is known as the Ledger of Imports and Exports, British North America, 1768–1772, CUST 16/1, PRO/TNA. A more recent attempt to assemble and compile data from the extant NOSL was organized in the 1930s by Lawrence A. Harper and others. See text in the next section.

Documentation

See the Appendixes to the essay in this chapter for a general discussion of the tables and the sources of the data, along with a key to abbreviations used in this chapter and general information on such matters as regional definitions, calendar differences, money, and weights and measures. In Tables Eg474–673, the unit of measure for vessels is the registered ton, one of three kinds of tons associated with ships and the shipping industry of the period – with one exception (see Table Eg634–673). As discussed in Appendix A to the essay in this chapter, the year of record ended on December 24 through 1751 and on January 4 thereafter. Exceptions are the period 1714–1717, for which the figures are annual averages for years ending June 23, and the period 1765–1767, for which the figures are annual averages for the year ending October 9.

The trade data in Tables Eg474–673 for these five ports of entry (POE) – Boston, New York, Philadelphia, James River, Lower Part (Hampton, Virginia), and Charleston – were compiled from colonial NOSL and related documents by Lawrence A. Harper and others. The NOSL used by Harper and his colleagues are in the Colonial Office Papers, PRO/TNA. With the exceptions listed hereafter, all of the data in these five tables come from the Harper project discussed in Appendix A to the essay in this chapter. All five tables are based on full returns for the entire year (all four quarters).

In addition to the NOSL, see the following. For 1714–1717, POE Boston, and 1715–1718, POE New York, see the report from the Commissioners for Trade and Plantations to the King, September 8, 1721, CO 324/10, folios 193v–194r, PRO/TNA. For 1729–1742, POE Philadelphia, see the yearly shipping returns published annually in the local newspapers (for example, for the year December 4, 1729, through December 3, 1730, see *The Pennsylvania Gazette*, January 5, 1730/31). Compare the compilation of these data in Helen Louise Klopfer, "Statistics of the Foreign Trade of Philadelphia, 1700–1860" (Ph.D. dissertation, University of Pennsylvania, 1936), Table XIII. For 1752, POE James River, Lower Part (Hampton, Virginia), see Francis Carroll Huntley, "The Seaborne Trade of Virginia in Mid-Eighteenth Century: Port Hampton," *Virginia Magazine of History and Biography* 59 (July 1951): 297–308, who depended on the Harper materials. For 1763 and 1764, POE New York, see Virginia D. Harrington, *The New York Merchant on the Eve of the Revolution,* Columbia University Studies in History, Economics and Public Law, number 404 (Columbia University Press, 1935), pp. 356–7. For 1768–1772, all POE, see the Ledger of Imports and Exports, British North America, 1768–1772, CUST 16/1, PRO/TNA.

Not part of the Harper compilation are the data for the following. For 1717–1766, POE Charleston, Converse D. Clowse, *Measuring Charleston's*

TABLE Eg474–513   Vessels clearing Boston – number and tonnage, by origin or destination: 1714–1772   *Continued*

Overseas Commerce, 1717–1767: Statistics from the Port's Naval Lists (University Press of America, 1981), pp. 97–104 (these are the mean values for each of the several periods; the tables in this source contain some mistakes in arithmetic, most of them minor, all of them corrected here). For 1725–1736, POE Charleston, *Charles-Town in South-Carolina, November 1, 1736. An Account of Sundry Goods Imported, and of Sundry Goods of the Produce of This Province Exported, from the Year 1724, to the Year 1735. With the Number of Vessels Entered and Cleared Each Year. And a Particular Account of the Last Year* (Lewis Timothy, 1736). For 1746–1748, POE Charleston, report in letter from Governor James Glen, at Charleston, to Board of Trade, May 31, 1749, CO 5/461, folio 43v, PRO/TNA. For 1719–1724 and 1730–1734, POE Philadelphia, for which see Arthur L. Jensen, *The Maritime Commerce of Colonial Philadelphia* (State Historical Society of Wisconsin for the Department of History, University of Wisconsin, 1963), pp. 290–1. For 1750–1754, POE Philadelphia, John J. McCusker, "Sources of Investment Capital in the Colonial Philadelphia Shipping Industry," *Journal of Economic History* 32 (March 1972): 146–57, as

revised and updated in McCusker, *Essays in the Economic History of the Atlantic World* (Routledge, 1997), pp. 245–57. For 1766 and 1767, POE Boston, and for 1765–1767, POE New York, POE Philadelphia, and POE James River, Lower Part (Hampton, Virginia), Fitzwilliam (Wentworth Woodhouse) Muniments, R 61/2, Sheffield Archives, Sheffield, England. See also the data presented in Harrington (1935), p. 358, where the tables are in considerable confusion, especially for Boston.

In several instances, the accounts in these sources combined data in ways different from those used in these five tables, and certain accommodations were necessary. Data are sometimes not available because the original source added numbers together which, for others years, are disaggregated. This is especially the case here for the years 1765–1767 where, for instance, the source added together the numbers for Great Britain and Ireland. In the table, the total is presented in the series for Great Britain. Similarly, data for Europe and Africa are given in the series for Europe, and so forth. Some of the data reported here silently correct clerical errors in the original sources.

TABLE Eg514–553   Vessels clearing New York – number and tonnage, by origin or destination: 1715–1772

Contributed by John J. McCusker

	Vessels									
	Outward									
Year(s)	Total	Great Britain	Ireland	Europe	Africa	Bahama Islands	Bermuda Islands	Caribbean	Thirteen Continental Colonies	Other American colonies
	Eg514	Eg515	Eg516	Eg517	Eg518	Eg519	Eg520	Eg521	Eg522	Eg523
	Number	Number	Number	Number	Number	Number	Number	Number	Number	Number
1715–1718	215	21	—	10	1	3	5	104	68	3
1726	211	12	—	8	—	—	3	95	90	5
1727	214	11	—	6	—	—	5	104	86	2
1733	223	9	5	6	—	4	6	103	85	6
1734	184	8	2	9	1	1	4	87	70	5
1735	207	12	3	17	—	3	1	95	73	5
1739	269	9	16	21	—	1	3	113	97	10
1754	322	31	23	19	4	3	3	180	51	12
1763	—	—	—	—	—	—	—	—	—	—
1764	—	—	—	—	—	—	—	—	—	—
1765	359	63	—	31	—	—	—	198	67	—
1766	403	59	—	52	—	—	—	211	81	—
1767	374	72	—	47	—	—	—	188	67	—
1768	480	56	30	45	2	4	7	156	125	55
1769	787	47	30	78	5	2	8	125	430	62
1770	612	46	29	58	2	8	4	189	188	88
1771	524	45	27	40	4	7	6	194	134	67
1772	700	39	19	48	9	5	3	199	324	54

	Vessels									
	Inward									
Year(s)	Total	Great Britain	Ireland	Europe	Africa	Bahama Islands	Bermuda Islands	Caribbean	Thirteen Continental Colonies	Other American colonies
	Eg524	Eg525	Eg526	Eg527	Eg528	Eg529	Eg530	Eg531	Eg532	Eg533
	Number	Number	Number	Number	Number	Number	Number	Number	Number	Number
1715–1718	—	—	—	—	—	—	—	—	—	—
1726	202	31	1	10	1	—	9	85	69	5
1727	215	17	—	7	—	2	11	95	87	3
1733	217	24	3	12	1	3	15	97	78	6
1734	213	18	4	24	—	6	19	78	71	5
1735	196	26	3	25	—	2	13	83	47	5
1739	261	27	4	22	—	1	14	105	93	11
1754	266	28	10	25	5	6	3	177	23	7
1763	—	—	—	—	—	—	—	—	—	—
1764	—	—	—	—	—	—	—	—	—	—

TABLE Eg514–553　Vessels clearing New York – number and tonnage, by origin or destination: 1715–1772
Continued

Vessels

Inward

Year(s)	Total	Great Britain	Ireland	Europe	Africa	Bahama Islands	Bermuda Islands	Caribbean	Thirteen Continental Colonies	Other American colonies
	Eg524	Eg525	Eg526	Eg527	Eg528	Eg529	Eg530	Eg531	Eg532	Eg533
	Number	Number	Number	Number	Number	Number	Number	Number	Number	Number
1765	294	72	—	36	—	—	—	161	25	—
1766	400	66	—	16	—	—	—	210	108	—
1767	327	81	—	16	—	—	—	191	39	—
1768	462	79	15	31	2	9	3	158	139	26
1769	725	41	18	39	1	4	2	179	394	47
1770	600	39	19	44	4	11	1	226	217	39
1771	557	63	13	27	0	9	4	220	184	37
1772	710	61	11	38	0	11	5	208	352	24

Tonnage

Outward

Year(s)	Total	Great Britain	Ireland	Europe	Africa	Bahama Islands	Bermuda Islands	Caribbean	Thirteen Continental Colonies	Other American colonies
	Eg534	Eg535	Eg536	Eg537	Eg538	Eg539	Eg540	Eg541	Eg542	Eg543
	Tons	Tons	Tons	Tons	Tons	Tons	Tons	Tons	Tons	Tons
1715–1718	7,464	1,461	—	630	40	75	107	3,608	1,406	137
1726	7,855	988	—	515	—	—	90	3,378	2,761	155
1727	8,052	1,030	—	465	—	—	160	4,149	2,138	110
1733	7,704	690	160	275	—	145	168	3,624	2,349	305
1734	6,374	645	160	475	60	20	90	2,771	1,959	278
1735	7,358	838	200	904	—	60	45	2,836	2,321	250
1739	10,012	795	820	1,040	—	20	78	4,333	2,451	505
1754	13,322	2,085	1,615	725	130	60	75	6,351	2,076	440
1763	15,741	2,079	1,460	1,000	70	35	115	7,507	2,450	1,025
1764	16,982	2,952	1,882	1,087	140	93	230	7,898	1,495	1,205
1765	17,570	5,165	—	1,592	—	—	—	7,825	2,988	—
1766	19,862	4,907	—	3,480	—	—	—	8,385	3,090	—
1767	19,875	5,588	—	3,820	—	—	—	6,697	3,770	—
1768	23,566	5,130	2,522	2,360	35	67	172	6,981	3,754	2,545
1769	26,859	3,955	2,515	3,278	205	35	127	5,466	9,068	2,210
1770	26,653	4,665	2,692	2,920	98	144	95	7,005	5,655	3,379
1771	25,433	4,830	2,476	2,029	115	135	153	7,708	4,968	3,019
1772	28,574	4,280	1,610	2,449	260	88	85	8,076	8,859	2,867

Tonnage

Inward

Year(s)	Total	Great Britain	Ireland	Europe	Africa	Bahama Islands	Bermuda Islands	Caribbean	Thirteen Continental Colonies	Other American colonies
	Eg544	Eg545	Eg546	Eg547	Eg548	Eg549	Eg550	Eg551	Eg552	Eg553
	Tons	Tons	Tons	Tons	Tons	Tons	Tons	Tons	Tons	Tons
1715–1718	—	—	—	—	—	—	—	—	—	—
1726	7,716	2,470	80	615	25	—	275	3,072	1,452	149
1727	7,672	1,473	—	420	—	40	305	3,775	1,753	135
1733	7,433	1,823	100	640	120	65	426	3,271	1,629	204
1734	7,442	1,350	215	1,571	—	145	525	2,707	1,366	241
1735	6,759	1,648	240	1,436	—	40	365	2,509	882	124
1739	9,738	2,224	360	1,320	—	20	426	3,643	2,069	321
1754	10,921	2,475	650	1,055	205	120	80	6,020	931	280
1763	11,129	3,980	550	1,390	65	205	200	4,124	615	—
1764	16,750	4,040	1,647	2,385	0	103	370	7,430	645	130

(continued)

TABLE Eg514–553   Vessels clearing New York – number and tonnage, by origin or destination: 1715–1772
Continued

					Tonnage				
					Inward				
	Total	Great Britain	Ireland	Europe	Africa	Bahama Islands	Bermuda Islands	Caribbean	Thirteen Continental Colonies	Other American colonies
	Eg544	Eg545	Eg546	Eg547	Eg548	Eg549	Eg550	Eg551	Eg552	Eg553
Year(s)	Tons	Tons	Tons	Tons	Tons	Tons	Tons	Tons	Tons	Tons
1765	14,941	5,770	—	1,828	—	—	—	6,530	813	—
1766	18,214	5,722	—	1,005	—	—	—	8,265	3,222	—
1767	17,559	7,787	—	1,180	—	—	—	6,922	1,670	—
1768	21,847	7,158	1,387	1,500	130	204	115	6,301	3,952	1,100
1769	26,650	3,785	1,435	2,700	30	42	90	6,964	9,884	1,720
1770	25,539	4,055	1,667	3,124	230	284	30	8,695	5,941	1,513
1771	25,042	6,850	1,411	1,344	0	210	105	8,191	5,416	1,515
1772	28,861	6,117	915	2,480	0	268	215	8,170	9,247	1,449

Sources
See the sources for Table Eg474–513.

Documentation
See the text for Table Eg474–513.

TABLE Eg554–593   Vessels clearing Philadelphia – number and tonnage, by origin or destination: 1719–1772
Contributed by John J. McCusker

					Vessels				
					Outward				
	Total	Great Britain	Ireland	Europe	Africa	Bahama Islands	Bermuda Islands	Caribbean	Thirteen Continental Colonies	Other American colonies
	Eg554	Eg555	Eg556	Eg557	Eg558	Eg559	Eg560	Eg561	Eg562	Eg563
Year(s)	Number	Number	Number	Number	Number	Number	Number	Number	Number	Number
1719	—	—	—	—	—	—	—	—	—	—
1720	—	—	—	—	—	—	—	—	—	—
1721	—	—	—	—	—	—	—	—	—	—
1722	—	—	—	—	—	—	—	—	—	—
1723	—	—	—	—	—	—	—	—	—	—
1724	—	—	—	—	—	—	—	—	—	—
1730	171	20	—	16	—	—	—	85	50	—
1730–1734	192	17	10	19	—	—	—	83	62	—
1733	185	12	17	20	—	—	2	87	45	2
1734	191	21	16	22	—	—	6	74	50	2
1734–1737	228	38	—	36	—	—	—	77	78	—
1740	317	61	—	45	—	—	—	115	96	—
1742	271	38	—	23	—	—	—	97	113	—
1750–1754	445	16	36	36	—	—	—	191	166	—
1765	732	60	—	41	—	—	—	212	419	—
1766	706	67	—	53	—	—	—	241	345	—
1767	661	75	—	60	—	—	—	222	304	—
1768	641	40	38	88	0	0	3	206	229	37
1769	678	37	32	136	1	0	0	202	246	24
1770	769	25	49	125	0	10	2	243	283	32
1771	741	27	25	79	3	13	3	230	332	29
1772	759	23	24	88	1	11	4	268	307	33

TABLE Eg554–593   Vessels clearing Philadelphia – number and tonnage, by origin or destination: 1719–1772
Continued

	Vessels									
	Inward									
Year(s)	Total	Great Britain	Ireland	Europe	Africa	Bahama Islands	Bermuda Islands	Caribbean	Thirteen Continental Colonies	Other American colonies
	Eg564	Eg565	Eg566	Eg567	Eg568	Eg569	Eg570	Eg571	Eg572	Eg573
	Number	Number	Number	Number	Number	Number	Number	Number	Number	Number
1719	—	—	—	—	—	—	—	—	—	—
1720	—	—	—	—	—	—	—	—	—	—
1721	—	—	—	—	—	—	—	—	—	—
1722	—	—	—	—	—	—	—	—	—	—
1723	—	—	—	—	—	—	—	—	—	—
1724	—	—	—	—	—	—	—	—	—	—
1730	161	23	—	4	—	—	—	73	61	—
1730–1734	175	23	6	10	—	—	—	72	65	—
1733	190	26	8	16	—	—	10	77	58	—
1734	210	24	11	17	—	—	12	79	68	—
1734–1737	209	42	—	21	—	—	—	70	76	—
1740	318	63	—	51	—	—	—	61	143	—
1742	229	33	—	13	—	—	—	65	118	—
1750–1754	—	—	—	—	—	—	—	—	—	—
1765	708	88	—	50	—	—	—	193	377	—
1766	693	84		50	—	—	—	221	338	—
1767	588	95	—	31	—	—	—	211	251	—
1768	528	60	15	63	0	0	3	139	218	30
1769	698	46	32	108	0	0	0	214	243	55
1770	750	42	26	154	0	11	1	221	274	21
1771	719	71	16	69	0	12	6	232	294	19
1772	730	63	12	88	0	10	2	247	281	21

	Tonnage									
	Outward									
Year(s)	Total	Great Britain	Ireland	Europe	Africa	Bahama Islands	Bermuda Islands	Caribbean	Thirteen Continental Colonies	Other American colonies
	Eg574	Eg575	Eg576	Eg577	Eg578	Eg579	Eg580	Eg581	Eg582	Eg583
	Tons	Tons	Tons	Tons	Tons	Tons	Tons	Tons	Tons	Tons
1719	4,514	—	—	—	—	—	—	—	—	—
1720	3,982	—	—	—	—	—	—	—	—	—
1721	3,711	—	—	—	—	—	—	—	—	—
1722	3,531	—	—	—	—	—	—	—	—	—
1723	3,942	—	—	—	—	—	—	—	—	—
1724	5,450	—	—	—	—	—	—	—	—	—
1730	—	—	—	—	—	—	—	—	—	—
1730–1734	—	—	—	—	—	—	—	—	—	—
1733	—	—	—	—	—	—	—	—	—	—
1734	—	—	—	—	—	—	—	—	—	—
1734–1737	—	—	—	—	—	—	—	—	—	—
1740	—	—	—	—	—	—	—	—	—	—
1742	—	—	—	—	—	—	—	—	—	—
1750–1754	25,252	1,136	2,491	1,739	—	—	—	12,682	7,204	—
1765	37,850	5,161	—	3,345	—	—	—	12,340	17,004	—
1766	39,262	1,830	4,830	4,455	300	317	242	13,494	10,834	2,960
1767	41,103	8,263	—	6,408	—	—	—	13,371	13,061	—
1768	36,944	4,134	3,482	7,255	0	0	100	12,019	8,116	1,838
1769	40,871	4,049	3,170	12,040	30	0	0	11,114	9,085	1,383
1770	47,292	3,208	4,791	10,940	0	126	75	13,842	12,370	1,940
1771	43,029	3,222	3,470	7,110	90	253	55	13,449	13,655	1,725
1772	44,822	3,123	2,491	8,415	20	282	125	15,674	12,872	1,820

(continued)

TABLE Eg554–593   Vessels clearing Philadelphia – number and tonnage, by origin or destination: 1719–1772
Continued

	Tonnage									
	Inward									
Year(s)	Total	Great Britain	Ireland	Europe	Africa	Bahama Islands	Bermuda Islands	Caribbean	Thirteen Continental Colonies	Other American colonies
	Eg584	Eg585	Eg586	Eg587	Eg588	Eg589	Eg590	Eg591	Eg592	Eg593
	Tons	Tons	Tons	Tons	Tons	Tons	Tons	Tons	Tons	Tons
1719	—	—	—	—	—	—	—	—	—	—
1720	—	—	—	—	—	—	—	—	—	—
1721	—	—	—	—	—	—	—	—	—	—
1722	—	—	—	—	—	—	—	—	—	—
1723	—	—	—	—	—	—	—	—	—	—
1724	—	—	—	—	—	—	—	—	—	—
1730	—	—	—	—	—	—	—	—	—	—
1730–1734	—	—	—	—	—	—	—	—	—	—
1733	—	—	—	—	—	—	—	—	—	—
1734	—	—	—	—	—	—	—	—	—	—
1734–1737	—	—	—	—	—	—	—	—	—	—
1740	—	—	—	—	—	—	—	—	—	—
1742	—	—	—	—	—	—	—	—	—	—
1750–1754	—	—	—	—	—	—	—	—	—	—
1765	35,279	9,845	—	1,180	—	—	—	11,234	13,020	—
1766	36,872	8,555	—	4,270	—	—	—	10,920	13,127	—
1767	36,741	12,294	—	2,845	—	—	—	11,945	9,657	—
1768	34,970	6,924	1,470	5,001	0	0	110	11,677	7,978	1,810
1769	42,333	5,504	2,995	9,685	0	0	0	11,726	9,160	3,263
1770	47,489	4,705	2,267	13,620	0	156	10	14,946	10,670	1,115
1771	41,740	8,157	1,545	6,345	0	208	155	13,397	11,058	875
1772	42,300	7,757	1,125	8,120	0	247	70	12,947	11,024	1,010

Sources

See the sources for Table Eg474–513.

Documentation

See the text for Table Eg474–513.

For comparable data for the years 1766–1775, see also Thomas M. Doerflinger, *A Vigorous Spirit of Enterprise: Merchants and Economic Development in Revolutionary Philadelphia* (University of North Carolina Press, 1986), p. 373.

TABLE Eg594–633   Vessels clearing James River, Lower Part – number and tonnage, by origin or destination: 1727–1772

Contributed by John J. McCusker

	Vessels									
	Outward									
Year	Total	Great Britain	Ireland	Europe	Africa	Bahama Islands	Bermuda Islands	Caribbean	Thirteen Continental Colonies	Other American colonies
	Eg594	Eg595	Eg596	Eg597	Eg598	Eg599	Eg600	Eg601	Eg602	Eg603
	Number	Number	Number	Number	Number	Number	Number	Number	Number	Number
1727	104	22	—	2	—	—	19	41	20	—
1731	101	16	—	5	—	—	13	53	14	—
1733	82	11	—	6	—	—	5	50	10	—
1739	98	6	—	7	—	—	8	44	33	—
1752	156	20	—	14	1	1	8	81	31	—
1765	224	31	—	13	—	—	—	111	69	—
1766	205	47	—	11	—	—	—	105	42	—
1767	200	29	—	11	—	—	—	119	41	—
1768	246	33	1	14	0	5	7	148	37	1
1769	266	29	1	20	0	6	3	146	59	2
1770	244	27	2	15	0	3	12	141	42	2
1771	301	34	3	20	0	3	5	180	56	0
1772	356	36	0	14	0	3	10	205	88	0

TABLE Eg594–633   Vessels clearing James River, Lower Part – number and tonnage, by origin or destination: 1727–1772   *Continued*

					Vessels				
					Inward				
Year	Total	Great Britain	Ireland	Europe	Africa	Bahama Islands	Bermuda Islands	Caribbean	Thirteen Continental Colonies	Other American colonies
	Eg604	Eg605	Eg606	Eg607	Eg608	Eg609	Eg610	Eg611	Eg612	Eg613
	Number	Number	Number	Number	Number	Number	Number	Number	Number	Number
1727	94	18	—	2	—	1	16	37	20	—
1731	88	21	—	1	—	—	5	46	15	—
1733	87	19	—	4	1	2	5	50	10	—
1739	102	21	—	5	—	—	9	40	29	—
1752	169	37	—	10	2	1	4	78	37	—
1765	241	60	—	5	—	—	—	86	90	—
1766	197	43	—	9	—	—	—	100	45	—
1767	183	42	—	7	—	—	—	98	36	—
1768	254	55	0	9	0	3	3	134	50	0
1769	281	59	1	15	0	7	9	134	50	6
1770	282	56	2	13	1	5	8	132	64	1
1771	317	62	1	10	0	5	6	156	77	0
1772	332	62	1	10	1	3	7	158	88	2

					Tonnage				
					Outward				
Year	Total	Great Britain	Ireland	Europe	Africa	Bahama Islands	Bermuda Islands	Caribbean	Thirteen Continental Colonies	Other American colonies
	Eg614	Eg615	Eg616	Eg617	Eg618	Eg619	Eg620	Eg621	Eg622	Eg623
	Tons	Tons	Tons	Tons	Tons	Tons	Tons	Tons	Tons	Tons
1727	4,577	2,046	—	60	—	—	483	1,366	622	—
1731	4,501	1,633	—	300	—	—	332	1,795	441	—
1733	3,769	1,110	—	440	—	—	140	1,664	415	—
1739	3,966	745	—	410	—	—	240	1,607	964	—
1752	8,008	2,285	—	1,195	25	15	220	3,462	806	—
1765	12,937	3,988	—	985	—	—	—	5,407	2,557	—
1766	13,975	6,085	—	861	—	—	—	5,858	1,171	—
1767	13,377	4,008	—	878	—	—	—	7,335	1,156	—
1768	15,776	5,252	200	1,209	0	115	205	7,376	1,369	50
1769	17,046	4,110	100	2,096	0	65	68	8,136	2,396	75
1770	13,851	3,184	270	1,405	0	30	306	7,410	1,156	90
1771	18,593	4,530	360	1,790	0	55	123	9,450	2,285	0
1772	22,293	5,454	0	1,155	0	60	235	11,930	3,459	0

(continued)

TABLE Eg594–633   Vessels clearing James River, Lower Part – number and tonnage, by origin or destination: 1727–1772   Continued

	Tonnage									
	Inward									
Year	Total	Great Britain	Ireland	Europe	Africa	Bahama Islands	Bermuda Islands	Caribbean	Thirteen Continental Colonies	Other American colonies
	Eg624	Eg625	Eg626	Eg627	Eg628	Eg629	Eg630	Eg631	Eg632	Eg633
	Tons	Tons	Tons	Tons	Tons	Tons	Tons	Tons	Tons	Tons
1727	4,023	1,785	—	130	—	120	421	1,273	294	—
1731	5,009	2,525	—	40	—	—	127	1,760	557	—
1733	4,816	2,285	—	440	25	60	131	1,769	351	—
1739	5,746	2,535	—	330	—	—	330	1,579	1,122	—
1752	10,557	4,912	—	1,015	140	15	120	3,580	775	—
1765	17,431	8,520	—	437	—	—	—	4,472	4,002	—
1766	13,004	5,674	—	866	—	—	—	5,100	1,364	—
1767	14,250	6,020	—	760	—	—	—	6,374	1,096	—
1768	19,673	8,411	0	1,065	0	35	75	8,152	1,935	0
1769	19,843	8,532	105	1,595	0	80	236	7,575	1,425	295
1770	18,915	8,320	195	1,080	103	55	198	6,298	2,656	10
1771	21,857	8,216	130	878	0	105	150	8,532	3,846	0
1772	23,966	9,623	170	1,050	150	80	185	8,598	4,025	85

Sources

See the sources for Table Eg474–513.

Documentation

See the text for Table Eg474–513. What the Customs referred to as POE James River, Lower Part, was popularly known as Hampton, Hampton Roads, Port Hampton, and – sometimes – Norfolk. Note that for 1768, the total tonnage inward in the source is not equal to the sum of its parts and differs, therefore, from the amount stated here. Compare CUST 16/1, p. 2, PRO/TNA.

TABLE Eg634–673   Vessels clearing Charleston – number and tonnage, by origin or destination: 1717–1772

Contributed by John J. McCusker

	Vessels									
	Outward									
Year(s)	Total	Great Britain	Ireland	Europe	Africa	Bahama Islands	Bermuda Islands	Caribbean	Thirteen Continental Colonies	Other American colonies
	Eg634	Eg635	Eg636	Eg637	Eg638	Eg639	Eg640	Eg641	Eg642	Eg643
	Number	Number	Number	Number	Number	Number	Number	Number	Number	Number
1717–1720 [1]	143	56	—	1	—	12	3	28	43	—
1724	129	68	—	3	—	10	7	15	26	—
1725	115	—	—	—	—	—	—	—	—	—
1726	131	—	—	—	—	—	—	—	—	—
1727	138	—	—	—	—	—	—	—	—	—
1728	126	—	—	—	—	—	—	—	—	—
1729	157	—	—	—	—	—	—	—	—	—
1730	186	—	—	—	—	—	—	—	—	—
1731	184	—	—	—	—	—	—	—	—	—
1731–1732	220	85	—	17	—	22	2	59	35	—
1732	177	—	—	—	—	—	—	—	—	—
1733	211	—	—	—	—	—	—	—	—	—
1734	215	—	—	—	—	—	—	—	—	—
1734–1738	216	79	—	17	—	34	1	23	62	—
1735	253	—	—	—	—	—	—	—	—	—
1736	217	—	—	—	—	—	—	—	—	—
1737	217	—	—	—	—	—	—	—	—	—
1738	198	—	—	—	—	—	—	—	—	—
1739	222	—	—	—	—	—	—	—	—	—
1740	257	—	—	—	—	—	—	—	—	—
1741	256	—	—	—	—	—	—	—	—	—
1742	190	—	—	—	—	—	—	—	—	—
1743	206	—	—	—	—	—	—	—	—	—
1744	230	—	—	—	—	—	—	—	—	—
1745	208	—	—	—	—	—	—	—	—	—

Note appears at end of table

TABLE Eg634–673   Vessels clearing Charleston – number and tonnage, by origin or destination: 1717–1772
Continued

	Vessels									
	Outward									
	Total	Great Britain	Ireland	Europe	Africa	Bahama Islands	Bermuda Islands	Caribbean	Thirteen Continental Colonies	Other American colonies
	Eg634	Eg635	Eg636	Eg637	Eg638	Eg639	Eg640	Eg641	Eg642	Eg643
Year(s)	Number	Number	Number	Number	Number	Number	Number	Number	Number	Number
1746	255	86	—	—	—	—		121	48	—
1747	235	105	—	—	—	—	—	93	37	—
1748	193	68	—	—	—	—	—	87	38	—
1758–1760	234	67	—	27	1	13	4	57	65	—
1762–1763	345	91	—	22	—	13	16	115	88	—
1766	384	95	—	43	1	18	15	117	95	—
1768	429	121	0	48	0	22	9	113	83	33
1769	433	109	0	56	0	16	8	113	106	25
1770	451	81	0	53	0	21	11	163	98	24
1771	487	119	0	26	1	25	12	163	124	17
1772	485	115	0	16	2	25	11	129	166	21

	Vessels									
	Inward									
	Total	Great Britain	Ireland	Europe	Africa	Bahama Islands	Bermuda Islands	Caribbean	Thirteen Continental Colonies	Other American colonies
	Eg644	Eg645	Eg646	Eg647	Eg648	Eg649	Eg650	Eg651	Eg652	Eg653
Year(s)	Number	Number	Number	Number	Number	Number	Number	Number	Number	Number
1717 1720 [1]	144	32	—	6	5	12	5	42	42	—
1724	138	44	—	7	5	10	6	26	40	—
1725	134	—	—	—	—	—	—	—	—	—
1726	146	—	—	—	—	—	—	—	—	—
1727	126	—	—	—	—	—	—	—	—	—
1728	141	—	—	—	—	—	—	—	—	—
1729	157	—	—	—	—	—	—	—	—	—
1730	165	—	—	—	—	—	—	—	—	—
1731	184	—	—	—	—	—	—	—	—	—
1731–1732	189	45	—	11	6	20	9	51	47	—
1732	182	—	—	—	—	—	—	—	—	—
1733	222	—	—	—	—	—	—	—	—	—
1734	209	—	—	—	—	—	—	—	—	—
1734–1738	217	37	—	19	9	28	3	43	78	—
1735	248	—	—	—	—	—	—	—	—	—
1736	229	—	—	—	—	—	—	—	—	—
1737	—	—	—	—	—	—	—	—	—	—
1738	—	—	—	—	—	—	—	—	—	—
1739	—	—	—	—	—	—	—	—	—	—
1740	—	—	—	—	—	—	—	—	—	—
1741	—	—	—	—	—	—	—	—	—	—
1742	—	—	—	—	—	—	—	—	—	—
1743	—	—	—	—	—	—	—	—	—	—
1744	—	—	—	—	—	—	—	—	—	—
1745	—	—	—	—	—	—	—	—	—	—
1746	—	—	—	—	—	—	—	—	—	—
1747	—	—	—	—	—	—	—	—	—	—
1748	—	—	—	—	—	—	—	—	—	—
1758–1760	249	51	—	17	13	18	11	57	82	—
1762–1763	368	47	—	30	6	27	23	129	106	—
1766	416	83	—	32	—	20	7	127	147	—
1768	448	139	11	18	0	21	9	129	88	33
1769	433	115	0	13	21	20	10	114	104	36
1770	455	61	5	20	0	22	15	184	115	33
1771	489	79	3	21	11	29	20	163	132	31
1772	452	79	11	24	25	22	14	120	138	19

Note appears at end of table

(continued)

TABLE Eg634–673   Vessels clearing Charleston – number and tonnage, by origin or destination: 1717–1772
Continued

Tonnage

Outward

Year(s)	Total	Great Britain	Ireland	Europe	Africa	Bahama Islands	Bermuda Islands	Caribbean	Thirteen Continental Colonies	Other American colonies
	Eg654	Eg655	Eg656	Eg657	Eg658	Eg659	Eg660	Eg661	Eg662	Eg663
	Tons	Tons	Tons	Tons	Tons	Tons	Tons	Tons	Tons	Tons
1717–1720 [1]	7,256	4,829	—	24	—	179	45	855	1,324	—
1724	7,892	6,025	—	100	—	292	131	446	898	—
1725	—	—	—	—	—	—	—	—	—	—
1726	—	—	—	—	—	—	—	—	—	—
1727	—	—	—	—	—	—	—	—	—	—
1728	—	—	—	—	—	—	—	—	—	—
1729	—	—	—	—	—	—	—	—	—	—
1730	—	—	—	—	—	—	—	—	—	—
1731	—	—	—	—	—	—	—	—	—	—
1731–1732	11,363	7,389	—	1,375	—	30	327	1,192	1,050	—
1732	—	—	—	—	—	—	—	—	—	—
1733	—	—	—	—	—	—	—	—	—	—
1734	—	—	—	—	—	—	—	—	—	—
1734–1738	12,954	7,572	—	1,540	—	601	43	978	2,220	—
1735	—	—	—	—	—	—	—	—	—	—
1736	—	—	—	—	—	—	—	—	—	—
1737	—	—	—	—	—	—	—	—	—	—
1738	—	—	—	—	—	—	—	—	—	—
1739	—	—	—	—	—	—	—	—	—	—
1740	—	—	—	—	—	—	—	—	—	—
1741	—	—	—	—	—	—	—	—	—	—
1742	—	—	—	—	—	—	—	—	—	—
1743	—	—	—	—	—	—	—	—	—	—
1744	—	—	—	—	—	—	—	—	—	—
1745	—	—	—	—	—	—	—	—	—	—
1746	16,293	10,555	—	—	—	—	—	4,018	1,720	—
1747	18,756	12,712	—	—	—	—	—	4,712	1,332	—
1748	13,953	8,465	—	—	—	—	—	4,299	1,189	—
1758–1760	16,887	8,266	—	2,559	118	290	125	3,023	2,506	—
1762–1763	21,891	10,709	—	2,273	—	329	463	4,848	3,269	—
1766	29,450	12,664	—	5,019	90	401	455	6,066	4,755	—
1768	31,551	15,873	0	5,515	0	345	293	5,808	2,852	865
1769	31,147	14,681	0	5,773	0	333	205	5,807	3,698	650
1770	29,976	11,727	0	6,291	0	690	343	7,374	3,012	539
1771	31,031	15,792	0	2,882	30	497	398	6,131	4,875	426
1772	31,548	15,610	0	1,774	290	452	323	5,749	6,724	626

Tonnage

Inward

Year(s)	Total	Great Britain	Ireland	Europe	Africa	Bahama Islands	Bermuda Islands	Caribbean	Thirteen Continental Colonies	Other American colonies
	Eg664	Eg665	Eg666	Eg667	Eg668	Eg669	Eg670	Eg671	Eg672	Eg673
	Tons	Tons	Tons	Tons	Tons	Tons	Tons	Tons	Tons	Tons
1717–1720 [1]	7,639	3,036	—	437	303	168	177	2,242	1,276	—
1724	8,441	4,045	—	510	390	262	113	1,263	1,858	—
1725	—	—	—	—	—	—	—	—	—	—
1726	—	—	—	—	—	—	—	—	—	—
1727	—	—	—	—	—	—	—	—	—	—
1728	—	—	—	—	—	—	—	—	—	—
1729	—	—	—	—	—	—	—	—	—	—
1730	—	—	—	—	—	—	—	—	—	—
1731	—	—	—	—	—	—	—	—	—	—
1731–1732	10,755	4,032	—	824	530	274	274	2,825	1,996	—

TABLE Eg634–673   Vessels clearing Charleston – number and tonnage, by origin or destination: 1717–1772
Continued

	Tonnage									
	Inward									
Year(s)	Total	Great Britain	Ireland	Europe	Africa	Bahama Islands	Bermuda Islands	Caribbean	Thirteen Continental Colonies	Other American colonies
	Eg664	Eg665	Eg666	Eg667	Eg668	Eg669	Eg670	Eg671	Eg672	Eg673
	Tons	Tons	Tons	Tons	Tons	Tons	Tons	Tons	Tons	Tons
1732	—	—	—	—	—	—	—	—	—	—
1733	—	—	—	—	—	—	—	—	—	—
1734	—	—	—	—	—	—	—	—	—	—
1734–1738	12,907	3,471	—	1,648	874	465	85	2,572	3,792	—
1735	—	—	—	—	—	—	—	—	—	—
1736	—	—	—	—	—	—	—	—	—	—
1737	—	—	—	—	—	—	—	—	—	—
1738	—	—	—	—	—	—	—	—	—	—
1739	—	—	—	—	—	—	—	—	—	—
1740	—	—	—	—	—	—	—	—	—	—
1741	—	—	—	—	—	—	—	—	—	—
1742	—	—	—	—	—	—	—	—	—	—
1743	—	—	—	—	—	—	—	—	—	—
1744	—	—	—	—	—	—	—	—	—	—
1745	—	—	—	—	—	—	—	—	—	—
1746	—	—	—	—	—	—	—	—	—	—
1747	—	—	—	—	—	—	—	—	—	—
1748	—	—	—	—	—	—	—	—	—	—
1758–1760	17,397	5,858	—	1,778	1,205	543	423	3,153	4,437	—
1762–1763	23,493	5,423	—	3,150	605	912	778	7,224	5,401	—
1766	27,801	10,949	—	4,062	—	484	290	6,977	5,039	—
1768	34,449	18,125	1,010	2,023	0	355	273	8,238	3,410	1,015
1769	29,096	14,551	0	1,310	2,215	245	395	6,123	3,071	1,186
1770	27,554	9,153	440	2,256	0	466	395	9,563	4,223	1,058
1771	31,592	11,878	310	2,361	993	517	606	8,208	5,788	931
1772	29,933	10,932	1,110	2,565	2,171	585	386	6,121	5,538	525

[1] Mean of 1717–1720 for clearances outward; mean of 1717–1718 for entrances inward.

Sources
See the sources for Table Eg474–513.

Documentation
See the text for Table Eg474–51.

In this table, the unit of measure for vessels is the registered ton, with one exception. In his introduction to the original data for the three years 1746–1748, Governor James Glen specified that these were cargo tons: "the amount of Tonnage [is] computed from the [vessels'] Cargoes and not taken from the Register" (CO 5/461, folio 43v, PRO/TNA). As a consequence, without the appropriate adjustment (discussed in Appendix A to the essay in this chapter), these data are not comparable with the other tonnage data in this table or any other table in this chapter. If the ratio proposed previously held true for the shipping that cleared Charleston during these years, then Governor Glen's tonnage figures need to be cut in half.

See also the account of shipping clearing outwards at POE Charleston, 1783–1788, in the letter from George Miller, at Charleston, to the Secretary of State for Foreign Affairs, January 28, 1790, BT 6/21, folios 311r–312r, PRO/TNA. Miller was the British consul at Charleston.

	Vessels							
	Total	Ships	Snows	Brigantines	Sloops	Schooners	Doggers	Cutters	Tonnage
1783	303	19	1	71	73	139	0	0	—
1784	673	90	10	148	163	259	1	2	50,961
1785	778	86	8	154	234	295	0	1	56,162
1786	800	81	5	149	262	302	0	1	56,405
1787	947	78	8	155	325	381	0	0	62,188
1788	803	77	10	134	275	307	0	0	56,977

If the vessels that cleared Charleston in 1783 were comparable in size on average to those that sailed out of the port over the next five years, then we can estimate the tonnage clearing outward in 1783 at roughly 21,400 registered tons.

TABLE Eg674–685   Vessels clearing specific colonial ports of entry, by origin or destination: 1730

Contributed by John J. McCusker

Origin or destination	Piscataqua; Salem and Marblehead		Boston		Rhode Island		New York		Perth Amboy		Philadelphia	
	Inward	Outward	Inward	Outward	Inward	Outward	Inward	Outward	Inward	Outward	Inward	Outward
	Eg674	Eg675	Eg676	Eg677	Eg678	Eg679	Eg680	Eg681	Eg682	Eg683	Eg684	Eg685
	Number	Number	Number	Number	Number	Number	Number	Number	Number	Number	Number	Number
Total	102	124	634	648	126	108	211	222	40	44	161	171
Great Britain	5	5	67	40	0	1	15	9	2	3	18	20
Ireland	3	1	4	0	0	0	1	0	0	0	4	0
Europe	9	27	13	20	1	1	1	7	0	3	0	6
Africa and Atlantic islands	2	2	18	15	1	1	3	1	2	4	4	10
Bahama Islands	0	0	0	0	0	0	0	1	0	0	0	0
Bermuda Islands	0	0	2	2	1	1	13	5	2	1	10	2
Caribbean	42	34	160	197	90	83	98	116	6	9	73	85
Thirteen Colonies	11	20	303	278	32	21	75	75	28	24	52	46
Other American colonies	30	35	67	96	1	0	5	8	0	0	0	2

Source

The Pennsylvania Gazette, January 5, 1730/31.

Documentation

See the Appendixes to the essay in this chapter for a general discussion of the tables and the sources of the data, along with a key to abbreviations used in this chapter and general information on matters such as regional definitions, calendar differences, money, and weights and measures.

"In this Paper we exhibit an Account for one Year, of all the Vessels entered and cleared, from and to What Places, in the Ports of Philadelphia, Amboy, New-York, Rhode-Island, Boston, Salem and New-Hampshire." The table obviously owed its origins to the colonial naval office shipping lists (NOSL) from these seven ports of entry (POE), but how they made their way to the editor of *The Pennsylvania Gazette*, who compiled them in such a timely fashion, and why they were compiled and presented in this way, we are not told. Nonetheless, they appear an authentic account from all seven of the POE, and they are interesting for several reasons. (Note that the data are for seven POE, but the figures for two of them – POE Piscataqua, New Hampshire, and POE Salem and Marblehead, Massachusetts – were conflated for the original table.) They are complete accounts from several POE for the same year thus allowing the kind of comparisons that are available to us all too infrequently. They report shipping data from POE not otherwise represented in this chapter and, in the instance of POE Rhode Island, not available at all. And, dated to 1730, they portray an earlier period in colonial commerce when, for instance, Boston dominated colonial trade, in this instance accounting for about 50 percent of clearances inward and outward for these ports. Clearly, this is not a picture of the entirety of colonial commerce; missing are Maryland, Virginia, and the Carolinas as well as other, northern POE. But the table still affords an important glimpse into the shipping of the colonies that earned their credits other than by the staples trades.

The precise dates for each of the seven sets of returns vary slightly: for POE Piscataqua and POE Salem and Marblehead, December 1, 1729, to December 3, 1730; for POE Boston, December 1, 1729, to December 5, 1730; for POE Rhode Island, December 1, 1729, to December 3, 1730; for POE New York, December 1, 1729, to December 5, 1730; for POE Perth Amboy, December 3, 1729, to December 2, 1730; and for POE Philadelphia, December 4, 1729, to December 3, 1730.

TABLE Eg686–687　Freight rates for tobacco from Maryland and Virginia to Great Britain: 1675–1775

Contributed by John J. McCusker

Year	Maryland Eg686 Pounds (£) sterling per freight ton	Virginia Eg687 Pounds (£) sterling per freight ton	Year	Maryland Eg686 Pounds (£) sterling per freight ton	Virginia Eg687 Pounds (£) sterling per freight ton	Year	Maryland Eg686 Pounds (£) sterling per freight ton	Virginia Eg687 Pounds (£) sterling per freight ton	Year	Maryland Eg686 Pounds (£) sterling per freight ton	Virginia Eg687 Pounds (£) sterling per freight ton
1675	—	7.00	1715	6.27	—	1740	9.25	10.00	1760	12.00	14.00
1678	—	6.50	1716	6.13	—	1741	8.91	10.00	1761	10.75	12.00
1680	—	6.50	1717	6.44	—	1742	9.00	9.50	1762	13.33	14.00
1682	6.50	—	1718	5.75	—	1743	9.00	8.00	1763	7.80	10.50
1683	—	5.50	1719	6.63	—	1744	10.64	—	1764	7.00	8.00
1684	—	5.25	1720	7.63	9.50	1745	12.40	16.00	1765	7.00	8.00
1686	6.50	—	1721	7.60	8.40	1746	13.50	16.00	1766	7.00	8.00
1688	—	6.00	1722	7.06	—	1747	15.47	—	1767	7.00	8.00
1690	—	15.00	1723	6.90	—	1748	10.23	14.00	1768	7.00	8.00
1691	—	17.50	1724	6.10	—	1749	7.00	8.00	1769	7.00	8.00
1692	12.75	—	1725	6.12	—	1750	7.00	—	1770	7.00	8.00
1697	6.50	8.00	1726	7.00	8.00	1751	6.93	—	1771	7.14	8.20
1698	7.00	—	1727	7.00	—	1752	7.00	8.00	1772	7.00	8.00
1700	6.00	—	1728	7.00	—	1753	6.89	8.00	1773	7.00	8.00
1702	6.00	—	1729	7.00	—	1754	7.00	8.00	1774	7.00	8.00
1703	15.00	—	1730	6.53	8.00	1755	6.88	8.00	1775	7.00	8.00
1704	13.00	—	1731	7.00	8.00	1756	8.89	12.00			
1705	14.89	—	1732	7.00	8.00	1757	13.14	14.70			
1706	15.00	—	1733	7.00	8.00	1758	12.18	14.00			
1707	16.30	—	1734	7.00	8.00	1759	12.00	10.00			
1708	15.02	—	1735	6.97	8.00						
1709	13.67	12.00	1736	7.00	8.00						
1710	—	10.67	1737	7.00	8.00						
1711	—	12.00	1738	6.91	8.00						
1712	12.36	8.00	1739	7.00	8.00						
1713	8.09	—									
1714	6.00	—									

Source

Stephen Gregg Hardy, "Trade and Economic Growth in the Eighteenth-Century Chesapeake" (Ph.D. dissertation, University of Maryland, 1999), pp. 439–56.

Documentation

See the Appendixes to the essay in this chapter for a general discussion of the tables and the sources of the data, along with a key to abbreviations used in this chapter and general information on matters such as regional definitions, calendar differences, money, and weights and measures.

Hardy collected and compiled the annual average rate per freight ton in pounds sterling charged to ship tobacco from Maryland and Virginia to ports in England. He used a variety of sources, but for Maryland he was able to draw on the official record of such rates posted by law from 1714 on as extracted and first published in John M. Hemphill II, "Freight Rates in the Maryland Tobacco Trade, 1705–1762," *Maryland Historical Magazine* 54 (March, June 1959): 36–58, 153–87.

Freight rates for tobacco were always quoted in sterling. In the colonial export trade, the freight ton of tobacco was always and everywhere the equivalent to four hogsheads of tobacco (Hardy 1999, p. 440). Compare John J. McCusker, "The Tonnage of Ships Engaged in British Colonial Trade during the Eighteenth Century," *Research in Economic History* 6 (1981): 73–105, as revised and updated in McCusker, *Essays in the Economic History of the Atlantic World* (Routledge, 1997), pp. 61–5 and elsewhere. This was so despite the increase in the size of tobacco hogsheads. See the text for Table Eg275–284.

Given that "the purpose of the [Maryland] law was to encourage competition among tobacco merchants by requiring them publicly to post their freight rate and conditions" (Hardy 1999, p. 439), and given that Virginia had no such law, it is tempting to explain the consistently lower rates for Maryland after 1714 as the consequence of its law.

TABLE Eg688–754 Commodities exported from British North America, by destination: 1770[1]

Contributed by John J. McCusker

Specific commodities (quantity or value)

Value, quantity, and destination	Totals (value)			Potash	Pearl ash	Spermaceti candles	Tallow candles	Coal	Castorium	Fish Dried	Fish Pickled	Flaxseed	Indian corn	Oats
	All goods	Reexports	Domestic products exported											
	Eg688	Eg689	Eg690	Eg691	Eg692	Eg693	Eg694	Eg695	Eg696	Eg697	Eg698	Eg699	Eg700	Eg701
	Pounds (£) sterling	Pounds (£) sterling	Pounds (£) sterling	Tons	Tons	Pounds	Pounds	Chaldrons	Pounds	Hundredweight	Barrels	Bushels	Bushels	Bushels
Total value	3,437,715	81,555 [2]	3,356,160	35,192	29,469	23,688	1,238	25	1,680	375,394	22,551	35,169	43,376	1,243
Total quantity	—	—	—	1,173	737	379,012	59,420	20	7,465	660,003	30,068	312,612	578,349	24,859
Great Britain	1,752,515	65,860	1,686,654	1,173	737	4,865	0	0	7,465	22,086	123	6,780	0	0
Ireland	118,777	4,698	114,079	0	0	450	0	0	0	450	25	305,083	150	0
Southern Europe	691,912	5,992	685,920	0	0	14,167	1,630	0	0	431,386	307	749	175,221	3,421
West Indies	848,934	4,755	844,179	0	0	351,625	57,550	20	0	206,081	29,582	0	402,958	21,438
Africa	21,678	297	21,382	0	0	7,905	240	0	0	0	31	0	20	0

Specific commodities (quantity or value)

Value, quantity, and destination	Wheat	Peas and beans	Ginseng	Hemp	Iron Pig	Bar	Cast	Wrought	Indigo	Whale Oil	Fins	Linseed oil	Copper ore	Lead ore
	Eg702	Eg703	Eg704	Eg705	Eg706	Eg707	Eg708	Eg709	Eg710	Eg711	Eg712	Eg713	Eg714	Eg715
	Bushels	Bushels	Pounds	Hundredweight	Tons	Tons	Tons	Tons	Pounds	Tuns	Pounds	Tuns	Tons	Tons
Total value	131,467	10,077	1,243	130	30,089	36,961	33	167	131,552	85,013	19,121	488	854	83
Total quantity	751,240 [3]	50,383	74,604	86	6,017	2,470	2	8	584,672	5,667	112,971	168	41	6
Great Britain	11,739	0	74,604	86	5,747	2,102	0	0	584,593	5,202	112,971	161	41	6
Ireland	149,985	0	0	0	267	85	0	0	0	22	0	0	0	0
Southern Europe	588,561	1,046	0	0	0	10	0	0	0	175	0	0	0	0
West Indies	955	49,337	0	0	0	273	2	8	83	268	0	7	0	0
Africa	0	0	0	0	0	0	0	0	0	0	0	0	0	0

Specific commodities (quantity or value)

Value, quantity, and destination	Bread and flour	Meal	Potatoes	Beef and pork	Butter	Cheese	New England rum	Rice	Rough rice	Domestic loaf sugar	Raw silk	Soap	Shoes
	Eg716	Eg717	Eg718	Eg719	Eg720	Eg721	Eg722	Eg723	Eg724	Eg725	Eg726	Eg727	Eg728
	Tons	Bushels	Bushels	Barrels	Pounds	Pounds	Gallons	Barrels	Bushels	Pounds	Pounds	Pounds	Pairs
Total value	504,553	443	127	66,035	3,492	933	21,836	340,693	615	333	542	2,165	394
Total quantity	45,868	4,430	3,382	31,075	167,613	55,997	349,381 [2]	151,418 [3]	8,200	10,648	541	86,585	3,149
Great Britain	263	0	0	0	0	0	600	74,073	0	0	541	0	0
Ireland	3,583	0	0	0	0	0	7,931	0	0	0	0	0	0
Southern Europe	18,501	0	0	244	0	0	45,310	36,296	0	600	0	550	0
West Indies	23,449	4,430	3,382	30,392 [3]	167,313	55,997	2,574	40,932 [3]	8,200	8,548	0	85,035	3,149
Africa	72	0	0	439	300	0	292,966	117	0	1,500	0	1,000	0

Specific commodities (quantity or value)

Value, quantity, and destination	Ship stuff Eg729 Barrels	Onions (value) Eg730 Pounds sterling	Pitch Eg731 Barrels	Tar Common Eg732 Barrels	Tar Green Eg733 Barrels	Turpentine Eg734 Barrels	Rosin Eg735 Barrels	Oil of turpentine Eg736 Barrels	Masts, yards, etc. Eg737 Tons	Walnut wood (value) Eg738 Pounds sterling	Pine, oak, cedar boards Eg739 Board feet	Pine timber Eg740 Tons	Oak timber Eg741 Tons
Total value	9,959	6,495	3,200	24,427	261	6,806	279	103	16,630	115	58,618	4,405	3,487
Total quantity	7,964	—	9,144	81,422	653	17,014	223	41	3,045	—	42,756,306	11,011	3,874
Great Britain	0	0	8,265	78,115	653	15,125	195	11	3,043	106	6,013,519	10,582	3,710
Ireland	0	0	0	0	0	0	0	0	0	9	329,741	50	10
Southern Europe	7,327	117	0	0	0	0	0	0	0	0	486,078	64	10
West Indies	640	6,379	822	3,173	0	1,807	23	30	2	0	35,922,168	315	144
Africa	0	0	57	134	0	82	0	0	0	0	4,800	0	0

Specific commodities (quantity or value)

Value, quantity, and destination	House frames Eg742 Number	Staves and heading Eg743 Number	Hoops Eg744 Number	Shook hogsheads Eg745 Number	Cattle Eg746 Number	Horses Eg747 Number	Sheep and hogs Eg748 Number	Poultry Eg749 Dozen	Furs (value) Eg750 Pounds sterling	Deer skins Eg751 Pounds	Tobacco (value) Eg752 Pounds sterling	Tallow and lard Eg753 Pounds	Beeswax Eg754 Pounds
Total value	3,260	61,619	8,668	7,835	14,328	60,228	2,479	1,177	91,486	57,750	906,638	3,857	6,426
Total quantity	163	20,546,326	3,852,383	62,678	3,184	6,692	12,797	2,615	—	799,807	—	185,143	128,523
Great Britain	0	4,921,020	18,912	0	0	0	0	0	91,486	799,622	904,982	800	62,794
Ireland	0	2,828,762	7,072	0	0	0	0	0	0	185	0	0	10,980
Southern Europe	0	1,680,403	0	549	0	0	0	0	0	0	0	0	50,529
West Indies	163	11,116,141	3,817,899	62,099	3,184	6,692	12,797	2,615	0	0	1,569	183,893	1,820
Africa	0	0	8,500	30	0	0	0	0	0	0	87	450	2,400

1 Values are expressed in pounds sterling; quantities are expressed in the units specified.

2 Figure disagrees with source; sum corrected to agree with sum of components and with original source. See text.

3 Figure recalculated; differs from source. See text.

Source

David Macpherson, *Annals of Commerce, Manufactures, Fisheries and Navigation ... of the British Empire and Other Countries, from the Earliest Accounts to ... 1801* (Nichols and Son et al., 1805), volume 3, pp. 572–3. Macpherson stated that these "accounts [were] copied from those in the custom-house [London]" (p. 569). A fuller version of this table was earlier published in John [Baker Holroyd], Lord Sheffield, *Observations on the Commerce of the American States*, 6th edition, enlarged (J. Debrett, 1784), Tables V and VI. Sheffield cited the table as prepared under the direction of, and signed by, Thomas Irving, "Inspector General of Imports and Exports of North America, and Register of Shipping," dated at the Custom House, Boston, October 1, 1771. The source of Irving's data was the Ledger of Imports and Exports, British North America, 1768–1772, CUST 16/1, PRO/TNA.

Documentation

See the Appendixes to the essay in this chapter for a general discussion of the tables and the sources of the data, along with a key to abbreviations used in this chapter and general information on such matters as regional definitions, calendar differences, money, and weights and measures. For additional information about the weights and measures used, see Sheffield (1784), Tables V and VI.

The table displays the quantity and the value in pounds sterling of selected commodities exported overseas from all of the colonies in British North America in the year 1770 (January 5, 1770, through January 4, 1771). (Thus these figures do not include exports "coastwise" from one of these colonies to another.) As he presented it, Macpherson omitted many of the minor commodities that Irving had included in his original table and as Sheffield had printed it – and, therefore, the totals in series Eg688–690 do not always add up. Just how relatively unimportant those commodities were can be appreciated when one compares the grand total value of exports in 1770 as Macpherson indicated £3,437,315 with the total of the various commodities he listed, £3,321,000 (96.6 percent). Macpherson's distinction between continental products exported (series Eg690) and commodities imported – almost all from the West Indies – and subsequently reexported (series Eg689) is detailed commodity by commodity in Irving's original table (q.v.). Macpherson also omitted "the fractional parts of the quantities" but did not change the values; his action explains some of the minor anomalies in his table. The data can be usefully be compared both with the published version of Irving's table and with the original data in CUST 16/1, PRO/TNA. See the similar compilation for 1768 – also based on the data in CUST 16/1 – among the George Chalmers Papers, Add. MS 15485, folios 29v–35r, BL.

Macpherson was mistaken in his statement that the unit values of each commodity were "the official valuation, and consequently ... considerably under the real amount" (Macpherson 1805, volume 3, p. 572 n.). (He probably thought that these data were compiled in the same way as the CUST 3 and CUST 14 data, for which see the discussion in Appendix A to the essay in this chapter.) As explained

(continued)

TABLE Eg688-754   Commodities exported from British North America, by destination: 1770   *Continued*

in the text to Table Eg461-473, Irving used actual colonial market prices. Where it is possible to check, the unit values are the prices that applied in the colonies in the late 1760s and early 1770s reduced to sterling. Compare the prices of these same commodities as compiled in Arthur Harrison Cole, *Wholesale Commodity Prices in the United States, 1700–1861* (Harvard University Press, 1938). See also Table Eg251-270. For additional information about the prices used, see Sheffield (1784), Tables V and VI.

Exports of beef and pork were stated sometimes in numbers of barrels and sometime by weight (in tons, hundredweight and pounds). Both were used in 1770, the former for exports to Europe and to Africa, the latter for exports to the West Indies (CUST 16/1, pp. 138, 139, 142, PRO/TNA). In his table, Irving priced the barrel of beef and pork at £2 2s 6d and the ton of beef at £22 10s 0d. At these prices, the barrel of beef and pork weighed an average of 221.6 pounds. See John J. McCusker, "The Tonnage of Ships Engaged in British Colonial Trade during the Eighteenth Century," *Research in Economic History* 6 (1981): 73–105, as revised and updated in McCusker, *Essays in the Economic History of the Atlantic World* (Routledge, 1997), pp. 70–5, Table 3.5. The figure for the quantity exported to the West Indies in the table has been converted to the number of barrels shipped.

Both Macpherson (1805, volume 3, p. 573) and Sheffield (1784, Table V) badly confuse the figures for the export of rice to the West Indies. Resort must be had to Irving's original account in CUST 16/1, p. 142, PRO/TNA. There the components are totaled to 38,966 barrels and "1966 bbls. [containing] 9006 cwt. 0 qr. 22 lbs." The total number of barrels, 40,932, is

the number reported in the table. Sheffield's and Macpherson's mistake in adding up the total quantity of wheat exported has also been corrected.

The considerable difference between the total value of commodities carefully calculated by Irving and the crude estimates created by James F. Shepherd and Gary M. Walton, *Shipping, Maritime Trade, and the Economic Development of Colonial America* (Cambridge University Press, 1972), pp. 115, demonstrates, again, the unreliability of Shepherd and Walton's enterprise. They figured commodity exports in 1770 at £2,983,000, a great deal less than the actual value of exports. For a discussion of some of the difficulties with their effort, see John J. McCusker and Russell R. Menard, *The Economy of British America,1607–1789*, 2nd edition (University of North Carolina Press, 1991), pp. 71–88, 199, and elsewhere.

There are other contemporary compilations of such data that, most likely, also emanated from Irving's office. Especially notable is a table showing the quantity and value – again in pounds sterling – of all exports from POE Philadelphia for the three years 1771-1773: "An Aggregate and Valuation of the Exports from the Port of Philadelphia; with the Number of Vessels and Tonnage Employed Therein Annually," Historical Society of Pennsylvania Miscellaneous Collections, Records of Boats and Cargoes, Box 13A, part i, Historical Society of Pennsylvania, Philadelphia, and as printed in *Pennsylvania Magazine; or, American Monthly Museum* 1 (February 1775): 72–3.

TABLE Eg755-765   Coal exported from James River, Virginia, by destination: 1758-1765

Contributed by John J. McCusker

Year	Total	Piscataqua	Salem and Marblehead	Boston	Nantucket	Rhode Island	New York	Philadelphia	New Castle	James River, lower part	West Indies
	Eg755	Eg756	Eg757	Eg758	Eg759	Eg760	Eg761	Eg762	Eg763	Eg764	Eg765
	Tons	Tons	Tons	Tons	Tons	Tons	Tons	Tons	Tons	Tons	Tons
1758	32	0	0	0	0	0	24	0	0	8	0
1760	194	0	0	0	0	0	182	0	0	0	12
1761	211	0	0	0	0	0	136	60	0	0	15
1762	531	0	0	288	0	156	40	47	0	0	0
1763	1,076	168	112	232	34	136	247	102	24	0	21
1765	712	214	161	60	0	256	0	21	0	0	0

Sources

The sources of these data are the records kept in each of the colonial ports of entry (POE) by the administrative clerk of the port, the colonial naval officer. The original quarterly reports of the naval officers – the naval officer shipping lists (NOSL) – and various accounts based on them survive in many places, in many forms. The most important contemporary compilation of these reports was made under the direction of Thomas Irving, the Boston-based Inspector General of Imports and Exports of North America, and is known as the Ledger of Imports and Exports, British North America, 1768-1772, CUST 16/1, PRO/TNA. A more recent attempt to assemble and compile data from the extant NOSL was organized in the 1930s by Lawrence A. Harper and others. These data come from the Harper materials and were assembled by Howard N. Eavenson, *The First Century and a Quarter of American Coal Industry* (Privately printed, 1942), pp. 32–4.

Documentation

See the Appendixes to the essay in this chapter for a general discussion of the tables and the sources of the data, along with a key to abbreviations used in this chapter and general information on matters such as regional definitions, calendar differences, money, and weights and measures.

This table reports the quantity of coal in net or short pounds (2,000 pounds) exported from the premier coal-exporting region of the Thirteen Continental Colonies. The period 1758-1765 is the only one for which we have all on the NOSL for both POE James River, Upper Part, and POE James River, Lower Part (Hampton). The several destinations recorded are other

British American POE. The source confused POE Piscataqua, New Hampshire, with the town of Piscataway, New Jersey, a mistake corrected here. The year of record ran from January 5 through January 4.

Comparisons with the complete returns for the years 1768-1772 in Table Eg766-810, based on CUST 16/1, PRO/TNA, indicate that the James River basin shipments constituted the bulk of the exports from the Thirteen Continental Colonies. Out of a total of 2,798 net or short tons recorded in those five years, 1,220 net tons were shipped from the Upper James, 180 from the Lower James, 117 from New Hampshire, and only minor quantities from other ports. Some of the last may have been used as ballast in arriving vessels and, if so, may originally have come from Great Britain. CUST 16/1, PRO/TNA, as reported the export of 1,100 tons from Nova Scotia. Thus, for the period 1768-1772, Virginia accounted for 71.1 percent of all coal exported from British North America.

The units of measure employed in the coal trade are many. Whereas the figures in this table are in short tons, imports and exports of coal have usually been recorded in long tons, chaldrons, and bushels. The long ton (2,240 pounds) continued to be used in the coal trade down into the late nineteenth century and early twentieth century. The chaldron of coal in the colonial period measured thirty-six bushels. The bushel of coal used at Philadelphia during the colonial period was the standard Winchester bushel of 2,150.42 cubic inches and weighed 80 pounds. Thus, the chaldron of coal weighed 2,880 pounds. "A load of cole" measured "144 bushels." John Relfe, "Estimate on Pennsylvania Furnaces," in a letter from Relfe, at Philadelphia,

TABLE Eg755–765   Coal exported from James River, Virginia, by destination: 1758–1765   *Continued*

to Nicholas Brown and Co., at Providence, Rhode Island, undated but in reply to a letter from the company to Relfe dated May 21, 1765, Brown Papers, P-H6, Calendared, volume 1, John Carter Brown Library, Brown University, and as mentioned in James B. Hedges, *The Browns of Providence Plantations* (Harvard University Press, 1952–1968), volume 1, p. 126. Thus the load was the equivalent of 4 chaldrons, 11,520 pounds, or about 103 hundredweight (the long hundredweight, 112 pounds). See John J. McCusker, "The Tonnage of Ships Engaged in British Colonial Trade during the Eighteenth Century,"

Research in Economic History 6 (1981): 73–105, as revised and updated in McCusker, *Essays in the Economic History of the Atlantic World* (Routledge, 1997), pp. 70-5, Table 3.5. The London chaldron of coal measured 2,987 pounds; the Newcastle chaldron (after the 1680s), nearly twice as much, or 5,956 pounds. For the weights and measures used in the British coal trade, see John U. Nef, *The Rise of the British Coal Industry,* London School of Economics and Political Science, Studies in Economic and Social History, volume 6 (Routledge, 1932), volume 2, pp. 367–78.

TABLE Eg766–810   Coal imported, by origin and port of entry: 1768–1772

Contributed by John J. McCusker

Totals and Imported coastwise from elsewhere in British North America

Year	Total Eg766	Total Eg767	Falmouth Eg768	Piscataqua Eg769	Salem and Marblehead Eg770	Boston Eg771	Rhode Island Eg772	New Haven Eg773	New London Eg774	New York Eg775	Philadelphia Eg776	Patuxent Eg777	North Potomac Eg778	Rappahannock Eg779	James River, Lower Part Eg780
	Tons	Tons	Tons	Tons	Tons	Tons	Tons	Tons	Tons	Tons	Tons	Tons	Tons	Tons	Tons
1768	470	470	0	130	101	153	0	0	0	0	86	0	0	0	0
1769	8,546	0	0	0	0	0	0	0	0	0	0	0	0	0	0
1770	4,757	199	0	0	14	0	76	0	0	0	69	40	0	0	0
1771	6,297	1,056	0	50	183	174	13	0	37	226	122	0	0	0	0
1772	286	286	0	0	82	204	0	0	0	0	0	0	0	0	0

Imported coastwise from elsewhere in British North America (continued)

Year	James River, Upper Part Eg781	York River Eg782	Roanoke Eg783	Brunswick Eg784	Charleston Eg785	Savannah Eg786	Sunbury Eg787	St. Augustine Eg788
	Tons	Tons	Tons	Tons	Tons	Tons	Tons	Tons
1768	0	0	0	0	0	0	0	0
1769	0	0	0	0	0	0	0	0
1770	0	0	0	0	0	0	0	0
1771	0	0	0	0	244	4	0	3
1772	0	0	0	0	0	0	0	0

Imported from Great Britain and Ireland

Year	Total Eg789	Falmouth Eg790	Piscataqua Eg791	Salem and Marblehead Eg792	Boston Eg793	Rhode Island Eg794	New Haven Eg795
	Tons	Tons	Tons	Tons	Tons	Tons	Tons
1768	—	—	—	—	—	—	—
1769	8,546	12	293	30	1,894	159	37
1770	4,558	3	158	162	989	208	69
1771	5,241	—	89	0	527	206	0
1772	—	—	—	—	—	—	—

Imported from Great Britain and Ireland (continued)

Year	New London Eg796	New York Eg797	Philadelphia Eg798	Patuxent Eg799	North Potomac Eg800	Rappahannock Eg801	James River, Lower Part Eg802	James River, Upper Part Eg803	York River Eg804	Roanoke Eg805	Brunswick Eg806	Charleston Eg807	Savannah Eg808	Sunbury Eg809	St. Augustine Eg810
	Tons	Tons	Tons	Tons	Tons	Tons	Tons	Tons	Tons	Tons	Tons	Tons	Tons	Tons	Tons
1768	—	—	—	—	—	—	—	—	—	—	—	—	—	—	—
1769	—	1,537	1,507	107	65	150	815	56	0	0	3	1,819	74	0	0
1770	0	337	1,119	65	0	0	432	0	0	0	34	901	69	15	0
1771	0	2,248	0	239	316	96	384	0	181	19	46	774	93	0	23
1772	—	—	—	—	—	—	—	—	—	—	—	—	—	—	—

Source

The Ledger of Imports and Exports, British North America, 1768–1772, pp. 26, 58, 76, 104, 147, 170, 206, 250, CUST 16/1, PRO/TNA.

Documentation

See the Appendixes to the essay in this chapter for a general discussion of the tables and the sources of the data, along with a key to abbreviations used in this chapter and general information on matters such as regional definitions, calendar differences, money, and weights and measures. Imports and exports of coal were recorded in long tons, chaldrons, and bushels. The figures in the table are in short tons or net tons (equal to 2,000 pounds). See the text for Table Eg755–765 for additional information. The year of record ran from January 5 through January 4. Note that Florida (POE St. Augustine) is included here as part of British North America but that it was not one of the Thirteen Continental Colonies.

This table reports the quantity of coal in net or short tons (2,000 tons) imported into the Thirteen Continental Colonies. The source was compiled under the direction of Thomas Irving, Inspector General of Imports and Exports and Register of Shipping, in his office in the Custom House, Boston, from the naval officer shipping lists (NOSL) sent to him at his command by the Customs authorities in the several ports of entry (POE) in British North America. Coastwise imports were those coming from the neighboring British North American colonies. For these ports and the records of their trade, see also the text for Table Eg474–513. The source is defective in that it lacks any record of imports into the colonies from Great Britain and Ireland for 1768 or 1772.

TABLE Eg811–815   Pig iron imported into England from British North America, by colony: 1723–1776

Contributed by John J. McCusker

Year	Total	Virginia and Maryland	New York	Pennsylvania	Other colonies	Year	Total	Virginia and Maryland	New York	Pennsylvania	Other colonies
	Eg811	Eg812	Eg813	Eg814	Eg815		Eg811	Eg812	Eg813	Eg814	Eg815
	Long tons	Long tons	Long tons	Long tons	Long tons		Long tons	Long tons	Long tons	Long tons	Long tons
1723	15	15	0	0	0	1750	2,924	2,509	76	318	21
1724	202	202	0	0	0	1751	3,210	2,950	33	200	27
1725	137	137	0	0	0	1752	2,979	2,762	41	156	20
1726	296	263	0	33	0	1753	2,738	2,347	97	243	51
1727	484	407	0	77	0	1754	3,245	2,591	116	513	25
1728	886	643	0	243	0	1755	3,441	2,133	457	836	15
1729	1,132	853	0	274	5	1756	3,011	2,468	201	234	108
1730	1,716	1,527	0	189	1	1757	2,699	2,462	157	80	0
1731	2,250	2,081	0	169	0	1758	3,717	3,448	49	195	25
1732	2,333	2,226	0	107	0	1759	1,672	1,429	103	128	12
1733	2,405	2,310	0	95	0	1760	3,265	3,123	51	61	30
1734	2,197	2,042	0	147	7	1761	2,766	2,512	76	149	29
1735	2,562	2,362	0	196	4	1762	1,782	1,733	19	7	23
1736	2,729	2,458	0	271	0	1763	2,565	2,325	108	132	0
1737	2,316	2,120	0	169	27	1764	2,555	1,837	371	307	40
1738	2,359	2,113	0	228	18	1765	2,965	2,071	564	301	29
1739	2,418	2,242	0	170	5	1766	2,588	1,741	548	299	0
1740	2,275	2,020	0	159	96	1767	3,313	2,070	357	785	101
1741	3,457	3,261	0	153	43	1768	2,953	1,718	520	665	50
1742	2,075	1,926	0	144	5	1769	3,402	1,616	864	634	288
1743	3,005	2,816	81	63	45	1770	4,232	1,572	1,031	1,381	248
1744	1,862	1,748	6	88	20	1771	5,334	2,624	778	1,553	379
1745	2,275	2,131	19	97	27	1772	3,705	1,879	756	706	364
1746	1,861	1,729	29	103	0	1773	2,937	1,581	984	209	163
1747	2,157	2,119	13	25	0	1774	3,445	1,458	1,533	323	131
1748	2,156	2,018	22	115	1	1775	2,997	1,467	1,015	385	130
1749	1,758	1,575	17	167	0	1776	311	208	43	0	60

Sources

The sources of the data are the Ledgers of Imports and Exports of England, 1723–1776, CUST 3/24–76, PRO/TNA, and contemporary accounts extracted from them. The data from 1723 through 1749 are from "An Account of the Quantity of Iron Imported [into England] from the British Colonies in America," 1711–1749, dated April 5, 1750, and signed by John Oxenford, the Inspector General of Imports and Exports. It is House of Lords, Main Papers, April 5, 1750, HLRO. For this account, see Great Britain, Parliament, House of Lords, *Journals of the House of Lords* (House of Lords, 1767 to date), volume 27, pp. 445, 451. The data for 1750–1755 are from a similar account printed in Harry Scrivenor, *A Comprehensive History of the Iron Trade, throughout the World, from the Earliest Records to the Present Period. With an Appendix, Containing Official Tables, and Other Public Documents* (Smith, Elder, 1841), p. 340. The data for 1756–1776 are taken directly from CUST 3/56-76, PRO/TNA.

Documentation

See the Appendixes to the essay in this chapter for a general discussion of the tables and the sources of the data, along with a key to abbreviations used in this chapter and general information on such matters as regional definitions, calendar differences, money, and weights and measures. Iron and iron goods were bought, sold, and shipped in terms of the long ton (2,240 pounds) and its subunits: the hundredweight, the quarter, and the pound. Note especially the discussion of the time periods used for compiling these records. For these accounts, the year of record ended on December 24 for 1699–1751; and on January 4 thereafter.

General Note on the Iron Trade

Raw iron in colonial commerce was described in two ways: as "pig iron" and as "bar iron." Pig iron was the product of the first step in the processing process, the crude result of a smelting that separated impurities and waste products from iron ore. Although some of the molten iron could be made into cast-iron articles, most of the initial output of the furnace was poured into molds forming pig iron, that is, rough bars of metal of a fairly standard size and shape (five to six feet long and about six inches square). The next step was to reheat the rough iron ingot at a refinery forge and hammer it into bars. Bar iron, too, had a distinctive shape: a rod of iron with two ends somewhat larger than the central shaft. Reheated again and again, the increasingly pliant bar of iron was hammered into a variety of forms, flattened or rolled into a sheet, cut or slit, drawn or plated. Bar iron was then sold to blacksmiths, who fabricated it into many different finished products – "wrought" iron goods. Unless specifically identified as a particular type of manufactured commodity (cast stove plates, fire backs, skillets, pots, and other hollow ware; wrought anchors, axes, nails, scythes, or kettles), fabricated iron ware was usually described in trade records as cast iron, if poured into forms, and wrought iron, if forged from malleable iron. The exception to this general rule was the English Inspector General's accounts, in which the term "wrought iron" seems to have included both cast iron and malleable iron products. Obviously, raw pig iron sold for less than raw bar iron – at a ratio of roughly 1:2 – and cast iron goods for less than wrought iron goods.

The statistical picture of iron in the Colonies can be reconstructed in part from data concerning colonial iron works and in part from records of colonial trade. The beginning of this industry came early in the various American Colonies: Virginia by 1622, Massachusetts by 1645, Connecticut by 1657, New Jersey by 1680, Maryland by 1715, Pennsylvania by 1716, and New York shortly before 1750. On the eve of the American Revolutionary War, the Colonies had at least eighty-two charcoal furnaces that each produced about 300 tons of pig iron for a total of 24,600 tons. There were also more than 175 iron forges, some being bloomeries that made bar iron directly from the ore. Most of them, however, were refinery forges that used pig iron. Each of the 175 forges produced roughly 150 tons of bar iron a year, or 26,250 tons in all. In addition, there were slitting mills and other iron works. See Arthur C. Bining, *British Regulation of the Colonial Iron Industry* (University of Pennsylvania Press, 1933), pp. 26–30, 122, 134; Bining, *Pennsylvania Iron Manufacture in the Eighteenth Century* (Pennsylvania Historical Commission, 1938); James A. Mulholland, *A History of Metals in Colonial America* (University of Alabama Press,

(continued)

TABLE Eg811–815 Pig iron imported into England from British North America, by colony: 1723–1776 *Continued*

1981), pp. 116, 192 nn. 80, 82. See also Paul F. Paskoff, *Industrial Evolution: Organization, Structure, and Growth of the Pennsylvania Iron Industry, 1750–1860*, Studies in Industry and Society, volume 3 (Johns Hopkins University Press, 1983). See also the data in series Eg413 and the maps and essay that are the source of those data, Lester J. Cappon, "Ironworks," in Lester J. Cappon, Barbara Bartz Petchenik, and John Hamilton Long, editors, *Atlas of Early American History: The Revolutionary Era, 1760–1790* (Princeton University Press, 1976), pp. 29, 105–6; and the discussion in John J. McCusker and Russell R. Menard, *The Economy of British America, 1607–1789*, 2nd edition (University of North Carolina Press, 1991), pp. 308–30.

Based on his study of colonial ironworks, Bining (1933, p. 134) presented comparative estimates of total iron production in the Thirteen Continental Colonies and total world production. "These estimates include pig iron, cast-iron wares made at blast furnaces, and bar iron produced at bloomeries directly from the ore."

Iron production of the Thirteen Continental Colonies, later the United States, and the world

[In long tons]

Year	Colonies	World
1700	1,500	100,000
1750	10,000	150,000
1775	30,000	210,000
1790	38,000	325,000
1800	45,000	400,000

The omission of New Jersey as a category from the ledgers compiled in the London office of the Inspector General of Imports and Exports – see Appendix A to the essay in this chapter – has a particularly unfortunate impact on data dealing with the iron trade because so much of the production of iron in the Colonies took place in that colony. As discussed in Appendix A, the lack of a series labeled "New Jersey" does not mean that the imports or exports of the colony did not make it into the trade records; they are simply recorded elsewhere. The imports and exports of eastern New Jersey passed through POE New York just as the imports and exports of western New Jersey passed through POE Philadelphia – at least as recorded in the Ledgers of Imports and Exports of England (CUST 3, PRO/TNA).

Some of the categories in Tables Eg811–1012 suffer potentially from double-counting, given the intercolonial coastwise trade in pig iron. See John J. McCusker, "The Tonnage of Ships Engaged in British Colonial Trade during the Eighteenth Century," *Research in Economic History* 6 (1981): 73–105, as revised and updated in McCusker, *Essays in the Economic History of the Atlantic World* (Routledge, 1997), p. 63. See, for instance, the text for series Eg815.

Table Eg811–815

Reported in this table are the quantities in long tons (2,240 pounds) of pig iron imported annually into England and Wales from British North America. It must be underscored that these data are the figures for imports into England and Wales, *not* figures for exports from the Colonies as they have too often been described. For these accounts, the year of record ended on December 24 for 1699–1751; and on January 4 thereafter.

All of these data originate in the Ledgers of Imports and Exports of England, CUST 2/1–10, CUST3/1–82, PRO/TNA, a source used repeatedly in this chapter. For a discussion of these sources, see John J. McCusker, "The Current Value of English Exports, 1697 to 1800," *William and Mary Quarterly*, 3rd series, 28 (October 1971): 607–28, as revised and updated in McCusker (1997), pp. 222–44. Oxenford's account drew directly from the ledgers in his office in the Custom House and, as Scrivenor (1841, p. 324) tells us, he also relied on accounts extracted from the ledgers by later Inspectors General for reports they had prepared at the request of the House of Commons. Many of the later returns were published in the sessional papers issued by the British Parliament. Note that the "new [1854] edition" of Scrivenor's book – and, thus, the twentieth-century reprints of it – omits all of the tabular material appended to the 1841 edition. For some years during that latter period, the totals in series Eg811 are different from the data given in Scrivenor (1841), pp. 343–4. Compare [Romaine] Elizabeth Boody Schumpeter, *English Overseas Trade Statistics, 1697–1808* (Clarendon Press, 1960), pp. 52–5, 56.

As Oxenford's account makes explicit, England imported no pig iron from British North America in the years 1711–1722. Of the nearly fifty thousand tons of pig iron imported into England and Wales from all of British America between 1711 and 1749, 92 percent came from Virginia and Maryland.

For data on the importation into Scotland of pig iron from the Thirteen Continental Colonies, 1750–1756 and 1761–1776, drawn from the Ledgers of Imports and Exports of Scotland by the Scottish Inspector General, see Scrivenor (1841), pp. 342–3. For these records, see the text for Table Eg443–460.

Series Eg815. These figures state the totals for pig iron imported from Newfoundland, Canada, New England, and the Carolinas. (The original source also recorded iron imports from various parts of the British West Indies.) It is probable that some of the iron imported into England and Wales from such places as Newfoundland and the British West Indies had actually been produced in, say, New Jersey or Virginia and subsequently shipped from there as ballast. No longer needed for the next leg of a voyage, the ballast was off-loaded, sold, and afterward reexported as freight (or ballast). In a similar way, some of the iron exported from Virginia and Maryland may have been imported into those Colonies from elsewhere to be used as ballast onboard tobacco ships. See McCusker (1997), p. 63. See also the text for Tables Eg755–765 and Eg867–872.

TABLE Eg816–850 Pig iron exported, by colony and destination: 1768–1772

Contributed by John J. McCusker

Total

Year	Total	Massachusetts	Rhode Island	New York	Pennsylvania	Maryland	Virginia
	Eg816	Eg817	Eg818	Eg819	Eg820	Eg821	Eg822
	Hundredweight	Hundredweight	Hundredweight	Hundredweight	Hundredweight	Hundredweight	Hundredweight
1768	71,134 [1]	1,077	2,220	31,119	12,102	6,422	17,494
1769	112,186	2,365	5,980	23,795	21,896	24,830	33,320
1770	133,079	1,020	6,957	26,490	31,947	35,150	31,515
1771	128,306 [2]	810	7,820	15,770	30,886	45,245	27,455
1772	98,098	1,521	6,325	26,755	9,408	33,405	20,684

To Great Britain

Year	Total	Massachusetts	Rhode Island	New York	Pennsylvania	Maryland	Virginia
	Eg823	Eg824	Eg825	Eg826	Eg827	Eg828	Eg829
	Hundredweight	Hundredweight	Hundredweight	Hundredweight	Hundredweight	Hundredweight	Hundredweight
1768	62,356 [1]	1,077	1,820	29,819	10,006	1,780	17,094
1769	93,866	1,360	2,310	14,960	21,676	20,240	33,320
1770	114,944	1,020	3,697	21,515	31,387	25,810	31,515
1771	101,316	810	2,760	10,300	29,986	30,005	27,455
1772	74,320	1,301	1,075	15,585	8,840	27,215	20,304

To Ireland

Year	Total	Massachusetts	Rhode Island	New York	Pennsylvania	Maryland	Virginia
	Eg830	Eg831	Eg832	Eg833	Eg834	Eg835	Eg836
	Hundredweight	Hundredweight	Hundredweight	Hundredweight	Hundredweight	Hundredweight	Hundredweight
1768	0	0	0	0	0	0	0
1769	930	370	0	40	220	300	0
1770	5,350	0	0	1,250	560	3,540	0
1771	1,280	0	0	700	—	580	0
1772	610	0	0	0	160	150	300

Coastwise to other continental colonies

Year	Total	Massachusetts	Rhode Island	New York	Pennsylvania	Maryland	Virginia
	Eg837	Eg838	Eg839	Eg840	Eg841	Eg842	Eg843
	Hundredweight	Hundredweight	Hundredweight	Hundredweight	Hundredweight	Hundredweight	Hundredweight
1768	8,838	0	400	1,300	2,096	4,642	400
1769	17,390	635	3,670	8,795	0	4,290	0
1770	12,725	0	3,260	3,725	0	5,740	0
1771	25,680 [2]	0	5,060	4,740	900	14,660	0
1772	22,688	220	5,250	11,170	8	6,040	0

To West Indies

Year	Total	Massachusetts	Rhode Island	New York	Pennsylvania	Maryland	Virginia
	Eg844	Eg845	Eg846	Eg847	Eg848	Eg849	Eg850
	Hundredweight	Hundredweight	Hundredweight	Hundredweight	Hundredweight	Hundredweight	Hundredweight
1768	0	0	0	0	0	0	0
1769	0	0	0	0	0	0	0
1770	60	0	0	0	0	60	0
1771	30	0	0	30	0	0	0
1772	480	0	0	0	400	0	80

[1] Includes 760 hundredweight exported by New Jersey.
[2] Includes 320 hundredweight exported by Connecticut.

Source

The Ledger of Imports and Exports, British North America, 1768–1772, CUST 16/1, PRO/TNA.

Documentation

See the Appendixes to the essay in this chapter for a general discussion of the tables and the sources of the data, along with a key to abbreviations used in this chapter and general information on matters such as regional definitions, calendar differences, money, and weights and measures. Also see the text for Table Eg811–815 for a general note on the iron trade. Note especially the implications for this table of the discussion there of the coastwise trade in iron.

This table reports the quantity of pig iron in hundredweight (112 pounds) exported from the Thirteen Continental Colonies to all destinations.

TABLE Eg851–860   Pig iron imported coastwise, by importing colony: 1768–1772

Contributed by John J. McCusker

	Total	Massachusetts	Rhode Island	Connecticut	New York	Pennsylvania	Maryland	Virginia	North Carolina	South Carolina
	Eg851	Eg852	Eg853	Eg854	Eg855	Eg856	Eg857	Eg858	Eg859	Eg860
Year	Hundredweight	Hundredweight	Hundredweight	Hundredweight	Hundredweight	Hundredweight	Hundredweight	Hundredweight	Hundredweight	Hundredweight
1768	12,447	1,654	0	360	1,920	4,523	430	3,560	0	0
1769	15,535	4,555	3,020	1,340	3,280	20	0	3,320	0	0
1770	14,127	2,710	3,405	1,640	740	2,872	0	2,700	0	60
1771	27,625	3,640	3,875	1,420	1,980	5,590	1,060	10,040	20	0
1772	25,768	5,680	9,620	620	4,770	160	0	4,918	0	0

Source

The Ledger of Imports and Exports, British North America, 1768–1772, CUST 16/1, PRO/TNA.

Documentation

See the Appendixes to the essay in this chapter for a general discussion of the tables and the sources of the data, along with a key to abbreviations used in this chapter and general information on matters such as regional definitions, calendar differences, money, and weights and measures. Also see the text for Table Eg811–815 for a general note on the iron trade. Note especially the implications for this table of the discussion there of the coastwise trade in iron.

This table reports the quantity of pig iron in hundredweight (112 pounds) imported into the Thirteen Continental Colonies coastwise from the other colonies in British North America, in the instance of this table the other Continental Colonies. In 1768–1772, none of the Thirteen Continental Colonies other than the ones listed here imported pig iron coastwise.

TABLE Eg861–866   Bar iron exported from England, by importing colony: 1711–1750

Contributed by John J. McCusker

	Total	New England	New York	Pennsylvania	Virginia and Maryland	Carolina
	Eg861	Eg862	Eg863	Eg864	Eg865	Eg866
Year	Long tons	Long tons	Long tons	Long tons	Long tons	Long tons
1711	226	201	10	13	2	0
1712	326	282	32	2	5	5
1713	302	211	49	7	8	27
1714	419	279	98	25	8	9
1715	511	373	111	8	17	2
1716	539	373	147	10	9	0
1717	207	141	43	9	10	4
1718	190	154	3	4	27	2
1729	405	338	58	4	1	4
1730	250	150	92	0	2	6
1731	365	243	102	5	4	11
1732	488	413	58	3	5	9
1733	465	371	55	2	12	25
1734	363	263	90	0	2	8
1735	218	101	108	0	3	6
1750	5	1	0	0	3	1

Sources

The sources of the data are the Ledgers of Imports and Exports of England, CUST 3/14-35, CUST 3/50, PRO/TNA, and contemporary accounts extracted from them. The detailed data through 1735 were printed in J[ohn] Leander Bishop, [Edwin T. Freedley, and Edward Young], *A History of American Manufactures from 1608 to 1860: Exhibiting the Origin and Growth of the Principal Mechanic Arts and Manufactures, from the Earliest Colonial Period to the Adoption of the Constitution; and Comprising Annals of the Industry of the United States in Machinery, Manufactures and Useful Arts, with a Notice of the Important Inventions, Tariffs, and the Results of Each Decennial Census*, 3rd edition (Edward Young, 1868), volume 1, p. 629. The data for 1750 are taken directly from CUST 3/50, PRO/TNA.

Documentation

See the Appendixes to the essay in this chapter for a general discussion of the tables and the sources of the data, along with a key to abbreviations used in this chapter and general information on matters such as regional definitions, calendar differences, money, and weights and measures. Note especially the discussion of the time periods used for compiling these records. For these accounts, the year of record began on December 25 and ended on December 24. Also see the text for Table Eg811–815 for a general note on the iron trade.

This table reports the quantity of bar iron in long tons (2,240 pounds) exported from England to the Thirteen Continental Colonies It must be underscored that these data are the figures for exports from England and Wales, *not* figures for imports into the Colonies, as they have too often been described. Data for the remaining years of the period through 1790 have yet to be compiled, but English exports of bar iron to the Thirteen Continental Colonies are thought to have been inconsequential after midcentury.

TABLE Eg867–872   Bar iron imported into England from British North America, by colony: 1718–1776

Contributed by John J. McCusker

Year	Total Eg867 Long tons	New England Eg868 Long tons	New York Eg869 Long tons	Pennsylvania Eg870 Long tons	Virginia and Maryland Eg871 Long tons	Other colonies Eg872 Long tons
1718	3	0	0	0	3	0
1719	1	0	0	0	1	0
1720	4	0	0	0	4	0
1721	15	0	0	0	15	0
1724	7	0	0	0	7	0
1726	2	1	0	0	(Z)	(Z)
1727	3	0	0	0	3	0
1729	(Z)	0	0	0	0	(Z)
1730	9	0	0	0	0	9
1733	1	0	1	0	0	0
1734	(Z)	0	0	0	0	(Z)
1735	55	0	0	11	44	0
1736	5	0	0	5	0	0
1740	5	(Z)	0	0	5	0
1741	5	0	0	0	5	0
1744	57	0	0	0	57	0
1745	4	0	0	0	4	0
1746	197	0	0	3	193	0
1747	83	0	0	0	83	0
1748	4	0	0	0	4	0
1750	6	0	0	0	6	0
1751	5	0	2	0	3	0
1752	82	0	0	65	17	0
1753	248	2	0	148	98	0
1754	271	0	7	110	154	0
1755	390	0	12	79	299	0
1756	181	0	2	31	148	0
1757	73	0	19	19	35	0
1758	355	0	0	10	341	4
1759	273	0	0	199	74	0
1760	127	0	0	29	98	0
1761	39	0	0	3	36	0
1762	113	0	0	3	107	3
1763	297	0	39	21	234	3
1764	761	0	241	272	247	1
1765	1,078	0	194	85	639	160
1766	1,256	9	400	88	744	15
1767	1,325	13	401	342	569	0
1768	1,988	7	909	357	712	3
1769	1,779	46	861	208	659	5
1770	1,716	9	984	93	598	32
1771	2,221	1	1,493	18	709	0
1772	961	0	561	0	382	18
1773	929	5	498	137	289	0
1774	642	0	284	114	244	0
1775	916	5	361	88	462	0
1776	28	0	0	0	28	0

(Z) Less than 10 hundredweight (1,120 pounds).

Sources

The sources of the data are the Ledgers of Imports and Exports of England, 1718–1776, CUST 3/20-76, PRO/TNA, and contemporary accounts extracted from them. The data from 1723 through 1749 are from "An Account of the Quantity of Iron Imported [into England] from the British Colonies in America," 1711–1749, dated April 5, 1750, and signed by John Oxenford, the Inspector General of Imports and Exports. It is House of Lords, Main Papers, April 5, 1750, HLRO. For this account, see Great Britain, Parliament, House of Lords, *Journals of the House of Lords* (House of Lords, 1767 to date), volume 27, pp. 445, 451. The data for 1750–1755 are from a similar account printed in Harry Scrivenor, *A Comprehensive History of the Iron Trade, throughout the World, from the Earliest Records to the Present Period,*

With an Appendix, Containing Official Tables, and Other Public Documents (Smith, Elder, 1841), p. 340. The data for 1756–1776 are taken directly from CUST 3/56-76, PRO/TNA.

Documentation

See the Appendixes to the essay in this chapter for a general discussion of the tables and the sources of the data, along with a key to abbreviations used in this chapter and general information on matters such as regional definitions, calendar differences, money, and weights and measures. Iron and iron goods were bought, sold, and shipped in terms of the long ton (2,240 pounds) and its subunits: the hundredweight, the quarter, and the pound. Note especially the discussion of the time periods used for compiling these records. For these accounts, the year of record ended on December 24 for 1699–1751; and on

(continued)

TABLE Eg867–872   Bar iron imported into England from British North America, by colony: 1718–1776   *Continued*

January 4 thereafter. See also the text for Table Eg811–815 for a general note on the iron trade.

Reported in this table are the quantities in long tons (2,240 pounds) of pig iron imported annually into England and Wales from British North America. It must be underscored that these data are the figures for imports into England and Wales, *not* figures for exports from the colonies as they have too often been described. For some years during that latter period, the totals in series Eg811 are different from the data given in Scrivenor (1841), pp. 343–4. Compare [Romaine] Elizabeth Boody Schumpeter, *English Overseas Trade Statistics, 1697–1808* (Clarendon Press, 1960), pp. 52–5, 56.

As Oxenford's account makes explicit, England imported no bar iron from British North America in the years 1711–1717, 1722–1723, 1725, 1728, 1731–1732, 1736–1737, 1738–1739, 1742–1743, and 1749. Of the 513 tons of bar iron imported into England and Wales from all of British America between 1711 and 1749, 84 percent of it came from Virginia and Maryland.

Series Eg872. These figures state the totals for bar iron imported from Newfoundland, Canada, and the Carolinas. (The original source also recorded iron imports from various parts of the British West Indies.) It is probable that some of the iron imported into England and Wales from such places as Newfoundland and the British West Indies had actually been produced in, say, New Jersey or Virginia and subsequently shipped from there as ballast. No longer needed for the next leg of a voyage, the ballast was off-loaded, sold, and afterward reexported as freight (or ballast). In a similar way, some of the iron exported from Virginia and Maryland may have been imported into those colonies from elsewhere to be used as ballast onboard tobacco ships. See John J. McCusker, "The Tonnage of Ships Engaged in British Colonial Trade during the Eighteenth Century," *Research in Economic History* 6 (1981): 73–105, as revised and updated in McCusker, *Essays in the Economic History of the Atlantic World* (Routledge, 1997), p. 63.

TABLE Eg873–886   Bar iron imported coastwise, by importing colony: 1768–1772

Contributed by John J. McCusker

Year	Total Eg873 Hundredweight	New Hampshire Eg874 Hundredweight	Massachusetts Eg875 Hundredweight	Rhode Island Eg876 Hundredweight	Connecticut Eg877 Hundredweight	New York Eg878 Hundredweight	New Jersey Eg879 Hundredweight
1768	16,905	1,500	7,977	2,322	271	236	145
1769	21,860	2,390	8,648	1,175	1,734	710	0
1770	28,338	3,717	13,052	1,240	2,295	120	0
1771	28,084	3,079	10,869	2,240	2,351	880	0
1772	33,156	4,169	14,367	2,304	1,588	220	6

Year	Pennsylvania Eg880 Hundredweight	Maryland Eg881 Hundredweight	Virginia Eg882 Hundredweight	North Carolina Eg883 Hundredweight	South Carolina Eg884 Hundredweight	Georgia Eg885 Hundredweight	Florida Eg886 Hundredweight
1768	684	45	71	1,401	1,775	317	161
1769	530	97	1,546	1,352	3,127	525	28
1770	166	0	2,105	1,186	3,961	324	172
1771	494	47	2,420	2,604	2,590	419	91
1772	940	16	4,540	1,749	2,778	352	127

Source

The Ledger of Imports and Exports, British North America, 1768–1772, CUST 16/1, PRO/TNA.

Documentation

See the Appendixes to the essay in this chapter for a general discussion of the tables and the sources of the data, along with a key to abbreviations used in this chapter and general information on matters such as regional definitions, calendar differences, money, and weights and measures. Also see the text for Table Eg811–815 for a general note on the iron trade. Especially important are the implications for this table of the discussion there of the coastwise trade in iron. Note that Florida is included here as part of British North America, but it was not one of the Thirteen Continental Colonies.

This table reports the quantity of bar iron in hundredweight (112 pounds) imported into the Thirteen Continental Colonies coastwise from the other colonies in British North America, in the instance of this table the other Continental Colonies.

The recorded importation into Massachusetts in 1770 included 154 bars. They were reduced to 1.75 tons and added to the total. "Eighty-six to ninety bars usually weighed a ton," according to Arthur C. Bining, *British Regulation of the Colonial Iron Industry* (University of Pennsylvania Press, 1933), p. 94 n. 75.

TABLE Eg887–936 Bar iron exported, by colony and destination: 1768–1772

Contributed by John J. McCusker

Total

Year	Total	Massachusetts	Rhode Island	Connecticut	New York	New Jersey	Pennsylvania	Maryland	Virginia	Other colonies
	Eg887	Eg888	Eg889	Eg890	Eg891	Eg892	Eg893	Eg894	Eg895	Eg896
	Hundredweight	Hundredweight	Hundredweight	Hundredweight	Hundredweight	Hundredweight	Hundredweight	Hundredweight	Hundredweight	Hundredweight
1768	83,787	1,137	3,199	223	4,422	140	24,034	35,280	14,958	356
1769	75,869	1,009	641	556	24,358	230	21,805	17,965	9,184	121
1770	78,262	1,029	720	180	33,629	108	22,967	14,823	4,453	353
1771	76,513	985	500	85	28,892	94	21,942	20,080	3,713	222
1772	60,916	1,110	354	538	17,245	140	22,008	17,272	2,091	158

To Great Britain

Year	Total	Massachusetts	Rhode Island	Connecticut	New York	New Jersey	Pennsylvania	Maryland	Virginia	Other colonies
	Eg897	Eg898	Eg899	Eg900	Eg901	Eg902	Eg903	Eg904	Eg905	Eg906
	Hundredweight	Hundredweight	Hundredweight	Hundredweight	Hundredweight	Hundredweight	Hundredweight	Hundredweight	Hundredweight	Hundredweight
1768	55,513	10	739	38	0	0	8,604 [2]	31,431	14,355	336
1769	43,105	124	98	0	17,090	0	4,415	12,925	8,453	0
1770	42,047	100	40	0	25,985	0	1,577	10,530	3,815	0
1771	42,300	2	20	0	23,650	0	200	15,531	2,897	0
1772	19,708	0	0	0	9,930	0	900	7,797	1,081	0

To the Thirteen Continental Colonies

Year	Total	Massachusetts	Rhode Island	Connecticut	New York	New Jersey	Pennsylvania	Maryland	Virginia	Other colonies
	Eg907	Eg908	Eg909	Eg910	Eg911	Eg912	Eg913	Eg914	Eg915	Eg916
	Hundredweight	Hundredweight	Hundredweight	Hundredweight	Hundredweight	Hundredweight	Hundredweight	Hundredweight	Hundredweight	Hundredweight
1768	24,403	1,107	2,400	171	3,874	140	12,621	3,714	356	20
1769	26,378	885	543	446	5,223	230	14,628	3,789	514	120
1770	28,983	929	640	0	4,674	108	18,776	3,200	484	172
1771	29,310	983	320	65	3,607	14	19,413	4,207	489	212
1772	35,848	1,110	314	504	4,805	100	19,253	8,875	729	158

To the West Indies

Year	Total	Massachusetts	Rhode Island	Connecticut	New York	New Jersey	Pennsylvania	Maryland	Virginia	Other colonies
	Eg917	Eg918	Eg919	Eg920	Eg921	Eg922	Eg923 [1]	Eg924	Eg925	Eg926
	Hundredweight	Hundredweight	Hundredweight	Hundredweight	Hundredweight	Hundredweight	Hundredweight	Hundredweight	Hundredweight	Hundredweight
1768	3,606	20	0	14	548	0	2,642	135	247	0
1769	4,826	0	0	110	1,385	0	2,652	461	217	1
1770	5,457	0	40	180	1,635	0	2,594	673	154	181
1771	3,980	0	120	20	935	80	2,196	302	327	0
1772	4,620	0	40	34	2,370	40	1,595	260	281	0

To other destinations

Year	Total	Massachusetts	Rhode Island	Connecticut	New York	New Jersey	Pennsylvania	Maryland	Virginia	Other colonies
	Eg927	Eg928	Eg929	Eg930	Eg931	Eg932	Eg933	Eg934	Eg935	Eg936
	Hundredweight	Hundredweight	Hundredweight	Hundredweight	Hundredweight	Hundredweight	Hundredweight	Hundredweight	Hundredweight	Hundredweight
1768	227	0	60	0	0	0	167	0	0	0
1769	1,560	0	0	0	660	0	110	790	0	0
1770	1,775	0	0	0	1,335	0	20	420	0	0
1771	923	0	40	0	700	0	133	40	0	10
1772	740	0	0	0	140	0	260	340	0	0

Notes appear on next page

(continued)

TABLE Eg887–936   Bar iron exported, by colony and destination: 1768–1772   *Continued*

[1] Includes exports through port of entry (POE) New Castle, Delaware: 45 hundredweight in 1768, 134 in 1770, and 40 in 1772.

[2] An additional 166 bars (38 hundredweight) were exported to Ireland. That sum is added to the total for the year.

Source

The Ledger of Imports and Exports, British North America, 1768–1772, CUST 16/1, PRO/TNA.

Documentation

See the Appendixes to the essay in this chapter for a general discussion of the tables and the sources of the data, along with a key to abbreviations used in this chapter and general information on matters such as regional definitions, calendar differences, money, and weights and measures. Also see the text for Table Eg811–815 for a general note on the iron trade. Note especially the implications for this table of the discussion there of the coastwise trade in iron.

This table reports the quantity of bar iron in hundredweight (112 pounds) exported from the Thirteen Continental Colonies to all destinations.

In several instances, exports were recorded in bars. They were reduced to hundredweight at a rate of 4.4 bars per hundredweight and included in the totals. "Eighty-six to ninety bars usually weighed a ton." Arthur C. Bining, *British Regulation of the Colonial Iron Industry* (University of Pennsylvania Press, 1933), p. 94 n. 75.

Series Eg896, Eg905, Eg915, Eg925, and Eg931. These series include exports from New Hampshire, North Carolina, South Carolina, Georgia, and Florida.

TABLE Eg937–992   Cast iron ware imported and exported, by colony and by origin or destination: 1768–1772

Contributed by John J. McCusker

				Imports				
				From other Continental Colonies				
	Total	New Hampshire	Massachusetts	Rhode Island	Connecticut	New York	New Jersey	Pennsylvania
	Eg937	Eg938	Eg939	Eg940	Eg941	Eg942	Eg943	Eg944
Year	Hundredweight	Hundredweight	Hundredweight	Hundredweight	Hundredweight	Hundredweight	Hundredweight	Hundredweight
1768	4,733	0	43	7	256	785	0	359
1769	3,824	40	44	194	1,581	318	116	155
1770	4,039	72	121	0	1,150	150	24	1,357 [1]
1771	4,884	402	138	97	2,364	422	10	45 [1]
1772	4,936	217	128	72	964	1,773	0	58

			Imports					
			From other Continental Colonies				**From Great Britain**	
	Maryland	Virginia	North Carolina	South Carolina	Georgia	Florida	Total	New Hampshire
	Eg945	Eg946	Eg947	Eg948	Eg949	Eg950	Eg951	Eg952
Year	Hundredweight	Hundredweight	Hundredweight	Hundredweight	Hundredweight	Hundredweight	Hundredweight	Hundredweight
1768	1,496	65	1,066	363	270	23	—	—
1769	285	391	633	67	0	0	2,621	0
1770	236	347	297	192	3	90	969	0
1771	266	290	532	313	5	0	968	0
1772	280	138	1,131	142	3	30	—	—

				Imports				
				From Great Britain				
	Massachusetts	Rhode Island	Connecticut	New York	New Jersey	Pennsylvania	Maryland	Virginia
	Eg953	Eg954	Eg955	Eg956	Eg957	Eg958	Eg959	Eg960
Year	Hundredweight	Hundredweight	Hundredweight	Hundredweight	Hundredweight	Hundredweight	Hundredweight	Hundredweight
1768	—	—	—	—	—	—	—	—
1769	0	0	0	0	0	231	1,426	528
1770	0	0	0	0	0	106	30	626
1771	8	0	0	0	0	0	0	733
1772	—	—	—	—	—	—	—	—

Notes appear at end of table

TABLE Eg937–992   Cast iron ware imported and exported, by colony and by origin or destination: 1768–1772
Continued

	Imports				Exports			
	From Great Britain				To other Continental Colonies			
	North Carolina	South Carolina	Georgia	Florida	Total	New Hampshire	Massachusetts	Rhode Island
	Eg961	Eg962	Eg963	Eg964	Eg965	Eg966	Eg967	Eg968
Year	Hundredweight	Hundredweight	Hundredweight	Hundredweight	Hundredweight	Hundredweight	Hundredweight	Hundredweight
1768	—	—	.	—	2,025	18	860	711
1769	6	359	71	0	3,926	29	1,972	1,422
1770	78	60	69	0	6,309	18	2,029	1,206
1771	178	0	49	0	5,503	11	1,714	2,795
1772	—	—	—	—	5,231	5	2,070	2,538

	Exports							
	To other Continental Colonies							
	Connecticut	New York	New Jersey	Pennsylvania	Maryland	Virginia	North Carolina	South Carolina
	Eg969	Eg970	Eg971	Eg972	Eg973	Eg974	Eg975	Eg976
Year	Hundredweight	Hundredweight	Hundredweight	Hundredweight	Hundredweight	Hundredweight	Hundredweight	Hundredweight
1768	41	20	0	188	51	99	2	35
1769	129	142	0	137	95	0	0	0
1770	37	61	0	356	2,513	0	0	89
1771	315	206	2	290 [2]	39	82	12	37
1772	77	180	0	311	4	8	8	30

	Exports							
	To other Continental Colonies		To the West Indies					
	Georgia	Florida	Total	New Hampshire	Massachusetts	Rhode Island	Connecticut	New York
	Eg977	Eg978	Eg979	Eg980	Eg981	Eg982	Eg983	Eg984
Year	Hundredweight	Hundredweight	Hundredweight	Hundredweight	Hundredweight	Hundredweight	Hundredweight	Hundredweight
1768	0	0	0	0	0	0	0	0
1769	0	0	165	0	10	65	0	0
1770	0	0	42	0	25	0	7	6
1771	0	0	97	0	0	21	0	20
1772	0	0	0	0	0	0	0	0

	Exports							
	To the West Indies							
	New Jersey	Pennsylvania	Maryland	Virginia	North Carolina	South Carolina	Georgia	Florida
	Eg985	Eg986	Eg987	Eg988	Eg989	Eg990	Eg991	Eg992
Year	Hundredweight	Hundredweight	Hundredweight	Hundredweight	Hundredweight	Hundredweight	Hundredweight	Hundredweight
1768	0	0	0	0	0	0	0	0
1769	0	70	0	0	20	0	0	0
1770	0	0	0	0	0	0	4	0
1771	0	3	53	0	0	0	0	0
1772	0	0	0	0	0	0	0	0

[1] Includes exports through port of entry (POE) New Castle, Delaware: 1 hundredweight in 1770, and 40 in 1771.

[2] Includes 3 hundredweight imported through POE New Castle, Delaware.

Source

The Ledger of Imports and Exports, British North America, 1768–1772, CUST 16/1, PRO/TNA.

Documentation

See the Appendixes to the essay in this chapter for a general discussion of the tables and the sources of the data, along with a key to abbreviations used in this chapter and general information on matters such as regional definitions, calendar differences, money, and weights and measures. Note that Florida is included here as part of British North America, but it was not one of the Thirteen Continental Colonies. Also see the text for Table Eg811–815 for a general note on the iron trade.

These data record in long hundredweight of 112 pounds the import and export of all sorts of cast iron ware measured not by type of commodity but by gross weight of all such commodities. The usual cast iron goods were "hollow ware such as pots, pans, skillets, sugar kettles, Dutch ovens, stoves, and firebacks," according to Arthur C. Bining, *British Regulation of the Colonial Iron Industry* (University of Pennsylvania Press, 1933), p. 80. The source is defective in that it lacks any record of imports into the colonies from Great Britain and Ireland for 1768 or 1772.

(continued)

TABLE Eg937–992   Cast iron ware imported and exported, by colony and by origin or destination: 1768–1772
Continued

The source also indicates additional minor quantities of cast iron ware exported to Southern Europe, Wine Islands, and West Indies. The source shows that the following items were imported and exported by count. In 1770, New Hampshire imported 4 pots from the other Continental Colonies; Massachusetts, 20; Connecticut, 103; New York, 52; and Pennsylvania, 130. In 1769, New York imported 100 pots from Great Britain; Pennsylvania, 231; Maryland, 34; Georgia, 71; and Florida, 2. In 1769, New Hampshire imported 187 pots from Great Britain; Massachusetts, 12 pots by count and another 250 in pound weight; and Maryland 107 pots by count. In 1771, Maryland imported from Great Britain 2,432 pots; North Carolina, 169; Georgia, 150; and Florida, 4. In 1770, Massachusetts exported 510 pots and 35 potash kettles; Rhode Island, 166 pots; Connecticut, 20 pots; and New York, 104 pots.

TABLE Eg993–1000   Wrought iron ware exported from England, by importing colony: 1711–1773
Contributed by John J. McCusker

Year	Total	New England	New York	Pennsylvania	Virginia and Maryland	Carolina	Georgia	Florida
	Eg993	Eg994	Eg995	Eg996	Eg997	Eg998	Eg999	Eg1000
	Hundredweight	Hundredweight	Hundredweight	Hundredweight	Hundredweight	Hundredweight	Hundredweight	Hundredweight
1711	10,309	4,597	567	988	3,014	1,143	—	—
1712	13,729	5,345	639	540	5,654	1,551	—	—
1713	11,176	4,883	986	1,040	2,860	1,407	—	—
1714	14,343	4,633	1,137	924	6,598	1,051	—	—
1715	17,802	5,796	1,380	988	8,947	691	—	—
1716	15,571	5,398	1,094	963	7,446	670	—	—
1717	15,705	3,819	1,145	1,147	8,728	866	—	—
1718	13,097	3,110	1,396	887	6,735	969	—	—
1729	16,357	7,394	1,904	851	4,866	1,342	—	—
1730	20,604	7,330	2,775	2,629	6,390	1,480	—	—
1731	26,753	9,727	2,628	2,946	9,682	1,770	—	—
1732	22,800	8,598	2,380	2,208	7,446	2,168	0	—
1733	22,643	7,105	1,610	2,420	8,815	2,693	0	—
1734	23,155	6,192	2,291	3,150	8,641	2,881	0	—
1735	23,845	6,544	2,137	2,102	9,709	3,353	0	—
1750	29,508	7,884	4,384	4,765	8,684	3,733	58	—
1758	35,549	3,455	6,280	8,687	10,128	6,849	150	—
1764	29,720	6,290	4,883	5,303	4,866	7,993	385	0
1769	33,685	2,907 [1]	620	1,565 [2]	21,734	5,773 [4]	878 [6]	208 [7]
1770	19,756	2,250	3,860	176	7,664	4,393	1,402	11
1771	59,186	4,209	11,497	— [3]	38,546	3,212 [5]	1,068	654 [8]
1773	56,988	2,634	5,972	19,652	12,554	12,155	1,855	2,166

[1] Plus 41 casks and 13 packs.

[2] Plus 1 cask.

[3] The import data for 1771 for port of entry (POE) Philadelphia are defective in the source.

[4] Plus 49 packs.

[5] Plus 5 casks and 4 cases.

[6] Plus 11 packs.

[7] Plus 7 packs.

[8] Plus 15 casks and 1 case.

Sources
1711–1764 and 1773. The source of the data is the Ledgers of Imports and Exports of England, 1711–1735, CUST 3/14-35, PRO/TNA, and contemporary accounts extracted from them. The detailed data through 1735 were printed in J[ohn] Leander Bishop, [Edwin T. Freedley, and Edward Young], *A History of American Manufactures from 1608 to 1860: Exhibiting the Origin and Growth of the Principal Mechanic Arts and Manufactures, from the Earliest Colonial Period to the Adoption of the Constitution; and Comprising Annals of the Industry of the United States in Machinery, Manufactures and Useful Arts, with a Notice of the Important Inventions, Tariffs, and the Results of Each Decennial Census*, 3rd edition (Edward Young, 1868), volume 1, p. 629. The data for 1750–1764 and 1773 are taken directly from CUST 3/50-64 and CUST 3/73, PRO/TNA.

1769–1771. The Ledger of Imports and Exports, British North America, 1768–1772, CUST 16/1, PRO/TNA.

Documentation
See the Appendixes to the essay in this chapter for a general discussion of the tables and the sources of the data, along with a key to abbreviations used in this chapter and general information on matters such as regional definitions, calendar differences, money, and weights and measures. For these accounts, the year of record ended on December 24 for 1711–1751; and on January 4 thereafter. Note that Florida is included here as part of British North America, but it was not one of the Thirteen Continental Colonies. Also see the text for Table Eg811–815 for a general note on the iron trade.

These data record the import and export of all sorts of wrought iron ware measured not by type of commodity but by the gross weight of such commodities (in long hundredweight of 112 pounds). The usual wrought iron goods, the product of skilled blacksmiths, were tools such as hoes, axes, shovels, sickles, and scythes. Of major importance were anchors and chain and other wares associated with the shipping industry. Then there were the myriad of smaller wrought iron goods used in the building of houses and the making of furniture. See Arthur C. Bining, *British Regulation of the Colonial Iron Industry* (University of Pennsylvania Press, 1933), p. 85 and elsewhere.

The data for 1769–1771 are from a different source and are of a different character from the data for the other years. They record imports into the Colonies, whereas the other data are the figures for exports from England and Wales. The latter are not figures for imports into the Colonies, as they have too often been described.

The footnotes to the table for the years 1769–1771 illustrate the all-too-common practice of entering manufactured goods in the Customs records by packaging rather than by weight or measure.

TABLE Eg1001–1012   Imports and exports of selected iron and steel products, by origin or destination: 1768–1772

Contributed by John J. McCusker

	Imports						Exports, coastwise					
	Coastwise				From Great Britain		Wrought iron				Axes	
Year	Wrought iron	Anchors	Scythes	Axes	Nails	Steel	To the Thirteen Continental Colonies	To the West Indies	Anchors	Scythes	To the Thirteen Continental Colonies	To the West Indies
	Eg1001	Eg1002	Eg1003	Eg1004	Eg1005	Eg1006	Eg1007	Eg1008	Eg1009	Eg1010	Eg1011	Eg1012
	Hundredweight	Number	Dozen	Number	Hundredweight	Hundredweight	Hundredweight	Hundredweight	Number	Dozen	Number	Number
1768	0	0	0	5,568	—	—	162 [6]	279	0 [8]	0	2,688	0
1769	1,289 [1]	12 [1]	102 [3]	6,665	3,161 [4]	2,126 [5]	1,101 [6]	0	0 [9]	400	5,606	4,059
1770	256 [1]	126 [1,2]	297	6,063	22,283 [4]	1,578 [5]	103 [7]	167	156	377	7,483	1,961
1771	513	109 [2]	340 [3]	7,144	5,668	1,599	391	153	70	540 [11]	7,574	2,385
1772	351	68	494	5,603	—	—	301	47	80 [10]	454	6,800	2,673

[1] Entries for wrought iron included anchors by weight that may not have been included in the number of anchors: 363 hundredweight in 1769 and 43 in 1770.

[2] Plus imports from Great Britain: 27 anchors in 1770 and 15 anchors in 1771.

[3] Plus imports from Great Britain: 46 bundles and 1 dozen scythes in 1769, and 129 bundles of scythes in 1771.

[4] Plus imports from Great Britain: 84 casks of nails in 1769 and 1,993 casks of nails in 1770. Also in 1770: 102 barrels of nails imported from other colonies.

[5] Plus 6 bundles and 41 faggots of steel in 1769 and 4,030 bars and 12.5 faggots of steel in 1770.

[6] All wrought iron exported consisted only of anchors, by weight.

[7] Entry for wrought iron included 110 hundredweight of anchors that may also have been included in the number of anchors.

[8] In addition to coastwise exports listed under wrought iron, 1 anchor was exported to the West Indies.

[9] The only anchors exported this year were 15 sent to Africa.

[10] Plus 36 anchors exported to the West Indies.

[11] Plus 30 dozen scythes exported to the West Indies.

Source

The Ledger of Imports and Exports, British North America, 1768–1772, CUST 16/1, PRO/TNA.

Documentation

See the Appendixes to the essay in this chapter for a general discussion of the tables and the sources of the data, along with a key to abbreviations used in this chapter and general information on matters such as regional definitions, calendar differences, money, and weights and measures. Also see the text for Table Eg811–815 for a general note on the iron trade.

These data record the import and export of a variety of iron and steel products into and out of the Thirteen Continental Colonies. The source is defective in that it lacks any record of imports into the Colonies from Great Britain and Ireland for 1768 or 1772. With a few exceptions, the table mostly reports the trade coastwise of the Thirteen Continental Colonies in the items specified. The two major exceptions are imported nails and imported steel, both of which came almost exclusively from Great Britain.

Because colonial imports of axes and scythes, to the extent that they were imported, came so predominantly from the other Colonies, and because almost all imported steel and nails came from Great Britain, no note has been taken of the negligible importation of these items from other places.

The footnotes illustrate the problems caused by the all-too-common practice of entering manufactured goods in the Customs records by nonstandard units of measure (for example, "bundles" rather than hundred-weight).

TABLE Eg1013–1026　Furs imported into England, by origin: 1700–1775　[Official values]

Contributed by John J. McCusker

		Atlantic Canada and Hudson's Bay					Thirteen Continental Colonies							
	Total	Total	Hudson's Bay	Canada	Newfoundland	Nova Scotia	Total	New England	New York	Pennsylvania	Virginia and Maryland	North and South Carolina	Georgia	Everywhere else
	Eg1013	Eg1014	Eg1015	Eg1016	Eg1017	Eg1018	Eg1019	Eg1020	Eg1021	Eg1022	Eg1023	Eg1024	Eg1025	Eg1026
Year	Pounds (£) sterling	Pounds (£) sterling	Pounds (£) sterling	Pounds (£) sterling	Pounds (£) sterling	Pounds (£) sterling	Pounds (£) sterling	Pounds (£) sterling	Pounds (£) sterling	Pounds (£) sterling	Pounds (£) sterling	Pounds (£) sterling	Pounds (£) sterling	Pounds (£) sterling
1700	16,284	2,583	2,360	—	223	—	11,129	2,435	4,962	723	2,433	576	—	2,572
1710	7,840	553	0	—	553	—	4,612	1,595	2,148	88	754	27	—	2,675
1720	19,377	10,296	9,839	—	457	—	8,832	2,119	5,393	849	467	4	—	249
1725	23,541	11,632	11,180	—	452	—	10,271	1,862	6,952	923	488	46	—	1,638
1730	22,348	12,991	12,335	—	500	156	6,813	2,010	2,611	1,642	493	57	—	2,544
1739	25,196	14,003	13,452	—	551	—	8,533	2,481	5,073	329	641	9	0	2,660
1750	22,817	8,563	8,143	—	420	0	8,928	1,015	5,710	1,909	282	12	0	5,326
1760	19,985	10,745	8,321	1,930	470	24	3,892	946	1,023	1,879	21	20	3	5,348
1765	49,293	35,008	9,770	24,512	648	78	10,917	2,811	5,565	1,927	70	491	53	3,368
1770	47,758	38,181	9,213	28,433	403	132	6,145	2,453	2,340	1,148	169	26	9	3,432
1775	53,709	42,249	5,640	34,486	1,913	210	8,701	1,642	3,939	2,866	63	128	63	2,759

Source

The source of the data is the Ledgers of Imports and Exports of England, CUST 3, PRO/TNA. The data were analyzed and compiled by Murray G. Lawson, *Fur: A Study in English Mercantilism, 1700–1775*, University of Toronto Studies, History and Economics Series, volume 9 (University of Toronto Press, 1943), pp. 108–9.

Documentation

See the Appendixes to the essay in this chapter for a general discussion of the tables and the sources of the data, along with a key to abbreviations used in this chapter and general information on matters such as regional definitions, calendar differences, money, and weights and measures. Note especially the discussion of the time periods used for compiling these records.

This table reports the official values in constant pounds sterling of all furs imported into England and Wales specifying the place from which they were exported. Two cautions need to be registered. It must be underscored that these data are the figures for imports into England and Wales, *not* figures for exports from the Colonies as they have too often been described. The valuations for each type of fur were fixed at the beginning of the eighteenth century and used uniformly across the century (see

Appendix A to the chapter essay). Whereas the market price for each type of fur changed over time, the values used in compiling these data did not change. Thus, the series presented here becomes in effect a measure of the changing volume of the trade. For a discussion of the source and these issues, see John J. McCusker, "The Current Value of English Exports, 1697 to 1800," *William and Mary Quarterly*, 3rd series, 28 (October 1971): 607–28, as revised and updated in McCusker, *Essays in the Economic History of the Atlantic World* (Routledge, 1997), pp. 222–44. See also Lawson (1943), pp. 76–9.

Note that Lawson worked from copies of the Customs ledgers obtained in the 1930s as part of a project organized by Lawrence A. Harper. Lawson stated that he deposited his original work sheets with that project. "The year 1739 was chosen instead of 1740 as our copy of the English Customs records for the latter year is not complete" (Lawson 1943, p. 108 n.).

Through 1751, the year of record ended December 24; thereafter, it ended January 4 of the following year.

Series Eg1026. This series includes trivial quantities of furs from other British colonies in the Western Hemisphere, some of which may have originated in the Colonies listed here, been exported from them, and then reexported to England and Wales.

TABLE Eg1027–1032 Indigo and silk exported from South Carolina and Georgia: 1747–1788[1]

Contributed by John J. McCusker

	Indigo			Silk		
	Total	South Carolina	Georgia	Total	South Carolina	Georgia
	Eg1027	Eg1028	Eg1029	Eg1030	Eg1031	Eg1032
Year	Thousand pounds	Thousand pounds	Thousand pounds	Pounds	Pounds	Pounds
1747 [2]	—	138.3	—	—	86	—
1748 [2]	—	62.2	—	—	60	—
1749 [2]	—	138.3	—	—	11	—
1750 [2]	—	63.1	—	—	72	—
1751 [2]	—	19.9	—	—	—	—
1752 [3]	—	3.8	—	—	5	—
1753	—	28.5	—	—	11	—
1754	—	129.6	—	—	—	—
1755	308.0	303.5	4.5	598	160	438
1756	232.1	222.8	9.3	368	100	268
1757	894.6	876.4	18.2	358	—	358
1758	572.6	563.0	9.6	358	—	358
1759	696.3	695.7	0.6	856	122	734
1760	519.3	507.6	11.7	558	—	558
1761	385.7	384.1	1.6	332	—	332
1762	264.4	255.3	9.1	380	—	380
1763	447.6	438.9	8.7	953	—	953
1764	543.3	529.1	14.2	898	—	898
1765	351.8	335.8	16.0	1,061	350	711
1766	506.2	491.8	14.4	—	—	1,084
1767	—	—	12.9	—	—	671
1768	586.3	566.6	19.7	—	—	541
1769	416.6	402.7	13.9	—	—	333
1770	573.1	550.8	22.3	—	—	291
1771	454.1	434.2	19.9	—	—	438
1772	865.6	853.7	11.9	—	—	485
1773 [4]	—	720.6	—	—	—	—
1774 [5]	—	815.1	—	—	—	—
1775 [6]	—	1,122.2	—	—	—	—
1783	—	299.8	—	—	—	—
1784	—	731.7	—	—	—	—
1785	—	654.8	—	—	—	—
1786	—	840.6	—	—	—	—
1787	—	974.1 [7]	—	—	—	—
1788	—	833.6 [7]	—	—	—	—

[1] Through 1751, the year of record ended December 24; thereafter, it ended January 4 of the following year, except as noted.

[2] For year ending March 24 of following year.

[3] For the period March 25, 1752, to January 4, 1753, a little more than nine months. See text.

[4] For year ending November 11. See text.

[5] For year ending November 7. See text.

[6] For 6½ months ending February 24. See text.

[7] For Charleston only.

Sources

The sources of these data are the records kept in each of the Colonial ports of entry (POE) by the administrative clerk of the port, the colonial naval officer. The original quarterly reports of the naval officers – the naval officer shipping lists (NOSL) – and various accounts based on them survive in many places, in many forms. The most important contemporary compilation of these reports was made under the direction of Thomas Irving, the Boston-based Inspector General of Imports and Exports of North America, and is known as the Ledger of Imports and Exports, British North America, 1768–1772, CUST 16/1, PRO/TNA. Two twentieth-century efforts attempted to assemble and compile the extant NOSL, the one organized in the 1930s by Lawrence A. Harper and his associates, the other in the 1970s, the work of Converse D. Clowse. See Clowse, *Measuring Charleston's Overseas Commerce, 1717–1767: Statistics from the Port's Naval Lists* (University Press of America, 1981). Data in this table not otherwise accounted for here are drawn from these two sources.

For POE Charleston, 1747–1765, the data from the NOSL are as compiled in the account enclosed in a letter from Governor Charles Montagu, at Charleston, to the Secretary of State, December 8, 1766, CO 5/390, folio 166r, PRO/TNA. There is a copy of the account in King's MS 206, folios 28r–29v, BL. (See also Lewis Cecil Gray, *History of Agriculture in the Southern United States to 1860*, Carnegie Institution of Washington, Publication number 430 (Carnegie Institution of Washington, 1933), volume 2, p. 1024.) For South Carolina, 1766–1775, the NOSL reports were compiled by Harper and his colleagues using, among other sources, CUST 16/1, PRO/TNA. For the years 1758–1760 and 1762–1763, see also the results of the same exercise performed independently by Clowse (1981, p. 70). For the year 1768, see also the account in *The South Carolina and American General Gazette*, September 2, 1768, as enclosed with and commented upon in the letter from Lieutenant Governor William Bull, at Charleston, to Secretary of State, September 6, 1768, CO 5/379, folios 56r, 60r–60v, PRO/TNA. For the year November 12, 1773, to November 7, 1774, see *The South-Carolina Gazette*, November 25, 1774.

(continued)

TABLE Eg1027-1032   Indigo and silk exported from South Carolina and Georgia: 1747-1788   *Continued*

For South Carolina, 1783-1788, see the account in the letter from George Miller, at Charleston, to the Secretary of State for Foreign Affairs, January 28, 1790, BT 6/21, folios 311r-312r, PRO/TNA. Miller was the British consul at Charleston. What appears to have been the source of Miller's data is the "statistical accounts of exports [prepared for and sent] to the general assembly" of South Carolina by port officials, copies of which can be found among the papers of the state legislature. See R[obert] Nicholas Olsberg and Helen Craig Carson, *Duties on Trade at Charleston, 1784-1789*, Pamphlet Accompanying South Carolina Archives Microcopy, number 6 (South Carolina Department of Archives and History, 1970), p. 11. Olsberg and Carson (pp. 18-21) presented the data for POE Charleston and POE Winyah (Georgetown) for 1783-1787 – though the numbers for the latter appear to have been only for part of the last year – and scattered returns for POE Port Royal for 1784-1786. The numbers from Olsberg and Carson agree precisely with Miller's numbers. Compare the data in Charles Gregg Singer, *South Carolina in the Confederation* (University of Pennsylvania, 1941), pp. 23-4.

The Georgia export figures for indigo and silk were compiled and certified by William Brown, Comptroller of POE Savannah, March 1, 1773: "An Aggregate and Valuation of Exports of Produce from the Province of Georgia . . . 1754 to 1773." The table was printed in Bernard Romans, *A Concise Natural History of East and West Florida* . . . (Published by the author, 1775), opposite p. 104; and in [George Walton, William Few, and Richard Howly], *Observations upon the Effects of Certain Late Political Suggestions* (Robert Aitken, 1781), p. 11. CUST 16/1, pp. 17, 46, 134, 192, 236, PRO/TNA, shows that, for the years 1768-1772, Brown recorded the export of raw silk to Great Britain, the only destination for such exported silk. In making his table, Brown incorrectly rounded down two of the numbers that he sent in a fuller form to Irving in Boston and that are recorded in detail in the Ledger of Imports and Exports, British North America, 1768-1772, CUST 16/1, PRO/TNA. The correctly rounded numbers appear here from that source.

Documentation

See the Appendixes to the essay in this chapter for a general discussion of the tables and the sources of the data, along with a key to abbreviations used in this chapter and general information on matters such as regional definitions, calendar differences, money, and weights and measures.

These data record the quantity in pounds weight (pounds avoirdupois) of indigo and silk exported from South Carolina and Georgia. The year of record is, usually, the year used by the Customs. The "year" 1752 began with March 25, 1752 and ended with January 4, 1753. For the remaining period, unless otherwise noted, the year of record ended January 4. For South Carolina, this regularly, and sometimes explicitly, reflected the exportation of the previous year's crop. The "crop year" was rarely coterminous with the Customs year. For the South Carolina account dated 1747-1765, the year of record ran from March 25 through March 24, through 1751. See George Miller's account of exports for the years 1783-1788 and, as he noted, for crop years 1782-1787 (BT 6/21, folios 311r-312r, PRO/TNA). Thus, even though the dating in the sources for the three years 1773-1774 suggests something less than a full year's accounting, it is highly likely that the export data represent a full year's export of indigo. See also, for the years running from June 24, 1748, through June 21, 1773, the annual exports of indigo from POE Charleston published in *The South-Carolina Gazette*, June 21, 1773. Note that these data are from midsummer to midsummer.

For indigo, the account in *The South Carolina and American General Gazette*, September 2, 1768, indicated that 522,840 pounds had been exported to Great Britain and 7,252 pounds to "N. America" for a total of 530,092 pounds exported since October 31, 1767, "when the first Vessel, with Rice of said Year's Crop, was cleared out." Governor William Bull commented that this was "a faithful list of our Exports for almost one whole year" (CO 5/379, folios 56r, PRO/TNA). See also CO 5/379, folios 28r-29r, PRO/TNA. Similarly, the account for the year November 12, 1773, to November 7, 1774, in *The South-Carolina Gazette*, November 25, 1774, indicated that 804,383 pounds were shipped to Great Britain and 10,692 pounds were shipped to North America.

These data demonstrate that, for 1768-1772, the only period when we are sure that we have figures for the entirety of both colonies, South

Carolina accounted for 97 percent of the indigo exported by them. The data for Georgia's export of indigo for the other years are stated explicitly to be for the entire colony. For South Carolina – with the exception of the period 1768-1772 – the data are for POE Charleston only. Over the years 1768-1772, POE Charleston dominated South Carolina's export trade in indigo. In that period, Charleston exported 92.2 percent of the colony's indigo. *The South-Carolina Gazette*, December 12, 1774, put the total amount of indigo exported from Charleston for the year at 599,115 pounds. If both this figure and the one for 1774 in the table are correct, Charleston accounted for 92.6 percent of the indigo exports that year.

The data as reported also seem to account for all of the destinations. The great bulk of indigo exported from South Carolina and Georgia went to Great Britain, but some minor quantities went to other Continental Colonies, only 1.6 percent of the total in 1768-1772. Thus, the apparent omission of coastwise shipments from the data presented here for South Carolina, 1747-1765, is unimportant. Georgia's coastwise shipments of indigo to other of the Thirteen Continental Colonies constituted 5.1 percent of Georgia's total exports of indigo for 1768-1772.

Sometimes the trade in indigo was recorded in terms of casks. George Miller's account of indigo exported in 1783 put the cask of indigo at 350 pounds (BT 6/21, folio 311r, PRO/TNA). (See also Olsberg and Carson 1970, p. 18.) Two different accounts of the export of indigo for the two years 1791-1792 state the amount, one in casks and the other in pounds. See also John Drayton, *A View of South-Carolina, as Respects Her Natural and Civil Concerns* (W[illiam] P. Young, 1802), p. 168, and Tench Coxe, *A View of the United States of America, in a Series of Papers, Written at Various Times, between the Years 1787 and 1794* (William Hall; Wrigley and Berriman, 1794), pp. 406, 416. For these two years, the casks averaged 342 pounds. Using the 350 pounds per cask figure, the number of casks is converted into pounds for several instances in this table: for Charleston, for 196 casks in 1768 and 302 casks in 1772; for Georgia, for 357 casks in 1768; and for South Carolina, 1783-1787.

Sometimes the trade in indigo was recorded in terms of chests or boxes. Two different accounts of the export of indigo for the two years 1783-1785 state the amount, one in chests and the other in pounds. See also Gray (1933), volume 2, p. 1024, citing François-Alexandre-Frédéric La Rochefoucauld-Liancourt, *Travels through the United States of North America, the Country of the Iroquois, and Upper Canada, in the Years 1795, 1796, and 1797; With an Authentic Account of Lower Canada*, translated by H[enry] Neuman (R. Phillips, 1799), volume 2, p. 501, with the data in series Eg1028. For these three years, the chests averaged 262 pounds. This figure is used to convert the five boxes exported in 1772 to an equivalent weight.

Although CUST 16/1, p. 14, PRO/TNA, does indeed record that 357 casks of indigo were exported from POE Savannah to Great Britain and Ireland in 1768 (in addition to some 19,700 pounds), this not only seems highly unlikely given the export levels of earlier and subsequent years, but it is directly contradicted by the account of the Comptroller of POE Savannah, William Brown, cited previously. The 357 casks are not included here as having been entered by mistake.

British Florida also exported minor amounts of indigo. The total exported from the three POE in the two colonies of East Florida and West Florida over the five years 1768 and 1772 came to less than 100,000 pounds of which roughly two thirds passed through POE St. Augustine. CUST 16/1, pp. 14, 44, 132, 190, 234, PRO/TNA.

For the quantity of raw silk cleared for export at POE Charleston, 1747, see the "8 boxes" in Governor James Glen's original account in the enclosure in his letter to the Board of Trade, Charleston, May 31, 1749, CO 5/461, folio 45v, PRO/TNA. The report was printed in [James Glen], *A Description of South Carolina; Containing, Many Curious and Interesting Particulars Relating to the Civil, Natural and Commercial History of That Colony, viz. The Succession of European Settlers There; . . . The Nature of the Climate; . . . The Culture and Produce of Rice, Indian Corn, and Indigo; . . . The State of Their Maritime Trade in the Years 1710, 1723, 1740 and 1748, with the Number or Tonnage of Shipping Employed . . . To Which Is Added, A Very Particular Account of Their Rice-Trade for Twenty Years, with Their Exports of Raw Silk and Imports of British Silk Manufactures for Twenty-Five Years* (Dodsley, 1761). A comparison of the two figures suggests that silk was shipped in boxes weighing 7.5 pounds each.

TABLE Eg1033-1037   Trade of raw silk and silk goods between England and the Carolinas: 1731-1755

Contributed by John J. McCusker

	Imports of raw silk into England	Exports of silk manufactures from England			
		Wrought	With worsted	With inkle	With grosgrain
	Eg1033	Eg1034	Eg1035	Eg1036	Eg1037
Year	Pounds	Pounds	Pounds	Pounds	Pounds
1731	0	970	537	0	0
1732	0	774	892	0	0
1733	0	1,015	1,341	0	0
1734	0	943	937	0	0
1735	0	1,487	864	0	0
1736	0	1,223	516	0	0
1737	0	691	790	0	0
1738	0	1,111	1,177	0	0
1739	0	1,273	877	0	0
1740	0	1,454	1,492	0	0
1741	0	2,798	2,452	440	7
1742	19	1,576	1,350	144	0
1743	0	1,427	1,262	122	0
1744	0	1,035	1,296	181	0
1745	0	544	615	184	40
1746	0	929	590	330	3
1747	0	1,313	2,050	386	0
1748	52	1,772	1,658	155	34
1749	46	1,772	1,065	74	0
1750	118	1,519	1,258	223	50
1751	0	2,404	1,933	291	0
1752	0	3,365	2,860	218	7
1753	11	3,027	2,236	190	0
1754	0	2,682	2,300	374	150
1755	6	3,416	2,634	337	0

Source

The source of the data is the Ledgers of Imports and Exports of England, 1731-1755, CUST 3/31-55, PRO/TNA. The data were published in [James Glen], *A Description of South Carolina; Containing, Many Curious and Interesting Particulars Relating to the Civil, Natural and Commercial History of That Colony, viz. The Succession of European Settlers There; ... The Nature of the Climate; ... The Culture and Produce of Rice, Indian Corn, and Indigo; ... The State of Their Maritime Trade in the Years 1710, 1723, 1740 and 1748, with the Number or Tonnage of Shipping Employed ... To Which Is Added, a Very Particular Account of Their Rice-Trade for Twenty Years, with Their Exports of Raw Silk and Imports of British Silk Manufactures for Twenty-Five Years* (R. and J. Dodsley, 1761), p. 96.

Documentation

See the Appendixes to the essay in this chapter for a general discussion of the tables and the sources of the data, along with a key to abbreviations used in this chapter and general information on matters such as regional definitions, calendar differences, money, and weights and measures. Note especially the discussion of the time periods used for compiling these records. Through the year 1751, the year of record ended December 24; thereafter, it ended January 4 of the following year. Although the source indicates that this was the case for these data through 1755, it seems highly unlikely. Nevertheless, the returns for each year represent the imports and exports for a full twelve months.

These data record the quantity in pounds weight (pounds avoirdupois) of raw silk imported into England from North and South Carolina and of silk goods exported from England to North and South Carolina. It must be underscored that these data are the figures for exports from and imports into England and Wales, *not* figures for exports from or imports into the colonies, as they have too often been described.

These data were not part of Governor James Glen's original report on South Carolina, for which see the enclosure in his letter to the Board of Trade, Charleston, May 31, 1749, CO 5/461, folios 37v-48v, PRO/TNA. A contemporary Charleston physician, George Milligen (fl. 1737-1775), owned the printed book (Glen 1761) and wrote an explanation of what transpired on the verso side of the leaf opposite the title page. Milligen stated that "the Governour lodged a copy of his letter in the ... Office [of the Secretary of the Province]. A Clerk of that office brought a Copy of it to England, and published it in this form without the Governour's Consent or Knowledge." The added material, "from page 64 to the end of the pamphlet are additions by the Clerk." See the facsimile reproduction of Milligen's copy of the book in Chapman J. Milling, editor, *Colonial South Carolina: Two Contemporary Descriptions*, South Caroliniana Sesquicentennial Series, number 1 (University of South Carolina Press, 1951), p. 2.

TABLE Eg1038–1045   Tobacco imported into England, by origin: 1697–1775[1]

Contributed by John J. McCusker

Year	Total	Virginia and Maryland	Carolina	Georgia	Pennsylvania	New England	New York	All other places
	Eg1038	Eg1039	Eg1040	Eg1041	Eg1042	Eg1043	Eg1044	Eg1045
	Thousand pounds	Thousand pounds	Thousand pounds	Thousand pounds	Thousand pounds	Thousand pounds	Thousand pounds	Thousand pounds
1697	35,632	35,329	1	—	118	1	27	156
1698	23,052	22,738	(Z)	—	22	2	7	283
1698	8,478	8,359	(Z)	—	67	(Z)	9	43
1699	31,253	30,641	3	—	65	16	32	496
1700	37,840	37,166	8	—	398	23	12	233
1701	32,189	31,754	0	—	270	44	1	120
1702	37,209	36,749	3	—	304	67	0	86
1703	20,075	19,451	2	—	313	113	3	193
1704	34,864	34,665	7	—	86	9	2	95
1705	15,661	15,573	0	—	47	9	0	32
1706	19,780	19,379	5	—	94	17	5	280
1707	28,088	27,684	6	—	83	192	46	77
1708	28,975	28,716	7	—	184	57	1	10
1709	34,547	34,467	1	—	65	0	2	12
1710	23,498	23,351	2	—	117	2	(Z)	26
1711	28,122	28,100	0	—	0	1	6	15
1712	30,523	30,502	0	—	7	4	4	6
1713	21,598	21,573	(Z)	—	0	12	2	11
1714	29,264	29,248	0	—	0	1	9	6
1715	17,810	17,783	0	—	18	(Z)	0	9
1716	28,316	28,305	(Z)	—	3	(Z)	0	8
1717	29,600	29,450	(Z)	—	102	47	(Z)	1
1718	31,840	31,740	4	—	94	1	0	(Z)
1719	33,684	33,503	1	—	177	2	(Z)	1
1720	34,526	34,138	8	—	365	4	1	10
1721	37,292	36,949	47	—	254	41	0	1
1722	28,543	28,383	8	—	140	0	1	10
1723	29,297	29,259	6	—	23	(Z)	2	7
1724	26,634	26,612	(Z)	—	13	0	1	9
1725	21,046	20,968	0	—	66	0	2	12
1726	32,311	32,159	0	—	142	1	0	9
1727	43,275	43,026	0	—	225	0	0	24
1728	42,588	42,328	1	—	155	1	0	103
1729	39,951	39,785	0	—	161	(Z)	0	5
1730	35,080	34,860	16	—	73	0	0	131
1731	41,595	41,194	2	—	90	0	0	309
1732	30,891	30,847	0	0	21	14	0	9
1733	40,085	39,854	0	0	169	0	0	62
1734	35,563	35,216	0	0	338	1	0	8
1735	40,069	39,818	0	0	250	0	0	1
1736	37,904	37,682	108	0	100	(Z)	0	14
1737	50,208	49,946	86	0	154	0	0	22
1738	40,120	39,868	0	0	226	0	0	26
1739	46,724	45,866	552	0	305	0	0	1
1740	36,002	35,372	49	0	427	48	0	106
1741	59,449	59,007	70	0	221	7	0	144
1742	43,467	42,838	558	0	30	(Z)	0	41
1743	56,767	55,666	515	0	18	0	0	568
1744	41,434	41,119	35	0	159	3	0	118
1745	41,073	40,897	0	0	166	0	0	10
1746	39,990	39,567	81	0	228	0	0	114
1747	51,289	50,765	287	0	107	124	0	6
1748	50,695	49,646	393	0	66	319	0	271
1749	44,648	44,190	321	0	122	0	0	15
1750	51,339	50,785	12	0	34	447	0	61
1751	45,979	45,745	162	0	67	4	0	(Z)
1752	57,250	56,591	83	0	68	505	0	3
1753	62,686	61,913	451	0	35	285	0	2
1754	58,867	57,977	836	0	46	0	0	8
1755	49,084	48,610	241	0	14	2	0	217
1756	33,291	32,943	289	0	1	(Z)	0	58
1757	42,232	41,542	369	0	0	0	0	321
1758	43,969	43,623	273	0	0	0	0	73
1759	34,782	34,652	120	0	4	0	0	6

Notes appear at end of table

TABLE Eg1038–1045   Tobacco imported into England, by origin: 1697–1775   *Continued*

Year	Total	Virginia and Maryland	Carolina	Georgia	Pennsylvania	New England	New York	All other places
	Eg1038	Eg1039	Eg1040	Eg1041	Eg1042	Eg1043	Eg1044	Eg1045
	Thousand pounds	Thousand pounds	Thousand pounds	Thousand pounds	Thousand pounds	Thousand pounds	Thousand pounds	Thousand pounds
1760	52,347	51,283	989	0	10	7	0	59
1761	47,075	45,818	796	0	450	0	0	11
1762	44,111	41,862	2,226	0	10	0	0	13
1763	65,179	64,500	647	0	6	0	0	27
1764	54,433	53,662	765	0	4	0	0	2
1765	48,320	47,600	704	0	0	3	0	13
1766	43,318	43,193	114	0	0	0	0	12
1767	39,145	39,096	44	0	0	0	0	4
1768	35,555	35,457	88	0	0	0	0	9
1769	33,797	33,552	203	1	0	0	0	41
1770	39,188	38,986	190	8	0	0	0	4
1771	58,093	56,888	1,136	35	0	0	0	34
1772	51,501	50,667	684	135	0	0	0	15
1773	55,929	54,915	964	50	0	0	0	(Z)
1774	56,057	54,785	1,191	71	0	0	0	10
1775	55,968	54,458	834	109	0	57	0	510

(Z) Less than 500 pounds.

[1] The year of record ended September 28 for 1697–1698; December 24 for 1699–1751; and January 4 thereafter. The second set of values shown covers the transition period, September 29 to December 24, 1698.

Sources

The sources of the data are the Ledgers of Imports and Exports of England, CUST 2/1-10, CUST 3/1-82, PRO/TNA, contemporary accounts extracted from them, and related documents as discussed here and in the source for Table Eg1046–1053. Most of the data were originally compiled by Jacob M. Price, "The Tobacco Trade and the Treasury, 1685–1733: British Mercantilism in Its Fiscal Aspects" (Ph.D. dissertation, Harvard University, 1954), volume 2, pp. 906-10.

Documentation

See the Appendixes to the essay in this chapter for a general discussion of the tables and the sources of the data, along with a key to abbreviations used in this chapter and general information on matters such as regional definitions, calendar differences, money, and weights and measures. Note especially the discussion of the time periods used for compiling these records.

General Note on the Tobacco Trade

Figures for the transatlantic shipment of tobacco in the eighteenth century are reasonably satisfactory, whereas those for the seventeenth century are less so, if only because the former were much more regularly and systematically collected and compiled (compare the text for Table Eg1054–1056). The English data presented here were initially collected by the Customs officers in the ports of England and Wales and were then transmitted to London, where they were compiled into annual totals under the direction of the Inspector General of Imports and Exports located in the Custom House. Almost all of the large post-1697 volumes survive in CUST 2 and CUST 3, PRO/TNA, but some do not. Two volumes from early in the eighteenth century, for 1705 and 1712, and all volumes from late in that century and early in the nineteenth century are missing, presumably destroyed in the 1814 Custom House fire. The figures for Scotland were compiled in a similar fashion in the offices of the Commissioners of the Customs in Edinburgh, but they do not survive from as early a period. It is thus fortunate that Scotland's tobacco imports were relatively minor in those years and that, as their relative importance grew, the Scottish statistics became more plentiful (see Table Eg1046–1053).

British imports of tobacco represented virtually all of colonial exports, certainly in the eighteenth century even if less so in the seventeenth century. Some discrepancies that might seem to challenge those notions exist. For instance, more tobacco by weight was shipped from colonial ports than arrived in Great Britain. The figures given in Tables Eg1038–1053 indicate the landed weight in Great Britain. Because tobacco lost moisture while crossing the Atlantic, the landed weight in Great Britain averaged about 5 percent less than the shipped weight in America. See Arthur Pierce Middleton, *Tobacco Coast: A Maritime History of Chesapeake Bay in the Colonial*

Era, edited by George Carrington Mason (The Mariners' Museum, 1953), p. 104; Rupert C. Jarvis, editor, *Customs Letter-Books of the Port of Liverpool, 1711–1813*, Remains Historical and Literary Connected with the Palatine Counties of Lancaster and Chester, 3rd series, volume 6 (Chetham Society, 1954), pp. 44-5. In 1733, the Inspector General of Imports and Exports, John Oxenford, reported to Parliament that, on average, the weight loss of the nearly ten thousand hogsheads of tobacco imported from Virginia through port of entry (POE) London between June and December the previous year measured 3.5 percent. Great Britain, Parliament, House of Commons, *The Report, with the Appendix, from the Committee of the House of Commons Appointed to Enquire into the Frauds and Abuses in the Customs, to the Prejudice of Trade, and the Diminution of the Revenue* (Printed for Richard Williamson and William Bowyer, 1733), p. 51.

There is also much talk about the failure of the colonists to obey British government laws and regulations that required the export of colonial tobacco only to Great Britain (England prior to 1707) and British colonies. The validity of British statistics as a reflection of the colonial tobacco trade depends, of course, on colonial obedience to those regulations. Although opportunities existed for illicit trade – once again, more in the seventeenth century and fewer in the eighteenth century – those who have studied the tobacco industry are uniform in determining that what smuggling there was mattered little in the larger scheme of things. Undeniably, some tobacco was shipped from the Colonies to foreign ports both in Europe and in the Western Hemisphere, but two factors militated against any statistically significant fraud. One was that enforcement of the applicable laws and regulations grew increasingly tight on both sides of the Atlantic. The other is that the physical size of the tobacco hogshead, large to begin with, grew ever larger over time. The text for Table Eg275–284 shows that it had grown to more than one thousand pounds by the middle of the eighteenth century. Heavy hogsheads were not easily shipped and even less easily smuggled. They required sizable vessels to transport them, major port and docking facilities to load and land them, and large-scale enterprises to manage the business. Vessels and cargo and the business itself were increasingly at risk of seizure by an increasingly rigorous imperial Customs administration. The threat of loss of ship and cargo stayed many a potentially wayward individual. As Jacob Price, the author of the text of this chapter in its earlier editions and the leading historian of the trade in tobacco over the last half-century, concluded, "there was undoubtedly some smuggling of tobacco but it does not seem likely to impair the validity of the colonial import statistics" (*Historical Statistics of the United States* (1975), p. 1161). See also the discussion in Lawrence A. Harper, *The English Navigation Laws: A Seventeenth Century Experiment in Social Engineering* (Columbia University Press, 1939); and John J. McCusker, *Mercantilism and the Economic History of the Early Modern Atlantic World* (Cambridge University Press, forthcoming).

Price went on to cite as an instructive example the shipment twice during the 1760s from Rhode Island to Suriname, the Dutch colony on the northeast

TABLE Eg1038–1045   Tobacco imported into England, by origin: 1697–1775   *Continued*

coast of South America, of between 150,000 and 200,000 pounds of tobacco grown in that colony, as clear a breech of British law as one might expect to find. See James B. Hedges, *The Browns of Providence Plantations* (Harvard University Press, 1952–1968), volume 1, pp. 30–9. Price then observed: "It need not be assumed that the colonists were averse to violating the law. It may be that violations on a significant scale were not good business. The fact that the 200,000 pounds of Rhode Island tobacco sent to Surinam went there illegally means little. It was a type of tobacco not in general demand and constituted less than one-third of one percent of the annual legal trade" (*Historical Statistics of the United States* (1975), p. 1162). The simple fact is that the great bulk of tobacco ended up where it was supposed to go, the ports in Great Britain and the British colonies – there to be recorded by the Customs authorities.

Table Eg1038–1045

The figures in this table record the annual total weight of all tobacco imported into English and Welsh POE – London and "the Outports" – from the Thirteen Continental Colonies and all other points of origin. It must be underscored that these data are the figures for imports into England and Wales, not figures for exports from the Colonies, as they have too often been described. (See Table Eg1057–1134 for British North American colonial export data.)

Series Eg1045. Includes tobacco imported from Portugal and the Madeira Islands, the rest of Europe, Turkey, Africa, the East Indies, Antigua, Barbados, Bermuda, Jamaica, St. Christopher, other places, and tobacco captured on the high seas as a prize of war.

TABLE Eg1046–1053   Tobacco imported into and reexported from Great Britain: 1697–1791[1]

Contributed by John J. McCusker

	Imports					Reexports		
		England						
	Total	Total	Via London	Via outports	Scotland	Total	England	Scotland
	Eg1046	Eg1047	Eg1048	Eg1049	Eg1050 [2]	Eg1051	Eg1052	Eg1053 [2]
Year	Million pounds	Million pounds	Million pounds	Million pounds	Million pounds	Million pounds	Million pounds	Million pounds
1697	—	36	26	10	—	—	18	—
1698	—	23	10	13	—	—	18	—
1699	—	31	18	13	—	—	22	—
1700	—	38	25	12	—	—	25	—
1701	—	32	21	11	—	—	21	—
1702	—	37	25	12	—	—	14	—
1703	—	20	0	11	—	—	17	—
1704	—	35	25	10	—	—	20	—
1705	—	16	0	0	—	—	11	—
1706	—	20	12	8	—	—	11	—
1707	—	28	15	13	—	—	21	—
1708	30	29	—	—	1	18	17	1
1709	36	35	—	—	1	22	21	1
1710	25	23	—	—	1	16	15	1
1711	30	28	—	—	1	16	15	1
1712	—	31	—	—	—	—	19	—
1713	—	22	—	—	—	—	17	—
1714	—	29	—	—	—	—	20	—
1715	20	18	—	—	2	15	13	2
1716	31	28	—	—	2	19	17	2
1717	32	30	—	—	2	21	19	2
1718	—	32	—	—	—	—	19	—
1719	—	34	—	—	—	—	20	—
1720	—	35	—	—	—	—	23	—
1721	41	37	—	—	4	30	26	4
1722	35	29	19	9	7	25	21	4
1723	34	29	21	9	5	24	22	1
1724	32	27	18	8	6	28	18	11
1725	25	21	14	7	4	16	13	3
1726	36	32	20	12	4	31	28	3
1727	50	43	28	16	7	32	26	5
1728	50	43	29	14	7	35	29	6
1729	47	40	27	13	7	38	31	7
1730	41	35	24	11	6	33	27	5
1731	46	42	29	13	4	34	29	5
1732	—	31	20	11	—	—	31	—
1733	—	40	27	13	—	—	26	—
1734	—	36	24	12	—	—	27	—
1735	—	40	26	14	—	—	33	—
1736	—	38	25	13	—	—	32	—
1737	—	50	32	19	—	—	41	—
1738	45	40	25	15	5	37	33	4
1739	53	47	31	16	7	43	38	5

Notes appear at end of table

TABLE Eg1046–1053   Tobacco imported into and reexported from Great Britain: 1697–1791   *Continued*

	Imports					Reexports		
		England						
	Total	Total	Via London	Via outports	Scotland	Total	England	Scotland
	Eg1046	Eg1047	Eg1048	Eg1049	Eg1050 [2]	Eg1051	Eg1052	Eg1053 [2]
Year	Million pounds	Million pounds	Million pounds	Million pounds	Million pounds	Million pounds	Million pounds	Million pounds
1740	41	36	19	17	5	42	35	7
1741	68	59	41	19	9	54	46	8
1742	53	43	24	19	10	52	44	8
1743	67	57	33	24	11	58	47	11
1744	52	41	24	17	11	51	42	10
1745	55	41	22	19	14	43	33	10
1746	52	40	19	21	12	49	32	16
1747	64	51	29	23	13	52	39	13
1748	—	51	28	23	—	—	43	—
1749	—	45	21	23	—	—	44	—
1750	—	51	26	26	—	—	33	—
1751	—	46	26	20	—	—	39	—
1752	78	57	33	24	21	69	49	20
1753	87	63	37	25	24	74	50	23
1754	79	59	33	26	20	73	53	20
1755	64	49	27	22	15	45	34	10
1756	46	33	19	14	12	38	26	12
1757	60	42	22	20	18	46	28	18
1758	70	44	24	20	26	43	26	17
1759	50	35	18	16	15	50	32	19
1760	85	52	28	24	32	64	40	25
1761	73	47	27	20	26	66	37	29
1762	71	44	22	22	27	62	36	25
1763	98	65	47	18	33	65	41	24
1764	81	54	37	17	26	85	54	31
1765	81	48	29	20	33	68	39	29
1766	73	43	27	16	29	63	33	30
1767	68	39	26	14	29	63	36	26
1768	69	36	23	12	33	67	31	36
1769	70	34	24	9	36	59	24	35
1770	78	39	27	12	39	73	33	40
1771	105	58	43	15	47	87	41	46
1772	97	51	36	15	45	94	50	44
1773	100	56	38	18	45	97	50	46
1774	97	56	—	—	41	79	45	34
1775	102	56	—	—	46	74	44	30
1776	15	7	—	—	7	40	17	24
1777	2	2	—	—	0	8	3	6
1778	12	9	—	—	3	4	2	2
1779	17	14	—	—	3	6	4	2
1780	17	12	—	—	5	6	3	3
1781	13	11	—	—	2	6	4	2
1782	10	7	—	—	3	3	3	1
1783	18	16	—	—	2	8	6	2
1784	44	40	—	—	4	31	28	3
1785	43	34	—	—	9	35	26	9
1786	45	38	—	—	8	27	21	6
1787	40	32	—	—	8	34	27	8
1788	49	39	—	—	10	16	7	9
1789	59	48	—	—	12	38	29	8
1790	58	47	—	—	11	37	28	9
1791	53	38	—	—	14	54	44	10

[1] Except as noted, the year of record ended September 28 for 1697–1698; December 24 for 1699–1751; and January 4 thereafter.

[2] For 1721–1731 and 1752–1754, the year of record ended September 28.

Sources

The sources of the data are the Ledgers of Imports and Exports of England, CUST 2/1-10, CUST 3/1-82, PRO/TNA, contemporary accounts extracted from them, and related documents as detailed here. The data for 1697–1775 were originally compiled in Jacob M. Price, "The Tobacco Trade and

the Treasury, 1685–1733: British Mercantilism in Its Fiscal Aspects" (Ph.D. dissertation, Harvard University, 1954), volume 2, pp. 906–10. The data for 1782–1791 were compiled by Jacob M. Price for the earlier editions of this chapter. The data for 1776–1782 are from Adam Anderson, *An Historical and Chronological Deduction of the Origin of Commerce, from the Earliest Accounts. Containing an History of the Great Commercial Interests of the British Empire...*, edited by William Combe, revised and corrected edition (J. White [et al.], 1787–1789), volume 4, pp. 453, 455.

(continued)

TABLE Eg1046–1053   Tobacco imported into and reexported from Great Britain: 1697–1791   *Continued*

Documentation

See the Appendixes to the essay in this chapter for a general discussion of the tables and the sources of the data, along with a key to abbreviations used in this chapter and general information on matters such as regional definitions, calendar differences, money, and weights and measures. Note especially the discussion of the time periods used for compiling these records. Also see the text for Table Eg1038–1045 for a general note on the tobacco trade.

The figures in this table record the total weight annually of all tobacco imported into the port of entry (POE) of Great Britain and reexported from them. The total imports include tobacco imported from a variety of places, but mostly from the Thirteen Continental Colonies. Nonetheless, it must be underscored that these data are the figures for imports into Great Britain, not figures for exports from the Thirteen Continental Colonies, as they have too often been described.

Total imports and reexports for 1708–1731 and 1752–1754 were obtained by adding figures not strictly comparable with each other. Scottish imports and reexports for 1708–1711 and 1715–1717 are averages of estimates for two separate groups of years.

For England and Wales, in addition to CUST 2/1–10 and CUST 3/1–82, PRO/TNA, Price consulted the following contemporary compilations: for 1703–1722, CO 390/5, number 47, PRO/TNA; the data for 1717–1722, confirmed in T 1/281, number 18, PRO/TNA, and in Add. MS 33038, folio 159, BL; for 1722 (London imports only), T 64/276B, number 327, PRO/TNA; for 1763–1769 (imports only), T 64/276B, number 328, PRO/TNA; for 1770–1773 (imports only), T 64/276B, number 332, PRO/TNA; for 1770–1771 (exports), from T 64/276, number 330, PRO/TNA; for 1772, 1774–1775 (imports and exports), T 17/20-21, PRO/TNA; and for 1783–1791, CUST 17/8-14, PRO/TNA. See also, for 1773–1782, Anderson (1787–1789), volume 4, p. 453.

For Scotland, Price's data came from the Ledgers of Imports and Exports of Scotland, 1755–1791, CUST 14/1-10, PRO/TNA, except as follows: for 1707–1711 (imports and exports), T 1/39, number 29, PRO/TNA; for 1715–1717 (imports and exports), from CO 390/5, number 13, PRO/TNA; for 1721–1724 (imports and exports), T 1/282, number 23, PRO/TNA; for 1725–1731, 1752–1754, 1763, 1769 (imports and exports), from T 36/13, PRO/TNA; for 1738–1747 (imports and exports), T 1/329, folio 125, PRO/TNA. See also, for 1773–1782, Anderson (1781–1789), volume 4, p. 455.

For these sources, see John J. McCusker, "The Current Value of English Exports, 1697 to 1800," *William and Mary Quarterly*, 3rd series, 28 (October 1971): 607–28, as revised and updated in McCusker, *Essays in the Economic History of the Atlantic World* (Routledge, 1997), pp. 222–44; and Jacob M. Price, "New Time Series for Scotland's and Britain's Trade with the Thirteen Colonies and States, 1740 to 1791," *William and Mary Quarterly*, 3rd series, 32 (April 1975): 307–25.

Data on tobacco exported from the Thirteen Continental Colonies and the United States from the late eighteen to the mid-nineteenth centuries are available in J[ames] D. B. De Bow, *The Industrial Resources, Statistics, Etc., of the United States, and More Particularly of the Southern and Western States: Embracing a View of Their Commerce, Agriculture, Manufactures, Internal Improvements, Slave and Free Labor, Slavery Institutions, Products, etc., of the South, Together with Historical and Statistical Sketches of the Different States and Cities of the Union, Statistics of the United States Commerce and Manufactures, from the Earliest Periods, Compared with Other Leading Powers, The Results of the Different Census Returns since 1790, and Returns of the Census of 1850, on Population, Agriculture and Industry, etc., with an Appendix*, 3rd edition (D. Appleton, 1854), volume 3, pp. 347–9.

TABLE Eg1054–1056   English colonial tobacco imported into England: 1615–1701[1]

Contributed by John J. McCusker

	Total	London	Outports		Total	London	Outports		Total	London	Outports
	Eg1054	Eg1055	Eg1056		Eg1054	Eg1055	Eg1056		Eg1054	Eg1055	Eg1056
Year(s)	Thousand pounds	Thousand pounds	Thousand pounds	Year(s)	Thousand pounds	Thousand pounds	Thousand pounds	Year(s)	Thousand pounds	Thousand pounds	Thousand pounds
1615	0.0	0.0	0.0	1630	458.2	360.6	97.5	1682	21,399.0	12,592.0	8,807.0
1616	2.5	2.3	0.2	1631	272.3	209.8	62.6	1683	—	—	13,495.0
1617	18.8	18.8	0.0	1637	—	1,537.4	—	1684	—	—	13,495.0
1618	49.7	49.5	0.2	1638	—	3,134.1	—	1686–1688	36,352.0	—	—
1619	45.8	45.8	0.0	1639	—	1,344.9	—	1689–1692	25,863.0	—	—
1620	119.0	118.0	1.0	1640	—	1,257.3	—	1693–1697	26,922.0	—	—
1621	73.8	73.8	0.0	1663	—	7,371.1	—	1698–1701	31,083.0	—	—
1622	61.6	59.4	2.2	1669	15,039.6	9,037.3	6,002.3				
1623	134.6	119.4	15.2	1672	17,559.0	10,539.0	7,020.0				
1624	203.0	187.4	15.6	1676	—	11,127.0	—				
1625	131.8	111.1	20.7	1677	—	11,735.0	—				
1626	333.1	213.3	119.8	1678	—	14,455.0	—				
1627	376.9	335.3	41.6	1679	—	12,983.0	—				
1628	552.9	420.1	132.8	1680	—	11,943.0	—				
1629	178.7	89.0	89.7	1681	—	14,472.0	—				

[1] The year of record ended September 28 except as follows: 1637–1640, March 24 of the following year; 1672–1682 and 1693–1695, December 24; and 1690–1692, November.

Sources

1615–1621. [Arthur Percival Newton, editor], "Lord Sackville's Papers Respecting Virginia, 1613–1631," *American Historical Review* 28 (April, June 1922): 526.

1622–1631. Neville [J.] Williams, "England's Tobacco Trade in the Reign of Charles I," *Virginia Magazine of History and Biography* 65 (October 1957): 419–20.

1637–1640. John R. Pagan, "Growth of the Tobacco Trade between London and Virginia, 1614–40," *Guildhall Studies in London History* 3 (April 1979): 253, citing "Tobaccoes entered in the porte of London in fower yeeres from Lady Day 1637," Add. MS 35865, folios 247-8, BL.

1663–1669. Compiled by Jacob. M. Price from CO 388/2 folios 7, 13, PRO/TNA; for outports, 1669, Lonsdale MS, BL.

1672–1682. Stanley Gray and V[ertrees] J. Wyckoff, "The International Tobacco Trade in the Seventeenth Century," *Southern Economic Journal* 7 (July 1940): 1–26.

(continued)

TABLE Eg1054–1056   English colonial tobacco imported into England: 1615–1701   *Continued*

1683–1684. Compiled by Jacob. M. Price from Sloane MS 1815, folios 34–37, BL.

1686–1701. Annual averages for four periods compiled by Robert Christopher Nash, "English Transatlantic Trade, 1660–1730: A Quantitative Study" (Ph.D. dissertation, University of Cambridge, 1982), pp. 80, 92–3, from the Chalmondeley (Houghton) Papers, Cambridge University Library.

Documentation

See the Appendixes to the essay in this chapter for a general discussion of the tables and the sources of the data, along with a key to abbreviations used in this chapter and general information on matters such as regional definitions, calendar differences, money, and weights and measures. Also see the text for Table Eg1038–1045 for a general note on the tobacco trade.

These figures present the annual total weight of all tobacco imported into English and Welsh ports (London and "the Outports," that is, all other ports besides London) from the English colonies in the seventeenth century. Although after the mid-1620s almost all imported tobacco came from the English colonies in the Western Hemisphere, in a few instances the figures from Gray and Wyckoff (1940, for example, p. 20), are known to include minor quantities of Spanish and Brazilian tobacco. In this and in other ways, these data are not as satisfactory as those given in Tables Eg1038–1053. The total imports for 1686 and 1688 were obtained by adding figures not strictly comparable with each other. Imports of the outports for 1682–1688 are averages of estimates for several years.

The figures for 1616–1621 are for tobacco imported into London and the Outports from "Virginia and Bermudos." An additional 685,030 pounds was imported from Spain. Note that the original series, which begins with the year 1615, indicates that no tobacco was imported from those colonies in that year, whereas a total of 102,277 pounds of Spanish tobacco was imported in that year. See also Vertrees J. Wyckoff, *Tobacco Regulation in Colonial Maryland*, Johns Hopkins University Studies in Historical and Political Science, Extra Volumes, new series, number 22 (Johns Hopkins University Press, 1936), p. 20 n. 2.

The annual averages that Nash compiled were developed from the accounts of receipts from the 1685 "New Impost" of three pence per pound on tobacco: Act of 1 James II, c. 4 (1685) as continued by subsequent acts and made perpetual by Act of 9 Anne, c. 16 (1710). The "View of the Impost on Tobacco," 1686–1713, is among the Customs and Excise Papers, "Papers Relating to the Produce of the Duties on Tobacco," p. 29, item number 6, Chalmondeley (Houghton) Papers, Cambridge University Library. To test the quality of these data, Nash (1982), pp. 92–3, compared the account for 1700–1713 with the imports recorded in the Ledgers of Imports and Exports of England, CUST 2/7-10, CUST 3/1-15, PRO/TNA, and found little difference between them (1.8 percent). From this he inferred that the data given here for the earlier years were also likely to be reliable.

Other data for 1686–1688 and 1693–1694 suggest that whereas London accounted for roughly half of tobacco imports in the former period, by the latter period, the ratio between London and the Outports was two thirds to one third. Sloane MS 1815, folios 34–37, BL; "Account of Exports and Imports, London and the Outports," 1693–1695, Parchment Collection, Sessional Papers, House of Lords, HLRO.

Although these data are reasonably satisfactory (see the text for Table Eg1038–1045), there are a variety of problems with them. For instance, any data for the late 1630s through the early 1660s, when the Dutch were actively engaged in the trade either as traders in the Chesapeake from their base at New Netherland or as importers at Amsterdam or the other Dutch ports, need carefully to be questioned. Alfred Rive, "The Consumption of Tobacco since 1600," *Economic History: A Supplement of The Economic Journal* 1 (January 1926): 60–1, suggested that the doubling of the London import figures between 1637 and 1638 may have been attributable to better English patrolling of the Channel, thus indicating the potential impact on these statistics of Dutch traders in the Chesapeake. Once strict regulations were in place from the mid- and late-1620s, others argue that, with the exception of the 1640s, the years of the Civil Wars, the laws excluding Spanish tobacco and those restricting tobacco shipments to London were "effectively executed" in Virginia and that "very little, if any, [tobacco] was shipped elsewhere" than to England. See George Louis Beer, *The Origins of the British Colonial System, 1578–1660* (Macmillan, 1908), pp. 176–219 (quotations,

pp. 208, 209). It needs also to be recognized that prior to these restrictions, the export of tobacco from Virginia and the other Colonies was not only countenanced but encouraged. Especially in the first decade of Virginia tobacco (1615–1624), the Crown's ambivalence is shown by provisions in its contracts with the Virginia Company and the Somers Islands Company such as the allowance for direct export to foreign ports in the November 1622 agreement as they "themselves shall thinke fitte." Susan Myra Kingsbury, editor, *The Records of the Virginia Company of London* (U.S. Government Printing Office, 1906–1935), volume 2, p. 86.

An alternative approach to assessing the adequacy of the early import figures as a measure of production and exports is to consider contemporary estimates of the amount of tobacco that could be or had been produced or imported. Proposals for limitations on tobacco importation included the following: 55,000 pounds in 1620; 200,000 pounds in 1625 and 1626; 250,000 pounds in 1627; 600,000 pounds in 1635; and 1,600,000 pounds in 1638. See Beer (1908), pp. 120, 138, 154, and 158; Philip Alexander Bruce, *Economic History of Virginia in the Seventeenth Century: An Inquiry into the Material Condition of the People, Based upon Original and Contemporaneous Records* (Macmillan, 1896), volume 1, p. 281. The 1620 agreement is especially interesting because under its provisions the two companies could and did decide in 1621 to import the entire allotment from Bermuda while shipping the Virginia crop of at least 50,000 pounds directly to the Netherlands. Kingsbury (1906–1935), volume 1, pp. 398, 405–6, 422, 482, 504–5. In 1628, Virginia wanted the Crown to take at least 500,000 pounds annually – with any excess to be exported to foreign markets; in 1634, the figure was 800,000 pounds; and by 1639, the colonists sought to reduce the tobacco crop to 1,500,000 that year and 1,300,000 pounds for each of the next two years. See R[obert] A. Brock, "A Succinct Account of Tobacco in Virginia, 1607–1790," in J[oseph] B. Killebrew, "Report on the Culture and Curing of Tobacco in the United States," U.S. Census Office, 10th Census (1880); *Report on the Productions of Agriculture as Returned at the Tenth Census (June 1, 1880), Embracing General Statistics and Monographs on Cereal Production, Flour-Milling, Tobacco Culture, Manufacture and Movement of Tobacco, [and] Meat Production*, 47th Congress, 2nd Session, House of Representatives, Miscellaneous Document 42, Part 3 (1884), pp. 215–16, 224; Bruce (1896), volume 1, p. 268. Comparing these figures for limitation and reduction from the late 1630s with the average annual importation into England, 1637–1640, of about 1,800,000, there seems more reason to agree with Beer than with his critics: "very little, if any, was shipped elsewhere" (Beer 1908, p. 209).

Another weakness of the figures for these series comes from their failure to distinguish the quantity of tobacco supplied by each colony; however, other data provide some opportunities to estimate the quantity contributed by the various colonies. Although, as indicated earlier, we cannot tell which tobacco came from Virginia and which from the Bermuda Islands for the six years 1616–1621, we do know that soon thereafter Virginia drew far ahead. See Beer (1908), p. 120; and Williams (1957), pp. 419–20. Virginia's tobacco production rose from about 20,000 pounds in 1619 to 18,157,000 in 1688 and 18,295,000 pounds in 1704. Brock (1880), p. 224. Bermuda's production increased to over 500,000 pounds in the 1670s and 1680s. Before the end of the century, Bermuda's exports to England had become negligible, and by the first quarter of the eighteenth century Bermuda was importing from Virginia some of the 20,000 pounds consumed there annually. George Louis Beer, *The Old Colonial System, 1660–1754* (Macmillan, 1912), volume 2, p. 91; Henry C. Wilkinson, *Bermuda in the Old Empire: A History of the Island from the Dissolution of the Somers Island Company until the End of the American Revolutionary War, 1684–1784* (Oxford University Press, 1950), p. 14; Michael J. Jarvis, "'In the Eye of All Trade': Maritime Revolution and the Transformation of Bermudian Society, 1612–1800" (Ph.D. dissertation, College of William and Mary, 1998), pp. 766–7.

In the meanwhile, Maryland, which probably had produced no more than 100,000 pounds annually by 1639, so increased its output that it contributed about 36 percent of the combined Virginia–Maryland total in 1688 – a percentage approximated not only at the turn of the seventeenth century but also during the period 1768–1772 (see series Eg1064–1065), thus suggesting the possibility that a similar one-third to two-thirds ratio applied across the entirety of the eighteenth century. See Wyckoff (1936), p. 49; Margaret Shove Morris, *Colonial Trade of Maryland, 1689–1715*, Johns Hopkins

(continued)

TABLE Eg1054–1056   English colonial tobacco imported into England: 1615–1701   *Continued*

University Studies in Historical and Political Science, series 32, number 3 (Johns Hopkins University Press, 1914), pp. 31–6.

Tobacco was also grown elsewhere in British America, though, as with Bermuda, the quantities involved had fallen off significantly by the last third of the seventeenth century. In the other mainland Colonies farther south, North Carolina was said to grow about 800,000 pounds of tobacco annually in the mid-1670s (2,000 hogsheads at 400 pounds per hogshead) – an amount that seems larger than the subsequent pattern of exports justifies. Letter from the Assembly of Carolina to the Lords Proprietors, October 11, 1677, as referred to in the letter from Thomas Miller, Collector of Customs of North Carolina, and Henry Hudson, Deputy Collector of Customs, at London, to the Commissioners of the Customs, January 21, 1679/80, CO 1/44, folio 18v, PRO/TNA. The West Indies (specifically Barbados) were said to have begun growing tobacco by the mid- to late-1620s; one report shows shipments in 1628 in excess of 100,000 pounds, but even by the end of the next decade cotton had begun to replace tobacco and by the middle of the century sugar had begun to take over as the predominant crop. See Beer (1908), p. 89 n. 2. Compare Henry Colt, "The Voyage of Sir Henry Colt," in V[incent] T. Harlow, editor, *Colonising Expeditions to the West Indies and Guiana, 1623–1667*, Works Issued by the Hakluyt Society, 2nd series, number 56 (Hakluyt Society, 1925), p. 101. At the end of the seventeenth century, Barbados, like Bermuda, was importing tobacco from the Chesapeake. Morris (1914), p. 36 n. 116.

Based on the fragmentary and difficult London Port Books, Dr. A. M. Millard compiled data on port of entry (POE) London's imports during the late sixteenth century and first third of the seventeenth century with some intriguing results as far as tobacco imports from the colonies are concerned. She took her data from the following: Records of the Exchequer, King's Remembrancer, Port of London, Port Book, Surveyor of Tunnage and Poundage Overseas, Imports by Denizens, Christmas 1620–Christmas 1621, E 190/24/4; Controller of Tunnage and Poundage Overseas, Imports by Denizens, Christmas 1625–Christmas 1626, E 190/31/3 (incomplete; ends November 4); Overseas Inwards, Christmas 1629–Christmas 1630, E 190/35/4; Waiters Overseas, Inwards, Christmas 1629–Christmas 1630, E 190/34/2; Surveyor of Tunnage and Poundage Overseas, Imports by Denizens, Christmas 1632–Christmas 1633, E 190/38/1; Surveyor General of Tunnage and Poundage Overseas, Imports by Denizens, Christmas 1633–Christmas 1634, E 190/38/5; Controller of Tunnage and Poundage Overseas, Imports by Denizens, Christmas 1639–Christmas 1640, E 190/43/5, PRO/TNA. See A[nnie] M. Millard, "The Import Trade of London, 1600–1640" (Ph.D. dissertation, University of London, 1956), pp. 303–13, and Tables 31–35 in Millard, "Analyses of Port Books Recording Merchandises Imported into the Port of London by English and Alien and Denizen Merchants for Certain Years between 1588 and 1640" (1960), unpublished manuscript, Library, PRO/TNA. For these records, see Neville [J.] Williams, "The London Port Books," *Transactions of the London and Middlesex Archaeological Society* 18 (1955): 13–26; and Donald [M.] Woodward, "The Port Books of England and Wales," *Maritime History* 3 (September 1973): 147–65.

Year	From where	Amount of tobacco (pounds)
1621	Virginia	24,397
	Bermuda	46,022
	Total	70,419
1626	Virginia	85,022
	Bermuda	6,977
	Total	91,999
1630	Virginia	270,030
	Bermuda	34,146
	St. Christopher	80,252
	Total	384,428
1633	Virginia	243,014
	West Indies	98,206
	Total	341,220
1634	Virginia	417,005
	Bermuda	64,410
	St. Christopher	24,896
	Barbados	4,506
	Providence Island	7,652
	Total	518,523
1640	Virginia	938,418
	St. Christopher	141,800
	Barbados	65,924
	Total	1,146,142

Compare "Tobaccoes entered in the porte of London in fower yeeres from Lady Day 1637," Add. MS 35865, folios 247–8, BL.

	Barbados	St. Christopher	Virginia
1637	124,365	263,599	1,067,262
1638	204,956	470,732	2,361,999
1639	208,100	107,312	1,091,773

It is probable that the figures for Virginia for 1637–1640 included tobacco imported from Maryland.

As a consequence of all these considerations, one can conclude that the quantities of tobacco imported into England during the seventeenth century, presented in Table Eg1054–1056, came mostly from the English colonies in the Western Hemisphere, almost all of it from Maryland and Virginia.

TABLE Eg1057–1134   Tobacco exported and imported, by colony and by origin or destination: 1768–1772

Contributed by John J. McCusker

						Exports							
						Total							
Year	Total	New Hampshire	Massachusetts	Rhode Island	Connecticut	New York	Pennsylvania	Maryland	Virginia	North Carolina	South Carolina	Georgia	Florida
	Eg1057	Eg1058	Eg1059	Eg1060	Eg1061	Eg1062	Eg1063	Eg1064	Eg1065	Eg1066	Eg1067	Eg1068	Eg1069
	Thousand pounds	Thousand pounds	Thousand pounds	Thousand pounds	Thousand pounds	Thousand pounds	Thousand pounds	Thousand pounds	Thousand pounds	Thousand pounds	Thousand pounds	Thousand pounds	Thousand pounds
1768	69,683.1	0.0	11.8	3.1	23.2	5.0	0.0	24,382.3	44,876.9	380.8	0.0	0.0	0.0
1769	84,207.3	0.0	46.7	11.2	29.3	12.6	1.2	25,790.8	57,445.2	554.7	310.4	5.2	0.0
1770	89,744.3	3.7	20.9	0.4	13.5	34.6	6.5	27,272.0	61,048.5	1,097.3	233.2	13.4	0.3
1771	112,921.2	4.4	58.0	11.4	5.0	48.2	4.4	38,963.0	71,468.7	1,886.6	436.6	34.9	0.0
1772	106,979.4	2.0	23.7	14.0	1.7	58.6	26.4	33,909.2	70,632.3	1,604.8	527.6	179.1	0.0

TABLE Eg1057–1134 Tobacco exported and imported, by colony and by origin or destination: 1768–1772
Continued

Exports

To Great Britain

Year	Total	New Hampshire	Massachusetts	Rhode Island	Connecticut	New York	Pennsylvania	Maryland	Virginia	North Carolina	South Carolina	Georgia	Florida
	Eg1070	Eg1071	Eg1072	Eg1073	Eg1074	Eg1075	Eg1076	Eg1077	Eg1078	Eg1079	Eg1080	Eg1081	Eg1082
	Thousand pounds	Thousand pounds	Thousand pounds	Thousand pounds	Thousand pounds	Thousand pounds	Thousand pounds	Thousand pounds	Thousand pounds	Thousand pounds	Thousand pounds	Thousand pounds	Thousand pounds
1768	69,519.1	0	0	0	0	0	0	24,382.3	44,769.7	367.1	0.0	0.0	0
1769	83,945.2	0	0	0	0	0	0	25,781.8	57,337.8	549.6	275.4	0.6	0
1770	89,321.4	0	0	0	0	0	0	27,266.8	60,811.1	1,084.7	145.5	13.3	0
1771	112,508.6	0	0	0	0	0	0	38,931.4	71,268.7	1,872.2	401.4	34.9	0
1772	106,574.0	0	0	0	0	0	0	33,902.0	70,449.4	1,573.4	479.0	170.2	0

Exports

To the West Indies

Year	Total	New Hampshire	Massachusetts	Rhode Island	Connecticut	New York	Pennsylvania	Maryland	Virginia	North Carolina	South Carolina	Georgia	Florida
	Eg1083	Eg1084	Eg1085	Eg1086	Eg1087	Eg1088	Eg1089	Eg1090	Eg1091	Eg1092	Eg1093	Eg1094	Eg1095
	Thousand pounds	Thousand pounds	Thousand pounds	Thousand pounds	Thousand pounds	Thousand pounds	Thousand pounds	Thousand pounds	Thousand pounds	Thousand pounds	Thousand pounds	Thousand pounds	Thousand pounds
1768	139.2	0	0.0	1.4	23.2	1.0	0	0.0	107.2	6.4	0.0	0.0	0
1769	102.3	0	0.3	2.3	13.9	1.3	0	1.2	78.2	3.4	0.1	1.6	0
1770	165.4	0	0.0	0.0	10.8	3.4	0	3.1	145.6	2.4	0.0	0.1	0
1771	181.7	0	0.0	0.0	2.9	0.0	1	15.3	160.5	2.0	0.0	0.0	0
1772	178.0	0	0.5	1.8	0.3	6.7	0	2.5	147.0	11.8	7.4	0.0	0

Exports

Coastwise

Year	Total	New Hampshire	Massachusetts	Rhode Island	Connecticut	New York	Pennsylvania	Maryland	Virginia	North Carolina	South Carolina	Georgia	Florida
	Eg1096	Eg1097	Eg1098	Eg1099	Eg1100	Eg1101	Eg1102	Eg1103	Eg1104	Eg1105	Eg1106	Eg1107	Eg1108
	Thousand pounds	Thousand pounds	Thousand pounds	Thousand pounds	Thousand pounds	Thousand pounds	Thousand pounds	Thousand pounds	Thousand pounds	Thousand pounds	Thousand pounds	Thousand pounds	Thousand pounds
1768	20.5	0.0	11.8	1.4	0.0	0.0	0.0	0.0	0.0	7.3	0.0	0.0	0.0
1769	155.2	0.0	45.5	6.6	15.4	10.6	1.2	7.8	29.2	1.0	34.9	3.0	0.0
1770	248.2	3.7	20.9	0.4	2.7	21.9	6.5	2.1	91.8	10.2	87.7	0.0	0.3
1771	197.5	4.4	55.6	9.9	2.1	29.1	1.1	16.3	39.5	12.4	27.1	0.0	0.0
1772	194.4	2.0	23.2	4.1	1.4	36.6	22.3 [1]	4.7	35.9	19.6	35.7	8.9	0.0

Exports

To Southern Europe and Africa

Year	Total	New Hampshire	Massachusetts	Rhode Island	Connecticut	New York	Pennsylvania	Maryland	Virginia	North Carolina	South Carolina	Georgia	Florida
	Eg1109	Eg1110	Eg1111	Eg1112	Eg1113	Eg1114	Eg1115	Eg1116	Eg1117	Eg1118	Eg1119	Eg1120	Eg1121
	Thousand pounds	Thousand pounds	Thousand pounds	Thousand pounds	Thousand pounds	Thousand pounds	Thousand pounds	Thousand pounds	Thousand pounds	Thousand pounds	Thousand pounds	Thousand pounds	Thousand pounds
1768	4.3	0	0.0	0.3	0	4.0	0.0	0	0	0.0	0.0	0	0
1769	4.6	0	0.9	2.3	0	0.7	0.0	0	0	0.7	0.0	0	0
1770	9.3	0	0.0	0.0	0	9.3	0.0	0	0	0.0	0.0	0	0
1771	33.4	0	2.4	1.5	0	19.1	2.3	0	0	0.0	8.1	0	0
1772	33.0	0	0.0	8.1	0	15.3	4.1	0	0	0.0	5.5	0	0

Notes appear at end of table

(continued)

TABLE Eg1057–1134   Tobacco exported and imported, by colony and by origin or destination: 1768–1772
Continued

							Imports, coastwise							
	Total	New Hampshire	Massachusetts	Rhode Island	Connecticut	New York	Pennsylvania	Maryland	Virginia	North Carolina	South Carolina	Georgia	Florida
	Eg1122	Eg1123	Eg1124	Eg1125	Eg1126	Eg1127	Eg1128	Eg1129	Eg1130	Eg1131	Eg1132	Eg1133	Eg1134
Year	Thousand pounds	Thousand pounds	Thousand pounds	Thousand pounds	Thousand pounds	Thousand pounds	Thousand pounds	Thousand pounds	Thousand pounds	Thousand pounds	Thousand pounds	Thousand pounds	Thousand pounds
1768	22.1	0.0	3.7	0.0	0.0	10.0	5.5	0.0	0	0.0	0.8	0.7	1.4
1769	95.2	10.6	38.1	0.0	1.2	34.4	4.7 [3]	0.0	0	1.0	0.2	0.0	5.0
1770	158.7	5.9	39.0	5.4	0.0	72.6	32.4	0.0	0	0.0	0.0	0.5	2.9
1771	141.5	12.2	39.3	7.2	1.0	66.7	14.8	0.1	0	0.0	0.0	0.2	0.0
1772	87.4 [2]	0.0	13.7	16.6	0.6	25.1	30.8	0.0	0	0.1	0.0 [2]	0.5	0.0

[1] Includes 14,589 pounds exported from Delaware

[2] Plus 5 pigtails.

[3] Includes 224 pounds imported by New Jersey.

Sources

The sources of these data are the records kept in each of the colonial ports of entry (POE) by the administrative clerk of the port, the colonial naval officer. The original quarterly reports of the naval officers – the naval officer shipping lists (NOSL) – and various accounts based on them survive in many places, in many forms. The most important contemporary compilation of these reports was made under the direction of Thomas Irving, the Boston-based Inspector General of Imports and Exports of North America, and is known as the Ledger of Imports and Exports, British North America, 1768–1772, CUST 16/1, PRO/TNA.

Documentation

See the Appendixes to the essay in this chapter for a general discussion of the tables and the sources of the data, along with a key to abbreviations used in this chapter and general information on matters such as regional definitions, calendar differences, money, and weights and measures. The year of record ran from January 5 through January 4. Note that Florida is included here as part of British North America, but it was not one of the Thirteen Continental Colonies. Also see the text for Table Eg1038–1045 for a general note on the tobacco trade.

These figures show the quantity of tobacco annually exported from the Thirteen Continental Colonies and Florida to all destinations and the quantity each of those colonies imported coastwise from one or more of its neighbors. Harper compiled the data as part of his 1930s Works Progress Administration program. There are minor problems with the accounts in the original source. Some export figures for 1768 and 1770 from Virginia, North Carolina, and South Carolina were shown in hogsheads or barrels. When the weights of these units were not indicated, Harper converted them to pounds using the average weights of these units as reflected in the shipments to Great Britain from the respective colonies for 1768–1772. The ledger also reported that in 1771 South Carolina exported to Great Britain 433 hogsheads totaling 40,333 pounds, implying that each hogshead weighed only 90 pounds or so. This is an obvious mistake. Because the hogshead figure is more comparable to other data shown here than the pounds figure, the former is assumed to be correct. It has been converted to pounds in the same manner as the 1770 export figures mentioned previously.

TABLE Eg1135–1141   Tobacco exported from Virginia, by port: 1745–1773

Contributed by John J. McCusker

Year	Total	James River, Upper Part	James River, Lower Part	York River	Rappahannock	South Potomac	Accomack
	Eg1135 [1]	Eg1136	Eg1137	Eg1138	Eg1139	Eg1140	Eg1141
	Hogsheads	Hogsheads	Hogsheads	Hogsheads	Hogsheads	Hogsheads	Hogsheads
1745	42,481	10,991	1,381	11,118	12,332	6,659	0
1746	40,242	10,779	1,372	11,015	10,745	6,311	0
1747	41,804	9,355	1,719	12,895	12,132	5,704	0
1748	46,783	12,489	3,170	11,089	13,052	6,983	0
1749	47,987	11,509	3,150	10,970	15,012	7,346	0
1750	48,567	12,974	2,218	13,802	14,331	5,242	0
1751	46,703	10,858	2,525	12,054	13,553	7,713	0
1752	48,380	13,530	1,423	12,623	14,299	6,505	0
1753	59,847	18,830	2,113	15,127	16,815	6,959	3
1754	50,803	13,900	1,181	14,878	13,512	7,332	0
1755	47,687	13,739	918	15,344	11,963	5,723	0
1756	28,452	7,262	1,096	6,918	8,531	4,645	0
1768	39,623	15,860	1,504	5,668	9,105	5,512	0
1769	50,222	17,825	1,993	8,225	9,920	9,143	3
1772	65,208	24,900 [2]	— [2]	8,634	14,549	10,716	0
1773	69,587	27,592	4,674	8,248	13,244	10,541	0

[1] Includes an additional 1,974, 3,113, 6,409, and 5,288 hogsheads in the years 1768, 1769, 1772, and 1773, respectively. See the text.

[2] The exports for both James River, Upper Part, and James River, Lower Part, were combined in the source and are given here together.

Sources

The sources of these data are the records kept in each of the six Virginia ports of entry (POE) by the administrative clerks of the ports, the colonial naval officers. The original quarterly reports of the naval officers – the naval officer shipping lists (NOSL) – and various accounts based on them survive in many places and in many forms, the details of which are discussed here. In this instance, the data have been compiled by James H. Soltow, *The Economic Role of Williamsburg*, Williamsburg Research Studies (Colonial Williamsburg, 1965), Table III, p. 22c.

TABLE Eg1135–1141   Tobacco exported from Virginia, by port: 1745–1773   *Continued*

Documentation

See the Appendixes to the essay in this chapter for a general discussion of the tables and the sources of the data, along with a key to abbreviations used in this chapter and general information on matters such as regional definitions, calendar differences, money, and weights and measures. Also see the text for Table Eg1038–1045 for a general note on the tobacco trade. The reporting periods ran from October of the previous year through October of the year specified.

The table presents the total number of hogsheads of tobacco exported annually from each of Virginia's ports of entry. For these data, Soltow drew on the following sources.

1745–1756. Edward D. Neill, *The Fairfaxes of England and America in the Seventeenth and Eighteenth Centuries, Including Letters from and to Hon. William Fairfax, President of Council of Virginia, and His Sons Col. George William Fairfax and Rev. Bryan, Eighth Lord Fairfax, the Neighbors and Friends of George Washington* (Joel Munsell, 1868), p. 225. The table records an additional eleven barrels exported from POE Accomack in either 1755 or 1756.

1768. Letter from Jerman Baker, at Bristol, to Thomas Adams, at London, January 8, 1769, Adams Family Papers, 1672–1792, Mss1AD198a, Virginia Historical Society, Richmond. Of the 15,860 hogsheads exported from POE James River, Upper Part, 9,600 hogsheads were said to be from the Appomattox River basin.

1769. *Virginia Gazette* (Rind), November 2, 1769, p. 2, column 2.

1772. *Virginia Gazette* (Purdie and Dixon), November 19, 1772, p. 2, column 1.

1773. *Virginia Gazette* (Purdie and Dixon), November 11, 1773, p. 2, column 2.

As indicated in the footnotes, for the years 1768–1773, there were a number of hogsheads of tobacco exported every year that the sources included among the totals but that were not allocated to one of the ports. These were exported in ships that were registered in Virginia ("free bottoms") and that were consequently exempt from all or part of some duties. Arthur Pierce Middleton, *Tobacco Coast: A Maritime History of Chesapeake Bay in the Colonial Era*, edited by George Carrington Mason (The Mariners' Museum, 1953), pp. 258–9. For the use of the phrase, see William Waller Hening, editor, *The Statutes at Large: Being a Collection of All the Laws of Virginia, from the First Session of the Legislature, in the Year 1619. Published Pursuant to an Act of the General Assembly of Virginia, Passed on the Fifth Day of February One Thousand Eight Hundred and Eight . . .* (Samuel Pleasants Jr. and the Editor, 1809–1823), volume 8, p. 252. Over that period, the amount involved averaged 7.2 percent of total tobacco exported.

The sources recorded only the number of hogsheads exported. For the average weight of tobacco hogsheads during this period, see Lorena S. Walsh's data presented in the text for Table Eg275–284.

TABLE Eg1142–1151   Tobacco exported from James River, Upper Part, to British ports, by destination: 1773–1775

Contributed by John J. McCusker

		England						Scotland		
	Total	Total	London	Bristol	Falmouth	Liverpool	Whitehaven	Total	Glasgow	Greenock
	Eg1142	Eg1143	Eg1144	Eg1145	Eg1146	Eg1147	Eg1148	Eg1149	Eg1150	Eg1151
Year and month	Hogsheads	Hogsheads	Hogsheads	Hogsheads	Hogsheads	Hogsheads	Hogsheads	Hogsheads	Hogsheads	Hogsheads
1773										
June	4,525	1,654	699	0	166	789	0	2,871	2,871	0
July	3,873	1,763	651	0	194	548	370	2,110	1,683	427
Aug	3,691	2,035	825	593	0	617	0	1,656	1,656	0
Sept	3,764	1,787	1,116	240	0	0	431	1,977	1,977	0
Oct	464	464	0	0	0	464	0	0	0	0
Nov	1,396	582	0	0	0	0	582	814	814	0
Dec	0	0	0	0	0	0	0	0	0	0
1774										
Jan	3,108	1,262	380	459	0	0	423	1,846	1,846	0
Feb	2,825	700	0	0	0	700	0	2,125	2,125	0
Mar	1,382	370	0	0	0	0	370	1,012	1,012	0
Apr	2,240	1,881	888	504	0	287	202	359	359	0
May	3,356	1,802	1,223	218	0	0	361	1,554	1,163	391
June	4,311	1,502	720	0	173	609	0	2,809	2,381	428
July	4,082	2,590	1,223	100	241	310	716	1,492	1,492	0
Aug	2,409	459	0	0	0	459	0	1,950	1,213	737
Sept	3,427	1,614	836	0	0	0	778	1,813	1,813	0
Oct	810	0	0	0	0	0	0	810	810	0
Nov	0	0	0	0	0	0	0	0	0	0
Dec	1,301	835	835	0	0	0	0	466	466	0
1775										
Jan	1,839	960	0	587 [2]	0	0	373	879	879	0
Feb	2,865	868	868	0	0	0	0	1,997	1,997	0
Mar	1,470	654	287	0	135	0	232	816	816	0
Apr	2,338	567	374	0	0	0	193	1,771	1,771	0
May	1,899	1,113	0	512	0	601	0	786	786	0
June	3,606	1,622	771	0	0	0	851	1,984	1,984	0
July	7,315	2,068	1,310	0	97	90	571	5,247	5,247	0
Aug	2,992	903	463	0	163	0	277	2,089	2,089	0
Sept	1,523 [1]	579	461	0	0	118 [3]	0	944	944 [4]	0

Notes appear on next page

(continued)

TABLE Eg1142-1151 Tobacco exported from James River, Upper Part, to British ports, by destination: 1773-1775
Continued

[1] The record for September is incomplete as indicated in the other footnotes and explained in the text.

[2] Date is not listed, but it must be January 1775.

[3] This manifest appears to be incomplete.

[4] One vessel is listed with a blank manifest.

Source

The source of these data is the records kept in one colonial port of entry – POE James River, Upper Part – by the administrative clerk of the port, the colonial naval officer, Lewis Burrell. His Manifest Book, June 2, 1773, to September 9, 1775, is in the Library of Virginia, Richmond. The analysis of data was prepared by Robert Polk Thomson, "The Tobacco Export of the Upper James River Naval District, 1773-75," *William and Mary Quarterly*, 3rd series, 18 (July 1961): 393-407.

Documentation

See the Appendixes to the essay in this chapter for a general discussion of the tables and the sources of the data, along with a key to abbreviations used in this chapter and general information on matters such as regional definitions, calendar differences, money, and weights and measures. Also see the text for Table Eg1038-1045 for a general note on the tobacco trade.

The table presents the total number of hogsheads of tobacco exported and their destinations monthly for 28 months from one of Virginia's most important POE, James River, Upper Part (that is, everything upriver from Jamestown).

In doing his job as clerk of the naval office, Burrell, like his colleagues at the other POE, kept a variety of records in addition to the naval officer shipping lists (NOSL) so often referenced in this chapter. From the manifests that ship captains submitted to him, Burrell copied into this "Manifest Book" all of the details of a ship, its projected voyage, and its cargo (for example, the number of tobacco hogsheads). John Mair, *Book-Keeping Methodiz'd: Or, A Methodical Treatise of Merchant-Accompts, According to the Italian Form . . .*, 7th edition (Printed by W. Sands, A. Murray, and J. Cochran, for W. Sands, A. Kincaid & J. Bell, and A. Donaldson, 1763), p. 408, defined "manifest" as "a note or memorial of a ship's cargo, shewing what is due to the master for freight from the several persons to whom the cargo belongs." Thomson extracted, organized, and analyzed this information. Reproduced here is only his Table I (Thomson, 1961, p. 402). William Bell Clark, William James Morgan, and Michael J. Crawford, editors, *Naval Documents of the American Revolution* (Naval History Division, 1964 to date), volume 1, pp. 1387-94, printed a truncated version of the Manifest Book, from December 10, 1774, on.

The table displays the volume of exports for part of 1773 and all of 1774 and 1775, the distribution among the British POE to which that tobacco was exported, and something of the seasonal character of the trade for the single largest Virginia port exporting tobacco. The export of tobacco from Virginia ended with the onset of nonexportation on September 10, 1775, which was agreed by the Continental Congress in the previous October as part of The Association. Upper James River alone accounted for almost a third of all tobacco imported into Great Britain. As Table Eg1046-1053 demonstrates, over the five years 1771-1775, British ports landed on average just over a hundred million pounds of tobacco annually. In 1774, at 1,047 pounds per hogsheads, the 25,847 hogsheads exported through Upper James River equaled 31.4 percent of that amount. In that same year, Glasgow merchants imported a total of 40,453 hogsheads of tobacco, of which Virginia counted for three quarters and Upper James River one quarter (counting Greenock as simply a holding port for Glasgow). [James Pagan], *Sketches of the History of Glasgow* (Robert Stuart, 1847), pp. 80-1 n.

Thomson's table presented only the number of hogsheads shipped. For the average weight of Virginia tobacco hogsheads during this period, see Lorena S. Walsh's data presented in the text for Table Eg275-284.

As a check on the data, Thomson compared the amounts recorded in the Manifest Book with what Burrell submitted in one of his extant NOSL (CO 5/1352, PRO/TNA). For the first quarter of 1774 (January 5 to April 4), the numbers from both agree completely with the exception of an additional four hogsheads recorded in the NOSL as exported coastwise to POE Piscataqua.

Thomson also compiled and presented comparable data from the NOSL for the first quarter of 1773 (T 1/498, folios 19 et seq., PRO/TNA).

London	1,577	Glasgow	3,715	Boston	7
Bristol	857	Greenock	0	Philadelphia	6
Falmouth	0	**Scotland**	**3,715**	**North America**	**13**
Hull	115				
Liverpool	1,049				
Whitehaven	290			**Grand Total**	**7,616**
England	**3,888**				

For the crop year 1766, POE James River, Upper Part, exported 8,234 hogsheads of tobacco to English and Welsh ports (2,470 of them to London) and 11,176 to Scottish ports, for a total of 19,410. *Virginia Gazette* (Purdie and Dixon), January 22, 1767, p. 3, column 1. See also the detailed listing of all goods exported through POE James River, Upper Part, year by year for 1764-1766 in *Virginia Gazette* (Purdie and Dixon), February 12, 1767, pp. 2-3.

TABLE Eg1152-1159 Tea exported from England, by importing colony: 1761-1775
Contributed by John J. McCusker

	Total	New England	New York	Pennsylvania	Virginia and Maryland	Carolina	Georgia	Florida
	Eg1152	Eg1153	Eg1154	Eg1155	Eg1156	Eg1157	Eg1158	Eg1159
Year	Pounds	Pounds	Pounds	Pounds	Pounds	Pounds	Pounds	Pounds
1761	56,110	6,992	3,837	144	22,244	22,893	0	0
1762	161,588	51,618	70,460	7,884	12,773	17,850	1,003	0
1763	188,785	37,525	83,870	18,281	23,481	22,860	2,768	0
1764	489,252	143,234	265,385	41,949	18,249	18,374	1,989	72
1765	518,424	175,389	226,232	54,538	23,280	36,067	2,918	0
1766	361,001	118,982	124,464	60,796	29,177	20,112	6,798	672
1767	480,376	152,435	177,111	87,741	36,088	24,261	2,325	415
1768	873,744	291,899	320,214	174,883	41,944	34,639	5,212	4,953
1769	229,439	86,004	4,282	81,729	37,355	12,982	4,426	2,661
1770	110,386	85,935	269	0	18,270	1,175	2,980	1,757
1771	362,257	282,857	1,035	495	32,961	36,385	5,420	3,104
1772	264,882	151,184	530	128	78,117	22,916	10,265	1,742
1773	739,221	206,312	208,385	208,191	26,491	83,959	5,070	813
1774	73,274	30,161	1,304	0	31,273	4,332	3,661	2,543
1775	22,198	8,005	0	0	8,825	0	0	5,368

TABLE Eg1152–1159   Tea exported from England, by importing colony: 1761–1775   *Continued*

Source

The source of the data is the Ledgers of Imports and Exports of England, 3/61-75, PRO/TNA.

Documentation

See the Appendixes to the essay in this chapter for a general discussion of the tables and the sources of the data, along with a key to abbreviations used in this chapter and general information on matters such as regional definitions, calendar differences, money, and weights and measures. Note that Florida is included here as part of British North America, but it was not one of the Thirteen Continental Colonies.

These figures show the annual total weight of all tea exported from England and Wales to the Thirteen Continental Colonies. Harper compiled the data as part of his 1930s Works Progress Administration program. The year of record ran from January 5 through January 4. It must be underscored that these data are the figures for exports from England, not figures for imports into the Thirteen Continental Colonies, as they have too often been described.

For the years 1768–1772, when fairly complete colonial import data and British export data are both available, a comparison of figures for the tea trade is possible. See Oliver M. Dickerson, *The Navigation Acts and the American Revolution* (University of Pennsylvania Press, 1951), pp. 87–91, 99–100 n. 80, which presents a compilation of the data from the Ledger of Imports and Exports, British North America, 1768–1772, CUST 16/1, PRO/TNA. The two sets of figures approximate each other closely, thus challenging claims that the colonists were engaged in the smuggling of tea during this period – at least from England. Contrast Arthur Meier Schlesinger, *The Colonial Merchants and the American Revolution, 1763–1776,* Columbia University Studies in History, Economics and Public Law, volume 78, number 182 (Columbia University, 1918), pp. 246-7.

TABLE Eg1160–1165   Rice exported from South Carolina and Georgia: 1698–1790[1]

Contributed by John J. McCusker

	Total		South Carolina			
	Weight	Quantity	Total	Charleston	Winyah (Georgetown) and Port Royal (Beaufort)	Georgia
	Eg1160	Eg1161	Eg1162	Eg1163	Eg1164	Eg1165
Year	Thousand pounds	Barrels	Barrels	Barrels	Barrels	Barrels
1698	10	—	—	—	—	—
1699	131	—	—	—	—	—
1700	394	—	—	—	—	—
1701	195	—	—	—	—	—
1702	613	—	—	—	—	—
1703	694	—	—	—	—	—
1704	760	—	—	—	—	—
1706	267	—	—	—	—	—
1707	561	—	—	—	—	—
1708	675	—	—	—	—	—
1709	1,511	—	—	—	—	—
1710	1,601	—	—	—	—	—
1711	1,181	—	—	—	—	—
1713	3,851	—	—	—	—	—
1714	3,139	—	—	—	—	—
1715	2,368	—	—	—	—	—
1716	4,585	—	—	—	—	—
1717	2,881	—	—	—	—	—
1718	2,957	—	—	—	—	—
1719	5,449	13,623	13,623	13,623	—	—
1720	6,486	—	—	—	—	—
1721	8,752	21,879	21,879	21,879	—	—
1722	9,424	23,559	23,559	23,559	—	—
1723	8,060	20,151	20,151	20,151	—	—
1724	8,654	—	—	—	—	—
1725	7,546	18,866	18,866	17,734	1,132	—
1726	10,045	24,501	24,501	23,031	1,470	—
1727	12,012	28,600	28,600	26,884	1,716	—
1728	13,707	31,878	31,878	29,965	1,913	—
1729	15,158	34,451	34,451	32,384	2,067	—
1730	19,973	44,385	44,385	41,722	2,663	—
1731	18,903	42,007	42,007	39,487	2,520	—
1732	17,745	39,434	39,434	37,068	2,366	—
1733	24,284	53,964	53,964	50,726	3,238	—
1734	14,516	32,259	32,259	30,323	1,936	—
1735	22,191	49,314	49,314	46,355	2,959	—
1736	25,358	56,352	56,352	52,971	3,381	—
1737	20,586	45,748	45,748	42,827	2,921	—
1738	16,432	36,515	36,515	34,324	2,191	—
1739	32,168	71,484	71,484	67,117	4,367	—

Note appears at end of table

(continued)

TABLE Eg1160-1165   Rice exported from South Carolina and Georgia: 1698-1790
Continued

	Total		South Carolina			
	Weight	Quantity	Total	Charleston	Winyah (Georgetown) and Port Royal (Beaufort)	Georgia
	Eg1160	Eg1161	Eg1162	Eg1163	Eg1164	Eg1165
Year	Thousand pounds	Barrels	Barrels	Barrels	Barrels	Barrels
1740	43,616	96,926	96,926	91,110	5,816	—
1741	39,308	86,391	86,006	80,846	5,160	385
1742	22,944	49,879	49,145	46,196	2,949	734
1743	36,317	78,102	78,102	73,416	4,686	—
1744	40,389	85,934	85,934	80,778	5,156	—
1745	30,131	63,433	63,433	59,627	3,806	—
1746	27,626	57,554	57,554	54,101	3,453	—
1747	26,360	54,351	54,351	51,090	3,261	—
1748	26,890	54,877	54,877	51,584	3,293	—
1749	24,216	48,921	48,921	45,986	2,935	—
1750	25,353	50,707	49,846	46,855	2,991	861
1751	32,751	64,854	87,076	81,852	5,225	—
1752	11,906	23,346	22,835	21,465	1,370	511
1753	28,943	56,200	55,248	51,933	3,315	952
1754	48,178	92,650	91,306	85,828	5,478	1,344
1755	52,707	100,395	98,096	92,210	5,886	2,299
1756	41,915	79,837	76,840	72,230	4,610	2,997
1757	36,752	70,003	67,005	62,985	4,020	2,998
1758	37,178	70,815	68,444	64,337	4,107	2,371
1759	31,929	60,818	57,215	53,782	3,433	3,603
1760	37,832	72,062	68,779	64,652	4,127	3,283
1761	56,217	107,081	102,415	96,270	6,145	4,666
1762	50,756	96,679	90,170	84,760	5,410	6,509
1763	61,945	117,990	110,288	103,671	6,617	7,702
1764	66,644	126,941	117,251	110,216	7,035	9,690
1765	60,394	115,037	102,813	96,644	6,169	12,224
1766	48,832	93,013	78,756	74,031	4,725	14,257
1767	64,077	122,052	110,771	104,125	6,646	11,281
1768	75,238	143,311	125,538	118,493	7,045	17,773
1769	69,469	132,322	115,582	108,682	6,900	16,740
1770	80,815	153,934	131,805	126,237	5,568	22,129
1771	78,951	150,383	125,151	119,942	5,209	25,232
1772	67,390	128,361	104,821	100,745	4,076	23,540
1773	86,469	164,704	135,043	126,940	8,103	29,661
1774	80,708	153,729	126,045	118,482	7,563	27,684
1783	—	—	26,935	24,255	2,680	—
1784	—	—	63,905	61,974	1,931	—
1785	—	—	66,862	63,732	3,130	—
1786	—	—	70,541	66,557	3,984	—
1787	—	—	—	65,195	—	—
1788	—	—	—	82,400	—	—
1789	—	—	—	100,000	—	—
1790	—	—	—	115,000	—	—

[1] Year of record and pounds per barrel varied over time; see text.

Sources

The sources of these data are the records kept in each of the colonial ports of entry (POE) by the administrative clerk of the port, the colonial naval officer. The original quarterly reports of the naval officers – the naval officer shipping lists (NOSL) – and various accounts based on them survive in many places, in many forms. The most important contemporary compilation of these reports was made under the direction of Thomas Irving, the Boston-based Inspector General of Imports and Exports of North America, and is known as the Ledger of Imports and Exports, British North America, 1768-1772, CUST 16/1, PRO/TNA. Two twentieth-century efforts attempted to assemble and compile the extant NOSL, the one organized in the 1930s by Lawrence A. Harper and his associates, the other in the 1970s, the work of Converse D. Clowse. See Clowse, *Measuring Charleston's Overseas Commerce, 1717-1767: Statistics from the Port's Naval Lists* (University Press of America, [1981]). Data in this table not otherwise accounted for here are drawn from these two sources. See Appendix A to the essay in this chapter, and the following comments.

For 1719 and 1721, see the report on the colony's production and export of rice prepared at the request of the Board of Trade by Francis Yonge, the colony's London agent, and sent in his letter to the Board of Trade, London, [February 5, 1722/23], CO 5/358, folios 272-9, PRO/TNA. See also [Francis Yonge], *A View of the Trade of South-Carolina, with Proposals Humbly Offer'd for Improving the Same* ([N.p.], 1723), p. 10. See also the letter from the Board of Trade to Yonge, December 7, 1722, CO 5/400, folio 155r, PRO/TNA.

For 1722-1723, see the account of William Hammerton, "Naval Officer," among the "Copies of Letters & papers &c. from Francis Nicholson Esqr. to Arthur Middleton Esqr. and Others concerning the Affairs of His Majties. Province of South Carolina," CO 5/387, folios 221v-222r, PRO/TNA.

For 1725-1742, figures newly compiled for this chapter, see *Port of Charles-Town in South-Carolina, November 1, 1736. An Account of Sundry Goods Imported, and of Sundry Goods of the Produce of This Province Exported, from the Year 1724,*

TABLE Eg1160–1165   Rice exported from South Carolina and Georgia: 1698–1790   *Continued*

to the Year 1735. With the Number of Vessels Entered and Cleared Each Year. And a Particular Account of the Last Year (Lewis Timothy, 1736); An Account of Sundry Goods Imported, and of Sundry Goods the Produce of this Province Exported, from the Several Ports of Charles-Town, George-Town, and Port-Royal, South-Carolina, from the First of November 1736, to the First of November 1737. With the Number of Vessels Entered and Cleared in Each Port (Lewis Timothy, 1738); Port of Charles-Town in South-Carolina. An Account of Sundry Goods Imported, and of Sundry Goods of the Produce of This Province Exported from this Port, from the First of November 1737, to the First of November 1738. With the Number of Vessels Entered Inwards, and from Whence Arriv'd, Cleared Outwards, and Where Bound (Lewis Timothy, 1738); South-Carolina. An Account of Sundry Goods Imported, and of Sundry Goods of the Province Exported, from the Several Ports within the Said Province, from the First of November 1738, to the First of November 1739. With the Number of Vessels Entered and Cleared at Each Port. As Also from Whence Arrived and Where Bound (Peter Timothy, 1739); and the associated handwritten accounts for the three years 1741–1742. All of these broadsides and the manuscript accounts are in the same volume: shelf mark Cup. 1247.n.69, Department of Printed Books, BL.

For POE Charleston, 1747–1765, the data from the NOSL are as compiled in the account enclosed in a letter from Governor Charles Montagu, at Charleston, to the Secretary of State, December 8, 1766, CO 5/390, folio 166r, PRO/TNA. There is a copy of the account in King's MS 206, folios 28r–29v, BL. For 1748, compare the figure in Governor James Glen's original report on South Carolina in the enclosure in his letter to the Board of Trade, Charleston, May 31, 1749, CO 5/461, folio 45v, PRO/TNA. It was printed in [James Glen], A Description of South Carolina; Containing, Many Curious and Interesting Particulars Relating to the Civil, Natural and Commercial History of That Colony, viz. The Succession of European Settlers There; . . . The Nature of the Climate; . . . The Culture and Produce of Rice, Indian Corn, and Indigo; . . . The State of Their Maritime Trade in the Years 1710, 1723, 1740 and 1748, with the Number or Tonnage of Shipping Employed . . . To Which Is Added, A Very Particular Account of Their Rice-Trade for Twenty Years, with Their Exports of Raw Silk and Imports of British Silk Manufactures for Twenty-Five Years (R. and J. Dodsley, 1761), pp. 50–5. Glen reported 55,000 barrels exported in 1748, a figure quite close to the estimated total in the table based on Montagu's number.

For South Carolina, 1783–1790, see the account in the letter from George Miller, at Charleston, to the Secretary of State for Foreign Affairs, January 28, 1790, BT 6/21, folios 311r–312r, PRO/TNA. Miller was the British consul at Charleston. What appears to have been the source of Miller's data is the "statistical accounts of exports [prepared for and sent] to the general assembly" of South Carolina by port officials copies of which can be found among the papers of the state legislature. See R[obert] Nicholas Olsberg and Helen Craig Carson, Duties on Trade at Charleston, 1784–1789, Pamphlet Accompanying South Carolina Archives Microcopy, number 6 (South Carolina Department of Archives and History, 1970), p. 11. Olsberg and Carson (pp. 18–21) presented the data for POE Charleston and POE Winyah (Georgetown) for 1783–1787 – though the numbers for the latter appear to have been only for part of the last year – and scattered returns for POE Port Royal for 1784–1786. The numbers for Charleston agree almost precisely with Miller's numbers, differing only for 1783 (22,224½ barrels) and for 1786 (65,857½ barrels) in ways that are obvious mistakes in copying. Compare John Drayton, A View of South-Carolina, as Respects Her Natural and Civil Concerns (W[illiam] P. Young, 1802), pp. 165–7, 173; and the data in Charles Gregg Singer, South Carolina in the Confederation (University of Pennsylvania Press, 1941), pp. 23–4.

Documentation

See the Appendixes to the essay in this chapter for a general discussion of the tables and the sources of the data, along with a key to abbreviations used in this chapter and general information on matters such as regional definitions, calendar differences, money, and weights and measures.

This table does two things in pursuit of as complete a picture as possible of rice exports from South Carolina and Georgia, the two major rice-producing colonies in British North America (and, afterward, the United States). It reports all available statistics for "clean," "merchantable" rice (not "rough" rice) exported from the four relevant POEs. It also attempts to formulate estimates of some of the missing values.

The statistics were recorded in terms of barrels; as with other staple commodities like tobacco and sugar, the size of the rice barrel was not constant

but grew larger over time. The conversion from barrels to pounds follows the protocol established in the text for Table Eg299. Note that rice was measured by the short hundredweight (100 pounds avoirdupois) in South Carolina and Georgia, and by the long hundredweight (112 pounds) in the northern Continental Colonies and in Great Britain.

By the end of the colonial period there were three POEs for South Carolina, Winyah (Georgetown), Charleston, and Port Royal (Beaufort); and two for Georgia, Savannah and Sunbury.

For 1698–1724, Harper calculated his figures on the assumption that, of the rice imported from the Thirteen Continental Colonies recorded in the English Inspector General's Ledgers of Imports and Exports, POE Charleston accounted for seven eighths of total exported. He based this calculation on the statement that this was the case in 1719 made by Francis Yonge, a member of the colonial Council and the colony's agent in London. See [Yonge], (1723), p. 10. Compare Yonge's submission by (almost) the same name – "A view of the Trade of S. Carolina, with proposals for improving the same" – to the Board of Trade, [February 5, 1722/23], CO 5/358, folios 272–279, PRO/TNA. Harper detected reinforcement for Yonge's suggestion in Edward Randolph's 1700 report that 10 percent of Charleston's exports went to the West Indies. See Randolph, at Charleston, to Board of Trade, May 27, 1700, CO 5/1260, folio 160r, PRO/TNA. Harper found corroboration of his calculations of Charleston exports in a comparison of them with English imports for 1717, 1718, 1719, and 1724. Exports for the transition period in 1698 – September 29 to December 24 – amounted to 1,597 pounds.

Hammerton's account for 1722 and 1723 distinguished between exports to Great Britain and "to the Plantations" (CO 5/387, folio 221v, PRO/TNA) as follows.

	To Great Britain	To Plantations	Total
1722	20,213	3,346	23,559
1723	16,878	3,273	20,151

In these two years, exports to Great Britain constituted about 85 percent of the total. His accounts further distinguished quantities exported coastwise colony by colony (CO 5/387, folio 222v, PRO/TNA). The largest portion, over 40 percent, went to Boston.

For most of the fifty years after 1724, with the exceptions noted here, Harper relied on the figures for POE Charleston developed from The South-Carolina Gazette (Charleston) by Charles Joseph Gayle, "The Nature and Volume of Exports from Charleston, 1724–1774," Proceedings of the South Carolina Historical Association [7] (1937): 30. When Gayle's figures were for less than twelve months (1750, 1756, 1757, 1763, and 1767), Harper extended the numbers to a full year, but on what basis does not appear. David L. Coon reviewed the table in Gayle, rechecking it against the original newspaper accounts that were Gayle's source, finding and correcting numerous errors and omissions. Compare the series presented with Coon's revised numbers for the years 1748, 1750–1752, 1754–1757, 1762–1765, in his The Development of Market Agriculture in South Carolina, 1670–1785 (Garland, 1989), pp. 349–51. The tables published in The South-Carolina Gazette are frequently for periods of less than a full year.

There are other data available to compare with the series presented here: for 1758, see the figures in The South-Carolina Gazette; for 1765, see the Charleston Year Book (1880) as copied in George K. Holmes, Rice Crop of the United States, 1712–1911, U.S. Department of Agriculture, Bureau of Statistics, Circular number 34 (U.S. Government Printing Office, 1912), p. 5; for 1766, see the Harper compilation of the POE Charleston NOSL; for 1768–1772, see CUST 16/1, PRO/TNA; for 1773 and 1774, see Lewis Cecil Gray, History of Agriculture in the Southern United States to 1860, Carnegie Institution of Washington, Publication number 430 (Carnegie Institution of Washington, 1933), volume 2, p. 1022. Harper extended Gray's partial figure for 1773 to complete the year. Compare the results of Harper's compilations with: J[ames] D. B. De Bow, The Industrial Resources, Statistics, Etc., of the United States, and More Particularly of the Southern and Western States: Embracing a View of Their Commerce, Agriculture, Manufactures, Internal Improvements, Slave and Free Labor, Slavery Institutions, Products, etc., of the South, Together with Historical and Statistical Sketches of the Different States and Cities of the Union, Statistics of the United States Commerce and Manufactures, from the Earliest Periods, Compared with Other Leading

(continued)

TABLE Eg1160-1165   Rice exported from South Carolina and Georgia: 1698-1790   *Continued*

Powers, The Results of the Different Census Returns since 1790, and Returns of the Census of 1850, on Population, Agriculture and Industry, etc., with an Appendix, 3rd edition (D. Appleton, 1854), volume 2, pp. 408–9; Gray (1933), volume 2, pp. 1020–3; Clowse (1981), pp. 57–8; Peter A. Coclanis, *The Shadow of a Dream: Economic Life and Death in the South Carolina Low Country, 1670–1720* (Oxford University Press, 1989); and Stephen G. Hardy, "Colonial South Carolina's Rice Industry and the Atlantic Economy: Patterns of Trade, Shipping, and Growth," in Jack P. Greene, Rosemary Brana-Shute, and Randy J. Sparks, editors, *Money, Trade, and Power: The Evolution of Colonial South Carolina's Plantation Society* (University of South Carolina Press, 2001), pp. 112–44. De Bow (1854), volume 2, pp. 409–10, continues the series through the mid-nineteenth century.

Compare, for the years running from June 24, 1748, through June 21, 1773, the annual exports of rice from POE Charleston published in *The South-Carolina Gazette,* June 21, 1773.

George Miller's account reported export data for 1783-1788. For 1789, he stated that the "returns . . . [had] not yet [been] brought up [but] the Rice will amount to near 100,000 Barrels." For "the Crop of 1789, the Shipping of which is just commenced, [the amount will be] about 115,000 Barrels of Rice." BT 6/21, folio 312r, PRO/TNA. Compare the account of rice exported from Charleston in 1785 as published in *The Pennsylvania Packet, and Daily Advertiser* (Philadelphia), March 20, 1786: 60,442 barrels, 6,542 half-barrels, equal to a total of 6,173 barrels.

Of considerable interest is Yonge's extrapolation based on his report to the Board of Trade, London, December 10, 1722, CO 5/358, folios 200v, PRO/TNA. See [Yonge], (1723), p. 10. According to him, the colony exported 13,623 barrels of rice in 1719 and 21,879 barrels in 1721. He allowed 800 barrels annually for domestic consumption and then calculated the average production in these years at 4,607 tons of rice. At his figure of 400 pounds per barrel, this suggests an annual average domestic consumption in South Carolina of roughly 15 pounds per person, white and black.

For South Carolina's two other POEs, it is necessary to estimate their exports for almost every year. POE Port Royal was established sometime after 1722, and POE Winyah was established in 1732, both of them carved out of territory that was previously part of POE Charleston. Even though few NOSL survive for either POE, some contemporary compilations from these same records help serve as the basis of the estimates. In 1737, POE Winyah exported 1,143 barrels, and POE Port Royal, 1,778 barrels – in the same period that POE Charleston witnessed the equivalent of 45,748 barrels exported. In 1739, POE Winyah exported 2,202 barrels and POE Port Royal, 2,165 barrels – in the same period that POE Charleston witnessed 67,117 barrels exported. See *An Account of Sundry Goods Imported, and of Sundry Goods the Produce of this Province Exported, from the Several Ports of Charles-Town, George-Town, and Port-Royal, South-Carolina, from the First of November 1736, to*

the First of November 1737. With the Number of Vessels Entered and Cleared in Each Port (Lewis Timothy, 1738); and *South-Carolina. An Account of Sundry Goods Imported, and of Sundry Goods of the Province Exported, from the Several Ports within the Said Province, from the First of November 1738, to the First of November 1739. With the Number of Vessels Entered and Cleared at Each Port. As Also from Whence Arrived and Where Bound* (Peter Timothy, 1739). Obviously, POE Charleston dominated the export trade of the colony; in these two years, the other POE averaged about 6.25 percent of the quantity that POE Charleston exported. For the period 1768-1772, the next time we have fully comparable data, Charleston's domination had increased. CUST 16/1, PRO/TNA. On average for these five years, POE Winyah and POE Port Royal exported 4.8 percent of Charleston's share. For the four postwar years, 1783-1786, the figure was 5.8 percent. Crudely put, one can say that during the years 1736-1786, POE Charleston accounted for 94 percent – and POE Port Royal and POE Winyah, 6 percent – of rice exported from South Carolina. Estimates of the rice exported from these two POE have been derived on this basis for all years 1725 and after, other than 1737, 1739, and 1768-1772.

Concerning these two POE, the British consul, George Miller, commented, "The exports from George Town and Beaufort are too inconsiderable to demand particular attention, as it is well understood that the imports of Rice &c. into Charleston from Georgia, are nearly on an equality with the exports of the same Articles from the two former ports." Letter from George Miller, at Charleston, to the Secretary of State for Foreign Affairs, January 28, 1790, BT 6/21, folios 308r-308v, PRO/TNA.

The Georgia rice export figures were compiled and certified by William Brown, Comptroller of POE, Savannah, March 1, 1773: "An Aggregate and Valuation of Exports of Produce from the Province of Georgia . . . 1754 to 1773." The table was printed in Bernard Romans, *A Concise Natural History of East and West Florida . . .* (Published by the author, 1775), opposite p. 104.; and in [George Walton, William Few, and Richard Howly], *Observations upon the Effects of Certain Late Political Suggestions* (Robert Aitken, 1781), p. 11. The estimated figures for 1773 and 1774 are based on the assumption that in those two years Georgia exported the same proportion of the amount exported by South Carolina, as was the case in 1772 (23.4 percent).

The year of record used by the Customs ended as follows: in 1698, on September 28; in 1699-1751, on December 24 (with the exceptions noted later); in 1752 and after, on January 4 of the following year. The exceptions are: for 1722-1723, the year ran from September 29 through September 28; and for the newly compiled figures for 1725-1742, the accounts were said to have run from November 1 to November 1 of their respective years – the crop year. The "crop year" was rarely coterminus with the Customs year. See, for example, George Miller's account of exports for the years 1783-1788 and, as he noted, for crop years 1782-1787 (BT 6/21, folios 311r-312r, PRO/TNA). See also the text for Table Eg474-513.

TABLE Eg1166–1170 Rice exported from Charleston, by destination: 1717–1772[1]

Contributed by John J. McCusker

Year	Total Eg1166 Barrels	Great Britain Eg1167 Barrels	Iberian Peninsula and the Mediterranean Sea region Eg1168 Barrels	Other colonies in British North America Eg1169 [2] Barrels	West Indies Eg1170 [2] Barrels
1717	10,849	7,530	—	1,985	1,334
1718	8,309	6,090	—	992	1,227
1719	14,010	9,157	—	3,206	1,647
1720	14,584	11,904	—	1,399	1,281
1722	23,559	20,213	—	2,057	1,289
1723	20,151	16,878	—	2,348	925
1724	20,165	16,682	—	2,199	1,284
1731	48,238	38,168	6,403	1,737	1,930
1732	39,111	26,589	9,458	1,460	1,604
1734	37,126	24,931	10,600	552	1,043
1735	44,356	27,795	15,020	677	864
1736	50,678	37,274	11,591	775	1,038
1737	36,505	31,152	4,278	461	614
1738	32,251	27,236	3,852	546	617
1758	64,122	40,736	12,424	5,149	5,813
1759	52,680	29,551	14,758	2,979	5,392
1760	63,038	32,188	15,144	6,221	9,485
1762	85,209	39,547	11,014	12,387	22,261
1763	104,394	56,359	14,342	16,194	17,499
1764	101,841	58,930	16,206	7,463	19,244
1766	92,492	45,210	28,251	4,283	14,748
1768	118,910	76,182	30,027	—[3]	12,701
1769	116,250	61,825	31,755	3,891	18,779
1770	133,314	56,980	34,429	8,574	33,331
1771	126,906	74,297	15,875	9,433	27,301
1772	108,015	74,521	9,708	5,879	17,907

[1] Data are for various terminal dates, primarily December 24, January 4 (of the following year), and October 31; see text.

[2] For 1758 and 1762–1766, exports to Bermuda and the Bahamas – included with the West Indies in the source – are presented here under series Eg1169 in order to ensure comparability with data from 1768 to 1772.

[3] Omitted in the source, perhaps as a result of a clerical error.

Sources

The sources of these data are the records kept in each of the colonial ports of entry (POE) by the administrative clerk of the port, the colonial naval officer. The original quarterly reports of the naval officers – the naval officer shipping lists (NOSL) – and various accounts based on them survive in many places, in many forms. The most important contemporary compilation of these reports was made under the direction of Thomas Irving, the Boston-based Inspector General of Imports and Exports of North America, and is known as the Ledger of Imports and Exports, British North America, 1768–1772, CUST 16/1, PRO/TNA. They were compiled by Converse D. Clowse, *Measuring Charleston's Overseas Commerce, 1717–1767: Statistics from the Port's Naval Lists* (University Press of America, 1981), pp. 59–64.

For 1722–1723, see the account of William Hammerton, "Naval Officer," among the "Copies of Letters & papers &c. from Francis Nicholson Esqr. to Arthur Middleton Esqr. and Others concerning the Affairs of His Majties. Province of South Carolina," CO 5/387, folios 221v–222r, PRO/TNA.

For 1764, see the account for the year November 2, 1763, to November 1, 1764, in *The South-Carolina Gazette*, November 5, 1764. This account specifies the destinations in considerable detail.

Documentation

See the Appendixes to the essay in this chapter for a general discussion of the tables and the sources of the data, along with a key to abbreviations used in this chapter and general information on matters such as regional definitions, calendar differences, money, and weights and measures.

These series report on the quantities of "clean," "merchantable" rice (not "rough" rice) exported from Charleston to various markets. For a discussion of this source and related records, see the text for Table Eg1160–1165. The tables in Clowse (1981), pp. 59–64, offer considerable detail within each of the categories used here.

The statistics were recorded in terms of barrels; as with other staple commodities like tobacco and sugar, the size of the rice barrel was not constant but grew larger over time. The conversion from barrels to pounds follows the protocol established in the text for Table Eg299. Note that rice was measured by the short hundredweight (100 pounds avoirdupois) in South Carolina and Georgia, and by the long hundredweight (112 pounds) in the northern Continental Colonies and in Great Britain.

Series Eg1166. There is no obvious explanation for the difference between these figures and those found in the Harper compilation, series Eg1163, other than the different sources employed. Clowse does not address the issue.

The number of barrels exported from Charleston "to the Plantations" in 1723 does not add up to the total shown. Presumably, the defect is in the number of barrels exported to Barbados, which should have been 381 rather than 308. CO 5/387, folio 222r, PRO/TNA.

TABLE Eg1171–1173   Pitch, tar, and turpentine exported from Charleston: 1712–1787[1]

Contributed by John J. McCusker

| | Pitch | Tar | Turpentine | | Pitch | Tar | Turpentine | | Pitch | Tar | Turpentine |
| | Eg1171 | Eg1172 | Eg1173 | | Eg1171 | Eg1172 | Eg1173 | | Eg1171 | Eg1172 | Eg1173 |
Year	Barrels	Barrels	Barrels	Year	Barrels	Barrels	Barrels	Year	Barrels	Barrels	Barrels
1712	4,580	2,037	—	1740	10,260	2,374	562	1760	6,315	1,646	2,834
1717	14,363	29,594	669	1741	12,694	1,925	2,159	1761 [2]	6,626	1,438	4,874
1718	20,208	32,007	605	1742	15,808	3,115	1,965	1762	4,924	2,052	1,878
1719	17,489	25,495	1,245	1743	9,755	2,206	2,012	1763 [2]	5,221	2,461	2,793
1720	24,453	10,025	75	1744	7,678	17,552	1,245	1764	7,459	3,158	1,643
1721	11,213	12,288	—	1745	8,823	1,286	988	1765 [2]	8,751	2,575	653
1722	13,536	17,434	—	1746	18,016	1,519	4,262	1767 [2]	15,612	4,224	3,674
1723	28,609	13,603	—	1747	13,737	4,422	5,162	1768 [3]	6,948	2,276	5,761
1724	32,720	12,220	469	1748	5,521	3,075	2,397	1769	5,256	5,127	3,201
1725	57,422	2,333	113	1749	7,796	3,765	1,582	1770	4,133	2,938	1,335
1726	29,776	8,322	715	1750 [2]	11,157	3,858	812	1771	7,429	3,401	1,353
1727	13,654	10,950	1,252	1751	11,441	5,070	1,401	1772	4,125	5,723	864
1728	3,186	2,269	1,232	1752	20,483	2,651	6,271	1774	4,326	3,266	3,282
1729	8,377	3,441	1,913	1753	15,220	6,008	6,496	1783	565	540	926
1730	10,825	2,014	1,073	1754	11,025	2,664	5,375	1784	4,877	2,489	7,331
1731	9,385	1,725	1,560	1755	5,869	3,143	2,171	1785	3,719	6,737	6,545
1732	32,593	4,575	2,466	1756 [2]	3,058	3,781	1,195	1786	3,789	5,056	6,628
1733	18,283	6,027	2,313	1757 [2]	4,962	2,500	337	1787	1,904	2,230	3,707
1734	28,874	7,336	4,552	1758	2,592	2,054	916				
1735	24,056	5,636	8,061	1759	7,250	2,426	1,744				
1736	11,836	1,491	5,192								
1737	11,987	8,501	4,411								
1738	16,788	5,417	845								
1739	7,890	2,722	33								

[1] Year of record varied over time; see text.

[2] Data cover only part of a year: 1750, 1761, and 1763, 11 months; 1756, 9 months; 1757 and 1765, 7 months; and 1767, 10 months.

[3] Exports coastwise to British North America omitted in the source, perhaps as a result of a clerical error.

Sources

The source of these data is the records kept in each of the colonial ports of entry (POE) by the administrative clerk of the port, the colonial naval officer. The original quarterly reports of the South Carolina naval officers – the naval officer shipping lists (NOSL) – and various accounts based on them survive in many places, in many forms. Important for South Carolina were the regular summaries of these accounts published in the Charleston newspapers, especially *The South-Carolina Gazette*. The most significant contemporary compilation of the NOSL was made under the direction of Thomas Irving, the Boston-based Inspector General of Imports and Exports of North America, and is known as the Ledger of Imports and Exports, British North America, 1768–1772, CUST 16/1, PRO/TNA. They are reported here from two twentieth-century efforts to assemble and compile the extant NOSL. One set of these data was collected by Lawrence A. Harper and others, as discussed in Appendix A to the essay in this chapter. The second set of data is as gathered in Converse D. Clowse, *Measuring Charleston's Overseas Commerce, 1717–1767: Statistics from the Port's Naval Lists* (University Press of America, 1981), pp. 65–9. Data in this table not otherwise accounted for below are drawn from these two sources.

For 1722–1723, see the account of William Hammerton, "Naval Officer," among the "Copies of Letters & papers &c. from Francis Nicholson Esqr. to Arthur Middleton Esqr. and Others concerning the Affairs of His Majties. Province of South Carolina," CO 5/387, folios 221v–222r, PRO/TNA. Clowse (1981, p. 65) assigns these data to the wrong years. See also Clowse, "The Charleston Export Trade, 1717–1737" (Ph.D. dissertation, Northwestern University, 1963), pp. 197–8.

For 1725–1742, these data are newly compiled for this chapter, from *Port of Charles-Town in South-Carolina, November 1, 1736. An Account of Sundry Goods Imported, and of Sundry Goods of the Produce of This Province Exported, from the Year 1724, to the Year 1735. With the Number of Vessels Entered and Cleared Each Year.*

And a Particular Account of the Last Year (Lewis Timothy, 1736); *An Account of Sundry Goods Imported, and of Sundry Goods the Produce of this Province Exported, from the Several Ports of Charles-Town, George-Town, and Port-Royal, South-Carolina, from the First of November 1736, to the First of November 1737. With the Number of Vessels Entered and Cleared in Each Port* (Lewis Timothy, 1738); *Port of Charles-Town in South-Carolina. An Account of Sundry Goods Imported, and of Sundry Goods of the Produce of This Province Exported from this Port, from the First of November 1737, to the First of November 1738. With the Number of Vessels Entered Inwards, and from Whence Arriv'd, Cleared Outwards, and Where Bound* ([Lewis Timothy, 1738]); *South-Carolina. An Account of Sundry Goods Imported, and of Sundry Goods of the Province Exported, from the Several Ports within the Said Province, from the First of November 1738, to the First of November 1739. With the Number of Vessels Entered and Cleared at Each Port. As Also from Whence Arrived and Where Bound* (Peter Timothy, 1739); and the associated handwritten accounts for the three years 1741–1742. (There are misprints in the reporting of the number of barrels of tar exported in 1736 and 1738; they are corrected here.) All of these broadsides and the manuscript accounts are in the same volume: shelf mark Cup. 1247.n.69, Department of Printed Books, BL.

The figures for POE Charleston, 1748, are from Governor James Glen's original report on South Carolina for which see the enclosure in his letter to the Board of Trade, Charleston, May 31, 1749, CO 5/461, folios 45r–45v, PRO/TNA. The report was printed in [James Glen], *A Description of South Carolina; Containing, Many Curious and Interesting Particulars Relating to the Civil, Natural and Commercial History of That Colony, viz. The Succession of European Settlers There; ... The Nature of the Climate; ... The Culture and Produce of Rice, Indian Corn, and Indigo; ... The State of Their Maritime Trade in the Years 1710, 1723, 1740 and 1748, with the Number or Tonnage of Shipping Employed ... To Which Is Added, A Very Particular Account of Their Rice-Trade for Twenty Years, with Their Exports of Raw Silk and Imports of British Silk Manufactures for Twenty-Five Years* (R. and J. Dodsley, 1761).

For 1768–1772, the data come from CUST 16/1, PRO/TNA.

For POE Charleston, 1774, see the account for the year November 12, 1773, to November 7, 1774, in *The South-Carolina Gazette*, November 25, 1774.

TABLE Eg1171–1173   Pitch, tar, and turpentine exported from Charleston: 1712–1787   *Continued*

For POE Charleston, 1783–1787, see R[obert] Nicholas Olsberg and Helen Craig Carson, *Duties on Trade at Charleston, 1784–1789*, Pamphlet Accompanying South Carolina Archives Microcopy, number 6 (South Carolina Department of Archives and History, [1970]), p. 18, based on "statistical accounts of exports [prepared by and sent] to the general assembly" of South Carolina by port officials copies of which can be found among the papers of the state legislature (p. 11). The numbers for 1783 agree almost precisely with the account in the letter from George Miller, at Charleston, to the Secretary of State for Foreign Affairs, January 28, 1790, BT 6/21, folios 311r–312r, PRO/TNA. Miller was the British consul at Charleston. The only difference is the number of barrels of turpentine (936), an obvious mistake in copying. Compare the data in Charles Gregg Singer, *South Carolina in the Confederation* (University of Pennsylvania, 1941), pp. 23–4. See also Tables Eg1027–1032, Eg1160–1165, and Eg1174–1179.

Documentation

See the Appendixes to the essay in this chapter for a general discussion of the tables and the sources of the data, along with a key to abbreviations used in this chapter and general information on such matters as regional definitions, calendar differences, money, and weights and measures. Except as noted, the year of record was as follows: for 1712–1751, ending December 24; and thereafter, January 4 of the following year. The exceptions are as follows: for 1722–1723, the year ran from September 29 through September 28; for the figures newly compiled here for 1725–1742 and 1747, the accounts were said to have run from November 1 to November 1 of their respective years; and in some instances (see footnotes), only a partial year's worth of data is included. See also the text for Table Eg474–513.

These series report the number of barrels exported of these three related products – "naval stores" – from Charleston. Where there are data for both "common tar" and "green tar," the numbers have been combined. "Regular tar or common tar was the usual grade shipped . . . . This product came from pine trees which had been cut for some time; green tar was made from recently-cut trees and was supposedly of superior quality." Clowse (1981), p. 66 n. Clowse's tables offer considerable detail within each of the categories used here.

The capacity of the barrels used to ship pitch, tar, and turpentine conformed in size to the 31.5 gallons stipulated in the legislation that enacted a bounty on the importation of these commodities from the colonies into England. Act of 3 and 4 Anne, c. 9 (1704). Thus the South Carolina legislature soon passed a law, December 18, 1714, that raised the legal gauge for such casks to 32 gallons (from the earlier legislated minimum of 28 gallons [1691; 1703]). Thomas Cooper and David J. McCord, editors, *The Statutes at Large of South Carolina*, 10 volumes (A. S. Johnson, 1836–1841), volume 2, pp. 615–7. Compare Helen Louise Klopfer, "Statistics of the Foreign Trade of Philadelphia, 1700–1860" (Ph.D. dissertation, University of Pennsylvania, 1936), pp. 71, 80–1, 97, and elsewhere.

Hammerton's account for 1722 and 1723 distinguished between exports to Great Britain and "to the Plantations" (CO 5/387, folio 221v, PRO/TNA) as follows:

		To Great Britain	To plantations	Total
1722	Pitch	10,163	1,050	11,213
	Tar	10,266	2,022	12,288
1723	Pitch	12,060	1,476	13,536
	Tar	15,792	1,642	17,434

For most of the fifty years after 1724 Harper relied on the figures for POE Charleston developed from *The South-Carolina Gazette* (Charleston) by Charles Joseph Gayle, "The Nature and Volume of Exports from Charleston, 1724–1774," *Proceedings of the South Carolina Historical Association* [7] (1937): 31. Questions have been raised about the errors and omissions in Gayle's tables but they have not been resolved for these series. In the instance of his

data for 1773 and 1774, Gayle's data are so suspect as to have been omitted from this table.

Compare the annual total numbers of barrels of naval stores exported from POE Charleston, 1747–1765, in the account enclosed in a letter from Gov. Charles Montagu, at Charleston, to the Secretary of State, 8 December 1766, CO 5/390, folio 166r, PRO/TNA. There is a copy of the account in King's MS 206, folios 28r–29v, BL. Although the numbers for each year vary slightly from the total of the three series in the table, the grand totals for the nineteen years in each of the two accounts differ by less than six tenths of one percent. The annual differences are probably owing to different reporting periods.

For the year 1768, the data are the same as set down in the account in *The South Carolina and American General Gazette*, September 2, 1768, as enclosed with and commented upon in the letter from Lt. Gov. William Bull, at Charleston, to Secretary of State, September 6, 1768, CO 5/379, folios 56r, 60r–60v, PRO/TNA.

The same sources noted above for the period 1725–1742 twice reported the numbers of barrels of the commodities exported from the other two South Carolina POE as follows:

Year	Port	Pitch	Tar	Turpentine
1737	POE Winyah	2,630	3,984	2,194
	POE Beaufort	0	18	0
1739	POE Winyah	205	22	0
	POE Beaufort	0	0	0

See *An Account of Sundry Goods Imported, and of Sundry Goods the Produce of this Province Exported, from the Several Ports of Charles-Town, George-Town, and Port-Royal, South-Carolina, from the First of November 1736, to the First of November 1737. With the Number of Vessels Entered and Cleared in Each Port* (Lewis Timothy, 1738); and *South-Carolina. An Account of Sundry Goods Imported, and of Sundry Goods of the Province Exported, from the Several Ports within the Said Province, from the First of November 1738, to the First of November 1739. With the Number of Vessels Entered and Cleared at Each Port. As Also from Whence Arrived and Where Bound* (Peter Timothy, 1739).

Olsberg and Carson, *Duties on Trade at Charleston*, pp. 19–21, also presented data for POE Winyah (Georgetown) for 1783–1787 – though the numbers for the latter appear to have been only for part of the last year – and scattered returns for POE Port Royal for 1784–1786:

Year	Port	Pitch	Tar	Turpentine
1783	POE Winyah	3,711	221	0
	POE Beaufort	0	0	0
1784	POE Winyah	1,234	120	401
	POE Beaufort	0	0	0
1785	POE Winyah	1,654	286	1,380
	POE Beaufort	0	0	0
1786	POE Winyah	266	55	778
	POE Beaufort	0	0	0

It must also be noted that North Carolina was by far the largest producer and exporter of naval stores among the Thirteen Continental Colonies. A tabulation of the commodities "Exported from North-Carolina, within the Year 1753," indicated 12,055 barrels of pitch, 61,528 barrels of tar, and 10,429 barrels of turpentine. "Account of the British Plantations in America," *London Magazine* 22 (August 1757): 400. In other words North Carolina was responsible for three quarters of the total number of barrels of these commodities in that year. Of the total number of barrels of pitch, tar, and turpentine exported from the two Carolinas in 1768–1771, North Carolina accounted for more than 90 percent. See Harry Roy Merrens, *Colonial North Carolina in the Eighteenth Century: A Study in Historical Geography* (University of North Carolina Press, 1964), pp. 90–1.

TABLE Eg1174–1179   Timber and timber products exported from Charleston and Savannah: 1717–1787[1]

Contributed by John J. McCusker

	Charleston			Savannah		
	Lumber	Shingles	Staves	Timber	Shingles	Staves
	Eg1174	Eg1175	Eg1176	Eg1177	Eg1178	Eg1179
Year	Board feet	Number	Number	Board feet	Number	Number
1717	14,000	24,000	34,600	—	—	—
1718	19,000	10,000	7,600	—	—	—
1719	13,000	—	—	—	—	—
1720	14,000	12,000	68,100	—	—	—
1724	24,000	60,000	15,400	—	—	—
1725	53,635	31,700	114,630	—	—	—
1726	55,694	93,000	202,628	—	—	—
1727	80,606	141,800	199,760	—	—	—
1728	39,900	136,600	194,210	—	—	—
1729	220,901	292,263	226,255	—	—	—
1730	67,023	75,000	72,454	—	—	—
1731	74,870	63,600	38,340	—	—	—
1732	124,850	95,300	70,510	—	—	—
1733	111,410	240,000	78,700	—	—	—
1734	197,000	134,000	113,875	—	—	—
1735	221,077	21,900	116,985	—	—	—
1736	204,690	206,300	95,350	—	—	—
1737	245,739	95,000	53,214	—	—	—
1738	411,378	330,000	60,300	—	—	—
1739	133,890	42,600	42,200	—	—	—
1747	649,230	—	195,644	—	—	—
1748	475,984	635,170	70,832	—	—	—
1749	425,485	—	89,863	—	—	—
1750	613,380	—	117,442	—	—	—
1751	160,144	—	59,615	—	—	—
1752	588,023	—	41,666	—	—	—
1753	450,564	—	115,282	—	—	—
1754	732,309	822,120	171,631	—	—	—
1755	286,718	952,880	170,412	387,849	240,690	203,225
1756 [2]	376,326	522,420	115,860	289,843	263,000	196,259
1757 [2]	224,893	664,100	136,235	270,396	178,400	182,268
1758	780,761	976,000	148,321	50,215	68,985	63,330
1759	936,506	1,319,000	176,332	278,066	808,580	102,959
1760	718,166	1,550,000	167,872	283,961	581,200	80,500
1761	452,960	1,354,500	237,547	307,690	606,650	50,969
1762	169,664	1,037,000	170,830	417,449	685,265	325,477
1763	863,721	1,506,000	384,662	917,384	1,470,120	594,356
1764	1,006,341	1,553,365	272,995	1,043,535	2,061,151	423,251
1765 [2]	1,119,856	—	307,284	1,879,454	3,722,050	661,416
1766	1,249,000	1,574,000	139,500	2,101,466	2,036,947	737,898
1767 [2]	450,118	1,717,800	240,813	1,767,199	2,570,725	748,166
1768	747,000	2,208,000	336,600	1,787,258	3,669,477	806,609
1769	777,000	1,924,000	207,500	1,634,331	3,474,588	747,903
1770	436,000	1,327,000	161,500	1,805,992	2,896,991	466,276
1771	616,000	1,188,000	132,000	2,159,072	2,224,598	403,253
1772	701,000	884,000	174,600	2,163,582	3,525,930	988,791
1774	441,580	1,612,520	137,100	—	—	—
1783	251,000	215,800	12,900	—	—	—
1784	705,200	1,072,000	402,100	—	—	—
1785	1,072,650	3,096,900	403,050	—	—	—
1786	1,758,100	3,104,200	836,300	—	—	—
1787	1,057,600	3,689,600	1,023,700	—	—	—

[1] Year of record varied over time; see text.

[2] Charleston data cover only part of a year, but see text: 1756, 9 months; 1757 and 1767, 10 months; and 1765, 7 months.

Sources

The sources of these data are the records kept in each of the colonial ports of entry (POE) by the administrative clerk of the port, the colonial naval officer.

The original quarterly reports of the South Carolina and Georgia naval officers – the naval officer shipping lists (NOSL) – and various accounts based on them survive in many places, in many forms. The most important contemporary compilation of these reports was made under the direction of Thomas Irving, the Boston-based Inspector General of Imports and Exports of North America, and is known as the Ledger of Imports and Exports, British North

TABLE Eg1174–1179   Timber and timber products exported from Charleston and Savannah: 1717–1787   *Continued*

America, 1768–1772, CUST 16/1, PRO/TNA. Two twentieth-century efforts attempted to assemble and compile the extant NOSL, the one organized in the 1930s by Lawrence A. Harper and his associates, the other in the 1970s, the work of Converse D. Clowse. See Clowse, *Measuring Charleston's Overseas Commerce, 1717–1767: Statistics from the Port's Naval Lists* (University Press of America, 1981). Data in this table not otherwise accounted for here are drawn from these two sources.

For 1725–1739, the data are newly compiled for this chapter, from *Port of Charles-Town in South-Carolina, November 1, 1736 An Account of Sundry Goods Imported, and of Sundry Goods of the Produce of This Province Exported, from the Year 1724, to the Year 1735. With the Number of Vessels Entered and Cleared Each Year. And a Particular Account of the Last Year* (Lewis Timothy, 1736); *An Account of Sundry Goods Imported, and of Sundry Goods the Produce of This Province Exported, from the Several Ports of Charles-Town, George-Town, and Port-Royal, South-Carolina, from the First of November 1736, to the First of November 1737. With the Number of Vessels Entered and Cleared in Each Port* (Lewis Timothy, 1738); *Port of Charles-Town in South-Carolina. An Account of Sundry Goods Imported, and of Sundry Goods of the Produce of This Province Exported from this Port, from the First of November 1737, to the First of November 1738. With the Number of Vessels Entered Inwards, and from Whence Arriv'd, Cleared Outwards, and Where Bound* (Lewis Timothy, 1738); and *South-Carolina. An Account of Sundry Goods Imported, and of Sundry Goods of the Province Exported, from the Several Ports within the Said Province, from the First of November 1738, to the First of November 1739. With the Number of Vessels Entered and Cleared at Each Port. As Also from Whence Arrived and Where Bound* (Peter Timothy, 1739). All of these broadsides are in the same volume: shelf mark Cup. 1247.n.69, Department of Printed Books, BL.

For POE Charleston, 1747–1765, the data from the NOSL are as compiled in the account enclosed in a letter from Governor Charles Montagu, at Charleston, to the Secretary of State, December 8, 1766, CO 5/390, folio 166r, PRO/TNA. There is a copy of the account in King's MS 206, folios 28r–29v, BL. For POE Charleston, the number of shingles exported in 1748 is as stated in Governor James Glen's original report on South Carolina for which see the enclosure in his letter to the Board of Trade, Charleston, May 31, 1749, CO 5/461, folio 45r, PRO/TNA. The report was printed in [James Glen], *A Description of South Carolina; Containing, Many Curious and Interesting Particulars Relating to the Civil, Natural and Commercial History of That Colony, viz. The Succession of European Settlers There; . . . The Nature of the Climate; . . . The Culture and Produce of Rice, Indian Corn, and Indigo; . . . The State of Their Maritime Trade in the Years 1710, 1723, 1740 and 1748, with the Number or Tonnage of Shipping employed . . . To Which Is Added, a Very Particular Account of Their Rice-Trade for Twenty Years, with Their Exports of Raw Silk and Imports of British Silk Manufactures for Twenty-Five Years* (R. and J. Dodsley, 1761).

For POE Charleston, 1774, see the account for the year November 12, 1773, to November 7, 1774, in *The South-Carolina Gazette*, November 25, 1774.

For POE Charleston, 1783–1787, see R[obert] Nicholas Olsberg and Helen Craig Carson, *Duties on Trade at Charleston, 1784–1789*, Pamphlet Accompanying South Carolina Archives Microcopy, number 6 (South Carolina Department of Archives and History, [1970]), p. 18, based on "statistical accounts of exports [prepared by and sent] to the general assembly" of South Carolina by port officials copies of which can be found among the papers of the state legislature (p. 11). The numbers for 1783 agree almost precisely with the account in the letter from George Miller, at Charleston, to the Secretary of State for Foreign Affairs, January 28, 1790, BT 6/21, folios 311r–312r, PRO/TNA. Miller was the British consul at Charleston. The only difference is the amount of timber (215,800), an obvious mistake in copying. Compare the data in Charles Gregg Singer, *South Carolina in the Confederation* ([University of Pennsylvania], 1941), pp. 23–4. See also Tables Eg1027–1032, Eg1160–1165, and Eg1171–1173.

The Georgia export figures, 1755–1772, were compiled and certified by William Brown, Comptroller of POE, Savannah, March 1, 1773: "An Aggregate and Valuation of Exports of Produce from the Province of Georgia . . . 1754 to 1773." The table was printed in Bernard Romans, *A Concise Natural History of East and West Florida . . .* (Published by the author,

1775), opposite p. 104; and in [George Walton, William Few, and Richard Howly], *Observations upon the Effects of Certain Late Political Suggestions* (Robert Aitken, 1781), p. 11.

Documentation

See the Appendixes to the essay in this chapter for a general discussion of the tables and the sources of the data, along with a key to abbreviations used in this chapter and general information on matters such as regional definitions, calendar differences, money, and weights and measures. Except where noted otherwise, the year of record ended December 24 for 1717–1751; and January 4 thereafter. The figures newly compiled here for 1725–1742 and 1747 are all from accounts that were said to have run from November 1 to November 1 of their respective years. Even though, as noted, the dating for several of the years suggests something less than a full year's accounting, it is highly likely that the export data represent a full year's exports. See also the text for Tables Eg474–513, Eg1027–1032, and Eg1160–1165.

These data record the quantities of timber products exported from the major POE of South Carolina and Georgia. While South Carolina had three POE and Georgia two, POE Charleston and POE Savannah accounted for most of the exports of both colonies. The earliest South Carolina accounts distinguish among "Pine and Cypress Timber," "Pine and Cypress Plank and Boards," and "Cedar Boards." The Georgia account speaks of "Timber of all Kinds." The words "lumber" and "timber" were the generic terms, as the Georgia reference suggests. "Board" and "plank" were distinguished by their relative thickness; boards were thinner, up to one and one quarter inches thick; timber over that thickness was accounted "plank." Series Eg1174 combines the South Carolina footage in the spirit of the Georgia reports. Note that timber and some of these timber products were frequently traded by the "thousand" (abbreviated by the Roman numeral "M"). Conventionally, this sometimes meant, not 1,000 units but 1,200 units, both in Great Britain and in the British colonies in the Western Hemisphere. The scholar who worked this out most carefully for Pennsylvania concluded that "staves, headings, and hoops were sold and shipped 1,200 pieces to the M; boards and planks, 1,000 feet to the M; and shingles and laths, 1,000 pieces to the M." Helen Louise Klopfer, "Statistics of the Foreign Trade of Philadelphia, 1700–1860" (Ph.D. dissertation, University of Pennsylvania, 1936), p. 27. See similar modes of counting involving the "hundred" and the "thousand" in Great Britain as discussed in Ronald Edward Zupko, *A Dictionary of Weights and Measures for the British Isles: The Middle Ages to the Twentieth Century*, Memoirs of the American Philosophical Society, volume 168 (American Philosophical Society, 1985), pp. 190–2, 408–9. On the subject of timber generally, see Donna J. Rilling, *Making Houses, Crafting Capitalism: Builders in Philadelphia, 1790–1850* (University of Pennsylvania Press, 2001).

For most of the fifty years after 1724, Harper relied on the figures for POE Charleston developed from *The South-Carolina Gazette* (Charleston) by Charles Joseph Gayle, "The Nature and Volume of Exports from Charleston, 1724–1774," *Proceedings of the South Carolina Historical Association* [7] (1937): 31. Questions have been raised about the errors and omissions in Gayle's tables, but they have not been resolved for these series. In the instance of his data for 1773 and 1774, Gayle's data are so suspect as to have been omitted from this table.

These same sources noted previously for the period 1725–1742 twice record the quantities of these commodities exported from the other two South Carolina POE as follows.

Year	Port	Lumber	Shingles	Staves
1737	POE Winyah	0	0	0
	POE Beaufort	12,730	8,250	23,500
1739	POE Winyah	0	0	14,621
	POE Beaufort	78,500	0	6,000

See *An Account of Sundry Goods Imported, and of Sundry Goods the Produce of this Province Exported, from the Several Ports of Charles-Town, George-Town, and Port-Royal, South-Carolina, from the First of November 1736,*

(continued)

TABLE Eg1174–1179   Timber and timber products exported from Charleston and Savannah: 1717–1787   *Continued*

to the *First of November 1737. With the Number of Vessels Entered and Cleared in Each Port* (Lewis Timothy, 1738); and *South-Carolina. An Account of Sundry Goods Imported, and of Sundry Goods of the Province Exported, from the Several Ports within the Said Province, from the First of November 1738, to the First of November 1739. With the Number of Vessels Entered and Cleared at Each Port. As Also from Whence Arrived and Where Bound* (Peter Timothy, 1739).

Olsberg and Carson ([1970]), pp. 19–21, also presented data for POE Winyah (Georgetown) for 1783–1787 – though the numbers for the latter appear to have been only for part of the last year – and scattered returns for POE Port Royal for 1784–1786:

Year	Port	Lumber	Shingles	Staves
1783	POE Winyah	11 tons	44,200	1,100
	POE Beaufort	0	0	0
1784	POE Winyah	54,100	164,000	4,672
	POE Beaufort	0	0	0
1785	POE Winyah	57,334	179,000	15,815
	POE Beaufort	0	0	0
1786	POE Winyah	27,841	107,000	8,000
	POE Beaufort	0	0	0

CHAPTER Eh

Confederate States of America

Editor: Roger L. Ransom

CONFEDERATE STATES OF AMERICA

Roger L. Ransom

The Confederate States of America existed as a self-proclaimed nation for only forty-nine months – from February 1861 to early April 1865 (see Table Eh-A). The initial steps toward establishing an independent country were taken when South Carolina seceded from the United States on December 20, 1860. Within three weeks, six other slave states – Mississippi, Florida, Alabama, Georgia, Louisiana, and Texas – had followed South Carolina's lead. On February 4, 1861, Jefferson Davis was sworn in as President of the Confederacy in Montgomery, Alabama. Following the bombardment of Fort Sumter in April 1861, four more slave states decided to join the Confederacy. Map Eh-B shows the territorial boundaries of the Confederate States of America as of June 1861.[1] The founders of the Confederacy had hoped that the remaining four states where slavery was legal in 1860 would also elect to leave the Union. Indeed, representatives from three of those "border" states – Kentucky, Maryland, and Missouri – were allotted seats in the Confederate Congress and actually sent representatives to Richmond. As events turned out, none of these states joined the Confederacy; however, communities in those states contributed men and supplies to the Confederate cause.[2] Both Union and Confederate troops occupied territory within each of these states at one time or another during the Civil War.

The Confederate government made few efforts to collect statistical data that encompassed the entire country. Indeed, after mid-1862, when Union troops captured New Orleans and thereafter controlled most of the Mississippi River, the Confederate states west of the Mississippi were physically separated from the seven Eastern states. The Department of the Trans-Mississippi West was virtually autonomous for the last two years of the war, governed by a military governor. Consequently, most of the statistical data that have been aggregated by historians for "the Confederacy" are based exclusively on data from the Eastern states.[3] The data presented in this chapter have been organized into four basic groups:

1. Statistics collected by the U.S. Census Offices of 1860 and 1870 for each of the states that seceded from the Union, for each of the border states, and summary totals for the states and territories that remained in the Union;
2. Statistics on the money supply and behavior of prices in the Confederacy;
3. Data on the revenues, expenditures, and debt of the Confederate government; and
4. Data on cotton trade and the Union blockades of Confederate commerce during the war.

The Resource Base of the Confederate States

The data presented in Tables Eh1–49 present a statistical cross section of the states that seceded from the United States in 1861 taken from the U.S. Census of 1860. A second look at the same states in 1870, five years after the surrender of Confederate armies, is taken from the U.S. Census of 1870. Totals for the free states of the Union are also presented for each census. An examination of the data presented in these tables reveals that the Northern states held an enormous edge in manpower and resources. Allowing for a division of resources to each side from the border states, the North had a manpower pool that was roughly twice that available to the South.[4] The Northern advantage in the production of manufactures was even larger; the manufacturing capacity of the states of New York and Massachusetts alone exceeded that for the entire South. Although the regional disparity in production of foodstuffs and agricultural output was less dramatic, the South's reliance on cash crops whose markets were outside the region made it vulnerable to economic pressures through a blockade of seagoing commerce. Finally, the data demonstrate how critical the states of the upper South – Arkansas, North Carolina, Tennessee, and particularly Virginia – were to the Confederate war effort. Those states accounted for between one third and one half of the economic resources of the Confederacy.

This sizable advantage of the North in terms of economic capacity provides a somewhat misleading guide to the extent to which the Union had a *military* superiority in 1861. It is important to recall that neither side was prepared for war. The U.S. Army numbered just over 16,000 officers and men in 1861, and at least a third of the men – and a higher fraction of officers – eventually fought for the South. At the outbreak of hostilities, neither the Union nor the Confederacy could immediately equip the men who

---

[1] On November 26, 1861, a convention met in Wheeling to form a new state of West Virginia. The map does not show the state of West Virginia, which was officially admitted to the Union on June 20, 1863.

[2] The fourth "slave" state was Delaware, which had 1,798 slaves and 19,829 free blacks out of a total population of 112,221.

[3] For the problems of getting statistics on the trans-Mississippi region, see Todd (1954) and Pecquet (1987).

Acknowledgments

Roger L. Ransom acknowledges the financial support from the Center for Social and Economic Policy, University of California, Riverside.

---

[4] Although accurate figures do not exist for the recruitment of troops from border states by the Confederacy, an educated guess would be that about 30 percent of the manpower went to the South, with the rest being available to the Union. See Hattaway and Jones (1983), p. 17; McPherson (1988), p. 293; and Ransom (1989), pp. 190–1.

TABLE Eh-A   Chronology of events in the history of the Confederate States of America: 1860–1865

1860

December 20	South Carolina secedes from the Union.

1861

January 9–February 1	Mississippi, Florida, Alabama, Georgia, Louisiana, and Texas secede from the Union.
February 4	Provisional Confederate Congress meets in Mobile, Alabama.
February 9	Confederate Congress elects Jefferson Davis of Mississippi as President of the Confederate States of America (CSA).
February 18	Jefferson Davis inaugurated as president.
February 19	Davis nominates Christopher Memminger as Secretary of the Treasury.
February 28	Confederate Congress authorizes "15 Million-Dollar Loan" at 8 percent payable in specie (see series Eh217).
March 9	Confederate Congress authorizes issuance of treasury notes "for such sum or sums as the exigencies of the public service may require."
April 6	Confederates fire on Fort Sumter, Charleston, SC.
April 17	Virginia secedes from the Union.
May 16	Confederate Congress authorizes "50 Million-Dollar Loan" at 8 percent. This was a "produce loan" that could be paid for by exchanging goods for bonds.
May 18	Confederate Congress votes to move its capital to Richmond, Virginia. Congress adjourns and reconvenes in Richmond on July 20.
May 20–June 8	North Carolina, Tennessee, and Arkansas secede from the Union.
July 21	First Battle of Bull Run: Confederates repulse Union advance on Richmond.
August 1	Confederate Congress imposes an export tax on cotton to back the 15 Million-Dollar Loan.
August 19	Confederate Congress authorizes "100 Million-Dollar Loan" and enacts the war tax to back interest payments on the loan (see series Eh216).
September 3–6	Confederate and Union troops enter Kentucky.
November 26	Convention meets in Wheeling to draft a constitution for the new state of West Virginia, comprising counties that had voted to secede from the Confederate State of Virginia.

1862

February 13	Confederate Congress enacts "An act to organize the clerical force of the Treasury Department."
March 9	Battle between USS Monitor and CSS Virginia (Merrimac).
April 6–7	Battle of Shiloh: Union Army of Tennessee advances into Mississippi.
April 16	Confederate Congress passes the Conscription Act.
April 29	New Orleans captured by the Union fleet.
June 25–July 1	Seven Days Battles: Union Army of the Potomac turned away from Richmond.
September 17	Battle of Antietam: Lee's invasion of Maryland turned back.
September 22	Lincoln issues a preliminary Emancipation Proclamation.
October 8	Battle of Perryville: Confederate invasion of Kentucky repulsed.
December 13	Battle of Fredricksburg: Army of the Potomac suffers major defeat.

1863

January 1	Lincoln issues the Emancipation Proclamation.
January 8	Confederate Congress authorizes "Erlanger loan" backed by cotton certificates (see series Eh221).
March 3	U.S. Congress enacts conscription.
March 26	Confederate Congress enacts "An Act to Regulate Impressments."
April 2	Bread riots in Richmond.
April 24	Confederate Congress enacts a revised war tax including a "tax-in-kind."
May 1–6	Battle of Chancellorsville: Lee's greatest victory – Stonewall Jackson is mortally wounded.
June 20	West Virginia officially enters the Union.
July 1–3	Battle of Gettysburg: Union Army turns back Lee's invasion of the North.
July 4	Vicksburg surrenders – Mississippi River is controlled by Union forces.
July 13–16	Draft riots in New York City.
September 19–20	Battle of Chickamauga: last major Confederate victory of the war – Union Army is besieged in Chattanooga.
November 24 – 25	Battle of Chattanooga: Union Army under Grant drives Confederates from Tennessee.

1864

February 17	Confederate Congress enacts "An Act to reduce the currency and to authorize a new issue of notes and bonds."
May 5–19	Battles of the Wilderness and Spotsylvania: Grant invades Virginia.
June 3	Battle of Cold Harbor: Union assault on Confederate lines repulsed with heavy losses.
June 8	Republican Party renominates Lincoln for president.

TABLE Eh-A   Chronology of events in the history of the Confederate States of America: 1860–1865   *Continued*

July 11	Confederate General Jubal Early reaches outskirts of Washington, D.C.
August 31	Democratic party nominates George McClellan for President.
September 2	Atlanta Falls to Union Army under Sherman.
November 8	Lincoln reelected.
November 30	Battle of Franklin (Tennessee): Union Army under Thomas and Schofield destroys the Confederate Army of Tennessee under Hood.
December 22	Savannah occupied by Union Army under Sherman.

1865

January 31	U.S. Congress approves Thirteenth Amendment abolishing slavery.
February 18	Charleston occupied by Sherman's army.
March 13	Confederate Congress passes Negro soldier bill – slaves can serve in CSA armies.
April 9	Lee surrenders the Army of Northern Virginia to Grant at Appomattox, Virginia.
April 14	Lincoln assassinated by John Wilkes Booth.
April 26	Joseph Johnston surrenders to Sherman.
May 10	Jefferson Davis captured near Abbeville, Georgia.
December 6	Thirteenth Amendment ratified, abolishing slavery.

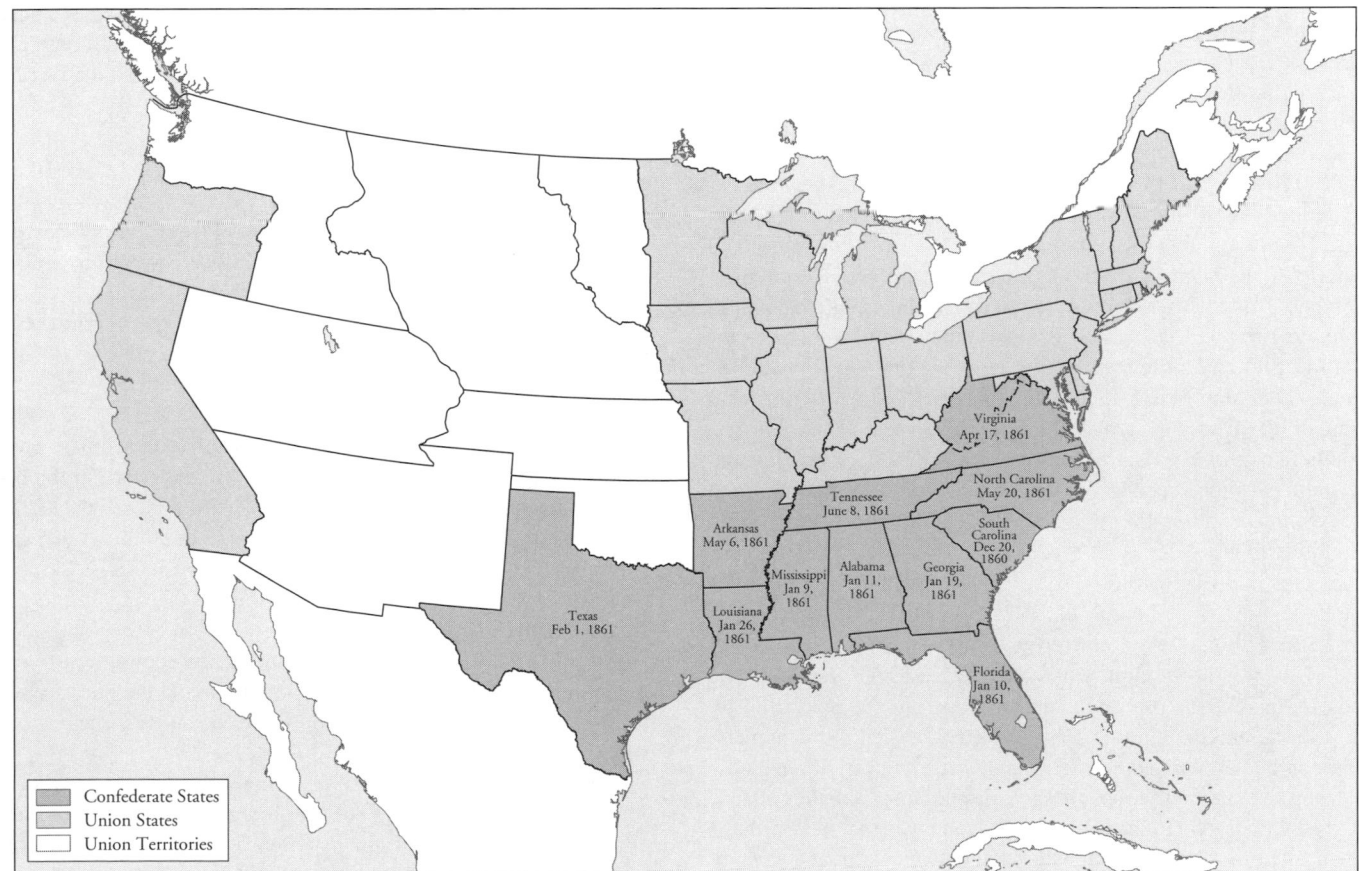

MAP Eh-B   The Confederate States of America, June 1860–1861

Source

William Thorndale and William Dollarhide, *Map Guide to the Federal Censuses, 1790–1920* (Genealogical Publishing, 1987), p. 8.

Documentation

The states of the Confederacy are named on the map together with the date in 1860 (South Carolina) or 1861 that they seceded from the Union. The State of Virginia, which then consisted of present-day Virginia and West Virginia, seceded in April 1861, but the counties in the northwest of the state that now constitute West Virginia later seceded from the Confederacy and were admitted as a separate and independent state of the Union in 1863.

were called to arms. Although time would eventually work in the Union's favor with regard to production of war materiel, it was not until 1864 that the Union military machine was finally able to tap the full potential of the Northern industrial economy. Thus, for much of the conflict, the South was able effectively to counter the Union military effort.

Northern critics of the antebellum South saw the region as a "backward" society. Yet that is not the picture of the Confederacy that emerges from a review of Tables Eh1–49. The South had levels of per capita wealth and income that compared favorably with the most well-developed economies of its day. Specializing in the production of cash crops for an export market, plantation slavery was the backbone of a globally successful if morally reprehensible economy that emerged as one of the wealthiest in the Western world by the middle of the nineteenth century.

The potential military prowess of the Confederacy can also be gleaned from evidence on its taxable property presented in Table Eh50–58. One of the facets of the Southern economy that emerges from these data is the enormous investment that Southern planters had made in their chattel labor. Almost half of the total value of assets reported in Table Eh50–58 was in the "value of Negroes."[5] An important point made by economic historians is that the market value of a slave is a reflection of the slave's productive capacity. Thus, our statistical picture suggests that on the eve of the Civil War the Southern economy was capable of producing more than enough food and basic consumption needs to sustain the population in a war, and Southerners were confident that they could purchase their military needs through the sale of cotton abroad. These expectations rested on the erroneous belief that this would be a short war. No one on either side foresaw a war of attrition that would require a massive mobilization of men and resources by both sides. The belief that the war would be relatively short was particularly damaging to the South, as time was on the side of the North. By the time Southerners realized that a quick victory was beyond their reach, the Union blockade was already seriously interfering with their efforts to secure arms and materiel for the military effort. Southern confidence that the interruption to the cotton trade would be only transitory encouraged planters to continue growing (and stockpiling) cotton rather than switching production to crops that might better serve the war effort.

It took the North four years of protracted fighting finally to put down the "War of the Rebellion." Contrasting the census data for 1870 with the data collected in 1860 reveals just how costly that effort was to the Southern states. Table Eh-C presents some indexes to illustrate the point. Farm values in the South fell by 42 percent, and the number of improved acres fell by 13 percent. The number of workstock in 1870 was still 21 percent below the 1860 figure. Output of foodstuffs fell significantly, and the collapse of production of Southern staples was even more dramatic. All this occurred during a period when the agricultural output and value of farms in the free states was undergoing a dramatic expansion. Yet the declines in output and the value of farms were not the most far-reaching changes in postbellum Southern agriculture. Table

---

[5] For the five cotton states – Alabama, Georgia, Louisiana, Mississippi, and South Carolina – the fraction of wealth in slaves reported in Table Eh50–58 is exactly 50 percent. This figure agrees with the value of slaves in these states derived by Ransom and Sutch from the number of slaves given in the 1860 Census and data on the estimated prices of slaves in 1860. See Ransom and Sutch (1988).

TABLE Eh-C Farms and farm output in the Confederate States – 1870 values as a percentage of 1860 values

Farms	
Number	148
Value	58
Improved acres	87
Workstock	79
Farm output	
Cotton	56
Tobacco	36
Wheat	77
Corn	66
Irish potatoes	84
Sweet potatoes	47

Sources
Tables Eh8–39.

Eh-C shows that from 1860 to 1870 the number of farms in the South *increased* by 48 percent. In fact, the number of farms with fewer than 50 tilled acres more than doubled over the decade, while the number of farms with more than 100 tilled acres *declined* by 17 percent. These figures confirm what most contemporaries claimed: small family farms were created from land that had been plantations run with slave labor before the war. The demise of the plantation and the rise of tenancy completely changed the institutional structure of the South after 1865.

Money, Prices, and Bonds

One of the advantages of a market society from the perspective of a historian is that it leaves us a record of prices paid for goods bought and sold. It was common for newspapers to quote prices of commodities for sale in local markets. In the larger commercial centers such as Richmond, Charleston, Mobile, or New Orleans, statistics on commerce in the city were often reported on a regular basis. Commercial magazines chronicled the prices and flows of commodities traded outside the region. Numerous scholars have sifted through these sources to construct indexes charting the behavior of prices in the Confederacy. Presented here are data from three price studies of the Confederacy: the studies by John Schwab (Table Eh166–193), Eugene Lerner (Table Eh128–130), and Thomas Berry (Tables Eh131–165). Although there are some differences in the data collected by each study, all three show the same trend. From its inception, the Confederate economy suffered from a high rate of inflation that eventually made the government currency worthless either as a store of value or as a medium of exchange.

In addition to the price series, Eugene Lerner constructed the first careful estimates of the Confederate money supply. For economists such as Lerner, the experience of the Confederacy offers an excellent laboratory to test the influence of the rapidly increasing stock of money on commodity prices. In a series of essays, Lerner argued that his data rather clearly showed that despite the distortions of the wartime economy, the fundamental cause of inflation was "the increase in the stock of money and the decrease in real output."[6] Figure Eh-D plots Lerner's monthly index of prices

---

[6] Lerner (1955), p. 37. Lerner elaborated on this theme in a series of essays based on his doctoral dissertation at the University of Chicago (1954a, 1954b, 1956).

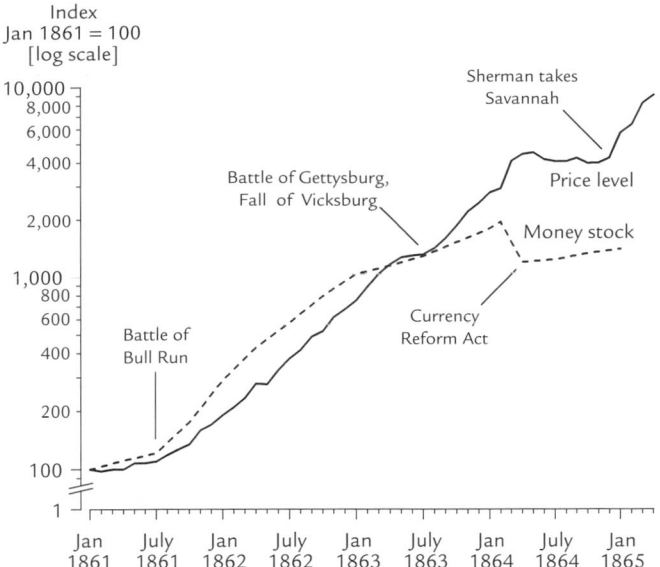

Index
Jan 1861 = 100
[log scale]

FIGURE Eh-D   Indexes of the Confederate money stock and price level: 1861–1865

Sources
Series Eh118 and Eh128.

together with an index of the amount of money in circulation constructed by John Godfrey from January 1861 through February 1865.[7] Because the data are plotted on a semilog scale, the slope of the lines in figure Eh-D represents the rate of increase of each variable. The inflationary problems of the Confederacy are immediately apparent. From mid-1861 to the end of the war, commodity prices rose by an average of about 10 percent per month.

At first glance, the data appear to confirm what Lerner claimed. The high rate of inflation that began in the spring of 1861 and continued through 1863 coincided with a rapid expansion of the money supply. The sharp reduction of the money supply associated with the Currency Reform Act in early 1864 corresponded with a break in inflation at about the same time.[8] However, more than monetary factors were at work here. The Confederate government tried to counteract the inflationary effects of its deficit finance by imposing price controls, rationing food in urban areas, and denouncing speculators who sought to profit from rising prices. Although these efforts clearly failed to halt inflation, the data presented in Figure Eh-D suggest that they were not entirely in vain. The rate of inflation through the end of 1863 (11.3 percent) was appreciably less than the rate of increase in the money supply (14.2 percent) over the same period. However, after the middle of 1863, inflation substantially outstripped the rate of increase in money. Various writers have suggested that in wartime, changes in the price level may also reflect people's confidence in the success of the government as the fortunes of war rise or fall. The Confederacy suffered severe

military setbacks during the last half of 1863, beginning with defeats at Gettysburg and Vicksburg and culminating with the fall of Chattanooga in December of that year. Although the period of relatively stable prices in mid-1864 coincided with a major monetary reform, this was also a period when Union forces seemed stalemated in Virginia and were struggling to capture Atlanta. If prices were sensitive to war news, the stalling of Union offensives would have contributed to a decline in inflationary pressures. Moreover, the behavior of the money supply does not provide a good explanation of the rapid inflation after Sherman's capture of Atlanta and his subsequent "march to the sea." Indeed, the statistical relationship between prices and war news is so powerful that Richard Burdekin and Farrokh Langdana argue "changes in the price level may have depended largely upon the people's confidence in the currency.... [I]t may have depended more fundamentally upon perceptions of the government's ability to bring about victory on the battlefield."[9]

Another economic signal of the effects of the war on people's confidence is the gold price of Confederate "graybacks," as the paper currency was nicknamed, in the financial markets of the South. Wesley Mitchell pioneered this sort of analysis with his work on the U.S. "greenbacks" during the war. For the Confederacy, figures for the price of gold in Richmond have been collected by John Schwab and Richard Todd, both of whom argued that news from the battlefield had an effect on the value of graybacks. More recently, George Davis and Gary Pecquet, W. O. Brown and Richard Burdekin, and Marc Weidenmier have studied both gold prices of Confederate graybacks and bond yields on domestic and foreign issues of the Confederate government to see how battle news affected prices in financial markets (see Tables Eh216–228). All of the studies found that the value of graybacks and bonds fluctuated with the changes in military fortunes.[10]

An example of creative – and highly successful – finance on the part of the Confederate Treasury was the issue of bonds on the Amsterdam market in early 1863 that were backed by cotton rather than gold. Called "Erlanger Bonds" after the French firm that underwrote the issues, these bonds sustained their value despite the obvious failures of the Confederate military effort in 1864. The weekly price quotations for both the Erlanger and gold-backed sterling bonds on the Amsterdam market are given in Table Eh221–222 and plotted in Figure Eh-E. Quotations for both cotton bonds and those backed with gold fell sharply in response to

---

[7] Because Godfrey's estimates of the money supply are more complete than those constructed by Lerner, series Eh124 is plotted rather than the estimates Lerner constructed in 1955 (Table Eh125–127). For more on the differences in the two series, see the text for each table.

[8] The Currency Reform Act of April 1864 stated that any currency outstanding could be exchanged on a three-for-two basis. This amounted to a 33 percent "tax" on those holding notes after April 1864. See Todd (1954), pp. 111–15; Davis and Pecquet (1990); and Burdekin and Langdana (1993).

---

[9] Burdekin and Langdana (1993), p. 374. The authors take care to point out that their results do not contradict a view that the fiscal deficit was an important element in generating inflation. Earlier writers on Confederate finance who argue that war events affected prices on the home front include Schwab (1899) and Todd (1954).

[10] Schwab (1899); Mitchell (1903, 1908); Todd (1954); Davis and Pecquet (1990); Brown and Burdekin (2000); and Weidenmier (2000). In addition to these studies of Confederate money and bond prices, work by McCandless (1996) and Willard, Guinnane, and Rosen (1996) have examined the impact of war news on the prices of Greenbacks and Union bonds. Davis and Pecquet found that prices of domestic bonds did not fluctuate in terms of nominal dollars. However, they note, "When the market yields of Confederate securities and the value of paper money are calculated in a gold basis, the impact of military events becomes apparent" (1990, p. 133). Davis and Pecquet also report that state and local bonds held their value better than the bonds issued by the Confederate government in Richmond, suggesting that investors believed their more local governments might make good on the debt regardless of the outcome of the war. The data for all three classes of bonds is in Table Eh216–220.

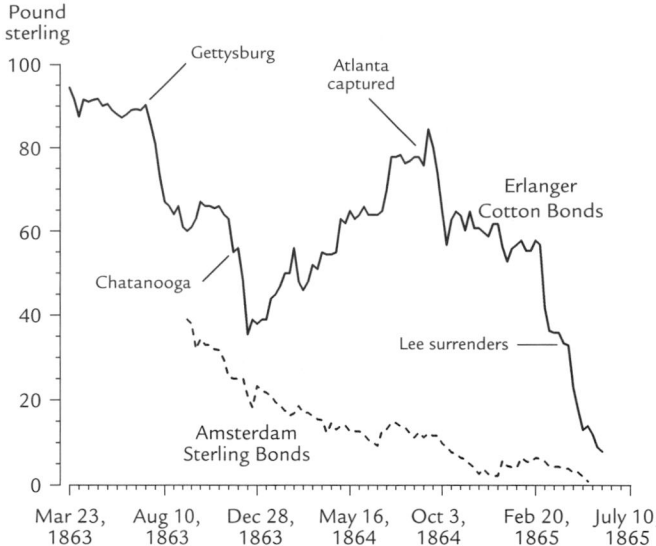

FIGURE Eh-E   Weekly prices of Confederate cotton bonds and sterling bonds in Amsterdam: 1863–1865

Source
Table Eh221–222.

Confederate reverses in the last half of 1863; however, the Erlanger issue staged a remarkable recovery through the first three quarters of 1864. Although the military fortunes of the Confederacy continued to sink – a fact reflected in the continued decline of gold bonds – the price of cotton rose sharply. Thus, the Erlanger bonds, which had fallen to as low as $35 (converted to gold dollars from pounds sterling) in December 1863, were trading at more than $80 just before the fall of Atlanta in September 1864. Equally remarkable was the fact that they were still trading at a price of $33 (or about one third their par value) the week that Richmond fell and Lee surrendered. As Marc Weidenmier (2000) observed, the option to buy cotton gave investors a hedge against the war risk.

Government Finances and the Cost of the War

The wartime finances of the Confederate government were chaotic at best, a situation that has confounded those scholars who try to estimate the costs associated with the Confederate war effort. The estimates of Richard Burdekin and Farrokh Langdana presented in Table Eh194–215 represent the most complete set of government accounts for the Confederacy currently available. Relying primarily on the reports of the Secretary of the Treasury, Burdekin and Langdana were able to reconstruct the "state of the Confederate Treasury" over the course of the war.

The problems of the Confederate Treasury are immediately apparent in the figures of Table Eh194–215. Efforts to raise money through taxes were feeble at best: only 6 percent of the $2.3 billion in revenues came from a combination of export and import duties, together with a "war tax" on commodities. Efforts at borrowing money were somewhat more successful: bond issues, call certificates, and bank loans accounted for 35 percent of all revenues. All but a tiny fraction of the remaining revenues were obtained through

issuance of treasury notes (which circulated as money) or non-interest-bearing notes. The deficits reflected by these notes fueled the inflation discussed earlier. Burdekin and Langdana (1993) estimate that the Confederate government spent a total of $2.01 billion between February 1861 and the beginning of October 1864. Just over $600 million – or about 30 percent of all expenditures – was spent to service the costs of government debt. Less than $50 million was spent on nonmilitary purchases of goods and services.

Do these figures from the budget represent the "cost" of the war to the South? Not exactly. An immediate problem posed by the figure just quoted is that it is reckoned in "nominal" Confederate dollars, uncorrected for the rapid inflation. Burdekin and Langdana offer a solution by estimating the costs for each year in "real" terms using Lerner's price index as a means of adjusting for inflation. Total expenditures would by their reckoning then amount to $282 million in 1860 U.S.-equivalent dollars, of which $276 million was related to military expenditures. This is a more accurate measure of the Richmond government's real level of expenditures, but it still falls far short of what an economist would regard as a measure of the total "cost" of the Civil War to the South. The most comprehensive attempt to measure the costs of the war is the analysis of Claudia Goldin and Frank Lewis (1975). They estimate that the Confederate government spent a total of $1.01 billion in 1860 U.S. dollars to fight the war.[11] To this they add $20.3 million for the costs of the draft and $1.49 billion to account for the decrease in the value of physical capital due to the war. This produces a figure of just over $2.5 billion (in 1860 prices) for what Goldin and Lewis term the *direct costs* of the war to the Confederacy.[12] This figure compares with their estimate of $1.8 billion of expenditures by the state and federal governments in the North and a total of $2.3 billion in direct costs to the Union.[13]

As Goldin and Lewis point out, these figures are still incomplete. To fully appreciate the "costs" of the war, one must include the *indirect* effects, which take into account the long-term effects from the war. The examination of the postwar census data in Tables Eh1–49 has already shown that the effects of the war in the Southern states were both large and long-lasting. Can one place a dollar value on these changes? Goldin and Lewis argue that the most appropriate measure would be the *forgone consumption* by each side as a result of the war (Goldin and Lewis 1975, pp. 304–5). By comparing the *actual* consumption paths of the North and South with those that would have existed without a war, Goldin and Lewis concluded

---

[11] The number cited in the text is considerably higher than the figure for direct expenditures reported in Table Eh194–215 for two reasons. First, Goldin and Lewis include state and local government expenditures in their estimate. Second, they insist that the value of expenditures reported by the authorities is biased downward owing to "the seizure of goods" by the Confederate Army, as well as "forced sales at lower than current prices" (1975, p. 307). Goldin and Lewis have adjusted the reported expenditures upward to correct for this bias. The details are presented in Goldin and Lewis (1975), pp. 306–9, especially Table 2.

[12] This figure does not include the human costs of the war, which the authors estimate to be $767 million. These costs bring their estimate of the total direct costs of the war for the Confederacy to $3.286 million (Goldin and Lewis 1975, p. 308, Table 2).

[13] Goldin and Lewis (1975), pp. 304–5, Table 1. It is interesting to note that, despite the much higher expenditures by the Union government, the total direct costs to the Union are less than those to the Confederacy because Goldin and Lewis estimate that there was no destruction of capital on the Union side.

that the *indirect costs* of the war would have added an additional $9.5 billion to the bill for the South and an additional $4.5 billion for the North. Several writers have criticized the assumptions of the Goldin–Lewis model and claimed that the estimates of indirect costs were far too high – especially with regard to the South.[14] However, although the exact magnitudes are in some dispute, all of the participants in the debate agree that the order of magnitude of costs from the war was enormous, and all agree that the South bore a far higher share of the burden than the North. While the economic effects on the North had largely disappeared by the end of the century, the South was still struggling to recover from the changes brought about by emancipation and the war.

Cotton and the Northern Blockade

A cornerstone of the Confederacy's war plans was to use its dominance in the production of raw cotton to its advantage in the conflict. Cotton was important in two respects. First, because Southern cotton was an essential raw material for the textile industries of Great Britain and Europe, Confederate leaders believed that this would provide them with an economic weapon that could be used to induce the European powers to intervene in the American conflict on the side of the South. Second, the funds earned by selling cotton abroad could finance the purchase of military supplies to equip the Confederate army.

On the eve of the Civil War, the United States accounted for roughly 80 percent of all cotton imported into Europe (Tables Eh95–110). Southerners were confident that a curtailment of Southern supply would drive up the price of cotton on the world market and create economic distress in Europe. They were correct in this assessment; by late 1864, the price of cotton in Liverpool had risen by a factor of ten (series Eh101). Hoping to improve their terms of trade, the Confederates imposed an embargo on cotton in the spring of 1861. Prices did rise, but what the Confederates had not anticipated was the possibility that the Union might cut off delivery of cotton sold at the higher price through a naval blockade. By the time Southern leaders realized their error and once again began to ship cotton to Europe, the window of opportunity was closing. The "cotton famine" did create economic hardships in Europe, but it did not have the results hoped for by the South. By 1863, when the Union blockade became effective, both the British and the French governments had decided to ride out the economic crisis rather than intervene in the war. By that time, the Confederates could no longer gain from the sale of a commodity they could not deliver to European buyers.

Notwithstanding the statistics on the decline in cotton exports, the effectiveness of the Union blockade in reducing the Confederate war effort remains a matter of considerable debate. Thanks

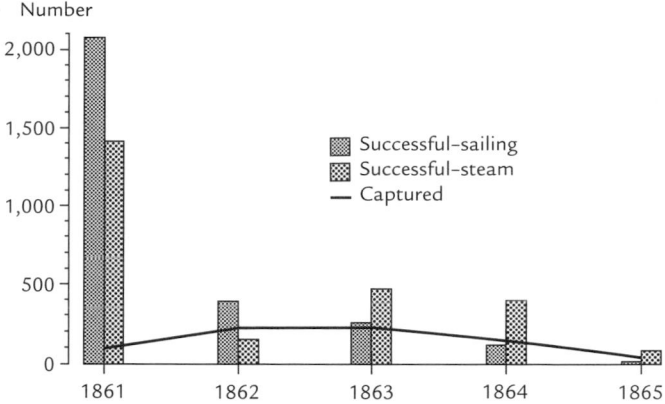

FIGURE Eh-F   Confederate blockade running – ships captured and successful runs: 1861–1865

Sources
Series Eh63–65.

to the work of Marcus Price, there is a fairly detailed record of trips to and from Southern ports during the war, together with the number of ships captured by the Union Navy.[15] These data are summarized in Figure Eh-F. Several conclusions can immediately be drawn from the data. First is the success of the Union blockade in reducing traffic to and from Southern ports by the end of 1861. The total number of "successful trips" fell from 3,485 in 1861 to 548 in 1862. On the other hand, the number of successful trips remained at about this level through 1864, suggesting that a steady flow of goods continued to get through the blockade. The data also clearly reveal how Southerners responded to the blockade. Early on it became apparent that steam-powered vessels were able to get through the blockade with far greater success than sailing ships. Indeed, by the end of 1863 virtually all of the goods coming from Bermuda or Cuba came on steamships, most of them built specifically for blockade running or refitted for that task. Finally, one can see that the Union Navy had managed to substantially raise the risks to blockade runners as early as 1862 through its ability to sink or capture Southern ships. By the end of the war, Union warships had captured 754 ships, and 172 others had been lost at sea.[16]

Most historians of the blockade have focused on the blockade runners themselves rather than the impact of the blockade on the Southern economy or war effort. The only serious quantitative study of the blockade is an article by Stanley Lebergott, who focuses on the extent to which the blockade shut down the exports of cotton from the South (Lebergott 1981). His research turned up two interesting facts. First was the continued commitment on the part of planters to grow cotton despite increasing evidence that it could not be sold outside the South. Lebergott estimates that the South grew 6.8 million bales of cotton during the war. Using data on captures and vessels that succeeded in running the

---

[14] In constructing their "counterfactual" world without a war, Goldin and Lewis projected the antebellum growth of the South into the future. Two objections to this procedure have been raised: (1) that the demand for cotton – which was a key element in antebellum growth – would not proceed unabated into the postwar era; and (2) that by comparing the actual path of Southern consumption with their counterfactual model, Goldin and Lewis were characterizing the effects of emancipation – which were substantial – as a "cost" of the war. For a discussion of these points, see Temin (1976, 1978), the reply to Temin by Goldin and Lewis (1978), and Ransom (1998).

---

[15] In addition to the articles by Price (1948, 1951–1952, 1955) that supply the data for the statistics in Table Eh59–94, the collection of documents in Vandiver (1947) provide useful information on the blockade.

[16] Many of the ships listed as "lost" were in fact victims of the blockade that had been forced to run aground or sank attempting to escape capture.

blockade, Lebergott estimates that 446,000 bales were smuggled to Europe (Lebergott 1981, p. 880, Table 7). In addition to this cotton, Lebergott argues that about two thirds of the 1.8 million bales of cotton consumed in the North were smuggled in from the South (Lebergott 1981, p. 882). Of the rest, 400,000 bales were consumed in the South and 3.3 million bales were destroyed during the war (Lebergott 1981, p. 883, Table 10). This leads Lebergott to the interesting conclusion that "the single group who did well . . . consisted of those who held 3.8 million bales at the end of the war. Like the survivors of a tontine they had seen the value of their stocks driven up as those of their fellow planters had been destroyed" (Lebergott 1981, pp. 884–5). Lebergott's estimates substantiate the view that only a few people in the South were able to capitalize on the earnings from its staple crop, and the earnings from cotton did little to support the Southern war effort.

Because of the emphasis on the need to import foreign supplies for the war, blockade historians have tended to overlook the impact of the blockade on the coastal trade of the South. Yet the greatest effect of the blockade may well have been to disrupt the internal commerce of the South. In 1860, the rail system of the South was still rudimentary and was geared to taking goods from the interior to the seaports. As observed in Figure Eh-F, the number of trips made to and from Southern ports fell by 85 percent between 1861 and 1862. A major part of that enormous decline was the virtual elimination of the coastal trade. The need for high-speed steamships to run the blockade put an emphasis on quick profits – profits gained in the lucrative trade with Bermuda and Havana, not the coastal trade. The result was a substantial decline in the South's ability to move goods within its economy. Figure Eh-G compares indexes for several commodity groups. As one would expect, prices on imported commodities rose sooner and faster than other commodities. Yet the index for food and sundries was also significantly above the average throughout the war. Finally, it is interesting to note that the prices of agricultural commodities remained below the average

for all commodities. Thus, although urban housewives found reason to complain of the rising cost of living in cities, farm families suffered a relative decline in the prices they received. There were very real shortages of many commodities throughout the South as a result of the war and the blockade. Yet the South as a whole was not running out of food, and shortages such as those observed in the cities were created as much by failures of the transportation network as by the absence of production. The blockade stretched the South's transportation system to the limit by preventing the use of coastal waterways to move goods.

Finally, the psychological effect of the shortages produced by the blockade was also significant. Southerners were forced to substantially alter their patterns of consumption – patterns that relied on imported goods and a network of transportation that was seriously encumbered by the blockade. Contemporary accounts are full of complaints about shortages in the cities, and in April 1863 there were "bread riots" in Richmond to protest the shortages. As Thomas Berry notes, the term "bread riot" is somewhat misleading because "bread as such was hardly involved at all. The loot covered such items as shoes, bacon, candles, hats, flour, coffee and calico, more or less in that order" (Berry 1985, p. 125). Beyond the frequent references to complaints, little has been done to study the actual effects of the Union blockade on Southern consumption patterns during the war. One of the few works that has carefully examined the effects of a wartime blockade is Avner Offer's study of Germany in World War I. Commenting on the food situation, he notes that although there was usually enough food available to meet minimal needs, "consumers had to break the law in order to acquire a good part of what they ate" (Offer 1989, p. 2). The situation in the South with regard to food may not have been as serious as it was in Germany, but there are strong parallels in Offer's analysis of effects of the British blockade of 1914–1919 and the effects of the Union blockade of the South in 1861–1865. Offer's conclusion that the blockade was a central reason for Germany's defeat in 1918 suggests that the Union's blockade may have been a central factor in its defeat of the South in 1865.

Conclusion

This essay has touched on a few problems that could be addressed with the data in this chapter. The list is no more than a beginning. Nor are the historical statistics of the Confederacy presented in this chapter by any means complete; we have barely scratched the surface of what may someday be available. Many of the statistical series assembled for this volume were constructed by scholars over the past four decades. That work involved molding thousands of fragments of data into composite series. There are still many fragments of data lying around. And there are still many questions to be answered.

Appendix: Suggestions for Further Reading

Donald and Wynelle Dodd (1973) have compiled an excellent source of census data on the fifteen antebellum slave states (plus West Virginia after 1860) from 1790 through 1970. This source relies completely on the published censuses and includes data by state for population, manufacturing, and agriculture, along with the decennial population from 1900 to 1970 of cities with at least 50,000 inhabitants in 1950.

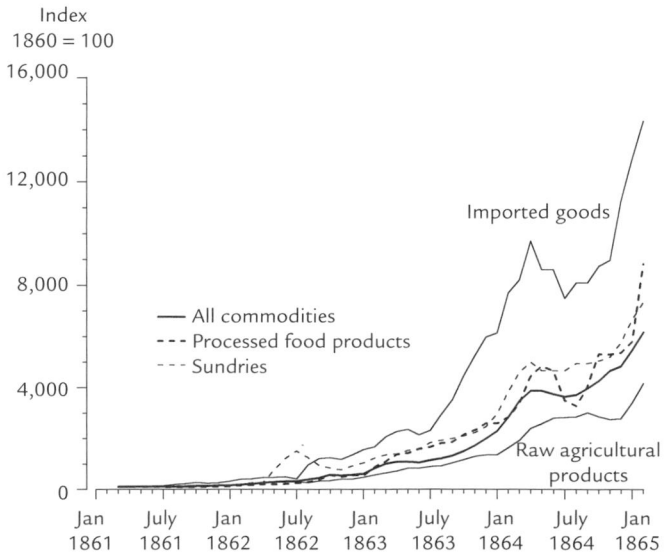

FIGURE Eh-G   Price indexes for the Confederate states: 1861–1865

Source
Three-month moving averages of series Eh166–170.

On the formation of the Confederacy and the confidence of Confederate leaders in the early period of the war, see Davis (1994) and Rable (1994). For an excellent and highly readable assessment of the Confederate war effort, see Gallagher (1997).

A considerable literature has grown up over the economic development of the Southern states before the Civil War. Douglass North (1961) provides an excellent analysis of the expansion of the cotton South and the key role that region played in the early growth of the United States. On the issue of slavery and the South, see Fogel and Engerman (1971), Chapter 4; Wright (1978, 1986); Fogel (1989); and Ransom (1989), Chapters 2 and 3. For Northern views on the South before the war, see Foner (1970), Chapter 3; Fogel and Engerman (1971), Chapter 5; Foner (1980); and Fogel (1989). There is a lengthy literature on the demise of the plantation, the rise of tenancy, and the changes that accompanied this transformation of Southern society. Roger Ransom and Richard Sutch (2000) provide an analysis of these changes and offer an extensive bibliography of the recent literature.

The best accounts of the efforts of the Confederate government to finance the war are Todd (1954) and Ball (1991). Both rely on the earlier work of John Schwab (1901). For a description of how the Confederate government secured the Erlanger bonds with pledges of cotton purchases during the war, see Gentry (1970) and Weidenmier (2000).

There are numerous accounts of blockade running. Among the best are Vandiver (1947) and Cochrane (1958). Two sources that deal more fully with the effects of the blockade are Owsley (1959) and Wise (1988). Stanley Lebergott (1981) offers the best quantitative assessment of the blockade.

References

Ball, D. B. 1991. *Financial Failure and Confederate Defeat*. University of Illinois Press.

Berry, Thomas Senior. 1985. *Richmond Commodity Prices: 1861–1865*. Bostwick Paper number 5. Bostwick Press.

Brown, William O., and Richard C. K. Burdekin. 2000. "Turning Points in the U.S. Civil War: A British Perspective." *Journal of Economic History* 60 (1): 216–31.

Burdekin, Richard C. K., and Farrokh K. Langdana. 1993. "War Finance in the Southern Confederacy." *Explorations in Economic History* 30 (July 1993): 352–77.

Cochrane, Hamilton. 1958. *Blockade Runners of the Confederacy*. Bobbs-Merrill.

Davis, George K., and Gary M. Pecquet. 1990. "Interest Rates in the Civil War South." *Journal of Economic History* 50 (March 1990): 133–48.

Davis, William C. 1994. *"A Government of Our Own": The Making of the Confederacy*. Free Press.

Dodd, Donald B., and Wynelle S. Dodd. 1973. *Historical Statistics of the South, 1790–1970*. University of Alabama Press.

Fogel, Robert W. 1989. *Without Consent or Contract: The Rise and Fall of American Slavery*. Norton.

Fogel, Robert W., and Stanley L. Engerman, editors. 1971. *The Reinterpretation of American Economic History*. Harper & Row.

Foner, Eric. 1970. *Free Soil, Free Men, and Free Labor: The Ideology of the Republican Party before the Civil War*. Oxford University Press.

Foner, Eric. 1980. *Politics and Ideology in the Age of the Civil War*. Oxford University Press.

Gallagher, Gary. 1997. *The Confederate War: How Popular Will, Nationalism, and Military Strategy Could Not Stave Off Defeat*. Harvard University Press.

Gentry, J. F. 1970. "A Confederate Success in Europe, the Erlanger Loans." *Journal of Southern History* 36: 157–8.

Goldin, Claudia Dale, and Frank Lewis. 1975. "The Economic Costs of the American Civil War: Estimates and Implications." *Journal of Economic History* 35 (June): 299–326.

Goldin, Claudia, and Frank Lewis. 1978. "The Post-Bellum Recovery of the South and the Cost of the Civil War: Comment." *Journal of Economic History* 38 (June): 299–326.

Hattaway, Herman, and Archer Jones. 1983. *How the North Won: A Military History of the Civil War*. University of Illinois Press.

Lebergott, Stanley. 1981. "Through the Blockade: The Profitability and Extent of Cotton Smuggling, 1861–1865." *Journal of Economic History* 41 (December): 867–87.

Lerner, Eugene M. 1954a. "The Monetary and Fiscal Programs of the Confederate Government, 1861–65." *Journal of Political Economy* 62 (December): 506–22.

Lerner, Eugene. 1954b. "Money, Prices and Wages in the Confederacy, 1861–65." Ph.D. dissertation, University of Chicago.

Lerner, Eugene M. 1955. "Money, Prices, and Wages in the Confederacy, 1861–1865." *Journal of Political Economy* 63 (1): 20–40.

Lerner, Eugene. 1956. "Inflation in the Confederacy, 1861–65." In Milton Friedman, editor. *Studies in the Quantity Theory of Money*. University of Chicago Press.

McCandless, G. T. 1996. "Money and the Civil War." *American Economic Review* 86: 661–71.

McPherson, James M. 1988. *Battle Cry of Freedom: The Civil War Era*. Oxford University Press.

Mitchell, Wesley G. 1903. *A History of the Greenbacks, with Special Reference to the Economic Consequences of Their Issue: 1862–1865*. Decennial Publications of the University of Chicago, second series, volume 9. University of Chicago Press.

Mitchell, Wesley G. 1908. *Gold, Prices, and Wages under the Greenback Standard*. University of California Publications in Economics, volume 1. University of California Press.

North, Douglass C. 1961. *The Economic Growth of the United States, 1790–1860*. Prentice-Hall.

Offer, Avner. 1985. *The First World War: An Agrarian Interpretation*. Oxford University Press.

Owsley, Frank L. 1959. *King Cotton Diplomacy: Foreign Relations of the Confederate States of America*. 2nd edition, revised by Harriet C. Owsley, editor. University of Chicago Press.

Pecquet, Gary M. 1987. "Money in the Trans-Mississippi Confederacy and the Confederate Currency Reform Act of 1864." *Explorations in Economic History* 24 (April): 218–43.

Price, Marcus W. 1948. "Ships That Tested the Blockade of the Carolina Ports, 1861–1865." *American Neptune* 8: 196–241.

Price, Marcus W. 1951–1952. "Ships That Tested the Blockade of the Gulf Ports, 1861–1865." *American Neptune* 11 (4) (1951): 262–90; 12 (1) (1952): 52–9; 12 (2) (1952): 154–61; 12 (3) (1952): 229–38.

Price, Marcus W. 1955. "Ships That Tested the Blockade of the Georgia and East Florida Ports, 1861–1865." *American Neptune* 15: 97–132.

Rable, George C. 1994. *The Confederate Republic: A Revolution against Politics*. University of North Carolina Press.

Ransom, Roger L. 1989. *Conflict and Compromise: The Political Economy of Slavery, Emancipation, and the American Civil War*. Cambridge University Press.

Ransom, Roger L. 1998. "The Economic Consequences of the American Civil War." In Murray Wolfson, editor. *The Political Economy of War and Peace*. Kluwer.

Ransom, Roger L., and Richard Sutch. 1988. "Capitalists without Capital: The Burden of Slavery and the Impact of Emancipation." *Agricultural History* (Fall): 119–47.

Ransom, Roger L., and Richard Sutch. 2000. *One Kind of Freedom: The Economic Consequences of Emancipation*. 2nd edition. Cambridge University Press.

Schwab, John C. 1899. "Prices in the Confederacy." *Political Science Quarterly* 14: 281–304.

Schwab, John C. 1901. *The Confederate States of America, 1861–1865: A Financial and Industrial History of the South during the Civil War*. Burt Franklin.

Temin, Peter. 1976. "The Post-Bellum Recovery of the South and the Cost of the Civil War." *Journal of Economic History* 36 (December): 898–907.

Temin, Peter. 1978. "Reply to Goldin and Lewis." *Journal of Economic History* 38 (June): 493.

Todd, Richard C. 1954. *Confederate Finance*. University of Georgia Press.

Vandiver, Frank, editor. 1947. *Confederate Blockade Running through Bermuda, 1861–1865*. University of Texas Press.

Weidenmier, Marc. 2000. "The Market for Confederate Bonds." *Explorations in Economic History* 37 (January): 76–97.

Willard, K., Timothy Guinnane, and H. Rosen. 1996. "Turning Points in the Civil War: Views from the Greenback Market." *American Economic Review* 86: 1001–18.

Wise, Stephen. 1988. *Lifeline of the Confederacy*. University of South Carolina Press.

Wright, Gavin. 1978. *The Political Economy of the Cotton South: Households, Markets, and Wealth in the Nineteenth Century*. Norton.

Wright, Gavin. 1986. *Old South, New South: Revolutions in the Southern Economy since the Civil War*. Basic Books.

POPULATION AND ECONOMY

Roger L. Ransom

TABLE Eh1–7   Population of the slave states, by state, race, and slave status: 1860–1870

Contributed by Roger L. Ransom

State	Total		White		Black		
					1860		
	1860	1870	1860	1870	Slave	Free	1870
	Eh1	Eh2	Eh3	Eh4	Eh5	Eh6	Eh7
	Number	Number	Number	Number	Number	Number	Number
Total, Confederate states	9,103,332	9,929,400	5,447,220	5,968,521	3,521,110	132,760	3,957,012
Alabama	964,201	996,992	526,271	521,384	435,080	2,690	475,510
Arkansas	435,450	484,471	324,143	362,115	111,115	144	122,169
Florida	140,424	187,748	77,747	96,057	61,745	932	91,689
Georgia	1,057,286	1,184,109	591,550	638,926	462,198	3,500	545,142
Louisiana	708,002	726,915	357,456	362,065	331,726	18,647	364,210
Mississippi	791,305	827,922	353,899	382,896	436,631	773	444,201
North Carolina	992,622	1,071,361	629,942	678,470	331,059	30,463	391,650
South Carolina	703,708	705,606	291,300	289,667	402,406	9,914	415,814
Tennessee	1,109,801	1,258,520	826,722	936,119	275,719	7,300	322,331
Texas	604,215	818,579	420,891	564,700	182,566	355	253,475
Virginia [1]	1,596,318	1,667,177	1,047,299	1,136,122	490,865	58,042	530,821
Total, border states	3,136,961	3,948,215	2,589,480	3,409,556	429,401	118,027	538,466
Delaware	112,216	125,015	90,589	102,221	1,798	19,829	22,794
Kentucky	1,155,684	1,321,011	919,484	1,098,692	225,483	10,684	222,210
Maryland	687,049	780,894	515,918	605,497	87,189	83,942	175,391
Missouri	1,182,012	1,721,295	1,063,489	1,603,146	114,931	3,572	118,071
Total, free states and territories	18,943,451	24,277,890	18,654,081	23,864,272	35	225,961	340,084

[1] Includes West Virginia in 1870.

Sources

Inter-University Consortium for Political and Social Research (ICPSR), Historical, Demographic, Economic and Social Data: The United States, 1790–1970, "1860 Data Set (County and State)," taken from U.S. Census Office, *Eighth Decennial Census of the United States, 1860,* "Population"; and "1870 Data Set (County and State)," taken from U.S. Census Office, *Ninth Census of the United States, 1870,* "Statistics on Population."

Documentation

The data in these series were collected by the census offices for 1860 and 1870 and reported in the *Compendium for the 1870 Census.*

Series Eh7. The Census Office in 1870 admitted to a serious undercount of the black population for that year. The problem is discussed in U.S. Census Office, *Compendium of the Eleventh Census, 1890,* part 1, pp. xxxv–xliii, where the 1890 Census Office estimates that the undercount of blacks was 9.5 percent. Although there is no question that the black population was undercounted in 1870, this is probably too large an adjustment. See the discussion in Roger Ransom and Richard Sutch, "The Economic Impact of the Civil War and of Emancipation on Southern Agriculture," *Explorations in Economic History* 12 (January 1975): 8–10.

TABLE Eh8-23 Farms, farm implements, livestock, and home manufactures in the slave states, by state: 1860–1870
Contributed by Roger L. Ransom

State	Farms		Improved acres		Value of Farms		Value of Farm implements and machinery		Livestock		Workstock		Swine		Value of total home manufactures	
	Eh8	Eh9	Eh10	Eh11	Eh12	Eh13	Eh14	Eh15	Eh16	Eh17	Eh18	Eh19	Eh20	Eh21	Eh22	Eh23
	1860	1870	1860	1870	1860	1870	1860	1870	1860	1870	1860	1870	1860	1870	1860	1870
	Number	Number	Number	Number	Dollars	Dollars	Dollars	Dollars	Dollars	Dollars	Number	Number	Number	Number	Dollars	Dollars
Total, Confederate states	496,745	733,724	56,794,333	49,567,528	1,850,708,493	1,078,746,888	85,084,373	47,258,384	253,839,192	297,459,737	3,424,598	2,690,333	15,562,867	9,305,947	14,411,986	9,901,124
Alabama	50,064	67,382	6,385,724	5,062,204	175,824,622	67,739,036	7,433,178	3,286,924	43,411,711	26,690,095	327,066	216,621	1,748,321	719,737	1,817,520	1,124,513
Arkansas	33,190	49,424	1,983,313	1,859,821	91,649,773	40,029,698	4,175,326	2,237,409	22,096,977	17,222,506	276,443	163,602	1,171,630	841,129	1,019,240	807,573
Florida	6,396	10,241	654,213	736,172	16,435,727	9,947,920	900,669	505,074	5,553,356	5,212,157	31,717	27,029	271,742	158,906	63,259	131,693
Georgia	53,897	69,956	8,062,758	6,831,856	157,072,803	94,559,468	6,844,387	4,614,701	38,372,734	30,156,317	306,327	223,535	2,036,116	988,565	1,431,413	1,113,080
Louisiana	17,281	28,481	2,707,108	2,045,640	204,789,662	68,215,421	18,648,225	7,159,333	24,546,940	15,929,188	231,003	153,582	634,525	338,391	502,100	64,416
Mississippi	37,007	68,023	5,065,755	4,209,146	190,760,367	81,716,576	8,826,512	4,456,633	41,891,692	29,940,238	333,897	234,253	1,532,768	814,381	1,382,144	505,298
North Carolina	67,022	93,565	6,517,284	5,258,742	143,301,065	78,211,083	5,873,942	4,082,111	31,130,805	21,993,367	250,560	198,855	1,883,214	1,075,215	2,045,372	1,603,513
South Carolina	28,456	51,889	4,572,060	3,010,539	139,652,508	44,808,763	6,151,657	2,282,946	23,934,465	12,443,511	160,210	103,117	965,779	395,928	815,117	312,191
Tennessee	77,741	118,141	6,795,337	6,843,278	271,358,985	218,743,747	8,465,792	8,199,487	60,211,425	55,084,075	519,385	414,162	2,347,321	1,828,630	3,174,977	2,773,820
Texas	37,363	61,125	2,650,781	2,964,836	88,101,320	60,149,950	6,259,452	3,396,793	42,825,447	37,425,194	561,524	618,233	1,371,532	1,202,443	584,217	293,308
Virginia [1]	86,468	113,627	11,400,000	10,745,294	371,761,661	314,625,226	11,505,233	7,036,973	47,803,049	45,363,089	426,466	337,344	1,599,919	942,622	1,576,627	1,171,719
Total, border states	204,073	301,365	17,530,411	20,846,587	699,529,115	921,229,517	21,014,493	30,639,642	133,374,469	173,263,637	1,358,585	1,306,538	5,120,624	4,425,265	4,164,434	3,518,256
Delaware	6,588	7,615	637,065	698,115	31,426,357	46,712,870	817,883	1,201,644	3,144,706	4,257,323	29,086	27,242	47,848	22,714	17,591	33,070
Kentucky	83,689	118,422	7,644,208	8,103,850	291,496,955	311,238,916	7,474,573	8,572,896	61,868,237	66,287,343	582,337	485,983	2,330,595	1,838,222	2,095,578	1,683,972
Maryland	25,244	27,000	3,002,267	2,914,007	145,973,677	170,369,684	4,010,529	5,268,676	14,667,853	18,433,698	137,759	122,017	387,756	257,899	67,003	63,608
Missouri	88,552	148,328	6,246,871	9,130,615	230,632,126	392,908,047	8,711,508	15,596,426	53,693,673	84,285,273	609,403	671,296	2,354,425	2,306,430	1,984,262	1,737,606
Total, free states and territories	1,231,863	1,585,248	88,476,737	117,876,095	4,084,780,666	7,262,827,456	141,394,284	258,980,403	716,769,440	1,054,553,083	4,872,050	5,593,185	12,859,376	11,403,357	5,843,253	10,003,952

[1] Includes West Virginia in 1870.

Source
U.S. Census Office, *Compendium of the Ninth Census of the United States, 1870*, pp. 690–711.

Documentation
The data in these series were collected by the Census Offices for 1860 and 1870 and reported in the *Compendium* for the 1870 Census.

Series Eh18–19. Includes horses, mules, asses, and working oxen.

TABLE Eh24-39   Selected crop outputs of the slave states, by state: 1860–1870

Contributed by Roger L. Ransom

State	Wheat 1860 Eh24 Bushels	Wheat 1870 Eh25 Bushels	Indian corn 1860 Eh26 Bushels	Indian corn 1870 Eh27 Bushels	Oats 1860 Eh28 Bushels	Oats 1870 Eh29 Bushels	Irish potatoes 1860 Eh30 Bushels	Irish potatoes 1870 Eh31 Bushels	Sweet potatoes 1860 Eh32 Bushels	Sweet potatoes 1870 Eh33 Bushels	Rice 1860 Eh34 Pounds	Rice 1870 Eh35 Pounds	Tobacco 1860 Eh36 Pounds	Tobacco 1870 Eh37 Pounds	Cotton 1860 Eh38 400-pound bales	Cotton 1870 Eh39 400-pound bales
Total, Confederate states	31,441,826	24,338,053	282,626,178	187,279,295	19,906,032	22,114,238	6,647,071	5,576,046	37,937,439	17,660,742	187,151,123	73,635,021	203,642,093	73,113,048	5,344,148	3,009,033
Alabama	1,218,444	1,055,068	33,226,282	16,977,948	682,179	770,866	491,646	162,512	5,439,917	1,871,360	493,465	222,945	232,914	152,742	989,955	429,482
Arkansas	957,601	741,736	17,823,588	13,382,145	475,268	528,777	418,010	422,196	1,566,540	890,631	16,831	73,021	989,980	594,886	367,393	247,968
Florida	2,808	—	2,834,391	2,225,056	46,899	114,204	18,766	10,218	1,129,759	789,456	223,704	401,687	828,815	157,405	65,135	39,789
Georgia	2,544,913	2,127,017	30,776,293	17,646,459	1,231,817	1,904,601	303,789	197,101	6,508,511	2,621,562	52,507,652	22,277,380	919,318	288,596	701,840	473,934
Louisiana	32,208	9,906	16,853,745	7,596,628	89,377	224	294,655	67,695	2,060,981	1,023,706	6,331,257	15,854,012	39,940	15,541	777,738	350,832
Mississippi	587,925	274,479	29,057,082	15,637,316	221,235	414,586	414,320	214,189	4,563,873	1,743,432	809,082	374,627	159,141	61,012	1,202,507	564,938
North Carolina	4,743,706	2,859,879	30,078,564	18,454,215	2,781,860	3,220,105	830,565	738,803	6,140,039	3,071,840	7,593,976	2,059,281	32,853,250	11,150,087	145,514	144,935
South Carolina	1,285,631	783,610	15,065,606	7,614,207	936,974	613,593	226,735	83,252	4,115,688	1,342,165	119,100,528	32,304,825	104,412	34,805	353,412	224,500
Tennessee	5,459,268	6,188,916	52,089,926	41,343,614	2,267,814	4,513,315	1,182,005	1,124,337	2,604,672	1,205,683	40,372	3,399	43,448,097	21,465,452	296,464	181,842
Texas	1,478,345	415,112	16,500,702	20,554,538	985,889	762,663	174,182	208,383	1,846,642	2,188,041	26,031	63,844	97,914	59,706	431,463	350,628
Virginia [1]	13,130,977	9,882,330	38,319,999	25,847,169	10,186,720	9,271,304	2,292,398	2,347,360	1,960,817	912,866	8,225	0	123,968,312	39,132,816	12,727	185
Total, border states	18,638,816	26,714,610	154,273,049	130,837,288	13,304,107	26,974,447	5,389,741	8,624,352	1,771,621	1,347,382	9,767	0	171,633,700	133,411,941	41,188	2,326
Delaware	912,941	895,477	3,892,337	3,010,390	1,046,910	554,388	377,931	362,724	142,213	85,309		0	9,699	250	0	0
Kentucky	7,394,809	5,728,704	64,043,633	50,091,006	4,617,029	6,620,103	1,756,531	2,391,062	1,057,557	802,114		0	108,126,840	105,305,869	0	1,080
Maryland	6,103,480	5,774,503	13,444,922	11,701,817	3,959,298	3,221,643	1,264,429	1,632,205	236,749	218,706		0	38,410,965	15,785,339	0	0
Missouri	4,227,586	14,315,926	72,892,157	66,034,075	3,680,870	16,578,313	1,990,850	4,238,361	335,102	241,253	9,767	0	25,086,196	12,320,483	41,188	1,246
Total, free states and territories	123,024,282	236,692,963	401,893,513	442,827,966	139,433,046	233,018,472	99,112,055	129,137,075	2,385,966	2,701,700	6,142	0	58,933,668	56,210,352	1,716	637

[1] Includes West Virginia in 1870.

Source

U.S. Census Office, *Compendium of the Ninth Census of the United States, 1870*, pp. 690–711.

Documentation

The data in these series were collected by the Census Offices for 1860 and 1870 and reported in the *Compendium* for the 1870 Census.

TABLE Eh40–49 Manufacturing in the slave states – establishments, capital invested, product value, and employment, by state: 1860–1870

Contributed by Roger L. Ransom

	Manufacturing establishments		Aggregate value of capital invested in manufactures		Aggregate value of manufactured products		Employed in manufacturing			
							Males		Females	
	1860	1870	1860	1870	1860	1870	1860	1870	1860	1870
	Eh40	Eh41	Eh42	Eh43	Eh44	Eh45	Eh46	Eh47	Eh48	Eh49
State	Number	Number	Dollars	Dollars	Dollars	Dollars	Number	Number	Number	Number
Total, Confederate states	20,631	33,360	95,922,489	109,882,904	155,611,631	223,094,828	98,583	133,612	12,138	12,422
Alabama	1,459	2,188	9,098,181	5,714,032	10,600,000	13,040,644	6,792	7,196	1,097	664
Arkansas	518	1,070	1,316,610	1,782,913	2,880,578	4,629,234	1,831	3,077	46	47
Florida	185	659	1,874,125	1,679,930	2,447,969	4,685,403	2,297	2,670	157	20
Georgia	1,890	3,836	10,900,000	13,930,125	16,900,000	31,196,115	9,492	15,078	2,083	1,498
Louisiana	1,744	2,557	7,151,172	18,313,974	15,600,000	24,161,905	7,873	23,637	916	4,210
Mississippi	976	1,731	4,384,492	4,501,714	6,590,687	8,154,758	4,572	5,500	203	191
North Carolina	3,689	3,642	9,693,703	8,140,473	16,700,000	19,021,327	12,104	11,339	2,113	1,422
South Carolina	1,230	1,584	6,931,756	5,400,418	8,615,195	9,858,981	6,096	7,099	898	578
Tennessee	2,572	5,317	14,400,000	15,595,295	18,000,000	34,362,636	11,582	17,663	946	1,089
Texas	983	2,399	3,272,450	5,284,110	6,577,202	11,517,302	3,338	7,450	111	157
Virginia [1]	5,385	8,377	26,900,000	29,539,920	50,700,000	62,466,523	32,606	32,903	3,568	2,546
Total, border states	10,305	23,873	68,952,887	156,812,875	131,292,902	354,224,233	65,310	125,357	10,453	14,520
Delaware	615	800	5,452,887	10,839,093	9,892,902	16,791,382	5,465	7,705	956	1,199
Kentucky	3,450	5,390	20,300,000	29,277,809	37,900,000	54,625,809	19,587	27,687	1,671	1,159
Maryland	3,083	5,812	23,200,000	36,438,729	41,700,000	76,593,613	21,630	34,061	6,773	8,278
Missouri	3,157	11,871	20,000,000	80,257,244	41,800,000	206,213,429	18,628	55,904	1,053	3,884
Total, free states and territories	108,573	192,601	840,802,835	1,838,098,898	1,589,814,669	3,634,358,730	870,973	1,347,749	247,766	296,564

[1] Includes West Virginia in 1870.

Sources

Inter-University Consortium for Political and Social Research (ICPSR), *Historical, Demographic, Economic and Social Data: The United States, 1790–1970*, "1860 Data Set (County and State)," taken from U.S.

Census Office, *Eighth Decennial Census of the United States, 1860*, "Manufacturing of the United States in 1860"; and "1870 Data Set (County and State)," taken from U.S. Census Office, *Ninth Decennial Census of the United States, 1860*, "Statistics of the Wealth and Industry of United States."

TABLE Eh50–58　Taxable property in the Confederacy, by state: 1861

Contributed by Roger L. Ransom

						Value			
	Total assessed taxable property	Capital invested in trade, merchandise, etc.	Bank capital	Railroad and other stocks	Money at interest	Real estate		Slaves	Slaves
						Total, including town lots	Town lots alone		
	Eh50	Eh51	Eh52	Eh53	Eh54	Eh55	Eh56	Eh57	Eh58
State	Thousand Confederate dollars	Thousand Confederate dollars	Thousand Confederate dollars	Thousand Confederate dollars	Thousand Confederate dollars	Thousand Confederate dollars	Thousand Confederate dollars	Thousand Confederate dollars	Number
Total	4,632,161	256,852	84,809	191,210	198,418	1,758,238	191,069	2,142,635	3,571,057
Alabama	494,966	41,363	5,000	20,976	22,578	143,766	—	261,284	435,473
Arkansas	138,442	2,865	—	142	1,336	68,662	5,228	65,439	109,065
Florida	67,752	2,003	381	6,369	2,121	13,593	—	38,285	63,809
Georgia	633,322	15,577	9,028	24,000	107,336	195,905	35,139	280,477	467,461
Louisiana	480,597	36,658	24,497	16,073	5,701	210,356	—	187,312	312,186
Mississippi	471,677	19,253	436	9,025	12,199	143,000	—	287,765	479,607
North Carolina	343,125	20,000	6,626	13,698	8,000	97,773	12,050	197,026	328,377
South Carolina	440,034	26,389	14,000	19,000	15,000	121,334	31,334	244,311	407,185
Tennessee	485,339	25,000	8,132	27,348	10,000	242,592	29,771	172,267	287,112
Texas	282,077	19,257	—	7,579	4,000	140,268	17,983	110,974	184,956
Virginia	794,830	48,489	16,708	47,000	10,147	374,990	59,564	297,496	495,826

Source

Richard C. Todd, *Confederate Finance* (University of Georgia Press, 1954), Appendix D, p. 199.

Documentation

In May 1861, Confederate States of America Secretary of the Treasury Christopher Memminger recommended that the Confederate Congress enact a direct tax on property in the Confederacy. The Congress reacted by instructing Memminger to collect information "regarding the value of property, the revenue system, and the amount collected during the fiscal year in each of the Confederate states . . . so as to enable it to lay a fair, equal, and convenient system of taxation" (Todd 1954, p. 131). On July 24, 1861, Memminger submitted his report, which included the data reproduced in these series. The data present an economic "snapshot" of the Confederacy in the summer of 1861.

TABLE Eh59–94 Confederate blockade running – ships engaged, ships lost, and successful runs, by vessel type and port: 1861–1865

Contributed by Roger L. Ransom

All ports

	Vessels engaged			Successful runs			Vessels captured			Vessels lost or destroyed		
	Total	Sail	Steam	Total	Sailing vessels	Steam vessels	Total	Sail	Steam	Total	Sail	Steam
	Eh59	Eh60	Eh61	Eh62	Eh63	Eh64	Eh65	Eh66	Eh67	Eh68	Eh69	Eh70
Year	Number	Number	Number	Number	Number	Number	Number	Number	Number	Number	Number	Number
1861	840	755	85	3,485	2,074	1,411	97	93	4	14	14	—
1862	534	420	114	548	394	154	232	194	38	58	46	12
1863	469	317	152	732	260	472	230	176	54	42	23	19
1864	348	188	160	519	118	401	153	113	40	50	13	37
1865	97	40	57	102	14	88	42	29	13	8	3	5

Carolina ports

	Vessels engaged		Successful runs		Vessels captured		Vessels lost or destroyed	
	Sail	Steam	Sailing vessels	Steam vessels	Sail	Steam	Sail	Steam
	Eh71	Eh72	Eh73	Eh74	Eh75	Eh76	Eh77	Eh78
Year	Number	Number	Number	Number	Number	Number	Number	Number
1861	265	28	563	130	33	—	7	—
1862	160	65	160	96	75	21	17	7
1863	56	96	45	392	33	29	3	14
1864	14	122	12	310	7	28	—	32
1865	5	27	2	25	3	10	—	3

East Florida and Georgia ports

	Vessels engaged		Successful runs		Vessels captured		Vessels lost or destroyed	
	Sail	Steam	Sailing vessels	Steam vessels	Sail	Steam	Sail	Steam
	Eh79	Eh80	Eh81	Eh82	Eh83	Eh84	Eh85	Eh86
Year	Number	Number	Number	Number	Number	Number	Number	Number
1861	88	17	216	906	13	—	2	—
1862	24	8	23	9	17	4	1	—
1863	39	8	20	9	21	3	6	1
1864	49	4	19	3	33	3	4	1
1865	1	1	—	—	1	1	—	—

Gulf ports

	Vessels engaged		Successful runs		Vessels captured		Vessels lost or destroyed	
	Sail	Steam	Sailing vessels	Steam vessels	Sail	Steam	Sail	Steam
	Eh87	Eh88	Eh89	Eh90	Eh91	Eh92	Eh93	Eh94
Year	Number	Number	Number	Number	Number	Number	Number	Number
1861	402	40	1,295	375	47	4	5	—
1862	236	41	211	49	102	13	28	5
1863	222	48	195	71	122	22	14	4
1864	125	34	87	88	73	9	9	4
1865	34	29	12	63	25	2	3	2

Sources

Marcus W. Price, "Ships That Tested the Blockade of the Carolina Ports, 1861–1865," *American Neptune* 8 (1948): 196–241; Marcus W. Price, "Ships That Tested the Blockade of the Gulf Ports, 1861–1865," *American Neptune* 11 (4) (1951): 262–90, 12 (1) (1952): 52–9, 12 (2) (1952): 154–61, and 12 (3) (1952): 229–38; Marcus W. Price, "Ships That Tested the Blockade of Georgia and East Florida, 1861–1865," *American Neptune* 15 (1955): 97–132.

Documentation

This table presents data on the frequency with which Southern ships "tested" the Union blockade between 1861 and 1865. The table presents a new tabulation of data compiled by Marcus Price and published in a series of three articles in the *American Neptune*. The table is organized into the groups of Confederate ports identified by Price.

For each of the three groups of ports, Price classified voyages that were "successful," those that resulted in a "capture" by Union forces, and those in which the vessel was either "lost" or destroyed by the Union Navy. In addition, his table indicates whether the vessel was powered by steam or sail. There was usually a notation of the location in cases where a vessel was captured. In addition to the information on trips, there is a summary table for each year indicating the number of vessels engaged from each of the three groups of ports.

Marcus Price drew on a large body of sources for his data. The government documents that form the basis of his study included the Records of the U.S. Department of State (National Archives record group number 59), General Records of the U.S. Department of the Treasury (National Archives record group number 56), Records of the U.S. Bureau of Customs (National Archives record group number 36), and Records of the Department of the U.S. Navy (National Archives record groups numbers 24 and 45), together with various records of the British and Confederate governments in the Library of Congress. Price consulted newspapers in Charleston, Mobile, Montgomery, New Orleans, and Savannah; in Liverpool and London; and in Havana, Cuba. Finally, he consulted a large body of private correspondence.

Price takes care to point out that "it is neither represented nor believed that these tabular reports contain the name of all vessels that tested the blockade.... Only those vessels have been listed whose entrances and/or clearances have been definitely established by the authorities cited" (Price 1951, p. 278). In addition to the incompleteness of existing government records, there were, according to one Confederate customs official, "a class of small, light-draught vessels from six to twenty tons burthen engaged in the trade with the Island of Cuba and the Bahamas" that regularly evaded detection by the authorities. Although these small craft doubtless plied the entire coast of the Confederacy, the list compiled by Price includes the vessels that accounted for most of the tonnage engaged in running the blockade.

Series Eh59–70, all ports. Totals for all of the trips included in the study.

Series Eh71–78, Carolina Ports. Includes towns along Albemarle Sound and Cape Fear, and the ports of Elizabeth City, New Bern, and Wilmington in North Carolina, together with ports of Charleston, Georgetown, Port Royal, and Santee in South Carolina.

Series Eh79–86, Georgia and East Florida Ports. With Savannah effectively blockaded and Jacksonville captured by Union troops early in the war, blockade running in this area was limited to coastal traffic putting in and out of small harbors and inlets. Relatively few of these vessels engaged in foreign trade.

Series Eh87–94, Gulf Ports. Includes Eagle Pass, Galveston, Matagorda, and Sabine, Texas; and Apalachicola, Chatahoochie, Pensacola, St. Marks, and Tampa Bay, Florida. New Orleans was one of the most active ports until its capture in April 1862, and the inlets and lakes around the mouth of the Mississippi remained busy throughout the war.

TABLE Eh95–102   Quantity and price of cotton imported into the United Kingdom: 1855–1875

Contributed by Roger L. Ransom

	Cotton imported into the United Kingdom							
	Bales of varying weight			400-pound bales				
	From the United States	From all other suppliers	Pounds of cotton	Total	From the United States	From all other suppliers	Liverpool price of cotton	New York price of cotton
	Eh95	Eh96	Eh97	Eh98	Eh99	Eh100	Eh101	Eh102
Year	Thousand bales	Thousand bales	Million pounds	Thousand 400-pound bales	Thousand 400-pound bales	Thousand 400-pound bales	Pence per pound	Cents per pound
1855	1,624	655	901	2,253	1,758	495	—	—
1856	1,758	710	1,021	2,553	1,921	632	—	—
1857	1,482	937	976	2,440	1,633	807	—	—
1858	1,803	639	1,026	2,564	2,004	560	—	—
1859	2,086	744	1,191	2,977	2,316	662	—	—
1860	2,581	786	1,436	3,590	2,861	728	5.97	11.00
1861	1,842	1,194	1,261	3,154	2,039	1,114	8.50	13.01
1862	72	1,373	533	1,333	79	1,253	18.37	31.29
1863	132	1,800	692	1,730	146	1,584	22.46	67.21
1864	198	2,389	896	2,240	218	2,022	27.17	101.50
1865	462	2,293	966	2,416	509	1,907	19.11	83.38
1866	1,163	2,586	1,354	3,385	1,280	2,104	15.30	43.20
1867	1,226	2,275	1,274	3,185	1,348	1,837	10.98	31.59
1868	1,269	2,391	1,292	3,230	1,394	1,836	10.52	24.85
1869	1,040	2,343	1,197	2,993	1,141	1,851	12.12	29.01
1870	1,664	1,798	1,321	3,303	1,826	1,477	9.89	23.98
1871	2,249	2,156	1,676	4,190	2,467	1,723	8.55	16.95
1872	1,404	2,477	1,373	3,432	1,538	1,895	10.78	20.48
1873	1,898	2,006	1,509	3,771	2,085	1,686	9.65	18.15
1874	1,958	1,957	1,520	3,800	2,159	1,641	8.36	17.00
1875	1,859	1,849	1,459	3,647	2,056	1,591	7.61	15.00

Sources

Cotton imports are from Thomas Ellison, *The Cotton Trade of Great Britain* (Frank Cass, 1886), Table 1; cotton prices are from M. B. Hammond, *The Cotton Industry* (Macmillan, 1897), Appendix.

Documentation

Tables Eh95–110 present data on the imports of cotton to Great Britain and Europe in the middle of the nineteenth century. Thomas Ellison's *The Cotton Trade of Great Britain* is the definitive source for the cotton trade not only of Britain but of Europe as well. The figures most often quoted by researchers from his 1886 study are from his data appendix on shipments of cotton into Great Britain from the United States and various other suppliers of cotton reported in bales. The difficulty with these numbers is that the weight of a "bale" of cotton varied widely between countries and over time, making it difficult to obtain meaningful totals by adding bales from different countries. The following table, computed from data given in Ellison (1866), p. 99, illustrates the point.

Pounds of cotton per bale in various countries – five-year averages: 1851–1881

Years	Total	United States	Brazil	West Indies	India	Egypt
1851–1855	401.4	425.5	181.9	210.0	383.0	280.4
1856–1860	423.6	444.5	181.0	205.7	385.0	351.9
1861–1865	387.6	441.9	180.1	200.0	355.9	457.9
1866–1870	375.5	439.4	162.7	189.7	360.1	435.8
1871–1875	390.2	438.2	157.7	209.4	362.9	504.2
1876–1881	428.7	445.0	170.7	172.8	373.8	572.9

Ellison's solution to this problem was to take the figures given in pounds of cotton and convert them into "bales of uniform weight of 400 lbs." (p. 91). Unfortunately, although he provides data for the total pounds of cotton imported into Britain, he does not provide the weight in pounds for individual suppliers.

Series Eh95 and Eh97. These series present the data reported by Ellison for the United States and all other countries (in bales) and for the total imported to the United Kingdom (in pounds).

Series Eh98–100. These series have been constructed from Ellison's data. For the United States, the number of reported bales were multiplied by the average weight of U.S. bales reported by Ellison to obtain the total weight of cotton from the U.S. in pounds, which was divided by 400 to obtain 400-pound bales. Although annual data are not available, the weight of a bale of U.S. cotton remained quite stable at just over 440 pounds during the period 1855 through 1875. Annual values for the weight of U.S. bales were obtained by interpolating the midpoint estimates of the five-year averages. The estimates for all other countries were obtained by subtracting the total weight in pounds of cotton imported from the United States from the weight of all imports and dividing the residual by 400. The total, series Eh98, was estimated directly from series Eh97.

TABLE Eh103–110   European cotton imports, by country of origin: 1860–1875

Contributed by Roger L. Ransom

	All countries	United States	Brazil	Egypt	Turkey	West Indies	India and East Indies	China and Japan
	Eh103	Eh104	Eh105	Eh106	Eh107	Eh108	Eh109	Eh110
Year	Thousand 400-pound bales	Thousand 400-pound bales	Thousand 400-pound bales	Thousand 400-pound bales	Thousand 400-pound bales	Thousand 400-pound bales	Thousand 400-pound bales	Thousand 400-pound bales
1860	4,837	4,058	48	135	21	23	552	—
1861	4,248	3,075	46	124	36	18	949	84
1862	1,439	102	65	182	58	20	1,010	2
1863	1,947	163	67	294	127	36	1,179	81
1864	2,635	241	127	427	188	39	1,374	239
1865	2,860	522	150	549	239	84	1,231	85
1866	4,015	1,555	222	279	161	77	1,706	15
1867	3,806	1,659	220	305	129	103	1,389	1
1868	4,316	1,946	309	355	145	85	1,476	—
1869	4,094	1,583	281	353	207	92	1,578	—
1870	4,213	2,345	217	379	136	79	1,057	—
1871	5,719	3,409	281	396	119	130	1,384	—
1872	4,885	2,234	377	489	138	121	1,526	—
1873	5,038	2,908	243	484	143	105	1,155	—
1874	5,469	3,177	252	532	93	98	1,317	—
1875	5,457	3,112	216	552	88	69	1,420	—

Source

Thomas Ellison, *The Cotton Trade of Great Britain* (Frank Cass, 1886), p. 91.

Documentation

These series present Ellison's estimates of the amount of cotton imported into "all countries of Europe." These estimates have been converted into uniform 400-pound bales and are thus comparable to the estimates for imports into Great Britain, shown in series Eh95–96.

See the text for Table Eh95–102 for additional information on the source and a discussion of bale weights.

MONEY AND PRICES

Roger L. Ransom

TABLE Eh111–117   Confederate money stock: 1860–1862   [Godfrey, nine states]

Contributed by Roger L. Ransom

		Total			Confederate currency	Bank notes	Deposits	State currency
		Total	Bank cash	In private hands				
		Eh111	Eh112	Eh113	Eh114	Eh115	Eh116	Eh117
Year	Month	Million Confederate dollars	Million Confederate dollars	Million Confederate dollars	Million Confederate dollars	Million Confederate dollars	Million Confederate dollars	Million Confederate dollars
1860	Jan	117	27	90	—	58	59	—
1860	Apr	115	26	89	—	58	57	—
1860	July	101	22	79	—	50	51	—
1860	Oct	93	16	77	—	44	46	—
1861	Jan	93	23	70	—	43	50	—
1861	Apr	109	33	76	—	50	59	—
1861	July	109	40	69	1	50	58	(Z)
1861	Oct	145	44	101	20	56	68	1
1862	Jan	222	62	160	68	64	87	3
1862	Apr	317	81	236	135	68	108	6

(Z) Less than $500,000.

Source
John Munro Godfrey, *Monetary Expansion in the Confederacy* (Arno Press, 1978), Table 6.1, p. 116.

Documentation
The most detailed and comprehensive estimates of the supply of money in the Confederacy are those of John Godfrey, which are presented in Tables Eh111–124. For many years, the definitive series on the supply of money in the Confederacy have been those constructed in 1955 by Eugene Lerner, presented in Table Eh125–127. Godfrey pointed out that Lerner's estimates – and those of other studies on the Confederate money supply data – were incomplete or deficient because not all relevant items were included in the definitions of the money stock; there were gaps in the data with regard to both dates and regions of the Confederate States of America (CSA); and data in reports were sometimes misinterpreted by researchers (Godfrey 1978, pp. 3–7).

Godfrey presents data for nine states from the inception of the CSA through April 1862 (Table Eh111–117) and for seven states through April 1865 (Table Eh118–124). The series in the two tables are the same except for the geographical coverage.

In addition to the data reproduced here, Godfrey also presents estimates of the "condition of banks" for each state in the tables (p. 137). Although his estimates are the best available, they do not account for money in the trans-Mississippi area of the Confederacy after 1862. Those areas, designated the Trans-Mississippi Department, were not authorized to issue currency, and reliable monetary statistics are not available. The most detailed discussion of the problems of money in that region can be found in Gary Pecquet, "Money in the Trans-Mississippi Confederacy and the Confederate Currency Reform Act of 1864," *Explorations in Economic History* 24 (April 1987): 218–43.

Godfrey identifies four components of the money supply: (1) Confederate currency, which in his definition includes bills issued by the Confederate government that bore no interest, interest-bearing treasury notes, and call certificates; (2) bank notes issued by state banks; (3) deposits in banks owned by individuals, businesses, banks, and governments; and (4) state currency that was issued by eight of the Confederate state governments during the war.

Series Eh111 and Eh118. Equals the sum of the four components just described: Confederate currency, bank notes, deposits in banks, and state currency. Also equals the sum of money in the hands of the public and cash held by banks.

TABLE Eh118–124   Confederate money stock: 1860–1865   [Godfrey, seven states]

Contributed by Roger L. Ransom

		Total			Confederate currency	Bank notes	Deposits	State currency
		Total	Bank cash	In private hands				
		Eh118	Eh119	Eh120	Eh121	Eh122	Eh123	Eh124
Year	Month	Million Confederate dollars	Million Confederate dollars	Million Confederate dollars	Million Confederate dollars	Million Confederate dollars	Million Confederate dollars	Million Confederate dollars
1860	Jan	74	15	59	—	42	32	
1860	Apr	71	15	56	—	40	31	—
1860	July	67	14	53	—	36	31	—
1860	Oct	60	12	48	—	33	27	—
1861	Jan	61	14	47	—	33	28	—
1861	Apr	68	19	49	—	36	32	—
1861	July	74	24	50	1	37	36	(Z)
1861	Oct	107	34	73	20	41	45	1

Note appears at end of table

(continued)

TABLE Eh118-124   Confederate money stock: 1860-1865   [Godfrey, seven states]   *Continued*

| | | | Total | | | | | |
		Total	Bank cash	In private hands	Confederate currency	Bank notes	Deposits	State currency
		Eh118	Eh119	Eh120	Eh121	Eh122	Eh123	Eh124
Year	Month	Million Confederate dollars	Million Confederate dollars	Million Confederate dollars	Million Confederate dollars	Million Confederate dollars	Million Confederate dollars	Million Confederate dollars
1862	Jan	176	42	134	68	49	56	3
1862	Apr	261	53	208	135	51	69	6
1862	July	352	62	290	214	52	76	10
1862	Oct	485	74	411	328	53	89	15
1863	Jan	632	84	548	456	53	104	19
1863	Apr	700	92	608	508	53	117	22
1863	July	784	101	683	576	53	130	25
1863	Oct	930	116	814	701	53	149	27
1864	Jan	1,096	133	963	845	54	168	29
1864	Feb	1,190	141	1,049	926	54	178	32
1864	Apr	730	47	683	632	54	10	34
1864	July	754	37	717	644	54	16	40
1864	Oct	812	43	769	690	54	22	46
1865	Jan	856	49	860	781	54	28	46

(Z) Less than $500,000.

Source

John Munro Godfrey, *Monetary Expansion in the Confederacy* (Arno Press, 1978), Table 6.3, pp. 118-19.

Documentation

See the text for Table Eh111-117.

TABLE Eh125-127   Confederate money stock: 1861-1864   [Lerner]

Contributed by Roger L. Ransom

		Total	Bank notes and deposits	Confederate government notes
		Eh125	Eh126	Eh127
Year	Month	Million Confederate dollars	Million Confederate dollars	Million Confederate dollars
1861	Jan	94.6	94.6	—
1861	Apr	121.8	121.8	—
1861	June	120.4	119.3	1.1
1861	Oct	170.8	146.3	24.5
1862	Jan	239.8	165.2	74.6
1862	Apr	282.1	151.1	131.0
1862	June	309.0	142.9	166.1
1862	Oct	468.8	181.5	287.3
1863	Jan	649.6	239.1	410.5
1863	Apr	818.8	257.1	561.7
1863	June	904.8	267.5	637.3
1863	Oct	1,067.1	274.7	792.4
1864	Jan	1,094.9	268.1	826.8

Source

Eugene Lerner, "Money, Prices and Wages in the Confederacy, 1861-65," *Journal of Political Economy* 43 (February 1955), Table 1, p. 21.

Documentation

Lerner's series on the money supply include only two components: (1) bank notes and deposits, including cash held by banks and interbank deposits; and (2) Confederate government notes, which include incomplete estimates of notes issued by states. The source of these estimates is not explained in detail, and the author is particularly unclear on the extent of geographical coverage of the data in these series. Texas, Arkansas, and Mississippi are not included in the estimate for January 1861, and data for these and several other states are incomplete for some years. Despite these drawbacks, Lerner's series have been the most widely used for monetary statistics on the Confederacy.

See the text for Table Eh111-117 for additional information.

TABLE Eh128–130   Prices and wage indexes for the eastern Confederacy: 1861–1865

Contributed by Roger L. Ransom

Year	Month	General index of prices Eh128 Jan–Apr 1861 = 100	Wage index Eh129 Jan 1861 = 100	Ratio of mean skilled wage to mean unskilled wage Eh130 Ratio	Year	Month	General index of prices Eh128 Jan–Apr 1861 = 100	Wage index Eh129 Jan 1861 = 100	Ratio of mean skilled wage to mean unskilled wage Eh130 Ratio
1861	Jan	101	100	3.76	1863	May	1,279	233	2.30
1861	Feb	99	100	4.28	1863	June	1,308	241	2.32
1861	Mar	101	99	3.92	1863	July	1,326	263	2.61
1861	Apr	101	101	4.73	1863	Aug	1,428	296	2.97
1861	May	109	107	4.25	1863	Sept	1,617	305	2.25
1861	June	109	105	3.03	1863	Oct	1,879	341	2.24
1861	July	111	100	4.25	1863	Nov	2,236	371	1.69
1861	Aug	120	100	3.37	1863	Dec	2,464	349	1.86
1861	Sept	128	106	—	1864	Jan	2,801	397	2.96
1861	Oct	136	101	5.30	1864	Feb	2,947	381	2.23
1861	Nov	161	116	—	1864	Mar	4,128	462	2.21
1861	Dec	172	114	—	1864	Apr	4,470	402	3.15
1862	Jan	193	121	3.38	1864	May	4,575	398	2.57
1862	Feb	211	112	3.38	1864	June	4,198	372	2.84
1862	Mar	236	118	3.98	1864	July	4,094	385	2.81
1862	Apr	281	119	4.02	1864	Aug	4,097	394	2.59
1862	May	278	122	3.72	1864	Sept	4,279	450	3.21
1862	June	331	127	3.09	1864	Oct	4,001	527	3.21
1862	July	380	122	3.15	1864	Nov	4,029	528	3.05
1862	Aug	419	136	3.38	1864	Dec	4,285	521	1.39
1862	Sept	493	139	3.00	1865	Jan	5,824	784	1.16
1862	Oct	526	160	2.30	1865	Feb	6,427	884	3.04
1862	Nov	624	166	2.49	1865	Mar	8,336	997	3.73
1862	Dec	686	177	2.38	1865	Apr	9,211	—	—
1863	Jan	762	201	2.91					
1863	Feb	900	207	2.62					
1863	Mar	1,051	212	2.77					
1863	Apr	1,178	237	2.46					

Source

Eugene Lerner, "Money, Prices and Wages in the Confederacy, 1861–65," *Journal of Political Economy* 43 (February 1955), Table 2, p. 24; Table 4, p. 32; and Table 5, p. 34.

Documentation

Eugene Lerner's study represents the most comprehensive attempt to chart the course of wages and prices in the Confederacy.

Lerner constructed an unweighted index of monthly prices in four cities: Richmond, Virginia; Fayetteville, Arkansas; Augusta, Georgia; and Wilmington, North Carolina. His description of the method by which he constructed the index in series Eh128 is as follows: "To construct these price series, the quotations for each item continuously listed in the newspapers were recorded. (About three times as many quotations were collected from these sources as could be used. Discontinuous series were rejected.) When only one quotation was available for a commodity in a given month, as occasionally happened, this figure was taken as typical of the commodity's price during that month. More often, two or three quotations were available. When I had two quotations for a given month, I took their simple average as typical of the price for the month. When I had three quotations, I gave equal weight to both the beginning and end of the month. (If I had quotations for, say, the first, fifteenth, and thirty-first, I averaged all three quotations. If I had quotations for the first, twenty-fifth, and twenty-eighth, I rejected the twenty-eighth and used only the figures for the first and twenty-fifth.) In most cases, however, at least one quotation a week was available, and the four quotations for the month were averaged" (Lerner 1955, p. 23, footnote 8).

Lerner used the following commodities when constructing the index in series Eh128:

Richmond – corn, rye, red wheat, flaxseed, hay, oats, cotton, tobacco, bacon, butter, lard, cornmeal, family flour, extrafine flour, superfine flour, Irish potatoes, rice, salt, sugar, coffee, molasses, tallow candles, adamantine candles, whiskey, sole leather, upper leather, beeswax, and lime.

Fayetteville – corn, rye, wheat, flaxseed, cotton, wool, bacon, lard, family flour, peas, molasses, New Orleans sugar, salt, tallow, iron, nails, peach brandy, apple brandy, cotton yarn, sheeting, green hides, beeswax, and spirits of turpentine.

Augusta – corn, wheat, hay, cotton, bacon, butter, eggs, chickens, lard, cornmeal, family flour, peas, rice, coffee, molasses, sugar, pork, salt, tea, beef, bagging, 4 × 4 sheeting, cotton yarn, 7 × 8 shirting, 3 × 4 shirting, cotton rope, New Orleans whiskey, apple brandy, peach brandy, nails, iron, dry hides, and starch.

Wilmington – corn, hay, cotton, bacon, beef, butter, eggs, chickens, live turkeys, dead turkeys, pork, lard, cornmeal, superfine flour, peanuts, sheeting, wool yarn, and beeswax (Lerner 1955, p. 23, footnote 9).

Lerner also constructed an index of wages for the "eastern" Confederacy, shown in series Eh129. His description of the sources is as follows: "The most fruitful source of quotations was the Tredegar Iron Works. . . . The University of North Carolina has the account-book of the Henry Gaist Flour and Saw Mill and the John Judge Sock and Yarn Factory. These include quotations for farm hands, butchers, and general labor. In the Moravian Archives at Winston Salem, North Carolina, the account-books of the Fries Cotton and Wool Company are available. Only the total pay roll and the number of people employed are listed. From this source the average take-home pay was recorded. The time book of the Atlanta, Georgia, arsenal, available at the National Archives in Washington, revealed figures for 1863 and 1864 for guards, machinists, carpenters, cartridge-makers, and superintendents. The accounts of the Central Laboratory of Georgia, also located in the National Archives, give data for 1863, 1864, and 1865 on carpenters, watchmen,

(continued)

TABLE Eh128–130   Prices and wage indexes for the eastern Confederacy: 1861–1865   *Continued*

overseers, bricklayers, brick-burners, and painters. In the Historical Commission of Columbia, South Carolina, the records for the building of the statehouse are available and reveal the figures for quarrymen, assistant quarrymen, blacksmiths, engineers, watchmen, carpenters, hostlers, architects, and railroad inspectors in 1862–63. The Graham Robinson Iron and Steel Works account-books at the University of Virginia reveal the wages paid to several workers in the mills, not classified by profession, throughout the war" (Lerner 1955, p. 31, footnote 37).

To compute the index in series Eh129, Lerner relied on the median: Because "the median is not affected by extreme values, it was the statistic used as typical of all wages in a trade 'in any given month.' The first quotation listed in 1861 was taken as the base, and successive monthly medians were expressed as a percentage of this value. For some occupations quotations were not available for 1861. To utilize the quotations that were available for

later years, I assumed that during 1861 wages increased in these trades as much as the average increase in all other trades. The first quotation for these occupations in 1862 was therefore given the value of 1.085, a base in 1861 was determined, and the successive monthly quotations were expressed as a percentage of this" (Lerner 1955, pp. 31–2).

Series Eh130. Equals the ratio of Lerner's index of skilled wages to his index of unskilled wages in the Confederacy. Neither series was published. His definition of skilled labor was as follows: "Engineers, bricklayers, machinists, foremen, boiler makers, pattern-makers, carpenters, blacksmiths and the highest figure found in a month for foundry and quarry help." He classified as unskilled trades "saw mill help, butchers, farm help, watchmen, overseers yarn-and-sock-factory help, isolated individuals in steel mills, and railroad inspectors" (Lerner 1955, p. 56).

TABLE Eh131   Monthly index of Richmond wholesale commodity prices: 1861–1865

Contributed by Roger L. Ransom

Year	Month	Index of Richmond prices Eh131 1860 = 100	Year	Month	Index of Richmond prices Eh131 1860 = 100	Year	Month	Index of Richmond prices Eh131 1860 = 100	Year	Month	Index of Richmond prices Eh131 1860 = 100
1861	Jan	96	1862	Jan	178	1863	Jan	631	1864	Jan	2,670
1861	Feb	100	1862	Feb	186	1863	Feb	912	1864	Feb	3,624
1861	Mar	99	1862	Mar	203	1863	Mar	1,154	1864	Mar	4,146
1861	Apr	103	1862	Apr	220	1863	Apr	1,284	1864	Apr	5,200
1861	May	104	1862	May	297	1863	May	1,388	1864	May	5,788
1861	June	108	1862	June	285	1863	June	1,340	1864	June	4,993
1861	July	121	1862	July	324	1863	July	1,488	1864	July	5,632
1861	Aug	124	1862	Aug	330	1863	Aug	1,429	1864	Aug	4,488
1861	Sept	134	1862	Sept	438	1863	Sept	1,461	1864	Sept	5,208
1861	Oct	154	1862	Oct	528	1863	Oct	1,646	1864	Oct	5,344
1861	Nov	164	1862	Nov	549	1863	Nov	2,110	1864	Nov	5,274
1861	Dec	187	1862	Dec	584	1863	Dec	2,020	1865	Feb	7,500

Source

Thomas Senior Berry, *Richmond Commodity Prices, 1861–1865,* Bostwick Paper number 5 (Bostwick Press, 1985), Table 1, p. 2.

Documentation

Thomas Senior Berry's monthly index of wholesale prices in Richmond is part of his study of prices in the Confederate capital during the Civil War. To measure price changes, Berry collected price quotations for thirty commodities primarily drawn from the columns of five Richmond dailies: the *Richmond Dispatch,* the *Richmond Enquirer,* the *Richmond Examiner,* the *Sentinel,* and the *Richmond Whig* (Berry 1985, p. 22). With regard to the sources, Berry explains: "In 1861 these journals contained fairly lively commercial and financial columns. As time went on, however, those columns shrank both in size and frequency of publication. It proved possible to assemble 18 reasonably continuous commodity price-series from 1861 through November 1864. Auction sales at Robinson, Adams and Company (Main Street at Ninth) helped in

the fall of the latter year. The fog lifted briefly with the appearance of a price list in the *Whig* of February 3, 1865."

By limiting the geographical scope, Berry's index of Richmond prices offers the best in-depth study of the behavior of a group of consistent commodity prices in a single market in the Confederacy.

Data from Berry's study are presented in Tables Eh131–165.

Series Eh131 is Berry's monthly index of prices for Richmond between April 1861 and November 1865. Berry is unclear on the definition of the base period, saying only that it is a "prewar base" of Richmond prices (Berry 1985, p. 1). Following the procedure employed by Lerner in his index of prices in the Eastern Confederacy (see series Eh128), Berry used unweighted medians of the array of prices to construct his price relatives. This lessens the undue influence that commodities such as coffee and flour – which soared to very high levels by late 1864 – would have on the overall index if one used means rather than medians to calculate the index.

TABLE Eh132-135   Wholesale commodity price indexes in Richmond, the eastern Confederacy, New York, and San Francisco: 1861–1865

Contributed by Roger L. Ransom

		Richmond	Eastern Confederacy	New York	San Francisco
		Eh132	Eh133	Eh134	Eh135
Year	Month	Jan–Apr 1861 = 100	Jan–Apr 1861 = 100	Jan–Apr 1861 = 100	Jan–Apr 1861 = 100
1861	Mar	100	100	100	100
1862	Mar	203	189	109	111
1863	Mar	1,154	670	156	115
1864	Mar	4,146	3,600	178	122
1865	Feb	7,500	5,155	240	150
1865	Nov	166	—	209	134

Source

Thomas Senior Berry, *Richmond Commodity Prices, 1861–1865,* Bostwick Paper number 5 (Bostwick Press, 1985), Table 2, p. 4.

Documentation

See the text for Table Eh131 for further discussion of the source.

Richmond's experience with inflation did not mirror that of the rest of the Confederacy or the United States during the war. To place series Eh131 in perspective, Berry constructed estimates of prices in three other cities in the Confederacy and the United States for a single month in the spring of each year from 1861 through 1865. These series present this comparison.

Series Eh132 is from the Richmond price quotations used to construct series Eh131. Series Eh133 is an index of prices in the eastern Confederacy constructed from the data collected by Eugene Lerner (see series Eh128). The two other series are for cities that Berry felt were representative of the northeastern and western areas of the United States during the war. Series Eh134 is a series of New York prices taken from George A. Warren and Frank A. Pearson, *Prices* (Wiley, 1933), p. 12. Berry adjusted the base period to correspond with the other series (Berry 1985, p. 5). Series Eh135 is a series of San Francisco prices taken from T. S. Berry, *Early California* (Bostwick Press, 1984), pp. 144–60.

TABLE Eh136–165 Monthly wholesale price quotations for selected commodities in Richmond: 1856–1865

Contributed by Roger L. Ransom

Year(s)	Month	Unprocessed agricultural products								Processed food products					
		Corn	Flaxseed	Hay	Oats	Potatoes, Irish	Rice	Rye	Wheat, white	Bacon	Butter, good	Corn meal	Flour, superfine	Molasses, New Orleans	Sugar, New Orleans, brown
		Eh136	Eh137	Eh138	Eh139	Eh140	Eh141	Eh142	Eh143	Eh144	Eh145	Eh146	Eh147	Eh148	Eh149
		Dollars per bushel	Dollars per bushel	Dollars per hundredweight	Dollars per bushel	Dollars per bushel	Dollars per pound	Dollars per bushel	Dollars per bushel	Dollars per pound	Dollars per pound	Dollars per bushel	Dollars per barrel	Dollars per gallon	Dollars per pound
1856–1860	—[1]	0.61	1.26	1.19	0.38	0.87	0.05	0.62	1.47	0.12	0.18	0.72	6.75	0.44	0.07
1861	Apr	0.64	1.25	1.25	0.32	1.22	0.05	0.62	1.55	0.17	0.14	0.75	7.88	0.42	0.06
1862	May	0.85	1.50	1.95	0.80	1.38 [3]	—	1.75	1.12	0.36	1.20	1.02	7.12	1.90	0.30
1863	Apr	7.50	4.00 [2]	8.25	5.25	12.00	0.26	2.62 [4]	6.50	1.15	2.88 [2]	6.50	32.00	9.50	1.17
1864	Apr	45.00	12.00	33.75	37.75	16.00	1.10	9.50 [4]	18.00 [4]	7.42	9.50	45.00	250.00	55.17	8.88
1865	Feb	67.50	—	—	—	80.00	1.50	—	—	9.00	12.00	72.50	1,200.00 [2]	—	15.00
1865	Nov	1.00	2.58	2.00	0.55	—	—	1.00	2.25	0.22	0.42	—	10.12	0.58	0.15

Year(s)	Month	Sundries										Imported goods				Agricultural staples	
		Beeswax, best	Candles, tallow	Cotton yarn	Hides	Lard	Leather, sole	Salt	Soap, country	Whiskey, common	Wool, unwashed	Coffee, Rio	Nails, cut	Cement, James River	Lime	Cotton	Tobacco
		Eh150	Eh151	Eh152	Eh153	Eh154	Eh155	Eh156	Eh157	Eh158	Eh159	Eh160	Eh161	Eh162	Eh163	Eh164	Eh165
		Dollars per pound	Dollars per pound	Dollars per pound	Dollars per pound	Dollars per pound	Dollars per pound	Dollars per bushel	Dollars per pound	Dollars per gallon	Dollars per pound	Dollars per pound	Dollars per hundredweight	Dollars per barrel	Dollars per barrel	Dollars per pound	Dollars per hundredweight
1856–1860	—[1]	0.30	0.14	0.22	0.10	0.12	0.24	1.67	0.10	0.23	0.24	0.15	3.59	1.62	1.19	0.12	2.98
1861	Apr	0.30	0.14	0.26	0.10	0.12	0.25	1.75	—	0.28	0.24	0.17	4.12	1.62	1.25	0.12	2.88
1862	May	0.30 [3]	0.26	0.70	0.14	0.38	1.00	5.50	—	1.50 [3]	0.92	0.82	10.50	2.75	2.25	0.10	3.38
1863	Apr	1.50 [4]	2.70	2.20	1.30	1.51	3.88	7.42	0.70	27.50	1.38	3.50	35.00 [4]	2.50 [4]	7.00	0.28 [2]	19.50
1864	Apr	5.50	7.17	10.70	2.75 [4]	8.74	10.50	20.00	3.25	70.00	4.50	14.05	120.00	—	22.50	2.40 [2]	24.00
1865	Feb	10.50	14.50	15.00	2.50	13.00	15.50	28.75	4.00	—	—	36.50	287.50	—	—	—	—
1865	Nov	—	0.22	—	—	0.28	—	1.88	0.12	2.25	0.42	0.29	—	—	2.75	—	8.75

[1] Prewar base price. See text.

[2] March.

[3] February.

[4] January.

Source

Thomas Senior Berry, *Richmond Commodity Prices, 1861–1865*, Bostwick Paper number 5 (Bostwick Press, 1985), Table 7, p. 24.

Documentation

See the text for Table Eh131 for further discussion of the source.

These series present monthly mean price quotations for the thirty commodities included in Berry's index of wholesale prices in Richmond. In addition to the price quotations given for specific months during the war, Berry provides a "prewar base" price, which is the median price for the period 1856–1860.

To facilitate comparisons of different kinds of commodities, the data have been grouped into five general categories: unprocessed agricultural products; processed food products; sundries; raw materials; imported goods; and the two agricultural staples of the South, cotton and tobacco.

TABLE Eh166–193 Monthly commodity price indexes for the Confederate states: 1861–1865 [Schwab]
Contributed by Roger L. Ransom

		Composite indexes of commodity groups						Unprocessed agricultural products					
		All commodities	Raw agricultural products	Processed food products	Sundries	Imported goods	Agricultural staples	Corn	Oats	Potatoes (Irish)	Potatoes (sweet)	Rice	Wheat
		Eh166	Eh167	Eh168	Eh169	Eh170	Eh171	Eh172	Eh173	Eh174	Eh175	Eh176	Eh177
Year	Month	1860 = 100	1860 = 100	1860 = 100	1860 = 100	1860 = 100	1860 = 100	1860 = 100	1860 = 100	1860 = 100	1860 = 100	1860 = 100	1860 = 100
1861	Feb	105	110	100	—	—	100	110	110	—	—	80	—
1861	Mar	100	100	100	100	130	120	100	120	100	60	80	90
1861	Apr	105	105	100	95	130	130	100	120	100	60	110	90
1861	May	110	115	110	105	130	115	80	140	120	80	110	90
1861	June	115	125	100	105	145	110	80	150	120	80	140	90
1861	July	110	120	105	140	150	—	110	—	—	—	50	—
1861	Aug	105	120	90	90	130	60	100	150	—	—	60	90
1861	Sept	140	160	80	180	280	—	120	160	—	—	60	—
1861	Oct	100	140	95	165	270	80	120	160	—	—	80	100
1861	Nov	160	180	120	150	270	70	170	230	—	—	80	—
1861	Dec	145	170	100	145	190	100	—	200	170	—	120	90
1862	Jan	185	160	130	200	340	110	—	160	—	—	140	90
1862	Feb	160	150	170	—	430	90	—	—	—	—	150	—
1862	Mar	230	230	190	230	450	125	180	240	—	—	150	—
1862	Apr	240	235	160	295	380	80	210	240	—	—	140	230
1862	May	315	260	255	300	570	90	200	—	200	—	—	—
1862	June	330	330	180	1,700	—	—	150	—	—	—	—	—
1862	July	340	290	225	1,645	420	—	210	290	—	—	—	—
1862	Aug	300	300	345	1,200	—	—	210	300	—	—	—	—
1862	Sept	555	190	—	920	1,500	190	—	—	—	—	—	190
1862	Oct	500	500	430	750	930	180	—	—	500	—	—	340
1862	Nov	680	360	710	840	1,300	295	360	—	—	—	280	350
1862	Dec	460	355	340	730	1,300	150	360	490	230	140	310	350
1863	Jan	610	495	645	1,200	1,500	230	430	610	500	600	380	340
1863	Feb	800	570	655	1,200	1,900	—	560	430	580	630	380	380
1863	Mar	1,100	645	1,350	1,300	1,625	220	560	730	1,100	300	560	380
1863	Apr	1,150	740	1,315	1,600	2,700	235	720	1,100	760	500	670	440
1863	May	1,015	795	1,465	1,300	2,500	400	840	1,200	600	450	750	440
1863	June	1,100	965	1,500	1,700	1,880	390	1,000	1,100	500	450	7,100	440
1863	July	1,050	740	1,800	1,800	2,050	405	—	1,200	500	500	1,000	500
1863	Aug	1,300	975	1,700	2,000	3,000	435	1,400	1,200	350	500	1,000	470
1863	Sept	1,300	1,055	1,950	2,000	3,800	360	1,300	1,200	400	680	910	480
1863	Oct	1,400	1,100	1,955	2,000	3,800	370	1,400	1,200	450	450	1,000	720
1863	Nov	1,800	1,350	2,550	2,300	5,800	620	1,700	1,500	610	810	940	1,200
1863	Dec	2,000	1,450	2,500	2,400	6,150	—	1,900	1,700	670	350	930	1,200
1864	Jan	2,200	1,300	2,750	2,700	6,000	1,500	2,000	1,500	650	830	940	1,100
1864	Feb	2,700	1,350	2,550	3,800	6,300	900	3,000	1,600	1,000	1,000	1,000	1,100
1864	Mar	3,600	2,250	3,200	5,000	10,850	1,035	3,700	2,000	1,600	1,300	2,500	1,100
1864	Apr	4,150	2,200	4,400	5,000	7,500	1,700	—	2,200	1,800	1,900	4,400	1,100
1864	May	3,900	2,750	5,750	5,000	10,850	1,700	—	2,000	2,000	—	3,800	1,100
1864	June	3,600	2,800	4,400	4,000	7,500	—	3,800	2,100	1,500	2,500	5,000	1,200
1864	July	3,750	2,850	3,800	5,000	7,500	1,100	4,200	2,800	1,500	2,500	3,700	1,700
1864	Aug	3,600	2,850	2,300	5,000	7,500	1,500	—	2,800	1,300	—	4,200	2,300
1864	Sept	3,800	2,850	3,750	4,850	9,300	1,200	7,300	2,800	2,800	2,700	3,800	2,300
1864	Oct	4,500	3,350	6,100	5,000	7,500	—	4,000	2,100	—	—	3,800	2,300
1864	Nov	4,500	2,400	6,100	5,300	9,450	1,400	4,000	2,100	1,600	1,800	2,500	2,300
1864	Dec	5,000	2,500	3,700	5,300	10,000	1,700	—	2,000	—	—	2,500	2,300
1865	Jan	5,000	3,450	6,300	6,700	14,350	2,100	4,300	2,400	2,300	1,600	3,900	3,000
1865	Feb	6,400	4,250	7,400	8,000	14,350	3,000	3,600	2,400	4,000	2,500	5,000	4,500
1865	Mar	7,100	4,800	12,800	—	—	—	—	—	2,500	—	10,600	—

(continued)

TABLE Eh166–193   Monthly commodity price indexes for the Confederate states: 1861–1865   [Schwab]   *Continued*

Year	Month	Processed food products						Sundries					Imported goods			Agricultural staples	
		Bacon	Butter	Corn meal	Flour	Molasses	Sugar	Candles (adamantine)	Candles (tallow)	Hides	Lard	Salt	Coffee	Nails	Tea	Cotton	Tobacco
		Eh178	Eh179	Eh180	Eh181	Eh182	Eh183	Eh184	Eh185	Eh186	Eh187	Eh188	Eh189	Eh190	Eh191	Eh192	Eh193
		1860 = 100	1860 = 100	1860 = 100	1860 = 100	1860 = 100	1860 = 100	1860 = 100	1860 = 100	1860 = 100	1860 = 100	1860 = 100	1860 = 100	1860 = 100	1860 = 100	1860 = 100	1860 = 100
1861	Feb	110	—	—	100	—	—	—	—	—	—	—	—	—	—	100	—
1861	Mar	110	110	100	100	100	160	90	110	100	100	—	120	140	—	100	140
1861	Apr	110	110	100	90	100	150	90	110	100	90	—	130	130	—	120	140
1861	May	120	140	100	120	100	150	90	110	100	110	—	130	130	—	100	130
1861	June	130	140	100	100	100	150	90	110	100	130	—	160	130	—	90	130
1861	July	130	160	110	100	100	120	—	—	—	140	—	190	110	—	—	—
1861	Aug	140	200	110	90	90	—	90	—	—	—	—	230	110	130	60	—
1861	Sept	190	180	—	80	70	100	—	—	—	180	—	280	—	—	—	—
1861	Oct	200	180	100	80	90	100	90	—	—	240	—	400	140	—	80	—
1861	Nov	210	180	—	120	120	100	—	—	—	150	—	350	190	—	70	—
1861	Dec	—	190	100	—	—	—	90	—	—	200	—	—	190	—	100	—
1862	Jan	220	210	—	120	130	180	220	200	—	190	—	490	190	—	110	—
1862	Feb	—	—	—	170	—	—	—	—	—	—	—	430	—	—	90	—
1862	Mar	230	230	150	150	250	230	210	190	—	250	920	450	380	450	90	160
1862	Apr	110	160	220	—	310	160	—	280	1,100	450	380	380	80	—		
1862	May	320	360	110	—	—	400	310	170	—	290	1,500	650	330	570	90	—
1862	June	330	370	170	180	—	1,000	—	—	—	—	1,700	—	—	—	—	—
1862	July	—	450	260	190	—	—	690	—	—	—	2,600	—	340	500	—	—
1862	Aug	300	390	—	280	410	—	1,200	—	—	290	2,000	—	—	—	—	—
1862	Sept	—	—	—	—	—	—	920	—	—	—	—	1,500	—	—	190	—
1862	Oct	—	600	—	430	—	—	—	750	—	—	—	—	—	930	180	—
1862	Nov	480	730	—	330	710	1,000	1,000	—	680	400	4,200	2,500	1,200	1,300	180	410
1862	Dec	460	610	340	310	850	—	1,100	730	730	350	—	2,300	1,300	1,100	150	—
1863	Jan	490	780	410	310	880	1,400	1,200	820	1,300	360	3,100	2,800	1,500	1,100	230	—
1863	Feb	830	890	430	350	880	1,400	1,200	800	1,300	670	4,300	2,300	1,500	—	—	—
1863	Mar	1,100	1,400	1,300	480	2,100	1,400	1,200	1,300	1,300	730	2,700	—	2,500	750	220	—
1863	Apr	1,200	1,300	930	500	2,100	1,700	1,600	1,900	1,300	1,200	3,100	2,700	2,700	640	190	280
1863	May	1,200	1,200	930	490	2,200	2,000	1,100	1,800	1,300	910	4,000	2,500	3,100	840	340	460
1863	June	1,200	930	1,000	470	2,000	2,000	1,700	1,500	2,300	1,100	3,800	—	3,100	660	360	420
1863	July	1,200	740	1,100	560	2,500	2,800	1,900	1,800	1,400	1,000	4,700	—	3,100	1,000	360	450
1863	Aug	1,400	950	1,000	510	2,800	2,400	2,000	2,000	1,400	1,300	4,200	2,900	3,100	—	440	430
1863	Sept	1,600	1,200	900	540	3,000	3,200	2,000	2,000	1,800	1,500	5,400	4,100	3,800	1,200	360	—
1863	Oct	1,900	1,300	910	710	3,000	3,600	2,000	2,000	1,800	1,700	6,300	6,300	3,800	1,200	—	370
1863	Nov	2,500	1,900	1,700	1,100	3,400	4,300	1,800	2,500	2,300	2,100	5,300	7,800	3,800	—	630	610
1863	Dec	2,600	1,700	1,500	1,200	3,500	4,800	2,400	2,800	2,000	2,400	5,500	7,900	4,400	—	—	—
1864	Jan	2,800	2,100	1,900	1,900	3,600	5,900	2,400	2,700	2,300	2,800	5,500	7,000	5,000	—	1,500	—
1864	Feb	4,200	3,100	2,700	2,400	5,900	1,400	2,400	3,200	5,000	3,800	5,600	10,700	6,300	1,500	—	900
1864	Mar	5,900	3,300	4,400	2,000	6,700	1,200	3,600	3,900	5,000	5,900	7,700	14,200	7,500	—	1,600	470
1864	Apr	4,800	4,300	5,300	3,500	9,800	1,300	3,200	4,000	5,000	6,500	9,100	14,200	7,500	2,200	1,700	—
1864	May	3,500	4,600	8,100	3,400	8,700	1,300	3,200	4,000	5,000	5,500	9,000	14,200	7,500	—	1,700	—
1864	June	3,400	3,100	5,000	3,800	9,900	1,100	3,200	4,000	3,200	4,500	9,000	13,000	7,500	2,400	—	—
1864	July	4,400	2,900	—	3,800	9,900	1,300	3,200	4,000	5,000	5,500	9,000	11,800	7,500	3,000	—	1,100
1864	Aug	5,000	2,900	—	2,300	5,200	1,300	3,200	4,000	5,000	5,000	10,600	12,500	7,500	3,000	1,500	—
1864	Sept	5,400	2,900	4,700	2,800	5,000	1,300	3,200	4,000	—	5,700	12,000	11,100	7,500	—	1,200	—
1864	Oct	7,200	2,900	5,800	6,400	10,000	1,400	3,200	4,000	5,000	5,500	12,600	11,800	7,500	2,500	—	—
1864	Nov	5,200	4,000	5,800	6,400	10,000	1,400	3,200	5,300	5,000	6,300	12,000	11,800	7,100	—	1,400	—
1864	Dec	5,000	3,800	6,000	—	—	1,400	3,500	5,300	5,000	7,300	12,900	11,800	7,500	10,000	1,700	—
1865	Jan	6,700	5,000	6,300	8,300	—	1,600	4,100	6,700	5,000	7,300	11,400	19,600	9,100	—	2,100	—
1865	Feb	6,700	6,400	6,500	8,300	8,800	1,700	8,000	6,700	5,000	8,400	17,200	19,600	9,100	—	4,000	2,000
1865	Mar	1,300	7,100	—	12,800	—	—	—	—	—	—	—	—	—	—	—	—

TABLE Eh166–193   Monthly commodity price indexes for the Confederate states: 1861–1865   [Schwab]   *Continued*

Sources

John C. Schwab, "Prices in the Confederacy," *Political Science Quarterly* 14 (1899), table following p. 282. Also John C. Schwab, *The Confederate States of America* (Burt Franklin, 1901).

Documentation

Series Eh166–171. Present composite indexes of all commodities and each commodity group. These indexes were computed from Schwab's estimates using the median value of the commodities in each group, so that they would correspond with the indexes computed by Eugene Lerner and Thomas Berry presented in Tables Eh128–131. Note that the commodities in Schwab's index correspond rather closely with those in the index constructed by Thomas Berry for Richmond (series Eh131). Comparisons of Schwab's data with those of Lerner's index for the Eastern Confederacy (series Eh128) and Berry's index for Richmond suggest that all three are very much in accord with each other.

Series Eh172–193. Present unweighted indexes of twenty-one commodities in the Confederacy from January 1861 through March 1865, constructed by John Schwab. These commodities were chosen, according to Schwab, "because their prices were most regularly and consistently quoted in the available market reports of the time" (Schwab 1899, p. 283). He reports that "the newspapers, diaries, memoirs and other books of those years available to the writer furnished about three thousand individual price quotations" (p. 283). Quotations from Charleston, Richmond, and areas of North Carolina were the most reliable, and that region of the Confederacy is most strongly represented in Schwab's data.

GOVERNMENT FINANCES

Roger L. Ransom

TABLE Eh194–215   Confederate government revenues and expenditures: 1861–1864

Contributed by Roger L. Ransom

Revenues from

Period	All sources	Treasury notes			Bond issues	Call certificates	Loans from banks	Customs	Export duties	War tax	Tax on notes
		All notes	Non-interest-bearing notes	Interest-bearing notes							
	Eh194	Eh195	Eh196	Eh197	Eh198	Eh199	Eh200	Eh201	Eh202	Eh203	Eh204
	Thousand Confederate dollars	Thousand Confederate dollars	Thousand Confederate dollars	Thousand Confederate dollars	Thousand Confederate dollars	Thousand Confederate dollars	Thousand Confederate dollars	Thousand Confederate dollars	Thousand Confederate dollars	Thousand Confederate dollars	Thousand Confederate dollars
Feb 17, 1861–May 1, 1861	1,121.7	—			—		—	732.5	—	—	—
May 2, 1861–Nov 16, 1861	60,711.8	32,199.5	30,178.4	2,021.1	18,043.0	—	9,813.5	217.2	1.3	—	—
Nov 17, 1861–Feb 18, 1861	77,216.5	63,590.8	63,590.8	—	13,109.6	—	—	321.3	—	—	—
Feb 18, 1862–Aug 1, 1862	170,693.7	114,989.3	92,189.4	22,799.9	6,460.7	37,585.2	—	166.5	—	10,539.9	—
Aug 2, 1862–Dec 31, 1862	285,786.7	214,305.6	123,365.5	90,940.1	34,937.6	22,157.6	—	502.0	—	6,124.6	—
Jan 1, 1863–Sept 30, 1863	601,522.9	391,623.5	382,781.3	8,842.2	154,840.6	23,475.1	—	934.8	8.1	4,129.0	—
Oct 1, 1863–Sept 30, 1863	691,393.3	265,690.9	265,690.9	—	273,016.1	40,155.5	—	441.1	14.3	59,406.7	—
Apr 1, 1864–Apr 1, 1864	415,191.6	277,577.0	277,577.0	—	30,751.5	20,973.2	—	59.0	4.3	42,294.3	14,440.6

Revenues from

| Period | Other taxes | Coin and bullion | Sequestration | Patent fund | Miscellaneous revenues |
| | Eh205 | Eh206 | Eh207 | Eh208 | Eh209 |
	Thousand Confederate dollars	Thousand Confederate dollars	Thousand Confederate dollars	Thousand Confederate dollars	Thousand Confederate dollars
Feb 17, 1861–May 1, 1861	—	—	—	—	—
May 2, 1861–Nov 16, 1861	—	—	—	—	437.3
Nov 17, 1861–Feb 18, 1861	—	—	—	—	194.8
Feb 18, 1862–Aug 1, 1862	—	—	—	—	952.1
Aug 2, 1862–Dec 31, 1862	—	2,539.8	—	13.9	5,205.6
Jan 1, 1863–Sept 30, 1863	—	—	1,862.6	10.8	24,638.4
Oct 1, 1863–Sept 30, 1863	595.0	—	3,000.8	27.0	49,045.8
Apr 1, 1864–Apr 1, 1864	939.1	1,653.2	1,238.7	0.9	25,259.9

Expenditures from

| Period | All sources | War Department | Navy Department | Civil and miscellaneous | Debt service | Taxes in kind |
| | Eh210 | Eh211 | Eh212 | Eh213 | Eh214 | Eh215 |
	Thousand Confederate dollars	Thousand Confederate dollars	Thousand Confederate dollars	Thousand Confederate dollars	Thousand Confederate dollars	Thousand Confederate dollars
Feb 17, 1861–May 1, 1861	993.3	—	—	—	—	—
May 2, 1861–Nov 16, 1861	70,666.7	66,018.7	2,902.3	1,745.7	—	—
Nov 17, 1861–Feb 18, 1861	94,823.9	86,825.7	4,698.2	3,300.0	—	—
Feb 18, 1862–Aug 1, 1862	163,258.3	145,532.1	7,005.3	5,186.7	5,534.1	—
Aug 2, 1862–Dec 31, 1862	253,713.5	195,479.6	13,554.0	8,486.7	36,193.2	—
Jan 1, 1863–Sept 30, 1863	519,368.6	377,988.2	38,437.7	11,685.9	91,256.7	6,000
Oct 1, 1863–Sept 30, 1863	383,110.6	238,572.4	10,853.7	5,637.6	128,046.8	34,000
Apr 1, 1864–Apr 1, 1864	614,938.8	246,367.4	15,554.8	10,456.3	342,560.3	22,000

Source

Richard C. K. Burdekin and Farrokh Langdana, "War Finance in the Confederacy, 1861–1865," *Explorations in Economic History* 30 (July 1993), Table 1, p. 354.

Documentation

These series present detailed data on revenues and expenditures of the Confederate government. The authors describe these as "raw" data taken from reports of the Secretary of War to the Confederate Congress. Christopher Memminger filed seven reports covering the period from February 1861 to April 1864, and his successor, George Trenholm, filed one report covering the period April 1, 1864, to October 1, 1864. Five of these reports are reprinted in H. D. Capers, *The Life and Times of C. G. Memminger* (Ever t Waddey, 1893), pp. 417–88.

The most complete description of the financial policies of the Confederate government is that in Richard C. Todd, *Confederate Finance* (University of Georgia Press, 1954). In addition, one might consult

TABLE Eh194-215   Confederate government revenues and expenditures: 1861-1864   *Continued*

John C. Schwab, *The Confederate States of America* (Burt Franklin, 1901), and D. B. Ball, *Financial Failure and Confederate Defeat* (University of Illinois Press, 1991).

Series Eh194. Equals the sum of series Eh195-209.

Series Eh195-197. The major source of revenue to the Confederate government was issuance of notes. Series Eh195 presents the amount of treasury notes in circulation, which is divided into non-interest-bearing notes and interest-bearing notes issued by the government. The authors note that the figures on interest-bearing notes in this table have been adjusted using the data of John Godfrey (see the text for Table Eh111-117).

Series Eh198-200. The Confederate government engaged in borrowing through the issuance of interest-bearing debt. Legislation authorizing the first major borrowing by the government – the so-called "15 Million-Dollar Loan" – was passed in February 1861. This was followed by a series of acts enabling the issuance of bonds and other interest-bearing debt. The reports of the Secretary of the Treasury identify the amount of funds obtained from the issuance of bonds, call certificates, and loans obtained by the Confederate government from banks.

Series Eh201-203. Confederate tax revenues came primarily from a customs duty of 12.5 percent enacted in March and August 1861; a duty levied on exports effective after August 1, 1861; and a "war tax" enacted on August 19, 1861, with a tax rate of 0.5 percent levied on taxable property plus some luxuries.

Series Eh204. The Currency Reform Act of April 1864 stated that any currency outstanding could be exchanged on a three-for-two basis. This amounted to a 33 percent "tax" on those holding notes after April 1864. Series Eh204 estimates the effect of this action.

Series Eh206-209. The Secretaries also reported several minor sources of revenues in addition to that obtained through taxes and borrowing. This includes coin and bullion donated by citizens to the government; revenues from the Sequestration Act of 1861, which required Southerners to exchange any "Northern-owned" property for certificates from the Confederate government; and revenues from the patent fund. Finally, the reports include a growing source of "miscellaneous" revenue.

Series Eh210. Equals the sum of series Eh211-214.

Series Eh215. On April 24, 1863, the Confederate government passed the Tithe Act, which imposed a tax-in-kind equal to one tenth of the agricultural output of 1863. Burdekin and Langdana suggest that "in the first nine months of 1863, the tax-in-kind is believed to have accounted for more than half of the average monthly tax revenues" and in the final reporting period "still accounted for between a quarter and a third of average monthly tax revenues" (pp. 358-9). Their estimate of the implicit value of revenues generated by the tax-in-kind is presented in this series.

TABLE Eh216–220   Bond yields on domestic loans in the Confederacy: 1862–1864

Contributed by Roger L. Ransom

Year	Month	"$100 Million" Bonds	"$15 Million" Bonds	City of Richmond bonds	State of Virginia bonds	Nominal rate on "$100 Million Loan"
		Eh216	Eh217	Eh218	Eh219	Eh220
		Percent	Percent	Percent	Percent	Percent
1862	Jan	12.71	—	—	—	8.000
1862	Feb	12.71	14.65	9.90	11.04	8.050
1862	Mar	—	15.25	9.77	10.61	—
1862	Apr	14.09	18.00	10.72	11.52	8.276
1862	May	15.40	—	10.87	11.39	8.150
1862	June	17.02	—	11.31	11.80	8.819
1862	July	16.43	18.86	10.82	—	8.156
1862	Aug	17.22	—	—	12.93	7.999
1862	Sept	17.23	—	11.51	12.93	7.998
1862	Oct	18.43	22.14	12.37	13.76	7.998
1862	Nov	26.92	30.35	16.64	20.19	7.998
1862	Dec	25.78	28.91	15.54	17.57	7.999
1863	Jan	23.90	27.15	14.53	16.40	7.999
1863	Feb	25.96	29.67	—	18.28	7.895
1863	Mar	38.01	40.56	22.24	26.98	7.998
1863	Apr	36.52	30.69	—	26.89	7.017
1863	May	39.71	29.36	23.62	27.54	7.392
1863	June	54.35	37.10	32.29	33.39	7.344
1863	July	57.50	39.83	34.49	34.49	7.246
1863	Aug	80.01	54.11	31.74	32.24	6.917
1863	Sept	83.14	57.17	28.71	37.92	7.338
1863	Oct	79.40	55.06	28.38	32.79	6.866
1863	Nov	116.49	71.28	40.65	38.93	6.819
1863	Dec	140.31	88.96	46.45	51.13	6.291
1864	Jan	140.06	98.72	—	51.44	6.372
1864	Feb	138.91	109.23	53.17	53.19	5.673
1864	Mar	147.15	123.70	56.87	74.74	6.626
1864	Apr	145.49	—	—	75.26	6.990
1864	June	—	—	—	—	7.395
1864	July	114.41	—	—	—	6.262
1864	Aug	128.82	—	—	—	6.522
1864	Sept	152.20	129.46	56.05	65.25	5.677
1864	Oct	159.11	—	—	—	5.665
1864	Nov	174.97	164.07	56.78	68.65	6.072
1864	Dec	218.68	209.12	73.15	68.97	5.899

Source

George K. Davis and Gary M. Pecquet, "Interest Rates in the Civil War South," *Journal of Economic History* 50 (March 1990), Table 2, p. 148.

Documentation

These series present estimates of interest rates in the Confederacy derived from data on bond prices and gold premiums. George Davis and Gary Pecquet argue that the nominal rate of interest in the Confederacy was effectively fixed by the availability of call certificates issued by the government at 6 percent (pp. 137-9). However, because the price of gold was free to vary, the yield can be expressed on a gold basis that could also vary. Drawing on price quotations from newspapers in Richmond and Wilmington, Davis and Pecquet constructed four series of "gold yields," presented in series Eh216-219. The gold yield of a bond was calculated as if the bond were held to maturity and the Confederate States of America government kept its promise to pay

in gold. The details of those calculations are in the appendix to their article (pp. 147-8). The very high yields reported in the last two years reflect the growing risk that the Confederate government would not, in fact, redeem the bonds.

Series Eh216–217. The Confederate Congress authorized two major offerings of bonds in early 1861. What is commonly called the "$100 Million Loan" bore an 8 percent coupon and the bonds were general obligations of the Confederate government. The "$15 Million Loan" also bore an 8 percent coupon; however, payment was guaranteed by revenues from the export duty on cotton.

Series Eh218–219. These series present gold yields for bond issues of the city of Richmond and the state of Virginia.

Series Eh220. The nominal rate of interest – expressed as the yield in Confederate dollars on the $100 Million Loan – is presented in this series.

TABLE Eh221-222 Weekly prices of Confederate cotton bonds and sterling bonds in Amsterdam: 1863-1865
Contributed by Roger L. Ransom

Year	Month	Day	Erlanger cotton bonds Eh221 Pounds sterling	Amsterdam sterling bonds Eh222 Pounds sterling	Year	Month	Day	Erlanger cotton bonds Eh221 Pounds sterling	Amsterdam sterling bonds Eh222 Pounds sterling
1863	Mar	23	94.50	—	1864	May	16	65.00	12.63
1863	Mar	30	91.75	—	1864	May	23	63.00	12.69
1863	Apr	6	87.50	—	1864	May	30	64.00	12.66
1863	Apr	13	91.63	—	1864	June	6	66.00	11.88
1863	Apr	20	91.00	—	1864	June	13	64.00	10.72
1863	Apr	27	91.50	—	1864	June	20	64.00	10.03
1863	May	4	91.75	—	1864	June	27	64.00	9.25
1863	May	11	90.00	—	1864	July	4	65.00	12.88
1863	May	18	90.50	—	1864	July	11	70.00	13.19
1863	May	25	89.00	—	1864	July	18	78.00	14.69
1863	June	1	88.00	—	1864	July	25	78.00	14.69
1863	June	8	87.25	—	1864	Aug	1	78.50	13.91
1863	June	15	88.00	—	1864	Aug	8	76.50	13.59
1863	June	22	89.00	—	1864	Aug	15	77.00	12.25
1863	June	29	89.25	—	1864	Aug	22	78.00	11.22
1863	July	6	89.00	—	1864	Aug	29	78.00	12.44
1863	July	13	90.25	—	1864	Sept	5	76.00	11.25
1863	July	20	86.00	—	1864	Sept	12	84.75	12.22
1863	July	27	81.00	—	1864	Sept	19	80.50	11.63
1863	Aug	3	73.00	—	1864	Sept	26	74.00	11.59
1863	Aug	10	67.00	—	1864	Oct	3	65.00	9.81
1863	Aug	17	66.00	—	1864	Oct	10	57.00	9.00
1863	Aug	24	64.00	—	1864	Oct	17	63.00	7.75
1863	Aug	31	66.00	—	1864	Oct	24	65.00	7.34
1863	Sept	7	61.00	—	1864	Oct	31	64.00	6.50
1863	Sept	14	60.00	39.00	1864	Nov	7	60.50	6.06
1863	Sept	21	61.00	38.00	1864	Nov	14	65.00	5.03
1863	Sept	28	63.00	32.00	1864	Nov	21	61.00	4.06
1863	Oct	5	67.00	34.38	1864	Nov	28	61.00	2.66
1863	Oct	12	66.00	33.00	1864	Dec	5	60.00	3.88
1863	Oct	19	66.00	32.94	1864	Dec	12	59.00	2.66
1863	Oct	26	65.50	31.94	1864	Dec	19	62.00	2.09
1863	Nov	2	66.00	31.75	1864	Dec	26	62.00	2.31
1863	Nov	9	64.00	29.50	1865	Jan	2	56.50	5.84
1863	Nov	16	63.00	25.50	1865	Jan	9	53.00	4.56
1863	Nov	23	55.00	25.00	1865	Jan	16	56.00	4.28
1863	Nov	30	56.00	25.00	1865	Jan	23	57.00	4.13
1863	Dec	7	48.00	25.13	1865	Jan	30	58.00	6.50
1863	Dec	14	35.50	21.00	1865	Feb	6	55.50	5.63
1863	Dec	21	39.00	18.25	1865	Feb	13	55.50	5.44
1863	Dec	28	38.00	23.33	1865	Feb	20	58.00	6.47
1864	Jan	4	39.00	22.25	1865	Feb	27	57.00	6.25
1864	Jan	11	39.00	21.75	1865	Mar	6	42.00	5.69
1864	Jan	18	44.00	21.00	1865	Mar	13	36.50	4.50
1864	Jan	25	45.00	19.50	1865	Mar	20	36.00	4.41
1864	Feb	1	47.00	18.75	1865	Mar	27	36.00	4.38
1864	Feb	8	50.00	17.50	1865	Apr	3	33.50	3.94
1864	Feb	15	50.00	16.33	1865	Apr	10	33.00	3.91
1864	Feb	22	56.00	16.88	1865	Apr	17	23.00	2.97
1864	Feb	29	48.00	18.63	1865	Apr	24	18.00	3.09
1864	Mar	7	46.00	17.00	1865	May	1	13.00	2.13
1864	Mar	14	48.00	17.00	1865	May	8	14.00	1.03
1864	Mar	21	52.00	16.25	1865	May	15	12.00	—
1864	Mar	28	51.00	15.50	1865	May	22	9.00	—
1864	Apr	4	55.00	15.31	1865	May	29	8.00	—
1864	Apr	11	54.50	12.31					
1864	Apr	18	54.50	14.56					
1864	Apr	25	55.00	13.06					
1864	May	2	63.00	13.88					
1864	May	9	62.00	14.06					

(continued)

TABLE Eh221–222   Weekly prices of Confederate cotton bonds and sterling bonds in Amsterdam: 1863–1865
Continued

Sources

Marc Weidenmier, "The Market for Confederate Bonds," *Explorations in Economic History* 37 (January 2000): 76–97, as well as worksheets provided by Weidenmier.

Documentation

In addition to funds borrowed at home, the Confederacy floated bonds in the London and Amsterdam financial markets. This table presents data on weekly price quotations of two series of foreign bonds issued by the Confederate government.

The bond prices presented in series Eh221 are for twenty-year bonds issued in March 1863 and payable in pounds sterling. These bonds, which were underwritten by the French firm Emile Erlanger and Company, offered the buyer the option of taking payment in sterling, or the bond holder could convert the value of the bond into "cotton certificates" once the Confederate government had received the funds from the issue of bonds. The cotton certificate guaranteed that bond holders could purchase cotton at a fixed price

of six pence per pound. At the time that the bonds were initially offered, cotton was selling at roughly 24 pence per pound, and by the end of the war the price was more than twice that level. The only problem with converting the bond to cotton was that the bondholder had to take delivery of the cotton within the Confederate states – and thus get past the Union blockade of the Southern coast.

Despite this drawback, the cotton collateral for the Erlanger loan bonds meant that these securities traded at prices substantially above the prices for other Confederate loans in Europe. To measure the effect of the cotton backing for Erlanger bonds, Weidenmier collected data for weekly prices on an unsecured sterling loan by the Confederate government traded on the Amsterdam capital market. These data are presented in series Eh222.

The data for both these series come from quotations in the *Amsterdamisch Effectenblad*. Quotations for the Erlanger bond first appeared in March 1863; those for the unsecured bond issue began in August of that year (Weidenmier 2000, pp. 76–7).

TABLE Eh223–228   Gold prices in the Confederacy: 1861–1865
Contributed by Roger L. Ransom

		Davis and Pecquet	Todd		Weidenmier		
			Low	High	Richmond	Houston	
						Old issue	New issue
		Eh223	Eh224	Eh225	Eh226	Eh227	Eh228
Year	Month	Confederate dollars	Confederate dollars	Confederate dollars	Confederate dollars	Confederate dollars	Confederate dollars
1861	Sept	—	—	—	1.14	1.00	—
1861	Oct	—	—	—	1.18	1.05	—
1861	Nov	—	—	—	1.20	1.10	—
1861	Dec	—	—	—	1.33	1.38	—
1862	Jan	—	1.25	1.25	1.33	1.50	—
1862	Feb	1.50	1.25	1.25	1.34	1.63	—
1862	Mar	1.55	1.30	1.30	1.58	1.75	—
1862	Apr	1.78	1.40	1.40	1.78	2.00	—
1862	May	1.80	1.50	1.50	2.00	2.00	—
1862	June	1.88	1.50	1.50	2.00	2.25	—
1862	July	1.88	1.50	1.50	2.00	2.50	—
1862	Aug	2.05	1.50	1.50	2.15	2.67	—
1862	Sept	2.05	2.50	2.50	2.40	2.88	—
1862	Oct	2.20	2.50	2.50	2.60	3.00	—
1862	Nov	3.30	3.00	3.00	3.30	2.75	—
1862	Dec	3.13	3.00	3.00	3.25	3.50	—
1863	Jan	2.90	3.00	3.00	3.13	4.42	—
1863	Feb	3.20	4.00	4.00	3.35	5.00	—
1863	Mar	4.75	5.00	5.00	5.13	4.88	—
1863	Apr	5.00	5.50	5.50	5.50	5.13	—
1863	May	5.25	5.50	5.50	6.25	7.00	—
1863	June	7.25	7.00	8.00	7.75	8.00	—
1863	July	7.75	9.00	9.00	9.13	8.25	—
1863	Aug	11.25	12.00	13.00	12.00	9.83	—
1863	Sept	11.25	12.00	13.00	12.25	11.75	—
1863	Oct	11.25	14.00	14.00	12.50	11.00	—
1863	Nov	16.71	15.00	17.00	14.63	13.50	—
1863	Dec	21.00	18.00	20.00	17.50	17.50	—
1864	Jan	20.88	20.00	20.50	20.83	22.33	—
1864	Feb	22.50	22.50	25.00	24.75	21.50	—
1864	Mar	22.00	23.00	24.50	21.63	21.50	—
1864	Apr	21.00	22.00	23.00	23.00	26.00	—
1864	May	—	18.00	21.00	19.63	33.75	—
1864	June	—	17.00	19.00	17.00	39.00	—
1864	July	17.00	20.00	23.00	17.67	33.83	—
1864	Aug	19.00	22.50	25.00	19.50	38.50	—

TABLE Eh223–228   Gold prices in the Confederacy: 1861–1865   *Continued*

Year	Month	Davis and Pecquet	Todd		Weidenmier		
			Low	High	Richmond	Houston	
						Old issue	New issue
		Eh223	Eh224	Eh225	Eh226	Eh227	Eh228
		Confederate dollars	Confederate dollars	Confederate dollars	Confederate dollars	Confederate dollars	Confederate dollars
1864	Sept	24.88	22.50	27.50	24.00	50.50	—
1864	Oct	26.38	26.00	27.00	24.00	51.50	—
1864	Nov	27.88	27.50	33.50	26.50	49.00	21.15
1864	Dec	34.63	34.00	49.00	34.58	47.67	20.67
1865	Jan	—	45.00	60.00	42.50	—	25.50
1865	Feb	—	45.00	65.00	45.00	—	25.00
1865	Mar	—	60.00	70.00	—	—	—
1865	Apr	—	60.00	60.00	—	—	—

Sources

George K. Davis and Gary M. Pecquet, "Interest Rates in the Civil War South," *Journal of Economic History* 50 (March 1990), Table 2, p. 148; Richard C. Todd, *Confederate Finance* (University of Georgia Press, 1954), p. 198; Marc Weidenmier, "The Market for Confederate Bonds." *Explorations in Economic History* 37 (January 2000): 76–97, as well as worksheets provided by Weidenmier.

Documentation

This table presents estimates of the price of gold expressed in Confederate dollars.

Series Eh223. George Davis and Gary Pecquet used this series in their calculations of yields presented in Table Eh216–220.

Series Eh224–225. Compiled by a Richmond banking firm and cited by Todd (1954), p. 198. Values were reported as ranges, recorded here in the separate series.

Series Eh226–227. Prices of gold in Richmond and Houston collected by Marc Weidenmier from a series of semiweekly newspaper quotations in those cities.

Series Eh228. Presents gold prices expressed in the "new issue" currency in Houston after the currency reform of 1864. These figures suggest that the old currency continued to circulate in the areas west of the Mississippi after the reform.

APPENDIXES

APPENDIX 1

Weights, Measures, and Monetary Values

Editors: Alan L. Olmstead and Richard Sutch

Weights and Measures

The data for most series in *Historical Statistics of the United States* are expressed in American units. This system of weights and measures was adapted and modified over time from the British Imperial System and is now known as the U.S. Customary System. Table Ap-A presents the official relationships within the U.S. Customary System. It should be noted that the British Imperial System and the U.S. system share many common terms (for example, "gallon" and "bushel"), but the measures are not always equivalent.

At this time, only three countries – Burma (Myanmar), Liberia, and the United States – have not adopted the International System of Units (SI, or metric system) as their official system of weights and measures. The SI (for *Système International*, the French name) was adopted in 1960 by the Eleventh General Conference on Weights and Measures. The key features of the International System are decimalization, a system of prefixes, and a standard defined in terms of invariable physical measures. Table Ap-B presents the standard system of prefixes used in the metric system.

The first U.S. Secretary of State, Thomas Jefferson, influenced by a proposal circulating in France, proposed a decimal system for weights, measures, and coinage of the United States in 1790. However, only his proposal for the coinage was adopted when two years later the U.S. mint introduced the world's first decimal coinage (a dollar of 100 cents). France adopted the decimal metric system in 1795. An international treaty signed by the United States in 1875 established the metric system as an international standard.

The U.S. Customary System has many drawbacks: its nondecimal nature makes it more complex to convert from one unit to another; it uses the same name for different units (e.g., ounce for both weight and liquid capacity, quart and pint for both liquid and dry capacity); and it has three different systems of weights (avoirdupois, troy, and apothecary). Although U.S. law has sanctioned the use of the metric system since 1866, SI has yet to displace the customary system in everyday use. While the United States does not use the metric system in its commercial activities, there is increasing acceptance of the metric system in science, medicine, government, and many sectors of industry. Important equivalencies are provided in Table Ap-C as an aid to users who might wish to convert data in this volume into the International System of weights and measures.

Table Ap-D provides more extensive information on units of measure for agricultural products, which have been sold and transported in a bewildering variety of different shipping containers. Before the middle years of the nineteenth century, most products were sold by volume, not weight. Article I, Section 8 of the U.S. Constitution gave Congress the power to establish legal weights and measures, but in practice the legal definition of these measures and the size of containers were left to the states until the late nineteenth century. It was not uncommon for different states to define a legal measure differently and to define a measure differently when used for different products. As farmers began to have access to weight scales and as products were sold more regularly over long distances, sales increasingly were based on weight. Tradition, however, dictated that quantities and prices continued to be denominated in volume measures (for example, bushels of corn). Conversion factors were used to equate volume measures and weight. At first these conversion factors were informal rules of thumb, but states began to legislate the legal weight of various volumes, crop by crop. Gradually over the nineteenth century, national standards began to emerge for most crops. Generally speaking, dry products are measured by bushels and liquid products are measured by gallons. The standard bushel that evolved in the United States is formally known as the "Winchester bushel" (see Table Ap-A).

Note that, in some cases, units of measure for particular data series may differ from the standard values presented in Tables Ap-A and Ap-D. As always, users should consult the table documentation.

Monetary Values

Many of the series in *Historical Statistics of the United States* give the (average) price of an item or the value of an aggregate such as total expenditure or total value of production. Generally speaking, these values are measured either in market prices of the year to which the data refer or in "real dollars," which are sometimes called "constant dollars." In the former case, the interpretation of the data is usually straightforward. The actual price or value of the item in the year it was sold or produced is presented in U.S. dollars. These are called current prices, market prices, or values in current dollars or nominal dollars. These terms are interchangeable. However, users should take notice of the specifics provided in the table documentation for the series in which they are interested.

From year to year, the value of the U.S. dollar has fluctuated, and over time there has been a general tendency for the value of the dollar to fall. It is often desired to make comparisons of the value of some item over time. Consider, for example, the Ford Motor Company, which was incorporated in 1903 by Henry Ford. In October 1908, Ford offered his Model-T for $850. What would that be equivalent to today? In 1914, Ford began paying his employees five dollars a day, nearly doubling the wages offered by other manufacturers. How much is that in today's terms?

There is no universally accepted answer to these questions.[1] Determining the relative value of an amount of money in one year

---

[1] A useful resource is Williamson (2002). Several of the examples given later in this appendix are from this source.

TABLE Ap-A   U.S. Customary System of weights and measures

Length			Volume		
foot	=	12 inches	**Dry measure**		
yard	=	3 feet	pint	=	16 ounces
furlong	=	660 feet	quart	=	2 pints
mile (statute)	=	5,280 feet	peck	=	8 quarts
			bucket	=	2 pecks
Geographic area			bushel	=	2 buckets
acre	=	4,840 square yards	bushel	=	2,150.42 cubic inches
square mile	=	640 acres	boardfoot (timber)		144 cubic inches
section	=	1 square mile	cord (firewood)	=	128 cubic feet
township	=	36 sections	**Liquid measure**		
Weight			pint	=	16 ounces
Avoirdupois			quart	=	2 pints
ounce	=	437.5 grains	gallon	=	4 quarts
pound	=	16 ounces	gallon	=	231 cubic inches
hundredweight (short)	=	100 pounds	barrel (beer and wine)	=	31 gallons
hundredweight (long)	=	112 pounds	barrel (proof spirits)	=	40 gallons
ton (short)	=	2,000 pounds	barrel (other liquids)	=	31.5 gallons
ton (long)	=	2,240 pounds	barrel (petroleum)	=	42 gallons
Troy			hogshead		63 gallons
ounce	=	480 grains	acre foot		43,560 cubic feet
pound	=	12 ounces	**Shipping capacity**		
pound	=	0.822857 pounds (avoirdupois)	ton (gross register)	=	100 cubic feet of enclosed space
			ton (net register)	=	100 cubic feet for cargo and passengers
			ton (shipping)	=	42 cubic feet for cargo

Source

L. J. Chisholm, *Units of Weight and Measure – International (Metric) and U.S. Customary*, U.S. National Bureau of Standards Miscellaneous Publication 286 (1967).

Documentation

The U.S. Customary System uses the following standard units: yard (length), acre (geographic area), pound (weight), bushel (volume, dry measure), and gallon (volume, liquid measure).

There are three systems of weights in the U.S. Customary System: avoirdupois, troy, and apothecary. The avoirdupois system is the most common. The troy system is used primarily for precious metals (for example, gold or silver). Conversion between the avoirdupois and troy systems can be made via the common unit, grains, of which there are 7,000 in an avoirdupois pound and 5,760 in a troy pound. The apothecary system, formerly used by pharmacists, is a variant of the troy system. In the apothecary system, the ounce (equivalent to a troy ounce) is divided into eight drams of sixty grains each, each dram containing three scruples. There is a parallel apothecary system of liquid measure, in which the fluid troy ounce is divided into eight fluidrams. The apothecary system continued in use into the early twentieth century, but it has been replaced in pharmacy by the use of metric units.

The U.S. Customary System has two units of volume, one for dry measure and one for liquid. Many terms are common to both, but with different meanings.

Many state laws fix the barrel for liquids at 31.5 gallons. Four states set a standard of 42 gallons for liquids.

Measures of shipping capacity are traditionally a measure of the cargo capacity of a merchant ship. Warships are measured by the weight of the volume of seawater they displace.

compared with another is a matter of often-subtle historical judgment, and the appropriate method will depend upon the context of the question. The value of the dollar fluctuates because prices fluctuate. If, on balance, prices rise, the value of the dollar falls. Of course, all prices do not rise or fall in lock-step with one another. The most common method of calculating an equivalent price is to use a price index that represents an average of the prices comprising a bundle of goods and services (see Chapter Cc). A common choice is the Consumer Price Index (CPI), which averages prices paid by urban consumers for a representative basket of goods and services (series Cc1). Price indexes such as the CPI are set equal to 100 in a base reference period. In this case, the base years when the index averages 100 are 1982–1984.

In 1908, the year of the first Model-T Ford, the CPI was 9.235. In 2001, the index number was 177.100 (series Cc1). Thus, average prices as measured by this index rose more than 19-fold (177.100/9.235 = 19.18). The $850 asking price is equivalent to $16,300 in 2001 (19.18 * 850 = 16,303). Before accepting this result, there are several points to consider.

First, the CPI is only one of many price indexes we might have chosen. Because any price index is only an average of prices for a finite list of goods, indexes will differ from each other, often widely. The CPI uses a list of goods and services purchased in 1993–1995 by urban consumers. Thus, the comparison just calculated represents the value of the Model-T in terms of the consumption goods included in the index. Another alternative would be to use a producer price index that represents the price of inputs that an automobile manufacturer might purchase. A third alternative would be to use a broad index such as the gross domestic product (GDP) deflator (see Table Ca149–158).

Second, when making such calculations over a relatively long time span, the representative bundle of goods will change, both in its make-up and in the inherent quality of the goods and services that are included. In practice, the goods included on the list are changed periodically, and the resulting averages are "spliced" together to form a long continuous series. The automobile purchaser of 1908 could not have purchased many of the goods and services on the 1993–1995 CPI list (frozen orange juice, television sets, modern medicines). You might ask, would you rather have $16,300 that you could spend on items obtainable in 2001 or $850 to spend on items obtainable in 1908? Which is a "better" car, the 1908 Model-T or a $16,300 Ford manufactured in 2001? Interpreting these converted prices is tricky business, and the further one goes into the past, the trickier the task becomes.

An alternative to using a price index to compare values over time is to compare the historical price with the typical wage of a worker

TABLE Ap-B   International System of weights and measures

Type of measure	Standard unit	
Length	meter	
Geographic area	are (100 square meters)	
Weight	gram	
Volume	liter (1,000 cubic centimeters)	

Metric prefix	Power of 10	Equivalent in American usage
tera- (T-)	10^{12}	trillion
giga- (G-)	10^9	billion
mega- (M-)	10^6	million
kilo- (k-)	10^3	thousand
hecto- (h-)	10^2	hundred
deka- (da-)	10	ten
deci- (d-)	10^{-1}	tenth
centi- (c-)	10^{-2}	hundredth
milli- (m-)	10^{-3}	thousandth
micro- (μ)	10^{-6}	millionth
nano- (n-)	10^{-9}	billionth

Note that "deka" is the U.S. spelling; the SI-approved spelling is "deca."

Source
U.S. National Institute of Standards and Technology, "Specifications, Tolerances, and Other Technical Requirements for Weighing and Measuring Devices," in *NIST Handbook 44 – 2000 Edition*, Appendix C.

Documentation
The Nineteenth General Conference on Weights and Measures in 1991 established a list of metric prefixes that reaches from yotta, at 10^{24} (one septillion), to yocto, at 10^{-24} (one septillionth). This table presents the most common metric prefixes, their numerical equivalents expressed as a power of ten, and the standard American usage for naming large numbers. To form a convenient unit of measure, one combines the appropriate prefix with the root name of the fundamental unit (for example, a kilogram is 1,000 grams).

The metric system is also designed to facilitate conversions between units used for length and volume because 1 cubic centimeter equals 1 milliliter. Similarly, volume and mass are linked by means of the following relationship, which holds for water under typical conditions: 1 milliliter equals 1 gram.

TABLE Ap-C   Conversion between U.S. and metric units

Length		
inch	=	2.54 centimeters
foot	=	30.48 centimeters
yard	=	0.9144 meters
mile (statute)	=	1.609344 kilometers
mile (nautical)	=	1.852 kilometers
Geographic area		
square foot	=	0.09290304 square meters
square yard	=	0.83612736 square meters
square mile	=	2.58998811 square kilometers
square mile	=	258.998811 hectares
acre	=	0.404685642 hectares
Weight		
pound (avoirdupois)	=	0.45359237 kilograms
short ton	=	0.90718474 tonnes (metric tons)
Volume		
bushel	=	35.2390702 liters
cubic foot	=	0.028316847 cubic meters
gallon	=	3.78541178 liters
42-gallon barrel	=	158.987295 liters
Temperature		

To convert from degrees Fahrenheit to degrees Celsius, subtract 32 and then divide by 1.8.

Source
U.S. National Institute of Standards and Technology, "Specifications, Tolerances, and Other Technical Requirements for Weighing and Measuring Devices," in *NIST Handbook 44 – 2000 Edition*, Appendix C.

Documentation
The equivalencies for length and weight are exact, as are those for a square foot and square yard; all others are precise to nine digits.

Note that in the United States, petroleum is sold by barrel; in international trade, it is sold by weight. The standard weight of a 42-gallon barrel of Arabian light crude oil is 136 kilograms. Petroleum products vary in density, so this weight should be considered an approximation.

at the same time or with per capita income. At the $5 for an 8-hour day that Ford offered workers in 1914, they would have had to work for 170 days before earning $850. Before this raise, the majority of workers had been earning $2.34 per 9-hour day (Raff 1988). At that rate, over 360 days of work would be required to equal the Model-T. In 2001, a worker earning the federal minimum wage ($5.15 per hour) would make only $7,000 (before tax) in 170 days and $15,000 in 360 days, still not enough to cover the price of a $16,300 automobile.

Begun in 1817, the Erie Canal was completed in 1825 at an approximate cost of $7 million. This waterway is regarded as one of the most important transportation investments of the nineteenth century (see Chapter Df). How does its cost compare with transportation projects of recent times? Using the CPI, it would be about $100 million, sufficient for only a few miles of interstate highway.

This calculation, however, trivializes the vast size of the undertaking represented by the Erie Canal project. An alternative to using a price index is to estimate the fraction of GDP accounted for by the project. Our estimate of GDP for 1825 is about $1 billion (series Ca10); thus, the canal cost 0.7 percent of an entire year's output. In 2001, GDP was more than $10 trillion, and 0.7 percent of that amount is $70 billion. As a comparison, the fiscal year 2001 budget of the U.S. Department of Transportation was approximately $60 billion.

References

Raff, Daniel M. G. 1988. "Wage Determination Theory and the Five-Dollar Day at Ford." *Journal of Economic History* 48 (June): 387–99.

Williamson, Samuel H. 2002. "What Is the Relative Value?" *Economic History Services,* at the EH.net Internet site.

TABLE Ap-D Conversion of crop units to pounds

Commodity	Unit	Approximate net weight in pounds
Alfalfa seed	Bushel	60
Apples	Bushel	48
Apples	Northwest boxes	44 [1]
Apricots	Brentwood lug	24 [2]
Artichokes	Carton	20–25
Asparagus	Crate	30
Avocados	Lug	12–15 [3]
Bananas	Folding box	40 [4]
Barley	Bushel	48
Beans – lima, unshelled	Bushel	28–32
Beans – lima, dry	Bushel	56
Beans – other, dry	Bushel	60
Beans – other, dry	Sack	100
Beans – snap	Bushel	28–32
Beets – bunched	1/2 crate; 2 dozen bunches	36–40
Beets – topped	Sack	25
Broccoli	Wirebound crate	20–25
Broomcorn	Bale	333.3
Brussels sprouts	Carton	25
Buckwheat	Bushel	48
Butter	Box	64
Cabbage	Bag	50
Cabbage	Flat crate (1.75 bushel)	50–60
Cabbage	Carton	53
Cabbage	Wirebound crates	50 [5]
Cabbage	Western crates	80 [6]
Cantaloupe	Jumbo crates	83 [7]
Cantaloupe	Crate	40
Carrots – bunched	Carton	55
Carrots – topped	Burlap sack	74–80
Carrots – without tops	Bushels	50
Cauliflower	W.G.A. crate	50–60
Cauliflower	Fiberboard box	23–35
Celery	Crate	60 [8]
Cherries	Campbell lug	16 [9]
Cherries	Lug	20
Clover seed	Bushel	60
Coffee	Bag	132.3
Corn – ear, husked	Bushel	70 [10]
Corn – meal	Bushel	50
Corn – oil	Gallon	7.7 [11]
Corn – shelled	Bushel	56
Corn – sweet corn	Wirebound crate	50
Corn – syrup	Gallon	11.72
Cotton	Bale, gross	500 [12]
Cotton	Bale, net	480 [12]
Cottonseed	Bushel	32 [13]

Commodity	Unit	Approximate net weight in pounds
Cottonseed oil	Gallon	7.7 [11]
Cowpeas	Bushel	60
Cranberries	Barrel	100 [14]
Cream – 40 percent butterfat	Gallon	8.38
Cucumbers	Bushel	48
Eggplant	Bushel	33
Eggs – average size	Case, 30 dozen	47
Figs – fresh	Box	6 [15]
Flaxseed	Bushel	56
Flour – various	Bag	100
Garlic	Carton	10
Grapefruit – California and Arizona	Box	67 [16, 17, 18]
Grapefruit – California desert valleys and Arizona	Carton	32 [19]
Grapefruit – California, other than desert valleys	Carton	33.5 [19]
Grapefruit – Florida	13/5 bushel boxes	85
Grapefruit – Florida and Texas	1/2 box mesh bag	40
Grapefruit – Texas	12/5 bushel boxes	80
Grapes – Eastern	12-quart basket	18–20
Grapes – Western	Lug	28 [20]
Grapes – Western	4-basket crate	20 [21]
Hempseed	Bushel	44
Hickory nuts	Bushel	50
Honey	Gallon	11.84
Honeydew melons	2/3 carton	28–32
Honeydew melons	Jumbo crates	44 [22]
Hops	Bale, gross	200
Horseradish roots	Bushel	35
Horseradish roots	Sack	50
Kale	Carton or crate	25
Lard	Tierce	375
Lemons	Box	76 [18, 23]
Lemons	Carton	38 [19]
Lentils	Bushel	60
Lettuce	Fiberboard box; carton	38–55
Lettuce – hot-house	24-quart basket	10
Lettuce – iceberg	Carton	43–52
Limes	Box	88
Limes – Florida	Box	80
Linseed oil	Gallon	7.7 [11]
Malt	Bushel	34
Maple syrup	Gallon	11.02
Milk	Gallon	8.6
Millet	Bushel	48–60

Notes appear at end of table

TABLE Ap-D Conversion of crop units to pounds *Continued*

Commodity	Unit	Approximate net weight in pounds	Commodity	Unit	Approximate net weight in pounds
Molasses	Gallon	11.74	Rice – rough	Barrel	162
Mustard seed	Bushel	58–60	Rutabagas	Bushel	56
			Rye	Bushel	56
Oats	Bushel	32			
Olive oil	Gallon	7.6 [11]	Sesame seed	Bushel	46
Olives	Lug	25–30	Shallots	Crate	20–35
Onions	Sack	50	Sorghum grain	Bushel	56 [20]
Onions – green bunched	Carton, 24 dozen bunches	10–16	Sorgo seed	Bushel	50
Oranges California and Arizona	Carton	37.5 [19]	Sorgo syrup	Gallon	11.55
Oranges – California and Arizona	Box	75 [16, 18]	Soybean oil	Gallon	7.7 [11]
Oranges – Florida	Box	90	Soybeans	Bushel	60
Oranges – Florida and Texas	Box	90 [24]	Spinach	Bushel	18–20
Oranges – Texas	Box	85	Strawberries	24-quart crate	36
			Sugarcane syrup	Gallon	11.45
Parsnips	Bushel	50	Sunflower seed	Bushel	24
Peaches	Bushel	48	Sunflower seed	Bushel	32
Peaches	Lug box	20 [20]	Sweet potatoes	Bushel	55 [29]
Peaches – California	Fruit box	18 [25]	Sweet potatoes	Crate	50
Peanut oil	Gallon	7.7 [11]			
Peanuts – unshelled, Runners	Bushel	21	Tangerines – Arizona and California	Box	75
Peanuts – unshelled, Spanish	Bushel	25			
Peanuts – unshelled, Virginia type	Bushel	17	Tangerines – Florida	Box	95
Pears – California	Bushel	48	Tobacco – Burley	Hogshead	975
Pears – Other	Bushel	50	Tobacco – Cigar-leaf	Case	250–365
Pears – Western	Box	46 [26]	Tobacco – Cigar-leaf	Bale	150–175
Peas – dry	Bushel	60	Tobacco – Dark air-cured	Hogshead	1150
Peas – green, unshelled	Bushel	28–30	Tobacco – Flue-cured	Hogshead	950
Peppers – green	Fiberboard carton	30–34	Tobacco – Kentucky and Tennessee fire-cured	Hogshead	1500
Peppers – green	Bushel	25–30			
Peppers – green	1 1/2 bushel carton	28	Tobacco – Maryland	Hogshead	775
Pineapples	Carton	40	Tobacco – Virginia fire-cured	Hogshead	1350
Plums and fresh prunes	Carton and lug	28	Tomatoes	Crate	60
Plums and fresh prunes	1/2-bushel basket	28–30	Tomatoes	2-layer flat	21
Plums and fresh prunes – California	4-basket crate	28–34 [27]	Tomatoes	Lug box	32 [20]
Potatoes	Bushel	60	Tomatoes – hot-house	12-quart basket	20
Potatoes	Barrel	165	Turnips – bunched	Crate	70–80 [6]
Potatoes	Box	50	Turnips – topped	Sack	50
Potatoes	Bag	100	Turpentine	Gallon	7.23
Rice – milled	Pocket or bag	100	Walnuts	Sack	50
Rice – rough	Bushel	45	Watermelons	Average or medium size	25
Rice – rough	Bag	100	Wheat	Bushel	60

[1] Approximate inside dimensions are $10\frac{1}{2}$ by $11\frac{1}{2}$ by 18 inches.

[2] Approximate inside dimensions are $4\frac{5}{8}$ by $12\frac{1}{2}$ by $16\frac{1}{8}$ inches.

[3] Approximate dimensions are $4\frac{1}{2}$ by $13\frac{1}{2}$ by $16\frac{1}{8}$ inches.

[4] Approximate inside dimensions are 13 by 12 by 32 inches.

[5] Inside dimensions vary. Common sizes are 13 by 13 by $22\frac{1}{8}$ inches, and 13 by $15\frac{1}{8}$ by 23 inches.

[6] Approximate inside dimensions are 13 by 18 by $21\frac{5}{8}$ inches.

[7] Approximate inside dimensions are 13 by 13 by $22\frac{1}{8}$ inches.

[8] Approximate inside dimensions are $9\frac{3}{4}$ by 16 by 20 inches.

[9] Approximate inside dimensions are $4\frac{1}{8}$ by $11\frac{1}{2}$ by 14 inches.

[10] The standard weight of 70 pounds is usually recognized as being about 2 measured bushels of corn, husked, on the ear, because it required 70 pounds to yield 1 bushel, or 56 pounds, of shelled corn.

[11] This is the weight commonly used in trade practices, the actual weight varying according to temperature conditions.

[12] For statistical purposes the bale of cotton is 500 pounds gross weight or 480 pounds net weight. Prior to August 1, 1946, the net weight was estimated at 478 pounds. Actual bale weights vary considerably, and the customary average weights of bales of foreign cotton differ from that of the American square bale.

[13] This is the average weight of cottonseed, although the legal weight in some states varies from this figure of 32 pounds.

[14] The cranberry barrel contains 5,826 cubic inches.

[15] Approximate inside dimensions are $1\frac{3}{4}$ by 11 by $16\frac{1}{8}$ inches.

[16] Approximate inside dimensions are $11\frac{1}{2}$ by $11\frac{1}{2}$ by 24 inches.

[17] Beginning with the 1993-1994 season, net weights for California desert valley and Arizona grapefruit were increased from 64 to 67 pounds, equal to the California other area net weight, making a 67 pound net weight apply to all of California.

[18] In California and Arizona for 1942–1953, the net weights as used by the U.S. Department of Agriculture were 77 pounds for oranges, 79 pounds for lemons, and 65 pounds for desert valley grapefruit. Grapefruit in California areas other than the desert valleys averaged 68 pounds. The weights effective 1954 reflected the shift from the "box" to the half-box carton as the container used.

[19] Approximate inside dimensions are $10\frac{1}{4}$ by $10\frac{11}{16}$ by $16\frac{3}{8}$ inches for oranges or lemons, and $9\frac{3}{4}$ by $10\frac{11}{16}$ by $16\frac{3}{8}$ inches for grapefruit.

[20] Approximate inside dimensions are $5\frac{3}{4}$ by $13\frac{1}{2}$ by $16\frac{1}{8}$ inches.

[21] Approximate inside dimensions are $4\frac{3}{4}$ by 16 by $16\frac{1}{8}$ inches.

[22] Approximate inside dimensions are $7\frac{3}{4}$ by 16 by $21\frac{7}{8}$ inches.

[23] Approximate inside dimensions are $9\frac{7}{8}$ by 13 by 25 inches.

[24] Approximate inside dimensions are 12 by 12 by 24 inches.

[25] Approximate inside dimensions vary. A common size is $4\frac{1}{2}$ by $11\frac{1}{2}$ by $16\frac{1}{8}$ inches.

[26] Approximate inside dimensions are $8\frac{1}{2}$ by $11\frac{1}{2}$ by 18 inches.

[27] Inside dimensions vary and range from 4 by 16 by $16\frac{1}{8}$ inches to 6 by 16 by $16\frac{1}{8}$ inches.

[28] Includes both sorghum grain (kafir, milo, hegari, and so forth) and sweet sorghum varieties.

[29] This average of 55 pounds indicates the usual weight of sweet potatoes when harvested. Much weight is lost in curing or drying, and the net weight when sold in terminal markets may be less than 55 pounds.

Sources

U.S. Department of Agriculture, Statistical Reporting Service, *Agricultural Statistics* (1967), pp. v–viii; and National Agricultural Statistics Service, *Agricultural Statistics, 2000*, pp. iv–ix.

APPENDIX 2
States and Census Regions

Editor: Monty Hindman

The United States is organized under a federal system of government, presently consisting of a national government plus fifty states and the District of Columbia. Each state has its own constitution and governance structure.

Statehood

Authority for admitting new states is vested in Congress by the Constitution's Article IV, Section 3. Once an area has achieved territorial status – a typical preliminary step on the route to statehood – the procedure for becoming a state usually involves three steps: first a territory petitions Congress through its territorial assembly; then Congress passes an enabling act authorizing the territory to write a constitution; finally, Congress passes an act admitting the state to the union. Both the enabling and admission acts require presidential approval.

Table Ap-E provides information concerning the timing of two important stages in that process: the date of legislation conferring territorial status (where applicable) and the effective date of admission to the United States.

There have been many deviations from the procedure just described; in fact, it is just one of the common routes taken to statehood. Three others can be noted.

- The thirteen original states were created through an entirely different political process. For such cases, the date of the state's ratification of the U.S. Constitution is given as the date of effective admission in Table Ap-E.
- Six states bypassed the territorial stage and were admitted directly. Four of them – Kentucky, Maine, Vermont, and West Virginia – had been part of other states prior to admission. California had been an unorganized area under military rule. And Texas was an independent republic before becoming a state.
- Eight states – Colorado, Montana, Nevada, North Dakota, Oklahoma, South Dakota, Utah, and Washington – were formally admitted through presidential proclamation, Congress having authorized this during the enabling phase for these states.

Census Regions

Many tables in *Historical Statistics of the United States* refer to census regions and divisions or rely on the two-letter state codes standardized by the U.S. Postal Service. Refer to Map Ap-F for the current state boundaries and the current census regional classification. Refer to Table Ap-E for a listing of the state codes.

The census regional classifications have a history. Through 1840, the decennial censuses tended not to organize statistical presentations along regional lines. Instead, state-level data were typically shown in tables that simply listed the states in north-to-south fashion. The Census Office introduced many changes to the tabular presentation of data in the 1850 Census, including the use of various regional groupings in summary tables that were published as part of a one-volume compendium. This change was one part of a wide-ranging census reform conducted against the backdrop of a deepening sectional crisis that gave regional summaries new salience.[1]

The use of regional tabulations and summaries was continued in subsequent censuses, with a fair bit of variation and experimentation in the groupings as new states were admitted to the nation. A five-region scheme used in the 1880 Census is generally consistent with modern categories, although various regroupings and minor adjustments to nomenclature have occurred since 1880 (see Table Ap-G). Beginning with the 1900 Census, the regional categories were standardized.

References

Anderson, Margo J. 1988. *The American Census: A Social History.* Yale University Press.

---

[1] For a discussion of the wider reforms and the political context, see Anderson (1988). For details on the regional classifications used in the nineteenth century, refer to the source for Table Ap-G.

TABLE Ap-E   Dates of territorial legislation and effective admission to the United States: 1787–1959

Name	Code	Territorial act Date	Territorial act Year	Effective admission Date	Effective admission Year	Name	Code	Territorial act Date	Territorial act Year	Effective admission Date	Effective admission Year
Delaware	DE	—	—	Dec 7	1787	Michigan	MI	Jan 11	1805	Jan 26	1837
Pennsylvania	PA	—	—	Dec 12	1787	Florida	FL	Mar 30	1822	Mar 3	1845
New Jersey	NJ	—	—	Dec 18	1787	Texas	TX	—	—	Dec 29	1845
Georgia	GA	—	—	Jan 2	1788	Iowa	IA	Jun 12	1838	Dec 28	1846
Connecticut	CT	—	—	Jan 9	1788	Wisconsin	WI	Apr 20	1836	May 29	1848
Massachusetts	MA	—	—	Feb 6	1788	California	CA	—	—	Sep 9	1850
Maryland	MD	—	—	Apr 28	1788	Minnesota	MN	Mar 3	1849	May 11	1858
South Carolina	SC	—	—	May 23	1788	Oregon	OR	Aug 14	1848	Feb 14	1859
New Hampshire	NH	—	—	Jun 21	1788	Kansas	KS	May 30	1854	Jan 29	1861
Virginia	VA	—	—	Jun 25	1788	West Virginia	WV	—	—	Jun 20	1863
New York	NY	—	—	Jul 26	1788	Nevada	NV	Mar 2	1861	Oct 31	1864
North Carolina	NC	—	—	Nov 21	1789	Nebraska	NE	May 30	1854	Mar 1	1867
Rhode Island	RI	—	—	May 29	1790	Colorado	CO	Feb 28	1861	Aug 1	1876
Vermont	VT	—	—	Mar 4	1791	North Dakota	ND	Mar 2	1861	Nov 2	1889
Kentucky	KY	—	—	Jun 1	1792	South Dakota	SD	Mar 2	1861	Nov 2	1889
Tennessee	TN	May 26	1790	Jun 1	1796	Montana	MT	May 26	1864	Nov 8	1889
Ohio	OH	Jul 13	1787	Mar 1	1803	Washington	WA	Mar 2	1853	Nov 11	1889
Louisiana	LA	Mar 26	1804	Apr 30	1812	Idaho	ID	Mar 3	1863	Jul 3	1890
Indiana	IN	May 7	1800	Dec 11	1816	Wyoming	WY	Jul 25	1868	Jul 10	1890
Mississippi	MS	Apr 7	1798	Dec 10	1817	Utah	UT	Sep 9	1850	Jan 4	1896
Illinois	IL	Feb 3	1809	Dec 3	1818	Oklahoma	OK	May 2	1890	Nov 16	1907
Alabama	AL	Mar 3	1817	Dec 14	1819	New Mexico	NM	Sep 9	1850	Jan 6	1912
Maine	ME	—	—	Mar 15	1820	Arizona	AZ	Feb 24	1863	Feb 14	1912
Missouri	MO	Jun 4	1812	Aug 10	1821	Alaska	AK	Aug 24	1912	Jan 3	1959
Arkansas	AR	Mar 2	1819	Jun 15	1836	Hawai'i	HI	Apr 30	1900	Aug 21	1959

Source

Peter B. Sheridan, *Admission of States into the Union after the Original Thirteen: A Brief History and Analysis of the Statehood Process* (Congressional Research Service, Library of Congress, April 2, 1985).

Documentation

This table does not provide dates for the legislation enabling a territory to write a constitution or for the admission legislation itself (as contrasted with the date of effective admission). Refer to the source for such details.

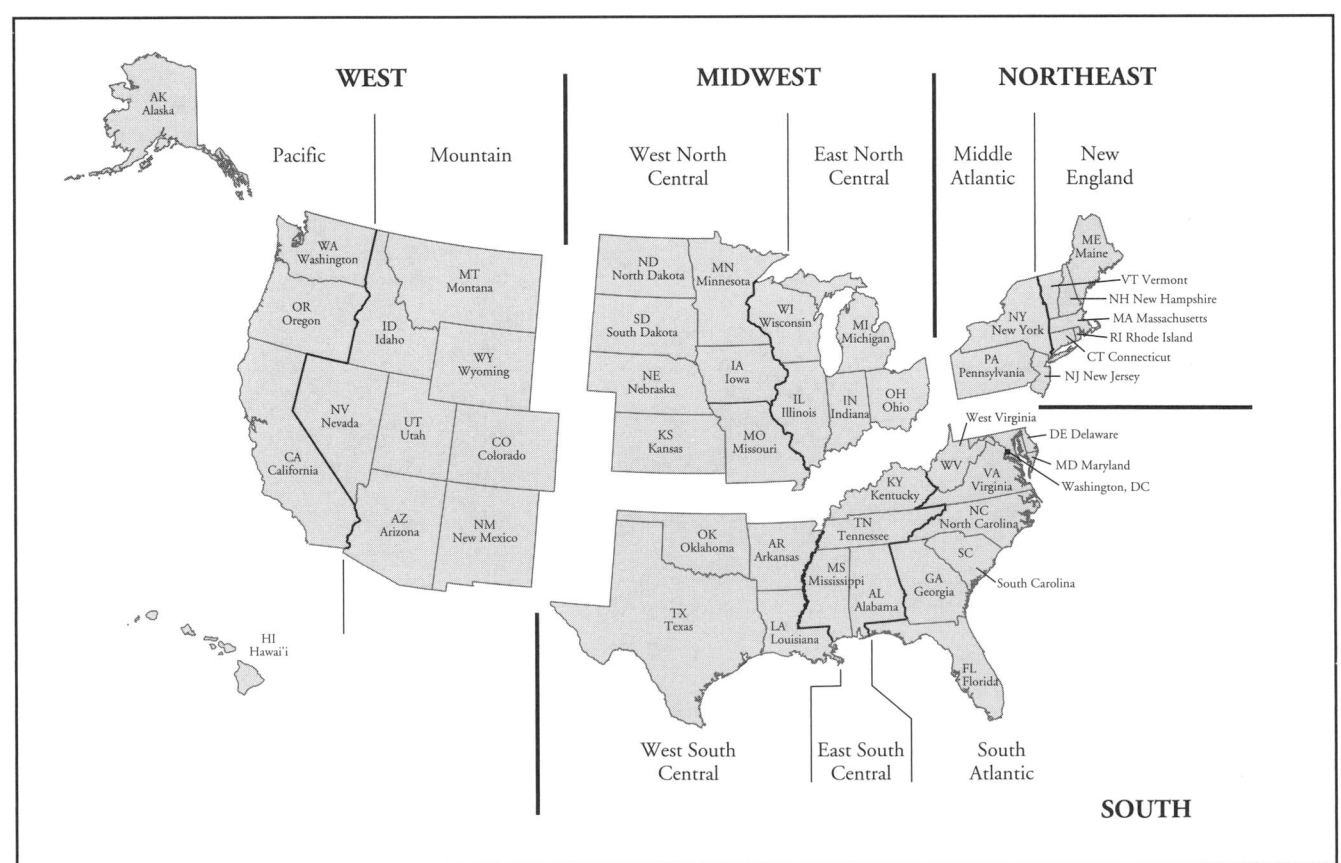

MAP Ap-F   Map of the United States, with current census regions and divisions

Source

U.S. Bureau of the Census, *Statistical Abstract of the United States* (2000), front flyleaf.

TABLE Ap-G Census regions and divisions: 1880–2000

1880–1890	1900	1910–1940	1950–2000
North Atlantic	**North Atlantic**	**North**	**Northeast**
	New England	New England	New England
			Maine
			New Hampshire
			Vermont
			Massachusetts
			Rhode Island
			Connecticut
	Southern North Atlantic	Middle Atlantic	Middle Atlantic
			New York
			New Jersey
			Pennsylvania
Northern Central	**North Central**		**Midwest**
	Eastern North Central	East North Central	East North Central
			Ohio
			Indiana
			Illinois
			Michigan
			Wisconsin
	Western North Central	West North Central	West North Central
			Minnesota
			Iowa
			Missouri
			North Dakota
			South Dakota
			Nebraska
			Kansas
South Atlantic	**South Atlantic**	**South**	**South**
	Northern South Atlantic	South Atlantic	South Atlantic
			Delaware
			Maryland
			District of Columbia
			Virginia
			West Virginia
	Southern South Atlantic		
			North Carolina
			South Carolina
			Georgia
			Florida
South Central	**South Central**		
	Eastern South Central	East South Central	East South Central
			Kentucky
			Tennessee
			Alabama
			Mississippi
	Western South Central	West South Central	West South Central
			Arkansas
			Louisiana
			Oklahoma
			Texas
Western	**Western**	**West**	**West**
	Rocky Mountain	Mountain	Mountain
			Montana
			Idaho
			Wyoming
			Colorado
			New Mexico
	Basin and Plateau		
			Arizona
			Utah
			Nevada
	Pacific	Pacific	Pacific
			Washington
			Oregon
			California
			Alaska
			Hawai'i

Source

U. S. Bureau of the Census, "Statistical Groupings of States and Counties," Chapter 6 in *Geographic Areas Reference Manual* (1994).

Documentation

Note that the Midwest region was designated as the North Central region until June 1984.

APPENDIX 3

Origin of *Historical Statistics of the United States*

Editor: Carmel Ullman Chiswick

Historical Statistics of the United States is the premier source of quantitative evidence on American economic, social, political, demographic, and institutional history. Introduced in 1949 as a time-series supplement to the *Statistical Abstract of the United States,* it has inspired similar efforts in countries around the world. At the time of this writing, when the current edition is a quarter-century out of date, *Historical Statistics of the United States* is still a basic reference generating hundreds of citations annually in academic, professional, and journalistic publications. This essay describes the origins of this influential work and how it evolved over time.

Historical Statistics of the United States was initially developed by the U.S. Census Bureau as an historical supplement to its *Statistical Abstract*, a convenient one-volume compendium of economic, social, political, and demographic data, reported for the United States as a whole and by state, compiled from data collected by the highly decentralized federal statistical system.[1] *Statistical Abstract* has been published annually (with only a few exceptions) since 1878 by various statistical units of the federal government.[2]

In 1943, it became the responsibility of the Statistical Reports Section in the Office of the Assistant Director for Statistical Standards, Bureau of the Census. Shortly thereafter, most of these historical statistics, generally uneven in coverage and quality, were dropped from the *Statistical Abstract* to make room for expanded coverage of contemporary subjects.

The Census Bureau developed the idea of supplements to the *Statistical Abstract* in the 1940s to satisfy a growing appetite for quantitative data. Statistics were becoming increasingly important as a form of evidence, especially in the social sciences, and new statistical methods were being developed to analyze quantitative data. Many public policy concerns of the time focused on the distribution of income and assets, stimulating interest in statistics that could facilitate comparisons between subgroups of the population. Other public policy concerns focused on the rate of economic growth and the international competitiveness of the United States. Economists, impressed by the wartime mobilization experience and hoping to avoid another Great Depression, were studying the determinants of economic growth and stability. The newly published theories of John Maynard Keynes generated an interest in national income growth as an aggregate phenomenon.

The first edition of *Historical Statistics of the United States* was published as a *Statistical Abstract* supplement in 1949, following on the heels of the *Cities Supplement* (1944) and the *County Data Book* (1947).[3] The *Cities Supplement* and the *County Data Book* reported up-to-date figures for small geographic areas, designed to reveal phenomena obscured by aggregation to the state and national levels. *Historical Statistics of the United States* was a companion volume designed to provide consistent time-series data for the national aggregates covering as long a period as possible.

Historical Statistics of the United States was originally envisioned as a serial that would be published at one-decade intervals, with mid-decade updates that would include adjusted data and new figures for recent years. The first edition of *Historical Statistics of the United States,* Volume I of the series, appeared in 1949, and the *Continuation to 1952* was published five years later. Volume II was published in 1960 as the second edition, *Historical Statistics of the United States: Colonial Times to 1957*, and was followed by the *Continuation to 1962.* Volume III, subtitled *Colonial Times to 1970*, was published in 1975 as the Bicentennial Edition (U.S. Bureau of the Census 1949b, 1954, 1960, 1965, and 1975). This third edition marked the end of Census Bureau publication of historical compendia. The present Millennial Edition has been prepared by the academic community (see the Preface).

---

[1] Nearly every governmental agency has its own statistical unit. The largest are the Bureau of the Census, the Bureau of Economic Analysis (both in the U.S. Department of Commerce), and the Bureau of Labor Statistics (in the U.S. Department of Labor). The Office of Statistical Policy, a small unit with fewer than seventy people, oversees the system from the Office of Regulatory Affairs, Office of Management and Budget (formerly the Bureau of the Budget).

[2] The Treasury Department's Bureau of Statistics was the first to publish the annual *Statistical Abstract of the United States* beginning in 1878. It was moved to the newly formed Department of Commerce and Labor in 1903 and remained in the Department of Commerce when it became a separate agency in 1912 (Duncan and Shelton 1978). The *Statistical Abstract* was issued by the Bureau of Foreign and Domestic Commerce from 1912 to 1938, after which it became the responsibility of the Bureau of the Census. Various initiatives over the years

have considered bringing the *Abstract* to a more central location in the federal system, but pragmatism and efficiency have prevailed over bureaucratic logic, and it remains at Census (Duncan and Shelton 1978; Goldfield 1998).

[3] These publications were merged in 1952 to become the *County and City Data Book*, which continues to be issued approximately every five years. The *Congressional District Data Book* was added later.

Acknowledgments

The spirit of two important teachers and mentors informs this essay: the late Morris B. Ullman, formerly of the U.S. Bureau of the Census, and the late Jonathan R. T. Hughes of Northwestern University. Carmella Chiswick acknowledges the helpful support of David Pemberton in the Census History Unit, Bureau of the Census, the suggestions of William Lerner and Edwin Goldfield, and the comments by Margo Anderson and Barry R. Chiswick.

Origins of *Historical Statistics*

The original *Historical Statistics of the United States* project at the Bureau of the Census was headed by Morris B. Ullman, at that time Chief of the Statistical Reports Section in the office of Morris H. Hansen, Statistical Assistant to the Director of the Bureau of the Census.[4] *Historical Statistics of the United States* was only one of many new statistical reporting projects developed at the Bureau of the Census by Ullman and Hansen, a team referred to as "The Two Morrises."[5] The Office of the Assistant Director at that time was a place of innovation and intellectual stimulation, where professionals on the Bureau of the Census staff interacted closely with academics and other nongovernmental researchers at the forefront of the rapidly advancing science of statistics. The Statistical Reports Section was designing and implementing new, user-friendly ways to disseminate data to a wider audience. The Statistical Methods Section was developing sampling theory and applying it to the survey activities of the Bureau of the Census, playing a major role in establishing the modern fields of statistics and sampling theory.[6] Hansen frequently testified before Congress about the Census Bureau's important new breakthroughs in data-processing technology, especially the potential savings of time and money promised by the development of computers (Scott 1968; Duncan and Shelton 1978).[7]

In this heady environment, one of Ullman's first initiatives was to place a return postcard in all copies of the 1942 *Statistical Abstract of the United States* requesting feedback on its use and soliciting suggestions for improvement. This informal survey indicated that most copies went to libraries and to governmental agencies where they provide quick access to statistics for the writers of term papers, speeches, and reports. Suggestions for improvement included requests for more and longer historical series as well as more breakdowns of the aggregate into data for smaller areas (Ullman 1949). Size limitations made it difficult to include either of these in the *Statistical Abstract of the United States* itself, but the idea of developing supplemental publications for this purpose was appealing. The first "trial balloon," no doubt benefiting from the new data-processing equipment that made it easier and less costly to produce small-area statistics, was the *Cities Supplement* published in 1945. Its success led to further work on the *County Data Book* that appeared in 1947. A time-series project was next in line, but its implementation was more ambitious and took longer to come into focus.

Like the *Statistical Abstract of the United States* itself, *Historical Statistics of the United States* was a collection of data from secondary sources in an era when every table had to be manually typeset. If it made relatively little direct use of new technology, it would benefit greatly from the statistical expertise of the Census Bureau staff.[8] This staff included not only professional statisticians but also specialists in the collection, design, and editing of statistical tables, experts who worked with a similarly specialized unit at the Government Printing Office on the production of statistical reports. These in-house skills were a major asset for the production of *Historical Statistics of the United States* at the Bureau of the Census.

Historical Statistics of the United States also required the expertise of nongovernment statisticians scattered in universities, research institutes, and foundations throughout the country. These individuals were collected into a variety of professional associations that, in their turn, formed umbrella organizations for purposes that crossed disciplinary boundaries. The Social Science Research Council (SSRC) was such an organization, formed in 1924 by seven professional associations in the social sciences.[9] The stated goals of the SSRC were to support basic research in the social sciences, to improve the infrastructure for social research, and to include the "human or social dimension" in the nation's scientific projects (Prewitt 2000).

When J. Frederick Dewhurst decided in 1945 to promote compilation of a source book of historical statistics, he turned to the American Economics Association (AEA), the American Statistical Association (ASA), and the SSRC for sponsorship. Dewhurst was the senior economist at the Twentieth Century Fund (TCF), a private foundation in New York focusing since the early 1930s on in-house projects to investigate "flaws in the economic system, and

---

[4] When Calvert L. Dedrick became Assistant Chief of the Division of Statistical Research in 1935, with a mission to upgrade its professional staff, his first appointment (in 1936) was Morris Hansen. Morris Ullman came to the Census Bureau in 1937 as a junior statistical technician and "trouble shooter," joining Hansen's Statistical Reports Section in the same year (1943) that it became responsible for the *Statistical Abstract of the United States* (Duncan and Shelton 1978).

[5] Both men subsequently left the Bureau of the Census, Morris Ullman in 1958 and Morris Hansen a decade later. Volume II was prepared by Herman P. Miller under the general direction of Edwin G. Goldfield, and Volume III was prepared by William Lerner. The basic structure and organization of the project remained the same, however, and "the two Morrises" are generally credited at the Bureau of the Census with the conception, organization, and implementation of the *Historical Statistics of the United States* project.

[6] The country's foremost probability theorists and mathematicians were brought in as advisers and consultants, and some of this talent was hired for the permanent staff. In 1942, Hansen began his long-term collaboration on sampling methods with William N. Hurwitz, who had come to the Bureau of the Census in 1940. Other staff in this section included W. Edwards Deming and William G. Madow, who, along with Hansen and Hurwitz, would soon publish seminal books in the new field of statistical sampling (Deming 1950; Hansen, Hurwitz, and Madow 1953). By the mid-1940s, the early results of this work were already appearing prominently in academic journals (Duncan and Shelton 1978).

[7] The large-scale data gathering efforts at the Bureau of the Census cried out for better forms of mechanization, and by the 1940s a tradition of innovating and developing data-processing machinery – mainly for keypunching and card sorting operations – was well established (Truesdell 1965). Hansen became interested in the development of the first civilian electronic computer, the UNIVAC, as early as 1944 (Duncan and Shelton 1978, p. 124). Upon consultation with scientists at the National Bureau of Standards (also in the Department of Commerce), a contract was signed to develop the UNIVAC in time to handle data tabulations for the 1950 Census. By 1949, James L. McPherson, formerly of the Population Division but since 1945 the "machine development officer" under Hansen, had started to write the first computer program in anticipation of delivery of the first computer (Scott 1968, p. 62).

[8] For most of its history, the permanent staff at the Census Bureau was minimal, and the decennial censuses had been carried out by a temporary work force. Budget cutting during the Great Depression further depleted the ranks, leaving the Bureau "with only a skeleton staff, many of whom had joined the agency in 1902 and had little technical training in statistics. In 1933, the Bureau had only 3 Ph.D.'s and only one professional man under forty-five years of age" (Eckler 1972). This changed dramatically in 1935, when Stuart A. Rice was made Assistant Director and set about selecting a cadre of academically trained statisticians.

[9] The participating organizations were the American Economic, Political Science, Historical, Sociological, Statistical, Psychological, and Anthropological Associations.

the positing of solutions to them" (Century Foundation 2000).[10] In the mid-1940s, Dewhurst was Research Director for *America's Needs and Resources*, a major TCF undertaking that analyzed historical trends in production, income, and consumption to assess the U.S. economy's economic potential (Dewhurst 1947). Drawing heavily on new time-series data being constructed elsewhere, most notably at the National Bureau of Economic Research (NBER) in New York, the TCF project exemplified a growing interest in research that used historical data and applied quantitative methods for policy analysis.

In a memorandum dated April 12, 1945, Dewhurst proposed a new project "involving the completion and publication of a comprehensive source book of economic statistics" to be accomplished cooperatively by the AEA and the ASA. At its April 1945 meeting, the Executive Committee of the AEA named three members to a committee "to explore the merits and feasibility of such a project," the Board of Directors of the ASA followed suit in May, and the Economic History Association was invited to participate as well.[11] Chaired by Dewhurst, it was called the "Joint Committee for a Source Book of Economic Statistics." The proposal was discussed by the SSRC Problems and Policy Committee, where "one member" suggested the possibility that the Census Bureau might be able to handle the preparation of such a book (Copeland 1946). The member was not identified in the minutes, but it may be noted that Phillip Hauser, one of the ASA members of the Joint Committee, was at that time Deputy Director of the Bureau of the Census.

The Dewhurst initiative struck a responsive chord at the Census Bureau in the Statistical Reports Section, where the historical supplement to the *Statistical Abstract of the United States* had been accepted in principle but not yet developed (Ullman 1949). By August 1945, letters had been exchanged between SSRC and the Bureau of the Census, the Secretary of Commerce had approved the project, and the Census Bureau had agreed to include the project in its budget request for the 1946–1947 fiscal year (Bell 1946, pp. 880–1; Copeland 1946). In November 1945, Dewhurst's Joint Committee met at the SSRC offices in New York City, and Hauser agreed that the Census Bureau would conduct "exploratory and planning work." Ullman's proposal for a time-series supplement to the *Statistical Abstract of the United States* thus became the basis of discussions between the Census Bureau and the committee members (U.S. Bureau of the Census 1946a). At its meeting in April 1946, the Joint Committee accepted the Census Bureau's proposal, declared the project feasible, and dissolved itself after only one year of existence.

The Bureau of the Census agreed to handle the publication, the working title of which was "Source Book on Economic Statistics." From the beginning, however, the Census Bureau recognized the ambitious scale of the project and the fact that its staffing requirements differed from those of their usual statistical reports. As observed in its report to the Joint Committee: "Because of the nature of the work involved, the amount of clerical work necessary for the preparation of the various chapters is greatly subordinated to the amount of professional effort needed. . . . It is, therefore, suggested that . . . the Joint Committee will recommend, and assist the Bureau in selecting and obtaining cooperation from, a sufficiently large number of consultants each of whom will be asked to prepare the material on a particular subject" (U.S. Bureau of the Census 1946a).

To implement this recommendation, the SSRC appointed a Committee on the Source Book of Historical Statistics (Advisory to the Bureau of the Census), again with Dewhurst as chairman. The members of this Advisory Committee were actively involved in the preparation of *Historical Statistics of the United States*, and their participation – as a committee and as individuals – is liberally acknowledged in the Introduction to the 1949 edition.

Even though it was common for research carried out by the federal government to draw on the expertise of advisory board members and to use nongovernment researchers as consultants, by all accounts the degree of collaboration between the Bureau of the Census and SSRC on *Historical Statistics of the United States* was unusually close and extensive (U.S. Bureau of the Census 1949b; Goldfield 1998; William Lerner, personal interview, Suitland, Maryland, August 5, 1998). The SSRC Committee on Research in Economic History, whose chairman (Arthur H. Cole of Harvard University) was a member of Dewhurst's committee, even provided a grant to support a full-time Executive Secretary. This position was filled by A. Benjamin Handler, who had been working with Dewhurst at TCF as Assistant Research Director for *America's Needs and Resources*. Handler would end up spending much of his time in Washington and worked so closely with Census on *Historical Statistics of the United States* that he is said to have functioned as a de facto member of the Statistical Reports Section.[12]

Scope and Format of *Historical Statistics*

Initial guidelines for the *Historical Statistics of the United States* project were clear that the goal was to produce a statistical source book, asserting explicitly that "text material will describe the statistical significance of the data but will not involve analysis of their economic or social significance" (U.S. Bureau of the Census 1946c). But the compilation of historical data itself is often an example of economic or social research. Many of the nongovernment economists, demographers, and sociologists recruited by the SSRC had acquired their expertise in historical statistics through just such analyses, and this kind of research was often the framework for assessing the importance of including a particular series.[13] Some controversy over the appropriate boundary between data reporting and substantive analysis was inevitable.

The pragmatic solution to this problem was to include detailed notes on the source of each series and to add a set of "substantive"

---

[10] Dewhurst would later become Executive Director of the Twentieth Century Fund, which was renamed the Century Foundation in the late 1990s.

[11] The three members of the joint committee named by AEA were Morris Copeland, Amos E. Taylor, and Stacy May. The three members named by ASA were Walter Mitchell, Phillip Hauser, and Theodore Yntema. The Economic History Association named Shepard B. Clough, W. B. Smith, and Harold Williamson as its three members.

[12] Handler was "primarily responsible for procurement of data and relationships with the agencies and individuals who contributed to the publication." Bruce L. Jenkinson and William Lerner in the Statistical Abstract unit at the Census Bureau had primary responsibility, respectively, for "planning and preparation of the report" and for "review and editing of the materials as to content, adequacy and coverage." Morris B. Ullman "supervised" the project and was involved with every aspect (U.S. Bureau of the Census 1949b).

[13] The *Historical Statistics of the United States* project itself was valued in large part because various public policy issues had aroused an interest in historical trends (Anderson 1988).

appendices for special topics. Source notes for each series and section would present "the concepts used, the principal points of comparability, some discussion of the methods used in preparing the series, other information available which is not shown in the supplement, and such cross-reference information as is needed" (U.S. Bureau of the Census 1946b).

The original estimate was that on average a page of tables would require nearly a page of text. Specialists would need to look elsewhere for more details, but *Historical Statistics of the United States* could serve as a reference to provide direction for this search. This function of the Bureau of the Census as a clearinghouse for statistical expertise was deemed so important that the notes for each series and section in *Historical Statistics of the United States* would include as a matter of policy the names of individual contributors both inside and outside of government.[14]

Topical coverage for *Historical Statistics of the United States* was to take as its point of departure the *Statistical Abstract of the United States*, to which it was a supplement. Coverage in the *Statistical Abstract* was itself based on a prior consensus as to which statistics were both interesting and accurate, and the presumption was that these same criteria would make it useful to carry them back historically.[15] This was not expected to be limiting, however, for if a "new" series were deemed worthy of being added to the *Supplement*, current data on the subject would be considered for inclusion in the *Statistical Abstract* (U.S. Bureau of the Census 1946a). The data from one should feed directly into the tables of the other, and series-by-series cross references were published both as an appendix to the *Statistical Abstract of the United States* and as source notes to the historical tables. The major exception would be "lapsed" historical series for which data were no longer collected, as in the size of the slave population, or for which the data had undergone important conceptual changes in construction, as in the early figures for housing and for manufacturing (U.S. Bureau of the Census 1946d; 1949b, Appendix II).

Coverage in *Historical Statistics of the United States* was generally to be confined to data for the continental United States as a whole, primarily for reasons of space but also because *Historical Statistics of the United States* was intended as a time-series supplement to the *Statistical Abstract of the United States* itself and not to its small-area supplements.[16] Anticipated exceptions included cases where subnational statistics would be essential to interpreting the aggregate (as in merchant marine statistics, reported separately by coast and inland waterways), where an aggregate would not be meaningful (as in data on rainfall or internal migration), or where a subnational series could be interpreted as an indicator of

the aggregate (as in prices on the New York Stock Exchange or the production of anthracite in Pennsylvania). Exceptions were also made for cases of important series that were available only for a limited geographical area, as for the early years in which figures were limited to the Atlantic seaboard (U.S. Bureau of the Census 1946d; 1949b, Appendix II).

Coverage in *Historical Statistics of the United States* was limited to series available on an annual or census-period basis that would extend back for at least twenty years. Some historical series were available on a monthly or quarterly basis, but it was decided that data presented at quarterly, monthly, or weekly intervals would be included only if they were deemed "of paramount importance." A substantive appendix on the turning points of business cycles would include "a few illustrative series of basic significance presented on a monthly or quarterly basis," but readers were cautioned that "this should not be counted upon to round out a subject or time-period presentation in the main part of the volume" (U.S. Bureau of the Census 1946d).

The order in which time series were arranged in a Census Bureau report generally depended on its purpose, arranged backward in time (beginning with the latest date) to give perspective for current data or forward in time (beginning with the earliest date) to show "historical progression or development" (U.S. Bureau of the Census 1949a, paragraph 1122).[17] *Historical Statistics of the United States* could be viewed either way, for while historians would find the forward ordering most natural, general readers writing a speech or report on current policy would typically focus on recent decades to provide a context for data in the *Statistical Abstract of the United States* (William Lerner, personal interview, August 5, 1998). The Census Bureau advisory committees were comprised mainly of historians and tended to favor forward ordering (Evans 1952). Because series varied widely in their earliest dates, however, forward ordering would have resulted in far more "white space" on the printed page and would have increased the publication's size and cost.[18] For these and related technical reasons, *Historical Statistics of the United States* used backward ordering (U.S. Bureau of the Census 1949a).

Evolution of *Historical Statistics*

By December 1946, the Bureau of the Census had prepared a plan for publishing 3,000 data series and was soliciting comments from outside experts that the SSRC had enlisted (U.S. Bureau of the Census 1946e). The experts, encouraged by the potential of the project, made suggestions for the inclusion of a number of additional series, some of which would have required major research projects in order to be developed. In the meantime, the Census Bureau funds for printing were set to expire in June 1947.[19] Ullman solved both

[14] This decision was not trivial, for many statistical experts were employed in governmental agencies in positions where their names did not appear in official publications. The introduction would also identify the main contributors for each major section, and because of the cumulative nature of this project, the later volumes would name the major contributors to all previous volumes as well.

[15] Items included in the *Statistical Abstract of the United States*, and in the federal statistical system in general, were in turn a reflection of the policy interests of the era. For an extensive and thoughtful discussion of this aspect of Census Bureau activity, see Anderson (1988).

[16] Early volumes of the *Statistical Abstract of the United States* had included historical data for many entries, but these had been shortened or dropped as the number of economic series included in each annual volume increased substantially. Dewhurst's idea for a volume with only historical data may have been in part a response to this change (Cole 1950).

[17] The *Statistical Abstract of the United States* was considered an exception because its time series were ordered forward instead of backward. The forward ordering had begun with the very earliest editions, and typesetting technology would have made the change very expensive (U.S. Bureau of the Census 1949a, paragraph 1122, footnote 8).

[18] According to Jenkinson of the Statistical Reports Section, "Because of the nature of the mass-presentation problem, the data could be presented in the least number of pages if all series were arranged with the most recent year first. Here also mass-production requirements, and the cost of printing, were the determining factors, rather than analytical considerations as such" (U.S. Bureau of the Census 1949a, paragraph 1122, footnote 9).

[19] This deadline had not been fully anticipated at the initiation of the project. Cost-cutting measures imposed by the new Congress elected in 1946 not only

problems by recasting the 1949 edition as an extended prospectus, the "first draft" of a multistage project, enabling subsequent editions to benefit from the feedback of users. Preparation of the 1949 and 1960 editions should thus be viewed as two phases of a single project, the first relying primarily on the federal statistical system and the second including relatively more contributions from experts in academia and research institutes.[20]

In the interest of speed, nearly all series in the 1949 edition were obtained within the federal government from individuals who already had a working relationship with the Statistical Reports Section.[21] Contributors were asked to document sources, define terms, and provide explanatory notes for all changes, revisions, and adjustments necessary to compile the time-series figures. The "selection, assembling, posting, correction, preparing of tables for the printer, and the writing of text" were concentrated between October 1946 and June 1947, when the volume went to the printer, and any series not in hand by that date was simply dropped (Ullman 1949). This meant that most of the included series would have a counterpart in the *Statistical Abstract of the United States*, but it also meant exclusion for most "lapsed" series for which data were no longer collected. Other topics were missing because data were not readily available and there was insufficient time for finding and evaluating appropriate material.[22] Of the three essays originally proposed as substantive appendices, only one was prepared in time to be included.[23]

Both the original prospectus for the 1949 edition and the final publication included 3,000 series arranged into fourteen major chapters. Many of the proposed series (and their corresponding chapters) had to be dropped, but the federal statisticians who responded in time provided more series than expected, and some of the planned chapters were split into two or more.[24] Often documenting their historical statistics for the first time, these statisticians uncovered a variety of unanticipated problems of fact and interpretation. The Census Bureau team (including Handler) focused on editing text for completeness and clarity. They fact-checked all notes and references, and by the time the final copy went to press, every source cited had been followed up by a member of the editorial staff in the Statistical Reports Section. The unexpectedly

large number of changes considerably lengthened the elapsed time between galley and page proofs, although they reveal a process of feedback that improved the quality of federal statistics beyond the Census Bureau itself (Ullman 1949). An appendix in the 1949 *Statistical Abstract of the United States* updated the historical series for the years 1946–1948 and cross-referenced each series with its counterpart in *Historical Statistics of the United States*.

Despite the obvious limitations of its scaled-down first effort, the 1949 edition of *Historical Statistics of the United States* was well received. It satisfied an immediate need while at the same time stimulating suggestions for improvement and expansion. By September 1950 (about one year after publication), an advisory committee chaired by G. Heberton Evans Jr. had been appointed by the Economic History Association at the request of the Census Bureau. Its report, issued two years later, contained general and specific recommendations for revisions, most of which would be implemented in the 1960 edition (Evans 1952). Many of the shortcomings identified in the Evans report were the direct consequence of the decision to scale down the production of the 1949 edition, and the recommended revisions brought the 1960 edition in line with the original plan.[25] Thus, while the 1960 edition would have a total of 8,000 series arranged in twenty-four chapters (a substantial increase over the 3,000 series and fourteen chapters in the 1949 edition), its Introduction characterizes it as "intended to achieve the purpose foreshadowed in the original volume" (U.S. Bureau of the Census 1960, p. ix).

The 1960 edition of *Historical Statistics of the United States* was also prepared in the Statistical Reports Section in cooperation with the SSRC. Funded by a grant from the Ford Foundation, SSRC engaged more than 125 specialists as consultants on various chapters. These individuals are cited by name in the Introduction. Herman P. Miller directed the project at the Bureau of the Census, served as Executive Secretary of the SSRC Committee on *Historical Statistics of the United States* chaired by Evans, and participated in the selection of consultants. The final product would go through a cycle of five printings, and some 40,000 copies would be sold before the supply was exhausted.

At mid-decade, the Census Bureau published its *Continuation to 1962 and Revisions* (U.S. Bureau of the Census 1965).[26] By then, however, policy interests had shifted and neither the Census Bureau nor the SSRC was prepared to devote major funding to the preparation of a new edition of *Historical Statistics of the United*

---

removed the possibility of a supplementary appropriation but also required that the project be completed before the end of the fiscal year (Cole 1950).

[20] The acknowledgments in the 1960 and 1975 editions include many nongovernmental sources, in marked contrast with the case for the 1949 edition. Nonetheless, the federal statistical system continued to be the major source of contributors for the 1960 and 1975 editions.

[21] An important exception was the work of the NBER, most notably the material on national income and product developed by Simon Kuznets and the appendix on business condition indicators prepared by Geoffrey H. Moore.

[22] Material on education and communications arrived too late to be properly evaluated, and the Department of Agriculture could not get the basic series on Sugar and Tobacco in time (Ullman 1949).

[23] The three appendices were to have been "Statistics of the Colonial Period," "Business Cycle Turning Points and Selected Indicators," and "Bibliography on Methodological Techniques Commonly Employed in Analysis of Time Series." The appendix actually published was "Monthly and Quarterly Indicators of Business Conditions," prepared at the NBER by Geoffrey H. Moore.

[24] The planned chapter on Population and Vital Statistics became two chapters and Extractive Industries was split into three. Omitted chapters were Land and Climate, Social Institutions and Activities, Communication and Power, Domestic Trade, Consumption, and an introductory chapter titled "Summary Measures of American Development." Some series planned for omitted chapters were included elsewhere, and others (notably Price Indexes and Wealth and Income) were given chapters of their own.

[25] The Introduction to the 1960 edition lists no fewer than thirteen new subject areas that did not appear in the 1949 edition. Yet of these only three (Services, Corporate Assets, and Research & Development) were actually missing from the original outline (1946e). The rest were present either as major chapters or as sections within a chapter.

[26] Shortly thereafter Ben J. Wattenberg, of Fairfield Publishers, Inc., combined the 1960 edition and its *Continuation* into a single up-to-date document titled *The Statistical History of the United States from Colonial Times to the Present* (*Statistical History* 1966). Census documents are in the public domain, and for several years Wattenberg had been republishing the *Statistical Abstract of the United States* under the title *U.S. Deskbook of Facts & Statistics*. In 1966 Wattenberg published *Statistical History of the United States* as a *Deskbook* supplement, interleaving the two Census Bureau publications by following each chapter of the 1960 edition of *Historical Statistics of the United States* with the corresponding chapter of its *Continuation* (Ben J. Wattenberg, personal interview, August 18, 2000). Because the Government Printing Office provided him with negatives for each page, his tables were exact replicas of the original publications.

States. The Bicentennial Edition, published in 1975, was eventually undertaken by the Statistical Reports Division as an updating exercise. Drawing on previous experience and on voluntary contributions from a network of experts already largely in place, the major chapter headings remained the same as in the 1960 edition. The 1975 publication encompassed some 12,500 time series, an increase of more than 50 percent over the 1960 edition. Some of these were excluded from earlier editions because they had yet to meet the twenty-year-minimum criterion for a historical series and others because they had not yet been "discovered or properly developed."[27]

Concluding Remarks

Historical Statistics of the United States was first developed in the mid-1940s by the Statistical Reports Section, Office of the Assistant Director for Statistical Standards, Bureau of the Census. The project fulfilled multiple goals of that unit. Produced as a supplement to the *Statistical Abstract of the United States*, it greatly expanded the *Abstract*'s coverage of time-series data. As part of the Census Bureau's mission to improve statistical reporting, it raised standards for historical statistics and correspondingly stimulated the development of statistical expertise. As a joint project between the Bureau of the Census and the SSRC, it created and enhanced a network of professional experts on historical statistics.

When Frederick Dewhurst first proposed developing a source book for economic statistics, modern research in quantitative history was in its infancy. Expertise in the collection of historical statistics was the domain of a few widely scattered individuals in the statistical units of various departments and agencies of the federal government as well as in academia. Today quantitative historical research occupies a central place in the social sciences, in no small part because of the signal role played by *Historical Statistics of the United States*.

References

Anderson, Margo J. 1988. *The American Census: A Social History*. Yale University Press.

Bell, James Washington. 1946. "Proceedings of the 58th Annual Meeting of the AEA: Report of the Secretary." *American Economic Review* 36 (2): 870–86.

Century Foundation. 2000. "The Fund's First 75 Years (1919–1994)." Internet site of the Century Foundation.

Cole, Arthur H. 1950. "Review of *Historical Statistics of the United States, 1789–1945: A Supplement to the Statistical Abstract of the United States*." *Review of Economics and Statistics* 32 (3): 273–4.

---

[27] Wattenberg again obtained the negatives from the Government Printing Office and reproduced the volume with a private publisher and his own "Introduction and User's Guide" (*Statistical History* 1976). By this time Bernan Press was also reissuing Census Bureau documents as "The U.S. DataBook Series" and reproduced yet another version of the Bicentennial Edition. In 1989 Kraus International Publications issued its own reprint of the Bicentennial Edition (*Historical Statistics of the United States, Colonial Times to 1970*, prepared by the U.S. Bureau of the Census, published by Kraus International Publications, White Plains, N.Y., 1989). In 1997 Cambridge University Press released an electronic version of the Bicentennial Edition on CD-ROM with no updating of series. The total number of copies issued by all these sources is unknown, but Census Bureau records show sales of some 38,000 copies for its version (King, telephone conversation, August 2, 2000). Even though the sales of the private publishing efforts is not known, the existence of these efforts points to a strong continuing demand for the publication well after the Census Bureau allowed it to fall out of print.

Copeland, Morris A. 1946. "Proceedings of the 58th Annual Meeting of the AEA: Progress Report on Source Book of Economic Statistics." *American Economic Review* 36 (2): 934–6.

Deming, W. Edwards. 1950. *Some Theory of Sampling*. Wiley.

Dewhurst, J. Frederick. 1947. *America's Needs and Resources: A Twentieth Century Fund Survey Which Includes Estimates for 1950 and 1960*. Twentieth Century Fund.

Dubester, Henry J. 1950. *Catalog of United States Census Publications, 1790–1945*. U.S. Government Printing Office.

Duncan, Joseph W., and William C. Shelton. 1978. *Revolution in United States Government Statistics, 1926–1976*. Office of Federal Statistical Policy and Standards, U.S. Department of Commerce. U.S. Government Printing Office.

Eckler, Ross. 1972. *The Bureau of the Census*. Praeger.

Evans, G. Heberton, Jr. 1952. "On the Revision of *Historical Statistics of the United States, 1789–1945*." Report of the Committee of the Economic History Association (Advisory to the Bureau of the Census), April 15, 1952.

Goldfield, Edwin G. 1998. Personal interview. Suitland, Maryland, August 6, 1998.

Hammack, David C. 1999. "The Politics of Numbers: *Historical Statistics of the United States* and Public Policy, 1945–2000." Presented to the 1999 Annual Meetings of the Social Science History Association.

Hansen, Morris H., William N. Hurwitz, and William G. Madow. 1953. *Sample Survey Methods and Theory*. 2 volumes. Wiley.

Prewitt, Kenneth. 2000. "SSRC: A Brief History of the Council." Internet site of the Social Science Research Council.

Scott, Ann Herbert. 1968. *Census, U.S.A.: Fact Finding for the American People, 1790–1970*. Seabury Press.

The Statistical History of the United States from Colonial Times to the Present. 1966. With an Introduction by Ben J. Wattenberg. Horizon Press.

The Statistical History of the United States from Colonial Times to the Present. 1976. With an Introduction and User's Guide by Ben J. Wattenberg. Basic Books.

Truesdell, Leon E. 1965. *The Development of Punch Card Tabulation in the Bureau of the Census: 1890–1940*. U.S. Government Printing Office.

Ullman, Morris B. 1949. "Statistical Abstract Program, with Special Reference to *Historical Statistics of the United States*." Presented to the American Statistical Association, Philadelphia Chapter, February 18.

U.S. Bureau of the Census. 1946a. "Report to Joint Committee on Status of Source Book Project." April 1. Mimeographed, 3 pages plus exhibits.

U.S. Bureau of the Census. 1946b. "Source Book of Historical Statistics (A Supplement to the *Statistical Abstract of the United States*)." September 9. Mimeographed, 3 pages.

U.S. Bureau of the Census. 1946c. "Source Book of Historical Statistics: General Description of Project." December 10. Mimeographed, 4 pages.

U.S. Bureau of the Census. 1946d. "Source Book of Historical Statistics: Basic Premises for Data Selection." December 10. Mimeographed, 6 pages. Reprinted with minor changes as "Appendix II. Statement of Basic Premises" in U.S. Bureau of the Census, *Historical Statistics of the United States, 1789–1945*. U.S. Government Printing Office, 1949.

U.S. Bureau of the Census. 1946e. "Source Book of Historical Statistics: Detailed Outline." December 10. Mimeographed, 21 pages.

U.S. Bureau of the Census. 1949a. *Bureau of the Census Manual of Tabular Presentation: An Outline of Theory and Practice in the Presentation of Statistical Data in Tables for Publication*. By Bruce L. Jenkinson. U.S. Government Printing Office.

U.S. Bureau of the Census. 1949b. *Historical Statistics of the United States, 1789–1945*. U.S. Government Printing Office.

U.S. Bureau of the Census. 1954. *Continuation to 1952 of Historical Statistics of the United States, 1789–1945 with Revisions of Selected Series*. U.S. Government Printing Office.

U.S. Bureau of the Census. 1960. *Historical Statistics of the United States: Colonial Times to 1957*. U.S. Government Printing Office.

U.S. Bureau of the Census. 1965. *Historical Statistics of the United States, Colonial Times to 1957: Continuation to 1962 and Revisions*. U.S. Government Printing Office.

U.S. Bureau of the Census. 1975. *Historical Statistics of the United States: Colonial Times to 1970*. U.S. Government Printing Office.

COPYRIGHT CITATIONS

Much of the statistical data reproduced here was taken from publications of the U.S. government and is not copy protected. The contributors to this volume have freely reproduced definitions and methodological descriptions of data and data sources from government publications, including earlier editions of *Historical Statistics of the United States*, without direct quotation or citation.

Data from sources other than the U.S. government may be under copyright. Cambridge University Press has made every effort to secure, where necessary, permission to reproduce such protected material. In almost every case, the permission requested was freely granted. In a few instances, however, the copyright owner requested a specific citation or acknowledgment. These citations are provided here. Cambridge University Press thanks all copyright owners for their generous permission to reproduce the data included in this edition of *Historical Statistics of the United States*.

Series Ab63 for 1800–1930. Ansley J. Coale and Melvin Zelnik, *New Estimates of Fertility and Population in the United States: A Study of Annual White Births from 1855 to 1960 and of Completeness of Enumeration in the Censuses from 1880 to 1960*, p. 36. Copyright 1963 by Princeton University Press. Used by permission of Princeton University Press.

Series Ab85 for 1800–1930. Ansley J. Coale and Norfleet W. Rives Jr., "A Statistical Reconstruction of the Black Population of the United States, 1880 1970: Estimates of True Numbers by Age and Sex, Birth Rates, and Total Fertility," *Population Index* 31, p. 26. Copyright 1973 by Ansley J. Coale. Used with permission courtesy of Ansley J. Coale.

Series Ab923 for 1850. Richard H. Steckel, "A Dreadful Childhood: The Excess Mortality of American Slaves," *Social Science History* 10. Copyright 1986 by the Social Science History Association (all rights reserved). Used by permission of Duke University Press.

Series Ad15. Robert W. Fogel, Ralph A. Galantine, and Richard L. Manning, editors, *Without Consent or Contract: The Rise and Fall of American Slavery, Evidence and Methods*, Table 4.2, p. 55. Copyright 1992, 1988 by Robert W. Fogel. Used by permission of W. W. Norton and Company.

Series Ag265–327 for 1950–1980; Ag395–433 for 1910, 1930, and 1970; Ag478–492 for 1890, 1910, 1930, 1960, 1970, and 1980; Ag547–654 for 1936, 1953, 1962, 1974, and 1983; and Ag700–703 for 1865–1983. Paul Stuart, *Nations within a Nation*, Tables 2.10, 2.11, 2.12, 2.13, 2.15, 3.3, 3.8, 3.14, 3.5, 3.16, 3.17, 4.16, and 4.17. Copyright 1987. Used by permission of Greenwood Publishing Group, Westport, Connecticut.

Series Ag718–720. Joane Nagel, *American Indian Ethnic Renewal*, Table 10. Copyright 1996 by Oxford University Press. Used by permission of Oxford University Press.

Series Ba4224–4233. Claudia Goldin, *Understanding the Gender Gap: An Economic History of American Women*, Table 3.1. Copyright 1990 by Oxford University Press. Used by permission of Oxford University Press.

Series Ba4641–4646. J. P. Robinson and G. Godbey, *Time for Life: The Surprising Ways Americans Use Their Time*, Tables 2 and 3. Copyright 1997 by the Pennsylvania State University. Used by permission of Pennsylvania State University.

Series Ba4778–4782. Price V. Fishback, *Soft Coal, Hard Choices: The Economic Welfare of Bituminous Coal Miners, 1890–1930*, pp. 103, 234–5. Copyright 1992 by Oxford University Press. Used by permission of Oxford University Press.

Series Bb209–218. Richard Sutch, "Appendix: The Value of the Slave Population, 1805–1860," in Roger Ransom and Richard Sutch, "Capitalists without Capital: The Burden of Slavery and the Impact of Emancipation," *Agricultural History* 62, Tables A.1 and A.4. Copyright 1988 by the Agricultural History Society. Used by permission of the University of California Press.

Series Bc450–453 for 1983–1997. Barry T. Hirsch and David A. Macpherson, *Union Membership and Earnings Data Book: Compilations from the Current Population Survey*, annual issues. Copyrights 1983 to 1997. Used by permission of the Bureau of National Affairs, Inc.

Series Bc586 for 1919–1966; Bc587 for 1877–1966; and Bc919 for 1869–1966. Abbott L. Ferriss, *Indicators of Trends in American Education*, Appendix D. Copyright 1969 by the Russell Sage Foundation, 112 East 64th Street, New York, New York 10021. Used by permission of the Russell Sage Foundation.

Series Bd664, Bd683, and Bd687. Peter A. Coclanis and John Komlos, "Nutrition and Economic Development in Post-Reconstruction South Carolina: An Anthropomorphic Approach," *Social Science History* 19. Copyright 1995 by the Social Science History Association (all rights reserved). Used by permission of Duke University Press.

Series Bf28–33. Stanley Lebergott, *The American Economy: Income, Wealth, and Want*, pp. 64–5. Copyright 1976 by Princeton University Press. Used by permission of Princeton University Press.

Series Bg551, Bg594, and Cd1–152. Stanley Lebergott, *Consumer Expenditures: New Measures and Old Motives*, Tables A1 and A2. Copyright 1996 by Princeton University Press. Used by permission of Princeton University Press.

Series Cb64–69 and Cj141. Milton Friedman and Anna J. Schwartz, *A Monetary History of the United States, 1867–1960*, Tables A1, A2, and B3. Copyright 1963 by Princeton University Press. Used by permission of Princeton University Press.

Series Da633 for 1946–1952. James Street, *The New Revolution in the Cotton Economy*, p. 133. Copyright 1955 by the University of North Carolina Press, renewed 1985 by James Harry Street. Used by permission of the University of North Carolina Press.

Series Db273–282 for 1887 and 1889–1917. Harden F. Taylor, *Survey of Marine Fisheries of North Carolina*. Copyright 1951. Used by permission of the University of North Carolina Press.

Series Dd368–369 for 1860–1914; Dd375–377 for 1870–1879; Dd406 for 1879–1889; Dd407 for 1860–1872; Dd429–430 for 1871–1914; Dd497; and Dd843 for 1860–1914. Edwin Frickey, *Production in the United States, 1860–1914*, pp. 8–9, 14–15, 54, 135–44, and 189–97. Copyright 1947. Used by permission of Harvard University Press.

Series Df22–24, Df625, Df632–638, and Df639–640. Erik F. Haites, James Mak, and Gary M. Walton, *Western River Transportation: The Era of Early Internal Development*, 1810–1860, Tables 16, A-1, A-2, A-3, G-1, and G-2, and Appendix B. Copyright 1975. Used by permission of the Johns Hopkins University Press.

INDEX

Note: The number before the colon is the volume; the number after the colon is the page. A number range indicates inclusive pages in the same volume. Numbers in italics refer to pages in essays; numbers not in italics refer to pages in statistical tables.

Numbers in italics refer to pages in essays; numbers not in italics refer to pages in statistical tables.

Numbers in italics refer to pages in essays; numbers not in italics refer to pages in statistical tables.

Numbers in italics refer to pages in essays; numbers not in italics refer to pages in statistical tables.

Numbers in italics refer to pages in essays; numbers not in italics refer to pages in statistical tables.

Numbers in italics refer to pages in essays; numbers not in italics refer to pages in statistical tables.

Numbers in italics refer to pages in essays; numbers not in italics refer to pages in statistical tables.

Numbers in italics refer to pages in essays; numbers not in italics refer to pages in statistical tables.

Numbers in italics refer to pages in essays; numbers not in italics refer to pages in statistical tables.

Numbers in italics refer to pages in essays; numbers not in italics refer to pages in statistical tables.

Numbers in italics refer to pages in essays; numbers not in italics refer to pages in statistical tables.

Mineral industries, 1:621–2, 1:772, *4:275–84. See*
    also Mining
  earnings, 2:272–3, 2:277–9
  employees, 2:111–14, 4:285
    female, 2:114
    full-time, 2:117–19
    by industry division, 4:286–7
    output, 3:467–9
    production, 2:115–16, 2:129–32
  establishments, 4:285
  expenses, 4:285
  fuel mineral production, 4:288–94
  hours of work, 2:305–8
  injuries and fatalities, 2:326–33, 2:335
  labor force, 2:110–11
  labor force participants engaged in, 2:101
    by nativity, 2:108–9
    by race, 2:104–7
    by sex, 2:102–7
  national income originating in, 3:32–5
  operations, 4:285
  patents granted, 3:430–44
  receipts of, 4:285
  union membership in, 2:347
  value added in, 4:285
  wages and salaries, 2:282–3, 2:292
  work stoppages, 2:359–61
Mineral production
  metal, 4:308–23
  nonmetal, 4:323–5
    cement, 4:323–8
    lime, 4:326–8
    pyrites, 4:323–5
    stone, 4:323–8
Mineral products
  patents granted, 3:430–44
  price indexes, producer and wholesale,
    3:173–4
Minerals
  American Indian land, 1:755–6
  operations, 4:285
Minimum wage, 2:284–5
Mining, 4:285–334. *See also* Mineral industries
  accidents, bituminous coal mining, 2:335
  business incorporations, 3:539–47
  clay, 4:326–8
  companies and corporations, 3:503–5, 3:522,
    3:558, 3:566–7
  employees, 4:286–7
    coal mining, 4:286–7
  gypsum, crude, 4:323–5
  industrial production indexes, 4:663–9
  injuries and fatalities, 2:326–9
  lime, 4:323–5
  limited liability companies, 3:522
  mergers, *3:487*, 3:553–6
  output, 3:467–9
  phosphate rock, 4:323–8
  potash, 4:323–5
  salt, 4:323–8
  sand and gravel, 4:323–8
  stone, 4:326–8
  sulfur, 4:323–8
  U.S. direct investment in foreign countries,
    5:473–8
Minnesota. *See* State data
Mississippi. *See* State data
Missouri. *See* State data
Modern Woodmen of America,
  2:888–92
Molybdenum
  imports and exports, 4:329–33
  production, 4:318–23
Monetary aggregates, *3:583–5,* 3:596–622
  definition, *3:585, 3:601*
  Divisia, 3:591–2, 3:621–2

Monetary aggregates (*continued*)
  Federal Reserve Board, 3:590–1, 3:619–21
  U.S. monetary gold stock, 3:584, 3:596–7
Monetary policy, *3:588–9, 3:592, 3:604–7,*
  3:623–31
  definition, *3:588, 3:608–13*
Monetary values, 3:592–3, 3:623, *5:809–12*
Money. *See also* Currency; Monetary policy
  colonial, *5:643–4*
  Confederate States of America, *5:776–8,*
    5:791–9
    money stock, 5:791–2
  during the Great Depression, 3:136–40
  high-powered, 3:631
  market rates, 3:820–5
  monetary aggregates, *3:583–5,* 3:596–622
  monetary standards, 3:592–3, 3:623
  stock, and components, 3:585–9, 3:598–607
  value of the dollar, 3:592–3, 3:623
Montana. *See* State data
Montserrat, U.S. population born in, 1:611
Monuments and tombstones, 3:267–70
Morocco, U.S. population born in, 1:610
Mortality rates, 1:467, 1:458–73, 1:487,
    1:695. See also Deaths and death
    rates
  decline, *1:385–7*
  infant, *1:388*
  maternal, 1:458–61
  neonatal, 1:458–61
Mortgages, *4:395–403,* 4:406–572
  conventional single-family
    delinquencies and foreclosures, 4:571–2
    terms, 4:565–8
  debt, 3:777
    by financing, 4:532–5
    by holder, 4:526–39
    by property type, 4:526–39
    by type, 4:526–31
  delinquencies, 4:569–72
  farm
    owner-operated, 4:74
  foreclosures, 4:569–72
  insurance, 4:550–5
  interest rates, 3:831
  multifamily residential property,
    4:547–9
  nonfarm residential, 4:526–39, 4:541,
    4:562–4
  nonfarm structure, 4:526–35
  one- to four-family homes, 4:540, 4:542–6
  by property, 3:777, 4:526–39, 4:545–6,
    4:549
  residential, *4:399–401,* 4:526–72
    nonfarm, 4:526–39
    secondary, 4:470–1, 4:556–9
  secondary residential, 4:470–1, 4:556–9
  securities related to, 4:560–2
  terms, 4:562–8
  by type of holder, 3:777
Motion picture attendance, 4:1123
Motor fuel. *See also* Gasoline
  consumption, 4:847–9
  fuel efficiency, vehicles, 4:346
  price indexes, consumer, 3:165–7
Motor vehicles, *4:762–6,* 4:806–57. *See also*
    Automobiles
  accidents, 4:843–4
  alternative-fuel, 4:346
  deaths and death rates, *4:765,* 4:843–6
  distance traveled, 4:835–40
  emissions
    carbon monoxide, 4:851
    lead, 4:854
    nitrogen oxide, 4:852
    organic compounds, volatile, 4:853

Motor vehicles (*continued*)
  factory sales, 4:831
  fatalities and injuries, 2:600–4, 4:840–2
    motor vehicle accidents, 4:843
  fuel consumption, 4:847–9
    by motor vehicle type, 4:837–40
  fuel efficiency, 4:346
  registrations, 4:830, 4:837–40
  speed, highway, 4:855
  thefts, 5:225
Motorcycles and bicycles, 3:267–70
Mountain States. *See* Regional data
Multifamily residential property. *See also*
    Housing
  houses for sale, 4:495–7
  mortgages, 4:547–9
Municipal solid waste disposal, *3:339–40*
Murder, prisoners executed for, 5:262–3. *See also*
    Homicides
Musculoskeletal conditions, 2:616–17
Museums, 2:885–7
Music, radio, and television consumption
  expenditures, 3:230–42
Musical instruments, commodity value, 3:267–70.
    See also Radios and musical instruments
Mutual funds, 3:771
Mutual savings banks, 3:671–82. *See also* Banks
  insured, 3:724–5

NAICS. *See* North American Industry
    Classification System
Nails, prices, 3:212–17
NAIRU. *See* Nonaccelerating inflation rate of
    unemployment
NASA. *See* National Aeronautics and Space
    Administration
National Aeronautics and Space Administration
    (NASA), 3:453–5
National Assessment of Educational Progress,
    2:425–30
National Banks, 3:641–9
National Collegiate Athletic Association,
    attendance, 4:1118–19
National Credit Union Administration, 3:691–2
National defense, 3:53–6
National Economic Recovery Party, 5:172–9
National Endowment for the Arts, 4:1122
National Endowment for the Humanities,
    4:1122
National Forest System, 4:377–81
National income, *3:3–19,* 3:21–69
  definition, *3:3*
National income and product accounts (NIPA),
    3:6–10
National Labor Relations Board
  elections and results, 2:352
  unfair practice complaints, 2:353
National Party, 5:172–9
National product, *3:3–19,* 3:21–69
National saving, *3:290*
  net, personal, corporate, and government,
    3:298–9
  rates, *3:290,* 3:312–13
National Science Foundation, 3:453–5
National security, federal government
    expenditures for, 5:95
National States Rights Party, 5:172–9
National wealth, 3:325–32
  estimating, *3:294–5*
  by type of asset, 3:325–9
Nativity. *See* Immigration; Population; *specific*
    countries of origin
NATO. *See* North Atlantic Treaty Organization
Natural gas, 4:335–9, 4:341–4
  fuel production, 4:288–91
Natural Law Party, 5:172–9

Numbers in italics refer to pages in essays; numbers not in italics refer to pages in statistical tables.

Numbers in italics refer to pages in essays; numbers not in italics refer to pages in statistical tables.

Numbers in italics refer to pages in essays; numbers not in italics refer to pages in statistical tables.

Numbers in italics refer to pages in essays; numbers not in italics refer to pages in statistical tables.

Numbers in italics refer to pages in essays; numbers not in italics refer to pages in statistical tables.

Numbers in italics refer to pages in essays; numbers not in italics refer to pages in statistical tables.

Numbers in italics refer to pages in essays; numbers not in italics refer to pages in statistical tables.

Numbers in italics refer to pages in essays; numbers not in italics refer to pages in statistical tables.

Numbers in italics refer to pages in essays; numbers not in italics refer to pages in statistical tables.

Numbers in italics refer to pages in essays; numbers not in italics refer to pages in statistical tables.